The new 1990 edition
provides fast access to
the answers—

- What's happening in
  world affairs

- The latest scientific
  information

- The earth's vital
  statistics

- Special articles by
  experts

- More sports pages
  than any other
  almanac

- More maps and
  illustrations

- Plus history, religion,
  taxes, cities and states,
  calendars, celebrities,
  travel, and much more!

If you need to know, turn to

INFORMATION PLEASE!

PROFILE OF THE UNITED STATES

This Profile was created by the editors of *Information Please* from many data sources. Most figures are approximate. For additional details about the United States, please refer to the appropriate sections of the *Information Please Almanac*. NOTE: Figures given are latest available at presstime.

GEOGRAPHY

Number of states: 50
Land area (1989): 3,615,100 sq. mi. Share of world land area: (1989): 6.2%
Northernmost point: Point Barrow, Alaska
Easternmost point: West Quoddy Head, Me.
Southernmost point: Ka Lae (South Cape), Hawaii
Westernmost point: Pochnoi Point, Alaska
Geographic center: In Butte County, S.D. (44″ 58′ N. lat., 103″ 46′ W. long.)

POPULATION

Total (est. mid-1989): 248,800,000
Center of population (1980): 1/4 mile west of De-Soto in Jefferson County, MO
Males (1987): 118,987,000
Females (1987): 124,928,000
White persons (1988): 207,696,000
Black and other persons (1987): 56,371,000
Breakdown by age groups (1987):
  Under 5 years: 18,252,000
  5-14 years: 34,146,000
  15-24 years: 38,481,000
  25-64 years: 123,200,000
  65 and over: 29,835,000
Centenarians (est. 1985): 25,000 (proj. 2,000): over 100,000 (proj. 2080): over 1 million
Median age (1987): 32.1
Rural population (1986): 56,300,000
Metropolitan population (1987): 187,072,000
Families (1987): 64,491,000
Average family size (1987): 3.19
Home ownership (1983): 54,724,000
Married couples (est. 1987): 52,613,000
Unmarried couples (est. 1989): 2,334,000
Single parents (1987): female, 6,297,000; male, 955,000
Widows (1987): 11,123,000
Widowers (1987): 2,120,000

VITAL STATISTICS

Births (1988): 3,913,000
Deaths (1987): 2,127,000
Marriages (1988): 2,389,000
Divorces (1988): 1,183,000
Infant Mortality Rate (est. 1988): 10/1,000
Legal abortions (est. 1985): 1,588,550
Life Expectancy (1986): White men, 72; white women, 78.8; black men, 65.5; black women, 73.6

CIVILIAN LABOR FORCE

Males (1988): 59,781,000 (94.5% employed)
Females (1988): 48,383,000 (94.6% employed)
Teenagers 16-19 (1988): 7,998,000 (82.2% employed)
Work at home (est. 1988): Full-time, 6 million, Part-time, 24.9 million.

INCOME AND CREDIT

Gross National Product (1988): $4,864,300,00 000
Personal income per capita (1988): $16,444
Median family income (1988): $30,992
Individual Shareholders (1985): 47,040,000
Number below poverty level (1987): white, 21,40 000; black and other minorities, 15,153,000
Credit market debt outstanding (1988): $10,33 000,000
Mortgage debt outstanding (1987): $2,908,00 000
Consumer credit outstanding (1987): $685,50 000

EDUCATION

Public elementary and secondary pupils (pro 1990): 40,572,000
Public elementary and secondary classroom teac ers (est. fall 1989): 2,340,000 (ca. 1,560,00 female, 780,000 male)
College enrollment, public and private (proj. 1990 12,585,000
Money spent on elementary and secondary educa tion (est. 1988): $171,690,000,000

CONVENIENCES

Households with radios (est. 1988): 99 million
Radio stations (standard and FM, 1987): 8,943
Television stations (1988): 1,362
Registered automobiles (est. 1988): 140,655,00
Households with telephones (March 1988): 85 million (92.9%)
Newspaper circulation (morning and evening, Sep 30, 1988): 62,694,816
Cable TV subscribers (1988): 42,800,000
Total TV homes (est. Jan. 1, 1988): 88,600,00
Homes with VCRs (May, 1988): 59%
Personal computers used at home (est. 1987): 1 970,000

CRIME

Total arrests (1988): 13,812,300; Males, 7,25 407; Under 18, 1,100,491; Females, 1,58 426; Under 18, 310,369
Child neglect and abuse cases (1985): 1,299,40
Prisoners under sentence of death (1988): 1,13
Law enforcement officers killed (1987): 147
Total murder victims (1988): 18,269
Households touched by crime (Total 1987): 2 254,000 (24.4%)
Violent crime (1987): 4,190,000 (4.6%)
Theft (1987): 15,667,00 (17.1%)

INFORMATION
PLEASE
ALMANAC®
ATLAS & YEARBOOK

43RD EDITION

HOUGHTON MIFFLIN COMPANY BOSTON

1990

Executive Editor
Otto Johnson
Associate Editor
Vera Dailey
Contributing Editors
Arthur Reed, Jr. (Current Events)
William E. Bruno (World Coun-
tries)
Dennis M. Lyons (Sports)
Staff
Manuscript Editors:
Daniel Kulkosky and
Lisa Zolesi
Maps
Maps copyright © Hammond
Incorporated.
Requests for map use should be
sent to Hammond Incorporated,
Maplewood, New Jersey 07040.

The Information Please Almanac invites comments and suggestions from readers. Because of
the many letters received, however, it is not possible to respond personally to every correspondent.
Nevertheless, all suggestions are most welcome,
and the editors will consider them carefully. (Information Please Almanac does not rule on bets
or wagers.)

ISBN (Hardcover): 0–395–51177–1
ISBN (Paperback): 0–395–51178–X–4
ISSN: 0073–7860

Previous editions of INFORMATION PLEASE were
published in 1988, 1987, 1986, 1985, and
1984 by Houghton Mifflin Company, in 1982 by
A&W Publishing Company, and in 1981, 1980,
and 1979 by Simon & Schuster, in 1978 and
1977 by Information Please Publishing, Inc., and
from 1947–1976 by Dan Golenpaul Associates.

Copies of Information Please Almanac may be or-
dered directly by mail from:
Customer Service Department
Houghton Mifflin Company
Burlington, Ma 01803
Phone toll-free, (800) 225-3362 for price and
shipping information. In Massachusetts phone:
272-1500.

INFORMATION PLEASE ALMANAC®
Editorial Office
Houghton Mifflin Company
215 Park Avenue South
New York, N.Y. 10003

Printed in the United States of America

WP Pa   BP Hbd 10 9 8 7 6 5 4 3 2 1

CONTENTS

SPECIAL ARTICLES

SPECIAL FEATURES

TABLE OF CONTENTS

18 *Index*

Hudson's Bay Company, 168
Huguenots, 112, 115
Humanism, 428–429
Humidity, relative, 679–81
Humphrey, Hubert H., 633
"Hundred Days," 117
Hundred Years' War, 111, 190, 273
Hungary, 202–03
 1956 uprisings, 130, 203
 See also Countries
Huns. *See* Mongols
Huron, Lake, 167, 470, 758
Hus, Jan, 111, 179, 436
Hurricanes, 669, 673–74, 678
Hussein, King, 215, 216, 284, 693
Hyde Park, N.Y. (F.D.R.), 633, 764
Hydroelectric plants, 610
Hydrogen, 532
 First use in balloon, 361
Hydrogen, heavy, 124, 557
Hydrogen bomb, 128, 257, 314

I

ICC, 651
Icecaps, Arctic, Antarctic, 568
Ice Cave, 475
Ice hockey. *See* Hockey
Iceland, 109, 203–04, 458, 460
 Island, 474
 Volcanoes, 461
 See also Countries
Ice skating. *See* Figure skating; Speed
 skating
I Ching, 429
Idaho, 752–53
 See also States of U.S.
Ikhnaton, 105
"Iliad,"–105
Illinois, 753
 See also States of U.S.
Illinois River, 478
IMF, 293
Immigration statistics, 805, 806
Impeachments, 136, 616–17, 619, 649
 Andrew Johnson, 649, 657
 Richard Nixon, 132, 663
Imperial gallon, 383
Imports:
 United States, 76, 150
 Value by country, 150
Inca Empire, 111, 112, 161, 171, 183, 241
Income:
 By occupation, 51, 62, 63
 Family, 51, 53
 Farm income, 68
 Household, 51, 53
 National income, 59
 Per capita, 50, 59, 778–87
 See also Revenue; Salaries; Wages
Income tax (city), 85
Income tax (federal), 69–70, 78–80
 Collections, 69, 78
 Established, 77, 118, 623
Incubation periods, animals, 562
Independence, Declaration of, 614–15
Independence Day, 578
Independence Hall, 630, 767
India, 115, 118, 128, 135, 157, 204–05, 238, 273
 Sikh rebellion, 134, 205
 Structures, 607
 See also Countries
Indiana, 753–54
 See also States of U.S.
Indianapolis, Ind., 753, 781
 See also Cities (U.S.)
Indianapolis "500," 955–56
Indian Ocean, 469
 Islands, 473, 474
 Volcanoes, 461
Indians (American):
 Births and birth rates, 813

Population of reservations, 806
 Reservations, 806
Indochina. *See* Cambodia; Laos;
 Vietnam
Indonesia, 205–06
 Volcanoes, 461
 See also Countries
Indus River, 204, 238, 471
Industrial Revolution, 115, 547
Industry:
 Employment, 61, 66
 Foreign countries, 146–50
 Hours and wages, 62, 63
 Plant and equipment costs, 53
 Production indexes, 52
 See also individual industries
Infantile paralysis. *See* Poliomyelitis
Infant mortality, 815, 817, 818, 819
Influenza, 122, 815
Information Agency, U.S., 652
Information bureaus, sports, 939
"Information Please" quiz show, 828
Ingatherng, Feast of, 578, 580
Inini, 190–91
Inquisition, 111, 113
Insulin, 132, 557, 713
Insurance:
 Life insurance, 53
 Unemployment, 586–87
Insured mail, 603
Intelligence testing, 557
Interest:
 Public debt, 69–70
Interior, U.S. Dept. of, 650
 Secretaries of, 643–46
Internal Revenue Service. *See* Taxes
International affairs, news events,
 1988–89. *See* Current Events
International Atomic Energy Agency,
 292
International Bank, 292
International Civil Aviation
 Organization, 292
International Court, 292
International Date Line, 576
International Development Association,
 292
International Development
 Cooperation Agency, U.S., 652
International Finance Corp., 292–93
International Labor Organization, 293
International mail, 604
International Maritime Organization,
 293
International Monetary Fund, 128,
 293
International organizations, U.S.
 contributions to, 70
Internationals, 119, 122
International System of Units, 381–85
International Telecommunication
 Union, 293
International Trade Commission, U.S.,
 652
Interplanetary probes, 354–55
Interstate commerce, 72
Interstate Commerce Commission,
 651
Inventions and discoveries, 557–58
Inventions & Technology, 545–58
Iolani Palace, 752
Ionian Islands, 198
Ionosphere, 339
Iowa, 754
 See also States of U.S.
IRA (Irish Republic Army), 133, 134,
 137, 209, 275
Iran, 133, 206–07
 Hostage crisis, 133, 207
 Map, 494
 Shah of, 133, 207
 War with Iraq, 133, 135, 207, 208
 See also Countries; News events
Iran-Contra affair, 135, 136
Iraq, 133, 208
 Israel and, 208

Map, 494
War with Iran, 133, 136, 207, 208
 See also Countries; News events
Ireland, Northern, 209, 271, 274–75
 See also United Kingdom
Ireland (island), 474
Ireland (republic), 122, 208–09
 See also Countries
Irish Republican Army, 133, 134,
 209, 275
Iron:
 As element, 533
 Economic statistics, 62, 76
"Iron Curtain," 128
Irrawaddy River, 164, 472
Irtish River, 471
Islam, 400, 580
 Number of Moslems, 397
Islamabad, Pakistan, 237
Islands, 473–74
 See also specific islands
Isle of Man, 278
Isle Royale National Park, 564
Isotopes of elements, 532–33, 557
Israel, 209–12
 Balfour Declaration, 122, 210
 Entebbe rescue, 132
 Independence (1948), 128, 210–12
 Invasion of Lebanon, 133, 212, 221
 Map, 494
 Wars with Arabs, 128, 130, 131,
 132, 133, 184, 208, 210–12,
 216
 See also Countries; Headline History
Israel, ancient, 105, 210, 397–98
Istanbul, Turkey, 269
 See also Constantinople
Italy, 212–13
 Structures, 606–7
 Volcanoes, 461
 World War I, 122
 World War II, 127
 See also Countries; Roman Empire
Ivory Coast, 213
 See also Countries
Ivy League, 871
Iwo Jima, 460

J

Jackson, Andrew, 654–55
 See also Headline History; Presidents
 (U.S.)
Jackson, Miss., 759
Jackson, Jesse, Rev., 693
Jacksonville, Fla., 781
 See also Cities (U.S.)
Jack the Ripper, 119
Jakarta, Indonesia, 206
Jamaica, 213–14
 See also Countries
James, Jesse, 647, 693
James River, 478
Jamestown, Va., 113, 458, 771
Jammu, 205
Japan, 214–15, 458
 China and, 119, 124, 127, 172,
 214, 215
 Islands, 214, 473, 474
 Russia and, 120, 215, 256
 Volcanoes, 214, 460
 War trial, 128
 World War I, 122
 World War II, 127, 128
 World War II peace treaty, 129, 215
 See also Countries
Japanese in U.S.:
 Births and birth rates, 813
 See also Nonwhite persons
Japan Sea, 214, 469
Japurá River, 472
Jarvis Island, 774
Java, 206, 473
 See also Indonesia
Javelin throw. *See* Track and Field

Ordering Information Please Almanac by Mail

Information Please Almanac is available in bookstores everywhere. Copies of the *Almanac* may also be ordered directly by mail from the publisher.

To order, write to: Customer Service Department, Houghton Mifflin Publishing Company, Burlington, Massachusetts 01803. Readers may phone Customer Service, Toll-Free (800) 225-3362 for the latest price and shipping information. In Massachusetts, telephone 272-1500. Please do not send orders to New York Editorial Office.

Other reference books published by Houghton Mifflin Company are: *The American Heritage Dictionary, The American Heritage Dictionary of Science* (Robert K. Barnhart), *Webster's II New Riverside University Dictionary, The Professional Secretary's Handbook, Roget's II: The New Thesaurus (Expanded Edition), Word Mysteries & Histories: From Quiche to Humble Pie, The American Heritage Larousse Spanish Dictionary, Contemporary Quotations,* and *Wall Street Words.*

FRONT FEATURES

A World at Risk—A Loss of Food Security

By Lester R. Brown, Christopher Flavin, and Sandra Postel

A dramatic 2.6-fold increase in grain production between 1950 and 1984 raised per capita consumption by nearly 40 percent. But since then growth has stopped. In each of the past two years, world grain production has fallen sharply, marking the first steep back-to-back annual declines on record. A monsoon failure in India in 1987 and drought-reduced harvests in North America and China in 1988 explain only part of the reduction. In several populous countries, including China, India, Indonesia, and Mexico, little or no progress has been made in expanding grain production since 1984.

This reversal in humanity's agricultural fortunes has occurred rather abruptly. For those accustomed to reading as recently as early 1988 of "a world awash in grain," the latest downturn in grain output may come as a surprise. Although not widely recognized at the time, the impressive growth in world production following the doubling of world grain prices in 1973 was achieved in part by plowing highly erodible land, and in part by drawing down water tables through overpumping for irrigation.

Farmers can overplow and overpump with impressive results in the short run, but for many the short run is drawing to a close. The result is a worldwide retrenchment in cultivated area and a dramatic slowdown in the spread of irrigation. As highly erodible cropland brought under the plow during the agricultural boom years of the seventies is taken out of cultivation, and as falling water tables in key food-producing countries force a reduction in irrigated area, the growth in world food output is slowing.

Evidence that environmental degradation in some regions is altering the food prospect and, in turn, the human prospect is unmistakable. In Africa, a deteriorating agricultural resource base, record population growth, and economic mismanagement lowered grain output per person throughout the seventies. During the eighties, mounting external debt reduced capital available for investment in agriculture, exacerbating the decline.

The social effects of agricultural adversity are now becoming highly visible throughout the continent. In mid-1988, the World Bank reported that "both the proportion and the total number of Africans with deficient diets have climbed and will continue to rise unless special action is taken." The Bank went on to say that "barely a quarter of Africans are living in countries where food consumption was increasing in the 1980s, down considerably from about two-thirds in the 1970s."

In Africa, the number of "food insecure" people, defined by the Bank as those not having enough food for normal health and physical activity, now totals over 100 million. Some 14.7 million Ethiopians, one third of the country, are undernourished; Nigeria is close behind, with 13.7 million undernourished people. The countries with 40 percent or more of their populations suffering from chronic food insecurity are Chad, Mozambique, Somalia, and Uganda. (See Table 1.) The Bank summarized its findings by noting that "Africa's food situation is not only serious, it is deteriorating."

The island of Madagascar, with a population of 11 million expanding by 3 percent per year, reveals in some detail how population growth and environmental deterioration are affecting people. As with the rest of Africa, per capita grain production peaked in 1967 and declined gradually until 1983 when the fall accelerated. Since then average grain consumption has fallen by nearly one fifth, pushing food intake below the survival level for many. Infant mortality, the most sensitive indicator of nutritional stress, rose from 75 to 133 per thousand between 1975 and 1985. Short of a miracle, the future of this country, with a birth rate among the world's highest and a rate of topsoil loss greater even than that of Ethiopia, is not bright.

This deterioration is not limited to Africa. In Latin America, which exported more grain than

Table 1. Food Insecurity in Selected African Countries, 1986

Country	Number of people (million)	Share of population (percent)
Ethiopia	14.7	34
Nigeria	13.7	13
Zaire	12.0	38
Tanzania	6.6	29
Kenya	6.2	29
Uganda	6.1	40
Mozambique	5.9	42
Algeria	4.1	18
Ghana	4.1	31
Sudan	3.4	15
Zambia	2.7	39
Mali	2.5	33
Chad	2.4	47
Morocco	2.4	11
Somalia	2.3	42

Source: World Bank, *Report of the Task Force on Food Security in Africa* (Washington, D.C.: 1988); World Bank, *World Development Report 1988* (New York: Oxford University Press, 1988).

Lester R. Brown is the President of Worldwatch Institute. Christopher Flavin and Sandra Postel are Associate Project Directors with the organization. Worldwatch is an independent, nonprofit research organization that was established to inform policy makers and the general public about the interdependence of the world economy and its environmental support systems. This article was excerpted with permission from *State of the World 1989*, copyright © 1989 by the Worldwatch Institute. The annual *State of the World* may be ordered from Worldwatch, 1776 Massachusetts Ave., N.W. Washington, D.C., 20036, $18.95 cloth, $9.95 paperback prepaid, or through bookstores in the United States or directly from the publishers, W.W. Norton & Company, Inc., 500 Fifth Ave., New York, N.Y. 10110. A list of other publications is available from Worldwatch.

North America did a mere half-century ago, per capita grain production has fallen 7 percent since reaching an all-time high in 1981. In its 1988 report "The Global State of Hunger and Malnutrition," the U.N.'s World Food Council reports that the share of malnourished preschoolers in Peru increased from 42 percent to 68 percent between 1980 and 1983. Infant deaths have risen in Brazil during the eighties. If recent trends in population growth, land degradation, and growth in external debt continue, Latin America's decline in food production per person will almost certainly continue into the nineties, increasing the number of hungry, malnourished people. The Council summarized its worldwide findings by noting that "earlier progress in fighting hunger, malnutrition and poverty has come to a halt or is being reversed in many parts of the world."

When domestic food production is inadequate, the ability of countries to import becomes the key to food sufficiency. . . . low-income grain-deficit countries must contend not only with an increase in grain prices, but also in many cases with unmanageable external debt, which severely limits their expenditures on food imports. . . .

The effect of higher grain prices on consumers is much greater in developing countries than in industrial ones. In the United States, for example, a $1 loaf of bread contains roughly 5¢ worth of wheat. If the price of wheat doubles, the price of the loaf would increase only to $1.05. In developing countries, however, where wheat is purchased in the market and ground into flour at home, a doubling of world grain prices translates into a doubling of prices to consumers. For those who already spend most of their income on food, such a rise can drive consumption below the survival level (See Table 2).

* * *

Already faced with a deteriorating food situation, the world is now confronted with climate change, an additional threat to food security. . . . With normal weather, the United States typically harvests more than 300 million tons of grain; Americans consume roughly 200 million tons and the rest is exported. Because this year's drought [1988] eliminated the share of harvest normally sold overseas, exports during the 1988-89 trade year will come entirely from reserves.

As noted earlier, climate change will not affect all countries in the same way. The projected rise of 1.5-4.5 degrees Celsius (3-8 degrees Fahrenheit) is a global average, but temperatures are expected to increase much more in the middle and higher latitudes and more over land than over the oceans. They are projected to change little near the equator, while gains in the higher latitudes could easily be twice the anticipated global average. This uneven distribution will affect world agriculture disproportionately, since most food is produced in the middle and higher latitudes of the northern hemisphere.

Though they remain sketchy, meteorological models suggest that two of the world's major food-producing regions—the North American agricultural heartland and a large area of central Asia—are likely to experience a decline in soil moisture during the summer growing season as a result of higher temperatures and increased evaporation. If the warming progresses as the models indicate, some of the land in the U.S. western Great Plains that now produces wheat would revert to range-land. The western Corn Belt would become semi-arid, with wheat or other drought-tolerant grains

Table 2. World Grain Prices, July 1988, Compared With July 1987

Grain	July 1987	July 1988	Change
	(current dollars)		(percent)
Wheat (price per bushel)	2.85	4.07	+43
Rice (price per ton)	212	305	+44
Corn (price per bushel)	1.94	3.22	+66

Source: International Monetary Fund, *International Financial Statistics* (Washington, D.C.: various months).

that yield 40 bushels per acre replacing corn that yields over 100 bushels.

On the plus side, as temperatures increase the winter wheat belt might migrate northward, allowing winter strains that yield 40 bushels per acre to replace spring varieties yielding 30 bushels. A longer growing season would also permit a northward extension of spring wheat production into areas such as Canada's Alberta province, thus increasing that nation's cultivated area. On balance, though, higher temperatures and increased summer dryness will reduce the North American grain harvest, largely because of their negative impact on the all-important corn crop.

* * *

A study from the National Center for Atmospheric Research in Boulder, Colorado, suggests that a rise in average temperatures will also increase the probability of extreme short-term heat waves. If these occur at critical times—such as the corn pollination period—they can have a much greater effect on crop yields than the relatively modest average temperature increase of a few degrees might indicate.

This vulnerability of corn, which accounts for two thirds of the U.S. grain harvest and one eighth of the world's, can cause wide year-to-year swings in the world grain crop. An examination of U.S. corn yields since 1950 shows five sharply reduced harvests over the past 38 years [to 1988]. The only pronounced drops before the eighties came in 1970, from an outbreak of corn blight, and in 1974, when a wet spring and late planting combined with an early frost to destroy a part of the crop before it matured.

Three harvests since 1950 have been sharply reduced by drought, all in the eighties. Each drop has been worse than the last. Compared with the preceding year, the 1980 corn yield per hectare was down by 17 percent, that in 1983 was down by 28 percent, and that in 1988 by a staggering 34 percent.

These three reduced harvests each occurred during one of the five warmest years globally of the last century. There is no way to conclusively link the drought-depressed U.S. harvests with the global warming, since annual weather variability is so much greater than the rise in average global temperatures measured during the eighties.

Among other things, the prospect of climate change increases uncertainty over future harvests, making decision more complicated for farmers and policymakers alike. . . .

Judging by the historical record, the odds are against severe back-to-back droughts, but with the warming now apparently under way, hot dry summers will become more frequent. In the event of another disastrous drought, U.S. grain exports would drop dramatically. The world would face a food emergency for which there is no precedent in the decades since North America emerged as its breadbasket. There would be a desperate effort to corner available supplies as world grain prices soared to record levels. In such a situation, preventing starvation among the world's poor would require affluent countries to reduce the amount of grain fed to livestock.

Asian and African countries, in particular, would find it impossible to feed their people without North American grain. Many of the world's major cities—Leningrad, Cairo, Lagos, Caracas, and Tokyo, for example—depend largely on grain from the United States and Canada. In an integrated world food economy, all countries suffer the consequences of poor harvests.

All available evidence indicates that the ranks of the hungry are expanding during the late eighties, reversing the trend of recent decades. Uncertainties and stresses from a changing climate are now being overlaid upon an already tightening food situation. In the absence of a major commitment by governments to slow population growth and strengthen agriculture, food insecurity and the social instability associated with it will preoccupy the political leaders of many countries during the nineties.

Senior Citizen Population Is Growing In Developing Countries

Although the low-fertility developed countries are known to have a large proportion of older citizens within their populations, the phenomenon is building unrecognized in developing countries as well, according to an analysis by the U.S. Bureau of the Census of the populations of 22 such countries. In fact, 58 percent of people aged 55 and older currently live in developing countries, and this proportion will increase as time goes on. Almost one million persons in the Third World reach the age of 55 each month; the resulting annual growth rate among the older population is slightly more than three percent, a rate three times that of the developed countries.

The data for the report come from the International Data Base on Aging, computerized files covering a wide variety of variables that are maintained and updated by the Center for International Research within the Bureau of the Census. The data, while not necessarily representative of the developing world as a whole, pertain to 10 countries in Asia, five in Africa, and seven in Latin America and the Caribbean; these countries were selected based on data availability, regional representation, and importance to the Agency for International Development.

Among the developing regions, the Caribbean has the "oldest" population: Twelve percent of its citizens are 55 and older, compared with 10 percent in Asia, nine percent in Latin America, and seven percent in Africa. The report notes that several factors tend to produce older populations in some countries within a region than in others, including a low-fertility rate and emigration of working-age individuals. The proportions can vary greatly among countries within a region; in Asia, for example, the share of the population 55 and older ranges from seven percent in Bangladesh to 17 percent in Hong Kong. Overall, proportions among individual countries range from five percent in Kenya to 22 percent in Uruguay.

The median age in almost all the countries in the study is currently younger than 25, and ranges from 19 in Kenya to 33 in Uruguay. However, these medians are expected to rise by 8-10 years over the next three decades; by the year 2020, countries such as Hong Kong and Singapore are expected to have median ages older than 45.

Although the majority of all persons 55 and older live in the developing world, 57 percent of those 75 and older are currently living in industrialized countries. However, this is the fastest growing group within the older population of the developing world, and by the turn of the century, the majority of people aged 75 and older (61 percent) will be living in developing nations, too.

Overall, average life expectancy at birth is 51 years in the developing world, but this average ranges from about 50 years in Bangladesh and Malawi to more than 75 years in Hong Kong, Costa Rica, and Jamaica. Although the life-span advantage that women in the developed world have over men is not as great in the developing world, women outlive men in all the countries studied except Bangladesh, where men live 2.3 years longer than women. The report attributes this reversal of the typical worldwide pattern to the low social status accorded women and to the preference that men often receive in the use of scarce resources ranging from medical care to education.

Nonetheless, in most developing countries, as in the developed world, the proportion of women in the older population increases with age. In only four countries—Bangladesh, Zimbabwe, Morocco and Tunisia—do men outnumber women at age 60 and older. Countries such as Hong Kong, Uruguay, and the Republic of Korea already show the large female imbalances at older ages that are seen in industrialized nations, and this pattern is expected to be present by the year 2020 in most of the other countries as well.

The aging of societies actually represents a success story, the report points out, because it means that infant mortality rates, the incidence of infectious diseases, and fertility rates are being reduced and that education and health are improving. However, the study also notes that older populations require different social support services than young populations and that developing nations will have to recognize and plan for these changes if they are to age gracefully.

Source: "Older Population Growing at Rapid Pace in Developing Countries," *Family Planning Perspectives*, Volume 21, Number 4, (July/August 1989), pp. 191–192. © The Alan Guttmacher Institute.

Third World Children

By Lawrence E. Bruce

Have you ever seen a child die? Every single day 40,000 mothers in developing countries stand by helplessly as their children perish from malnutrition and easily preventable diseases. Tragically, one in every three deaths in the world is that of a child under five years old.

Introducing organ transplants, gene therapy, or even building bigger, better hospitals won't prevent the deaths of hundreds of thousands of children. The problem is not lack of scientific knowledge or technology. In fact the money devoted to improving hospitals in developing countries usually reduces the amount of aid that reaches the poor. Educating mothers on newborns' nutritional needs and training them to use basic medical skills, such as keeping sick children from becoming dehydrated, are key to eradicating the children's suffering. Through the support of international organizations and growing concern among government officials in developing countries, these programs have begun reducing child mortality.

In 1950, 23.2 million children perished before their fifth birthday. Today that figure has dropped to 14 million. An impressive improvement, but the number of children dying from preventable causes is still too high. The death of even one child is a horrible loss.

Dehydration from diarrhea remains the leading cause of child mortality. Children often contract illnesses that cause diarrhea from contaminated drinking water or poor sanitation and don't receive the immediate medical care that the illness requires. In a scene repeated more than 3 million times a year, a two-year-old girl in Bangladesh is stricken with an acute intestinal infection. Fluid pours from her body, and her skin becomes flaccid. Urination stops and blood pressure falls. Shock sets in, and in a few hours the lifeless child becomes another grim statistic.

Such tragedies are easily prevented by oral rehydration therapy (ORT), introduced in the Sixties by scientists treating cholera in Calcutta. ORT is a simple solution of water, salt, and sugar that allows the body to reabsorb fluid, thus stopping the dehydration process. The therapy's cost: only ten cents. A large part of the medical community, however, clings to the impractical and expensive intravenous or drug treatment recommended in standard textbooks. This is because ORT therapy isn't taught to health workers, and most medical students don't receive hands-on training in the use of ORT. In communities where ORT is available, only 6 percent of health professionals are trained to teach mothers how to administer this medicine. Still, the message is slowly reaching the people: In 1980 fewer than 1 percent of children with diarrhea were treated with ORT; today 25 percent receive this treatment.

Estimates reveal that approximately 3.3 million children under age five die each year from preventable diseases such as measles, tetanus, whooping cough, polio, diphtheria, and tuberculosis. These children could be saved if they simply were given the proper vaccines. The main problem: Although plenty of vaccine is available, many parents do not understand the importance of getting their children inoculated. To address this problem teachers, religious leaders, community organizations, trade unions, women's groups, and government institutions are being mobilized to educate parents about the benefits of vaccination.

In the Dominican Republic 20,000 trained volunteers go house to house to inoculate children. In Senegal traditional storytellers beat the drums to announce the arrival of immunization teams. And in Chad camels rigged with solar-powered refrigeration devices carry serums to remote areas. By the year 2000 health organizations hope to reduce vaccine-preventable deaths from 3.3 million to fewer than 250,000.

Immunization alone, however, cannot save all of the children who die. A vaccine can't protect against malnutrition, responsible for one-third of child deaths worldwide. Surprisingly, the cause is not necessarily a shortage of food. More often it is the result of a lack of simple information available to mothers about proper nutrition during their children's crucial early years.

In Guatemala, for example, many children are fed primarily sugared water and tortillas. As a result, their bellies are bloated and their hair is thin and sparse. Suffering from poor nutrition, these children are unable to fight repeated infections, and many die. What should we do? Institute basic health services; raise the literacy rates of women, the primary caretakers of children; and teach nutrition and hygiene to children in schools. The answers aren't complicated—and they work.

When the diseases that kill babies are conquered, the fight to stay alive will no longer consume the energy of most of the world's women. This is when real national development will begin. Studies show that once women are relieved of these burdens, they begin to engage in income-generating activities: forming co-ops to farm rice in Indonesia and marketing crafts in Peru. Wage-earning mothers, assured of the health of the children they already have, also welcome the idea of spacing pregnancies at least two years apart. Fewer children are born, but the ones who arrive survive. Thus the cycle of poverty and disease is broken.   □

Lawrence E. Bruce is president of the U.S. Committee for UNICEF, the United Nations Children's Fund.

PROFILE OF THE WORLD

GEOGRAPHY

Total area: 510,072,000 sq km; (196,887,792 sq. mi.); 361,132,000 sq km (139,396,952 sq mi.) (70.8%) is water and 148,940,000 sq km (57,490,840 sq mi.) (29.2%) is land

Comparative area: land area about 16 times the size of the U.S.

Land boundaries: 442,000 km (274,482 mi.)

Coastline: 359,000 km (222,939 mi.)

Maritime claims:
Contiguous zone: generally 24 nm, but varies from 4 nm to 24 nm
Continental shelf: generally 200 nm, but some are 200 meters in depth
Exclusive fishing zone: most are 200 nm, but varies from 12 nm to 200 nm
Extended economic zone: 200 nm, only Madagascar claims 150 nm
Territorial sea: generally 12 nm, but varies from 3 nm to 200 nm

Disputes: 13 international land boundary disputes—Argentina-Uruguay, Bangladesh-India, Brazil-Paraguay, Brazil-Uruguay, Cambodia-Vietnam, China-India, China-U.S.S.R., Ecuador-Peru, El Salvador-Honduras, French Guiana-Suriname, Guyana-Suriname, Guyana-Venezuela, Qatar-UAE

Climate: two large areas of polar climates separated by two rather narrow temperate zones from a wide equatorial band of tropical to subtropical climates

Terrain: highest elevation is Mt. Everest at 8,848 meters (29,108 ft) and lowest elevation is the Dead Sea at 392 meters (1,290 ft) below sea level; greatest ocean depth is the Marianas Trench at 10,924 meters (35,839 ft)

Natural resources: the oceans represent the last major frontier for the discovery and development of natural resources

Land use: 10% arable land; 1% permanent crops; 24% meadows and pastures; 31% forest and woodland; 34% other; includes 1.6% irrigated

Environment: large areas subject to severe weather (tropical cyclones), natural disasters (earthquakes, landslides, tsunamis, volcanic eruptions), industrial disasters, pollution (air, water, acid rain, toxic substances), loss of vegetation (overgrazing, deforestation, desertification), loss of wildlife resources, soil degradation, soil depletion, erosion

PEOPLE

Population: 5,242,874,000 (July 1989), growth rate 1.8% (1989)

Birth rate: 27 births/1,000 population (1989)

Death rate: 10 deaths/1,000 population (1989)

Infant mortality rate: 71 deaths/1,000 live births (1989)

Life expectancy at birth: 60 years male, 64 years female (1989)

Total fertility rate: 3.5 children born/woman (1989)

This section is reprinted with permission from *The World Factbook, 1989,* published by the Directorate of Intelligence of the Central Intelligence Agency. Metric conversions by *Information Please Almanac.*

Literacy: 77% men; 66% women (1980)

Labor force: 1,939,000,000 (1984)

Organized labor: n.a.

GOVERNMENT

Administrative divisions: 247 nations, dependencies, and geographic entities

Legal system: varies among each of the entities; 162 parties to the United Nations International Court of Justice (ICJ) or World Court

Diplomatic representation: there are 159 members of the U.N

ECONOMY

Overview: In 1988 the world economy grew at an estimated 3.4%, nearly double the average annual rate of 1.8% in the period 1986-87. This growth was dominated by the technologically advanced countries—the United States, Japan, and those of Western Europe—which together account for three-fifths of the gross world product (GWP) of $18.5 trillion; these countries, led by Japan, grew in the aggregate at about 4.0%. In contrast, the Soviet Union grew at 1.5% and Eastern Europe (including Yugoslavia) at 1.6%. Experience in the developing countries was mixed, with the newly industrializing countries generally continuing their rapid progress, and others struggling with debt, inflation and inadequate investment. The year 1988 witnessed a marked reduction in world tensions, which could yield sizable economic benefits in the 1990s. However, the addition of nearly 100,000,000 people a year to an already overcrowded globe will exacerbate the problems of pollution, desertification, underemployment, and poverty.

GWP (gross world product): $18.5 trillion, per capita $3,600 real growth rate 3.4% (1988 est.)

Inflation rate (consumer prices): 10.9% (1987)

Unemployment rate: % n.a.

Exports: $2,358 billion (f.o.b., 1987); *commodities*—n.a. *partners*—in value, about 70% of exports from industrial countries

Imports: $2,410 billion (c.i.f., 1987); *commodities*—n.a. *partners*—in value, about 75% of imports by the industrial countries

External debt: $1,008 billion for less developed countries (1988 est.)

Industrial production: growth rate 5.4% (1987)

Electricity: 2,771,613,200 kW capacity; 10,977,966 million kWh produced, 2,135 kWh per capita (1988)

Industries: agriculture, chemicals, energy, machinery, electronics, equipment, manufacturing, metals, mining

Agriculture: cereals (wheat, maize, rice), sugar, livestock products, tropical crops, fruit, vegetables, fish

Aid: n.a.

COMMUNICATIONS

Ports: Mina al Ahmadi (Kuwait), Chiba, Houston, Kawasaki, Kobe, Marseille, New Orleans, New York, Rotterdam, Yokohama

The Hundredth and First Congress

Composition of 100th and 101th Congresses

	100th Congress				101th Congress			
	Dem.	Rep.	Male	Female	Dem.	Rep.	Male	Female
Senate	54	46	98	2	55	45	98	2
House	258	171	411	24	255 [1]	176 [2]	404	27

1. One seat vacant in California, and 2 in Texas, as of August 31, 1989. 2. One vacant seat in Mississippi.

The Senate

Senior Senator is listed first. The dates in the first column indicate period of service. The date given in parentheses after the Senator's name is year of birth. All terms are for six years and expire in January. Mailing address of Senators: The Senate, Washington, D.C. 20510.

ALABAMA
1979–91 Howell T. Heflin (D) (1921)
1987–93 Richard C. Shelby (D) (1934)
ALASKA
1968–91 Ted Stevens (R) (1923)
1981–93 Frank H. Murkowski (R) (1933)
ARIZONA
1977–95 Dennis DeConcini (D) (1937)
1987–93 John McCain (R) (1936)
ARKANSAS
1975–93 Dale Bumpers (D) (1925)
1979–91 David H. Pryor (D) (1934)
CALIFORNIA
1969–93 Alan Cranston (D) (1914)
1983–95 Pete Wilson (R) (1933)
COLORADO
1979–91 William L. Armstrong (R) (1937)
1987–93 Timothy E. Wirth (D) (1939)
CONNECTICUT
1981–93 Christopher J. Dodd (D) (1944)
1989–95 Joseph I. Lieberman (D) (1942)
DELAWARE
1971–95 William V. Roth, Jr. (R) (1921)
1973–91 Joseph R. Biden, Jr. (D) (1942)
FLORIDA
1987–93 Bob Graham (D) (1936)
1989–95 Connie Mack III (R) (1940)
GEORGIA
1972–91 Sam Nunn (D) (1938)
1987–93 Wyche Fowler, Jr. (D) (1940)
HAWAII
1963–93 Daniel K. Inouye (D) (1924)
1977–95 Spark M. Matsunaga (D) (1916)
IDAHO
1973–91 James A. McClure (R) (1924)
1981–93 Steven D. Symms (R) (1938)
ILLINOIS
1981–93 Alan J. Dixon (D) (1927)
1985–91 Paul Simon (D) (1928)
INDIANA
1977–95 Richard G. Lugar (R) (1932)
1989–93 Dan Coats (R) (1943)
IOWA
1981–93 Charles E. Grassley (R) (1933)
1985–91 Tom Harkin (D) (1939)
KANSAS
1969–93 Robert J. Dole (R) (1923)
1978–91 Nancy Landon Kassebaum (R) (1932)
KENTUCKY
1974–93 Wendell H. Ford (D) (1924)
1985–91 Mitch McConnell (R) (1942)

LOUISIANA
1972–91 J. Bennett Johnson (D) (1932)
1987–93 John B. Breaux (D) (1944)
MAINE
1979–91 William S. Cohen (R) (1940)
1980–95 George J. Mitchell (D) (1933)
MARYLAND
1977–95 Paul Sarbanes (D) (1933)
1987–93 Barbara A. Mikulski (D) (1936)
MASSACHUSETTS
1962–95 Edward M. Kennedy (D) (1932)
1985–91 John F. Kerry (D) (1943)
MICHIGAN
1976–95 Donald W. Riegle, Jr. (D) (1938)
1979–91 Carl Levin (D) (1934)
MINNESOTA
1978–91 Rudy Boschwitz (R) (1930)
1978–89 David F. Durenberger (R) (1934)
MISSISSIPPI
1978–91 Thad Cochran (R) (1937)
1989–95 Trent Lott (R) (1941)
MISSOURI
1976–95 John C. Danforth (R) (1936)
1987–91 Christopher S. (Kit) Bond (R) (1939)
MONTANA
1978–91 Max Baucus (D) (1941)
1989–95 Conrad Burns (R) (1935)
NEBRASKA
1979–91 J. James Exon (D) (1921)
1989–95 Robert Kerrey (D) (1943)
NEVADA
1987–93 Harry M. Reid (D) (1939)
1989–95 Dick Bryan (D) (1937)
NEW HAMPSHIRE
1979–91 Gordon J. Humphrey (R) (1940)
1980–95 Warren B. Rudman (R) (1930)
NEW JERSEY
1979–91 Bill Bradley (D) (1943)
1982–95 Frank R. Lautenberg (D) (1924)
NEW MEXICO
1973–91 Pete V. Domenici (R) (1932)
1983–95 Jeff Bingaman (D) (1943)
NEW YORK
1977–95 Daniel P. Moynihan (D) (1927)
1981–93 Alfonse M. D'Amato (R) (1937)
NORTH CAROLINA
1973–91 Jesse Helms (R) (1921)
1986–93 Terry Sanford (D) (1917)
NORTH DAKOTA
1960–95 Quentin N. Burdick (D) (1908)
1987–93 Kent Conrad (D) (1948)

OHIO
1974–93 John H. Glenn, Jr. (D) (1921)
1976–95 Howard M. Metzenbaum (D) (1917)
OKLAHOMA
1979–91 David L. Boren (D) (1941)
1981–93 Don Nickles (R) (1948)
OREGON
1967–91 Mark O. Hatfield (R) (1922)
1969–93 Bob Packwood (R) (1932)
PENNSYLVANIA
1977–95 John Heinz (R) (1938)
1981–93 Arlen Specter (R) (1930)
RHODE ISLAND
1961–91 Claiborne Pell (D) (1918)
1976–95 John H. Chafee (R) (1922)
SOUTH CAROLINA
1956–91 Strom Thurmond (R) (1902)
1966–93 Ernest F. Hollings (D) (1922)
SOUTH DAKOTA
1979–91 Larry Pressler (R) (1942)
1987–93 Thomas A. Daschle (D) (1947)
TENNESSEE
1977–95 James R. Sasser (D) (1936)
1985–91 Albert Gore, Jr. (D) (1948)

TEXAS
1971–95 Lloyd M. Bentsen (D) (1921)
1985–91 Phil Gramm (R) (1942)
UTAH
1974–93 E.J. (Jake) Garn (R) (1932)
1977–95 Orrin G. Hatch (R) (1934)
VERMONT
1975–93 Patrick J. Leahy (D) (1940)
1989–95 James M. Jeffords (R) (1934)
VIRGINIA
1979–91 John W. Warner (R) (1927)
1989–95 Charles Robb (D) (1939)
WASHINGTON
1987–93 Brock Adams (D) (1927)
1989–95 Slade Gorton (R) (1928)
WEST VIRGINIA
1959–95 Robert C. Byrd (D) (1918)
1985–91 John D. (Jay) Rockefeller IV (D) (1937)
WISCONSIN
1981–93 Robert W. Kasten, Jr. (R) (1942)
1989–95 Herbert Kohl (D) (1935)
WYOMING
1977–95 Malcolm Wallop (R) (1933)
1979–91 Alan K. Simpson (R) (1931)

The House of Representatives

The numerals indicate the Congressional Districts of the states; the designation AL means At Large. All terms end January 1991. Mailing address of Representatives: House of Representatives, Washington, D.C. 20515

ALABAMA
(7 Representatives)
1. H.L. (Sonny) Callahan (R)
2. William L. Dickinson (R)
3. Glen Browder (D)
4. Thomas Bevill (D)
5. Ronald G. Flippo (D)
6. Ben Erdreich (D)
7. Claude Harris (D)

ALASKA
(1 Representative)
AL Don Young (R)

ARIZONA
(5 Representatives)
1. John J. (Jay) Rhodes III (R)
2. Morris Udall (D)
3. Bob Stump (R)
4. Jon Kyl (R)
5. Jim Kolbe (R)

ARKANSAS
(4 Representatives)
1. Bill Alexander (D)
2. Tommy F. Robinson (R)
3. John Hammerschmidt (R)
4. Beryl Anthony (D)

CALIFORNIA
(45 Representatives)
1. Douglas H. Bosco (D)
2. Wally Herger (R)
3. Robert T. Matsui (D)
4. Vic Fazio (D)
5. Nancy Pelosi (D)
6. Barbara Boxer (D)
7. George Miller (D)
8. Ronald V. Dellums (D)
9. Fortney H. (Pete) Stark (D)
10. Don Edwards (D)
11. Tom Lantos (D)
12. Thomas J. Campbell (R)
13. Norman Y. Mineta (D)
14. Norman D. Shumway (R)
15. Vacant
16. Leon E. Panetta (D)
17. Charles Pashayan, Jr. (R)
18. Richard H. Lehman (D)
19. Robert J. Lagomarsino (R)
20. William M. Thomas (R)
21. Elton Gallegly (R)
22. Carlos J. Moorhead (R)
23. Anthony C. Beilenson (D)
24. Henry A. Waxman (D)
25. Edward R. Roybal (D)
26. Howard L. Berman (D)
27. Mel Levine (D)
28. Julian C. Dixon (D)
29. Augustus F. Hawkins (D)
30. Matthew G. Martinez (D)
31. Mervyn M. Dymally (D)
32. Glenn M. Anderson (D)
33. David Dreier (R)
34. Esteban Edward Torres (D)
35. Jerry Lewis (R)
36. George E. Brown, Jr. (D)
37. Al McCandless (R)
38. Robert K. Dornan (R)
39. William E. Dannemeyer (R)
40. Christopher Cox (R)
41. Wiliam Lowery (R)
42. Dana Rohrabacher (R)
43. Ron Packard (R)
44. James Bates (D)
45. Duncan L. Hunter (R)

COLORADO
(6 Representatives)
1. Patricia Schroeder (D)
2. David E. Skaggs (D)
3. Ben Nighthorse Campbell (D)
4. Hank Brown (R)
5. Joel Hefley (R)
6. Daniel L. Schaefer (R)

CONNECTICUT
(6 Representatives)
1. Barbara B. Kennelly (D)
2. Sam Gejdenson (D)
3. Bruce A. Morrison (D)
4. Christopher H. Shays (R)
5. John G. Rowland (R)
6. Nancy L. Johnson (R)

DELAWARE
(1 Representative)
AL Thomas R. Carper (D)

FLORIDA
(19 Representatives)
1. Earl D. Hutto (D)
2. William Grant (R)
3. Charles E. Bennett (D)
4. Craig James (R)
5. Bill McCollum (R)
6. Cliff Stearns (R)
7. Sam Gibbons (D)
8. C.W. Bill Young (R)
9. Michael Bilirakis (R)
10. Andy Ireland (R)
11. Bill Nelson (D)
12. Tom Lewis (R)
13. Porter Goss (R)
14. Harry Johnston (D)
15. E. Clay Shaw, Jr. (R)
16. Larry Smith (D)
17. William Lehman (D)
18. Ileana Ros-Lehtineor (R)
19. Dante B. Fascell (D)

GEORGIA
(10 Representatives)
1. Robert Lindsay Thomas (D)
2. Charles Hatcher (D)
3. Richard Ray (D)
4. Ben Jones (D)
5. John Lewis (D)
6. Newt Gingrich (R)
7. George (Buddy) Darden (D)
8. J. Roy Rowland (D)
9. Edgar L. Jenkins (D)
10. Doug Barnard, Jr. (D)

HAWAII
(2 Representatives)
1. Patricia Saiki (R)
2. Daniel Akaka (D)

IDAHO
(2 Representatives)
1. Larry E. Craig (R)
2. Richard H. Stallings (D)

ILLINOIS
(22 Representatives)
1. Charles A. Hayes (D)
2. Gus Savage (D)
3. Marty Russo (D)
4. George Sangemeister (D)
5. William O. Lipinski (D)
6. Henry J. Hyde (R)
7. Cardiss Collins (D)
8. Dan Rostenkowski (D)
9. Sidney R. Yates (D)
10. John Edward Porter (R)

11. Frank Annunzio (D)
12. Philip M. Crane (R)
13. Harris W. Fawell (R)
14. J. Dennis Hastert (R)
15. Edward R. Madigan (R)
16. Lynn Martin (R)
17. Lane Evans (D)
18. Robert H. Michel (R)
19. Terry L. Bruce (D)
20. Richard Durbin (D)
21. Jerry Costello (D)
22. Glenn Poshard (D)

INDIANA
(10 Representatives)
1. Peter Visclosky (D)
2. Philip R. Sharp (D)
3. John P. Hiler (R)
4. Jill Long (D)
5. Jim Jontz (D)
6. Daniel Burton (R)
7. John T. Meyers (R)
8. Frank McCloskey (D)
9. Lee H. Hamilton (D)
10. Andrew Jacobs, Jr. (D)

IOWA
(6 Representatives)
1. Jim Leach (R)
2. Thomas J. Tauke (R)
3. Dave R. Nagle (D)
4. Neal Smith (D)
5. Jim Ross Lightfoot (R)
6. Fred Grandy (R)

KANSAS
(5 Representatives)
1. Pat Roberts (R)
2. James Slattery (D)
3. Jan Meyers (R)
4. Dan Glickman (D)
5. Bob Whittaker (R)

KENTUCKY
(7 Representatives)
1. Carroll Hubbard, Jr. (D)
2. William H. Natcher (D)
3. Romano L. Mazzoli (D)
4. Jim Bunning (R)
5. Harold Rogers (R)
6. Larry J. Hopkins (R)
7. Carl C. Perkins (D)

LOUISIANA
(8 Representatives)
1. Robert L. Livingston, Jr. (R)
2. Corrine C. (Lindy) Boggs (D)
3. W.J. (Billy) Tauzin (D)
4. Jim McCrery (R)
5. Thomas J. (Jerry) Huckaby (D)
6. Richard Baker (R)
7. Jimmy Hayes (D)
8. Clyde Holloway (R)

MAINE
(2 Representatives)
1. Joseph E. Brennan (D)
2. Olympia J. Snowe (R)

MARYLAND
(8 Representatives)
1. Roy Dyson (D)
2. Helen Delich Bentley (R)
3. Benjamin L. Cardin (D)
4. Thomas McMillen (D)
5. Steny H. Hoyer (D)
6. Beverly B. Byron (D)
7. Kweisi Mfume (D)
8. Constance A. Morella (R)

MASSACHUSETTS
(11 Representatives)
1. Silvio O. Conte (R)
2. Richard Neal (D)
3. Joseph D. Early (D)
4. Barney Frank (D)
5. Chester G. Atkins (D)
6. Nicholas Mavroules (D)
7. Edward J. Markey (D)
8. Joseph P. Kennedy II (D)
9. Joe Moakley (D)
10. Gerry E. Studds (D)
11. Brian J. Donnelly (D)

MICHIGAN
(18 Representatives)
1. John Conyers, Jr. (D)
2. Carl D. Pursell (R)
3. Howard Wolpe (D)
4. Fred Upton (R)
5. Paul B. Henry (R)
6. Bob Carr (D)
7. Dale E. Kildee (D)
8. Bob Traxler (D)
9. Guy Vander Jagt (R)
10. Bill Schuette (R)
11. Robert W. Davis (R)
12. David E. Bonior (D)
13. George W. Crockett, Jr. (D)
14. Dennis M. Hertel (D)
15. William D. Ford (D)
16. John D. Dingell (D)
17. Sander M. Levin (D)
18. William S. Broomfield (R)

MINNESOTA
(8 Representatives)
1. Timothy J. Penny (D)
2. Vin Weber (R)
3. Bill Frenzel (R)
4. Bruce F. Vento (D)
5. Martin Sabo (D)
6. Gerry Sikorski (D)
7. Arlan Strangeland (R)
8. James L. Oberstar (D)

MISSISSIPPI
(5 Representatives)
1. Jamie L. Whitten (D)
2. Mike Espy (D)
3. G.V. (Sonny) Montgomery (D)
4. Michael Parker (D)
5. Vacant

MISSOURI
(9 Representatives)
1. William L. Clay (D)
2. Jack Buechner (R)
3. Richard A. Gephardt (D)
4. Ike Skelton (D)
5. Alan Wheat (D)
6. E. Thomas Coleman (R)
7. Mel Hancock (R)
8. William Emerson (R)
9. Harold L. Volkmer (D)

MONTANA
(2 Representatives)
1. Pat Williams (D)
2. Ron Marlenee (R)

NEBRASKA
(3 Representatives)
1. Douglas K. Bereuther (R)
2. Peter Hoagland (D)
3. Virginia Smith (R)

NEVADA
(2 Representatives)
1. James H. Bilbray (D)
2. Barbara F. Vucanovich (R)

NEW HAMPSHIRE
(2 Representatives)
1. Robert C. Smith (R)
2. Chuck Douglas (R)

NEW JERSEY
(14 Representatives)
1. James J. Florio (D)
2. William J. Hughes (D)
3. Frank Pallone (D)
4. Christopher H. Smith (R)
5. Marge Roukema (R)
6. Bernard J. Dwyer (D)
7. Matthew J. Rinaldo (R)
8. Robert A. Roe (D)
9. Robert G. Torricelli (D)
10. Donald Payne (D)
11. Dean A. Gallo (R)
12. James Courter (R)
13. H. James Saxton (R)
14. Frank Guarini (D)

NEW MEXICO
(3 Representatives)
1. Steve Schiff (R)
2. Joseph R. Skeen (R)
3. William Richardson (D)

NEW YORK
(34 Representatives)
1. George J. Hochbreuckner (D)
2. Thomas J. Downey (D)
3. Robert J. Mrazek (D)
4. Norman F. Lent (R)
5. Raymond J. McGrath (R)
6. Floyd H. Flake (D)
7. Gary L. Ackerman (D)
8. James H. Scheuer (D)
9. Thomas J. Manton (D)
10. Charles E. Schumer (D)
11. Edolphus Towns (D)
12. Major R. Owens (D)
13. Stephen J. Solarz (D)
14. Guy V. Molinari (R)
15. S. William Green (R)
16. Charles B. Rangel (D)
17. Ted Weiss (D)
18. Robert Garcia (D)
19. Elliott Engel (D)
20. Nita Lowey (D)
21. Hamilton Fish, Jr. (R)
22. Benjamin A. Gilman (R)
23. Michael McNulty (D)
24. Gerald B.H. Solomon (R)
25. Sherwood Boehlert (R)
26. David O'B. Martin (R)
27. James Walsh (R)
27. James Walsh (R)
28. Matther F. McHugh (D)
29. Frank Horton (R)
30. Louise M. Slaughter (D)
31. L. William Paxon (R)
32. John L. LaFalce (D)
33. Henry J. Nowak (D)
34. Amory Houghton, Jr. (R)

NORTH CAROLINA
(11 Representatives)
1. Walter B. Jones (D)
2. Tim Valentine (D)
3. Martin Lancaster (D)
4. David E. Price (D)
5. Stephen L. Neal (D)
6. Howard Coble (R)
7. Charlie Rose (D)
8. W.G. (Bill) Hefner (D)
9. J. Alex McMillan (R)
10. Cass Ballenger (R)
11. James McClure Clarke (D)

NORTH DAKOTA
(1 Representative)
AL Byron L. Dorgan (D)

OHIO
(21 Representatives)
1. Thomas A. Luken (D)
2. Willis D. Gradison, Jr. (R)
3. Tony P. Hall (D)
4. Michael G. Oxley (R)
5. Paul Gillmor (R)
6. Bob McEwen (R)
7. Michael DeWine (R)
8. Donald E. (Buz) Lukens (R)
9. Marcy Kaptur (D)

10. Clarence E. Miller (R)
11. Dennis E. Eckart (D)
12. John R. Kasich (R)
13. Don J. Pease (D)
14. Tom Sawyer (D)
15. Chalmers Wylie (R)
16. Ralph Regula (R)
17. James A. Traficant, Jr. (D)
18. Douglas Applegate (D)
19. Edward F. Feighan (D)
20. Mary Rose Oakar (D)
21. Louis Stokes (D)

OKLAHOMA
(6 Representatives)
1. James M. Inhofe (R)
2. Mike Synar (D)
3. Wesley W. Watkins (D)
4. Dave McCurdy (D)
5. Mickey Edwards (R)
6. Glenn English (D)

OREGON
(5 Representatives)
1. Les AuCoin (D)
2. Robert F. Smith (R)
3. Ronald L. Wyden (D)
4. Peter A. De Fazio (D)
5. Denny Smith (R)

PENNSYLVANIA
(23 Representatives)
1. Thomas M. Foglietta (D)
2. William H. Gray III (D)
3. Robert A. Borski (D)
4. Joseph P. Kolter (D)
5. Richard T. Schulze (R)
6. Gus Yatron (D)
7. Curt Weldon (R)
8. Peter H. Kostmayer (D)
9. E.G. Shuster (R)
10. Joseph M. McDade (R)
11. Paul E. Kanjorski (D)
12. John P. Murtha (D)
13. Lawrence Coughlin (R)
14. William J. Coyne (D)
15. Don Ritter (R)
16. Robert S. Walker (R)
17. George W. Gekas (R)
18. Doug Walgren (D)
19. William F. Goodling (R)
20. Joseph M. Gaydos (D)
21. Tom Ridge (R)
22. Austin J. Murphy (D)
23. William F. Clinger (R)

RHODE ISLAND
(2 Representatives)
1. Ronald Machtley (R)
2. Claudine J. Schneider (R)

SOUTH CAROLINA
(6 Representatives)
1. Arthur Ravenel, Jr. (R)
2. Floyd Spence (R)
3. Butler Derrick (D)
4. Elizabeth J. Patterson (D)
5. John M. Spratt, Jr. (D)
6. Robin Tallon (D)

SOUTH DAKOTA
(1 Representative)
AL Tim Johnson (D)

TENNESSEE
(9 Representatives)
1. James H. Quillen (R)
2. James Duncan (R)
3. Marilyn Lloyd (D)
4. James Cooper (D)
5. Robert Clement (D)
6. Bart Gordon (D)
7. Don Sundquist (R)
8. John Tanner (D)
9. Harold E. Ford (D)

TEXAS
27 Representatives)
1. Jim Chapman (D)
2. Charles Wilson (D)
3. Steven Bartlett (R)
4. Ralph M. Hall (D)
5. John Bryant (D)
6. Joe L. Barton (R)
7. William Archer (R)
8. Jack Fields (R)
9. Jack Brooks (D)
10. J.J. Pickle (D)
11. Marvin Leath (D)
12. Vacant
13. William Sarpalius (D)
14. Greg Laughlin (D)
15. E. (Kika) de la Garza (D)
16. Ronald D. Coleman (D)
17. Charles W. Stenholm (D)
18. Vacant
19. Larry Combest (R)
20. Henry B. Gonzalez (D)
21. Lamar Smith (R)
22. Thomas D. Delay (R)
23. Albert G. Bustamante (D)
24. Martin Frost (D)

25. Michael A. Andrews (D)
26. Richard Armey (R)
27. Solomon P. Ortiz (D)

UTAH
(3 Representatives)
1. James V. Hansen (R)
2. Wayne Owens (D)
3. Howard C. Nielson (R)

VERMONT
(1 Representative)
AL Peter Smith (R)

VIRGINIA
(10 Representatives)
1. Herbert H. Bateman (R)
2. Owen B. Pickett (D)
3. Thomas J. Bliley, Jr. (R)
4. Norman Sisisky (D)
5. L.F. Payne (D)
6. James R. Olin (D)
7. D. French Slaughter (R)
8. Stan Parris (R)
9. Frederick C. Boucher (D)
10. Frank R. Wolf (R)

WASHINGTON
(8 Representatives)
1. John R. Miller (R)
2. Al Swift (D)
3. Jolene Unsoeld (D)
4. Sid W. Morrison (R)
5. Thomas S. Foley (D)
6. Norman D. Dicks (D)
7. James McDermott (D)
8. Rodney Chandler (R)

WESTWEST VIRGINIA
(4 Representatives)
1. Alan B. Mollohan (D)
2. Harley O. Staggers, Jr. (D)
3. Robert Wise (D)
4. Nick J. Rahall (D)

WISCONSIN
(9 Representatives)
1. Les Aspin (D)
2. Robert W. Kastenmeier (D)
3. Steve Gunderson (R)
4. Gerald D. Kleczka (D)
5. James Moody (D)
6. Thomas E. Petri (R)
7. David P. Obey (D)
8. Toby Roth (R)
9. F. James Sensenbrenner, Jr. (R)

WYOMING
(1 Representative)
AL Craig Thomas (R)

Characteristics of Voters in 1988 Presidential Election

(in thousands)

Characteristic	Persons of voting age	Persons reporting they voted		Persons reporting they did not vote	Characteristic	Persons of voting age	Persons reporting they voted		Persons reporting they did not vote
		Total	Percent				Total	Percent	
Male	84,531	47,704	56.4	36,826	North and West	117,373	69,129	58.9	48,243
Female	93,568	54,519	58.3	39,048	South	60,725	33,094	54.5	27,631
White	152,848	90,357	59.1	62,492	Education				
Black	19,692	10,144	51.5	9,548	8 years or less	19,145	7,025	36.7	12,120
Spanish origin[1]	12,893	3,710	28.8	9,183	9-11 years	21,052	8,698	41.3	12,354
Age: 18-20	10,742	3,570	33.2	7,172	12 years	70,033	38,328	54.7	31,706
21-24	14,827	5,684	38.3	9,142	13-15 years	34,264	22,090	64.5	12,174
25-34	42,677	20,468	48.0	22,210	16 or more	33,604	26,083	77.6	7,521
35-44	35,186	21,550	61.2	13,636	Employed	113,836	66,510	58.4	47,327
45-54	24,277	16,170	66.6	8,107	Unemployed	5,809	2,243	38.6	3,565
55-64	21,585	14,964	69.3	6,621	Not in labor force	58,453	33,471	57.3	24,983
65-74	17,578	12,840	73.0	4,738	**Total**	178,098	102,224	57.4	75,875
75 and over	11,226	6,978	62.2	4,248					

NOTE: Persons of Spanish origin may be of any race. *Source:* Department of Commerce, Bureau of Commerce, Bureau of the Census, *Current Population Survey,* November 1988.

Senate and House Standing Committees, 101st Congress

Committees of the Senate

Agriculture, Nutrition, and Forestry (19 members)
Chairman: Patrick J. Leahy (Vt.)
Ranking Rep.: Richard G. Luger (Ind.)
Appropriations (29 members)
Chairman: Robert C. Byrd (W.Va.)
Ranking Rep.: Mark O. Hatfield (Ore.)
Armed Services (19 members)
Chairman: Sam Nunn (Ga.)
Ranking Rep.: John Warner (Va.)
Banking, Housing, and Urban Affairs (21 members)
Chairman: Donald W. Riegle (Mich.)
Ranking Rep.: E. J. (Jake) Garn (Utah)
Budget (23 members)
Chairman: James R. Sasser (Tenn.)
Ranking Rep.: Pete V. Domenici (N.M.)
Commerce, Science, and Transportation
  (20 members)
Chairman: Ernest F. Hollings (S.C.)
Ranking Rep.: John C. Danforth (Mo.)
Energy and Natural Resources (19 members)
Chairman: J. Bennett Johnston (La.)
Ranking Rep.: James A. McClure (Idaho)
Environment and Public Works (16 members)
Chairman: Quentin N. Burdick (N.D.)
Ranking Rep.: John H. Chafee (R.I.)
Finance (20 members)
Chairman: Lloyd M. Bentsen (Texas)
Ranking Rep.: Bob Packwood (Ore.)
Foreign Relations (19 members)
Chairman: Claiborne Pell (R.I.)
Ranking Rep.: Jesse Helms (N.C.)
Governmental Affairs (14 members)
Chairman: John Glenn (Ohio)
Ranking Rep.: William V. Roth, Jr. (Del.)
Judiciary (14 members)
Chairman: Joseph R. Biden, Jr. (Del)
Ranking Rep.: Strom Thurmond (S.C.)
Labor and Human Resources (16 members)
Chairman: Edward M. Kennedy (Mass.)
Ranking Rep.: Orrin G. Hatch (Utah)
Rules and Administration (16 members)
Chairman: Wendell H. Ford (Ky.)
Ranking Rep.: Ted Stevens (Alas.)
Small Business (19 members)
Chairman: Dale Bumpers (Ark.)
Ranking Rep.: Rudy Boschwitz (Minn.)
Veterans' Affairs (11 members)
Chairman: Alan Cranston (Calif.)
Ranking Rep: Frank H. Murkowski (Alas.)

Select and Special Committees

Aging (19 members)
Chairman: David H. Pryor (Ark.)
Ranking Rep.: John Heinz (Pa.)
Ethics (6 members)
Chairman: Howell T. Heflin (Ala.)
Ranking Rep.: Warren Rudman (N.H.)
Indian Affairs (8 members)
Chairman: Daniel K. Inouye (Hawaii)
Ranking Rep.: Frank H. Murkowski (Alas.)
Intelligence (15 members)
Chairman: David L. Boren (Okla.)
Ranking Rep.: William S. Cohen (Me.)

Committees of the House

Agriculture (43 members)
Chairman: E. (Kika) de la Garza (Texas)
Ranking Rep.: Edward R. Madigan (Ill.)

Appropriations (57 members)
Chairman: Jamie L. Whitten (Miss.)
Ranking Rep.: Silvio O. Conte (Mass.)
Armed Services (52 members)
Chairman: Les Aspin (Wis.)
Ranking Rep.: William L. Dickinson (Ala.)
Banking, Finance, and Urban Affairs (52 members)
Chairman: Henry B. Gonzalez (Texas)
Ranking Rep.: Chalmers P. Wylie (Ohio)
Budget (36 members)
Chairman: Leon E. Panetta (Calif.)
Ranking Rep.: Bill Frenzel (Minn.)
District of Columbia (11 members)
Chairman: Ronald V. Dellums (Calif.)
Ranking Rep.: Stanford E. Parris (Va.)
Education and Labor (35 members)
Chairman: Augustus F. Hawkins (Calif.)
Ranking Rep.: William F. Goodling (Pa.)
Energy and Commerce (43 members)
Chairman: John D. Dingell (Mich.)
Ranking Rep.: Norman Lent (N.Y.)
Foreign Affairs (45 members)
Chairman: Dante B. Fascell (Fla.)
Ranking Rep.: William S. Broomfield (Mich.)
Government Operations (39 members)
Chairman: John Conyers, Jr. (Mich.)
Ranking Rep.: Frank Horton (N.Y.)
House Administration (20 members)
Chairman: Frank Annunzio (Ill.)
Ranking Rep.: Newt Gingrich (Ga.)
Interior and Insular Affairs (41 members)
Chairman: Morris K. Udall (Ariz.)
Ranking Rep.: Don Young (Alas.)
Judiciary (35 members)
Chairman: Jack Brooks (Texas)
Ranking Rep.: Hamilton Fish, Jr. (N.Y.)
Merchant Marine and Fisheries (43 members)
Chairman: Walter B. Jones (N.C.)
Ranking Rep.: Robert W. Davis (Mich.)
Post Office and Civil Service (21 members)
Chairman: William D. Ford (Mich.)
Ranking Rep.: Benjamin Gilman (N.Y.)
Public Works and Transportation (51 members)
Chairman: Glenn Anderson (Calif.)
Ranking Rep.: John P. Hammerschmidt (Ark.)
Rules (13 members)
Chairman: Vacant
Ranking Rep.: James H. Quillen (Tenn.)
Science, Space, and Technology (48 members)
Chairman: Robert A. Roe (N.J.)
Ranking Rep.: Robert S. Walker (Pa.)
Small Business (43 members)
Chairman: John J. LaFalce (N.Y.)
Ranking Rep.: Joseph M. McDade (Pa.)
Standards of Official Conduct (12 members)
Chairman: Julian C. Dixon (Calif.)
Ranking Rep.: John T. Myers (Ind.)
Veterans' Affairs (34 members)
Chairman: G. V. (Sonny) Montgomery (Miss.)
Ranking Rep.: Bob Stump (Ariz.)
Ways and Means (36 members)
Chairman: Dan Rostenkowski (Ill.)
Ranking Rep.: William Archer (Texas)

Select Committees

Aging (62 members)
Chairman: Edward Roybal (Calif.)
Ranking Rep.: Matthew J. Rinaldo (N.J.)

Children, Youth, and Families (30 members)
Chairman: George Miller (Calif.)
Ranking Rep.: Thomas Bliley (Va.)
Hunger (25 members)
Chairman: Vacant
Ranking Rep.: William Emerson (Mo.)

Intelligence (20 members)
Chairman: Anthony C. Beilenson (Calif.)
Ranking Rep.: Henry Hyde (Ill.)
Narcotics Abuse and Control (27 members)
Chairman: Charles B. Rangel (N.Y.)
Ranking Rep.: Lawrence Coughlin (Pa.)

Speakers of the House of Representatives

Dates served	Congress	Name and state	Dates served	Congress	Name and state
1789–1791	1	Frederick A. C. Muhlenberg (Pa.)	1863–1869	38–40	Schuyler Colfax (Ind.)
1791–1793	2	Jonathan Trumbull (Conn.)	1869–1869	40	Theodore M. Pomeroy (N.Y.)[5]
1793–1795	3	Frederick A. C. Muhlenberg (Pa.)	1869–1875	41–43	James G. Blaine (Me.)
1795–1799	4–5	Jonathan Dayton (N.J.)[1]	1875–1876	44	Michael C. Kerr (Ind.)[6]
1799–1801	6	Theodore Sedgwick (Mass.)	1876–1881	44–46	Samuel J. Randall (Pa.)
1801–1807	7–9	Nathaniel Macon (N.C.)	1881–1883	47	J. Warren Keifer (Ohio)
1807–1811	10–11	Joseph B. Varnum (Mass.)	1883–1889	48–50	John G. Carlisle (Ky.)
1811–1814	12–13	Henry Clay (Ky.)[2]	1889–1891	51	Thomas B. Reed (Me.)
1814–1815	13	Langdon Cheves (S.C.)	1891–1895	52–53	Charles F. Crisp (Ga.)
1815–1820	14–16	Henry Clay (Ky.)[3]	1895–1899	54–55	Thomas B. Reed (Me.)
1820–1821	16	John W. Taylor (N.Y.)	1899–1903	56–57	David B. Henderson (Iowa)
1821–1823	17	Philip P. Barbour (Va.)	1903–1911	58–61	Joseph G. Cannon (Ill.)
1823–1825	18	Henry Clay (Ky.)	1911–1919	62–65	Champ Clark (Mo.)
1825–1827	19	John W. Taylor (N.Y.)	1919–1925	66–68	Frederick H. Gillett (Mass.)
1827–1834	20–23	Andrew Stevenson (Va.)[4]	1925–1931	69–71	Nicholas Longworth (Ohio)
1834–1835	23	John Bell (Tenn.)	1931–1933	72	John N. Garner (Tex.)
1835–1839	24–25	James K. Polk (Tenn.)	1933–1934	73	Henry T. Rainey (Ill.)[7]
1839–1841	26	Robert M. T. Hunter (Va.)	1935–1936	74	Joseph W. Byrns (Tenn.)[8]
1841–1843	27	John White (Ky.)	1936–1940	74–76	William B. Bankhead (Ala.)[9]
1843–1845	28	John W. Jones (Va.)	1940–1947	76–79	Sam Rayburn (Tex.)
1845–1847	29	John W. Davis (Ind.)	1947–1949	80	Joseph W. Martin, Jr. (Mass.)
1847–1849	30	Robert C. Winthrop (Mass.)	1949–1953	81–82	Sam Rayburn (Tex.)
1849–1851	31	Howell Cobb (Ga.)	1953–1955	83	Joseph W. Martin, Jr. (Mass.)
1851–1855	32–33	Linn Boyd (Ky.)	1955–1961	84–87	Sam Rayburn (Tex.)[10]
1855–1857	34	Nathaniel P. Banks (Mass.)	1962–1971	87–91	John W. McCormack (Mass.)[11]
1857–1859	35	James L. Orr (S.C.)	1971–1977	92–94	Carl Albert (Okla.)[12]
1859–1861	36	Wm. Pennington (N.J.)	1977–1987	95–99	Thomas P. O'Neill, Jr. (Mass.)[13]
1861–1863	37	Galusha A. Grow (Pa.)	1987–1989	100–101	James C. Wright, Jr. (Tex.)[14]
			1989–	101–	Thomas S. Foley (Wash.)

1. George Dent (Md.) was elected Speaker pro tempore for April 20 and May 28, 1798. 2. Resigned during second session of 13th Congress. 3. Resigned between first and second sessions of 16th Congress. 4. Resigned during first session of 23rd Congress. 5. Elected Speaker and served the day of adjournment. 6. Died between first and second sessions of 44th Congress. During first session, there were two Speakers pro tempore: Samuel S. Cox (N.Y.), appointed for Feb. 17, May 12, and June 19, 1876, and Milton Sayler (Ohio), appointed for June 4, 1876. 7. Died in 1934 after adjournment of second session of 73rd Congress. 8. Died during second session of 74th Congress. 9. Died during third session of 76th Congress. 10. Died between first and second sessions of 87th Congress. 11. Not a candidate in 1970 election. 12. Not a candidate in 1976 election. 13. Not a candidate in 1986 election. 14. Resigned during first session of 101st Congress. *Source: Congressional Directory.*

Floor Leaders of the Senate

Democratic	Republican
Gilbert M. Hitchcock, Neb. (Min. 1919–20)	Charles Curtis, Kan. (Maj. 1925–29)
Oscar W. Underwood, Ala. (Min. 1920–23)	James E. Watson, Ind. (Maj. 1929–33)
Joseph T. Robinson, Ark. (Min. 1923–33, Maj. 1933–37)	Charles L. McNary, Ore. (Min. 1933–44)
Alben W. Barkley, Ky. (Maj. 1937–46, Min. 1947–48)	Wallace H. White, Jr., Me. (Min. 1944–47, Maj. 1947–48)
Scott W. Lucas, Ill. (Maj. 1949–50)	Kenneth S. Wherry, Neb. (Min. 1949–51)
Ernest W. McFarland, Ariz. (Maj. 1951–52)	Styles Bridges, N. H. (Min. 1951–52)
Lyndon B. Johnson, Tex. (Min. 1953–54, Maj. 1955–60)	Robert A. Taft, Ohio (Maj. 1953)
Mike Mansfield, Mont. (Maj. 1961–77)	William F. Knowland, Calif. (Maj. 1953–54, Min. 1955–58)
Robert C. Byrd, W. Va. (Maj. 1977–81, Min. 1981–86, Maj. 1987–88))	Everett M. Dirksen, Ill. (Min. 1959–69)
George John Mitchell, Me. (Maj. 1989–)	Hugh Scott, Pa. (Min. 1969–1977)
	Howard H. Baker, Jr., Tenn. (Min. 1977–81, Maj. 1981–84)
	Robert J. Dole, Kan. (Maj. 1985–86, Min. 1987–)

NOTE: Min. = Minority Leader; Maj. = Majority Leader. *Source:* United States Senate, Secretary for the Majority.

Presidential Election of 1988

Principal Candidates for President and Vice President
Republican: George H. Bush; J. Danforth Quayle
Democratic: Michael S. Dukakis; Lloyd Bentsen

State	Total	Bush Rep.	Per-cent	Dukakis Dem.	Per-cent	Plurality	Electoral vote R	Electoral vote D
Alabama	1,378,476	815,576	59.17	549,506	39.86	266,070	9	—
Alaska	200,116	119,251	59.59	72,584	36.27	46,667	3	—
Arizona	1,171,873	702,541	59.95	454,029	38.74	248,512	7	—
Arkansas	827,738	466,578	56.37	349,237	42.19	117,341	6	—
California	9,887,065	5,054,917	51.13	4,702,233	47.56	352,684	47	—
Colorado	1,372,394	728,177	53.06	621,453	45.28	106,724	8	—
Connecticut	1,443,394	750,241	51.98	676,584	46.87	73,657	8	—
Delaware	249,891	139,639	55.88	108,647	43.48	30,992	3	—
D.C.	192,877	27,590	14.30	159,407	82.65	131,817	—	3
Florida	4,302,313	2,618,885	60.87	1,656,701	38.51	962,184	21	—
Georgia	1,809,672	1,081,331	59.75	714,792	39.50	366,539	12	—
Hawaii	354,461	158,625	44.75	192,364	54.27	33,739	—	4
Idaho	408,968	253,881	62.08	147,272	36.01	106,609	4	—
Illinois	4,559,120	2,310,939	50.69	2,215,940	48.60	94,999	24	—
Indiana	2,168,621	1,297,763	59.84	860,643	39.69	437,120	12	—
Iowa	1,225,614	545,355	44.50	670,557	54.71	125,202	—	8
Kansas	993,044	554,049	55.79	422,636	42.56	131,413	7	—
Kentucky	1,322,517	734,281	55.52	580,368	43.88	153,913	9	—
Louisiana	1,628,202	883,702	54.27	717,460	44.06	166,242	10	—
Maine	555,035	307,131	55.34	243,569	43.88	63,562	4	—
Maryland	1,714,358	876,167	51.11	826,304	48.20	49,863	10	—
Massachusetts	2,632,805	1,194,635	45.38	1,401,415	53.23	206,780	—	13
Michigan	3,669,163	1,965,486	53.57	1,675,783	45.67	289,703	20	—
Minnesota	2,096,790	962,337	45.90	1,109,471	52.91	147,134	—	10
Mississippi	931,527	557,890	59.89	363,921	39.07	193,969	7	—
Missouri	2,093,713	1,084,953	51.82	1,001,619	47.84	83,334	11	—
Montana	365,674	190,412	52.07	168,936	46.20	21,476	4	—
Nebraska	661,465	397,956	60.16	259,235	39.19	138,721	5	—
Nevada	350,067	206,040	58.86	132,738	37.92	73,302	4	—
New Hampshire	451,074	281,537	62.41	163,696	36.29	117,841	4	—
New Jersey	3,099,553	1,743,192	56.24	1,320,352	42.60	422,840	16	—
New Mexico	521,287	270,341	51.86	244,497	46.90	25,844	5	—
New York[1]	6,485,683	3,081,871	47.52	3,347,882	51.62	266,011	—	36
North Carolina	2,134,370	1,237,258	57.97	890,167	41.71	347,091	13	—
North Dakota	297,261	166,559	56.03	127,739	42.97	38,820	3	—
Ohio	4,393,699	2,416,549	55.00	1,939,629	44.15	476,920	23	—
Oklahoma	1,171,036	678,367	57.93	483,423	41.28	194,944	8	—
Oregon	1,201,694	560,126	46.61	616,206	51.28	56,080	—	7
Pennsylvania	4,536,251	2,300,087	50.70	2,194,944	48.39	105,143	25	—
Rhode Island	404,620	177,761	43.93	225,123	55.64	47,362	—	4
South Carolina	986,009	606,443	61.50	370,554	37.58	235,889	8	—
South Dakota	312,991	165,415	52.85	145,560	46.51	19,855	3	—
Tennessee	1,636,250	947,233	57.89	679,794	41.55	267,439	11	—
Texas	5,427,410	3,036,829	55.95	2,352,748	43.35	684,081	29	—
Utah	647,008	428,442	66.22	207,343	32.05	221,099	5	—
Vermont	243,328	124,331	51.10	115,775	47.58	8,556	3	—
Virginia	2,191,609	1,309,162	59.74	859,799	39.23	449,363	12	—
Washington	1,865,253	903,835	48.46	933,516	50.05	29,681	—	10
West Virginia	653,311	310,065	47.46	341,016	52.20	30,951	—	6
Wisconsin	2,191,608	1,047,499	47.80	1,126,794	51.41	79,295	—	11
Wyoming	176,551	106,867	60.53	67,113	38.01	39,754	3	—
Total	91,594,809	48,886,097	53.37	41,809,074	45.65	7,077,023	426	112

1. Bush figure is combined Republican and Conservative Party votes; Dukakis figure is combined Democratic and Liberal Party votes. NATIONAL TOTALS OF OTHER CANDIDATES FOR PRESIDENT: Ronald E. Paul, Libertarian, 432,179; Lenora B. Fulani, New Alliance, 217,219; David Duke, Populist, 47,047; Eugene J. McCarthy, Consumer, 30,905; James C. Griffin, American Independent; 27,818; Lyndon H. LaRouche, National Economic, 25,562; William A. Marra, Right to Life, 20,504; Ed Winn, Workers League, 18,693; James Mac Warren, Socialist Workers, 15,604; Herbert Lewin, Peace & Freedom, 10,370; Earl Dodge, Prohibition, 8,002; Larry Holmes, Workers World, 7,846; Willa Kenoyer, Socialist, 3,882; Delmar Dennis, American, 3,475; Jack Herer, GrassRoots, 1,949; Louie G. Youngkeit, Independent, 372; John G. Martin, Third World Assembly, 236; write-ins and None of the Above, 27,975. Source: Federal Elections 88, Federal Election Commission.

The Governors of the Fifty States

State	Governor	Current term[1]	State	Governor	Current term[1]
Ala.	Guy Hunt (R)	1987–91	Mont.	Stanley Stephens (R)	1989–93
Alaska	Steve Cowper (D)	1986–90[2]	Neb.	Kay A. Orr (R)	1987–91
Ariz.	Rose Mofford (D)	1988–91	Nev.	Richard H. Byran (D)	1987–91
Ark.	Bill Clinton (D)	1987–91	N.H.	Judd Gregg (R)	1989–93
Calif.	George Deukmejian (R)	1987–91	N.J.	Thomas H. Kean (R)	1986–90
Colo.	Roy Romer (D)	1987–91	N.M.	Garrey E. Carruthers (R)	1987–91
Conn.	William A. O'Neill (D)	1987–91	N.Y.	Mario M. Cuomo (D)	1987–91
Del.	Michael Castle (R)	1989–93	N.C.	James G. Martin (R)	1989–93
Fla.	Bob Martinez (R)	1987–91	N.D.	George A. Sinner (D)	1989–93
Ga.	Joe Frank Harris (D)	1987–91	Ohio	Richard F. Celeste (D)	1987–91
Hawaii	John Waihee (D)	1986–90[2]	Okla.	Henry Bellmon (R)	1987–91
Idaho	Cecil D. Andrus (D)	1987–91	Ore.	Neil Goldschmidt (D)	1987–91
Ill.	James R. Thompson (R)	1987–91	Pa.	Robert P. Casey (D)	1987–91
Ind.	B. Evan Bayh III (R)	1989–93	R.I.	Edward D. DiPrete (R)	1989–92
Iowa	Terry E. Branstad (R)	1987–91	S.C.	Carroll A. Campbell, Jr. (R)	1987–91
Kan.	Mike Hayden (R)	1987–91	S.D.	George Mickelson (R)	1987–91
Ky.	Wallace Wilkinson (D)	1987–91[2]	Tenn.	Ned Ray McWherter (D)	1987–91
La.	Charles (Buddy) Roemer (D)	1988–92[3]	Tex.	William P. Clements (R)	1987–91
Me.	John R. McKernan, Jr. (R)	1987–91	Utah	Norman H. Bangerter (R)	1989–93
Md.	William Donald Schaefer (D)	1987–91	Vt.	Madeline M. Kunin (D)	1989–93
Mass.	Michael S. Dukakis (D)	1987–91	Va.	Gerald L. Baliles (D)	1986–90
Mich.	James J. Blanchard (D)	1987–91	Wash.	Booth Gardner (D)	1989–93
Minn.	Rudy Perpich (D)	1987–91	W. Va.	Gaston Caperton (D)	1989–93
Miss.	Ray Mabus (D)	1988–92	Wis.	Tommy G. Thompson (R)	1987–91
Mo.	John D. Ashcroft (R)	1989–93	Wyo.	Mike J. Sullivan (D)	1987–91

1. Except where indicated, all terms begin in January. 2. December. 3. March.

Black Elected Officials

Year	U.S. and State Legislatures[1]	City and County Offices[2]	Law Enforcement[3]	Education[4]	Total
1970 (Feb.)	182	715	213	362	1,472
1975 (Apr.)	299	1,878	387	939	3,503
1976 (Apr.)	299	2,274	412	994	3,979
1977 (July)	316	2,497	447	1,051	4,311
1978 (July)	316	2,595	454	1,138	4,503
1979 (July)	315	2,647	486	1,136	4,584
1980 (July)	326	2,832	526	1,206	4,890
1981 (July)	343	2,863	549	1,259	5,014
1982 (July)	342	2,951	563	1,259	5,115
1983 (July)	366	3,197	607	1,369	5,559
1984 (Jan.)	396	3,259	636	1,363	5,654
1985 (Jan.)	407	3,517	661	1,431	6,016[5]
1986 (Jan.)	420	3,824	676	1,504	6,424[5]
1987 (Jan.)	440	3,966	728	1,547	6,681
1988 (July)	436	4,105	738	1,550	6,829
1989 (Jan.)	448	4,406	759	1,612	7,225

1. Includes elected State administrators. 2. County commissioners and councilmen, mayors, vice mayors, aldermen, regional officials, and other. 3. Judges, magistrates, constables, marshals, sheriffs, justices of the peace, and other. 4. Members of State education agencies, college boards, school boards, and other. 5. Includes Black elected officials in the Virgin Islands. *Source:* Joint Center for Political Studies, Washington, D.C., *Black Elected Officials: A National Roster*, Copyright.

Annual Salaries of Federal Officials

President of the U.S.	$200,000[1]	Secretaries of the Army, Navy, Air Force	89,500
Vice President of the U.S.	115,000[2]	Senators and Representatives	89,500
Cabinet members	99,500	President Pro Tempore of Senate	89,500
Under secretaries of executive departments	82,500	Majority and Minority Leader of the Senate	89,500
Deputy Secretaries of State, Defense, Treasury	89,500	Majority and Minority Leader of the House	89,500
Deputy Attorney General	89,500	Speaker of the House	115,800
Under Secretary of Transportation	82,500	Chief Justice of the United States	115,000
		Associate Justices of the Supreme Court	110,000

1. Plus taxable $50,000 for expenses and a nontaxable sum (not to exceed $100,000 a year) for travel expenses. 2. Plus taxable $10,000 for expenses. NOTE: All salaries shown above are taxable. Data are as of August 1989. President Bush has proposed increases but the measure has not been voted on as yet. *Source: Federal Register*, Vol. 53, No. 2.

BUSINESS & ECONOMY

Eight Forecasts for U.S. Banking

By Burnham P. Beckwith

Cash money may become illegal in the future for all but very small transactions, suggests a noted social scientist and futurist.

There are eight major reforms that I predict will be largely or entirely completed before the year 2100. These reforms will transform the monetary and banking system far more radically than all earlier reforms since the creation of the system.

Most of these reforms are already being achieved. The order in which they are described below is not meant to indicate the precise chronological order in which they are to be begun or completed. Most of them will occur simultaneously.

Cash Will Be Replaced

The use of bank checks and check substitutes to make monetary payments has been growing almost steadily in the United States since 1800. It is estimated that in 1980 about 80% of all legal payments were made by check. This percentage will continue to rise until all payments of over $10, and many for smaller amounts, are made by check or by electronic fund transfer.

*　　*　　*

One of the first new steps in this direction will be the gradual withdrawal from circulation of large-denomination paper money. By 2050, no paper money with a value (in 1985 values) of more than $10 will remain in circulation. This reform alone will have a significant effect on crime because many illegal payments are made in large-denomination paper money.

After all large-denomination paper money has been withdrawn from circulation or declared invalid, the U.S. government will gradually limit the use of cash to pay rent, buy autos, or make any other payment of more than some increasingly small maximum amount. By 2100, all such use of cash will be prohibited. . . .

Bank Records Will Be Used to Prevent Crime

The use of checks leaves bank records that can be used, and increasingly will be used, by government agencies to enforce payment of taxes and to prevent and detect all crimes involving the theft or payment of money. For instance, restrictions on the use of cash will eventually not only make it almost impossible for dealers in illegal drugs to buy or sell such drugs, but will make it impossible for all criminals to obtain or spend illegal income. . . .

To facilitate such police review, the government will require that each person have only one personal checking account and that he receive all income and make all payments through this account. As a result, each person will receive periodic bank statements on standardized statement forms designed to make all unusual or suspicious entries conspicuous to the police. . . .

A Demand-Deposit and Check-Handling Monopoly

The third major reform will be the creation of a single national agency for checking accounts. This new agency will not be a commercial bank because it will make no loans.

The function of holding demand deposits and clearing checks (and check substitutes) on such deposits will be taken from all other financial institutions and will be entrusted to the new agency, which will have no function other than debiting and crediting the demand deposits of its millions of depositors. It will not accept savings deposits, create demand deposits, make loans, or perform any function other than holding demand deposits and transferring them from one bank account to another by simple accounting entries. This central clearinghouse will need only one giant computer and will probably employ fewer than 1,000 workers. . . .

*　　*　　*

A Security-Brokerage Monopoly

Most of the arguments for concentrating all transfers of demand accounts in a single national office can be used to justify a like concentration of all security transfers. It is just as wasteful to spend money on transporting securities from one brokerage office to another as to spend money on transporting checks from one bank to another. Therefore, in time, a single national security-brokerage agency that holds, and transfers titles to, all securities will be created, probably before the year 2100. The prices paid will probably be determined automatically by a computer complex programmed to fix prices that balance supply and demand.

*　　*　　*

Burnham P. Beckwith was an economist and independent writer who had written several books and essays on future social, political, and economic trends. He was the author of *The Future of Money and Banking* (B.P. Beckwith, 1987. Out of print.) Mr. Beckwith died in February 1989.

This article is excerpted with permission from *The Futurist,* March-April 1989. Copyright © 1989 World Future Society. *The Futurist* is a publication of The World Future Society, 4916 Saint Elmo Ave., Bethesda, Md. 20814.

This article expresses the opinion of the author, not *Information Please Almanac,* and is presented herein because it challenges much of current economic thought. It is reprinted with the permission of the author's estate.

The deposit of all securities in the vaults of a single national brokerage agency will not only save the high costs of locating, counting, verifying, and transporting these securities whenever they are transferred from one owner to another, but will also greatly reduce both storage costs and losses from thefts, embezzlement, and fire. If anyone tries to sell securities he does not own, the national brokerage agency will find it easy to detect this illegal effort, or to reverse the sale after it has been found to be illegal. No seller will be paid in cash, and illegal demand-deposit payments will be easily reversible. Moreover, no sale will be completed unless the buyer has adequate funds in his demand account, which will be held by the affiliated national check-handling agency.

* * *

Direct Bank-Deposit Debiting and Crediting

In the United States, the vast majority of firms that pay wages by check still give or send wage checks to their employees and also send dividend and interest checks to their stock and bond holders. This is very uneconomical because it requires the check recipients to take or mail such checks to their banks for deposit.

This wasteful system is certain to be replaced gradually by a system in which firms send wages, dividend, interest, rent, and most other check payments directly to the payees' banks. The creation of a single national demand-deposit and check-handling monopoly will greatly facilitate such direct payment to payees' banks because all payees and payors will have their demand deposits in the same office.

* * *

. . . A growing number of U.S. firms have begun to pay wages and salaries directly to the employees' bank accounts. I predict that, by the year 2050, all wage, dividend, and interest payments will be so paid.

* * *

Under the coming U.S. system, firms will send their invoices directly to the creditor's bank, which will also be the debtor's bank after creation of the national check-clearing agency. Payment by check will then require no action by the debtor and will be achieved by bookkeeping entries in one office only.

Such direct payment of debts will grow until, by 2100, the vast majority of debts to business firms will be paid in this manner. It will probably begin here with automatic direct collection of recurring debts to public utilities, landlords, mortgage holders, and installment-debt creditors. Social Security taxes and personal-income taxes will also soon be collected by direct debits to payees' bank accounts. . . .

It may seem that direct debiting could be easily abused. But all fraudulent or improper debits would be accompanied by improper credits, and both could easily be reversed when proven improper. Any deliberate or repeated practice of fraud would soon become obvious, and perpetrators could easily be penalized by suitable fines debited to their accounts.

Electronic Fund Transfers Will Expand

Electronic fund transfer (EFT) will rapidly grow as a substitute for the use of checks. The use of EFT has been growing for some time. For instance, many Social Security benefits are now paid by direct electronic transfer of government funds to personal checking accounts. . . .

By 2050, most public-utility accounting offices, banks, insurance companies, and large retail stores will be electronically linked to one or more commercial banks so these firms will be able to directly debit and credit their customers' demand accounts. Retail-store customers will carry credit cards that will be used by store cashiers to debit customers' accounts at the moment of purchase. By the year 2100, all retail purchases of more than some small maximum amount ($5?) will be made in this way.

* * *

Independent Banks Will Radically Decline

. . . This trend is easily predicted for several reasons.

First, the number and relative importance of small, independent banks has long been declining. The number of banking offices operated by U.S. chain banks grew almost steadily from 2,500 in 1925 to more than 40,000 in 1984, a period during which the number of one-office banks declined by more than 50%.

Second, chain banking has developed much further in advanced countries other than America. . . .

. . . The chief reason there are still so many small banks is that the states, with federal approval and support, have protected small, mostly rural, banks by not allowing competition from out-of-state and/or big-city banks, despite the fact that the latter are more efficient.

Third, one-office banks are relatively inefficient. Whenever chain banks are allowed to compete with one-unit banks, they grow much faster than the latter because they can operate more cheaply. They enjoy all the economies of large-scale management and operation. . . . The chain banks pass some of these savings on to their customers, who therefore increasingly prefer to deal with chain banks.

Fourth, restrictions on chain banking will gradually be weakened. . . . As bankers, borrowers, voters, and politicians become more aware of the growing advantages of branch banking, they will gradually relax or end all legal restrictions on such banking. By 2050, all limitations on chain banking in the nation will probably have been eliminated.

* * *

The Private Creation of Money Will End

Since banks do not have to give out cash when they make new loans, but merely create new demand deposits, they can loan more money than actually exists and benefit by charging interest. In other words, banks can and do create money for profit.

The making of a new, additional bank loan always achieves three quite distinct results: It increases the supply of money in circulation, it increases the assets of the borrower, and it creates additional income for the bank. Individual banks make new loans, thereby increasing the supply of money, in order to increase their interest income.

But the creation of money and demand deposits y banks or other private agencies will gradually e reduced and, before the year 2100, prohibited y law, for the following reasons:

First, the creation of money has long been generally recognized as a natural function of government, because private creation of money enables rivate persons to enrich themselves at the expense of the public. It is obvious that successful ounterfeiters so enrich themselves. It will eventually be generally recognized that bankers and borowers of new bank money also do so.

Second, whenever bankers or their borrowers end new money, they tend to raise price levels nd thereby reduce the purchasing power of, and onsumption by, the general public. The private reation of new bank money makes it far more difcult for any government to properly control the rowth of the total quantity of money in circulation nd the resulting price levels. And failure to properly control the quantity of money in circulation as often resulted in a severe business depression nd heavy unemployment, or in runaway inflation nd a business boom.

Third, the creation of demand deposits that are ot backed 100% by cash creates the risk that anks may fail whenever depositors demand more ash than is in reserve behind such deposits. The wer the reserves, the greater the risk that the ommercial banking system may become insolent, and the mere threat of such insolvency may cause or deepen a serious economic recession. . . .

The best way to prevent banks from creating money and causing inflation is to require that all bank money—i.e., demand deposits and bank notes—or at least all new, additional bank money, be backed 100% by money created by the government. Then the function of creating new money will be entrusted to an independent government monetary agency. The adoption of 100% cash reserves will also end the risk of bank runs.

To enable the commercial banks to build up 100% reserves behind all demand deposits and bank notes, without a reduction in their earnings, the U.S. government will probably print the required amount of new reserve money and give it to banks free of charge. This new paper money will be legal tender only for interbank transactions.

* * *

Making Economic Behavior Rational

Nearly all of the eight major monetary and banking reforms predicted above will occur gradually and simultaneously over several decades. Only the creation of a single national demand-deposit-holding and check-clearing agency will probably require a sudden drastic compulsory change in the system. And even this radical reform can be largely achieved gradually and without government coercion if free competition results in the survival of only one national chain of commercial banks. □

Unemployment and the Older Worker

Source: Monthly Labor Review, February 1989.

Workers age 55 and over consistently have the west rates of unemployment of any labor force roup. However, the data do not fully depict the xtent of their problems in the job market, especially as compared to those of other groups. For exmple, by definition, workers who retire after unuccessfully seeking employment are out of the bor force. Thus, they are not counted among the nemployed.

Older unemployed workers under the age of 62, ke their younger counterparts, have strong labor orce attachments. These persons typically look for ull-time rather than part-time jobs. Until age 62, hen they become eligible for Social Security reirement benefits, these workers rarely can afford retire or to take only part-time jobs; thus, they enerally continue seeking full-time employment ntil they find it. By contrast, unemployed persons ge 62 and over—particularly those over 65—often ok for part-time or temporary jobs, search for ork less intensively than younger persons, and nd their job search by retiring rather than finding job. The latter option is made possible by the vailability of retirement benefits, although the mount of such benefits may be quite small.

Commonly available data show that the average umber of weeks of unemployment increases with ge, and some analysts have concluded that older orkers have a more difficult time finding a job an do younger ones. However, this conclusion is roblematic because (1) other sources of data on e duration of unemployment suggest that ounger persons may require about as much time older ones to find a job, and (2) the data reflect ot only employers' demand for specific types of orkers, but also the available supply of workers. lder workers may seek different work schedules wage arrangements than younger ones, or they ay have better nonwork (usually retirement) op-tions. These differences affect whether, how long, and how intensely individuals will look for work.

Permanent displacement from jobs probably occurs about as frequently to older workers as to others. Much permanent job loss is the result of plant closings and other actions from which seniority affords little or no protection. Also, large-scale layoffs occur most often in declining industries, in which workers are older, on average, than they are in growing industries.

When an older worker loses a job, that worker typically gives up a considerable amount of tenure and, along with the tenure, a substantial pay premium. If the individual must find employment in a different occupation, the wages he or she will receive will often be at the level of an "inexperienced" applicant for the position. On the other hand, a substantial proportion of job losers do obtain jobs with wages that match or even exceed the wages in their lost jobs. Displacement late in one's career, however, can lead to premature retirement, which is often seen as a socially acceptable alternative to prolonged unemployment.

Older men who lose jobs tend to experience greater losses of earnings than do older women upon reemployment. This is because the men's wages were typically far higher to begin with. For example, when women lose factory jobs, these jobs are typically in textiles, apparel, or leather products industries, in which average wages for production workers are about $6 to $7 per hour. The factory jobs men lose are more often in industries such as steel, machinery, or automobile manufacturing, in which average wages range from $10 to $15 per hour. Older women who are reentering the labor force experience problems related to outdated skills and lack of confidence. The principal labor market problem facing reentrants is very low earnings compared to those of men. □

Consumer Price Indexes
(1982-84 = 100)

Year	All items	En-ergy	Food	Shel-ter	Apparel[1]	Transporta-tion	Medical care	Fuel oil	Electric-ity	Utility (gas)	Tele-phone	Com mod ties
1960	29.6	22.4	30.0	25.2	45.7	29.8	22.3	13.5	29.9	17.6	58.3	33
1970	38.8	25.5	39.2	35.5	59.2	37.5	34.0	16.5	31.8	19.6	58.7	41
1975	53.8	42.1	59.8	48.8	72.5	50.1	47.5	34.9	50.0	31.1	71.7	5
1980	82.4	86.0	86.8	81.0	90.9	83.1	74.9	87.7	75.8	65.7	77.7	8
1986	109.6	88.2	109.0	115.8	105.9	102.3	122.0	74.1	110.4	99.7	117.2	10
1987	113.6	88.6	113.5	121.3	110.6	105.4	130.1	75.8	110.0	95.1	116.5	10

1. Includes upkeep. *Source: Statistical Abstract of the United States 1989.*

Consumer Price Index for All Urban Consumers
(1984 = 100)

Group	March 1989	March 1988	Group	March 1989	March 1988
All items	122.3	116.5	Fuel oil, coal, bottled gas	81.5	80.5
Food	123.5	115.9	House operation[1]	110.5	108.3
Alcoholic beverages	121.8	117.4	House furnishings	105.1	104.7
Apparel and upkeep	119.3	114.3	Transportation	111.9	106.5
Men's and boys' apparel	115.9	111.6	Medical care	146.1	136.3
Women's and girls' apparel	119.4	115.3	Personal care	123.6	118.1
Footwear	114.1	107.3	Tobacco products	159.2	142.8
Housing, total	121.5	117.0	Entertainment	124.7	119.0
Rent	138.6	132.9	Personal and educational		
Gas and electricity	104.8	101.7	expenses	154.6	145.0

1. Combines house furnishings and operation. *Source:* Department of Labor, Bureau of Labor Statistics.

Consumer Price Index for Urban Wage Earners and Clerical Workers
(1982-84 = 100)

Effective January 1978, the Consumer Price Index was revised, with two indexes now being produced: A new index for Urban Consumers covers 80% of the non-institutional population; the other index, the Consumer Price Index for Urban Wa Earners and Clerical Workers, covers about half of those included in the new index and is a major revision of the one th had been published for many years.

	1989[1]	1988[2]	1980[4]	1975[4]	1970[4]	1965[4]	1960[4]	1955[4]	195
All items	120.8	115.1	247.0	161.2	116.3	94.5	88.7	80.2	72
Food total	123.3	115.7	255.3	175.4	114.9	94.4	88.0	81.6	
Apparel and upkeep	118.4	113.9	177.4	142.3	116.1	93.7	89.6	84.1	79
Housing total	119.6	115.4	263.2	166.8	118.9	94.9	90.2	82.3	72
Rent	123.0	118.4	191.3	137.3	110.1	96.9	91.7	84.3	70
Gas and electricity	104.6	101.4	301.2	169.6	107.3	99.4	98.6	87.5	81
Fuel oil, coal, bottled gas	81.2	80.2	557.2	253.3	110.1	94.6	89.2	82.3	72
House operation[3]	110.0	107.8	202.9	158.1	113.4	95.3	93.8	89.9	
House furnishings	104.5	104.1	172.6	144.4	111.4	97.1	99.3	99.2	95
Transportation	111.6	106.2	250.5	150.6	112.7	95.9	89.6	77.4	68
Medical care	146.5	136.5	267.2	168.6	120.6	89.5	79.1	64.8	53
Personal care	123.5	117.7	212.7	150.7	113.2	95.2	90.1	77.9	68
Entertainment	124.1	118.2	203.7	144.4	113.4	95.9	87.3	76.7	74

1. March 1989. 2. March 1988. 3. Combines house furnishings and operation. 4. 1967 = 100. *Source:* Department of Lab Bureau of Labor Statistics.

Per Capita Personal Income

Year	Amount	Year	Amount	Year	Amount	Year	Amount	Year	Amou
1935	$474	1965	$2,773	1974	$5,428	1979	$8,638	1984	$13,1
1945	1,223	1970	3,893	1975	5,851	1980	9,910	1985	13,8
1950	1,501	1971	4,132	1976	6,402	1981	10,949	1986	14,6
1955	1,881	1972	$4,493	1977	7,043	1982	11,480	1987	15,4
1960	2,219	1973	4,980	1978	7,729	1983	12,098	1988[1]	16,4

1. Preliminary. *Source:* Department of Commerce, Bureau of Economic Analysis.

Total Family Income
(figures in percent)

Income range	White				Black and other races			
	1987	1980	1970	1960	1987	1980	1970	1960
Families (thousands)[1]	56,044	52,710	46,535	41,123	9,089	7,599	5,413	4,333
Under $2,500	1.3	1.6	5.6	15.1	4.6	5.0	15.6	39.8
$2,500 to $7,499	4.8	8.6	25.8	52.9	15.1	22.5	41.4	48.9
$7,500 to $12,499	7.4	13.1	33.4	24.6	13.9	18.5	25.6	9.9
$12,500 to $14,999	4.4	6.8	11.5	3.3	5.0	7.4	6.5	0.9
$15,000 to $19,999	9.3	14.1	13.8	2.2	10.8	12.8	7.4	0.3
$20,000 to $24,999	9.1	14.2	4.9	0.9	9.5	10.6	2.1	0.3
$25,000 to $34,999	18.1	20.8	3.2	—	13.9	12.9	1.1	—
$35,000 to $49,999	21.2	13.6	1.2	1.1	13.9	7.6	0.3	—
$50,000 and over	24.4	7.2	0.6	—	13.2	2.8	0.1	—
Median income	$32,274	$21,904	$10,236	$5,835	$20,236	$13,843	$6,516	$3,230

1. As of March 1988. *Source:* Department of Commerce, Bureau of the Census.

Median Weekly Earnings of Full-Time Workers by Occupation and Sex

Occupation	Men		Women		Total	
	Number of workers (in thousands)	Median weekly earnings	Number of workers (in thousands)	Median weekly earnings	Number of workers (in thousands)	Median weekly earnings
Managerial and prof. specialty	12,086	$674	10,129	$476	22,215	$559
Executive, admin, and managerial	6,302	686	4,547	442	10,849	556
Professional specialty	5,783	661	5,582	493	11,365	561
Technical, sales, and admin. support	9,201	481	15,535	310	24,735	358
Technicians and related support	1,604	512	1,313	405	2,918	458
Sales occupations	4,575	507	3,252	264	7,827	404
Administrative support, incl. clerical	3,021	418	10,970	310	13,991	323
Service occupations	4,317	298	4,516	211	8,833	246
Private household	0	(1)	309	153	309	153
Protective service	1,594	423	245	364	1,839	417
Service, except private household and protective	2,723	255	3,962	212	6,685	225
Precision production, craft, and repair	10,116	453	857	277	10,973	437
Mechanics and repairers	3,612	447	137	347	3,749	442
Construction trades	3,628	434	69	(1)	3,697	432
Other precision production, craft, and repair	2,876	476	651	267	3,527	436
Operators, fabricators, and laborers	11,023	358	3,878	242	14,901	316
Machine operators, assemblers, and inspectors	4,554	367	3,033	238	7,587	302
Transportation and material moving occupations	3,647	399	210	293	3,857	394
Handlers, equipment cleaners, helpers, and laborers	2,822	297	635	244	3,457	289
Farming, forestry, and fishing	1,143	245	164	204	1,307	238

1. Data not shown where base is less than 100,000. NOTE: Figures are for the fourth quarter of 1988. *Source:* U.S. Department of Labor, Bureau of Labor Statistics, "Employment and Earnings," January 1989.

Consumer Credit
(installment credit outstanding; in billions of dollars, seasonally adjusted)

Holder	1988	1987	1986	1985	1984	1983	1980	1975
Commercial banks	318.9	282.9	263.0	241.6	209.2	169.3	145.6	83.0
Finance companies	145.2	140.3	133.9	111.0	89.5	83.0	61.9	32.7
Credit unions	86.1	80.1	76.2	71.9	65.5	53.0	43.7	25.5
Retailers[1]	43.5	41.0	39.4	39.2	37.2	34.2	26.1	16.7
Other[2]	65.8	63.5	59.5	54.0	41.2	28.4	20.3	9.2
Total	**659.5**	**607.7**	**572.1**	**517.8**	**442.5**	**367.9**	**297.6**	**167.0**

1. Excludes 30-day charge credit held by retailers, oil and gas companies, and travel and entertainment companies. 2. Includes mutual savings banks, savings and loan associations, and gasoline companies. *Source:* Federal Reserve Bulletin.

The Public Debt

Year	Gross debt Amount (in millions)	Per capita	Year	Gross debt Amount (in millions)	Per capita
1800 (Jan. 1)	$ 83	$ 15.87	1950	$256,087 [2]	$1,688.30
1860 (June 30)	65	2.06	1955	272,807 [2]	1,650.63
1865	2,678	75.01	1960	284,093 [2]	1,572.31
1900	1,263	16.60	1965	313,819 [2]	1,612.70
1920	24,299	228.23	1970	370,094 [2]	1,807.09
1925	20,516	177.12	1975	533,189	2,496.90
1930	16,185	131.51	1980	907,701	3,969.55
1935	28,701	225.55	1985	1,823,103	7,598.51
1940	42,968	325.23	1987	2,350,277	9,607.59
1945	258,682	1,848.60	1988	2,602,338	10,534.12

1. Preliminary, Sept. 30, 1988. 2. Adjusted to exclude issues to the international Monetary Fund and other international lending institutions to conform to the budget presentation. *Source:* Department of the Treasury, Financial Management Service.

Gross National Product or Expenditure
(in billions)

Item	1988	1987	1986	1985	1984	1980	1970	1960	1950
Gross national product	$4,864.3	$4,526.7	$4,235.0	$3,998	$3,774	$2,626	$982	$506	$28
GNP in constant (1982) dollars[1]	3,996.1	3,847.0	3,713.3	3,585	3,492	1,481	1,075	737	53
Personal consumption expenditures	3,227.5	3,012.1	2,799.8	2,601	2,423	1,673	619	325	19
Durable goods	451.1	421.9	402.4	359	331	212	85	43	3
Nondurable goods	1,046.9	997.9	939.4	905	872	676	265	151	9
Services	1,729.6	1,592.3	1,458.0	1,336	1,220	785	269	131	6
Gross private domestic investment	766.5	712.9	671.0	661	674	395	141	76	5
Residential structures	229.7	226.9	218.3	192	179	105	36	24	2
Nonresidential structures	142.8	139.5	137.4	458	428	109	38	18	
Producers' durable equipment	345.6	307.3	299.5	303	280	190	64	30	1
Change in business inventories	48.4	39.2	15.7	11	67	−6	4	4	
Net export of goods and services	−94.6	−123.0	−105.5	−79	−59	23	4	4	
Government purchases	964.9	924.7	869.7	815	737	535	219	100	3
Federal	381.0	382.0	366.2	354	313	199	96	54	1
National defense	298.4	295.3	277.8	259	237	132	74	44	1
Other	82.6	86.7	88.4	95	76	67	22	9	
State and local	583.9	542.8	503.5	461	424	336	123	47	2
Implicit price deflator[1]	n.a.	n.a.	n.a.	112	108	177	91	69	5

1. For 1950, 1960, 1970, and 1980 GNP in constant (1972) dollars. NOTE: n.a. = not available. *Source:* Department of Commerce, Bureau of Economic Analysis.

Producer Price Indexes by Major Commodity Groups
(1982 = 100)

Commodity	1988	1987	1985[1]	1980[1]	1975[1]	1970
All commodities	106.9	102.8	308.7	268.8	174.9	110.4
Farm products	104.8	95.4	230.5	249.4	186.7	111.0
Processed foods	112.8	107.9	260.4	241.2	182.6	112.1
Textile products and apparel	109.2	105.1	210.4	183.5	137.9	107.1
Hides, skins, and leather products	131.5	120.4	286.1	248.9	148.5	110.3
Fuels and related products and power	66.8	70.2	633.6	574.0	245.1	106.2
Chemicals and allied products	116.4	106.5	303.2	260.3	181.3	102.2
Rubber and plastic products	109.4	103.0	245.9	217.4	150.2	108.3
Lumber and wood products	118.9	112.7	303.6	288.9	176.9	113.6
Pulp, paper, and allied products	130.4	121.8	327.2	249.2	170.4	108.2
Metals and metal products	118.7	107.1	314.9	286.4	185.6	116.6
Machinery and equipment	113.2	110.4	298.9	239.8	161.4	111.4
Furniture and household durables	113.1	110.0	221.6	187.7	139.7	107.5
Nonmetallic mineral products	111.2	110.0	347.8	283.0	174.0	112.9
Transportation equipment	114.2	112.6	269.5 [2]	207.0 [2]	141.5 [2]	104.6
Miscellaneous products	n.a.	n.a.	300.9	258.8	147.7	109.9

[1]1967 = 100 [2]Dec. 1968 = 100 NOTE: n.a. = not available. *Source:* Department of Commerce, Bureau of Economic Analysis.

Weekly Earnings of Full-Time Women Workers

Major occupation group	1988 weekly earnings	% Men's weekly earnings
Managerial and professional specialty	$465	69.8
Executive, administrative, and managerial	430	63.0
Professional specialty	485	74.5
Technical, sales, and administrative support	305	64.6
Technicians and related support	384	75.3
Sales occupations	264	54.1
Administrative support, including clerical	305	73.0
Service occupations	208	69.6
Precision production, craft, and repair	302	67.7
Operators, fabricators, and laborers	238	67.6
Machine operators, assemblers, and inspectors	236	64.5
Transportation and material moving	286	72.6
Handlers, equipment cleaners, helpers, and laborers	237	82.6
Farming, forestry, and fishing	201	85.9
Total; all occupations	315	70.2

1. Median usual weekly earnings. Half the workers earn more and half the workers usually earn less each week. *Source:* U.S. Department of Labor, Bureau of Labor Statistics.

Median Family Income

(in current dollars)

Year	Income	Percent change	Year	Income	Percent change
1960	$ 5,620	—	1983	24,580	4.9
1970	9,867	—	1984	25,948	5.1
1975	13,719	—	1985	27,144	5.0
1980	21,023	6.9	1986	28,236	4.0
1981	22,388	6.5	1987	29,744	5.3
1982	23,433	4.7	1988	30,992	4.0

Source: U.S. Department of Labor, Bureau of Labor Statistics, *Employment and Earnings.*

Expenditures for New Plant and Equipment[1]

(in billions of dollars)

Year	Manufacturing	Transportation[2]	Total nonmanufacturing	Total
1950	$7.73	$2.87	$18.08	$25.81
1955	12.50	3.10	24.58	37.08
1960	16.36	3.54	32.63	48.99
1965	25.41	5.66	45.39	70.79
1970	36.99	7.17	69.16	106.15
1975	53.66	9.95	108.95	162.60
1980	112.33	16.60	202.15	314.47
1982	120.68	14.79	226.79	347.47
1983	116.20	13.97	227.15	343.35
1984	138.82	16.52	260.16	398.99
1985	153.48	18.02	278.46	431.94
1986	142.69	18.80	284.54	427.23
1987	145.90	18.85	294.77	440.66
1988	165.70	21.35	316.70	482.40

1. Data exclude agriculture. 2. Transportation is included in total nonmanufacturing. NOTE: This series was revised in June 1989. *Source:* Department of Commerce, Bureau of Economic Analysis.

New Housing Starts[1] and Mobile Homes Shipped

(in thousands)

Year	No. of units started	Year	No. of units started	Year	Mobile homes shipped
1900	189	1970	1,469	1965	216
1910	387	1975	1,171	1970	401
1920	247	1979	1,760	1975	213
1925	937	1980	1,313	1980	222
1930	330	1981	1,100	1981	241
1935	221	1982	1,072	1982	240
1940	603	1983	1,712	1983	296
1945	326	1984	1,756	1984	295
1950	1,952	1985	1,745	1985	284
1955	1,646	1986	1,807	1986	244
1960[1]	1,296	1987	1,623	1987	233
1965	1,510	1988[2]	1,488	1988	218

1. Prior to 1960, starts limited to nonfarm housing; from 1960 on, figures include farm housing. 2. As of 1988 data for housing starts no longer includes public housing starts and only includes private housing starts. *Sources:* Department of Commerce, Housing Construction Statistics, 1900–1965, and Construction Reports, Housing Starts, 1970–83, Manufactured Housing Institute, 1965–76; National Conference of States on Building Codes and Standards.

Life Insurance in Force

(in millions of dollars)

As of Dec. 31	Ordinary	Group	Industrial	Credit	Total
1915	$16,650	$100	$4,279	—	$21,029
1930	78,756	9,801	17,693	73	106,413
1945	101,550	22,172	27,675	365	151,762
1950	149,071	47,793	33,415	3,844	234,168
1955	216,812	101,345	39,682	14,493	373,332
1960	341,881	175,903	39,563	29,101	586,448
1965	499,638	308,078	39,818	53,020	900,554
1970	734,730	551,357	38,644	77,392	1,402,123
1980	1,760,474	1,579,355	35,994	165,215	3,541,038
1985	3,247,289	2,561,595	28,250	215,973	6,053,107
1987	4,139,071	3,043,782	26,668	242,977	7,452,498
1988	4,511,608	3,232,080	25,456	251,015	8,020,159

Source: American Council of Life Insurance.

Farm Indexes

(1977 - 100)

Year	Prices paid by farmers[1]	Prices rec'd by farmers[2]	Ratio
1950	37	56	151
1955	40	51	128
1960	44	52	118
1965	49	54	115
1970	56	60	109
1975	90	101	113
1980	137	134	97
1985	163	128	79
1987	162	127	78
1988	168	130	77

1. Commodities, interest, and taxes and wage rates. 2. All crops and livestock. *Source:* Department of Agriculture, National Agricultural Statistics Service.

Estimated Annual Retail and Wholesale Sales by Kind of Business
(in millions of dollars)

Kind of business	1988	1987	Kind of business	1988	1987
Retail trade, total	1,629,150	1,521,417	Furniture and home furnishings	27,985	25,18
Building materials, hardware, garden supply, and mobile home dealers	88,894	81,549	Lumber and other construction materials	55,652	57,28
Automotive dealers	369,028	334,429	Electrical goods	104,083	97,68
Furniture, home furnishings, and equipment stores	92,952	84,562	Hardware, plumbing, heating, and supplies	46,995	44,22
General merchandise group stores	183,783	176,023	Machinery, equipment, supplies	209,185	187,73
Food stores	331,892	314,605	Scrap and waste materials	(s)	(s)
Gasoline service stations	101,916	98,680	Nondurable goods, total	805,586	757,29
Apparel and accessory stores	82,028	77,998	Total, (excluding farm-product raw materials)	679,570	655,09
Eating and drinking places	157,504	147,717	Paper and paper products	51,653	44,25
Drug and proprietary stores	58,729	54,958	Drugs, drug proprietaries, and druggists' sundries	36,469	32,78
Liquor stores	19,143	19,458	Apparel, piece goods, & notions	50,234	45,41
Merchant wholesale trade, total	1,588,330	1,482,975	Groceries and related products	223,897	222,37
Total (excluding farm-product raw materials)	1,462,314	1,380,775	Beer, wine, distilled alcoholic beverages	43,725	43,35
Durable goods, total	782,744	725,683	Miscellaneous nondurable goods	111,340	106,47
Motor vehicles and automotive parts and supplies	164,046	152,231	Tobacco and tobacco products	(s)	(s)

NOTE: (S) = does not meet publication standards. *Source:* Department of Commerce, Bureau of the Census.

Shareholders in Public Corporations

Characteristic	1985	1983	1981	1980	1975	1970	1965
Individual shareholders (thousands)	47,040	42,360	32,260	30,200	25,270	30,850	20,12
Owners of shares listed on New York Stock Exchange (thousands)	25,263	26,029	25,504A	23,804	17,950	18,290	12,43
Adult shareowner incidence in population	1 in 4	1 in 4	1 in 5	1 in 5	1 in 6	1 in 4	1 in
Median household income	$36,800	$33,200	$29,200	$27,750	$19,000	$13,500	$9,50
Adult shareowners with household income: under $10,000 (thousands)	2,151	1,460	2,164	1,742	3,420	8,170	10,08
$10,000 and over (thousands)	40,999	36,261	26,913	25,715	19,970	20,130	8,41
Adult female shareowners (thousands)	22,509	20,385	14,154	13,696	11,750	14,290	9,43
Adult male shareowners (thousands)	22,484	19,226	15,785	14,196	11,630	14,340	9,06
Median age	44	45	46	46	53	48	4

NOTE: Latest figures available. *Source:* New York Stock Exchange.

50 Most Active Stocks in 1988

Stock	Share volume	Stock	Share volume	Stock	Share volume
American Tel. & Tel. (1)	349,170,800	Texas Utilities	190,464,900	Gillette Co. (23)	153,609,70
Int'l Business Machines (2)	315,528,100	Digital Equipment (20)	188,034,400	USX Corp. (7)	150,020,70
General Electric (3)	302,526,300	Philips Petroleum (15)	186,580,800	Chrysler Corp. (17)	149,316,58
Occidental Petroleum (19)	296,741,100	Centerior Energy	185,313,300	Dow Chemical (27)	148,570,90
Southern Co. (36)	281,728,200	Baxter International[1] (30)	182,539,100	Mobil Corp. (18)	148,320,40
Exxon Corp. (8)	273,550,100	Sears, Roebuck (21)	180,723,700	Upjohn Company	145,058,00
Texaco Inc. (5)	269,247,700	GTE Corp. (50)	180,477,200	Unisys Corp. (48)	143,532,90
Pacific Gas & Electric (14)	244,973,000	SCEcorp[2]	175,955,800	National Semiconductor (16)	140,068,20
RJR Nabisco (25)	244,899,500	Navistar International (6)	175,150,000	Coca-Cola Co. (22)	138,774,20
Ford Motor (11)	240,824,200	Niagara Mohawk Power	171,686,700	Hewlett-Packard (24)	134,636,60
Union Carbide (12)	230,571,400	Varity Corporation	165,054,600	Tandem Computers	133,718,60
Houston Industries	227,427,500	Citicorp (41)	163,412,500	Zayre Corp.	133,543,70
Philadelphia Electric	221,241,400	Pillsbury Co.	161,354,600	Motorola, Inc. (40)	133,399,70
Eastman Kodak (10)	218,141,800	Morris (Philip) (13)	160,614,000	USF&G Corp.	133,374,90
American Express (4)	215,856,900	Inco Limited	156,059,800	Detroit Edison (31)	132,890,20
American Electric Power	214,880,100	BellSouth Corp.	155,393,100	Polaroid Corp.	132,835,70
General Motors (9)	197,069,600	Tenneco Inc.	155,342,400		

NOTE: 1988 ranking in parentheses, if among top 50. 1. Formerly Baxter Travenol. 2. Formerly Southern California Edison. *Source:* New York Stock Exchange.

50 Companies With Largest Number of Stockholders

Company	Stockholders	Company	Stockholders
American Tel. & Tel.	2,702,000	Chrysler Corp.	206,000
General Motors	1,725,000	du Pont de Nemours	206,000
BellSouth Corp.	1,491,000	Detroit Edison	203,000
Bell Atlantic	1,280,000	Ohio Edison	194,000
NYNEX Corp.	1,249,000	Chevron Corp.	192,000
Southwestern Bell	1,169,000	Texaco Inc.	190,000
American Information Tech.	1,164,000	Eastman Kodak	174,000
Pacific Telesis Group	1,027,000	Consolidated Edison	171,000
US WEST	1,007,000	Niagara Mohawk Power	162,000
International Business Machines	834,000	Tenneco Inc.	161,000
Exxon Corporation	735,000	Amoco Corp.	159,000
General Electric	531,000	Atlantic Richfield	158,000
GTE Corporation	440,000	Centerior Energy Corp.	158,000
BCE Inc.[1]	372,000	Northeast Utilities	158,000
Sears, Roebuck	352,000	Southern California Edison	153,000
Pacific Gas & Electric	302,000	USX Corp.	151,000
Southern Company	291,000	Pennsylvania Power & Light	140,000
Philadelphia Electric	290,000	Union Electric	140,000
Ford Motor	270,000	BankAmerica Corp.	138,000
Mobil Corp.	247,000	Westinghouse Electric	113,000
American Electric Power	238,000	Allied-Signal	111,000
Commonwealth Edison	237,000	CMS Energy	104,000
Public Service Enterprises	213,000	Long Island Lighting	93,000
Dominion Resources	208,000	ITT Corp.	91,000
Occidental Petroleum	207,000	Middle South Utilities	88,000

1. Formerly Bell Canada Enterprises. NOTE: As of Dec. 31, 1988. *Source:* New York Stock Exchange.

New York Stock Exchange Seat Sales for Cash, 1988

	Price				Price		
Month	High	Low	Number	Month	High	Low	Number
January	$625	—	1	July	$700	—	2
February	650	$625	5	August	650	$580	6
March	750	700	2	September	700	620	3
April	750	675	2	October	—	—	—
May	820	800	3	November	665	—	1
June	665	—	1	December	675	620	6

NOTE: In addition, there were nine private seat sales, ranging from a high of 790,000 and a low of 650,000. *Source:* New York Stock Exchange.

Largest Businesses, 1988

(in millions of dollars)

Source: FORTUNE 500 and SERVICE 500 © 1989 The Time Inc. Magazine Company. All rights reserved.

50 LARGEST INDUSTRIAL CORPORATIONS

	Sales	Assets
General Motors	121,085.4	164,063.1
Ford Motor	92,445.6	143,366.5
Exxon	79,557.0	74,293.0
Int'l Business Machines	59,681.0	73,037.0
General Electric	49,414.0	110,865.0
Mobil	48,198.0	38,820.0
Chrysler	35,472.7	48,566.8
Texaco	33,544.0	26,337.0
E.I. du Pont de Nemours	32,514.0	30,719.0
Philip Morris	25,860.0	36,960.0
Chevron	25,196.0	33,968.0
Amoco	21,150.0	29,919.0
Shell Oil	21,070.0	27,169.0
Occidental Petroleum	19,417.0	20,747.0
Procter & Gamble	19,336.0	14,820.0
United Technologies	18,087.8	12,748.3
Atlantic Richfield	17,626.0	21,514.0
Eastman Kodak	17,034.0	22,964.0
Boeing	16,962.0	12,608.0
RJR Nabisco	16,956.0	17,751.0
Dow Chemical	16,682.0	16,239.0
Xerox	16,441.0	26,441.0
USX	15,792.0	19,474.0
Tenneco	15,707.0	17,376.0
McDonnell Douglas	15,072.0	11,885.0
Pepsico	13,007.0	11,135.3
Westinghouse Electric	12,499.5	16,937.3
Rockwell International	11,946.3	9,208.5
Allied-Signal	11,909.0	10,005.0
Digital Equipment	11,475.4	10,111.6
Phillips Petroleum	11,304.0	11,968.0
Goodyear Tire & Rubber	10,810.4	8,618.3
Lockheed	10,667.0	6,643.0
Minnesota Mining & Mfg.	10,581.0	8,922.0

Caterpillar	10,435.0	9,686.0
Sara Lee	10,423.8	5,012.1
Weyerhaeuser	10,004.2	15,387.1
Unisys	9,902.0	11,534.6
Hewlett-Packard	9,831.0	7,497.0
Aluminum Co. of America	9,795.3	10,537.5
General Dynamics	9,551.0	6,118.1
International Paper	9,533.0	9,462.0
Georgia-Pacific	9,509.0	7,115.0
Conagra	9,475.0	3,042.9
Johnson & Johnson	9,000.0	7,119.0
Anheuser-Busch	8,924.1	7,109.8
Unocal	8,853.0	9,508.0
Sun	8,612.0	8,616.0
Coca-Cola	8,337.8	7,450.6
Union Carbide	8,324.0	8,441.0

25 LARGEST RETAILING COMPANIES

	Sales	Assets
Sears Roebuck	50,251.0	77,951.6
K Mart	27,301.0	12,126.0
Wal-Mart Stores	20,649.0	6,359.7
Kroger	19,053.0	4,614.0
American Stores	18,478.4	7,010.4
J.C. Penney	14,833.0	12,254.0
Safeway Stores	13,612.4	4,371.7
Dayton Hudson	12,204.0	6,523.0
May Department Stores	11,921.0	8,144.0
Great Atlantic & Pacific Tea	9,531.8	2,243.2
Winn-Dixie Stores	9,007.7	1,514.0
F.W. Woolworth	8,088.0	3,535.0
Southland	7,950.3	4,861.5
Marriott	7,370.0	5,981.0
Melville	6,780.4	2,736.2
Albertson's	6,773.1	1,591.0
R.H. Macy	5,729.1	5,514.6
McDonald's	5,566.3	8,158.7
Montgomery Ward Holding	5,371.0	3,825.0
Walgreen	4,883.5	1,511.9
Publix Super Markets	4,803.7	1,173.2
SSC Holdings	4,669.6	1,993.1
Federated Department Stores	4,541.7	7,912.8
Price	4,140.5	993.4
The Limited	4,070.8	2,145.5

10 LARGEST TRANSPORTATION COMPANIES

	Operating revenues	Assets
United Parcel Service	11,032.1	6,935.5
UAL	9,014.6	6,700.7
AMR	8,824.3	9,722.4
CSX	8,668.0	13,026.0
Texas Air	8,572.9	8,198.7
Delta Air Lines	6,915.4	5,748.4
Union Pacific	6,794.0	12,228.0
USAir Group	5,707.0	5,348.9
NWA	5,650.4	4,372.0
Santa Fe Southern Pacific	4,934.9	6,824.3

10 LARGEST DIVERSIFIED FINANCIAL COMPANIES

	Assets	Revenues
American Express	142,704.0	22,934.
Federal Nat'l Mortgage Ass'n	112,258.0	10,635.
Salomon	85,256.0	6,146.
Aetna Life & Casualty	81,414.6	24,296.
Merrill Lynch	64,402.7	10,547.
Cigna	55,824.5	17,889.
Travelers Corp.	53,332.0	18,986.
ITT	41,941.0	19,355.
Morgan Stanley Group	40,050.8	4,108.
American International Group	37,408.7	13,613.2

10 LARGEST LIFE INSURANCE COMPANIES

	Assets	Premium and annuity income
Prudential of America	116,197.0	14,396.
Metropolitan Life	94,232.0	15,487.
Equitable Life Assurance	50,415.5	4,917.
Aetna Life	48,884.9	8,266.
Teachers Insurance & Annuity	38,631.4	3,064.
New York Life	35,153.8	6,929.
Connecticut General Life	31,095.5	2,732.
Travelers	30,672.2	4,200.
John Hancock Mutual Life	28,315.2	4,865.
Northwestern Mutual Life	25,349.0	3,542.

10 LARGEST COMMERCIAL BANKS

	Assets	Deposits
Citicorp	207,666.0	124,072.
Chase Manhattan Corp.	97,455.1	64,056.
Bankamerica Corp.	94,647.0	77,150.
J.P. Morgan & Co.	83,923.0	42,469.
Security Pacific Corp.	77,870.0	47,653.
Chemical Banking Corp.	67,349.0	47,966.
Manufacturers Hanover Corp.	66,710.0	41,714.
First Interstate Bancorp	58,193.9	44,148.
Bankers Trust New York Corp.	57,942.3	32,490.
Bank of New York Co.	47,388.1	32,706.
Wells Fargo & Co.	46,616.5	35,068.
First Chicago Corp.	44,432.0	32,018.

10 LARGEST UTILITIES

	Assets	Operating revenues
GTE	31,103.9	16,459.
Bellsouth	28,472.4	13,596.
NYNEX	25,362.0	12,661.
Bell Atlantic	24,729.2	10,880.
US West	22,415.9	9,220.
Pacific Telesis Group	21,191.0	9,483.
Pacific Gas & Electric	21,067.7	7,645.
Southwestern Bell	20,985.1	8,452.
Southern	19,729.0	7,235.
American Information Tech.	19,163.0	9,903.

New Business Concerns and Business Failures

Formations and Failures	1987[1]	1986	1985	1984	1983	1982	1981	198
Business formations								
Index, net formations (1967 = 100)	120.9	120.4	120.9	121.3	117.5	113.2	118.6	122.
New Incorporations (1,000)	68.5	703	662	635	600	567	582	53
Failures, number (1,000)	61.2	61.6	57.1	52.0	31.3	24.9	16.8	11.
Rate per 10,000 concerns	102	120	115	107	110	88	61	4

1. Preliminary. *Sources:* U.S. Bureau of Economic Analysis and Dun & Bradstreet Corporation.

50 Leading Stocks in Market Value

Stock	Market value (millions)	Listed shares (millions)	Stock	Market value (millions)	Listed shares (millions)
Exxon Corp.	$79,311	1,812.8	American Information Technologies		
International Business Machines	72,148	592.6	(Ameritech)	$14,066	146.9
General Electric	41,348	926.6	Texaco Inc.	14,023	274.3
American Telephone & Telegraph	30,872	1,073.8	NYNEX Corp.	13,520	204.5
Merck & Co.	26,193	455.5	Pacific Telesis	13,364	432.8
General Motors	26,160	312.8	Bristol-Myers	13,092	289.3
Morris (Philip)	24,411	239.6	Digital Equipment	12,806	130.2
Ford Motor	23,356	462.5	Hewlett-Packard	12,608	236.8
du Pont de Nemours	21,125	239.4	Eli Lilly	12,484	146.0
RJR Nabisco	20,884	229.5	Southwestern Bell	12,148	300.9
Mobil Corp.	19,754	434.2	American Int'l Group	11,762	173.6
BellSouth Corp.	19,377	485.9	PepsiCo, Inc.	11,429	287.5
Amoco Corp.	19,346	257.9	American Express	11,167	419.4
Dow Chemical	19,113	217.8	U S WEST	11,159	193.2
Coca-Cola Co.	18,592	416.6	Abbott Laboratories	10,989	228.3
Atlantic Richfield	17,561	217.8	Anheuser-Busch	10,402	330.2
Wal-Mart Stores	17,507	562.5	Dun & Bradstreet	10,153	189.3
Eastman Kodak	16,914	374.8	Royal Dutch Petroleum	10,106	88.6
Johnson & Johnson	16,332	191.9	McDonald's Corp.	10,024	208.8
Sears, Roebuck	15,667	383.3	Kellogg Co.	9,902	154.1
Chevron Corp.	15,651	342.1	Schlumberger Ltd.	9,901	303.5
GTE Corp.	15,513	348.6	Westinghouse Electric	9,649	183.4
American Home Products	14,935	179.4	Pfizer Inc.	9,575	165.4
Procter & Gamble	14,773	169.8	Boeing Co.	9,412	155.2
Minnesota Mining & Manufacturing	14,633	236.0	Ralston Purina	9,379	114.6
Bell Atlantic	14,207	199.7	**Total**	**$908,803**	**16,720.2**

NOTE: As of Dec. 31, 1988. *Source:* New York Stock Exchange.

Top 50 Banks in the World

Bank	Country	Deposits (U.S. dollars)	Bank	Country	Deposits (U.S. dollars)
Dai-ichi Kangyo Bank Ltd., Tokyo	Japan	312,465,781,696 [1]	Citibank NA, New York	United States	104,996,000,000
Sumitomo Bank Ltd., Osaka	Japan	296,000,827,700 [1]	Hongkong and Shanghai Banking		
Fuji Bank, Ltd., Tokyo	Japan	283,585,351,200 [1]	Corp., Hong Kong	Hong Kong	101,841,280,000 [1]
Mitsubishi Bank Ltd., Tokyo	Japan	269,427,020,100 [2]	Nippon Credit Bank, Ltd. Tokyo	Japan	96,733,830,308
Sanwa Bank Ltd., Osaka	Japan	269,032,279,492 [1]	Commerzbank, Frankfurt	Germany	94,904,206,676 [1]
Industrial Bank of Japan, Ltd., Tokyo	Japan	215,397,605,132 [2]	Union Bank of Switzerland,		
Norinchukin Bank, Tokyo	Japan	210,759,455,544	Zurich	Switzerland	93,750,145,230 [2]
Mitsubishi Trust & Banking Corp.,			Swiss Bank Corp., Basle	Switzerland	89,572,067,935 [2]
Tokyo	Japan	185,955,516,200 [2]	Midland Bank Plc, London	United Kingdom	86,753,264,000 [1]
Sumitomo Trust & Banking Co., Ltd.,			Westdeutsche Landesbank		
Osaka	Japan	177,932,182,096 [2]	Girozentrale, Duesseldorf	Germany	86,730,534,166 [1]
Tokai Bank Ltd., Nagoya	Japan	175,600,895,540 [1]	Bayerische Vereinsbank, Munich	Germany	85,089,724,160 [1]
Mitsui Trust & Banking Co., Ltd.			Lloyds Bank Plc, London	United Kingdom	82,911,264,000 [1]
Tokyo	Japan	161,228,496,316	Shoko Chukin Bank, Tokyo	Japan	81,968,920,352
Mitsui Bank, Ltd., Tokyo	Japan	159,039,606,488 [1]	Kyowa Bank, Ltd., Tokyo	Japan	81,096,761,040 [2]
Banque Nationale de Paris	France	158,549,122,000 [1]	Zenshinren Bank, Tokyo	Japan	77,741,067,948
Barclays Bank Plc, London	United Kingdom	157,357,472,000 [1]	Banca Nazionale del Lavoro, Rome	Italy	76,309,515,000 [1]
Deutsche Bank, Frankfurt	Germany	154,974,576,400 [1]	Saitama Bank Ltd., Urawa	Japan	76,037,495,240 [2]
National Westminister Bank Plc,			Royal Bank of Canada, Montreal	Canada	72,146,963,596 [1]
London	United Kingdom	153,645,648,000 [1]	Bayerische Hypotheken-und		
Credit Lyonnais, Paris	France	148,842,971,595 [1]	Wechsel-Bank, Munich	Germany	70,527,672,594 [1]
Long-Term Credit Bank of Japan, Ltd.			Bank of America NT&SA, San		
Tokyo	Japan	147,426,607,488 [2]	Francisco	United States	69,640,000,000
Credit Agricole Mutuel, Paris	France	141,973,000,000 [2]	Bayerische Landesbank Girozentrale,		
Taiyo Kobe Bank, Ltd., Kobe	Japan	138,986,023,792 [2]	Munich	Germany	68,858,720,000 [1]
Daiwa Bank, Ltd., Osaka	Japan	134,466,778,400 [2]	Credit Suisse, Zurich	Switzerland	66,549,571,095 [2]
Bank of Tokyo, Ltd.	Japan	132,147,474,612 [2]	Chuo Trust & Banking Co., Ltd.,		
Yasuda Trust & Banking Co. Ltd.,			Tokyo	Japan	66,142,311,624 [2]
Tokyo	Japan	131,788,381,988	Amsterdam-Rotterdam Bank,		
Societe Generale, Paris	France	123,187,087,000 [1]	Amsterdam	Netherlands	64,270,884,000 [1]
Dresdner Bank, Frankfurt	Germany	120,317,120,000 [1]	Bank of Yokohama, Ltd.	Japan	62,917,505,496 [2]
Toyo Trust & Banking Co., Ltd.,			Rabobank Nederland, Utrecht	Netherlands	62,616,528,000 [1]
Tokyo	Japan	105,384,007,332			

NOTE: As of Dec. 31, 1988. 1. Consolidated data. 2. Data are not consolidated for affiliates more than 50% owned. *Source: American Banker, July 24, 1989.* Reprinted by permission of American Banker/Bond Buyer.

National Labor Organizations With Membership Over 100,000

Members[1]	Union
1,102,675	Automobile, Aerospace and Agricultural Implement Workers of America, International Union, United
145,000	Bakery, Confectionery, and Tobacco Workers International Union
105,000	Boilermakers, Iron Ship Builders, Blacksmiths, Forgers and Helpers, International Brotherhood of
105,000	Bricklayers and Allied Craftsmen, International Union of
140,000	Bridge, Structural and Ornamental Iron Workers, International Association of
609,000	Carpenters and Joiners of America, United Brotherhood of
265,834	Clothing and Textile Workers Union, Amalgamated
700,000	Communications Workers of America
1,900,000	Education Association, National (Ind.)
845,000	Electrical Workers, International Brotherhood of
180,000	Electronic, Electrical, Salaried, Machine and Furniture Workers, International Union of
160,000	Fire Fighters, International Association of
1,235,000	Food and Commercial Workers International Union, United
210,000	Government Employees, American Federation of
185,585	Graphic Communications International Union
301,300	Hotel and Restaurant Employees and Bartenders, International Union
570,000	Laborers' International Union of North America
190,000	Ladies' Garment Workers' Union, International
315,000	Letter Carriers, National Association of
767,000	Machinists and Aerospace Workers, International Association of
230,000	Mine Workers of America, United (Ind.)
192,662	Nurses' Association, American (Ind.)
125,000	Office and Professional Employees International Union
108,000	Oil, Chemical and Atomic Workers International Union
360,000	Operating Engineers, International Union of
133,000	Painters and Allied Trades of the United States and Canada, International Brotherhood of
232,000	Paper Workers International Union, United
325,000	Plumbing and Pipe Fitting Industry of the United States and Canada, United Association of Journeymen and Apprentices of the
365,000	Postal Workers Union, American
180,000	Retail, Wholesale, and Department Store Union
100,000	Rubber, Cork, Linoleum, and Plastic Workers of America, United
925,000	Service Employees International Union
144,000	Sheet Metal Workers' International Association
1,200,000	State, County and Municipal Employees of America, American Federation of
655,000	Steelworkers of America, United
700,000	Teachers, American Federation of
1,700,000	Teamsters, Chauffeurs, Warehousemen and Helpers of America, International Brotherhood of
165,000	Transit Union, Amalgamated*
200,000	Transportation • Communications International Union
100,000	Transportation Union, United

1. Data are for 1988. *Did not reply. NOTE: Figures are most recent available.

Persons in the Labor Force

Year	Labor force[1] Number (thousands)	% working-age population	Percent of labor force in[2] Farm occupation	Nonfarm occupation	Year	Labor force[1] Number (thousands)	% working-age population	Percent of labor force in[2] Farm occupation	Nonfarm occupation
1830	3,932	45.5	70.5	29.5	1910	37,371	52.2	31.0	69.0
1840	5,420	46.6	68.6	31.4	1920	42,434	51.3	27.0	73.0
1850	7,697	46.8	63.7	36.3	1930	48,830	49.5	21.4	78.6
1860	10,533	47.0	58.9	41.1	1940	52,789	52.2	17.4	82.6
1870	12,925	45.8	53.0	47.0	1950	60,054	53.5	11.6	88.4
1880	17,392	47.3	49.4	50.6	1960	69,877	55.3	6.0	94.0
1890	23,318	49.2	42.6	57.4	1970	82,049	58.2	3.1	96.9
1900	29,073	50.2	37.5	62.5	1980	106,085	62.0	2.2	97.8

1. For 1830 to 1930, the data relate to the population and gainful workers at ages 10 and over. For 1940 to 1960, the data relate to the population and labor force at ages 14 and over; for 1970 and 1980, the data relate to the population and labor force at age 16 and over. For 1940 to 1980, the data include the Armed Forces. 2. The farm and nonfarm percentages relate only to the experienced civilian labor force. *Source:* Department of Commerce, Bureau of the Census.

Corporate Profits[1]

(in billions of dollars)

em	1989[2]	1988	1987	1986	1985	1980	1975	1970
omestic industries	243.8	245.7	222.3	207.2	190.8	161.9	107.6	62.4
Financial	31.7	30.5	30.1	26.1	21.0	26.9	11.8	12.1
Nonfinancial	212.2	215.1	192.1	181.1	169.7	134.9	95.8	50.2
Manufacturing	112.9	114.1	96.8	69.4	73.0	72.9	52.6	26.6
Wholesale and retail trade	34.3	39.7	42.8	52.1	49.7	23.6	21.3	9.5
Other	23.4	22.7	17.6	17.2	14.0	38.4	21.9	14.1
est of world	42.3	37.1	36.4	31.2	31.8	29.9	13.0	6.5
otal	286.1	282.8	258.7	238.4	222.6	191.7	120.6	68.9

. Corporate profits with inventory valuation adjustment. 2. Preliminary. *Source:* U.S. Bureau of Economic Analysis, *Survey f Current Business.*

National Income by Type

(in billions of dollars)

Type of share	1988	1987	1985	1980	1975	1970	1965	1960	1950
lational income	$3,968.4	$3,678.7	$3,222.3	$2,121.4	$1,215.0	$800.5	$564.3	$414.5	$241.1
ompensation of employees	2,904.7	2,683.4	2,368.2	1,596.5	931.1	603.9	393.8	294.2	154.6
Wages and salaries	2,436.9	2,248.4	1,965.8	1,343.6	805.9	542.0	358.9	270.8	146.8
Supplements to wages and salaries	467.8	435.0	402.4	252.9	125.2	61.9	35.0	23.4	7.8
roprietors' income[1][2]	324.5	312.9	254.4	130.6	87.0	66.9	57.3	46.2	37.5
Business and professional	288.2	270.0	225.2	107.2	63.5	50.0	42.4	34.2	24.0
Farm	36.3	43.0	29.2	23.4	23.5	16.9	14.8	12.0	13.5
ental income of persons	19.3[1]	18.4[1]	7.6[1]	31.8	22.4	23.9	19.0	15.8	9.4
orporate profits[1][2]	328.4	310.4	280.7	182.7	95.9	69.4	76.1	49.9	37.7
let interest	391.5	353.6	311.4	179.8	78.6	36.4	18.2	8.4	2.0

. Includes capital consumption adjustment. 2. Includes inventory valuation adjustment. *Source:* Department of Commerce, ureau of Economic Analysis.

Per Capita Personal Income by States

tate	1988[1]	1987	1986	1980	State	1988[1]	1987	1986	1980
labama	$12,604	$11,944	$11,323	$ 7,465	Montana	$12,670	$12,291	$11,846	$ 8,342
laska	19,514	18,353	18,016	13,007	Nebraska	15,184	14,300	13,727	8,895
rizona	14,887	14,241	13,640	8,854	Nevada	17,440	16,412	15,380	10,848
rkansas	12,172	11,537	11,050	7,113	New Hampshire	19,016	17,906	16,321	9,150
alifornia	18,855	17,846	16,863	11,021	New Jersey	21,882	20,313	18,866	10,966
olorado	16,417	15,605	15,234	10,143	New Mexico	12,481	11,898	11,435	7,940
onnecticut	22,761	21,192	19,625	11,532	New York	19,299	18,005	16,958	10,179
elaware	17,699	16,407	15,457	10,059	North Carolina	14,128	13,325	12,438	7,780
.C.	21,667	20,084	19,071	12,251	North Dakota	12,720	12,971	12,449	8,642
lorida	16,546	15,584	14,607	9,246	Ohio	15,485	14,598	13,898	9,399
eorgia	14,980	14,306	13,459	8,021	Oklahoma	13,269	12,607	12,318	9,018
awaii	16,898	15,683	14,625	10,129	Oregon	14,982	14,019	13,331	9,309
daho	12,657	11,859	11,224	8,105	Pennsylvania	16,168	15,200	14,242	9,353
linois	17,611	16,417	15,533	10,454	Rhode Island	16,793	15,633	14,564	9,227
ndiana	14,721	13,937	13,136	8,914	South Carolina	12,764	12,027	11,268	7,392
owa	14,764	14,284	13,375	9,226	South Dakota	12,475	12,545	11,811	7,800
ansas	15,905	15,152	14,494	9,880	Tennessee	13,659	12,876	12,002	7,711
entucky	12,795	12,008	11,342	7,679	Texas	14,640	13,889	13,480	9,439
ouisiana	12,193	11,515	11,197	8,412	Utah	12,013	11,389	10,994	7,671
laine	14,976	13,984	12,786	7,760	Vermont	15,382	14,325	13,342	7,957
laryland	19,314	18,167	16,863	10,394	Virginia	17,640	16,486	15,461	9,413
lassachusetts	20,701	19,050	17,657	10,103	Washington	16,569	15,630	14,979	10,256
lichigan	16,387	15,418	14,816	9,801	West Virginia	11,658	10,992	10,531	7,764
linnesota	16,787	15,910	14,995	9,673	Wisconsin	15,444	14,720	13,983	9,364
lississippi	10,992	10,303	9,699	6,573	Wyoming	13,718	12,719	12,775	11,018
lissouri	15,492	14,648	13,923	8,812	**United States**	**16,444**	**15,482**	**14,636**	**9,494**

. Preliminary. *Source:* U.S. Department of Commerce, Bureau of Economic Analysis, *Survey of Current Business.*

The Federal Budget—Receipts and Outlays
(in billions of dollars)

Description	1990[1]	1989[1]	1988	Description	1990[1]	1989[1]	1988
RECEIPTS BY SOURCE				Natural resources and environment	14.4	16.5	14.6
Individual income taxes	466.7	425.2	401.2	Agriculture	15.9	20.9	17.2
Corporation income taxes	117.4	107.0	94.5	Commerce and housing credit	8.3	20.0	18.8
Social insurance taxes and				Transportation	28.3	28.0	27.3
contributions:	391.5	363.9	334.3	Community and regional development	6.4	6.3	5.3
Employment taxes and				Education, training, employment,			
contributions	364.4	336.0	305.1	and social services	39.5	36.4	31.9
Unemployment insurance	22.4	23.1	24.6	Health	52.2	49.8	44.5
Other retirement contributions	4.7	4.7	4.7	Medicare	94.9	86.7	78.9
Excise taxes	35.3	34.0	35.2	Income security	136.8	136.9	129.3
Estate and gift taxes	8.1	7.8	7.6	Social security	246.7	232.3	219.3
Customs duties	18.0	16.3	16.2	Veterans benefits and services	29.9	29.2	29.4
Miscellaneous receipts	22.4	21.4	19.9	Administration of justice	10.6	9.4	9.2
Total budget receipts	**1,059.3**	**975.5**	**909.0**	General government	10.0	10.0	9.5
OUTLAYS BY FUNCTION				Net interest	170.1	165.7	151.7
National defense	303.0	298.3	290.4	Allowances	−0.4	—	—
International affairs	17.3	10.7	10.5	Undistributed offsetting receipts	−42.0	−36.9	−37.0
General science, space, and technology	14.9	12.6	10.8	**Total outlays**	**1,151.8**	**1,137.0**	**1,064.0**
Energy	2.3	4.1	2.3	**Total budget deficit**	**−92.5**	**−161.5**	**−155.0**

1. Estimated. NOTE: The fiscal year is from Oct. 1 to Sept. 30. *Source:* Executive Office of the President, Office of Management and Budget.

Foreign Assistance
(in millions of dollars)

	Non-military programs			Military programs		
Calendar years	Net new grants	Net new credits	Net other assistance	Net grants	Net credits	Total net assistance[1]
1945–1950[2]	$18,413	$8,086	—	$ 1,525	—	$28,023
1951–55	10,459	550	$ 541	13,286	$ 7	24,842
1956–60	8,291	1,462	2,226	13,269	42	25,290
1961–65	9,384	5,538	576	8,295	−16	23,777
1966–70	8,808	9,238	−564	13,296	192	30,970
1971–75	12,939	5,479	−725	16,940	2,044	36,677
1976–80	14,277	10,919	−286	5,662	6,959	37,531
1981–1985	29,025	7,072	−2	9,296	10,836	56,277
1987	7,344	−2,657	−27	3,131	334	8,125
1988	7,296	159	−23	3,578	−4,205	6,805
Total postwar period	**134,093**	**46,154**	**1,721**	**92,402**	**17,406**	**291,776**

1. Excludes investment in international nonmonetary financial institutions of $18,449 million. 2. Includes transactions after V-J Day (Sept. 2, 1945). NOTE: Detail may not add to total due to rounding. *Source:* Department of Commerce, Bureau of Economic Analysis.

Women in the Civilian Labor Force
(16 years of age and over; in thousands)

Labor force status	1988	1987	1986	1985	1984	1983
In the labor force:	54,742	53,658	52,413	51,050	49,709	48,503
16 to 19 years of age	3,872	3,875	3,824	3,767	3,810	3,868
20 years and over	50,870	49,783	48,589	47,283	45,900	44,636
Employed	51,696	50,334	48,706	47,259	45,915	44,047
16 to 19 years of age	3,313	3,260	3,149	3,105	3,122	3,043
20 years and over	48,383	47,075	45,557	44,154	42,793	41,004
Unemployed	3,046	3,324	3,707	3,791	3,794	4,457
16 to 19 years of age	558	616	675	661	687	825
20 years and over	2,488	2,709	3,032	3,129	3,107	3,632
Not in the labor force:	42,014	42,195	42,376	42,686	43,068	43,181
Women as percent of labor force	45.0	44.8	44.5	44.2	43.8	43.5
Total civilian noninstitutional population	96,756	95,853	94,789	93,736	92,778	91,684

Source: Department of Labor, Bureau of Labor Statistics, annual averages.

Employed Persons 16 Years and Over, by Race and Major Occupational Groups
(number in thousands)

Race and occupational group	1988 Number	1988 Percent distribution	1987 Number	1987 Percent distribution
WHITE				
Managerial and professional specialty	26,408	26.5	25,107	25.7
Executive, administrative, & managerial	13,022	13.0	12,200	12.5
Professional specialty	13,386	13.4	12,907	13.2
Technical, sales, & administrative support	31,178	31.2	30,949	31.6
Technicians & related support	3,019	3.0	2,914	3.0
Sales occupations	12,495	12.5	12,295	12.6
Administrative support, including clerical	15,664	15.7	15,740	16.1
Service occupations	12,105	12.1	11,916	12.2
Precision production, craft, and repair	12,305	12.3	12,262	12.5
Operators, fabricators, and laborers	14,665	14.7	14,340	14.7
Farming, forestry, fishing	3,150	3.2	3,214	3.3
Total	99,812	100.0	97,789	100.0
BLACK				
Managerial and professional specialty	1,794	15.4	1,712	15.1
Executive, administrative, & managerial	789	6.8	741	6.6
Professional specialty	1,005	8.6	972	8.6
Technical, sales, & administrative support	3,239	27.8	3,099	27.4
Technicians & related support	329	2.8	283	2.5
Sales occupations	839	7.2	806	7.1
Administrative support, including clerical	2,071	17.8	2,010	17.8
Service occupations	2,698	23.1	2,614	23.1
Precision production, craft, and repair	1,029	8.8	996	8.8
Operators, fabricators, and laborers	2,672	22.9	2,659	23.5
Farming, forestry, and fishing	226	1.9	229	2.0
Total	11,658	100.0	11,309	100.0

Source: Department of Labor, Bureau of Labor Statistics.

Mothers Participating in Labor Force
(figures in percentage)

Year	Mothers with children Under 18 years	Mothers with children 6 to 17 years	Mothers with children Under 6 years[1]
1955	27.0	38.4	18.2
1965	35.0	45.7	25.3
1975	47.4	54.8	38.9
1980	56.6	64.4	46.6
1981	58.1	65.5	48.9
1982	58.5	65.8	49.9
1983	58.9	66.3	50.5
1984	60.5	68.2	52.1
1985	62.1	69.9	53.5
1986	62.8	70.4	54.4
1987	64.7	72.0	56.7
1988	65.0	73.3	56.1

1. May also have older children. NOTE: For 1950 and 1955 data are for April; for 1965 and 1975–88, data are for March. *Source:* Department of Labor, Bureau of Labor Statistics.

Women in the Labor Force

Year[1]	Number (thousands)	% Female population aged 16 and over[1]	% of Labor force population aged 16 and over[1]
1900	5,319	18.8	18.3
1910	7,445	21.5	19.9
1920	8,637	21.4	20.4
1930	10,752	22.0	22.0
1940	12,845	25.4	24.3
1950	18,408	33.9	29.0
1960[2]	23,268	37.8	32.5
1970	31,580	43.4	37.2
1980	45,611	51.6	42.0
1985	51,200	54.5	43.7
1987	53,818	56.1	44.3
1988	54,904	56.6	44.5

1. For 1900–1930, data relate to population and labor force aged 10 and over; for 1940, to population and labor force aged 14 and over; beginning 1950, to population and labor force aged 16 and over. 2. Beginning in 1960, figures include Alaska and Hawaii. *Sources:* Department of Commerce, Bureau of the Census, and Department of Labor, Bureau of Labor Statistics.

Persons Below the Poverty Level, 1960-1986

(in thousands)

Year	All persons	White	Black	Spanish origin[1]	Year	All persons	White	Black	Spanish origin[1]
1960	39,851	28,309	—	—	1978	24,497	16,259	7,625	2,607
1965	33,185	22,496	—	—	1979	26,072	17,214	8,050	2,921
1970	25,420	17,484	7,548	—	1980	29,272	19,699	8,579	3,491
1971	25,559	17,780	7,396	—	1981	31,822	21,553	9,173	3,713
1972	24,460	16,203	7,710	—	1982	34,398	23,517	9,697	4,301
1973	22,973	15,142	7,388	2,366	1983[2]	35,303	23,984	9,882	4,633
1974	23,370	15,736	7,182	2,575	1984	33,700	22,955	9,490	4,806
1975	25,877	17,770	7,545	2,991	1985	33,064	22,860	8,926	5,236
1976	24,975	16,713	7,595	2,783	1986	32,370	22,183	8,983	5,117
1977	24,720	16,416	7,726	2,700	1987	32,546	21,409	9,683	5,470

1. Persons of Spanish origin may be of any race. 2. Revised. *Source:* U.S. Department of Commerce, Bureau of the Census.

Manufacturing Industries—Gross Average Weekly Earnings and Hours Worked

	1988		1987		1985		1980		1975		1970	
Industry	Earnings	Hours worked	Earnings	Hours worked	Earnings	Hours worked	Earnings	Hours worked	Earnings	Hours worked	Earnings	Hours worked
All manufacturing	$417.99	41.1	$406.31	41.0	$385.56	40.5	$288.62	39.7	$189.51	39.4	$133.73	39.8
Durable goods	447.26	41.8	433.68	41.5	415.71	41.2	310.78	40.1	205.09	39.9	143.07	40.3
Primary metal industries	529.74	43.6	516.34	43.1	484.72	41.5	391.78	40.1	246.80	40.0	159.17	40.5
Iron and steel foundries	478.73	43.6	458.82	42.8	429.62	40.8	328.00	40.0	220.99	40.4	151.03	40.6
Nonferrous foundries	403.50	41.9	399.61	41.8	388.74	41.8	291.27	39.9	190.03	39.1	138.16	39.7
Fabricated metal products	428.03	41.8	416.25	41.5	398.96	41.3	300.98	40.4	201.60	40.0	143.67	40.7
Hardware, cutlery, hand tools	421.64	41.5	409.12	41.2	396.42	40.7	275.89	39.3	187.07	39.3	132.33	40.1
Other hardware	437.60	41.4	422.91	40.9	385.40	41.3	195.42	39.4	133.46	40.2		
Structural metal products	391.41	40.9	379.03	40.8	369.00	41.0	291.85	40.2	202.61	40.2	142.61	40.4
Electric and electronic equipment	415.33	41.0	404.91	40.9	384.48	40.6	276.21	39.8	180.91	39.5	130.54	39.8
Machinery, except electrical	467.32	42.6	454.49	42.2	427.04	41.5	328.00	41.0	219.22	40.9	154.95	41.1
Transportation equipment	570.47	42.7	545.62	42.1	542.72	42.7	379.61	40.6	242.61	40.3	163.22	40.3
Motor vehicles and equipment	612.05	43.5	574.01	42.3	584.64	43.5	394.00	40.0	262.68	40.6	170.07	40.3
Lumber and wood products	346.58	40.3	341.04	40.6	326.36	39.8	252.18	38.5	167.35	39.1	117.51	39.7
Furniture and fixtures	312.05	39.4	306.03	39.9	283.29	39.4	209.17	38.1	142.13	37.9	108.58	39.2
Nondurable goods	378.68	40.2	368.23	40.2	342.86	39.5	255.45	39.0	168.78	38.8	120.43	39.1
Textile mill products	302.91	41.1	300.84	41.9	266.39	39.7	203.31	40.1	133.28	39.2	97.76	39.9
Apparel and other textile products	225.09	36.9	220.75	37.1	208.00	36.3	161.42	35.4	111.97	35.1	84.37	35.3
Leather and leather products	235.50	37.5	230.89	38.1	217.09	37.3	169.09	36.7	120.80	37.4	92.63	37.2
Food and kindred products	368.04	40.4	358.58	40.2	341.60	40.0	271.95	39.7	184.17	40.3	127.98	40.5
Tobacco manufactures	579.49	39.8	531.69	38.5	448.26	37.2	294.89	38.1	171.38	38.0	110.00	37.8
Paper and allied products	502.85	43.2	495.63	43.4	466.34	43.1	330.85	42.2	207.58	41.6	144.14	41.9
Printing and publishing	400.14	38.0	390.64	38.0	365.31	37.7	279.36	37.1	198.32	37.0	147.78	37.7
Chemicals and allied products	535.94	42.3	523.25	42.3	484.78	41.9	344.45	41.5	219.63	40.9	153.50	41.6
Petroleum and allied products	668.22	44.4	639.62	43.9	603.72	43.0	422.18	41.8	267.07	41.6	182.76	42.7

Source: Department of Labor, Bureau of Labor Statistics.

Nonmanufacturing Industries—Gross Average Weekly Earnings and Hours Worked

Industry	1988 Earnings	1988 Hours worked	1987 Earnings	1987 Hours worked	1985 Earnings	1985 Hours worked	1975 Earnings	1975 Hours worked	1970 Earnings	1970 Hours worked
Bituminous coal and lignite mining	675.11	42.4	$658.86	42.0	$630.77	41.4	$284.53	39.2[2]	$186.41	40.8
Metal mining	557.94	42.3	546.00	42.0	547.24	40.9	250.72	42.3	165.68	42.7
Nonmetallic minerals	498.49	45.4	480.93	45.2	451.68	44.5	213.09	43.4	155.11	44.7
Telephone communications	555.90	41.3	545.57	41.3	512.52	41.1	221.18	38.4	131.60	39.4
Radio and TV broadcasting	412.49	35.9	394.22	36.3	381.39	37.1	214.50	39.0	147.45	38.2
Electric, gas, and sanitary services	594.46	41.6	572.70	41.5	534.59	41.7	246.79	41.2	172.64	41.5
Local and suburban transportation	350.49	38.6	344.04	38.7	309.85	38.3	196.89	40.1	142.30	42.1
Wholesale trade	377.95	38.1	367.10	38.2	358.36	38.7	188.75	38.6	137.60	40.0
Retail trade	183.62	29.1	179.32	29.3	177.31	29.7	108.22	32.4	82.47	33.8
Hotels, tourist courts, motels	199.68	31.2	187.88	30.7	176.90	30.5	89.64	31.9	68.16	34.6
Laundries and dry cleaning plants	216.83	34.2	209.99	34.2	198.70	34.2	106.05	35.0	77.47	35.7
General building contracting	454.41	37.4	439.45	37.4	414.78	37.1	254.88	36.0	184.40	36.3

Source: Department of Labor, Bureau of Labor Statistics.

Median Income Comparisons of Year-Round Workers by Educational Attainment 1987

(persons 25 years and over)

Years of school completed	Median income Women	Median income Men	Income gap in dollars	Women's income as a percent of men's	Percent men's income exceeded women's
Elementary school:					
Less than 8 years	$9,927	$14,903	$4,976	66	50
8 years	12,174	18,939	6,765	64	55
High School:					
1 to 3 years	12,940	21,269	8,329	61	64
4 years	16,461	25,394	8,933	65	54
College:					
1 to 3 years	29,536	19,843	9,693	67	49
4 years or more	22,554	34,380	11,826	66	52

Source: Department of Commerce, Bureau of the Census. NOTE: Data are latest available.

Characteristics of Households With Female Householder, 1988

Characteristics	Number of households	Income bracket	Number of households
All female householders	28,293,000	3 persons	40,084,000
MARITAL STATUS		4 persons or more	3,960,000
Married, husband present	3,061,000	**RELATED CHILDREN UNDER 18**	
Married, husband absent	2,768,000	No related children	19,653,000
Widowed	9,628,000	1 or more related children	8,640,000
Divorced	6,527,000	**TOTAL HOUSEHOLD INCOME[2]**	
Single (never married)	6,310,000	Under $2,500	1,194,000
RACE AND SPANISH ORIGIN		$2,500 to $4,999	2,920,000
OF HOUSEHOLDER		$5,000 to $7,499	3,694,000
White	22,542,000	$7,500 to $9,999	2,561,000
Black	5,136,000	$10,000 to $14,999	4,066,000
Spanish origin[1]	1,832,000	$15,000 to $24,999	5,660,000
SIZE OF HOUSEHOLD		$25,000 to $49,000	6,182,000
1 person	13,101,000	$50,000 and over	2,017,000
2 persons	7,149,000	Median income	14,600
		Mean income	20,532

1. Persons of Spanish origin may be of any race. 2. Income during previous calendar year. *Source:* Department of Commerce, Bureau of the Census.

Unemployment by Marital Status, Sex, and Race[1]

Marital status and race	Men		Women	
	Number	Unemployment rate	Number	Unemployment rate
White, 16 years and over	2,595,000	4.4	2,007,000	4.3
Married, spouse present	1,090,000	2.9	952,000	3.5
Widowed, divorced, or separated	337,000	5.8	423,000	5.0
Single (never married)	1,168,000	7.7	632,000	5.7
Black, 16 years and over	780,000	11.9	642,000	9.8
Married, spouse present	206,000	6.4	143,000	5.9
Widowed, divorced, or separated	123,000	13.2	172,000	9.3
Single (never married)	452,000	18.9	326,000	14.4
Total, 16 years and over	3,499,000	5.2	2,730,000	4.9
Married, spouse present	1,356,000	3.2	1,141,000	3.7
Widowed, divorced, or separated	472,000	6.9	608,000	5.7
Single (never married)	1,671,000	9.2	981,000	7.1

1. April, 1989. *Source:* U.S. Department of Labor, Bureau of Labor Statistics.

Earnings Distribution of Year-Round, Full-Time Workers, by Sex, 1987

(persons 15 years old and over as of March 1988)

Earnings group	Number		Distribution (percent)		Likelihood of a woman in each earnings group (percent)[1]
	Women	Men	Women	Men	
$2,999 or less	572,000	708,000	1.9	1.5	1.3
$3,000 to $4,999	350,000	380,000	1.2	0.8	1.5
$5,000 to $6,999	1,059,000	760,000	3.6	1.6	2.3
$7,000 to $9,999	2,754,000	1,982,000	9.2	4.2	2.2
$10,000 to $14,999	7,111,000	5,564,000	23.9	11.8	2.0
$15,000 to $19,999	6,601,000	6,205,000	22.1	13.2	1.7
$20,000 to $24,999	4,685,000	6,536,000	15.7	13.9	1.1
$25,000 to $49,999	6,164,000	19,455,000	20.7	41.3	0.5
$50,000 and over	512,000	5,507,000	1.7	11.7	0.1
Total	**29,809,000**	**47,080,000**	**100.0**	**100.0**	—

Figures obtained by dividing percentages for women by percentages for men. Figures may not add to totals because of rounding.
Source: Department of Commerce, Bureau of the Census.

Comparison of Median Earnings of Year-Round, Full-Time Workers 15 Years and Over, by Sex, 1960 to 1987

Year	Median earnings		Earnings gap in current dollars	Women's earnings as a percent of men's	Percent men's earnings exceeded women's	Earnings gap in constant 1987 dollars
	Women	Men				
1960	$3,257	$5,368	$2,111	60.7	64.8	$8,102
1965	3,828	6,388	2,560	60.0	66.9	9,232
1970	5,323	8,966	3,643	59.4	68.4	10,666
1975	7,504	12,758	5,254	58.8	70.0	11,094
1979	10,169	17,045	6,876	59.7	67.6	10,759
1980	11,197	18,612	7,415	60.2	66.2	10,223
1981	12,001	20,260	8,259	59.2	68.8	10,321
1982	13,014	21,077	8,063	61.7	62.0	9,492
1983	13,915	21,881	7,966	63.6	57.2	9,086
1984	14,780	23,218	8,438	63.7	57.1	9,226
1985	15,624	24,195	8,571	64.7	54.9	9,049
1986	16,232	25,256	9,024	64.3	55.6	9,353
1987	16,909	26,008	9,099	65.0	53.8	9,099

Source: Department of Commerce, Bureau of the Census.

Occupations of Employed Women
(16 years of age and over. Figures are percentage)

Occupations	1988[1]	1987[1]	1986[1]	1985[1]	1984[1]	1983[1]	1982[1]
Managerial and professional	25.2	24.4	23.7	23.4	22.5	21.9	21.7
Technical, sales, administrative support	44.6	45.1	45.6	45.5	45.6	45.8	45.7
Service occupations	17.9	18.1	18.3	18.5	18.7	18.9	19.0
Precision production, craft and repair	2.3	2.3	2.4	2.4	2.4	2.3	1.9
Operators, fabricators, laborers	8.9	9.0	8.9	9.1	9.6	9.7	10.3
Farming, forestry, fishing	1.1	1.1	1.1	1.2	1.2	1.3	1.4

1. Annual averages. NOTE: Details may not add up to totals because of rounding. *Source:* Department of Labor.

Employed and Unemployed Workers by Full- and Part-Time Status, Sex, and Age: 1970 to 1987
(In thousands)

	1988	1987	1986	1985	1984	1980	1975	1970
Total 16 yr and over								
Employed	114,968	112,440	109,597	107,150	105,005	99,303	85,846	78,678
Full time	95,214	92,957	90,529	88,535	86,544	82,564	71,585	66,752
Part time	19,754	19,483	19,069	18,615	18,461	16,742	14,260	11,924
Unemployed	6,701	7,425	8,237	8,312	8,539	7,637	7,929	4,093
Full time	5,357	5,979	6,708	6,793	7,057	6,269	6,523	3,206
Part time	1,343	1,446	1,529	1,519	1,481	1,369	1,408	889
Men, 20 yr and over								
Employed	59,781	58,726	57,569	56,562	55,769	53,101	48,018	45,581
Full time	55,353	54,381	53,317	52,425	51,624	49,699	45,051	43,138
Part time	4,427	4,345	4,252	4,137	4,145	3,403	2,966	2,444
Unemployed	2,987	3,369	3,751	3,715	3,932	3,353	3,476	1,638
Full time	2,778	3,147	3,508	3,479	3,685	3,167	3,255	1,502
Part time	209	222	243	236	247	186	223	137
Women, 20 yr. and over								
Employed	48,383	47,074	45,556	44,154	42,793	38,492	30,726	26,952
Full time	37,299	36,121	34,812	33,604	32,404	29,391	23,242	20,654
Part time	11,084	10,953	10,744	10,550	10,388	9,102	7,484	6,297
Unemployed	2,487	2,709	3,032	3,129	3,107	2,615	2,684	1,349
Full time	1,987	2,178	2,468	2,536	2,556	2,135	2,210	1,077
Part time	500	530	565	593	551	480	474	271
Both sexes 16–19 yr.								
Employed	6,805	6,640	6,472	6,434	6,444	7,710	7,104	6,144
Full time	2,562	2,454	2,400	2,507	2,516	3,474	3,292	2,960
Part time	4,243	4,185	4,073	3,927	3,928	4,237	3,810	3,183
Unemployed	1,226	1,347	1,454	1,468	1,499	1,669	1,767	1,106
Full time	592	653	733	777	816	966	1,057	626
Part time	634	694	721	690	683	701	709	480

Source: U.S. Dept. of Labor, Bureau of Labor Statistics.

Work Stoppages Involving 1,000 Workers or More[1]

Year	Work stoppages	Workers involved (thousands)	Man-days idle (thousands)	Year	Work stoppages	Workers involved (thousands)	Man-days idle (thousands)
1950	424	1,698	30,390	1980	187	795	20,844
1955	363	2,055	21,180	1981	145	729	16,908
1960	222	896	13,260	1982	96	656	9,061
1965	268	999	15,140	1983	81	909	17,461
1970	381	2,468	52,761	1984	68	391	8,499
1975	235	965	17,563	1985	61	584	7,079
1977	298	1,212	21,258	1986	72	900	11,861
1978	219	1,006	23,774	1987	46	174	4,456
1979	235	1,021	20,409	1988	40	118	4,381

1. The number of stoppages and workers relate to stoppages that began in the year. Days of idleness include all stoppages in effect. Workers are counted more than once if they were involved in more than one stoppage during the year. *Source:* U.S. Department of Labor. Bureau of Labor Statistics, *Monthly Labor Review. July 1989.*

Leading Advertising Agencies in World Billings

(in thousands of dollars)

Agency	1988	1987
Saatchi & Saatchi Advertising	$5,035,973	$4,609,437
McCann-Erickson	4,381,000	3,468,495 [1]
FCB-Publicis	4,052,000 [2]	3,225,000 [2]
Backer Spielvogel Bates Worldwide	3,804,784	3,244,388
Young & Rubicam	3,757,000	3,100,000
J. Walter Thompson	3,686,616 [2]	3,020,829 [1]
Lintas: Worldwide	3,591,000 [2]	2,900,000 [1]
Ogilvy & Mather Worldwide	3,482,638	3,088,606
D'Arcy Masius Benton & Bowles	3,003,000	2,424,000
Leo Burnett Co.	2,865,087	2,461,794

1. Restated 1987 billings. 2. Estimated. *Source: Ad Week Magazine*, Top 30 Worldwide Agencies, May 15, 1989 edition. Copyright © Ad Week Magazine Network 1989. All rights reserved.

Unemployment Rate, 1988

Race and age	Women[1]	Men[1]
All races:	5.6	5.5
16 to 19 years	14.4	16.0
20 years and over	4.9	4.8
White	4.7	4.7
16 to 19 years	12.3	13.9
20 years and over	4.1	4.1
Minority races:	10.5	10.3
16 to 19 years	28.6	29.3
20 years and over	9.3	8.9

1. Annual averages. *Source:* Bureau of Labor Statistics, Department of Labor.

Unemployment Rate in the Civilian Labor Force

Year	Unemployment Rate	Year	Unemployment Rate
1920	5.2	1976	7.7
1922	6.7	1978	6.0
1924	5.0	1979	5.8
1926	1.8	1980	7.1
1928	4.2	1981	7.6
1930	8.7	1982	9.7
1932	23.6	1983	9.6
1934	21.7	1984	7.5
1936	16.9	1985	7.2
1938	19.0	1986	7.0
1940	14.6	1987	6.2
1942	4.7	1988	5.5
1944	1.2	Jan.	5.8
1946	3.9	Feb.	5.7
1948	3.8	March	5.6
1950	5.3	April	5.5
1952	3.0	May	5.6
1954	5.5	June	5.4
1956	4.1	July	5.4
1958	6.8	Aug.	5.6
1960	5.5	Sept.	5.4
1962	5.5	Oct.	5.3
1964	5.2	Nov.	5.4
1966	3.8	Dec.	5.3
1968	3.6	1989	
1970	4.9	Jan.	5.4
1972	5.6	Feb.	5.1
1974	5.6	March	5.0
		April	5.3

NOTE: Estimates prior to 1940 are based on sources other than direct enumeration. *Source:* Department of Labor, Bureau of Labor Statistics.

Employment and Unemployment

(in millions of persons)

Category	1989[2]	1988	1987	1985	1980	1975	1970	1950	1945	1932	1929
EMPLOYMENT STATUS[1]											
Civilian noninstitutional population	186.3	184.6	182.8	178.2	167.7	153.2	137.1	105.0	94.1	—	—
Civilian labor force	124.1	121.7	119.9	115.5	106.9	93.8	82.8	62.2	53.9	—	—
Civilian labor force participation rate	66.6	65.9	65.6	64.8	63.8	61.2	60.4	59.2	57.2	—	—
Employed	117.5	115.0	112.4	107.2	99.3	85.8	78.7	58.9	52.8	38.9	47.6
Employment-population ratio	63.1	62.3	61.5	60.1	59.2	56.1	57.4	56.1	56.1	—	—
Agriculture	3.1	3.2	3.2	3.2	3.4	3.4	3.5	7.2	8.6	10.2	10.5
Nonagricultural industries	114.4	111.8	109.2	104.0	95.9	82.4	75.2	51.8	44.2	28.8	37.2
Unemployed	6.6	6.7	7.4	8.3	7.6	7.9	4.1	3.3	1.0	12.1	1.6
Unemployment rate	5.3	5.5	6.2	7.2	7.1	8.5	4.9	5.3	1.9	23.6	3.2
Not in labor force	62.2	62.9	62.9	62.7	60.8	59.4	54.3	42.8	40.2	—	—
INDUSTRY											
Total nonagricultural employment	108.5	105.6	102.2	97.5	90.4	76.9	70.9	45.2	40.4	23.6	31.3
Goods-producing industries	25.6	25.2	24.7	24.9	25.7	22.6	23.6	18.5	17.5	8.6	13.3
Mining	0.7	0.7	0.7	0.9	1.0	0.8	0.6	0.9	0.8	0.7	1.1
Construction	5.3	5.1	5.0	4.7	4.3	3.5	3.6	2.4	1.1	1.0	1.5
Manufacturing: Durable goods	11.6	11.4	11.2	11.5	12.2	10.7	11.2	8.1	9.1	—	—
Nondurable goods	8.1	8.0	7.8	7.8	8.1	7.6	8.2	7.1	6.5	—	—
Services-producing industries	82.9	80.3	77.5	72.7	64.7	54.3	47.3	26.7	22.9	15.0	18.0
Transportation and public utilities	5.7	5.5	5.4	5.2	5.1	4.5	4.5	4.0	3.9	2.8	3.9
Trade, Wholesale	6.2	6.0	5.8	5.7	5.3	4.4	4.0	2.6	1.9	—	—
Retail	19.5	19.1	18.5	17.4	15.0	12.6	11.0	6.8	5.4	—	—
Finance, insurance, and real estate	6.8	6.7	6.5	6.0	5.2	4.2	3.6	1.9	1.5	1.3	1.5
Services	26.9	25.6	24.2	22.0	17.9	13.9	11.5	5.4	4.2	2.9	3.4
Federal government	3.0	3.0	2.9	2.9	2.9	2.7	2.7	1.9	2.8	0.6	0.5
State and local government	14.7	14.4	14.1	13.5	13.4	11.9	9.8	4.1	3.1	2.7	2.5

1. For 1929–45, figures on employment status relate to persons 14 years and over; beginning in 1950, 16 years and over.
2. As of June; seasonally adjusted; industry data are preliminary. *Source:* Bureau of Labor Statistics.

Livestock on Farms (in thousands)

Type	1989	1988	1987	1985	1980	1975	1970	1965	1960	1950
Cattle[1]	99,484	98,994	102,000	109,749	111,242	132,028	112,369	109,000	96,236	77,963
Dairy cows[1]	10,298	10,307	10,502	10,805	10,758	11,220	13,303	16,981	19,527	23,853
Sheep[1]	10,802	10,774	10,324	10,443	12,699	14,515	20,423	25,127	33,170	29,826
Swine[2]	52,485	53,795	50,920	54,073	67,318	54,693	57,046	56,106	59,026	58,937
Chickens[2]	5,706,264	5,003,000	4,646,000	374,008	400,585	384,101	422,000	401,000	369,000	457,000
Turkeys[3]	259,440	240,349	207,216	3,159	3,749	3,014	6,715	6,100	5,633	5,124

1. As of Jan. 1. 2. As of Jan. 1 the previous year for 1945–60 and Dec. 1 for 1965–87. 3. Turkey breeder hens for 1975–85 as of Dec. 1 the previous year. *Source:* Department of Agriculture, Statistical Reporting Service, Economic Research Service.

Agricultural Output by States, 1988 Crops

State	Corn (1,000 bu)	Wheat (1,000 bu)	Cotton (1,000 ba[1])	Potatoes (1,000 cwt)	Tobacco (1,000 lb)	Cattle[2] (1,000 head)	Swine[3] (1,000 head)
Alabama	7,480	8,600	380	1,139	—	1,750	n.a.
Alaska	—	—	—	—	—	9.5	n.a.
Arizona	2,210	7,730	1,120.0	1,246	—	960	n.a.
Arkansas	6,000	56,710	1,050.0	—	—	1,850	n.a.
California	27,115	43,785	2,853.2	16,765	—	4,650	n.a.
Colorado	128,000	79,540	—	20,156	—	2,700	n.a.
Connecticut	—	—	—	113	2,848	77	n.a.
Delaware	9,800	3,276	—	1,806	—	29	n.a.
Florida	3,770	2,035	30.0	8,173	17,152	1,970	n.a.
Georgia	31,000	21,500	370.0	—	85,880	1,520	1,125
Hawaii	—	—	—	—	—	199	n.a.
Idaho	6,500	75,520	—	99,320	—	1,570	n.a.
Illinois	700,800	67,500	—	736	—	2,050	n.a.
Indiana	415,000	35,000	—	756	10,600	1,360	5,600
Iowa	898,800	1,050	—	289	—	4,650	4,100
Kansas	143,750	323,000	0.8	—	—	5,860	13,500
Kentucky	80,300	20,520	—	—	337,250	2,450	1,420
Louisiana	11,875	11,070	950.0	20	—	1,125	850
Maine	—	—	—	22,000	—	113	n.a.
Maryland	27,300	9,010	—	460	12,900	320	n.a.
Massachusetts	—	—	—	572	836	70	n.a.
Michigan	112,000	26,040	—	8,610	—	1,225	n.a.
Minnesota	347,800	51,730	—	13,557	—	2,900	1,130
Mississippi	9,000	20,700	1,830.0	—	—	1,350	4,300
Missouri	153,520	77,500	310.0	—	4,100	4,400	2,900
Montana	2,200	59,970	—	2,156	—	2,350	n.a.
Nebraska	818,400	72,000	—	2,818	—	5,450	3,900
Nevada	—	1,340	—	2,480	—	500	n.a.
New Hampshire	—	—	—	—	—	55	n.a.
New Jersey	5,880	1,395	—	1,170	—	80	n.a.
New Mexico	8,525	6,960	128.0	3,060	—	1,320	n.a.
New York	41,225	4,950	—	6,420	—	1,702	n.a.
North Carolina	78,120	24,000	132.0	2,904	552,970	825	2,500
North Dakota	22,040	103,390	—	14,375	—	1,800	n.a.
Ohio	255,000	46,000	—	1,697	14,838	1,820	2,000
Oklahoma	6,840	172,800	290.0	—	—	5,100	n.a.
Oregon	3,002	51,800	—	20,735	—	1,360	n.a.
Pennsylvania	59,150	9,010	—	3,690	18,175	1,920	830
Rhode Island	19,430	—	—	300	—	7.0	n.a.
South Carolina	—	14,030	148.0	1,600	100,125	620	n.a.
South Dakota	132,000	38,006	—	91	—	3,500	1,640
Tennessee	38,690	21,500	590.0	3,397	90,830	2,300	900
Texas	129,600	89,600	5,260.0	1,617	—	13,600	n.a.
Utah	2,728	6,768	—	—	—	760	n.a.
Vermont	—	—	—	2,048	—	297	n.a.
Virginia	23,305	10,400	3.5	63,250	90,950	1,700	n.a.
Washington	13,600	124,620	—	—	—	1,290	n.a.
West Virginia	2,320	414	—	20,000	2,945	490	n.a.
Wisconsin	130,650	5,152	—	447	5,725	4,230	1,300
Wyoming	6,466	5,340	—	—	—	1,290	n.a.
U.S. Total	4,921,191	1,811,261	15,445.5	349,973	1,348,124	99,524	52,345

1. 480-lb net-weight bales. 2. Number on farms as of Jan. 1, 1989. 3. Number on farms as of Dec. 1, 1988. n.a. = not available. *Source:* Department of Agriculture, Statistical Reporting Service.

Farm Income
(in millions of dollars)

Year	Cash receipts from marketings Crops	Livestock, livestock products	Government payments	Total cash income
1925	5,545	5,476	—	11,021
1930	3,868	5,187	—	9,055
1935	2,977	4,143	$573	7,693
1940	3,469	4,913	723	9,105
1945	9,655	12,008	742	22,405
1950	12,356	16,105	283	28,744
1955	13,523	15,967	229	29,719
1960[1]	15,023	18,989	702	34,714
1965	17,479	21,886	2,463	41,828
1970	20,977	29,532	3,717	54,226
1975[1]	45,813	43,089	807	89,709
1980[1]	71,746	67,991	1,286	141,023
1982[1]	72,338	70,257	3,492	146,087
1983	67,129	69,438	9,295 [2]	150,362
1984[1]	69,471	72,966	8,430	150,867
1985[1]	74,270	69,845	7,704	151,819
1986[1]	63,778	71,534	11,813	147,125
1987[1]	63,478	75,717	16,747	155,942

1. Figures revised. 2. Includes value of PIK commodities. *Source:* Department of Agriculture, Economic Research Service. NOTE: Figures are latest available.

Per Capita Consumption of Principal Foods[1]

Food	1987	1986	1985
Red meat[2]	135.4	140.2	144.1
Poultry	87.8	72.0	69.7
Fish (edible weight)	15.4	14.7	14.4
Eggs	31.6	31.7	32.2
Fluid milk and cream[3]	235.7	237.5	238.5
Ice cream	18.3	18.4	18.1
Cheese (excluding cottage)	24.0	23.0	22.5
Butter (actual weight)	4.6	4.6	4.9
Margarine (actual weight)	10.5	11.4	10.8
Total fats and oils	62.7	64.1	64.0
Selected fresh fruits (farm weight)	101.7	96.6	89.6
Peanuts (shelled)	6.3	6.4	6.3
Selected fresh vegetable	78.6	79.9	78.8
White potatoes[4]	118.6	124.3	124.3
Sugar (refined)	62.2	60.2	63.0
Corn sweeteners (dry weight)	68.8	67.1	66.5
Flour and cereal products	173.8	164.5	159.8
Soft drinks (gal)	n.a.	30.3	29.1
Coffee	7.6	7.6	7.6
Cocoa (chocolate liquor equivalent)	3.9	3.8	3.7

1. As of August 1988. Except where noted, consumption is from commercial sources and is in terms of retail weight. 2. Skeletal meat; excludes edible offals. 3. Includes milk and cream produced and consumed on farms. 4. Farm-weight equivalent of fresh and processed use. NOTE: Data are latest available.

Government Employment and Payrolls

Year and function	Employees (in thousands) Total	Federal[1]	State	Local	October payrolls (in millions) Total	Federal[1]	State	Local
1940	4,474	1,128	3,346		$566	177	$389	
1945	6,677	3,496	3,181		1,059	591	468	
1950	6,402	2,117	1,057	3,228	1,528	613	218	696
1955	7,432	2,378	1,199	3,855	2,265	846	326	1,093
1960	8,808	2,421	1,527	4,860	3,333	1,118	524	1,691
1965	10,589	2,588	2,028	5,973	4,884	1,484	849	2,551
1970	13,028	2,881	2,755	7,392	8,334	2,428	1,612	4,294
1975	14,973	2,890	3,271	8,813	13,224	3,584	2,653	6,987
1978	15,628	2,885	3,539	9,204	16,483	4,344	3,483	8,656
1979	15,971	2,869	3,699	9,403	18,077	4,728	3,869	9,480
1980	16,213	2,898	3,753	9,562	19,935	5,205	4,285	10,445
1981	15,968	2,865	3,726	9,377	21,193	5,239	4,668	11,287
1982	15,841	2,848	3,744	9,249	23,173	5,959	5,022	12,192
1983	16,034	2,875	3,816	9,344	24,525	6,302	5,346	12,878
1984	16,436	2,942	3,898	9,595	26,904	7,137	5,815	13,952
1985	16,690	3,021	3,984	9,685	28,945	7,580	6,329	15,036
1986	16,933	3,019	4,068	9,846	30,670	7,561	6,810	12,298
1987, total	17,281	3,091	4,115	10,076	32,382	7,924	7,298	17,160
National defense and international relations	1,099	1,099	(2)	(2)	2,898	2,898	(2)	(2)
Postal service	807	807	(2)	(2)	1,966	1,966	(2)	(2)
Education	7,404	15	1,804	5,584	12,352	37	2,758	9,557
Instructional employees	4,153	n.a.	553	3,600	8,674	n.a.	1,275	7,398
Highways	557		251	302	1,018	15	505	498
Health and Hospitals	1,664	265	691	708	3,024	631	1,252	1,141
Police protection	791	73	82	636	1,731	213	195	1,322
Local fire protection	335	(2)	(2)	335	629	(2)	(2)	629
Sewerage and sanitation	226	n.a.	1	225	404	n.a.	2	402
Parks and recreation	298	24	37	237	371	52	50	268
Natural resources	439	243	158	38	968	635	283	50
Financial administration	467	134	133	200	843	289	258	296
All other	3,196	428	958	1,810	6,180	1,190	1,994	2,997

1. Civilians only. 2. Not applicable. NOTE: n.a. = not available. Detail may not add to totals because of rounding. *Source:* Department of Commerce, Bureau of the Census.

Receipts and Outlays of the Federal Government

(in millions of dollars)

From 1789 to 1842, the federal fiscal year ended Dec. 31; from 1844 to 1976, on June 30; and beginning 1977, on Sept. 30.

Year	Customs (including tonnage tax)[1]	Internal revenue		Miscellaneous taxes and receipts	Total receipts	Net receipts[2]
		Income and profits tax	Other			
1789–1791	$ 4	—	—	—	$ 4	$ 4
1800	9	—	$ −1	$ 1	11	11
1810	9	—	—	1	9	9
1820	15	—	—	3	18	18
1830	22	—	—	3	25	25
1840	14	—	—	6	20	20
1850	40	—	—	4	44	44
1860	53	—	—	3	56	56
1865	85	—	209	39	334	334
1870	195	—	185	32	411	411
1880	187	—	124	23	334	334
1890	230	—	143	31	403	403
1900	233	—	295	39	567	567
1910	334	—	290	52	675	675
1915	210	$ 80	335	72	698	683
1918	180	2,314	872	299	3,665	3,645
1929	602	2,331	607	493	4,033	3,862
1933	251	746	858	225	2,080	1,997
1939	319	2,189	2,972	188	5,668	4,979
1943	324	16,094	6,050	934	23,402	21,947
1944	431	34,655	7,030	3,325	45,441	43,563
1945	355	35,173	8,729	3,494	47,750	44,362
1950	423	28,263	11,186	1,439	41,311	36,422
1956[4]	705	56,639	20,564	389	78,297	74,547
1960	1,123	67,151	28,266	1,190	97,730	92,492
1965	1,478	79,792	39,996	1,598	122,863	116,833
1970	2,494	138,689	65,276	3,424	209,883	193,743
1975	3,782	202,146	108,371	6,711	321,010	280,997
1980	7,482	359,927	192,436	12,797	572,641	520,050
1985	12,079	474,074	311,092	18,576	815,821	733,996
1986	13,323	412,102	323,779	19,887	([5])	769,091
1987	15,085	476,483	343,268	19,307	([5])	854,143
1988	16,198	495,376	377,469	19,909	([5])	908,953

Year	Department of Defense (Army, 1789–1950)	Department of the Navy	Interest on public debt	All other	Net outlays[3]	Surplus (+) or deficit (−)
1789–1791	$ 1	—	$ 2	$ 1	$ 4	—
1800	3	$ 3	3	1	11	—
1810	2	2	3	1	8	$ +1
1820	3	4	5	6	18	—
1830	5	3	2	5	15	+10
1840	7	6	—	11	24	−4
1850	9	8	4	18	40	+4
1860	16	12	3	32	63	−7
1865	1,031	123	77	66	1,298	−964
1870	58	22	129	101	310	+101
1880	38	14	96	120	268	+66
1890	45	22	36	215	318	+85
1900	135	56	40	290	521	+46
1910	190	123	21	359	694	−19
1915	202	142	23	379	746	−63
1918	4,870	1,279	190	6,339	12,677	−9,032
1929	426	365	678	1,658	3,127	+734
1933	435	349	689	3,125	4,598	−2,602

	Outlays					
Year	Department of Defense (Army, 1789–1950)	Department of the Navy	Interest on public debt	All other	Net outlays[3]	Surplus (+) or deficit (−)
1939	695	673	941	6,533	8,841	−3,862
1943	42,526	20,888	1,808	14,146	79,368	−57,420
1944	49,438	26,538	2,609	16,401	94,986	−51,423
1945	50,490	30,047	3,617	14,149	98,303	−53,941
1950	5,789	4,130	5,750	23,875	39,544	−3,122
1956[4]	35,693	—	6,787	27,981	70,460	+4,087
1960	43,969	—	9,180	39,075	92,223	+269
1965	47,179	—	11,346	59,904	118,430	−1,596
1970	78,360	—	19,304	98,924	196,588	−2,845
1975	87,471	—	32,665	205,969	326,105	−45,108
1980	136,138	—	74,860	368,013	579,011	−58,961
1985	244,054	—	178,945	513,810	936,809	−202,813
1986	273,369	—	135,284	581,136	989,789	−220,698
1987	282,016	—	138,519	581,612	1,002,147	−148,004
1988	290,349	—	151,711	621,995	1,064,055	−155,102

1. Beginning 1933, tonnage tax is included in "Other receipts." 2. Net receipts equal total receipts less (a) appropriations to federal old-age and survivors' insurance trust fund beginning fiscal year 1939 and (b) refunds of receipts beginning fiscal year 1933. 3. Includes Air Force 1950–65 (in millions): 1950—$3,521; 1956—$16,750; 1960—$19,065; 1965—$18,471. 4. Beginning 1956, computed on unified budget concepts; not strictly comparable with preceding figures. 5. Net receipts are now the total receipts. Public Law 99-177 moved two social security trust funds off-budget. Source: Department of the Treasury, Financial Management Service.

Contributions to International Organizations
(for fiscal year 1988 in millions of dollars)

Organization	Amount[1]	Organization	Amount[1]
United Nations and Specialized Agencies		International Institute for Cotton	1.95
United Nations	$ 147.95	Others (36 Programs, less than $1 million)	6.10
Food and Agriculture Organization	25.00	Special Voluntary Programs	
International Atomic Energy Agency	33.82	Consultative Group on International	
International Civil Aviation Organization	6.92	Agricultural Research	42.00
International Labor Organization	26.71	Intergovernmental Committee for Migration	6.24
International Telecommunication Union	5.18	International Atomic Energy Agency Technical	
United Nations Industrial Development		Assistance Fund	21.56[2]
Organization	12.50	International Fund for Agricultural Development	30.00
World Health Organization	62.86	OAS Special Development Assistance Fund	4.80
World Meteorological Organization	5.76	OAS Special Multilateral Fund (Education and	
Others (7 Programs, less than $1 million)	3.04	Science)	5.40
Peacekeeping Forces		OAS Special Projects Fund (Mar del Plata)	1.50
United Nations Force in Cyprus	7.31	PAHO Special Health Promotion Funds	5.00
United Nations Disengagement Observer Force		United Nations Children's Fund	53.90
(UNDOF) and UNIFIL	29.40	United Nations Development Program	108.00
Multinational Force and Observers	24.38	United Nations Environment Program	7.84
Inter-American Organizations		U.N./FAO World Food Program	234.64[3]
Organization of American States	38.12	U.N. Fund for Drug Abuse Control	5.52
Inter-American Institute for Cooperation on		U.N. High Commissioner for Refugees Program:	
Agriculture	11.03	Regular Programs (5)	84.66
Inter-American Tropical Tuna Commission	2.68	Special Programs (7)	26.46
Pan American Health Organization	32.56	United Nations Relief and Works Agency:	
Others (4 Programs, less than $1 million)	.54	Regular Program	61.30
Regional Organizations		Special Emergency Programs	2.00
NATO Civilian Headquarters (and MBFR)	21.10	WHO Special Programs	15.00
Organization for Economic Cooperation and		WMO Voluntary Cooperation Program	1.96
Development	34.09	Others (12 Programs, less than $1 million)	4.36
Others (3 Programs, less than $1 million)	1.42	Total U.S. Contributions	$1,271.33
Other International Organizations			
Customs Cooperation Council	1.91		
General Agreement on Tariffs and Trade	6.86		

1. Estimated. 2. Includes cash, commodities and services, and $7.84 million for the Safeguards Program and other non-proliferation activities. 3. Includes cash, commodities and services, and $56.8 million for the International Emergency Food Reserve.

Social Welfare Expenditures Under Public Programs
(in millions of dollars)

Year and source of funds	Social insurance	Public aid	Health and medical programs[1]	Veterans' programs	Education	Housing	Other social welfare	All health and medical care[2]	Total social welfare	Total social welfare as: Percent of gross national product	Percent of total gov't outlays
FEDERAL											
1960	14,307	2,117	1,737	5,367	868	144	417	2,918	24,957	5.0	28.1
1965	21,807	3,594	2,781	6,011	2,470	238	812	4,625	37,712	5.7	32.6
1970	45,246	9,649	4,775	8,952	5,876	582	2,259	16,600	77,337	8.1	40.1
1975	99,715	27,205	8,513	16,570	8,629	2,541	4,264	34,645	167,436	11.5	53.8
1980	191,162	48,666	12,886	21,254	13,452	6,608	8,786	68,989	303,276	11.5	53.2
1981	224,574	55,946	13,596	23,229	13,372	6,045	7,304	80,505	344,066	11.6	54.0
1982	250,551	52,485	14,598	24,463	11,917	7,176	6,500	90,776	367,691	12.0	52.5
1983	274,212	55,895	15,594	25,561	12,397	8,087	7,046	100,274	398,792	12.0	51.9
1984	288,743	58,480	16,622	25,970	13,010	10,226	7,349	103,927	420,399	11.3	50.2
1985	313,108	61,985	18,630	26,704	13,796	11,088	7,548	118,955	452,860	11.5	47.8
1986	326,588	65,615	19,926	27,072	15,022	10,164	7,977	125,730	472,364	11.3	47.6
STATE AND LOCAL											
1960	4,999	1,984	2,727	112	16,758	33	723	3,478	27,337	5.5	60.1
1965	6,316	2,690	3,466	20	25,638	80	1,254	4,911	39,464	6.0	60.4
1970	9,446	6,839	5,132	127	44,970	120	1,886	8,791	68,519	7.1	64.0
1975	23,298	14,122	9,195	449	72,234	631	2,683	17,847	122,612	8.4	63.7
1980	38,592	23,133	14,771	212	107,597	601	4,813	31,309	189,720	7.2	66.5
1981	42,821	26,477	17,124	212	114,773	688	4,679	36,327	206,774	7.0	63.1
1982	52,481	28,367	19,195	245	121,957	778	5,154	40,738	228,178	7.4	62.6
1983	56,846	29,935	20,382	265	129,416	1,003	5,438	42,854	243,285	7.3	60.1
1984	52,378	32,206	20,383	301	139,046	1,306	5,946	44,540	251,569	6.8	58.9
1985	59,420	34,792	22,430	338	152,622	1,540	6,398	48,587	277,540	7.0	59.0
1986	63,816	37,464	24,408	373	163,495	1,872	6,728	53,884	298,158	7.1	58.2
TOTAL											
1960	19,307	4,101	4,464	5,479	17,626	177	1,139	6,395	52,293	10.5	38.4
1965	28,123	6,283	6,246	6,031	28,108	318	2,066	9,535	77,175	11.7	42.2
1970	54,691	16,488	9,907	9,078	50,846	701	4,145	25,391	145,856	15.2	48.2
1975	123,013	41,326	17,708	17,019	80,863	3,172	6,947	52,492	290,047	20.0	57.4
1980	229,754	71,799	27,657	21,466	121,050	7,210	13,599	100,298	492,534	18.7	57.4
1981	267,395	82,424	30,720	23,441	128,145	6,734	11,983	116,832	550,841	18.6	56.9
1982	303,033	80,852	33,793	24,708	133,874	7,954	11,654	131,514	595,869	19.4	55.7
1983	331,058	85,830	35,976	25,826	141,813	9,090	12,484	143,128	642,077	19.3	54.5
1984	341,120	90,685	37,006	26,275	152,056	11,532	13,295	148,467	671,969	18.2	52.8
1985	372,529	96,777	41,060	27,042	166,418	12,627	13,946	167,542	730,399	18.5	51.2
1986	390,404	103,079	44,334	27,445	178,518	12,036	14,705	179,614	770,522	18.4	47.9
PERCENT OF TOTAL, BY TYPE											
1960	36.9	7.8	8.5	10.5	33.7	0.3	2.2	12.2	100.0	(3)	(3)
1965	36.4	8.1	8.1	7.8	36.4	0.4	2.7	12.4	100.0	(3)	(3)
1970	37.5	11.3	6.7	6.2	34.9	0.5	3.0	17.2	100.0	(3)	(3)
1975	42.4	14.2	6.1	5.9	27.9	1.1	2.4	18.1	100.0	(3)	(3)
1980	46.6	14.6	5.6	4.4	24.6	1.5	2.8	20.4	100.0	(3)	(3)
1984[2]	50.9	13.4	5.6	3.9	22.6	1.5	2.0	23.1	100.0	(3)	(3)
1985	51.0	13.2	5.6	3.7	22.8	1.7	1.9	22.9	100.0	(3)	(3)
1986	50.7	13.4	5.8	3.6	23.2	1.6	1.9	23.3	100.0	(3)	(3)
FEDERAL PERCENT OF TOTAL											
1960	74.1	51.6	38.9	98.0	4.9	81.2	36.6	45.6	47.7	(3)	(3)
1965	77.5	57.2	44.5	99.7	8.8	74.9	39.3	48.5	48.9	(3)	(3)
1970	82.7	58.5	48.2	98.6	11.6	82.9	54.5	65.4	53.0	(3)	(3)
1975	81.1	65.8	48.1	97.4	10.7	80.1	61.4	66.0	57.7	(3)	(3)
1980	83.2	67.8	46.6	99.0	11.1	91.7	64.6	68.8	61.6	(3)	(3)
1984[2]	84.7	64.2	43.6	99.0	8.5	87.4	54.7	70.0	62.4	(3)	(3)
1985	84.0	64.0	45.4	98.8	8.3	87.8	54.1	71.0	62.0	(3)	(3)
1986	83.6	63.7	44.9	98.6	8.4	84.4	54.2	70.0	61.3	(3)	(3)

1. Excludes program parts of social insurance, public aid, veterans, and other social welfare. 2. Combines health and medical programs with medical services provided in connection with social insurance, public aid, veterans, and other social welfare programs. 3. Not applicable. NOTE: Figures are latest available. *Source:* Department of Health and Human Services. *Social Security Bulletin,* November 1988 and earlier issues.

Domestic Freight Traffic by Major Carriers

(in millions of ton-miles)[1]

Year	Railroads Ton-miles	Railroads % of total	Inland waterways[2] Ton-miles	Inland waterways[2] % of total	Motor trucks Ton-miles	Motor trucks % of total	Oil pipelines Ton-miles	Oil pipelines % of total	Air carriers Ton-miles	Air carriers % of total
1940	379,201	61.3	118,057	19.1	62,043	10.0	59,277	9.6	14	—
1945	690,809	67.3	142,737	13.9	66,948	6.5	126,530	12.3	91	—
1950	596,940	56.2	163,344	15.4	172,860	16.3	129,175	12.1	318	—
1955	631,385	49.5	216,508	17.0	223,254	17.5	203,244	16.0	481	—
1960	579,130	44.1	220,253	16.8	285,483	21.7	228,626	17.4	778	—
1965	708,700	43.3	262,421	16.0	359,218	21.9	306,393	18.7	1,910	0.1
1970	771,168	39.8	318,560	16.4	412,000	21.3	431,000	22.3	3,274	0.2
1975	759,000	36.7	342,210	16.5	454,000	22.0	507,300	24.6	3,732	0.2
1980	932,000	37.2	420,000	16.9	567,000	22.6	588,000	23.1	4,528	0.2
1982	810,000	35.8	351,000	15.5	525,000	23.2	571,000	25.3	4,476	0.2
1983	841,000	36.0	359,000	15.4	575,000	24.6	556,000	23.8	5,870	0.3
1985	895,000	36.4	382,000	15.6	610,000	24.9	564,000	22.9	6,080	0.2
1986	889,000	35.5	393,000	15.7	634,000	25.4	578,000	23.1	7,100	0.3
1987	972,000	36.8	411,000	15.6	661,000	25.1	587,000	22.2	8,670	0.3
1988[3]	1,034,000	37.0	434,000	15.5	704,000	25.2	612,000	21.9	9,300	0.3

1. Mail and express included, except railroads for 1970. 2. Rivers, canals, and domestic traffic on Great Lakes. 3. Preliminary.
Source: For 1987 on, *Transportation in America, 7th Edition,* Eno Foundation for Transportation.

Tonnage Handled by Principal U.S. Ports

(Over 10 million tons annually; in thousands of tons)

Port	1987	1986	Port	1987	1986
New Orleans	167,917	149,082	Chicago	20,705	24,330
New York	154,536	157,801	Port Arthur, Texas	20,615	18,880
Houston	112,546	101,659	Boston, Port of	19,829	21,036
Valdez Harbor, Alaska	106,867	101,118	Newport News, Va.	19,264	18,531
Baton Rouge, La.	73,401	77,184	Huntington, W. Va.	18,772	20,852
Corpus Christi, Texas	53,539	50,105	Seattle	18,552	17,098
Long Beach, Calif.	45,898	42,718	Paulsboro, N.J.	17,936	18,295
Tampa Harbor, Fla.	44,303	39,909	Tacoma Harbor, Wash.	17,129	16,173
Los Angeles	40,460	39,859	Toledo Harbor	16,211	17,819
Norfolk Harbor, Va.	39,993	44,069	Lorain Harbor, Ohio	14,372	11,427
Baltimore Harbor, Md.	37,488	35,432	Detroit	14,129	15,219
Philadelphia	37,336	35,661	Port Everglades, Fla.	14,045	11,536
Texas City, Texas	37,233	35,480	Freeport, Texas	13,980	13,370
Duluth–Superior, Minn.	36,462	29,155	Cleveland	13,914	12,188
Mobile, Ala.	32,384	37,576	Anacortes, Wash.	13,687	12,747
Lake Charles, La.	31,730	30,921	Jacksonville, Fla.	13,483	12,442
Beaumont, Texas	29,758	27,454	San Juan, P.R.	13,452	12,361
Pittsburgh	28,840	26,709	Indiana Harbor, Ind.	13,335	14,014
Marcus Hook, Pa.	28,154	30,554	Savannah, Ga.	13,201	12,041
Pascagoula, Miss.	27,824	23,700	Cincinnati, Ohio	11,995	12,276
St. Louis (Metropolitan)	27,571	28,003	New Castle, Del.	11,292	9,940
Portland, Ore.	26,812	25,590	Memphis, Tenn.	11,200	10,985
Richmond, Calif.	21,431	18,833			

Source: Department of the Army, Corps of Engineers.

Annual Railroad Carloadings

Year	Total	Year	Total	Year	Total	Year	Total
1920	33,754,000	1950	38,903,000	1975	22,929,843 [1]	1984	20,945,536 [1]
1930	30,173,000	1955	32,761,707 [1]	1980	22,223,000 [1]	1985	19,501,242 [1]
1935	22,015,000	1960	30,441,000	1981	21,342,987 [1]	1986	19,588,666
1940	36,358,000	1965	29,248,000	1982	18,584,760 [1]	1987	20,602,204
1945	41,918,000	1970	27,160,000	1983	19,013,250 [1]	1988	22,139,542

[1]Only Class 1 railroads. *Source:* Association of American Railroads.

Estimated Motor Vehicle Registration, 1988
(in thousands; including publicly owned vehicles)

State	Autos[1]	Trucks and buses	Motor-cycles	Total	State	Autos[1]	Trucks and buses	Motor-cycles	Total
Alabama	2,758	894	50	3,652	Montana	413	231	22	644
Alaska	225	129	9	354	Nebraska	887	445	30	1,332
Arizona	1,783	715	57	2,498	Nevada	624	233	17	857
Arkansas	961	520	17	1,481	New Hampshire	724	190	33	914
California	16,473	4,808	661	21,281	New Jersey	5,048	593	58	5,641
Colorado	2,227	853	117	3,080	New Mexico	799	477	37	1,276
Connecticut	2,498	166	62	2,664	New York	8,764	1,270	226	10,034
Delaware	385	112	9	497	North Carolina	3,542	1,474	62	5,016
Dist. of Col.	252	16	2	268	North Dakota	387	267	24	654
Florida	8,822	2,224	213	11,046	Ohio	7,177	1,601	268	8,778
Georgia	3,708	1,522	80	5,230	Oklahoma	1,991	946	71	2,937
Hawaii	614	84	24	693	Oregon	1,689	571	78	2,260
Idaho	626	393	44	1,019	Pennsylvania	6,331	1,538	194	7,869
Illinois	6,428	1,448	248	7,876	Rhode Island	554	118	25	672
Indiana	2,774	962	95	3,736	South Carolina	1,793	610	31	2,403
Iowa	1,987	779	208	2,766	South Dakota	418	271	31	689
Kansas	1,512	694	80	2,206	Tennessee	3,304	831	77	4,135
Kentucky	1,832	930	36	2,762	Texas	8,330	3,897	215	12,209
Louisiana	1,984	943	39	2,927	Utah	760	359	45	1,119
Maine	698	226	41	924	Vermont	345	121	19	466
Maryland	2,769	600	51	3,369	Virginia	3,623	1,106	67	4,729
Massachusetts	3,433	498	110	3,931	Washington	2,801	1,122	138	3,923
Michigan	5,556	1,524	224	7,080	West Virginia	831	385	24	1,216
Minnesota	2,546	717	150	3,263	Wisconsin	2,373	714	189	3,087
Mississippi	1,341	413	24	1,754	Wyoming	290	203	21	493
Missouri	2,665	1,088	66	3,753	**Total**	**140,655**	**42,813**	**4,719**	**183,468**

1. Includes taxicabs. NOTE: Figures are latest available. *Source:* Department of Transportation, Federal Highway Administration.

Passenger Car Production by Make

Companies and models	1988	1987	1985	1980	1975	1970
American Motors Corporation	—	16,004	109,919	164,725	323,704	276,127
Chrysler Corporation						
Plymouth	313,700	321,585	369,487	293,342	443,550	699,031
Dodge	511,133	414,684	482,388	263,169	354,482	405,699
Chrysler	248,012	357,148	414,193	82,463	102,940	158,614
Imperial	—	—	—	—	1,930	10,111
Total	1,072,845	1,093,417	1,266,068	638,974	902,902	1,273,455
Ford Motor Company						
Ford	1,304,819	1,317,786	1,098,627	929,627	1,301,414	1,647,918
Mercury	293,766	328,432	374,446	324,528	405,104	310,463
Lincoln	207,156	184,158	163,077	52,793	101,520	58,771
Total	1,805,741	1,830,376	1,636,150	1,306,948	1,808,038	2,017,152
General Motors Corporation						
Chevrolet	1,381,967	1,515,571	1,691,254	1,737,336	1,687,091	1,504,614
Pontiac	806,356	657,281	702,617	556,429	523,469	422,212
Oldsmobile	562,920	601,774	1,168,982	783,225	654,342	439,632
Buick	484,851	552,567	1,001,461	783,575	535,820	459,931
Cadillac	265,030	275,881	322,765	203,991	278,404	152,859
Total	3,501,124	3,603,074	4,887,079	4,064,556	3,679,126	2,979,248
Checker Motors Corporation	—	—	—	3,197	3,181	4,146
Volkswagen of America	35,998	66,696	96,458	197,106	—	—
Honda	366,354	324,065	238,159	145,337	—	—
Mazda	163,289	4,200				
Nissan	109,897	117,334	43,810	—	—	—
Toyota	55,480	43,744				
Industry total	7,110,728	7,098,910	8,184,821	6,375,506	6,716,951	6,550,128

Source: Motor Vehicle Manufacturers Association of the United States.

Motor Vehicle Data

	1987	1986	1980	1970	1960
U.S. passenger cars and taxis registered (thousands)	137,324	135,431	121,724	89,280	61,671
Total mileage of U.S. passenger cars (millions)	1,357,191	1,301,214	1,111,596	916,700	588,083
Total fuel consumption of U.S. passenger cars (millions of gallons)	70,787	71,216	71,883	67,820	41,169
World registration of cars, trucks, and buses (thousands)	515,386	499,731	411,113	246,368	126,955
U.S. registration of cars, trucks, and buses (thousands)	179,044	176,191	155,796	108,418	73,858
U.S. share of world registration of cars, trucks, and buses	34.7%	35.3%	37.9%	44.0%	58.2%

Source: Motor Vehicle Manufacturers Association of the U.S.

Domestic Motor Vehicles Sales

(in thousands)

Type of Vehicle	1987	1986	1985	1984	1983	1982	1980	1975
Passenger Cars								
Passenger car factory sales	7,085	7,516	8,002	7,621	6,739	5,049	6,400	6,713
Passenger car (new) retail sales[1]	10,278	11,460	11,042	10,390	9,182	7,982	8,979	8,640
Domestic[2]	7,081	8,215	8,205	7,952	6,795	5,759	6,581	7,050
Subcompact[3]	1,101	1,325	1,297	2,322	1,776	1,489	1,604	700
Compact[3]	2,388	2,461	2,563	1,336	1,110	1,257	1,659	2,336
Standard[3]	1,565	1,888	1,882	1,817	1,825	1,377	1,358	1,956
Intermediate[3]	2,026	2,540	2,464	2,484	2,071	1,641	1,957	2,058
Imports[4]	3,197	3,245	2,838	2,439	2,387	2,223	2,398	1,587
Trucks								
Truck and bus factory sales	3,821	3,393	3,357	3,075	2,414	1,906	1,667	2,272
Truck and bus retail sales[5]	4,174	4,031	3,984	3,538	2,709	2,248	2,232	2,351
Light duty (up to 14,000 GVW)[6]	3,885	3,766	3,700	3,261	2,521	2,064	1,964	2,076
Med. duty (14,000-26,000 GVW)[6]	55	51	53	61	48	46	92	169
Heavy duty (over 26,000 GVW)[6]	234	214	231	216	141	138	176	106
Motorcycles								
Motorcycles (new) retail sales[7]	935	1,045	1,260	1,305	1,185	990	1,070	940
All-terrain vehicles	395	465	550	550	425	250	n.a.	n.a.
All-terrain vehicle imports	320	498	683	635	430	275	n.a.	n.a.
Motorcycle imports total[8]	318	550	733	441	540	917	1,120	948

1. Based on data from U.S. Dept. of Commerce. 2. Includes domestic models produced in Canada and Mexico. 3. Beginning 1980, cars produced in U.S. by foreign manufacturers are included. 4. Excludes domestic models produced in Canada. 5. Excludes motorcoaches and light-duty imports from foreign manufacturers. Includes imports sold by franchised dealers of U.S. manufacturers. Starting in 1986 includes sales of trucks over 10,000 lbs. GVW by foreign manufacturers. 6. Gross vehicle weight (fully loaded vehicles). 7. Estimates by Motorcycle Industry Council Inc., Costa Mesa, Calif. Includes all-terrain vehicles and scooters. Excludes mopeds/motorized bicycles. 8. *Source:* Motorcycle Industry Council Inc. Data from U.S. Dept. of Commerce. Excludes mopeds/motorized bicycles and all-terrain vehicles. NOTE: n.a. = not available. *Source: Statistical Abstract of the United States 1989.*

Domestic and Export Factory Sales of Motor Vehicles

(in thousands)

	From plants in United States								
	Passenger cars			Motor trucks and buses			Total motor vehicles		
Year	Total	Domestic	Exports	Total	Domestic	Exports	Total	Domestic	Exports
1970	6,547	6,187	360	1,692	1,566	126	8,239	7,753	486
1975	6,713	6,073	640	2,272	2,003	269	8,985	8,076	909
1980	6,400	5,840	560	1,667	1,464	203	8,067	7,304	763
1983	6,739	6,201	538	2,414	2,260	154	9,153	8,461	692
1984	7,621	7,030	591	3,075	2,884	191	10,696	9,914	782
1985	8,002	7,337	665	3,357	3,126	231	11,359	10,463	896
1986	7,516	6,869	647	3,393	3,130	263	10,909	9,999	910
1987	7,085	6,487	598	3,821	3,509	312	10,906	9,996	910
1988	7,105	6,437	668	4,120	3,795	325	11,225	10,232	993

Source: Motor Vehicle Manufacturers Association of the U.S.

U.S. Direct Investment in EEC Countries, 1988

(in millions of dollars)

Countries	All industries	Petroleum	Manufacturing	Wholesale	Banking	Finance & Insurance	Services	Other services
Belgium	$7,224	$551	$3,897	$1,477	$412	$780	$ 73	$ 34
Denmark	1,191	(¹)	265	513	41	174	(¹)	−1
France	12,495	926	8,047	2,377	235	446	176	287
Germany, West	21,673	2,043	14,200	1,114	1,678	1,921	−21	739
Greece	194	45	107	33	−24	(¹)	(¹)	5
Ireland	5,743	−9	4,138	16	9	1,662	−66	−7
Italy	9,075	401	6,561	1,153	253	481	170	56
Luxembourg	756	3	456	5	199	93	0	0
Netherlands	15,367	2,212	6,073	2,419	173	3,178	887	427
Portugal	425	(¹)	194	105	104	(¹)	(¹)	8
Spain	4,368	96	2,626	757	477	26	274	111
United Kingdom	47,991	9,327	18,867	2,805	2,271	12,850	1,312	558
Total	$126,502	$15,695	$65,431	$12,774	$5,829	$21,634	$2,922	$2,216

1. Suppressed to avoid disclosure of data of individual companies. *Source: Survey of Current Business,* June 1989.

Balance of International Payments

(in billions of dollars)

Item	1988	1987	1985	1980	1975	1970	1965	1960	1955
Exports of goods and services (excluding transfers under military grants)	$529.8	$446.1	$358.5	$344.7	$155.7	$65.7	$41.1	$28.9	$19.9
Merchandise, adjusted, excluding military	319.2	250.3	214.4	224.0	107.1	42.5	26.5	19.7	14.4
Transfers under U.S. military agency sales contracts	10.0	11.2	9.0	8.2	3.9	1.5	0.8	0.3	0.2
Receipts of income on U.S. investments abroad	107.8	104.7	90.0	75.9	25.4	11.8	7.4	4.6	2.6
Other services	92.7	79.9	45.0	36.5	19.3	9.9	6.4	4.3	2.7
Imports of goods and services	−641.7	−575.6	−461.2	−333.9	−132.6	−60.0	−32.8	−23.7	−17.8
Merchandise, adjusted, excluding military	−446.5	−409.8	−339.0	−249.3	−98.0	−39.9	−21.5	−14.8	−11.5
Direct defense expenditures	−14.6	−14.1	−12.0	−10.7	−4.8	4.9	−3.0	−3.1	−2.9
Payments of income on foreign assets in U.S.	−105.5	−82.4	−65.0	−43.2	−12.6	−5.5	−2.1	−1.2	−0.5
Other services	−75.0	−69.3	−46.0	−30.7	−17.2	−9.8	−6.2	−4.6	−2.8
Unilateral transfers, excluding military grants, net	−14.6	−14.2	−15.0	−7.0	−4.6	−3.3	−2.9	−2.3	−2.5
U.S. Government assets abroad, net	−3.6	9.1	−32.4	−84.8	−3.5	−1.6	−1.6	−1.1	−0.3
U.S. private assets abroad, net	−81.5	−86.4	−26.0	−71.5	−35.4	−10.2	−5.3	−5.1	−1.3
U.S. assets abroad, official reserve, net	−82.1	−76.2	−4.0	−8.2	−0.6	2.5	1.2	2.1	0.2
Foreign assets in U.S., net	219.3	218.0	127.1	50.3	15.6	6.4	0.7	2.3	−1.4
Statistical discrepancy	−10.6	1.9	23.0	29.6	5.5	−0.2	−0.5	−1.0	0.4
Balance on goods and services	−111.9	−129.5	−103.0	10.8	23.1	5.7	8.3	5.1	2.2
Balance on goods, services, and remittances	−116.2	−133.5	−106.4	8.4	21.3	4.1	7.2	4.5	1.6
Balance on current account	−126.5	−143.7	−118.0	3.7	18.4	2.4	5.4	2.8	−0.3

NOTE: — denotes debits. *Source:* Department of Commerce, Bureau of Economic Analysis.

Foreign Investors in U.S. Business Enterprises

	Number				Investment outlays (millions of dollars)			
	1988¹	1987	1986	1985	1988¹	1987	1986	1985
Investments, total	1,012	978	1,040	753	$65,019	$40,310	$39,177	$23,106
Acquisitions	646	543	555	390	60,003	33,933	31,450	20,083
Establishments	366	435	485	363	5,016	6,377	7,728	3,023
Investors, total	1,090	1,051	1,121	817	65,019	40,310	39,177	23,106
Foreign direct investors	416	480	476	320	16,400	11,773	8,602	4,225
U.S. affilates	674	571	645	497	48,619	28,536	30,575	18,881

1. Figures are preliminary. *Source:* U.S. Department of Commerce, *Survey of Current Business,* May 1989.

Imports of Leading Commodities
(value in millions of dollars)

Commodity	1988	1987
Food and live animals	$20,106.6	$22,224
Cattle, except for breeding	594.4	417
Meat and preparations	2,738.4	3,037
Dairy products and eggs	401.5	479
Fish	5,326.7	5,026
Grains and feed for animals	1010.6	880
Vegetables and fruit	4,661.9	5,133
Sugar, cane or beet	436.4	481
Coffee	2,288.3	2,846
Cocoa beans	405.3	545
Tea	129.6	122
Beverages and tobacco	4,139.0	4,461
Alcoholic beverages	3,414.3	3,553
Tobacco, unmanufactured	444.7	624
Crude materials, inedible, except fuels	13,397.5	12,299
Hides and skins, except fur skins	101.8	85
Fur skins, undressed	154.0	220
Crude rubber	1,022.6	837
Wood—simply worked	3,179.2	3,464
Paper base stocks	2,662.8	2,131
Textile fibers and wastes	523.4	469
Industrial diamonds	159.2	119
Ores and metal scrap	3,263.8	2,666
Iron ore and concentrates	485.5	478
Nonferrous metal ores and concentrates	1,600.7	1,303
Precious metal ores and concentrates, except gold	327.3	308
Mineral fuels and related materials	51,087.8	46,723
Petroleum products	38,175.2	43,936
Natural gas	2,576.6	2,580
Animal and vegetable oils and fats	849.0	629
Chemicals	19,875.6	17,036
Organic chemicals	6,952.9	5,685
Inorganic chemicals	3,595.9	3,199
Medicinal and pharmaceutical products	1,859.2	1,484
Fertilizers, manufactured	1,021.1	868
Machinery and transport equipment	197,053.3	182,807
Machinery	117,281.0	102,262
Transport equipment	79,772.4	80,545
Automobiles, buses, trucks	55,327.9	58,604
Motor vehicle parts	16,019.1	14,143
Aircraft and parts	5,168.4	4,512
Misc. manufactured goods	61,636.0	69,037
Paper and manufactures	8,336.1	7,613
Glass, glassware, and pottery	2,974.4	3,094
Gem diamonds	4,305.8	3,441
Metals and manufactures	9,030.7	8,512
Iron and steel-mill products	10,273.7	9,177
Nonferrous metals	10,302.3	8,154
Precious metals, except gold	1,746.9	1,618
Textile yarn and thread	707.9	782
Clothing	21,517.5	21,960
Footwear	8,041.4	7,654
Scientific and contolling instruments	5,173.3	4,621
Printed matter	1,583.2	1,569
Clocks and watches	1,908.6	1,744
Baby carriages, toys, games and sporting goods	6,719.0	6,438
Artworks and antiques	2,044.1	1,978
Other transactions	12,672.4	12,500
Total	**441,282.4**	**424,082**

Exports of Leading Commodities
(value in millions of dollars)

Commodity	1987	1986
Food and live animals	$26,414.7	$19,179
Meat and preparations	2,429.6	1,768
Dairy products and eggs	496.3	385
Grains and preparations	12,281.4	8,058
Wheat, including wheat flour	5,080.4	3,248
Rice	801.8	576
Corn	5,190.6	3,314
Vegetables and fruit	3,488.2	2,956
Feed for animals	3,425.6	2,692
Beverages and tobacco	4,548.3	3,667
Cigarettes	2,645.4	2,047
Tobacco	1,251.7	1,090
Crude materials, inedible, except fuels	25,135.0	20,416
Hides and skins, except fur skins	1,638.8	1,450
Soybeans	4,815.9	4,343
Synthetic rubber	857.7	761
Logs and lumber	4,086.8	3,008
Pulpwood and wood pulp	4,001.8	3,084
Raw cotton, excluding wastes	1,975.1	1,631
Ores and metal scrap	4,279.3	3,018
Mineral fuels and related materials	8,185.8	7,713
Coal	3,959.6	3,430
Petroleum and products	3,679.2	3,922
Animal and vegetable oils and fats	1,453.7	981
Soybean oil	487.0	271
Chemicals	32,299.6	26,381
Chemical elements and compounds	12,950.2	10,679
Medicines and pharmaceuticals	3,941.3	3,182
Fertilizers	2,497.8	2,259
Plastic materials and resins	7,276.8	5,492
Machinery and transport equipment	135,134.8	108,596
Machinery	88,432.0	69,637
Power generating machinery	12,817.5	10,193
Aircraft engines, parts	3,679.2	3,036
Automotive engines, parts	1,631.0	1,216
Agricultural machinery, including tractors, and parts	1,955.7	1,493
Office machines, computers	23,127.9	18,692
Metalworking machinery	1,924.5	1,606
Textile and leather machinery	819.9	661
Transport equipment	46,702.8	38,959
Motor vehicles and parts	25,178.0	20,879
Aircraft, spacecraft, accessories	20,003.7	16,904
Misc. manufactured goods	24,513.9	19,409
Tires and tubes	771.6	514
Paper and manufactures	3,892.1	3,180
Nonmetallic mineral manufactures	2,861.1	2,289
Metals and manufactures	4,372.9	3,534
Iron and steel-mill products	2,016.6	1,223
Nonferrous base metals	3,041.4	1,853
Other manufactures of metal	2,828.3	3,534
Textile yarns and fabrics	3,649.5	2,933
Clothing	1,574.3	624
Scientific instruments	8,888.9	7,388
Photographic supplies	1,589.3	1,472
Printed matter	1,917.8	1,562
Other transactions	27,482.9	20,381
Total	**320,385.4**	**252,866**

Source: Department of Commerce, Bureau of the Census, Foreign Trade Division.

History of the Income Tax in the United States

Source: Touche Ross & Co.

The nation had few taxes in its early history. From 1791 to 1802, the United States Government was supported by internal taxes on distilled spirits, carriages, refined sugar, tobacco and snuff, property sold at auction, corporate bonds, and slaves. The high cost of the War of 1812 brought about the nation's first sales taxes on gold, silverware, jewelry, and watches. In 1817, however, Congress did away with all internal taxes, relying on tariffs on imported goods to provide sufficient funds for running the Government.

In 1862, in order to support the Civil War effort, Congress enacted the nation's first income tax law. It was a forerunner of our modern income tax in that it was based on the principles of graduated, or progressive, taxation and of withholding income at the source. During the Civil War, a person earning from $600 to $10,000 per year paid tax at the rate of 3%. Those with incomes of more than $10,000 paid taxes at a higher rate. Additional sales and excise taxes were added, and an "inheritance" tax also made its debut. In 1866, internal revenue collections reached their highest point in the nation's 90-year history—more than $310 million, an amount not reached again until 1911.

The Act of 1862 established the office of Commissioner of Internal Revenue. The Commissioner was given the power to assess, levy, and collect taxes, and the right to enforce the tax laws through seizure of property and income and through prosecution. His powers and authority remain very much the same today.

In 1868, Congress again focused its taxation efforts on tobacco and distilled spirits and eliminated the income tax in 1872. It had a short-lived revival in 1894 and 1895. In the latter year, the U.S. Supreme Court decided that the income tax was unconstitutional because it was not apportioned among the states in conformity with the Constitution.

By 1913, with the 16th Amendment to the Constitution, the income tax had become a permanent fixture of the U.S. tax system. The amendment gave Congress legal authority to tax income and resulted in a revenue law that taxed incomes of both individuals and corporations. In fiscal year 1918, annual internal revenue collections for the first time passed the billion-dollar mark, rising to $5.4 billion by 1920. With the advent of World War II, employment increased, as did tax collections—to $7.3 billion. The withholding tax on wages was introduced in 1943 and was instrumental in increasing the number of taxpayers to 60 million and tax collections to $43 billion by 1945.

In 1981, Congress enacted the largest tax cut in U.S. history, approximately $750 billion over six years. The tax reduction, however, was offset by two tax acts; in 1982 and 1984, which attempted to raise approximately $265 billion.

On Oct. 22, 1986, President Reagan signed into law one of the most far-reaching reforms of the United States tax system since the adoption of the income tax. The Tax Reform Act of 1986, as it was called, attempted to be revenue neutral by increasing business taxes and correspondingly decreasing individual taxes by approximately $120 billion over a five-year period.

On December 22, 1987, the President signed into law the Revenue Act of 1987. The Act, which imposed a two-year $23-billion tax increase, was small in scope compared to the Tax Reform Act of 1986.

Internal Revenue Service

The Internal Revenue Service (IRS), a bureau of the U.S. Treasury Department, is the federal agency charged with the administration of the tax laws passed by Congress. The IRS functions through a national office in Washington, 7 regional offices, 63 district offices, and 10 service centers.

Operations involving most taxpayers are carried out in the district offices and service centers. District offices are organized into Resources Management, Examination, Collection, Taxpayer Service, Employee Plans and Exempt Organizations, and Criminal Investigation. All tax returns are filed with the service centers, where the IRS computer operations are located.

IRS service centers are processing an ever increasing number of returns and documents. In 1988 the number of returns and supplemental documents processed totaled 194 million. This represented a 0.6% increase over 1987.

In prior years, all processing of documents was performed by hand. This process was time consuming and costly. In an attempt to improve the speed and efficiency of the manual processing procedure, the IRS began testing an electronic return filing system beginning with the filing of 1985 returns.

The two most significant results of the test were that refunds for the electronically filed returns were issued more quickly and the tax processing error rate was significantly lower when compared to paper returns.

Electronic filing of individual income tax returns with refunds became an operational program in selected areas for the 1987 processing year. In 1988, the I.R.S. expanded the program to 16 district offices with 2,500 preparers, software firms, and communication firms transmitting 583,000 returns.

In addition to the expansion of the electronic filing program for individual returns, the I.R.S. also tested an electronic fund transfer/direct deposit system and an electronic/magnetic media filing system for fiduciary and partnership returns.

Internal Revenue Service

	1988	1987	1986	1985	1970	1960	1950
U.S. population (in thousands)	246,590	244,344	241,995	239,714	204,878	180,671	152,271
Number of IRS employees	114,873	102,188	95,880	92,254	68,683	51,047	55,551
Cost to govt. of collecting $100 in taxes	$0.54	$0.49	$0.49	$0.48	$0.45	$0.40	$0.59
Tax per capita	$3,792.15	$3,627.22	$3,232.51	$3,098.99	$955.31	$507.96	$255.84
Collections by principal sources (in thousands of dollars)							
Total IRS collections	$935,106,594	$886,290,590	$782,251,812	$742,871,541	$195,722,096	$91,744,803	$38,957,132
Income and profits taxes							
Individual	473,666,566	465,452,486	416,568,384	396,659,558	103,651,585	44,945,711	17,153,308
Corporation	109,682,554	102,858,985	80,441,620	77,412,769	35,036,983	22,179,414	10,854,351
Employment taxes	318,038,990	277,000,469	244,374,767	225,214,568	37,449,188	11,158,589	2,644,575
Estate and gift taxes	7,784,445	7,667,670	7,194,956	6,579,703	3,680,076	1,626,348	706,227
Alcohol taxes	NOTE 4	11,097,677	5,647,485	5,398,100	4,746,382	3,193,714	2,219,202
Tobacco taxes	NOTE 4	note 2	4,607,845	4,483,193	2,094,212	1,931,504	1,328,464
Manufacturers' excise taxes	NOTE 3	10,221,574	9,927,742	10,020,574	6,683,061	4,735,129	1,836,053
All other taxes	25,934,040	11,991,729	13,489,014	17,103,077	2,380,609	2,004,394	2,214,951

NOTE: For fiscal year ending September 30th. NOTE 2: Alcohol and tobacco tax collections are included in the "All other taxes" amount. NOTE 3: Manufacturers' excise taxes are included in the "All other taxes" amount. NOTE 4: Alcohol and tobacco tax collections are now collected and reported by the Bureau of Alcohol, Tobacco, and Firearms.

Auditing Tax Returns

Most taxpayers' contacts with the IRS arise through the auditing of their tax returns. The Service has been empowered by Congress to inquire about all persons who may be liable for any tax and to obtain for review the books and/or records pertinent to those taxpayers' returns. A wide-ranging audit operation is carried out in the 63 district offices by 17,323 field agents and 3,569 office auditors.

Selecting Returns for Audit

The primary method used by the IRS in selecting returns for audits is a computer program that measures the probability of tax error in each return. The data base (established by an in-depth audit of randomly selected returns in various income categories) consists of approximately 200–250 individual items of information taken from each return. These 200–250 variables individually or in combination are weighted as relative indicators of potential tax change. Returns are then scored according to the weights given the combinations of variables as they appear on each return. The higher the score, the greater the tax change potential. Other returns are selected for examination on the basis of claims for refund, multi-year audits, related return audits, and other audits initiated by the IRS as a result of informants' information, special compliance programs, and the information document matching program.

In 1988, the IRS recommended additional tax and penalties on 861,545 returns, totaling $20 billion.

The Appeals Process

The IRS attempts to resolve tax disputes through an administrative appeals system. Taxpayers who, after audit of their tax returns, disagree with a proposed change in their tax liabilities are entitled to an independent review of their cases. Taxpayers are able to seek an immediate, informal appeal with the Appeals Office. If, however, the dispute arises from a field audit and the amount in question exceeds $2,500, a taxpayer must submit a written protest. Alternatively, the taxpayer can wait for the examiner's report and then request consideration by the Appeals Office and file a protest if necessary. Taxpayers may represent themselves or be represented by an attorney, accountant, or any other advisor authorized to practice before the IRS. Taxpayers can forego their right to the above process and await receipt of a deficiency notice. At this juncture, taxpayers can either (1) not pay the deficiency and petition the Tax Court by a required deadline or (2) pay the deficiency and file a claim for refund with the District Director's office. If the claim is denied, a suit for refund may be brought either in the District Court or the Claims Court within a specified period.

Federal Individual Income Tax

The Federal individual income tax is levied on the world-wide income of U.S. citizens and resident aliens and on certain types of U.S. source income of non-residents. For a non-itemizer, "tax table income" is adjusted gross income (*see* below) less $2,000 for each personal exemption and the standard deduction (*see* below). If a taxpayer itemizes, tax table income is adjusted gross income minus total itemized deductions and personal exemptions. Previous law provided 5 tax brackets, with a top rate of 38.5 percent. For the 1989 tax year, there are only 2 tax brackets, 15% and 28%. In addition there are two separate 5% surtaxes for high-income taxpayers.

Tax Brackets—1989
Taxable Income

Joint Return	Single Taxpayer	Rate
$0 –$ 30,950	$0 –$18,550	15%
30,951 – 74,850	18,551 – 44,900	28
74,851 –155,320 [1]	44,901 – 93,130 [1]	33
155,321[1] and up	93,131[1] and up	28

1. Increase this figure by $11,200 for each personal exemption.

Who Must File a Return[1]

You must file a return if you are:	and your gross income is at least:
Single (legally separated, divorced, or married living apart from spouse with dependent child) and are under 65	$5,100
Single (legally separated, divorced, or married living apart from spouse with dependent child) and are 65 or older	$5,850
A person who can be claimed as a dependent on your parent's return, and who has taxable dividends, interest, or other unearned income	$500
Head of household under age 65	$6,550
Head of household over age 65	$7,150
Married, filing jointly, living together at end of year (or at date of death of spouse), and both are under 65	$9,200
Married, filing jointly, living together at end of year (or at date of death of spouse), and one is 65 or older	$9,800
Married, filing jointly, living together at end of year (or at date of death of spouse), and both are 65 or older	$10,400
Married, filing separate return, or married but not living together at end of year	$2,000
A person with income from sources within U.S. possessions	$2,000
Self-employed and your net earnings from self-employment were at least $400	
A person who received any advance earned income credit payments from their employer during the year	
A person who owes minimum tax, individual retirement arrangement tax, investment credit recapture tax or social security tax on unreported tips	

1. In 1989.

Adjusted Gross Income

Gross income consists of wages and salaries, unemployment compensation, tips and gratuities, interest, dividends, annuities, rents and royalties, up to 1/2 of Social Security Benefits if the recipient's income exceeds a base amount, and certain other types of income. Among the items excluded from gross income, and thus not subject to tax, are public assistance benefits and interest on exempt securities (mostly state and local bonds). Under the 1986 act, both the 60 percent of net capital gains exclusion and the $100 ($200 on a joint return) eligible dividends received exclusion have been eliminated.

Adjusted gross income is determined by subtracting from gross income: alimony paid, penalties on early withdrawal of savings, reimbursed employee business expenses, payments to an I.R.A. (reduced proportionately based upon adjusted gross income levels if taxpayer is an active participant in an employer maintained retirement plan), payments to a Keogh retirement plan and self-employed health insurance payments (25% limit). Unreimbursed business expenses and job related moving expenses are now treated as itemized deductions.

Itemized Deductions

Taxpayers may itemize deductions or take the standard deduction. The standard deduction replaces the zero bracket amount. The standard deduction amounts for 1989 are as follows: Married filing jointly and surviving spouses $5,200; Heads of household $4,550; Single $3,100; and Married filing separate returns $2,500. Tax payers who are age 65 or over or are blind are entitled to an additional standard deduction of $750 for single taxpayers and $600 for a married taxpayer.

In itemizing deductions, the following are major items that may be deducted in 1989: state and local income and property taxes, charitable contributions, employee moving expenses, medical expenses (exceeding 7.5% of adjusted gross income), casualty losses (only the amount over the $100 floor which exceeds 10% of adjusted gross income), interest payments (only 20% of personal interest payments are deductible) and miscellaneous deductions (deductible only to the extent by which cumulatively they exceed 2% of adjusted gross income).

Personal Exemptions

Personal exemptions are available to the taxpayer for himself, his spouse, and his dependents. The 1989 amount is $2,000 for each individual. Under the 1986 act, no exemption is allowed a taxpayer who can be claimed as a dependent on another taxpayer's return. Additional personal exemptions for taxpayers age 65 or over or blind have been eliminated.

Credits

Taxpayers can reduce their income tax liability by claiming the benefit of certain tax credits. Each dollar of tax credit offsets a dollar of tax liability. The following are a few of the available tax credits:

Certain lower-income households with dependent children may claim an Earned Income Credit of up to $910 on $6,500 of earned income. This maximum credit will be reduced if earned income or adjusted gross income exceeds $10,240, and the credit will be zero for families with incomes over $19,340. The earned income credit is a refundable credit.

A credit for Child and Dependent Care Expenses is available for amounts paid to care for a child or other dependent so that the taxpayer can work. The credit is between 20% and 30% (depending on adjusted gross income) of up to $2,400 of employment-related expenses for one qualifying child or dependent and up to $4,800 of expenses for two or more qualifying individuals.

The elderly and those under 65 who are retired under total disability may be entitled to a credit of up to $750 (if single) or $1,125 (if married and filing jointly). No credit is available if the taxpayer is single and has adjusted gross income of $17,500 or more, or $5,000 or more in nontaxable Social Security benefits. Similarly, the credit is unavailable to a married couple if their adjusted gross income exceeds $25,000 or if their nontaxable Social Security benefits equal or exceed $7,500.

Other tax credits available to taxpayers include the targeted jobs credit, and the foreign tax credit. The 1986 act eliminated the investment tax credit and the contibutions to candidates for public office credit.

Federal Income Tax Comparisons

Taxes at Selected Rate Brackets After Standard Deductions and Personal Exemptions[1]

Adjusted gross income	Single return listing no dependents				Joint return listing two dependents			
	1989	1988	1987	1975	1989	1988	1987	1975
$ 10,000	$ 735	$ 758	$ 762	$ 1,506	$ -910	$ -700[2]	$ -450[2]	$ 829
20,000	2,235	2,258	2,262	4,153	1,020	1,080	1,176	2,860
30,000	4,561	4,694	4,901	8,018	2,520	2,580	2,676	5,804
40,000	7,361	7,494	8,300	12,765	4,020	4,080	4,259	9,668
50,000	10,161	10,389	11,800	18,360	6,272	6,549	7,059	14,260

1. For comparison purposes, tax rate schedules were used. 2. Refund based on earned income credit for families with dependent children.

Federal Corporation Taxes

Corporations are taxed under a graduated tax rate structure as shown in the chart below. For tax years beginning on or after July 1, 1987, the benefits of the lower rates are phased out for corporations with taxable income between $100,000 and $335,000 and totally eliminated for corporations with income equal to or in excess of $335,000.

If the corporation qualifies, it may elect to be an S corporation. If it makes this election, the corporation will not (with certain exceptions) pay corporate tax on its income. Its income is instead passed through and taxed to its shareholders. There are several requirements a corporation must meet to qualify as an S corporation including having 35 or fewer shareholders, and having only one class of stock.

Tax Years Beginning on or After July 1, 1987

Taxable income	Tax rate
$0–$50,000	15%
$50,001–75,000	25
75,001–100,000	34
100,001–335,000	39
335,001 and up	34

State Corporation Income and Franchise Taxes

All states but Nevada, South Dakota, Texas, Washington, and Wyoming impose a tax on corporation net income. The majority of states impose the tax at flat rates ranging from 2.35% to 11.5%. Several states have adopted a graduated basis of rates for corporations.

Nearly all states follow the federal law in defining net income. However, many states provide for varying exclusions and adjustments.

A state is empowered to tax all of the net income of its domestic corporations. With regard to non-resident corporations, however, it may only tax the net income on business carried on within its boundaries. Corporations are, therefore, required to apportion their incomes among the states where they do business and pay a tax to each of these states. Nearly all states provide an apportionment to their domestic corporations, too, in order that they not be unduly burdened.

Several states tax unincorporated businesses separately.

Federal Estate and Gift Taxes

A Federal Estate Tax Return must be filed for the estate of every U.S. citizen or resident whose gross estate, if the decedent died in 1989, exceeds $600,000. An estate tax return must also be filed for the estate of a non-resident, if the value of his gross estate in the U.S. is more than $60,000 at the date of death. The estate tax return is due nine months after the date of death of the decedent, but a reasonable extension of time to file may be obtained for good reason. Tax due is to be paid when the return is filed. The executor of an estate with an interest in closely held business that comprises at least 35% of the adjusted gross estate may pay estate tax attributable to the business in from two to ten equal annual installments. In such a case, a 5-year extension for the payment of estate taxes may be exercised for that portion of the tax attributable to a closely held business.

Under the unified federal estate and gift tax structure, individuals who made taxable gifts during the calendar year are required to file a gift tax return by April 15 of the following year.

A unified credit of $192,800 (during 1989) is available to offset both estate and gift taxes. Any part of the credit used to offset gift taxes is not available to offset estate taxes. As a result, although they are still taxable as gifts, lifetime transfers no longer cushion the impact of progressive estate tax rates. Lifetime transfers and transfers made at death are cumulated for estate tax rate purposes.

Gift taxes are computed by applying the uniform rate schedule to lifetime taxable transfers (after deducting the unified credit) and subtracting the taxes payable for prior taxable periods. In general, estate taxes are computed by applying the uniform rate schedule to cumulated transfers and subtracting the gift taxes paid. An appropriate adjustment is made for taxes on lifetime transfers—such as certain gifts within three years of death—in a decedent's estate.

Among the deductions allowed in computing the amount of the estate subject to tax are funeral expenditures, administrative costs, claims and bequests to religious, charitable, and fraternal organizations or government welfare agencies, and state inheritance taxes. For transfers made after 1981 during life or death, there is an unlimited marital deduction.

An annual gift tax exclusion is provided that permits tax-free gifts to each donee of $10,000 for each year. A husband and wife who agree to treat gifts to third persons as joint gifts can exclude up to $20,000 a year to each donee. An unlimited exclusion for medical expenses and school tuition paid for the benefit of any donee is also available.

Federal Estate and Gift Taxes
Unified Rate Schedule, 1989[1]

If the net amount is:		Tentative tax is:		
From	To	Tax +	%	On excess over
$ 0	$ 10,000	$ 0	18	$ 0
10,001	20,000	1,800	20	10,000
20,001	40,000	3,800	22	20,000
40,001	60,000	8,200	24	40,000
60,001	80,000	13,000	26	60,000
80,001	100,000	18,200	28	80,000
100,001	150,000	23,800	30	100,000
150,001	250,000	38,800	32	150,000
250,001	500,000	70,800	34	250,000
500,001	750,000	155,800	37	500,000
750,001	1,000,000	248,300	39	750,000
1,000,001	1,250,000	345,800	41	1,000,000
1,250,001	1,500,000	448,300	43	1,250,000
1,500,001	2,000,000	555,800	45	1,500,000
2,000,001	2,500,000	780,800	49	2,000,000
2,500,001	3,000,000	1,025,800	53	2,500,000
3,000,001 and up	—	1,290,800	55	3,000,000

1. The estate and gift tax rates are combined in the single rate schedule effective for the estates of decedents dying, and for gifts made, after Dec. 31, 1976.

Recent Legislation

On November 10, 1988, the President signed into law the Technical and Miscellaneous Revenue Act of 1988 (the "Act"). Changes imposed by the Act include:

Exclusion of Interest Earned on U.S. Savings Bonds Used to Finance Higher Education

Generally, the new law provides that interest earned on a "qualified" U.S. Series EE savings bond which is used to pay higher education tuition and fees for a taxpayer, spouse, or dependent is excluded from a taxpayer's gross income.

Children Filing on Parents' Return

For post-1988 tax year, parents may elect to include on their return the unearned income of a child under age 14 whose income is between $500 and $5,000. The income must consist solely of interest and dividends. The child does not have to file a tax return if the election is made.

Who Shoulders the U.S. Federal Income Tax Burden?

The top earning half of the population continues to pay well over 90% of the Federal individual tax bill, according to Tax Foundation analysis of preliminary I.R.S. data for 1987.

Although 1987 total receipts increased by $4 billion, the income tax distribution reveals that those earning $50,000 or more paid $24 billion more income tax in 1987 while the under $50,000 income groups experienced a tax reduction of $20 billion.

In 1987, the top five percent of earners paid an average tax of $29,820, up 71% from 1979. The top ten percent paid $19,214, a 68% increase over what they paid in 1979.

While the top ten percent, or 10.7 million earners paid well over half the total income tax in 1987, their adjusted gross income ranged down to $54,700. It still takes millions of basically middle and upper-middle income taxpayers to pay the bulk of the total income tax bill.

Taxpayer Bill of Rights—What It Means to You

By the editors of Professional Corporation Advisor

A section of the Technical and Miscellaneous Revenue Act of 1988 that provides major procedural safeguards for taxpayers—both individual and business—is the so-called "Taxpayer Bill of Rights." The following is a detailed look at some of its most significant portions. Unless otherwise noted, these rules are in effect from the date they were signed into law—November 10, 1988.

● **Taxpayer Interviews.** Before the Bill of Rights, the IRS claimed the right to directly interview taxpayers whose returns were under audit. For corporations, this generally meant the responsible corporate officer or employee. The Service sometimes insisted on this right even though the taxpayer had retained a qualified representative—a CPA, attorney, or other person authorized to practice before the Treasury Department.

The Bill of Rights sets forth the legal rights you can claim regarding a taxpayer interview. First, either at or before any interview, the IRS must explain to you the audit process and your rights. Second, if at any point during the interview you indicate a desire to retain or consult with a qualified representative, the interview must be halted until you arrange to do so. Third, if you do retain a qualified representative, you cannot be compelled to accompany him or her to the audit meeting unless the Service issues an administrative summons.

In addition, the Service must select a reasonable time and place to conduct the audit. (Congress has requested that within the year the IRS publish rules specifying what is "reasonable.") Another provision allows you to make an audio recording of the interview. The Service also has this right, but it must advise you beforehand and supply you with a copy or transcript if you request one and pay the associated expenses. Provisions relating to taxpayer interviews are effective for interviews on or after February 8, 1989.

● **Levy and Distraint.** These rather cumbersome words spell sure trouble for taxpayers. They refer to the drastic actions the IRS can take to collect unpaid taxes. Because there have been a number of cases in which taxpayers were erroneously subjected to this remedy—with the potential for causing irreparable harm—Congress wanted to ensure that the Service was providing adequate time for taxpayers to resolve any misunderstandings before property was seized. Under the new rules, the Service must wait at least 30 days (rather than 10) after it notifies a taxpayer of a seizure action. The notice has to be brief and simple and written in nontechnical terms.

In addition, the Service cannot levy and sell property if the expense of doing so would exceed either the property's fair market value or the amount of the tax deficiency. To ensure that taxpayers are given enough time to state why the levy

may have been improper, banks and other financial institutions must wait at least 21 days after notice of levy is served before turning an account balance over to the Service.

Finally, the Service must release the levy if (1) the tax liability was satisfied; (2) releasing the levy would make it easier to collect the tax liability; (3) you have entered into an installment agreement with the Service to pay off the liability; (4) the levy is causing you "economic hardship;" or (5) if the fair market value of the property is greater than the tax liability, and it would not jeopardize the Service's collection of the tax and the related costs. These provisions will apply to levies served on or after July 1, 1989.

● **Installment Payment of Taxes.** The IRS is now authorized—but not required—to enter into installment payment agreements with taxpayers if such an arrangement will facilitate collection of unpaid taxes. When it does enter into such agreements, the IRS cannot reverse itself and demand immediate payment unless it proves that (1) the taxpayer provided the Service with inaccurate or incomplete information; (2) the installment was not paid on time; (3) other tax liabilities were not paid when due; (4) the taxpayer does not respond to reasonable IRS requests for current financial information; or (5) the Service determines that collection of the tax is in jeopardy.

● **Action for Damages.** Under prior law, taxpayers generally had no remedy if an action by an IRS employee damaged them—even if the employee intentionally disregarded IRS rules and regulations. The Bill of Rights now allows you to sue the government in federal district court if an IRS employee intentionally disregards the tax code or regulations in collecting a tax liability (but not in determining the amount of tax). You may be able to recover up to $100,000 if legal proceedings are begun within two years. The Service cannot prevent you from filing on the grounds that you were partially responsible, but damages can be reduced if your actions could have reasonably mitigated the injury.

● **Reliance on Written Advice.** Before the Bill of Rights, the burden of risk of relying on erroneous IRS advice was borne by taxpayers. Congress felt this was particularly inequitable, especially in regard to written advice from IRS, which could still subject you to a penalty if you filed an incorrect return while relying on IRS guidance. The Service must now abate any portion of the penalty that was imposed due to erroneous written IRS advice. The safeguard applies to written responses to specific written requests when it is reasonable for the taxpayer to rely on such advice. But this provision assumes that the taxpayer has provided the IRS with accurate information when requesting advice.

● **Cost and Fee Awards.** Under prior law, a taxpayer who won a tax case in federal court was permitted to receive litigation costs if the government's position was not substantially justified. The Bill of Rights expands this rule to cover certain administrative proceedings. □

Major State Taxes and Rates
as of July 1, 1989

State	Income taxes		General Sales and Use Tax	Gasoline Tax (per gallon)	Cigarette Tax (per pack of 20)	Property Tax
	Corporate	Individual				
Alabama	5% F	2 to 5%F	4%a	11 cents	16.5 cents	X
Arizona	2.5 to 10.5F	2 to 8F	5a	17	15	X
Arkansas	1 to 6	1 to 7	4a	13.5	21	X
California	9.3(q)	1 to 9.3q	4.75a	9	35	X
Colorado	5 to 5.4b	5q	3a	18e	20	X
Connecticut	11.5c, g	1 to 14d	8	20e	40	X
Georgia	6	1 to 6	4a	7.5 + 3% of retail	12	X
Hawaii	4.4 to 6.4	2 to 10	4	16 to 22.5	40% wholesale	
Idaho	8	2 to 8.2	5	18	18	X
Illinois	4.8p	2.5	5a, o	13e	20e	X
Indiana	3.4 f	3.4	5	15	15.5	X
Iowa	6 to 12F, h, q	.4 to 9.98F, q	4a	20	31	
Kansas	4.5g	3.65 to 8.75F, n	4.25a	15e	24	X
Kentucky	3 to 7.25	2 to 6F	5a	15l	3.001	X
Louisiana	4 to 8F	2 to 6F	4a	16	16	
Maine	3.5 to 8.93q	2 to 8	5	17	28	X
Maryland	7	2 to 5	5	18.5	13	X
Massachusetts	j	5k	5	11l	26	X
Michigan	2.35	4.6	4	15	25	X
Minnesota	9.5q	6 to 8.5o, q	6a	20	38	X
Mississippi	3 to 5	3 to 5	6	18b	18	
Missouri	5F, c	1.5 to 6F	4.225a, b	11	13	X
Nebraska	4.75 to 6.65	3.1 to 4.8q	4a	22.3l	27	
New Jersey	9g	2 to 3.5	6	10.5	27	X
New Mexico	4.8 to 7.6	1.8 to 8.5	4.75a	16.2	15	X
New York	9c, q	4 to 7.875b, r	4a	8	33	
North Carolina	7	3 to 7	3a	15.7l	2	X
North Dakota	3 to 10.5F, q	3.24 to 14.57F, h, m	6	17	30b	X
Ohio	5.1 to 8.9c	.743 to 6.9	5a	14.8e	18	X
Oklahoma	5	.5 to 10F, n	4a	17	23	
Pennsylvania	8.5	2.1	6	12	18	X
Rhode Island	9	22.96% of Federal Income tax	6	20l	37	X
South Carolina	5	2.75 to 7	5	16	7	X
Tennessee	6	6d	5.5a	20	13	
Utah	5	2.6 to 7.35F, h	5.094a, b	19	23	X
Vermont	5.5 to 8.25	25% of Federal Income tax	4	16b	17	X
Virginia	6c	2 to 5.75	3.5a	17.5	2.5	X
West Virginia	9.45b	3 to 6.5q	6	15.5	17	
Wisconsin	7.9	4.9 to 6.93q	5a	20.8l	30	X
Florida	5.5q		6a	4	24	X
Nevada	These 5 states have no corporate Income tax	These 7 states have no Individual income tax	5.75a	16.25	15e	X
South Dakota			4a	18	23	
Texas			6a	15	26	
Washington			6.5a	18	34b	X
Wyoming			3a	9	12	X
Alaska	1 to 9.4q		These 5 states have no general sales tax	8	16e	X
Delaware	8.7			16	14	
Montana	6.75g, s	2 to 11F		20	16e	X
New Hampshire	8	5d		14	21	X
Oregon	6.6	5 to 9F, h		16e	27	X

X. Indicates state levies a property tax. F. Allows Federal Income Tax as a deduction. a. Local taxes are additional. b. Future reduction scheduled under current law. c. Alternative methods of calculation may be required. d. In Connecticut, New Hampshire, and Tennessee, rates apply to income from interest and dividends only. Capital gains are taxed at 7% in Connecticut. e. Future increases scheduled under current law. f. A supplemental net income tax is imposed at 4.5%. g. Corporate surtax is imposed: Connecticut, 20%; Kansas, 2.25%; Montana, 4%; New Jersey's rate is .375% beginning July 31, 1989. h. Deductions limited. j. Excise tax is imposed equal to the greater of $400; or the sum of a tax on net worth or the value of tangible property not taxed locally, plus 9.5% of net income. k. Tax of 10% on income derived from intangibles, and 5% on all other income. l. Tax rate is periodically adjusted administratively. m. Optional tax of 17% of taxpayer's adjusted Federal income tax liability. n. In Kansas and Oklahoma, the higher rates apply to taxpayers deducting Federal income tax. o. Additional tax is imposed on income over specified levels, varying with filing status. p. Additional 2.5% personal property replacement tax. q. Alternative minimum tax is imposed. r. Qualified taxpayers may elect to pay alternative taxes at varying rates. s. 7% rate for corporations using water's edge apportionment. *Source:* Compiled by Tax Foundation from data reported by Commerce Clearing House through July 15, 1989.

Sales Tax Rates in Selected Cities, July 1989[1]

City	Percent rate	City	Percent rate	City	Percent rate
Albuquerque, N.M.	.5	Kansas City, Mo.[4]	2	Roanoke, Va.	1
Atlanta, Ga.[4]	2	Lincoln, Neb.	1.5	Sacramento, Calif.[2 4]	1.75
Austin, Tex.[4]	1.75	Los Angeles[4 2]	1.75	St. Louis[4]	1.875
Baton Rouge, La.[3]	3.5	Minneapolis, Minn.	.5	Salt Lake City, Utah[4]	1.16
Berkeley, Calif.[2,4]	2.25	Mobile, Ala.	3	San Antonio, Tex.[4]	2
Birmingham, Ala.	3	Montgomery, Ala.	4	San Diego, Calif.[2 4]	2.25
Bismarck, N.D.	1	New Orleans[3]	5.0	San Francisco[2 4]	1.75
Chicago[4]	4	New York[4]	4.25	Sante Fe, N.M.	.875
Colorado Springs, Colo.	3.5	Nome, Alaska	4	Seattle[4]	1.6
Dallas[4]	2	Norfolk, Va.	1	Shreveport, La.[3]	4.5
Denver[4]	4.1	Oakland, Calif.[2,4]	2.25	Spokane, Wash.[4]	1.3
El Paso[4]	2	Oklahoma City	2	Springfield, Ill.	2.25
Fayetteville, Ark.	2	Omaha, Neb.	1.5	Topeka, Kan.	1.0
Houston[4]	2	Pasadena, Calif.[4 2]	1.75	Tucson, Ariz.	2
Huntsville, Ala.	3	Phoenix, Ariz.[4]	1.7	Tulsa, Okla.	3
Ithaca, N.Y.	3	Rapid City, S.D.	2	Washington, D.C.	6
Jefferson City, Mo.[4]	2	Richmond, Va.	1	Yonkers, N.Y.[4]	4.25

1. Excludes state sales taxes. Includes county taxes if applicable. 2. Combined city and county rate. 3. Includes Parish School Board tax. 4. Includes tax imposed for public transit or transportation purposes. *Source:* Tax Foundation, Inc. Compiled from Commerce Clearing House reports.

State and Local Taxes Paid by a Family of Four in Selected Large Cities, 1987

City	Total Taxes Paid by Gross Family Income Level			Percent of Income by Income Level		
	$20,000	$35,000	$50,000	$20,000	$35,000	$50,000
Albuquerque, N.M.	1,504	2,594	4,056	7.5	7.4	8.1
Atlanta	1,897	3,388	5,263	9.5	9.7	10.5
Baltimore	2,148	3,767	5,669	10.7	10.8	11.3
Bridgeport	2,742	4,374	6,514	13.7	12.5	13.0
Burlington	1,570	2,709	4,225	7.8	7.7	8.4
Charleston, W.V.	1,560	2,695	4,393	7.8	7.7	8.8
Charlotte	1,663	2,887	4,562	8.3	8.2	9.1
Chicago	1,707	2,821	4,150	8.5	8.1	8.3
Cleveland	1,832	3,260	4,940	9.2	9.3	9.9
Columbia	1,568	2,918	4,739	7.8	8.3	9.5
Des Moines	2,027	3,586	5,569	10.1	10.2	11.1
Detroit	2,400	4,102	6,139	12.0	11.7	12.3
Honolulu	1,905	3,380	5,240	9.5	9.7	10.5
Indianapolis	1,648	2,672	3,936	8.2	7.6	7.9
Jackson, Miss.	1,508	2,685	4,300	7.5	7.7	8.6
Louisville	1,800	3,104	4,610	9.0	8.9	9.2
Memphis	1,601	2,366	3,222	8.0	6.8	6.4
Milwaukee	2,542	4,671	7,009	12.7	13.3	14.0
Newark	2,706	4,711	6,906	13.5	13.5	13.8
New York City	1,913	3,932	6,462	9.6	11.2	12.9
Norfolk	1,619	2,757	4,283	8.1	7.9	8.6
Omaha	1,642	2,714	4,237	8.2	7.8	8.5
Philadelphia	2,527	4,173	5,799	12.6	11.9	11.6
Portland, Maine	1,570	3,055	5,140	7.9	8.7	10.3
Portland, Ore.	2,281	4,008	6,163	11.4	11.5	12.3
Providence	2,297	3,865	6,168	11.5	11.0	12.3
St. Louis	1,557	2,607	3,998	7.8	7.4	8.0
Salt Lake City	1,866	3,304	5,168	9.3	9.4	10.3
Sioux Falls, S.D.	1,912	2,903	3,991	9.6	8.3	8.0
Washington, DC	2,086	3,797	5,623	10.4	10.8	11.2

NOTE: Data based on average family of four (one wage earner, wife or husband, and two school age children) owning their own home and living in a city where taxes apply. Comprises State and local sales, income, auto, and real estate taxes. *Source:* Government of the District of Columbia, Department of Finance and Revenue, *Tax Rates and Tax Burdens in the District of Columbia: a Nationwide Comparison.*

Income Tax Rates in Selected Cities, July 1989[1]

City	Percent rate	Year begun	City	Percent rate	Year begun
Akron, Ohio	2	1962	Kettering, Ohio	1.75	1968
Allentown, Pa.	1.045	1958	Lakewood, Ohio	1.5	1968
Altoona, Pa.	1	1948	Lancaster, Pa	0.5	1959
Baltimore[3]	([2])	1966	Lansing, Mich	1	1968
Bethlehem, Pa.	1	1957	Lexington, Ky.	2	1952
Birmingham, Ala.	1	1970	Lorain, Ohio	1.5	1967
Canton, Ohio	2	1954	Louisville, Ky.	1.45	1948
Cincinnati	2.1	1954	Mansfield, Ohio	1.75	1966
Cleveland	2	1967	New York	2.2–3.4	1966
Cleveland Heights, Ohio	2	1968	Owensboro, Ky.	1	1960
Columbus, Ohio	2	1947	Parma, Ohio	2	1967
Covington, Ky.	2.5	1956	Philadelphia	4.96	1939
Dayton, Ohio	2.25	1949	Pittsburgh	1.625	1954
Detroit	3	1965	Pontiac, Mich.	1	1968
District of Columbia	6–9.5	1947	Reading, Pa.	1	1969
Elyria, Ohio	1	1969	Saginaw, Mich.	1	1965
Erie, Pa.	1	1948	St. Louis	1	1948
Euclid, Ohio	2	1967	Scranton, Pa.	2.2	1948
Flint, Mich.	1	1965	Springfield, Ohio	2	1948
Fort Wayne, Ind.[3]	1	1973	Toledo, Ohio	2.25	1946
Gadsden, Ala.	2	1956	Warren, Ohio	1.5	1952
Grand Rapids, Mich.	1	1967	Wilkes-Barre, Pa.	3	1966
Hamilton, Ohio	1.75	1960	Wilmington, Del.	1.25	1970
Harrisburg, Pa.	1	1966	York, Pa.	1	1965
Kansas City, Mo.	1	1964	Youngstown, Ohio	2	1948

1. Excludes school district income taxes in Pennsylvania and Louisville, Ky. 2. Tax is 50% of state income tax. 3. County-level tax. NOTE: All cities above, except the District of Columbia and Baltimore, tax income earned in their jurisdictions by nonresidents. Rates shown apply to residents' income. However, the nonresident rate is the same in cities in Alabama, Delaware, Kentucky, Missouri, Ohio, and Pennsylvania—except Philadelphia, Scranton, and Pittsburgh. *Source:* Tax Foundation, compiled from Commerce Clearing House, as of June 1, 1989.

Labor Firsts in America

Source: U.S. Department of Labor.

The first . . .

Labor organization was formed by the Boston shoemakers and coopers guilds, which obtained a three-year charter (1648).

Women's labor organization was established by maidservants in New York City to protest abuses they suffered from their mistresses' husbands (1734).

National labor union that still exists today is the International Typographical Union (1850).

Union of federal employees was formed by New York City letter carriers (1863).

State to create a permanent agency to mediate labor disputes was New York (1886).

Federal arbitration law was passed (1888).

State to study occupational safety was Massachusetts (1850), which also passed the first legislation requiring factory safeguards (1877) and factory inspections (1879).

Pension was established by the Plymouth Colony for disabled soldiers (1638).

Federal government pension was established to assist wounded and disabled Revolutionary soldiers (1776).

Private pension plan offered by a company was established by the American Express Company (1875).

Legislation dealing with child labor was a Massachusetts Bay colony court order calling for town magistrates to investigate the possibility of "teaching the boys and girls in all towns the spinning of the yarn" (1640).

State law restricting child labor was in Massachusetts. It states that no child under the age of 15 shall work in "manufacturing establishments" unless the child attended school for at least three of the 12 months preceding any year of employment (1836).

Dispute that may be labeled a strike occurred in Jamestown, Va., as Polish workers protested against being denied the right to vote (1619).

Criminal prosecution of strikers came after a strike of cartmen in New York City (1677).

Strike of national importance occurred when railroad workers on several eastern and midwestern lines struck to protest wage cuts (1877).

National general strike, and the first designated "May Day" strike, occurred when approximately 340,000 workers demonstrated for an eight-hour day in several cities (1886).

Massive strike by federal employees was by postal workers (1970).

Fixed wage rates were set by the governor of Virginia and the Council of London Company (1621).

States to have equal pay legislation for women were Michigan and Montana (1919).

Minimum wage of 25 cents per hour was established by the Fair Labor Standards Act (1938).

Anti-discrimination law against women was in Illinois (1872).

Workers' compensation agreement was made between Captain William Kidd, the pirate, and his crew. "If any man should Loose a Leg or Arm in ye said service, he should six hundred pieces of Eight, or six able slaves." (1695).

CAREER PLANNING KIT

The Job Outlook for 2000

Source: U.S. Department of Labor, Bureau of Labor Statistics.

Generally, occupations in which current participants have the most education are projected to have the most rapid growth rates. Jobs are expected to continue to be available for those with only a high school education. Persons with less than a high school education will find it more difficult to find a job—particularly a job with good pay and chances for advancement—than those with more education. The fact that large numbers of young people continue to drop out of high school clearly signals that an important problem remains. Blacks and Hispanics are disproportionately represented among those with less education and are projected to account for an increasing share of workers. Given this trend, the declining college enrollment of blacks, as indicated by recent data, is unfortunate.

Despite the faster than average employment growth for occupations requiring at least a bachelor's degree, the surplus of college graduates that began in the early 1970s is expected to continue through the end of the century. However, the balance between supply and demand for new college graduates is expected to improve considerably as we enter the 1990s, partly because of the decline of college graduates stemming from the shrinkage of the college-age population.

Occupations that are generally filled by young workers, such as food service, retail sales, and construction labor, are projected to continue to generate many jobs, and the declining number of young workers could offer an opportunity to improve the labor market for young people and other groups.

The Department of Labor projections also carry with them the implication of change in the patterns of employment. Women and blacks have traditionally been highly concentrated in certain occupations. Although some improvements have occurred in the past decade, the future offers a chance for further improvement because employment growth is projected to be most rapid in occupations not traditionally filled by Hispanics, blacks, or, to some extent, women—the groups that will provide most of the labor force growth.

Although the number of white men in the labor force will grow by 5 million, an increase of only 8.8%, blacks are expected to increase 23%, adding 3.6 million members to the labor force. Women in the labor force are projected to rise 25%, up more than 13 million. The Asian and other races group (which includes American Indians, Alaskan Natives, Asians, and Pacific Islanders) are projected to grow 70%, adding nearly 2.4 million workers. Altogether, blacks, women, Asians and other races, and Hispanics should account for more than 90% of all labor force growth. In should be noted that 23% of the new workers will be immigrants.

Fastest Growing Jobs
(Numbers in thousands)

Occupation	Employment		Change in employment, 1986-2000		% Job growth
	1986	Projected, 2000	Number	Percent	
Legal assistants	61	125	64	103.7	0.3
Medical assistants	132	251	119	90.4	.6
Physical therapists	61	115	53	87.5	.2
Physical and corrective therapy assistants and aides	36	65	29	81.6	.1
Data processing equipment repairers	69	125	56	80.4	.3
Homemaker-home health aides	138	249	111	80.1	.5
Podiatrists	13	23	10	77.2	0
Computer systems analysts	331	582	251	75.6	1.2
Medical record technicians	40	70	30	75.0	.1
Employment interviewers	75	129	54	71.2	.3
Computer programmers	479	813	335	69.9.	1.6
Radiologic technologists and technicians	115	190	75	64.7	.3
Dental hygienists	87	141	54	62.6	.3
Dental assistants	155	244	88	57.0	.4
Physician assistants	26	41	15	56.7	.1
Operations research analysts	38	59	21	54.1	.1
Occupational therapists	29	45	15	52.2	.1
Peripheral electronic data processing equipment operators	46	70	24	50.8	.1
Data entry keyers, composing	29	43	15	50.8	.1
Optometrists	37	55	18	49.2	.1

Source: U.S. Department of Labor, Bureau of Labor Statistics.

Largest Job Growth

(Numbers in thousands)

Occupation	Employment		Change in employment, 1986-2000		% Job growth
	1986	Projected, 2000	Number	Percent	
Salespersons, retail	3,579	4,780	1,201	33.5	5.6
Waiters and waitresses	1,702	2,454	752	44.2	3.5
Registered nurses	1,406	2,018	612	43.6	2.9
Janitors and cleaners	2,676	3,280	604	22.6	2.8
General managers and top executives	2,383	2,965	582	24.2	2.7
Cashiers	2,165	2,740	575	26.5	2.7
Truckdrivers	2,211	2,736	525	23.8	2.5
General office clerks	2,361	2,824	462	19.6	2.2
Food counter and related workers	1,500	1,949	449	29.9	2.1
Nursing aides, orderlies, and attendants	1,224	1,658	433	35.4	2.0
Secretaries	3,234	3,658	424	13.1	2.0
Guards	794	1,177	383	48.3	1.8
Accountants and auditors	945	1,322	376	39.8	1.8
Computer programmers	479	813	335	69.9	1.6
Food preparation workers	949	1,273	324	34.2	1.5
Teachers, kindergarten and elementary	1,527	1,826	299	19.6	1.4
Receptionists and information clerks	682	964	282	41.4	1.3
Computer systems analysts	331	582	251	75.6	1.2
Cooks, restaurant	520	759	240	46.2	1.1
Licensed practical nurses	631	869	238	37.7	1.1
Gardeners and groundskeepers	767	1,005	238	31.1	1.1
Maintenance repairers	1,039	1,270	232	22.3	1.1
Stock clerks	1,087	1,312	225	20.7	1.0
First-line clerical supervisors and managers	956	1,161	205	21.4	1.0
Dining room and cafeteria attendants	433	631	197	45.6	.9
Electrical and electronics engineers	401	592	192	47.8	.9
Lawyers	527	718	191	36.3	.9

Source: U.S. Department of Labor, Bureau of Labor Statistics.

Employment Forecasts

The Department of Labor expects jobs to rise by 21 million in the 1986-2000 period. The increase—more than 19 percent, or 1.3 percent a year—represents a slowing of employment growth compared to 1972-86, when it was 2.2 percent a year.

Service-producing industries will account for nearly all of the growth. A large increase in jobs is projected for both wholesale and retail trade, a continuation of past trends. Almost 4.9 million new wage and salary jobs are expected in retail trade and more than 1.5 million in wholesale trade. The finance, insurance, and real estate industries are projected to add more than 1.6 million jobs. However, this represents a considerable slowing in this sector when compared with the nearly 2.4 million jobs added over the previous 14 years. The service industries themselves will expand by more than 10 million jobs; health care services will be important contributors as they continue to produce new services that greatly add to their overall demand and employment growth. Federal Government employment is expected to remain stable, but State and local governments are expected to add 1.5 million.

Among major groups in the goods-producing industries, the forecast shows increasing employment only in construction, in which employment will rise 890,000. Because of improved productivity, manufacturing employment is projected to decline by more than 800,000 jobs during the same period even though output is expected to increase 2.3 percent a year. However, many manufacturing industries are projected to grow, some quite rapidly, despite the overall decline. It is important to note that manufacturing as a whole will still provide more than 15 percent of all wage and salary employment in the year 2000. Employment gains are expected in the printing and publishing, drugs and pharmaceutical products, computers, plastics products, and instruments industries. Generally, the manufacturing industries expected to decline in employment have been declining for years; these include basic steel, leather goods, shoes, tobacco, some of the textile and most of the basic metal processing industries, and many of the food processing industries.

The problem of jobs for displaced workers is one for which no easy solution has been found. Although much occupational mobility exists in our economy, it is concentrated among the young. Some displaced workers will obtain related jobs near their homes and maintain their standard of living, but others will require further training or education or need to relocate. Some of those displaced may not find similar employment anywhere, given the occupational shifts that are projected to occur between now and 2000, particularly if they lack the education and training required for the emerging jobs. □

How To Write A Successful Résumé

Source: *The Professional Secretary's Handbook,* Copyright © 1984, Houghton Mifflin Company.

The Résumé

Your personal résumé should be thought of as a marketing tool for selling yourself to a prospective employer. Since you will have limited page space on which to present everything relevant about your work history, you should go back to the "who," "what," "where," "when," "why" formula and be concise and clear in your presentation and format. A lot of people out there are looking for jobs—all of them with résumés in one form or another. An employer may have to look through as many as 100 résumés of applicants for the same job before selecting the people to be interviewed. Therefore, your résumé must be eye-catching and brief so that a person scanning a page can immediately pick out your best assets and work experience.

If you have a career objective, you may want to state it on your résumé. There are two schools of thought on this subject, however. If you state your job objective, you may be limiting or categorizing yourself into a specific job market. There may be a job out there that can combine all of your skills with a title that does not even resemble your career objective. On the other hand, you may have determined in your research that you definitely want the particular type of job atmosphere associated with the title that you are seeking.

The Format

You may put identical information into several different formats and thereby present totally different images with each. The choice of formats will depend on the way you want to focus attention on your proficiencies.

Guidelines

The appearance of your résumé is almost as important as its content, for your resume is a reflection of your professionalism. As such, it should project a businesslike image. Here are a few general guidelines for résumé preparation that will help you:

(1) Paper should be 8 1/2″ × 11″ and white or off-white. If you are going to use colored paper, it should be conservative in tone or shade.

(2) Use a high-quality copying process such as offset printing or laser printing.

(3) Don't include personal information other than your name, address, and telephone number. Employers do not need to know your marital status, height, weight, sex, etc. Most of that can be determined at your interview.

(4) Use the active voice throughout and be careful not to change tenses in the body of the résumé.

(5) Try to keep the format pleasing to the eye. Avoid overuse of underlining and capitalization.

(6) Spell out names of organizations and agencies. Titles also should be spelled out.

(7) Proofread your résumé carefully. In fact, have someone else proofread it for you a final time before you have it printed. There is nothing more embarrassing than finding a mistake on your résumé after having given it to a prospective employer.

The Chronological Résumé

The chronological format is one of the most commonly used. It starts with your latest job experience and works backward. It is easy to follow and focuses on your career development. Since tasks for each position are detailed separately in the chronological format, try not to repeat elements of job descriptions. Only the inclusive years should be used to designate employment dates; there is no need to specify the months. If you want to highlight skills instead of chronological work history, you should not use this format.

The Functional Résumé

If you want to highlight your skills as opposed to the individual tasks for each position that you have held, you may want to use the functional résumé for your resume. This format details your skills under the specific function areas that you choose to highlight. A disadvantage to the use of this format is the possibility that your interviewer might want to relate your duties to each previously held job. However, this format may give you an opportunity to cover each position in more detail at your interview.

If you have had more than three or four jobs or if your experience looks scattered, this is an excellent format to use. Because the functional résumé focuses on your marketable skills rather than on your job history, it also can be used advantageously if you are worried that a prospective employer will be concerned with too many moves.

Where To Find Your Niche

The newspaper. This is probably the first place that people look when they are trying to get information on available jobs. Look through all the jobs. One suiting all of your qualifications might be listed in any section of the classifieds.

Be sure to keep a file on all of the ads that you have answered so that you do not answer the same ad twice, and also so that you remember what positions you have applied for.

Trade journals and speciality publications. If you are looking for a job in a specialized industry, you may want to check out the classifieds in professional trade journals. Your local library will have trade journals and speciality publications available for you to browse through.

Employment agencies. If you are going to use an employment agency to find a job, be sure to find one that specializes in the jobs that you are seeking. Agencies screen and test job candidates before sending them on interviews. Hence, an agency interview should be treated exactly like an interview with a prospective employer.

The Application Cover Letter

When you answer an ad through the mail, you should always send a descriptive cover letter with your résumé. The letter should be brief and formal while at the same time sparking the interest of the prospective employer. Try to give a reason why you should be interviewed for the advertised position. Never prepare a cover form letter for photocopying and submission to numerous firms. Such letters indicate that the sender is lazy and uninterested in taking the time to write personally to a prospective employer.

Résumé

PROFILE

Margaret E. Longford
321 State Street Apartment 39
City, US 98765
(800) 555-1212

Experience

November 1975 - December 1983	Allied College Publications, Inc. College Textbook Division/Science Associate Editor, Acquisitions
July 1969 - November 1975	Howe & Row Publishers, Inc. College Textbook Department Assistant Editor, Life Sciences
March 1967 - July 1969	LangData Incorporated College Division Editorial Assistant

Experience Summary

Sixteen years' experience in line editing of college science textbooks . Author
acquisitions . Production & Scheduling . Cost estimation . Budgets . Contracts .
Revisions . Manuscript Review . Liaison with Typesetters, Artists, Designers,
and Printers . Public Relations & Marketing Support . Liaison with Sales Personnel

Education

1964 - 1967	MBA	Taft Graduate School of Business Management
1960 - 1964	BA (cum laude)	Hartfield College Major: Biology
1956 - 1960	diploma	Stonleigh School for Girls

Languages

French (fluent)
German (fluent)
Russian (scientific only)

Publications List

Available upon request

References

Available upon request

Helpful Hints for the Interview

Source: U.S. Department of Labor, Employment and Training Administration

A job interview is your showcase for merchandising your talents. During the interview an employer judges your qualifications, appearance, and general fitness for the job opening. It is your opportunity to convince the employer that you can make a real contribution.

Equally important, it gives you a chance to appraise the job, the employer, and the firm. It enables you to decide if the job meets your career needs and interests and whether the employer is of the type and caliber you want to work for.

Before each interview, though, you should assume that the job you are applying for is precisely the one you want—because it may be. To present your qualifications most advantageously, you will need to prepare in advance. You should have the needed papers ready and the necessary information about yourself firmly in mind; and you should know how to act at the interview to make it an effective device for selling your skills.

Preparing for the Interview

Assemble all the papers that you may need. The main item will be your background and work experience inventory. It contains all the facts and figures you could possibly be asked—either in filling in the job application form, or in the job interview. Don't forget to take copies of your résumé, even though you may have already submitted one. Take your social security card, recent school records, military separation papers, and union card, if you have one. If your work is the sort you can show in an interview (such as artwork, publications, or procedures), take along a few samples. Be careful not to leave your only copy of something, as it could get lost.

Additional Pointers

* Learn all you can about the company where you are going for an interview—its product or service, standing in the industry, number and kinds of jobs available, and hiring policies.
* Know what you have to offer—what education and training you have had, what work you have done, and what you can do.
* Know what kind of job you want and why you want to work for the firm where you are applying.
* Bring along the names, addresses, and business affiliations of three persons (not relatives) who are familiar with your work and character. If you are a recent graduate, you can list your teachers. Ask references for permission to use their names.
* As you are filling in the job application, be aware that it in itself offers an excellent opportunity to convince an employer that you are a valuable person to hire. It is not only a chance to describe your accomplishments, but it also shows how clearly you can think and write, and how well you can present important details.
* Learn the area salary scale for the type of work you are seeking. If you have the required skill and experience, don't hesitate to state your salary expectations in filling in the application blank. On the other hand, if for any reason you don't want to commit yourself then, simply write "Open" in the space for salary desired. If asked, say you prefer to wait until the job interview to discuss salary.

* Never take anyone with you to the interview.
* Allow as much uninterrupted time for the interview as may be required. (For example, do not park your car in a limited-time space.)
* Dress conservatively. Avoid either too formal or too casual dress.

You and the Interview

* Be pleasant and friendly but businesslike.
* Let the employer control the interview. Your answers should be frank and brief but complete, without rambling. Avoid dogmatic statements.
* Be flexible and willing but give the employer a clear idea of your job preferences.
* Stress your qualifications without exaggeration. The employer's questions or statements will indicate the type of person wanted. Use these clues in presenting your qualifications. For example, if you are being interviewed for an engineering position and the employer mentions that the job will require some customer contact work, use this clue to emphasize any work, experience, or courses you have had in this kind of skill.
* If you have not sent your resume in advance, present it, or your work records, references, personal data, work samples, or other materials to support your statements when the employer requests them.
* In discussing your previous jobs and work situations, avoid criticizing former employers or fellow workers.
* Don't discuss your personal, domestic, or financial problems unless you are specifically asked. Answer only what relates to the job.
* Don't be in a hurry to ask questions unless the employer invites them. But don't be afraid to ask what you need to know. If the employer offers you a job, be sure you understand exactly what your duties will be. Also find out what opportunities for advancement will be open. A definite understanding about the nature of your job will avoid future disappointment for either you or your employer.
* Be prepared to state the salary you want, but not until the employer has introduced the subject. Be realistic in discussing salary. But don't sell yourself short.
* If the employer does not definitely offer you a job or indicate when you will hear about it, ask when you may call to learn the decision.
* If the employer asks you to call or return for another interview, make a note of the time, date, and place.
* Thank the employer for the interview. If the firm cannot use you, ask about other employers who may need a person with your qualifications.

The Fastest Declining Jobs

(1) Electrical and electronics assemblers; (2) Electronic semiconductor processors; (3) Railroad conductors and yardmasters; (4) Railroad brake, signal, and switch operators; (5) Gas and petroleum plant and system occupations; (6) Industrial truck and tractor operators; (7) Shoe sewing-machine operators and tenders; (8) Telephone station installers and repairers; (9) Chemical equipment controllers, operators, and tenders; and (10) Chemical plant and system operators.

Information Please Almanac is not responsible and assumes no responsibility for any action undertaken by anyone utilizing the first aid procedures which follow.

The Heimlich Maneuver[1]

Food-Choking

What to look for: Victim cannot speak or breathe; turns blue; collapses.
To perform the Heimlich Maneuver when the victim is standing or sitting:
1. Stand behind the victim and wrap your arms around his waist.
2. Place the thumb side of your fist against the victim's abdomen, slightly above the navel and below the rib cage.
3. Grasp your fist with the other hand and press your fist into the victim's abdomen with a quick upward thrust. Repeat as often as necessary.
4. If the victim is sitting, stand behind the victim's chair and perform the maneuver in the same manner.
5. After the food is dislodged, have the victim seen by a doctor.
When the victim has collapsed and cannot be lifted:
1. Lay the victim on his back.
2. Face the victim and kneel astride his hips.
3. With one hand on top of the other, place the heel of your bottom hand on the abdomen slightly above the navel and below the rib cage.
4. Press into the victim's abdomen with a quick upward thrust. Repeat as often as necessary
5. Should the victim vomit, quickly place him on his side and wipe out his mouth to prevent aspira-

tion (drawing of vomit into the throat).
6. After the food is dislodged, have the victim seen by a doctor.
NOTE: If you start to choke when alone and help is not available, an attempt should be made to self-administer this maneuver.

Burns[2]

First Degree: Signs/Symptoms—reddened skin. **Treatment**—Immerse quickly in cold water or apply ice until pain stops.
Second Degree: Signs/Symptoms—reddened skin, blisters. **Treatment**—(1) Cut away loose clothing. (2) Cover with several layers of cold moist dressings or, if limb is involved, immerse in cold water for relief of pain. (3) Treat for shock.
Third Degree: Signs/Symtoms—skin destroyed, tissues damaged, charring. **Treatment**—(1) Cut away loose clothing (do not remove clothing adhered to skin). (2) Cover with several layers of sterile, cold, moist dressings for relief of pain and to stop burning action. (3) Treat for shock.

Poisons[2]

Treatment—(1) Dilute by drinking large quantities of water. (2) Induce vomiting except when poison is corrosive or a petroleum product. (3) Call the poison control center or a doctor.

Shock[2]

Shock may accompany any serious injury: blood loss, breathing impairment, heart failure, burns. Shock can kill—treat as soon as possible and con-

The Heimlich Maneuver

Courtesy of New York City Department of Health

tinue until medical aid is available.

Signs/Symptoms—(1) Shallow breathing. (2) Rapid and weak pulse. (3) Nausea, collapse, vomiting. (4) Shivering. (5) Pale, moist skin. (6) Mental confusion. (7) Drooping eyelids, dilated pupils.

Treatment—(1) Establish and maintain an open airway. (2) Control bleeding. (3) Keep victim lying down. Exception: Head and chest injuries, heart attack, stroke, sun stroke. If no spine injury, victim may be more comfortable and breathe better in a semi-reclining position. If in doubt, keep the victim flat. Elevate the feet unless injury would be aggravated. Maintain normal body temperature. Place blankets under and over victim.

Frostbite[2]

Most frequently frostbitten: toes, fingers, nose, and ears. It is caused by exposure to cold.

Signs/Symptoms—(1) Skin becomes pale or a grayish-yellow color. (2) Parts feel cold and numb. (3) Frozen parts feel doughy.

Treatment—(1) Until victim can be brought inside, he should be wrapped in woolen cloth and kept dry. (2) Do not rub, chafe, or manipulate frostbitten parts. (3) Bring victim indoors. (4) Place in warm water (102° to 105°) and make sure it remains warm. Test water by pouring on inner surface of your forearm. Never thaw if the victim has to go back out into the cold which may cause the affected area to be refrozen. (5) Do not use hot water bottles or a heat lamp, and do not place victim near a hot stove. (6) Do not allow victim to walk if feet are affected. (7) Once thawed, have victim gently exercise parts. (8) For serious frostbite, seek medical aid for thawing because pain will be intense and tissue damage extensive.

Heat Cramps[2]

Affects people who work or do strenous exercises in a hot environment. To prevent it, such people should drink large amounts of cool water and add a pinch of salt to each glass of water

Signs/Symptoms—(1) Painful muscle cramps in legs and abdomen. (2) Faintness. (3) Profuse perspiration.

Treatment—(1) Move victim to a cool place. (2) Give him sips of salted drinking water (one teaspoon of salt to one quart of water). (3) Apply manual pressure to the cramped muscle.

Heat Exhaustion[2]

Signs/Symptoms—(1) Pale and clammy skin. (2) Profuse perspiration. (3) Rapid and shallow breathing. (4) Weakness, dizziness, and headache.

Treatment—(1) Care for victim as if he were in shock. (2) Remove victim to a cool area, do not allow chilling. (3) If body gets too cold, cover victim.

Heat Stroke[2]

Signs/Symptoms—(1) Face is red and flushed. (2) Victim becomes rapidly unconscious. (3) Skin is hot and dry with no perspiration.

Treatment—(1) Lay victim down with head and shoulders raised. (2) Reduce the high body temperature as quickly as possible. (3) Apply cold applications to the body and head. (4) Use ice and fan if available. (5) Watch for signs of shock and treat accordingly. (6) Get medical aid as soon as possible.

Artificial Respiration[3]

(Mouth-to-Mouth Breathing—In Cases Like Drowning, Electric Shock or Smoke Inhalation.)

There is need for help in breathing when breathing movements stop or lips, tongue, and fingernails become blue. When in doubt, apply artificial respiration until you get medical help. No harm can result from its use and delay may cost the patient his life. Start immediately. Seconds count. Clear mouth and throat of any obstructions with your fingers.

For Adults: Place patient on back with face up.

Lift the chin and tilt the head back. If air passage is still closed, pull chin up by placing fingers behind the angles of the lower jaw and pushing forward.

Take deep breath, place you mouth over patient's mouth, making leak-proof seal.

Pinch patient's nostrils closed.

Blow into patient's mouth until you see his chest rise.

—OR—

Take deep breath, place your mouth over patient's nose, making leak-proof seal.

Seal patient's mouth with your hand.

Blow into patient's nose until you see his chest rise.

Remove your mouth and let patient exhale.

Repeat about 12 times a minute. (If the patient's stomach rises markedly, exert moderate hand pressure on the stomach just below the rib cage to keep it from inflating.)

For Infants and Small Children: Place your mouth over patient's mouth and nose. Blow into mouth and nose until you see patient's chest rise normally.

Repeat 20 to 30 times per minute. (Don't exaggerate the tilted position of an infant's head.)

NOTE: For emergency treatment of heart attack, cardiopulmonary resuscitation (CPR) is recommended. Instruction in CPR can be obtained through local health organizations or schools.

Sources: 1. New York City Department of Health. NOTE Heimlich Maneuver, T.M. Pending. 2. *First Aid*, Mining Enforcement and Safety Administration, U.S. Department of the Interior. 3. *Health Emergency Chart*, Council on Family Health.

NUTRITION & HEALTH

AIDS Watch: The Arsenal Gets Larger

By Margie Patlak

In 1983, when the cause of AIDS was found to be a virus, the pharmaceutical industry was openly gloomy about the prospects for treating the disease. It hadn't had much success with drugs aimed at viruses—only five antiviral drugs had been developed. A large part of the problem was—and is—the sheer intimacy of the relationship between viruses and the cells they infect. The challenge lies in making drugs that attack the virus without harming the cell. HIV, the AIDS virus, presents a particularly tough problem. It not only takes up residence in cells but slips its genes right into their DNA, making it even more difficult for a drug to distinguish between the two.

Now [1989], six years after the AIDS virus was identified, the horizon looks a little brighter. More than 25 potential anti-HIV compounds are in various stages of testing. No single drug can promise a cure—none can actually rid the body of HIV. But researchers speak more hopefully about using combinations of drugs to keep the virus in check. "We used to say everybody with AIDS is going to die and there's nothing we can do about it," says Mathilde Krim of the American Foundation for AIDS Research. "Now we say AIDS is a treatable disease. How well it can be treated remains to be seen."

The progress in AIDS drug development stems in part from advances in understanding the virus's biology. Basic research has shed light on the key events in the virus's life cycle—from the time it first introduces itself to a cell to when it co-opts it into becoming a virus factory. Each of these steps offers drugmakers an opportunity to intercept the virus and cut short its path of destruction. The very first step involves the binding of the virus to a cell. Cells targeted by the AIDS virus have molecules called CD4 receptors on their surface. The AIDS virus, for its part, is studded with proteins that serve as the binding site for these receptors. Attachment gains the virus entry into the cell and launches the infection.

The most intriguing of the drugs developed to block this process is a synthetic, free-floating version of the receptor, called soluble CD4. It essentially acts as a decoy: it sticks to all the binding sites on the virus before they have a chance to bind to the real CD4 receptors on the cells. Smothered by the drug, the virus can't get a fix on the cells and therefore can't infect them. "It's a very exciting, promising new drug," says Paul Volberding, director of the AIDS program at San Francisco General Hospital and one of several investigators now testing CD4 in AIDS patients.

The strategy just described uses CD4 to keep virus out of healthy cells. But in an interesting twist, the drug could be used to search out virus-inhabited cells as well. When the AIDS virus lurks inside a cell, it apparently "marks" the surface of that cell with the very same protein that acts as the binding site for CD4. So to attack the virus in these cells, researchers at the National Institutes of Health and the University of Texas have linked soluble CD4 to lethal poisons. In the laboratory dish at least, the drugs act as guided missiles, carrying their poisonous cargo right to the infected cells, while sparing healthy ones.

"These drugs are more likely to get to the right cells than any other substance we have to date," says John McGowan of the National Institute of Allergy and Infectious Diseases. But it remains to be seen if the toxic bullets perform in humans as well as they do in the laboratory.

Another drug that appears to stop HIV from binding to cells—at least in the laboratory—is a sugarlike compound called dextran sulfate. This drug, which is imported from Japan, made headlines last summer when AIDS patients pressured the Food and Drug Administration into relaxing import restrictions on it. Exactly how dextran sulfate works is still unclear, but the drug is known to carry a strong negative charge. Flossie Wong-Staal of the National Cancer Institute speculates that the compound somehow comes between HIV and its target cells and uses its negative charge like an electronic shield to repel the virus, which is also negatively charged. The drug has "striking activity" in the laboratory, says Volberding, and it is now being tested in patients.

Once HIV enters a cell, it sheds its protein coat, revealing its naked thread of genetic material. In HIV that genetic material is in the form of RNA. Using its RNA as a template, the virus must then transcribe its genetic message into DNA, to make it compatible with the cell's own genetic machinery. It is this transcription process—without which the virus cannot reproduce—that is targeted by zidovudine, better known as AZT. The drug tricks the virus by providing a compound that looks like one of the building blocks HIV needs to build its DNA chains. But the building block is a fake; it lacks the attachment point for the next block in the sequence, so the chain can't be completed.

AZT is still the only anti-HIV drug approved by the Food and Drug Administration. But it has been dogged by its toxicity. About half of all patients with advanced AIDS have to give up the drug because of severe anemia, liver problems, and other side effects. The hope is that a second generation of AZT-like drugs—compounds designated by abbreviations like ddI, d4T, and AZDU—will turn out to be less damaging. "It would be a major step forward to find a drug that equals AZT in action with less toxicity," says Volberding.

After the AIDS virus has inserted its genes into a cell, it's in the driver's seat. It can now turn the cell into a factory that churns out viral proteins and then assembles them into new virus particles. Eventually these offspring burst forth from the cell to seek out and infect new targets.

Interferons, substances normally made in the body in response to infection, are known to thwart these steps in the life cycle of certain viruses. Now it's hoped that they will also stop the AIDS virus in its tracks. National Institutes of Health immunologist H. Clifford Lane recently tested alpha interferon on a small group of patients and found the results promising for those who were in the early stages of infection. The drug boosted their white blood cells and lowered amounts of an HIV marker, a protein made by the virus that circulates in the blood. Both these findings suggest that interferon is stemming the tide of new virus escaping into the bloodstream.

Moreover, studies suggest that combining alpha interferon with AZT works better—and at lower, less toxic doses—than using either alone. "If I had an HIV infection today," says Krim, who pioneered interferon research in the 1970s, "I'd treat myself with alpha interferon and AZT." All AIDS investigators may not share her conviction that the combination of these two drugs is the answer. But most

do agree that a multipronged attack on HIV, using several drugs with different targets, probably offers AIDS patients their best shot at a normal life span. "In AIDS no single therapy is going to work," says McGowan, "so we need to have as many different kinds of drugs as possible in the arsenal."

There's no guarantee, of course, that the drugs now being tested will pan out: results that look spectacular in the lab may not translate into real improvements in the clinic, or a drug's side effects may prove to be intolerable. But these drugs are only the first to be examined—numerous others are waiting in the wings. Many of these compounds attack quite different stages in the virus's life cycle. Some appear to prevent the virus from uncoating when it enters a cell, for example. Others seem to work further along the assembly line—they stop infected cells from making and trimming the proteins prior to assembling them into new viral packages. "We're just beginning," says McGowan. "There are many important drugs in development with equal or better potential than the ones we see now." □

Understanding AIDS

The Acquired Immune Deficiency Syndrome, or AIDS, was first reported in the United States in mid-1981. The total AIDS cases in the United States (including U.S. territories) as of June 30, 1989, were 99,936, and of these cases, 58,014 deaths were reported. According to World Health Organization projections in June 1989, there will be 5.5 million new cases of AIDS worldwide in the next decade. It is estimated that 500,000 persons around the globe have AIDS, and that 5 to 10 million people are infected with the HIV virus.

AIDS is characterized by a defect in natural immunity against disease. People who have AIDS are vulnerable to serious illnesses which would not be a threat to anyone whose immune system was functioning normally. These illnesses are referred to as "opportunistic" infections or diseases: in AIDS patients the most common of these are Pneumocystis carinii pneumonia (PCP), a parasitic infection of the lungs; and a type of cancer known as Kaposi's sarcoma (KS). Other opportunistic infections include unusually severe infections with yeast, cytomegalovirus, herpes virus, and parasites such as Toxoplasma or Cryptosporidia. Milder infections with these organisms do not suggest immune deficiency.

AIDS is caused by a virus usually known as human immunodeficiency virus, or HIV. Symptoms of full-blown AIDS include a persistent cough, fever, and difficulty in breathing. Multiple purplish blotches and bumps on the skin may indicate Kaposi's sarcoma. The virus can also cause brain damage.

People infected with the virus can have a wide range of symptoms—from none to mild to severe. At least a fourth to a half of those infected will develop AIDS within four to ten years. Many experts think the percentage will be much higher.

AIDS is spread by sexual contact, needle sharing, or less commonly through transfused blood or its components. The risk of infection with the virus is increased by having multiple sexual partners, either homosexual or heterosexual, and sharing of needles among those using illicit drugs. The occurrence of the syndrome in hemophilia patients and persons receiving transfusions provides evidence for transmission through blood. It may be transmit-

ted from infected mother to infant before, during, or shortly after birth (probably through breast milk).

The need for education about AIDS reflects the medical consensus that a means of arresting the disease will come no sooner than five or 10 years. In the past two years, scientists have discovered how AIDS infects brain cells and have identified genes that affect the AIDS virus. But efforts to devise a treatment or vaccine are complicated by the fact that AIDS is caused by two, perhaps three, similar viruses, and that the virus mutates frequently.

Even symptomatic relief has come from just one drug, zidovudine (formerly known as AZT). While not a cure, AZT stops the virus from reproducing. Most researchers believe that more than one drug will be necessary—one to suppress the AIDS virus, another to reconstitute the victim's damaged immune system. The cost of treatment can be very expensive.

With no cure in sight, prudence could save thousands of people in the U.S. who have yet to be exposed to the virus. Their fate will depend less on science than on the ability of large numbers of human beings to change their behavior in the face of growing danger. Experts believe that couples who have had a totally monogamous relationship for the past decade are safe. A negative blood test would be near-certain evidence of safety.

People who should be tested for AIDS include gay men and intravenous drug users, their sex partners, and anyone who has had several sex partners, if their sexual history is unknown, during any one of the last five years. Anyone who tests positive should see a physician immediately for a medical evaluation. Persons testing positive should inform their sex partners and should use a condom during sex. They should not donate blood, body organs, other tissue or sperm, nor should they share toothbrushes, razors, or other implements that could become contaminated with blood.

Information about where to go for confidential testing for the presence of the AIDS virus is provided by local and state health departments. There is a National AIDS Hot Line: (800) 342-2437 for recorded information about AIDS, or (800) 433-0366 for specific questions. □

AIDS Clinical Trials Information Service

A new federal AIDS Clinical Trials Information Service has been established to provide current information, free of charge, about AIDS drug testing. Dial 1-800-TRIALS-A Monday through Friday from 9:00 a.m. to 7:00 p.m. E.S.T.

Among the services, callers may request to speak with a Spanish-speaking health specialist or may obtain computer printouts from searches of the clinical trials database. The service is confidential.

The new service is part of a coordinated AIDS Public Health Service information effort. It is sponsored by the National Institute of Allergy and Infectious Diseases, in cooperation with the Centers for Disease Control, which sponsors the National AIDS Clearinghouse. The service will complement a database on all AIDS therapies in clinical trials now being developed by the Food and Drug Administration. Plans are under way to make all this information available through the National Library of Medicine's on-line services. (*Source:* The National Foundation for Infectious Diseases.) ☐

New AIDS Treatment Studies

In 1989, The FDA authorized clinical testing of two experimental treatments—a vaccine and an anti-viral drug, for people infected with the AIDS virus (HIV).

VaxSyn HIV-1, which in August 1987 became the first experimental vaccine to be cleared for clinical testing to prevent AIDS infection, will now be studied as a means of boosting the immune systems of HIV-infected people who have not yet shown symptoms of the disease. The genetically engineered vaccine contains a protein found on the surface of the AIDS virus.

Its developer, MicroGeneSys Inc., West Haven, Conn., will sponsor this new study, which will be conducted at Walter Reed Army Medical Center in Washington, D.C.

An anti-viral drug, SC48334, will be tested as a treatment for people with AIDS or advanced AIDS-related complex. The studies sponsored by the drug's manufacturer, G.D. Searle & Co. of Chicago, Ill., will be conducted at six test centers around the country. ☐

Another Promising AIDS Drug

Scientists at the National Cancer Institute in Bethesda, Md., have reported that persons infected with the AIDS virus showed improved immune functions after taking the experimental drug, DDI (dideoxyinosine) during a pilot study. DDI is manufactured by the Bristol-Myers Company, New York City. The drug appears to be less toxic than AZT. ☐

Focus on Sexually Transmitted Diseases

According to the National Institute of Allergy and Infectious Diseases (NIAID), sexually transmitted diseases (STDs) are a growing public health problem. More than 20 infectious agents are transmitted by sexual means and the STDs they cause are associated with a wide variety of acute and chronic health problems. The economic impact alone is estimated to be billions of dollars annually in the United States.

The National Institute of Allergy and Infectious Diseases created a STD branch in 1989 to direct research at prevention and control of STDs and their complications.

A few U.S. statistics put STDs in perspective:

● More than 4 million Americans are newly infected each year with *Clamydia*.

● About 2 million new cases of gonorrhea occur each year.

● About 1 million American women develop pelvic inflammatory disease.

● Approximately 500,000 new cases of genital herpes are identified each year, and it is estimated that 30 million Americans are affected by this painful, recurrent, and currently incurable disease.

● Genital warts are caused by the human papillomavirus (HPV), and about a million new cases are diagnosed each year.

● Syphilis, one of the world's oldest known STDs, has decreased in some populations but risen in others. In 1987, the largest single-year increase in cases of primary and secondary syphilis in more than a quarter of a century was reported with increases predominating among heterosexual men and women, particularly among blacks and hispanics. The incidence of congenital syphilis increased more than 20% to 10.5 cases per 100,000 live births. ☐

Cuba Quarantines AIDS Patients

Cuba is the only country in the world to require both mandatory testing of its population for the AIDS virus and the mandatory quarantining of its AIDS patients. The government has screened about one-third of its population and should complete the testing of its 10 million people in the next few years.

Those who test positive are sent to the government quarantine center in Havana where they are kept apart from the rest of the population.

Cuba has the lowest AIDS-infection rate in Latin America. Less than 300 persons have been quarantined so far. The government also requires foreigners to be tested for AIDS before entering the country.

The United States and other nations have condemned this totalitarian policy. ☐

Helping a Person With AIDS

No one will require more support and more love than your friend with AIDS. Feel free to offer what you can, without fear of becoming infected. You need to take precautions such as wearing rubber gloves only when blood is present.

If you don't know anyone with AIDS, but you'd still like to offer a helping hand, become a volunteer. You can be sure your help will be appreciated by a person with AIDS.

This might mean dropping by a supermarket to pick up groceries or just being there to talk. Above all, keep an upbeat attitude. It will help you and everyone face the disease more comfortably.

Dietary Guidelines for Americans

Source: FDA Consumer.

The "Dietary Guidelines for Americans" were made public in September 1985 by the U.S. Department of Agriculture and the Department of Health and Human Services. They are intended to provide healthy Americans with sensible, uncomplicated guidance on the kinds of foods they should be eating. Basically, their advice to Americans is: concentrate on eating a balanced and varied diet that provides the nutrients essential to good health, increase consumption of starch and fiber, but reduce fat, sugar, sodium, and alcohol.

The guidelines differ little from those announced by USDA and HHS in 1980. The advisory committee concluded that no recent nutrition research was persuasive enough to warrant any major changes. Not enough is known to describe an "ideal" diet for every individual because nutrition needs vary according to a person's sex, age, health, body size, and other factors. So the guidelines are aimed at those Americans who are in good health. They do not apply to people with diseases or conditions that affect nutritional needs.

More than 40 different nutrients—in the form of vitamins, minerals, amino acids (from proteins), essential fatty acids (from fats and oils), and calories from carbohydrates, fats, and proteins—are needed for good health. However, no one can be expected to keep track of all of them. Instead, most people generally can expect to satisfy their nutritional requirements by eating a variety of foods.

The guidelines do not suggest specific goals for such substances as fats and dietary fiber because of the need for more research. Instead, the guidelines state that "for the U.S. population as a whole, increasing starch and fiber in our diets and reducing calories (primarily from fats, sugars, and alcohol) is sensible. These suggestions are especially appropriate for people who have other risk factors for chronic diseases, such as a family history of obesity, premature heart disease, diabetes, high blood pressure, high blood cholesterol levels, or for those who use tobacco, particularly cigarette smokers."

Here are the guidelines and the rationale for each of them:

Eat a variety of foods

Most foods have more than one nutrient, but no single food provides all the essential nutrients. That is achieved by eating a balanced, varied diet that emphasizes the major food groups—fruits and vegetables; cereals and other foods made from grains; dairy products; and meats, fish, poultry, eggs, and dry beans and peas.

For example, dairy products such as milk are a source of protein, fats, sugar, vitamin A, riboflavin and other B vitamins, calcium, phosphorus, and other nutrients. But they provide little iron. Meat provides protein, several B vitamins, iron and zinc but little calcium. Vitamins A and C, folic acid, fiber, and various minerals are obtained from fruit and vegetables. Whole-grain and enriched breads, cereals, and other grain products provide B vitamins, iron, protein, and fiber.

Although there are some exceptions, a varied diet based on these food groups will satisfy the nutrient requirements of most healthy individuals without the need for supplements. "There are no known advantages and some potential harm in

consuming excessive amounts of any nutrient," the guidelines stress. "Large dose supplements of any nutrient should be avoided. You will rarely need to take vitamin or mineral supplements if you eat a variety of foods."

However, there are some exceptions. Iron supplements often are needed by women in their childbearing years. Pregnant and breast-feeding women have an increased need for certain nutrients, notably iron, folic acid, vitamin A, and calcium. Infants also have special nutritional needs. Breast-feeding is recommended for the first three to six months because infants absorb nutrients from breast milk better than cow's milk. Breast milk also contains substances that provide immunity to some diseases until the infant's body is able to produce these substances itself.

After three to six months, babies can start taking solid foods. Prolonged breast- or bottle-feeding without solid foods or iron supplements can result in iron deficiency, the guidelines point out. Flavoring baby foods with salt and sugar is also discouraged.

Elderly people also have to be extra careful about getting enough of all the essential nutrients because many older people eat less. The guidelines stress meals based on the basic food groups and a reduction in the consumption of fats, oils, sugars, sweets, alcohol, and other foods that are high in calories but low in other nutrients. Some elderly men and women who take certain medications that affect nutrient intake also may require supplements. Such supplements, however, should be taken only under the guidance of a physician.

Maintain a Desirable Weight

Experts estimate that one-third or more of all adult Americans are overweight and that, at any given time, more than 20 million Americans are resorting to diets to shed excess weight. Obesity is a major health concern in the United States, for it increases the risk of such chronic diseases as high blood pressure, heart disease, stroke, and diabetes.

Although many Americans keep searching for easy paths to losing weight, most such efforts are doomed to failure, in the view of most nutrition experts. Losing weight and not regaining it, the guidelines suggest, means eating foods high in nutritional value but with fewer calories, getting more exercise, and shedding weight at a sensible, gradual rate, a pound or two each week.

The guidelines warn that diets of less than 800 calories a day can be hazardous and should be followed only under medical supervision. Severely restricted, low-calorie diets make it extremely difficult to obtain the nutrients essential to maintaining good health, and they can have adverse effects. The guidelines warned: "Some people have developed kidney stones, disturbing psychological changes, and other complications while following such diets. A few people have died suddenly and without warning."

Frequent use of laxatives, induced vomiting, and other extreme measures should not be used to lose weight, according to the guidelines. Such actions can cause imbalances that can lead to irregular heartbeats and even death.

The emphasis should be on keeping body weight

t a reasonable level for one's sex, age, and height. Severe weight loss—below what is recommended—also is discouraged. Some people have suffered nutrient deficiencies, infertility, hair loss, skin changes, cold intolerance, severe constipation, psychiatric disturbances, and other complications from excessive weight losses. A doctor should be seen about any sudden, unexplained loss of weight.

Avoid Too Much Fat, Saturated Fat, and Cholesterol

The American diet generally is high in fat and cholesterol compared to some countries, and Americans tend to have high blood cholesterol levels. High blood cholesterol is one of the risk factors for heart attack. Nutritionists lack enough research data to make specific recommendations about how much fat and cholesterol the general public should eat, but the guidelines urge a sensible reduction in total fat—especially saturated fat—and cholesterol.

Among the suggested ways of doing this is to trim excess fat off meats and to eat lean meat, fish, poultry, and dry beans and peas as protein sources; use low-fat dairy products; eat moderate amounts of eggs and organ meats; limit intake of foods high in saturated fat, such as butter, cream, heavily hydrogenated fats, shortenings, and foods with palm and coconut oils; and broil or bake, rather than fry, foods.

The effect of diet on blood cholesterol levels varies among individuals. Some people—for reasons not completely understood—can eat foods high in saturated fat and cholesterol and maintain reasonable blood cholesterol levels, while others on low-fat, low-cholesterol diets still end up with high cholesterol levels. Heredity is believed to play a role. Acknowledging the controversy over what recommendations would be appropriate for the general public, the guidelines state that it would be "sensible" for Americans to reduce their daily consumption of fat. This is especially appropriate, the guidelines say, for individuals who have other cardiovascular risk factors, such as smoking or family histories of premature heart disease, high blood pressure, and diabetes. The guidelines do not suggest complete avoidance of any foods, because many foods that contain fat and cholesterol also provide high-quality protein and many essential vitamins and minerals.

Eat Foods With Adequate Starch and Fiber

The guidelines favor a moderate increase in consumption of fiber-containing foods. The American diet generally is low in fiber, yet there is evidence that fiber can help reduce chronic constipation, diverticular disease, and some types of "irritable bowel." Fruits, whole-grain breads and cereals, vegetables, dry beans and peas, and nuts are good sources of starch and fiber.

Carbohydrates and fat are major sources of energy (calories). If Americans cut back on fat consumption, energy needs can still be met from carbohydrates, especially the complex carbohydrates. "Carbohydrates are especially helpful in weight reduction diets, because, ounce for ounce, they contain about half as many calories as fats do," the guidelines said.

Simple carbohydrates like sugar provide calories but little other nutritional benefit. In contrast, complex carbohydrates—such as starch in bread and other grain products, beans, peas, nuts, seeds, fruits, and vegetables—contain other essential nutrients. Also, eating more foods with complex carbohydrates adds dietary fiber.

(Dietary fiber describes parts of plant foods that generally are not digestible by humans. Foods differ in the kinds of fiber they contain. Wheat bran has several kinds of fiber and has laxative properties but does not affect blood cholesterol levels. Other kinds of fiber have no laxative effects but seem to reduce blood cholesterol.)

Although in recent years there have been studies suggesting that the risk of colon cancer is greater among those with low-fiber diets, the guidelines state that more research is needed before definitive judgments can be made.

Avoid Too Much Sugar

It is not necessary to avoid eating simple sugars. It would, in fact, be difficult, because sugars are naturally present in many foods and are added to many processed products, usually in the form of sucrose, glucose, maltose, dextrose, lactose, fructose, corn sweeteners, honey and syrups. The major health concern with excess sugar consumption is tooth decay, especially when sugars (and starches, as well) are consumed between meals. The guidelines discourage eating sweets between meals. The guidelines also restate the age-old advice about proper dental hygiene, brushing after meals, drinking fluoridated water, and using fluoridated toothpastes and mouth rinses.

Avoid Too Much Sodium

Sodium is essential to the human body, but most Americans consume far more than they need, especially from table salt (which is 40 percent sodium). An intake of 1,100 to 3,300 milligrams a day is generally recommended. Salt is not the only source, for a wide variety of sodium compounds is used in many processed foods and beverages. The principal concern with high sodium consumption is for people with hypertension (high blood pressure) and those who may be susceptible to it.

If You Drink Alcoholic Beverages, Do So In Moderation

In urging moderate use of alcohol, the guidelines also support the national effort to discourage drinking and driving. From a nutritional standpoint, alcohol is high in calories but provides virtually no other nutritional benefit. The guidelines note that one or two standard-sized drinks daily appear to cause no harm in healthy adults.

Overweight people should be aware that alcohol adds calories. Heavy drinkers especially can suffer appetite loss, and this can lead to nutritional deficiencies and other health problems, such as cirrhosis of the liver and some types of cancer.

Pregnant women are advised by the National Institute of Alcohol Abuse and Alcoholism to refrain from drinking alcohol because excessive consumption may lead to birth defects or other problems during pregnancy. The level of consumption at which risks to an unborn child occur has not been established, the guidelines declare. □

Fat, Cholesterol, and Your Health

For the U.S. population as a whole, it is sensible to reduce daily intake of total fat, saturated fat, and cholesterol. Why? High blood cholesterol levels increase the risk of heart disease and the blood cholesterol level of many Americans is undesirably high. Eating a diet high in fat—especially saturated fatty acids and cholesterol—causes elevated blood cholesterol levels in many people.

For many, high blood cholesterol levels can be reduced by eating diets lower in saturated fatty acids and cholesterol. However, some people can eat diets high in total fat, saturated fatty acids, and cholesterol and still maintain normal blood cholesterol. Others have high blood cholesterol levels even on lowfat, low-cholesterol diets.

For adults, blood cholesterol is considered to be high if it measures more than 200 to 240 milligrams of cholesterol per deciliter of blood, depending on age. Ask your doctor to check your blood cholesterol.

Fat and Cholesterol

Fat is the most concentrated source of food energy (calories). Each gram of fat supplies about 9 calories, compared with about 4 calories per gram of protein or carbohydrate and 7 calories per gram of alcohol. In addition to providing energy, fat aids in the absorption of certain vitamins. Some fats provide linoleic acid, an essential fatty acid which is needed by everyone in small amounts.

Butter, margarine, shortening, and oil are obvious sources of fat. Well-marbled meats, poultry skin, whole milk, cheese, ice-cream, nuts, seeds, salad dressings, and some baked products also provide a lot of fat.

Cholesterol is a fat-like substance found in the body cells of humans and animals. Cholesterol is needed to form hormones, cell membranes, and other body substances. The body is able to make the cholesterol it needs for these functions. Cholesterol is not needed in the diet.

Cholesterol is present in all animal tissues—meat, poultry, and fish—in milk and milk products, and in egg yolks. Both the lean and fat of meats and the meat and skin of poultry contain cholesterol. Cholesterol is *not* found in foods of plant origin such as fruits, vegetables, grains, nuts, seeds, and dry beans and peas.

Fatty Acids are the basic chemical units in fat. They may be either "saturated," "monounsaturated," or "polyunsaturated." All dietary fats are made up of *mixtures* of these fatty acid types.

Saturated fatty acids are found in largest proportions in fats of animal origin. These include the fats in whole milk, cream, cheese, butter, meat, and poultry. Saturated fatty acids are also found in large amounts in some vegetable oils, including coconut and palm.

Monounsaturated fatty acids are found in fats of

Meat, Poultry, Fish

		Total fat grams	Saturated fatty acids grams	Cholesterol milligrams
Beef arm, roasted:				
Lean and fat	3 oz.	16	8	80
Lean only	3 oz.	6	3	77
Ground beef, cooked:				
Regular	3 oz. patty	17	7	77
Lean	3 oz. patty	15	6	80
Pork rib, roasted:				
Lean and fat	3 oz.	20	7	69
Lean only	3 oz.	12	4	67
Beef liver, fried	3 oz.	9	2	372
Chicken, light and dark meat, roasted:				
With skin	3 oz.	12	3	75
Without skin	3 oz.	6	2	76
Halibut fillets, broiled, with margarine	3 oz.	6	1	48
Tuna salad	1/2 cup	10	2	40
Crabs, hard-shell, steamed	2 med.	2	0	96
Dry beans, cooked	1/2 cup	1	trace	0
Peanut butter	2 tbsp.	16	2	0
Egg, large, cooked	1 yolk	6	2	274
	1 white	trace	0	0

Source: USDA, Human Nutrition Information Service.

Milk, Cheese, Yogurt

		Total fat grams	Saturated fatty acids grams	Cholesterol milligrams
Milk:				
Whole	1 cup	8	5	33
2% fat	1 cup	5	3	18
Skim	1 cup	1	trace	5
Buttermilk	1 cup	2	1	9
Yogurt:				
Lowfat plain	8 oz. carton	4	2	14
Lowfat fruit-flavored	8-oz. carton	2	2	10
Cottage cheese:				
Creamed	1 cup	9	6	31
Lowfat	1 cup	4	3	19
Cheese:				
Natural Cheddar	1 oz.	9	6	30
Mozzarella, part skim milk	1 oz.	5	3	15
Process American	1 oz.	9	6	27
Macaroni and cheese	3/4 cup	17	7	32
Vanilla ice cream	1/2 cup	7	4	30
Vanilla ice milk	1/2 cup	3	2	9

Source: USDA, Human Nutrition Information Service.

both plant and animal origin. Olive oil and peanut oil are the most common examples of fat with mostly monounsaturated fatty acids. Also, most margarines and hydrogenated vegetable shortenings tend to be high in monounsaturated fatty acids.

Polyunsaturated fatty acids are found in largest proportions in fats of plant origin. Sunflower, corn, soybean, cottonseed, and safflower oils are vegetable fats that usually contain a high proportion of polyunsaturated fatty acids. Some fish are also sources of polyunsaturated fatty acids.

NOTE: *All* fats, whether they contain mainly saturated fatty acids, monounsaturated fatty acids, or polyunsaturated fatty acids, provide the same number of calories. ☐

New FDA Sulfite Proposal

FDA has proposed that sulfites in many canned, frozen, dehydrated, and other commercially prepared foods be generally recognized as safe (GRAS) within certain levels and that manufacturers must declare on food labels levels of sulfites greater than 10 parts per million.

The term sulfites refers to six sulfur-based chemicals that have been used for many years as preservatives, as antioxidants to prevent discoloration, and as disinfection agents for food containers, among other uses.

The new proposal would establish limits on sulfite levels and require that stores selling products such as dried fruit and shrimp in bulk would have to use counter signs, cards, or other displays stating that the bulk products have been treated with sulfites.

A small minority of people are sulfite-sensitive and may suffer adverse reactions ranging from hives, nausea and diarrhea to shortness of breath and even death.

In 1986, the FDA banned the use of sulfites on fresh fruits and vegetables, particularly those

Fats and Sweets

		Total fat	Saturated fatty acids	Cholesterol
		grams	grams	milligrams
Butter	1 tbsp.	11	7	31
Margarine:				
Soft	1 tbsp.	11	2	0
Stick	1 tbsp.	11	2	0
Vegetable oil (corn)	1 tbsp.	14	2	0
Salad dressing:				
Mayonnaise	1 tbsp.	11	2	8
Mayonnaise-type	1 tbsp.	5	1	4
Italian, low-calorie	1 tbsp.	trace	trace	0
Italian	1 tbsp.	9	1	0
Cream:				
Sour	1 tbsp.	3	2	5
Light (table)	1 tbsp.	3	2	10
Nondairy, frozen	1 tbsp.	2	1	0
Cream cheese	1 oz. (2 tbsp.)	10	6	31
Cake, frosted, devil's food	1/12 8"-layer	11	5	50
Brownie	1 brownie	6	1	18
Pie, apple	1/6 pie	18	5	2

Source: USDA, Human Nutrition Information Service.

served at salad bars, and in 1987 proposed banning their use on fresh, pre-cut potatoes and processed potato products that are served or sold unpackaged or unlabeled to consumers. The FDA decided that these unlabeled items were a risk for those sensitive to sulfites. ☐

Facts on Sodium

What is sodium?

Sodium is a mineral that occurs naturally in some foods and is added to many foods and beverages. Most of the sodium in the American diet comes from table salt, which is 40% sodium and 60% chloride. One teaspoon of salt contains about 2,000 milligrams of sodium.

Why Is Sodium Important?

Sodium attracts water into the blood vessels and helps maintain normal blood volume and blood pressure. Sodium is also needed for the normal function of nerves and muscles.

How Much Sodium Do I Need?

Although some sodium is essential to your health, you need very little. The National Research Council of the National Academy of Sciences suggests that a "safe and adequate" range of sodium intake per day is about 1,100 to 3,300 milligrams for

adults. This is well below the amount that most American adults consume.

Sodium in Processed Foods

Most of the sodium in processed foods is added to preserve and/or flavor them. Salt is the major source of sodium added to these foods. It is added to most canned and some frozen vegetables, smoked and cured meats, pickles, and sauerkraut. Salt is used in most cheeses, sauces, soups, salad dressings, and in many breakfast cereals. Sodium is also found in many other ingredients used in food processing. Examples of sodium-containing ingredients, and their uses in foods are: baking powder—leavening agent; baking soda—leavening agent; monosodium glutamate—flavor enhancer; sodium benzoate—preservative; sodium caseinate—thickener and binder; sodium citrate—buffer, used to control acidity in soft drinks and fruit drinks; sodium nitrate—curing agent in meat, provides color, prevents botulism (a food poisoning); sodium phosphate—emulsifier, stabilizer, buffer; sodium propionate—mold inhibitor; sodium saccharin—artificial sweetener.

About Condiments

Watch out for commercially prepared condiments, sauces, and seasonings when preparing and serving foods for you and your family. Many, like those that follow, are high in sodium: onion salt, celery salt, garlic salt, seasoned salt, meat tenderizer, bouillon, baking powder, baking soda, monosodium glutamate (msg), soy sauce, steak sauce, barbecue sauce, catsup, mustard, Worcestershire sauce, salad dressings, pickles, chili sauce, relish.

The link between salt and sodium may be a little hard to understand at first. If you remember that

Salt-Sodium Conversions

1/4 tsp. salt = 500 mg sodium
1/2 tsp. salt = 1,000 mg sodium
3/4 tsp. salt = 1,500 mg sodium
1 tsp. salt = 2,000 mg sodium

1 teaspoon of salt provides 2,000 milligrams of sodium, however, you can estimate the amount of sodium that you add to foods during cooking and preparation, or even at the table.

Sodium Content of Some Foods

This table shows the sodium content of some types of foods. The ranges are rough guides; individual food items may be higher or lower in sodium.

Foods	Approximate sodium content (in milligrams)
Breads, Cereals, and Grain Products	
Cooked cereal, pasta, rice (unsalted)	Less than 5 per 1/2 cup
Ready-to-eat cereal	100-360 per oz.
Bread, whole-grain or enriched	110-175 per slice
Biscuits and muffins	170-390 each
Vegetables	
Fresh or frozen vegetables (cooked without added salt)	Less than 70 per 1/2 cup
Vegetables, canned or frozen with sauce	140-460 per 1/2 cup
Fruit	
Fruits (fresh, frozen, or canned)	Less than 10 per 1/2 cup
Milk, Cheese, and Yogurt	
Milk and yogurt	120-160 per cup
Buttermilk (salt added)	260 per cup
Natural cheeses	110-450 per 1-1/2-oz. serving
Cottage cheese (regular and lowfat)	450 per 1/2 cup
Process cheese and cheese spreads	700-900 per 2-oz. serving
Meat, Poultry, and Fish	
Fresh meat, poultry, finfish	Less than 90 per 3-oz. serving
Cured ham, sausages, luncheon meat, frankfurters, canned meats	750-1,350 per 3-oz. serving
Fats and Dressings	
Oil	None
Vinegar	Less than 6 per tbsp.
Prepared salad dressings	80-250 per tbsp.
Unsalted butter or margarine	1 per tsp.
Salted butter or margarine	45 per tsp.
Salt pork, cooked	360 per oz.
Condiments	
Catsup, mustard, chili sauce, tartar sauce, steak sauce	125-275 per tbsp.
Soy sauce	1,000 per tbsp.
Salt	2,000 per tsp.
Snack and Convenience Foods	
Canned and dehydrated soups	630-1,300 per cup
Canned and frozen main dishes	800-1,400 per 8-oz. serving
Unsalted nuts and popcorn	Less than 5 per oz.
Salted nuts, potato chips, corn chips	150-300 per oz.
Deep-fried pork rind	750 per oz.

Source: FDA, Human Nutrition Information Service.

Some Major Points About The Table

Unprocessed grains are naturally low in sodium. Ready-to-eat cereals vary widely in sodium content.

Fresh, frozen, and canned fruits and fruit juices are low in sodium. Most canned vegetables, vegetable juices, and frozen vegetables with sauce are higher in sodium than fresh or frozen ones cooked without salt.

A serving of milk or yogurt is lower in sodium than most natural cheeses, which vary widely in their sodium content. Process cheeses, cheese

foods, and cheese spreads contain more sodium than natural cheeses.

Most fresh meats, poultry, and fish are low in sodium. Canned poultry are higher. Most cured and processed meats such as hotdogs, sausage, and luncheon meats are even higher in sodium.

Most "convenience" foods are quite high in sodium. Frozen dinners and combination dishes, canned soups, and dehydrated mixes for soups, sauces, and salad dressings contain a lot of sodium. Condiments are also high in sodium.

Facts on Fiber

Dietary fiber is the parts of plants that humans can't digest.

There are several types of fiber, such as cellulose, pectin, lignin, and gums. Plants differ in the types and amounts of fiber they contain.

Different types of fiber function differently in the body. It is important to eat a variety of plant foods to benefit from effects of different kinds of fiber.

Some kinds of fiber have a laxative effect, producing softer, bulkier stools and more rapid movement of wastes through the intestine. Fiber is helpful in preventing and treating constipation and diverticular disease.

The possible benefits of dietary fiber for colon cancer, heart disease, diabetes, and obesity are being studied. Whether such benefits exist is not yet known.

It is not clear exactly how much and what types of fiber we need in our diets daily. However, for most Americans, a moderate increase in dietary fiber by eating more fiber-containing foods like those listed on this page is desirable.

There is no reason to take fiber supplements or to add fiber to foods that already contain it.

Some fiber foods are: whole-grain breads; whole-grain breakfast cereals; whole-wheat pasta; vegetables, especially with edible skins, stems, seeds; dry beans and peas; whole fruits, especially with edible skins or seeds; nuts and seeds.

High Fiber Food Sources
(4 grams or more per serving)

Food source	Serving
Breads and cereals	
All Bran*	1/3 cup-1 oz
Bran Buds*	1/3 cup-1 oz
Bran Chex	2/3 cup-1 oz
Corn bran	2/3 cup-1 oz
Cracklin' Bran	1/3 cup-1 oz
100% Bran*	1/2 cup-1 oz
Raisin Bran	3/4 cup-1 oz
Bran, unsweetened*	1/4 cup
Wheat germ, toasted, plain	1/4 cup-1 oz
Legumes (Cooked portions)	
Kidney beans	1/2 cup
Lima beans	1/2 cup
Navy beans	1/2 cup
Pinto beans	1/2 cup
White beans	1/2 cup
Fruits	
Blackberries	1/2 cup
Dried prunes	3

*Indicates foods that have 6 or more grams of fiber per serving. *Source:* National Cancer Institute.

What Are Whole Grains?

Whole grains are products that contain the entire grain, or all the grain that is edible. They include the bran and germ portions which contain most of the fiber, vitamins, and minerals, as well as the starchy endosperm.

Some examples are whole wheat, cracked wheat, bulgur, oatmeal, whole cornmeal, popcorn, brown rice, whole rye, and scotch barley.

Whole grain doesn't have to mean bread or cereal. Try these: brown rice, corn tortillas, unbuttered popcorn, scotch barley—in soups, tabbouleh—a bulgar wheat salad, whole-wheat pasta.

Recognizing the *Real* Whole Wheat

All whole-wheat bread is brown, but not all brown bread is whole wheat.

By law, bread that is labeled "whole wheat" must be made from 100 percent whole-wheat flour. "Wheat bread" may be made from varying proportions of enriched white flour and whole-wheat flour. The type of flour present in the largest amount is listed first on the ingredient label. Sometimes a dark color is provided by caramel coloring, also listed on the label.

The milling of the wheat to produce white flour results in the loss of nutrients as the bran and germ are removed. Enrichment replaces four important nutrients: iron, thiamin, riboflavin, and niacin. But flours made from the whole grain contain more of other nutrients, such as folic acid, vitamin B_6, vitamin E, phosphorus, magnesium, and zinc, than enriched white flour.

You don't have to switch to whole-wheat bread to increase your intake of whole grains.

Many products on the market are made of a mixture of whole-grain flours and enriched flour. Try those listed below for variety in taste and texture, as well as a bonus of fiber and nutrients. Or, try substituting whole-grain flour for half the amount of white flour when you bake quick breads or cookies.

Bran muffins; cornbread, from whole, ground cornmeal; cracked wheat bread; graham crackers; oatmeal bread; pumpernickel bread; rye bread. □

Mixing Antacids and RX Drugs Can Spell Trouble

Although many consumers take antacids almost casually, these drugs are not as harmless as they may seem. For one thing, antacids can affect the way other drugs behave in the body. They can speed the absorption of some prescription drugs—possibly causing an overdose—and slow it for others, thus reducing their effectiveness.

Among the drugs absorbed faster are: salicylates (for example, aspirin); indomethacin and naproxen, both used to treat arthritis; pseudoephedrine, a nasal decongestant; sulfadiazine, an infection fighter; and levodopa, a mainstay of Parkinson's disease therapy.

In other cases, the effectiveness of prescription drugs such as the antibiotic tetracycline, the heart drug digoxin, and the tuberculosis drug isoniazid are delayed.

Check with your physician first, to be safe.

Alcohol Facts

About two-thirds of Americans 18 or older drink alcoholic beverages, and about three-quarters of students in the 10th and 12th grades also indulge. Long-term alcohol abuse lops 10 years or so off the lifespan and prematurely ages the brain by about the same.

One-half of the traffic deaths that occur on U.S. highways are alcohol related.

Facts on Cocaine and Crack

Source: National Institute on Drug Abuse.

What is Cocaine?

Cocaine is a white powder that comes from the leaves of the South American coca plant. Users call it by a variety of names, including coke, C, snow, blow, toot, nose candy, and The Lady. The drug sold on the street is often a mixture of cocaine with other substances, which stretch the supply and increase the seller's profits. Cocaine belongs to a class of drugs known as stimulants, which tend to give a temporary illusion of limitless power and energy.

What is Crack?

Crack is a form of cocaine that has been chemically altered so that it can be smoked. Because the processing converts the cocaine into a chemical "base" (as opposed to an acid or a salt), crack belongs to a category of cocaine known as freebase. In the past, most freebase cocaine was processed using ether, a highly flammable solvent. Today, baking soda and heat are used to convert cocaine into freebase, eliminating the processing step involving ether. The product still contains some impurities found in the original cocaine, along with excess baking soda. When heated, the mixture makes a crackling sound.

Crack looks like small lumps or shavings of soap but has the texture of porcelain. In some parts of the country, the lumps of crack are called "rock" or "readyrock." In other areas, the drug is sold in 3-inch sticks with ridges that are referred to as "french fries" or "teeth." There are also reports that crack is being pressed into pills.

In many cities, the price of cocaine has dropped to all-time lows while the purity of the drug has increased. A gram of the drug can be purchased for $70 to $100 in some places. Since cocaine can be purchased in even smaller amounts, it can be even less expensive for the beginning user.

Crack, the smokable form of cocaine, can be purchased for $5 to $10 per dose. This low price is of national concern because even youngsters can afford to buy the drug.

How They Affect the Body

The immediate effects include dilated pupils and a narrowing of blood vessels. Cocaine and crack also cause increases in blood pressure, heart rate, breathing rate, and body temperature. Users lose their appetites and have trouble sleeping. Those who snort cocaine often have a runny nose. Cocaine and crack initially elevate mood, temporarily filling the user with a sense of exhilaration and well-being. As these effects wear off, however, the user's mind and body slide into a depression that is characterized by a "let down" feeling, dullness, tenseness, and edginess.

The Danger of Taking These Drugs

Addiction is among the most common and devastating problems caused by cocaine and crack. The effects of addiction can linger for a lifetime—relapse to drug use is always a possibility.

Besides addiction, however, cocaine and crack can also cause medical problems. On occasion, even death. In some people, a single dose of cocaine can produce seizures or heart and respiratory failure. The risk of such complications become greater for all users as the amount and frequency of drug use increase.

Users who share needles or other paraphernalia to inject cocaine face other potentially life threatening risks. These individuals may infect themselves with the organisms that cause hepatitis or acquired immunodeficiency syndrome (AIDS). In addition, users may pass these organisms on to their sexual partners or unborn babies.

Effects On the Brain

Cocaine and crack can cause brain seizures, a disturbance of the brain's electrical signals, some of which regulate the heart and muscles controlling breathing. Over time, studies in animals have shown, the brain appears to become more and more sensitive to cocaine. As a result, the threshold at which seizures occur is lowered. Repeated use of the drug without experiencing problems does not guarantee freedom from seizures in the future.

Risks Run By Pregnant Women

If the drugs are used during the early months of pregnancy, they may cause miscarriages or still births. Later, the drugs may cause premature labor or premature delivery. Sometimes, when the drug causes the placenta to separate early, the lives of both mother and baby are in danger due to bleeding and shock.

Some cocaine-exposed babies have suffered strokes before birth or heart attacks after delivery. Infants born to cocaine-using mothers may have malformed kidneys and genitals and can be at risk for having seizures or succumbing to crib death (sudden infant death syndrome).

In addition, nursing mothers can pass cocaine along to their babies, and may cause them to suffer some of the same heart and brain problems as adults.

Treatment Programs

The long-lasting craving for these drugs make addiction hard to treat without assistance. But there are many treatment programs throughout the country that can help people get off and stay off cocaine or crack. The goal of recovery program is to improve self-image and promote healthy living without drugs. Supportive family members or close friends of the person in treatment can often help make recovery a success. Many recovering individuals also find continuing strength and support in attending meetings of Cocaine Anonymous or Narcotics Anonymous, which are modeled after the Alcoholics Anonymous program. These groups are listed in the phone book.

A phone call to the National Institute on Drug Abuse's information and treatment referral hotline could help you or someone you care about get off cocaine or crack.

Call 1-800-662-HELP.

Lyme Disease Cases Rise

Lyme disease, an infection caused by the bites of ticks, has increased significantly in recent years and is now the most common tick-transmitted illness in the U.S. and worldwide. Lyme disease can result in conditions such as facial paralysis, cardiac disorders and, especially, arthritis. Eighty percent of cases occur between May and August. In 1988 more than 5,000 cases of Lyme disease were reported in 43 states. The actual number of cases is far greater, however; incorrect diagnosis and, in many states, the failure to require notification of the disease to public health authorities significantly impair case calculation.

Additional information is found in *Lyme Disease*, a report published by the American Council on Science and Health (ACSH), an independent scientific organization. To obtain a copy of *Lyme Disease*, send $2.00 with a self-addressed, stamped (75¢ postage) #10 envelope to: Lyme Disease, ACSH, 1995 Broadway, New York, N.Y. 10023. □

Mean Heights and Weights and Recommended Energy Intake

Category	Age (years)	Weight (lb)	Weight (kg)	Height (in.)	Height (cm)	Energy needs (with range) (kcal)	Energy needs (with range) (MJ)
Infants	0.0–0.5	13	6	24	60	kg × 115 (95–145)	kg × .48
	0.5–1.0	20	9	28	71	kg × 105 (80–135)	kg × .44
Children	1–3	29	13	35	90	1300 (900–1800)	5.5
	4–6	44	20	44	112	1700 (1300–2300)	7.1
	7–10	62	28	52	132	2400 (1650–3300)	10.1
Males	11–14	99	45	62	157	2700 (2000–3700)	11.3
	15–18	145	66	69	176	2800 (2100–3900)	11.8
	19–22	154	70	70	177	2900 (2500–3300)	12.2
	23–50	154	70	70	178	2700 (2300–3100)	11.3
	51–75	154	70	70	178	2400 (2000–2800)	10.1
	76 +	154	70	70	178	2050 (1650–2450)	8.6
Females	11–14	101	46	62	157	2200 (1500–3000)	9.2
	15–18	120	55	64	163	2100 (1200–3000)	8.8
	19–22	120	55	64	163	2100 (1700–2500)	8.8
	23–50	120	55	64	163	2000 (1600–2400)	8.4
	51–75	120	55	64	163	1800 (1400–2200)	7.6
	76 +	120	55	64	163	1600 (1200–2000)	6.7
Pregnancy						+ 300	
Lactation						+ 500	

The energy allowances for the young adults are for men and women doing light work. The allowances for the two older age groups represent mean energy needs over these age spans, allowing for a 2% decrease in basal (resting) metabolic rate per decade and a reduction in activity of 200 kcal/day for men and women between 51 and 75 years, 500 kcal for men over 75 years, and 400 kcal for women over 75. The customary range of daily energy output is shown for adults in parentheses, and is based on a variation in energy needs of ± 400 kcal at any one age, emphasizing the wide range of energy intakes appropriate for any group of people. Energy allowances for children through age 18 are based on median energy intakes of children these ages followed in longitudinal growth studies. The values in parentheses are 10th and 90th percentile of energy intake, to indicate the range of energy consumption among children of these ages. NOTE: kg—kilogram; cm—centimeter; kcal—kilocalorie; MJ—megajoule. 1 kcal is equivalent to 4.18 kilojoules. 1 megajoule is equal to 1000 kilojoules. *Source: Recommended Dietary Allowances*, Ninth Edition (1980), with the permission of the National Academy of Sciences, Washington, D.C.

Desirable Weights[1]

Height[2] (in.)	Height[2] (cm)	Weight[3] Men (lb)	Weight[3] Men (kg)	Weight[3] Women (lb)	Weight[3] Women (kg)
58	147	— —	— —	102 (92–119)	46 (42–54)
60	152	— —	— —	107 (96–125)	49 (44–57)
62	158	123 (112–141)	56 (51–64)	113 (102–131)	51 (46–59)
64	163	130 (118–148)	59 (54–67)	120 (108–138)	55 (49–63)
66	168	136 (124–156)	62 (56–71)	128 (114–146)	58 (52–66)
68	173	145 (132–166)	66 (60–75)	136 (122–154)	62 (55–70)
70	178	154 (140–174)	70 (64–79)	144 (130–163)	65 (59–74)
72	183	162 (148–184)	74 (67–84)	152 (138–173)	69 (63–79)
74	188	171 (156–194)	78 (71–88)	— —	— —
76	193	181 (164–204)	82 (74–93)	— —	— —

1. Desirable weights for men and women of different heights, based on evidence from insurance statistics of weight in relation to longevity. According to the National Center for Health Statistics, the average American male adult is 70 in. tall (178 cm) and the average female is 64 in. tall (163 cm). Accordingly, the average desirable weights are 154 lb (70 kg) and 120 lb (55 kg) throughout adult life. 2. Without shoes. 3. Without clothes. Average weight ranges in parentheses. *Source: Recommended Dietary Allowances*, 9th Edition (1980), with permission of the National Academy of Sciences, Washington, D.C.

Recommended Daily Dietary Allowances[1]

Designed for the maintenance of good nutrition of practically all healthy persons in the U.S. (revised 1980)

Persons	Age (years)	Wgt. (lbs)	(kg)	Hgt. (in.)	(cm)	Fat-Soluble Vitamins			Water-Soluble Vitamins				
						Vitamin A μg R.E.[2]	Vitamin D (μg)[3]	Vitamin E (mgα T.E.)[4]	Ascorbic Acid (mg)	Folacin (μg)	Niacin[5] (mg)	Riboflavin (mg)	Thiamin (mg)
Infants	0.0–0.5	13	6	24	60	420	10	3	35	30	6	0.4	0.3
	0.5–1.0	20	9	28	71	400	10	4	35	45	8	0.6	0.5
Children	1–3	29	13	35	90	400	10	5	45	100	9	0.8	0.7
	4–6	44	20	44	112	500	10	6	45	200	11	1.0	0.9
	7–10	62	28	52	132	700	10	7	45	300	16	1.4	1.2
Males	11–14	99	45	62	157	1,000	10	8	50	400	18	1.6	1.4
	15–18	145	66	69	176	1,000	10	10	60	400	18	1.7	1.4
	19–22	154	70	70	177	1,000	7.5	10	60	400	19	1.7	
	23–50	154	70	70	178	1,000	5	10	60	400	18	1.6	1.4
	51+	154	70	70	178	1,000	5	10	60	400	16	1.4	1.2
Females	11–14	101	46	62	157	800	10	8	50	400	15	1.3	1.1
	15–18	120	55	64	163	800	10	8	60	400	14	1.3	1.1
	19–22	120	55	64	163	800	7.5	8	60	400	14	1.3	1.1
	23–50	120	55	64	163	800	5	8	60	400	13	1.2	1.0
	51+	120	55	64	163	800	5	8	60	400	13	1.2	1.0
Pregnant	—	—	—	—	—	+200	+5	+2	+20	+400	+2	+0.3	+0.4
Lactating	—	—	—	—	—	+400	+5	+3	+40	+100	+5	+0.5	+0.5

Persons	Age (years)	Wgt. (lbs)	(kg)	Hgt. (in.)	(cm)	Water-Soluble Vitamins		Minerals					
						Vitamin B₁ (mg)	Vitamin B₁₂ (μg)	Calcium (mg)	Phosphorus (mg)	Iodine (μg)	Iron (mg)	Magnesium (mg)	Zinc (mg)
Infants	0.0–0.5	13	6	24	60	0.3	0.5 [6]	360	240	40	10	50	3
	0.5–1.0	20	9	28	71	0.6	1.5	540	360	50	15	70	5
Children	1–3	29	13	35	90	0.9	2.0	800	800	70	15	150	10
	4–6	44	20	44	112	1.3	2.5	800	800	90	10	200	10
	7–10	62	28	52	132	1.6	3.0	800	800	120	10	250	10
Males	11–14	99	45	62	157	1.8	3.0	1,200	1,200	150	18	350	15
	15–18	145	66	69	176	2.0	3.0	1,200	1,200	150	18	400	15
	19–22	154	70	70	177	2.2	3.0	800	800	150	10	350	15
	23–50	154	70	70	178	2.2	3.0	800	800	150	10	350	15
	51+	154	70	70	178	2.2	3.0	800	800	150	10	350	15
Females	11–14	101	46	62	157	1.8	3.0	1,200	1,200	150	18	300	15
	15–18	120	55	64	163	2.0	3.0	1,200	1,200	150	18	300	15
	19–22	120	55	64	163	2.0	3.0	800	800	150	18	300	15
	23–50	120	55	64	163	3.0	3.0	800	150	150	18	300	15
	51+	120	55	64	163	2.0	3.0	800	800	150	10	300	15
Pregnant	—	—	—	—	—	+0.6	+1.0	+400	+400	+25	[7]	+150	+5
Lactating	—	—	—	—	—	+0.5	+1.0	+400	+400	+50	[7]	+150	+10

1. Allowances provide for individual variances among most normal persons living in the United States under usual environmental stresses. 2. Retinol equivalents. 1. Retinol equivalent = 1 μg retinol. 3. As cholecalciferol. 10 μg cholecalciferol = 400 I.U. vitamin D. 4. αtocopherol equivalents. 1 mg d-α-tocopherol = 1 α T.E. 5. 1 NE (niacin equivalent) is equal to 1 mg of niacin or 60 mg of dietary tryptophan. 6. The RDA for vitamin B12 in infants is based on average concentration of the vitamin in human milk. 7. Cannot be met by ordinary diets: use of supplemental iron is recommended. NOTE: mg—milligram; μg—microgram; IU—International Units; lbs—pounds; Wgt.—Weight; Hgt.—Height. *Source: Recommended Dietary Allowances,* Ninth Edition (1980), with the permission of the National Academy of Sciences, Washington, D.C. Most recent. A 1985 revision was not adapted.

HEADLINE HISTORY

In any broad overview of history, arbitrary compartmentalization of facts is self-defeating (and makes locating interrelated people, places, and things that much harder). Therefore, Headline History is designed as a "timeline"—a chronology that highlights both the march of time and interesting, sometimes surprising, juxtapositions.

Also see related sections of *Information Please*, particularly Inventions and Discoveries, Countries of the World, etc.

B.C.
Before Christ or Before Common Era (B.C.E.)

5 billion B.C. Planet Earth formed.
3 billion B.C. First signs of primeval life (bacteria and blue-green algae) appear in oceans.
600 million B.C. Earliest date to which fossils can be traced.
1.7 million B.C. First discernible hominids (*Australopithecus* and *Homo habilis*). Early hunters and food-gatherers.
500,000 B.C. *Homo erectus* (crude chopping tools).
70,000 B.C. Neanderthal man (use of fire and advanced tools).
35,000 B.C. Neanderthal man being replaced by later groups of *Homo sapiens* (i.e. Cro-Magnon man, etc.).
18,000 B.C. Cro-Magnons being replaced by later cultures.
15,000 B.C. Migrations across Bering Straits into the Americas.
10,000 B.C. Semi-permanent agricultural settlements in Old World.
10,000-4,000 B.C. Development of settlements into cities and development of skills such as the wheel, pottery and improved methods of cultivation in Mesopatamia and elsewhere.

NOTE: For futher information on the geographic development in Earth's prehistory, read pages 531-532 in the Science section.

4500-3000 B.C. Sumerians in the Tigris and Euphrates valleys develop a city-state civilization; first phonetic writing (**c.3500 B.C.**). Egyptian agriculture develops. Western Europe is neolithic, without metals or written records. Earliest recorded date in Egyptian calendar (**4241 B.C.**). First year of Jewish calendar (**3760 B.C.**). Copper used by Egyptians and Sumerians.
3000-2000 B.C. Pharaonic rule begins in Egypt. Cheops, 4th dynasty (**2700–2675 B.C.**). The Great Sphinx of Giza. Earliest Egyptian mummies. Papyrus. Phoenician settlements on coast of what is now Syria and Lebanon. Semitic tribes settle in Assyria. Sargon, first Akkadian king, builds Mesopotamian empire. The Gilgamesh epic (**c.3000 B.C.**). Abraham leaves Ur (**c.2000 B.C.**). Systematic astronomy in Egypt, Babylon, India, China.
2000-1500 B.C. Hyksos invaders drive Egyptians from Lower Egypt (**17th century B.C.**). Amosis I frees Egypt from Hyksos (**c.1600 B.C.**). Assyrians rise to power—cities of Ashur and Nineveh. Twenty-four-character alphabet in Egypt. Israelites enslaved in Egypt. Cuneiform inscriptions used by Hittites. Peak of Minoan culture on Isle of Crete—earliest form of written Greek. Hammurabi, king of Babylon, develops oldest existing code of laws (**18th century B.C.**). In Britain, Stonehenge erected on some unknown astronomical rationale.
1500-1000 B.C. Ikhnaton develops monotheistic religion in Egypt (**c.1375 B.C.**). His successor, Tutankhamen, returns to earlier gods. Moses leads Israelites out of Egypt into Canaan—Ten Commandments. Greeks destroy Troy (**c.1193 B.C.**). End of Greek civilization in Mycenae with invasion of Dorians. Chinese civilization develops under Shang dynasty. Olmec civilization in Mexico—stone monuments; picture writing.
1000-900 B.C. Solomon succeeds King David, builds Jerusalem temple. After Solomon's death, kingdom divided into Israel and Judah. Hebrew elders begin to write Old Testament books of Bible. Phoenicians colonize Spain with settlement at Cadiz.
900-800 B.C. Phoenicians establish Carthage (**c.810 B.C.**). The *Iliad* and the *Odyssey*, perhaps composed by Greek poet Homer.
800-700 B.C. Prophets Amos, Hosea, Isaiah. First recorded Olympic games (**776 B.C.**). Legendary founding of Rome by Romulus (**753 B.C.**). Assyrian

Brontosaur

Moses

Egyptian chariots
(1500 B.C.)

105

ANCIENT EMPIRES

The Egyptian Empire (1400 BC)
Alexander's Empire (323 BC)
The Roman Empire (120 AD)
Path of the Crusaders (1000-1200 AD)

ASIA

ARABIA

Indus R.

Persepolis

Susa
Tigris Assur
Euphrates Babylon
Ur

Red Sea

Berenice

Caspian Sea

Mt. Ararat

Damascus
Antioch Jerusalem
Issus Tyre Gaza
Tarsus Cyprus Memphis
Smyrna Nile R.
Troy Crete Alexandria
Byzantium Thebes
Sinope
Black Sea

SARMATIA

MACEDONIA
Mt. Pela
Olympus Athens
Sparta

Cyrene

AFRICA

Mediterranean Sea

GERMANIA

Danube Vienna
R.

ETRUSCANS
Florence
Genoa Rome
Pompeii
Sicily
Syracuse
Carthage

EUROPE

GAUL

Cologne
Rhine R.
Paris

London

Sardinia

Taraco
Valencia
New Carthage

Miles 0 200 400
Kilometers 0 600

Some Ancient Civilizations

Name	Approximate dates	Location	Major cities
Akkadian	2350–2230 B.C.	Mesopotamia, parts of Syria, Asia Minor, Iran	Akkad, Ur, Erich
Assyrian	1800–889 B.C.	Mesopotamia, Syria	Assur, Nineveh, Calah
Babylonian	1728–1686 B.C. (old) 625–539 B.C. (new)	Mesopotamia, Syria, Palestine	Babylon
Cimmerian	750–500 B.C.	Caucasus, northern Asia Minor	—
Egyptian	2850–715 B.C.	Nile valley	Thebes, Memphis, Tanis
Etruscan	900–396 B.C.	Northern Italy	—
Greek	900–200 B.C.	Greece	Athens, Sparta, Thebes, Mycenae, Corinth
Hittite	1640–1200 B.C.	Asia Minor, Syria	Hattusas, Nesa
Lydian	700–547 B.C.	Western Asia Minor	Sardis, Miletus
Mede	835–550 B.C.	Iran	Media
Minoan	3000–1100 B.C.	Crete	Knossos
Persian	559–330 B.C.	Iran, Asia Minor, Syria	Persepolis, Pasargadae
Phoenician	1100–332 B.C.	Palestine (colonies: Gibraltar, Carthage Sardinia)	Tyre, Sidon, Byblos
Phrygian	1000–547 B.C.	Central Asia Minor	Gordion
Roman	500 B.C.–A.D. 300	Italy, Mediterranean region, Asia Minor, western Europe	Rome, Byzantium
Scythian	800–300 B.C.	Caucasus	—
Sumerian	3200–2360 B.C.	Mesopotamia	Ur, Nippur

king Sargon II conquers Hittites, Chaldeans, Samaria (end of Kingdom of Israel). Earliest written music. Chariots introduced into Italy by Etruscans.

700–600 B.C. End of Assyrian Empire (**616 B.C.**)—Nineveh destroyed by Chaldeans (Neo-Babylonians) and Medes (**612 B.C.**). Founding of Byzantium by Greeks (**c.660 B.C.**). Building of the Acropolis in Athens. Solon, Greek lawgiver (**640–560 B.C.**). Sappho of Lesbos, Greek poetess, Lao-Tse, Chinese philosopher and founder of Taoism (born **c.604 B.C.**).

600–500 B.C. Babylonian king Nebuchadnezzar builds empire, destroys Jerusalem (**586 B.C.**). Babylonian Captivity of the Jews (starting **587 B.C.**). Hanging Gardens of Babylon. Cyrus the Great of Persia creates great empire, conquers Babylon (**539 B.C.**), frees the Jews. Athenian democracy develops. Aeschylus, Greek dramatist (**525–465 B.C.**). Confucius (**551–479 B.C.**) develops philosophy-religion in China. Buddha (**563–483 B.C.**) founds Buddhism in India.

500–400 B.C. Greeks defeat Persians: battles of Marathon (**490 B.C.**), Thermopylae (**480 B.C.**), Salamis (**480 B.C.**). Peloponnesian Wars between Athens and Sparta (**431–404 B.C.**)—Sparta victorious. Pericles comes to power in Athens (**462 B.C.**). Flowering of Greek culture during the Age of Pericles (**450–400 B.C.**). Sophocles, Greek dramatist (**496–c.406 B.C.**). Hippocrates, Greek "Father of Medicine" (born **460 B.C.**). Xerxes I, king of Persia (rules **485–465 B.C.**).

400–300 B.C. Pentateuch—first five books of the Old Testament evolve in final form. Philip of Macedon assassinated (**336 B.C.**) after conquering Greece; succeeded by son, Alexander the Great (**356–323 B.C.**), who destroys Thebes (**335 B.C.**), conquers Tyre and Jerusalem (**332 B.C.**), occupies Babylon (**330 B.C.**), invades India, and dies in Babylon. His empire is divided among his generals; one of them, Seleucis I, establishes Middle East empire with capitals at Antioch (Syria) and Seleucia (in Iraq). Trial and execution of Greek philosopher Socrates (**399 B.C.**). Dialogues recorded by his student, Plato. Euclid's work on geometry (**323 B.C.**). Aristotle, Greek philosopher (**384–322 B.C.**). Demosthenes, Greek orator (**384–322 B.C.**). Praxiteles, Greek sculptor (**400–330 B.C.**).

300–251 B.C. First Punic War (**264–241 B.C.**): Rome defeats the Carthaginians and begins its domination of the Mediterranean. Temple of the Sun at Teotihuacan, Mexico (**c.300 B.C.**). Invention of Mayan calendar in

**Confucius
(551-479 B.C.)**

**Plato
(427?-347 B.C.)**

**Archimedes
(287-212 B.C.)**

Yucatán—more exact than older calendars. First Roman gladiatorial games (264 B.C.). Archimedes, Greek mathematician (287–212 B.C.).

250–201 B.C. Second Punic War (219–201 B.C.): Hannibal, Carthaginian general (246–142 B.C.), crosses the Alps (218 B.C.), reaches gates of Rome (211 B.C.), retreats, and is defeated by Scipio Africanus at Zama (202 B.C.). Great Wall of China built (c.215 B.C.).

200–151 B.C. Romans defeat Seleucid King Antiochus III at Thermopylae (191 B.C.)—beginning of Roman world domination. Maccabean revolt against Seleucids (167 B.C.).

150–101 B.C. Third Punic War (149–146 B.C.): Rome destroys Carthage, killing 450,000 and enslaving the remaining 50,000 inhabitants. Roman armies conquer Macedonia, Greece, Anatolia, Balearic Islands, and southern France. Venus de Milo (c.140 B.C.). Cicero, Roman orator (106–43 B.C.).

100–51 B.C. Julius Caesar (100–44 B.C.) invades Britain (55 B.C.) and conquers Gaul (France) (c.50 B.C.). Spartacus leads slave revolt against Rome (71 B.C.). Romans conquer Seleucid empire. Roman general Pompey conquers Jerusalem (63 B.C.). Cleopatra on Egyptian throne (51–31 B.C.). Chinese develop use of paper (c.100 B.C.). Virgil, Roman poet (70–19 B.C.). Horace, Roman poet (65–8 B.C.).

50–1 B.C. Caesar crosses Rubicon to fight Pompey (50 B.C.). Herod made Roman governor of Judea (47 B.C.). Caesar murdered (44 B.C.). Caesar's nephew, Octavian, defeats Mark Antony and Cleopatra at Battle of Actium (31 B.C.), and establishes Roman empire as Emperor Augustus—rules 27 B.C.—A.D. 14. Birth of Jesus Christ (variously given from 4 B.C. to A.D. 7). Ovid, Roman poet (43 B.C.—A.D. 18).

A.D.

The Christian or Common Era (C.E.)

**Jesus Christ
(4? B.C.-29? B.C.)**

1–49 After Augustus, Tiberius becomes emperor (dies, 37), succeeded by Caligula (assassinated, 41), who is followed by Claudius. Crucifixion of Jesus (probably 30). Han dynasty in China founded by Emperor Kuang Wu Ti. Buddhism introduced to China.

50–99 Claudius poisoned (54), succeeded by Nero (commits suicide, 68). Missionary journeys of Paul the Apostle (34–60). Jews revolt against Rome, Jerusalem destroyed (70). Roman persecutions of Christians begin (64). Colosseum built in Rome (71–80). Trajan (rules 98–116); Roman empire extends to Mesopotamia, Arabia, Balkans. First Gospels of St. Mark, St. John, St. Matthew.

100–149 Hadrian rules Rome (117–138); codifies Roman law, establishes postal system, builds wall between England and Scotland. Jews revolt under Bar Kokhba (122–135); final *Diaspora* (dispersion) of Jews begins.

150–199 Marcus Aurelius (rules Rome 161–180). Oldest Mayan temples in Central America (c.200)., Mayan civilization develops writing, astronomy, mathematics.

200–249 Goths invade Asia Minor (c.220). Roman persecutions of Christians increase. Persian (Sassanid) empire re-established. End of Chinese Han dynasty.

250–299 Increasing invasions of the Roman empire by Franks and Goths. Buddhism spreads in China.

300–349 Constantine the Great (rules 312–337) reunites eastern and western Roman empires, with new capital (Constantinople) on site of Byzantium (330); issues Edict of Milan legalizing Christianity (313); becomes a Christian on his deathbed (337). Council of Nicaea (325) defines orthodox Christian doctrine. First Gupta dynasty in India (c.320).

350–399 Huns (Mongols) invade Europe (c.360). Theodosius the Great (rules 392–395)—last emperor of a united Roman empire. Roman empire permanently divided in 395: western empire ruled from Rome; eastern empire ruled from Constantinople.

400–449 Western Roman empire disintegrates under weak emperors. Alaric king of the Visigoths, sacks Rome (410). Attila, Hun chieftain, attacks Roman provinces (433). St. Patrick returns to Ireland (432). St. Augustine's *City of God* (411).

450–499 Vandals destroy Rome (455). Western Roman empire ends as Odoacer, German chieftain, overthrows last Roman emperor, Romulus Augustulus, and becomes king of Italy (476). Ostrogothic kingdom of Italy established by Theodoric the Great (493). Clovis, ruler of the Franks, is converted to Christianity (496). First schism between western and eastern churches (484). Peak of Mayan culture in Mexico (c.460).

500–549 Eastern and western churches reconciled (519). Justinian I, the

Great (**483–565**), becomes Byzantine emperor (**527**), issues his first code of civil laws (**529**), conquers North Africa, Italy, and part of Spain. Plague spreads through Europe (from **542**). Arthur, semi-legendary king of the Britons (killed, **c.537**). Boëthius, Roman scholar (executed, **524**).

550–599 Beginnings of European silk industry after Justinian's missionaries smuggle silkworms out of China (**553**). Mohammed, founder of Islam (**570–632**). Buddhism in Japan (**c.560**). St. Augustine of Canterbury brings Christianity to Britain (**597**). After killing about half the population, plague in Europe subsides (**594**).

600–649 Mohammed flees from Mecca to Medina (the *Hegira*); first year of the Muslim calendar (**622**). Muslim empire grows (**634**). Arabs conquer Jerusalem (**637**), destroy Alexandrian library (**641**), conquer Persians (**641**). Fatima, Mohammed's daughter (**606–632**).

650–699 Arabs attack North Africa (**670**), destroy Carthage (**697**). Venerable Bede, English monk (**672–735**).

700–749 Arab empire extends from Lisbon to China (by **716**). Charles Martel, Frankish leader, defeats Arabs at Tours/Poitiers, halting Arab advance in Europe (**732**). Charlemagne (**742–814**).

750–799 Caliph Harun al-Rashid rules Arab empire (**786–809**): the "golden age" of Arab culture. Vikings begin attacks on Britain (**790**), land in Ireland (**795**). Charlemagne becomes king of the Franks (**771**). City of Machu Picchu flourishes in Peru.

800–849 Charlemagne (Charles the Great) crowned first Holy Roman Emperor in Rome (**800**). Arabs conquer Crete, Sicily, and Sardinia (**826–827**). Charlemagne dies (**814**), succeeded by his son, Louis the Pious, who divides France among his sons (**817**).

850–899 Norsemen attack as far south as the Mediterranean but are repulsed (**859**), discover Iceland (**861**). Alfred the Great becomes king of Britain (**871**), defeats Danish invaders (**878**). Russian nation founded by Vikings under Prince Rurik, establishing capital at Novgorod (**855–879**).

900–949 Vikings discover Greenland (**c.900**). Arab Spain under Abd ar-Rahman III becomes center of learning (**912–961**).

950–999 Eric the Red establishes first Viking colony in Greenland (**982**). Mieczyslaw I becomes first ruler of Poland (**960**). Hugh Capet elected King of France in **987**; Capetian dynasty to rule until **1328**. Musical notation systematized (**c.990**). Vikings and Danes attack Britain (**988–999**). Holy Roman Empire founded by Otto I, King of Germany since **936**, crowned by Pope John XII in **962**.

11th century A.D.

c.1000 Hungary and Scandinavia converted to Christianity. Viking raider Leif Ericson discovers North America, calls it *Vinland*. Chinese invent gunpowder. *Beowulf*, Old English epic.

1009 Moslems destroy Holy Sepulchre in Jerusalem.

1013 Danes control England. Canute takes throne (**1016**), conquers Norway (**1028**), dies (**1035**); kingdom divided among his sons: Harold Harefoot (England), Sweyn (Norway), Hardecanute (Denmark).

1040 Macbeth murders Duncan, king of Scotland.

1053 Robert Guiscard, Norman invader, establishes kingdom in Italy, conquers Sicily (**1072**).

1054 Final separation between Eastern (Orthodox) and Western (Roman) churches.

1055 Seljuk Turks, Asian nomads, move west, capture Baghdad, Armenia (**1064**), Syria, and Palestine (**1075**).

1066 William of Normandy invades England, defeats last Saxon king, Harold II, at Battle of Hastings, crowned William I of England ("the Conqueror").

1073 Emergence of strong papacy when Gregory VII is elected. Conflict with English and French kings and German emperors will continue throughout medieval period.

1095 (*See* special material on "The Crusades.")

**Viking Discovery
of Greenland (c.900)**

12th century A.D.

1150–67 Universities of Paris and Oxford founded in France and England.

1162 Thomas à Becket named Archbishop of Canterbury, murdered by Henry II's men (**1170**). Troubadours (wandering minstrels) glorify romantic concepts of feudalism.

1189 Richard I ("the Lionhearted") succeeds Henry II in England, killed in France (**1199**), succeeded by King John.

13th century A.D.

1211 Genghis Khan invades China, captures Peking (**1214**), conquers Persia (**1218**), invades Russia (**1223**), dies (**1227**).

The
MOSLEM WORLD
about 732

..... Territory overrun by Moslems

▨ The Byzantine Empire

Scale of Miles

0   300   600   900

1215 King John forced by barons to sign Magna Carta at Runneymede, limiting royal power.

1233 The Inquisition begins as Pope Gregory IX assigns Dominicans responsibility for combatting heresy. Torture used (**1252**). Ferdinand and Isabella establish Spanish Inquisition (**1478**). Tourquemada, Grand Inquisitor, forces conversion or expulsion of Spanish Jews (**1492**). Forced conversion of Moors (**1499**). Inquisition in Portugal (**1531**). First Protestants burned at the stake in Spain (**1543**). Spanish Inquisition abolished (**1834**).

1241 Mongols defeat Germans in Silesia, invade Poland and Hungary, withdraw from Europe after Ughetai, Mongol leader, dies.

1251 Kublai Khan governs China, becomes ruler of Mongols (1259), establishes Yuan dynasty in China (1280), invades Burma (1287), dies (1294).

1271 Marco Polo of Venice travels to China, in court of Kublai Khan (1275–1292), returns to Genoa (1295) and writes *Travels*.

1295 English King Edward I summons the Model Parliament.

**John Wycliffe
(1320-1384)**

14th century A.D.

1312-37 Mali Empire reaches its height in Africa under King Mansa Musa.

1337-1453 Hundred Years' War—English and French kings fight for control of France.

c.1325 The beginning of the Renaissance in Italy: writers Dante, Petrarch, Boccaccio; painter Giotto. Development of *No* drama in Japan. Aztecs establish capital on site of modern Mexico City. Peak of Moslem culture in Spain. Small cannon in use.

1347-1351 At least 25 million people die in Europe's "Black Death" (bubonic plague).

1368 Ming dynasty begins in China.

1376-82 John Wycliffe, pre-Reformation religious reformer and followers translate Latin Bible into English.

1378 The Great Schism (to 1417)—rival popes in Rome and Avignon, France, fight for control of Roman Catholic Church.

c.1387 Chaucer's *Canterbury Tales*.

15th century A.D.

1415 Henry V defeats French at Agincourt. Jan Hus, Bohemian preacher and follower of Wycliffe, burned at stake in Constance as heretic.

1418-60 Portugal's Prince Henry the Navigator sponsors exploration of Africa's coast.

1428 Joan of Arc leads French against English, captured by Burgundians (1430) and turned over to the English, burned at the stake as a witch after ecclesiastical trial (1431).

1438 Inca rule in Peru.

1450 Florence becomes center of Renaissance arts and learning under the Medicis.

1453 Turks conquer Constantinople, end of the Byzantine empire. Hundred Years' War between France and England ends.

1455 The Wars of the Roses, civil wars between rival noble factions, begin in England (to 1485). Having invented printing with movable type at Mainz, Germany, Johann Gutenberg completes first Bible.

1462 Ivan the Great rules Russia until 1505 as first czar; ends payment of tribute to Mongols.

1492 Moors conquered in Spain by troops of Ferdinand and Isabella. Columbus discovers Caribbean islands, returns to Spain (1493). Second voyage to Dominica, Jamaica, Puerto Rico (1493–1496). Third voyage to Orinoco (1498). Fourth voyage to Honduras and Panama (1502–1504).

1497 Vasco da Gama sails around Africa and discovers sea route to India (1498). Establishes Portuguese colony in India (1502). John Cabot, employed by England, reaches and explores Canadian coast. Michelangelo's *Bacchus* sculpture.

**Joan of Arc
(1412-1431)**

**Christopher Columbus
(1451-1506)**

THE CRUSADES (1096–1291)

In 1095 at Council of Clermont, Pope Urban II calls for war to rescue Holy Land from Moslem infidels. *First Crusade* (1096)—about 500,000 peasants led by Peter the Hermit prove so troublesome that Byzantine Emperor Alexius ships them to Asia Minor; only 25,000 survive return after massacre by Seljuk Turks. Followed by organized army, led by nobility, which reaches Constantinople (1097), conquers Jerusalem (1099), Acre (1104), establishes Latin Kingdom protected by Knights of St. John the Hospitaller (1100), and Knights Templar (1123). Seljuk Turks start series of counterattacks (1144). *Second Crusade* (1146) led by King Louis VIII of France and Emperor Conrad III. Crusaders perish in Asia Minor (1147).

Saladin controls Egypt (1171), unites Islam in Holy War (*Jihad*) against Christians, recaptures Jerusalem (1187). *Third Crusade* (1189) under kings of France, England, and Germany fails to reduce Saladin's power. *Fourth Crusade* (1200–1204)—French knights sack Greek Christian Constantinople, establish Latin empire in Byzantium. Greeks reestablish Orthodox faith (1262).

Children's Crusade (1212)—Only 1 of 30,000 French children and about 200 of 20,000 German children survive to return home. Other Crusades—against Egypt (1217), *Sixth* (1228), *Seventh* (1248), *Eighth* (1270). Mamelukes conquer Acre; end of the Crusades (1291).

16th century A.D.

**Michelangelo Buonarreti
(1475-1564)**

**Martin Luther
(1483-1546)**

1501 First black slaves in America brought to Spanish colony of Santo Domingo.

c.1503 Leonardo da Vinci paints the *Mona Lisa*.

1506 St. Peter's Church started in Rome; designed and decorated by such artists and architects as Bramante, Michelangelo, da Vinci, Raphael, and Bernini before its completion in **1626**.

1509 Henry VIII ascends English throne. Michelangelo paints the ceiling of the Sistine Chapel.

1517 Turks conquer Egypt, control Arabia. Martin Luther posts his 95 theses denouncing church abuses on church door in Wittenberg—start of the Reformation in Germany.

1519 Ulrich Zwingli begins Reformation in Switzerland. Hernando Cortes conquers Mexico for Spain. Charles I of Spain is chosen Holy Roman Emperor Charles V. Portuguese explorer Fernando Magellan sets out to circumnavigate the globe.

1520 Luther excommunicated by Pope Leo X. Suleiman I ("the Magnificent") becomes Sultan of Turkey, invades Hungary (**1521**), Rhodes (**1522**), attacks Austria (**1529**), annexes Hungary (**1541**), Tripoli (**1551**), makes peace with Persia (**1553**), destroys Spanish fleet (**1560**), dies (**1566**). Magellan reaches the Pacific, is killed by Philippine natives (**1521**). One of his ships under Juan Sebastián del Cano continues around the world, reaches Spain (**1522**).

1524 Verrazano, sailing under the French flag, explores the New England coast and New York Bay.

1527 Troops of the Holy Roman Empire attack Rome, imprison Pope Clement VII—the end of the Italian Renaissance. Castiglione writes *The Courtier*. The Medici expelled from Florence.

1532 Pizarro marches from Panama to Peru, kills the Inca chieftain, Atahualpa, of Peru (**1533**). Machiavelli's *Prince* published posthumously.

1535 Reformation begins as Henry VIII makes himself head of English Church after being excommunicated by Pope. Sir Thomas More executed as traitor for refusal to acknowledge king's religious authority. Jacques Cartier sails up the St. Lawrence River, basis of French claims to Canada.

1536 Henry VIII executes second wife, Anne Boleyn. John Calvin establishes Presbyterian form of Protestantism in Switzerland, writes *Institutes of the Christian Religion*. Danish and Norwegian Reformations. Michelangelo's *Last Judgment*.

1541 John Knox leads Reformation in Scotland, establishes Presbyterian church (**1560**).

1543 Publication of *On the Revolution of Heavenly Bodies* by Polish scholar Nicolaus Copernicus—giving his theory that the earth revolves around the sun.

1545 Council of Trent to meet intermittently until **1563** to define Catholic dogma and doctrine, reiterate papal authority.

1547 Ivan IV ("the Terrible") crowned as Czar of Russia, begins conquest of Astrakhan and Kazan (**1552**), battles nobles (boyars) for power (**1564**), kills his son (**1580**), dies, and is succeeded by a son who gives power to Boris Godunov (**1584**).

1553 Roman Catholicism restored in England by Queen Mary I, who rules until **1558**. Religious radical Michael Servetus burned as heretic in Geneva by order of John Calvin.

1554 Benvenuto Cellini completes the bronze *Perseus*.

1556 Akbar the Great becomes Mogul emperor of India, conquers Afghanistan (**1581**), continues wars of conquest (until **1605**).

1558 Queen Elizabeth I ascends the throne (rules to **1603**). Restores Protestantism, establishes state Church of England (Anglicanism). Renaissance will reach height in England—Shakespeare, Marlowe, Spenser.

1561 Persecution of Huguenots in France stopped by Edict of Orleans. French religious wars begin again with massacre of Huguenots at Vassy. St. Bartholomew's Day Massacre—thousands of Huguenots murdered (**1572**). Amnesty granted (**1573**). Persecution continues periodically until Edict of Nantes (**1598**) gives Huguenots religious freedom (until **1685**).

1568 Protestant Netherlands revolts against Catholic Spain; independence will be acknowledged by Spain in **1648**. High point of Dutch Renaissance—painters Rubens, Van Dyck, Hals, and Rembrandt.

1570 Japan permits visits of foreign ships. Queen Elizabeth I excommunicated by Pope. Turks attack Cyprus and war on Venice. Turkish fleet defeated at Battle of Lepanto by Spanish and Italian fleets (**1571**). Peace of Constantinople (**1572**) ends Turkish attacks on Europe.

**Anthony Van Dyck
(1599-1641)**

1580 Francis Drake returns to England after circumnavigating the globe. Knighted by Queen Elizabeth I (**1581**). Montaigne's *Essays* published.
1583 William of Orange rules The Netherlands; assassinated on orders of Philip II of Spain (**1584**).
1587 Mary, Queen of Scots, executed for treason by order of Queen Elizabeth I. Monteverdi's *First Book of Madrigals.*
1588 Defeat of the Spanish Armada by English. Henry, King of Navarre and Protestant leader, recognized as Henry IV, first Bourbon king of France. Converts to Roman Catholicism in 1593 in attempt to end religious wars.
1590 Henry IV enters Paris, wars on Spain (**1595**), marries Marie de Medici (**1600**), assassinated (**1610**). Spenser's *The Faerie Queen*, El Greco's *St. Jerome.* Galileo's experiments with falling objects.
1598 Boris Godunov becomes Russian Czar. Tycho Brahe describes his astronomical experiments.

Francis Bacon
(1561-1626)

17th century A.D.

1600 Giordano Bruno burned as a heretic. Ieyasu rules Japan, moves capital to Edo (Tokyo). Shakespeare's *Hamlet* begins his most productive decade. English East India Company established to develop overseas trade.
1607 Jamestown, Virginia, established—first permanent English colony on American mainland.
1609 Samuel de Champlain establishes French colony of Quebec.
1611 Gustavus Adolphus elected King of Sweden. King James Version of the Bible published in England. Rubens paints his *Descent from the Cross.*
1614 John Napier discovers logarithms.
1618 Start of the Thirty Years' War (to **1648**)—Protestant revolt against Catholic oppression; Denmark, Sweden, and France will invade Germany in later phases of war. Kepler proposes his Third Law of planetary motion.
1620 Pilgrims, after three-month voyage in *Mayflower*, land at Plymouth Rock. Francis Bacon's *Novum Organum.*
1633 Inquisition forces Galileo to recant his belief in Copernican theory.
1642 English Civil War. Cavaliers, supporters of Charles I, against Roundheads, parliamentary forces. Oliver Cromwell defeats Royalists (**1646**). Parliament demands reforms. Charles I offers concessions, brought to trial (**1648**), beheaded (**1649**). Cromwell becomes Lord Protector (**1653**). Rembrandt paints his *Night Watch.*
1644 End of Ming Dynasty in China—Manchus come to power. Descartes' *Principles of Philosophy.* John Milton's *Areopagitica* on the freedom of the press.
1648 End of the Thirty Years' War. German population about half of what it was in **1618** because of war and pestilence.
1658 Cromwell dies; his son, Richard, resigns and Puritan government collapses.
1660 English Parliament calls for the restoration of the monarchy; invites Charles II to return from France.
1661 Charles II is crowned King of England. Louis XIV begins personal rule as absolute monarch; starts to build Versailles.

Giordano Bruno
(1548-1600)

George Washington
(1732-1799)

THE FOUNDING OF THE AMERICAN NATION

Colonization of America begins: Jamestown, Va. (**1607**); Pilgrims in Plymouth (**1620**); Massachusetts Bay Colony (**1630**) New Netherland founded by Dutch West India Company (**1623**), captured by English (**1664**). Delaware established by Swedish trading company (**1638**), absorbed later by Penn family. Proprietorships by royal grants to Lord Baltimore (Maryland, **1632**); Captain John Mason (New Hampshire, **1635**); Sir William Berkeley and Sir George Carteret (New Jersey, **1663**); friends of Charles II (the Carolinas, **1663**); William Penn (Pennsylvania, **1682**); James Oglethorpe and others (Georgia, **1732**).

Increasing conflict between colonists and Britain on western frontier because of royal edict limiting western expansion (**1763**), and regulation of colonial trade and increased taxation of colonies (Writs of Assistance allow search for illegal shipments, **1761**; Sugar Act, **1764**; Currency Act, **1764**; Stamp Act, **1765**; Quartering Act, **1765**; Duty Act, **1767**.) Boston Massacre (**1770**). Lord North attempts conciliation (**1770**). Boston Tea Party (**1773**), followed by punitive measures passed by Parliament—the "Intolerable Acts."

First Continental Congress (**1774**) sends "Declaration of Rights and Grievances" to king, urges colonies to form Continental Association. Paul Revere's Ride and Lexington and Concord battle between Massachusetts minutemen and British (**1775**).

Second Continental Congress (**1775**), while sending "olive branch" to the king, begins to raise army, appoints Washington commander-in-chief, and seeks alliance with France. Some colonial legislatures urge their delegates to vote for independence. Declaration of Independence (July 4, **1776**).

Major Battles of the Revolutionary War: *Long Island:* Howe defeats Putnam's division of Washington's Army in Brooklyn Heights, but Americans escape across East River (**1776**). *Trenton and Princeton:* Washington defeats Hessians at Trenton. British at Princeton, winters at Morristown (**1776–77**). Howe winters in Philadelphia; Washington at Valley Forge (**1777–78**). Burgoyne surrenders British army to General Gates at *Saratoga* (**1777**).

France recognizes American independence (**1778**). The War moves south: Savannah captured by British (**1778**); Charleston occupied (**1780**); Americans fight successful guerrilla actions under Marion, Pickens, and Sumter. In the West, George Rogers Clark attacks Forts Kaskaskia and Vincennes (**1778–1779**), defeating British in the region. Cornwallis surrenders at *Yorktown*, Virginia (Oct. 19, **1781**). By **1782**, Britain is eager for peace because of conflicts with European nations. *Peace of Paris* (**1783**): Britain recognizes American independence.

HUDSON'S BAY COMPANY

Lake Superior

L. Michigan

Lake Huron

Lake Erie

Lake Ontario

Ottawa R.

QUEBEC

(1774-1783)

Detroit

Ft. Niagara

Ft. Oswego

St. Lawrence R.

Quebec

Montreal

Champlain

Crown Point

Ft. Ticonderoga

L. George

Saratoga

Oriskany

Mohawk R.

Cherry Valley

Albany

Concord

Lexington

Cambridge

Boston

Charlestown

Portsmouth

N.H.

MASSA

(MAINE)

Falmouth (Portland)

St. John R.

Proclamation Line of 1763

MTS.

Connecticut

CONN.

R.I.

Newport

New London

LONG I.

Brooklyn

New York

N.J.

West Point

Stony Pt.

Hudson

Del. R.

Morristown

Wyoming Valley

Susquehanna

Princeton

Trenton

Monmouth

NEW YORK

INDIAN

PENNSYLVANIA

Ft. Pitt (Pittsburg)

Valley Forge

Brandywine

Germantown

Philadelphia

Wilmington

DEL.

Baltimore

Potomac R.

MARYLAND

Mt. Vernon

VIRGINIA

James R.

Richmond

Roanoke R.

Williamsburg

Yorktown

Norfolk

Ohio R.

Kanawha R.

Boonesborough

Harrodsburg

Holston R.

Watauga R.

COUNTRY

1763

Proclamation Line

APP

A

L

A

C

H

I

A

N

Cape Fear R.

Guilford Court House

Pee Dee R.

NORTH CAROLINA

New Bern

Moore's Creek Bridge

Cowpens

King's Mt.

Camden

Santee R.

Wilmington

SOUTH CAROLINA

Savannah R.

Chattahoochee R.

GEORGIA

Charleston

Altamaha R.

Savannah

EAST FLORIDA

Atlantic Ocean

The UNITED STATES during the REVOLUTION

1664 British take New Amsterdam from the Dutch. English limit "Nonconformity" with re-established Anglican Church. Isaac Newton's experiments with gravity.

1665 Great Plague in London kills 75,000.

1666 Great Fire of London. Molière's *Misanthrope.*

1683 War of European powers against the Turks (to 1699). Vienna withstands three-month Turkish siege; high point of Turkish advance in Europe.

1685 James II succeeds Charles II in England, calls for freedom of conscience (1687). Protestants fear restoration of Catholicism and demand "Glorious Revolution." William of Orange invited to England and James II escapes to France (1688). William III and his wife, Mary, crowned. In France, Edict of Nantes of 1598, granting freedom of worship to Huguenots (French Protestants), is revoked by Louis XIV; thousands of Protestants flee.

1689 Peter the Great becomes Czar of Russia—attempts to westernize nation and build Russia as a military power. Defeats Charles XII of Sweden at Poltava (1709). Beginning of the French and Indian Wars (to 1763), campaigns in America linked to a series of wars between France and England for domination of Europe.

1690 William III of England defeats former King James II and Irish rebels at Battle of the Boyne in Ireland. John Locke's *Human Understanding.*

**John Locke
(1632-1704)**

18th century A.D.

1701 War of the Spanish Succession begins—the last of Louis XIV's wars for domination of the continent. The Peace of Utrecht (1714) will end the conflict and mark the rise of the British Empire. Called Queen Anne's War in America, it ends with the British taking New Foundland, Acadia, and Hudson's Bay Territory from France, and Gibraltar and Minorca from Spain.

1704 Deerfield (Conn.) Massacre of English colonists by French and Indians. Bach's first cantata. Jonathan Swift's *Tale of a Tub. Boston News Letter*—first newspaper in America.

1707 United Kingdom of Great Britain formed—England, Wales, and Scotland joined by parliamentary Act of Union.

1729 J. S. Bach's *St. Matthew Passion.* Isaac Newton's *Principia* translated from Latin into English.

1735 John Peter Zenger, New York editor, acquitted of libel in New York, establishing press freedom.

1740 Capt. Vitus Bering, Dane employed by Russia, discovers Alaska.

1746 British defeat Scots under Stuart Pretender Prince Charles at Culloden Moor. Last battle fought on British soil.

1751 Publication of the *Encyclopédie* begins in France, the "bible" of the Enlightenment.

1755 Samuel Johnson's *Dictionary* first published. Great earthquake in Lisbon, Portugal—over 60,000 die.

1756 Seven Years' War (French and Indian War in America) (to 1763), in which Britain and Prussia defeat France, Spain, Austria, and Russia. France loses North American colonies; Spain cedes Florida to Britain in exchange for Cuba. In India, over 100 British prisoners die in "Black Hole of Calcutta."

1757 Beginning of British Empire in India as Robert Clive, British commander, defeats Nawab of Bengal at Plassey.

**Catherine II
(1729-1796)**

1759 British capture Quebec from French. Voltaire's *Candide.* Haydn's *Symphony No. 1.*

1762 Catherine II ("the Great") becomes Czarina of Russia. J. J. Rousseau's *Social Contract.* Mozart tours Europe as six-year-old prodigy.

1765 James Watt invents the steam engine.

1769 Sir William Arkwright patents a spinning machine—an early step in the Industrial Revolution.

1772 Joseph Priestley and Daniel Rutherford independently discover nitrogen. Partition of Poland—in 1772, 1793, and 1795, Austria, Prussia, and Russia divide land and people of Poland, end its independence.

1775 The American Revolution (*see* "The Founding of the American Nation"). Priestley discovers hydrochloric and sulfuric acids.

1776 Adam Smith's *Wealth of Nations.* Edward Gibbon's *Decline and Fall of the Roman Empire.* Thomas Paine's *Common Sense.* Fragonard's *Washerwoman.* Mozart's *Haffner Serenade.*

1778 Capt. James Cook discovers Hawaii. Franz Mesmer uses hypnotism.

1781 Immanuel Kant's *Critique of Pure Reason.* Herschel discovers Uranus.

1783 End of Revolutionary War (*see* special material on "The Founding of

Napoleon Bonaparte
(1769-1821)

the American Nation"). William Blake's poems. Beethoven's first printed works.

1784 Crimea annexed by Russia. John Wesley's *Deed of Declaration*, the basic work of Methodism.

1785 Russians settle Aleutian Islands.

1787 The Constitution of the United States signed. Lavoisier's work on chemical nomenclature. Mozart's *Don Giovanni*.

1788 French *Parlement* presents grievances to Louis XVI who agrees to convening of Estates-General in **1789**—not called since **1613**. Goethe's *Egmont*. Laplace's *Laws of the Planetary System*.

1789 French Revolution (*see* special material on the "French Revolution"). In U.S., George Washington elected President with all 69 votes of the Electoral College, takes oath of office in New York City. Vice President: John Adams. Secretary of State: Thomas Jefferson. Secretary of Treasury: Alexander Hamilton.

1790 H.M.S. *Bounty* mutineers settle on Pitcairn Island. Aloisio Galvani experiments on electrical stimulation of the muscles. Philadelphia temporary capital of U.S. as Congress votes to establish new capital on Potomac. U.S. population about 3,929,000, including 698,000 slaves. Lavoisier formulates *Table of 31 chemical elements*.

1791 U.S. Bill of Rights ratified. Boswell's *Life of Johnson*.

1794 Kosciusko's uprising in Poland quelled by the Russians. In U.S., Whiskey Rebellion in Pennsylvania as farmers object to liquor taxes. U.S. Navy and Post Office Department established.

1796 Napoleon Bonaparte, French general, defeats Austrians. In the U.S., Washington's Farewell Address (**Sept. 17**); John Adams elected President; Thomas Jefferson, Vice President. Edward Jenner introduces smallpox vaccination.

1798 Napoleon extends French conquests to Rome and Egypt.

1799 Napoleon leads coup that overthrows Directory, becomes First Consul—one of three who rule France.

19th century A.D.

Thomas Jefferson
(1743-1826)

1800 Napoleon conquers Italy, firmly establishes himself as First Consul in France. In the U.S., Federal Government moves to Washington. Robert Owen's social reforms in England. William Herschel discovers infrared rays. Alessandro Volta produces electricity.

1801 Austria makes temporary peace with France. United Kingdom of Great Britain and Ireland established with one monarch and one parliament. Catholics excluded from voting.

1803 U.S. negotiates Louisiana Purchase from France: For $15 million, U.S. doubles its domain, increasing its territory by 827,000 sq. mi. (2,144,500 sq km), from Mississippi River to Rockies and from Gulf of Mexico to British North America.

1804 Haiti declares independence from France; first black nation to gain freedom from European colonial rule. Napoleon proclaims himself emperor of France, systematizes French law under *Code Napoleon*. In the U.S. Alexander Hamilton is mortally wounded in duel with Aaron Burr. Lewis and Clark expedition begins exploration of what is now northwestern U.S.

1805 Lord Nelson defeats the French-Spanish fleets in the Battle of Trafalgar. Napoleon victorious over Austrian and Russian forces at the Battle of Austerlitz.

1807 Robert Fulton makes first successful steamboat trip on *Clermont* between New York City and Albany.

1808 French armies occupy Rome and Spain, extending Napoleon's empire. Britain begins aiding Spanish guerrillas against Napoleon in Peninsular War. In the U.S., Congress bars importation of slaves. Beethoven's *Fifth* and *Sixth Symphonies* performed.

1812 Napoleon's Grand Army invades Russia in June. Forced to retreat in winter, most of Napoleon's 600,000 men are lost. In the U.S., war with

Alexander Hamilton
(1755-1804)

FRENCH REVOLUTION (1789–1799)

Revolution begins when Third Estate (Commons) delegates swear not to disband until France has a constitution. Paris mob storms Bastille, symbol of royal power (**July 14, 1789**). National Assembly votes for Constitution, Declaration of the Rights of Man, a limited monarchy, and other reforms (**1789–90**). Legislative Assembly elected, Revolutionary Commune formed, and French Republic proclaimed (**1792**). War of the First Coalition—Austria, Prussia, Britain, Netherlands, and Spain fight to restore French nobility (**1792–97**). Start of series of wars between France and European powers that will last, almost without interruption, for 23 years. Louis XVI and Marie Antoinette executed. Committee of Public Safety begins Reign of Terror as political control measure. Interfactional rivalry leads to mass killings. Danton and Robespierre executed. Third French Constitution sets up Directory government (**1795**).

Britain declared over freedom of the seas for U.S. vessels. U.S.S. *Constitution* sinks British frigate. (*See* special material on the "War of 1812.")

1814 French defeated by allies (Britain, Austria, Russia, Prussia, Sweden, and Portugal) in War of Liberation. Napoleon exiled to Elba, off Italian coast. Bourbon King Louis XVIII takes French throne. George Stephenson builds first practical steam locomotive.

1815 Napoleon returns: "Hundred Days" begin. Napoleon defeated by Wellington at Waterloo, banished again to St. Helena in South Atlantic. Congress of Vienna: victorious allies change the map of Europe.

1817 Simón Bolívar establishes independent Venezuela, as Spain loses hold on South American countries. Bolívar named President of Colombia (1819). Peru, Guatemala, Panama, and Santo Domingo proclaim independence from Spain (1821).

1820 Missouri Compromise—Missouri admitted as slave state but slavery barred in rest of Louisiana Purchase north of 36°30' N.

1822 Greeks proclaim a republic and independence from Turkey. Turks invade Greece. Russia declares war on Turkey (1828). Greece also aided by France and Britain. War ends and Turks recognize Greek independence (1829). Brazil becomes independent of Portugal. Schubert's *Eighth Symphony* ("The Unfinished").

1823 U.S. Monroe Doctrine warns European nations not to interfere in Western Hemisphere.

1824 Mexico becomes a republic, three years after declaring independence from Spain. Beethoven's *Ninth Symphony.*

**Charles Dickens
(1812-1870)**

1825 First passenger-carrying railroad in England.

1830 French invade Algeria. Louis Philippe becomes "Citizen King" as revolution forces Charles X to abdicate. Mormon church formed in U.S. by Joseph Smith.

1831 Polish revolt against Russia fails. Belgium separates from the Netherlands. In U.S., Nat Turner leads unsuccessful slave rebellion.

1833 Slavery abolished in British Empire.

1834 Charles Babbage invents "analytical engine," precursor of computer. McCormick patents reaper.

1836 Boer farmers start "Great Trek"—Natal, Transvaal, and Orange Free State founded in South Africa. Mexican army besieges Texans in Alamo. Entire garrison, including Davy Crockett and Jim Bowie, wiped out. Texans gain independence from Mexico after winning Battle of San Jacinto. Dicken's *Pickwick Papers.*

1837 Victoria becomes Queen of Great Britain. Mob kills Elijah P. Lovejoy, Illinois abolitionist publisher.

1839 First Opium War (to 1842) between Britain and China, over importation of drug into China.

1840 Lower and Upper Canada united.

1841 U.S. President Harrison dies (April 4) one month after inauguration; John Tyler becomes first Vice President to succeed to Presidency.

1844 Democratic convention calls for annexation of Texas and acquisition of Oregon ("Fifty-four-forty-or-fight"). Five Chinese ports opened to U.S. ships. Samuel F. B. Morse patents telegraph.

**Henry Clay
(1777-1852)**

1845 Congress adopts joint resolution for annexation of Texas.

1846 Failure of potato crop causes famine in Ireland. U.S. declares war on Mexico. California and New Mexico annexed by U.S. Brigham Young leads Mormons to Great Salt Lake. W.T. Morton uses ether as anesthetic. Sewing machine patented by Elias Howe.

1848 Revolt in Paris: Louis Philippe abdicates; Louis Napoleon elected President of French Republic. Revolutions in Vienna, Venice, Berlin, Milan, Rome, and Warsaw. Put down by royal troops in 1848–49. U.S.-Mexico War ends; Mexico cedes claims to Texas, California, Arizona, New Mexico, Utah, Nevada. U.S. treaty with Britain sets Oregon Territory boundary at 49th parallel. Karl Marx and Friedrich Engels' *Communist Manifesto.*

1849 California gold rush begins.

1850 Henry Clay opens great debate on slavery, warns South against secession.

1851 Herman Melville's *Moby Dick.* Harriet Beecher Stowe's *Uncle Tom's Cabin.*

1852 South African Republic established. Louis Napoleon proclaims himself Napoleon III ("Second Empire").

WAR OF 1812

British interference with American trade, impressment of American seamen, and "War Hawks" drive for western expansion lead to war. American attacks on Canada foiled; U.S. Commodore Perry wins battle of Lake Erie (1813). British capture and burn Washington (1814) but fail to take Fort McHenry at Baltimore. Andrew Jackson repulses assault on New Orleans after treaty of Ghent ends war (1815). War settles little but strengthens U.S. as independent nation.

**Dred Scott
(1795?-1858)**

**Abraham Lincoln
(1809-1865)**

**Ulysses S. Grant
(1822-1885)**

1853 Crimean War begins as Turkey declares war on Russia. Commodore Perry reaches Tokyo.

1854 Britain and France join Turkey in war on Russia. In U.S., Kansas-Nebraska Act permits local option on slavery; rioting and bloodshed. Japanese allow American trade. Antislavery men in Michigan form Republican Party. Tennyson's *Charge of the Light Brigade.* Thoreau's *Walden.*

1855 Armed clashes in Kansas between pro- and anti-slavery forces. Florence Nightingale nurses wounded in Crimea. Walt Whitman's *Leaves of Grass.*

1856 Flaubert's *Madame Bovary.*

1857 Supreme Court, in Dred Scott decision, rules that a slave is not a citizen. Financial crisis in Europe and U.S. Great Mutiny (Sepoy Rebellion) begins in India. India placed under crown rule as a result.

1858 Pro-slavery constitution rejected in Kansas. Abraham Lincoln makes strong antislavery speech in Springfield, Ill.: ". . . this Government cannot endure permanently half slave and half free." Lincoln-Douglas debates. First trans-Atlantic telegraph cable completed by Cyrus W. Field.

1859 John Brown raids Harpers Ferry; is captured and hanged. Work begins on Suez Canal. Unification of Italy starts under leadership of Count Cavour, Sardinian premier. Joined by France in war against Austria. Edward Fitzgerald's *Rubaiyat of Omar Khayyam.* Charles Darwin's *Origin of Species.* J. S. Mill's *On Liberty*

1861 U.S. Civil War begins as attempts at compromise fail (*see* special material on "The Civil War"). Congress creates Colorado, Dakota, and Nevada territories; adopts income tax; Lincoln inaugurated. Serfs emancipated in Russia. Pasteur's theory of germs. Independent Kingdom of Italy proclaimed under Sardinian King Victor Emmanuel II.

1863 French capture Mexico City; proclaim Archduke Maximilian of Austria emperor.

1865 Lincoln fatally shot at Ford's Theater by John Wilkes Booth. Vice President Johnson sworn as successor. Booth caught and dies of gunshot wounds; four conspirators are hanged. Joseph Lister begins antiseptic surgery. Gregor Mendel's Law of Heredity. Lewis Carroll's *Alice's Adventures in Wonderland.*

1866 Alfred Nobel invents dynamite (patented in Britain 1867). Seven Weeks' War: Austria defeated by Prussia and Italy.

1867 Austria-Hungary Dual Monarchy established. French leave Mexico; Maximilian executed. Dominion of Canada established. U.S. buys Alaska from Russia for $7,200,000. South African diamond field discovered. Volume I of Marx's *Das Kapital.* Strauss's *Blue Danube.*

1868 Revolution in Spain; Queen Isabella deposed, flees to France. In U.S., Fourteenth Amendment giving civil rights to blacks is ratified. Georgia under military government after legislature expels blacks.

1869 First U.S. transcontinental rail route completed. James Fisk and Jay Gould attempt to control gold market causes Black Friday panic. Suez Canal opened. Mendeleev's periodic table of elements.

1870 Franco-Prussian War (to 1871): Napoleon III capitulates at Sedan. Revolt in Paris; Third Republic proclaimed.

THE CIVIL WAR
(The War Between the States or the War of the Rebellion)

Apart from the matter of slavery, the Civil War arose out of both the economic and political rivalry between an agrarian South and an industrial North and the issue of the right of states to secede from the Union.

1861 After South Carolina secedes (**Dec. 20, 1860**), Mississippi, Florida, Alabama, Georgia, Louisiana, and Texas follow, forming the Confederate States of America, with Jefferson Davis as president (**Jan.-March**). War begins as Confederates fire on Fort Sumter (**April 12**). Lincoln calls for 75,000 volunteers. Southern ports blockaded by superior Union naval forces. Virginia, Arkansas, Tennessee, and North Carolina secede to complete 11-state Confederacy. Union army advancing on Richmond repulsed at first Battle of Bull Run (**July**).

1862 Edwin M. Stanton named Secretary of War (**Jan.**). Grant wins first important Union victory in West, at Fort Donelson; Nashville falls (**Feb.**). Ironclads, Union's *Monitor* and Confederate's *Virginia (Merrimac)* duel at Hampton Roads (**March**). New Orleans falls to Union fleet under Farragut; city occupied (**April**). Grant's army escapes defeat at Shiloh. Memphis falls as Union gunboats control upper Mississippi (**June**). Confederate general Robert E. Lee victorious at second Battle of Bull Run (**Aug.**). Union army under McClellan

halts Lee's attack on Washington in the Battle of Antietam (**Sept.**). Lincoln removes McClellan for lack of aggressiveness. Burnside's drive on Richmond fails at Fredericksburg (**Dec.**). Union forces under Rosecrans chase Bragg through Tennessee; battle at Murfreesboro (**Oct.-Jan. 1863**).

1863 Lee defeats Hooker at Chancellorsville; "Stonewall" Jackson, Confederate general, dies (**May**). Confederate invasion of Pennsylvania stopped at Gettysburg by George Meade—Lee loses 20,000 men—the greatest battle of the War (**July**). It and the Union victory at Vicksburg mark the war's turning point. Union general George H. Thomas, the "Rock of Chickamauga," holds Bragg's forces on Georgia-Tennessee border (**Sept.**). Sherman, Hooker, and Thomas drive Bragg back to Georgia. Tennessee restored to the Union (**Nov.**).

1864 Ulysses S. Grant named commander-in-chief of Union forces (**March**). In the Wilderness campaign, Grant forces Lee's Army of Northern Virginia back toward Richmond (**May-June**). Sherman's Atlanta campaign and "march to the sea" (**May-Sept.**). Farragut's victory at Mobile Bay (**Aug.**). Hood's Confederate army defeated at Nashville. Sherman takes Savannah (**Dec.**).

1865 Sheridan defeats Confederates at Five Forks; Confederates evacuate Richmond (**April**). On April 9, Lee surrenders to Grant at Appomattox.

1871 France surrenders Alsace-Lorraine to Germany; war ends. German Empire proclaimed with Prussian King as Kaiser Wilhelm I. Fighting with Apaches begins in American West. Boss Tweed corruption exposed in New York. The Chicago Fire, with 250 deaths and $196-million damage. Stanley meets Livingston in Africa.

1872 Congress gives amnesty to most Confederates. Jules Verne's *Around the World in 80 Days.*

1873 Economic crisis in Europe. U.S. establishes gold standard.

1875 First Kentucky Derby.

1876 Sioux kill Gen. George A. Custer and 264 troopers at Little Big Horn River. Alexander Graham Bell patents the telephone.

1877 After Presidential election of **1876**, Electoral Commission gives disputed Electoral College votes to Rutherford B. Hayes despite Tilden's popular majority. Russo-Turkish war (ends in **1878** with power of Turkey in Europe broken). Reconstruction ends in the American South. Thomas Edison patents phonograph.

1878 Congress of Berlin revises Treaty of San Stefano ending Russo-Turkish War; makes extensive redivision of southeastern Europe. First commercial telephone exchange opened in New Haven, Conn.

1880 U.S.-China treaty allows U.S. to restrict immigration of Chinese labor.

1881 President Garfield fatally shot by assassin; Vice President Arthur succeeds him. Charles J. Guiteau convicted and executed (in **1882**).

1882 Terrorism in Ireland after land evictions. Britain invades and conquers Egypt. Germany, Austria, and Italy form Triple Alliance. In U.S., Congress adopts Chinese Exclusion Act. Rockefeller's Standard Oil Trust is first industrial monopoly. In Berlin, Robert Koch announces discovery of tuberculosis germ.

1883 Congress creates Civil Service Commission. Brooklyn Bridge and Metropolitan Opera House completed.

1885 British Gen. Charles G. "Chinese" Gordon killed at Khartoum in Egyptian Sudan.

1886 Bombing at Haymarket Square, Chicago, kills seven policemen and injures many others. Eight alleged anarchists accused—three imprisoned, one commits suicide, four hanged. (In **1893**, Illinois Governor Altgeld, critical of trial, pardons three survivors.) Statue of Liberty dedicated. Geronimo, Apache Indian chief, surrenders.

1887 Queen Victoria's Golden Jubilee. Sir Arthur Conan Doyle's first Sherlock Holmes story, "A Study in Scarlet."

1888 Historic March blizzard in Northeast U.S.—many perish, property damage exceeds $25 million. George Eastman's box camera (the Kodak). J.B. Dunlop invents pneumatic tire. Jack the Ripper murders in London.

1889 Second (Socialist) International founded in Paris. Indian Territory in Oklahoma opened to settlement. Thousands die in Johnstown, Pa., flood. Mark Twain's *A Connecticut Yankee in King Arthur's Court.*

1890 Congress votes Sherman Antitrust Act. Sitting Bull killed in Sioux uprising.

1892 Battle between steel strikers and Pinkerton guards at Homestead, Pa.; union defeated after militia intervenes. Silver mine strikers in Idaho fight non-union workers; U.S. troops dispatched. Diesel engine patented.

1894 Sino-Japanese War begins (ends in **1895** with China's defeat). In France, Capt. Alfred Dreyfus convicted on false treason charge (pardoned in **1906**). In U.S., Jacob S. Coxey of Ohio leads "Coxey's Army" of unemployed on Washington. Eugene V. Debs calls general strike of rail workers to support Pullman Company strikers; strike broken, Debs jailed for six months. Thomas A. Edison's kinetoscope given first public showing in New York City.

1895 X-rays discovered by German physicist, Wilhelm Roentgen.

1896 Supreme Court's *Plessy v. Ferguson* decision—"separate but equal" doctrine. Alfred Nobel's will establishes prizes for peace, science, and literature. Marconi receives first wireless patent in Britain. William Jennings Bryan delivers "Cross of Gold" speech at Democratic Convention

Geronimo
(1829-1909)

Samuel Clemens
(Mark Twain)
(1835-1910)

Thomas A. Edison
(1847-1931)

SPANISH-AMERICAN WAR (1898–1899)

War fires stoked by "jingo journalism" as American people support Cuban rebels against Spain. American business sees economic gain in Cuban trade and resources and American power zones in Latin America. Outstanding events: Submarine mine explodes U.S. battleship *Maine* in Havana Harbor **(Feb. 15)**; 260 killed; responsibility never fixed. Congress declares independence of Cuba **(April 19).** Spain declares war on U.S. **(Apr. 24);** Congress **(Apr. 25)** formally declares nation has been at war with Spain since Apr. 21. Commodore

George Dewey wins seven-hour battle of Manila Bay **(May 1).** Spanish fleet destroyed off Santiago, Cuba **(July 3);** city surrenders **(July 17).** Treaty of Paris (ratified by Senate **1899**) ends war. U.S. given Guam and Puerto Rico and agrees to pay Spain $20 million for Philippines. Cuba independent of Spain; under U.S. military control for three years until **May 20, 1902.** Yellow fever is eradicated and political reforms achieved.

**Marie Curie
(1867–1934)**

**Theodore Roosevelt
(1858–1919)**

**Albert Einstein
(1879-1955)**

in Chicago. First modern Olympic games held in Athens, Greece.

1898 Chinese "Boxers," anti-foreign organization, established. They stage uprisings against Europeans in 1900; U.S. and other Western troops relieve Peking legations. Spanish-American War (*see* special material on the "Spanish-American War"). Pierre and Marie Curie discover radium and polonium.

1899 Boer War (or South African War). Conflict between British and Boers (descendants of Dutch settlers of South Africa). Causes rooted in longstanding territorial disputes and in friction over political rights for English and other "uitlanders" following 1886 discovery of vast gold deposits in Transvaal. (British victorious as war ends in 1902.) Casualties: 5,774 British dead, about 4,000 Boers. Union of South Africa established in 1908 as confederation of colonies; becomes British dominion in 1910.

20th century A.D.

1900 Hurricane ravages Galveston, Tex.; 6,000 drown. Sigmund Freud's *The Interpretation of Dreams.*

1901 Queen Victoria dies; succeeded by son, Edward VII. As President McKinley begins second term, he is shot fatally by anarchist Leon Czolgosz. Theodore Roosevelt sworn in as successor.

1902 Enrico Caruso's first gramophone recording.

1903 Wright brothers, Orville and Wilbur, fly first powered, controlled, heavier-than-air plane at Kitty Hawk, N.C. Henry Ford organizes Ford Motor Company.

1904 Russo-Japanese War—competition for Korea and Manchuria: In 1905, Port Arthur surrenders to Japanese and Russia suffers other defeats; President Roosevelt mediates Treaty of Portsmouth, N.H., ending war with concessions for Japan. *Entente Cordiale:* Britain and France settle their international differences. General theory of radioactivity by Rutherford and Soddy. New York City subway opened.

1905 General strike in Russia; first workers' soviet set up in St. Petersburg. Sailors on battleship *Potemkin* mutiny; reforms including first Duma (parliament) established by Czar's "October Manifesto." Albert Einstein's special theory of relativity and other key theories in physics. Franz Lehar's *Merry Widow.*

1906 San Francisco earthquake and three-day fire; 500 dead. Roald Amundsen, Norwegian explorer, fixes magnetic North Pole.

1907 Second Hague Peace Conference, of 46 nations, adopts 10 conventions on rules of war. Financial panic of 1907 in U.S.

1908 Earthquake kills 150,000 in southern Italy and Sicily. U.S. Supreme Court, in Danbury Hatters' case, outlaws secondary union boycotts.

1909 North Pole reached by American explorers Robert E. Peary and Matthew Henson.

1910 Boy Scouts of America incorporated.

1911 First use of aircraft as offensive weapon in Turkish-Italian War. Italy defeats Turks and annexes Tripoli and Libya. Chinese Republic proclaimed after revolution overthrows Manchu dynasty. Sun Yat-sen named president. Mexican Revolution: Porfirio Diaz, president since 1877, replaced by Francisco Madero. Triangle Shirtwaist Company fire in New York; 145 killed. Richard Strauss's *Der Rosenkavalier.* Irving Berlin's *Alexander's Ragtime Band.* Amundsen reaches South Pole.

1912 Balkan Wars (1912–13) resulting from territorial disputes: Turkey defeated by alliance of Bulgaria, Serbia, Greece, and Montenegro; London peace treaty (1913) partitions most of European Turkey among the victors. In second war (1913), Bulgaria attacks Serbia and Greece and is defeated after Romania intervenes and Turks recapture Adrianople. *Titanic* sinks on maiden voyage; over 1,500 drown.

1913 Suffragettes demonstrate in London. Garment workers strike in New York and Boston; win pay raise and shorter hours. Sixteenth Amendment (income tax) and 17th (popular election of U.S. senators) adopted. Bill creating U.S. Federal Reserve System becomes law. Stravinsky's *The Rite of Spring.*

1914 World War I begins (*see* special material on "World War I"). Panama Canal officially opened. Congress sets up Federal Trade Commission, passes Clayton Antitrust Act. U.S. Marines occupy Veracruz, Mexico, intervening in civil war to protect American interests.

1915 U.S. protests German submarine actions and British blockade of Germany. U.S. banks lend $500 million to France and Britain. D. W. Griffith's film *Birth of a Nation.* Albert Einstein's *General Theory of Relativity.*

1916 Congress expands armed forces. Tom Mooney arrested for San Francisco bombing (pardoned in 1939). Pershing fails in raid into Mexico in

The Partition of Africa ~ 1914

EUROPE

TANGIER (Sp.)
Casablanca
MADEIRA IS. (Port.)
Algiers
TUNISIA
Tripoli
Suez Canal
MOROCCO
ALGERIA
CANARY IS. (Spain)
RIO DE ORO
LIBYA
Cairo
SAHARA
EGYPT (Br. Protect.)
ARABIA
FRENCH WEST AFRICA
ANGLO EGYPTIAN SUDAN
Red Sea
ERITREA
Massawa
Khartum
Adua
F.R. SOMALILAND
GAMBIA (Br.)
PORT. GUINEA
Senegal
Niger
Lake Chad
BR. SOMALILAND
SIERRA LEONE (Br.)
NIGERIA (Br.)
FRENCH EQUATORIAL AFRICA
White Nile
Blue Nile
ETHIOPIA
LIBERIA
IVORY COAST
GOLD COAST (Br.)
TOGOLAND (Ger.)
RIO MUNI (Sp.)
CAMEROONS (Ger.)
Congo R.
UGANDA
ITAL. SOMALILAND

EQUATOR

BELGIAN CONGO
L. Victoria Nyanza
BRITISH EAST AFRICA
KENYA
Mombasa
Lake Tanganyika
GERMAN EAST AFRICA
ZANZIBAR (Br.)
ANGOLA (Port.)
RHODESIA
NYASALAND
PORT. EAST AFRICA
MADAGASCAR (Fr.)
GERMAN SOUTHWEST AFRICA
BECHUANALAND
UNION OF SOUTH AFRICA
TRANSVAAL
ORANGE FREE STATE
NATAL
Capetown
CAPE COLONY

KEY

British	Italian
French	Portuguese
German	Belgian
Spanish	

European Colonies in Africa ~ 1878

ALGERIA
SENEGAL
GAMBIA
ANGOLA
MOZAMBIQUE
CAPE COLONY

quest of rebel Pancho Villa. U.S. buys Virgin Islands from Denmark for $25 million. President Wilson re-elected with "he kept us out of war" slogan. "Black Tom" explosion at munitions dock in Jersey City, N.J., $40,000,000 damages; traced to German saboteurs. Margaret Sanger opens first birth control clinic. Easter Rebellion in Ireland put down by British troops.

**Vladimir Lenin
(1870-1924)**

1917 First U.S. combat troops in France as U.S. declares war (**April 6**). Russian Revolution—climax of long unrest under czars. February Revolution—Czar forced to abdicate, liberal government created. Kerensky becomes prime minister and forms provisional government (**July**). In October Revolution, Bolsheviks seize power in armed coup d'état led by Lenin and Trotsky. Kerensky flees. Revolutionaries execute the czar and his family (**1918**). Reds set up Third International in Moscow (**1919**). Balfour Declaration promises Jewish homeland in Palestine. Sigmund Freud's *Introduction to Psychoanalysis*.

1918 Russian Civil War between Reds (Bolsheviks) and Whites (anti-Bolsheviks); Reds win in **1920**. Allied troops (U.S., British, French) intervene (**March**); leave in **1919**. Japanese hold Vladivostok until **1922**. World-wide influenza epidemic strikes; by **1920**, nearly 20 million are dead. In U.S. alone, 500,000 perish.

1919 Third International (Comintern) establishes Soviet control over international Communist movements. Paris peace conference. Versailles Treaty, incorporating Wilson's draft Covenant of League of Nations, signed by Allies and Germany; rejected by U.S. Senate. Congress formally ends war in **1921**. Eighteenth (Prohibition) Amendment adopted. Alcock and Brown make first trans-Atlantic non-stop flight.

**Woodrow Wilson
(1856–1924)**

1920 League of Nations holds first meeting at Geneva, Switzerland. U.S. Dept. of Justice "red hunt" nets thousands of radicals; aliens deported. Women's suffrage (19th) amendment ratified. First Agatha Christie mystery. Sinclair Lewis's *Main Street*.

1921 Reparations Commission fixes German liability at 132 billion gold marks. German inflation begins. Major treaties signed at Washington Disarmament Conference limit naval tonnage and pledge to respect territorial integrity of China. Irish Free State formed in southern Ireland as self-governing dominion of British Empire. In U.S., Nicola Sacco and Bartolomeo Vanzetti, Italian-born anarchists, convicted of armed robbery murder; case stirs world-wide protests; they are executed in **1927**.

1922 Mussolini marches on Rome; forms Fascist government. Irish Free State officially proclaimed.

1923 Adolf Hitler's "Beer Hall Putsch" in Munich fails; in **1924** he is sentenced to five years in prison where he writes *Mein Kampf;* released after eight months. Occupation of Ruhr by French and Belgian troops to enforce reparations payments. Widespread Ku Klux Klan violence in U.S. George Gershwin's *Rhapsody in Blue.*

WORLD WAR I (1914–1918)

Imperial, territorial, and economic rivalries lead to the "Great War" between the Central Powers (Austria-Hungary, Germany, Bulgaria, and Turkey) and the Allies (U.S., Britain, France, Russia, Belgium, Serbia, Greece, Romania, Montenegro, Portugal, Italy, Japan). About 10 million combatants killed, 20 million wounded.

1914 Austrian Archduke Francis Ferdinand and wife assassinated in Sarajevo by Serbian nationalist, Gavrilo Princip (**June 28**). Austria declares war on Serbia (**July 28**). Germany declares war on Russia (**Aug. 1**), on France (**Aug. 3**), invades Belgium (**Aug. 4**). Britain declares war on Germany (**Aug. 4**). Germans defeat Russians in Battle of Tannenberg on Eastern Front (**Aug.**). First Battle of the Marne (**Sept.**). German drive stopped 25 miles from Paris. By end of year, war on the Western Front is "positional" in the trenches.

1915 German submarine blockade of Great Britain begins (**Feb.**). Dardanelles Campaign—British land in Turkey (**April**), withdraw from Gallipoli (**Dec. to Jan. 1916**). Germans use gas at second Battle of Ypres (**April–May**). *Lusitania* sunk by German submarine—1,198 lost, including 128 Americans (**May 7**). On Eastern Front, German and Austrian "great offensive" conquers all of Poland and Lithuania; Russians lose 1 million men (by **Sept. 6**). "Great Fall Offensive" by Allies results in little change from 1914 (**Sept.–Oct.**). Britain and France declare war on Bulgaria (**Oct. 14**).

1916 Battle of Verdun—Germans and French each lose about 350,000 men (**Feb.**). Extended submarine warfare begins (**March**). British-German sea battle of Jutland (**May**); British lose more ships, but German fleet never ventures forth again. On Eastern front, the Brusilov offensive demoralizes Russians, costs them 1 million men (**June–Sept.**). Battle of the Somme—British lose over 400,000; French, 200,000; Germans, about 450,000; all with no strategic results (**July–Nov.**). Romania declares war on Austria-Hungary (**Aug. 27**). Bucharest captured (**Dec.**).

1917 U.S. declares war on Germany (**April 6**). Submarine warfare at peak (**April**). On Italian Front, Battle of Caporetto—Italians retreat, losing 600,000 prisoners and deserters (**Oct.–Dec.**). On Western Front, Battles of Arras, Champagne, Ypres (third battle), etc. First large British tank attack (**Nov.**). U.S. declares war on Austria-Hungary (**Dec. 7**). Armistice between new Russian Bolshevik government and Germans (**Dec. 15**).

1918 Great offensive by Germans (**March–June**). Americans' first important battle role at Château-Thierry—as they and French stop German advance (**June**). Second Battle of the Marne (**July–Aug.**)—start of Allied offensive at Amiens, St. Mihiel, etc. Battles of the Argonne and Ypres panic German leadership (**Sept.–Oct.**). British offensive in Palestine (**Sept.**). Germans ask for armistice (**Oct. 4**). British armistice with Turkey (**Oct.**). German Kaiser abdicates (**Nov.**). Hostilities cease on Western Front (**Nov. 11**).

TERRITORIAL CHANGES,
following WORLD WAR I

Territory lost

by Germany   by Russia

by Bulgaria   by Austria-Hungary

1924 Death of Lenin; Stalin wins power struggle, rules as Soviet dictator until death in 1953. Italian Fascists murder Socialist leader Giacomo Matteotti. Interior Secretary Albert B. Fall and oilmen Harry Sinclair and Edward L. Doheny are charged with conspiracy and bribery in the Teapot Dome scandal, involving fraudulent leases of naval oil reserves. In 1931, Fall is sentenced to year in prison; Doheny and Sinclair acquitted of

**Charles A. Lindbergh
(1902–1974)**

**Herbert C. Hoover
(1874–1964)**

bribery. Nathan Leopold and Richard Loeb convicted in "thrill killing" of Bobby Franks in Chicago; defended by Clarence Darrow; sentenced to life imprisonment. (Loeb killed by fellow convict in **1936**; Leopold paroled in **1958**, dies in **1971**.)

1925 Nellie Tayloe Ross elected governor of Wyoming; first woman governor elected in U.S. Locarno conferences seek to secure European peace by mutual guarantees. John T. Scopes convicted and fined for teaching evolution in a public school in Tennessee "Monkey Trial"; sentence set aside. John Logie Baird, Scottish inventor, transmits human features by television. Adolf Hitler publishes Volume I of *Mein Kampf*.

1926 General strike in Britain brings nation's activities to standstill. U.S. marines dispatched to Nicaragua during revolt; they remain until **1933**. Gertrude Ederle of U.S. is first woman to swim English Channel.

1927 German economy collapses. Socialists riot in Vienna; general strike follows acquittal of Nazis for political murder. Trotsky expelled from Russian Communist Party. Charles A. Lindbergh flies first successful solo non-stop flight from New York to Paris. Ruth Snyder and Judd Gray convicted of murder of Albert Snyder; they are executed at Sing Sing prison in **1928**. *The Jazz Singer*, with Al Jolson, first part-talking motion picture.

1928 Kellogg-Briand Pact, outlawing war, signed in Paris by 65 nations. Alexander Fleming discovers penicillin. Richard E. Byrd starts expedition to Antarctic; returns in **1930**.

1929 Trotsky expelled from U.S.S.R. Lateran Treaty establishes independent Vatican City. In U.S., stock market prices collapse, with U.S. securities losing $26 billion—first phase of Depression and world economic crisis. St. Valentine's Day gangland massacre in Chicago.

1930 Britain, U.S., Japan, France, and Italy sign naval disarmament treaty. Nazis gain in German elections. Cyclotron developed by Ernest O. Lawrence, U.S. physicist.

1931 Spain becomes a republic with overthrow of King Alfonso XIII. German industrialists finance 800,000-strong Nazi party. British parliament enacts statute of Westminster, legalizing dominion equality with Britain. Mukden Incident begins Japanese occupation of Manchuria. In U.S., Hoover proposes one-year moratorium of war debts. Harold C. Urey discovers heavy hydrogen. Gangster Al Capone sentenced to 11 years in prison for tax evasion (freed in **1939**; dies in **1947**).

1932 Nazis lead in German elections with 230 Reichstag seats. Famine in U.S.S.R. In U.S., Congress sets up Reconstruction Finance Corporation to stimulate economy. Veterans march on Washington—most leave after Senate rejects payment of cash bonuses; others removed by troops under Douglas MacArthur. U.S. protests Japanese aggression in Manchuria. Amelia Earhart is first woman to fly Atlantic solo. Charles A. Lindbergh's baby son kidnapped, killed. (Bruno Richard Hauptmann arrested in **1934**, convicted in **1935**, executed in **1936**.)

1933 Hitler appointed German chancellor, gets dictatorial powers. Reichstag fire in Berlin; Nazi terror begins. (*See* special material on "The Holocaust.") Germany and Japan withdraw from League of Nations. Giuseppe Zangara executed for attempted assassination of President-elect

THE HOLOCAUST (1933–1945)

"Holocaust" is the term describing the Nazi annihilation of about 6 million Jews (two thirds of the pre-World War II European Jewish population), including 4,500,000 from Russia, Poland, and the Baltic; 750,000 from Hungary and Romania; 290,000 from Germany and Austria; 105,000 from The Netherlands; 90,000 from France; 54,000 from Greece, etc.

The Holocaust was unique in its being *genocide*—the systematic destruction of a people solely because of religion, race, ethnicity, nationality, or homosexuality—on an unmatched scale. Along with the Jews, another 9 to 10 million people—Gypsies, Slavs (Poles, Ukrainians, and Belorussians)—were exterminated.

The only comparable act of genocide in modern times was launched in April 1915, when an estimated 600,000 Armenians were massacred by the Turks.

1933 Hitler named German Chancellor **(Jan.)**. Dachau, first concentration camp, established **(March)**. Boycotts against Jews begin **(April)**.
1935 Anti-Semitic Nuremberg Laws passed by Reichstag **(Sept.)**.
1937 Buchenwald concentration camp opens **(July)**.

1938 Extension of anti-Semitic laws to Austria after annexation **(March)**. *Kristallnacht* (Night of Broken Glass)—anti-Semitic riots in Germany and Austria **(Nov. 9)**. 26,000 Jews sent to concentration camps; Jewish children expelled from schools **(Nov.)**. Expropriation of Jewish property and businesses **(Dec.)**.
1940 As war continues, Nazi acts against Jews extended to German-conquered areas.
1941 Deportation of German Jews begins; massacres of Jews in Odessa and Kiev—68,000 killed **(Nov.)**; in Riga and Vilna—almost 60,000 killed **(Dec.)**.
1942 Unified Jewish resistance in ghettos begins **(Jan.)**. 300,000 Jews from Warsaw Ghetto deported to Treblinka death camp **(July)**.
1943 Warsaw Ghetto uprisings **(Jan. and April)**; Ghetto exterminated **(May)**.
1944 476,000 Hungarian Jews sent to Auschwitz **(May–June)**. D-day **(June 6)**. Soviet Army liberates Maidanek death camp **(July)**. Nazis try to hide evidence of death camps **(Nov.)**.
1945 Americans liberate Buchenwald and British liberate Bergen-Belsen camps **(April)**. Nuremberg War Crimes Trial **(Nov. 1945 to Oct. 1946)**.

The German Attack on Soviet Russia, 1941-1943

Axis occupied areas and Finland, June 22, 41

Russian areas held by Axis—Apr. 15, '43

Retaken by Russia after Nov. 19, '42
(185,300 SQ. miles)

Arctic Ocean

SWEDEN

FINLAND

Murmansk

White Sea

Archangel

Viipuri

Lake Ladoga

Leningrad

Vologda

Sverdlovst

Baltic Sea

ESTONIA

Novgorod

L. Ilmen

Kalinin

Dmitrov

Gorki

Kazan

Ufa

Riga

LATVIA

Velikiye Luki

Mozhaisk

Moscow

LITHUANIA

Vilna

Vitebsk

Vyazma

Ryazan

Kuibyshev

Minsk

Smolensk

Tula

Bialystok

BATTLE LINE as of April 15, 1943

Orel

Michurinsk

Volga

POLAND

Brest-Litovsk

Dnieper

Kursk

Voronezh

Saratov

Zhitomir

Kiev

Kharkov

BATTLE LINE as of Nov. 19, 1942

Tarnopol

RETAKEN by AXIS

Stalingrad

Dniepropetrovsk

Stalino

Tanganrog

Rostov

Astrakhan

Odessa

ROUMANIA

Kerch

CRIMEA

Maikop

Grozny

BULGARIA

Sevastopol

Novorossiisk

Tuapse

Makhach Kala

Black Sea

Istanbul

Batum

Tiflis

Baku

DARDANELLES

Caspian Sea

TURKEY

IRAN

The Pacific Theater of War
1941–1945

Legend:
- Japanese territory 1942
- Area retained by Japan after World War II
- Allied drives, 1942–45

Roosevelt in which Chicago Mayor Cermak is fatally shot. Roosevelt inaugurated ("the only thing we have to fear is fear itself"); launches New Deal. Prohibition repealed. U.S.S.R. recognized by U.S.

1934 Chancellor Dollfuss of Austria assassinated by Nazis. Hitler becomes Führer. U.S.S.R. admitted to League of Nations. Dionne sisters, first quintuplets to survive beyond infancy, born in Canada.

1935 Saar incorporated into Germany after plebiscite. Nazis repudiate Versailles Treaty, introduce compulsory military service. Mussolini invades Ethiopia; League of Nations invokes sanctions. Roosevelt opens second phase of New Deal in U.S., calling for social security, better housing, equitable taxation, and farm assistance. Huey Long assassinated in Louisiana.

1936 Germans occupy Rhineland. Italy annexes Ethiopia. Rome-Berlin Axis proclaimed (Japan to join in 1940). Trotsky exiled to Mexico. King George V dies; succeeded by son, Edward VIII, who soon abdicated to marry American-born divorcée, and is succeeded by brother, George VI. Spanish civil war begins. (Franco's fascist forces defeat Loyalist forces by 1939, when Madrid falls.) War between China and Japan begins, to continue through World War II. Japan and Germany sign anti-Comintern pact; joined by Italy in 1937.

**Amelia Earhart
(1898-1937)**

1937 Hitler repudiates war guilt clause of Versailles Treaty; continues to build German power. Italy withdraws from League of Nations. U.S. gunboat *Panay* sunk by Japanese in Yangtze River. Japan invades China, conquers most of coastal area. Amelia Earhart lost somewhere in Pacific on round-the-world flight.

1938 Hitler marches into Austria; political and geographical union of Germany and Austria proclaimed. Munich Pact—Britain, France, and Italy agree to let Germany partition Czechoslovakia. Douglas "Wrong-Way" Corrigan flies from New York to Dublin.

1939 Germany occupies Bohemia and Moravia; renounces pacts with Poland and England and concludes 10-year non-aggression pact with U.S.S.R. Russo-Finnish War begins; Finns to lose one-tenth of territory in 1940 peace treaty. World War II begins (*see* special material on "World War II"). In U.S., Roosevelt submits $1,319-million defense budget, proclaims U.S. neutrality, and declares limited emergency. Einstein writes FDR about feasibility of atomic bomb. New York World's Fair opens.

1940 Trotsky assassinated in Mexico. Estonia, Latvia, and Lithuania annexed by U.S.S.R. U.S. trades 50 destroyers for leases on British bases in Western Hemisphere. Selective Service Act signed.

WORLD WAR II (1939–1945)

Axis powers (Germany, Italy, Japan, Hungary, Romania, Bulgaria) vs. Allies (U.S., Britain, France, U.S.S.R., Australia, Belgium, Brazil, Canada, China, Denmark, Greece, Netherlands, New Zealand, Norway, Poland, South Africa, Yugoslavia).

1939 Germany invades Poland and annexes Danzig; Britain and France give Hitler ultimatum **(Sept. 1)**, declare war **(Sept. 3)**. Disabled German pocket battleship *Admiral Graf Spee* blown up off Montevideo, Uruguay, on Hitler's orders **(Dec. 17)**. Limited activity ("Sitzkrieg") on Western Front.

1940 Nazis invade Netherlands, Belgium, and Luxembourg **(May 10)**. Chamberlain resigns as Prime Minister; Churchill takes over **(May 10)**. Germans cross French frontier **(May 12)** using air/tank/infantry "Blitzkrieg" tactics. Dunkerque evacuation—about 335,000 out of 400,000 Allied soldiers rescued from Belgium by British civilian and naval craft **(May 26–June 3)**. Italy declares war on France and Britain; invades France **(June 10)**. Germans enter Paris; city undefended **(June 14)**. France and Germany sign armistice at Compiègne **(June 22)**. Nazis bomb Coventry, England **(Nov. 14)**.

1941 Germans launch attacks in Balkans. Yugoslavia surrenders—General Mihajlovic continues guerrilla warfare; Tito leads left-wing guerrillas **(April 17)**. Nazi tanks enter Athens; remnants of British Army quit Greece **(April 27)**. Hitler attacks Russia **(June 22)**. Atlantic Charter—FDR and Churchill agree on war aims **(Aug. 14)**. Japanese attacks on Pearl Harbor, Philippines, Guam force U.S. into war; U.S. Pacific fleet crippled **(Dec. 7)**. U.S. and Britain declare war on Japan. Germany and Italy declare war on U.S.; Congress declares war on those countries **(Dec. 11)**.

1942 British surrender Singapore to Japanese **(Feb. 15)**. U.S. forces on Bataan peninsula in Philippines surrender **(April 9)**. U.S. and Filipino troops on Corregidor island in Manila Bay surrender to Japanese **(May 6)**. Village of Lidice in Czechoslovakia razed by Nazis **(June 10)**. U.S. and Britain

land in French North Africa **(Nov. 8)**.

1943 Casablanca Conference—Churchill and FDR agree on unconditional surrender goal **(Jan. 14–24)**. German 6th Army surrenders at Stalingrad—turning point of war in Russia **(Feb. 1–2)**. Remnants of Nazis trapped on Cape Bon, ending war in Africa **(May 12)**. Mussolini deposed; Badoglio named premier **(July 25)**. Allied troops land on Italian mainland after conquest of Sicily **(Sept. 3)**. Italy surrenders **(Sept. 8)**. Nazis seize Rome **(Sept. 10)**. Cairo Conference: FDR, Churchill, Chiang Kai-shek pledge defeat of Japan, free Korea **(Nov. 22–26)**. Teheran Conference: FDR, Churchill, Stalin agree on invasion plans **(Nov. 28–Dec. 1)**.

1944 U.S. and British troops land at Anzio on west Italian coast and hold beachhead **(Jan. 22)**. U.S. and British troops enter Rome **(June 4)**. D-Day—Allies launch Normandy invasion **(June 6)**. Hitler wounded in bomb plot **(July 20)**. Paris liberated **(Aug. 25)**. Athens freed by Allies **(Oct. 13)**. Americans invade Philippines **(Oct. 20)**. Germans launch counteroffensive in Belgium—Battle of Bulge **(Dec. 16)**.

1945 Yalta Agreement signed by FDR, Churchill, Stalin—establishes basis for occupation of Germany, returns to Soviet Union lands taken by Germany and Japan; U.S.S.R. agrees to friendship pact with China **(Feb. 11)**. Mussolini killed at Lake Como **(April 28)**. Admiral Doenitz takes command in Germany; suicide of Hitler announced **(May 1)**. Berlin falls **(May 2)**. V-E Day—Germany signs unconditional surrender terms at Rheims **(May 7)**. Potsdam Conference—Truman, Churchill, Atlee (after **July 28**), Stalin establish council of foreign ministers to prepare peace treaties; plan German postwar government and reparations **(July 17–Aug. 2)**. A-bomb blasts Hiroshima **(Aug. 6)**. U.S.S.R. declares war on Japan **(Aug. 8)**. Nagasaki hit by A-bomb **(Aug. 9)**. Japan surrenders **(Aug. 14)**. V-J Day—Japanese sign surrender terms aboard battleship *Missouri* **(Sept. 2)**.

D-Day, June 6, 1944

1941 Japanese surprise attack on U.S. fleet at Pearl Harbor brings U.S. into World War II. Manhattan Project (atomic bomb research) begins. Roosevelt enunciates "four freedoms," signs lend-lease act, declares national emergency, promises aid to U.S.S.R.

1942 Declaration of United Nations signed in Washington. Women's military services established. Enrico Fermi achieves nuclear chain reaction. Japanese and persons of Japanese ancestry moved inland from Pacific Coast. Coconut Grove nightclub fire in Boston kills 491.

1943 President freezes prices, salaries, and wages to prevent inflation. Income tax withholding introduced.

1944 G.I. Bill of Rights enacted. Bretton Woods Conference creates International Monetary Fund and World Bank. Dumbarton Oaks Conference—U.S., British Commonwealth, and U.S.S.R. propose establishment of United Nations.

1945 Yalta Conference (Roosevelt, Churchill, Stalin) plans final defeat of Germany (Feb.). Germany surrenders (May 7). San Francisco Conference establishes U.N. (April–June). FDR dies (April 12). Potsdam Conference (Truman, Churchill, Stalin) establishes basis of German reconstruction (July–Aug). Japan surrenders (Sept. 2).

Winston Churchill, Franklin D. Roosevelt, and Joseph V. Stalin at Yalta

1946 First meeting of U.N. General Assembly opens in London (Jan. 10). League of Nations dissolved (April). Italy abolishes monarchy (June). Verdict in Nuremberg war trial: 12 Nazi leaders (including 1 tried in absentia) sentenced to hang; 7 imprisoned; 3 acquitted (Oct. 1). Goering commits suicide a few hours before 10 other Nazis are executed (Oct. 15). Winston Churchill's "Iron Curtain" speech warns of Soviet expansion.

1947 Britain nationalizes coal mines (Jan. 1). Peace treaties for Italy, Romania, Bulgaria, Hungary, Finland signed in Paris (Feb. 10). Soviet Union rejects U.S. plan for U.N. atomic-energy control (March 4). Truman Doctrine proposed—the first significant U.S. attempt to "contain" communist expansion (March 12). Marshall Plan for European recovery proposed—a coordinated program to help European nations recover from ravages of war (June). (By 1951, this "European Recovery Program" had cost $11 billion.) India and Pakistan gain independence from Britain (Aug. 15). Cominform (Communist Information Bureau) founded under Soviet auspices to rebuild contacts among European Communist parties, missing since dissolution of Comintern in 1943 (Sept.). (Yugoslav party expelled in 1948 and Cominform disbanded in 1956.)

1948 Gandhi assassinated in New Delhi by Hindu fanatic (Jan. 30). Communists seize power in Czechoslovakia (Feb. 23–25). Burma and Ceylon granted independence by Britain. Organization of American States (OAS) Charter signed at Bogotá, Colombia (April 30). Nation of Israel proclaimed; British end Mandate at midnight; Arab armies attack (May 14). Berlin airlift begins (June 21); ends May 12, 1949. Stalin and Tito break (June 28). Independent Republic of Korea is proclaimed, following election supervised by U.N. (Aug. 15). Verdict in Japanese war trial: Tojo and six others sentenced to hang (hanged Dec. 23); 18 imprisoned (Nov. 12). United States of Indonesia established as Dutch and Indonesians settled conflict (Dec. 27). Alger Hiss, former U.S. State Department official, indicted on perjury charges after denying passing secret documents to communist spy ring. Convicted in second trial (1950) and sentenced to five-year prison term.

Harry S. Truman (1884–1972)

1949 Cease-fire in Palestine (Jan. 7). Truman proposes Point Four Program to help world's backward areas (Jan. 20). Israel signs armistice with Egypt (Feb. 24). Start of North Atlantic Treaty Organization (NATO)—treaty signed by 12 nations (April 4). German Federal Republic (West Germany) established (Sept. 21). Truman discloses Soviet Union has set off atomic explosion (Sept. 23). Communist People's Republic of China formally proclaimed by Chairman Mao Zedong. (Oct. 1).

1950 Truman orders development of hydrogen bomb (Jan. 31). Korean War (*see* special material on the "Korean War"). Assassination attempt on

---

KOREAN WAR (1950–1953)

1950 North Korean Communist forces invade South Korea (June 25). U.N. calls for cease-fire and asks U.N. members to assist South Korea (June 27). Truman orders U.S. forces into Korea (June 27). North Koreans capture Seoul (June 28). Gen. Douglas MacArthur designated commander of unified U.N. forces (July 8). Pusan Beachhead—U.N. forces counterattack and capture Seoul (Aug.–Sept.), capture Pyongyang, North Korean capital (Oct.). Chinese Commu- nists enter war (Oct. 26), force U.N. retreat toward 39th parallel (Dec.).

1951 Gen. Matthew B. Ridgeway replaces MacArthur after he threatens Chinese with massive retaliation (April 11). Armistice negotiations (July) continue with interruptions until June 1953.

1953 Armistice signed (June 26). Chinese troops withdraw from North Korea (Oct. 26, 1958), but over 200 violations of armistice noted in 1959.

President Truman by Puerto Rican nationalists (**Nov. 1**). Brink's robbery in Boston; almost $3 million stolen (**Jan. 17**).

1951 Six nations agree to Schuman Plan to pool European coal and steel (**March 19**)—in effect Feb. 10, 1953. Julius and Ethel Rosenberg sentenced to death for passing atomic secrets to Russians (**March**). Japanese peace treaty signed in San Francisco by 49 nations (**Sept. 8**). Color television introduced in U.S.

1952 George VI dies; his daughter becomes Elizabeth II (**Feb. 6**). NATO conference approves European army (**Feb.**). AEC announces "satisfactory" experiments in hydrogen-weapons research; eyewitnesses tell of blasts near Enewetak (**Nov.**).

1953 Gen. Dwight D. Eisenhower inaugurated President of United States (**Jan. 20**). Stalin dies (**March 5**). Malenkov becomes Soviet Premier; Beria, Minister of Interior; Molotov, Foreign Minister (**March 6**). Dag Hammarskjold begins term as U.N. Secretary-General (**April 10**). Edmund Hillary, of New Zealand, and Tenzing Norkay, of Nepal, reach top of Mt. Everest (**May 29**). East Berliners rise against Communist rule; quelled by tanks (**June 17**). Egypt becomes republic ruled by military junta (**June 18**). Julius and Ethel Rosenberg executed in Sing Sing prison (**June 19**). Korean armistice signed (**July 27**). Moscow announces explosion of hydrogen bomb (**Aug. 20**).

1954 First atomic submarine *Nautilus*, launched (**Jan. 21**). Five U.S. Congressmen shot on floor of House as Puerto Rican nationalists fire from spectators' gallery; all five recover (**March 1**). Army *vs.* McCarthy inquiry—Senate subcommittee report blames both sides (**Apr. 22–June 17**). Dien Bien Phu, French military outpost in Vietnam, falls to Vietminh army (**May 7**). (*see* special material on the "Vietnam War.") U.S. Supreme Court (in *Brown* v. *Board of Education of Topeka*) unanimously bans racial segregation in public schools (**May 17**). Eisenhower launches world atomic pool without Soviet Union (**Sept. 6**). Eight-nation Southeast Asia defense treaty (SEATO) signed at Manila (**Sept. 8**). West Germany is granted sovereignty, admitted to NATO and Western European Union (**Oct. 23**). Dr. Jonas Salk starts innoculating children against polio. Algerian War of Independence against France begins (**Nov.**); France struggles to maintain colonial rule until 1962 when it agrees to Algeria's independence.

1955 Nikolai A. Bulganin becomes Soviet Premier, replacing Malenkov (**Feb. 8**). Churchill resigns; Anthony Eden succeeds him (**April 6**). Federal Republic of West Germany becomes a sovereign state (**May 5**). Warsaw

Dwight D. Eisenhower
(1890–1969)

Joseph Stalin
(1879–1953)

VIETNAM WAR (1950–1975)

U.S., South Vietnam, and Allies versus North Vietnam and National Liberation Front (Viet Cong). Outstanding events:

1950 President Truman sends 35-man military advisory group to aid French fighting to maintain colonial power in Vietnam.

1954 After defeat of French at Dienbienphu, Geneva Agreements (**July**) provide for withdrawal of French and Vietminh to either side of demarcation zone (DMZ) pending reunification elections, which are never held. Presidents Eisenhower and Kennedy (from **1954** onward) send civilian advisors and, later, military personnel to train South Vietnamese.

1960 Communists from National Liberation Front in South.

1963 Ngo Dinh Diem, South Vietnam's premier, slain in coup (**Nov. 1**).

1961–1963 U.S. military advisors rise from 2,000 to 15,000.

1964 North Vietnamese torpedo boats reportedly attack U.S. destroyers in Gulf of Tonkin (**Aug. 2**). President Johnson orders retaliatory air strikes. Congress approves Gulf of Tonkin resolution (**Aug. 7**) authorizing President to take necessary steps to "maintain peace."

1965 U.S. planes begin combat missions over South Vietnam. In **June**, 23,000 American advisors committed to combat. By end of year over 184,000 U.S. troops in area.

1966 B-52s bomb DMZ, reportedly used by North Vietnam for entry into South (**July 31**).

1967 South Vietnam National Assembly approves election of Nguyen Van Thieu as President (**Oct. 21**).

1968 U.S. has almost 525,000 men in Vietnam. In Tet offensive (**Jan.–Feb.**), Viet Cong guerrillas attack Saigon, Hue, and some provincial capitals. President Johnson orders halt to U.S. bombardment of North Vietnam (**Oct. 31**). Saigon and N.L.F. join U.S. and North Vietnam in Paris peace talks.

1969 President Nixon announces Vietnam peace offer (**May 14**)—begins troop withdrawals (**June**). Viet Cong forms Provisional Revolutionary Government. U.S. Senate calls for curb on commitments (**June 25**). Ho Chi Minh, 79, North Vietnam president, dies (**Sept. 3**); collective leadership chosen. Some 6,000 U.S. troops pulled back from Thailand and 1,000 marines from Vietnam (announced **Sept. 30**). Massive demonstrations in U.S. protest or support war policies (**Oct. 15**).

1970 Nixon announces sending of troops to Cambodia (**April 30**). Last U.S. troops removed from Cambodia (**June 29**).

1971 Congress bars use of combat troops, but not air power, in Laos and Cambodia (**Jan. 1**). South Vietnamese troops, with U.S. air cover, fail in Laos thrust. Many American ground forces withdrawn from Vietnam combat. *New York Times* publishes Pentagon papers, classified material on expansion of war (**June**).

1972 Nixon responds to North Vietnamese drive across DMZ by ordering mining of North Vietnam ports and heavy bombing of Hanoi-Haiphong area (**April 1**). Nixon orders "Christmas bombing" of north to get North Vietnamese back to conference table (**Dec.**).

1973 President orders halt to offensive operations in North Vietnam (**Jan. 15**). Representatives of North and South Vietnam, U.S., and N.L.F. sign peace pacts in Paris, ending longest war in U.S. history (**Jan. 27**).

1974 Both sides accuse each other of frequent violations of cease-fire agreement.

1975 Full-scale warfare resumes. Communists victorious (**April 30**). South Vietnam Premier Nguyen Van Thieu resigns (**April 21**). American troops evacuated (**April 30**). More than 140,000 Vietnamese refugees leave by air and sea, many to settle in U.S. Provisional Revolutionary Government takes control (**June 6**).

1976 Election of National Assembly paves way for reunification of North and South.

**Yuri A. Gagarin
(1934-1968)**

**Fidel Castro
(Aug. 13, 1926)**

Pact, east European mutual defense agreement, signed (**May 14**). Argentina ousts Perón (**Sept. 19**). President Eisenhower suffers coronary thrombosis in Denver (**Sept. 24**). Martin Luther King, Jr., leads black boycott of Montgomery, Ala., bus system (**Dec. 1**); desegregated service begun (**Dec. 21**). AFL and CIO become one organization—AFL-CIO (**Dec. 5**).

1956 Nikita Khrushchev, First Secretary of U.S.S.R. Communist Party, denounces Stalin's excesses (**Feb. 24**). First aerial H-bomb tested over Namu islet, Bikini Atoll—10 million tons TNT equivalent (**May 21**). Worker's uprising against Communist rule in Poznan, Poland, is crushed (**June 28–30**). Egypt takes control of Suez Canal (**July 26**). Israel launches attack on Egypt's Sinai peninsula and drives toward Suez Canal (**Oct. 29**). British and French invade Egypt at Port Said (**Nov. 5**). Cease-fire forced by U.S. pressure stops British, French, and Israeli advance (**Nov. 6**). Revolt starts in Hungary—Soviet troops and tanks crush anti-Communist rebellion (**Nov.**).

1957 Eisenhower Doctrine calls for aid to Mideast countries which resist armed aggression from Communist-controlled nations (**Jan. 5**). Eisenhower sends troops to Little Rock, Ark., to quell mob and protect school integration (**Sept. 24**). Russians launch *Sputnik I,* first earth-orbiting satellite—the Space Age begins (**Oct. 4**).

1958 Army's Jupiter-C rocket fires first U.S. earth satellite, *Explorer I,* into orbit (**Jan. 31**). Egypt and Syria merge into United Arab Republic (**Feb. 1**). European Economic Community (Common Market) established by Rome Treaty becomes effective **Jan. 1, 1958**. Khrushchev becomes Premier of Soviet Union as Bulganin resigns (**Mar. 27**). Gen. Charles de Gaulle becomes French premier (**June 1**), remaining in power until 1969. New French constitution adopted (**Sept. 28**), de Gaulle elected president of 5th Republic (**Dec. 21**). Eisenhower orders U.S. Marines into Lebanon at request of President Chamoun, who fears overthrow (**July 15**).

1959 Cuban President Batista resigns and flees—Castro takes over (**Jan. 1**). Tibet's Dalai Lama escapes to India (**Mar. 31**). St. Lawrence Seaway opens, allowing ocean ships to reach Midwest (**April 25**).

1960 American U-2 spy plane, piloted by Francis Gary Powers, shot down over Russia (**May 1**). Khrushchev kills Paris summit conference because of U-2 (**May 16**). Powers sentenced to prison for 10 years (**Aug. 19**)—freed in **February 1962** in exchange for Soviet spy. Top Nazi murderer of Jews, Adolf Eichmann, captured by Israelis in Argentina (**May 23**)—executed in Israel in **1962**. Communist China and Soviet Union split in conflict over Communist ideology. Belgium starts to break up its African colonial empire, gives independence to Belgian Congo (Zaire) on **June 30**. Cuba begins confiscation of $770 million of U.S. property (**Aug. 7**).

1961 U.S. breaks diplomatic relations with Cuba (**Jan. 3**). John F. Kennedy inaugurated President of U.S. (**Jan. 20**). Kennedy proposes Alliance for Progress—10-year plan to raise Latin American living standards (**Mar. 13**). Moscow announces putting first man in orbit around earth, Maj. Yuri A. Gagarin (**April 12**). Cuba invaded at Bay of Pigs by an estimated 1,200 anti-Castro exiles aided by U.S.; invasion crushed (**April 17**). First U.S. spaceman, Navy Cmdr. Alan B. Shepard, Jr., rockets 116.5 miles up in 302-mile trip (**May 5**). Virgil Grissom becomes second American astronaut, making 118-mile-high, 303-mile-long rocket flight over Atlantic (**July 21**). Gherman Stepanovich Titov is launched in Soviet spaceship *Vostok II:* makes 17 1/2 orbits in 25 hours, covering 434,960 miles before landing safely (**Aug. 6**). East Germans erect Berlin Wall between East and West Berlin to halt flood of refugees (**Aug. 13**). U.S.S.R. fires 50-megaton hydrogen bomb, biggest explosion in history (**Oct. 29**).

1962 Lt. Col. John H. Glenn, Jr., is first American to orbit earth—three times in 4 hr 55 min (**Feb. 20**). Adolf Eichmann hanged in Israel for his part in Nazi extermination of six million Jews (**May 31**). France transfers sovereignty to new republic of Algeria (**July 3**). Cuban missile crisis—U.S.S.R. to build missile bases in Cuba; Kennedy orders Cuban blockade, lifts blockade after Russians back down (**Aug.–Nov.**). James H. Meredith, escorted by Federal marshals, registers in University of Mississippi (**Oct. 1**). Pope John XXIII opens Second Vatican Council (**Oct. 11**)—Council holds four sessions, finally closing Dec. 8, 1965. Cuba releases 1,113 prisoners of 1961 invasion attempt (**Dec. 24**).

1963 France and West Germany sign treaty of cooperation ending four centuries of conflict (**Jan. 22**). Pope John XXIII dies (**June 3**)—succeeded June 21 by Cardinal Montini, who becomes Paul VI. U.S. Supreme Court rules no locality may require recitation of Lord's Prayer or Bible verses in public schools (**June 17**). Civil rights rally held by 200,000 blacks and whites in Washington, D.C. (**Aug. 28**). Washington-to-Moscow "hot line" communications link opens, designed to reduce risk of accidental war **(Aug. 30)**. President Kennedy shot and killed by sniper in Dallas, Tex. Lyndon B. Johnson becomes President same day **(Nov. 22)**. Lee Harvey Oswald, accused assassin of President Kennedy, is shot and killed by Jack Ruby, Dallas nightclub owner **(Nov. 24)**.

1964 U.S. Supreme Court rules that Congressional districts should be roughly equal in population **(Feb. 17)**. Jack Ruby convicted of murder in slaying of Lee Harvey Oswald; sentenced to death by Dallas jury **(March 14)**— conviction reversed Oct. 5, 1966; Ruby dies Jan. 3, 1967, before second trial can be held. Three civil rights workers—Schwerner, Goodman, and Cheney—murdered in Mississippi **(June)**. Twenty-one arrests result in trial and conviction of seven by Federal jury. President's Commission on the Assassination of President Kennedy issues Warren Report concluding that Lee Harvey Oswald acted alone.

**John F. Kennedy
(1917-1963)**

1965 Rev. Dr. Martin Luther King, Jr., and more than 2,600 other blacks arrested in Selma, Ala., during three-day demonstrations against voter-registration rules **(Feb. 1)**. Malcolm X, black-nationalist leader, shot to death at Harlem rally in New York City **(Feb. 21)**. U.S. Marines land in Dominican Republic as fighting persists between rebels and Dominican army **(April 28)**. Medicare, senior citizens' government medical assistance program, begins **(July 1)**. Blacks riot for six days in Watts section of Los Angeles: 34 dead, over 1,000 injured, nearly 4,000 arrested, fire damage put at $175 million **(Aug. 11–16)**. Power failure in Ontario plant blacks out parts of eight northeastern states of U.S. and two provinces of southeastern Canada **(Nov. 9)**.

1966 Black teen-agers riot in Watts, Los Angeles; two men killed and at least 25 injured **(March 15)**. Michael E. De Bakey implants artificial heart in human for first time at Houston hospital; plastic device functions and patient lives **(April 21)**.

1967 Three Apollo astronauts—Col. Virgil I. Grissom, Col. Edward White II, and Lt. Cmdr. Roger B. Chaffee—killed in spacecraft fire during simulated launch **(Jan. 27)**. Israeli and Arab forces battle; six-day war ends with Israel occupying Sinai Peninsula, Golan Heights, Gaza Strip, and east bank of Suez Canal **(June 5)**. Red China announces explosion of its first hydrogen bomb **(June 17)**. Racial violence in Detroit; 7,000 National Guardsmen aid police after night of rioting. Similar outbreaks occur in New York City's Spanish Harlem, Rochester, N.Y., Birmingham, Ala., and New Britain, Conn. **(July 23)**. Thurgood Marshall sworn in as first black U.S. Supreme Court justice **(Oct. 2)**. Dr. Christian N. Barnard and team of South African surgeons perform world's first successful human heart transplant **(Dec. 3)**—patient dies 18 days later.

**Lyndon B. Johnson
(1908–1973)**

1968 North Korea seizes U.S. Navy ship *Pueblo;* holds 83 on board as spies **(Jan. 23)**. President Johnson announces he will not seek or accept presidential renomination **(March 31)**. Martin Luther King, Jr., civil rights leader, is slain in Memphis **(April 4)**—James Earl Ray, indicted in murder, captured in London on **June 8**. In 1969 Ray pleads guilty and is sentenced to 99 years. Sen. Robert F. Kennedy is shot and critically wounded in Los Angeles hotel after winning California primary **(June 5)**—dies **June 6**. Sirhan B. Sirhan convicted 1969. Czechoslovakia is invaded by Russians and Warsaw Pact forces to crush liberal regime **(Aug. 20)**.

1969 Richard M. Nixon is inaugurated 37th President of the U.S. **(Jan. 20)**. Apollo 11 astronauts—Neil A. Armstrong, Edwin E. Aldrin, Jr., and Michael Collins—take man's first walk on moon **(July 20)**. Sen. Edward M. Kennedy pleads guilty to leaving scene of fatal accident at Chappaquiddick, Mass. **(July 18)** in which Mary Jo Kopechne was drowned—gets two-month suspended sentence **(July 25)**.

**Martin Luther King, Jr.
(1929-1968)**

1970 Biafra surrenders after 32-month fight for independence from Nigeria **(Jan. 12)**. Rhodesia severs last tie with British Crown and declares itself a racially segregated republic **(March 1)**. Four students at Kent State University in Ohio slain by National Guardsmen at demonstration protesting April 30 incursion into Cambodia **(May 4)**. Senate repeals Gulf of Tonkin resolution **(June 24)**.

1971 Supreme Court rules unanimously that busing of students may be ordered to achieve racial desegregation **(April 20)**. Anti-war militants attempt to disrupt government business in Washington **(May 3)**—police and military units arrest as many as 12,000; most are later released. Twenty-sixth Amendment to U.S. Constitution lowers voting age to 18. U.N. seats Communist China and expels Nationalist China **(Oct. 25)**.

1972 President Nixon makes unprecedented eight-day visit to Communist China **(Feb.)**. Britain takes over direct rule of Northern Ireland in bid for peace **(March 24)**. Gov. George C. Wallace of Alabama is shot by Arthur H. Bremer at Laurel, Md., political rally **(May 15)**. Five men are apprehended by police in attempt to bug Democratic National Commit-

Richard M. Nixon
(Jan. 9, 1913)

tee headquarters in Washington D.C.'s Watergate complex—start of the Watergate scandal (**June 17**). Supreme Court rules that death penalty is unconstitutional (**June 29**). Eleven Israeli athletes at Olympic Games in Munich are killed after eight members of an Arab terrorist group invade Olympic Village; five guerrillas and one policeman are also killed (**Sept. 5**).

1973 Great Britain, Ireland, and Denmark enter European Common Market (**Jan. 1**). Nixon, on national TV, accepts responsibility, but not blame, for Watergate; accepts resignations of advisers H. R. Haldeman and John D. Ehrlichman, fires John W. Dean III as counsel. (**April 30**). Greek military junta abolishes monarchy and proclaims republic (**June 1**). U.S. bombing of Cambodia ends, marking official halt to 12 years of combat activity in Southeast Asia (**Aug. 15**). Fourth and biggest Arab-Israeli War begins as Egyptian and Syrian forces attack Israel as Jews mark Yom Kippur, holiest day in their calendar. (**Oct. 6**). Spiro T. Agnew resigns as Vice President and then, in Federal Court in Baltimore, pleads no contest to charges of evasion of income taxes on $29,500 he received in 1967, while Governor of Maryland. He is fined $10,000 and put on three years' probation (**Oct. 10**). In the "Saturday Night Massacre," Nixon fires special Watergate prosecutor Archibald Cox and Deputy Attorney General William D. Ruckelshaus; Attorney General Elliot L. Richardson resigns (**Oct. 20**). Egypt and Israel sign U.S.-sponsored cease-fire accord (**Nov. 11**).

1974 Patricia Hearst, 19-year-old daughter of publisher Randolph Hearst, kidnapped by Symbionese Liberation Army. (**Feb. 5**). House Judiciary Committee adopts three articles of impeachment charging President Nixon with obstruction of justice, failure to uphold laws, and refusal to produce material subpoenaed by the committee (**July 30**). Richard M. Nixon announces he will resign the next day, the first President to do so (**Aug. 8**). Vice President Gerald R. Ford of Michigan is sworn in as 38th President of the U.S. (**Aug. 9**). Ford grants "full, free, and absolute pardon" to ex-President Nixon (**Sept. 8**).

1975 John N. Mitchell, H. R. Haldeman, John D. Ehrlichman, and Robert C. Mardian found guilty of Watergate cover-up. Mitchell, Haldeman, and Ehrlichman are sentenced on Feb. 21 to 30 months-8 years in jail and Mardian to 10 months-3 years (**Jan. 1**). American merchant ship *Mayaguez*, seized by Cambodian forces, is rescued in operation by U.S. Navy and Marines, 38 of whom are killed (**May 15**). *Apollo* and *Soyuz* spacecraft take off for U.S.-Soviet link-up in space (**July 15**). President Ford escapes assassination attempt in Sacramento, Calif., (**Sept. 5**). President Ford escapes second assassination attempt in 17 days. (**Sept. 22**).

1976 Supreme Court rules that blacks and other minorities are entitled to retroactive job seniority (**March 24**). Ford signs Federal Election Campaign Act (**May 11**). Supreme Court rules that death penalty is not inherently cruel or unusual and is a constitutionally acceptable form of punishment (**July 3**). Nation celebrates Bicentennial (**July 4**). Israeli airborne commandos attack Uganda's Entebbe Airport and free 103 hostages held by pro-Palestinian hijackers of Air France plane; one Israeli and several Ugandan soldiers killed in raid (**July 4**). Mysterious disease that eventually claims 29 lives strikes American Legion convention in Philadelphia (**Aug. 4**). Jimmy Carter elected U.S. President (**Nov. 2**).

1977 First woman Episcopal priest ordained (**Jan. 1**). Scientists identify previously unknown bacterium as cause of mysterious "legionnaire's disease" (**Jan. 18**). Carter pardons Vietnam draft evaders (**Jan. 21**). Scientists report using bacteria in lab to make insulin (**May 23**). Supreme Court rules that states are not required to spend Medicaid funds on elective abortions (**June 20**). Deng Xiaoping, purged Chinese leader, restored to power as "Gang of Four" is expelled from Communist Party (**July 22**). Nuclear-proliferation pact, curbing spread of nuclear weapons, signed by 15 countries, including U.S. and U.S.S.R. (**Sept. 21**).

1978 President chooses Federal Appeals Court Judge William H. Webster as F.B.I. Director (**Jan. 19**). Rhodesia's Prime Minister Ian D. Smith and three black leaders agree on transfer to black majority rule (**Feb. 15**). Former Italian Premier Aldo Moro kidnapped by left-wing terrorists who kill five bodyguards (**March 16**); he is found slain (**May 9**). U.S. Senate approves Panama Canal neutrality treaty (**March 16**); votes treaty to turn canal over to Panama by year 2000 (**April 18**). Californians in referendum approve Proposition 13 for nearly 60% slash in property tax revenues (**June 6**). Supreme Court, in Bakke case, bars quota system in college admissions but affirms constitutionality of programs giving advantage to minorities (**June 28**). Pope Paul VI, dead at 80, mourned (**Aug. 6**); new Pope, John Paul I, 65, dies unexpectedly after 34 days in office (**Sept. 28**); succeeded by Karol Cardinal Wojtyla of Poland as John Paul II (**Oct. 16**). "Framework for Peace" in Middle East signed by

Viking I and II
(Launched 1975)

Voyager I and II
(Launched 1977)

Egypt's President Anwar el-Sadat and Israel Premier Menachem Begin after 13-day conference at Camp David led by President Carter (Sept. 17).

1979 Oil spills pollute ocean waters in Atlantic and Gulf of Mexico (Jan. 1, June 8, July 21). Ohio agrees to pay $675,000 to families of dead and injured in Kent State University shootings (Jan. 4). Vietnam and Cambodian insurgents it backs announce fall of Phnom Penh, Cambodian capital, and collapse of Pol Pot regime (Jan. 7). Shah leaves Iran after year of turmoil (Jan. 16); revolutionary forces under Moslem leader, Ayatollah Ruhollah Khomeini, take over (Feb. 1 et seq.). Conservatives win British election; Margaret Thatcher new Prime Minister (March 28). Nuclear power plant accident at Three Mile Island, Pa., releases radioactivity (March 28). Carter and Brezhnev sign SALT II agreement (June 14). Nicaraguan President Gen. Anastasio Somoza Debayle resigns and flees to Miami (July 17); Sandinistas form government (July 19). Earl Mountbatten of Burma, 79, British World War II hero, and three others killed by blast on fishing boat off Irish coast (Aug. 27); two I.R.A. members accused (Aug. 30). Iranian militants seize U.S. Embassy in Teheran and hold hostages (Nov. 4). Soviet invasion of Afghanistan stirs world protests (Dec. 27).

Margaret Thatcher
(Oct. 13, 1925)

1980 Six U.S. Embassy aides escape from Iran with Canadian help (Jan. 29). F.B.I.'s undercover operation "Abscam" (for Arab scam) implicates public officials (Feb. 2). U.S. breaks diplomatic ties with Iran (April 7). Eight U.S. servicemen are killed and five are injured as helicopter and cargo plane collide in abortive desert raid to rescue American hostages in Teheran (April 25). Supreme Court upholds limits on Federal aid for abortions (June 30). Shah of Iran dies at 60 (July 27). Anastasio Somoza Debayle, ousted Nicaragua ruler, and two aides assassinated in Asunción, Paraguay capital (Sept. 17). Iraq troops hold 90 square miles of Iran after invasion (Sept. 19). Ronald Reagan elected President in Republican sweep (Nov. 4). Three U.S. nuns and lay worker found shot in El Salvador (Dec. 4). John Lennon of Beatles shot dead in New York City (Dec. 8).

Sally K. Ride
(May 26, 1951)

1981 U.S.-Iran agreement frees 52 hostages held in Teheran since Nov. 4, 1979 (Jan. 18); hostages welcomed back in U.S. (Jan. 25). Ronald Reagan takes oath as 40th President (Jan. 20). President Reagan wounded by gunman, with press secretary and two law-enforcement officers (March 30). Pope John Paul II wounded by gunman (May 14). Supreme Court rules, 4-4, that former President Nixon and three top aides may be required to pay monetary damages for unconstitutional wiretap of home telephone of former national security aide (June 22). Reagan nominates Judge Sandra Day O'Connor, 51, of Arizona as first woman on Supreme Court (July 7). More than 110 die in collapse of aerial walkways in lobby of Hyatt Regency Hotel in Kansas City; 188 injured (July 18). Air controllers strike, disrupting flights (Aug. 3); Government dismisses strikers (Aug. 11).

1982 British overcome Argentina in Falklands war (April 2-June 15). Israel invades Lebanon in attack on P.L.O. (June 4). John W. Hinckley, Jr. found not guilty because of insanity in shooting of President Reagan (June 21). Alexander M. Haig, Jr. resigns as Secretary of State (June 25). Equal rights amendment fails ratification (June 30). Lebanese Christian Phalangists kill hundreds of people in two Palestinian refugee camps in West Beirut (Sept. 15). Princess Grace, 52, dies of injuries when car plunges off mountain road; daughter, Stephanie, 17, suffers serious injuries (Sept. 14). Leonid I. Brezhnev, Soviet leader, dies at 75 (Nov. 10). Yuri V. Andropov, 68, chosen as successor (Nov. 15). Artificial heart implanted for first time in Dr. Barney B. Clark, 61, at University of Utah Medical Center in Salt Lake City (Dec. 2); Barney Clark dies (March 23, 1983).

1983 Pope John Paul II signs new Roman Catholic code incorporating changes brought about by Second Vatican Council (Jan. 25). Second space shuttle, *Challenger*, makes successful maiden voyage, which includes the first U.S. space walk in nine years (April 4). U.S. Supreme Court declares many local abortion restrictions unconstitutional (June 15). Sally K. Ride, 32, first U.S. woman astronaut in space as a crew member aboard space shuttle *Challenger* (June 18). U.S. admits shielding former Nazi Gestapo chief, Klaus Barbie, 69, the "butcher of Lyons," wanted in France for war crimes (Aug. 15). Benigno S. Aquino, Jr., 50, political rival of Philippines President Marcos, slain in Manila (Aug. 21). South Korean Boeing 747 jetliner bound for Seoul apparently strays into Soviet airspace and is shot down by a Soviet SU-15 fighter after it had tracked the airliner for two hours; all 269 aboard are killed, including 61 Americans (Aug. 30). Terrorist explosion kills 237 U.S. Marines in Beirut (Oct. 23). U.S. and Caribbean allies invade Grenada (Oct. 25).

Space Shuttle Columbia
(Launched April 12, 1981)

Indira Gandhi
(1917-1984)

1984 Bell System broken up (**Jan. 1**). France gets first deliveries of Soviet natural gas (**Jan. 1**). Syria frees captured U.S. Navy pilot, Lieut. Robert C. Goodman, Jr. (**Jan. 3**). U.S. and Vatican exchange diplomats after 116-year hiatus (**Jan. 10**). Reagan orders U.S. Marines withdrawn from Beirut international peacekeeping force (**Feb. 7**). Yuri V. Andropov dies at 69; Konstantin U. Chernenko, 72, named Soviet Union leader (**Feb. 9**). Italy and Vatican agree to end Roman Catholicism as state religion (**Feb. 18**). Reagan ends U.S. role in Beirut by relieving Sixth Fleet from peacekeeping force (**March 30**). First baby born from frozen embryo in Australia (**April 10**). Congress rebukes President Reagan on use of federal funds for mining Nicaraguan harbors (**April 10**). Gunman fires from Libyan Embassy into London crowd, killing British policewoman (**April 17**). Soviet Union withdraws from summer Olympic games in U.S., and other bloc nations follow (**May 7 et seq.**). World Court rules against U.S. on mining of Nicaraguan harbors (**May 10**). Federal judge finds U.S. negligent in 1950 atomic tests (**May 10**). José Napoleón Duarte, moderate, elected president of El Salvador (**May 11**). Three hundred slain as Indian Army occupies Sikh Golden Temple in Amritsar (**June 6**). Thirty-ninth Democratic National Convention, in San Francisco, nominates Walter F. Mondale and Geraldine A. Ferraro (**July 16–19**). Thirty-third Republican National Convention, at Dallas, renominates President Reagan and Vice President Bush (**Aug. 20–25**). Brian Mulroney and Conservative party win Canadian election in landslide (**Sept. 4**). British Prime Minister Margaret Thatcher nearly killed by I.R.A. assassination attempt (**Oct. 12**). Indian Prime Minister Indira Gandhi assassinated by two Sikh bodyguards; 1,000 killed in anti-Sikh riots; son Rajiv succeeds her (**Oct. 31**). President Reagan re-elected in landslide with 59% of vote (**Nov. 7**). Toxic gas leaks from Union Carbide plant in Bhopal, India, killing 2,000 and injuring 150,000 (**Dec. 3**).

Ronald W. Reagan
(Feb. 6, 1911)

1985 U.S. and Soviet Union reach compromise agreement on resuming negotiations on limiting and reducing nuclear arms and preventing arms race in space (**Jan. 8**). Two thousand refugee Ethiopian Jews perish in Sudan (**Jan. 18**). Ronald Reagan, 73, takes oath for second term as 40th President (**Jan. 20**). New Zealand bars U.S. ship when Washington refuses to say whether she carries nuclear arms (**Feb. 4**). Border of Gibraltar reopened under Spain-Britain agreement (**Feb. 5**). Worldwide Conservative Rabbinical Assembly approves women in clergy (**Feb. 14**). General Westmoreland settles libel action against CBS (**Feb. 18**). Prime Minister Margaret Thatcher addresses Congress, endorsing Reagan's policies (**Feb. 20**). Uruguay ends military rule after 12 years (**March 1**). Kidnapped U.S. drug agent and his pilot slain in Mexico (**March 6**). U.S. S.R. leader Chernenko dies at 73 and is replaced by Mikhail Gorbachev, 54 (**March 11**). Secretary of Labor Raymond J. Donovan, facing New York fraud trial, resigns; first sitting Cabinet member to be indicted (**March 15**). Civilian rule returns to Brazil after 12 years (**March 15**). Tens of thousands mark 40th anniversary of liberation of Buchenwald death camp (**April 13**). Reagan target of wide attacks by Jewish leaders and others over visit to Bitburg Cemetery, West Germany, where SS troops are buried (**April 18 et seq. May 5**). Philadelphia police firebomb home of MOVE, organization of armed blacks, and fire spreads to neighboring homes; 11 dead and 200 homeless (**May 13**). Thirty-eight killed in Brussels football riot (**May 29**). Two Shiite Moslem gunmen capture TWA airliner with 133 aboard, 104 of them Americans (**June 14**); 39 remaining hostages freed in Beirut (**June 30**). Supreme Court, 5-4, bars public school teachers from parochial schools (**July 1**). Arthur James Walker, 50, retired naval officer, convicted by federal judge of participating in Soviet spy ring (**Aug. 9**). Spy scandal flares up in West Germany as top counterintelligence officer defects to East Germany (**Aug. 23**). Thousands dead in Mexico earthquake (**Sept. 19**). French government shaken by scandal over sinking of antinuclear ship off New Zealand (**Sept. 22**). Israelis bomb P.L.O. headquarters in Tunis in retaliation for slaying of three Israelis in Cyprus (**Oct. 1**). P.L.O. terrorists hijack *Achille Lauro,* Italian cruise ship, with 80 passengers, plus crew (**Oct. 7**); American, Leon Klinghoffer, killed (**Oct. 8**). Italian government toppled by political crisis over hijacking of *Achille Lauro* (**Oct. 16**). John A. Walker and son, Michael I. Walker, 22, sentenced in Navy espionage case (**Oct. 28**). Volcano eruption leaves 25,000 dead and missing in Colombia (**Nov. 14**). Reagan and Gorbachev meet at summit (**Nov. 19**); agree to step up arms control talks and renew cultural contacts (**Nov. 21**). Terrorists seize Egyptian Boeing 737 airliner after takeoff from Athens (**Nov. 23**); 59 dead as Egyptian forces storm plane on Malta (**Nov. 24**). U.S. budget-balancing bill enacted (**Dec. 12**). Newfoundland plane crash kills 248 U.S. soldiers (**Dec. 12**). Terrorists kill 19 at Rome and Vienna airports (**Dec. 30**); Reagan accuses Libya of aiding attackers.

Mikhail S. Gorbachev
(March 2, 1931)

1986 Spain and Portugal join Common Market (**Jan. 1**). President freezes Libyan assets in U.S. (**Jan. 8**). Supreme Court bars racial bias in trial jury selection (**Jan. 14**). Britain and France plan Channel tunnel (**Jan. 20**). *Voyager 2* spacecraft reports secrets of Uranus (**Jan. 26**). Space shuttle *Challenger* explodes after launch at Cape Canaveral, Fla., killing all seven aboard (**Jan. 28**); space agency reports solid-fuel booster rocket lost power before blast (**Jan. 31**) Haiti President Jean-Claude Duvalier flees to France (**Feb. 7**). President Marcos flees Philippines after ruling 20 years, as newly elected Corazon Aquino succeeds him (**Feb. 26**). Prime Minister Olaf Palme of Sweden shot dead (**Feb. 28**). Seven baseball players suspended over drug use (**Feb. 28**). Kurt Waldheim service as Nazi army officer revealed (**March 3**). Leo M. Frank, Georgia lynching victim, pardoned posthumously on killing charge (**March 11**). Worldwide Marcos fortune identified by Philippines (**March 13**). Union Carbide agrees to settlement with victims of Bhopal gas leak in India (**March 22**). U.S. forces clash with Libyans during Navy maneuvers in Gulf of Sidra (**March 24** et seq.). Two scientific teams report finding AIDS viruses (**March 26**). Halley's Comet yields information on return visit (**April 10**). U.S. planes attack Libyan "terrorist centers" (**April 14**). Desmond Tutu elected Archbishop in South Africa (**April 14**). Three hostages slain in Lebanon in reprisal for bombing of Libya (**April 17**). Major nuclear accident at Soviet Union's Chernobyl power station alarms world (**April 28** et seq.). Bangladesh river ferry with 1,000 aboard capsizes (**May 26**). Ex-Navy analyst, Jonathan Jay Pollard, 31, guilty as spy for Israel (**June 4**). Final report on shuttle blast inquiry faults management policies (**June 9**). Supreme Court reaffirms abortion rights (**June 11**). Millions of blacks strike in South Africa on anniversary of 1976 Soweto uprising (**June 16**). World Court rules U.S. broke international law in mining Nicaraguan waters (**June 27**). Supreme Court voids automatic provisions of budget-balancing law (**July 7**). Jerry A. Whitworth, ex-Navy radioman, convicted as spy (**July 24**). Moslem captors release Rev. Lawrence Martin Jenco (**July 26**). Senate Judiciary Committee approves William H. Rehnquist to be Chief Justice of U.S. (**Aug. 14**). Mexican police torture U.S. narcotics agent (**Aug. 14**). House votes arms appropriations bill rejecting Administration's "star wars" policy (**Aug. 15**). Volcano gas from lake bottom kills 1,500 in Cameroon (**Aug. 25**). Three Lutheran church groups in U.S. set to merge (**Aug. 29**). Nicholas Daniloff, correspondent for *U.S. News & World Report,* detained in Moscow on espionage charges (**Aug. 30**); released and allowed to leave Soviet Union (**Sept. 29**). In apparent U.S.-Soviet agreement, Gennadi F. Zakharov, accused spy, allowed to leave U.S. (**Sept. 30**). Congress overrides Reagan veto of stiff sanctions against South Africa (**Sept. 29 and Oct. 2**). Reagan and Gorbachev deadlocked in two-day arms control conference at Reykjavik (**Oct. 12**). Congress approves immigration bill barring hiring of illegal aliens, with amnesty provision (**Oct. 17**). Reagan signs $11.7-billion budget reduction measure (**Oct. 21**). He approves sweeping revision of U.S. tax code (**Oct. 22**). Democrats triumph in elections, gaining eight seats to win Senate majority (**Nov. 4**). Secret initiative to send arms to Iran revealed (**Nov. 6** et seq.); Reagan denies exchanging arms for hostages and halts arms sales (**Nov. 19**); diversion of funds from arms sales to Nicaraguan contras revealed (**Nov. 25**). Walkers, father and son, sentenced in naval spy ring (**Nov. 6**). Ivan F. Boesky penalized $100 million for illegal insider Wall Street trading (**Nov. 14**). Soviet lifts ban on Andrei D. Sakharov, rights activist (**Dec. 19**). Hotel fire kills 96 in Puerto Rico (**Dec. 31**).

1987 William Buckley, U.S. hostage in Lebanon, reported slain (**Jan. 20**). Gorbachev demands Communist Party reforms (**Jan. 27**). Senate report on Iran-Contra affair finds Administration officials deceived one another and Congress (**Jan. 29**). U.S. charges three Wall Street traders with making millions in illegal inside trading (**Feb. 12**). Soviet writers' union posthumously reinstates Boris Pasternak (**Feb. 23**). Soviet ends nuclear test moratorium (**Feb. 26**). President removes Donald Regan as Chief of Staff, replacing him with Howard H. Baker, Jr. (**Feb. 27**). French sentence Georges Ibrahim Abdallah, Lebanese terrorist, to life in two killings (**Feb. 28**). Reagan names F.B.I. chief William H. Webster C.I.A. head (**March 3**). Reagan admits "mistake" in Iran-Contra affair (**March 4**). Death toll 134 as British ferry capsizes at Belgian port (**March 7**). Appeals Court reverses $2-million libel judgment against Washington Post (**March 13**). New ceramic material made into powerful new superconductor (**March 17**). Two terrorists slay Italian Air Force general (**March 20**). F.D.A. approves drug AZT for treating AIDS victims (**March 20**). Congress overrides Reagan veto of highway bill (**March 27**). South Africa outlaws protests to win freedom for detainees (**April 11**). Reagan imposes 100% retaliatory tariff on many Japanese imports (**April 17**).

Corazon C. Aquino
(Jan. 25, 1933)

Kurt Waldheim
(Dec. 21, 1918)

Col. Oliver North
(Oct. 7, 1943)

Daniel Ortega
(Nov. 11, 1945)

Argentine army blocks antigovernment rebellion **(April 17)**. Gene altered bacteria tested in experiment to aid agriculture **(April 24)**. U.S. puts Austrian President Kurt Waldheim on list of those banned from country **(April 27)**. Nicaraguan rebels kill Benjamin Ernest Linder, 27 American volunteer worker **(April 28)**. Quebec accepts Canadian con stitution as "distinct society" **(May 1)**. Supreme Court rules Rotary clubs must admit women **(May 4)**. Thousands of aliens seek legal status under new amnesty law **(May 5)**. First Soviet ship attacked in Persian Gulf **(May 8)**. Ulster police slay nine attackers in police station battle **(May 8)**. Three-way heart transplant performed **(May 12)**. Soviet launches world's most powerful rocket **(May 16)**. Iraqi missiles kill 37 in attack on U.S. frigate *Stark* in Persian Gulf **(May 17)**; Iraqi president apologizes **(May 18)**. Former Labor. Secretary Ramond J. Donovan acquitted in construction fraud **(May 25)**. Lebanon's Prime Minister Rashid Karami 55, assassinated ,**(June 1)**. Three U.S. agencies investigate charges of fraud against TV evangelical PTL Ministry **(June 10)**. Prime Minister Thatcher wins rare third term in Britain **(June 11)**. Robert B. Anderson 77, former Treasury Secretary, sentenced for tax evasion **(June 25)**. Su preme Court Justice Lewis F. Powell, Jr., retires **(June 26)**. Klaus Barbie 73, Gestapo wartime chief in Lyons, sentenced to life by French court for war crimes **(July 4)**. Marine Lieut. Col. Oliver L. North tells Congres sional inquiry higher officials approved his secret Iran-Contra opera tions **(July 7–10)**. Admiral John M. Poindexter, former National Security Adviser, testifies he authorized use of Iran arms sale profits to aid Con tras **(July 15–22)**. Portugal gets majority government **(July 19)**. Secre tary of State George P. Shultz testifies he was deceived repeatedly on Iran-Contra affair **(July 23–24)**. India and Sri Lanka sign pact to end four years of ethnic violence **(July 29)**. Soviet sentences three Chernobyl offi cials for safety violations in nuclear disaster **(July 29)**. Defense Secretary Caspar W. Weinberger tells inquiry of official deception and intrigue **(July 31, Aug. 3)**. Hundreds killed in clashes at Moslem holy site of Mecca **(Aug. 1)**. Five regional presidents agree on peace accord for Cen tral America **(Aug. 7)**. Reagan says Iran arms-Contra policy went astray and accepts responsibility **(Aug. 12)**. Charles Glass, ABC correspondent escapes from Beirut kidnappers **(Aug. 18)**. Jewels retrieved from wreck age of liner *Titanic* **(Aug. 20)**. Black miners end strike in South Afric without pay improvements **(Aug. 30)**. Twenty ships attacked as Iran and Iraq resume "tanker war" in Persian Gulf **(Sept. 3)**. Soviet sentence Mathias Rust, 19, German pilot who flew single-engine plane across bor der to Red Square **(Sept. 4)**. Pope John Paul II visits North Americ **(Sept. 10)**; celebrates mass for Indians in Canada's Far North **(Sept. 20)** Ceremonies in Philadelphia celebrate 200th year of U.S. Constitution **(Sept. 17)**. National Football League players strike **(Sept. 23)**; walkout ends without new contract **(Oct. 15)**. Severe earthquake strikes Los An geles, leaving 100 injured and six dead **(Oct. 1)**. Wall Street industria average plunges 508 points, worst stock market drop in history **(Oct 19)**. Senate, 58-42, rejects Robert H. Bork as Supreme Court Justice **(Oct. 23)**.

1988 U.S. and Canada reach free-trade agreement **(Jan. 2)**. Oil spill pollute drinking water for 750,000 in Pittsburgh suburban area **(Jan. 3 et seq.**. Three former Mexican police officials indicted in death of U.S. drug agen **(Jan. 6)**. West German women arrested in disco bombing fatal to tw U.S. servicemen **(Jan. 11)**. U.S. and Soviet sign accord on science re search **(Jan. 12)**. Taiwan President Chiang Ching-kuo dead at 77 **(Jan 13)**. Supreme Court, 5-3, backs public school officials' power to censo student activities **(Jan. 13)**. Leslie F. Manigat, former professor, electe Haiti president **(Jan. 24)**. Aspirin found to cut heart attacks **(Jan. 26** Senate approves Appeals Court Judge Anthony M. Kennedy for Su preme Court **(Feb. 3)**. Lyn Nofziger, former Reagan advisor, convicte of violating Federal ethics law **(Feb. 11)**. Palestinian gunman, Ibrahir Mohammed Khaled, sentenced to 30 years for part in 1985 Rome ai port attack **(Feb. 12)**. Marine Lieut. Col. William R. Higgins abducte in Lebanon **(Feb. 17)**. TV evangelist, Rev. Jimmy Swaggart, quits pulpi after revelations of sexual misbehavior **(Feb. 21)**. Longest Olympic win ter games end at Calgary, Alberta **(Feb. 28)**. General strike by oppe nents of General Noriega paralyzes Panama **(March 2 et seq.)**. Nin killed in Soviet plane hijacking **(March 10)**. Robert C. McFarlane, for mer National Security Adviser, pleads guilty in Iran-Contra case **(Marc 11)**. Israel fights Palestinian uprising **(March 13 et seq.)**. First U.S. blac archbishop chosen to head Atlanta archdiocese **(March 15)**. Top figure indicted in Iran-Contra affair **(March 16)**. Irish mobs kill two British so diers **(March 19)**. Black workers strike in South Africa **(March 21)**. Con gress overrides Reagan veto of civil rights bill **(March 22)**. Arizona Gov Evan Mecham removed from office after impeachment trial **(April 4**

Gunmen hijack Kuwaiti airliner (**April 5** et seq.). Li Peng, electrical engineer, is new Chinese Prime Minister (**April 9**). Khalil al-Wazir, P.L.O. official, assassinated in Tunisia (**April 16**). Supreme Court upholds taxation of municipal bonds (**April 20**). Israel court dooms John Demjanjuk, 68, "Ivan the Terrible," for Nazi war crimes (**April 25**). Polish workers lose nine-day strike (**May 2**). Amnesty program for immigrants ends (**May 4**). Scientists decipher second genetic code (**May 12**). Hungarian Reds oust Janos Kadar as party head (**May 22**). Reagan-Gorbachev summit in Moscow ends without major results (**May 29** et seq.). Heat wave kills 450 in India (**June 3**). Million blacks start three-day protest strike in South Africa (**June 6**). Soviet court clears executed Bolsheviks (**June 13**). Federal court in New Jersey finds cigarette company liable in death (**June 13**). Supreme Court rules against private-club membership restrictions (**June 20**). Justices, in rebuff to Reagan, uphold special-prosecutor law (**June 29**). Soviet conference votes political overhaul (**July 1**). U.S. Navy ship shoots down Iranian airliner in Persian Gulf, mistaking it for jet fighter; 290 killed (**July 3**). Attorney General Meese announces resignation (**July 5**); former Gov. Dick Thornburgh of Pennsylvania succeeds him (**July 11**). Terrorists kill nine tourists on Aegean cruise (**July 11**). Democratic convention nominates Gov. Michael Dukakis of Massachusetts for President and Texas Senator Lloyd Bentsen for Vice President (**July 17** et seq.). U.S. judge sentences Carlos Lehder Rivas, Colombia drug leader, to life in prison (**July 20**). Flash floods kill thousands in China (**Aug. 2**). Reagan signs sweeping measure aimed at unfair trading (**Aug. 3**). Secretary of State Shultz unhurt in Bolivia bombing (**Aug. 8**). Reagan signs law to compensate interned Japanese-Americans (**Aug. 10**). Republicans nominate Vice President George Bush for President and Indiana Senator Dan Quayle for Vice President (**Aug. 15** et seq.). Plane blast kills Pakistan President Mohammad Zia ul-Haq (**Aug. 17**). I.R.A. bomb kills eight British soldiers in Ulster (**Aug. 20**). More than 40 killed as three jets collide in midair in air show at West German base (**Aug. 28**). Donor nations allot millions in flood relief aid to Bangladesh (**Sept. 6**). U.S. warns homeowners of radon peril (**Sept. 12**). Lieut. Gen. Prosper Avril assumes power in Haiti as army replaces Lieut. Gen. Henri Namphy (**Sept. 18**); new cabinet almost entirely civilian (**Sept. 19**). Michael K. Deaver, Reagan friend, sentenced for lying about lobbying (**Sept. 23**). Space shuttle *Discovery* in orbit as civilian space program resumes after *Challenger* disaster (**Sept. 29**). Gorbachev named Soviet President (**Oct. 1**). Foes defeat Pinochet in Chile's Presidential plebiscite (**Oct. 5**). Dozens perish in Algerian rioting (**Oct. 7**). U.S. and Philippines sign military-base treaty (**Oct. 17**). Computer "virus" disrupts network. Computer science graduate student blamed (**Nov. 2** et seq.). Republicans sweep 40 states in election. Vice President Bush beats Gov. Michael S. Dukakis (**Nov. 8**). Independent Palestine proclaimed by Yasir Arafat, P.L.O. chairman, recognizes Israel, at least implicitly, for first time (**Nov. 15**). Soviet space shuttle *Buran* succeeds in debut completing two orbits (**Nov. 15**). U.S. Air Force unveils stealth bomber (**Nov. 22**). Soviet legislature approves political restructuring and new national legislature (**Dec. 1**). Benazir Bhutto, first Islamic woman Prime Minister, chosen to lead Pakistan's government (**Dec. 1**). Earthquake in Soviet Armenia kills 25,000, injures 15,000, and leaves at least 400,000 homeless (**Dec. 7**). Two Soviet astronauts set record for staying in space 366 days (**Dec. 21**). Pan-Am 747 explodes from terrorist bomb and crashes in Lockerbie, Scotland, killing all 259 aboard and 11 on ground (**Dec. 21**).

George H. Bush
(June 12, 1924)

Michael S. Dukakis
(Nov. 3, 1933)

PICTURE CREDITS. The following credits list the names of organizations and individuals who have contributed illustrations to HEADLINE HISTORY. The editors wish to thank all of them for their assistance. The credits are arranged alphabetically by picture source, then picture title and page number in HEADLINE HISTORY. Credits: AIP Niels Bohr Library, **Marie Curie** and **Albert Einstein**, p. 120; British Information Services, **Margaret Thatcher**, p. 133; Dukakis for President Committee, Inc., **Michael S. Dukakis**, p. 137; Embassy of The Philippines, **Corazon C. Aquino**, p. 135; Harry S. Truman Library, **Harry S. Truman**, p. 128; John Fitzgerald Kennedy Library, Boston, **John F. Kennedy**, p. 131; Matthew Kalmenott, **Brontosaur**, p. 105; NASA Photos, **Charles A. Lindbergh**, p. 124, **Voyager and Viking**, p. 132, **Space Shuttle Columbia**, p. 133, **Sally K. Ride**, p. 132; National Portrait Gallery, Smithsonian Institution, **Theodore Roosevelt**, p. 120; Novosti Photos, **Vladimir Lenin**, p. 122, **Yuri A. Gagarin**, p. 130; **Mikhail S. Gorbachev**, p. 134; The Library of Congress Picture Collection, **Christopher Columbus**, p. 111, **Dred Scott**, p. 118, **Geronimo**, p. 119, **Woodrow Wilson**, p. 122, **Herbert C. Hoover**, p. 124, **Amelia Earhart**, p. 127, **Dwight D. Eisenhower**, p. 129, **Lyndon B. Johnson**, p. 131, **Richard M. Nixon**, p. 132; The Permanent Mission of India to the U.N., **Indira Gandhi**, p. 134; The Permanent Mission of Nicaragua to the U.N., **Daniel Ortega**, p. 136; Republican National Committee, **Ronald W. Reagan**, p. 134, **George H. Bush**, p. 137; U.S. Army Photos, **D-Day, Yalta Conference**, p. 128, **Joseph Stalin**, p. 129; AP/Wide World Photos, Inc., **Martin Luther King, Jr.**, p. 131, **Col. Oliver North**, p. 136; U.N. Photo, **Fidel Castro**, p. 130, U.N. Photo by D. Burnett, **Kurt Waldheim**, p. 134. MAP CREDITS: Maps on pp. 110, 114, 121, 123, 125, and 126 from *An Encyclopedia of World History*, by William L. Langer, The Fifth Edition, Copyright 1940, 1948, 1952, and © 1967, 1972 by Houghton Mifflin Company. Reprinted by permission of Houghton Mifflin Company.

WORLD STATISTICS

Area and Population by Country
Mid-1989 Estimates

Country	Area[1]	Population	Country	Area[1]	Population
Afghanistan	249,999	14,800,000	Honduras	43,277	5,000,000
Albania	11,100	3,200,000	Hungary	35,919	10,600,000
Algeria	919,591	24,900,000	Iceland	39,768	200,000
Angola	481,351	8,500,000	India[3]	1,269,340	835,000,000
Antigua and Barbuda	171	71,000	Indonesia	735,355	184,600,000
Argentina	1,068,297	31,900,000	Iran	636,293	53,900,000
Australia	2,967,894	16,800,000	Iraq	167,924	18,100,000
Austria	32,374	7,600,000	Ireland	27,136	3,500,000
Bahamas	5,380	243,000	Israel	8,019	4,500,000
Bahrain	240	500,000	Italy	116,303	57,600,000
Bangladesh	55,598	114,700,000	Ivory Coast	322,460	12,100,000
Barbados	166	257,000	Jamaica	4,243	2,500,000
Belgium	11,749	9,900,000	Japan	143,750	123,200,000
Belize	8,867	200,000	Jordan	37,737	4,000,000
Benin	43,483	4,700,000	Kenya	224,960	24,100,000
Bhutan	18,147	1,500,000	Korea, North	46,540	22,500,000
Bolivia	424,162	7,100,000	Korea, South	38,025	43,200,000
Botswana	231,804	1,200,000	Kuwait	6,880	2,100,000
Brazil	3,286,472	147,400,000	Laos	91,429	3,900,000
Brunei	2,226	300,000	Lebanon	4,015	3,300,000
Bulgaria	42,823	9,000,000	Lesotho	11,720	1,700,000
Burkina Faso[2]	105,869	8,500,000	Liberia	43,000	2,500,000
Burundi	10,747	5,500,000	Libya	679,359	4,100,000
Cambodia	69,880	6,800,000	Luxembourg	998	400,000
Cameroon	183,568	10,800,000	Madagascar	226,657	11,600,000
Canada	3,851,790	26,300,000	Malawi	45,747	8,700,000
Cape Verde	1,557	400,000	Malaysia	127,316	17,400,000
Central African Republic	240,534	2,800,000	Maldives	115	200,000
Chad	495,753	4,900,000	Mali	478,764	8,900,000
Chile	292,257	13,000,000	Malta	122	400,000
China, People's Republic of	3,705,390	1,103,900,000	Mauritania	397,954	2,000,000
Colombia	439,735	31,200,000	Mauritius	790	1,100,000
Comoros	694	400,000	Mexico	761,601	86,700,000
Congo	132,046	2,200,000	Mongolia	604,247	2,100,000
Costa Rica	19,575	3,000,000	Morocco	172,413	25,600,000
Cuba	42,803	10,500,000	Mozambique	309,494	15,200,000
Cyprus	3,572	700,000	Myanmar	261,220	40,800,000
Czechoslovakia	49,370	15,600,000	Nepal	54,362	18,700,000
Denmark	16,629	5,100,000	Netherlands	14,405	14,900,000
Dijibouti	8,494	400,000	New Zealand	103,736	3,347,000
Dominica	290	100,000	Nicaragua	50,193	3,500,000
Dominican Republic	18,816	7,000,000	Niger	489,189	7,400,000
Ecuador	109,483	10,500,000	Nigeria	356,667	115,600,000
Egypt	386,660	54,800,000	Norway	125,181	4,200,000
El Salvador	8,124	5,100,000	Oman	82,030	1,400,000
Equatorial Guinea	10,830	347,000	Pakistan[4]	310,403	110,400,000
Ethiopia	471,776	49,800,000	Panama	29,761	2,400,000
Fiji	7,055	800,000	Papua New Guinea	178,259	3,900,000
Finland	130,119	5,000,000	Paraguay	157,047	4,200,000
France	211,207	56,100,000	Peru	496,222	21,400,000
Gabon	103,346	1,100,000	Philippines	115,830	64,900,000
Gambia	4,361	800,000	Poland	120,725	38,200,000
Germany, East	41,826	16,600,000	Portugal	35,553	10,400,000
Germany, West	95,976	62,000,000	Qatar	4,247	400,000
Ghana	92,099	14,600,000	Romania	91,699	23,200,000
Greece	50,944	10,000,000	Rwanda	10,169	7,000,000
Grenada	133	85,000	St. Lucia	238	200,000
Guatemala	42,042	8,900,000	St. Vincent and the Grenadines	150	100,000
Guinea	94,927	7,100,000	Saudi Arabia	829,996	14,700,000
Guinea-Bissau	13,948	1,000,000	Senegal	75,750	7,200,000
Guyana	83,000	800,000	Sierra Leone	27,699	4,100,000
Haiti	10,714	6,400,000	Singapore	224	2,700,000

Country	Area[1]	Population	Country	Area[1]	Population
Solomon Islands	10,983	312,200	Uganda	91,134	17,000,000
Somalia	246,200	8,200,000	U.S.S.R.	8,649,496	289,000,000
South Africa	471,443	38,500,000	United Arab Emirates	32,278	1,700,000
Spain	194,896	39,200,000	United Kingdom	94,525	57,300,000
Sri Lanka	25,332	16,900,000	United States	3,615,105	248,800,000
Sudan	967,495	24,500,000	Uruguay	68,037	3,000,000
Suriname	63,037	400,000	Vanuatu	5,700	200,000
Swaziland	6,704	800,000	Venezuela	352,143	18,800,000
Sweden	173,731	8,500,000	Vietnam	127,243	66,800,000
Switzerland	15,941	6,600,000	Western Samoa	1,097	200,000
Syria	71,498	12,100,000	Yemen, People's Democratic Republic of	128,559	2,500,000
Taiwan	13,885	20,000,000			
Tanzania	364,898	26,300,000	Yemen Arab Republic	75,290	6,900,000
Thailand	198,456	55,600,000	Yugoslavia	98,766	23,700,000
Togo	21,927	3,400,000	Zaire	905,563	34,900,000
Trinidad and Tobago	1,981	1,200,000	Zambia	290,584	8,100,000
Tunisia	63,170	7,900,000	Zimbabwe	150,803	10,100,000
Turkey	301,381	55,400,000			

1. Square miles. 2. Formerly Upper Volta. 3. Includes the Indian-held part of Jammu and Kashmir. 4. Excludes the Pakistani-held part of Jammu and Kashmir. *Source: 1988 World Population Data Sheet,* Population Reference Bureau, Inc., Washington, D.C.

Some Large Cities of the World

Census figures and population estimates in the following table are based on data reflecting different years. Some cities include metropolitan areas or contiguous suburbs, while others report only those residing within precise geographical or physical boundaries. Therefore, the ratings in this listing must be considered approximate.

City	Population	Year[1]	City	Population	Year[1]
Addis Ababa, Ethiopia	1,423,111	1984E	Chicago	3,009,530	1986E
Ahmedabad, India	2,548,057	1981E	Chittagong, Bangladesh	1,388,476 [2]	1981C
Alexandria, Egypt	2,893,000	1986E	Chongqing (Chungking), China	3,890,000	1983E
Algiers	1,483,000	1987E	Cologne, West Germany	914,000	1986E
Amman, Jordan	972,000	1986E	Copenhagen	1,358,540	1985E
Amsterdam	679,100	1986E	Cordoba, Argentina	1,000,000	1983E
Ankara, Turkey	3,462,880	1985C	Cuenca, Ecuador	201,490	1987E
Antwerp, Belgium	483,199	1986E	Damascus, Syria	1,292,000	1987E
Athens	3,027,000	1981C	Delhi, India	5,729,283 [2]	1981E
Auckland, New Zealand	324,400	1988E	Dhaka, Bangladesh	4,470,000	1986E
Baghdad, Iraq	4,648,609	1985E	Dnepropetrovsk, U.S.S.R.	1,166,000	1986E
Baku, U.S.S.R.	1,722,000	1986E	Donetsk, U.S.S.R.	1,081,000	1986E
Bandung, Indonesia	1,602,000	1983E	Dresden, East Germany	519,769	1986E
Bangalore, India	2,921,751 [2]	1981E	Dublin	550,000	1982E
Bangkok	5,174,682	1984E	Düsseldorf, West Germany	561,200	1986E
Barcelona	1,752,627	1987E	Edinburgh, Scotland	439,700	1985E
Barranquilla, Colombia	1,120,001	1985E	Edmonton, Canada	785,465	1986C
Beirut, Lebanon	500,000	1989E	Essen, West Germany	617,700	1986E
Belfast, Northern Ireland	303,800	1987E	Florence, Italy	435,698	1984E
Belgrade, Yugoslavia	1,250,000	1982E	Frankfurt, West Germany	593,400	1986E
Belo Horizonte, Brazil	2,122,073	1985E	Fukuoka, Japan	1,160,440	1986E
Berlin[3]	3,094,586	1986E	Geneva	161,473	1988E
Bern, Switzerland	136,292	1988E	Genoa, Italy	738,099	1984E
Birmingham, England	1,004,100	1986E	Glasgow, Scotland	733,000	1985E
Bogotá, Colombia	4,208,000	1985E	Gorky, U.S.S.R.	1,409,000	1986E
Bombay	8,243,405	1981E	Guadalajara, Mexico	3,000,000	1980C
Brisbane, Australia	1,215,000	1985E	Guatemala City	1,250,000	1982E
Brussels	976,536	1986E	Guayaquil, Ecuador	1,572,615	1987E
Bucharest	2,014,359	1987E	The Hague	440,000	1986E
Budapest	2,076,000	1986E	Haifa, Israel	223,400	1986E
Buenos Aires	3,000,000	1983E	Hamburg, West Germany	1,575,700	1986E
Cairo	12,560,000	1987E	Harbin, China	3,730,000	1983E
Calcutta	9,194,018	1981E	Havana	2,013,746	1986E
Calgary, Canada	671,326 [2]	1986C	Helsinki, Finland*	487,749	1987E
Cali, Colombia	1,654,000	1985E	Ho Chi Minh City (Saigon), Vietnam	3,450,000	1979E
Canton, China	6,840,000	1983E	Hyderabad, India	2,545,836 [2]	1981C
Cape Town, South Africa	1,912,000	1985E	Hyderabad, Pakistan	795,000 [2]	1981C
Caracas, Venezuela	3,000,000 [2]	1981E	Ibadan, Nigeria	1,060,000	1983E
Casablanca, Morocco	2,158,369 [2]	1984E	Istanbul	5,858,558	1985C

City	Population	Year[1]	City	Population	Year[1]
Jakarta, Indonesia	7,636,000	1983E	Port-au-Prince, Haiti[2]	738,342	1984E
Jerusalem[4]	468,400	1986E	Porto Alegre, Brazil	1,275,483	1985E
Johannesburg, South Africa	1,609,000	1985E	Prague	1,193,500	1986E
Kanpur, India	1,639,064[2]	1981E	Pusan, South Korea	3,500,000	1985E
Karachi, Pakistan	5,208,100	1981C	Pyongyang, North Korea	1,500,000	1982E
Kharkov, U.S.S.R.	1,567,000	1986E	Quebec	625,304	1986C
Kiev, U.S.S.R.	2,495,000	1986E	Quezon City, Philippines	1,326,000	1984E
Kinshasa, Zaire	2,653,558	1984E	Quito, Ecuador	1,137,705	1987E
Kobe, Japan	1,410,000	1986E	Recife, Brazil	1,289,627	1985E
Kuala Lumpur, Malaysia	1,000,000	1980E	Rio de Janeiro	5,615,149	1985E
Kuilbyshev, U.S.S.R.	1,267,000	1986E	Riyadh, Saudi Arabia	1,250,000	1980E
Lagos, Nigeria	1,097,000	1983E	Rome	2,826,733	1984E
Lahore, Pakistan	2,952,700	1981C	Rosario, Argentina	950,000	1983E
La Paz, Bolivia	992,592	1985E	Rotterdam	571,400	1986E
Lausanne, Switzerland	124,022	1988E	Salvador, Brazil	1,811,367	1985E
Leipzig, East Germany	553,660	1986E	San José, Costa Rica	278,500	1984E
Leningrad	4,904,000	1986E	Santiago, Chile	4,804,200	1986E
Liege, Belgium	210,324	1986E	Santo Domingo, Dominican Republic	1,410,000	1983E
Lima	5,330,800	1987E	São Paulo, Brazil	10,099,086	1985E
Lisbon	827,800	1985E	Sapporo, Japan	1,542,979	1986
Liverpool, England	483,000	1986E	Seoul, South Korea	9,600,000	1985
Lódz, Poland	847,900	1986E	Seville, Spain	645,817	1987E
London	6,775,200	1986E	Shanghai	11,940,000	1983E
Los Angeles	3,259,340	1986E	Sheffield, England	539,000	1985E
Lyons, France	410,455	1982E	Shenyang, China	5,210,000	1983E
Madras, India	4,289,347[2]	1981E	Singapore, Singapore	2,600,000	1988E
Madrid	3,158,800	1987E	Sofia, Bulgaria	1,114,962	1986E
Managua	682,111	1985E	Stockholm	1,435,000	1986E
Manchester, England	172,600	1986E	Stuttgart, West Germany	564,200	1986E
Manila	1,728,400	1984E	Surabaja, Indonesia	2,289,000	1983E
Marseilles, France	868,435	1982E	Sverdjovsk, U.S.S.R.	1,315,000	1986E
Mecca, Saudi Arabia	750,000	1980E	Sydney	3,531,000	1985E
Medellin, Colombia	2,069,000	1985E	Taipei, Taiwan	2,507,620	1986E
Melbourne	2,965,900	1985E	Tashkent, U.S.S.R.	2,077,000	1986E
Mexico City	12,900,000	1980C	Tbilisi, U.S.S.R.	1,174,000	1986E
Milan, Italy	1,535,722	1984E	Teheran	6,037,656	1986E
Minsk, U.S.S.R.	1,510,000	1986E	Tel Aviv, Israel	320,300	1986E
Monterrey, Mexico	2,700,000	1980C	Tianjin (Tientsin), China	7,850,000	1983E
Montevideo, Uruguay	1,325,000	1982E	Tokyo	8,354,615	1986E
Montreal	2,921,357	1986C	Toronto	3,427,168[2]	1986C
Moscow	8,714,000	1986E	Tripoli, Libya	587,400	1980E
Munich, West Germany	1,269,400	1986E	Tunis, Tunisia	600,000	1981E
Nagoya, Japan	2,116,381	1986E	Turin, Italy	1,049,997	1984E
Nanjing (Nanking), China	4,560,000	1983E	Valparaiso, Chile	277,900	1986E
Nantes, France	237,789	1982E	Valencia, Spain	774,748	1987E
Naples, Italy	1,206,955	1984E	Vancouver, Canada	1,380,729	1986C
New York	7,262,700	1986E	Venice	340,873	1984C
Nice, France	331,165	1982E	Vienna	1,550,000	1983E
Novosibirsk, U.S.S.R.	1,405,000	1986E	Volgograd, U.S.S.R.	974,000	1985E
Odessa, U.S.S.R.	1,132,000	1986E	Warsaw	1,659,400	1986E
Osaka, Japan	2,636,249	1986E	Washington, D.C.	626,000	1986E
Oslo	450,308	1988E	Wellington, New Zealand	829,200	1988E
Ottawa	819,263	1986C	Winnipeg, Canada	671,326[2]	1986C
Palermo	716,149	1984E	Yangon, Myanmar	2,458,712	1983E
Panama City, Panama	440,000	1987E	Yokohama, Japan	2,992,926	1986E
Paris	2,150,000	1983E	Zurich	346,879	1988E
Peking (Beijing)	9,330,000	1983E			

1. E = estimated; C = census. 2. Figure is for metropolitan area and may include suburbs or some rural population. 3. West Berlin, 1,879,000; East Berlin, 1,215,586 1986E. 4. Includes East Jerusalem. NOTE: The population of many other cities will be found throughout the World History section under individual countries. *See* Table of Contents.

Global Population Is on the Rise

The global population growth rate has reversed its 20-year decline and is now on the upswing. New figures show the rate at 1.8 percent, up from 1.7 percent in 1988. In part, this rise reflects continued declines in death rates in some regions not matched by similar trends in birthrates. In some countries, such as China and India, and in parts of Africa, birthrates actually have risen somewhat, according to *World-Watch* magazine, published by Worldwatch Institute, Washington, D.C.

Estimates of World Population by Regions

Year	North America[1]	Latin America[2]	Europe[3]	U.S.S.R.	Asia[4]	Africa	Oceania	World total
1650	1	7	103	(5)	257	100	2	470
1750	1	10	144	(5)	437	100	2	694
1850	26	33	274	(5)	656	100	2	1,091
1900	81	63	423	(5)	857	141	6	1,571
1950	166	164	392	180	1,380	219	13	2,513
1960	199	215	425	214	1,683	275	16	3,027
1970	226	283	460	244	2,091	354	19	3,678
1980	252	365	484	266	2,618	472	23	4,478
1983	259	390	489	272	2,771	516	24	4,722
1984	262	398	491	275	2,785	532	24	4,766
1985	264	410	492	278	2,831	566	24	4,865
1986	267	419	493	280	2,876	583	25	4,942
1987	270	421	495	284	2,930	601	25	5,026
1988	272	429	497	286	2,995	623	26	5,128
1989	275	438	499	289	3,061	646	26	5,234

Estimated population in millions

1. U.S. (including Alaska and Hawaii), Bermuda, Canada, Greenland, and St. Pierre and Miquelon. 2. Mexico, Central and South America, and Caribbean Islands. 3. Includes Russia 1650–1900. 4. Excludes Russia (U.S.S.R.). 5. Included in Europe. NOTE: From 1930 on European Turkey included in Asia not Europe. *Sources:* W.F. Willcox, 1650–1900; United Nations, 1930–70. United States Department of Commerce, Bureau of the Census, 1983, 1984; *1986, 1987, 1988,* and *1989 World Population Data Sheet,* Population Reference Bureau, Inc., Washington, D.C.

World's 20 Most Populous Countries: 1989 and 2100

	1989			2100	
Rank	Country	Population	Rank	Country	Population
1.	China	1,103,900,000	1.	India	1,631,800,000
2.	India	835,000,000	2.	China	1,571,400,000
3.	USSR	289,000,000	3.	Nigeria	508,800,000
4.	United States	248,800,000	4.	USSR	375,900,000
5.	Indonesia	184,600,000	5.	Indonesia	356,300,000
6.	Brazil	147,400,000	6.	Pakistan	315,800,000
7.	Japan	123,200,000	7.	United States	308,700,000
8.	Nigeria	115,300,000	8.	Bangladesh	297,100,000
9.	Bangladesh	114,700,000	9.	Brazil	293,200,000
10.	Pakistan	110,400,000	10.	Mexico	195,500,000
11.	Mexico	86,700,000	11.	Ethiopia	173,300,000
12.	Vietnam	66,800,000	12.	Vietnam	168,100,000
13.	Philippines	64,900,000	13.	Iran	163,800,000
14.	Germany, West	61,500,000	14.	Zaire	138,900,000
15.	Italy	57,600,000	15.	Japan	127,900,000
16.	United Kingdom	57,300,000	16.	Philippines	125,100,000
17.	France	56,100,000	17.	Tanzania	119,600,000
18.	Thailand	55,600,000	18.	Kenya	116,400,000
19.	Turkey	55,400,000	19.	Burma	111,700,000
20.	Egypt	54,800,000	20.	Egypt	110,500,000

Sources: 1989 World Population Data Sheet of the Population Reference Bureau, Inc; *2100,* World Bank.

Nigeria Opts for Smaller Families

Often among Africa's most progressive nations, Nigeria is now in the forefront of population issues with the recent announcement it has set a national goal to limit family size at four children by the year 2000. Nigeria has come to a realization other African governments inevitably will have to: its large and rapidly growing population is overwhelming the country's economic and environmental resources, according to *World-Watch* magazine.

Chief among the goals of this policy is the commitment to reduce the population growth rate from 3.3 percent per year to 2 percent by 2000, by encouraging at least 80 percent of Nigerian mothers to limit themselves voluntarily to four children. (Families now average six children.) Sharply scaling back the number of women who get married before the age of 18 will contribute to this objective.

Expectation of Life by Age and Sex for Selected Countries

Country	Period	Males						Females					
		0	1	10	20	40	60	0	1	10	20	40	60
NORTH AMERICA													
U.S.	1984	71.20	71.10	62.30	52.70	34.30	17.90	78.20	78.00	69.20	59.40	40.10	22.50
Canada	1980–1982	71.88	71.67	62.92	53.39	34.72	17.96	78.98	78.65	68.97	60.08	40.73	22.85
Mexico	1979	62.10	—	—	—	—	—	66.00	—	—	—	—	—
Trinidad & Tobago	1980–1985	66.88	67.34	58.97	49.39	31.13	15.84	71.62	71.64	63.18	53.44	34.55	18.42
CENTRAL AND SOUTH AMERICA													
Brazil	1980–1985	60.90	—	—	—	—	—	66.00	—	—	—	—	—
Chile	1985	65.03	67.85	59.48	49.91	31.91	16.57	71.69	73.46	64.88	55.15	36.33	19.62
Costa Rica	1980–1985	70.50	—	—	—	—	—	75.70	—	—	—	—	—
Ecuador	1974–1979	59.51	63.26	57.41	48.65	32.12	16.52	61.83	65.37	59.22	50.34	33.46	17.42
Guatemala	1979–1980	55.11	59.09	54.38	45.55	30.56	16.57	59.43	62.98	58.74	49.79	33.01	17.50
Panama	1980–1985	69.20	70.16	62.37	53.01	35.02	18.55	72.85	73.60	65.71	56.17	37.56	20.28
Peru	1980–1985	56.80	—	—	—	—	—	60.50	—	—	—	—	—
Uruguay	1974–1976	65.66	68.27	59.83	50.24	31.78	16.04	72.41	74.52	66.08	56.37	37.37	20.02
Venezuela	1985	66.68	68.45	60.31	50.92	33.07	17.30	72.80	74.16	65.90	56.23	37.31	20.30
EUROPE													
Austria	1985	70.40	70.33	61.57	51.99	33.41	17.02	77.36	77.07	68.27	58.44	39.05	21.01
Belgium	1979–1982	70.04	69.99	61.26	51.64	32.98	16.26	76.79	76.61	67.88	58.08	38.82	20.93
Cyprus	1979–1981	72.26	72.63	63.82	54.01	34.57	17.28	75.99	76.04	67.17	57.31	37.70	19.51
Czechoslovakia	1984	67.11	67.30	58.68	48.97	30.29	14.81	74.31	74.30	65.90	56.07	36.64	18.89
Denmark	1984–1985	71.60	71.20	62.40	52.70	34.00	17.20	77.50	77.00	68.20	58.40	39.10	21.60
Finland	1985	70.07	69.54	60.71	51.03	32.40	16.12	78.49	77.94	69.07	59.21	39.71	21.34
France	1983–1985	71.04	70.74	61.99	52.37	33.92	17.76	79.19	78.78	70.00	60.20	40.94	22.84
Germany, East	1985	69.52	69.27	60.60	50.94	32.26	15.77	75.42	75.05	66.31	56.48	37.16	19.24
Germany, West	1983–1985	71.18	70.95	62.18	52.50	33.64	16.92	77.79	77.45	68.66	58.83	39.44	21.36
Greece	1980	72.15	72.82	54.13	54.48	35.58	18.17	76.35	76.78	68.24	58.43	38.95	20.63
Hungary	1985	65.60	66.08	57.32	47.62	29.58	15.12	73.57	73.93	65.15	55.32	36.22	19.15
Ireland	1980–1982	70.14	69.94	61.25	51.58	32.63	15.90	75.62	75.35	66.58	56.75	37.26	19.55
Italy	1981	71.05	71.15	62.38	52.76	33.75	16.97	77.78	77.72	68.93	59.09	39.62	21.41
Netherlands	1984–1985	72.94	72.63	63.85	54.08	34.91	17.55	79.67	79.23	70.40	60.53	41.03	22.86
Norway	1984–1985	72.80	72.48	63.72	54.05	35.10	17.93	79.51	79.12	70.32	60.47	40.95	22.65
Poland	1985	66.50	66.87	58.16	48.49	30.24	15.14	74.81	74.99	66.24	56.40	37.08	19.4
Portugal	1979–1982	68.35	69.10	60.66	51.31	33.09	16.74	75.20	75.72	67.17	57.46	38.27	20.2
Spain	1980	72.55	72.63	64.01	54.36	35.51	18.63	78.59	78.50	69.79	59.98	40.56	22.2
Sweden	1985	73.79	73.33	64.48	54.70	35.70	18.34	79.68	79.18	70.31	60.46	41.03	22.70
Switzerland	1984–1985	73.50	73.10	64.30	54.70	35.70	18.60	80.00	79.50	70.70	60.90	41.50	23.1
U.S.S.R.	1984–1985	62.87	63.74	55.66	46.12	28.86	14.79	72.73	73.40	65.29	55.55	36.58	19.4
United Kingdom													
England and Wales	1983–1985	71.80	71.58	62.79	53.07	33.89	16.75	77.74	77.40	68.59	58.74	39.24	21.3
Northern Ireland	1983	69.25	69.30	60.57	50.93	32.13	15.62	75.65	75.40	66.63	56.80	37.44	19.0
Scotland	1985	70.05	69.76	60.97	51.27	32.26	15.68	75.83	75.49	66.71	56.86	37.45	19.9
Yugoslavia	1980–1981	67.69	68.98	60.43	50.77	32.21	16.19	73.23	74.43	65.86	56.07	36.76	19.0
ASIA													
Bangladesh	1984	54.90	62.40	58.80	49.80	31.90	16.20	54.70	60.30	57.80	49.30	32.10	16.0
India	1976–1980	52.50	58.60	54.80	45.80	28.30	14.10	52.10	58.60	56.60	47.80	31.20	15.9
Iran	1976	55.75	60.78	53.87	45.19	29.19	14.58	55.04	60.14	54.38	44.97	30.47	15.3
Israel	1984	73.10	73.00	64.30	54.60	35.60	18.40	76.60	76.60	67.90	58.00	38.50	20.4
Japan	1985	74.84	74.28	65.53	55.80	36.68	19.38	80.46	79.87	71.06	61.18	41.69	23.2
Korea, South	1978–1979	62.70	63.73	55.62	46.21	28.13	12.74	69.07	71.02	63.46	53.86	35.04	17.8
Pakistan	1976–1978	59.04	66.46	61.34	52.30	34.77	19.25	59.20	65.58	60.68	51.98	35.23	19.2
Sri Lanka	1981	67.78	68.99	60.99	51.64	33.19	17.74	71.66	72.67	64.75	55.36	36.96	19.5
Syria	1976–1979	63.77	66.92	59.88	50.69	32.74	16.16	64.70	67.06	60.14	50.90	32.84	16.2
AFRICA													
Egypt	1980–1985	56.80	—	—	—	—	—	59.50	—	—	—	—	—
Kenya	1980–1985	51.20	—	—	—	—	—	54.70	—	—	—	—	—
South Africa	1980–1985	51.80	—	—	—	—	—	55.20	—	—	—	—	—
OCEANIA													
Australia	1985	72.32	72.13	63.39	53.78	35.02	17.80	78.76	78.46	69.67	59.85	40.44	22.3
New Zealand	1985	70.97	70.84	62.10	52.62	33.86	16.93	76.83	76.57	67.85	58.10	38.84	21.1

1. Provisional. 2. Excluding nomadic Indian tribes. 3. Excluding tribal Indian population. 4. Estimates prepared by the Population Division of the United Nations. 5. Excluding data for Faeroe Islands and Greenland. 6. Including relevant data relating to Berlin. No separate data have been supplied. 7. Including data for East Jerusalem and Israeli residents in certain other territories under occupation by Israeli military forces since June 1967. 8. Japanese nationals in Japan only. 9. Excluding full-blooded aborigines. NOTE: Figures are latest available as of August 1989. *Source:* United Nations *Demographic Yearbook, 1986.*

Crude Birth and Death Rates for Selected Countries
(per 1,000 population)

Country	Birth rates					Death rates				
	1987	1986	1985	1980	1975	1987	1986	1985	1980	1975
Australia	15.1	15.0	15.7	15.3	16.9	7.2	7.3	7.5	7.4	7.9
Austria	11.4	11.4	11.4	12.0	12.5	11.2	11.4	11.9	12.2	12.8
Belgium	11.8	11.8	11.5	12.7	12.2	10.6	11.1	11.2	11.6	12.2
Canada	14.4	14.5	14.8	15.4	15.8	7.2	7.2	7.2	7.2	7.4
Cuba	17.4	16.3	18.0	14.1	n.a.	6.3	6.2	6.4	5.7	n.a.
Czechoslovakia	13.8	14.2	14.5	16.4	19.6	11.5	11.8	11.8	12.1	11.5
Denmark	11.0	10.8	10.6	11.2	14.2	11.3	11.4	11.4	10.9	10.1
El Salvador	n.a.	n.a.	n.a.	34.7	38.9	n.a.	n.a.	n.a.	7.9	7.9
Finland	12.0	12.3	12.8	13.1	13.9	9.7	9.6	9.8	9.3	9.3
France	13.8	14.1	13.9	14.8	14.1	9.5	9.9	10.1	10.2	10.6
Germany, East	13.6	13.4	13.7	14.6	10.8	12.9	13.4	13.5	14.2	14.3
Germany, West	10.5	10.2	9.6	10.0	9.7	11.2	11.5	11.5	11.6	12.1
Greece	10.6	11.3	11.7	15.4	15.7	9.5	9.2	9.4	9.1	8.9
Hong Kong	12.4	13.1	14.0	16.9	n.a.	4.8	4.7	4.6	5.1	n.a.
Hungary	11.9	12.1	12.2	13.9	18.4	13.4	13.8	13.9	13.6	12.4
Ireland	16.6	17.3	17.5	21.9	21.5	8.8	9.5	9.0	9.7	10.6
Israel	22.7	23.1	23.5	24.1	28.2	n.a.	6.8	6.6	6.7	7.1
Italy	9.6	n.a.	10.1	11.2	14.8	9.3	n.a.	9.5	9.7	9.9
Japan	11.1	11.4	11.9	13.7	17.2	6.2	6.2	6.2	6.2	6.4
Luxembourg	11.5	11.9	11.2	11.5	11.2	10.9	10.9	11.8	11.5	12.2
Malta	15.4	15.8	14.2	16.0	18.3	8.4	8.2	7.4	8.8	8.8
Mauritius	19.1	18.3	18.8	27.0	25.1	6.6	6.7	6.8	7.2	8.1
Mexico	n.a.	n.a.	n.a.	35.3	37.5	n.a.	n.a.	n.a.	6.2	7.2
Netherlands	12.7	12.7	12.3	12.8	13.0	8.3	8.6	8.5	8.1	8.3
New Zealand	16.8	16.3	15.6	n.a.	18.4	8.4	8.3	8.4	n.a.	8.1
Norway	13.0	12.6	12.3	12.5	14.1	10.7	9.8	10.7	10.1	9.9
Panama	25.7	25.9	26.6	26.8	32.3	n.a.	n.a.	n.a.	n.a.	n.a.
Poland	16.1	16.9	18.2	19.5	18.9	10.0	10.0	10.3	9.8	8.7
Portugal	12.0	12.4	12.5	16.4	19.1	9.3	9.4	9.6	9.9	10.4
Singapore	16.8	14.8	16.6	17.3	17.8	5.0	5.0	5.2	5.2	5.1
Spain	n.a.	n.a.	n.a.	16.1	19.1	n.a.	n.a.	n.a.	7.7	8.2
Sweden	12.5	12.2	11.8	11.7	12.6	11.1	11.1	11.3	11.0	10.8
Switzerland	11.7	11.7	11.6	11.3	12.3	9.1	9.2	9.2	9.2	8.7
Tunisia	n.a.	31.1	n.a.	35.2	36.6	n.a.	n.a.	n.a.	n.a.	n.a.
United Kingdom	13.6	13.3	13.3	13.5	12.5	11.2	11.6	11.8	11.8	11.9
United States	15.7	15.5	15.7	16.2	14.0	8.7	8.7	8.7	8.9	8.9
Yugoslavia	15.3	15.4	15.9	17.0	18.2	9.2	9.1	9.1	9.0	8.7

NOTE: n.a. = not available. Source: United Nations, Monthly Bulletin of Statistics, May 1989.

Legal Abortions in Selected Countries, 1977–1985

Country	1977	1978	1979	1980	1981	1982	1983	1984	1985
Bulgaria	141,702	147,667	147,888	155,876	152,370	147,791	134,165	131,140	132,041
Canada	—	—	65,043	65,751	65,053	66,254	61,750	62,291	60,956
Cuba	—	—	106,549	103,974	108,559	126,745	116,956	139,588	138,671
Czechosolvakia	88,989	92,545	94,486	100,170	103,517	107,638	108,662	113,802	119,325
Denmark	25,662	23,699	23,193	23,334	22,779	21,462	20,791	20,742	19,919
Finland	17,772	16,928	15,849	15,037	14,120	13,861	13,360	13,642	—
France	150,931	150,417	156,810	171,218	180,695	181,122	182,862	180,789	173,300
Germany, West	54,309	73,548	82,788	87,702	87,353	91,064	86,529	86,298	83,538
Greece	45	45	137	117	109	—	220	193	180 [1]
Hungary	89,096	83,545	80,767	80,882	78,421	78,682	78,599	82,191	81,970
Iceland	456	455	556	523	597	613	687	—	—
India	247,049	312,754	—	346,327	—	500,624	492,696	561,033	—
Israel	—	—	15,925	14,708	14,514	16,829	15,593	18,948	18,406
Italy	—	—	187,752	220,263	224,377	231,308	231,401 [1]	227,809 [1]	—
Netherlands	—	—	—	—	20,897	20,187	19,700	18,700 [1]	—
New Zealand	—	—	—	5,945	6,758	6,903	7,198	7,275	7,130
Norway	15,528	14,783	14,456	13,531	13,845	13,496	13,646	14,070	14,599
Poland	216,533	223,288	220,431	133,835	130,070	141,177	130,980	132,844	135,564
Singapore	16,443	17,246	16,999	18,219	18,890	15,548	19,100	22,190	23,512
Sweden	31,462	31,918	34,709	34,887	33,294	32,604	31,014	30,755	30,838
United Kingdom	109,960	119,273	128,365	136,782	171,455	171,417	170,620	179,102	180,983
United States	1,079,430	1,157,776	—	—	—	1,573,920 [2]	—	1,577,180 [2]	1,588,550 [2]

1. Provisional. 2 Figures are from The Alan Guttmacher Institute. NOTE: Data latest available as of August 1989. Source: United Nations, Demographic Yearbook, 1986.

Cost of Living of United Nations Personnel in Selected Cities as Reflected by Index of Retail Prices, 1988

(New York City, December 1988 = 100)

City	Index	City	Index	City	Index
Abu Dhabi	102 [1]	Dar es Salaam	84 [1]	Nassau	110
Addis Ababa	87 [1]	Geneva	137	New Delhi	56
Algiers	109 [1]	Guatemala City	82	Panama City	84
Amman	79	The Hague	101	Paris	107
Ankara	59	Helsinki	123	Port-au-Prince	92
Athens	91	Islamabad	73	Quito	64
Baghdad	127 [1]	Jakarta	86	Rabat	77
Bangkok	71	Kabul	100	Rome	101
Beirut	66	Kathmandu	55	Roseau	92
Belgrade	77	Kingston	68	San Salvador	80
Bogota	81	Kinshasa	97 [1]	Santiago	65
Bonn	116	La Paz	65	Seoul	107
Brazzaville	93 [1]	Lagos	69 [1]	Sofia	78
Brussels	96	Lima	68	Sydney	94
Budapest	49	London	111	Tokyo	154
Buenos Aires	67	Madrid	102	Tripoli	151 [1]
Cairo	84	Managua	67	Tunis	64
Caracas	59	Manila	74	Valetta	82
Colombo	64	Mexico City	66	Vienna	114
Copenhagen	111	Montevideo	77	Warsaw	48
Dhaka	67	Montreal	87	Washington. D.C.	91
Dakar	104 [1]	Nairobi	68	Yangon	97

1. Calculated on the basis of cost of Government or subsidized housing which is normally lower than prevailing rentals. *Source:* United Nations, *Monthly Bulletin of Statistics, March 1989.*

Consumer Price Indexes for Selected Countries

(1967=100)

Country	Total Indexes[1]				Annual percent change 1986–1987	Indexes for Selected Items, 1987			
	1987	1986	1985	1980		Food[2]	Cloth-ing	Hous-ing[3]	Trans-portation
Australia	520.8	480.1	—	295.5	8.5	486.0	495.2	576.5	(n.a.)
Austria	266.1	262.4	258.0	203.3	1.4	235.6	218.7	315.1	284.4
Canada	378.5	362.6	348.4	243.5	4.4	427.7	259.2	377.7	386.1
France	491.9	477.2	464.8	294.2	3.3	493.2	466.9	518.9	562.1
Germany, West	212.4	211.9	212.4	175.8	0.3	185.9	218.4	234.0	222.4
Italy	850.8	812.5	767.3	403.2	4.7	758.3	957.6	822.4	988.6
Japan	325.2	324.9	322.9	281.8	—	327.4	360.2	275.3	280.6
Netherlands	291.9	292.4	291.4	237.4	−0.5	227.5	302.4	315.9	279.7
Sweden	451.9	433.8	416.2	270.6	4.2	539.1	277.7	501.6	(n.a.)
United Kingdom	645.8	619.9	599.5	423.6	4.2	654.5	348.0	699.0	642.7
United States	340.4	328.4	—	246.8	3.7	333.0	200.6	371.0	316.8

1. Includes other items not shown separately. 2. Restaurant meals, alcohol, and tobacco are included for some countries, excluded for others. 3. Includes shelter, utilities, and household furnishings and operations. However, actual coverage and measurements vary significantly from country to country. NOTE: n.a. = not available. *Source:* United States Department of Labor, Bureau of Labor Statistics.

Labor Force Participation Rates by Sex[1]

Country	Female				Male				Females as percent of total labor force			
	1987	1986	1985	1980	1987	1986	1985	1980	1987	1986	1985	1980
Canada	50.9	49.7	48.5	46.2	70.1	69.5	68.7	73.0	43.2	42.8	44.9	39.7
France	n.a.	39.6 [2]	39.7	40.0	n.a.	62.0 [2]	62.2	68.6	n.a.	41.6 [2]	41.6	39.4
Germany, West	n.a.	36.0 [2]	35.5 [2]	36.7	n.a.	64.1 [2]	63.7 [2]	68.9	n.a.	39.0 [2]	38.9 [2]	38.0
Italy	28.6 [2]	28.3	27.8	27.9	61.6 [2]	62.3	62.5	66.0	33.6	33.2	32.7	31.7
Japan	46.2	46.2	46.3	45.7	74.9	75.4	75.9	77.9	39.6	39.4	39.3	38.4
Sweden	61.6 [2]	60.3 [2]	59.7	58.0	71.0 [2]	70.7 [2]	70.5	73.6	47.7 [2]	47.3 [2]	47.1	45.1
United Kingdom	45.9 [2]	44.9 [2]	44.4 [2]	44.8	68.2 [2]	67.5 [2]	68.0 [2]	72.8	42.4 [2]	42.1 [2]	41.7 [2]	40.4
United States	52.5	51.4	50.4	47.7	71.5	71.0	70.9	72.0	44.8	44.4	44.1	42.4

1. Labor force of all ages as percent of population, 15–64 years old. 2. Preliminary. *Source: Statistical Abstract of the United States 1989.*

Unemployment Figures for Selected Countries: 1983-1988

(In thousands except for percentages)

Country	1988 No.	1988 %	1987 No.	1987 %	1986 No.	1986 %	1985 No.	1985 %	1984 No.	1984 %	1983 No.	1983 %
Australia	576.2	7.2	628.8	8.1	609.9	8.1	601.6	8.3	642.1	9.0	697.0	10.0
Austria[1]	158.6	5.3	164.5	5.6	152.0	5.2	139.5	4.8	130.5	4.5	127.4	4.5
Belgium[1 2 8]	459.4	10.9	500.8	11.9	516.8	12.3	557.4	13.5	595.0	14.4	589.5	14.3
Canada	1,047.0	7.8	1,167.0	8.9	1,236.0	9.6	1,327.9	10.5	1,399.0	11.3	1,448.0	11.9
Chile	285.8	8.1	343.6	7.9	374.3	8.8	273.4	17.0	285.0	18.4	279.0	19.0
Cyprus[1]	7.4	n.a.	8.7	3.4	9.2	3.7	8.3	3.3	8.0	3.3	7.8	3.3
Denmark	243.9	8.7	219.4	8.0	217.3	8.0	247.8	9.2	276.3	10.3	283.0	10.6
Finland[3]	116.0	4.5	130.0	5.1	140.0	5.4	163.2	6.3	158.0	6.2	156.0	6.1
Germany, West[1]	2,236.6	8.7	2,232.5	8.9	2,228.0	9.0	2,304.0	9.3	2,265.6	9.1	2,258.2	9.1
Hong-Kong	n.a.	n.a.	47.5	1.7	76.3	2.8	83.6	3.2	101.0	3.9	113.9	4.5
Ireland[4]	241.4	18.6	247.3	19.0	236.4	18.2	230.6	17.7	214.2	16.2	192.7	14.7
Israel[5]	n.a.	n.a.	90.0	6.1	104.0	7.1	97.0	6.7	85.0	5.9	63.0	4.5
Italy	2,885.0	12.0	2,832.0	12.0	2,611.0	n.a.	2,471.0	10.6	2,391.0	10.4	2,264.0	9.9
Japan	1,550.0	2.5	1,730.0	2.9	1,670.0	2.8	1,564.3	2.6	1,600.0	2.7	1,560.0	2.64
Korea	435.0	2.5	519.0	3.1	611.0	3.8	619.0	4.0	567.0	3.8	614.0	4.1
Netherlands[1 2]	682.2	n.a.	685.5	11.5	710.7	12.0	761.0	15.6	822.4	17.6	800.6	17.1
Norway	69.3	3.2	45.0	2.1	40.0	1.9	51.0	2.5	61.0	3.0	67.0	3.3
Philippines[6]	n.a.	n.a.	2,085.0	n.a.	1,438.0	6.4	1,316.0	6.1	1,231.0	6.1	850.0	4.1
Portugal	262.2	5.7	319.6	7.1	381.6	8.4	384.7	8.5	381.0	8.3	354.8	7.7
Puerto Rico[7]	n.a.	n.a.	171.0	16.8	188.0	18.9	211.0	21.8	198.0	20.7	220.0	23.4
Sweden	72.0	1.6	84.0	1.9	117.0	2.1	125.0	2.8	136.0	3.1	151.0	3.5
Switzerland[1 8]	22.2	0.7	24.7	0.8	25.7	0.8	30.3	1.0	35.2	1.1	26.3	0.9
United Kingdom[1 9]	2,370.4	8.4	2,953.4	10.6	3,289.1	11.9	3,271.2	13.5	3,159.8	13.1	3,104.7	12.9
United States	6,701.0	5.5	7,425.0	6.2	8,237.0	7.0	8,312.0	7.2	8,539.0	7.5	10,717.0	9.6
Yugoslavia[1]	1,131.8	14.1	1,080.6	13.6	1,086.7	13.9	1,040.0	13.8	974.8	13.3	910.3	12.8

1. Employment office statistics. All others labor force sample surveys unless otherwise indicated. 2. Scope of series revised as of 1983. 3. Scope of series revised as of 1983 and 1986. 4. Excluding agriculture, fishing and private domestic services. 5. Including persons who did not work in the country during the previous 12 months. 6. Average of less than 12 months. 7. Excluding people temporarily laid off. 8. Scope of series revised as of 1984. 9. Excluding persons temporarily laid off. Excluding adult students registered for vacation employment. NOTE: n.a.= not available. Source: United Nations, Monthly Bulletin of Statistics, July 1989.

Public Expenditure for Education for Selected Countries

Country	Year	Percent of total expenditure	Percent of GNP	Country	Year	Percent of total expenditure	Percent of GNP
Algeria	1986	14.6[1]	6.1[1]	Mexico	1986	n.a.	2.1[2]
Argentina	1986	7.5[2]	1.8[2]	Morocco	1983	22.0	7.9
Australia	1985	12.8	6.4	Nepal	1985	10.8	3.0
Bangladesh	1986	10.5[2]	2.1[2]	Netherlands	1984	16.8	6.9
Brazil	1985	17.2[3]	3.3[3]	Nigeria	1986	12.0[6]	1.8[6]
Canada	1986	15.5	7.7	Philippines	1986	n.a.	1.7
Chile	1985	15.3	4.5	Poland	1986	11.5[5]	3.8[4 5]
China	1986	n.a.	2.3	Portugal	1986	n.a.	4.4
Czechoslovakia	1986	8.1	5.2[4]	Romania	1985	n.a.	2.1
Egypt	1985	11.5	5.5	Soviet Union	1986	n.a.	7.0[4]
Ethiopia	1986	9.9	3.9	Spain	1986	13.3	3.2
France	1984	n.a.	6.1	Tanzania	1985	19.0[2]	4.3[2]
Germany, E.	1986	n.a.	5.5[4 5]	Thailand	1985	n.a.	3.9
Germany, W.	1985	9.2	4.6	Turkey	1986	n.a.	2.1
Hungary	1986	6.4	5.7	UK	1984	11.3	5.2
India	1985	9.4	3.6	US	1983	n.a.	6.7
Indonesia	1981	9.3	2.0	Venezuela	1985	21.3	6.8
Italy	1986	8.6[2]	4.7[2]	Yugoslavia	1986	n.a.	3.8
Japan	1985	17.9	5.1	Zaire	1980	32.3[5]	3.4[5]
Korea, S	1986	27.3	4.5	Zimbabwe	1985	16.0	7.9

1. Expenditure of the Ministry of Basic and Secondary Education only. 2. Ministry of Education expenditures only. 3. Excludes municipalities. 4. Percent of net material product. 5. Current expenditures only. 6. Federal government expenditures only. n.a. = not available. NOTE: Expenditure includes both capital and current expenditures on public education and subsidized private education except as noted above. Source: United Nations Educational, Scientific and Cultural Organization, Paris, France, Statistical Yearbook (Copyright). From Statistical Abstract of the United States 1989.

Energy, Petroleum, and Coal, by Country

Country	Energy consumed[1] (coal equiv.) Total (mil. metric tons) 1986	1980	Per capita (kilograms) 1986	1980	Electric energy production[2] (bil. kwh) 1986	1980	Crude petroleum production[3] (mil. metric tons) 1986	1980	Coal production[4] (mil. metric tons) 1986	1980
Algeria	28.5	24.8	1,273	1,327	12.7	7.1	27.9	47.4	(Z)[5]	(Z)
Argentina	53.9	49.3	1,737	1,746	49.0	39.7	22.3	25.3	.4	.4
Australia[6]	106.5	91.2	6,700	6,195	127.7	96.1	25.3	18.9	133.4	72.5
Austria	30.2	30.5	4,024	4,058	44.1	42.0	1.1	1.5	(Z)	—
Bahrain	6.6	4.4	14,664	12,651	3.0	1.7	2.1	2.4	(NA)	—
Bangladesh	6.4	3.8	62	44	5.1	2.7	(Z)	(Z)	(X)	(X)
Belgium	55.3	59.1	5,577	5,997	57.6	53.6	(X)	(X)	5.6[7]	6.3
Brazil	105.4	92.5	761	763	201.6	139.5	28.8	9.1	7.4	5.2
Bulgaria	52.7	47.3	5,780	5,254	41.8	34.8	.3[5]	.3[5]	.2	.3
Canada	249.1	254.2	9,694	10,547	468.6	377.5	72.1	70.4	30.5	20.2
Chile	11.3	11.4	921	1,025	14.8	11.8	1.5	1.6	1.0	1.0
China	742.8	562.8	706	571	444.1	300.6	130.6	05.9	840.0[5]	95.8
Colombia	22.8	23.8	779	923	27.0	22.9	15.7	6.5	10.7[5]	4.9
Cuba	14.4	13.6	1,424	1,394	13.2	9.9	.9	.3	(X)	(X)
Czechoslovakia	97.8	97.4	6,258	6,364	84.8	72.7	.1	.1	25.7[7]	28.3[7]
Denmark	27.3	26.9	5,331	5,254	30.7	27.1	3.6	.3	(X)	(X)
Ecuador	6.3	5.7	656	708	5.3	3.4	14.6	10.4	(NA)	(NA)
Egypt	33.7	20.1	702	488	25.1	18.9	40.2	29.4	(X)	(X)
Ethiopia	.8	.9	19	27	.8	.7	(X)	(X)	(NA)	(NA)
Finland	27.6	26.4	5,623	5,514	46.9[8]	38.7[8]	(X)	(X)	(X)	(X)
France[9]	212.8	237.3	3,881	4,409	343.0[8]	246.4[8]	2.9	1.2	16.3[7]	20.2[7]
Germany, East	133.3	121.8	7,944	7,276	115.3	98.8	(Z)	.1	(Z)	(Z)
Germany, West	344.5	359.4	5,672	5,829	406.4	368.8	5.6[10]	4.6	87.1	94.5
Greece	24.3	20.1	2,455	2,088	28.2	22.7	1.3	(Z)	(X)	(X)
Hong Kong	10.0	7.3	1,764	1,448	21.4	12.6	(NA)	(NA)	(X)	(X)
Hungary	39.9	40.6	3,735	3,787	28.1	23.9	2.0	2.0	2.3[8]	3.1[7]
India	210.2	139.4	272	202	202.6	119.3	31.1	9.4	166.1	109.1
Indonesia	47.5	34.7	280	230	29.9	14.2	71.0	77.6	1.7	.3
Iran	52.8	45.7[11]	1,150	1,177[11]	36.8	22.4[1]	93.4[5]	72.7[11]	.8[5]	.9[5]
Iraq	11.1	10.7	678	807	18.9	11.4	82.7	130.1	(NA)	(NA)
Ireland	13.0	11.1	3,556	3,268	12.3	10.9	(X)	(X)	.1	.1
Israel	11.0	8.8	2,546	2,273	16.3	12.5	(Z)	(Z)	(X)	(X)
Italy[12]	184.2	174.9	3,211	3,112	189.0	185.7	2.5	1.8	(Z)	(Z)[5]
Japan	440.2	434.8	3,625	3,726	671.8	577.5	.6	.4	16.0	18.0
Korea North	57.9	48.5	2,771	2,713	50.0	35.0	(X)	(X)	39.5[5]	36.0[5]
Korea South	68.2	52.3	1,625	1,373	69.8	40.1	(X)	(X)	24.3	18.6
Kuwait[13]	14.7	6.9	7,773	5,019	17.3	9.4	71.5	84.1	(X)	n.a.
Libya	13.5	7.3	3,597	2,456	9.0	4.8	49.7	88.3	(X)	(X)
Malaysia	16.7	12.2	1,048	882	16.1	10.2	24.5	13.2	(X)	(X)
Mexico	129.8	118.6	1,604	1,709	97.5[8]	67.0[8]	126.2[5]	99.9	8.5[5]	7.0[8]
Morocco	7.3	6.4	323	319	7.2	4.9	(Z)[5]	(Z)	.8[5]	.7[8]
Myanmar	3.2	2.2	85	62	2.2	1.3	1.4[5]	1.6	.1[5]	(Z)
Netherlands	104.8	93.0	7,200	6,543	67.1	64.8	4.6	1.3	(Z)[14]	(Z)[14]
New Zealand	13.1	10.0	3,910	3,152	28.2	22.0	1.3[5]	.3[6]	2.1[5]	2.0
Nigeria	16.9	11.0	171	136	9.9	7.2	72.8	104.2	.1	.2[5]
Norway[15]	27.5	26.3	6,618	6,423	96.4	84.1	40.5	24.6	.6	.3
Pakistan	25.6	16.6	249	191	25.8	15.3	1.9	.5	2.1	1.5
Peru	10.6	12.0	524	693	12.8	9.8	8.8	9.6	.2[5]	.1[5]
Philippines	13.7	16.7	246	346	22.3	17.9	.3	.5	1.2	.3
Poland	176.2	176.8	4,700	4,935	140.3	121.9	.2	.3	192.1	193.1
Portugal	13.5	11.2	1,318	1,153	20.2	15.3	(X)	(X)	.2	.2
Romania	103.9	100.0	4,483	4,505	71.6	67.5	10.5[5]	11.5	8.7[5]	8.1
Saudi Arabia[13]	49.8	25.3	4,148	2,745	32.9	18.9	251.7	495.9	(NA)	n.a.
South Africa[16]	106.2	90.2	2,779	2,751	123.3	90.4	(X)	(X)	175.7	116.6
Soviet Union	1,797.2	1,473.1	6,389	5,549	1,598.9	293.9	615.0	603.2	512.9	492.9
Spain	85.3	88.4	2,199	2,359	127.7	110.5	1.9	1.6	16.0[7]	13.1[57]
Sudan	1.5	1.5	67	82	1.1	1.0	(X)	(X)	(X)	n.a.
Sweden	40.8	44.5	4,893	5,376	138.0	96.7	(Z)	(Z)	(Z)	(Z)
Switzerland[17]	25.6	23.3	3,990	3,636	54.9[8]	48.1[8]	(X)	(X)	(X)	(X)
Syria	13.1	7.3	1,198	835	7.0	3.8	9.3	8.3	(X)	(X)
Taiwan[8]	49.8	37.9	2,550	2,127	63.4	42.0	.1	.2	1.7	2.6
Tanzania	.9	.8	38	44	.9	.7	(X)	(X)	(Z)[6]	(Z)
Thailand	23.6	17.3	451	372	25.9	15.1	1.1	(Z)	(Z)	(Z)
Trinidad and Tobago	9.1	7.5	7,587	6,992	3.3	2.0	8.7	11.0	(NA)	n.a.

Country	Energy consumed[1] (coal equiv.) Total (mil. metric tons) 1986	1980	Per capita (kilograms) 1986	1980	Electric energy production[2] (bil. kwh) 1986	1980	Crude petroleum production[3] (mil. metric tons) 1986	1980	Coal production[4] (mil. metric tons) 1986	1980
Tunisia	5.2	4.1	712	639	4.2	2.8	5.2	5.6	(X)	(X)
Turkey	49.0	31.9	974	718	39.7	23.3	2.4	2.3	3.5	3.6
United Arab Emirates	9.7	16.8	6,991	17,188	6.7	6.3	66.2[5]	82.8	(NA)	n.a.
United Kingdom	302.3	271.0	5,363	4,850	298.2	284.9	121.2	78.9	108.1[7]	30.1[7]
United States	2,278.1	2,364.5	9,489	10,386	2,583	2,354	428.2	24.2	738.9	10.4
Venezuela	60.1	49.0	3,380	3,140	46.7	35.9	94.0	14.8	.1	(Z)
Vietnam	7.3	6.6	120	122	5.2	3.8	(NA)	n.a.	5.5[5]	5.2
Yugoslavia	56.9	48.0	2,440	2,152	77.4	59.4	4.2	4.2	.4	.4
Zaire	2.1	2.0	67	69	4.6	4.2	1.3[5]	1.0	.1[5]	.1
Zambia	1.9	2.3	281	403	10.1[8]	9.2	(X)	(X)	.6	.6
World, total	9,321.9	8,544.3	1,896	1,919	9,962	8,247	2,800	2,979	3,195	2,728

—Represents zero. n.a. = not available. X = Not applicable. Z = Less than 50,000 metric tons. 1. Based on apparent consumption of coal, lignite, petroleum products, natural gas, and hydro, nuclear, and geothermal electricity. 2. Comprises production by utilities generating primarily for public use, and production by industrial establishments generating primarily for own use. Relates to production at generating centers, including station use and transmission losses. 3. Includes shale oil, but excludes natural gasoline. 4. Excludes lignite and brown coal, except as noted. 5. United Nations Statistical Office estimate. 6. For year ending June 30 of year shown. 7. Includes slurries. 8. Net production, i.e. excluding station use. 9. Includes Monaco. 10. Includes inputs other than crude petroleum and natural gas liquids. 11. For year ending March 20 of year shown. 12. Includes San Marino. 13. Includes share of consumption in the Neutral Zone. 14. Includes patent fuel and hard coal briquettes. 15. Includes Svalbard and Jan Mayen Islands. 16. Includes Botswana, Lesotho, Namibia, and Swaziland. 17. Includes Liechtenstein. 18. *Source:* U.S. Bureau of the Census. Data from Republic of China publications. *Source:* Except as noted, Statistical Office of the United Nations, New York, N.Y., *Energy Statistics Yearbook, 1986* (copyright). From: *Statistical Abstract of the United States, 1989.*

Wheat, Rice, and Corn—Production for Selected Countries

(in thousands of metric tons)

Country	Wheat 1986	1985	1984	Rice 1986	1985	1984	Corn 1986	1985	1984
Argentina	8,100	8,500	13,000	405	400	476	12,400	12,600	9,500
Australia	17,356	16,550	18,580	687	864	635	228	311	210
Belgium[2]	1,265	1,204[1]	1,330	n.a.	n.a.	n.a.	58	90[1]	39[1]
Brazil	5,433	4,247	1,830	10,339	9,019	9,023	20,510	22,017	21,174
Canada	31,580	23,900	21,199	n.a.	n.a.	n.a.	6,694	7,393	7,024
China: Mainland[3]	89,022	85,286	87,682	177,000	171,479	181,028	16,560	62,250	72,690
Egypt	1,929	1,874[1]	1,815	2,450[1]	2,312[1]	2,230	3,801	3,982[1]	3,600
France	26,587	29,030	32,844	60	61	42	10,792	11,839	10,321
Germany, West	10,406	9,866	10,223	n.a.	n.a.	n.a.	1,302	1,204	1,026
Greece	2,200	1,792	2,646	102	106	91	2,070	1,800	1,992
Hungary	5,803	6,573	7,300	44	36	30	7,214	6,798	6,700
India	46,885	44,229	45,148	90,000	91,500[3]	91,000	8,000	7,000[3]	7,750
Indonesia	n.a.	n.a.	n.a.	39,275	38,660[3]	37,500	5,767	5,300	4,000
Iran	7,128	6,000[3]	5,500[3]	1,569	1,100	1,230	50[3]	50[1]	50
Iraq	1,100[1]	650[1]	300	145[1]	105[3]	95	36[1]	32[3]	25
Italy	9,070	8,516	10,005	1,082	1,064	1,027	6,560	6,352	6,781
Japan	876	874	741	14,559	14,578	14,848	1	(4)	3
Korea, South	5[1]	11	17	7,790	7,855	7,970	113	132	133
Mexico	4,772	5,228	4,262	523	988	635	12,154	15,013	14,050
Myanmar	246	206	191	15,000[3]	15,400[1]	14,500	350[3]	403	360
Pakistan	13,923	11,600[1]	11,053	5,241	4,500[1]	5,009	1,067	1,030[3]	1,100
Soviet Union	92,300	83,000[3]	76,000[3]	2,600	2,600[3]	2,500[3]	12,500	15,000[3]	13,000[3]
Sweden	1,714	1,378	1,776	n.a.	n.a.	n.a.	n.a.	n.a.	n.a.
Thailand	n.a.	n.a.	n.a.	19,100	19,521	19,200	4,197	4,686	4,150
United Kingdom	13,874	11,700	14,960	n.a.	n.a.	n.a.	1[3]	1[3]	1[3]
United States	56,792	65,992	70,638	6,097	6,171	6,216	209,632	225,180	194,475
Vietnam	n.a.	n.a.	n.a.	16,197	15,600[2]	15,416	600[1]	500[1]	475
Yugoslavia	4,776	4,859	5,596	48	36	36	12,502	9,891	11,265
World, total	535,842	510,029	521,682	475,533	465,970	469,959	480,609	490,155	449,255

1. Unofficial figure. 2. Includes Luxembourg. 3. FAO estimate. 4. None or negligible. NOTES: Rice data cover rough and paddy. Data for each country pertain to the calendar year in which all or most of the crop was harvested. n.a. = not available. *Source:* Food and Agriculture Organization of the United Nations, Rome, Italy, 1986. *FAO Production Yearbook, vol. 40* (copyright). From: *Statistical Abstract of the United States, 1989.*

Wheat, Rice and Corn Exports and Imports, 1984-1986

(in thousands of metric tons. Countries listed are the 10 leading exporters or importers in 1986)

Exporters	1986	1985	1984	Importers	1986	1985	1984
WHEAT				**WHEAT**			
United States	24,555	24,810	42,243	Soviet Union	14,125	20,309	26,700
Australia	16,109	15,704	10,535	China, Mainland	6,882	6,135	10,539
Canada	15,957	16,983	21,091	Japan	5,620	5,510	5,978
France	13,367	16,943	13,617	Italy	5,259	4,534	4,019
Argentina	4,030	9,583	7,245	Egypt	4,660	4,524	4,520
United Kingdom	3,987	1,886	2,175	South Korea	3,449	2,986	2,649
West Germany	2,143	1,045	1,803	West Germany	2,393	3,083	1,593
Hungary	1,670	2,002	1,271	Iran	2,350	2,700	2,604
Soviet Union	1,100	1,250	1,621	Algeria	2,300	3,030	2,006
Greece	546	345	1,011	Brazil	2,250	4,041	4,868
RICE				**RICE**			
Thailand	4,524	4,062	4,616	Brazil	1,310	339	—
United States	2,392	1,940	2,141	Iraq	525	550	510
Pakistan	1,316	719	1,265	Vietnam	500	422	284
China, Mainland	990	1,046	1,370	Soviet Union	493	321	150
Italy	676	727	536	Iran	400	420	588
Myanmar	500	470	720	Senegal	378	336	371
Uruguay	261	242	152	Ivory Coast	375	342	321
India	250	250	200	Saudi Arabia	375	428	490
Australia	178	341	246	Hong Kong	368	378	366
Indonesia	138	259	—	China, Mainland	330	213	103
CORN				**CORN**			
United States	27,099	44,033	49,104	Japan	14,653	14,225	14,170
Argentina	7,375	7,069	5,518	Soviet Union	6,900	16,600	12,200
France	5,799	4,457	5,208	South Korea	3,671	3,406	3,065
China, Mainland	5,643	6,338	952	China, Mainland	3,664	3,108	3,015
Thailand	3,981	2,752	3,117	Brazil	2,225	262	254
South Africa	1,800	400	40	Egypt	2,140	1,907	1,582
Yugoslavia	1,798	900	685	Netherlands	1,977	2,374	2,229
Greece	580	209	48	Mexico	1,704	3,066	2,498
Hungary	478	228	198	United Kingdom	1,482	1,455	1,473
Zimbabwe	436	189	2	Belgium-Luxembourg	1,466	1,930	2,860

—Represents or rounds to zero. *Source:* U.S. Dept. of Agriculture, Economic Research Service. Data from Food and Agricultur Organization of the United Nations, Rome, Italy, *FOA Trade Yearbook.* From *Statistical Abstract of the United States 198!*

Passenger Car Production[1]
(in thousands, monthly averages)

Country	1987	1986	1985	1984	1983	1982	1981
Argentina[2]	—	11.7	9.6	11.9	11.0	9.2	11.5
Australia[2]	25.2	26.5	31.8	28.4	30.3	31.3	26.4
Austria	0.6	0.6	0.6	0.6	0.5	0.6	0.6
Brazil[2]	33.1	39.9	38.3	55.5	57.1	57.2	50.4
Canada	—	88.4	89.6	86.1	80.9	67.3	66.9
Czechoslovakia	14.5	15.4	15.2	15.0	14.9	14.5	15.1
France	248.5	227.7	232.0	242.5	269.0	257.2	246.1
Germany, East	18.1	18.2	17.5	16.8	15.7	15.2	15.0
Germany, West	361.7	356.1	347.1	315.3	322.9	314.3	299.2
India	12.9	10.8	7.8	7.3	5.7	5.3	5.1
Italy	142.7	136.9	112.8	119.7	116.3	108.0	104.5
Japan	657.6	650.9	637.1	589.4	596.0	573.5	581.2
Korea, South[2]	64.8	38.1	21.8	13.9	10.7	8.3	6.0
Mexico[2]	19.0	16.5	23.8	20.6	17.8	27.0	30.8
Netherlands	10.4	9.9	9.0	9.1	8.9	7.6	6.5
Poland	24.5	24.2	23.6	23.2	22.4	19.0	20.0
Romania	—	10.3	11.2	10.4	7.5	8.7	7.7
Spain	119.3	108.2	101.4	94.8	92.5	78.7	73.1
Sweden[3]	—	34.6	33.4	26.2	31.2	26.9	25.5
U.S.S.R.	108.3	109.9	111.0	110.6	109.6	108.9	110.3
United Kingdom	95.2	84.9	87.3	75.8	87.1	74.0	79.6
United States[4]	590.4	626.3	666.8	635.2	565.1	422.8	521.1
Yugoslavia	25.8[1]	17.5	19.1	15.6	14.0	13.2	15.0

1. Vehicles built on imported chassis or assembled from imported parts are excluded except for those countries marked. 2 Including assembly. 3. Deliveries. 4. Factory sales. *Source:* United Nations, *Monthly Bulletin of Statistics, January 1989.*

Meat—Production by Country
(in thousands of metric tons)

Country	1986, est.	1985	1980	Country	1986, est.	1985	1980
Argentina	3,136	3,104	3,220	Japan	2,109	2,087	1,893
Australia[1]	2,232	2,086	2,332	Mexico	2,369	2,256	1,036
Brazil	3,029	3,021	3,115	Poland	2,461	2,192	2,397
China	19,538	17,977	12,664	Soviet Union	14,385	14,023	12,698
France	3,912	3,879	3,823	United Kingdom	2,329	2,419	2,305
Germany, West	5,053	4,845	4,766	United States	17,831	17,874	17,680
Italy	2,404	2,458	2,305	World, total	114,941	112,175	103,014

Year ending June 30. NOTE: Covers beef and veal (incl. buffalo meat), pork (incl. bacon and ham), and mutton and lamb incl. goat meat). Refers to meat from animals slaughtered within the national boundaries irrespective of origin of animals, and relates to commercial and farm slaughter. In terms of carcass weight. Excludes lard, tallow, and edible offals. NOTE: Data are most recent available. *Source:* Office of the United Nations, New York, NY, *Statistical Yearbook.* (Copyright.) From: *Statistical Abstract of the United States 1989.*

Crude Steel Production and Consumption

Country	Production (mil. metric tons)			Consumption					
				Total (mil. metric tons)			Per capita (kilograms)		
	1985	1984	1983	1985	1984	1983	1985	1984	1983
Argentina	2.8	2.5	2.8	n.a.	2.7	3.6	n.a.	88	120
Australia	6.3[1]	4.6[1]	5.4[4]	5.8	5.7	4.9	336	369	318
Austria	4.7	4.9	4.4	1.8	1.9	2.0	235	257	263
Bangladesh	.1	.1	z	.5	.4	.3	5	4	3
Belgium	10.8	11.4	10.3	2.8[2]	3.6[2]	5.8	275[2]	354[2]	564[2]
Brazil	9.1	10.8	8.2	n.a.	9.3	7.9	n.a.	70	61
Bulgaria	2.9	2.9	2.8	3.0	2.9	3.2	336	323	353
Canada	13.5	14.7	128	11.9	13.2	11.0	448	479	443
China: Mainland	46.8	43.5	40.1	66.6	57.9	51.7	63	55	50
Czechoslovakia	15.0	14.8	15.0	11.0	10.8	11.1	709	700	719
France	19.1	19.0	17.6	14.2	15.2	15.0	258	276	275
Germany, East	7.9	7.6	7.2	9.5	8.9	n.a.	574	536	n.a.
Germany, West	39.2	39.3	35.7	29.3	29.9	29.8	481	489	486
Greece	1.0	.8	.9[35]	1.6	1.5	2.0	164	149	207
India	11.1	10.3	10.1	n.a.	n.a.	12.1	n.a.	n.a.	16
Italy	23.9	24.1	21.8	20.7	20.9	18.2	362	367	319
Japan	105.3	105.6	97.2	66.7	68.3	59.6	553	571	500
Korea, North	6.5	6.5	3.5[3]	8.4	6.3	6.1	413	319	320
Korea, South	4.9	5.1	5.1	n.a.	8.1	8.9	n.a.	198	222
Mexico	7.2	7.3	6.7	8.3	8.6	7.5	105	113	100
Netherlands	3.4	3.5	2.9	4.2	4.2	3.4	305	295	237
Nigeria	.3	.2	.1[5]	.9	.6	.9	9	7	10
Poland	15.4	15.2	16.2	15.2	15.3	14.9	409	416	406
Romania	13.8	14.4	12.6	10.9	11.5	10.9	480	509	482
South Africa	8.6	7.8	7.0[5]	n.a.	5.4[6]	4.6	n.a.	172[6]	130
Soviet Union	154.7	154.2	152.5	n.a.	n.a.	n.a.	n.a.	n.a.	n.a.
Spain	14.7	13.4	13.3	9.9	6.5	9.3	257	170	244
Sweden	4.9	4.7	4.2[5]	3.2	3.7	3.5	384	441	419
Turkey	3.1	2.8	2.5	n.a.	5.1	4.2	n.a.	105	88
United Kingdom	15.7	15.1	5.0	14.4	14.4	14.1	254	255	249
United States	80.1[4]	83.9[4]	76.8[4]	107.3	113.3	94.5	448	479	403
Venezuela	3.1	2.8	2.2[5]	3.2	3.0	2.6	186	177	158
Yugoslavia	2.1	2.0	2.0	5.1	5.0	5.3	221	217	231
World	678.9	677.1	642.0	n.a.	n.a.	n.a.	n.a.	n.a.	n.a.

Year ending June 30. 2. Luxembourg included with Belgium. 3. Data from U.S. Bureau of Mines. 4. Excludes steel for castings made in foundries operated by producers not producing ingots. 5. Estimated. 6. Includes Botswana, Lesotho, Namibia, and Swaziland. n.a. = not available. Z less than 50,000 metric tons. NOTE: Production data cover both ingots and steel for castings and exclude wrought (puddled) iron. Consumption data represent apparent consumption (i.e. production plus imports minus exports) and do not take into account changes in stock. *Source:* Statistical Office of the United Nations, New York, NY, *Statistical Yearbook.* (Copyright.) NOTE: Figures are latest available.

Sugar—A New Energy Resource

More sugar cane is grown every year than any other crop. It also produces a sizable pile of agricultural waste, but newly emerging technologies for converting this waste into usable energy can become an important source of electric power for the developing world, according to *World-Watch* magazine.

Value of Exports and Imports
(in millions of U.S. dollars)

Country	Exports[1]	Imports[1]	Country	Exports[1]	Imports
Afghanistan	552[2]	1,404[2]	Libya	10,841[5]	—[5]
Algeria	8,186[3]	7,029[3]	Madagascar	332[3]	302
Argentina	6,360[3]	5,818[3]	Malawi	295	412
Australia	32,734	33,245	Malaysia	20,771	16,585
Austria	31,088	36,608	Mali	260[3]	493[3]
Bahamas	2,545[3]	3,233[3]	Malta	604[3]	1,138[3]
Bahrain	2,384[3]	2,717[3]	Mauritania	428[3]	382
Bangladesh	1,194[3]	2,419[3]	Mauritius	901[3]	1,013[3]
Barbados	176	582	Mexico	20,658	18,954
Belgium-Luxembourg	92,786	92,578	Morocco	2,827[3]	4,230[3]
Benin	167[4]	288[4]	Myanmar	138	244
Bolivia	598	595	Netherlands	103,561	99,800
Brazil	26,225[3]	15,061[3]	New Zealand	8,806	7,305
Bulgaria	17,223	16,582	Nicaragua	247[2]	770[3]
Burkina Faso	83[2]	405[2]	Nigeria	7,383[3]	3,917[3]
Burundi	153	204	Norway	22,509	23,221
Cameroon	924	1,271	Oman	3,776[3]	1,823[3]
Canada	112,855	107,742	Pakistan	4,497	6,590
Cape Verde	4[2]	110[2]	Panama	280	678
Central African Republic	131[2]	252[2]	Papua-New Guinea	1,399	1,164
Chile	7,048	4,924	Paraguay	379[3]	590[3]
Colombia	4,642	3,907	Peru	2,672	2,556
Congo	673[2]	528[2]	Phillippines	7,035	8,731
Costa Rica	1,189	1,409	Poland	13,960	12,243
Cuba	5,401[3]	7,612[3]	Portugal	10,526	15,855
Cyprus	608[3]	1,484[3]	Qatar	—[3]	1,161
Czechoslovakia	24,946	24,251	Romania	12,543[2]	10,590[3]
Denmark	27,879	26,514	Rwanda	101	368
Dominican Republic	720[3]	1,782[3]	Saudi Arabia	20,085[2]	19,113[3]
Ecuador	2,165	1,714	Senegal	606[3]	1,023[3]
Egypt	4,352[3]	16,226[3]	Sierra Leone	132[3]	137
El Salvador	591[3]	994[3]	Singapore	39,305	43,862
Ethiopia	358[3]	1,102[3]	Solomon Islands	67[2]	63
Fiji	343	454	Somalia	91[5]	112
Finland	22,151	21,843	Spain	40,067	60,576
France	162,988	177,518	Sri Lanka	1,466	2,227
Gabon	1,271[2]	866[2]	Sudan	504[3]	—
Gambia	35[2]	100[2]	Suriname	241[2]	244
Germany, East	29,870[3]	28,786[3]	Sweden	50,010	45,851
Germany, West	322,524	248,880	Switzerland	50,733	56,384
Ghana	909[3]	919[3]	Syria	1,345	2,231
Greece	6,535[3]	13,056[3]	Tanzania	282[3]	928
Guatemala	419[3]	592[3]	Thailand	11,546[3]	12,849
Guyana	243[3]	—[3]	Togo	242	487
Haiti	153[3]	—[3]	Tonga	7[3]	48
Honduras	854[2]	875[2]	Trinidad	1,405	1,123
Hungary	9,971	9,366	Tunisia	2,395	3,688
Iceland	1,424	1,574	Turkey	10,127[3]	14,149
India	11,596[3]	16,754[3]	Uganda	386[4]	—
Indonesia	17,136[3]	12,370[3]	U.S.S.R.	110,559	107,229
Iran	12,378[5]	—[5]	United Arab Emirates	—[3]	8,055
Iraq	9,785[6]	6,636[6]	U.K.	145,151	189,471
Ireland	18,738	15,568	U.S.	321,843	459,494
Israel	9,145	12,506	Uruguay	1,405	1,177
Italy	137,114	138,665	Vanuatu	18[3]	70
Ivory Coast	3,110[3]	2,241[3]	Venezuela	8,402[3]	7,951
Jamaica	821	1,433	Western Samoa	15	75
Japan	264,959	187,343	Yemen, Democratic	29[2]	483
Jordan	734[3]	2,703[3]	Yemen, Arab	8[5]	1,123
Kenya	961[3]	1,756[3]	Yugoslavia	12,597	13,154
Korea, South	60,696	51,811	Zaire	970[3]	756
Kuwait	8,357[3]	5,299[3]	Zambia	—	835
Liberia	382[3]	308[3]	Zimbabwe	1,419[3]	1,046

1. 1988 unless otherwise indicated. 2. 1986. 3. 1987. 4. 1984. 5. 1985. 6. 1983. *Source:* United Nations, *Monthly Bulletin of Statistics,* July 1989.

COUNTRIES OF THE WORLD

AFGHANISTAN

Republic of Afghanistan
President: Lt. Gen. Najibullah (1986)
Area: 250,000 sq mi. (647,500 sq km)
Population (est. mid-1988): 14,800,000 (Average annual rate of natural increase: 2.6%)
Density per square mile: 59
Capital: Kabul
Largest cities (est. 1983): Kabul, 750,000; Kandahar, 225,000; Herat, 150,000
Monetary unit: Afghani
Languages: Pushtu and Dari Persian (both official)
Religion: Islam (Sunni, 74%; Shiite, 25%; other 1%)
National name: Jamhouri Afghanistan
Literacy rate: 12%
Economic summary: Gross national product (1986): $3.08 billion, $220 per capita. Average annual growth rate (1976–79): 2.5%. Land used for agriculture: 58%; labor force: 68%; principal products: wheat, cotton, fruits, nuts, wool. Labor force in industry: 10%; major products: carpets and textiles. Natural resources: natural gas, oil, coal, copper, sulfur, lead, zinc, iron, salt, precious and semi-precious stones. Exports: fresh and dried fruits, nuts, natural gas, carpets. Imports: petroleum products and food supplies. Major trading partners: U.S.S.R., Soviet bloc countries, Japan, and China.

Geography. Afghanistan, approximately the size of Texas, lies wedged between the U.S.S.R., China, Pakistan, and Iran. The country is split east to west by the Hindu Kush mountain range, rising in the east to heights of 24,000 feet (7,315 m). With the exception of the southwest, most of the country is covered by high snow-capped mountains and is traversed by deep valleys.

Government. A Marxist "people's republic" was created by Noor Taraki's coup of April 27, 1978. In May 1986, Lt. Gen. Najibullah, head of the secret police, became general secretary of the Central Committee of the People's Democratic Party of Afghanistan, replacing Babrak Karmal. Najibullah became President in Nov. 1986.

History. Darius I and Alexander the Great were the first conquerors to use Afghanistan as the gateway to India. Islamic conquerors arrived in the 7th century and Genghis Khan and Tamerlane followed in the 13th and 14th centuries.

In the 19th century, Afghanistan became a battleground in the rivalry of imperial Britain and Czarist Russia for the control of Central Asia. The Afghan Wars (1838–42 and 1878–81) fought against the British by Dost Mohammed and his son and grandson ended in defeat.

Afghanistan regained autonomy by the Anglo-Russian agreement of 1907 and full independence by the Treaty of Rawalpindi in 1919. Emir Amanullah founded the kingdom in 1926.

Taraki's attempts to create a Marxist state with Soviet aid brought armed resistance from conservative Muslim opposition.

Taraki was succeeded by Prime Minister Hafizullah Amin. Amin was replaced by Babrak Karmal, who had called for Soviet troops under a mutual defense treaty. Pakistan and other Moslem nations called for a U.N. Security Council session and charged that Amin had been executed on Dec.

27 by Soviet troops already present in Kabul. The Council's call for immediate withdrawal of Soviet troops was vetoed by the U.S.S.R. on Jan. 8, 1980.

The Soviet invasion was met with unanticipated fierce resistance from the Afghan population, resulting in a bloody war. Soviet troops were estimated by Western sources to number about 110,000 in Afghanistan. Pitted against the Soviets' bombers, helicopter gunships, heavy artillery and mechanized infantry were upward of 90,000 Afghan tribesmen who called themselves "mujahedeen," or "holy warriors." In the early fighting, many of the guerrillas were armed only with flintlock rifles, but later they acquired more modern weapons, including rockets that they used to attack Soviet installations.

Soviet saturation bombing has demolished many villages in several regions of the country. The nation's population was reported to have shrunk by as much as one third, with at least four million having fled to Iran or Pakistan and up to one million killed in the war.

In April 1988, the U.S.S.R., U.S.A., Afghanistan, and Pakistan signed accords calling for an end to outside aid to the warring factions, in return for Soviet withdrawal by 1989. This took place in February of that year but the U.S. and the U.S.S.R. have continued to aid the warring Communist and mujahedeen factions.

ALBANIA

People's Socialist Republic of Albania
President of Presidium: Ramiz Alia (1982)
Premier: Adil Carcani (1982)
Area: 11,100 sq mi. (28,748 sq km)
Population (est. mid-1989): 3,200,000 (average annual rate of natural increase: 2.0%)
Density per square mile: 287
Capital and largest city (est. 1983): Tirana, 206,100
Monetary unit: Lek
Language: Albanian, Greek
Religions: nonreligious, 55%; Islam, 21%; atheist, 19%, Christian, 5%
National name: Republika Popullore Socialiste e Shqipërisë
Literacy rate 75%
Economic summary: Gross national product (1986 est.): $2.9 billion. Average annual growth rate (1970–78): 4.2%. Per capita income (1986 est.): $930. Land used for agriculture: 39%; labor force: 61%; principal products: wheat, corn, potatoes, sugar beets, cotton, tobacco. Labor force in industry: 40%; major products: textiles, timber, construction materials, fuels, semi-processed minerals. Exports: minerals, metals, fuels, foodstuffs, agricultural materials. Imports: machinery, equipment, and spare parts, minerals, metals, fuels, construction materials, foodstuffs. Major trading partners: Greece, Yugoslavia, Czechoslovakia, Poland, Hungary, Bulgaria, Romania, W. and E. Germany, France, Italy

Geography. Albania is situated on the eastern shore of the Adriatic Sea, with Yugoslavia to the north and east and Greece to the south. Slightly larger than Maryland, it is a mountainous country, mostly over 3,000 feet (914 m) above sea level, with a narrow, marshy coastal plain crossed by several rivers. The centers of population are contained in the interior mountain plateaus and basins.

Government. Albania is ruled by the Albanian Workers (Communist) Party, headed by a Politburo which hands down all policy decisions. President Ramiz Alia became First Secretary of the party and the Politburo upon the death in 1985 of Enver Hoxha, who wielded absolute power for four decades.

History. Albania proclaimed its independence on Nov. 28, 1912, after a history of Roman, Byzantine, and Turkish domination.

Largely agricultural, Albania is one of the poorest countries in Europe. A battlefield in World War I, after the war it became a republic in which a conservative Moslem landlord, Ahmed Zogu, proclaimed himself President in 1925, and then proclaimed himself King Zog I in a monarchy in 1928. He ruled until Italy annexed Albania in 1939. Communist guerrillas under Enver Hoxha seized power in 1944, near the end of World War II.

His regime closed all of the nation's 2,169 churches and mosques in 1967 in a move to make Albania "the first atheist state in the world."

Hoxha died on April 11, 1985, at the age of 78. His successor as Communist party chief was Ramiz Alia, 59, who had been President since 1982.

ALGERIA

Democratic and Popular Republic of Algeria
President: Chadli Bendjedid (1979)
Prime Minister: Kasdi Merbah (1988)
Area: 919,595 sq mi. (2,381,751 sq km)
Population (est. mid-1989): 24,900,000 (average annual rate of natural increase: 3.2%)
Density per square mile: 27
Capital: Algiers
Largest cities (est. 1987): Algiers, 1,483,000; Oran, 590,000; Constantine, 438,000; Annaba, 310,000
Monetary unit: Dinar
Languages: Arabic (official), French, Berber
Religion: Islam (Sunni)
National name: République Algérienne Democratique et Populaire—El Djemhouria El Djazaïria Demokratia Echaabia
Literacy rate 80%
Economic summary: Gross domestic product (est. 1986): $59 billion, $2,600 per capita. Real growth rate: 2%. Land used for agriculture: 16%; labor force: 30%; principal products: wheat, barley, oats, wine, citrus fruits, olives, livestock. Labor force in industry: 40%; major products: petroleum, gas, petrochemicals, fertilizers, iron and steel, textiles, transport equipment. Natural resources: petroleum, natural gas, iron ore, phosphates, lead, zinc, mercury, uranium. Exports: petroleum and gas, iron, wine, phosphates. Imports: food, capital and consumer goods. Major trading partners: U.S., West Germany, France, Italy, Belgium, Netherlands, Canada.

Geography. Nearly four times the size of Texas, Algeria is bordered on the west by Morocco and on the east by Tunisia and Libya. To the south are Mauritania, Mali, and Niger. Low plains cover small areas near the Mediterranean coast, with 68% of the country a plateau between 2,625 and 5,250 feet (800 and 1,600 m) above sea level. The highest point is Mount Tahat in the Sahara, which rises 9,850 feet (3,000 m).

Government. Algeria is governed by the President whose term runs for 5 years. A new Constitution was approved on Feb. 23, 1989.

A National Popular Assembly of 295 members exercises legislative power, serving for a five-year term. The National Liberation Front, which led the struggle for independence from France, is the only legal party.

History. As ancient Numidia, Algeria became a Roman colony at the close of the Punic Wars (146 B.C.). Conquered by the Vandals about A.D. 440, it fell from a high state of civilization to virtual barbarism, from which it partly recovered after invasion by the Moslems about 650.

In 1492 the Moors and Jews, who had been expelled from Spain, settled in Algeria. Falling under Turkish control in 1518, Algiers served for three centuries as the headquarters of the Barbary pirates. The French took Algeria in 1830 and made it a part of France in 1848.

On July 5, 1962, Algeria was proclaimed independent. In October 1963, Ahmed Ben Bella was elected President. He began to nationalize foreign holdings and aroused opposition. He was overthrown in a military coup on June 19, 1965, by Col. Houari Boumediène, who suspended the Constitution and sought to restore financial stability.

Boumediène died in December 1978 after a long illness. Chadli Bendjedid, Secretary-General of the National Liberation Front, took the presidency in a smooth transition of power. On July 4, 1979, he released from house arrest former President Ahmed Ben Bella, who had been confined for 14 years since his overthrow.

Algeria, chosen by Iran to represent it in negotiations in November 1980 with the United States, was able to secure the eventual release of 52 Americans who had been held hostage in the U.S. Embassy in Teheran. The hostages were flown to Algiers on Jan. 20, 1981, and turned over to U.S. custody, ending 444 days in captivity.

ANDORRA

Principality of Andorra
Episcopal Co-Prince: Msgr. Joan Martí y Alanis, Bishop of Seo de Urgel, Spain
French Co-Prince: François Mitterrand, President of France (1981)
First Syndic: Francesc Cerqueda Pasquet (1982)
Area: 175 sq mi. (453 sq km)
Population (est. 1988): 49,422 (average annual growth rate: 2.75%)
Density per square mile: 282
Capital (est. 1986): Andorra la Vella, 15,639
Monetary units: French franc and Spanish peseta
Languages: Catalán (official); French, Spanish
Religion: Roman Catholic
National names: Les Vallées d'Andorre-Valls d'Andorra
Literacy rate 100%
Economic summary: Land used for agriculture: 58%; labor force: 20%; principal products: oats, barley, cattle, sheep. Labor force in industry: 80%; major products: tobacco products and electric power; tourism. Natural resources: water power, mineral water. Major trading partners: Spain and France.

Geography. Andorra lies high in the Pyrenees

Mountains on the French-Spanish border. The country is drained by the Valira River.

Government. A General Council of 28 members, elected for four years, chooses the First Syndic and Second Syndic. In 1976 the Andorran Democratic Party, the principality's first political party, was formed.

History. An autonomous and semi-independent co-principality, Andorra has been under the joint suzerainty of the French state and the Spanish bishops of Urgel since 1278.

ANGOLA

People's Republic of Angola
President: José Eduardo dos Santos (1979)
Area: 481,350 sq mi. (1,246,700 sq km)
Population (est. mid-1989): 8,500,000 (average annual rate of natural increase: 2.6%)
Density per square mile: 18
Capital and largest city (est. 1983): Luanda, 525,000
Monetary unit: Kwanza
Languages: Bantu, Portuguese (official)
Religions: Roman Catholic, 69%; Protestant, 20%; traditional, 10%
Literacy rate: 20%
Economic summary: Gross domestic product (1987 est.): $4.7 billion. $600 per capita; stagnant growth. Principal agricultural products: coffee, sisal, corn, cotton, sugar, tobacco, bananas, cassava. Major industrial products: oil, diamonds, processed fish, tobacco, textiles, cement, processed food and sugar, brewing. Natural resources: diamonds, gold, iron, oil. Exports: oil, coffee, diamonds, fish and fish products, iron ore, timber, corn. Imports: machinery and electrical equipment, bulk iron, steel and metals, textiles, clothing, food. Major trading partners: Brazil, U.S.S.R., Cuba, Portugal, U.S.

Geography. Angola, more than three times the size of California, extends for more than 1,000 miles (1,-609 km) along the South Atlantic in southwestern Africa. Zaire is to the north and east; Zambia to the east, and South-West Africa (Namibia) to the south. A plateau averaging 6,000 feet (1,829 m) above sea level rises abruptly from the coastal lowlands. Nearly all the land is desert or savanna, with hardwood forests in the northeast.

Government. A Marxist "people's republic" is the recognized government, but large areas in the east and south are held by the Union for the Total Independence of Angola (Unita), led by Jonas Savimbi. President José Eduardo dos Santos heads the official party, the Popular Movement for the Liberation of Angola-Workers Party. The Popular Movement won out over Savimbi's group and a third element in an internal struggle after Portugal granted its former colony independence on Nov. 11, 1975. Elections promised at the time of independence have never taken place, and the government relies heavily on Soviet support and Cuban troops, while Savimbi receives aid from South Africa and the U.S.

History. Discovered by the Portuguese navigator Diego Cao in 1482, Angola became a link in trade with India and the Far East. Later it was a major source of slaves for Portugal's New World colony of Brazil. Development of the interior began after the Treaty of Berlin in 1885 fixed the colony's borders, and British and Portuguese investment pushed mining, railways, and agriculture.

Following World War II, independence movements began but were sternly suppressed by military force. The April revolution of 1974 brought about a reversal of Portugal's policy, and the next year President Francisco da Costa Gomes signed an agreement to grant independence to Angola. The plan called for election of a constituent assembly and a settlement of differences by the MPLA and the National Front for the Liberation of Angola (FNLA) and the National Union for the Total Independence of Angola (UNITA).

The Organization of African Unity, recognized the MPLA government led by Agostinho Neto on Feb. 11, 1976, and the People's Republic of Angola became the 47th member of the organization.

Although militarily victorious, Neto's regime had yet to consolidate its power in opposition strongholds in the east and south.

In March 1977 and May 1978, Zairean refugees in Angola invaded Zaire's Shaba Province, bringing charges by Zairean President Mobutu Sese Seko that the unsuccessful invasions were Soviet-backed with Angolan help. Angola, the U.S.S.R., and Cuba denied complicity.

Neto died in Moscow of cancer on Sept. 10, 1979. The Planning Minister, José Eduardo dos Santos, was named President.

The South-West Africa People's Organization, or Swapo, the guerrillas fighting for the independence of the disputed territory south of Angola also known as Namibia, fought from bases in Angola and the South African armed forces also maintained troops there both to fight the SWAPO guerrillas and to assist the UNITA guerrillas against Angolan and Cuban troops.

In February 1986, President Reagan, following a repeal of an earlier ban on military aid to Joseph Savimbi's UNITA rebels, resumed military aid.

In December 1988, Angola, Cuba, and South Africa signed agreements calling for Cuban withdrawal from Angola and South African withdrawal from Namibia by July 1991 and independence for Namibia. In June 1989, the Angolan government and UNITA agreed on a truce.

ANTIGUA AND BARBUDA

Sovereign: Queen Elizabeth II
Governor-General: Sir Wilfred E. Jacobs (1981)
Prime Minister: Vere Bird (1981)
Area: 170 sq mi. (442 sq km)
Population (est. mid-1988): 80,000 (average annual growth rate: 1%)
Density per square mile: 377
Capital and largest city (est. 1983): St. John's, 30,000
Monetary unit: East Caribbean dollar
Language: English
Religions: Anglican and Roman Catholic
Literacy rate: 90%
Member of Commonwealth of Nations
Economic summary: Gross national product (1986): $130 million. Average annual growth rate (1983–86): 7%. Per capita income (1986): $1,750. Land used for agriculture: 25%; principal product: cotton. Major industry: tourism. Exports: clothing, rum, lobsters. Imports: fuel, food, machinery. Major trading partners: U.K., U.S.

Geography. Antigua, the larger of the two main islands located 295 miles (420 km) south-southeast of San Juan, P.R., is low-lying except for a range of hills in the south that rise to their highest point at Boggy Peak (1,330 ft; 405 m). As a result of its relative flatness, Antigua suffers from cyclical drought, despite a mean annual rainfall of 44 inches. Barbuda is a coral island, well-wooded.

Government. Executive power is held by the Cabinet, presided over by Prime Minister Vere C. Bird. A 17-member Parliament is elected by universal suffrage. The Antigua Labour Party, led by Prime Minister Bird, holds 15 seats and the remaining one is held by an independent member, H. Frank, who has been appointed opposition leader.

History. Antigua was discovered by Christopher Columbus in 1493 and named for the Church of Santa Maria la Antigua in Seville. Colonized by Britain in 1632, it joined the West Indies Federation in 1958. With the breakup of the Federation, it became one of the West Indies Associated States in 1967, self-governing in internal affairs. Full independence was granted Nov. 1, 1981.

ARGENTINA

Argentine Republic
President: Carlos S. Menem (1989)
Area: 1,072,067 sq mi. (2,776,654 sq km)
Population (est. mid-1988): 31,900,000 (average annual rate of natural increase: 1.4%)
Density per square mile: 30
Capital: Buenos Aires
Largest cities (est. 1983): Buenos Aires, 3,000,000; Córdoba, 1,000,000; Rosario, 950,000; La Plafa, 450,000; San Miguel de Tucumán, 400,000
Monetary unit: Austral
Language: Spanish
Religion: Predominantly Roman Catholic
National name: República Argentina
Literacy rate 94%
Economic summary: Gross domestic product (1986): $77.2 billion; $2,150 per capita; real growth rate: 5.3%. Land used for agriculture: 65%; labor force: 12%; principal products: grains, oilseeds, livestock products. Labor force in industry: 31%; major products: processed foods, motor vehicles, consumer durables, textiles, chemicals. Natural resources: minerals, lead, zinc, tin, copper, iron, manganese oil, uranium. Exports: meats, corn, wheat, wool, hides. Imports: machinery, fuel and lubricating oils, iron and steel, chemical products. Major trading partners: U.S., Brazil, Italy, West Germany, Netherlands, Soviet Union, France, Bolivia.

Geography. With an area slightly less than one third of the United States and second in South America only to its eastern neighbor, Brazil, in size and population, Argentina is a plain, rising from the Atlantic to the Chilean border and the towering Andes peaks. Aconcagua (23,034 ft.; 7,021 m) is the highest peak in the world outside Asia. It is bordered also by Bolivia and Paraguay on the north, and by Uruguay on the east.

The northern area is the swampy and partly wooded Gran Chaco, bordering on Bolivia and Paraguay. South of that are the rolling, fertile pampas, rich for agriculture and grazing and supporting most of the population. Next southward is Patagonia, a region of cool, arid steppes with some wooded and fertile sections.

Government. Argentina is a federal union of 22 provinces, one national territory, and the Federal District. Under the Constitution of 1853 (restored by a Constituent National Convention in 1957), the President and Vice President are elected every six years by popular vote through an electoral college. The President appoints his Cabinet. The Vice President presides over the Senate but has no other powers. The Congress consists of two houses: a 46-member Senate and a 254-member Chamber of Deputies.

History. Discovered in 1516 by Juan Díaz de Solís, Argentina developed slowly under Spanish colonial rule. Buenos Aires was settled in 1580; the cattle industry was thriving as early as 1600.

Invading British forces were expelled in 1806–07, and when Napoleon conquered Spain, the Argentinians set up their own government in the name of the Spanish King in 1810. On July 9, 1816, independence was formally declared.

As in World War I, Argentina proclaimed neutrality at the outbreak of World War II, but in the closing phase declared war on the Axis on March 27, 1945, and became a founding member of the United Nations. Juan D. Perón, an army colonel, emerged as the strongman of the postwar era, winning the Presidential elections of 1946 and 1951.

Opposition to Perón's increasing authoritarianism, led to a coup by the armed forces that sent Perón into exile in 1955. Argentina entered a long period of military dictatorships with brief intervals of constitutional government.

The former dictator returned to power in 1973 and his wife was elected Vice-President.

After Peron's death in 1974, his widow became the hemisphere's first woman chief of state, but was deposed in 1976 by a military junta.

In December 1981, Lt. Gen. Leopoldo Galtieri, commander of the army, was named president.

On April 2, 1982, Galtieri landed thousands of troops on the Falkland Islands on and reclaimed the Malvinas, their Spanish name, as national territory. By May 21, 5,000 British marines and para troops landed from the British armada, and regained control of the islands.

Galtieri resigned three days after the surrender of the island garrison on June 14. Maj. Gen. Reynaldo Bignone, took office as President on July 1. Civilian rule was promised by early 1984 and on July 16 Bignone lifted the six-year ban on political parties.

In the presidential election of October 1983, Raúl Alfonsín, leader of the middle-class Radical Civic Union, handed the Peronist Party its first defeat since its founding.

Among the enormous problems facing Alfonsín after eight years of mismanagement under military rule was a $45-billion foreign debt, the developing world's third largest. In some circles, fears were voiced that the new civilian government might repudiate the debt, triggering a wholesale repudiation by debtor countries that could bring on worldwide financial collapse. But after cliffhanging negotiations with American, European and Japanese banks representing the country's private creditors, the Alfonsín government agreed on June 29, 1984, to pay $350 million in overdue interest and was moving toward austerity measures.

With the arrears mounting at the rate of $150 million a month, the debt to foreign creditors mounted to $48 billion by mid-1985, and more than $1 billion was past due. On June 11, the Alfonsín government reached agreement with the International Monetary Fund on an austerity program designed to put Argentina into a position to pay its way internationally and keep current with its debt obligations. The agreement opened the door for up to $1.2 billion of new loans to Argentina. A key requirement of the pact was that inflation, which had been running at 1,010%, be brought down to 150% by April 1986.

Three days later, on June 14, President Alfonsin announced an "economy of war" to bring the inflation rate down. The program combined the creation of a new currency—the austral, meaning southern—to replace the peso, wage and price controls and a halt to the government's deficit spending. In April 1986, the austral was devalued to spur exports.

Twin economic problems of growing unemployment and quadruple-digit inflation led to a Peronist victory in the elections of May 1989. Inflation of food prices led to riots that induced Alfonsin to step down in June 1989, six months early, in favor of the Peronist, Carlos Menem.

AUSTRALIA

Commonwealth of Australia
Sovereign: Queen Elizabeth II
Governor-General: William Hayden (1989)
Prime Minister: Robert J. L. Hawke (1983)
Area: 2,966,150 sq mi. (7,682,300 sq km)
Population (est. mid-1988): 16,800,000 (average annual rate of natural increase: 0.8%)
Density per square mile: 6
Capital (est. 1986): Canberra, 289,000
Largest cities (est. 1985 for metropolitan area): Sydney, 3,531,000; Melbourne, 2,965,900; Brisbane, 1,215,-000; Adelaide, 1,013,000; Perth, 1,083,400
Monetary unit: Australian dollar
Language: English
Religions: Roman Catholic, 28%; Anglican, 28%; Uniting Church (combined Methodist-Presbyterian), 14%
Literacy rate: 99%
Member of Commonwealth of Nations
Economic summary: Gross domestic product (1986): $196 billion, $12,190 per capita; average annual real growth rate (1986): 1.25% Land used for agriculture: 64%; labor force: 6% (1986); principal products: wool, meat, cereals, sugar, sheep, cattle, dairy products. Labor force in industry: 16% (1986); major products: machinery, motor vehicles, iron and steel, chemicals. Natural resources: iron ore, bauxite, zinc, lead, tin, coal, oil, gas, copper, nickel, uranium. Exports: wheat, wool, coal. Imports: meat; iron ore; capital equipment. Major trading partners: Japan, U.S., U.K., New Zealand, West Germany, ASEAN.

Geography. The continent of Australia, with the island state of Tasmania, is approximately equal in area to the United States (excluding Alaska and Hawaii), and is nearly 50% larger than Europe (excluding the U.S.S.R.).

Mountain ranges run from north to south along the east coast, reaching their highest point in Mount Kosciusko (7,308 ft; 2,228 m). The western half of the continent is occupied by a desert plateau that rises into barren, rolling hills near the west coast. It includes the Great Victoria Desert to the south and the Great Sandy Desert to the north. The Great Barrier Reef, extending about 1,245 miles (2,000 km), lies along the northeast coast.

The island of Tasmania (26,178 sq mi.; 67,800 sq km) is off the southeastern coast.

Government. The Federal Parliament consists of a bicameral legislature. The House of Representatives has 148 members elected for three years by popular vote. The Senate has 76 members elected by popular vote for six years. One half of the Senate is elected every three years. Voting is compulsory at 18. Supreme federal judicial power is vested in the High Court of Australia in the Federal Courts, and in the State Courts invested by Parliament with Federal jurisdiction. The High Court consists of seven justices, appointed by the Governor-General in Council. Each of the states has its own judicial system.

History. Dutch, Portuguese, and Spanish ships sighted Australia in the 17th century; the Dutch landed at the Gulf of Carpentaria in 1606. Australia was called New Holland, Botany Bay, and New South Wales until about 1820.

Captain James Cook, in 1770, claimed possession for Great Britain.

Free settlers established six colonies: New South Wales (1786), Tasmania (then Van Diemen's Land) (1825), Western Australia (1829), South Australia (1834), Victoria (1851), and Queensland (1859).

The six colonies became states and in 1901 federated into the Commonwealth of Australia with a Constitution that incorporated British parliamentary tradition and U.S. federal experience. Australia became known for liberal legislation: free compulsory education, protected trade unionism with industrial conciliation and arbitration, the "Australian" ballot facilitating selection, the secret ballot, women's suffrage, maternity allowances, and sickness and old age pensions.

In the election of 1983, Robert Hawke, head of the Labor Party, became Prime Minister. The Labor government was reelected in a Federal election in December 1984.

By mid-1982, however, world recession was slowing the resources boom. Low resource prices were an issue in the election of 1987 but Hawke was able secure re-election on a platform of diversifying the economy.

Australian External Territories

Norfolk Island (13 sq mi.; 36.3 sq km) was placed under Australian administration in 1914. Population in 1988 was about 1,800.

The Ashmore and Cartier Islands (.8 sq mi.), situated in the Indian Ocean off the northwest coast of Australia, came under Australian administration in 1934. In 1938 the islands were annexed to the Northern Territory. On the attainment of self-government by the Northern Territory in 1978, the islands which are uninhabited were retained as Commonwealth Territory.

The Australian Antarctic Territory (2,360,000 sq mi.; 6,112,400 sq km), comprises all the islands and territories, other than Adélie Land, situated south of lat. 60° S and lying between long. 160° to 45° E. It came under Australian administration in 1936.

Heard Island and the McDonald Islands (158 sq mi.; 409.2 sq km), lying in the sub-Antarctic, were placed under Australian administration in 1947. The islands are uninhabited.

Christmas Island (52 sq mi.; 134.7 sq km) is situated in the Indian Ocean. It came under Australian administration in 1958. Population in 1988 was about 2,000.

Coral Sea Islands (400,000 sq mi.; 1,036,000 sq km, but only a few sq mi. of land) became a territory of Australia in 1969. There is no permanent population on the islands.

AUSTRIA

Republic of Austria
President: Kurt Waldheim (1986)
Chancellor: Franz Vranitzky (1986)
Area: 32,375 sq mi. (83,851 sq km)
Population (est. mid-1989): 7,600,000 (average annual rate of natural increase: 0.1%)
Density per square mile: 235
Capital: Vienna
Largest cities (est. 1983): Vienna, 1,550,000; Graz, 240,000; Linz, 200,000; Salzburg, 135,000; Innsbruck, 115,000; Klagenfurt, 85,000
Monetary unit: Schilling
Language: German
Religion: Roman Catholic, 89%
Literacy rate: 98%
National name: Republik Österreich
Economic summary: Gross national product (1988 est.): $120.3 billion, $15,800 per capita; average annual growth rate (1988): 4.2%. Land used for agriculture: 42%; principal products: livestock, forest products, grains, sugar beets, potatoes. Labor force in industry: 35%; principal products: iron and steel, chemicals, machinery, paper and pulp. Natural resources: iron ore, petroleum, timber, magnesite, aluminum, coal, lignite, cement, copper, hydropower. Exports: iron and steel products, timber, paper, textiles, electrotechnical machines, chemical products. Imports: machinery, chemicals, foodstuffs, textiles and clothing, petroleum. Major trading partners: West Germany, Italy, Switzerland, U.S., Eastern Europe.

Geography. Slightly smaller than Maine, Austria includes much of the mountainous territory of the eastern Alps (about 75% of the area). The country contains many snowfields, glaciers, and snow-capped peaks, the highest being the Grossglockner (12,530 ft; 3,819 m). The Danube is the principal river. Forests and woodlands cover about 40% of the land area.

Almost at the heart of Europe, Austria has as its neighbors Italy, Switzerland, West Germany, Czechoslovakia, Hungary, Yugoslavia, and Liechtenstein.

Government. Austria is a federal republic composed of nine provinces (Bundesländer), including Vienna. The President is elected by the people for a term of six years. The bicameral legislature consists of the Bundesrat, with 58 members chosen by the provincial assemblies, and the Nationalrat, with 183 members popularly elected for four years. Presidency of the Bundesrat revolves every six months, going to the provinces in alphabetical order.

History. Settled in prehistoric times, the Central European land that is now Austria was overrun in pre-Roman times by various tribes, including the Celts. Charlemagne conquered the area in 788 and encouraged colonization and Christianity. In 1252, Ottokar, King of Bohemia, gained possession, only to lose the territories to Rudolf of Hapsburg in 1278. Thereafter, until World War I, Austria's history was largely that of its ruling house, the Hapsburgs.

Austria emerged from the Congress of Vienna in 1815 as the Continent's dominant power. The *Ausgleich* of 1867 provided for a dual sovereignty, the empire of Austria and the kingdom of Hungary, under Francis Joseph I, who ruled until his death on Nov. 21, 1916. He was succeeded by his grand-nephew, Charles I.

During World War I, Austria-Hungary was one of the Central Powers with Germany, Bulgaria, and Turkey, and the conflict left the country in political chaos and economic ruin. Austria, shorn of Hungary, was proclaimed a republic in 1918, and the monarchy was dissolved in 1919.

A parliamentary democracy was set up by the Constitution of Nov. 10, 1920. On March 12, 1938, German troops occupied the country, and Hitler proclaimed its *Anschluss* (union) with Germany, annexing it to the Third Reich.

After World War II, the U.S. and Britain declared the Austrians a "liberated" people. But the Russians prolonged the occupation. Finally Austria concluded a state treaty with the U.S.S.R. and the other occupying powers and regained its independence on May 15, 1955. The second Austrian republic, established Dec. 19, 1945, on the basis of the 1920 Constitution (amended in 1929), was declared by the federal parliament to be permanently neutral.

Vienna has since become a headquarters for several international organizations such as OPEC.

On June 8, 1986, former UN Secretary-General Kurt Waldheim was elected to the ceremonial office of President in a campaign marked by controversy over his alleged links to Nazi war-crimes in Yugoslavia.

BAHAMAS

Commonwealth of the Bahamas
Sovereign: Queen Elizabeth II
Governor-General: Sir Henry M. Taylor (1988)
Prime Minister: Lynden O. Pindling (1967)
Area: 5,380 sq mi. (13,939 sq km)
Population (est. 1988): 242,983 (average annual rate of natural increase, 1989: 1.2%)
Density per square mile: 46
Capital and largest city (est. 1984 for metropolitan area): Nassau, 139,000
Monetary unit: Bahamian dollar
Language: English
Religions: Baptist, 29%; Anglican, 23%; Roman Catholic, 23%; Methodist, 7%
Literacy rate: 95%
Member of Commonwealth of Nations
Economic summary: Gross domestic product (1986 est.): $2.1 billion; $8,950 per capita; real growth rate, 2%. Principal agricultural products: fruits, vegetables. Major industrial products: fish, refined petroleum, pharmaceutical products; tourism. Natural resources: salt, aragonite. Exports: lobster, fish, pharmaceuticals, cement, rum. Imports: foodstuffs, manufactured goods, fuels. Major trading partners: U.S., U.K., Nigeria, Canada.

Geography. The Bahamas are an archipelago of about 700 islands and 2,400 uninhabited islets and cays lying 50 miles off the east coast of Florida. They extend from northwest to southeast for about 760 miles (1,223 km). Only 22 of the islands are inhabited; the most important is New Providence (80 sq mi.; 207 sq km), on which Nassau is situated. Other islands include Grand Bahama, Abaco, Eleuthera, Andros, Cat Island, San Salvador (or Watling's Island), Exuma, Long Island, Crooked Island, Acklins Island, Mayaguana, and Inagua.

The islands are mainly flat, few rising above 200 feet (61 m). There are no fresh water streams. There are several large brackish lakes on several islands including Inagua and New Providence.

Government. The Bahamas moved toward greater autonomy in 1968 after the overwhelming victory in general elections of the Progressive Liberal Party, led by Prime Minister Lynden O. Pindling. The black leader's party won 29 seats in the House of Assembly to only 7 for the predominantly white United Bahamians, who had controlled the islands for decades before Pindling became Premier in 1967.

With its new mandate from the 85%-black population, Pindling's government negotiated a new Constitution with Britain under which the colony became the Commonwealth of the Bahama Islands in 1969. On July 10, 1973, The Bahamas became an independent nation as the Commonwealth of the Bahamas.

In the 1987 election, Pindling's Progressive Liberal Party won 31 of 49 seats in Parliament; the Free National Movement, 16.

History. The islands were reached by Columbus in October 1492, and were a favorite pirate area in the early 18th century. The Bahamas were a crown colony from 1717 until they were granted internal self-government in 1964.

BAHRAIN

State of Bahrain
Emir: Sheik Isa ibn-Sulman al-Khalifa (1961)
Prime Minister: Sheik Khalifa bin Sulman al-Khalifa (1970)
Area: 240 sq mi. (620 sq km)
Population (est. mid-1989): 500,000 (average annual rate of natural increase: 2.8%)
Density per square mile: 1,968.5
Capital (est. 1982): Manama, 150,000
Monetary unit: Bahrain dinar
Languages: Arabic (official), English
Religion: Islam
Literacy rate : 40%
Economic summary: Gross domestic product (1984): $3.7 billion, $8,110 per capita; real growth rate (1987): 3.5%. Land used for agriculture: 10%; labor force: 5%; principal products: eggs, vegetables, fruits. Labor force in industry: 90%; major products: oil, aluminum, fish. Natural resources: oil, fish. Exports: oil, natural gas, aluminum, fish. Imports: machinery, oil-industry equipment, motor vehicles, foodstuffs. Major trading partners: Saudi Arabia, U.S., U.K., Japan.

Geography. Bahrain is an archipelago in the Persian Gulf off the coast of Saudi Arabia. The islands for the most part are level expanses of sand and rock.

Government. A new Constitution was approved in 1973. It created the first elected parliament in the country's history. Called the National Council, it consisted of 30 members elected by male citizens

for four-year terms, plus up to 16 Cabinet ministers as ex-officio members. In August 1975, the Amir dissolved the National Council.

History. A sheikdom that passed from the Persians to the al-Khalifa family from Arabia in 1782, Bahrain became, by treaty, a British protectorate in 1820. It has become a major Middle Eastern oil center and, through use of oil revenues, is one of the most developed of the Persian Gulf sheikdoms. The Emir, Sheik Isa ibn-Sulman al-Khalifa, who succeeded to the post in 1961, is a member of the original ruling family. Bahrain announced its independence on Aug. 14, 1971.

BANGLADESH

People's Republic of Bangladesh
President: H. M. Ershad (1983)
Vice President: A.K.M. Nurul Islam (1986)
Area: 55,598 sq mi. (143,998 sq km)
Population (est. mid-1988): 114,700,000 (average annual rate of natural increase: 2.8%)
Density per square mile: 2,063
Capital and largest city (est 1986): Dhaka, 4,470,000
Monetary unit: Taka
Principal languages: Bengali (official), English
Religions: Islam, (official) 83%; Hindu, 16%
Literacy rate: 29%
Member of Commonwealth of Nations
Economic summary: Gross domestic product (1985): $15.6 billion, $150 per capita; real growth rate 4.5%. Land used for agriculture: 73%; labor force, 75%; principal products: rice, jute, tea, sugar, wheat. Labor force in industry, 11%; major products: jute goods, textiles, leather, sugar, fertilizer, paper, pharmaceuticals. Natural resources: natural gas. Exports: jute goods, jute, tea, leather, garments. Imports: food grains, fuels, raw cotton, fertilizer, manufactured goods. Major trading partners: U.S., Japan, Singapore, U.K., China, India.

Geography. Bangladesh, on the northern coast of the Bay of Bengal, is surrounded by India, with a small common border with Burma in the southeast. It is approximately the size of Wisconsin. The country is low-lying riverine land traversed by the many branches and tributaries of the Ganges and Brahmaputra rivers. Elevations averages less than 600 feet (183 m) above sea level. Tropical monsoons and frequent floods and cyclones inflict heavy damage in the delta region.

Government. On Oct. 15, 1986, Ershad was elected President, in an election boycotted by the opposition, for a five-year term. Martial law ended in November. Parliamentary elections held in March 1988, though boycotted by the opposition and much of the population, gave Ershad's Jatiya Party 250 of 300 seats.

History. The former East Pakistan was part of imperial British India until Britain withdrew in 1947. The two Pakistans were united by religion (Islam), but their peoples were separated by culture, physical features, and 1,000 miles of Indian territory. Bangladesh consists primarily of East Bengal (West Bengal is part of India and its people are primarily Hindu) plus the Sylhet district of the Indian state of Assam. For almost 25 years after independence from Britain, its history was as part of Pakistan (*see* Pakistan).

The East Pakistanis unsuccessfully sought greater autonomy from West Pakistan. The first general elections in Pakistani history, in December 1970, saw virtually all 171 seats of the region (out of 300 for both East and West Pakistan) go to Sheik Mujibur Rahman's Awami League.

Attempts to write an all-Pakistan Constitution to replace the military regime of Gen. Yahya Khan failed. Yahya put down a revolt in March 1971. An estimated one million Bengalis were killed in the fighting or later slaughtered. Ten million more took refuge in India.

In December 1971, India invaded East Pakistan, routed the West Pakistani occupation forces, and created Bangladesh. In February 1974, Pakistan agreed to recognize the independence of Bangladesh.

On March 24, 1982, Gen. Hossain Mohammad Ershad, army chief of staff, took control in a bloodless coup. Ershad assumed the office of President in 1983.

BARBADOS

Sovereign: Queen Elizabeth II
Governor-General: Sir Hugh Springer (1984)
Prime Minister: L. Erskine Sandiford (1987)
Area: 166 sq. mi. (431 sq km)
Population (est. mid-1988): 257,000 (average annual rate of natural increase (1989): 1.2%.
Density per square mile: 1,560
Capital and largest city (est. 1988): Bridgetown, 102,000
Monetary unit: Barbados dollar
Language: English
Religions: Anglican, 70%; Methodist, 9%; Roman Catholic, 4%
Literacy rate: 99%
Member of Commonwealth of Nations
Economic summary: Gross domestic product (1986): $1,231 million. $4,870 per capita; real growth rate (1986): 2.5%. Land used for agriculture: 86%; principal products: sugar cane, subsistence foods. Major industrial products: light manufactures, sugar milling, tourism. Exports: sugar and sugar cane byproducts, clothing, electrical parts. Imports: foodstuffs, machinery, manufactured goods. Major trading partners: U.S., Caribbean nations, U.K., Canada.

Geography. An island in the Atlantic about 300 miles (483 km) north of Venezuela, Barbados is only 21 miles long (34 km) and 14 miles across (23 km) at its widest point. It is circled by fine beaches and narrow coastal plains. The highest point is Mount Hillaby (1,105 ft; 337 m) in the north central area.

Government. The Barbados legislature dates from 1627. It is bicameral, with a Senate of 21 appointed members and an Assembly of 27 elected members.

The major political parties are the Democratic Labor Party (24 seats in Assembly), led by Prime Minister L. Erskine Sandiford; Barbados Labor Party (3 seats), led by Henry Deb. Forde.

History. Barbados, with a population 90% black, was settled by the British in 1627. It became a crown colony in 1885. It was a member of the Federation of the West Indies from 1958 to 1962. Britain granted the colony independence on Nov. 30, 1966, and it became a parliamentary democracy.

While retaining membership in the Commonwealth of Nations and economic ties with Britain, Barbados seeks broader economic and political relations with Western Hemisphere countries. Diplomatic ties with Cuba were established in 1972.

BELGIUM

Kingdom of Belgium
Sovereign: King Baudouin I (1951)
Premier: Wilfried Martens (1981)
Area: 11,781 sq mi. (30,513 sq km)
Population (est. mid-1989): 9,900,160 (average annual rate of natural increase: 0.1%)
Density per square mile: 841
Capital: Brussels
Largest cities (est. 1986): Brussels, 976,536; Ghent, 234,251; Charleroi, 210,324; Liège, 201,749; Antwerp, 483,199; Bruges, 117,201
Monetary Unit: Belgian franc
Languages: Flemish, 57%; French, 32%; bilingual (Brussels), 10%; German, 0.7%.
Religion: Roman Catholic, 75%
National name: Royaume de Belgique—Koninkrijk van België
Literacy rate: 98%
Economic summary: Gross national product (1986): $114.9 billion, $11,650 per capita; real growth rate (1986): 2.8%. Land used for agriculture: 46%; labor force: 5%; principal products: livestock, poultry, grain, sugar beets, flax, tobacco, potatoes, vegetables, fruits. Labor force in industry: 37%; major products: fabricated metal, iron and steel, machinery, textiles, chemicals, food processing. Exports: (Belg.-Luxembourg Econ. Union) iron and steel products, chemicals, pharmaceuticals, textile products. Imports: (Belg.-Luxembourg Econ. Union) nonelectrical machinery, motor vehicles, textiles, chemicals, fuels. Major trading partners: West Germany, France, Netherlands, U.K., U.S., Italy.

Geography. A neighbor of France, West Germany, the Netherlands, and Luxembourg, Belgium has about 40 miles of seacoast on the North Sea at the Strait of Dover. In area, it is approximately the size of Maryland. The northern third of the country is a plain extending eastward from the seacoast. North of the Sambre and Meuse Rivers is a low plateau; to the south lies the heavily wooded Ardennes plateau, attaining an elevation of about 2,300 feet (700 m).

The Schelde River, which rises in France and flows through Belgium, emptying into the Schelde estuaries, enables Antwerp to be an ocean port.

Government. Belgium, a parliamentary democracy under a constitutional monarch, consists of nine provinces. Its bicameral legislature has a Senate, with its 181 members elected for four years—106 by general election, 50 by provincial councillors and 25 by the Senate itself. The 212-member Chamber of Representatives is directly elected for four years by proportional representation. There is universal suffrage, and those who do not vote are fined.

Belgium joined the North Atlantic Alliance in 1949 and is a member of the European Community. NATO and the European Community have their headquarters in Brussels.

The sovereign, Baudouin I, was born Sept. 7, 1930, the son of King Leopold III and Queen Astrid. He became King on July 17, 1951, after the abdication of his father. He married Doña Fabiola de Mora y Aragón on Dec. 15, 1960. Since he has no children, his brother, Prince Albert, is heir to the throne.

History. Belgium occupies part of the Roman province of Belgica, named after the Belgae, a people of ancient Gaul. The area was conquered by Julius Caesar in 57–50 B.C., then was overrun by the Franks in the 5th century. It was part of Charlemagne's empire in the 8th century, then in the next century was absorbed into Lotharingia and later into the Duchy of Lower Lorraine. In the 12th century it was partitioned into the Duchies of Brabant and Luxembourg, the Bishopric of Liège, and the domain of the Count of Hainaut, which included Flanders.

In the 16th century, Belgium, with most of the area of the Low Countries, passed to the Duchy of Burgundy and was the marriage portion of Archduke Maximilian of Hapsburg and the inheritance of his grandson, Charles V, who incorporated it into his empire. Then, in 1555, they were united with Spain.

By the treaty of Utrecht in 1713, the country's sovereignty passed to Austria. During the wars that followed the French Revolution, Belgium was occupied and later annexed to France. But with the downfall of Napoleon, the Congress of Vienna in 1815 gave the country to the Netherlands. The Belgians revolted in 1830 and declared their independence.

Germany's invasion of Belgium in 1914 set off World War I. The Treaty of Versailles (1919) gave the areas of Eupen, Malmédy, and Moresnet to Belgium. Leopold III succeeded Albert, King during World War I, in 1934. In World War II, Belgium was overwhelmed by Nazi Germany, and Leopold III was made prisoner. When he attempted to return in 1950, Socialists and Liberals revolted. He abdicated July 16, 1951, and his son, Baudouin, became King the next day.

Despite the increasingly strong divisions between the French- and Flemish-speaking communities, a Christian Democrat-Liberal coalition that took office in December 1981 came close to setting a record for longevity among the 32 governments that had ruled Belgium since World War II. Headed by Prime Minister Wilfried Martens—the fifth government he had led since 1979—it survived several serious political challenges, including the implementation of an unpopular economic austerity program in 1983 and the deployment of NATO cruise missiles in March 1985.

Strife between French and Flemish speakers almost toppled the government in 1986 and 1987. Elections in Dec. 1987 saw Marten's coalition barely holding on in the face of a resurgent Socialist opposition.

BELIZE

Sovereign: Queen Elizabeth II
Governor-General: Dame Minita Gordon (1981)
Prime Minister: Manuel Esquivel (1984)
Area: 8,867 sq mi. (22,965 sq km)
Population (est. mid-1989): 200,000 (average annual rate of natural increase: 3.0%)
Density per sq mi.: 20
Capital (est. 1985): Belmopan, 5,000

Largest city (est. 1985): Belize City, 47,000
Monetary unit: Belize dollar
Languages: English (official) and Spanish, Maya, Carib
Religions: Roman Catholic, 62%; Anglican, 12%; Methodist, 6%; Baha'i, 2.5%
Literacy rate: 93%
Member of Commonwealth of Nations
Economic summary: Gross domestic product (1985): $193 million, $1,190 per capita; real growth rate (1984): 1.5%. Land used for agriculture: 4%; labor force: 30%; principal products: sugar cane, citrus fruits, corn, molasses, rice, bananas, livestock. Labor force in industry: 10%; major products: timber, processed foods, furniture, rum, soap. Natural resource: timber. Exports: sugar, molasses, clothing, lumber, citrus fruits, fish. Imports: fuels, transportation equipment, foodstuffs, textiles, machinery. Major trading partners: U.S., U.K., Trinidad and Tobago, Canada.

Geography. Belize (formerly British Honduras) is situated on the Caribbean Sea south of Mexico and east and north of Guatemala. In area, it is about the size of New Hampshire. Most of the country is heavily forested with various hardwoods. Mangrove swamps and cays along the coast give way to hills and mountains in the interior. The highest point is Victoria Peak, 3,681 feet (1,122 m).

Government. Formerly the colony of British Honduras, Belize became a fully independent commonwealth on Sept. 21, 1981, after having been self-governing since 1964. Executive power is nominally wielded by Queen Elizabeth II through an appointed Governor-General but effective power is held by the Prime Minister, who is responsible to a 28-member parliament elected by universal suffrage.

History. Once a part of the Mayan empire, the area was deserted until British timber cutters began exploiting valuable hardwoods in the 17th century. Efforts by Spain to dislodge British settlers, including a major naval attack in 1798, were defeated. The territory was formally named a British colony in 1862 but administered by the Governor of Jamaica until 1884.

Guatemala has long made claims to the territory and refused to recognize Britain's efforts to grant independence to Belize. Fear of Guatemala caused many inhabitants to oppose independence until a tentative agreement was reached between Britain, Belize, and Guatemala in March 1981 that would offer access to the Caribbean through Belizean territory for Guatemala. The agreement broke down, however, and 1,600 British troops remained to protect the new state after the flag-raising ceremony on Sept. 21, 1981.

BENIN

People's Republic of Benin
President: General Mathieu Kerekou (1972)
Area: 43,483 sq mi. (112,622 sq km)
Population (est. mid-1989): 4,700,000 (average annual rate of natural increase: 3.0%)
Density per square mile: 107
Capital (est. 1984): Porto-Novo, 208,000
Largest city (est. 1982): Cotonou, 490,000
Monetary unit: Franc CFA
Ethnic groups: Fons and Adjas, Baribas, Yorubas, Mahis

Languages: French, African languages
Religions: indigenous, 70%; Christian, 15%; Islam, 15%
National name: Republique Populaire du Benin
Literacy rate (1981): 20%
Economic summary: Gross national product (1986 est.): $1.4 billion. $340 per capita; real growth rate (1986 est.): −0.2%. Per capita income (1985): $270. Labor force in agriculture: 60%; principal products: oil palms, peanuts, cotton, coffee, tobacco, corn, rice, livestock, fish. Major industrial products: processed palm oil, palm kernel oil, textiles, beverages. Natural resources: low-grade iron ore, limestone, some offshore oil. Exports: palm and agricultural products. Imports: clothing, consumer goods, lumber, fuels, foodstuffs, machinery, transportation equipment. Major trading partners: France and other Western European countries.

Geography. This West African nation on the Gulf of Guinea, between Togo on the west and Nigeria on the east, is about the size of Tennessee. It is bounded also by Burkina Faso and Niger on the north. The land consists of a narrow coastal strip that rises to a swampy, forested plateau and then to highlands in the north. A hot and humid climate blankets the entire country.

Government. The change in name from Dahomey to Benin was announced by President Mathieu Kerekou on November 30, 1975. Benin commemorates an African kingdom that flourished in the 17th century. At the same time, Kerekou announced the formation of a political organization, the Party of the People's Revolution of Benin, to mark the first anniversary of his declaration of a "new society" guided by Marxist-Leninist principles.

History. One of the smallest and most densely populated states in Africa, Benin was annexed by the French in 1893. The area was incorporated into French West Africa in 1904. It became an autonomous republic within the French Community in 1958, and on Aug. 1, 1960, was granted its independence within the Community.

Gen. Christophe Soglo deposed the first president, Hubert Maga, in an army coup in 1963. He dismissed the civilian government in 1965, proclaiming himself chief of state. A group of young army officers seized power in December 1967, deposing Soglo. They promulgated a new Constitution in 1968.

In December 1969, Benin had its fifth coup of the decade, with the army again taking power. In May 1970, a three-man presidential commission was created to take over the government. The commission had a six-year term; each member serves as president for two years. Maga turned over power as scheduled to Justin Ahomadegbe in May 1972, but six months later yet another army coup ousted the triumvirate and installed Lt. Col. Mathieu Kerekou as President.

BHUTAN

Kingdom of Bhutan
Ruler: King Jigme Singye Wangchuk (1972)
Area: 18,000 sq mi. (46,620 sq km)
Population (est. mid-1989): 1,500,000 (average annual rate of natural increase: 2.1%)
Density per square mile: 85
Capital (est. 1984): Thimphu, 30,000
Monetary unit: Ngultrum

Language: Dzongkha
Religions: Buddhist, 75%; Hindu, 25%
National name: Druk-yul
Literacy rate: 15%
Economic summary: Gross domestic product: $300 million, $218 per capita; real growth rate (1986): 6.7%. Labor force in agriculture: 95%; principal products: rice, barley, wheat, potatoes, fruit. Major industrial product: cement. Natural resources: timber, hydroelectric power. Exports: fruits and vegetables, timber, coal, cement. Imports: fuels, machinery, vehicles. Major trading partner: India.

Geography. Mountainous Bhutan, half the size of Indiana, is situated on the southeast slope of the Himalayas, bordered on the north and east by Tibet and on the south and west by India. The landscape consists of a succession of lofty and rugged mountains running generally from north to south and separated by deep valleys. In the north, towering peaks reach a height of 24,000 feet (7,315 m).

Government. Bhutan is a constitutional monarchy. The King rules with a Council of Ministers and a Royal Advisory Council. There is a National Assembly (Parliament), which meets semiannually, but no political parties.

History. British troops invaded the country in 1865 and negotiated an agreement under which Britain undertook to pay an annual allowance to Bhutan on condition of good behavior. A treaty with India in 1949 increased this subsidy and placed Bhutan's foreign affairs under Indian control.

In the 1960s, Bhutan undertook modernization, abolishing slavery and the caste system, emancipating women and enacting land reform. In 1985, Bhutan made its first diplomatic links with non-Asian countries.

BOLIVIA

Republic of Bolivia
President: Jaime Paz Zamora (1989)
Area: 424,162 sq mi. (1,098,581 sq km)
Population (est. mid-1989): 7,100,000 (average annual rate of natural increase: 2.6%. (Indian, 53%; mestizo, 32%; white, 15%)
Density per square mile: 17
Judicial capital (est. 1985): Sucre, 86,609
Administrative capital (est. 1985): La Paz, 992,592
Largest cities (est. 1985): Santa Cruz, 441,717; Cochabamba, 317,251; Oruro, 178,393
Monetary unit: Boliviano
Languages: Spanish, Quechua, Aymara
Religion: Roman Catholic, 94%; others, 3%
National name: República de Bolivia
Literacy rate: 63%
Economic summary: Gross domestic product (est. 1987): $3.87 billion. $610 per capita; real growth rate: 2.7%. Labor force in agriculture: 50%; principal products: potatoes, corn, rice, sugar cane, bananas, coffee. Labor force in industry: 19%; major products: refined petroleum, processed foods, tin, textiles, clothing. Natural resources: petroleum, natural gas, tin, lead, zinc, copper, tungsten, bismuth, antimony, gold, sulfur, silver, iron ore. Exports: tin, lead, zinc, silver, antimony, coffee, sugar, cotton, soya beans, leather, citrus, natural gas. Imports: foodstuffs, chemicals, capital goods, pharmaceuticals, transport equipment. Major trading partners: U.S., Argentina, U.K., Brazil, Netherlands.

Geography. Landlocked Bolivia, equal in size to California and Texas combined, lies to the west of Brazil. Its other neighbors are Peru and Chile on the west and Argentina and Paraguay on the south.

The country is a low alluvial plain throughout 60% of its area toward the east, drained by the Amazon and Plata river systems. The western part, enclosed by two chains of the Andes, is a great plateau—the Altiplano, with an average altitude of 12,000 feet (3,658 m). More than 80% of the population lives on the plateau, which also contains La Paz. At an altitude of 11,910 feet (3,630 m), it is the highest capital city in the world.

Lake Titicaca, half the size of Lake Ontario, is one of the highest large lakes in the world, at an altitude of 12,507 feet (3,812 m). Islands in the lake hold ruins of the ancient Incas.

Government. President Victor Paz Estensoro was inaugurated on Aug. 7, 1985, after the Congress, at a raucous session, chose him over Hugo Banzer, the candidate who had received the most votes in a popular election on July 14. Banzer won 28.6% of the 1.7 million votes tallied and Paz won 26.4%. Under the Constitution, if no Presidential candidate receives 50% of the vote, Congress chooses between the top two vote-getters.

History. Famous since Spanish colonial days for its mineral wealth, modern Bolivia was once a part of the ancient Incan Empire. After the Spaniards defeated the Incas in the 16th century, Bolivia's predominantly Indian population was reduced to slavery. The country won its independence in 1825 and was named after Simón Bolívar, the famed liberator.

Since 1825 Bolivia has had more than 60 revolutions, 70 Presidents, and 11 Constitutions.

Harassed by internal strife, Bolivia lost great slices of territory to three neighbor nations. Several thousand square miles and its outlet to the Pacific were taken by Chile after the War of the Pacific (1879–84). In 1903 a piece of Bolivia's Acre province, rich in rubber, was ceded to Brazil. And in 1938, after a war with Paraguay, Bolivia gave up claim to nearly 100,000 square miles of the Gran Chaco.

In 1965 a guerrilla movement mounted from Cuba and headed by Maj. Ernesto (Ché) Guevara began a revolutionary war. With the aid of U.S. military advisers, the Bolivian army, helped by the peasants, smashed the guerrilla movement, wounding and capturing Guevara on Oct. 8, 1967, and shooting him to death the next day.

Faltering steps toward restoration of civilian government were halted abruptly on July 17, 1980, when Gen. Luis Garcia Meza Tejada seized power. A series of military leaders followed before the military moved, in 1982, to return the government to civilian rule. Hernán Siles Zuazo was inaugurated President on Oct. 10, 1982.

Under Siles' left-of-center government, the country was regularly shut down by work stoppages, the bulk of Bolivia's natural resources—natural gas, gold, lithium, potassium and tungsten—were either sold on the black market or left in the ground, the country had the lowest per-capita income in South America, and inflation approached 3,000 percent. In 1985, the 73-year-old Siles decided he was unable to carry on and quit a year early.

No candidate won a majority in the elections in 1985 and Victor Paz Estensoro, 77, was picked by Congress to become President. During his administration, inflation continued to rise and the currency collapsed. Drastic economic measures were taken toward the end of the year, including a wage freeze and a cutback of government price subsidies, which lowered the inflation rate to about 276%. The economy showed signs of growth in 1987, for the first time since 1980.

BOPHUTHATSWANA

See South Africa

BOTSWANA

Republic of Botswana
President: Quett K. Masire (1980)
Area: 231,800 sq mi. (600,360 sq km)
Population (est. mid-1986): 1,200,000 (average annual rate of natural increase: 3.4%)
Density per square mile: 5
Capital and largest city (est. 1984): Gaborone, 79,000
Monetary unit: Pula
Languages: English, Setswana
Religions: Christian, 48%; traditional, 49%
Member of Commonwealth of Nations
Literacy rate: 59%
Economic summary: Gross domestic product (FY1985): $905 million, $880 per capita; real growth rate (FY1985): 6%. Land used for agriculture: 77%; principal products: livestock, sorghum, corn, millet, cowpeas, beans. Major industrial products: diamonds, copper, nickel, salt, soda ash, potash, coal, frozen beef; tourism. Natural resources: diamonds, copper, nickel, salt, soda ash, potash, coal, natural gas. Exports: diamonds, cattle, animal products, copper, nickel. Imports: foodstuffs, vehicles, textiles, petroleum products. Major trading partners: South Africa, U.K., U.S., Switzerland.

Geography. Twice the size of Arizona, Botswana is in south central Africa, bounded by South-West Africa, Zambia, Zimbabwe, and South Africa. Most of the country is near-desert, with the Kalahari occupying the western part of the country. The eastern part is hilly, with salt lakes in the north.

Government. The Botswana Constitution provides, in addition to the unicameral National Assembly, for a House of Chiefs, which has a voice on bills affecting tribal affairs. There is universal suffrage.

The major political parties are the Democratic Party (29 of 34 elective seats in 36-man Legislative Assembly), led by President Quett Masire; National Front (4 seats), led by Kenneth Koma; People's Party (1 seat), led by Kenneth Nkhwa.

History. Botswana is the land of the Batawana tribes, which, when threatened by the Boers in Transvaal, asked Britain in 1885 to establish a protectorate over the country, then known as Bechuanaland. In 1961, Britain granted a Constitution to the country. Self-government began in 1965, and on Sept. 30, 1966, the country became independent. Since 1975, it has been an associate member of the European Common Market.

BRAZIL

Federative Republic of Brazil
President: José Sarney (1985)[1]
Area: 3,286,470 sq mi. (8,511,957 sq km)
Population (est. mid-1989): 147,400,000 (average annual
rate of natural increase: 2.0%) (approx.: white, 60%;
mestizo, 26%; black, 11%)
Density per square mile: 45
Capital: Brasilia, (est. 1985) 1,576,657
Largest cities (est. 1985): São Paulo, 10,099,086; Rio de
Janeiro, 5,615,149; Salvador, 1,811,367; Belo
Horizonte, 2,122,073; Recife, 1,289,627; Porto Alegre,
1,275,483
Monetary unit: Cruzado
Language: Portuguese
Religion: Roman Catholic, 88%; Protestant, 6%
National name: República Federativa de Brasil
Literacy rate: 74%
Economic summary: Gross national product (1986): $270
billion, $1,880 per capita; real growth rate (1986):
8.2%. Land used for agriculture; 27%; labor force: 35%;
principal products: coffee, sugar cane, oranges, cocoa,
soybeans, tobacco, cattle. Labor force in industry: 25%;
major products: steel, chemicals, petrochemicals,
machinery, motor vehicles, cement, lumber. Natural
resources: iron ore, manganese, bauxite, nickel, other
industrial metals, hydropower, timber. Exports: coffee,
iron ore, soybeans, sugar, beef, transport equipment,
footwear, orange juice. Imports: wheat, copper, petroleum,
machinery, chemicals, pharmaceuticals. Major trading
partners: U.S., West Germany, Japan, Saudi Arabia.

Geography. Brazil covers nearly half of South
America, extends 2,965 miles (4,772 km) north-
south, 2,691 miles (4,331 km), east-west, and borders every nation on the continent except Chile
and Ecuador. It is the fifth largest country in the
world, ranking after the U.S.S.R., Canada, China,
and the U.S.

More than a third of Brazil is drained by the Amazon and its more than 200 tributaries. The Amazon is navigable for ocean steamers to Iquitos,
Peru, 2,300 miles (3,700 km) upstream. Southern
Brazil is drained by the Plata system—the Paraguay, Uruguay, and Paraná Rivers. The most important stream entirely within Brazil is the São
Francisco, navigable for 1,000 miles (1,903 km), but
broken near its mouth by the 275-foot (84 m) Paulo
Afonso Falls.

Government. The military took control in 1964,
ousting the last elected civilian President and installing a series of military men (with the Congress
ratifying the junta's choice). Election of a civilian
President by the 686-member electoral college
took place in January 1985.

A new constitution in 1988 provided for the
president to be elected for a five-year term through
direct, compulsory and secret suffrage. The National Congress maintains a bicameral structure—
a Senate, whose members serve eight-year terms,
and a Chamber of Deputies, elected for four-year
terms.

History. Brazil is the only Latin American nation
deriving its language and culture from Portugal.
Adm. Pedro Alvares Cabral claimed the territory
for the Portuguese in 1500. He brought to Portugal
a cargo of wood, pau-brasil, from which the land
received its name. Portugal began colonization in
1532 and made the area a royal colony in 1549.

During the Napoleonic wars, King João VI, then
Prince Regent, fled the country in 1807 in advance
of the French armies and in 1808 set up his court

in Rio de Janeiro. João was drawn home in 1820 by
a revolution, leaving his son as Regent. When Portugal sought to reduce Brazil again to colonial status, the prince declared Brazil's independence on
Sept. 7, 1822, and became Pedro I, Emperor of
Brazil.

Harassed by his parliament, Pedro I abdicated in
1831 in favor of his five-year-old son, who became
Emperor in 1840 as Pedro II. The son was a popular monarch, but discontent built up and, in 1889,
following a military revolt, he had to abdicate. Although a republic was proclaimed, Brazil was
under two military dictatorships during the next
four years. A revolt permitted a gradual return to
stability under civilian Presidents.

The President during World War I, Wenceslau
Braz, cooperated with the Allies and declared war
on Germany.

In World War II, Brazil cooperated with the
Western Allies, welcoming Allied air bases, patrol-
ling the South Atlantic, and joining the invasion of
Italy after declaring war on the Axis.

Gen. João Baptista de Oliveira Figueiredo, became President in 1979 and pledged a return to democracy in 1985.

The electoral college's choice of Tancredo Neves
on Jan. 15, 1985, as the first civilian President since
1964 brought a nationwide wave of optimism, but
the 75-year-old President-elect was hospitalized
and underwent a series of intestinal operations.
The civilian government was inaugurated on
schedule on March 15, but only Neves' Vice Presidential running mate, José Sarney, was sworn in,
and he was widely distrusted because he had previously been a member of the governing military regime's political party. When Neves died on April
21, Sarney became President.

Congressional elections in Nov. 1986 gave pro-
Sarney candidates a large majority.

Economically, Brazil's $93-billion foreign debt
was the Third World's largest, and inflation
reached a staggering 229% annual rate in 1984, almost double the 115% rate in 1983. But tough austerity measures imposed by the International Monetary Fund appeared to be taking hold and, by
mid-1984, Brazilian economists said the country's
recession had ended and Brazil was on the road to
recovery.

In 1985 the GNP increased by 8.3% and in February 1986, President Sarney announced an across-
the-board price and wage freeze that failed to stop
a resurgence of inflation to about 600%.

1. An election in Nov. 1989 will choose a new president who
will take office in March 1990.

BRUNEI

State of Brunei
Sultan: Haji Hassanal Bolkiah
Area: 2,226 sq mi. (5,765 sq km)
Population (est. mid-1989): 300,000 (average annual rate
of natural increase: 2.7%)
Density per square mile: 115
Capital and largest city (est. 1987): Bandar Seri Begawan,
56,300
Monetary unit: Brunei dollar
Ethnic groups: Malay, 65%; Chinese, 25%; other, 1.0%
Languages: Malay (official), Chinese, English
Religions: Islam, 60%; Christian, 8%; Buddhist and local,
32%

Literacy rate: 45%
Member of Commonwealth of Nations
Economic summary: Gross domestic product (1986): $2.943 billion, $10,970 per capita. Land used for agriculture: 3%; labor force: 5%; principle agricultural products: fruit, rice, pepper. Labor force in industry: 50%; major industrial products: crude petroleum, liquified natural gas. Natural resources: petroleum, natural gas, timber. Exports: crude petroleum, liquified natural gas. Imports: machinery, transport equipment, manufactured goods, foodstuffs. Major trading partners: Japan, U.S., U.K., Singapore, South Korea.

Geography. About the size of Delaware, Brunei is an independent sultanate on the northwest coast of the island of Borneo in the South China Sea, wedged between the Malaysian states of Sabah and Sarawak. Three quarters of the thinly populated country is covered with tropical rain forest; there are rich oil and gas deposits.

Government. Sultan Haji Hassanal Bolkiah is ruler of the state, a former British protectorate which became fully sovereign and independent on New Year's Day, 1984, presiding over a Privy Council and Council of Ministers appointed by himself. The Constitution provides for a three-tiered system of indirect elections, but the last elections were held in 1965. The only known opposition leader is in exile. In 1985, the Brunei National Democratic Party (BDNP) was formed but was dissolved by the sultan in 1988.

History. Brunei (pronounced broon-eye) was a powerful state from the 16th to the 19th century, ruling over the northern part of Borneo and adjacent island chains. But it fell into decay and lost Sarawak in 1841, becoming a British protectorate in 1888 and a British dependency in 1905.

The Sultan regained control over internal affairs in 1959, but Britain retained responsibility for the state's defense and foreign affairs until the end of 1983, when the sultanate became fully independent.

Sultain Bolkiah was crowned in 1968 at the age of 22, succeeding his father, Sir Omar Ali Saifuddin, who had abdicated. During his reign, exploitation of the rich Seria oilfield has made the sultanate wealthy. The majority of the population lives in and around the capital, situated on the Brunei River nine miles from its mouth.

BULGARIA

People's Republic of Bulgaria
Chairman of the State Council: Todor Zhivkov (1971)
Prime Minister (Chairman of Council of Ministers): Georgy Atanasov (1986)
Area: 42,823 sq mi. (110,912 sq km)
Population (est. mid-1989): 9,000,000 (average annual rate of natural increase: 0.1%) (Bulgarian, 88%; Turkish, 9%)
Density per square mile: 210.2
Capital: Sofia
Largest cities (est. 1986): Sofia, 1,114,962; Plovdiv, 342,-131; Varna, 302,211; Ruse, 183,746; Burgas, 182,570
Monetary unit: Lev
Language: Bulgarian
Religions: atheist, 65%; Eastern Orthodox, 27%; Muslim, 8%

National name: Narodna Republika Bulgariya
Literacy rate: 98%
Economic summary: Gross national product (1986): $61.2 billion, $6,800 per capita; real growth rate (1986): 2.2%. Labor force in agriculture: 17%; principal products: grains, tobacco, fruits, vegetables. Labor force in industry: 27%; major products: processed agricultural products, machinery, electronics, chemicals. Natural resources: metals, minerals, timber. Exports: machinery and transport equipment, fuels, minerals, raw materials, agricultural products. Imports: machinery and transportation equipment, fuels, raw materials, metals, agricultural raw materials. Major trading partners: U.S.S.R., Soviet bloc countries.

Geography. Two mountain ranges and two great valleys mark the topography of Bulgaria, a country the size of Tennessee. Situated on the Black Sea in the eastern part of the Balkan peninsula, it shares borders with Yugoslavia, Romania, Greece, and Turkey. The Balkan belt crosses the center of the country, almost due east-west, rising to a height of 7,800 feet (2,377 m). The Rhodope range breaks off from the Balkans in the west, curves, and then straightens out to run nearly parallel along the southern border. Between the two ranges, is the valley of the Maritsa, Bulgaria's principal river. Between the Balkan range and the Danube, which forms most of the northern boundary with Romania, is the Danubian tableland.

Southern Dobruja, a fertile region of 2,900 square miles (7,511 sq km), below the Danube delta, is an area of low hills, fens, and sandy steppes.

Government. The present Constitution has been in effect since May 18, 1971. The National Assembly, consisting of 400 members elected for five-year terms, is the governing body. It elects the State Council and the Council of Ministers.

The Communist Party is led by the chairman of the State Council, Todor Zhivkov.

History. The first Bulgarians, a tribe of wild horsemen akin to the Huns, crossed the Danube from the north in A.D. 679 and subjugated the Slavic population of Moesia. They adopted a Slav dialect and Slavic customs and twice conquered most of the Balkan peninsula between 893 and 1280. After the Serbs subjected their kingdom in 1330, the Bulgars gradually fell prey to the Turks, and from 1396 to 1878 Bulgaria was a Turkish province. In 1878, Russia forced Turkey to give the country its independence; but the European powers, fearing that Bulgaria might become a Russian dependency, intervened. By the Treaty of Berlin in 1878, Bulgaria became autonomous under Turkish sovereignty.

In 1887, Prince Ferdinand of Saxe-Coburg-Gotha was elected ruler of Bulgaria; on Oct. 5, 1908, he declared the country independent and took the title of Tsar.

Bulgaria joined Germany in World War I and lost. On Oct. 3, 1918, Tsar Ferdinand abdicated in favor of his son, Tsar Boris III. Boris assumed dictatorial powers in 1934–35. When Hitler awarded Bulgaria southern Dobruja, taken from Romania in 1940, Boris joined the Nazis in war the next year and occupied parts of Yugoslavia and Greece. Later the Germans tried to force Boris to send his troops against the Russians. Boris resisted and died under mysterious circumstances on Aug. 28, 1943.

Simeon II, infant son of Boris, became nominal ruler under a regency. Russia declared war on Bulgaria on Sept. 5, 1944. An armistice was agreed to three days later, after Bulgaria had declared war on Germany. Russian troops streamed in the next day.

A Soviet-style people's republic was established in 1947. Since then, Bulgaria acquired the reputation of being the most slavishly loyal to Moscow of all the East European Communist countries.

BURKINA FASO

President of the Popular Front: Blaise Compaore (1987)
Area: 105,870 sq mi. (274,200 sq km)
Population (est. mid-1989): 8,700,000 (average annual rate of natural increase: 2.8%)
Density per square mile: 82
Capital and largest city (est. 1985): Ouagadougou, 442,-000
Monetary unit: Franc CFA
Ethnic groups: Mossis, Bobos, Lobis, Fulanis
Languages: French, African languages
Religions: Animist, 65%; Islam, 25%; Roman Catholic, 10%
National name: Burkina Faso
Literacy rate: 13%
Economic summary: Gross domestic product (1985): $1.2 billion, $170 per capita; real growth rate (1985): 13%. Labor force in agriculture: 82%; principal products: millet, sorghum, corn, rice, livestock, peanuts, sugar cane, cotton. Major industrial products: processed agricultural products, light industrial items, brick, brewed products. Natural resources: manganese, limestone, marble, gold, uranium, bauxite, copper. Exports: livestock, peanuts, cotton. Imports: textiles, food and consumer goods, transport equipment, machinery, fuels. Major trading partners: Ivory Coast, France, Ghana, Western European nations.

Geography. Slightly larger than Colorado, Burkina Faso, formerly known as Upper Volta, is a landlocked country in West Africa. Its neighbors are the Ivory Coast, Mali, Niger, Benin, Togo, and Ghana. The country consists of extensive plains, low hills, high savannas, and a desert area in the north.

Government. The former French colony has been governed by a series of military leaders since a coup in November 1980 overthrew the last elected president. All political parties were banned.

History. The country, called Upper Volta by the French, consists chiefly of the lands of the Mossi Empire, where France established a protectorate over the Kingdom of Ouagadougou in 1897. Upper Volta became a separate colony in 1919, was partitioned among Niger, the Sudan, and the Ivory Coast in 1933 and was reconstituted in 1947. An autonomous republic within the French Community, it became independent on Aug. 5, 1960.

President Maurice Yameogo was deposed on Jan. 3, 1966, by a military coup led by Col. Sangoulé Lamizana, who dissolved the National Assembly and suspended the Constitution. A new Constitution was adopted later that year and a new Assembly was elected. However, dissension within the Volta Democratic Union, the major party, led to renewed military rule. Constitutional rule returned in 1978 with the election of an Assembly and a presidential vote in June in which Gen. Lamizana won by a narrow margin over three other candidates.

On Nov. 25, 1980, there was a bloodless coup which placed Gen. Lamizana under house arrest. Col. Sayé Zerbo took charge as the President of the

Military Committee of Reform for National Progress. Maj. Jean-Baptiste Ouedraogo toppled Zerbo in another coup on Nov. 7, 1982. Captain Thomas Sankara, in turn, deposed Ouedraogo a year later. His government changed the country's name on Aug. 3, 1984, to Burkina Faso (the "land of upright men") to sever ties with its colonial past. He was overthrown and killed by Blaise Compaore in 1987.

MYANMAR (BURMA)

Union of Myanmar
Head of State (Chairman): Gen. Saw Maung (1988)
Area: 261,220 sq mi. (676,560 sq km)
Population (est. mid-1989): 40,800,000 (average annual rate of natural increase: 2.3%) (Burmese, 68%; Shan, 7%; Karen, 6%, 16% others)
Density per square mile: 156
Capital: Yangon
Largest cities (est. 1983): Yangon, 2,458,712; Mandalay, 532,895; Moulmein, 219,991; Bassein, 144,092
Monetary unit: Kyat
Language: Burmese, minority languages
Religions: Buddhist, 89%; Christian, 5%; Islam, 3%
National name: Pyidaungsu Myanmar Naingngandau
Literacy rate: 78%
Economic summary: Gross domestic product (1986): $8 billion, $210 per capita; real growth rate (1986 est.): 3.7%. Labor force in agriculture: 66%; principal products: legumes, sugar cane, corn, rice, peanuts. Labor force in industry: 12%; major products: textiles, footwear, processed agricultural products, wood and wood products, refined petroleum. Natural resources: timber, nickel, cobalt, copper, gold, precious stones, crude oil and natural gas. Exports: rice, teak, beans, ores. Imports: machinery, transportation and construction equipment, manufactured goods. Major trading partners: Singapore, West Germany, U.K., Japan, Singapore.

Geography. Myanmar occupies the northwest portion of the Indochinese peninsula. India lies to the northwest and China to the northeast. Bangladesh, Laos, and Thailand are also neighbors. The Bay of Bengal touches the southwestern coast.

Slightly smaller than Texas, the country is divided into three natural regions: the Arakan Yoma, a long, narrow mountain range forming the barrier between Myanmar and India; the Shan Plateau in the east, extending southward into Tenasserim; and the Central Basin, running down to the flat fertile delta of the Irrawaddy in the south. This delta contains a network of intercommunicating canals and nine principal river mouths.

Government. On March 2, 1962, the government of U Nu was overthrown and replaced by a Revolutionary Council, which assumed all power in the state. Gen. U Ne Win, as chairman of the Revolutionary Council, became the chief executive.

A new Constitution was approved in 1973 and took effect Jan. 4, 1974. In 1972, Ne Win and his colleagues resigned their military titles. In 1974, Ne Win dissolved the Revolutionary Council and became President under the new Constitution. He voluntarily relinquished the presidency on Nov. 9, 1981.

History. In 1612, the British East India Company sent agents to Burma, but the Burmese long resisted efforts of British traders, and Dutch and Portuguese as well, to establish posts on the Bay of Bengal. By the Anglo-Burmese War in 1824–26

and two following wars, the British East India Company expanded to the whole of Burma by 1886. Burma was annexed to India. It became a separate colony in 1937.

During World War II, Burma was a key battleground; the 800-mile Burma Road was the Allies' vital supply line to China. The Japanese invaded the country in December 1941, and by May 1942 had occupied most of it, cutting the Burma Road. After one of the most difficult campaigns of the war, Allied forces liberated most of Burma prior to the Japanese surrender in August 1945.

Burma became independent on Jan. 4, 1948. In 1951 and 1952 the Socialists achieved power, and Burma became the first Asian country to introduce social legislation.

In 1968, after the government had made headway against the Communist and separatist rebels, the military regime adopted a policy of strict nonalignment and followed "the Burmese Way" to socialism. But the insurgents continued active.

In July 1988, Ne Win announced his resignation from the Burmese Socialist Program Party (BSPP), the only legal political party, effectively retiring from politics. The continuing problems of guerrilla insurgencies, failed economy, and violent unrest were the causes.

He was succeeded by U Sein Lwin who was forced out of office by widespread protests in August. Former Attorney General U Maung Maung was subsequently named President on August 19. Unrest continued and the civilian government was overthrown in Sept. 1988 by a military junta led by General Saw Maung, an associate of U Ne Win. He changed the name of the party to the National Unity Party and abolished the parliament.

BURUNDI

Republic of Burundi
President: Maj. Pierre Buyoya (1987)
Prime Minister: Adrien Sibomana (1988)
Area: 10,747 sq mi. (27,834 sq km)
Population (est. mid-1989): 5,500,000 (average annual rate of natural increase: 3.3%)
Density per square mile: 508
Capital and largest city (1986): Bujumbura, 272,600
Monetary unit: Burundi franc
Languages: Kirundi (official), French
Religions: Roman Catholic, 62%; Protestant, 5%; indigenous, 32%
National name: Republika Y'Uburundi
Literacy rate: 30%
Economic summary: Gross domestic product (1986): $1.33 billion, $240 per capita; real growth rate (1986): 4%. Principal agricultural products: coffee, tea, cotton, bananas, sorghum. Major industrial products: light consumer goods. Natural resources: nickel, kaolin, gold, unexploited copper and platinum deposits. Exports: coffee, tea, cotton, hides and skins. Imports: textiles, food, transport equipment, petroleum products. Major trading partners: U.S., Western Europe, Finland.

Geography. Wedged among Tanzania, Zaire, and Rwanda in east central Africa, Burundi occupies a high plateau divided by several deep valleys. It is equal in size to Maryland.

Government. Legislative and executive power is vested in the president.

Burundi's first Constitution, approved July 11, 1974, placed UPRONA (Unity and National Progress), the only political party, in control of national policy.

History. Burundi was once part of German East Africa. An integrated society developed among the Watusi, a tall, warlike people and nomad cattle raisers, and the Bahutu, a Bantu people, who were subject farmers. Belgium won a League of Nations mandate in 1923, and subsequently Burundi, with Rwanda, was transferred to the status of a United Nations trust territory.

In 1962, Burundi gained independence and became a kingdom under Mwami Mwambutsa IV. His son deposed him in 1966 to rule as Ntaré V.

Premier Micombero overthrew the Mwami, a few months later, installing himself as president.

One of Africa's worst tribal wars, which became genocide, occurred in Burundi in April 1972, following the return of Ntare V. He was given a safe-conduct promise in writing by President Micombero but was "judged and immediately executed" by the Burundi leader. His return was apparently attended by an invasion of exiles of Burundi's Hutu tribe. Whether Hutus living in Burundi joined the invasion is unclear, but after it failed, the victorious Tutsis proceeded to massacre some 100,000 persons in six weeks, with possibly 100,000 more slain by summer.

On Nov. 1, 1976, a military coup led by Lt. Col. Jean-Baptiste Bagaza ousted Micombero, who was serving his second term. Bagaza assumed the presidency Nov. 3, suspended the Constitution, and announced that a 30-member Supreme Revolutionary Council would be the governing body.

Bagaza was elected head of the only legal political party in 1979 and re-elected to a second five-year term as party chieftain in 1984, but was overthrown in 1987.

CAMBODIA

People's Republic of Kampuchea
President: Heng Samrin (1979)
Prime Minister: Hun Sen (1985)
Area: 69,884 sq mi. (181,000 sq km)
Population (est. mid-1988): 6,800,000 (average annual rate of natural increase: 3%)
Density per square mile: 98
Capital and largest city (est. 1980 for metropolitan area): Phnom Penh, 500,000
Monetary unit: Riel
Ethnic groups: Khmer, 90%; Chinese, 5%; other minorities 5%
Languages: Khmer (official), French
Religion: Theravada Buddhist, 5% others
Literacy rate: 48%
Economic summary: Gross national product (1971): $500 million. Principal agricultural products: rice, rubber, corn. Major industrial products: fish, wood and wood products, milled rice, rubber, cement. Natural resources: timber, gemstones, iron ore, manganese, phosphate. Exports: natural rubber, rice, pepper, wood. Imports: foodstuffs, fuel, machinery. Major trading partners: Vietnam, U.S.S.R., Eastern Europe, Japan, India.

Geography. Situated on the Indochinese peninsula, Cambodia is bordered by Thailand and Laos on the north and Vietnam on the east and south. The Gulf of Siam is off the western coast. The country, the size of Missouri, consists chiefly of a large alluvial plain ringed in by mountains and on the east by the Mekong River. The plain is centered on Lake Tonle Sap, which is a natural storage basin of the Mekong.

Government. A bloodless coup toppled Prince Sihanouk in 1970. It was led by Lon Nol and Prince Sisowath Sirik Matak, Sihanouk's cousin. Sihanouk moved to Peking to head a government-in-exile. On Oct. 9, 1970, Lon Nol proclaimed himself President.

The Lon Nol regime was overthrown in April 1975 by Pol Pot, a leader of the Communist Khmer Rouge forces, who instituted a xenophobic reign of terror. Pol Pot was in turn ousted on Jan. 8, 1979, by Vietnamese forces. A new government led by Heng Samrin was installed.

History. Cambodia came under Khmer rule about A.D. 600. Under the Khmers, magnificent temples were built at Angkor. The Khmer kingdom once ruled over most of Southeast Asia, but attacks by the Thai and the Vietnamese almost annihilated the empire until the French joined Cambodia, Laos, and Vietnam into French Indochina.

Under Norodom Sihanouk, enthroned in 1941, and particularly under Japanese occupation during World War II, nationalism revived. After the ouster of the Japanese, the Cambodians sought independence, but the French returned in 1946, granting the country a Constitution in 1947 and independence within the French Union in 1949. Sihanouk won full military control during the French-Indochinese War in 1953. He abdicated in 1955 in favor of his parents, remaining head of the government, and when his father died in 1960, became chief of state without returning to the throne. In 1963, he sought a guarantee of Cambodia's neutrality from all parties to the Vietnam War.

On March 18, 1970, while Sihanouk was abroad trying to get North Vietnamese and the Vietcong out of border sanctuaries near Vietnam, anti-Vietnamese riots occurred, and Sihanouk was overthrown.

North Vietnamese and Vietcong units in border sanctuaries began moving deeper into Cambodia, threatening rapid overthrow of the new regime headed by Lon Nol. President Nixon sent South Vietnamese and U.S. troops across the border on April 30. U.S. ground forces, limited to 30-kilometer penetration, withdrew by June 30.

The Vietnam peace agreement of 1973 stipulated withdrawal of foreign forces from Cambodia, but fighting continued between Hanoi-backed insurgents and U.S.-supplied government troops. U.S. air support for the government forces was ended by Congress on Aug. 15, 1973.

Fighting reached a quick climax early in 1975, as government troops fell back in bitter fighting, Lon Nol fled by air April 1, leaving the government under the interim control of Premier Long Boret. On April 16, the government's capitulation ended the five-year war, but not the travails of war-ravaged Cambodia.

A new Constitution was proclaimed in December 1975, establishing a 250-member People's Assembly, a State Presidium headed by Pol Pot, and a Supreme Judicial Tribunal. Samphan replaced Sihanouk as head of state in April 1976, and the former monarch became a virtual prisoner until freed by Pol Pot in 1979.

In the next two years, from 2 million to 4 million Cambodians are estimated to have died under the brutality of the Pol Pot regime. Border clashes with Vietnam developed into a Vietnamese invasion and by the end of 1978 the Pol Pot government appeared to be collapsing.

Despite the capture of Phnom Penh on Jan. 8, fighting continued in isolated areas. Retreating Pol Pot forces and refugees totaling 40,000 were driven into Thailand by May.

At a meeting in Kuala Lumpur, Malaysia, on June 22, 1982, Sihanouk formed an alliance with Son Sann, his former prime minister, and Khieu Samphan, Pol Pot's representative, to oppose the Heng Samrin regime installed in Phnom Penh by the Vietnamese.

While Sihanouk remained in exile, about 9,000 noncommunist troops loyal to him and another 15,000 under Son Sann joined about 35,000 communist Pol Pot forces fighting the 170,000 Vietnamese troops supporting the Heng Samrin government. The Cambodian insurgents suffered a major defeat in March 1985 when Vietnamese forces overran their camps in Cambodia and forced them into Thailand. Resistance forces were able to switch to hit-and-run tactics and operate effectively inside the country.

The Vietnamese plan to withdraw by early 1990 has led to negotiations to have a political settlement in place by then. The main issues are the status of the Heng Samrin government and the objections raised by Sihanouk, the Heng Samrin government, and the U.S. to the Khmer Rouge, with their record of atrocities during the Pol Pot regime, entering a new government.

CAMEROON

Republic of Cameroon
President: Paul Biya (1982)
Area: 183,569 sq mi. (475,442 sq km)
Population (est. mid-1989): 10,800,000 (average annual rate of natural increase: 2.6%)
Density per square mile: 59
Capital: Yaoundé
Largest cities (est. 1985): Douala, 852,700; Yaoundé, 583,500
Monetary unit: Franc CFA
Languages: French and English (both official); Foulbé, Bamiléke, Ewondo, Donala, Mungaka, Bassa
Religions: Roman Catholic, 35%; Animist, 12%; Islam, 35%; Protestant, 18%
National name: République du Cameroun
Literacy rate: 65%
Economic summary: Gross domestic product (FY87 est.): $12.6 billion, $1,230 per capita; real growth rate ('86 est.): 5.5%. Land used for agriculture: 33%; labor force: 74%; principal products: coffee, cocoa, timber, corn, peanuts. Labor force in industry: 11%. Major products. crude oil, small manufacturing, consumer goods, aluminum. Natural resources: timber, some oil, bauxite, hydropower potential. Exports: cocoa, coffee, timber, aluminum, petroleum. Imports: consumer goods, machinery, food, beverages, tobacco, fuel. Major trading partners: France, U.S., Western European nations.

Geography. Cameroon is a West African nation on the Gulf of Guinea, bordered by Nigeria, Chad, the Central African Republic, the Congo, Equatorial Guinea, and Gabon. It is nearly twice the size of Oregon.

The interior consists of a high plateau, rising to 4,500 feet (1,372 m), with the land descending to a lower, densely wooded plateau and then to swamps and plains along the coast. Mount Cameroon (13,350 ft.; 4,069 m), near the coast, is the highest elevation in the country. The main rivers are the Benue, Nyong, and Sanaga.

Government. After a 1972 plebiscite, a unitary nation was formed out of East and West Cameroon to replace the former Federal Republic. A Constitution was adopted, providing for election of a president every five years and of a 120-seat National Assembly (later increased to 180), whose nominal five-year term can be extended or shortened by the president. The Cameroon People's Democratic Movement is the only political party.

History. The Republic of Cameroon is inhabited by Hamitic and Semitic peoples in the north, where Islam is the principal religion, and by Bantu peoples in the central and southern regions, where native animism prevails. The tribes were conquered by many invaders.

The land escaped colonial rule until 1884, when treaties with tribal chiefs brought the area under German domination. After World War I, the League of Nations gave the French a mandate over 80% of the area, and the British 20% adjacent to Nigeria. After World War II, when the country came under a U.N. trusteeship in 1946, self-government was granted, and the Cameroun People's Union emerged as the dominant party by campaigning for reunification of French and British Cameroon and for independence. Accused of being under Communist control, it waged a campaign of revolutionary terror from 1955 to 1958, when it was crushed. In British Cameroon, unification was pressed also by the leading party, the Kamerun National Democratic Party, led by John Foncha.

France set up Cameroun as an autonomous state in 1957, and the next year its legislative assembly voted for independence by 1960. In 1959 a fully autonomous government of Cameroun was formed under Ahmadou Ahidjo. Cameroun became an independent republic on Jan. 1, 1960, adopted a Constitution in a referendum in February, and chose a National Assembly in April. The Assembly elected Ahidjo president. A federal Constitution was approved in 1961, and the Federal Republic of Cameroon came into being in October, headed by Ahidjo and Foncha.

CANADA

Sovereign: Queen Elizabeth II
Governor General: Jeanne Sauvé (1984)
Prime Minister: Brian Mulroney (1984)
Area: 3,851,809 sq mi. (9,976,186 sq km)
Population (est. mid-1988): 26,300,000 (British, 40%; French, 27%; other European, 20%; 1.5% aborigine) (average annual rate of natural increase: 0.8%)
Density per square mile: 7
Capital: Ottawa, Ont.
Largest cities (1986 census; metropolitan areas): Toronto, 3,427,168; Montreal, 2,921,357; Vancouver, 1,380,-729; Ottawa, 819,263; Edmonton, 785,465; Calgary, 671,326; Winnipeg, 625,304; Quebec, 603,627; Hamilton, 557,029; St. Catherines-Niagara, 343,258
Monetary Unit: Canadian dollar
Languages: English, French
Religions: Roman Catholic, 46%; Protestant, 41%; no religion, 7%; Eastern Orthodox, 2%; Jewish, 1%; other, 1.3%
Literacy rate: 99%
Economic Summary: Gross domestic product: (1986) $412.8 billion; $15,910 per capita; real growth rate (FY87): 4.4%. Land use for agriculture: 7%; labor force: 4%; Principal products; wheat, barley, oats, livestock. Labor force in industry: 17%. Major products;

transportation equipment, petroleum, chemicals, wood products. Exports: wheat, petroleum, lumber and wood products, ores, motor vehicles. Imports: electronic equipment, chemicals. Major trading partners: U.S., Japan, U.K., U.S.S.R., West Germany.

Geography. Covering most of the northern part of the North American continent and with an area larger than that of the United States, Canada has an extremely varied topography. In the east the mountainous maritime provinces have an irregular coast line on the Gulf of St. Lawrence and the Atlantic. The St. Lawrence plain, covering most of southern Quebec and Ontario, and the interior continental plain, covering southern Manitoba and Saskatchewan and most of Alberta, are the principal cultivable areas. They are separated by a forested plateau rising from lakes Superior and Huron.

Westward toward the Pacific, most of British Columbia, Yukon, and part of western Alberta are covered by parallel mountain ranges including the Rockies. The Pacific border of the coast range is ragged with fiords and channels. The highest point in Canada is Mount Logan (19,850 ft; 6,050 m), which is in the Yukon.

Canada has an abundance of large and small lakes. In addition to the Great Lakes on the U.S. border, there are 9 others that are more than 100 miles long (161 km) and 35 that are more than 50 miles long (80 km).

The two principal river systems are the Mackenzie and the St. Lawrence. The St. Lawrence, with its tributaries, is navigable for over 1,900 miles (3,058 km).

Government. Canada, a self-governing member of the Commonwealth of Nations, is a federation of 10 provinces (Alberta, British Columbia, Manitoba, New Brunswick, Newfoundland, Nova Scotia, Ontario, Prince Edward Island, Quebec, and Saskatchewan) and two territories (Northwest Territories and Yukon) whose powers were spelled out in the British North America Act of 1867. With the passing of the Constitution Act of 1981, the act and the Constitutional amending power were transferred from the British government to Canada so that the Canadian Constitution is now entirely in the hands of the Canadians.

Actually the Governor General acts only with the advice of the Canadian Prime Minister and the Cabinet, who also sit in the federal Parliament. The Parliament has two houses: a Senate of 104 members appointed for life, and a House of Commons of 295 members apportioned according to provincial population. Elections are held at least every five years or whenever the party in power is voted down in the House of Commons or considers it expedient to appeal to the people. The Prime Minister is the leader of the majority party in the House of Commons—or, if no single party holds a majority, the leader of the party able to command the support of a majority of members of the House. Laws must be passed by both houses of Parliament and signed by the Governor General in the Queen's name.

The 10 provincial governments are nominally headed by Lieutenant Governors appointed by the federal government, but the executive power in each actually is vested in a Cabinet headed by a Premier, who is leader of the majority party. The provincial legislatures are composed of one-house assemblies whose members are elected for four-year terms. They are known as Legislative Assem-

Canadian Governors General and Prime Ministers Since 1867

Term of office	Governor General	Term	Prime Minister	Party
1867–1868	Viscount Monck[1]	1867–1873	Sir John A. MacDonald	Conservative
1869–1872	Baron Lisgar	1873–1878	Alexander Mackenzie	Liberal
1872–1878	Earl of Dufferin	1878–1891	Sir John A. MacDonald	Conservative
1878–1883	Marquess of Lorne	1891–1892	Sir John J. C. Abbott	Conservative
1883–1888	Marquess of Lansdowne	1892–1894	Sir John S. D. Thompson	Conservative
1888–1893	Baron Stanley of Preston	1894–1896	Sir Mackenzie Bowell	Conservative
1893–1898	Earl of Aberdeen	1896	Sir Charles Tupper	Conservative
1898–1904	Earl of Minto	1896–1911	Sir Wilfrid Laurier	Liberal
1904–1911	Earl Grey	1911–1917	Sir Robert L. Borden	Conservative
1911–1916	Duke of Connaught	1917–1920	Sir Robert L. Borden	Unionist
1916–1921	Duke of Devonshire	1920–1921	Arthur Meighen	Unionist
1921–1926	Baron Byng of Vimy	1921–1926	W. L. Mackenzie King	Liberal
1926–1931	Viscount Willingdon	1926	Arthur Meighen	Conservative
1931–1935	Earl of Bessborough	1926–1930	W. L. Mackenzie King	Liberal
1935–1940	Baron Tweedsmuir	1930–1935	Richard B. Bennett	Conservative
1940–1946	Earl of Athlone	1935–1948	W. L. Mackenzie King	Liberal
1946–1952	Viscount Alexander	1948–1957	Louis S. St. Laurent	Liberal
1952–1959	Vincent Massey	1957–1963	John G. Diefenbaker	Conservative
1959–1967	George P. Vanier	1963–1968	Lester B. Pearson	Liberal
1967–1973	Roland Michener	1968–1979	Pierre Elliott Trudeau	Liberal
1974–1979	Jules Léger	1979–1980	Charles Joseph Clark	Conservative
1979–1984	Edward R. Schreyer	1980–1984	Pierre Elliott Trudeau	Liberal
1984–	Jeanne Sauvé	1984–1984	John Turner	Liberal
		1984–	Brian Mulroney	Conservative

1. Became Governor General of British North America in 1861.

blies, except in Newfoundland, where it is the House of Assembly, and in Quebec, where it is the National Assembly.

The judicial system consists of a Supreme Court in Ottawa (established in 1875), with appellate jurisdiction, and a Supreme Court in each province, as well as county courts with limited jurisdiction in most of the provinces. The Governor General in Council appoints these judges.

History. The Norse explorer Leif Ericson probably reached the shores of Canada (Labrador or Nova Scotia) in A.D. 1000, but the history of the white man in the country actually began in 1497, when John Cabot, an Italian in the service of Henry VII of England, reached Newfoundland or Nova Scotia. Canada was taken for France in 1534 by Jacques Cartier. The actual settlement of New France, as it was then called, began in 1604 at Port Royal in what is now Nova Scotia; in 1608, Quebec was founded. France's colonization efforts were not very successful, but French explorers by the end of the 17th century had penetrated beyond the Great Lakes to the western prairies and south along the Mississippi to the Gulf of Mexico. Meanwhile, the English Hudson's Bay Company had been established in 1670. Because of the valuable fisheries and fur trade, a conflict developed between the French and English; in 1713, Newfoundland, Hudson Bay, and Nova Scotia (Acadia) were lost to England.

During the Seven Years' War (1756–63), England extended its conquest, and the British Maj. Gen. James Wolfe won his famous victory over Gen. Louis Montcalm outside Quebec on Sept. 13, 1759. The Treaty of Paris in 1763 gave England control.

At that time the population of Canada was almost entirely French, but in the next few decades, thousands of British colonists emigrated to Canada from the British Isles and from the American colonies. In 1849, the right of Canada to self-government was recognized. By the British North America Act of 1867, the Dominion of Canada was created through the confederation of Upper and Lower Canada, Nova Scotia, and New Brunswick. Prince Edward Island joined the Dominion in 1873.

In 1869 Canada purchased from the Hudson's Bay Company the vast middle west (Rupert's Land) from which the provinces of Manitoba (1870), Alberta, and Saskatchewan (1905) were later formed. In 1871, British Columbia joined the Dominion. The country was linked from coast to coast in 1885 by the Canadian Pacific Railway.

During the formative years between 1866 and 1896, the Conservative Party, led by Sir John A. MacDonald, governed the country, except during the years 1873–78. In 1896, the Liberal Party took over and, under Sir Wilfrid Laurier, an eminent French Canadian, ruled until 1911.

By the Statute of Westminster in 1931 the British Dominions, including Canada, were formally declared to be partner nations with Britain, "equal in status, in no way subordinate to each other," and bound together only by allegiance to a common Crown.

Newfoundland became Canada's 10th province on March 31, 1949, following a plebiscite. Canada includes two territories—the Yukon Territory, the area north of British Columbia and east of Alaska, and the Northwest Territories, including all of Canada north of 60° north latitude except Yukon and the northernmost sections of Quebec and Newfoundland. This area includes all of the Arctic north of the mainland, Norway having recognized Canadian sovereignty over the Svendrup Islands in the Arctic in 1931.

The Liberal Party, led by William Lyon Mackenzie King, dominated Canadian politics from 1921 until 1957, when it was succeeded by the Progressive Conservatives. The Liberals, under the leadership of Lester B. Pearson, returned to power in 1963. Pearson remained Prime Minister until 1968, when he retired and was replaced by a former law professor, Pierre Elliott Trudeau. Trudeau main-

Population by Provinces and Territories

Province	1981 (Census)	1983 (June Estimate)
Alberta	2,237,724	2,352,300
British Columbia	2,744,467	2,825,000
Manitoba	1,026,241	1,046,300
New Brunswick	696,403	706,600
Newfoundland	567,681	576,200
Nova Scotia	847,442	859,300
Ontario	8,625,107	8,816,000
Prince Edward Island	122,506	123,900
Quebec	6,438,403	6,514,900
Saskatchewan	968,313	992,000
Northwest Territories	45,741	48,600
Yukon Territory	23,153	22,200
Total	**24,343,181**	**24,883,400**

Source: Statistics Canada.

tained Canada's defensive alliance with the United States, but began moving toward a more independent policy in world affairs.

Trudeau set about creating what he termed a "just society," stressing domestic reforms. His election was considered in part a response to the most serious problem confronting the country, the division between French- and English-speaking Canadians, which had led to a separatist movement in the predominantly French province of Quebec. Trudeau, himself a French Canadian, supported programs for bilingualism and an increased measure of provincial autonomy, although he would not tolerate the idea of separatism. In 1974, the provincial government voted to make French the official language of Quebec.

Conflicts over the law establishing French as the dominant language in Quebec, particularly in schooling, kept separatism as a national issue, but by-elections in 1977 produced easy victories for Trudeau's ruling Liberals in four Quebec seats in the national legislature, and polls showed a decline in separatist support both in the province and elsewhere in Canada.

Economic problems appeared to take precedence over politics in 1978, as the Sun Life Assurance Company of Canada, the nation's largest insurance firm, announced that it would move its headquarters from Montreal to Toronto. Many businesses had left the province earlier, but Sun Life was the first to cite the language law as the reason for its departure.

Despite Trudeau's removal of price and wage controls in 1978, continuing inflation and a high rate of unemployment caused him to delay elections until May 22, 1979, the first time since 1935 that a Canadian government had retained office for the allowable five-year term. The delay gave Trudeau no advantage—the Progressive Conservatives under Charles Joseph Clark defeated the Liberals everywhere except in Quebec, New Brunswick, and Newfoundland.

Clark took office as the head of Canada's fifth minority government in the last 20 years, needing the support of 26 New Democratic Party members and six Social Credit members to obtain an absolute majority in the 282-seat House.

Clark's government collapsed after only six months when a motion to the Tory budget carried by 139-133 on Dec. 13, 1979. On the same day, the Quebec law making French the exclusive official language of the province—an issue which had been expected to provide Clark's first major in-

ternal test—was voided by the Canadian Supreme Court.

In national elections Feb. 18, 1980, the resurgent Liberals under Trudeau scored an unexpectedly big victory, winning 146 seats (147 when a vacancy was filled a month later), while the Conservatives fell from 136 to 103 and the New Democrats won 32 seats.

Resolving a dispute that had occupied Trudeau since the beginning of his tenure, Queen Elizabeth II, in Ottawa on April 17, 1982, signed the Constitution Act, cutting the last legal tie between Canada and Britain. Since 1867, the British North America Act required British Parliament approval for any Canadian constitutional change.

The new charter was approved by the federal House of Commons, 246–24, on Dec. 2, 1981, and by a 59–23 vote of the Senate six days later. The Constitution retains Queen Elizabeth as Queen of Canada and keeps Canada's membership in the Commonwealth.

Ending an era, Trudeau retired on June 30, 1984, after 16 years as prime minister, except for the nine-month interruption in 1979–80.

His successor as Liberal Party leader and Prime Minister, John N. Turner, called an early election for a new Parliament after polls showed the Liberals had made a big comeback from the last months of Trudeau's term, despite Canada's continuing recession and 11.2% unemployment, the highest in 40 years.

In the national election on Sept. 4, 1984, the Progressive Conservative Party scored an overwhelming victory, fundamentally changing the country's political landscape. The Conservatives, led by Brian Mulroney, a 45-year-old corporate lawyer, won the highest political majority in Canadian history, Mulroney was sworn in as Canada's 18th Prime Minister on Sept. 17.

The dominant foreign issue was a free-trade pact with the U.S., a treaty bitterly opposed by the Liberal and New Democratic parties. The conflict led to elections in Nov. 1988 that solidly re-elected Mulroney and gave him a mandate to proceed with the agreement.

CAPE VERDE

Republic of Cape Verde

President: Aristides Pereira (1975)
Premier: Maj. Pedro Pires (1975)
Area: 1,557 sq mi. (4,033 sq km)
Population: (est. mid-1989): 400,000 (average annual rate of natural increase: 2.5%)
Density per square mile: 237
Capital (est. 1982): Praia, 37,676
Largest city (est. 1982): Mindelo, 50,000
Monetary unit: Cape Verde escudo
Language: Portuguese, Criuolo
Religion: Roman Catholic fused with indigenous beliefs, 98%
National name: República de Cabo Verde
Literacy rate: 37%
Economic summary: Gross national product (1985): $140 million. Average annual growth rate (1970–79): 4.8%. Per capita income (1985): $420. Principal agricultural products: bananas, corn, sugar cane, beans. Major industry: fishing, salt mining. Natural resources: salt, siliceous rock. Exports: fish, textiles, bananas, salt. Imports: machinery, petroleum products, corn, rice. Major trading partners: Portugal, U.K., Japan, Angola, Zaire.

Geography: Cape Verde, only slightly larger than

Rhode Island, is an archipelago in the Atlantic 385 miles (620 km) west of Dakar, Senegal.

The islands are divided into two groups: Barlavento in the north, comprising Santo Antão (291 sq mi.; 754 sq km), Boa Vista (240 sq mi.; 622 sq km), São Nicolau (132 sq mi.; 342 sq km), São Vicente (88 sq mi.; 246 sq km), Sal (83 sq mi.; 298 sq km), and Santa Luzia (13 sq mi.; 34 sq km); and Sotavento in the south, consisting of São Tiago (383 sq mi.; 992 sq km), Fogo (184 sq mi.; 477 sq km), Maio (103 sq mi.; 267 sq km), and Brava (25 sq mi.; 65 sq km). The islands are mostly mountainous, with the land deeply scarred by erosion. There is an active volcano on Fogo.

Government. The islands became independent on July 5, 1975, under an agreement negotiated with Portugal in 1974. The 56-member National Assembly chose Aristides Pereira as President and Maj. Pedro Pires as Premier. All members of the Assembly belong to the African Party for the Independence of Portuguese Guinea and Cape Verde, then the only party that entered candidates in the election. It is committed to union with Guinea-Bissau, another former Portuguese colony.

History. Uninhabited upon their discovery in 1456, the Cape Verde islands became part of the Portuguese empire in 1495. A majority of their modern inhabitants are of mixed Portuguese and African ancestry. A coaling station developed during the 19th century on the island of São Vicente has grown in recent years to an oil and gasoline storage depot for ships and aircraft.

CENTRAL AFRICAN REPUBLIC

Head of Government: Gen. André Kolingba (1981)
Area: 241,313 sq mi. (625,000 sq km)
Population (est. mid-1989): 2,800,000 (average annual rate of natural increase: 2.5%)
Density per square mile: 12
Capital and largest city (est. 1985): Bangui, 473,000
Monetary unit: Franc CFA
Ethnic groups: Mandja-Baya, Banda, Mbaka, Azande, Yakoma, Mbanziri, Sango
Languages: French (official) and Sango
Religions: Protestant and Roman Catholic with animist influence, 40%; indigenous, 24%; Islam, 15%; other, 11%
National name: République Centrafricaine
Literacy rate: 33%
Economic summary: Gross national product (1987): $1.2 billion. Average annual growth rate (1980–87): 3%. Per capita income (1987): $350. Land used for agriculture: 8%; labor force: 85%; principal products: cotton, coffee, peanuts, food crops, livestock. Major industrial products: timber, textiles, soap, cigarettes, diamonds, processed food, brewed beverages. Natural resources: diamonds, uranium, timber. Exports: diamonds, cotton, timber, coffee. Imports: machinery and electrical equipment, petroleum products, textiles. Major trading partners: France, Japan, U.S., Western Europe, Algeria, Yugoslavia.

Geography. Situated about 500 miles north (805 km) of the equator, the Central African Republic is a landlocked nation bordered by Cameroon, Chad, the Sudan, Zaire, and the Congo. Twice the size of New Mexico, it is covered by tropical forests in the south and semidesert land in the east. The Ubangi and Shari are the largest of many rivers.

Government. On Dec. 4, 1976, the Central African Republic became the Central African Empire.

Marshal Jean-Bédel Bokassa, who had ruled the republic since he took power in a military coup Dec. 31, 1965, was declared Emperor Bokassa I. He was overthrown in a coup on Sept. 20, 1979. Former President David Dacko, returned to power and changed the country's name back to the Central African Republic. An army coup on Sept. 1, 1981, deposed Dacko and suspended the Constitution and all political parties. A Military Committee of National Redress was set up to run the country. A new constitution was enacted on Nov. 21, 1986 that extended Kolingba's term another six years and allowed for parliamentary elections in which the Centrafrican Democratic Assembly would be the only party.

History. As the colony of Ubangi-Shari, what is now the Central African Republic was united with Chad in 1905 and joined with Gabon and the Middle Congo in French Equatorial Africa in 1910. After World War II a rebellion in 1946 forced the French to grant self-government. In 1958 the territory voted to become an autonomous republic within the French Community, but on Aug. 13, 1960, President David Dacko proclaimed the republic's independence from France.

Dacko undertook to move the country into Peking's orbit, but was overthrown in a coup on Dec. 31, 1965, by the then Col. Jean-Bédel Bokassa, Army Chief of Staff. In August 1977, the U.S. State Department protested the Emperor's jailing of American and British newsmen.

Bokassa staged an elaborate coronation ceremony on the first anniversary of the Empire. The cost of the ceremony was one fourth of the annual foreign-exchange earnings of the country.

CHAD

Republic of Chad
President: Hissen Habré (1982)
Area: 495,752 sq mi. (1,284,000 sq km)
Population (est. mid-1988): 4,900,000 (average annual rate of natural increase, 2.0%)
Density per square mile: 10
Capital and largest city (est. 1986): N'djamena, 511,700
Monetary unit: Franc CFA
Ethnic groups: Baguirmiens, Kanembous, Saras, Massas, Arabs, Toubous, Goranes
Languages: French and Arabic (official), many tribal languages
Religions: Islam, 44%; Christian, 33%; traditional, 23%
National name: République du Tchad
Literacy rate: 17%
Economic summary: Gross domestic product (1986 est.): $817 billion, $160 per capita; real growth rate: −2.0%. Land used for agriculture: 38%; labor force: 85%; principal products: cotton, cattle, sugar, subsistence crops. Labor force in industry: 4%; major products: livestock and livestock products, beer, food processing, textiles, cigarettes. Natural resources: petroleum, unexploited uranium, kaolin. Exports: cotton, livestock and animal products, fish. Imports: food, motor vehicles and parts, petroleum products, machinery, cement, textiles. Major trading partners: France, Nigeria, and central African countries.

Geography. A landlocked country in north central Africa, Chad is about 85% the size of Alaska. Its neighbors are Niger, Libya, the Sudan, the Central African Republic, Cameroon, and Nigeria.

Lake Chad, from which the country gets its name, lies on the western border with Niger and

Nigeria. In the north is a desert that runs into the Sahara.

Government. Hissen Habré became president of Chad on June 7, 1982, by overthrowing Goukouni Oueddei.

History. Chad was absorbed into the colony of French Equatorial Africa, as part of Ubangi-Shari, in 1910. France began the country's development after 1920, when it became a separate colony. In 1946, French Equatorial Africa was admitted to the French Union. By referendum in 1958 the Chad territory became an autonomous republic within the French Union.

An independence movement led by the first Premier and President, François (later Ngarta) Tombalbaye, achieved complete independence on Aug. 11, 1960.

Tombalbaye was killed in the 1975 coup and was succeeded by Gen. Félix Malloum, who faced a Libyan-financed rebel movement throughout his tenure in office. A ceasefire backed by Libya, Niger, and the Sudan early in 1978 failed to end the fighting, and French military aid was increased.

Nine rival groups meeting in Lagos, Nigeria, in March 1979 agreed to form a provisional government headed by Goukouni Oueddei, a former rebel leader. Fighting broke out again in Chad in March 1980, when Defense Minister Hissen Habré challenged Goukouni and seized the capital. By the year's end, Libyan troops supporting Goukouni recaptured N'djamena, and Libyan President Muammar el-Qaddafi, in January 1981, proposed a merger of Chad with Libya.

The Libyan merger proposal was rejected and Libyan troops withdrew from Chad but in 1983 poured back into the barren northern part of the country in support of Goukouni. France, in turn, sent troops into southern Chad in support of Habré.

A Qaddafi-Goukouni break in Nov. 1986 led to the defection of his troops. Government troops then launched an offensive in early 1987 that drove the Libyans out of most of the country.

CHILE

Republic of Chile
President: Gen. Augusto Pinochet (1973)
Area: 292,132 sq mi. (756,622 sq km)
Population (est. mid-1989): 13,000,000 (average annual rate of natural increase: 1.6%)
Density per square mile: 44
Capital: Santiago
Largest cities (est. 1986): Santiago, 4,804,200; Valparaiso, 277,900; Concepción, 292,700; Antofagasta, 203,100; Talcahuano, 229,500; Temuca, 215,400
Monetary unit: Peso
Language: Spanish
Religion: Roman Catholic, 89%; Protestant, 11%; small jewish pop.
National name: República de Chile
Literacy rate: 96%
Economic summary: Gross domestic product (1986): $16.4 billion, $1,300 per capita; real growth rate (1986): 5.7%. Land used for agriculture: 23%; labor force 13%; principal products: wheat, corn, sugar beets, vegetables, wine, livestock. Labor force in industry: 15%; major products: processed fish, transportation equipment, iron and steel, pulp, paper. Natural resources: copper, timber, iron ore, nitrates. Exports: copper, iron ore, paper and

wood products, fruits. Imports: sugar, wheat, vehicles, petroleum, capital goods. Major trading partners: U.S., Japan, West Germany, Brazil, Argentina, Venezuela.

Geography. Situated south of Peru and west of Bolivia and Argentina, Chile fills a narrow 1,800-mile (2,897 km) strip between the Andes and the Pacific. Its area is nearly twice that of Montana.

One third of Chile is covered by the towering ranges of the Andes. In the north is the mineral-rich Atacama Desert, between the coastal mountains and the Andes. In the center is a 700-mile-long (1,127 km) valley, thickly populated, between the Andes and the coastal plateau. In the south, the Andes border on the ocean.

At the southern tip of Chile's mainland is Punta Arenas, the southernmost city in the world, and beyond that lies the Strait of Magellan and Tierra del Fuego, an island divided between Chile and Argentina. The southernmost point of South America is Cape Horn, a 1,390-foot (424-m) rock on Horn Island in the Wollaston group, which belongs to Chile.

The Juan Fernández Islands, in the South Pacific about 400 miles (644 km) west of the mainland, and Easter Island, about 2,000 miles (3,219 km) west, are Chilean possessions.

Government. The 1980 Constitution calls for a 1989 plebiscite to confirm if the sitting president (Pinochet) would serve until 1997, when open elections would be held. A Congress is to be elected in 1990.

Leftist parties were abolished immediately after the 1973 military coup that ousted President Salvador Allende Gossens. Other parties were placed "in recess," and on March 12, 1977, the government officially dissolved them.

History. Chile was originally under the control of the Incas in the north and the fierce Araucanian people in the south. In 1541, a Spaniard, Pedro de Valdivia, founded Santiago. Chile won its independence from Spain in 1818 under Bernardo O'Higgins and an Argentinian, José de San Martin. O'Higgins, dictator until 1823, laid the foundations of the modern state with a two-party system and a centralized government.

The dictator from 1830 to 1837, Diego Portales, fought a war with Peru in 1836–39 that expanded Chilean territory. The Conservatives were in power from 1831 to 1861. Then the Liberals, winning a share of power for the next 30 years, disestablished the church and limited presidential power. Chile fought the War of the Pacific with Peru and Bolivia from 1879 to 1883, winning Antofagasta, Bolivia's only outlet to the sea, and extensive areas from Peru. A revolt in 1890 led by Jorge Montt overthrew, in 1891, José Balmaceda and established a parliamentary dictatorship that existed until a new Constitution was adopted in 1925. Industrialization began before World War I and led to the formation of Marxist groups.

Juan Antonio Ríos, President during World War II, was originally pro-Nazi but in 1944 led his country into the war on the side of the U.S.

A small abortive army uprising in 1969 raised fear of military intervention to prevent a Marxist, Salvador Allende Gossens, from taking office after his election to the presidency on Sept. 4, 1970, with 36.3% of the vote in a three-way battle. Dr. Allende was the first President in a non-Communist country freely elected on a Marxist-Leninist program.

Allende quickly established relations with Cuba and the People's Republic of China and nationalized several American companies.

Allende's overthrow and death in an army assault on the presidential palace in September 1973 ended a 46-year era of constitutional government in Chile, which had boasted the longest such record in Latin America.

The takeover was led by a four-man junta headed by Army Chief of Staff Augusto Pinochet Ugarte, who assumed the office of President.

Committed to "exterminate Marxism," the junta embarked on a right-wing dictatorship. It suspended parliament, banned political activity, and broke relations with Cuba.

The Human Rights Commission of the Organization of American States charged the junta with "most grave violations" of basic liberties. In July, Chile denied entry to a U.N. investigatory panel. On June 9, 1978, the government reversed that policy to permit the U.N. Human Rights Commission to send an investigative mission to Chile.

In 1977, Pinochet, in a speech marking his fourth year in power, promised elections by 1985 if conditions warranted. Earlier, he had abolished DINA, the secret police, and decreed an amnesty for political prisoners, an action Amnesty International said might affect only 200–400 of some 1,500 political prisoners.

Pinochet was inaugurated on March 11, 1981, for an eight-year term as President. The 1989 plebiscite resulted in a defeat for Pinochet. He will step down in January 1990 in favor of a successor who will be elected Dec. 1989.

CHINA

People's Republic of China
President: Gen. Yang Shangkun (1988)
Premier: Li Peng (1987)
Area: 3,691,521 sq mi. (9,561,000 sq km)[1]
Population (est. mid-1989): 1,103,900,000 (average rate of natural increase: 1.4%)
Density per square mile: 298
Capital: Beijing
Largest cities (est. 1983): Shanghai, 11,940,000; Beijing (Peking) 9,330,000; Tianjin (Tientsin) 7,850,000; Canton, 6,840,000; Wuhan, 5,940,000; Shenyang (Mukden), 5,210,000; Nanjing (Nanking), 4,560,000; Chongqing (Chungking), 3,890,000; Harbin; 3,730,000
Monetary unit: Yuan
Languages: Chinese, (Mandarin, Cantonese, and local dialects)
Religions: Non-religious, 59%; folk religions, 20%; atheist, 12%
National name: Zhonghua Renmin Gongheguo
Literacy rate: 76.5%
Economic summary: Gross national product (1987 est.); $286 billion, $280 per capita. Land used for agriculture: 41%; labor force: 61%; principal products: rice, wheat, grains, cotton. Major industrial products: iron and steel, textiles, armaments, petroleum. Natural resources: coal, natural gas, limestone, marble, metals, hydropower potential. Exports: agricultural products, oil, minerals, metals, manufactured goods. Imports: grains, chemical fertilizer, steel, industrial raw materials, machinery and equipment. Major trading partners: Japan, Hong Kong, U.S., West Germany, Singapore, Canada, U.S.S.R., Italy.

1. Including Manchuria and Tibet.

Geography. China, which occupies the eastern part of Asia, is slightly larger in area than the U.S. Its coastline is roughly a semicircle. The greater part of the country is mountainous, and only in the lower reaches of the Yellow and Yangtze Rivers are there extensive low plains.

The principal mountain ranges are the Tien Shan, to the northwest; the Kunlun chain, running south of the Taklimakan and Gobi Deserts; and the Trans-Himalaya, connecting the Kunlun with the borders of China and Tibet. Manchuria is largely an undulating plain connected with the north China plain by a narrow lowland corridor. Inner Mongolia contains the relatively fertile southern and eastern portions of the Gobi. The large island of Hainan (13,500 sq mi.; 34,380 sq km) lies off the southern coast.

Hydrographically, China proper consists of three great river systems. The northern part of the country is drained by the Yellow River (Huang Ho), 2,109 miles long (5,464 km) and mostly unnavigable. The central part is drained by the Chang Jiang (Yangtze Kiang), the third longest river in the world 2,432 miles (6,300 km). The Zhujiang (Si Kiang) in the south is 848 miles long (2,197 km) and navigable for a considerable distance. In addition, the Amur (1,144 sq mi.; 2,965 km) forms part of the northeastern boundary.

Government. With 2,978 deputies, elected for four-year terms by universal suffrage, the National People's Congress is the chief legislative organ. A State Council has the executive authority. The Congress elects the Premier and Deputy Premiers. All ministries are under the State Council, headed by the Premier.

The Communist Party controls the government.

History. By 2000 B.C.; the Chinese were living in the Huang Ho basin, and they had achieved an advanced stage of civilization by 1200 B.C. The great philosophers Lao-tse, Confucius Mo Ti, and Mencius lived during the Chou dynasty (1122–249 B.C.). The warring feudal states were first united under Emperor Ch'in Shih Huang Ti, during whose reign (246–210 B.C.) work was begun on the Great Wall. Under the Han dynasty (206 B.C.–A.D. 220), China prospered and traded with the West.

In the T'ang dynasty (618–907), often called the golden age of Chinese history, painting, sculpture, and poetry flourished, and printing made its earliest known appearance.

The Mings, last of the native rulers (1368–1644), overthrew the Mongol, or Yuan, dynasty (1280–1368) established by Kublai Khan. The Mings in turn were overthrown in 1644 by invaders from the north, the Manchus.

China closely restricted foreign activities, and by the end of the 18th century only Canton and the Portuguese port of Macao were open to European merchants. Following the Anglo-Chinese War of 1839–42, however, several treaty 'ports were opened, and Hong Kong was ceded to Britain. Treaties signed after further hostilities (1856–60) weakened Chinese sovereignty and removed foreigners from Chinese jurisdiction. The disastrous Chinese-Japanese War of 1894–95 was followed by a scramble for Chinese concessions by European powers, leading to the Boxer Rebellion (1900), suppressed by an international force.

The death of the Empress Dowager Tzu Hsi in 1908 and the accession of the infant Emperor Hsüan T'ung (Pu-Yi) were followed by a nation-

Provinces and Regions of China

Name	Area (sq mi.)	Area (sq km)	Capital
Provinces			
Anhui (Anhwei)	54,015	139,900	Hefei (Hofei)
Fujian (Fukien)	47,529	123,100	Fuzhou (Fukien)
Gansu (Kansu)	137,104	355,100	Lanzhou (Lanchow)
Guangdong (Kwangtung)	89,344	231,400	Canton
Guizhou (Kweichow)	67,181	174,000	Guiyang (Kweiyang)
Hebei (Hopei)	81,479	211,030	Shijiazhuang (Shitikiachwang)
Heilongjiang (Heilungkiang)[1]	178,996	463,600	Harbin
Henan (Honan)	64,479	167,000	Zhengzhou (Chengchow)
Hubei (Hupeh)	72,394	187,500	Wuhan
Hunan	81,274	210,500	Changsha
Jiangsu (Kiangsu)	40,927	106,000	Nanjing (Nanking)
Jiangxi (Kiangsi)	63,629	164,800	Nanchang
Jilin (Kirin)[1]	72,201	187,000	Changchun
Liaoning[1]	53,301	138,050	Shenyang
Quinghai (Chinghai)	278,378	721,000	Xining (Sining)
Shaanxi (Shensi)	75,598	195,800	Xian (Sian)
Shandong (Shantung)	59,189	153,300	Jinan (Tsinan)
Shanxi (Shansi)	60,656	157,100	Taiyuan
Sichuan (Szechwan)	219,691	569,000	Chengdu (Chengtu)
Yunnan	168,417	436,200	Kunming
Zhejiang (Chekiang)	39,305	101,800	Hangzhou (Hangchow)
Autonomous Region			
Guangxi Zhuang (Kwangsi Chuang)	85,096	220,400	Nanning
Nei Monggol (Inner Mongolia)[1]	454,633	1,177,500	Hohhot (Huhehot)
Ningxia Hui	30,039	77,800	Yinchuan (Yinchwan)
Xinjiang Uygur (Sinkiang Uighur)[1]	635,829	1,646,800	Urumqi (Urumchi)
Xizang (Tibet)	471,660	1,221,600	Lhasa

1. Together constitute (with Taiwan) what has been traditionally known as Outer China, the remaining territory forming the historical China Proper. NOTE: Names are in Pinyin, with conventional spelling in parentheses.

wide rebellion led by Dr. Sun Yat-sen, who became first President of the Provisional Chinese Republic in 1911. The Manchus abdicated on Feb. 12, 1912. Dr. Sun resigned in favor of Yuan Shih-k'ai, who suppressed the republicans but was forced by a serious rising in 1915–16 to abandon his intention of declaring himself Emperor. Yuan's death in June 1916 was followed by years of civil war between rival militarists and Dr. Sun's republicans.

Nationalist forces, led by Gen. Chiang Kai-shek and with the advice of Communist experts, soon occupied most of China, setting up a Kuomintang regime in 1928. Internal strife continued, however, and Chiang broke with the Communists.

An alleged explosion on the South Manchurian Railway on Sept. 18, 1931, brought invasion of Manchuria by Japanese forces, who installed the last Manchu Emperor, Henry Pu-Yi, as nominal ruler of the puppet state of "Manchukuo." Japanese efforts to take China's northern provinces in July 1937 were resisted by Chiang, who meanwhile had succeeded in uniting most of China behind him. Within two years, however, Japan seized most of the ports and railways. The Kuomintang government retreated first to Hankow and then to Chungking, while the Japanese set up a puppet government at Nanking headed by Wang Jingwei.

Japan's surrender in 1945 touched off civil war between Nationalist forces under Chiang and Communist forces led by Mao Zedong, the party chairman. Despite U. S. aid, the Chiang forces were overcome by the Maoists, backed by the Soviet bloc, and were expelled from the mainland. The Mao regime, established in Peking as the new capital, proclaimed the People's Republic of China on Oct. 1, 1949, with Zhou Enlai as Premier.

After the Korean War began in June 1950, China led the Communist bloc in supporting North Korea, and on Nov. 26, 1950, the Mao regime intervened openly.

In 1958, Mao undertook the "Great Leap Forward" campaign, which combined the establishment of rural communes with a crash program of village industrialization. These efforts also failed, causing Mao to lose influence to Liu Shaoqi, who became President in 1959, to Premier Zhou, and to Party Secretary Deng Xiaoping.

China exploded its first atomic (fission) bomb in 1964 and produced a fusion bomb in 1967.

Mao moved to Shanghai, and from that base he and his supporters waged what they called a Cultural Revolution. In the spring of 1966 the Mao group formed Red Guard units dominated by youths and students, closing the schools to free the students for agitation.

The Red Guards campaigned against "old ideas, old culture, old habits, and old customs." Often they were no more than uncontrolled mobs, and brutality was frequent. Early in 1967 efforts were made to restore control. The Red Guards were urged to return home. Schools started opening.

Persistent overtures by the Nixon Administration resulted in the dramatic announcement in July that Henry Kissinger, President Richard M. Nixon's national security adviser, had secretly visited Peking and reached agreement on a visit by the President to China.

The movement toward reconciliation, which signaled the end of the U.S. containment policy toward China, provided irresistible momentum for Chinese admission to the U.N. Despite U.S. opposition to expelling Taiwan (Nationalist China), the world body overwhelmingly ousted Chiang in seating Peking.

President Nixon went to Peking for a week early in 1972, meeting Mao as well as Zhou. The summit ended with a historic communiqué on February 28, in which both nations promised to work toward improved relations.

In 1973, the U.S. and China agreed to set up "liaison offices" in each other's capitals, which constituted de facto diplomatic relations. Full diplomatic relations were barred by China as long as the U.S. continued to recognize Nationalist China.

On Jan. 8, 1976, Zhou died. His successor, Vice Premier Deng Xiaoping was supplanted within a month by Hua Guofeng, former Minister of Public Security. Hua became permanent Premier in April. In October he was named successor to Mao as Chairman of the Communist Party.

After Mao died on Sept. 10, a campaign against his widow, Jiang Qing, and three of her "radical" colleagues began. The "Gang of Four" was denounced for having undermined the party, the government, and the economy.

Jiang was brought to trial in 1980 and sentenced on Jan. 25, 1981, to die within two years unless she showed repentance, in which case she would be imprisoned for life.

At the Central Committee meeting of 1977, Deng was reinstated as Deputy Premier, Chief of Staff of the Army, and member of the Central Committee of the Politburo.

At the same time, Jiang Qing, Wang Hongwen, Zhang Chunqiao, and Yao Wenyuan—the notorious "Gang of Four"—were removed from all official posts and banished from the party.

In May 1978, expulsion of ethnic Chinese by Vietnam produced an open rupture. Peking sided with Cambodia in the border fighting that flared between Vietnam and Cambodia, charging Hanoi with aggression.

On Aug. 12, 1978, China and Japan signed a treaty of peace and friendship. Peking and Washington then announced that they would open full diplomatic relations on Jan. 1, 1979 and the Carter Administration abrogated the Taiwan defense treaty. Deputy Premier Deng sealed the agreement with a visit to the United States that coincided with the opening of embassies in both capitals on March 1.

On Deng's return from the U.S. Chinese troops invaded Vietnam to avenge alleged violations of Chinese territory. The action was seen as a reaction to Vietnam's invasion of Cambodia.

The first People's Congress in five years confirmed Zhao Ziyang, an economic planner, as Premier replacing Hua Guofeng, who had held the post since 1976.

After the Central Committee meeting of June 27–29, 1981, Hu Yaobang, a Deng protégé, was elevated to the party chairmanship, replacing Hua Guofeng. Deng became chairman of the military commission of the central committee, giving him control over the army. The committee's 215 members concluded the session with a statement holding Mao Zedong responsible for the "grave blunder" of the Cultural Revolution.

Under Deng Xiaoping's leadership, meanwhile, China's Communist ideology was almost totally reinterpreted and sweeping economic changes were set in motion in the early 1980s. The Chinese scrapped the personality cult that idolized Mao Zedong, muted Mao's old call for class struggle and exportation of the Communist revolution, and imported Western technology and management techniques to replace the Marxist tenets that retarded modernization.

Also under Deng's leadership, the Chinese Communists worked out an arrangement with Britain for the future of Hong Kong after 1997. The flag of China will be raised but the territory will retain its present social, economic and legal system.

The removal of Hu Yaobang as party chairman in January 1987 was a sign of a hard-line resurgence. He was replaced by former Premier Zhao Ziyang. Conflict between hard-liners and moderates continued and reached a violent climax in 1989. Student demonstrations calling for accelerated liberalization were crushed by military force in June, resulting in several hundred deaths. This was followed by a purge of moderates, including party leader Zhao Ziyang, who was replaced with Jiang Zemin.

COLOMBIA

Republic of Colombia

President: Virgilio Barco Vargas (1986)*
Population (est. mid-1989): 31,200,000 (average annual rate of natural increase, 2.0%) (mestizo, 58%; white, 20%; 14% mulatto; 17%, Black/Black-Indian; 1% Indian)
Density per square mile: 71
Capital: Bogotá
Largest cities (est. 1985): Bogotá, 4,208,000; Medellín, 2,069,000; Cali, 1,654,000; Baranquilla, 1,120,000; Bucaramanga, 545,000; Cartagena, 530,000
Monetary unit: Peso
Language: Spanish
Religion: Roman Catholic
National name: República de Colombia
Literacy rate (1985): 88%
Economic summary: Gross national product (est. 1987): $34 billion, $390 per capita; real growth rate 5.3%. Land used for agriculture: 35%; labor force: 26%; principal products: coffee, bananas, rice, corn, sugar cane, cotton, tobacco, sorghum. Labor force in industry: 21%; major products: textiles, processed food, beverages, chemicals, cement. Natural resources: petroleum, natural gas, coal, iron ore, nickel, gold, silver. Exports: coffee, fuel oil, cotton, bananas. Imports: machinery, electrical equipment, chemical products, metals and metal products, transportation equipment. Major trading partners: U.S., West Germany, Japan, Venezuela, Netherlands, Brazil.

Geography. Colombia, in the northwestern part of South America, is the only country on that continent that borders on both the Atlantic and Pacific Oceans. It is nearly equal to the combined areas of California and Texas.

Through the western half of the country, three Andean ranges run north and south, merging into one at the Ecuadorean border. The eastern half is a low, jungle-covered plain, drained by spurs of the Amazon and Orinoco, inhabited mostly by isolated, tropical-forest Indian tribes. The fertile plateau and valley of the eastern range are the most densely populated parts of the country.

Government. Colombia's President, who appoints his own Cabinet, serves for a four-year term. The Senate, the upper house of Congress, has 114 members elected for four years by direct vote. The House of Representatives of 199 members is directly elected for four years.

History. Spaniards in 1510 founded Darien, the first permanent European settlement on the American mainland. In 1538 the Spaniards established the colony of New Granada, the area's name until 1861. After a 14-year struggle, in which Simón Bolívar's Venezuelan troops won the battle of Boyacá in Colombia on Aug. 7, 1819, independence was attained in 1824. Bolívar united Colombia, Venezuela, Panama, and Ecuador in the Republic of Greater Colombia (1819–30), but lost Venezuela and Ecuador to separatists. Bolívar's Vice President, Francisco de Paula Santander, founded the Liberal Party as the Federalists while Bolívar established the Conservatives as the Centralists.

Santander's presidency (1832–36) re-established order, but later periods of Liberal dominance (1849–57 and 1861–80), when the Liberals sought to disestablish the Roman Catholic Church, were marked by insurrection and even civil war. Rafael Nuñez, in a 15-year-presidency, restored the power of the central government and the church, which led in 1899 to a bloody civil war and the loss in 1903 of Panama over ratification of a lease to the U.S. of the Canal Zone. For 21 years, until 1930, the Conservatives held power as revolutionary pressures built up.

The Liberal administrations of Enrique Olaya Herrera and Alfonso López (1930–38) were marked by social reforms that failed to solve the country's problems, and in 1946, insurrection and banditry broke out, claiming hundreds of thousands of lives by 1958. Laureano Gómez (1950–53); the Army Chief of Staff, Gen. Gustavo Rojas Pinilla (1953–56), and a military junta (1956–57) sought to curb disorder by repression.

Julio César Turbay Ayala, Liberal Party candidate in 1978, won a narrow victory—approximately 140,000 of a total of nearly 2.5 million votes—over the Conservative Party candidate. The Liberals also retained control of both the Senate and House.

Government efforts to stamp out the Movement of April 19 (M-19), an urban guerrilla organization, intensified in 1981 with the capture of some of the leaders. In 1986 three of its founders were killed in separate gun battles. The Liberals won a solid majority in 1982, but a party split enabled Belisario Betancur Cuartas, the Conservative candidate, to win the presidency on May 31. After his inauguration, he ended the state of siege that had existed almost continuously for 34 years and renewed the general amnesty of 1981.

In May 1986, the liberal Virgilio Barco Vargas was elected by a record-breaking margin.

*Election to be held in May 1990.

COMOROS

Federal Islamic Republic of the Comoros
President: Ahmed Abdallah Abderemane (1978)
Area: 690 sq mi. (1,787 sq km)
Population (est. 1989): 400,000 (average annual rate of natural increase: 3.3%)
Density per square mile: 640
Capital and largest city (est. 1980): Moroni (on Grande Comoro), 20,000
Monetary unit: Franc CFA
Languages: French, Arabic
Religions: Islam, 86%; Roman Catholic, 14%.
National name: République Fédéral Islamique des Comores
Literacy rate (1981): 15%

Economic summary: Gross national product (1986): $163 million, $390 per capita; real growth rate 2.1%. Principal agricultural products: perfume essences, copra, coconuts, cloves, vanilla, cinnamon, yams; major industrial products: perfume distillations. Exports: perfume essences, vanilla, copra, cloves. Imports: foodstuffs, fuels, chemicals, cotton textiles, cement. Major trading partners: France, Kenya, Pakistan, West Germany, Reunion, China.

Geography. The Comoros Islands—Grande Comoro, Anjouan, Mohéli, and Mayotte (which retains ties to France)—are an archipelago of volcanic origin in the Indian Ocean between Mozambique and Madagascar.

Government. A coup by foreign mercenaries on May 13, 1978, deposed President Ali Soilih, who had held power since 1975. A "political and military directorate" headed by Ahmed Abdallah Abderemane and Mohammed Ahmed governed until the adoption of a constitution on Oct. 1 ushered in a republic. With the resignation of Ahmed two days later, Abdallah became president.

History. Under French rule since 1886, the Comoros declared themselves independent July 6, 1975. However, Mayotte, with a Christian majority, voted against joining the other, mainly Islamic, islands, in the move to independence and remains French.

A month after independence, Justice Minister Ali Soilih staged a coup with the help of mercenaries, overthrowing the new nation's first president, Ahmed Abdallah. Soilih lowered the voting age to 14, destroyed all records and killed many Comorans. He was overthrown on May 13, 1978, when a small boatload of French mercenaries, some of whom had aided him three years earlier, seized government headquarters.

CONGO

People's Republic of the Congo
President: Col. Denis Sassou-Nguessou (1979)
Prime Minister: Ange-Edouard Poungui (1984)
Area: 132,046 sq mi. (342,000 sq km)
Population (est. mid-1989): 2,200,000 (average annual rate of natural increase: 3.4%)
Density per sq mile: 16.7
Capital and largest city (est. 1984): Brazzaville, 595,102
Monetary unit: Franc CFA
Ethnic groups: Kongo, Teke, Boubangi
Languages: French, Lingala, Kokongo
Religions: traditional, 42%; Christian, 50%; Muslim, 2%
National name: République Populaire du Congo
Literacy rate: 80%
Economic summary: Gross domestic product (1985): ca. $1.8 billion, $1,140 per capita; real growth rate 2.5% (1984). Principal agricultural products: sugar cane, bananas, coffee, cocoa, peanuts. Labor force in industry: 20%; major products: refined oil, cigarettes, cement, beverages, milled sugar. Natural resources: wood, potash, petroleum, natural gas. Exports: oil, lumber, tobacco, wood, coffee. Imports: machinery, transportation equipment, manufactured consumer goods, iron and steel, foodstuffs. Major trading partners: France, U.S., Italy, Spain, Brazil, West Germany.

Geography. The Congo is situated in west Central Africa astride the Equator. It borders on Gabon, Cameroon, the Central African Republic, Zaire, and the Angola exclave of Cabinda, with a short stretch of coast on the South Atlantic. Its area is nearly three times that of Pennsylvania.

Most of the inland is tropical rain forest, drained by tributaries of the Zaire (Congo) River, which flows south along the eastern border with Zaire to Stanley Pool. The narrow coastal plain rises to highlands separated from the inland plateaus by the 200-mile-wide Niari River Valley, which gives passage to the coast.

Government. Since the coup of September 1968 the country has been governed by a military regime. The Congolese Labor Party is the only party.

History. The inhabitants of the former French Congo, mainly Bantu peoples with Pygmies in the north, were subjects of several kingdoms in earlier times.

The Frenchman Pierre Savorgnan de Brazza signed a treaty with Makoko, ruler of the Bateke people, in 1880, which established French control. The area, with Gabon and Ubangi-Shari, was constituted the colony of French Equatorial Africa in 1910. It joined Chad in supporting the Free French cause in World War II. The Congo proclaimed its independence without leaving the French Community in 1960.

Maj. Marien Ngouabi, head of the National Council of the Revolution, took power as president on Jan. 1, 1969. He was sworn in for a second five-year term in 1975. A visit to Moscow by Ngouabi in March ended with the signing of a Soviet-Congolese economic and technical aid pact.

A four-man commando squad assassinated Ngouabi in Brazzaville on March 18, 1977. Five days later the assassination of Émile Cardinal Biayenda, Archbishop of Brazzaville, was announced. Former President Alphonse Massamba-Débat, accused of plotting both deaths, was executed.

Col. Joachim Yhombi-Opango, Army Chief of Staff, assumed the presidency on April 4. In June, the new government agreed to resume diplomatic relations with the U.S., ending a 12-year rift. Yombhi-Opango resigned on Feb. 4, 1979, and was replaced by Col. Denis Sassou-Neguessou.

COSTA RICA

Republic of Costa Rica
President: Oscar Arias Sanchez (1986)*
Area: 19,652 sq mi. (50,898 sq km)
Population (est. mid-1989): 3,000,000 (average annual rate of natural increase: 2.5%)
Density per square mile: 151
Capital and largest city (est. 1984): San José, 278,500
Monetary unit: Colón
Language: Spanish
Religion: Roman Catholic
National name: República de Costa Rica
Literacy rate (1984): 93%
Economic summary: Gross domestic product (1986 est.): $4.2 billion, $1,530 per capita; real growth rate (1987 est.): 3%. Land used for agriculture: 58%; labor force: 35%; principal products: bananas, coffee, sugar cane, rice, corn, livestock. Labor force in industry: 21%; major products: processed foods, textiles and clothing, construction materials, fertilizer. Natural resource: timber, hydropower potential. Exports: coffee, bananas, beef, sugar, cocoa. Imports: manufactured products, machinery, chemicals, foodstuffs, fuels, fertilizer. Major trading

partners: U.S., Central American countries, West Germany, Japan.

Geography. This Central American country lies between Nicaragua to the north and Panama to the south. Its area slightly exceeds that of Vermont and New Hampshire combined.

Most of Costa Rica is tableland, from 3,000 to 6,000 feet (914 to 1,829 m) above sea level. Cocos Island (10 sq mi.; 26 sq km), about 300 miles (483 km) off the Pacific Coast, is under Costa Rican sovereignty.

Government. Under the 1949 Constitution, the president and the one-house Legislative Assembly of 57 members are elected for terms of four years.

The army was abolished in 1949. There is a civil guard and a rural guard.

History. Costa Rica was inhabited by 25,000 Indians when Columbus discovered it and probably named it in 1502. Few of the Indians survived the Spanish conquest, which began in 1563. The region was administered as a Spanish province. Costa Rica achieved independence in 1821 but was absorbed for two years by Agustín de Iturbide in his Mexican Empire. It was established as a republic in 1848.

Except for the military dictatorship of Tomás Guardia from 1870 to 1882, Costa Rica has enjoyed one of the most democratic governments in Latin America.

Rodrigo Carazo Odio, leader of a four-party coalition called the Unity Party, won the presidency in February 1978. His tenure was marked by a disastrous decline in the economy, which forced postponement of foreign debt payments at the end of 1981. Luis Alberto Monge Alvarez, a former union organizer and cofounder of the National Liberation Party, swept to victory in the Feb. 7, 1982, national elections.

On Feb. 2, 1986, Oscar Arias Sanchez won the national elections on a neutralist platform, defeating Rafael Angel Calderon, who was a stronger supporter of U.S. policies in Central America. Arias initiated a policy of preventing contra usage of Costa Rican territory.

*Elections in Feb. 1990.

CUBA

Republic of Cuba
President: Fidel Castro Ruz (1976)
Area: 44,218 sq mi. (114,524 sq km)
Population (est. mid-1989): 10,500,000 (average annual rate of natural increase: 1.1%)
Density per square mile: 236
Capital: Havana
Largest cities (est. 1986): Havana, 2,013,746; Santiago de Cuba, 358,764; Camagüey, 260,782; Holguin, 194,728; Santa Clara, 178,278
Monetary unit: Peso
Language: Spanish
Religion: Roman Catholic, 40%; non-religious, 49%; atheist, 6%
National name: República de Cuba
Literacy rate: 96%
Economic summary: Gross national product (in 1974 dollars): $18.7 billion, $1,800 per capita; real growth rate (1987 est.): 0%. Land used for agriculture: 52%; labor force: 17%; principal products: sugar, tobacco, coffee, rice, fruits. Labor force in industry: 52%; major products: processed sugar and tobacco, refined oil products, textiles, chemicals, processed food, metals, light consumer products. Natural resources: metals, primarily

nickel, timber. Exports: coffee, sugar, nickel, shellfish, tobacco. Imports: capital goods, industrial raw materials, petroleum, foodstuffs. Major trading partners: U.S.S.R., other Communist bloc countries, Spain, Japan.

Geography. The largest island of the West Indies group (equal in area to Pennsylvania), Cuba is also the westernmost—just west of Hispaniola (Haiti and the Dominican Republic), and 90 miles (145 km) south of Key West, Fla., at the entrance to the Gulf of Mexico.

The island is mountainous in the southeast and south central area (Sierra Maestra). Elsewhere it is flat or rolling.

Government. Since 1976, elections have been held every five years to elect the National Assembly, which in turn elects the 31-member Council of States, its President, First Vice-President, five Vice-Presidents, and Secretary. Fidel Castro is President of the Council of State and of the government and First Secretary of the Communist Party of Cuba, the only political party.

History. Arawak Indians inhabiting Cuba when Columbus discovered the island in 1492 died off from diseases brought by sailors and settlers. By 1511, Spaniards under Diego Velásquez were founding settlements that served as bases for Spanish exploration. Cuba soon after served as an assembly point for treasure looted by the conquistadores, attracting French and English pirates.

Black slaves and free laborers were imported to work sugar and tobacco plantations, and waves of chiefly Spanish immigrants maintained a European character in the island's culture. Early slave rebellions and conflicts between colonials and Spanish rulers laid the foundation for an independence movement that turned into open warfare from 1867 to 1878. The poet, José Marti, in 1895 led the struggle that finally ended Spanish rule, thanks largely to U.S. intervention in 1898 after the sinking of the battleship *Maine* in Havana harbor.

A treaty in 1899 made Cuba an independent republic under U.S. protection. The U.S. occupation, which ended in 1902, suppressed yellow fever and brought large American investment. From 1906 to 1909, Washington invoked the Platt Amendment to the treaty, which gave it the right to intervene in order to suppress any revolt. U.S. troops came back in 1912 and again in 1917 to restore order. The Platt Amendment was abrogated in 1934.

Fulgencio Batista, an army sergeant, led a revolt in 1934 that overthrew the regime of President Gerado Machado.

Batista's Cuba was a police state. Corrupt officials took payoffs from American gamblers who operated casinos, demanded bribes from Cubans for various public services and enriched themselves with raids on the public treasury. Dissenters were murdered and their bodies dumped in gutters.

Fidel Castro Ruz, a hulking, bearded attorney in his 30s, landed in Cuba on Christmas Day 1956 with a band of 12 fellow revolutionaries, evaded Batista's soldiers, and set up headquarters in the jungled hills of the Sierra Maestra range. By 1958 his force had grown to about 2,000 guerrillas, for the most part young and middle class. Castro's brother, Raul, and Ernesto (Ché) Guevara, an Argentine physician, were his top lieutenants. Businessmen and landowners who opposed the Batista regime gave financial support to the rebels. The United States, meanwhile, cut off arms shipments to Batista's army.

The beginning of the end for Batista came when the rebels routed 3,000 government troops and captured Santa Clara, capital of Las Villas province 150 miles from Havana, and a trainload of Batista reinforcements refused to get out of their railroad cars. On New Year's Day 1959, Batista flew to exile in the Dominican Republic and Castro took over the government. Crowds cheered the revolutionaries on their seven-day march to the capital.

The United States initially welcomed what looked like the prospect for a democratic Cuba, but a rude awakening came within a few months when Castro established military tribunals for political opponents, jailed hundreds, and began to veer leftward. Castro disavowed Cuba's 1952 military pact with the United States. He confiscated U.S. investments in banks and industries and seized large U.S. landholdings, turning them first into collective farms and then into Soviet-type state farms. The United States broke relations with Cuba on Jan. 3, 1961. Castro thereupon forged an alliance with the Soviet Union.

From the ranks of the Cuban exiles who had fled to the United States, the Central Intelligence Agency recruited and trained an expeditionary force, numbering less than 2,000 men, to invade Cuba, with the expectation that the invasion would spark an uprising of the Cuban populace against Castro. The invasion was planned under the Eisenhower administration and President John F. Kennedy gave the go-ahead for it in the first months of his administration, but rejected a CIA proposal for U.S. planes to provide air support. The landing at the Bay of Pigs on April 17, 1961, was a fiasco. Not only did the invaders fail to receive any support from the populace, but Castro's tanks and artillery made short work of the small force.

A Soviet attempt to change the global power balance by installing in Cuba medium-range missiles—capable of striking targets in the United States with nuclear warheads—provoked a crisis between the superpowers in 1962 that had the potential of touching off World War III. After a visit to Moscow by Cuba's war minister, Raul Castro, work began secretly on the missile launching sites.

Denouncing the Soviets for "deliberate deception," President Kennedy on Oct. 22 announced that the U.S. navy would enforce a "quarantine" of shipping to Cuba and search Soviet bloc ships to prevent the missiles themselves from reaching the island. After six days of tough public statements on both sides and secret diplomacy, Soviet Premier Nikita Khrushchev on Oct. 28 ordered the missile sites dismantled, crated and shipped back to the Soviet Union, in return for a U.S. pledge not to attack Cuba. Limited diplomatic ties were reestablished on Sept. 1, 1977.

Emigration increased dramatically after April 1, 1980, when Castro, irritated by the granting of asylum to would-be refugees by the Peruvian embassy in Havana, removed guards and allowed 10,000 Cubans to swarm into the embassy grounds.

As an airlift began taking the refugees to Costa Rica, Castro opened the port of Mariel to a "freedom flotilla" of ships and yachts from the United States, many of them owned or chartered by Cuban-Americans to bring out relatives. More than 125,000 Cubans poured out of Mariel in a mass exodus. It wasn't until after they had reached the United States that it was discovered that the regime had opened prisons and mental hospitals to permit criminals, homosexuals and others unwanted in Cuba to join the refugees.

For most of President Ronald Reagan's first term, U.S.-Cuban relations were frozen, with Secretary of State Alexander Haig calling Havana the "source" of troubles in Central America. But late in 1984, an agreement was reached between the two countries. Cuba would take back more than 2,700 Cubans who had come to the United States in the Mariel exodus but were not eligible to stay in the country under U.S. immigration law because of criminal or psychiatric disqualification. The United States, in exchange, would reinstitute regular immigration for Cubans to the United States. Castro cancelled it when the U.S. began the Radio Marti broadcasts in May 1985 to bring a non-Communist view to the Cuban people.

As the first step in the accord, 23 Cuban aliens were moved from Atlanta Federal Penitentiary on Feb. 21, 1985 and flown to Havana.

After a machinegun attack by leftist rebels in June 1985 killed 13 diners—including six Americans—at an outdoor cafe in El Salvador, President Reagan listed Cuba with Iran, Libya, North Korea and Nicaragua in what he called "a confederation of terrorist states".

In January 1987, the U.S. withdrew its chief of mission when Cuba excluded him from diplomatic functions.

CYPRUS

Republic of Cyprus
President: Dr. George Vassiliou (1988)
Area: 3,572 sq mi (9,251 sq km)
Population (est. mid-1989): 700,000 (average annual rate of natural increase: 1.0%) (Greek, 80%; Turkish, 18%)
Density per square mile: 195
Capital and largest city (est. 1982): Nicosia, 123,298
Monetary unit: Cyprus pound
Languages: Greek, Turkish, English
Religions: Greek Orthodox, 82%; Islam, 18%
National name: Kypriaki Dimokratia—Kibris Cumhuriyeti
Member of Commonwealth of Nations
Literacy rate (1981): 89%
Economic summary: Gross national product (1985): $3.7 billion. Average annual growth rate (1970–78): 1.4%. Per capita income (1983): $3,270. Land used for agriculture: 57%; labor force: 22% (in Greek area); principal products: vine products, citrus, potatoes, other vegetables. Labor force in industry: 33% (in Greek area); major products: beverages, footwear, clothing, cement, asbestos mining. Natural resources: copper, asbestos, gypsum, building stone, marble, clay, salt. Exports: food and beverage, clothing, machinery. Imports: manufactured goods, machinery and transportation equipment, petroleum products, foodstuffs. Major trading partners: U.K., Lebanon, Italy, Turkey, Arab countries, Japan, West Germany.

Geography. The third largest island in the Mediterranean (one and one half times the size of Delaware), Cyprus lies off the southern coast of Turkey and the western shore of Syria. Most of the country consists of a wide plain lying between two mountain ranges that cross the island. The highest peak is Mount Olympus at 6,406 feet (1,953 m).

Government. Under the republic's Constitution, for the protection of the Turkish minority the vice president as well as three of the 10 Cabinet ministers must be from the Turkish community, while the House of Representatives is elected by each community separately, 70% Greek Cypriote and 30% Turkish Cypriote representatives.

The Greek and Turkish communities are self-governing in questions of religion, education, and culture. Other governmental matters are under the jurisdiction of the central government. Each community is entitled to a Communal Chamber. The Greek Communal Chamber, which had 23 members, was abolished in 1965 and its function was absorbed by the Ministry of Education. The Turkish Communal Chamber, however, has continued to function.

History. Cyprus was the site of early Phoenician and Greek colonies. For centuries its rule passed through many hands. It fell to the Turks in 1571, and a large Turkish colony settled on the island.

In World War I, on the outbreak of hostilities with Turkey, Britain annexed the island. It was declared a crown colony in 1925.

For centuries the Greek population, regarding Greece as its mother country, has sought self-determination and reunion with it *(enosis).* The resulting quarrel with Turkey threatened NATO. Cyprus became an independent nation on Aug. 16, 1960, with Britain, Greece, and Turkey as guarantor powers.

Archbishop Makarios, president since 1959, was overthrown July 15, 1974, by a military coup led by the Cypriot National Guard. The new regime named Nikos Giorgiades Sampson as president and Bishop Gennadios as head of the Cypriot Church to replace Makarios. The rebels were led by rightist Greek officers who supported *enosis.*

Diplomacy failed to resolve the crisis. Turkey invaded Cyprus by sea and air July 20, 1974, asserting its right to protect the Turkish Cypriote minority.

Geneva talks involving Greece, Turkey, Britain, and the two Cypriote factions failed in mid-August, and the Turks subsequently gained control of 40% of the island. Greece made no armed response to the superior Turkish force, but bitterly suspended military participation in the NATO alliance.

The tension continued after Makarios returned to become President on Dec. 7, 1974. He offered self-government to the Turkish minority, but rejected any solution "involving transfer of populations and amounting to partition of Cyprus."

Turkish Cypriots proclaimed a separate state under Rauf Denktash in the northern part of the island in Nov. 1983, and proposed a "biregional federation."

Makarios died on Aug. 3, 1977, and Spyros Kyprianou was elected to serve the remainder of his term. Kyprianou was subsequently re-elected in 1978 and 1983.

Kyprianou's victory in the legislative elections on December 8, 1985, was seen as a vote of support for his hard-line approach to reunification talks, which remained deadlocked, support that dwindled enough by 1988 for George Vassiliou to defeat Kyprianou. Vassiliou has conducted some informal talks with Denktask, leader of the Turkish Cypriots.

CZECHOSLOVAKIA

Czechoslovak Socialist Republic
President: Gustav Husak (1975)
Premier: Ladislav Adamec (1988)
Area: 49,374 sq mi. (127,896 sq km)
Population (est. mid-1989): 15,600,000 (average annual rate of natural increase: 0.2%) (Czech, 64%; Slovak, 30%)
Density per square mile: 317
Capital: Prague
Largest cities (est. 1986): Prague, 1,193,500; Bratislava, 417,100; Brno, 385,700; Ostrova, 327,800; Kosice, 222,200

Monetary unit: Koruna
Languages: Czech, Slovak, Hungarian
Religions: Roman Catholic, 67%; atheist, 20%;
Czechoslovak Church, 4%
National name: Ceskoslovenská Socialistická Republika
Literacy rate (1981): 100%
Economic summary: Gross national product (1986 est.);
$143.9 (1986 dollars) billion, $9280 per capita; real
growth rate (1986 est.); 1.4%. Labor force in agriculture:
12.3%; principal products: wheat, rye, oats, corn, barley,
potatoes, sugar beets, hogs, cattle, horses. Labor force in
industry: 37%; major products: iron and steel, machinery
and equipment, cement, textiles, motor vehicles,
armaments, chemicals, ceramics. Natural resources:
coal/coke, timber, lignite, uranium, magnesite. Exports:
machinery, chemicals, vehicles, consumer goods. Imports:
machinery, equipment, fuels, raw materials, food,
consumer goods. Major trading partners: U.S.S.R. and
Soviet bloc, Yugoslavia, West Germany, Austria

Geography. Czechoslovakia lies in central Europe,
a neighbor of East and West Germany, Poland, the
U.S.S.R., Hungary, and Austria. It is equal in size
to New York State. The principal rivers—the Elbe,
Danube, Oder, and Moldau—are vital commercially to this landlocked country, for both water-
borne commerce and agriculture, which flourishes
in fertile valleys irrigated by these rivers and their
tributaries.

Government. Since 1969 the supreme organ of the
state has been the Federal Assembly, which has
two equal chambers: the Chamber of People, with
200 deputies, and the Chamber of Nations, with
150 deputies (75 from the Czech Socialist Republic
and 75 from the Slovak Socialist Republic). The
chief executive is the President, who is elected by
the Federal Assembly for a five-year term. The
Premier and his Cabinet are appointed by the
President but are responsible to the Federal Assembly. The leader of the Czechoslovak Communist Party is General Secretary Milos Jakes.

History. Probably about the 5th century A.D., Slavic
tribes from the Vistula basin settled in the region
of modern Czechoslovakia. Slovakia came under
Magyar domination. The Czechs founded the kingdom of Bohemia, the Premyslide dynasty, which
ruled Bohemia and Moravia from the 10th to the
16th century. One of the Bohemian kings, Charles
IV, Holy Roman Emperor, made Prague an imperial capital and a center of Latin scholarship. The
Hussite movement founded by Jan Hus (1369?–
1415) linked the Slavs to the Reformation and revived Czech nationalism, previously under German domination. A Hapsburg, Ferdinand I, ascended the throne in 1526. The Czechs rebelled
in 1618. Defeated in 1620, they were ruled for the
next 300 years as part of the Austrian Empire.

In World War I, Czech and Slovak patriots, notably Thomas G. Masaryk and Milan Stefanik, promoted Czech-Slovak independence from abroad
while their followers fought against the Central
Powers. On Oct. 28, 1918, Czechoslovakia proclaimed itself a republic. Shortly thereafter Masaryk was unanimously elected first President.

Hitler provoked the country's German minority
in the Sudetenland to agitate for autonomy. At the
Munich Conference on Sept. 30, 1938, France and
the U.K., seeking to avoid World War II, agreed
that the Nazis could take the Sudetenland. Dr. Eduard Beneš, who had succeeded Masaryk, resigned
on Oct. 5, 1938, and fled to London. Czechoslovakia became a state within the German orbit and
was known as Czecho-Slovakia. In March 1939, the
Nazis occupied the country.

Soon after Czechoslovakia was liberated in
World War II and the government returned in
April 1945, it was obliged to cede Ruthenia to the
U.S.S.R. In 1946, a Communist, Klement Gottwald,
formed a six-party coalition Cabinet. Pressure from
Moscow increased until Feb. 23–25, 1948, when
the Communists seized complete control in a coup.
Following constituent assembly elections in which
the Communists and their allies were unopposed,
a new Constitution was adopted.

The "people's democracy" was converted into a
"socialist" state by a new Constitution adopted
June 11, 1960.

After the death of Stalin and the relaxing of Soviet controls, Czechoslovakia witnessed a nationalist awakening. In 1968 conservative Stalinists were
driven from power and replaced by more liberal,
reform-minded Communists.

Soviet military maneuvers on Czechoslovak soil
in May 1968 were followed in July by a meeting of
the U.S.S.R. with Poland, Bulgaria, East Germany,
and Hungary in Warsaw that demanded an accounting, which Prague refused. Czechoslovak-
Soviet talks on Czechoslovak territory, at Cierna,
in late July led to an accord. But the Russians
charged that the Czechoslovaks had reneged on
pledges to modify their policies, and on Aug. 20–
21, troops of the five powers, estimated at 600,000,
executed a lightning invasion and occupation.

Soviet secret police seized the top Czechoslovak
leadership and detained it for several days in Moscow. But Soviet efforts to establish a puppet regime
failed. President Ludvik Svoboda negotiated an accord providing for a gradual troop withdrawal in
return for "normalization" of political policy.

Czechoslovakia signed a new friendship treaty
with the U.S.S.R. that codified the "Brezhnev doctrine," under which Russia can invade any Eastern
European socialist nation that threatens to leave
the satellite camp.

One of the most vigorous of the Eastern European groups formed to support human rights in the
wake of the 1975 Helsinki Conference on Security
and Cooperation in Europe was the Czech "Charter 77," an association of 240 intellectuals who
signed a New Year manifesto protesting the suppression of freedom. Detentions of the signers
began immediately, and a second manifesto appeared on January 8 with 300 signatures condemning the official reaction to the first.

Enough of the group remained in May 1981 for
the government to jail 36 persons as part of the precautions against any show of sympathy for Polish
workers. The Czech Communist Party was among
the most severe of the Eastern European states in
condemning what Husak called an attempted
"counterrevolutionary coup" in Poland.

DENMARK

Kingdom of Denmark
Sovereign: Queen Margrethe II (1972)
Premier: Poul Schlüter (1982)
Area: 16,631 sq mi. (43,075 sq km)[1]
Population (est. mid-1989): 5,100,000 (average annual
rate of natural increase: 0.0%)
Density per square mile: 309
Capital: Copenhagen
Largest cities (est. 1985): Copenhagen, 1,358,540;
Aarhus, 252,071; Odense, 171,468; Alborg, 154,750
Monetary unit: Krone
Language: Danish, small German-speaking minority
Religion: Lutheran (established)

National name: Kongeriget Danmark
Literacy rate: 100%
Economic summary: Gross national product (1987): $102.9 billion. Average annual growth rate (1985–7): 2.2%. Per capita income (1984): $11,290. Labor force in agriculture: 6%; principal products: meat, dairy products, fish, grains. Labor force in industry: 23%; major products; industrial and construction equipment, electronics, chemicals, textiles. Natural resources: oil, zinc, lead, coal, molybdenum, cryolite, uranium. Exports: meat and dairy products, fish, industrial machinery, textiles and clothing, chemical products, transportation equipment. Imports: industrial raw materials, fuel, machinery and equipment, transport equipment, petroleum, chemicals. Major trading partners: West Germany, Sweden, U.K., U.S., Norway.

1. Excluding Faeroe Islands and Greenland.

Geography. Smallest of the Scandinavian countries (half the size of Maine), Denmark occupies the Jutland peninsula, which extends north from Germany between the tips of Norway and Sweden. To the west is the North Sea and to the east the Baltic.

The country also consists of several Baltic islands; the two largest are Sjaelland, the site of Copenhagen, and Fyn. The narrow waters off the north coast are called the Skagerrak and those off the east, the Kattegat.

Government. Denmark has been a constitutional monarchy since 1849. Legislative power is held jointly by the Sovereign and parliament. The Constitution of 1953 provides for a unicameral parliament called the Folketing, consisting of 179 popularly elected members who serve for four years. The Cabinet is presided over by the Sovereign, who appoints the Prime Minister.

The Sovereign, Queen Margrethe II, was born April 16, 1940, and became Queen—the first in Denmark's history—Jan. 15, 1972, the day after her father, King Frederik IX, died at 72 in the 25th year of his reign. Margrethe was the eldest of his three daughters (by Princess Ingrid of Sweden). The nation's Constitution was amended in 1953 to permit her to succeed her father in the absence of a male heir to the throne. (Denmark was ruled six centuries ago by Margrethe I, but she was never crowned Queen since there was no female right of succession.)

History. Denmark emerged with establishment of the Norwegian dynasty of the Ynglinger in Jutland at the end of the 8th century. Danish mariners played a major role in the raids of the Vikings, or Norsemen, on Western Europe and particularly England. The country was Christianized by St. Ansgar and Harald Blaatand (Bluetooth)—the first Christian king—in the 10th century. Harald's son, Sweyn, conquered England in 1013. His son, Canute the Great, who reigned from 1014 to 1035, united Denmark, England, and Norway under his rule; the southern tip of Sweden was part of Denmark until the 17th century. On Canute's death, civil war tore the country until Waldemar I (1157–82) re-established Danish hegemony over the north.

In 1282, the nobles won the Great Charter, and Eric V was forced to share power with parliament and a Council of Nobles. Waldemar IV (1340–75) restored Danish power, checked only by the Hanseatic League of north German cities allied with ports from Holland to Poland. His daughter, Margrethe, in 1397 united under her rule Denmark, Norway, and Sweden. But Sweden later achieved autonomy and in 1523, under Gustavus I, independence.

Denmark supported Napoleon, for which it was punished at the Congress of Vienna in 1815 by the loss of Norway to Sweden. In 1864, Bismarck, together with the Austrians, made war on the little country as an initial step in the unification of Germany. Denmark was neutral in World War I.

In 1940, Denmark was invaded by the Nazis. King Christian X reluctantly cautioned his countrymen to accept the occupation, but there was widespread resistance against the Nazis. In 1944, Iceland declared its independence from Denmark, ending a union that had existed since 1380.

Liberated by British troops in May 1945, the country staged a fast recovery in both agriculture and manufacturing and was a leader in liberalizing trade. It joined the United Nations in 1945 and NATO in 1949.

The Social Democrats largely ran Denmark after the war but were ousted in 1973 in an election dominated by protests against high taxes. A minority government was formed by the Liberal Democrats, with their leader, Poul Hartling, as Premier. After losing a vote of confidence in January 1975, Hartling resigned and was succeeded by Anker Jørgensen, a Social Democrat who was Premier in 1972–73.

Disputes over economic policy led to elections in 1981 that led to Poul Schülter coming to power in early 1982. Further disputes over his pro-NATO posture led to elections in May, 1988 that marginally confirmed his position, despite previous losses in the general election of Sept., 1987.

Outlying Territories of Denmark

FAEROE ISLANDS

Status: Autonomous part of Denmark
Lagmand (President): Jogran Sundstein (1989)
Area: 540 sq mi. (1,399 sq km)
Population (1988): 46,853 (average annual growth rate: 1.0%)
Density per square mile: 87
Capital (est. 1982): Thorshavn, 12,750
Monetary unit: Faeroese krone
Literacy rate: 99%
Economic summary: Gross national product (1986): $803 million. Average annual growth rate (1970–79): 5.6 %. Per capita income (1980): $10,620. Principal agricultural products: sheep and cattle. Major industrial product: fish. Exports: fish and fish products. Imports: machinery and transport equipment, foodstuffs, petroleum and petroleum products. Major trading partners: Denmark, U.S., U.K., West Germany

This group of 18 islands, lying in the North Atlantic about 200 miles (322 km) northwest of the Shetland Islands, joined Denmark in 1386 and has since been part of the Danish kingdom. The islands were occupied by British troops during World War II, after the German occupation of Denmark.

The Faeroes have home rule under a bill enacted in 1948; they also have two representatives in the Danish Folketing.

GREENLAND

Status: Autonomous part of Denmark
Premier: Jonathan Motzfeldt (1983)

Area: 840,000 sq mi. (incl. 708,069 sq mi. covered by icecap) (2,175,600 sq km)
Population (1988): 54,790 (average annual growth rate: 13%)
Capital (est. 1982): Godthaab, 10,000
Monetary unit: Krone
Literacy rate: 99%
Economic summary: Gross national product (1986): $470 million. Average annual growth rate (1970–79): 4.4%. Per capita income (1980): $8,290. Principal agricultural products: hay, sheep, garden produce. Major industries: mining, slaughtering, fishing, sealing. Natural resources: metals, cryolite, iron ore, coal, uranium, fish. Exports: fish and fish products, metalic ores and concentrates. Imports: petroleum and petroleum products, machinery and transport equipment, foodstuffs. Major trading partners: Denmark, U.S., Finland, West Germany, U.K.

Greenland, the world's largest island, was colonized in 985–86 by Eric the Red. Danish sovereignty, which covered only the west coast, was extended over the whole island in 1917. In 1941 the U.S. signed an agreement with the Danish minister in Washington, placing it under U.S. protection during World War II but maintaining Danish sovereignty. A definitive agreement for the joint defense of Greenland within the framework of NATO was signed in 1951. A large U.S. air base at Thule in the far north was completed in 1953.

Under 1953 amendments to the Danish Constitution, Greenland became part of Denmark, with two representatives in the Danish Folketing. On May 1, 1979, Greenland gained home rule, with its own local parliament (Landsting), replacing the Greenland Provincial Council.

In February 1982, Greenlanders voted to withdraw from the European Community, which they had joined as part of Denmark in 1973. Danish Premier Anker Jørgensen said he would support the request, but with reluctance.

Greenland is the world's only source of natural cryolite, important in making aluminum.

DJIBOUTI

Republic of Djibouti
President: Hassan Gouled Aptidon (1977)
Prime Minister: Barkat Gourad Hamadou (1978)
Area: 8,490 sq mi. (22,000 sq km)
Population (est. mid-1989): 400,000 (average annual rate of natural increase: 3.0%)
Density per square mile: 46
Capital (est. 1980): Djibouti, 200,000
Monetary unit: Djibouti franc
Languages: Arabic, French, Afar, Somali, Issa
Religions: Islam (Sunni), 94%; Christian, 6%
National name: Jumhouriyya Djibouti
Literacy rate: 20%
Economic summary: Gross domestic product (1986): $333 million, $1,067 per capita. Average annual growth rate (1970–79): −4.9%. Principal agricultural products: goats, sheep, camels. Industries: port and maritime support, construction. Exports: hides, cattle, coffee (in transit from Ethiopia). Imports: machinery, transport equipment, foodstuffs. Major trading partners: France, Ethiopia, Japan, Belgium, U.K., Saudi Arabia, Yemen

Geography. Djibouti lies in northeastern Africa on the Gulf of Aden at the southern entrance to the Red Sea. It borders on Ethiopia and Somalia. The country, the size of Massachusetts, is mainly a stony desert, with scattered plateaus and highlands.

Government. On May 8, 1977, the population of the French Territory of the Afars and Issas voted by more than 98% for independence. Voters also approved a 65-member interim Constituent Assembly. France transferred sovereignty to the new nation of Djibouti on June 27. Later in the year it became a member of the Organization of African Unity and the Arab League. The People's Progress Assembly is the only legal political party.

History. The territory that is now Djibouti was acquired by France between 1843 and 1886 by treaties with the Somali sultans. Small, arid, and sparsely populated, Djibouti is important chiefly because of the capital city's port, the terminal of the Djibouti-Addis Ababa railway that carries 60% of Ethiopia's foreign trade.

Originally known as French Somaliland, the colony voted in 1958 and 1967 to remain under French rule. It was renamed the Territory of the Afars and Issas in 1967 and took the name of its capital city on attaining independence.

Somali rebels in Ethiopia's Ogaden Province cut the railway to Djibouti in June 1977 and there was fear that the new nation might be absorbed by Somalia. In July 1980, Djibouti granted base rights to United States ships and planes in exchange for undisclosed amounts of aid.

DOMINICA

Commonwealth of Dominica
President: Sir Clarence Seignoret (1985)
Prime Minister: Mary Eugenia Charles (1980)
Area: 290 sq mi. (751 sq km)
Population: (est. mid-1989): 100,000 (average annual rate of natural increase: 2.1%)
Density per square mile: 287
Capital and largest city (est. 1981): Roseau, 20,000
Monetary unit: East Caribbean dollar
Languages: English and French patois
Religions: Roman Catholic, Anglican, Methodist
Member of Commonwealth of Nations
Literacy rate: 80%
Economic summary: Gross domestic product (1985): $91 million, $1,090 per capita; real growth rate (1986 est.): 1.2%. Labor force in agriculture: 40%; principal products: bananas, citrus fruits, coconuts, cocoa. Major industries: agricultural processing; tourism. Exports: bananas, lime juice, cocoa, coconut oil, soap. Imports: machinery and equipment, foodstuffs, manufactured goods, chemicals. Major trading partners: U.K., Caribbean countries, U.S.

Geography. Dominica is an island of the Lesser Antilles in the Caribbean south of Guadeloupe and north of Martinique.

Government. Dominica is a republic, with a president elected by the House of Assembly as head of state and a prime minister appointed by the president on the advice of the Assembly. The Freedom Party (17 of 21 seats in the Assembly) is led by Prime Minister Mary Eugenia Charles. The Opposition Democratic Labor Party holds three seats and the United Dominica Labor Party one.

History. Discovered by Columbus in 1493, Dominica was claimed by Britain and France until 1815, when Britain asserted sovereignty. Dominica, along with other Windward Isles, became a self-governing member of the West Indies Associated States in free association with Britain in 1967.

Full independence was granted on Nov. 3, 1978, and the first Prime Minister, Patrick R. John, declared a socialist course for the new republic.

Dissatisfaction over the slow pace of reconstruction after Hurricane David struck the island in September 1979 brought a landslide victory for the opposition Freedom Party in July 1980. The vote gave the prime ministership to Mary Eugenia Charles, a strong advocate of free enterprise. The Freedom Party won again in 1985 elections, giving Miss Charles a second five-year term as prime minister.

DOMINICAN REPUBLIC

President: Joaquin Balaguer (1986)
Area: 18,704 sq mi. (48,442 sq km)
Population (est. mid-1989): 7,000,000 (average annual rate of natural increase: 2.5%) (approx.): mulatto, 75%; white, 15%; Negro, 10%
Density per square mile: 373
Capital: Santo Domingo
Largest cities (est. 1983): Santo Domingo, 1,410,000; Santiago de los Caballeros, 285,000
Monetary unit: Peso
Language: Spanish
Religion: Roman Catholic
National name: República Dominicana
Literacy rate: 74%
Economic summary: Gross domestic product (1986 est.): $5.6 billion, $800 per capita; real growth rate (1986 est.): 2.0%. Land used for agriculture: 73%; labor force: 49%; principal products: sugar cane, coffee, cocoa, tobacco, bananas, corn. Labor force in industry: 18%; major products: processed sugar, textiles, nickel, silver, and gold mining. Natural resources: nickel, bauxite, gold, silver. Exports: sugar, nickel, coffee, tobacco, gold, cocoa. Imports: foodstuffs, petroleum, industrial raw materials, capital equipment. Major trading partners: U.S., Venezuela, Mexico.

Geography. The Dominican Republic in the West Indies, occupies the eastern two thirds of the island of Hispaniola, which it shares with Haiti. Its area equals that of Vermont and New Hampshire combined.

Crossed from northwest to southeast by a mountain range with elevations exceeding 10,000 feet (3,048 m), the country has fertile, well-watered land in the north and east, where nearly two thirds of the population lives. The southwest part is arid and has poor soil, except around Santo Domingo.

Government. The president is elected by direct vote every four years. Legislative powers rest with a Senate and a Chamber of Deputies, both elected by direct vote, also for four years. All citizens must vote when they reach 18 years of age, or even earlier if they are married.

History. The Dominican Republic was discovered by Columbus in 1492. He named it La Española, and his son, Diego, was its first viceroy. The capital, Santo Domingo, founded in 1496, is the oldest European settlement in the Western Hemisphere. Spain ceded the colony to France in 1795, and Haitian blacks under Toussaint L'Ouverture conquered it in 1801.

In 1808 the people revolted and the next year captured Santo Domingo, setting up the first republic. Spain regained title to the colony in 1814. In 1821 the people overthrew Spanish rule, but in 1822 they were reconquered by the Haitians. They revolted again in 1844, threw out the Haitians, and established the Dominican Republic, headed by Pedro Santana. Uprisings and Haitian attacks led Santana to make the country a province of Spain from 1861 to 1865. The U.S. Senate refused to ratify a treaty of annexation. Disorder continued until the dictatorship of Ulíses Heureaux; in 1916, when disorder broke out again, the U.S. sent in a contingent of marines, who remained until 1934.

A sergeant in the Dominican army trained by the marines, Rafaél Leonides Trujillo Molina, overthrew Horacio Vásquez in 1930 and established a dictatorship that lasted until his assassination 31 years later.

A new Constitution was adopted in 1962, and the first free elections since 1924 put Juan Bosch, a leftist leader, in office. A planned program of reforms with U.S. support was cut off by a right-wing military coup that replaced Bosch with a civilian triumvirate.

Leftists rebelled April 24, 1965, and President Lyndon Johnson sent in marines and troops. After an OAS ceasefire request May 6, a compromise installed Hector Garcia-Godoy as provisional president. Joaquin Balaguer won in free elections in 1966 against Bosch, and a peacekeeping force of 9,000 U.S. troops and 2,000 from other countries withdrew. Balaguer restored political and economic stability.

Balaguer's longtime support for free elections faltered in May 1978, when the army suspended the counting of ballots as he trailed in a fourth-term bid. After a warning from President Jimmy Carter, however, Balaguer accepted the victory of Antonio Guzmán of the opposition Dominican Revolutionary Party.

Salvador Jorge Blanco of the Dominican Revolutionary Party was elected President on May 16, 1982, defeating Balaguer and Bosch. Austerity measures imposed by the International Monetary Fund, including sharply higher prices for food and gasoline, provoked rioting in the spring of 1984 that left more than 50 dead.

Saying he feared they would provoke "some kind of revolution," Blanco dragged his feet about putting into effect further IMF demands for higher prices and taxes and devaluation of the peso, and came within weeks of defaulting on several big loans.

Balaguer was elected President in May 1986 and aimed economic policy at diversifying the economy. On April 30, 1987, Blanco asked for political asylum in Venezuela after charges of corruption during his term were levelled against him.

ECUADOR

Republic of Ecuador
President: Rodrigo Borja Cevallos (1988)
Area: 109,484 sq mi. (270,670 sq km)
Population (est. mid-1988): 10,500,000 (average annual rate of natural increase: 2.6%)
Density per square mile: 95
Capital: Quito
Largest cities (est. 1987): Guayaquil, 1,572,615; Quito, 1,137,705; Cuenca, 201,490

Monetary unit: Sucre
Languages: Spanish, Quéchua
Religion: Roman Catholic, 95%
National name: República del Ecuador
Literacy rate: 85%
Economic summary: Gross national product (1986). $13.1 billion, $1,310 per capita; real growth rate: 1.7%. Land used for agriculture: 26%; labor force: 52%; principal products: bananas, cocoa, coffee, sugar cane, fruits, corn, potatoes, rice. Labor force in industry: 13%; major products: processed foods, textiles, fish, petroleum. Natural resources: petroleum, fish, silver, gold. Exports: petroleum, shrimp, bananas, coffee, cocoa, fish products. Imports: agricultural and industrial machinery, industrial raw materials, foodstuffs, chemical products, transportation and communication equipment. Major trading partners: U.S., EEC, Brazil, Chile, Japan.

Geography. Ecuador, equal in area to Nevada, is in the northwest part of South America fronting on the Pacific. To the north is Colombia and to the east and south is Peru. Two high and parallel ranges of the Andes, traversing the country from north to south, are topped by tall volcanic peaks. The highest is Chimborazo at 20,577 feet (6,272 m).

The Galápagos Islands (or Colón Archipelago) (3,029 sq mi.; 7,845 sq km) in the Pacific Ocean about 600 miles (966 km) west of the South American mainland, became part of Ecuador in 1832.

Government. A 1978 Constitution returned Ecuador to civilian government after eight years of military rule. The President is elected to a term of four years and a House of Representatives of 71 members is popularly elected for the same period.

History. The tribes in the northern highlands of Ecuador formed the Kingdom of Quito around A.D. 1000. It was absorbed, by conquest and marriage, into the Inca Empire. Pizarro conquered the land in 1532, and through the 17th century a thriving colony was built by exploitation of the Indians. The first revolt against Spain occurred in 1809. Ecuador then joined Venezuela, Colombia, and Panama in a confederacy known as Greater Colombia.

On the collapse of this union in 1830, Ecuador became independent. Subsequent history was one of revolts and dictatorships; it had 48 presidents during the first 131 years of the republic. Conservatives ruled until the Revolution of 1895 ushered in nearly a half century of Radical Liberal rule, during which the church was disestablished and freedom of worship, speech, and press was introduced.

A three-man military junta which had taken power in a 1976 coup, agreed to a free presidential election on July 16, 1978. Jaime Roldós Aguilera won the runoff on April 29, 1979.

The 40-year-old President died in the crash of a small plane May 24, 1981. Vice President Osvaldo Hurtado Larrea became President. León Febres Cordero, was installed President in August 1984. Combined opposition parties won a majority in the 71-member Congress large enough to block significant action, a majority increased in the June 1986 elections.

Problems with the military plagued Febres in 1986-87, and he faced two rebellions.

In 1988, Rodrigo Borja was elected President. He was also able to form a coalition in the House, confirming a leftward shift in the government and promising smoother executive-legislative relations.

EGYPT

Arab Republic of Egypt
President: Hosni Mubarak (1981)
Premier: Dr. Atef Sedki (1986)
Area: 386,900 sq. mi. (1,002,000 sq km)
Population (est. mid-1989): 54,800,000 (average annual rate of natural increase: 2.8%)
Density per square mile: 142
Capital: Cairo
Largest cities (est. 1987): Cairo, 12,560,000; **(1986 est.):** Alexandria, 2,893,000; Giza, 1,670,800; Shubra el Khema, 533,300; El Mahalla el Kubra, 385,300
Monetary unit: Egyptian pound
Language: Arabic
Religions: Islam, 93%; Christian (mostly Copt), 7%
Literacy rate: 43%
Economic summary: Gross national product (1987, in 1980 dollars): $34 billion, $655 per capita; real growth rate (1987): 3%. Land used for agriculture: 5%; labor force: 40–45%; principal products: cotton, wheat, rice, corn. Labor force in industry: 20%; major products: textiles, processed foods, chemicals, fertilizer, petroleum and petroleum products. Natural resources: iron ore, phosphates, petroleum, gypsum. Exports: cotton, petroleum, cement. Imports: foodstuffs, machinery, fertilizers, woods. Major trading partners: U.S., Western Europe, Japan, Eastern Europe.

Geography. Egypt, at the northeast corner of Africa on the Mediterranean Sea, is bordered on the west by Libya, on the south by the Sudan, and on the east by the Red Sea and Israel. It is nearly one and one half times the size of Texas.

The historic Nile flows through the eastern third of the country. On either side of the Nile valley are desert plateaus, spotted with oases. In the north, toward the Mediterranean, plateaus are low, while south of Cairo they rise to a maximum of 1,015 feet (309 m) above sea level. At the head of the Red Sea is the Sinai Peninsula, between the Suez Canal and Israel.

Navigable throughout its course in Egypt, the Nile is used largely as a means of cheap transport for heavy goods. The principal port is Alexandria.

The Nile delta starts 100 miles (161 km) south of the Mediterranean and fans out to a sea front of 155 miles between the cities of Alexandria and Port Said. From Cairo north, the Nile branches into many streams, the principal ones being the Damietta and the Rosetta.

Except for a narrow belt along the Mediterranean, Egypt lies in an almost rainless area, in which high daytime temperatures fall quickly at night.

Government. Executive power is held by the President, who is elected every six years and can appoint one or more Vice Presidents.

The National Democratic Party, led by President Hosni Mubarak, is the dominant political party. Elections on April 6, 1987 confirmed its huge majority (348 of 448 seats). There is also a three-party alliance, that includes the Muslim Brotherhood, that forms the main opposition (60 seats). The New Wafd is the third largest party (35 seats).

History. Egyptian history dates back to about 4000 B.C., when the kingdoms of upper and lower Egypt, already highly civilized, were united. Egypt's "Golden Age" coincided with the 18th and 19th dynasties (16th to 13th centuries B.C.), during which the empire was established. Persia conquered Egypt in 525 B.C.; Alexander the Great subdued it in 332 B.C.; and then the dynasty of the Ptolemies ruled the land until 30 B.C., when Cleopatra, last of the line, committed suicide and Egypt became a Roman province. From 641 to 1517 the Arab caliphs ruled Egypt, and then the Turks took it for their Ottoman Empire.

Napoleon's armies occupied the country from 1798 to 1801. In 1805, Mohammed Ali, leader of a band of Albanian soldiers, became Pasha of Egypt. After completion of the Suez Canal in 1869, the French and British took increasing interest in Egypt.

British troops occupied Egypt in 1882, and British resident agents became its actual administrators, though it remained under nominal Turkish sovereignty. In 1914, this fiction was ended, and Egypt became a protectorate of Britain.

Egyptian nationalism forced Britain to declare Egypt an independent, sovereign state on Feb. 28, 1922, although the British reserved rights for the protection of the Suez Canal and the defense of Egypt. In 1936, by an Anglo-Egyptian treaty of alliance, all British troops and officials were to be withdrawn, except from the Suez Canal Zone. When World War II started, Egypt remained neutral. British imperial troops finally ended the Nazi threat to Suez in 1942 in the battle of El Alamein, west of Alexandria.

In 1951, Egypt abrogated the 1936 treaty and the 1899 Anglo-Egyptian condominium of the Sudan (*See* Sudan). Rioting and attacks on British troops in the Suez Canal Zone followed, reaching a climax in January 1952. The army, led by Gen. Mohammed Naguib, seized power on July 23, 1952. Three days later, King Farouk abdicated in favor of his infant son. The monarchy was abolished and a republic proclaimed on June 18, 1953, with Naguib holding the posts of Provisional President and Premier. He relinquished the latter in 1954 to Gamal Abdel Nasser, leader of the ruling military junta. Naguib was deposed seven months later and Nasser confirmed as President in a referendum on June 23, 1956.

Nasser's policies embroiled his country in continual conflict. In 1956, the U.S. and Britain withdrew their pledges of financial aid for the building of the Aswan High Dam. In reply, Nasser nationalized the Suez Canal and expelled British oil and embassy officials. Israel, barred from the Canal and exasperated by terrorist raids, invaded the Gaza Strip and the Sinai Peninsula. Britain and France, after demanding Egyptian evacuation of the Canal Zone, attacked Egypt on Oct. 31, 1956. Worldwide pressure forced Britain, France, and Israel to halt the hostilities. A U.N. emergency force occupied the Canal Zone, and all troops were evacuated in the spring of 1957.

On Feb. 1, 1958, Egypt and Syria formed the United Arab Republic, which was joined by Yemen in an association known as the United Arab States. However, Syria withdrew from the United Arab Republic in 1961 and Egypt dissolved its ties with Yemen in the United Arab States.

On June 5, 1967, Israel invaded the Sinai Peninsula, the East Bank of the Jordan River, and the zone around the Gulf of Aqaba. A U.N. ceasefire on June 10 saved the Arabs from complete rout.

Nasser declared the 1967 cease-fire void along the Canal in April 1969 and began a war of attrition. The U.S. peace plan of June 19, 1970, resulted in Egypt's agreement to reinstate the cease-fire for at least three months, (from August) and to accept Israel's existence within "recognized and secure" frontiers that might emerge from U.N.-mediated talks. In return, Israel accepted the principle of withdrawing from occupied territories.

Then, on Sept. 28, 1970, Nasser died, at 52, of a heart attack. The new President was Anwar el-Sadat, an associate of Nasser and a former newspaper editor.

The Aswan High Dam, whose financing by the U.S.S.R. was its first step into Egypt, was completed and dedicated in January 1971.

In July 1972, Sadat ordered the expulsion of Soviet "advisors and experts" from Egypt because the Russians had not provided the sophisticated weapons he felt were needed to retake territory lost to Israel in 1967.

The fourth Arab-Israeli war broke out Oct. 6, 1973, while Israelis were commemorating Yom Kippur, the Jewish high holy day. Egypt swept deep into the Sinai, while Syria strove to throw Israel off the Golan Heights.

A U.N.-sponsored truce was accepted on October 22. In January 1974, both sides agreed to a settlement negotiated by U.S. Secretary of State Henry A. Kissinger that gave Egypt a narrow strip along the entire Sinai bank of the Suez Canal. In June, President Nixon made the first visit by a U.S. President to Egypt and full diplomatic relations were established. The Suez Canal was cleared and reopened on June 5, 1975.

Kissinger pursued "shuttle diplomacy" between Cairo and Jerusalem to extend areas of agreement. Israel yielded on three points—the possession of the Mitla and Giddi passes in the Sinai and the Abu Rudeis oil field in the peninsula—and both sides committed themselves to annual renewal of the U.N. peacekeeping force in the Sinai.

In the most audacious act of his career, Sadat flew to Jerusalem at the invitation of Prime Minister Menachem Begin and pleaded before Israel's Knesset on Nov. 20, 1977, for a permanent peace settlement. The Arab world reacted with fury—only Morocco, Tunisia, Sudan, and Oman approved.

Egypt and Israel signed a formal peace treaty on March 26, 1979. The pact ended 30 years of war and established diplomatic and commercial relations.

Egyptian and Israeli officials met in the Sinai desert on April 26, 1979, to implement the peace treaty calling for the phased withdrawal of occupation forces from the peninsula. By mid-1980, two thirds of the Sinai was transferred, but progress here was not matched—the negotiation of Arab autonomy in the Gaza Strip and the West Bank.

Sadat halted further talks in August 1980 because of continued Israeli settlement of the West Bank. On October 6 1981, Sadat was assassinated by extremist Muslim soldiers at a parade in Cairo. Vice President Hosni Mubarak, a former Air Force chief of staff, was confirmed by the parliament as president the next day.

Although feared unrest in Egypt did not occur in the wake of the assassination, and Israel completed the return of the Sinai to Egyptian control on April 25, 1982, Mubarak was unable to revive the autonomy talks. Israel's invasion of Lebanon in June imposed a new strain on him, and brought a marked cooling in Egyptian-Israeli relations, but not a disavowal of the peace treaty.

During 1985, pressures by Moslem fundamentalists to implement Islamic law in Egypt increased. In response, the government began putting all mosques under control of the minister for religious endowments. In July, authorities arrested at least

45 fundamentalists including Sheik Hafez Salama, the fundamentalist cleric spearheading the campaign for immediate application of *sharia*, the Islamic legal code dating back 1,300 years.

In February 1986, a riot by the security forces had to be quelled by the army; an incident that underscored Mubarak's dependence on the army in the face of growing Islamic fundamentalism and increasing discontent with the failing economy.

Suez Canal. The Suez Canal, in Egyptian territory between the Arabian Desert and the Sinai Peninsula, is an artificial waterway about 100 miles (161 km) long between Port Said on the Mediterranean and Suez on the Red Sea. Construction work, directed by the French engineer Ferdinand de Lesseps, was begun April 25, 1859, and the Canal was opened Nov. 17, 1869. The cost was 432,807,882 francs. The concession was held by an Egyptian joint stock company, *Compagnie Universelle du Canal Maritime de Suez*, in which the British government held 353,504 out of a total of 800,000 shares. The concession was to expire Nov. 17, 1968, but the company was nationalized July 26, 1956, by unilateral action of the Egyptian government.

The Canal was closed in June 1967 after the Arab-Israeli conflict. With the help of the U.S. Navy, work was begun on clearing the Canal in 1974, after the cease-fire ending the Arab-Israeli war. It was reopened to traffic June 5, 1975.

EL SALVADOR

Republic of El Salvador
President: Alfredo Christiani (1989)
Area: 8,260 sq mi. (21,393 sq km)
Population (est. mid-1989): 5,100,000 (average annual rate of natural increase: 2.7%)
Density per square mile: 620
Capital: San Salvador
Largest cities (est. 1985): San Salvador, 459,902; Santa Ana, 137,879; Mejicanos, 91,465; San Miguel, 88,520
Monetary unit: Colón
Language: Spanish
Religion: Roman Catholic
National name: República de El Salvador
Literacy rate: 69%
Economic summary: Gross domestic product (1985 est.): $4.36 billion, $870 per capita. Average annual growth rate (1973–82): 0.6%. Land used for agriculture: 64%; labor force: 40%; principal products: coffee, cotton, corn, sugar, rice, sorghum. Labor force in industry: 16%; major products: processed foods, clothing and textiles, petroleum products. Natural resources: hydro- and geothermal power, crude oil. Exports: coffee, cotton, sugar, shrimp. Imports: machinery, automotive vehicles, petroleum, foodstuffs, fertilizer. Major trading partners: U.S., Guatemala, Japan, West Germany, Mexico, Costa Rica, Venezuela.

Geography. Situated on the Pacific coast of Central America, El Salvador has Guatemala to the west and Honduras to the north and east. It is the smallest of the Central American countries, its area equal to that of Massachusetts, and the only one without an Atlantic coastline.

Most of the country is a fertile volcanic plateau about 2,000 feet (607 m) high. There are some active volcanoes and many scenic crater lakes.

Government. A new Constitution enacted in 1983

vests executive power in a President elected for a nonrenewable, five-year term, and legislative power in a 60-member National Assembly elected by universal suffrage and proportional representation. Judicial power is vested in a Supreme Court, composed of a President and nine magistrates elected by the Assembly, and subordinate courts.

History. Pedro de Alvarado, a lieutenant of Cortés, conquered El Salvador in 1525. El Salvador, with the other countries of Central America, declared its independence from Spain on Sept. 15, 1821, and was part of a federation of Central American states until that union was dissolved in 1838. Its independent career for decades thereafter was marked by numerous revolutions and wars against other Central American republics.

On Oct. 15, 1979, a junta deposed the President, Gen. Carlos Humberto Romero, seeking to halt increasingly violent clashes between leftist and rightist forces.

On Dec. 4, 1980, three American nuns and an American lay worker were killed in an ambush near San Salvador, causing the Carter Administration to suspend all aid pending an investigation. The naming of José Napoleón Duarte, a moderate civilian, as head of the governing junta brought a resumption of U.S. aid.

Defying guerrilla threats, voters on March 28, 1982, elected a rightist majority to a constituent assembly that dismissed Duarte and replaced him with a centrist physician, Dr. Alvaro Alfredo Magaña. The rightist majority repealed the laws permitting expropriation of land, and critics charged that the land-reform program begun under Duarte was dead. Even though fighting continued, with reports of government violations of human rights, the Reagan Administration asked certification of El Salvador's eligibility for resumed foreign aid, and this was approved by Congress.

In an election closely monitored by American and other foreign observers, Duarte was elected President in May 1984.

Duarte's Christian Democratic Party scored an unexpected electoral triumph in national legislative and municipal elections held in March 1985, a winning majority in the new National Assembly. The rightist parties that had been dominant in the previous Constituent Assembly demanded that the vote be nullified, but the army high command rejected their assertion the voting had been fraudulent. The army's refusal to support the rightists was interpreted as a turning point in El Salvador's struggle for political stability.

At the same time, U.S. officials said that while the rebels still were far from being defeated, there had been marked improvement in the effectiveness of government troops in the civil war against antigovernment guerrillas that has been waged mainly in the countryside. The rebels responded by initiating a campaign of urban terror; killing and kidnapping pro-government figures. In 1986, Duarte called for a new round of talks with the rebels. This was seen as an attempt to revive a popularity that was falling due to his perceived failure to improve the economy, implement promised social programs or end the war. These broke down in September. Duarte's inability to find solutions led to the right-wing ARENA party controlling half the seats in the National Assembly, in the elections of March, 1988. The decisive victory of Alfredo Christiani, the ARENA candidate for president, gives the right-wing party effective control of the country, given their political control of most of the municipalities.

EQUATORIAL GUINEA

Republic of Equatorial Guinea
President: Col. Teodoro Obiang Nguema Mbasogo (1979)
Prime Minister: Capt. Cristino Seriche Bioko
Area: 10,830 sq mi. (28,051 sq km)
Population (mid-1988): 346,839 (average annual rate of natural increase: 1.9%)
Density per square mile: 33
Capital and largest city (est. 1983): Malabo, 37,500
Monetary unit: CFA Franc
Languages: Spanish, pidgin English, Fang, Bubi, N'Dowe
Religions: Roman Catholic, Protestant, traditional
National name: República de Guinea Ecuatorial
Literacy rate: 55%
Economic summary: Gross national product (1986): $75 million, $300 per capita. Land used for agriculture: 13%; labor force: 76%; principal products: cocoa, wood, coffee; rice, yams. Natural resource: wood, crude oil. Exports: cocoa, wood, coffee. Imports: foodstuffs, textiles, machinery. Major trading partner: Spain

Geography. Equatorial Guinea, formerly Spanish Guinea, consists of Rio Muni (10,045 sq mi.; 26,117 sq km), on the western coast of Africa, and several islands in the Gulf of Guinea, the largest of which is Bioko (formerly Fernando Po) (785 sq mi.; 2,033 sq km). The other islands are Annobón, Corisco, Elobey Grande, and Elobey Chico. The total area is twice that of Connecticut.

Government. The Constitution of 1973 was suspended after a coup on Aug. 3, 1979. A Supreme Military Council, headed by the president, exercises all power. Political parties were banned until Aug. 1987.

History. Fernando Po and Annobón came under Spanish control in 1778. From 1827 to 1844, with Spanish consent, Britain administered Fernando Po, but in the latter year Spain reclaimed the island. Río Muni was given to Spain in 1885 by the Treaty of Berlin.

Negotiations with Spain led to independence on Oct. 12, 1968.

In 1969, anti-Spanish incidents in Río Muni, including the tearing down of a Spanish flag by national troops, caused 5,000 Spanish residents to flee for their safety, and diplomatic relations between the two nations became strained. A month later, President Masie Nguema Biyogo Negue Ndong charged that a coup had been attempted against him. He seized dictatorial powers and arrested 80 opposition politicians and even several of his Cabinet ministers and the secretary of the National Assembly.

A coup on Aug. 3, 1979, deposed Masie, and a junta led by Lieut. Col. Teodoro Obiang Nguema Mbasogo took over the government. Obiang expelled Soviet technicians and reinstated cooperation with Spain.

ETHIOPIA

People's Democratic Republic of Ethiopia
President: Mengistu Haile Mariam (1987)
Prime Minister: Fikre Selassie Wagderess (1987)
Area: 472,432 sq mi. (1,223,600 sq km)
Population (est. mid-1989): 49,800,000 (average annual rate of natural increase: 2.1%)
Density per square mile: 105
Capital: Addis Ababa
Largest cities (est. 1984): Addis Ababa, 1,423,111; Asmara, 275,385

Monetary unit: Birr
Languages: Amharic (official), Galligna, Tigrigna
Religions: Ethiopian Orthodox, 40%; Islam, 35%; traditional, 15%
Literacy rate: 35%
Economic summary: Gross domestic product (FY87 est.): $5.4 billion, $110 per capita. Average annual growth rate (1973–82): 2.6%. Land used for agriculture: 54%; labor force: 90%; principal products: coffee, barley, wheat, corn, sugar cane, cotton, oilseeds, livestock. Labor force in industry: 10%; Major industrial products: cement, cotton textiles, refined sugar, processed foods, refined oil. Natural resources: potash, salt, gold, platinum, copper. Exports: coffee, hides and skins, oilseeds. Imports: petroleum, foodstuffs. Major trading partners: U.S.S.R., U.S., W. Germany, Italy, Japan, Djibouti, South Yemen.

Geography. Ethiopia is in east central Africa, bordered on the west by the Sudan, the east by Somalia and Djibouti, the south by Kenya, and the north by the Red Sea. It is nearly three times the size of California.

Over its main plateau land, Ethiopia has several high mountains, the highest of which is Ras Dashan at 15,158 feet (4,620 m). The Blue Nile, or Abbai, rises in the northwest and flows in a great semicircle east, south, and northwest before entering the Sudan. Its chief reservoir, Lake Tana, lies in the northwestern part of the plateau.

Government. On Feb. 22, 1987, a new constitution came into effect. It establishes a Communist civilian government with a national assembly, the Shengo, which elected Mengistu as president for a five-year term. The Workers Party of Ethiopia is the only party.

History. Black Africa's oldest state, Ethiopia can trace 2,000 years of recorded history. Its now deposed royal line claimed descent from King Menelik I, traditionally believed to have been the son of the Queen of Sheba and King Solomon. The present nation is a consolidation of smaller kingdoms that owed feudal allegiance to the Ethiopian Emperor.

Hamitic peoples migrated to Ethiopia from Asia Minor in prehistoric times. Semitic traders from Arabia penetrated the region in the 7th century B.C. Its Red Sea ports were important to the Roman and Byzantine Empires. Coptic Christianity came to the country in A.D. 341, and a variant of that communion became Ethiopia's state religion.

Ancient Ethiopia reached its peak in the 5th century, then was isolated by the rise of Islam and weakened by feudal wars. Modern Ethiopia emerged under Emperor Menelik II, who established its independence by routing an Italian invasion in 1896. He expanded Ethiopia by conquest.

Disorders that followed Menelik's death brought his daughter to the throne in 1917, with his cousin, Tafari Makonnen, as Regent, heir presumptive, and strongman. When the Empress died in 1930, Tafari was crowned Emperor Haile Selassie I.

As Regent, Haile Selassie outlawed slavery. As Emperor, he worked for centralization of his diffuse realm, in which 70 languages are spoken, and for moderate reform. In 1931, he granted a Constitution, revised in 1955, that created a parliament with an appointed Senate and an elected Chamber of Deputies, and a system of courts. But basic power remained with the Emperor.

Bent on colonial empire, fascist Italy invaded Ethiopia on Oct. 3, 1935, forcing Haile Selassie into exile in May 1936. Ethiopia was annexed to Eritrea, then an Italian colony, and Italian Somaliland to form Italian East Africa, losing its independence for the first time in recorded history. In 1941, British troops routed the Italians, and Haile Selassie returned to Addis Ababa.

Deep discontent erupted in the fall of 1973. A long drought had caused famine that killed 100,000 peasants and drove thousands of others to cities, where food was scarce and inflation was rampant. Charges of mismanagement of drought relief sparked riots in Addis Ababa in 1974, and unpaid troops in Asmara, capital of Eritrea, mutinied to protest conditions.

In August 1974, the Armed Forces Committee nationalized Haile Selassie's palace and estates and directed him not to leave Addis Ababa. On Sept. 12, 1974, he was deposed after nearly 58 years as Regent and Emperor. The 82-year-old "Lion of Judah" was placed under guard. Parliament was dissolved and the Constitution suspended.

On Aug. 27, 1975, Haile Selassie died in a small apartment in his former Addis Ababa palace where he had been treated as a state prisoner. He was 83.

Lt. Col. Mengistu Haile Mariam was named head of state Feb. 2, 1977, to replace Brig. Gen. Teferi Benti, who was killed in a factional fight of the Dirgue after having ruled since 1974. The government was losing its fight to hold Eritrea and in the southeastern region of Ogaden, Somali guerrillas backed by Somali regular forces threatened the ancient city of Harar. In October, the U.S.S.R. announced it would end military aid to Somalia and henceforth back its new ally, Ethiopia. This, together with the intervention of Cuban troops in Ogaden, turned the tide for Mengistu. By March 1978, the badly beaten Somalis had retreated to their homeland. This brought an end to large-scale fighting with Somalia, but border skirmishing continued intermittently.

The Marxist government still had not quelled the Eritrean secessionists in the north by 1988. In addition, a secessionist struggle was going on in Tigre, the province adjoining Eritrea. The government lost ground in both provinces and both sides agreed to cease-fire negotiations.

A Communist regime was formally proclaimed on Sept. 10, 1984, with Mengistu as party leader. After enduring years of drought, the country in 1986 was in the throes of the worst famine in more than a decade. The spring rains of 1987 marked a pause to the famine, which, however, resumed in 1988.

FIJI

President: Ratu Sir Penaia Ganilau (1987)
Prime Minister: Ratu Sir Kamisese Mara (1987)
Area: 7,078 sq mi. (18,333 sq km)
Population (est. mid-1989): 800,000 (average annual rate of natural increase: 2.4%) (Indian, 49%; Fijian, 47%)
Density per square mile: 98.9
Capital (1985): Suva (on Viti Levu), 75,000
Monetary unit: Fiji dollar
Languages: Fijian, Hindustani, English
Religions: Christian, 50%; Hindu, 41%; Islam, 8%
Literacy rate (1985): 80%
Economic summary: Gross domestic product (1986): $1.18 billion, $1,660 per capita, real growth rate 2.7%. Labor force in agriculture: 44%; principal products: sugar, copra, rice, ginger. Labor force in industry: 16%; major industrial products: refined sugar, gold, lumber. Natural resources: timber, fish, gold, copper. Exports: sugar, copra. Imports: foodstuffs, machinery, manufactured goods, fuels, chemicals. Major trading partners: U.K., Australia, Japan, New Zealand

Geography. Fiji consists of more than 330 islands in the southwestern Pacific Ocean about 1,960 miles (3,152 km) from Sydney, Australia. The two largest islands are Viti Levu (4,109 sq mi.; 10,642 sq km) and Vanua Levu (2,242 sq mi.; 5,807 sq km). The island of Rotuma (18 sq mi.; 47 sq km), about 400 miles (644 km) to the north, is a dependency of Fiji. Overall, Fiji is nearly as large as New Jersey.

The largest islands in the group are mountainous and volcanic, with the tallest peak being Mount Victoria (4,341 ft; 1,323 m) on Viti Levu. The islands in the south have dense forests on the windward side and grasslands on the leeward.

Government. An April, 1987, election brought the newly formed Fijian Labor Party to power. Riots by ethnic Fijians against the Indian-dominated government sparked coups by the Fijian-dominated army in May, 1987 and Sept., 1987. The new government is structured to preserve Fijian control.

History. In 1874, an offer of cession by the Fijian chiefs was accepted, and Fiji was proclaimed a possession and dependency of the British Crown.

During World War II, the archipelago was an important air and naval station on the route from the U.S. and Hawaii to Australia and New Zealand.

Fiji became independent on Oct. 10, 1970. The next year it joined the five-island South Pacific Forum, which intends to become a permanent regional group to promote collective diplomacy of the newly independent members. The Forum also includes Western Samoa, Tonga, Nauru, and the self-governing segments of the Cook Islands.

In Oct., 1987, Brig. Gen. Sitiveni Rabuka, the coup leader, declared Fiji a republic and removed it from the British Commonwealth.

FINLAND

Republic of Finland
President: Mauno H. Koivisto (1982)
Premier: Harri Holkeri (1987)
Area: 130,119 sq mi. (337,009 sq km)
Population (est. mid-1989): 5,000,000 (average annual rate of natural increase: 0.3%) (Finnish, 93%; Swedish, 6%)
Density per square mile: 38
Capital: Helsinki
Largest cities (est. 1987): Helsinki, 487,749; Tampere, 170,097; Espoo, 162,106; Turku, 160,974
Monetary unit: Markka
Languages: Finnish, Swedish
Religions: Lutheran, 90%; Eastern Orthodox, 1%
National name: Suomen Tasavalta—Republiken Finland
Literacy rate: almost 100%
Economic summary: Gross national product (1986): $70.35 billion, $14,190 per capita; real growth rate (1986): 3.2%. Land used for agriculture: 8%; labor force: 10%; principal products: dairy and meat products, cereals, sugar beets, potatoes. Labor force in industry: 23%; major products: metal manufactures, forestry and wood products, refined copper, ships, electronics. Natural resource: timber. Exports: timber, paper and pulp, ships, machinery, iron and steel, clothing, footwear. Imports: petroleum and petroleum products, chemicals, transportation equipment, machinery, textile yarns, foodstuffs, fodder grain. Major trading partners: W. Germany, Sweden, U.S.S.R., U.K., U.S.

Geography. Finland stretches 700 miles (1,127 km) from the Gulf of Finland on the south to Soviet Petsamo, north of the Arctic Circle. The U.S.S.R. extends along the entire eastern frontier while Norway and Sweden lie on her western border. In area, Finland is three times the size of Ohio.

Off the southwest coast are the Aland Islands, controlling the entrance to the Gulf of Bothnia. Finland has more than 200,000 lakes.

The Swedish-populated Aland Islands (581 sq mi.; 1,505 sq km) have an autonomous status under a law passed in 1921.

Government. The president, chosen for six years by the popularly elected Electoral College of 301 members, appoints the Cabinet. The one-chamber Diet, the Eduskunta, consists of 200 members elected for four-year terms by proportional representation.

History. At the end of the 7th century, the Finns came to Finland from their Volga settlements, taking the country from the Lapps, who retreated northward. The Finns' repeated raids on the Scandinavian coast impelled Eric IX, the Swedish King, to conquer the country in 1157 and bring it into contact with Western Christendom. By 1809 the whole of Finland was conquered by Alexander I of Russia, who set up Finland as a Grand Duchy.

The first period of Russification (1809–1905) resulted in a lessening of the powers of the Finnish Diet. The Russian language was made official, and the Finnish military system was superseded by the Russian. The pace of Russification was intensified from 1908 to 1914. When Russian control was weakened as a consequence of the March Revolution of 1917, the Diet on July 20, 1917, proclaimed Finland's independence, which became complete on Dec. 6, 1917.

Finland rejected Soviet territorial demands, and the U.S.S.R. attacked on Nov. 30, 1939. The Finns made an amazing stand of three months and finally capitulated, ceding 16,000 square miles (41,440 sq km) to the U.S.S.R. Under German pressure, the Finns joined the Nazis against Russia in 1941, but were defeated again and ceded the Petsamo area to the U.S.S.R. In 1948, a 20-year treaty of friendship and mutual assistance was signed by the two nations and renewed for another 20 years in 1970.

After 25 years in office, President Urho K. Kekkonen resigned in October 1981 because of ill health. Premier Mauno Koivisto, leader of the Social Democratic Party, was elected President on Jan. 26, 1982, winning decisively over a conservative rival with support from Finnish Communists. On Feb. 17, Kalevi Sorsa, a Social Democrat, took office as Premier, heading the same center-left coalition Koivisto had led but elections on Mar. 16, 1987 brought the conservative National Coalition Party into the government.

FRANCE

French Republic
President: François Mitterrand (1981)
Premier: Michel Rocard (1988)
Area: 211,208 sq mi. (547,026 sq km)
Population (est. mid-1989): 56,100,000 (average annual rate of natural increase: 0.4%)
Density per square mile: 266
Capital: Paris
Largest cities (est. 1983): Paris, 2,150,000; **(1982 est.):**

Marseilles, 868,435; Lyons, 410,455; Toulouse, 344, 917; Nice, 331,165; Nantes, 237,789; Strasbourg, 247, 068; Bordeaux, 201,965
Monetary unit: Franc
Language: French, declining regional dialects
Religion (est.): Roman Catholic, 76%
National name: République Française
Literacy rate (1981): 99%
Economic summary: Gross domestic product (1986): $724.1 billion, $13,020 per capita; real growth rate (1986): 2.0%. Land used for agriculture, 60%; labor force: 7%; principal products: cereals, feed grains, livestock and dairy products, wine, fruits, vegetables, potatoes. Labor force in industry: 30%; major products: chemicals, automobiles, processed foods, iron and steel, aircraft, textiles, clothing. Natural resources: coal, iron ore, bauxite, fish, forests. Exports: textiles and clothing, chemicals, machinery and transport equipment, agricultural products. Imports: machinery, crude petroleum, chemicals, agricultural products. Major trading partners: West Germany, Italy, U.S., Belgium-Luxembourg, U.K., Netherlands.

Geography. France (80% the size of Texas) is second in size to the U.S.S.R. among Europe's nations. In the Alps near the Italian and Swiss borders is Europe's highest point—Mont Blanc (15,781 ft; 4,810 m). The forest-covered Vosges Mountains are in the northeast, and the Pyrenees are along the Spanish border.

Except for extreme northern France, which is part of the Flanders plain, the country may be described as four river basins and a plateau. Three of the streams flow west—the Seine into the English Channel, the Loire into the Atlantic, and the Garonne into the Bay of Biscay. The Rhône flows south into the Mediterranean. For about 100 miles (161 km), the Rhine is France's eastern border.

West of the Rhône and northeast of the Garonne lies the central plateau, covering about 15% of France's area and rising to a maximum elevation of 6,188 feet (1,886 m). In the Mediterranean, about 115 miles (185 km) east-southeast of Nice, is Corsica (3,367 sq mi.; 8,721 sq km).

Government. The president is elected for seven years by universal suffrage. He appoints the premier, and the Cabinet is responsible to Parliament. The president has the right to dissolve the National Assembly or to ask Parliament for reconsideration of a law. The Parliament consists of two houses: the National Assembly and the Senate.

History. The history of France, as distinct from ancient Gaul, begins with the Treaty of Verdun (843), dividing the territories corresponding roughly to France, Germany, and Italy among the three grandsons of Charlemagne. Julius Caesar had conquered part of Gaul in 57–52 B.C., and it remained Roman until Franks invaded it in the 5th century.

Charles the Bald, inheritor of *Francia Occidentalis*, founded the Carolingian dynasty, which ruled over a kingdom increasingly feudalized. By 987, the crown passed to Hugh Capet, a princeling who controlled only the Ile-de-France, the region surrounding Paris. For 350 years, an unbroken Capetian line added to its domain and consolidated royal authority until the accession in 1328 of Philip VI, first of the Valois line. France was then the most powerful nation in Europe, with a population of 15 million.

The missing pieces in Philip's domain were the French provinces still held by the Plantagenet kings of England, who also claimed the French

Rulers of France

Name	Born	Ruled[1]	Name	Born	Ruled[1]
CAROLINGIAN DYNASTY			**FIRST REPUBLIC**		
Pepin the Short	c. 714	751–768	National Convention	—	1792–1795
Charlemagne[2]	742	768–814	Directory (Directoire)	—	1795–1799
Louis I the Debonair[3]	778	814–840			
Charles I the Bald[4]	823	840–877	**CONSULATE**		
Louis II the Stammerer	846	877–879	Napoleon Bonaparte[15]	1769	1799–1804
Louis III[5]	c. 863	879–882			
Carloman[5]	?	879–884	**FIRST EMPIRE**		
Charles II the Fat[6]	839	884–887	Napoleon I	1769	1804–1815[16]
Eudes (Odo), Count					
of Paris	?	888–898	**RESTORATION OF**		
Charles III the Simple[8]	879	893–923[9]	**HOUSE OF BOURBON**		
Robert I[10]	c. 865	922–923	Louis XVIII le Désiré	1755	1814–1824
Rudolf (Raoul), Duke			Charles X	1757	1824–1830[17]
of Burgundy	?	923–936			
Louis IV d'Outremer	c. 921	936–954	**BOURBON-ORLEANS LINE**		
Lothair	941	954–986	Louis Philippe		
Louis V the Sluggard	c. 967	986–987	("Citizen King")	1773	1830–1848[18]
CAPETIAN DYNASTY			**SECOND REPUBLIC**		
Hugh Capet	c. 940	987–996	Louis Napoleon[19]	1808	1848–1852
Robert II the Pious[11]	c. 970	996–1031			
Henry I	1008	1031–1060	**SECOND EMPIRE**		
Philip I	1052	1060–1108	Napoleon III		
Louis VI the Fat	1081	1108–1137	(Louis Napoleon)	1808	1852–1870[20]
Louis VII the Young	c.1121	1137–1180			
Philip II (Philip Augustus)	1165	1180–1223	**THIRD REPUBLIC (PRESIDENTS)**		
Louis VIII the Lion	1187	1223–1226	Louis Adolphe Thiers	1797	1871–1873
Louis IX (St. Louis)	1214	1226–1270	Marie E. P. M.		
Philip III the Bold	1245	1270–1285	de MacMahon	1808	1873–1879
Philip IV the Fair	1268	1285–1314	François P. J. Grévy	1807	1879–1887
Louis X the Quarreler	1289	1314–1316	Sadi Carnot	1837	1887–1894
John I[12]	1316	1316	Jean Casimir-Périer	1847	1894–1895
Philip V the Tall	1294	1316–1322	François Félix Faure	1841	1895–1899
Charles IV the Fair	1294	1322–1328	Émile Loubet	1838	1899–1906
			Clement Armand Fallières	1841	1906–1913
HOUSE OF VALOIS			Raymond Poincaré	1860	1913–1920
Philip VI	1293	1328–1350	Paul E. L. Deschanel	1856	1920–1920
John II the Good	1319	1350–1364	Alexandre Millerand	1859	1920–1924
Charles V the Wise	1337	1364–1380	Gaston Doumergue	1863	1924–1931
Charles VI			Paul Doumer	1857	1931–1932
the Well-Beloved	1368	1380–1422	Albert Lebrun	1871	1932–1940
Charles VII	1403	1422–1461			
Louis XI	1423	1461–1483	**VICHY GOVERNMENT**		
Charles VIII	1470	1483–1498	**(CHIEF OF STATE)**		
Louis XII the Father			Henri Philippe Pétain	1856	1940–1944
of the People	1462	1498–1515			
Francis I	1494	1515–1547	**PROVISIONAL GOVERNMENT**		
Henry II	1519	1547–1559	**(PRESIDENTS)**		
Francis II	1544	1559–1560	Charles de Gaulle	1890	1944–1946
Charles IX	1550	1560–1574	Félix Gouin	1884	1946–1946
Henry III	1551	1574–1589	Georges Bidault	1899	1946–1947
HOUSE OF BOURBON			**FOURTH REPUBLIC (PRESIDENTS)**		
Henry IV of Navarre	1553	1589–1610	Vincent Auriol	1884	1947–1954
Louis XIII	1601	1610–1643	René Coty	1882	1954–1959
Louis XIV the Great	1638	1643–1715			
Louis XV the Well-Beloved	1710	1715–1774	**FIFTH REPUBLIC (PRESIDENTS)**		
Louis XVI	1754	1774–1792[13]	Charles de Gaulle	1890	1959–1969
Louis XVII (Louis Charles	1785	1793–1795	Georges Pompidou	1911	1969–1974
de France)[14]			Valéry Giscard d'Estaing	1926	1974–1981
			François Mitterrand	1916	1981–

1. For Kings and Emperors through the Second Empire, year of end of rule is also that of death, unless otherwise indicated. 2. Crowned Emperor of the West in 800. His brother, Carloman, ruled as King of the Eastern Franks from 768 until his death in 771. 3. Holy Roman Emperor 814–840. 4. Holy Roman Emperor 875–877 as Charles II. 5. Ruled jointly 879–882. 6. Holy Roman Emperor 881–887 as Charles III. 7. Died 888. 8. King 893–898 in opposition to Eudes. 9. Died 929. 10. Not counted in regular line of Kings of France by some authorities. Elected by nobles but killed in Battle of Soissons. 11. Sometimes called Robert I. 12. Posthumous son of Louis X; lived for only five days. 13. Executed 1793. 14. Titular King only. He died in prison according to official reports, but many pretenders appeared during the Bourbon restoration. 15. As First Consul, Napoleon held the power of government. In 1804, he became Emperor. 16. Abdicated first time June 1814. Re-entered Paris March 1815, after escape from Elba; Louis XVIII fled to Ghent. Abdicated second time June 1815. He named as his successor his son, Napoleon II, who was not acceptable to the Allies. He died 1821. 17. Died 1836. 18. Died 1850. 19. President; became Emperor in 1852. 20. Died 1873.

crown. Beginning in 1338, the Hundred Years' War eventually settled the contest. English longbows defeated French armored knights at Crécy (1346) and the English also won the second landmark battle at Agincourt (1415), but the final victory went to the French at Castillon (1453).

Absolute monarchy reached its apogee in the reign of Louis XIV (1643–1715), the Sun King, whose brilliant court was the center of the Western world.

Revolution plunged France into a blood bath beginning in 1789 and ending with a new authoritarianism under Napoleon Bonaparte, who had successfully defended the infant republic from foreign attack and then made himself First Consul in 1799 and Emperor in 1804.

The Congress of Vienna (1815) sought to restore the pre-Napoleonic order in the person of Louis XVIII, but industrialization and the middle class, both fostered under Napoleon, built pressure for change, and a revolution in 1848 drove Louis Phillipe, last of the Bourbons, into exile.

A second republic elected as its president Prince Louis Napoleon, a nephew of Napoleon I, who declared the Second Empire in 1852 and took the throne as Napoleon III. His opposition to the rising power of Prussia ignited the Franco-Prussian War (1870–71), ending in his defeat and abdication.

A new France emerged from World War I as the continent's dominant power. But four years of hostile occupation had reduced northeast France to ruins. The postwar Third Republic was plagued by political instability and economic chaos.

From 1919, French foreign policy aimed at keeping Germany weak through a system of alliances, but it failed to halt the rise of Adolf Hitler and the Nazi war machine. On May 10, 1940, mechanized Nazi troops attacked, and, as they approached Paris, Italy joined with Germany. The Germans marched into an undefended Paris and Marshal Henri Philippe Pétain signed an armistice June 22. France was split into an occupied north and an unoccupied south, the latter becoming a totalitarian state with Pétain as its chief.

Allied armies liberated France in August 1944. The French Committee of National Liberation, formed in Algiers in 1943, established a provisional government in Paris headed by Gen. Charles de Gaulle. The Fourth Republic was born Dec. 24, 1946.

The Empire became the French Union; the National Assembly was strengthened and the presidency weakened; and France joined the North Atlantic Treaty Organization. A war against communist insurgents in Indochina was abandoned after the defeat at Dien Bien Phu. A new rebellion in Algeria threatened a military coup, and on June 1, 1958, the Assembly invited de Gàulle to return as premier with extraordinary powers. He drafted a new Constitution for a Fifth Republic, adopted Sept. 28, which strengthened the presidency and reduced legislative power. He was elected president Dec. 21.

De Gaulle took France out of the NATO military command in 1967 and expelled all foreign-controlled troops from the country. He later went on to attempt to achieve a long-cherished plan of regional reform. This, however, aroused wide opposition. He decided to stake his fate on a referendum. At the voting in April 1969, the electorate defeated the plan.

His successor Georges Pompidou continued the de Gaulle policies of seeking to expand France's influence in the Mideast and Africa, selling arms to South Africa (despite the U.N. embargo), to Libya, and to Greece, and in 1971 he endorsed British entry into the Common Market.

Pompidou died of cancer in April 1974 and the special election to choose a successor was won by Valéry Giscard d'Estaing.

Socialist François Mitterrand attained a stunning victory in the May 10, 1981, Presidential election over the Gaullist alliance that had held power since 1958.

The victors immediately moved to carry out campaign pledges to nationalize major industries, halt nuclear testing, suspend nuclear power plant construction, and impose new taxes on the rich. On Feb. 11, 1982, the nationalization bills became law.

The Socialists' policies during Mitterrand's first two years created a 12% inflation rate, a huge trade deficit, and devaluations of the franc. In early 1983, Mitterand, embarked on an austerity program to control inflation and reduce the trade deficit. He increased taxes and slashed government spending. A halt in economic growth, declining purchasing power for the average Frenchman, and an increase in unemployment to 10% followed. Mitterand sank lower and lower in the opinion polls.

In mid-1984, Mitterrand moved toward the political center. He appointed a new Premier, Laurent Fabius who ended the Socialist-Communist coalition. He proposed cuts that would reduce the French worker's income and social security taxes by 5 to 8%. Mitterrand promised further tax cuts.

In March, 1986, a center-right coalition led by Jacques Chirac won a slim majority in legislative elections. Chirac became Premier initiating a period of "co-habitation" between him and the Socialist President, Mitterrand, a cooperation marked by sparring over Chirac's plan to denationalize major industries and effect a harder line on security issues and on New Caledonia.

Mitterrand's decisive re-election in May, 1987, led to Chirac being replaced as Premier by Michel Rocard, a Socialist. Mitterrand called legislative elections for June, 1987 that gave the Socialists a plurality.

Overseas Departments

Overseas Departments elect representatives to the National Assembly, and the same administrative organization as that of mainland France applies to them.

FRENCH GUIANA (including ININI)

Status: Overseas Department
Prefect: Jacques Dewatre (1986)
Area: 35,126 sq mi. (90,976 sq km)
Population (est. mid 1988): 91,641 (average annual growth rate: 3.3%)
Capital (est. 1982): Cayenne, 37,097
Monetary unit: Franc
Language: French
Religion: Roman Catholic
Literacy rate: 82%
Economic summary: Gross national product (1982): $210 million. Average annual growth rate (1970–79): 0.4%. Per capita income (1982): $3,230. Labor force in agriculture: 18%; principal agricultural products: rice, corn, manioc, cocoa, bananas, sugar cane. Labor force in industry: 21%; major industrial products: timber, rum, rosewood essence, gold mining, processed shrimp. Natural resources: bauxite, timber, cinnabar, low-grade iron ore. Exports: shrimp, timber, rum, rosewood essence. Imports: food, consumer and producer goods, petroleum. Major

trading partners: U.S., France, Trinidad, Japan.

French Guiana, lying north of Brazil and east of Suriname on the northeast coast of South America, was first settled in 1604. Penal settlements, embracing the area around the mouth of the Maroni River and the Iles du Salut (including Devil's Island), were founded in 1852; they have since been abolished.

During World War II, French Guiana at first adhered to the Vichy government, but the Free French took over in 1943. French Guiana accepted in 1958 the new Constitution of the French Fifth Republic and remained an Overseas Department of the French Republic.

GUADELOUPE

Status: Overseas Department
Prefect: Yves Bonnet (1986)
Area: 687 sq mi. (1,779 sq km)
Population (est. mid-1988): 338,730 (average annual growth rate: 0.8%)
Capital (est. 1983): Basse-Terre, 35,000
Largest city (est. 1982): Pointe-à-Pitre, 50,000
Monetary unit: Franc
Language: French, Creole patois
Religions: Roman Catholic
Literacy rate: over 70%
Economic summary: Gross national product (1984): $998 million, $3,630 per capita; real growth rate (avg. '79–'80): 15.7%. Land used for agriculture: 36%; labor force: 21%; principal agricultural products: sugar cane, bananas, rum, tobacco. Major industries: construction, public works, sugar, rum, tourism. Exports: sugar, fruits and vegetables, bananas. Imports: foodstuffs, clothing, consumer goods, petroleum. Major trading partner: France.

Guadeloupe, in the West Indies about 300 miles (483 km) southeast of Puerto Rico, was discovered by Columbus in 1493. It consists of the twin islands of Basse-Terre and Grande-Terre and five dependencies—Marie-Galante, Les Saintes, La Désirade, St. Barthélemy, and the northern half of St. Martin. The volcano Soufrière (4,813 ft; 1,467 m), also called La Grande Soufrière, is the highest point on Guadeloupe. Violent activity in 1976 and 1977 caused thousands to flee their homes.

French colonization began in 1635. In 1958, Guadeloupe voted in favor of the new Constitution of the French Fifth Republic and remained an Overseas Department of the French Republic.

MARTINIQUE

Status: Overseas Department
Prefect: Edouard LaCroix (1986)
Area: 431 sq mi. (1,116 sq km)
Population (est. mid-1988): 351,105 (average annual growth rate: 1.7%)
Capital (est. 1984): Fort-de-France, 97,814
Monetary unit: Franc
Languages: French, Creole patois
Religion: Roman Catholic
Literacy rate (1981): 70%
Economic summary: Gross domestic product (1984): $1.3 billion, $3.650 per capita. Average annual growth rate (1970–79): 4.3%. Per capita income (1983): $4,040. Land used for agriculture: 48%; labor force: 13%; principal agricultural products: sugar cane, bananas, rum, pineapples. Labor force in industry: 7%; major industries: sugar, rum, refined oil, cement, tourism. Natural resource: fish. Exports: bananas, refined petroleum products, rum,

sugar, pineapples. Imports: foodstuffs, clothing and other consumer goods, petroleum products, construction materials. Major trading partners: France, U.S.

Martinique, lying in the Lesser Antilles about 300 miles (483 km) northeast of Venezuela, was probably discovered by Columbus in 1502 and was taken for France in 1635. Following the Franco-German armistice of 1940, it had a semiautonomous status until 1943, when authority was relinquished to the Free French. The area, administered by a Prefect assisted by an elected council, is represented in the French Parliament. In 1958, Martinique voted in favor of the new Constitution of the French Fifth Republic and remained an Overseas Department of the French Republic.

RÉUNION

Status: Overseas Department
Prefect: Jean Anciaux (1986)
Area: 970 sq mi. (2,510 sq km)
Population (est. mid-1988): 557,441 (average annual growth rate, 1.4%)
Capital (est. 1986): Saint-Denis, 109,072
Monetary unit: Franc
Languages: French, Creole
Religion: Roman Catholic
Economic summary: Gross national product (1983): $2.06 billion. Average annual growth rate (1970–79): −0.9%. Principal agricultural products: rum, vanilla, bananas, perfume plants. Major industrial products: rum, cigarettes, processed sugar. Exports: sugar, perfume essences, rum, molasses. Imports: manufactured goods, foodstuffs, beverages, machinery and transportation equipment, petroleum products. Major trading partners: France, Mauritius.

Discovered by Portuguese navigators in the 16th century, the island of Réunion, then uninhabited, was taken as a French possession in 1642. It is located about 450 miles (724 km) east of Madagascar, in the Indian Ocean. In 1958, Réunion approved the Constitution of the Fifth French Republic and remained an Overseas Department of the French Republic.

ST. PIERRE AND MIQUELON

Status: Overseas Department
Prefect: Bernard Leurguin (1986)
Area: 93 sq mi. (242 sq km)
Population (est. 1983): 6,000
Capital (est. 1981): Saint Pierre, 5,800
Economic summary: Major industries: fishing, canneries. Exports: fish, pelts. Imports: food, petroleum. Major trading partners: Canada, France, U.S., U.K., Portugal.

The sole remnant of the French colonial empire in North America, these islands were first occupied by the French in 1604. Their only importance arises from proximity to the Grand Banks, located 10 miles south of Newfoundland, making them the center of the French Atlantic cod fisheries. On July 19, 1976, the islands became an Overseas Department of the French Republic.

Overseas Territories

Overseas Territories are comparable to Departments, except that their administrative organization includes a locally-elected government.

FRENCH POLYNESIA

Status: Overseas Territory

High Commissioner: Bernard Gerard (1986)
Area: 1,544 sq mi. (4,000 sq km)
Population (est. mid-1988): 190,939 (average annual growth rate: 2.7%)
Monetary unit: Pacific financial community franc
Language: French
Religions: Protestant, 47%; Roman Catholic, 40%
Capital (est. 1983): Papeete (on Tahiti), 23,496
Economic summary: Gross national product (1983): $1.3 billion. Average annual growth rate (1970–78): 2.8%. Per capita income (1983): $7,620. Principal agricultural product: copra. Major industries: tourism, maintenance of French nuclear test base. Exports: coconut products, mother of pearl, vanilla. Imports: fuels, foodstuffs, equipment. Major trading partners: France, U.S.

The term French Polynesia is applied to the scattered French possessions in the South Pacific—Mangareva (Gambier), Makatea, the Marquesas Islands, Rapa, Rurutu, Rimatara, the Society Islands, the Tuamotu Archipelago, Tubuai, Raivavae, and the island of Clipperton—which were organized into a single colony in 1903. There are 120 islands, of which 25 are uninhabited.

The High Commissioner is assisted by a Council of Government and a popularly elected Territorial Assembly. The principal and most populous island—Tahiti, in the Society group—was claimed as French in 1768. In 1958, French Polynesia voted in favor of the new Constitution of the French Fifth Republic and remained an Overseas Territory of the French Republic. The natives are mostly Maoris.

The Pacific Nuclear Test Center on the atoll of Mururoa, 744 miles (1,200 km) from Tahiti, was completed in 1966.

MAYOTTE

Status: Territorial collectivity
Prefect: Guy DuPuis (1986)
Area: 146 sq mi. (378 sq km)
Population (est. 1985): 66,282
Capital (est. 1985): Dzaoudzi, 5,675
Principal products: vanilla, essential oils, copra

The most populous of the Comoro Islands in the Indian Ocean, with a Christian majority, Mayotte voted in 1974 and 1976 against joining the other, predominantly Moslem islands, in declaring themselves independent. It continues to retain its ties to France.

NEW CALEDONIA AND DEPENDENCIES

Status: Overseas Territory
High Commissioner: Ferdinand Wibaux (1986)
Area: 7,374 sq mi. (19,103 sq km)[1]
Population (est. mid-1989): 200,000 (average annual growth rate: 1.8%)
Capital (est. 1983): Nouméa, 60,112
Monetary unit: Pacific financial community franc
Languages: French, Melanesian and Polynesian dialects
Religion: Christian
Literacy rate: Not known
Economic summary: Gross national product (1983): $1.21 billion. Average annual growth rate (1970–78): −4.9%. Per capita income (1983): $8,050. Principal agricultural products: coffee, copra, beef, wheat, vegetables. Major industrial output: nickel. Natural resources: nickel, chromite, iron ore. Exports: nickel, chrome. Imports: mineral fuels, machinery, transport equipment, foodstuffs. Major trading partners: France, Japan, U.S., Australia.

1. Including dependencies.

New Caledonia (6,466 sq mi.; 16,747 sq km), about 1,070 miles (1,722 km) northeast of Sydney, Australia, was discovered by Capt. James Cook in 1774 and annexed by France in 1853. The government also administers the Isle of Pines, the Loyalty Islands (Uvéa, Lifu, and Maré), the Belep Islands, the Huon Island group, and Chesterfield Islands.

The natives are Melanesians; about one third of the population is white and one fifth Indochinese and Javanese. The French National Assembly on July 31, 1984, voted a bill into law that granted internal autonomy to New Caledonia and opened the way to possible eventual independence. This touched off ethnic tensions and violence between the natives and the European settlers, with the natives demanding full independence and sovereignty while the settlers wanted to remain part of France. In June, 1988, France resumed direct administration of the territory and promised a referendum on self-determination in 1998. This was agreed to by organizations representing the natives and the French settlers.

SOUTHERN AND ANTARCTIC LANDS

Status: Overseas Territory
Administrator: Claude Pieri
Area: 3,004 sq mi. (7,781 sq km)
Capital: Port-au-Français

This territory is uninhabited except for the personnel of scientific bases. It consists of Adélie Land (166,752 sq mi.; 431,888 sq km) on the Antarctic mainland and the following islands in the southern Indian Ocean: the Kerguelen and Crozet archipelagos and the islands of Saint-Paul and New Amsterdam.

WALLIS AND FUTUNA ISLANDS

Status: Overseas Territory
Administrator Superior: Bernard Lesterlin (1986)
Area: 106 sq mi. (274 sq km)
Population (est. 1985): 12,391
Capital (1980): Wallis (on Uvea), 600

The two islands groups in the South Pacific between Fiji and Samoa were settled by French missionaries at the beginning of the 19th century. A protectorate was established in the 1880s. Following a referendum by the Polynesian inhabitants, the status was changed to that of an Overseas Territory in 1961.

GABON

Gabonese Republic
President: Omar Bongo (1967)
Premier: Léon Mébiame (1975)
Area: 103,346 sq mi. (267,667 sq km)
Population (est. mid-1989): 1,100,000 (average annual rate of natural increase: 1.1%) (Fang, Mpongwe, Mbete, Punu)
Density per square mile: 11
Capital and largest city (est. 1983): Libreville, 257,000
Monetary unit: Franc CFA
Ethnic groups: Bateke, Obamba, Bakota, Shake, Pongwés, Adumas, Chiras, Punu, and Lumbu
Languages: French (official) and Bantu dialects
Religions: Roman Catholic, 65%, Protestant, 19%
National name: République Gabonaise
Member of French Community
Literacy rate: 65%
Economic summary: Gross domestic product (1986): $3.3

$3,300 per capita; real growth rate (1986): ▲2.0%. Labor force in agriculture: 65%; principal products: sugar cane, coffee, wood, palm oil, rice, bananas, peanuts. Labor force in industry: 30%; major products: petroleum, natural gas, processed wood, manganese, uranium. Natural resources: wood, petroleum, iron ore, manganese, uranium. Exports: crude petroleum, wood and wood products, minerals. Imports: mining and road-building machinery, electrical equipment, foodstuffs, textiles, transport vehicles. Major trading partners: France, U.S., West Germany.

Geography. This West African land with the Atlantic as its western border is also bounded by Equatorial Guinea, Cameroon, and the Congo. Its area is slightly less than Kentucky's.

From mangrove swamps on the coast, the land becomes divided plateaus in the north and east and mountains in the north. Most of the country is covered by a dense tropical forest.

Government. The president is elected for a seven-year term. Legislative powers are exercised by a National Assembly, which is elected for a seven-year term. After his conversion to Islam in 1973, President Bongo changed his given name, Albert Bernard, to Omar. The Parti Démocratique Gabonais (all National Assembly seats) is led by President Bongo. He was re-elected without opposition in 1973 and in 1980.

History. Little is known of Gabon's history, even in oral tradition, but Pygmies are believed to be the original inhabitants. Now there are many tribal groups in the country, the largest being the Fang people who constitute a third of the population.

Gabon was first visited by the Portuguese navigator Diego Cam in the 15th century. In 1839, the French founded their first settlement on the left bank of the Gabon Estuary and gradually occupied the hinterland during the second half of the 19th century. It was organized as a French territory in 1888 and became an autonomous republic within the French Union after World War II and an independent republic on Aug. 17, 1960.

Immense resources in oil, uranium, manganese, and iron help give Gabon's inhabitants a per capita annual income of $2,890, one of the highest in black Africa. To speed exploitation of a billion-ton iron ore reserve in the Belinga-Mekambo region, the government began work in 1969 on a 350-mile railroad leading from the coast into the area. The project was initiated by President León Mba, who died in 1967, and has been continued by his hand-picked successor, Omar Bongo.

In 1974, Bongo negotiated 60% control of an iron-ore venture half-owned by the Bethlehem Steel Corp. In October of that year, he visited Peking and concluded an economic and technical agreement with China.

GAMBIA

Republic of the Gambia
President: Sir Dawda K. Jawara (1970)
Area: 4,093 sq mi. (10,600 sq km)
Population (est. mid-1989): 800,000 (average annual rate of natural increase: 2.5%)
Density per square mile: 191
Capital (est. 1983): Banjul, 44,188
Monetary unit: Dalasi
Languages: Native tongues, English (official)
Religions: Islam, 90%, Christian, 9%, traditional 1%

Member of Commonwealth of Nations
Literacy rate: 12%
Economic summary: Gross domestic product (1985): $125 million, $260 per capita; real growth rate (1986–87): 6%. Land used for agriculture: 25%; labor force: 75%; principal products: peanuts, rice, palm kernels. Major industrial products: processed peanuts. Natural resources: fish. Exports: peanuts and peanut products, fish. Imports: textiles, foodstuffs, tobacco, machinery, petroleum products. Major trading partners: U.S., EEC, Africa.

Geography. Situated on the Atlantic coast in westernmost Africa and surrounded on three sides by Senegal, Gambia is twice the size of Delaware. The Gambia River flows for 200 miles (322 km) through Gambia on its way to the Atlantic. The country, the smallest on the continent, averages only 20 miles (32 km) in width.

Government. The president's five-year term is linked to the 35-member unicameral House of Representatives, from which he appoints his Cabinet members and the vice president.

The major political party is the People's Progressive Party (27 seats in House of Representatives), led by President Jawara.

History. During the 17th century, Gambia was settled by various companies of English merchants. Slavery was the chief source of revenue until it was abolished in 1807. Gambia became a crown colony in 1843 and an independent nation within the Commonwealth of Nations on Feb. 18, 1965.

Full independence was approved in a 1970 referendum, and on April 24 of that year Gambia proclaimed itself a republic.

President Dawda K. Jawara won overwhelming re-election to his fifth term on May 5, 1982, in a vote that was also seen as an endorsement of his proposal for a confederation with Senegal.

GERMANY, EAST

German Democratic Republic
Chairman of Council of State: Erich Honecker (1976)
Chairman of Council of Ministers: Willi Stoph (1976)
Area: 41,767 sq mi. (108,177 sq km)[1]
Population (est. mid-1988): 16,600,000 (average annual growth rate: 0.0%)
Density per square mile: 397.4
Capital: Berlin (eastern sector)
Largest cities (est. 1986): East Berlin, 1,215,586; Leipzig, 553,660; Dresden, 519,769; Karl-Marx Stadt, 315,452; Magdeburg, 288,965; Rostock, 238,011
Monetary unit: Mark of the Deutsche Demokratische Republik
Language: German
Religions: Protestant, 53%; Roman Catholic, 8%
National name: Deutsche Demokratische Republik
Literacy rate: 100%
Economic summary: Gross national product (1986): $187.5 billion, $11,300 per capita; real growth rate (1986): 2.0%. Land used for agriculture: 60%; labor force: 11%; principal products: grains, potatoes, sugar beets, meat and dairy products. Labor force in industry: 38%; major products: steel, chemicals, machinery, electrical and precision engineering products. Natural resources: brown coal, potash, bauxite. Exports: machinery and equipment, chemical products, textiles, clothing. Imports: raw materials, fuels, agricultural

products, machinery and equipment. Major trading partners: U.S.S.R., Soviet bloc, West Germany.

1. Including East Berlin (156 square miles), which has been incorporated into the German Democratic Republic.

Geography. East Germany lies on the Baltic Sea with Poland to the east and Czechoslovakia to the south. The border with West Germany is roughly a line running south from Lübeck for about 250 miles. The main river is the Elbe, which flows from Dresden in the southeast to the North Sea in the northwest. The Oder and Neisse Rivers form the border with Poland. Most of the country, which is the size of Tennessee, is situated in the north German plain.

Government. The People's Chamber, composed of 500 deputies elected for five-year terms, chooses the chairman and Council of State and the chairman and Council of Ministers, which carries on executive functions.

History. (For history before 1945, *see* Germany, West.) The area now occupied by East Germany, as well as adjacent areas in Eastern Europe, consists of Mecklenburg, Brandenburg, Lusatia, Saxony, and Thuringia. Soviet armies conquered the five territories by 1945. In the division of 1945 they were allotted to the U.S.S.R. Soviet forces created a State controlled by the secret police with a single party, the Socialist Unity (Communist) Party. The Russians appropriated East German plants to restore their war-ravaged industry.

When the Federal Republic of Germany was established in West Germany, the East German states adopted a more centralized constitution for the Democratic Republic of Germany, and it was put into effect on Oct. 7, 1949. The U.S.S.R. thereupon dissolved its occupation zone, but Soviet troops remained. The Western Allies declared that the East German Republic was a Soviet creation undertaken without self-determination and refused to recognize it. It was recognized only within the Soviet bloc.

Talks between the two German states on normalization began in 1970, with the East seeking recognition of its existence and the West wanting easing of pressure on Berlin, and rapprochement between the two Germanys accelerated with agreement on a variety of issues (for details, *see* Germany, West). By 1973, normal relations were established, and the two states entered the United Nations.

The 25-year diplomatic hiatus between East Germany and the U.S. ended Sept. 4, 1974, with the establishment of formal relations.

The East German government has repeatedly challenged the Western powers' right of access to Berlin, most recently at the time of President Carter's July 15, 1978, visit to West Berlin. Autobahn traffic between the city and West Germany was deliberately slowed and, as in a similar 1977 case, the U.S., U.K., and France protested to the U.S.S.R. and the East Germans that such action was illegal under the 1971 Four Power Agreement.

Chairman of the Council of State Erich Honecker gave strong backing to the Soviet Union's stern policy toward Poland as the workers' demand for democratic rights advanced in 1980 and 1981. On Oct. 28, 1980, he closed the border, which had been open between the two states for 10 years, permitting only certified relatives or invited friends to visit. Five million Poles had visited East Germany in the previous year, largely to find cheaper and more abundant consumer goods.

In February 1981, Honecker, in a surprise gesture, declared at his party's 16th Congress that German reunification might eventually be possible, something the Communist regime had ruled out 10 years earlier. He also eased border restrictions on exchanges with West Germany imposed a few months before, and made a long-delayed long-planned milestone visit to West Germany in Sept. 1987.

GERMANY, WEST

Federal Republic of Germany
President: Richard von Weizsäcker (1984)
Chancellor: Helmut Kohl (1982)
Area: 96,010 sq mi. (248,667 sq km)[1]
Population (census 1987): 61,082,800, includes West Berlin. (average annual growth rate: −0.1%)
Density per square mile: 640
Capital (est. 1985): Bonn, 292,600
Largest cities (1986): Hamburg, 1,575,700; Munich, 1,269,400; Cologne, 914,000; Essen, 617,700; Frankfurt, 593,400; Dortmund, 569,800; Dusseldorf, 561,200; Stuttgart, 564,200; Bremen, 524,700; Hannover, 506,400; West Berlin, 2,014,100 (1987 census)
Monetary unit: Deutsche Mark
Language: German
Religions: Protestant, 49%; Roman Catholic, 45%
National name: Bundesrepublik Deutschland
Literacy rate: 99%
Economic summary: Gross national product (1985): $908.3 billion, $14,890 per capita; real growth rate (1986): 2.2%. Land used for agriculture: 50%; labor force: 5%; principal products: grains, potatoes, sugar beets. Labor force in industry: 41%; major products: chemicals, machinery, vehicles. Natural resources: iron ore, timber, coal. Exports: machines and machine tools, chemicals, motor vehicles, iron and steel products. Imports: manufactured and agricultural products, raw materials, fuels. Major trading partners: France, Netherlands, Belgium-Luxembourg, Italy, U.S., U.K.

1. Excluding West Berlin (184 square miles with 1986 population of 1,879,000).

Geography. The Federal Republic of Germany occupies the western half of the central European area historically regarded as German. This was the part of Germany occupied by the United States, Britain, and France after World War II, when the eastern half of prewar Germany was split roughly between a Soviet-occupied zone, which became the present German Democratic Republic, and an area annexed by Poland.

West Germany's neighbors are France, Belgium, Luxembourg, and the Netherlands on the west, Switzerland and Austria on the south, Czechoslovakia and East Germany on the east, and Denmark on the north.

The northern plain, the central hill country, and the southern mountain district constitute the main physical divisions of West Germany, which is slightly smaller than Oregon. The Bavarian plateau in the southwest averages 1,600 feet (488 m) above sea level, but it reaches 9,721 feet (2,962 m) in the Zugspitze Mountains, the highest point in the country.

Important navigable rivers are the Danube, rising in the Black Forest and flowing east across Bavaria into Austria, and the Rhine, which rises in Switzerland and flows across the Netherlands in two channels to the North Sea and is navigable by

Rulers of Germany and Prussia

Name	Born	Ruled[1]	Name	Born	Ruled[1]
KINGS OF PRUSSIA			Karl Doenitz[6]	1891	1945–1945
Frederick I[2]	1657	1701–1713			
Frederick William I	1688	1713–1740	**GERMAN FEDERAL REPUBLIC**		
Frederick II the Great	1712	1740–1786	**(WEST) (PRESIDENTS)**		
Frederick William II	1744	1786–1797	Theodor Heuss	1884	1949–1959[9]
Frederick William III	1770	1797–1840	Heinrich Luebke	1895	1959–1969[8]
Frederick William IV	1795	1840–1861	Gustav Heinemann[10]	1899	1969–1974
William I	1797	1861–1871[3]	Walter Scheel	1919	1974–1979
			Karl Carstens	1914	1979–1984
EMPERORS OF GERMANY			Richard von Weizsäcker	1920	1984–
William I	1797	1871–1888			
Frederick III	1831	1888–1888	**GERMAN DEMOCRATIC REPUBLIC**		
William II	1859	1888–1918[4]	**(EAST)**		
			Wilhelm Pieck[5]	1876	1949–1960
HEADS OF THE REICH			Walter Ulbricht[11]	1893	1960–1973
Friedrich Ebert[5]	1871	1919–1925	Willi Stoph[12]	1914	1973–1976
Paul von Hindenburg[5]	1847	1925–1934	Erich Honecker[12]	1912	1976–
Adolf Hitler[6][7]	1889	1934–1945			

1. Year of end of rule is also that of death, unless otherwise indicated. 2. Was Elector of Brandenburg (1688–1701) as Frederick III. 3. Became Emperor of Germany in 1871. 4. Died 1941. 5. President. 6. Führer. 7. Named Chancellor by President Hindenburg in 1933. 8. Died 1972. 9. Died 1963. 10. Died 1976. 11. Chairman of Council of State. Died 1973. 12. Chairman of Council of State.

ocean-going and coastal vessels as far as Cologne. The Elbe, which also empties into the North Sea, is navigable within Germany for smaller vessels. The Weser, flowing into the North Sea, and the Main and Mosel (Moselle), both tributaries of the Rhine, are also important.

Government. Under the Constitution of May 23, 1949, the Federal Republic was established as a parliamentary democracy. The Parliament consists of the Bundesrat, an upper chamber representing and appointed by the 10 Länder, or states (plus West Berlin), and the Bundestag, a lower house elected for four years by universal suffrage. Each house has non-voting representatives from West Berlin. A federal assembly composed of Bundestag deputies and deputies from the state parliaments elects the President of the Republic for a five-year term; the Bundestag alone chooses the Chancellor, or Prime Minister. Each of the Länder and West Berlin have a legislature popularly elected for a four-year or five-year term.

The major political parties are the Christian Democratic Union-Christian Social Union (223 of 497 seats in the Bundestag), led by Chancellor Helmut Kohl; Social Democratic Party (186 seats) led by Hans-Jochen Vogel; and the Free Democratic Party (46 seats), led by Otto Count Larbsdorff, the Greens (42 seats). Kohl's government is a coalition with the Free Democrats.

History. Immediately before the Christian era, when the Roman Empire had pushed its frontier to the Rhine, what is now Germany was inhabited by several tribes believed to have migrated from Central Asia between the 6th and 4th centuries B.C. One of these tribes, the Franks, attained supremacy in western Europe under Charlemagne, who was crowned Holy Roman Emperor A.D. 800. By the Treaty of Verdun (843), Charlemagne's lands east of the Rhine were ceded to the German Prince Louis. Additional territory acquired by the Treaty of Mersen (870) gave Germany approximately the area it maintained throughout the Middle Ages. For several centuries after Otto the Great was crowned King in 936, the German rulers were also usually heads of the Holy Roman Empire.

Relations between state and church were changed by the Reformation, which began with Martin Luther's 95 theses, and came to a head in 1547, when Charles V scattered the forces of the Protestant League at Mühlberg. Freedom of worship was guaranteed by the Peace of Augsburg (1555), but a Counter Reformation took place later, and a dispute over the succession to the Bohemian throne brought on the Thirty Years' War (1618–48), which devastated Germany and left the empire divided into hundreds of small principalities virtually independent of the Emperor.

Meanwhile, Prussia was developing into a state of considerable strength. Frederick the Great (1740–86) reorganized the Prussian army and defeated Maria Theresa of Austria in a struggle over Silesia. After the defeat of Napoleon at Waterloo (1815), the struggle between Austria and Prussia for supremacy in Germany continued, reaching its climax in the defeat of Austria in the Seven Weeks' War (1866) and the formation of the Prussian-dominated North German Confederation (1867).

The architect of German unity was Otto von Bismarck, a conservative, monarchist, and militaristic Prussian Junker who had no use for "empty phrase-making and constitutions." From 1862 until his retirement in 1890 he dominated not only the German but also the entire European scene. He unified all Germany in a series of three wars against Denmark (1864), Austria (1866), and France (1870–71), which many historians believe were instigated and promoted by Bismarck in his zeal to build a nation through "blood and iron."

On Jan. 18, 1871, King Wilhelm I of Prussia was proclaimed German Emperor in the Hall of Mirrors at Versailles. The North German Confederation, created in 1867, was abolished, and the Second German Reich, consisting of the North and South German states, was born. With a powerful army, an efficient bureaucracy, and a loyal bourgeoisie, Chancellor Bismarck consolidated a powerful centralized state.

Wilhelm II dismissed Bismarck in 1890 and embarked upon a "New Course," stressing an intensified colonialism and a powerful navy. His chaotic foreign policy culminated in the diplomatic isolation of Germany and the disastrous defeat in World War I (1914–18).

The Second German Empire collapsed following the defeat of the German armies in 1918, the naval mutiny at Kiel, and the flight of the Kaiser to the Netherlands on November 10. The Social Democrats, led by Friedrich Ebert and Philipp Scheidemann, crushed the Communists and established a moderate republic with Ebert as President.

The Weimar Constitution of 1919 provided for a President to be elected for seven years by universal suffrage and a bicameral legislature, consisting of the Reichsrat, representing the states, and the Reichstag, representing the people. It contained a model Bill of Rights. It was weakened, however, by a provision that enabled the President to rule by decree.

President Ebert died Feb. 28, 1925, and on April 26, Field Marshal Paul von Hindenburg was elected president.

The mass of Germans regarded the Weimar Republic as a child of defeat, imposed upon a Germany whose legitimate aspirations to world leadership had been thwarted by a world conspiracy. Added to this were a crippling currency debacle, a tremendous burden of reparations, and acute economic distress.

Adolf Hitler, an Austrian war veteran and a fanatical nationalist, fanned discontent by promising a Greater Germany, abrogation of the Treaty of Versailles, restoration of Germany's lost colonies, and destruction of the Jews. When the Social Democrats and the Communists refused to combine against the Nazi threat, President Hindenburg made Hitler chancellor on Jan. 30, 1933.

With the death of Hindenburg on Aug. 2, 1934, Hitler repudiated the Treaty of Versailles and began full-scale rearmament. In 1935 he withdrew Germany from the League of Nations, and the next year he reoccupied the Rhineland and signed the anti-Comintern pact with Japan, at the same time strengthening relations with Italy. Austria was annexed in March 1938. By the Munich agreement in September 1938 he gained the Czech Sudetenland, and in violation of this agreement he completed the dismemberment of Czechoslovakia in March 1939. But his invasion of Poland on Sept. 1, 1939, precipitated World War II.

On May 8, 1945, Germany surrendered unconditionally to Allied and Soviet military commanders, and on June 5 the four-nation Allied Control Council became the *de facto* government of Germany. (For details of World War II, *see* Headline History.)

At the Berlin (or Potsdam) Conference (July 17–Aug. 2, 1945) President Truman, Premier Stalin, and Prime Minister Clement Attlee of Britain set forth the guiding principles of the Allied Control Council. They were Germany's complete disarmament and demilitarization, destruction of its war potential, rigid control of industry, and decentralization of the political and economic structure. Pending final determination of territorial questions at a peace conference, the three victors agreed in principle to the ultimate transfer of the city of Königsberg (now Kaliningrad) and its adjacent area to the U.S.S.R. and to the administration by Poland of former German territories lying generally east of the Oder-Neisse Line.

For purposes of control Germany was divided in 1945 into four national occupation zones, each headed by a Military Governor.

The Western powers were unable to agree with the U.S.S.R. on any fundamental issue. Work of the Allied Control Council was hamstrung by repeated Soviet vetoes; and finally, on March 20, 1948, Russia walked out of the Council. Meanwhile, the U.S and Britain had taken steps to merge their zones economically (Bizone); and on May 31, 1948, the U.S., Britain, France, and the Benelux countries agreed to set up a German state comprising the three Western Zones.

The U.S.S.R. reacted by clamping a blockade on all ground communications between the Western Zones and Berlin, an enclave in the Soviet Zone The Western Allies countered by organizing a gigantic airlift to fly supplies into the beleaguered city, assigning 60,000 men to it. The U.S.S.R. was finally forced to lift the blockade on May 12, 1949

The Federal Republic of Germany was proclaimed on May 23, 1949, with its capital at Bonn. In free elections, West German voters gave a majority in the Constituent Assembly to the Christian Democrats, with the Social Democrats largely making up the opposition. Konrad Adenauer became chancellor, and Theodor Heuss of the Free Democrats was elected first president.

Agreements in Paris in 1954 giving the Federal Republic full independence and complete sovereignty came into force on May 5, 1955. Under it, West Germany and Italy became members of the Brussels treaty organization created in 1948 and renamed the Western European Union. West Germany also became a member of NATO. In 1955 the U.S.S.R. recognized the Federal Republic. The Saar territory, under an agreement between France and West Germany, held a plebiscite and despite economic links to France voted to rejoin West Germany. It became a state of West Germany on Jan. 1, 1957.

In 1963, Chancellor Adenauer concluded a treaty of mutual cooperation and friendship with France and then retired. He was succeeded by his chief inner-party critic, Ludwig Erhard, who was followed in 1966 by Kurt Georg Kiesinger. He, in turn, was succeeded in 1969 by Willy Brandt, former mayor of West Berlin.

The division between West Germany and East Germany was intensified when the Communists erected the Berlin Wall in 1961. In 1968, the East German Communist leader, Walter Ulbricht, imposed restrictions on West German movements into West Berlin. The Soviet-bloc invasion of Czechoslovakia in August 1968 added to the tension.

A treaty with the U.S.S.R. was signed in Moscow in August 1970 in which force was renounced and respect for the "territorial integrity" of present European states declared.

Three months later, West Germany signed a similar treaty with Poland, renouncing force and setting Poland's western border as the Oder-Neisse Line. It subsequently resumed formal relations with Czechoslovakia in a pact that "voided" the Munich treaty that gave Nazi Germany the Sudetenland.

Both German states were admitted to the United Nations in 1973.

Brandt, winner of a Nobel Peace Prize for his foreign policies, was forced to resign in 1974 when an East German spy was discovered to be one of his top staff members. Succeeding him was a moderate Social Democrat, Helmut Schmidt.

Helmut Schmidt, Brandt's successor as chancellor, staunchly backed U.S. military strategy in Europe nevertheless, staking his political fate on the strategy of placing U.S. nuclear missiles in Germany unless the Soviet Union reduced its arsenal of intermediate missiles.

The chancellor also strongly opposed nuclear freeze proposals and won 2-1 support for his stand at the convention of Social Democrats in April. The Free Democrats then deserted the Socialists after losing ground in local elections and joined with the Christian Democrats to unseat Schmidt and install Helmut Kohl as chancellor in 1982.

Kohl's tenure has seen a dwindling of the nuclear freeze issue after the deployment of the U.S. missiles. U.S.-Soviet negotiations in 1987 produced a treaty setting up the removal of medium- and short-range missiles from Europe. An economic upswing in 1986 led to Kohl's re-election.

BERLIN

Status: West Berlin: State of West Germany; East Berlin: capital of East Germany
Governing Mayor, West Berlin: Walter Momper (SDP) (1989)
Mayor, East Berlin: Erhard Krack
Area: 340 square miles (West Berlin, 184; East Berlin, 156)
Population (est. 1986): 3,094,600 (West Berlin, 1,879,-000; East Berlin, 1,215,600)

Berlin, the capital of prewar Germany, lies entirely within the borders of East Germany. After the war, the city was occupied by the forces of the U.S., Britain, France, and the U.S.S.R. The three western sectors, now known as West Berlin, contain 55% of the area and 60% of the population.

West Berlin is a state of the Federal Republic of Germany, but supreme authority remains in the hands of the three Western powers in accordance with postwar agreements. The government is composed of the governing mayor, the 11-member Senate (his Cabinet), and the House of Representatives, a popularly elected legislative body that elects the governing mayor and the Senate.

East Berlin is governed by a City Assembly elected by Communist Party members, and a Magistrate (City Council) chosen by the Assembly and headed by the mayor. In violation of the Four Power Agreements, the Soviet Sector has been incorporated into the German Democratic Republic and is now the capital of that country.

Major anti-Communist riots broke out in East Berlin in June 1953 and, since Aug. 13, 1961, the Soviet Sector has been sealed off by a Communist-built wall, 26 1/2 miles (43 km) long, running through the city. It was built to stem the flood of refugees seeking freedom in the West, 200,000 having fled in 1961 before the wall was erected.

GHANA

Republic of Ghana
Chairman of Provisional National Defense Council: Flight Lt. Jerry John Rawlings (1981)
Area: 92,100 sq mi. (238,537 sq km)
Population (est. mid-1989): 14,600,000 (average annual rate of natural increase: 3.1%)
Density per square mile: 158
Capital: Accra
Largest cities (est. 1984): Accra, 859,600; Kumasi, 348,900; Tamale, 136,800
Monetary unit: Cedi
Languages: English (official), Native tongues (Brong Ahafo, Twi, Fanti, Ga, Ewe, Dagbani)
Religions: Christian 40–50%; Islam 10–20%, and Animist
Literacy rate: 45% (in English)
Member of Commonwealth of Nations

Economic summary: Gross national product (1986 est.): $5.7 billion, real growth rate (1986 est.): 5.3%. Per capita income (1984): $380. Land used for agriculture: 27%; labor force: 55%; principal products: cocoa, coconuts, coffee, cassava, yams, rice, rubber. Labor force in industry: 19%; major products: mining products, cocoa products, aluminum. Natural resources: gold, diamonds, bauxite, manganese, timber, fish. Exports: cocoa beans and products, gold, timber, manganese ore. Imports: textiles and manufactured goods, food, fuels, transport equipment. Major trading partners: U.K., U.S., Nigeria, U.S.S.R., Switzerland, Netherlands.

Geography. A West African country bordering on the Gulf of Guinea, Ghana has the Ivory Coast to the west, Burkina Faso to the north, and Togo to the east. It compares in size to Oregon.

The coastal belt, extending about 270 miles (435 km), is sandy, marshy, and generally exposed. Behind it is a gradually widening grass strip. The forested plateau region to the north is broken by ridges and hills. The largest river is the Volta.

Government. Ghana returned to military rule after two years of constitutional government when Flight Lt. Jerry Rawlings, who led a coup in 1979 and stepped down voluntarily, seized power on Dec. 31, 1981. Rawlings heads a Provisional National Defense Council, which exercises all power.

History. Created an independent country on March 6, 1957, Ghana is the former British colony of the Gold Coast. The area was first seen by Portuguese traders in 1470. They were followed by the English (1553), the Dutch (1595), and the Swedes (1640). British rule over the Gold Coast began in 1820, but it was not until after quelling the severe resistance of the Ashanti in 1901 that it was firmly established. British Togoland, formerly a colony of Germany, was incorporated into Ghana by referendum in 1956. As the result of a plebiscite, Ghana became a republic on July 1, 1960.

Premier Kwame Nkrumah attempted to take leadership of the Pan-African Movement, holding the All-African People's Congress in his capital, Accra, in 1958 and organizing the Union of African States with Guinea and Mali in 1961. But he oriented his country toward the Soviet Union and China and built an autocratic rule over all aspects of Ghanaian life.

In February 1966, while Nkrumah was visiting Peking and Hanoi, he was deposed by a military coup led by Gen. Emmanuel K. Kotoka.

A series of military coups followed and on June 4, 1979, Flight Lieutenant Jerry Rawlings overthrew Lt. Gen. Frederick Akuffo's military rule on June 4, 1979. Rawlings permitted the election of a civilian president to go ahead as scheduled the following month, and Hilla Limann, candidate of the People's National Party, took office. Charging the civilian government with corruption and repression, Rawlings staged another coup on Dec. 31, 1981. As chairman of the Provisional National Defense Council, Rawlings instituted an austerity program and reduced budget deficits.

On July 11, 1985, a relative of Rawlings, Michael Agbotui Soussoudis, 39, and Sharon M. Scranage, 29, who had been a low-level clerk in the Central Intelligence Agency station in the West African country, were arrested in the United States on espionage charges. Reagan Administration officials said the American woman had given Soussoudis, her Ghanian lover, information about the agency's operations in Ghana and that as a result, at least one

CIA informant had been murdered and the CIA feared reprisals would be taken by the Rawlings government against as many as 10 others.

GREECE

Hellenic Republic
President: Christos Sartzetakis (1985)
Premier: Tzannis Tzannetakis (1989)
Area: 50,961 sq mi. (131,990 sq km)
Population (est. mid-1988): 10,000,000 (average annual rate of natural increase: 0.1%)
Density per square mile: 197
Capital: Athens
Largest cities (1981 census): Athens, 3,027,000; Salonika, 706,000; Patras, 150,000; Larissa, 102,000; Heraklion, 111,000; Volos, 107,000.
Monetary unit: Drachma
Language: Greek
Religion: Greek Orthodox
National name: Elliniki Dimokratia
Literacy rate: 95%
Economic summary: Gross national product (1986): $39.5 billion, $3,950 per capita; real growth rate (1986): 0.7%. Land used for agriculture: 71%; labor force: 27%; principal products: grains, fruits, vegetables, olives, olive oil, tobacco, cotton, livestock, dairy products. Labor force in industry: 29%; major products: textiles, chemicals, food processing. Natural resources: bauxite, iron, forests. Exports: fruits, textiles, tobacco. Imports: machinery and automotive equipment, petroleum, consumer goods, chemicals, foodstuffs. Major trading partners: West Germany, Netherlands, Italy, France, Saudi Arabia, U.S.A., U.K.

Geography. Greece, on the Mediterranean Sea, is the southernmost country on the Balkan Peninsula in southern Europe. It is bordered on the north by Albania, Yugoslavia, and Bulgaria; on the west by the Ionian Sea; and on the east by the Aegean Sea and Turkey. It is slightly smaller than Alabama.

North central Greece, Epirus, and western Macedonia all are mountainous. The main chain of the Pindus Mountains rises to 9,000 feet (2,743 m) in places, separating Epirus from the plains of Thessaly. Mt. Olympus, rising to 9,570 feet (2,909 m) in the north near the Aegean Sea, is the highest point in the country. Greek Thrace is mostly a lowland region separated from European Turkey by the lower Evros River.

Among the many islands are the Ionian group off the west coast; the Cyclades group to the southeast; other islands in the eastern Aegean, including the Dodecanese Islands, Euboea, Lesbos, Samos, and Chios; and Crete, the fourth largest Mediterranean island.

Government. A referendum in December 1974, five months after the collapse of a military dictatorship, ended the Greek monarchy and established a republic. Ceremonial executive power is held by the president; the Premier heads the government and is responsible to a 300-member unicameral Parliament.

History. Greece, with a recorded history going back to 766 B.C., reached the peak of its glory in the 5th century B.C., and by the middle of the 2nd century B.C., it had declined to the status of a Roman province. It remained within the Eastern Roman Empire until Constantinople fell to the Crusaders in 1204.

In 1453, the Turks took Constantinople, and by 1460 Greece was a Turkish province. The insurrection made famous by the poet Lord Byron broke out in 1821, and in 1827 Greece won independence with sovereignty guaranteed by Britain, France, and Russia.

The protecting powers chose Prince Otto of Bavaria as the first king of modern Greece in 1832 to reign over an area only slightly larger than the Peloponnese Peninsula. Chiefly under the next king, George I, chosen by the protecting powers in 1863, Greece acquired much of its present territory. During his 57-year reign, a period in which he encouraged parliamentary democracy, Thessaly, Epirus, Macedonia, Crete, and most of the Aegean islands were added from the disintegrating Turkish empire. An unsuccessful war against Turkey after World War I brought down the monarchy, to be replaced by a republic in 1923.

Two military dictatorships and a financial crisis brought George II back from exile, but only until 1941, when Italian and German invaders defeated tough Greek resistance. After British and Greek troops liberated the country in October 1944, Communist guerrillas staged a long campaign in which the government received U.S. aid under the Truman Doctrine, the predecessor of the Marshall Plan.

A military junta seized power in April 1967, sending young King Constantine II into exile December 14. Col. George Papadopoulos, as premier, converted the government to republican form in 1973 and as President ended martial law. He was moving to restore democracy when he was ousted in November of that year by his military colleagues. The regime of the "colonels," which had tortured its opponents and scoffed at human rights, resigned July 23, 1974, after having bungled an attempt to seize Cyprus.

Former Premier Karamanlis returned from exile to become premier of Greece's first civilian government since 1967.

On Jan. 1, 1981, Greece became the 10th member of the European Community. On Oct. 18, the first Socialist government in Greek history won power, and Andreas Papandreou became the new Premier.

Double-digit inflation and scandals in the Socialist government led to them losing their majority in the elections of June 1989. The opposition New Democracy Party did not gain a majority, however, leading to the creation of a NDP-Communist coalition that will initiate an investigation of the scandals and then call new elections.

GRENADA

State of Grenada
Sovereign: Queen Elizabeth II
Governor General: Paul Scoon (1978)
Prime Minister: Herbert A. Blaize (1984)
Area: 133 sq mi. (344 sq km)
Population (est. mid-1988): 85,000 (black, 84%; mixed, 11%) (average annual growth rate, 1.9%)
Density per square mile: 751.9
Capital and largest city (est. 1981): St. George's, 4,800
Monetary unit: East Caribbean dollar
Ethnic groups: Caribs and Indians
Language: English
Religions: Roman Catholic, 64%; Anglican, 21%
Member of Commonwealth of Nations
Literacy rate: 85%
Economic summary: Gross domestic product (1986): $129 million, $1,520 per capita; real growth rate (1986):

4.3%. Land used for agriculture: 44%; labor force: 24%; principal products: spices, cocoa, bananas. Exports: nutmeg, cocoa beans, bananas, mace. Imports: foodstuffs, machinery, building materials. Major trading partners: U.K., Trinidad, U.S.

Geography. Grenada (the first "a" is pronounced as in "gray") is the most southerly of the Windward Islands, about 100 miles (161 km) from the South American coast. It is a volcanic island traversed by a mountain range, the highest peak of which is Mount St. Catherine (2,756 ft.; 840 m).

Government. A Governor-General represents the sovereign, Elizabeth II. The Prime Minister is the head of government, chosen by a 15-member House of Representatives elected by universal suffrage every five years.

History. Grenada was discovered by Columbus in 1498. After more than 200 years of British rule, most recently as part of the West Indies Associated States, it became independent Feb. 7, 1974, with Eric M. Gairy as Prime Minister.

Prime Minister Maurice Bishop, a protégé of Cuba's President Castro, was killed in a military coup on Oct. 19, 1983. At the request of five members of the Organization of Eastern Caribbean States, President Reagan ordered an invasion of Grenada on Oct. 25 involving over 1,900 U.S. troops and a small military force from Barbados, Dominica, Jamaica, St. Lucia, and St. Vincent. The troops met strong resistance from Cuban military personnel on the island. Reagan said he ordered the invasion to protect some 1,000 American citizens on the island, and to help restore democratic institutions in that country. A centrist coalition led by Herbert A. Blaize, a 66-year-old lawyer, won 14 of the 15 seats in Parliament in an election in December 1984, and Blaize became Prime Minister.

1. Elections due at end of 1989.

GUATEMALA

Republic of Guatemala
President: Marco Vinicio Cerezo Arévalo (1986)
Area: 42,042 sq mi. (108,889 sq km)
Population (est. mid-1988): 8,900,000 (average annual rate of natural increase: 3.1%)
Density per square mile: 213
Capital and largest city (est. 1982): Guatemala City, 1,250,000
Monetary unit: Quetzal
Languages: Spanish, Indian dialects
Religion: Roman Catholic, Protestant, Mayan.
National name: República de Guatemala
Literacy rate (1983): 51%
Economic summary: Gross domestic product (1986): $9.2 billion, $1,120 per capita; real growth rate: 2,590. Land used for agriculture: 28%; labor force. 5.7%; principal products: corn, beans, coffee, cotton, cattle, sugar, bananas, fruits and vegetables, timber. Labor force in industry: 14%; principal products: prepared foods, textiles, construction materials, tires, pharmaceuticals. Natural resources: nickel, timber, shrimp. Exports: coffee, cotton, sugar, fruits and vegetables, bananas. Imports: manufactured products, machinery, transportation equipment, chemicals, fuels. Major trading partners: U.S., Central American nations, Caribbean, Mexico.

Geography. The northernmost of the Central American nations, Guatemala is the size of Tennes-

see. Its neighbors are Mexico on the north, west, and east and Belize, Honduras, and El Salvador on the east. The country consists of two main regions—the cool highlands with the heaviest population and the tropical area along the Pacific and Caribbean coasts. The principal mountain range rises to the highest elevation in Central America and contains many volcanic peaks. Volcanic eruptions are frequent.

The Petén region in the north contains important resources and archaeological sites of the Mayan civilization.

Government. On December 8, 1985, Marco Vinicio Cerezo Arévalo, a left-of-center Christian Democrat, won in elections that were generally free from military interference. A 100-seat Congress was also elected.

Both the President and the Congress are elected for five-year terms and the President may not be re-elected.

History. Once the site of the ancient Mayan civilization, Guatemala, conquered by Spain in 1524, set itself up as a republic in 1839. From 1898 to 1920, the dictator Manuel Estrada Cabrera ran the country, and from 1931 to 1944, Gen. Jorge Ubico Castaneda was the strongman. In 1944 the National Assembly elected Gen. Federico Ponce president, but he was overthrown in October. In December, Dr. Juan José Arévalo was elected as the head of a leftist regime that continued to press its reform program. Jacobo Arbenz Guzmán, administration candidate with leftist leanings, won the 1950 elections.

Arbenz expropriated the large estates, including plantations of the United Fruit Company. With covert U.S. backing, a revolt was led by Col. Carlos Castillo Armas, and Arbenz took refuge in Mexico. Castillo Armas became president but was assassinated in 1957. Constitutional government was restored in 1958, and Gen. Miguel Ydigoras Fuentes was elected president.

A wave of terrorism, by left and right, began in 1967, and in August 1968 U.S. Ambassador John Gordon Mein was killed when he resisted kidnappers. Fear of anarchy led to the election in 1970 of Army Chief of Staff Carlos Araña Osorio, who had put down a rural guerrilla movement at the cost of nearly 3,000 lives. Araña, surprisingly, pledged social reforms when he took office. Another military candidate, Gen. Kjell Laugerud, won the presidency in 1974 amid renewed political violence.

The administration of Gen. Romeo Lucas Garcia, elected president in 1978, ended in a coup by a three-man military junta on March 23, 1982. Lucas Garcia was charged by Amnesty International with responsibility for at least 5,000 political murders in a reign of brutality and corruption that brought a cutoff of U.S. military aid in 1978. Hopes for improvement under the junta faded when Gen. José Efraín Ríos Montt took sole power in June.

President Oscar Mejía Victores, another general, seized power from Rios Montt in an August 1983 coup and pledged to turn over power to an elected civilian President in 1985. A constituent assembly was elected on July 1, 1984, to write a new Constitution.

Attempts by President Cerezo to improve social programs and raise taxes on the wealth have been hampered by right-wing opposition and military coup attempts.

GUINEA

Republic of Guinea
President: Brig. Gen. Lansana Conté (1984)
Area: 94,925 sq mi. (245,857 sq km)
Population (est. mid-1989): 7,100,000 (average annual rate of natural increase: 2.4%)
Density per square mile: 69
Capital and largest city (est. 1983): Conakry, 656,000
Monetary unit: Guinean franc
Languages: French (official), native tongues (Malinké, Susu, Fulani)
Religions: Islam, 85%; 10% Christian, 5% indigenous
National name: République de Guinée
Literacy rate: 28%
Economic summary: Gross national product (1986): $1.7 billion, $250 per capita; real growth rate (1987 est.): 6.0%. Principal agricultural products: rice, cassava, millet, corn, coffee, bananas, pineapples. Major industrial products: bauxite, alumina, light manufactured and processed goods, diamonds. Natural resources: bauxite, iron ore, diamonds, gold, water power. Exports: bauxite, alumina, pineapples, bananas, coffee. Imports: petroleum, machinery, transport equipment, foodstuffs, textiles. Major trading partners: U.S., U.S.S.R., France, W. Germany, Italy.

Geography. Guinea, in West Africa on the Atlantic, is also bordered by Guinea-Bissau, Senegal, Mali, the Ivory Coast, Liberia, and Sierra Leone. Slightly smaller than Oregon, the country consists of a coastal plain, a mountainous region, a savanna interior, and a forest area in the Guinea Highlands. The highest peak is Mount Nimba at about 6,000 feet (1,829 m).

Government. Military government headed by President Lansana Conté, who promoted himself from colonel to brigadier general after a 1984 coup.

History. Previously part of French West Africa, Guinea achieved independence by rejecting the new French Constitution, and on Oct. 2, 1958, became an independent state with Sékou Touré as president. Touré led the country into being the first avowedly Marxist state in Africa. Diplomatic relations with France were suspended in 1965, with the Soviet Union replacing France as the country's chief source of economic and technical assistance.

In 1966, when a Ghanaian military coup deposed Kwame Nkrumah as President, Touré welcomed him to Guinea and declared him joint president and party leader. The titles proved to be only honorary.

Prosperity came in 1960 after the start of exploitation of bauxite deposits. Touré was re-elected to a seven-year term in 1974 and again in 1981.

After 26 years as President, Touré died in the United States in March 1984, following surgery. A week later, a military regime headed by Col. Lansana Conté took power with a promise not to shed any more blood after Touré's harsh rule. Conté became President and his co-conspirator in the coup, Col. Diara Traoré, became Prime Minister, but Conté later demoted Traoré to Education Minister. Traoré tried to seize power on July 4, 1985, while Conté was out of the country, but his attempted coup was crushed by troops loyal to Conté.

GUINEA-BISSAU

Republic of Guinea-Bissau
President of the Council of State: João Bernardo Vieira (1980)
Area: 13,948 sq mi. (36,125 sq km)
Population (est. mid-1989): 1,000,000 (average annual rate of natural increase: 1.9%)
Density per square mile: 69
Capital and largest city (est. 1980): Bissau, 110,000
Monetary unit: Guinea-Bissau peso
Language: Portugese Criolo, African languages
Religions: traditional, 65%; Islam, 30%; Christian, 5%
National name: Républica da Guiné-Bissau
Literacy rate: 9%
Economic summary: Gross national product (1985): $150 million. Annual growth rate (1983): −5.1%. Per capita income (1985): $170. Labor force in agriculture: 90%; principal products: palm oil, root crops, rice, coconuts, peanuts. Major industries: food processing, beer, soft drinks. Natural resources: potential bauxite deposits; fish and timber. Exports: peanuts, coconuts, shrimp, fish, wood. Imports: foodstuffs, manufactured goods, fuels, transportation equipment. Major trading partners: Portugal, Spain, and other Eur. countries.

Geography. A neighbor of Senegal and Guinea in West Africa, on the Atlantic coast, Guinea-Bissau is about half the size of South Carolina.

The country is a low-lying coastal region of swamps, rain forests, and mangrove-covered wetlands, with about 25 islands off the coast. The Bijagos archipelago extends 30 miles (48 km) out to sea. Internal communications depend mainly on deep estuaries and meandering rivers, since there are no railroads. Bissau, the capital, is the main port.

Government. After the overthrow of Louis Cabral in November 1980, the nine-member Council of the Revolution formed an interm government. In 1982, they formed a new government consisting of the President, 2 Vice-Presidents, 18 ministers and 10 state secretaries.

History. Guinea-Bissau was discovered in 1446 by the Portuguese Nuno Tristao, and colonists in the Cape Verde Islands obtained trading rights in the territory. In 1879 the connection with the Cape Verde Islands was broken. Early in the 1900s the Portuguese managed to pacify some tribesmen, although resistance to colonial rule remained.

The African Party for the Independence of Guinea-Bissau and Cape Verde was founded in 1956 and several years later began guerrilla warfare that grew increasingly effective. By 1974 the rebels controlled most of the countryside, where they formed a government that was soon recognized by scores of countries. The military coup in Portugal in April 1974 brightened the prospects for freedom, and in August the Lisbon government signed an agreement granting independence to the province as of Sept. 10. The new republic took the name Guinea-Bissau. Its government was immediately recognized by the United States.

In November 1980, Prémier João Bernardo Vieira headed a coup that deposed Luis Cabral, President since 1974. A Revolutionary Council assumed the powers of government, with Vieira as its head.

GUYANA

Cooperative Republic of Guyana
President: Desmond Hoyte (1985)
Area: 83,000 sq mi. (214,969 sq km)
Population (est. mid-1988): 800,000 (average annual rate of natural increase: 2.0%) (East Indian, 51%; African, 30%; mixed 13%; Amerindian, 4%)

Density per square mile: 9
Capital and largest city (est. 1981): Georgetown, 200,000
Monetary unit: Guyana dollar
Languages: English (official), Hindi, Urdu, Creole
Religions: Hindu, 34%; Protestant, 18%; Islam, 9%; Roman Catholic, 18%; Anglican, 16%
Member of Commonwealth of Nations
Literacy rate: 86%
Economic summary: Gross domestic product (1986): $519 million. $680 per capita real growth rate: 0.3%. Labor force in agriculture: 34%; principal products: sugar, rice. Labor force in industry: 22%; major products: bauxite, alumina. Natural resources: bauxite, gold, diamonds, hardwood timber, shrimp. Exports: sugar, bauxite, alumina, rice, timber. Imports: fuels, machinery. Major trading partners: U.K., U.S., Trinidad, Venezuela.

Geography. Guyana is situated on the northern coast of South America east of Venezuela, west of Suriname, and north of Brazil. The country consists of a low coastal area and the Guiana Highlands in the south. There is an extensive north-south network of rivers. Guyana is the size of Idaho.

Government. Guyana, formerly British Guiana, proclaimed itself a republic on Feb. 23, 1970, ending its tie with Britain while remaining in the Commonwealth.

Guyana has a unicameral legislature, the National Assembly, with 53 members directly elected for five-year terms and 12 elected by local councils. A 24-member Cabinet is headed by the President.

History. British Guiana won internal self-government in 1952. The next year the People's Progressive Party, headed by Cheddi B. Jagan, an East Indian dentist, won the elections and Jagan became Prime Minister. British authorities deposed him for alleged Communist connections. A coalition ousted Jagan in 1964, installing a moderate Socialist, Forbes Burnham, a black, as Prime Minister. On May 26, 1966, the country became an independent member of the Commonwealth and resumed its traditional name, Guyana.

After ruling Guyana for 21 years, Burnham died on Aug. 6 1985, in a Guyana hospital after a throat operation. Desmond Hoyte, the country's Prime Minister succeeded him under the Guyanese constitution.

HAITI

Republic of Haiti
President: Lt. Gen. Prosper Avril (1989)
Area: 10,714 sq mi. (27,750 sq km)
Population (est. mid-1988): 6,400,000 (average annual rate of natural increase: 2%)
Density per square mile: 596
Capital and largest city (est. 1984): Port-au-Prince, city, 461,464; urban area, 738,342
Monetary unit: Gourde
Languages: French, Creole
Religion: Roman Catholic, 80%; Baptist, 10%
National name: République d'Haïti
Literacy rate: 23%
Economic summary: Gross domestic product (1986): $2.1 billion, $350 per capita; real growth rate: 1.0%. Land used for agriculture: 51%; labor force: 66%; principal products: coffee, sugar cane, corn, sorghum. Labor force in industry: 9%; major products: refined sugar, textiles, flour, cement, light assembly products. Natural resource:

bauxite. Exports: coffee, light industrial products, sugar, cocoa, sisal. Imports: consumer goods, foodstuffs, industrial equipment, petroleum products. Major trading partner: U.S.

Geography. Haiti, in the West Indies, occupies the western third of the island of Hispaniola, which it shares with the Dominican Republic. About the size of Maryland, Haiti is two thirds mountainous, with the rest of the country marked by great valleys, extensive plateaus, and small plains. The most densely populated region is the Cul-de-Sac plain near Port-au-Prince.

Government. Duvalier fled the country in February, 1986 after strong unrest. His Chief of Staff, Lt. Gen. Henri Namphy, established a governing council with himself as head. A new constitution was enacted in March, 1987. The army stopped the first scheduled elections in November and army-sponsored elections led to the election of Leslie Manigat in Jan., 1988. He was overthrown in June 1988 in a military coup led by Namphy, after the former attempted to dismiss him. He was in turn overthrown by Lt. Gen. Prosper Avril.

History. Discovered by Columbus, who landed at Môle Saint Nicolas on Dec. 6, 1492, Haiti in 1697 became a French possession known as Saint Domingue. An insurrection among a slave population of 500,000 in 1791 ended with a declaration of independence by Pierre-Dominique Toussaint l'Ouverture in 1801. Napoleon Bonaparte suppressed the independence movement, but it eventually triumphed in 1804 under Jean-Jacques Dessalines, who gave the new nation the aboriginal name Haiti.

Its prosperity dissipated in internal strife as well as disputes with neighboring Santo Domingo during a succession of 19th-century dictatorships, a bankrupt Haiti accepted a U.S. customs receivership from 1905 to 1941. Direct U.S. rule from 1915 to 1934 brought a measure of stability and a population growth that made Haiti the most densely populated nation in the hemisphere.

In 1949, after four years of democratic rule by President Dumarsais Estimé, dictatorship returned under Gen. Paul Magloire, who was succeeded by François Duvalier in 1957.

Duvalier established a dictatorship. Duvalier's son, Jean-Claude, or "Baby Doc," succeeded his father in 1971 as ruler of the poorest nation in the Western Hemisphere.

The ruling council that took power upon the exile of Duvalier was criticized for the inclusion of former Duvalier aides.

HONDURAS

Republic of Honduras
President: José Azcona Hoyo (1986)
Area: 43,277 sq mi. (112,088 sq km)
Population (est. mid-1989): 5,000,000 (average annual rate of natural increase: 3.2%) (90% mestizo)
Density per square mile: 115
Capital and largest city (1985): Tegucigalpa, 571,400
Monetary unit: Lempira
Languages: Spanish, some Indian dialects, English in Bay Islands Department
Religion: Roman Catholic
National name: República de Honduras

Literacy rate: 56%
Economic summary: Gross domestic product (1986): $2.6 billion, $560 per capita; real growth rate (1987 est.): 3.5%. Labor force in agriculture: 62%; principal products: bananas, coffee, sugar cane, seafood, citrus, tobacco. Labor force in industry: 12%; major products: processed agricultural products, textiles and clothing, wood products. Natural resources: timber, gold, silver, lead, zinc, antimony. Exports: bananas, coffee, lumber, meat, petroleum products, tobacco, sugar, shrimp and lobster. Imports: manufactured goods, machinery, transportation equipment, chemicals, petroleum. Major trading partners: U.S., Caribbean countries, Western Europe, Japan, Latin America.

Geography. Honduras, in the north central part of Central America, has a 400-mile (644-km) Caribbean coastline and a 40-mile (64-km) Pacific frontage. Its neighbors are Guatemala to the west, El Salvador to the south, and Nicaragua to the east. Honduras is slightly larger than Tennessee.

Generally mountainous, the country is marked by fertile plateaus, river valleys, and narrow coastal plains.

Government. José Azcona Hoyo was elected to succeed Roberto Suazo Córdova. He was inaugurated on January 27, 1986. There is a 134-member National Congress.

History. Columbus discovered Honduras on his last voyage in 1502. Honduras, with four other countries of Central America, declared its independence from Spain in 1821 and was part of a federation of Central American states until 1838. In that year it seceded from the federation and became a completely independent country.

U.S. Marines intervened in 1903 and 1923. In 1931, 1932, and 1937, major revolutions were crushed by force.

In July 1969, El Salvador invaded Honduras after Honduran landowners had deported several thousand Salvadorans. The fighting left 1,000 dead and tens of thousands homeless. By threatening economic sanctions and military intervention, the OAS induced El Salvador to withdraw.

Although parliamentary democracy returned with the election of Roberto Suazo Córdova as President in 1982 after a decade of military rule, Honduras faced severe economic problems and tensions along its border with Nicaragua. "Contra" rebels, waging a guerrilla war against the Sandinista regime in Nicaragua, used Honduras as a training and staging area. At the same time, the United States used Honduras as a site for military exercises and built bases to train both Honduran and Salvadoran troops. Honduras received $1 billion in U.S. economic and military aid from 1982–87.

1. A successor to be elected in Nov. 1989.

HUNGARY

Hungarian People's Republic
President: Bruno Straub (1988)
Premier: Miklós Németh (1988)
Area: 35,919 sq mi. (93,030 sq km)
Population (est. mid-1989): 10,600,000 (average annual rate of natural increase: −0.2%)
Density per square mile: 294
Capital: Budapest
Largest cities (est. 1986): Budapest, 2,076,000; Miskolc, 211,700; Debrecen, 211,800; Szeged, 182,100; Pécs, 177,100
Monetary unit: Forint
Language: Magyar
Religions: Roman Catholic, 67%; Protestant, 25%; atheist, 7%
National name: Magyar Népköztársaság
Literacy rate: 99%
Economic summary: Gross national product (1986): $84 billion, $7,910 per capita; real growth rate: 1.3%. Land used for agriculture: 71%; labor force: 29%; principal products: corn, wheat, potatoes, sugar beets, vegetables, wine grapes, fruits. Labor force in industry: 32%; major products: steel, chemicals, pharmaceuticals, textiles, transport equipment. Natural resources: some bauxite and iron. Exports: machinery and tools, industrial and consumer goods, raw materials. Imports: machinery, raw materials. Major trading partners: U.S.S.R., Warsaw Pact countries, West Germany, Yugoslavia, Austria, and Italy.

Geography. This central European country the size of Indiana is bordered by Austria to the west, Czechoslovakia to the north, the U.S.S.R. and Romania to the east, and Yugoslavia to the south.

Most of Hungary is a fertile, rolling plain lying east of the Danube River and drained by the Danube and Tisza rivers. In the extreme northwest is the Little Hungarian Plain. South of that area is Lake Balaton (250 sq mi.; 648 sq km).

Government. Hungary is a People's Republic with legislative power vested in the unicameral National Assembly, whose 352 members are elected directly for four-year terms. The supreme body of state power is the 21-member Presidential Council elected by the National Assembly. The supreme administrative body is the Council of Ministers, headed by the Premier.

The Hungarian Socialist Workers (Communist) Party, led by Károly Grósz, is the only political party.

History. About 2,000 years ago, Hungary was part of the Roman provinces of Pannonia and Dacia. In A.D. 896 it was invaded by the Magyars, who founded a kingdom. Christianity was accepted during the reign of Stephen I (St. Stephen) (997–1038).

The peak of Hungary's great period of medieval power came during the reign of Louis I the Great (1342–82), whose dominions touched the Baltic, Black, and Mediterranean seas.

War with the Turks broke out in 1389, and for more than 100 years the Turks advanced through the Balkans. When the Turks smashed a Hungarian army in 1526, western and northern Hungary accepted Hapsburg rule to escape Turkish occupation. Transylvania became independent under Hungarian princes. Intermittent war with the Turks was waged until a peace treaty was signed in 1699.

After the suppression of the 1848 revolt against Hapsburg rule, led by Louis Kossuth, the dual monarchy of Austria-Hungary was set up in 1867.

The dual monarchy was defeated with the other Central Powers in World War I. After a short-lived republic in 1918, the chaotic Communist rule of 1919 under Béla Kun ended with the Romanians occupying Budapest on Aug. 4, 1919. When the Romanians left, Adm. Nicholas Horthy entered the capital with a national army. The Treaty of Trianon of June 4, 1920, cost Hungary 68% of its land and 58% of its population. Meanwhile, the National Assembly had restored the legal continuity of the old monarchy; and, on March 1, 1920, Horthy was elected Regent.

Following the German invasion of Russia on June 22, 1941, Hungary joined the attack against the Soviet Union, but the war was not popular and Hungarian troops were almost entirely withdrawn from the eastern front by May 1943. German occupation troops set up a puppet government after Horthy's appeal for an armistice with advancing Soviet troops on Oct. 15, 1944, had resulted in his overthrow. The German regime soon fled the capital, however, and on December 23 a provisional government was formed in Soviet-occupied eastern Hungary. On Jan. 20, 1945, it signed an armistice in Moscow. Early the next year, the National Assembly approved a constitutional law abolishing the thousand-year-old monarchy and establishing a republic.

By the Treaty of Paris (1947), Hungary had to give up all territory it had acquired since 1937 and to pay $300 million reparations to the U.S.S.R., Czechoslovakia, and Yugoslavia. In 1948 the Communist Party, with the support of Soviet troops seized control. Hungary was proclaimed a People's Republic and one-party state in 1949. Industry was nationalized, the land collectivized into state farms, and the opposition terrorized by the secret police.

The terror, modeled after that of the U.S.S.R., reached its height with the trial of Jozsef Cardinal Mindszenty, Roman Catholic primate. He confessed to fantastic charges under duress of drugs or brainwashing and was sentenced to life imprisonment in 1949. Protests were voiced in all parts of the world.

On Oct. 23, 1956, anti-Communist revolution broke out in Budapest. To cope with it, the Communists set up a coalition government and called former Premier Imre Nagy back to head it. But he and most of his ministers were swept by the logic of events into the anti-Communist opposition, and he declared Hungary a neutral power, withdrawing from the Warsaw Treaty and appealing to the United Nations for help.

One of his ministers, János Kádár, established a counter-regime and asked the U.S.S.R. to send in military power. Soviet troops and tanks suppressed the revolution in bloody fighting after 190,000 people had fled the country and Mindszenty, freed from jail, had taken refuge in the U.S. Embassy.

Kádár was succeeded as Premier, but not party secretary, by Gyula Kallai in 1965. Continuing his program of national reconciliation, Kádár emptied prisons, reformed the secret police, and eased travel restrictions.

Hungary developed the reputation of being the freest East European state.

After 15 years' asylum in the U.S. Embassy, Mindszenty, under an agreement between the Vatican and the Hungarian regime, was allowed to travel into exile to Rome in 1971. In a move applauded by Kádár, Pope Paul VI removed Mindszenty from his honorary post as Primate of Hungary in 1974. The Cardinal died in Vienna in 1975.

Relations with the U.S. improved in 1972 when World War II debt claims between the two nations were settled. On Jan. 6, 1978, the U.S. returned to Hungary, over anti-Communist protests, the 977-year-old crown of St. Stephen, held at Fort Knox since World War II.

An emerging struggle between reformists and hard-liners was illustrated by the creation of a four-man Presidium composed of both. A party congress in October will determine the leader of the party.

ICELAND

Republic of Iceland
President: Mrs. Vigdis Finnbogadottir (1980)
Prime Minister: Steingrimur Hermannsson (1987)
Area: 39,709 sq mi. (102,846 sq km)
Population (est. mid-1988): 200,000 (average annual rate of natural increase: 1.0%)
Density per square mile: 6.0
Capital and largest city (est. 1983): Reykjavik, 91,394
Monetary unit: M.N. króna
Language: Icelandic
Religion: Evangelical Lutheran
National name: Lydveldid Island
Literacy rate: 99.9%
Economic summary: Gross domestic product (1986): $3.9 billion, $16,200 per capita; real growth rate: 6.3%. Labor force in agriculture: 11%; fishing and fish processing: 13.0%; principal agricultural products: livestock, hay, fodder, cheese. Labor force in industry: 17%; major products: processed aluminum, fish. Natural resources: fish, diatomite, hydroelectric and geothermal power. Exports: fish, animal products, aluminum. Imports: petroleum products, machinery and transportation equipment, food, textiles. Major trading partners: U.S., U.S.S.R., Western European countries.

1. Including some offshore islands.

Geography. Iceland, an island about the size of Kentucky, lies in the north Atlantic Ocean east of Greenland and just touches the Arctic Circle. It is one of the most volcanic regions in the world.

Small fresh-water lakes are to be found throughout the island, and there are many natural phenomena, including hot springs, geysers, sulfur beds, canyons, waterfalls, and swift rivers. More than 13% of the area is covered by snowfields and glaciers, and most of the people live in the 7% of the island comprising fertile coastlands.

Government. The president is elected for four years by popular vote. Executive power resides in the prime minister and his Cabinet. The Althing (Parliament) is composed of 63 members in two houses. They elect 22 of themselves to constitute the Upper House, the remaining 41 representing the Lower House.

History. Iceland was first settled shortly before 900, mainly by Norse. A Constitution drawn up about 930 created a form of democracy and provided for an Althing, or General Assembly.

In 1262–64, Iceland came under Norwegian rule and passed to ultimate Danish control through the formation of the Union of Kalmar in 1483. In 1874, Icelanders obtained their own Constitution. In 1918, Denmark recognized Iceland as a separate state with unlimited sovereignty but still nominally under the Danish king.

On June 17, 1944, after a popular referendum, the Althing proclaimed Iceland an independent republic.

The British occupied Iceland in 1940, immediately after the German invasion of Denmark. In 1942, the U.S. took over the burden of protection. Iceland refused to abandon its neutrality in World War II and thus forfeited charter membership in the United Nations, but it cooperated with the Allies throughout the conflict. Iceland joined the North Atlantic Treaty Organization in 1949.

Iceland unilaterally extended its territorial waters from 12 to 50 nautical miles in 1972, precipitating a running dispute with Britain known as the "cod war." Icelandic warships harassed British trawlers, which then received aid from British gunboats; some trawlers were shelled, and Icelandic and British warships collided in 1973. The World Court ruled in 1974 that the 50-mile limit could not be applied unilaterally, but Iceland rejected the ruling.

An agreement calling for registration of all British trawlers fishing within 200 miles of Iceland and a 24-hour time limit on incursions was finally reached in 1976.

INDIA

Republic of India
President: Ramaswamy Venkataraman (1987)
Prime Minister: Rajiv Gandhi (1984)
Area: 1,229,737 sq mi. (3,185,019 sq km)
Population (est. mid-1989): 835,000,000 (average annual rate of natural increase: 2.2%)
Density per square mile: 658
Capital (1980 census): New Delhi, 619,417
Largest cities (1981 est.): Calcutta, 9,194,018; Greater Bombay, 8,243,405; Delhi, 5,729,283; Madras, 4,289,347; Bangalore, 2,921,751; Ahmedabad, 2,548,-057; Kanpur, 1,639,064
Monetary unit: Rupee
Principal languages: Hindi (official), English (official), Bengali, Gujarati, Kashmiri, Malayalam, Marathi, Oriya, Punjabi, Tamil, Telugu, Urdu, Kannada, Assamese (all recognized by the Constitution)
Religions: Hindu, 83%; Islam, 11%; Christian, 3%; Sikh, 2%
National name: Bharat
Literacy rate: 36%
Member of Commonwealth of Nations
Economic summary: Gross national product (FY87): $200 billion; $250 per capita; real growth (FY87 est): 4.8%. Land used for agriculture: 60%; labor force: 67%; principal products: rice, wheat, oilseeds, cotton, tea, opium poppy (for pharmaceuticals). Major industrial products: jute, processed food, steel, machinery, transport machinery, cement. Natural resources: iron ore, coal, manganese, mica, bauxite, limestone, textiles. Exports: diamonds, iron goods, textiles and clothing, tea, crude oil. Imports: machinery and transport equipment, petroleum, edible oils, fertilizers. Major trading partners: U.S., U.S.S.R., Japan, Saudi Arabia, U.K.

Geography. One third the area of the United States, the Republic of India occupies most of the subcontinent of India in south Asia. It borders on China in the northeast. Other neighbors are Pakistan on the west, Nepal and Bhutan on the north, and Burma and Bangladesh on the east.

The country contains a large part of the great Indo-Gangetic plain, which extends from the Bay of Bengal on the east to the Afghan frontier on the Arabian Sea on the west. This plain is the richest and most densely settled part of the subcontinent. Another distinct natural region is the Deccan, a plateau of 2,000 to 3,000 feet (610 to 914 m) in elevation, occupying the southern portion of the subcontinent.

Forming a part of the republic are several groups of islands—the Laccadives (14 islands) in the Arabian Sea and the Andamans (204 islands) and the Nicobars (19 islands) in the Bay of Bengal.

India's three great river systems, all rising in the Himalayas, have extensive deltas. The Ganges flows south and then east for 1,540 miles (2,478 km) across the northern plain to the Bay of Bengal; part of its delta, which begins 220 miles (354 km) from

the sea, is within the republic. The Indus, starting in Tibet, flows northwest for several hundred miles in the Kashmir before turning southwest toward the Arabian Sea; it is important for irrigation in Pakistan. The Brahmaputra, also rising in Tibet, flows eastward, first through India and then south into Bangladesh and the Bay of Bengal.

Government. India is a federal republic. It is also a member of the Commonwealth of Nations, a status defined at the 1949 London Conference of Prime Ministers, by which India recognizes Queen as head of the Commonwealth. Under the Constitution effective Jan. 26, 1950, India has a parliamentary type of government.

The constitutional head of the state is the President, who is elected every five years. He is advised by the Prime Minister and a Cabinet based on a majority of the bicameral Parliament, which consists of a Council of States (Rajya Sabha), representing the constituent units of the republic and a House of the People (Lok Sabha), elected every five years by universal suffrage.

History. The Aryans, or Hindus, who invaded India between 2400 and 1500 B.C. from the northwest found a land already well civilized. Buddhism was founded in the 6th century B.C. and spread through northern India.

In 1526, Moslem invaders founded the great Mogul empire, centered on Delhi, which lasted, at least in name, until 1857. Akbar the Great (1542–1605) strengthened this empire and became the ruler of a greater portion of India than had ever before acknowledged the suzerainty of one man. The long reign of his great-grandson, Aurangzeb (1658–1707), represents both the culmination of Mogul power and the beginning of its decay.

Vasco da Gama, the Portuguese explorer, visited India first in 1498, and for the next 100 years the Portuguese had a virtual monopoly on trade with the subcontinent. Meanwhile, the English founded the East India Company, which set up its first factory at Surat in 1612 and began expanding its influence, fighting the Indian rulers and the French, Dutch, and Portuguese traders simultaneously.

Bombay, taken from the Portuguese, became the seat of English rule in 1687. The defeat of French and Islamic armies by Lord Clive in the decade ending in 1760 laid the foundation of the British Empire in India. From then until 1858, when the administration of India was formally transferred to the British Crown following the Sepoy Mutiny of native troops in 1857, the East India Company suppressed native uprisings and extended British rule.

After World War I, in which the Indian states sent more than 6 million troops to fight beside the Allies, Indian nationalist unrest rose to new heights under the leadership of a little Hindu lawyer, Mohandas K. Gandhi, called Mahatma Gandhi. His tactics called for nonviolent revolts against British authority. He soon became the leading spirit of the All-India Congress Party, which was the spearhead of revolt. In 1919 the British gave added responsibility to Indian officials, and in 1935 India was given a federal form of government and a measure of self-rule.

In 1942, with the Japanese pressing hard on the eastern borders of India, the British War Cabinet tried and failed to reach a political settlement with nationalist leaders. The Congress Party took the position that the British must quit India. In 1942, fearing mass civil disobedience, the government of

India carried out widespread arrests of Congress leaders, including Gandhi.

Gandhi was released in 1944 and negotiations for a settlement were resumed. Finally, in February 1947, the Labor government announced its determination to transfer power to "responsible Indian hands" by June 1948 even if a Constitution had not been worked out.

Lord Mountbatten as Viceroy, by June 1947, achieved agreement on the partitioning of India along religious lines and on the splitting of the provinces of Bengal and the Punjab, which the Moslems had claimed.

The Indian Independence Act, passed quickly by the British Parliament, received royal assent on July 18, 1947, and on August 15 the Indian Empire passed into history.

Jawaharlal Nehru, leader of the Congress Party, was made Prime Minister. Before an exchange of populations could be arranged, bloody riots occurred among the communal groups, and armed conflict broke out over rival claims to the princely state of Jammu and Kashmir. Peace was restored only with the greatest difficulty. In 1949 a Constitution, along the lines of the U.S. Constitution, was approved making India a sovereign republic. Under a federal structure the states were organized on linguistic lines.

The dominance of the Congress Party contributed to stability. In 1956 the republic absorbed the former French settlements. Five years later, it forcibly annexed the Portuguese enclaves of Goa, Damao, and Diu.

Nehru died in 1964. His successor, Lal Bahadur Shastri, died on Jan. 10, 1966. Nehru's daughter, Indira Gandhi, became Prime Minister, and she continued his policy of nonalignment.

In 1971 the Pakistani Army moved in to quash the independence movement in East Pakistan that was supported by clandestine aid from India, and some 10 million Bengali refugees poured across the border into India, creating social, economic, and health problems. After numerous border incidents, India invaded East Pakistan and in two weeks forced the surrender of the Pakistani army. East Pakistan was established as an independent state and renamed Bangladesh.

In the summer of 1975, the world's largest democracy veered suddenly toward authoritarianism when a judge in Allahabad, Mrs. Gandhi's home constituency, found her landslide victory in the 1971 elections invalid because civil servants had illegally aided her campaign. Amid demands for her resignation, Mrs. Gandhi decreed a state of emergency on June 26 and ordered mass arrests of her critics, including all opposition party leaders except the Communists.

In 1976, India and Pakistan formally renewed diplomatic relations.

Despite strong opposition to her repressive measures and particularly the resentment against compulsory birth control programs, Mrs. Gandhi in 1977 announced parliamentary elections for March. At the same time, she freed most political prisoners.

The landslide victory of Morarji R. Desai unseated Mrs. Gandhi and also defeated a bid for office by her son, Sanjay.

Mrs. Gandhi staged a spectacular comeback in the elections of January 1980.

In 1984, Mrs. Gandhi ordered the Indian Army to root out a band of Sikh holy men and gunmen who were using the holiest shrine of the Sikh religion, the Golden Temple in Amritsar, as a base for terrorist raids in a violent campaign for greater political autonomy in the strategic Punjab border state. As many as 1,000 people were reported killed in the June 5–6 battle, including Jarnall Singh Bhindranwale, the Khomeini-like militant leader, and 93 soldiers. The perceived sacrilege to the Golden Temple kindled outrage among many of India's 14 million Sikhs and brought a spasm of mutinies and desertions by Sikh officers and soldiers in the army.

On Oct. 31, 1984, Mrs. Gandhi was assassinated by two men identified by police as Sikh members of her bodyguard. The ruling Congress I Party chose her second son, Rajiv Gandhi, to succeed her as Prime Minister.

On July 24, Rajiv Gandhi and moderate Sikh leaders agreed on a package of steps to ease Sikh hostility toward the government and end the turmoil in the state of Punjab. A key element called for a change in the Punjab boundaries to increase the Sikh population within the state and give it greater political influence. Prime Minister Gandhi also yielded to demands for more lenient treatment of Sikhs arrested in riots over the last three years. Violence continued unabated with about 1,000 people being killed in 1986 and the first half of 1987 and Gandhi established direct rule on May 11, 1987, dissolving the local government.

1. Parliamentary elections due in late-1989.

Native States. Most of the 560-odd native states and subdivisions of pre-1947 India acceded to the new nation, and the central government pursued a vigorous policy of integration. This took three forms: merger into adjacent provinces, conversion into centrally administered areas, and grouping into unions of states. Finally, under a controversial reorganization plan effective Nov. 1, 1956, the unions of states were abolished and merged into adjacent states, and India became a union of 15 states and 8 centrally administered areas. A 16th state was added in 1962, and in 1966, the Punjab was partitioned into two states.

Resolution of the territorial dispute over Kashmir grew out of peace negotiations following the two-week India-Pakistan war of 1971. After sporadic skirmishing, an accord reached July 3, 1972, committed both powers to withdraw troops from a temporary cease-fire line after the border was fixed. Agreement on the border was reached Dec. 7, 1972.

In April 1975, the Indian Parliament voted to make the 300-year-old kingdom of Sikkim a full-fledged Indian state, and the annexation took effect May 16.

Situated in the Himalayas, Sikkim was a virtual dependency of Tibet until the early 19th century. Under an 1890 treaty between China and Great Britain, it became a British protectorate, and was made an Indian protectorate after Britain quit the subcontinent.

INDONESIA

Republic of Indonesia
President: Suharto (1969)[1]
Area: 735,268 sq mi. (1,904,344 sq km)[2]
Population (est. mid-1989): 184,600,000 (average annual rate of natural increase: 2.0%)

Density per square mile: 251
Capital: Jakarta
Largest cities (est. 1983): Jakarta, 7,636,000; Surabaja, 2,289,000; Bandung, 1,602,000; Medan, 1,966,000; Semarang, 1,269,000
Monetary unit: Rupiah
Languages: Bahasa Indonesia (official), Dutch, English, and more than 60 regional languages
Religions: Islam, 87%; Christian, 10%; Hindu Buddhist, 3%
National name: Republik Indonesia
Literacy rate: 64%
Economic summary: Gross national product (1987 est.): $59 billion, $330 per capita; real growth rate (1987 est.): 2.0%. Land used for agriculture: 18%; labor force: 55%; principal products: rice, cassava, sugarcane, rubber, coffee. Labor force in industry: 10%; major products: oil, textiles, food and beverages, light manufactures, cement, fertilizer, rubber. Natural resources: oil, timber, nickel, natural gas, tin, bauxite, copper. Exports: petroleum and liquid natural gas, timber, rubber, coffee, tin. Imports: rice, wheat, textiles, chemicals, machinery, transport equipment, iron and steel. Major trading partners: Japan, U.S., Singapore, Saudi Arabia, West Germany.

1. General Suharto served as Acting President of Indonesia from 1967 to 1969. 2. Includes West Irian (former Netherlands New Guinea), renamed Irian Jaya in March 1973 (159, 355 sq mi.; 412,731 sq km), and former Portuguese Timor (5,763 sq mi.; 14,925 sq km), annexed in 1976.

Geography. Indonesia is part of the Malay archipelago in Southeast Asia with an area nearly three times that of Texas. It consists of the islands of Sumatra, Java, Madura, Borneo (except Sarawak and Brunei in the north), the Celebes, the Moluccas, Irian Jaya, and about 30 smaller archipelagos, totaling 13,677 islands, of which about 6,000 are inhabited. Its neighbor to the north is Malaysia and to the east Papua New Guinea.

A backbone of mountain ranges extends throughout the main islands of the archipelago. Earthquakes are frequent, and there are many active volcanoes.

Government. The President is elected by the People's Consultative Assembly, whose 1000 members include the functioning legislative arm, the 500-member House of Representatives. Meeting at least once every five years, the Assembly has broad policy functions. The House, 100 of whose members are appointed by the President, meets at least once annually. General Suharto was elected unopposed to a fifth five-year term in 1988.

History. Indonesia is inhabited by Malayan and Papuan peoples ranging from the more advanced Javanese and Balinese to the more primitive Dyaks of Borneo. Invasions from China and India contributed Chinese and Indian admixtures.

During the first few centuries of the Christian era, most of the islands came under the influence of Hindu priests and traders, who spread their culture and religion. Moslem invasions began in the 13th century, and most of the area was Moslem by the 15th. Portuguese traders arrived early in the 16th century but were ousted by the Dutch about 1595. After Napoleon subjugated the Netherlands homeland in 1811, the British seized the islands but returned them to the Dutch in 1816. In 1922 the islands were made an integral part of the Netherlands kingdom.

During World War II, Indonesia was under Japanese military occupation with nominal native self-government. When the Japanese surrendered to the Allies, President Sukarno and Mohammed Hatta, his Vice President, proclaimed Indonesian independence from the Dutch on Aug. 17, 1945. Allied troops—mostly British Indian troops—fought the nationalists until the arrival of Dutch troops. In November 1946, the Dutch and the Indonesians reached a draft agreement contemplating formation of a Netherlands-Indonesian Union, but differences in interpretation resulted in more fighting between Dutch and Indonesian forces.

On Nov. 2, 1949, Dutch and Indonesian leaders agreed upon the terms of union. The transfer of sovereignty took place at Amsterdam on Dec. 27, 1949. In February 1956 Indonesia abrogated the Union with the Netherlands and in August 1956 repudiated its debt to the Netherlands. In 1963, Netherlands New Guinea was transferred to Indonesia and renamed West Irian. In 1973 it became Irian Jaya.

Hatta and Sukarno, the co-fathers of Indonesian independence, split after it was achieved over Sukarno's concept of "guided democracy." Under Sukarno, the country's leading political figure for almost a half century, the Indonesian Communist Party gradually gained increasing influence.

After an attempted coup was put down by General Suharto, the army chief of staff, and officers loyal to him, thousands of Communist suspects were sought out and killed all over the country. Suharto took over the reins of government, gradually eased Sukarno out of office, and took full power in 1967. Under President Suharto, Indonesia has been strongly anticommunist. It also has been politically stable and has made progress in economic development.

Indonesia invaded the former Portuguese half of the island of Timor in 1975, and annexed the territory in 1976. On a visit to Jakarta in July 1984, Secretary of State George P. Shultz expressed concern about reports of human rights abuses being carried out by Indonesian forces in East Timor. More than 100,000 Timorese, a sixth of the mostly Catholic population, were reported to have died from famine, disease, and fighting since the annexation.

IRAN

Islamic Republic of Iran
President: Hashemi Rafsanjani (1989)
Prime Minister: Mir Hussein Moussavi (1981)
Area: 636,293 sq mi. (1,648,000 sq km)
Population (est. mid-1989): 53,000,000 (average annual rate of natural increase: 3.4%) (Persian, Azerbaijani, Kurdish)
Density per square mile: 85
Capital: Teheran
Largest cities (est. 1986): Teheran, 6,037,658; Isfahan, 1,422,308; Mashed, 2,038,388; Tabriz, 1,566,932
Monetary unit: Rial
Languages: Farsi (Persian), Kurdish, Arabic
Religions: Shi'ite Moslem, 93%; Sunni Moslem, 5%
Literacy rate: 48%
Economic summary: Gross national product (1987): $86.4 billion, $1,756 per capita; real growth rate (1987): 1.3%. Land used for agriculture: 35%; Labor force: 33%; principal products: wheat, barley, rice, sugar beets, cotton, dates, raisins, sheep, goats. Labor force in industry: 21%; major products: crude and refined oil, textiles, cement, processed foods, steel and copper fabrication. Natural resources: oil, gas, iron, copper. Exports: petroleum, carpets. Imports: machinery, military supplies, foodstuffs, pharmaceuticals. Major trading partners: Japan, West Germany, Netherlands, U.K., Italy, Spain, Turkey.

Geography. Iran, a Middle Eastern country south of the Caspian Sea and north of the Persian Gulf, is three times the size of Arizona. It shares borders with Iraq, Turkey, the U.S.S.R., Afghanistan, and Pakistan.

In general, the country is a plateau averaging 4,000 feet (1,219 m) in elevation. There are also maritime lowlands along the Persian Gulf and the Caspian Sea. The Elburz Mountains in the north rise to 18,603 feet (5,670 m) at Mt. Damavend. From northwest to southeast, the country is crossed by a desert 800 miles (1,287 km) long.

Government. The Pahlavi dynasty was overthrown on Feb. 11, 1979, by followers of the Ayatollah Ruhollah Khomeini. After a referendum endorsed the establishment of a republic, Khomeini drafted a Constitution calling for a President to be popularly elected every four years, an appointed Prime Minister, and a unicameral National Consultative Assembly, popularly elected every four years.

Khomeini also instituted a Revolutionary Council to insure the adherence to Islamic principles in all phases of Iranian life. The Council formally handed over its powers to the Assembly after the organization of the legislature in July 1980, but continued to exercise power behind the scenes.

History. Oil-rich Iran was called Persia before 1935. Its key location blocks the lower land gate to Asia and also stands in the way of traditional Russian ambitions for access to the Indian Ocean. After periods of Assyrian, Median, and Achaemenidian rule, Persia became a powerful empire under Cyrus the Great, reaching from the Indus to the Nile at its zenith in 525 B.C. It fell to Alexander in 331–30 B.C. and to the Seleucids in 312–02 B.C., and a native Persian regime arose about 130 B.C. Another Persian regime arose about A.D. 224, but it fell to the Arabs in 637. In the 12th century, the Mongols took their turn ruling Persia, and in the early part of the 18th century, the Turks occupied the country.

An Anglo-Russian convention of 1907 divided Persia into two spheres of influence. British attempts to impose a protectorate over the entire country were defeated in 1919. Two years later, Gen. Reza Pahlavi seized the government and was elected hereditary Shah in 1925. Subsequently he did much to modernize the country and abolished all foreign extraterritorial rights.

Increased pro-Axis activity led to Anglo-Russian occupation of Iran in 1941 and deposition of the Shah in favor of his son, Mohammed Reza Pahlavi.

Ali Razmara became premier in 1950 and pledged to restore efficient and honest government, but he was assassinated after less than nine months in office and Mohammed Mossadegh took over. Mossadegh was ousted in August 1953, by Fazollah Zahedi, whom the Shah had named premier.

Opposition to the Shah spread, despite the imposition of martial law in September 1978, and massive demonstrations demanded the return of the exiled Ayatollah Ruhollah Khomeini. Riots and strikes continued despite the appointment of an opposition leader, Shahpur Bakhtiar, as premier on Dec. 29. The Shah and his family left Iran on Jan. 16, 1979, for a "vacation," leaving power in the hands of a regency council.

Khomeini returned on Feb. 1 to a nation in turmoil as military units loyal to the Shah continued to support Bakhtiar and clashed with revolutionaries. Khomeini appointed Mehdi Bazargan as premier of the provisional government and in two days of fighting, revolutionaries forced the military to capitulate on Feb. 11.

The new government began a program of nationalization of insurance companies, banks, and industries both locally and foreign-owned. Oil production fell amid the political confusion.

Khomeini, ignoring opposition, proceeded with his plans for revitalizing Islamic traditions. He urged women to return to the veil, or chador; banned alcohol and mixed bathing, and prohibited music from radio and television broadcasting, declaring it to be "no different from opium."

Revolutionary militants invaded the U.S. Embassy in Teheran on Nov. 4, 1979, seized staff members as hostages, and precipitated an international crisis.

Khomeini refused all appeals, even a unanimous vote by the U.N. Security Council demanding immediate release of the hostages.

Iranian hostility toward Washington was reinforced by the Carter administration's economic boycott and deportation order against Iranian students in the U.S., the break in diplomatic relations and ultimately an aborted U.S. raid in April aimed at rescuing the hostages.

As the first anniversary of the embassy seizure neared, Khomeini and his followers insisted on their original conditions: guarantee by the U.S. not to interfere in Iran's affairs, cancellation of U.S. damage claims against Iran, release of $8 billion in frozen Iranian assets, an apology, and the return of the assets held by the former imperial family.

These conditions were largely met and the 52 American hostages were released on Jan. 20, ending 444 days in captivity.

From the release of the hostages onward, President Bani-Sadr and the conservative clerics of the dominant Islamic Republican Party clashed with growing frequency. He was stripped of his command of the armed forces by Khomeini on June 6 and ousted as President on June 22. On July 24, Prime Minister Mohammed Ali Rajai was elected overwhelmingly to the Presidency.

Rajai and Prime Minister Mohammed Javad Bahonar were killed on Aug. 30 by a bomb in Bahonar's office. Hojatolislam Mohammed Ali Khamenei, a clergyman, leader of the Islamic Republican Party and spokesman for Khomeini, was elected President on Oct. 2, 1981.

The sporadic war with Iraq regained momentum in 1982, as Iran launched an offensive in March and regained much of the border area occupied by Iraq in late 1980. Khomeini rejected Iraqi bids for a truce, insisting that Iraq's President Saddam Hussein must leave office first.

Iran continued to be at war with Iraq well into 1988. Although Iraq expressed its willingness to cease fighting, Iran stated that it would not stop the war until Iraq agreed to make payment for war damages to Iran, and punish the Iraqi government leaders involved in the conflict. The fighting, spread into the Persian Gulf in 1984, with Iraq attacking tankers loading at Iran's Kharg Island, and Iran striking back at tankers calling at Saudi Arabia and the smaller, oil-rich Arab Gulf states. The latter has led to clashes with the U.S. Navy.

On July 20, 1988, Khomeini, after a series of Iranian military reverses, agreed to cease-fire negotiations with Iraq. A cease-fire went into effect Aug. 20, 1988.

Khomeini died in June 1989. He was replaced as the supreme religious leader by President Ali Khamenei.

IRAQ

Republic of Iraq
President: Saddam Hussein (1979)
Area: 167,920 sq mi. (434,913,000 sq km)
Population (est. mid-1989): 18,100,000 (average annual rate of natural increase: 3.8%) (Arab, 77%; Kurds, 19%)
Density per square mile: 108
Capital: Baghdad
Largest cities (est. 1985): Baghdad, 4,648,609; Basra, 616,700; Mosul, 570,926
Monetary unit: Iraqi dinar
Languages: Arabic (official) and Kurdish
Religions: Islam, 97%; Christian, 3%
National name: Al Jumhouriya Al Iraqia
Literacy rate: about 55%
Economic summary: Gross national product (1987 est.): $40 billion, $2,400 per capita; real growth rate: −15%. Land used for agriculture, 22%; labor force, 44%; principal products: dates, livestock, wheat, barley, sugarcane, rice. Labor force in industry: 26%; major products: petroleum, shoes, beer, textiles. Natural resources: oil, natural gas, gypsum, sulfur. Exports: petroleum, foodstuffs. Imports: manufactured goods, machinery, chemicals, livestock. Major trading partners: France, Italy, Japan, West Germany, Brazil, U.K., U.S., Turkey, Soviet bloc.

Geography. Iraq, a triangle of mountains, desert, and fertile river valley, is bounded on the east by Iran, on the north by Turkey, the west by Syria and Jordan, and the south by Saudi Arabia and Kuwait. It is twice the size of Idaho.

The country has arid desertland west of the Euphrates, a broad central valley between the Euphrates and Tigris, and mountains in the northeast. The fertile lower valley is formed by the delta of the two rivers, which join about 120 miles (193 km) from the head of the Persian Gulf. The gulf coastline is 26 miles (42 km) long. The only port for seagoing vessels is Basra, which is on the Shatt-al-Arab River near the head of the Persian Gulf.

Government. Since the coup d'etat of July 1968, Iraq has been governed by the Arab Ba'ath Socialist Party through a Council of Command of the Revolution headed by the President. There is also a Council of Ministers headed by the President.

History. From earliest times Iraq was known as Mesopotamia—the land between the rivers—for it embraces a large part of the alluvial plains of the Tigris and Euphrates.

An advanced civilization existed by 4000 B.C. Sometime after 2000 B.C. the land became the center of the ancient Babylonian and Assyrian empires. It was conquered by Cyrus the Great of Persia in 538 B.C., and by Alexander in 331 B.C. After an Arab conquest in A.D. 637–40, Baghdad became capital of the ruling caliphate. The country was cruelly pillaged by the Mongols in 1258, and during the 16th, 17th, and 18th centuries was the object of repeated Turkish-Persian competition.

Nominal Turkish suzerainty imposed in 1638 was replaced by direct Turkish rule in 1831. In World War I, an Anglo-Indian force occupied most of the country, and Britain was given a mandate over the area in 1920. The British recognized Iraq as a kingdom in 1922 and terminated the mandate in 1932 when Iraq was admitted to the League of Nations. In World War II, Iraq generally adhered to its 1930 treaty of alliance with Britain, but in 1941, British troops were compelled to put down a pro-Axis revolt led by Premier Rashid Ali.

Iraq became a charter member of the Arab League in 1945, and Iraqi troops took part in the Arab invasion of Palestine in 1948.

Faisal II, born on May 2, 1935, succeeded his father, Ghazi I, who was killed in an automobile accident on April 4, 1939. Faisal and his uncle, Crown Prince Abdul-Ilah, were assassinated in August 1958 in a swift revolutionary coup that brought to power a military junta headed by Abdul Karem Kassim. Kassim, in turn, was overthrown and killed in a coup staged March 8, 1963, by the Ba'ath Socialist Party.

Abdel Salam Arif, a leader in the 1958 coup, staged another coup in November 1963, driving the Ba'ath members of the revolutionary council from power. He adopted a new constitution in 1964. In 1966, he, two Cabinet members, and other supporters died in a helicopter crash. His brother, Gen. Abdel Rahman Arif, assumed the presidency, crushed the opposition, and won an indefinite extension of his term in 1967. His regime was ousted in July 1968 by a junta led by Maj. Gen. Ahmed Hassan al-Bakr.

A long-standing dispute over control of the Shatt al-Arab waterway between Iraq and Iran broke into full-scale war on Sept. 20, 1980. Iraqi planes attacked Iranian airfields and the Abadan refinery, and Iraqi ground forces moved into Iran.

Despite the smaller size of its armed forces, Iraq took and held the initiative by seizing Abadan and Khurramshahr together with substantial Iranian territory by December and beating back Iranian counterattacks in January. Peace efforts by the Islamic nations, the nonaligned, and the United Nations failed as 1981 wore on and the war stagnated.

In 1982, the Iraqis fell back to their own country and dug themselves in behind sandbagged defensive fortifications. With massive firepower, they turned back wave after wave of attacking Iranian troops and revolutionary guards, many of them in their teens. From the beginning of the war in September 1980 to September 1984, foreign military analysts estimated that more than 100,000 Iranians and perhaps 50,000 Iraqis had been killed.

The Iraqis clearly wanted to end the war, but the Iranians refused. In March of 1985, Iraq apparently won the largest battle of the long war, crushing a major Iranian offensive in the southern marshes in a week of heavy fighting that killed an estimated 30,000 Iranians and perhaps 10,000 Iraqis.

In February 1986, Iranian forces gained on two fronts; on the Fao peninsula in the south and in the northern mountains, but Iraq retook most of the lost ground in 1988 and the war continued a stalemate. In August, Iraq and Iran agreed to hold direct talks after a ceasefire takes effect.

IRELAND

President: Patrick J. Hillery (1976)
Taoiseach (Prime Minister): Charles J. Haughey (1987)
Area: 26,600 sq mi. (68,394 sq km)
Population (est. mid-1989): 3,500,000 (average annual rate of natural increase: 0.8%)
Density per square mile: 131
Capital: Dublin
Largest cities (est. 1982): Dublin, 550,000; Cork, 140,000; Limerick, 60,000
Monetary unit: Irish pound (punt)
Languages: Irish, English

Religions: Roman Catholic, 94%; Protestant, 5%
National name: Eire
Literacy rate: 99%
Economic summary: Gross national product (1987): $27.8 billion. Average annual growth rate (1985–87): 0.2%; Per capita Income (1987): $7,480. Land used for agriculture, 85%; labor force in agriculture and fishing: 13%; principal products: cattle and dairy products, pigs, poultry and eggs, sheep and wool, horses, barley, sugar beets. Labor force in industry: 21%; major products: processed foods, metals and engineering, electronics, beverages and tobacco, chemicals. Natural resources: zinc, lead, natural gas, barite, copper, gypsum, limestone, dolomite, peat, silver. Exports: livestock, dairy products, machinery, chemicals, processed foods, data processing equipment, raw materials and minerals. Imports: grains, petroleum products, machinery, chemicals, textile yarn, cereals. Major trading partners: U.K., Western European countries, U.S.

Geography. Ireland is situated in the Atlantic Ocean and separated from Britain by the Irish Sea. Half the size of Arkansas, it occupies the entire island except for the six counties which make up Northern Ireland.

Ireland resembles a basin—a central plain rimmed with mountains, except in the Dublin region. The mountains are low, with the highest peak, Carrantuohill in County Kerry, rising to 3,415 feet (1,041 m).

The principal river is the Shannon, which begins in the north central area, flows south and southwest for about 240 miles (386 km), and empties into the Atlantic.

Government. Ireland is a parliamentary democracy. The National Parliament (Oireachtas) consists of the president and two Houses, the House of Representatives (Dáil Éireann) and the Senate (Seanad Éireann), whose members serve for a maximum term of five years. The House of Representatives has 166 members elected by proportional representation; the Senate has 60 members of whom 11 are nominated by the prime minister, 6 by the universities and the remaining 43 from five vocational panels. The prime minister (Taoiseach), who is the head of government, is appointed by the president on the nomination of the House of Representatives, to which he is responsible.

History. In the Stone and Bronze Ages, Ireland was inhabited by Picts in the north and a people called the Erainn in the south, the same stock, apparently, as in all the isles before the Anglo-Saxon invasion of Britain. About the fourth century B.C., tall, red-haired Celts arrived from Gaul or Galicia. They subdued and assimilated the inhabitants and established a Gaelic civilization.

By the beginning of the Christian Era, Ireland was divided into five kingdoms—Ulster, Connacht, Leinster, Meath, and Munster. St. Patrick introduced Christianity in 432 and the country developed into a center of Gaelic and Latin learning. Irish monasteries, the equivalent of universities, attracted intellectuals as well as the pious and sent out missionaries to many parts of Europe and, some believe, to North America.

Norse depredations along the coasts, starting in 795, ended in 1014 with Norse defeat at the Battle of Clontarf by forces under Brian Boru. In the 12th century, the Pope gave all Ireland to the English Crown as a papal fief. In 1171, Henry II of England was acknowledged "Lord of Ireland," but local sectional rule continued for centuries, and English control over the whole island was not reasonably ab-

solute until the 17th century. By the Act of Union (1801), England and Ireland became the "United Kingdom of Great Britain and Ireland."

A steady decline in the Irish economy followed in the next decades. The population had reached 8.25 million when the great potato famine of 1846–48 took many lives and drove millions to emigrate to America. By 1921 it was down to 4.3 million.

In the meantime, anti-British agitation continued along with demands for Irish home rule. The advent of World War I delayed the institution of home rule and resulted in the Easter Rebellion in Dublin (April 24–29, 1916), in which Irish nationalists unsuccessfully attempted to throw off British rule. Guerrilla warfare against British forces followed proclamation of a republic by the rebels in 1919.

The Irish Free State was established as a dominion on Dec. 6, 1922, with the six northern counties as part of the United Kingdom. Ireland was neutral in World War II.

In 1948, Éamon de Valera, American-born leader of the Sinn Fein, who had won establishment of the Free State in 1921 in negotiations with Britain's David Lloyd George, was defeated by John A. Costello, who demanded final independence from Britain. The Republic of Ireland was proclaimed on April 18, 1949. It withdrew from the Commonwealth but in 1955 entered the United Nations. Since 1949 the prime concern of successive governments has been economic development.

Through the 1960s, two antagonistic currents dominated Irish politics. One sought to bind the wounds of the rebellion and civil war. The other was the effort of the outlawed extremist Irish Republican Army to bring Northern Ireland into the republic. Despite public sympathy for unification of Ireland, the Dublin government dealt rigorously with IRA guerrillas caught inside the republic's borders.

In the elections of June 11, 1981, Garret M. D. FitzGerald, leader of the Fine Gael, was elected Prime Minister by 81 to 78 with the support of 15 Labor Party members and one independent Socialist added to his own party's 65 members. Other independents abstained, among them Kieran Doherty, a prisoner in Northern Ireland's Maze Prison, who with another prisoner had won election to the Southern Parliament (the Republic's Constitution extends citizenship to anyone born in Northern Ireland). Doherty died after a hunger strike on Aug. 3, one of nine Maze prisoners to do so.

FitzGerald resigned Jan. 27, 1982, after his presentation of an austerity budget aroused the opposition of independents who had backed him previously. Former Prime Minister Haughey was sworn in on March 9 and presented a budget with nearly a $1 billion deficit, with additional public spending aimed at stimulating the lagging economy. FitzGerald was re-elected Prime Minister on Dec. 14, 1982 but was unable to solve the problem of unemployment and the elections of 1987 brought Haughey back into power on March 10.

ISRAEL

State of Israel
President: Chaim Herzog (1988)
Prime Minister: Yitzhak Shamir (1988) (term ends Nov., 1992)

Area: 8,020 sq mi. (20,772 sq km)
Population (est. mid-1988): 4,500,000[1] (average annual rate of natural increase: 1.6%)
Density per square mile: 559
Capital: Jerusalem[2]
Largest cities (est. 1986): Jerusalem, 468,400[3]; Tel Aviv, 320,300; Haifa, 223,400
Monetary unit: Shekel
Languages: Hebrew, Arabic, English
Religions: Jewish, 82%, Islam, 14%, Christian, 2.3%, Druze and others, 1.7%
National name: Medinat Yisra'el
Literacy rate: 92%
Economic summary: Gross national product (1988): $35 billion. Annual growth rate (1987–8): 1.1%. Per capita income (1986): $7,830. Land used for agriculture: 62%; labor force: 6%; principal products: citrus and other fruits, vegetables, beef, dairy and poultry products. Labor force in industry: 25%; major products: processed foods, cut diamonds, clothing and textiles, chemicals, metal products, transport and electrical equipment, plastics. Natural resources: sulfur, rock salt, phosphates, potash, bromine. Exports: polished diamonds, citrus and other fruits, clothing and textiles, processed foods, high technology products, computerized medical equipment, military hardware, fertilizer and chemical products. Imports: rough diamonds, chemicals, oil, machinery, iron and steel, cereals, textiles, vehicles, ships. Major trading partners: U.S., West Germany, U.K., Switzerland, France, Italy, Belgium, Luxembourg.

1. Excludes West Bank, Gaza Strip, East Jerusalem. 2. Not recognized by U.S. which recognizes Tel Aviv. 3. Includes East Jerusalem.

Geography. Israel, slightly smaller than Massachusetts, lies at the eastern end of the Mediterranean Sea. It is bordered by Egypt on the west, Syria and Jordan on the east, and Lebanon on the north.

Northern Israel is largely a plateau traversed from north to south by mountains and broken by great depressions, also running from north to south.

The maritime plain of Israel is remarkably fertile. The southern Negev region, which comprises almost half the total area, is largely a wide desert steppe area. The National Water Project irrigation scheme is now transforming it into fertile land. The Jordan, the only important river, flows from the north through Lake Hule (Waters of Merom) and Lake Kinneret (Sea of Galilee or Sea of Tiberias), finally entering the Dead Sea, 1,290 feet (393 m) below sea level. This "sea," which is actually a salt lake (394 sq mi.; 1,020 sq km), has no outlet, its water balance being maintained by evaporation.

Government. Israel, which does not have a written constitution, has a republican form of government headed by a president elected for a five-year term by the Knesset. He may serve no more than two terms. The Knesset has 120 members elected by universal suffrage under proportional representation for four years. The government is administered by the Cabinet, which is headed by the prime minister.

The Knesset decided in June 1950 that Israel would acquire a constitution gradually through the years by the enactment of fundamental laws. Israel grants automatic citizenship to every Jew who desires to settle within its borders, subject to control of the Knesset.

History. Palestine, cradle of two great religions and homeland of the modern state of Israel, was known to the ancient Hebrews as the "Land of Canaan." Palestine's name derives from the Philistines, a people who occupied the southern coastal part of the country in the 12th century B.C.

A Hebrew kingdom established in 1000 B.C. was later split into the kingdoms of Judah and Israel; they were subsequently invaded by Assyrians, Babylonians, Egyptians, Persians, Macedonians, Romans, and Byzantines. The Arabs took Palestine from the Byzantine Empire A.D. 634–40. With the exception of a Frankish Crusader kingdom from 1099 to 1187, Palestine remained under Moslem rule until the 20th century (Turkish rule from 1516), when British forces under Gen. Sir Edmund Allenby defeated the Turks and captured Jerusalem Dec. 9, 1917. The League of Nations granted Britain a mandate to govern Palestine, effective in 1923.

Jewish colonies—Jews from Russia established one as early as 1882—multiplied after Theodor Herzl's 1897 call for a Jewish state. The Zionist movement received official approval with the publication of a letter Nov. 2, 1917, from Arthur Balfour, British Foreign Secretary, to Lord Rothschild, a British Jewish leader. Balfour promised support for the establishment of a Jewish homeland in Palestine on the understanding that the civil and religious rights of non-Jewish Palestinians would be safeguarded.

A 1937 British proposal called for an Arab and a Jewish state separated by a mandated area incorporating Jerusalem and Nazareth. Arabs opposed this, demanding a single state with minority rights for Jews, and a 1939 British White Paper retreated, offering instead a single state with further Jewish immigration to be limited to 75,000. Although the White Paper satisfied neither side, further discussion ended on the outbreak of World War II, when the Jewish population stood at nearly 500,000, or 30% of the total. Illegal and legal immigration during the war brought the Jewish population to 678,000 in 1946, compared with 1,269,000 Arabs. Unable to reach a compromise, Britain turned the problem over to the United Nations in 1947, which on November 29 voted for partition—despite strong Arab opposition.

Britain did not help implement the U.N. decision and withdrew on expiration of its mandate May 14, 1948. Zionists had already seized control of areas designated as Jewish, and, on the day of British departure, the Jewish National Council proclaimed the State of Israel.

U.S. recognition came within hours. The next day, Jordanian and Egyptian forces invaded the new nation. At the cease-fire Jan. 7, 1949, Israel increased its original territory by 50%, taking western Galilee, a broad corridor through central Palestine to Jerusalem, and part of modern Jerusalem. (In April 1950, Jordan annexed areas of eastern and central Palestine that had been designated for an Arab state, together with the old city of Jerusalem).

Chaim Weizmann and David Ben-Gurion became Israel's first president and prime minister. The new government was admitted to the U.N. May 11, 1949.

The next clash with Arab neighbors came when Egypt nationalized the Suez Canal in 1956 and barred Israeli shipping. Coordinating with an Anglo-French force, Israeli troops seized the Gaza Strip and drove through the Sinai to the east bank of the Suez Canal, but withdrew under U.S. and U.N. pressure. In 1967, Israel threatened retaliation against Syrian border raids, and Syria asked Egyptian aid. Egypt demanded the removal of U.N. peace-keeping forces from Suez, staged a national mobilization, closed the Gulf of Aqaba, and moved troops into the Sinai. Starting with simultaneous air attacks against Syrian, Jordanian, and Egyptian air bases on June 5, Israel during a six-day war totally defeated its Arab enemies. Expanding its territory by 200%, Israel at the cease-fire held the Golan Heights, the West Bank of the Jordan River, the Old City, and all of the Sinai and the east bank of the Suez Canal.

Israel insisted that Jerusalem remain a unified city and that peace negotiations be conducted directly, something the Arab states had refused to do because it would constitute a recognition of their Jewish neighbor.

Egypt's President Gamal Abdel Nasser renounced the 1967 cease-fire in 1969 and began a "war of attrition" against Israel, firing Soviet artillery at Israeli forces on the east bank of the canal. Nasser died of a heart attack on Sept. 28, 1970, and was succeeded by Anwar el-Sadat.

In the face of Israeli reluctance even to discuss the return of occupied territories, the fourth Mideast war erupted Oct. 6, 1973, with a surprise Egyptian and Syrian assault on the Jewish high holy day of Yom Kippur. Initial Arab gains were reversed when a cease-fire took effect two weeks later, but Israel suffered heavy losses in manpower.

U.S. Secretary of State Henry A. Kissinger arranged a disengagement of forces on both the Egyptian and Syrian fronts. Geneva talks, aimed at a lasting peace, foundered, however, when Israel balked at inclusion of the Palestine Liberation Organization, a group increasingly active in terrorism directed against Israel.

A second-stage Sinai withdrawal signed by Israel and Egypt in September 1975 required Israel to give up the strategic Mitla and Gidi passes and to return the captured Abu Rudeis oil fields. Egypt guaranteed passage of Israeli cargoes through the reopened Suez Canal, and both sides renounced force in the settlement of disputes. Two hundred U.S. civilian technicians were stationed in a widened U.N. buffer zone to monitor and warn either side of truce violations.

A dramatic breakthrough in the tortuous history of Mideast peace efforts occurred Nov. 9, 1977, when Egypt's President Sadat declared his willingness to go anywhere to talk peace. Prime Minister Menachem Begin on Nov. 15 extended an invitation to the Egyptian leader to address the Knesset. Sadat's arrival in Israel four days later raised worldwide hopes. But optimism ebbed even before Begin was invited to Ismailia by Sadat, December 25–26.

An Israeli peace plan unveiled by Begin on his return, and approved by the Knesset, offered to end military administration in the West Bank and the Gaza Strip, with a degree of Arab self-rule but no relinquishment of sovereignty by Israel. Sadat severed talks on Jan. 18 and, despite U.S. condemnation, Begin approved new West Bank settlements by Israelis.

A PLO raid on Israel's coast on March 11, 1978, killed 30 civilians and provoked a full-scale invasion of southern Lebanon by Israel three days later to attack PLO bases. Israel withdrew three months later, turning over strongpoints to Lebanese Christian militia wherever possible rather than to a U.N. peacekeeping force installed in the area.

On March 14, 1979, after a visit by Carter, the Knesset approved a final peace treaty, and 12 days later Begin and Sadat signed the document, together with Carter, in a White House ceremony. Israel began its withdrawal from the Sinai on May 25 by handing over the coastal town of El Arish and the two countries opened their border on May 29.

One of the most difficult periods in Israel's history began with a confrontation with Syria over the placing by Syria of Soviet surface-to-air missiles in the Bekaa Valley of Lebanon in April 1981. President Reagan dispatched Philip C. Habib to prevent a clash. While Habib was seeking a settlement, Begin ordered a bombing raid against an Iraqi nuclear reactor on June 7, invoking the theory of preemptive self-defense because he said Iraq was planning to make nuclear weapons to attack Israel.

Although Israel withdrew its last settlers from the Sinai in April 1982 and agreed to a Sinai "peace patrol" composed of troops from four West European nations, the fragile peace engineered by Habib in Lebanon was shattered on June 9 by a massive Israeli assault on southern Lebanon. The attack was in retaliation for what Israel charged was a PLO attack that critically wounded the Israeli ambassador to London six days earlier.

Israeli armor swept through UNIFIL lines in southern Lebanon, destroyed PLO strongholds in Tyre and Sidon, and reached the suburbs of Beirut on June 10. As Israeli troops ringed Moslem East Beirut, where 5,000 PLO guerrillas were believed trapped, Habib sought to negotiate a safe exit for them. The Arab world loudly protested the entire action, estimated by Lebanon to have cost the lives of 10,000 civilians by mid-July.

A U.S.-mediated accord between Lebanon and Israel, signed on May 17, 1983, provided for Israeli withdrawal from Lebanon. Israeli withdrawal was conditioned on withdrawal of Syrian troops from the Bekaa Valley, however, and the Syrians refused to leave. Israel eventually withdrew its troops from the Beirut area, but kept them in southern Lebanon. Lebanon, under pressure from Syria, canceled the accord in March 1984.

Prime Minister Begin resigned on Sept. 15, 1983. On Oct. 10, Likud Party stalwart Yitzhak Shamir was elected Prime Minister.

After a close election, the two major parties worked out a carefully balanced power-sharing agreement and the Knesset, on Sept. 14, 1984 approved a national unity government including both the Labor Alignment and the Likud bloc.

By the anniversary of the invasion of Lebanon in June of 1985, Israel had withdrawn most—but not all—of its troops from the country. Israeli combat units left, but military advisers remained in a security zone along Israel's northern frontier.

The Peres government decided in May to exchange 1,150 Palestinian prisoners—including terrorists—for three Israeli soldiers who had been held since the Lebanon war by the Popular Front for the Liberation of Palestine. Another development dividing Israelis was the verdict by a three-judge court on July 10 convicting three Jewish settlers of murder and 12 others of different violent crimes against Arabs.

In one hopeful development, the coalition government declared an economic emergency on July 1 and imposed sweeping austerity measures intended to break the country's 260% inflation. Key elements were an 18.8% devaluation of the shekel, price increases in such government-subsidized products as gasoline, dismissal of 9,000 government employees, government spending cuts and a wage and price freeze. By the end of Peres' term in October, 1986, the shekel had been revalued and stabilized and inflation was down to less than 20%.

Differences in the approach to take to peace talks started to strain the government in 1987.

In Dec. 1987, riots by Gazan Palestinians led to the current general uprising throughout the occupied territories which consists of low-level violence and civil disobedience. As a consequence, in 1988 the PLO formally declared an independent state. Also, in response to their ostensible recognition of Israel in that year, the U.S. established low-level diplomatic contacts with the PLO.

A deadlock in the elections of Dec. 1988 led to a continuation of the Likud-Labor national unity government.

ITALY

Italian Republic
President: Francesco Cossiga (1985)
Premier: Giulio Andreotti (1989)
Area: 116,500 sq mi. (301,278 sq km)
Population (est. mid-1989): 57,600,000 (average annual rate of natural increase: 0%)
Density per square mile: 495
Capital: Rome
Largest cities (1984): Rome, 2,826,733; Milan, 1,535,722; Naples, 1,206,955; Turin, 1,049,997; Genoa, 738,099; Palermo, 716,149; Bologna, 442,307; Florence, 435,698; Catania, 377,707; Bari, 368,216.
Monetary unit: Lira
Language: Italian
Religion: Roman Catholic, almost 100%
National name: Repubblica Italiana
Literacy rate: 93%
Economic summary: Gross national product (1987): $743.3 billion, $12,955 per capita; real growth rate (1987): 2.5%. Land used for agriculture: 59%; labor force: 10%; principal products: grapes, olives, citrus fruits, vegetables, wheat, corn. Labor force in industry: 30%; major products: machinery, autos, textiles, shoes, chemicals. Natural resources: mercury, potash, sulfur, fish, gas, marble. Exports: Engineering, chemicals, textiles, metals, shoes, food. Imports: engineering, chemicals, food, metals. Major trading partners: West Germany, France, United States, United Kingdom, Switzerland.

Geography. Italy is a long peninsula shaped like a boot bounded on the west by the Tyrrhenian Sea and on the east by the Adriatic. Slightly larger than Arizona, it has for neighbors France, Switzerland, Austria, and Yugoslavia.

Approximately 600 of Italy's 708 miles (1,139 km) of length are in the long peninsula that projects into the Mediterranean from the fertile basin of the Po River. The Apennine Mountains, branching off from the Alps between Nice and Genoa, form the peninsula's backbone, and rise to a maximum height of 9,560 feet (2,912 m) at the Gran Sasso d'Italia (Corno). The Alps form Italy's northern boundary.

Several islands form part of Italy. Sicily (9,926 sq mi.; 25,708 sq km) lies off the toe of the boot, across the Strait of Messina, with a steep and rockbound northern coast and gentler slopes to the sea in the west and south. Mount Etna, an active volcano, rises to 10,741 feet (3,274 m), and most of Sicily is more than 500 feet (3,274 m) in elevation. Sixty-two miles (100 km) southwest of Sicily lies Pantelleria (45 sq mi.; 117 sq km), and south of that are Lampedusa and Linosa. Sardinia (9,301 sq mi.; 24,090 sq km), which is just south of Corsica and about 125 miles (200 km) west of the mainland, is mountainous, stony, and unproductive.

Italy has many northern lakes, lying below the snow-covered peaks of the Alps. The largest are Garda (143 sq mi.; 370 sq km), Maggiore (83 sq mi.; 215 sq km), and Como (55 sq mi.; 142 sq km).

The Po, the principal river, flows from the Alps on Italy's western border and crosses the Lombard plain to the Adriatic.

Government. The president is elected for a term of seven years by Parliament in joint session with regional representatives. The president nominates the premier and, upon the premier's recommendations, the members of the Cabinet. Parliament is composed of two houses: a Senate with 315 elective members and a Chamber of Deputies of 630 members elected by the people for a five-year term.

History. Until A.D. 476, when the German Odoacer became head of the Roman Empire in the west, the history of Italy was largely the history of Rome. From A.D. 800 on, the Holy Roman Emperors, Popes, Normans, and Saracens all vied for control over various segments of the Italian peninsula. Numerous city states, such as Venice and Genoa, and many small principalities flourished in the late Middle Ages.

In 1713, after the War of the Spanish Succession, Milan, Naples, and Sardinia were handed over to Austria, which lost some of its Italian territories in 1735. After 1800, Italy was unified by Napoleon, who crowned himself King of Italy in 1805; but with the Congress of Vienna in 1815, Austria once again became the dominant power in Italy.

Austrian armies crushed Italian uprisings in 1820-1821, and 1831. In the 1830s Giuseppe Mazzini, brilliant liberal nationalist, organized the Risorgimento (Resurrection), which laid the foundation for Italian unity.

Disappointed Italian patriots looked to the House of Savoy for leadership. Count Camille di Cavour (1810–61), Premier of Sardinia in 1852 and the architect of a united Italy, joined England and France in the Crimean War (1853–56), and in 1859, helped France in a war against Austria, thereby obtaining Lombardy. By plebiscite in 1860, Modena, Parma, Tuscany, and the Romagna voted to join Sardinia. In 1860, Giuseppe Garibaldi conquered Sicily and Naples and turned them over to Sardinia. Victor Emmanuel II, King of Sardinia, was proclaimed King of Italy in 1861.

Allied with Germany and Austria-Hungary in the Triple Alliance of 1882, Italy declared its neutrality upon the outbreak of World War I on the ground that Germany had embarked upon an offensive war. In 1915, Italy entered the war on the side of the Allies.

Benito (Il Duce) Mussolini, a former Socialist, organized discontented Italians in 1919 into the Fascist Party to "rescue Italy from Bolshevism." He led his Black Shirts in a march on Rome and, on Oct. 28, 1922, became premier. He transformed Italy into a dictatorship, embarking on an expansionist foreign policy with the invasion and annexation of Ethiopia in 1935 and allying himself with Adolf Hitler in the Rome-Berlin Axis in 1936. He was executed by Partisans on April 28, 1945 at Dongo on Lake Como.

Following the overthrow of Mussolini's dictatorship and the armistice with the Allies (Sept. 3, 1943), Italy joined the war against Germany as a co-belligerent. King Victor Emmanuel III abdicated May 9, 1946, and left the country after having installed his son as King Humbert II. A plebiscite rejected monarchy, however, and on June 13, King Humbert followed his father into exile.

The peace treaty of Sept. 15, 1947, required Italian renunciation of all claims in Ethiopia and Greece and the cession of the Dodecanese to Greece and of five small Alpine areas to France. Much of the Istrian Peninsula, including Fiume and Pola, went to Yugoslavia.

The Trieste area west of the new Yugoslav territory was made a free territory (until 1954, when the city and a 90-square-mile zone were transferred to Italy and the rest to Yugoslavia).

Scandal brought the long reign of the Christian Democrats to an end when Italy's 40th premier since World War II, Arnaldo Forlani, was forced to resign in the wake of disclosure that many high-ranking Christian Democrats and civil servants belonged to a secret Masonic lodge known as "P-2."

When the Socialists deserted the coalition, Forlani was forced to resign on May 26, 1981, leaving to Giovanni Spadolini of the small Republican Party the task of forming a new government. He was succeeded by Amintore Fanfani, a Christian Democrat, the following year. Bettino Craxi, a Socialist, became Premier in 1983.

Craxi was forced to resign on June 27, 1986 following the loss of a key secret-ballot vote in Parliament. After a month of political wrangling, Craxi was able to form a new government on condition that his term end in March, 1987.

Disputes over who Craxi's successor would be led to general elections in June, 1987 in which the Socialists and the Christian Democrats gained at the expense of the Communists and the smaller parties. Giovanni Goria, a Christian Democrat, became the new Premier. Budget disputes led to Goria being replaced by Ciriaco De Mita in April, 1988.

IVORY COAST

Republic of Côte d'Ivoire
President: Félix Houphouët-Boigny (1960)
Area: 124,502 sq mi. (322,462 sq km)
Population (est. mid-1989): 12,100,000 (average annual rate of natural increase: 3.6%)
Density per square mile: 97
Capital: Yamoussoukro[1]
Monetary unit: Franc CFA
Ethnic groups: 60 different groups: principals are Baoule, Bete, Senoufou, Malinke, Agni
Languages: French and African languages (Diaula esp.)
Religions: folk beliefs, 44%; Christian, 32%; Islam, 24%
National name: République de la Côte d'Ivoire
Literacy rate: 35%
Economic summary: Gross domestic product (1987 est.): $10.4 billion, $970 per capita; real growth rate (1987): −3%. Labor force in agriculture: 85%; principal products: coffee, cocoa, sugar, corn, cotton. Major industrial products: food, cement, bananas, pineapples. Natural resources: diamonds, iron ore, oil refining, auto assembly, textiles, timber. Exports: coffee, cocoa, tropical woods. Imports: raw materials, consumer goods, fuels. Major trading partners: France, U.S., Western European countries, Nigeria.

1. Not recognized by U.S. which recognizes Abidjan.

Geography. The Ivory Coast, in western Africa on the Gulf of Guinea, is a little larger than New Mexico. Its neighbors are Liberia, Guinea, Mali, Burkina Faso, and Ghana.

The country consists of a coastal strip in the south, dense forests in the interior, and savannas in the north. Rainfall is heavy, especially along the coast.

Government. The government is headed by a President who is elected every five years by popular vote, together with a National Assembly of 175 members.

The Parti Démocratique de la Côte d'Ivoire, a member of the Rassemblement Démocratique Africain, is the only political party.

History. The Ivory Coast attracted both French and Portuguese merchants in the 15th century. French traders set up establishments early in the 19th century, and in 1842, the French obtained territorial concessions from local tribes, gradually extending their influence along the coast and inland. The area was organized as a territory in 1893, became an autonomous republic in the French Union after World War II, and achieved independence on Aug. 7, 1960.

The Ivory Coast formed a customs union in 1959 with Dahomey (Benin), Niger, and Burkina Faso. The country is one of the most prosperous and stable in West Africa.

JAMAICA

Sovereign: Queen Elizabeth II
Governor-General: Sir Florizel Glasspole (1973)
Prime Minister: Michael Manley (1989)
Area: 4,411 sq mi. (11,424 sq km)
Population (est. mid-1988): 2,500,000 (average annual rate of natural increase: 1.7%)
Density per square mile: 586
Capital and largest city (est. 1982): Kingston, 104,000
Monetary unit: Jamaican dollar
Language: English
Religions: Protestant, 71%; Roman Catholic, 10%; Rastafarian, 7%
Member of Commonwealth of Nations
Literacy rate: 76%
Economic summary: Gross domestic product (1986): $2.4 billion. Average annual rate of natural increase: 1.7%. Land used for agriculture: 43%; labor force: 33% (includes fishing and mining); principal products: sugar cane, citrus fruits, bananas, spices, coconuts, coffee, cocoa. Labor force in industry: 13%; major products: bauxite, textiles, processed foods, light manufactures. Natural resources: bauxite, gypsum. Exports: alumina, bauxite, sugar, clothing, citrus fruits, rum, cocoa. Imports: fuels, machinery, transport and electrical equipment, food, fertilizer. Major trading partners: U.S., U.K., Netherlands Antilles, Venezuela.

Geography. Jamaica is an island in the West Indies, 90 miles (145 km) south of Cuba and 100 miles (161 km) west of Haiti. It is a little smaller than Connecticut.

The island is made up of a plateau and the Blue Mountains, a group of volcanic hills, in the east. Blue Mountain (7,402 ft.; 2,256 m) is the tallest peak.

Government. The legislature is a 60-member House of Representatives elected by universal suffrage and an appointed Senate of 21 members. The Prime Minister is appointed by the Governor-General and must, in the Governor-General's opinion, be the person best able to command the confidence of a majority of the members of the House of Representatives.

History. Jamaica was inhabited by Arawak Indians when Columbus discovered it in 1494 and named it St. Iago. It remained under Spanish rule until 1655, then became a British possession. The island prospered from wealth brought by buccaneers to their base, Port Royal, the capital, until the city disappeared in the sea in 1692 after an earthquake. The Arawaks died off from disease and exploitation, and slaves, mostly black, were imported to work sugar plantations. Abolition of the slave trade (1807), emancipation of the slaves (1833), and a gradual drop in sugar prices led to depressed economic conditions that resulted in an uprising in 1865.

The following year Jamaica's status was changed to that of a colony, and conditions improved considerably. Introduction of banana cultivation made the island less dependent on the sugar crop for its well-being.

On May 5, 1953, Jamaica attained internal autonomy, and in 1958 it led in organizing the West Indies Federation. This effort at Caribbean unification failed. A nationalist labor leader, Sir Alexander Bustamente, led a campaign for withdrawal from the Federation. As the result of a popular referendum in 1961, Jamaica became independent on Aug. 6, 1962.

Michael Manley became Prime Minister in 1972 and initiated a socialist program and in 1977, the government bought 51% of the Kaiser and Reynolds bauxite operations.

The Labor Party defeated Manley's People's National Party in 1980 and its capitalist-oriented leader, Edward P.G. Seaga, became Prime Minister. He instituted measures to encourage private investment.

Like other Caribbean countries, Jamaica was hard-hit by the 1981–82 recession. By 1984, austerity measures that Seaga instituted in the hope of bringing the economy back into balance included elimination of government subsidies. Devaluation of the Jamaican dollar made Jamaican products more competitive on the world market and Jamaica achieved record growth in tourism and agriculture. Manufacturing also grew. But at the same time, the cost of many foods went up 50% to 75% and thousands of Jamaicans fell deeper into poverty.

The PNP decisively won local elections in mid-July, 1987, signaling a weakening in Seaga's position. In 1989, Manley swept back into power with a clear-cut victory in 1989. He has indicated that he would pursue more centrist policies than he did in his previous administration.

JAPAN

Emperor: Akihito (1989)
Prime Minister: Toshiki Kaifu (1989)
Area: 143,574 sq mi. (371,857 sq km)
Population (est. mid-1989): 123,200,000 (average annual rate of natural increase: 0.5%)
Density per square mile: 857
Capital: Tokyo

Largest cities (est. 1986): Tokyo, 8,354,615; Yokohama, 2,992,926; Osaka, 2,636,249; Nagoya, 2,116,381; Sapporo, 1,542,979; Kyoto, 1,479,218; Kobe, 1,410,000; Fukuoka, 1,160,440; Kitakyusho, 1,056,402; Kawasaki, 1,088,624
Monetary unit: Yen
Language: Japanese
Religions: Shintoist, Buddhist
National name: Nippon
Literacy rate (1981): 99%
Economic summary: Gross national product (1986): $2,644 billion, $21,820 per capita; real growth rate (1986): 3.8%. Land used for agriculture, 15%; labor force, including fishing, 8%; principal products: rice, vegetables, fruits, sugar. Labor force in industry: 33%; major products: machinery and equipment, metals and metal products, textiles, autos, consumer electronics, chemicals, electrical and electronic equipment. Natural resource: fish. Exports: machinery and equipment, automobiles, metals and metal products, textiles. Imports: fossil fuels, metal ore, raw materials, foodstuffs, machinery and equipment. Major trading partners: U.S., Middle East, Western Europe, Indonesia, China, Australia, Canada, South Korea, Taiwan

Geography. An archipelago extending more than 1,744 miles (2,790 km) from northeast to southwest in the Pacific, Japan is separated from the east coast of Asia by the Sea of Japan. It is approximately the size of Montana.

Japan's four main islands are Honshu, Hokkaido, Kyushu, and Shikoku. The Ryukyu chain to the southwest was U.S.-occupied and the Kuriles to the northeast are Russian-occupied. The surface of the main islands consists largely of mountains separated by narrow valleys. There are about 60 more or less active volcanoes, of which the best-known is Mount Aso. Mount Fuji, seen on postcards, is not active.

Government. Japan's Constitution, promulgated on Nov. 3, 1946, replaced the Meiji Constitution of 1889. The 1946 Constitution, sponsored by the U.S. during its occupation of Japan, brought fundamental changes to the Japanese political system, including the abandonment of the Emperor's divine rights. The Diet (Parliament) consists of a House of Representatives of 511 members, elected for four years, and a House of Councilors of 252 members, half of whom are elected every three years for six-year terms. Executive power is vested in the Cabinet, which is headed by a Prime Minister, nominated by the Diet from its members.

On Jan. 7, 1989, Emperor Hirohito, Japan's longest-reigning monarch died and was succeed by his son, Akihito (born 1933). He was married in 1959 to Michiko Shoda (the first time a crown prince married a commoner). They have two sons, Hiro and Aya, and a daughter, Nori.

History. A series of legends attributes creation of Japan to the sun goddess, from whom the later emperors were allegedly descended. The first of them was Jimmu Tenno, supposed to have ascended the throne in 660 B.C.

Recorded Japanese history begins with the first contact with China in the 5th century A.D. Japan was then divided into strong feudal states, all nominally under the Emperor, but with real power often held by a court minister or clan. In 1185, Yoritomo, chief of the Minamoto clan, was designated Shogun (Generalissimo) with the administration of the islands under his control. A dual government system—Shogun and Emperor—continued until 1867.

First contact with the West came about 1542, when a Portuguese ship off course arrived in Japanese waters. Portuguese, traders, Jesuit missionaries, and Spanish, Dutch, and English traders followed. Suspicious of Christianity and of Portuguese support of a local Japanese revolt, the shoguns prohibited all trade with foreign countries; only a Dutch trading post at Nagasaki was permitted. Western attempts to renew trading relations failed until 1853, when Commodore Matthew Perry sailed an American fleet into Tokyo Bay.

Japan now quickly made the transition from a medieval to a modern power. Feudalism was abolished and industrialization was speeded. An imperial army was established with conscription. The shogun system was abolished in 1868 by Emperor Meiji, and parliamentary government was established in 1889. After a brief war with China in 1894–95, Japan acquired Formosa (Taiwan), the Pescadores Islands, and part of southern Manchuria. China also recognized the independence of Korea (Chosen), which Japan later annexed (1910).

In 1904–05, Japan defeated Russia in the Russo-Japanese War, gaining the territory of southern Sakhalin (Karafuto) and Russia's port and rail rights in Manchuria. In World War I Japan seized Germany's Pacific islands and leased areas in China. The Treaty of Versailles then awarded it a mandate over the islands.

At the Washington Conference of 1921–22, Japan agreed to respect Chinese national integrity. The series of Japanese aggressions that was to lead to the nation's downfall began in 1931 with the invasion of Manchuria. The following year, Japan set up this area as a puppet state, "Manchukuo," under Emperor Henry Pu-Yi, last of China's Manchu dynasty. On Nov. 25, 1936, Japan joined the Axis by signing the anti-Comintern pact. The invasion of China came the next year and the Pearl Harbor attack on the U.S. on Dec. 7, 1941.

(For details of World War II (1939–45), *see* Headline History.)

Japan surrendered formally on Sept. 2, 1945, aboard the battleship *Missouri* in Tokyo Bay after atomic bombs had hit Hiroshima and Nagasaki. Southern Sakhalin and the Kurile Islands reverted to the U.S.S.R., and Formosa (Taiwan) and Manchuria to China. The Pacific islands remained under U.S. occupation. General of the Army Douglas MacArthur was appointed Supreme Commander for the Allied Powers on Aug. 14, 1945.

A new Japanese Constitution went into effect in 1947. In 1949, many of the responsibilities of government were returned to the Japanese. Full sovereignty was granted to Japan by the Japanese Peace Treaty in 1951.

The treaty took effect on April 28, 1952, when Japan returned to full status as a nation. It was admitted into the United Nations in 1958.

Following the visit of Prime Minister Eisaku Sato to Washington in 1969, the U.S. agreed to return Okinawa and other Ryukyu Islands to Japan in 1972, and both nations renewed the security treaty in 1970.

When President Nixon opened a dialogue with Peking in 1972, Prime Minister Kakuei Tanaka, who succeeded Sato in 1972, quickly established diplomatic relations with the mainland Chinese and severed ties with Formosa.

Announcement on June 19, 1981 that Japan's gross national product grew at a rate of nearly 5% for the fiscal year ending March 31 brought new demands for increased imports of manufactured goods by Japan, which international trade experts charged was still creating barriers against trade despite repeated promises by Tokyo to relax such restrictions.

The same figure was agreed to by Japan for the following year, and for the first time, Japanese automobile exports declined for the 12-month period ending March 31, 1982. In an effort to remove nontariff trade barriers, which U.S. businessmen held responsible for their inability to increase sales in Japan, the Suzuki government appointed a special ombudsman with authority to cut red tape.

Under continued U.S. prodding, Tokyo announced an increase in defense spending with the 1987 budget reaching the target figure of 1% of the gross national product.

Suzuki was defeated in 1982 by Yasuhiro Nakasone who is considered pro-Western and better relations with the United States have ensued. Despite some opposition to his pro-Western policies in general, his Liberal Democratic party won decisively in the elections of July 7, 1986 and he was granted another year beyond his four-year limit which would have expired in October, 1986. Noboru Takeshita succeeded him in November 1987.

In 1989, an influence-peddling scandal shook the LDP and led to Takeshita's resignation. He was succeeded by Sousuke Uno.

JORDAN

The Hashemite Kingdom of Jordan
Ruler: King Hussein I (1952)
Prime Minister: Zaid bin-Shaker (1989)
Area: 37,297 sq mi. (96,599 sq km)[1]
Population (est. mid-1989): 4,000,000[1] (average annual rate of natural increase: 3.5%)
Density per square mile: 105
Capital: Amman
Largest cities (est. 1986): Amman, 972,000; Zarka, 392,220; Irbid, 271,000; Salt, 134,100
Monetary unit: Jordanian dinar
Languages: Arabic, English
Religions: Islam (Sunni), 95%; Christian, 5%
National name: Al Mamlaka al Urduniya al Hashemiyah
Literacy rate: 75%
Economic summary: Gross national product (1986): $5.5 billion, $2,070 per capita; real growth rate (1986): 2.0%. Land used for agriculture: 4%; labor force: 4%; principal products: wheat, fruits, vegetables, olive oil. Labor force in industry: 20%; major products: phosphate, refined petroleum products, cement. Natural resources: phosphate, potash. Exports: phosphates, fruits, and vegetables, foodstuffs, fertilizer. Imports: petroleum products, textiles, capital goods, motor vehicles, foodstuffs. Major trading partners: U.S., Japan, Saudi Arabia, Iraq, U.K., W. Germany.

1. Includes territory occupied by Israel in 1967 war.

Geography. The Middle East kingdom of Jordan is bordered on the west by Israel and the Dead Sea, on the north by Syria, on the east by Iraq, and on the south Saudi Arabia. It is comparable in size to Indiana.

Arid hills and mountains make up most of the country. The southern section of the Jordan River flows through the country.

Government. Jordan is a constitutional monarchy with a bicameral parliament. Its Chamber of Deputies is elected for four years by the people and the members of the Senate are appointed by the King. A new law will changed the number of the members of parliament in 1989. There is now a 30-member Senate and a 74-member Chamber of Deputies.

All political parties were banned in 1957.

History. In biblical times, the country that is now Jordan contained the lands of Edom, Moab, Ammon, and Bashan. In A.D. 106 it became part of the Roman province of Arabia and in 633–36 was conquered by the Arabs.

Taken from the Turks by the British in World War I, Jordan (formerly known as Transjordan) was separated from the Palestine mandate in 1920, and in 1921, placed under the rule of Abdullah ibn Hussein.

In 1923, Britain recognized Jordan's independence, subject to the mandate. In 1946, grateful for Jordan's loyalty in World War II, Britain abolished the mandate. That part of Palestine occupied by Jordanian troops was formally incorporated by action of the Jordanian Parliament in 1950.

King Abdullah was assassinated in 1951. His son Talal was deposed as mentally ill the next year. Talal's son Hussein, born Nov. 14, 1935, succeeded him.

From the beginning of his reign, Hussein had to steer a careful course between his powerful neighbor to the west, Israel, and rising Arab nationalism, frequently a direct threat to this throne. Riots erupted when he joined the Central Treaty Organization (the Baghdad Pact) in 1955, and he incurred further unpopularity when Britain, France, and Israel attacked the Suez Canal in 1956, forcing him to place his army under nominal command of the United Arab Republic of Egypt and Syria.

The 1961 breakup of the UAR eased Arab national pressure on Hussein, who was the first to recognize Syria after it reclaimed its independence. Jordan was swept into the 1967 Arab-Israeli war, however, and lost the old city of Jerusalem and all of its territory west of the Jordan river, the West Bank. Embittered Palestinian guerrilla forces virtually took over sections of Jordan in the aftermath of defeat, and open warfare broke out between the Palestinians and government forces in 1970.

Despite intervention of Syrian tanks, Hussein's Bedouin army defeated the Palestinians, suffering heavy casualties.

In October 1974, Hussein concurred in an Arab summit resolution calling for an independent Palestinian state and endorsing the Palestine Liberation Organization as the "sole legitimate representative of the Palestinian people." This apparent reversal of policy changed with the growing disillusion of Arab states with the P.L.O., however, and by 1977 Hussein referred again to the unity of people on both banks of the Jordan.

As Egypt and Israel neared final agreement on a peace treaty early in 1979, Hussein met with Yassir Arafat, the PLO leader, on March 17 and issued a joint statement of opposition. Although the U.S. pressed Jordan to break Arab ranks on the issue,

Hussein elected to side with the great majority, cutting ties with Cairo and joining the boycott against Egypt.

In September 1980, Jordan declared itself with Iraq in its conflict with Iran and, despite threats from Syria, opened ports to war shipments for Iraq.

In April 1983, Jordan rejected the American-sponsored Palestine peace plan.

An attempt to enlist Arafat in a new peace process collapsed in early 1986. Hussein then began a rapproachment with President Assad of Syria.

In 1988, Hussein formally renounced all claims to the West Bank, thus implicitly acknowledging Palestinian claims to statehood and torpedoing USA-sponsored efforts at a Palestinian confederation with Jordan.

KAMPUCHEA

See Cambodia

KENYA

Republic of Kenya
President: Daniel arap Moi (1978)
Area: 224,960 sq mi. (582,646 sq km)
Population (est. mid-1989): 24,100,000 (average annual rate of natural increase: 4.1%)
Density per square mile: 107
Capital: Nairobi
Largest cities (est. 1985): Nairobi, 1,000,000; Mombasa, 700,000
Monetary unit: Kenyan shilling
Languages: English (official), Swahili (national), and several other languages spoken by 40 ethnic groups
Religions: Protestant, 38%; Roman Catholic, 28%; traditional, 26%; Islam, 6%
Literacy rate: 59%
Member of Commonwealth of Nations
National name: Jamhuri ya Kenya
Economic summary: Gross domestic product (1986): $5.0 billion, $230 per capita; real growth rate (1986 est.): 5.0%. Land used for agriculture: 20%; labor force in agriculture: 11%; principal products: coffee, sisal, tea, pyrethrum, cotton, livestock. Labor force in industry: 18%; major products: textiles, processed foods, consumer goods, refined oil. Natural resources: gold, limestone, minerals, wildlife. Exports: coffee, tea, foodstuffs, refined petroleum. Imports: machinery, transport equipment, crude oil, iron and steel products. Major trading partners: Western European countries, Japan, U.S., Uganda, U.K., Rwanda, Middle East.

Geography. Kenya lies on the equator in east central Africa on the coast of the Indian Ocean. It is twice the size of Nevada. Kenya's neighbors are Tanzania, Uganda, the Sudan, Ethiopia, and Somalia.

In the north, the land is arid; the southwestern corner is in the fertile Lake Victoria Basin; and a length of the eastern depression of Great Rift Valley separates western highlands from those that rise from the lowland coastal strip. Large game reserves have been developed.

Government. Under its Constitution Kenya has a one-house National Assembly of 188 members, elected for five years by universal suffrage and 12 nominated and 2 ex-officio, for a total of 202. Since 1969, the president has been chosen by a general election.

The Kenya African National Union (KANU), led by the president, is the only political party allowed.

President Jomo Kenyatta died in his sleep on Aug. 22, 1978. Vice President Daniel arap Moi was elected to succeed him on Oct. 10.

History. Kenya, formerly a British colony and protectorate, was made a crown colony in 1920. The whites' domination of the rich plateau area, the White Highlands, long regarded by the Kikiyu people as their territory, was a factor leading to native terrorism, called the Mau Mau movement, in 1952. In 1954 the British began preparing the territory for African rule and independence. In 1961 Jomo Kenyatta was freed from banishment to become leader of the Kenya African National Union.

Internal self-government was granted in 1963; Kenya became independent on Dec. 12, 1963, with Kenyatta as its first president.

Moi's tenure has been marked by a consolidation of power which has included the harassment of political opponents, the banning of secret ballots, and his declaration that KANU was more powerful than the Assembly or the courts.

KIRIBATI

Republic of Kiribati
President: Ieremia Tabai (1979)
Area: 277 sq mi. (717 sq km)
Population (est. 1988): 67,638 (average annual growth rate: 1.7%)
Density per square mile: 245
Capital (1985): Tarawa, 21,393
Monetary unit: Australian dollar
Language: English
Religions: Roman Catholic, 48%; Protestant, 45%
Member of Commonwealth of Nations
Literacy rate: 90%
Economic summary: Gross domestic product (1985): $20 million, $310 per capita. Principal agricultural products: copra, vegetables. Exports: fish, copra. Imports: foodstuffs, fuel, transportation equipment. Major trading partners: New Zealand, Australia, Japan, American Samoa, Western Europe.

Geography. Kiribati, formerly the Gilbert Islands, consists of three widely separated main groups of Southwest Pacific islands, the Gilberts on the equator, the Phoenix Islands to the east, and the Line Islands further east. Ocean Island, producer of phosphates until it was mined out in 1981, is also included in the two million square miles of ocean, which give Kiribati an important fishery resource.

Government. The president holds executive power. The legislature consists of a House Assembly with 39 members.

History. A British protectorate since 1892, the Gilbert and Ellice Islands became a colony in 1915–16. The two island groups were separated in 1975 and given internal self-government.

Tarawa and others of the Gilbert group were occupied by Japan during World War II. Tarawa was the site of one of the bloodiest battles in U.S. Marine Corps history when Marines landed in November 1943 to dislodge the Japanese defenders.

Princess Anne, representing Queen Elizabeth II, presented the independence documents to the new government on July 12, 1979.

KOREA, NORTH

Democratic People's Republic of Korea
President: Marshal Kim Il Sung (1972)
Premier: Yong Hyong Muk (1989)
Area: 46,768 sq mi. (121,129 sq km)
Population (est. mid-1989): 22,500,000 (average annual rate of natural increase: 2.4%)
Density per square mile: 484
Capital and largest city (est. 1982): Pyongyang, 1,500,-000
Monetary unit: Won
Language: Korean
Religions: atheist, 68%; traditional, 16%
National name: Choson Minjujuui Inmin Konghwaguk
Literacy rate: 95% (est.)
Economic summary: Gross national product (1986): $19 billion, $910 per capita. Land used for agriculture: 19%; labor force, 48%; principal products: corn, rice, vegetables. Major industrial products: machines, electric power, chemicals, textiles, fertilizers, metallurgical products. Natural resources: coal, iron ore, hydroelectric power. Exports: minerals, chemical and metallurgical products. Imports: machinery and equipment, petroleum, foodstuffs, coking coal. Major trading partners: U.S.S.R., China, Japan.

Geography. Korea is a 600-mile (966 km) peninsula jutting from Manchuria and China (and a small portion of the U.S.S.R.) into the Sea of Japan and the Yellow Sea off eastern Asia. North Korea occupies an area slightly smaller than Pennsylvania north of the 38th parallel.

The country is almost completely covered by a series of north-south mountain ranges separated by narrow valleys. The Yalu River forms part of the northern border with Manchuria.

Government. The elected Supreme People's Assembly, as the chief organ of government, chooses a Presidium and a Cabinet. The Cabinet, which exercises executive authority, is subject to approval by the Assembly and the Presidium.

The Korean Workers (Communist) Party, led by President Kim Il Sung, is the only political party.

History. According to myth, Korea was founded in 2333 B.C. by Tangun. In the 17th century, it became a vassal of China and was isolated from all but Chinese influence and contact until 1876, when Japan forced Korea to negotiate a commercial treaty, opening the land to the U. S. and Europe. Japan achieved control as the result of its war with China (1894–95) and with Russia (1904–05) and annexed Korea in 1910. Japan developed the country but never won over the Korean nationalists.

After the Japanese surrender in 1945, the country was divided into two occupation zones, the U.S.S.R. north of and the U.S. south of the 38th parallel. When the cold war developed between the U.S. and U.S.S.R., trade between the zones was cut off. In 1948, the division between the zones was made permanent with the establishment of separate regimes in the north and south. By mid-1949, the U.S. and U.S.S.R. withdrew all troops. The Democratic People's Republic of Korea (North Korea) was established on May 1, 1948. The Communist Party, headed by Kim Il Sung, was established in power.

On June 25, 1950, the North Korean army launched a surprise attack on South Korea. On June 26, the U.N. Security Council condemned the invasion as aggression and ordered withdrawal of the invading forces. On June 27, President Harry S. Truman ordered air and naval units into action to enforce the U.N. order. The British government did the same, and soon a multinational U.N. command was set up to aid the South Koreans. The North Korean invaders took Seoul and pushed the South Koreans into the southeast corner of their country.

Gen. Douglas MacArthur, U.N. commander, made an amphibious landing at Inchon on September 15 behind the North Korean lines, which resulted in the complete rout of the North Korean army. The U.N. forces drove north across the 38th parallel, approaching the Yalu River. Then Communist China entered the war, forcing the U.N. forces into headlong retreat. Seoul was lost again, then regained; ultimately the war stabilized near the 38th parallel but dragged on for two years while the belligerents negotiated. An armistice was agreed to on July 27, 1953.

President Carter, visiting Seoul from June 29 to July 1, 1979, proposed that the U.S., North Korea, and South Korea meet "to promote dialogue and reduce tensions in the area," possibly leading to reunification of the two Koreas. Pyongyang's official party newspaper rejected the proposal, saying the North favors reunification talks but without the "alien interference" of the U.S.

Kim again rejected as a "foolish burlesque" an invitation on Jan. 12, 1981, by South Korea's military chief, Chun Doo Hwan, to hold reunification talks in Seoul. Kim refused again when Chun repeated the invitation on March 3 during his inauguration as President of the Southern republic.

KOREA, SOUTH

Republic of Korea
President: Roh Tae Woo (1987)
Premier: Kang Young Hoon (1988)
Area: 38,031 sq mi. (98,500 sq km)
Population (est. mid-1988): 43,200,000 (average annual rate of natural increase: 3%)
Density per square mile: 133
Capital: Seoul
Largest cities (est. 1985): Seoul, 9,900,000; Pusan, 3,650,000; Taegu, 2,000,000; Inchon, 1,600,000
Monetary unit: Won
Language: Korean
Religions: Buddhist, 19%; Protestant, 16%; Roman Catholic, 5%
National name: Taehan Min'guk
Literacy rate: 95%
Economic summary: Gross national product (1987): $118 billion, $2,800 per capita; real growth rate (avg. '83–'87): 10.1%. Land used for agriculture: 22%; labor force, including fishing, 24%; principal products: rice, barley. Labor force in industry: 27%; major products: clothing and textiles, processed foods, chemical fertilizers, chemicals, automobiles, steel, electronics equipment. Natural resources: iron and copper ore, tungsten, graphite, limestone, coal, gold, silver. Exports: Textiles, electric and electronics, ships, and steel. Imports: oil, grains, chemicals, machinery, electronics. Major trading partners: U.S., Japan.

Geography. Slightly larger than Indiana, South Korea lies below the 38th parallel on the Korean peninsula. It is mountainous in the east; in the west and south are many harbors on the mainland and offshore islands.

Government. Constitutional amendments enacted in Sept. 1987 called for direct election of a President, who would be limited to a single five-year term, and increased the powers of the National Assembly vis a vis the President.

The National Assembly was expanded from 276 to 299 seats, filled by proportional representation.

History. South Korea came into being in the aftermath of World War II as the result of a 1945 agreement making the 38th parallel the boundary between a northern zone occupied by the U.S.S.R. and a southern zone occupied by U.S. forces. (For details, see North Korea.)

Elections were held in the U.S. zone in 1948 for a national assembly, which adopted a republican Constitution and elected Syngman Rhee president. The new republic was proclaimed on August 15 and was recognized as the legal government of Korea by the U.N. on Dec. 12, 1948.

On June 25, 1950, South Korea was attacked by North Korean Communist forces. U.S. armed intervention was ordered on June 27 by President Harry S. Truman, and on the same day the U.N. invoked military sanctions against North Korea. Gen. Douglas MacArthur was named commander of the U.N. forces. U.S. and South Korean troops fought a heroic holding action but, by the first week of August, they had been forced back to a 4,000-square-mile beachhead in southeast Korea.

There stood off superior North Korean forces until September 15, when a major U.N. amphibious attack was launched far behind the Communist lines at Inchon, port of Seoul. By September 30, U.N. forces were in complete control of South Korea. They then invaded North Korea and were nearing the Manchurian and Siberian borders when several hundred thousand Chinese Communist troops entered the conflict in late October. U.N. forces were then forced to retreat below the 38th parallel.

On May 24, 1951, U.N. forces recrossed the parallel and had made important new inroads into North Korea when truce negotiations began on July 10. An armistice was finally signed at Panmunjom on July 27, 1953, leaving a devastated Korea in need of large-scale rehabilitation.

The U.S. and South Korea signed a mutual-defense treaty on Oct. 1, 1953.

Rhee, president since 1948, resigned in 1960 in the face of rising disorders. PoSun Yun was elected to succeed him, but political instability continued. In 1961, Gen. Park Chung Hee took power and subsequently built up the country. The U.S. stepped up military aid, building up South Korea's armed forces to 600,000 men. The South Koreans sent 50,000 troops to Vietnam, at U.S. expense.

Park's assassination on Oct. 26, 1979, by Kim Jae Kyu, head of the Korean Central Intelligence Agency, brought a liberalizing trend as Choi Kyu Hah, the new President, freed imprisoned dissidents. The release of opposition leader Kim Dae jung in February 1980 generated anti-government demonstrations that turned into riots by May. Choi resigned on Aug. 16. Chun Doo Wha, head of a military Special Committee for National Security Measures, was the sole candidate as the electoral college confirmed him as President on Aug. 27.

Elected to a full seven-year term on Feb. 11, Chun had visited Washington on Feb. 2 to receive President Reagan's assurance that U.S. troops would remain in South Korea. General elections on March 25 gave the ruling Democratic Justice Party a majority of the National Assembly.

Debate over the Presidential succession in 1988 was the main dispute in 1986-87 with Chun wanting election by the electoral college and the opposition demanding a direct popular vote, charging that Chun could manipulate the college. On April 13, 1987, Chun declared a close on the debate but when, in June, he appointed Roh Toe Woo, the DJP chairman as his successor, violent protests broke out. Roh, and later, Chun, agreed that direct elections should be held. A split in the opposition led to Roh's election on Dec. 16, 1987, with 36.6% of the vote.

Legislative elections deprived Roh's DJP of its Assembly majority in April, 1988. Roh declared his willingness to share leadership posts with the opposition.

KUWAIT

State of Kuwait
Emir: Sheik Jaber al-Ahmad al-Sabah (1977)
Prime Minister: Sheik Sa'ad Abdullah al-Salim (1978)
Area: 6,880 sq mi. (17,820 sq km)
Population (est. mid-1989): 2,100,000 (average annual rate of natural increase: 2.8%)
Density per square mile: 304
Capital (est. 1980): Kuwait, 60,525
Largest city (est. 1980): Hawalli, 152,402
Monetary unit: Kuwaiti dinar
Languages: Arabic and English
Religions: Islam, 85% (Sunni, 45%; Shiite, 30%; other, 10%); 15% others
National name: Dawlat al Kuwayt
Literacy rate: about 71%
Economic summary: Gross domestic product (1987): $16.9 billion, $9,040 per capita; real growth rate (1987): 3%. Land used for agriculture: 8%. Labor force in industry: 22%; major products: crude and refined oil, fertilizer, chemicals, building materials, shrimp. Natural resources: petroleum, fish, shrimp. Exports: crude and refined petroleum, shrimp. Imports: foodstuffs, automobiles, building materials, machinery, textiles. Major trading partners: U.S., Japan, Italy, Netherlands, Iraq, W. Germany.

Geography. Kuwait is situated northeast of Saudi Arabia at the northern end of the Persian Gulf, south of Iraq. It is slightly larger than Hawaii. The low-lying land is mainly sandy and barren.

Government. Sheik Jaber al-Ahmad al-Sabah rules as Emir of Kuwait and appoints the Prime Minister, who appoints his Cabinet (Council of Ministers). The National Assembly was suspended on July 3, 1986. There are no political parties in Kuwait.

History. Kuwait obtained British protection in 1897 when the Sheik feared that the Turks would take over the area. In 1961, Britain ended the protectorate, giving Kuwait independence, but agreed to give military aid on request. Iraq immediately threatened to occupy the area and Sheik Sabah al-Salem al-Sabah called in British troops in 1961. Soon afterward the Arab League sent in troops, replacing the British. The prize was oil.

Oil was discovered in the 1930s. Kuwait proved to have 20% of the world's known oil resources. It has been a major producer since 1946, the world's second largest oil exporter. The Sheik, who gets half the profits, devotes most of them to the education, welfare, and modernization of his kingdom. In 1966, Sheik Sabah designated a relative, Jaber al-Ahmad al-Sabah, as his successor.

By 1968, the sheikdom had established a model welfare state, and it sought to establish dominance among the sheikdoms and emirates of the Persian Gulf.

A worldwide decline in the price of oil reduced Kuwait's oil income from $18.4 billion in 1980 to only $9 billion in 1984. During the same period Kuwait's support for Iraq in its war with Iran sparked terrorist attacks in Kuwait by radical Shiite Moslem supporters of Iran's Ayatollah Khomeini. The risk of Iranian attack prompted Kuwait to obtain U.S. protection for its tankers in 1987.

In May 1985, a suicide bomber drove into the motorcade of Sheik Jaber al-Ahmad al-Sabah, the ruler. The Sheik escaped with minor cuts and bruises but five people, including the suicide bomber, were killed. In July, bombs exploded in two popular cafes, killing nine people and wounding 56.

LAOS

Lao People's Democratic Republic
President (acting): Phuomi Vongvichit (1986)
Chairman of the Council of Ministers: Kaysone Phomvihane (1975)
Area: 91,429 sq mi. (236,800 sq km)
Population (est. mid-1989): 3,900,000 (average annual rate of natural increase: 2.5%)
Density per square mile: 43
Capital and largest city (est. 1984): Vientiane, 200,000
Monetary unit: Kip
Languages: Lao (official), French, English
Religions: Buddhist, 58%; tribal, 34%
Literacy rate: 85%
Economic summary: Gross national product: (1986 est.): $660 million, $180 per capita. Land used for agriculture, 7%; labor force, 90%; principal products: rice, corn, vegetables. Major industrial products: tin, timber, tobacco, textiles, electric power. Natural resources: tin, timber, hydroelectric power. Exports: electric power, forest products, tin concentrates, coffee. Imports: rice, foodstuffs, petroleum products, machinery, transport equipment. Major trading partners: Thailand, Malaysia, Vietnam, China, Japan, France, Vietnam

Geography. A landlocked nation in Southeast Asia occupying the northwestern portion of the Indochinese peninsula, Laos is surrounded by China, Vietnam, Cambodia, Thailand, and Burma. It is twice the size of Pennsylvania.

Laos is a mountainous country, especially in the north, where peaks rise above 8,000 feet (2,438 m). Dense forests cover the northern and eastern areas. The Mekong River, which forms the boundary with Burma and Thailand, flows entirely through the country for 300 miles (483 km) of its course.

Government. Laos is a people's democratic republic with executive power in the hands of the premier. The monarchy was abolished Dec. 2, 1975, when the Pathet Lao ousted a coalition government and King Sisavang Vatthana abdicated. The King was appointed "Supreme Adviser" to the President, the former Prince Souphanouvong. Former Prince Souvanna Phouma, Premier since 1962, was made an "adviser" to the government. The Lao People's Revolutionary Party (Pathet Lao), led by Chairman Kaysone Phomvihane, is the only political party.

History. Laos became a French protectorate in 1893, and the territory was incorporated into the union of Indochina. A strong nationalist movement developed during World War II, but France reestablished control in 1946 and made the King of Luang Prabang constitutional monarch of all Laos. France granted semiautonomy in 1949 and then, spurred by the Viet Minh rebellion in Vietnam, full independence within the French Union in 1950. In 1951, Prince Souphanouvong organized the Pathet Lao, a Communist independence movement, in North Vietnam. The Viet Minh in 1953 established the Pathet Lao in power at Samneua. Viet Minh and Pathet Lao forces invaded central Laos, and civil war resulted.

By the Geneva agreements of 1954 and an armistice of 1955, two northern provinces were given the Pathet Lao, the royal regime the rest. Full sovereignty was given the kingdom by the Paris agreements of Dec. 29, 1954. In 1957, Prince Souvanna Phouma, the royal Premier, and the Pathet Lao leader, Prince Souphanouvong, the Premier's half-brother, agreed to reestablishment of a unified government, with Pathet Lao participation and integration of Pathet Lao forces into the royal army. The agreement broke down in 1959, and armed conflict broke out again.

In 1960, the struggle became three-way as Gen. Phoumi Nosavan, controlling the bulk of the royal army, set up in the south a pro-Western revolutionary government headed by Prince Boun Gum. General Phoumi took Vientiane in December, driving Souvanna Phouma into exile in Cambodia. The Soviet bloc supported Souvanna Phouma. In 1961, a cease-fire was arranged and the three princes agreed to a coalition government headed by Souvanna Phouma.

But North Vietnam, the U.S. (in the form of Central Intelligence Agency personnel), and China remained active in Laos after the settlement. North Vietnam used a supply line (Ho Chi Minh trail) running down the mountain valleys of eastern Laos into Cambodia and South Vietnam, particularly after the U.S.-South Vietnamese incursion into Cambodia in 1970 stopped supplies via Cambodian seaports.

An agreement, reached in 1973 revived coalition government. The Communist Pathet Lao seized complete power in 1975, installing Souphanouvong as president and Kaysone Phomvihane as premier. Since then other parties and political groups have been moribund and most of their leaders have fled the country.

In July 1985, Laos agreed to help the United States search for U.S. servicemen missing since the Indochina war.

In 1985, border clashes between Laos and Thailand intensified, with over 120 skirmishes reported in 1984 and 1985.

LEBANON

Republic of Lebanon
President: Vacant
Premier: Disputed
Area: 4,015 sq mi. (10,400 sq km)
Population (est. mid-1989): 3,300,000 (average annual rate of natural increase: 2.1%)
Density per square mile: 822
Capital: Beirut
Largest cities (est. 1989): Beirut, 500,000; Tripoli, 300,-000

Monetary unit: Lebanese pound
Languages: Arabic (official), French, English
Religions: Islam, 75% (5 sects); Christian, 25% (21 sects)
National name: Al-Joumhouriya al-Lubnaniya
Literacy rate: 75%
Economic summary: Gross domestic product (1985): $1.8 billion. Per capita income: n.a. Land used for agriculture: 31%; labor force: 11%; principal products: fruits, wheat, corn, barley, potatoes, tobacco, olives, onions. Labor force in industry: 79%; major products: processed foods, textiles, cement, chemicals, refined oil. Exports: fruits, vegetables, textiles. Imports: metals, machinery, foodstuffs. Major trading partners: U.S., Western European and Arab countries.

Geography. Lebanon lies at the eastern end of the Mediterranean Sea north of Israel and west of Syria. It is four fifths the size of Connecticut.

The Lebanon Mountains, which parallel the coast on the west, cover most of the country, while on the eastern border is the Anti-Lebanon range. Between the two lies the Bekaa Valley, the principal agricultural area.

Government. Lebanon is governed by a President, elected by Parliament for a six-year term, and a Cabinet of Ministers appointed by the President but responsible to Parliament.

Parliament has 99 members elected for a four-year term by universal suffrage and chosen by proportional division of religious groups.

History. After World War I, France was given a League of Nations mandate over Lebanon and its neighbor Syria, which together had previously been a single political unit in the Ottoman Empire. France divided them in 1920 into separate colonial administrations, drawing a border that separated predominantly Moslem Syria from the kaleidoscope of religious communities in Lebanon in which Maronite Christians were then dominant. After 20 years of the French mandate regime, Lebanon's independence was proclaimed on Nov. 26, 1941, but full independence came in stages. Under an agreement between representatives of Lebanon and the French National Committee of Liberation, most of the powers exercised by France were transferred to the Lebanese government on Jan. 1, 1944. The evacuation of French troops was completed in 1946.

Civil war broke out in 1958, with Moslem factions led by Kamal Jumblat and Saeb Salam rising in insurrection against the Lebanese government headed by President Camille Chamoun, a Maronite Christian. At Chamoun's request, President Eisenhower on July 15 sent U.S. troops to reestablish the government's authority.

Clan warfare between various factions in Lebanon goes back centuries. The hodgepodge includes Maronite Christians, who since independence have dominated the government; Sunni Moslems, who have prospered in business and shared political power; the Druse, a secretive Islamic splinter group; and at the bottom of the heap until recently, Shiite Moslems.

A new—and bloodier—Lebanese civil war that broke out in 1975 resulted in the addition of still another ingredient in the brew—the Syrians. In the fighting between Lebanese factions, 40,000 Lebanese were estimated to have been killed and 100,000 wounded between March 1975 and November 1976. At that point, a Syrian-dominated Arab Deterrent Force intervened and brought large-scale fighting to a halt.

Palestinian guerrillas staging raids on Israel from

Lebanese territory drew punitive Israeli raids on Lebanon, and two large-scale Israeli invasions. The Israelis withdrew in June after the U.N. Security Council created a 6,000-man peacekeeping force for the area, called UNIFIL. As they departed, the Israelis turned their strongpoints over to a Christian militia that they had organized, instead of to the U.N. force.

The second Israeli invasion came on June 6, 1982, and this time it was a total one. It was in response to an assassination attempt by Palestinian terrorists on the Israeli ambassador in London.

A U.S. special envoy, Philip C. Habib, negotiated the dispersal of most of the PLO to other Arab nations and Israel pulled back some of its forces. The violence seemed to have come to an end when, on Sept. 14, Bashir Gemayel, the 34-year-old President-elect, was killed by a bomb that destroyed the headquarters of his Christian Phalangist Party.

The day after Gemayel's assassination, Israeli troops moved into west Beirut in force. On Sept. 17 it was revealed that Christian militiamen had massacred hundreds of Palestinians in two refugee camps but Israel denied responsibility.

On Sept. 20, Amin Gemayel, older brother of Bashir Gemayel, was elected President by the parliament.

The massacre in the refugee camps prompted the return of a multinational peacekeeping force composed of U.S. Marines and British, French, and Italian soldiers. Their mandate was to support the central Lebanese government, but they soon found themselves drawn into the struggle for power between different Lebanese factions. During their stay in Lebanon, 260 U.S. Marines and about 60 French soldiers were killed, most of them in suicide bombings of the Marine and French Army compounds on Oct. 23, 1983. The multinational force left in the spring of 1984.

During 1984, Israeli troops remained in southern Lebanon and Syrian troops remained in the Bekaa Valley. By the third anniversary of the invasion, June 6, 1985, all Israeli troops had withdrawn except for several hundred "advisers" to a Christian militia trained and armed by the Israelis.

During 1985, the long-deprived Shiites shouldered aside the traditional urban upper class of Sunni oligarchs as the dominant Moslem faction in west Beirut. The more extremist Shiite factions such as Hizbullah (Party of God), inspired by Iran's Ayatollah Ruhollah Khomeini, wanted to establish an Iranian-style religious state in Lebanon and were virulently anti-Israel and anti-U.S. They later defeated the moderate Amal Faction of the Shiites in Beirut's southern suburbs in 1988. Hizbullah has conducted hit-and-run warfare against the Christian militia and its Israeli advisers in southern Lebanon.

Events since the Israeli withdrawal included Shiite-PLO fighting resulting from PLO attempts to reestablish its old power base in areas now held by Shiite militia.

In July 1986, Syrian observers took position in Beirut to monitor a peacekeeping agreement. The agreement broke down and fighting between Shiite and Druze militia in West Beirut became so intense that Syrian troops moved in force in February 1987, suppressing militia resistance.

Amin Gemayel's Presidency expired on Sept. 23, 1988. The impossibility of setting up elections led Gemayel to designate a government under army chief Gen. Michael Aoun. Aoun's government was rejected by Prime Minister Selim al-Hoss who established a rival government in Muslim West Beirut. The inability of the Parliament to assemble a quorum finished the disappearance of the image of a central government in Lebanon.

LESOTHO

Kingdom of Lesotho
Sovereign: King Moshoeshoe II (1966)
Chairman, Military Council: Maj. Gen. Justin Lekhanya (1986)
Area: 11,720 sq mi. (30,355 sq km)
Population (est. mid-1989): 1,600,000 (average annual rate of natural increase: 2.8%)
Density per square mile: 147
Capital and largest city (est. 1983): Maseru, 70,000
Monetary unit: Loti
Languages: English and Sesotho (official); also Zulu and Xhosa
Religions: Roman Catholic, 44%; Lesotho Evangelical Church, 30%; Anglican, 12%
Member of Commonwealth of Nations
Literacy rate: 65%
Economic summary: Gross domestic product (1984): $247 million, $163 per capita; real growth rate: 3.5%. Land used for agriculture: 76%; labor force: 86%; principal products: corn, wheat, sorghum, barley. Labor force in industry: 2%. Natural resources: diamonds. Exports: wool, mohair, wheat, cattle, diamonds, hides and skins. Imports: foodstuffs, building materials, clothing, vehicles, machinery. Major trading partner: South Africa.

Geography. Mountainous Lesotho, the size of Maryland, is surrounded by the Republic of South Africa in the east central part of that country except for short borders on the east and south with two discontinuous units of the Republic of Transkei. The Drakensberg Mountains in the east are Lesotho's principal chain. Elsewhere the region consists of rocky tableland.

Government. In January, 1986, following an economic crisis caused by a South African blockade, the military overthrew Chief Johnathan and established a Military Council and a Council of Ministers that would exercise a policy less tolerant of anti-apartheid activists within its borders.

The King has also been given greater powers.

History. Lesotho (formerly Basutoland) was constituted a native state under British protection by a treaty signed with the native chief Moshesh in 1843. It was annexed to Cape Colony in 1871, but in 1884 it was restored to direct control by the Crown.

The colony of Basutoland became the independent nation of Lesotho on Oct. 4, 1966.

In the 1970 elections, Ntsu Mokhehle, head of the Basutoland Congress Party, claimed a victory, but Jonathan declared a state of emergency, suspended the Constitution, and arrested Mokhehle. The major issue in the election was relations with South Africa, with Jonathan for close ties to the surrounding white nation, while Mokhehle was for a more independent policy. Jonathan jailed 45 opposition politicians, declared the King had "technically abdicated" by siding with the opposition party, exiled him to the Netherlands, and named his Queen and her seven-year-old son as Regent.

The King returned after a compromise with Jonathan in which the new Constitution would name him head of state but forbid his participation in politics.

LIBERIA

Republic of Liberia
President: Gen. Samuel K. Doe (1980)
Area: 43,000 sq mi. (111,370 sq km)
Population (est. mid-1989): 2,500,000 (average annual rate of natural increase: 3.2%)
Density per square mile: 58
Capital and largest city (est. 1984): Monrovia, 425,000
Monetary unit: Liberian dollar
Languages: English (official) and tribal dialects
Religions: traditional, 75%; Christian, 10%; Islam, 15%
Literacy rate: 20%
Economic summary: Gross domestic product (1986): $711 million, $310 per capita; real growth rate (1986): −0.7%. Land used for agriculture: 6%; labor force: 71%; principal products: rubber, rice, palm oil, cassava, coffee, cocoa. Labor force in industry: 5%; major products: iron ore, diamonds, processed rubber, processed food, construction materials. Natural resources: iron ore, rubber, timber, diamonds. Exports: iron ore, rubber, timber, diamonds. Imports: machinery, petroleum products, transport equipment, foodstuffs. Major trading partners: U.S., West Germany, Netherlands, Italy, Belgium.

Geography. Lying on the Atlantic in the southern part of West Africa, Liberia is bordered by Sierra Leone, Guinea, and the Ivory Coast. It is comparable in size to Tennessee.

Most of the country is a plateau covered by dense tropical forests, which thrive under an annual rainfall of about 160 inches a year.

Government. Since April 25, 1980, Liberia had been under military rule by the 17-member People's Redemptive Council, which suspended the Constitution after overthrowing the civilian government. On July 22, 1984, the Council was replaced with an interim, appointed National Assembly in a step toward return of civilian rule.

History. Liberia was founded in 1822 as a result of the efforts of the American Colonization Society to settle freed American slaves in West Africa. In 1847, it became the Free and Independent Republic of Liberia.

The government of Africa's first republic was modeled after that of the United States, and Joseph J. Roberts of Virginia was elected the first president. He laid the foundations of a modern state and initiated efforts, never too successful but pursued for more than a century, to bring the aboriginal inhabitants of the territory to the level of the emigrants. The English-speaking descendants of U.S. blacks, known as Americo-Liberians, were the intellectual and ruling class. The indigenous inhabitants, divided, constitute 99% of the population.

After 1920, considerable progress was made toward opening up the interior, a process that was spurred in 1951 by the establishment of a 43-mile (69-km) railroad to the Bomi Hills from Monrovia.

In July 1971, while serving his sixth term as president, William V. S. Tubman died following surgery and was succeeded by his long-time associate, Vice President William R. Tolbert, Jr.

Tolbert was ousted in a military coup carried out April 12, 1980, by army enlisted men led by Master Sgt. Samuel K. Doe. Tolbert and 27 other high officials were executed. Doe and his colleagues based their action on the grievances of "native" Liberians against corruption and misrule by the Americo-Liberians who had ruled the country since its founding.

In November 1985, an attempted coup against Doe following a disputed re-election, was bloodily put down and the coup leader, a former associate of Doe's, was executed.

LIBYA

Socialist People's Libyan Arab Jamahiriya
Head of State: Col. Muammar el-Qaddafi (1969)
Secretary-General of the General People's Committee: Omar Mustafa el-Montassir (1987)
Area: 679,536 sq mi. (1,759,998 sq km)
Population (est. mid-1989): 4,000,000 (average annual rate of natural increase: 3.5%)
Density per square mile: 6
Capital: Tripoli
Largest cities (est. 1980): Tripoli, 587,400; Benghazi, 267,700
Monetary unit: Libyan dinar
Language: Arabic
Religion: Islam
National name: Al-Jumhuria al-Arabia al-Libya
Literacy rate: 50%
Economic summary: Gross national product (1986): ca. $20 billion, $5,410 per capita; real growth rate: 0%. Land used for agriculture: 9%; labor force: 18%; principal products: wheat, barley, olives, dates, citrus fruits, peanuts. Labor force in industry: 31%; major products: petroleum, processed foods, textiles, handicrafts. Natural resources: petroleum, natural gas. Export: petroleum. Imports: machinery, foodstuffs, manufactured goods. Major trading partners: Italy, West Germany, U.K., France, Spain, Japan.

Geography. Libya stretches along the northeastern coast of Africa between Tunisia and Algeria on the west and Egypt on the east; to the south are the Sudan, Chad, and Niger. It is one sixth larger than Alaska.

A greater part of the country lies within the Sahara. Along the Mediterranean coast and farther inland is arable plateau land.

Government. In a bloodless coup d'etat on Sept. 1, 1969, the military seized power in Libya. King Idris I, who had ruled since 1951, was deposed and the Libyan Arab Republic proclaimed. The official name was changed in 1977 to the Socialist People's Libyan Arab Jamahiriya. The Revolutionary Council that had governed since the coup was renamed the General Secretariat of the General People's Congress. The Arab Socialist Union Organization is the only political party.

History. Libya was a part of the Turkish dominions from the 16th century until 1911. Following the outbreak of hostilities between Italy and Turkey in that year, Italian troops occupied Tripoli; Italian sovereignty was recognized in 1912.

Libya was the scene of much desert fighting during World War II. After the fall of Tripoli on Jan. 23, 1943, it came under Allied administration. In 1949, the U.N. voted that Libya should become independent by 1952.

Discovery of oil in the Libyan Desert promised financial stability and funds for economic development.

The Reagan Administration, accusing Libya of supporting international terrorism, closed the Libyan embassy in Washington on May 6, 1981. After talks with Libyan officials in July, the U.S. concluded that no improvement in relations was possible, although U.S. oil companies remained active in Libya and 2,000 U.S. citizens continued to work there.

On Aug. 19, 1981, two U.S. Navy F-14's shot down two Soviet-made SU-22's of the Libyan air force that had attacked them in air space above the Gulf of Sidra, claimed by Libya but held to be international by the U.S. In December, Washington asserted that Libyan "hit squads" had been dispatched to the U.S. and security was drastically tightened around President Reagan and other officials. Reagan requested remaining American citizens to leave Libya and nearly all did by Dec. 15. When the Mobil Oil Company abandoned its operations in April 1982, only four U.S. firms were still in Libya, using Libyan or third-country personnel.

Qaddafi's troops also supported rebels in Chad but suffered major military reverses in 1987.

In December 1985, Qaddafi lauded as "heroic" a terrorist attack on Rome and Vienna airports that killed 20 people.

On March 24, 1986, U.S. and Libyan forces skirmished in the Gulf of Sidra, with two Libyan patrol boats being sunk.

On April 14, after a Libyan-backed attack on a West Berlin disco in which two people, including an American serviceman, were killed, Reagan ordered an air raid on Libyan military installations.

LIECHTENSTEIN

Principality of Liechtenstein
Ruler: Prince Franz Josef II (1938)
Prime Minister: Hans Brunhart (1978)
Area: 61 sq mi. (157 sq km)
Population (est. 1985): 27,825 (average annual growth rate: 0.9%)
Density per square mile: 459.0
Capital and largest city (est. 1986): Vaduz, 4,920
Monetary unit: Swiss franc
Language: German
Religions: Roman Catholic, 86%; Protestant, 9%
Literacy rate: 100%
Economic summary: Gross national product: Economy is tied to Switzerland, no breakdown available. Per capita income (1985 est.): $16,500. Labor force in agriculture: 4%; principal products: livestock, vegetables, corn, wheat, potatoes, grapes. Labor force in industry: 54%; major products: high-technology products, building equipment, food products, machinery, industrial goods. Natural resources: timber, hydroelectric power, salt. Exports: manufactured metal products, machines and instruments, chemical products. Imports: raw materials, machinery, processed foods and goods. Major trading partners: Switzerland and other Western European countries.

Geography. Tiny Liechtenstein, not quite as large as Washington, D.C., lies on the east bank of the Rhine River south of Lake Constance between Austria and Switzerland. It consists of low valley land and Alpine peaks. Falknis (8,401 ft; 2,561 m) and Naatkopf (8,432 ft; 2,570 m) are the tallest.

Government. The Constitution of 1921, amended in 1972, provides for a legislature, the Landtag, of 25 members elected by direct male suffrage.

Prince Hans Adam has been defacto ruler since 1984, when his father, Prince Franz Josef II, relinquished his responsibilities but not his title to the throne.

History. Founded in 1719, Liechtenstein was a member of the German Confederation from 1815 to 1866, when it became an independent principality. It abolished its army in 1868 and has managed to stay neutral and undamaged in all European wars since then. In a referendum on July 1, 1984, male voters granted women the right to vote, a victory for Prince Hans Adam.

LUXEMBOURG

Grand Duchy of Luxembourg
Ruler: Grand Duke Jean (1964)
Premier: Jacques Santer (1984)
Area: 999 sq mi. (2,586 sq km)
Population (est. mid-1989): 400,000 (Luxembourgian, French, German) (average annual rate of natural increase: 0.1%)
Density per square mile: 379
Capital and largest city (est. 1982): Luxembourg, 80,000
Monetary unit: Luxembourg franc
Languages: Luxermbourgish, French, German
Religion: Mainly Roman Catholic
National name: Grand-Duché de Luxembourg
Literacy rate: 100%
Economic summary: Gross national product (1986): $4.6 billion, $12,570 per capita; real growth rate: 2.5%. Land used for agriculture: 45%; labor force: 4%; principal products: livestock, dairy products, wine. Labor force in industry: 25%; major products: banking, steel, plastics, synthetic fibers. Natural resource: Iron ore. Exports: steel, plastics, chemicals, textiles. Imports: machinery, chemicals, consumer goods. Major trading partners: European Common Market countries.

Geography. Luxembourg is a neighbor of Belgium on the west, West Germany on the east, and France on the south. The Ardennes Mountains extend from Belgium into the northern section of Luxembourg.

Government. Luxembourg's unicameral legislature, the Chamber of Deputies, consists of 59 members elected for five years.

History. Sigefroi, Count of Ardennes, an offspring of Charlemagne, was Luxembourg's first sovereign ruler. In 1060, the country came under the rule of the House of Luxembourg. From the 15th to the 18th century, Spain, France, and Austria held it in turn. The Congress of Vienna in 1815 made it a Grand Duchy and gave it to William I, King of the Netherlands. In 1839 the Treaty of London ceded the western part of Luxembourg to Belgium.

The eastern part, continuing in personal union with the Netherlands and a member of the German Confederation, became autonomous in 1848 and a neutral territory by decision of the London Conference of 1867, governed by its Grand Duke. Germany occupied the duchy in World Wars I and II. Allied troops liberated the enclave in 1944.

In 1961, Prince Jean, son and heir of Grand Duchess Charlotte, was made head of state, acting for his mother. She abdicated in 1964, and Prince Jean became Grand Duke. Grand Dutchess Charlotte died in 1985.

By a customs union between Belgium and Luxembourg, which came into force on May 1, 1922, to last for 50 years, customs frontiers between the two countries were abolished. On Jan. 1, 1948, a customs union with Belgium and the Netherlands (Benelux) came into existence. On Feb. 3, 1958, it became an economic union.

MADAGASCAR

Democratic Republic of Madagascar
President and Head of State: Didier Ratsiraka (1975)
Prime Minister: Lt. Col. Victor Ramahatra (1988)
Area: 226,660 sq mi. (587,050 sq km)
Population (est. mid-1989): 11,600,000 (average annual rate of natural increase: 3.1%)
Density per square mile: 51
Capital and largest city (est. 1983): Antananarivo, 700,-000
Monetary unit: Malagasy franc
Languages: Malagasy, French
Ethnic groups: Merina (or Hova), Betsimisaraka, Betsileo, Tsimihety, Antaisaka, Sakalava, Antandroy
Religions: traditional, 47%; Roman Catholic, 26%; Protestant, 23%; Islam, 2%
National name: Repoblika Demokratika Malagasy
Literacy rate: 53%
Economic summary: Gross domestic product (1986): $2.7 billion, $267 per capita; real growth rate: 0.7%. Land used for agriculture: 63%; labor force: 26%; principal products: rice, livestock, coffee, vanilla, sugar, cloves, cotton, sisal, peanuts, tobacco. Labor force in industry: 15%; major products: processed food, textiles, assembled automobiles, soap, mining products. Natural resources: graphite, chromium, ilmenite, semiprecious stones. Exports: coffee, cloves, vanilla, graphite, cotton products. Imports: consumer goods, foodstuffs, crude petroleum. Major trading partners: France, U.S., U.S.S.R., Indonesia.

Geography. Madagascar lies in the Indian Ocean off the southeast coast of Africa opposite Mozambique. The world's fourth-largest island, it is twice the size of Arizona. The country's low-lying coastal area gives way to a central plateau. The once densely wooded interior has largely been cut down.

Government. The Constitution of Dec. 30, 1975, approved by referendum following a military coup, provides for direct election by universal suffrage of a president for a seven-year term, a Supreme Council of the Revolution as a policy-making body, a unicameral People's National Assembly of 137 members (elected for five-year terms), and a military Committee for Development. The new constitution followed a period of martial rule that began with the suspension of the republic's original bicameral legislature in 1972.

History. The present population is of black and Malay stock, with perhaps some Polynesian, called Malagasy. The French took over a protectorate in 1885, and then in 1894–95 ended the monarchy, exiling Queen Rànavàlona III to Algiers. A colonial administration was set up, to which the Comoro Islands were attached in 1908, and other territories later. In World War II, the British occupied Madagascar, which retained ties to Vichy France.

An autonomous republic within the French Community since 1958, Madagascar became an independent member of the Community in 1960. In May 1973, an army coup led by Maj. Gen. Gabriel Ramanantsoa ousted Philibert Tsiranana, president since 1959.

With unemployment and inflation both high, Ramanantsoa resigned Feb. 5, 1975. His leftist-leaning successor, Interior Minister Richard Ratsimandrava, an Army lieutenant colonel, was killed six days later by a machine-gun ambush in Antananarivo, the capital.

On June 15, 1975, Comdr. Didier Ratsiraka was named President. He announced that he would follow a socialist course and, after nationalizing banks and insurance companies, declared all mineral resources nationalized.

MALAWI

Republic of Malawi
President: Hastings Kamuzu Banda (1966)
Area: 45,747 sq mi. (118,484 sq km)
Population (est. mid-1989): 8,700,000 (average annual rate of natural increase: 3.3%)
Density per square mile: 168.3
Capital (est. 1986): Lilongwe, 202,900
Largest city (est. 1986): Blantyre, 378,100
Monetary unit: Kwacha
Languages: English and Chichewa (National); also Tombuka
Religions: Christian, 57%; traditional, 19%; Islam, 16%
Member of Commonwealth of Nations
Literacy rate: 25%
Economic summary: Gross domestic product (1986): $1.23 billion, $170 per capita; growth rate (1986): −0.3%. Land used for agriculture: 45%; labor force: 52%; principal products: tobacco, tea, sugar, corn, peanuts. Labor force in industry: 16%; major products: food, beverages, tobacco, textiles, processed wood, consumer goods. Natural resource: limestone. Exports: tobacco, sugar, tea. Imports: machinery, transport equipment, building and construction materials, fuel. Major trading partners: U.K., U.S., Japan, West Germany, South Africa.

Geography. Malawi is a landlocked country the size of Pennsylvania in southeastern Africa, surrounded by Mozambique, Zambia, and Tanzania. Lake Malawi, formerly Lake Nyasa, occupies most of the country's eastern border. The north-south Rift Valley is flanked by mountain ranges and high plateau areas.

Government. Under a Constitution that came into effect on July 6, 1966, the president is the sole head of state; there is neither a prime minister nor a vice president. The National Assembly has 107 members.

There is only one national party—the Malawi Congress Party led by President Hastings K. Banda, who was designated President for life in 1970.

History. The first European to make extensive explorations in the area was David Livingstone in the 1850s and 1860s. In 1884, Cecil Rhodes's British South African Company received a charter to develop the country. The company came into conflict with the Arab slavers in 1887–89. After Britain annexed the Nyasaland territory in 1891, making it a protectorate in 1892, Sir Harry Johnstone, the first high commissioner, using Royal Navy gunboats, wiped out the slavers.

Nyasaland became the independent nation of Malawi on July 6, 1964. Two years later, it became a republic within the Commonwealth of Nations.

Dr. Hastings K. Banda, Malawi's first Prime Minister, became its first President. He pledged to follow a policy of "discretionary nonalignment." Banda alienated much of black Africa by maintaining good relations with South Africa. He argued that his landlocked country had to rely on South Africa for access to the sea and trade.

MALAYSIA

Paramount Ruler: Azlan Muhibuddin Shah, Sultan of Perak (1989)
Prime Minister: D.S. Mahathir Bin Mohamed (1981)
Area: 128,328 sq mi. (332,370 sq km)
Population (est. mid-1989): 17,400,000 (average annual rate of natural increase: 2.5%) (Malay, 59%; Chinese, 32%, Indian, 9%)
Density per square mile: 137
Capital: Kuala Lumpur
Largest cities (est. 1980 by U.N.): Kuala Lumpur, 1,000,-000; George Town (Pinang), 300,000; Ipoh, 275,000
Monetary unit: Ringgit
Languages: Malay (official), Chinese, Tamil, English
Religions: Islam, (official), 53%; Buddhist, 17%; Chinese folk religions, 12%; Hindu, 7%; Christian, 6%
Member of Commonwealth of Nations
Literacy rate: 65%
Economic summary: Gross domestic product (1986 est.): $25.8 billion; $1,600 per capita; annual growth rate: 1.8%. Labor force: in agriculture, 35%; principal products: rice, rubber, palm products. Major industrial products: processed rubber, timber, and palm oil, tin, petroleum, light manufactures, electronics equipment. Natural resources: tin, oil, copper, timber. Exports: natural rubber, palm oil, tin, timber, petroleum. Imports: machinery, transport equipment, chemicals. Major trading partners: Japan, Singapore, U.S., Western European countries.

Geography. Malaysia is at the southern end of the Malay Peninsula in southeast Asia. The nation also includes Sabah and Sarawak on the island of Borneo to the southeast. Its area slightly exceeds that of New Mexico.

Most of Malaysia is covered by dense jungle and swamps, with a mountain range running the length of the peninsula. Extensive forests provide ebony, sandalwood, teak, and other woods.

Government. Malaysia is a sovereign constitutional monarchy within the Commonwealth of Nations. The Paramount Ruler is elected for a five-year term by the hereditary rulers of the states from among themselves. He is advised by the prime minister and his cabinet. There is a bicameral legislature. The Senate, whose role is comparable more to that of the British House of Lords than to the U.S. Senate, has 68 members, partly appointed by the Paramount Ruler to represent minority and special interests, and partly elected by the legislative assemblies of the various states.

The House of Representatives, is made up of 180 members, who are elected for five-year terms.

History. Malaysia came into existence on Sept. 16, 1963, as a federation of Malaya, Singapore, Sabah (North Borneo), and Sarawak. In 1965, Singapore withdrew from the federation. Since 1966, the 11 states of former Malaya have been known as West Malaysia, and Sabah and Sarawak have been known as East Malaysia.

The Union of Malaya was established April 1, 1946, being formed from the Federated Malay States of Negri Sembilan, Pahang, Perak, and Selangor; the Unfederated Malay States of Johore, Kedah, Kelantan, Perlis, and Trengganu; and two of the Straits Settlements—Malacca and Penang. The Malay states had been brought under British administration during the late 19th and early 20th centuries.

It became the Federation of Malaya on Feb. 1, 1948, and the Federation attained full independence within the Commonwealth of Nations in 1957.

Sabah, constituting the extreme northern portion of the island of Borneo, was a British protectorate administered under charter by the British North Borneo Company from 1881 to 1946, when it assumed the status of a colony. It was occupied by Japanese troops from 1942 to 1945.

Sarawak extends along the northwestern coast of Borneo for about 500 miles (805 km). In 1841, part of the present territory was granted by the Sultan of Brunei to Sir James Brooke. Sarawak continued to be ruled by members of the Brooke family until the Japanese occupation.

From 1963, when Malaysia became independent, it was the target of guerrilla infiltration from Indonesia, but beat off invasion attempts. In 1966, when Sukarno fell and the Communist Party was liquidated in Indonesia, hostilities ended.

In the late 1960s, the country was torn by communal rioting directed against Chinese and Indians, who controlled a disproportionate share of the country's wealth. Beginning in 1968, the government moved to achieve greater economic balance through a rural development program.

Malaysia felt the impact of the "boat people" fleeing Vietnam early in 1978. Because the refugees were mostly ethnic Chinese, the government was apprehensive about any increase of a minority that previously had been the source of internal conflict in the country. In April 1988, it announced that starting in April 1989 it would accept no more refugees.

In April 1987, Prime Minister Mahathir barely fended off a challenge that would have removed him as head of his party.

MALDIVES

Republic of Maldives
President: Maumoon Abdul Gayoom (1978)
Area: 115 sq mi. (298 sq km)
Population (est. mid-1989): 200,000 (average annual rate of natural increase: 3.7%)
Density per square mile: 1,822
Capital and largest city (est. 1985): Malé, 53,800
Monetary unit: Maldivian rufiyaq
Language: Divehi
Religion: Islam
Literacy rate: 94%
Economic summary: Gross domestic product (1985): $68.3 million. $440 per capita; real growth rate: 10%. Principal agricultural products: coconuts, tropical fruits. Labor force in industry: 26%, major products: fish, processed coconuts. Natural resource: fish, coconuts. Export: fish, clothing, ambergris. Imports: rice, foodstuffs. Major trading partners: Japan, Sri Lanka, Singapore, U.S., Thailand, Switzerland.

Geography. The Republic of Maldives is a group of atolls in the Indian Ocean about 417 miles (671 km) southwest of Sri Lanka. Its 1,300 coral islets stretch over an area of 35,200 square miles (90,000 sq km).

Government. The 9-member Cabinet is headed by the president. The Majlis (Parliament) is a unicameral legislature consisting of 48 members. Eight of these are appointed by the president. The others are elected for five-year terms, 2 from the capital island of Malé and 2 from each of the 19 administrative atolls.

There are no political parties in the Maldives.

History. The Maldives (formerly called the Maldive Islands) are inhabited by an Islamic seafaring people. Originally the islands were under the suzerainty of Ceylon. They came under British protection in 1887 and were a dependency of the then colony of Ceylon until 1948. The independence agreement with Britain was signed July 26, 1965.

For centuries a sultanate, the islands adopted a republican form of government in 1952, but the sultanate was restored in 1954. In 1968, however, as the result of a referendum, a republic was again established in the islands.

Ibrahim Nasir, president since 1968, was removed from office by the Majlis in November 1978 and replaced by Maumoon Abdul Cayoom. A national referendum confirmed the new leader.

MALI

Republic of Mali
President of the Republic: Gen. Moussa Traoré
Area: 478,819 sq mi. (1,240,142 sq km)
Population (est. mid-1989): 8,900,000 (average annual rate of natural increase: 2.9%)
Density per square mile: 19
Capital and largest city (est. 1981): Bamako, 750,000
Monetary unit: Franc CFA
Ethnic groups: Bambara, Peul, Soninke, Malinke, Songhai, Dogon, Senoufo, Minianka, Berbers, and Moors
Languages: French (official), African languages
Religions: Islam, 90%; traditional, 9%; Christian, 1%
National name: République de Mali
Literacy rate: 10%
Economic summary: Gross domestic product (1985): $1.1 billion, $150 per capita; real growth rate (avg. 1965-85): 1.4%. Principal agricultural products: millet, sorghum, corn, rice, sugar, cotton, peanuts, livestock. Major industrial products: consumer goods, phosphates, gold, fish. Natural resources: bauxite, iron ore, maganese, phosphate, salt, limestone, gold. Exports: livestock, peanuts, dried fish, cotton, skins. Imports: textiles, vehicles, petroleum products, machinery, sugar, cereals. Major trading partners: Western Europe; also U.S.S.R., and China.

Geography. Most of Mali, in West Africa, lies in the Sahara. A landlocked country four fifths the size of Alaska, it is bordered by Guinea, Senegal, Mauritania, Algeria, Niger, Burkina Faso, and the Ivory Coast.

The only fertile area is in the south, where the Niger and Senegal Rivers provide irrigation.

Government. The army overthrew the government on Nov. 19, 1968, and formed a provisional government. The Military Committee of National Liberation consists of 14 members and forms the decision-making body.

In late 1969 an attempted coup was foiled, and Lt. Moussa Traoré, president of the Military Committee took over as chief of state and later as head of government, ousting Capt. Yoro Diakité as Premier.

The Malian People's Democratic Union, established in 1976, is the only political party.

History. Subjugated by France by the end of the 19th century, this area became a colony in 1904 (named French Sudan in 1920) and in 1946 became part of the French Union. On June 20, 1960, it became independent and, under the name of Sudanese Republic, was federated with the Republic of Senegal in the Mali Federation. However, Senegal seceded from the Federation on Aug. 20, 1960, and the Sudanese Republic then changed its name to the Republic of Mali on September 22.

In the 1960s, Mali concentrated on economic development, continuing to accept aid from both Soviet bloc and Western nations, as well as international agencies. In the late 1960s, it began retreating from close ties with China. But a purge of conservative opponents brought greater power to President Modibo Keita, and in 1968 the influence of the Chinese and their Malian sympathizers increased. By a treaty signed in Peking in 1968, China agreed to help build a railroad from Mali to Guinea, providing Mali with vital access to the sea.

Mali, with Mauritania, the Ivory Coast, Senegal, Dahomey (Benin), Niger, and Burkina Faso signed a treaty establishing the Economic Community for West Africa.

A six-year sub-Sahara drought devastated Mali before disastrously heavy rains began in 1974. Emergency shipments from a dozen nations and international organizations helped alleviate a famine that affected 1.8 million Malians and killed thousands.

Mali and Burkina Faso fought a brief border war from December 25 to 29, 1985.

MALTA

Republic of Malta
President: Dr. Vincent Tabone (1989)
Prime Minister: Edward Fenech Adami (1987)
Area: 122 sq mi. (316 sq km)
Population (est. mid-1989): 400,000 (average annual rate of natural increase: 0.7%)
Density per square mile: 2,833
Capital (est. 1987): Valetta, 9,300
Largest city (est. 1987): Birkirkara, 20,300
Monetary unit: Maltese lira
Languages: Maltese and English
Religion: Roman Catholic
National name: Repubblika Ta Malta
Member of Commonwealth of Nations
Literacy rate: 83%
Economic summary: Gross domestic product (1986): $1.5 billion, $4,110 per capita; real growth rate: 4.0%. Land used for agriculture, 41%; labor force: 4%; principal products: potatoes, wheat, barley, citrus, vegetables, hogs, poultry. Labor force in industry: 37%; major products: textiles, wine, beer, processed foods, plastics, electronic equipment. Natural resources: limestone, salt. Exports: textiles, yarns, manufactured goods, ships, printed matter. Imports: manufactured goods, machinery, transport equipment. Major trading partners: West Germany, U.K., Italy.

Geography. The five Maltese islands—with a combined land area smaller than Philadelphia—are in the Mediterranean about 60 miles (97 km) south of the southeastern tip of Sicily.

Government. The government is headed by a Prime Minister, responsible to a 69-member House of Representatives elected by universal suffrage.

The major political parties are the Nationalists (35 of 69 seats in the House,) led by Prime Minister Edward Fenech Adami; Malta Labor Party (34 seats), led by Carmelo Mifsud Bonnici.

History. The strategic importance of Malta was recognized by the Phoenicians, who occupied it, as did in their turn the Greeks, Carthaginians, and Romans. The apostle Paul was shipwrecked there in A.D. 58.

The Knights of St. John (Malta), who obtained the three habitable Maltese islands of Malta, Gozo, and Comino from Charles V in 1530, reached their highest fame when they withstood an attack by superior Turkish forces in 1565.

Napoleon seized Malta in 1798, but the French forces were ousted by British troops the next year, and British rule was confirmed by the Treaty of Paris in 1814.

Malta was heavily attacked by German and Italian aircraft during World War II, but was never invaded by the Axis.

Malta became an independent nation on Sept. 21, 1964, and a republic Dec. 13, 1974, but remained in the British Commonwealth. The Governor-General, Sir Anthony Mamo, was sworn in as first president and Dom Mintoff became prime minister.

After 13 years in office, Mintoff resigned as Prime Minister on Dec. 22, 1984, giving way to chosen successor, Carmelo Mifsud Bonnici, who had been Senior Deputy Prime Minister. Fenech Adami's election ended 16 years of Labor rule.

miles (592 km) of coastline on the Atlantic Ocean. It is bordered by Morocco on the north, Algeria and Mali on the east, and Senegal on the south.

The country is mostly desert, with the exception of the fertile Senegal River valley in the south and grazing land in the north.

Government. An Army coup on July 10, 1978, deposed Moktar Ould Daddah, who had been President since Mauritania's independence in 1960. President Mohammed Khouna Ould Haldala, who seized power in the 1978 coup, was in turn deposed in a Dec. 12, 1984, coup by army chief of staff Maaouye Ould Sidi Ahmed Taya, who assumed the title of President.

History. Mauritania was first explored by the Portuguese. The French organized the area as a territory in 1904.

Mauritania became an independent nation on Nov. 28, 1960, and was admitted to the United Nations in 1961 over the strenuous opposition of Morocco, which claimed the territory. With Moors, Arabs, Berbers, and blacks frequently in conflict, the government in the late 1960s sought to make Arab culture dominant to unify the land.

Mauritania acquired administrative control of the southern part of the former Spanish Sahara when the colonial administration withdrew in 1975, under an agreement with Morocco and Spain. Mauritanian troops moved into the territory but encountered resistance from the Polisario Front, a Saharan independence movement backed by Algeria. The task of trying to pacify the area proved a heavy burden. Mauritania signed a peace agreement with the Polisario insurgents in August 1979, withdrew from the territory and renounced territorial claims.

Increased military spending and rising casualties in Western Sahara contributed to the discontent that brought down the civilian government of Ould Daddah in 1978. A succession of military rulers has followed.

MAURITANIA

Islamic Republic of Mauritania
Chief of State and Head of Government: Col. Maaouye Ould Sidi Ahmed Taya (1984)
Area: 397,953 sq mi. (1,030,700 sq km)
Population (est. mid-1989): 2,000,000 (average annual rate of natural increase: 2.7%)
Density per square mile: 5.3
Capital and largest city (est. 1981): Nouakchott, 175,000
Monetary unit: Ouguyia
Ethnic groups: Moors, Black/moor mix, 70%; Blacks, 30%.
Languages: Arabic and French
Religion: Islam
National name: République Islamique de Mauritanie
Literacy rate: 17%
Economic summary: Gross national product (1985 est.): $971 million, $540 per capita. Principal agricultural products: livestock, millet, maize, wheat, dates, rice. Major industrial products: iron ore, processed fish. Natural resources: copper, iron ore, gypsum, fish. Exports: iron ore, fish, copper. Imports: foodstuffs, petroleum, capital goods. Major trading partners: France, Western Europe, Senegal, U.S.

Geography. Mauritania, three times the size of Arizona, is situated in northwest Africa with about 350

MAURITIUS

Sovereign: Queen Elizabeth II
Governor-General: Sir Veerasamy Ringadoo (1986)
Prime Minister: Aneerood Jugnauth (1982)
Area: 787 sq mi. (2,040 sq km)
Population (est. mid-1988): 1,100,000 (average annual rate of natural increase: 1.3%) (Indian, 51%; Creole, 33%)
Density per square mile: 1,419
Capital and largest city (est. 1980): Port Louis, 155,000
Monetary unit: Mauritian rupee
Languages: English (official), French, Creole, Hindi, Urdu, Chinese
Religions: Hindu, 52%, Roman Catholic, 26%; Islam, 13%
Member of Commonwealth of Nations
Literacy rate: 83%
Economic summary: Gross domestic product (1987 est.): $1.5 billion. Average annual growth rate (1984–88): 6.8%. Per capita income (1988): $1,460. Land used for agriculture: 62%; labor force: 28%; principal products: sugar cane. Labor force in industry: 24%; major products: processed sugar and tea, molasses, rum, textiles. Natural resources: fish. Exports: sugar, tea, molasses. Imports: foodstuffs, manufactured goods. Major trading partners: U.K., France, S. Africa, U.S.

Geography. Mauritius is a mountainous island in the Indian Ocean east of Madagascar.

Government. Mauritius is a member of the British Commonwealth, with Queen Elizabeth II as head of state. She is represented by a governor-general, who chooses the prime minister from the unicameral Legislative Assembly. The Legislative Assembly has 70 members, 62 of whom are elected by direct suffrage. The remaining 8 are chosen from among the unsuccessful candidates.

History. Mauritius was seized from France by British troops in 1810 and ceded to Britain by the Treaty of Paris in 1814. Until 1903, Mauritius and the Seychelles were administered as a single colony. The colony of Mauritius became an independent nation on March 12, 1968.

The nation has an Indian majority, descendants of laborers imported from India to work the sugar plantations after the abolition of slavery in 1834. The native blacks speak French and are Roman Catholics.

The Labor Party government of Sir Seewoosagur Ramgoolam, who had ruled Mauritius since independence, was toppled in a 1982 election by the Movement Militant Mauricien, which had campaigned for recovery of Diego Garcia island, separated from Mauritius during the colonial period and leased by Britain to the United States for a naval base. But an Alliance Party coalition, including the Labor Party, regained power at the end of 1983 and brought back Ramgoolam as Prime Minister. He was succeeded by Aneerood Jugnauth of his party in 1982.

MEXICO

United Mexican States
President: Carlos Salinas de Gortari (1988)
Area: 761,600 sq mi. (1,972,547 sq km)
Population (est. mid-1989): 86,700,000 (average annual rate of natural increase: 2.4%) (55%, mestizo; 29%, indian; 15%, white)
Density per square mile: 114
Capital: Mexico City
Largest cities (1980 census): Mexico City, 12,900,000; Guadalajara, 3,000,000; Monterrey, 2,700,000; Ciudad Juarez, 1,120,000; Puebla de Zaragoza, 1,100,000; Leon, 1,000,000
Monetary unit: Peso
Languages: Spanish, Indian languages
Religion: Mostly Roman Catholic
Official name: Estados Unidos Mexicanos
Literacy rate: 88%
Economic summary: Gross national product (1988): $173.5 billion. Annual growth rate (1988): 1.1%. Per capita income (1988): $7,252.9. Land used for agriculture, 52%; labor force: 26%; principal products: corn, cotton, sugar cane, fruits. Labor force in industry: 17%; major products: processed foods, chemicals, basic metals and metal products, petroleum. Natural resources: petroleum, silver, copper, gold, lead, zinc, natural gas, timber. Exports: cotton, shrimp, cattle and meat, coffee, machinery, petroleum. Imports: machinery, equipment, industrial vehicles, intermediate goods. Major trading partners: U.S., Japan, Western European countries.

Geography. The United States' neighbor to the south, Mexico is about one fifth its size. Baja California in the west, an 800-mile (1,287-km) peninsula, forms the Gulf of California. In the east are the Gulf of Mexico and the Bay of Campeche, which is formed by Mexico's other peninsula, the Yucatán.

The center of Mexico is a great, high plateau, open to the north, with mountain chains on east and west and with ocean-front lowlands lying outside of them.

Government. The President, who is popularly elected for six years and is ineligible to succeed himself, governs with a Cabinet of secretaries. Congress has two houses—a 400-member Chamber of Deputies, elected for three years, and a 64-member Senate, elected for six years.

Each of the 31 states has considerable autonomy, with a popularly elected governor, a legislature, and a local judiciary. The President of Mexico appoints the mayor of the Federal District.

History. At least two civilized races—the Mayas and later the Toltecs—preceded the wealthy Aztec empire, conquered in 1519–21 by the Spanish under Hernando Cortés. Spain ruled for the next 300 years until 1810 (the date was Sept. 16 and is now celebrated as Independence Day), when the Mexicans first revolted. They continued the struggle and finally won independence in 1821.

From 1821 to 1877, there were two emperors, several dictators, and enough presidents and provisional executives to make a new government on the average of every nine months. Mexico lost Texas (1836), and after defeat in the war with the U.S. (1846–48) it lost the area comprising the present states of California, Nevada, and Utah, most of Arizona and New Mexico, and parts of Wyoming and Colorado.

In 1855, the Indian patriot Benito Juárez began a series of liberal reforms, including the disestablishment of the Catholic Church, which had acquired vast property. A subsequent civil war was interrupted by the French invasion of Mexico (1861), the crowning of Maximilian of Austria as Emperor (1864), and then his overthrow and execution by forces under Juárez, who again became President in 1867.

The years after the fall of the dictator Porfirio Diaz (1877–80 and 1884–1911) were marked by bloody political-military strife and trouble with the U.S., culminating in the punitive expedition into northern Mexico (1916–17) in unsuccessful pursuit of the revolutionary Pancho Villa. Since a brief period of civil war in 1920, Mexico has enjoyed a period of gradual agricultural, political, and social reforms. Relations with the U.S. were again disturbed in 1938 when all foreign oil wells were expropriated. Agreement on compensation was finally reached in 1941.

The last year of José López Portillo's presidency was shadowed by economic problems caused by falling oil prices.

Miguel de la Madrid Hurtado, candidate of the ruling Partido Revolucionario Institucional, won the July 4 election for a six-year term.

During 1983 and 1984, Mexico suffered its worst financial crisis in 50 years, leading to critically high unemployment and an inability to pay its foreign debt. The collapse of oil prices in 1986 cut into Mexico's export earnings and worsened the situation.

In an election held on July 7, 1985, the ruling Institutional Party declared it had won all seven contested governorships and an overwhelming majority in the national Chamber of Deputies. Accusations of vote fraud by the ruling party intensified after state elections in 1986 in which it claimed a victory amidst reports of election irregularities such as ballot stuffing.

Although the PRI's candidate, Carlos Salinas de Gortari, won the presidential election, the opposition parties on the left and the right showed unprecedented strength. This continued in mid-1989 when the ruling PRI acknowledged an unprecedented defeat in a gubernatorial election.

MONACO

Principality of Monaco
Ruler: Prince Rainier III (1949)
Minister of State: Jean Ausseil (1986)
Area: 0.73 sq mi. (465 acres)
Population (est. 1987): 28,000 (average annual growth
  rate: 1.2%)
Density per square mile: 38,356.2
Capital: Monaco-Ville
Monetary unit: French franc
Languages: French, Monégasque, Italian
Religion: Roman Catholic
National name: Principauté de Monaco
Literacy rate: 99%

Geography. Monaco is a tiny, hilly wedge driven into the French Mediterranean coast nine miles east of Nice.

Government. Prince Albert of Monaco gave the principality a Constitution in 1911, creating a National Council of 18 members popularly elected for five years. The head of government is the Minister of State.

Prince Rainier III, born May 31, 1923, succeeded his grandfather, Louis II, on the latter's death, May 9, 1949. Rainier was married April 18, 1956, to Grace Kelly, U.S. actress. A daughter, Princess Caroline Louise Marguerite, was born on Jan. 23, 1957 (married to Philippe Junot June 28, 1978 and divorced in 1980; married to Stefano Casiraghi Dec. 29, 1983, and gave birth to a son, Andrea Albert, June 9, 1984); a son, Prince Albert Louis Pierre, on March 14, 1958; and Princess Stéphanie Marie Elisabeth, on Feb. 1, 1965. Princess Grace died Sept. 14, 1982, of injuries received the day before when the car she was driving went off the road near Monte Carlo. She was 52. Her daughter Stéphanie suffered neck injuries.

The special significance attached to the birth of descendants to Prince Rainier stems from a clause in the Treaty of July 17, 1919, between France and Monaco stipulating that in the event of vacancy of the Crown, the Monégasque territory would become an autonomous state under a French protectorate.

The National and Democratic Union (all 18 seats in National Council), led by Auguste Medecin, is the only political party.

History. The Phoenicians, and after them the Greeks, had a temple on the Monacan headland honoring Hercules. From *Monoikos*, the Greek surname for this mythological strong man, the principality took its name. After being independent for 800 years, Monaco was annexed to France in 1793 and was placed under Sardinia's protection in 1815. In 1861, it went under French guardianship but continued to be independent.

By a treaty in 1918, France stipulated that the French government be given a veto over the succession to the throne.

Monaco is a little land of pleasure with a tourist business that runs as high as 1.5 million visitors a year. It had popular gaming tables as early as 1856. Five years later, a 50-year concession to operate the games was granted to François Blanc, of Bad Homburg. This concession passed into the hands of a private company in 1898.

Monaco's practice of providing a tax shelter for French businessmen resulted in a dispute between the countries. When Rainier refused to end the practice, France retaliated with a customs tax. In 1967, Rainier took control of the Société des Bains de Mer, operator of the famous Monte Carlo gambling casino, in a program to increase hotel and convention space. He paid $8 million to Greek shipping magnate Aristotle Onassis for his shares.

MONGOLIA

Mongolian People's Republic
**Chairman of Presidium of the Great People's Khural
  (President):** Jambyn Batmunkh (1984)
Chairman of Council of Ministers (Premier): Dumagiin
  Sodnom (1984)
Area: 604,250 sq mi. (1,565,000 sq km)
Population (est. mid-1989): 2,100,000 (average annual
  rate of natural increase: 2.9%)
Density per square mile: 4
Capital and largest city (est. 1985): Ulan Bator, 488,200
Monetary unit: Tugrik
Language: Mongolian
Religion: Lamaistic Buddhism
National name: Bugd Nairamdakh Mongol Ard Uls
Literacy rate: about 90%
Economic summary: Gross domestic product (1985): $1.67
  billion. $880 per capita (1985 est.), average real growth
  rate (1976-85 est.): 3.6%. Principal agricultural
  products: livestock, wheat, oats, barley. Major industrial
  products: animal products, building materials, coal.
  Natural resources: coal, copper, molybdenum. Exports:
  livestock, animal products, wool, nonferrous metals.
  Imports: machinery and equipment, clothing, petroleum.
  Major trading partners: U.S.S.R. and Soviet bloc countries.

Geography. Mongolia lies in eastern Asia between Soviet Siberia on the north and China on the south. It is slightly larger than Alaska.

The productive regions of Mongolia—a tableland ranging from 3,000 to 5,000 feet (914 to 1,524 m) in elevation—are in the north, which is well drained by numerous rivers, including the Hovd, Onon, Selenga, and Tula.

Much of the Gobi Desert falls within Mongolia.

Government. The Mongolian People's Republic is a socialist state. The highest organ of state power is the Great People's Khural (Parliament), which is elected for a term of four years and is convened once a year. The Great People's Khural elects the Presidium, which consists of a chairman, two vice chairmen, a secretary, and six members. The Council of Ministers is set up by the Great People's Khural and consists of a chairman, vice chairmen, and ministers.

The Mongolian People's Revolutionary Party, led by President Jambyn Batmunkh, is the only political party.

History. The Mongolian People's Republic, formerly known as Outer Mongolia, is a Soviet satellite. It contains the original homeland of the historic Mongols, whose power reached its zenith during the 13th century under Kublai Khan. The area accepted Manchu rule in 1689, but after the Chinese Revolution of 1911 and the fall of the Manchus in 1912, the northern Mongol princes expelled the Chinese officials and declared independence under the Khutukhtu, or "Living Buddha."

In 1921, Soviet troops entered the country and facilitated the establishment of a republic by Mongolian revolutionaries in 1924 after the death of the last Living Buddha. China, meanwhile, continued to claim Outer Mongolia but was unable to back the claim with any strength. Under the 1945 Chinese-Russian Treaty, China agreed to give up Outer Mongolia, which, after a plebiscite, became a nominally independent country.

Allied with the U.S.S.R. in its dispute with China, Mongolia has mobilized troops along its borders since 1968 when the two powers became involved in border clashes on the Kazakh-Sinkiang frontier to the west and on the Amur and Ussuri Rivers. A 20-year treaty of friendship and cooperation, signed in 1966, entitled Mongolia to call upon the U.S.S.R. for military aid in the event of invasion.

MOROCCO

Kingdom of Morocco
Ruler: King Hassan II (1961)
Prime Minister: Azzedine Laraki (1986)
Area: 172,413 sq mi. (446,550 sq km)
Population (est. mid-1989): 25,600,000 (average annual rate of natural increase: 2.6%)
Density per square mile: 149
Capital: Rabat
Largest cities (1984): Casablanca, 2,158,369; Rabat, 556,000; Fez, 548,206; Marrakech, 482,603
Monetary unit: Dirham
Languages: Arabic, French, Berber dialects
Religions: Islam
National name: al-Mamlaka al-Maghrebia
Literacy rate: 28%
Economic summary: Gross domestic product (1985): $11.9 billion, $510 per capita; real growth rate (1987 est.): 5.7%. Land used for agriculture; 47%; labor force: 50%; products: barley, wheat, citrus fruits, vegetables. Labor force in industry, 15%; major products: textiles, chemicals. Natural resources: phosphates, lead, manganese, fisheries. Exports: phosphates, citrus fruits, vegetables, canned fruits and vegetables, canned fish, carpets. Imports: capital goods, fuels, foodstuffs, iron and steel. Major trading partners: France, West Germany, Italy, Saudi Arabia, Benelux.

Geography. Morocco, about one tenth larger than California, is just south of Spain across the Strait of Gibraltar and looks out on the Atlantic from the northwest shoulder of Africa. Algeria is to the east and Mauritania to the south.

On the Atlantic coast there is a fertile plain. The Mediterranean coast is mountainous. The Atlas Mountains, running northeastward from the south to the Algerian frontier, average 11,000 feet (3,353 m) in elevation.

Government. The King, after suspending the 1962 Constitution and dissolving Parliament in 1965, promulgated a new Constitution in 1972. He continued to rule by decree until June 3, 1977, when the first free elections since 1962 took place. The 306-member Chamber of Deputies has 204 elected seats, with the balance chosen by local councils and groups.

History. Morocco was once the home of the Berbers, who helped the Arabs invade Spain in A.D. 711 and then revolted against them and gradually won control of large areas of Spain for a time after 739.

The country was ruled successively by various native dynasties and maintained regular commercial relations with Europe, even during the 17th and 18th centuries when it was the headquarters of the famous Salé pirates. In the 19th century, there were frequent clashes with the French and Spanish. Finally, in 1904, France and Spain divided Morocco into zones of French and Spanish influence, and these were established as protectorates in 1912.

Meanwhile, Morocco had become the object of big-power rivalry, which almost led to a European war in 1905 when Germany attempted to gain a foothold in the rich mineral country. By terms of the Algeciras Conference (1906), Morocco was internationalized economically, and France's privileges were limited.

The Tangier Statute, concluded by Britain, France, and Spain in 1923, created an international zone at the port of Tangier, permanently neutralized and demilitarized. In World War II, Spain occupied the zone, ostensibly to ensure order, but was forced to withdraw in 1945.

Sultan Mohammed V was deposed by the French in 1953 and replaced by his uncle, but nationalist agitation forced his return in 1955. On his death on Feb. 26, 1961, his son, Hassan, became King.

France and Spain recognized the independence and sovereignty of Morocco in 1956. Later the same year, the Tangier international zone was abolished.

In 1975, tens of thousands of Moroccans crossed the border into Spanish Sahara to back their government's contention that the northern part of the territory was historically part of Morocco. At the same time, Mauritania occupied the southern half of the territory in defiance of Spanish threats to resist such a takeover. Abandoning its commitment to self-determination for the territory, Spain withdrew, and only Algeria protested.

When Mauritania signed a peace treaty with the Algerian-backed Polisario Front in August 1979, Morocco occupied and assumed administrative control of the southern part of the Western Sahara, in addition to the northern part it already occupied. Under pressure from other African leaders, Hassan agreed in mid-1981 to a cease-fire with a referendum under international supervision to decide the fate of the Sahara territory, but the referendum was never carried out.

King Hassan, startled the Reagan Administration in mid-August 1984 by signing a treaty of union with Col. Muammar el-Qaddafi, the Libyan leader.

The Moroccans described the treaty as the culmination of a process in which Libya had withdrawn its support for the Polisario in the Western Sahara, and Morocco had agreed to refrain from sending troops to help the French in Chad.

King Hassan became the second Arab leader to meet with an Israeli leader when, on July 21, 1986, Israeli Prime Minister Shimon Peres came to Morocco. Libyan criticism of the meeting led to King Hassan's abrogation of the treaty with Libya.

MOZAMBIQUE

People's Republic of Mozambique
President: Joaquim Chissano (1986)
Prime Minister: Dr. Mario Machungo (1986)
Area: 303,073 sq mi. (799,380 sq. km.)
Population (est. mid-1989): 15,200,000 (average annual rate of natural increase: 2.6%)
Density per square mile: 49
Capital and largest city (est. mid-1986): Maputo, 882,800
Monetary unit: Metical
Languages: Portuguese (official), Bantu languages
Religions: traditional, 60%; Christian, 30%; Islam, 10%
National name: República Popular de Moçambique
Literacy rate: 17%
Economic summary: Gross national product (1987 est.): $1.3 billion; average annual growth rate (est. '86-'87): 3.0%. Principal agricultural products: cotton, cashew nuts, sugar, tea, copra, peanuts. Labor force in industry: 5%; major products: processed foods, petroleum products, beverages, textiles, tobacco. Natural resources: bauxite, coal, iron ore, copper, diamonds. Exports: cashew nuts, cotton, sugar, shrimp, petroleum products, tea, copra, prawns, citrus, textiles. Imports: refined petroleum, machinery, vehicles, consumer goods, arms. Major trading partners: U.S., Western Europe, Eastern Europe, U.S.S.R.

Geography. Mozambique stretches for 1,535 miles (2,470 km) along Africa's southeast coast. It is nearly twice the size of California. Tanzania is to the north; Malawi, Zambia, and Zimbabwe to the west; and South Africa and Swaziland to the south.

The country is generally a low-lying plateau broken up by 25 sizable rivers that flow into the Indian Ocean. The largest is the Zambezi, which provides access to central Africa. The principal ports are Maputo and Beira, which is the port for Zimbabwe.

Government. After having been under Portuguese colonial rule for 470 years, Mozambique became independent on June 25, 1975. It is a Marxist state. The first President, Samora Moises Machel, headed the National Front for the Liberation of Mozambique (FRELIMO) in its 10-year guerrilla war for independence. He died in a plane crash on Oct. 19, 1986 and was succeeded by his Foreign Minister, Joaquim Chissano.

History. Mozambique was discovered by Vasco da Gama in 1498, although the Arabs had penetrated into the area as early as the 10th century. It was first colonized in 1505, and by 1510, the Portuguese had control of all the former Arab sultanates on the east African coast.

FRELIMO was organized in 1963. Guerrilla activity had become so extensive by 1973 that Portugal was forced to dispatch 40,000 troops to fight the rebels. A cease-fire was signed in September 1974, when Portugal agreed to grant Mozambique independence.

On Jan. 25, 1985, Mozambique's celebration of a decade of independence from Portugal was not a happy one. The Marxist government was locked in a five-year-old, stalemated, paralyzing war with anti-government guerrillas, known as the MNR, backed by the white minority government in South Africa. At the same time, like those in much of eastern Africa, the peasants who make up most of the population suffered from the consequences of four years of drought, with thousands reported starving.

MYANMAR
See Burma

NAMIBIA
See South Africa

NAURU

Republic of Nauru
President and Head Chief: Hammer DeRoburt (1968)
Area: 8.2 sq mi. (21 sq km)
Population (est. 1988): 8,902 (average annual growth rate: 1.7%)
Density per square mile: 1,086
Capital: Yaren
Monetary unit: Australian dollar
Languages: Nauruan and English
Religions: Protestant, 58%; Roman Catholic, 24%; Confucian and Taoist, 8%
Special relationship within the Commonwealth of Nations
Literacy rate: 99%
Economic summary: Gross national product (1984): $160 million. Per capita income (1984): $20,000. Major industrial products: phosphates. Natural resources: phosphates. Exports: phosphates. Imports: foodstuffs, fuel, machinery. Major trading partners: Australia, New Zealand, U.K., Japan.

Geography. Nauru (pronounced NAH oo roo) is an island in the Pacific just south of the equator, about 2,500 miles (4,023 km) southwest of Honolulu.

Government. Legislative power is invested in a popularly elected 18-member Parliament, which elects the President from among its members. Executive power rests with the President, who is assisted by a five-member Cabinet.

History. Nauru was annexed by Germany in 1888. It was placed under joint Australian, New Zealand, and British mandate after World War I, and in 1947 it became a U.N. trusteeship administered by the same three powers. On Jan. 31, 1968, Nauru became an independent republic.

NEPAL

Kingdom of Nepal
Ruler: King Birendra Bir Bikram Shah Deva (1972)
Prime Minister: Marich Man Singh Shrestha (1986)
Area: 54,463 sq mi. (141,059 sq km)
Population (est. mid-1989): 18,700,000 (average annual rate of natural growth: 2.5%)
Density per square mile: 344
Capital and largest city (est. 1980): Katmandu, 400,000
Monetary unit: Nepalese rupee
Languages: Nepali (official), Newari, Bhutia
Religions: Hindu, 90%; Buddhist, 5%; Islam, 3%
Literacy rate: 23%
Economic summary: Gross domestic product (FY87): $2.4 billion, $180 per capita; real growth rate (FY87): 4.2%. Labor force in agriculture: 93%; principal products: rice, maize, wheat, millet, jute, sugar cane, oilseed, potatoes.

Labor force in industry: 2%; major products: sugar, lumber, jute, cigarettes, cement. Natural resources: water, timber, hydroelectric potential. Exports: rice and food products, jute, and timber. Imports: textiles, manufactured goods, construction materials, fuel. Major trading partners: India, Japan.

Geography. A landlocked country the size of Arkansas, lying between India and the Tibetan Autonomous Region of China, Nepal contains Mount Everest (29,108 ft.; 8,872 m), the tallest mountain in the world. Along its southern border, Nepal has a strip of level land that is partly forested, partly cultivated. North of that is the slope of the main section of the Himalayan range, including Everest and many other peaks higher than 20,000 feet (6,096 m).

Government. A new Constitution promulgated by King Mahendra in 1962 provided for a unicameral legislature called the National Panchayat. All political parties were banned in 1960.

History. The Kingdom of Nepal was unified in 1768 by King Prithwi Narayan Shah. A commercial treaty was signed with Britain in 1792, and in 1816, after more than a year's hostilities, the Nepalese agreed to allow British residents to live in Katmandu, the capital. In 1923, Britain recognized the absolute independence of Nepal. Between 1846 and 1951, the country was ruled by the Rana family, which always held the office of prime minister. In 1951, however, the King took over all power and proclaimed a constitutional monarchy.

Mahendra Bir Bikram Shah became King in 1955. Nepal and China settled their differences in 1956, and thereafter Nepal accepted economic aid from the Chinese. The U.S. and the U.S.S.R. also provide aid.

After Mahendra, who had ruled since 1955, died of a heart attack in 1972, Prince Birendra, at 26, succeeded to the throne.

In the first election in 22 years, on May 2, 1980, voters approved the continued autocratic rule by the King with the advice of a partyless Parliament. The King, however, permitted the election of a new legislature, in May 1986, to which the Prime Minister and Cabinet are responsible.

A dispute with India over the renewal of a trade and transit treaty led to India closing most of the border crossings, causing severe economic disruption.

THE NETHERLANDS

Kingdom of the Netherlands
Sovereign: Queen Beatrix (1980)
Premier: Ruud Lubbers (1982)[1]
Area: 16,041 sq. mi. (41,548 sq. km.)
Population (est. mid-1989): 14,900,000 (average annual rate of natural increase: 0.4%)
Density per square mile: 1,031
Capital: Amsterdam; seat of government: The Hague
Largest cities (est. 1986): Amsterdam, 679,100; Rotterdam, 571,400; 's-Gravenhage, 444,000; Utrecht, 229,900; Eindhoven, 190,800
Monetary unit: Guilder
Language: Dutch
Religions: Roman Catholic, 36%; Dutch Reformed, 19%; unaffiliated, 27%
National name: Koninkrijk der Nederlanden
Literacy rate: 99%
Economic summary: Gross domestic product (1986): $175.3 billion. $12,050 per capita; real growth rate

(1986): 1.7%. Land used for agriculture: 60%; labor force, 6%; principal products: wheat, barley, sugar beets, potatoes, meat and dairy products. Labor force in industry: 28%; major products: metal fabrication, textiles, chemicals, electronic equipment, petroleum, fishing. Exports: foodstuffs, machinery, natural gas, chemicals, petroleum products, textiles. Imports: machinery, crude petroleum, chemicals, textiles, mineral ores. Major trading partners: West Germany, Belgium, France, U.K., U.S.

1. Resigned May 1989. Staying in office until general elections in September 1989.

Geography. The Netherlands, on the coast of the North Sea, has West Germany to the east and Belgium to the south. It is twice the size of New Jersey.

Part of the great plain of north and west Europe, the Netherlands has maximum dimensions of 190 by 160 miles (360 by 257 km) and is low and flat except in Limburg in the southeast, where some hills rise to 300 feet (92 m). About half the country's area is below sea level, making the famous Dutch dikes a requisite to the use of much land. Reclamation of land from the sea through dikes has continued through recent times.

All drainage reaches the North Sea, and the principal rivers—Rhine, Maas (Meuse), and Schelde—have their sources outside the country. The Rhine is the most heavily used waterway in Europe.

Government. The Netherlands and its former colony of the Netherlands Antilles form the Kingdom of the Netherlands.

The Netherlands is a constitutional monarchy with a bicameral Parliament. The Upper Chamber has 75 members elected for six years by representative bodies of the provinces, half of the members retiring every three years. The Lower Chamber has 150 members elected by universal suffrage for four years. The two Chambers have the right of investigation and interpellation; the Lower Chamber can initiate legislation and amend bills.

The Sovereign, Queen Beatrix Wilhelmina Armgard, born Jan. 31, 1938, was married on March 10, 1966, to Claus von Amsberg, a former West German diplomat. The marriage drew public criticism because of the bridegroom's service in the German army during World War II. In 1967, Beatrix gave birth to a son, Willem-Alexander Claus George Ferdinand, the first male heir to the throne since 1884. She also has two other sons, Johan Friso Bernhard Christian David, born in 1968, and Constantijn Christof Frederik Aschwin, born the next year.

History. Julius Caesar found the low-lying Netherlands inhabited by Germanic tribes—the Nervii, Frisii, and Batavi. The Batavi on the Roman frontier did not submit to Rome's rule until 13 B.C., and then only as allies.

A part of Charlemagne's empire in the 8th and 9th centuries A.D., the area later passed into the hands of Burgundy and the Austrian Hapsburgs, and finally in the 16th century came under Spanish rule.

When Philip II of Spain suppressed political liberties and the growing Protestant movement in the Netherlands, a revolt led by William of Orange broke out in 1568. Under the Union if Utrecht (1579), the seven northern provinces became the Republic of the United Netherlands.

The Dutch East India Company was established in 1602, and by the end of the 17th century Holland was one of the great sea and colonial powers of Europe.

The nation's independence was not completely established until after the Thirty Years' War (1618–48), after which the country's rise as a commercial and maritime power began. In 1814, all the provinces of Holland and Belgium were merged into one kingdom, but in 1830 the southern provinces broke away to form the Kingdom of Belgium. A liberal Constitution was adopted by the Netherlands in 1848.

In spite of its neutrality in World War II, the Netherlands was invaded by the Nazis in May 1940, and the East Indies were later taken by the Japanese. The nation was liberated in May 1945. In 1948, after a reign of 50 years, Queen Wilhelmina resigned and was succeeded by her daughter Juliana.

In 1949, after a four-year war, the Netherlands granted independence to the East Indies, which became the Republic of Indonesia. In 1963, it turned over the western half of New Guinea to the new nation, ending 300 years of Dutch presence in Asia. Attainment of independence by Suriname on Nov. 25, 1975, left the Dutch Antilles as the Netherlands' only overseas territory.

Prime Minister Van Agt lost his narrow majority in elections on May 26, 1981, in which the major issue was the deployment of U.S. cruise missiles on Dutch soil. Public opposition to the missiles forced the Netherlands, along with Belgium, to reverse its position in 1982 despite the Prime Minister's personal support for the NATO decision to deploy the new weapons in Western Europe. Van Agt lost his centrist coalition in May 1982 in a dispute over economic policy, and was succeeded by Ruud Lubber as Premier. Lubber announced on November 1, 1985 to accept the deployment of the U.S. missiles.

Netherlands Autonomous Country

NETHERLANDS ANTILLES

Status: Part of the Kingdom of the Netherlands
Governor: Prof. R. A. Romer (1986)
Premier: Maria Liberia Peters
Area: 383 sq mi. (993 sq km)
Population (est. mid-1988): 200,000 (average annual growth rate: 1.4%)
Capital (est. 1978): Willemstad, 152,000
Literacy rate: 95%
Economic summary: Gross national product (1984): $1.36 billion. Average annual growth rate (1984): 1.0%. Per capita income: $9,140. Principal agricultural products: pigs, goats. Major industries: oil refining, tourism. Natural resource: phosphate. Export: petroleum. Import: petroleum. Major trading partners: U.S., Venezuela.

Geography. The Netherlands Antilles comprise two groups of Caribbean islands 500 miles (805 km) apart: one, about 40 miles (64 km) off the Venezuelan coast, consists of Curaçao (173 sq mi.; 448 sq km), Bonaire (95 sq mi.; 246 sq km), the other, lying to the northeast, consists of three small islands with a total area of 34 square miles (88 sq km).
Government. There is a constitutional government formed by the Governor and Cabinet and an elected Legislative Council. The area has complete autonomy in domestic affairs.

ARUBA

Status: Part of the Kingdom of the Netherlands
Governor: F. B. Tromp
Prime Minister: J. H. A. Eman
Area: 75 sq mi. (193 sq km)

Population: (est. mid-1988): 62,322 (average annual growth rate: 0.29%)
Capital: (1986): Oranjestad, 19,800
Literacy rate: 95%
Economic summary: Gross national product (1986): $378 million. Real growth rate (1986): −31%. Per capita income, $6,100. Little agriculture. Major industries: tourism, light manufacturing (tobacco, beverages, consumer goods.

Geography. Aruba, an island slightly larger than Washington D.C., lies 18 miles (28.9 km) off the coast of Venezuela in the southern Caribbean.
Government. The governmental structure comprises the Governor, appointed by the Queen for a term of six years; the Legislature consisting of 21 members elected by universal suffrage for terms not exceeding four years; and the Council of Ministers, presided over by the Prime Minister, which holds executive power.

NEW ZEALAND

Sovereign: Queen Elizabeth II
Governor-General: Sir Paul Reeves (1985)
Prime Minister: Geoffrey Palmer (1989)
Area: 103,884 sq mi. (269,062 sq km) (excluding dependencies)
Population (est. mid-1989): 3,347,000 (average annual growth rate: 0.8%) (European, 87%; Maori, 9%)
Density per square mile: 33
Capital: Wellington
Largest cities (est. 1988): Auckland, 324,400; Wellington, 829,000; Christchurch, 299,400
Monetary unit: New Zealand dollar
Languages: English, Maori
Religions: Church of England, 26%; Presbyterian, 17%; Roman Catholic, 14%
Member of Commonwealth of Nations
Literacy rate: 99.5%
Economic summary: Gross domestic product (1988): $38.5 billion. Average annual growth rate (1980–88): 2.1%. Per capita income (1988): $1,150. Labor force in agriculture: 10%; principal products: wool, meat, dairy products, livestock. Labor force in industry: 21%; major products: processed foods, textiles, machinery, transport equipment, wood and paper products, financial services. Natural resources: forests, coal, gold. Exports: meat, dairy products, wool. Imports: machinery, minerals, chemicals, consumer goods. Major trading partners: Japan, Australia, U.K., U.S.

Geography. New Zealand, about 1,250 miles (2,012 km) east of Australia, consists of two main islands and a number of smaller, outlying islands so scattered that they range from the tropical to the antarctic. The country is the size of Colorado.

New Zealand's two main components are North Island and South Island, separated by Cook Strait, which varies from 16 to 190 miles (26 to 396 km) in width. North Island (44,281 sq mi.; 114,688 sq km) is 515 miles (829 km) long and volcanic in its south-central part. This area contains many hot springs and beautiful geysers. South Island (58,093 sq mi.; 150,461 sq km) has the Southern Alps along its west coast, with Mount Cook (12,349 ft; 3,764 m) the highest point.

The largest of the outlying islands are the Auckland Islands (234 sq mi.; 606 sq km), Campbell Island (44 sq mi.; 114 sq km), the Antipodes Islands (24 sq mi.; 62 sq km), and the Kermadec Islands (13 sq mi.; 34 sq km).

Government. New Zealand was granted self-government in 1852, a full parliamentary system and ministries in 1856, and dominion status in 1907. The Queen is represented by a Governor-General, and the Cabinet is responsible to a unicameral Parliament of 97 members, who are elected by popular vote for three years.

History. New Zealand was discovered and named in 1642 by Abel Tasman, a Dutch navigator. Captain James Cook explored the islands in 1769. In 1840, Britain formally annexed them.

From the first, the country has been in the forefront in instituting social welfare legislation. It adopted old age pensions (1898); a national child welfare program (1907); social security for the aged, widows, and orphans, along with family benefit payments; minimum wages; a 40-hour week and unemployment and health insurance (1938); and socialized medicine (1941).

The New Zealand Labor Party, headed by David Lange, swept Sir Robert Muldoon's conservative National Party from power in a parliamentary election on July 14, 1984. Lange's campaign promise to ban American nuclear-powered and nuclear-armed naval vessels from New Zealand waters provoked a crisis in the 33-year-old Anzus alliance of the United States, Australia and New Zealand. After New Zealand refused to let a U.S. warship make a port call on the ground it might be carrying nuclear weapons, Secretary of State George P. Shultz on July 17, 1985, accused New Zealand of undermining the U.S. nuclear deterrent and weakening its own security.

Cook Islands and Overseas Territories

The Cook Islands (93 sq mi.; 241 sq km) were placed under New Zealand administration in 1901. They achieved self-governing status in association with New Zealand in 1965. Population in 1978 was about 19,600. The seat of government is on Rarotonga Island.

The island's chief exports are citrus juice, clothing, canned fruit, and pineapple juice. Nearly all of the trade is with New Zealand.

Niue (100 sq mi.; 259 sq km) was formerly administered as part of the Cook Islands. It was placed under separate New Zealand administration in 1901 and achieved self-governing status in association with New Zealand in 1974. The capital is Alofi. Population in 1980 was about 3,300.

Niue exports passion fruit, copra, plaited ware, honey, and limes. Its principal trading partner is New Zealand.

The Ross Dependency (160,000 sq mi.; 414,400 sq km), an Antarctic region, was placed under New Zealand administration in 1923.

Tokelau (4 sq mi.; 10 sq km) was formerly administered as part of the Gilbert and Ellice Islands colony. It was placed under New Zealand administration in 1925. Its population is about 1,600.

NICARAGUA

Republic of Nicaragua
President: Daniel Ortega (1985)
Area: 50,180 sq mi. (130,000 sq km)

Population (est. mid-1989): 3,500,000 (average annual rate of natural increse: 3.5%) (mestizo, 70%; white, 17%; black, 9%; Indian, 4%)
Density per square mile: 70
Capital and largest city (est. 1985): Managua, 682,111
Monetary unit: Cordoba
Language: Spanish
Religion: Roman Catholic, 91%
National name: República de Nicaragua
Literacy rate: 87%
Economic summary: Gross domestic product (1986): $2.0 billion, $600 per capita; real growth rate (1987 est.): −3%. Land used for agriculture: 53%; labor force: 44%; principal products: cotton, coffee, sugar cane, rice, corn, beans, cattle. Labor force in industry: 13%; major products: processed foods, chemicals, metal products, clothing and textiles, beverages, footware. Natural resources: timber, fisheries. Exports: coffee, cotton, seafood, bananas, food and nonfood agricultural products. Imports: machinery, chemicals and pharmaceuticals, transport equipment, clothing, petroleum. Major trading partners: Mexico, West Germany, Japan, France, Cuba, Central America, Caribbean.

Geography. Largest but most sparsely populated of the Central American nations, Nicaragua borders on Honduras to the north and Costa Rica to the south. It is slightly larger than New York State.

Nicaragua is mountainous in the west, with fertile valleys. A plateau slopes eastward toward the Caribbean.

Two big lakes—Nicaragua, about 100 miles long (161 km), and Managua, about 38 miles long (61 km)—are connected by the Tipitapa River. The Pacific coast is volcanic and very fertile. The Caribbean coast, swampy and indented, is aptly called the "Mosquito Coast."

Government. After an election on Nov. 4, 1984, Daniel Ortega began a six-year term as President on Jan. 10, 1985. The major political parties are the Sandinista National Liberation Front (61 of 96 members of the National Assembly), led by President Ortega; the Democratic Conservative Party (14 seats); Independent Liberal Party (9 seats); Popular Social Christian Party (2 seats) and three small Marxist-Leninist groups with two seats each.

History. Nicaragua, which established independence in 1838, was first visited by the Spaniards in 1522. The chief of the country's leading Indian tribe at that time was called Nicaragua, from whom the nation derived its name. A U.S. naval force intervened in 1909 after two American citizens had been executed, and a few U.S. Marines were kept in the country from 1912 to 1925. The Bryan-Chamorro Treaty of 1916 (terminated in 1970) gave the U.S. an option on a canal route through Nicaragua, and naval bases. Disorder after the 1924 elections brought in the marines again.

A guerrilla leader, Gen. César Augusto Sandino, began fighting the occupation force in 1927. He fought the U.S. troops until their withdrawal in 1933. They trained Gen. Anastasio (Tacho) Somoza García to head a National Guard. In 1934, Somoza assassinated Sandino and overthrew the Liberal President Juan Batista Sacassa, establishing a military dictatorship with himself as president. He spurred the economic development of the country, meanwhile enriching his family through estates in the countryside and investments in air and shipping lines. On his assassination in 1956, he was succeeded by his son Luis, who alternated with trusted family friends in the presidency until his death in 1967. Another son, Maj. Gen. Anastasio Somoza

Debayle, became President in 1967.

Sandinista guerrillas, leftists who took their name from Gen. Sandino, launched an offensive in May 1979.

After seven weeks of fighting, Somoza fled the country on July 17, 1979. The Sandinistas assumed power on July 19, promising to maintain a mixed economy, a non-aligned foreign policy, and a pluralist political system. However, the prominence of Cuban President Fidel Castro at the celebration of the first anniversary of the revolution and a five-year delay in holding elections increased debate over the true political color of the Sandinistas.

On Jan. 23, 1981, the Reagan Administration suspended U.S. aid, charging that Nicaragua, with the aid of Cuba and the Soviet Union, was supplying arms to rebels in El Salvador. The Sandinistas denied the charges. Later that year, Nicaraguan guerrillas known as "contras," began a war to overthrow the Sandinistas.

The elections were finally held on Nov. 4, 1984, with Daniel Ortega Saavedra, the Sandinista junta coordinator, winning 63% of the votes cast for President. He began a six-year term on Jan. 10, 1985.

Meanwhile, the war between the Sandinistas and the U.S.-backed contras continued, and on Feb. 21, 1985, President Reagan denounced the Sandinista regime and said his objective was to "remove it in the sense of its present structure." On May 1, Reagan ordered an embargo on U.S. trade with Nicaragua, telling Congress that the policies and actions of the Sandinistas constituted a threat to U.S. security.

In October 1985, Nicaragua suspended civil liberties and in June 1986, Congress voted $100 million in aid, military and non-military, to the contras.

The war intensified in 1986-87, with the resupplied contras establishing themselves inside the country. Negotiations sponsored by the Contadora (neutral Latin American) nations, but a peace plan sponsored by Arias, the Costa Rican president, led to a treaty signed by the Central American leaders in August 1987, that called for an end to outside aid to guerrillas and negotiations between hostile parties. Congress later cut off military aid to the contras. Although the two sides agreed to a cease-fire in March, 1988, further negotiations were inconclusive.

Although the fighting died down, Nicaragua still has to contend with a crippled economy, with annual inflation reaching 20,000 percent in 1988.

Economic summary: Gross domestic product (1985 est.): $1.2 billion. Average annual growth rate (1985 est.): −3.1%. Per capita income (1983): $300. Land used for agriculture: 10%; labor force: 90%; principal products: peanuts, cotton, livestock, millet, sorghum, bananas, rice. Major industrial products: uranium, cement, bricks, light industrial products. Natural resources: uranium, coal, iron ore. Exports: uranium, peanuts, livestock, hides, skins. Imports: fuels, machinery, transport equipment, foodstuffs, consumer goods. Major trading partners: France, Nigeria, Japan, Algeria, U.S.

Geography. Niger, in West Africa's Sahara region, is four fifths the size of Alaska. It is surrounded by Mali, Algeria, Libya, Chad, Nigeria, Benin, and Burkina Faso.

The Niger River in the southwest flows through the country's only fertile area. Elsewhere the land is semiarid.

Government. After a military coup on April 15, 1974, Gen. Seyni Kountché suspended the Constitution and instituted rule by decree. Previously, the President was elected by direct universal suffrage for a five-year term and a National House of Assembly of 50 members was elected for the same term. He died on Nov. 10, 1987, and Col. Saibou, his Chief of Staff, succeeded him.

The Parti Progressiste Nigérien-Rassemblement Démocratique Africain, the only political party, was dissolved in 1974.

History. Niger was incorporated into French West Africa in 1896. There were frequent rebellions, but when order was restored in 1922, the French made the area a colony. In 1958, the voters approved the French Constitution and voted to make the territory an autonomous republic within the French Community. The republic adopted a Constitution in 1959 and the next year withdrew from the Community, proclaiming its independence.

The 1974 army coup ousted President Hamani Diori, who had held office since 1960. He was charged with having mishandled relief for the terrible drought that had devastated Niger and five neighboring sub-Saharan nations for several years. An estimated 2 million people were starving in Niger, but 200,000 tons of imported food, half U.S.-supplied, substantially ended famine conditions by the year's end. The new President, Lt. Col. Seyni Kountché, Chief of Staff of the army, installed a 12-man military government. A predominantly civilian government was formed by Kountché in 1976.

NIGER

Republic of Niger
Chief of State: Brigadier Ali Saibou (1987)
Area: 489,206 sq mi. (1,267,044 sq km)
Population (est. mid-1989): 7,400,000 (average annual rate of natural increase: 2.9%)
Density per square mile: 15
Capital and largest city (est. 1983): Niamey, 399,100
Monetary unit: Franc CFA
Ethnic groups: Hausa, 54%; Djerma and Songhai, 24%; Peul, 11%
Languages: French (official); Hausa, Songhai; Arabic
Religions: Islam, 80%; Animist and Christian, 20%
National name: République du Niger
Literacy rate: 21%

NIGERIA

Federal Republic of Nigeria
President: Gen. Ibrahim Badamasi Babangida (1985)
Area: 356,700 sq mi. (923,853 sq km)
Population (est. mid-1989): 115,600,000 (average annual rate of natural increase: 2.9%)
Density per square mile: 323
Capital: Lagos; Abuja (capital-as of 1990)
Largest cities (est. 1983): Lagos, 1,097,000; Ibadan, 1,060,000; Ogbomosho, 527,400; Kano, 487,100
Monetary unit: Naira
Languages: English (official) Hausa, Yoruba, Ibo
Religions: Islam, 47%; Christian, 34%; Animist, 18%
Member of Commonwealth of Nations
Literacy rate: 30%
Economic summary: Gross domestic product (1985): $53.4

billion, $520 per capita; growth rate (1986 est.): −3.4%. Land used for agriculture: 57%; labor force: 55%; principal products: peanuts, cotton, cocoa, grains, fish, yams, cassava, livestock. Labor force in industry: 19%; major products: crude oil, natural gas, coal, tin, processed rubber, cotton, petroleum, hides, textiles, cement, chemicals. Natural resources: petroleum, tin, columbite, iron ore, coal, limestone, timber. Exports: oil, cocoa, palm products, rubber, timber, tin. Imports: machinery and transport equipment, manufactured goods, chemicals, wheat. Major trading partners: U.K., Western European countries, U.S.

Geography. Nigeria, one third larger than Texas and black Africa's most populous nation, is situated on the Gulf of Guinea in West Africa. Its neighbors are Benin, Niger, Cameroon, and Chad.

The lower course of the Niger River flows south through the western part of the country into the Gulf of Guinea. Swamps and mangrove forests border the southern coast; inland are hardwood forests.

Government. After 12 years of military rule, a new Constitution re-established democratic government in 1979, but it lasted four years. The military again took over from the democratically elected civilian government on Dec. 31, 1983. The arms of the military government include an Armed Forces Ruling Council, a National Council of State, and National Council of Ministers. The various ministers make up the Federal Executive Council. There are state military governors.

History. Between 1879 and 1914, private colonial developments by the British, with reorganizations of the Crown's interest in the region, resulted in the formation of Nigeria as it exists today. During World War I, native troops of the West African frontier force joined with French forces to defeat the German garrison in the Cameroons.

Nigeria became independent on Oct. 1, 1960. Organized as a loose federation of self-governing states, the independent nation faced an overwhelming task of unifying a country with 250 ethnic and linguistic groups.

Rioting broke out again in 1966, the military commander was seized, and Col. Yakubu Gowon took power. Also in that year, the Moslem Hausas in the north massacred the predominantly Christian Ibos in the east, many of whom had been driven from the north. Thousands of Ibos took refuge in the Eastern Region. The military government there asked Ibos to return to the region and, in May 1967, the assembly voted to secede from the federation and set up the Republic of Biafra. Civil war broke out.

In January 1970, after 31 months of civil war, Biafra surrendered to the federal government.

Gowon's nine-year rule was ended in 1975 by a bloodless coup that made Army Brigadier Muritala Rufai Mohammed the new chief of state. Mohammed was assassinated the next year 1976 by a group of seven young officers, who failed to seize control of the government.

The return of civilian leadership was established with the election of Alhaji Shehu Shagari, as president in 1979.

A coup on December 31, 1983, restored military rule. The military regime headed by Maj. Gen. Mohammed Buhari was overthrown in a bloodless coup on Aug. 27, 1985, led by Maj. Gen. Ibrahim Babangida, who proclaimed himself president.

NORWAY
Kingdom of Norway
Sovereign: King Olav V (1957)
Prime Minister: Gro Harlem Brundtland (1986)
Area: 125,049 sq mi. (323,877 sq km)
Population (1988): 4,200,000 (average annual growth rate: 0.3%)
Density per square mile: 34
Capital: Oslo
Largest cities (1988): Oslo, 450,308; Bergen, 209,912; Trondheim, 135,542; Stavanger, 96,316
Monetary unit: Krone
Language: Norwegian
Religion: Evangelical Lutheran (state), 88%
National name: Kongeriket Norge
Literacy rate: 100%
Economic summary: Gross national product (1987): $82.6 billion. Est. annual growth rate (1987–88): 0.5%. Per capita income (1987): $17,300. Land used for agriculture: 3%; labor force, including fishing: 7%; principal products: dairy products, livestock, grain, potatoes, furs, wool. Labor force in industry: 17%; major products: oil and gas, fish, pulp and paper, ships, aluminum, iron, steel, nickel, fertilizers, transportation equipment, hydroelectric power, petrochemicals. Natural resources: fish, timber, hydroelectric power, ores, oil, gas. Exports: oil, natural gas, fish products, chemicals, pulp and paper, aluminum. Imports: machinery, motor vehicles, foodstuffs, iron and steel, textiles and clothing. Major trading partners: U.K., Sweden, West Germany, U.S., Denmark, Netherlands.

Geography. Norway is situated in the western part of the Scandinavian peninsula. It extends about 1,100 miles (1,770 km) from the North Sea along the Norwegian Sea to more than 300 miles (483 km) above the Arctic Circle, the farthest north of any European country. It is slightly larger than New Mexico. Sweden borders on most of the eastern frontier, with Finland and the U.S.S.R. in the northeast.

Nearly 70% of Norway is uninhabitable and covered by mountains, glaciers, moors, and rivers. The hundreds of deep fiords that cut into the coastline give Norway an overall oceanfront of more than 12,000 miles (19,312 km). Nearly 50,000 islands off the coast form a breakwater and make a safe coastal shipping channel.

Government. Norway is a constitutional hereditary monarchy. Executive power is vested in the King together with a Cabinet, or Council of State, consisting of a Prime Minister and at least seven other members. The Storting, or Parliament, is composed of 165 members elected by the people under proportional representation. The Storting discusses and votes on political and financial questions, but divides itself into two sections (Lagting and Odelsting) to discuss and pass on legislative matters. The King cannot dissolve the Storting before the expiration of its term.

The sovereign is Olav V, born July 2, 1903, only son of Haakon VII and Princess Maud (1869–1938), third daughter of Edward VII of England. He succeeded to the throne on the death of his father Sept. 20, 1957. He married Princess Märtha of Sweden (1901–1954) on March 21, 1929. Their children are Princess Ragnhild Alexandra (born 1930), Princess Astrid (born 1932), and Crown Prince Harald (born 1937). In 1968, the Crown Prince married Sonja Haraldsen, a commoner.

History. Norwegians, like the Danes and Swedes, are of Teutonic origin. The Norsemen, also known as Vikings, ravaged the coasts of northwestern Europe from the 8th to the 11th century.

In 1815, Norway fell under the control of Sweden. The union of Norway, inhabited by fishermen, sailors, merchants, and peasants, and Sweden, an aristocratic country of large estates and tenant farmers, was not a happy one, but it lasted for nearly a century. In 1905, the Norwegian Parliament arranged a peaceful separation and invited a Danish prince to the Norwegian throne—King Haakon VII. A treaty with Sweden provided that all disputes be settled by arbitration and that no fortifications be erected on the common frontier.

When World War I broke out, Norway joined with Sweden and Denmark in a decision to remain neutral and to cooperate in the joint interest of the three countries. In World War II, Norway was invaded by the Germans on April 9, 1940. It resisted for two months before the Nazis took over complete control. King Haakon and his government fled to London, where they established a government-in-exile. Maj. Vidkun Quisling, whose name is now synonymous with traitor or fifth columnist, was the most notorious Norwegian collaborator with the Nazis. He was executed by the Norwegians on Oct. 24, 1945.

Despite severe losses in the war, Norway recovered quickly. The country led the world in social experimentation. A neighbor of the U.S.S.R., Norway sought to retain good relations with the Soviet Union without losing its identity with the West. It entered the North Atlantic Treaty Organization in 1949.

Verification of U.S. and Soviet oil strikes in separated areas of Norway's sector of the North Sea bottom led the Storting in 1975 to impose stiff tax and royalty rates on concession holders. Following discovery of a North Sea field expected to produce 900,000 barrels a day by 1984, Parliament in 1976 approved establishment of a national refining and distributing company to market petroleum products at home and abroad.

Dependencies of Norway

Svalbard (24,208 sq mi.; 62,700 sq km), in the Arctic Ocean about 360 miles north of Norway, consists of the Spitsbergen group and several smaller islands, including Bear Island, Hope Island, King Charles Land, and White Island (or Gillis Land). It came under Norwegian administration in 1925. The population in 1986 was 3,942 of which 1,387 were Norwegians.

Bouvet Island (23 sq mi.; 60 sq km), in the South Atlantic about 1,600 miles south-southwest of the Cape of Good Hope, came under Norwegian administration in 1928.

Jan Mayen Island (147 sq mi.; 380 sq km), in the Arctic Ocean between Norway and Greenland, came under Norwegian administration in 1929.

Peter I Island (96 sq mi.; 249 sq km), lying off Antarctica in the Bellinghausen Sea, came under Norwegian administration in 1931.

Queen Maud Land, a section of Antarctica, came under Norwegian administration in 1939.

OMAN

Sultanate of Oman
Sultan: Qabus Bin Said (1970)
Area: 82,030 sq mi. (212,458 sq km)[1]
Population (est. mid-1989): 1,400,000 (average annual rate of natural increase: 3.3%)
Density per square mile: 17
Capital and largest city (est. 1981): Muscat, 70,000
Monetary unit: Omani rial
Language: Arabic (official); also English and Indian languages
Religion: Islam, 86%
National name: Saltonat Uman
Literacy rate: 20%
Economic summary: Gross domestic product (1986 est.): $7.5 billion, $5,900 per capita. Principal agricultural products: dates, fruit, cereal, livestock. Major industries: petroleum drilling, fishing, construction. Natural resources: oil, marble, copper, limestone. Exports: oil. Imports: machinery and transport equipment, food, mineral fuels. Major trading partners: U.K., U.S., China, Japan, Korea, Thailand.

1. Excluding the Kuria Muria Islands.

Geography. Oman is a 1,000-mile-long (1,700-km) coastal plain at the southeastern tip of the Arabian peninsula lying on the Arabian Sea and the Gulf of Oman. The interior is a plateau. The country is the size of Kansas.

Government. The Sultan of Oman (formerly called Muscat and Oman), an absolute monarch, is assisted by a council of ministers, six specialized councils, a consultative council and personal advisers.

There are no political parties.

History. Although Oman is an independent state under the rule of the Sultan, it has been under British protection since the early 19th century.

Muscat, the capital of the geographical area known as Oman, was occupied by the Portuguese from 1508 to 1648. Then it fell to Persian princes and later was regained by the Sultan.

The Kuria Muria Islands, formerly part of Aden, were given to Oman by the British in 1967.

In a palace coup on July 23, 1970, the Sultan, Sa'id bin Taimur, who had ruled since 1932, was overthrown by his son, who promised to establish a modern government and use new-found wealth to aid the people of this very isolated state.

PAKISTAN

Islamic Republic of Pakistan
President: Gulam Ishaq Khan (1988)
Prime Minister: Benazir Bhutto (1988)
Area: 310,400 sq mi. (803,936 sq km)[1]
Population (est. mid-1989): 110,400,000 (average annual growth rate: 2.9%)
Density per square mile: 356
Capital (1981 census): Islamabad, 201,000
Largest cities (1981 census for metropolitan area): Karachi, 5,208,100; Lahore, 2,952,700; Faisalabad, (Lyallpur) 1,920,000; Rawalpindi, 920,000; Hyderabad, 795,000
Monetary unit: Pakistan rupee
Principal languages: Urdu (national), English (official), Punjabi, Sindhi, Pashtu, and Baluchi
Religions: Islam, 97%; Hindu, Christian, Buddhist, Parsi
Literacy rate: 26%
Economic summary: Gross national product (1987): $33

billion, $330 per capita; real growth rate (1987): 5.2%
Land used for agriculture: 25%; labor force: 49%;
principal products: wheat, rice, cotton, sugarcane. Labor
force in industry: 14%; major products: cotton textiles,
processed foods, tobacco, chemicals, natural gas. Natural
resources: natural gas, limited petroleum, iron ore.
Exports: raw and manufactured cotton, rice, carpets,
leather, fish. Imports: food grains, edible oil, crude oil,
machinery, chemicals, transport equipment. Major trading
partners: U.S., U.K., West Germany, Saudi Arabia, Japan.

1. Excluding Kashmir and Jammu. 2. Does not include about
3 million refugees from Afghanistan.

Geography. Pakistan is situated in the western part
of the Indian subcontinent, with Afghanistan and
Iran on the west, India on the east, and the Arabian
Sea on the south.

Nearly twice the size of California, Pakistan consists of towering mountains, including the Hindu
Kush in the west, a desert area in the east, the Punjab plains in the north, and an expanse of alluvial
plains. The 1,000-mile-long (1,609 km) Indus River
flows through the country from the Kashmir to the
Arabian Sea.

Government. Pakistan is a federal republic with a
bicameral legislature.

History. Pakistan was one of the two original successor states to British India. For almost 25 years
following independence in 1947, it consisted of two
separate regions East and West Pakistan, but now
comprises only the western sector. It consists of
Sind, Baluchistan, the former North-West Frontier
Province, western Punjab, the princely state of Ba-
hawalpur, and several other smaller native states.

The British became the dominant power in the
region in 1797 following Lord Clive's military victory, but rebellious tribes kept the northwest in
turmoil. In the northeast, the formation of the Moslem League in 1906 estranged the Moslems from
the Hindus. In 1930, the league, led by Mohammed
Ali Jinnah, demanded creation of a Moslem state
wherever Moslems were in the majority. He supported Britain during the war. Afterward, the
league received almost a unanimous Moslem vote
in 1946 and Britain agreed to the formation of Pakistan as a separate dominion.

Pakistan was proclaimed a republic March 23,
1956. Iskander Mirza, then Governor General, was
elected Provisional President and H. S. Suhra-
wardy became the first non-Moslem League Prime
Minister.

The election of 1970 set the stage for civil war
when Sheik Muuibur told East Pakistanis to stop
paying taxes to the central government. West Pakistan troops moved in and fighting began. The independent state of Bangladesh, or Bengali nation,
was proclaimed March 26, 1971.

The intervention of Indian troops protected the
new state and brought President Yahya Kahn
down. Bhutto took over and accepted Bangladesh
as an independent entity.

Diplomatically, 1976 saw the resumption of formal relations between India and Pakistan.

Pakistan's first elections under civilian rule took
place in March 1977 and provoked bitter opposition protest when Bhutto's party was declared to
have won 155 of the 200 elected seats in the 216-
member National Assembly. A rising tide of violent
protest and political deadlock led to a military
takeover on July 5. Gen. Mohammed Zia ul-Haq
became Chief Martial Law Administrator.

Bhutto was tried and convicted for the 1974
murder of a political opponent, and despite worldwide protests was executed on April 4, 1979, touching off riots by his supporters. Zia declared himself
President on Sept. 16, 1978, a month after Fazel
Elahi Chaudhry left office upon the completion of
his 5-year term.

A measure of representative government was restored with the election of a new National Assembly in February 1985, although leaders of opposition parties were banned from the election and it
was unclear what powers Zia would yield to the
legislature.

On December 30, 1985, Zia ended martial law.
In May 1988, Zia deposed Prime Minister Mohammed Junejo and dissolved the National Assembly
on the grounds that they had not moved quickly
enough to establish Islamic law or deal with ethnic
strife.

On August 19, 1988, President Zia was killed in
a midair explosion of a Pakistani Air Force plane.
Senate leader, Gulam Ishaq Khan assumed power
as Acting President until elections can be held.

Elections at the end of 1988 brought longtime
Zia opponent Benazir Bhutto, daughter of Zulfikar
Bhutto, into office as Prime Minister.

PANAMA

Republic of Panama
President: Manuel Solis Palma (1988)
Area: 29,761 sq mi. (77,082 sq km)
Population (est. mid-1989): 2,400,000 (average annual
rate of natural increase: 2.2%) (mestizo, 70%; black,
12%; white, 12%; Indian, 6%)
Density per square mile: 80
Capital and largest city (est. 1987): Panama City, 440,-
000
Monetary unit: Balboa
Language: Spanish (official); many bilingual in English
Religions: Roman Catholic, 89%; Protestant, 6%
National name: República de Panamá
Literacy rate: 90%
Economic summary: Gross domestic product (1986): $5.1
billion, $2,290 per capita; real growth rate (1986):
−2.7%. Land used for agriculture: 24%; labor force:
29%; principal products: bananas, corn, sugar, rice,
coffee. Labor force in industry: 16%; major industrial
products: refined petroleum, sugar. Natural resources:
copper, mahogany, shrimp. Exports: bananas, refined
petroleum, sugar, shrimp, coffee. Imports: petroleum,
manufactured goods, machinery and transportation
equipment, food. Major trading partners: U.S., Central
America and the Caribbean, Western Europe, Mexico,
Japan.

Geography. The southernmost of the Central
American nations, Panama is south of Costa Rica
and north of Colombia. The Panama Canal bisects
the isthmus at its narrowest and lowest point, allowing passage from the Caribbean Sea to the Pacific Ocean.

Panama is slightly smaller than South Carolina.
It is marked by a chain of volcanic mountains in the
west, moderate hills in the interior, and a low range
on the east coast. There are extensive forests in the
fertile Caribbean area.

Government. In 1972, a new Constitution was approved by a new 505-seat National Assembly of Community Representatives (corregidores), which was created in the first election in five years. The Charter provides for indirect election of the President by the Assembly for a six-year term.

History. Visited by Columbus in 1502 on his fourth voyage and explored by Balboa in 1513, Panama was the principal transshipment point for Spanish treasure and supplies to and from South and Central America in colonial days. In 1821, when Central America revolted against Spain, Panama joined Colombia, which already had declared its independence. For the next 82 years, Panama attempted unsuccessfully to break away from Colombia. After U. S. proposals for canal rights over the narrow isthmus had been rejected by Colombia, Panama proclaimed its independence with U.S. backing in 1903.

For canal rights in perpetuity, the U.S. paid Panama $10 million and agreed to pay $250,000 each year, increased to $430,000 after devaluation of the U.S. dollar in 1933 and was further increased under a revised treaty signed in 1955. In exchange, the U.S. got the Canal Zone—a 10-mile-wide strip across the isthmus—and a considerable degree of influence in Panama's affairs.

Panama and the U.S. agreed in 1974 to negotiate the eventual reversion of the canal to Panama, despite strongly expressed opposition in the U.S. Congress. The texts of two treaties—one governing the transfer of the canal and the other guaranteeing its neutrality after transfer—were negotiated by August 1977 and were signed by Pres. Omar Torrijos Herara and President Carter in Washington on September 7. A Panamanian referendum approved the treaties by more than two thirds on October 23, but further changes were insisted upon by the U.S. Senate.

The principal change was a reservation specifying that despite the neutrality treaty's specification that only Panama shall maintain forces in its territory after transfer of the canal Dec. 31, 1999, the U.S. should have the right to use military force to keep the canal operating if it should become obstructed. The Senate approved the treaties in March-April, 1978. On June 16, Carter and Torrijos exchanged instruments of ratification in Panama City.

The basic treaty provides an increase from $2.3 million a year in royalties to $10 million a year during the transition period, with an additional annual payment of $10 million if it can be obtained from tolls. It also requires the use of more Panamanians as canal employees in the interim and pledges the U.S. not to pursue the development of another canal without the agreement of Panama.

Nicolas Ardito Barletta, Panama's first directly elected President in 16 years, was inaugurated on Oct. 11, 1984, for a five-year term. He lacked the necessary support to solve the country's economic crisis and resigned September 28, 1985. He was replaced by Vice President Eric Arturo Delvalle.

In June, 1986, reports surfaced that the behind-the-scenes strongman, Gen. Manuel Noriega, was involved in drug trafficking and the murder of an opposition leader. In 1987, Noriega was accused by his ex-Chief of Staff of assassinating Torrijos in 1981. He was indicted in the U.S. for drug trafficking but when Delvalle attempted to fire him, he forced the National Assembly to replace Delvalle with Manuel Solis Palma. Despite protests and U.S. economic sanctions, Noriega remains in power.

The crisis continued when Noreiga called presidential elections for when the current term expires. Despite massive fraud by Noreiga, the opposition seemed headed to a landslide. Noreiga annulled the elections and suppressed protests by the opposition.

Panama Canal. First conceived by the Spaniards in 1524, when King Charles V of Spain ordered a survey of a waterway across the Isthmus, a construction concession was granted by the Colombian government in 1878 to St. Lucien N. B. Wyse, representing a French company. Two years later, the French Canal Company, inspired by Ferdinand de Lesseps, began construction of what was to have been a sea-level canal. The effort ended in bankruptcy nine years later and the United States ultimately paid the French $40 million for their rights and assets.

The U.S. project, built on territory controlled by the United States, and calling for the creation of an interior lake connected to both oceans by locks, got under way in 1904. Completed in 1914, the Canal is 40.27 miles long and lifts ships 85 feet above sea level through a series of three locks on the Pacific and Atlantic sides. Enlarged in later years, each lock now measures 1,000 feet in length, 110 feet in width, and 40 feet in depth of water.

PAPUA NEW GUINEA

Sovereign: Queen Elizabeth II
Governor General: Sir Kingsford Díbela (1983)
Prime Minister: Rabbie Namaliu (1988)
Area: 178,704 sq mi. (462,840 sq km)
Population (est. mid-1989): 3,900,000 (average annual rate of natural increase: 2.7%)
Density per square mile: 22
Capital and largest city (est. 1986): Port Moresby, 145,000
Monetary unit: Kina
Languages: English, Melanesian pidgin, Hiri Motu, and 717 distinct native languages
Religions: over half Christian, remainder indigenous.
Member of Commonwealth of Nations
Literacy rate: 32%
Economic summary: Gross domestic product (1985): $2.4 billion, $700 per capita; real growth rate (1985): 4.4%. Labor force in agriculture, including fishing: 54%; principal products: coffee, copra, palm oil, cocoa, tea, coconuts. Major industrial products: coconut oil, plywood, wood chips, gold, silver. Natural resources: copper, gold, silver, timber, natural gas. Exports: gold, copper, coffee and cocoa beans, copra, timber. Imports: food, machinery, transport equipment, fuels. Major trading partners: Australia, U.K., Japan, West Germany, Singapore.

Geography. Papua New Guinea occupies the eastern half of the island of New Guinea, just north of Australia, and many outlying islands. The Indonesian province of Irian Jaya is to the west. To the north and east are the islands of Manus, New Britain, New Ireland, and Bougainville, all part of Papua New Guinea.

Papua New Guinea is about one tenth larger than California. Its mountainous interior has only recently been explored. The high-plateau climate is temperate, in contrast to the tropical climate of the coastal plains. Two major rivers, the Sepik and the Fly, are navigable for shallow-draft vessels.

Government. Papua New Guinea attained independence Sept. 16, 1975, ending a United Nations trusteeship under the administration of Australia. Parliamentary democracy was established by a Constitution that invests power in a 109-member national legislature.

History. The eastern half of New Guinea was first visited by Spanish and Portuguese explorers in the 16th century, but a permanent European presence was not established until 1884, when Germany declared a protectorate over the northern coast and Britain took similar action in the south. Both nations formally annexed their protectorates and, in 1901, Britain transferred its rights to a newly independent Australia. Australian troops invaded German New Guinea in World War I and retained control under a League of Nations mandate that eventually became a United Nations trusteeship, incorporating a territorial government in the southern region, known as Papua.

Australia granted limited home rule in 1951 and, in 1964, organized elections for the first House of Assembly. Autonomy in internal affairs came nine years later.

PARAGUAY

Republic of Paraguay
President: Gen. Andres Rodriguez (1989)
Area: 157,047 sq mi. (406,752 sq km)
Population (est. mid-1989): 4,200,000 (average annual rate of natural increase: 2.9%) (mestizo, 91%; white, 2%; Indian, 3%)
Density per square mile: 26
Capital and largest city (est. 1985): Asunción, 477,000
Monetary unit: Guarani
Languages: Spanish (official), Guaraní
Religion: Roman Catholic (official)
National name: República del Paraguay
Literacy rate: 84%
Economic summary: Gross domestic product (1986): $3.8 billion. Average annual growth rate (1985): 4.5%. Per capita income (1986): $950. Labor force in agriculture: 44%; principal products: soybeans, cotton, hides, sweet potatoes, tobacco, corn, rice, sugar cane. Labor force in industry: 34%; major products: packed meats, crushed oilseeds, beverages, textiles, light consumer goods, cement. Natural resources: Copper, gold and silver, iron ore, coal, timber, fish. Exports: cotton, soybeans, meat products, tobacco, timber, coffee, hides. Imports: fuels and lubricants, machinery and motors, motor vehicles, beverages, tobacco, foodstuffs. Major trading partners: Argentina, Brazil, West Germany, U.S., Netherlands, Switzerland, Algeria

Geography. California-size Paraguay is surrounded by Brazil, Bolivia, and Argentina in south central South America. Eastern Paraguay, between the Paraná and Paraguay Rivers, is upland country with the thickest population settled on the grassy slope that inclines toward the Paraguay River. The greater part of the Chaco region to the west is covered with marshes, lagoons, dense forests, and jungles.

Government. The President is elected by popular vote for five years. The legislature is bicameral, consisting of a Senate of 30 members and a Chamber of Representatives of 60 members. There is also a Council of State, whose members are nominated by the government.

History. In 1526 and again in 1529, Sebastian Cabot explored Paraguay when he sailed up the Paraná and Paraguay Rivers. From 1608 until their expulsion from the Spanish dominions in 1767, the Jesuits maintained an extensive establishment in the south and east of Paraguay. In 1811, Paraguay revolted against Spanish rule and became a nominal republic under two Consuls.

Actually, Paraguay was governed by three dictators during the first 60 years of independence. The third, Francisco López, waged war against Brazil and Argentina in 1865–70, a conflict in which the male population was almost wiped out. A new Constitution in 1870, designed to prevent dictatorships and internal strife, failed to do so, and not until 1912 did a period of comparative economic and political stability begin.

After World War II, politics became particularly unstable.

Stroessner ruled under a state of siege until 1965, when the dictatorship was relaxed and exiles returned. The Constitution was revised in 1967 to permit Stroessner to be re-elected.

Although oil exploration begun by U.S. companies in the Chaco boreal in 1974 has been fruitless, Paraguay found prosperity in another form of energy when construction started in 1978 on the Itaipu Dam on the Parana River as a joint Paraguayan-Brazilian project. The largest hydroelectric development in the world when completed, Itaipu will generate 12.6 megawatts of electricity, surpassing the U.S. Grand Coulee Dam.

The Stroessner regime was criticized by the U.S. State Department during the Carter administration as a violator of human rights, but unlike Argentina and Uruguay, Paraguay did not suffer cuts in U.S. military aid. The criticism is credited with having reduced the number of political prisoners to a "few hundred."

The government was forced to devalue the guarani as a condition for IMF help for the ailing economy.

Stroessner was overthrown by an army leader, Gen. Andres Rodriguez, in 1989. Rodriguez won in Paraguay's first multi-candidate elections in decades. He has promised to hand over power to an elected civilian successor in 1993.

PERU

Republic of Peru
President: Alan Garcia Pérez (1985)[1]
Premier: Armando Villanueva (1988)
Area: 496,222 sq mi. (1,285,216 sq km)
Population (mid-1989): 21,400,000 (average annual rate of natural increase: 2.1%) (white and mestizo, 52%; Indian, 46%)
Density per square mile: 43
Capital: Lima
Largest cities (est. 1987): Lima, 5,330,800; Arequipa, 572,000; Callao, 545,000; Trujillo, 476,000; Chiclayo, 379,000
Monetary unit: Inti
Languages: Spanish, Quéchua, Aymara, and other native languages
Religion: Roman Catholic
National name: República del Perú
Literacy rate: est. 80%

Economic summary: Gross domestic product (1986): $19.8 billion, $980 per capita; real growth rate (1986): 8.5%. Land used for agriculture: 24%; labor force: 37%; principal products: wheat, potatoes, beans, rice, sugar, cotton, coffee. Labor force in industry: 19%; major products: processed minerals, fish meal, refined petroleum, textiles. Natural resources: silver, gold, iron, copper, fish, petroleum, timber. Exports: copper, fish products, cotton, sugar, coffee, lead, silver, zinc, wool, oil, iron ore. Imports: machinery, foodstuffs, chemicals, pharmaceuticals. Major trading partners: U.S., Japan, Western European, and Latin American countries.

1. Elections in 1990.

Geography. Peru, in western South America, extends for nearly 1,500 miles (2,414 km) along the Pacific Ocean. Colombia and Ecuador are to the north, Brazil and Bolivia to the east, and Chile to the south.

Five sixths the size of Alaska, Peru is divided by the Andes Mountains into three sharply differentiated zones. To the west is the coastline, much of it arid, extending 50 to 100 miles (80 to 160 km) inland. The mountain area, with peaks over 20,000 feet (6,096 m), lofty plateaus, and deep valleys, lies centrally. Beyond the mountains to the east is the heavily forested slope leading to the Amazonian plains.

Government. The President, elected by universal suffrage for a five-year term, holds executive power. A Senate of 60 members and a Chamber of Deputies of 180 members, both elected for five-year terms, share legislative power.

History. Peru was once part of the great Incan empire and later the major vice-royalty of Spanish South America. It was conquered in 1531–33 by Francisco Pizarro. On July 28, 1821, Peru proclaimed its independence, but the Spanish were not finally defeated until 1824. For a hundred years thereafter, revolutions were frequent, and a new war was fought with Spain in 1864–66.

Peru emerged from 20 years of dictatorship in 1945 with the inauguration of President José Luis Bustamante y Rivero after the first free election in many decades. But he served for only three years and was succeeded in turn by Gen. Manual A. Odria, Manuel Prado y Ugarteche, and Fernando Belaúnde Terry. On Oct. 3, 1968, Belaúnde was overthrown by Gen. Juan Velasco Alvarado.

In 1975, Velasco was replaced in a bloodless coup by his Premier, Gen. Francisco Morales Bermudez, who promised to restore civilian government. In elections held on May 18, 1980, Belaunde Terry, the last previous civilian President and the candidate of the conservative parties that have traditionally ruled Peru, was elected President again. By the end of his five-year term in 1985, the country was in the midst of acute economic and social crisis.

But Peru's fragile democracy survived this period of stress and when he left office in 1985 Belaunde Terry was the first elected President to turn over power to a constitutionally elected successor since 1945. Alan Garcia Pérez, a 36-year-old Social Democrat, was inaugurated President on July 28, 1985. In his inaugural address, he said Peru would limit payments on its foreign debt to no more than 10% of its export earnings, instead of the terms demanded by the International Monetary Fund.

The savage war with the Sendero Luminoso guerrillas, a Maoist group, continued unabated with much of Peru remaining under military control.

THE PHILIPPINES

Republic of the Philippines
President: Corazon C. Aquino (1986)
Vice President: Salvador H. Laurel (1986)
Area: 115,830 sq mi. (300,000 sq km)
Population (est. mid-1989): 64,900,000 (average annual rate of natural increase: 2.8%)
Density per square mile: 560
Capital: Manila
Largest cities (est. 1984): Manila, 1,728,400[1]; Quezon City, 1,326,000; Cebu, 552,200
Monetary unit: Peso
Languages: Filipino (based on Tagalog), English; regional languages: Tagalog, Ilocano, Cebuano, others
Religions: Roman Catholic, 85%; Islam, 4%; Aglipayan (Independent Philippine Christian), 4%; Protestant, 3%
National name: Republika ng Pilipinas
Literacy rate: 88%
Economic summary: Gross domestic product (1986): $33.1 billion, $540 per capita; real growth rate (1987 est.): 5.1%. Land used for agriculture: 41%; labor force: 50%; principal products: rice, corn, coconuts, sugar cane, bananas, tobacco. Labor force in industry: 20%; major products: textiles, pharmaceuticals, chemicals, food processing, electronics assembly. Natural resources: forests, metallic and non-metallic minerals. Exports: electronic equipment, coconut products, sugar, logs and lumber, copper concentrates, bananas, garments, nickel. Imports: petroleum, industrial equipment, wheat. Major trading partners: U.S., Japan.

1. Metropolitan area population is 7,500,000.

Geography. The Philippine Islands are an archipelago of over 7,000 islands lying about 500 miles (805 km) off the southeast coast of Asia. The overall land area is comparable to that of Arizona. The northernmost island, Y'Ami, is 65 miles (105 km) from Taiwan, while the southernmost, Saluag, is 40 miles (64 km) east of Borneo.

Only about 7% of the islands are larger than one square mile, and only one third have names. The largest are Luzon in the north (40,420 sq mi.; 104,687 sq km), Mindanao in the south (36,537 sq mi.; 94,631 sq km), Samar (5,124 sq mi.; 13,271 sq km).

The islands are of volcanic origin, with the larger ones crossed by mountain ranges. The highest peak is Mount Apo (9,690 ft; 2,954 m) on Mindanao.

Government. On February 2, 1987, the Filipino people voted for a new Constitution that established a 24-seat Senate and a 250-seat House of Representatives and gave President Aquino a six-year term. It limits the powers of the President, who can't be re-elected.

History. Fernando Magellan, the Portuguese navigator in the service of Spain, discovered the Philippines in 1521. Twenty-one years later, a Spanish exploration party named the group of islands in honor of Prince Philip, later Philip II of Spain. Spain retained possession of the islands for the next 350 years.

The Philippines were ceded to the U.S. in 1899 by the Treaty of Paris after the Spanish-American War. Meanwhile, the Filipinos, led by Emilio Aguinaldo, had declared their independence. They continued guerrilla warfare against U.S. troops until the capture of Aguinaldo in 1901. By 1902, peace was established except among the Moros.

The first U.S. civilian Governor-General was William Howard Taft (1901–04). The Jones Law (1916) provided for the establishment of a Philippine Legislature composed of an elective Senate and House of Representatives. The Tydings-McDuffie Act (1934) provided for a transitional period until 1946, at which time the Philippines would become completely independent.

Under a Constitution approved by the people of the Philippines in 1935, the Commonwealth of the Philippines came into being, with Manuel Quezon y Molina as president.

On Dec. 8, 1941, the Philippines were invaded by Japanese troops. Following the fall of Bataan and Corregidor, Quezon established a government-in-exile, which he headed until his death in 1944. He was succeeded by Vice President Sergio Osmeña.

U.S. forces led by Gen. Douglas MacArthur reinvaded the Philippines in October 1944 and, after the liberation of Manila in February 1945, Osmeña re-established the government.

The Philippines achieved full independence on July 4, 1946. Manual A. Roxas y Acuña was elected first president. Subsequent presidents have been Elpidio Quirino (1948–53), Ramón Magsaysay (1953–57), Carlos P. García (1957–61), Diosdado Macapagal (1961–65), Ferdinand E. Marcos (1965–86).

Marcos, who had freed the last of the national leaders still in detention, former Senator Benigno S. Aquino, Jr., in 1980 and permitted him to go to the United States, ended eight years of martial law on January 17, 1981.

Despite having been warned by First Lady Imelda Marcos that he risked being killed if he came back, opposition leader Aquino returned to the Philippines from self-exile on Aug. 21, 1983. He was shot to death as he was being escorted from his plane by military police at Manila International Airport. The government contended the assassin was a small-time hoodlum allegedly hired by communists, who was in turn shot dead by Filipino troops, but there was widespread suspicion that the Marcos government was involved in the murder.

The assassination sparked huge anti-government rallies and violent clashes between demonstrators and police, which continued intermittently through most of 1984, and helped the fragmented opposition parties score substantial gains in the May 14, 1984, elections for a National Assembly with greater power than a previous interim parliament.

On Jan. 23, 1985, one of Marcos's closest associates, Gen. Fabian C. Ver, the armed forces chief of staff, and 25 others were charged with the 1983 assassination of Aquino. Their trial dragged on through most of the year, with defense attorneys charging the evidence against Ver and the other defendants was fabricated.

In an attempt to re-secure American support, Marcos set Presidential elections for Feb. 7, 1986. After Ver's acquittal, and with the support of the Catholic church, Corazon Aquino, widow of Benigno Aquino, declared her candidacy. Marcos was declared the winner but the vote was widely considered to be rigged and anti-Marcos protests continued. The defection of Defense Minister Juan Enrile and Lt. Gen. Fidel Ramos signaled an end of military support for Marcos, who fled into exile in the U.S. on Feb. 25, 1986.

The Aquino government survived coup attempts by Marcos supporters and other right-wing elements including one, in November, by Enrile. Legislative elections on May 11, 1987, gave pro-Aquino candidates a large majority.

The growth of the Communist insurgency in the Philippines remains a matter of increasing concern, both in Manila and Washington.

POLAND

Polish People's Republic

President of the Council of State: Gen. Wojciech Jaruzelski (1985)
Prime Minister: Tadeusz Mazowiecki (1989)
Area: 120,727 sq mi. (312,683 sq km)
Population (est. mid-1989): 38,200,000 (average annual rate of natural increase: 6%)
Density per square mile: 316
Capital: Warsaw
Largest cities (est. 1986): Warsaw, 1,659,400; Lodz, 847,900; Krakow, 740,100; Wroclaw, 637,200; Poznan, 575,100; Gdansk, 464,600; Szczecin, 392,300
Monetary unit: Zloty
Language: Polish
Religions: Roman Catholic.
National name: Polska Rzeczpospolita Ludowa
Literacy rate: 98%
Economic summary: Gross national product (1987): $151.0 billion. Average annual growth rate (1987): 2.1%. Per capita income (1987): $3,998. Labor force in agriculture: 29%; principal products: grains, sugar beets, potatoes, hogs and other livestock. Labor force in industry: 28%; major products: iron and steel, chemicals, textiles, processed foods, transport equipment. Natural resources: coal, sulfur, copper, natural gas. Exports: coal, machinery and equipment, chemicals, industrial products. Imports: machinery and equipment, fuels, raw materials, agricultural and food products. Major trading partners: Communist bloc countries, U.K., Italy, U.S., West Germany, France.

Geography. Poland, a country the size of New Mexico in north central Europe, borders on East Germany to the west, Czechoslovakia to the south, and the U.S.S.R. to the east. In the north is the Baltic Sea.

Most of the country is a plain with no natural boundaries except the Carpathian Mountains in the south and the Oder and Neisse Rivers in the east. Other major rivers, which are important to commerce, are the Vistula, Warta, and Bug.

Government. The 1952 Constitution describes Poland as a people's republic. The supreme organ of state authority is the Sejm (Parliament), which is composed of 460 members elected for four years. A 100-seat Senate was established in 1989.

History. Little is known about Polish history before the 11th century, when King Boleslaus I (the Brave) ruled over Bohemia, Saxony, and Moravia. Meanwhile, the Teutonic knights of Prussia conquered part of Poland and barred the latter's access to the Baltic. The knights were defeated by Wladislaus II at Tannenberg in 1410 and became Polish vassals, and Poland regained a Baltic shoreline. Poland reached the peak of power between the 14th and 16th centuries, scoring military successes against the Russians and Turks. In 1683, John III (John Sobieski) turned back the Turkish tide at Vienna.

An elective monarchy failed to produce strong central authority, and Prussia, and Austria were able to carry out a first partition of the country in 1772, a second in 1792, and a third in 1795. For more than a century thereafter, there was no Polish state, but the Poles never ceased their efforts to regain their independence.

Poland was formally reconstituted in November 1918, with Marshal Josef Pilsudski as Chief of State. In 1919, Ignace Paderewski, the famous pianist and patriot, became the first premier. In 1926, Pilsudski seized complete power in a coup and ruled dictatorially until his death on May 12, 1935, when he was succeeded by Marshal Edward Smigly-Rydz.

Despite a 10-year nonaggression pact signed in 1934, Hitler attacked Poland on Sept. 1, 1939. Russian troops invaded from the east on September 17, and on September 28 a German-Russian agreement divided Poland between Russia and Germany. Wladyslaw Raczkiewicz formed a government-in-exile in France, which moved to London after France's defeat in 1940.

All of Poland was occupied by Germany after the Nazi attack on the U.S.S.R. in June 1941.

The legal Polish government soon fell out with the Russians, and, in 1944, a Communist-dominated Polish Committee of National Liberation received Soviet recognition. Moving to Lublin after that city's liberation, it proclaimed itself the Provisional Government of Poland. Some former members of the Polish government in London joined with the Lublin government to form the Polish Government of National Unity, which Britain and the U.S. recognized.

On Aug. 2, 1945, in Berlin, President Harry S. Truman, Joseph Stalin and Prime Minister Clement Attlee of Britain established a new *de facto* western frontier for Poland along the Oder and Neisse Rivers. (The border was finally agreed to by West Germany in a nonagression pact signed Dec. 7, 1970.) On Aug. 16, 1945, the U.S.S.R. and Poland signed a treaty delimiting the Soviet-Polish frontier. Under these agreements, Poland was shifted westward. In the east it lost 69,860 square miles (180,934 sq km) with 10,772,000 inhabitants; in the west it gained (subject to final peace-conference approval) 38,986 square miles (100,973 sq km) with a prewar population of 8,621,000.

A New Constitution in 1952 made Poland a "people's democracy" of the Soviet type. In 1955, Poland, became a member of the Warsaw Treaty Organization, and its foreign policy became identical with that of the U.S.S.R. The government undertook persecution of the Roman Catholic Church as a remaining source of opposition.

Wladyslaw Gomulka was elected leader of the United Workers (Communist) Party in 1956. He denounced the Stalinist terror, ousted many Stalinists, and improved relations with the church. Most collective farms were dissolved, and the press became freer.

A strike that began in shipyards and spread to other industries in August 1980 produced a stunning victory for workers when the economically hard-pressed government accepted for the first time in a Marxist state the right of workers to organize in independent unions.

Led by Solidarity, a free union founded by Lech Walesa, workers launched a drive for liberty and improved conditions. A national strike for a five-day week in January 1981 led to the dismissal of Premier Pinkowski and the naming of the fourth Premier in less than a year, Gen. Wojciech Jaruzelski.

Antistrike legislation was approved on Dec. 2 and martial law declared on Dec. 13, when Walesa and other Solidarity leaders were arrested. Ten days later, President Reagan ordered sanctions against the Polish government, stopping food shipments and cutting commercial air traffic. The sanc-

tions were lifted in early 1987.

Despite demands for declaring Poland in default, Congress in February authorized payment of $3.5 million in interest charges to U.S. banks that had given loans to Poland for food purchases.

Martial law was formally ended in 1984 but the government retained emergency powers. On July 21, 1984, the Parliament marked the 40th anniversary of Communist rule in Poland by enacting an amnesty bill authorizing the release of 652 political prisoners—virtually all except for those charged with high treason, espionage, and sabotage—and 35,000 common criminals. On September 10, 1986, the government freed all 225 remaining political prisoners.

The abduction and murder in October 1984 of a pro-Solidarity, Roman Catholic priest, the Rev. Jerzy Popieluszko, jolted the government as no other event had since the start of the Solidarity movement in 1980. After a 25-day trial before a five-judge tribunal, four state security policemen were convicted on Feb. 7, 1985, and sentenced to prison terms of 14 to 25 years for the murder.

Increasing opposition to the government because of the failing economy led to a new wave of strikes in 1988. Unable to totally quell the dissent, it relegalized Solidarity and allowed them to compete in elections.

Solidarity won a stunning victory, taking almost all the seats in the Senate and all of the 169 seats they were allowed to contest in the Sejm. This has given them substantial influence in the new government.

PORTUGAL

Republic of Portugal
President: Mario Soares (1986)
Prime Minister: Anibal Cavaco Silva (1987)
Area: 35,550 sq mi. (92,075 sq km)
Population (est. mid-1989): 10,400,000 (average annual rate of natural increase: 0.3%)
Density per square mile: 293
Capital: Lisbon
Largest cities (est. 1985): Lisbon, 827,800; Opporto, 344,500
Monetary unit: Escudo
Language: Portuguese
Religion: Roman Catholic 97%, 1% Protestant, 2% other.
National name: República Portuguesa
Literacy rate: 80%
Economic summary: Gross national product (1987): $35.0 billion, $3,393 per capita; real growth rate (1987): 3.7%. Land used for agriculture: 44%; labor force: 22%; principal products: grains, potatoes, olives, wine grapes. Labor force in industry: 35%; major products: textiles, footwear, wood pulp, paper, cork, metal products, refined oil, chemicals, canned fish, wine. Natural resources: fish, cork, tungsten, iron ore. Exports: cotton, textiles, cork and cork products, canned fish, wine, timber and timber products, resin. Imports: petroleum, cotton, foodgrains, industrial machinery, iron and steel, chemicals. Major trading partners: Western European countries, U.S.

Geography. Portugal occupies the western part of the Iberian Peninsula, bordering on the Atlantic Ocean to the west and Spain to the north and east. It is slightly smaller than Indiana.

The country is crossed by many small rivers, and also by three large ones that rise in Spain, flow into the Atlantic, and divide the country into three geographic areas. The Minho River, part of the northern boundary, cuts through a mountainous area that extends south to the vicinity of the Douro River. South of the Douro, the mountains slope to the plains about the Tejo River. The remaining division is the southern one of Alentejo.

The Azores, stretching over 340 miles (547 km) in the Atlantic, consist of nine islands divided into three groups, with a total area of 902 square miles (2,335 sq km). The nearest continental land is Cape da Roca, Portugal, about 900 miles (1,448 km) to the east. The Azores are an important station on Atlantic air routes, and Britain and the U.S. established air bases there during World War II. Madeira, consisting of two inhabited islands, Madeira and Porto Santo, and two groups of uninhabited islands, lies in the Atlantic about 535 miles (861 km) southwest of Lisbon. The Madeiras are 307 square miles (796 sq km) in area.

Government. The Constitution of 1976, revised in 1982, provides for popular election of a President for a five-year term and for a legislature, the Assembly of the Republic, for four years.

History. Portugal was a part of Spain until it won its independence in the middle of the 12th century. King John I (1385–1433) unified his country at the expense of the Castilians and the Moors of Morocco. The expansion of Portugal was brilliantly coordinated by John's son, Prince Henry the Navigator. In 1488, Bartolomew Diaz reached the Cape of Good Hope, proving that the Far East was accessible by sea. In 1498, Vasco da Gama reached the west coast of India. By the middle of the 16th century, the Portuguese Empire was in West and East Africa, Brazil, Persia, Indochina, and Malaya.

In 1581, Philip II of Spain invaded Portugal and held it for 60 years, precipitating a catastrophic decline of Portuguese commerce. Courageous and shrewd explorers, the Portuguese proved to be inefficient and corrupt colonizers. By the time the Portuguese dynasty was restored in 1640, Dutch, English, and French competitors began to seize the lion's share of the world's colonies and commerce. Portugal retained Angola and Mozambique in Africa, and Brazil (until 1822).

The corrupt King Carlos, who ascended the throne in 1889, made Joao Franco the Premier with dictatorial power in 1906. In 1908, Carlos and his heir were shot dead on the streets of Lisbon. The new King, Manoel II, was driven from the throne in the Revolution of 1910 and Portugal became a French-style republic.

Traditionally friendly to Britain, Portugal fought in World War I on the Allied side in Africa as well as on the Western Front. Weak postwar governments and a revolution in 1926 brought Antonio Oliveira Salazar to power. He kept Portugal neutral in World War II but gave the Allies naval and air bases after 1943.

Portugal lost the tiny remnants of its Indian empire—Goa, Daman, and Diu—to Indian military occupation in 1961, the year an insurrection broke out in Angola. For the next 13 years, Salazar, who died in 1970, and his successor, Marcello Caetano, fought independence movements amid growing world criticism. Leftists in the armed forces, weary of a losing battle, launched a successful revolution on April 25, 1974.

In 1980, President General Antonia Ramalho Eanes won a second four-year term with 57% of the popular vote.

In late-1985, a PSP-PSD split ended the Soares coalition government. Cavaco Silva, an advocate of free-market economics, was the Social Decmocratic candidate. His party emerged with a plurality, unseating the Socialists.

In July, 1987, the governing Social Democratic Party was swept back into office with 50.22% of the popular vote, giving Portugal its first majority Government since democracy was restored in 1974.

Portuguese Overseas Territory

After the April 1974 revolution, the military junta moved to grant independence to the territories, beginning with Portuguese Guinea in September 1974, which became the Republic of Guinea-Bissau.

Mozambique and Angola followed, leaving only Portuguese Timor and Macao of the former empire. Despite Lisbon's objections, Indonesia annexed Timor.

MACAO

Status: Territory
Governor: Carlos Melancia (1987)
Area: 6 sq mi. (15.5 sq km)
Population (est. 1988): 432,232 (average annual growth rate: 1.5%)
Capital (1970 census): Macao, 241,413
Monetary unit: Patacá
Literacy rate (1981): 99% (excluding Chinese)
Economic summary: Gross domestic product (1987 est.): $2.0 billion, $4,350 per capita; real growth rate (1987 est.): 8%. Principal agricultural products: rice and vegetables. Major industrial products: clothing, textiles, plastics, furniture. Exports: textiles and clothing. Imports: raw materials, foodstuffs. Major trading partners: Hong Kong, China, U.S., West Germany, France.

Macao comprises the peninsula of Macao and the two small islands of Taipa and Colôane on the South China coast, about 35 miles (53 km) from Hong Kong. Established by the Portuguese in 1557, it is the oldest European outpost in the China trade, but Portugal's sovereign rights to the port were not recognized by China until 1887. The port has been eclipsed in importance by Hong Kong, but it is still a busy distribution center and also has an important fishing industry. Portugal will return Macao to China in 1999.

QATAR

State of Qatar
Emir: Sheikh Khalifa bin Hamad al-Thani (1972)
Area: 4,000 sq mi. (11,437 sq km)
Population (est. mid-1989): 400,000 (average annual rate of natural increase: 2.7%)
Density per square mile: 103
Capital (est. 1981): Doha, 190,000
Monetary unit: Qatari riyal
Language: Arabic; English is also widely spoken
Religion: Islam, 94%; Christian, 6%
Literacy rate: 70%

Economic summary: Gross national product (1985): $5.1 billion. Average annual growth rate (1970–79): −1.2%. Per capita income (1985): $15,723. Major industrial product: oil. Natural resources: oil, gas. Export: oil. Major trading partners: Japan, U.K., W. Germany, France, India.

Geography. Qatar occupies a small peninsula that extends into the PGulf from the east side of the Arabian Peninsula. Saudi Arabia is to the west and the United Arab Emirates to the south. The country is mainly barren.

Government. Qatar, one of the Arabian Gulf states, lies between Bahrain and United Arab Emirates. For a long time, it was under Turkish protection, but in 1916, the Emir accepted British protection. After the discovery of oil in the 1940s and its exploitation in the 1950s and 1960s, political unrest spread to the sheikhdoms. Qatar declared its independence in 1971. The next year the current Sheikh, Khalifa bin Hamad al-Thani, ousted his cousin in a bloodless coup.

ROMANIA

Socialist Republic of Romania
President: Nicolae Ceausescu (1974)
Premier: Constantin Dascalescu (1982)
Area: 91,700 sq mi. (237,500 sq km)
Population (est. mid-1989): 23,200,000 (Romanian, 89%; Hungarian, 8%; Germans, 1.5%; 1.5% others) (average annual rate of natural increase: 0.5%)
Density per square mile: 250.8
Capital: Bucharest
Largest cities (est. July 1, 1986): Bucharest, 2,014,359 (1987); Brasov, 351,493; Constanta, 327,676; Timisoara, 325,272; Iasi, 313,060; Cluj-Napoca, 310,017; Galati, 295,372
Monetary unit: Leu
Languages: Romanian, Magyar
Religions: Romanian Orthodox, 80%; Roman Catholic, 6%; 4% others
National name: Republica Socialista România
Literacy rate: 98%
Economic summary: Gross national product (1986): $138 billion, $6,030 per capita; real growth rate (1986): 3.8%. Land used for agriculture: 66%; labor force: 28%; principal products: corn, wheat, livestock. Labor force in industry: 37%; major products: steel, cement, metal production and processing, chemicals, food processing, textiles. Natural resources: oil, timber, natural gas, coal. Exports: machinery, minerals and metals, foodstuffs, lumber, fuel, manufactures. Imports: machinery, minerals, fuels, agricultural products, consumer goods. Major trading partners: U.S.S.R., East Germany, West Germany, Iran, Egypt, Italy.

Geography. A country in southeastern Europe slightly smaller than Oregon, Romania is bordered on the west by Hungary and Yugoslavia, on the north and east by the U.S.S.R., on the east by the Black Sea, and on the south by Bulgaria.

The Carpathian Mountains divide Romania's upper half from north to south and connect near the center of the country with the Transylvanian Alps, running east and west.

North and west of these ranges lies the Transylvanian plateau, and to the south and east are the plains of Moldavia and Walachia. In its last 190 miles (306 km), the Danube River flows through Romania only. It enters the Black Sea in northern Dobruja, just south of the border with the Soviet Union.

Government. The supreme body of state power and the sole legislative body is the Grand National Assembly, with 369 members elected for five-year terms. It elects a State Council, which provides for the continuity of state power and settles problems between sessions of the Assembly. The supreme executive and administrative body is the Council of Ministers elected by the Assembly. The office of President was created in 1974.

The Communist Partry, led by Secretary General Nicolae Ceausescu, is the only political party.

History. Most of Romania was the Roman province of Dacia from about A.D. 100 to 271. From the 6th to the 12th century, wave after wave of barbarian conquerors overran the native Daco-Roman population. By the 16th century, the main Romanian principalities of Moldavia and Walachia had become satellites within the Ottoman Empire, although they retained much independence. After the Russo-Turkish War of 1828–29, they became Russian protectorates. The nation became a kingdom in 1881 after the Congress of Berlin.

King Ferdinand ascended the throne in 1914. At the start of World War I, Romania proclaimed its neutrality, but later joined the Allied side and in 1916 declared war on the Central Powers. The armistice of Nov. 11, 1918, gave Romania vast territories from Russia and the Austro-Hungarian Empire.

The gains of World War I, making Romania the largest Balkan state, included Bessarabia, Transylvania, and Bukovina. The Banat, a Hungarian area, was divided with Yugoslavia.

In 1925, Crown Prince Carol renounced his rights to the throne, and when King Ferdinand died in 1927, Carol's son, Michael (Mihai) became King under a regency. However, Carol returned from exile in 1930, was crowned King Carol II, and gradually became a powerful political force in the country. In 1938, he abolished the democratic Constitution of 1923.

In 1940, the country was reorganized along Fascist lines, and the Fascist Iron Guard became the nucleus of the new totalitarian party. On June 27, the Soviet Union occupied Bessarabia and northern Bukovina. By the Axis-dictated Vienna Award of 1940, two fifths of Transylvania went to Hungary, after which Carol dissolved Parliament and granted the new premier, Ion Antonescu, full power. He abdicated and again went into exile.

Romania subsequently signed the Axis Pact on Nov. 23, 1940, and the following June joined in Germany's attack on the Soviet Union, reoccupying Bessarabia. Following the invasion of Romania by the Red Army in August 1944, King Michael led a coup that ousted the Antonescu government. An armistice with the Soviet Union was signed in Moscow on Sept. 12, 1944.

A Communist-dominated government bloc won elections in 1946, Michael abdicated on Dec. 30, 1947, and Romania became a "people's republic." In 1955, Romania joined the Warsaw Treaty Organization and the United Nations. A decade later, with the adoption of a new Constitution emphasizing national autonomy, and especially after Nicolae Ceausescu came to power in 1967, Bucharest became an increasingly dissident voice in the Soviet bloc.

Despite his liberal international record, at home Ceausescu has harshly suppressed dissidents calling for freedom of expression in the wake of the Helsinki agreements.

RWANDA

Republic of Rwanda
President: Maj. Gen. Juvénal Habyarimana (1973)
Area: 10,169 sq mi. (26,338 sq km)
Population (est. mid-1989): 7,000,000 (average annual rate of natural increase: 3.4%)
Density per square mile: 687
Capital and largest city (est. 1981): Kigali, 155,000
Monetary unit: Rwanda franc
Languages: Kinyarwanda and French
Religions: Roman Catholic, 56%; Protestant, 12%; Islam, 9%; Animist, 23%
National name: Repubulika y'u Rwanda
Literacy rate: 49%
Economic summary: Gross domestic product (1985): $.84 billion, $290 per capita; real growth rate (est. 1985): 7.5%. Land used for agriculture: 48%; labor force: 93%; principal products: coffee, tea, bananas, yams, beans. Labor force in industry: less than 2%; major products: processed foods, light consumer goods, minerals. Natural resources: cassiterite, wolfram. Exports: coffee, tea, tungsten, tin. Imports: textiles, foodstuffs, machinery, and equipment. Major trading partners: Belgium, West Germany, Kenya, Japan, France, U.S.

Geography. Rwanda, in east central Africa, is surrounded by Zaire, Uganda, Tanzania, and Burundi. It is slightly smaller than Maryland.

Steep mountains and deep valleys cover most of the country. Lake Kivu in the northwest, at an altitude of 4,829 feet (1,472 m) is the highest lake in Africa. Extending north of it are the Virunga Mountains, which include Volcan Karisimbi (14,-187 ft.; 4,324 m), Rwanda's highest point.

Government. Grégoire Kayibanda was President from 1962 until he was overthrown in a bloodless coup on July 5, 1973, by the military led by Gen. Juvénal Habyarimana.

In a plebiscite in December 1978, Habyarimana was elected to a five-year term as president and a new constitution adopted that provides for an elected Assembly and a single official party, the National Revolutionary Development Movement.

History. Rwanda, which was part of German East Africa, was first visited by European explorers in 1854. During World War I, it was occupied in 1916 by Belgian troops. After the war, it became a Belgian League of Nations mandate, along with Burundi, under the name of Ruanda-Urundi. The mandate was made a U.N. trust territory in 1946. Until the Belgian Congo achieved independence in 1960, Ruanda-Urundi was administered as part of that colony.

Ruanda became the independent nation of Rwanda on July 1, 1962.

ST. KITTS AND NEVIS

Federation of St. Kitts and Nevis
Sovereign: Queen Elizabeth II
Governor General: Sir Clement Athelston Arrindell (1985)
Prime Minister: Kennedy Alphonse Simmonds (1980)
Area: St. Kitts 65 sq mi. (169 sq km); Nevis 35 sq mi. (93 sq km)
Total population (est. mid-1989): 45,000 (average annual rate of natural increase, est. 1989: 1.3%)
Capital: Basseterre (on St. Kitts), 19,000
Largest town on Nevis: Charlestown, 1,771
Monetary unit: East Caribbean dollar

Economic summary: Gross domestic product (1986 est.): $70 million, $1,870 per capita; real growth rate (est. 1986): 4.5%. Principal agricultural products: sugar, cotton. Major industries: tourism, sugar processing, salt extraction. Exports: sugar, molasses. Imports: foodstuffs, manufactured goods. Major trading partners: U.S., U.K., Japan, Trinidad.

St. Christopher-Nevis, now St. Kitts and Nevis, was formerly part of the West Indies Associated States which were established in 1967 and consisted of Antigua and St. Kitts-Nevis-Anguilla of the Leeward Islands, and Dominica, Grenada, St. Lucia, and St. Vincent of the Windward Islands. Statehood for St. Vincent was held up until 1969 because of local political uncertainties. (Grenada, became independent in 1974, Dominica in 1978, St. Lucia and St. Vincent in 1979, and Antigua (known as Antigua and Barbuda) in 1981.) Anguilla's association with St. Christopher-Nevis ended in 1980.

Two members of the Leeward group—the British Virgin Islands and Montserrat—did not become Associated States.

St. Christopher-Nevis, now St. Kitts and Nevis, became independent on September 19, 1983.

ST. LUCIA

Sovereign: Queen Elizabeth II
Governor-General: Sir Vincent Floissac (1988)
Prime Minister: John Compton (1982)
Area: 238 sq mi. (616 sq km)
Population (est. mid-1989): 200,000 (average annual rate of natural increase: 2.2%)
Density per square mile: 627
Capital (est. 1972): Castries, 45,000
Monetary unit: East Caribbean dollar
Languages: English and patois
Religions: Roman Catholic, 91%; Protestant, 7%; Anglican, 3%
Member of Commonwealth of Nations
Literacy rate: 78%
Economic summary: Gross domestic product (1986): $158 million, $1,180 per capita; real growth rate (1986): 6.1%. Labor force in agriculture: 44%; principal products: bananas, coconuts, sugar, cocoa, spices. Major industrial products: clothing, assembled electronics, beverages. Exports: bananas, cocoa. Imports: foodstuffs, machinery and equipment, fertilizers, petroleum products. Major trading partners: U.K., U.S., Caribbean countries.

Geography. One of the Windward Isles of the Eastern Caribbean, St. Lucia lies just south of Martinique. It is of volcanic origin. A chain of wooded mountains runs from north to south, and from them flow many streams into fertile valleys.

Government. A Governor-General represents the sovereign, Queen Elizabeth II. A Prime Minister is head of government, chosen by a 17-member House of Assembly elected by universal suffrage for a maximum term of five years.

History. Discovered by Spain in 1503 and ruled by Spain and then France, St. Lucia became a British territory in 1803. With other Windward Isles, St. Lucia was granted home rule in 1967 as one of the West Indies Associated States. On Feb. 22, 1979, St. Lucia achieved full independence in ceremonies boycotted by the opposition St. Lucia Labor

Party, which had advocated a referendum before cutting ties with Britain.

Unrest and a strike by civil servants forced Prime Minister John Compton to hold elections in July, in which his United Workers Party lost its majority for the first time in 15 years.

A Labor Party government was ousted in turn by Compton and his followers, in elections in May 1982.

Formerly dependent on a single crop, bananas, St. Lucia has sought to lower its chronic unemployment and payments deficit. The government provided tax incentives to a U.S. corporation, Amerada Hess, to facilitate location of a $150-million oil refinery and transshipment terminal on the island.

ST. VINCENT AND THE GRENADINES

Sovereign: Queen Elizabeth II
Governor-General: Henry H. Williams (1988)
Prime Minister: James Mitchell (1984)
Area: 150 sq mi. (389 sq km)
Population (est. mid-1989): 100,000 (average annual rate of natural increase: 1.9%)
Density per square mile: 700
Capital and largest city (est. 1984): Kingstown, 18,378
Monetary unit: East Caribbean dollar
Language: English, some French patois
Religions: Anglican, 47%; Methodist, 28%; Roman Catholic, 13%
Member of Commonwealth of Nations
Literacy rate: 85%
Economic summary: Gross domestic product (1986 est.): $95.0 million, $900 per capita; real rate (est. 1986): 3.1%. Land used for agriculture: 56%; labor force: 29%; principal products: bananas, arrowroot, coconuts. Major industry: food processing. Exports: bananas, arrowroot, copra. Imports: foodstuffs, machinery and equipment, chemicals, fuels, clothing. Major trading partners: U.K., U.S., Canada, Caribbean nations.

Geography. St. Vincent, chief island of the chain, is 18 miles (29 km) long and 11 miles (18 km) wide. One of the Windward Islands in the Lesser Antilles, it is 100 miles (161 km) west of Barbados. The island is mountainous and well forested. The Grenadines, a chain of nearly 600 islets with a total area of only 17 square miles (27 sq km), extend for 60 miles (96 km) from northeast to southwest between St. Vincent and Grenada, southernmost of the Windwards.

St. Vincent is dominated by the volcano La Soufrière, part of a volcanic range running north and south, which rises to 4,048 feet (1,234 m). The volcano erupted over a 10-day period in April 1979, causing the evacuation of the northern two thirds of the island. (There is also a volcano of the same name on Basse-Terre, Guadeloupe, which became violently active in 1976 and 1977.)

Government. A Governor-General represents the sovereign, Queen Elizabeth II. A Prime Minister, elected by a 13-member unicameral legislature, holds executive power.

History. Discovered by Columbus in 1498, and alternately claimed by Britain and France, St. Vincent became a British colony by the Treaty of Paris in 1783. The islands won home rule in 1969 as part of the West Indies Associated States and achieved full independence Oct. 26, 1979. Prime Minister

Milton Cato's government quelled a brief rebellion Dec. 8, 1979 attributed to economic problems following the eruption of La Soufrière in April, 1979. Unlike a 1902 eruption which killed 2,000, there was no loss of life but widespread losses to agriculture.

SAN MARINO

Most Serene Republic of San Marino
Co-Regents: Two selected every six months by Grand and General Council
Area: 23.6 sq mi. (62 sq km)
Population (est. 1988): 22,986 (mostly Italian) (average annual growth rate: 0.8%)
Density per square mile: 974.6
Capital and largest city (est. 1982 for metropolitan area): San Marino, 4,500
Monetary unit: Italian lira
Language: Italian
Religion: Roman Catholic
National name: Repubblica di San Marino
Literacy rate: 98%
Economic summary: Gross national product (1980): $176 million. Per capita income (1980): $8,250. Land used for agriculture: 17%; principal products: wheat and other grains, grapes, fruits, vegetables. Major industrial products: textiles, paper, leather, cement and other building materials. Exports: building stone, lime, chestnuts, wheat, hides, baked goods. Imports: manufactured consumer goods. Major trading partner: Italy.

Geography. One tenth the size of New York City, San Marino is surrounded by Italy. It is situated in the Apennines, a little inland from the Adriatic Sea near Rimini.

Government. The country is governed by two co-regents. Executive power is exercised by ten ministers. In 1959, the Grand Council granted women the vote.

History. According to tradition, San Marino was founded about A.D. 350 and had good luck for centuries in staying out of the many wars and feuds on the Italian peninsula. It is the oldest republic in the world.

A person born in San Marino remains a citizen and can vote no matter where he lives.

SÃO TOMÉ AND PRÍNCIPE

Democratic Republic of São Tomé and Principe
President: Manuel Pinto da Costa (1975)
Prime Minister: Celestino Rochada Costa (1988)
Area: 370 sq mi. (958 sq km)
Population (est. mid-1988): 100,000 (average annual growth rate: 2.7%)
Density per square mile: 326
Capital and largest city (est. 1984): São Tomé, 34,997
Monetary unit: Dobra
Language: Portuguese
Religions: Roman Catholic, Evangelical Protestant, Seventh-Day Adventist
Literacy rate: 54%
Economic summary: Gross domestic product $37.7 million; $340 per capita; annual growth rate (1987 est.): 1.8%. Principal agricultural products: cocoa, copra, coconuts, palm oil, coffee, bananas. Major industrial products: shirts, soap, beer, processed fish and shrimp. Exports: cocoa, coffee, copra, palm oil. Imports:

foodstuffs, textiles, machinery, electrical equipment, fuels, lubricants. Major trading partners: Netherlands, Portugal, East Germany, West Germany, U.S.

Geography. The tiny volcanic islands of São Tomé and Príncipe lie in the Gulf of Guinea about 150 miles (240 km) off West Africa. São Tomé (about 330 sq mi.; 859 sq km) is covered by a dense mountainous jungle, out of which have been carved large plantations. Príncipe (about 40 sq. mi.; 142 sq km) consists of jagged mountains. Other islands in the republic are Pedras Tinhosas and Rolas.

Government. The Constitution grants supreme power to a People's Assembly composed of members elected for four years. The Assembly chooses the President of the republic from candidates named by the Movement for the Liberation of São Tomé and Príncipe, the only legal party.

History. São Tomé and Príncipe were discovered, by Portuguese navigators in 1471 and settled by the end of the century. Intensive cultivation by slave labor made the islands a major producer of sugar during the 17th century but output declined until the introduction of coffee and cacao in the 19th century brought new prosperity. The island of São Tomé was the world's largest producer of cacao in 1908 and the crop is still the most important. An exile liberation movement was formed in 1953 after Portuguese landowners quelled labor riots by killing several hundred African workers.

The Portuguese revolution of 1974 brought the end of the overseas empire and the new Lisbon government transferred power to the liberation movement on July 12, 1975. Most of the 4,000 Portuguese inhabitants departed during the transition period.

SAUDI ARABIA

Kingdom of Saudi Arabia
Ruler and Prime Minister: King Fahd bin 'Abdulaziz (1982)
Area: 865,000 sq mi. (2,250,070 sq km)
Population (est. mid-1989): 14,700,000 (average annual rate of natural increase: 3.4%)
Density per square mile: 18
Capital: Riyadh
Largest cities (est. 1980): Jeddah, 1,500,000; Riyadh, 1,250,000; Mecca, 750,000
Monetary unit: Riyal
Language: Arabic
Religion: Islam
National name: Al-Mamlaka al-'Arabiya as-Sa'udiya
Literacy rate: 52%
Economic summary: Gross domestic product (1987): $85.0 billion, $6,030 per capita; growth rate (1987): −10%. Labor force in agriculture: 30%; principal products: dates, grains, livestock. Labor force in industry: 29%; major products: petroleum, cement, plastic products, steel. Natural resource: oil. Exports: petroleum and petroleum products, wheat. Imports: manufactured goods, transport equipment, construction materials, processed food. Major trading partners: U.S., Western European countries, Japan, West Germany, Bahrain.

Geography. Saudi Arabia occupies most of the Arabian Peninsula, with the Red Sea and the Gulf of Aqaba to the west, the Arabian Gulf to the east. Neighboring countries are Jordan, Iraq, Kuwait, Qatar, the United Arab Emirates, the Sultanate of Oman, the Yemen Arab Republic, and the People's Democratic Republic of Yemen.

A narrow coastal plain on the Red Sea rims a mountain range that spans the length of the western coastline. These mountains gradually rise in elevation from north to south. East of these mountains is a massive plateau which slopes gently downward toward the Arabian Gulf. Part of this plateau is covered by the world's largest sand desert, the Rub Al-Khali, or Empty Quarter. Saudi Arabia's oil region lies primarily along the Arabian Gulf.

Government. Saudi Arabia is a monarchy based on the Sharia (Islamic law), as revealed in the Koran (the holy book) and the Hadith (teachings and sayings of the prophet Mohammed). A Council of Ministers was formed in 1953, which acts as a Cabinet under the leadership of the King. There are 21 Ministries.

Royal and ministerial decrees account for most of the promulgated legislation, treaties, and conventions. There are no political parties.

History. Mohammed united the Arabs in the 7th century, and his followers, led by the caliphs, founded a great empire, with its capital at Medina. Later, the caliphate capital was transferred to Damascus and then Baghdad, but Arabia retained its importance because of the holy cities of Mecca and Medina. In the 16th and 17th centuries, the Turks established at least nominal rule over much of Arabia, and in the middle of the 18th century, it was divided into separate principalities.

The Kingdom of Saudi Arabia is almost entirely the creation of King Ibn Saud (1882–1953). A descendant of earlier Wahabi rulers, he seized Riyadh, the capital of Nejd, in 1901 and set himself up as leader of the Arab nationalist movement. By 1906 he had established Wahabi dominance in Nejd. He conquered Hejaz in 1924–25, consolidating it and Nejd into a dual kingdom in 1926. In 1932, Hejaz and Nejd became a single kingdom, which was officially named Saudi Arabia. A year later the region of Asir was incorporated into the kingdom.

Oil was discovered in 1936, and commercial production began during World War II. Saudi Arabia was neutral until nearly the end of the war, but it was permitted to be a charter member of the United Nations. The country joined the Arab League in 1945 and took part in the 1948–49 war against Israel.

On Ibn Saud's death in 1953, his eldest son, Saud, began an 11-year reign marked by an increasing hostility toward the radical Arabism of Egypt's Gamal Abdel Nasser. In 1964, the ailing Saud was deposed and replaced by the Premier, Crown Prince Faisal, who gave vocal support but no military help to Egypt in the 1967 Mideast war.

Faisal's assassination by a deranged kinsman in 1975 shook the Middle East, but failed to alter his kingdom's course. His successor was his brother, Prince Khalid. Khalid gave influential support to Egypt during negotiations on Israeli withdrawal from the Sinai desert.

King Khalid died of a heart attack June 13, 1982, and was succeeded by his half-brother, Prince Fahd bin 'Abdulaziz, 60, who had exercised the real power throughout Khalid's reign. King Fahd, a pro-Western modernist, chose his 58-year-old half-brother, Abdullah, as Crown Prince.

Saudi Arabia and the smaller, oil-rich Arab states on the Persian Gulf, fearful that they might become Ayatollah Ruhollah Khomeini's next targets if Iran conquered Iraq, made large financial contributions to the Iraqi war effort. They began being dragged into the conflict themselves in the spring of 1984, when Iraq and Iran extended their ground war to attacks on Gulf shipping. First, Iraq attacked tankers loading at Iran's Kharg Island terminal with air-to-ground missiles, then Iran struck back at tankers calling at Saudi Arabia and other Arab countries.

President Reagan ordered the sale, at the end of May, of 400 Stinger antiaircraft missiles to Saudi Arabia. Shortly afterward, Saudi fighter planes shot down two Iranian planes as they approached a foreign tanker over the Gulf. The Saudis were directed to the targets by a U.S. Air Force AWAC plane.

At the same time, cheating by other members of the Organization of Petroleum Exporting Countries, competition from nonmember oil producers, and conservation efforts by consuming nations combined to drive down the world price of oil. Saudi Arabia has one-third of all known oil reserves, but falling demand and rising production outside OPEC combined to reduce its oil revenues from $120 billion in 1980 to $43 billion in 1984 to less the $25 billion in 1985, threatening the country with domestic unrest and undermining its influence in the Gulf area.

Saudi Arabia broke relations with Iran in April 1988 over the issues of riots by Iranian pilgrims in Mecca in July, 1987 and Iranian naval attacks on Saudi vessels in the Persian Gulf.

SENEGAL

Republic of Senegal
President: Abdou Diouf (1981)
Area: 75,954 sq mi. (196,722 sq km)
Population (est. mid-1989): 7,200,000 (average annual rate of natural increase: 2.6%)
Density per square mile: 95
Capital and largest city (est. 1982): Dakar, 975,000
Monetary unit: Franc CFA
Ethnic groups: Wolofs, Sereres, Peuls, Tukulers, and others
Languages: French (official); Wolof, Serer, other ethnic dialects
Religions: Islam, 91%; indigenous, 6%; Christian, 2%
National name: République du Sénegal
Literacy rate: 23%
Economic summary: Gross national product (1985): $2.4 billion. Average annual growth rate (1986): 4.5%. Per capita income (1985): $370. Land used for agriculture: 57%; labor force: 77%; principal products: peanuts, millet, corn, rice, sorghum. Major industrial products: processed food, phosphates, refined petroleum, peanut oil, fertilizer, cement, and fish. Natural resources: fish, phosphate, iron ore. Exports: peanuts, phosphate rock, canned fish. Imports: foodstuffs, consumer goods, machinery, transport equipment, petroleum. Major trading partners: France, Western European countries, African neighbors.

Geography. The capital of Senegal, Dakar, is the westernmost point in Africa. The country, slighty smaller than South Dakota, surrounds The Gambia on three sides and is bordered on the north by Mauritania, on the east by Mali, and on the south by Guinea and Guinea-Bissau.

Senegal is mainly a low-lying country, with a semidesert area in the north and northeast and forests in the southwest. The largest rivers include the Senegal in the north and the Casamance in the south tropical climate region.

Government. There is a National Assembly of 120 members, elected every five years. There is universal suffrage and a constitutional guarantee of equality before the law.

History. The Portuguese had some stations on the banks of the Senegal River in the 15th century, and the first French settlement was made at Saint-Louis about 1650. The British took parts of Senegal at various times, but the French gained possession in 1840 and organized the Sudan as a territory in 1904. In 1946, together with other parts of French West Africa, Senegal became part of the French Union. On June 20, 1960, it became an independent republic federated with the Sudanese Republic inthe Mali Federation, from which it withdrew two months later.

In 1973, Senegal joined with six other states to create the West African Economic Community.

Senegal exists in a confederation with The Gambia.

SEYCHELLES

Republic of Seychelles
President: France-Albert René (1977)
Area: 175 sq mi. (453 sq km)
Population (est. mid-1988): 100,000 (average annual rate of natural increase: 1.8%)
Density per square mile: 629
Capital: Victoria, 24,000
Monetary unit: Seychelles rupee
Languages: English and French (official); Creole
Religions: Roman Catholic, 90%; Anglican, 8%.
Member of Commonwealth of Nations
Literacy rate: 65%
Economic summary: Gross domestic product (1985): $175 million, $2,670 per capita; real growth rate (1985): 6%. Land used for agriculture: 22%; labor force: 12%; principal products: vanilla, copra, cinnamon. Labor force in industry: 55%; major products: processed copra and vanilla, coconut oil. Exports: cinnamon, vanilla, copra. Imports: food, tobacco, manufactured goods, machinery, petroleum products, textiles, transport equipment. Major trading partners: U.K., Bahrain, Japan, Pakistan, Reunion, South Africa.

Geography. Seychelles consists of an archipelago of about 100 islands in the Indian Ocean northeast of Madagascar. The principal islands are Mahé (55 sq mi.; 142 sq km), Praslin (15 sq mi.; 38 sq km), and La Digue (4 sq mi.; 10 sq km). The Aldabra, Farquhar, and Desroches groups are included in the territory of the republic.

Government. Seized from France by Britain in 1810, the Seychelles Islands remained a colony until June 29, 1976. The state is an independent republic within the Commonwealth.

On June 5, 1977, Prime Minister Albert René ousted the islands' first President, James Mancham, suspending the Constitution and the 25-member National Assembly. Mancham, whose "lavish spending" and flamboyance were cited by René in seizing power, charged that Soviet influence was at work. The new president denied this and, while more left than his predecessor, pledged to keep the Seychelles in the nonaligned group of countries.

An unsuccessful attempted coup against René attracted international attention when a group of 50 South African mercenaries posing as rugby players attacked the Victoria airport on Nov. 25, 1981. They caused extensive damage before they hijacked an Air India plane and returned to South Africa, where all but five were freed. Only after widespread international protest did the Pretoria government, which denied any responsibility for the attack, reverse the decision and order all the mercenaries tried as hijackers.

cers, but the then Prime Minister Stevens called in troops of neighboring Guinea's army, under a 1970 mutual defense pact, to guard his residence. After perfunctorily blaming the U.S. for the coup attempt, Stevens switched Governors-General, changed the Constitution, and ended up with a republic, of which he was first president. He was accused of taking "sweeping dictatorial powers," but was re-elected in 1978. Dr. Stevens' picked successor, Major-General Joseph Saidu Momoh was elected unopposed on Oct. 1, 1985.

SIERRA LEONE

Republic of Sierra Leone
President: Maj. Gen. Joseph Saidu Momoh (1985)
Area: 27,700 sq mi. (71,740 sq km)
Population (est. mid-1989): 4,100,000 (average annual rate of natural increase: 2.4%)
Density per square mile: 143.2
Capital and largest city (est. 1985): Freetown, 500,000
Monetary unit: Leone
Languages: English (official), Mende, Temne, Krio
Religions: Islam, 30%; indigenous, 30%; Christian, 10%; other, 30%
Member of Commonwealth of Nations
Literacy rate: 24%
Economic summary: Gross domestic product (FY87) $965 million, $247 per capita; real growth rate (FY87): 1.8%. Land used for agriculture: 56%; labor force: 65%; principal products: coffee, cocoa, ginger, rice. Labor force in industry: 22%; major products: diamonds, bauxite, rutile, beverages, cigarettes, construction goods. Natural resources: diamonds, bauxite, iron ore. Exports: diamonds, iron ore, palm kernels, cocoa, coffee. Imports: food, petroleum products, chemicals, machinery. Major trading partners: U.K., U.S., Western European countries, Japan.

Geography. Sierra Leone, on the Atlantic Ocean in West Africa, is half the size of Illinois. Guinea, in the north and east, and Liberia, in the south, are its neighbors.

Mangrove swamps lie along the coast, with wooded hills and a plateau in the interior. The eastern region is mountainous.

Government. Sierra Leone became an independent nation on April 27, 1961, and declared itself a republic on April 19, 1971.

Sierra Leone became a one party state under the aegis of the All People's Congress Party in April 1978.

History. The coastal area of Sierra Leone was ceded to English settlers in 1788 as a home for blacks discharged from the British armed forces and also for runaway slaves who had found asylum in London. The British protectorate over the hinterland was proclaimed in 1896.

After elections in 1967, the British Governor-General replaced Sir Albert Margai, head of SLPP, which had held power since independence, with Dr. Stevens, head of APC, as prime minister. The Army took over the government; then another coup in April 1968 restored civilian rule and put the military leaders in jail.

A coup attempt early in 1971 by the army commander was apparently foiled by loyal army offi-

SINGAPORE

Republic of Singapore
Prime Minister: Lee Kuan Yew (1959)
Area: 220 sq mi. (570 sq km)
Population (est. mid-1989): 2,700,000 (average annual rate of natural increase: 1.2%) (Chinese, 76%; Malay, 15%; Indian, 7%)
Density per square mile: 11,972
Capital (est. mid-1988): Singapore, 2,600,000
Monetary unit: Singapore dollar
Languages: Malay, Chinese (Mandarin), Tamil, English
Religions: Islam, Christian, Buddhist, Hindu, Taoist
Member of Commonwealth of Nations
Literacy rate: 86%
Economic summary: Gross national product (1987): $39.2 billion. Annual growth rate (1986-7): 3.5%. Per capita income (1987): $14,435. Land used for agriculture: 11%; labor force; 1%; principal products: poultry, hogs, vegetables, fruits. Labor force in industry: 25%; major industries: petroleum refining, ship repair, rubber processing, electronics, financial services, biotechnology. Exports: petroleum products, rubber, manufactured goods, electronics. Imports: capital equipment, manufactured goods, petroleum. Major trading partners: U.S., Japan, Malaysia, Hong Kong, Saudi Arabia, West Germany, China, Thailand.

Geography. The Republic of Singapore consists of the main island of Singapore, off the southern tip of the Malay Peninsula between the South China Sea and the Indian Ocean, and 54 nearby islands.

There are extensive mangrove swamps extending inland from the coast, which is broken by many inlets.

Government. There is a Cabinet, headed by the Prime Minister, and a Parliament of 79 members elected by universal suffrage.

The People's Action Party, led by Prime Minister Lee Kuan Yew, is the ruling political party in Parliament, holding all but two seats.

History. Singapore, founded in 1819 by Sir Stamford Raffles, became a separate crown colony of Britain in 1946, when the former colony of the Straits Settlements was dissolved. The other two settlements—Penang and Malacca—were transferred to the Union of Malaya, and the small island of Labuan was transferred to North Borneo. The Cocos (or Keeling) Islands were transferred to Australia in 1955 and Christmas Island in 1958.

Singapore attained full internal self-government in 1959. On Sept. 16, 1963, it joined Malaya, Sabah (North Borneo), and Sarawak in the Federation of Malaysia. It withdrew from the Federation on Aug. 9, 1965, and proclaimed itself a republic the next month.

SOLOMON ISLANDS

Sovereign: Queen Elizabeth II
Governor-General: Sir George Lepping (1988)
Prime Minister: Solomon Mamaloni (1989)
Area: 11,500 sq mi. (29,785 sq km)
Population (est. mid-1988): 312,196 (average annual rate of natural increase (1989 est.): 3.6%)
Density per square mile: 29
Capital and largest city (est. 1986): Honiara (on Guadalcanal), 30,499
Monetary unit: Solomon Islands dollar
Languages: English, Melanesian dialects
Religions: Anglican, 34%; Roman Catholic, 19%; South Seas Evangelical, 25%; other Protestant, 15%
Member of British Commonwealth
Literacy rate: 60%
Economic summary: Gross domestic product (1986): $115 million, $380 per capita. Principal agricultural products: copra, palm oil, rice, cocoa, yams, pigs. Major industrial products: processed fish, timber, jute, soap, canned meat, handicrafts. Natural resources: fish, timber, gold, bauxite. Exports: fish, timber, copra, palm oil. Imports: machinery and transport equipment, foodstuffs, fuel, manufactured goods. Major trading partners: Japan, Australia, U.K.

Geography. Lying east of New Guinea, this island nation consists of the southern islands of the Solomon group: Guadalcanal, Malaita, Santa Isabel, San Cristóbal, Choiseul, New Georgia, and numerous smaller islands.

Government. After 85 years of British rule, the Solomons achieved independence July 7, 1978. The Crown is represented by a Governor-General and legislative power is vested in a unicameral legislature of 38 members, led by the Prime Minister.

History. Discovered in 1567 by Alvaro de Mendana, the Solomons were not visited again for about 200 years. In 1886, Great Britain and Germany divided the islands between them. In 1914, Australian forces took over the German islands and the Solomons became an Australian mandate in 1920. In World War II, most of the islands were occupied by the Japanese. American forces landed on Guadalcanal on Aug. 7, 1942. The islands were the scene of several important U.S. naval and military victories. They are still largely undeveloped, with only 60 miles of paved road and fewer than 2,500 motor vehicles.

SOMALIA

Somali Democratic Republic
President: Maj. Gen. Mohamed Siad Barre (1969)
Prime Minister: Lt. Gen. Muhammad Ali Samator (1987)
Area: 246,199 sq mi. (637,655 sq km)
Population (est. mid-1989): 8,200,000 (average annual rate of natural increase: 2.6%)
Density per square mile: 34
Capital and largest city (est. 1982): Mogadishu, 700,000
Monetary unit: Somali shilling
Language: Somali (official), Arabic, English, Italian
Religion: Islam (Sunni)
National name: Al Jumhouriya As-Somalya al-Dimocradia
Literacy rate: 60%
Economic summary: Gross national product (1985): $1.47 billion. Average annual growth rate: 4.7%. Per capita income (1985): $250. Labor force in agriculture: 30%; principal products: livestock, bananas, sorghum, cereals, sugar cane, maize. Labor force in industry: 3%; a few small industries: sugar refining, textiles, petroleum refining. Natural resources: uranium. Exports: livestock, skins and hides, bananas. Imports: textiles, cereals, construction materials and equipment, machinery, petroleum products, transport equipment. Major trading partners: Saudi Arabia, Italy, U.S.

Geography. Somalia, situated in the Horn of Africa, lies along the Gulf of Aden and the Indian Ocean. It is bounded by Djibouti in the northwest, Ethiopia in the west, and Kenya in the southwest. In area it is slightly smaller than Texas.

Generally arid and barren, Somalia has two chief rivers, the Shebelle and the Juba.

Government. Maj. Gen. Mohamed Siad Barre took power on Oct. 21, 1969, in a coup that established a Supreme Revolutionary Council as the governing body, replacing a parliamentary government. On July 1, 1976, Barre dissolved the Council, naming its members to the Somali Socialist Party, organized that day as the nation's only legal political party. In December 1979, a 171-member People's Assembly was elected under a new Constitution adopted in August. The Assembly confirmed Barre as President for a six-year term. He was re-elected in 1986.

History. From the 7th to the 10th century, Arab and Persian trading posts were established along the coast of present-day Somalia. Nomadic tribes occupied the interior, occasionally pushing into Ethiopian territory. In the 16th century, Turkish rule extended to the northern coast and the Sultans of Zanzibar gained control in the south.

After British occupation of Aden in 1839, the Somali coast became its source of food. The French established a coaling station in 1862 at the site of Djibouti and the Italians planted a settlement in Eritrea. Egypt, which for a time-claimed Turkish rights in the area, was succeeded by Britain. By 1920, a British protectorate and an Italian protectorate occupied what is now Somalia. The British ruled the entire area after 1941, with Italy returning in 1950 to serve as United Nations trustee for its former territory.

In mid-1960, Britain and Italy granted independence to their respective sectors, enabling the two to join as the Republic of Somalia on July 1. Somalia broke diplomatic relations with Britain in 1963 when the British granted the Somali-populated Northern Frontier District of Kenya to the Republic of Kenya.

On Oct. 15, 1969, President Abdi Rashid Ali Shermarke was assassinated and the army seized power, dissolving the legislature and arresting all government leaders. Maj. Gen. Mohamed Siad Barre, as President of a renamed Somali Democratic Republic, leaned heavily toward the U.S.S.R.

In 1977, Somalia openly backed rebels in the easternmost area of Ethiopia, the Ogaden desert, which had been seized by Ethiopia at the turn of the century.

Somalia acknowledged defeat in an eight-month war against the Ethiopians, having lost much of it's 32,000-man army and most of its tanks and planes. In March 1978, the U.S. agreed to supply $7 million in food over six months, in addition to $6 million in emergency food relief provided in December. The U.S. refused to consider weapons sales, however, unless Somalia gave up all claims to northern Kenya, the Ogaden, and the Republic of Djibouti, all once claimed as "Greater Somalia." Barre refused to do this.

A U.S. announcement on Jan. 9, 1980, that bases for U.S. ships and planes in the Indian Ocean would be sought in Somalia, Oman, and Kenya, brought a request from Somalia for $1 billion worth of modern arms and an equal amount of economic aid. In August, an agreement was signed giving the U.S. use of military bases in Somalia in return for $25 million in military aid in 1981 and more in subsequent years. In 1988, guerrillas in the north went on the offensive and threatened the northern regional capital.

SOUTH AFRICA

Republic of South Africa
President: (acting): F.W. de Klerk (1989)
Area: 471,440 sq mi. (1,221,030 sq km)
Population (est. mid-1989): 38,500,000 (average annual rate of natural increase: 2.6%) (black, 68%; white, 18%; colored [mixed], 11%; Asian, 3%)
Density per square mile: 82.1[1]
Administrative capital: Pretoria
Legislative capital: Cape Town
Judicial capital: Bloemfontein
Largest cities (est. 1985): Johannesburg, 1,609,000; Cape Town, 1,912,000; Durban, 1,000,000; Pretoria, 823,000.
Monetary unit: Rand
Languages: English, Afrikaans (official); Xhosa, Zulu, other African tongues
Religions (1984): Dutch Reformed, 40%; Anglican, 11%; Roman Catholic, 8%; other Christian, 25%
National name: Republic of South Africa
Literacy rate: 99% (whites), 60-70% blacks (govt. est.)
Economic summary: Gross domestic product (1987): $60 billion, $1,700 per capita; real growth rate (1987): 2.4%. Labor force in agriculture: 30%; principal products: corn, wool, wheat, sugar cane, tobacco, citrus fruits. Labor force in industry: 36%; major products: gold, coal, diamonds, assembled automobiles, machinery, textiles, iron and steel, chemicals, fertilizer. Natural resources: gold, diamonds, platinum, uranium, coal, iron ore, asbestos, manganese. Exports: gold, wool, diamonds, corn, uranium, sugar, fruits, hides and skins, asbestos, fish products. Imports: motor vehicle parts, machinery, metals, petroleum products, chemicals, textiles. Major trading partners: U.S., West Germany, Japan, U.K., African nations.

1. Excluding Namibia (South-West Africa).

Geography. South Africa, on the continent's southern tip, is washed by the Atlantic Ocean on the west and by the Indian Ocean on the south and east. Its neighbors are South-West Africa (Namibia) in the northwest, Zimbabwe and Botswana in the north, and Mozambique and Swaziland in the northeast. The kingdom of Lesotho forms an enclave within the southeastern part of South Africa. Bophuthatswana, Transkei, Ciskei, and Venda are independent states within South Africa, which occupies an area nearly three times that of California.

The country has a high interior plateau, or veld, nearly half of which averages 4,000 feet (1,219 m) in elevation.

There are no important mountain ranges, although the Great Escarpment, separating the veld from the coastal plain, rises to over 11,000 feet (3,350 m) in the Drakensberg Mountains in the east. The principal river is the Orange, rising in Lesotho and flowing westward for 1,300 miles (2,092 km) to the Atlantic.

The southernmost point of Africa is Cape Agulhas, located in Cape Province about 100 miles (161 km) southeast of the Cape of Good Hope.

Government. A new Constitution in 1984 created a new office of Executive State President, with potentially authoritarian powers. Pieter W. Botha, Prime Minister since 1978, was sworn in as President on Sept. 14, 1984. The President has the power to act at his own discretion (e.g. appoint cabinet members) as well as power that has to exercised in consultation with the cabinet (e.g. declare war, ratify treaties).

The new Constitution brought whites, Indians, and coloreds (mixed-race) into a racially divided Parliament made up of three separate chambers for different racial groups. It provides for selection of the President by an Electoral College made up of representatives from the three chambers.

Ten "Bantustans," or black homelands, have unicameral legislatures elected by black voters.

History. The Dutch East India Company landed the first settlers on the Cape of Good Hope in 1652, launching a colony that by the end of the 18th century numbered only about 15,000. Known as Boers or Afrikaners, speaking a Dutch dialect known as Afrikaans, the settlers as early as 1795 tried to establish an independent republic.

After occupying the Cape Colony in that year, Britain took permanent possession in 1814 at the end of the Napoleonic wars, bringing in 5,000 settlers. Anglicization of government and the freeing of slaves in 1833 drove about 12,000 Afrikaners to make the "great trek" north and east into African tribal territory, where they established the republics of the Transvaal and the Orange Free State.

The discovery of diamonds in 1867 and gold nine years later brought an influx of "outlanders" into the republics and spurred Cecil Rhodes to plot annexation. Rhodes's scheme of sparking an "outlander" rebellion to which an armed party under Leander Starr Jameson would ride to the rescue misfired in 1895, forcing Rhodes to resign as prime minister of the Cape colony. What British expansionists called the "inevitable" war with the Boers eventually broke out on Oct. 11, 1899.

The defeat of the Boers in 1902 led in 1910 to the Union of South Africa, composed of four provinces, the two former republics and the old Cape and Natal colonies. Louis Botha, a Boer, became the first Prime Minister.

Jan Christiaan Smuts brought the nation into World War II on the Allied side against Nationalist opposition, and South Africa became a charter member of the United Nations in 1945, but refused to sign the Universal Declaration of Human Rights. Apartheid—racial separation—dominated domestic politics as the Nationalists gained power and imposed greater restrictions on Bantus, Coloreds, and Asians.

Afrikaner hostility to Britain triumphed in 1961 with the declaration on May 31 of the Republic of South Africa and the severing of ties with the Commonwealth. Nationalist Prime Minister H. F. Verwoerd's government in 1963 asserted the power to restrict freedom of those who opposed rigid racial laws. Three years later, amid increasing racial tension and criticism from the outside world, Verwoerd was assassinated. His Nationalist successor, Balthazar J. Vorster, launched a campaign of conciliation toward conservative black African states, offering development loans and trade concessions.

A scandal led to Vorster's resignation on June 4, 1978. Pieter W. Botha succeeded him as Prime Minister, and became President on Sept. 14, 1984.

South Africa's policy of apartheid—or racial separation—excluded the country's black majority from participation in the country's government and kept blacks at the bottom rung of the economic ladder. Protests against apartheid by militant blacks, beginning in the latter half of 1984, led to a state of emergency being declared twice, the first on July 20, 1985, covered 36 cities and towns and gave the police powers to make arrests without warrants and to detain people indefinitely. The second, declared on June 12, 1986, covered the whole nation. It gave the police a similar extension of powers and banned "subversive" press reports. It was extended for another year in June 1988.

Elections on May 7, 1987 increased the power of Botha's Nationalist party while enabling the far-right Conservative Party to replace the liberal Progressives as the official opposition. The results of the whites-only vote indicated a strong conservative reaction against Botha's policy of limited reform.

A stroke led Botha to step down as leader of his party in 1989 in favor of Frederick de Klerk. This has led to the possibility that de Klerk will succeed Botha as President when general elections take place in September 1989.

BOPHUTHATSWANA

Republic of Bophuthatswana
President: Kgosi Lucas Mangope (1977)
Area: 15,573 sq mi. (40,333 sq km)
Population (est. 1988): 1,300,000 (average annual growth rate: 2.8%)
Density per square mile: 83.5
Capital: Mmabatho
Largest city (est. 1987): Mabopane, 100,000
Monetary unit: South African rand
Languages: Setswana, English, Afrikaans
Religions: Methodist, Lutheran, Anglican, Presbyterian, Dutch Reformed, Roman Catholic, A.M.E.

Geography. Bophuthatswana consists of seven discontinuous areas within the boundaries of South Africa, most of them share a common border with Botswana.

Government. The republic has a 108-member Legislative Assembly, three quarters of whom are elected and the others appointed. President Mangope's Democratic Party is the majority party.

History. Bophuthatswana was given independence by South Africa on Dec. 6, 1977, following Transkei as the second "homeland" to be established by Pretoria. The new state and Transkei are recognized only by South Africa and each other.

Mangope, as chief minister in the pre-independence period, sought linkage of the six units into a consolidated area, but was unable to achieve his objective. A second issue, the citizenship of Tswanas in South Africa who wished to remain South African nationals, was settled by enabling them to have citizenship in South African homelands not yet independent.

About two thirds of the population of Bophuthatswana live permanently or as migrants in white areas of South Africa.

Economy. Bophuthatswana is richer than many other South African homelands, as it has more than half of the republic's platinum deposits. All foreign trade is included with South Africa's, and it is economically dependent at present on that country.

CISKEI

Republic of Ciskei
President: Chief Lennox Leslie Wongama Sebe (1981)
Area: 3,282 sq mi. (8,500 sq km)
Population (est. 1982): 675,000
Density per square mile: 205.7
Capital (est. 1980): Zwelitsha, 30,750
Largest city (est. 1981): Mdantsane, 159,000
Monetary unit: South African rand
Languages: Xhosa (official) and English
Religions: Methodist, Lutheran, Anglican, and Bantu Christian

Geography. Ciskei is surrounded by South Africa on three sides, with the Indian Ocean on the south. From a subtropical coastal strip, the land rises through grasslands to the mountainous escarpment that edges the South African interior plateau.

Government. Legislative power is vested in a National Assembly with 22 elected seats. Thirty-three hereditary chiefs complete the membership of the Assembly. The President holds executive power. South Africa's State President retains the power to legislate by proclamation and has veto power over the budget. The Ciskei National Independence Party holds all elective seats in the Assembly.

History. Oral tradition ascribes the origin of the Cape Nguni peoples to the central lakes area of Africa. They arrived in what is now Ciskei in the mid-17th century. White settlers from the Cape Colony first entered the territory a century later, but the Dutch East India Colony sought unsuccessfully to discourage white penetration. Nine wars between whites and the inhabitants, by now known as Xhosas, occurred between 1779 and 1878.

A Ciskeian territorial authority was established in 1961, with 84 chiefs and an executive council exercising limited self-government. In 1972, 20 elected members were added to the legislative assembly and a chief minister and six cabinet members elected by the assembly to function as an executive.

A proposed Constitution was approved by referendum on Oct. 30, 1980, and independence ceremonies held on Dec. 4. No government outside South Africa recognized the new state.

Economy. A subsistence agricultural economy has been superseded by commuter and migratory labor, which accounted for 64% of national income in 1977. There is some light industry and a potential for exploitation of limestone and other minerals.

NAMIBIA (SOUTH-WEST AFRICA)

Status: Mandate
Area: 318,261 sq mi. (824,296 sq km)
Population (est. 1988): 1,301,598 (average annual growth rate: 5.3%)
Density per square mile: 2
Administrator-General: Louis Pienaar (1986)
Capital (est. 1980): Windhoek, 85,000
Summer capital (est. 1980): Swakopmund, 17,500
Monetary unit: South African rand
National name: Suidwes-Afrika/Namibië; South-West Africa/Namibia
Literacy rate: 100% whites/28% non-whites
Economic summary: Gross national product (1983): $1.5 billion. Average annual growth rate (1970–85): −0.3%. Land used for agriculture: 30%; labor force: 60%;

principal products: corn, millet, sorghum, livestock. Labor force in industry: 19%; major products: canned meat, dairy products, tanned leather, textiles, clothing. Natural resources: diamonds, copper, lead, zinc, uranium, fish. Exports: diamonds, copper, lead, zinc, beef cattle, karakul pelts. Imports: construction materials, fertilizer, grain, foodstuffs. Major trading partner: South Africa.

Geography. The mandate, bounded on the north by Angola and Zambia and on the east by Botswana and South Africa, was discovered by the Portuguese explorer Diaz in the late 15th century. It is for the most part a portion of the high plateau of southern Africa with a general elevation of from 3,000 to 4,000 feet.

History. The territory became a German colony in 1884 but was taken by South African forces in 1915, becoming a South African mandate by the terms of the Treaty of Versailles in 1920.

South Africa's application for incorporation of the territory was rejected by the U.N. General Assembly in 1946 and South Africa was invited to prepare a trusteeship agreement instead. By a law passed in 1949, however, the territory was brought into much closer association with South Africa—including representation in its Parliament.

In 1969, South Africa extended its laws to the mandate over the objection of the U.N., particularly its black African members. When South Africa refused to withdraw them, the Security Council condemned it.

Under a 1974 Security Council resolution, South Africa was required to begin the transfer of power to the Namibians by May 30, 1975, or face U.N. action, but 10 days before the deadline Prime Minister Balthazar J. Vorster rejected U.N. supervision. He said, however, that his government was prepared to negotiate Namibian independence, but not with the South-West African People's Organization, the principal black separatist group. Meanwhile, the all-white legislature of South-West Africa eased several laws on apartheid in public places.

Despite international opposition, the Turnhalle Conference in Windhoek drafted a constitution to organize an interim government based on racial divisions, a proposal overwhelmingly endorsed by white voters in the territory in 1977. At the urging of ambassadors of the five Western members of the Security Council—the U.S., Britain, France, West Germany, and Canada—South Africa on June 11 announced rejection of the Turnhalle constitution and acceptance of the Western proposal to include the South-West Africa People's Organization (SWAPO) in negotiations.

Although negotiations continued between South Africa, the western powers, neighboring black African states, and internal political groups, there was still no agreement on a final independence plan. A new round of talks aimed at resolving the 18-year-old conflict ended in a stalemate on July 25, 1984. Dr. Willie van Niekerk, South Africa's Administrator-General in the territory, met in the remote Cape Verde Islands with leaders of the insurgents, including SWAPO leader Sam Nujoma, to "explore the possibilities of bringing about a cessation of violent and armed activities in South-West Africa."

As policemen wielding riot sticks charged demonstrators in a black, South-West Africa township, South Africa handed over limited powers to a new, multiracial administration in the former German colony on June 17, 1985. Installation of the new government ended South Africa's direct rule, but South Africa retained an effective veto over the new government's decisions along with responsibility for the territory's defense and foreign policy, and South Africa's efforts to quell the insurgents seeking independence continued.

An agreement between South Africa, Angola and Cuba arranged for elections for a Constituent Assembly in Nov. 1989 which will establish a new government.

TRANSKEI

Republic of Transkei
President: Chief Tutor N. Ndamase (1986)
Head of Military Council: Maj. Gen. Bantu Holomisa (1987)
Area: 15,831 sq mi. (41,002 sq km)
Population (est. 1986): 3,609,962 (growth rate: 2.2%)
Density per square mile: 151.6
Capital (est. 1989): Umtala, 57,796
Monetary unit: South African rand
Languages: English, Xhosa, Southern Sotho
Religions: Christian, 66%; tribal, 24%
Economic summary: Gross domestic product: $150 million. Per capita income: $86. Principal agricultural products: tea, corn, sorghum, dry beans. Major industrial products: timber, textiles. Natural resource: timber. Exports: timber, tea, sacks. Imports: foodstuffs, machines, equipment. Major trading partner: South Africa.

Geography. Transkei occupies three discontinuous enclaves within southeast South Africa that add up to twice the size of Massachusetts. It has a 270-mile (435 km) coastline on the Indian Ocean. The capital, Umtala, is connected by rail to the South African port of East London, 100 miles (161 km) to the southwest.

Government. Transkei was granted independence by South Africa as of Oct. 26, 1976. A constitution called for organization of a parliament composed of 77 chiefs and 75 elected members, with a ceremonial president and executive power in the hands of a prime minister.

The Organization of African States and the chairman of the United Nations Special Committee Against Apartheid denounced the new state as a sham and urged governments not to recognize it.

History. British rule was established over the Transkei region between 1866 and 1894, and the Transkeian Territories were formed in 1903. Under the Native Land Act of 1913, the Territories were reserved for black occupation. In 1963, Transkei was given internal self-government and a legislature that elected Paramount Chief Kaiser Matanzima as Chief Minister, a post he retained in elections in 1968 and 1973. Instability led to a coup in Dec. 1987.

Economy. Some 60% of Transkei is cultivated, producing corn, wheat, beans, and sorghum. Grazing is important. Some light industry has been established.

VENDA

Republic of Venda
President: Frank Ravele (1988)
Area: 2,510 sq mi. (6,500 sq km)
Population (est. 1982): 400,000 (average annual growth rate: 2.4%)
Density per square mile: 214.5
Capital: Thohoyandou

Largest town (est. 1980): Makearela, 2,500
Monetary unit: South African rand
Languages: Venda, English, Afrikaans
Religions: Christian, tribal
Economic summary: Gross domestic product: $156 million.
Per capita income: $312. Principal agricultural products:
meat, tea, fruit, sisal, corn. Major industrial products:
timber, graphite, magnetite.

Geography. Venda is composed of two noncontiguous territories in northeast South Africa with a total area of about half that of Connecticut. It is mountainous but fertile, well-watered land, with a climate ranging from tropical to subtropical.

Government. The third of South Africa's homelands to be granted independence, Venda became a separate republic on Sept. 13, 1979, unrecognized by any government other than South Africa and its sister homelands, Transkei and Bophuthatswana. The President is popularly elected. An 84-seat legislature is half elected, half appointed.

History. The first European reached Venda in 1816, but the isolation of the area prevented its involvement in the wars of the 19th century between blacks and whites and with other tribes. Venda came under South African administration after the Boer War in 1902. Limited home rule was granted in 1962. Chief Patrick R. Mphephu, leader of one of the 27 tribes that historically made up the Venda nation, became Chief Minister of the interim government in 1973 and President upon independence in 1979.

SOVIET UNION

Union of Soviet Socialist Republics
President: Mikhail S. Gorbachev (1989)
Chairman of Council of Ministers (Premier): Nikolai I.
Ryzhkov (1985)
Area: 8,649,489 sq mi. (22,402,200 sq km)
Population (est. mid-1989): 289,000,000 (average annual rate of natural increase: 1.0%) (Russian, 52%; Ukrainian, 17%; Uzbek, 5%; Byelorussian, 4%; Kazak, 3%; Tatar, 2%)
Density per square mile: 33
Capital: Moscow
Largest cities (est. 1986): Moscow, 8,714,000; Leningrad, 4,904,000; Kiev, 2,495,000; Tashkent, 2,077,000; Baku, 1,722,000; Kharkov, 1,567,000; Minsk, 1,510,-000; Gorky, 1,409,000; Novosibirsk, 1,405,000; Sverdlovsk, 1,315,000; Kuibyshev, 1,267,000; Dnepropetrovsk, 1,166,000; Tbilisi, 1,174,000; Odessa, 1,132,000; Yerevan, 1,148,000; Omsk, 1,122,-000; Chelyabinsk, 1,107,000; Donetsk, 1,081,000
Monetary unit: Ruble
Languages: *See* Population, above
Religions: Russian Orthodox (predominant), Islam, Roman Catholic, Jewish, Lutheran, atheist
National name: Soyuz Sovyetskikh Sotsialisticheskikh Respublik
Literacy rate: 99%
Economic summary: Gross national product (1986): $2,357 billion, $8,735 per capita; average annual real growth rate of GNP (1971–86): 2.5%. Land used for agriculture: 27%; labor force: 23%; principal products: wheat, rye, corn, oats, potatoes, sugar beets, cotton and flax, cattle, pigs, sheep. Labor force in industry: 77%; major products: ferrous and nonferrous metals, fuels and power, building materials, chemicals, machinery. Natural resources: fossil fuels, water power, timber, manganese, lead, zinc, nickel, mercury, potash, phosphate. Exports: petroleum and petroleum products, natural gas, machinery and equipment, manufactured goods. Imports: grain, machinery and equipment, foodstuffs, raw materials, consumer manufactures. Major trading partners: 67%, Soviet bloc; 22%, Western industrialized countries; 11% less developed countries.

Geography. The U.S.S.R. is the largest unbroken political unit in the world, occupying more than one seventh of the land surface of the globe. The greater part of its territory is a vast plain stretching from eastern Europe to the Pacific Ocean. This plain, relieved only occasionally by low mountain ranges (notably the Urals), consists of three zones running east and west: the frozen marshy tundra of the Arctic; the more temperate forest belt; and the steppes or prairies to the south, which in southern Soviet Asia become sandy deserts.

The topography is more varied in the south, particularly in the Caucasus between the Caspian and Black Seas, and in the Tien-Pamir mountain system bordering Afghanistan, Sinkiang, and Mongolia. Mountains (Stanovoi and Kolyma) and great rivers (Amur, Yenisei, Lena) also break up the sweep of the plain in Siberia.

In the west, the major rivers are the Volga, Dnieper, Don, Kama, and Southern Bug.

Government. The Soviet Union is a Communist state. The creation of a new supreme legislature—the 2,250-member Congress of Peoples Deputies—was approved at the 19th Communist Party Conference which opened on June 28, 1988. The new representative body has 1,500 members elected from territorial and national districts, and 750 deputies elected at the congresses or plenary sessions of governing bodies of party, trade union, cooperative, women, and other officially recognized organizations. All the deputies are elected for a five-year term. The first elections were held in March 1989. The Congress meets annually to decide important constitutional, political, and socioeconomic issues, and also selects the President who serves as the country's Chief Executive Officer.

The Congress of Peoples Deputies elects from its members, a small (542) standing government body—the bicameral Supreme Soviet which considers and decides all legislative, administrative, and monitoring questions. It reports to the Congress of People Deputies.

In addition, the administrative Council of Ministers carries out the daily operations of the government.

The Communist Party of the Soviet Union is the only party. It is the basic power in the country and has a membership of 19,000,000.

History. Tradition says the Viking Rurik came to Russia in A.D. 862 and founded the first Russian dynasty in Novgorod. The various tribes were united by the spread of Christianity in the 10th and 11th centuries; Vladimir "the Saint" was converted in 988. During the 11th century, the grand dukes of Kiev held such centralizing power as existed. In 1240, Kiev was destroyed by the Mongols, and the Russian territory was split into numerous smaller dukedoms, early dukes of Moscow extended their dominions through their office of tribute collector for the Mongols.

In the late 15th century, Duke Ivan III acquired

Republics of the U.S.S.R.

Republic and capital	Area sq mi.	Population est. 1986 (thousands)
Russian S.F.S.R. (Moscow)	6,593,391	144,000
Ukraine (Kiev)	233,089	50,900
Kazakhstan (Alma-Ata)	1,064,092	16,000
Byelorussia (Minsk)	80,154	10,000
Uzbekistan (Tashkent)	158,069	18,500
Georgia (Tbilsi)	26,872	5,271
Azerbaijan (Baku)	33,475	6,700
Lithuania[1] (Vilnius)	25,174	3,600
Moldavia (Kishinev)	13,012	4,100
Latvia[1] (Riga)	24,595	2,600
Kirghizia (Frunze)	76,641	4,000
Tadzhikistan (Duschambe)	55,019	4,600
Armenia (Erevan)	11,506	3,343
Turkmenistan (Ashkhabad)	188,417	3,200
Estonia[1] (Tallinn)	17,413	1,542

1. Soviet jurisdiction not recognized by the United States.

Novgorod and Tver and threw off the Mongol yoke. Ivan IV, the Terrible (1533–84), first Muscovite Tsar, is considered to have founded the Russian state. He crushed the power of rival princes and boyars (great landowners), but Russia remained largely medieval until the reign of Peter the Great (1689–1725), grandson of the first Romanov Tsar, Michael (1613–45). Peter made extensive reforms aimed at westernization and, through his defeat of Charles XII of Sweden at the Battle of Poltava in 1709, he extended Russia's boundaries to the west.

Catherine the Great (1762–96) continued Peter's westernization program and also expanded Russian territory, acquiring the Crimea and part of Poland. During the reign of Alexander I (1801–25), Napoleon's attempt to subdue Russia was defeated (1812–13), and new territory was gained, including Finland (1809) and Bessarabia (1812). Alexander originated the Holy Alliance, which for a time crushed Europe's rising liberal movement.

Alexander II (1855–81) pushed Russia's borders to the Pacific and into central Asia. Serfdom was abolished in 1861, but heavy restrictions were imposed on the emancipated class. Revolutionary strikes following Russia's defeat in the war with Japan forced Nicholas II (1894–1917) to grant a representative national body (Duma), elected by narrowly limited suffrage. It met for the first time in 1906, little influencing Nicholas in his reactionary course.

World War I demonstrated tsarist corruption and inefficiency and only patriotism held the poorly equipped army together for a time. Disorders broke out in Petrograd (now Leningrad) in March 1917, and defection of the Petrograd garrison launched the revolution. Nicholas II was forced to abdicate on March 15, 1917, and he and his family were killed by revolutionists on July 16, 1918.

A provisional government under the successive premierships of Prince Lvov and a moderate, Alexander Kerensky, lost ground to the radical, or Bolshevik, wing of the Socialist Democratic Labor Party. On Nov. 7, 1917, the Bolshevik revolution, engineered by N. Lenin[1] and Leon Trotsky, overthrew the Kerensky government and authority was vested in a Council of People's Commissars, with Lenin as Premier.

The humiliating Treaty of Brest-Litovsk (March 3, 1918) concluded the war with Germany, but civil war and foreign intervention delayed Communist control of all Russia until 1920. A brief war with Poland in 1920 resulted in Russian defeat.

The Union of Soviet Socialist Republics was established as a federation on Dec. 30, 1922.

The death of Lenin on Jan. 21, 1924, precipitated an intraparty struggle between Joseph Stalin, General Secretary of the party, and Trotsky, who favored swifter socialization at home and fomentation of revolution abroad. Trotsky was dismissed as Commissar of War in 1925 and banished from the Soviet Union in 1929. He was murdered in Mexico City on Aug. 21, 1940, by a political agent.

Stalin further consolidated his power by a series of purges in the late 1930s, liquidating prominent party leaders and military officers. Stalin assumed the premiership May 6, 1941.

Soviet foreign policy, at first friendly toward Germany and antagonistic toward Britain and France and then, after Hitler's rise to power in 1933, becoming anti-Fascist and pro-League of Nations, took an abrupt turn on Aug. 24, 1939, with the signing of a nonaggression pact with Nazi Germany. The next month, Moscow joined in the German attack on Poland, seizing territory later incorporated into the Ukrainian and Byelorussian S.S.R.'s. The war with Finland, 1939–40, added territory to the Karelian S.S.R. set up March 31, 1940; the annexation of Bessarabia and Bukovina from Romania became part of the new Moldavian S.S.R. on Aug. 2, 1940; and the annexation of the Baltic republics of Estonia, Latvia, and Lithuania in June 1940 (still unrecognized by the U.S.) created the 14th, 15th, and 16th Soviet Republics. (The number of so-called "Union" republics was reduced to 15 in 1956 when the Karelian S.S.R. became one of the 20 Autonomous Soviet Socialist Republics based on ethnic groups.)

The Soviet-German collaboration ended abruptly with a lightning attack by Hitler on June 22, 1941, which seized 500,000 square miles of Russian territory before Soviet defenses, aided by U.S. and British arms, could halt it. The Soviet resurgence at Stalingrad from November 1942 to February 1943 marked the turning point in a long battle, ending in the final offensive of January 1945.

Then, after denouncing a 1941 nonaggression pact with Japan in April 1945, when Allied forces were nearing victory in the Pacific, the Soviet Union declared war on Japan on Aug. 8, 1945, and quickly occupied Manchuria, Karafuto, and the Kurile islands.

The U.S.S.R. built a cordon of Communist states running from Poland in the north to Albania and Bulgaria in the south, including East Germany, Czechoslovakia, Hungary, and Romania, composed of the territories Soviet troops occupied at the war's end. With its Eastern front solidified, the Soviet Union launched a political offensive against the non-Communist West, moving first to block the Western access to Berlin. The Western powers countered with an airlift, completed unification of West Germany, and organized the defense of Western Europe in the North Atlantic Treaty Organization.

1. N. Lenin was the pseudonym taken by Vladimir Ilich Ulyanov. It is sometimes given as Nikolai Lenin or V.

Rulers of Russia Since 1533

Name	Born	Ruled[1]	Name	Born	Ruled[1]
Ivan IV the Terrible	1530	1533–1584	Alexander II	1818	1855–1881
Theodore I	1557	1584–1598	Alexander III	1845	1881–1894
Boris Godunov	c.1551	1598–1605	Nicholas II	1868	1894–1917[7]
Theodore II	1589	1605–1605			
Demetrius I[2]	?	1605–1606	**PROVISIONAL GOVERNMENT**		
Basil IV Shuiski	?	1606–1610[3]	**(PREMIERS)**		
"Time of Troubles"	—	1610–1613	Prince Georgi Lvov	1861	1917–1917
Michael Romanov	1596	1613–1645	Alexander Kerensky	1881	1917–1917
Alexis I	1629	1645–1676			
Theodore III	1656	1676–1682	**POLITICAL LEADERS**		
Ivan V[4]	1666	1682–1689[5]	N. Lenin	1870	1917–1924
Peter I the Great[4]	1672	1682–1725	Aleksei Rykov	1881	1924–1930
Catherine I	c.1684	1725–1727	Vyacheslav Molotov	1890	1930–1941
Peter II	1715	1727–1730	Joseph Stalin[8]	1879	1941–1953
Anna	1693	1730–1740	Georgi M. Malenkov	1902	1953–1955
Ivan VI	1740	1740–1741[6]	Nikolai A. Bulganin	1895	1955–1958
Elizabeth	1709	1741–1762	Nikita S. Khrushchev	1894	1958–1964
Peter III	1728	1762–1762	Leonid I. Brezhnev	1906	1964–1982
Catherine II the Great	1729	1762–1796	Yuri V. Andropov	1914	1982–1984
Paul I	1754	1796–1801	Konstantin U. Chernenko	1912	1984–1985
Alexander I	1777	1801–1825	Mikhail S. Gorbachev	1931	1985–
Nicholas I	1796	1825–1855			

1. For Tsars through Nicholas II, year of end of rule is also that of death, unless otherwise indicated. 2. Also known as Pseudo-Demetrius. 3. Died 1612. 4. Ruled jointly until 1689, when Ivan was deposed. 5. Died 1696. 6. Died 1764. 7. Killed 1918. 8. General Secretary of Communist Party, 1924–53.

Stalin died on March 6, 1953, and was succeeded the next day by G. M. Malenkov as Premier. His chief rivals for power—Lavrenti P. Beria (chief of the secret police), Nikolai A. Bulganin, and Lazar M. Kaganovich—were named first deputies. Beria was purged in July and executed on Dec. 23, 1953.

The new power in the Kremlin was Nikita S. Khrushchev, First Secretary of the party.

Khrushchev formalized the Eastern European system into a Council for Mutual Economic Assistance (Comecon) and a Warsaw Pact Treaty Organization as a counterweight to NATO.

In its technological race with the U.S., the Soviet Union exploded a hydrogen bomb in 1953, developed an intercontinental ballistic missile by 1957, sent the first satellite into space (Sputnik I) in 1957, and put Yuri Gagarin in the first orbital flight around the earth in 1961.

Khrushchev's downfall stemmed from his decision to place Soviet nuclear missiles in Cuba and then, when challenged by the U.S., backing down and removing the weapons. He was also blamed for the ideological break with China after 1963.

Khrushchev was forced into retirement on Oct. 15, 1964, and was replaced by Leonid I. Brezhnev as First Secretary of the Party and Aleksei N. Kosygin as Premier.

President Nixon visited the U.S.S.R. for summit talks in May 1972, concluding agreements on strategic-arms limitation and a declaration of principles on future U.S.-Soviet relations.

Presidents Gerald R. Ford and Brezhnev met in Vladivostok in November 1974 and reached tentative agreements to be incorporated into a treaty at the Geneva SALT talks in 1975. They proposed a ceiling of 2,400 ICBM's for each side, of which no more than 1,320 could have MIRV's.

President Carter, actively pursuing both human rights and disarmament, joined with the Soviet Union in September 1977 to declare that the SALT I accord, which would have expired Oct. 1 without further action, be maintained in effect while the two sides sought a new agreement (SALT II).

Brezhnev's 1977 election to the presidency followed publication of a new Constitution supplanting the one adopted in 1936. It specified the dominance of the Communist Party, previously unstated.

Carter and the ailing Brezhnev signed the SALT II treaty in Vienna on June 18, 1979, setting ceilings on each nation's arsenal of intercontinental ballistic missiles. Doubts about Senate ratification grew, and became a certainty on Dec. 27, when Soviet troops invaded Afghanistan. Despite protests from the Moslem and Western worlds, Moscow insisted that Afghan President Hafizullah Amin had asked for aid in quelling a rebellion.

In the face of evidence that Amin had been liquidated by Soviet advisers before the troops arrived, the Soviet Union vetoed a Security Council resolution on Jan. 7, 1980, that called for a withdrawal. Carter ordered a freeze on grain exports and high-technology equipment.

On Jan. 20, Carter called for a world boycott of the Summer Olympic Games scheduled for Moscow. The boycott, less than complete, nevertheless marred the first Olympics to be held in Moscow as the United States, Canada, Japan, and to a partial extent all the western allies except France and Italy shunned the event.

The Soviet Union maintained a stony defense in the face of criticism from Western Europe and the U.S., and a summit meeting of 37 Islamic nations that unanimously condemned the "imperialist invasion" of Afghanistan.

Despite the tension between Moscow and Washington, Strategic Arms Reduction Talks (START) began in Geneva between U.S. and Soviet delegations in mid-1982. Negotiations on intermediate missile reduction also continued in Geneva.

On November 10, 1982, Soviet radio and television announced the death of Leonid Brezhnev.

Yuri V. Andropov, who formerly headed the K.G.B., was chosen to succeed Brezhnev as General Secretary. By mid-June 1983, Andropov had assumed all of Brezhnev's three titles.

The Soviet Union broke off both the START talks and the parallel negotiations on European-based missiles in November 1983 in protest against the deployment of medium-range U.S. missiles in Western Europe.

After months of illness, Andropov died in February 1984. Konstantin U. Chernenko, a 72-year-old party stalwart who had been close to Brezhnev, succeeded him as General Secretary and, by mid-April, had also assumed the title of President. In the months following Chernenko's assumption of power, the Kremlin took on a hostile mood toward the West of a kind rarely seen since the height of the cold war 30 years before. Led by Moscow, all the Soviet bloc countries except Romania boycotted the 1984 Summer Olympic Games in Los Angeles—tit-for-tat for the U.S.-led boycott of the 1980 Moscow Games, in the view of most observers.

After 13 months in office, Chernenko died on March 10, 1985. He had been ill much of the time and left only a minor imprint on Soviet history.

Chosen to succeed him as Soviet leader was Mikhail S. Gorbachev, at 54 the youngest man to take charge of the Soviet Union since Stalin. Under Gorbachev, the Soviet Union began its long-awaited shift to a new generation of leadership. Unlike his immediate predecessors, Gorbachev did not also assume the title of President but wielded power from the post of party General Secretary. In a surprise move, Gorbachev elevated Andrei Gromyko, 75, for 28 years the Soviet Union's stony-faced Foreign Minister, to the largely ceremonial post of President. He installed a younger man with no experience in foreign affairs, Eduard Shevardnadze, 57, as Foreign Minister.

A new round of U.S. Soviet arms reduction negotiations began in Geneva in March 1985, this time involving three types of weapons systems—strategic, or long-range, missiles and bombers; medium-range systems in Europe, and space-based systems. In the new talks, the two sides differed sharply on how to approach the three-part negotiations, with the United States putting the focus on cuts in land-based weapons while the Soviet Union made curbing space weapons its first priority.

After months of quiet negotiations, Reagan and Gorbachev agreed to meet in Geneva on Nov. 19-20,1985—the 11th postwar meeting between the leaders of the two superpowers. Expectations for concrete results were low because the Geneva arms talks appeared to be at an impasse, with both sides repeating old slogans.

The Soviet Union took much criticism in early 1986 over the April 24 meltdown at the Chernobyl nuclear plant and its reluctance to give out any information on the accident.

In October, 1986, a potential agreement on strategic weapons reduction broke down over Soviet insistence that SDI be terminated as the price of such an agreement, but by Dec., 1987 the superpowers signed an accord eliminating medium-range missiles in Europe at the Reagan-Gorbachev summit in Washington.

In June 1987, Gorbachev obtained the support of the Central Committee for proposals that would loosen some government controls over the economy and in June, 1988, an unusually open party conference approved several resolutions for changes in the structure of the Soviet system. These included a shift of some power from the Party to local soviets, a ten-year limit on the terms of elected government and party officials, and an alteration in the office of the President to give it real power in domestic and foreign policy. Gorbachev was elected President in 1989. The elections to the Congress were the first competitive elections in the Soviet Union since 1917. Dissident candidates won a surprisingly large minority although pro-Government deputies maintained a strong lock on the Supreme Soviet.

SPAIN

Kingdom of Spain
Ruler: King Juan Carlos I (1975)
Prime Minister: Felipe González Márquez (1982)
Area: 194,885 sq mi. (504,750 km)[1]
Population (est. mid-1989): 39,200,000 (average annual growth rate: 0.5%) (Spanish, Basque, Catalan, Galician)
Density per square mile: 201
Capital: Madrid
Largest cities (est. 1987): Madrid, 3,158,800; Barcelona, 1,752,627; Valencia, 774,748; Seville, 645,817
Monetary unit: Peseta
Languages: Spanish, Basque, Catalan, Galician
Religion: Roman Catholic
National name: Reino de España
Literacy rate: 97%
Economic summary: Gross national product (1987 est.): $282.2 billion, $7,240 per capita; real growth rate (1987): 3.1%. Land used for agriculture: 62%; labor force: 19%; principal products: cereals, vegetables, citrus fruits, wine, olives and olive oil, livestock. Labor force in industry: 35%; major products: processed foods, textiles, footwear, petro-chemicals, steel, automobiles, ships. Natural resources: coal, lignite, water power, uranium, mercury, pyrites, fluorospar, gypsum, iron ore, zinc, lead, tungsten, copper. Exports: fresh fruits, iron and steel products, textiles, footwear, automobiles, fruits and vegetables, wine. Imports: machinery and transportation equipment, chemicals, fuels, automobiles, iron, steel. Major trading partners: Western European nations, U.S., Middle Eastern countries.

1. Including the Balearic and Canary Islands.

Geography. Spain occupies 85% of the Iberian Peninsula in southwestern Europe, which it shares with Portugal; France is to the northeast, separated by the Pyrenees. The Bay of Biscay lies to the north, the Atlantic Ocean to the west, and the Mediterranean Sea to the south and east; Africa is less than 10 miles (16 km) south at the Strait of Gibraltar.

A broad central plateau slopes to the south and east, crossed by a series of mountain ranges and river valleys.

Principal rivers are the Ebro in the northeast, the Tajo in the central region, and the Guadalquivir in the south.

Off Spain's east coast in the Mediterranean are the Balearic Islands (1,936 sq mi.; 5,014 sq km), the largest of which is Majorca. Sixty miles (97 km) west of Africa are the Canary Islands (2,808 sq mi.; 7,273 sq km).

Government. King Juan Carlos I (born Jan. 5, 1938) succeeded Generalissimo Francisco Franco Bahamonde as Chief of State Nov. 27, 1975.

The Cortes, or Parliament, consists of a Chamber of Deputies of 350 members and a Senate of 208, all elected by universal suffrage. The new Cortes, replacing one that was largely appointed or elected by special constituencies, was organized under a constitution adopted by referendum Dec. 6, 1978.

History. Spain, originally inhabited by Celts, Iberians and Basques, became a part of the Roman Empire in 206 B.C., when it was conquered by Scipio Africanus. In A.D. 412, the barbarian Visigothic leader Ataulf crossed the Pyrenees and ruled Spain, first in the name of the Roman emperor and then independently. In 711, the Moslems under Tariq entered Spain from Africa and within a few years completed the subjugation of the country. In 732, the Franks, led by Charles Martel, defeated the Moslems near Poitiers, thus preventing the further expansion of Islam in southern Europe. Internal dissension of Spanish Islam invited a steady Christian conquest from the north.

Aragon and Castile were the most important Spanish states from the 12th to the 15th century, consolidated by the marriage of Ferdinand II and Isabella I in 1469. The last Moslem stronghold, Granada, was captured in 1492. Roman Catholicism was established as the official state religion and the Jews (1492) and the Moslems (1502) expelled.

In the era of exploration, discovery, and colonization, Spain amassed tremendous wealth and a vast colonial empire through the conquest of Peru by Pizarro (1532–33) and of Mexico by Cortés (1519–21). The Spanish Hapsburg monarchy became for a time the most powerful in the world. In 1588, Philip II sent his Invincible Armada to invade England, but its destruction cost Spain its supremacy on the seas and paved the way for England's colonization of America. Spain then sank rapidly to the status of a second-rate power and never again played a major role in European politics. Its colonial empire in the Americas and the Philippines vanished in wars and revolutions during the 18th and 19th centuries.

In World War I, Spain maintained a position of neutrality. In 1923, Gen. Miguel Primo de Rivera became dictator. In 1930, King Alfonso XIII revoked the dictatorship, but a strong antimonarchist and republican movement led to his leaving Spain in 1931. The new Constitution declared Spain a workers' republic, broke up the large estates, separated church and state, and secularized the schools. The elections held in 1936 returned a strong Popular Front majority, with Manuel Azaña as President.

On July 18, 1936, a conservative army officer in Morocco, Francisco Franco Bahamonde, led a mutiny against the government. The civil war that followed lasted three years and cost the lives of nearly a million people. Franco was aided by Fascist Italy and Nazi Germany, while Soviet Russia helped the Loyalist side. Several hundred leftist Americans served in the Abraham Lincoln Brigade on the side of the republic. The war ended when Franco took Madrid on March 28, 1939.

Franco became head of the state, national chief of the Falange Party (the governing party), and Premier and Caudillo (leader). In a referendum in 1947, the Spanish people approved a Franco-drafted succession law declaring Spain a monarchy again. Franco, however, continued as Chief of State.

In 1969, Franco and the Cortes designated Prince Juan Carlos Alfonso Victor María de Borbón (who married Princess Sophia of Greece on May 14, 1962) to become King of Spain when the provisional government headed by Franco came to an end. He is the grandson of Alfonso XIII and the son of Don Juan, pretender to the throne.

Franco died of a heart attack on Nov. 20, 1975, after more than a year of ill health, and Juan Carlos was proclaimed King seven days later.

Over strong rightist opposition, the government legalized the Communist Party in advance of the 1977 elections. Premier Adolfo Suaraz Gonzalez's Union of the Democratic Center, a coalition of a dozen centrist and rightist parties, claimed 34.3% of the popular vote in the election.

Under pressure from Catalonian and Basque nationalists, Suárez granted home rule to these regions in 1979, but centrists backed by him did poorly in the 1980 elections for local assemblies in the two areas. Economic problems persisted, along with new incidents of terrorism, and Suárez resigned on Jan. 29, 1981 and was succeded by Leopoldo Calvo Sotelo.

With the overwhelming election of Prime Minister Felipe González Márquez and his Spanish Socialist Workers Party in the Oct. 20, 1982, parliamentary elections, the Franco past was finally buried. The thrust of Gonzalez, a pragmatic moderate, was to modernize rather than radicalize Spain. As promised, the Socialists did not carry out widespread nationalization of private industry, but did seek to nationalize the high-tension power grid.

A treaty admitting Spain, along with Portugal, to the European Economic Community was to take effect on Jan. 1, 1986. Later that year, in June, Spain voted to remain in NATO, but outside of its military command and Gonzalez's Socialists retained their majority in national elections.

SRI LANKA

Democratic Socialist Republic of Sri Lanka
President: Ranasinghe Premadasa (1988)
Prime Minister: Hondoval D. B. Wijetunga (1989)
Area: 25,332 sq mi. (65,610 sq km)
Population (est. mid-1989): 16,900,000 (average annual rate of natural increase: 1.6%)
Density per square mile: 666
Capital: Sri Jayewardenepura Kotte (Colombo)
Largest cities (est. 1984): Colombo, 664,000; Dehiwela, 188,000; Moratuwa, 138,000; Jaffna, 138,000
Monetary unit: Sri Lanka rupee
Languages: Sinhala, Tamil, English
Religions: Buddhist, 69%; Hindu, 15%; Islam, 8%; Christian, 8%
Member of Commonwealth of Nations
Literacy rate: 87%
Economic summary: Gross domestic product (1988): $7.1 billion. Average annual growth rate (1987): 4.5%. Per capita income (1988): $430. Land used for agriculture: 25%; labor force: 53%; principal products: tea, coconuts, rubber, rice, spices. Labor force in industry: 15%; major products: consumer goods, textiles, chemicals, paper and paper products. Natural resources: limestone, graphite, gems. Exports: textiles, tea, rubber, petroleum products, gems and jewelry. Imports: petroleum, machinery, transport equipment, sugar. Major trading partners: Egypt, Iraq, Saudi Arabia, U.S., U.K., West Germany, Japan, Singapore, India.

Geography. An island in the Indian Ocean off the southeast tip of India, Sri Lanka is about half the size of Alabama. Most of the land is flat and rolling;

mountains in the south central region rise to over 8,000 feet (2,438 m).

Government. Ceylon became an independent country in 1948 after British rule and reverted to the traditional name (resplendent island) on May 22, 1972. A new Constitution was adopted in 1978, replacing that of 1972.

The new Constitution set up the National State Assembly, a 168-member unicameral legislature that serves for six years unless dissolved earlier.

History. Following Portuguese and Dutch rule, Ceylon became an English crown colony in 1798. The British developed coffee, tea, and rubber plantations and granted six Constitutions between 1798 and 1924. The Constitution of 1931 gave a large measure of self-government.

Ceylon became a self-governing dominion of the Commonwealth of Nations in 1948.

Presidential elections were held in December 1982, and won by J.R. Jayewardene.

Tension between the Tamil minority and the Sinhalese majority continued to build and erupted in bloody violence in 1983 that has grown worse since. There are about 2.6 million Tamils in Sri Lanka, while the Sinhalese make up about three-quarters of the 16-million population. Tamil extremists are fighting for a separate nation.

Negotiations broke down in late 1986. A string of Tamil atrocities in early 1987 brought on a government offensive in May-June against guerilla base areas. Although it was largely successful, the increased intensity of the civil war dimmed hopes for a settlement.

An accord signed in July, 1987, between Jayewardene and Prime Minister Gandhi of India called for: the disarming of Tamil militants, amnesty for Tamil guerrillas, Tamil and English to share official status with Sinhala, greater political autonomy for Tamil-dominated areas, the closure of Tamil bases in India and an Indian peacekeeping force to help guarantee the accord. This led to fighting between Indian troops and Tamils in the north and violence by extreme Sinhala nationalists in the south.

SUDAN

Republic of the Sudan
Prime Minister: Brig. Omar Hassam Ahmed Bashir (1989)
Area: 967,491 sq mi. (2,505,802 sq km)
Population (est. mid-1989): 24,500,000 (average annual rate of natural increase: 2.8%)
Density per square mile: 25
Capital: Khartoum
Largest cities (est. 1988): Khartoum, 817,000; Omdurman, 527,000; Port Sudan, 207,000
Monetary unit: Sudanese pound
Languages: Arabic, English, tribal dialects
Religions: Islam, 73%; Animist, 18%; Christian, 9%
National name: Jamhuryat.es-Sudan
Literacy rate: 20%
Economic summary: Gross domestic product (1985): $4.55 billion, $200 per capita. Average annual growth rate (1970–79): 1.5%. Land used for agriculture: 29%; labor force: 80%; principal products: cotton, peanuts, sesame seeds, gum arabic, sorghum, wheat, beans, barley. Labor force in industry: 10%; major products: cement, textiles,

pharmaceuticals, shoes, processed foods. Natural resources: some iron ore, copper, chrome, industrial metals. Exports: cotton, peanuts, gum arabic, groundnuts. Imports: textiles, petroleum products, vehicles, tea, wheat. Major trading partners: U.K., West Germany, Saudi Arabia, U.S., Netherlands, France.

Geography. The Sudan, in northeast Africa, is the largest country on the continent, measuring about one fourth the size of the United States. Its neighbors are Chad and the Central African Republic on the west, Egypt and Libya on the north, Ethiopia on the east, and Kenya, Uganda, and Zaire on the south. The Red Sea washes about 500 miles of the eastern coast.

The country extends from north to south about 1,200 miles (1,931 km) and west to east about 1,000 miles (1,609 km). The northern region is a continuation of the Libyan Desert. The southern region is fertile, abundantly watered, and, in places, heavily forested. It is traversed from north to south by the Nile, all of whose great tributaries are partly or entirely within its borders.

Government. A multi-party democracy was established. Elections were held in April, 1986.

The three main parties in the 264-seat Parliament are the National Islamic Front (51 seats), Umma Party (99 seats) and the Democratic Unionist Party (63 seats). They formed a consensus government in May 1988.

History. The early history of the Sudan (known as the Anglo-Egyptian Sudan between 1898 and 1955) is linked with that of Nubia, where a powerful local kingdom was formed in Roman times with its capital at Dongola. After conversion to Christianity in the 6th century, it joined with Ethiopia and resisted Mohammedanization until the 14th century. Thereafter the area was broken up into many small states until 1820–22, when it was conquered by Mohammed Ali, Pasha of Egypt. Egyptian forces were evacuated during the Mahdist revolt (1881–98), but the Sudan was reconquered by the Anglo-Egyptian expeditions of 1896–98, and in 1899 became an Anglo-Egyptian condominium, which was reaffirmed by the Anglo-Egyptian treaty of 1936.

Egypt and Britain agreed in 1953 to grant self-government to the Sudan under an appointed Governor-General. An all-Sudanese Parliament was elected in November-December 1953, and an all-Sudanese government was formed. In December 1955, the Parliament declared the independence of the Sudan, which, with the approval of Britain and Egypt, was proclaimed on Jan. 1, 1956.

In October 1969, Maj. Gen. Gaafar Mohamed Nimeiri, the president of the Council for the Revolution, took over as prime minister. He was elected the nation's first president in 1971.

In 1976, a third coup was attempted against Nimeiri. Nimeiri accused President Muammar el Qaddafi of Libya of having instigated the attempt and broke relations with Libya.

On April 6, 1985, while out of the country on visits to the United States and Egypt, Nimeiry lost power on April 6, 1985, in the same way he gained it 16 years previously—by a military coup headed by his Defense Minister, Gen. Abdel Rahman Siwar el-Dahab.

Among the problems that the new government faced were a debilitating civil war with rebels in the south of the country, other sectarian and tribal conflicts, and the famine that affected more than four million Sudanese.

The government's inability to cope with the war led to disaffections within the army and a military coup in June 1989. The new leader, Brigadier Bashir, dissolved the constitution, parliament and all political parties.

SURINAME

Republic of Suriname
President: Ramsewak Shankar (1988)
Vice President and Prime Minister: Henck Aaron (1988)
Area: 63,251 sq mi. (163,820 sq km)
Population (est. mid-1989): 400,000 (average annual rate of natural increase: 2.1%) (Indo-Pakistani, 37%; Creole, 31%; Indonesian, 15%; Bush Negro, 10%)
Density per square mile: 6.3
Capital and largest city (est. 1982): Paramaribo, 100,000
Monetary unit: Suriname guilder
Languages: Dutch, Surinamese (lingua franca), English also widely spoken
Religions: Protestant, Roman Catholic, Hindu, Islam
Literacy rate: 65%
Economic summary: Gross domestic product (1986): $904 million, $2,290 per capita; real growth rate (1986): −2.0%. Land used for agriculture: 0.3%; labor force: 11%; principal products: rice. Labor force in industry: 15%; major products: aluminum, alumina, processed foods, lumber. Natural resources: bauxite, iron ore, timber, fish, shrimp. Exports: bauxite, alumina, aluminum, rice, shrimp, lumber and wood products. Imports: capital equipment, petroleum, iron and steel, cotton, flour, meat, dairy products. Major trading partners: U.S., Trinidad, Netherlands, Norway.

Geography. Suriname lies on the northeast coast of South America, with Guyana to the west, French Guiana to the east, and Brazil to the south. It is about one tenth larger than Michigan. The principal rivers are the Corantijn on the Guyana border, the Marowijne in the east, and the Suriname, on which the capital city of Paramaribo is situated. The Tumuc-Humac Mountains are on the border with Brazil.

Government. Suriname, formerly known as Dutch Guiana, became an independent republic on Nov. 25, 1975. Elections in November 1987 gave the Front for Democracy and Development coalition an overwhelming majority in the 51-seat National Assembly. The coalition elected Shankar and Aaron as President and Vice-President in January, 1988.

A draft constitution approved in September, 1987, gave the military a continuing behind-the-scenes role in the government.

History. England established the first European settlement on the Suriname River in 1650 but transferred sovereignty to the Dutch in 1667 in the Treaty of Breda, by which the British acquired New York. Colonization was confined to a narrow coastal strip, and until the abolition of slavery in 1863, African slaves furnished the labor for the plantation economy. After 1870, laborers were imported from British India and the Dutch East Indies.

In 1948, the colony was integrated into the Kingdom of the Netherlands and two years later was granted full home rule in other than foreign affairs and defense. After race rioting over unemployment and inflation, the Netherlands offered complete independence in 1973. Henck A. E. Aaron,

leader of a coalition of Creole (Surinamese of African descent) parties, advocated independence, while Jaggernath Lachmon, leader of the Surinamese of East Indian descent, urged delay.

Aaron retained power in the first post-independence elections in 1977. He had promised early elections when Army sergeants and a lieutenant staged a coup on Feb. 25 and installed a civilian, Dr. Henk R. Chin A Sen, as Prime Minister. A subsequent military intervention made Henk Chin A Sen president, abolishing the legislature and instituting a military government.

In mid-1986, Ronnie Brunswijk, a former army private, began a guerilla insurgency in eastern Suriname.

SWAZILAND

Kingdom of Swaziland
Ruler: King Mswati III (1986)
Prime Minister: Sotsha Dlamini (1986)
Area: 6,704 sq mi. (17,363 sq km)
Population (est. mid-1989): 800,000 (average annual rate of natural increase: 3.4%)
Density per square mile: 114
Capital (est. 1986): Mbabane, 40,000
Monetary unit: Lilangeni
Languages: English and Swazi (official)
Religions: Christian, 77%; Animist, 27%
Member of Commonwealth of Nations
Literacy rate (1985): 68%
Economic summary: Gross national product (1986 est.): $478 million, $690 per capita; real growth rate (1986 est.): 10%. Land used for agriculture: 75%; labor force: 36%; principal products: corn, livestock, sugar cane, citrus fruits, cotton, rice, pineapples. Labor force in industry: 25%; major products: milled sugar, ginned cotton, processed meat and wood. Natural resources: asbestos, diamonds. Exports: sugar, wood products, iron ore, asbestos, citrus fruits, cotton. Imports: motor vehicles, fuels and lubricants, foodstuffs, chemicals. Major trading partners: South Africa, U.K., U.S.

Geography. Swaziland, 85% the size of New Jersey, is surrounded by South Africa and Mozambique. The country consists of a high veld in the west and a series of plateaus descending from 6,000 feet (1,829 m) to a low veld of 1,500 feet (457 m).

Government. In 1967, a new Constitution established King Sobhuza II as head of state and provided for an Assembly of 24 members elected by universal suffrage, together with a Senate of 12 members—half appointed by the Assembly and half by the King. In 1973, the King renounced the Constitution, suspended political parties, and took total power for himself. In 1977, he replaced the Parliament with an assembly of tribal leaders. The Parliament reconvened in 1979.

History. Bantu peoples migrated southwest to the area of Mozambique in the 16th century. A number of clans broke away from the main body in the 18th century and settled in Swaziland. In the 19th century they organized as a tribe, partly because they were in constant conflict with the Zulu. Their ruler, Mswazi, applied to the British in the 1840s for help against the Zulu. The British and the Transvaal governments guaranteed the independence of Swaziland in 1881.

South Africa held Swaziland as a protectorate from 1894 to 1899, but after the Boer War, in 1902, Swaziland was transferred to British administration. The Paramount Chief was recognized as the native authority in 1941.

In 1963, the territory was constituted a protectorate, and on Sept. 6, 1968, it became the independent nation of Swaziland.

King Sobhuza died in August 1982.

SWEDEN

Kingdom of Sweden
Sovereign: King Carl XVI Gustaf (1973)
Prime Minister: Ingvar Carlsson (1986)
Area: 173,800 sq mi. (449,964 sq km)
Population (est. mid-1989): 8,500,000 (average annual rate of natural increase: 0.2%)
Density per square mile: 49
Capital: Stockholm
Largest cities (est. 1986): Stockholm, 1,435,000; Göteborg, 704,000; Malmö, 458,000
Monetary unit: Krona
Language: Swedish
Religion: Swedish Lutheran, 95%
National name: Konungariket Sverige
Literacy rate: 99.5%
Economic summary: Gross domestic product (1986): $105.5 billion, $12,590 per capita; growth rate (1986): 1.4%. Labor force in agriculture: 5%. Principal agricultural products: dairy products, grains, sugar beets, potatoes, wood. Labor force in industry: 31%; major products: machinery, instruments, metal products, automobiles. Natural resources: forests, iron ore, hydroelectric power, unmined uranium. Exports: machinery, motor vehicles, wood pulp, paper products, iron and steel products. Imports: machinery, petroleum, yarns, foodstuffs, iron and steel, chemicals. Major trading partners: Norway, West Germany, U.K., Denmark, Finland, U.S.

Geography. Sweden occupies the eastern part of the Scandinavian peninsula, with Norway to the west, Finland and the Gulf of Bothnia to the east, and Denmark and the Baltic Sea in the south. It is one tenth larger than California.

The country slopes eastward and southward from the Kjölen Mountains along the Norwegian border, where the peak elevation is Kebnekaise at 6,965 feet (2,123 m) in Lapland. In the north are mountains and many lakes. To the south and east are central lowlands and south of them are fertile areas of forest, valley, and plain.

Along Sweden's rocky coast, chopped up by bays and inlets, are many islands, the largest of which are Gotland and Oland.

Government. Sweden is a constitutional monarchy. Under the 1975 Constitution, the Riksdag is the sole governing body. The prime minister is the political chief executive.

In 1967, agreement was reached on part of a new Constitution after 13 years of work. It provided for a single-house Riksdag of 350 members (later amended to 349 seats) to replace the 104-year old bicameral Riksdag. The members are popularly elected for three years. Ninety-two present members of the Riksdag are women.

The King, Carl XVI Gustaf, was born April 30, 1946, and succeeded to the throne Sept. 19, 1973, on the death at 90 of his grandfather, Gustaf VI Adolf. Carl Gustaf was married on June 19, 1976, to Silvia Sommerlath, a West German commoner. They have three children: Princess Victoria, born July 14, 1977; Prince Carl Philip, born May 13,

1979; and Princess Madeleine, born June 10, 1982. Under the new Act of Succession, effective Jan. 1, 1980, the first child of the reigning monarch, regardless of sex, is heir to the throne.

History. The earliest historical mention of Sweden is found in Tacitus' *Germania*, where reference is made to the powerful king and strong fleet of the Suiones. Toward the end of the 10th century, Olaf Sköttkonung established a Christian stronghold in Sweden. Around 1400, an attempt was made to unite the northern nations into one kingdom, but this led to bitter strife between the Danes and the Swedes.

In 1520, the Danish King, Christian II, conquered Sweden and in the "Stockholm Bloodbath" put leading Swedish personalities to death. Gustavus Vasa (1523–60) broke away from Denmark and fashioned the modern Swedish state.

Sweden played a leading role in the second phase (1630–35) of the Thirty Years' War (1618–48). By the Treaty of Westphalia (1648), Sweden obtained western Pomerania and some neighboring territory on the Baltic. In 1700, a coalition of Russia, Poland, and Denmark united against Sweden and by the Peace of Nystad (1721) forced it to relinquish Livonia, Ingria, Estonia, and parts of Finland.

Sweden emerged from the Napoleonic Wars with the acquisition of Norway from Denmark and with a new royal dynasty stemming from Marshal Jean Bernadotte of France, who became King Charles XIV (1818–44). The artificial union between Sweden and Norway led to an uneasy relationship, and the union was finally dissolved in 1905.

Sweden maintained a position of neutrality in both World Wars.

An elaborate structure of welfare legislation, imitated by many larger nations, began with the establishment of old-age pensions in 1911. Economic prosperity based on its neutralist policy enabled Sweden, together with Norway, to pioneer in public health, housing, and job security programs.

Forty-four years of Socialist government were ended in 1976 with the election of a conservative coalition headed by Thorbjörn Fälldin, a 50-year-old sheep farmer.

Fälldin resigned on Oct. 5, 1978, when his conservative parties partners demanded less restrictions on nuclear power, and his successor, Ola Ullsten, resigned a year later after failing to achieve a consensus on the issue. Returned to office by his coalition partners, Fälldin said he would follow the course directed by a national referendum. On March 23, 1980, voters backed the development of 12 nuclear plants and use of them for at least 25 years to supply 40% of national energy needs while the search for alternative sources continued.

Olof Palme and the Socialists were returned to power in the election of 1982.

In February 1986, Palme was killed by an unknown assailant. His death shocked the world. His assailant was arrested in 1989.

SWITZERLAND

Swiss Confederation
President: Jean-Pascal Delamuraz (1989)
Vice President: Arnold Koller (1989)
Area: 15,941 sq mi. (41,288 sq km)
Population (est. mid-1989): 6,600,000 (average annual

rate of natural increase: 0.3%) (Swiss, 85%; Italian, 8%; German, 2%; Spanish, 2%; French, 1%—figures by place of birth)
Density per square mile: 414.0
Capital: Bern
Largest cities (est. 1988): Zurich, 346,879; Basel, 171,574; Geneva, 161,473; Bern, 136,292; Lausanne, 124,022
Monetary unit: Swiss franc
Languages: German, 65%; French, 18%; Italian, 10%; Romansch, 1%
Religions: Roman Catholic, 48%; Protestant, 44%
National name: Schweiz/Suisse/Svizzera/Svizra
Literacy rate: 99.5%
Economic summary: Gross national product (1987): $178.6 billion. Average annual growth rate (1987): 4.5%. Per capita income (1987): $16,981. Land used for agriculture: 26%; labor force: 6%; principal products: cheese and other dairy products, livestock, fruits, grains, wine. Labor force in industry: 39%; major products: watches and clocks, precision instruments, machinery, chemicals, pharmaceuticals, textiles, generators, turbines. Natural resources: water power, timber, salt. Exports: electrical machinery, chemicals, precision instruments, textiles, foodstuffs, textile yarns, dyestuffs, chemicals. Imports: transport equipment, metals and metal products, foodstuffs, chemicals, textile yarns. Major trading partners: West Germany, France, U.S., Italy, U.K., Japan

Geography. Switzerland, in central Europe, is the land of the Alps. Its tallest peak is the Dufourspitze at 15,203 feet (4,634 m) on the Swiss side of the Italian border, one of 10 summits of the Monte Rose massif in the Apennines. The tallest peak in all of the Alps, Mont Blanc (15,771 ft; 4,807 m), is actually in France.

Most of Switzerland comprises a mountainous plateau bordered by the great bulk of the Alps on the south and by the Jura Mountains on the northwest. About one fourth of the total area is covered by mountains and glaciers.

The country's largest lakes—Geneva, Constance (Bodensee), and Maggiore—straddle the French, German-Austrian, and Italian borders, respectively.

The Rhine, navigable from Basel to the North Sea, is the principal inland waterway. Other rivers are the Aare and the Rhône.

Switzerland, twice the size of New Jersey, is surrounded by France, West Germany, Austria, Liechtenstein, and Italy.

Government. The Swiss Confederation consists of 23 sovereign cantons, of which three are divided into six half-cantons. Federal authority is vested in a bicameral legislature. The Ständerat, or State Council, consists of 46 members, two from each canton. The lower house, the Nationalrat, or National Council, has 200 deputies, elected for four-year terms.

Executive authority rests with the Bundesrat, or Federal Council, consisting of seven members chosen by parliament. The parliament elects the President, who serves for one year and is succeeded by the Vice President. The federal government regulates foreign policy, railroads, postal service, and the national mint. Each canton reserves for itself important local powers.

A constitutional amendment adopted in 1971 by referendum gave women the vote in federal elections and the right to hold federal office. An equal rights amendment was passed in a national referendum June 14, 1981, barring discrimination against women under canton as well as federal law.

History. Called Helvetia in ancient times, Switzerland in the Middle Ages was a league of cantons of the Holy Roman Empire. Fashioned around the nucleus of three German forest districts of Schwyz, Uri, and Unterwalden, the Swiss Confederation slowly added new cantons. In 1648 the Treaty of Westphalia gave Switzerland its independence from the Holy Roman Empire.

French revolutionary troops occupied the country in 1798 and named it the Helvetic Republic, but Napoleon in 1803 restored its federal government. By 1815, the French- and Italian-speaking peoples of Switzerland had been granted political equality.

In 1815, the Congress of Vienna guaranteed the neutrality and recognized the independence of Switzerland. In the revolutionary period of 1847, the Catholic cantons seceded and organized a separate union called the *Sonderbund.* In 1848 the new Swiss Constitution established a union modeled upon that of the U.S. The Federal Constitution of 1874 established a strong central government while maintaining large powers of control in each canton.

National unity and political conservatism grew as the country prospered from its neutrality. Its banking system became the world's leading repository for international accounts. Strict neutrality was its policy in World Wars I and II. Geneva was the seat of the League of Nations (later the European headquarters of the United Nations) and of a number of international organizations.

In 1971, the Swiss Supreme Court ruled that Swiss banks must show U.S. tax officials records of U.S. citizens suspected of tax fraud, thus significantly modifying a 1934 law that had seemed to forbid any bank disclosures.

SYRIA

Syrian Arab Republic
President: Hafez al-Assad (1971)
Premier: Mahmoud al-Zubi (1987)
Area: 71,498 sq mi. (185,180 sq km)
Population (est. mid-1989): 12,100,000 (average annual rate of natural increase: 3.8%)
Density per square mile: 169
Capital: Damascus
Largest cities (est. 1987): Damascus, 1,292,000; Aleppo, 1,216,000; Homs, 431,000; Hama, 214,000; Latakia, 241,000
Monetary unit: Syrian pound
Language: Arabic
Religions: Islam, 90%; Christian, 10%
National name: Al-Jamhouriya al Arabiya As-Souriya
Literacy rate: 55%
Economic summary: Gross domestic product (1985): $20.3 billion, $1,970 per capita; real growth rate (1985): 0.7%. Land used for agriculture: 76%; labor force: 29%; principal products: Cotton, wheat, barley, tobacco, sheep, goats. Labor force in industry: 32%; major products: textiles, cement, petroleum, processed food. Natural resources: chrome, manganese, asphalt, iron ore, rock salt, phosphate, oil, natural gas. Exports: petroleum, textiles, tobacco. Imports: machinery and metal products, fuels, foodstuffs. Major trading partners: Italy, Romania, U.S.S.R., U.S., Iran, Libya, France, West Germany.

Geography. Slightly larger than North Dakota, Syria lies at the eastern end of the Mediterranean

Sea. It is bordered by Lebanon and Israel on the west, Turkey on the north, Iraq on the east, and Jordan on the south.

Coastal Syria is a narrow plain, in back of which is a range of coastal mountains, and still farther inland a steppe area. In the east is the Syrian Desert, and in the south is the Jebel Druze Range. The highest point in Syria is Mount Hermon (9,232 ft; 2,814 m) on the Lebanese border.

Government. Syria's first permanent Constitution was approved in 1973, replacing a provisional charter that had been in force for 10 years. It provided for an elected People's Council as the legislature.

In the first election in 10 years, in 1973, the Ba'ath Arab Socialist Party of President Hafez al-Assad, running on a unified National Progressive ticket with the Communist and Socialist parties, won 70% of the vote and a commensurate proportion of the seats in the People's Assembly. In 1977 and 1981 elections, the ruling Ba'athists won by similar margins.

History. Ancient Syria was conquered by Egypt about 1500 B.C., and after that by Hebrews, Assyrians, Chaldeans, Persians, and Greeks. From 64 B.C. until the Arab conquest in A.D. 636, it was part of the Roman Empire except during brief periods. The Arabs made it a trade center for their extensive empire, but it suffered severely from the Mongol invasion in 1260 and fell to the Ottoman Turks in 1516. Syria remained a Turkish province until World War I.

A secret Anglo-French pact of 1916 put Syria in the French zone of influence. The League of Nations gave France a mandate over Syria after World War I, but the French were forced to put down several nationalist uprisings. In 1930, France recognized Syria as an independent republic, but still subject to the mandate. After nationalist demonstrations in 1939, the French High Commissioner suspended the Syrian Constitution. In 1941, British and Free French forces invaded Syria to eliminate Vichy control. During the rest of World War II, Syria was an Allied base.

Again in 1945, nationalist demonstrations broke into actual fighting, and British troops had to restore order. Syrian forces met a series of reverses while participating in the Arab invasion of Palestine in 1948. In 1958, Egypt and Syria formed the United Arab Republic, with Gamal Abdel Nasser of Egypt as President. However, Syria became independent again on Sept. 29, 1961, following a revolution.

In the war of 1967, Israel quickly vanquished the Syrian army. Before acceding to the U.N. ceasefire, the Israeli forces took over control of the fortified Golan Heights commanding the Sea of Galilee.

Syria joined Egypt in attacking Israel in October 1973 in the fourth Arab-Israeli war, but was pushed back from initial successes on the Golan Heights to end up losing more land. However, in the settlement worked out by U.S. Secretary of State Henry A. Kissinger in 1974, the Syrians recovered all the territory lost in 1973 and a token amount of territory, including the deserted town of Quneitra, lost in 1967.

Syrian troops, in Lebanon since 1976 as part of an Arab peacekeeping force whose other members subsequently departed, intervened increasingly during 1980 and 1981 on the side of Moslem Lebanese in their clashes with Christian militants supported by Israel. When Israeli jets shot down Syrian helicopters operating in Lebanon in April 1981, Syria moved Soviet-built surface-to-air (SAM 6) missiles into Lebanon's Bekaa Valley. Israel demanded that the missiles be removed because they violated a 1976 understanding between the governments. The demand, backed up by bombing raids, prompted the Reagan Administration to send veteran diplomat Philip C. Habib as a special envoy to avert a new conflict between the nations.

Habib's carefully engineered cease-fire was shattered by a new Israeli invasion in June 1982, when Israeli aircraft bombed Bekaa Valley missile sites, claiming to destroy all of them along with 25 Syrian planes that had sought to defend the sites. On the ground, Syrian army units were driven back by Israeli armor along the Lebanese coast. The Syrians, who were equipped with Soviet weapons, were outfought everywhere by U.S.-equipped Israelis.

Nevertheless, while the Israelis overran most of the rest of Lebanon, the Syrians retained their positions in the Bekaa Valley. Over the next three years, as the Israelis gradually withdrew their forces, the Syrians remained. As the various Lebanese factions fought each other, the Syrians became the dominant force in the country, both militarily and politically.

The extent of Syrian influence in Lebanaon was demonstrated dramatically after Lebanese Shiite extremists hijacked a TWA airliner from Athens to Beirut on June 14, 1985. President al-Assad played the key role in delicate, many-sided negotiations that obtained the release of the 39 American hostages from the plane 17 days later.

TAIWAN

Republic of China
President: Lee Teng-hui (1988)
Premier: Yu Kuo-hwa
Area: 13,895 sq mi. (35,988 sq km)
Population (est. mid-1989): 20,000,000 (average annual rate of natural increase: 1.1%)
Density per square mile: 1,604
Capital: Taipei
Largest cities (est. 1986): Taipei, 2,507,620; Kaohsiung, 1,302,849; Taichung, 674,936; Tainan, 639,888; Chilung (Keelung), 351,524
Monetary unit: New Taiwan dollar
Languages: Chinese (Mandarin) and various dialects
Religions: Chinese Folk, 49%; Buddhist, 43%; Christian, 7%
Literacy rate: 92%
Economic summary: Gross national product (1986): $72.8 billion. Real growth rate (1985–7): 8.0%. Per capita income (1986): $3,750. Land used for agriculture: 30%; labor force: 20%; principal products: rice, yams, sugar cane, bananas, pineapples, citrus fruits. Labor force in industry: 42%; major products: textiles, clothing, chemicals, processed foods, electronic equipment, cement, ships, plywood. Natural resources: coal, natural gas, limestone, marble. Exports: textiles, electrical machinery, plywood. Imports: machinery, basic metals, crude oil, chemicals. Major trading partners: U.S., Japan, Saudi Arabia.

Geography. The Republic of China today consists of the island of Taiwan, an island 100 miles (161 km) off the Asian mainland in the Pacific; two offshore island, Quemoy and Matsu; and the nearby islets of the Pescadores chain. It is slightly larger than the combined areas of Massachusetts and Connecticut.

Taiwan is divided by a central mountain range that runs from north to south, rising sharply on the east coast and descending gradually to a broad western plain, where cultivation is concentrated.

Government. The President and the Vice President are elected by the National Assembly for a term of six years. There are five major governing bodies called Yuans: Executive, Legislative, Judicial, Control, and Examination. Taiwan's internal affairs are administered by the Taiwan Provincial Government under the supervision of the Provincial Assembly, which is popularly elected.

The majority and ruling party is the Kuomintang (KMT) (Nationalist Party) led by President Lee Teng-hui. The main opposition party is the Democratic Progressive Party (DPP).

History. Taiwan was inhabited by aborigines of Malayan descent when Chinese from the areas now designated as Fukien and Kwangtung began settling it beginning in the 7th century, becoming the majority.

The Portuguese explored the area in 1590, naming it The Beautiful (Formosa). In 1624 the Dutch set up forts in the south, the Spanish in the North. The Dutch threw out the Spanish in 1641 and controlled the island until 1661, when the Chinese General Koxinga took it over, established an independent kingdom, and expelled the Dutch. The Manchus seized the island in 1683 and held it until 1895, when it passed to Japan after the first Sino-Japanese War. Japan developed and exploited it, and it was heavily bombed by American planes during World War II, after which it was restored to China.

After the defeat of its armies on the mainland, the Nationalist Government of Generalissimo Chiang Kai-shek retreated to Taiwan in December 1949. With only 15% of the population consisting of the 1949 immigrants, Chiang dominated the island, maintaining a 600,000-man army in the hope of eventually recovering the mainland. Japan renounced its claim to the island by the San Francisco Peace Treaty of 1951.

By stationing a fleet in the Strait of Formosa the U.S. prevented a mainland invasion in 1953.

The "China seat" in the U.N., which the Nationalists held with U.S. help for over two decades was lost in October 1971, when the People's Republic of China was admitted and Taiwan ousted by the world body.

Chiang died at 87 of a heart attack on April 5, 1975. His son, Chiang Ching-kuo, continued as Premier and dominant power in the Taipei regime. He assumed the presidency in 1978, and Sun Yunhsuan became Premier.

President Carter's announcement that the U.S. would recognize only the People's Republic of China after Jan. 1, 1979, and that the U.S. defense treaty with the Nationalists would end aroused protests in Taiwan and in the U.S. Congress. Against Carter's wishes, Congress, in a bill governing future relations with Taiwan, guaranteed U.S. action in the event of an attack on the island. The legislation also provided for the continuation of trade and other relations through an American Institute in Taipei, housed in the former American Embassy.

Although the U.S. had assured Taiwan of continuing arms aid, a communiqué on Aug. 17, 1982,

signed by Washington and Peking and promising a gradual reduction of such aid, cast a shadow over Taiwan. The striking success of the DPP in legislative elections in December 1986 marked a slight loosening of the KMT's hold on power.

TANZANIA

United Republic of Tanzania
President: Ali Hassan Mwinyi (1985)
Prime Minister: Joseph Warioba (1985)
Area: 364,900 sq mi. (945,087 sq km)[1]
Population (est. mid-1989): 26,300,000 (average annual rate of natural increase: 3.6%)
Density per square mile: 72
Capital and largest city (est. 1984): Dar es Salaam, 1,-400,000
Monetary unit: Tanzanian shilling
Languages: Swahili, English, local languages
Religions: Christian, 33%; Islam, 33%; Animist, 33%
Member of Commonwealth of Nations
Literacy rate: 85%
Economic summary: Gross domestic product (FY87): $4.9 billion, $240 per capita; real growth rate (FY87): 3.5%. Land used for agriculture: 45%; labor force: 90%; Principal products: coconuts, maize, rice, wheat, cotton, coffee, sisal, cashew nuts, pyrethrum, cloves. Major industrial products: textiles, light manufactures, refined oil, processed agricultural products, diamonds, cement, fertilizer. Natural resources: hydroelectric potential, unexploited iron and coal. Exports: coffee, cotton, sisal, diamonds, cloves, cashew nuts. Imports: manufactured goods, textiles, machinery and transport equipment, crude oil, foodstuffs. Major trading partners: West Germany, U.K., U.S., Iran.

1. Including Zanzibar.

Geography. Tanzania is in East Africa on the Indian Ocean. To the north are Uganda and Kenya; to the west, Burundi, Rwanda, and Zaire; and to the south, Mozambique, Zambia, and Malawi. Its area is three times that of New Mexico.

Tanzania contains three of Africa's best-known lakes—Victoria in the north, Tanganyika in the west, and Nyasa in the south. Mount Kilimanjaro in the north, 19,340 feet (5,895 m), is the highest point on the continent.

Government. Under the republican form of government, Tanzania has a President elected by universal suffrage who appoints the Cabinet ministers. The 244-member National Assembly is composed of 119 elected members from the mainland, 50 elected from Zanzibar, 10 members appointed by the President (from both Tanganyika and Zanzibar), 5 national members (elected by the National Assembly after nomination by various national institutions), 20 members elected by Zanzibar's House of Representatives, 25 Regional Commissioners sitting as *ex officio* members, and 15 seats reserved for women (elected by the National Assembly).

The Tanganyika African National Union, the only authorized party on the mainland, and the Afro-Shirazi Party, the only party in Zanzibar and Pemba, merged in 1977 as the Revolutionary Party (Chama Cha Mapinduzi) and elected Julius K. Nyerere as its head.

History. Arab traders first began to colonize the

area in A.D. 700. Portuguese explorers reached the coastal regions in 1500 and held some control until the 17th century, when the Sultan of Oman took power. With what are now Burundi and Rwanda, Tanganyika became the colony of German East Africa in 1885. After World War I, it was administered by Britain under a League of Nations mandate and later as a U.N. trust territory.

Although not mentioned in old histories until the 12th century, Zanzibar was believed always to have had connections with southern Arabia. The Portuguese made it one of their tributaries in 1503 and later established a trading post, but they were driven out by Arabs from Oman in 1698. Zanzibar was declared independent of Oman in 1861 and, in 1890, it became a British protectorate.

Tanganyika became independent on Dec. 9, 1961; Zanzibar, on Dec. 10, 1963. On April 26, 1964, the two nations merged into the United Republic of Tanganyika and Zanzibar. The name was changed to Tanzania six months later.

An invasion by Ugandan troops in November 1978 was followed by a counterattack in January 1979, in which 5,000 Tanzanian troops were joined by 3,000 Ugandan exiles opposed to President Idi Amin. Within a month, full-scale war developed.

Nyerere kept troops in Uganda in open support of former Ugandan President Milton Obote, despite protests from opposition groups, until the national elections in December 1980. Although Obote asked that the Tanzanians remain after his victory in order to control guerrilla resistance, Nyerere ordered their withdrawal in May 1981, citing the $1-million-a-month drain on his precarious finances.

In November 1985, Nyerere stepped down as President. Ali Hassan Myinyi, his Vice-President, succeeded him. Nyerere remained chariman of the party.

THAILAND

Kingdom of Thailand
Ruler: King Bhumibol Adulyadej (1946)
Prime Minister: Maj. General Chatichai Choonharan (1988)
Area: 198,455 sq mi. (514,000 sq km)
Population (est. mid-1989): 55,600,000 (average annual rate of natural increase: 1.7%) (incl. 2.5 million of Chinese descent born in Thailand)
Density per square mile: 280
Capital and largest city (est. 1984): Bangkok, 5,174,682
Monetary unit: Baht
Languages: Thai (Siamese), Chinese, English
Religions: Buddhist, 95%; Islam, 4%
National name: Thailand
Literacy rate (1985): 85.5%
Economic summary: Gross national product (1988): $53 billion. Average annual growth rate (1981–87): approx. 5%. Per capita income (1988): $950. Land used for agriculture: 38%; labor force; 65%; principal products: rice, rubber, corn, tapioca, sugar, coconuts. Labor force in industry: 10%; major products: processed food, textiles, wood, cement, tin, tungsten, jewelry. Natural resources: fish, natural gas, forests, fluorite, tin, tungsten. Exports: rice, tapioca, sugar, rubber, tin, textiles, jewelry. Imports: machinery and transport equipment, fertilizer, crude oil, fuels and lubricants, base metals, chemicals. Major trading partners: Japan, U.S., Singapore, Malaysia, Netherlands, U.K., Hong Kong, W. Germany.

Geography. Thailand occupies the western half of the Indochinese peninsula and the northern two thirds of the Malay peninsula in southeast Asia. Its neighbors are Burma on the north and west, Laos on the north and northeast, Cambodia on the east, and Malaysia on the south. Thailand is about the size of France.

Most of the population is supported in the fertile central alluvial plain, which is drained by the Chao Phraya River and its tributaries.

Government. King Bhumibol Adulyadej, who was born Dec. 5, 1927, second son of Prince Mahidol of Songkhla, succeeded to the throne on June 9, 1946, when his brother, King Ananda Mahidol, died of a gunshot wound. He was married on April 28, 1950, to Queen Sirikit; their son, Vajiralongkorn, born July 28, 1952, is the Crown Prince.

Thailand is a constitutional monarchy with a 357-member Parliament.

History. The Thais first began moving down into their present homeland from the Asian continent in the 6th century A.D. and by the end of the 13th century ruled most of the western portion. During the next 400 years, the Thais fought sporadically with the Cambodians and the Burmese. The British obtained recognition of paramount interest in Thailand in 1824, and in 1896 an Anglo-French accord guaranteed the independence of Thailand.

A coup in 1932 changed the absolute monarchy into a representative government with universal suffrage. After five hours of token resistance on Dec. 8, 1941, Thailand yielded to Japanese occupation and became one of the springboards in World War II for the Japanese campaign against Malaya.

After the fall of its pro-Japanese puppet government in July 1944, Thailand pursued a policy of passive resistance against the Japanese, and after the Japanese surrender, Thailand repudiated the declaration of war it had been forced to make against Britain and the U.S. in 1942.

Thailand's major problem in the late 1960s was suppressing guerrilla action by Communist invaders in the north.

Although Thailand had received $2 billion in U.S. economic and military aid since 1950 and had sent troops (paid by the U.S.) to Vietnam while permitting U.S. bomber bases on its territory, the collapse of South Vietnam and Cambodia in the spring of 1975 brought rapid changes in the country's diplomatic posture.

At the Thai government's insistence, the U.S. agreed to withdraw all 23,000 U.S. military personnel remaining in Thailand by March 1976. Diplomatic relations with China were established in 1975. Meanwhile, overtures toward an accommodation with the new regime in South Vietnam were initiated.

After three years of civilian government ended with a military coup on Oct. 6, 1976, Thailand reverted to military rule. Political parties, banned after the coup, gained limited freedom in 1980. The same year, the National Assembly elected Gen. Prem Tinsulanonda as prime minister. General elections on April 18, 1983, and July 27, 1986 resulted in Prem continuing as prime minister over a coalition government.

Refugees from Laos, Cambodia, and Vietnam flooded into Thailand in 1978 and 1979, and despite efforts by the United States and other Western countries to resettle them, a total of 130,000 Laotian and Vietnamese refugees were living in camps along the Cambodian border in mid-1980. A drive by Vietnamese occupation forces on western Cambodian areas loyal to the Pol Pot government, culminating in invasions of Thai territory in late June, drove an estimated 100,000 Cambodians across the line as refugees, adding to the 200,000 of their countrymen already in Thailand. The total of 430,000 were being fed by United Nations and church relief organizations but the Thai government complained of the burden of their presence.

The Vietnamese incursions, notwithstanding Hanoi's claim that the troops were only seeking guerrillas hidden in the refugee camps, prompted a Thai appeal to Washington for military aid. In July, 35 reconditioned tanks and other weapons were flown to Thailand.

On April 3, 1981, a military coup against the Prem government failed. Another coup attempt on Sept. 9, 1985, was crushed by loyal troops after 10 hours of fighting in Bangkok. Four persons were killed and about 60 wounded.

General elections in 1988 led to Prem stepping down in favor of Chatichai Choonharan.

TOGO

Republic of Togo
President: Gen. Gnassingbé Eyadema (1967)
Area: 21,925 sq mi. (56,785 sq km)
Population (est. mid-1989): 3,400,000 (average annual rate of natural increase: 3.5%)
Density per square mile: 157
Capital and largest city (est. 1982): Lomé, 285,000
Monetary unit: Franc CFA
Languages: Ewé, Mina (south), Kabyé, Cotocoli (north), French (official), and many dialects
Religions: Animist, 46%; Christian, 37%; Islam, 17%
National name: République Togolaise
Literacy rate: 18%
Economic summary: Gross national product (1985): $696 million, $240 per capita; real growth rate (1985): 4.7%. Land used for agriculture: 26%; labor force: 78%; principal products: yams, manioc, millet, sorghum, cocoa, coffee, peanuts. Labor force in industry: 22%; major products: phosphate, textiles, processed food. Natural resources: marble, phosphate, limestone. Exports: phosphate, cocoa, coffee. Imports: consumer goods, fuels, machinery, foodstuffs. Major trading partners: France, U.K., Japan, Netherlands, W. Germany.

Geography. Togo, twice the size of Maryland, is on the south coast of West Africa bordering on Ghana to the west, Burkina Faso to the north and Benin to the east.

The Gulf of Guinea coastline, only 32 miles long (51 km), is low and sandy. The only port is at Lomé. The Togo hills traverse the central section.

Government. The government of Nicolas Grunitzky was overthrown in a bloodless coup on Jan. 13, 1967, led by Lt. Col. Etienne Eyadema (now Gen. Gnassingbé Eyadema). A National Reconciliation Committee was set up to rule the country. In April, however, Eyadema dissolved the Committee and took over as President. In December 1979, a 67-member National Assembly was voted in by national referendum. The Assembly of the Togolese People is the only political party.

History. Freed slaves from Brazil were the first traders to settle in Togo. Established as a German colony (Togoland) in 1884, the area was split between the British and the French as League of Na-

tions mandates after World War I and subsequently administered as U. N. trusteeships. The British portion voted for incorporation with Ghana.

Togo became independent on April 27, 1960. Sylvanus Olympio, its first President, was assassinated in 1963 and succeeded by Nicolas Grunitzky.

TONGA

Kingdom of Tonga
Sovereign: King Taufa'ahau Tupou IV (1965)
Prime Minister: Prince Fatafehi Tu'ipelehake (1965)
Area: 290 sq mi. (751 sq km)
Population (est. mid 1989): 99,620 (average annual growth rate: 0.8%)
Density per square mile: 344
Capital (est. 1986): Nuku'alofa, 28,899
Monetary unit: Pa'anga
Languages: Tongan, English
Religions: Free Wesleyan, 47%; Roman Catholic, 16%; Free Church of Tonga, 14%; Mormon, 9%; Church of Tonga, 9%
Member of Commonwealth of Nations
Literacy rate: 95%
Economic summary: Gross national product (1985): $100 million. Average annual growth rate (1970–78): 1.2%. Per capita income (1985): $1,030. Land used for agriculture: 80%; labor force: 75%; principal products: vanilla, coffee, ginger, black pepper, coconuts, bananas, copra. Major industrial products: copra, desiccated coconut. Natural resources: fish. Exports: copra, coconut products, bananas. Imports: manufactures, foodstuffs, machinery, petroleum. Major trading partners: New Zealand, Australia, Fiji, U.K.

Geography. Situated east of the Fiji Islands in the South Pacific, Tonga (also called the Friendly Islands) consists of some 150 islands, of which 36 are inhabited.

Most of the islands contain active volcanic craters; others are coral atolls.

Government. Tonga is a constitutional monarchy. Executive authority is vested in the Sovereign, a Privy Council, and a Cabinet headed by the Prime Minister. Legislative authority is vested in the Legislative Assembly.

History. The present dynasty of Tonga was founded in 1831 by Taufa'ahau Tupou, who took the name George I. He consolidated the kingdom by conquest and in 1875 granted a Constitution.

In 1900, his great-grandson, George II, signed a treaty of friendship with Britain, and the country became a British protected state. The treaty was revised in 1959.

Queen Salote Tupou reigned from 1918 to 1964 and was succeeded by her son, who became King Taufa'ahau Tupou IV.

Tonga became independent on June 4, 1970.

TRANSKEI

See South Africa

TRINIDAD AND TOBAGO

Republic of Trinidad and Tobago
President: Noor Hassanali (1987)
Prime Minister: A.N.R. Robinson (1986)

Area: 1,980 sq mi. (5,128 sq km)
Population (est. mid-1989): 1,200,000 (average annual rate of natural increase: 2.0%) (black, 41%; East Indian, 41%; mixed, 16%)
Density per square mile: 628
Capital and largest city (est. 1981): Port-of-Spain, 125,-000
Monetary unit: Trinidad and Tobago dollar
Languages: English (official); Hindi, French, Spanish
Religions: Christian, 64%; Hindu, 25%; Islam, 6%
Member of Commonwealth of Nations
Literacy rate: 95%
Economic summary: Gross domestic product (1986): $5 billion, $4,160 per capita; real growth rate (1986): − 6.4%. Land used for agriculture: 33%; labor force: 11%; principal products: sugar cane, cocoa, coffee, citrus. Labor force in industry: 33%; major products: petroleum, processed food, cement; tourism. Natural resources: petroleum. Exports: petroleum, ammonia, fertilizer. Imports: chemicals, foodstuffs, machinery and equipment. Major trading partners: U.S., Caribbean, Western Europe.

Geography. Trinidad and Tobago lies in the Caribbean Sea off the northeast coast of Venezuela. The area of the two islands is slightly less than that of Delaware.

Trinidad, the larger, is mainly flat and rolling, with mountains in the north that reach a height of 3,085 feet (940 m) at Mount Aripo. Tobago is heavily forested with hardwood trees.

Government. The legislature consists of a 24-member Senate and a 36-member House of Representatives.

The political parties are the National Alliance for Reconstruction, led by Prime Minister A.N.R. Robinson (33 seats in the House of Representatives); People's National Movement (3 seats).

History. Trinidad was discovered by Columbus in 1498 and remained in Spanish possession, despite raids by other European nations, until it capitulated to the British in 1797 during a war between Britain and Spain.

Trinidad was ceded to Britain in 1802, and in 1899 it was united with Tobago as a colony. From 1958 to 1962, Trinidad and Tobago was a part of the West Indies Federation, and on Aug, 31, 1962, it became independent.

On Aug. 1, 1976, Trinidad and Tobago cut its ties with Britain and became a republic, remaining within the Commonwealth and recognizing Queen Elizabeth II only as head of that organization.

TUNISIA

Republic of Tunisia

President: Gen. Zine al-Abidine Ben Ali (1987)
Prime Minister: Hedi Baccouche (1987)
Area: 63,379 sq mi. (164,152 sq km)
Population (est. mid-1989): 7,900,000 (average annual rate of natural increase: 2.4%)
Density per square mile: 125
Capital and largest city (est. 1981): Tunis, 600,000
Monetary unit: Tunisian dinar
Languages: Arabic, French
Religion: Islam (Sunni); 99.4%

National name: Al-Joumhouria Attunisia
Literacy rate: 64%
Economic summary: Gross domestic product (1987 est.): $9.3 billion, $1,230 per capita; real growth rate (1987 est.): 3.5%. Land used for agriculture: 49%; labor force: 32%; principal products: wheat, olives, citrus fruits, grapes, dates. Labor force in industry: 21%; major products: crude oil, olive oil, textiles, and leather, chemical fertilizers, petroleum. Natural resources: oil, phosphates, iron ore, lead, zinc. Exports: petroleum, phosphates, textiles. Imports: machinery and equipment, consumer goods, foodstuffs. Major trading partners: France, West Germany, Italy, U.S.

Geography. Tunisia, at the northernmost bulge of Africa, thrusts out toward Sicily to mark the division between the eastern and western Mediterranean Sea. Twice the size of South Carolina, it is bordered on the west by Algeria and by Libya on the south.

Coastal plains on the east rise to a north-south escarpment which slopes gently to the west. Saharan in the south, Tunisia is more mountainous in the north, where the Atlas range continues from Algeria.

Government. Executive power is vested by the Constitution in the president, elected for five years and eligible for re-election to two additional terms. Legislative power is vested in a House of Deputies elected by universal suffrage.

In 1975, the National Assembly amended the Constitution to make Habib Bourguiba president for life. At 71, Bourguiba was re-elected to a fourth five-year term when he ran unopposed in 1974. He was deposed by Gen. Zine Ben Ali in 1987. Ben Ali was elected to a five-year term in April 1989.

History. Tunisia was settled by the Phoenicians and Carthaginians in ancient times. Except for an interval of Vandal conquest in A.D. 439–533, it was part of the Roman Empire until the Arab conquest of 648–69. It was ruled by various Arab and Berber dynasties until the Turks took it in 1570–74. French troops occupied the country in 1881, and the Bey signed a treaty acknowledging a French protectorate.

Nationalist agitation forced France to grant internal autonomy to Tunisia in 1955 and to recognize Tunisian independence and sovereignty in 1956. The Constituent Assembly deposed the Bey on July 25, 1957, declared Tunisia a republic, and elected Habib Bourguiba as president.

Bourguiba maintained a pro-Western foreign policy that earned him enemies. Tunisia refused to break relations with the U.S. during the Israeli-Arab war in June 1967.

Tunisia ended its traditionally neutral role in the Arab world when it joined with the majority of Arab League members to condemn Egypt for concluding a peace treaty with Israel. The Tunisian capital was offered as the temporary headquarters of the League, following the expulsion of Egypt.

Developments in 1986-87 were characterized by a consolidation of power by the 84-year-old Bourguiba and his failure to arrange for a successor. This issue was settled when the then-Prime Minister, Gen. Ben Ali, deposed Bourguiba on the grounds that the latter's "senility and lingering illness" rendered him unfit to rule. Ben Ali succeeded him as per the Constitution and promised democratic reforms.

TURKEY

Republic of Turkey
President: Kenan Evren (1982)
Prime Minister: Turgut Özal (1983)
Area: 300,947 sq mi. (incl. 9,121 in Europe) (779,452 sq km)
Population (est. mid-1989): 55,400,000 (average annual rate of natural increase: 2.2%)
Density per square mile: 184
Capital: Ankara
Largest cities (1985 census): Istanbul, 5,858,558; Ankara, 3,462,880; Izmir, 2,316,843; Adana, 1,757,102; Bursa, 1,327,762; Gaziantep, 953,859
Monetary unit: Turkish Lira
Language: Turkish
Religion: Islam (Sunni), 99.2%
National name: Türkiye Cumhuriyeti
Literacy rate: 80%
Economic summary: Gross national product (1988): $67.1 billion. Average annual growth rate (1988): 5.4%. Per capita income (est. 1987): $1,309. Land used for agriculture: 46%; labor force: 56%; principal products: cotton, tobacco, cereals, sugar beets, fruits, nuts. Labor force in industry: 14%; major products: textiles, coal, minerals, processed foods, steel, petroleum. Natural resources: coal, chromite, copper, boron, oil. Exports: cotton, tobacco, fruits, nuts, livestock products, textiles. Imports: crude oil, machinery, transport equipment, metals, mineral fuels, fertilizer, chemicals. Major trading partners: West Germany, Iraq, France, Italy, U.S.S.R., U.S., U.K., Iran, Japan.

Geography. Turkey is at the northeastern end of the Mediterranean Sea in southeast Europe and southwest Asia. To the north is the Black Sea and to the west the Aegean Sea. Its neighbors are Greece and Bulgaria to the west, the U.S.S.R. to the north, Iran to the east, and Syria and Iraq to the south. Overall, it is a little larger than Texas.

The Dardanelles, the Sea of Marmara, and the Bosporus divide the country.

Turkey in Europe comprises an area about equal to the state of Massachusetts. It is hilly country drained by the Maritsa River and its tributaries.

Turkey in Asia, or Anatolia, about the size of Texas, is roughly a rectangle in shape with its short sides on the east and west. Its center is a treeless plateau rimmed by mountains.

Government. The President is elected by the Grand National Assembly for a seven-year term and is not eligible for re-election.

In a military coup on Sept. 12, 1980, led by Gen. Kenan Evren, the Chief of General Staff, Premier Süleyman Demirel was ousted, the Grand National Assembly dissolved and the Constitution suspended. Demirel, former Premier Bülent Ecevit, and some 100 legislators and political figures were detained, but later released. Martial law was declared and all political parties were dissolved. New elections were held in 1983 and a new Assembly was established.

The Prime Minister and his Council of Ministers hold the executive power although the President has the right to veto legislation.

History. The Ottoman Turks first appeared in the early 13th century in Anatolia, subjugating Turkish and Mongol bands pressing against the eastern borders of Byzantium. They gradually spread through the Near East and Balkans, capturing Constantinople in 1453 and storming the gates of Vienna two centuries later. At its height, the Ottoman Empire stretched from the Persian Gulf to western Algeria.

Defeat of the Turkish navy at Lepanto by the Holy League in 1571 and failure of the siege of Vienna heralded the decline of Turkish power. By the 18th century, Russia was seeking to establish itself as the protector of Christians in Turkey's Balkan territories. Russian ambitions were checked by Britain and France in the Crimean War (1854–56), but the Russo-Turkish War (1877–78) gave Bulgaria virtual independence and Romania and Serbia liberation from their nominal allegiance to the Sultan.

Turkish weakness stimulated a revolt of young liberals known as the Young Turks in 1909. They forced Sultan Abdul Hamid to grant a constitution and install a liberal government. Reforms were no barrier to further defeats, however, in a war with Italy (1911–12) and the Balkan Wars (1912–13). Under the influence of German military advisors, Turkey signed a secret alliance with Germany on Aug. 2, 1914, that led to a declaration of war by the Allied powers and the ultimate humiliation of the occupation of Turkish territory by Greek and other Allied troops.

In 1919, the new Nationalist movement, headed by Mustafa Kemal, was organized to resist the Allied occupation and, in 1920, a National Assembly elected him President of both the Assembly and the government. Under his leadership, the Greeks were driven out of Smyrna, and other Allied forces were withdrawn.

The present Turkish boundaries (with the exception of Alexandretta, ceded to Turkey by France in 1939) were fixed by the Treaty of Lausanne (1923) and later negotiations. The caliphate and sultanate were separated, and the sultanate was abolished in 1922. On Oct. 29, 1923, Turkey formally became a republic, with Mustafa Kemal, who took the name Kemal Atatürk, as its first President. The caliphate was abolished in 1924, and Atatürk proceeded to carry out an extensive program of reform, modernization, and industrialization.

Gen. Ismet Inönü was elected to succeed Atatürk in 1938 and was re-elected in 1939, 1943, and 1946. Defeated in 1950, he was succeeded by Celâl Bayar. In 1939, a mutual assistance pact was concluded with Britain and France. Neutral during most of World War II Turkey, on Feb. 23, 1945, declared war on Germany and Japan, but took no active part in the conflict.

Turkey became a full member of NATO in 1952.

Turkey invaded Cyprus by sea and air July 20, 1974, following the failure of diplomatic efforts to resolve the crisis caused by the ouster of Archbishop Makarios.

Talks in Geneva involving Greece, Turkey, Britain, and Greek Cypriot and Turkish Cypriot leaders brokers down in mid-August. Turkey unilaterally announced a cease-fire August 16, after having gained control of 40% of the island. Turkish Cypriots established their own state in the north on Feb. 13, 1975.

U.S.-Turkish relations, excellent for a generation, were seriously damaged when Congress voted to end arms sales to Turkey in 1975 because arms the U.S. had supplied for mutual defense had been used in the invasion of Cyprus.

In July 1975, after a 30-day warning, Turkey took over control of all the U.S. installations except the big joint defense base at Incirlik, which it reserved for "NATO tasks alone."

The establishment of military government in September 1980 stopped the slide toward anarchy and brought some improvement in the economy. The military regime was criticized, however, for suppression of human rights.

A Constituent Assembly, consisting of the six-member National Security Council and members appointed by them, drafted a new Constitution that was approved by an overwhelming (91.5%) majority of the voters in a Nov. 6, 1982, referendum. Prime Minister Turgut Özal's Motherland Party came to power in parliamentary elections held in late 1983. Özal was re-elected in November 1987.

TUVALU

Sovereign: Queen Elizabeth II
Governor-General: Tupua Leupena (1986)
Prime Minister: Tomasi Puapua (1981)
Area: 10 sq mi. (26 sq km)
Population (est. mid-1988): 8,475 (average annual growth rate: 1.7%)
Density per square mile: 848
Capital and largest city (est. 1981): Funafuti, 2,500
Monetary unit: Australian dollar
Languages: Tuvaluan, English
Member of the Commonwealth of Nations
Literacy rate: 50%
Economic summary: Gross national product (1984): $4 million. Per capita income (1984): $450. Principal agricultural products: copra and coconuts. Export: copra. Imports: food and fuels. Major trading partners: Australia, U.K., Fiji, New Zealand

Geography. Formerly the Ellice Islands, Tuvalu consists of nine small islands scattered over 500,000 square miles of the western Pacific, just south of the equator.

Government. Official executive power is vested in a Governor-General, representing the Queen, who is appointed by her on the recommendation of the Tuvalu government. Actual executive power lies with a Prime Minister, who is responsible to a House of Assembly composed of eight elected members.

History. The Ellice Islands became a British protectorate in 1892 and were annexed by Britain in 1915–16 as part of the Gilbert and Ellice Islands Colony. The Ellice Islands were separated in 1975, given home rule, and renamed Tuvalu. Full independence was granted on Sept. 30, 1978.

UGANDA

Republic of Uganda
President: Yoweri Museveni (1986)
Prime Minister: Dr. Samson Kiseka (1986)
Area: 91,343 sq mi. (236,880 sq km)
Population (est. mid-1989): 17,000,000 (average annual rate of natural increase: 3.4%)
Density per square mile: 187
Capital and largest city (est. 1980): Kampala, 458,000
Monetary unit: Ugandan shilling
Languages: English (official), Swahili, Luganda, Ateso, Luo
Religions: Christian, 63%; Islam, 16%
Member of Commonwealth of Nations
Literacy rate: 52%
Economic summary: Gross national product (1984): $6.2 billion. Average annual growth rate (1983): 5.0%. Per capita income (1984): $434. Land used for agriculture: 57%; labor force: 90%; principal products: coffee, tea, cotton, sugar. Labor force in industry: 3%; major products: sugar, beer, tobacco, cotton textiles, cement. Natural resources: copper, cobalt, limestone, salt. Exports: coffee, cotton. Imports: petroleum products, machinery, transport equipment, metals, food. Major trading partners: U.S., U.K., Kenya, Spain.

Geography. Uganda, twice the size of Pennsylvania, is in east Africa. It is bordered on the west by Zaire, on the north by the Sudan, on the east by Kenya, and on the south by Tanzania and Rwanda.

The country, which lies across the Equator, is divided into three main areas—swampy lowlands, a fertile plateau with wooded hills, and a desert region. Lake Victoria forms part of the southern border.

Government. The country has been run by the National Reistance Movement (NRM) since January, 1986.

History. Uganda was first visited by European explorers as well as Arab traders in 1844. An Anglo-German agreement of 1890 declared it to be in the British sphere of influence in Africa, and the Imperial British East Africa Company was chartered to develop the area. The company did not prosper financially, and in 1894 a British protectorate was proclaimed.

Uganda became independent on Oct. 9, 1962.

Sir Edward Mutesa was elected the first President and Milton Obote the first Prime Minister of the newly independent country. With the help of a young army officer, Col. Idi Amin, Prime Minister Obote seized control of the government from President Mutesa four years later.

On Jan. 25, 1971, Col. Amin deposed President Obote. Obote went into exile in Tanzania. Amin expelled Asian residents and launched a reign of terror against Ugandan opponents, torturing and killing tens of thousands. In 1976, he had himself proclaimed President for Life. In 1977, Amnesty International estimated that 300,000 may have died under his rule, including church leaders and recalcitrant cabinet ministers.

After Amin held military exercises on the Tanzanian border, angering Tanzania's President Julius Nyerere, a combined force of Tanzanian troops and Ugandan exiles loyal to former President Obote invaded Uganda and chased Amin into exile.

After a series of interim administrations, President Obote led his People's Congress Party to victory in 1980 elections that opponents charged were rigged.

Obote continued Amin's human rights abuses. The U.S. reported in August 1984 that the abuses included large-scale massacres.

On July, 27, 1985, army troops staged a coup taking over the government. Obote fled into exile. The military regime installed Gen. Tito Okello as chief of state.

The National Resistance Army (NRA), an anti-Obote group led by Yoweri Musevni, kept fighting after being excluded from the new regime. They seized Kampala on January 29, 1986, and Musevni was declared President but strife still continues in the nothern part of the country.

UNION OF SOVIET SOCIALIST REPUBLICS

See Soviet Union

UNITED ARAB EMIRATES

President: Sheikh Zayed Bin Sultan Al-Nahayan (1971)
Prime Minister: Sheik Rashid Bin Said al-Maktoum (1979)
Area: 32,000 sq mi. (82,880 sq km)
Population (est. mid-1989): 1,700,000 (Arab, 42%; South Asian, 50%) (average annual rate of natural increase: 2.3%)
Density per square mile: 53
Capital and largest city (est. 1981): Abu Dhabi, 225,000
Monetary unit: Dirham
Language: Arabic; Farsi and English widely spoken
Religion: Islam (Sunni, 80%; Shiite, 20%)
Literacy rate: 68%
Economic summary: Gross national product (1987 est.): $22 billion, $11,900 per capita; real growth rate (1987 est.): 3.0%. Land used for agriculture: 2%; labor force: 5%; principal products: vegetables, dates, tobacco, fruit. Labor force in industry: 85%; major products: fish, light manufactures, petroleum, construction materials. Natural resources: oil. Exports: petroleum, dates, fish. Imports: consumer goods, food. Major trading partners: Japan, Western Europe, U.S.

Geography. The United Arab Emirates, in the eastern part of the Arabian Peninsula, extends along part of the Gulf of Oman and the southern coast of the Persian Gulf. The nation is the size of Maine. Its neighbors are Saudi Arabia in the west and south, Qatar in the north, and Oman in the east. Most of the land is barren and sandy.

Government. The United Arab Emirates was formed in 1971 by seven emirates known as the Trucial States—Abu Dhabi (the largest), Dubai, Sharjah, Ajman, Fujairah, Ras al Khaimah and Umm al-Qaiwain.

The loose federation allows joint policies in foreign relations, defense, and development, with each member state keeping its internal local system of government headed by its own ruler. A 40-member legislature consists of eight seats each for Abu Dhabi and Dubai, six seats each for Ras al Khaimah and Sharjah, and four each for the others. It is a member of the Arab League.

History. Originally the area was inhabited by a seafaring people who were converted to Islam in the seventh century. Later, a dissident sect, the Carmathians, established a powerful sheikdom, and its army conquered Mecca. After the sheikdom disintegrated, its people became pirates.

Threatening the sultanate of Muscat and Oman early in the 19th century, the pirates provoked the intervention of the British, who in 1820 enforced a partial truce and in 1853 a permanent truce. Thus what had been called the Pirate Coast was renamed the Trucial Coast.

UNITED KINGDOM

United Kingdom of Great Britain and Northern Ireland
Sovereign: Queen Elizabeth II (1952)
Prime Minister: Margaret Thatcher (1979)
Area: 94,247 sq mi. (244,100 sq km)
Population (est. mid-1989): 57,300,000 (average annual rate of natural increase: 0.2%) (English, Scottish, Welsh, Northern Irish)
Density per square mile: 606
Capital: London, England
Largest cities (est. mid-1986): Greater London, 6,775,-200; Birmingham, 1,004,100; Glasgow, 733,800; Leeds, 710,900; Sheffield, 534,300; Liverpool, 483,000; Bradford 463,100; Edinburgh, 439,700; Bristol, 391,-500; Manchester, 172,600
Monetary unit: Pound sterling (£)
Languages: English, Welsh, Scots Gaelic
Religions: Church of England (established church); Church of Wales (disestablished); Church of Scotland (established church—Presbyterian); Church of Ireland (disestablished); Roman Catholic; Methodist; Congregational; Baptist; Jewish
Literacy rate: 99.5%
Economic summary: Gross national product (1986): $556.8 billion, $9,800 per capita; real growth rate (1987 est.): 4.3%. Land used for agriculture: 77%, principal products: wheat, barley, potatoes, sugar beets, livestock, dairy products. Major industrial products: machinery and transport equipment, metals, processed food, paper, textiles, chemicals, clothing. Natural resources: coal, oil, gas. Exports: machinery, transport equipment, chemicals, petroleum. Imports: foodstuffs, petroleum, machinery, chemicals, crude materials. Major trading partners: Western European nations, U.S.

Geography. The United Kingdom, consisting of England, Wales, Scotland, and Northern Ireland, is twice the size of New York State. England, in the southeast part of the British Isles, is separated from Scotland on the north by the granite Cheviot Hills; from them the Pennine chain of uplands extends south through the center of England, reaching its highest point in the Lake District in the northwest. To the west along the border of Wales—a land of steep hills and valleys—are the Cambrian Mountains, while the Cotswolds, a range of hills in Gloucestershire, extend into the surrounding shires.

The remainder of England is plain land, though not necessarily flat, with the rocky sand-topped moors in the southwest, the rolling downs in the south and southeast, and the reclaimed marshes of the low-lying fens in the east central districts.

Scotland is divided into three physical regions—the Highlands, the Central Lowlands, containing two-thirds of the population, and the Southern Uplands. The western Highland coast is intersected throughout by long, narrow sea-lochs, or fiords. Scotland also includes the Outer and Inner Hebrides and other islands off the west coast and the Orkney and Shetland Islands off the north coast.

Wales is generally hilly; the Snowdon range in the northern part culminates in Mount Snowdon (3,560 ft, 1,085 m), highest in both England and Wales.

Important rivers flowing into the North Sea are the Thames, Humber, Tees, and Tyne. In the west are the Severn and Wye, which empty into the Bristol Channel and are navigable, as are the Mersey and Ribble.

Government. The United Kingdom is a constitutional monarchy, with a Queen and a Parliament that has two houses: the House of Lords with about 830 hereditary peers, 26 spiritual peers, about 270 life peers and peeresses, and 9 law-lords, who are hereditary, or life, peers, and the House of Commons, which has 650 popularly elected members.

Rulers of England and Great Britain

Name	Born	Ruled[1]	Name	Born	Ruled[1]
SAXONS[2]			**HOUSE OF YORK**		
Egbert[3]	c.775	828–839	Edward IV	1442	1461–1483[5]
Ethelwulf	?	839–858	Edward V	1470	1483–1483
Ethelbald	?	858–860	Richard III	1452	1483–1485
Ethelbert	?	860–866			
Ethelred I	?	866–871	**HOUSE OF TUDOR**		
Alfred the Great	849	871–899	Henry VII	1457	1485–1509
Edward the Elder	c.870	899–924	Henry VIII	1491	1509–1547
Athelstan	895	924–939	Edward VI	1537	1547–1553
Edmund I the Deed-doer	921	939–946	Jane (Lady Jane Grey)[6]	1537	1553–1553
Edred	c.925	946–955	Mary I ("Bloody Mary")	1516	1553–1558
Edwy the Fair	c.943	955–959	Elizabeth I	1533	1558–1603
Edgar the Peaceful	943	959–975			
Edward the Martyr	c.962	975–979	**HOUSE OF STUART**		
Ethelred II the Unready	968	979–1016	James I[7]	1566	1603–1625
Edmund II Ironside	c.993	1016–1016	Charles I	1600	1625–1649
DANES			**COMMONWEALTH**		
Canute	995	1016–1035	Council of State	—	1649–1653
Harold I Harefoot	c.1016	1035–1040	Oliver Cromwell[8]	1599	1653–1658
Hardecanute	c.1018	1040–1042	Richard Cromwell[8]	1626	1658–1659[9]
SAXONS			**RESTORATION OF HOUSE OF STUART**		
Edward the Confessor	c.1004	1042–1066	Charles II	1630	1660–1685
Harold II	c.1020	1066–1066	James II	1633	1685–1688[10]
			William III[11]	1650	1689–1702
HOUSE OF NORMANDY			Mary II[11]	1662	1689–1694
William I the Conqueror	1027	1066–1087	Anne	1665	1702–1714
William II Rufus	c.1056	1087–1100			
Henry I Beauclerc	1068	1100–1135	**HOUSE OF HANOVER**		
Stephen of Boulogne	c.1100	1135–1154	George I	1660	1714–1727
			George II	1683	1727–1760
HOUSE OF PLANTAGENET			George III	1738	1760–1820
Henry II	1133	1154–1189	George IV	1762	1820–1830
Richard I Coeur de Lion	1157	1189–1199	William IV	1765	1830–1837
John Lackland	1167	1199–1216	Victoria	1819	1837–1901
Henry III	1207	1216–1272			
Edward I Longshanks	1239	1272–1307	**HOUSE OF SAXE-COBURG**[12]		
Edward II	1284	1307–1327	Edward VII	1841	1901–1910
Edward III	1312	1327–1377			
Richard II	1367	1377–1399[4]	**HOUSE OF WINDSOR**[12]		
			George V	1865	1910–1936
HOUSE OF LANCASTER			Edward VIII	1894	1936–1936[13]
Henry IV Bolingbroke	1367	1399–1413	George VI	1895	1936–1952
Henry V	1387	1413–1422	Elizabeth II	1926	1952–
Henry VI	1421	1422–1461[5]			

1. Year of end of rule is also that of death, unless otherwise indicated. 2. Dates for Saxon kings are still subject of controversy. 3. Became King of West Saxons in 802; considered (from 828) first King of all England. 4. Died 1400. 5. Henry VI reigned again briefly 1470–71. 6. Nominal Queen for 9 days; not counted as Queen by some authorities. She was beheaded in 1554. 7. Ruled in Scotland as James VI (1567–1625). 8. Lord Protector. 9. Died 1712. 10. Died 1701. 11. Joint rulers (1689–1694). 12. Name changed from Saxe-Coburg to Windsor in 1917. 13. Was known after his abdication as the Duke of Windsor, died 1972.

Supreme legislative power is vested in Parliament, which sits for five years unless sooner dissolved.

The executive power of the Crown is exercised by the Cabinet, headed by the Prime Minister. The latter, normally the head of the party commanding a majority in the House of Commons, is appointed by the Sovereign, with whose consent he or she in turn appoints the rest of the Cabinet. All ministers must be members of one or the other house of Parliament; they are individually and collectively responsible to the Crown and Parliament. The Cabinet proposes bills and arranges the business of Parliament, but it depends entirely on the votes in the House of Commons. The Lords cannot hold up "money" bills, but they can delay other bills for a maximum of one year.

By the Act of Union (1707), the Scottish Parliament was assimilated with that of England, and Scotland is now represented in Commons by 71 members. The Secretary of State for Scotland, a member of the Cabinet, is responsible for the administration of Scottish affairs.

Ruler. Queen Elizabeth II, born April 21, 1926, elder daughter of King George VI and Queen Elizabeth, succeeded to the throne on the death of her father on Feb. 6, 1952; married Nov. 20, 1947, to Prince Philip, Duke of Edinburgh, born June 10,

Area and Population of United Kingdom

Subdivision	Area sq mi	Area sq km	Population (est. mid-1986)
England and Wales	58,381	151,207	50,075,000
Scotland	30,414	78,772	5,121,000
Northern Ireland	5,452	14,121	1,575,200 [1]
Total	94,247	244,100	56,771,200

1. Estimated mid-1987.

1921; their children are Prince Charles[1] (heir presumptive), born Nov. 14, 1948; Princess Anne, born Aug. 15, 1950; Prince Andrew, born Feb. 19, 1960; and Prince Edward, born March 10, 1964. The Queen's sister is Princess Margaret, born Aug. 21, 1930. Prince William Arthur Philip Louis, son of the Prince and Princess of Wales and second in line to the throne, was born June 21, 1982. A second son, Prince Henry Charles Albert David, was born Sept. 15, 1984, and is third in line.

History. Roman invasions of the 1st century B.C. brought Britain into contact with the Continent. When the Roman legions withdrew in the 5th century A.D., Britain fell easy prey to the invading hordes of Angles, Saxons, and Jutes from Scandinavia and the Low Countries. Seven large kingdoms were established, and the original Britons were forced into Wales and Scotland. It was not until the 10th century that the country finally became united under the kings of Wessex. Following the death of Edward the Confessor (1066), a dispute about the succession arose, and William, Duke of Normandy, invaded England, defeating the Saxon King, Harold II, at the Battle of Hastings (1066). The Norman conquest introduced Norman law and feudalism.

The reign of Henry II (1154–89), first of the Plantagenets, saw an increasing centralization of royal power at the expense of the nobles, but in 1215 John (1199–1216) was forced to sign the Magna Carta, which awarded the people, especially the nobles, certain basic rights. Edward I (1272–1307) continued the conquest of Ireland, reduced Wales to subjection and made some gains in Scotland. In 1314, however, English forces led by Edward II were ousted from Scotland after the Battle of Bannockburn. The late 13th and early 14th centuries saw the development of a separate House of Commons with tax-raising powers.

Edward III's claim to the throne of France led to the Hundred Years' War (1338–1453) and the loss of almost all the large English territory in France. In England, the great poverty and discontent caused by the war were intensified by the Black Death, a plague that reduced the population by about one third. The Wars of the Roses (1455–85), a struggle for the throne between the House of York and the House of Lancaster, ended in the victory of Henry Tudor (Henry VII) at Bosworth Field (1485).

During the reign of Henry VIII (1509–47), the Church in England asserted its independence from the Roman Catholic Church. Under Edward VI and Mary, the two extremes of religious fanaticism

1. The title Prince of Wales, which is not inherited, was conferred on Prince Charles by his mother on July 26, 1958. The investiture ceremony took place on July 1, 1969. The previous Prince of Wales was Prince Edward Albert, who held the title from 1911 to 1936 before he became Edward VIII.

were reached, and it remained for Henry's daughter, Elizabeth I (1558-1603), to set up the Church of England on a moderate basis. In 1588, the Spanish Armada, a fleet sent out by Catholic King Philip II of Spain, was defeated by the English and destroyed during a storm. During Elizabeth's reign, England became a world power.

Elizabeth's heir was a Stuart—James VI of Scotland—who joined the two crowns as James I (1603-25). The Stuart kings incurred large debts and were forced either to depend on Parliament for taxes or to raise money by illegal means. In 1642, war broke out between Charles I and a large segment of the Parliament; Charles was defeated and executed in 1649, and the monarchy was then abolished. After the death in 1658 of Oliver Cromwell, the Lord Protector, the Puritan Commonwealth fell to pieces and Charles II was placed on the throne in 1660. The struggle between the King and Parliament continued, but Charles II knew when to compromise. His brother, James II (1685-88), possessed none of his ability and was ousted by the Revolution of 1688, which confirmed the primacy of Parliament. James's daughter, Mary, and her husband, William of Orange, were now the rulers.

Queen Anne's reign (1702-14) was marked by the Duke of Marlborough's victories over France at Blenheim, Oudenarde, and Malplaquet in the War of the Spanish Succession. England and Scotland meanwhile were joined by the Act of Union (1707). Upon the death of Anne, the distant claims of the elector of Hanover were recognized, and he became King of Great Britain and Ireland as George I.

The unwillingness of the Hanoverian kings to rule resulted in the formation by the royal ministers of a Cabinet, headed by a Prime Minister, which directed all public business. Abroad, the constant wars with France expanded the British Empire all over the globe, particularly in North America and India. This imperial growth was checked by the revolt of the American colonies (1775-81).

Struggles with France broke out again in 1793 and, during the Napoleonic Wars, which ended at Waterloo in (1815).

The Victorian era, named after Queen Victoria (1837-1901), saw the growth of a democratic system of government that had begun with the Reform Bill of 1832. The two important wars in Victoria's reign were the Crimean War against Russia (1853-56) and the Boer War (1899-1902), the latter enormously extending Britain's influence in Africa.

Increasing uneasiness at home and abroad marked the reign of Edward VII (1901-10). Within four years after the accession of George V in 1910, Britain entered World War I when Germany invaded Belgium. The nation was led by coalition Cabinets, headed first by Herbert Asquith and then, starting in 1916, by the Welsh statesman David Lloyd George. Postwar labor unrest culminated in the general strike of 1926.

King Edward VIII succeeded to the throne on Jan. 20, 1936, at his father's death, but abdicated on Dec. 11, 1936 (in order to marry an American divorcee, Wallis Warfield Simpson) in favor of his brother, who became George VI.

The efforts of Prime Minister Neville Chamberlain to stem the rising threat of Nazism in Germany failed with the German invasion of Poland on Sept. 1, 1939, which was followed by Britain's entry into World War II on September 3. Allied reverses in the spring of 1940 led to Chamberlain's resignation

British Prime Ministers Since 1770

Name	Term	Name	Term
Lord North (Tory)	1770–1782	Marquis of Salisbury (Conservative)	1886–1892
Marquis of Rockingham (Whig)	1782–1782	William E. Gladstone (Liberal)	1892–1894
Earl of Shelburne (Whig)	1782–1783	Earl of Rosebery (Liberal)	1894–1895
Duke of Portland (Coalition)	1783–1783	Marquis of Salisbury (Conservative)	1895–1902
William Pitt, the Younger (Tory)	1783–1801	Earl Balfour (Conservative)	1902–1905
Henry Addington (Tory)	1801–1804	Sir H. Campbell-Bannerman (Liberal)	1905–1908
William Pitt, the Younger (Tory)	1804–1806	Herbert H. Asquith (Liberal)	1908–1915
Baron Grenville (Whig)	1806–1807	Herbert H. Asquith (Coalition)	1915–1916
Duke of Portland (Tory)	1807–1809	David Lloyd George (Coalition)	1916–1922
Spencer Perceval (Tory)	1809–1812	Andrew Bonar Law (Conservative)	1922–1923
Earl of Liverpool (Tory)	1812–1827	Stanley Baldwin (Conservative)	1923–1924
George Canning (Tory)	1827–1827	James Ramsay MacDonald (Labor)	1924–1924
Viscount Goderich (Tory)	1827–1828	Stanley Baldwin (Conservative)	1924–1929
Duke of Wellington (Tory)	1828–1830	James Ramsay MacDonald (Labor)	1929–1931
Earl Grey (Whig)	1830–1834	James Ramsay MacDonald (Coalition)	1931–1935
Viscount Melbourne (Whig)	1834–1834	Stanley Baldwin (Coalition)	1935–1937
Sir Robert Peel (Tory)	1834–1835	Neville Chamberlain (Coalition)	1937–1940
Viscount Melbourne (Whig)	1835–1841	Winston Churchill (Coalition)	1940–1945
Sir Robert Peel (Tory)	1841–1846	Clement R. Attlee (Labor)	1945–1951
Earl Russell (Whig)	1846–1852	Sir Winston Churchill (Conservative)	1951–1955
Earl of Derby (Tory)	1852–1852	Sir Anthony Eden (Conservative)	1955–1957
Earl of Aberdeen (Coalition)	1852–1855	Harold Macmillan (Conservative)	1957–1963
Viscount Palmerston (Liberal)	1855–1858	Sir Alec Frederick Douglas-Home	
Earl of Derby (Conservative)	1858–1859	(Conservative)	1963–1964
Viscount Palmerston (Liberal)	1859–1865	Harold Wilson (Labor)	1964–1970
Earl Russell (Liberal)	1865–1866	Edward Heath (Conservative)	1970–1974
Earl of Derby (Conservative)	1866–1868	Harold Wilson (Labor)	1974–1976
Benjamin Disraeli (Conservative)	1868–1868	James Callaghan (Labor)	1976–1979
William E. Gladstone (Liberal)	1868–1874	Margaret Thatcher (Conservative)	1979–
Benjamin Disraeli (Conservative)	1874–1880		
William E. Gladstone (Liberal)	1880–1885		
Marquis of Salisbury (Conservative)	1885–1886		
William E. Gladstone (Liberal)	1886–1886		

and the formation of another coalition war Cabinet by the Conservative leader, Winston Churchill, who led Britain through most of World War II. Churchill resigned shortly after V-E Day, May 7, 1945, but then formed a "caretaker" government that remained in office until after the parliamentary elections in July, which the Labor Party won overwhelmingly. The government formed by Clement R. Attlee began a moderate socialist program.

For details of World War II (1939–45), *see* Headline History.

In 1951, Churchill again became Prime Minister at the head of a Conservative government. George VI died Feb. 6, 1952, and was succeeded by his daughter Elizabeth II.

Churchill stepped down in 1955 in favor of Sir Anthony Eden, who resigned on grounds of ill health in 1957, and was succeeded by Harold Macmillan and Sir Alec Douglas-Home. In 1964, Harold Wilson led the Labor Party to victory.

A lagging economy brought the Conservatives back to power in 1970. Prime Minister Edward Heath won Britain's admission to the European Community.

Margaret Thatcher became Britain's first woman Prime Minister as the Conservatives won 339 seats on May 3, 1979.

An Argentine invasion of the Falkland Islands on April 2, 1982, involved Britain in a war 8,000 miles from the home islands. Although Argentina had long claimed the Falklands, known as the Malvinas in Spanish, negotiations were in progress until a month before the invasion. The Thatcher government responded to the invasion with a 40-ship task force, which sailed from Portsmouth on April 5. U.S. efforts to settle the dispute failed and United Nations efforts collapsed as the Argentine military government ignored Security Council resolutions calling for a withdrawal of its forces.

When more than 11,000 Argentine troops on the Falklands surrendered on June 14, 1982, Mrs. Thatcher declared her intention to garrison the islands indefinitely, together with a naval presence.

The military victory bolstered Conservative fortunes at least temporarily, but economic problems continued for the government. Unemployment had risen to a record 2.91 million by mid-June.

In the general election of June 9, 1983, Prime Minister Thatcher and her Conservative party won a landslide victory over the Laborites and other opponents. The Tories seized 58 seats in the House of Commons, giving the Labor party its worst defeat since 1922.

Although there were continuing economic problems and foreign policy disputes, an upswing in the economy in 1986-87 led Thatcher to call elections for June 11 in which she won a near-unprecedented third consecutive term.

NORTHERN IRELAND

Status: Part of United Kingdom
Secretary of State: Thomas Jeremy King
Area: 5,452 sq mi. (14,121 sq km)
Population (est. mid-1987): 1,575,200

Density per square mile: 279.7
Capital and largest city (est. mid-1987): Belfast, 303,800
Monetary unit: British pound sterling
Languages: English, Gaelic
Religions: Roman Catholic, 28%; Presbyterian, 22.9%; Church of Ireland, 19%; Methodist, 4%

Geography. Northern Ireland comprises the counties of Antrim, Armagh, Down, Fermanagh, Londonderry, and Tyrone, which make up predominantly Protestant Ulster and form the northern part of the island of Ireland, westernmost of the British Isles. It is slightly larger than Connecticut.

Government. Northern Ireland is an integral part of the United Kingdom (it has 12 representatives in the British House of Commons), but under the terms of the government of Ireland Act in 1920, it had a semiautonomous government. But in 1972, after three years of internal strife which resulted in over 400 dead and thousands injured, Britain suspended the Ulster parliament. The Ulster counties became governed directly from London after an attempt to return certain powers to an elected Assembly in Belfast.

The Northern Ireland Assembly was dissolved in 1975 and a Constitutional Convention was elected to write a Constitution acceptable to Protestants and Catholics. The convention failed to reach agreement and closed down the next year.

History. Ulster was part of Catholic Ireland until the reign of Elizabeth I (1558–1603) when, after crushing three Irish rebellions, the crown confiscated lands in Ireland and settled in Ulster the Scot Presbyterians who became rooted there. Another rebellion in 1641–51, crushed as brutally by Oliver Cromwell, resulted in the settlement of Anglican Englishmen in Ulster. Subsequent political policy favoring Protestants and disadvantaging Catholics encouraged further settlement in Northern Ireland.

But the North did not separate from the South until William Gladstone presented in 1886 his proposal for home rule in Ireland as a means of settling the Irish Question. The Protestants in the North, although they had grievances like the Catholics in the South, feared domination by the Catholic majority. Industry, moreover, was concentrated in the north and dependent on the British market.

When World War I began, civil war threatened between the regions. Northern Ireland, however, did not become a political entity until the six counties accepted the Home Rule Bill of 1920. This set up a semiautonomous Parliament in Belfast and a Crown-appointed Governor advised by a Cabinet of the Prime Minister and eight ministers, as well as a 12-member representation in the House of Commons in London.

As the Republic of Ireland gained its sovereignty, relations improved between North and South, although the Irish Republican Army, outlawed in recent years, continued the struggle to end the partition of Ireland. In 1966–69, communal rioting and street fighting between Protestants and Catholics occurred in Londonderry, fomented by extremist nationalist Protestants, who feared the Catholics might attain a local majority, and by Catholics demonstrating for civil rights.

Rioting, terrorism, and sniping killed more than 2,200 people from 1969 through 1984 and the religious communities, Catholic and Protestant, became hostile armed camps. British troops were brought in to separate them but themselves became a target of Catholics.

In 1973, a new British charter created a 78-member Assembly elected by proportional representation that gave more weight to Catholic strength. It created a Province Executive with committee chairmen of the Assembly heading all government departments except law enforcement, which remained under London's control. Assembly elections in 1973 produced a majority for the new Constitution that included Catholic assemblymen.

Ulster's leaders agreed in 1973 to create an 11-member Executive Body with six seats assigned to Unionists (Protestants) and four to members of Catholic parties. Unionist leader Brian Faulkner headed the Executive. Also agreed to was a Council of Ireland, with 14 seats evenly divided between Dublin and Belfast, which could act only by unanimous vote.

Although the Council lacked real authority, its creation sparked a general strike by Protestant extremists in 1974. The two-week strike caused Faulkner's resignation from the Executive and resumption of direct rule from London.

In April 1974, London instituted a new program that responded to some Catholic grievances, but assigned more British troops to cut off movement of arms and munitions to Ulster's violence-racked cities.

Violence continued unabated, with new heights reached early in 1976 when the Brtish government announced the end of special privileges for political prisoners in Northern Ireland. British Prime Minister James Callaghan visited Belfast in July and pledged that Ulster would remain part of the United Kingdom unless a clear majority wished to separate.

In October 1977, the 1976 Nobel Prize for Peace was awarded to Mairead Corrigan and Betty Williams for their campaign for peace in Northern Ireland. Intermittent violence continued, however, and on Aug. 27, 1979, an I.R.A. bomb killed Earl Mountbatten as he was sailing off southern Ireland.

New talks aimed at a restoration of home rule in Northern Ireland began and quickly ended in January 1980. In May, Mrs. Thatcher met with the new Prime Minister of the Irish Republic, Charles Haughey, but she insisted that the future of Ulster must be decided only by its people and the British Parliament. Haughey declared that an internal solution "cannot and will not succeed."

Civil disturbances reached new heights in the summer of 1981 as Irish nationalist prisoners went on hunger strikes in Maze Prison to attain their demands for "political" status.

Ten nationalists died before the strike ended in August as families of fasters asked that they be fed.

On November 15, 1985, Mrs. Thatcher signed an agreement with Irish Prime Minister Garrett Fitzgerald giving Ireland a consultative role in the affairs of Northern Ireland. It was met with intense disapproval by the Ulster Unionists.

Dependencies of the United Kingdom

ANGUILLA

Status: Dependency
Governor: G.O. Whittaker (1987)
Area: 35 sq mi. (91 sq km)
Population (1988): 6,875
Monetary unit: East Caribbean dollar
Literacy: 80%

Anguilla was originally part of the West Indies Associated States as a component of St. Kitts-Nevis-Anguilla.

In 1967, Anguilla declared its independence from the St. Kitts-Nevis-Anguilla federation. Britain however, did not recognize this action. In February 1969, Anguilla voted to cut all ties with Britain and become an independent republic. In March, Britain landed troops on the island and, on March 30, a truce was signed. In July 1971, Anguilla became a dependency of Britain and two months later Britain ordered the withdrawal of all its troops.

A new Constitution for Anguilla, effective in February 1976, provides for separate administration and a government of elected representatives. The Associated State of St. Kitts-Nevis-Anguilla ended Dec. 19, 1980.

BERMUDA

Status: Self-governing dependency
Governor: Sir Desmond Langley (1988)
Premier: John Swan (1982)
Area: 20 sq mi. (52 sq km)
Population (est. 1988): 58,317 (average annual growth rate: 0.2%)
Capital (est. 1985): Hamilton, 1,700
Monetary unit: Bermuda dollar
Literacy rate: 98%
Economic summary: Gross domestic product (FY86): $1.15 billion, $19,800 per capita. Principal agricultrual products: bananas, vegetables, citrus fruits, dairy products. Labor force in industry: 6.2%; major products: structural concrete, paints, perfumes, furniture. Natural resource: limestone. Exports: semi-tropical produce, light manufactures. Imports: foodstuffs, fuel, machinery. Major trading partners: U.S., U.K., Canada.

Bermuda is an archipelago of about 360 small islands, 580 miles (934 km) east of North Carolina. The largest is (Great) Bermuda, or Long Island. Discovered by Juan de Bermúdez, a shipwrecked Spaniard, early in the 16th century, the islands were settled in 1612 by an offshoot of the Virginia Company and became a crown colony in 1684.

In 1940, sites on the islands were leased for 99 years to the U.S. for air and navy bases. Bermuda is also the headquarters of the West Indies and Atlantic squadron of the Royal Navy.

In 1968, Bermuda was granted a new Constitution, its first Prime Minister, and autonomy, except for foreign relations, defense, and internal security. The predominantly white United Bermuda Party has retained power in four elections against the opposition—the black-led Progressive Laborites—although Bermuda's population is 60% black. Serious rioting occurred in December 1977 after two blacks were hanged for a series of murders, including the 1973 assassination of the Governor, Sir Richard Sharples, and British troops were summoned to restore order.

BRITISH ANTARCTIC TERRITORY

Status: Dependency
High Commissioner: William Hugh Fullerton (1988)
Area: 500,000 sq mi. (1,395,000 sq km)
Population (1986): no permanent residents

The British Antarctic Territory consists of the South Shetland Islands, South Orkney Islands, and

Nearby Graham Land on the Antarctic continent, largely uninhabited. They are dependencies of the British crown colony of the Falkland Islands but received a separate administration in 1962, being governed by a British-appointed High Commissioner who is Governor of the Falklands.

BRITISH INDIAN OCEAN TERRITORY

Status: Dependency
Commissioner: R. Edis
Administrator: R. Crompton
Administrative headquarters: Victoria, Seychelles
Area: 85 sq mi, (220 sq km)

This dependency, consisting of the Chagos Archipelago and other small island groups, was formed in 1965 by agreement with Mauritius and the Seychelles. There is no permanent civilian population in the territory.

BRITISH VIRGIN ISLANDS

Status: Dependency
Governor: Mark Herdman (1986)
Area: 59 sq mi. (153 sq km)
Population (est. 1988): 12,075
Capital (est. 1986): Road Town (on Tortola): 2,479
Monetary unit: U.S. dollar

Some 36 islands in the Caribbean Sea northeast of Puerto Rico and west of the Leeward Islands, the British Virgin Islands are economically interdependent with the U.S. Virgin Islands to the south. They were formerly part of the administration of the Leeward Islands. They received a separate administration in 1956 as a crown colony. In 1967 a new Constitution was promulgated that provided for a ministerial system of government headed by the Governor. The principal islands are Tortola, Virgin Gorda, Anegada and Jost Van Dyke.

CAYMAN ISLANDS

Status: Dependency
Governor: Alan James Scott
Area: 100 sq mi. (259 sq km)
Population (est. 1988): 23,037
Capital (est. 1987): Georgetown (on Grand Cayman), 10,-000
Monetary unit: Cayman Islands dollar

This dependency consists of three islands—Grand Cayman (76 sq mi; 197 sq km), Cayman Brac (22 sq mi; 57 sq km), and Little Cayman (20 sq mi; 52 sq km)—situated about 180 miles (290 km) northwest of Jamaica. They were dependencies of Jamaica until 1959, when they became a unit territory within the Federation of the West Indies. In 1962, upon the dissolution of the Federation, the Cayman Islands became a British dependency. The islands' chief export is turtle products.

CHANNEL ISLANDS

Status: Crown dependencies
Lieutenant Governor of Jersey: Adm. Sir William Pillar (1985)
Lieutenant Governor of Guernsey: Sir Alexander Boswell (1985)

Area: 120 sq mi. (311 sq km)
Population (1988): 133,960
Capital of Jersey: St. Helier
Capital of Guernsey: St. Peter Port
Monetary units: Guernsey pound; Jersey pound

This group of islands, lying in the English Channel off the northwest coast of France, is the only portion of the Duchy of Normandy belonging to the English Crown, to which it has been attached since the conquest of 1066. It was the only British possession occupied by Germany during World War II.

For purposes of government, the islands are divided into the Bailiwick of Jersey (45 sq mi.; 117 sq km) and the Bailiwick of Guernsey (30 sq mi.; 78 sq km), including Alderney (3 sq mi.; 7.8 sq km); Sark (2 sq mi.; 5.2 sq km), Herm, Jethou, etc. The islands are administered according to their own laws and customs by local governments. Acts of Parliament in London are not binding on the islands unless they are specifically mentioned. The Queen is represented in each Bailiwick by a Lieutenant Governor.

FALKLAND ISLANDS AND DEPENDENCIES

Status: Dependency
Governor: William Hugh Fullerton (1988)
Acting Chief Executive: D. G. P. Taylor
Area: 4,700 sq mi. (12,173 sq km)
Population est. (1988): 1,821
Capital (est. 1986): Stanley (on East Falkland), 1,231
Monetary unit: Falkland Island pound

This sparsely inhabited dependency consists of a group of islands in the South Atlantic, about 250 miles (402 km) east of the South American mainland. The largest islands are East Falkland and West Falkland. Dependencies are South Georgia Island (1,450 sq mi.; 3,756 sq km), the South Sandwich Islands, and other islets. Three former dependencies—Graham Land, the South Shetland Islands, and the South Orkney Islands—were established as a new British dependency, the British Antarctic Territory, in 1962.

The chief industry is sheep raising and, apart from the production of wool, hides and skins, and tallow, there are no known resources. The whaling industry is carried on from South Georgia Island. The chief export is wool.

GIBRALTAR

Status: Self-governing dependency
Governor: Sir Peter Terry
Chief Minister: J. Bossano
Area: 2.25 sq mi. (5.8 sq km)
Population (1988): 29,141
Monetary unit: Gibraltar pound
Literacy rate: 99%
Economic summary: Gross national product (FY85 est.): $129 million. Exports: re-exports of tobacco, petroleum, wine. Imports: manufactured goods, fuels, foodstuffs. Major trading partners: U.K., Morocco, Portugal, Netherlands.

Gibraltar, at the south end of the Iberian Peninsula, is a rocky promonotory commanding the western entrance to the Mediterranean. Aside from its strategic importance, it is also a free port, naval base, and coaling station. It was captured by the Arabs crossing from Africa into Spain in A.D. 711. In the 15th century, it passed to the Moorish ruler of Granada and later became Spanish. It was captured by an Anglo-Dutch force in 1704 during the War of the Spanish Succession and passed to Great Britain by the Treaty of Utrecht in 1713. Most of the inhabitants of Gibraltar are of Spanish, Italian, and Maltese descent.

Spanish efforts to recover Gibraltar culminated in a referendum in 1967 in which the residents voted overwhelmingly to retain their link with Britain. Spain sealed Gibraltar's land border in 1969 and did not open communications until April 1980, after the two governments had agreed to solve their dispute in keeping with a United Nations resolution calling for restoration of the "Rock" to Spain.

HONG KONG

Status: Dependency
Governor: Sir David Wilson (1987)
Area: 398 sq mi. (1,031 sq km)
Population (est. mid-1989): 5,700,000 (average annual rate of natural increase: 0.5%)
Density per square mile: 14,218
Capital (1976 census): Victoria (Hong Kong Island), 501,-700
Monetary unit: Hong Kong dollar
Literacy rate: 75%
Economic summary: Gross domestic product (1986): $41.8 billion, $7,550 per capita; real growth rate (1987 est.): 12.0%. Land used for agriculture: 14%. labor force, 3%; principal products: vegetables, rice, dairy products. Labor force in industry: 45%; major industrial products: textiles, clothing, toys, transistor radios, watches, electronic components. Exports: clothing, textiles, toys, watches, transistor radios, electronic components. Imports: raw materials, consumer goods, food. Major trading partners: U.S., U.K., Japan, West Germany, China, Taiwan.

The crown colony of Hong Kong comprises the island of Hong Kong (32 sq mi.; 83 sq km), Stonecutters' Island, Kowloon Peninsula, and the New Territories on the adjoining mainland. The island of Hong Kong, located at the mouth of the Pearl River about 90 miles (145 km) southeast of Canton, was ceded to the Britain in 1841.

Stonecutters' Island and Kowloon were annexed in 1860, and the New Territories, which are mainly agricultural lands, were leased from China in 1898 for 99 years. Hong Kong was attacked by Japanese troops Dec. 7, 1941, and surrendered the following Christmas. It remained under Japanese occupation until August 1945.

After two years of painstaking negotiation, authorities of Britain and the People's Republic of China agreed in 1984 that Hong Kong would return to Chinese sovereignty on June 30, 1997, when Britain's lease on the New Territories expires. They also agreed that the vibrant capitalist enclave on China's coast would retain its status as a free port and its social, economic, and legal system as a special administrative region of China. Current laws will remain basically unchanged.

Under a unique "One Country, Two Systems" arrangement, the Chinese government promised that Hong Kong's lifestyle would remain unchanged for 50 years, and that freedoms of speech, press, assembly, association, travel, right to strike and religious belief would be guaranteed by law.

Hong Kong will continue to have its own finances and issue its own travel documents, and Peking will not levy taxes.

ISLE OF MAN

Status: Self-Governing Crown Dependency
Lieutenant Governor: Maj. Gen. Laurence A.W. New
Area: 227 sq mi. (588 sq km)
Population (1988): 64,576
Capital (1986): Douglas, 20,368
Monetary unit: Isle of Man pound

Situated in the Irish Sea, equidistant from Scotland, Ireland, and England, the Isle of Man is administered according to its own laws by a government composed of the Lieutenant Governor, a Legislative Council, and a House of Keys, one of the most ancient legislative assemblies in the world.

The chief exports are beef and lamb, fish, and livestock.

LEEWARD ISLANDS

See British Virgin Islands; Montserrat

MONTSERRAT

Status: Dependency
Governor: Christopher John Turner (1987)
Area: 40 sq mi. (104 sq km)
Population (1988): 12,078
Capital (est. 1988): Plymouth, 3,000
Monetary unit: East Caribbean dollar

The island of Montserrat is in the Lesser Antilles of the West Indies. Until 1956, it was a division of the Leeward Islands. It did not join the West Indies Associated States established in 1967.

The chief exports are cattle, potatoes, cotton, lint, recapped tires, mangoes, tomatoes.

PITCAIRN ISLAND

Status: Dependency
Governor: R. A. C. Byatt
Island Magistrate: B. Young
Area: 1.75 sq mi. (4.5 sq km)
Population (1987): 57
Capital: Adamstown

Pitcairn Island, in the South Pacific about midway between Australia and South America, consists of the island of Pitcairn and the three uninhabited islands of Henderson, Duicie, and Oeno. The island of Pitcairn was settled in 1790 by British mutineers from the ship *Bounty,* commanded by Capt. William Bligh. It was annexed as a British colony in 1838. Overpopulation forced removal of the settlement to Norfolk Island in 1856, but about 40 persons soon returned.

The colony is governed by a 10-member Council presided over by the Island Magistrate, who is elected for a three-year term.

ST. HELENA

Status: Dependency
Governor: Francis E. Baker (1984)
Area: 120 sq mi. (310 sq km)
Population (1988): 8,624
Capital (1987): Jamestown, 1,330
Monetary unit: Pound sterling

St. Helena is a volcanic island in the South Atlantic about 1,100 miles (1,770 km) from the west coast of Africa. It is famous as the place of exile of Napoleon (1815–21).

It was taken for England in 1659 by the East India Company and was brought under the direct government of the Crown in 1834.

St. Helena has two dependencies: Ascension (34 sq mi.; 88 sq km), an island about 700 miles (1,127 km) northwest of St. Helena; and Tristan da Cunha (40 sq mi.; 104 sq km), a group of six islands about 1,500 miles (2,414 km) south-southwest of St. Helena.

TURKS AND CAICOS ISLANDS

Status: Dependency
Governor: Michael Bradley (1987)
Area: 193 sq mi. (500 sq km)
Population (1988): 9,295
Capital (est. 1988): Grand Turk, 3,146
Monetary unit: U.S. dollar

These two groups of islands are situated at the southeast end of the Bahamas. The principal islands in the Turks group are Grand Turk and Salt Cay; the principal ones in the Caicos group are South Caicos, East Caicos, Middle (or Grand) Caicos, North Caicos, Providenciales, and West Caicos.

The Turks and Caicos Islands were dependencies of Jamaica until 1959, when they became a unit territory within the Federation of the West Indies. In 1962, when Jamaica became independent, the Turks and Caicos became a British crown colony. The present Constitution has been in force since 1969.

Chief exports in 1974 were crayfish (73%) and conch (25%).

VIRGIN ISLANDS

See British Virgin Islands

UNITED STATES

The United States of America
President: George Bush (1989)
Area: 3,540,939 sq mi. (9,171,032 sq km)
Population (est. mid-1989): 248,800,000 (average annual rate of natural increase: 0.7%)
Density per square mile: 69
Capital (1986 est.): Washington, D.C., 626,000
Largest cities (1986 est.): New York, 7,262,700; Los Angeles, 3,259,340; Chicago, 3,009,530; Houston, 1,728,910; Philadelphia, 1,642,900; Detroit, 1,086,220
Monetary unit: Dollar
Language: predominantly English, sizable Spanish-speaking minority
Religions: Protestant (78.7 million members); Roman Catholic (52.3 million members); Jewish (5.8 million members)
Literacy rate: 96%
Economic summary: Gross national product (1988): $4,864.3 billion, per capita income (1988): $16,444.

Annual growth rate (1988): 7.5%. Labor force in agriculture: 2.7%; principal products: corn, wheat, barley, oats, sugar, potatoes, soybeans, fruits, beef, veal, pork. Labor force in non-agricultural occupations: 97.3%. Major industrial products: petroleum products, fertilizers, cement, pig iron and steel, plastics and resins, newsprint, motor vehicles, machinery, natural gas, electricity. Natural resources: coal, oil, water power, copper, gold, silver, minerals, timber. Exports: machinery, chemicals, aircrafts, military equipment, cereals, motor vehicles, grains. Imports: crude and partly refined petroleum, machinery, automobiles. Major trading partners: Canada, Japan, United Kingdom, West Germany, Mexico, Saudi Arabia.

Government. The president is elected for a four-year term and may be re-elected only once. In 1989, the bicameral Congress consisted of the 100-member Senate (55 Democrats, 45 Republicans), elected to a six-year term with one-third of the seats becoming vacant every two years, and the 435-member House of Representatives (255 Democrats, 176 Republicans),[1] elected every two years. The minimum voting age is 18.

1. As of August 1989 there were 4 vacant House seats.

URUGUAY

Oriental Republic of Uruguay
President: Julio Maria Sanguinetti (1985)
Area: 68,040 sq mi. (176,224 sq km)
Population (est. mid-1989): 3,000,000 (average annual rate of natural increase: 0.8%)
Density per square mile: 44
Capital and largest city (est. 1982): Montevideo, 1,325,-000
Monetary unit: Peso
Language: Spanish
Religion: Roman Catholic, 60%
National name: Republica Oriental del Uruguay
Literacy rate: 96%
Economic summary: Gross domestic product (1987 est.): $6.9 billion, $2,330 per capita; real growth rate (1987 est.): 4.0%. Land used for agriculture: 86%; labor force: 11%; principal products: livestock, grains, sugar. Labor force in industry: 29%; major products: processed meats, wool and hides, textiles, shoes, handbags and leather wearing apparel, cement, refined petroleum. Natural resources: hydroelectric power potential. Exports: meat, hides, wool, textiles. Imports: crude petroleum, transportation equipment, chemicals, machinery, metals. Major trading partners: U.S., Brazil, Argentina, Nigeria, Western Europe.

Geography. Uruguay, on the east coast of South America south of Brazil and east of Argentina, is comparable in size to the State of Washington.

The country consists of a low, rolling plain in the south and a low plateau in the north. It has a 120-mile (193 km) Atlantic shore line, a 235-mile (378 km) frontage on the Rio de la Plata, and 270 miles (435 km) on the Uruguay River, its western boundary.

Government. After elections in November 1984, Julio Maria Sanguinetti was inaugurated as President on March 1, 1985, ending 12 years of military rule. Under the Constitution, Presidents serve a single five-year term. The bicameral Congress, dissolved by the military in 1973, also was restored in 1985.

History. Juan Díaz de Solis, a Spaniard, discovered Uruguay in 1516, but the Portuguese were first to settle it when they founded Colonia in 1680. After a long struggle, Spain wrested the country from Portugal in 1778. Uruguay revolted against Spain in 1811, only to be conquered in 1817 by the Portuguese from Brazil. Independence was reasserted with Argentine help in 1825, and the republic was set up in 1828.

Independence, however, did not restore order, and a revolt in 1836 touched off nearly 50 years of factional strife, with occasional armed intervention from Argentina and Brazil.

Uruguay, made prosperous by meat and wool exports, founded a welfare state early in the 20th century. A decline began in the 1950s as successive governments struggled to maintain a large bureaucracy and costly social benefits. Economic stagnation and political frustration followed.

A military coup ousted the civilian government in 1973. The military dictatorship that followed used fear and terror to demoralize the population, taking thousands of political prisoners, probably the highest proportion of citizens jailed for political reasons anywhere in the world.

Under the generals, the country's worst economic crisis in decades produced 66% inflation, 30% unemployment and a foreign debt of $5 billion. Per capita income sank to $1,100.

After ruling for 12 years, the military regime permitted election of a civilian government in November 1984 and relinquished rule in March 1985.

VANUATU

Republic of Vanuatu
President: Fred Timakata (1989)
Prime Minister: Fr. Walter Lini (1980)
Area: 5,700 sq mi. (14,763 sq km)
Population (est. mid-1989): 200,000 (average annual rate of natural increase: 3.2%)
Density per square mile: 28
Capital (est. 1987): Port Vila, 15,100
Monetary unit: Vatu
Religions: Presbyterian, 47%; Roman Catholic, 15%; Anglican, 15%; other Christian, 10%; Animist, 9%
Literacy rate: 10-20%
Economic Summary: Gross domestic product (1986): $84 million, $580 per capita; real growth rate (1986): −1.0%. Principal agricultural products: copra, cocoa, coffee. Exports: copra, cocoa, coffee, frozen fish. Imports: food, machinery. Major trading partners: France, New Zealand, Japan, Australia, Netherlands.

Geography. Formerly known as the New Hebrides, Vanuatu is an archipelago of some 80 islands lying between New Caledonia and Fiji in the South Pacific. Largest of the islands is Espiritu Santo (875 sq mi.; 2,266 sq km); others are Efate, Malekula, Malo, Pentecost, and Tanna. The population is largely Melanesian of mixed blood.

Government. The constitution by which Vanuatu achieved independence on July 30, 1980, vests executive authority in a President, elected by an electoral college for a five-year term. A unicameral legislature of 39 members exercises legislative power.

History. The islands were discovered by Pedro Fernandes de Queiros of Portugal in 1606 and were charted and named by the British navigator James Cook in 1774. Conflicting British and French interests were resolved by a joint naval commission that administered the islands from 1887. A condominium government was established in 1906.

The islands' plantation economy, based on imported Vietnamese labor, was prosperous until the 1920s, when markets for its products declined. The New Hebrides escaped Japanese occupation in World War II and the French population was among the first to support the Gaullist Free French movement.

A brief rebellion by French settlers and plantation workers on Espiritu Santo led by Jimmy Stevens in May 1980 threatened the scheduled independence of the islands. Britain sent a company of Royal Marines and France a contingent of 50 policemen to quell the revolt, which the new government said was financed by the Phoenix Foundation, a right-wing U.S. group. With the British and French forces replaced by soldiers from Papua New Guinea, independence ceremonies took place on July 30. The next month it was reported that Stevens had been arrested and the revolt quelled.

VATICAN CITY STATE

Ruler: Pope John Paul II (1978)
Area: 0.17 sq mi. (0.44 sq km)
Population (est. 1988): 752 (mostly Italian)
Density per square mile: 4,424
Monetary unit: Lira
Languages: Latin and Italian
Religion: Roman Catholic
National name: Stato della Città del Vaticano

Geography. The Vatican City State is situated on the Vatican hill, on the right bank of the Tiber River, within the commune of Rome.

Government. The Pope has full legal, executive, and judicial powers. Executive power over the area is in the hands of a Commission of Cardinals appointed by the Pope. The College of Cardinals is the Pope's chief advisory body, and upon his death the cardinals elect his successor for life. The cardinals themselves are created for life by the Pope.

In the Vatican the central administration of the Roman Catholic Church throughout the world (Holy See) is carried on by the Secretariat of State, nine Congregations, three tribunals, twelve councils, and five offices. In its diplomatic relations, the Holy See is represented by the Papal Secretary of State.

History. The Vatican City State, sovereign and independent, is the survivor of the papal states that in 1859 comprised an area of some 17,000 square miles (44,030 sq km). During the struggle for Italian unification, from 1860 to 1870, most of this area became part of Italy.

By an Italian law of May 13, 1871, the temporal power of the Pope was abrogated, and the territory of the Papacy was confined to the Vatican and Lateran palaces and the villa of Castel Gandolfo. The Popes consistently refused to recognize this arrangement and, by the Lateran Treaty of Feb. 11, 1929, between the Vatican and the Kingdom of Italy, the exclusive dominion and sovereign jurisdiction of the Holy See over the city of the Vatican was again recognized, thus restoring the Pope's temporal authority over the area.

The first session of Ecumenical Council Vatican II was opened by John XXIII on Oct. 11, 1962, to plan and set policies for the modernization of the Roman Catholic Church. Pope Paul VI continued the Council, opening the second session on Sept. 29, 1963.

On Aug. 26, 1978, Cardinal Albino Luciani was chosen by the College of Cardinals to succeed Paul VI, who had died of a heart attack on Aug. 6. The new Pope, who took the name John Paul I, was born on Oct. 17, 1912, at Forno di Canale in Italy.

(For a listing of all the Popes, *see* the Index.)

Only 34 days after his election, John Paul I died of a heart attack, ending the shortest reign in 373 years. On Oct. 16, Cardinal Karol Wojtyla, 58, was chosen Pope and took the name John Paul II.

A visit to the Irish Republic and to the United States in September and October 1979, followed by a 12-nation African tour in May 1980 and a visit in July to Brazil, the most populous Catholic nation, further established John Paul's image as a "people's" Pope. On May 13, 1981, a Turkish terrorist shot the Pope in St. Peter's Square, the first assassination attempt against the Pontiff in modern times. Mehmet Ali Agca was sentenced on July 22 to life imprisonment by an Italian Court.

The Pontiff traveled to Britain and Argentina in 1982. He also made a visit to Poland.

On June 3, 1985, the Vatican and Italy ratified a new church-state treaty, known as a concordat, replacing the Lateran Pact of 1929. The new accord affirmed the independence of Vatican City but ended a number of privileges the Catholic Church had in Italy, including its status as the state religion. The treaty ended Rome's status as a "sacred city."

VENEZUELA

Republic of Venezuela
President: Carlos Andrés Pérez (1989)
Area: 352,143 sq mi. (912,050 sq km)
Population (est. mid-1989): 19,100,000 (average annual rate of natural increase: 2.4%) (mestizo, 67%; white, 21%; black, 10%; Indian, 2%)
Density per square mile: 54
Capital: Caracas
Largest cities (est. 1981 for metropolitan area): Caracas, 3,000,000; Maracaibo, 890,000; Valencia, 616,000; Barquisimeto, 498,000
Monetary unit: Bolivar
Language: Spanish, Indian dialects in interior
Religion: Roman Catholic
National name: Republica de Venezuela
Literacy rate: 88.4%
Economic summary: Gross domestic product (1986): $53.9 billion, $3,030 per capita; real growth rate (1986): 2.2%. Land used for agriculture, 24%; labor force, 16%; principal products: rice, coffee, corn, sugar, bananas, dairy and meat products. Labor force in industry, 28%; principal products: refined petroleum products, iron and steel, paper products, cement, textiles, transport equipment. Natural resources: petroleum, natural gas,

iron ore, hydroelectric power. Exports: petroleum, iron ore. Imports: industrial machinery and equipment, manufactures, chemicals, foodstuffs. Major trading partners: U.S., Canada, Japan, Netherlands, Antilles, W. Germany.

Geography. Venezuela, a third larger than Texas, occupies most of the northern coast of South America on the Caribbean Sea. It is bordered by Colombia to the west, Guyana to the east, and Brazil to the south.

Mountain systems break Venezuela into four distinct areas: (1) the Maracaibo lowlands; (2) the mountainous region in the north and northwest; (3) the Orinoco basin, with the llanos (vast grass-covered plains) on its northern border and great forest areas in the south and southeast; (4) the Guiana Highlands, south of the Orinoco, accounting for nearly half the national territory. About 80% of Venezuela is drained by the Orinoco and its tributaries.

Government. Venezuela is a federal republic consisting of 20 states, the Federal District, two territories and 72 islands in the Caribbean. There is a bicameral Congress, the 50 members of the Senate and the 201 members of the Chamber of Deputies being elected by popular vote to five-year terms. The President is also elected for five years. He must be a Venezuelan by birth and over 30 years old. He is not eligible for re-election until 10 years after the end of his term.

History. Columbus discovered Venezuela on his third voyage in 1498. A subsequent Spanish explorer gave the country its name, meaning "Little Venice." There were no important settlements until Caracas was founded in 1567. Simón Bolívar, who led the liberation of much of the continent from Spain, was born in Caracas in 1783. With Bolívar taking part, Venezuela was one of the first South American colonies to revolt against Spain, in 1810, but it was not until 1821 that independence was won. Federated at first with Colombia and Ecuador, the country set up a republic in 1830 and then sank for many decades into a condition of revolt, dictatorship, and corruption.

From 1908 to 1935, Gen. Juan Vicente Gómez ruled tyrannically, picking satellites to alternate with him in the presidential palace. Thereafter, there was a struggle between democratic forces and those backing a return to strong-man rule. Dr. Rómulo Betancourt and the liberal Acción Democrática Party won a majority of seats in a constituent assembly to draft a new Constitution in 1946. A well-known writer, Rómulo Gallegos, candidate of Betancourt's party, easily won the presidential election of 1947. But, the army ousted Gallegos the next year and instituted a military junta.

The country overthrew the dictatorship in 1958 and thereafter enjoyed democratic government. Rafael Caldera Rodríguez, President from 1969 to 1974, legalized the Communist Party and established diplomatic relations with Moscow. In 1974, President Carlos Andrés Perez took office.

In 1976, Venezuela nationalized 21 oil companies, mostly subsidiaries of U.S. firms, offering compensation of $1.28 billion. Oil income in that year was $9.9 billion, and although production decreased 2.2%, revenue remained at the same level in 1977 because of higher prices, largely financing an ambitious social welfare program.

Despite difficulties at home, Pérez continued to play an active foreign role in extending economic aid to Latin neighbors, in backing the human-rights policy of President Carter, and in supporting Carter's return of the Panama Canal to Panama.

Opposition Christian Democrats capitalized on Pérez's domestic problems to elect Luis Herrera Campíns President in Venezuela's fifth consecutive free election, on Dec. 3, 1978.

Herrera Campins at first supported U.S. policy in Central America, lining up behind the government of El Salva but he later shifted toward a "political solution" that would include the insurgents. In March 1982, he assailed Reagan's policy as "interventionist."

When the Falklands war broke out, Venezuela became one of the most vigorous advocates of the Argentine cause and one of the sharpest critics of the U.S. decision to back Britain.

Jaime Lusinchi of the Democratic Action party won the country's sixth consecutive free election, on Dec. 4, 1983, and was inaugurated President in March 1984. In 1985, he reached a debt-rescheduling agreement with Venezuela's creditors for its $21-billion debt.

VIETNAM

Socialist Republic of Vietnam
President: Vo Chi Cong (1987)
Premier: Do Muoi (1988)
Area: 127,246 sq mi. (329,566 sq km)
Population (est. mid-1989): 66,800,000 (average annual rate of natural increase: 2.6%)
Density per square mile: 525
Capital: Hanoi
Largest cities (est. 1979): Ho Chi Minh City (Saigon),[1] 3,450,000; Hanoi, 2,600,000; Haiphong, 1,280,000; (est. 1973); Da Nang, 492,200; Nha Trang, 216,200; Qui Nho'n, 213,750; Hué 209,000
Monetary unit: Dong
Languages: Vietnamese (official), French, English, Khmer, Chinese
Religions: Buddhist, Roman Catholic, Islam, Taoist, Confucian, Animist
National name: Công Hòa Xa Hôi Chú Nghia Viêt Nam
Literacy rate: 78%
Economic summary: Gross national product (1986 est.): $12.4 billion, $200 per capita. Land used for agriculture: 23%; labor force: 70%; principal products: rice, rubber, fruits and vegetables, corn, sugar cane, fish. Labor force in industry, 5%; major products: processed foods, textiles, cement, chemical fertilizers, glass, tires. Natural resources: phosphates, forests, coal. Exports: agricultural products, coal, minerals. Imports: petroleum, steel products, railroad equipment, chemicals, medicines, raw cotton, fertilizer, grain. Major trading partners: U.S.S.R., Singapore, Japan, Eastern Europe.

1. Includes suburb of Cholon.

Geography. Vietnam occupies the eastern and southern part of the Indochinese peninsula in Southeast Asia, with the South China Sea along its entire coast. China is to the north and Laos and Cambodia to the west. Long and narrow on a north-south axis, Vietnam is about twice the size of Arizona.

The Mekong River delta lies in the south and the Red River delta in the north. Heavily forested mountain and plateau regions make up most of the country.

Government. Less than a year after the capitulation of the former Republic of Vietnam (South Vietnam) on April 30, 1975, a joint National Assembly convened with 249 deputies representing the North and 243 representing the South. The Assembly set July 2, 1976, as the official reunification date. Hanoi became the capital, with North Vietnamese President Ton Duc Thang becoming President of the new Socialist Republic of Vietnam and North Vietnamese Premier Pham Van Dong becoming its head of government. By 1981, the National Assembly had increased to 496 members. Truong Chinh succeeded Thang in 1981.

Dang Cong san Vietnam (Communist Party), led by General Secretary Nguyen Van Linh, is the ruling political party. There are also the Socialist Party and the Democratic Party.

History. The Vietnamese are descendants of Mongoloid nomads from China and migrants from Indonesia. They recognized Chinese suzerainty until the 15th century, an era of nationalistic expansion, when Cambodians were pushed out of the southern area of what is now Vietnam.

A century later, the Portuguese were the first Europeans to enter the area. France established its influence early in the 19th century and within 80 years conquered the three regions into which the country was then divided—Cochin-China in the south, Annam in the center, and Tonkin in the north.

France first unified Vietnam in 1887, when a single governor-generalship was created, followed by the first physical links between north and south—a rail and road system. Even at the beginning of World War II, however, there were internal differences among the three regions.

Japan took over military bases in Vietnam in 1940 and a pro-Vichy French administration remained until 1945. A veteran Communist leader, Ho Chi Minh, organized an independence movement known as the Vietminh to exploit a confused situation. At the end of the war, Ho's followers seized Hanoi and declared a short-lived republic, which ended with the arrival of French forces in 1946.

Paris proposed a unified government within the French Union under the former Annamite emperor, Bao Dai. Cochin-China and Annam accepted the proposal, and Bao Dai was proclaimed emperor of all Vietnam in 1949. Ho and the Vietminh withheld support, and the revolution in China gave them the outside help needed for a war of resistance against French and Vietnamese troops armed largely by the U.S.

A bitter defeat at Dien Bien Phu in northwest Vietnam on May 5, 1954, broke the French military campaign and brought the division of Vietnam at the conference of Geneva that year.

In the new South, Ngo Dinh Diem, Premier under Bao Dai, deposed the monarch in 1955 and established a republic with himself as President. Diem used strong U.S. backing to create an authoritarian regime that suppressed all opposition but could not eradicate the Northern-supplied Communist Viet Cong.

Skirmishing grew into a full-scale war, with escalating U.S. involvement. A military coup, U.S.-inspired in the view of many, ousted Diem Nov. 1, 1963, and a kaleidoscope of military governments followed. The most savage fighting of the war occurred in early 1968, during the Tet holidays.

Although the Viet Cong failed to overthrow the Saigon government, U.S. public reaction to the apparently endless war forced a limitation of U.S. troops to 550,000 and a new emphasis on shifting the burden of further combat to the South Vietnamese. Ho Chi Minh's death on Sept. 3, 1969, brought a quadrumvirate to replace him but no flagging in Northern will to fight.

U.S. bombing and invasion of Cambodia in the summer of 1970—an effort to destroy Viet Cong bases in the neighboring state—marked the end of major U.S. participation in the fighting. Most American ground troops were withdrawn from combat by mid-1971 as heavy bombing of the Ho Chi Minh trail from North Vietnam appeared to cut the supply of men and matériel to the South.

Secret negotiations for peace by Secretary of State Henry A. Kissinger with North Vietnamese officials during 1972 after heavy bombing of Hanoi and Haiphong brought the two sides near agreement in October. When the Northerners demanded the removal of the South's President Nguyen Van Thieu as their price, President Nixon ordered the "Christmas bombing" of the North. The conference resumed and a peace settlement was signed in Paris on Jan. 27, 1973. It called for release of all U.S. prisoners, withdrawal of U.S. forces, limitation of both sides' forces inside South Vietnam, and a commitment to peaceful reunification.

Despite Chinese and Soviet endorsement, the agreement foundered. U.S. bombing of Communist-held areas in Cambodia was halted by Congress in August 1973, and in the following year Communist action in South Vietnam increased.

An armored attack across the 17th parallel in January 1975 panicked the South Vietnamese army and brought the invasion within 40 miles of Saigon by April 9. Thieu resigned on April 21 and fled, to be replaced by Vice President Tran Van Huong, who quit a week later, turning over the office to Gen. Duong Van Minh. "Big Minh" surrendered Saigon on April 30, ending a war that took 1.3 million Vietnamese and 56,000 American lives, at the cost of $141 billion in U.S. aid.

On May 3, 1977, the U.S. and Vietnam opened negotiations in Paris to normalize relations. One of the first results was the withdrawal of U.S. opposition to Vietnamese membership in the United Nations, formalized in the Security Council on July 20. Two major issues remained to be settled, however: the return of the bodies of some 2,500 U.S. servicemen missing in the war and the claim by Hanoi that former President Nixon had promised reconstruction aid under the 1973 agreement. Negotiations failed to resolve these issues.

The new year also brought an intensification of border clashes between Vietnam and Cambodia and accusations by China that Chinese residents of Vietnam were being subjected to persecution. Peking cut off all aid and withdrew 800 technicians. By June, 133,000 ethnic Chinese were reported to have fled Vietnam, and a year later as many as 500,000 of the 1.8 million Vietnamese of Chinese ancestry were believed to have escaped.

Hanoi was undoubtedly preoccupied with a continuing war in Cambodia, where 60,000 Vietnamese troops were aiding the Heng Samrin regime in suppressing the last forces of the pro-Chinese Pol Pot regime. In early 1979, Vietnam was conducting a two-front war, defending its northern border against a Chinese invasion and at the same time supporting its army in Cambodia.

Despite Hanoi's claims of total victory, resistance in Cambodia continued through 1984. Vietnam's second conflict, on its border with China, also flared sporadically.

The Hanoi government agreed in July 1984 to resume technical talks with U.S. officials on the possible whereabouts of the 2,490 Americans still listed as missing, most of them believed dead. In August 1985, the North Vietnamese turned over to an American team 26 numbered crates described as containing the remains of 26 U.S. servicemen.

Economic troubles continued, with the government seeking to reschedule its $1.4-billion foreign hard-currency debt, owed mainly to Japan and the International Monetary Fund. In late 1987, a shuffle of the Vietnamese Politburo brought in new leaders who are expected to slightly relax the government grip on the economy and crack down on corruption within the party.

The exodus of the Vietnamese boat people also continued, despite a growing tendency by passing ships not to help the Vietnamese fleeing their country by boat.

In 1988, Vietnam also began limited troop withdrawals from Laos and Cambodia. The government has undertaken to withdraw completely from Cambodia by mid-1990.

(For a Vietnam War chronology, see Headline History.)

WESTERN SAMOA

Independent State of Western Samoa
Head of State: Malietoa Tanumafili II (1962)
Prime Minister: Tofilau Eti Alesana (1988)
Area: 1,093 sq mi. (2,831 sq km)
Population (1989): 165,000 (average annual growth rate: 2.4%)
Density per square mile: 183
Capital and largest city (1980): Apia, 33,400
Monetary unit: Tala
Languages: Samoan and English
Religions: Congregational, 50%; Roman Catholic, 22%; Methodist, 16%
National name: Samoa i Sisifo
Member of Commonwealth of Nations
Literacy rate: 90%
Economic summary: Gross domestic product (1986 est.): $110 million. $520 per capita. Land used for agriculture: 50%; labor force: 50%; principal products: copra, cocoa, bananas, timber. Labor force in industry: 10%; major products: timber, light industrial products. Natural resource: timber. Exports: copra, cocoa, bananas, timber. Imports: food, manufactured goods, machinery. Major trading partners: New Zealand, Australia, U.S., Fiji, Japan

Geography. Western Samoa, the size of Rhode Island, is in the South Pacific Ocean about 2,200 miles (3,540 km) south of Hawaii midway to Sydney, Australia, and about 800 miles (1,287 km) northeast of Fiji. The larger islands in the Samoan chain are mountainous and of volcanic origin. There is little level land except in the coastal areas, where most cultivation takes place.

Government. Western Samoa has a 47-member Legislature, consisting mainly of the titleholders (chiefs) of family groups, with two members elected by universal suffrage to represent those not belonging to such groups. When the present Head of State dies, successors will be elected by the Legislature for five-year terms.

History. The Samoan islands were discovered in the 18th century and visited by Dutch and French traders. Toward the end of the 19th century, conflicting interests of the U.S., Britain, and Germany resulted in a treaty signed in 1899. It recognized the paramount interests of the U.S. in those islands east of 171° west longitude (American Samoa) and Germany's interests in the other islands (Western Samoa); the British withdrew in return for recognition of their rights in Tonga and the Solomons.

New Zealand occupied Western Samoa in 1914, and was granted a League of Nations mandate. In 1947, the islands became a U.N. trust territory administered by New Zealand.

Western Samoa became independent on Jan. 1, 1962.

YEMEN

People's Democratic Republic of Yemen
President: Haider Abubaker Al-Attas (1986)
Area: 128,560 sq mi. (332,970 sq km)
Population (est. mid-1989): 2,500,000 (average annual rate of natural increase: 3.4%)
Density per square mile: 21.62[1]
National capital and largest city (est. 1981): Aden, 365,000
Administrative capital: Aden
Monetary unit: Yemen dinar
Language: Arabic
Religion: Islam (Sunni)
National name: Jumhurijah al-Yemen al Dimuqratiyah al Sha'abijah
Literacy rate: 25%
Economic summary: Gross national product (1985 est.): $1.1 billion, $500 per capita. Land used for agriculture: 28%. Principal agricultural products: cotton, cereal, coffee, dates, livestock. Major industrial products: refined oil products, salt, fish meal, cloth. Natural resources: fish, petroleum. Exports: cotton, hides and skins, dried fish. Imports: foodstuffs, manufactured goods. Major trading partners: U.K., Japan, Yemen Arab Republic, Australia, UAE.

Geography. Formerly known as Southern Yemen, the People's Democratic Republic of Yemen extends along the southern part of the Arabian Peninsula on the Gulf of Aden and the Indian Ocean. It is comparable in size to Nevada. The Yemen Arab Republic is to the northwest, Saudi Arabia to the north, and Oman to the east.

A 700-mile (1,130-km) narrow coastal plain gives way to a mountainous region and then a plateau area.

Government. On June 22, 1969, President Qahtan Mohammed al Shaabi resigned and was replaced by a five-man Presidential Council.

A Constitution published in 1970 changed the state's name from Southern Yemen and established a 111-seat legislature, the People's Supreme Council of which al-Attas is chairman, and thus head of state. The only legal political party is the Yemeni Socialist Party.

History. The People's Republic of Southern Yemen was established Nov. 30, 1967, when Britain granted independence to the Federation of South Arabia. This Federation consisted of the state (once the colony) of Aden and 16 of the 20 states of the Protectorate of South Arabia (once the Aden Protectorate). The four states of the Protectorate that did not join the Federation later became part of Southern Yemen.

Salim Robea Ali, chairman of the Presidential Council since its establishment in 1969, was ousted and executed June 26, 1978, two days after the assassination of President Ahmed Hussein al-Ghashmi of the Yemen Arab Republic. Premier Ali Nasir Muhammad al-Husani assumed the added duty of Council head.

Abdul Fattah Ismail was elected President by the Supreme Council on Dec. 27, 1978 and reversed Robea's movement toward reconciliation with the Yemen Arab Republic and an accommodation with Saudi Arabia. His sudden resignation on April 21, 1980, was reported to have stemmed from the new Soviet desire to win friends in the Yemen Arab Republic and Saudi Arabia.

In December 1985, a purge of Ismail's hardline faction led to a brief civil war in which Ismail was killed but al-Husani was overthrown by Haider al-Attas, an Ismail ally.

YEMEN ARAB REPUBLIC

President: Col. Ali Abdullah Saleh (1978)
Premier: Abdulaziz Abdulghani (1983)
Area: 75,290 sq mi. (195,000 sq km)
Population (est. mid-1989): 6,900,000 (average annual rate of natural increase: 3.5%)
Density per square mile: 92
Capital and largest city (est. 1986): San'a', 427,185
Monetary unit: Rial
Language: Arabic
Religion: Islam (Shiite, 60%; Sunni, 40%)
National name: Al Jamhuriya al Arabiya Yamaniya
Literacy rate: 15% (est.)
Economic summary: Gross domestic product (1986): $3.2 billion, $505 per capita; real growth rate (1986): 0.2%. Land used for agriculture: principal products: wheat, sorghum, cattle, sheep, cotton, fruits. Major industrial products: crude oil, cotton, textiles, leather goods, handicrafts. Natural resources: oil, rock salt, marble; some coal, nickel, copper. Exports: cotton, coffee, hides, vegetables. Imports: textiles and other manufactured consumer goods, sugar, grain, flour. Major trading partners: France, Yemen (Aden), Japan, Saudi Arabia.

Geography. The Yemen Arab Republic, also known as North Yemen, occupies the southwestern tip of the Arabian Peninsula, with its western coast on the Red Sea opposite Ethiopia. Its neighbors are Saudi Arabia to the north and east and the People's Democratic Republic of Yemen to the south. Its area is slightly less than that of South Dakota.

A north-south coastal plain 20–50 miles wide (32–80 km) lies in the west; eastward, there are the interior highlands, which attain a height of 12,000 feet (3,660 m), and the expanse of the Rub 'al-Khali Desert.

Government. The country's first permanent Constitution was submitted to the National Assembly in 1971. It provided for a 179-member legislature, the Consultative Council, 20 of whose members would be chosen by the President and the rest elected every four years. A five-man executive Presidential Council was to be chosen by the Consultative Council.

In 1974, the army ousted the government in a bloodless coup and suspended the Constitution and its various legislative bodies.

History. The history of Yemen dates back to the Minaean kingdom (1200–650 B.C.). It accepted Islam in A.D. 628, and in the 10th century came under the control of the Rassite dynasty of the Zaidi sect. The Turks occupied the area from 1538 to 1630 and from 1849 to 1918. The sovereign status of Yemen was confirmed by treaties signed with Saudi Arabia and Britain in 1934.

Yemen joined the Arab League in 1945 and established diplomatic relations with the U.S. in 1946.

In 1962, a military revolt of elements favoring President Gamal Abdel Nasser of Egypt broke out. A ruling junta proclaimed a republic, and Yemen became an international battleground, with Egypt and the U.S.S.R. supporting the revolutionaries, and King Saud of Saudi Arabia and King Hussein of Jordan the royalists. The civil war continued until the war between the Arab states and Israel broke out in June 1967. Nasser had to pull out many of his troops and agree to a cease-fire and withdrawal of foreign forces. The war finally ended with the defeat of the royalists in mid-1969.

In 1977, Col. Ibrahim al-Hamidi was assassinated after three years as head of government and was succeeded by Lt. Col. Ahmed Hussein al-Ghashmi as head of the Presidential Council. On June 24, 1978, al-Ghashmi was killed by a bomb as he received the credentials of a new ambassador from the People's Democratic Republic of Yemen. The People's Council elected Col. Ali Abdullah Saleh as President on July 17.

In 1984, the Hunt Oil Co. of Dallas discovered oil in North Yemen, the first time it has been found in the desolate Arab state, one of the world's poorest nations. Construction of a pipeline began in 1986 and exports began in 1988.

YUGOSLAVIA

Socialist Federal Republic of Yugoslavia
President: Janez Drnovšek (1989)
President of Federal Executive Council (Premier): Ante Marković (1989)
Area: 98,766 sq mi. (255,804 sq km)
Population (est. mid-1989): 23,700,000 (average annual rate of natural increase: 0.6%) (Serbian, 36%; Croatian, 20%; Moslem, 9%; Slovene, 8%; Albanian, 8%; Macedonian, 6%, Montenegrin, 3%)
Density per square mile: 240
Capital: Belgrade
Largest cities (est. 1982): Belgrade, 1,250,000; Zagreb, 765,000; Skopje, 505,000; Sarajevo, 450,000; Ljubljana, 255,000; Split, 200,000
Monetary unit: Dinar
Languages: Serbo-Croatian, Slovene, Macedonian (all official)
Religions: Eastern Orthodox, 50%; Roman Catholic, 30%; Islam, 10%
National name: Socijalisticka Federativna Republika Jugoslavija

Literacy rate: 90%
Economic summary: Gross national product (1986): $145.0 billion, $6,220 per capita; real growth rate 3.0%. Land used for agriculture: 56%; labor force: 22%; principal products: corn, wheat, tobacco, sugar beets. Labor force in industry: 27%; major products: wood, processed food, nonferrous metals, machinery, textiles. Natural resources: coal, timber, copper, iron, lead, zinc, bauxite. Exports: leather goods, textiles, machinery. Imports: machinery, chemicals, iron, and steel. Major trading partners: U.S.S.R., West Germany, Italy, U.S., Czechoslovakia.

Geography. Yugoslavia fronts on the eastern coast of the Adriatic Sea opposite Italy. Its neighbors are Austria, Italy, and Hungary to the north, Romania and Bulgaria to the east, and Greece and Albania to the south. It is slightly larger than Wyoming.

About half of Yugoslavia is mountainous. In the north, the Dinaric Alps rise abruptly from the sea and progress eastward as a barren limestone plateau called the Karst. Montenegro is a jumbled mass of mountains, containing also some grassy slopes and fertile river valleys. Southern Serbia, too, is mountainous. A rich plain in the north and northeast, drained by the Danube, is the most fertile area of the country.

Government. Yugoslavia is a federal republic composed of six socialist republics—Serbia (which includes the provinces of Vojvodina and Kosovo), Croatia, Slovenia, Bosnia-Herzegovina, Macedonia, and Montenegro. Actual administration is carried on by the Federal Executive Council and its secretaries.

The League of Communists and the Socialist Alliance of the Working People are the major political parties.

History. Yugoslavia was formed Dec. 4, 1918, from the patchwork of Balkan states and territories where World War I began with the assassination of Archduke Ferdinand of Austria at Sarajevo on June 28, 1914. The new Kingdom of Serbs, Croats, and Slovenes included the former kingdoms of Serbia and Montenegro; Bosnia-Herzegovina, previously administered jointly by Austria and Hungary; Croatia-Slavonia, a semi-autonomous region of Hungary, and Dalmatia, formerly administered by Austria. King Peter I of Serbia became the first monarch, his son acting as Regent until his accession as Alexander I on Aug. 16, 1921.

Croatian demands for a federal state forced Alexander to assume dictatorial powers in 1929 and to change the country's name to Yugoslavia. Serbian dominance continued despite his efforts, amid the resentment of other regions. A Macedonian associated with Croatian dissidents assassinated Alexander in Marseilles, France, on Oct. 9, 1934, and his cousin, Prince Paul, became Regent for the King's son, Prince Peter.

Paul's pro-Axis policy brought Yugoslavia to sign the Axis Pact on March 25, 1941, and opponents overthrew the government two days later. On April 6 the Nazis occupied the country, and the young King and his government fled. Two guerrilla armies —the Chetniks under Draza Mihajlovic supporting the monarchy and the Partisans under Tito (Josip Broz) leaning toward the U.S.S.R.—fought the Nazis for the duration of the war. In 1943, Tito established an Executive National Committee of Liberation to function as a provisional government.

Tito won the election held in the fall of 1945, as monarchists boycotted the vote. A new Assembly abolished the monarchy and proclaimed the Federal People's Republic of Yugoslavia, with Tito as Prime Minister.

Ruthlessly eliminating opposition, the Tito government executed Mihajlovic in 1946. With Soviet aid, Tito annexed the greater part of Italian Istria under the 1947 peace treaty with Italy but failed in his claim to the key port of Trieste. Zone B of the former free territory of Trieste went to Yugoslavia in 1954.

Tito broke with the Soviet bloc in 1948 and Yugoslavia has since followed a middle road, combining orthodox Communist control of politics and general overall economic policy with a varying degree of freedom in the arts, travel, and individual enterprise. Tito, who became President in 1953 and President for life under a revised Constitution adopted in 1963, has played a major part in the creation of a "non-aligned" group of states, the so-called "third world."

The Marshal supported his one-time Soviet mentors in their quarrel with Communist China, but even though he imprisoned the writer Mihajlo Mihajlov and other dissenters at home, he criticized Soviet repression of Czecholovakia in 1968.

Tito's death on May 4, 1980, three days before his 88th birthday, removed from the scene the last World War II leader. A rotating presidency designed to avoid internal dissension was put into effect immediately, and the feared clash of Yugoslavia's multiple nationalities and regions appeared to have been averted. A collective presidency, rotated annually among the six republics and two autonomous provinces of the federal republic, continued to govern according to a constitutional change made in 1974.

Demonstrations by ethnic Albanians in Kosovo for freedom from Serb rule were met with a forcible response from Serb authorities under the direction of Serb leader Slobodan Miloslovic. In 1988–89, Miloslovic has mobilized Serb sentiment not only against the Albanians but also against the central government, raising the spectre of further divisiveness within Yugoslavia.

ZAIRE

Republic of Zaire
President: Mobutu Sese Seko (1965)
Prime Minister: Kengo Wa Dondo (1988)
Area: 905,365 sq mi. (2,344,885 sq km)
Population (est. mid-1989): 34,900,000 (average annual rate of natural increase: 3.1%)
Density per square mile: 38
Capital: Kinshasa
Largest cities (est. 1984): Kinshasa, 2,653,558; Lubumbashi, 543,268; Mbuji-Mayi, 423,363; Kananga, 290,898
Monetary unit: Zaire
Languages: French (official), English, Bantu dialects, mainly Swahili, Lingala, Ishiluba, and Kikongo
Religions: Roman Catholic 48%, Protestant 29%, Islam 10%; syncretic and traditional, 10%
Ethnic groups: Bantu, Sudanese, Nilotics, Pygmies, Hamites
National name: République du Zaïre
Literacy rate: 55% male, 37% female

Economic summary: Gross domestic product (1986): $4.5 billion, $140 per capita; real growth rate (1986): 1.4%. Land used for agriculture: 7%; labor force: 75%, principal products: coffee, palm oil, rubber, sugar, cotton, cocoa, bananas, plantains, vegetables, fruits. Major industrial products: processed and unprocessed minerals, consumer goods. Natural resources: copper, cobalt, zinc, industrial diamonds, manganese, tin, gold, silver, bauxite, iron, coal, crude oil, 13% of world hydroelectric potential. Exports: copper, cobalt, diamonds, petroleum, coffee. Imports: consumer goods, foodstuffs, mining and other machinery, transport equipment. Major trading partners: Belgium, France, U.S., West Germany.

Geography. Zaire is situated in west central Africa and is bordered by the Congo, the Central African Republic, the Sudan, Uganda, Rwanda, Burundi, Tanzania, Zambia, Angola, and the Atlantic Ocean. It is one quarter the size of the U.S.

The principal rivers are the Ubangi and Bomu in the north and the Zaire (Congo) in the west, which flows into the Atlantic. The entire length of Lake Tanganyika lies along the eastern border with Tanzania and Burundi.

Government. Under the Constitution approved by referendum in 1967 and amended in 1974, the third Constitution since 1960, the president and a unicameral Legislature are elected by universal suffrage for five-year terms.

In 1971, the government proclaimed that the Democratic Republic of the Congo would be known as the Republic of Zaire, since the Congo River's name had been changed to the Zaire. In addition, President Joseph D. Mobutu took the name Mobutu Sese Seko and Katanga Province became Shaba.

There is only one political party: the Popular Movement of the Revolution, led by President Mobutu.

History. Formerly the Belgian Congo, this territory was inhabited by ancient Negrito peoples (Pygmies), who were pushed into the mountains by Bantu and Nilotic invaders. The American correspondent Henry M. Stanley navigated the Congo River in 1877 and opened the interior to exploration. Commissioned by King Leopold II of the Belgians, Stanley made treaties with native chiefs that enabled the King to obtain personal title to the territory at the Berlin Conference of 1885.

Criticism of forced labor under royal exploitation prompted Belgium to take over administration of the Congo, which remained a colony until agitation for independence forced Brussels to grant freedom on June 30, 1960. Moise Tshombe, Premier of the then Katanga Province seceded from the new republic on July 11, and another mining province, South Kasai, followed. Belgium sent paratroopers to quell the civil war, and with President Joseph Kasavubu and Premier Patrice Lumumba of the national government in conflict, the United Nations flew in a peacekeeping force.

Kasavubu staged an army coup in 1960 and handed Lumumba over to the Katangan forces. A U.N. investigating commission found that Lumumba had been killed by a Belgian mercenary in the presence of Tshombe. Dag Hammarskjold, U.N. Secretary-General, died in a plane crash en route to a peace conference with Tshombe on Sept. 17, 1961.

U.N. Secretary-General U Thant submitted a national reconciliation plan in 1962 that Tshombe rejected. Tshombe's troops fired on the U.N. force in December, and in the ensuing conflict Tshombe capitulated on Jan. 14, 1963. The peacekeeping force withdrew, and, in a complete about-face, Kasavubu named Tshombe Premier to fight a spreading rebellion. Tshombe used foreign mercenaries and, with the help of Belgian paratroops airlifted by U.S. planes, defeated the most serious opposition, a Communist-backed regime in the northeast.

Kasavubu abruptly dismissed Tshombe in 1965 and was himself ousted by Gen. Joseph-Desiré Mobutu, Army Chief of Staff. The new President nationalized the Union Minière, the Belgian copper mining enterprise that had been a dominant force in the Congo since colonial days. The plane carrying the exiled Tshombe was hijacked in 1967 and he was held prisoner in Algeria until his death from a heart attack was announced June 29, 1969.

Mobutu eliminated opposition to win election in 1970 to a term of seven years, which was renewed in a 1977 election. He invited U.S., South African, and Japanese investment to replace Belgian interests. In 1975, he nationalized much of the economy, barred religious instruction in schools, and decreed the adoption of African names.

On March 8, 1977, invaders from Angola calling themselves the Congolese National Liberation Front pushed into Shaba and threatened the important mining center of Kolwezi. France and Belgium responded to Mobutu's pleas for help with weapons, but the U.S. gave only nonmilitary supplies.

In April, France flew 1,500 Moroccan troops to Shaba to defeat the invaders, who were, Mobutu charged, Soviet-inspired, and Cuban-led. U.S. intelligence sources, however, confirmed Soviet and Cuban denials of any participation and identified the rebels as former Katanga gendarmes who had fled to Angola after their 1963 defeat.

On May 15, 1978, a new assault from Angola resulted in the capture of Kolwezi and the death of 100 whites and 300 blacks. In this second invasion, France and Belgium intervened directly as 1,000 Foreign Legion paratroopers repelled the Katangese and 1,750 Belgian soldiers helped evacuate 2,000 Europeans. The U.S. supplied 18 air transports for both the troop movement and the evacuation. This time President Carter himself backed Mobutu's renewed assertions of Soviet-Cuban participation.

In 1984 and 1985, Zaire and Angola signed bilateral agreements aimed at improved relations, including an agreement not to support rebels in each other's country.

ZAMBIA

Republic of Zambia
President: Kenneth D. Kaunda (1964)
Prime Minister: Kebby Musokotwane (1985)
Area: 290,586 sq mi. (752,618 sq km)
Population (est. mid-1989): 8,100,000 (average annual rate of natural increase: 3.7%)
Density per square mile: 28
Capital: Lusaka
Largest cities (est. 1982): Lusaka, 650,000; Kitwe, 345,000; Ndola, 325,000; Chingola, 195,000
Monetary unit: Kwacha
Languages: English and local dialects
Religions: Animist, Roman Catholic, Protestant.

Member of Commonwealth of Nations
Literacy rate: 55.5%
Economic summary: Gross domestic product (1986 est.): $2.1 billion, $300 per capita; real growth rate (1986 est.): 1.2%. Land used for agriculture: 54%; labor force: 85%; principal products: corn, tobacco, fruits, sugar cane. Labor force in industry: 6%; major products: copper, cobalt, chemicals, zinc, fertilizers. Natural resources: copper, zinc, lead, cobalt, coal. Exports: copper, zinc, lead, cobalt, tobacco. Imports: manufactured goods, machinery and transport equipment, foodstuffs. Major trading partners: Western Europe, Japan, South Africa, U.S.

Geography. Zambia, a landlocked country in south central Africa, is about one tenth larger than Texas. It is surrounded by Angola, Zaire, Tanzania, Malawi, Mozambique, Zimbabwe, Botswana, and SouthWest Africa (Namibia). The country is mostly a plateau that rises to 8,000 feet (2,434 m) in the east.

Government. Zambia (formerly Northern Rhodesia) is governed by a president, elected by universal suffrage, and a Legislative Assembly, consisting of 125 members elected by universal suffrage and up to 10 additional members nominated by the president.

In 1972, the Assembly passed a law making the ruling United National Independence Party, led by President Kenneth D. Kaunda, the only legal political party.

History. Empire builder Cecil Rhodes obtained mining concessions in 1889 from King Lewanika of the Barotse and sent settlers to the area soon thereafter. It was ruled by the British South Africa Company, which he established, until 1924, when the British government took over the administration.

From 1953 to 1964, Northern Rhodesia was federated with Southern Rhodesia and Nyasaland in the Federation of Rhodesia and Nyasaland. On Oct. 24, 1964, Northern Rhodesia became the independent nation of Zambia.

Kenneth Kaunda, the first president, kept Zambia within the Commonwealth of Nations. The country's economy, dependent on copper exports, was threatened when Rhodesia declared its independence from British rule in 1965 and defied U.N. sanctions, which Zambia supported, an action that deprived Zambia of its trade route through Rhodesia. The U.S., Britain, and Canada organized an airlift in 1966 to ship gasoline into Zambia. In 1967, Britain agreed to finance new trade routes for Zambia.

Kaunda visited China in 1967, and China later agreed to finance a 1,000-mile railroad from the copper fields to Dar es Salaam in Tanzania. A pipeline was opened in 1968 from Ndola in Zambia's copper belt to the Indian Ocean at Dar es Salaam, ending the three-year oil drought.

In 1969, Kaunda announced the nationalization of the foreign copper-mining industry, with Zambia to take 51% (over $1 billion, estimated), and an agreement was reached with the companies on payment. He then announced a similar takeover of foreign oil producers.

Zambia suffered heavy damage from bombing raids from the former Rhodesian air force on Zimbabwean guerrilla bases and on its transportation links. These actions, combined with falling prices for copper and cobalt, forced Kaunda to declare a state of economic austerity in January 1981.

A strike by copper-belt workers, in 1981, directed partly against cuts in consumer subsidies and partly at UNIP, the regime's single party, brought a quick victory for the workers after they shut down production. In February, Kaunda installed a new Prime Minister and a new party chief, both more acceptable to the powerful copper-belt unions, and in April, UNIP readmitted union leaders who had been expelled at the time of the strike.

ZIMBABWE

Republic of Zimbabwe
Executive President: Robert Mugabe (1987)
Area: 150,699 sq mi. (390,308 sq km)
Population (est. mid-1989): 10,100,000 (average annual rate of natural increase: 3.6%) (black, 98%; white, 2%)
Density per square mile: 67
Capital: Harare
Largest cities (est. 1983 for metropolitan area): Harare, 681,000; Bulawayo, 429,000
Monetary unit: Zimbabwean dollar
Languages: English (official), Ndebele, Shona
Religions: Christian, 25%; Animist 24%; Syncretic 50%
Literacy rate: 77%
Economic summary: Gross domestic product (1986): $4.9 billion, $540 per capita; real growth rate (1986): 0.2%. Land used for agriculture: 19%; labor force: 74%; principal agricultural products: tobacco, corn, sugar, tea, cotton, livestock. Labor force in industry: 10%; major products: steel, textiles, chemicals, vehicles, gold, copper. Natural resources: gold, copper, chrome, nickel, tin, asbestos. Exports: gold, tobacco, asbestos, copper, meat, chrome, nickel, corn, sugar. Imports: machinery, petroleum products, transport equipment. Major trading partners: South Africa, UK

Geography. Zimbabwe, a landlocked country in south central Africa, is slightly smaller than California. It is bordered by Botswana on the west, Zambia on the north, Mozambique on the east, and South Africa on the south.

A high veld up to 6,000 feet (1,829 m) crosses the country from northeast to southwest. This is flanked by a somewhat lower veld that contains ranching country. Tropical forests that yield hardwoods lie in the southeast.

In the north, on the border with Zambia, is the 175-mile-long (128-m) Kariba Lake, formed by the Kariba Dam across the Zambezi River. It is the site of one of the world's largest hydroelectric projects.

Government. An amendment to the Constitution in October, 1987 created the position of Executive President that would combine Presidential and Prime Ministerial functions. Prime Minister Mugabe was the sole candidate and was elected to this post December 30. On December 22, the long negotiated ZANU-ZAPU merger was promulgated with ZAPU head Joshua Nkomo becoming a Vice President of ZANU. In August, 1987, the Parliament voted to abolish the 20 whites-only seats that had existed since 1980. The remaining 80 members selected replacements who were obliged to support Mugabe's ZANU party.

History. Zimbabwe was colonized by Cecil Rhodes's British South Africa Company at the end of the 19th century. In 1923, European settlers voted to become the self-governing British colony of Southern Rhodesia rather than merge with the Union of South Africa. After a brief federation with Northern Rhodesia and Nyasaland in the post-World War II period, Southern Rhodesia chose to remain a colony when its two partners voted for independence in 1963.

On Nov. 11, 1965, the white-minority government of Rhodesia unilaterally declared its independence from Britain.

In 1967, the U.N. imposed mandatory sactions against Rhodesia. The country moved slowly toward meeting the demands of black Africans. The white-minority regime of Prime Minister Ian Smith withstood British pressure, economic sanctions, guerrilla attacks, and a right-wing assault.

On March 1, 1970, Rhodesia formally proclaimed itself a republic, and within the month nine nations, including the U.S., closed their consulates there.

Heightened guerrilla war and a withdrawal of South African military aid—particularly helicopters—marked the beginning of the collapse of Smith's 11 years of resistance in the spring of 1976. Under pressure from South Africa, Smith agreed with the U.S. that majority rule should come within two years.

In the fall, Smith met with black nationalist leaders in Geneva. The meeting broke up six weeks later when the Rhodesian Premier insisted that whites must retain control of the police and armed forces during the transition to majority rule. A British proposal called for Britons to take over these powers.

Divisions between Rhodesian blacks—Bishop Abel Muzorewa of the African National Congress and Ndabaningi Sithole as moderates versus Robert Mugabe and Joshua Nkomo of the Patriotic Front as advocates of guerrilla force—sharpened in 1977 and no agreement was reached. In July, with white residents leaving in increasing numbers and the economy showing the strain of war, Smith rejected outside mediation and called for general elections in order to work out an "internal solution" of the transfer of power.

On March 3, 1978, Smith, Muzorewa, Sithole, and Chief Jeremiah Chirau signed an agreement to transfer power to the black majority by Dec. 31, 1978. They constituted themselves an Executive Council, with chairmanship rotating but Smith retaining the title of Prime Minister. Blacks were named to each cabinet ministry, serving as co-

ministers with the whites already holding these posts. African nations and the Patriotic Front leaders immediately denounced the action, but Western governments were more reserved, although none granted recognition to the new regime.

White voters ratified a new constitution on Jan. 30, 1979, enfranchising all blacks, establishing a black majority Senate and Assembly, and changing the country's name to Zimbabwe Rhodesia. A general election on April 24 gave Muzorewa's party 67.3% of the vote.

Muzorewa agreed to negotiate with Mugabe and Nkomo in British-sponsored talks beginning Sept. 9. By December, all parties accepted a new draft constitution, a cease-fire, and a period of British administration pending a general election.

In voting completed on Feb. 29, 1980, Mugabe's ZANU-Patriotic Front party won 57 of the 80 Assembly seats reserved for blacks. Nkomo's ZAPU-Patriotic Front party won 20 seats and Muzorewa's United African National Council only three. In an earlier vote on Feb. 14, the Rhodesian Front won all 20 seats reserved for whites in the Assembly.

At a ceremony on April 18, Prince Charles of Britain handed to President-elect Rev. Canaan Banana the symbols of independence. Mugabe, a Marxist, had already pledged his support for continuation of the existing free-market economy.

On April 18, 1980, Britain formally recognized the independence of Zimbabwe.

In January 1981, Mugabe dismissed Nkomo as Home Minister and his onetime rival left the government in protest. At the same time, the Prime Minister discharged Edgar Z. Tekere, Manpower and Planning Minister, who had been tried and acquitted of the murder of a white farmer.

Mugabe survived both tests and scored an unprecedented triumph when, in response to his appeal for economic aid, Western nations pledged $1.8 billion for the next three years.

The 1985 harvest was good in Zimbabwe and the country could feed itself. But political turmoil and civil strife continued. In what Western analysts viewed as a free and fair election, President Mugabe's African National Union increased its sizeable majority in the House of Assembly but Mugabe was frustrated because it did not win the 70 seats he sought to cement one-party rule. After the election, Mugabe cracked down on Nkomo's ZAPU-Patriotic Front party.

Pressure on ZAPU has alternated with efforts to bring about a ZANU-ZAPU union as part of Mugabe's plans for one-party rule.

(For late reports, see Current Events of 1989)

The World's Moslems

According to a report in *Population Today*, published by the Population Reference Bureau, Inc., Moslems are the world's fastest growing religious group. Nearly one in every five persons is Moslem, an estimated world population of 984 million in 1988. In the late 20th century, there are more Moslems in Asian and African countries than in the Arab nations which saw the rise of Islam in the 7th century A.D. If the current high levels of fertility continue, almost one-quarter of the world's population could be Moslem around the year 2020.

There are 40 countries, including the world's fifth most populous, Indonesia, and Albania in Europe, with a population of 50% to 100% Moslem, and another seven countries, including Nigeria and Malaysia, ranging from 25% to 49% Moslem. In addition, there are nine countries each with more than 2 million Moslems who total less than 25% of their total population, such as the Soviet Union, China, Yugoslavia, and India. □

UNITED NATIONS

The 159 Members of the United Nations

Country	Joined U.N.[1]	Country	Joined U.N.[1]	Country	Joined U.N.[1]
Afghanistan	1946	Germany, West	1973	Panama	1945
Albania	1955	Ghana	1957	Papua New Guinea	1975
Algeria	1962	Greece	1945	Paraguay	1945
Angola	1976	Grenada	1974	Peru	1945
Antigua and Barbuda	1981	Guatemala	1945	Philippines	1945
Argentina	1945	Guinea	1958	Poland	1945
Australia	1945	Guinea-Bissau	1974	Portugal	1955
Austria	1955	Guyana	1966	Qatar	1971
Bahamas	1973	Haiti	1945	Romania	1955
Bahrain	1971	Honduras	1945	Rwanda	1962
Bangladesh	1974	Hungary	1955	St. Kitts and Nevis	1983
Barbados	1966	Iceland	1946	St. Lucia	1979
Belgium	1945	India	1945	St. Vincent and the Grenadines	1980
Belize	1981	Indonesia	1950	São Tomé and Príncipe	1975
Benin	1960	Iran	1945	Saudi Arabia	1945
Bhutan	1971	Iraq	1945	Senegal	1960
Bolivia	1945	Ireland	1955	Seychelles	1976
Botswana	1966	Israel	1949	Sierra Leone	1961
Brazil	1945	Italy	1955	Singapore	1965
Brunei	1984	Ivory Coast	1960	Solomon Islands	1978
Bulgaria	1955	Jamaica	1962	Somalia	1960
Burkina Faso	1960	Japan	1956	South Africa	1945
Burundi	1962	Jordan	1955	Spain	1955
Byelorussian S.S.R.	1945	Kenya	1963	Sri Lanka	1955
Cambodia	1955	Kuwait	1963	Sudan	1956
Cameroon	1960	Laos	1955	Suriname	1975
Canada	1945	Lebanon	1945	Swaziland	1968
Cape Verde	1975	Lesotho	1966	Sweden	1946
Central African Republic	1960	Liberia	1945	Syria	1945
Chad	1960	Libya	1955	Tanzania	1961
Chile	1945	Luxembourg	1945	Thailand	1946
China[2]	1945	Madagascar	1960	Togo	1960
Colombia	1945	Malawi	1964	Trinidad and Tobago	1962
Comoros	1975	Malaysia	1957	Tunisia	1956
Congo	1960	Maldives	1965	Turkey	1945
Costa Rica	1945	Mali	1960	Uganda	1962
Cuba	1945	Malta	1964	Ukrainian S.S.R.	1945
Cyprus	1960	Mauritania	1961	U.S.S.R.	1945
Czechoslovakia	1945	Mauritius	1968	United Arab Emirates	1971
Denmark	1945	Mexico	1945	United Kingdom	1945
Djibouti	1977	Mongolia	1961	United States	1945
Dominica	1978	Morocco	1956	Uruguay	1945
Dominican Republic	1945	Mozambique	1975	Vanuatu	1981
Ecuador	1945	Myanmar	1948	Venezuela	1945
Egypt	1945	Nepal	1955	Vietnam	1977
El Salvador	1945	Netherlands	1945	Western Samoa	1976
Equatorial Guinea	1968	New Zealand	1945	Yemen Arab Republic	1947
Ethiopia	1945	Nicaragua	1945	Yemen, People's Dem.	
Fiji	1970	Niger	1960	Republic of	1967
Finland	1955	Nigeria	1960	Yugoslavia	1945
France	1945	Norway	1945	Zaire	1960
Gabon	1960	Oman	1971	Zambia	1964
Gambia	1965	Pakistan	1947	Zimbabwe	1980
Germany, East	1973				

1. The U.N. officially came into existence on Oct. 24, 1945. 2. On Oct. 25, 1971, the U.N. voted membership to the People's Republic of China, which replaced the Republic of China (Taiwan) in the world body.

Six Official Languages Used by U.N.

There are six official working languages recognized by the United Nations. They are Chinese, English, French, Russian, and Spanish, which have been in use since the world body was organized, and Arabic, which was added by the General Assembly in 1973 and by the Security Council in 1982.

Member Countries' Assessments to U.N. Budget, 1989

Country	Total	Country	Total	Country	Total
Afghanistan	$74,708	Germany, East	9,562,547	Panama	149,415
Albania	74,708	Germany, West	60,363,583	Papua New Guinea	74,708
Algeria	1,120,610	Ghana	74,708	Paraguay	224,123
Angola	74,708	Greece	2,988,296	Peru	448,243
Antigua and Barbuda	74,708	Grenada	74,708	Philippines	672,365
Argentina	4,930,687	Guatemala	149,415	Poland	4,183,614
Australia	11,729,062	Guinea	74,708	Portugal	1,344,732
Austria	5,528,347	Guinea-Bissau	74,708	Qatar	373,538
Bahamas	149,415	Guyana	74,708	Romania	1,419,440
Bahrain	149,415	Haiti	74,708	Rwanda	74,708
Bangladesh	74,708	Honduras	74,708	Saint Kitts and Nevis	74,708
Barbados	74,708	Hungary	1,568,854	St. Lucia	74,708
Belgium	8,740,766	Iceland	224,123	St. Vincent and the Grenadines	74,708
Belize	74,708	India	2,764,173	São Tomé and Príncipe	74,708
Benin	74,708	Indonesia	1,120,610	Saudi Arabia	7,620,155
Bhutan	74,708	Iran	5,154,810	Senegal	74,708
Bolivia	74,708	Iraq	896,488	Seychelles	74,708
Botswana	74,708	Ireland	1,344,732	Sierra Leone	74,708
Brazil	10,832,573	Israel	1,568,854	Singapore	821,781
Brunei Darussalam	298,831	Italy	29,808,254	Solomon Islands	74,708
Bulgaria	1,120,610	Jamaica	74,708	Somalia	74,708
Burkina Faso	74,708	Japan	85,017,027	South Africa	3,361,832
Burundi	74,708	Jordan	74,708	Spain	14,567,943
Byelorussian SSR	2,465,343	Kenya	74,708	Sri Lanka	74,708
Cambodia	74,708	Kuwait	2,166,513	Sudan	74,708
Cameroon	74,708	Laos	74,708	Suriname	74,708
Canada	23,091,430	Lebanon	74,708	Swaziland	74,708
Cape Verde	74,708	Lesotho	74,708	Sweden	9,039,595
Central African Republic	74,708	Liberia	74,708	Syria	298,831
Chad	74,708	Libya	2,091,807	Tanzania	74,708
Chile	597,658	Luxembourg	448,243	Thailand	747,073
China	5,901,883	Madagascar	74,708	Togo	74,708
Colombia	1,045,903	Malawi	74,708	Trinidad and Tobago	373,538
Comoros	74,708	Malaysia	821,781	Tunisia	224,123
Congo	74,708	Maldives	74,708	Turkey	2,396,146
Costa Rica	149,415	Mali	74,708	Uganda	74,708
Cote D'Ivoire	149,415	Malta	74,708	Ukrainian SSR	9,338,425
Cuba	672,365	Mauritania	74,708	U.S.S.R.	74,632,698
Cyprus	149,415	Mauritius	74,708	United Arab Emirates	1,419,440
Czechoslovakia	4,930,687	Mexico	7,022,495	United Kingdom	36,307,798
Denmark	5,154,810	Mongolia	74,708	United States	216,286,625
Djibouti	74,708	Morocco	298,831	Uruguay	298,831
Dominica	74,708	Mozambique	74,708	Vanuatu	74,708
Dominican Republic	224,123	Myanmar	74,708	Venezuela	4,258,322
Ecuador	224,123	Nepal	74,708	Vietnam	74,708
Egypt	522,951	Netherlands	12,326,721	Western Samoa	74,708
El Salvador	74,708	New Zealand	1,792,977	Yemen Arab Republic	74,708
Equatorial Guinea	74,708	Nicaragua	74,708	Yemen, People's Dem. Republic of	74,708
Ethiopia	74,708	Niger	74,708	Yugoslavia	3,436,539
Fiji	74,708	Nigeria	1,494,148	Zaire	74,708
Finland	3,810,077	Norway	4,108,906	Zambia	74,708
France	46,692,128	Oman	149,415	Zimbabwe	149,461
Gabon	224,123	Pakistan	448,243	**TOTAL**	776,604,569
Gambia	74,708				

United Nations Headquarters

The first regular session of the General Assembly held at Central Hall, Westminster, London, voted that interim headquarters of the Organization should be located in New York. From London the U.N. moved to Hunter College in the Bronx. In August 1946, an interim headquarters was set up at Lake Success on Long Island. The New York City building at Flushing Meadows, site of the 1939 World's Fair, was converted for the use of the General Assembly. The search for a permanent home ended in December 1946, when the General Assembly accepted an offer from John D. Rockefeller, Jr., of $8,500,000[1] for the purchase of the present Headquarters site—an 18-acre tract in Manhattan, alongside the East River. The U.S. Government lent the U.N. $65,000,000 interest free, which is being repaid in annual installments.

Architectural plans drawn up by an international Board of Design were approved by the Assembly, and construction began in September 1948. By mid-1950, the 39-story Secretariat Building was ready for occupancy, and in the spring of 1951 "United Nations, New York" became the Organization's permanent address.

1. This amount paid for two-thirds of the land; New York City gave one-third.

Preamble of the United Nations Charter

The Charter of the United Nations was adopted at the San Francisco Conference of 1945. The complete text may be obtained by writing to the United Nations Sales Section, United Nations, New York, N.Y. 10017, and enclosing $1.

We the peoples of the United Nations determined to save succeeding generations from the scourge of war, which twice in our lifetime has brought untold sorrow to mankind, and

To reaffirm faith in fundamental human rights, in the dignity and worth of the human person, in the equal rights of men and women and of nations large and small, and

To establish conditions under which justice and respect for the obligations arising from treaties and other sources of international law can be maintained, and

To promote social progress and better standards of life in larger freedom, and for these ends

To practice tolerance and live together in peace with one another as good neighbors, and

To unite our strength to maintain international peace and security, and

To insure, by the acceptance of principles and the institution of methods, that armed force shall not be used, save in the common interest, and

To employ international machinery for the promotion of the economic and social advancement of all peoples, have resolved to combine our efforts to accomplish these aims.

Accordingly, our respective Governments, through representatives assembled in the city of San Francisco, who have exhibited their full powers found to be in good and due form, have agreed to the present Charter of the United Nations and do hereby establish an international organization to be known as the United Nations.

Principal Organs of the United Nations

Secretariat

This is the directorate on U.N. operations, apart from political decisions. All members contribute to its upkeep. Its staff of over 6,000 specialists is recruited from member nations on the basis of as wide a geographical distribution as possible. The staff works under the Secretary-General, whom it assists and advises.

Secretaries-General

Javier Pérez de Cuéllar, Peru, Jan. 1, 1982.
Kurt Waldheim, Austria, Jan. 1, 1972, to Dec. 31, 1981.
U Thant, Burma, Nov. 3, 1961, to Dec. 31, 1971.
Dag Hammarskjöld, Sweden, April 11, 1953, to Sept. 17, 1961.
Trygve Lie, Norway, Feb. 1, 1946, to April 10, 1953.

General Assembly

The General Assembly is the world's forum for discussing matters affecting world peace and security, and for making recommendations concerning them. It has no power of its own to enforce decisions.

The Assembly is composed of the 51 original member nations and those admitted since, a total of 159. Each nation has one vote. On important questions including international peace and security, a two-thirds majority of those present and voting is required. Decisions on other questions are made by a simple majority.

The Assembly's agenda can be as broad as the Charter. It can make recommendations to member nations, the Security Council, or both. Emphasis is given on questions relating to international peace and security brought before it by any member, the Security Council, or nonmembers.

The Assembly also maintains a broad program of international cooperation in economic, social, cultural, educational, and health fields, and for assisting in human rights and freedoms.

Among other duties, the Assembly has functions relating to the trusteeship system, and considers and approves the U.N. Budget. Every member contributes to operating expenses according to its means.

Security Council

The Security Council is the primary instrument for establishing and maintaining international peace. Its main purpose is to prevent war by settling disputes between nations.

Under the Charter, the Council is permitted to dispatch a U.N. force to stop aggression. All member nations undertake to make available armed forces, assistance, and facilities to maintain international peace and security.

Any member may bring a dispute before the Security Council or the General Assembly. Any nonmember may do so if it accepts the charter obligations of pacific settlement.

The Security Council has 15 members. There are five permanent members: the United States, the Soviet Union, Britain, France, and China; and 10 temporary members elected by the General Assembly for two-year terms, from five different regions of the world.

Voting on procedural matters requires a nine-vote majority to carry. However, on questions of substance, the vote of each of the five permanent members is required.

Current temporary members are (term expires Dec. 31, 1989): Algeria, Brazil, Nepal, Senegal, and Yugoslavia; (term expires Dec. 31, 1990): Canada, Colombia, Ethiopia, Finland, and Malaysia.

Economic and Social Council

This council is composed of 54 members elected by the General Assembly to 3-year terms. It works closely with the General Assembly as a link with groups formed within the U.N. to help peoples in such fields as education, health, and human rights. It insures that there is no overlapping and sets up commissions to deal with economic conditions and collect facts and figures on conditions over the world. It issues studies and reports and may make recommendations to the Assembly and specialized agencies.

Functional Commissions

Statistical Commission; Population Commission; Commission for Social Development; Commission on Human Rights; Commission on the Status of Women; Commission on Narcotic Drugs.

Regional Commissions

Economic Commission for Europe (ECE); Economic and Social Commission for Asia and the Pacific (ESCAP); Economic Commission for Latin America and the Caribbean (ECLAC); Economic Commission for Africa (ECA); Economic and Social Commission for Western Asia (ESCWA).

Trusteeship Council

This council supervises territories administered by various nations and placed under an international trusteeship system by the United Nations. Each nation is charged with developing the self-government of the territory and preserving and advancing the cultural, political, economic, and other forms of welfare of the people.

The Trusteeship Council is currently composed of 5 members: 1 member—the United States—that administers a trust territory, and 4 members—China, France, the Soviet Union, and the United Kingdom—that are permanent members of the Security Council but do not administer trust territories.

The following countries ceased to be administering members because of the independence of territories they had administered: Italy and France in 1960, Belgium in 1962, New Zealand and the United Kingdom in 1968 and Australia in 1975. France and the U.K. became nonadministering members.

As of December 1985, there was only one trust territory: the Trust Territory of the Pacific Islands (administered by the United States).

International Court of Justice

The International Court of Justice sits at The Hague, the Netherlands. Its 15-judge bench was established to hear disputes among states, which must agree to accept its verdicts. Its judges, charged with administering justice under international law, deal with cases ranging from disputes over territory to those concerning rights of passage.

Following are the members of the Court and the years in which their terms expire on Feb. 5:

President: Jose Maria Ruda, Argentina (1991)
Vice President: Keba Mbaye, Senegal V.P. (1991)
Robert Y. Jennings, United Kingdom (1991)
Gilbert Guillaume, France (1991)
Raghunandan Swarup Pathak, India (1991)
Taslim Olawale Elias, Nigeria (1994)
Jens Evensen, Norway (1994)
Ni Zhengyu, China (1994)
Manfred Lachs, Poland (1994)
Shigeru Oda, Japan (1994)
Roberto Ago, Italy (1997)
Mohamed Shahabuddeen, Guyana (1997)
Stephen Schwebel, United States (1997)
Mohammed Bedjaoui, Algeria (1997)
Nikolai Tarassov, U.S.S.R. (1997)

Agencies of the United Nations

INTL. ATOMIC ENERGY AGENCY (IAEA)

Established: Statute for IAEA, approved on Oct. 26, 1956, at a conference held at U.N. Headquarters, New York, came into force on July 29, 1957. The Agency is under the aegis of the U.N., but unlike the following, it is not a specialized agency.

Purpose: To promote the peaceful uses of atomic energy; to ensure that assistance provided by it or at its request or under its supervision or control is not used in such a way as to further any military purpose.

Headquarters: Vienna International Center, P.O. Box 100, A-1400 Vienna, Austria

FOOD AND AGRICULTURE ORGANIZATION OF THE UNITED NATIONS (FAO)

Established: October 16, 1945, when constitution became effective.

Purpose: To raise nutrition levels and living standards; to secure improvements in production and distribution of food and agricultural products.

Headquarters: Via delle Terme di Caracalla, 00100, Rome, Italy.

GENERAL AGREEMENT ON TARIFFS AND TRADE (GATT)

Established: Jan. 1, 1948.

Purpose: An International Trade Organization (ITO) was originally planned. Although this agency has not materialized, some of its objectives have been embodied in an international commercial treaty, the General Agreement on Tariffs and Trade. Its purpose is to sponsor trade negotiations.

Headquarters: Centre William Rappard, 154 Rue de Lausanne, 1211, Geneva 21, Switzerland.

INTERNATIONAL BANK FOR RECONSTRUCTION AND DEVELOPMENT (IBRD) (WORLD BANK)

Established: December 27, 1945, when Articles of Agreement drawn up at Bretton Woods Conference in July 1944 came into force. Began operations on June 25, 1946.

Purpose: To assist in reconstruction and development of economies of members by facilitating capital investment and by making loans to governments and furnishing technical advice.

Headquarters: 1818 H St., N.W., Washington, D.C. 20433.

INTL. CIVIL AVIATION ORGANIZATION (ICAO)

Established: April 4, 1947, after working as a provisional organization since June 1945.

Purpose: To study problems of international civil aviation; to establish international standards and regulations; to promote safety measures, uniform regulations for operation, simpler procedures at international borders, and the use of new technical methods and equipment. It has evolved standards for meteorological services, traffic control, communications, radio beacons and ranges, search and rescue organization, and other facilities. It has brought about much simplification of customs, immigration, and public health regulations as they apply to international air transport. It drafts international air law conventions, and is concerned with economic aspects of air travel.

Headquarters: International Aviation Square, 1000 Sherbrooke St. West, Montreal, Quebec, H3A 2R2, Canada.

INTL. DEVELOPMENT ASSOCIATION (IDA)

Established: Sept. 24, 1960. An affiliate of the World Bank, IDA has the same officers and staff as the Bank.

Purpose: To further economic development of its members by providing finance on terms which bear less heavily on balance of payments of members than those of conventional loans.

Headquarters: 1818 H St., N.W., Washington, D.C. 20433.

INTERNATIONAL FINANCE CORPORATION (IFC)

Established: Charter of IFC came into force on July 20, 1956. Although IFC is affiliated with the World Bank, it is a separate legal entity, and its funds are entirely separate from those of the Bank. However, membership in the Corporation is open only to Bank members.

Purpose: To further economic development by encouraging the growth of productive private enterprise in its member countries, particularly in the less developed areas; to invest in productive private enterprises in association with private investors, without government guarantee of repayment where sufficient private capital is not available on reasonable terms; to serve as a clearing house to bring together investment opportunities, private capital (both foreign and domestic), and experienced management.

Headquarters: 1818 H St., N.W., Washington, D.C. 20433.

INTERNATIONAL FUND FOR AGRICULTURAL DEVELOPMENT (IFAD)

Established: June 18, 1976. Began operations in December 1977.

Purpose: To mobilize additional funds for agricultural and rural development in developing countries through projects and programs directly benefiting the poorest rural populations.

Headquarters: 107 Via del Serafico, 00142, Rome, Italy.

INTERNATIONAL LABOR ORGANIZATION (ILO)

Established: April 11, 1919, when constitution was adopted as Part XIII of Treaty of Versailles. Became specialized agency of U.N. in 1946.

Purpose: To contribute to establishment of lasting peace by promoting social justice; to improve labor conditions and living standards through international action; to promote economic and social stability. The U.S. withdrew from the ILO in 1977 and resumed membership in 1980.

Headquarters: 4, route des Morillons, CH-1211 Geneva 22, Switzerland.

INTERNATIONAL MARITIME ORGANIZATION (IMO)

Established: March 17, 1958.

Purpose: To give advisory and consultative help to promote international cooperation in maritime navigation and to encourage the highest standards of safety and navigation. Its aim is to bring about a uniform system of measuring ship tonnage; systems now vary widely in different parts of the world. Other activities include cooperation with other U.N. agencies on matters affecting the maritime field.

Headquarters: 4 Albert Embankment, London SE 1 7SR England.

INTERNATIONAL MONETARY FUND (IMF)

Established: Dec. 27, 1945, when Articles of Agreement drawn up at Bretton Woods Conference in July 1944 came into force. Fund began operations on March 1, 1947.

Purpose: To promote international monetary cooperation and expansion of international trade; to promote exchange stability; to assist in establishment of multilateral system of payments in respect of currency transactions between members.

Headquarters: 700 19th St., N.W., Washington, D.C. 20431.

INTERNATIONAL TELECOMMUNICATION UNION (ITU)

Established: 1865. Became specialized agency of U.N. in 1947.

Purpose: To extend technical assistance to help members keep up with present day telecommunication needs; to standardize communications equipment and procedures; to lower costs. It also works for orderly sharing of radio frequencies and makes studies and recommendations to benefit its members.

Headquarters: Place des Nations, 1211 Geneva 20, Switzerland.

UNITED NATIONS EDUCATIONAL, SCIENTIFIC, AND CULTURAL ORGANIZATION (UNESCO)

Established: Nov. 4, 1946, when twentieth signatory to constitution deposited instrument of acceptance with government of U.K.

Purpose: To promote collaboration among nations through education, science, and culture in order to further justice, rule of law, and human rights and freedoms without distinction of race, sex, language, or religion.

Headquarters: UNESCO House. Place de Fontenoy, 7e, Paris, France.

UNITED NATIONS INDUSTRIAL DEVELOPMENT ORGANIZATION (UNIDO)

Established: Nov. 17, 1966. Became specialized agency of the U.N. in 1985.

Purpose: To promote and accelerate the industrialization of the developing countries.

Headquarters: UNIDO, Vienna International Centre, P.O. Box 300, A-1400 Vienna, Austria.

UNIVERSAL POSTAL UNION (UPU)

Established: Oct. 9, 1874. Became specialized agency of U.N. in 1947.

Purpose: To facilitate reciprocal exchange of correspondence by uniform procedures by all UPU members; to help governments modernize and speed up mailing procedures.

Headquarters: Weltpoststrasse 4, Berne, Switzerland.

WORLD HEALTH ORGANIZATION (WHO)

Established: April 7, 1948, when 26 members of the U.N. had accepted its constitution, adopted July 22, 1946, by the International Health Conference in New York City.

Purpose: To aid attainment by all people of highest possible level of health.

Headquarters: 20 Avenue Appia, 1211 Geneva 27, Switzerland.

WORLD INTELLECTUAL PROPERTY ORGANIZATION (WIPO)

Established: April 26, 1970, when its Convention came into force. Originated as International Bureau of Paris Union (1883) and Berne Union (1886), later succeeded by United International Bureau for the Protection of Intellectual Property (BIRPI). Became a specialized agency of the U.N. in December 1974.

Purpose: To promote legal protection of intellectual property, including artistic and scientific works, artistic performances, sound recordings, broadcasts, inventions, trademarks, industrial designs, and commercial names.

Headquarters: 34 Chemin des Colombettes, 1211 Geneva 20, Switzerland.

WORLD METEOROLOGICAL ORGANIZATION (WMO)

Established: March 23, 1950, succeeding the International Meteorological Organization, a nongovernmental organization founded in 1878.

Purpose: To promote international exchange of weather reports and maximum standardization of observations; to help developing countries establish weather services for their own economic needs; to fill gaps in observation stations; to' promote meterological investigations affecting jet aircraft, satellites, energy resources, etc.

Headquarters: 41 Avenue Giuseppe Motta, Geneva, Switzerland.

MEDIA

Leading Magazines: United States and Canada

Magazine	Circulation[1]	Magazine	Circulation[1]
American Health—Fitness of Body and Mind	981,626	Omni	925,345
Better Homes and Gardens	8,143,083	1,001 Home Ideas	1,536,706
Bon Appetit	1,344,050	Outdoor Life	1,514,400
Business Week (North America)	879,334	Parents Magazine	1,772,633
Car and Driver	935,315	Penthouse	2,108,256
Changing Times, The Kiplinger Magazine	1,040,677	People Weekly	3,349,401
Chatelaine	998,231	Playboy	3,555,663
Conde Nast Traveler	753,381	Popular Mechanics	1,668,096
Cosmopolitan	2,760,010	Prevention	3,136,447
Country Home	972,178	Psychology Today	931,859
Country Living	1,833,816	Reader's Digest	16,452,422
Discover	1,030,228	Reader's Digest (Canadian English Edition)	1,261,705
Ebony	1,764,993	Redbook	3,950,489
Elle	826,877	Rodale's Organic Gardening	1,086,406
Esquire	753,730	Rolling Stone	1,273,681
Essence	850,007	Self	1,229,791
Family Circle	5,922,530	Sesame Street Magazine	1,260,274
The Family Handyman	1,260,373	Seventeen	1,752,308
Field & Stream	2,032,020	Smithsonian	2,262,015
Glamour	2,190,027	Soap Opera Digest	1,147,884
Globe	1,525,745	Southern Living	2,288,695
Golf Digest	1,314,434	Sport	947,005
Golf Magazine	937,232	Sports Illustrated	3,329,415
Good Housekeeping	5,217,147	Star	3,682,796
Gourmet	806,304	Sunset, The Magazine of Western Living	1,430,860
Harper's Bazaar	753,262	Teen	1,093,051
Health	1,026,164	Time	4,648,454
Home Magazine	923,493	Travel & Leisure	1,125,788
Home Mechanix	1,229,727	Traveler	796,678
Hot Rod	884,668	True Story	1,300,829
House Beautiful	890,745	TV Guide	16,302,705
Jet	852,913	TV Guide (Canada)	804,838
Ladies' Home Journal	5,086,714	U.S. News & World Report	2,300,197
Life	1,749,936	US Magazine	1,379,602
McCall's	5,142,463	Vogue	1,202,471
Mademoiselle	1,283,242	Weekly World News	990,177
Money	1,821,625	Weight Watchers Magazine	1,003,347
Motor Trend	784,919	Woman's Day	5,571,573
Nation's Business	855,424	The Workbasket	1,402,785
National Enquirer	4,285,707	Workbench	845,673
National Examiner	1,120,434	Working Woman	905,358
National Geographic Magazine	10,574,562	Yankee	1,003,948
New Woman	1,332,586	YM	887,571
Newsweek	3,227,391		

1. Average total paid circulation for the six-month period ending December 31, 1987. The table lists magazines with combined newsstand and subscription circulation of over 750,000. *Source:* Audit Bureau of Circulations. Publishers' Statements for six-month period ending December 31, 1988.

Major U.S. Daily Newspapers[1]

City and newspaper	Net paid circulation			
	Morning[2]	All-Day[2]	Evening[2]	Sunday
Akron, Ohio: *Beacon Journal*	152,929		—	221,258
Albany, N.Y.: *Times-Union* (M & S); *Knickerbocker News* (E)	103,125		—	168,163
Albuquerque, N.M.: *Journal* (M & S); *Tribune* (E)	119,400 [4]		40,636 [4]	154,646 [4]
Allentown, Pa.: *Call* (M & S)	136,973			182,776
Asbury Park, N.J.: *Press*	—		144,526	210,242
Atlanta: *Constitution* (M); *Journal* (E); *Journal and Constitution* (S)	282,442 [3]		184,583 [3]	665,186
Atlantic City, N.J.: *Press*	77,134			92,196

City and newspaper	Net paid circulation			
	Morning[2]	All-Day[2]	Evening[2]	Sunday
Augusta, Ga.: *Chronicle* (M); *Herald* (E);				
Chronicle—Herald (S)	66,540[3]		14,045[3]	89,693
Austin, Tex.: *American-Statesman*	172,766		—	217,844
Bakersfield, Calif.: *Californian*	82,248[4]		—	90,546[4]
Baltimore: *Sun*	231,990[3]		170,252[3]	485,269
Bangor, Me.: *News*	79,448[3]		—	96,147[5]
Baton Rouge, La.: *Advocate* (M & S); *State-Times* (E)	77,259		28,004	132,152
Bergen County (Hackensack), N.J.; *Record* (E);				
Sunday Record	—		155,433[34]	227,775[4]
Beaumont, Tex.: *Enterprise*	66,886		—	81,099
Binghamton, N.Y.: *Press & Sun-Bulletin* (M & S)	68,248		—	92,033
Birmingham, Ala.: *Post-Herald* (M); *News* (E & S)	63,021[3]		172,510[3]	209,047
Boston: *Globe*	509,573[3]		—	787,385
Herald	360,046[3]		—	251,851
Christian Science Monitor	177,504[3]		—	—
Bridgeport, Conn.: *Telegram* (M); *Post* (E); *Sunday Post*	20,084[34]		56,117[34]	90,955[4]
Buffalo, N.Y.: *News*	—	320,003[3]		384,157
Camden, N.J.: *Courier-Post*	—		103,497[4]	103,832[4]
Canton, Ohio: *Repository*	—		56,672[4]	76,138[4]
Cedar Rapids, Iowa: *Gazette*	70,124		—	81,722
Charleston, S.C.: *News & Courier* (M);				
Evening Post; News & Courier Post (S)	78,460[3]		37,512	121,469
Charleston, W. Va.: *Gazette* (M); *Daily Mail* (E);				
Gazette-Mail (S)	55,456		50,917	105,753
Charlotte, N.C.: *Observer*	235,739		—	292,828
Chattanooga, Tenn.: *Times* (M); *News-Free Press* (E & S)	47,784		57,233	110,686
Chicago: *Tribune*	740,154[3]		—	1,137,447
Sun-Times	554,670[3]		—	595,311
Daily Herald (M); *Sunday Herald*	88,500			87,400
Cincinnati: *Enquirer* (M & S); *Post* (E)	196,883		109,262	337,413
Cleveland: *Plain Dealer*	447,822[3]		—	570,737
Colorado Springs, Colo.: *Gazette Telegraph*	105,167[3]		—	117,743
Columbia, S.C.: *State*	139,963		—	164,104
Columbus, Ohio: *Dispatch*	257,366		—	380,375
Corpus Christi, Tex.: *Caller* (M); *Caller-Times* (S)	67,628[4]		—	88,808[4]
Dallas: *News*	419,000		—	534,843
Times-Herald	—	222,147	—	333,713
Wall Street Journal (Southwest edition)	200,234[3]		—	—
Davenport, Iowa: *Quad City Times*	—	55,183	—	82,855
Dayton, Ohio: *News*	179,823		—	228,581
Daytona Beach, Fla.: *News-Journal*	92,394		—	108,259
Denver: *Post*	241,386		—	401,843
Rocky Mountain News	365,493		—	411,023
Des Moines, Iowa: *Register*	210,744		—	355,356
Detroit: *News*	—	676,025[3]	—	820,655
Free Press	629,275[3]		—	693,943
Duluth, Minn.: *News-Tribune*	61,715		—	83,077
Erie, Pa.: *News* (M); *Times* (E); *Times-News* (S)	29,711[3]		40,825[3]	102,492
El Paso, Tex.: *Times* (M & S); *Herald-Post* (E)	61,641[4]		29,439[4]	98,104[4]
Evansville, Ind.: *Courier* (M); *Press* (E); *Courier & Press* (S)	62,888		36,475	115,626
Fayetteville, N.C.: *Times* (M); *Observer* (E);				
Observer-Times (S)	27,991[34]		43,456[34]	75,523[4]
Flint, Mich.: *Journal*	—		107,130[3]	123,937
Fort Lauderdale, Fla.: *Sun-Sentinel* (M); *News* (E);				
News & Sun-Sentinel (S)	232,650[3]		31,607[3]	340,474
Fort Myers, Fla.: *News-Press*	91,958		—	118,664
Fort Wayne, Ind.: *Journal-Gazette* (M & S); *News-Sentinel* (E)	61,777		55,675	137,023
Fort Worth: *Star-Telegram*	141,868[3]		112,887[3]	323,785
Fresno, Calif.: *Bee*	144,384[4]		—	174,108[4]
Gary, Ind.: *Post-Tribune*	73,969		—	88,364
Grand Rapids, Mich.: *Press*	—		142,059	186,302
Green Bay, Wis.: *Press-Gazette*	—		55,848	79,642
Greensboro, N.C.: *News & Record*	114,958		—	129,604
Greensburg, Pa.: *Tribune-Review*	52,484		—	81,501
Greenville, S.C.: *News* (M); *Piedmont* (E); *News & Piedmont* (S)	86,506[3]		25,658[3]	134,188
Harrisburg, Pa.: *Patriot* (M); *Evening News;*				
Sunday Patriot-News	54,794[3]		51,440[3]	170,332
Hartford, Conn.: *Courant*	225,418		—	312,020

City and newspaper	Net paid circulation			
	Morning[2]	All-Day[2]	Evening[2]	Sunday
Honolulu: *Advertiser* (M); *Star-Bulletin* (E);				
Star-Bulletin & Advertiser (S)	98,025		96,074	203,752
Houston: *Chronicle*	—	427,844	—	585,845
Post	322,193		—	362,847
Huntsville, Ala.: *News* (M); *Times* (E & S)	15,400[3]		58,675[3]	77,339
Indianapolis: *Star* (M & S); *News* (E)	230,787[4]		113,957[4]	406,099[4]
Jackson, Miss.: *Clarion-Ledger* (M); *News* (E);				
Clarion Ledger-News (S)	80,044[3]		21,749[3]	120,428
Jacksonville, Fla.: *Florida Times-Union* (M); *Journal* (E);				
Times-Union & Journal (S)	173,272		32,529[3 6]	235,642
Kalamazoo, Mich.: *Gazette*	—		62,045	78,436
Kansas City, Mo.: *Times* (M); *Star* (E & S)	275,016		175,941[3]	414,689
Knoxville, Tenn.: *Journal* (E); *News-Sentinel* (M & S)	100,353		42,156	166,574
Lakeland, Fla.: *Ledger*	84,517[4]		—	102,906[4]
Lancaster, Pa.: *Intelligencer-Journal* (M); *New Era* (E);				
News (S)	43,731[4]		55,067[4]	103,100[4]
Lansing, Mich.: *State-Journal*	68,379		—	87,307
Las Vegas, Nev.: *Review-Journal*	—	134,491[3]	—	159,770
Sun	53,948		—	58,731
Lexington, Ky.: *Herald-Leader*	122,579		—	154,114
Lincoln, Neb.: *Star* (M); *Journal* (E); *Journal & Star* (S)	37,855		42,714	81,792
Little Rock, Ark.: *Gazette*	187,197		—	225,254
Democrat	105,717		—	199,513
Long Beach, Calif.: *Press-Telegram*	124,749[3]		4,708[3]	148,169
Long Island (Melville), N.Y.: *Newsday*	—	697,509[3]	—	707,787
Los Angeles: *Times*	1,119,840[3]		—	1,423,310
Herald-Examiner	238,392[3]		—	183,122
News	183,402[3]		—	201,533
Louisville, Ky.: *Courier-Journal*	235,414		—	326,767
Macon, Ga.: *Telegraph and News*	73,134		—	99,964
Madison, Wis.: *State Journal* (M & S); *Capital Times* (E)	80,498[3]		27,206[3]	151,805
Melbourne, Fla.: *Today*	78,429		—	105,787
Memphis, Tenn.: *Commercial Appeal*	212,808		—	289,834
Miami, Fla.: *Herald*	442,976		47,205[7]	546,801
Middletown, N.Y.: *Times Herald-Record* (M);				
Sunday Record (S)	82,878		—	97,174
Milwaukee: *Sentinel* (M); *Journal* (E & S)	176,154[3]		275,778[3]	506,517
Minneapolis: *Star & Tribune*	403,300		—	650,317
Mobile, Ala.: *Register* (M); *Press* (E); *Press-Register* (S)	56,736[3 4]		43,650[3 4]	107,180[4]
Modesto, Calif.: *Bee*	79,058[4]		—	86,587[4]
Montgomery, Ala. *Advertiser* (M); *Journal* (E);				
Journal & Advertiser (S)	51,524[3]		17,183[3]	80,263
Naperville, Ill.: *Wall Street Journal* (Midwest edition)	531,080[3]		—	—
Nashville, Tenn.: *Tennessean* (M & S); *Banner* (E)	126,762		63,078	258,969
New Haven, Conn.: *Register*	103,507		—	139,506
New Orleans: *Times-Picayune*	—	281,851[3 4]	—	338,987[4]
New York: *News*	1,230,186[3]		—	1,526,413
Times	1,117,376[3]		—	1,663,530
Post	535,407[3]		—	402,136
Wall Street Journal (Eastern edition)	797,779[3]		—	—
National edition	1,931,410[3]		—	—
Women's Wear Daily	62,062[3]		—	—
Newark, N.J.: *Star-Ledger*	458,049[3]		—	675,980[3]
Newport News—Hampton, Va.: *Press* (M & S);				
Times Herald (E)	75,744[3 4]		31,460[3 4]	116,842[4]
Norfolk-Portsmouth-Virginia Beach-Chesapeake, Va.:				
Virginian-Pilot (M); *Ledger-Star* (E);				
Virginian-Pilot/Ledger-Star (S)	149,346[3 4]		80,590[3 4]	232,060[4]
Oakland, Calif.: *Tribune* (M & S)	142,456[3]		—	138,803
Oklahoma City: *Oklahoman* (M & S)	229,008[3]		—	323,118
Omaha, Neb.: *World-Herald*	121,742[3]		96,825[3]	285,419
Orange County (Santa Ana), Calif.: *Register*	—	344,965[3]	—	392,695
Orlando, Fla.: *Sentinel*	—	273,544[3]	—	377,935
Palo Alto, Calif.: *Wall Street Journal* (Western edition)	402,317[3]		—	—
Peninsula Times Tribune	—		47,982	51,046
Peoria, Ill.: *Journal Star*	—	93,443[3]	—	115,740
Philadelphia: *Inquirer* (M & S); *Daily News* (E)	500,136[3]		—	1,010,530
Phoenix, Ariz.: *Republic* (M & S); *Gazette* (E)	372,209[4]		112,223[4]	566,510[4]

City and newspaper	Morning[2]	All-Day[2]	Evening[2]	Sunday
Pittsburgh: *Post-Gazette, Sun-Telegraph* (M); *Press* (E & S)	166,942[3]		227,434[3]	560,199
Pontiac, Mich.: *Oakland Press*	—	74,139	—	81,414
Portland, Me.: *Press-Herald* (M); *Express* (E)	58,924		24,681	
Maine Sunday Telegram	—			410,420
Portland, Ore.: *Oregonian*		327,603		
Providence, R.I.: *Journal Bulletin;* Journal (S)	—	199,507	—	261,760
Quincy, Mass.: *Patriot-Ledger*	—		87,123[3][4]	96,997[4][8]
Raleigh, N.C.: *News & Observer* (M & S); *Times* (E)	141,974[4]		22,069[3][4]	187,534[4]
Reading, Pa.: *Times* (M); *Eagle* (E & S)	46,058[3]		32,806[3]	112,747
Reno, Nev.: *Gazette Journal*	63,448		—	75,958
Richmond, Va.: *Times-Dispatch* (M & S); *News-Leader* (E)	140,774		105,340	246,806
Riverside, Calif.: *Press-Enterprise* (M & S)	149,634		—	157,514
Roanoke, Va.: *Times & World-News*	82,125[3]		41,885[3]	126,725
Rochester, N.Y.: *Democrat & Chronicle* (M & S); *Times-Union* (E)	127,720[3]		90,472[3]	258,804
Rockford, Ill.: *Register Star*	74,080		—	88,462
Sacramento, Calif.: *Bee*	251,120[4]		—	306,574[4]
Union	83,272[4]		—	80,070[4]
St. Louis: *Post-Dispatch*	378,225[3]		—	560,618
St. Paul: *Pioneer Press & Dispatch*		191,638[3]		254,241
St. Petersburg, Fla.: *Times*	375,870[4]		—	471,472[4]
Salt Lake City, Utah: *Tribune* (M & S);	111,356		—	141,180
Deseret News (E & S)	—		60,682	66,988
San Antonio: *Express News*	—	181,225	—	272,631
Light	—	159,605	—	233,134
San Bernardino, Calif.: *Sun*	86,316		—	94,690
San Diego, Calif.: *Union* (M & S); *Tribune* (E)	269,190[4]		122,094[4]	437,784[4]
San Francisco: *Chronicle* (M); *Examiner* (E);				
Examiner & Chronicle (S)	556,196[3]		135,444[3]	700,989
San Gabriel Valley, Calif.: *Tribune* (M); *Tribune-News* (S)	59,877		—	81,540
San Jose, Calif.: *Mercury-News*	—	277,010[3]	—	331,998
Santa Rosa, Calif.: *Press Democrat*	84,736		—	92,430
Sarasota, Fla.: *Herald-Tribune* (M & S)	133,926[4]		—	161,445[4]
Seattle: *Post-Intelligencer* (M); *Times* (E); combined (S)	204,827[3]		236,563[3]	504,993
Shreveport, La.: *Times* (M & S); *Journal* (E)	76,988		19,118	104,926
South Bend-Mishawaka, Ind.: *Tribune*			90,253	126,514
Spokane, Wash.: *Spokesman-Review* (M & S); *Daily Chronicle* (E)	95,284[3]		26,274[3]	139,838
Springfield, Ill.: *State Journal-Register*	—	68,336	—	76,448
Springfield, Mass.: *Union News; Republican* (S)	—	112,229	—	158,648
Springfield, Mo.: *News-Leader*	61,997[4]		—	97,581[4]
Staten Island, N.Y.: *Advance* (E&S)	—		76,972[3]	88,823
Syracuse, N.Y.: *Post-Standard* (M); *Herald-Journal* (E);				
Herald-American (S)	83,201		95,791	226,207
Tacoma, Wash.: *News-Tribune*	117,246[4]		—	129,436[4]
Tampa, Fla.: *Tribune* (M); *Tribune & Times* (S)	287,289[4]		—	382,842[4]
Toledo, Ohio: *Blade*	—		154,592	219,289
Topeka, Kan.: *Capital-Journal*	67,680		—	77,516
Trenton, N.J.: *Times* (M&S)	75,289		—	90,566
Trentonian (M&S)	68,679[3]		—	64,773
Tucson, Ariz.: *Star* (M & S); *Citizen* (E)	90,498[4]		57,247[4]	171,212[4]
Tulsa, Okla.: *World* (M & S); *Tribune* (E)	126,909[4]		68,990[4]	238,495[4]
Walnut Creek, Calif.: *Contra Costa Times*	85,945		—	95,329
Washington, D.C.: *Post*	812,419[3]		—	1,149,856
Times	103,652		—	—
USA Today	1,341,811[9]		—	—
West Palm Beach, Fla.: *Post*	179,759[3]		—	225,826
Wichita, Kan.: *Eagle-Beacon*	120,070		—	196,168
Wilmington, Del.: *Journal; Sunday News Journal*	—		120,132[4]	137,035[4]
Winston-Salem, N.C.: *Journal*	94,652		—	105,935
Worcester, Mass.: *Telegram* (M & S); *Gazette* (E)	58,388[3][4]		71,542[3][4]	131,175[4]
Youngstown, Ohio: *Vindicator*	—		90,608[4]	138,056[4]

1. Listing is of cities in which any one edition of a newspaper exceeds an average net paid circulation of 75,000; newspapers of smaller circulation in those cities are also included. 2. Unless otherwise indicated, figures are average Monday-through-Saturday circulation for six-month period ending March 31, 1988. 3. Average Monday-through-Friday circulation. 4. Three-month average for period ending March 31, 1988. 5. Week-end edition. 6. (10-1-88 to 10-28-88) 7. (10-1-88 to 12-31-88) 8. Saturday edition. 9. Average Monday through Thursday circulation. n.a. = not available.

English Language Daily and Sunday U.S. Newspapers
(number of newspapers as of Feb. 1, 1989; circulation as reported for Sept. 30, 1988)

State	Morning papers and circulation		Evening papers and circulation		Total M and E and circulation		Sunday papers and circulation	
Alabama	15	298,519	12	456,914	27	755,433	20	750,377
Alaska	3	64,727	5	60,817	8	125,544	4	137,725
Arizona[1]	6	463,786	13	272,456	19	736,242	11	790,506
Arkansas[1]	9	338,284	24	204,031	32	542,315	16	617,206
California[1][2]	51	4,899,288	71	1,674,519	120	6,573,807	66	6,523,494
Colorado	9	807,075	17	153,511	26	960,586	11	1,133,100
Connecticut[1]	11	566,256	14	298,668	23	864,924	11	819,601
Delaware	2	95,883	1	46,359	3	142,242	2	164,313
D.C.	2	866,448	0	0	2	866,448	1	1,112,349
Florida[1][2]	30	2,678,909	17	350,766	46	3,029,675	36	3,657,671
Georgia	14	656,011	23	486,700	37	1,142,711	17	1,240,505
Hawaii	2	102,376	4	141,669	6	244,045	5	259,273
Idaho	4	105,047	8	98,868	12	203,915	9	242,711
Illinois[1]	15	1,802,680	58	836,649	71	2,639,329	26	2,733,845
Indiana	12	604,990	61	935,855	73	1,540,845	20	1,321,305
Iowa[1]	11	428,170	27	303,661	37	731,831	11	746,184
Kansas	7	282,116	39	257,761	46	539,877	17	493,648
Kentucky	6	415,351	18	243,670	24	659,021	13	671,154
Louisiana[1]	14	490,772	15	301,051	28	791,823	21	903,032
Maine	5	225,104	4	65,964	9	291,068	2	184,628
Maryland	8	417,133	6	285,197	14	702,330	7	643,613
Massachusetts[1]	7	1,245,299	38	856,918	44	2,102,217	12	1,724,335
Michigan[1]	13	1,124,065	41	1,408,353	52	2,532,418	16	2,454,767
Minnesota[1]	11	651,481	15	288,022	25	939,503	13	1,115,650
Mississippi	6	187,753	17	216,257	23	404,010	14	369,256
Missouri	10	821,632	36	451,143	46	1,272,775	19	1,298,994
Montana	5	136,403	6	49,429	11	185,832	7	187,283
Nebraska	4	188,605	15	279,910	19	468,515	7	434,337
Nevada[1]	4	187,878	5	84,294	8	272,172	4	294,135
New Hampshire	1	70,772	8	149,361	9	220,133	4	146,734
New Jersey	11	1,058,960	12	621,332	23	1,680,292	18	1,890,546
New Mexico	3	148,026	16	163,222	19	311,248	13	278,491
New York[1]	25	6,271,148	48	1,396,712	71	7,667,860	35	5,834,296
North Carolina	12	823,011	43	630,040	55	1,453,051	30	1,367,378
North Dakota[1]	5	135,529	5	51,493	10	187,022	7	181,671
Ohio[1]	11	1,348,919	76	1,415,931	87	2,764,850	33	2,848,985
Oklahoma	10	421,896	40	316,690	50	738,586	42	870,744
Oregon[1]	5	300,813	16	356,770	20	657,583	10	661,399
Pennsylvania[1]	37	1,727,991	58	1,574,770	93	3,302,761	28	3,096,101
Rhode Island	1	98,150	6	196,270	7	294,420	3	301,296
South Carolina	10	513,807	7	133,593	17	647,400	13	684,457
South Dakota	5	108,523	7	63,359	12	171,882	4	136,799
Tennessee[1]	9	566,879	20	401,565	28	968,444	16	1,061,333
Texas[1][2]	37	2,343,953	73	1,230,993	106	3,574,946	97	4,504,944
Utah	1	108,372	5	172,711	6	281,083	6	320,458
Vermont	4	96,241	4	32,688	8	128,929	3	97,821
Virginia[3]	16	1,988,087	21	540,042	35	2,528,129	15	948,520
Washington[1]	8	529,425	19	633,490	26	1,162,915	16	1,655,983
West Virginia	9	242,396	14	195,599	23	437,995	10	388,863
Wisconsin	7	362,869	29	822,155	36	1,151,257	15	1,099,889
Wyoming	6	65,734	4	29,688	10	95,422	4	72,484
Total	**529**	**40,452,815**	**1,141**	**22,242,001**	**1,642**	**62,694,816**	**840**	**61,474,189**
Total U.S., Sept. 30, 1987	511	39,123,807	1,166	23,702,466	1,645	62,826,273	820	60,111,863
Total U.S., Sept. 30, 1986	499	37,441,125	1,188	25,060,911	1,657	62,502,036	802	58,924,518
Total U.S., Sept. 30, 1985	482	36,361,561	1,220	26,404,671	1,676	62,766,232	798	58,825,978
Total U.S., Sept. 30, 1984	458	35,424,418	1,257	27,657,322	1,688	63,081,740	783	57,573,979
Total U.S., Sept. 30, 1983	446	33,842,142	1,284	28,802,461	1,701	62,644,603	722	56,747,436
Total U.S., Sept. 30, 1982	434	33,174,087	1,310	29,313,090	1,711	62,487,177	768	56,260,764
Total U.S., Sept. 30, 1981	408	30,552,316	1,352	30,878,429	1,730	61,430,745	755	55,180,004
Total U.S., Sept. 30, 1980	387	29,414,036	1,388	32,787,804	1,745	62,201,840	736	54,676,173
Total U.S., Sept. 30, 1979	382	28,574,879	1,405	33,648,161	1,763	62,223,040	720	54,379,923

1. "All-day" newspapers are listed in morning and evening columns but only once in the total, and their circulations are divided between morning and evening figures. Adjustments have been made in state and U.S. total figures. 2. Includes one Spanish language daily. 3. Includes nationally circulated daily. Circulation counted only in the state indicated. *Source: Editor and Publisher International Yearbook, 1989.*

See the Entertainment and Culture section for additional Media information.

Chemical Arms Control

By Joe Poyer

History

The first such measure was embodied in the Hague Convention of 1899 and was broken less than 15 years later by Germany. The 1925 Geneva Convention, which forbade chemical warfare, not only lacked a means of enforcement but was twisted by its signatories to mean no first use. Ten years later it was broken by Italy, when that country caused, according to official Soviet estimates, nearly 15,000 casualties in Ethiopia. While Japan tested chemical weapons against the Chinese and Germany used poison gases in their extermination camps to kill more than six million people, only vast arsenals of chemical and nerve gases on both sides prevented their use during World War II as combat weapons.

Since 1945, chemical weapons—CS,[1] CN[2] and BZ[3] incapacitating gases—have been used in Vietnam by U.S. and allied forces; in Yemen (1962), Red China (1969), Laos (1975), Iraq and Iran (1980 to 1988), Afghanistan (1981 to 1988) and the Ethiopian-Eritrean Civil War (1978 to 1988) by Soviet or Soviet-client forces. While no verifiable samples of poison gases have been returned from these areas, sufficient documentation has been gathered by a number of agencies, including the International Red Cross, to provide strong circumstantial evidence of their use. During the 1967 and 1973 Arab-Israeli Wars, chemical weapons were stockpiled by Egyptian forces but were never used. Vietnam used chemical weapons in Cambodia (1978) and to repel invading Red Chinese forces in 1979. Iraq has more recently used mustard gas against Iranian forces in their long-running Gulf war, and has the dubious distinction of being the first country ever to use nerve agents (GA or Tabun) against an enemy. In late 1986 Reuter's news service reported the use of chemical warfare agents by Libya against Chadian troops.

The 40-nation Conference on Disarmament, including the Soviet Union, which has met in Geneva since 1980, finally accepted the principle of a complete ban on chemical weapons and defenses in 1984. But the question of implementing such a consensus has stalled on means of verification, without which such an agreement is meaningless. In April 1987 the Soviets accepted, in principle, verification by onsite observers of the destruction of existing stocks and the inspection, on 48-hour notice, of the destruction of chemical warfare agents and manufacturing plants. In December 1987 the U.S. and U.S.S.R. traded official inspection teams to verify on-site the other's mechanisms, equipment and facilities to dispose of chemical munitions.[5]

Why Chemical Weapons?

The weapons are available, and so there is a danger they will be used under the right circumstances. The Soviets' chemical weapons industry is extensive and productive and includes the Sverdlovsk and the Shikhany chemical warfare proving grounds, plus up to 14 production centers that produce Sarin, Soman, and the new V-series agents. They also produce blistering agents like mustard gas and Lewisite, hydrogen cyanide (blood agent), phosgene (choking agent), and several disabling agents that appear to be widely used in Afghanistan, such as Blue X.[4] The Soviets manufacture both persistent (remains active for days to weeks or until decontamination procedures are applied) and nonpersistent (becomes harmless within a few hours) chemicals. The Soviet Union is also investigating binary weapon systems; in their December 1987 announcement, they stated that if the U.S. continues to produce binary chemical munitions, they will have no choice but to do so as well.

Compared to other weaponry, chemical aerial bombs, rockets, and artillery shells are inexpensive to produce and therefore attractive to third-world nations. Small and efficient processing plants can turn out chemical weapons by the ton. The Stockholm International Peace Research Institute reported that the Iraqis are manufacturing the nerve agent Tabun in fertilizer factories bought from West Germany. Iran, in turn, threatened

---

1. CS: Causes eyes to smart and tear; choking. 2. CN: Causes eyes to smart and tear, short acting. 3. BZ: Hallucinogenic LSD derivative (U.S.). 4. Unknown composition. Incapacitating variously estimated for 1-2 and 8-12 hours (U.S.S.R.) 5. In July 1989, the U.S. and the Soviet Union reached an agreement on the key elements of a treaty to ban chemical weapons. Both countries will submit their recommendations to the Conference on Disarmament in Geneva.—Ed.

Japan's Forgotten Chemical Weapons Factory

During WW II, Japan produced poison gas in secret factories located on the tiny island of Okunoshima near Hiroshima where the first atomic bomb fell. Many Japanese civilians died in producing the chemical weapons and at least 6,000 today are still suffering from the effects of their exposure to toxic substances during their wartime work.

During the occupation of Japan, U.S. military forces found substantial evidence of Japan's use of chemical weapons, but did not disclose it, and those responsible for the atrocities were never tried for war crimes.

The full story is documented by Yuki Tanaka in the *Bulletin of Atomic Scientists*, October 1988.—Ed.

to retaliate by producing its own chemical weapons.

Much of a chemical weapon's effectiveness lies in the panic and disorientation it produces in unprotected soldiers and civilians. Modern chemical warfare agents (nerve gases as opposed to blister, blood or choking chemical compounds) sprang from insecticide research. Classes of organic chemicals known as organophosphorous compounds, which inhibit the production of cholinesterase, are widely used for insect control. In higher concentrations, they are lethal to mammals.

Symptoms compiled by Colonel Charles W. Lewis, Chief of the Dermatology Section, Brooke Army Medical Center, from interviews with Laotian refugees in 1979 included ". . . sweating, tearing, excessive salivation, difficulty in breathing, nausea, vomiting, dizziness, weakness, convulsion, and death." Similar symptoms were reported to the International Red Cross among gassed populations in Yemen.

Nerve gases dispersed in aerial bombs or by artillery shells in aerosol form will carry downwind for extended distances. Anyone not wearing protective clothing and gas masks or under cover in sealed, airtight structures would be killed when the aerosol touched bare skin, was inhaled, entered the body through a wound or through the digestive tract.

There is the perception that the use of chemical warfare will so shock and disorient the enemy that your own troops will gain an advantage. In actual fact, the reverse is almost always true after the initial attacks. After the Germans used gas successfully for the first time at Ypres in April 1915, the British replied in October of the same year with an equally devastating attack. From then on, gas warfare became a serious nuisance but gained neither side much advantage other than a mutual reduction in combat efficiency.

The noted British military historian J.B.S. Haldane cited 150,000 casualties on all sides caused by mustard gas. Of this number, less than 4,000 died (2.6 percent) and 700 suffered permanent physical handicap. Of the 275,000 American casualties in World War I, 68,700 (25 percent) were caused by gas warfare; of this total, only about two percent

died—1,375. Many of the others suffered mild to severe impairment of vision, respiration and skin disease for the rest of their lives. But most gassed soldiers were returned to duty within a few days. Iranian deaths due to Iraqi chemical attacks are estimated to be some 10,000 out of an estimated 1.5 million dead and wounded in the entire war as of mid 1987. The advantage gained by the use of chemical warfare is quickly negated by the other side's procurement of similar weapons, as experience during World War I shows.

Protection

Defeating nerve gases and chemical agents from CN to mustard gas requires protective clothing and an efficient gas mask. The clothing has to be airtight, and the mask must fit snugly and filter all air through canisters of chemicals that deactivate the chemical agent being used. Such clothing is hot, claustrophobic and clumsy. It is hard to manipulate equipment and weapons, and harder still to walk or run. Exertion produces more body heat, which increases the discomfort inside the protective clothing. Visibility is hampered by gas masks that steam up. Hearing is reduced by the thick material of the hood.

Protecting the individual soldier is relatively easy, as long as sufficient protective gear is available and suitable early warning instrumentation is in place. Buildings can be gas-proofed with sealing techniques and the maintenance of positive air pressure slightly above ambient. All it takes is money. Dr. Thomas J. Welch has stated, "Most [American] forces can survive an initial enemy chemical warfare attack. We have sufficient protective material to resupply our troops to sustain a few days of operations under chemical warfare conditions." Dr. Welch also pointed out that such protective measures degrade performance and thus operational effectiveness. "Therefore, we need a credible counterforce.

If the soldier can be protected, the civilian in the zone of attack, which includes most of metropolitan Central and Western Europe, cannot be. To provide millions of civilians with protective suits would be prohibitively expensive. The warring powers issued gas masks to their civilian populations during World War II, but a gas mask costs pennies in relation to the full body protective gear required today. It is axiomatic, then, that if chemical weapons are ever employed on a large scale, civilians will bear the brunt of the casualties. □

This article is reprinted with permission from the *International Combat Arms—The Journal of Defense Technology*, Volume 6, Number 6. Copyright © 1988 by Peterson Publishing Company, Los Angeles, California. Joe Poyer is a Field Editor for the *International Combat Arms*. The facts expressed herein are the sole responsibility of the author.

America's Forgotten Veterans

During a three-year duration, June 21, 1950, to July 27, 1953, the United States fought one of its toughest wars under the UN flag in Korea. During this period, 5,720,00 Americans served in the Armed Forces. Of those servicemen and women, 34,000 were killed in action, 8,000 of whom were missing in action, and later declared dead, and 20,000 others died of nonbattle causes, for a total of 54,000 deaths in service. In addition, 103,000 were wounded, and 7,000 were captured or interned. Only 4,000 of the latter were returned by the enemy. The rest are MIAs.

That the total deaths for three years fighting

comes close to the ten-year total for Vietnam demonstrates the savageness of the fighting.

After the war, Korean veterans returned home and quietly integrated themselves into their communities. No special recognition was given. They had served in a "Forgotten War."

Legislation was enacted in 1986 to authorize erection of a memorial in the Washington, D.C., area by the American Battle Monuments Commission primarily through private contributions. Over $3.2 million in private contributions have been received. Hyundai Motors America has contributed over $1 million.

Highest Ranking Officers in the Armed Forces

ARMY[1]

Generals; Colin L. Powell, Chairman of the Joint Chiefs of Staff; Carl E. Vuono, Chief of Staff; Robert RisCassi, Vice Chief of Staff; Glenn K. Otis, Supreme Allied Commander, Europe; John R. Galvin, James J. Lindsay, Louis C. Menetrey, John Voss, Louis C. Wagner, Jr., Frederick F. Werner, Jr.

AIR FORCE

Generals: Duane H. Cassidy, Hohn T. Chain, Jr., Michael J. Dugan, Alfred G. Hansen, Monroe W. Hatch, Jr., Robert T. Herres, William L. Kirk, Merrill A. McPeak, John L. Piotrowski, Bernard P. Randolph, Robert H. Reed, Thomas C. Richards, Robert D. Russ, John A. Shaud, Larry D. Welch.

NAVY

Admirals: Carlisle A.H. Trost, Chief of Naval Operations; Frank B. Kelso, II; Huntington Hardisty; Powell F. Carter, Jr.; David E. Jeremiah; Leon A. Edney; Bruce DeMars; James R. Hoggs; Jonathan T. Howe.

MARINE CORPS

Generals: Alfred M. Gray, Commandmant of the Marine Corps; Joseph J. Went, Assistant Commandmant of the Marine Corps.
Lieutenant Generals: Keith A. Smith, Joseph J. Went, Frank E. Petersen, Stephen G. Olmstead, Edwin J. Godfrey, Ernest T. Cook, Jr., Charles H. Pitman, William G. Carson, Jr., William R. Etnyre, John I. Hudson, Carl E. Mundy, Jr.

COAST GUARD

Admiral: Adm. Paul A. Yost, Jr., Commandant.
Vice Admirals: Clyde T. Lusk, Jr., Vice Commandant; Howard B. Thorsen, Commander Atlantic Area; Clyde E. Robbins, Commander, Pacific Area.

1. On March 15, 1978, George Washington, the commander of the Continental Army in the American Revolution and our first President, was promoted posthumously to the newly-created rank of General of the Armies of the United States. Congress authorized this title to make it clear that Washington is the Army's senior general. *Source:* Department of Defense.

History of the Armed Services

Source: Department of Defense.

U.S. Army

On June 14, 1775, the Continental Congress "adopted" the New England Armies—a mixed force of volunteers besieging the British in Boston—appointing a committee to draft "Rules and regulations for the government of the Army" and voting to raise 10 rifle companies as a reinforcement. The next day, it appointed Washington commander-in-chief of the "Continental forces to be raised for the defense of liberty," and he took command at Boston on July 3, 1775. The Continental Army that fought the Revolution was our first national military organization, and hence the Army is the senior service. After the war, the army was radically reduced but enough survived to form a small Regular Army of about 700 men under the Constitution, a nucleus for expansion in the 1790s to successfully meet threats from the Indians and from France. From these humble beginnings, the U.S. Army has developed, normally expanding rapidly by absorbing citizen soldiers in wartime and contracting just as rapidly after each war.

U.S. Navy

The antecedents of the U.S. Navy go back to September 1775, when Gen. Washington commissioned 7 schooners and brigantines to prey on British supply vessels bound for the Colonies or Canada. On Oct. 13, 1775, a resolve of the Continental Congress called for the purchase of 2 vessels for the purpose of intercepting enemy transports. With its passage a Naval Committee of 7 men was formed, and they rapidly obtained passage of legislation calling for procurement of additional vessels. The Continental Navy was supplemented by privateers and ships operated as state navies, but soon after the British surrender it was disestablished.

In 1794, because of dissatisfaction with the payment of tribute to the Barbary pirates, Congress

authorized construction of 6 frigates. The first, *United States*, was launched May 10, 1797, but the Navy still remained under the control of the Secretary of War until April 1798, when the Navy Department was created under the Secretary of the Navy with Cabinet rank.

U.S. Air Force

Until creation of the National Military Establishment in September 1947, which united the services under one department, military aviation was a part of the U.S. Army. In the Army, aeronautical operations came under the Signal Corps from 1907 to 1918, when the Army Air Service was established. In 1926, the Army Air Corps came into being and remained until 1941, when the Army Air Forces succeeded it as the Army's air arm. On Sept. 18, 1947, the U.S. Air Force was established as an independent military service under the National Military Establishment. At that time, the name "Army Air Forces" was abolished.

U.S. Coast Guard

Our country's oldest continuous seagoing service, the U.S. Coast Guard, traces its history back to 1790, when the first Congress authorized the construction of ten vessels for the collection of revenue. Known first as the Revenue Marine, and later as the Revenue Cutter Service, the Coast Guard received its present name in 1915 under an act of Congress combining the Revenue Cutter Service with the Life-Saving Service. In 1939, the Lighthouse Service was also consolidated with this unit. The Bureau of Marine Inspection and Navigation was transferred temporarily to the Coast Guard in 1942, permanently in 1946. Through its antecedents, the Coast Guard is one of the oldest organizations under the federal government and, until the Navy Department was established in 1798, served as the only U.S. armed force afloat. In times of peace, it operates under the Department of Transportation, serving as the nation's primary agency for promoting marine safety and enforcing federal maritime laws. In times of war, or on direction of the President, it is attached to the Navy Department.

U.S. Marine Corps

Founded in 1775 and observing its official birthday on Nov. 10, the U.S. Marine Corps was developed to serve on land, on sea, and in the air.

Marines have fought in every U.S. war. From an initial two battalions in the Revolution, the Corps reached a peak strength of six divisions and five aircraft wings in World War II. Its present strength is three active divisions and aircraft wings and a Reserve division/aircraft wing team. In 1947, the National Security Act set Marine Corps strength at not less than three divisions and three aircraft wings.

Service Academies

U.S. Military Academy

Source: U.S. Military Academy.

Established in 1802 by an act of Congress, the U.S. Military Academy is located on the west bank of the Hudson River some 50 miles north of New York City. To gain admission a candidate must first secure a nomination from an authorized source. These sources, and the number of cadetships allocated to each, are:

Congressional

Representatives	5 each
Senators	5 each
Other: Vice Presidential	5
District of Columbia	5
Puerto Rico	6
Am. Samoa, Guam, Virgin Is.	1 each

Military-Service-Connected Nominations (Each Class)

Presidential	100
Enlisted members of Army	85
Enlisted members of Army Reserve/ National Guard	85
Sons and daughters of deceased and disabled veterans (approximately)	10
Honor military, naval schools and ROTC	20
Sons and daughters of persons awarded the Medal of Honor	(unlimited)

Any number of applicants can meet the requirements for a *nomination* in these categories. *Appointments* (offers of admission), however, can only be made to the number of applicants shown above.

Candidates may be nominated for vacancies during the year preceding the day of admission, which occurs in early July. The best time to apply is during the junior year in high school.

Candidates must be citizens of the U.S., be unmarried, be at least 17 but not yet 22 years old on July 1 of the year admitted, have a secondary-school education or its equivalent, and be able to meet the academic, medical, and physical aptitude requirements. Academic qualification is determined by an analysis of entire scholastic record, and performance on either the American College Testing (ACT) Assessment Program Test or the College Entrance Examination Board Scholastic Aptitude Test (SAT). Entrance requirements and procedures for appointment are described in the Admissions Bulletin, available without charge from Admissions, U.S. Military Academy, West Point, N.Y. 10996-1797.

Cadets are members of the Regular Army. As such they receive full scholarships and annual salaries from which they pay for their uniforms, textbooks, and incidental expenses. Upon successful completion of the four-year course, the graduate receives the degree of Bachelor of Science and is commissioned a second lieutenant in the Regular Army with a requirement to serve as an officer for a minimum of five years.

U.S. Naval Academy

Source: U.S. Naval Academy.

The Naval School, established in 1845 at Fort Severn, Annapolis, Md., was renamed the U.S. Naval Academy in 1850. A four-year course was adopted a year later.

The Superintendent is a rear admiral. A civilian academic dean heads the academic program. A captain heads the 4,525-man Brigade of Midshipmen and military, professional, and physical training. The faculty is half military and half civilian.

Graduates are awarded the Bachelor of Science or Bachelor of Science in Engineering and are commissioned as officers in the U.S. Navy or Marine Corps.

Midshipmen are nominated for an appointment from several official sources, which are summarized below. The numbers represent the total each nominator may have at the academy at any one time. Five each from the Vice President, U.S. Senators, U.S. Representatives, the delegate from Washington, D.C., and the Resident Commissioner of Puerto Rico. Delegates from Guam and the Virgin Islands nominate two each, with one each from the Governor of Puerto Rico, the delegate from American Samoa, and the Office of the Administrator of the Panama Canal Commission.

Annual nominations are from several other sources: Presidential nominations for 100 sons and daughters of career military personnel; 85 each from the regular Navy and Marine corps, and the Navy and Marine Corps reserve; 20 from NROTC/NJROTC/MCJROTC and Honor Military and Naval schools; 65 sons and daughters of disabled veterans or POWs, 600 qualified alternates; and an unlimited number of sons and daughters of Medal of Honor recipients.

To have basic eligibility for admission, candidates must be citizens of the U.S., of good moral character, at least 17 and not more than 22 years of age on July 1 of their entering year, and unmarried.

In order to be considered for admission, a candidate must obtain a nomination from one of the sources of appointments listed above. The Admissions Board at the Naval Academy examines the candidate's school record, College Board or ACT scores, recommendations from school officials, extracurricular activities, and evidence from other sources concerning his or her character, leadership potential, academic preparation, and physical fitness. Qualification for admission is based on all of the above factors.

Tuition, board, lodging, and medical and dental care are provided. Midshipmen receive over $500 a month for books, uniforms, and personal needs.

For general information or answers to specific questions, write: Superintendent, U.S. Naval Academy, (Attention: Candidate Guidance), Annapolis, Md. 21402-5018.

U.S. Air Force Academy

Source: U.S. Air Force Academy.

The bill establishing the Air Force Academy was signed by President Eisenhower on April 1, 1954. The first class of 306 cadets was sworn in on July 11, 1955, at Lowry Air Force Base, Denver, the Academy's temporary location. The Cadet Wing moved into the Academy's permanent home north of Colorado Springs, Colorado, in 1958.

Cadets receive four years of academic, military, and physical education to prepare them for leadership as officers in the Air Force. The Academy is authorized a total of 4,546 cadets. Each new class averages 1,400. The candidates for the Academy must be at least 17 but less than 22 on July 1 of the year for which they enter the Academy, must be a United States citizen, never married, and be able to meet the mental and physical requirements. A candidate is required to take the following examinations and tests: (1) the Service Academies' Qualifying Medical Examination; (2) either the American College Testing (ACT) Assessment Program test or the College Entrance Examination Board Scholastic Aptitude Test (SAT); and (3) a Physical Aptitude Examination.

Each new cadet must deposit $1,000 at the time of admission to the Academy, otherwise cadets receive their entire education at government expense and, in addition, are paid $525 per month base pay. From this sum, they pay for their uniforms, textbooks, tailoring, laundry, entertainment tickets, etc. Upon completion of the four-year course, leading to a Bachelor of Science degree, a cadet who meets the qualifications is commissioned a second lieutenant in the regular U.S. Air Force. About 70 percent enter pilot or navigator training. For details on admissions, write: Director of Cadet Admissions (RRS), HQ USAF Academy, Colorado Springs, CO 80840-5651.

U.S. Coast Guard Academy

Source: U.S. Coast Guard Academy.

The U.S. Coast Guard Academy, New London, Conn., was founded on July 31, 1876, to serve as the "School of Instruction" for the Revenue Cutter Service, predecessor to the Coast Guard.

The J.C. Dobbin, a converted schooner, housed the first Coast Guard Academy, and was succeeded in 1878 by the barque Chase, a ship built for cadet training. First winter quarters were in a sail loft at New Bedford, Mass. The school was moved in 1900 to Curtis Bay, Md., to provide a more technical education, and in 1910 was moved back to New England to Fort Trumbull, New London, Conn. In 1932 the Academy moved to its present location in New London.

The Academy today offers a four-year curriculum for the professional and academic training of cadets, which leads to a Bachelor of Science degree and a commission as ensign in the Coast Guard.

Cadets receive appointment through nationwide competition, which includes either the December administration of the College Entrance Examination Board tests, or the American College Testing (ACT) Program tests. Applications must be submitted to the Coast Guard not later than December 15 and to the College Entrance Examination Board, 30 days prior to the tests.

Women were admitted to the Coast Guard Academy for the first time during 1976 as members of the Class of 1980. Candidates must be between 17 and 22 years of age, physically sound, and unmarried. They must agree to remain unmarried until graduation and to serve at least five years on active duty. Cadets receive one-half of an Ensign's base pay per year to cover their uniform and incidental expenses and are furnished their rations and quarters. Applications may be made to Director of Admissions, U.S. Coast Guard Academy, New London, Conn. 06320.

U.S. Merchant Marine Academy

Source: U.S. Merchant Marine Academy.

The U.S. Merchant Marine Academy, situated at Kings Point, N.Y., on the north shore of Long Island, was dedicated Sept. 30, 1943. It is maintained by the Department of Transportation under direction of the Maritime Administration.

The Academy has a complement of approximately 840 men and women representing every state, D.C., the Canal Zone, Puerto Rico, Guam, American Samoa, and the Virgin Islands. It is also authorized to admit up to 12 candidates from the Western Hemisphere and 30 other foreign students at any one time.

Candidates are nominated by Senators and members of the House of Representatives. Nominations to the Academy are governed by a state and territory quota system based on population and the results of the College Entrance Examination Board tests.

A candidate must be a citizen not less than 17 and not yet 22 years of age by July 1 of the year in which admission is sought. Fifteen high school credits, including 3 units in mathematics (from algebra, geometry and/or trigonometry), 1 unit in science (physics or chemistry) and 3 in English are required.

The course is four years and includes one year of practical training aboard a merchant ship. Study includes marine engineering, navigation, satellite navigation and communications, electricity, ship construction, naval science and tactics, economics, business, languages, history, etc.

Upon completion of the course of study, a graduate receives a Bachelor of Science degree, a license as a merchant marine deck or engineering officer, and a commission as an Ensign in the Naval Reserve.

The National Guard

Source: Departments of the Army and the Air Force, National Guard Bureau.

The National Guard of the U.S. originated in 1636 with the Old North, South and East Regiments of the Colonial Militia in Massachusetts Bay Colony. It is the oldest military force in the country. Guardmembers have served this country at home and overseas in every major conflict in which the U.S. has been involved.

As of April 1989, the Army National Guard had 451,589 individuals, making it the eleventh largest army in the world. In that same time period, the Air National Guard had 114,642 people, ranking the air "arm" of the National Guard as the fifth largest Air Force in the world.

In peacetime, the National Guard is commanded by the governors of the respective states/territories and may be called to state active duty by the governor to assist in state emergencies, disasters, and civil disturbances. During a war or national emergency, the National Guard may be called to active duty by the President or Congress. The National Guard serves as the primary source of augmentation for the Army and the Air Force.

The Army Guard operated in fiscal year 1987 with $4.98 billion dollars, the Air Guard $3.1 billion. Although a substantial portion of National Guard funding comes from the federal government, the respective states and territories provide fiscal support in such areas as state missions, recruiting and training administration, armory construction, and funding for state-salaried employees.

The Army National Guard is made up of 3,000 units located in 2,600 communities throughout the 50 states, Puerto Rico, Guam, the Virgin Islands and the District of Columbia.

The Army National Guard provides 43% of the total Army's combat capability and approximately 20 percent of its support units. The Army Guard consists of 10 combat divisions, 14 separate combat brigades, 4 divisional roundout brigades, 4 armored cavalry regiments, 3 medical brigades, 5 special forces groups, 1 infantry scout group (arctic reconnaissance) and 17 major command headquarters units.

The Army National Guard is crucial to the nation's first-line of defense. Over half of the Army's divisional capability is in the Army National Guard. Of the Army's 28 divisions, ten are solely Guard divisions with an additional eight requiring Guard units of battalion or brigade size to bring them to their full combat potential.

The Army National Guard's force structure is broken down into: 10 divisions, 14 separate brigades, five divisional roundout brigades, three armored cavalry regiments, and two special forces groups. In addition, the Army Guard has the Army's only infantry scout group (arctic reconnaissance).

The Air National Guard has 91 flying units and 549 mission support units which, upon mobilization, would be gained by one of six major commands of the USAF. The gaining major commands are Tactical Air Command (TAC), Strategic Air Command (SAC), Military Airlift Command (MAC), Air Force Communications Command (AFCC), Pacific Air Forces (PACAF), and Alaskan Air Command (AAC).

The Air National Guard is a vital contributor to the Total Air Force mission. By the close of fiscal year 89, the Air Guard will be performing:

- 86 percent of the Total Air Force air defense mission,
- 50 percent of all Air Force tactical reconnaissance,
- 36 percent of tactical airlift,
- and will represent 26 percent of all U.S. Air Force fighters.

In the mission support areas, the Air National Guard comprises:

- 67 percent of the total Air Forces' combat communications units;
- 68 percent of its engineering and installation forces;
- 40 percent of base services;
- and 24 percent of the U.S. Air Force civil engineering units.

The National Guard Bureau, a joint, Federal agency located in Washington D.C., formulates and administers National Guard programs to ensure the continued development and maintenance of Army and Air Guard units. Functioning as both an operating and staff agency, the National Guard Bureau serves as the channel of communications between the 54 states and U.S. territories and the Departments of the Army and Air Force. The Chief, National Guard Bureau is nominated by the President and confirmed by the Senate. The current Chief, National Guard Bureau, is Lt. General Herbert R. Temple, Jr., of California.

The National Guard offers its young men and women a broad spectrum of educational opportunities. These not only include skill training associated with their military assignment, but in many instances embrace civilian occupations as well. The list of skills is not limited to those that are equipment oriented but includes management, medical, and other career fields. Some of these educational opportunities may even be pursued in civilian institutions, specifically that of the Clinical Specialist, which is compatible with a Licensed Practical Nurse or Licensed Vocational Nurse.

If openings exist, men and women between the ages of 17 and 35 may enlist for a period of four or six years followed by a 4 or 2 year inactive reserve period. The time required on inactive reserve duty status is contingent upon an enlistee's initial service obligation. (Initial service obligation plus inactive duty status must meet time requirement of eight years.) While on inactive status, the service member is subject to recall should the need arise.

A woman between the ages of 17 and 35 who has no previous military experience may also enlist in the National Guard for a period of six years. Women in the Army National Guard will receive basic training at either Fort McClellan, Ala., Fort Dix, N.J., or Fort Jackson, S.C.; women in the Air National Guard train at Lackland Air Force Base, Tex. Advanced training takes place at appropriate training centers.

Guard members receive a full day's pay of their military rank for each unit training assembly attended. Additionally, they receive a day's pay of their military rank for each day of their 15 days of annual training, plus any other days on active duty for training at military schools or special assignments. All such training counts toward retirement eligibility at age 60 with 20 or more years of qualifying service.

Veterans' Benefits

Although benefits of various kinds date back to Colonial days, veterans of World War I were the first to receive disability compensation, allotments for dependents, life insurance, medical care, and vocational rehabilitation. In 1940, these benefits were slowly broadened. On March 15, 1989, the Veterans Administration became the Department of Veterans Affairs.

The following benefits available to veterans require certain minimum periods of active duty during qualifying periods of service and, except for service personnel, are applicable only to those whose discharges are not dishonorable.

For information or assistance in applying for veterans benefits, write, call, or visit a VA Regional Office. Consult your local telephone directory under United States Government, Department of Veterans Affairs (VA) for the address and telephone number. Toll-free telephone service is available in all 50 States. Former POW's may call a toll-free number (800-821-8139) in Washington, D.C.

Unemployment allowances. Every effort is being made to secure employment for Vietnam veterans. Unemployment benefits are administered by the U.S. Department of Labor.

Loans. GI loans are made for a variety of purposes, such as: to buy or build a home; to purchase a manufactured home with or without a lot; and to refinance a home presently owned and occupied by the veteran. When the purpose of a refinancing loan is to lower the interest rate on an existing guaranteed loan then prior occupancy by the veteran or spouse will suffice. VA will guarantee the lender against loss up to 50% on loans of $45,000 or less and the lesser of $36,000 or 40% (never less than $22,500), on loans of more than $45,000. On mobile home loans, the amount of the guarantee is 40% of the loan to a maximum of $20,000. The interest rate may not exceed the maximum rate set by VA and in effect when the loan is made.

Compensation and rehabilitation benefits. These are available to those having some service-connected illness or disability.

Disability compensation. VA pays from $73 to $1,468 per month, and for specific conditions up to $4,195 per month, plus allowances for dependents, where the disability is rated 30% or more.

Vocational Rehabilitation. VA provides professional counseling, training and other assistance to help compensably service-disabled veterans who have an employment handicap to achieve maximum independence in daily living and, to the extent possible, to obtain and maintain suitable employment. Generally, a veteran may receive up to 48 months of this assistance during the 12 years from the date he or she is notified of entitlement to VA compensation. All the expenses of a veteran's rehabilitation program are paid by VA. In addition, the veteran receives a subsistence allowance which varies based on the rate of training and number of dependents. For example, a single veteran training full time would receive $310 monthly.

Vocational Training for VA Pension Recipients. Veterans who are awarded pension during the period from February 1, 1985, through January 31, 1992, may participate in a program of vocational training essentially identical to that provided in VA's vocational rehabilitation program. Participants do not receive any direct payments, such as subsistence allowance, while in training.

Medical and dental care. This includes care in VA and, in certain instances, in non-VA, or other federal hospitals. It also covers outpatient treatment at a VA field facility or, in some cases, by an approved private physician or dentist. Full domiciliary care is also provided where necessary. Nursing home care may be provided at certain VA medical facilities or in approved community nursing homes. Hospital and other medical care may also be provided for the spouse and child dependents of a veteran who is permanently and totally disabled due to a service-connected disability; or for survivors of a veteran who dies from a service-connected disability; or for survivors of a veteran who at the time of death had a total disability, permanent in nature, resulting from a service-connected disability. These latter benefits are usually provided in nonfederal facilities. Eligibility criteria for these benefits vary and certain veterans must agree to make a copayment for the care they receive from VA. Veterans and/or their dependents or survivors should always apply in advance. Contact the nearest VA medical facility.

Readjustment Counseling. VA provides readjustment counseling to veterans of the Vietnam Era in need of assistance in resolving post-war readjustment problems in the areas of employment, family, education, and personal readjustment including post-traumatic stress disorder. Services are provided at community-based Vet Centers and at VA Medical Centers in certain locations. Services include individual family and group counseling, employment and educational counseling, and assistance in obtaining referrals to various governmental and nongovernmental agencies with an interest in assisting Vietnam Era veterans. All Vietnam Era veterans are eligible for services except those with a type of discharge which may limit eligibility for VA services. Certain types of discharges are subject to special adjudication to determine eligibility. Contact the nearest Vet Center or VA facility to determine location of Vet Center.

Dependents' educational assistance. VA pays $376 a month for up to 45 months of schooling to sons and daughters of veterans who died of service-connected causes or who were permanently and totally disabled from service-connected causes or died while permanently and totally disabled or who are missing in action, captured in the line of duty, or forcibly detained or interned in line of duty by a foreign power for more than 90 days. Students must usually be between 18 and 26.

Spouses of veterans whose deaths are adjudged to be service-connected, and spouses of veterans who are permanently and totally disabled due to service-connected causes or who are prisoners of war or are missing in action are also eligible for this educational benefit.

Veterans readjustment education. Most education and training assistance for Vietnam Era veterans expires on Dec. 31, 1989. Veterans and servicepersons who initially entered the military on or after Jan. 1, 1977, and before July 1, 1985, may receive educational assistance under a contributory plan. Individuals contribute $25 to $100 from military pay, up to a maximum of $2,700. This amount is matched by the Federal Government on a 2 for 1 basis. Participants, while on active duty, may make a lump sum contribution. Participants receive monthly payments for the number of months they contributed, or for 36 months, whichever is less. No initial enrollments are permitted after March 31, 1987.

Veterans Educational Assistance Act of 1984. This Act established a program of education benefits for individuals entering military after June 30, 1985. Servicepersons entering active duty after that date will have their basic pay reduced by $100 a month for the first 12 months of their service, unless they specifically elect not to participate in the program. Servicepersons eligible for post-Korean GI Bill benefits as of December 31, 1989, and who serve 3 years in active duty service after July 1, 1985, are also eligible for the new program, but will not have their basic pay reduced. Servicepersons who, after December 31, 1976, received commissions as officers from service academies or scholarship senior ROTC programs are not eligible for this program.

Active duty for three years (two years, if the initial obligated period of active duty is less than three years), or two years active duty plus four years in the Selected Reserve or National Guard will entitle an individual to $300 a month basic benefits. There is also a targeted, discretionary kicker of up to an additional $400 available. A supplemental benefit of up to an additional $300 with a targeted, discretionary kicker of up to $300 more is also available for certain additional active duty service.

An educational entitlement program is also available for members of the Selected Reserve. Eligibility applies to individuals who, after June 30, 1985 enlist, re-enlist, or extend an enlistment for a six-year period. Benefits may be paid to eligible members of the Selected Reserve who complete their initial period of active duty training. Full-time payments are $140 a month for 36 months.

Veterans' Benefits Improvement Act of 1984. Veterans awarded 100 percent disability compensation based upon unemployability during the period February 1, 1985, through January 31, 1992, for whom a vocational goal is feasible are required to participate in a rehabilitation program. Necessary training expenses, special equipment, etc., toward a definite job objective are paid for, plus a monthly allowance up to $310, with increased amounts for dependents, in addition to compensation. In addition, all veterans granted an unemployability rating before February 1, 1985, the start of the special program period, may receive special assistance in securing employment under the Vocational Rehabilitation Program. Any veteran with an unemployability rating who secures gainful employment during the special program period will be protected from reduction until such veteran has worked continuously for 12 months.

Pensions. Pension benefits are payable for wartime veterans permanently and totally disabled from non-service-connected causes. These benefits are based on need. Surviving spouses and orphans of wartime veterans have the same eligibility status, based on the veteran's honorable wartime service and their need.

Insurance. The VA life insurance programs have approximately 7.4 million policyholders with total coverage of about $213 billion. Detailed information on NSLI (National Service Life Insurance), USGLI (United States Government Life Insurance), and VMLI (Veterans Mortgage Life Insurance) may be obtained at any VA Office. Information regarding SGLI (Servicemen's Group Life Insurance) and VGLI (Veterans Group Life Insurance) may be obtained from the Office of Servicemen's Group Life Insurance, 213 Washington St., Newark, N.J. 07102

Burial benefits. Burial is provided in any VA national cemetery with available grave space to any deceased veteran of wartime or peacetime service, other than for training, who was discharged under conditions other than dishonorable. Laws of the Congress extend eligibility for burial in a national cemetery to the veteran's spouse, widow, widower, minor children, and under certain conditions, unmarried adult children.

Headstone or marker. A government headstone or marker is furnished for any deceased veteran of wartime or peacetime service, other than for training, who was discharged under conditions other than dishonorable and is interred in a national, state veterans', or private cemetery. VA also will furnish markers to veterans' eligible dependents interred in a national or state veterans' cemetery.

The Battle of Tokyo

The change in the American bombing campaign against Tokyo to incendiary bombs instead of explosive bombs produced horrifyingly effective results. On March 9, 1945, 279 American B 29s—each carrying 6–8 tons of incendiaries—devastated Tokyo. A quarter of the total area of the city, nearly 16 square miles, was burnt out, and over 267,000 buildings were destroyed. Civilian casualties totaled approximately 185,000, while American attackers lost only 14 aircraft. In the next ten days the United States dropped nearly 10,000 tons of incendiaries, devastating not only Tokyo but the cities of Osaka, Kobe, and Nagoya as well.

For three months early in 1945 the use of explosive bombs had had disappointing results, but civilian morale declined badly after the Tokyo fire-raid. Over 8 1/2 million people fled into the countryside, causing war production to practically cease. More than 600 major war factories were destroyed by bombing.

The Kamikazes

During the 13th century, a great typhoon off the coast of Japan nearly destroyed the ships of an invading Mongol army. This seeming intervention by Providence was considered a "Divine Wind" or Kamikaze by the Japanese people.

In late 1944, the United States was in the process of recapturing the Philippine Islands from Japan. In a desperate act to prevent it, Japanese military leaders authorized the formation of a Special Attack Force whose mission was to destroy American aircraft carriers. Each member of this special unit had volunteered to sacrifice his life by diving a bomb-laden plane into the deck of a U.S. flattop.

The suicide fliers were called the Kamikaze, named after the Divine Wind that had saved their country from invasion in the past.

By the end of the war, over 1,200 Kamikaze pilots had sunk 34 U.S. ships, damaged 288 others and caused over 15,000 casualties.

U.S. Casualties in Major Wars

War	Branch of service	Numbers engaged	Battle deaths	Other deaths	Total deaths	Wounds not mortal	Total casualties[1]
Revolutionary War	Army	n.a.	4,044	n.a.	n.a.	6,004	n.a.
1775 to 1783	Navy	n.a.	342	n.a.	n.a.	114	n.a.
	Marines	n.a.	49	n.a.	n.a.	70	n.a.
	Total	**n.a.**	**4,435**	**n.a.**	**n.a.**	**6,188**	**n.a.**
War of 1812	Army	n.a.	1,950	n.a.	n.a.	4,000	n.a.
1812 to 1815	Navy	n.a.	265	n.a.	n.a.	439	n.a.
	Marines	n.a.	45	n.a.	n.a.	66	n.a.
	Total	**286,730**	**2,260**	**n.a.**	**n.a.**	**4,505**	**n.a.**
Mexican War	Army	n.a.	1,721	11,550	13,271	4,102	17,373
1846 to 1848	Navy	n.a.	1	n.a.	n.a.	3	n.a.
	Marines	n.a.	11	n.a.	n.a.	47	n.a.
	Total	**78,718**	**1,733**	**n.a.**	**n.a.**	**4,152**	**n.a.**
Civil War[2]	Army	2,128,948	138,154	221,374	359,528	280,040	639,568
1861 to 1865	Navy	84,415	2,112	2,411	4,523	1,710	6,233
	Marines		148	312	460	131	591
	Total	**2,213,363**	**140,414**	**224,097**	**364,511**	**281,881**	**646,392**
Spanish-American War	Army	280,564	369	2,061	2,430	1,594	4,024
1898	Navy	22,875	10	0	10	47	57
	Marines	3,321	6	0	6	21	27
	Total	**306,760**	**385**	**2,061**	**2,446**	**1,662**	**4,108**
World War I	Army	4,057,101	50,510	55,868	106,378	193,663	300,041
1917 to 1918	Navy	599,051	431	6,856	7,287	819	8,106
	Marines	78,839	2,461	390	2,851	9,520	12,371
	Total	**4,734,991**	**53,402**	**63,114**	**116,516**	**204,002**	**320,518**
World War II	Army[3]	11,260,000	234,874	83,400	318,274	565,861	884,135
1941 to 1946	Navy	4,183,466	36,950	25,664	62,614	37,778	100,392
	Marines	669,100	19,733	4,778	24,511	67,207	91,718
	Total	**16,112,566**	**291,557**	**113,842**	**405,399**	**670,846**	**1,076,245**
Korean War	Army	2,834,000	27,704	9,429	37,133	77,596	114,729
1950 to 1953	Navy	1,177,000	458	4,043	4,501	1,576	6,077
	Marines	424,000	4,267	1,261	5,528	23,744	29,272
	Air Force	1,285,000	1,200	5,884	7,084	368	7,452
	Total	**5,720,000**	**33,629**	**20,617**	**54,246**	**103,284**	**157,530**
War in Southeast Asia[4]	Army	4,386,000	30,904	7,270	38,174	96,802	134,976
	Navy[5]	1,842,000	1,634	916	2,552	4,178	6,730
	Marines	794,000	13,079	1,750	14,829	51,392	66,221
	Air Force	1,740,000	1,765	815	2,580	931	3,511
	Total	**8,744,000**	**47,382**	**10,753**	**58,135**	**153,303**	**211,438**

1. Excludes captured or interned and missing in action who were subsequently returned to military control. 2. Union forces only. Totals should probably be somewhat larger as data or disposition of prisoners are far from complete. Final Confederate deaths, based on incomplete returns, were 133,821, to which should be added 26,000–31,000 personnel who died in Union prisons. 3. Army data include Air Force. 4. As of Nov. 11, 1986. 5. Includes a small number of Coast Guard of which 5 were battle deaths. NOTE: All data are subject to revision. For wars before World War I, information represents best data from available records. However, due to incomplete records and possible difference in usage of terminology, reporting systems, etc., figures should be considered estimates. n.a. = not available. *Source:* Department of Defense.

The Fire-Bombing of Dresden

Early in 1945 Allied forces obliterated the greater part of one of the most beautiful cities in Europe, killing at least 35,000 people and perhaps 135,000.

The fire-bombing of Dresden was launched by the British Royal Air Force with 800 aircraft in the night of February 13–14 and continued by the U.S. 8th Air Force with 400 aircraft in daylight on February 14, with 200 on February 15, with 400 again on March 2, and, finally, with 572 on April 17. The raids allegedly were intended to promote the Soviet advance by destroying a center of communications important to the German defense of the Eastern Front, but, in fact, they did nothing to help the Red Army militarily and may have been motivated as retribution for the German bombing of Coventry earlier in the war.

Casualties in World War I

Country	Total mobilized forces	Killed or died[1]	Wounded	Prisoners or missing	Total casualties
Austria-Hungary	7,800,000	1,200,000	3,620,000	2,200,000	7,020,000
Belgium	267,000	13,716	44,686	34,659	93,061
British Empire[2]	8,904,467	908,371	2,090,212	191,652	3,190,235
Bulgaria	1,200,000	87,500	152,390	27,029	266,919
France[2]	8,410,000	1,357,800	4,266,000	537,000	6,160,800
Germany	11,000,000	1,773,700	4,216,058	1,152,800	7,142,558
Greece	230,000	5,000	21,000	1,000	27,000
Italy	5,615,000	650,000	947,000	600,000	2,197,000
Japan	800,000	300	907	3	1,210
Montenegro	50,000	3,000	10,000	7,000	20,000
Portugal	100,000	7,222	13,751	12,318	33,291
Romania	750,000	335,706	120,000	80,000	535,706
Russia	12,000,000	1,700,000	4,950,000	2,500,000	9,150,000
Serbia	707,343	45,000	133,148	152,958	331,106
Turkey	2,850,000	325,000	400,000	250,000	975,000
United States	4,734,991	116,516	204,002	—	320,518

1. Includes deaths from all causes. 2. Official figures. NOTE: For additional U.S. figures, *see* the table on U.S. Casualties in Major Wars in this section.

Casualties in World War II

Country	Men in war	Battle deaths	Wounded
Australia	1,000,000	26,976	180,864
Austria	800,000	280,000	350,117
Belgium	625,000	8,460	55,513[1]
Brazil[2]	40,334	943	4,222
Bulgaria	339,760	6,671	21,878
Canada	1,086,343[7]	42,042[7]	53,145
China[3]	17,250,521	1,324,516	1,762,006
Czechoslovakia	—	6,683[4]	8,017
Denmark	—	4,339	—
Finland	500,000	79,047	50,000
France	—	201,568	400,000
Germany	20,000,000	3,250,000[4]	7,250,000
Greece	—	17,024	47,290
Hungary	—	147,435	89,313
India	2,393,891	32,121	64,354
Italy	3,100,000	149,496[4]	66,716
Japan	9,700,000	1,270,000	140,000
Netherlands	280,000	6,500	2,860
New Zealand	194,000	11,625[4]	17,000
Norway	75,000	2,000	—
Poland	—	664,000	530,000
Romania	650,000[5]	350,000[6]	—
South Africa	410,056	2,473	—
U.S.S.R.	—	6,115,000[4]	14,012,000
United Kingdom	5,896,000	357,116[4]	369,267
United States	16,112,566	291,557	670,846
Yugoslavia	3,741,000	305,000	425,000

1. Civilians only. 2. Army and Navy figures. 3. Figures cover period July 7, 1937–Sept. 2, 1945, and concern only Chinese regular troops. They do not include casualties suffered by guerrillas and local military corps. 4. Deaths from all causes. 5. Against Soviet Russia; 385,847 against Nazi Germany. 6. Against Soviet Russia; 169,822 against Nazi Germany. 7. National Defense Ctr., Canadian Forces Hq., Director of History. NOTE: The figures in this table are unofficial estimates obtained from various sources.

Military Pensions

The Military Reform Act of 1986 changed pensions for anyone entering the armed forces after August 1, 1986. Under the new law, those who retire after 20 years (and usually go on to a new career) will receive 40 percent of base pay for the three highest years. It rises to 75 percent after 30 years of service.

The bill also provided for annual cost-of-living increases.

Early retirement pensions are adjusted up to a base of 50 percent at age 62, with a 1 percent penalty added after the cost-of-living adjustment for each year of service less than 30 years.

U.S. Military Actions Other Than Declared Wars

Hawaii (1893): U.S. Marines, ordered to land by U.S. Minister John L. Stevens, aided the revolutionary Committee of Safety in overthrowing the native government. Stevens then proclaimed Hawaii a U.S. protectorate. Annexation, resisted by the Democratic administration in Washington, was not formally accomplished until 1898.

China (1900): Boxers (a group of Chinese revolutionists) occupied Peking and laid siege to foreign legations. U.S. troops joined an international expedition which relieved the city.

Panama (1903): After Colombia had rejected a proposed agreement for relinquishing sovereignty over the Panama Canal Zone, revolution broke out, aided by promoters of the Panama Canal Co. Two U.S. warships were standing by to protect American privileges. The U.S. recognized the Republic of Panama on November 6.

Dominican Republic (1904): When the Dominican Republic failed to meet debts owed to the U.S. and foreign creditors, President Theodore Roosevelt declared the U.S. intention of exercising "international police power" in the Western Hemisphere whenever necessary. The U.S. accordingly administered customs and managed debt payments of the Dominican Republic from 1905 to 1907.

Nicaragua (1911): The possibility of foreign control over Nicaragua's canal route led to U.S. intervention and agreement. The U.S. landed Marines in Nicaragua (Aug. 14, 1912) to protect American interests there. A small detachment remained until 1933.

Mexico (1914): Mexican dictator Victoriano Huerta, opposed by President Woodrow Wilson, had the support of European governments. An incident involving unarmed U.S. sailors in Tampico led to the landing of U.S. forces on Mexican soil. Veracruz was bombarded by the Navy to prevent the landing of munitions from a German vessel. At the point of war, both powers agreed to mediation by Argentina, Brazil, and Chile. Huerta abdicated, and Venustiano Carranza succeeded to the presidency.

Haiti (1915): U.S. Marines imposed a military occupation. Haiti signed a treaty making it a virtual protectorate of the U.S. until troops were withdrawn in 1934.

Mexico (1916): Raids by Pancho Villa cost American lives on both sides of the border. President Carranza consented to a punitive expedition led by Gen. John J. Pershing, but antagonism grew in Mexico. Wilson withdrew the U.S. force when war with Germany became imminent.

Dominican Republic (1916): Renewed intervention in the Dominican Republic with internal administration by U.S. naval officers lasted until 1924.

Korea (1950): In this undeclared war, which terminated with the July 27, 1953, truce at Panmunjom and the establishment of a neutral nations' supervisory commission, the U.S. and 15 member-nations of the U.N. came to the aid of the Republic of South Korea, whose 38th-parallel border was crossed by the invading Russian Communist-controlled North Koreans, who were later joined by the Chinese Communists.

Lebanon (1958 and 1983): Fearful of the newly formed U.A.R. abetting the rebels of his politically and economically torn country, President Camille Chamoun appealed to the U.S. for military assistance. U.S. troops landed in mid-July and left before the end of the year, after internal and external quiet were restored. In September 1983, President Reagan ordered Marines to join an international peacekeeping force in Beirut. On October 23, 241 were killed in the terrorist bombing of the Marine compound. On February 7, 1984, Reagan ordered the Marine contingent withdrawn. He ended the U.S. role in Beirut on March 30 by releasing the Sixth Fleet from the international force.

Dominican Republic (1965): On April 28, when a political coup-turned-civil war endangered the lives of American nationals, President Lyndon B. Johnson rushed 400 marines into Santo Domingo, the beginning of an eventual U.S. peak-commitment of 30,000 troops, constituting the preponderant military strength of the OAS-created Inter-American Peace Force, and 6,500 troops, including 5,000 Americans, remained until after the peaceful inauguration of President Joaquin Balaguer on July 1, 1966, and the entire force left the country on September 20.

Vietnam: This longest war in U.S. history began with economic and technical assistance after 1954 Geneva accords ending the Indochinese War. By 1964 it had escalated into a major conflict.

This involvement spanning the administrations of five Presidents led to domestic discontent in the late 1960s. By April 1969, U.S. troop strength reached a peak of 543,400. Peace negotiations began in Paris in 1968 but proved fruitless. Finally, on Jan. 27, 1973, a peace accord was signed in Paris by the U.S., North and South Vietnam, and the Vietcong. Within 60 days, U.S. POWs were returned, and the U.S. withdrew all military forces from South Vietnam.

Grenada (1983): A left-wing military coup resulted in the intervention of a 1,900-man United States contingent, supported by token forces from Caribbean allies, which engaged an 800-man Cuban Force and secured the island within a few days. The American combat force was brought home two months later although a small noncombat unit was left behind to assist in peacekeeping functions.

Defense Budget by Major Categories
(In billions of dollars)

Major Missions and Programs	1987 actual	1988 actual	1989 estimate	1990 estimate
Strategic forces[1]	21.1	19.8	21.2	23.4
General purpose forces	114.9	114.9	112.8	117.8
Intelligence and communications	27.7	28.3	29.6	31.7
Airlift and sealift	7.1	4.4	5.4	6.3
Guard and reserve	15.7	16.9	17.2	17.2
Research and development[2]	27.5	28.4	29.1	32.1
Central supply and maintenance	22.7	24.3	25.3	27.0
Training, medical, and other general personnel activities	35.5	37.3	38.5	40.0
Administration and associated activities	6.6	6.7	6.9	5.9
Support of other nations	0.7	0.8	1.0	1.1
Special operations forces		2.0	3.2	3.1
Total	279.5	283.8	290.2	305.6

1. Excludes strategic systems development included in the research and development category. 2. Excludes research and development in other program areas on systems approved for production.

Budget Outlays for National Defense Functions
(In billions)

Item	1988	1987	1986	1985	1984	1983	1980	1975	1970
Defense Dept., military	281.9	273.9	265.6	245.4	220.8	204.4	131.0	85.9	80.2
Military personnel	76.3	72.0	71.5	67.8	64.2	60.9	40.9	32.2	29.0
Operation, maintenance	84.5	76.2	75.2	72.3	67.4	64.9	44.8	26.3	21.6
Procurement	77.2	80.7	76.5	70.4	61.9	53.6	29.0	16.0	21.6
Research and development	34.8	33.5	32.3	27.1	23.1	20.6	13.1	8.9	7.2
Military construction	5.9	5.8	5.0	4.3	3.7	3.5	2.5	1.5	1.2
Family housing	3.1	2.9	2.8	2.6	2.4	2.1	1.7	1.1	.6
Other[1]	.1	3.4	1.4	.8	−1.8	1.2	1.0	.1	1.0
Atomic energy activities[2]	8.0	7.4	7.4	7.1	6.1	5.2	2.9	1.5	1.4
Defense-related activities[3]	.5	.5	.3	.3	.5	.3	.1	.8	.1
Total	290.3	281.9	273.4	252.7	227.4	209.9	134.0	86.5	81.7

1. Revolving and management funds, trust funds, special foreign currency program, allowances, and offsetting receipts. 2. Defense activities only. 3. Includes civil defense activities. *Source:* Office of Management and Budget.

Average Military Strength[1]

Year	Army	Air Force	Navy	Marine Corps	Total
1942	1,992	[2]	416	89	2,498
1943	5,224	[2]	1,206	232	6,662
1944	7,507	[2]	2,386	398	10,290
1945	8,131	[2]	3,205	473	11,809
1950	632	415	412	80	1,539
1953	1,536	971	809	237	3,554
1954	1,477	939	767	242	3,425
1955	1,311	958	692	217	3,178
1960	871	828	617	173	2,489
1965	966	844	669	190	2,668
1970	1,432	834	732	295	3,293
1975	779	628	545	193	2,145
1980	762	561	525	185	2,033
1985	781	602	571	198	2,151
1988	772	576	593	197	2,138

1. In thousands. Data represent averages of month-end strengths. 2. Air Force data prior to June 30, 1948 included with Army data. NOTE: Detail may not add to totals due to rounding. *Source:* Department of Defense.

U.S. Strategic Nuclear Forces, End of 1988

Type	Name	Launchers	Year deployed	Warheads × yield (megatons)	Total Warheads	Total megatons
ICBMs						
LGM-30F	Minuteman II	450	1966	1 × 1.2	450	540.0
LGM-30G	Minuteman III	500			1,500	403.5
	Mk-12	(200)	1970	3 × .170 (MIRV)	(600)	(102.0)
	Mk-12A	(300)	1979	3 × .335 (MIRV)	(900)	(301.5)
LGM-118A	MX/Peacekeeper	50	1986	10 × .300 (MIRV)	500	150
Total		**1,000**			**2,450**	**1,093.5**
SLBMs						
UGM-73A	Poseidon C-3	224	1971	10 × .050 (MIRV)	2,240	112.0
UGM-96A	Trident I C-4	384	1979	8 × .100 (MIRV)	3,072	307.2
Total		**608**			**5,312**	**419.2**
Bombers/weapons						
B-1B		90	1986	ALCM .05-.150	1,614	242.1
B-52G/H		180	1958/61	SRAM .170	1,140	193.8
FB-111A		48	1969	Bombs .500	2,484	1,242.0
Total		**318**			**5,238**	**1,677.9**
Grand total		**1,926**			**13,000**	**3,190.6**

ALCM—air-launched cruise missile; **AS**—air-to-surface missile; **ICBM**—intercontinental ballistic missile, range of 5,760-15,360 kilometers; **MIRV**—multiple independently targetable reentry vehicles; **SLBM**—submarine-launched ballistic missile; **SRAM**—short-range attack missile; **SSBN**—nuclear-powered ballistic missile submarine.

Reprinted by permission of the BULLETIN OF THE ATOMIC SCIENTISTS, a magazine of science and world affairs. Copyright © 1989 by the Educational Foundation for Nuclear Science, 6042 S. Kimbark Acve., Chicago, Ill. 60637.

During 1988 the United States deployed almost 600 new strategic weapons. These include 200 warheads for final 20 silo-based MX missiles at Warren Air Force Base, Wyoming, and 400 B83 bombs for B-1B and B52 bombers. As the B-1B's problems are corrected, the aircraft's capacity to carry ordnance increases.

Due to retirements, however, warhead totals on U.S. strategic forces declined for the first time since 1981. Retirements included two ballistic missile submarines: The USS *Andrew Jackson* (SSBN 619) was removed from service on April 1 to comply with a congressional mandate in the fiscal 1988 defense authorization bill. The real purpose of the mandate was to bring SLBM numbers down closer to the SALT II limits. And the Defense Department decided not to overhaul the USS *John Adams* (SSBN 620), which was removed from service October 1. No new Trident submarines were deployed in 1988; the ninth Trident is scheduled for introduction into service at the end of 1989.

Also retired were about 20 Minuteman III missiles, which were removed from silos to make room for the MX missiles.

The bomber force underwent dramatic changes. On October 1, four B-52G squadrons were assigned conventional missions: these 69 aircraft were the ones not modified to carry ALCMs. Because of this change, several special nuclear weapons storage areas were deactivated—at Mather Air Force Base in California, Andersen in Guam, and Loring in Maine—and the storage area at Barksdale in Louisiana was reduced. B-52H bombers continued to be configured to carry cruise missiles. By year's end 72 of the 96 were finished, leaving the last 24 for completion in 1989. But there are no Advanced Cruise Missiles to deploy yet because the program is behind schedule, so the same 1,614 ALCMs may be spread across the larger number of modified B-52s.

U.S. strategic warheads have increased by 70 percent since the signing of the SALT I Treaty (1972) and by 22 percent during the Reagan administration. Soviet strategic warheads have increased by 324 percent since SALT I and by 46 percent during the Reagan administration.

Soviet Strategic Nuclear Forces, End of 1988

Type	Name	Launchers	Year deployed	Warheads × yield (megatons)	Total Warheads	Total megatons
ICBMs						
SS-11	Sego					
M2		160	1973	1 × 1.1	160	176
M3		210	1973	3 × 350 (MRV)	630	220.5
SS-13 M2	Savage	60	1973	1 × .750	60	45
SS-17 M3	Spanker	120	1979	4 × .750 (MIRV)	480	360
SS-18 M4	Satan	308	1979	10 × .550 (MIRV)	3,080	1,694
SS-19 M3	Stiletto	350	1979	6 × .550 (MIRV)	2,100	1,155
SS-24	Scalpel	20	1987	10 × .550 (MIRV)	200	110
SS-25	Sickle	150	1985	1 × .550	150	82.5
Total		**1,378**			**6,860**	**3,843.0**
SLBMs						
SS-N-6 M3	Serb	240	1973	2 × 1 (MRV)	480	480
SS-N-8 M1/M2	Sawfly	286	1973	1 × 1.5	286	429

Type	Name	Launchers	Year deployed	Warheads × yield (megatons)	Total Warheads	Total megatons
SS-N-17	Snipe	12	1980	1 × 1	12	12
SS-N-18 M1-3	Stingray	224	1978	7 × .500 (MIRV)	1,568	784
SS-N-20	Sturgeon	100	1983	10 × .200 (MIRV)	1,000	200
SS-N-23	Skiff	64	1986	4 × .100 (MIRV)	256	25.6
Total		**926**			**3,602**	**1,930.6**
Bombers/weapons						
Tu-95	Bear A	15	1956	2 bombs	30	90
Tu-95	Bear B/C	25	1962	4 bombs or 1 AS-3	100	125
Tu-95	Bear G	45	1984	4 bombs and 2 AS-4	270	184
Tu-142	Bear H	75	1984	8 AS-15 ALCMs or bombs	600	150
Tu-160	Blackjack	10	1988	6 AS-15 ALCMs and 4 bombs	100	50
Total		**170**			**1,100**	**599**
Grand total		**2,474**			**11,562**	**6,372.6**

ALCM—air-launched cruise missile; **AS**—air-to-surface missile; **ICBM**—intercontinental ballistic missile, range of 5,760-15,360 kilometers; **MIRV**—multiple independently targetable reentry vehicles; **MRV**—multiple reentry vehicles; **SLBM**—submarine-launched ballistic missile; **SRAM**—short-range attack missile; **SSBN**—nuclear-powered ballistic missile submarine.

Reprinted by permission of the BULLETIN OF THE ATOMIC SCIENTISTS, a magazine of science and world affairs, Copyright © 1989 by the Educational Foundation for Nuclear Science, 6042 S. Kimbark Ave., Chicago, Ill. 60637.

In 1988, the Soviet Union continued to deploy new weapons in all three "legs" of its triad. About 25 SS-25s were deployed and 10 more rail-mobile SS-24s were fielded. The fifth Typhoon and fourth Delta IV submarines became operational, while the next units of each model were launched. One more Yankee ballistic missile submarine was withdrawn; the MIRVing of the submarine force continued, with SS-N-20 and SS-N-23 SLBMs. Bear B/C bombers continued to be converted to the G model, and 20 new H models were deployed during the year with an additional 160 new AS-15 long-range ALCMs. In a major development, the first of what could be a sizable force of Blackjack bombers were deployed.

Soviet strategic warheads have increased by 324 percent since the SALT I Treaty was signed in 1972 and by 46 percent during the Reagan administration. The United States has acquired 70 percent more warheads since SALT I and 22 percent more under Ronald Reagan. The United States still has more warheads than the Soviets (13,000), but only about half the megatonnage.

The Medal of Honor

Often called the Congressional Medal of Honor, it is the Nation's highest military award for "uncommon valor" by men and women in the armed forces. It is given for actions that are above and beyond the call of duty in combat against an armed enemy. The medal was first awarded by the Army on March 25, 1863, and then by the Navy on April 3, 1863. President Reagan awarded the last Medal of Honor to retired Master Sargeant Roy Benavidez, a Vietnam veteran, on February 24, 1981.

Recipients of the medal receive $200 per month for life, a right to burial at Arlington National Cemetary, admission for them or their children to a service academy if they qualify and quotas permit, and free travel on government aircraft to almost anywhere in the world, on a space-available basis.

In 1989, medals were restored to William F. Cody (Buffalo Bill) and four other scouts who had them revoked in 1917 due to a new ruling.

Medal of Honor Recipients[1]

	Total	Army	Navy	Marines	Air Force	Coast Guard
Civil War	1,520	1,196	307	17	—	—
Indian Wars (1861–98)	428	428	—	—	—	—
Korean Expedition (1871)	15	—	9	6	—	—
Spanish-American War	109	30	64	15	—	—
Philippines/Samoa (1899–1913)	91	70	12	9	—	—
Boxer Rebellion (1900)	59	4	22	33	—	—
Dominican Republic (1904)	3	—	—	3	—	—
Nicaragua (1911)	2	—	—	2	—	—
Mexico (Veracruz) (1914)	55	—	46	9	—	—
Haiti (1915)	6	—	—	6	—	—
Misc. (1865–1920)	166	1	161	4	—	—
World War I	123	95	21	7	—	—
Haitian Action (1919–20)	2	—	—	2	—	—
Misc. (1920–1940)	18	2	15	1	—	—
World War II	433	294	57	81	—	1
Korean War	131	78	7	42	4	—
Vietnam War	238	155	14	57	12	—
Total	**3,399***	**2,353**	**735**	**294**	**16**	**1**

1. Total number of actual medals awarded is 3,417. This includes nine awarded to Unknown Soldiers, and some soldiers received more than one medal. *Source:* The Congressional Medal of Honor Society, New York, N.Y.

Arms Control Treaties and Agreements Since World War II

Name	Parties	Effective date	Description
Antarctic Treaty	13 nations, including U.S., U.S.S.R.	June 23, 1961 (signed Dec. 1, 1959)	Internationalized and demilitarized Antarctica
Hot Line Agreement	U.S., U.S.S.R.	June 20, 1963	Established direct radio and wire telegraph link between governments
Hot Line Modernization	U.S., U.S.S.R.	Sept. 30, 1971	Established satellite link
Partial Test Ban Treaty	Original parties: U.K., U.S., U.S.S.R.; most nations except France and China have signed	Oct. 10, 1963	Banned nuclear weapon testing in atmosphere, outer space, under water
Outer Space Treaty	89 signers, including U.S., U.S.S.R.	Oct. 10, 1967	Banned weapons of mass destruction from space, demilitarized celestial bodies
Tlatelolco Treaty and Protocols	Latin American nations except Argentina, Brazil; China, France, U.S., U.S.S.R.	April 22, 1968 (signed Feb. 14, 1967; protocols 1971, 1981)	Banned nuclear weapons from Latin America
Non-Proliferation Treaty	138 nations; notable exceptions: Argentina, Brazil, China, France, India, Israel, Pakistan, South Africa	March 5, 1970 (signed in 1968)	Aimed to prevent spread of nuclear weapons, promote peaceful uses of nuclear energy and nuclear disarmament
Seabed Arms Control Treaty	U.K., U.S., U.S.S.R., and others; not France and China	May 18, 1972 (signed Feb. 11, 1971)	Banned weapons of mass destruction from seabed outside 12-mile zone
Accident Measures Agreement	U.S., U.S.S.R.	Sept. 30, 1971	Prevention, notification of accidental launch
Biological Weapons Convention	U.K., U.S., U.S.S.R., and others; not France and China	March 26, 1975 (signed April 10, 1972)	Banned bacteriological and toxin weapons
SALT I—Anti-Ballistic Missile Treaty	U.S., U.S.S.R.	Oct. 3, 1972	Limited antiballistic missile systems to two sites, prohibited them for territorial defense
SALT I—Interim Agreement on Offensive Weapons	U.S., U.S.S.R.	Oct. 3, 1972	Set temporary limits on strategic offensive forces
SALT I—ABM Protocol	U.S., U.S.S.R.	May 24, 1976 (signed July 3, 1974)	Limited ABMs to one site
Threshold Test Ban Treaty	U.S., U.S.S.R.	Signed July 3, 1974; not ratified	Limited nuclear tests to 150 kilotons
Peaceful Nuclear Explosions Treaty	U.S., U.S.S.R.	Signed May 28, 1976; not ratified	Governed explosions other than weapons tests
SALT II	U.S., U.S.S.R.	Signed June 18, 1979; not ratified	Would have limited offensive nuclear weapons: 2,400, then 2,250 delivery vehicles, with further sublimits
Stockholm Accord on Confidence-Building Measures	U.S., U.S.S.R., and 33 European nations	Sept. 22, 1986	Provided for notification, observation of conventional military exercises, Atlantic to Urals
Nuclear Risk Reduction Centers Agreement	U.S., U.S.S.R.	Sept. 15, 1987	Established high-speed communication centers in both capitals
Intermediate-Range Nuclear Forces Treaty	U.S., U.S.S.R.	June 1, 1988	Banned ground-based nuclear missiles with ranges of 300-3,500 miles

Source: U.S. Arms Control and Disarmament Agency, *Arms Control and Disarmament Agreements*, 1982 ed., and recent reports.
Reprinted by permission of the BULLETIN OF THE ATOMIC SCIENTISTS, a magazine of science and world affairs. Copyright © 1989 by the Educational Foundation for Nuclear Science, 6042 S. Kimbark Ave., Chicago, Ill. 60637.

Nuclear Pursuits

	United States	Soviet Union	Britain	France	China
Number of warheads in stockpile	22,500	33,000	300	450	350
Number of known test explosions (end of 1988)	910	635	41	172	34
First fission test, type/yield	July 16, 1945 plutonium/23 kt.	Aug. 29, 1949 plutonium/20 kt.	Oct. 3, 1952 plutonium/25 kt.	Feb. 13, 1960 plutonium/60-70 kt.	Oct. 16, 1964 uranium 235/20 kt.
First test of boosted fission weapon	May 8, 1951	Aug. 12, 1953	May 15, 1957?	Sept. 24, 1966	May 9, 1966
First multistage thermonuclear (hydrogen bomb) test, yield	Oct. 31, 1952 10.4 mt.	Nov. 22, 1955 1.6 mt.	Nov. 8, 1957? ? mt.	Aug. 24, 1968 2.6 mt.	June 17, 1967 3 mt.
First airdrop explosion of nuclear weapon, aircraft used	Aug. 6, 1945 B-29	Nov. 6, 1955 Tu-4 Bull	Oct. 11, 1956 Valiant	July 19, 1966 Mirage IV-A	May 14, 1965 Hong 6
Number of known atmospheric tests	212	179	21	48	22
Largest atmospheric test	Feb. 28, 1954 15 mt.	Oct. 30, 1961 58 mt.	1957-58 ? mt.	Aug. 24, 1968 2.6 mt.	Nov. 17, 1976 4 mt.
First underground test	July 26, 1957	Feb. 2, 1962	March 1, 1962	Nov. 7, 1961	Sept. 22, 1969
Largest underground test	Nov. 6, 1971 5 mt.	Oct. 27, 1973 2.8-4 mt.	Dec. 5, 1985 less than 150 kt.	July 25, 1979 120 kt.	June 5, 1987 ?
Atomic bomb developers	J. Robert Oppenheimer, Gen. Leslie Groves	Igor V. Kurchatov	William Penney	Gen. Charles Ailleret, Pierre Guillaumat	Nie Rongzhen, Liu Jie, Li Jue
Hydrogen bomb developers	Stanislaw Ulam, Edward Teller	Andrei Sakharov, Igor Tamm	William Penney	Robert Dautray	Dong Jiaxian, Yu Min
Current test sites	Nevada	Kazakhstan, Novaya Zemlya	Nevada	Mururoa atoll, Fangataufa atoll	Lop Nur (Malan)
First operational ICBM	Oct. 31, 1959 Atlas D	1960 SS-6	n.a.	Aug. 2, 1971 S-2 IRBM	1979 Dong Feng-5
First nuclear-powered naval vessel enters service	Jan. 1955 *Nautilus* SSN	Aug. 1958 *November* SSN	1963 *Dreadnought* SSN	Jan. 1971 *Redoutable* SSBN	1974 *Han* SSN
First SSBN patrol with Polaris-type SLBM, vessel, missile	Nov. 15, 1960 *Washington* Polaris A1	1968 *Yankee* SS-N-6	June 1968 *Resolution* Polaris A3	Jan. 1972 *Redoutable* M1	1986 *Xia* CSS-N-3
First MIRVed missile deployed	Aug. 19, 1970 Minuteman III	1974 SS-18 or 19?	1993-94 Trident II	April 1985 M4 SLBM	n.a.
Final assembly plant	Pantex near Amarillo, Texas	Chelyabinsk in the Urals	Burghfield Royal Ordnance near Reading	Valduc in Côte-d'Or	Jiquuan in Gansu province
Chief design labs	Los Alamos in New Mexico, Lawrence Livermore in California	Sungul Radiological Institute in the Urals, Kyshtim? others?	Aldermaston near Reading	Limeil-Valenton in Val-de-Marne	Ninth Academy in Haiyan, Quinhai province
Current directors, developers	James Watkins, Energy Secretary; Siegfried Hecker, dir., Los Alamos; John Nuckolls, dir., Livermore	Lev D. Ryabev, minister of Medium Machine Building	Donald Spiers, controller of Establishments, Research and Nuclear; Tom McLean, dir., Aldermaston	Roger Baleras, dir., Direction des Applications Militaires	?

"Boosted": small quantities of tritium and deuterium incorporated in fission weapon to increase efficiency of yield; **kt.**: kilotons; **mt**: megatons; **ICBM**: intercontinental ballistic missile; **IRBM**: intermediate-range ballistic missile; **SSN**: nuclear-powered submarine; **SSBN**: nuclear-powered ballistic missile submarine; **SLBM**: submarine-launched ballistic missile

Reprinted by Permission of the BULLETIN OF THE ATOMIC SCIENTISTS, a magazine of science and world affairs. Copyright © 1989 by the Educational Foundation for Nuclear Science, 6042 S. Kimbark Ave., Chicago, Ill. 60637.

Travel Warning on Drugs Abroad

Source: gist, 1989, Bureau of Public Affairs, Department of State

Background: In 1988, 2,658 Americans were arrested abroad; more than 900 of them were held on charges of using, possessing, or trafficking in illegal narcotics. Thirty-seven percent of all American arrests on drug charges involved marijuana and frequently resulted in stiff fines or prison sentences. Although drug laws and enforcement policies vary in different countries, American travelers should be aware of the serious consequences resulting from the possession or sale of any type of narcotics. Penalties for drug violations are severe in foreign countries and may include lengthy prison sentences without parole. In addition, many countries do not permit bail in drug-trafficking cases.

Statistics on drug arrests: Americans were arrested on drug-related charges in 64 countries in 1988. As in 1987, the five nations that accounted for the majority of all drug arrests were Mexico, Jamaica, the Bahamas, the Federal Republic of Germany, and the Dominican Republic. Drug charges filed in Mexico alone accounted for nearly 23% of the worldwide total.

Travel advice: The global war on drugs is heating up. Many countries are increasing their efforts to stop the flow of illegal narcotics. Americans traveling abroad mistakenly believe that as U.S. citizens they are immune from prosecution under foreign laws or that buying or carrying small amounts of drugs cannot result in arrest. In reality, Americans have been jailed abroad for possessing as little as one-third of an ounce of marijuana. Travelers should be particularly wary of persons who ask them to carry a package or drive a car across a border; they might unknowingly become narcotics traffickers. The U.S. Customs Service will inspect baggage of travelers returning to the U.S.; this applies not only to hand baggage and packages but also to articles mailed back to the U.S.

Persons required to take a medication containing narcotic drugs should carry a doctor's certificate attesting to that fact and should keep medicines in their original and labeled containers. To avoid potential problems, travelers carrying such medicines should consult the embassies of the countries they will visit before leaving the U.S. In Saudi Arabia, for example, narcotics include alcohol, amphetamines, barbiturates, codeine, captagon, and many other drugs or substances that may not be considered narcotics in the US.

Facts about drug arrests abroad:
- Once travelers leave U.S. jurisdiction, they are not covered by U.S. laws and have no U.S. constitutional rights.
- Few foreign countries provide trial by jury.
- Pretrial detention may involve months of confinement in primitive prison conditions.
- Trials frequently involve lengthy delays or postponements and are conducted in the language of the foreign country.
- Sentences for possession or trafficking in drugs can range from 2 to 25 years and may include heavy fines.
- In some countries—for example Turkey, Egypt, Malaysia, and Thailand—conviction may lead to a life sentence or even the death penalty. In Saudi Arabia, drug smugglers and traffickers convicted of a second offense receive the death penalty.
- Several countries have stiffened their penalties for drug violations and imposed stricter enforcement of existing drug laws. In the Bahamas, individuals convicted of possessing even small amounts of marijuana or cocaine for personal use receive harsh sentences, including a minimum of 6 months in prison, a $2,000 fine, or both. And those convicted of possessing larger amounts can receive life imprisonment. There also are stiff penalties for possessing illegal drugs while in the Dominican Republic; legislation imposes 5-20 years' imprisonment on anyone caught bringing narcotics into or out of the country. Proposed laws in Mexico will increase the maximum sentence for drug trafficking from 15 to 25 years.

What U.S. consular officers abroad can do:
- Ensure insofar as possible that the detainee's rights under local law are fully observed and that humane treatment is accorded under internationally accepted standards;
- Visit the U.S. citizen as soon as possible after the foreign government has notified the US embassy or consulate of the arrest;
- Provide the detainee with a list of local attorneys from which to select defense counsel; and
- Contact family and/or friends for financial or medical aid and food, if requested to do so by the detainee.

What U.S. consular officers abroad cannot do:
- Demand a U.S. citizen's release;
- Represent the detainee at trial, give legal counsel, or pay legal fees or other related expenses with U.S. Government funds; or
- Intervene in a foreign country's court system or judicial process to obtain special treatment.

Help available in the U.S.: The Citizens Emergency Center in the Department of State's Bureau of Consular Affairs:
- Provides emergency services relating to the welfare of Americans arrested or detained abroad;
- Transmits messages to incarcerated Americans or their next of kin in the US; and
- Helps arrange the transfer of private funds to US posts abroad for delivery to Americans for legal fees, medical treatment, or dietary supplements.

Assistance from the Citizens Emergency Center is available Monday through Friday from 8:15 a.m. to 10 p.m. and on Saturday from 9 a.m. to 3 p.m. (Eastern time) at (202) 647-5225. After hours and on Sundays and holidays, a duty officer is available for emergencies at (202) 634-3600.

U.S. Passport and Customs Information

Source: Department of State, Bureau of Consular Affairs and Department of the Treasury, Customs Service.

Passports

With a few exceptions, a passport is required for all U.S. citizens to depart and enter the United States and to enter most foreign countries. A valid U.S. passport is the best documentation of U.S. citizenship available. Persons who travel to a country where a U.S. passport is not required should be in possession of documentary evidence of their U.S. citizenship and identity to facilitate reentry into the United States. Travelers should check passport and visa requirements with consular officials of the countries to be visited well in advance of their departure date.

Application for a passport may be made at a passport agency; to a clerk of any Federal court or State court of record; or a judge or clerk of any probate court accepting applications; or at a post office selected to accept passport applications. Passport agencies are located in Boston, Chicago, Honolulu, Houston, Los Angeles, Miami, New Orleans, New York, Philadelphia, San Francisco, Seattle, Stamford, Conn., and Washington, D.C.

All persons are required to obtain individual passports in their own names. Neither spouses nor children may be included in each others' passports. Applicants between the ages of 13 and 18 must appear in person before the clerk or agent executing the application. For children under the age of 13, a parent or legal guardian may execute an application for them.

First time passport applicants must apply in person. Applicants must present evidence of citizenship (e.g., a certified copy of birth certificate), personal identification (e.g., a valid driver's license), two identical black and white or color photographs taken within six months (2 × 2 inches, with the image size measured from the bottom of the chin to the top of the head [including hair] not less than 1 inch nor more than 1 3/8 inches on a plain white or off-white background, vending machine photographs not acceptable), plus a completed passport application (DSP-11). If you were born abroad, you may also use as proof of citizenship: a Certificate of Naturalization, a Report of Birth abroad of a Citizen of the United States of America or a Certification of Birth. A fee of $35 plus a $7 execution fee is charged for adults 18 years and older for a passport valid for ten years from the date of issue. The fee for minor children under 18 years of age is $20 for a five-year passport plus $7 for the execution of the application.

You may apply for a passport by mail if you have been the bearer of a passport issued within 12 years prior to the date of a new application, are able to submit your most recent U.S. passport with your new application, and your previous passport was not issued before your 16th birthday. If you are eligible to apply by mail, include your previous passport, a completed, signed, and dated DSP-82 "Application for Passport by Mail," new photographs, and the passport fee of $35. The $7 execution fee is not required when applying by mail. Mail the application and attachments to one of the 13 passport agencies.

Passports may be presented for amendment to show a married name or legal change of name or to correct descriptive data. Any alterations to the passport by the bearer *other than* in the spaces provided for change of address and next of kin data are forbidden.

Loss, theft or destruction of a passport should be reported to Passport Services, 1425 K Street, N.W., Washington, D.C. 20524 immediately, or to the nearest passport agency. If you are overseas, report to the nearest U.S. Embassy or consulate and to local police authorities. Your passport is a valuable citizenship and identity document. It should be carefully safeguarded. Its loss could cause you unnecessary travel complications as well as significant expense. It is advisable to photocopy the data page of your passport and keep it in a place separate from your passport to facilitate the issuance of a replacement passport should one be necessary.

Customs

United States residents must declare all articles acquired abroad and in their possession at the time of their return. In addition, articles acquired in the U.S. Virgin Islands, American Samoa, or Guam and not accompanying you must be declared at the time of your return. The wearing or use of an article acquired abroad does *not* exempt it from duty. Customs declaration forms are distributed on vessels and planes, and should be prepared in advance of arrival for presentation to the customs inspectors.

If you have not exceeded the duty-free exemption allowed, you may make an oral declaration to the customs inspector. A written declaration is necessary when (1) total fair retail value of articles exceeds $1,400 ($400 tax-free exemption plus $1,000 dutiable at a flat 10% rate) (keep your sales slips); (2) over 1 liter of liquor, 200 cigarettes, or 100 cigars are included; (3) items are not intended for your personal or household use, or articles brought home for another person; and (4) when a customs duty or internal revenue tax is collectible on any article in your possession.

An exception to the above are regulations applicable to articles purchased in the U.S. Virgin Islands, American Samoa, or Guam where you may receive a customs exemption of $800. Not more than $400 of this exemption may be applied to merchandise obtained elsewhere than in these islands. Five liters of alcoholic beverages and 1000 cigarettes may be included provided not more than one liter and 200 cigarettes were acquired elsewhere than in these islands. Articles acquired in and sent from these islands to the United States may be claimed under your duty-free personal exemption if properly declared at the time of your return.

Articles accompanying you, in excess of your personal exemption, up to $1000 will be assessed at a flat rate of duty of 10% based on fair retail value in country of acquisition. (If articles were acquired in the insular possessions, the flat rate of duty is 5% and these goods may accompany you or be shipped home.) These articles must be for your personal use or for use as gifts and not for sale. This provision may be used every 30 days, excluding the day of your last arrival. Any items which have a "free" duty rate will be excluded before duty is calculated.

Other exemptions include in part: automobiles, boats, planes, or other vehicles taken abroad for noncommercial use. Foreign-made personal articles (e.g., watches, cameras, etc.) taken abroad should be registered with Customs before departure. Customs will register *only* serially numbered foreign-made items. Gifts of not more than $50 can be shipped back to the United States tax and duty free ($100 if mailed from the Virgin Islands, American Samoa, or Guam). Household effects and tools of trade which you take out of the United States are duty free at time of return.

Prohibited and restricted articles include in part: absinthe, narcotics and dangerous drugs, obscene articles and publications, seditious and treasonable materials, hazardous articles (e.g., fireworks, dangerous toys, toxic and poisonous substances, and switchblade knives), biological materials of public health or veterinary importance, fruit, vegetables and plants, meats, poultry and products thereof, birds, monkeys, and turtles.

If you understate the value of an article you declare, or if you otherwise misrepresent an article in your declaration, you may have to pay a penalty in addition to payment of duty. Under certain circumstances, the article could be seized and forfeited if the penalty is not paid.

If you fail to declare an article acquired abroad, not only is the article subject to seizure and forfeiture, but you will be liable for a personal penalty in an amount equal to the value of the article in the United States. In addition, you may also be liable to criminal prosecution.

If you carry more than $10,000 into or out of the United States in currency (either United States or foreign money), negotiable instruments in bearer form, or travelers checks, a report must be filed with United States Customs at the time you arrive or depart with such amounts.

As U.S. restrictions on travel to Cuba, North Korea, Vietnam, and Cambodia have been eased, the Office of Foreign Assets Control (FAC) issued a general license, effective March 21, 1977, which allows visitors to those countries to purchase a maximum of $100 worth of goods. This amount is based on retail value in the country where acquired. These articles must be for personal use—not for resale—and must accompany the traveler on his entry into the U.S. This allowance may be used only once every 6 months.

Foreign Embassies in the United States

Source: U.S. Department of State

Embassy of the Democratic Republic of Afghanistan, 2341 Wyoming Ave., N.W., Washington, D.C. 20008. Phone: (202) 234-3770.

Embassy of the Democratic & Popular Republic of Algeria, 2118 Kalorama Rd., N.W., Washington, D.C. 20008. Phone: (202) 328-5300.

Embassy of Antigua & Barbuda, 3400 International Dr., N.W., Suite 2H, Washington, D.C. 20008. Phone: (202) 362-5211.

Embassy of the Argentine Republic, 1600 New Hampshire Ave., N.W., Washington, D.C. 20009. Phone: (202) 939-6400.

Embassy of Australia, 1601 Massachusetts Ave., N.W., Washington, D.C. 20036. Phone: (202) 797-3000.

Embassy of Austria, 2343 Massachusetts Ave., N.W., Washington, D.C. 20008. Phone: (202) 483-4474.

Embassy of the Commonwealth of the Bahamas, 600 New Hampshire Ave., N.W., Suite 865, Washington, D.C. 20037. Phone: (202) 944-3390.

Embassy of the State of Bahrain, 3502 International Dr., N.W., Washington, D.C. 20008. Phone: (202) 342-0741.

Embassy of the People's Republic of Bangladesh, 2201 Wisconsin Ave., N.W., Washington, D.C. 20007. Phone: (202) 342-8372.

Embassy of Barbados, 2144 Wyoming Ave., N.W., Washington, D.C. 20008. Phone: (202) 939-9218.

Embassy of Belgium, 3330 Garfield St., N.W., Washington, D.C. 20008. Phone: (202) 333-6900.

Embassy of Belize, 3400 International Dr., N.W., Suite 2J, Washington, D.C. 20008. Phone: (202) 363-4505.

Embassy of the People's Republic of Benin, 2737 Cathedral Ave., N.W., Washington, D.C. 20008. Phone: (202) 232-6656.

Embassy of Bolivia, 3014 Massachusetts Ave., N.W., Washington, D.C. 20008. Phone: (202) 483-4410.

Embassy of the Republic of Botswana, 4301 Connecticut Ave., N.W., Suite 404, Washington, D.C. 20008. Phone: (202) 244-4990.

Brazilian Embassy, 3006 Massachusetts Ave., N.W., Washington, D.C. 20008. Phone: (202) 745-2700.

Embassy of the State of Brunei Darussalam, 2600 Virginia Ave., N.W., Suite 300, Washington, D.C. 20037. Phone: (202) 342-0159.

Embassy of the People's Republic of Bulgaria, 1621 22nd St., N.W., Washington, D.C. 20008. Phone: (202) 387-7969.

Embassy of Burkina Faso, 2340 Massachusetts Ave., N.W., Washington, D.C. 20008. Phone: (202) 332-5577.

Embassy of the Republic of Burundi, 2233 Wisconsin Ave., N.W., Suite 212, Washington, D.C. 20007. Phone: (202) 342-2574.

Embassy of the Republic of Cameroon, 2349 Massachusetts Ave., N.W., Washington, D.C. 20008. Phone: (202) 265-8790.

Embassy of Canada, 1746 Massachusetts Ave., N.W., Washington, D.C. 20036. Phone: (202) 785-1400.

Embassy of the Republic of Cape Verde, 3415 Massachusetts Ave., N.W., Washington, D.C. 20007. Phone: (202) 965-6820.

Embassy of Central African Republic, 1618 22nd St. N.W., Washington, D.C. 20008. Phone: (202) 483-7800.

Embassy of the Republic of Chad, 2002 R St., N.W., Washington, D.C. 20009. Phone: (202) 462-4009.

Embassy of Chile, 1732 Massachusetts Ave., N.W., Washington, D.C. 20036. Phone: (202) 785-1746.

Embassy of the People's Republic of China, 2300 Connecticut Ave., N.W., Washington, D.C. 20008. Phone: (202) 328-2500.

Embassy of Colombia, 2118 Leroy Pl., N.W., Washington, D.C. 20008. Phone: (202) 387-8338.

Embassy of the Federal and Islamic Republic of Comoros, c/o Permanent Mission of the Federal and Islamic Republic of Comoros to the United Nations, 336 E. 45th St., New York, N.Y. 10017. Phone: (212) 972-8010.

Embassy of the People's Republic of the Congo, 4891 Colorado Ave., N.W., Washington, D.C. 20011. Phone: (202) 726-5500.

Embassy of Costa Rica, 1825 Connecticut Ave.,

N.W., Suite 211, Washington, D.C. 20009. Phone: (202) 234-2945.

Embassy of the Republic of Cote d'Ivoire, 2424 Massachusetts Ave., N.W., Washington, D.C. 20008. Phone: (202) 797-0300.

Embassy of the Republic of Cyprus, 2211 R St. N.W., Washington, D.C. 20008. Phone: (202) 462-5772.

Embassy of the Czechoslovak Socialist Republic, 3900 Linnean Ave., N.W., Washington, D.C. 20008. Phone: (202) 363-6315.

Cuban Interests Section, 2630 and 2639 16th St., N.W., Washington, D.C. 20009. Phone: (202) 797-8518.

Royal Danish Embassy, 3200 Whitehaven St., N.W., Washington, D.C. 20008. Phone: (202) 234-4300.

Embassy of the Republic of Djibouti, 1430 K St. N.W., Suite 600, Washington, D.C. 20006. Phone: (202) 347-0254.

Embassy of the Commonwealth of Dominica, 205 Yoakum Pkwy. #823, Alexandria, Va. 22304. Phone: (703) 751-6939.

Embassy of the Dominican Republic, 1715 22nd St., N.W., Washington, D.C. 20008. Phone: (202) 332-6280.

Embassy of Ecuador, 2535 15th St., N.W., Washington, D.C. 20009. Phone: (202) 234-7200.

Embassy of the Arab Republic of Egypt, 2310 Decatur Pl., N.W., Washington, D.C. 20008. Phone: (202) 232-5400.

Embassy of El Salvador, 2308 California St., N.W., Washington, D.C. 20008. Phone: (202) 265-3480.

Embassy of Equatorial Guinea, 801 Second Ave., Suite 1403, New York, N.Y. 10017. Phone: (212) 599-1523.

Legation of Estonia, 9 Rockefeller Plaza, New York, N.Y. 10020. Phone: (212) 247-1450.

Embassy of Ethiopia, 2134 Kalorama Rd., N.W., Washington, D.C. 20008. Phone: (202) 234-2281.

Embassy of Fiji, 2233 Wisconsin Ave., N.W., Suite 240, Washington, D.C. 20007. Phone: (202) 337-8320.

Embassy of Finland, 3216 New Mexico Ave., N.W., Washington, D.C. 20016. Phone: (202) 363-2430.

Embassy of France, 4101 Reservoir Rd., N.W., Washington, D.C. 20007. Phone: (202) 944-6000.

Embassy of the Gabonese Republic, 2034 20th St., N.W., Washington, D.C. 20009. Phone: (202) 797-1000.

Embassy of The Gambia, 1030 15th St., N.W., Suite 720, Washington, D.C. 20005. Phone: (202) 842-1356.

Embassy of the German Democratic Republic, 1717 Massachusetts Ave., N.W., Washington, D.C., 20036. Phone: (202) 232-3134.

Embassy of the Federal Republic of Germany, 4645 Reservoir Rd., N.W., Washington, D.C. 20007. Phone: (202) 298-4000.

Embassy of Ghana, 3512 International Dr., N.W., Washington, D.C. 20008 (202) 686-4520.

Embassy of Greece, 2221 Massachusetts Ave., N.W., Washington, D.C. 20008. Phone (202) 667-3168.

Embassy of Grenada, 1701 New Hampshire Ave., N.W., Washington, D.C. 20009. Phone: (202) 265-2561.

Embassy of Guatemala, 2220 R St., N.W., Washington, D.C. 20008. Phone: (202) 745-4952.

Embassy of the Republic of Guinea, 2112 Leroy Pl., N.W., Washington, D.C. 20008. Phone: (202) 483-9420.

Embassy of the Republic of Guinea-Bissau, c/o of the Permanent Mission of the Republic of Guinea-Bissau to the United Nations, 211 E. 43rd St., Suite 604, New York, N.Y. 10017. Phone: (212) 661-3977.

Embassy of Guyana, 2490 Tracy Pl., N.W. Washington, D.C. 20008. Phone: (202) 265-6900.

Embassy of Haiti, 2311 Massachusetts Ave., N.W., Washington, D.C. 20008. Phone: (202) 332-4090.

Apostolic Nunciature of the Holy See, 3339 Massachusetts Ave., N.W., Washington, D.C. 20008. Phone: (202) 333-7121.

Embassy of Honduras, 4301 Connecticut Ave., N.W., Suite 100, Washington, D.C. 20008. Phone: (202) 966-7700.

Embassy of the Hungarian People's Republic, 3910 Shoemaker St., N.W., Washington, D.C. 20008. Phone: (202) 362-6730.

Embassy of Iceland, 2022 Connecticut Ave., N.W., Washington, D.C. 20008. Phone: (202) 265-6653.

Embassy of India, 2107 Massachusetts Ave., N.W., Washington, D.C. 20008. Phone: (202) 939-7000.

Embassy of the Republic of Indonesia, 2020 Massachusetts Ave., N.W., Washington, D.C. 20036. Phone: (202) 775-5200.

Embassy of the Republic of Iraq, 1801 P St., N.W., Washington, D.C. 20036. Phone: (202) 483-7500.

Embassy of Ireland, 2234 Massachusetts Ave., N.W., Washington, D.C. 20008. Phone: (202) 462-3939.

Embassy of Israel, 3514 International Dr., N.W., Washington, D.C. 20008. Phone: (202) 364-5500.

Embassy of Italy, 1601 Fuller St., N.W., Washington, D.C. 20009. Phone: (202) 328-5500.

Embassy of Jamaica, 1850 K St., N.W., Suite 355, Washington, D.C. 20006. Phone: (202) 452-0660.

Embassy of Japan, 2520 Massachusetts Ave., N.W., Washington, D.C. 20008. Phone: (202) 939-6700.

Embassy of the Hashemite Kingdom of Jordan, 3504 International Dr., N.W., Washington, D.C. 20008. Phone: (202) 966-2664.

Embassy of Kenya, 2249 R St., N.W., Washington, D.C. 20008. Phone: (202) 387-6101.

Embassy of Korea, 2370 Massachusetts Ave., N.W., Washington, D.C. 20008. Phone: (202) 939-5600.

Embassy of the State of Kuwait, 2940 Tilden St., N.W., Washington, D.C. 20008. Phone: (202) 966-0702.

Embassy of the Lao People's Democratic Republic, 2222 S St., N.W., Washington, D.C. 20008. Phone: (202) 332-6416.

Legation of Latvia, 4325 17th St., N.W., Washington, D.C. 20011. Phone: (202) 726-8213/8214.

Embassy of Lebanon, 2560 28th St., N.W., Washington, D.C. 20008. Phone: (202) 939-6300.

Embassy of the Kingdom of Lesotho, 2511 Massachusetts Ave., N.W., Washington, D.C. 20008. Phone: (202) 797-5534.

Embassy of Liberia, 5201 16th St., N.W., Washington, D.C. 20011. Phone: (202) 723-0437.

Legation of Lithuania, 2622 16th St., N.W., Washington, D.C. Phone: (202) 234-5860/2639.

Embassy of Luxembourg, 2200 Massachusetts

Ave., N.W., Washington, D.C. 20008. Phone: (202) 265-4171.

Embassy of the Democratic Republic of Madagascar, 2374 Massachusetts Ave., N.W., Washington, D.C. 20008. Phone: (202) 265-5525.

Malawi Embassy, 2408 Massachusetts Ave., N.W., Washington, D.C. 20008. Phone: (202) 797-1007.

Embassy of Malaysia, 2401 Massachusetts Ave., N.W., Washington, D.C. 20008. Phone: (202) 328-2700.

Embassy of the Republic of Mali, 2130 R St., N.W., Washington, D.C. 20008. Phone: (202) 332-2249.

Embassy of Malta, 2017 Connecticut Ave., N.W., Washington, D.C. 20008. Phone: (202) 462-3611.

Embassy of the Islamic Republic of Mauritania, 2129 Leroy Pl., N.W., Washington, D.C. 20008. Phone: (202) 232-5700.

Embassy of Mauritius, 4301 Connecticut Ave., N.W., Suite 134, Washington, D.C. 20008. Phone: (202) 244-1491.

Embassy of Mexico, 2829 16th St., N.W., Washington, D.C. 20009. Phone: (202) 234-6000.

Embassy of Morocco, 1601 21st St., N.W., Washington, D.C. 20009. Phone: (202) 462-7979.

Embassy of the People's Republic of Mozambique, 1990 M St., N.W., Suite 570, Washington, D.C. 20036. Phone: (202) 293-7146.

Embassy of the Socialist Republic of the Union of Myanmar, 2300 S St., N.W., Washington, D.C. 20008. Phone: (202) 332-9044.

Royal Nepalese Embassy, 2131 Leroy Pl., N.W., Washington, D.C. 20008. Phone: (202) 667-4550.

Embassy of the Netherlands, 4200 Linnean Ave., N.W., Washington, D.C. 20008. Phone: (202) 244-5300.

Embassy of New Zealand, 37 Observatory Circle, N.W., Washington, D.C. 20008. Phone: (202) 328-4800.

Embassy of Nicaragua, 1627 New Hampshire Ave., N.W., Washington, D.C. 20009. Phone: (202) 387-4371.

Embassy of the Republic of Niger, 2204 R St., N.W., Washington, D.C. 20008. Phone: (202) 483-4224.

Embassy of the Federal Republic of Nigeria, 2201 M St., N.W., Washington, D.C. 20037. Phone: (202) 822-1500.

Royal Norwegian Embassy, 2720 34th St., N.W., Washington, D.C. 20008. Phone: (202) 333-6000.

Embassy of the Sultanate of Oman, 2342 Massachusetts Ave., N.W., Washington, D.C. 20008. Phone: (202) 387-1980.

Embassy of Pakistan, 2315 Massachusetts Ave., N.W., Washington, D.C. 20008. Phone: (202) 939-6200.

Embassy of Panama, 2862 McGill Terrace, N.W., Washington, D.C. 20008. Phone: (202) 483-1407.

Embassy of Papua New Guinea, 1330 Connecticut Ave., N.W., Suite 350, Washington, D.C. 20036. Phone: (202) 659-0856.

Embassy of Paraguay, 2400 Massachusetts Ave., N.W., Washington, D.C. 20008. Phone: (202) 483-6960.

Embassy of Peru, 1700 Massachusetts Ave., N.W., Washington, D.C. 20036. Phone: (202) 833-9860.

Embassy of the Philippines, 1617 Massachusetts Ave., N.W., Washington, D.C. 20036. Phone: (202) 483-1414.

Embassy of the Polish People's Republic, 2640 16th St., N.W., Washington, D.C. 20009. Phone: (202) 234-3800.

Embassy of Portugal, 2125 Kalorama Rd., N.W., Washington, D.C. 20008. Phone: (202) 328-8610.

Embassy of the State of Qatar, 600 New Hampshire Ave., N.W., Suite 1180, Washington, D.C. 20037. Phone: (202) 338-0111.

Embassy of the Socialist Republic of Romania, 1607 23rd St., N.W., Washington, D.C. 20008. Phone: (202) 232-4747.

Embassy of the Republic of Rwanda, 1714 New Hampshire Ave., N.W., Washington, D.C. 20009. Phone: (202) 232-2882.

Embassy of Saint Kitts and Nevis, 2501 M St., N.W., Suite 540, Washington, D.C. 20037. Phone: (202) 833-3550.

Embassy of Saint Lucia, 2100 M St., N.W., Suite 309, Washington, D.C. 20037. Phone: (202) 463-7378.

Embassy of São Tomé and Príncipe, 801 Second Ave., Suite 1504, New York, N.Y. 10017 Phone: (212) 697-4211.

Embassy of Saudi Arabia, 601 New Hampshire Ave., N.W., Washington, D.C. 20037. Phone: (202) 342-3800.

Embassy of the Republic of Senegal, 2112 Wyoming Ave., N.W., Washington, D.C. 20008. Phone: (202) 234-0540.

Embassy of the Republic of Seychelles, c/o Permanent Mission of the Republic of Seychelles to the United Nations, 820 Second Ave., Suite 927, New York, N.Y. 10017. Phone: (212) 687-9766.

Embassy of Sierra Leone, 1701 19th St., N.W., Washington, D.C. 20009. Phone: (202) 939-9261.

Embassy of the Republic of Singapore, 1824 R St., N.W., Washington, D.C. 20009. Phone: (202) 667-7555.

Embassy of the Somali Democratic Republic, 600 New Hampshire Ave., N.W., Suite 710, Washington, D.C. 20037. Phone: (202) 342-1575.

Embassy of South Africa, 3051 Massachusetts Ave., N.W., Washington, D.C. 20008. Phone: (202) 232-4400.

Embassy of Spain, 2700 15th St., N.W., Washington, D.C. 20009. Phone: (202) 265-0190.

Embassy of the Democratic Socialist Republic of Sri Lanka, 2148 Wyoming Ave., N.W., Washington, D.C. 20008. Phone: (202) 483-4025.

Embassy of the Republic of the Sudan, 2210 Massachusetts Ave., N.W., Washington, D.C. 20008. Phone: (202) 338-8565.

Embassy of the Republic of Suriname, 4301 Connecticut Ave., N.W., Suite 108, Washington, D.C. 20008. Phone: (202) 244-7488.

Embassy of the Kingdom of Swaziland, 4301 Connecticut Ave., N.W., Washington, D.C. 20008. Phone: (202) 362-6683.

Embassy of Sweden, 600 New Hampshire Ave., N.W., Suite 1200, Washington, D.C. 20037. Phone: (202) 944-5600.

Embassy of Switzerland, 2900 Cathedral Ave., N.W., Washington, D.C. 20008. Phone: (202) 745-7900.

Embassy of the Syrian Arab Republic, 2215 Wyoming Ave., N.W., Washington, D.C. 20008. Phone: (202) 232-6313.

Embassy of the United Republic of Tanzania, 2139 R St., N.W., Washington, D.C. 20008. Phone: (202) 939-6125.

Embassy of Thailand, 2300 Kalorama Rd., N.W.,

N.W., Washington, D.C. 20008. Phone: (202) 483-7200.

Embassy of the Republic of Togo, 2208 Massachusetts Ave., N.W., Washington, D.C. 20008. Phone: (202) 234-4212.

Embassy of Trinidad and Tobago, 1708 Massachusetts Ave., N.W., Washington, D.C. 20036. Phone: (202) 467-6490.

Embassy of Tunisia, 1515 Massachusetts Ave., N.W., Washington, D.C. 20005. Phone: (202) 862-1850.

Embassy of the Republic of Turkey, 1606 23rd St., N.W., Washington, D.C. 20008. Phone: (202) 387-3200.

Embassy of the Republic of Uganda, 5909 16th St., N.W., Washington, D.C. 20011. Phone: (202) 726-7100.

Embassy of the Union of Soviet Socialist Republics, 1125 16th St., N.W., Washington, D.C. 20036. Phone: (202) 628-7551.

Embassy of the United Arab Emirates, 600 New Hampshire Ave., N.W., Suite 740, Washington, D.C. 20037. Phone: (202) 338-6500.

United Kingdom of Great Britain & Northern Ireland British Embassy, 3100 Massachusetts Ave., N.W., Washington, D.C. 20008. Phone: (202)

462-1340.

Embassy of Uruguay, 1918 F St., N.W., Washington D.C. 20006. Phone: (202) 331-1313.

Embassy of Venezuela, 2445 Massachusetts Ave., N.W., Washington, D.C. 20008. Phone: (202) 797-3800.

Embassy of Western Samoa, c/o Permanent Mission of Samoa to the United Nations, 820 Second Ave., New York, N.Y., 10017. Phone: (212) 599-6196.

Embassy of the Yemen Arab Republic, 600 New Hampshire Ave., N.W., Suite 840, Washington, D.C. 20037. Phone: (202) 965-4760.

Embassy of the Socialist Federal Republic of Yugoslavia, 2410 California St., N.W., Washington, D.C. 20008. Phone: (202) 462-6566.

Embassy of the Republic of Zaire, 1800 New Hampshire Ave., N.W., Washington, D.C. 20009. Phone: (202) 234-7690.

Embassy of the Republic of Zambia, 2419 Massachusetts Ave., N.W., Washington, D.C. 20008. Phone: (202) 265-9717.

Embassy of Zimbabwe, 2852 McGill Terrace, N.W., Washington, D.C. 20008. Phone: (202) 332-7100.

Diplomatic Personnel To and From the U.S.

Country	U.S. Representative to[1]	Rank	Representative from[2]	Rank
Afghanistan	Jon Glassman	Cd'A.	Mr. Miagol	Min.
Algeria	Christopher W. S. Ross	Amb.	Abderrahmane Bensid	Amb.
Antigua and Barbuda	(Vacancy)		Edmund Hawkins Lake	Amb.
Argentina	Terance A. Todman	Amb.	Enrique J.A. Candioti	Amb.
Australia	Laurence W. Lane, Jr.	Amb.	Michael John Cook	Amb.
Austria	Henry A. Grunwald	Amb.	Friedrich Hoess	Amb.
Bahamas	Carol Boyd Hallett	Amb.	Margaret E. McDonald	Amb.
Bahrain	Dr. Sam H. Zakhem	Amb.	Ghazi Mohamed Algosaibi	Amb.
Bangladesh	Willard A. DePree	Amb.	A.H.S. Ataul Karim	Amb.
Barbados	(Vacancy)		Sir William Douglas	Amb.
Belgium	Maynard W. Gitman	Amb.	Herman Dehennin	Amb.
Belize	Robert G. Rich, Jr.	Amb.	Edward A. Laing	Amb.
Benin	Walter E. Stadtler	Amb.	Theophile Nata	Amb.
Bolivia	Robert S. Gelbard	Amb.	Carlos E. Delius	Amb
Botswana	John F. Kordek	Amb.	Botsweletse Kingsley Sebele	Amb.
Brazil	Harry W. Shlaudeman	Amb.	Marcilio Marques Moreira	Amb.
Brunei	Thomas C. Ferguson	Amb.	Dato Paduka Haji Mohd Suni	Amb.
Bulgaria	Sol Polansky	Amb.	Velichko F. Velichkov	Amb.
Burkina Faso	David H. Shinn	Amb.	Paul-Désiré Kabore	Amb.
Burundi	James Daniel Phillips	Amb.	Edouard Kadigiri	Amb.
Cameroon	Mark L. Edelman	Amb.	Paul Pondi	Amb.
Canada	(Vacancy)		Derek H. Burney	Amb.
Cape Verde	Vernon D. Penner, Jr.	Amb.	Jose Luis Fernandes Lopes	Amb.
Central African Republic	David C. Fields	Amb.	Christian Lingama-Toleque	Amb.
Chad	Robert L. Pugh	Amb.	Mahamat Ali Adoum	Amb.
Chile	Charles A. Gillespie Jr.	Amb.	Octavio Errazuriz	Amb.
China	James R. Lilley	Amb.	Han Xu	Amb.
Colombia	Thomas E. McNamara	Amb.	Victor Mosquera	Amb.
Comoros	Patricia Gates Lynch	Amb.	Amini Ali Moumin	Amb.
Congo, People's Republic of	Leonard G. Shurtleff	Amb.	Benjamin Bounkoulou	Amb.
Costa Rica	Deane R. Hinton	Amb.	Danilo Jimenez	Amb.
Cyprus	Bill K. Perrin	Amb.	Andrew J. Jacovides	Amb.
Czechoslovakia	Julian M. Niemczyk	Amb.	Miroslav Houstecky	Amb.
Denmark	Keith L. Brown	Amb.	Ulrik Federspiel	Min.
Djibouti	Robert S. Barrett IV		Roble Olhaye	Amb.
Dominica	(Vacancy)	Amb.	McDonald P. Benjamin	Amb.
Dominican Republic	Paul D. Taylor	Amb.	Eduardo Leon	Amb.
Ecuador	Richard N. Holwill	Amb.	Jaime Moncayo	Amb.
Egypt	Frank G. Wisner	Amb.	El Sayed Abdel Raouf El Reedy	Amb.
El Salvador	William G. Walker	Amb.	Ernesto Rivas-Gallont	Amb.
Equatorial Guinea	Chester E. Norris, Jr.	Amb.	Damaso Obiang Ndong	Amb.

Country	U.S. Representatives to[1]	Rank	Representative from[2]	Rank
Ethiopia	Robert G. Houdek	Cd'A.	Girma Amare	Consul.
Fiji	Leonard Rochwarger	Amb.	Abdul H. Yusuf	Consul.
Finland	Rockwell A. Schnabel	Amb.	Jukka Valtasaari	Amb.
France	Walter J. P. Curley	Amb.	Emmanuel de Margerie	Amb.
Gabon	Warren Clark, Jr.	Amb.	Jean Robert Odzaga	Amb.
Gambia	Herbert E. Horowitz	Amb.	Ousman A, Sallah	Amb.
Germany (East)	Richard C. Barkley	Amb.	Dr. Gerhard Herder	Amb.
Germany (West)	Vernon A. Walters	Amb.	Juergen Ruhfus	Amb.
Ghana	Stephen R. Lyne	Amb.	Eric K. Otoo	Amb.
Greece	Robert V. Keeley	Amb.	George D. Papoulias	Amb.
Grenada	James F. Cooper	Cd'A.	Albert O. Xavier	Amb.
Guatemala	James H. Michel	Amb.	Rodolfo Rohrmoser V.	Amb.
Guinea	Samuel E. Lupo	Amb.	Dr. Kekoura Camara	Amb.
Guinea-Bissau	John Dale Blacken	Amb.	Alfredo Lopes Cabral	Amb.
Guyana	Theresa A. Tull	Amb.	Dr. Cedric Hilburn Grant	Amb.
Haiti	Brunson McKinley	Amb.	Pierre Francois Benoit	Amb.
Holy See	Frank Shakespeare	Amb.	Most Rev. Pio Laghi	Pro-Nuncio
Honduras	Everett Ellis Briggs	Amb.	Jorge Ramon Hernandez-Alcerro	Amb.
Hungary	Mark Palmer	Amb.	Dr. Vencel Hazi	Amb.
Iceland	L. Nicholas Ruwe	Amb.	Ingvi S. Ingvarsson	Amb.
India	John R. Hubbard	Cd'A.	P.K. Kaul	Amb.
Indonesia	John C. Monjo	Amb.	Abdul Rachman Ramly	Amb.
Iraq	April C. Glaspie	Amb.	Abdul-Amir Ali Al-Anbari	Amb.
Ireland	Margaret M. O. Heckler	Amb.	Padraic N. MacKernan	Amb.
Israel	William A. Brown	Amb.	Moshe Arad	Amb.
Italy	Maxwell M. Rabb	Amb.	Rinaldo Petrignani	Amb.
Ivory Coast	Dennis Kux	Amb.	Charles Gomis	Amb.
Jamaica	Michael G. Sotirhos	Amb.	Keith Johnson	Amb.
Japan	Michael H. Armacost	Amb.	Nobuo Matsunaga	Amb.
Jordan	Roscoe S. Suddarth	Amb.	Hussein A. Hammami	Amb.
Kenya	Elinor G. Constable	Amb.	Denis D. Afande	Amb.
Korea, South	(Vacancy)	Amb.	Tong-Jin Park	Amb.
Kuwait	W. Nathaniel Howell	Amb.	Shaikh Saud Nasir Al-Sabah	Amb.
Laos	Harriet W. Isom	Cd'A.	Doñe Somvorachit	1st Secy.
Lebanon	John T. McCarthy	Amb.	Dr. Abdallah Bouhabib	Amb.
Lesotho	Robert M. Smalley	Amb.	W. T. Van Tonder	Amb.
Liberia	James K. Bishop	Amb.	Eugenia A. Wordsworth-Stevenson	Amb.
Luxembourg	Jean B. S. Gerard	Amb.	Andre Philippe	Amb.
Madagascar	Patricia Gates Lynch	Amb.	Leon M. Rajaobelina	Amb.
Malawi	George A. Trail, III	Amb.	Robert Mbaya	Amb.
Malaysia	(Vacancy)	Amb.	Albert S. Talalla	Amb.
Mali	Robert M. Pringle	Amb.	Nouhoum Samassekou	Amb.
Malta	Peter R. Sommer	Amb.	Salv. J. Stellini	Amb.
Mauritania	William H. Twaddell	Amb.	Abdellah Ould Daddah	Amb.
Mauritius	Ronald D. Palmer	Amb.	Chitmansing Jesseramsing	Amb.
Mexico	John D. Negroponte	Amb.	Gustavo Petricioli Iturbide	Amb.
Morocco	Michael Ussery	Amb.	Ali Bengelloun	Amb.
Mozambique	Melissa F. Wells	Amb.	Valeriano Ferrao	Amb.
Myanmar (Burma)	Burton Levin	Amb.	U. Myo Aung	Amb.
Nepal	Milton Frank	Amb.	Mohan Man Sainju	Amb.
Netherlands	John S. Shad	Amb.	Richard H. Fein	Amb.
New Zealand	Paul M. Cleveland	Amb.	Harold Huyton Francis	Amb.
Nicaragua	(Vacancy)	Amb.	Leonor de Huper	Min.
Niger	Carl C. Cundiff	Amb.	Moumouni Adamou Djermakoye	Amb.
Nigeria	Princeton N. Lyman	Amb.	Hamzat Ahmadu	Amb.
Norway	Robert D. Stuart, Jr.	Amb.	Kjeld Vibe	Amb.
Oman	(Vacancy)	Amb.	Awadh Bader Al-Shanfari	Amb.
Pakistan	Robert B. Oakley	Amb.	Jamsheed K.A. Marker	Amb.
Panama	Arthur H. Davis	Amb.	Juan B. Sosa	Amb.
Papua New Guinea	Everett E. Bierman	Amb.	Renagi R. Lohia	Amb.
Paraguay	Timothy L. Towell	Amb.	Marcos Martinez Mendieta	Amb.
Peru	Alexander F. Watson	Amb.	Cesar G. Atala	Amb.
Philippines	Nicholas Platt	Amb.	Emmanuel Pelaez	Amb.
Poland	John R. Davis, Jr.	Amb.	Jan Kinast	Amb.
Portugal	Robert M. Rowell	Amb.	Joao Eduardo M. Pereira Bastos	Amb.
Qatar	Joseph Ghougassian	Amb.	Ahmed Adbulla Zaid Al-Mahmoud	Amb.
Romania	Roger Kirk	Amb.	Ion Stoichici	Amb.
Rwanda	Leonard H. O. Spearman, Sr.	Amb.	Aloys Uwimana	Amb.
Saint Kitts and Nevis	(Vacancy)		Erstein M. Edwards	Amb.

Country	U.S. Representatives to[1]	Rank	Representative from[2]	Rank
Saint Lucia	(Vacancy)		Dr. Joseph Edsel Edmunds	Amb.
Saudi Arabia	(Vacancy)	Amb.	Prince Bandar Bin Sultan	Amb.
Senegal	George E. Moose	Amb.	Ibra Deguene Ka	Amb.
Seychelles	James Moran	Amb.	Marc R. Marengo	2nd Secy.
Sierra Leone	Cynthia S. Perry	Amb.	Dr. George Carew	Amb.
Singapore	Daryl Arnold	Amb.	Tommy T.B. Koh	Amb.
Solomon Islands	Everette Bierman	Amb.	Francis Saemala	Amb.
Somalia	T. Frank Crigler	Amb.	Abdullahi Ahmed Addou	Amb.
South Africa	(Vacancy)	Amb.	Piet G.J. Koornhof	Amb.
Spain	(Vacancy)	Amb.	Julian Santamaria	Amb.
Sri Lanka	James W. Spain	Amb.	W. Susanta DeAlwis	Amb.
Sudan	G. Norman Anderson	Amb.	Hassan Elamin El-Bashir	Amb.
Suriname	Richard Howland	Amb.	Willem A. Undenhout	Amb.
Swaziland	Mary A. Ryan	Amb.	Absalom Vusani Mamba	Amb.
Sweden	Charles E. Rednam	Amb.	Count Wilhelm Wachtmeister	Amb.
Switzerland	Philip D. Winn	Amb.	Edouard Brunner	Amb.
Syria	Edward P. Djerejian	Amb.	Bushra Kanafani	Min.
Tanzania	Donald K. Petterson	Amb.	Asterius M. Hyera	Amb.
Thailand	Daniel A. O'Donohue	Amb.	Vitthya Vejjajiva	Amb.
Togo	Rush W. Taylor Jr.	Amb.	Ellom-Kodjo Schuppius	Amb.
Trinidad and Tobago	Charles A. Gargano	Amb.	Angus Albert Khan	Amb.
Tunisia	Robert H. Pelletreau, Jr.	Amb.	Dr. Abdelaziz Hamzaoui	Amb.
Turkey	Robert Strausz-Hupé	Amb.	Dr. Sukru Elekdag	Amb.
Uganda	John A. Burroughs, Jr.	Amb.	Stephen Kapimpina Katena-Apuli	Amb.
U.S.S.R.	Jack F. Matlock, Jr.	Amb.	Yuriy V. Dubinin	Amb.
United Arab Emirates	David L. Mack	Amb.	Ahmed S. Al-Mokarrab	Amb.
United Kingdom	Henry E. Catto	Amb.	Sir Antony Acland	Amb.
Uruguay	Malcolm R. Wilkey	Amb.	Dr. Hector Luisi	Amb.
Venezuela	Otto J. Reich	Amb.	Simon Alberto Consalvi	Amb.
Yemen Arab Republic	Charles F. Dunbar	Amb.	Mohsin A. Alaini	Amb.
Yugoslavia	Warren Zimmerman	Amb.	Zivorad Kovacevic	Amb.
Zaire	William C. Harrop	Amb.	Mushobekwa Kalimba Wa Katana	Amb.
Zambia	Jeffrey Davidow	Amb.	Lazarous Kapambwe	Consl.
Zimbabwe	James Wilson Rawlings	Amb.	Jonathan Watawunashe	Consl.

1. As of May 1989. 2. As of May 1989. NOTE: Amb.=Ambassador; Cd'A.=Charge d'Affaires; Secy.=Secretary; Consl.=Counselor; Min.=Minister; P.O.=Principal Officer. *Source:* U.S. Department of State.

Consular Assistance Abroad

Source: U.S. Department of State.

U.S. consular officers are located at U.S. Embassies and consulates in most countries abroad. Consular officers can advise you of any adverse conditions in the places you are visiting and can help you in emergencies. If you plan more than a short stay in one place or if you are in an area experiencing civil unrest or some natural disaster, it is advisable to register with the nearest U.S. Embassy or consulate. This will make it easier should someone at home need to locate you urgently or in the unlikely event that you need to be evacuated due to an emergency. It will also facilitate the issuance of a new passport should yours be lost or stolen.

Should you find yourself in any legal difficulty, contact a consular officer immediately. Consular officers cannot serve as attorneys or give legal advice but they can provide lists of local attorneys and help you find legal representation. Consular officers cannot get you out of jail. However, if you are arrested, ask permission to notify a consular official—it is your right. American consular officials will visit you, advise you of your rights under local laws, ensure that you aren't held under inhumane conditions, and contact your family and friends for you if you desire. They can transfer money, and will try to get relief for you, including food and clothing in countries where this is a problem. If you become destitute overseas, consular officers can help you get in touch with your family, friends, bank, or employer and inform them how to wire funds to you.

Travel Advisories

Source: U.S. Department of State.

The Department of State tries to alert American travelers to adverse conditions abroad—including violence—through the travel advisory program. In consultation with our embassies and consulates overseas, and various bureaus of the Department of State, the Office of Overseas Citizens Services in the Bureau of Consular Affairs issues travel advisories about conditions in specific countries. Advisories generally do not pertain to isolated international terrorist incidents since these can occur anywhere and at any time. The majority of these advisories deal with short-term or temporary difficulties which Americans may encounter when they go abroad. Some mention conditions of political or civil unrest which could pose a threat to personal safety.

There are only a few advisories in effect which advise avoiding all travel to a particular country because of a high incidence of terrorism within the region or because a long-term problem exists. Most of the security-related advisories do not recommend against travel to an entire country but suggest avoiding specific areas within a country where unrest is endemic.

Ask about current travel advisories for specific countries at any of the 13 regional U.S. passport agencies and at U.S. Embassies and consulates abroad. Travel advisories are also widely disseminated to interested organizations, travel associations, and airlines.

State and City Tourism Offices

The following is a selected list of state, tourism offices. Where a toll-free 800 number is available, it is given. However, the numbers are subject to change.

ALABAMA
Bureau of Tourism & Travel
532 S. Perry St.
Montgomery, AL 36104
205-261-4169 or
1-800-ALABAMA

ALASKA
Alaska Division of Tourism
P.O. Box E
Juneau, AK 99811
907-465-2010

ARIZONA
Arizona Office of Tourism
1100 West Washington
Phoenix, AZ 85007
602 542-TOUR

ARKANSAS
Arkansas Department of Parks
and Tourism
1 Capitol Mall
Little Rock, AR 72201
501-682-7777 or
1-800-482-8999 or
1-800-643-8383
(Out of state)

CALIFORNIA
California Office of Tourism
Department of Commerce
1121 L Street
Suite 103
Sacramento, CA 95814
Write or phone for free 200-
page Guide Information
Packet: (Outside Calif.) 800-
862-2543; X-100

COLORADO
Colorado Tourism Board
1625 Broadway, Suite 1700
Denver, CO 80202
303-592-5410
For a vacation planning kit,
call Toll-free 1-800-433-2656

CONNECTICUT
Tourism Promotion Service
CT Dept. of Economic Development
865 Brook Street
Rocky Hill, CT 06067-3405
203-566-3948 or 800-CT
BOUND (nationwide, except
CT)

DELAWARE
Delaware Tourism Office
Delaware Development Office
99 Kings Highway
P.O. Box 1401
Dover, DE 19903
302-736-4271 or
1-800-441-8846

DISTRICT OF COLUMBIA
Washington Convention and
Visitors Association
1212 New York Ave., NW
Washington, D.C. 20005
202-789-7000

FLORIDA
Department of Commerce Visitors Inquiry
126 Van Buren St.
Tallahassee, FL 32399-2000
904-487-1462

GEORGIA
Tourist Division
P.O. Box 1776
Atlanta, GA 30301
404-656-3590

HAWAII
Hawaii Visitors Bureau
2270 Kalakaua Ave., Suite 801
Honolulu, HI 96815
808-923-1811

IDAHO
Department of Commerce
700 W. State St.
Second Floor
Boise, ID 83720
208-334-2470 or
1-800-635-7820

ILLINOIS
Illinois Department of Commerce and Community Affairs, Bureau of Tourism
620 East Adams Street
Springfield, IL 62701
217-782-7139

INDIANA
Indiana Dept. of Commerce
Tourism Division
1 North Capitol, Suite 700
Indianapolis, IN 46204-2288
317-232-8860

IOWA
Iowa Department of Economic
Development
Bureau of Tourism and Visitors
200 East Grand Avenue
Des Moines, IA 50309
515-281-3100

KANSAS
Travel & Tourism Development
Division
Department of Commerce
400 W. 8th St., 5th Floor
Topeka, KS 66603
913-296-2009

KENTUCKY
Department of Travel Development
Capital Plaza Tower
Frankfort, KY 40601
502-564-4930 or
1-800-225-TRIP
(Continental United States and
provinces of Ontario and
Quebec, Canada)

LOUISIANA
Office of Tourism
P.O. Box 94291
Baton Rouge, LA 70804-9291
504-342-8119 or
1-800-33GUMBO

MAINE
Maine Publicity Bureau
97 Winthrop St., P.O. Box
2300
Hallowell, ME 04347-2300
207-289-2423

MARYLAND
Office of Tourism Development
217 E. Redwood St.
Baltimore, MD 21202
301-333-6611

MASSACHUSETTS
Office of Travel and Tourism
100 Cambridge St., 13th Floor
Boston, MA 02202
617-727-3201

MICHIGAN
Travel Bureau
Department of Commerce
P.O. Box 30226
Lansing, MI 48909
1-800-5432-YES

Average Daily Temperatures (°F) in Tourist Cities

Location	January High	January Low	April High	April Low	July High	July Low	October High	October Low
U.S. CITIES (See Weather and Climate Section)								
CANADA								
Ottawa	21	3	51	31	81	58	54	37
Quebec	18	2	45	29	76	57	51	37
Toronto	30	16	50	34	79	59	56	40
Vancouver	41	32	58	40	74	54	57	44
MEXICO								
Acapulco	85	70	87	71	89	75	88	74
Mexico City	66	42	78	52	74	54	70	50
OVERSEAS								
Australia (Sydney)	78	65	71	58	60	46	71	56
Austria (Vienna)	34	26	57	41	75	59	55	44
Bahamas (Nassau)	77	65	81	69	88	75	85	73
Bermuda (Hamilton)	68	58	71	59	85	73	79	69
Brazil (Rio de Janeiro)	84	73	80	69	75	63	77	66
Denmark (Copenhagen)	36	29	50	37	72	55	53	42
Egypt (Cairo)	65	47	83	57	96	70	86	65
France (Paris)	42	32	60	41	76	55	59	44
Germany (Berlin)	35	26	55	38	74	55	55	41
Greece (Athens)	54	42	67	52	90	72	74	60
Hong Kong	64	56	75	67	87	78	81	73
India (Calcutta)	80	55	97	76	90	79	89	74
Italy (Rome)	54	39	68	46	88	64	73	53
Israel (Jerusalem)	55	41	73	50	87	63	81	59
Japan (Tokyo)	47	29	63	46	83	70	69	55
Nigeria (Lagos)	88	74	89	77	83	74	85	74
Netherlands (Amsterdam)	40	34	52	43	69	59	56	48
Puerto Rico (San Juan)	81	67	84	69	87	74	87	73
South Africa (Cape Town)	78	60	72	53	63	45	70	52
Spain (Madrid)	47	33	64	44	87	62	66	48
United Kingdom (London)	44	35	56	40	73	55	58	44
United Kingdom (Edinburgh)	43	35	50	39	65	52	53	44
U.S.S.R. (Moscow)	21	9	47	31	76	55	46	34
Venezuela (Caracas)	75	56	81	60	78	61	79	61
Yugoslavia (Belgrade)	37	27	64	45	84	61	65	47

MINNESOTA
Minnesota Office of Tourism
375 Jackson St.
250 Skyway Level
Farm Credit Services Bldg.
St. Paul, MN 55101
612-296-5029 or
1-800-328-1461 (U.S. Toll-Free) and (Minnesota Toll-Free) 1-800-652-9747

MISSISSIPPI
Division of Tourism
Department of Economic Development
P.O. Box 849
Jackson, MS 39205
601-359-3414 or
1-800-647-2290

MISSOURI
Missouri Division of Tourism
Truman State Office Bldg.
301 W. High St.
P.O. Box 1055
Jefferson City, MO 65102
314-751-4133

MONTANA
Travel Montana
Department of Commerce
1424 9th Ave.
Helena, MT 59620
406-444-2654 or
1-800-541-1447

NEBRASKA
Dept. of Economic Development
Division of Travel and Tourism
301 Centennial Mall South
P.O. Box 94666
Lincoln, NE 68509
402-471-3796 or
1-800-742-7595 or
1-800-228-4307 (out of state)

NEVADA
Commission on Tourism
Capitol Complex
Carson City, NV 89710
1-800-Nevada-8

NEW HAMPSHIRE
Office of Vacation Travel
P.O. Box 856
Concord, NH 03301
603-271-2666
or for recorded weekly events, ski conditions, foliage reports
1-800-258-3608
Toll free number is for northeast only

NEW JERSEY
Division of Travel and Tourism
CN-826
Trenton, NJ 08625
609-292-2470

NEW MEXICO
New Mexico Tourism
& Travel Division ED & TD
Room 119, Joseph M. Montoya Bldg.
1100 St. Francis Dr.
Santa Fe, NM 87503
505-827-0291 or
1-800-545-2040

NEW YORK
Division of Tourism
1 Commerce Plaza
Albany, NY 12245
Toll free from anywhere in the U.S. and its territorial possessions 1-800-225-5697. From Canada, call (518) 474-4116

NORTH CAROLINA
Travel and Tourism Division
Department of Commerce
430 North Salisbury St.
Raleigh, NC 27611
919-733-4171 or 1-800-VISIT NC

NORTH DAKOTA
North Dakota Tourism Promotion
Liberty Memorial Building
Capitol Grounds
Bismarck, ND 58505
701-224-2525 or 1-800-437-2077 (out of state) 1-800-537-8879 (Canada)

OHIO
Ohio Division of Travel and Tourism
P.O. Box 1001
Columbus, OH 43266-0101
614-466-8844 (Business Office) 1-800-BUCKEYE (National Toll-Free Travel Hotline)

OKLAHOMA
Oklahoma Tourism and Recreation Dept.
Literature Distribution Center
P.O. Box 60000
Oklahoma City, OK 73146
405-521-2409 (In Oklahoma City area) or nationwide at 1-800-652-6552

OREGON
Tourism Division
Oregon Economic Development
595 Cottage St., NE
Salem, OR 97310
503-373-1270 or

1-800-547-7842 (Out of state); 1-800-543-8838 (in-state)

PENNSYLVANIA
Bureau of Travel Development
453 Forum Building
Harrisburg, PA 17120
717-787-5453 (Business Office) 1-800-VISIT PA, ext. 275 (Consumer Information)

RHODE ISLAND
Rhode Island Tourism Division
7 Jackson Walkway
Providence, RI 02903
401-277-2601 or 1-800-556-2484 (For residents from Maine to Virginia/West Virginia and Northern Ohio)

SOUTH CAROLINA
South Carolina Division of Tourism
Box 71
Columbia, SC 29202
803-734-0235

SOUTH DAKOTA
Department of Tourism
Capitol Lake Plaza
Pierre, South Dakota 57501
605-773-3301 or 1-800-843-1930 out of SD; 1-800-952-2217 in SD

TENNESSEE
Department of Tourist Development
P.O. Box 23170
Nashville, TN 37202
615-741-2158

TEXAS
Travel Information Services
State Highway Department
P.O. Box 5064
Austin, TX 78763-5064
512-463-8971

UTAH
Utah Travel Council
Council Hall, Capitol Hill

Salt Lake City, UT 84114
801-538-1030

VERMONT
Agency of Development and Community Affairs
Travel Division
134 State St.
Montpelier, VT 05602
802-828-3236

VIRGINIA
Virginia Division of Tourism
202 North Ninth Street
Suite 500
Richmond, VA 23219
804-786-4484

WASHINGTON
Washington State Dept. of Trade and Economic Development
101 General Administration Bldg.
AX-13
Olympia, WA 98504
206-753-5630

WASHINGTON, D.C.
See District of Columbia

WEST VIRGINIA
Dept. of Commerce
State Capitol Complex
Charleston, WV 25305
304-348-2286 or 1-800-CALL-WVA

WISCONSIN
Department of Development
Division of Tourism Development
Box 7606
Madison, WI 53707
Toll free in WI and neighbor states 1-800-ESCAPES others: 608-266-2161 Nationally 1-800-432-TRIP

WYOMING
Wyoming Travel Commission
I-25 at College Drive
Cheyenne, WY 82002-0660
307-777-7777 or 1-800-225-5996

Avoiding Motion Sickness

(*Source:* American Council on Science and Health)

The Food and Drug Administration suggests the following:

(1) Place yourself where there is the least motion: on deck and amidships on a ship, in the front seat of a car, and over the wing of a plane.

(2) When traveling in a vehicle where seat belts are not necessary, lie on your back, in a semireclined position, and keep your head as still as possible. In an automobile, do this only to the extent possible without removing your seat belt. Safety must take priority over motion sickness.

(3) Don't watch the waves or fast-moving scenery.

(4) Avoid food and tobacco odors.

(5) Don't overindulge in food or alcohol the night before a trip.

When buying over-the-counter remedies for motion sickness, read the labels carefully. Some are unsuitable for children. All are unsuitable if you have certain medical problems or if you're the one who will be driving or piloting the vehicle in question (they cause drowsiness). If you must take other medications, consult your doctor before using motion sickness remedies; some drugs should not be mixed because they magnify or antagonize each other's effects.

Additional Information

The booklet, *Your Trip Abroad*, contains some valuable information on loss and theft of a passport as well as other travel tips. To obtain a copy, write to the Superintendent of Documents, U.S. Government Printing Office, Washington, D.C. 20402 and ask for publication #8969. The single copy price is $1.

Road Mileages Between U.S. Cities[1]

Cities	Birmingham	Boston	Buffalo	Chicago	Cleveland	Dallas	Denver
Birmingham, Ala.	—	1,194	947	657	734	653	1,318
Boston, Mass.	1,194	—	457	983	639	1,815	1,991
Buffalo, N.Y.	947	457	—	536	192	1,387	1,561
Chicago, Ill.	657	983	536	—	344	931	1,050
Cleveland, Ohio	734	639	192	344	—	1,205	1,369
Dallas, Tex.	653	1,815	1,387	931	1,205	—	801
Denver, Colo	1,318	1,991	1,561	1,050	1,369	801	—
Detroit, Mich.	754	702	252	279	175	1,167	1,301
El Paso, Tex.	1,278	2,358	1,928	1,439	1,746	625	652
Houston, Tex.	692	1,886	1,532	1,092	1,358	242	1,032
Indianapolis, Ind.	492	940	510	189	318	877	1,051
Kansas City, Mo.	703	1,427	997	503	815	508	616
Los Angeles, Calif.	2,078	3,036	2,606	2,112	2,424	1,425	1,174
Louisville, Ky.	378	996	571	305	379	865	1,135
Memphis, Tenn.	249	1,345	965	546	773	470	1,069
Miami, Fla.	777	1,539	1,445	1,390	1,325	1,332	2,094
Minneapolis, Minn.	1,067	1,402	955	411	763	969	867
New Orleans, La.	347	1,541	1,294	947	1,102	504	1,305
New York, N.Y.	983	213	436	840	514	1,604	1,780
Omaha, Neb.	907	1,458	1,011	493	819	661	559
Philadelphia, Pa.	894	304	383	758	432	1,515	1,698
Phoenix, Ariz.	1,680	2,664	2,234	1,729	2,052	1,027	836
Pittsburgh, Pa.	792	597	219	457	131	1,237	1,411
St. Louis, Mo.	508	1,179	749	293	567	638	871
Salt Lake City, Utah	1,805	2,425	1,978	1,458	1,786	1,239	512
San Francisco, Calif.	2,385	3,179	2,732	2,212	2,540	1,765	1,266
Seattle, Wash.	2,612	3,043	2,596	2,052	2,404	2,122	1,373
Washington, D.C.	751	440	386	695	369	1,372	1,635

Cities	Detroit	El Paso	Houston	Indianapolis	Kansas City	Los Angeles	Louisville
Birmingham, Ala.	754	1,278	692	492	703	2,078	378
Boston, Mass.	702	2,358	1,886	940	1,427	3,036	996
Buffalo, N.Y.	252	1,928	1,532	510	997	2,606	571
Chicago, Ill.	279	1,439	1,092	189	503	2,112	305
Cleveland, Ohio	175	1,746	1,358	318	815	2,424	379
Dallas, Tex.	1,167	625	242	877	508	1,425	865
Denver, Colo.	1,310	652	1,032	1,051	616	1,174	1,135
Detroit, Mich.	—	1,696	1,312	290	760	2,369	378
El Paso, Tex.	1,696	—	756	1,418	936	800	1,443
Houston, Tex.	1,312	756	—	1,022	750	1,556	981
Indianapolis, Ind.	290	1,418	1,022	—	487	2,096	114
Kansas City, Mo.	760	936	750	487	—	1,609	519
Los Angeles, Calif.	2,369	800	1,556	2,096	1,609	—	2,128
Louisville, Ky.	378	1,443	981	114	519	2,128	—
Memphis, Tenn.	756	1,095	586	466	454	1,847	396
Miami, Fla.	1,409	1,957	1,237	1,225	1,479	2,757	1,111
Minneapolis, Minn.	698	1,353	1,211	600	466	2,041	716
New Orleans, La.	1,101	1,121	365	839	839	1,921	725
New York, N.Y.	671	2,147	1,675	729	1,216	2,825	785
Omaha, Neb.	754	1,015	903	590	204	1,733	704
Philadelphia, Pa.	589	2,065	1,586	647	1,134	2,743	703
Phoenix, Ariz.	1,986	402	1,158	1,713	1,226	398	1,749
Pittsburgh, Pa.	288	1,778	1,395	360	847	2,456	416
St. Louis, Mo.	529	1,179	799	239	255	1,864	264
Salt Lake City, Utah	1,721	877	1,465	1,545	1,128	728	1,647
San Francisco, Calif.	2,475	1,202	1,958	2,299	1,882	403	2,401
Seattle, Wash.	2,339	1,760	2,348	2,241	1,909	1,150	2,355
Washington, D.C.	526	1,997	1,443	565	1,071	2,680	601

1. These figures represent estimates and are subject to change.

Road Mileages Between U.S. Cities

Cities	Memphis	Miami	Minne-apolis	New Orleans	New York	Omaha	Phila-delphia
Birmingham, Ala.	249	777	1,067	347	983	907	894
Boston, Mass.	1,345	1,539	1,402	1,541	213	1,458	304
Buffalo, N.Y.	965	1,445	955	1,294	436	1,011	383
Chicago, Ill.	546	1,390	411	947	840	493	758
Cleveland, Ohio	773	1,325	763	1,102	514	819	432
Dallas, Tex.	470	1,332	969	504	1,604	661	1,515
Denver, Colo.	1,069	2,094	867	1,305	1,780	559	1,698
Detroit, Mich.	756	1,409	698	1,101	671	754	589
El Paso, Tex.	1,095	1,957	1,353	1,121	2,147	1,015	2,065
Houston, Tex.	586	1,237	1,211	365	1,675	903	1,586
Indianapolis, Ind.	466	1,225	600	839	729	590	647
Kansas City, Mo.	454	1,479	466	839	1,216	204	1,134
Los Angeles, Calif.	1,847	2,757	2,041	1,921	2,825	1,733	2,743
Louisville, Ky.	396	1,111	716	725	785	704	703
Memphis, Tenn.	—	1,025	854	401	1,134	658	1,045
Miami, Fla.	1,025	—	1,801	892	1,328	1,683	1,239
Minneapolis, Minn.	854	1,801	—	1,255	1,259	373	1,177
New Orleans, La.	401	892	1,255	—	1,330	1,043	1,241
New York, N.Y.	1,134	1,328	1,259	1,330	—	1,315	93
Omaha, Neb.	658	1,683	373	1,043	1,315	—	1,233
Philadelphia, Pa.	1,045	1,239	1,177	1,241	93	1,233	—
Phoenix, Ariz.	1,464	2,359	1,644	1,523	2,442	1,305	2,360
Pittsburgh, Pa.	810	1,250	876	1,118	386	932	304
St. Louis, Mo.	295	1,241	559	696	968	459	886
Salt Lake City, Utah	1,556	2,571	1,243	1,743	2,282	967	2,200
San Francisco, Calif.	2,151	3,097	1,997	2,269	3,036	1,721	2,954
Seattle, Wash.	2,363	3,389	1,641	2,606	2,900	1,705	2,818
Washington, D.C.	902	1,101	1,114	1,098	229	1,170	140

Cities	Phoenix	Pitts-burgh	St. Louis	Salt Lake City	San Francisco	Seattle	Wash-ington
Birmingham, Ala.	1,680	792	508	1,805	2,385	2,612	751
Boston, Mass.	2,664	597	1,179	2,425	3,179	3,043	440
Buffalo, N.Y.	2,234	219	749	1,978	2,732	2,596	386
Chicago, Ill.	1,729	457	293	1,458	2,212	2,052	695
Cleveland, Ohio	2,052	131	567	1,786	2,540	2,404	369
Dallas, Tex.	1,027	1,237	638	1,239	1,765	2,122	1,372
Denver, Colo.	836	1,411	871	512	1,266	1,373	1,635
Detroit, Mich.	1,986	288	529	1,721	2,475	2,339	526
El Paso, Tex.	402	1,778	1,179	877	1,202	1,760	1,997
Houston, Tex.	1,158	1,395	799	1,465	1,958	2,348	1,443
Indianapolis, Ind.	1,713	360	239	1,545	2,299	2,241	565
Kansas City, Mo.	1,226	847	255	1,128	1,882	1,909	1,071
Los Angeles, Calif.	398	2,456	1,864	728	403	1,150	2,680
Louisville, Ky.	1,749	416	264	1,647	2,401	2,355	601
Memphis, Tenn.	1,464	810	295	1,556	2,151	2,363	902
Miami, Fla.	2,359	1,250	1,241	2,571	3,097	3,389	1,101
Minneapolis, Minn.	1,644	876	559	1,243	1,997	1,641	1,114
New Orleans, La.	1,523	1,118	696	1,743	2,269	2,626	1,098
New York, N.Y.	2,442	386	968	2,282	3,036	2,900	229
Omaha, Neb.	1,305	932	459	967	1,721	1,705	1,178
Philadelphia, Pa.	2,360	304	886	2,200	2,954	2,818	140
Phoenix, Ariz.	—	2,073	1,485	651	800	1,482	2,278
Pittsburgh, Pa.	2,073	—	599	1,899	2,653	2,517	241
St. Louis, Mo.	1,485	599	—	1,383	2,137	2,164	836
Salt Lake City, Utah	651	1,899	1,383	—	754	883	2,110
San Francisco, Calif.	800	2,653	2,137	754	—	817	2,864
Seattle, Wash.	1,482	2,517	2,164	883	817	—	2,755
Washington, D.C.	2,278	241	836	2,110	2,864	2,755	—

Air Distances Between U.S. Cities in Statute Miles

Cities	Birming-ham	Boston	Buffalo	Chicago	Cleveland	Dallas	Denver
Birmingham, Ala.	—	1,052	776	578	618	581	1,095
Boston, Mass.	1,052	—	400	851	551	1,551	1,769
Buffalo, N. Y.	776	400	—	454	173	1,198	1,370
Chicago, Ill.	578	851	454	—	308	803	920
Cleveland, Ohio	618	551	173	308	—	1,025	1,227
Dallas, Tex.	581	1,551	1,198	803	1,025	—	663
Denver, Colo.	1,095	1,769	1,370	920	1,227	663	—
Detroit, Mich.	641	613	216	238	90	999	1,156
El Paso, Tex.	1,152	2,072	1,692	1,252	1,525	572	557
Houston, Tex.	567	1,605	1,286	940	1,114	225	879
Indianapolis, Ind.	433	807	435	165	263	763	1,000
Kansas City, Mo.	579	1,251	861	414	700	451	558
Los Angeles, Calif.	1,802	2,596	2,198	1,745	2,049	1,240	831
Louisville, Ky.	331	826	483	269	311	726	1,038
Memphis, Tenn.	217	1,137	803	482	630	420	879
Miami, Fla.	665	1,255	1,181	1,188	1,087	1,111	1,726
Minneapolis, Minn.	862	1,123	731	355	630	862	700
New Orleans, La.	312	1,359	1,086	833	924	443	1,082
New York, N. Y.	864	188	292	713	405	1,374	1,631
Omaha, Neb.	732	1,282	883	432	739	586	488
Philadelphia, Pa.	783	271	279	666	360	1,299	1,579
Phoenix, Ariz.	1,456	2,300	1,906	1,453	1,749	887	586
Pittsburgh, Pa.	608	483	178	410	115	1,070	1,320
St. Louis, Mo.	400	1,038	662	262	492	547	796
Salt Lake City, Utah	1,466	2,099	1,699	1,260	1,568	999	371
San Francisco, Calif.	2,013	2,699	2,300	1,858	2,166	1,483	949
Seattle, Wash.	2,082	2,493	2,117	1,737	2,026	1,681	1,021
Washington, D.C.	661	393	292	597	306	1,185	1,494

Cities	Detroit	El Paso	Houston	Indian-apolis	Kansas City	Los Angeles	Louisville
Birmingham, Ala.	641	1,152	567	433	579	1,802	331
Boston, Mass.	613	2,072	1,605	807	1,251	2,596	826
Buffalo, N. Y.	216	1,692	1,286	435	861	2,198	483
Chicago, Ill.	238	1,252	940	165	414	1,745	269
Cleveland, Ohio	90	1,525	1,114	263	700	2,049	311
Dallas, Tex.	999	572	225	763	451	1,240	726
Denver, Colo.	1,156	557	879	1,000	558	831	1,038
Detroit, Mich.	—	1,479	1,105	240	645	1,983	316
El Paso, Tex.	1,479	—	676	1,264	839	701	1,254
Houston, Tex.	1,105	676	—	865	644	1,374	803
Indianapolis, Ind.	240	1,264	865	—	453	1,809	107
Kansas City, Mo.	645	839	644	453	—	1,356	480
Los Angeles, Calif.	1,983	701	1,374	1,809	1,356	—	1,829
Louisville, Ky.	316	1,254	803	107	480	1,829	—
Memphis, Tenn.	623	976	484	384	369	1,603	320
Miami, Fla.	1,152	1,643	968	1,024	1,241	2,339	919
Minneapolis, Minn.	543	1,157	1,056	511	413	1,524	605
New Orleans, La.	939	983	318	712	680	1,673	623
New York, N. Y.	482	1,905	1,420	646	1,097	2,451	652
Omaha, Neb.	669	878	794	525	166	1,315	580
Philadelphia, Pa.	443	1,836	1,341	585	1,038	2,394	582
Phoenix, Ariz.	1,690	346	1,017	1,499	1,049	357	1,508
Pittsburgh, Pa.	205	1,590	1,137	330	781	2,136	344
St. Louis, Mo.	455	1,034	679	231	238	1,589	242
Salt Lake City, Utah	1,492	689	1,200	1,356	925	579	1,402
San Francisco, Calif.	2,091	995	1,645	1,949	1,506	347	1,986
Seattle, Wash.	1,938	1,376	1,891	1,872	1,506	959	1,943
Washington, D.C.	396	1,728	1,220	494	945	2,300	476

Source: National Geodetic Survey.

Air Distances Between U.S. Cities in Statute Miles

Cities	Memphis	Miami	Minne-apolis	New Orleans	New York	Omaha	Phila-delphia
Birmingham, Ala.	217	665	862	312	864	732	783
Boston, Mass.	1,137	1,255	1,123	1,359	188	1,282	271
Buffalo, N. Y.	803	1,181	731	1,086	292	883	279
Chicago, Ill.	482	1,188	355	833	713	432	666
Cleveland, Ohio	630	1,087	630	924	405	739	360
Dallas, Tex.	420	1,111	862	443	1,374	586	1,299
Denver, Colo.	879	1,726	700	1,082	1,631	488	1,579
Detroit, Mich.	623	1,152	543	939	482	669	443
El Paso, Tex.	976	1,643	1,157	983	1,905	878	1,836
Houston, Tex.	484	968	1,056	318	1,420	794	1,341
Indianapolis, Ind.	384	1,024	511	712	646	525	585
Kansas City, Mo.	369	1,241	413	680	1,097	166	1,038
Los Angeles, Calif.	1,603	2,339	1,524	1,673	2,451	1,315	2,394
Louisville, Ky.	320	919	605	623	652	580	582
Memphis, Tenn.	—	872	699	358	957	529	881
Miami, Fla.	872	—	1,511	669	1,092	1,397	1,019
Minneapolis, Minn.	699	1,511	—	1,051	1,018	290	985
New Orleans, La.	358	669	1,051	—	1,171	847	1,089
New York, N. Y.	957	1,092	1,018	1,171	—	1,144	83
Omaha, Neb.	529	1,397	290	847	1,144	—	1,094
Philadelphia, Pa.	881	1,019	985	1,089	83	1,094	—
Phoenix, Ariz.	1,263	1,982	1,280	1,316	2,145	1,036	2,083
Pittsburgh, Pa.	660	1,010	743	919	317	836	259
St. Louis, Mo.	240	1,061	466	598	875	354	811
Salt Lake City, Utah	1,250	2,089	987	1,434	1,972	833	1,925
San Francisco, Calif.	1,802	2,594	1,584	1,926	2,571	1,429	2,523
Seattle, Wash.	1,867	2,734	1,395	2,101	2,408	1,369	2,380
Washington, D.C.	765	923	934	966	205	1,014	123

Cities	Phoenix	Pitts-burgh	St. Louis	Salt Lake City	San Francisco	Seattle	Wash-ington
Birmingham, Ala.	1,456	608	400	1,466	2,013	2,082	661
Boston, Mass.	2,300	483	1,038	2,099	2,699	2,493	393
Buffalo, N. Y.	1,906	178	662	1,699	2,300	2,117	292
Chicago, Ill.	1,453	410	262	1,260	1,858	1,737	597
Cleveland, Ohio	1,749	115	492	1,568	2,166	2,026	306
Dallas, Tex.	887	1,070	547	999	1,483	1,681	1,185
Denver, Colo.	586	1,320	796	371	949	1,021	1,494
Detroit, Mich.	1,690	205	455	1,492	2,091	1,938	396
El Paso, Tex.	346	1,590	1,034	689	995	1,376	1,728
Houston, Tex.	1,017	1,137	679	1,200	1,645	1,891	1,220
Indianapolis, Ind.	1,499	330	231	1,356	1,949	1,872	494
Kansas City, Mo.	1,049	781	238	925	1,506	1,506	945
Los Angeles, Calif.	357	2,136	1,589	579	347	959	2,300
Louisville, Ky.	1,508	344	242	1,402	1,986	1,943	476
Memphis, Tenn.	1,263	660	240	1,250	1,802	1,867	765
Miami, Fla.	1,982	1,010	1,061	2,089	2,594	2,734	923
Minneapolis, Minn.	1,280	743	466	987	1,584	1,395	934
New Orleans, La.	1,316	919	598	1,434	1,926	2,101	966
New York, N. Y.	2,145	317	875	1,972	2,571	2,408	205
Omaha, Neb.	1,036	836	354	833	1,429	1,369	1,014
Philadelphia, Pa.	2,083	259	811	1,925	2,523	2,380	123
Phoenix, Ariz.	—	1,828	1,272	504	653	1,114	1,983
Pittsburgh, Pa.	1,828	—	559	1,668	2,264	2,138	192
St. Louis, Mo.	1,272	559	—	1,162	1,744	1,724	712
Salt Lake City, Utah	504	1,668	1,162	—	600	701	1,848
San Francisco, Calif.	653	2,264	1,744	600	—	678	2,442
Seattle, Wash.	1,114	2,138	1,724	701	678	—	2,329
Washington, D.C.	1,983	192	712	1,848	2,442	2,329	—

Source: National Geodetic Survey.

Air Distances Between World Cities in Statute Miles

Cities	Berlin	Buenos Aires	Cairo	Calcutta	Cape Town	Caracas	Chicago
Berlin	—	7,402	1,795	4,368	5,981	5,247	4,405
Buenos Aires	7,402	—	7,345	10,265	4,269	3,168	5,598
Cairo	1,795	7,345	—	3,539	4,500	6,338	6,129
Calcutta	4,368	10,265	3,539	—	6,024	9,605	7,980
Cape Town, South Africa	5,981	4,269	4,500	6,024	—	6,365	8,494
Caracas, Venezuela	5,247	3,168	6,338	9,605	6,365	—	2,501
Chicago	4,405	5,598	6,129	7,980	8,494	2,501	—
Hong Kong	5,440	11,472	5,061	1,648	7,375	10,167	7,793
Honolulu, Hawaii	7,309	7,561	8,838	7,047	11,534	6,013	4,250
Istanbul	1,078	7,611	768	3,638	5,154	6,048	5,477
Lisbon	1,436	5,956	2,363	5,638	5,325	4,041	3,990
London	579	6,916	2,181	4,947	6,012	4,660	3,950
Los Angeles	5,724	6,170	7,520	8,090	9,992	3,632	1,745
Manila	6,132	11,051	5,704	2,203	7,486	10,620	8,143
Mexico City	6,047	4,592	7,688	9,492	8,517	2,232	1,691
Montreal	3,729	5,615	5,414	7,607	7,931	2,449	744
Moscow	1,004	8,376	1,803	3,321	6,300	6,173	4,974
New York	3,965	5,297	5,602	7,918	7,764	2,132	713
Paris	545	6,870	1,995	4,883	5,807	4,736	4,134
Rio de Janeiro	6,220	1,200	6,146	9,377	3,773	2,810	5,296
Rome	734	6,929	1,320	4,482	5,249	5,196	4,808
San Francisco	5,661	6,467	7,364	7,814	10,247	3,904	1,858
Shanghai, China	5,218	12,201	5,183	2,117	8,061	9,501	7,061
Stockholm	504	7,808	2,111	4,195	6,444	5,420	4,278
Sydney, Australia	10,006	7,330	8,952	5,685	6,843	9,513	9,272
Tokyo	5,540	11,408	5,935	3,194	9,156	8,799	6,299
Warsaw	320	7,662	1,630	4,048	5,958	5,517	4,667
Washington, D.C.	4,169	5,218	5,800	8,084	7,901	2,059	597

Cities	Hong Kong	Honolulu	Istanbul	Lisbon	London	Los Angeles	Manila
Berlin	5,440	7,309	1,078	1,436	579	5,724	6,132
Buenos Aires	11,472	7,561	7,611	5,956	6,916	6,170	11,051
Cairo	5,061	8,838	768	2,363	2,181	7,520	5,704
Calcutta	1,648	7,047	3,638	5,638	4,947	8,090	2,203
Cape Town, South Africa	7,375	11,534	5,154	5,325	6,012	9,992	7,486
Caracas, Venezuela	10,167	6,013	6,048	4,041	4,660	3,632	10,620
Chicago	7,793	4,250	5,477	3,990	3,950	1,745	8,143
Hong Kong	—	5,549	4,984	6,853	5,982	7,195	693
Honolulu, Hawaii	5,549	—	8,109	7,820	7,228	2,574	5,299
Istanbul	4,984	8,109	—	2,012	1,552	6,783	5,664
Lisbon	6,853	7,820	2,012	—	985	5,621	7,546
London	5,982	7,228	1,552	985	—	5,382	6,672
Los Angeles, Calif.	7,195	2,574	6,783	5,621	5,382	—	7,261
Manila	693	5,299	5,664	7,546	6,672	7,261	—
Mexico City	8,782	3,779	7,110	5,390	5,550	1,589	8,835
Montreal	7,729	4,910	4,789	3,246	3,282	2,427	8,186
Moscow	4,439	7,037	1,091	2,427	1,555	6,003	5,131
New York	8,054	4,964	4,975	3,364	3,458	2,451	8,498
Paris	5,985	7,438	1,400	904	213	5,588	6,677
Rio de Janeiro	11,021	8,285	6,389	4,796	5,766	6,331	11,259
Rome	5,768	8,022	843	1,161	887	6,732	6,457
San Francisco	6,897	2,393	6,703	5,666	5,357	347	6,967
Shanghai, China	764	4,941	4,962	6,654	5,715	6,438	1,150
Stockholm	5,113	6,862	1,348	1,856	890	5,454	5,797
Sydney, Australia	4,584	4,943	9,294	11,302	10,564	7,530	3,944
Tokyo	1,794	3,853	5,560	6,915	5,940	5,433	1,866
Warsaw	5,144	7,355	863	1,715	899	5,922	5,837
Washington, D.C.	8,147	4,519	5,215	3,562	3,663	2,300	8,562

Source: Encyclopaedia Britannica.

Air Distances Between World Cities in Statute Miles

Cities	Mexico City	Montreal	Moscow	New York	Paris	Rio de Janeiro	Rome
Berlin	6,047	3,729	1,004	3,965	545	6,220	734
Buenos Aires	4,592	5,615	8,376	5,297	6,870	1,200	6,929
Cairo	7,688	5,414	1,803	5,602	1,995	6,146	1,320
Calcutta	9,492	7,607	3,321	7,918	4,883	9,377	4,482
Cape Town, South Africa	8,517	7,931	6,300	7,764	5,807	3,773	5,249
Caracas, Venezuela	2,232	2,449	6,173	2,132	4,736	2,810	5,196
Chicago	1,691	744	4,974	713	4,134	5,296	4,808
Hong Kong	8,782	7,729	4,439	8,054	5,985	11,021	5,768
Honolulu	3,779	4,910	7,037	4,964	7,438	8,285	8,022
Istanbul	7,110	4,789	1,091	4,975	1,400	6,389	843
Lisbon	5,390	3,246	2,427	3,364	904	4,796	1,161
London	5,550	3,282	1,555	3,458	213	5,766	887
Los Angeles	1,589	2,427	6,003	2,451	5,588	6,331	6,732
Manila	8,835	8,186	5,131	8,498	6,677	11,259	6,457
Mexico City	—	2,318	6,663	2,094	5,716	4,771	6,366
Montreal	2,318	—	4,386	320	3,422	5,097	4,080
Moscow	6,663	4,386	—	4,665	1,544	7,175	1,474
New York	2,094	320	4,665	—	3,624	4,817	4,281
Paris	5,716	3,422	1,544	3,624	—	5,699	697
Rio de Janeiro	4,771	5,097	7,175	4,817	5,699	—	5,684
Rome	6,366	4,080	1,474	4,281	697	5,684	—
San Francisco	1,887	2,539	5,871	2,571	5,558	6,621	6,240
Shanghai, China	8,022	7,053	4,235	7,371	5,754	11,336	5,677
Stockholm	5,959	3,667	762	3,924	958	6,651	1,234
Sydney, Australia	8,052	9,954	9,012	9,933	10,544	8,306	10,136
Tokyo	7,021	6,383	4,647	6,740	6,034	11,533	6,135
Warsaw	6,365	4,009	715	4,344	849	6,467	817
Washington, D.C.	1,887	488	4,858	205	3,829	4,796	4,434

Cities	San Francisco	Shanghai	Stockholm	Sydney	Tokyo	Warsaw	Washington
Berlin	5,661	5,218	504	10,006	5,540	320	4,169
Buenos Aires	6,467	12,201	7,808	7,330	11,408	7,662	5,218
Cairo	7,364	5,183	2,111	8,952	5,935	1,630	5,800
Calcutta	7,814	2,117	4,195	5,685	3,194	4,048	8,084
Cape Town, South Africa	10,247	8,061	6,444	6,843	9,156	5,958	7,901
Caracas, Venezuela	3,904	9,501	5,420	9,513	8,799	5,517	2,059
Chicago	1,858	7,061	4,278	9,272	6,299	4,667	597
Hong Kong	6,897	764	5,113	4,584	1,794	5,144	8,147
Honolulu	2,393	4,941	6,862	4,943	3,853	7,355	4,519
Istanbul	6,703	4,962	1,348	9,294	5,560	863	5,215
Lisbon	5,666	6,654	1,856	11,302	6,915	1,715	3,562
London	5,357	5,715	890	10,564	5,940	899	3,663
Los Angeles	347	6,438	5,454	7,530	5,433	5,922	2,300
Manila	6,967	1,150	5,797	3,944	1,866	5,837	8,562
Mexico City	1,887	8,022	5,959	8,052	7,021	6,365	1,887
Montreal	2,539	7,053	3,667	9,954	6,383	4,009	488
Moscow	5,871	4,235	762	9,012	4,647	715	4,858
New York	2,571	7,371	3,924	9,933	6,740	4,344	205
Paris	5,558	5,754	958	10,544	6,034	849	3,829
Rio de Janeiro	6,621	11,336	6,651	8,306	11,533	6,467	4,796
Rome	6,240	5,677	1,234	10,136	6,135	817	4,434
San Francisco	—	6,140	5,361	7,416	5,135	5,841	2,442
Shanghai, China	6,140	—	4,825	4,899	1,097	4,951	7,448
Stockholm	5,361	4,825	—	9,696	5,051	501	4,123
Sydney, Australia	7,416	4,899	9,696	—	4,866	9,696	9,758
Tokyo	5,135	1,097	5,051	4,866	—	5,249	6,772
Warsaw	5,841	4,951	501	9,696	5,249	—	4,457
Washington, D.C.	2,442	7,448	4,123	9,758	6,772	4,457	—

Source: Encyclopaedia Britannica.

ASTRONOMY

A Soviet View of a Lunar Base

By Vladislav V. Shevchenko

The Apollo 10 Command Module orbits the far side of the Moon some 60 miles from the lunar surface. NASA photo.

After a lengthy silence about the Moon, specialists have again turned their attention to our planet's natural satellite. They predict that the last decade of our century may mark a new "lunar renaissance."

The last *Apollo* expedition left the Moon in December 1972. The last flight of robotic spacecraft to the Moon, *Luna 24*, returned to Earth with samples of lunar material in 1976. Launches of new lunar spacecraft are not expected earlier than the end of the 1980s or the beginning of the 1990s.

Perhaps by the 50th anniversary of the launch of Earth's first artificial satellite [*Sputnik* was launched in 1957], the scientific lunar bases will begin to function. Although the project may not be realized before 2000, lunar specialists already consider it necessary to set the strategy of exploration of the Moon toward the creation of a multiglobal civilization.

The scientific desirability of lunar laboratories is unquestioned. They can aid in studying the origin and evolution of the solar system, including Earth's early history; they can provide new measurements of near and deep space; and they can support unique experiments in physics, chemistry, biology, and other sciences. Less clear are practical questions about how to realize the project and justify the expenditures it requires.

Calculations show that for large constructions in near-Earth orbits, it is more sensible to use lunar materials. Projects such as building solar power satellites are impractical without using lunar resources and lunar industry.

A Museum of Universal Antiquities

Despite intensive study of the Moon by spacecraft in the 1960s and 1970s, many questions remain unsolved. The Moon retains valuable information about the early steps in the evolution of the solar system—processes that took place in the first five hundred million years of its existence.

During its formation the lunar crust may have melted to a depth of at least several kilometers. If a similar process occurred on Earth, it would be important to understanding the formation of the core and mantle. More than that, intensive bombardment by falling comets and meteorites, traces of which are clearly visible on the Moon, could have greatly influenced the evolution of Earth's continents more than 3.8 billion years ago. We can determine the age of the Moon's most ancient (bedrock) areas and how the bedrock changed depending on depth using samples from the ancient intrusions and lower parts of the crust.

Such samples may be found among the ejecta of gigantic circular structures called basins. Lunar basins, part of which are filled with maria [*mare*, from the Latin for *sea*, is a dark, smooth region on the Moon's surface] probably were formed by impacting bodies with diameters up to 200 kilometers (124.28 mi.). These giant basins were formed in the earliest period of lunar history—from 4.25 to 3.85 billion years ago.

Detailed research on the Moon's ancient regolith [the surface layer of loose rock fragments and dust] in the open plains, as well as the study of natural exposures of the deeper layers, may give us unique data about the earliest events in our planet's history. Recently we have learned that fragments thrown out from the Moon by large impacts can be found on Earth's surface. Meteorites recently found in Antarctica are parts of lunar bedrock. We can probably assume the reciprocal: perhaps on the Moon the traces of gigantic ejecta from Earth can be found in noticeable layers.

On the Moon, we might search for a layer of regolith 65 million years old. One of the biggest ecological catastrophes in Earth's history corresponds to this period. More than half of the plant and animal species on our planet at that time, including the dinosaurs, were destroyed. Because geochemical analysis showed a high content of the rare metal iridium in the rocks of that period, scientists have speculated that those tragic events are connected with the intensive bombardment of Earth by comets or asteroids. The high iridium content is more characteristic of these cosmic bodies than of Earth's surface materials. Study of the lunar surface may find places where substances were thrown out from Earth.

In recent years, a new subject has attracted interest—the atypical bright formations on the lunar surface. They are not expressed in relief, and their borders do not correspond to topographic features. Their light or dark structures look like turbulent pictures of a gaseous atmosphere.

Scientists have confirmed a connection between these albedo (reflectivity) anomalies and magnetic anomalies. The nature of this relationship is still un-

solved. One interesting hypothesis suggests that these structures are the traces of the fall of comet nuclei on the Moon's surface. A lunar base would permit detailed on-site study of such structures related to global catastrophes in the inner solar system.

Sampling the Lunar Surface

The investigation of the first samples brought back to Earth showed that lunar regolith contained tracks of fast and heavy particles of solar and galactic origin. The tracks of these particles allowed us to estimate the time materials were exposed on the surface and to establish the history of soil transport. Knowing the time of irradiation and the speed of erosion, we can calculate the solar particle flux in the past and try to determine the solar activity at that time.

So far, only surface samples or drilled columns no more than two meters deep have been collected and studied by this method. To use field geology methods effectively on the Moon, samples of the ancient layered regolith hundreds of meters thick have to be taken. These can be found inside deep cracks or craters where the steep slopes prohibit the accumulation of overlying regolith.

Material for a Lunar Base

The first use of local material that the designers of lunar settlements will consider will be for life support. The use of volatiles [easily evaporated substances, such as water] and internal lunar processes has intrinsic scientific value as well as very practical meaning for the lunar base.

Although the lunar interior is supposed to be solid to a depth of hundreds of kilometers, the so-called lunar transient phenomena have frequently been observed. [Many observers have reported glowing red spots, gas emissions, and possible ash ventings from the Moon's surface, but the nature of these phenomena is not understood.] Unfortunately, most of these sightings were visual. But gas emitted from the lunar interior is verified by exper-

Astronaut Alan L. Bean is photographed with tools and carrier for the Apollo Lunar Hand Tools (ALHT) during extravehicular activity on the surface of the Moon. NASA photo.

iments left on the Moon and also by mass spectrometers on the *Apollo 15* and *16* orbiting spacecraft.

The connection between the transient phenomena and internal activity is indirectly confirmed by several coincidences of surface effects and interior seismic activity. These processes may be occurring along a system of very deep faults inside the Moon. The driving mechanism could be tides raised by Earth.

It is interesting that the Moon's surface is completely dry. However, two spectrograms of transient phenomena show the presence of hydrogen and carbon in the assumed discharge of subsurface gases. If these outflows are coming from reservoirs located relatively close to the surface, then under certain conditions these gases might accumulate on the surface. So, according to the hypothesis, on the inner sides of polar craters, never illuminated by sunlight, there could be methane, carbon dioxide, hydrogen sulfide and water ice.

An optimistic view might be that layers of water ice mixed with carbon dioxide, methane, argon, and other components can reach a thickness of several meters. But at the same time, some laboratory work has shown that the rate of erosion of water ice by interplanetary and magnetospheric particles is approximately equal to the expected rate of formation of water ice layers. Thus, even in the coldest lunar polar regions, permanently shadowed from sunlight, significant accumulation of water ice is not very probable. The question of the existence of lunar polar ice can be solved by specialized experiments on board a spacecraft equipped with a gamma spectrometer and an electromagnetic probe.

We can make more certain predictions about retrieving oxygen and water from the Moon's surface rocks. Three principal rock-forming minerals contain significant amounts of oxygen in different combinations: pyroxene—44 percent, plagioclase—46 percent and ilmenite—32 percent.

The most promising prospect from the technological point of view is the method of deriving water vapor from lunar surface rocks rich in ilmenite. Heating the mineral ore to temperatures of about 1,000 degrees Celsius starts the process, which releases about 10 percent of the ore's oxygen. If the ilmenite soil were used as a raw material, then the resulting product would be pure iron.

Solar radiation could be the first source of energy for a lunar base. But we should not rule out other sources such as nuclear energy that do not depend on a day/night cycle.

The lunar soil should be used for construction of different facilities. Engineers and architects believe that the fine lunar dust, abundant on the surface, would be wonderful material for concrete.

21st Century Lunar Settlements

The first studies of permanently occupied lunar bases appeared more than twenty years ago. The International Astronautical Federation established a special committee to coordinate work on scientific laboratories on the Moon. The joint work of scientific organizations from many countries in studying Antarctica served as a pattern.

After concluding their lunar missions in the '70s, the leading space powers concentrated on near-Earth space using piloted spaceflight. Starting from accumulated experience and predictions for the future, a group of experts at the Johnson Space Center in Houston concluded that in a few decades the term "near-Earth space" will include the Moon. The great possibilities of lunar industry will drive development of all near-Earth space inside the lunar orbit. Therefore, the establishment of a lunar base is once again an urgent subject.

There are several possible versions of such a base. In the simplest one an automatic facility for industrial processing of the lunar soil will land in the Ocean of Storms, near the equator. After the station processes a defined amount of the necessary resources, it will be supplemented by a habitable module. By remote control from Earth, a lunar rover will transport the habitable module into a specially built or existing depression, where a layer of lunar regolith will protect it from radiation as well as from rapid cooling at night.

When the first inhabitants land, the automatic equipment will fully supply the base with oxygen and water from local resources, although the hydrogen will initially be supplied from Earth. Later trips will bring necessary equipment and other crew members, up to a total of twelve people.

A more ambitious program will require a series of reconnaissance and technological trips with both automated and piloted flights. A large station orbiting Earth is assumed for the transportation node, and all lunar operations will be controlled from an orbiting station around the Moon.

Each module of the lunar settlements could consist of an aluminum cylinder located at a depth of about three meters and covered with a layer of soil two to five meters deep. The foundation for life support will be a closed ecological system regenerating water and air. Since oxygen will be supplied from local resources, it will be necessary to transport from Earth only nitrogen and water or hydrogen for producing water under lunar conditions.

It is possible to grow plants on lunar soil in a special greenhouse. Plants will supply sufficient oxygen for breeding small domestic animals (such as rabits) to provide the inhabitants of the base with balanced nutrition.

The forms of scientific and industrial facilities correspond to their functions. Absence of atmosphere and low gravity will allow us to construct light and economical structures of huge dimensions. For example, a telescope on the Moon with a mirror diameter of 25 meters (82 ft) would give a resolution of 0.0001 arc seconds. [One arc second equals 1/3,600 of a degree. The circle of the sky is divided into 360 degrees.] Using this telescope in the lunar conditions would enable us to observe planets of nearby stars or details in the centers of nearby galaxies.

Accomplishing such a grandiose project would require significant financial resources. International cooperation will substantially decrease the investment required by each individual country. I had an opportunity to discuss lunar bases with experts from Johnson Space Center, the initiators of the project. During these discussions, as well as in their publications, these scientists have emphasized uniting the efforts of different countries, primarily the leading space powers, not only to accomplish scientific goals but also to further develop space for peaceful purposes. □

Vladislav V. Shevchenko is Chief, Lunar and Planetary Research Department, Sternberg State Astronomical Institute, Moscow University and is chairman of the Lunar Task Group of the International Astronomical Union's Working Group on Solar System Nomenclature. This article is reprinted from the *Planetary Report,* November-December 1988, and is published with permission of the author and The Planetary Society.

Astronomical Terms

Planet is the term used for a body in orbit around the Sun. Its origin is Greek; even in antiquity it was known that a number of "stars" did not stay in the same relative positions to the others. There were five such restless "stars" known—Mercury, Venus, Mars, Jupiter, and Saturn—and the Greeks referred to them as *planetes,* a word which means "wanderers." That the earth is one of the planets was realized later. The additional planets were discovered after the invention of the telescope.

Satellite (or *moon*) is the term for a body in orbit around a planet. As long as our own Moon was the only moon known, there was no need for a general term for the moons of planets. But when Galileo Galilei discovered the four main moons of the planet Jupiter, Johannes Kepler (in a letter to Galileo) suggested "satellite" (from the Latin *satelles,* which means attendant) as a general term for such bodies. The word is used interchangeably with "moons": astronomers speak and write about the moons of Neptune, Saturn, etc. A satellite may be any size.

Orbit is the term for the path traveled by a body in space. It comes from the Latin *orbis,* which means circle, circuit, etc., and *orbita,* which means a rut or a wheel track. Theoretically, four mathematical figures are possible orbits: two are open (hyperbola and parabola) and two are closed (ellipse and circle), but in reality all closed orbits are ellipses. These ellipses can be nearly circular, as are the orbits of most planets, or very elongated, as are the orbits of most comets. In these orbits, the Sun is in one focal point of the ellipse, and the other focal point is empty. In the orbits of satellites, the planet stands in one focal point of the orbit. The *primary* of an orbit is the body in the focal point. For planets, the point of the orbit closest to the Sun is the *perihelion,* and the point farthest from the Sun is the *aphelion.* For orbits around the Earth, the corresponding terms are *perigee* and *apogee;* for orbits around other planets, corresponding terms are coined when necessary.

Two heavenly bodies are in *inferior* or *superior conjunction* when they have the same Right Ascension, or are in the same meridian; that is, when one is due north or south of the other. If the bodies appear near each other as seen from the Earth, they will rise and set at the same time. They are in *opposition* when they are opposite each other in the heavens: when one rises as the other is setting. *Greatest elongation* is the greatest apparent angular distance from the Sun, when a planet is most favorably suited for observation. Mercury can be seen with the naked eye only at about this time. An *occultation* of a planet or star is an eclipse of it by some other body, usually the Moon.

Stars are the basic units of population in the universe. Our Sun is the nearest star. Stars are very large (our Sun has a diameter of 865,400 miles—a comparatively small star). Stars are composed of intensely hot gasses, deriving their energy from nuclear reactions going on in their interiors.

Galaxies are immense systems containing billions of stars. All that you can see in the sky (with a very few exceptions) belongs to our galaxy—a system of roughly 200 billion stars. The few exceptions are other galaxies. Our own galaxy, the rim of which we see as the "Milky Way," is about 100,000 light-years in diameter and about 10,000 light-years in thickness. Its shape is roughly that of a thick lens; more precisely it is a "spiral nebula," a term first used for other galaxies when they were discovered and before it was realized that these were separate and distant galaxies. The spiral galaxy nearest to ours is in the constellation Andromeda. It is somewhat larger than our own galaxy and is visible to the naked eye.

Recent developments in radio astronomy have revealed additional celestial objects that are still incompletely understood.

Quasars ("quasi-stellar" objects), originally thought to be peculiar stars in our own galaxy, are now believed to be the most remote objects in the Universe. Spectral studies of quasars indicate that some are 9 billion light years away and moving away from us at the incredible rate of 150,000 miles per second. Quasars emit tremendous amounts of light and microwave radiation. Although they appear to be far smaller than ordinary galaxies, some quasars emit as much as 100 times more energy. Some astronomers believe that quasars are the cores of violently exploding galaxies.

Pulsars are believed to be rapidly spinning neutron stars, so crushed by their own gravity that a million tons of their matter would hardly fill a thimble. Pulsars are so named because they emit bursts of radio energy at regular intervals. Some have pulse rates as rapid as 10 per second.

A *black hole* is the theoretical end-product of the total gravitational collapse of a massive star or group of stars. Crushed even smaller than an incredibly dense neutron star, such a body may become so dense that not even light can escape its gravitational field. It has been suggested that black holes may be detectable in proximity to normal stars when they draw matter away from their visible neighbors. Strong sources of X-rays in our galaxy and beyond may also indicate the presence of black holes. One possible black hole now being studied is the invisible companion to a supergiant star in the constellation Cygnus.

Origin of the Universe

Evidence uncovered in recent years tends to confirm that the universe began its existence about 15 billion years ago as a dense, hot globule of gas expanding rapidly outward. At that time, the universe contained nothing but hydrogen and a small amount of helium. There were no stars and no planets. The first stars probably began to condense out of the primordial hydrogen when the universe was about 100 million years old and continued to form as the universe aged. The Sun arose in this way 4.6 billion years ago. Many stars came into being before the Sun was formed; many others formed after the Sun appeared. This process continues, and through telescopes we can now see stars forming out of compressed pockets of hydrogen in outer space.

Birth and Death of a Star

When a star begins to form as a dense cloud of gas, the individual hydrogen atoms fall toward the center of the cloud under the force of the star's gravity. As they fall, they pick up speed, and their energy increases. The increase in energy heats the gas. When this process has continued for some millions of years, the temperature reaches about 20 million degrees Fahrenheit. At this temperature, the hydrogen within the star ignites and burns in a continuing series of nuclear reactions in which all the elements in the universe are manufactured from hydrogen and helium. The onset of these re-

Astronomical Constants

Light-year (distance traveled by light in one year)	5,880,000,000,000 mi.
Parsec (parallax of one second, for stellar distances)	3.259 light-yrs.
Velocity of light	186,281.7 mi./sec.
Astronomical unit (A.U.), or mean distance earth-to-sun	ca. 93,000,000 mi.[1]
Mean distance, earth to moon	238,860 mi.
General precession	50".26
Obliquity of the ecliptic	$23° 27'8".26–0".4684(t–1900)$[2]
Equatorial radius of the earth	3963.34 statute mi.
Polar radius of the earth	3949.99 statute mi.
Earth's mean radius	3958.89 statute mi.
Oblateness of the earth	1/297
Equatorial horizontal parallax of the moon	57' 2".70
Earth's mean velocity in orbit	18.5 mi./sec.
Sidereal year	365d.2564
Tropical year	365d.2422
Sidereal month	27d.3217
Synodic month	29d.5306
Mean sidereal day	23h56m4s.091 of mean solar time
Mean solar day	24h3m56s.555 of sidereal time

1. Actual mean distance derived from radar bounces: 92,935,700 mi. The value of 92,897,400 mi. (based on parallax of 8".80) is used in calculations. 2. *t* refers to the year in question, for example, 1990.

actions marks the birth of a star. When a star begins to exhaust its hydrogen supply, its life nears an end. The first sign of old age is a swelling and reddening of its outer regions. Such an aging, swollen star is called a red giant. The Sun, a middle-aged star, will probably swell to a red giant in 5 billion years, vaporizing the earth and any creatures that may be left on its surface. When all its fuel has been exhausted, a star cannot generate sufficient pressure at its center to balance the crushing force of gravity. The star collapses under the force of its own weight; if it is a small star, it collapses gently and remains collapsed. Such a collapsed star, at its life's end, is called a white dwarf. The Sun will probably end its life in this way. A different fate awaits a large star. Its final collapse generates a violent explosion, blowing the innards of the star out into space. There, the materials of the exploded star mix with the primeval hydrogen of the universe. Later in the history of the galaxy, other stars are formed out of this mixture. The Sun is one of these stars. It contains the debris of countless other stars that exploded before the Sun was born.

Supernova 1987A

On Feb. 24, 1987, Canadian astronomer Ian Shelter at the Las Campas Observatory in Chile discovered a supernova—an exploding star—from a photograph taken on Feb. 23 of the Large Megallanic Cloud, a galaxy some 160,000 light years away from Earth. Astronomers believe that the dying star was Sanduleak −69°202, a 10-million-year-old blue supergiant.

Supernova 1987A was the closest and best studied supernova in almost 400 years. The last known one was observed by Johannes Kepler in 1604, four years before the telescope was invented.

On January 18 1989, astronomers reported evidence that they had sighted the birth of a pulsar, an extremely dense star spinning about 2,000 times per second in the debris left over from the explosion of supernova 1987A. If this discovery is confirmed, it would mark the first time the creation of a pulsar has been observed. However, no one has seen it since that night.

Formation of the Solar System

The sun's age was calculated in 1989 to be 4.49 billion years old, less than the 4.7 billion years previously believed. It was formed from a cloud of hydrogen mixed with small amounts of other substances that had been manufactured in the bodies of other stars before the Sun was born. This was the parent cloud of the solar system. The dense hot gas at the center of the cloud gave rise to the Sun; the outer regions of the cloud—cooler and less dense—gave birth to the planets.

Our solar system consists of one star (the Sun), nine planets and all their moons, several thousand minor planets called asteroids or planetoids, and an equally large number of comets.

The Sun

All the stars, including our Sun, are gigantic balls of superheated gas, kept hot by atomic reactions in their centers. In our Sun, this atomic reaction is hydrogen fusion: four hydrogen atoms are combined to form one helium atom. The temperature at the core of our Sun must be 20 million degrees centigrade, the surface temperature is around 6,000 degrees centigrade, or about 11,000 degrees Fahrenheit. The diameter of the sun is 865,400 miles, and its surface area is approximately 12,000 times that of the Earth. Compared with other stars, our Sun is just a bit below average in size and temperature. Its fuel supply (hydrogen) is estimated to last for another 5 billion years.

Our Sun is not motionless in space; in fact it has two proper motions. One is a seemingly straight-line motion in the direction of the constellation Hercules at the rate of about 12 miles per second. But since the Sun is a part of the Milky Way system and since the whole system rotates slowly around its own center, the Sun also moves at the rate of 175 miles per second as part of the rotating Milky Way system.

In addition to this motion, the Sun rotates on its axis. Observing the motion of sun spots (darkish areas which look like enormous whirling storms) and solar flares, which are usually associated with

OUR PLACE IN THE GALAXY

THE MILKY WAY GALAXY. Our sun is one of 200-billion stars banded together by gravity in an enormous spiral disk called the Milky Way Galaxy. The arrow indicates our position three-fifths of the way out from the center. It takes light 100,000 years to traverse our Galaxy, one of billions of galaxies in the universe. Copyright © 1984, Hansen Planetarium, Salt Lake City, Utah. Reproduced with Permission.

sun spots, has shown that the rotational period of our Sun is just short of 25 days. But this figure is valid for the Sun's equator only; the sections near the Sun's poles seem to have a rotational period of 34 days. Naturally, since the Sun generates its own heat and light, there is no temperature difference between poles and equator.

What we call the Sun's "surface" is technically known as the photosphere. Since the whole Sun is a ball of very hot gas, there is really no such thing as a surface; it is a question of visual impression. The next layer outside the photosphere is known as the chromosphere, which extends several thousand miles beyond the photosphere. It is in steady motion, and often enormous prominences can be seen to burst from it, extending as much as 100,000 miles into space. Outside the chromosphere is the corona. The corona consists of very tenuous gases (essentially hydrogen) and makes a magnificent sight when the Sun is eclipsed.

The Moon

Mercury and Venus do not have any moons. Therefore, the Earth is the planet nearest the Sun to be orbited by a moon.

The next planet farther out, Mars, has two very small moons. Jupiter has four major moons and twelve minor ones. Saturn, the ringed planet, has fifteen known moons, of which one (Titan) is larger than the planet Mercury. Uranus has five known moons (four of them large) as well as rings, while Neptune has one large and one small moon. Pluto has one moon, discovered in 1978. Some astronomers still consider Pluto to be a "runaway moon" of Neptune.

Our own Moon, with a diameter of 2,160 miles, is one of the larger moons in our solar system and

is especially large when compared with the planet that it orbits. In fact, the common center of gravity of the Earth-Moon system is only about 1,000 miles below the Earth's surface. The closest our Moon can come to us (its perigee) is 221,463 miles; the farthest it can go away (its apogee) is 252,710 miles. The period of rotation of our Moon is equal to its period of revolution around the Earth. Hence from Earth we can see only one hemisphere of the Moon. Both periods are 27 days, 7 hours, 43 minutes and 11.47 seconds. But while the rotation of the Moon is constant, its velocity in its orbit is not, since it moves more slowly in apogee than in perigee. Consequently, some portions near the rim which are not normally visible will appear briefly. This phenomenon is called "libration," and by taking advantage of the librations, astronomers have succeeded in mapping approximately 59% of the lunar surface. The other 41% can never be seen from the earth but has been mapped by American and Russian Moon-orbiting spacecraft.

Though the Moon goes around the Earth in the time mentioned, the interval from new Moon to new Moon is 29 days, 12 hours, 44 minutes and 2.78 seconds. This delay of nearly two days is due to the fact that the Earth is moving around the Sun, so that the Moon needs two extra days to reach a spot in its orbit where no part is illuminated by the Sun, as seen from Earth.

If the plane of the Earth's orbit around the Sun (the ecliptic) and the plane of the Moon's orbit around the Earth were the same, the Moon would be eclipsed by the Earth every time it is full, and the Sun would be eclipsed by the Moon every time the Moon is "new" (it would be better to call it the "black Moon" when it is in this position). But because the two orbits do not coincide, the Moon's shadow normally misses the Earth and the Earth's

The Brightest Stars

Star	Constellation	Mag.	Dist. (l.-y.)	Star	Constellation	Mag.	Dist. (l.-y.)
Sirius	Canis Major	−1.6	8	Antares	Scorpius	1.2	170
Canopus	Carina	−0.9	650	Fomalhaut	Piscis Austrinus	1.3	27
Alpha Centauri	Centaurus	+0.1	4	Deneb	Cygnus	1.3	465
Vega[1]	Lyra	0.1	23	Regulus	Leo	1.3	70
Capella	Auriga	0.2	42	Beta Crucis	Crux	1.5	465
Arcturus	Boötes	0.2	32	Eta Carinae	Carina	1–7	—
Rigel	Orion	0.3	545	Alpha-one Crucis	Crux	1.6	150
Procyon	Canis Minor	0.5	10	Castor	Gemini	1.6	44
Achernar	Eridanus	0.6	70	Gamma Crucis	Crux	1.6	
Beta Centauri	Centaurus	0.9	130	Epsilon Canis Majoris	Canis Major	1.6	325
Altair	Aquila	0.9	18	Epsilon Ursae Majoris	Ursa Major	1.7	50
Betelgeuse	Orion	0.9	600	Bellatrix	Orion	1.7	215
Aldebaran	Taurus	1.1	54	Lambda Scorpii	Scorpius	1.7	205
Spica	Virgo	1.2	190	Epsilon Carinae	Carina	1.7	325
Pollux	Gemini	1.2	31	Mira	Cetus	2–10	250

1. In 1984, the discovery of a possible planetary system around Vega was reported.

shadow misses the Moon. The inclination of the two orbital planes to each other is 5 degrees. The tides are, of course, caused by the Moon with the help of the Sun, but in the open ocean they are surprisingly low, amounting to about one yard. The very high tides which can be observed near the shore in some places are due to funnelling effects of the shorelines. At new Moon and at full Moon the tides raised by the Moon are reinforced by the Sun; these are the "spring tides." If the Sun's tidal power acts at right angles to that of the Moon (quarter moons) we get the low "neap tides."

Our Planet Earth

The Earth, circling the Sun at an average distance of 93 million miles, is the fifth largest planet and the third from the Sun. It orbits the Sun at a speed of 67,000 miles per hour, making one revolution in 365 days, 5 hours, 48 minutes, and 45.51 seconds. The Earth completes one rotation on its axis every 23 hours, 56 minutes, and 4.09 seconds. Actually a bit pear-shaped rather than a true sphere, the Earth has a diameter of 7,927 miles at the Equator and a few miles less at the poles. It has an estimated mass of about 6.6 sextillion tons, with an average density of 5.52 grams per cubic centimeter. The Earth's surface area encompasses 196,949,970 square miles of which about three-fourths is water.

Origin of the Earth. The Earth, along with the other planets, is believed to have been born 4.5 billion years ago as a solidified cloud of dust and gases left over from the creation of the Sun. For perhaps 500 million years, the interior of the Earth stayed solid and relatively cool, perhaps 2000° F. The main ingredients, according to the best available evidence, were iron and silicates, with small amounts of other elements, some of them radioactive. As millions of years passed, energy released by radioactive decay—mostly of uranium, thorium, and potassium—gradually heated the Earth, melting some of its constituents. The iron melted before the silicates and, being heavier, sank toward the center. This forced upward the silicates that it found there. After many years, the iron reached the center, almost 4,000 miles deep, and began to accumulate. No eyes were around at that time to view the turmoil which must have taken place on the face of the Earth—gigantic heaves and bubbling of the surface, exploding volcanoes, and flowing lava covering everything in sight. Finally, the iron in the center accumulated as the core. Around it, a thin but fairly stable crust of solid rock formed as the Earth cooled. Depressions in the crust were natural basins in which water, rising from the interior of the planet through volcanoes and fissures, collected to form the oceans. Slowly the Earth acquired its present appearance.

The Earth Today. As a result of radioactive heating over millions of years, the Earth's molten *core* is probably fairly hot today, around 11,000° F. By comparison, lead melts at around 800° F. Most of the Earth's 2,100-mile-thick core is liquid, but there is evidence that the center of the core is solid. The liquid outer portion, about 95% of the core, is constantly in motion, causing the Earth to have a magnetic field that makes compass needles point north and south. The details are not known, but the latest evidence suggests that planets which have a magnetic field probably have a solid core or a partially liquid one.

Outside the core is the Earth's *mantle*, 1,800 miles thick, and extending nearly to the surface. The mantle is composed of heavy silicate rock, similar to that brought up by volcanic eruptions. It is somewhere between liquid and solid, slightly yielding, and therefore contributing to an active, moving Earth. Most of the Earth's radioactive material is in the thin *crust* which covers the mantle, but some is in the mantle and continues to give off heat. The crust's thickness ranges from 5 to 25 miles.

Scientists recently discovered that the Earth's core is not a perfect sphere. X-ray like images of inside the Earth show that there are vast mountains six to seven miles high and deep valleys on the core. These features are in an upside down relationship to the Earth's surface.

Continental Drift. A great deal of recent evidence confirms the long-disputed theory that the continents of the Earth, made mostly of relatively light granite, float in the slightly yielding mantle, like logs in a pond. For many years it had been noticed that if North and South America could be pushed

Data for Sun, Moon, and Planets

	Mean distance from Sun in millions of miles	Period of revolution around the Sun	Eccentricity of orbit	Inclination to ecliptic ° '		Diameter (miles)	Period of rotation on axis	Inclination of equator to orbit plane °	Surface gravity (earth = 1)	Density $H_2O = 1$	Number of satellites	Mean velocity in orbit (mi./sec.)	Max. stellar mag.
Sun	—	—	—		—	865,400	24d. 64²	7.2	28	1.4	0		−26.7
Moon	—	(27d. 322)¹	0.05	5	8	2,160	27d. 322	6.7	0.16	3.3	0	0.63	−12.6
Mercury	36.00	87d. 969	0.21	7	0	3,100	58. 66d	7	0.28	3.8	0	30	−1.2
Venus	67.27	224d. 701	0.01	3	24	7,700	243. 2d	—	0.85	5.1	0	22	−4.4
Earth	93.00	365d. 256	0.02	0	0	7,927³	23h 56m	23.4	1.00	5.5	1	18.5	—
Mars	141.71	1y. 881	0.09	1	51	4,200	24h 37m	25.2	0.38	4.0	2	15	−2.8
Jupiter	483.88	11y. 862	0.05	1	18	88,700³	9h 50m²	3.1	2.6	1.3	16	8	−2.5
Saturn	887.14	29y. 458	0.06	2	29	75,100³	16h 39m²	26.8	1.2	0.7	21+	6	−0.4
Uranus	1783.98	84y. 013	0.05	0	46	32,000	16. 8h	97	1.1	1.3	15	4	+5.7
Neptune	2795.46	164y. 794	0.01	1	46	27,700	17h 50m	29	1.4	2.2	8	3	+7.8
Pluto	3675.27	248y. 430	0.25	17	9	1,420(?)	6d 8h(?)	—	—	>1.0	1	<3	+14

1. Period of revolution around the earth. 2. Voyager 1 and 2 data. 3. The equatorial diameters of the earth, Jupiter, and Saturn are given; polar diameters are: earth 7,900.0 mi., Jupiter 82,789 mi., Saturn 67,170 mi. OTHER DATA ON THE EARTH: Equatorial circumference, 24,902.4 mi.; total area, 196,949,970 sq. mi.; mass, 6.6 sextillion tons; mean diameter, 7,917.8 mi.

toward western and southern Europe and western Africa, they would fit like pieces in a jigsaw puzzle. Today, there is little question—the continents have drifted widely and continue to do so.

In 10 million years, the world as we know it may be unrecognizable, with California drifting out to sea, Florida joining South America, and Africa moving farther away from Europe and Asia.

The Earth's Atmosphere. The thin blanket of atmosphere that envelops the Earth extends several hundred miles into space. From sea level—the very bottom of the ocean of air—to a height of about 60 miles, the air in the atmosphere is made up of the same gases in the same ratio: about 78% nitrogen, 21% oxygen, and the remaining 1% being a mixture of argon, carbon dioxide, and tiny amounts of neon, helium, krypton, xenon, and other gases. The atmosphere becomes less dense with increasing altitude: more than three-fourths of the Earth's huge envelope is concentrated in the first 5 to 10 miles above the surface. At sea level, a cubic foot of the atmosphere weighs about an ounce and a quarter. The entire atmosphere weighs 5,700,000,000,000,000 tons, and the force with which gravity holds it in place causes it to exert a pressure of nearly 15 pounds per square inch. Going out from the Earth's surface, the atmosphere is divided into five regions. The regions, and the heights to which they extend, are: *Troposphere,* 0 to 7 miles (at middle latitudes); *stratosphere,* 7 to 30 miles; *mesosphere,* 30 to 50 miles; *thermosphere,* 50 to 400 miles; and *exosphere,* above 400 miles. The boundaries between each of the regions are known respectively as the *tropopause, stratopause, mesopause,* and *thermopause.* Alternate terms often used for the layers above the troposphere are *ozonosphere* (for stratosphere) and *ionosphere* for the remaining upper layers.

The Seasons. Seasons are caused by the 23.4 degree tilt of the Earth's axis, which alternately turns the North and South Poles toward the Sun. Times when the Sun's apparent path crosses the Equator are known as *equinoxes.* Times when the Sun's apparent path is at the greatest distance from the Equator are known as *solstices.* The lengths of the days are most extreme at each solstice. If the Earth's axis were perpendicular to the plane of the Earth's orbit around the Sun, there would be no seasons, and the days always would be equal in length. Since the Earth's axis is at an angle, the Sun strikes the Earth directly at the Equator only twice a year: in March (vernal equinox) and September (autumnal equinox). In the Northern Hemisphere, spring begins at the vernal equinox, summer at the summer solstice, fall at the autumnal equinox, and winter at the winter solstice. The situation is reversed in the Southern Hemisphere.

Mercury

Mercury is the planet nearest the Sun. Appropriately named for the wing-footed Roman messenger of the gods, Mercury whizzes around the Sun at a speed of 30 miles per second, completing one circuit in 88 days. The planet rotates on its axis over a period of nearly 59 days. Daytime on cratered Mercury is hot, about 800 degrees F., although at night the temperature may fall to room temperature. Mercury has no moons, but it does have a trace of atmosphere and a weak magnetic field, according to findings of Mariner 10. Until this spacecraft flew by Mercury in 1974 and 1975, very little was known about the planet, primarily because of its short angular distance from the Sun as seen from Earth, which puts it too close to the Sun to be easily observed.

● Mercury is a naked eye object at morning or evening twilight when it is at greatest elongation.

Venus

Although Venus is Earth's nearest neighbor, little is known about this planet because it is permanently covered by thick clouds. In 1962, Soviet and American space probes, coupled with Earth-based radar and infrared spectroscopy, began slowly unraveling some of the mystery surrounding Venus. According to the latest results, Venus' atmosphere is about 96% carbon dioxide, exerting a pressure

PLANET SIZES

PLANET SIZES. Shown from left to right: Mercury, Venus, Earth, Mars, Jupiter, Saturn, Uranus, Neptune, and Pluto. The sizes of the planets vary greatly from tiny Pluto (smaller than our moon) to giant Jupiter. If Jupiter were the size of a basketball, the Earth would be the size of a grape and Pluto would only be as large as a grape seed.

Although larger and more massive than all the other planets and moons combined, Jupiter still has 50 times too little mass to be a star. The great red spot, larger than two Earths, is a giant cyclonic storm in Jupiter's turbulent atmosphere. Copyright © 1984 Hansen Planetarium, Salt Lake City, Utah. Reproduced with Permission.

at the surface 90.5 times greater than Earth's. Walking on Venus would be as difficult as walking a half-mile beneath the ocean. Because of the thick blanket of carbon dioxide, a "greenhouse effect" exists on Venus: Venus intercepts twice as much of the Sun's light as does the Earth. The light enters freely through carbon dioxide gas and is changed to heat radiation in molecular collisions. But carbon dioxide prevents the heat from escaping. Consequently, the temperature of the surface of Venus is over 800 degrees F., hot enough to melt lead. The atmosphere appears to have five distinct layers and to flash almost continuously with lightning. Radar bounced off the planet recently revealed what appear to be large craters and an immense, 900-mile-long canyon. Venus rotates in retrograde motion for a reason not yet known.

In March 1982, the Soviet *Venera 13* and *14* landing craft made the first actual test samples of the Venusian surface by x-ray fluorescence spectroscopy which gave an element-by-element analysis. The terrestrial samples revealed a terrain of basaltic uplands and lowlands.

The unmanned NASA spacecraft *Magellan* was launched on May 4, 1989, from the shuttle *Atlantis.* It will arrive at Venus August 1990 and will map up to 90% of the planet. (*Also see* Space Section).

● Venus is the brightest of all the planets and is often visible in the morning or evening, when it is frequently referred to as the Morning Star or Evening Star. At its brightest, it can sometimes be seen with the naked eye in full daylight, if one knows where to look.

Mars

Mars, on the other side of the Earth from Venus, is Venus' direct opposite in terms of physical properties. Its atmosphere is cold, thin, and transparent, and readily permits observation of the planet's fea-

tures. We know more about Mars than any other planet except Earth. Mars is a forbidding, rugged planet with huge volcanoes and deep chasms. The largest volcano, Olympus Mons rises 78,000 feet above the surface, higher than Mount Everest. The plains of Mars are pockmarked by the hits of thousands of meteors over the years. Most of our information about Mars comes from the Mariner 9 spacecraft, which orbited the planet in 1971. Mariner 9, photographing 100% of the planet, uncovered spectacular geological formations, including a Martian Grand Canyon that dwarfs the one on Earth. The spacecraft's cameras also recorded what appeared to be dried riverbeds, suggesting the onetime presence of water on the planet. The latter idea gives encouragement to scientists looking for life on Mars, for where there is water, there may be life. However, by 1979, no evidence of life has been found. Temperatures near the equator range from −17 degrees F. in the daytime to −130 degrees F. at night. Mars rotates upon its axis in nearly the same period as Earth—24 hours, 37 minutes—so that a Mars day is almost identical to an Earth day. Mars takes 687 days to make one trip around the Sun. Because of its eccentric orbit Mars' distance from the Sun can vary by about 36 million miles. Its distance from Earth can vary by as much as 200 million miles. The atmosphere of Mars is much thinner than Earth's; atmospheric pressure is about 1% that of our planet. Its gravity is one-third of Earth's. Major constituents are carbon dioxide and nitrogen. Water vapor and oxygen are minor constituents. Mars' polar caps, composed mostly of carbon dioxide, recede and advance according to the Martian seasons. Mars was named for the Roman god of war, because when seen from Earth its distinct red color reminded the ancient people of blood. We know now that the reddish hue reflects the oxidized (rusted) iron in the surface material. The landing of two robot Viking spacecraft on the surface of Mars in 1976 provided more information about Mars in a few months than in all the time that has gone before.

In 1988, the Soviet Union launched two spacecraft to study the geology, climate, and atmosphere of Mars, and explore its moon, Phobos. The attempt was unsuccesful as contact was lost with both spacecraft.

Jupiter

Jupiter, with an equatorial diameter of 88,000 miles, is the largest of a group of planets which differ markedly from the terrestrial planets. The others in the group are Saturn, Uranus, and Neptune. All are large, with very dense atmospheres, and indeed may be giant balls of gas without any perceptible surfaces. They all whirl rapidly around their axes, but more slowly around the Sun, resulting in short days and long years. They have many moons. Majestic Jupiter, named for the king of the Roman gods, rotates so fast that it is greatly flattened at the poles. According to Pioneers 10 and 11, which flew past Jupiter in 1974 and 1975, this planet is a whirling ball of liquid hydrogen with perhaps an Earth-sized iron core. Other atmospheric constituents are helium, methane, and ammonia. Its clouds are probably ammonia ice crystals, becoming ammonia droplets deeper towards the "surface." Temperatures range from perhaps minus 300 degrees F. at the tops of the cloud decks to 100,000 degrees F. or more deep down at the center. The pressure at the center of the planet is estimated to be a crushing 10 million pounds per square inch. The Great Red Spot, a 13,000-mile-wide storm that may have been raging for thousands of years, was found by Voyagers 1 and 2 in 1979 to be cooler at the top than the surrounding clouds, indicating that the Red Spot may tower high above them. Jupiter has 16 satellites. The four largest moons, called Galilean moons, are Europa, Ganymede, Io, and Callisto. *Voyagers 1 and 2* found them to be very different from each other in terms of surface relief, volcanic activity, and other characteristics.

In 1989, evidence from ground-based infrared spectra of Io indicated that the Jovian moon has hydrogen sulfide (H_2S) on its surface and in its atmosphere. It is the first time that the presence of H_2S has been detected outside the Earth.

• Even when nearest the Earth, Jupiter is still almost 400 million miles away. But because of its size, it may rival Venus in brilliance when near. Jupiter's four large moons may be seen through field glasses, moving rapidly around Jupiter and changing their position from night to night.

Saturn

Saturn, the second largest planet in the solar system, is the least dense. It would float in an ocean if there were one big enough to hold it. Aside from its rings, Saturn is very similar to Jupiter except that it is probably colder, being twice as far from the Sun. Recent radar observations of Saturn's rings indicate that they are no more than 10 miles thick, and probably composed of chunks of rock and ice averaging a meter in size. Saturn's ring system begins about 7000 miles from the planet's disk, and extends out to about 35,000 miles. Recent observations have shown Saturn to have between 21 and 23 moons, more than any other planet. The two *Voyager* probes that examined Jupiter in 1979 flew by Saturn in 1980 and 1981.

• Saturn is the last of the planets visible to the naked eye. Saturn is never an object of overwhelming brilliance, but it looks like a bright star. The rings can be seen with a small telescope.

Uranus

Uranus is the seventh planet from the sun, twice as far out as Saturn. The axis of Uranus is tilted at 97 degrees, so it goes around the Sun nearly lying on its side. In 1977, American astronomers made the startling discovery that Uranus has rings, like Saturn.

The first *Voyager* to Uranus took extensive readings of the planet in January 1986. The information received drastically altered perceptions of the planet. Readings of the atmosphere confirmed previous theories that under the cloud layer a hot ocean of superheated water exists. The pressure caused by the thick atmosphere keeps the water, with a temperature that reaches thousands of degrees, from boiling away and the heat keeps the pressure from solidifying the water. This discovery suggested that Uranus differs in composition from Jupiter and Saturn and that the planet may have formed from a coalescence of comets, as comets and the atmosphere and ocean of Uranus are similarly constituted. Other discoveries about the planetary atmosphere were that the pole facing the sun was no hotter than the pole facing away from the sun and that four large methane clouds in the atmosphere were being blown around the planet in the same direction as the planet's rotation, exactly opposite the way in which they should have blown, according to calculations made based on observed conditions.

Another observation was that the planet's magnetic field is 60 degrees out of sync with the poles of the planet. Explanations for this unique feature included the possibility that Uranus may be experiencing a shift of north and south magnetic poles or that the churning of the ocean or of the molten core of the planet has generated this peculiar field. There is, however, insufficent information for any definite conclusions to be drawn.

Voyager 2 also expanded the body of information pertaining to the rings and moons of Uranus. A tenth ring was discovered and the rings were discovered to be formed not of fine particles of ice and dust like Saturn but of chunky objects of rock and large ice "boulders".

In addition to the new ring, ten new moons, smaller in diameter and closer to the planet than the five known moons—Oberon, Titania, Umbriel, Ariel, and Miranda—were discovered.

The *Voyager* craft took the first close-up pictures of Uranus's five largest moons, with surprising results. The pictures of Oberon showed surprising activity going on underneath its icy surface. Titania and Ariel were seen to have large rift-valleys scarring the surface, evidence of some sort of eruption of frozen water from within their surfaces. The surface of Umbriel proved to be inexplicably darker than the other moons with no signs of recent crustal activity. Miranda was the biggest surprise with an unparalled variety of terrain features that caused scientists to label it as a "bizarre hybrid." Uranus can—on rare occasions—become bright enough to be seen with the naked eye, if one knows exactly where to look; normally, a good set of field glasses or a small portable telescope is required.

THE SOLAR SYSTEM

THE SOLAR SYSTEM. Orbiting around the Sun are Mercury, Venus, Earth, Mars, Jupiter, Saturn, Uranus, Neptune, and Pluto. Our Solar System was born nearly five billion years ago out of a cloud of interstellar gas and dust. Gravity caused this nebula to contract and flatten into a spinning disk. Near the center, where the density was greatest, a body formed which was so massive that its internal pressures ignited and sustained a nuclear reaction, creating a star we call the Sun. Elsewhere in the cloud, smaller bodies coalesced and cooled—nine planets, perhaps fifty moons, millions of asteroids, and billions of comets. Within our Milky Way Galaxy, there may be billions of other solar systems. Copyright © 1984 Hansen Planetarium, Salt Lake City, Utah. Reproduced with Permission.

Neptune

Little was known about the giant blue planet Neptune until *Voyager 2* encountered the planet in August 1989. Located 2.8 billion miles from the Sun, it is a frozen world with a turbulent atmosphere. The *Voyager* spacecraft discovered several, possibly five, rings orbiting the planet, a Great Dark Spot (a storm system the size of Mars), a magnetic field, and six additional moons, making the total eight.

Voyager's data confirmed that Neptune's largest moon, Triton, has a nitrogen-rich atmosphere with lesser amounts of methane closer to its icy pink surface.

Pluto

Pluto, the outermost and smallest planet in the solar system, looks more like a terrestrial planet than a gaseous planet. But so little is known about it, that it is difficult to classify. Appropriately named for the Roman god of the underworld, it must be frozen, dark, and dead.

In 1978, light curve studies gave evidence of a moon some 500-600 miles in diameter revolving around Pluto with the same period as Pluto's rotation. Therefore, it stays over the same point on Pluto's surface. In addition, it keeps the same face toward the planet. Recent estimates indicate Pluto's diameter is about 1,420 miles, making the pair more like a double planet than any other in the solar system. Previously, the Earth-Moon system held this distinction. The density of Pluto is slightly greater than that of water.

There is evidence that Pluto has an atmosphere containing methane and polar ice caps that increase and decrease in size with the planet's seasons.

Pluto was predicted by calculation when Percival Lowell noticed irregularities in the orbits of Uranus and Neptune. Clyde Tombaugh discovered the planet in 1930, precisely where Lowell predicted it would be. The name Pluto was chosen because the first two letters represent the initials of Percival Lowell.

• Pluto has the most eccentric orbit in the solar system, bringing it at times closer to the Sun than Neptune. Pluto is now approaching the perihelion of its orbit, and for the rest of this century will be closer to the Sun than Neptune. Even then, it can be seen only with a large telescope.

The Asteroids

Between the orbits of Mars and Jupiter are an estimated 30,000 pieces of rocky debris, known collectively as the asteroids, or planetoids. The first and, incidentally, the largest was discovered during the New Year's night of 1801 by the Italian astronomer Father Piazzi, and its orbit was calculated by the German mathematician Karl Friedrich Gauss. (Gauss invented a new method of calculating orbits on that occasion.) A German amateur astronomer, the physician Olbers, discovered the second asteroid. The number now known, catalogued, and named is around 1,600; the estimated total is about 20 times that figure. A few asteroids do not move in orbits beyond the orbit of Mars, but in orbits which cross the orbit of Mars. The first of them was named Eros because of this peculiar orbit. It had become the rule to bestow female names on the asteroids, but when it was found that Eros crossed the orbit of a major planet, it received

a male name. Since then around two dozen orbit-crossers have been discovered, and they are often referred to as the "male asteroids." A few of them—Albert, Adonis, Apollo, Amor, and Icarus—cross the orbit of the Earth, and two of them may come closer than our Moon; but the crossing is like a bridge crossing a highway, not like two highways intersecting. Hence there is very little danger of collision from these bodies. They are all small, three to five miles in diameter, and therefore very difficult objects to identify, even when quite close. Some scientists believe the asteroids represent the remains of an exploded planet.

Comets

Comets, according to the noted astronomer, Fred L. Whipple, are enormous "snowballs" of frozen gases (mostly carbon dioxide, methane, and water vapor) and contain very little solid material. The whole behavior of comets can then be explained as the behavior of frozen gas being heated by the Sun. When the comet Kohoutek made its first appearance to man in 1973, its behavior seemed to confirm this Whipple theory of the make-up of comets.

Since comets appear in the sky without any warning, people in classical times and especially during the Middle Ages believed that they had a special meaning, which, of course, was bad. Since a natural catastrophe of some sort of a military conflict occurs every year, it was quite simple to blame the comet that happened to be visible. But even in the past, there were some people who used logical reasoning. When, in Roman times, a comet was blamed for the loss of a battle and hence was called a "bad omen," a Roman writer observed that the victors in the battle probably did not think so.

Up until the middle of the sixteenth century, comets were believed to be phenomena of the upper atmosphere; they were usually "explained" as "burning vapors" which had risen from "distant swamps." That nobody had ever actually seen burning vapors rise from a swamp did not matter.

But a large comet which appeared in 1577 was carefully observed by Tycho Brahe, a Danish astronomer who is often, and with the best of reasons, called "eccentric" but who insisted on precise measurements for everything. It was Tycho Brahe's accumulation of literally thousands of precise measurements which later enable his younger collaborator, Johannes Kepler, to discover the laws of planetary motion. Measuring the motion of the comet of 1577, Tycho Brahe could show that it had been far beyond the atmosphere, even though he could not give figures for the distance. Tycho Brahe's work proved that comets were astronomical and not meteorological phenomena.

In 1682, the second Astronomer Royal of Great Britain, Dr. Edmond Halley, checked the orbit of a bright comet that was in the sky then and compared it with earlier comet orbits which were known in part. Halley found that the comet of 1682 was the third to move through what appeared to be the same orbit. And the three appearances were roughly 76 years apart. Halley concluded that this was the same comet, moving around the Sun in a closed orbit, like the planets. He predicted that it would reappear in 1758 or 1759. Halley himself died in 1742, but a large comet appeared sixteen years after his death as predicted and was immediately referred to as "Halley's comet."

In the Spring of 1973, the discovery of comet Kohoutek, apparently headed for a close-

Christmastime rendezvous with the Sun, created worldwide excitement. The comet was a visual disappointment, but turned out to be a treasure trove of information on these little-understood celestial objects. Given an unprecedented advance notice of nine months on the advent of the fiery object, scientists were able to study the comet in visible, ultraviolet and infrared light; with optical telescopes, radio telescopes, and radar. They observed it from the ground, from high-flying aircraft, with instruments aboard unmanned satellites, with sounding rockets, and telescopes and cameras on the Earth-orbiting Skylab space station.

Halley's Comet appeared again in 1986, sparking a worldwide effort to study it up close. Five satellites in all took readings from the comet at various distances. Two Soviet craft, *Vega 1* and *Vega 2*, went in close to provide detailed pictures of the comet, including the first of the comet's core. The European Space Agency's craft, *Giotto*, entered the comet itself, coming to within 450 miles of the comet's center and successfully passing through its tail. In addition, two Japanese craft, the *Suisei* and the *Sakigake*, passed at a longer distance in order to analyze the cloud and tail of the comet and the effect of solar radiation upon it. The United States declined to launch a similar mission, citing budgetary constraints imposed by the shuttle program. A space telescope was to study Halley's Comet but was destroyed in the *Challenger* disaster.

The information gained included measurements of the size of the nucleus, an idea of its configuration and the rate of its rotation. The gas and dust of the comet were analyzed as was the material of the tail. This information is considered important because comets are believed to be debris from the formation of the solar system and to have changed little since then.

Astronomers refer to comets as "periodic" or as "non-periodic" comets, but the latter term does not mean that these comets have no period; it merely means that their period is not known. The actual periods of comets run from 3.3 years (the shortest known) to many thousands of years. Their orbits are elliptical, like those of the planets, but they are very eccentric, long and narrow ellipses. Only comet Schwassmann-Wachmann has an orbit which has such a low eccentricity (for a cometary orbit) that it could be the orbit of a minor planet.

When a comet, coming from deep space, approaches the Sun, it is at first indistinguishable from a minor planet. Somewhere between the orbits of Mars and Jupiter its outline becomes fuzzy; it is said to develop a "coma" (the word used here is the Latin word *coma*, which means "hair," not the phonetically identical Greek word which means "deep sleep"). Then, near the orbit of Mars, the comet develops its tail, which at first trails behind. This grows steadily as the comet comes closer and closer to the Sun. As it rounds the Sun (as first noticed by Girolamo Fracastoro) the tail always points away from the Sun so that the comet, when moving away from the Sun, points its tail ahead like the landing lights of an airplane.

The reason for this behavior is that the tail is pushed in these directions by the radiation pressure of the Sun. It sometimes happens that a comet loses its tail at perihelion; it then grows another one. Although the tail is clearly visible against the black of the sky, it is very tenuous. It has been said that if the tail of Halley's comet could be compressed to the density of iron, it would fit into a small suitcase.

Although very low in mass, comets are among the largest members of the solar system. The nucleus of a comet may be up to 10,000 miles in diameter; its coma between 10,000 and 50,000 miles in diameter; and its tail as long as 28 million miles.

Meteors and Meteorites

The term "meteor" for what is usually called a "shooting star" bears an unfortunate resemblance to the term "meteorology," the science of weather and weather forecasting. This resemblance is due to an ancient misunderstanding which wrongly considered meteors an atmospheric phenomenon. Actually, the streak of light in the sky that scientists call a meteor is essentially an astronomical phenomenon: the entry of a small piece of cosmic matter into our atmosphere.

The distinction between "meteors" and "fireballs" (formerly also called "bolides") is merely one of convenience; a fireball is an unusually bright meteor. Incidentally, it also means that a fireball is larger than a faint meteor.

Bodies which enter our atmosphere become visible when they are about 60 miles above the ground. The fact that they grow hot enough to emit light is not due to the "friction" of the atmosphere, as one can often read. The phenomenon responsible for the heating is one of compression. Unconfined air cannot move faster than the speed of sound. Since the entering meteorite moves with 30 to 60 times the speed of sound, the air simply cannot get out of the way. Therefore, it is compressed like the air in the cylinder of a Diesel engine and is heated by compression. This heat—or part of it—is transferred to the moving body. The details of this process are now fairly well understood as a result of re-entry tests with ballistic-missile nose cones.

The average weight of a body producing a faint "shooting star" is only a small fraction of an ounce. Even a bright fireball may not weigh more than 2 or 3 pounds. Naturally, the smaller bodies are worn to dust by the passage through the atmosphere; only rather large ones reach the ground. Those that are found are called meteorites. (The "meteor," to repeat, is the term for the light streak in the sky.)

The largest meteorite known is still imbedded in the ground near Grootfontein in SW Africa and is estimated to weight 70 tons. The second largest known is the 34-ton Anighito (on exhibit in the Hayden Planetarium, New York), which was found by Admiral Peary at Cape York in Greenland. The largest meteorite found in the United States is the Willamette meteorite (found in Oregon, weight ca. 15 tons), but large portions of this meteorite weathered away before it was found. Its weight as it struck the ground may have been 20 tons.

All these are iron meteorites (an iron meteorite normally contains about 7% nickel), which form one class of meteorites. The other class consists of the stony meteorites, and between them there are the so-called "stony irons." The so-called "tektites" consist of glass similar to our volcanic glass obsidian, and because of the similarity, there is doubt in a number of cases whether the glass is of terrestrial or of extra-terrestrial origin.

Though no meteorite larger than the Grootfontein is actually known, we do know that the Earth has, on occasion, been struck by much larger bodies. Evidence for such hits are the meteorite craters, of which an especially good example is located

The 88 Recognized Constellations

In astronomical works, the Latin names of the constellations are used. The letter N or S following the Latin name indicates whether the constellation is located to the north or south of the Zodiac. The letter Z indicates that the constellation is within the Zodiac.

Latin name	Letter	English version	Latin name	Letter	English version	Latin name	Letter	English version
Andromeda	N	Andromeda	Delphinus	N	Dolphin	Pavo	S	Peacock
Antlia	S	Airpump	Dorado	S	Swordfish	Pegasus	N	Pegasus
Apus	S	Bird of Paradise			(Goldfish)	Perseus	N	Perseus
Aquarius	Z	Water Bearer	Draco	N	Dragon	Phoenix	S	Phoenix
Aquila	N	Eagle	Equuleus	N	Filly	Pictor	S	Painter (or his
Ara	S	Altar	Eridanus	S	Eridanus (river)			Easel)
Aries	Z	Ram	Fornax	S	Furnace	Pisces	Z	Fishes
Auriga	N	Charioteer	Gemini	Z	Twins	Piscis		
Boötes	N	Herdsmen	Grus	S	Crane	Austrinus	S	Southern Fish
Caelum	S	Sculptor's Tool	Hercules	N	Hercules	Puppis	S	Poop (of Argo)[1]
Camelopardalis	N	Giraffe	Horologium	S	Clock	Pyxis	S	Mariner's
Cancer	Z	Crab	Hydra	N	Sea Serpent			Compass
Canes Venatici	N	Hunting Dogs	Hydrus	S	Water Snake	Reticulum	S	Net
Canis Major	S	Great Dog	Indus	S	Indian	Sagitta	N	Arrow
Canis Minor	S	Little Dog	Lacerta	N	Lizard	Sagittarius	Z	Archer
Capricornus	Z	Goat (or Sea-	Leo	Z	Lion	Scorpius	Z	Scorpion
		Goat)	Leo Minor	N	Little Lion	Sculptor	S	Sculptor
Carina	S	Keel (of Argo)[1]	Lepus	S	Hare	Scutum	N	Shield
Cassiopeia	N	Cassiopeia	Libra	Z	Scales	Serpens	N	Serpent
Centaurus	S	Centaur	Lupus	S	Wolf	Sextans	S	Sextant
Cepheus	N	Cepheus	Lynx	N	Lynx	Taurus	Z	Bull
Cetus	S	Whale	Lyra	N	Lyre (Harp)	Telescopium	S	Telescope
Chameleon	S	Chameleon	Mensa	S	Table	Triangulum	N	Triangle
Circinus	S	Compasses			(mountain)	Triangulum	S	Southern
Columba	S	Dove	Microscopium	S	Microscope	Australe		Triangle
Coma Berenices	N	Berenice's Hair	Monoceros	S	Unicorn	Tucana	S	Toucan
Corona Australis	S	Southern Crown	Musca	S	Southern Fly	Ursa Major	N	Big Dipper
Corona Borealis	N	Northern Crown	Norma	S	Rule	Ursa Minor	N	Little Dipper
Corvus	S	Crow (Raven)			(straightedge)	Vela	S	Sail (of Argo)[1]
Crater	S	Cup	Octans	S	Octant	Virgo	Z	Virgin
Crux	S	Southern Cross	Ophiuchus	N	Serpent-Bearer	Volans	S	Flying Fish
Cygnus	N	Swan	Orion	S	Orion	Vulpecula	N	Fox

1. The original constellation Argo Navis (the Ship Argo) has been divided into Carina, Puppis, and Vela. Normally the brightest star in each constellation is designated by alpha, the first letter of the Greek alphabet, the second brightest by beta, the second letter of the Greek alphabet, and so forth. But the Greek letters run through Carina, Puppis, and Vela as if it were still one constellation.

near the Cañon Diablo in Arizona. Another meteor crater in the United States is a rather old crater near Odessa, Texas. A large number of others are known, especially in eastern Canada, and for many "probables," meteoric origin has now been proved.

The meteor showers are caused by multitudes of very small bodies travelling in swarms. The Earth travels in its orbit through these swarms like a car driving through falling snow. The point from which the meteors seem to emanate is called the *radiant* and is named for the constellation in that area. The Perseid meteor shower in August is the most spectacular of the year, boasting at peak roughly 60 meteors per hour under good atmospheric conditions. The presence of a bright moon diminishes the number of visible meteors.

The Constellations

Constellations are groupings of stars which form patterns that can be easily recognized and remembered, for example, Orion and the Big Dipper. Actually, the stars of the majority of all constellations do not "belong together." Usually they are at greatly varying distances from the Earth and just happen to lie more or less in the same line of sight as seen from our solar system. But in a few cases the stars of a constellation are actually associated; most of the bright stars of the Big Dipper travel together and form what astronomers call an open cluster.

If you observe a planet, say Mars, for one complete revolution, you will see that it passes successively through twelve constellations. All planets (except Pluto at certain times) can be observed only in these twelve constellations, which form the so-called Zodiac, and the Sun also moves through the Zodiacal signs, though the Sun's apparent movement is actually caused by the movement of the Earth.

Although the constellations are due mainly to the optical accident of line of sight and have no real significance, astronomers have retained them as reference areas. It is much easier to speak of a star in Orion than to give its geometrical position in the sky. During the Astronomical Congress of 1928, it was decided to recognize 88 constellations. A description of their agreed-upon boundaries was published at Cambridge, England, in 1930, under the title *Atlas Céleste*.

The Auroras

The "northern lights" *(Aurora borealis)* as well as the "southern lights" *(Aurora australis)* are upper-atmosphere phenomena of astronomical origin. The auroras center around the magnetic (not the geographical) poles of the Earth, which explains why, in the Western Hemisphere, they have been seen as far to the south as New Orleans and Florida while the equivalent latitude in the Eastern Hemisphere never sees an aurora. The northern magnetic pole happens to be in the Western Hemisphere.

The lower limit of an aurora is at about 50 miles. Upper limits have been estimated to be as high as 400 miles. Since about 1880, a connection between the auroras on Earth and the sun spots has been suspected and has gradually come to be accepted. It was said that the sun spots probably eject "particles" (later the word *electrons* was substituted) which on striking the Earth's atmosphere, cause the auroras. But this explanation suffered from certain difficulties. Sometimes a very large sun spot group on the Sun, with individual spots bigger than the Earth itself, would not cause an aurora. Moreover, even if a sun spot caused an aurora, the time that passed between the appearance of the one and the occurrence of the other was highly unpredictable.

This problem of the time lag is, in all probability, solved by the discovery of the Van Allen layer by artificial satellite *Explorer I.* The Van Allen layer is a double layer of charged sub-atomic particles around the Earth. The inner layer, with its center some 1,500 miles from the ground, reaches from about 40° N. to about 40° S. and does not touch the atmosphere. The outer layer, much larger and with its center several thousand miles from the ground, does touch the atmosphere in the vicinity of the magnetic poles.

It seems probable that the "leakage" of electrons from the outer Van Allen layer causes the auroras. A new burst of electrons from the Sun seems to be caught in the outer layer first. Under the assumption that all electrons are first caught in the outer layer, the time lag can be understood. There has to be an "overflow" from the outer layer to produce an aurora.

The Atmosphere

Astronomically speaking, the presence of our atmosphere is deplorable. Though reasonably transparent to visible light, the atmosphere may absorb as much as 60% of the visible and near-visible light. It is opaque to most other wave-lengths, except certain fairly short radio waves. In addition to absorbing much light, our atmosphere bends light rays entering at a slant (for a given observer) so that the true position of a star close to the horizon is not what it seems to be. One effect is that we see the Sun above the horizon before it actually is. And the unsteady movement of the atmosphere causes the "twinkling" of the stars, which may be romantic but is a nuisance when it comes to observing.

The composition of our atmosphere near the ground is 78% nitrogen and 21% oxygen, the remaining 1% consisting of other gases, most of it argon. The composition stays the same to an altitude of at least 70 miles (except that higher up two impurities, carbon dioxide and water vapor, are missing), but the pressure drops very fast. At 18,000 feet, half of the total mass of the atmosphere is below, and at 100,000 feet, 99% of the mass of the atmosphere is below. The upper limit of the atmosphere is usually given as 120 miles; no definitive figure is possible, since there is no boundary line between the incredibly attenuated gases 120 miles up and space.

Astronomical Telescopes

Optical telescopes used in astronomy are of two basic kinds: refracting and reflecting. In the *refractor telescope*, a lens is used to collect light from a distant object and bring it to a focus. A second lens, the eyepiece, then magnifies the image which may be examined visually or photographed directly. The *reflector telescope* uses a concave mirror instead of a lens, which reflects the light rays back toward the upper end of the telescope where they are magnified and observed or photographed. Most large optical telescopes now being built are reflectors.

Radio telescopes are used to study radio waves coming from outside the Earth's atmosphere. The waves are gathered by an antenna or "dish," which is a parabolic reflecting surface made of metal or finely meshed wire. Radio signals have been received from the Sun, Moon, and planets, and from the center of our galaxy and other galaxies. Radio signals are the means by which the distant and mysterious quasars and pulsars were recently discovered.

Very Large Telescope

In December 1987, the European Southern Observatory (ESO) agreed to build a super telescope called the Very Large Telescope in the mountains of northern Chile. It will be the world's largest ground-based optical telescope and will consist of four 8-meter (26.24 ft) telescopes whose mirrors will combine their images to simulate a single mirror of 16-meter (52.49 ft) diameter.

It will take at least ten years to complete construction of the super telescope and will cost about $235 million.

TAU Project

NASA's Jet Propulsion Laboratory is studying the possibility of sending a spacecraft billions of miles beyond the planets at speeds of more than a quarter of a million miles an hour to directly measure the distance to stars in our galaxy and to neighboring galaxies.

Named the TAU Project for Thousand Astronomical Units, it would begin taking measurements of star distances as far away as the center of our galaxy about 10 years after it is launched.

An astronomical unit (AU) is the average distance from the Earth to the Sun, or 93 million miles. The planning also includes the option of viewing the entire solar system as a unit and taking measurements of the solar magnetic field and probing the nature of the interstellar plasma.

TAU would continue its observations of distances to stars in our galaxy and to neighboring ones for a period of 50 years. Not one team, but generations of scientists would work on the TAU Project.

The project would use a 50,000-lb, 40-meter (131-ft) long ion propulsion system to boost the 11,000-lb science spacecraft to about 225,000 mph by the time its is about six billion miles from Earth.

TAU would eventually enter the Oort cloud, an area of 50,000 to 100,000 AU from the sun, where, in theory, the primitive objects left over from the formation of the solar system that could become comets still orbit the sun.

The Hubble Space Telescope shown in orbit after its launching by the Space shuttle. NASA illustration.

The Edwin P. Hubble Space Telescope will be able to peer far out in space and back in time, producing imagery of unprecedented clarity, of galaxies, star systems, and some of the universe's more intriguing objects: quasars, pulsars, and exploding galaxies. It will distinguish fine details—in planetary atmospheres or nearby star fields—with ten times the clarity of the best ground observatories. When pointed at Jupiter, for example, the telescope will provide images comparable to those from Voyager flybys.

The Space Telescope has a primary mirror 2.4 m (94 inches) in diameter. The mirror is almost half the diameter of the 5-m (200 inch) telescope at Mt. Palomar, the most powerful ground-based telescope in the western world.

Once in orbit at 600 km (370 statute miles) alti-

tude, the Hubble Telescope will become the principal tool for exploring the universe through this decade and the next. It will be operated from the Goddard Space Flight Center in Greenbelt, Maryland, in support of astronomers working at the Goddard-managed Space Telescope Science Institute at Johns Hopkins University in nearby Baltimore.

The Space telescope will view galaxies and quasars over distances up to 14 billion light years. Seeing that far will show us the universe as it was early in its lifetime and will reveal how matter has evolved over the eons. It will also teach us more about the large structure of the universe, providing clues as to whether the universe will continue to expand.

Conversion of Universal Time (U. T.) to Civil Time

U.T.	E.D.T.[1]	E.S.T.[2]	C.S.T.[3]	M.S.T.[4]	P.S.T.[5]	U.T.	E.D.T.[1]	E.S.T.[2]	C.S.T.[3]	M.S.T.[4]	P.S.T.[5]
00	*8P	*7P	*6P	*5P	*4P	12	8A	7A	6A	5A	4A
01	*9P	*8P	*7P	*6P	*5P	13	9A	8A	7A	6A	5A
02	*10P	*9P	*8P	*7P	*6P	14	10A	9A	8A	7A	6A
03	*11P	*10P	*9P	*8P	*7P	15	11A	10A	9A	8A	7A
04	M	*11P	*10P	*9P	*8P	16	N	11A	10A	9A	8A
05	1A	M	*11P	*10P	*9P	17	1P	N	11A	10A	9A
06	2A	1A	M	*11P	*10P	18	2P	1P	N	11A	10A
07	3A	2A	1A	M	*11P	19	3P	2P	1P	N	11A
08	4A	3A	2A	1A	M	20	4P	3P	2P	1P	N
09	5A	4A	3A	2A	1A	21	5P	4P	3P	2P	1P
10	6A	5A	4A	3A	2A	22	6P	5P	4P	3P	2P
11	7A	6A	5A	4A	3A	23	7P	6P	5P	4P	3P

1. Eastern Daylight Time. 2. Eastern Standard Time, same as Central Daylight Time. 3. Central Standard Time, same as Mountain Daylight Time. 4. Mountain Standard Time, same as Pacific Daylight Time. 5. Pacific Standard Time. NOTES: *denotes previous day. N = noon. M = midnight.

Eclipses of the Sun and the Moon, 1990

Jan. 26. Annular eclipse of the Sun. Visible south of New Zealand, Antarctica, and South America except northwestern part.

Feb. 9. Total eclipse of the Moon. The beginning of the umbral phase visible in New Zealand, Australia, all of Asia, western Pacific Ocean, Alaska, Arctic regions, Europe except Iberian peninsula, Africa except northwest extension and southwest coast, Indian Ocean, Wilkes Land; the end visible in western half of Australia, Asia, Philippine Sea, Arctic regions, Greenland, Europe, Africa, eastern Atlantic Ocean, Indian Ocean, and portions of Antarctica.

July 22. Total eclipse of the Sun. Visible in northeastern Europe, North of Greenland, North Asia, arctic regions, northwestern part of North America, and the Hawaiian Islands.

Aug. 6. Partical eclipse of the Moon. The beginning of the umbral phase visible in Antarctica, the Pacific Ocean, California, southern Alaska, eastern Siberia and southeastern Asia, eastern Indian Ocean, Australia, and New Zealand; the end visible in Antarctica, western Pacific Ocean, all of Asia except the west, southern half of the Middle East, east coast of Africa, Indian Ocean, Australia, and New Zealand.

Phenomena, 1990

Configurations of Sun, Moon, and Planets

NOTE: The hour listings are in Universal Time. For conversion to United States time zones, see conversion table above.

JANUARY

d	h	
2	18	Neptune in conjunction with Sun
4	11	FIRST QUARTER
4	17	Earth at perihelion
6	21	Saturn in conjunction with Sun
7	19	Moon at perigee
9	02	Mercury in inferior conjunction
9	08	Ceres 0°·6 S of Moon
10	00	Jupiter 4° S of Moon
11	05	FULL MOON
13	21	Mercury 3° N of Neptune
18	21	LAST QUARTER
18	23	Venus in inferior conjunction
19	16	Moon at apogee
20	03	Mercury stationary
22	08	Antares 0°·3 N of Moon
23	15	Mars 4° N of Moon
24	13	Uranus 3° N of Moon
24	20	Mercury 5° N of Moon
24	23	Neptune 4° N of Moon
25	10	Saturn 3° N of Moon
26	19	NEW MOON (Eclipse)
27	23	Mercury 0°·8 N of Neptune

FEBRUARY

1	01	Mercury greatest elong. W (25°)

2	03	Moon at perigee
2	19	FIRST QUARTER
3	15	Mercury 0°·2 N of Saturn
4	06	Mercury 7° S of Venus
5	10	Ceres 0°·3 N of Moon
6	04	Jupiter 4° S of Moon
6	10	Ceres stationary
7	05	Venus 7° N of Saturn
8	04	Venus stationary
9	14	Mars 0°·2 S of Uranus
9	19	FULL MOON (Eclipse)
14	17	Venus 7° N of Saturn
16	13	Moon at apogee
17	06	Mars 1°·5 S of Neptune
17	19	LAST QUARTER
18	16	Antares 0°·3 N of Moon
21	00	Uranus 3° N of Moon
21	10	Neptune 4° N of Moon
21	16	Mars 2° N of Moon
22	00	Saturn 3° N of Moon
22	04	Venus 8° N of Moon
22	13	Venus greatest brilliancy
23	01	Pluto stationary
24	01	Mercury 2° S of Moon
24	19	Jupiter stationary
25	09	NEW MOON
28	08	Moon at perigee
28	17	Mars 1°·0 S of Saturn

MARCH

4	02	FIRST QUARTER
4	20	Ceres 1°·1 N of Moon
5	09	Jupiter 4° S of Moon
11	11	FULL MOON
12	14	Vesta in conjunction with Sun
16	08	Moon at apogee
16	17	Juno stationary
18	00	Antares 0°·2 N of Moon
19	15	LAST QUARTER
20	01	Mercury in superior conjunction
20	11	Uranus 3° N of Moon
20	20	Neptune 4° N of Moon
20	21	Equinox
21	14	Saturn 2° N of Moon
22	18	Mars 0°·4 S of Moon
23	07	Venus 2° N of Moon
26	20	NEW MOON
28	08	Moon at perigee
30	07	Venus greatest elong. W (46°)

APRIL

1	18	Jupiter 3° S of Moon
2	10	FIRST QUARTER
10	03	FULL MOON
12	20	Moon at apogee

13 15 Mercury greatest elong. E (20°)
13 23 Uranus stationary
14 07 Antares 0°.1 S of Moon
16 11 Neptune stationary
16 19 Uranus 3° N of Moon
17 04 Neptune 3° N of Moon
18 01 Saturn 1°.8 N of Moon
18 07 LAST QUARTER
20 20 Mars 3° S of Moon
22 01 Venus 4° S of Moon
23 15 Mercury stationary
25 04 NEW MOON
25 17 Moon at perigee
29 08 Jupiter 3° S of Moon

MAY

1 20 FIRST QUARTER
4 00 Mercury in inferior conjunction
5 02 Saturn stationary
7 05 Pluto at opposition
8 03 Juno at opposition
9 20 FULL MOON
10 00 Moon at apogee
11 13 Antares 0°.2 S of Moon
14 00 Uranus 3° N of Moon
14 10 Neptune 3° N of Moon
15 08 Saturn 1°.5 N of Moon
16 07 Mercury stationary
17 20 LAST QUARTER
19 20 Mars 6° S of Moon
21 20 Venus 7° S of Moon
23 03 Mercury 9° S of Moon
24 03 Moon at perigee
24 12 NEW MOON
25 11 Pallas in conjunction with Sun
27 02 Jupiter 2° S of Moon
31 03 Mercury greatest elong. W (25°)
31 08 FIRST QUARTER

JUNE

6 04 Moon at apogee
7 19 Antares 0°.2 S of Moon
8 11 FULL MOON
10 05 Uranus 2° N of Moon
10 15 Neptune 3° N of Moon
11 12 Saturn 1°.4 N of Moon
16 05 LAST QUARTER
17 16 Mars 7° S of Moon
18 02 Mercury 4° N of Aldebaran
20 11 Venus 7° S of Moon
21 11 Moon at perigee
21 16 Solstice
22 19 NEW MOON
23 22 Jupiter 1°.6 S of Moon
29 15 Uranus at opposition
29 22 FIRST QUARTER

JULY

2 17 Mercury in superior conjunction
3 15 Venus 4° N of Aldebaran
3 16 Moon at apogee
4 05 Earth at aphelion
5 02 Antares 0°.2 S of Moon
5 11 Neptune at opposition
7 09 Uranus 2° N of Moon

7 16 Juno stationary
7 20 Neptune 3° N of Moon
8 01 FULL MOON
8 14 Saturn 1°.5 N of Moon
14 18 Saturn at opposition
15 06 Jupiter in conjunction with Sun
15 11 LAST QUARTER
16 08 Mars 8° S of Moon
19 11 Moon at perigee
20 03 Venus 4° S of Moon
22 03 NEW MOON (Eclipse)
23 18 Mercury 3° N of Moon
29 06 Mercury 0°.04 N of Regulus
29 14 FIRST QUARTER
31 02 Pluto stationary
31 08 Moon at apogee

AUGUST

1 09 Antares 0°.1 S of Moon
3 14 Uranus 2° N of Moon
4 02 Neptune 3° N of Moon
4 18 Saturn 1°.6 N of Moon
6 14 FULL MOON (Eclipse)
9 05 Venus 7° S of Pollux
11 20 Mercury greatest elong. E (27°)
12 23 Venus 0°.04 N of Jupiter
13 16 LAST QUARTER
13 19 Mars 7° S of Moon
15 10 Moon at perigee
18 13 Jupiter 0°.4 S of Moon
19 00 Venus 0°.5 N of Moon
20 13 NEW MOON
20 16 Ceres in conjunction with Sun
22 12 Mercury 0°.2 N of Moon
25 00 Mercury stationary
28 03 Moon at apogee
28 08 FIRST QUARTER
28 17 Antares 0°.2 S of Moon
30 21 Uranus 2° N of Moon
31 09 Neptune 3° N of Moon

SEPTEMBER

1 00 Saturn 1°.7 N of Moon
5 02 FULL MOON
6 21 Venus 0°.8 N of Regulus
8 04 Mercury in inferior conjunction
9 11 Moon at perigee
10 23 Mars 6° S of Moon
11 21 LAST QUARTER
14 15 Mercury 3° S of Venus
14 19 Uranus stationary
15 06 Jupiter 0°.3 N of Moon
16 16 Mercury stationary
17 20 Mercury 2° N of Moon
19 01 NEW MOON
23 03 Saturn stationary
23 07 Equinox
23 16 Neptune stationary
24 04 Mercury greatest elong. W (18°)
24 22 Moon at apogee
25 01 Antares 0°.4 S of Moon
25 07 Mars 4° N of Aldebaran
27 02 FIRST QUARTER
27 06 Uranus 2° N of Moon
27 18 Neptune 3° N of Moon
28 08 Saturn 1°.5 N of Moon

OCTOBER

4 12 FULL MOON
6 18 Moon at perigee
8 19 Mars 5° S of Moon
11 04 LAST QUARTER
12 20 Jupiter 1°.0 N of Moon
18 16 NEW MOON
20 12 Mars stationary
22 04 Mercury in superior conjunction
22 08 Antares 0°.6 S of Moon
22 16 Moon at apogee
24 15 Uranus 1°.9 N of Moon
25 02 Neptune 3° N of Moon
25 17 Saturn 1°.1 N of Moon
26 20 FIRST QUARTER

NOVEMBER

1 15 Venus in superior conjunction
2 22 FULL MOON
3 23 Moon at perigee
5 02 Mars 3° S of Moon
9 07 Jupiter 1°.6 N of Moon
9 13 LAST QUARTER
10 09 Pluto in conjunction with Sun
13 10 Mars 6° N of Aldebaran
15 20 Vesta at opposition
17 03 Mercury 3° N of Antares
17 09 NEW MOON
18 15 Antares 0°.7 S of Moon
18 20 Mercury 1°.7 N of Moon
19 03 Moon at apogee
20 04 Mars closest approach
20 23 Uranus 1°.6 N of Moon
21 10 Neptune 2° N of Moon
22 04 Saturn 0°.6 N of Moon
25 13 FIRST QUARTER
27 21 Mars at opposition
30 13 Jupiter stationary

DECEMBER

1 23 Mars 3° S of Moon
2 08 FULL MOON
2 11 Moon at perigee
6 07 Mercury greatest elong. E (21°)
6 16 Jupiter 2° N of Moon
9 02 LAST QUARTER
10 08 Mercury 1°.3 S of Uranus
10 11 Juno in conjunction with Sun
14 18 Mercury stationary
15 21 Antares 0°.7 S of Moon
16 04 Moon at apogee
17 04 NEW MOON
18 05 Mercury 0°.6 N of Uranus
18 18 Neptune 2° N of Moon
18 23 Mercury 1°.4 N of Venus
19 10 Venus 0°.6 S of Uranus
19 15 Saturn 0°.2 N of Moon
22 03 Solstice
23 03 Venus 1°.8 S of Neptune
24 08 Mercury in inferior conjunction
25 03 FIRST QUARTER
29 01 Mars 2° S of Moon
31 00 Moon at perigee
31 16 Uranus in conjunction with Sun
31 19 FULL MOON

SPACE

Mars: Back to the Frontier

By Carl Sagan

The surface of Mars taken by Viking Lander 2 at its Utopia Planitia landing site on May 18, 1979. It shows a thin coating of water ice on the rocks and soil. The time the frost appeared corresponds almost exactly with the buildup of frost one Martian year (23 Earth months) ago. It remained on the surface for about 100 days. NASA photo and data.

Mars is the most Earthlike other world we know. Its hundreds of ancient river valleys point to an earlier epoch that was still more clement. Did life arise on primordial Mars as it did on primordial Earth? Are there fossils or extant life forms awaiting us? How did a warm, wet world become frigid and desiccated? Is there a useful lesson here about climatic instability of Earth? With almost no ozone in the martian atmosphere, ultraviolet light from the Sun strikes the planet unimpeded and, apparently, destroys all the organic matter near the surface. Is this a cautionary tale for us, who are carelessly burning holes in our own ozone layer? Mars is an awesome world with monumental and enigmatic landforms, occasional planetwide dust storms, two tiny organic-rich moons and a surface area equal to all the continents of Earth. It has much to teach us.

But if the exploration of Mars were our only objective, I would recommend sending smart robots—they're much cheaper, they can go to more dangerous locations, and no human lives are risked (although humans are better explorers than any likely robot). For me, the chief reason to send humans is political. The *Apollo* program was fundamentally an American response to the orbital flight of Yuri Gagarin, and a demonstration to the world that the US was fully capable of building rockets that could reliably convey nuclear warheads halfway around the world. The US and the USSR have now booby-trapped the planet with nearly 60,000 nuclear weapons. They have fully demonstrated their talent for mass annihilation. Today, I think, their obligation is different: to demonstrate that they can work together on behalf of the human species; that high technology need not be a gun aimed at our own heads, but a bridge to a new world. Dreams are maps.

There are many other reasons for human missions to Mars, and they are listed in The Planetary

Society's Mars Declaration. One that I find compelling is revitalizing a dispirited and unravelling NASA. Virtually all NASA's historic expeditions of exploration and discovery—*Apollo, Mariner, Surveyor, Lunar Orbiter, Pioneer, Viking, Voyager*—were carried out, or at least designed, under the umbrella of the *Apollo* program. But since 1978, long before the *Challenger* disaster, NASA has not launched a single mission—not one—to the Moon or planets. The Mars goal provides a coherent focus for the US civilian space program, including precursor robotic missions to Mars, its moons and other worlds; space science in general; long-duration human spaceflight in microgravity and in "artificial" gravity; forecasting solar flares; and giving a crisp set of objectives for the long-delayed US space station. It unifies NASA's diverse constituencies—field centers, industry, science, technology and a public longing for a grand exploratory vision.

Naturally, there are some objections (O), but I think they all have answers (A).

O: A human mission to Mars is too expensive.

A: It is estimated to cost as much as a single major strategic weapons system.

O: The Russians will steal our technology.

A: Since the USSR is about a decade ahead of the US in long-duration human spaceflight, has been spectacularly successful in its recent Venus and Halley's Comet missions and has a launch booster far more powerful than any American rocket now available, technology transfer, if it occurs, is likely to flow both ways.

O: NASA isn't ready for such ambitious cooperation; it could be a technological embarrassment for the US.

A: With a presidential endorsement and congressional support, NASA will again be capable of legendary achievements.

O: We'll be left high and dry if the Russians pull out midway through the project.

A: We proceed by slow steps—exchanging scientists on the *Phobos* and *Mars Observer* robotic missions, designing collaborative but largely independent balloon, rover and sample return missions. We have plenty of time to build mutual confidence.

O: If we're going by slow steps, let's establish a lunar base first. We can use it to test Mars hardware.

A: For exploration and science, for the technical and human challenge, and in terms of public interest, Mars is far more interesting than the Moon. Mars hardware can be better tested in Earth orbit and on Earth. With finite resources, commitment to a lunar base is likely to delay the Mars goal for decades.

O: If we're after major cooperative projects with the Soviets, why not do them here on Earth?

A: This is the means to bring such projects to pass, as the Soviets have stressed.

O: Such a commitment will make strategic confrontation between the superpowers more difficult.

A: Exactly.

O: Considering what we're doing with *this* planet, can we be trusted with another?

Carl Sagan is the David Duncan Professor of Astronomy and Space Sciences and Director of the Laboratory for Planetary Studies at Cornell University, as well as President of The Planetary Society. In 1984, Dr. Sagan was first to advocate a joint piloted US/Soviet expedition to Mars. © 1988 by Carl Sagan. All Rights Reserved. First published in *The Chicago Tribune*. Reprinted by permission of the author.

The ice seen in this picture, like that which formed one Martian year ago, is extremely thin, perhaps no more than one-thousandth of an inch thick. NASA photo and data.

A: This is an open question. But making peace with our enemies, transforming nuclear-armed missiles into vessels of exploration, turning hatred and suspicion into cooperation suggests a hopeful answer.

During the Washington summit last December [1987], General Secretary Gorbachev was asked what could be done to heal the wounds that divide our two nations. His immediate answer was a joint US/Soviet human expedition to Mars. With prior and subsequent endorsements of the idea by leading presidential candidates of both parties, a bill passed by the House to begin establishing the bureaucratic machinery for joint Mars exploration, and a stunningly ecumenical range of American leaders signing the Mars Declaration, there seems to be a chance of actually achieving this dream in the next two decades.

There's plenty of housework to be done here on Earth, and our commitment to it must be steadfast. But we're the kind of species that needs a frontier. Every time humanity stretches itself, turns a new corner, it receives a jolt of productive vitality that can last for centuries or millennia.

There's a new world next door. And we know how to get there. □

According to Soviet sources, the second large module of for *Mir* will allow dockings with the new Soviet space shuttle. Artwork: *The Soviet Year in Space 1988,* Teledyne Brown Engineering.

Future Mir Modules

According to *AD ASTRA,* the magazine of the National Space Society, Soviet space planners are preparing a series of modules for attachment to *Mir.* First to be attached is the "Energy" module, which will augment *Mir*'s electrical power and expand the station's living quarters. "Energy" will also carry a large airlock to support cosmonaut spacewalks.

Three other modules are being readied: "Technology," built to hold new equipment for carrying out microgravity processing; "Priorda," equipped with remote sensing devices developed in cooperation with Bulgaria, Hungary, the German Democratic Republic, and Czechoslovakia; and "Medilab," which will be used to perform biomedical research on both human and animal subjects. The latter module may be permanently staffed by a biological doctor who will be rotated after three-month stints.

Soviets Launch "Snowstorm"

The successful test flight of the Soviet Union's first reusable space shuttle *Buran* (Russian for "snowstorm") (Shown at left on launch pad. Novosti photo) was made on Nov. 15, 1988. The unmanned flight circled the Earth for two orbits and lasted 3 hr 25 min.

The Soviet and American space shuttles closely resemble each other in size and appearance and

Photo left: Soviet astronaut, Col. Vladimir Titov, 41, mission commander, and **photo right:** Col. Titov and Musa Manarov, 37, flight engineer, who together set a record single-mission endurance flight aboard the space station *Mir* on December 21, 1989, after spending 366 days in space. The longest U.S. space mission was 84 days aboard *Skylab:* Nov. 16, 1973–Feb. 8, 1974.

The Soviet space station *Mir (Peace)* was launched on Feb. 20, 1986. It is 43 ft long (13.10 m), has a diameter of 13.7 ft (4.14 m), and weighs 46,300 lb. Its two solar panels span about 100 ft (30 m). The Soviet Union has placed seven space stations in orbit since 1971. The *Mir* is equipped with six docking ports so it can be docked simultaneously with six spacecraft, including passenger, cargo, and research ships.

The Soviets launched the world's first space station, *Salyut 1,* on April 19, 1971. The *Salyuts* were 49.2 ft long (14.98 m) and 13.8 ft (4.16 m) maximum diameter. Photos by Tass and Novosti.

have similar delta wings and vertical tail structures. Some major differences between the two shuttles are that the Soviet craft has no large rocket engines of its own. It uses the giant disposable *Energiya* rocket for most of its propulsion, and has only small rockets for maneuvering. The United States space shuttles have three reusable main engines to help lift it into orbit. The *Buran* also has larger payload capabilities than NASA's orbiters.

Unlike the American version, the *Buran* is designed for fully automatic flight, from takeoff to landing, a difficult engineering feat. By comparison, U.S. astronauts take control of their shuttles when making the final landing approach.

The crew cabin of *Buran* can accommodate two to four astronauts and has seats for six passengers or other crew members. The U.S. space shuttle can accommodate up to eight crew members. The Soviet shuttle will be adapted for docking with an advanced second-generation *Mir-2* space station.

The Soviet craft is 19 ft (5.6 m) in diameter compared with NASA's shuttle, 17 ft (5.2 m). The wingspan is 79.2 ft (24 m). NASA's orbiter is 78.6 ft (23.79 m). *Buran's* length is 119 ft (36 m), the U.S. shuttle is 122.2 ft long (37.24 m).

Is There Ice on the Moon?

Unlike the rest of the Moon's surface, the temperature of its polar regions remains permanently about −390° to −315° F and some of its craters remain perpetually in the dark. Some scientists have speculated that ice may have accumulated in the dark craters over long eons of time.

NASA would like to launch a polar lunar orbiter known as the *Lunar Observer* in the mid-1990s to study the unknown regions of the Moon's poles and search for water, ice, and other useful volatiles that may exist on the Moon.

The Mars Observer

A NASA mission is underway to launch an unmanned spacecraft to Mars in 1992. The craft will be launched from a NASA space shuttle.

After a one-year cruise, the spacecraft will arrive at and begin orbiting Mars. The scientific mission will last for one Martian year, or nearly two years. This will allow the spacecraft to study how Mars' atmosphere and surface change throughout the planet's seasons.

U.S. Unmanned Planetary and Lunar Programs

Lunar Orbiter. Series of spacecraft designed to orbit the Moon, taking pictures and obtaining data in support of the subsequent manned Apollo landings. The U.S. launched five *Lunar Orbiters* between Aug. 10, 1966 and Aug. 2, 1967.

Mariner. Designation for a series of spacecraft designed to fly past or orbit the planets, particularly Mercury, Venus, and Mars. *Mariners* provided the early information on Venus and Mars. *Mariner 9*, orbiting Mars in 1971, returned the most startling photographs of that planet to date, and helped pave the way for a *Viking* landing in 1976. *Mariner 10* explored Venus and Mercury in 1973 and was the first probe to use a planet's gravity to whip it toward another.

Pioneer. Designation for the United States' first series of sophisticated interplanetary spacecraft. *Pioneers 10* and *11* reached Jupiter in 1973 and 1974 and continued on to explore Saturn and the other outer planets. *Pioneer 11*, renamed *Pioneer Saturn*, examined the Saturn system in September 1979. Significant discoveries were the finding of a small new moon and a narrow new ring. In 1986, *Pioneer 10* was the first man-made object to escape the solar system. *Pioneer Venus 1* and *2* reached Venus in 1978 and provided detailed information about that planet's surface and atmosphere.

Ranger. NASA's earliest moon exploration program. Spacecraft were designed for a crash landing on the Moon, taking pictures and returning scientific data up to the moment of impact. Provided the first closeup views of the lunar surface. The *Rangers* provided more than 17,000 closeup pictures, giving us more information about the Moon in a few years than in all the time that had gone before.

Surveyor. Series of unmanned spacecraft designed to land gently on the Moon and provide information on the surface in preparation for the manned lunar landings. Their legs were instrumented to return data on the surface hardness of the Moon. *Surveyor* dispelled the fear that Apollo spacecraft might sink several feet or more into the lunar dust.

Viking. Designation for two spacecraft designed to conduct detailed scientific examination of the planet Mars, including a search for life. *Viking 1* landed on July 20, 1976; *Viking 2*, Sept. 3, 1976. More was learned about the Red Planet in a few short months than in all the time that had gone before. But the question of life on Mars remains unresolved.

Voyager. Designation for two spacecraft designed to explore Jupiter and the other outer planets. *Voyager 1* and *Voyager 2* passed Jupiter in 1979 and sent back startling color TV images of that planet and its moons. They took a total of about 33,000 pictures. *Voyager 1* passed Saturn November 1980. *Voyager 2* passed Saturn August 1981 and Uranus January 1986. It will have passed Neptune on Aug. 24, 1989.

Notable Unmanned Lunar and Interplanetary Probes

Spacecraft	Launch date	Destination	Remarks
Pioneer 3 (U.S.)	Dec. 6, 1958	Moon	Max. alt.: 66,654 mi. Discovered outer Van Allen layer.
Luna 2 (U.S.S.R.)	Sept. 12, 1959	Moon	Impacted on Sept. 14. First space vehicle to reach moon.
Luna 3 (U.S.S.R.)	Oct. 4, 1959	Moon	Flew around Moon and transmitted first pictures of lunar far side, Oct. 7.
Mariner 2 (U.S.)	Aug. 27, 1962	Venus	Venus probe. Successful mid-course correction. Passed 21,648 mi. from Venus Dec. 14, 1962. Reported 800° F. surface temp. Contact lost Jan. 3, 1963 at 54 million mi.
Mariner 4 (U.S.)	Nov. 28, 1964	Mars	Transmitted first close-up pictures on June 14, 1965, from altitude of 6,000 mi.
Ranger 7 (U.S.)	July 28, 1964	Moon	Impacted near Crater Guericke 68.5 h after launch. Sent 4,316 pictures during last 15 min of flight as close as 1,000 ft above lunar surface.
Luna 9 (U.S.S.R.)	Jan. 31, 1966	Moon	3,428 lb. Instrument capsule of 220 lb soft-landed Feb. 3, 1966. Sent back about 30 pictures.
Surveyor 1 (U.S.)	May 30, 1966	Moon	Landed June 2, 1966. Sent almost 10,400 pictures, a number after surviving the 14-day lunar night.
Lunar Orbiter 1 (U.S.)	Aug. 10, 1966	Moon	Orbited Moon Aug. 14. 21 pictures sent.
Surveyor 3 (U.S.)	April 17, 1967	Moon	Soft-landed 65 h after launch on Oceanus Procellarum. Scooped and tested lunar soil.
Venera 4 (U.S.S.R.)	June 12, 1967	Venus	Arrived Oct. 17. Instrument capsule sent temperature and chemical data.
Surveyor 5 (U.S.)	Sept. 8, 1967	Moon	Landed near lunar equator Sept. 10. Radiological analysis of lunar soil. Mechanical claw for digging soil.
Surveyor 7 (U.S.)	Jan. 6, 1968	Moon	Landed near Crater Tycho Jan. 10. Soil analysis. Sent 3,343 pictures.
Pioneer 9 (U.S.)	Nov. 8, 1968	Sun Orbit	Achieved orbit. Six experiments returned solar radiation data.
Venera 5 (U.S.S.R.)	Jan. 5, 1969	Venus	Landed May 16, 1969. Returned atmospheric data.
Mariner 6 (U.S.)	Feb. 24, 1969	Mars	Came within 2000 mi. of Mars July 31, 1969. Sent back data & TV pictures.
Luna 16 (U.S.S.R.)	Sept. 12, 1970	Moon	Soft-landed Sept. 20, scooped up rock, returned to Earth Sept. 24.
Luna 17 (U.S.S.R.)	Nov. 10, 1970	Moon	Soft-landed on Sea of Rains Nov. 17. Lunokhod 1, self-propelled vehicle, used for first time. Sent TV photos, made soil analysis, etc.

Spacecraft	Launch date	Destination	Remarks
Mariner 9 (U.S.)	May 30, 1971	Mars	First craft to orbit Mars, Nov. 13. 7,300 pictures, 1st closeups of Mars' moon. Transmission ended Oct. 27, 1972.
Luna 20 (U.S.S.R.)	Feb. 14, 1972	Moon	Soft-landed Feb. 21 in Sea of Fertility. Returned Feb. 25 with rock samples.
Pioneer 10 (U.S.)	March 3, 1972	Jupiter	620-million-mile flight path through asteroid belt passed Jupiter Dec. 3, 1973, to give man first closeup of planet. In 1986, it became first man-made object to escape solar system.
Luna 21 (U.S.S.R.)	Jan. 8, 1973	Moon	Soft-landed Jan. 16. Lunokhod 2 (moon-car) scooped up soil samples, returned them to Earth Jan. 27.
Mariner 10 (U.S.)	Nov. 3, 1973	Venus, Mercury	Passed Venus Feb. 5, 1974. Arrived Mercury March 29, 1974, for man's first closeup look at planet. First time gravity of one planet (Venus) used to whip spacecraft toward another (Mercury).
Viking 1 (U.S.)	Aug. 20, 1975	Mars	Carrying life-detection labs. Landed July 20, 1976, for detailed scientific research, including pictures. Designed to work for only 90 days, it operated for almost 6 1/2 years before it went silent in November 1982.
Viking 2 (U.S.)	Sept. 9, 1975	Mars	Like Viking 1. Landed Sept. 3, 1976. Functioned 3 1/2 years.
Luna 24 (U.S.S.R.)	Aug. 9, 1976	Moon	Soft-landed Aug. 18, 1976. Returned soil samples Aug. 22, 1976.
Voyager 1 (U.S.)	Sept. 5, 1977	Jupiter, Saturn	Fly-by mission. Reached Jupiter in March 1979; passed Saturn Nov. 1980; passed Uranus 1986.
Voyager 2 (U.S.)	Aug. 20, 1977	Jupiter, Saturn, Uranus	Launched before *Voyager 1*. Encountered Jupiter in July 1979; flew by Saturn Aug. 1981; passed Uranus January 1986; scheduled to pass Neptune Aug. 24, 1989.
Pioneer Venus 1 (U.S.)	May 20, 1978	Venus	Arrived Dec. 4 and orbited Venus, photographing surface and atmosphere.
Pioneer Venus 2 (U.S.)	Aug. 8, 1978	Venus	Four-part multi-probe, landed Dec. 9.
Venera 13 (U.S.S.R.)	Oct. 30, 1981	Venus	Landed March 1, 1982. Took first X-ray fluorescence analysis of the planet's surface. Transmitted data 2 hours 7 minutes.
VEGA 1 (U.S.S.R.)	Deployed on Venus, June 10, 1985	Encounter with	In flyby over Venus while enroute to encounter with Halley's Comet, VEGA 1 and 2 dropped scientific capsules
VEGA 2 (U.S.S.R.)	Deployed on Venus, June 14, 1985	Halley's comet	onto Venus to study atmosphere and surface material. Encountered Halley's Comet on March 6 and March 9, 1986. Took TV pictures, and studied comet's dust particles.
Suisei (Japan)	Encountered Hally's Comet March 8, 1986	Halley's Comet	Spacecraft made fly-by of comet and studied atmosphere with ultraviolet camera. Observed rotation nucleus.
Sakigake (Japan)	Encountered Halley's Comet March 10, 1986	Halley's Comet	Spacecraft made fly-by to study solar wind and magnetic fields. Detected plasma waves.
Giotto (ESA)	Encountered Halley's Comet March 13, 1986	Halley's Comet	European Space Agency spacecraft made closest approach to comet. Studied atmosphere and magnetic fields. Sent back best pictures of nucleus.
Phobos Mission (U.S.S.R.)	July 7 and July 12, 1988	Mars and Phobos	Two spacecraft to probe Martian moon Phobos starting April 1989. Were to study orbit, soil chemistry, send TV pictures and data of planet. Contact was lost with Phobos 1 in August 1988 and later with Phobos 2 in March 1989 after it reached the Martian moon.
Magellan (U.S.)	May 4, 1989	Venus	To arrive at Venus on Aug. 10, 1990 and make a geologic map of planet with a powerful radar.
Galileo (U.S.)	Oct. 12, 1989[1]	Jupiter	To study Jupiter's atmosphere and its moons during 22-month mission.
Hubble Space Telescope (U.S., E.S.A.)[2]	Dec. 11, 1989[1]	Earth Orbit	Will study distant stars and galaxies and search for evidence of planets in other solar systems.

1. Tentative launch date. To be deployed by Space Shuttle. 2. European Space Agency (E.S.A.) responsible for furnishing the solar arrays, the Faint Object Camera, and will participate in flight operations aspects of the mission.

MAGELLAN
Venus Radar Mapper

On May 4, 1989, NASA'S unmanned spacecraft *Magellan* was launched from the shuttle *Discovery*. It was the first time a space probe was launched from a shuttle. *Magellan* is a spacecraft equipped with an imaging radar system designed to "see" through Venus' thick cloud-like cover and obtain detailed photographlike images of 90% of the planet's surface. Upon reaching the planet on August 10, 1990, the spacecraft will be placed in an elliptical orbit, circling Venus once every 3.1 hours and the radar will operate once each orbit for approximately 40 minutes, from an altitude of 190 to 1060 miles (300 to 1,700 kilometers). The mapping will continue for 243 days.

Notable Manned Space Flights

Designation and country	Date	Astronauts	Flight time (h/min)	Remarks
Vostok 1(U.S.S.R.)	April 12, 1961	Yuri A. Gagarin	1/48	First manned orbital flight
MR III (U.S.)	May 5, 1961	Alan B. Shepard, Jr.	0/15	Range 486 km (302 mi.), peak 187 km (116.5 mi.); capsule recovered. First American in space.
Vostok 2 (U.S.S.R.)	Aug. 6–7, 1961	Gherman S. Titov	25/18	First long-duration flight
MA VI (U.S.)	Feb. 20, 1962	John H. Glenn, Jr.	4/55	First American in orbit
MA IX (U.S.)	May 15–16, 1963	L. Gordon Cooper, Jr.	34/20	Longest Mercury flight
Vostok 6 (U.S.S.R.)	June 16–19, 1963	Valentina V. Tereshkova	70/50	First orbital flight by female cosmonaut
Voskhod 1 (U.S.S.R.)	Oct. 12, 1964	Vladimir M. Komarov; Konstantin P. Feoktistov; Boris G. Yegorov	24/17	First 3-man orbital flight; also first flight without space suits
Voskhod 2 (U.S.S.R.)	March 18, 1965	Alexei A. Leonov; Pavel I. Belyaev	26/2	First "space walk" (by Leonov), 10 min
GT III (U.S.)	March 23, 1965	Virgil I. Grissom; John W. Young	4/53	First manned test of Gemini spacecraft
GT IV (U.S.)	June 3–7, 1965	James A. McDivitt; Edward H. White, 2d	97/48	First American "space walk" (by White), lasting slightly over 20 min
GT VIII (U.S.)	March 16-17, 1966	Neil A. Armstrong; David R. Scott	10/42	First docking between manned spacecraft and an unmanned space vehicle (an orbiting Agena rocket).
Apollo 7 (U.S.)	Oct. 11–22, 1968	Walter M. Schirra, Jr.; Donn F. Eisele; R. Walter Cunningham	260/9	First manned test of Apollo command module; first live TV transmissions from orbit
Soyuz 3 (U.S.S.R.)	Oct. 26-30, 1968	Georgi T. Bergeovoi	94/51	First manned rendezvous and possible docking by Soviet cosmonaut
Apollo 8 (U.S.)	Dec. 21-27, 1968	Frank Borman; James A. Lovell, Jr.; William A. Anders	147/00	First spacecraft in circumlunar orbit; TV transmissions from this orbit
Apollo 9 (U.S.)	Mar. 3-13, 1969	James A. McDivitt; David R. Scott; Russell L. Schweikart	241/1	First manned flight of Lunar Module
Apollo 10 (U.S.)	May 18–26, 1969	Thomas P. Stafford; Eugene A. Cernan; John W. Young	192/3	First descent to within 9 miles of moon's surface by manned craft
Apollo 11 (U.S.)	July 16–24, 1969	Neil A. Armstrong; Edwin E. Aldrin, Jr.; Michael Collins	195/18	First manned landing and EVA on Moon; soil and rock samples collected; experiments left on lunar surface
Soyuz 6 (U.S.S.R.)	Oct. 11–16, 1969	Gorgiy Shonin; Valriy Kabasov	118/42	Three spacecraft and seven men put into earth orbit simultaneously for first time
Apollo 12 (U.S.)	Nov. 14–24, 1969	Charles Conrad, Jr.; Richard F. Gordon, Jr.; Alan Bean	244/36	Manned lunar landing mission; investigated Surveyor 3 spacecraft; collected lunar samples. EVA time: 15 h 30 min
Apollo 13 (U.S.)	April 11-17, 1970	James A. Lovell, Jr.; Fred W. Haise, Jr.; John L. Swigert, Jr.	142/54	Third manned lunar landing attempt; aborted due to pressure loss in liquid oxygen in service module and failure of fuel cells
Apollo 14 (U.S.)	Jan. 31–Feb. 9, 1971	Alan B. Shepard; Stuart A. Roosa; Edgar D. Mitchell	216/42	Third manned lunar landing; returned largest amount of lunar material
Soyuz 11 (U.S.S.R.)	June 6–30, 1971	Georgiy Tomofeyevich Dobrovolskiy; Vladislav Nikolayevich Volkov; Viktor Ivanovich Patsyev	569/40	Linked up with first space station, Salyut 1. Astronauts died just before re-entry due to loss of pressurization in spacecraft
Apollo 15 (U.S.)	July 26–Aug. 7, 1971	David R. Scott; James B. Irwin; Alfred M. Worden	295/12	Fourth manned lunar landing; first use of Lunar Rover propelled by Scott and Irwin; first live pictures of LM lift-off from Moon; exploration time: 18 hours
Apollo 16 (U.S.)	April 16–27, 1972	John W. Young; Thomas K. Mattingly; Charles M. Duke, Jr.	265/51	Fifth manned lunar landing; second use of Lunar Rover Vehicle, propelled by Young and Duke. Total exploration time on the Moon was 20 h 14 min, setting new record. Mattingly's in-flight "walk in space" was 1 h 23 min. Approximately 213 lb of lunar rock returned
Apollo 17 (U.S.)	Dec. 7-19, 1972	Eugene A. Cernan; Ronald E. Evans; Harrison H. Schmitt	301/51	Sixth and last manned lunar landing; third to carry lunar rover. Cernan and Schmitt, during three EVA's, completed total of 22 h 05 min 3 sec. USS Ticonderoga recovered crew and about 250 lbs of lunar samples
Skylab SL-2 (U.S.)	May 25-June 22, 1973	Charles Conrad, Jr.; Josep P. Kerwin; Paul J. Weitz	672/50	First manned Skylab launch. Established Skylab Orbital Assembly and conducted scientific and medical experiments
Skylab SL-3 (U.S.)	July 28-Sept. 25, 1973	Alan L. Bean, Jr.; Jack R. Lousma; Owen K. Garriott	1427/9	Second manned Skylab launch. New crew remained in space for 59 days, continuing scientific and medical experiments and earth observations from orbit

Designation and country	Date	Astronauts	Flight time (h/min)	Remarks
Skylab SL-4 (U.S.)	Nov. 16, 1973-Feb. 8, 1974	Gerald Carr; Edward Gibson; William Pogue	2017/16	Third manned Skylab launch; obtained medical data on crew for use in extending the duration of manned space flight; crews "walked in space" 4 times, totaling 44 h 40 min. Longest space mission yet—84 d 1 h 16 min. Splashdown in Pacific, Feb. 9, 1974
Apollo/Soyuz Test Project (U.S. and U.S.S.R.)	July 15–24, 1975 (U.S.)	U.S.: Brig. Gen. Thomas P. Stafford, Vance D. Brand, Donald K. Slayton	216/05	World's first international manned rendezvous and docking in space; aimed at developing a space rescue capability
	July 15–21, 1975 (U.S.S.R)	U.S.S.R.: Col. A. A. Leonov, V. N. Kubasov	223/35	Apollo and Soyuz docked and crewmen exchanged visits on July 17, 1975. Mission duration for Soyuz: 142 h 31 min. For Apollo: 217 h, 28 min.
Columbia (U.S.)	April 12–14, 1981	Capt. Robert L. Crippen; John W. Young	54/20	Maiden voyage of *Space Shuttle*, the first spacecraft designed specifically for re-use up to 100 times
Salyut 7 (U.S.S.R.)	Feb. 8, 1984— Oct. 2, 1985	Leonid Kizim; Vladimir Solovyov; Oleg Atkov	237 days	Record Soviet team endurance flight in orbiting space station
Mir (U.S.S.R.)	Feb. 8, 1987— Dec. 29, 1987	Yuri V. Romanenko[2]	326.5 days	Record Soviet single endurance flight in orbiting space station.
Mir (U.S.S.R.)	Dec. 21, 1988— Dec. 21, 1989	Col. Vladimir Titov and Musa Manarov[3]	366 days	Record Soviet team endurance flight in orbiting space station.

1. Approximate time. NOTE: The letters MR stand for Mercury (capsule) and Redstone (rocket); MA, for Mercury and Atlas (rocket); GT, for Gemini (capsule) and Titan-II (rocket). The first astronaut listed in the Gemini and Apollo flights is the command pilot. The Mercury capsules had names: MR-III was *Freedom 7*, MR-IV was *Liberty Bell 7*, MA-VI was *Friendship 7*, MA-VII was *Aurora 7*, MA-VIII was *Sigma 7*, and MA-IX was *Faith 7*. The figure 7 referred to the fact that the first group of U.S. astronauts numbered seven men. Only one Gemini capsule had a name: GT-III was called *Molly Brown* (after the Broadway musical *The Unsinkable Molly Brown*); thereafter the practice of naming the capsules was discontinued. 2. Returned to earth with two fellow cosmonauts, Aleksandr P. Aleksandrov and Anatoly Levchenko, who had spent a shorter stay aboard the *Mir*. 3. Also returned to earth with French astronaut Jean-Loup Chrétien who spent 3-1/2 weeks aboard the *Mir*.

U.S. Manned Space Flight Projects

Mercury. *Project Mercury*, America's first manned space program, was designed to further knowledge about man's capabilities in space. *Mercury 3* put the first American, Alan B. Shepard, into space. *Mercury 9*, with astronaut Gordon L. Cooper, was the longest flight.

Gemini. *Gemini* was an extension of *Project Mercury*, to determine the effects of prolonged space flight on man—two weeks or longer. "Walks in space" provided invaluable information for astronauts' later walks on the Moon. The *Gemini* spacecraft, twice as large as the *Mercury* capsule, accommodated two astronauts.

Apollo. *Apollo* was the designation for the United States' effort to land a man on the Moon and return him safely to Earth. The goal was successfully accomplished with *Apollo 11* on July 20, 1969, culminating eight years of rehearsal and centuries of dreaming. Astronauts Neil A. Armstrong and Col. Edwin E. Aldrin, Jr., scooped up and brought back the first lunar rocks ever seen on Earth—about 47 pounds. Six *Apollo* flights followed, ending with *Apollo 17* in December, 1972. The last three *Apollos* carried mechanized vehicles called lunar rovers for wide-ranging surface exploration of the Moon by astronauts. The rendezvous and docking of an *Apollo* spacecraft with a Russian *Soyuz* craft in Earth orbit on July 18, 1975, closed out the *Apollo* program.

Skylab. America's first Earth-orbiting space station. *Project Skylab* was designed to demonstrate that men can work and live in space for prolonged periods without ill effects. Originally the spent third stage of a Saturn 5 moon rocket, *Skylab* measured 118 feet from stem to stern, and carried the most varied assortment of experimental equipment ever assembled in a single spacecraft. Three three-man crews visited the space stations, spending more than 740 hours observing the Sun and bringing home more than 175,000 solar pictures. These were the first recordings of solar activity above Earth's obscuring atmosphere. *Skylab* also evaluated systems designed to gather information on Earth's resources and environmental conditions. *Skylab* biomedical findings indicated that man adapts well to space for at least a period of three months, provided he has a proper diet and adequately programmed exercise, sleep, work, and recreation periods. *Skylab* orbited Earth at a distance of about 300 miles. Five years after the last *Skylab* mission, the 77-ton space station's orbit began to deteriorate faster than expected, owing to unexpectedly high sunspot activity. On July 11, 1979, the parts of *Skylab* that did not burn up in the atmosphere came crashing down on parts of Australia and the Indian Ocean. No one was hurt.

Space Shuttle. The *Space Shuttle* (also known as the National Space Transportation System or STS) is a manned spacecraft design developed by NASA to reduce the cost of using space for commercial, scientific, and defense needs. The *Shuttle* is a manned rocket which, after depositing its payload in space, can be flown back to Earth like a conventional airplane and be available for re-use. Although most of its cargoes will be unmanned, the *Shuttle* can serve as an inhabited Earth-orbiting laboratory for up to 30 days. The NASA orbiter is 122.2 feet long and has a wingspan of 78.6 feet.

The *Space Shuttle Columbia* was successfully launched on April 12, 1981. It made five flights (the first four were test runs), the last completed on November 16, 1982.

The second shuttle, *Challenger*, made its maiden flight on April 4, 1983. In April 1984, crew members of the *Challenger* captured, repaired, and returned the Solar Max satellite to orbit, making it the first time a disabled satellite had been repaired in space. The third shuttle, *Discovery*, made its first flight on August 30, 1984. The fourth space shuttle, *Atlantis*, made its maiden flight on Oct. 3, 1985.

A tragedy occurred on Jan. 28, 1986, when the shuttle *Challenger* exploded, killing the crew of seven 73 seconds after takeoff. It was the world's worst space flight disaster.

The first U.S. space mission since the *Challenger* disaster was launched 32 months later on Sept. 29, 1988, with the flight of *Discovery*. It had a crew of five and deployed a TDRS (Tracking Data Relay Satellite) communications satellite.

A new orbiter, the *Endeavour*, named after British explorer James Cook's first ship, is being built to replace the *Challenger*.

Soviet Manned Space Flight Programs

Vostok. The Soviets' first manned capsule, roughly spherical, used to place the first six cosmonauts in Earth orbit (1961–65).

Voskhod. Adaptation of the *Vostok* capsule to accommodate two and three cosmonauts. *Voskhod 1* orbited three persons, and *Voskhod 2* orbited two persons performing the world's first manned extravehicular activity.

Soyuz. Late-model manned spacecraft with provisions for three cosmonauts and a "working compartment" accessible through a hatch. Soyuz is the Russian word for "union". Since 1973, all *Soyuz* spacecraft have carried two cosmonauts. *Soyuz 19*, launched July 15, 1975, docked with the American *Apollo* spacecraft.

Spaceflight Visionaries

Konstantin E. Tsiolkovsky

Konstantin Eduardovich Tsiolkovsky, a deaf, provincial schoolteacher, is the acknowledged founder of theoretical cosmonautics. He pioneered the development of rocket and space research in the Soviet Union. Tsiolkovsky made many contributions to early space flight literature, and his classic article on astronautics, "The Investigation of Universal Space by Means of Reactive Devices" was published in 1903, the same year the Wright brothers made their famous flight. He also built the first wind tunnel in Russia for the testing of aerodynamic designs.

Konstantin E. Tsiolkovsky was born on September 17, 1857, in Izhevskoye, Ryazan Province, and died on September 19, 1935, at the age of seventy-eight. During his lifetime, details of his research were essentially unknown outside the Soviet Union. Photo reproduced by Novosti Press Agency.

Robert H. Goddard

Robert Hutchings Goddard is generally acknowledged to be the father of modern rocketry. He began his study of rockets in 1909 and he received a basic patent for a rocket apparatus as early as 1914. While a physics professor at Clark University, he conducted experimental and theoretical research on rocket devices. Goddard launched the world's first liquid-fuel rocket from a farm near Auburn, Mass., on March 16, 1926. (Above photo). In 1935, he became the first person to fire a liquid-fuel rocket faster than the speed of sound. Goddard was a brilliant inventor and he developed many rocket devices including the first automatic rocket steering mechanism.

Robert H. Goddard was born on Oct. 5, 1882, in Worcester, Mass., and he died on Aug. 10, 1945, at the age of sixty-three. Photo Smithsonian Institution.

Salyut. Earth-orbiting space station intended for prolonged occupancy and re-visitation by cosmonauts. They are usually launched by Soviet Proton rockets. *Salyut 1* was launched April 19, 1971. *Salyut 2,* launched April 3, 1973, malfunctioned in orbit and was never occupied. *Salyut 3* was launched June 25, 1974. *Salyut 4* was launched Dec. 26, 1974. *Salyut 5* was launched June 22, 1976. *Salyut 6* was launched on Sept. 29, 1977. *Salyut 7* was launched on April 19, 1982 and is still in orbit. A record breaking Russian endurance flight was set (Feb. 8, 1984-Oct. 2, 1985) when Soviet astronauts spent 237 days in orbit aboard *Salyut-7.*

Mir. A new Soviet space station, to be permanently manned, was launched into orbit on Feb. 20, 1986. Since that time, two space endurance records have been set in the *Mir.* On Dec. 29, 1987, Col. Yuri Romanenko set a single-mission record of 326.5 days in space. On Dec. 21, 1989, Col. Vladimir Titov and Musa Manarov returned to Earth after spending 366 days aboard the orbiting space station.

GALILEO
Long-Term Study of Jupiter

Galileo is a project to orbit Jupiter and send an instrumented probe into the giant planet's atmosphere. The Galileo mission will allow scientists to study—at close range and for almost two years—the largest planet in the solar system, its satellites and massive energy field. The project is named after the Italian astronomer Galileo Galilei, who on Jan. 7, 1610, discovered three of Jupiter's moons and later on January 13th discovered a fourth satellite. These four "Galilean" satellites—Io, Europa, Ganymede, and Callisto, are major targets for the mission. The spacecraft will study the chemical composition and physical state of Jupiter's atmosphere and the four moons, as well as the structure and dynamics of the Jovian magnetosphere.

During the 22-month life of the mission, the orbiter will complete 10 orbits of Jupiter while making a close flyby of at least one Galilean satellite on each orbit.

If all goes as planned, the spacecraft will be carried to Earth orbit by the space shuttle and launched toward Jupiter in October 1989. After a six-year journey, it will reach the planet in 1995. A comprehensive article about the Galileo mission was published in the 1988 edition of *Information Please Almanac.*

ULYSSES
International Solar Polar Mission

Ulysses is an international project to study the poles of the Sun and interstellar space above and below the poles. *Ulysses,* formerly called the International Solar Polar Mission, will launch a single 814-lb (370-kg) spacecraft into an orbit at right angles to the solar system's ecliptic plane. (The ecliptic is the plane in which the Earth and most of the planets orbit the Sun). This special orbit will allow the spacecraft to examine for the first time the regions of the Sun's north and south poles. Besides examining the Sun's energy fields, instruments on *Ulysses* will study other phenomena from the Milky Way and beyond.

While scientists have studied the Sun for centuries, they know very little about matter reaching the solar system from other nearby stars. This is because particles reaching the Sun's magnetic field from beyond the solar system are greatly changed by the Sun's magnetic field and by collision with particles flowing outward from the Sun. No spacecraft has ever left the solar system to make actual measurements of the interstellar medium.

It is hoped that the *Ulysses* spacecraft will be launched from a space shuttle in the fall of 1990.

THE CRAF/CASSINI MISSION

These projects combine two missions that will both use NASA's new *Mariner Mark II* spacecraft and greatly reduce the total cost. NASA plans to launch CRAF in 1995 and follow it with the Cassini mission in 1996.

Comet Rendezvous Asteroid Flyby (CRAF)

This mission will send a spacecraft to encounter an asteroid, and then to rendezvous with a comet and fly alongside it for nearly three years. CRAF will launch a heavily instrumented penetrator/lander into the comet's nucleus to measure temperatures and chemical composition. Other instruments will collect data on the comet's nucleus, its coma, and its dust and ion cloud and tail.

CRAF will be launched aboard a *Titan IV-Centaur* expendable launch vehicle in August 1995. The spacecraft would encounter an asteroid named 449 Hamburga in January 1998 en route to the comet. CRAF would take photographs and other scientific measurements during the encounter period. The asteroid is about 55 miles (88 kilometers) in diameter and is a carbonaceous type.

The spacecraft will subsequently arrive at a rendezvous point with Comet Kopff in August 2000. CRAF will fire its penetrator/lander at the comet in August 2001, and will continue to fly beside it for two and two-thirds years. The mission will end on March 31, 2003. It will mark the first time a spacecraft will have flown in formation with a comet.

Comet Kopff is named for August Adalbert Kopff, who discovered it on August 22, 1906. The comet travels between a region from just inside the orbit of Jupiter inward to perihelion near the orbit of Mars, 140 million miles (220 million kilometers) from the Sun. The CRAF spacecraft will fly within six miles (10 kilometers) of the comet's nucleus.

All of the phenomena associated with comets will be the target of CRAF's instruments. □

The Cassini Mission

The ringed planet Saturn, its major moon Titan, and complex system of at least 16 other satellites[i] will be the destination for NASA's and the European Space Agency's Cassini Mission. Cassini is named for the Italian-French astronomer, Gian Domenico Cassini, who discovered four of Saturn's major moons and a dark, narrow gap ("Cassini's Division") splitting the planet's rings.

Early during the spacecraft's four-year tour orbiting Saturn, it will launch a parachuted probe descending through Titan's dense atmosphere to the surface of the satellite which has unique organic-like chemistry that could provide clues to the origin of life on Earth.

Current plans call for Cassini to be launched in April 1996. NASA would provide the expendable Titan-Centaur launch vehicle and the Cassini orbiter spacecraft and the European Space Agency

THE SPACE STATION *FREEDOM*. An artist's depiction of the United States' first permanently manned space station, *Freedom,* being assembled. It would be over 500 ft long (153 m) and would have four modules for living and working. Additional modules could be added when required and it eventually could be possible to house as many as 30 astronauts.

Freedom would be assembled in orbit almost 300 miles above the earth from materials brought aloft by space shuttles making 20 trips in two years' time. NASA would like funding to begin its construction in late 1995.

(*See* "Skylab/Space Station Differences," *Information Please Almanac,* 1989, for additional information.)

(ESA) would contribute the Titan probe. NASA and ESA member countries would provide science instruments for both the orbiter and probe.

In order to reach Saturn, Cassini will first execute flybys of the Earth and Jupiter to gain "gravity assist" boosts in velocity to send it on its way. The first flyby of Earth will take place 26 months after launch, followed by the Jupiter flyby some 19 months later. During the first leg of its trip, before its first Earth flyby, Cassini will navigate through part of the asteroid belt and could perform an encounter with the asteroid Maja in March 1997. Maja is a carbonaceous, or "C" type asteroid about 50 miles (78 kilometers) in diameter. Two small asteroids are being considered as possible additional targets, but only one of them could be visited.

The spacecraft's final encounter before proceeding to Saturn will be with Jupiter, which it will pass at a distance of about 2.2 million miles (3.6 million kilometers). Its flight path will take it for 130 days down through a region that no spacecraft has explored more than briefly—the giant planet's magnetotail. Cassini will fly down the magnetotail[2] of Jupiter, performing studies complementing NASA's CRAF mission and the Galileo mission to Jupiter.

Upon reaching Saturn in October 2002, the spacecraft will begin the first of some three dozen highly elliptical orbits during the remainder of its mission. Eighty-five days later, it will release its probe to Titan. Eleven days later, the probe will enter Titan's dense atmosphere and descend to the surface by parachute.

Because of the dense atmosphere shrouding the moon Titan, little is known of its surface—whether it is solid or covered with liquid oceans. At Titan, scientists hope to gain a better understanding of abundances of elements and compounds in its atmosphere, winds, and temperatures, and its surface state and composition.

After relaying to Earth data from the Titan probe's experiments, Cassini will continue with orbits of Saturn and flybys of most of the planet's 16 or more moons. In addition to 36 close encounters with Titan, the spacecraft's orbits will allow it to study Saturn's polar regions after examining the planet's equatorial zone. □

---

1. The International Astronomical Union has officially recognized 17 Saturnian moons. Photographs from *Voyager* flybys suggest that others may exist. 2. A tube of Jupiter's energy field, which trails away from the sun for several million miles.

Famous Firsts in Aviation

Cayley's Helicopter

Sir George Cayley's Helicopter design

Sir George Cayley of England (1773-1857) designed the first practical helicopter in 1842-43. His remarkable machine had twin contra-rotating rotors which served as wings and two pusher-type propellers at the back to give the aircraft forward motion.

Cayley designed and built the first successful man-carrying glider in 1853 and sent his coachman aloft in it on its first flight. He also formulated the basic principles of modern aerodynamics and is the father of British aeronautics.

1782 **First balloon flight.** Jacques and Joseph Montgolfier of Annonay, France, sent up a small smoke-filled balloon about mid-November.

1783 **First hydrogen-filled balloon flight.** Jacques A. C. Charles, Paris physicist, supervised construction by A. J. and M. N. Robert of a 13-ft diameter balloon that was filled with hydrogen. It got up to about 3,000 ft and traveled about 16 mi. in a 45-min flight (Aug. 27).

First human balloon flights. A Frenchman, Jean Pilâtre de Rozier made the first captive-balloon ascension (Oct. 15). With the Marquis d'Arlandes, Pilâtre de Rozier made the first free flight, reaching a peak altitude of about 500 ft, and traveling about 5 1/2 mi. in 20 min (Nov. 21).

1784 **First powered balloon.** Gen. Jean Baptiste Marie Meusnier developed the first propeller-driven and elliptically-shaped balloon—the crew cranking three propellers on a common shaft to give the craft a speed of about 3 mph.

First woman to fly. Mme. Thible, a French opera singer (June 4).

1793 **First balloon flight in America.** Jean Pierre Blanchard, a French pilot, made it from Philadelphia to near Woodbury, Gloucester County, N.J., in a little over 45 min (Jan. 9).

1794 **First military use of the balloon.** Jean Marie Coutelle, using a balloon built for the French Army, made two 4-hr observation ascents. The military purpose of the ascents seems to have been to damage the enemy's morale.

1797 **First parachute jump.** André-Jacques Garnerin dropped from about 6,500 ft over Monceau Park in Paris in a 23-ft diameter parachute

made of white canvas with a basket attached (Oct. 22).

1843 **First air transport company.** In London, William S. Henson and John Stringfellow filed articles of incorporation for the Aerial Transit Company (March 24). It failed.

1852 **First dirigible.** Henri Giffard, a French engineer, flew in a controllable (more or less) steam-engine powered balloon, 144 ft long and 39 ft in diameter, inflated with 88,000 cu ft of coal gas. It reached 6.7 mph on a flight from Paris to Trappe (Sept. 24).

1860 **First aerial photographers.** Samuel Archer King and William Black made two photos of Boston, still in existence.

1872 **First gas-engine powered dirigible.** Paul Haenlein, a German engineer, flew in a semi-rigid-frame dirigible, powered by a 4-cylinder internal-combustion engine running on coal gas drawn from the supporting bag.

1873 **First transatlantic attempt.** *The New York Daily Graphic* sponsored the attempt with a 400,000 cu ft balloon carrying a lifeboat. A rip in the bag during inflation brought collapse of the balloon and the project.

1897 **First successful metal dirigible.** An all-metal dirigible, designed by David Schwarz, a Hungarian, took off from Berlin's Tempelhof Field and, powered by a 16-hp Daimler engine, got several miles before leaking gas caused it to crash (Nov. 13).

1900 **First Zeppelin flight.** Germany's Count Ferdinand von Zeppelin flew the first of his long series of rigid-frame airships. It attained a speed of 18 mi. per h and got 3 1/2 mi. before its steering gear failed (July 2).

Moy's Aerial Steamer

Thomas Moy's Aerial Steamer, 1875

Thomas Moy, a British Engineer, invented a steam-powered monoplane with 15-foot tandem wings and two large fan-shaped propellers. He named his flying machine "The Aerial Steamer." Moy demonstrated his airplane at London's Crystal Palace in 1875. While his pilotless aircraft never actually flew, it was able to rise about six inches off the ground under its own power while attached to a tether on a circular track.

Dec. 17, 1903. Orville Wright at the controls, Wilbur runs alongside him. (National Air and Space Museum, Smithsonian Institution)

1903 **First successful heavier-than-air machine flight.** Aviation was really born on the sand dunes at Kitty Hawk, N.C., when Orville Wright crawled to his prone position between the wings of the biplane he and his brother Wilbur had built, opened the throttle of their homemade 12-hp engine and took to the air. He covered 120 ft in 12 sec. Later that day, in one of four flights, Wilbur stayed up 59 sec and covered 852 ft (Dec. 17).

1904 **First airplane maneuvers.** Orville Wright made the first turn with an airplane (Sept. 15); 5 days later his brother Wilbur made the first complete circle.

1905 **First airplane flight over half an hour.** Orville Wright kept his craft up 33 min 17 sec (Oct. 4).

1906 **First European airplane flight.** Alberto Santos-Dumont, a Brazilian, flew a heavier-than-air machine at Bagatelle Field, Paris (Sept. 13).

1908 **First airplane fatality.** Lt. Thomas E. Selfridge, U.S. Army Signal Corps, was in a group of officers evaluating the Wright plane at Fort Myer, Va. He was up about 75 ft with Orville Wright when the propeller hit a bracing wire and was broken, throwing the plane out of control, killing Selfridge and seriously injuring Wright (Sept. 17).

1909 **First cross-Channel flight.** Louis Blériot flew in a 25-hp Blériot VI monoplane from Les Baraques near Calais, France, and landed near Dover Castle, England, in a 26.61-mi. (38-km) 37-min flight across the English Channel (July 25).

1910 **First licensed woman pilot.** Baroness Raymonde de la Roche of France, who learned to fly in 1909, received ticket No. 36 on March 8.

First flight from shipboard. Lt. Eugene Ely, USN, took a Curtiss plane off from the deck of cruiser *Birmingham* at Hampton Roads, Va., and flew to Norfolk (Nov. 14). The following January, he reversed the process, flying from Camp Selfridge to the deck of the armored cruiser *Pennsylvania* in San Francisco Bay (Jan. 18).

1911 **First U.S. woman pilot.** Harriet Quimby, a magazine writer, who got ticket No. 37.

1912 **First woman's cross-Channel flight.** Harriet Quimby flew from Dover, England, across the English Channel, and landed at Hardelot, France (25 mi. south of Calais) in a Blériot monoplane

Harriet Quimby was the leading woman aviator of her day. (Leslie's Weekly Illustrated Newspaper)

loaned to her by Louis Blériot (April 16). She was later killed in a flying accident over Dorchester Bay during a Harvard-Boston aviation meet on July 1, 1912.

1913 **First multi-engined aircraft.** Built and flown by Igor Ivan Sikorsky while still in his native Russia.

1914 **First aerial combat.** In August, Allied and German pilots and observers started shooting at each other with pistols and rifles—with negligible results.

1915 **First air raids on England.** German Zeppelins started dropping bombs on four English communities (Jan. 19).

1918 **First U.S. air squadron.** The U.S. Army Air Corps made its first independent raids over enemy lines, in DH-4 planes (British-designed) powered with 400-hp American-designed Liberty engines (April 8).

First regular airmail service. Operated for the Post Office Department by the Army, the first regular service was inaugurated with one round trip a day (except Sunday) between Washington, D.C., and New York City (May 15).

1919 **First transatlantic flight.** The NC-4, one of four Curtiss flying boats commanded by Lt. Comdr. Albert C. Read, reached Lisbon, Portugal, (May 27) after hops from Trepassy Bay, Newfoundland, to Horta, Azores (May 16–17), to Ponta Delgada (May 20). The Liberty-powered craft was piloted by Walter Hinton.

First nonstop transatlantic flight. Capt. John Alcock and Lt. Arthur Whitten Brown, British World War I flyers, made the 1,900 mi. from St. John's, Newfoundland, to Clifden, Ireland, in 16 h 12 min in a Vickers-Vimy bomber with two 350-hp Rolls-Royce engines (June 15–16).

First lighter-than-air transatlantic flight. The British dirigible R-34, commanded by Maj. George H. Scott, left Firth of Forth, Scotland, (July 2) and touched down at Mineola, L.I., 108 h later. The eastbound trip was made in 75 h (completed July 13).

First scheduled London-Paris passenger service (using airplanes). Aircraft Travel and Transport inaugurated London-Paris service (Aug. 25). Later the company started the first trans-channel mail service on the same route (Nov. 10).

1921 **First naval vessel sunk by aircraft.** Two battleships being scrapped by treaty were sunk by bombs dropped from Army planes in demonstration put on by Brig. Gen. William S. Mitchell (July 21).

First helium balloon. The C-7, non-rigid Navy dirigible was first to use non-inflammable helium as lifting gas, making a flight from Hampton Roads, Va., to Washington, D.C. (Dec. 1).

1922 **First member of Caterpillar Club.** Lt. (later Maj. Gen.) Harold Harris bailed out of a crippled plane he was testing at McCook Field, Dayton, Ohio (Oct. 20), and became the first man to join the Caterpillar Club—those whose lives have been saved by parachute.

1923 **First nonstop transcontinental flight.** Lts. John A. Macready and Oakley Kelly flew a single-engine Fokker T-2 nonstop from New York to San Diego, a distance of just over 2,500 mi. in 26 h 50 min (May 2–3).

First autogyro flight. Juan de la Cierva, a brilliant Spanish mathematician, made the first successful flight in a rotary wing aircraft in Madrid (June 9).

1924 **First round-the-world flight.** Four Douglas Cruiser biplanes of the U.S. Army Air Corps took off from Seattle under command of Maj. Frederick Martin (April 6). 175 days later, two of the planes (Lt. Lowell Smith's and Lt. Erik Nelson's) landed in Seattle after a circuitous route—one source saying 26,345 mi., another saying 27,553 mi.

1926 **First polar flight.** Then-Lt. Cmdr. Richard E. Byrd, acting as navigator, and Floyd Bennett as pilot, flew a trimotor Fokker from Kings Bay, Spitsbergen, over the North Pole and back in 15 1/2 h (May 8–9).

1927 **First solo, nonstop transatlantic flight.** Charles Augustus Lindbergh lifted his Wright-powered Ryan monoplane, *Spirit of St. Louis*, from Roosevelt Field, L.I., to stay aloft 33 h 39 min and travel 3,600 mi. to Le Bourget Field outside Paris (May 20–21).

Charles A. Lindbergh and *The Spirit of St. Louis*. (National Air and Space Museum, Smithsonian Institution)

First transatlantic passenger. Charles A. Levine was piloted by Clarence D. Chamberlin from Roosevelt Field, L.I., to Eisleben, Germany, in a Wright-powered Bellanca (June 4–5).

1928 **First east-west transatlantic crossing.** Baron Guenther von Huenefeld, piloted by German Capt. Hermann Koehl and Irish Capt. James Fitzmaurice, left Dublin for New York City (April 12) in a single-engine all-metal Junkers monoplane. Some 37 h later, they crashed on Greely Island, Labrador. Rescued.

First U.S.-Australia flight. Sir Charles Kingsford-Smith and Capt. Charles T. P. Ulm, Australians, and two American navigators, Harry W. Lyon and James Warner, crossed the Pacific from Oakland to Brisbane. They went via Hawaii and the Fiji Islands in a trimotor Fokker (May 31–June 8).

First transarctic flight. Sir Hubert Wilkins, an Australian explorer and Carl Ben Eielson, who served as pilot, flew from Point Barrow, Alaska, to Spitsbergen (mid-April).

1929 **First of the endurance records.** With Air Corps Maj. Carl Spaatz in command and Capt. Ira Eaker as chief pilot, an Army Fokker, aided by refueling in the air, remained aloft 150 h 40 min at Los Angeles (Jan. 1–7).

First round-the-world airship flight. The LZ-127, known as the *Graf Zeppelin*, flew 21,300 miles in 20 days and 4 hours. Also set distance record (August).

First blind flight. James H. Doolittle proved the feasibility of instrument-guided flying when he took off and landed entirely on instruments (Sept. 24).

First rocket-engine flight. Fritz von Opel, a German auto maker, stayed aloft in his small rocket-powered craft for 75 sec, covering nearly 2 mi. (Sept. 30).

First South Pole flight. Comdr. Richard E. Byrd, with Bernt Balchen as pilot, Harold I. June, radio operator, and Capt. A. C. McKinley, photographer, flew a trimotor Fokker from the Bay of Whales, Little America, over the South Pole and back (Nov. 28–29).

1930 **First Paris–New York nonstop flight.** Dieudonné Coste and Maurice Bellonte, French pilots, flew a Hispano-powered Breguet biplane from Le Bourget Field to Valley Stream, L.I., in 37 h 18 min. (Sept. 2–3).

Chuck Yeager alongside the Bell X-1 named *Glamorous Glennis* after his wife. (National Air and Space Museum, Smithsonian Institution)

1931 **First flight into the stratosphere.** Auguste Piccard, a Swiss physicist, and Charles Knipfer ascended in a balloon from Augsburg, Germany, and reached a height of 51,793 ft in a 17-h flight that terminated on a glacier near Innsbruck, Austria (May 27).

First nonstop transpacific flight. Hugh Herndon and Clyde Pangborn took off from Sabishiro Beach, Japan, dropped their landing gear, and flew 4,860 mi. to near Wenatchee, Wash., in 41 h 13 min. (Oct. 4–5).

1932 **First woman's transatlantic solo.** Amelia Earhart, flying a Pratt & Whitney Wasp-powered Lockheed Vega, flew alone from Harbor Grace, Newfoundland, to Ireland in approximately 15 h (May 20–21).

First westbound transatlantic solo. James A. Mollison, a British pilot, took a de Havilland Puss Moth from Portmarnock, Ireland, to Pennfield, N.B. (Aug. 18).

First woman airline pilot. Ruth Rowland Nichols, first woman to hold three international records at the same time—speed, distance, altitude—was employed by N.Y.-New England Airways.

1933 **First round-the-world solo.** Wiley Post took a Lockheed Vega, *Winnie Mae*, 15,596 mi. around the world in 7 d 18 h 49 1/2 min (July 15–22).

1937 **First successful helicopter.** Hanna Reitsch, a German pilot, flew Dr. Heinrich Focke's FW-61 in free, fully controlled flight at Bremen (July 4).

1939 **First turbojet flight.** Just before their invasion of Poland, the Germans flew a Heinkel He-178 plane powered by a Heinkel S3B turbojet (Aug. 27).

1942 **First American jet plane flight.** Robert Stanley, chief pilot for the Bell Aircraft Corp., flew the Bell XP-59 *Airacomet* at Muroc Army Base, Calif. (Oct. 1).

1947 **First piloted supersonic flight in an airplane.** Capt. Charles E. Yeager, U.S. Air Force, flew the X-1 rocket-powered research plane built by Bell Aircraft Corp., faster than the speed of sound at Muroc Air Force Base, California (Oct. 14).

1949 **First round-the-world nonstop flight.** Capt. James Gallagher and USAF crew of 13 flew a Boeing B-50A Superfortress around the world nonstop from Ft. Worth, returning to same point: 23,452 mi. in 94 h 1 min, with 4 aerial refuelings enroute (Feb. 27–March 2).

1950 **First nonstop transatlantic jet flight.** Col. David C. Schilling (USAF) flew 3,300 mi. from England to Limestone, Maine, in 10 h 1 min (Sept. 22).

1951 **First solo across North Pole.** Charles F. Blair, Jr., flew a converted P-51 (May 29).

1952 **First jetliner service.** De Havilland Comet flight inaugurated by BOAC between London and Johannesburg, South Africa (May 2). Flight, including stops, took 23 h 38 min.

First transatlantic helicopter flight. Capt. Vincent H. McGovern and 1st Lt. Harold W. Moore piloted 2 Sikorsky H-19s from Westover, Mass., to Prestwick, Scotland (3,410 mi.). Trip was made in 5 steps, with flying time of 42 h 25 min (July 15–31).

First transatlantic round trip in same day. British Canberra twin-jet bomber flew from Aldergrove, Northern Ireland, to Gander, Newfoundland, and back in 7 h 59 min flying time (Aug. 26).

1955 **First transcontinental round trip in same day.** Lt. John M. Conroy piloted F-86 Sabrejet across U.S. (Los Angeles–New York) and back—5,085 mi.—in 11 h 33 min 27 sec (May 21).

1957 **First round-the-world, nonstop jet plane flight.** Maj. Gen. Archie J. Old, Jr., USAF, led a flight of 3 Boeing B-52 bombers, powered with 8 10,000-lb. thrust Pratt & Whitney Aircraft J57 engines around the world in 45 h 19 min; distance 24,325 mi.; average speed 525 mph. (Completed Jan. 18.)

1958 **First transatlantic jet passenger service.** BOAC, New York to London (Oct. 4). Pan American started daily service, N.Y. to Paris (Oct. 26).

First domestic jet passenger service. National Airlines inaugurated service between New York and Miami (Dec. 10).

1968 **Prototype of world's first supersonic** airliner, the Soviet-designed Tupolev Tu-144 made first flight, Dec. 31. It first achieved supersonic speed on June 5, 1969.

1973 **First female pilot of a U.S. major scheduled airline.** Emily H. Warner became employed by Frontier Airlines on January 29 as second officer on a Boeing 737.

1976 **First regularly-scheduled commercial supersonic transport (SST) flights begin.** Air France and British Airways inaugurate service (January 21). Air France flies the Paris-Rio de Janeiro route; B.A., the London-Bahrain. Both airlines begin SST service to Washington, D.C. (May 24).

1977 **First successful man-powered aircraft.** Paul MacCready, an aeronautical engineer from Pasadena, Calif., was awarded the Kremer Prize for creating the world's first successful man-powered aircraft. The *Gossamer Condor* was flown by Bryan Allen over the required 3-mile course on Aug. 23.

1978 **First successful transatlantic balloon flight.** Three Albuquerque, N.M., men, Ben Abruzzo, Larry Newman, and Maxie Anderson, completed the crossing (Aug. 16. Landed, Aug. 17) in their hot air balloon, *Double Eagle II.*

1979 **First man-powered aircraft to fly across the English Channel.** The Kremer Prize for the Channel crossing was won by Bryan Allen who flew the *Gossamer Albatross* from Folkestone, England to Cap Gris-Nez, France, in 2 h 55 min (June 12).

1980 First successful balloon flight over the North Pole. Sidney Conn and his wife Eleanor, in hot-air balloon *Joy of Sound* (April 11).

First nonstop transcontinental balloon flight, and also record for longest overland voyage in a balloon. Maxie Anderson and his son, Kris, completed four-day flight from Fort Baker, Calif., to successful landing outside Matane, Quebec, on May 12 in their helium-filled balloon, *Kitty Hawk*.

First long-distance solar-powered flight. Janice Brown, 98-lb former teacher, flew tiny experimental solar-powered aircraft, *Solar Challenger* six miles in 22-min near Marana, Ariz. (Dec. 3). The craft was powered by a 2.75-hp engine.

First solar-powered aircraft to fly across the English Channel. Stephen R. Ptacek flew the 210-lb *Solar Challenger* at the average speed of 30 mph

from Cormeilles-en-Vexin near Paris to the Royal Manston Air Force Base on England's southeastern coast in 5 h 30 min (July 7).

1984 First solo transatlantic balloon flight. Joe W. Kittinger landed Sept. 18 near Savona, Italy, in his helium-filled balloon *Rosie O'Grady's Balloon of Peace* after a flight of 3,535 miles from Caribou, Me.

1986 First nonstop flight around the world without refueling. From Edwards AFB, Calif., Dick Rutan and Jeana Yeager flew in *Voyager* around the world (24,986.727 mi.), returning to Edwards in 216 h 3 min 44 s (Dec. 14–23).

1987 First Transatlantic Hot-Air Balloon Flight. Richard Branson and Per Lindstrand flew 2,789.6 miles from Sugarloaf Mt., Maine, to Ireland in the hot-air balloon *Virgin Atlantic Flyer* (July 2-4).

Five Easy Steps to Set an Aviation Record

Source: National Aeronautic Association.

It's easy to attempt your own aviation record. The National Aeronautic Association, the U.S. sanctioning body for all World and National Records, can supply you with a brochure about its record's program and how you can go about setting your own record. You need only follow five easy steps.

1. Contact the NAA at 1763 R St. NW, Washington, D.C. 20009 (202-265-8720, and tell us that you are interested in setting a record. The Secretary of NAA's Contest and Records Board will help you with subsequent steps.

2. The prospective contestant must apply for and be granted a sanction by NAA. The sanction gives the contestant the exclusive right within the United Sates to attempt the record. To provide adequate time for planning, the sanction request must be submitted at least 30 days prior to the start of the record attempt.

3. The contestant must possess an FAI Sporting license valid for the year in which the attempt is to be made. The license is available from NAA at a cost of $12.50.

4. When the sanction is granted, the contestant will be put in contact with the NAA officials who are available to assist the contestant in developing plans and resolving all technical matters.

5. When the contestant is ready and the appointed official observers are present, the record attempt is made. The NAA directing official will coordinate all details, and will insure compliance with all rules of the international governing body, the Federation Aeronautique Internationale (FAI). That's all it takes.

World's 50 Busiest Airports in 1988

Airport	Passengers[1]	Airport	Passengers[1]
1. Chicago Ill. (O'Hare)	56,280,545	26. Philadelphia/Wilmington	15,427,317
2. Atlanta, Georgia	47,649,470	27. Houston, (International)	15,388,667
3. Los Angeles (International)	44,873,113	28. Orlando, (International)	14,781,222
4. Dallas/Ft. Worth, Texas	41,875,444	29. Phoenix, Arizona	14,771,236
5. London (Heathrow Airport)	34,742,100	30. Las Vegas, (International)	14,644,962
6. Denver, Colorado	32,355,000	31. Seattle/Tacoma, (international)	14,445,482
7. New York (Kennedy Airport)	30,192,477	32. Rome (Fiumicino)	13,701,783
8. Tokyo, Japan	29,927,027	33. Amsterdam (Schiphol)	13,231,722
9. San Francisco/Oakland	29,812,440	34. Charlotte, N.C. (International)	12,978,582
10. New York (La Guardia)	24,225,913	35. Hong Kong, Hong Kong	12,667,434
11. Miami Fla. (International)	24,036,104	36. Memphis (International)	10,815,549
12. New York NY/Newark, NJ	23,475,254	37. Washington (Dulles Airport)	10,784,767
13. Boston, Massachusetts	23,283,047	38. Copenhagen, Denmark	10,622,814
14. Paris, France (Orly)	20,427,446	39. Sydney, N.S.W., Australia	10,537,076
15. Honolulu, Oahu, Hawaii	20,380,282	40. Mexico City, Mexico	10,327,348
16. St. Louis, Missouri	20,362,606	41. Salt Lake City, Utah	10,163,883
17. Frankfurt, Fed. Rep. of Germany	19,802,229	42. Zurich, Switzerland	10,114,237
18. Detroit (Metro Wayne Co.)	19,746,992	43. San Diego (International)	10,101,030
19. London (Gatwick Airport)	19,372,600	44. Fukuoka, Japan	10,027,862
20. Osaka, Japan	19,291,209	45. Singapore, Singapore	10,022,621
21. Toronto Ont. (Pearson Airport)	17,962,401	46. Tampa/St. Petersburg, Florida	10,008,089
22. Minneapolis/St Paul, Minn	17,858,986	47. Duesseldorf, Fed. Rep. of Germany	9,456,468
23. Pittsburgh, Pa	17,457,801	48. Kansas City (International)	9,445,778
24. Paris, France (Charles De Gaulle)	16,040,641	49. Baltimore, Maryland	9,146,286
25. Washington (National Airport)	15,439,860	50. Munich. Fed. Rep. of Germany	9,125,266

1. Enplaned, deplaned, and transfer, in millions. *Source:* Airport Operators Council International, June 1988. Figures and rank are latest available as of mid-1989.

America's Hottest Fighter Jets

By Gerard Varni

F-14A

F-16

F-14 TOMCAT

The F-14 Tomcat is a carrier-based multipurpose fighter, whose main task is fleet air defense. Armed with Sidewinder, Sparrow, and Phoenix air-to-air missiles, the variable-wing Tomcat is a potent aerial dueler. The F-14 crew comprises a pilot and radar intercept officer seated in tandem. The first Tomcat, an F-14A, joined the fleet in 1972.

The F-14A (Plus) made its debut in 1984. Currently undergoing flight tests is the F-14D, an upgraded model, has vastly improved radar and advanced digital avionics. The F-14D also carries new ECM equipment, the JTIDS (joint tactical information distribution system) and an IRST (infrared search and track) set.

Dimensions: Length: 62.8 feet (19.1 meters); Height: 16 feet (4.88 meters); Unswept Wingspan: 64.1 feet (19.54 meters); Swept Wingspan: 38.2 feet (11.65 meters).

Maximum Level Speed at Altitude: Mach 2.4.

Weight: 40,100 lb. (18,190 kg) when empty.

Range: Tactical combat radius (loaded with six Sparrow and nine Sidewinder air-to-air missiles) is approximately 920 miles. Combat service ceiling for the A(Plus) and D versions is 80,000 feet.

Armament: Various combinations of Sidewinder, Sparrow and Phoenix air-to-air missiles. The F-14D will also accept the advanced medium-range air-to-air missile (AMRAAM). Various combinations of bombs to a maximum external weapon load of 14,500 pounds (6,577 kg). One General Electric M61A1 Vulcan 20 mm cannon with 675 rounds of ammunition.

First Flight: F-14A: December 21, 1970. F-14 (Plus) September 29, 1986.

Prime Contractor: Grumman Corporation.

F-16 FALCON

The F-16 Fighting Falcon is a multipurpose fighter that is proficient at both close-in aerial combat and visual ground attack. Since its maiden flight in 1976 more than 2,000 F-16s, in various configurations, have been delivered to 14 countries other than the United States. The first production versions of the Fighting Falcon, the single-seat F-16A and the two-seat F-16B, fulfilled the roles of air-to-air and air-to-surface combatants.

Subsequent variants of the F-16, designated C (single-seat) and D (two-seat fighter/trainer), re-sulted from the Air Force's multinational staged improvement program (MSIP), which was instituted in 1980. F-16C/Ds are fitted with advanced avionics and systems that allow beyond-visual-range intercept and ground attack at night and in bad weather.

The F-16 is the current aircraft of choice for the USAF flight demonstration team, also known as the Thunderbirds.

Dimensions: Length: 47.64 feet (14.53 meters); Height: 16.43 feet (5.01 meters); Wingspan: 32.83 feet (10.01 meters) with missiles.

Maximum Level Speed at Altitude: Mach 2.03.

Weight: F-16C, 16,794 lb (7,618 kg) when empty; F-16D, 17,408 lb (7,896 kg) when empty.

Range: Combat radius fully loaded is 575 miles. Unrefueled ferry range (with drop tanks) is approximately 2,400 miles. Combat service ceiling is 50,000 feet.

Armament: Various combinations of rockets, missiles and bombs distributed over nine ordnance stations. There is a single mounting for an air-to-air missile at each wing tip, in addition to six hardpoints beneath the wings and a single hardpoint beneath the centerline of the fuselage.

A typical ordnance mix would include a combination of Sidewinders, cluster bombs, air-to-surface missiles, rockets and conventional bombs. The F-16C has successfully test fired the AMRAAM, and Norwegian F-16s carry Penguin antiship missiles. The GE M61A1 Vulcan 20 mm cannon can also be used for ground attack and air-to-air combat.

First Flight: F-16A, December 8, 1976; F-16B, August 8, 1977; F-16C, July 19, 1984 (delivered); F-16D, September 1984 (delivered).

Prime Contractor: General Dynamics Corporation.

F-15 EAGLE

The F-15 Eagle is a single-seat, twin-engine aircraft whose primary mission is air superiority, although it also possesses an excellent air-to-ground weapons delivery capability. The F-15 combines the most advanced fire-control system ever built with three air-to-air weapons for optimum combat efficiency. It is also capable of carrying conventional ordnance on multiple racks without off-loading any of its air-to-air missiles.

Original versions of the Eagle included the

F-15

F-15A single-seat aircraft and the F-15B two-seat trainer. After 1979, Eagles with greater range and weapons capability were designated F-15C/D. The C and D versions are single-seat fighters. In 1987 the Air Force took delivery of its first F-15E, a dual-role attack/air-superiority fighter. The two-seat F-15E is able to perform long-range interdiction missions and can deliver a variety of air-to-ground ordnance at night and in bad weather. Export versions of the F-15 have been delivered to Saudi Arabia and Israel.

Dimensions: Length: 63.8 feet (19.45 meters) Height: 18.5 feet (5.64 meters) Wingspan: 42.8 feet (13.05 meters)

Maximum Level Speed at Altitude: Mach 2.5.
Weight: 40,000 lb. (18,144 kg) when empty.

Range: The F-15 Eagle has an unrefueled ferry range of approximately 3,200 miles (5,100 km). The aircraft has in-flight refueling capability, and its unrefueled range can be increased with the addition of three external conformal fuel tanks. Combat service ceiling is 60,000 feet.

Variations: F-15A, Original single-seat design; F-15B, Two-seat trainer first delivered in 1973; F-15C/D, Eagle versions since 1979 with more sophisticated radar, greater combat radius and ability to carry advanced medium-range air-to-air missile (AMRAAM) and Maverick laser-guided missile. F-15E: Two-seat Strike Eagle dual-role fighter features greater variety of air-to-ground ordnance than C/D versions. Delivered to the Air Force in 1988.

Armament: C/D versions: Air-to-air weapons include the Aim-7 Sparrow, Aim-9 Sidewinder and the Aim-120 AMRAAM. More than 23,000 pounds of bombs and rockets can be delivered from three air-to-ground weapon stations. **E version:** Air-to-air weapons include the Aim-7 Sparrow, Aim-9 Sidewinder and Aim-120 AMRAAM. Air-to-ground weapons include the AGM-65 Maverick laser-guided missile, the Mk. 20 Rockeye bomb and a host of additional bombs and rockets. Guidance for laser-guided bombs is provided by LANTIRN target-designating system.

First Flight: F-15A: July 27, 1972; F-15B: July 7, 1973; F-15C: February 26, 1979; F-15D: June 19, 1979.

Prime Contractor: McDonnell Douglas Corporation.

F-18

F/A-18 HORNET

The F/A-18 is a carrier-based fighter/attack weapon system flown by the U.S. Navy and Marine Corps. It has also been selected for multimission service by Canada, Australia, and Spain.

The initial F/A-18A is a single-seat twin-jet aircraft for all-weather fighter escort and light attack. It performs fleet air defense as a secondary mission. A limited number of two-seat F/A-18B Hornets were also produced as training aircraft. The F/A-18 is capable of catapult launch and arrested landings with little or no wind over deck. Its weapon system and aerodynamic performance allow it to replace both the F-4 and A-7 with superior overall performance in both missions.

Dimensions: Length: 56 feet (17.1 meters); Height: 15.2 feet (4.6 meters); Wingspan: 40.7 feet (12.4 meters).

Maximum Level Speed at Altitude: Mach 1.8.
Weight: 21,830 lb. (9,900 kg) when empty.

Range: The Hornet has an unrefueled ferry range of more than 2,300 miles (3,700 km) and a combat radius of more than 460 miles (740 km) on internal fuel with a full complement of air-to-air missiles; its radius exceeds 630 miles on the interdiction mission. The F/A-18 has in-flight refueling capability and is able to carry three external fuel tanks for additional range. Combat service ceiling is 50,000 feet (15,250 meters).

Variations: F/A-18A: Single seat; F/A-18B, Two-seat trainer; F/A-18C, Single seat; F/A-18D, Two seat.

The C & D versions are similar to their predecessors, but are designed to carry up to six AMRAAMs and four Maverick missiles. F/A-18R: Reconnaissance.

Armament: The Hornet can carry more than 17,000 pounds (7,700 kg) of ordnance, and it has an all-weather, air-to-air radar as well as a fire-control system for accurate delivery of conventional or guided weapons in the air-to-ground role.

The F/A-18 has nine weapon stations: two wingtip stations for Sidewinders; two outboard wing stations for air-to-ground weapons, Sparrows or Sidewinders; two inboard wing stations for fuel tanks or air-to-ground weapons; two nacelle fuselage stations for Sparrows or sensor pods; one centerline station for fuel or air-to-ground weapons. The M62 20 mm gun is mounted in the nose.

First Flight: November 18, 1978.
Prime Contractor: McDonnell Douglas Corporation.

This article is reprinted with permission from the *International Combat Arms—The Journal of Defense Technology*, Volume 7, Number 1. Copyright © 1988 by Peterson Publishing Company, Los Angeles, California. Gerard Varni is Senior Editor for the *International Combat Arms*. The facts expressed herein are the sole responsibility of the author.

The World's Fastest Aircraft

The Lockheed SR-71 A/B "Blackbird," produced in January 1966 was moth-balled in October 1989. It is the world's fastest and highest flying production aircraft built.

The Blackbird was unarmed and had a crew of two seated in tandem. The dimensions are: span 55 ft 7 in.; length 107 ft 5 in.; and height 18 ft 6 in. Its estimated maximum speed at 78,750 ft is over Mach 3, and its operational ceiling is above 80,000 ft. In a reconnaissance mission, the SR-71 could cover up to a 100,000-sq-mi. area in one hour. The aircraft was assigned to the 9th Strategic Reconnaissance Wing, Beale AFB, California. USAF Photo.

World Class Helicopter Records

Selected records. *Source:* National Aeronautic Association.

Great Circle Distance Without Landing
International: 2,213.04 mi.; 3,561.55 km.
Robert G. Ferry (U.S.) in Hughes YOH-6A helicopter powered by Allison T-63-A-5 engine; from Culver City, Calif., to Ormond Beach, Fla., April 6–7, 1966.

Distance, Closed Circuit
International: 1,739.96 mi.; 2,800.20 km.
Jack Schweibold (U.S.) in Hughes YOH-6A helicopter powered by Allison T-62-A-5 engine; Edwards Air Force Base, Calif., March 26, 1966.

Altitude
International: 40,820 ft; 12,442 m.
Jean Boulet (France) in Alouette SA 315-001 "Lama" powered by Artouste IIIB 735 KW engine; Istres, France, June 21, 1972.

Altitude in Horizontal Flight
International: 36,122 ft; 11,010 m.
CWO James K. Church, (U.S.) in Sikorsky CH-54B helicopter powered by 2 P&W JFTD-12 engines; Stratford, CT., Nov. 4, 1971.

Speed Around the World
35.40 mph; 56.97 kph.
H. Ross Perot, Jr., pilot; J.W. Coburn, co-pilot (U.S.) in Bell 206 L-II Long Ranger, powered by one Allison 250-C28B of 435 hp. Elapsed time: 29 days 3 h 8 min 13 sec, Sept. 1–30, 1982.

The First Manned Helicopter Flights

Professor Charles Richet made a successful ascent of about two feet in a tethered aircraft with four biplane rotors at Douai, France, on September 19, 1907. The helicopter, designed by Louis and Jacques Breguet, was named the *Gyroplane*.

Paul Cornu, another French aviator, made a six-foot-high, 20-second free flight in a tandem-rotor helicopter that he built at Lisieux on November 13, 1907.

Active Pilot Certificates Held[1]

(as of January 1)

Year	Total	Airline transport	Com-mercial	Private
1970	720,028	31,442	176,585	299,491
1975	733,728	41,002	192,425	305,848
1980	814,667	63,652	182,097	343,276
1985	722,376	79,192	155,929	320,086
1987	699,653	91,287	143,635	300,949
1988	694,016	96,968	143,030	299,786

1. Includes other pilot categories—helicopter, glider and lighter-than-air (17,319), and students (136,913). *Source:* Department of Transportation, Federal Aviation Administration.

Absolute World Records
(Maximum Performance in Any Class)
Source: National Aeronautic Association.

These official Absolute World Records are the supreme achievements of all the hundreds of records open to flying machines. They are the most outstanding of all the major types, and thus warrant the highest respect.

All types of airplanes are eligible for these few very special records. Airplanes may be powered by piston, turboprop, turbojet, rocket engines or a combination. They may be landplanes, seaplanes or amphibians; they may be lightplanes, business planes, military or commercial airplanes.

Over the years, many different categories of aircraft have held these records. In the past, the cost of developing high-performance aircraft has been so great that only airplanes created for military purposes have held these records. There have been two exceptions to this situation.

Most recently and most dramatically, the Rutan designed "Voyager" shattered the theory that only a complicated military behemoth could hold an Absolute World Record. The Voyager team and its nonstop, non-refueled flight around the world proved that the dreams of dedicated individuals, combined with creative engineering, new technology, and hard work, could conquer the world.

The other exception was the X-15 rocket-powered research airplane. Holder of one record, it was used for both civilian and military research during its highly productive lifetime.

Within the seven basic categories of Absolute Records for airplanes, again the Voyager stands out as a special achievement. This amateur, hand-built, experimental aircraft deserves special recognition because the others were are all military/civilian aircraft designed and built by major government facilities. They are: the little-known Soviet E-266M, a rocket-boosted version of the MiG-25 "Foxbat" interceptor, which holds the absolute altitude record, the aforementioned North American X-15 which holds the record for carrier-launched altitude, and the Lockheed SR-71 "Blackbird" photoreconnaisance airplane which holds three records for speed and altitude.

As evidence of the exceptional status of these records, note that several are more than 10 years old. Since the performance of many new government-backed airplanes which might be superior to these is wrapped in a blanket of national security, the breaking of some of these records will depend as much on political considerations as on technical ones.

Speed Around The World, Nonstop, Nonrefueled

Speed (mph)	Date	Type plane	Pilots	Place
115.65	Dec. 14-23, 1986	*Voyager*	Dick Rutan & Jeana Yeager (U.S.)	Edwards AFB, Calif.—Edwards AFB, Calif.

Distance, Great Circle Without Landing, also Distance, Closed Circuit Without Landing

Distance (mi.)	Date	Pilots	Place
24,986.727	Dec. 14-23, 1986	Dick Rutan & Jeana Yeager (U.S.)	Edwards AFB, Calif.—Edwards AFB, Calif.

Speed Over a Straight Course

Speed (mph)	Date	Type plane	Pilot	Place
2,193.16	July 28, 1976	Lockheed SR-71A	Capt. Eldon W. Joersz (USAF)	Beale AFB, Calif.

Speed Over A Closed Circuit

Speed (mph)	Date	Type plane	Pilot	Place
2,092.294	July 27, 1976	Lockheed SR-71A	Maj. Adolphus H. Bledsoe, Jr. (USAF)	Beale, AFB, Calif.

Altitude

Height (ft)	Date	Type plane	Pilot	Place
123,523.58	Aug. 31, 1977	MIG-25, E-266M	Alexander Fedotov (U.S.S.R.)	U.S.S.R.

Altitude in Horizontal Flight

Height (ft)	Date	Pilot	Place
85,068.997	July 28, 1976	Capt. Robert C. Helt (USAF)	Beale AFB, Calif.

Altitude, Aircraft Launched From A Carrier Airplane

Height (ft)	Date	Type plane	Pilot	Place
314,750.00	July 17, 1962	N. American X-15-1	Maj. Robert H. White (USAF)	Edwards AFB, Calif.

GREAT DISASTERS

The following lists are not all-inclusive due to space limitations. Only disasters involving great loss of life and/or property, historical interest, or unusual circumstances are listed. For later disasters see *Current Events* of 1989.

Earthquakes and Volcanic Eruptions

A.D. 79 Aug. 24, Italy: eruption of Mt. Vesuvius buried cities of Pompeii and Herculaneum, killing thousands.

1556 Jan. 24, Shaanxi (Shensi) Province, China: most deadly earthquake in history; 830,000 killed.

1755 Nov. 1, Portugal: one of the most severe of recorded earthquakes leveled Lisbon and was felt as far away as southern France and North Africa; 10,000–20,000 killed in Lisbon.

1883 Aug. 26–28, Netherlands Indies: eruption of Krakatau; violent explosions destroyed two thirds of island. Sea waves occurred as far away as Cape Horn, and possibly England. Estimated 36,000 dead.

1902 May 8, Martinique, West Indies: Mt. Pelée erupted and wiped out city of St. Pierre; 40,000 dead.

1908 Dec. 28, Messina, Sicily: about 85,000 killed and city totally destroyed.

1915 Jan. 13, Avezzano, Italy: earthquake left 29,980 dead.

1920 Dec. 16, Gansu (Kansu) Province, China: earthquake killed 200,000.

1923 Sept. 1, Japan: earthquake destroyed third of Tokyo and most of Yokohama; more than 140,000 killed.

1933 March 10, Long Beach, Calif.: 117 left dead by earthquake.

1935 May 31, India: earthquake at Quetta killed an estimated 50,000.

1939 Jan. 24, Chile: earthquake razed 50,000 sq mi.; about 30,000 killed.

Dec. 27, Northern Turkey: severe quakes destroyed city of Erzincan; about 100,000 casualties.

1950 Aug. 15, India: earthquake affected 30,000 sq mi. in Assam; 20,000–30,000 believed killed.

1963 July 26, Skoplje, Yugoslavia: four fifths of city destroyed; 1,011 dead, 3,350 injured.

1964 March 27, Alaska: strongest earthquake ever to strike North America hit 80 miles east of Anchorage; followed by seismic wave 50 feet high that traveled 8,445 miles at 450 miles per hour; 117 killed.

1970 May 31, Peru: earthquake left 50,000 dead, 17,000 missing.

1972 April 10, Iran: 5,000 killed in earthquake 600 miles south of Teheran.

Dec. 22, Managua, Nicaragua: earthquake devastated city, leaving up to 6,000 dead.

1976 Feb. 4, Guatemala: earthquake left over 23,000 dead.

July 28, Tangshan, China: earthquake devastated 20-sq.-mi. area of city leaving estimated 242,000 dead.

Aug. 17, Mindanao, Philippines: earthquake and tidal wave left up to 8,000 dead or missing.

1977 March 4, Bucharest: earthquake razed most of downtown Bucharest; 1,541 reported dead, over 11,000 injured.

1978 Sept. 16, Tabas, Iran: earthquake destroyed city in eastern Iran, leaving 25,000 dead.

1980 Nov. 23, Naples, Italy: 2,735 killed when earthquake struck southern Italy.

1982 Dec. 13, Yemen: 2,800 reported dead in earthquake.

1985 Sept. 19–20, Mexico: earthquake registering 8.1 on Richter scale struck central and southwestern regions, devastating part of Mexico City and three coastal states. An estimated 25,000 killed.

Nov. 14–16, Colombia: eruption of Nevada del Ruiz, 85 miles northwest of Bogotá, caused mud slides which buried most of the town of Armero and devastated Chinchiná. An estimated 25,000 were killed.

1988 Dec. 7, Armenia: An earthquake measuring 6.9 on the Richter scale killed nearly 25,000, injured 15,000, and left at least 400,000 homeless.

Floods, Avalanches, and Tidal Waves

1228 Holland: 100,000 persons reputedly drowned by sea flood in Friesland.

1642 China: rebels destroyed Kaifeng seawall; 300,000 drowned.

1896 June 15, Sanriku, Japan: earthquake and tidal wave killed 27,000.

1953 Northwest Europe: storm followed by floods devastated North Sea coastal areas. Netherlands was hardest hit with 1,794 dead.

1959 Dec. 2, Frejus, France: flood caused by collapse of Malpasset Dam left 412 dead.

1960 Agadir, Morocco: 10,000–12,000 dead as earthquake set off tidal wave and fire, destroying most of city.

1962 Jan. 10, Peru: avalanche down Huascaran, extinct Andean volcano, killed more than 3,000 persons.

1963 Oct. 9, Italy: landslide into the Vaiont Dam; flood killed about 2,000.

1966 Oct. 21, Aberfan, Wales: avalanche of coal, waste, mud, and rocks killed 144 persons, including 116 children in school.

1969 Jan. 18–26, Southern California: floods and mudslides from heavy rains caused widespread property damage; at least 100 dead. Another downpour (Feb. 23–26) caused further floods and mudslides; at least 18 dead.

1970 Nov. 13, East Pakistan: 200,000 killed by cyclone-driven tidal wave from Bay of Bengal. Over 100,000 missing.

1971 Sept. 29, Orissa State, India: cyclone and tidal wave off Bay of Bengal killed as many as 10,000.

1972 Feb. 26, Man, W. Va.: more than 118 died when slag-pile dam collapsed under pressure of torrential rains and flooded 17-mile valley.

June 9–10, Rapid City, S.D.: flash flood caused 237 deaths and $160 million in damage.

June 20, Eastern Seaboard: tropical storm Agnes, in 10-day rampage, caused widespread flash floods. Death toll was 129, 115,000 were left homeless, and damage estimated at $3.5 billion.

370

Worst United States Disasters

Aircraft

1979 **May 25, Chicago:** American Airlines DC-10 left engine upon take-off and crashed seconds later, killing all 272 persons aboard and three on the ground in worst U.S. air disaster.

Dam

1928 **March 12, Santa Paula, Calif.:** collapse of St. Francis Dam left 450 dead.

Earthquake

1906 **April 18, San Francisco:** earthquake accompanied by fire razed more than 4 sq mi.; more than 500 dead or missing.

Explosion

1947 **April 16-18, Texas City, Tex.:** most of city destroyed, 561 dead following explosion on ship.

Fire

1871 **Oct. 8, Peshtigo, Wis.:** over 1,200 lives lost and 2 billion trees burned in forest fire.

Flood

1889 **May 31, Johnstown, Pa.:** more than 2,200 died in flood.

Hurricane

1900 **Aug. 27-Sept. 15, Galveston, Tex.:** over 6,000 died from devastation due to both winds and tidal wave.

Marine

1865 **April 27, *Sultana*:** boiler explosion on Mississippi River steamboat near Memphis, 1,547 killed.

Mine

1907 **Dec. 6, Monongha, W. Va.:** coal mine explosion killed 361.

Oil Spill

1989 **Mar. 24, Prince William Sound, Alaska:** Tanker, *Exxon Valdez*, hit an undersea reef and released 10 million plus gallons of oil into the waters, causing the worst oil spill in U.S. history.

Railroad

1918 **July 9, Nashville, Tenn.:** 101 killed in a two-train collision near Nashville.

Submarine

1963 **April 10, *Thresher*:** atomic-powered submarine sank in North Atlantic: 129 dead.

Tornado

1925 **March 18, Great Tri-State Tornado:** Missouri, Illinois, and Indiana; 695 deaths. Eight additional tornadoes in Kentucky, Tennessee, and Alabama raised day's toll to 792 dead.

1976 **Aug. 1, Loveland, Colo.:** Flash flood along Route 34 in Big Thompson Canyon left 139 dead.
1977 **Nov. 19, Andhra Pradesh State, India:** cyclone and flood from Bay of Bengal left 7,000–10,000 dead.
1988 **August-September, Bangladesh:** Heaviest monsoon in 70 years innundates three-fourths of country, killing more than 1,300 people and leaving 30 million homeless. Damage is estimated at over $1 billion.

Storms and Weather

(For U.S. tornadoes and hurricanes, see Index)

1864 **Oct. 5, India:** most of Calcutta denuded by cyclone; 70,000 killed.
1930 **Sept. 3, Santo Domingo:** hurricane killed about 2,000 and injured 6,000.
1934 **Sept. 21, Japan:** hurricane killed more than 4,000 on Honshu.
1942 **Oct. 16, India:** cyclone devastated Bengal; about 40,000 lives lost.
1963 **May 28–29, East Pakistan:** cyclone killed about 22,000 along coast.
 Oct. 2–7, Caribbean: Hurricane Flora killed up to 7,000 in Haiti and Cuba.
1965 **May 11–12 and June 1–2, East Pakistan:** cyclones killed about 47,000.
 Dec. 15, Karachi, Pakistan: cyclone killed about 10,000.
1974 **Sept. 20, Honduras:** Hurricane Fifi struck north-

ern section of country, leaving 8,000 dead, 100,000 homeless.
 Dec. 25, Darwin, Australia: cyclone destroyed nearly the entire city, causing mass evacuation.
1977 **Nov. 19, India:** cyclone struck state of Andhra Pradesh, killing 10,000.

Fires and Explosions

1666 **Sept. 2, England:** "Great Fire of London" destroyed St. Paul's Church, etc. Damage £10 million.
1835 **Dec. 16, New York City:** 530 buildings destroyed by fire.
1871 **Oct. 8, Chicago:** the "Chicago Fire" burned 17,450 buildings, killed 250 persons; $196 million damage.
1872 **Nov. 9, Boston:** fire destroyed 800 buildings; $75-million damage.
1876 **Dec. 5, New York City:** fire in Brooklyn Theater killed more than 300.
1881 **Dec. 8, Vienna:** at least 620 died in fire at Ring Theatre.
1894 **Sept. 1, Minnesota:** forest fire over 480-square-mile area destroyed six towns and killed 480 people.
1900 **May 1, Scofield, Utah:** explosion of blasting powder in coal mine killed 200.
 June 30, Hoboken, N.J.: piers of North German Lloyd Steamship line burned; 326 dead.
1903 **Dec. 30, Chicago:** Iroquois Theatre fire killed 602.

Nuclear Power Plant Accidents

1952 Dec. 12, Chalk River, near Ottawa, Canada: A partial meltdown of the reactor's uranium fuel core resulted after the accidental removal of four control rods. Although millions of gallons of radioactive water accumulated inside the reactor, there were no injuries.

1957 Oct. 7, Windscale Pile No. 1, north of Liverpool, England: Fire in a graphite-cooled reactor spewed radiation over the countryside, contaminating a 200 sq mi area.

South Ural Mountains: Explosion of radioactive wastes at Soviet nuclear weapons factory 12 miles from city of Kyshtym forces the evacuation of over 10,000 people from a contaminated area. No casualties were reported by Soviet officials.

1979 March 28, Three Mile Island, near Harrisburg, Pa.: One of two reactors lost its coolant, which caused the radioactive fuel to overheat and caused a partial meltdown. Some radioactive material was released.

1986 April 16, Chernobyl, near Kiev, U.S.S.R.: Explosion and fire in the graphite core of one of four reactors released radioactive material which spread over part of the Soviet Union, Eastern Europe, Scandinavia, and later Western Europe, in the worst such accident to date.

1906 March 10, France: explosion in coal mine in Courrières killed 1,060.

1907 Dec. 19, Jacobs Creek, Pa.: explosion in coal mine left 239 dead.

1909 Nov. 13, Cherry, Ill.: explosion in coal mine killed 259.

1911 March 25, New York City: fire in Triangle Shirtwaist Factory fatal to 145.

1913 Oct. 22, Dawson, N.M.: coal mine explosion left 263 dead.

1917 April 10, Eddystone, Pa.: explosion in munitions plant killed 133.
Dec. 6, Canada: 1,600 people died when French ammunition ship *Mont Blanc* collided with Belgium steamer in Halifax Harbor.

1930 April 21, Columbus, Ohio: fire in Ohio State Penitentiary killed 320 convicts.

1937 March 18, New London, Tex.: explosion destroyed schoolhouse; 294 killed.

1942 April 26, Manchuria: explosion in Honkeiko Colliery killed 1,549.
Nov. 28, Boston: Cocoanut Grove nightclub fire killed 491.

1944 July 6, Hartford, Conn.: fire and ensuing stampede in main tent of Ringling Brothers Circus killed 168, injured 487.
July 17, Port Chicago, Calif.: 322 killed as ammunition ships explode.
Oct. 20, Cleveland: liquid-gas tanks exploded, killing 130.

1946 Dec. 7, Atlanta: fire in Winecoff Hotel killed 119.

1948 Dec. 3, Shanghai: Chinese passenger ship *Kiangya*, carrying refugees fleeing Communist troops during civil war, struck an old mine, exploded, and sank off Shanghai. Over 3,000 people are believed killed.

1949 Sept. 2, China: fire on Chongqing (Chungking) waterfront killed 1,700.

1954 May 26, off Quonset Point, R.I.: explosion and fire aboard aircraft carrier *Bennington* killed 103 crewmen.

1956 Aug. 7, Colombia: about 1,100 reported killed when seven army ammunition trucks exploded at Cali.
Aug. 8, Belgium: 262 died in coal mine fire at Marcinelle.

1960 Jan. 21, Coalbrook, South Africa: coal mine explosion killed 437.
Nov. 13, Syria: 152 children killed in moviehouse fire.

1961 Dec. 17, Niteroi, Brazil: circus fire fatal to 323.

1962 Feb. 7, Saarland, West Germany: coal mine gas explosion killed 298.

1963 Nov. 9, Japan: explosion in coal mine at Omuta killed 447.

1965 May 28, India: coal mine fire in state of Bihar killed 375.
June 1, near Fukuoka, Japan: coal mine explosion killed 236.

1967 May 22, Brussels: fire in L'Innovation, major department store, left 322 dead.
July 29, off North Vietnam: fire on U.S. carrier *Forrestal* killed 134.

1969 Jan. 14, Pearl Harbor, Hawaii: nuclear aircraft carrier *Enterprise* ripped by explosions; 27 dead, 82 injured.

1970 Nov. 1, Saint-Laurent-du-Pont, France: fire in dance hall killed 146 young people.

1972 May 13, Osaka, Japan: 118 people died in fire in nightclub on top floor of Sennichi department store.
June 6, Wankie, Rhodesia: explosion in coal mine killed 427.

1973 Nov. 29, Kumamoto, Japan: fire in Taiyo department store killed 101.

1974 Feb. 1, Sao Paulo, Brazil: fire in upper stories of bank building killed 189 persons, many of whom leaped to death.

1975 Dec. 27, Dhanbad, India: explosion in coal mine followed by flooding from nearby reservoir left 372 dead.

1977 May 28, Southgate, Ky.: fire in Beverly Hills Supper Club; 167 dead.

1978 July 11, Tarragona, Spain: 140 killed at coastal campsite when tank truck carrying liquid gas overturned and exploded.
Aug. 20, Abadan, Iran: nearly 400 killed when arsonists set fire to crowded theater.

1982 Dec. 18–21, Caracas, Venezuela: power-plant fire leaves 128 dead.

1986 Dec. 31, San Juan, P. R.: arson fire in Dupont Plaza Hotel set by three hotel employees kills 96.

1989 April 19, off Puerto Rico: A gun turret on the battleship *Iowa* exploded during a test-firing while participating in training excercises in the Atlantic about 330 miles northeast of Puerto Rico; 47 crew members were killed. *Also see* Wartime Disasters, *U.S.S. Mississippi*.
June 3, Ural Mountains: Liquified petroleum gas leaking from a pipeline running alongside the Trans-Siberian railway near Uta, 720 miles east of Moscow, exploded and destroyed two passing passenger trains. About 500 travelers were killed and 723 injured of an estimated 1,200 passengers on both trains.

Shipwrecks

1833 May 11, *Lady of the Lake:* bound from England to Quebec, struck iceberg; 215 perished.

1853 Sept. 29 *Annie Jane:* emigrant vessel off coast of Scotland; 348 died.

1898 Nov. 26, *City of Portland:* Loss of 157 off Cape Cod.

1904 June 15, *General Slocum:* excursion steamer burned in East River, New York; 1,021 perished.

1912 March 5, *Principe de Asturias:* Spanish steamer struck rock off Sebastien Point; 500 drowned. April 15, *Titanic:* sank after colliding with iceberg; 1,513 died.

1914 May 29, *Empress of Ireland:* sank after collision in St. Lawrence River; 1,024 perished.

1915 July 24, *Eastland:* Great Lakes excursion steamer overturned in Chicago River; 812 died.

1928 Nov. 12, *Vestris:* British steamer sank in gale off Virginia; 110 died.

1931 June 14: French excursion steamer overturned in gale off St. Nazaire; approximately 450 died.

1934 Sept. 8, *Morro Castle:* 134 killed in fire off Asbury Park, N.J.

1939 May 23, *Squalus:* submarine with 59 men sank off Hampton Beach, N.H.; 33 saved. June 1, Submarine *Thetis:* sank in Liverpool Bay, England; 99 perished.

1942 Oct. 2, *Queen Mary:* rammed and sank a British cruiser; 338 aboard the cruiser died.

1945 April 9: U.S. ship, loaded with aerial bombs, exploded at Bari, Italy; at least 360 killed.

1947 November, Yingkow: Unidentified Chinese troopship evacuating Nationalist troops from Manchuria sank, killing an estimated 6,000 persons.

1949 Sept. 17, *Noronic:* Canadian Great Lakes cruise ship burned at Toronto dock; about 130 died.

1952 April 26, *Hobson:* minesweeper collided with aircraft carrier *Wasp* and sank during night maneuvers in mid-Atlantic; 176 persons lost.

1953 Jan. 9, *Chang Tyong-Ho:* South Korean ferry foundered off Pusan; 249 reported dead. Jan. 31, *Princess Victoria:* British ferry sank in Irish Sea; 133 lost.

1956 July 25, *Andrea Doria:* Italian liner collided with Swedish liner *Stockholm* off Nantucket Island, Mass., sinking next day; 52, mostly passengers on Italian ship, dead or unaccounted for; over 1,600 rescued.

1962 April 8, *Dara,* British liner, exploded and sank in Persian Gulf; 236 persons dead. Caused by time bomb.

1963 May 4: U.A.R. ferry capsized and sank in upper Nile; over 200 died.

1968 Late May, *Scorpion:* nuclear submarine sank in Atlantic 400 miles S.W. of Azores; 99 dead. (Located Oct. 31.)

1970 Dec. 15: ferry in Korean Strait capsized; 261 lost.

1976 Oct. 20, Luling, La.: *George Prince,* Mississippi River ferry, rammed by Norwegian tanker *Frosta;* 77 dead.

1983 May 25, *10th of Ramadan,* Nile steamer, caught fire and sank in Lake Nasser, near Aswan, Egypt; 272 dead and 75 missing.

1987 March 9, Belgium: British ferry capsizes after leaving Belgian port of Zeebrugge with 500 abroad; 134 drowned. Water rushing through open bow is believed to be probable cause.

1987 Dec. 20. Manila: Over 1,500 people killed when passenger ferry *Dona Paz* collided with oil tanker *Victor* off Mindoro Is., 110 miles south of Manila.

1989 April 7, Norwegian Sea: Fourty-two seamen died when Soviet Mike-class nuclear-powered submarine sank more than 300 miles off coast of Norway after an undersea accident and fire. Twenty-seven crew members were rescued.

Aircraft Accidents

1921 Aug. 24, England: *AR-2* British dirigible, broke in two on trial trip near Hull; 62 died.

1925 Sept. 3, Caldwell, Ohio: U.S. dirigible *Shenandoah* broke apart; 14 dead.

1930 Oct. 5, Beauvais, France: British dirigible R 101 crashed, killing 47.

1933 April 4, New Jersey Coast: U.S. dirigible *Akron* crashed; 73 died.

1937 May 6, Lakehurst, N.J.: German zeppelin *Hindenburg* destroyed by fire at tower mooring; 36 killed.

1945 July 28, New York City: U.S. Army bomber crashed into Empire State Building; 13 dead.

1952 Jan. 22, Elizabeth, N.J.: 29 killed, including former Secretary of War Robert P. Patterson, when airliner hit apartments; seven of dead were on ground.

1953 June 18, near Tokyo: crash of U.S. Air Force "Globemaster" killed 129 servicemen.

1960 Dec. 16, New York City: United and Trans World planes collided in fog, crashed in two boroughs, killing 134 in air and on ground.

1961 Feb. 15, near Brussels: 72 on board and farmer on ground killed in crash of Sabena plane; U.S.

THE WORST MARINE DISASTER IN U.S. HISTORY.

The Mississippi sidewheeler *Sultana* had a total capacity of 376 passengers and crew. On this occasion, the ship was jammed with some 2,400 Union soldiers who had recently been released from Confederate prison camps. The Civil War had ended several weeks before and the troops were cheerfully looking forward to returning home. There were about 100 civilian passengers aboard, men, women, and children, who occupied first-class cabins. The boat also had a cargo of horses, mules, hogs, and, surprisingly, a live ten-foot alligator that was kept in a wooden crate. On April 27, 1865, eight miles out of Memphis, Tennessee, the boiler exploded and the ship burst into flames. During the night, the *Sultana* burned down to the water line, while its survivors clung to floating debris. Some passengers were trapped aboard the flaming ship and died in the inferno. During the shipboard fire, one desperate individual managed to kill the alligator with a knife and used the crate to float to safety. Exactly how many people died in the disaster is not known. At least 1,547 lives were lost, exceeding the total of 1,513 for the 1912 sinking of the *Titanic.* The death toll may have been much higher.

Space Accidents

1967 **Jan. 27, Apollo 1:** A fire aboard the space capsule on the ground at Cape Kennedy, Fla. killed astronauts Virgil L. Grissom, Edward H. White, and Roger Chaffee.

April 23-24, Soyuz 1: Vladimir M. Komarov was killed when his craft crashed after its parachute lines, released at 23,000 feet for re-entry, became snarled.

1971 **June 6-30, Soyuz 11:** Three cosmonauts, Georgi T. Dolrovolsky, Vladislav N. Volkov, and Viktor I. Patsayev, found dead in the craft after its automatic landing. Apparently the cause of death was loss of pressurization in the space craft during re-entry into the earth's atmosphere.

1986 **Jan 28, Challenger Space Shuttle:** Exploded 73 seconds after lift off, killing all seven crew members. They were: Christa McAuliffe, Francis R. Scobee, Michael J. Smith, Judith A. Resnick, Ronald E. McNair, Ellison S. Onizuka, and Gregory B. Jarvis. A booster leak ignited the fuel, causing the explosion.

---

figure skating team wiped out.

1966 **March 5, Japan:** British airliner caught fire and crashed into Mt. Fuji; 124 dead.

Dec. 24, Binh Thai, South Vietnam: crash of military-chartered plane into village killed 129.

1970 **Nov. 14, Huntington, W. Va.:** chartered plane carrying 43 players and coaches of Marshall University football team crashed; 75 dead.

1971 **July 30, Morioka, Japan:** Japanese Boeing 727 and F-86 fighter collided in mid-air; toll was 162.

Sept. 4, near Juneau, Alaska: Alaska Airlines Boeing 727 crashed into Chilkoot Mountains; 111 killed.

1972 **Aug. 14, East Berlin, East Germany:** Soviet-built East German Ilyushin plane crashed, killing 156.

Dec. 3, Santa Cruz de Tenerife, Canary Islands: Spanish charter jet carrying West German tourists crashed on take-off; all 155 aboard killed.

Dec. 30, Miami, Fla.: Eastern Airlines Lockheed 1011 TriStar Jumbo jet crashed into Everglades; 101 killed, 75 survived.

1973 **Jan. 22, Kano, Nigeria:** 171 Nigerian Moslems returning from Mecca and five crewmen died in crash.

1973 **Feb. 21:** Civilian Libyan Arab Airlines Boeing 727 shot down by Israeli fighters over Sinai after it had strayed off course; 108 died, five survived. Officials claimed that the pilot had ignored fighters' warnings to land.

April 10, Hochwald, Switzerland: British airliner carrying tourists to Swiss fair crashed in blizzard; 106 dead.

July 11, Paris: Boeing 707 of Varig Airlines, en route to Rio de Janeiro, crashed near airport, killing 122 of 134 passengers.

1974 **March 3, Paris:** Turkish DC-10 jumbo jet crashed in forest shortly after take-off; all 346 passengers and crew killed.

Dec. 4, Colombo, Sri Lanka: Dutch DC-8 carrying Moslems to Mecca crashed on landing approach, killing all 191 persons aboard.

1975 **April 4, near Saigon, Vietnam:** Air Force Galaxy C-5A crashed after take-off, killing 172, mostly Vietnamese children.

Aug. 3, Agadir, Morocco: Chartered Boeing 707, returning Moroccan workers home after vacation in France, plunged into mountainside; all 188 aboard killed.

1976 **Sept. 10, Zagreb, Yugoslavia:** midair collision between British Airways Trident and Yugoslav charter DC-9 fatal to all 176 persons aboard; worst mid-air collision on record.

1977 **March 27, Santa Cruz de Tenerife, Canary Islands:** Pan American and KLM Boeing 747s collided on runway. All 249 on KLM plane and 333 of 394 aboard Pan Am jet killed. Total of 582 is highest for any type of aviation disaster.

1978 **Jan. 1, Bombay:** Air India 747 with 213 aboard exploded and plunged into sea minutes after takeoff.

Sept. 25, San Diego, Calif.: Pacific Southwest plane collided in midair with Cessna. All 135 on airliner, 2 in Cessna, and 7 on ground killed for total of 144.

Nov. 15, Colombo, Sri Lanka: Chartered Icelandic Airlines DC-8, carrying 249 Moslem pilgrims from Mecca, crashed in thunderstorm during landing approach; 183 killed.

1979 **Nov. 26, Jidda, Saudi Arabia:** Pakistan International Airlines 707 carrying pilgrims returning from Mecca crashed on take-off; all 156 aboard killed.

Nov. 28, Mt. Erebus, Antarctica: Air New Zealand DC-10 crashed on sightseeing flight; 257 killed.

1980 **March 14, Warsaw:** LOT Polish Airlines Ilyushin 62 crashed while attempting landing; 22 boxers and officials of a U.S. amateur boxing team killed along with 65 others.

April 25, Santa Cruz de Tenerife, Canary Islands: Chartered Boeing 727 carrying 138 British vacationers and crew of 8 crashed into mountain while approaching for landing; all killed.

Aug. 19, Riyadh, Saudi Arabia: all 301 aboard Saudi Arabian jet killed when burning plane made safe landing but passengers were unable to escape.

1981 **Dec. 1, Ajaccio, Corsica:** Yugoslav DC-9 Super 80 carrying tourists crashed into mountain on landing approach, killing all 178 aboard.

1983 **June 28, near Cuenca, Ecuador:** Ecuadorean jetliner crashed in mountains, killing 119.

Aug. 30, near island of Sakhalin off Siberia, South Korean civilian jetliner shot down by Soviet fighter after it strayed off course into Soviet airspace. All 269 people aboard killed.

Nov. 26, Madrid: A Columbian Avianca Boeing 747 crashed near Mejorada del Campó Airport killing 183 persons aboard. Eleven people survived the accident.

1985 **June 23:** Air-India Boeing 747 exploded over the Atlantic off the coast of Ireland, all 329 aboard killed.

Aug. 12, Japan Air Lines Boeing 747 crashed into a mountain, killing 520 of the 524 aboard.

Dec. 12, A chartered Arrow Air DC-8, bringing American soldiers home for Christmas, crashed on takeoff from Gander, Newfoundland. All 256 aboard died.

1987 **May 9, Poland:** Polish airliner, Ilyushin 62M on charter flight to New York, crashes after take-off from Warsaw killing 183.

Aug. 16, Detroit: Northwest Airlines McDonnell Douglas MD-30 plunges to heavily traveled boulevard, killing 156. Girl 4, only survivor.

Nov. 26: South African Airways Boeing 747 goes down south of Mauritius in rough seas; 160 die.

Nov. 29: Korean Air Boeing 747 jetliner explodes from bomb planted by North Korean agents and crashes into sea off Burma, killing all 115 aboard.

1988 **July 3, Persian Gulf:** U.S. Navy cruiser *Vincennes* shot down Iran Air A300 Airbus, killing 290 persons, after mistaking it for an attacking jet fighter.

Aug. 28, Ramstein Air Force Base, West Germany: Three jets from Italian Air Force acrobatic team collided in mid-air during air show and crashed, killing 70 persons, including the pilots and spectators on the ground. It is worst air-show disaster in history.

Dec. 21, Lockerbie, Scotland: A New-York-bound Pan-Am Boeing 747 exploded in flight from a terrorist bomb and crashed into Scottish village, killing all 259 aboard and 11 persons on the ground. Passengers included 38 Syracuse University students and many U.S. military personnel.

1989 **Feb. 24, UAL 811:** About 100 miles southwest of Hawaii, a 10- × 40-ft hole blew open in the fuselage of a United Airlines Boeing 747. Nine passengers were sucked out of the jet liner to their deaths 20,000 ft over the Pacific; 27 other passengers were injured.

June 7, Paramaribo, Suriname: A Surinam Airways DC-8 carrying 174 passengers and nine crew members crashed into the jungle while making a third attempt to land in a thick fog, killing 168 aboard.

Railroad Accidents

1904 **Aug. 7, Eden, Colo.:** Train derailed on bridge during flash flood; 96 killed.

1910 **March 1, Wellington, Wash.:** two trains swept into canyon by avalanche; 96 dead.

1915 **May 22, Gretna, Scotland:** two passenger trains and troop train collided; 227 killed.

1917 **Dec. 12, Modane, France:** nearly 550 killed in derailment of troop train near mouth of Mt. Cenis tunnel.

1918 **Nov. 1, New York City:** derailment of subway train in Malbone St. tunnel in Brooklyn left 92 dead.

1939 **Dec. 22, near Magdeburg, Germany:** more than 125 killed in collision; 99 killed in another wreck near Friedrichshafen.

1943 **Dec. 16, near Rennert, N.C.:** 72 killed in derailment and collision of two Atlantic Coast Line trains.

1944 **March 2, near Salerno, Italy:** 521 suffocated when Italian train stalled in tunnel.

1949 **Oct. 22, near Nowy Dwor, Poland:** more than 200 reported killed in derailment of Danzig-Warsaw express.

1950 **Nov. 22, Richmond Hill, N.Y.:** 79 died when one Long Island Rail Road commuter train crashed into rear of another.

1951 **Feb. 6, Woodbridge, N.J.:** 85 died when Pennsylvania Railroad commuter train plunged through temporary overpass.

1952 **Oct. 8, Harrow-Wealdstone, England:** two express trains crashed into commuter train; 112 dead.

1953 **Dec. 24, near Sakvice, Czechoslovakia:** two trains crashed; over 100 dead.

1957 **Sept. 1, near Kendal, Jamaica:** about 175 killed when train plunged into ravine.

Sept. 29, near Montgomery, West Pakistan: express train crashed into standing oil train; nearly 300 killed.

Dec. 4, St. John's, England: 92 killed, 187 injured as one commuter train crashed into another in fog.

1960 **Nov. 14, Pardubice, Czechoslovakia:** two trains collided; 110 dead, 106 injured.

1962 **May 3, near Tokyo:** 163 killed and 400 injured when train crashed into wreckage of collision between inbound freight train and outbound commuter train.

1963 **Nov. 9, near Yokohama, Japan:** two passenger trains crashed into derailed freight, killing 162.

1964 **July 26, Custoias, Portugal:** passenger train derailed; 94 dead.

1970 **Feb. 4, near Buenos Aires:** 236 killed when express train crashed into standing commuter train.

1972 **July 21, Seville, Spain:** head-on crash of two passenger trains killed 76.

Oct. 6, near Saltillo, Mexico: train carrying religious pilgrims derailed and caught fire, killing 204 and injuring over 1,000.

Oct. 30, Chicago: two Illinois Central commuter trains collided during morning rush hour; 45 dead and over 200 injured.

1974 **Aug. 30, Zagreb, Yugoslavia:** train entering station derailed, killing 153 and injuring over 60.

1977 **Feb. 4, Chicago:** 11 killed and over 180 injured when elevated train hit rear of another, sending two cars to street.

1981 **June 6, Near Mansi, India:** Driver of train carrying over 500 passengers, braked to avoid hitting cow, causing train to plunge off a bridge into Baghmati River; 268 passengers were reported killed, but at least 300 more were missing.

1982 **Jan. 26, Algeria:** Derailment on Algiers—Oran line leaves up to 120 dead.

July 11, Tepic, Mexico: Nogales-Guadalajara train plunges down mountain gorge killing 120.

1988 **Dec. 12, South London:** A commuter train crashed into the rear of a stopped train killing 33 and injuring more than 110 passengers.

1989 **Jan. 15, Maizdi Khan, Bangladesh:** A train carrying Muslim pilgrims crashed head-on with a mail train killing at least 110 persons and injuring as many as 1,000. Many people were riding on the roof of the trains and between the cars.

Oil Spills

1978 **March 16, off Portsall, France:** Wrecked supertanker *Amoco Cadiz* spilled 68 million gallons causing widespread environmental damage over 100 miles of coast of Brittany. Is world's largest tanker disaster.

1979 **June 8, Gulf of Mexico:** Exploratory oil well, Ixtoc 1, blew out, spilling an estimated 140 million gallons of crude into the open sea. Although it is the largest known oil spill, it had a low environmental impact.

Sports

1955 June 11, Le Mans, France: Racing car in Grand Prix hurtled into grandstand, killing 82 spectators.

1964 May 24, Lima, Peru: More than 300 soccer fans killed and over 500 injured during riot and panic following unpopular ruling by referee in Peru vs. Argentina soccer game. It is worst soccer disaster on record.

1971 Jan. 2, Glasgow, Scotland: Sixty-six persons killed in a crush at the Glasgow Rangers home stadium when fans trying to leave encountered fans trying to return to the stadium after hearing that a late goal had been scored.

1982 Oct. 20, Moscow: According to *Sovietsky Sport*, as many as 340 persons were killed at Lenin Stadium when exiting soccer fans collided with returning fans after final goal was scored. All the fans had been crowded into one section of stadium by police.

1985 May 11, Bradford, England: 56 persons burned to death and over 200 injured when fire engulfed the main grandstand at Bradford's soccer stadium.

May 29, Brussels, Belgium: Drunken group of British soccer fans supporting Liverpool club stormed stand filled with Italian supporters of Juventus team before European Champion's Cup final. While British fans attacked rival spectators at the Heysel Stadium, concrete retaining wall collapsed and 39 persons were crushed or trampled to death, 32 of them Italians. More than 400 persons were injured.

1988 March 12, Katmandu, Nepal: Some 80 soccer fans seeking cover during a violent hail storm at the national stadium were trampled to death in a stampede because the stadium doors were locked.

1989 April 15, Sheffield, England: Ninety-four people were killed and 170 injured at Hillsborough stadium when throngs of Liverpool soccer fans, many without tickets, collapsed a stadium barrier in a mad rush to see the game between Liverpool and Nottingham Forest. It was Britain's worst soccer disaster.

Miscellaneous

1980 Jan. 20, Sincelejo, Colombia: Bleachers at a bullring collapsed, leaving 222 dead.

March 30, Stavanger, Norway: Floating hotel in North Sea collapsed, killing 123 oil workers.

1981 July 18, Kansas City, Mo.: suspended walkway in Hyatt Regency Hotel collapses; 113 dead, 186 injured.

1984 Dec. 3, Bhopal, India: Toxic gas, methyl isocyanate, seeped from Union Carbide insecticide plant, killing more than 2,000; injuring about 150,000.

1987 Sept. 18, Goiânia, Brazil: 244 people contaminated with cesium-137 removed from steel cylinder taken from cancer-therapy machine in abandoned clinic and sold as scrap. Four people died in worst radiation disaster in Western Hemisphere.

1988 July 6, North Sea off Scotland: 166 workers killed in explosion and fire on Occidental Petroleum's Piper Alpha rig in North Sea off Scottish coast; 64 survivors rescued. It is the world's worst offshore oil disaster.

Wartime Disasters

1915 May 6: Despite German warnings, the Cunard Liner *Lusitania* sailed from New York for Liverpool, England, on May 1st and was sunk off the coast of Ireland by a German submarine. 1,198 passengers and crew, 128 of them Americans, died. Unknown to the passengers, the ship was carrying a cargo of small arms. The disaster contributed to the entry of the United States into World War I.

1916 Feb. 26: 3,100 people died when the French cruiser *Provence* was sunk by a German submarine in the Mediterranean.

1943 November, Gilbert Islands: While battleship *U.S.S. Mississippi* was bombarding Makin Atoll in Pacific during WW II, an accidental gun turret explosion killed 43 of her crew.

1944 Sept. 12, South China Sea: U.S. submarines torpedoed and sank two Japanese troop ships[1], the *Kachidoki Maru* and the *Rakuyo Maru*. Unknown to the submarines, the Japanese, in disregard for the rules of treatment of prisoners of war, had forced 2,000 British, Australian, and American POWs into the holds of the ships which were designed to hold only 300 troops. Later, when the subs discovered the tragedy, they sought to rescue as many survivors as possible. Japanese vessels picked up most of *Kachidoki Maru*'s prisoners but abandoned those from the *Rakuyo Maru*, taking only the Japanese survivors. Of the 1,300 POWs aboard the *Rakuyo Maru*, 159 were rescued, but only seven lived.

Oct. 24, South China Sea: The *Arisan Maru*[1] carrying 1,800 American prisoners was torpedoed by a U.S. submarine and sunk. The Japanese destroyer escort rescued Japanese military and civilian personnel and left the POWs to their fate. It is estimated that only ten prisoners survived the disaster.

Dec. 17-18, Philippine Sea: A typhoon struck U.S. Third Fleet's Task Force 38, sank three destroyers, damaged seven other ships, destroyed 186 aircraft, and killed 800 officers and men.

1945 Jan. 30: 7,700 persons died in world's largest marine disaster when the Nazi passenger ship *Wilhelm Gustoff* carrying Germans fleeing Poland was torpedoed in the Baltic by a Soviet submarine.

May 3, *Cap Arcona:* Several days before World War II ended in Europe, the German passenger ship carrying about 6,000, of which an estimated 5,000 were concentration camp prisoners, was sunk by British aircraft. An estimated 5,000 persons were killed, most of them prisoners who were about to gain their freedom.

July 29, near Leyte Gulf: The heavy cruiser *Indianapolis* was torpedoed and sunk by a Japanese submarine. Of the crew of 1,199 men, only 316 survived. Several days earlier, the *Indianapolis* had delivered a lead cylinder containing uranium (U-235) and the firing mechanism for the first atomic bomb to Tinian Island. Had the ship been sunk earlier while delivering its special cargo, WW II would have ended differently.

---

1. The ships had no identification that they were transporting prisoners of war.

Simplified diagram of a nuclear reactor. Laurel Cook, Boston, Ma.

Largest Nuclear Power Plants in the United States

(over a million kilowatts)

Plant	Operating utility	Capacity (kilowatts)	Year operative
South Texas 1, TX	Houston Lighting & Power	1,250,000	1988
Palo Verde 1, AZ	Arizona Public Service	1,221,000	1986
Palo Verde 2, AZ	Arizona Public Service	1,221,000	1986
Palo Verde 3, AZ	Arizona Public Service	1,221,000	1988
Perry 1, OH	Cleveland Electric Illumination	1,205,000	1987
Sequoyah 1, TN	Tennessee Valley Authority	1,148,000	1981
Sequoyah 2, TN	Tennessee Valley Authority	1,148,000	1982
Callaway, MO	Union Electric	1,145,000	1984
Grand Gulf 1, MS	System Energy Resources	1,142,000	1985
Millstone 3, CT	Northeast Nuclear Energy	1,142,000	1986
Catawba 1, SC	Duke Power Co.	1,129,000	1985
Catawba 2, SC	Duke Power Co.	1,129,000	1986
McGuire 1, NC	Duke Power Co.	1,129,000	1981
McGuire 2, NC	Duke Power Co.	1,129,000	1984
Wolf Creek 1, KS	Wolf Creek Nuclear Operating	1,128,000	1985
Braidwood 1, IL	Commonwealth Edison	1,120,000	1988
Braidwood 2, IL	Commonwealth Edison	1,120,000	1988
Salem 1, DE	Public Service Electric & Gas	1,106,000	1977
Salem 2, DE	Public Service Electric & Gas	1,106,000	1981
Byron 1, IL	Commonwealth Edison	1,105,000	1985
Byron 2, IL	Commonwealth Edison	1,105,000	1987
Trojan, OR	Portland General Electric	1,095,000	1976
Fermi 2, OH	Detroit Edison	1,093,000	1988
Diablo Canyon 2	Pacific Gas & Electric	1,087,000	1986
Nine Mile Point 2, NY	Niagara Mohawk Power	1,080,000	1988
San Onofre 3, CA	Southern California Edison	1,080,000	1984
Vogtle 1, GA	Georgia Power	1,079,000	1987
Waterford 3, LA	Louisiana Power & Light	1,075,000	1985
Diablo Canyon 1, CA	Pacific Gas & Electric	1,073,000	1985
San Onofre 2, CA	Southern California Edison	1,070,000	1983
Hope Creek 1, DE	Public Service Electric & Gas	1,067,000	1986
Browns Ferry 1, AL	Tennessee Valley Authority	1,065,000	1974
Browns Ferry 2, AL	Tennessee Valley Authority	1,065,000	1975
Browns Ferry 3, AL	Tennessee Valley Authority	1,065,000	1977

Plant	Operating utility	Capacity (kilowatts)	Year operative
Cook 2, MI	Indiana & Michigan Power	1,060,000	1978
Limerick 1, PA	Philadelphia Electric	1,055,000	1986
Peach Bottom 2, PA	Philadelphia Electric	1,051,000	1974
Zion 1, IL	Commonwealth Edison	1,040,000	1973
Zion 2, IL	Commonwealth Edison	1,040,000	1974
La Salle 1, IL	Commonwealth Edison	1,036,000	1984
La Salle 2, IL	Commonwealth Edison	1,036,000	1984
Peach Bottom 3, PA	Philadelphia Gas & Electric	1,035,000	1974
Susquehanna 1, PA	Pennsylvania Power & Light	1,032,000	1983
Susquehanna 2, PA	Pennsylvania Power & Light	1,032,000	1985

Source: Nuclear Regulatory Commission.

Energy Overview

Source: Energy Information Administration

Energy Prices

Since the mid-1970s, changes in fossil fuel prices have become more frequent and more pronounced. Prior to the Arab oil embargo of 1973-74, the composite real price (in 1982 constant dollars) per million Btu of crude oil, natural gas, and coal had gradually declined from $1.12 in 1949 to a post-World War II low of $0.75 in 1969. In 1974, the real price rose to $1.25, eventually peaking at $2.92 in 1981 after a second round of crude oil price increases.

Thereafter, overproduction of crude oil began to affect energy prices and, when crude oil prices plunged in 1986, the composite real price of the major fossil fuels fell to $1.45. In 1987, the composite price declined slightly, to $1.44, and in 1988 it fell to $1.26.

Throughout the 40-year period, changes in the real price of oil dominated movements in the composite index. The real price of oil trended downward between 1949 and 1970 and then rose sharply in 1973-74 and again in 1979-81. Thereafter, in the face of shrinking demand and excess production, price trends reversed sharply. The precipitous declines in 1986 and 1988 brought the real price of oil to $1.78 per million Btu, the lowest level since 1973.

Prices of coal and natural gas were much less volatile than those of oil. Coal markets are generally more competitive than oil markets, where the output and pricing policies of OPEC were a major influence throughout much of the 1970s and 1980s. Natural gas prices are subject to substantial State and Federal regulation. Throughout the 1970s, regulation dampened the response of natural gas prices relative to oil price movement.

However, the 1986 and 1988 declines in crude oil prices were severe enough to trigger declines in the prices of the other fossil fuels, higher energy prices, but, following the price declines in 1986 and 1988, grew to a record level of 29 quadrillion Btu. Transportation sector consumption grew more slowly over the 40-year period but also attained a record level (22 quadrillion Btu) in 1988.

Changing Patterns of Trade

From 1958 forward, the United States consumed more energy than it produced, and the difference was met by energy imports. Net imports of energy (primarily petroleum) grew rapidly through 1973, as demand for cheap foreign oil eroded quotas on petroleum imports. In 1973, net imports of petroleum totaled 13 quadrillion Btu.

The Arab oil embargo of 1973-74, coupled with increases in the price of crude oil, interrupted growth in petroleum net imports, but nevertheless they climbed to a peak of 18 quadrillion Btu in 1977. That year, U.S. dependence on petroleum net imports also peaked, at 47% of consumption.

A second round of price increases, in 1979-81, suppressed demand for foreign oil. In 1985, petroleum net imports totaled 9 quadrillion Btu, and U.S. dependence fell to 27% of consumption. That was the last year in which the ratio of petroleum net imports to petroleum consumption declined. In 1988, as the price of crude oil continued to be repressed, net imports of petroleum rose to over 13 quadrillion Btu, and U.S. dependence on foreign sources of oil reached 37%. However, because of the decline in oil prices, the value of crude oil and petroleum product net imports fell from $37.6 billion in 1987 to $35.2 billion in 1988.

Natural gas trade was limited to border countries until the advent of shipping natural gas in liquefied form. In 1988, natural gas net imports surpassed 1 quadrillion Btu for only the second time since 1949. Net imports of natural gas were valued at close to $3 billion.

Throughout the 1949-to-1988 period, the United States was a net exporter of coal. In 1988, net exports totaled 2 quadrillion Btu. Net exports of coal (including coal coke) were valued at nearly $4 billion.

Consumption

Energy consumption more than doubled during the 1949-73 period, increasing from 30 quadrillion Btu in 1949 to 74 quadrillion Btu in 1973, and the U.S. economy grew at about the same rate. The domestic energy market was dominated by rapid growth in petroleum and natural gas consumption, which more than tripled during the period.

After the 1973 oil price shock, energy consumption fluctuated, rising to a peak of 79 quadrillion Btu in 1979 before returning, in the mid-1980s, to about the same level as in 1973. In contrast, the economy registered a net expansion of about one-third.

Consumption by Sector

Growth in electric utility consumption continued during the 1970s and 1980s despite rising energy prices. In 1988, that sector's consumption reached an all-time high of almost 29 quadrillion Btu. However, only 9 quadrillion Btu were sold to consumers; the remainder was used to generate, transmit, and distribute the electricity.

The transportation and residential and commercial sectors accounted for most of the growth in energy consumption during the 1949-88 period. Residential and commercial consumption leveled off in response to particularly natural gas. In 1988, the real price of crude oil per million Btu was $1.78, 52 percent below the 1985 price. The real price of natural gas fell 38%, to $1.26, during the 4-year period. The decline in the real price of bituminous coal and lignite was smaller—a decrease of 20%, to $0.83, in the 4-year period.

Production

Historically, three fossil fuels have accounted for the bulk of domestic energy production, which by 1988 totaled 66 quadrillion Btu. Coal accounted for the largest share of domestic energy production in 1949-51 and, after a long hiatus, again in 1984-88.

In the interim, first crude oil and then natural gas dominated domestic production. In 1988, coal production reached a record 21 quadrillion Btu. Crude oil production and dry natural gas production totaled 17 quadrillion Btu each. Natural gas plant liquids accounted for another 2 quadrillion Btu.

Electricity generation increased throughout 1949-88, registering only one year-to-year decline (during the recession in 1982). Nuclear-based generation increased to the record level of 6 quadrillion Btu in 1988. Since the mid-1970s, coal and nuclear fuels have provided increasing shares of fuel input for power generation, displacing substantial quantities of both petroleum and natural gas.

Hydroelectric generation accounted for over 1 quadrillion Btu of electricity in 1949 and from the 1970s through 1987 provided about 3 quadrillion Btu per year. In 1988, the second consecutive year of drought, hydroelectric generation totaled only 2.3 quadrillion Btu, the lowest level since 1966.

Other sources of renewable energy still provide only a small part of total domestic energy supplied. Generation of electricity from geothermal energy totaled 0.2 quadrillion Btu in 1988, and generation of electricity from wood, waste, wind, photovoltaic, and solar thermal energy totaled 0.02 quadrillion Btu.

Production of Crude Petroleum by Countries

(in thousands of 42-gallon barrels)

Area and country	Est. 1989[1]	1988[1]	Est. percent change	Area and country	Est. 1989[1]	1988[1]	Est. percent change
Western Hemisphere	5,782,695	5,868,835	1.5	Syria	91,250	85,140	6.8
Argentina	166,075	158,775	0.8	United Arab Emirates	583,635	367,555	58.8
Bolivia	6,570	6,570	0.0	Yemen, North	69,715	48,910	42.5
Brazil	202,575	214,255	−5.5	Yemen, South	3,650	3,650	0.0
Canada	574,510	570,130	0.8	Asia Pacific	1,179,315	1,131,500	4.2
Chile	8,760	9,125	−4.0	Australia	196,735	197,830	−0.6
Columbia	153,300	112,785	37.7	Brunei	52,560	55,480	−5.3
Ecuador	106,215	112,785	−5.8	Burma	5,475	5,475	0.0
Mexico	958,855	966,155	−0.8	India	233,600	225,570	3.6
Peru	52,195	55,845	−6.5	Indonesia	438,000	401,500	9.1
Trinidad and Tobago	56,575	53,290	6.2	Japan	4,380	5,110	−14.3
United States	2,897,140	3,042,420	−4.5	Malaysia	205,130	197,100	4.1
Venezuela	597,140	575,240	3.8	New Zealand	10,220	10,220	0.0
Western Europe	1,341,010	1,510,075	−11.2	Pakistan	16,425	16,790	−2.2
Austria	8,395	8,030	4.5	Thailand	13,505	13,505	0.0
Denmark	39,055	35,770	9.2	Africa	1,829,745	1,763,305	5.4
France	24,090	25,185	−4.3	Algeria	224,840	205,860	9.2
West Germany	28,105	28,470	−1.3	Angola/Cabinda[3]	165,710	163,885	1.1
Greece	8,030	8,030	0.0	Cameroon	65,700	63,510	3.4
Italy	21,535	29,565	−27.2	Congo	49,275	48,910	0.7
Netherlands	25,915	29,565	−12.3	Egypt	315,725	316,090	−0.1
Norway	490,560	397,120	23.5	Gabon	68,985	63,875	8.0
Spain	10,220	11,315	−9.7	Ivory Coast	4,015	5,110	−21.4
Turkey	18,615	17,520	6.3	Libya	383,250	365,000	5.0
United Kingdom	666,490	920,165	−27.6	Nigeria	501,510	455,155	10.2
Middle East	5,288,850	4,541,330	20.1	Tunisia	38,325	36,500	5.0
Bahrain	15,695	14,965	4.9	Zaire	10,585	10,585	0.0
Iran	1,070,180	689,850	55.1	Communist Bloc	5,692,175	5,710,790	−0.3
Iraq	967,615	962,870	0.5	China	1,017,620	988,055	3.0
Kuwait	418,655	420,845	−0.5	Romania	68,620	68,620	0.0
Neutral Zone[2]	146,730	84,680	73.3	U.S.S.R.	4,526,000	4,574,180	−1.1
Oman	229,950	213,890	7.5	Other communist	79,935	79,935	0.0
Qatar	155,125	136,145	24.9				
Saudi Arabia	1,700,170	1,511,830	12.5	**World Total**	**21,278,040**	**20,499,495**	**3.8**

1. Based on Jan.–Feb. average. 2. Shared by Kuwait and Saudi Arabia. 3. An enclave in West Africa on Atlantic coast between the Congo and Angola. Totals may not add up due to rounding.

Crude Oil Imports[1] and Petroleum Products by Country of Origin, 1979–1988

(thousand barrels per day)

	Organization of Petroleum Exporting Countries (OPEC)									
Year	Nigeria	Saudi Arabia	Vene-zuela	Other OPEC[2]	Total OPEC	Arab Members of OPEC[3]	Canada	Mexico	United Kingdom	Virgin Is./ Puerto Rico
1979	1,080	1,354	688	2,510	5,633	438	418	196	353	948
1980	857	1,259	478	1,699	4,293	347	506	169	256	794
1981	620	1,128	403	1,165	3,315	358	497	370	169	693
1982	512	551	409	663	2,136	397	632	442	154	538
1983	299	336	420	788	1,843	471	802	374	178	644
1984	215	324	544	953	2,037	547	714	388	184	847
1985	293	167	602	759	1,821	696	755	295	114	605
1986	440	685	788	915	2,828	721	642	342	152	753
1987	535	751	801	968	3,055	1,273	765	585	346	158
1988[4]	568	1,061	775	1,017	3,421	1,826	892	670	301	112

1. Imports minus exports. NOTE: Sum of components may not equal total due to independent rounding. 2. Includes Algeria, Ecuador, Gabon, Indonesia, Iran, Iraq, Kuwait, Libya, Qatar, and United Arab Emirates. Prior to 1988, imports from the Neutral Zone between Kuwait and Saudi Arabia are included in imports from Saudi Arabia. From 1988 forward, those imports are included in imports from "Other OPEC." 3. Includes Algeria, Iraq, Kuwait, Libya, Qatar, Saudi Arabia, and United Arab Emirates. 4. Preliminary. *Source:* 1978-1980—Energy Information Administration, Energy Data Reports, *P.A.D. Districts Supply/ Demand, Annual.* 1981-1986—Energy Information Administration, *Petroleum Supply Annual.* 1988—Energy Information Administration, *Petroleum Supply Monthly,* December 1988.

Exports of Crude Oil and Petroleum Products by Country of Destination, 1979–1988

(Thousand Barrels per Day)

Year	Canada	Japan	Mexico	Nether-lands	Belgium[1]	Italy	United Kingdom	France	Brazil	Virgin Is./ Puerto Rico
1979	100	34	21	28	19	15	7	13	7	170
1980	108	32	28	23	20	14	7	11	4	220
1981	89	38	26	42	12	22	5	15	1	221
1982	85	68	53	85	17	32	14	24	8	211
1983	76	104	24	49	22	35	8	23	2	144
1984	83	92	35	37	21	39	14	18	1	152
1985	74	108	61	44	26	30	14	11	3	161
1986	85	110	56	58	30	39	8	11	3	112
1987	83	120	70	39	17	42	6	12	2	126
1988[2]	84	124	70	26	25	29	9	12	3	150

1. Including Luxembourg. 2. Preliminary. NOTE: Sum of components may not equal total due to independent rounding. *Source:* 1978 through 1980—Energy Information Administration, Energy Data Reports, *Petroleum Statement, Annual.* 1981 through 1986—Energy Information Administration, *Petroleum Supply Annual.* 1987-88—Energy Information Administration, *Petroleum Supply Monthly.*

U.S. Motor Vehicle Fuel Consumption and Related Data

(1987 estimate)

Type of vehicle	Total travel (million vehicle miles)	Number of registered vehicles	Average miles traveled per vehicle	Fuel consumed (thousand gallons)	Average fuel con-sumption per vehicle (gallons)	Average miles per gallon
All passenger vehicles	1,372,372	142,811,459	9,610	71,888,323	503	19.09
Total personal passenger vehicles	1,367,046	142,209,404	9,613	70,984,079	499	19.26
Cars	1,357,191	137,323,632	9,883	70,786,979	515	19.17
Motorcycles	9,855	4,885,772	2,017	197,100	40	50.00
All buses	5,326	602,055	8,846	904,244	1,502	5.89
All cargo vehicles	551,955	41,118,762	13,423	55,859,924	1,359	9.88
Single unit trucks	465,621	39,700,248	11,728	39,332,505	991	11.84
Combinations	86,334	1,418,514	60,862	16,527,419	11,651	5.22
All motor vehicles	1,924,327	183,930,221	10,462	127,748,247	695	15.06

Source: Department of Transportation, Federal Highway Administration.

WEIGHTS & MEASURES

Measures and Weights

Source: Department of Commerce, National Bureau of Standards.

The International System (Metric)

The International System of Units is a modernized version of the metric system, established by international agreement, that i.e. provides a logical and interconnected framework for all measurements in science, industry, and commerce. The system is built on a foundation of seven basic units, and all other units are derived from them. (Use of metric weights and measures was legalized in the United States in 1866, and our customary units of weights and measures are defined in terms of the meter and kilogram.)

Length. Meter. The meter is defined as 1,650,-763.73 wavelengths in vacuum of the orange-red line of the spectrum of krypton-86.

Time. Second. The second is defined as the duration of 9,192,631,770 cycles of the radiation associated with a specified transition of the cesium 133 atom.

Mass. Kilogram. The standard for the kilogram is a cylinder of platinum-iridium alloy kept by the International Bureau of Weights and Measures at Paris. A duplicate at the National Bureau of Standards serves as the mass standard for the United States. The kilogram is the only base unit still defined by a physical object.

Temperature. Kelvin. The kelvin is defined as the fraction 1/273.16 of the thermodynamic temperature of the triple point of water; that is, the point at which water forms an interface of solid, liquid and vapor. This is defined as 0.01° C on the Centigrade or Celsius scale and 32.02° F on the Fahrenheit scale. The temperature 0° K is called "absolute zero."

Electric Current. Ampere. The ampere is defined as that current that, if maintained in each of two long parallel wires separated by one meter in free space, would produce a force between the two wires (due to their magnetic fields) of 2×10^{-7} newton for each meter of length. (A newton is the unit of force which when applied to one kilogram mass would experience an acceleration of one meter per second per second.)

Luminous Intensity. Candela. The candela is defined as the luminous intensity of 1/600,000 of a square meter of a cavity at the temperature of freezing platinum (2,042K).

Amount of Substance. Mole. The mole is the amount of substance of a system that contains as many elementary entities as there are atoms in 0.012 kilogram of carbon-12.

Tables of Metric Weights and Measures

LINEAR MEASURE

10 millimeters (mm) = 1 centimeter (cm)
10 centimeters = 1 decimeter (dm) = 100 millimeters
10 decimeters = 1 meter (m) = 1,000 millimeters
10 meters = 1 dekameter (dam)
10 dekameters = 1 hectometer (hm) = 100 meters
10 hectometers = 1 kilometer (km) = 1,000 meters

AREA MEASURE

100 square millimeters (mm²) = 1 sq centimeter (cm²)
10,000 square centimeters = 1 sq meter (m²) = 1,000,000 sq millimeters
100 square meters = 1 are (a)
100 ares = 1 hectare (ha) = 10,000 sq meters
100 hectares = 1 sq kilometer (km²) = 1,000,000 sq meters

VOLUME MEASURE

10 milliliters (ml) = 1 centiliter (cl)
10 centiliters = 1 deciliter (dl) = 100 milliliters
10 deciliters = 1 liter (1) = 1,000 milliliters
10 liters = 1 dekaliter (dal)
10 dekaliters = 1 hectoliter (hl) = 100 liters
10 hectoliters = 1 kiloliter (kl) = 1,000 liters

CUBIC MEASURE

1,000 cubic millimeters (mm³) = 1 cu centimeter (cm³)
1,000 cubic centimeters = 1 cu decimeter (dm³) = 1,000,000 cu millimeters
1,000 cubic decimeters = 1 cu meter (m³) = 1 stere = 1,000,000 cu centimeters = 1,000,000,000 cu millimeters

WEIGHT

10 milligrams (mg) = 1 centigram (cg)
10 centigrams = 1 decigram (dg) = 100 milligrams
10 decigrams = 1 gram (g) = 1,000 milligrams
10 grams = 1 dekagram (dag)
10 dekagrams = 1 hectogram (hg) = 100 grams
10 hectograms = 1 kilogram (kg) = 1,000 grams
1,000 kilograms = 1 metric ton (t)

Tables of Customary U.S. Weights and Measures

LINEAR MEASURE

12 inches (in.) = 1 foot (ft)
3 feet = 1 yard (yd)
5 1/2 yards = 1 rod (rd), pole, or perch (16 1/2 ft)
40 rods = 1 furlong (fur) = 220 yds = 660 ft
8 furlongs = 1 statute mile (mi.) = 1,760 yds = 5,280 ft
3 land miles = 1 league
5,280 feet = 1 statute or land mile
6,076.11549 feet = 1 international nautical mile

AREA MEASURE

144 square inches = 1 sq ft
9 square feet = 1 sq yd = 1,296 sq in.
30 1/4 square yards = 1 sq rd = 272 1/4 sq ft
160 square rods = 1 acre = 4,840 sq yds = 43,560 sq ft
640 acres = 1 sq mi.
1 mile square = 1 section (of land)
6 miles square = 1 township = 36 sections = 36 sq mi.

CUBIC MEASURE

1,728 cubic inches = 1 cu ft
27 cubic feet = 1 cu yd

LIQUID MEASURE

When necessary to distinguish the liquid pint or quart from the dry pint or quart, the word "liquid" or the abbreviation "liq" should be used in combination with the name or abbreviation of the liquid unit.

4 gills (gi) = 1 pint (pt) (= 28.875 cu in.)
2 pints = 1 quart (qt) (= 57.75 cu in.)
4 quarts = 1 gallon (gal) (= 231 cu in.) = 8 pts = 32 gills

APOTHECARIES' FLUID MEASURE

60 minims (min.) = 1 fluid dram (fl dr) (= 0.2256 cu in.)
8 fluid drams = 1 fluid ounce (fl oz) (= 1.8047 cu in.)
16 fluid ounces = 1 pt (= 28.875 cu in.) = 128 fl drs
2 pints = 1 qt (= 57.75 cu in.) = 32 fl oz = 256 fl drs
4 quarts = 1 gal (= 231 cu in.) = 128 fl oz = 1,024 fl drs

DRY MEASURE

When necessary to distinguish the dry pint or quart from the liquid pint or quart, the word "dry" should be used in combination with the name or abbreviation of the dry unit.

2 pints = 1 qt (=67.2006 cu in.)
8 quarts = 1 peck (pk) (=537.605 cu in.) = 16 pts
4 pecks = 1 bushel (bu) (= 2,150.42 cu in.) = 32 qts

AVOIRDUPOIS WEIGHT

When necessary to distinguish the avoirdupois dram from the apothecaries dram, or to distinguish the avoirdupois dram or ounce from the fluid dram or ounce, or to distinguish the avoirdupois ounce or pound from the troy or apothecaries, ounce or pound, the word "avoirdupois" or the abbreviation "avdp" should be used in combination with the name or abbreviation of the avoirdupois unit.
(The "grain" is the same in avoirdupois, troy, and apothecaries weights.)

27 11/32 grains = 1 dram (dr)
16 drams = 1 oz = 437 1/2 grains
16 ounces = 1 lb = 256 drams = 7,000 grains
100 pounds = 1 hundredweight (cwt)[1]
20 hundredweights = 1 ton (tn) = 2,000 lbs[1]

In "gross" or "long" measure, the following values are recognized:

112 pounds = 1 gross or long cwt[1]
20 gross or long hundredweights = 1 gross or long ton = 2,240 lbs[1]

1. When the terms "hundredweight" and "ton" are used unmodified, they are commonly understood to mean the 100-pound hundredweight and the 2,000-pound ton, respectively; these units may be designated "net" or "short" when necessary to distinguish them from the corresponding units in gross or long measure.

UNITS OF CIRCULAR MEASURE

Second (″) = —
Minute (′) = 60 seconds
Degree (°) = 60 minutes
Right angle = 90 degrees
Straight angle = 180 degrees
Circle = 360 degrees

TROY WEIGHT

24 grains = 1 pennyweight (dwt)
20 pennyweights = 1 ounce troy (oz t) = 480 grains
12 ounces troy = 1 pound troy (lb t) = 240 pennyweights = 5,760 grains

APOTHECARIES' WEIGHT

20 grains = 1 scruple (s ap)
3 scruples = 1 dram apothecaries' (dr ap) = 60 grains
8 drams apothecaries = 1 ounce apothecaries' (oz ap) = 24 scruples = 480 grains
12 ounces apothecaries = 1 pound apothecaries' (lb ap) = 96 drams apothecaries' = 288 scruples = 5,760 grains

GUNTER'S OR SURVEYOR'S CHAIN MEASURE

7.92 inches = 1 link (li)
100 links = 1 chain (ch) = 4 rods = 66 ft
80 chains = 1 statute mile = 320 rods = 5,280 ft

Metric and U.S. Equivalents

1 angstrom[1] (light wave measurement)	0.1 millimicron 0.000 1 micron 0.000 000 1 millimeter 0.000 000 004 inch	1 decimeter	3.937 inches
		1 dekameter	32.808 feet
		1 fathom	6 feet 1.8288 meters
1 cable's length	120 fathoms 720 feet 219.456 meters	1 foot	0.3048 meter
1 centimeter	0.3937 inch	1 furlong	10 chains (surveyor's) 660 feet 220 yards 1/8 statute mile 201.168 meters
1 chain (Gunter's or surveyor's)	66 feet 20.1168 meters		

1 inch	2.54 centimeters		

Length/Distance		Capacities or Volumes	
1 inch	2.54 centimeters	**CAPACITIES OR VOLUMES**	
1 kilometer	0.621 mile	1 barrel, liquid	31 to 42 gallons[2]
1 league (land)	3 statute miles 4.828 kilometers	1 barrel, standard for fruits, vegetables, and other dry commodities except cranberries	7,056 cubic inches 105 dry quarts 3.281 bushels, struck measure
1 link (Gunter's or surveyor's)	7.92 inches 0.201 168 meter		
1 meter	39.37 inches 1.094 yards	1 barrel, standard, cranberry	5.286 cubic inches 86 45/64 dry quarts 2.709 bushels, struck measure
1 micron	0.001 millimeter 0.000 039 37 inch	1 bushel (U.S.) struck measure	2,150.42 cubic inches 35.238 liters
1 mil	0.001 inch 0.025 4 millimeter	1 bushel, heaped (U.S.)	2,747.715 cubic inches 1.278 bushels, struck measure[3]
1 mile (statute or land)	5,280 feet 1.609 kilometers	1 cord (firewood)	128 cubic feet
1 mile (nautical international)	1.852 kilometers 1.151 statute miles 0.999 U.S. nautical miles	1 cubic centimeter	0.061 cubic inch
		1 cubic decimeter	61.024 cubic inches
1 millimeter	0.03937 inch	1 cubic foot	7.481 gallons 28.316 cubic decimeters
1 millimicron (mμ)	0.001 micron 0.000 000 039 37 inch	1 cubic inch	0.554 fluid ounce 4.433 fluid drams 16.387 cubic centimeters
1 nanometer	0.001 micrometer or 0.000 000 039 37 inch		
		1 cubic meter	1.308 cubic yards
1 point (typography)	0.013 837 inch 1/72 inch (approximately) 0.351 millimeter	1 cubic yard	0.765 cubic meter
		1 cup, measuring	8 fluid ounces 1/2 liquid pint
1 rod, pole, or perch	16 1/2 feet 5.0292 meters	1 dram, fluid or liquid (U.S.)	1/8 fluid ounces 0.226 cubic inch 3.697 milliliters 1.041 British fluid drachms
1 yard	0.9144 meter		

AREAS OR SURFACES

1 acre	43,560 square feet 4,840 square yards 0.405 hectare	1 dekaliter	2.642 gallons 1.135 pecks
		1 gallon (U.S.)	231 cubic inches 3.785 liters 0.833 British gallon 128 U.S. fluid ounces
1 are	119.599 square yards 0.025 acre		
1 hectare	2.471 acres	1 gallon (British Imperial)	277.42 cubic inches 1.201 U.S. gallons 4.546 liters 160 British fluid ounces
1 square centimeter	0.155 square inch		
1 square decimeter	15.5 square inches		
1 square foot	929.030 square centimeters	1 gill	7.219 cubic inches 4 fluid ounces 0.118 liter
1 square inch	6.4516 square centimeters		
1 square kilometer	0.386 square mile 247.105 acres	1 hectoliter	26.418 gallons 2.838 bushels
1 square meter	1.196 square yards 10.764 square feet	1 liter	1.057 liquid quarts 0.908 dry quart 61.024 cubic inches
1 square mile	258.999 hectares		
1 square millimeter	0.002 square inch	1 milliliter	0.271 fluid dram 16.231 minims 0.061 cubic inch
1 square rod, square pole or square perch	25.293 square meters		
1 square yard	0.836 square meters	1 ounce, fluid or liquid (U.S.)	1.805 cubic inch 29.574 milliliters 1.041 British fluid ounces

1 peck	8.810 liters	1 hundredweight, net or short	100 pounds 45.359 kilograms
1 pint, dry	33.600 cubic inches 0.551 liter	1 kilogram	2.205 pounds
1 pint, liquid	28.875 cubic inches 0.473 liter	1 microgram [µg (the Greek letter mu in combination with the letter g)]	0.000 001 gram
1 quart, dry (U.S.)	67.201 cubic inches 1.101 liters 0.969 British quart	1 milligram	0.015 grain
1 quart, liquid (U.S.)	57.75 cubic inches 0.946 liter 0.833 British quart	1 ounce, avoirdupois	437.5 grains 0.911 troy or apothecaries, ounce 28.350 grams
1 quart (British)	69.354 cubic inches 1.032 U.S. dry quarts 1.201 U.S. liquid quarts	1 ounce, troy or apothecaries	480 grains 1.097 avoirdupois ounces 31.103 grams
1 tablespoon, measuring	3 teaspoons 4 fluid drams 1/2 fluid ounce	1 pennyweight	1.555 grams
1 teaspoon, measuring	1/3 tablespoon 1 1/3 fluid drams	1 point	0.01 carat 2 milligrams
1 assay ton[4]	29.167 grams	1 pound, avoirdupois	7,000 grains 1.215 troy or apothecaries pounds 453.592 37 grams
1 carat	200 milligrams 3.086 grains		
1 dram, apothecaries'	60 grains 3.888 grams	1 pound, troy or apothecaries	5,760 grains 0.823 avoirdupois pound 373.242 grams
1 dram, avoirdupois	27 11/32 (=27.344) grains 1.772 grams	1 ton, gross or long[5]	2,240 pounds 1.12 net tons 1.016 metric tons
1 grain	64.798 91 milligrams	1 ton, metric	2,204.623 pounds 0.984 gross ton 1.102 net tons
1 gram	15.432 grains 0.035 ounce, avoirdupois		
1 hundredweight, gross or long[5]	112 pounds 50.802 kilograms	1 ton, net or short	2,000 pounds 0.893 gross ton 0.907 metric ton

1. The angstrom is basically defined as 10^{-10} meter. 2. There is a variety of "barrels" established by law or usage. For example, federal taxes on fermented liquors are based on a barrel of 31 gallons; many state laws fix the "barrel for liquids" at 31 1/2 gallons; one state fixes a 36-gallon barrel for cistern measurement; federal law recognizes a 40-gallon barrel for "proof spirits"; by custom, 42 gallons comprise a barrel of crude oil or petroleum products for statistical purposes, and this equivalent is recognized "for liquids" by four states. 3. Frequently recognized as 1 1/4 bushels, struck measure. 4. Used in assaying. The assay ton bears the same relation to the milligram that a ton of 2,000 pounds avoirdupois bears to the ounce troy; hence the weight in milligrams of precious metal obtained from one assay ton of ore gives directly the number of troy ounces to the net ton. 5. The gross or long ton and hundredweight are used commercially in the United States to only a limited extent, usually in restricted industrial fields. These units are the same as the British "ton" and "hundredweight."

Miscellaneous Units of Measure

Acre: An area of 43,560 square feet. Originally, the area a yoke of oxen could plow in one day.

Agate: Originally a measurement of type size (5 1/2 points). Now equal to 1/14 inch. Used in printing for measuring column length.

Ampere: Unit of electric current. A potential difference of one volt across a resistance of one ohm produces a current of one ampere.

Astronomical Unit (A.U.): 93,000,000 miles, the average distance of the earth from the sun. Used in astronomy.

Bale: A large bundle of goods. In the U.S., the approximate weight of a bale of cotton is 500 pounds. The weight varies in other countries.

Board Foot (fbm): 144 cubic inches (12 in. × 12 in. × 1 in.). Used for lumber.

Bolt: 40 yards. Used for measuring cloth.

Btu: British thermal unit. Amount of heat needed to increase the temperature of one pound of water by one degree Fahrenheit (252 calories).

Carat (c): 200 milligrams or 3.086 grains troy.

Originally the weight of a seed of the carob tree in the Mediterranean region. Used for weighing precious stones. *See also* Karat.

Chain (ch): a chain 66 feet or one-tenth of a furlong in length, divided into 100 parts called links. One mile is equal to 80 chains. Used in surveying and sometimes called Gunter's or surveyor's chain.

Cubit: 18 inches or 45.72 cm. Derived from distance between elbow and tip of middle finger.

Decibel: Unit of relative loudness. One decibel is the smallest amount of change detectable by the human ear.

Ell, English: 1 1/4 yards or 1/32 bolt. Used for measuring cloth.

Freight Ton (also called Measurement Ton): 40 cubic feet of merchandise. Used for cargo freight.

Great Gross: 12 gross or 1728.

Gross: 12 dozen or 144.

Hand: 4 inches or 10.16 cm. Derived from the width of the hand. Used for measuring the height of horses at withers.

Hertz: Modern unit for measurement of electromagnetic wave frequencies (equivalent to "cycles per second").

Hogshead (hhd): 2 liquid barrels or 14,653 cubic inches.

Horsepower: The power needed to lift 33,000 pounds a distance of one foot in one minute (about 1/2 times the power an average horse can exert). Used for measuring power of steam engines, etc.

Karat (kt): A measure of the purity of gold, indicating how many parts out of 24 are pure. For example, 18 karat gold is 3/4 pure. Sometimes spelled *carat*.

Knot: Not a distance, but the rate of speed of one nautical mile per hour. Used for measuring speed of ships.

League: Rather indefinite and varying measure, but usually estimated at 3 miles in English-speaking countries.

Light-Year: 5,880,000,000,000 miles, the distance light travels in a year at the rate of 186,281.7 miles per second. (If an astronomical unit were represented by one inch, a light-year would be represented by about one mile.) Used for measurements in interstellar space.

Magnum: Two-quart bottle. Used for measuring wine, etc.

Ohm: Unit of electrical resistance. A circuit in which a potential difference of one volt produces a current of one ampere has a resistance of one ohm.

Parsec: Approximately 3.26 light-years of 19.2 trillion miles. Term is combination of first syllables of *par*allax and *sec*ond, and distance is that of imaginary star when lines drawn from it to both earth and sun form a maximum angle or parallax of one second (1/3600 degree). Used for measuring interstellar distances.

Pi (π): 3.14159265+. The ratio of the circumference of a circle to its diameter. For practical purposes, the value is used to four decimal places: 3.1416.

Pica: 1/6 inch or 12 points. Used in printing for measuring column width, etc.

Pipe: 2 hogsheads. Used for measuring wine and other liquids.

Point: .013837 (approximately 1/72) inch or 1/12 pica. Used in printing for measuring type size.

Quintal: 100,000 grams or 220.46 pounds avoirdupois.

Quire: Used for measuring paper. Sometimes 24 sheets but more often 25. There are 20 quires in a ream.

Ream: Used for measuring paper. Sometimes 480 sheets, but more often 500 sheets.

Roentgen: Dosage unit of radiation exposure produced by X-rays.

Score: 20 units.

Sound, Speed of: Usually placed at 1,088 ft per second at 32° F at sea level. It varies at other temperatures and in different media.

Span: 9 inches or 22.86 cm. Derived from the distance between the end of the thumb and the end of the little finger when both are outstretched.

Square: 100 square feet. Used in building.

Stone: Legally 14 pounds avoirdupois in Great Britain.

Therm: 100,000 Btu's.

Township: U. S. land measurement of almost 36 square miles. The south border is 6 miles long. The east and west borders, also 6 miles long, follow the meridians, making the north border slightly less than 6 miles long. Used in surveying.

Tun: 252 gallons, but often larger. Used for measuring wine and other liquids.

Watt: Unit of power. The power used by a current of one ampere across a potential difference of one volt equals one watt.

Kelvin Scale

Absolute zero, −273.16° on the Celsius (Centigrade) scale, is 0° Kelvin. Thus, degrees Kelvin are equivalent to degrees Celsius plus 273.16. The freezing point of water, 0° C. and 32° F., is 273.16° K. The conversion formula is K° = C° + 273.16.

Conversion of Miles to Kilometers and Kilometers to Miles

Miles	Kilometers	Miles	Kilometers	Miles	Kilometers	Kilometers	Miles	Kilometers	Miles	Kilometers	Miles
1	1.6	8	12.8	60	96.5	1	0.6	8	4.9	60	37.2
2	3.2	9	14.4	70	112.6	2	1.2	9	5.5	70	43.4
3	4.8	10	16.0	80	128.7	3	1.8	10	6.2	80	49.7
4	6.4	20	32.1	90	144.8	4	2.4	20	12.4	90	55.9
5	8.0	30	48.2	100	160.9	5	3.1	30	18.6	100	62.1
6	9.6	40	64.3	1,000	1609	6	3.7	40	24.8	1,000	621
7	11.2	50	80.4			7	4.3	50	31.0		

Bolts and Screws: Conversion from Fractions of an Inch to Millimeters

Inch	mm	Inch	mm	Inch	mm	Inch	mm
1/64	0.40	17/64	6.75	33/64	13.10	49/64	19.45
1/32	0/79	9/32	7.14	17/32	13.50	25/32	19.84
3/64	1.19	19/64	7.54	35/64	13.90	51/64	20.24
1/16	1.59	5/16	7.94	9/16	14.29	13/16	20.64
5/64	1.98	21/64	8.33	37/64	14.69	53/64	21.03
3/32	2.38	11/32	8.73	19/32	15.08	27/32	21.43
7/64	2.78	23/64	9.13	39/64	15.48	55/64	21.83
1/8	3.18	3/8	9.53	5/8	15.88	7/8	22.23
9/64	3.57	25/64	9.92	41/64	16.27	57/64	22.62
5/32	3.97	13/32	10.32	21/32	16.67	29/32	23.02
11/64	4.37	27/64	10.72	43/64	17.06	59/64	23.42
3/16	4.76	7/16	11.11	11/64	17.46	15/16	23.81
13/64	5.16	29/64	11.51	45/64	17.86	61/64	24.21
7/32	5.56	15/32	11.91	23/32	18.26	31/32	24.61
15/64	5.95	31/64	12.30	47/64	18.65	63/64	25.00
1/4	6.35	1/2	12.70	3/4	19.05	1	25.40

U.S.—Metric Cooking Conversions

U.S. customary system				Metric			
Capacity		Weight		Capacity		Weight	
1/5 teaspoon	1 milliliter	1 fluid oz	30 milliliters	1 milliliter	1/5 teaspoon	1 gram	.035 ounce
1 teaspoon	5 ml		28 grams	5 ml	1 teaspoon	100 grams	3.5 ounces
1 tablespoon	15 ml	1 pound	454 grams	15 ml	1 tablespoon	500 grams	1.10 pounds
1/5 cup	50 ml			34 ml	1 fluid oz	1 kilogram	2.205
1 cup	240 ml						pounds
2 cups (1 pint)	470 ml			100 ml	3.4 fluid oz		35 oz
4 cups (1 quart)	.95 liter			240 ml	1 cup		
4 quarts (1 gal.)	3.8 liters			1 liter	34 fluid oz		
					4.2 cups		
					2.1 pints		
					1.06 quarts		
					0.26 gallon		

Cooking Measurement Equivalents

16 tablespoons	=	1 cup
12 tablespoons	=	3/4 cup
10 tablespoons + 2 teaspoons	=	2/3 cup
8 tablespoons	=	1/2 cup
6 tablespoons	=	3/8 cup
5 tablespoons + 1 teaspoon	=	1/3 cup
4 tablespoons	=	1/4 cup
2 tablespoons	=	1/8 cup
2 tablespoons + 2 teaspoons	=	1/6 cup
1 tablespoon	=	1/16 cup
2 cups	=	1 pint
2 pints	=	1 quart
3 teaspoons	=	1 tablespoon
48 teaspoons	=	1 cup

Prefixes and Multiples

Prefix	Symbol	Equivalent	Multiple/submultiple	Prefix	Symbol	Equivalent	Multiple/submultiple
atto	a	quintillionth part	10^{-18}	deci	d	tenth part	10^{-1}
femto	f	quadrillionth part	10^{-15}	deka	da	tenfold	10
pico	p	trillionth part	10^{-12}	hecto	h	hundredfold	10^2
nano	n	billionth part	10^{-9}	kilo	k	thousandfold	10^3
micro	μ	millionth part	10^{-6}	mega	M	millionfold	10^6
milli	m	thousandth part	10^{-3}	giga	G	billionfold	10^9
centi	c	hundredth part	10^{-2}	tera	T	trillionfold	10^{12}

Common Formulas

Circumference

Circle: $C = \pi d$, in which π is 3.1416 and d the diameter.

Area

Triangle: $A = \dfrac{ab}{2}$, in which a is the base and b the height.

Square: $A = a^2$, in which a is one of the sides.

Rectangle: $A = ab$, in which a is the base and b the height.

Trapezoid: $A = \dfrac{h(a+b)}{2}$, in which h is the height, a the longer parallel side, and b the shorter.

Regular pentagon: $A = 1.720a^2$, in which a is one of the sides.

Regular hexagon: $A = 2.598a^2$, in which a is one of the sides.

Regular octagon: $A = 4.828a^2$, in which a is one of the sides.

Circle: $A = \pi r^2$, in which π is 3.1416 and r the radius.

Volume

Cube: $V = a^3$, in which a is one of the edges.

Rectangular prism: $V = abc$, in which a is the length, b the width, and c the depth.

Pyramid: $V = \dfrac{Ah}{3}$, in which A is the area of the base and h the height.

Cylinder: $V = \pi r^2 h$, in which π is 3.1416, r the radius of the base, and h the height.

Cone: $V = \dfrac{\pi r^2 h}{3}$, in which π is 3.1416, r the radius of the base, and h the height.

Sphere: $V = \dfrac{4\pi r^3}{3}$, in which π is 3.1416 and r the radius.

Miscellaneous

Distance in feet traveled by falling body: $d = 16t^2$, in which t is the time in seconds.

Speed of sound in feet per second through any given temperature of air: $V = \dfrac{1087 \sqrt{273+t}}{16.52}$, in which t is the temperature Centigrade.

Cost in cents of operation of electrical device: $C = \dfrac{Wtc}{1000}$, in which W is the number of watts, t the time in hours, and c the cost in cents per kilowatt-hour.

Conversion of matter into energy (Einstein's Theorem): $E = mc^2$, in which E is the energy in ergs, m the mass of the matter in grams, and c the speed of light in centimeters per second. ($c^2 = 9.10^{20}$).

Decimal Equivalents of Common Fractions

1/2	.5000	1/10	.1000	2/7	.2857	3/11	.2727	5/9	.5556	7/11	.6364
1/3	.3333	1/11	.0909	2/9	.2222	4/5	.8000	5/11	.4545	7/12	.5833
1/4	.2500	1/12	.0833	2/11	.1818	4/7	.5714	5/12	.4167	8/9	.8889
1/5	.2000	1/16	.0625	3/4	.7500	4/9	.4444	6/7	.8571	8/11	.7273
1/6	.1667	1/32	.0313	3/5	.6000	4/11	.3636	6/11	.5455	9/10	.9000
1/7	.1429	1/64	.0156	3/7	.4286	5/6	.8333	7/8	.8750	9/11	.8182
1/8	.1250	2/3	.6667	3/8	.3750	5/7	.7143	7/9	.7778	10/11	.9091
1/9	.1111	2/5	.4000	3/10	.3000	5/8	.6250	7/10	.7000	11/12	.9167

Conversion Factors

To change	To	Multi- ply by	To change	To	Multi- ply by
acres	hectares	.4047	liters	pints (dry)	1.8162
acres	square feet	43,560	liters	pints (liquid)	2.1134
acres	square miles	.001562	liters	quarts (dry)	.9081
atmospheres	cms. of mercury	76	liters	quarts (liquid)	1.0567
BTU	horsepower-hour	.0003931	meters	feet	3.2808
BTU	kilowatt-hour	.0002928	meters	miles	.0006214
BTU/hour	watts	.2931	meters	yards	1.0936
bushels	cubic inches	2150.4	metric tons	tons (long)	.9842
bushels (U.S.)	hectoliters	.3524	metric tons	tons (short)	1.1023
centimeters	inches	.3937	miles	kilometers	1.6093
centimeters	feet	.03281	miles	feet	5280
circumference	radians	6.283	miles (nautical)	miles (statute)	1.1516
cubic feet	cubic meters	.0283	miles (statute)	miles (nautical)	.8684
cubic meters	cubic feet	35.3145	miles/hour	feet/minute	88
cubic meters	cubic yards	1.3079	millimeters	inches	.0394
cubic yards	cubic meters	.7646	ounces avdp.	grams	28.3495
degrees	radians	.01745	ounces	pounds	.0625
dynes	grams	.00102	ounces (troy)	ounces (avdp)	1.09714
fathoms	feet	6.0	pecks	liters	8.8096
feet	meters	.3048	pints (dry)	liters	.5506
feet	miles (nautical)	.0001645	pints (liquid)	liters	.4732
feet	miles (statute)	.0001894	pounds ap or t	kilograms	.3782
feet/second	miles/hour	.6818	pounds avdp	kilograms	.4536
furlongs	feet	660.0	pounds	ounces	16
furlongs	miles	.125	quarts (dry)	liters	1.1012
gallons (U.S.)	liters	3.7853	quarts (liquid)	liters	.9463
grains	grams	.0648	radians	degrees	57.30
grams	grains	15.4324	rods	meters	5.029
grams	ounces avdp	.0353	rods	feet	16.5
grams	pounds	.002205	square feet	square meters	.0929
hectares	acres	2.4710	square kilometers	square miles	.3861
hectoliters	bushels (U.S.)	2.8378	square meters	square feet	10.7639
horsepower	watts	745.7	square meters	square yards	1.1960
hours	days	.04167	square miles	square kilometers	2.5900
inches	millimeters	25.4000	square yards	square meters	.8361
inches	centimeters	2.5400	tons (long)	metric tons	1.016
kilograms	pounds avdp or t	2.2046	tons (short)	metric tons	.9072
kilometers	miles	.6214	tons (long)	pounds	2240
kilowatts	horsepower	1.341	tons (short)	pounds	2000
knots	nautical miles/hour	1.0	watts	Btu/hour	3.4129
knots	statute miles/hour	1.151	watts	horsepower	.001341
liters	gallons (U.S.)	.2642	yards	meters	.9144
liters	pecks	.1135	yards	miles	.0005682

Fahrenheit and Celsius (Centigrade) Scales

Zero on the Fahrenheit scale represents the temperature produced by the mixing of equal weights of snow and common salt.

	F	C
Boiling point of water	212°	100°
Freezing point of water	32°	0°
Absolute zero	−459.6°	−273.1°

Absolute zero is theoretically the lowest possible temperature, the point at which all molecular motion would cease.

To convert Fahrenheit to Celsius (Centigrade), subtract 32 and multiply by 5/9.

To convert Celsius (Centigrade) to Fahrenheit, multiply by 9/5 and add 32.

° Centi- grade	° Fahren- heit	° Centi- grade	° Fahren- heit
−273.1	−459.6	30	86
−250	−418	35	95
−200	−328	40	104
−150	−238	45	113
−100	−148	50	122
−50	−58	55	131
−40	−40	60	140
−30	−22	65	149
−20	−4	70	158
−10	14	75	167
0	32	80	176
5	41	85	185
10	50	90	194
15	59	95	203
20	68	**100**	**212**
25	77		

Roman Numerals

Roman numerals are expressed by letters of the alphabet and are rarely used today except for formality or variety.

There are three basic principles for reading Roman numerals:

1. A letter repeated once or twice repeats its value that many times. (XXX=30, CC=200, etc.).

2. One or more letters placed after another letter of greater value increases the greater value by the amount of the smaller. (VI=6, LXX=70, MCC=1200, etc.).

3. A letter placed before another letter of greater value decreases the greater value by the amount of the smaller. (IV=4, XC=90, CM=900, etc.).

Letter	Value	Letter	Value	Letter	Value	Letter	Value	Letter	Value
I	1	VII	7	XXX	30	LXXX	80	$\bar{V}$	5,000
II	2	VIII	8	XL	40	XC	90	$\bar{X}$	10,000
III	3	IX	9	L	50	C	100	$\bar{L}$	50,000
IV	4	X	10	LX	60	D	500	$\bar{C}$	100,000
V	5	XX	20	LXX	70	M	1,000	$\bar{D}$	500,000
VI	6							$\bar{M}$	1,000,000

Mean and Median

The mean, also called the average, of a series of quantities is obtained by finding the sum of the quantities and dividing it by the number of quantities. In the series 1,3,5,18,19,20,25, the mean or average is 13—i.e., 91 divided by 7.

The median of a series is that point which so divides it that half the quantities are on one side, half on the other. In the above series, the median is 18.

The median often better expresses the common-run, since it is not, as is the mean, affected by an excessively high or low figure. In the series 1,3,4, 7,55, the median of 4 is a truer expression of the common-run than is the mean of 14.

Prime Numbers Between 1 and 1,000

	2	3	5	7	11	13	17	19	23
29	31	37	41	43	47	53	59	61	67
71	73	79	83	89	97	101	103	107	109
113	127	131	137	139	149	151	157	163	167
173	179	181	191	193	197	199	211	223	227
229	233	239	241	251	257	263	269	271	277
281	283	293	307	311	313	317	331	337	347
349	353	359	367	373	379	383	389	397	401
409	419	421	431	433	439	443	449	457	461
463	467	479	487	491	499	503	509	521	523
541	547	557	563	569	571	577	587	593	599
601	607	613	617	619	631	641	643	647	653
659	661	673	677	683	691	701	709	719	727
733	739	743	751	757	761	769	773	787	797
809	811	821	823	827	829	839	853	857	859
863	877	881	883	887	907	911	919	929	937
941	947	953	967	971	977	983	991	997	(1009)

Definitions of Gold Terminology

The term "fineness" defines a gold content in parts per thousand. For example, a gold nugget containing 885 parts of pure gold, 100 parts of silver, and 15 parts of copper would be considered 885-fine.

The word "karat" indicates the proportion of solid gold in an alloy based on a total of 24 parts. Thus, 14-karat (14K) gold indicates a composition of 14 parts of gold and 10 parts of other metals.

The term "gold-filled" is used to describe articles of jewelry made of base metal which are covered on one or more surfaces with a layer of gold alloy. No article having a gold alloy portion of less than one twentieth by weight may be marked "gold-filled." Articles may be marked "rolled gold plate" provided the proportional fraction and fineness designations are also shown.

Electroplated jewelry items carrying at least 7 millionths of an inch of gold on significant surfaces may be labeled "electroplate." Plate thicknesses less than this may be marked "gold flashed" or "gold washed."

Portraits and Designs of U.S. Paper Currency[1]

Currency	Portrait	Design on back	Currency	Portrait	Design on back
$1	Washington	ONE between obverse and reverse of Great Seal of U.S.	$50	Grant	U.S. Capitol
			$100	Franklin	Independence Hall
$2[2]	Jefferson	Monticello	$500	McKinley	Ornate FIVE HUNDRED
$2[3]	Jefferson	"The Signing of the Declaration of Independence"	$1,000	Cleveland	Ornate ONE THOUSAND
			$5,000	Madison	Ornate FIVE THOUSAND
$5	Lincoln	Lincoln Memorial	$10,000	Chase	Ornate TEN THOUSAND
$10	Hamilton	U.S. Treasury Building	$100,000[4]	Wilson	Ornate ONE HUNDRED THOUSAND
$20	Jackson	White House			

1. Denominations of $500 and higher were discontinued in 1969. 2. Discontinued in 1966. 3. New issue, April 13, 1976. 4. For use only in transactions between Federal Reserve System and Treasury Department.

WRITER'S GUIDE

A Concise Guide to Style

From *Webster's II New Riverside University Dictionary.* © 1984 by Houghton Mifflin Company.

This section discusses and illustrates the basic conventions of American capitalization, punctuation, and italicization.

Capitalization

Capitalize the following: **1.** the first word of a sentence: Some spiders are poisonous; others are not. Are you my new neighbor?
2. the first word of a direct quotation, except when the quotation is split: Joyce asked, "Do you think that the lecture was interesting?" "No," I responded, "it was very boring." Tom Paine said, "The sublime and the ridiculous are often so nearly related that it is difficult to class them separately."
3. the first word of each line in a poem in traditional verse: Half a league, half a league,/Half a league onward,/All in the valley of Death/Rode the six hundred.—Alfred, Lord Tennyson
4. the names of people, of organizations and their members, of councils and congresses, and of historical periods and events: Marie Curie, Benevolent and Protective Order of Elks, an Elk, Protestant Episcopal Church, an Episcopalian, the Democratic Party, a Democrat, the Nuclear Regulatory Commission, the U.S. Senate, the Middle Ages, World War I, the Battle of Britain.
5. the names of places and geographic divisions, districts, regions, and locales: Richmond, Vermont, Argentina, Seventh Avenue, London Bridge, Arctic Circle, Eastern Hemisphere, Continental Divide, Middle East, Far North, Gulf States, East Coast, the North, the South Shore.
Do not capitalize words indicating compass points unless a specific region is referred to: Turn north onto Interstate 91.
6. the names of rivers, lakes, mountains, and oceans: Ohio River, Lake Como, Rocky Mountains, Atlantic Ocean.
7. the names of ships, aircraft, satellites, and space vehicles: U.S.S. *Arizona, Spirit of St. Louis,* the spy satellite Ferret-D, Voyager II, the space shuttle Challenger.
8. the names of nationalities, races, tribes, and languages: Spanish, Maori, Bantu, Russian.
9. words derived from proper names, except in their extended senses: the Byzantine Empire. *But:* byzantine office politics.
10. words indicating family relationships when used with a person's name as a title: Aunt Toni and Uncle Jack. *But:* my aunt and uncle, Toni and Jack Walker.
11. a title (i.e., civil, judicial, military, royal and noble, religious, and honorary) when preceding a name: Justice Marshall, General Jackson, Mayor Daley, Queen Victoria, Lord Mountbatten, Pope John Paul II, Professor Jacobson, Senator Byrd.
12. all references to the President and Vice President of the United States: The President has entered the hall. The Vice President presides over the Senate.
13. all key words in titles of literary, dramatic, artistic, and musical works: the novel *The Old Man and the Sea,* the short story "Notes from Underground," an article entitled "On Passive Verbs," James Dickey's poem "In the Tree House a Night," the play *Cat on a Hot Tin Roof,* Van Gogh's *Wheat Field and Cypress Trees,* Beethoven's *Emperor Concerto.*
14. *the* in the title of a newspaper if it is a part of the title: *The Wall Street Journal. But:* the New York *Daily News.*
15. the first word in the salutation and in the complimentary close of a letter: My dear Carol Yours sincerely.
16. epithets and substitutes for the names of people and places: Old Hickory, Old Blood and Guts The Oval Office, the Windy City.
17. words used in personifications: When is not Death at watch/Within those secret waters?/What wants he but to catch/Earth's heedless sons and daughters?—Edmund Blunden
18. the pronoun *I:* I told them that I had heard the news.
19. names for the Deity and sacred works: God the Almighty, Jesus, Allah, the Supreme Being, the Bible, the Koran, the Talmud.
20. days of the week, months of the year, holidays, and holy days: Tuesday, May, Independence Day, Passover, Ramadan, Christmas.
21. the names of specific courts: The Supreme Court of the United States, the Massachusetts Appeals Court, the United States Court of Appeals for the First Circuit.
22. the names of treaties, accords, pacts, laws and specific amendments: Panama Canal Treaty, Treaty of Paris, Geneva Accords, Warsaw Pact countries, Sherman Antitrust Law, Labor Management Relations Act, took the Fifth Amendment.
23. registered trademarks and service marks Day-Glo, Comsat.
24. the names of geologic eras, periods, epochs, and strata and the names of prehistoric divisions Paleozoic Era, Precambrian, Pleistocene, Age of Reptiles, Bronze Age, Stone Age.
25. the names of constellations, planets, and stars: Milky Way, Southern Crown, Saturn, Jupiter Uranus, Polaris.
26. genus but not species names in binomial nomenclature: *Rana pipiens.*
27. New Latin names of classes, families, and all groups higher than genera in botanical and zoological nomenclature: Nematoda.
But do not capitalize derivatives from such names: nematodes.
28. many abbreviations and acronyms: Dec. Tues., Lt. Gen., M.F.A., UNESCO, MIRV.

Italicization

Use italics to:
1. indicate titles of books, plays, and epic poems

War and Peace, The Importance of Being Earnest, Paradise Lost.

2. indicate titles of magazines and newspapers: *New York* magazine, *The Wall Street Journal,* the New York *Daily News.*

3. set off the titles of motion pictures and radio and television programs: *Star Wars, All Things Considered, Masterpiece Theater.*

4. indicate titles of major musical compositions: Handel's *Messiah,* Adam's *Giselle.*

5. set off the names of paintings and sculpture: *Mona Lisa, Pietà.*

6. indicate words, letters, or numbers that are referred to: The word *hiss* is onomatopoeic. *Can't* means *won't* in your lexicon. You form your *n*'s like *u*'s. A *6* looks like an inverted *9.*

7. indicate foreign words and phrases not yet assimilated into English: *C'est la vie* was the response to my complaint.

8. indicate the names of plaintiff and defendant in legal citations: *Roe* v. *Doe.*

9. emphasize a word or phrase: When you appear on the national news, you are *somebody.*

Use this device sparingly.

10. distinguish New Latin names of genera, species, subspecies, and varieties in botanical and zoological nomenclature: *Homo sapiens.*

11. set off the names of ships and aircraft but not space vehicles: U.S.S. *Arizona, Spirit of St. Louis,* Voyager II, the space shuttle Challenger, the spy satellite Ferret-D.

Punctuation

Apostrophe. 1. indicates the possessive case of singular and plural nouns, indefinite pronouns, and surnames combined with designations such as *Jr., Sr.,* and *II:* my sister's husband, my three sisters' husbands, anyone's guess, They answer each other's phones, John Smith, Jr.'s car.

2. indicates joint possession when used with the last of two or more nouns in a series: Doe and Roe's report.

3. indicates individual possession or authorship when used with each of two or more nouns in a series: Smith's, Roe's, and Doe's reports.

4. indicates the plurals of words, letters, and figures used as such: 60's and 70's; *x*'s, *y*'s, and *z*'s.

5. indicates omission of letters in contractions: aren't, that's, o'clock.

6. indicates omission of figures in dates: the class of '63.

Brackets. 1. enclose words or passages in quoted matter to indicate insertion of material written by someone other than the author: A tough but nervous, tenacious but restless race [the Yankees]; materially ambitious, yet prone to introspection. . . .—Samuel Eliot Morison

2. enclose material inserted within matter already in parentheses: (Vancouver [B.C.] January 1, 19—).

Colon. 1. introduces words, phrases, or clauses that explain, amplify, or summarize what has gone before: Suddenly I realized where we were: Rome.

There are two cardinal sins from which all the others spring: impatience and laziness.—Franz Kafka

2. introduces a long quotation: In his original draft of the *Declaration of Independence,* Jefferson wrote: "We hold these truths to be sacred and undeniable; that all men are created equal and independent, that from that equal creation they derive

rights inherent and inalienable. . . ."

3. introduces a list: We need the following items: pens, paper, pencils, blotters, and erasers.

4. separates chapter and verse numbers in Biblical references: James 1:4.

5. separates city from publisher in footnotes and bibliographies: Chicago: Riverside Press, 1983.

6. separates hour and minute(s) in time designations: 9:30 a.m., a 9:30 meeting.

7. follows the salutation in a business letter: Gentlemen:

Comma. 1. separates the clauses of a compound sentence connected by a coordinating conjunction: A difference exists between the musical works of Handel and Haydn, and it is a difference worth noting.

The comma may be omitted in short compound sentences: I heard what you said and I am furious. I got out of the car and I walked and walked.

2. separates *and* or *or* from the final item in a series of three or more: Red, yellow, and blue may be mixed to produce all colors.

3. separates two or more adjectives modifying the same noun if *and* could be used between them without altering the meaning: a solid, heavy gait. *But:* a polished mahogany dresser.

4. sets off nonrestrictive clauses or phrases (i.e., those that if eliminated would not affect the meaning of the sentences): The burglar, who had entered through the patio, went straight to the silver chest.

The comma should not be used when a clause is restrictive (i.e., essential to the meaning of the sentence): The burglar who had entered through the patio went straight to the silver chest; the other burglar searched for the wall safe.

5. sets off words or phrases in apposition to a noun or noun phrase: Plato, the famous Greek philosopher, was a student of Socrates.

The comma should not be used if such words or phrases precede the noun: The Greek philosopher Plato was a student of Socrates.

6. sets off transitional words and short expressions that require a pause in reading or speaking: Unfortunately, my friend was not well traveled. Did you, after all, find what you were looking for? I live with my family, of course.

7. sets off words used to introduce a sentence: No, I haven't been to Paris. Well, what do you think we should do now?

8. sets off a subordinate clause or a long phrase that precedes a principal clause: By the time we found the restaurant, we were starved. Of all the illustrations in the book, the most striking are those of the tapestries.

9. sets off short quotations and sayings: The candidate said, "Actions speak louder than words." "Talking of axes," said the Duchess, "chop off her head!"—Lewis Carroll

10. indicates omission of a word or words: To err is human; to forgive, divine.

11. sets off the year from the month in full dates: Nicholas II of Russia was shot on July 16, 1918.

But note that when only the month and the year are used, no comma appears: Nicholas II of Russia was shot in July 1918.

12. sets off city and state in geographic names: Atlanta, Georgia, is the transportation center of the South. 34 Beach Drive, Bedford, VA 24523.

13. separates series of four or more figures into thousands, millions, etc.: 67,000; 200,000.

14. sets off words used in direct address: I tell you, folks, all politics is applesauce.—Will Rogers Thank you for your expert assistance, Dolores.

15. Separates a tag question from the rest of a sentence: You forgot your keys again, didn't you?

16. sets off sentence elements that could be misunderstood if the comma were not used: Some time after, the actual date for the project was set.

17. follows the salutation in a personal letter and the complimentary close in a business or personal letter: Dear Jessica, Sincerely yours.

18. sets off titles and degrees from surnames and from the rest of a sentence: Walter T. Prescott, Jr.; Gregory A. Rossi, S.J.; Susan P. Green, M.D., presented the case.

Dash. 1. indicates a sudden break or abrupt change in continuity: "If—if you'll just let me explain—" the student stammered. And the problem—if there really is one—can then be solved.

2. sets apart an explanatory, a defining, or an emphatic phrase: Foods rich in protein—meat, fish, and eggs—should be eaten on a daily basis.

More important than winning the election, is governing the nation. That is the test of a political party—the acid, final test.—Adlai E. Stevenson

3. sets apart parenthetical matter: Wolsey, for all his faults—and he had many—was a great statesman, a man of natural dignity with a generous temperament. . . .—Jasper Ridley

4. marks an unfinished sentence: "But if my bus is late—" he began.

5. sets off a summarizing phrase or clause: The vital measure of a newspaper is not its size but its spirit—that is its responsibility to report the news fully, accurately, and fairly.—Arthur H. Sulzberger

6. sets off the name of an author or source, as at the end of a quotation: A poet can survive everything but a misprint.—Oscar Wilde

Ellipses. 1. indicate, by three spaced points, omission of words or sentences within quoted matter: Equipped by education to rule in the nineteenth century, . . . he lived and reigned in Russia in the twentieth century.—Robert K. Massie

2. indicate, by four spaced points, omission of words at the end of a sentence: The timidity of bureaucrats when it comes to dealing with . . . abuses is easy to explain. . . .—*New York*

3. indicate, when extended the length of a line, omission of one or more lines of poetry:

  Roll on, thou deep and dark blue
    ocean—roll!

 . . . .

  Man marks the earth with ruin—his
    control
  Stops with the shore.—Lord Byron

4. are sometimes used as a device, as for example, in advertising copy:

  To help you Move and Grow
    with the Rigors of
  Business in the 1980's . . .
    and Beyond.—*Journal of Business Strategy*

Exclamation Point. 1. terminates an emphatic or exclamatory sentence: Go home at once! You've got to be kidding!

2. terminates an emphatic interjection: Encore!

Hyphen. 1. indicates that part of a word of more than one syllable has been carried over from one line to the next:

  During the revolution, the nation was
  beset with problems—looting, fighting, and famine.

2. joins the elements of some compounds: greatgrandparent, attorney-at-law, ne'er-do-well.

3. joins the elements of compound modifiers preceding nouns: high-school students, a fire-and-brimstone lecture, a two-hour meeting.

4. indicates that two or more compounds share a single base: four- and six-volume sets, eight- and nine-year olds.

5. separates the prefix and root in some combinations; check the Dictionary when in doubt about the spelling: anti-Nazi, re-elect, co-author, re-form/reform, re-cover/recover, re-creation/-recreation.

6. substitutes for the word *to* between typewritten inclusive words or figures: pp. 145-155, the Boston-New York air shuttle.

7. punctuates written-out compound numbers from 21 through 99: forty-six years of age, a person who is forty-six, two hundred fifty-nine dollars.

Parentheses. 1. enclose material that is not essential to a sentence and that if not included would not alter its meaning: After a few minutes (some say less) the blaze was extinguished.

2. often enclose letters or figures to indicate subdivisions of a series: A movement in sonata form consists of the following elements: (1) the exposition, (2) the development, and (3) the recapitulation.

3. enclose figures following and confirming written-out numbers, especially in legal and business documents: The fee for my services will be two thousand dollars ($2,000.00).

4. enclose an abbreviation for a term following the written-out term, when used for the first time in a text: The patient is suffering from acquired immune deficiency syndrome (AIDS).

Period. 1. terminates a complete declarative or mild imperative sentence: There could be no turning back as war's dark shadow settled irrevocably across the continent of Europe.—W. Bruce Lincoln. Return all the books when you can. Would you kindly affix your signature here.

2. terminates sentence fragments: Gray clouds—and what looks like a veil of rain falling behind the East German headland. A pair of ducks. A tired or dying swan, head buried in its back feathers, sits on the sand a few feet from the water's edge.—Anthony Bailey

3. follows some abbreviations: Dec., Rev., St., Blvd., pp., Co.

Question Mark. 1. punctuates a direct question: Have you seen the new play yet? Who goes there? *But:* I wonder who said "Nothing is easy in war." I asked if they planned to leave.

2. indicates uncertainty: Ferdinand Magellan (1480?-1521), Plato (427?-347 B.C.).

Quotation Marks. 1. Double quotation marks enclose direct quotations: "What was Paris like in the Twenties?" our daughter asked. "Ladies and Gentlemen," the Chief Usher said, "the President of the United States." Robert Louis Stevenson said that "it is better to be a fool than to be dead." When advised not to become a lawyer because the profession was already overcrowded, Daniel Webster replied, "There is always room at the top."

2. Double quotation marks enclose words or phrases to clarify their meaning or use or to indicate that they are being used in a special way: This was the border of what we often call "the West" or "the Free World." "The Windy City" is a name for Chicago.

3. Double quotation marks set off the translation of a foreign word or phrase: *die Grenze,* "the border."

4. Double quotation marks set off the titles of series of books, of articles or chapters in publications, of essays, of short stories and poems, of individual radio and television programs, and of songs and short musical pieces: "The Horizon Concise History" series; an article entitled "On Reflexive

Verbs in English"; Chapter Nine, "The Prince and the Peasant"; Pushkin's "The Queen of Spades"; Tennyson's "Ode on the Death of the Duke of Wellington"; "The Bob Hope Special"; Schubert's "Death and the Maiden."

5. Single quotation marks enclose quotations within quotations: The blurb for the piece proclaimed, "Two years ago at Geneva, South Vietnam was virtually sold down the river to the Communists. Today the spunky little . . . country is back on its own feet, thanks to 'a mandarin in a sharkskin suit who's upsetting the Red timetable.' "—Frances FitzGerald

Put commas and periods inside quotation marks; put semicolons and colons outside. Other punctuation, such as exclamation points and question marks, should be put inside the closing quotation marks only if part of the matter quoted.

Semicolon. 1. separates the clauses of a compound sentence having no coordinating conjunction: Do not let us speak of darker days; let us rather speak of sterner days.—Winston Churchill

2. separates the clauses of a compound sentence in which the clauses contain internal punctuation, even when the clauses are joined by conjunctions: Skis in hand, we trudged to the lodge, stowed our lunches, and donned our boots; and the rest of our party waited for us at the lifts.

3. separates elements of a series in which items already contain commas: Among those at the diplomatic reception were the Secretary of State; the daughter of the Ambassador to the Court of St. James's, formerly of London; and two United Nations delegates.

4. separates clauses of a compound sentence joined by a conjunctive adverb, such as *however, nonetheless,* or *hence:* We insisted upon a hearing; however, the Grievance Committee refused.

5. may be used instead of a comma to signal longer pauses for dramatic effect: But I want you to know that when I cross the river my last conscious thought will be of the Corps; and the Corps; and the Corps.—General Douglas MacArthur

Virgule. 1. separates successive divisions in an extended date: fiscal year 1983/84.

2. represents *per:* 35 km/hr, 1,800 ft/sec.

3. means *or* between the words *and* and *or:* Take water skis and/or fishing equipment when you visit the beach this summer.

4. separates two or more lines of poetry that are quoted and run in on successive lines of a text: The student actress had a memory lapse when she came to the lines "Double, double, toil and trouble/Fire burn and cauldron bubble/Eye of newt and toe of frog/Wool of bat and tongue of dog" and had to leave the stage in embarrassment.

Forms of Address[1]

Source: *Webster's II New Riverside University Dictionary.* Copyright © 1984 by Houghton Mifflin Company.

Academics

Dean, college or university. *Address:* Dean _____. *Salutation:* Dear Dean _____.

President. *Address:* President _____ _____. *Salutation:* Dear President _____.

Professor, college or university. *Address:* Professor _____. *Salutation:* Dear Professor _____.

Clerical and Religious Orders

Abbot. *Address:* The Right Reverend _____ O.S.B. Abbot of _____. *Salutation:* Right Reverend Abbot or Dear Father Abbot.

Archbishop, Eastern Orthodox. *Address:* The Most Reverend Joseph, Archbishop of _____. *Salutation:* Your Eminence.

Archbishop, Roman Catholic. The Most Reverend _____, Archbishop of _____. *Salutation:* Your Excellency.

Archdeacon, Episcopal. *Address:* The Venerable _____, Archdeacon of _____. *Salutation:* Venerable Sir or Dear Archdeacon _____.

Bishop, Episcopal. *Address:* The Right Reverend _____, Bishop of _____. *Salutation:* Right Reverend Sir or Dear Bishop _____.

Bishop, other Protestant. *Address:* The Reverend _____. *Salutation:* Dear Bishop _____.

Bishop, Roman Catholic. *Address:* The Most Reverend _____, Bishop of _____. *Salutation:* Your Excellency or Dear Bishop _____.

Brotherhood, Roman Catholic. *Address:* Brother _____, C.F.C. *Salutation:* Dear Brother or Dear Brother Joseph.

Brotherhood, superior of. *Address:* Brother Joseph C.F.C. Superior. *Salutation:* Dear Brother Joseph.

Cardinal. *Address:* His Eminence Joseph Cardinal Stone. *Salutation:* Your Eminence.

Clergyman/woman, Protestant. *Address:* The Reverend _____ or The Reverend _____, D.D. *Salutation:* Dear Mr./Ms. _____ or Dear Dr. _____.

Dean of a cathedral, Episcopal. *Address:* The Very Reverend _____, Dean of _____. *Salutation:* Dear Dean _____.

Monsignor. *Address:* The Right Reverend Monsignor _____. *Salutation:* Dear Monsignor.

Patriarch, Greek Orthodox. *Address:* His All Holiness Patriarch Joseph. *Salutation:* Your All Holiness.

Patriarch, Russian Orthodox. *Address:* His Holiness the Patriarch of _____. *Salutation:* Your Holiness.

Pope. *Address:* His Holiness The Pope. *Salutation:* Your Holiness or Most Holy Father.

Priest, Roman Catholic. *Address:* The Reverend _____, S.J. *Salutation:* Dear Reverend Father or Dear Father.

Rabbi, man or woman. *Address:* Rabbi _____ or _____ D.D.. *Salutation:* Dear Rabbi _____ or Dear Dr. _____.

Sisterhood, Roman Catholic. *Address:* Sister _____, C.S.J. *Salutation:* Dear Sister or Dear Sister _____.

Sisterhood, superior of. *Address:* The Reverend Mother Superior, S.C. *Salutation:* Reverend Mother.

Diplomats

Ambassador, U.S. *Address:* The Honorable _____ The Ambassador of the United States. *Sal-*

utation: Sir/Madam or Dear Mr./Madam Ambassador.

Ambassador to the U.S. *Address:* His/Her Excellency _____ _____, The Ambassador of _____. *Salutation:* Excellency or Dear Mr./Madam Ambassador.

Chargé d'Affaires, U.S. *Address:* The Honorable _____, United States Chargé d'Affaires. *Salutation:* Dear Mr./Ms. _____.

Consul, U.S. *Address:* _____ _____, Esq., United States Consul. *Salutation:* Dear Mr./Ms. _____.

Minister, U.S. or to U.S. *Address:* The Honorable _____, The Minister of _____. *Salutation:* Sir/Madam or Dear Mr./Madame Minister.

Secretary General, United Nations. *Address:* His/Her Excellency _____, Secretary General of the United Nations. *Salutation:* Dear Mr./Madam/Madame Secretary General.

United Nations Representative (Foreign). *Address:* His/Her Excellency _____ _____ Representative of _____ to the United Nations. *Salutation:* Excellency or My dear Mr./Madame _____.

United Nations Representative (U.S.) *Address:* The Honorable _____ _____, United States Representative to the United Nations. *Salutation:* Sir/Madam or Dear Mr./Ms. _____.

Government Officials

Assemblyman. *Address:* The Honorable _____ _____. *Salutation:* Dear Mr./Ms. _____.

Associate Justice, U.S. Supreme Court. *Address:* Mr./Madam Justice _____. *Salutation:* Dear Mr./Madam Justice or Sir/Madam.

Attorney General, U.S. *Address:* The Honorable _____ _____, Attorney General of the United States. *Salutation:* Dear Mr./Madam or Attorney General.

Cabinet member: *Address:* The Honorable _____ _____, Secretary of _____. *Salutation:* Sir/Madam or Dear Mr./Madam Secretary.

Chief Justice, U.S. Supreme Court. *Address:* The Chief Justice of the United States. *Salutation:* Dear Mr. Chief Justice.

Commissioner (federal, state, local). *Address:* The Honorable _____ _____. *Salutation:* Dear Mr./Ms. _____.

Governor. *Address:* The Honorable _____ _____, Governor of _____. *Salutation:* Dear Governor _____.

Judge, Federal: *Address:* The Honorable _____, Judge of the United States District Court for the _____, District of _____. *Salutation:* Sir/Madam or Dear Judge _____.

Judge, state or local. *Address:* The Honorable _____ _____, Judge of the Court of _____. *Salutation:* Dear Judge _____.

Lieutenant Governor. *Address:* The Honorable _____ _____, Lieutenant Governor of _____. *Salutation:* Dear Mr./Ms. _____.

Mayor. *Address:* The Honorable _____ _____, Mayor of _____. *Salutation:* Dear Mayor _____.

President, U.S. *Address:* The President. *Salutation:* Dear Mr. President.

President, U.S., former. *Address:* The Honorable _____ _____. *Salutation:* Dear Mr. _____.

Representative, state. *Address:* The Honorable _____ _____. *Salutation:* Dear Mr./Ms. _____.

Representative, U.S. *Address:* The Honorable _____ _____, United States House of Representatives. *Salutation:* Dear Mr./Ms. _____.

Senator, state. *Address:* The Honorable _____ _____, The State Senate, State Capitol. *Salutation:* Dear Senator _____.

Senator, U.S. *Address:* The Honorable _____ _____, United States Senate. *Salutation:* Dear Senator _____.

Speaker, U.S. House of Representatives. *Address:* The Honorable _____ _____, Speaker of the House of Representatives. *Salutation:* Dear Mr./Madam Speaker.

Vice President, U.S. *Address:* The Vice President of the United States. *Salutation:* Sir or Dear Mr. Vice President.

Military and Naval Officers

Rank. *Address:* Full rank, USN (or USCG, USAF, USA, USMC). *Salutation:* Dear (full rank) _____.

Professions

Attorney. *Address:* Mr./Ms. _____ _____, Attorney at law or _____ _____, Esq. *Salutation:* Dear Mr./Ms. _____.

Dentist. *Address:* _____ _____, D.D.S. *Salutation:* Dear Dr. _____.

Physician. *Address:* _____ _____, M.D. *Salutation:* Dear Dr. _____.

Veterinarian. *Address:* _____ _____, D.V.M. *Salutation:* Dear Dr. _____.

1. Forms of address do not always follow set guidelines; the type of salutation is often determined by the relationship between correspondents or by the purpose and content of the letter. However, a general style applies to most occasions. In highly formal salutations, when the addressee is a woman, "Madam" should be substituted for "Sir." When the salutation is informal, "Ms.," "Miss," or "Mrs." should be substituted for "Mr." If a woman addressee has previously indicated a preference for a particular form of address, that form should be used.

Telephone Solicitations

For your protection, don't buy anything over the telephone unless you initiate the call, you know who you have reached, and you believe the seller is reputable. To check on a company's reputation, call the Better Business Bureau or consumer protection office where the company is located. Be wary of any caller who insists on an immediate purchase decision. Ask for the name, address, and phone number where you can reach the caller after considering the solicitation. Don't be lured into buying otherwise unwanted merchandise by offers of promotional gifts or prizes.

Get the offer in writing before you buy. Look to see if there are conditions or restrictions that you were not told about on the phone.

Never give your credit card or social security number over the telephone as a verification of your identity. Don't use your credit card number to purchase anything unless you initiated the call or you know exactly with whom you are talking.

Reference Books And Other Sources

This cannot be a record of all the thousands of available sources of information. Nevertheless, these selected references will enable the reader to locate additional facts about many subjects covered in the *Information Please Almanac*. The editors have chosen sources that they believe will be helpful to the general reader.

General References

Encyclopedias are a unique category, since they attempt to cover most subjects quite thoroughly. The most valuable multivolume encyclopedias are the **Encyclopaedia Britannica** and the **Encyclopedia Americana**. Useful one-volume encyclopedias are the **New Columbia Encyclopedia** and the **Random House Encyclopedia**.

Dictionaries and similar "word books" are also unique: **The American Heritage Dictionary, Second College Edition**, containing 200,000 definitions and specialized usage guidance; **The American Heritage Illustrated Encyclopedic Dictionary**, containing 180,000 entries, 275 boxed encyclopedic features, and 175 colored maps of the world; **Webster's Third New International Dictionary, Unabridged; Webster's II New Riverside University Dictionary**, containing 200,000 definitions plus hundreds of word history paragraphs; and the multivolume **Oxford English Dictionary**, providing definitions in historical order. **Roget's II The New Thesaurus**, containing thousands of synonyms grouped according to meaning, assists writers in choosing just the right word. The quick reference set—**The Word Book II** (over 40,000 words spelled and divided), **The Right Word II** (a concise thesaurus), and **The Written Word II** (a concise guide to writing, style, and usage)—are based on **The American Heritage Dictionary** and are intended for the busy reader needing information fast. Two excellent books of quotations are **Bartlett's Familiar Quotations** and **The Oxford Dictionary of Quotations**.

There are a number of useful atlases: the **New York Times Atlas of the World**, a number of historical atlases (Penguin Books), **Oxford Economic Atlas of the World**, **Rand McNally Cosmopolitan World Atlas: New Census Edition**, and **Atlas of the Historical Geography of the United States** (Greenwood). Many contemporary road atlases of the United States and foreign countries are also available.

A source of information on virtually all subjects is the United States Government Printing Office (GPO). For information, write: Superintendent of Documents, Washington, D.C. 20402.

For help on any subject, consult: **Subject Guide to Books in Print, The New York Times Index**, and the **Reader's Guide to Periodical Literature** in your library.

Specific References

AIDS: Resource Guide (Government Printing Office)
America Votes (Congressional Quarterly, Inc.)
American Indian, Reference Encyclopedia of the (B. Klein Publications)
American Revolution, The (American Heritage)
Anatomy, Gray's (Saunders)
Antiques and Collectibles Price List, the Kovels' (Crown)
Architectural & Building Technology, Dictionary of (Elsevier)
Architecture, Encyclopedia of World (VanNostrand Reinhold)
Art, History of (Prentice-Hall)
Art, Oxford Companion to (Oxford University Press)
Art, Who's Who in American (R.R. Bowker)
Art Directory, American (R.R. Bowker)
Associations, Encyclopedia of (Gale Research Co.)
Astronomy, Peterson First Guide (Houghton Mifflin)
Authors, 1000–1900, European (H.W. Wilson)
Authors, Twentieth Century (H.W. Wilson)
Automobile Facts and Figures (Kallman)
Automobile Year Book (Motorbooks International)
Ballet & Modern Dance: A Concise History (Princeton Book Co.)
Banking and Finance, Encyclopedia of (Bankers Publishing Co.)
Baseball Encyclopedia (Macmillan)
Biographical Dictionary, Chambers (Cambridge University Press)
Biography Yearbook, Current (H.W. Wilson)
Birds, Field Guide to the, Peterson Field Guide Series (Houghton Mifflin)
Black Americans, Who's Who Among (Who's Who Among Black Americans, Inc.)
Book Review Digest, 1905– (H.W. Wilson)
Catholic Encyclopedia, New (Publishers Guild)
Chemistry, Encyclopedia of (VanNostrand Rinehold)
Chemistry, Lange's Handbook of, 13th Edition (McGraw Hill)
Christian Church, Oxford Dictionary of the (Oxford University Press)
Citizens Band: Radio Rules and Regulations (AMECO)
College Cost Book, 1986-87, The (The College Board)
Composers, Great 1300–1900 (H.W. Wilson)
Composers Since 1900 (H.W. Wilson)
Computer Science and Technology, Encyclopedia of (Dekker)
(Computer software) Yellow Book: A Parent's Guide to Teacher Tested Educational Software (NEA Computer Services Staff)
Computer Terms, Dictionary of (Barron)
Condo and Co-op Information Book, Complete (Houghton Mifflin)
Congressional Quarterly Almanac (Congressional Quarterly, Inc.)
Consumer Reports (Consumers Union)
Costume, The Dictionary of (Scribners)
Drama, Classical, Greek and Roman (Barron)
Cultural Literacy, The Dictionary of (Houghton Mifflin)
Drama, 20th Century, England, Ireland, the United States (Random House)
Ecology Information and Organizations, Guide to (H.W. Wilson)
Energy Factbook (McGraw-Hill)

Environmental Progress and Challenges: EPA's Update (Government Printing Office)

Environmental Science (Saunders College Publishing)

Europa Year Book (Gale Research Co.)

Fact Books, The Rand McNally (Rand)

Facts, Famous First (H.W. Wilson)

Facts on File (Facts on File, Inc.)

Film: A Reference Guide (Greenwood)

(Film) Guide to Movies on Video-cassette (Consumers Reports)

(Finance) Touche Ross Guide to Personal Financial Management (Prentice-Hall)

Food and Drink, Dictionary of American (Ticknor & Fields)

Football Made Easy (Jonathan David)

Games, Book of (Jazz Press)

Gardening, Encyclopedia of (Houghton Mifflin)

Gardening, Taylor's Pocket Guides (Houghton Mifflin)

Geography, Dictionary of (Penguin Books)

Government Manual, U.S. (U.S. Office of the Federal Register, Government Printing Office)

History, Album of American (Scribner's)

History, Dictionary of American (Rowman)

History, Documents of American (Prentice-Hall)

History, Encyclopedia of Latin-American (Greenwood)

History, Encyclopedia of World (Houghton Mifflin)

Hockey, the Illustrated History: An Official Publication of the National Hockey League (Doubleday)

How the World Works, A Guide to Science's Greatest Discoveries (Quill/William Morrow)

Infomania, The Guide to Essential Electronic Services (Houghton Mifflin Company)

Islam, Dictionary of (Orient Book Distributors)

Jazz in the Seventies, Encyclopedia of (Horizon)

Jewish Concepts, Encyclopedia of (Hebrew Publishers)

Legal Word Book, The (Houghton Mifflin)

Libraries, World Guide to (K. G. Saur)

Library Directory, American (R.R. Bowker)

Literary Market Place (R. R. Bowker)

Literature, Oxford Companion to American (Oxford University Press)

Literature, Oxford Companion to Classical (Oxford University Press)

Literature, Oxford Companion to English (Oxford University Press)

(Literature) Reader's Adviser: A Layman's Guide to Literature (R.R. Bowker)

Literature, Reader's Encyclopedia of American (T.Y. Crowell)

Medical Encyclopedia, Home (Fawcett)

Medical & Health Sciences Word Book (Houghton Mifflin)

Museums of the World (K.G. Saur)

Music and Musicians, Handbook of American (Da Capo)

Music, Concise Oxford Dictionary of (Oxford University Press)

Music, Harvard Dictionary of (Harvard University Press)

Musical Terms, Dictionary of (Gordon Press)

Mystery Writers, Twentieth Century Crime and (St. Martin's Press)

Mythology (Little, Brown and Co.)

National Park Guide (Rand McNally)

New Nations: A Student Handbook (Shoe String)

Numismatics (Oxford University Press)

Occupational Outlook Handbook (U.S. Bureau of Labor Statistics, Government Printing Office)

Operas, New Milton Cross Complete Stories of the Great (Doubleday)

Physics, Handbook of, 2nd Edition (McGraw Hill)

Pocket Data Book, U.S.A. (U.S. Department of Commerce, Bureau of the Census, Government Printing Office)

Poetry, Granger's Index to (Columbia University Press)

Politics, Almanac of American (Barone & Co.)

Politics, Who's Who in American (R.R. Bowker)

Pop/Rock, Dictionary of American (Schirmer Books)

Prescription & Non-Prescription Drugs, Complete Guide to (HP Books)

Radon, A Citizen's Guide to (Government Printing Office)

Religions, The Facts on File Dictionary of (Facts on File)

Robert's Rules of Order Revised (Morrow & Co.)

Science, American Men and Women of (R.R. Bowker)

Science and Technology, Asimov's Biographical Encyclopedia of (Doubleday)

Scientific Encyclopedia, VanNostrand's (VanNostrand Reinhold)

Secondary Schools, Guide to Independent 1986-87 (Peterson's Guides)

Secretary's Handbook, The Professional (Houghton Mifflin)

Shakespeare, The Riverside (Houghton Mifflin)

Ships, Boats, & Vessels, Illustrated Encyclopedia of (Overlook Press)

Social Security, Facts and Figures About (Government Printing Office)

Stamp Collecting As a Hobby (Sterling)

Stars and Planets, Field Guide to the (Houghton Mifflin)

States, Book of the (Council of State Governments)

Statesman's Year-Book (St. Martin's)

Theater, Oxford Companion to the (Oxford University Press)

Theater, Who's Who in the (Gale Research Co.)

(Travel) The Birnbaum Guides (Houghton Mifflin)

United Nations, Demographic Yearbook (Unipub)

United Nations, Statistical Yearbook of the (Unipub)

United States, Historical Statistics of the Colonial Times to 1970 (Revisionist Press)

United States, Statistical Abstract of the (U.S. Department of Commerce, Bureau of the Census, Government Printing Office)

Vitamin Book: A No-Nonsense Consumer Guide (Bantam)

Washington Information Directory (Congressional Quarterly, Inc.)

The Way Things Work (Houghton Mifflin)

Who's Who in America (Marquis)

Wines, Dictionary of American (Morrow)

Women, Notable American (Harvard University Press)

World War I (American Heritage)

World War II (American Heritage)

Writer's Market (Writers Digest)

Zip Code and Post Office Directory, National (U.S. Postal Service, Government Printing Office)

See the full range of publications of Dun & Bradstreet and Standard & Poor's for corporate financial and stockholder information.

For detailed information on American colleges and universities, see the many publications of the American Council on Education.

Also see many other specialized Who's Who volumes not listed here for biographies of famous people in many fields.

Major Religions of the World

Judaism

The determining factors of Judaism are: descendance from Israel, the *Torah,* and Tradition.

The name Israel (Jacob, a patriarch) also signifies his descendants as a people. During the 15th–13th centuries B.C., Israelite tribes, coming from South and East, gradually settled in Palestine, then inhabited by Canaanites. They were held together by Moses, who gave them religious unity in the worship of *Jahweh,* the God who had chosen Israel to be his people.

Under Judges, the 12 tribes at first formed an amphictyonic covenant. Saul established kingship (circa 1050 B.C.), and under David, his successor (1000–960 B.C.), the State of Israel comprised all of Palestine with Jerusalem as religio-political center. A golden era followed under Solomon (965–926 B.C.), who built *Jahweh* a temple.

After Solomon's death, the kingdom separated into Israel in the North and Judah in the South. A period of conflicts ensued, which ended with the conquest of Israel by Assyria in 722 B.C. The Babylonians defeated Judah in 586 B.C., destroying Jerusalem and its temple, and deporting many to Babylon.

The era of the kings is significant also in that the great prophets worked in that time, emphasizing faith in *Jahweh* as both God of Israel and God of the universe, and stressing social justice.

When the Persians permitted the Jews to return from exile (539 B.C.), temple and cult were restored in Jerusalem. The Persian rulers were succeeded by the Seleucides. The Maccabaean revolt against these Hellenistic kings gave independence to the Jews in 128 B.C., which lasted till the Romans occupied the country.

Important groups that exerted influence during these times were the Sadducees, priests in the temple in Jerusalem; the Pharisees, teachers of the Law in the synagogues; Essenes, a religious order (from whom Dead Sea Scrolls, discovered in 1947, came); Apocalyptists, who were expecting the heavenly Messiah; and Zealots, who were prepared to fight for national independence.

When the latter turned against Rome in A.D. 66, Roman armies under Titus suppressed the revolt,

Estimated Membership of the Principal Religions of the World

Statistics of the world's religions are only very rough approximations. Aside from Christianity, few religions, if any, attempt to keep statistical records; and even Protestants and Catholics employ different methods of counting members. All persons of whatever age who have received baptism in the Catholic Church are counted as members, while in most Protestant Churches only those who "join" the church are numbered. The compiling of statistics is further complicated by the fact that in China one may be at the same time a Confucian, a Taoist, and a Buddhist. In Japan, one may be both a Buddhist and a Shintoist.

Religion	North America[1]	South America	Europe[2]	Asia	Africa	Oceania[3]	World
Total Christians	232,557,080	402,245,550	516,975,400	213,784,490	282,526,720	21,431,200	1,669,520,440
Roman Catholics	94,274,950	377,753,520	265,741,690	100,028,160	106,487,220	7,557,820	951,843,360
Protestants	93,637,200	14,502,350	82,528,950	64,563,390	74,678,880	7,570,210	337,480,980
Orthodox	5,871,470	718,760	126,025,450	3,286,550	25,363,450	508,670	161,774,350
Anglicans	7,262,000	1,228,900	32,696,330	634,240	23,282,850	5,236,620	70,340,940
Other Christians	31,511,460	8,042,020	9,982,980	45,272,150	52,714,320	557,880	148,080,810
Muslims	2,689,480	664,820	40,881,040	583,068,050	253,153,340	98,480	880,555,210
Nonreligious	22,785,380	13,772,620	138,741,370	687,044,510	1,556,150	2,909,630	866,759,660
Hindus	855,800	683,660	595,560	659,629,900	1,424,610	305,920	663,495,450
Buddhists	186,560	483,020	512,690	310,627,030	11,750	15,120	311,836,170
Atheists	1,116,880	2,687,590	79,439,700	145,705,630	245,530	516,080	229,711,410
Chinese folk religionists	103,840	51,540	47,750	172,053,490	8,780	12,830	172,278,230
New Religionists	1,126,150	382,170	34,730	110,347,300	13,920	7,290	111,911,560
Tribal religionists	54,750	1,151,840	150	24,487,890	66,268,630	77,270	92,040,570
Jews	8,117,900	1,003,770	4,515,760	4,207,840	237,610	86,460	18,169,340
Sikhs	150,340	6,050	217,810	16,783,630	22,890	6,670	17,187,390
Shamanists	110	300	200,750	12,179,470	900	110	12,381,640
Confucians	18,980	500	1,210	6,166,910	450	110	6,188,160
Baha'is	319,890	596,540	79,010	2,424,340	1,210,650	61,460	4,691,890
Jains	1,960	2,020	9,950	3,495,920	45,020	820	3,555,690
Shintoists	1,290	610	430	3,376,240	50	410	3,379,030
Other religionists	674,950	6,812,590	330,860	309,750	66,600	26,730	8,221,480
Total Population	270,761,380	430,495,190	782,584,170	2,915,692,390	606,793,600	25,556,590	5,071,883,320

1. Includes Central America and West Indies. 2. Includes the U.S.S.R. and other countries with established Marxist ideology where continuing religious adherence is difficult to estimate. 3. Includes Australia and New Zealand, as well as islands of the South Pacific. *Source: Britiannica Book of the Year, 1989.*

destroying Jerusalem and its temple in A.D. 70. The Jews were scattered in the *diaspora* (Dispersion), subject to oppressions until the Age of the Enlightenment (18th century) brought their emancipation, although persecutions did not end entirely.

The fall of the Jerusalem temple was an important event in the religious life of the Jews, which now developed around *Torah* (Law) and synagogue. Around A.D. 100 the Sacred Scriptures were codified. Synagogue worship became central, with readings from *Torah* and prophets. Most important prayers are the *Shema* (Hear) and the Prayer of the 18 Benedictions.

Religious life is guided by the commandments contained in the *Torah:* circumcision and *Sabbath,* as well as other ethical and ceremonial commandments.

The *Talmud,* based on the *Mishnah* and its interpretations, took shape over many centuries in the Babylonian and Palestinian Schools. It was a strong binding force of Judaism in the Dispersion.

In the 12th century, Maimonides formulated his "13 Articles of Faith," which carried great authority. Fundamental in this creed are: belief in God and his oneness *(Sherma),* belief in the changeless *Torah,* in the words of Moses and the prophets, belief in reward and punishment, the coming of the Messiah, and the resurrection of the dead.

Judaism is divided into theological schools, the main divisions of which are Orthodox, Conservative, and Reform.

Christianity

Christianity is founded upon Jesus Christ, to whose life the New Testament writings testify. Jesus, a Jew, was born in about 7 B.C. and assumed his public life, after his 30th year, in Galilee. The Gospels tell of many extraordinary deeds that accompanied his ministry. He proclaimed the Kingdom of God, a future reality that is at the same time already present. Nationalistic-Jewish expectations of the Messiah he rejected. Rather, he referred to himself as the "Son of Man," the Christ, who has power to forgive sins now and who shall also come as Judge at the end of time. Jesus set forth the religio-ethical demands for participation in the Kingdom of God as change of heart and love of God and neighbor.

At the Last Supper he signified his death as a sacrifice, which would inaugurate the New Covenant, by which many would be saved. Circa A.D. 30 he died on a cross in Jerusalem. The early Church carried on Jesus' proclamation, the apostle Paul emphasizing his death and resurrection.

The person of Jesus is fundamental to the Christian faith since it is believed that in his life, death, and resurrection, God's revelation became historically tangible. He is seen as the turning point in history, and man's relationship to God as determined by his attitude to Jesus.

Historically Christianity thus arose out of Judaism, claiming fulfillment of the promises of the Old Testament in Jesus. The early Church designated itself as "the true Israel," which expected the speedy return of Jesus. The mother church was at Jerusalem, but churches were soon founded in many other places. The apostle Paul was instrumental in founding and extending a Gentile Christianity that was free from Jewish legalism.

The new religion spread rapidly throughout the eastern and western parts of the Roman Empire. In coming to terms with other religious movements within the Empire, Christianity began to take definite shape as an organization in its doctrine, liturgy, and ministry circa A.D. 200. In the 4th century the Catholic Church had taken root in countries stretching from Spain in the West to Persia and India in the East. Christians had been repeatedly subject to persecution by the Roman state, but finally gained tolerance under Constantine the Great (A.D. 313). Since that time, the Church became favored under his successors and in 380 the Emperor Theodosius proclaimed Christianity the State religion. Paganism was suppressed and public life was gradually molded in accordance with Christian ethical demands.

It was in these years also that the Church was able to achieve a certain unity of doctrine. Due to differences of interpretation of basic doctrines concerning Christ, which threatened to divide the Catholic Church, a standard Christian Creed was formulated by bishops at successive Ecumenical Councils, the first of which was held in A.D. 325 (Nicaea). The chief doctrines formulated concerned the doctrine of the Trinity, i.e., that there is one God in three persons: Father, Son, and Holy Spirit (Constantinople, A.D. 381); and the nature of Christ as both divine and human (Chalcedon, A.D. 541).

Through differences and rivalry between East and West the unity of the Church was broken by schism in 1054. In 1517 a separation occurred in the Western Church with the Reformation. From the major Protestant denominations [Lutheran, Presbyterian, Anglican (Episcopalian)], many Free Churches separated themselves in an age of individualism.

In the 20th century, however, the direction is toward unity. The Ecumenical Movement led to the formation of the World Council of Churches in 1948 (Amsterdam), which has since been joined by many Protestant and Orthodox Churches.

Through its missionary activity Christianity has spread to most parts of the globe.

Eastern Orthodoxy

Eastern Orthodoxy comprises the faith and practice of Churches stemming from ancient Churches in the Eastern part of the Roman Empire. The term covers Orthodox Churches in communion with the See of Constantinople, Uniate Churches in communion with Rome, and Nestorian and Monophysite Churches.

The Orthodox, Catholic, Apostolic Church is the direct descendant of the Byzantine State Church and consists of a series of independent national

U. S. Church Membership

Religious group	Members
Protestant bodies and others	79,296,394
Roman Catholics	53,496,862
Jewish congregations[1]	5,943,700
Old Catholic, Polish National Catholic, Armenian churches	829,007
Buddhists	100,000
Miscellaneous	192,065
Subtotal[2]	143,830,806
Moslems[3]	1,500,000
Total	145,330,806

1. Includes Orthodox, Conservative, and Reform. 2. As reported in the *1989 Yearbook of American & Canadian Churches* from statistics furnished by 219 religious bodies in the United States. 3. Figure from staff member, Population Reference Bureau, Inc.

churches that are united by Doctrine, Liturgy, and Hierarchical organization (deacons and priests, who may either be married or be monks before ordination, and bishops, who must be celibates). The heads of these Churches are patriarchs or metropolitans; the Patriarch of Constantinople is only "first among equals." Rivalry between the Pope of Rome and the Patriarch of Constantinople, aided by differences and misunderstandings that existed for centuries between the Eastern and Western parts of the Empire, led to a schism in 1054. Repeated attempts at reunion have failed in past centuries. The mutual excommunication pronounced in that year was lifted in 1965, however, and because of greater interaction in theology between Orthodox Churches and those in the West, a climate of better understanding has been created in the 20th century. First contacts were with Anglicans and Old Catholics. Orthodox Churches belong to the World Council of Churches.

The Eastern Orthodox Churches recognize only the canons of the seven Ecumenical Councils (325–787) as binding for faith and they reject doctrines that have been added in the West.

The central worship service is called the Liturgy, which is understood as representation of God's acts of salvation. Its center is the celebration of the Eucharist, or Lord's Supper.

In their worship *icons* (sacred pictures) are used that have a sacramental meaning as representation. The Mother of Christ, angels, and saints are highly venerated.

The number of sacraments in the Orthodox Church is the same as in the Western Catholic Church.

Orthodox Churches are found in the Balkans and the Soviet Union also, since the 20th century, in Western Europe and other parts of the world, particularly in America.

Eastern Orthodoxy also includes the Uniate Churches that recognize the authority of the Pope but keep their own traditional liturgies and those Churches dating back to the 5th century that emancipated themselves from the Byzantine State Church: the Nestorian Church in the Near East and India with approximately half a million members and the Monophysite Churches with some 17 million members (Coptic, Ethiopian, Syrian, Armenian, and the Mar Thoma Church in India).

Roman Catholicism

Roman Catholicism comprises the belief and practice of the Roman Catholic Church. The Church stands under the authority of the Bishop of Rome, the Pope, and is ruled by him and bishops who are held to be, through ordination, successors of Peter and the Apostles, respectively. Fundamental to the structure of the Church is the juridical aspect: doctrine and sacraments are bound to the power of jurisdiction and consecration of the hierarchy. The Pope, as the head of the hierarchy of archbishops, bishops, priests, and deacons, has full ecclesiastical power, granted him by Christ, through Peter. As successor to Peter, he is the Vicar of Christ. The powers that others in the hierarchy possess are delegated.

Roman Catholics believe their Church to be the one, holy, catholic, and apostolic Church, possessing all the properties of the one, true Church of Christ.

The faith of the Church is understood to be identical with that taught by Christ and his Apostles and contained in Bible and Tradition, i.e. the original deposit of faith, to which nothing new may be added. New definitions of doctrines, such as the Immaculate Conception of Mary (1854) and the bodily Assumption of Mary (1950), have been declared by Popes, however, in accordance with the principle of development (implicit-explicit doctrine).

At Vatican Council I (1870) the Pope was proclaimed "endowed with infallibility, *ex cathedra*, i.e., when exercising the office of Pastor and Teacher of all Christians."

The center of Roman Catholic worship is the celebration of the Mass, the Eucharist, which is the commemoration of Christ's sacrificial death and of his resurrection. Other sacraments are Baptism, Confirmation, Confession, Matrimony, Ordination, and Extreme Unction, seven in all. The Virgin Mary and saints, and their relics, are highly venerated and prayers are made to them to intercede with God, in whose presence they are believed to dwell.

The Roman Catholic Church is the largest Christian organization in the world, found in most countries. Some 8 million belong to the Uniate rites, the vast majority to the Latin rite.

Since Vatican Council II (1962–65), and the effort to "update" the Church, many interesting changes and developments have been taking place.

Protestantism

Protestantism comprises the Christian churches that separated from Rome during the Reformation in the 16th century, initiated by an Augustinian monk, Martin Luther. "Protestant" was originally applied to followers of Luther, who protested at the Diet of Spires (1529) against the decree which prohibited all further ecclesiastical reforms. Subsequently, Protestantism came to mean rejection of attempts to tie God's revelation to earthly institutions, and a return to the Gospel and the Word of God as sole authority in matters of faith and practice. Central in the biblical message is the justification of the sinner by faith alone. The Church is understood as a fellowship and the priesthood of all believers stressed.

The Augsburg Confession (1530) was the principal statement of Lutheran faith and practice. It became a model for other Confessions of Faith, which in their turn had decisive influence on Church polity. Major Protestant denominations are the Lutheran, Reformed (Calvinist), Presbyterian, and Anglican (Episcopal). Smaller ones are the Mennonite, Schwenkfeldians, and Unitarians. In Great Britain and America there are the Congregationalists, Baptists, Quakers, Methodists, and other free church types of communities. (In regarding themselves as being faithful to original biblical Christianity, these Churches differ from such religious bodies as Unitarians, Mormons, Jehovah's Witnesses, and Christian Scientists, who either teach new doctrines or reject old ones.)

Since the latter part of the 19th century, national councils of churches have been established in many countries, e.g. the Federal Council of Churches of Christ in America in 1908. Denominations across countries joined in federations and world alliances, beginning with the Anglican Lambeth Conference in 1867.

Protestant missionary activity, particularly strong in the last century, resulted in the founding of many younger churches in Asia and Africa. The Ecumenical Movement, which originated with Protestant missions, aims at unity among Christians and churches.

Islam

Islam is the religion founded in Arabia by Mohammed between 610 and 632. Its more than 600 million adherents are found in countries stretching from Morocco in the West to Indonesia in the East.

Mohammed was born in A.D. 570 at Mecca and belonged to the Quraysh tribe, which was active in caravan trade. At the age of 25 he joined the caravan trade from Mecca to Syria in the employment of a rich widow, Khadiji, whom he married. Critical of the idolatry of the inhabitants of Mecca, he began to lead a contemplative life in the deserts. There he received a series of revelations. Encouraged by Khadiji, he gradually became convinced that he was given a God-appointed task to devote himself to the reform of religion and society. Idolatry was to be abandoned.

The *Hegira (Hijra)* (migration) of Mohammed from Mecca, where he was not honored, to Medina, where he was well received, occurred in 622 and marks the beginning of the Muslim era. In 630 he marched on Mecca and conquered it. He died at Medina in 632. His grave there has since been a place of pilgrimage.

Mohammed's followers, called Moslems, revered him as the prophet of *Allah* (God), beside whom there is no other God. Although he had no close knowledge of Judaism and Christianity, he considered himself succeeding and completing them as the seal of the Prophets. Sources of the Islamic faith are the *Qur'an*, regarded as the uncreated, eternal Word of God, and Tradition *(hadith)* regarding sayings and deeds of the prophet.

Islam means surrender to the will of *Allah*. He is the all-powerful, whose will is supreme and determines man's fate. Good deeds will be rewarded at the Last Judgment in paradise and evil deeds will be punished in hell.

The Five Pillars, primary duties, of Islam are: witness; confessing the oneness of God and of Mohammed, his prophet; prayer, to be performed five times a day; almsgiving to the poor and the mosque (house of worship); fasting during daylight hours in the month of Ramadan; and pilgrimage to Mecca at least once in the Moslem's lifetime.

Islam, upholding the law of brotherhood, succeeded in uniting an Arab world that had disintegrated into tribes and castes. Disagreements concerning the succession of the prophet caused a great division in Islam between *Sunnis* and *Shias.* Among these, other sects arose *(Wahhabi).* Doctrinal issues also led to the rise of different schools of thought in theology. Nevertheless, since Arab armies turned against Syria and Palestine in 635, Islam has expanded successfully under Mohammed's successors. Its rapid conquests in Asia and Africa are unsurpassed in history. Turning against Europe, Moslems conquered Spain in 713. In 1453 Constantinople fell into their hands and in 1529 Moslem armies besieged Vienna. Since then, Islam has lost its foothold in Europe.

In modern times it has made great gains in Africa.

Hinduism

In India alone there are more than 300 million adherents of Hinduism. In contrast to other religions, it has no founder. Considered the oldest religion in the world, it dates back, perhaps, to prehistoric times.

Hinduism is hard to define, there being no common creed, no one doctrine to bind Hindus together. Intellectually there is complete freedom of belief, and one can be monotheist, polytheist, or atheist. What matters is the social system: a Hindu is one born into a caste.

As a religion, Hinduism is founded on the sacred scriptures, written in Sanskrit and called the *Vedas (Veda-*knowledge). There are four Vedic books, among which the *Rig Veda* is the most important. It speaks of many gods and also deals with questions concerning the universe and creation. The dates of these works are unknown (1000 B.C.?).

The *Upanishads* (dated 1000–300 B.C.), commentaries on the Vedic texts, have philosophical speculations on the origin of the universe, the nature of deity, of *atman* (the human soul), and its relationship to *Brahman* (the universal soul).

Brahman is the principle and source of the universe who can be indicated only by negatives. As the divine intelligence, he is the ground of the visible world, a presence that pervades all beings. Thus the many Hindu deities came to be understood as manifestations of the one *Brahman* from whom everything proceeds and to whom everything ultimately returns. The religio-social system of Hinduism is based on the concept of reincarnation and transmigration in which all living beings, from plants below to gods above, are caught in a cosmic system that is an everlasting cycle of becoming and perishing.

Life is determined by the law of *karma,* according to which rebirth is dependent on moral behavior in a previous phase of existence. The doctrine of transmigration thus provides a rationale for the caste system. In this view, life on earth is regarded as transient *(maya)* and a burden. The goal of existence is liberation from the cycle of rebirth and redeath and entrance into the indescribable state of what in Buddhism is called *nirvana* (extinction of passion).

Further important sacred writings are the Epics *(puranas),* which contain legendary stories about gods and men. They are the *Mahabharata* (composed between 200 B.C. and A.D. 200) and the *Ramayana.* The former includes the *Bhagavad-Gita* (Song of the Lord), its most famous part, that tells of devotion to *Krishna* (Lord), who appears as an *avatar* (incarnation) of the god *Vishnu,* and of the duty of obeying caste rules. The work begins with a praise of the *yoga* (discipline) system.

The practice of Hinduism consists of rites and ceremonies, performed within the framework of the caste system and centering on the main socioreligious occasions of birth, marriage, and death. There are many Hindu temples, which are dwelling places of the deities and to which people bring offerings. There are also places of pilgrimages, the chief one being Benares on the Ganges, most sacred among the rivers in India.

In modern times work has been done to reform and revive Hinduism. One of the outstanding reformers was Ramakrishna (1836–86), who inspired many followers, one of whom founded the Ramakrishna mission, which seeks to convert others to its religion. The mission is active both in India and in other countries.

Buddhism

Founded in the 6th century B.C. in northern India by Gautama Buddha, who was born in southern Nepal as son to a king. His birth is surrounded by many legends, but Western scholars agree that he lived from 563 to 483 B.C. Warned by a sage that his son would become an ascetic or a universal monarch, the king confined him to his home. He was able to escape and began the life of a homeless wanderer in search of peace, passing through many disappointments until he finally came to the Tree of Enlightenment, under which he lived in meditation till enlightenment came to him and he became a Buddha (enlightened one).

Now he understood the origin of suffering, summarized in the *Four Noble Truths,* which constitutes the foundation of Buddhism. The Four are the truth of suffering, which all living beings must endure; of the origin of suffering, which is craving and which leads to rebirth; that it can be destroyed; and of the way that leads to cessation of pain, i.e., the *Noble Eightfold Way,* which is the rule of practical Buddhism: right views, right intention, right speech, right action, right livelihood, right effort, right concentration, and right ecstasy.

Nirvana is the goal of all existence, the state of complete redemption, into which the redeemed enters. Buddha's insight can free every man from the law of reincarnation through complete emptying of the self.

The nucleus of Buddha's church or association was originally formed by monks and lay-brothers, whose houses gradually became monasteries used as places for religious instruction. The worship service consisted of a sermon, expounding of Scripture, meditation, and confession. At a later stage pilgrimages to the holy places associated with the Buddha came into being, as well as veneration of relics.

In the 3rd century B.C., King Ashoka made Buddhism the State religion of India but, as centuries-passed, it gradually fell into decay through splits, persecutions, and the hostile Brahmans. Buddhism spread to countries outside India, however.

At the beginning of the Christian era, there occurred a split that gave rise to two main types: *Hinayana* (Little Vehicle), or southern Buddhism, and *Mahayana* (Great Vehicle), or northern Buddhism. The former type, more individualistic, survived in Ceylon and southern Asia. *Hinayana* retained more closely the original teachings of the Buddha, which did not know of a personal god or soul. *Mahayana,* more social, polytheistic, and developing a pluralistic pompous cult, was strong in the Himalayas, Tibet, Mongolia, China, Korea, and Japan.

In the present century, Buddhism has found believers also in the West and Buddhist associations have been established in Europe and the U.S.

Confucianism

Confucius (K'ung Fu-tzu), born in the state of Lu (northern China), lived from 551 to 479 B.C. Tradition, exaggerating the importance of Confucius in life, has depicted him as a great statesman but, in fact, he seems to have been a private teacher. Anthologies of ancient Chinese classics, along with his own Analects *(Lun Yu),* became the basis of Confucianism. These Analects were transmitted as a collection of his sayings as recorded by his students, with whom he discussed ethical and social problems. They developed into men of high moral standing, who served the State as administrators.

In his teachings, Confucius emphasized the importance of an old Chinese concept *(li),* which has the connotation of proper conduct. There is some disagreement as to the religious ideas of Confucius, but he held high the concepts handed down from centuries before him. Thus he believed in Heaven *(T'ien)* and sacrificed to his ancestors. Ancestor

worship he indeed encouraged as an expression of filial piety, which he considered the loftiest of virtues.

Piety to Confucius was the foundation of the family as well as the State. The family is the nucleus of the State, and the "five relations," between king and subject, father and son, man and wife, older and younger brother, and friend and friend, are determined by the virtues of love of fellow men, righteousness, and respect.

An extension of ancestor worship may be seen in the worship of Confucius, which became official in the 2nd century B.C. when the emperor, in recognition of Confucius' teachings as supporting the imperial rule, offered sacrifices at his tomb.

Mencius (Meng Tse), who lived around 400 B.C., did much to propagate and elaborate Confucianism in its concern with ordering society. Thus, for two millennia, Confucius' doctrine of State, with its emphasis on ethics and social morality, rooted in ancient Chinese tradition and developed and continued by his disciples, has been standard in China and the Far East.

With the revolution of 1911 in China, however, students, burning Confucius in effigy, called for the removal of "the old curiosity shop."

Shintoism

Shinto, the Chinese term for the Japanese *Kami no Michi,* i.e., the Way of the Gods, comprises the religious ideas and cult indigenous to Japan. *Kami,* or gods, considered divine forces of nature that are worshipped, may reside in rivers, trees, rocks, mountains, certain animals, or, particularly, in the sun and moon. The worship of ancestors, heroes, and deceased emperors was incorporated later.

After Buddhism had come from Korea, Japan's native religion at first resisted it. Then there followed a period of compromise and amalgamation with Buddhist beliefs and ceremonies, resulting, since the 9th century A.D., in a syncretistic religion, a Twofold Shinto. Buddhist deities came to be regarded as manifestations of Japanese deities and Buddhist priests took over most of the Shinto shrines.

In modern times Shinto regained independence from Buddhism. Under the reign of the Emperor Meiji (1868–1912) it became the official State religion, in which loyalty to the emperor was emphasized. The line of succession of emperors is traced back to the first Emperor Jimmu (660 B.C.) and beyond him to the Sun-goddess *Amaterasuomikami.*

The centers of worship are the shrines and temples in which the deities are believed to dwell and believers approach them through *torii* (gateways). Most important among the shrines is the imperial shrine of the Sun-goddess at Ise, where state ceremonies were once held in June and December. The *Yasukuni* shrine of the war dead in Tokyo is also well known.

Acts of worship consist of prayers, clapping of hands, acts of purification, and offerings. On feast days processions and performances of music and dancing take place and priests read prayers before the gods in the shrines, asking for good harvest, the well-being of people and emperor, etc. In Japanese homes there is a god-shelf, a small wooden shrine that contains the tablets bearing the names of ancestors. Offerings are made and candles lit before it.

After World War II the Allied Command ordered the disestablishment of State Shinto. To be distinguished from State Shinto is Sect Shinto, consisting of 13 recognized sects. These have arisen in modern times. Most important among them is *Tenrikyo* in Tenri City (Nara), in which healing by faith plays a central role.

Taoism

Taoism, a religion of China, was, according to tradition, founded by Lao Tse, a Chinese philosopher, long considered one of the prominent religious leaders from the 6th century B.C.

Data about him are for the most part legendary, however, and the *Tao Te Ching* (the classic of the Way and of its Power), traditionally ascribed to him, is now believed by many scholars to have originated in the 3rd century B.C. The book is composed in short chapters, written in aphoristic rhymes. Central are the word *Tao*, which means way or path and, in a deeper sense, signifies the principle that underlies the reality of this world and manifests itself in nature and in the lives of men, and the word *Te* (power).

The virtuous man draws power from being absorbed in *Tao*, the ultimate reality within an everchanging world. By non-action and keeping away from human striving it is possible for man to live in harmony with the principles that underlie and govern the universe. *Tao* cannot be comprehended by reason and knowledge, but only by inward quiet.

Besides the *Tao Te Ching*, dating from approximately the same period, there are two Taoist works, written by Chuang Tse and Lieh Tse.

Theoretical Taoism of this classical philosophical movement of the 4th and 3rd centuries B.C. in China differed from popular Taoism, into which it gradually degenerated. The standard of theoretical Taoism was maintained in the classics, of course, and among the upper classes it continued to be alive until modern times.

Religious Taoism is a form of religion dealing with deities and spirits, magic and soothsaying. In the 2nd century A.D. it was organized with temples, cult, priests, and monasteries and was able to hold its own in the competition with Buddhism that came up at the same time.

After the 7th century A.D., however, Taoist religion further declined. Split into numerous sects, which often operate like secret societies, it has become a syncretistic folk religion in which some of the old deities and saints live on.

Roman Catholic Pontiffs

St. Peter, of Bethsaida in Galilee, Prince of the Apostles, was the first Pope. He lived first in Antioch and then in Rome for 25 years. In AD 64 or 67, he was martyred. St. Linus became the second Pope.

Name	Birthplace	Reigned From	Reigned To	Name	Birthplace	Reigned From	Reigned To
St. Linus	Tuscia	67	76	St. Innocent I	Albano	401	417
St. Anacletus (Cletus)	Rome	76	88	St. Zozimus	Greece	417	418
				St. Boniface I	Rome	418	422
St. Clement	Rome	88	97	St. Celestine I	Campania	422	432
St. Evaristus	Greece	97	105	St. Sixtus III	Rome	432	440
St. Alexander I	Rome	105	115	St. Leo I (the Great)	Tuscany	440	461
St. Sixtus I	Rome	115	125				
St. Telesphorus	Greece	125	136	St. Hilary	Sardinia	461	468
St. Hyginus	Greece	136	140	St. Simplicius	Tivoli	468	483
St. Pius I	Aquileia	140	155	St. Felix III (II)²	Rome	483	492
St. Anicetus	Syria	155	166	St. Gelasius I	Africa	492	496
St. Soter	Campania	166	175	Anastasius II	Rome	496	498
St. Eleutherius	Epirus	175	189	St. Symmachus	Sardinia	498	514
St. Victor I	Africa	189	199	St. Hormisdas	Frosinone	514	523
St. Zephyrinus	Rome	199	217	St. John I	Tuscany	523	526
St. Callistus I	Rome	217	222	St. Felix IV (III)	Samnium	526	530
St. Urban I	Rome	222	230	Boniface II	Rome	530	532
St. Pontian	Rome	230	235	John II	Rome	533	535
St. Anterus	Greece	235	236	St. Agapitus I	Rome	535	536
St. Fabian	Rome	236	250	St. Silverius	Campania	536	537
St. Cornelius	Rome	251	253	Vigilius	Rome	537	555
St. Lucius I	Rome	253	254	Pelagius I	Rome	556	561
St. Stephen I	Rome	254	257	John III	Rome	561	574
St. Sixtus II	Greece	257	258	Benedict I	Rome	575	579
St. Dionysius	Unknown	259	268	Pelagius II	Rome	579	590
St. Felix I	Rome	269	274	St. Gregory I (the Great)	Rome	590	604
St. Eutychian	Luni	275	283				
St. Caius	Dalmatia	283	296	Sabinianus	Tuscany	604	606
St. Marcellinus	Rome	296	304	Boniface III	Rome	607	607
St. Marcellus I	Rome	308	309	St. Boniface IV	Marsi	608	615
St. Eusebius	Greece	309¹	309¹	St. Deusdedit (Adeodatus I)	Rome	615	618
St. Meltiades	Africa	311	314				
St. Sylvester I	Rome	314	335	Boniface V	Naples	619	625
St. Marcus	Rome	336	336	Honorius I	Campania	625	638
St. Julius I	Rome	337	352	Severinus	Rome	640	640
Liberius	Rome	352	366	John IV	Dalmatia	640	642
St. Damasus I	Spain	366	384	Theodore I	Greece	642	649
St. Siricius	Rome	384	399	St. Martin I	Todi	649	655
St. Anastasius I	Rome	399	401	St. Eugene I³	Rome	654	657

Name	Birthplace	Reigned From	Reigned To
St. Vitalian	Segni	657	672
Adeodatus II	Rome	672	676
Donus	Rome	676	678
St. Agatho	Sicily	678	681
St. Leo II	Sicily	682	683
St. Benedict II	Rome	684	685
John V	Syria	685	686
Conon	Unknown	686	687
St. Sergius I	Syria	687	701
John VI	Greece	701	705
John VII	Greece	705	707
Sisinnius	Syria	708	708
Constantine	Syria	708	715
St. Gregory II	Rome	715	731
St. Gregory III	Syria	731	741
St. Zachary	Greece	741	752
Stephen II (III)[4]	Rome	752	757
St. Paul I	Rome	757	767
Stephen III (IV)	Sicily	768	772
Adrian I	Rome	772	795
St. Leo III	Rome	795	816
Stephen IV (V)	Rome	816	817
St. Paschal I	Rome	817	824
Eugene II	Rome	824	827
Valentine	Rome	827	827
Gregory IV	Rome	827	844
Sergius II	Rome	844	847
St. Leo IV	Rome	847	855
Benedict III	Rome	855	858
St. Nicholas I (the Great)	Rome	858	867
Adrian II	Rome	867	872
John VIII	Rome	872	882
Marinus I	Gallese	882	884
St. Adrian III	Rome	884	885
Stephen V (VI)	Rome	885	891
Formosus	Portus	891	896
Boniface VI	Rome	896	896
Stephen VI (VII)	Rome	896	897
Romanus	Gallese	897	897
Theodore II	Rome	897	897
John IX	Tivoli	898	900
Benedict IV	Rome	900	903
Leo V	Ardea	903	903
Sergius III	Rome	904	911
Anastasius III	Rome	911	913
Landus	Sabina	913	914
John X	Tossignano	914	928
Leo VI	Rome	928	928
Stephen VII (VIII)	Rome	928	931
John XI	Rome	931	935
Leo VII	Rome	936	939
Stephen VIII (IX)	Rome	939	942
Marinus II	Rome	942	946
Agapitus II	Rome	946	955
John XII	Tusculum	955	964
Leo VIII[5]	Rome	963	965
Benedict V[5]	Rome	964	966
John XIII	Rome	965	972
Benedict VI	Rome	973	974
Benedict VII	Rome	974	983
John XIV	Pavia	983	984
John XV	Rome	985	996
Gregory V	Saxony	996	999
Sylvester II	Auvergne	999	1003
John XVII	Rome	1003	1003
John XVIII	Rome	1004	1009
Sergius IV	Rome	1009	1012
Benedict VIII	Tusculum	1012	1024
John XIX	Tusculum	1024	1032
Benedict IX[6]	Tusculum	1032	1044
Sylvester III	Rome	1045	1045

Name	Birthplace	Reigned From	Reigned To
Benedict IX (2nd time)	—	1045	1045
Gregory VI	Rome	1045	1046
Clement II	Saxony	1046	1047
Benedict IX (3rd time)	—	1047	1048
Damasus II	Bavaria	1048	1048
St. Leo IX	Alsace	1049	1054
Victor II	Germany	1055	1057
Stephen IX (X)	Lorraine	1057	1058
Nicholas II	Burgundy	1059	1061
Alexander II	Milan	1061	1073
St. Gregory VII	Tuscany	1073	1085
Bl. Victor III	Benevento	1086	1087
Bl. Urban II	France	1088	1099
Paschal II	Ravenna	1099	1118
Gelasius II	Gaeta	1118	1119
Callistus II	Burgundy	1119	1124
Honorius II	Flagnano	1124	1130
Innocent II	Rome	1130	1143
Celestine II	Città di Castello	1143	1144
Lucius II	Bologna	1144	1145
Bl. Eugene III	Pisa	1145	1153
Anastasius IV	Rome	1153	1154
Adrian IV	England	1154	1159
Alexander III	Siena	1159	1181
Lucius III	Lucca	1181	1185
Urban III	Milan	1185	1187
Gregory VIII	Benevento	1187	1187
Clement III	Rome	1187	1191
Celestine III	Rome	1191	1198
Innocent III	Anagni	1198	1216
Honorius III	Rome	1216	1227
Gregory IX	Anagni	1227	1241
Celestine IV	Milan	1241	1241
Innocent IV	Genoa	1243	1254
Alexander IV	Anagni	1254	1261
Urban IV	Troyes	1261	1264
Clement IV	France	1265	1268
Bl. Gregory X	Piacenza	1271	1276
Bl. Innocent V	Savoy	1276	1276
Adrian V	Genoa	1276	1276
John XXI[7]	Portugal	1276	1277
Nicholas III	Rome	1277	1280
Martin IV[8]	France	1281	1285
Honorius IV	Rome	1285	1287
Nicholas IV	Ascoli	1288	1292
St. Celestine V	Isernia	1294	1294
Boniface VIII	Anagni	1294	1303
Bl. Benedict XI	Treviso	1303	1304
Clement V	France	1305	1314
John XXII	Cahors	1316	1334
Benedict XII	France	1334	1342
Clement VI	France	1342	1352
Innocent VI	France	1352	1362
Bl. Urban V	France	1362	1370
Gregory XI	France	1370	1378
Urban VI	Naples	1378	1389
Boniface IX	Naples	1389	1404
Innocent VII	Sulmona	1404	1406
Gregory XII	Venice	1406	1415
Martin V	Rome	1417	1431
Eugene IV	Venice	1431	1447
Nicholas V	Sarzana	1447	1455
Callistus III	Jativa	1455	1458
Pius II	Siena	1458	1464
Paul II	Venice	1464	1471
Sixtus IV	Savona	1471	1484
Innocent VIII	Genoa	1484	1492
Alexander VI	Jativa	1492	1503

Name	Birthplace	Reigned From	Reigned To	Name	Birthplace	Reigned From	Reigned To
Pius III	Siena	1503	1503	Bl. Innocent XI	Como	1676	1689
Julius II	Savona	1503	1513	Alexander VIII	Venice	1689	1691
Leo X	Florence	1513	1521	Innocent XII	Spinazzola	1691	1700
Adrian VI	Utrecht	1522	1523	Clement XI	Urbino	1700	1721
Clement VII	Florence	1523	1534	Innocent XIII	Rome	1721	1724
Paul III	Rome	1534	1549	Benedict XIII	Gravina	1724	1730
Julius III	Rome	1550	1555	Clement XII	Florence	1730	1740
Marcellus II	Montepulciano	1555	1555	Benedict XIV	Bologna	1740	1758
Paul IV	Naples	1555	1559	Clement XIII	Venice	1758	1769
Pius IV	Milan	1559	1565	Clement XIV	Rimini	1769	1774
St. Pius V	Bosco	1566	1572	Pius VI	Cesena	1775	1799
Gregory XIII	Bologna	1572	1585	Pius VII	Cesena	1800	1823
Sixtus V	Grottammare	1585	1590	Leo XII	Genga	1823	1829
Urban VII	Rome	1590	1590	Pius VIII	Cingoli	1829	1830
Gregory XIV	Cremona	1590	1591	Gregory XVI	Belluno	1831	1846
Innocent IX	Bologna	1591	1591	Pius IX	Senegallia	1846	1878
Clement VIII	Florence	1592	1605	Leo XIII	Carpineto	1878	1903
Leo XI	Florence	1605	1605	St. Pius X	Riese	1903	1914
Paul V	Rome	1605	1621	Benedict XV	Genoa	1914	1922
Gregory XV	Bologna	1621	1623	Pius XI	Desio	1922	1939
Urban VIII	Florence	1623	1644	Pius XII	Rome	1939	1958
Innocent X	Rome	1644	1655	John XXIII	Sotto il Monte	1958	1963
Alexander VII	Siena	1655	1667	Paul VI	Concesio	1963	1978
Clement IX	Pistoia	1667	1669	John Paul I	Forno di Canale	1978	1978
Clement X	Rome	1670	1676	John Paul II	Wadowice, Poland	1978	

1. Or 310. 2. He should be called Felix II, and his successors of the same name should be numbered accordingly. The discrepancy was caused by the erroneous insertion in some lists of the name of St. Felix of Rome, Martyr. 3. He was elected during the exile of St. Martin I, who endorsed him as Pope. 4. After St. Zachary died, a Roman priest named Stephen was elected but died before his consecration as Bishop of Rome. His name is not included in all lists for this reason. In view of this historical confusion, the *National Catholic Almanac* lists the true Stephen II as Stephen II (III), the true Stephen III as Stephen III (IV), etc. 5. Confusion exists concerning the legitimacy of claims. If the deposition of John was invalid, Leo was an antipope until after the end of Benedict's reign. If the deposition of John was valid, Leo was the legitimate Pope and Benedict an antipope. 6. If the triple removal of Benedict IX was not valid, Sylvester III, Gregory VI, and Clement II were antipopes. 7. Elimination was made of the name of John XX in an effort to rectify the numerical designation of Popes named John. The error dates back to the time of John XV. 8. The names of Marinus I and Marinus II were construed as Martin. In view of these two pontificates and the earlier reign of St. Martin I, this pontiff was called Martin IV. *Source: National Catholic Almanac,* from *Annuarto Pontificio.*

Books of the Bible

OLD TESTAMENT

Genesis	[1]Tobit	Baruch
Exodus	[1]Judith	Ezekiel
Leviticus	Esther	Daniel
Numbers	[1]1 Maccabees	Hosea
Deuteronomy	[1]2 Maccabees	Joel
Joshua	Job	Amos
Judges	Psalms	Obadiah
Ruth	Proverbs	Jonah
I Samuel	Ecclesiastes	Micah
2 Samuel	Song of Songs/Solomon	Nahum
I Kings	Wisdom	Habakkuk
2 Kings	Sirach/Ecclesiasticus	Zephaniah
I Chronicles	Isaiah	Haggai
2 Chronicles	Jeremiah	Zechariah
Ezra	Lamentations	Malachi
Nehemiah	Ezekiel	

NEW TESTAMENT

Matthew	Ephesians	Hebrews
Mark	Phillipians	James
Luke	Colossians	1 Peter
John	1 Thessalonians	2 Peter
Acts	2 Thessalonians	1 John
Romans	1 Timothy	2 John
1 Corinthians	2 Timothy	3 John
2 Corinthians	Titus	Jude
Galatians	Philemon	Revelation

1. These books are generally not accepted in the Protestant canon of Scripture, and Protestants refer to them as "Apocrypha." Catholic bibles include these books and refer to them as "Deuterocanonical." These disputed books were included in pre-Reformation Bibles.

IDEAS AND BELIEFS

Introduction

THIS section explains many of the ideas and beliefs which people have held at different periods in history. Beliefs may be true or false, meaningful or totally meaningless, regardless of the degree of conviction with which they are held. Since man has been moved to action so often by his beliefs they are worth serious study. The section throws a vivid light on human history.

Man has always felt a deep need for emotional security, a sense of "belonging." This need has found expression in the framing of innumerable religious systems, nearly all of which have been concerned with man's relation to a divine ruling power. In the past, people have been accustomed to think of their own religion as true and of all others as false. Latterly we have come to realize that in man's religious strivings there is common ground, for our need in the world today is a morality whereby human beings may live together in harmony.

There is also to be found in man an irresistible curiosity which demands an explanation of the world in which he finds himself. This urge to make the world intelligible takes him into the realm of science where the unknown is the constant challenge. Science is a creative process, always in the making, since the scientist's conjectures are constantly being submitted to severe critical tests.

A

Acupuncture, a quasi-medical system originating in China and based on the supposedly therapeutic effects of implanting fine gold needles in the spinal cord and other specific parts of the body. The site of needle implantation is decided according to traditional texts. The apparent lack of any logical relationship between the implantation sites and any known physiological or anatomical systems within the body has caused acupuncture to be held in low regard by Western medicine. Indeed it is certainly true that acupuncture and other similar practices tend to flourish in parts of the world where orthodox medicine has made little progress or where doctors and trained staff are scarce.

Recent years however have seen a curious and unexpected revival of interest in acupuncture in Europe and America, prompted in large part by the considerable press publicity which has surrounded a number of major surgical operations performed without anesthesia upon human patients and which have been witnessed by sceptical Western specialists. Considerable controversy still surrounds acupuncture and is likely to continue for many years—possibly because it is hard to envisage a theory to explain its effects which is consistent with orthodox medicine. No doubt the immensely powerful effects of suggestion and hypnosis need to be taken into account. Some recent discoveries on the psychology and physiology of pain which show that severe wound pain may be alleviated by electrical stimulation of the nerve endings in the site of the wound may also have some relevance. It is tempting to take the line that acupuncture is based on some "forgotten" or "hidden" medical system and to assume that it is only because Western scientists are blinkered and hidebound that it is not being incorporated in a big way into European and American hospitals. But there are always two sides to an argument; whereas the first reports from Western specialists visiting China were filled with grudging acceptance and genuine puzzlement, some recent visitors have brought back less enthusiastic reports. It is clear that the full story about acupuncture, its nature and its practical value has not yet been told.

Adlerian Psychology. In 1911 the Viennese psychoanalyst Alfred Adler (1870–1937) together with his colleague Carl Gustav Jung broke with their friend Sigmund Freud over disputes concerning the latter's theoretic approach to psychoanalysis. Jung and Adler were themselves shortly also to part company, each to set up and develop his own "school" of psychoanalysis. Adler's system of psychotherapy is based on the idea, not of sex as a driving force as in the case of Freud, but on the concept of "compensation" or a drive for power in an attempt to overcome the "inferiority complex" which he held to be universal in human beings. The child naturally feels inferior to adults, but bullying, making him feel insignificant or guilty or contemptible, even spoiling, which makes him feel important within the family but relatively unimportant outside, increases this feeling. Or the child may have physical defects: he may be small or underweight, have to wear glasses, become lame, be constantly ill, or stupid at school. In these ways he develops a sense of inferiority which for the rest of his life he develops a technique to overcome.

This may be done in several ways: he may try to become capable in the very respects in which he feels incompetent—hence many great orators have originally had speech defects; many painters poor eyesight; many musicians have been partially deaf; like Nietzsche, the weakling, he may write about the superman, or like Sandow, the strong man, be born with poor health.

On the other hand he may overdo his attempt and overcompensate. Hence we have the bully who is really a coward, the small man who is self-assertive to an objectionable degree (Hitler, Napoleon, Stalin, and Mussolini were all small men) or the foreigner who like three of these men wanted to be the hero of his adopted country—Hitler the Austrian, Napoleon the Italian, Stalin the Georgian.

But what about the man who can do none of these things, who continues to fail to compensate? He, says Adler, becomes a neurotic because neurosis is an excuse which means "I could have done so-and-so but . . ." It is the unconscious flight into illness—the desire to be ill. Adler's treatment involves disclosing these subterfuges we play on ourselves so that we can deal with the real situation in a more realistic way. Adlerian psychoanalysis still attracts supporters, but its golden days were when the founder was at the head of the movement in the U.S.A., when his views were considered to provide a more "acceptable" theory of the mind than the enormously controversial theories of Freud with their strong sexual orientation.

Adventists, a group of American religious sects, the most familiar being the Seventh-Day Adventist Church, which observes Saturday as the true Sabbath. With (1987) more than 5 million members throughout the world, it shares with other Adventists a belief in the imminent second coming of Christ (a doctrine fairly widespread in the U.S.A. during the early decades of the 19th cent. when the end of the world was predicted by William Miller for 1843, then for 1844). Modern Adventists content themselves with the conviction that the "signs" of the Advent are multiplying, the "blessed event" which will solve the world's ills. Believers will be saved, but the sects differ as to whether the unjust will be tortured in hell, annihilated, or merely remain asleep eternally.

Agnosticism. *See* **God and Man.**

Albigenses, also known as Cathari. French heretical sect (named after the town of Albi in Provence) which appeared in the 11th cent. to challenge the Catholic Church on the way true Christians should lead their lives. They followed a life of extreme asceticism in contrast to the local clergy and their faith was adopted by the mass of the population, especially in Toulouse. Condemned as heretics by Pope Innocent III, the sect was exterminated in the savage Albigensian Crusade (1208–29), initially led by Simon de Montfort. (In his thoroughness, de Montfort also succeeded in destroying the high culture of the Troubadours.)

Alchemy, ancient art associated with magic and astrology in which modern chemistry has its roots. The earliest mention of alchemy comes from ancient Egypt but its later practitioners attributed its origins to such varied sources as the fallen angels of the Bible, to Moses and Aaron, but most commonly to Hermes Trismegistus, often identified with the Egyptian god Thoth, whose knowledge of the divine art was handed down only to the sons of kings (cf, the phrase "hermetically sealed"). Its main object was the transmutation of metals. Egyptian speculation concerning this reached its height during the 6th cent. in the Alexandrian period. Brought to Western Europe by the Moslems, one of its most famous Arab exponents was Jabir (*c.* 760–*c.* 815), known to the Latins as Geber, who had a laboratory at Kufa on the Tigris. One school of early Greek philosophy held that there was ultimately only one elemental matter of which everything was composed. Such men as Albertus Magnus (1206–80) and Roger Bacon (1214–94) assumed that, by removing impurities, this *materia prima* could be obtained. Although Bacon's ideas were in many ways ahead of his time, he firmly believed in the philosopher's stone, which

could turn base metals into gold, and in an elixir of life which would give eternal youth. Modern science has, of course, shown in its researches into radioactivity, the possibility of transmutation of certain elements, but this phenomenon has little bearing on either the methods of the alchemist or the mysteries with which he surrounded them. In line with the current considerable revival of interest in the occult, alchemy appears to be staging a comeback, at least as a literary if not an experimental topic.

Anabaptists. *See* **Baptists.**

Analytical Psychology, the name given by Carl Gustav Jung (1875–1961) of Zürich to his system of psychology, which, like Adler's (*see* **Adlerian Psychology**), took its origin from Freud's psychoanalysis from which both diverged in 1911. Briefly, Jung differed from Freud: (1) in believing that the latter had laid too much emphasis on the sexual drive as the basic one in man and replacing it with the concept of *libido* or life energy of which sex forms a part; (2) in his theory of types: men are either extrovert or introvert (*i.e.* their interest is turned primarily outwards to the world or inwards to the self), and they apprehend experience in four main ways, one or other of which is predominant in any given individual—sensing, feeling, thinking, or intuiting; (3) in his belief that the individual's unconscious mind contains not only repressed materials which, as Freud maintained, were too unpleasant to be allowed into awareness, but also faculties which had not been allowed to develop—*e.g.,* the emotional side of the too rational man, the feminine side of the too masculine one; (4) in the importance he attaches to the existence of a collective unconscious at a still deeper level which contains traces of ancient ways of thought which mankind has inherited over the centuries. These are the *archetypes* and include primitive notions of magic, spirits and witches, birth and death, gods, virgin mothers, resurrection, etc. In the treatment of the neuroses Jung believed in the importance of *(a)* the present situation which the patient refuses to face; *(b)* the bringing together of conscious and unconscious and integrating them.

In the 1940s and '50s interest in Jung's ideas waned, at least in academic circles, as the emphasis among experimental psychologists shifted closer and closer to the "hard" scientific line. This was also true in the field of psychoanalysis where the Jungian as opposed to the Freudian point of view became progressively less popular. At the present time this trend is beginning to reverse, and while Jung's offbeat views on astrology, telepathy, etc., are still unfashionable, a reappraisal of the significance of his views on the nature of the unconscious is taking place and many psychologists feel that his contribution to our understanding of the nature of human mental processes has been greatly underrated. *See also* **Psychoanalysis.**

Anarchism, a political philosophy which holds, in the words of the American anarchist Josiah Warren (1798–1874), an early follower of Robert Owen, that "every man should be his own government, his own law, his own church." The idea that governmental interference or even the mere existence of authority is inherently bad is as old as Zeno, the Greek Stoic philosopher, who believed that compulsion perverts the normal nature of man. William Godwin's *Enquiry Concerning Political Justice* (1793) was the first systematic exposition of the doctrine. Godwin (father-in-law of Shelley) claimed that man is by nature sociable, cooperative, rational, and good when given the choice to act freely; that under such conditions men will form voluntary groups to work in complete social harmony. Such groups or communities would be based on equality of income, no state control, and no property: this state of affairs would be brought about by rational discussion and persuasion rather than by revolution.

The French economist Proudhon (1809–65) was the first to bring anarchism to the status of a mass movement. In his book *What is Property?* he stated bluntly that "property is theft" and "governments are the scourge of God". He urged the formation of cooperative credit banks where money could be had without interest and goods would be exchanged at cost value at a rate representing the hours of work needed to produce each commodity. Like Godwin, he disapproved of violence but, unlike Marx, disapproved of trade unions as representing organized groups.

In communistic anarchism these ideas were combined with a revolutionary philosophy, primarily by the Russians Michael Bakunin (1814–76) and Peter Kropotkin (1842–1921) who favored training workers in the technique of "direct action" to overthrow the state by all possible means, including political assassination. In 1868 anarchists joined the First International which broke up a few years later after a bitter struggle between Bakuninists and Marxists. Subsequently small anarchist groups murdered such political figures as Tsar Alexander II of Russia, King Humbert of Italy, Presidents Carnot of France and McKinley of America, and the Empress Elizabeth of Austria.

Anarchism and communism differ in three main ways: (1) anarchism forms no political party, rejects all relationship with established authority, and regards democratic reform as a setback; (2) communism is against capitalism, anarchism against the state as such; (3) both have the final goal of a classless society, but anarchism rejects the idea of an intermediate period of socialist state control accepted by communism. Philosophical anarchists, such as the American writer Henry David Thoreau (1817–62), were primarily individualists who believed in a return to nature, the non-payment of taxes, and passive resistance to state control; in these respects Thoreau strongly influenced Gandhi as did the Christian anarchist Tolstoy.

Anarchism has traditionally been criticized as being impractical—*e.g.,* in a non-authoritarian society, who is going to look after the sewers or clean the streets?—and there is a good deal of force to this argument. In fact anarchistic ideas became progressively less fashionable in the first half of this century. A curious and probably significant revival of interest has taken place in the past decade, however, probably because of a growing sense of disillusion, particularly on the part of young people, with the progress of orthodox political systems. *See also* **Syndicalism.**

Anglo-Catholicism. To Queen Elizabeth I the Church of England was that of the "middle way" in which human reason and commonsense took their place beside Scripture and Church authority. The extent to which these various factors are stresses creates the distinctions between "high" and "low" church. Anglo-Catholics tend to reject the term "Protestant" and stress the term "Catholic" and, although few accept the infallibility of the Pope, some Anglo-Catholic churches have introduced much or all of the Roman ritual and teach Roman dogmas.

Animism. To early man and in primitive societies the distinction between animate and inanimate objects was not always obvious—it is not enough to say that living things move and nonliving things do not, for leaves blow about in the wind and streams flow down a hillside. In the religions of early societies, therefore, we find a tendency to believe that life exists in all objects from rocks and pools to seas and mountains. This belief is technically known as *animatism,* which differs from *animism,* a somewhat more sophisticated view which holds that natural objects have no life in themselves but may be the abode of dead people, spirits, or gods who occasionally give them the appearance of life. The classic example of this, of course, is the assumption that an erupting volcano is an expression of anger on the part of the god who resides in it. Such beliefs may seem absurd today, but it is worth realizing that we are not entirely free of them ourselves when we ascribe "personalities" of a limited kind to motor cars, boats, dolls, or models which incur our pleasure or anger depending upon how well they "behave".

Anthropomorphism, the attribution of human form, thoughts or motives to non-human entities or life forms from gods to animals. At one end this can be summed up in the once widespread image of God as a "white-bearded old gentleman sitting on a cloud." At the other end is the very common tendency to invest domestic animals and pets with man-like wishes and personalities. At both extremes the belief could be seriously misleading. Firstly, it could be very unwise to assume that God, if he exists, necessarily thinks as humans do and has human interests at heart. Secondly, we shall learn very little about animal behavior if we look upon them as mere extensions of our own personality, and we do them less than justice if we see them simply as human beings of diminutive intelligence.

Anthroposophy, a school of religious and philosophical thought based on the work of the German educationist and mystic Rudolf Steiner (1861–1925). Steiner was originally an adherent of Madame Blavatsky's theosophical movement (*cf* **Theosophy**) but in 1913 broke away to form his own splinter group, the Anthroposophical Society, following ideological disputes over the alleged "divinity" of the Indian boy Krishnamurtl. Steiner was much influenced by the German poet and scientist, Goethe, and believed that an appreciation and love for art was one of the keys to spiritual development. One of the first tasks of his new movement was the construction of a vast temple of arts and sciences, known as the Goetheanum, to act as the headquarters of the society. This structure, which was of striking and revolutionary architectural style, was unfortunately burnt down in 1922 to be replaced by an even more imaginative one which today is one of the most interesting buildings of its kind in the world. Anthroposophy, which ceased to expand greatly following its founder's death, is nevertheless well-established in various parts of the world with specialized, and often very well equipped, schools and clinics which propagate the educational and therapeutic theories of the movement. These, which include the allegedly beneficial powers of music, colored lights, etc., have made little impact on modern educational ideas, but the schools have acquired a reputation

for success in the training of mentally handicapped children, though one suspects that these
successes are due to the patience and tolerance
exercised in these establishments rather than to
the curative value of color or music "therapy"
itself. Despite its apparent eccentricities, anthroposophy has made its mark on art and architecture, the outstanding modern painter Kandinsky,
for example, being particularly influenced by Steiner's ideas and teachings.

Anticlericalism, resentment of priestly powers and
privileges, traceable in England to Wyclif's insistence in the 14th cent. on the right of all men to
have access to the Scriptures. The translation of
the Bible into the common tongue was a great
landmark in the history of the Bible and the English language. Wyclif's principles were condemned
by the Roman Church of his time but were readily
accepted during the Reformation. Tudor anticlericalism arose from motives ranging from a greedy
desire to plunder the riches of the Church to a genuine dislike of the powers of the priesthood whose
spiritual courts still had the right to decide on
points of doctrine or morals in an age when the layman felt he was well able to decide for himself. In
innumerable ways the Church was permitted to ex-
tort money from the laity. It is generally agreed,
says Trevelyan, that the final submission of church
to state in England was motivated quite as much
by anticlericalism as by Protestantism. The rise of
the Reformed churches in England satisfied the
people generally and anticlericalism never became
the fixed principle of permanent parties as happened in France and Italy from the time of Voltaire
onwards.

Antisemitism, a term first applied about the middle
of the last century to those who were anti-Jewish
in their outlook. Although this attitude was prevalent for religious reasons throughout the Middle
Ages, modern antisemitism differed *(a)* in being
largely motivated by economic or political conditions, and *(b)* in being doctrinaire with a pseudo-
scientific rationale presented by such men as Go-
bineau (1816–82) and Houston Stewart Chamberlain (1855–1927), and later by the Nazi and
Fascist "philosophers". Beginning in Russia and
Hungary with the pogroms of 1882 it gradually
spread south and westwards where, in France, the
Dreyfus case provided an unsavory example in
1894. Thousands of Jews from Eastern Europe
fled to Britain and America during this period; for
in these countries antisemitism has rarely been
more than a personal eccentricity. During the last
war the murder of six million Jews by the Nazis
and their accomplices led to a further exodus to
various parts of the world and finally to the creation of the state of Israel.

The individual Jew-hater makes unconscious
use of the psychological processes of projection
and displacement: his greed or sexual guilt is projected on to the Jew (or Negro or Catholic) because he cannot bear to accept them as his own
emotions, and his sense of failure in life is blamed
on his chosen scapegoat rather than on his own
inadequacy.

But there are social causes too and politicians
in some lands are well versed in the technique of
blaming unsatisfactory conditions (which they
themselves may have in part produced) upon minority groups and persuading others to do the
same. Historically, the Jew is ideally suited for this
role of scapegoat: (1) in the Middle Ages when
usury was forbidden to Christians but not to Jews,
the latter often became moneylenders incurring
the opprobrium generally associated with this
trade (*e.g.,* to the simple-minded Russian peasant
the Jew often represented, not only the "Christ-
killer", but also the moneylender or small shop-
keeper to whom he owed money); (2) many trades
being closed to Jews, it was natural that they concentrated in others, thus arousing suspicions of
"influence" (*i.e.* Jews are felt to occupy a place in
certain trades and professions which far exceeds
their numerical proportion to the population as a
whole); (3) even with the ending of ghetto life,
Jews often occupy *en masse* some parts of cities
rather than others and this may lead to resentment on the part of the original inhabitants who
begin to feel themselves dispossessed; (4) Jews
tend to form a closed society and incur the suspicions attached to all closed societies within which
social contacts are largely limited to members;
marriage outside the group is forbidden or
strongly disapproved of, and the preservation,
among the orthodox, of cultural and religious barriers tends to isolate them from their fellow citizens. Discrimination is a common phenomenon.
There is often prejudice against minority groups
if they are perceived as "exclusive" or " foreign."
See **Zionism.**

Aquarius, one of the twelve "signs of the Zodiac".
This has recently achieved special significance in
the mythology of our time because of the pronouncements of astrologers that the world is shifting out of the 2000-years-old cycle of the Age of
Pisces, the fish, into that of Aquarius the water-
carrier. The exact date of the transition is a matter
of astrological controversy, but the consensus is
that it began in 1960 and will be completed sometime in the 24th century. The Aquarian Age is predicted to be one of peace and harmony, replacing
the era of strife which, ironically, has marked the
dominance of the Christian symbol of the fish.
Such speculations are totally without scientific
backing and are mentioned here only to draw attention to the grip which astrological and other
mythical concepts still have on human thinking.
One of the first spaceships to carry man to the
moon, for example, was named Aquarius by its
crew. *See also* **Astrology.**

Arianism, formed the subject of the first great controversy within the Christian Church over the doctrine of Arius of Alexandria (d. 336) who denied
the divinity of Christ. The doctrine, although at
first influential, was condemned at the Council of
Nicaea (325), called by the Emperor Constantine,
at which Arius was opposed by Athanasius, also
of Alexandria, who maintained the now orthodox
view that the Son is of one substance with the Father. Arius was banished but the heresy persisted
until the 7th cent., especially among the barbar-
ians, the Goths, Vandals and Lombards. Disbelief
in the divinity of Christ has formed part of the doctrine of many minor sects since, notably in **Unitarianism** *(q.v.).*

Assassins, a sect of Moslem Shi'ites, founded by the
Persian Hasan i Sabbath (*c.* 1090), which for
more than two centuries established a rule of terror all over Persia and Syria. The coming of the
Mongols in 1256 destroyed them in Persia and
the Syrian branch suffered a similar fate at the
hands of the then Mamluk sultan of Egypt, *c.*
1270. It was a secret order, ruled over by a grand
master, under whom the members were strictly organized into classes, according to the degree of

initiation into the secrets of the order. The devotees, belonging to one of the lower groups, carried out the actual assassinations under strict laws of obedience, and total ignorance of the objects and ritual of the society. It is believed that the latter were given ecstatic visions under the influence of hashish, whence the term *hashshashin*, which became corrupted to "assassin".

Associationism. In psychology, the Associationist school of the 19th cent. accepted the association of ideas as the fundamental principle in mental life. It was represented in Britain by the two Mills and Herbert Spencer, in Germany by J. F. Herbart (1776–1841). To these, mental activity was nothing but the association of "ideas" conceived of as units of both thought and feeling—the emotion of anger or the perception of a chair were both "ideas"—and apart from them the self did not exist. Personality was simply a series of these units coming and going, adding to or cancelling each other out, in accordance with rigid and mechanistic scientific laws.

Astrology was once the best available theory for explaining the course of human life and bears much the same historical relationship to astronomy as alchemy does to chemistry. Originally it was divided into the two branches of Natural Astrology which dealt with the movements of the heavenly bodies and their calculations, and Judicial Astrology which studied the alleged influence of the stars and the planets on human life and fate. It was the former that developed into modern astronomy; the latter was, and remains, a primitive myth.

Astrology owes most to the early Babylonians (or Chaldeans) who, being largely nomadic in an environment which permitted an unobstructed view of the sky, readily accepted the idea that divine energy is manifested in the movements of the sun and planets. Gradually this concept became enlarged and the relative positions of the planets both in relation to each other and to the fixed stars became important together with the idea of omens—that, if a particular event occurred while the planets were in a particular position, the recurrence of that position heralded a recurrence of the same sort of event. Soon the planets became associated with almost every aspect of human life. They were bound up with the emotions, with parts of the body, so that astrology played quite a large part in medicine up to late medieval times. Not only was the position of the planet to be considered but also the particular sign of the zodiac (or house of heaven) it was occupying, and it was believed possible to foretell the destiny of an individual by calculating which star was in the ascendant (*i.e.* the sign of the zodiac nearest the eastern horizon and the star which arose at that precise moment) at the time of his birth. Astrology was popular among the Egyptians, the Romans (whose authorities found the Chaldean astrologers a nuisance and expelled them from time to time), and during the Middle Ages when astrologers were often highly respected.

Despite the apparent absurdity of astrological beliefs—for example, how could the pattern of light from stars billions of miles away possibly influence the temperament of single individuals on earth—a substantial number of intelligent and well-educated people take its study in all seriousness. The most interesting "convert" was the psychologist and philosopher, Carl Jung, who conducted a complex experiment in which he compared the "birth signs" of happily married and divorced couples and claimed to find that those most favorably matched in astrological terms were also those more likely to have permanent wedded bliss. Jung's findings were subsequently shown to have been based on a simple statistical fallacy, which did not prevent the brilliant but eccentric psychologist from offering them up as evidence in support of his own theory of "synchronicity" *(q.v.)*, an involved and vaguely metaphysical notion which suggests that events in the universe may be significantly related in a "non-causal" fashion. To add fuel to the controversy however, the French mathematician, Michel Gauquelin, has recently offered up fresh data which apparently supports the general astrological view. In a carefully controlled study he noticed statistically significant correspondences between certain astrological signs and the professions of a large number of Frenchmen whose birth time and date were accurately recorded. Gauquelin claims to have repeated his study on a second large sample of his fellow countrymen, though he has been unable to use English people as the exact times of birth are not recorded on their birth certificates! This apparent shot in the arm for astrology is still a matter of great scientific controversy, though Gauquelin's work has been given support from the distinguished British psychologist. H. J. Eysenck, who has pronounced his statistical data to to be incontrovertible. Both scientists, however, carefully refrain from discussing the implications of these curious findings, and the controversy will no doubt increase rather than decrease in the near future.

Atheism. *See* **God and Man.**

Atlantis, a mythical continent supposed to have lain somewhere between Europe and America and a center of advanced civilization before it was inundated by some great natural catastrophe in pre-Christian times. There is little, if any, serious historical or archaeological evidence for its existence, but the legend of the Golden Land destroyed when the waters of the Atlantic closed over it has remarkable staying power and is believed by large numbers of people. Plato wrote convincingly about the wonders of Atlantis in his dialogues *Timaeus* and *Critias*, while other writers have suggested that the biblical story of the Flood is based on fragmentary accounts of the Atlantean deluge. The lost continent is also of occult significance, largely as the result of the writings of W. Scott-Elliott whose book, *The Story of Atlantis* (recently republished by the Theosophical Society), alleged that by clairvoyance he had been able to contact the spirits of Atlanteans who had been destroyed because of their addiction to black magic. There even exists in Britain today a minor but ardent religious group, the "Atlanteans", who hold that Atlantis still exists today, but on a different metaphysical plane, and that it is possible to communicate with it via individuals with supposedly mediumistic powers (*see* **Spiritualism**). Members of the Atlanteans meet regularly to hear "trance addresses" by one of the high priests of Atlantis, Helio-Arconaphus. Such beliefs are essentially harmless and merely reflect the great variety of religious attitudes which human beings enjoy.

Atomism. In philosophy, the atomists were a group of early Greek thinkers, the most important of whom were Leucippus (fl. *c.* 440 B.C.) and his younger contemporary Democritus (*c.* 460–370 B.C.). Prior to these men, although it had been agreed that matter must be composed of tiny ultimate particles and that change must be due to the manner in which these mingled or separated from each other, it was supposed that there existed different types of particle for each material—*e.g.* for flesh, wood, hair, bone. The atomists taught that atoms were all made of a single substance and differed only in the connections (pictured as hooks, grooves, points, etc.) which enabled them to join each other in characteristic ways. Theirs was the first move towards modern atomic theory and a predecessor of the modern concept of chemical linkages.

Authoritarianism, a dictatorial form of government as contrasted with a democratic one based on popular sovereignty. Its alleged advantages are the avoidance of the delays and inefficiency said to be characteristic of the latter.

Automatism, the production of material, written or spoken in "automatic" fashion—*i.e.,* apparently not under the conscious or volitional control of the individual. This psychologically perplexing phenomenon has occurred from time to time throughout the history of literature and art, and while it has occasionally produced work of great merit (much of William Blake's poetry, Coleridge's "Kubla Khan", etc.) the bulk of it is indifferent and often simply rubbish. Spiritualists claim that the work is produced under the direct guidances of the spirit world, and their argument has attracted considerable attention through the compositions of the pianist Rosemary Brown who, with little or no academic background in musical theory, has produced a number of "original" piano pieces allegedly composed by Beethoven, Mozart, etc., from the astral plane. While few music critics doubt Mrs. Brown's honesty and integrity, most consider her work to be clever pastiche and barely comparable in quality to the masterworks of the dead composers. Nevertheless automatism wants some explaining, and most psychologists today defer judgment, taking the view that it serves to remind us of the fund of material which lies in the unconscious mind, and which is prone to pop up from time to time without warning. Rather similar is the case of Matthew Manning, a young English student who produced clever and artistically intriguing drawings and sketches, allegedly guided by the hands of famous dead artists.

B

Baconian Method, the use of the inductive (as opposed to the deductive or Aristotelian) method of reasoning as proposed by Francis Bacon in the 17th cent. and J. S. Mill in the 19th cent. Deduction argues from supposedly certain first principles (such as the existence of God or Descartes's "I think, therefore I am") what the nature of the universe and its laws *must* be, whereas the only means of obtaining true knowledge of the universe, in Bacon's view, was by the amassing of facts and observations so that when enough were obtained the certain truth would be known in the same way that a child's numbered dots in a playbook joined together by a pencilled line create a picture. However, this is not the way science progresses in practice. Bacon underrated the importance of hypothesis and theory and overrated the reliability of the senses. In discussing the scientific tradition, Sir Karl Popper in his book, *Conjecture*

and Refutations, says: "The most important function of observation and reasoning, and even of intuition and imagination, is to help us in the critical examination of those bold conjectures which are the means by which we probe into the unknown." Two of the greatest men who clearly saw that there was no such thing as an inductive procedure were Galileo and Einstein.

Bahá'i Faith, a faith which teaches the unity of all religions and the unity of mankind. It arose in Iran from the teachings of the Bab (Mirza Ali Mohammed, 1820–50) and the Bahá'u'lláh (Mirza Husain Ali, 1817–92), thought to be manifestations of God, who in his essence is unknowable. Emphasis is laid on service to others. It has communities in many states and is surprisingly strong in England with a substantial following among university students. Its aims—universal peace, love, fellowship, sexual equality, etc.—are so laudable that it is hard to disagree with anything in the movement. Since the ruling Ayatollah Khomeini's fundamentalist Islamic regime came to power in Iran in 1979 members of the faith have been persecuted. The movement is now guided and administered by an elected order, "The Universal House of Justice". Today (1988) the movement has some 3-4 million followers.

Baptists, a Christian denomination whose distinctive doctrines are that members can only be received by baptism "upon the confession of their faith and sins" and that "baptism is no wise appertaineth to infants." Baptism is therefore by total immersion of adults. Modern Baptists base their doctrines upon the teaching of the Apostles and some hold that the Albigenses *(q.v.)* maintained the true belief through what they regarded as the corruption of the Roman Church in medieval times. On the other hand any connection with the Anabaptist movement during the Reformation is rejected and the beginning of the modern Church is traced to John Smyth, a minister of the Church of England who in Amsterdam came under the influence of the Arminians *(q.v.)* and Mennonites. Smyth died in 1612 when the first Baptist church in England was built at Newgate. This, the "General" Baptist Church, rejected Calvinistic beliefs and held the Arminian doctrine of redemption open to all, but some years later a split occurred with the formation of the "Particular" Baptist Church which was Calvinist in doctrine. In 1891 the two bodies were united in the Baptist Union and today the sect is spread throughout the world, notably in the United States.

The Anabaptist movements of Germany, Switzerland, and Holland also practiced adult baptism in addition to a primitive communism and demanded social reforms. Persecuted by both Catholics and Protestants, their leader, Thomas Münzer, and many others were burned at the stake (1525). However, this sect was noted for its violence under a religious guise, and its taking over of the state of Münster in 1533 was characterized by wild licentiousness, since, as Antinomians, they believed that the "elect" could do no wrong. A revival begun by Menno Simons (d. 1561), a Dutch religious reformer, led to the formation of the Mennonite sect which, while rejecting infant baptism, gave up the objectionable features of the Anabaptists. This reformed sect still exists as small agricultural groups in the original strongholds of the movement and in the United States.

Beat Generation, a term first used by the American

writer Jack Kerouac (d. 1969), author of *The Town and the City* and *On the Road,* to define various groups spread across the face of the country, but notably in New York and San Francisco, who, belonging to the post-war generation, represented a complex of attitudes. Briefly, these were: rejection of the values of the past and lack of conviction in the possibility of a future for humanity—hence an acceptance of nothing but the immediate present in terms of experience and sensations; rebellion against organized authority, not out of any political conviction (as in the case of anarchism), but rather from lack of any interest or desire to control events, nature, or people; contempt for the "Square"—the orthodox individual who, stuck firmly in his rut, "plays it safe" and remains confident of the rightness and decency of his moral values.

The Beat Generation of the 1940s and '50s gave way to the Love generation or Flower people, with their flowers, beads, and cowbells. Their social philosophy was the same—living in the present, unconventionally, seeking personal freedom, believing drugs to be essential, claiming to be acting against the rat race, dissociating themselves from politics, taking a superficial interest in the religions of the East, borrowing much of their language, music, and ideas on dress from the American hippy, yet believing in the creation of a new and gentler society based on different forms and values.

Both the Beat and Love generations were forerunners in America of an increasing and certainly welcome social awareness on the part of American students. This led in turn to the "campus revolutions" which were disruptive in their early stages but were also influential as part of the wave of public protest against the American involvement in Vietnam.

Behaviorism, a school of psychology founded in 1914 by J. B. Watson (1878–1958), an animal psychologist at Johns Hopkins University, Baltimore. Its main tenet was that the method of introspection and the study of mental states were unscientific and should be replaced by the study of behavior. When animals or human beings were exposed to specific stimuli and their responses objectively recorded, or when the development of a child, as seen in its changing behavior, was noted, these alone were methods which were truly scientific. Watson contributed an important idea to psychology and did a great deal towards ridding it of the largely philosophical speculations of the past. But he also went to absurd extremes, as in his view that thought is nothing but subvocal speech, consisting of almost imperceptible movements of the tongue, throat, and larynx (*i.e.,* when we think, we are really talking to ourselves), and his further opinion that heredity is, except in grossly abnormal cases, of no importance. He claimed that by "conditioning", the ordinary individual could be made into any desired type, regardless of his or her inheritance.

The work of Ivan Pavlov had begun about 1901, but was unknown in America until about ten years later, and it was through another Russian, Vladimir Bekhterev, that the concept of "conditioning" was introduced into the country. Bekhterev's book *Objective Psychology,* describing his new science of "reflexology", was translated in 1913 and played a great part in the development of Behaviorist ideas. The conditioned reflex became central to Watson's theory of learning and habit, formation (*e.g.,* he showed that a year-old child, at first unafraid of white rats, became afraid of them when they came to be associated with a loud noise behind the head). Finally all behavior, including abnormal behavior, came to be explained in terms of conditioned responses; these were built up by association on the infant's three innate emotions of fear, rage, and love, of which the original stimuli were, for the first, loud noises and the fear of falling; for the second, interference with freedom of movement; and for the third, patting and stroking.

Because of its considerable theoretical simplicity and its implicit suggestion that human behavior could be easily described (and even modified or controlled), Pavlovian psychology appeared very attractive to the Communist regime in Russia, and before long it became the "official" dogma in universities and research laboratories. Whereas in America and Western Europe its severe limitations became gradually apparent, in Russia these were ignored or disguised for ideological reasons with the inevitable outcome that Soviet psychology failed to evolve and, at one stage, seemed to be no more than a pallid offshoot of physiology. The recent liberalization which has been taking place throughout Soviet society has led to a considerable broadening of scientific horizons and Pavlovian ideas are no longer looked upon with such unquestioning reverence. In non-Communist countries simple Watsonian behaviorism has evolved into more sophisticated studies of animal learning, largely pioneered by the Harvard psychologist, Skinner. These techniques, which have shown that animals, from monkeys to rats, may be taught to solve a remarkable range of physical problems (such as pressing complex sequences of buttons or levers to escape from a cage) have themselves turned out to be rather disappointing in terms of advancing our general understanding of the workings of the human and animal brain. There is a growing feeling among psychologists that the real keys to the understanding of mankind will only be found through the study of man himself, and not his simpler animal cousins. *See also* **Gestalt Psychology**

Benthamism. *See* **Utilitarianism.**

Bolshevism, an alternative name for **Communism** *(q.v.),* usually used in the West in a derogatory sense. When the Russian Social Democratic Party at a conference held in London in 1903 split over the issue of radicalism or moderation, it was the radical faction headed by Lenin (who subsequently led the 1917 Revolution and became first Head of State of the Soviet Union) which polled the majority of votes. The Russian for majority is *bolshinstro* and for minority *menshinstro;* hence the radicals became known as Bolsheviki and the moderates as Mensheviki, anglicized as Bolsheviks and Mensheviks. *See* **Communism, Marxism.**

Bushido, the traditional code of honour of the Samurai or Japanese military caste corresponding to the European concept of knighthood and chivalry from which it took its separate origin in the 12th cent. Even today it is a potent influence among the upper classes, being based on the principles of simplicity, honesty, courage, and justice which together form a man's idea of personal honour.

C

Cabala, originally a collection of Jewish doctrines about the nature of the Universe, supposedly handed down by Moses to the Rabbis, which evolved into a kind of mystical interpretation of the Old Testament. Students of the history of religious belief have found its origins to be in fact extremely obscure, and some aspects appear to have been lifted from ancient Egyptian sources. Skilled Cabalists hold that the system contains a key to biblical interpretation based on the numerical values of the words and letters of the Scriptures which reveal hidden depths of meaning behind the allegorical Old Testament stories.

Calvinism, the branch of Protestantism founded basically (although preceded by Zwingli and others) by Jean Chauvin (1509–64), who was born in Noyon in Picardy. John Calvin, as he is usually called, from the Latin form of his name, Calvinius, provided in his *Institutions of the Christian Religion* the first logical definition and justification of Protestantism, thus becoming the intellectual leader of the Reformation as the older Martin Luther was its emotional instigator. The distinctive doctrine of Calvinism is its dogma of predestination which states that God has unalterably destined some souls to salvation to whom "efficacious grace and the gift of perseverance" is granted and others to eternal damnation. Calvinism, as defined in the Westminster Confession, is established in the Reformed or Presbyterian churches of France, Holland, Scotland, etc., as contrasted with the Lutheran churches, and its harsh but logical beliefs inspired the French Huguenots, the Dutch in their fight against Spanish Catholic domination, and the English Puritans. The rule set up under Calvin's influence in Geneva was marred by the burning at the stake of the anatomist Servetus for the heresy of "pantheism", or, as we should say, Unitarianism.

Perhaps its greatest single influence outside the Church was the result of Calvinist belief that to labor industriously was one of God's commands. This changed the medieval notions of the blessedness of poverty and the wickedness of usury, proclaimed that men should shun luxury and be thrifty, yet implied that financial success was a mark of God's favor. In this way it was related to the rise of capitalism either as cause or effect. Max Weber, the German sociologist, believed that Calvinism was a powerful incentive to, or even cause of, the rise of **capitalism** *(q.v.):* Marx, Sombart, and in England, Tawney, have asserted the reverse view—that Calvinism was a result of developing capitalism, being its ideological justification.

Capitalism is an economic system under which the means of production and distribution are owned by a relatively small section of society which runs them at its own discretion for private profit. There exists, on the other hand, a propertyless class of those who exist by the sale of their labor power. Capitalism arose towards the end of the 18th cent. in England where the early factory owners working with small-scale units naturally approved of free enterprise and free trade. But free enterprise has no necessary connection with capitalism; by the beginning of this century monopolies were developing and state protection against foreign competition was demanded. Capitalism is opposed by those who believe in socialism, first, for the moral reasons that it leads to economic inequality and the exploitation of labour and the consuming public, and that public welfare rather than private profit should motivate the economic system; secondly, for the practical reason that capitalism leads to recurrent economic crises. The recent world economic crisis has led to great hopes on the part of Marxists and Communists that capitalism is now involved in its final death throes. It is worth commenting however, that the European war of the 1940s, the great depression of the 30s, the first world war and the Russian Revolution were also, in their turn, confidently held up by Communists as heralding capitalism's imminent collapse.

Cartomancy, the art of fortunes or predicting the future by playing cards or by the Tarot pack. The elegant Tarot cards number 78 in all and are probably medieval in origin. They are rich in symbolism and include trump cards depicting the devil, the pope, death, the moon, the wheel of fortune, etc., and are an interesting part of our cultural mythology. There is no evidence whatsoever that they can be used in any objective way to divine the future, and professional fortune tellers and clairvoyants who use them almost certainly rely on a little native, basic psychology to achieve their results.

Characterology, the attempt made over many centuries to classify people into personality types on the basis of physical or psychological characteristics. The first attempt was made by Hippocrates in the 5th cent. B.C. who classified temperaments into the *sanguine* (or optimistic), the *melancholic*, the *choleric* (or aggressive), and the *phlegmatic* (or placid); these were supposed to result from the predominance of the following "humors" in the body: red blood, black bile, yellow bile, or phlegm respectively. Theophrastus, a pupil of Aristotle, described, with examples, thirty extreme types of personality (*e.g.* the talkative, the boorish, the miserly, etc.); these were basically literary and imaginative but about the same time "physiognomy" arose which attempted to interpret character from the face. Physiognomy became of importance again during the Renaissance and there are still those today who believe in it in spite of the fact that, broadly speaking, there is no connection whatever between facial features and personality (i.e. although it may be possible to tell from the features that a man is an idiot or some extreme abnormal type and some idea of character may be obtained from an individual's characteristic facial expressions, it is not possible to tell (as Johann Lavater, the best-known physiognomist of the late 18th cent. believed) from the shape of the nose, height of the brow, or dominance of the lower jaw, whether anyone is weak, intellectual or determined). The contention of the 19th cent. Italian criminologist Cesare Lombroso that criminals show typical facial characteristics—prominent cheekbones and jaw, slanting eyes, receding brow, large ears of a particular shape—was disproved by Karl Pearson early this century when he found that 3,000 criminals showed no significant differences of features, carefully measured from a similar number of students at Oxford and Cambridge.

It has, however, been noted that people in general tend to be intellectual or emotional, inward- or outward-looking, and this observation is reflected in the classification of the Scottish psychologist, Alexander Bain (d. 1903), into intellectual, artistic, and practical; Nietzsche's Apollonian and

Dionysian types; William James's "tender" and "toughminded"; and C. G. Jung's introvert and extrovert. Careful experiments have shown that these are not clear-cut and that most individuals fall in between the extremes.

Some connection has been found between temperament and body-build. The German psychiatrist Ernst Kretschmer (b. 1888) showed that manic-depressive patients and normal people who are extroverted and tend to alternate in mood (as do manic-depressives to an exaggerated degree) were usually short and stout or thick-set in build; schizophrenics and normal people, who both show shyness, serious or introverted reactions, were usually tall and slender. The former of "pyknic" body-build are "cyclothyme" in temperament, the latter with "schizothyme" temperament are of two bodily types—the tall and thin or "asthenic" and the muscularly well-proportioned or "athletic". The American Sheldon has confirmed these observations on the whole and gone into further details. According to him the basic body types are: (1) *endomorphic* (rounded build), corresponding to Kretschmer's pyknic, normally associated with the *viscerotonic* temperament (relaxed, sociable); (2) *mesomorphic* (squarish, athletic build), normally associated with the *somatotonic* temperament (energetic, assertive); and (3) *ectomorphic* (linear build) normally associated with the *cerebrotonic* temperament (anxious, submissive, restless). Glandular and metabolic factors have considerable effect on human personality and also, to some extent, on physique. It is not too surprising, therefore, to find an association between body build (or "somatotype" as Sheldon termed it) and general mood. However, Sheldon's original clear-cut and oversimplified categories of body-type are no longer looked upon as reliable indicators of personality.

Chauvinism, a term applied to any excessive devotion to cause, particularly a patriotic or military one. The word is derived from Nicholas Chauvin whose excessive devotion to Napoleon made him a laughing-stock.

Chirognomy, the attempt to read character from the lines in the hand (as contrasted with chiromancy or palmistry, in which an attempt is made to tell the future in the same way) is an ancient practice which, like astrology *(q.v.)* has no discernible scientific basis but a very considerable popular following. As with astrology, where it is hard to see what kind of link could exist between the constellations and human behavior, so it is equally hard to see how the configuration of lines on the hand could be paralleled by psychological attributes. This argument might be thought of as irrelevant if palmistry, etc. actually had predictive power, but the plain fact is that when put to a scientific test, practitioners of these arts turn out to show no abilities beyond those with which a normally perceptive individual is equipped.

Chiropractice, the art of manipulation of the joints, in particular the spine, as a means of curing disease, is a slightly fashionable quasimedical practice. Few qualified doctors employ its questionable principles though, as with its neighbor osteopathy, it seems on occasions to be a useful complement to medical treatment. Much controversy surrounds the status of practitioners of fringe medicine of this kind. In America osteopathy (bone manipulation) which seems beneficial in many cases for the condition known as prolapsed or "slipped" disc, is becoming gradually merged into orthodox medical practice.

Christadelphians, a religious denomination formed in the U.S.A. in the late 1840s by John Thomas, an Englishman. They strive to represent the simple apostolic faith of the 1st century and hold that the Scriptures are the wholly inspired, infallible Word of God. They believe in the mortality of mankind—the teaching of the immortality of the soul is not of Bible origin and that salvation is dependent of belief followed by a baptism of total immersion in water. They believe in the imminent, personal return of Jesus Christ to the earth to judge the living and the dead and reward the righteous with Eternal life.

Christian Science claims that it is a religion based on the words and works of Christ Jesus. It draws its authority from the Bible, and its teachings are set forth in *Science and Health with Key to the Scriptures* by Mary Baker Eddy (1821–1910) the discoverer and founder of Christian Science. A distinctive part of Christian Science is its healing of physical disease as well as sin by spiritual means alone.

The Church of Christ, Scientist, was founded in 1879 when 15 students of Mrs. Eddy met with their teacher and voted to organize a church designed to commemorate the words and works of the Master, which should reinstate primitive Christianity and its lost element of healing.

A few years later the church took its present and permanent form as The Mother Church, The First Church of Christ, Scientist, in Boston, Massachusetts, which together with its branch churches and societies throughout the world, constitutes the Christian Science denomination. Now (1987) more than 100 years after its founding there are some 2,700 branches in 60 countries, as well as numerous informal groups not yet organized and about 300 organizations at universities and colleges.

Church of England. There is some evidence of possible continuity with the Christianity of Roman Britain, but in the main the Church derives from the fusion of the ancient Celtic church with the missionary church of St. Augustine, who founded the See of Canterbury in A.D. 597. To archbishop Theodore in 673 is ascribed its organization in dioceses with settled boundaries, and in parishes. St. Augustine's church was in communion with Rome from the first, but the Church of England was not brought within papal jurisdiction until after the Norman conquest, and was at no time under the complete domination of Rome. It remains the Catholic Church of England without break of continuity, but during the Reformation the royal supremacy was accepted and that of the pope repudiated. Its traditional forms of worship are embodied in the Book of Common Prayer, but the Alternative Service Book of 1980 is now widely used. In 1986 Easter communicants were estimated *c.* 1,650,000. The Anglican Church in 1987 was deeply divided over the ordination of women priests.

The **Anglican Communion** comprises the churches in all parts of the world which are in communion with the Church of England (In the U.S. it is the Episcopal Church). All the bishops of the Anglican Communion meet every ten years in the Lambeth Conference (first held in 1867), over which the Archbishop of Canterbury by custom presides as *primus inter pares*. At the 1968 Conference observers and laymen were admitted for the first time. The last Conference was held in 1978. The next will meet in 1988.

Clairvoyance. *See* **Telepathy.**

Communism, ideally refers to the type of society in which all property belongs to the community and social life is based on the principle "from each according to his ability, to each according to his needs." There would be public ownership of all enterprises and all goods would be free. Since no such society as yet exists, the word in practice refers to the attempt to achieve such a society by initially overthrowing the capitalist system and establishing a dictatorship of the proletariat (Marx identified the dictatorship with a democratic constitution). Communists believe that their first task is the establishment of socialism under which there remain class distinctions, private property to some extent, and differences between manual and brain workers. The state is regulated on the basis "from each according to his ability, to each according to his work". Lenin applied Marx's analysis to the new conditions which had arisen in 20th-cent. capitalist society. Marxism-Leninism develops continuously with practice since failure to apply its basic principles to changed circumstances and times would result in errors of dogmatism. Mao Tse-tung worked out the techniques of revolutionary action appropriate to China; Che Guevara the guerrilla tactics appropriate to the peasants of Latin America. His counsel "It is not necessary to wait until conditions for making revolution exist; the insurrection can create them", was the opposite of Mao Tse-tung's "Engage in no battle you are not sure of winning", and Lenin's "Never play with insurrection". Two fundamental principles of communism are (1) peaceful coexistence between countries of different social systems, and (2) the class struggle between oppressed and oppressing classes and between oppressed and oppressor nations. Maoism, for example, holds that it is a mistake to lay one-sided stress on peaceful transition towards socialism otherwise the revolutionary will of the proletariat becomes passive and unprepared politically and organizationally for the tasks ahead.

In Russia the civil war developed *after* the revolution; in China the communists fought their civil war *before* they seized power: the Yugoslav partisans won their own guerrilla war *during* their stand against the fascist powers—differences which had important political consequences. Russia suffered three decades of isolationism and totalitarian suppression ("an isolated and besieged fortress") before the advent of Gorbachev has heralded a new openness (*glasnost*) in Soviet politics. Mao Tse-tung held to the orthodox Leninist view about capitalism and communism, regarded détente as a dangerous illusion, and compromise and "revisionism" as a fatal error. The ideological dispute between these two great communist powers which lasted from the '60s to the '80s is ending with the improvement in inter-party relations and today a movement towards détente is taking place. Communist parties in some countries, *e.g.,* Italy, are taking the democratic road to socialism and believe that a communist government should be installed by the ballot box. *See also,* **Marxism, Trotskyism.**

Congregationalists, the oldest sect of Nonconformists who hold that each church should be independent of external ecclesiastical authority. They took their origin from the Brownists of Elizabeth's days. Robert Browne (*c.* 1550–*c.* 1633), an Anglican clergyman, who had come to reject bishops was forced with his followers to seek refuge, first in Holland and then in Scotland where he was imprisoned by the Kirk. In later life he changed his views and is disowned by Congregationalists because of his reversion to Anglicanism. His former views were spread by Henry Barrow and John Greenwood who, under an Act passed in 1592 "for the punishment of persons obstinately refusing to come to church" (and largely designed for the suppression of this sect), were hanged at Tyburn. They had preached *(a)* that the only head of the church is Jesus Christ; *(b)* that, contrary to Elizabethan doctrine, the church had no relationship to the state; *(c)* that the only statute-book was the Bible whereas the Articles of Religion and Book of Common Prayer were mere Acts of Parliament; *(d)* that each congregation of believers was independent and had the power of choosing its own ministers. The body fled once more to Holland and were among the Pilgrims who set sail in the *Mayflower* for America in 1620 while those who remained were joined by Puritans fleeing from Charles I. They became free once more to live in England under the Commonwealth only to be repressed again under Charles II. Finally full liberty of worship was granted under William III. In 1833 the Congregational Union of England and Wales was formed which had no legislative power. It had issued a Declaration of Faith by which no minister was bound; he was responsible to his own church and to nobody else. The sect is widespread both in Britain and the U.S.A. where it is held in special honor because of its connection with the Pilgrim Fathers. In 1972 the Congregational Church in England and Wales and the Presbyterian Church of England decided to unite to form the United Reformed Church. The majority of members who did not join comprise the Congregational Federation.

Coptic Church, the sect of Egyptian Christians who holding "Monophysite" opinions (*i.e.,* refusing to grant the two natures, God and Man, of Christ) were declared heretical by the Council of Chalcedon in 451. They practice circumcision and have dietary laws. Their language is a direct descendant of ancient Egyptian. Like the Armenians, they are regarded as an heretical branch of Eastern Christianity. Their religious head is the patriarch of Alexandria.

Cynics, a school of philosophy founded in the time of Alexander the Great by Diogenes. Choosing to live like a dog by rejecting all conventions of religion, manners, or decency, and allegedly living in a tub, Diogenes unwittingly brought on his school the title "Cynic", meaning not "cynical", as the word is understood today, but "canine". His teacher, Antisthenes, who had been a disciple of Socrates, decided, after the latter's death, that all philosophy was useless quibbling and man's sole aim should be simple goodness. He believed in a return to nature, despised luxury, wanted no government, no private property, and associated with working men and slaves. Far from being cynics in the modern sense, Diogenes and Antisthenes were virtuous anarchists rather like old Tolstoy (except that in the practice of their beliefs they were more consistent).

D

Deism. *See* **God and Man.**

Demonism, Demons, and the Devil. Demons are ethereal beings of various degrees of significance and power which are believed to be implicated in men's good, but especially evil, fortune. They are common to most cultures. From the anthropological point of view the demon arose as a widespread concept in the following ways: (1) as a psychological projection into the outer world of man's own good or evil emotions and thoughts; (2) as a survival of primitive animism *(q.v.),* thus spirits are believed to haunt places, trees, stones, and other natural objects; (3) when by warlike invasion the gods of the vanquished become the devils of the conquerors (as when the Jews occupied Canaan); (4) as a primitive belief that spirits of the dead continue after death to hover near their former habitation, and not always entirely welcome to the living; (5) the conception of a supreme source of evil (the Devil or Satan) which took shape among the Jews during their sojourn in Babylon under the influence of Zoroastrianism *(q.v.),* a religion in which the struggle between the two spirits, Good and Evil, reached its height in the imagination of the ancient world. The Satan of the Old Testament was first regarded as one of God's servants (in the Book of Job he goes up and down the earth to see whether God's commands are obeyed), but when the Jews returned from their captivity he had become identified with Ahriman, the spirit of evil, who was in continual conflict with Ahursa Mazda, the spirit of good. As Dr. Margaret Murray has pointed out, the primitive mind ascribed both good and evil to one power alone; the division into God and the Devil, priest and witch, belongs to a higher stage of civilization. The worship of evil itself, or of its personification in Satan, is a curious practice which seems to have developed hand-in-hand with Christianity and to have received steady support from a small but measurable minority. Many of the ceremonies involved in Satanism or in the so-called Black Mass appear to have been no more than opportunities for sexual excesses of one kind or another—such indulgences being traditionally barred to devout Christians. The alleged power of sex as a form of magic was propagated by the talented but rather mad poet, Aleister Crowley (1875–1947), who scandalized pre-war Europe with his very well-publicized dabblings into Satanism. The self-styled "wickedest man in the world", Crowley was a pathetic rather than shocking figure and died a drug addict. He can hardly be said to have significantly advanced the cause of Demonology, though it has to be admitted that he tried very hard.

Determinism and Free Will. The question of whether man is, or is not, free to mold his own destiny is one which has exercised the minds of philosophers since Greek mythology conceived of the Fates as weaving a web of destiny from which no man can free himself. Socrates emphasized that man could through knowledge influence his destiny while ignorance made him the plaything of fate; Plato went further in pointing out that man can, and does, defeat the purposes of the universe and its divine Creator. It is our duty to live a good life, but we can live a foolish and wicked one if we chose. Aristotle wrote "Virtue is a disposition or habit involving deliberate purpose or choice". If this were not so morality would be a sham.

The Problem for Theology. The last of the great philosophers of Antiquity and one of the great influences in molding Catholic theology was Plotinus (*c.* 204–70). Soul, he taught, is free, but once enmeshed in the body loses its freedom in the life of sense. Nevertheless, man is free to turn away from sensuality and towards God who is perfect freedom; for even when incarnated in matter the soul does not entirely lose the ability to rescue itself. This conception was carried over into the beliefs of the early Christian Apologists because it appeared to be in line with the teaching of Jesus that He had come to save man from sin. Sin implies guilt, and guilt implies the freedom to act otherwise; furthermore an all-good God cannot be responsible for the sin in the world which must be man's responsibility and this again implies freedom. Pelagius (*c.* 355–*c.* 425), a Welsh priest, not only believed in free will but questioning the doctrine of original sin, said that when men act righteously it is through their own moral effort, and God rewards them for their virtues in heaven. This belief became fairly widespread and was declared a heresy by the Church, being attacked notably by St. Augustine (354–430), a contemporary of Pelagius, who believed in predestination—that, since the sin of Adam, God had chosen who in all future history would be saved and who damned. This represents one tradition in Christianity: the determinism which leads to Calvinism *(q.v.)*. St. Thomas Aquinas (1227–74), the greatest figure of scholasticism and one of the principal saints in the Roman Catholic Church, compromised between the two positions in the sense that, believing man to be free, he yet held that Adam's sin was transmitted to all mankind and only divine grace can bring salvation. But even when God wishes to bestow his salvation, the human will must cooperate. God foresees that some will not accept the offer of grace and predestines them to eternal punishment.

The Problem for Philosophy. With the Renaissance, thinkers began to free themselves from the domination of the Church and so study the world objectively and freely without preconceptions. But the more man turned to science, the more he discovered that the world was ruled by apparently inexorable laws and, since the scientist must believe that every event has a cause, he was led back to determinism. Man as part of the universe was subject to law too and all that existed was a vast machine. Francis Bacon (1561–1626) separated the fields of religion and science but left man subject completely to the will of God. Thomas Hobbes (1588–1679) was a rigid determinist and materialist although, having had trouble with the Church in France whence, as a royalist, he had fled, he took care to announce that the Christian God is the Prime Mover.

Modern philosophy begins with René Descartes (1596–1650), a Frenchman who tried to reconcile the mechanical scientific universe of his time with the spiritual need for freedom. He did this by separating completely mind and body; the former, he said, is free, the latter completely determined. But, by admitting that the will can produce states of body, he was left with the problem of how this could happen—a problem which the so-called Occasionists solved to their own satisfaction by stating that the will is free and God so arranges the universe that what a person wills happens. Baruch Spinoza (1632–77), a Dutch Jew whose independence of thought had led to his excommunication from the Amsterdam Synagogue in 1656, was a complete determinist. He asserted that God and Nature are one, everything that happens is a manifestation of God's inscrutable nature, and it is logically impossible that things could be other than they are. Thus both Hobbes and Spinoza were determinists for entirely opposed reasons. The former as a materialist, the latter because he believed in the absolute perfection and universality of God. Yet the great religious mystic and mathematician Blaise Pascal (1623–62) held that, no matter what reason and cold logic may indicate we *know* from direct religious experience that we are free. John Calvin (1509–64) and Martin Luther (1483–1546) were both determinists. *See* **Calvinism.**

To the more practical British philosophers, John Locke (1632–1704) and David Hume (1711–76), free will was related to personality. Locke believed that God had implanted in each individual certain desires and these determine the will; the desires are already there, but we use our will to satisfy them. Hume argued that a man's behavior is the necessary result of his character and if he had a different character he would act otherwise. Accordingly, when a man's actions arise from his own nature and desires he is free. He is not free when external events compel him to act otherwise (*e.g.*, if he strikes another because his own nature is such he is free as he is not if he is compelled to do so against his desire). Leibnitz (1646–1716), although as a German metaphysical philosopher holding very different general views, said much the same thing—that choice is simply selecting the desire that is strongest. But most of the 18th cent. thinkers after Voltaire, with the great exceptions of Rousseau and the later German philosophers Kant, Fichte, Schopenhauer, and Hegel, who were initially influenced by him, accepted determinism. Rousseau (1712–78) began to stem the tide by his declaration that man is a free soul striving to remain free and only prevented from being so by society and the cold science which stifles his feeling heart. Once again the will became important as Kant (1724–1804) asserted that belief in freedom is a moral necessity although it cannot be proved by reason; the moral nature of man shows that there is a "transcendental" world beyond the senses where freedom applies. Fichte and Schelling found freedom in the Absolute ego or God, of whom each individual was part and thus also free. Hegel (1770–1831) saw the whole universe as evolving towards self-awareness and freedom in man although this could only be fully realized in a society that makes for freedom. Even God himself only attains full consciousness and self-realization through the minds of such individuals as are free. This is the goal of the dialectical process. (*See* **Dialectical Materialism.**)

The Scientist's View. For the scientist the law of cause and effect is a useful hypothesis since, by and large, it is necessary for him to assume that all events are caused. Nevertheless the modern tendency is to think in terms of statistical probability rather than relentless mechanistic causality, and, although the free will problem does not concern the scientist as such, it is clear that freedom and determinism (assuming the terms to have any meaning at all) are not necessarily opposed. In sociology, for example, we *know* that certain actions will produce certain results upon the behavior of

people in general, *e.g.*, that raising the bank rate will discourage business expansion. But this does not mean that Mr. Brown who decides in the circumstances not to add a new wing to his factory is not using his free will. Even in the case of atoms, as Dr. Bronowski has pointed out, the observed results of allowing gas under pressure in a cylinder to rush out occur because most of the atoms are "obeying" the scientific "law" relating to such situations. But this does not mean that some atoms are not busy rushing across the stream or even against it—they are, but the general tendency is outwards and that is what we note. Lastly, the modern philosophical school of Logical Analysis would probably ask, not whether Freewill or Determinism is the true belief, but whether the question has any meaning. For what scientific experiment could we set up to prove one or the other true? The reader will note that some of the philosophers mentioned above are using the words to mean quite different concepts.

Dialectical Materialism, the combination of Hegel's dialectic method with a materialist philosophy produced by Karl Marx (1818–83) and his friend Friedrich Engels (1820–95). It is the philosophical basis of **Marxism** *(q.v.)* and **Communism** *(q.v.)* "Dialectic" to the ancient Greek philosophers meant a kind of dialogue or conversation, as used particularly by Socrates, in which philosophical disputes were resolved by a series of successive contradictions: a thesis is put forward and the opposing side holds its contradiction or antithesis until in the course of argument a synthesis is reached in which the conflicting ideas are resolved.

From Thesis through Antithesis to Synthesis. Hegel in the 19th century put forward the view that this process applies to the course of nature and history as they strive towards the perfect state. But to him, as to the Greeks, the conflict was in the field of ideas. The "universal reason" behind events works through the ideas held by a particular society until they are challenged by those of another which supersedes them and in turn, usually by war, becomes the agent of universal reason until the arrival of a new challenger. Hegel therefore regarded war as an instrument of progress and his Prussian compatriots found no difficulty in identifying their own state as the new agent of progress by universal conquest. Feuerbach, Lassalle, and other early socialists were impressed by some of Hegel's ideas: *e.g.*, that societies evolved (with the assumption that finally their own ideal society would be achieved) and that truth, morals, and concepts were relative so that a type of society that was "good" at one time was not necessarily so at another. But Marx and Engels in effect turned Hegel upside-down, accepted his dialectic but rejected his belief that ideas were the motive force. On the contrary, they said, ideas are determined by social and economic change as a result of materialistic forces. (*See* **Calvinism,** where it is pointed out that the Marxist view is not that Calvin changed men's economic ideas but rather that a developing capitalism unconsciously changed his.) The historical materialism of Marxism purports to show that the inexorable dialectic determines that feudalism is displaced by capitalism and capitalism by creating a proletariat (its antithesis) inevitably leads to socialism and a classless society. The state, as a tool of the dominant class, withers away. Dialectical materialism is applied in all spheres. As a philosophy there is little to be said for it save that it has shown us the close dependence of man's thoughts upon current material and social conditions. But as a battle cry or a rationalization of Marxism it wields immense power over the minds of men. *See* **Marxism.**

Dianetics. *See* **Scientology.**

Doukhobors, a religious sect of Russian origin, founded by a Prussian sergeant at Kharkov in the middle of the 18th century, and now mainly settled in Canada. Like many other sects they belong to that type of Christianity which seeks direct communication with God and such bodies tend to have certain traits in common, such as belief in the "inner light", opposition to war and authority in general, and often ecstasies which show themselves in physical ways such as shaking, speaking in strange tongues (glossolalia), and other forms of what to the unbeliever seem mass hysteria. Liturgy, ritual, or ceremony is non-existent. The Doukhobors were persecuted in Tsarist Russia, but in 1898 Tolstoy used his influence to have them removed to Canada where the government granted them uninhabited land in what is now Saskatchewan and seven or eight thousand settled down in peace which they enjoyed for many years. Recently, however, their practices have caused difficulties once more; for even the most tolerant government which is prepared to accept pacifism, total dependence on communally-owned agriculture, refusal to engage in commerce, non-payment of taxes, rejection of the marriage ceremony and separation "when love ceases", finds it difficult to tolerate, as civilization advances ever closer to Doukhobor communities, their proneness to "put off these troublesome disguises which we wear"— *i.e.,* to walk about naked in the communities of their more orthodox neighbors. What the future of the Doukhobors in their various sects (for even they have their differences) will be it is impossible to say, but it is difficult to believe that these simple people can long resist the pressure of modern civilization.

Dowsing. *See* **Radiesthesia.**

Druidism, the religion of Celtic Britain and Gaul of which Druids were the priesthood. They were finally wiped out by the Roman general Suetonius Paulinus about A.D. 58 in their last stronghold, the island of Anglesey. There are two sources of our present beliefs in Druidism: (1) the brief and factual records of the Romans, notably Pliny and Julius Caesar, which tell us that they worshipped in sacred oak groves and presumably practiced a religion doing reverence to the powers of nature which must have had its roots in early stone age times and had many cruel rites, *e.g.,* human sacrifice; (2) the beliefs put forward by William Stukeley, an amateur antiquarian who from 1718 did valuable work by his studies of the stone circles at Stonehenge and Avebury. However, influenced by the Romantic movement, he later put forward the most extravagant theories which unfortunately are those popularly accepted by those without archaeological knowledge today. Stonehenge and Avebury were depicted as the temples of the "white-haired Druid bard sublime" and an attempt was made to tie up Druidism with early Christianity, above all with the concept of the Trinity. In fact, these circles have no connection with the Druids. They may have made ceremonial use of them but recent evidence suggests that the megalithic stones at Stonehenge belong to a Bronze Age culture (2100–1600 B.C.). Nor have Druidism and Christianity any relationship. Almost nothing is known of the religion. Yet such were its romantic associations that, even today, one hears of "Druidic" ceremonies practiced at the appropriate time of year on Primrose Hill in the heart of London (though whether seriously or with tongue in cheek, one does not know). In Wales the name Druid survives as the title for the semi-religious leaders of the annual festivals of Celtic poetry, drama, and music known as Eisteddfods. Lingering, but now tenuous, druidic connections are to be found in all Celtic parts including Cornwall and Brittany where Eisteddfods are also held.

Dualism, any philosophical or theological theory which implies that the universe has a double nature, notably Plato's distinction between appearance and reality, soul and body, ideas and material objects, reason and the evidence of the senses, which infers that behind the world as we perceive it there lies an "ideal" world which is more "real" than that of mere appearance. In religions such as Zoroastrianism or the Gnostic and Manichaeism heresies, it was believed that the universe was ruled by good and evil "principles"—in effect that there was a good god and a bad one. In psychology, dualism refers to the philosophical theories which believe mind and body to be separate entities. The opposite of dualism is monism which asserts the essential unity of the substance of the universe.

An essential problem in the dualistic view lies in the question as to how and where the two separate and distinct properties of the universe interact. Where, for example, does the "mind" actually mesh with the physical mechanics of the brain and body—where does the ghost sit in his machine? Descartes decided that mind and body must interact somewhere and he selected the pineal gland (an apparently functionless part of the brain) as the spot. But this did nothing to explain how two *totally different* aspects of nature can possibly influence each other, and today most philosophers and psychologists reject dualistic views of life and personality as posing more problems than they solve. *See also* **Psychology, Occam's Razor.**

E

Education. Education was no great problem to primitive man, but as societies became more complex people began to ask themselves such questions as: *What* should young people be taught? *How* should they be taught? Should the aim of their education be to bring out their individual qualities or rather to make them good servants of the state?

The first teachers were priests who knew most about the traditions, customs, and lore of their societies and thus the first schools were in religious meeting places. This was notably true of the Jews who learned from the rabbis in the synagogue.

The Greeks. We begin, as always, with the Greeks whose city-states, based on slavery, educated men (not women) for the sort of life described in Plato's *Dialogues*—the leisured life of gentlemen arguing the problems of the universe at their banquets or in the market-place. This made it necessary to learn debate and oratory (or rhetoric) especially for those who proposed to take up politics. The Sophist philosophy taught the need to build up convincing arguments in a persuasive manner, to learn the rules of logic and master the laws and customs of the Athenians, and to know the literature of the past so that illustrations might be drawn from it. These strolling philosophers who taught for a fee were individualists showing the student how to advance himself at all costs within his community.

Socrates had a more ethical approach, believing that education was good in itself, made a man happier and a better citizen, and emphasized his position as a member of a group. His method of teaching, the dialectic or "Socratic" method, involved argument and discussion rather than overwhelming others by rhetoric and is briefly mentioned under **Dialectical Materialism** *(q.v.)*. Today this method is increasingly used in adult education where a lecture is followed by a period of discussion in which both lecturer and audience participate; for psychologists have shown that people accept ideas more readily when conviction arises through their own arguments than when they are passively thrust down their throats.

Socrates' pupil Plato produced in his book *The Republic* one of the first comprehensive systems of education and vocational selection. Believing that essentially men have very different and unequal abilities he considered that in an idealistic or utopian society they should be put into social classes corresponding to these differences, and suggested the following method: (1) For the first 18 years of a boy's life he should be taught gymnastics and sports, playing and singing music, reading and writing, a knowledge of literature, and if he passed this course sent on to the next stage; those who failed were to become tradesmen and merchants. (2) From 18–20 those successful in the first course were to be given two years of cadet training, the ones thought incapable of further education being placed in the military class as soldiers. (3) The remainder, who were to become the leaders of society, proceeded with advanced studies in philosophy, mathematics, science, and art. Such education was to be a state concern, state supported and controlled, selecting men and training them for service in the state according to their abilities.

Plato's pupil Aristotle even suggested that the state should determine shortly after birth which children should be allowed to live and destroy the physically or mentally handicapped; that marriage should be state-controlled to ensure desirable offspring. However, in their time the leisured and individualistic Sophists held the field and few accepted the educational views of Plato or his pupil.

Rome. The Romans were not philosophers and most of their culture came from Greece. Administration was their chief aptitude and Quintilian (A.D. *c.* 35–*c.* 95) based his higher education on the earlier classical tuition in public speaking, but he is important for emphasizing the training of character and for his humanistic approach to the method of teaching that caused his *Institutio oratoria* to be influential for centuries later—indeed one might almost say up to the time of the great Dr. Arnold of Rugby. Education, he believed, should begin early but one must "take care that the child not old enough to love his studies does not come to hate them" by premature forcing; studies must be made pleasant and interesting and students encouraged by praise rather than discouraged when they sometimes fail; play is to be approved of as a sign of a lively disposition and

because gloomy, depressed children are not likely to be good students; corporal punishment should never be used because "it is an insult as you will realize if you imagine it yourself". The world became interested not in *what* he taught but *how* he taught it: he was the pioneer of humanistic education and character-training from Vittorino d. Feltre (1378–1446) of Mantua, through Milton and Pope who commended his works to the modern educationists who have studied their pupils as well as their books.

The Middle Ages: The Religious View. With the development of Christianity education once more became a religious problem. The earliest converts had to be taught Christian doctrine and were given instruction in "catechumenal" schools before admission to the group, but as the religion came increasingly into contact with other religions or heresies a more serious training was necessary, and from these newer "catechetical" schools, where the method used was the catechism (*i.e.*, question and answer as known to all Presbyterian children today), the Apologists arose among whom were Clement of Alexandria and the great Origen. From this time education became an instrument of the church and in 529 the Emperor Justinian ordered all pagan schools to be closed.

As typical of the best in medieval education while the lamp of civilization burned low during the Dark Ages, after the fall of Roman power, and survived only in the monasteries, we may mention St Benedict (*c.* 480–*c.* 547) of Monte Cassino. There, in southern Italy, a rule was established which became a part of monastic life in general. Monastic schools were originally intended for the training of would-be monks, but later others were admitted who simply wanted some education; thus two types of schools developed: one for the *interni* and the other for *externi* or external pupils. Originally studies were merely reading in order to study the Bible, writing to copy the sacred books, and sufficient calculation to be able to work out the advent of holy days or festivals. But by the end of the 6th century the "seven liberal arts" (grammar, rhetoric, dialectic, arithmetic, geometry, music and astronomy) were added.

The Renaissance. The close of the Middle Ages saw the development of two types of secular school. One came with the rise of the new merchant class and the skilled trader whose "guilds" or early trade unions established schools to train young men for their trades but ultimately gave rise to burgher or town schools; the other was the court school founded and supported by the wealthy rulers of the Italian cities—Vittorio da Feltre (mentioned above) presided over the most famous at Mantua.

These Renaissance developments are paralleled in northern Europe by the Protestant reformers who, having with Martin Luther held that everyone should know how to read his Bible in order to interpret it in his own way, were logically committed to popular education, compulsory and universal. In theory this was intended for biblical study, but writing, arithmetic, and other elementary subjects were taught and Luther said that, even if heaven and hell did not exist, education was important. Universal education is a Protestant conception.

Views of Philosophers. From this period onwards people were free to put forward any ideas about education, foolish or otherwise, and to create their own types of school. Of English philosophers who theorized about, but did not practice education we may mention the rationalist Francis Bacon (1561–1626) who saw learning as the dissipation of all prejudices and the collection of concrete facts; the materialist and totalitarian Hobbes (1588–1679) who, as a royalist, believed that the right to determine the kind of education fit for his subjects is one of the absolute rights of the sovereign power or ruler; the gentlemanly Locke (1632–1704) whose ideal was a sound mind in a sound body to be attained by hard physical exercise, wide experience of the world, and enough knowledge to meet the requirements of the pupil's environment. The end result would be one able to get on with his fellows, pious but wise in the ways of the world, independent and able to look after himself, informed but reticent about his knowledge. Classics and religious study were not to be carried to excess, since Locke held that these subjects had been overrated in the past. Locke's pupil was the well-to-do, civilized young man of the 17th century who knew how to behave in society.

Jean-Jacques Rousseau (1712–78), a forerunner of the Romantic movement *(q.v.),* which despised society and its institutions, put emotion at a higher level than reason. His book *Emile* describes the education of a boy which is natural and spontaneous. Society, he holds, warps the growing mind and therefore·the child should be protected from its influences until his development in accordance with his own nature is so complete that he cannot be harmed by it. During the first 4 years the body should be developed by physical training; from 5 to 12 the child would live in a state of nature such that he could develop his powers of observation and his senses; from 13, books would be used and intellectual training introduced, although only in line with the child's own interests, and he would be given instruction only as he came to ask for it. Moral training and contact with his fellows to learn the principles of sympathy, kindness, and helpfulness to mankind would be given between 15 and 20. Girls, however, should be educated to serve men in a spirit of modesty and restraint. His own five children he deposited in a foundling hospital.

Summary. Broadly speaking, then, there have been four main attitudes to education: (1) religious, with a view to a life beyond death; (2) state-controlled education, with a view to uniform subservience to authority; (3) "gentlemanly" education, with a view to social graces and easy congress in company; (4) the "child-centered" education, which attempts to follow the pupil's inner nature. It is unnecessary to mention the ordinary method of attempting to instill facts without any considerable degree of cooperation between pupil and teacher in order that the former may, with or without interest, follow some occupation in adult life; for this the philosophers did not consider. Today there remain the two fundamental principles: education for the advantage of the state and its ideology or education for individual development and freedom.

Four educationists of the modern period who have influenced us in the direction of freedom were Johann Pestalozzi of Switzerland (1746–1827) who, by trying to understand children, taught the "natural, progressive, and harmonious development of all the powers and capacities of the human being"; Friedrich Froebel (1782–1852) of Germany, the founder of the Kindergarten who, like Pestalozzi, was influenced by Rousseau but realized the need to combine complete personal development with social adjustment; Maria Montessori (1869–1952) whose free methods have revolutionized infant teaching; John Dewey (1859–1952) who held that the best interests of the group are served when the individual develops his own particular talents and nature.

Eleatics, the philosophers of Elea in ancient Greece who, at the time when Heraclitus (*c.* 535–475 B.C.) was teaching that change is all that exists and nothing is permanent, were asserting that change is an illusion. Of the three leaders of this school, Xenophanes asserted that the universe was a solid immovable mass forever the same; Parmenides explained away change as an inconceivable process, its appearance being due to the fact that what we see is unreal; and Zeno (the best-known today) illustrated the same thesis with his famous argument of the arrow which, at any given moment of its flight, must be where it is since it cannot be where it is not. But if it is where it is, it cannot move, this is based, of course, on the delusion that motion is discontinuous. The Eleatics were contemporaries of Socrates.

Empiricism. While not a single school of philosophy, empiricism is an approach to knowledge which holds that if a man wants to know what the universe is like the only correct way to do so is to go and look for himself, to collect facts which come to him through his senses. It is, in essence, the method of science as contrasted with rationalism *(q.v.)* which in philosophy implies that thinking or reasoning without necessarily referring to external observations can arrive at truth. Empiricism is typically an English attitude, for among the greatest empirical philosophers were John Locke, George Berkeley, and David Hume. *See* Rationalism.

Epicureanism. The two great schools of the Hellenistic period (*i.e.* the late Greek period beginning with the empire of Alexander the Great) were the Stoics and Epicureans, the former founded by Zeno of Citium (not to be confused with Zeno the Eleatic) *(q.v.),* the latter by Epicurus, born in Samos in 342 B.C. Both schools settled in Athens, where Epicurus taught that "pleasure is the beginning and end of a happy life." However, he was no sensualist and emphasized the importance of moderation in all things because excesses would lead to pain instead of pleasure and the best of all pleasures were mental ones. Pleasures could be active or passive but the former contain an element of pain since they are the process of satisfying desire not yet satiated. The latter involving the absence of desire are the more pleasant. In fact, Epicurus in his personal life was more stoical than many Stoics and wrote "when I live on bread and water I spit on luxurious pleasures." He disapproved of sexual enjoyment and thought friendship one of the highest of all joys. A materialist who accepted the atomic theory of Democritus, he was not a determinist, and if he did not disbelieve in the gods he regarded religion and the fear of death as the two primary sources of unhappiness.

Epiphenomenalism. *See* **Mind and Matter.**

Erastianism, the theory that the state has the right to decide the religion of its members, wrongly attributed to Erastus of Switzerland (1524–83) who was believed to have held this doctrine. The term has usually been made use of in a derogatory sense—*e.g.,* by the Scottish churches which held that the "call" of the congregation was the only way to elect ministers at a time when, about the turn of the 17th and 18th century, they felt that copalianism was being foisted on them. "Episcopalianism" (*i.e.* Anglicanism) with its state church, ecclesiastical hierarchy, and system of livings presented by patrons was to them "Erastian" in addition to its other "unscriptural practices."

Essenes, a Jewish sect which, during the oppressive rule of Herod (d. 4 B.C.), set up monastic communities in the region of the Dead Sea. They refused to be bound by the scriptural interpretations of the Pharisees and adhered rigorously to the letter of Holy Writ, although with additions of their own which cause them by orthodox Jews today to be regarded as a break-away from Judaism. Among their practices and beliefs were purification through baptism, renunciation of sexual pleasures, scrupulous cleanliness, strict observance of the Mosaic law, communal possession, asceticism. Akin in spirit, although not necessarily identical with them, were the writers of Apocalyptic literature preaching that the evils of the present would shortly be terminated by a new supernatural order heralded by a Messiah who would reign over a restored Israel. The casting out of demons and spiritual healing formed part of these general beliefs which were in the air at that time. The sect has an importance far beyond its size or what has been known about it in the past since the discovery from 1947 onwards of the Dead Sea Scrolls of the Qumran community occupying a monastery in the same area as the Essenes and holding the same type of belief. These scrolls with their references to a "Teacher of Righteousness" preceding the Messiah have obvious relevance to the sources of early Christianity and have given rise to speculations as to whether Jesus might have been influenced by views which, like His own, were unacceptable to orthodox Jews but in line with those of the Dead Sea communities. They seem to show that early Christianity was not a sudden development but a gradual one which had its predecessors.

Eugenics, a 19th century movement largely instigated by the British scientist and mathematician, Sir Francis Galton. Galton argued that many of the most satisfactory attributes of mankind—intelligence, physical strength, resistance to disease, etc.—were genetically determined and thus handed down in the normal process of inheritance. From this he reasoned that selective mating of physically "superior" individuals, and its converse, the controlled limitation on the breeding of criminals or the insane, would lead inevitably to a progressive improvement in the overall standards of the human race. In their simplest form these proposals are incontestable, though they do of course introduce marked restrictions on the choice of the individual for marriage and procreation. Worse yet is the way in which the argument can be misapplied or elaborated—as it was in Nazi Germany—to include the sterilization of alcoholics, confirmed criminals and even epileptics. Nevertheless there remains the feeling that there are some aspects of eugenics which intuitively at any rate make good sense and of course the widespread application of birth control is itself an enactment of eugenic principles.

Evangelicalism, the belief of those Protestant sects which hold that the essence of the Gospel consists in the doctrine of salvation by faith in the atoning death of Christ and not by good works or the sacraments; that worship should be "free" rather than liturgical through established forms; that ritual is unacceptable and superstitious. Evangelicals are Low Churchmen.

Evangelism, the preaching of the Gospel, emphasising the necessity for a new birth or conversion. The evangelistic fervor of John Wesley and George Whitefield (*see* Methodism) aroused the great missionary spirit of the late 18th and 19th century. George Fox, founder of the Society of Friends *(q.v.),* was also an evangelist. Evangelists can be Low, High, or Middle Churchmen.

Existentialism, a highly subjective philosophy which many people connect with such names as Jean-Paul Sartre (1905–80) or Albert Camus (1913–60) and assume to be a post-war movement associated with disillusion and a sordid view of life. However, existentialism stems from Sören Kierkegaard (1813–55), the Danish "religious writer"—his own description of himself—in such works as *Either/Or, Fear and Trembling,* and *Concluding Unscientific Postscript.* Between the two wars translations of Kierkegaard into German influenced Martin Heidegger's great work *Being and Time* and the other great existentialist Karl Jaspers; it has strongly influenced modern Protestant theology notably in Karl Barth, Reinhold Niebuhr, and Paul Tillich and beyond that field the French philosopher Gabriel Marcel, the Spanish writer Unamuno in his well-known *The Tragic Sense of Life,* and Martin Buber of Israel in his *I and Thou.* We have it on Heidegger's authority that "Sartre is no philosopher" even if it is to his works that modern existentialists often turn.

Existentialism is extremely difficult for the non-metaphysically-minded to understand. It deals, not with the nature of the universe of what are ordinarily thought of as philosophical problems but describes an attitude to life or God held by the individual. Briefly, its main essentials are: (1) it distinguishes between *essence, i.e.,* that aspect of an entity which can be observed and known—and its *existence*—the fact of its having a place in a changing and dangerous world which is what really matters; (2) existence being basic, each self-aware individual can grasp his own existence on reflection in his own immediate experience of himself and his situation as a free being in the world; what he finds is not merely a knowing self but a self that fears, hopes, believes, wills, and is aware of its need to find a purpose, plan, and destiny in life; (3) but we cannot grasp our existence by thought alone; thus the fact "all men must die" relates to the essence of man but it is necessary to be involved, to draw the conclusion as a person that "I too must die" and experience its impact on our own individual existence; (4) because of the preceding, it is necessary to abandon our attitude of objectivity and theoretical detachment when faced by the problems relating to the ultimate purpose of our own life and the basis of our own conduct; life remains closed to those who take no part in it because it can have no significance; (5) it follows that the existentialist cannot be rationalist in his outlook for this is merely an escape into thought from the serious problems of existence; none of the important aspects of life—failure, evil, sin, folly—nor (in the view of Kierkegaard) even the existence of God or the truth of Christianity—can be proved by reason. "God does not exist; He is eternal," was how he expressed it; (6) life is short and limited in space and time, therefore it is foolish to discuss in a leisurely fashion matters of life and death as if there were all eternity to argue them in. It is necessary to make a leap into the unknown, *e.g.,* accepting Christ (in the case of the Christian existentialist) by faith in the sense of giving and risking the self utterly. This means complete commitment, not a dependence on arguments as to whether certain historical events did, or did not, happen.

To summarize: existentialism of whatever type seems to the outsider to be an attitude to life concerning itself with the individual's ultimate problems (mine, not yours); to be anti-rationalist and anti-idealist (in the sense of being, as it seems to the believer, practical)—in effect it seems to say "life is too short to fool about with argument, you must dive in and become committed" to something. Sartre who called himself an "atheist existentialist" was apparently committed to the belief that "hell is other people," but for most critics the main argument against existentialist philosophy is that it often rests on a highly specialized personal experience and, as such, is incommunicable.

Existential Psychology, a new if rather diffuse movement in modern psychology with no specific founder but with a number of figures who have, perhaps against their will, acquired leader status. One of the key figures is the British psychiatrist, R. D. Laing, whose radical views on psychotherapy are counted as being heretical by the vast majority of his medical colleagues. Laing holds that many so-called neurotic and psychotic conditions are essentially not "abnormal" and merely represent extreme strategies by which an individual may adjust to environmental and personal stress. Instead of attempting to suppress or eliminate the psychosis in the traditional manner, one should lead the patient through it thus allowing the individual's "unconscious plan" for his own adjustment to be fulfilled.

Exorcism, the removal or ejection of an evil spirit by a ritual or prayer. It is easy to forget that the concept of insanity as representing a disorder of the brain, analogous to physical sickness of the body, is fairly recent in origin. Barely two centuries ago it was considered to be appropriate treatment to put lunatics into chains and beat them daily in the hope that the malevolent beings inhabiting them might be persuaded to depart. Tragically, many of the symptoms of severe forms of mental disorder induce such an apparent change in the personality of the individual as to suggest that an alien individual has indeed taken over their body, and this belief is still common in many parts of the world. Most religious systems have developed some ritual or set of rituals for expelling these demons, and while, not surprisingly, the practice of exorcism by the clergy has declined dramatically in the past century, it is still brought into play now and again in such circumstances as alleged hauntings, poltergeist phenomena, etc. From a scientific point of view, exorcism must be counted as a superstitious rite, but its suggestive power in cases of hysteria, and perhaps even more serious mental illnesses, cannot be completely ruled out. General interest in the topic has been stimulated in part by the resurgence of the practice of Black Magic and witchcraft, largely in the form of experimental dabbling by young people, who no doubt become disillusioned when it fails to live up to its promise. Testimony to the pulling-power of this remnant of our superstitious past is the fact that a sensational and terrifying novel, *The Exorcist,* which its author claimed was based on fact, topped the best-seller lists in 1972, and the even more horrific movie-version became one of the most successful (in box office terms) films of all time. The Church of England, incidentally, takes anything but a dismissive line on the matter, and in fact employs a number of ordained priests as "licensed exorcists". These services are apparently much in demand.

F

Fabian Society. In 1848 (the year of *The Communist Manifesto* by Marx and Engels) Europe was in revolt. In most countries the workers and intellectuals started bloody revolutions against the feudal ruling classes which were no less violently suppressed; hence on the continent socialism took on a Marxist tinge which to some extent it still retains. But at the same time England was undergoing a slow but nonviolent transition in her political and industrial life which led the workers in general to look forward to progress through evolution. Marxism never became an important movement in England even though it took its origin there. There were many reasons for this: the agitation of the Chartists, the writings of Mill, Ruskin, and Carlyle; the reforms of Robert Owen; the religious movement led by the Wesleys; the cooperative societies; the Christian socialists. Furthermore legislation stimulated by these bodies had led to an extension of the franchise to include a considerable number of wage-earners, remedial measures to correct some of the worst abuses of the factory system, recognition of the trade unions, etc.

This was the background against which the Fabian Society was founded in 1884 with the conviction that social change could be brought about by gradual parliamentary means. (The name is derived from Quintus Fabius Maximus, the Roman general nicknamed "Cunctator," the delayer, who achieved his successes in defending Rome against Hannibal by refusing to give direct battle.) It was a movement of brilliant intellectuals, chief among whom were Sidney and Beatrice Webb, H. G. Wells, G. B. Shaw, Graham Wallas, Sidney Olivier, and Edward Pease. The Society itself was basically a research institution which furnished the intellectual information for social reform and supported all contributing to the gradual attainment by parliamentary means of socialism.

The Webbs's analysis of society emphasized that individualist enterprise in capitalism was a hang-over from early days and was bound to defeat itself since socialism is the inevitable accompaniment of modern industrialism; the necessary result of popular government is control of their economic system by the people themselves. Utopian schemes had been doomed to failure because they were based on the fallacy that society is static and that islands of utopias could be formed in the midst of an unchanging and antagonistic environment. On the contrary, it was pointed out, society develops: "The new becomes old, often before it is consciously regarded as new." Social reorganization cannot usefully be hastened by violent means but only through methods consonant with this natural historical progression—gradual, peaceful, and democratic. The Fabians were convinced that men are rational enough to accept in their common interest developments which can be demonstrated as necessary; thus public opinion will come to see that socialization of the land and industries is essential in the same way that they came to accept the already-existing acts in respect of housing, insurance, medical care, and conditions of work.

The Society collaborated first in the formation of the Independent Labour Party and then with the more moderate Labour Party and the trade unions and Cooperative movement. But in general it disapproved of independent trade union action since change should come from the government and take political form. The class war of Marx was rejected and so too was the idea of the exclusive role of the working class—reform must come from the enlightened cooperation of all classes—not from their opposition.

Faith Healing, the belief and practice of curing physical and mental ills by faith in some supernatural power, either allegedly latent in the individual (as with Christian Science) or drawn in some way from God. It is a characteristic of faith healing that it is supposed to be publicly demonstrable—*i.e.,* a "healer" will hold public meetings and invite sick people to come up to be cured on the platform. In the emotionally charged atmosphere which the healer generates, it is not unusual for people to show immediate and striking improvement in their illness, but the almost invariable rule is for relapses to occur within days· or hours after the event. When remission is more permanent, the illness is generally hysterical in origin and will often return to the individual in some other form. Spiritualists claim that the healing in such cases is done not by "faith" but by direct intervention of the spirits of doctors, etc., who have died and passed on to another world. Perhaps the world's most famous faith healer in recent years was Harry Edwards (d. 1976), who had literally millions of letters from all parts of the world asking for the healing attention of his spirit guides. Many doctors, while remaining immensely sceptical about the origins and extent of this kind of therapy, are inclined to admit that it might have benefits when the sickness is mildly hysterical in origin. The real danger, of course, comes when patients seek unorthodox therapy before consulting their doctor.

Fascism. From the end of medieval times with the opening up of the world, the liberation of the mind and the release of business enterprise, a new spirit arose in Europe exemplified in such movements as the Renaissance, the Reformation, the struggle for democracy, the rise of capitalism, and the Industrial Revolution. With these movements there developed a certain tradition, which, in spite of hindrances and disagreement or failures, was universally held by both right- and left-wing parties however strongly they might fail to agree on the best means of attaining what was felt to be a universal ideal. The hard core of this tradition involved: belief in reason and the possibility of human progress; the essential sanctity and dignity of human life; tolerance of widely different religious and political views; reliance on popular government and the responsibility of the rulers to the ruled; freedom of thought and criticism; the necessity of universal education; impartial justice and the rule of law; the desirability of universal peace. Fascism was the negation of every aspect of this tradition and took pride in being so. Emotion took the place of reason, the "immutable, beneficial, and fruitful inequality of classes" and the right of a self-constituted élite to rule them replaced universal suffrage because absolute authority "quick, sure, unanimous" led to action rather than talk. Contrary opinions are not allowed and justice is in the service of the state; war is desirable to advance the power of the state; and racial inequality made a dogma. Those who belong to the "wrong"

religion, political party, or race are outside the law.

The attacks on liberalism and exaltation of the state derive largely from Hegel and his German followers; the mystical irrationalism from such 19th century philosophers as Schopenhauer, Nietzsche, and Bergson; from Sorel (*see* **Syndicalism**) came the idea of the "myth", and an image which would have the power to arouse the emotions of the masses and from Sorel also the rationale of violence and justification of force. But these philosophical justifications of fascism do not explain why it arose at all and why it arose where it did—in Italy, Germany, and Spain. These countries had one thing in common—disillusionment. Germany had lost the 1914–18 war, Italy had been on the winning side but was resentful about her small gains. Spain had sunk to the level of a third-rate power, and people were becoming increasingly restive under the reactionary powers of the Catholic Church, the landed aristocracy, and the army. In Marxist theory, fascism is the last fling of the ruling class and the bourgeoisie in their attempt to hold down the workers.

Italian Fascism. The corporate state set up by Benito Mussolini in Italy claimed to be neither capitalist nor socialist, and after its inception in 1922 the Fascist Party became the only recognized one. Its members wore black shirts, were organized in military formations, used the Roman greeting of the outstretched arm, and adopted as their slogan "Mussolini is always right". Membership of the Party was not allowed to exceed a number thought to be suited to the optimum size of a governing class and new candidates were drawn, after strict examinations, from the youth organizations. The Blackshirts, a Fascist militia, existed separately from the army and were ruled by Fascist headquarters.

At the head of government was Mussolini, "Il Duce" himself, a cabinet of fourteen ministers selected by him and approved by the King to supervise the various functions of government, and the Grand Council or directorate of the Fascist Party, all the members of which were chosen by the Duce. Parliament, which was not allowed to initiate legislation but only to approve decrees from above, consisted of a Senate with life membership and a Chamber of Fasci and Corporations composed of nominated members of the Party, the National Council of Corporations, and selected representatives of the employers' and employees' confederations. Private enterprise was encouraged and protected but rigidly controlled; strikes were forbidden, but a Charter of Labour enforced the collaboration of workers and employers whose disputes were settled in labor courts presided over by the Party. All decisions relating to industry were government-controlled (*e.g.,* wages, prices, conditions of employment and dismissal, the expansion or limitation of production), and some industries such as mining, shipping, and armaments were largely state-owned.

Italian Fascism served as a model in other countries, notably for the German National Socialist Party, in Spain and Japan, and most European nations between the wars had their small fascist parties, the British version led by Sir Oswald Mosley being known as the British Union which relied on "strong-arm tactics", marches and violence. The Public Order Act of 1936 was passed to deal with it. Although fascism in all countries has certain recognizable characteristics, it would be wrong to think of it as an international movement taking fixed forms and with a clearly thought-out rationale as in the case of communism. There have been minor revivals of interest in Fascism in Italy—presumably as a counter move against the considerable inroads being made by the Communist Party in that country and more recently in France with the emergence of the National Front led by M. Le Pen. Spain, however, has reverted to democracy since the death of Franco. *See* **Nazism.**

Fatalism. *See* **Determinism.**

Fetichism, originally a practice of the natives of West Africa and elsewhere of attributing magical properties to an object which was used as an amulet, for putting spells on others, or regarded as possessing dangerous powers. In psychology the term refers to a sexual perversion in which objects such as shoes, brassières, hair, etc., arouse sexual excitement.

Feudalism. The feudal system took its origins from Saxon times and broadly speaking lasted until the end of the 13th cent. It was a military and political organization based on land tenure, for, of course, society throughout this period was based almost entirely on agriculture. The activities of men divided them into three classes or estates. The First Estate was the clergy, responsible for man's spiritual needs; the Second was the nobility, including kings and emperor as well as the lesser nobles; the Third was composed of all those who had to do with the economic and mainly agricultural life of Europe. The praying men, the fighting men and administrators, and the toilers were all held to be dependent on each other in a web of mutual responsibilities.

The theory of feudalism, although it by no means always worked out in practice, was as follows: the earth was God's and therefore no man owned land in the modern sense of the word. God had given the Pope spiritual charge of men, and secular power over them to the emperor from whom kings held their kingdoms, and in turn the dukes and counts received the land over which they held sway from the king. Members of the second estate held their lands on the condition of fulfilling certain obligations to their overlord and to the people living under them, so when a noble received a fief or piece of land he became the vassal of the man who bestowed it. To him he owed military service for a specified period of the year, attendance at court, and giving his lord counsel. He undertook to ransom his lord when he fell into enemy hands and to contribute to his daughter's dowry and at the knighting of his son. In return the lord offered his vassal protection and justice, received the vassal's sons into his household and educated them for knighthood.

The system was complicated by the fact that large fiefs might be subdivided and abbots often governed church lands held in fief from nobles. The serf or toiling man dwelt on the land of a feudal noble or churchman where he rendered service by tilling the soil or carrying out his craft for his manorial lord in return for protection, justice, and the security of his life and land. He was given a share in the common lands or pastures from which he provided for his own needs. In the modern sense he was not free (although at a later stage he could buy his freedom) since he was attached to the soil and could not leave without the lord's permission. On the other hand he could neither be deprived of his land nor lose his livelihood. Feudal tenures were abolished in England by statute in 1660, although they had for long been inopera-

tive. In Japan a feudal system existed up to 1871, in Russia until 1917, and many relics of it still linger on (*e.g.* the *mezzadria* system of land tenure in parts of Italy).

Flying Saucers. In June 1947 an American private pilot, Kenneth Arnold, saw a series of wingless objects flying through the air at a speed which he estimated at thousands of miles an hour. He later told the press that the objects "flew as a saucer would if you skipped it across the water," and the phrase "flying saucers" was erroneously born. What Arnold actually saw has never been satisfactorily explained—it was probably a flight of jet fighters reflecting the sun's rays in a way that made them appear as discs—but since that date literally hundreds of thousands of people all over the world have reported the sighting of strange objects in the sky, coming in a bewildering range of shapes and sizes. Initially the American Air Force launched an official enquiry—Project Bluebook—to attempt to solve the mystery of these "unidentified flying objects" or "U.F.O.s," which finally folded in 1969 after concluding that the bulk of the sightings were probably misinterpretations of natural phenomena and that there was no evidence for the commonly held view that earth was being visited by spacecraft from some other planetary system. A rather similar conclusion was arrived at by the famous University of Colorado project—the Condon Committee—which published its findings in 1968. Despite this clear-cut official attitude, belief in the existence of flying saucers and their origin as alien space vehicles is exceedingly widespread and is held very strongly by people in all walks of life. In 1959 this striking social phenomenon attracted the attention of the psychologist C. G. Jung. He noticed that the press were inclined to report statements that saucers existed when made by prominent people and not publish contrary statements made by equally prominent people. He concluded that flying saucers were in some way welcome phenomena and in his brilliant little book. *Flying Saucers—A Modern Myth,* he hypothesized that the U.F.O.s were the modern equivalent of "signs in the skies." It was Jung's contention that the saucers were looked upon as the harbingers of advanced alien civilizations who had come to save the world from its descent into nuclear catastrophe—archangels in modern dress in fact.

Whatever the validity of this imaginative view of U.F.O.s, it is undeniably true that they exercise a great fascination for millions of people, some of whom invest them with definite religious significance. The best example of the open incorporation of flying saucers into a religious belief system is to be found in the Aetherius Society, an international organization with headquarters in Los Angeles but founded by a former London clerk, George King. Mr. King, who claims to be the mediumistic link between earth and the largely benevolent beings from outer space, regularly relays messages—notably from a Venusian known as Aetherius—to enthusiastic congregations at religious meetings. The sect, which is entirely sincere and dedicated in its beliefs, also makes pilgrimages to the tops of various mountains which have been "spiritually charged" with the aid of the spacebeings in their flying saucers.

Odd though such ideas may seem to most people, they can be readily understood within the context of the very marked decline in orthodox religious belief which we have seen in the past two decades. To an increasing number of people, many of whom feel a desperate need for spiritual guidance and enlightenment, the concepts of the traditionally Western religions seem somehow unsatisfactory. Many therefore turn to cults and splinter groups which use ideas and terminology which to them seem more at home in the twentieth century than those that sprung to life thousands of years ago. To members of the Aetherius Society, for example, the idea that Jesus Christ lives on Venus and rides around in a flying saucer is neither blasphemous nor ludicrous. As long as empty churches testify to the growing, if perhaps only temporary loss of contact between orthodox religions and the man-in-the-street, then one can expect such offbeat ideas as the cults surrounding flying saucers, to expand and flourish.

Freemasonry, a widespread, influential secret organization of English origin. Although it can be traced back to the Middle Ages when itinerant working masons in England and Scotland were organized in lodges with secret signs for the recognition of fellow-members, modern freemasonry first arose in England in the early decades of the 18th century. The first Grand Lodge was founded in London in 1716 and Freemasons' Hall was opened in 1776. With its clubs for discussion and social enjoyment (women were excluded) it met a need and became a well-known feature of English life. The movement quickly spread abroad to places which had direct trade links with England. The graded lodge structure, the social prestige conferred by membership, the symbolism, ritual and ceremony, and the emphasis on mutual help have had a lasting appeal. Interest in the occult had more appeal on the Continent than in England. Until a decade or so ago, membership conferred definite business and social advantages, particularly in small communities where the leading middle-class figures were generally members. Recently this advantage has markedly declined and freemason lodges nowadays tend to be little more than worthy charitable organizations. Fear of secret societies has given freemasonry many opponents; it was condemned by the Roman Catholic Church, banned by fascist dictators, and denounced by the Comintern. A statement from the congregation for the doctrine of the faith in 1981 reminded Catholics that under Article 2335 of the Code of Canon Law they are forbidden under pain of excommunication from joining masonic or similar associations.

Freudian theory. *See* **Psychoanalysis.**

Friends, The Society of. *See* **Quakers.**

Fundamentalism is a term covering a number of religious movements which adhere with the utmost rigidity to orthodox tenets; for example the Old Testament statement that the earth was created by God in six days and six nights would be held to be factual rather than allegorical or symbolic. Although the holding of rigid beliefs in the literal truth of the Bible might seem to be frequently contrary to modern scientific findings, the fundamentalists at least do not have the problems of compromise and interpretation to face, and to some people this is no doubt a great attraction. A factor influencing the present troubles in Northern Ireland is the narrow and intolerant form of fundamentalism represented by the extreme brand of Presbyterianism practiced there.

G

Gestalt Psychology. In the latter half of the 19th cent. it became evident to psychologists that in principle there was no good reason why "mental" events should not be just as measurable and manageable as "physical" ones. Intensive studies of learning, memory, perception, and so on were therefore undertaken and the beginnings of an empirical science of psychology were underway. In the early part of the 20th cent. the experiments of Pavlov (*see* **Behaviorism**) and his co-workers suggested that the behavior of an animal, or even men, might ultimately be reduced to a descriptive account of the activities of nervous reflex loops—the so-called conditioned reflexes. With the publication of Watson's important book on Behaviorism in 1914 it looked as though the transfer of psychological studies from the field of philosophy to that of science could now take place. Actually the over-simplified picture of cerebral and mental pictures which Behaviorism offered was rather comparable to the billiard ball view of the universe so fashionable in Victorian science. Just as Behaviorism implied that there was a fundamental building block (the conditioned reflex) from which all mental events could be constructed, so Victorian physics assumed that the entire universe could be described in terms of a vast collection of atoms pushing each other around like billiard balls. The development of nuclear physics was to shatter the latter dream and at the same time a challenge to the naïve "reflex psychology" came from the Gestalt experimental school.

The founders of this school were Max Wertheimer, Kurt Koffka and Wolfgang Köhler, three young psychologists who in 1912 were conducting experiments—notably in vision—which seemed to expose the inadequacies of the behaviorist position. The Pavlov-Watson view, as we have said, implied that complex sensory events were no more than a numerical sum of individual nervous impulses. Wertheimer's group proposed that certain facts of perceptual experiences (ruled out of court as subjective and therefore unreliable by Watson) implied that the whole *(Gestalt)* was something more than simply the sum of its parts. For example, the presentation of a number of photographs, each slightly different, in rapid series gives rise to cinematographic motion. In basic terms, the eye has received a number of discrete, "still" photographs, and yet "motion" is perceived. What, they asked, was the sensory input corresponding to this motion? Some processes within the brain clearly *added* something to the total input as defined in behaviorist terms. An obvious alternative—in a different sense modality—is that of the arrangement of musical notes. A cluster of notes played one way might be called a tune; played backwards they may form another tune, or may be meaningless. Yet in all cases the constituent parts are the same, and yet their relationship to one another is evidently vital. Once again the whole is something more than the simple sum of the parts.

The implications of all this appeared to be that the brain was equipped with the capacity to organize sensory input in certain well-defined ways, and that far from being misleading and scientifically unjustifiable, human subjective studies of visual experience might reveal the very principles of organization which the brain employs. Take a field of dots, more or less randomly distributed; inspection of the field will soon reveal certain patterns or clusters standing out—the constellations in the night sky are a good illustration. There are many other examples, and Wertheimer and his colleagues in a famous series of experiments made some effort to catalogue them and reduce them to a finite number of "Laws of Perceptual Organization" which are still much quoted today.

Ghosts, belief in ghosts is one of the most common features of supernatural and mystical philosophy. At its roots it is based on the assumption that Man is essentially an individual created of two separate and distinct substances, mind and body. Most religious systems hold to this dualistic view (*see* **Dualism**), arguing that whereas the body is transient and destructible, the mind or spirit is permanent and survives the death of its physical host. The discarnate spirit is normally assumed to progress to some other realm ("Heaven," "Nirvana," "The Spirit World," etc.) whereupon it loses contact with the mortal world. Occasionally, however, for one reason or another, the spirits may not progress and may become trapped and unable to escape the material world. Traditionally this is supposed to occur when the death of the individual is precipitated by some great tragedy—murder, suicide, etc.—when the site of the tragedy is supposed to be haunted by the earthbound spirit. Although the library of the Society for Psychical Research is crammed with supposedly authentic accounts of hauntings of this kind, scientific interest in ghosts has been waning rapidly in recent years. At one time, in particular in the latter part of the 19th cent., with the upsurge of scientific interest in Spiritualism *(q.v.),* there were even at-·tempts to call up ghosts in the laboratory. These led to spectacular opportunities for fraud on the part of Spiritualist mediums and the like, but in the long run added little to the cause of science. As we have said, belief in ghosts is largely dependent upon a parallel belief that the mind or soul of man is something essentially separate from the body. With the decline in belief of this notion (it is now almost totally dismissed by most scientists and philosophers) has come an inevitable decline in belief in ghosts.

Gnosticism. Among the many heresies of early Christianity, especially during its first two centuries, was a group which came under the heading of Gnosticism. This was a system or set of systems which attempted to combine Christian beliefs with others derived from Oriental and Greek sources, especially those which were of a mystical and metaphysical nature, such as the doctrines of Plato and Pythagoras. There were many Gnostic sects, the most celebrated being the Alexandrian school of Valentius (fl. *c.* 136–*c.* 160). "Gnosis" was understood not as meaning "knowledge" or "understanding" as we understand these words, but "revelation." As in other mystical religions, the ultimate object was individual salvation; sacraments took the most varied forms. Many who professed themselves Christians accepted Gnostic doctrines and even orthodox Christianity contains some elements of Gnostic mysticism. It was left to the bishops and theologians to decide at what point Gnosticism ceased to be orthodox and a difficult task this proved to be. Two of the greatest, Clement of Alexandria and his pupil Origen, unwittingly slipped into heresy when they tried to show that such men as Socrates and Plato, who were in quest of truth, were Christian in intention, and by their lives and works had prepared the way for

Christ. Thus they contradicted Church doctrine which specifically said *Extra ecclesiam nulla salus*—outside the Church there is no salvation.

God and Man. The idea of gods came before the idea of God and even earlier in the evolution of religious thought there existed belief in spirits (*see* **Animism**). It was only as a result of a long period of development that the notion of a universal "God" arose, a development particularly well documented in the Old Testament. Here we are concerned only with the views of philosophers, the views of specific religious bodies being given under the appropriate headings. First, however, some definitions.

Atheism is the positive disbelief in the existence of a God. **Agnosticism** (a term coined by T. H. Huxley, the 19th cent. biologist and contemporary of Darwin) signifies that one cannot know whether God exists or not. **Deism** is the acceptance of the existence of God, not through revelation, but as a hypothesis required by reason. **Theism** also accepts the existence of God, but, unlike Deism, does not reject the evidence of revelation (*e.g.,* in the Bible or in the lives of the saints). **Pantheism** is the identification of God with all that exists (*i.e.,* with the whole universe). **Monotheism** is the belief in one God, **polytheism** the belief in many (*see also* **Dualism**).

Early Greek Views. Among the early Greek philosophers, Thales (*c.* 624–565 B.C.) of Miletus, in Asia Minor, Anaximander (611–547 B.C.), his pupil, and Anaximenes (b. *c.* 570 B.C.), another Miletan, were men of scientific curiosity and their speculations about the origin of the universe were untouched by religious thought. They founded the scientific tradition of critical discussion. Heraclitus of Ephesus (*c.* 540–475 B.C.), was concerned with the problem of change. How does a thing change and yet remain itself? For him all things are flames—processes. "Everything is in flux, and nothing is at rest." Empedocles of Agrigentum in Sicily (*c.* 500–*c.* 430 B.C.) introduced the idea of opposition and affinity. All matter is composed of the so-called four elements—*earth, water, air,* and *fire*—which are in opposition or alliance with each other. All these were materialist philosophers who sought to explain the working of the universe without recourse to the gods.

Socrates, Plato, and Aristotle. Socrates (470–899 B.C.) was primarily concerned with ethical matters and conduct rather than the nature of the universe. For him goodness and virtue come from knowledge. He obeyed an "inner voice" and suffered death rather than give up his philosophy. He believed in the persistence of life after death and was essentially a monotheist. Plato (427–347 B.C.) was chiefly concerned with the nature of reality and thought in terms of absolute truths which were unchanging, logical, and mathematical. (*See* **Mind and Matter**.) Aristotle (384–322 B.C.) took his views of matter not from Democritus (atomic view) but from Empedocles (doctrine of four elements), a view which came to fit in well with orthodox medieval theology. Matter is conceived of as potentially alive and striving to attain its particular form, being moved by divine spirit or mind *(nous).* (An acorn, for example, is matter which contains the form "oak-tree" towards which it strives.) Thus there is a whole series from the simplest level of matter to the perfect living individual. But there must be a supreme source of all movement upon which the whole of Nature depends, a Being that Aristotle describes as the "Unmoved Mover", the ultimate cause of all becoming in the universe. This Being is pure intelligence, a philosopher's God, not a personal one. Unlike Plato, Aristotle did not believe in survival after death, holding that the divine, that is the immortal element in man, is mind.

Among the later Greek thinkers the Epicureans were polytheists whose gods, however, were denied supernatural powers. The Stoics built up a materialist theory of the universe, based on the Aristotelian model. To them God was an all-pervading force, related to the world as the soul is related to the body, but they conceived of it as material. They developed the mystical side of Plato's idealism and were much attracted by the astrology coming from Babylonia. They were pantheists. The Sceptics were agnostics.

From *Pagan to Christian Thought.* Philo, "the Jew of Alexandria," who was about 20 years older than Jesus, tried to show that the Jewish scriptures were in line with the best in Greek thought. He introduced the *Logos* as a bridge between the two systems. Philo's God is remote from the world, above and beyond all thought and being, and as His perfection does not permit direct contact with matter the divine *Logos* acts as intermediary between God and man. Plotinus (204–70), a Roman, and the founder of Neoplatonism, was the last of the great pagan philosophers. Like Philo, he believed that God had created the world indirectly through emanations—beings coming from Him but not of Him. The world needs God but God does not need the world. Creation is a fall from God, especially the human soul when enmeshed in the body and the world of the senses, yet (*see* **Determinism**) man has the ability to free himself from sense domination and turn towards God. Neoplatonism was the final stage of Greek thought drawing inspiration from the mystical side of Plato's idealism and its ethics from Stoicism.

Christianity: The Fathers and the Schoolmen. It was mainly through St. Augustine (354–430), Bishop of Hippo in North Africa, that certain of the doctrines of Neoplatonism found their way into Christianity. Augustine also emphasized the concept of God as all good, all wise, all knowing, transcendent, the Creator of the universe out of nothing. But, he added, since God knows everything, everything is determined by Him forever. This is the doctrine of predestination and its subsequent history is discussed under **Determinism**.

In the early centuries of Christianity, as we have seen, some found it difficult to reconcile God's perfection with His creation of the universe and introduced the concept of the *Logos* which many identified with Christ. Further, it came to be held that a power of divine origin permeated the universe, namely the Holy Spirit or Holy Ghost. Some theory had to be worked out to explain the relationships of these three entities whence arose the conception of the Trinity. God is One; but He is also Three: Father, Son (the *Logos* or Christ), and Holy Ghost.

This doctrine was argued by the Apologists and the Modalists. The former maintained that the *Logos* and the Holy Spirit were emanations from God and that Jesus was the *Logos* in the form of a man. The Modalists held that all three Persons of the Trinity were God in three forms or modes; the *Logos* is God creating, the Holy Spirit God reasoning, and God is God being. This led to a long discussion as to whether the *Logos* was an emanation from God or God in another form: was the *Logos* of like *nature* with God or of the same *substance?* This was resolved at the Council of Nicaea (325) when Athanasius formulated the orthodox doctrine against Arius *(q.v.):* that the one God is a Trinity of the same substance, three Persons of the same nature—Father, Son, and Holy Ghost.

St. Thomas Aquinas (1227–74), influenced greatly by Aristotle's doctrines, set the pattern for all subsequent Catholic belief even to the present time. He produced rational arguments for God's existence: *e.g.,* Aristotle's argument that, since movement exists, there must be a prime mover, the Unmoved Mover or God; further, we can see that things in the universe are related in a scale from the less to the more complex, from the less to the more perfect, and this leads us to suppose that at the peak there must be a Being with absolute perfection. God is the first and final cause of the universe, absolutely perfect, the Creator of everything out of nothing. He reveals Himself in his Creation and rules the universe through His perfect will. How Aquinas dealt with the problem of predestination is told under **Determinism**.

Break with Medieval Thought. Renaissance thinkers, free to think for themselves, doubted the validity of the arguments of the Schoolmen but most were unwilling to give up the idea of God (nor would it have been safe to do so). Mystics (*see* **Mysticism**) or near-mystics such as Nicholas of Cusa (c. 1401–64) and Jacob Boehme (1575–1624) taught that God was not to be found by reason but was a fact of the immediate intuition of the mystical experience. Giordano Bruno held that God was immanent in the infinite universe. He is the unity of all opposites, a unity without opposites, which the human mind cannot grasp. Bruno was burned at the stake in 1600 at the instigation of the Inquisition (a body which, so we are told, never caused pain to anyone since it was the civil power, not the Inquisition, that carried out the unpleasant sentences) for his heresy.

Francis Bacon, who died in 1626, separated, as was the tendency of that time, science from religion. The latter he divided into the two categories of natural and revealed theology. The former, through the study of nature, may give convincing proof of the existence of a God but nothing more. Of revealed theology he said: "We must quit the small vessel of human reason . . . as we are obliged to obey the divine law, though our will murmurs against it, so we are obliged to believe in the word of God, though our reason is shocked at it." Hobbes (d. 1679) was a complete materialist and one feels that his obeisance to the notion was politic rather than from conviction. However, he does mention God as starting the universe in motion; infers that God is corporeal but denies that His nature can be known.

From Descartes Onwards. Descartes (1596–1650) separated mind and body as different entities but believed that the existence of God could be deduced by the fact that the idea of him existed in the mind. Whatever God puts into man, including his ideas, must be real. God is self-caused, omniscient, omnipotent, eternal, all goodness and truth. But Descartes neglected to explain how mind separate from body can influence body, or God separate from the world can influence matter.

Spinoza (1632–77) declared that all existence is embraced in one substance—God, the all-in-all. He was a pantheist and as such was rejected by his Jewish brethren. But Spinoza's God has neither personality nor consciousness, intelligence nor purpose, although all things follow in strict law from His nature. All the thoughts of everyone in the world, make up God's thoughts.

Bishop Berkeley (1685–1753) took the view that things exist only when they are perceived, and this naturally implies that a tree, for example, ceases to exist when nobody is looking at it. This problem was solved to his own satisfaction by assuming that God, seeing everything, prevented objects from disappearing when we were not present. The world is a creation of God but it is a spiritual or mental world, not a material one.

Hume (1711–76), who was a sceptic, held that human reason cannot demonstrate the existence of God and all past arguments to show that it could were fallacious. Yet we must believe in God since the basis of all hope, morality, and society is based upon the belief. Kant (1724–1804) held a theory similar to that of Hume. We cannot know by reason that God exists, nor can we prove on the basis of argument anything about God. But we can form an idea of the whole of the universe, the one Absolute Whole, and personify it. We need the idea of God on which to base our moral life, although this idea of God is transcendent, *i.e.,* goes beyond experience.

William James (1842–1910), the American philosopher (*see* **Pragmatism**), held much the same view: God cannot be proved to exist, but we have a will to believe which must be satisfied, and the idea works in practice. Hegel (1770–1831) thought of God as a developing process, beginning with "the Absolute" or First Cause and finding its highest expression in man's mind, or reason. It is in man that God most clearly becomes aware of Himself. Finally Comte (1798–1857), the positivist, held that religion belongs to a more primitive state of society and, like many modern philosophers, turned the problem over to believers as being none of the business of science.

Golden Dawn, Order of, a strange but intellectually influential secret society founded in 1887 by three former Rosicrucians *(q.v.).* The Society, which was but one of the large number of occult organizations which flourished in the latter half of the 19th cent., was particularly interesting because it attracted so many scholarly eccentrics to its ranks. These included the poet W. B. Yeats, the actress Florence Farr, the writers Arthur Machen and Algernon Blackwood and the poetess Dion Fortune. A member with a less savory reputation was the notorious Aleister Crowley who was ultimately expelled from the order for practising Black Magic. Essentially the movement, like others of its kind, professed to offer important secrets of occult knowledge, and taught its followers the basic principles of White, as opposed to Black Magic. Mainly harmless in their aims and activities, societies such as this served largely as pastimes for individuals of intellectual and academic standing who found the concepts and rituals of the Established Church too dull for their inquisitive minds. Most members of the Order of the Golden Dawn, either became disillusioned when the white magic, which they had so arduously studied, failed to provide any genuine supernatural results and gave up in disgust, or broke away to form their own rival groups. Though these often had equally glamorous names and rituals, they tended to be no more successful and themselves vanished into the mists of obscurity. Today so-called White Magic has become fashionable with many young people, no doubt as the result of the almost total collapse of the authority of orthodox religion, but it is noticeable that such interest is generally to be found among the less well-educated and intelligent. White Magic had its intellectual heyday in the 19th century and it is unlikely ever to attract such sustained academic interest again.

Good and Evil.

Early Philosophers' Views. The early Greek philosophers were chiefly concerned with the laws of the universe, consequently it was common belief that knowledge of these laws, and living according to them, constituted the supreme good. Heraclitus, for example, who taught that all things carried with them their opposites, held that good and evil were like two notes in a harmony, necessary to each other. "It is the opposite which is good for us". Democritus, like Epicurus *(q.v.),* held that the main goal of life is happiness, but happiness in moderation. The good man is not merely the one who *does* good but who always *wants* to do so: "You can tell the good man not by his deeds alone but by his desires." Such goodness brings happiness, the ultimate goal. On the other hand, many of the wandering Sophist teachers taught that good was merely social convention, that there are no absolute principles of right and wrong, that each man should live according to his desires and make his own moral code. To Socrates knowledge was the highest good because doing wrong is the result of ignorance: "no man is voluntarily bad." Plato and Aristotle, differing in many other respects, drew attention to the fact that man is composed of three parts: his desires and appetites, his will, and his reason. A man whose reason rules his will and appetites is not only a good but a happy man; for happiness is not an aim in itself but a by-product of the good life. Aristotle, however, emphasized the goal of self-realization, and thought that if the goal of life is (as Plato had said) a rational attitude towards the feelings and desires, it needs to be further defined. Aristotle defined it as the "Golden Mean"—the good man is one who does not go to extremes but balances one extreme against another. Thus courage is a mean between cowardice and foolhardiness. The later philosophers Philo and Plotinus held that evil was in the very nature of the body and its senses. Goodness could only be achieved by giving up the life of the senses and, freed from the domination of the body, turning to God, the source of goodness.

Christian Views. St. Augustine taught that everything in the universe is good. Even those things which appear evil are good in that they fit with the harmony of the universe like shadows in a painting. Man should turn his back on the pleasures of the world and turn to the love of God. Peter Abelard (1079–1142) made the more sophisticated distinction when he suggested that the wrongness of an act lies not in the act itself, but in the intention of the doer: "God considers not what is done but in what spirit it is done; and the merit or praise of the agent lies not in the deed but in the intention." If we do what we believe to be right, we may err, but we do not sin. The only sinful man is he who deliberately sets out to do what he knows to be wrong. St. Thomas Aquinas agreed with Aristotle in that he believed the highest good to be realization of self as God has ordained, and he also agreed with Abelard that intention is important. Even a good act is not good unless the doer intended it to have good consequences. Intention will not make a bad act good, but it is the only thing that will make a good act genuinely good.

In general, Christianity has had difficulties in solving the problem of the existence of evil; for even when one accepts that the evil men do is somehow tied up with the body, it is still difficult to answer the question: how could an all-good God create evil? This is answered in one of two ways: *(a)* that Adam was given free will and chose to sin (an answer which still does not explain how sin could exist anywhere in the universe of a God who created everything); *(b)* by denying the reality of evil as some Christians have chosen to do (*e.g.,* Christian Science *q.v.*). The Eastern religions, on the other hand (*see* **Zoroastrianism**), solved the problem in a more realistic way by a dualism which denied that their gods were the creators of the whole universe and allowed the existence of at least two gods, one good and one evil. In Christianity there is, of course, a Devil, but it is not explained from where his evil nature came.

Later Philosophic Views. Hobbes equated good with pleasure, evil with pain. They are relative to the individual man in the sense that "one man's meat is another man's poison." Descartes believed that the power to distinguish between good and evil given by God to man is not complete, so that man does evil through ignorance. We act with insufficient knowledge and on inadequate evidence. Locke, believing that at birth the mind is a blank slate, held that men get their opinions of right and wrong from their parents. By and large, happiness is good and pain is evil. But men do not always agree over what is pleasurable and what not. Hence laws exist and these fall into three categories: (1) the divine law; (2) civil laws; (3) matters of opinion or reputation which are enforced by the fact that men do not like to incur the disapproval of their friends. We learn by experience that evil brings pain and good acts bring pleasure and, basically, one is good because not to be so would bring discomfort.

Kant (*see* **God and Man**) found moral beliefs to be inherent in man whether or not they can be proved by reason. There is a categorical imperative which makes us realize the validity of two universal laws: (1) "always act in such a way that the maxim determining your conduct might well become a universal law; act so that you can will that everybody shall follow the principle of your action; (2) "always act so as to treat humanity, whether in thine own person or in that of another, in every case as an end and never as a means."

Schopenhauer (1788–1860) was influenced by Buddhism and saw the will as a blind, impelling striving, and desire as the cause of all suffering. The remedy is to regard sympathy and pity as the basis of all morality and to deny one's individual will. This is made easier if we realise that everyone is part of the Universal Will and therefore the one against whom we are struggling is part of the same whole as ourselves.

John Stuart Mill and Jeremy Bentham were both representatives of the Utilitarian school, believing that good is the greatest good (happiness) of the greatest number (*see* **Utilitarianism**). Lastly, there is the view held mostly by political thinkers that good is what is good for the state or society in general.

Graphology, the study of the analysis of human handwriting. There are two approaches to this topic and it is important to separate them clearly. The first involves the attempt on the part of an expert to decide from looking at a signature *(a)* to whom it belongs, and *(b)* whether or not it is forgery. This art is a legitimate, though tricky area of study, and graphologists have been called in as expert witnesses in courts of law. The second approach involves attempts to detect such tenuous variables as character from a study of an individual's handwriting, and the facts here are altogether less clear. Psychologists find it difficult enough to assess character or personality in a face-to-face interview and even when they are equipped with a range of special tests. The general opinion here would seem to be that some slight information might be revealed by a careful study of handwriting, but that the overall effect would be too unreliable for this kind of graphology to be of practical value.

Gurdjieff, Russian-Greek mystic who set up an occult commune near Paris in the 1930s, to which were attracted a host of the intellectual and literary avant-garde of the time. His teachings, which are immensely obscure, are presented in allegorical form in a lengthy philosophical novel, *All and Everything,* which has the peculiar sub-title "Beelzebub's Tales to his Grandson." Opinions as to the merits of Gurdjieff's ideas are strikingly varied: some commentators hold that he was one of the century's leading philosophers, others that he was a brazen confidence trickster with a vivid personality and the gift of making trivial observations sound pregnant with meaning. The truth probably lies somewhere in between the two extremes and, despite the fact that a number of highly intelligent individuals still espouse his cause two decades after his death, most people continue to find his books largely unreadable and his philosophy muddled and pretentious.

H

Homoeopathy, a branch of fringe medicine whose motto *Similia Similibus Curantur* (like cures like) sums up its controversial approach to therapy. In essence the homoeopathists claim that a disease can be treated by administering quite minute doses of a substance which produce symptoms (in the healthy person) similar to those induced by the disease itself. The founder and popularizer of this unusual approach to medicine was the German Samuel Hahnemann who was born in 1775, a friend of the physician Mesmer who propagated hypnotherapy. Hahnemann lived to see his ideas spread across the civilized world and despite the grave theoretical difficulties implicit in the question of how the very minute dosages actually achieve any result at all, it remained a respectable approach of medicine until the latter half of the last century. Even today a number of qualified doctors still employ homeopathic ideas within the framework of the national health service, and the late King George V was treated by the eminent homoeopathist, Sir John Weir, but it seems nevertheless to be in slow but steady decline. This is probably due not to any revealed deficiences in homoeopathy itself, but rather to the extraordinary advances which have been made in orthodox medicine in the last few decades.

Humanism, the term applied to (1) a system of education based on the Greek and Latin classics; and (2) the vigorous attitudes that accompanied the end of the Middle Ages and were represented at different periods by the Renaissance, the Reformation, the Industrial Revolution, and the struggle for democracy. These include: release from ecclesiastical authority, the liberation of the intellect, faith in progress, the belief that man himself can improve his own conditions without supernatural help and, indeed has a duty to do so. "Man is the measure of all things" is the keynote of humanism. The humanist has faith in man's intellectual and spiritual resources not only to bring knowledge and understanding of the world but to solve the moral problems of how to use that knowledge. That man should show respect to man irrespective of class, race or creed is fundamental to the humanist attitude to life. Among the fundamental moral principles he would count those of freedom, justice, tolerance and happiness.

I

I Ching, the Chinese "Book of Changes" which is supposed to provide a practical demonstration of the truths of ancient Chinese philosophy. The method consists of casting forty-nine sticks into two random heaps, or more simply, of tossing three coins to see if there is a preponderance of heads or tails. The coins are cast six times whereupon the head-tail sequence achieved is referred to a coded series of phrases in the book, which are supposed to relate in some way to the question held in the mind when the sticks or coins are being cast. The phrases are without exception vague, and platitudinous remarks such as "Evil people do not further the perseverance of the superior man," etc., abound. Consequently it is not difficult to read into such amorphous stuff a suitable "interpretation" or answer to one's unspoken question. The I Ching might well be looked upon as an entertaining parlor game, but it is currently a great fad in Europe and America and is taken with great seriousness by an astonishing number of people.

Idealism, in a philosophical sense, the belief that there is no matter in the universe, that all that exists is mind or spirit. *See* **Mind and Matter** and **Realism.**

Illuminati, a secret society founded in 1776 by Adam Weishaupt, a Bavarian professor of canon law at Ingolstadt, in an attempt to combat superstition and ignorance by founding an association for rational enlightenment and the regeneration of the world. "He tried to give the social ideals of the Enlightenment realization by conspiratorial means" (J. M. Roberts, *The Mythology of the Secret Societies,* 1972). Under conditions of secrecy it sought to penetrate and control the Masonic lodges for subversive purposes. Among its members were Goethe and Schiller. The order spread to Austria, Italy and Hungary but was condemned by the Roman Catholic Church and dissolved in 1785 by the Bavarian government.

Immortality. The belief in a life after death has been widely held since the earliest times. It has certainly not been universal, nor has it always taken a form which everyone would find satisfying. In the early stages of human history or prehistory everything contained a spirit (*see* **Animism**) and it is obvious from the objects left in early graves that the dead were expected to exist in some form after death. The experience of dreams, too, seemed to suggest to the unsophisticated that there was a part of man which could leave his body and wander elsewhere during sleep. In order to save space, it will be helpful to classify the various types of belief

which have existed in philosophical thought regarding this problem: (1) There is the idea that, although *something* survives bodily death, it is not necessarily eternal. Thus most primitive peoples were prepared to believe that man's spirit haunted the place around his grave and that food and drink should be set out for it, but that this spirit did not go on forever and gradually faded away. (2) The ancient Greeks and Hebrews believed for the most part that the souls of the dead went to a place of shades there to pine for the world of men. Their whining ghosts spent eternity in a dark, uninviting region in misery and remorse. (3) Other people, and there were many more of these, believed in the transmigration of souls with the former life of the individual determining whether his next life would be at a higher or lower level. Sometimes this process seems to have been thought of as simply going on and on, by others (*e.g.,* in Hinduism and Buddhism) as terminating in either non-sentience or union with God but in any case in annihilation of the self as self. Believers in this theory were the Greek philosophers Pythagoras, Empedocles, Plato (who believed that soul comes from God and strives to return to God, according to his own rather confused notions of the deity. If it fails to free itself completely from the body it will sink lower and lower from one body to another.) Plotinus held similar views to Plato, and many other religious sects in addition to those mentioned have believed in transmigration. (4) The belief of Plato and Aristotle that if souls continue to exist after death there is no reason why they should not have existed before birth (this in part is covered by (3), but some have pointed out that eternity does not mean "from now on," but the whole of the time before and after "now"—nobody, however, so far as one knows, held that *individual* souls so exist. (5) The theory that the soul does not exist at all and therefore immortality is meaningless: this was held by Anaximenes in early Greek times; by Leucippus, Democritus, and the other Greek atomists; by the Epicureans from the Greek Epicurus to the Roman Lucretius; by the British Hobbes and Hume; by Comte of France; and William James and John Dewey of America. (6) The thesis, held notably by Locke and Kant, that although we cannot prove the reality of soul and immortality by pure reason, belief in them should be held for moral ends. (For the orthodox Christian view *see* **God and Man, Determinism and Free-will.**) From this summary we can see that many philosophies and religions (with the important exceptions of Islam and Christianity) without denying a future life do deny the permanence of the individual soul in anything resembling its earthly form (*see* **Spiritualism, Psychic Research**).

J

Jainism. The Jains are a small Indian sect, largely in commerce and finance, numbering about 2 million. Their movement founded by Vardhamana, called Mahavira (the great hero), in the 6th cent. B.C. arose rather earlier than Buddhism in revolt against the ritualism and impersonality of **Hinduism** *(q.v.).* It rejects the authority of the early Hindu Vedas and does away with many of the Hindu deities whose place is largely taken by Jainism's twenty-four immortal saints; it despises caste distinctions and modifies the two great

Hindu doctrines of *karma* and transmigration. Jain philosophy is based on *ahimsa,* the sacredness of all life, regarding even plants as the brethren of mankind, and refusing to kill even the smallest insect.

Jehovah's Witnesses, a religious body who consider themselves to be the present-day representatives of a religious movement which has existed since Abel "offered unto God a more excellent sacrifice than Cain, by which he obtained witness that he was righteous." Abel was the first "witness," and amongst others were Enoch, Noah, Abraham, Moses, Jeremiah, and John the Baptist. Preeminent among witnesses, of course, was Jesus Christ who is described in the Book of Revelation as "the faithful and true witness." Thus they see themselves as "the Lord's organization," in the long line of those who through the ages have preserved on earth the true and pure worship of God or, as the Witnesses prefer to call Him, "Jehovah-God."

So far as other people are aware, the movement was founded by Charles Taze Russell (Pastor Russell) of Allegany, Pittsburgh, in 1881 under the name, adopted in 1896, of the Watch Tower Bible and Tract Society, which has continued as the controlling organization of Jehovah's Witnesses. Its magazine, *The Watch Tower Announcing Jehovah's Kingdom,* first published in 1879, and other publications are distributed by the zealous members who carry out the house-to-house canvassing. The movement has a strong leadership.

Their teaching centers upon the early establishment of God's new world on earth, preceded by the second coming of Christ. Witnesses believe this has already happened and that Armageddon "will come as soon as the Witness is completed." The millenial period will give sinners a second chance of salvation and "millions now living will never die" (the title of one of their pamphlets).

The dead will progressively be raised to the new earth until all the vacant places left after Armageddon are filled. There is, however, some doubt about the "goatish souls" who have made themselves unpleasant to the Witnesses, those who have accepted (or permitted to be accepted) a blood-transfusion contrary to the Scriptures, and others who have committed grave sins.

Every belief held by the movement, it is asserted, can be upheld, chapter and verse, by reference to the Scriptures. Witnesses regard the doctrine of the Trinity as devised by Satan. In both wars Witnesses have been in trouble for their refusal to take part in war, and it is only fair to add that six thousand suffered for the same reason in German concentration camps.

Jensenism, name given to the minority group of psychologists and educationalists who, in general, support the view of the American professor, Arthur Jensen. The latter's studies of individual variation in learning and of the genetic factor in mental ability has led him to argue that heredity is more crucial in determining intellectual ability than environment. By implication this has put him and his colleagues at the center of a divisive "race and intelligence" controversy which has acquired some political overtones. In 1978 Professor H. J. Eysenck was physically assaulted by students at a university lecture because he was reputed to be supporting the Jensenist position.

L

Lamaism, the religion of Tibet. Its beliefs and worship derive from the Mahayana form of Buddhism which was introduced into Tibet in 749. The emphasis laid by its founder on the necessity for self-discipline and conversion through meditation and the study of philosophy deteriorated into formal monasticism and ritualism. The Dalai Lama, as the reincarnated Buddha, was both king and high priest, a sort of pope and emperor rolled into one. Under him was a hierarchy of officials in which the lowest order was that of the monks who became as numerous as one man in every six or seven of the population. The main work carried out by this vast church-state was the collection of taxes to maintain the monasteries and other religious offices. Second in power to the Dalai Lama was the Panchen or Tashi Lama believed to be a reincarnation of Amitabha, another Buddha. The last Dalai Lama fled to India in 1959 when the Chinese entered his country. For a brief period following his departure, the Panchen Lama surprised the Western world by publicly welcoming the Communist invasion, but he later renounced the regime and the suppression of Lamaism in Tibet continued unchecked.

Logical Positivism, a school of philosophy founded in Vienna in the 1920s by a group known as "the Vienna circle". Their work was based on that of Ernst Mach, but dates in essentials as far back as Hume. Of the leaders of the group, Schlick was murdered by a student; Wittgenstein came to Britain, and Carnap went to America following the entry of the Nazis. Briefly the philosophy differs from all others in that, while most people have believed that a statement might be *(a)* true, or *(b)* false, logical positivists consider there to be a third category; a statement may be meaningless. There are only two types of statement which can be said to have meaning: (1) those which are tautological, *i.e.,* those in which the statement is merely a definition of the subject, such as "a triangle is a three-sided plane figure" ("triangle" and "three-sided plane figure" are the same thing); and (2) those which can be tested by sense experience. This definition of meaningfulness excludes a great deal of what has previously been thought to be the field of philosophy; in particular it excludes the possibility of metaphysics. Thus the question as to whether there is a God or whether free will exists is strictly meaningless for it is neither a tautological statement nor can it be tested by sense experience.

Luddites, a group of peasants and working men who deliberately destroyed spinning and farm machinery in England in the early part of the 19th century, fearing that such devices would destroy their livelihood. Their name was taken from the eccentric Ned Lud who had done the same in a less organized way two or three decades earlier. The Luddites' worst fears were of course not realized, for far from putting human beings out of work the Industrial Revolution created jobs for a vastly increased population. Luddism, dormant for over a century, is beginning to appear again, if in muted form. Public anxiety about the rapid growth in computer technology is manifesting itself in the form of such groups as the Society for the Abolition of Data Processing Machines, which while not of course dedicated to the physical destruction of computers, urge for social and even governmental checks on the development of such things as "data banks." These are vast computer memory stores listing comprehensive records concerning all the people living in a city or country and able to cross-reference them in a way that has never previously been possible. Luddism is of considerable historical and social significance.

Lycanthropy, the belief that men may, by the exercise of magical powers or because of some inherited affliction, occasionally transform into wolves. The so-called werewolf is an important feature of mid-European folklore and much the same can be said of the were-tigers and were-bears of Africa and the Far East. There is, needless to say, no such thing as a genuine werewolf known to biology, but it is not hard to see how legends of their existence could arise. There are a number of mental illnesses in which men may deliberately or unconsciously mimic the actions of animals and there are a number of endocrinological disorders which may cause gross changes in the features of the individuals, including the excessive growth of hair. In times when the physiological bases of such afflictions were not properly understood, sufferers from such complaints could easily be persuaded, either by themselves or others, that they were in fact wolfmen. Once the mythology of lycanthropy is established in a society, then of course it will be used by unscrupulous individuals for their own ends—for example revenge killings by people dressed as animals—thus helping to perpetuate the legend.

M

Magic, a form of belief originating in very early days and based on the primitive's inability to distinguish between similarity and identity. The simplest example would perhaps be the fertility rites in which it is believed that a ceremony involving sexual relations between men and women will bring about fertility in the harvest. Or the idea that sticking pins in an image of an individual will bring about harm or even death to the real person. Magic is regarded by some as a form of early science in that man in his efforts to control Nature had recourse to magical practices when the only methods he knew had failed to bring the desired results. It filled a gap. By others magic is regarded as an elementary stage in the evolution of religion. It can be said to have served a purpose there too. Yet magic differs from religion, however closely at times it may come to be related with it in this important respect: religion depends upon a power *outside and beyond* human beings, whereas magic depends upon nothing but the casting of a spell or the performance of a ceremony—the result follows automatically.

The idea that "like produces like" is at the roots of imitative magic, and it is interesting to note that in some languages (*e.g.,* Hebrew and Arabic) there is no word for "resembles" or "similar to." Hence one says "All thy garments are myrrh" instead of "are *like* myrrh." It follows that an event can be compelled by imitating it. One engages in swinging, not for pleasure, but to produce a wind as the swing does; ball games are played to get rainy weather because the black ball represents dark

rainclouds; other ball games, in which one attempts to catch the ball in a cup or hit it with a stick, represent the sexual act (as some gentlemen at Lords (cricket grounds, London) may be distressed to hear) and bring about fertility; in medicine until a few centuries ago herbs were chosen to cure a disease because in some respects their leaves or other parts looked like the part of the body affected (*e.g.,* the common wildflower still known as "eyebright" was used in bathing the eyes because the flower looks like a tiny eye). *See* **Witchcraft, Demonism.**

Malthusianism, the theory about population growth put forward by the Rev. Thomas Malthus (1766–1834) in *An Essay on Population* (1798). His three main propositions were (1) "Population is necessarily limited by means of subsistence." (2) "Population invariably increases where means of subsistence increase unless prevented by some very powerful and obvious checks." (3) "These checks, and the checks which repress the superior power of population, and keep its effects on a level with the means of subsistence, are all resolvable into moral restraint, vice and misery." In other words, no matter how great the food supply may become, human reproductive power will always adjust itself so that food will always be scarce in relation to population; the only means to deal with this is by "moral restraint" (*i.e.,* chastity or not marrying), "vice" (*i.e.,* birth-control methods), or misery (*i.e.,* starvation). More specifically, Malthus claimed that while food increases by arithmetical progression, population increases by geometrical progression. It is true that these gloomy predictions did not take place in Malthus's time largely owing to the opening up of new areas of land outside Europe, the development of new techniques in agriculture, the growth of international trade to poorer areas, the increased knowledge of birth-control, and developments in medical science which reduced the misery he had predicted. Furthermore, we now know that as a society becomes industrialized its birth-rate tends to fall. Growth in the world's population has increased from about 465 million in 1650 to *c.* 5,000 million in 1988.

Manichaeism, an Asiatic religion which developed from Zoroastrianism *(q.v.)* and shows the influence of Buddhism and Gnosticism *(q.v.),* being founded by Mani, a Persian who was born in Babylonia, *c.* 216 A.D. Mani presented himself to Shapur I as the founder of a new religion which was to be to Babylonia what Buddhism was to India or Christianity to the West. His aspiration was to convert the East and he himself made no attempt to interfere directly with Christianity although he represented himself as the Paraclete (the Holy Ghost or "Comforter") and, like Jesus, had twelve disciples. His success in Persia aroused the fury of the Zoroastrian priests who objected to his reforming zeal towards their religion and in 276 Mani was taken prisoner and crucified.

Of Mani's complicated system little can be said here, save that it is based on the struggle of two eternal conflicting principles. God and matter, or light and darkness. Although its founder had no intention of interfering with the West, after his death his followers soon spread the religion from Persia and Mesopotamia to India and China. (Manichaeism flourished in China until the 11th cent.) It reached as far as Spain and Gaul and influenced many of the bishops in Alexandria and in Carthage where for a time St. Augustine accepted Manichaeism. Soon the toleration accorded it under Constantine ended and it was treated as a heresy and violently suppressed. Yet it later influenced many heresies, and even had some influence on orthodox Catholicism which had a genius for picking up elements in other religions which had been shown to appeal to worshippers provided they did not conflict unduly with fundamental beliefs.

Marxism. The sociological theories founded by Karl Marx and Friedrich Engels on which modern communist thought is based. Marx and Engels lived in a period of unrestrained capitalism when exploitation and misery were the lot of the industrial working classes, and it was their humanitarianism and concern for social justice which inspired their work. Marx wrote his *Communist Manifesto* in Brussels in 1848 and in his great work. *Das Kapital* (1867), he worked out a new theory of society. Marx showed that all social systems are economically motivated and change as a result of technical and economic changes in methods of production. The driving force of social change Marx found to be in the struggle which the oppressed classes wage to secure a better future. Thus in his celebrated theory of historical materialism he interpreted history in terms of economics and explained the evolution of society in terms of class struggle. (*See* **Dialectical Materialism.**) "In the social production of their means of existence," he wrote, "men enter into definite and unavoidable relations which are independent of their will. These productive relationships correspond to the particular stage in the development of their material productive forces." Marx's theory of historical materialism implies that history is propelled by class struggle with communism and the classless society as the final stage when man will have emancipated himself from the productive process. Marx was the first to put socialism on a rational and scientific basis, and he foretold that socialism would inevitably replace capitalism. His prophecy, however, came to realization not in the advanced countries as he had envisaged but in backward Russia and China. *See also* **Communism.**

Mesmerism, a rapidly vanishing name to denote the practice of hypnosis, which owes its popularity, though not its discovery, to the Austrian physician, Anton Mesmer (1733–1815). Mesmer's contribution was the realization that a large number of what we would today call psychosomatic or hysterical conditions could be cured (or at least temporarily alleviated) by one or another form of suggestion. Mesmer himself relied on the idea of what he called "animal magnetism," a supposedly potent therapeutic force emanating from the living body which could be controlled by the trained individual. Mesmer used wands and impressive gadgetry to dispense the marvellous force and he effected a remarkable number of cures of complaints, hitherto looked upon as incurable or totally mysterious in origin—the most typical of these being hysterical blindness, paralysis or deafness, nervous skin conditions, and so on. Hypnosis, which is a valid if very poorly understood psychological phenomenon even today, would probably have been developed much further had not efficient general anaesthetics such as ether, nitrous oxide, etc., been discovered, thus greatly diminishing its role as a pain reliever in surgery. Mesmer, who was three parts charlatan, never really troubled to think deeply about the cause of his undoubted success.

The first man to treat hysteria as a formal class of illness and who made a scientific attempt to treat it with hypnosis was Ambrose Liébeault (1823–1904). He and his colleague Hippolyte Bernheim (1840–1919) believed: *(a)* that hysteria was produced by suggestion, and particularly by autosuggestion on the part of the patient, and *(b)* that suggestion was a normal trait found in varying degrees in everyone. These conclusions are true, but as Freud showed later are far from being the whole truth.

Messianism. Most varieties of religious belief rely on the assumption that the deity is a supernatural being either permeating the universe or dwelling in some other sphere, and normally inaccessible to man. Where divine intervention is necessary, the deity is traditionally believed to nominate a human being—in the case of Christianity, for example, Jesus is believed to be the actual son of God. Messianic cults introduce a novel variant on the traditional theme. In these a human being is held to be God himself. He may either nominate himself for this role, relying on his own personality or native talent to acquire the necessary following, or for one reason or another large numbers of people may alight on one individual and declare him the Messiah. While it might seem that beliefs of this kind would be confined to earlier epochs in man's recorded history, this is in fact not the case. In the past century, and even within recent decades, a number of individuals have been held by groups to be actually divine. Among these were the Dutchman Lourens van Voorthuizen, a former fisherman who declared himself to be God in 1950 and got large numbers to accept his claim; the Anglican priest Henry James Prince, who did much the same thing in 1850; and of course the famous Negro George Baker, who convinced hundreds of thousands of other Negroes that he was "Father Divine." To simple people the idea that God is to be found on earth and that one may even be personally introduced to him, is an obviously attractive one. The trouble is that all self-styled gods to this present date have sooner or later seriously disappointed their supporters by performing that most human of acts—dying.

Metapsychology. Not to be confused with parapsychology *(q.v.)*. The branch or off-shoot of psychology which goes beyond empirical and experimental studies to consider such philosophical matters as the nature of mind, the reality of free will and the mind/body problem. It was originally used by Freud as a blanket descriptive term denoting all mental processes, but this usage is now obsolete.

Methodism, the religious movement founded by John Wesley in 1738, at a time when the Anglican Church was in one of its periodic phases of spiritual torpor, with the simple aim of spreading "scriptural holiness" throughout the land. Up to that time Wesley had been a High Churchman but on a visit to Georgia in the United States he was much impressed by the group known as Moravians *(q.v.),* and on his return to England was introduced by his brother Charles, who had already become an adherent, to Peter Böhler, a Moravian minister in England. Passing through a period of spiritual commotion following the meeting, he first saw the light at a small service in Aldersgate in May 1738 "where one was reading Luther's preface to the Epistle to the Romans" and from this time forth all Wesley's energies were devoted to the single object of saving souls.

Soon Whitefield, a follower with Calvinist views, was preaching throughout the country and Charles

Wesley was composing his well-known hymns; John's abilities at this time were taken up in organizing the movement described as "People called Methodists." They were to be arranged in "societies" which were united into "circuits" under a minister, the circuits into "districts" and all knit together into a single body under a conference of ministers which has met annually since 1744. Local lay preachers were also employed and to maintain interest the ministers were moved from circuit to circuit each year.

The class-meeting was the unit of the organization where members met regularly under a chosen leader to tell their "experiences" upon which they were often subjected to severe cross-examination.

Methodism, especially after Wesley's death in 1791, began, like other movements, to develop schisms. These were the long-standing differences which the Baptist movement *(q.v.)* had shown too between Arminian and Calvinist sections—*i.e.*, between those who did and those who did not accept the doctrine of predestination. In the case of the Methodists, this led to a complete break in 1811. Then there were differences associated with the status of the laity, or the relationship of the movement with the Anglican Church. The "Methodist New Connection" of 1797 differed only in giving the laity equal representation with the ministers but the more important break of the Primitive Methodists in 1810 gave still more power to the laity and reintroduced the "camp-meeting" type of service. Finally in 1932, at a conference in the Albert Hall in London, the Wesleyan Methodists, the Primitive Methodists, and the United Methodists became one Church, the Methodist Church.

Mind and Matter.

Early Greek Views: Idealism and Dualism. Primitive peoples could see that there is a distinction between those things which move and do things by themselves and others, such as stones, which do not. Following the early state of **Animism** *(q.v.),* in which spirits were believed to have their abode in everything, they began to differentiate between matter or substance and a force which seems to move it and shape it into objects and things. Thus to the Greek Parmenides (fl. *c.* 475 B.C.), who was a philosopher of pure reason, thought or mind was the creator of what we observe and in some way not quite clear to himself it seemed that mind was the cause of everything. This is perhaps the first expression of the movement known as Idealism which says, in effect, that the whole universe is mental—a creation either of our own minds or the mind of God. But from Anaxagoras (488–428 B.C.) we have the clearer statement that mind or *nous* causes all movement but is distinct from the substance it moves. He does not, however, think in terms of individual minds but rather of a kind of generalized mind throughout the universe which can be used as an explanation of anything which cannot be explained otherwise. This is the position known as Dualism *(q.v.)* which holds that both mind and matter exist and interact but are separate entities.

Most people in practice are dualists since, rightly or wrongly, mind and body are thought of as two different things: it is the "common-sense" (although not necessarily the true) point of view. Plato in a much more complex way was also a dualist although he held that the world of matter we observe is in some sense not the genuine world. The real world is the world of ideas and the tree we see is not real but simply matter upon which

mind or soul has imprinted the idea of a tree. Everything that exists has its corresponding form in the world of ideas and imprints its pattern upon matter. Mind has always existed and, having become entangled with matter, is constantly seeking to free itself and return to God.

Plato's pupil Aristotle had a much more scientific outlook and held that, although it was mind which gave matter its form, mind is not *outside* matter, as Plato had thought, but *inside* it as its formative principle. Therefore there could be no mind without matter and no matter without mind; for even the lowest forms of matter have some degree of mind which increases in quantity and quality as we move up the scale to more complex things.

So far, nobody had explained how two such different substances as matter and mind could influence each other in any way, and this remains, in spite of attempts to be mentioned later, a basic problem in philosophy.

Two later ideas, one of them rather foolish and the other simply refusing to answer the question, are typified by the Stoics and some members of the Sceptic school. The first is that only matter exists and what we call mind is merely matter of a finer texture, a view which as an explanation is unlikely to satisfy anyone; the other, that of some Sceptics, is that we can know nothing except the fleeting images or thoughts that flicker through our consciousness. Of either mind or matter we know nothing.

Renaissance Attitude. Christian doctrines have already been dealt with (*see* **God and Man, Determinism and Free-will**), and the past and future of the soul is dealt with under **Immortality.** Nor need we mention the Renaissance philosophers who were really much more concerned about how to use mind than about its nature. When they did consider the subject they usually dealt with it, as did Francis Bacon, by separating the sphere of science from that of religion and giving the orthodox view of the latter because there were still good reasons for not wishing to annoy the Church.

17th-cent. Views: Hobbes, Descartes, Guelincx, Spinoza, Locke, Berkeley. Thomas Hobbes in the 17th cent. was really one of the first to attempt a modern explanation of mind and matter even if his attempt was crude. As a materialist he held that all that exists is matter and hence our thoughts, ideas, images, and actions are really a form of motion taking place within the brain and nerves. This is the materialist theory which states that mind does not exist.

Thus there are three basic theories of the nature of mind and body: idealism, dualism, and materialism, and we may accept any one of the three. But, if we accept dualism, we shall have to explain precisely the relationship between body and mind. In some of his later writings Hobbes seems to suggest that mental processes are the effects of motion rather than motion itself; *i.e.,* they exist, but only as a result of physical processes just as a flame does on a candle. This theory of the relationship is known as *epiphenomenalism.*

Descartes, the great French contemporary of Hobbes, was a dualist who believed that mind and matter both exist and are entirely different entities; therefore he had to ask himself how, for example, the desire to walk leads to the physical motion of walking. His unsatisfactory answer was that, although animals are pure automatons, man is different in that he has a soul which resides in the pineal gland (a tiny structure in the brain which today we know to be a relic of evolution with no present function whatever). In this gland the mind comes in contact with the "vital spirits" of the body and thus there is interaction between the two. This theory is known as *interactionism,* and since we do not accept its basis in the function of the pineal gland, we are simply left with the notion of interaction but without the explanation of how it takes place.

One of Descartes's successors, Arnold Guelinex, produced the even more improbable theory of *psychophysical parallelism* sometimes known as the theory of the "two clocks". Imagine you have two clocks, each keeping perfect time, then supposing you saw one and heard the other, every time one points to the hour the other will strike, giving the impression that the first event causes the second, although in fact they are quite unrelated. So it is with the body and mind in Guelinex's view, each is "wound up" by God in the beginning in such a way as to keep time with the other so that when I have the desire to walk, purely unrelated physical events in my legs cause them to move at the same time. A variety of this theory is *occasionism,* which says that whenever something happens in the physical world, God affects us so that we *think* we are being affected by the happening.

The trouble about all these theories is *(a)* that they really explain nothing, and *(b)* that they give us a very peculiar view of God as a celestial showman treating us as puppets when it would surely have been easier to create a world in which mind and matter simply interacted by their very nature. Spinoza, too, believed in a sort of psychophysical parallelism in that he did not think that mind and body interacted. But since in his theory everything is God, mind and matter are simply two sides of the same penny.

John Locke, another contemporary, thought of the mind as a blank slate upon which the world writes in the form of sensations, for we have no innate or inborn ideas and mind and matter do interact although he does not tell us how. All we know are sensations—*i.e.,* sense impressions. Bishop Berkeley carried this idea to its logical conclusion: if we know nothing but sensations, we have no reason to suppose that matter exists at all. He was, therefore, an idealist.

18th cent. Views: Hume, Kant. David Hume went further still and pointed out that, if all we know are sensations, we cannot prove the existence of matter but we cannot prove the existence of mind either. All we can ever know is that ideas, impressions, thoughts, follow each other. We do not even experience a self or personality because every time we look into our "minds" all we really experience are thoughts and impressions. Hume was quick to point out that this was not the same as saying that the self did not exist; it only proved that we cannot know that it does.

Kant made it clear that, although there is a world outside ourselves, we can never know what it is really like. The mind receives impressions and forms them into patterns which conform not to the thing-in-itself but to the nature of mind. Space and time, for example, are not realities but only the form into which our mind fits its sensations. In other words our mind shapes impressions which are no more like the thing in itself than the map of a battlefield with pins showing the position of various army groups at any given moment is like the battlefield. This, of course, is true. From physics and physiol-ogy we know that the sounds we hear are "really" waves in the air, the sights we see "really" electromagnetic waves. What guarantee do we have that the source is "really" like the impression received in our brain? Kant was the leader of the great German Idealist movement of the 18th cent. which in effect said: "why bother about matter when all we can ever know is mental?"

19th and 20th cent. Views. The Englishman Bradley, and the Frenchman Henri Bergson in the 19th and early 20th cent. both held in one form or another the belief that mind in some way creates matter and were, therefore, idealists, whereas Comte, the positivist *(q.v.),* and the Americans William James and John Dewey, held that mind is a form of behavior. Certain acts (*e.g.,* reflexes) are "mindless" because they are deliberate; others which are intended may be described for the sake of convenience as "minded" (*i.e.,* purposeful). But like the majority of modern psychologists—insofar as they take any interest in the subject—they regarded mind as a process going on in the living body. Is there any reason, many now ask, why we should think of mind as being any different in nature from digestion? Both are processes going on in the body, the one in the brain the other in the stomach and intestines. Why should we regard them as "things"?

Mithraism, a sun-religion which originated in Persia with the worship of the mythical Mithra, the god of light and of truth. It was for two centuries one of early Christianity's most formidable rivals, particularly in the West since the more philosophical Hellenic Christianity of the East had little to fear from it. (Arnold Toynbee has described Mithraism as "a pre-Zoroastrian Iranian paganism—in a Hellenic dress"; Manichaeism as "Zoroastrianism—in a Christian dress".) Mithraism was a mystery-faith with secret rites known only to devotees. It appealed to the soldiers of the Roman Army which explains its spread to the farthest limits of the Roman empire and its decline as the Romans retreated. The religion resembled Zoroastrianism *(q.v.)* in that it laid stress on the constant struggle between good and evil and there are a number of parallels with Christianity. *e.g.,* a miraculous birth, death, and a glorious resurrection, a belief in heaven and hell and the immortality of the soul, a last judgment. Both religions held Sunday as the holy day of the week, celebrated 25 December (date of the pagan winter solstice festival) as the birthday of the founder; both celebrated Easter, and in their ceremonies made use of bell, holy water, and the candle. Mithraism reached its height about 275 A.D. and afterwards declined both for the reason given above and, perhaps, because it excluded women, was emotional rather than philosophical, and had no general organization to direct its course. Yet even today, from the Euphrates to the Tyne, traces of the religion remain and antiquarians are familiar with the image of the sun-god and the inscription *Deo Soli Mithrae, Invicto, Seculari* (dedicated to the sun-god of Mithra, the unconquered). Mithraism enjoyed a brief revival of popular interest in the mid-1950s when workers excavating the foundations of the skyscraper, Bucklersbury House in the City of London, found the well-preserved remains of a Roman Mithraic temple. A campaign to save the temple as a national monument resulted in its now being on open display on a site in front of the skyscraper.

Monasticism. When in the 4th cent. A.D. Constantine

in effect united state and church there were naturally many who hastened to become Christians for the worldly benefits they expected it to bring in view of the new situation. But there were others who, in their efforts to escape from wordly involvement, went into the deserts of North Africa and Syria to live as hermits and so in these regions there grew up large communities of monks whose lives of renunciation made a considerable impression on the Christian world. They were men of all types but the two main groups were those who preferred to live alone and those who preferred a community life. Among the first must be included St. Anthony, the earliest of the hermits, who was born in Egypt c. 250 and who lived alone in a hut near his home for fifteen years and then in the desert for a further twenty. As his fame spread Anthony came forth to teach and advocate a life of extreme austerity, until by the end of his life the Thebaid (the desert around Thebes) was full of hermits following his example. (Not unnaturally, he was constantly assailed by lustful visions which he thoughtfully attributed to Satan.) In the Syrian desert St. Simeon Stylites and others were stimulated to even greater austerities and Simeon himself spent many years on the top of a pillar in a space so small that it was only possible to sit or stand. With some of these men it is obvious that ascetic discipline had become perverted into an unpleasant form of exhibitionism.

The first monastery was founded by Pachomius of Egypt c. 315 and here the monks had a common life with communal meals, worship, and work mainly of an agricultural type. In the Eastern part of the Empire St. Basil (c. 360) tried to check the growth of the extreme and spectacular practices of the hermits by organizing monasteries in which the ascetic disciplines of fasting, meditation, and prayer, would be balanced by useful and healthy activities. His monasteries had orphanages and schools for boys—not only those who were intended for a monkish life. But the Eastern Church in general continued to favor the hermitic life and ascetic extremes. Originally a spontaneous movement, the monastic life was introduced to the West by St. Athanasius in 339 who obtained its recognition from the Church of Rome and St. Augustine introduced it into North Africa beyond Egypt. The movement was promoted also by St. Jerome, St. Martin of Tours, who introduced it into France, and St. Patrick into Ireland. The monastery of Iona was founded by St. Columba in 566. But it must be remembered that the Celtic Church had a life of its own which owed more to the Egyptian tradition than to Rome. Unlike the more elaborate monasteries of the Continent those of the early Celtic Church were often little more than a cluster of stone beehive huts, an oratory, and a stone cross. It had its own religious ceremonies and its own art (notably its beautifully carved crosses and the illuminated manuscripts such as the Lindisfarne Gospel (c. 700) and the Irish Book of Kells dating from about the same time). The Scottish St. Ninian played a major part in introducing Egyptian texts and art to Britain where, mixed with Byzantine influences and the art of the Vikings, it produced a typical culture of its own. Strangely enough, it was the relatively primitive Celts who played almost as large a part in preserving civilization in Europe during the Dark Ages as the Italians have since. It was St. Columbanus (c. 540–615) who founded the great monasteries of Annegray, Luxeuil, and Fontaine in the Vosges country, St. Gall in Switzer-

land, and Bobbio in the Apennines. So, too, it was the Anglo-Saxon Alcuin (c. 735–804) who was called from York by Charlemagne to set up a system of education throughout his empire; the most famous of the monastic schools he founded was at Tours. Among those influenced by him was the philosopher John Scotus Erigena.

Meanwhile from the south, as the disintegrating Roman empire became increasingly corrupt, St. Benedict of Nursia (c. 480–c. 543) fled the pleasures of Rome to lead a hermit's life near Subiaco. Here he founded some small monasteries, but c. 520 made a new settlement, the great monastery of Monte Cassino in southern Italy, where he established a "Rule" for the government of monks. This included both study and work and emphasized that education was necessary for the continuance of Christianity. As his influence spread his Rule was adopted by other monasteries, and schools became part of monastic life. It is not possible to describe the many different orders of monks and nuns formed since, nor the mendicant orders of friars (e.g., Franciscans, Dominicans, Carmelites, Augustinians). Outside the Roman Catholic Church, both Eastern Orthodox and Anglican Christians owe much to the monastic movement. Monasticism, of course, is not peculiar to Christianity and forms a major aspect of Buddhism, especially in the form of Lamaism in Tibet (q.v.).

Monophysitism, a heresy of the 5th cent. which grew out of a reaction against Nestorianism (q.v.). The majority of Egyptian Christians were Monophysites (Mono-physite = one nature)—i.e. they declared Christ's human and divine nature to be one and the same. This view was condemned at the Council of Chalcedon (A.D. 451) which pronounced that Jesus Christ, true God and true man, has two natures, at once perfectly distinct and inseparably joined in one person and partaking of the one divine substance. However, many continued to hold Monophysite opinions, including the Coptic Church (q.v.), declaring the Council to be unoecumenical (i.e. not holding the views of the true and universal Christian Church).

Montanism, a Phrygian form of primitive Puritanism with many peculiar tenets into which the early Christian theologian Tertullian (c. 150–c. 230) was driven by his extremist views that the Christian should keep himself aloof from the world and hold no social intercourse whatever with pagans. The sect had immediate expectation of Christ's second coming and indulged in prophetic utterance which they held to be inspired by the Holy Ghost but which their enemies put down to the work of the Devil.

Moral Re-Armament, a campaign launched in 1938 by an American evangelist of Lutheran background, Frank N. D. Buchman (1878–1961), founder of the Oxford Group Movement, and at first associated with the First Century Church Fellowship, a fundamentalist Protestant revivalist movement. On a visit to England in 1920 Buchman preached "world-changing through life-changing" to undergraduates at Oxford, hence the name Oxford Group. This revivalist movement was based on Buchman's conviction that world civilization was breaking down and a change had to be effected in the minds of men.

Two of the Group's most typical practices were group confession of sins openly and the "quiet time" set aside during the day to receive messages from the Almighty as to behavior and current problems. In the eyes of non-Groupers the confession (often of trivial sins) appeared to be exhibitionist and there was felt to be a certain snobbery about the movement which made it strongly conscious of the social status of the converts.

The Oxford Group gave way to Moral Rearmament, the third phase of Buchmanism. M.R.A. men and women lay stress on the four moral absolutes of honesty, purity, love, and unselfishness. They believe they have the ideas to set the pattern for the changing world and, indeed, claim to have aided in solving many international disputes—political, industrial, and racial. Theologians complained of the Groups that their movement lacked doctrine and intellectual content; M.R.A. is no different in this respect.

The peak of public interest in M.R.A. was probably reached in the 1950s. Like so many movements of its kind it relied heavily for its motive force on the dynamism of its founder and leader. With the death of Dr. Buchman and the unexpected demise at an early age of his most promising protege and successor-designate, the journalist Peter Howard, the movement began to lose its public impact. The phrase "moral re-armament" was coined by the English scientist W.H. Bragg and appropriated by Buchman.

Moravian Church, a revival of the Church of the "Bohemian Brethren" which originated (1457) among some of the followers of Jan Hus. It developed a kind of Quakerism that rejected the use of force, refused to take oaths, and had no hierarchy. It appears to have been sympathetic toward Calvinism but made unsuccessful approaches to Luther. As a Protestant sect it was ruthlessly persecuted by Fedinand II and barely managed to survive. However, in the 18th century the body was re-established by Count Zinzendorf who offered it a place of safety in Saxony where a town called Herrnhut (God's protection) was built and this became the center from which Moravian doctrine was spread by missionaries all over the world. Their chief belief (which had a fundamental influence on John Wesley—*see* Methodism) was that faith is a direct illumination from God which assures us beyond all possibility of doubt that we are saved, and that no goodness of behavior, piety, or orthodoxy is of any use without this "sufficient sovereign, saving grace."

Mysticism, a religious attitude which concerns itself with direct relationship with God, "reality" as contrasted with appearance or the "ultimate" in one form or another. All the higher religions have had their mystics who have not always been regarded without suspicion by their more orthodox members, and, as Bertrand Russell points out, there has been a remarkable unity of opinion among mystics which almost transcends their religious differences. Thus, characteristic of the mystical experience in general, have been the following features; (1) a belief in insight as opposed to analytical knowledge which is accompanied in the actual experience by the sense of a mystery unveiled, a hidden wisdom become certain beyond the possibility of doubt: this is often preceded by a period of utter hopelessness and isolation described as "the dark night of the soul"; (2) a belief in unity and a refusal to admit opposition or division anywhere; this sometimes appears in the form of what seem to be contradictory statements: "the way up and the way down is one and the same" (Heraclitus). There is no distinction between subject and object, the act of perception and the thing perceived; (3) a denial of the reality of time, since if all is one the distinction of past and future must be illusory; (4) a denial of the reality of evil (which does not maintain, *e.g.,* that cruelty is good but that it does not exist in the world of reality as opposed to the world of phantoms from which we are liberated by the insight of the vision). Among the great mystics have been Meister Eckhart and Jakob Boehme, the German religious mystics of the 13th and 16th cent. respectively, Acharya Sankara of India, and St. Theresa and St. John of the Cross of Spain. Mystical movements within the great religions have been: the Zen *(q.v.)* movement within Buddhism; Taoism in China; the Cabalists and Hasidim in Judaism; the Sufis within Islam; some of the Quakers within Christianity.

Mystery Religions. *See* **Orphism.**

N

Natural Law, the specifically Roman Catholic doctrine that there is a natural moral law, irrespective of time and place, which man can know through his own reason. Originally a product of early rational philosophy, the Christian form of the doctrine is basically due to St. Thomas Aquinas who defined natural law in relation to eternal law, holding that the eternal law is God's reason which governs the relations of all things in the universe to each other. The natural law is that part of the eternal law which relates to man's behavior. Catholic natural law assumes that the human reason is capable of deriving ultimate rules for right behavior, since there are in man and his institutions certain stable structures produced by God's reason which man's reason can know to be correct and true. Thus, the basis of marriage, property, the state, and the contents of justice are held to be available to man's natural reason. The rules of positive morality and civil law are held to be valid only insofar as they conform to the natural law, which man is not only capable of knowing but also of obeying.

Protestant theologians criticize this notion. Thus Karl Barth and many others hold that sinful and fallen man cannot have any direct knowledge of God or His reason or will without the aid of revelation. Another theologian, Reinhold Niebuhr, points out that the principles of the doctrines are too inflexible and that although they are the product of a particular time and circumstance, they are regarded as if they were absolute and eternal. In fact, as most social scientists would also agree, there is no law which can be regarded as "natural" for all men at all times. Nor does it seem sensible to suppose that all or even many men possess either the reason to discern natural law or the ability to obey it; whether or not we accept man's free will (and all Protestant sects do not), we know as a fact of science that people are not always fully responsible for their actions and some not at all.

Nazism, the term commonly used for the political and social ideology of the German National Socialist Party inspired and led by Hitler. The term *Nazi* was an abbreviation of Nazional-socialistische Deutsche Arbeiterpartei. Since 1945, neo-Nazi organizations have emerged in Germany, more recently, in South Africa.

Neoplatonism. *See* **Determinism and Free Will** and **God and Man.**

Nestorian Heresy. The 5th cent. of the Christian Church saw a battle of personalities and opinions waged with fanatical fury between St. Cyril, the patriarch of Alexandria, and Nestorius, patriarch of Constantinople. Nestorius maintained that Mary should not be called the mother of God, as she was only the mother of the human and not of the divine nature of Jesus. This view was contradicted by Cyril (one of the most unpleasant saints who ever lived) who held the orthodox view. In addition to his utter destruction of Nestorius by stealthy and unremitting animosity Cyril was also responsible for the lynching of Hypatia, a distinguished mathematician and saintly woman, head of the Neoplatonist school at Alexandria. She was dragged from her chariot, stripped naked, butchered and torn to pieces in the church, and her remains burned. As if this were not enough Cyril took pains to stir up pogroms against the very large Jewish colony of Alexandria. At the Council of Ephesus (A.D. 431) the Western Bishops quickly decided for Cyril. This Council (reinforced by the Council of Chalcedon in 451) clarified orthodox Catholic doctrine (*see* **Monophysitism**). Nestorius became a heretic, was banished to Antioch where he had a short respite of peace, but later, and in spite of his weakness and age, was dragged about from one place to another on the borders of Egypt. We are assured that his tongue was eaten by worms in punishment for the wicked words he had spoken, but later the Nestorian church flourished in Syria and Persia under the protection of the rulers of Persia and missions were sent to India and China.

Nihilism, the name commonly given to the earliest Russian form of revolutionary anarchism. It originated in the early years of Tsar Alexander II (1818–81), the liberator of the serfs, who, during his attempts to bring about a constitutional monarchy, was killed by a bomb. The term "nihilist", however, was first used in 1862 by Turgenev in his novel *Fathers and Children.* See **Anarchism.**

Nominalism. Early medieval thinkers were divided into two schools, those who regarded "universals" or abstract concepts as mere names without any corresponding realities (Nominalists), and those who held the opposite doctrine **(Realism)** that general concepts have an existence independent of individual things. The relation between universals and particulars was a subject of philosophical dispute all through the Middle Ages.

The first person to hold the nominalist doctrine was probably Roscelin or Roscellinus in the late 11th cent., but very little is known of him and none of his works remains except for a single letter to Peter Abelard who was his pupil. Roscelin was born in France, accused twice of heresy but recanted and fled to England where he attacked the views of Anselm, according to whom Roscelin used the phrase that universals were a *flatus voci* or breath of the voice. The most important nominalist was the Englishman William of Occam in the 13th cent. who, once and for all, separated the two schools by saying in effect that science is about things (the nominalist view) whereas logic, philosophy, and religion are about terms or concepts (the Platonic tradition). Both are justified, but we must distinguish between them. The proposition "man is a species" is not a proposition of logic or philosophy but a scientific statement since we cannot say whether it is true or false without knowing about man. If we fail to realize that words are conventional signs and that it is important to decide whether or not they have a meaning and refer to something, then we shall fall into logical fallacies of the type: "Man is a species, Socrates is a man, therefore Socrates is a species." This, in effect, is the beginning of the modern philosophy of logical analysis which, to oversimplify, tells us that a statement is not just true or untrue, it may also be meaningless. Therefore, in all the philosophical problems we have discussed elsewhere there is the third possibility that the problem we are discussing has no meaning because the words refer to nothing and we must ask ourselves before going any further "what do we mean by God", and has the word "free will" any definite meaning?

O

Occam's Razor, the philosophical maxim by which William of Occam, the 14th cent. Franciscan has become best-known. This states in the form which is most familiar: "Entities are not to be multiplied without necessity" and as such does not appear in his works. He did, however, say something much to the same effect: "It is vain to do with more what can be done with fewer." In other words, if everything in some science can be interpreted without assuming this or that hypothetical entity, there is no ground for assuming it. This is Bertrand Russell's version and he adds: "I have myself found this a most fruitful principle in logical analysis."

Occultism. *see,* **Alchemy, Astrology,** and **Theosophy.**

Orgonomy, a pseudo-psychological theory advanced by the German psychiatrist Wilhelm Reich (1897–1957), a pupil of Freud, who was expelled from Germany for attacking the Nazis and who started life afresh in the U.S.A. like so many of his colleagues. Moving quickly away from orthodox psychoanalytic theories, Reich became increasingly obsessed with the view that all living things were permeated with a unique force or energy which he termed "orgone" and which he believed could be photographed and measured with a geiger counter. The key to the successful flow of orgone throughout the body was sexual intercourse and the resulting orgasm (hence "orgone"). Reich achieved a substantial following for his increasingly bizarre views and when he was sentenced to two-years' imprisonment in 1956 for alleged medical malpractice a "civil rights" controversy developed which has not died down to this date. His unfortunate and rather tragic death in prison has fanned the emotional issues and granted him the important role of martyr to his cause.

Orphism. The Greeks in general thought very little of their gods, regarding them as similar human beings with human failings and virtues although on a larger scale. But there was another aspect of Greek religion which was passionate, ecstatic, and secret, dealing with the worship of various figures among whom were Bacchus or Dionysus, Orpheus, and Demeter and Persephone of the Eleusinian Mysteries. Dionysus (or Bacchus) was originally a god from Thrace where the people were primitive farmers naturally interested in fertility cults. Dionysus was the god of fertility who only later came to be associated with wine and the divine madness it produces. He assumed the form of a man or a bull and his worship by the time it arrived in Greece became associated with women (as was the case in most of the Mystery Religions) who spent nights on the hills dancing and possibly drinking wine in order to stimulate ecstasy; an unpleasant aspect of the cult was the tearing to pieces of wild animals whose flesh was eaten raw. Although the cult was disapproved of by the orthodox and, needless to say, by husbands, it existed for a long time.

This primitive and savage religion in time was modified by that attributed to Orpheus whose cult was more spiritualized, ascetic, and substituted mental for physical intoxication. Orpheus may have been a real person or a legendary hero and he, too, is supposed to have come from Thrace, but his name indicates that he, or the movement associated with him, came from Crete and originally from Egypt, which seems to have been the source of many of its doctrines. Crete, it must be remembered, was the island through which Egypt influenced Greece in other respects. Orpheus is said to have been a reformer who was torn to pieces by the Maenad worshippers of Dionysus. The Orphics believed in the transmigration of souls and that the soul after death might obtain either eternal bliss or temporary or permanent torment according to its way of life upon earth. They held ceremonies of purification and the more orthodox abstained from animal food except on special occasions when it was eaten ritually. Man is partly earthly, partly heavenly, and a good life increases the heavenly part so that, in the end, he may become one with Bacchus and be called a "Bacchus".

The religion had an elaborate theology. As the Bacchic rites were reformed by Orpheus, so the Orphic rites were reformed by Pythagoras (*c.* 582 –*c.* 507 B.C.) who introduced the mystical element into Greek philosophy, which reached its heights in Plato. Other elements entered Greek life from Orphism. One of these was feminism which was notably lacking in Greek civilization outside the Mystery Religions. The other was the drama which arose from the rites of Dionysus. The mysteries of Eleusis formed the most sacred part of the Athenian state religion, and it is clear that they had to do with fertility rites also, for they were in honour of Demeter and Persephone and all the myths speak of them as being associated with the supply of corn to the country. Without being provocative, it is accepted by most anthropologists and many theologians that Christianity, just as it accepted elements of Gnossticism and Mithraism, accepted elements from the Mystery Religions as they in turn must have done from earlier cults. The miraculous birth, the death and resurrection the sacramental feast of bread and wine, symbolizing the eating of the flesh and drinking of the blood of the god, all these are common elements in early religions and not just in one. None of this means that what we are told about Jesus is not true, but it surely does mean: *(a)* that Christianity was not a sudden development; *(b)* that the early Church absorbed many of the elements of other religions; *(c)* that perhaps Jesus Himself made use of certain symbols which He knew had a timeless significance for man and invested them with new meaning.

P

Pantheism. *See* **God and Man.**

Papal Infallibility. The basis of papal infallibility is *(a)* that every question of morals and faith is not dealt with in the Bible so it is necessary that there should be a sure court of appeal in case of doubt, and this was provided by Christ when he established the Church as His Teaching Authority upon earth; *(b)* ultimately this idea of the teaching function of the Church shapes the idea of papal infallibility which asserts that the Pope, when speaking officially on matters of faith or morals, is protected by God against the possibility of error. The doctrine was proclaimed in July 1870.

Infallibility is a strictly limited gift which does not mean that the Pope has extraordinary intelligence, that God helps him to find the answer to every conceivable question, or that Catholics have to accept the Pope's views on politics. He can make mistakes or fall into sin, his scientific or historical opinions may be quite wrong, he may write books that are full of errors. Only in two limited spheres is he infallible and in these only when he speaks officially as the supreme teacher and lawgiver of the Church, defining a doctrine that must be accepted by all its members. When, after studying a problem of faith or morals as carefully as possible, and with all available help from expert consultants, he emerges with the Church's answer—on these occasions it is not strictly an answer, it is *the* answer.

Historically speaking, the Roman Catholic Church of the early 19th century was at its lowest ebb of power. Pope Pius IX, in fear of Italian nationalism, revealed his reactionary attitude by the feverish declaration of new dogmas, the canonization of new saints, the denunciation of all modern ideals in the Syllabus of Errors, and the unqualified defence of his temporal power against the threat of Garibaldi. It is not too much to say that everything regarded as important by freedom-loving and democratic people was opposed by the papacy at that time. In 1870, after a long and sordid struggle, the Vatican Council, convened by Pius IX, pronounced the definition of his infallibility. Döllinger, a German priest and famous historian of the Church, was excommunicated because, like many others, he refused to accept the new dogma. It is difficult not to doubt that there was some connection between the pronouncement of the Pope's infallibility and his simultaneous loss of temporal power.

After the humanism of the Second Vatican Council (1962–5) Pope Paul's encyclical *Humanae Vitae* (1968), condemning birth control, came as a great disappointment to the many people (including theologians, priests, and laymen) who had expected there would be a change in the Church's teaching. The Church's moral guidance on this controversial issue, however, does not involve the doctrine of infallibility. (The Roman Catholic Church teaches that papal pronouncements are infallible only when they are specifically defined as such.) That there is unlikely to be any immediate softening of the Church's line on infallibility was made clear in July 1973 when the Vatican's Sacred Congregation for the Doctrine of the Faith published a document strongly reaffirming papal infallibility. The document also reminded Catholics of their obligation to accept the Catholic Church's unique claims to authenticity.

Parapsychology, the name given to the study of psychical research *(q.v.)* as an academic discipline, and chosen to denote the topic's supposed status as a branch of psychology. The impetus behind parapsychology came from the psychologist William MacDougall who persuaded Duke University in North Carolina to found a department of parapsychology under J. B. Rhine. Throughout the 1930s and '40s the work of Rhine and his colleagues, who claimed to have produced scientific evidence for the existence of ESP, attracted worldwide attention. Increasing reservations about the interpretation of Rhine's results and an apparent lack of any readily repeatable experiments, however, gradually eroded scientific confidence in the topic. The academic status of parapsychology is at the present time exceedingly uncertain. Rhine retired from university life in 1965 and the world-famous parapsychology laboratory at Duke University was closed. On the other hand the American Association for the Advancement of Science recently admitted the Parapsychology Association (the leading organization for professional parapsychologists) as an affiliated member society. An American government body, the National Institute of Mental Health, has also officially supported some medical research into alleged telepathic dreams, the first "official" grant support of this kind. In Britain a poll of readers in the weekly journal, *New Scientist,* revealed a very high interest in the subject matter of parapsychology, and active research is currently going on at the Dept. of Psychology at Cambridge. Stories of intensive parapsychological research in Soviet Russia are however without foundation and are not supported by Western parapsychologists who have visited Russia.

Parsees. *See* **Zoroastrianism.**

Pavlovian theory. *See* **Behaviorism.**

Pentecostalism, a religious movement within the Protestant churches, holding the belief that an essential feature of true Christianity is a vigorous and profound spiritual or mystical experience which occurs after, and seemingly reinforces the initial conversion. The origins of modern Pentecostalism appear to lie in the occasion on 1 January 1901 when a member of a Bible College in Topeka, Kansas, one Agnes N. Ozman, spontaneously began to speak in an apparently unknown language at one of the college's religious meetings. This "speaking in tongues" was assumed to be evidence of her conversion and "spirit baptism", and became a feature of most Pentecostal meetings in due course. The movement spread rapidly across America, particularly in rural communities, and also was a strong feature of Welsh religious life in the early part of the century. Pentecostal services are enthusiastic and rousing with a strong emphasis on music and participation on the part of the congregation. Pentecostalism is evangelistic in nature and seems to be gaining in strength at the present time, at the expense of more orthodox and staid versions of Christianity. The fiery character Aimee Semple McPherson was one of its most prominent evangelists.

Phrenology, a psychological "school" founded in 1800 by two Germans, Franz Josef Gall and Johann Gaspar Spurzheim. Gall was an anatomist who believed there to be some correspondence between mental faculties and the shape of the head. He tested these ideas in prisons and mental hospitals and began to lecture on his findings, arousing a great deal of interest throughout both Europe and America, where his doctrines were widely accepted. Phrenology became fashionable, and people would go to "have their bumps read" as later men and women of fashion have gone to be psychoanalyzed. Roughly speaking, Gall divided the mind into thirty-seven faculties such as destructiveness, suavity, self-esteem, conscientiousness, and so on, and claimed that each of these was located in a definite area of the brain. He further claimed that the areas in the brain corresponded to "bumps" on the skull which could be read by the expert, thus giving a complete account of the character of the subject. In fact, *(a)* no such faculties are located in the brain anywhere, for this is simply not the way the brain works; *(b)* the faculties described by Gall are not pure traits which cannot be further analysed and are based on a long outdated psychology; *(c)* the shape of the brain bears no specific relationship to the shape of the skull. Phrenology is a pseudo-science; there is no truth in it whatever. But, even so, like astrology, it still has its practitioners.

Physiocrats. A French school of economic thought during the 18th cent., known at the time as *Les Economistes* but in later years named physiocrats by Du Pont de Nemours, a member of the School. Other members were Quesnay, Mirabeau, and the great financier Turgot. The physiocrats held the view, common to the 18th cent., and deriving ultimately from Rousseau, of the goodness and bounty of nature and the goodness of man "as he came from the bosom of nature". The aim of governments, therefore, should be to conform to nature; and so long as men do not interfere with each other's liberty and do not combine among themselves, governments should leave them free to find their own salvation. Criminals, madmen, and monopolists should be eliminated. Otherwise the duty of government is *laissez-faire, laissez passer.* From this follows the doctrine of free trade between nations on grounds of both justice and economy; for the greater the competition the more will each one strive to economize the cost of his labour to the general advantage. Adam Smith, although not sharing their confidence in human nature, learned much from the physiocrats, eliminated their errors, and greatly developed their teaching.

Physiognomy. *See* **Characterology.**

Plymouth Brethren, a religious sect founded by John Nelson Darby, a minister of the Protestant Church of Ireland, and Edward Cronin a former Roman Catholic, in 1827. Both were dissatisfied with the lack of spirituality in their own and other churches and joined together in small meetings in Dublin every Sunday for "the breaking of bread". Soon the movement began to spread through Darby's travels and writings and he finally settled in Plymouth, giving the popular name to the "Brethren". Beginning as a movement open to all who felt the need to "keep the unity of the Spirit", it soon exercized the right to exclude all who had unorthodox views and split up into smaller groups. Among these the main ones were the "Exclusives", the Kellyites, the Newtonites, and "Bethesda" whose main differences were over problems of church government or prophetical powers. Some of these are further split among themselves. Readers of *Father and Son* by Sir Edmund Gosse, which describes life with his father, the eminent naturalist Philip Gosse, who belonged to the Brethren, will recall how this basically kind, honest, and learned man was led through their teachings to acts of unkindness (*e.g.,* in refusing to allow his son and other members of his household to celebrate Christmas and throwing out the small tokens they had secretly bought), and lack of scientific rigor (*e.g.,* in refusing for religious reasons alone to accept Darwinism when all his evidence pointed towards it).

Today, the majority of Brethren belong to the "Open Brethren" assemblies and, unlike the "Exclusives" hold that the Lord's Supper (a commemorative act of "breaking the bread" observed once a week) is for all Christians who care to join them. Baptism is required and Brethren believe in the personal premillennial second coming of Christ.

Poltergeist, allegedly a noisy type of spirit which specializes in throwing things about, making loud thumpings and bangings, and occasionally bringing in "apports", *i.e.,* objects from elsewhere. Most so-called poltergeist activities are plain frauds, but the others are almost invariably associated with the presence in the house of someone (often, but not always a child) who is suffering from an adolescent malaise or an epileptic condition. The inference is that those activities which are not simply fraudulent are either due to some unknown influence exuded by such mentally disturbed people, or that they are actually carried out by ordinary physical means by such people when in an hysterical state—*i.e.,* unconsciously. The second hypothesis is much the more probable. *See* **Psychic Research.**

Polytheism. *See* **God and Man.**

Positivism, also known as the **Religion of Humanity,** was founded by Auguste Comte (1798–1857), a famous mathematician and philosopher born in Montpellier, France. His views up to the end of the century attracted many and it would have been impossible throughout that time to read a book on philosophy or sociology that did not mention them, but today his significance is purely of historical interest. In his *Cours de Philosophie Positive* (1830) he put forward the thesis that mankind had seen three great stages in human thought: (1) the theological, during which man seeks for supernatural causes to explain nature and invents gods and devils; (2) the metaphysical, through which he thinks in terms of philosophical and metaphysical abstractions; (3) the last positive or scientific stage when he will proceed by experimental and objective observation to reach in time "positive truth".

Broadly speaking, there is little to complain of in this analysis; for there does seem to have been some sort of general direction along these lines. However, Comte was not satisfied with having reached this point and felt that his system demanded a religion and, of course, one that was "scientific". This religion was to be the worship of Humanity in place of the personal Deity of earlier times, and for it he supplied not only a Positive Catechism but a treatise on Sociology in which he declared himself the High Priest of the cult. Since, as it stood, the religion was likely to appear somewhat abstract to many, Comte drew up a list óf historical characters whom he regarded as worthy of the same sort of adoration as Catholics accord to their saints. The new Church attracted few members, even among those who had a high regard for Comte's scientific work, and its only significant adherents were a small group of Oxford scholars and some in his own country. Frederic Harrison was the best-known English adherent and throughout his life continued to preach Comtist doctrines in London to diminishing audiences.

Pragmatism, a typically American school of philosophy which comes under the heading of what Bertrand Russell describes as a "practical" as opposed to a "theoretical" philosophy. Whereas the latter, to which most of the great philosophical systems belong, seeks disinterested knowledge for its own sake, the former *(a)* regards action as the supreme good, *(b)* considers happiness an effect and knowledge a mere instrument of successful activity.

The originator of pragmatism is usually considered to have been the psychologist William James (1842–1910) although he himself attributed its basic principles to his life-long friend, the American philosopher, Charles Sanders Peirce (1839–1914). The other famous pragmatist is John Dewey, best-known in Europe for his works on education (for although American text-books on philosophy express opinions to the contrary, few educated people in Europe have taken the slightest interest in pragmatism and generally regard it as an eccentricity peculiar to Americans). James in his book *The Will to Believe* (1896) points out that we are often compelled to take a decision where no adequate theoretical grounds for a decision exist; for even to do nothing is to decide. Thus in religion we have a right to adopt a believing attitude although not intellectually fully convinced. We should believe truth and shun error, but the failing of the sceptical philosopher is that he adheres only to the latter rule and thus fails to believe various truths which a less cautious man will accept. If believing truth and avoiding error are equally important, then it is a good idea when we are presented with an alternative to believe one of the possibilities at will, since we then have an even chance of being right, whereas we have none if we suspend judgment. The function of philosophy, according to James, is to find out what difference it makes to the individual if a particular philosophy or world-system is true: "An idea is 'true' so long as to believe it is profitable to our lives" and, he adds, the truth is only the expedient in our way of thinking . . . in the long run and on the whole of course". Thus "if the hypothesis of God works satisfactorily in the widest sense of the word, it is true". Bertrand Russell's reply to this assertion is: "I have always found that the hypothesis of Santa Claus 'works satisfactorily in the widest sense of the word'; therefore 'Santa Claus exists' is true, although Santa Claus does not exist." Russell adds that James's concept of truth simply omits as unimportant the question whether God really *is* in His heaven; if He is a useful hypothesis that is enough. "God the Architect of the Cosmos is forgotten; all that is remembered is belief in God, and its effects upon the creatures inhabiting our petty planet. No wonder the Pope condemned the pragmatic defence of religion."

Predestination. *See* **Calvinism.**

Presbyterianism, a system of ecclesiastical government of the Protestant churches which look back to John Calvin as their Reformation leader. The ministry consists of presbyters who are all of equal rank. Its doctrinal standards are contained in the *Westminster Confession of Faith* (1647) which is, in general, accepted by English, Scottish, and American Presbyterians as the most thorough and logical statement in existence of the Calvinist creed.

The Presbyterian tradition includes uncompromising stress upon the Word of God contained in the Scriptures of the Old and New Testaments as the supreme rule of faith and life, and upon the value of a highly trained ministry, which has given the Church of Scotland a high reputation for scholarship and has in turn influenced the standard of education in Scotland. The unity of the Church is guaranteed by providing for democratic representation in a hierarchy of courts (unlike the Anglican Church, which is a hierarchy of persons). The local kirk session consists of the minister and popularly elected elders (laymen). Ministers, elected by their flocks, are ordained by presbyters (ministers already ordained). Above the kirk session is the court of the presbytery which has jurisdiction over a specified area; above that the court of synod which rules over many presbyteries; and finally the General Assembly which is the Supreme Court of the Church with both judicial and legislative powers, and over which the Moderator of the General Assembly presides. The function of the elders is to help the minister in the work and government of the kirk. The episcopacy set up by James VI and I, and maintained by Charles I was brought to an end by the Glasgow Assembly (1638), but General Assemblies were abolished by Oliver Cromwell and at the Restoration Charles II reestablished episcopacy. The Covenanters who resisted were hunted down, imprisoned, transported, or executed over a period of nearly thirty years before William of Orange came to the throne and Presbyterianism was re-established (1690). Today Presbyterians no less than other Christian communities are looking at Christianity as a common world religion in the sense that the principles which unite them are greater than those which divide them. A small but significant step in the direction of international Christian unity was made in 1972 when the Presbyterian and Congregationalist Churches in England were merged to form the United Reformed Church. *See* **Calvinism.**

Psychic Research is a general term for the various approaches to the scientific investigation of the paranormal, in particular supposed extrasensory powers of the mind, but also manifestations such as ghosts, poltergeists, spiritualistic phenomena, etc. In recent years the word parapsychology has also come into use, particularly for the investigation of ESP in a laboratory setting, but it is really part of psychic research as the subject's fascinating history reveals.

For all recorded history, and no doubt very much earlier, man has been puzzled at his apparent ability to perceive features of the universe without the use of the normal senses—mind-to-mind contact, dreams about the future which come true, etc. He has also been intrigued by the notion that in addition to the natural world of people and things, there exists in parallel, a *supernatural* world of ghosts, spirits and other similar strange manifestations. Belief in such oddities has been tremendously widespread and still forms one of the major casual conversational topics raised when people see each other socially today. Of course, until the 19th cent. or thereabouts such phenomena, while bizarre, unpredictable and possibly frightening, were not at odds with man's view of himself and his world as revealed through basic religious beliefs. Man was supposed to be in essence a supernatural being with eternal life, and the world was seen as the happy hunting ground of dynamic evil forces which could intervene directly in the lives of humans. The rise of material science in the 19th cent. however began to shake the orthodox religious framework, and as a result in due course scientists began to question the basis of all supernatural powers and manifestations, putting forward the reasonable argument: "if such things *are* real then they should be demonstrable in scientific terms—just as all other aspects of the universe are."

Once having advanced this argument, the next step was to carry it to its conclusion and set about the systematic investigation of the phenomena to see whether they *did* conform in any way to the immensely successful framework of 19th cent. science, and from this step psychic research was born. In fact one can date its origins rather precisely—to 1882 when a group of scholars formed the Society for Psychical Research in London—an organization which still exists today. The first experiments in this slightly eccentric field of science were haphazard and tended to be confined to spiritualistic phenomena such as table tapping, mediumistic messages, ectoplasmic manifestations, etc., which were having a great wave of popularity among the general public at the time. In fact what one might term as the first phase of psychic research—it has gone through three phases in its history—was really heavily tied up with Spiritualism. Before ridiculing it for this, it is only fair to point out that many of the most eminent figures of the time—the great physicists Sir Oliver Lodge and Sir William Crookes, Alfred Russell Wallace, co-discoverer with Darwin of the theory of evolution by natural selection, the brilliant author and creator of Sherlock Holmes, Sir Arthur Conan Doyle, and many others—became convinced Spiritualists as the result of their early experiments. Nevertheless, despite the ardent support of such intellectual giants, medium after medium was in due course detected in fraud sometimes of the most blatant kind—and the majority of scientists gradually became more critical and less likely to be taken in by even the subtlest of trickery. As a result, interest slowly shifted from the séance room to a different realm, and as it did so the first phase of psychic research drew to a close.

The second phase was, broadly speaking, the era of the ghost hunter. With the idea of spirits materializing in laboratories seeming intrinsically less and less credible, scientists began to study what struck them at the time to be basically more "plausible" matters—haunted houses, poltergeist phenomena and so on. For some reason the idea of a house dominated by a psychic presence as the result of some tragic history seemed (at the turn of the century) *somehow* scientifically and philosophically more acceptable than did the old Spiritualist notions about direct communication with the spirit world. The key figure in the "ghost hunting" era was Mr. Harry Price, an amateur magician who became the scourge of fraudulent mediums, but who staked his name and credibility on the authenticity of the alleged poltergeist phenomena at Borley Rectory in Suffolk, which became world famous through his book, *The Most Haunted House in England*. The ancient rectory's catalogue of ghosts and marvels allegedly witnessed by numerous "reliable witnesses" seemed irrefutable. Unfortunately investigations by the Society for Psychical Research some years after Price's death now make it seem certain that Price was responsible for faking some of the Borley phenomena himself, and with these disclosures scientifically "respectable" ghost hunting took a nasty tumble. Thus, with an increasingly critical attitude developing among scientists, haunted houses and poltergeists gradually began to shift out of favor to usher in the third phase of psychic research.

The date of the commencement of this phase can be identified as 1927 when the Parapsychology Laboratory at Duke University in North Carolina was formed by Dr. J. B. Rhine. Here the emphasis was on laboratory studies along the traditional lines of experimental psychology; spirit forms and poltergeists were ignored in favor of the routine testing of literally thousands of people for telepathy, precognition (the ability to see into the future), etc., almost always involving card tests which could be rigidly controlled and the results statistically analysed. By the 1940s Rhine was claiming irrefutable evidence of telepathy achieved by these means, but once again critical forces began to gather and it was pointed out that results obtained in Rhine's laboratory rarely seemed to be replicable in other scientists' laboratories in different parts of the world. In fact the failure of ESP experiments of this kind to be easily repeatable has turned out to be crucial and has led to a growing scepticism on the part of uncommitted scientists who now question whether psychic research and parapsychology have really advanced our understanding of the world of the paranormal in any way. At the present time the topic is in a highly controversial phase.

Although Rhine's university parapsychology laboratory closed with his retirement in 1965 research in the field has continued ever since, especially with the work of Dr. Helmut Schmidt who has made important contributions. In recent years a new Chair and research laboratory has been introduced at the University of Utrecht in the Netherlands.

To sum up the topic one could say that in a curious way, while the third phase of psychic research is now drawing to a close, the evidence suggests that a fourth phase is appearing, and that this may well feature a return to the study of the more sensational and dramatic phenomena reminiscent of the Victorian séance room. If this is so, a century after its foundation the wheel will have turned full circle and psychic research will be back where it started, without in the opinion of most scientists, having solved any of the basic questions which it had set out to answer. *See* **Parapsychology, Poltergeist, Telepathy, Spiritualism.**

Psychoanalysis, an approach to the study of human personality involving the rigorous probing, with the assistance of a specially trained practitioner, of an individual's personal problems, motives, goals and attitudes to life in general. Often, and quite understandably, confused with psychology (of which it is merely a part), psychoanalysis has an interesting historical background and has attracted the interest of philosophers, scientists and medical experts since it emerged as a radical and controversial form of mental therapy at the turn of the century. The traditionally accepted founder is the great Austrian Sigmund Freud, but he never failed to acknowledge the impetus that had been given to his own ideas by his talented friend, the physiologist Joseph Breuer, who for most of his working life had been interested in the curious phenomena associated with hypnosis. Breuer had successfully cured the hysterical paralysis of a young woman patient and had noticed that under hypnosis the girl seemed to be recalling emotional experiences, hitherto forgotten, which bore some relationship to the symptoms of her illness. Developing this with other patients Breuer then found that the mere recalling and discussing of the emotional events under hypnosis seemed to produce a dramatic alleviation of the symptoms—a phenomenon which came to be known as *catharsis*. Breuer also noticed another curious side-effect, that his women patients fell embarrassingly and violently in love with him, and he gradually dropped the practice of "mental catharsis", possibly feeling that it was a bit too dangerous to handle. This left the field clear for Freud, whose brilliant mind began to search beyond the therapeutic aspects of the topic to see what light might be thrown on the nature of human personality and psychological mechanisms in general. The most important question concerned the "forgotten" emotional material which turned up, apparently out of the blue, during the hypnotic session. Freud rightly saw that this posed problems for the current theories of memory, for how could something once forgotten (a) continue to have an effect on the individual without his being aware of it, and (b) ultimately be brought back to conscious memory again. It must be remembered that at this time memory was considered to be a fairly simple process—information was stored in the brain and was gradually eroded or destroyed with the passage of time and the decay of brain cells. Once lost, it was believed, memories were gone for ever, or at best only partially and inaccurately reproducible. Furthermore, human beings were supposed to be rational (if frequently wilful) creatures who never did anything without thinking about it (if only briefly) beforehand and without being well aware of their reasons for so doing. It was within this framework that Freud had his great insight, one which many people believe to be one of the most important ideas given to mankind. This was simply the realization that the human mind was not a simple entity controlling the brain and body more or less at will, but a complex system made up of a number of integrated parts with at least two major subdivisions—the conscious and the unconscious. The former concerned itself with the normal round of human behavior, including the larger part of rational thought, conversation, etc., and large areas of memory. The latter was principally devoted to the automatic control of bodily functions, such as respiration, cardiac activity, various types of emotional behavior not subject to much conscious modification and a large storehouse of relevant "memories" again not normally accessible to the conscious mind. Occasionally, Freud proposed, an exceedingly unpleasant emotional or otherwise painful event might be so troublesome if held in the conscious mind's store, that it would get shoved down into the unconscious or "repressed" where it would cease to trouble the individual in his normal life. The advantages of this mechanism are obvious, but they also brought with them hazards. With certain kinds of memory, particularly those involving psychological rather than physical pain—as for example a severe sexual conflict or marital problem—repression might be used as a device to save the individual from facing his problem in the "real" world, where he might be able ultimately to solve it, by merely hiding it away in the unconscious and thus pretending it did not exist. Unfortunately, Freud believed, conflicts of this kind were not snuffed out when consigned to the basements of the mind, but rather tended to smolder on, affecting the individual in various ways which he could not understand. Repressed marital conflicts might give rise to impotence, for example, or even to homosexual behavior. Guilt at improper social actions similarly repressed might provoke nervous tics, local paralysis, etc. etc. Following this line of reasoning, Freud argued that if the unwisely repressed material could be dredged up and the individual forced to face the crisis instead of denying it, then dramatic alleviations of symptoms and full recovery should follow.

To the great psychologist and his growing band of followers the stage seemed to be set for a dramatic breakthrough not only in mental therapy but also in a general understanding of the nature of human personality. To his pleasure—for various reasons he was never too happy about hypnosis—Freud discovered that with due patience, skill and guidance an individual could be led to resurrect the material repressed in his unconscious mind in the normal, as opposed to the hypnotic state. This technique, involving long sessions consisting of intimate discussions between patient and therapist became known as psychoanalysis, and it has steadily evolved from its experimental beginnings in the medical schools and universities of Vienna to being a major system of psychotherapy with a worldwide following and important theoretical connotations. Psychoanalysis, as practiced today, consists of a number of meetings between doctor and patient in which the latter is slowly taught to approach and enter the *territory* of his subconscious mind, and examine the strange and "forgotten" material within. A successful analysis, it is claimed, gives the individual greater insight into his own personality and a fuller understanding of the potent unconscious forces which are at work within him and in part dictating his goals.

Freud's initial ideas were of course tentative, and meant to be so. He was however a didactic and forceful personality himself, unwilling to compromise on many points which became controversial as the technique and practice of psychoanalysis developed. The outcome was that some of his early followers, notably the equally brilliant Carl Jung and Alfred Adler, broke away to found their own "schools" or versions of psychoanalysis, with varying degrees of success. Today, psychoanalysis is coming under increasingly critical scrutiny, and its claims are being treated with a good deal of reservation. Notable antagonists include the English psychologist Professor H. J. Eysenck who points out that there is little if any solid experimental data indicating that psychoanalysis is a valid method of treating or curing mental illness. Analysts respond by saying that their system is closer to an art than a craft and not amenable to routine scientific experiment. The controversy will no doubt continue for some time to come, but whatever its validity as therapy, the basic ideas behind psychoanalysis—notably the reality and power of the unconscious mind—are beyond question and have given human beings definite and major insights into the greatest enigma of all—the workings of the human mind.

Psychometry, the supposed talent or faculty of divining something about the history and previous owners of an object by holding it in the hand. A common feature of modern Spiritualistic practice, and to a certain extent synonymous with clairvoyance, psychometry is based on an ancient magical assumption that objects somehow take on traces or "memories" of their surroundings which are detectable by specially sensitive individuals. Controlled scientific tests on people claiming to have this power have however proved totally negative. *See also* **Psychic Research.**

Pyramidology, a curious belief that the dimensions of the Great Pyramid at Giza, if studied carefully, reveal principles of fundamental historical and religious significance. The perpetrator of this was a Victorian publisher, John Taylor, who discovered that if you divide the height of the pyramid into twice the side of its base you get a number very similar to *pi*—a number of considerable mathematical importance. Later discoveries in the same vein include the finding that the base of the pyramid (when divided by the width of a single casing stone) equals exactly 365—number of days in the year. Many books have been written on the interpretation of the dimensions of the pyramid, none of which has any scientific or archaeological validity. Pyramidology is simply a classic example of the well-known fact that hunting through even a random array of numbers will turn up sequences which appear to be "significant"—always provided that one carefully selects the numbers one wants and turns a blind eye to those that one doesn't! A peculiar variant of pyramidology has recently arisen through the publication of a claim that razor blades kept beneath a cardboard model of a pyramid never lose their cutting edge! Scientific tests have shown that this is not so, but the belief persists—implicit testimony to the mystical power of certain common emblems and symbols.

Pyrrhonism, a sceptical philosophy which doubts everything.

Q

Quakers, a religious body founded in England in the 17th cent. by George Fox (1624–91). The essence of their faith is that every individual who believes has the power of direct communication with God who will guide him into the ways of truth. This power comes from the "inner light" of his own heart, the light of Christ, Quakers meet for worship avoiding all ritual, without ordained ministers or prepared sermons; there is complete silence until someone is moved by the Holy Spirit to utter his message.

In the early days Quakers gave vent to violent outbursts and disturbed church services. Friends had the habit of preaching at anyone who happened to be nearby, their denunciation of "steeple-houses" and references to the "inner light," their addressing everyone as "thee" and "thou," their refusal to go beyond "yea" and "nay" in making an assertion and refusing to go further in taking an oath, must have played some part in bringing about the savage persecutions they were forced to endure. Many emigrated to Pennsylvania, founded by William Penn in 1682, and missionaries were sent to many parts of the world. The former violence gave way to gentleness. Friends not only refused to take part in war but even refused to resist personal violence. They took the lead in abolishing slavery, worked for prison reform and better education. As we know them today Quakers are quiet, sincere, undemonstrative people, given to a somewhat serious turn of mind. The former peculiarities of custom and dress have been dropped and interpretation of the Scriptures is more liberal. Although Quakers refuse to take part in warfare, they are always ready to help the victims of war, by organizing relief, helping refugees in distress, or sending their ambulance units into the heat of battle.

Quietism, a doctrine of extreme asceticism and contemplative devotion, embodied in the works of Michael Molinos, a 17th century Spanish priest, and condemned by Rome. It taught that the chief duty of man is to be occupied in the continual contemplation of God, so as to become totally independent of outward circumstances and the influence of the senses. Quietists taught that when this stage of perfection is reached the soul has no further need for prayer and other external devotional practices. Similar doctrines have been taught in the Moslem and Hindu religions. *See* **Yoga.**

R

Radiesthesia, the detection, either by some "psychic" faculty or with special equipment, of radiations alleged to be given off by all living things and natural substances such as water, oil, metal, etc. The word radiesthesia is in fact a fancy modern name for the ancient practice of "dowsing," whereby an individual is supposed to be able to detect the presence of hidden underground water by following the movements of a hazel twig held in his hands. Dowsers, or water diviners, as they are sometimes called, claim also to be able to detect the presence of minerals and, hard though it may seem to believe, have actually been hired by major oil companies to prospect for desert wells—though without any notable success. The theory of dowsing is that all things give off a unique radiation signal which the trained individual (via his twig, pendulum, or whatever) can "tune in" to, a theory which, while not backed up by any data known to orthodox sciences, is at least not too fantastically far-fetched. It is when radiesthesists claim to be able to detect the presence of oil, water, or precious metals by holding their pendulum *over a map* of the territory and declare that it is not necessary for them to visit the area in person to find the required spot that the topic moves from the remotely possible to the absurdly improbable. Some practitioners of this art state that they are able to perform even more marvellous feats such as determining the sex of chickens while still in the egg, or diagnosing illness by studying the movements of a pendulum held over a blood sample from the sick individual. Such claims when put to simple scientific test have almost invariably turned out as fiascos. Yet belief in dowsing, water-divining, and the like is still very widespread.

There is an important link between radiesthesia and the pseudo-science of *radionics,* which holds that the twig or pendulum can be superseded by complicated equipment built vaguely according to electronic principles. A typical radionic device consists of a box covered with knobs, dials, etc., by which the practitioner "tunes in" to the "vibration" given off by an object, such as a blood spot, a piece of hair, or even a signature. By the proper interpretation of the readings from the equipment the illness, or even the mental state, of the individual whose blood, hair, or signature is being tested, may be ascertained. The originator of radionics seems to have been a Dr. Albert Abrams who engaged in medical practice using radionic devices in America in the 1920s and '30s. The principal exponent in England was the late George de la Warr who manufactured radionic boxes for diagnosis and treatment of illnesses, and even a "camera" which he believed to be capable of photographing thought. In a sensational court case in 1960 a woman who had purchased one of the diagnostic devices sued de la Warr for fraud. After a long trial the case was dismissed, the Judge commenting that while he had no good evidence that the device worked as claimed, he felt that de la Warr seriously believed in its validity and thus was not guilty of fraud or misrepresentation.

Ranters, a fanatical antinomian (the doctrine that Christians are not bound to keep the law of God) and pantheistic sect in Commonwealth England. The name was also applied to the Primitive Methodists because of their noisy preaching.

Rationalism is defined as "the treating of reason as the ultimate authority in religion and the rejection of doctrines not consonant with reason." In practice, rationalism had a double significance: (1) the doctrine was defined above, and (2) a 19th cent. movement which was given to what was then known as "free-thought," "secularism," or agnosticism—*i.e.,* it was in the positive sense anti-religious and was represented by various bodies such as the Secular Society, the National Secular Society, and the Rationalist Press Association (founded in 1899).

In the first sense, which implies a particular philosophical attitude to the universe and life, rationalism is not easy to pin down although, at first sight, it would appear that nothing could be simpler. Does it mean the use of pure reason and logic or does it mean, on the other hand, the use of what is generally called the "scientific method" based on a critical attitude to existing beliefs? If we are thinking in terms of the use of pure reason and logic then the Roman Catholic Church throughout most of its history has maintained, not that the whole truth about religion can be discovered by reason, but as St. Thomas Aquinas held, the basis of religion—*e.g.* the existence of God—can be rationally demonstrated. Nobody could have made more use of logic than the schoolmen of the Middle Ages, yet not many people today would accept their conclusions, nor would many non-Catholics accept St. Thomas's proofs of the existence of God even when they themselves are religious. The arguments of a First Cause or Prime Mover or the argument from Design on the whole leave us unmoved, partly because they do not lead up to the idea of a *personal God,* partly because we rightly distrust logic and pure reason divorced from facts and know that, if we begin from the wrong assumptions or premises, we can arrive at some very strange answers. If the existence of a Deity can be proved by reason, then one can also by the use of reason come to the conclusions, or rather paradoxes, such as the following: God is by definition all good, all knowing, all powerful—yet evil exists (because if it does not exist then it cannot be wrong to say "there is no God"). But if evil exists, then it must do so either because of God (in which case He is not all good) or in spite of God (in which case He is not all powerful).

Arguments of this sort do not appeal to the modern mind for two historical reasons: (1) many of us have been brought up in the Protestant tradition which—at least in one of its aspects—insists that we must believe in God by faith rather than by logic and in its extreme form insists on God as revealed by the "inner light"; (2) our increasing trust in the scientific method of observation, experiment and argument. Thus, no matter what Aristotle or St. Thomas may say about a Prime Mover or a First Cause, we remain unconvinced since at least one scientific theory suggests that the universe did not have a beginning and if scientific investigation proved this to be so, then we should be entirely indifferent to what formal logic had to say.

The secularist and rationalist movements of the 19th cent. were anti-religious—and quite rightly so—because at that time there were serious disabilities imposed even in Britain by the Established Church on atheism or agnosticism and freedom of thought. They are of little significance now because very little is left, largely thanks to their efforts, of these disabilities.

Finally, although most people are likely to accept the scientific method as the main means of discovering truth, there are other factors which equally make us doubt the value of "pure" logic and reason unaided by observation. The first of these is the influence of Freud which shows that much of our reasoning is mere rationalizing—*e.g.*, we are more likely to become atheists because we hated our father than because we can prove that there is no God. The second is the influence of a movement in philosophy which, in the form of logical positivism or logical analysis, makes us doubt whether metaphysical systems have any meaning at all. Today, instead of asking ourselves whether Plato was right or wrong, we are much more likely to ask whether he did anything but make for the most part meaningless noises. Religion is in a sense much safer today than it ever was in the 19th cent. when it made foolish statements over matters of science that could be *proved* wrong; now we tend to see it as an emotional attitude to the universe or God (a "feeling of being at home in the universe," as William James put it) which can no more be proved or disproved than being in love.

Realism is a word which has so many meanings, and such contradictory ones, in various spheres, that it is difficult to define. We shall limit ourselves to its significance in philosophy. In philosophy, "realism" has two different meanings, diametrically opposed. (1) The most usual meaning is the one we should least expect from the everyday sense of the word—*i.e.*, it refers to all those philosophies from Plato onwards which maintained that the world of appearance is illusory and that ideas, forms, or universals are the only true realities, belonging to the world beyond matter and appearance—the world of God or mind. In early medieval times St. Thomas Aquinas was the chief exponent of this doctrine which was held by the scholastics as opposed to the Nominalists *(q.v.)*. (2) In its modern everyday meaning "realism" is the belief that the universe is real and not a creation of mind, that there is a reality that causes the appearance, the "thing-in-itself" as Kant described it. Material things may not really be what they appear to be

(*e.g.* a noise is not the "bang" we experience but a series of shock-waves passing through the atmosphere), yet, for all that, we can be sure that matter exists and it is very possible (some might add) that mind does not.

Reformation, the great religious movement of the 16th century, which resulted in the establishment of Protestantism. John Wyclif (d. 1384), Jan Hus (d. 1415) and others had sounded the warning note, and when later on Luther took up the cause in Germany, and Zwingli in Switzerland, adherents soon became numerous. The wholesale vending of indulgences by the papal agents had incensed the people, and when Luther denounced these things he spoke to willing ears. After much controversy, the reformers boldly prepounded the principles of the new doctrine, and the struggle for religious supremacy grew bitter. They claimed justification (salvation) by faith, and the use as well as the authority of the Scriptures, rejecting the doctrine of transubstantiation, the adoration of the Virgin and Saints, and the headship of the Pope. Luther was excommunicated. But the Reformation principles spread and ultimately a great part of Germany, as well as Switzerland, the Low Countries, Scandinavia, England, and Scotland were won over to the new faith. In England Henry VIII readily espoused the cause of the Reformation, his own personal quarrel with the Pope acting as an incentive. Under Mary there was a brief and sanguinary reaction, but Elizabeth gave completeness to the work which her father had initiated. *See* **Calvinism, Presbyterianism, Baptists, Methodism.**

Renaissance is defined in the *Oxford English Dictionary* as: "The revival of art and letters, under the influence of classical models, which began in Italy in the 14th century." It is a term which must be used with care for the following reasons: (1) Although it was first used in the form *rinascita* (rebirth) by Vasari in 1550 and people living at that time certainly were aware that something new was happening, the word had no wide currency until used by the Swiss historian Jacob Burckhardt in his classic *The Civilization of the Renaissance in Italy* (1860). (2) The term as used today refers not only to art in its widest sense but to a total change in man's outlook on life which extended into philosophical, scientific, economic, and technical fields. (3) Spreading from Italy there were Renaissance movements in France, Spain, Germany, and northern Europe, all widely different with varying delays in time. As the historian Edith Sichel says: "Out of the Italian Renaissance there issued a new-born art; out of the Northern Renaissance there came forth a new-born religion. There came forth also a great school of poetry, and a drama the greatest that the world had seen since the days of Greece. The religion was the offspring of Germany and the poetry that of England."

The real cause of the Renaissance was not the fall of Constantinople, the invention of printing, or the discovery of America, though these were phases in the process; it was, quite simply, money. The birth of a new merchant class gave rise to individualist attitudes in economic affairs which prepared the way for individualism and humanism. The new wealthy class in time became patrons of the arts whereas previously the Church had been the sole patron and controller. Thus the artist became more free to express himself, more respected, and being more well-to-do could afford to ignore the Church and even, in time, the views of his patrons.

It is true that art continued to serve to a considerable extent the purposes of faith, but it was judged from the standpoint of art. Medieval art was meant to elevate and teach man: Renaissance art to delight his senses and enrich his life. From this free and questing spirit acquired from economic individualism came the rise of modern science and technology; here Italy learned much from the Arab scholars who had translated and commented upon the philosophical, medical, and mathematical texts of antiquity, while denying themselves any interest in Greek art and literature. Arabic-Latin versions of Aristotle were in use well into the 16th cent. The Byzantine culture, though it had preserved the Greek tradition and gave supremacy to Plato, had made no move forward. But the Greek scholars who fled to Italy after the fall of Constantinople brought with them an immense cargo of classical manuscripts. The recovery of these Greek masterpieces, their translation into the vernaculars, and the invention of printing, made possible a completer understanding of the Greek spirit. It was the bringing together of the two heritages, Greek science, and Greek literature, that gave birth to a new vision. But it was not only Aristotle and Plato who were being studied but Ovid, Catullus, Horace, Pliny and Lucretius. What interested Renaissance man was the humanism of the Latin writers, their attitude to science, their scepticism.

The period *c.* 1400–1500 is known as the **Early Renaissance.** During this time such painters as Masaccio, Uccello, Piero della Francesca, Botticelli, and Giovanni Bellini were laying the foundations of drawing and painting for all subsequent periods including our own. They concerned themselves with such problems as anatomy, composition, perspective, and representation of space, creating in effect a grammar or textbook of visual expression. The term **High Renaissance** is reserved for a very brief period when a pure, balanced, classical harmony was achieved and artists were in complete control of the techniques learned earlier. The High Renaissance lasted only from *c.* 1500 to 1527 (the date of the sack of Rome), yet that interval included the earlier works of Michelangelo, most of Leonardo's, and all the Roman works of Raphael.

Romantic Movement or Romanticism is the name given not so much to an individual way of thinking but to the gradual but radical transformation of basic human values that occurred in the Western world round about the latter part of the 18th cent. It was a great breakthrough in European consciousness and arose through the writings of certain men living during the half-century or more following, say, 1760. It arose then because both time and place were propitious for the birth of these new ideas. There was a revolution in basic values—in art, morals, politics, religion, etc. The new view was of a world transcending the old one, infinitely larger and more varied.

To understand the Romantic movement it is necessary first to take note of the climate of thought preceding the great change; then to account for its beginning in Germany where it did during the latter part of the 18th century, and finally to appraise the writings of those men whose ideas fermented the new awakening. Briefly, the shift was away from French classicism and from belief in the all-pervasive power of human reason (the Enlightenment) towards the unfettered freedom that the new consciousness was able to engender. What mattered was to live a passionate and vigorous life, to dedicate oneself to an ideal, no matter what the cost (*e.g.,* Byron).

The ideas of the Enlightenment (*e.g.,* Fontenelle, Voltaire, Montesquieu) had been attacked by the Germans Hamann and Herder and by the ideas of the English philosopher Hume, but Kant, Schiller, and Fichte, Goethe's novel *Wilhelm Meister,* and the French Revolution all had profound effects on the aesthetic, moral, social, and political thought of the time. Friedrich Schlegel (1772–1829) said: "There is in man a terrible unsatisfied desire to soar into infinity; a feverish longing to break through the narrow bonds of individuality." Romanticism undermined the notion that in matters of value there are objective criteria which operate between men. Henceforth there was to be a resurgence of the human spirit, deep and profound, that is still going on.

Rosicrucians, an ancient mystical society founded in the 16th cent. by Christian Rosenkreuz which attempted to forge a theoretical link between the great Egyptian religions and the Church of Rome, drawing rituals and philosophy from both camps. The Society did not long survive the death of its founder (he managed to reach the age of 106 incidentally) but has been revived in succeeding centuries by a series of rivalling factions. Perhaps the most famous of these is the Rosicrucian Order (A.M.O.R.C) which has become well-known in the Western world as a result of its heavy advertising in the popular press. Founded by the American H. Spencer Lewis, this offers a simple and good-natured doctrine preaching the Brotherhood of Man, the reincarnation of the soul and the immense latent potential of the human mind. As with many American-based organizations of this kind, the boundary between business and religion is hard to define. It is probably best summed up as a modern secret society which serves an important function in the lives of many people of mystical inclinations.

S

Salvation Army. The religious movement which in 1878 became known by this name arose from the Christian Mission meetings which the Rev. William Booth and his devoted wife had held in the East End of London for the previous thirteen years. Its primary aim was, and still is, to preach the gospel of Jesus Christ to men and women untouched by ordinary religious efforts. The founder devoted his life to the salvation of the submerged classes whose conditions at that time were unspeakably dreadful. Originally his aim had been to convert people and then send them on to the churches, but he soon found that few religious bodies would accept these "low-class" men and women. So it was that social work became part of their effort. Practical help like the provision of soup kitchens, accompanied spiritual ministration. Soon, in the interests of more effective "warfare" against social evils, a military form of organization, with uniforms, brass bands, and religious songs, was introduced. Its magazine *The War Cry* gave as its aim "to carry the Blood of Christ and the Fire of the Holy Ghost into every part of the world.'

General Booth saw with blinding clarity that conversion must be accompanied by an improvement of external conditions. Various books had earlier described the terrible conditions of the slums, but in 1890 he produced a monumental survey entitled *In Darkest England and The Way Out.* From that time forward the Army was accepted and its facilities made use of by the authorities. Today the Army's spiritual and social activities have spread to countries all over the world; every one, no matter what class, color, or creed he belongs to is a "brother for whom Christ died."

Sceptics. From Thales of Miletus (*c.* 624–565 B.C.) to the Stoics in the 4th cent. B.C. philosophers had been trying to explain the nature of the universe; each one produced a different theory and each could, apparently, prove that he was right. This diversity of views convinced the Sceptic school founded by Pyrrho (*c.* 360–270 B.C.) that man is unable to know the real nature of the world or how it came into being. In place of a futile search for what must be forever unknowable, the Sceptics recommended that men should be practical, follow custom, and accept the evidence of their senses.

Schoolmen. From the time of Augustine to the middle of the 9th cent. philosophy, like science, was dead or merely a repetition of what had gone before. But about that time there arose a new interest in the subject, although (since by then Western Europe was entirely under the authority of the Catholic Church) the main form it took was an attempt to justify Church teaching in the light of Greek philosophy. Those who made this attempt to reconcile Christian beliefs with the best in Plato and Aristotle were known as "schoolmen" and the philosophies which they developed were known as "scholasticism." Among the most famous schoolmen must be counted John Scotus Erigena (*c.* 800 –*c.* 877), born in Ireland and probably the earliest; St. Anselm, archbishop of Canterbury (1033–1109); the great Peter Abelard whose school was in Paris (1079–1142); Bernard of Chartres, his contemporary; and the best-known of all, St. Thomas Aquinas of Naples (1225–74), who was given the name of the "Angelic Doctor."

The philosophies of these men are discussed under various headings (**God and Man, Determinism and Free Will**), but being severely limited by the Church their doctrines differed from each other much less than those of later philosophical schools. However, one of the great arguments was between the orthodox Realists *(q.v.)* and the Nominalists *(q.v.)* and a second was between the Thomists (or followers of St. Thomas Aquinas) and the Scotists (followers of John Duns Scotus—not to be confused with John Scotus Erigena). The two latter schools were known as the Ancients, while the followers of William of Occam, the Nominalist, were known as the Terminalists. All became reconciled in 1482 in face of the threat from humanism of which the great exponent was Erasmus of Rotterdam (1466–1536).

Scientology, an unusual quasi-philosophical system started by the American science-fiction writer L. Ron Hubbard, which claims to be able to effect dramatic improvement in the mental and physical well-being of its adherents. Originally developed in the United States as "Dianetics, the modern science of mental health," it was hailed in Hubbard's first book to be "a milestone for Man comparable to his discovery of fire and superior to his inventions of the wheel and the arch." Such extravagant statements exemplify the literature of the movement, which in the late 1950s began to expand in England when its founder came to live in East Grinstead. Followers of Dianetics and Scientology advance within the cult through a series of levels or grades, most reached by undertaking courses

of training and tuition, payment for which may amount to hundreds and, in total, even thousands of pounds. These courses consist largely of mental exercises known as "processing" and "auditing" (now called "pastoral counselling" since more emphasis has recently been laid on the religious aspect). One of the principal goals of a Scientologist is the attainment of the state known as "Clear" (roughly speaking, one "cleared" of certain mental and physical handicaps) when it is believed he (she) will be a literally superior being, equipped with a higher intelligence and a greater command over the pattern of his (her) own life. The Scientologists' claims that their movement is a genuine religion have generally been met with resistance from establishment bodies. In 1967 the Home Office announced that its centers would no longer be recognized as educational establishments and foreigners arriving for its courses would not be granted student status. In 1980 the Home Office lifted this ban. The international headquarters have been moved from East Grinstead to Los Angeles.

Shakers, members of a revivalist group, styled by themselves "The United Society of Believers in Christ's Second Appearing," who seceded from Quakerism in 1747 though adhering to many of the Quaker tenets. The community was joined in 1758 by Ann Lee, a young convert from Manchester, who had "revelations" that she was the female Christ; "Mother Ann" was accepted as their leader. Under the influence of her prophetic visions she set out with nine followers for "Immanuel's land" in America and the community settled near Albany, capital of New York state. They were known as the "Shakers" in ridicule because they were given to involuntary movements in moments of religious ecstasy. Central to their faith was the belief in the dual role of God through the male and female Christ: the male principle came to earth in Jesus; the female principle, in "Mother Ann." The sexes were equal and women preached as often as men at their meetings which sometimes included sacred dances—nevertheless the two sexes, even in dancing, kept apart. Their communistic way of living brought them economic prosperity, the Shakers becoming known as good agriculturists and craftsmen, noted for their furniture and textiles. After 1860, however, the movement began to decline and few, if any, are active today.

Shamans, the medicine men found in all primitive societies who used their magical arts to work cures, and protect the group from evil influences. The *shaman* was a man apart and wore special garments to show his authority. Shamanism with its magical practices, incantations, trances, exhausting dances, and self-torture is practiced even today by tribes.

Shiites or Shia, a heretical Moslem sect in Persia, opposed by the orthodox Sunnites. The dispute, which came almost immediately after the death of the Prophet and led to bitter feuding, had little to do with matters of doctrine as such but with the succession. After Mohammed's death, there were three possible claimants: Ali, the husband of his daughter Fatima, and two others, one of whom gave up his claim in favor of the other, Omar. The orthodox selected Omar, who was shortly assassinated, and the same happened to his successor as Ali was passed over again. The Shiites are those who maintain that Ali was the true vicar of the Prophet, and that the three orthodox predecessors were usurpers.

Sikhism. The Sikh community of the Punjab, which has played a significant part in the history of modern India, came into being during a period of religious revival in India in the 15th and 16th cent. It was originally founded as a religious sect by Guru (teacher) Nanak (1469–1538) who emphasized the fundamental truth of all religions, and whose mission was to put an end to religious conflict. He condemned the formalism both of Hinduism and Islam, preaching the gospel of universal toleration, and the unity of the Godhead, whether He be called Allah, Vishnu, or God. His ideas were welcomed by the great Mogul Emperor Akbar (1542–1605). Thus a succession of Gurus were able to live in peace after Nanak's death; they established the great Sikh center at Amritsar, compiled the sacred writings known as the *Adi Granth,* and improved their organization as a sect. But the peace did not last long, for an emperor arose who was a fanatical Moslem, in face of whom the last Guru, Govind Singh (1666–1708), whose father was put to death for refusal to embrace Islam, had to make himself a warrior and instil into the Sikhs a more aggressive spirit. A number of ceremonies were instituted by Govind Singh; admission to the fraternity was by special rite; caste distinctions were abolished; hair was worn long; the word singh, meaning lion, was added to the original name. They were able to organize themselves into 12 *misls* or confederacies but divisions appeared with the disappearance of a common enemy and it was not until the rise of Ranjit Singh (1780–1839) that a single powerful Sikh kingdom was established, its influence only being checked by the English, with whom a treaty of friendship was made. After the death of Ranjit Singh two Anglo-Sikh wars followed, in 1845–46, and 1848–49, which resulted in British annexation of the Punjab and the end of Sikh independence. In the two world wars the Sikhs proved among the most loyal of Britain's Indian subjects. The partitioning of the continent of India in 1947 into two states, one predominantly Hindu and the other predominantly Moslem, presented a considerable problem in the Punjab, which was divided in such a way as to leave 2 million Sikhs in Pakistan, and a considerable number of Moslems in the Indian Punjab. Although numbering less than 2 per cent of the population (*c.* 8 million) the Sikhs are a continuing factor in Indian political life. Demands for Sikh independence led to the storming by Indian troops of the Golden Temple at Amritsar on June 6, 1984. In October 1984, Mrs. Gandhi was assassinated by Sikh extremists.

Spiritualism is a religion which requires to be distinguished from psychical research *(q.v.)* which is a scientific attempt carried on by both believers and non-believers to investigate psychic phenomena including those not necessarily connected with "spirits"—*e.g.,* telepathy or clairvoyance and precognition. As a religion (although for that matter the whole of history is filled with attempts to get in touch with the "spirit world") Spiritualism begins with the American Andrew Jackson Davis who in 1847 published *Nature's Divine Revelations,* a book which is still widely read. In this Davis states that on the death of the physical body, the human spirit remains alive and moves on to one or another of a considerable range of worlds or "spheres" where it commences yet another stage of existence. Since the spirit has not died, but exists with full (and possibly even expanded) consciousness, there should be no reason, Davis ar-

gues, why it should not make its presence known to the beings it has temporarily left behind on earth. In 1847, the year of the publication of Davis's book, two young girls, Margaret and Kate Fox, living in a farmhouse at Hydesville, New York, began apparently to act as unwitting mediums for attempts at such between-worlds communication. The girls were the focus for strange rappings and bangs which it was alleged defied normal explanation and which spelt out, in the form of a simple alphabetical code, messages from the spirits of "the dead." The Fox sisters were later to confess that they had produced the raps by trickery, but by that time the fashion had spread across the world and before long "mediums" in all lands were issuing spirit communications (often in much more spectacular form). In the late 19th cent. Spiritualism went into a phase of great expansion and for various reasons attracted the attention of many scientists. Among these were Sir William Crookes, Sir Oliver Lodge, Professor Charles Richet, Alfred Russell Wallace, to say nothing of the brilliant and shrewd creator of Sherlock Holmes, Sir Arthur Conan Doyle. Today many people find it astonishing that people of such brilliance should find the phenomena of the séance room of more than passing interest, but the commitment of the Victorian scientists is understandable if we realize that Spiritualists, after all, claim to do no more than demonstrate as fact what all Christians are called on to believe—that the human personality survives bodily death. Furthermore, at the time of the late 19th cent. peak of Spiritualism, much less was known about human psychology and about the great limitations of sensory perception in typical séance conditions, when lights are dimmed or extinguished and an emotionally charged atmosphere generated. Today the most striking phenomena of the séance room—the alleged materialization of spirit people and the production of such half-spiritual, half-physical substances as ectoplasm—are rarely if ever produced at Spiritualist meetings. Some say that the most probable explanation for this is that too many fraudulent mediums have been caught out and publicly exposed for the profession to be worth the risks. The movement today, which still has a large and often articulate following, now concentrates on the less controversial areas of "mental mediumship," clairvoyance and the like, or on the very widespread practice of "spirit healing." Where people are not deliberately deluded by bogus mediums acting for monetary reward (a practice which largely died out with the "death" of ectoplasm) Spiritualism probably has an important role to play in the life of many people whose happiness has been removed by the death of a much loved relative or spouse. It does not deserve the violent attacks that are often made on it by orthodox clergy who allege that Spiritualists are communicating not with the souls of the departed but with the devil or his emissaries.

Stoics, the followers of Zeno, a Greek philosopher in the 4th century B.C., who received their name from the fact that they were taught in the Stoa Poikile or Painted Porch of Athens. They believed that since the world is the creation of divine wisdom and is governed by divine law, it is man's duty to accept his fate. Zeno conceived virtue to be the highest good and condemned the passions. (*See* **God and Man, Determinism and Free Will** for a more detailed account of their beliefs.)

Swedenborgianism. The Church of the New Jerusalem, based on the writings of Emanuel Swedenborg (1688–1772), was founded by his followers eleven years after his death. The New Church is regarded by its members not as a sect but as a new dispensation bearing the same relationship to Christianity as Christianity does to Judaism.

Synchronicity, an attempt by the psychologist, Carl Gustav Jung, to explain the apparently significant relationship between certain events in the physical universe which seem to have no obvious "causal" link. This rather involved concept is easily understood if one realizes that almost all scientific and philosophical beliefs are based on the notion that the continuous process of change which is taking place in ourselves and in the universe around us is dependent upon a principle known as causality. We can express this another way by saying that an object moves because it has been pushed or pulled by another. We see because light strikes the retina and signals pass up the nervous system to the brain. A stone falls to the ground because the earth's gravity is pulling it towards its center, etc., etc. For all practical purposes every event can be looked upon as being "caused" by some other prior event and this is obviously one of the most important principles of the operation of the universe. Jung, however, felt that there is a sufficiently large body of evidence to suggest that events may be linked in a significant (*i.e.*, non-chance) way without there being any true causal relationship between them. The classic example he held to be the supposed predictive power of astrology by which there appears to be a relationship between the stellar configurations and the personality and life-pattern of individuals on earth. Jung was scientist enough to realize that there could be no causal connection between the aspect of the stars and the lives of people billions of miles from them, yet felt the evidence for astrology was strong enough to demand an alternative non-causal explanation. The trouble with synchronicity, which has not made much impact on the world of physics or of psychology, is that it is not really an explanation at all but merely a convenient word to describe some puzzling correspondences. The real question, of course, is whether there really are events occurring which are significantly but not *causally* linked, and most scientists today would hold that there were probably not. Still it was typical of the bold and imaginative mind of Jung to tackle head-on one of the principal mysteries of existence and come up with a hypothesis to attempt to meet it.

Syndicalism, a form of socialist doctrine which aims at the ownership and control of all industries by the workers, contrasted with the more conventional type of socialism which advocates ownership and control by the state. Since syndicalists have preferred to improve the conditions of the workers by direct action, *e.g.*, strikes and working to rule, rather than through the usual parliamentary procedures, they have been closely related to anarchists *(q.v.)* and are sometimes described as anarcho-syndicalists. Under syndicalism there would be no state; for the state would be replaced by a federation of units based on functional economic organization rather than on geographical representation. The movement had bodies in the United Kingdom, where guild socialism was strongly influenced by its doctrines, in France, Germany, Italy, Spain, Argentina, and Mexico, but these gradually declined after the first world war losing many members to the communists. Fascism *(q.v.)* was also strongly influenced by the revolutionary syndicalism of Georges Sorel in making use of his concept of the "myth of the general strike" as an emotional image or ideal goal to spur on the workers; with Mussolini the "myth" became that of the state. Mussolini was also influenced by Sorel's doctrine of violence and the justification of force. Syndicalism had a certain influence in the Labour Party in its early days, but was crushed by men like Ernest Bevin who began to fear that by involving the workers in direct responsibility for their industries, it would put them at a disadvantage when bargaining for wages.

T

Telepathy and Clairvoyance. Telepathy is the alleged communication between one mind and another other than through the ordinary sense channels. Clairvoyance is the supposed faculty of "seeing" objects or events which, by reason of space and time or other causes, are not discernible through the ordinary sense of vision. Such claims have been made from time immemorial but it was not until this century that the phenomena were investigated scientifically. The first studies were undertaken by the Society for Psychical Research, which was founded in 1882 with Professor Henry Sidgwick as its first president. Since then it has carried out a scholarly program of research without—in accordance with its constitution—coming to any corporate conclusions. In America the center of this research was the Parapsychology Laboratory at Duke University (*see* **Parapsychology**) where at one time it was claimed clear scientific evidence for extra-sensory perception (ESP) had been obtained. These claims have been treated with great reservation by the majority of scientists but despite the belief that the study of ESP was going into eclipse, there remains a small but measurable residue of interest in scientific research in this area. It would be odd if some scientists were not interested in ESP because of the enormous weight of anecdotal evidence which has built up over centuries to support it. The weakness of the scientific as opposed to the casual evidence is however exemplified by the failure of ESP researchers to produce a reliable "repeatable" experiment.

Theism. *See* **God and Man.**

Theosophy (Sanskrit *Brahma Vidya* = divine wisdom), a system of thought that draws on the mystical teachings of those who assert the spiritual nature of the universe, and the divine nature of man. It insists that man is capable of intuitive insight into the nature of God. The way to wisdom, or self-knowledge, is through the practice of **Yoga** *(q.v.)*. Theosophy has close connections with Indian thought through Vedic, Buddhist, and Brahmanist literature. The modern Theosophical Society was founded by Mme H. P. Blavatsky and others in 1875, and popularized by Mrs. Annie Besant.

Transcendental Meditation, popularized in the West by the Maharishi Mahesh Yogi, who achieved sensational worldwide publicity by his "conversion" of the Beatles a few years ago. This is a simple meditational system which it is claimed is an aid to relaxation and the reduction of psychological and physical stress. It is reported that the technique can be taught in under five minutes provided that someone trained by the Maharishi is the teacher. The pupil or would-be meditator is given a mantra—a meaningless word which acts as a focal point for the imagination—letting his thoughts flow freely while sitting in a comfortable position. Extraordinary claims are made on behalf of the system. As with most cults, religious and occult systems, there is an initial psychological benefit to anyone who becomes deeply involved. Nevertheless, apart from this simple "participation-effect", there is some evidence that the body's autonomic functions (heart rate, respiratory cycle, brain waves, etc.) can be modified by certain individuals including yogis. Whether it is ultimately beneficial to be able to modify these autonomic functions or not is another matter. The TM movement in Britain is based at Mentmore Towers in Buckinghamshire.

Transmigration of Souls. *See* **Immortality.**

Transubstantiation, the conversion in the Eucharist of the bread and wine into the body and blood of Christ—a doctrine of the Roman Catholic Church.

Trotskyism, a form of communism supporting the views of Leon Trotsky, the assumed name of Lev Bronstein (1879–1940) who, in 1924, was ousted from power by Stalin and later exiled and assassinated in Mexico. Trotsky held that excessive Russian nationalism was incompatible with genuine international communism and that Stalin was concentrating on the economic development of the Soviet Union to an extent which could only lead to a bureaucratic state with a purely nationalist outlook. After the Hungarian uprising in 1956, which was ruthlessly suppressed by the Soviet Armed Forces, a wave of resignations from Western Communist parties took place, many of the dissidents joining the Trotskyist movement.

U

Ufology, cultish interest in the study of strange and unexplained aerial phenomena (unidentified flying objects, hence UFOs). *See* **Flying Saucers.**

Unitarianism has no special doctrines, although clearly, as the name indicates, belief is in the single personality of God, *i.e.,* anti-trinitarian. This general statement, however, can be interpreted with varying degrees of subtlety. Thus Unitarian belief may range from a sort of Arianism which accepts that, although Christ was not of divine nature, divine powers had been delegated to him by the Father, to the simple belief that Christ was a man like anyone else, and his goodness was of the same nature as that of many other great and good men. Indeed, today many Unitarians deny belief in a personal God and interpret their religion in purely moral terms, putting their faith in the value of love and the brotherhood of man. The Toleration Act (1689) excluded Unitarians but from 1813 they were legally tolerated in England. Nevertheless attempts were made to turn them out of their chapels on the ground that the preachers did not hold the views of the original founders of the endowments. But this ended with the Dissenting Chapels Act of 1845. In America no such difficulties existed, and in the Boston of the 19th cent. many of the great literary figures were openly Unitarian in both belief and name: *e.g.,* Emerson, Longfellow, Lowell, and Oliver Wendell Holmes.

Utilitarianism, a school of moral philosophy of which the main proponents were J. S. Mill (1806–73) and Jeremy Bentham (1748–1832). Bentham based his ethical theory upon the utilitarian principle that the greatest happiness of the greatest number is the criterion of morality. What is good is pleasure or happiness; what is bad is pain. If we act on this basis of self-interest (pursuing what we believe to be our own happiness), then what we do will automatically be for the general good. The serious failing of this thesis is (1) that it makes no distinction between the quality of one pleasure and another, and (2) that Bentham failed to see that the law might not be framed and administered by men as benevolent as himself. J. S. Mill accepted Bentham's position in general but seeing its failings emphasized (1) that self-interest was an inadequate basis for utilitarianism and suggested that we should take as the real criterion of good the social consequences of the act; (2) that some pleasures rank higher than others and held that those of the intellect are superior to those of the senses. Not only is the social factor emphasized, but emphasis is also placed on the nature of the act.

Utopias. The name "utopia" is taken from a Greek word meaning "nowhere" and was first used in 1516 by Sir Thomas More (1478–1535) as the title of his book referring to a mythical island in the south Pacific where he sited his ideal society. Since then it has been used of any ideal or fanciful society, and here a few will be mentioned. (The reader may recall that Samuel Butler's 19th century novel, describing an imaginary society in New Zealand where criminals were treated and the sick punished, was entitled *Erewhon* which is the word "nowhere" in reverse.) It should be noted that not all utopias were entirely fanciful—*e.g.,* Robert Owen's and François Fourier's beliefs, although found to be impractical, were, in fact, tried out.

Sir Thomas More. More wrote at a time when the rise of the wool-growing trade had resulted in farming land being turned over to pasture and there was a great wave of unemployment and a rise in crime among the dispossessed. More began to think in terms of the medieval ideal of small co-operative communities in which class interests and personal gain played a decreasing part, a society which would have the welfare of the people at heart both from the physical and intellectual points of view. His utopia was one in which there was no private property, because the desire for acquisition and private possessions lay at the root of human misery. There was, therefore, only common ownership of land and resources. Each class of worker was equipped to carry out its proper function in the economic scheme and each was fairly rewarded for its share in production so that there was neither wealth nor poverty to inspire conflict. Nobody was allowed to idle, until the time came for him to retire when he became free to enjoy whatever cultural pleasures he wished, but since the system was devoid of the waste associated with competition, the working day would be only six hours. There was to be compulsory schooling and free medical care for everybody, full religious toleration, complete equality of the sexes, and a modern system of dealing with crime which was free from vindictiveness and cruelty. Government was to be simple and direct by democratically elected officials whose powers would be strictly limited and the public expenditure kept under close scrutiny. It will be seen that More was far in advance of his age, and to most democratically minded people in advance of an earlier utopia, Plato's *Republic*, which is described under the heading of Education.

James Harrington. James Harrington published his book *The Commonwealth of Oceana* in 1656 and offered it to Oliver Cromwell for his consideration but without tangible results. Better than any other man of his time Harrington understood the nature of the economic revolution which was then taking place, and, like More, saw the private ownership of land as the main cause of conflict. He put forward the theory that the control of property, particularly in the shape of land, determines the character of the political structure of the state; if property were universally distributed among the people the sentiment for its protection would naturally result in a republican form of government. The Commonwealth of Oceana was a society "of laws and not of men"—*i.e.,* it was to be legally based and structured so as to be independent of the good or ill will of any individuals controlling it. Thus there must be a written constitution, a two-house legislature, frequent elections with a secret ballot, and separation of powers between legislature and executive—all today familiar features of parliamentary democracy, but unique in his time.

Saint-Simon. The utopias of the late 18th and 19th century come, of course, into the period of the Industrial Revolution and of laissez-faire capitalism. Individual enterprise and complete freedom of competition formed the outlook of the ruling class. Naturally the utopias of this period tended to have a strongly socialist tinge since such theories are obviously produced by those who are not satisfied with existing conditions. Saint-Simon's *New Christianity* (1825) is one such, and by many, Claude Henri, Comte de Saint-Simon (1760–1825) is regarded as the founder of French socialism. His book urged a dedication of society to the principle of human brotherhood and a community which would be led by men of science motivated by wholly spiritual aims. Production property was to be nationalized (or "socialized" as he describes the process) and employed to serve the public good rather than private gain; the worker was to produce according to his capacity and to be rewarded on the basis of individual merit; the principle of inheritance was to be abolished since it denied the principle of reward for accomplishment on which the society was to be founded. Saint-Simon's proposals were not directed towards the poorer classes alone, but to the conscience and intellect of all. He was deeply impressed with the productive power of the new machines and his scheme was, first and foremost, intended as a method of directing that power to the betterment of humanity as a whole.

Fourier. François Marie Charles Fourier (1772–1837), although by conviction a philosophical anarchist who held that human beings are naturally good if allowed to follow their natural desires, was the originator of what, on the face of it, one would suppose to be the most regimented of the utopias. It consisted of a system of "phalanxes" or cooperative communities each composed of a group of workers and technicians assured of a minimum income and sharing the surplus on an equitable basis. Agriculture was to be the chief occupation of each phalanx and industrial employment planned and so carefully assigned that work would become pleasant and creative rather than burdensome. One of his ideas was that necessary work should receive the highest pay, useful work the next, and pleasant work the least pay. The land was to be scientifically cultivated and natural resources carefully conserved. Most of the members' property was to be privately owned, but the ownership of each phalanx was to be widely diffused among members by the sale of shares. Such "parasitic and unproductive" occupations as stockbroker, soldier, economist, middleman and philosopher would be eliminated and the education of children carried out along vocational lines to train them for their future employment.

The strange thing was that Fourier's suggestions appealed to many in both Europe and the United States and such men (admittedly no economic or technical experts) as Emerson, Thoreau, James Russell Lowell, and Nathaniel Hawthorne strongly supported them. An American Fourier colony known as Brook Farm was established and carried on for eight years when it was dissolved after a serious fire had destroyed most of its property.

Robert Owen. Robert Owen (1771–1858), a wealthy textile manufacturer and philanthropist, established communities founded on a kind of utopian socialism in Lanarkshire, Hampshire, and in America. Of his New Lanark community an American observer wrote: "There is not, I apprehend, to be found in any part of the world, a manufacturing community in which so much order, good government, tranquillity, and rational happiness prevail." The workers in Lanark were given better housing and education for their children, and it was administered as a cooperative self-supporting community in Scotland. Later in life Owen returned to sponsoring legislation that would remove some of the worst evils of industrial life in those days: reduction of the working day to twelve hours, prohibition of labor for children under the age of ten, public schools for elementary education, and so on. But he lived to see few of his reforms adopted. He also promoted the creation of cooperative societies, the formation of trade unions, labor banks, and exchanges, the workers' educational movement, and even an Anglo-American federation.

V

Vegetarianism, a way of life practiced by those who abstain from meat. Strict vegetarians (Vegans) also exclude all animal products (*e.g.* butter, eggs, milk) from their diet.

Vitalism, the philosophical doctrine that the behavior of the living organism is, at least in part, due to a vital principle which cannot possibly be explained wholly in terms of physics and chemistry. This belief was held by the rationalist thinker C. E. M. Joad (1891–1953) and is implicit in Henri Bergson's (1859–1941) theory of creative evolution. It was maintained by Bergson that evolution, like the work of an artist, is creative and therefore unpredictable; that a vague need exists beforehand within the animal or plant before the means of satisfying the need develops. Thus we might assume that sightless animals developed the need to become aware of objects before they were in physical contact with them and that this ultimately led to the origins of organs of sight. Earlier this century a form of vitalism described as "emergent evolution" was put forward. This theory maintains that when two or more simple entities come together there may arise a new property which none of them previously possessed. Today biologists would say that it is the *arrangement* of atoms that counts, different arrangements exhibiting different properties, and that biological organization is an essentially dynamic affair.

W

Witchcraft. There are various interpretations and definitions of witchcraft from that of Pennethorne Hughes who states that "witchcraft, as it emerges into European history and literature, represents the old paleolithic fertility cult, plus the magical idea, plus various parodies of contemporary religions" to that of the fanatical Father Montague Summers who says that Spiritualism and witchcraft are the same thing. A leading authority on witchcraft, however, the late Dr. Margaret Murray, distinguishes between Operative Witchcraft (which is really Magic *(q.v.)* and Ritual Witchcraft which, she says, "embraces the religious beliefs and ritual of the people known in late medieval times as 'witches.' " That there were such people we know from history and we know, too, that many of them—the great majority of them women—were tortured or executed or both. Many innocent people perished, especially after the promulgation of the bull *Summis desiderantes* by Pope Innocent VIII in 1484. Himself "a man of scandalous life," according to a Catholic historian, he wrote to "his dear sons," the German professors of theology, Johann Sprenger and Heinrich Kraemer, "witches are hindering men from performing the sexual act and women from conceiving . . ." and delegated them as Inquisitors "of these heretical pravities." In 1494 they codified in the *Malleus Maleficarum* (Hammer of Witches) the ecclesiastical rules for detecting acts of witchcraft. Dr. Murray points out that there have ordinarily been two theories about witchcraft: (1) that there were such things as witches, that they possessed supernatural powers and that the evidence given at their trials was substantially correct; (2) that the witches were simply poor silly creatures who either deluded themselves into believing that they had certain powers or, more frequently, were tortured into admitting things that they did not do. She herself accepts a third theory: that there were such beings as witches, that they really did what they admitted to doing, but that they did not possess supernatural powers. They were in fact believers in the old religion of pre-Christian times and the Church took centuries to root them out. That there existed "covens" of witches who carried out peculiar rites Dr. Murray has no doubt whatever. The first to show that witchcraft was a superstition and that the majority of so-called witches were people suffering from mental illness was the physician Johann Weyer of Cleves (1515–88). His views were denounced by the Catholic Church. Few people realize how deeply the notion of witchcraft is implanted in our minds and how seriously its power is still taken. For example, the Witchcraft Act was not repealed in England until the 1950s. Furthermore, as recently as 1944, when the allied armies were invading Europe, the Spiritualist medium Mrs. Helen Duncan was charged with witchcraft and actually sent to prison—a prosecution which brought forth caustic comments from the then prime minister, Winston Churchill. *See also* **Demonism.**

Y

Yoga, a Hindu discipline which teaches a technique for freeing the mind from attachment to the senses, so that once freed the soul may become fused with the universal spirit (*atman* or Brahman), which is its natural goal. This is the sole function of the psychological and physical exercises which the Yogi undertakes, although few ever reach the final stage of *Samadhi* or union with Brahman which is said to take place in eight levels of attainment. These are: (1) *Yama,* which involves the extinction of desire and egotism and their replacement by charity and unselfishness; (2) *Niyama,* during which certain rules of conduct must be adopted, such as cleanliness, the pursuit of devotional studies, and the carrying out of rituals of purification; (3) *Asana,* or the attainment of correct posture and the reduction to a minimum of all bodily movement (the usual posture of the concentrating Yogi is the "lotus position" familiar from pictures); (4) *Pranayama,* the right control of the life-force or breath in which there are two stages at which the practitioner hopes to arrive, the first being complete absorption in the act of breathing which empties the mind of any other thought, the second being the ability almost to cease to breathe which allegedly enables him to achieve marvellous feats of endurance; (5) *Pratyahara* or abstraction which means the mind's complete withdrawal from the world of sense; (6) *Dharana* in which an attempt is made to think of one thing only which finally becomes a repetition of the sacred syllable OM; (7) *dhyana,* meditation, which finally leads to (8) *Samadhi* the trance state which is a sign of the complete unity of soul with reality.

Yoga is very old, and when the sage Patanjali (*c.* 300 B.C.) composed the book containing these instructions, the *Yoga Sutras,* he was probably collecting from many ancient traditions. Some of the claims made by Yogis seem, to the Western mind, frankly incredible; but in the West and especially in recent years Yoga methods have been used at the lower levels in order to gain improved self-control, better posture, and improved health. Whether it achieves these ends is another matter, but the genuine Yogi regards this as a perversion of the nature and purpose of the discipline.

Z

Zen Buddhism, a Buddhist sect which is believed to have arisen in 6th cent. China but has flourished chiefly in Japan; for some reason it has of recent years begun to attract attention in the West thanks to the voluminous writings of Dr. D. T. Suzuki and the less numerous but doubtless much-read books of Mr. Christmas Humphreys. But the fact that these writings exist does not explain their being read, nor why of all possible Eastern sects this particular one should be chosen in our times. What is Zen's attraction and why should anyone take the trouble to read about something (the word "something" is used for reasons that will become evident) that is not a religion, has no doctrine, knows no God and no afterlife, no good and no evil, and possesses no scriptures but has to be taught by parables which seem to be purposely meaningless? One of the heroes of Zen is the fierce-looking Indian monk Boddhidharma (fl. *c.* 516–34) who brought Buddhism to China, of whom it is recounted that when the Emperor asked him how much merit he had acquired by supporting the new creed, the monk shouted at him: "None whatever!" The emperor then wished to know what was the sacred doctrine of the creed and again the monk shouted: "It is empty—there is nothing sacred!" Dr. Suzuki, having affirmed that there is no God in Zen, goes on to state that this does not mean that Zen denies the existence of God because "neither denial nor affirmation concerns Zen." The most concrete statement he is prepared to make is that the basic idea of Zen is to come in touch with the inner workings of our being, and to do this in the most direct way possible without resorting to anything external or superadded. Therefore anything that has the semblance of an external authority is rejected by Zen. Absolute faith is placed in a man's own inner being. Apparently the intention is that, so far from indulging in inward meditations or such practices as the Yogi uses, the student must learn to act spontaneously, without thinking, and without self-consciousness or hesitation. This is the main purpose of the *koan,* the logically insoluble riddle which the pupil must try to solve. One such is the question put by master to pupil: "A girl is walking down the street, is she the younger or the older sister?" The correct answer, it seems, is to say nothing but put on a mincing gait, to *become* the girl, thus showing that what matters is the experience of being and not its verbal description. Another *koan*: "What is the Buddha?" "Three pounds of flax" is attributed to T'ungshan in the 9th cent. and a later authority's comment is that "none can excel it as regards its irrationality which cuts off all passages to speculation." Zen, in effect, teaches the uselessness of trying to use words to discuss the Absolute.

Zen came to Japan in the 13th cent., more than five centuries after Confucianism or the orthodox forms of Buddhism, and immediately gained acceptance while becoming typically Japanese in the process. One of the reasons why it appealed must have been that its spontaneity and insistence on action without thought, its emphasis on the uselessness of mere words, and such categories as logical opposites, had an inevitable attraction for a people given to seriousness, formality, and logic to a degree which was almost stifling. Zen must have been to the Japanese what nonsense rhymes and nonsense books, like those of Edward Lear and Lewis Carroll, were to the English intellectuals. Lear's limericks, like some of the *koans,* end up with a line which, just at the time when one expects a point to be made, has no particular point at all, and *Alice in Wonderland* is the perfect example of a world, not without logic, but with a crazy logic of its own which has no relationship with that of everyday life. Therefore Zen began to impregnate every aspect of life in Japan, and one of the results of its emphasis on spontaneous action rather than reason was its acceptance by the Samurai, the ferocious warrior class, in such activities as swordsmanship, archery, Japanese wrestling, and later Judo and the Kamikaze dive-bombers. But much of Japanese art, especially landscape gardening and flower-arrangement, was influenced similarly, and Zen is even used in Japanese psychiatry. The very strict life of the Zen monks is based largely on doing things, learning through experience; the periods of meditation in the Zendo hall are punctuated by sharp slaps on the face administered by the abbot to those who are unsatisfactory pupils. Dr. Suzuki denies that Zen is nihilistic, but it is probably its appearance of nihilism and its appeal to the irrational and spontaneous which attracts the Western world at a time when to many the world seems without meaning and life over-regimented. However, it has influenced such various aspects of Western life as philosophy (Heidegger), psychiatry (Erich Fromm and Hubert Benoit), writing (Aldous Huxley), and painting (Die Zen Gruppe in Germany).

Zionism, a belief in the need to establish an autonomous Jewish home in Palestine which, in its modern form, began with Theodor Herzl (1860–1904), a Hungarian journalist working in Vienna. Although Herzl was a more or less assimilated Jew, he was forced by the Dreyfus case and the pogroms in Eastern Europe to conclude that there was no real safety for the Jewish people until they had a state of their own. The Jews, of course, had always in a religious sense thought of Palestine as a spiritual homeland and prayed "next year in Jerusalem," but the religious had thought of this in a philosophical way as affirming old loyalties, not as recommending the formation of an actual state. Therefore Herzl was opposed both by many of the religious Jews and, at the other extreme, by those who felt themselves to be assimilated and in many cases without religious faith. Even after the Balfour Declaration of 1917, there was not a considerable flow of Jews to Palestine, which at that time was populated mainly by Arabs. But the persecutions of Hitler changed all this and, after bitter struggles, the Jewish state was proclaimed in 1948. Today Zionism is supported by the vast majority of the Jewish communities everywhere (although strongly disapproved of in the Soviet Union as "Western imperialism") and Zionism is now an active international force concerned with protecting the welfare and extending the influence of Israel.

Zoroastrianism, at one time one of the great world religions, competing in the 2nd cent. A.D. on almost equal terms from its Persian home with Hellenism and the Roman Imperial Government. Under the Achaemenidae (*c.* 550–330 B.C.) Zoroastrianism was the state religion of Persia. Alexander's conquest in 331 B.C. brought disruption but the religion flourished again under the Sassanian dynasty (A.D. *c.* 226–640). With the advance of the Mohammedan Arabs in the 7th cent. Zoroastrianism finally gave way to Islam. A number of devotees fled to India there to become the Parsees. In Persia itself a few scattered societies remain.

The name Zoroaster is the Greek rendering of Zarathustra, the prophet who came to purify the ancient religion of Persia. It is thought that he lived at the beginning of the 6th cent. B.C. He never claimed for himself divine powers but was given them by his followers. The basis of Zoroastrianism is the age-long war between good and evil, Ahura Mazda heading the good spirits and Ahriman the evil ones. Morality is very important since by doing right the worshipper is supporting Ahura Mazda against Ahriman, and the evil-doers will be punished in the last days when Ahura Mazda wins his inevitable victory.

The sacred book of this religion is the *Avesta.* If Zoroastrianism has little authority today, it had a very considerable influence in the past. Its doctrines penetrated into Judaism *(q.v.)* and, through Gnosticism, Christianity. The worship of Mithra by the Romans was an impure version of Zoroastrianism. Manichaeism *(q.v.)* was a Zoroastrian heresy and the Albigensianism of medieval times was the last relic of a belief which had impressed itself deeply in the minds of men.

GEOGRAPHY

EASTERN UNITED STATES EARTHQUAKES (1534-1984)

MASSENA, NY,
ATTICA, NY, 1944
1929
BLUE MOUNTAIN
LAKE, NY, 1983
CAPE ANN, MA, 175?
Boston
Chicago
WILKES-BARRE, PA, 1954
NEW YORK CITY, NY, 1884
LANCASTER, PA, 1984
St. Louis
ANNA, OH, 1937
GILES COUNTY, VA, 1897
NEW MADRID,
MO, 1811-12
Memphis
Dallas
CHARLESTON, SC, 1886
New Orleans
Houston
CHARLESTON, MO,
1895
Miami

LEGEND
Intensity Epicenter
- I-IV
- V-VI
- VII-IX
- X-XII

Fig. 1. *Source:* U.S. Geological Survey.

Why Experts Expect a Catastrophic Eastern Earthquake

By Robert L. Ketter, Director,
National Center for Earthquake Engineering Research

It is generally accepted that the outmost shell of the earth is composed of a dozen or so, very large and relatively rigid, crustal plates. These plates range from 70-150 kilometers thick, and they move slowly and continuously with respect to each other—approximately several centimeters per year.

In the central Atlantic Ocean, along the mid-Atlantic ridge, the plates are moving apart and a new oceanic crust is continually being formed as molten lava rises within the mantle. At the boundaries of other plates, different situations exist. In some areas one plate is forced downward under another. In others: for example, along the San Andreas fault in California; plates slide relative to each other in a "stick-slip" type of motion. (Corresponding sudden releases of energy are responsible for the earthquakes which occur in the California region.)

About 95% of the world's earthquakes occur along or near the boundaries of these crustal plates. However, many very destructive ones occur within the plates themselves—far away from the boundaries. The reasons for this intraplate seismic activity are not readily apparent.

Currently, the accepted explanation is the following: More than several hundred million years ago the central part of the United States was pushed upward by molten rock from the underlying mantle. This material was heavier than the surrounding rocks, and when the upwelling ceased, the entire region subsided. Seas covered the area, laying down thick layers of sediment which eventually hardened into limestone, sandstone, and shale. Later, during the various cycles of plate movement, rifting—faulting—took place. Still later, molten rock moved upward along these faults, cooling before it reached the surface. Once again, the ocean advanced over the area, depositing sands, clays, and gravels. At the present moment, due to the continual spreading that is occurring in the mid-Atlantic, these ancient faults are subjected to east-west compressive forces. These forces acting on these faults are responsible for

454

Fig. 2. *Source:* Central United States Earthquake Consortium, Yearly Meeting, 1985.

most intraplate earthquakes. Unfortunately, we do not know the magnitude or distribution of the forces that exist, or even the locations of all of the ancient faults. We, therefore, cannot predict with any certainty when or where the next crustal fracture—and therefore the next earthquake—will occur.

Figure 1 shows the locations of all known earthquakes that have occurred in the eastern and central parts of the United States since 1534.

The number of occurrence, however, is not the only—or necessarily the best—indicator of the earthquake threat that exists for this region. As stated in the Earthquake Hazards Reduction Act of 1977, Public Law 95-124: "All 50 states are vulnerable to the hazards of earthquakes, and at least 39 of them are subject to major or moderate seismic risk. . . ." Many of these states are in the East.

The largest earthquakes, or series of earthquakes, known to have occurred in North America were intraplate earthquakes that occurred in the Mississippi Valley near New Madrid, Missouri, in 1811 and 1812. It has been estimated that three had surface-wave Magnitudes of 8.6, 8.4, and 8.8 on the Richter scale. Church bells 1000 miles away in Boston rang; the earth was observed to "roll" in waves a few feet in height; large areas of land were uplifted, while much land sank; existing lakes drained, and others were created; and sand blows spread debris over large areas, where it is still visible today.

Another major north American intraplate earth-

quake occurred in 1886 in Charleston, South Carolina. There, the Magnitude was 7.7.

The earthquake problem in the central and eastern part of the United States is compounded by the fact that rocks in these regions of the country transmit seismic energy much more efficiently than do those that exist on the west coast. For example, the damage area for the 1811 New Madrid earthquake, which had a similar Magnitude as the San Francisco earthquake of 1906, resulted in an area of similar damage that was 15 times larger.

Another factor that must be taken into account: Large numbers of people live and work in these parts of the country. Further, very few structures have been designed or built for these circumstances. The consequences of a major seismic event, therefore, would be felt by many.

While undoubtedly there can be found exceptions to this general statement—all of the major earthquakes that have occurred in the eastern and central parts of the United States have exhibited precursor activities. With that in mind, consider that over 2000 earthquakes were recorded in and around the New Madrid area between 1974 and 1983—and I should here note that they are still occurring. I think that you will have to agree with me that it would be difficult for anyone to say that this region is not a prime candidate for a future major seismic event.

The most frequently asked, and the least satisfactorily answered, questions concerning earthquakes is, "When will the next major one happen?" Unfortunately, seismology cannot now, nor will it be able in the near future to answer that question in a deterministic fashion: that is, accurately predict when an earthquake will occur. A probabilistic assessment, however, is possible, and this has been done for New Madrid as well as a number of other potentially active sites. Based on those calculations, the probability of a destructive earthquake occurring at a given, singular, geographic site in the eastern part of the county within the next 15 to 25 years is relatively low. However, the probability of one occurring *somewhere in the eastern United States* before the year 2000 can be considered better than 75 to 95 percent. Before the year 2010, nearly 100 percent.

Johnson and Nava have estimated the probability of occurrence of two large New Madrid earthquakes for two separate time periods—by the end of the century, and by the year 2035. The earthquakes they considered were presumed to have surface-wave Magnitudes of 6.3 and 8.3 on the Richter scale, the latter corresponding to one of the 1811 quakes. It was found that the probability of occurrence between now and year 2000 for the smaller earthquake would be 40 to 60 percent; for the larger, only 0.3 percent to 1 percent. By the year 2035, however, there would be an 86 to 97 percent probability of occurrence for the smaller one, and a 2.7 percent to 4 percent probability of occurrence for the larger.

Figure 2 is a generalized isoseismal map for the larger of the two postulated New Madrid earthquakes. Shown are the intensities of shaking that would be experienced.

The Roman numerals are Modified Mercalli Intensity values, and indicate the perceived amount of shaking that will occur. For example, for an Intensity of VI: that is, for Chicago, Pittsburgh, Knoxville, etc.; the shaking would be felt by everyone. Many people would be frightened; dishes, glassware, and some windows would be broken; church and school bells would ring; and trees and bushes would shake visibly. In region VIII: that is, for St. Louis, Carbondale, and Nashville, there would be general fright and signs of panic; some masonry walls would fall and frame-houses, if not securely bolted down, would move on their foundations; branches would break on trees, and cracks would appear in wet soil and on steep slopes. In the general vicinity of the epicenter where the Intensity has been projected to be X, that is, in Memphis: most masonry and frame structures would be destroyed with their foundations; there would be serious damage to dams, dikes, and embankments; and there would be large landslides. Railroad tracks would be bent.

Should the postulated event occur at night, when most people are in their homes—which are primarily of wood construction—it is estimated that in the six cities nearest to the event—Memphis, Paducah, Carbondale, Evansville, Poplar Bluff, and Little Rock—there would result 676 deaths due to structural failure. If the event occurred during the daylight hours, that number would increase to 4,907 deaths.

Damage to transportation systems would seriously hamper rescue and relief efforts. Railway networks would be similarly affected. Riverports would be extensively disrupted, and there would be partial or limited availability of major airport facilities. These six cities would experience serious impairment or loss of their utility systems (electric, water, gas, and sewers).

Were the earthquake to occur at a time when high water conditions existed, flooding of low-lying areas would take place. Widespread individual or small-group structural fires would occur, but it is unlikely that there would result giant fires, or conflagrations. For this six-city region of major impact, four hundred and sixty thousand (460,000) persons would require shelter due to damaged residences. Finally, it is estimated that restoration and replacement costs would exceed $51 billion.

All of the consequences thus far described are "local" consequences. Equally of national importance would be the consequences felt by areas remote to the site, if the epicenter were located in the vicinity of one of the major pipeline routes, or if that route passed through an area where major soil liquefaction took place. In all likelihood such an earthquake would disrupt the distribution of flow of transport crude oil and natural gas. Not only would there be the potential for serious environmental contaminations, but it would be reasonable to expect significant energy distribution outages to heavily populated areas located several hundred miles away.

While—as I indicated earlier—the probability of an earthquake occurring at a singular particular site in the immediate future is not large, the probability of one occurring somewhere within the eastern part of the country is quite large. Moreover, the over-all consequences of such an event could be enormous.

Destructive earthquakes have occurred in the past, and will undoubtedly occur in the future. The only real uncertainties are when will they occur, and where. It is important that we be prepared in order to mitigate against the effects of such catastrophic events. A number of things can be done, and the role of Washington will be of major importance during the first several days—and later. Today's program should provide answers as to how well prepared we are to handle the problems that will necessarily follow.

It is to be understood that *for the purposes of illustration* it has been postulated that there will occur a major destructive earthquake in the Memphis, Tennessee, area. While that area is a reasonable one for such postulation, we could equally well have chosen other locations for the epicentral site. □

Robert L. Ketter was director of the National Center for Earthquake Engineering Research at the State University of New York at Buffalo from its inception in September 1986 until his death in April 1989. He was also leading professor of engineering and applied sciences at the university, and distinguished service professor of the State University of New York. Dr. Ketter was recognized internationally for his contributions toward the reduction of earthquake hazards, and for his deep concern for earthquake risk in the eastern United States.

The National Center for Earthquake Engineering Research (NCEER) is the first such national center sponsored by the National Science Foundation. The Center was proposed by researchers at a consortium of institutions including the University at Buffalo, City University of New York, Columbia University, Cornell University, Lamont-Doherty Geological Observatory of Columbia University, Lehigh University, Princeton University, and Rensselaer Polytechnic Institute, and involves individual researchers from throughout the Country, and the world.

The National Center's focus is to minimize damage caused by earthquakes through a system of research, implementation of findings, public education, and transfer of technology. Additionally, the Center addresses the socioeconomic issues of earthquakes such as emergency preparedness, response, and recovery.

The Severity of an Earthquake

(Source: U.S. Dept. of the Interior, Geological Survey.)

The Richter Magnitude Scale

The Richter magnitude scale was developed in 1935 by Charles F. Richter of the California Institute of Technology as a mathematical device to compare the size of earthquakes. The magnitude of an earthquake is determined from the logarithm of the amplitude of waves recorded by seismographs. Adjustments are included in the magnitude formula to compensate for the variation in the distance between the various seismographs and the epicenter of the earthquakes. On the Richter Scale, magnitude is expressed in whole numbers and decimal fractions. For example, a magnitude of 5.3 might be computed for a moderate earthquake, and a strong earthquake might be rated as magnitude 6.3.

Because of the logarithmic basis of the scale, each whole-number increase in magnitude represents a tenfold increase in measured amplitude; as an estimate of energy, each whole number step in the magnitude scale corresponds to the release of about 31 times more energy than the amount associated with the preceding whole number value.

Earthquakes with magnitudes of about 2.0 or less are usually called microearthquakes; they are not commonly felt by people and are generally recorded only on local seismographs. Events with magnitudes of about 4.5 or greater—there are several thousand such shocks annually—are strong enough to be recorded by sensitive seismographs all over the world.

Great earthquakes, such as the 1906 Good Friday earthquake in San Francisco, have magnitudes of 8.0 or higher. On the average, one earthquake of such size occurs somewhere in the world each year. Although the Richter Scale has no upper limit, the largest known shocks have had magnitudes in the 8.8 to 8.9 range.

The Richter Scale is not used to express damage. An earthquake in a densely populated area which results in many deaths and considerable damage may have the same magnitude as a shock in a remote area that does nothing more than frighten the wildlife. Large-magnitude earthquakes that occur beneath the oceans may not even be felt by humans.

The Modified Mercalli Intensity Scale

The effect of an earthquake on the Earth's surface is called the intensity. The intensity scale consists of a series of certain key responses such as people awakening, movement of furniture, damage to chimneys, and finally—total destruction. Although numerous *intensity scales* have been developed over the last several hundred years to evaluate the effects of earthquakes, the one currently used in the United States is the Modified Mercalli (MM) Intensity Scale. It was developed in 1931 by the American seismologists Harry Wood and Frank Neumann. This scale, composed of 12 increasing levels of intensity that range from imperceptible shaking to catastrophic destruction, is designated by Roman numerals. It does not have a mathematical basis; instead it is an arbitrary ranking based on observed effects.

The Modified Mercalli Intensity value assigned to a specific site after an earthquake has a more meaningful measure of severity to the nonscientist than the magnitude because intensity refers to the effects actually experienced at that place. After the occurrence of widely-felt earthquakes, the Geological Survey mails questionnaires to postmasters in the disturbed area requesting the information so that intensity values can be assigned. The results of this postal canvass and information furnished by other sources are used to assign an intensity value, and to compile isoseismal maps that show the extent of various levels of intensity within the felt area. The maximum observed intensity generally occurs near the epicenter.

The *lower* numbers of the intensity scale generally deal with the manner in which the earthquake is felt by people. The *higher* numbers of the scale are based on observed structural damage. Structural engineers usually contribute information for assigning intensity values of VIII or above.

The Mexico City earthquake on September 19, 1985, was assigned an intensity of IX on the Mercalli Scale.

The following is an abbreviated description of the 12 levels of Modified Mercalli intensity.

I. Not felt except by a very few under especially favorable conditions.

II. Felt only by a few persons at rest, especially on upper floors of buildings. Delicately suspended objects may swing.

III. Felt quite noticeably by persons indoors, especially on upper floors of buildings. Many people do not recognize it as an earthquake. Standing motor cars may rock slightly. Vibration similar to the passing of a truck. Duration estimated.

IV. Felt indoors by many, outdoors by few during the day. At night, some awakened. Dishes, windows, doors disturbed; walls make cracking sound. Sensation like heavy truck striking building. Standing motor cars rocked noticeably.

V. Felt by nearly everyone; many awakened. Some dishes, windows broken. Unstable objects overturned. Pendulum clocks may stop.

VI. Felt by all, many frightened. Some heavy furniture moved; a few instances of fallen plaster. Damage slight.

VII. Damage negligible in buildings of good design and construction; slight to moderate in well-built ordinary structures; considerable damage in poorly built or badly designed structures; some chimneys broken.

VIII. Damage slight in specially designed structures; considerable damage in ordinary substantial buildings with partial collapse. Damage great in poorly built structures. Fall of chimneys, factory stacks, columns, monuments, walls. Heavy furniture overturned.

IX. Damage considerable in specially designed structures; well-designed frame structures thrown out of plumb. Damage great in substantial buildings, with partial collapse. Buildings shifted off foundations.

X. Some well-built wooden structures destroyed; most masonry and frame structures destroyed with foundations. Rails bent.

XI. Few, if any (masonry) structures remain standing. Bridges destroyed. Rails bent greatly.

XII. Damage total. Lines of sight and level are distorted. Objects thrown into the air.

World Geography
Explorations and Discoveries
(All years are A.D. unless B.C. is specified.)

Country or place	Event	Explorer or discoverer	Date
AFRICA			
Sierra Leone	Visited	Hanno, Carthaginian seaman	c. 520 B.C.
Congo River	Mouth discovered	Diogo Cão, Portuguese	c. 1484
Cape of Good Hope	Rounded	Bartolomeu Diaz, Portuguese	1488
Gambia River	Explored	Mungo Park, Scottish explorer	1795
Sahara	Crossed	Dixon Denham and Hugh Clapperton, English explorers	1822–23
Zambezi River	Discovered	David Livingstone, Scottish explorer	1851
Sudan	Explored	Heinrich Barth, German explorer	1852–55
Victoria Falls	Discovered	Livingstone	1855
Lake Tanganyika	Discovered	Richard Burton and John Speke, British explorers	1858
Congo River	Traced	Sir Henry M. Stanley, British explorer	1877
ASIA			
Punjab (India)	Visited	Alexander the Great	327 B.C.
China	Visited	Marco Polo, Italian traveler	c. 1272
Tibet	Visited	Odoric of Pordenone, Italian monk	c. 1325
Southern China	Explored	Niccolò dei Conti, Venetian traveler	c. 1440
India	Visited (Cape route)	Vasco da Gama, Portuguese navigator	1498
Japan	Visited	St. Francis Xavier of Spain	1549
Arabia	Explored	Carsten Niebuhr, German explorer	1762
China	Explored	Ferdinand Richthofen, German scientist	1868
Mongolia	Explored	Nikolai M. Przhevalsky, Russian explorer	1870–73
Central Asia	Explored	Sven Hedin, Swedish scientist	1890–1908
EUROPE			
Shetland Islands	Visited	Pytheas of Massilia (Marseille)	c. 325 B.C.
North Cape	Rounded	Ottar, Norwegian explorer	c. 870
Iceland	Colonized	Norwegian noblemen	c. 890–900
NORTH AMERICA			
Greenland	Colonized	Eric the Red, Norwegian	c. 985
Labrador; Nova Scotia (?)	Discovered	Leif Ericson, Norse explorer	1000
West Indies	Discovered	Christopher Columbus, Italian	1492
North America	Coast discovered	Giovanni Caboto (John Cabot), for British	1497
Pacific Ocean	Discovered	Vasco Núñez de Balboa, Spanish explorer	1513
Florida	Explored	Ponce de León, Spanish explorer	1513
Mexico	Conquered	Hernando Cortés, Spanish adventurer	1519–21
St. Lawrence River	Discovered	Jacques Cartier, French navigator	1534
Southwest U. S.	Explored	Francisco Coronado, Spanish explorer	1540–42
Colorado River	Discovered	Hernando de Alarcón, Spanish explorer	1540
Mississippi River	Discovered	Hernando de Soto, Spanish explorer	1541
Frobisher Bay	Discovered	Martin Frobisher, English seaman	1576
Maine Coast	Explored	Samuel de Champlain, French explorer	1604
Jamestown, Va.	Settled	John Smith, English colonist	1607
Hudson River	Explored	Henry Hudson, English navigator	1609
Hudson Bay (Canada)	Discovered	Henry Hudson	1610
Baffin Bay	Discovered	William Baffin, English navigator	1616
Lake Michigan	Navigated	Jean Nicolet, French explorer	1634

Country or place	Event	Explorer or discover	Date
Arkansas River	Discovered	Jacques Marquette and Louis Jolliet, French explorers	1673
Mississippi River	Explored	Sieur de La Salle, French explorer	1682
Bering Strait	Discovered	Vitus Bering, Danish explorer	1728
Alaska	Discovered	Vitus Bering	1741
Mackenzie River (Canada)	Discovered	Sir Alexander Mackenzie, Scottish-Canadian explorer	1789
Northwest U. S.	Explored	Meriwether Lewis and William Clark	1804–06
Northeast Passage (Arctic Ocean)	Navigated	Nils Nordenskjöld, Swedish explorer	1879
Greenland	Explored	Robert Peary, American explorer	1892
Northwest Passage	Navigated	Roald Amundsen, Norwegian explorer	1906
SOUTH AMERICA			
Continent	Visited	Columbus, Italian	1498
Brazil	Discovered	Pedro Alvarez Cabral, Portuguese	1500
Peru	Conquered	Francisco Pizarro, Spanish explorer	1532–33
Amazon River	Explored	Francisco Orellana, Spanish explorer	1541
Cape Horn	Discovered	Willem C. Schouten, Dutch navigator	1615
OCEANIA			
Papua New Guinea	Visited	Jorge de Menezes, Portuguese explorer	1526
Australia	Visited	Abel Janszoon Tasman, Dutch navigator	1642
Tasmania	Discovered		
Australia	Explored	John McDouall Stuart, English explorer	1828
Australia	Explored	Robert Burke and William Wills, Australian explorers	1861
New Zealand	Sighted (and named)	Abel Janszoon Tasman	1642
New Zealand	Visited	James Cook, English navigator	1769
ARCTIC, ANTARCTIC, AND MISCELLANEOUS			
Ocean exploration	Expedition	Magellan's ships circled globe	1519–22
Galápagos Islands	Visited	Diego de Rivadeneira, Spanish captain	1535
Spitsbergen	Visited	Willem Barents, Dutch navigator	1596
Antarctic Circle	Crossed	James Cook, English navigator	1773
Antarctica	Discovered	Nathaniel Palmer, U. S. whaler (archipelago) and Fabian Gottlieb von Bellingshausen, Russian admiral (mainland)	1820–21
Antarctica	Explored	Charles Wilkes, American explorer	1840
North Pole	Reached	Robert E. Peary, American explorer	1909
South Pole	Reached	Roald Amundsen, Norwegian explorer	1911

The Continents

A continent is defined as a large unbroken land mass completely surrounded by water, although in some cases continents are (or were in part) connected by land bridges.

The hypothesis first suggested late in the 19th century was that the continents consist of lighter rocks that rest on heavier crustal material in about the same manner that icebergs float on water. That the rocks forming the continents are lighter than the material below them and under the ocean bottoms is now established. As a consequence of this fact, Alfred Wegener (for the first time in 1912) suggested that the continents are slowly moving, at a rate of about one yard per century, so that their relative positions are not rigidly fixed. Many geologists that were originally skeptical have come to accept this theory of Continental Drift.

When describing a continent, it is important to remember that there is a fundamental difference between a deep ocean, like the Atlantic, and shallow seas, like the Baltic and most of the North Sea, which are merely flooded portions of a continent. Another and entirely different point to remember is that political considerations have often overridden geographical facts when it came to naming continents.

Geographically speaking, Europe, including the British Isles, is a large western peninsula of the continent of Asia; and many geographers, when referring to Europe and Asia, speak of the Eurasian Continent. But traditionally, Europe is counted as a separate continent, with the Ural and the Caucasus mountains forming the line of demarcation between Europe and Asia.

To the south of Europe, Asia has an odd-shaped peninsula jutting westward, which has a large number of political subdivisions. The northern section is taken up by Turkey; to the south of Turkey there are Syria, Iraq, Israel, Jordan, Saudi Arabia, and a number of smaller Arab countries. All this is part of Asia. Traditionally, the island of Cyprus in the Mediterranean is also considered to be part of Asia, while the island of Crete is counted as European.

The large islands of Java, Borneo, and Sumatra and the smaller islands near them are counted as part of "tropical Asia," while New Guinea is counted as related to Australia. In the case of the Americas, the problem arises as to whether they should be considered one or two continents. There are good arguments on both sides, but since there is now a land bridge between North and South America (in the past it was often flooded) and since no part of the sea east of the land bridge is deep ocean, it is more logical to consider the Americas as one continent.

Politically, based mainly on history, the Americas are divided into North America (from the Arctic to the Mexican border), Central America (from Mexico to Panama, with the Caribbean islands), and South America. Greenland is considered a section of North America, while Iceland is traditionally counted as a European island because of its political ties with the Scandinavian countries.

The island groups in the Pacific are often called "Oceania," but this name does *not* imply that scientists consider them the remains of a continent.

The seven continents are North America, South America, Europe, Asia, Africa, Australia, and Antarctica.

Volcanoes of the World

About 500 volcanoes have had recorded eruptions within historical times. Almost two thirds of these are in the Northern Hemisphere. Most volcanoes occur at the boundaries of the earth's crustal plates, such as the famous "Ring of Fire" that surrounds the Pacific Ocean plate. Of the world's active volcanoes, about 60% are along the perimeter of the Pacific, about 17% on mid-oceanic islands, about 14% in an arc along the south of the Indonesian islands, and about 9% in the Mediterranean area, Africa, and Asia Minor. Many of the world's volcanoes are submarine and have unrecorded eruptions.

Pacific "Ring of Fire"
NORTHWEST
Japan: At least 33 active vents.

Aso (5,223 ft; 1,592 m), on Kyushu, has one of the largest craters in the world.

Asama (over 8,300 ft; 2,530 m), on Honshu, is continuously active; violent eruption in 1783.

Azuma (nearly 7,700 ft; 2,347 m), on Honshu, erupted in 1900.

Chokai (7,300 ft; 2,225 m), on Honshu, erupted in 1974 after having been quiescent since 1861.

Fujiyama (Fujisan) (12,385 ft; 3,775 m), on Honshu, southwest of Tokyo. Symmetrical in outline, snow-covered. Regarded as a sacred mountain.

On-take (3,668 ft; 1,118 m), on peninsula of Kyushu. Strong smoke emissions and explosions began November 1973 and continued through 1974.
U.S.S.R.: Kamchatka peninsula, 14–18 active volcanoes. Klyuchevskaya (Kluchev) (15,500 ft; 4,724 m) reported active in 1974.

Kurile Islands: At least 13 active volcanoes and several submarine outbreaks.

SOUTHWEST
New Zealand: Mount Tarawera (3,645 ft; 1,112 m), on North Island, had a severe eruption in 1886 that destroyed the famous Pink and White sinter terraces of Rotomahana, a hot lake.

Ngauruhoe (7,515 ft; 2,291 m), on North Island, emits steam and vapor constantly. Erupted 1974.

Papua New Guinea: Karkar Island (4,920 ft; 1,500 m). Mild eruptions 1974.
Philippine Islands: About 100 eruptive centers; Hibok Hibok, on Camiguin, erupted September 1950 and again in December 1951, when about 750 were reported killed or missing; eruptions continued during 1952–53.

Taal (4,752 ft; 1,448 m), on Luzon. Major eruption in 1965 killed 190; erupted again, 1968.
Volcano Islands: Mount Suribachi (546 ft; 166 m), on Iwo Jima. A sulfurous steaming volcano. Raising of U.S. flag over Mount Suribachi was one of the dramatic episodes of World War II.

NORTHEAST
Alaska: Mount Wrangell (14,163 ft; 4,317 m) and Mount Katmai (about 6,700 ft; 2,042 m). On June 6, 1912, a violent eruption (Nova Rupta) of Mount Katmai occurred, during which the "Valley of Ten Thousand Smokes" was formed.
Aleutian Islands: There are 32 active vents known and numerous inactive cones. Akutan Island (over 4,000 ft; 1,220 m) erupted in 1974, with ash and debris rising over 300 ft.

Great Sitkin (5,741 ft; 1,750 m). Explosive activity February–September 1974, accompanied by earthquake originating at volcano that registered 2.3 on Richter scale.
Augustine Island: Augustine volcano (4,000 ft; 1,220 m) erupted March 27, 1986. It last erupted in 1976.
California, Oregon, Washington: Lassen Peak (10,453 ft; 3,186 m) in California is one of two observed active volcanoes in the U.S. outside Alaska and Hawaii. The last period of activity was 1914–17. Mt. St. Helens (9,677 ft; 2,950 m) in the Cascade Range of southwest Washington became active on March 27, 1980, and erupted on May 18 after being inactive since 1857. From April 15 through May 1, 1986, weak activity began for the first time in two years. Other mountains of volcanic origin include Mount Shasta (California), Mount Hood (Oregon), Mount Mazama (Oregon)—the mountain containing Crater Lake, Mount Rainier (Washington), and Mount Baker (Washington), which has

been steaming since October 1975, but gives no sign of an impending eruption.

SOUTHEAST

Chile and Argentina: About 25 active or potentially active.

Colombia: Huila (nearly 18,900 ft; 5,760 m), a vapor-emitting volcano, and Tolima (nearly 18,500 ft; 5,640 m). Eruption of Puracé (15,600 ft; 4,755 m) in 1949 killed 17 people. Nevado del Ruiz (16,200 ft; 4,938 m.), erupted Nov. 13, 1985, sending torrential floods of mud and water engulfing the town of Armero and killing more than 22,000 people.

Ecuador: Cayambe (nearly 19,000 ft; 5,791 m). Almost on the equator.

Cotopaxi (19,344 ft; 5,896 m). Perhaps highest active volcano in the world. Possesses a beautifully formed cone.

Reventador (11,434 ft; 3,485 m). Observed in active state in late 1973.

El Salvador: Izalco ("beacon of Central America") (7,830 ft; 2,387 m) first appeared in 1770 and is still growing (erupted in 1950, 1956; last erupted in October–November 1966). San Salvador (6,187 ft; 1,886 m) had a violent eruption in 1923. Conchagua (about 4100 ft; 1,250 m) erupted with considerable damage early in 1947.

Guatemala: Santa Maria Quezaltenango (12,361 ft; 3,768 m). Frequent activity between 1902–08 and 1922–28 after centuries of quiescence. Most dangerously active vent of Central America. Other volcanoes include Tajumulco (13,814 ft; 4,211 m) and Atitlán (11,633 ft; 3,546 m).

Mexico: Boquerón ("Big Mouth"), on San Benedicto, about 250 mi. south of Lower California. Newest volcano in Western Hemisphere, discovered September 1952.

Colima (about 14,000 ft; 4,270 m), in group that has had frequent eruptions.

Orizaba (Citlaltépetl) (18,701 ft; 5,700 m).

Parícutin (7,450 ft; 2,270 m). First appeared in February 1943. In less than a week, a cone over 140 ft high developed with a crater one quarter mile in circumference. Cone grew more than 1,500 ft (457 m) in 1943. Erupted 1952.

Popocatépetl (17,887 ft; 5,452 m). Large, deep, bell-shaped crater. Not entirely extinct; steam still escapes.

El Chinchonal (7,300 ft; 1,005.6 m) about 15 miles from Pichucalco. Long inactive, it erupted in March 1982.

Nicaragua: Volcanoes include Telica, Coseguina, and Momotombo. Between Momotombo on the west shore of Lake Managua and Coseguina overlooking the Gulf of Fonseca, there is a string of more than 20 cones, many still active. One of these, Cerro Negro, erupted in July 1947, with considerable damage and loss of life, and again in 1971.

Concepción (5,100 ft; 1,555 m). Ash eruptions 1973–74.

Mid-oceanic Islands

Canary Islands: Pico de Teide (12,192 ft; 3,716 m), on Tenerife.

Cape Verde Islands: Fogo (nearly 9,300 ft; 2,835 m). Severe eruption in 1857; quiescent until 1951.

Caribbean: La Soufrière (4,813 ft; 1,467 m), on Basse-Terre, Guadeloupe. Also called La Grande Soufrière. Violent activity in July–August 1976 caused evacuation of 73,000 people; renewed activity in April 1977 again caused thousands to flee their homes.

La Soufrière (4,048 ft; 1,234 m), on St. Vincent. Major eruption in 1902 killed over 1,000 people. Eruptions over 10-day period in April 1979 caused evacuation of northern two thirds of island.

Comoros: One volcano, Karthala (nearly 8,000 ft; 2,440 m), is visible for over 100 miles. Last erupted in 1904.

Hawaii: Mauna Loa ("Long Mountain") (13,680 ft; 4,170 m), on Hawaii, discharges from its high side vents more lava than any other volcano. Largest volcanic mountain in the world in cubic content. Area of crater is 3.7 sq mi. Violent eruption in June 1950, with lava pouring 25 miles into the ocean. Last major eruption in March 1984.

Mauna Kea (13,796 ft; 4,205 m), on Hawaii. Highest mountain in state.

Kilauea (4,090 ft; 1,247 m) is a vent in the side of Mauna Loa, but its eruptions are apparently independent. One of the most spectacular and active craters. Crater has an area of 4.14 sq mi. Earthquake in July 1975 caused major eruption. Eruptions began in September 1977 and reached a height of 980 ft (300 m). Activity ended Oct. 1. Became active again in January 1983, exploding in earnest in March 1983 forming the volcanic cone Pu'u O which has erupted periodically ever since. In July 1986, lava began flowing from a new place in Kilauea's East Rift Zone.

Iceland: At least 25 volcanoes active in historical times. Very similar to Hawaiian volcanoes. Askja (over 4,700 ft; 1,433 m) is the largest.

Lesser Antilles (West Indian Islands): Mount Pelée (over 4,500 ft; 1,370 m), northwestern Martinique. Eruption in 1902 destroyed town of St. Pierre and killed approximately 40,000 people.

Réunion Island (east of Madagascar): Piton de la Fournaise (Le Volcan) (8,610 ft; 2,624 m). Large lava flows. Last erupted in 1972.

Samoan archipelago: Savai'i Island had an eruption in 1905 that caused considerable damage. Niuafoo (Tin Can), in the Tonga Islands, has a crater that extends 6,000 feet below and 600 feet above water.

Indonesia

Sumatra: Ninety volcanoes have been discovered; 12 are now active. The most famous, Krakatau, is a small volcanic island in the Sunda Strait. Numerous volcanic discharges occurred in 1883. One extremely violent explosion caused the disappearance of the highest peak and the northern part of the island. Fine dust was carried around the world in the upper atmosphere. Over 36,000 persons lost their lives in resultant tidal waves that were felt as far away as Cape Horn. Active in 1972.

Mediterranean Area

Italy: Mount Etna (10,902 ft; 3,323 m), eastern Sicily. Two new craters formed in eruptions of February–March 1947. Worst eruption in 50 years occurred November 1950–January 1951. Erupted again in 1974, 1975, 1977, 1978, 1979, and 1983.

Stromboli (about 3,000 ft; 914 m), Lipari Islands (north of Sicily). Called "Lighthouse of the Mediterranean." Reported active in 1971.

Mount Vesuvius (4,200 ft; 1,280 m), southeast of Naples. Only active volcano on European mainland. Pompeii buried by an eruption, A.D. 79.

Continued on page 464

The Pacific Ocean "Ring of Fire"

Volcanic Activity in the Solar System

(*Source:* U.S. Dept. of Interior, Geological Survey.)

From the 1976-1979 *Viking* mission, scientists have been able to study the volcanoes on Mars, and their studies are very revealing when compared with those of volcanoes on Earth. For example, Martian and Hawaiian volcanoes have gently sloping flanks, large multiple-collapse pits at their centers, and appear to be built of fluid lavas that have left their numerous flow features on their flanks. The most obvious difference between the two is size. The Martian shields are enormous. They can grow to over 17 miles in height and more than 350 miles across, in contrast to a maximum height of about 6 miles and width of 74 miles for the Hawaiian shields.

Source: U.S. Department of the Interior, U.S. Geological Survey.

Surtsey
Hekla
60°

Mt. Katmai
ishaldin
Mt. St. Helens
Mt. Rainier
Mt. Shasta
Mt. Adams
40°
Lassen Peak
Fayal
Mauna Loa
La Palma
ilauea
Parícutin
Fogo
Cerro Negro
Mt. Pelée
Irazú
0°
Cotopaxi
El Misti
Azul
40°
Tarawera
Burney
60°
120°
60°
0°

Earth's Volcanic Origin

In July 1979, *Voyager-2* spacecraft images taken of Io, a moon of Jupiter, captured volcanoes in the actual process of eruption. The volcanic plumes photographed rose to some 60 to 100 miles above the surface of the moon. Thus active volcanism is taking place, at present, on at least one planetary body in addition to our Earth.

More than 80 percent of the Earth's surface—above and below sea level—is of volcanic origin. Gaseous emissions from volcanic vents over hundreds of millions of years formed the Earth's earliest oceans and atmosphere. Over geologic eons, countless volcanic eruptions have produced mountains, plateaus, and plains which erosion and weathering have transformed into fertile soils.

Antarctica

The discovery of two small active volcanoes in 1982 brings to five the total number known on Antarctica. The new ones, 30 miles apart, are on the Weddell Sea side of the Antarctic Peninsula. The largest, Mount Erebus (13,000 ft; 3,962 m), rises from McMurdo Sound. Mount Melbourne (9,000 ft; 2,743 m) is in Victoria Land. The fifth, off the northern tip of the Antarctic Peninsula, is a crater known as Deception Island.

Principal Types of Volcanoes

(*Source:* U.S. Dept. of Interior, Geological Survey.)

The word "volcano" comes from the little island of Vulcano in the Mediterranean Sea off Sicily. Centuries ago, the people living in this area believed that Vulcano was the chimney of the forge of Vulcan—the blacksmith of the Roman gods. They thought that the hot lava fragments and clouds of dust erupting from Vulcano came from Vulcan's forge. Today, we know that volcanic eruptions are not supernatural but can be studied and interpreted by scientists.

Geologists generally group volcanoes into four main kinds—cinder cones, composite volcanoes, shield volcanoes, and lava domes.

Cinder Cones

Cinder cones are the simplest type of volcano. They are built from particles and blobs of congealed lava ejected from a single vent. As the gas-charged lava is blown violently into the air, it breaks into small fragments that solidify and fall as cinders around the vent to form a circular or oval cone. Most cinder cones have a bowl-shaped crater at the summit and rarely rise more than a thousand feet or so above their surroundings. Cinder cones are numerous in western North America as well as throughout other volcanic terrains of the world.

Composite Volcanoes

Some of the Earth's grandest mountains are composite volcanoes—sometimes called *stratovolcanoes*. They are typically steep-sided, symmetrical cones of large dimension built of alternating layers of lava flows, volcanic ash, cinders, blocks, and bombs and may rise as much as 8,000 feet above their bases. Some of the most conspicuous and beautiful mountains in the world are composite volcanoes, including Mount Fuji in Japan, Mount Cotopaxi in Ecuador, Mount Shasta in California, Mount Hood in Oregon, and Mount St. Helens and Mount Rainier in Washington.

Most composite volcanoes have a crater at the summit which contains a central vent or a clustered group of vents. Lavas either flow through breaks in the crater wall or issue from fissures on the flanks of the cone. Lava, solidified within the fissures, forms *dikes* that act as ribs which greatly strengthen the cone.

The essential feature of a composite volcano is a conduit system through which magma from a reservoir deep in the Earth's crust rises to the surface. The volcano is built up by the accumulation of material erupted through the conduit and increases in size as lava, cinders, ash, etc., are added to its slopes.

Shield Volcanoes

Shield volcanoes, the third type of volcano, are built almost entirely of fluid lava flows. Flow after flow pours out in all directions from a central summit vent, or group of vents, building a broad, gently sloping cone of flat, domical shape, with a profile much like that of a warrior's shield. They are built up slowly by the accretion of thousands of flows of highly fluid basaltic (from *basalt*, a hard, dense dark volcanic rock) lava that spread widely over great distances, and then cool as thin, gently dipping sheets. Lavas also commonly erupt from vents along fractures (rift zones) that develop on the flanks of the cone. Some of the largest volcanoes in the world are shield volcanoes. In northern California and Oregon, many shield volcanoes have diameters of 3 or 4 miles and heights of 1,500 to 2,000 feet. The Hawaiian Islands are composed of linear chains of these volcanoes, including Kilauea and Mauna Loa on the island of Hawaii.

In some shield-volcano eruptions, basaltic lava pours out quietly from long fissures instead of central vents and floods the surrounding countryside with lava flow upon lava flow, forming broad plateaus. Lava plateaus of this type can be seen in Iceland, southeastern Washington, eastern Oregon, and southern Idaho.

Lava Domes

Volcanic or lava domes are formed by relatively small, bulbous masses of lava too viscous to flow any great distance; consequently, on extrusion, the lava piles over and around its vent. A dome grows largely by expansion from within. As it grows its outer surface cools and hardens, then shatters, spilling loose fragments down its sides. Some domes form craggy knobs or spines over the volcanic vent, whereas others form short, steep-sided lava flows known as "coulees." Volcanic domes commonly occur within the craters or on the flanks of large composite volcanoes. The nearly circular Novarupta Dome that formed during the 1912 eruption of Katmai Volcano, Alaska, measures 800 feet across and 200 feet high. The internal structure of this dome—defined by layering of lava fanning upward and outward from the center—indicates that it grew largely by expansion from within. Mount Pelée in Martinique, West Indies, and Lassen Peak and Mono domes in California, are examples of lava domes.

Submarine Volcanoes

Submarine volcanoes and volcanic vents are common features on certain zones of the ocean floor. Some are active at the present time and, in shallow water, disclose their presence by blasting steam and rock-debris high above the surface of the sea. Many others lie at such great depths that the tremendous weight of the water above them results in high, confining pressure and prevents the formation and release of steam and gases. Even very large, deepwater eruptions may not disturb the ocean floor.

The famous black sand beaches of Hawaii were created virtually instantaneously by the violent interaction between hot lava and sea water.

Plate-Tectonics Theory—The Lithosphere Plates of the Earth

World Population, Land Areas, and Elevations

Area	Estimated population, mid-1989	Approximate Land area sq mi.	Percent of total land area	Population density per sq mi.	Elevation, feet	
					Highest	Lowest
WORLD	5,234,000,000	58,433,000	100.0	89.6	Mt. Everest, Asia, 29,108	Dead Sea, Asia, 1,290 below sea level
ASIA, incl. Philippines, Indonesia, and European and Asiatic Turkey; excl. Asiatic U.S.S.R.	3,061,000,000	10,644,000	18.2	287.6	Mt. Everest, Tibet-Nepal, 29,108	Dead Sea, Israel-Jordan, 1,290 below sea level
AFRICA	646,000,000	11,707,000	20.0	55.2	Mt. Kilimanjaro, Tanzania, 19,340	Lake Assal, Djibouti, 571 below sea level
NORTH AMERICA, including Hawaii, Central America, and Caribbean region	423,000,000	9,360,000	16.0	45.2	Mt. McKinley; Alaska, 20,320	Death Valley, Calif., 282 below sea level
SOUTH AMERICA	290,000,000	6,883,000	11.8	42.1	Mt. Aconcagua, Arg.-Chile, 23,034	Valdes Peninsula, 131 below sea level
ANTARCTICA	—	6,000,000	10.3	—	Vinson Massif, Sentinel Range, 16,863	Sea level
EUROPE, incl. Iceland; excl. European U.S.S.R. and European Turkey	499,000,000	1,905,000	3.3	261.9	Mont Blanc, France, 15,781	Sea level
OCEANIA, incl. Australia, New Zealand, Melanesia, Micronesia, and Polynesia[2]	26,000,000	3,284,000	5.6	7.9	Mauna Kea, Hawaii, 13,796	Lake Eyre, Australia, 38 below sea level
U.S.S.R., both European and Asiatic	289,000,000	8,647,000	14.8	33.4	Communism Peak, Pamir, 24,590	Caspian Sea, 96 below sea level

1. In computing density per square mile, the area of Antarctica is omitted. 2. Although Hawaii is geographically part of Oceania, its population is included in the population figure for North America. *Source:* Population Reference Bureau, Inc.

Plate-Tectonics Theory

(*Source:* U.S. Dept. of the Interior, Geological Survey.)

According to the generally accepted "plate-tectonics" theory, scientists believe that the Earth's surface is broken into a number of shifting slabs or plates, which average about 50 miles in thickness. These plates move relative to one another above a hotter, deeper, more mobile zone at average rates as great as a few inches per year. Most of the world's active volcanoes are located along or near the boundaries between shifting plates and are called "plate-boundary" volcanoes. However, some active volcanoes are not associated with plate boundaries, and many of these so-called "intra-plate" volcanoes form roughly linear chains in the interior of some oceanic plates. The Hawaiian Islands provide perhaps the best example of an "intra-plate" volcanic chain, developed by the northwest-moving Pacific plate passing over an inferred "hot spot" that initiates the magma-generation and volcano-formation process. The peripheral areas of the Pacific Ocean Basin, containing the boundaries of several plates, are dotted by many active volcanoes that form the so-called "Ring of Fire." The "Ring" provides excellent examples of "plate-boundary" volcanoes, including Mount St. Helens.

The accompanying figure on page 464 shows the boundaries of lithosphere plates that are active at present. The double lines indicate zones of spreading from which plates are moving apart. The lines with barbs show zones of underthrusting (subduction), where one plate is sliding beneath another. The barbs on the lines indicate the overriding plate. The single line defines a strike-slip fault along which plates are sliding horizontally past one another. The stippled areas indicate a part of a continent, exclusive of that along a plate boundary, which is undergoing active extensional, compressional, or strike-slip faulting.

Latitude and Longitude of World Cities
(and time corresponding to 12:00 noon, eastern standard time)

City	Lat. ° '	Long. ° '	Time
Aberdeen, Scotland	57 9 n	2 9 w	5:00 p.m.
Adelaide, Australia	34 55 s	138 36 e	2:30 a.m.[1]
Algiers	36 50 n	3 0 e	6:00 p.m.
Amsterdam	52 22 n	4 53 e	6:00 p.m.
Ankara, Turkey	39 55 n	32 55 e	7:00 p.m.
Asunción, Paraguay	25 15 s	57 40 w	1:00 p.m.
Athens	37 58 n	23 43 e	7:00 p.m.
Auckland, New Zealand	36 52 s	174 45 e	5:00 a.m.[1]
Bangkok, Thailand	13 45 n	100 30 e	midnight[1]
Barcelona	41 23 n	2 9 e	6:00 p.m.
Belém, Brazil	1 28 s	48 29 w	2:00 p.m.
Belfast, Northern Ireland	54 37 n	5 56 w	5:00 p.m.
Belgrade, Yugoslavia	44 52 n	20 32 e	6:00 p.m.
Berlin	52 30 n	13 25 e	6:00 p.m.
Birmingham, England	52 25 n	1 55 w	5:00 p.m.
Bogotá, Colombia	4 32 n	74 15 w	12:00 noon
Bombay	19 0 n	72 48 e	10:30 p.m.
Bordeaux, France	44 50 n	0 31 w	6:00 p.m.
Bremen, W. Germany	53 5 n	8 49 e	6:00 p.m.
Brisbane, Australia	27 29 s	153 8 e	3:00 a.m.[1]
Bristol, England	51 28 n	2 35 w	5:00 p.m.
Brussels	50 52 n	4 22 e	6:00 p.m.
Bucharest	44 25 n	26 7 e	7:00 p.m.
Budapest	47 30 n	19 5 e	6:00 p.m.
Buenos Aires	34 35 s	58 22 w	2:00 p.m.
Cairo	30 2 n	31 21 e	7:00 p.m.
Calcutta	22 34 n	88 24 e	10:30 p.m.
Canton, China	23 7 n	113 15 e	1:00 a.m.[1]
Cape Town, South Africa	33 55 s	18 22 e	7:00 p.m.
Caracas, Venezuela	10 28 n	67 2 w	1:00 p.m.
Cayenne, French Guiana	4 49 n	52 18 w	1:00 p.m.
Chihuahua, Mexico	28 37 n	106 5 w	11:00 a.m.
Chongqing, China	29 46 n	106 34 e	1:00 a.m.[1]
Copenhagen	55 40 n	12 34 e	6:00 p.m.
Córdoba, Argentina	31 28 s	64 10 w	2:00 p.m.
Dakar, Senegal	14 40 n	17 28 w	5:00 p.m.
Darwin, Australia	12 28 s	130 51 e	2:30 a.m.[1]
Djibouti	11 30 n	43 3 e	8:00 p.m.
Dublin	53 20 n	6 15 w	5:00 p.m.
Durban, South Africa	29 53 s	30 53 e	7:00 p.m.
Edinburgh, Scotland	55 55 n	3 10 w	5:00 p.m.
Frankfurt	50 7 n	8 41 e	6:00 p.m.
Georgetown, Guyana	6 45 n	58 15 w	1:15 p.m.
Glasgow, Scotland	55 50 n	4 15 w	5:00 p.m.
Guatemala City, Guatemala	14 37 n	90 31 w	11:00 a.m.
Guayaquil, Ecuador	2 10 s	79 56 w	12:00 noon
Hamburg	53 33 n	10 2 e	6:00 p.m.
Hammerfest, Norway	70 38 n	23 38 e	6:00 p.m.
Havana	23 8 n	82 23 w	12:00 noon
Helsinki, Finland	60 10 n	25 0 e	7:00 p.m.
Hobart, Tasmania	42 52 s	147 19 e	3:00 a.m.[1]
Iquique, Chile	20 10 s	70 7 w	1:00 p.m.
Irkutsk, U.S.S.R.	52 30 n	104 20 e	1:00 a.m.
Jakarta, Indonesia	6 16 s	106 48 e	0:30 a.m.[1]
Johannesburg, South Africa	26 12 s	28 4 e	7:00 p.m.
Kingston, Jamaica	17 59 n	76 49 w	12:00 noon
Kinshasa, Zaire	4 18 s	15 17 e	6:00 p.m.
La Paz, Bolivia	16 27 s	68 22 w	1:00 p.m.
Leeds, England	53 45 n	1 30 w	5:00 p.m.
Leningrad	59 56 n	30 18 e	8:00 p.m.
Lima, Peru	12 0 s	77 2 w	2:00 noon
Lisbon	38 44 n	9 9 w	5:00 p.m.
Liverpool, England	53 25 n	3 0 w	5:00 p.m.
London	51 32 n	0 5 w	5:00 p.m.
Lyons, France	45 45 n	4 50 e	6:00 p.m.
Madrid	40 26 n	3 42 w	6:00 p.m.
Manchester, England	53 30 n	2 15 w	5:00 p.m.
Manila	14 35 n	120 57 e	1:00 a.m.[1]
Marseilles, France	43 20 n	5 20 e	6:00 p.m.
Mazatlán, Mexico	23 12 n	106 25 w	10:00 a.m.
Mecca, Saudi Arabia	21 29 n	39 45 e	8:00 p.m.
Melbourne	37 47 s	144 58 e	3:00 a.m.[1]
Mexico City	19 26 n	99 7 w	11:00 a.m.
Milan, Italy	45 27 n	9 10 e	6:00 p.m.
Montevideo, Uruguay	34 53 s	56 10 w	2:00 p.m.
Moscow	55 45 n	37 36 e	8:00 p.m.
Munich, Germany	48 8 n	11 35 e	6:00 p.m.
Nagasaki, Japan	32 48 n	129 57 e	2:00 a.m.[1]
Nagoya, Japan	35 7 n	136 56 e	2:00 a.m.[1]
Nairobi, Kenya	1 25 s	36 55 e	8:00 p.m.
Nanjing (Nanking), China	32 3 n	118 53 e	1:00 a.m.[1]
Naples, Italy	40 50 n	14 15 e	6:00 p.m.
Newcastle-on-Tyne, Eng.	54 58 n	1 37 w	5:00 p.m.
Odessa, U.S.S.R.	46 27 n	30 48 e	8:00 p.m.
Osaka, Japan	34 32 n	135 30 e	2:00 a.m.[1]
Oslo	59 57 n	10 42 e	6:00 p.m.
Panama City, Panama	8 58 n	79 32 w	12:00 noon
Paramaribo, Surinam	5 45 n	55 15 w	1:30 p.m.
Paris	48 48 n	2 20 e	6:00 p.m.
Peking	39 55 n	116 25 e	1:00 a.m.[1]
Perth, Australia	31 57 s	115 52 e	1:00 a.m.[1]
Plymouth, England	50 25 n	4 5 w	5:00 p.m.
Port Moresby, Papua New Guinea	9 25 s	147 8 e	3:00 a.m.[1]
Prague	50 5 n	14 26 e	6:00 p.m.
Reykjavik, Iceland	64 4 n	21 58 w	4:00 p.m.
Rio de Janeiro	22 57 s	43 12 w	2:00 p.m.
Rome	41 54 n	12 27 e	6:00 p.m.
Salvador, Brazil	12 56 s	38 27 w	2:00 p.m.
Santiago, Chile	33 28 s	70 45 w	1:00 p.m.
Sao Paulo, Brazil	23 31 s	46 31 w	2:00 p.m.
Shanghai, China	31 10 n	121 28 e	1:00 a.m.[1]
Singapore	1 14 n	103 55 e	0:30 a.m.[1]
Sofia, Bulgaria	42 40 n	23 20 e	7:00 p.m.
Stockholm	59 17 n	18 3 e	6:00 p.m.
Sydney, Australia	34 0 s	151 0 e	3:00 a.m.[1]
Tananarive, Madagascar	18 50 s	47 33 e	8:00 p.m.
Teheran, Iran	35 45 n	51 45 e	8:30 p.m.
Tokyo	35 40 n	139 45 e	2:00 a.m.[1]
Tripoli, Libya	32 57 n	13 12 e	7:00 p.m.
Venice	45 26 n	12 20 e	6:00 p.m.
Veracruz, Mexico	19 10 n	96 10 w	11:00 a.m.
Vienna	48 14 n	16 20 e	6:00 p.m.
Vladivostok, U.S.S.R.	43 10 n	132 0 e	3:00 a.m.[1]
Warsaw	52 14 n	21 0 e	6:00 p.m.
Wellington, New Zealand	41 17 s	174 47 e	5:00 a.m.[1]
Yangon, Myanmar	16 50 n	96 0 e	11:30 p.m.
Zürich	47 21 n	8 31 e	6:00 p.m.

1. On the following day.

Highest Mountain Peaks of the World

(For U.S. peaks, see Index)

Mountain peak	Range	Location	Height feet	Height meters
Everest[1]	Himalayas	Nepal-Tibet	29,108	8,872
Godwin Austen (K-2)	Karakoram	Kashmir	29,064	8,858
Kanchenjunga	Himalayas	Nepal-Sikkim	28,208	8,598
Lhotse	Himalayas	Nepal-Tibet	27,890	8,501
Makalu	Himalayas	Tibet-Nepal	27,790	8,470
Dhaulagiri I	Himalayas	Nepal	26,810	8,172
Manaslu	Himalayas	Nepal	26,760	8,156
Cho Oyu	Himalayas	Nepal	26,750	8,153
Nanga Parbat	Himalayas	Kashmir	26,660	8,126
Annapurna I	Himalayas	Nepal	26,504	8,078
Gasherbrum I	Karakoram	Kashmir	26,470	8,068
Broad Peak	Karakoram	Kashmir	26,400	8,047
Gasherbrum II	Karakoram	Kashmir	26,360	8,033
Gosainthan	Himalayas	Tibet	26,291	8,013
Gasherbrum III	Karakoram	Kashmir	26,090	7,952
Annapurna II	Himalayas	Nepal	26,041	7,937
Gasherbrum IV	Karakoram	India	26,000	7,925
Kangbachen	Himalayas	Nepal	25,925	7,902
Gyachung Kang	Himalayas	Nepal	25,910	7,897
Himal Chuli	Himalayas	Nepal	25,895	7,893
Disteghil Sar	Karakoram	Kashmir	25,868	7,885
Nuptse	Himalayas	Nepal	25,850	7,829
Kunyang Kish	Karakoram	Kashmir	25,760	7,852
Dakum (Peak 29)	Himalayas	Nepal	25,760	7,852
Masherbrum	Karakoram	Kashmir	25,660	7,821
Nanda Devi	Himalayas	India	25,645	7,817
Chomolonzo	Himalayas	Nepal-Tibet	25,640	7,815
Rakaposhi	Karakoram	Kashmir	25,550	7,788
Batura	Karakoram	Kashmir	25,540	7,785
Kanjut Sar	Karakoram	Kashmir	25,460	7,760
Kamet	Himalayas	India-Tibet	25,447	7,756
Namche Barwa	Himalayas	Tibet	25,445	7,756
Dhaulagiri II	Himalayas	Nepal	25,427	7,750
Saltoro Kangri	Karakoram	India	25,400	7,742
Gurla Mandhata	Himalayas	Tibet	25,355	7,728
Ulugh Muztagh	Kunlun	Tibet	25,341	7,724
Trivor	Karakoram	Kashmir	25,330	7,721
Jannu	Himalayas	Nepal	25,294	7,710
Tirich Mir	Hindu Kush	Pakistan	25,230	7,690
Saser Kangri	Karakoram	India	25,170	7,672
Makalu II	Himalayas	Nepal	25,130	7,660
Chogolisa	Karakoram	India	25,110	7,654
Dhaulagiri IV	Himalayas	Nepal	25,064	7,639
Fang	Himalayas	Nepal	25,013	7,624
Kula Kangri	Himalayas	Bhutan	24,783	7,554
Changtse	Himalayas	Tibet	24,780	7,553
Muztagh Ata	Muztagh Ata	China	24,757	7,546
Skyang Kangri	Himalayas	Kashmir	24,750	7,544
Communism Peak	Pamir	U.S.S.R.	24,590	7,495
Victory Peak	Pamir	U.S.S.R.	24,406	7,439
Sia Kangri	Himalayas	Kashmir	24,340	7,419
Chamlang	Himalayas	Nepal	24,012	7,319
Alung Gangri	Himalayas	Tibet	23,999	7,315
Chomo Lhari	Himalayas	Tibet-Bhutan	23,996	7,314
Muztagh (K-5)	Kunlun	China	23,891	7,282
Amne Machin	Kunlun	China	23,490	7,160
Gaurisankar	Himalayas	Nepal-Tibet	23,440	7,145
Lenin Peak	Pamir	U.S.S.R.	23,405	7,134
Korzhenevski Peak	Pamir	U.S.S.R.	23,310	7,105
Kangto	Himalayas	Tibet	23,260	7,090
Dunagiri	Himalayas	India	23,184	7,066
Pauhunri	Himalayas	India-Tibet	23,180	7,065
Aconcagua	Andes	Argentina-Chile	23,034	7,021
Revolution Peak	Pamir	U.S.S.R.	22,880	6,974
Kangchenjhan	Himalayas	India	22,700	6,919
Siniolchu	Himalayas	India	22,620	6,895

Mountain peak	Range	Location	Height (feet)	Height (meters)
Ojos des Salado	Andes	Argentina-Chile	22,588	6,885
Bonete	Andes	Argentina-Chile	22,546	6,872
Simvuo	Himalayas	India	22,346	6,811
Tup	Andes	Argentina	22,309	6,800
Kungpu	Himalayas	Bhutan	22,300	6,797
Falso-Azufre	Andes	Argentina-Chile	22,277	6,790
Moscow Peak	Pamir	U.S.S.R.	22,260	6,785
Veladero	Andes	Argentina	22,244	6,780
Pissis	Andes	Argentina	22,241	6,779
Mercedario	Andes	Argentina-Chile	22,211	6,770
Huascarán	Andes	Peru	22,198	6,766
Tocorpuri	Andes	Bolivia-Chile	22,162	6,755
Karl Marx Peak	Pamir	U.S.S.R.	22,067	6,726
Llullaillaco	Andes	Argentina-Chile	22,057	6,723
Libertador	Andes	Argentina	22,047	6,720
Kailas	Himalayas	Tibet	22,027	6,714
Lingtren	Himalayas	Nepal-Tibet ·	21,972	6,697
Incahuasi	Andes	Argentina-Chile	21,719	6,620
Carnicero	Andes	Peru	21,689	6,611
Kurumda	Pamir	U.S.S.R.	21,686	6,610
Garmo Peak	Pamir	U.S.S.R.	21,637	6,595
Sajama	Andes	Bolivia	21,555	6,570
Ancohuma	Andes	Bolivia	21,490	6,550
El Muerto	Andes	Argentina-Chile	21,456	6,540
Nacimiento	Andes	Argentina	21,302	6,493
Illimani	Andes	Bolivia	21,184	6,457
Antofalla	Andes	Argentina-Chile	21,129	6,440
Coropuña	Andes	Peru	21,079	6,425
Cuzco (Ausangate)	Andes	Peru	20,995	6,399
Toro	Andes	Argentina-Chile	20,932	6,380
Parinacota	Andes	Bolivia-Chile	20,768	6,330
Chimboraso	Andes	Ecuador	20,702	6,310
Salcantay	Andes	Peru	20,575	6,271
General Manuel Belgrano	Andes	Argentina	20,505	6,250
Chañi	Andes	Argentina	20,341	6,200
Caca Aca	Andes	Bolivia	20,328	6,196
McKinley	Alaska	Alaska	20,320	6,194
Vudor Peak	Pamir	U.S.S.R.	20,118	6,132
Condoriri	Andes	Bolivia	20,095	6,125
Solimana	Andes	Peru	20,069	6,117
Nevada	Andes	Argentina	20,023	6,103

Oceans and Seas

Name	Area (sq mi.)	Area (sq km)	Average depth (feet)	Average depth (meters)	Greatest known depth (feet)	Greatest known depth (meters)	Place greatest known depth
Pacific Ocean	64,000,000	165,760,000	13,215	4,028	35,820	10,918	Mindanao Deep
Atlantic Ocean	31,815,000	82,400,000	12,880	3,926	30,246	9,219	Puerto Rico Trough
Indian Ocean	25,300,000	65,526,700	13,002	3,963	24,460	7,455	Sunda Trench
Arctic Ocean	5,440,200	14,090,000	3,953	1,205	18,456	5,625	77° 45' N; 175° W
Mediterranean Sea[1]	1,145,100	2,965,800	4,688	1,429	15,197	4,632	Off Cape Matapan, Greece
Caribbean Sea	1,049,500	2,718,200	8,685	2,647	22,788	6,946	Off Cayman Islands
South China Sea	895,400	2,319,000	5,419	1,652	16,456	5,016	West of Luzon
Bering Sea	884,900	2,291,900	5,075	1,547	15,659	4,773	Off Buldir Island
Gulf of Mexico	615,000	1,592,800	4,874	1,486	12,425	3,787	Sigsbee Deep
Okhotsk Sea	613,800	1,589,700	2,749	838	12,001	3,658	146° 10' E; 46° 50' N
East China Sea	482,300	1,249,200	617	188	9,126	2,782	25° 16' N; 125° E
Hudson Bay	475,800	1,232,300	420	128	600	183	Near entrance
Japan Sea	389,100	1,007,800	4,429	1,350	12,276	3,742	Central Basin
Andaman Sea	308,100	797,700	2,854	870	12,392	3,777	Off Car Nicobar Island
North Sea	222,100	575,200	308	94	2,165	660	Skagerrak
Red Sea	169,100	438,000	1,611	491	7,254	2,211	Off Port Sudan
Baltic Sea	163,000	422,200	180	55	1,380	421	Off Gotland

1. Includes Black Sea and Sea of Azov. NOTE: For Caspian Sea, *see* Large Lakes of World elsewhere in this section.

World's Greatest Man-Made Lakes[1]

Name of dam	Location	Millions of cubic meters	Thousands of acre-feet	Year completed
Owen Falls	Uganda	204,800	166,000	1954
Kariba	Zimbabwe	181,592	147,218	1959
Bratsk	U.S.S.R.	169,270	137,220	1964
High Aswan (Sadd-el-Aali)	Egypt	168,000	136,200	1970
Akosombo	Ghana	148,000	120,000	1965
Daniel Johnson	Canada	141,852	115,000	1968
Guri (Raul Leoni)	Venezuela	136,000	110,256	1986
Krasnoyarsk	U.S.S.R.	73,300	59,425	1967
Bennett W.A.C.	Canada	70,309	57,006	1967
Zeya	U.S.S.R.	68,400	55,452	1978
Cabora Bassa	Mozambique	63,000	51,075	1974
LaGrande 2	Canada	61,720	50,037	1982
LaGrande 3	Canada	60,020	48,659	1982
Ust'—Ilimsk	U.S.S.R.	59,300	48,075	1980
Volga—V.I. Lenin	U.S.S.R.	58,000	47,020	1955
Caniapiscau	Canada	53,790	43,608	1981
Pati (Chapetón)	Argentina	53,700	43,535	UC
Upper Wainganga	India	50,700	41,103	1987
São Felix	Brazil	50,600	41,022	1986
Bukhtarma	U.S.S.R.	49,740	40,325	1960
Atatürk (Karababa)	Turkey	48,700	39,482	UC
Cerros Colorados	Argentina	48,000	38,914	1973
Irkutsk	U.S.S.R.	46,000	37,290	1956
Tucuruí	Brazil	36,375	29,489	1984
Vilyuy	U.S.S.R.	35,900	29,104	1967
Sanmenxia	China	35,400	28,700	1960
Hoover	Nevada/Arizona	35,154	28,500	1936
Sobridinho	Brazil	34,200	27,726	1981
Glen Canyon	Arizona	33,304	27,000	1964
Jenpeg	Canada	31,790	25,772	1975

1. Formed by construction of dams. NOTE: UC = under construction. *Source:* Department of the Interior, Bureau of Reclamation and *International Water Power and Dam Construction.*

Large Lakes of the World

Name and location	Area sq mi.	Area sq km	Length mi.	Length km	Maximum depth feet	Maximum depth meters
Caspian Sea, U.S.S.R.-Iran[1]	152,239	394,299	745	1,199	3,104	946
Superior, U.S.-Canada	31,820	82,414	383	616	1,333	406
Victoria, Tanzania—Uganda	26,828	69,485	200	322	270	82
Aral, U.S.S.R.	25,659	66,457	266	428	223	68
Huron, U.S.-Canada	23,010	59,596	247	397	750	229
Michigan, U.S.	22,400	58,016	321	517	923	281
Tanganyika, Tanzania-Zaire	12,700	32,893	420	676	4,708	1,435
Baikal, U.S.S.R.	12,162	31,500	395	636	5,712	1,741
Great Bear, Canada	12,000	31,080	232	373	270	82
Nyasa, Malawi-Mozambique-Tanzania	11,600	30,044	360	579	2,316	706
Great Slave, Canada	11,170	28,930	298	480	2,015	614
Chad,[2] Chad-Niger-Nigeria	9,946	25,760	—	—	23	7
Erie, U.S.-Canada	9,930	25,719	241	388	210	64
Winnipeg, Canada	9,094	23,553	264	425	204	62
Ontario, U.S.-Canada	7,520	19,477	193	311	778	237
Balkash, U.S.S.R.	7,115	18,428	376	605	87	27
Ladoga, U.S.S.R.	7,000	18,130	124	200	738	225
Onega, U.S.S.R.	3,819	9,891	154	248	361	110
Titicaca, Bolivia-Peru	3,141	8,135	110	177	1,214	370
Nicaragua, Nicaragua	3,089	8,001	110	177	230	70
Athabaska, Canada	3,058	7,920	208	335	407	124
Rudolf, Kenya	2,473	6,405	154	248	—	—
Reindeer, Canada	2,444	6,330	152	245	—	—
Eyre, South Australia	2,400[3]	6,216	130	209	varies	varies
Issyk-Kul, U.S.S.R.	2,394	6,200	113	182	2,297	700
Urmia,[2] Iran	2,317	6,001	81	130	49	15
Torrens, South Australia	2,200	5,698	130	209	—	—
Vänern, Sweden	2,141	5,545	87	140	322	98

Name and location	Area		Length		Maximum depth	
	sq mi.	sq km	mi.	km	feet	meters
Winnipegosis, Canada	2,086	5,403	152	245	59	18
Mobutu Sese Seko, Uganda	2,046	5,299	100	161	180	55
Nettilling, Baffin Island, Canada	1,950	5,051	70	113	—	—
Nipigon, Canada	1,870	4,843	72	116	—	—
Manitoba, Canada	1,817	4,706	140	225	22	7
Great Salt, U.S.	1,800	4,662	75	121	15/25	5/8
Kioga, Uganda	1,700	4,403	50	80	about 30	9
Koko-Nor, China	1,630	4,222	66	106	—	—

1. The Caspian Sea is called "sea" because the Romans, finding it salty, named it *Mare Caspium*. Many geographers, however, consider it a lake because it is land-locked. 2. Figures represent high-water data. 3. Varies with the rainfall of the wet season. It has been reported to dry up almost completely on occasion.

Principal Rivers of the World

(For other U.S. rivers, see Index)

River	Source	Outflow	Approx. length	
			miles	km
Nile	Tributaries of Lake Victoria, Africa	Mediterranean Sea	4,180	6,690
Amazon	Glacier-fed lakes, Peru	Atlantic Ocean	3,912	6,296
Mississippi-Missouri-Red Rock	Source of Red Rock, Montana	Gulf of Mexico	3,880	6,240
Yangtze Kiang	Tibetan plateau, China	China Sea	3,602	5,797
Ob	Altai Mts., U.S.S.R.	Gulf of Ob	3,459	5,567
Yellow (Huang Ho)	Eastern part of Kunlan Mts., west China	Gulf of Chihli	2,900	4,667
Yenisei	Tannu-Ola Mts., western Tuva, U.S.S.R.	Arctic Ocean	2,800	4,506
Paraná	Confluence of Paranaiba and Grande rivers	Río de la Plata	2,795	4,498
Irtish	Altai Mts., U.S.S.R.	Ob River	2,758	4,438
Congo	Confluence of Lualaba and Luapula rivers, Zaire	Atlantic Ocean	2,716	4,371
Heilong (Amur)	Confluence of Shilka (U.S.S.R.) and Argun (Manchuria) rivers	Tatar Strait	2,704	4,352
Lena	Baikal Mts., U.S.S.R.	Arctic Ocean	2,652	4,268
Mackenzie	Head of Finlay River, British Columbia, Canada	Beaufort Sea (Arctic Ocean)	2,635	4,241
Niger	Guinea	Gulf of Guinea	2,600	4,184
Mekong	Tibetan highlands	South China Sea	2,500	4,023
Mississippi	Lake Itasca, Minnesota	Gulf of Mexico	2,348	3,779
Missouri	Confluence of Jefferson, Gallatin, and Madison rivers, Montana	Mississippi River	2,315	3,726
Volga	Valdai plateau, U.S.S.R.	Caspian Sea	2,291	3,687
Madeira	Confluence of Beni and Maumoré rivers, Bolivia-Brazil boundary	Amazon River	2,012	3,238
Purus	Peruvian Andes	Amazon River	1,993	3,207
São Francisco	Southwest Minas Gerais, Brazil	Atlantic Ocean	1,987	3,198
Yukon	Junction of Lewes and Pelly rivers, Yukon Territory, Canada	Bering Sea	1,979	3,185
St. Lawrence	Lake Ontario	Gulf of St. Lawrence	1,900	3,058
Rio Grande	San Juan Mts., Colorado	Gulf of Mexico	1,885	3,034
Brahmaputra	Himalayas	Ganges River	1,800	2,897
Indus	Himalayas	Arabian Sea	1,800	2,897
Danube	Black Forest, W. Germany	Black Sea	1,766	2,842

River	Source	Outflow	Approx. length	
			miles	km
Euphrates	Confluence of Murat Nehri and Kara Su rivers, Turkey	Shatt-al-Arab	1,739	2,799
Darling	Central part of Eastern Highlands, Australia	Murray River	1,702	2,739
Zambezi	11°21′S, 24°22′E, Zambia	Mozambique Channel	1,700	2,736
Tocantins	Goiás, Brazil	Pará River	1,677	2,699
Murray	Australian Alps, New South Wales	Indian Ocean	1,609	2,589
Nelson	Head of Bow River, western Alberta, Canada	Hudson Bay	1,600	2,575
Paraguay	Mato Grosso, Brazil	Paraná River	1,584	2,549
Ural	Southern Ural Mts., U.S.S.R.	Caspian Sea	1,574	2,533
Ganges	Himalayas	Bay of Bengal	1,557	2,506
Amu Darya (Oxus)	Nicholas Range, Pamir Mts., U.S.S.R.	Aral Sea	1,500	2,414
Japurá	Andes, Colombia	Amazon River	1,500	2,414
Salween	Tibet, south of Kunlun Mts.	Gulf of Martaban	1,500	2,414
Arkansas	Central Colorado	Mississippi River	1,459	2,348
Colorado	Grand County, Colorado	Gulf of California	1,450	2,333
Dnieper	Valdai Hills, U.S.S.R.	Black Sea	1,419	2,284
Ohio-Allegheny	Potter County, Pennsylvania	Mississippi River	1,306	2,102
Irrawaddy	Confluence of Nmai and Mali rivers, northeast Burma	Bay of Bengal	1,300	2,092
Orange	Lesotho	Atlantic Ocean	1,300	2,092
Orinoco	Serra Parima Mts., Venezuela	Atlantic Ocean	1,281	2,062
Pilcomayo	Andes Mts., Bolivia	Paraguay River	1,242	1,999
Xi Jiang (Si Kiang)	Eastern Yunnan Province, China	China Sea	1,236	1,989
Columbia	Columbia Lake, British Columbia, Canada	Pacific Ocean	1,232	1,983
Don	Tula, R.S.F.S.R., U.S.S.R.	Sea of Azov	1,223	1,968
Sungari	China-North Korea boundary	Amur River	1,215	1,955
Saskatchewan	Canadian Rocky Mts.	Lake Winnipeg	1,205	1,939
Peace	Stikine Mts., British Columbia, Canada	Great Slave River	1,195	1,923
Tigris	Taurus Mts., Turkey	Shatt-al-Arab	1,180	1,899

Highest Waterfalls of the World

Waterfall	Location	River	Height	
			feet	meters
Angel	Venezuela	Tributary of Caroni	3,281	1,000
Tugela	Natal, South Africa	Tugela	3,000	914
Cuquenán	Venezuela	Cuquenán	2,000	610
Sutherland	South Island, N.Z.	Arthur	1,904	580
Takkakaw	British Columbia	Tributary of Yoho	1,650	503
Ribbon (Yosemite)	California	Creek flowing into Yosemite	1,612	491
Upper Yosemite	California	Yosemite Creek, tributary of Merced	1,430	436
Gavarnie	Southwest France	Gave de Pau	1,384	422
Vettisfoss	Norway	Mörkedola	1,200	366
Widows' Tears (Yosemite)	California	Tributary of Merced	1,170	357
Staubbach	Switzerland	Staubbach (Lauterbrunnen Valley)	984	300

Waterfall	Location	River	Height feet	Height meters
Middle Cascade (Yosemite)	California	Yosemite Creek, tributary of Merced	909	277
King Edward VIII	Guyana	Courantyne	850	259
Gersoppa	India	Sharavati	829	253
Kaieteur	Guyana	Potaro	822	251
Skykje	Norway	In Skykjedal (valley of Inner Hardinger Fjord)	820	250
Kalambo	Tanzania-Zambia	—	720	219
Fairy (Mount Rainier Park)	Washington	Stevens Creek	700	213
Trummelbach	Switzerland	Trummelbach (Lauterbrunnen Valley)	700	213
Aniene (Teverone)	Italy	Tiber	680	207
Cascata delle Marmore	Italy	Velino, tributary of Nera	650	198
Maradalsfos	Norway	Stream flowing into Ejkisdalsvand (lake)	643	196
Feather	California	Fall River	640	195
Maletsunyane	Lesotho	Maletsunyane	630	192
Bridalveil (Yosemite)	California	Yosemite Creek	620	189
Multnomah	Oregon	Multnomah Creek, tributary of Columbia	620	189
Vøringsfos	Norway	Bjoreia	597	182
Nevada (Yosemite)	California	Merced	594	181
Skjeggedal	Norway	Tysso	525	160
Marina	Guyana	Tributary of Kuribrong, tributary of Potaro	500	152
Tequendama	Colombia	Funza, tributary of Magdalena	425	130
King George's	Cape of Good Hope, South Africa	Orange	400	122
Illilouette (Yosemite)	California	Illilouette Creek, tributary of Merced	370	113
Victoria	Rhodesia-Zambia boundary	Zambezi	355	108
Handöl	Sweden	Handöl Creek	345	105
Lower Yosemite	California	Yosemite	320	98
Comet (Mount Rainier Park)	Washington	Van Trump Creek	320	98
Vernal (Yosemite)	California	Merced	317	97
Virginia	Northwest Territories, Canada	South Nahanni, tributary of Mackenzie	315	96
Lower Yellowstone	Wyoming	Yellowstone	310	94

NOTE: Niagara Falls (New York-Ontario), though of great volume, has parallel drops of only 158 and 167 feet.

Large Islands of the World

Island	Location and status	Area sq mi.	Area sq km
Greenland	North Atlantic (Danish)	839,999	2,175,597
New Guinea	Southwest Pacific (Irian Jaya, Indonesian, west part; Papua New Guinea, east part)	316,615	820,033
Borneo	West mid-Pacific (Indonesian, south part; British protectorate, and Malaysian, north part)	286,914	743,107
Madagascar	Indian Ocean (Malagasy Republic)	226,657	587,042
Baffin	North Atlantic (Canadian)	183,810	476,068
Sumatra	Northeast Indian Ocean (Indonesian)	182,859	473,605
Honshu	Sea of Japan-Pacific (Japanese)	88,925	230,316
Great Britain	Off coast of NW Europe (England, Scotland, and Wales)	88,758	229,883
Ellesmere	Arctic Ocean (Canadian)	82,119	212,688
Victoria	Arctic Ocean (Canadian)	81,930	212,199
Celebes	West mid-Pacific (Indonesian)	72,986	189,034
South Island	South Pacific (New Zealand)	58,093	150,461
Java	Indian Ocean (Indonesian)	48,990	126,884
North Island	South Pacific (New Zealand)	44,281	114,688

Island	Location and status	Area sq mi.	Area sq km
Cuba	Caribbean Sea (republic)	44,218	114,525
Newfoundland	North Atlantic (Canadian)	42,734	110,681
Luzon	West mid-Pacific (Philippines)	40,420	104,688
Iceland	North Atlantic (republic)	39,768	102,999
Mindanao	West mid-Pacific (Philippines)	36,537	94,631
Ireland	West of Great Britain (republic, south part; United Kingdom, north part)	32,597	84,426
Hokkaido	Sea of Japan—Pacific (Japanese)	30,372	78,663
Hispaniola	Caribbean Sea (Dominican Republic, east part; Haiti, west part)	29,355	76,029
Tasmania	South of Australia (Australian)	26,215	67,892
Sri Lanka (Ceylon)	Indian Ocean (republic)	25,332	65,610
Sakhalin (Karafuto)	North of Japan (U.S.S.R.)	24,560	63,610
Banks	Arctic Ocean (Canadian)	23,230	60,166
Devon	Arctic Ocean (Canadian)	20,861	54,030
Tierra del Fuego	Southern tip of South America (Argentinian, east part; Chilean, west part)	18,605	48,187
Kyushu	Sea of Japan—Pacific (Japanese)	16,223	42,018
Melville	Arctic Ocean (Canadian)	16,141	41,805
Axel Heiberg	Arctic Ocean (Canadian)	15,779	40,868
Southampton	Hudson Bay (Canadian)	15,700	40,663

Principal Deserts of the World

Desert	Location	Approximate size	Approx. elevation, ft
Atacama	North Chile	400 mi. long	7,000–13,500
Black Rock	Northwest Nevada	About 1,000 sq mi.	2,000–8,500
Colorado	Southeast California from San Gorgonio Pass to Gulf of California	200 mi. long and a maximum width of 50 mi.	Few feet above to 250 below sea level
Dasht-e-Kavir	Southeast of Caspian Sea, Iran	—	2,000
Dasht-e-Lut	Northeast of Kerman, Iran	—	1,000
Gobi (Shamo)	Covers most of Mongolia	500,000 sq mi.	3,000–5,000
Great Arabian	Most of Arabia	1,500 mi. long	—
An Nafud (Red Desert)	South of Jauf	400 mi. by avg of 140 mi.	3,000
Dahna	Northeast of Nejd	400 mi. by 30 mi.	—
Rub' al-Khali	South portion of Nejd	Over 200,000 sq. mi.	—
Syrian (Al-Hamad)	North of lat. 30° N	—	1,850
Great Australian	Western portion of Australia	About one half the continent	600–1,000
Great Salt Lake	West of Great Salt Lake to Nevada—Utah boundary	About 110 mi. by 50 mi.	4,500
Kalahari	South Africa—South-West Africa	About 120,000 sq mi.	Over 3,000
Kara Kum (Desert of Kiva)	Southwest Turkmen, U.S.S.R.	115,000 sq mi.	—
Kyzyl Kum	Uzbek and Kazakh, U.S.S.R.	Over 100,000 sq. mi.	160 near Lake Aral to 2,000 in southeast
Libyan	Libya, Egypt, Sudan	Over 500,000 sq mi.	—
Mojave	North of Colorado Desert and south of Death Valley, southeast California	15,000 sq mi.	2,000
Nubian	From Red Sea to great west bend of the Nile, Sudan	—	2,500
Painted Desert	Northeast Arizona	Over 7,000 sq mi.	High plateau, 5,000
Sahara	North Africa to about lat. 15° N and from Red Sea to Atlantic Ocean	3,200 mi. greatest length along lat. 20° N; area over 3,500,000 sq mi.	440 below sea level to 11,000 above; avg elevation, 1,400–1,600
Takla Makan	South central Sinkiang, China	Over 100,000 sq mi.	—
Thar (Indian)	Pakistan-India	Nearly 100,000 sq mi.	Over 1,000

Interesting Caves and Caverns of the World

Aggtelek. In village of same name, northern Hungary. Large stalactitic cavern about 5 miles long.

Altamira Cave. Near Santander, Spain. Contains animal paintings (Old Stone Age art) on roof and walls.

Antiparos. On island of same name in the Grecian Archipelago. Some stalactites are 20 ft long. Brilliant colors and fantastic shapes.

Blue Grotto. On island of Capri, Italy. Cavern hollowed out in limestone by constant wave action. Now half filled with water because of sinking coast. Name derived from unusual blue light permeating the cave. Source of light is a submerged opening, light passing through the water.

Carlsbad Caverns. Southeast New Mexico. Largest underground labyrinth yet discovered. Three levels: 754, 900, and 1,320 ft below the surface.

Fingal's Cave. On island of Staffa off coast of western Scotland. Penetrates about 200 ft inland. Contains basaltic columns almost 40 ft high.

Ice Cave. Near Dobsina, Czechoslovakia. Noted for its beautiful crystal effects.

Jenolan Caves. In Blue Mountain plateau, New South Wales, Australia. Beautiful stalactitic formations.

Kent's Cavern. Near Torquay, England. Source of much information on Paleolithic man.

Luray Cavern. Near Luray, Va. Has large stalactitic and stalagmitic columns of many colors.

Mammoth Cave. Limestone cavern in central Kentucky. Cave area is about 10 miles in diameter but has at least 150 miles of irregular subterranean passageways at various levels. Temperature remains fairly constant at 54° F.

Peak Cavern or Devil's Hole. Derbyshire, England. About 2,250 ft into a mountain. Lowest part is about 600 ft below the surface.

Postojna (Postumia) Grotto. Near Postumia in Julian Alps, about 25 miles northeast of Trieste. Stalactitic cavern, largest in Europe. Piuca (Pivka) River flows through part of it. Caves have numerous beautiful stalactites.

Singing Cave. Iceland. A lava cave; name derived from echoes of people singing in it.

Wind Cave. In Black Hills of South Dakota. Limestone caverns with stalactites and stalagmites almost entirely missing. Variety of crystal formations called "boxwork."

Wyandotte Cave. In Crawford County, southern Indiana. A limestone cavern with five levels of passages; one of the largest in North America. "Monumental Mountain," approximately 135 ft high, is believed to be one of the world's largest underground "mountains."

U.S. Geography

Miscellaneous Data for the United States

Source: Department of the Interior, U.S. Geological Survey.

Highest point: Mount McKinley, Alaska	20,320 ft (6,198 m)
Lowest point: Death Valley, Calif.	282 ft (86 m) below sea level
Approximate mean altitude	2,500 ft (763 m)
Points farthest apart (50 states):	
Log Point, Elliot Key, Fla., and Kure Island, Hawaii	5,859 mi. (9,429 km)
Geographic center (50 states):	
In Butte County, S.D. (west of Castle Rock)	44° 58′ N. lat. 103° 46′ W. long.
Geographic center (48 conterminous states):	
In Smith County, Kan. (near Lebanon)	39° 50′ N. lat. 98° 35′ W. long.
Boundaries:	
Between Alaska and Canada	1,538 mi. (2,475 km)
Between the 48 conterminous states and Canada (incl. Great Lakes)	3,987 mi. (6,416 km)
Between the United States and Mexico	1,933 mi. (3,111 km)

Extreme Points of the United States (50 States)

Extreme point	Latitude	Longitude	Distance[1] mi.	km
Northernmost point: Point Barrow, Alaska	71°23′ N	156°29′ W	2,057	3,311
Easternmost point: West Quoddy Head, Me.	44°49′ N	66°57′ W	1,788	2,997
Southernmost point: Ka Lae (South Cape), Hawaii	18°55′ N	155°41′ W	3,463	5,573
Westernmost point: Pochnoi Point, Alaska (Semisopochnoi Island)	51°17′ N	172°09′ E	3,372	5,426

1. From geographic center of United States (incl. Alaska and Hawaii), west of Castle Rock, S.D., 44°58′ N. lat., 103°46′ W long.

Highest, Lowest, and Mean Altitudes in the United States

State	Altitude, ft[1]	Highest point	Altitude, ft	Lowest point	Altitude, ft
Alabama	500	Cheaha Mountain	2,405	Gulf of Mexico	Sea level
Alaska	1,900	Mount McKinley	20,320	Pacific Ocean	Sea level
Arizona	4,100	Humphreys Peak	12,633	Colorado River	70
Arkansas	650	Magazine Mountain	2,753	Ouachita River	55
California	2,900	Mount Whitney	14,494	Death Valley	282[2]
Colorado	6,800	Mount Elbert	14,433	Arkansas River	3,350
Connecticut	500	Mount Frissell, on south slope	2,380	Long Island Sound	Sea level
Delaware	60	On Ebright Road	442	Atlantic Ocean	Sea level
D.C.	—	Tenleytown, at Reno Reservoir	410	Potomac River	1
Florida	100	Sec. 30, T6N, R20W[3]	345	Atlantic Ocean	Sea level
Georgia	600	Brasstown Bald	4,784	Atlantic Ocean	Sea level
Hawaii	3,030	Puu Wekiu, Mauna Kea	13,796	Pacific Ocean	Sea level
Idaho	5,000	Borah Peak	12,662	Snake River	710
Illinois	600	Charles Mound	1,235	Mississippi River	279
Indiana	700	Franklin Township, Wayne County	1,257	Ohio River	320
Iowa	1,100	Sec. 29, T100N, R41W[4]	1,670	Mississippi River	480
Kansas	2,000	Mount Sunflower	4,039	Verdigris River	679
Kentucky	750	Black Mountain	4,139	Mississippi River	257
Louisiana	100	Driskill Mountain	535	New Orleans	8[2]
Maine	600	Mount Katahdin	5,267	Atlantic Ocean	Sea level
Maryland	350	Backbone Mountain	3,360	Atlantic Ocean	Sea level
Massachusetts	500	Mount Greylock	3,487	Atlantic Ocean	Sea level
Michigan	900	Mount Curwood	1,980	Lake Erie	570
Minnesota	1,200	Eagle Mountain	2,301	Lake Superior	605
Mississippi	300	Woodall Mountain	806	Gulf of Mexico	Sea level
Missouri	800	Taum Sauk Mountain	1,772	St. Francis River	230
Montana	3,400	Granite Peak	12,799	Kootenai River	1,800
Nebraska	2,600	Johnson Township, Kimball County	5,426	Missouri River	840
Nevada	5,500	Boundary Peak	13,140	Colorado River	479
New Hampshire	1,000	Mount Washington	6,288	Atlantic Ocean	Sea level
New Jersey	250	High Point	1,803	Atlantic Ocean	Sea level
New Mexico	5,700	Wheeler Peak	13,161	Red Bluff Reservoir	2,842
New York	1,000	Mount Marcy	5,344	Atlantic Ocean	Sea level
North Carolina	700	Mount Mitchell	6,684	Atlantic Ocean	Sea level
North Dakota	1,900	White Butte	3,506	Red River	750
Ohio	850	Campbell Hill	1,549	Ohio River	455
Oklahoma	1,300	Black Mesa	4,973	Little River	289
Oregon	3,300	Mount Hood	11,239	Pacific Ocean	Sea level
Pennsylvania	1,100	Mount Davis	3,213	Delaware River	Sea level
Rhode Island	200	Jerimoth Hill	812	Atlantic Ocean	Sea level
South Carolina	350	Sassafras Mountain	3,560	Atlantic Ocean	Sea level
South Dakota	2,200	Harney Peak	7,242	Big Stone Lake	966
Tennessee	900	Clingmans Dome	6,643	Mississippi River	178
Texas	1,700	Guadalupe Peak	8,749	Gulf of Mexico	Sea level
Utah	6,100	Kings Peak	13,528	Beaverdam Wash	2,000
Vermont	1,000	Mount Mansfield	4,393	Lake Champlain	95
Virginia	950	Mount Rogers	5,729	Atlantic Ocean	Sea level
Washington	1,700	Mount Rainier	14,410	Pacific Ocean	Sea level
West Virginia	1,500	Spruce Knob	4,861	Potomac River	240
Wisconsin	1,050	Timms Hill	1,951	Lake Michigan	581
Wyoming	6,700	Gannett Peak	13,804	Belle Fourche River	3,099
United States	2,500	Mount McKinley (Alaska)	20,320	Death Valley (California)	282[2]

1. Approximate mean altitude. 2. Below sea level. 3. Walton County. 4. Osceola County. *Source:* Department of the Interior, U.S. Geological Survey.

The Continental Divide

The Continental Divide is a ridge of high ground which runs irregularly north and south through the Rocky Mountains and separates eastward-flowing from westward-flowing streams. The waters which flow eastward empty into the Atlantic Ocean, chiefly by way of the Gulf of Mexico; those which flow westward empty into the Pacific.

Mason and Dixon's Line

Mason and Dixon's Line (often called the Mason-Dixon Line) is the boundary between Pennsylvania and Maryland, running at a north latitude of 39°43'19.11". The greater part of it was surveyed from 1763–67 by Charles Mason and Jeremiah Dixon, English astronomers who had been appointed to settle a dispute between the colonies. As the line was partly the boundary between the free and the slave states, it has come to signify the division between the North and the South.

Latitude and Longitude of U.S. and Canadian Cities
(and time corresponding to 12:00 noon, eastern standard time)

City	Lat. n ° ′	Long. w ° ′	Time	City	Lat. n ° ′	Long. w ° ′	Time
Albany, N.Y.	42 40	73 45	12:00 noon	Memphis, Tenn	35 9	90 3	11:00 a.m.
Albuquerque, N.M.	35 05	106 39	10:00 a.m.	Miami, Fla.	25 46	80 12	12:00 noon
Amarillo, Tex.	35 11	101 50	11:00 a.m.	Milwaukee	43 2	87 55	11:00 a.m.
Anchorage, Alaska	61 13	149 54	7:00 a.m.	Minneapolis	44 59	93 14	11:00 a.m.
Atlanta	33 45	84 23	12:00 noon	Mobile, Ala.	30 42	88 3	11:00 a.m.
Austin, Tex.	30 16	97 44	11:00 a.m.	Montgomery, Ala.	32 21	86 18	11:00 a.m.
Baker, Ore.	44 47	117 50	9:00 a.m.	Montpelier, Vt.	44 15	72 32	12:00 noon
Baltimore	39 18	76 38	12:00 noon	Montreal, Que.	45 30	73 35	12:00 noon
Bangor, Me.	44 48	68 47	12:00 noon	Moose Jaw, Sask.	50 37	105 31	10:00 a.m.
Birmingham, Ala.	33 30	86 50	11:00 a.m.	Nashville, Tenn.	36 10	86 47	11:00 a.m.
Bismarck, N.D.	46 48	100 47	11:00 a.m.	Nelson, B.C.	49 30	117 17	9:00 a.m.
Boise, Idaho	43 36	116 13	10:00 a.m.	Newark, N.J.	40 44	74 10	12:00 noon
Boston	42 21	71 5	12:00 noon	New Haven, Conn.	41 19	72 55	12:00 noon
Buffalo, N.Y.	42 55	78 50	12:00 noon	New Orleans	29 57	90 4	11:00 a.m.
Calgary, Alberta	51 1	114 1	10:00 a.m.	New York	40 47	73 58	12:00 noon
Carlsbad, N.M.	32 26	104 15	10:00 a.m.	Nome, Alaska	64 25	165 30	6:00 a.m.
Charleston, S.C.	32 47	79 56	12:00 noon	Oakland, Calif.	37 48	122 16	9:00 a.m.
Charleston, W. Va.	38 21	81 38	12:00 noon	Oklahoma City	35 26	97 28	11:00 a.m.
Charlotte, N.C.	35 14	80 50	12:00 noon	Omaha, Neb.	41 15	95 56	11:00 a.m.
Cheyenne, Wyo.	41 9	104 52	10:00 a.m.	Ottawa, Ont.	45 24	75 43	12:00 noon
Chicago	41 50	87 37	11:00 a.m.	Philadelphia	39 57	75 10	12:00 noon
Cincinnati	39 8	84 30	12:00 noon	Phoenix, Ariz.	33 29	112 4	10:00 a.m.
Cleveland	41 28	81 37	12:00 noon	Pierre, S.D.	44 22	100 21	11:00 a.m.
Columbia, S.C.	34 0	81 2	12:00 noon	Pittsburgh	40 27	79 57	12:00 noon
Columbus, Ohio	40 0	83 1	12:00 noon	Port Arthur, Ont.	48 30	89 17	12:00 noon
Dallas	32 46	96 46	11:00 a.m.	Portland, Me.	43 40	70 15	12:00 noon
Denver	39 45	105 0	10:00 a.m.	Portland, Ore.	45 31	122 41	9:00 a.m.
Des Moines, Iowa	41 35	-93 37	11:00 a.m.	Providence, R.I.	41 50	71 24	12:00 noon
Detroit	42 20	83 3	12:00 noon	Quebec, Que.	46 49	71 11	12:00 noon
Dubuque, Iowa	42 31	90 40	11:00 a.m.	Raleigh, N.C.	35 46	78 39	12:00 noon
Duluth, Minn.	46 49	92 5	11:00 a.m.	Reno, Nev.	39 30	119 49	9:00 a.m.
Eastport, Me.	44 54	67 0	12:00 noon	Richfield, Utah	38 46	112 5	10:00 a.m.
El Centro, Calif.	32 38	115 33	9:00 a.m.	Richmond, Va.	37 33	77 29	12:00 noon
El Paso	31 46	106 29	10:00 a.m.	Roanoke, Va.	37 17	79 57	12:00 noon
Eugene, Ore.	44 3	123 5	9:00 a.m.	Sacramento, Calif.	38 35	121 30	9:00 a.m.
Fargo, N.D.	46 52	96 48	11:00 a.m.	St. John, N.B.	45 18	66 10	1:00 p.m.
Flagstaff, Ariz.	35 13	111 41	10:00 a.m.	St. Louis	38 35	90 12	11:00 a.m.
Fort Worth, Tex.	32 43	97 19	11:00 a.m.	Salt Lake City, Utah	40 46	111 54	10:00 a.m.
Fresno, Calif.	36 44	119 48	9:00 a.m.	San Antonio	29 23	98 33	11:00 a.m.
Grand Junction, Colo.	39 5	108 33	10:00 a.m.	San Diego, Calif.	32 42	117 10	9:00 a.m.
Grand Rapids, Mich.	42 58	85 40	12:00 noon	San Francisco	37 47	122 26	9:00 a.m.
Havre, Mont.	48 33	109 43	10:00 a.m.	San Jose, Calif.	37 20	121 53	9:00 a.m.
Helena, Mont.	46 35	112 2	10:00 a.m.	San Juan, P.R.	18 30	66 10	1:00 p.m.
Honolulu	21 18	157 50	7:00 a.m.	Santa Fe, N.M.	35 41	105 57	10:00 a.m.
Hot Springs, Ark.	34 31	93 3	11:00 a.m.	Savannah, Ga.	32 5	81 5	12:00 noon
Houston, Tex.	29 45	95 21	11:00 a.m.	Seattle	47 37	122 20	9:00 a.m.
Idaho Falls, Idaho	43 30	112 1	10:00 a.m.	Shreveport, La.	32 28	93 42	11:00 a.m.
Indianapolis	39 46	86 10	12:00 noon	Sioux Falls, S.D.	43 33	96 44	11:00 a.m.
Jackson, Miss.	32 20	90 12	11:00 a.m.	Sitka, Alaska	57 10	135 15	9:00 a.m.
Jacksonville, Fla.	30 22	81 40	12:00 noon	Spokane, Wash.	47 40	117 26	9:00 a.m.
Juneau, Alaska	58 18	134 24	9:00 a.m.	Springfield, Ill.	39 48	89 38	11:00 a.m.
Kansas City, Mo.	39 6	94 35	11:00 a.m.	Springfield, Mass.	42 6	72 34	12:00 noon
Key West, Fla.	24 33	81 48	12:00 noon	Springfield, Mo.	37 13	93 17	11:00 a.m.
Kingston, Ont.	44 15	76 30	12:00 noon	Syracuse, N.Y.	43 2	76 8	12:00 noon
Klamath Falls, Ore.	42 10	121 44	9:00 a.m.	Tampa, Fla.	27 57	82 27	12:00 noon
Knoxville, Tenn.	35 57	83 56	12:00 noon	Toledo, Ohio	41 39	83 33	12:00 noon
Las Vegas, Nev.	36 10	115 12	9:00 a.m.	Toronto, Ont.	43 40	79 24	12:00 noon
Lewiston, Idaho	46 24	117 2	9:00 a.m.	Tulsa, Okla.	36 09	95 59	11:00 a.m.
Lincoln, Neb.	40 50	96 40	11:00 a.m.	Victoria, B.C.	48 25	123 21	9:00 a.m.
London, Ont.	43 2	81 34	12:00 noon	Virginia Beach, Va.	36 51	75 58	12:00 noon
Long Beach, Calif.	33 46	118 11	9:00 a.m.	Washington, D.C.	38 53	77 02	12:00 noon
Los Angeles	34 3	118 15	9:00 a.m.	Wichita, Kan.	37 43	97 17	11:00 a.m.
Louisville, Ky.	38 15	85 46	12:00 noon	Wilmington, N.C.	34 14	77 57	12:00 noon
Manchester, N.H.	43 0	71 30	12:00 noon	Winnipeg, Man.	49 54	97 7	11:00 a.m.

Named Summits in the U.S. Over 14,000 Feet Above Sea Level

Name	State	Height	Name	State	Height	Name	State	Height
Mt. McKinley	Alaska	20,320	Castle Peak	Colo.	14,265	Mt. Eolus	Colo.	14,083
Mt. St. Elias	Alaska	18,008	Quandary Peak	Colo.	14,265	Windom Peak	Colo.	14,082
Mt. Foraker	Alaska	17,400	Mt. Evans	Colo.	14,264	Mt. Columbia	Colo.	14,073
Mt. Bona	Alaska	16,500	Longs Peak	Colo.	14,255	Mt. Augusta	Alaska	14,070
Mt. Blackburn	Alaska	16,390	Mt. Wilson	Colo.	14,246	Missouri Mtn.	Colo.	14,067
Mt. Sanford	Alaska	16,237	White Mtn.	Calif.	14,246	Humboldt Peak	Colo.	14,064
Mt. Vancouver	Alaska	15,979	North Palisade	Calif.	14,242	Mt. Bierstadt	Colo.	14,060
South Buttress	Alaska	15,885	Mt. Cameron	Colo.	14,238	Sunlight Peak	Colo.	14,059
Mt. Churchill	Alaska	15,638	Shavano Peak	Colo.	14,229	Split Mtn.	Calif.	14,058
Mt. Fairweather	Alaska	15,300	Crestone Needle	Colo.	14,197	Handies Peak	Colo.	14,048
Mt. Hubbard	Alaska	14,950	Mt. Belford	Colo.	14,197	Culebra Peak	Colo.	14,047
Mt. Bear	Alaska	14,831	Mt. Princeton	Colo.	14,197	Mt. Lindsey	Colo.	14,042
East Buttress	Alaska	14,730	Mt. Yale	Colo.	14,196	Ellingwood Point	Colo.	14,042
Mt. Hunter	Alaska	14,573	Mt. Bross	Colo.	14,172	Little Bear Peak	Colo.	14,037
Browne Tower	Alaska	14,530	Kit Carson Mtn.	Colo.	14,165	Mt. Sherman	Colo.	14,036
Mt. Alverstone	Alaska	14,500	Mt. Wrangell	Alaska	14,163	Redcloud Peak	Colo.	14,034
Mt. Whitney	Calif.	14,494	Mt. Shasta	Calif.	14,162	Mt. Langley	Calif.	14,026
University Peak	Alaska	14,470	El Diente Peak	Colo.	14,159	Conundrum Peak	Colo.	14,022
Mt. Elbert	Colo.	14,433	Point Success	Wash.	14,158	Mt. Tyndall	Calif.	14,019
Mt. Massive	Colo.	14,421	Maroon Peak	Colo.	14,156	Pyramid Peak	Colo.	14,018
Mt. Harvard	Colo.	14,420	Tabeguache Mtn.	Colo.	14,155	Wilson Peak	Colo.	14,017
Mt. Rainier	Wash.	14,410	Mt. Oxford	Colo.	14,153	Wetterhorn Peak	Colo.	14,015
Mt. Williamson	Calif.	14,370	Mt. Sill	Calif.	14,153	North Maroon Peak	Colo.	14,014
La Plata Peak	Colo.	14,361	Mt. Sneffels	Colo.	14,150	San Luis Peak	Colo.	14,014
Blanca Peak	Colo.	14,345	Mt. Democrat	Colo.	14,148	Middle Palisade	Calif.	14,012
Uncompahgre Peak	Colo.	14,309	Capitol Peak	Colo.	14,130	Mt. Muir	Calif.	14,012
Crestone Peak	Colo.	14,294	Liberty Cap	Wash.	14,112	Mt. of the Holy Cross	Colo.	14,005
Mt. Lincoln	Colo.	14,286	Pikes Peak	Colo.	14,110	Huron Peak	Colo.	14,003
Grays Peak	Colo.	14,270	Snowmass Mtn.	Colo.	14,092	Thunderbolt Peak	Calif.	14,003
Mt. Antero	Colo.	14,269	Mt. Russell	Calif.	14,088	Sunshine Peak	Colo.	14,001
Torreys Peak	Colo.	14,267						

Source: Department of the Interior, U.S. Geological Survey.

Rivers of the United States

(350 or more miles long)

Alabama-Coosa (600 mi.; 966 km): From junction of Oostanula and Etowah R. in Georgia to Mobile R.

Altamaha-Ocmulgee (392 mi.; 631 km): From junction of Yellow R. and South R., Newton Co. in Georgia to Atlantic Ocean.

Apalachicola-Chattahoochee (524 mi.; 843 km): From Towns Co. in Georgia to Gulf of Mexico in Florida.

Arkansas (1,459 mi.; 2,348 km): From Lake Co. in Colorado to Mississippi R. in Arkansas.

Brazos (923 mi.; 1,490 km): From junction of Salt Fork and Double Mountain Fork in Texas to Gulf of Mexico.

Canadian (906 mi.; 1,458 km): From Las Animas Co. in Colorado to Arkansas R. in Oklahoma.

Cimarron (600 mi.; 966 km): From Colfax Co. in New Mexico to Arkansas R. in Oklahoma.

Colorado (1,450 mi.; 2,333 km): From Rocky Mountain National Park in Colorado to Gulf of California in Mexico.

Colorado (862 mi.; 1,387 km): From Dawson Co. in Texas to Matagorda Bay.

Columbia (1,243 mi.; 2,000 km): From Columbia Lake in British Columbia to Pacific Ocean (entering between Oregon and Washington).

Colville (350 mi.; 563 km): From Brooks Range in Alaska to Beaufort Sea.

Connecticut (407 mi.; 655 km): From Third Connecticut Lake in New Hampshire to Long Island Sound in Connecticut.

Cumberland (720 mi.; 1,159 km): From junction of Poor and Clover Forks in Harlan Co. in Kentucky to Ohio R.

Delaware (390 mi.; 628 km): From Schoharie Co. in New York to Liston Point, Delaware Bay.

Gila (649 mi.; 1,044 km): From Catron Co. in New Mexico to Colorado R. in Arizona.

Green (360 mi.; 579 km): From Lincoln Co. in Kentucky to Ohio R. in Kentucky.

Green (730 mi.; 1,175 km): From Sublette Co. in Wyoming to Colorado R. in Utah.

Illinois (420 mi.; 676 km): From St. Joseph Co. in Indiana to Mississippi R. at Grafton in Illinois.

James (sometimes called *Dakota*) (710 mi.; 1,143 km): From Wells Co. in North Dakota to Missouri R. in South Dakota.

Kanawha-New (352 mi.; 566 km): From junction of North and South Forks of New R. in North Carolina, through Virginia and West Virginia (New River becoming Kanawha River), to Ohio River.

Koyukuk (470 mi.; 756 km): From Brooks Range in Alaska to Yukon R.

Kuskokwim (724 mi.; 1,165 km): From Alaska Range in Alaska to Kuskokwim Bay.

Licking (350 mi.; 563 km): From Magoffin Co. in Kentucky to Ohio R. at Cincinnati in Ohio.

Little Missouri (560 mi.; 901 km): From Crook Co. in Wyoming to Missouri R. in North Dakota.

Milk (625 mi.; 1,006 km): From junction of forks in Alberta Province to Missouri R.

Coastline of the United States

State	Lengths, statute miles		State	Lengths, statute miles	
	General coastline[1]	Tidal shoreline[2]		General coastline[1]	Tidal shoreline[2]
Atlantic Coast:			Gulf Coast:		
Maine	228	3,478	Florida (Gulf)	770	5,095
New Hampshire	13	131	Alabama	53	607
Massachusetts	192	1,519	Mississippi	44	359
Rhode Island	40	384	Louisiana	397	7,721
Connecticut	—	618	Texas	367	3,359
New York	127	1,850	Total Gulf coast	1,631	17,141
New Jersey	130	1,792	Pacific Coast:		
Pennsylvania	—	89	California	840	3,427
Delaware	28	381	Oregon	296	1,410
Maryland	31	3,190	Washington	157	3,026
Virginia	112	3,315	Hawaii	750	1,052
North Carolina	301	3,375	Alaska (Pacific)	5,580	31,383
South Carolina	187	2,876	Total Pacific coast	7,623	40,298
Georgia	100	2,344	Arctic Coast:		
Florida (Atlantic)	580	3,331	Alaska (Arctic)	1,060	2,521
Total Atlantic coast	2,069	28,673	Total Arctic coast	1,060	2,521
			States Total	12,383	88,633

1. Figures are lengths of general outline of seacoast. Measurements made with unit measure of 30 minutes of latitude on charts as near scale of 1:1,200,000 as possible. Coastline of bays and sounds is included to point where they narrow to width of unit measure, and distance across at such point is included. 2. Figures obtained in 1939–40 with recording instrument on largest-scale maps and charts then available. Shoreline of outer coast, offshore islands, sounds, bays, rivers, and creeks is included to head of tidewater, or to point where tidal waters narrow to width of 100 feet. *Source:* Department of Commerce, National Oceanic and Atmospheric Administration, National Ocean Service.

Mississippi (2,340 mi.; 3,766 km): From Lake Itasca in Minnesota to mouth of Southwest Pass in La.

Mississippi-Missouri-Red Rock (3,710 mi.; 5,970 km): From source of Red Rock R. in Montana to mouth of Southwest Pass in Louisiana.

Missouri (2,315 mi.; 3,726 km): From junction of Jefferson R., Gallatin R., and Madison R. in Montana to Mississippi R. near St. Louis.

Missouri-Red Rock (2,540 mi.; 4,090 km): From source of Red Rock R. in Montana to Mississippi R. near St. Louis.

Mobile-Alabama-Coosa (645 mi.; 1,040 km): From junction of Etowah R. and Oostanula R. in Georgia to Mobile Bay.

Neosho (460 mi.; 740 km): From Morris Co. in Kansas to Arkansas R. in Oklahoma.

Niobrara (431 mi.; 694 km): From Niobrara Co. in Wyoming to Missouri R. in Nebraska.

Noatak (350 mi.; 563 km): From Brooks Range in Alaska to Kotzebue Sound.

North Canadian (800 mi.; 1,290 km): From Union Co. in New Mexico to Canadian R. in Oklahoma.

North Platte (618 mi.; 995 km): From Jackson Co. in Colorado to junction with So. Platte R. in Nebraska to form Platte R.

Ohio (981 mi.; 1,579 km): From junction of Allegheny R. and Monongahela R. at Pittsburgh to Mississippi R. between Illinois and Kentucky.

Ohio-Allegheny (1,306 mi.; 2,102 km): From Potter Co. in Pennsylvania to Mississippi R. at Cairo in Illinois.

Osage (500 mi.; 805 km): From east-central Kansas to Missouri R. near Jefferson City in Missouri.

Ouachita (605 mi.; 974 km): From Polk Co. in Arkansas to Red R. in Louisiana.

Pearl (411 mi.; 661 km): From Neshoba County in Mississippi to Gulf of Mexico (Mississippi-Louisiana).

Pecos (926 mi.; 1,490 km): From Mora Co. in New Mexico to Rio Grande in Texas.

Pee Dee-Yadkin (435 mi.; 700 km): From Watauga Co. in North Carolina to Winyah Bay in South Carolina.

Pend Oreille-Clark Fork (531 mi.; 855 km): Near Butte in Montana to Columbia R. on Washington-Canada border.

Porcupine (569 mi.; 916 km): From Yukon Territory, Canada, to Yukon R. in Alaska.

Potomac (383 mi.; 616 km): From Garrett Co. in Md. to Chesapeake Bay at Point Lookout in Md.

Powder (375 mi.; 603 km): From junction of forks in Johnson Co. in Wyoming to Yellowstone R. in Montana.

Red (1,290 mi.; 2,080 km): From source of Tierra Blanca Creek in Curry County, New Mexico to Mississippi R. in Louisiana.

Red (officially called *Red River of the North*) (545 mi.; 877 km): From junction of Otter Tail R. and Bois de Sioux R. in Minnesota to Lake Winnipeg in Manitoba.

Republican (445 mi.; 716 km): From junction of North Fork and Arikaree R. in Nebraska to junction with Smoky Hill R. in Kansas to form the Kansas R.

Rio Grande (1,760 mi.; 2,840 km): From San Juan Co. in Colorado to Gulf of Mexico.

Roanoke (380 mi.; 612 km): From junction of forks in Montgomery Co. in Virginia to Albemarle Sound in North Carolina.

Sabine (380 mi.; 612 km): From junction of forks in Hunt Co. in Texas to Sabine Lake between Texas and Louisiana.

Sacramento (377 mi.; 607 km): From Siskiyou Co. in California to Suisun Bay.

Saint Francis (425 mi.; 684 km): From Iron Co. in Missouri to Mississippi R. in Arkansas.

Salmon (420 mi.; 676 km): From Custer Co. in Idaho to Snake R.

San Joaquin (350 mi.; 563 km): From junction of forks in Madera Co. in California to Suisun Bay.

San Juan (360 mi.; 579 km): From Archuleta Co. in Colorado to Colorado R. in Utah.

Santee-Wateree-Catawba (538 mi.; 866 km): From McDowell Co. in North Carolina to Atlantic Ocean in South Carolina.
Smoky Hill (540 mi.; 869 km): From Cheyenne Co. in Colorado to junction with Republican R. in Kansas to form Kansas R.
Snake (1,038 mi.; 1,670 km): From Ocean Plateau in Wyoming to Columbia R. in Washington.
South Platte (424 mi.; 682 km): From Park Co. in Colorado to junction with North Platte R. in Nebraska to form Platte R.
Susquehanna (444 mi.; 715 km): From Otsego Lake in New York to Chesapeake Bay in Maryland.
Tanana (659 mi.; 1,060 km): From Wrangell Mts. in Yukon Territory, Canada, to Yukon R. in Alaska.
Tennessee (652 mi.; 1,049 km): From junction of Holston R. and French Broad R. in Tennessee to Ohio R. in Kentucky.
Tennessee-French Broad (870 mi.; 1,400 km): From Bland Co. in Virginia to Ohio R. at Paducah in Kentucky.
Tombigbee (525 mi.; 845 km): From junction of forks in Itawamba Co. in Mississippi to Mobile R. in Alabama.
Trinity (360 mi.; 579 km): From junction of forks in Dallas Co. in Texas to Galveston Bay.
Wabash (512 mi.; 824 km): From Darke Co. in Ohio to Ohio R. between Illinois and Indiana.
Washita (500 mi.; 805 km): From Hemphill Co. in Texas to Red R. in Oklahoma.
White (722 mi.; 1,160 km): From Madison Co. in Arkansas to Mississippi R.
Wisconsin (430 mi.; 692 km): From Vilas Co. in Wisconsin to Mississippi R.
Yellowstone (692 mi.; 1,110 km): From Park Co. in Wyoming to Missouri R. in North Dakota.
Yukon (1,979 mi.; 3,185 km): From junction of Lewes R. and Pelly R. in Yukon Territory, Canada, to Bering Sea in Alaska.

Geysers in The United States

Geysers are natural hot springs that intermittently eject a column of water and steam into the air. They exist in many parts of the volcanic regions of the world such as Japan and South America but their greatest development is in Iceland, New Zealand, and Yellowstone National Park.

There are 120 named geysers in Yellowstone National Park, Wyoming, and perhaps half that number unnamed. Most of the geysers and the 4,000 or more hot springs are located in the western portion of the park. The most important are the following:

Norris Geyser Basin has 24 or more active geysers; the number varies. There are scores of steam vents and hot springs. *Valentine* is highest, erupting 50-75 ft at intervals varying from 18 hr to 3 days or more. *Minuté* erupts 15-20 ft high, several hours apart. Others include *Steamboat, Fearless, Veteran, Vixen, Corporal, Whirligig, Little Whirligig,* and *Pinwheel.*

Lower Geyser Basin has at least 18 active geysers. *Fountain* throws water 50-75 ft in all directions at unpredictable intervals. *Clepsydra* erupts violently from four vents up to 30 ft. *Great Fountain* plays every 8 to 15 hr in spurts from 30 to 90 ft high.

Midway Geyser Basin has vast steaming terraces of red, orange, pink and other colors; there are pools and springs, including the beautiful *Grand Prismatic Spring. Excelsior* crater discharges boiling water into Firehole River at the rate of 6 cu ft per second.

Giant erupts up to 200 ft at intervals of 2 1/2 days to 3 mo; eruptions last about 1 1/2 hr. *Daisy* sends water up to 75 ft but is irregular and frequently inactive.

Old Faithful sends up a column varying from 116 to 175 ft at intervals of about 65 min, varying from 33 to 90 min. Eruptions last about 4 min, during which time about 12,000 gal are discharged.

Giantess seldom erupts, but during its active periods sends up streams 150-200 ft.

Lion Group: *Lion* plays up to 60 ft every 2-4 days when active; *Little Cub* up to 10 ft every 1-2 hr. *Big Cub* and *Lioness* seldom erupt.

Castle usually erupts twice daily to a height of 75 ft.

Mammoth Hot Springs: There are no geysers in this area. The formation is travertine. Sides of a hill are steps and terraces over which flow the steaming waters of hot springs laden with minerals. Each step is tinted by algae to many shades of orange, pink, yellow, brown, green, and blue. Terraces are white where no water flows.

Loihi: Hawaii's Newest Volcano

Source: Department of the Interior/U.S. Geological Survey.

Hawaii's worldwide image as an idyllic tropical paradise is well deserved. What is less well known, however, is that the islands exist only because of nearly continuous volcanic activity.

Since the beginning of a historical record early in the 19th century, eruptions have occurred frequently at Mauna Loa and Kilauea; these two volcanoes on the Big Island are among the most active in the world. Nearby Loihi Seamount, off the Big Island's south coast, is the newest Hawaiian volcano, not yet visible above the ocean surface.

Loihi rises 10,100 feet above the ocean floor to within 3,100 feet of the water surface. Recent detailed mapping shows Loihi to be similar in form to Kilauea and Mauna Loa. Photographs taken by deep-sea camera show that Loihi's summit area has fresh-appearing, coherent pillow-lava flows and talus blocks. Examination of samples dredged from Loihi indicates that the pillow-lava fragments have fresh glassy crusts, indicative of their recent formation. The exact ages of the sampled Loihi flows are not yet known, but certainly some cannot be more than a few hundred years old. In fact, the occurrence of earthquake swarms at Loihi during 1971-1972, 1975, and 1984-85 suggests major submarine eruptions or magma intrusions into the upper part of Loihi. Thus Loihi appears to be a historically active, but as yet submarine, volcano.

Studies of Loihi provide a unique opportunity to decipher the youthful submarine stage in the formation and evolution of Hawaiian volcanoes. When might the still-growing Loihi emerge above the surface of the Pacific to become Hawaii's newest volcano island? It will almost certainly take several tens of thousands of years, if the growth rate for Loihi is comparable to that of other Hawaiian volcanoes.

UNITED STATES

POLYCONIC PROJECTION

SCALE OF MILES

0   50   100   200   300   400

SCALE OF KILOMETERS

0   100   200   300   400

Capitals of Countries .... ☆

State Capitals .... △

International Boundaries ....

© Copyright HAMMOND INCORPORATED, Maplewood, N. J.

CANADA

CONIC PROJECTION

SCALE OF KILOMETERS
0 100 200 300 400 500

SCALE OF MILES
0 100 200 300 400 500

⊕ Capitals of Countries
⊛ Provincial & Territorial
    Capitals
● Administrative Centers

MIDDLE AMERICA

BONNE PROJECTION

Copyright by C. S. HAMMOND & Co., N. Y.

SCALE OF MILES

0   200   400   600

KILOMETERS

0   200   400   600

Capitals of Countries ⊛

Other Capitals ⊛

International Boundaries

AFRICA

LAMBERT AZIMUTHAL EQUAL-AREA PROJECTION

SCALE OF MILES
0   100   200   400   600   800

SCALE OF KILOMETERS
0   200   400   600   800

Capitals of Countries☆
Other Capitals......◉
Canals..............

International Boundaries.-..-..-
Mountain Peaks........▲

CAPE VERDE

Ribeira Grande   Santo Antão   Sal Rei
Mindelo   São Nicolau   Sta. Maria
Santa Luzia   Boa Vista
São   Maio
Vicente   São Tiago   Praia
Fogo
Brava

0   20   40   60 MI.
0   20   40   60 KM.

AFRICA 1939

British
French
Italian
Portuguese
Spanish
Belgian
Mandates

MOROCCO
IFNI
RIO DE ORO
ALGERIA
TUNISIA
LIBYA
EGYPT
FRENCH WEST AFRICA
GAMBIA
PORT. GUINEA
SIERRA LEONE
LIBERIA
GOLD COAST
TOGO
NIGERIA
CAMEROONS
RIO MUNI
FRENCH EQUATORIAL AFRICA
ANGLO-EGYPTIAN SUDAN
FR. SOM.
ITALIAN EAST AFRICA
SOM. PROT.
BELGIAN CONGO
UGANDA
KENYA
TANGANYIKA
NYASALAND
NO. RHODESIA
SO. RHODESIA
ANGOLA
SOUTH-WEST AFRICA
BECH. PROT.
SWAZILAND
UNION OF SOUTH AFRICA
BASUTOLAND
MOZAMBIQUE
MADAGASCAR

ATLANTIC OCEAN

INDIAN OCEAN

ANGOLA
NAMIBIA (SOUTH-WEST AFRICA)
BOTSWANA
Kalahari Desert
ZAMBIA
ZIMBABWE
MOZAMBIQUE
MALAWI
TANZANIA
SOUTH AFRICA
CAPE PROVINCE
ORANGE FREE STATE
TRANSVAAL
BOPHUTHATSWANA
NATAL
TRANSKEI
SWAZILAND

Kinshasa
Luanda
Windhoek
Gaborone
Pretoria
Johannesburg
Bloemfontein
Cape Town
Maputo
Harare
Lusaka
Lilongwe
Dodoma
Dar es Salaam
Antananarivo

Tropic of Capricorn

Longitude West of Greenwich 20°
Longitude East of Greenwich

BARENTS SEA

Salekhard

Northkapp (North Cape)

Vadsø

Kolguyev I.

Naryan Mar

Vorkuta

Berezovo

Ob'

Surgut

Ob'

Tobol'sk

Irtysh

Murmansk

KANIN PEN.

Chesnakova

Pechora

KOLA PEN.

Kirov

Kandalaksha

Bay of Mezen'

Mezen'

Usl Tsilma

Khanty-Mansiysk

Krasnoural'sk

Nizhniy Tagil

S

Kem'

Archangel

Mezen'

Pechora

Kirovgrad

Tyumen'

Sverdlovsk

FINLAND

White Sea

Northern Dvina

Syktyvkar

Zlatoust

O

C

I

A

Chelyabinsk

Oulu

Onega

Onega

Nyandoma

Kotlas

Kamp

L

Velikiy Ustyug

Bereznik

Vorkuta

Perm

Sarapul

Izhevsk

Kama Res.

Cherdyn

Ufa

Magnitogorsk

I

A

L

I

S

Kustanay

L. Onega

Petrozavodsk

Kirov (Vyatka)

Kotel'nich

Votkinsk Res.

Troitsk

Helsinki

Gulf of Finland

Vyborg

LENINGRAD

Cherepovets

Vologda

Rybinsk Res.

Kostroma

Gor'kiy Res.

Volga

Naberezhnye Chelny

Kuybyshev Res.

Belaya

Orenburg

50°

Tallinn

Narva

Kingisepp

Rybinsk

Yaroslavl'

Ivanovo

Balakhna

Kazan'

Ul'yanovsk

ESTONIAN S.S.R.

Pärnu

L. Peipus

Pskov

L. Il'men

Kalinin

Dzerzhinsk

Gor'kiy

Res.

Kuybyshev

Orenburg

Riga

Cēsis

Velikiye Luki

MOSCOW (Moskva)

Orekhovo Zuyevo

Oka

ATVIAN S.S.R.

Rēzekne

Serpukhov

Penza

Ural'sk

Aktyubinsk

HUANIAN S.S.R.

Daugavpils

Vitebsk

Smolensk

Kaluga

Tula

Michurinsk

Tambov

Temir

Kaunas

WHITE

Bryansk

Orel

Saratov

Emba

Chelkar

Vilna

RUSSIAN

Minsk

Voronezh

Engel's

Volgograd

Grodno

S.S.R.

Bobruysk

Kursk

Don

Res.

Stoltsy

Pinsk

Gomel

Volgograd (Stalingrad)

Brest

Millerovo

Tsimlyansk Res.

Volga

Astrakhan'

Lublin

Kiev Res.

Khar'kov

Donets

Voroshilovgrad

Shakhty

Port Shevchenko

Zhitomir

Poltava

Dneprodzerzhinsk

Kramatorsk

UKRAINIAN

Kremenchug

Makeyevka

Rostov

L. Manych-Gudilo

Elista

Gur'yev

Vinnitsa

Kirovograd

Dnepropetrovsk

Zaporozh'ye

Donetsk

Don

Chernovtsy

Krivoy Rog

Kakhovka Res.

Taganrog

Mariupol'

Nikolayev

Kherson

Sea of Azov

Krasnodar

Armavir

Pyatigorsk

Makhachkala

Kishinev

Odessa

Belgorod Dnestrovskiy

CRIMEA

Kerch

Novorossiysk

Maykop

Kislovodsk

Karachayevsk

Groznyy

OMANIA

Sulina

Galati

Simferopol'

Sevastopol'

Yalta

Tuapse

Sochi

Ordzhonikidze

Caucasus

Braila

Bucharest

Constanta

Sukhumi

GEORGIAN S.S.R.

Tbilisi

AZERBAIDZHAN S.S.R.

Baku

BLACK SEA

Sinop

Samsun

Trabzon

Batumi

Kutaisi

ARMENIAN S.S.R.

Erivan

Nakhichevan'

Dzhulfa

CASPIAN SEA

Krasnovodsk

Sofia

BULGARIA

Burgas

ISTANBUL

Ereğli

Erzurum

IRAN

EUROPE

LAMBERT AZIMUTHAL EQUAL AREA PROJECTION

SCALE OF MILES

0   100   200   300   400   500

SCALE OF KILOMETERS

0   100   200   300   400   500

Capitals of Countries .... ☆

International Boundaries .... —·—·—

Canals ....

TURKEY

Ankara

Eskişehir

Kayseri

Sivas

Maraş

Konya

Tarsus

Adana

Mersin

Antalya

Antakya

Aleppo

Latakia

SYRIA

CYPRUS

Nicosia

Larnaca

Copyright by C.S. HAMMOND & CO., N.Y.

ASIA

LAMBERT AZIMUTHAL EQUAL-AREA PROJECTION

SCALE OF MILES
0   150   300   600   900   1200

SCALE OF KILOMETERS
0   150   300   600   900   1200

Capitals of Countries .... ☆
International Boundaries ....
Canals ....

© Copyright HAMMOND INCORPORATED, Maplewood, N.J.

TIME ZONES OF THE WORLD

NOTE: Standard time zones in the U.S.S.R. are always advanced one hour.

STANDARD — TIME — ZONES

Areas not using zone system.

Areas using half hour deviations.

THE WORLD

MERCATOR PROJECTION

Capitals of Countries..............●

THE YEAR IN PICTURES

PHOTO CREDITS: All photos in this section are credited to AP/World Wide Photos unless otherwise noted.

SWORN IN—President George Bush takes the oath of office as Vice President Quayle looks on.

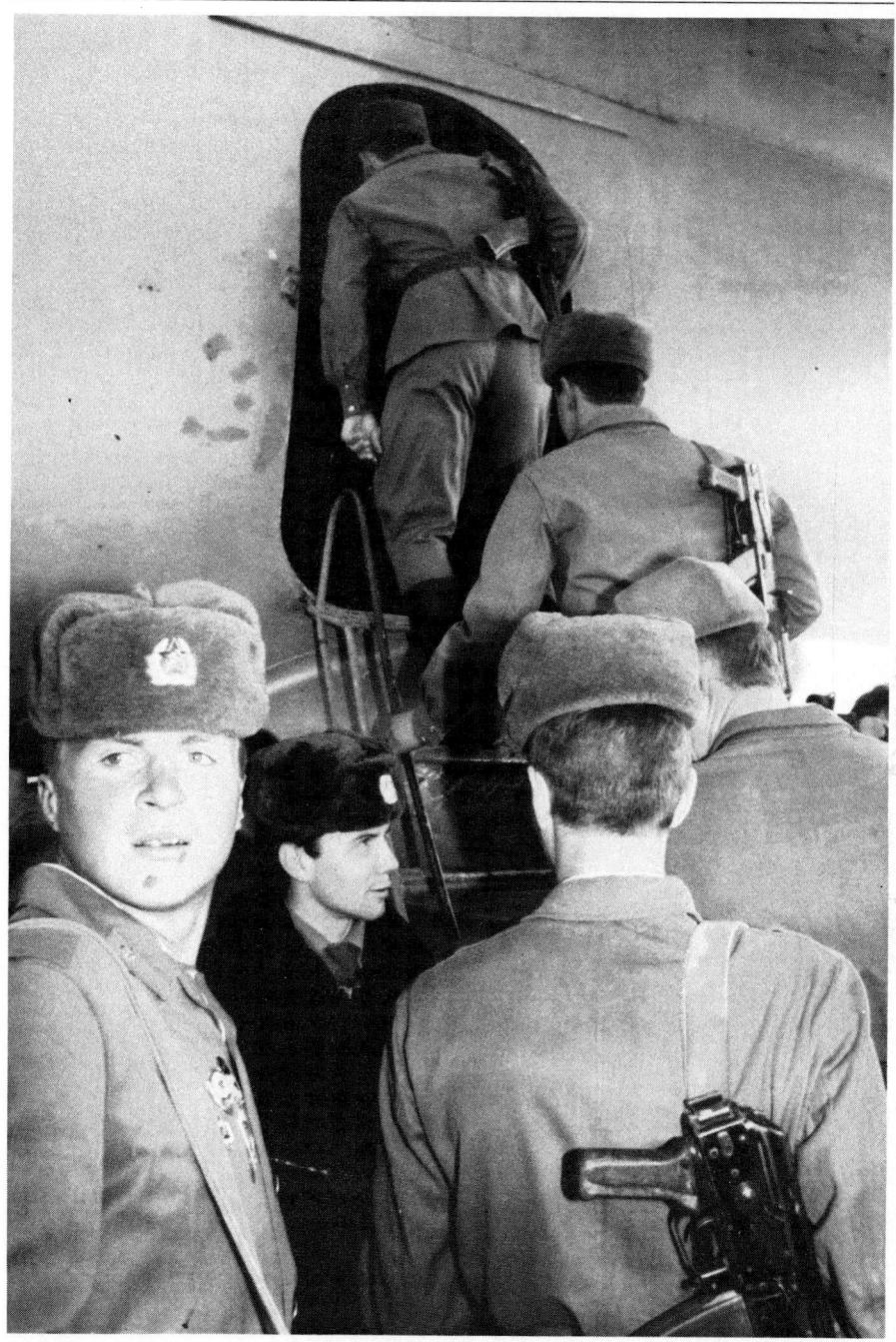

FAREWELL—The last Soviet soldiers to leave Afghanistan board a military transport plane at Kabul airport for their return home.

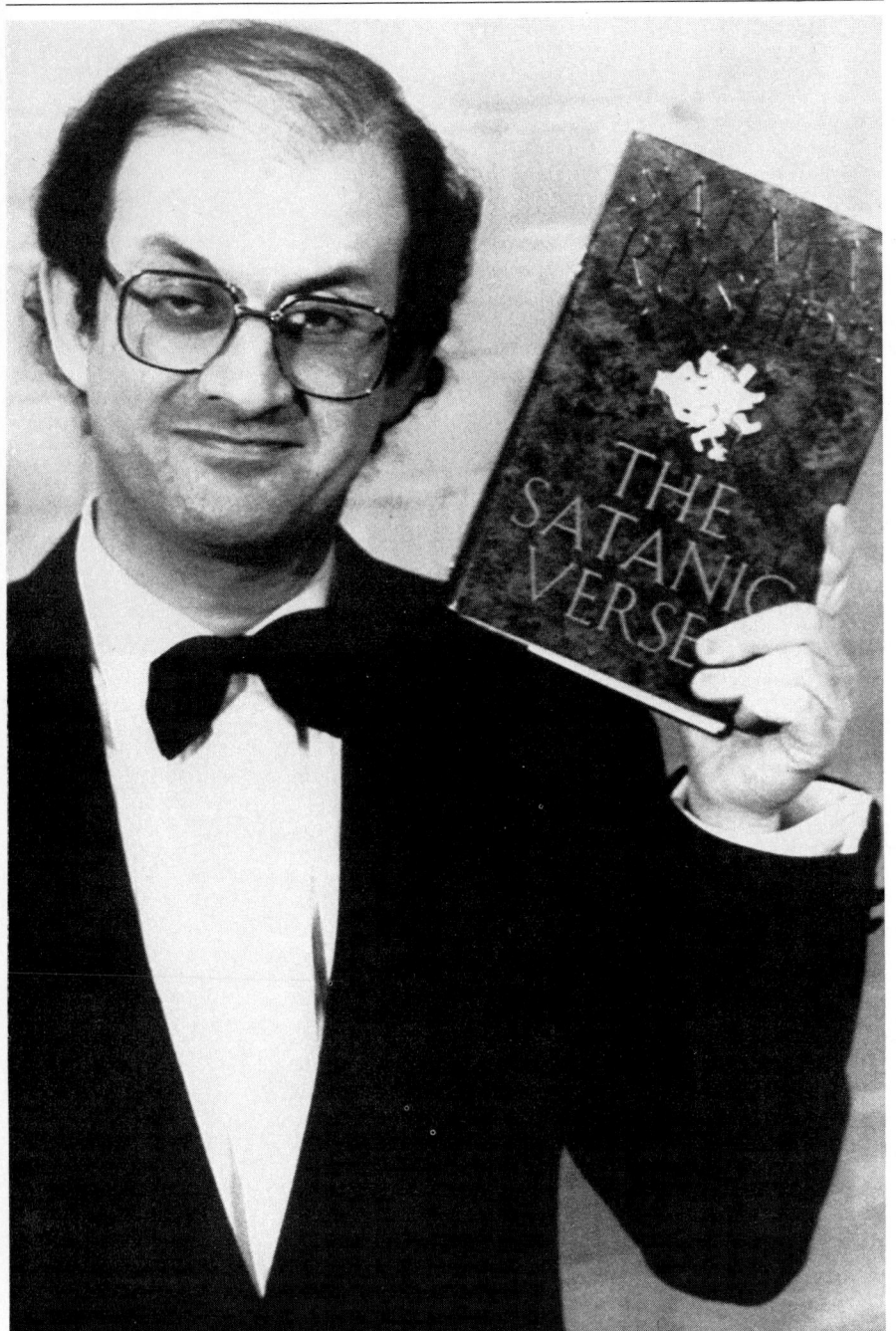

THREATENED—Salman Rushdie, target of a Khomeini death threat, with his controversial book "The Satanic Verses" which Moslems consider blasphemous.

BURIED—Japanese court musicians add a traditional touch at Emperor Hirohito's funeral.

DEFEATED—The Senate rejects John G. Tower as Defense Secretary by a 53 to 47 vote.

BIG SPILL—The tanker *Exxon Valdez* spewing an estimated 10 million plus gallons of crude oil into Prince William Sound, after running aground outside Valdez, Alaska.

HISTORY REPRISED—A re-enactment of George Washington's swearing-in ceremony, at the Federal Hall National Memorial in New York, marks the bicentennial of the United States' first presidential inaugural.

ELECTIONEERING—Supporters of maverick Communist Boris Yeltsin hold mass rally in Moscow prior to the Soviet's election for a new Congress of People's Deputies.

PICKETED—Eastern Airlines employees and union supporters rally in support of a machinists' strike against the airline.

CORDIAL—Britain's Prime Minister Margaret Thatcher and Soviet leader Mikhail Gorbachev share a laugh during his visit to London.

DEFIANCE—A Chinese citizen stands in the way of a column of tanks in Beijing, stopping their advance until he was pulled away by bystanders.

GODDESS—Beijing university students unveil their symbol of democracy in Tiananmen Square during the height of their protest demonstrations.

CRUSHED—A surge of Liverpool fans are jammed against fencing at the Hillsborough Stadium in Sheffield. As a result, 94 people died in England's worst soccer disaster.

DEAD—The Ayatollah Khomeini, Iran's leader for a decade, died June 3 in a Tehran hospital.

FREE—Oliver North avoids prison but is fined $150,000 and put on two years' probation.

FIREWORKS—France celebrates the bicentennial of her revolution with fireworks at Versailles.

STEPS DOWN—House Speaker Jim Wright steps down as Speaker and resigns from the House in the aftermath of his investigation by the House Ethics Committee.

RESTRICTED—Pro-choice advocates demonstrate in front of the Supreme Court building prior to its decision restricting abortion rights.

HANDSHAKE—President George Bush talks with Polish leader General Wojciech Jaruzelski during his stopover in Poland during a ten-day tour through Europe.

BURNING QUESTION—Gregory "Joey" Johnson, in whose name flag burning has been ruled constitutionally protected by the Supreme Court, holds a flag sent to him by a well-wisher.

FATAL CRASH—A National Transportation Safety Board investigator examines the wreckage of United Airlines' DC-10 that crashed at the Sioux City airport, killing 109 people.

NORTH AMERICA

LAMBERT AZIMUTHAL EQUAL-AREA PROJECTION

SCALE OF MILES

0   200   400   600   800   1000

SCALE OF KILOMETERS

0   200   400   600   800   1000

Capitals .... ⊙
International Boundaries .... _ _ _
Canals ....

© Copyright HAMMOND INCORPORATED, Maplewood, N.J.

CROSSWORD PUZZLE GUIDE

First Aid to Crossword Puzzlers

We cannot begin to list all the odd words you will meet with in your daily and Sunday crossword puzzles, for such words run into many thousands. But we have tried to include those that turn up most frequently, as well as many others that should be of help to you when you are unable to go any further.

Also, we do not guarantee that the definitions in your puzzle will be exactly the same as ours, although we have checked every word with a standard dictionary and have followed its definition.

In nearly every case, we have used as the key word the principal noun of the definition, rather than any adjective, adjective phrase, or noun used as an adjective. And, to simplify your searching, we have grouped the words according to the number of spaces you have to fill.

For a list of Foreign Phrases, *see* Index. For Rulers of England and Great Britain, France, Germany and Prussia, and Russia, *see* Countries of the World.

Words of Two Letters

Ambary, DA
And (French, Latin), ET
Article (Arabic), AL
  (French), LA, LE, UN
  (Spanish), EL, LA, UN
At the (French), AU
  (Spanish), AL
Behold, LO
Bird: Hawaiian, OO
Birthplace: Abraham's, UR
Bone, OS
Buddha, FO
Butterfly: Peacock, IO
Champagne, AY
Chaos, NU
Chief: Burmese, BO
Coin: Roman, AS
  Siamese, AT
Concerning, RE
Dialect: Chinese, WU
Double (Egy. relig.), KA
Drama: Japanese, NO
Egg (comb. form), OO
Esker, OS
Eye (Scotch), EE
Factor: Amplification, MU
Fifty (Greek), NU
Fish: Carplike, ID
Force, OD
Forty (Greek), MU
From (French, Latin, Spanish), DE

(Latin prefix), AB
From the (French), DU
God: Babylonian, EA, ZU
  Egyptian sun, RA
  Hindu unknown, KA
  Semitic, EL
Goddess: Babylonian, AI
  Greek earth, GE
Gold (heraldry), OR
Gulf: Arctic, OB
Heart (Egy. relig.), AB
Indian: South American, GE
King: Of Bashan, OG
Language: Artificial, RO
  Assamese, AO
Lava: Hawaiian, AA
Letter: Greek, MU, NU, PI, XI
  Hebrew, HE, PE
Lily: Palm, TI
Measure: Annamese, LY
  Chinese, HO, HU, KO, LI, MU, PU,
    TO, TU
  Japanese, GO, JO, MO, RI, SE, TO
  Metric land, AR
  Netherlands, EL
  Portuguese, PE
  Siamese, WA
  Swedish, AM
  Type, EM, EN
Monk: Buddhist, BO
Month: Jewish, AB

Mouth, OS
Mulberry: Indian, AL
Native: Burmese, WA
Note: Of Scale, DO, FA, MI, LA, RE, TI
Of (French, Latin, Spanish), DE
Of the (French), DU
One (Scotch), AE
Pagoda: Chinese, TA
Plant: East Indian fiber, DA
Ridge: Sandy, AS, OS
River: Russian, OB
Sloth: Three-toed, AI
Soul (Egy. relig.), BA
Sound: Hindu mystic, OM
Suffix: Comparative, ER
The. *See* Article
To the: French, AU
  Spanish, AL
Tree: Buddhist sacred, BO
Tribe: Assamese, AO
Type: Jumbled, PI
Weight: Annamese, TA
  Chinese, LI
  Danish, ES
  Japanese, MO
  Roman, AS
Whirlwind: Faeroe Is., OE
Yes (German), JA
  (Italian, Spanish), SI
  (Russian), DA

Words of Three Letters

Adherent: IST
Again, BIS
Age, ERA
Antelope: African, GNU, KOB
Apricot: Japanese, UME
Article (German), DAS, DEM, DEN,
  DER, DES, DIE, EIN
  (French), LES, UNE
  (Spanish), LAS, LOS, UNA
Banana: Polynesian, FEI
Barge, HOY
Bass: African, IYO
Beak, NEB, NIB
Beard: Grain, AWN
Beetle: June, DOR
Being, ENS
Berry: Hawthorn, HAW
Beverage: Hawaiian, AVA
Bird: Australian, EMU
  Crowlike, JAY
  Extinct, MOA

Fabulous, ROC
Frigate, IWA
Parson, POE, TUE, TUI
Sea, AUK
Blackbird, ANI, ANO
Born, NEE
Bronze: Roman, AES
Bugle: Yellow, IVA
By way of, VIA
Canton: Swiss, URI
Cap: Turkish, FEZ
Catnip, NEP
Character: In "Faerie Queene," UNA
Coin: Afghan, PUL
  Albanian, LEK
  British Guiana, BIT
  Bulgarian, LEV, LEW
  French, ECU, SOU
  Indian, PIE
  Japanese, SEN, YEN
  Korean, WON

Lithuanian, LIT
Macao, Timor, AVO
Palestinian, MIL
Persian, PUL
Peruvian, SOL
Rumanian, BAN, LEU, LEY
Scandinavian, ORE
Siamese, ATT
  See also Money of account
Collection: Facts, ANA
Commune: Belgian, ANS, ATH
  Netherlands, EDE, EPE
Community: Russian, MIR
Constellation: Southern, ARA
Contraction: Poetic, EEN, EER, OER
Covering: Apex of roof, EPI
Crab: Fiddler, UCA
Crag: Rocky, TOR
Cry: Crow, rook, raven, CAW
Cup: Wine, AMA
Cymbal, Oriental, TAL, ZEL

Disease: Silkworm, UJI
Division: Danish territorial, AMT
Geologic, EON
Doctrine, ISM
Dowry, DOT
Dry (French), SEC
Dynasty: Chinese, CHI, HAN, SUI, WEI, YIN
Eagle: Sea, ERN
Earth (comb. form), GEO
Egg: Louse, NIT
Eggs: Fish, ROE
Emmet, ANT
Enzyme, ASE
Equal (comb. form), ISO
Extension: building, ELL
Far (comb. form), TEL
Farewell, AVE
Fiber: Palm, TAL
Finial, EPI
Fish: Carplike, IDE
Pikelike, GAR
Flatfish, DAB
Fleur-de-lis, LIS, LYS
Food: Hawaiian, POI
Formerly, NEE
Friend (French), AMI
Game: Card, LOO
Garment: Camel-hair, ABA
Gateway, DAR
Gazelle: Tibetan, GOA
Genus: Ducks, AIX
Grasses, POA
Grasses (maize), ZEA
Herbs or shrubs, IVA
Lizards, UTA
Rodents (incl. house mice), MUS
Ruminants (incl. cattle), BOS
Swine, SUS
Gibbon: Malay, LAR
God: Assyrian, SIN
Babylonian, ABU, ANU, BEL, HEA, SIN, UTU
Irish sea, LER
Phrygian, MEN
Polynesian, ORO
Goddess: Babylonian, AYA
Etruscan, UNI
Hindu, SRI, UMA, VAC
Teutonic, RAN
Governor: Algerian, DEY
Turkish, BEY
Grampus, ORC
Grape, UVA
Grass: Meadow, POA
Gypsy, ROM
Hail, AVE
Hare: Female, DOE
Hawthorn, HAW
Hay: Spread for drying, TED
Herb: Japanese, UDO
Perennial, PIA
Used for blue dye, WAD
Herd: Whales, GAM, POD
Hero: Spanish, CID
High (music), ALT
Honey (pharm.), MEL
Humorist: American, ADE
I (Latin), EGO
I love (Latin), AMO
Indian: Algonquian, FOX, SAC, WEA
Chimakuan, HOH
Keresan, SIA
Mayan, MAM
Shoshonean, UTE
Siouan, KAW, OTO
South American, ITE, ONA, URO, URU, YAO
Tierra del Fuego, ONA
Wakashan, AHT
Ingot, PIG
Inlet: Narrow, RIA
Island: Cyclades, IOS
Dodecanese, COS, KOS
(French), ILE
River, AIT

Jackdaw, DAW
John (Gaelic), IAN
Keelbill, ANI, ANO
Kiln, OST
King: British legendary LUD
Kobold, NIS
Lace: To make, TAT
Lamprey, EEL
Language: Artificial, IDO
Bantu, ILA
Siamese, LAO, TAI
Leaf: Palm, OLA, OLE
Leaving, ORT
Left: Cause to turn, HAW
Letter: Greek, CHI, ETA, PHI, PSI, RHO, TAU
Hebrew, MEM, NUN, SIN, TAV, VAU
Lettuce, COS
Life (comb. form), BIO
Lily: Palm, TOI
Lizard, EFT
Louse: Young, NIT
Love (Anglo-Irish), GRA
Lute: Oriental, TAR
Macaw: Bralizian, ARA
Marble, TAW
Match: Shooting (French), TIR
Meadow, LEA
Measure: Abyssinian, TAT
Algerian, PIK
Annamese, GON, MAU, NGU, VUO, SAO, TAO, TAT
Arabian, DEN, SAA
Belgian, VAT
Bulgarian, OKA, OKE
Chinese, FEN, TOU, YIN
Cloth, ELL
Cyprus, OKA, OKE, PIK
Czech, LAN, SAH
Danish, FOD, MIL, POT
Dominican Republic, ONA
Dutch, old, AAM
East Indian, KIT
Egyptian, APT, HEN, PIK, ROB
Electric, MHO, OHM
Energy, ERG
English, PIN
Estonian, TUN
French, POT
German, AAM
Greek, PIK
Hebrew, CAB, HIN, KOR, LOG
Hungarian, AKO
Icelandic, FET
Indian, GAZ, GUZ, JOW, KOS
Japanese, BOO, CHO, KEN, RIN, SHO, SUN, TAN
Malabar, ADY
Metric land, ARE
Netherlands, KAN, KOP, MUD, VAT, ZAK
Norwegian, FOT, POT
Persian, GAZ, GUZ, MOU, ZAR, ZER
Polish, CAL
Rangoon, DHA, LAN
Roman, PES, URN
Russian, FUT, LOF
Scotch, COP
Siamese, KEN, NIU, RAI, SAT, SEN, SOK, WAH, YOT
Somaliland, TOP
Spanish, PIE
Straits Settlements, PAU, TUN
Swedish, ALN, FOT, MIL, REF, TUM
Swiss, POT
Tunisian, SAA
Turkish, OKA, OKE, PIK
Wire, MIL
Württemberg, IMI
Yarn, LEA
Yugoslavian, OKA, RIF
Milk, LAC
Milkfish, AWA
Moccasin, PAC
Money: Yap stone, FEI
Money of Account: Anglo-Saxon, ORA,

ORE
French, SOU
Indian, LAC
Japanese, RIN
Oman, GAJ
Virgin Islands, BIT
See also Coin
Monkey: Capuchin, SAI
Morsel, ORT
Mother: Peer Gynt's, ASE
Mountain: Asia Minor, IDA
Mulberry: Indian, AAL, ACH, AWL
Muttonbird: New Zealand, OII
Nahoor, SNA
Native: Mindanao, ATA
Neckpiece, BOA
Newt, EFT
No (Scotch), NAE
Note: Guido's highest, ELA
Of scale, SOL
Nursemaid: Oriental, AMA, IYA
Ocher: Yellow, SIL
One (Scotch), YIN
Ornament: Pagoda, TEE
Oven: Polynesian, UMU
Ox: Tibetan, YAK
Pagoda: Chinese, TAA
Parrot: Hawk, HIA
New Zealand, KEA
Part: Footlike, PES
Particle: Electrified, ION
Pasha, DEY
Pass: Mountain, COL
Paste: Rice, AME
Pea: Indian split, DAL
Peasant: Philippine, TAO
Penpoint, NEB, NIB
Piece out, EKE
Pigeon, NUN
Pine: Textile screw, ARA
Pistol (slang), GAT
Pit: Baking, IMU
Plant: Pepper, AVA
Play: By Capek, RUR
Poem: Old French, DIT
Porgy: Japanese, TAI
Priest: Biblical high, ELI
Prince Ethiopian, RAS
Pseudonym: Dickens', BOZ
Queen: Fairy, MAB
Quince: Bengal, BEL
Record: Ship's, LOG
Refuse: Flax (Scotch), PAB, POB
Resin, LAC
Resort, SPA
Revolver (slang), GAT
Right: Cause to turn, GEE
River: Scotch or English, DEE
(Spanish), RIO
Swiss, AAR
Room: Harem, ODA
Rootstock: Fern, ROI
Rose (Persian), GUL
Ruff: Female, REE
Rule: Indian, RAJ
Sailor, GOB, TAR
Saint: Female (abbr.), STE
Mohammedan, PIR
Salt, SAL
Sash: Japanese, OBI
Scrap, ORT
Seed: Poppy, MAW
Small, PIP
Self, EGO
Serpent: Vedic sky, AHI
Sesame, TIL
Sheep: Female, EWE
Indian, SHA
Male, RAM
Sheepfold (Scotch), REE
Shelter, LEE
Shield, ECU
Shooting match (French), TIR
Shrew: European, ERD
Shrub: Evergreen, YEW
Silkworm, ERI

Snake, ASP, BOA
Soak, RET
Son-in-law: Mohammed's, ALI
Sorrel: Wood, OCA
Spade: Long, narrow, LOY
Spirit: Malignant, KER
Spot: Playing-card, PIP
Spread for drying, TED
Spring: Mineral, SPA
Sprite: Water, NIX
Statesman: Japanese, ITO
Stern: Toward, AFT
Stomach: Bird's, MAW
Street (French), RUE
Summer (French), ETE
Sun, SOL
Swamp, BOG, FEN
Swan: Male, COB
Tea: Chinese, CHA
Temple: Shinto, SHA
The. *See* Article
Thing (law), RES
Title: Etruscan, LAR
   Monk's, FRA
   Portuguese, DOM
   Spanish, DON
   Turkish, AGA, BEY
Tool: Cutting, ADZ, AXE
   Mining, GAD
   Piercing, AWL
Tree: Candlenut, AMA
   Central American, EBO
   East Indian, SAJ, SAL

Evergreen, YEW
Hawaiian, KOA, KOU
Indian, BEL, DAR
Linden, LIN
New Zealand, AKE
Philippine, DAO, TUA, TUI
Rubber, ULE
South American, APA
Tribe: New Zealand, ATI
Turmeric, REA
Twice, BIS
Twin: Siamese, ENG
Uncle (dialect), EAM, EME
Veil: Chalice, AER, AIR
Vessel: Wine, AMA
Vestment: Ecclesiastical, ALB
Vetch: Bitter, ERS
Victorfish, AKU
Vine: New Zealand, AKA
   Philippine, IYO
Wallaba, APA
Wapiti, ELK
Water (French), EAU
Waterfall, LIN
Watering place: Prussian, EMS
Weave: Designating plain, UNI
Weight: Annamese, CAN
   Bulgarian, OKA, OKE
   Burmese, MOO, VIS
   Chinese, FEN, HAO, KIN, SSU, TAN,
      YIN
   Cyprus, OKA, OKE
   Danish, LOD, ORT, VOG

East Indian, TJI
Egyptian, KAT, OKA, OKE
English, for wool, TOD
German, LOT
Greek, MNA, OKA, OKE
Indian, SER
Japanese, FUN, KIN, RIN, SHI
Korean, KON
Malacca, KIP
Mongolian, LAN
Netherlands, ONS
Norwegian, LOD
Polish, LUT
Rangoon, PAI
Roman, BES
Russian, LOT
Siamese, BAT, HAP, PAI
Swedish, ASS, ORT
Turkish, OKA, OKE
Yugoslavian, OKA, OKE
Whales: Herd, GAM, POD
Wildebeest, GNU
Wing, ALA
Witticism, MOT
Wolframite, CAL
Worm: African, LOA
Wreath: Hawaiian, LEI
Yale, ELI
Yam: Hawaiian, HOI
Yes (French), OUI
Young: Bring forth, EAN
Z (letter), ZED

Words of Four Letters

Aborigine: Borneo, DYAK
Agave, ALOE
Animal: Footless, APOD
Ant: White, ANAI, ANAY
Antelope: African, ASSE, BISA, GUIB,
   KOBA, KUDU, ORYX, POKU, PUKU,
   TOPI, TORA
Apoplexy: Plant, ESCA
Apple, POME
Apricot, ANSU
Ardor, ELAN
Armadillo, APAR, PEBA, PEVA, TATU
Ascetic: Mohammedan, SUFI
Association: Chinese, TONG
Astronomer: Persian, OMAR
Avatar: Of Vishnu, RAMA
Axillary, ALAR
Band: Horizontal (heraldry), FESS
Barracuda, SPET
Bark: Mulberry, TAPA
Base: Column, DADO
Bearing (heraldry), ORLE
Beer: Russian, KVAS
Beige, ECRU
Being, ESSE
Beverage: Japanese rice, SAKE
Bird: Asian, MINA, MYNA
   Egyptian sacred, IBIS
   Extinct, DODO, MAMO
   Flightless, KIWI
   Gull-like, TERN
   Hawaiian, IIWI, MAMO
   Parson, KOKO
   Unfledged, EYAS
Birds: As class, AVES
Black, EBON
   (French), NOIR
Blackbird: European, MERL
Boat: Flat-bottomed, DORY
Bone: Forearm, ULNA
Bones, OSSA
Box, Japanese, INRO
Bravo (rare), EUGE
Buffalo: Indian wild, ARNA
Bull (Spanish), TORO
Burden, ONUS
Cabbage: Sliced, SLAW

Caliph: Mohammedan, OMAR
Canoe: Malay, PRAU, PROA
Cap: Military, KEPI
Cape, NESS
Capital: Ancient Irish, TARA
Case: Article, ETUI
Cat: Wild, BALU, EYRA
Chalcedony, SARD
Chamber: Indian ceremonial, KIVA
Channel: Brain, ITER
Cheese: Dutch, EDAM
Chest: Sepulchral stone, CIST
Chieftain: Arab, EMIR
Church: Part of, APSE, NAVE
   (Scotch), KIRK
Claim (law), LIEN
Cluster: Flower, CYME
Coin: Chinese, TAEL, YUAN
   German, MARK
   Indian, ANNA
   Iranian, RIAL
   Italian, LIRA
   Moroccan, OKIA
   Siamese, BAHT
   South American, PESO
   Spanish, DURO, PESO
   Turkish, PARA
Commune: Belgian, AATH
Composition: Musical, OPUS
Compound: Chemical, DIOL
Constellation: Southern, PAVO
Council: Russian, DUMA
Counsel, REDE
Covering: Seed, ARIL
Cross: Egyptian, ANKH
Cry: Bacchanalian, EVOE
Cup (Scotch), TASS
Cupbearer, SAKI
Dagger, DIRK
   Malay, KRIS
Dam: River, WEIR
Dash, ELAN
Date: Roman, IDES
Dawn: Pertaining to, EOAN
Dean: English, INGE
Decay: In fruit, BLET
Deer: Sambar, MAHA

Disease: Skin, ACNE
Disk: Solar, ATEN
Dog: Hunting, ALAN
Drink: Hindu intoxicating, SOMA
Duck, SMEE, SMEW, TEAL
Dynasty: Chinese, CHEN, CHIN, CHOU,
   CHOW, HSIA, MING, SUNG, TANG,
   TSIN
   Mongol, YUAN
Eagle: Biblical, GIER
   Sea, ERNE
Egyptian: Christian, COPT
Ear: Pertaining to, OTIC
Entrance: Mine, ADIT
Esau, EDOM
Escutcheon: Voided, ORLE
Eskers, OSAR
Evergreen: New Zealand, TAWA
Fairy: Persian, PERI
Family: Italian, ESTE
Far (comb. form), TELE
Farewell, VALE
Father (French), PERE
Fennel: Philippine, ANIS
Fever: Malarial, AGUE
Fiber: East Indian, JUTE
Firn, NEVE
Fish: Carplike, DACE
   Hawaiian, ULUA
   Herringlike, SHAD
   Mackerellike, CERO
   Marine, HAKE
   Sea, LING, MERO, OPAH
   Spiny-finned, GOBY
Food: Tropical, TARO
Foot: Metric, IAMB
Formerly, ERST
Founder: Of Carthage, DIDO
France: Southern, MIDI
Furze, ULEX
Gaelic, ERSE
Gaiter, SPAT
Game: Card, FARO, SKAT
Garlic: European wild, MOLY
Garment: Hindu, SARI
   Roman, TOGA
Gazelle, CORA

Gem, JADE, ONYX, OPAL, RUBY
Genus: Amphibians (incl. frogs), RANA
 Amphibians (incl. tree toads), HYLA
 Antelopes, ORYX
 Auks, ALCA, URIA
 Bees, APIS
 Birds (American ostriches), RHEA
 Birds (cranes), CRUS
 Birds (magpies), PICA
 Birds (peacocks), PAVO
 Cetaceans, INIA
 Ducks (incl. mallards), ANAS
 Fishes (burbots), LOTA
 Fishes (incl. bowfins), AMIA
 Geese (snow geese), CHEN
 Gulls, XEMA
 Herbs, ARUM, GEUM
 Insects (water scorpions), NEPA
 Lilies, ALOE
 Mammals (mankind), HOMO
 Orchids, DISA
 Owls, ASIO, BUBO, OTUS
 Palms, NIPA
 Sea birds, SULA
 Sheep, OVIS
 Shrubs, Eurasian, ULEX
 Shrubs (hollies), ILEX
 Shrubs (incl. Virginia Willow), ITEA
 Shrubs, tropical, EVEA
 Snakes (sand snakes), ERYX
 Swans, OLOR
 Trees, chocolate, COLA
 Trees (ebony family), MABA
 Trees (incl. maples), ACER
 Trees (olives), OLEA
 Trees, tropical, EVEA
 Turtles, EMYS
Goat: Wild, IBEX, KRAS, TAHR, TAIR, THAR
God: Assyrian, ASUR
 Babylonian, ADAD, ADDU, ENKI, ENZU, IRRA, NABU, NEBO, UTUG
 Celtic, LLEU, LLEW
 Hindu, AGNI, CIVA, DEVA, DEWA, KAMA, RAMA, SIVA, VAYU
 Phrygian, ATYS
 Semitic, BAAL
 Teutonic, HLER
Goddess: Babylonian, ERUA, GULA
 Hawaiian, PELE
 Hindu, DEVI, KALI, SHRI, VACH
Gooseberry: Hawaiian, POHA
Gourd, PEPO
Grafted (heraldry), ENTE
Grandfather (obsolete), AIEL
Grandparents: Pertaining to, AVAL
Grass: Hawaiian, HILO
Gray (French), GRIS
Green (heraldry), VERT
Groom: Indian, SYCE
Half (prefix), DEMI, HEMI, SEMI
Hamlet, DORP
Hammer-head: Part of, PEEN
Handle, ANSA
Harp: Japanese, KOTO
Hartebeest, ASSE, TORA
Hautboy, OBOE
Hawk: Taken from nest (falconry), EYAS
Hearing (law), OYER
Heater: For liquids, ETNA
Herb: Aromatic, ANET, DILL
 Fabulous, MOLY
 Perennial, GEUM, SEGO
 Pot, WORT
 Used for blue dye, WADE, WOAD
Hill: Flat-topped, MESA
 Sand, DENE, DUNE
Hoarfrost, RIME
Hog: Immature female, GILT
Holly, ILEX
House: Cow, BYRE
 (Spanish), CASA
Ice: Floating, FLOE
Image, ICON, IKON

Incarnation: Of Vishnu, RAMA
Indian: Algonquian, CREE, SAUK
 Central American, MAYA
 Iroquoian, ERIE
 Mexican, CORA
 Peruvian, CANA, INCA, MORO
 Shoshonean, HOPI
 Siouan, OTOE
 Southwestern, HOPI, PIMA, YUMA, ZUNI
Insect: Immature, PUPA
Instrument: Stringed, LUTE, LYRE
Ireland, EIRE, ERIN
Jacket: English, ETON
Jail (British), GAOL
Jar, OLLA
Judge: Mohammedan, CADI
Juniper: European, CADE
Kiln, OAST, OVEN
King: British legendary, LUDD, NUDD
Kiss, BUSS
Knife: Philippine, BOLO
Koran: Section of, SURA
Laborer: Spanish American, PEON
Lake: Mountain, TARN
 (Scotch), LOCH
Lamp: Miner's, DAVY
Landing place: Indian, GHAT
Language: Buddhist, PALI
 Japanese, AINU
Latvian, LETT
Layer: Of iris, UVEA
Leaf: Palm, OLAY, OLLA
Legislature: Ukrainian, RADA
Lemur, LORI
Leopard, PARD
Let it stand, STET
Letter: Greek, BETA, IOTA, ZETA
 Hebrew, AYIN, BETH, CAPH, KOPH, RESH, SHIN, TETH, YODH
 Papal, BULL
Lily, ALOE
Literature: Hindu sacred, VEDA
Lizard, GILA
 Monitor, URAN
Loquat, BIWA
Magistrate: Genoese or Venetian, DOGE
Man (Latin), HOMO
Mark: Omission, DELE
 armoset: South American, MICO
Meadow: Fertile, VEGA
Measure: Electric, VOLT, WATT
 Force, DYNE
 Hebrew, OMER
 Printing, PICA
 Spanish or Portuguese, VARA
 Swiss land, IMMI
Medley, OLIO
Merganser, SMEW
Milk (French), LAIT
Molding, GULA
 Curved, OGEE
Mongoose: Crab-eating, URVA
Monk: Tibetan, LAMA
Monkey: African, MONA, WAAG
 Ceylonese, MAHA
 Cochin-China, DOUC
 South American, SAKI, TITI
Monkshood, ATIS
Month: Jewish, ADAR, ELUL, IYAR
Mother (French), MERE
Mountain: Thessaly, OSSA
Mouse: Meadow, VOLE
Mythology: Norse, EDDA
Nail (French), CLOU
Native: Philippine, MORO
Nest: Of pheasants, NIDE
Network, RETE
No (German), NEIN
Noble: Mohammedan, AMIR
Notice: Death, OBIT
Novel: By Zola, NANA
Nursemaid: Oriental AMAH, AYAH, EYAH
Nut: Philippine, PILI

Oak: Holm, ILEX
Oil (comb. form), OLEO
Ostrich: American, RHEA
Oven, KILN, OAST
Owl: Barn, LULU
Ox: Celebes wild, ANOE
 Extinct wild, URUS
Palm, ATAP, NIPA, SAGO
Parliament, DIET
Parrot: New Zealand, KAKA
Pass: Indian mountain, GHAT
Passage: Closing (music), CODA
Peach: Clingstone, PAVY
Peasant: Indian, RYOT
 Old English, CARL
Pepper: Australasian, KAVA
Perfume, ATAR
Persia, IRAN
Person: Extraordinary, ONER
Pickerel or pike, ESOX
Pitcher, EWER
Plant: Aromatic, NARD
 Century, ALOE
 Indigo, ANIL
 Pepper, KAVA
Platform: Raised, DAIS
Plum: Wild, SLOE
Pods: Vegetable, OKRA, OKRO
Poem: Epic, EPOS
Poet: Persian, OMAR
 Roman, OVID
Poison, BANE
 Arrow, INEE
Porkfish, SISI
Portico: Greek, STOA
Premium, AGIO
Priest: Mohammedan, IMAM
Prima donna, DIVA
Prong: Fork, TINE
Pseudonym: Lamb's, ELIA
Queen: Carthaginian, DIDO
 Hindu, RANI
Rabbit, CONY
Race: Of Japan, AINU
Rail: Ducklike, COOT
 North American, SORA
Redshank, CLEE
Refuse: After pressing, MARC
Regiment: Turkish, ALAI
Reliquary, ARCA
Resort: Italian, LIDO
Ridges: Sandy, ASAR, OSAR
River: German, ELBE, ODER
 Italian, ADDA
 Siberian, LENA
Road: Roman, ITER
Rockfish: California, RENA
Rodent: Mouselike, VOLE
 South American, PACA
Rootstock, TARO
Salamander, NEWT
Salmon: Silver, COHO
 Young, PARR
Same (Greek), HOMO
 (Latin), IDEM
Sauce: Fish, ALEC
School: English, ETON
Seaweed, AGAR, ALGA, KELP
Secular, LAIC
Sediment, SILT
Seed: Dill, ANET
 Of vetch, TARE
Serf, ILOT
Sesame, TEEL
Settlement: Eskimo, ETAH
Shark: Atlantic, GATA
 European, TOPE
Sheep: Wild, UDAD
Sheltered, ALEE
Shield, EGIS
Ship: Jason's, ARGO
 Left side of, PORT
 Two-masted, BRIG
Shrine: Buddhist, TOPE
Shrub: New Zealand, TUTU

Sign: Magic, RUNE
Silkworm, ERIA
Skin: Beaver, PLEW
Skink: Egyptian, ADDA
Slave, ESNE
Sloth: Two-toed, UNAU
Smooth, LENE
Snow: Glacial, NEVE
Soapstone, TALC
Society: African secret, EGBO, PORO
Son: Of Seth, ENOS
Song (German), LIED
   Unaccompanied, GLEE
Sound: Lung, RALE
Sour, ACID
Sow: Young, GILT
Spike: Brad-shaped, BROB
Spirit: Buddhist evil, MARA
Stake: Poker, ANTE
Star: Temporary, NOVA
Starch: East Indian, SAGO
Stone: Precious, OPAL
Strap: Bridle, REIN
Strewn (heraldry), SEME
Sweetsop, ATES, ATTA
Sword: Fencing, EPEE, FOIL
Tambourine: African, TAAR
Tapir: Brazilian, ANTA
Tax, CESS
Tea: South American, MATE
Therefore (Latin), ERGO
Thing: Extraordinary, ONER
Three (dice, cards, etc.), TREY
Thrush: Hawaiian, OMAO

Tide, NEAP
Tipster: Racing, TOUT
Tissue, TELA
Title: Etruscan, LARS
   Hindu, BABU
   Indian, RAJA
   Mohammedan, EMIR, IMAM
   Persian, BABA
   Spanish, DONA
   Turkish, AGHA, BABA
Toad: Largest-known, AGUA
   Tree, HYLA
Tool: Cutting, ADZE
Track: Deer, SLOT
Tract: Sandy, DENE
Tree: Apple, SORB
   Central American, EBOE
   East Indian, TEAK
   Eucalyptus, YATE
   Guiana and Trinidad, MORA
   Javanese, UPAS
   Linden, LIME, LINN, TEIL, TILL
   Sandarac, ARAR
   Sassafras, AGUE
   Tamarisk salt, ATLE
Tribe: Moro, SULU
Trout, CHAR
Urchin: Street, ARAB
Vessel: Arab, DHOW
Vestment: Ecclesiastical, COPE
Vetch, TARE
Vine: East Indian, SOMA
Violinist: Famous, AUER
Vortex, EDDY

Wampum, PEAG
Wapiti, STAG
Waste: Allowance for, TRET
Watchman: Indian, MINA
Water (Spanish), AGUA
Waterfall, LINN
Wavy (heraldry), ONDE, UNDE
Wax, CERE
   Chinese, PELA
Weed: Biblical, TARE
Weight: Ancient, MINA
   Danish (pl.), ESER
   East Asian, TAEL
   Greek, MINA
   Siamese, BAHT
Well done (rare), EUGE
Whale, CETE
   Killer, ORCA
   White, HUSE, HUSO
Whirlpool, EDDY
Wife: Of Geraint, ENID
Willow: Virginia, ITEA
Wine, PORT
Winged, ALAR
   (Heraldry), AILE
Wings, ALAE
Withered, SERE
Without (French), SANS
Wool: To comb, CARD
Work, OPUS
Wrong: Civil, TORT
Young: Bring forth, YEAN

Words of Five Letters

Abode of dead: Babylonian, ARALU
Aborigine: Borneo DAYAK
Aftersong, EPODE
Aloe, AGAVE
Animal: Footless, APODE
Ant, EMMET
Antelope: African, ADDAX, BEISA, CAAMA, ELAND, GUIBA,
   ORIBI, TIANG
   Goat, GORAL, SEROW
   Indian, SASIN
   Siberian, SAIGA
Arch: Pointed, OGIVE
Armadillo, APARA, POYOU, TATOU
Arrowroot, ARARU
Artery: Trunk, AORTA
Association: Russian, ARTEL
   Secret, CABAL
Author: English, READE
Automaton, GOLEM, ROBOT
Award: Motion-picture, OSCAR
Basket: Fishing, CREEL
Beer: Russian, KVASS
Bible: Mohammedan, KORAN
Bird: Asian, MINAH, MYNAH
   Indian, SHAMA
   Larklike, PIPIT
   Loonlike, GREBE
   Oscine, VIREO
   South American, AGAMI
   Swimming, GREBE
Black: (French), NOIRE
   (Heraldry), SABLE
Blackbird: European, MERLE, OUSEL, OUZEL
Block: Glacial, SERAC
Blue (heraldry), AZURE
Boat: Eskimo, BIDAR, UMIAK
Bobwhite, COLIN, QUAIL
Bone (comb. form), OSTEO
   Leg, TIBIA
   Thigh, FEMUR
Broom: Twig, BESOM
Brother (French), FRERE
   Moses, AARON
Canoe: Eskimo, BIDAR, KAYAK
Cape: Papal, FANON, ORALE
Caravansary, SERAI

Card: Old playing, TAROT
Caterpillar: New Zealand, AWETO
Catkin, AMENT
Cavity: Stone, GEODE
Cephalopod, SQUID
Cetacean, WHALE
Chariot, ESSED
Cheek: Pertaining to, MALAR
Chieftain: Arab, EMEER
Child (Scotch), BAIRN
Cigar, CLARO
Coating: Seed, TESTA
Cockatoo: Palm, ARARA
Coin: Costa Rican, COLON
   Danish, KRONE
   Ecuadorian, SUCRE
   English, GROAT, PENCE
   French, FRANC
   German, KRONE, TALER
   Hungarian, PENGO
   Icelandic, KRONA
   Indian, RUPEE
   Iraqi, DINAR
   Norwegian, KRONE
   Polish, ZLOTY
   Russian, COPEC, KOPEK, RUBLE
   Swedish, KRONA
   Turkish, ASPER
   Yugoslav, DINAR
Collar: Papal, FANON, ORALE
   Roman, RABAT
Commune: Italian, TREIA
Composition: Choral, MOTET
Compound: Chemical, ESTER
Conceal (law), ELOIN
Council: Ecclesiastical, SYNOD
Court: Anglo-Saxon, GEMOT
   Inner, PATIO
Crest: Mountain, ARETE
Crown: Papal, TIARA
Cuttlefish, SEPIA
Date: Roman, NONES
Decree: Mohammedan, IRADE
   Russian, UKASE
Deposit: Loam, LOESS
Desert: Gobi, SHAMO

Devilfish, MANTA
Disease: Cereals, ERGOT
Disk, PATEN
Dog: Wild, DHOLE, DINGO
Dormouse, LEROT
Drum, TABOR
Duck: Sea, EIDER
Dynasty: Chinese, CHING, LIANG, SHANG
Earthquake, SEISM
Eel, ELVER, MORAY
Ermine: European, STOAT
Ether: Crystalline, APIOL
Fabric: Velvetlike, PANNE
Fabulist, AESOP
Family: Italian, CENCI
Fiber: West Indian, SISAL
Fig: Smyrna, ELEME, ELEMI
Figure: Of speech, TROPE
Finch: European, SERIN
Fish: American small, KILLY
Flower: Garden, ASTER
Friend (Spanish), AMIGO
Fruit: Tropical, MANGO
Fungus: Rye, ERGOT
Furze, GORSE
Gateway, TORAN, TORII
Gem, AGATE, BERYL, PEARL, TOPAZ
Genus: Barnacles, LEPAS
  Bears, URSUS
  Birds (loons), GAVIA
  Birds (nuthatches), SITTA
  Cats, FELIS
  Dogs, CANIS
  Fishes (chiros), ELOPS
  Fishes (perch), PERCA
  Geese, ANSER
  Grasses, STIPA
  Grasses (incl. oats), AVENA
  Gulls, LARUS
  Hares, rabbits, LEPUS
  Hawks, BUTEO
  Herbs, old world, INULA
  Herbs, trailing or climbing, APIOS
  Herbs, tropical, TACCA, URENA
  Horses, EQUUS
  Insects (olive flies), DACUS
  Lice, plant, APHIS
  Lichens, USNEA
  Lizards, AGAMA
  Moles, TALPA
  Mollusks, OLIVA
  Monkeys, CEBUS
  Palms, ARECA
  Pigeons, GOURA
  Plants (amaryllis family), AGAVE
  Ruminants (goats), CAPRA
  Shrubs, Asiatic, SABIA
  Shrubs (heath), ERICA
  Shrubs (incl. raspberry), RUBUS
  Shrubs, tropical, IXORA, TREMA, URENA
  Ticks, ARGAS
  Trees (of elm family), TREMA, ULMUS
  Trees, tropical, IXORA, TREMA
Goat: Bezoar, PASAN
God: Assyrian, ASHIR, ASHUR, ASSUR
  Babylonian, DAGAN, SIRIS
  Gaelic, DAGDA
  Hindu, BHAGA, INDRA, SHIVA
  Japanese, EBISU
  Philistine, DAGON
  Phrygian. ATTIS
  Teutonic, AEGIR, GYMIR
  Welsh, DYLAN
Goddess: Babylonian, ISTAR, NANAI
  Hindu, DURGA, GAURI, SHREE
Group: Of six, HEXAD
Grove: Sacred to Diana, NEMUS
Growing out, ENATE
Guitar: Hindu, SITAR
Gull: PEWEE, PEWIT
Hartebeest, CAAMA
Headdress: Jewish or Persian, TIARA
  Liturgical, MITER, MITRE
Heath, ERICA
Herb: Grasslike marsh, SEDGE
Heron, EGRET

Hog: Young, SHOAT, SHOTE
Image, EIKON
Indian: Cariban, ARARA
  Iroquoian, HURON
  Mexican, AZTEC, OPATA, OTOMI
  Muskhogean, CREEK
  Siouan, OSAGE, TETON
  Spanish American, ARARA, CARIB
Inflorescence: Racemose, AMENT
Insect: Immature, LARVA
Intrigue, CABAL
Iris: Yellow, SEDGE
Juniper, GORSE, RETEM
Kidneys: Pertaining to, RENAL
King: British legendary, LLUDD
Kite: European, GLEDE
Kobold, NISSE
Land: Cultivated, ARADA, ARADO
Landholder (Scotch), LAIRD, THANE
Language: Dravidian, TAMIL
Lariat, LASSO, REATA
Laughing, RIANT
Lawgiver: Athenian, DRACO, SOLON
Leaf: Calyx, SEPAL
  Fern, FROND
Lemur, LORIS
Letter: English, AITCH
  Greek, ALPHA, DELTA, GAMMA, KAPPA, OMEGA,
    SIGMA, THETA
  Hebrew, ALEPH, CHETH, GIMEL, SADHE, ZAYIN
Lichen, USNEA
Lighthouse, PHARE
Lizard: Old World, AGAMA
Loincloth, DHOTI
Louse: Plant, APHID
Macaw: Brazilian, ARARA
Mahogany: Philippine, ALMON
Mammal: Badgerlike, RATEL
  Civetlike, GENET
  Giraffelike, OKAPI
  Raccoonlike, COATI
Man (French), HOMME
Marble, AGATE
Mark: Insertion, CARET
Market place: Greek, AGORA
Marsupial: Australian, KOALA
Measure: Electric, FARAD, HENRY
  Energy, JOULE
  Metric, LITER, STERE
  Printing, AGATE
  Russian, VERST
Mixture: Smelting, MATTE
Mohicans: Last of, UNCAS
Molding: Convex, OVOLO, TORUS
Mole, TALPA
Monkey: African, PATAS
  Capuchin, SAJOU
  Howling, ARABA
Monkshood, ATEES
Month: Jewish, NISAN, SIVAN, TEBET
Museum (French), MUSEE
Musketeer, ATHOS
Native: Aleutian, ALEUT
  New Zealand, MAORI
Neckpiece: Ecclesiastical, AMICE
Nerve (comb. form), NEURO
Nest: Eagle's or hawk's, AERIE
  Insect's, NIDUS
Net: Fishing, SEINE
Newsstand, KIOSK
Nitrogen, AZOTE
Noble: Mohammedan, AMEER
Nodule: Stone, GEODE
Nostrils, NARES
Notched irregularly, EROSE
Nymph: Mohammedan, HOURI
Official: Roman, EDILE
Oleoresin, ELEMI
Opening: Mouthlike, STOMA
Oration: Funeral, ELOGE
Ostiole, STOMA
Page: Left-hand, VERSO
  Right-hand, RECTO
Palm, ARECA, BETEL
Park: Colorado, ESTES
Perfume, ATTAR

Philosopher: Greek, PLATO
Pillar: Stone, STELA, STELE
Pinnacle: Glacial, SERAC
Plain, LLANO
Plant: Century, AGAVE
  Climbing, LIANA
  Dwarf, CUMIN
  East Asian perennial, RAMIE
  Medicinal, SENNA
  Mustard family, CRESS
Plate: Communion, PATEN
Poem: Lyric, EPODE
Point: Lowest, NADIR
Poplar, ABELE, ALAMO, ASPEN
Porridge: Spanish American, ATOLE
Post: Stair, NEWEL
Priest: Mohammedan, IMAUM
Protozoan, AMEBA
Queen: (French), REINE
  Hindu, RANEE
Rabbit, CONEY
Rail, CRAKE
Red (heraldry), GULES
Religion: Moslem, ISLAM
Resin, ELEMI
Revoke (law), ADEEM
Rich man, MIDAS, NABOB
Ridge: Sandy, ESKAR, ESKER
River: French, LOIRE, SEINE
Rockfish: California, REINA
Rootstock: Fragrant, ORRIS
Ruff: Female, REEVE
Sack: Pack, KYACK
Salt: Ethereal, ESTER
Saltpeter, NITER, NITRE
Salutation: Eastern, SALAM
Sandpiper: Old World, TEREK
Scented, OLENT
School: Fish, SHOAL
  French public, LYCEE
Scriptures: Mohammedan, KORAN
Seaweeds, ALGAE
Seed: Aromatic, ANISE
Seraglio, HAREM, SERAI
Serf, HELOT
Sheep: Wild, AUDAD
Sheeplike, OVINE
Shield, AEGIS
Shoe: Wooden, SABOT
Shoots: Pickled bamboo, ACHAR
Shot: Billiard, CAROM, MASSE
Shrine: Buddhist, STUPA
Shrub: Burning bush, WAHOO
  Ornamental evergreen, TOYON
  Used in tanning, SUMAC
Silk: Watered, MOIRE
Sister (French), SOEUR
  (Latin), SOROR
Six: Group of, HEXAD
Skeleton: Marine, CORAL

Slave, HELOT
Snake, ABOMA, ADDER, COBRA, RACER
Soldier: French, POILU
  Indian, SEPOY
Sour, ACERB
Spirit: Air, ARIEL
Staff: Shepherd's, CROOK
Starwort, ASTER
Steel (German), STAHL
Stockade: Russian, ETAPE
Stop (nautical), AVAST
Storehouse, ETAPE
Subway: Parisian, METRO
Tapestry, ARRAS
Tea: Paraguayan, YERBA
Temple: Hawaiian, HEIAU
Terminal: Positive, ANODE
Theater: Greek, ODEON, ODEUM
Then (French), ALORS
Thread: Surgical, SETON
Thrush: Wilson's, VEERY
Title: Hindu, BABOO
  Indian, RAJAH, SAHEB, SAHIB
  Mohammedan, EMEER, IMAUM
Tree: Buddhist sacred, PIPAL
  East Indian cotton, SIMAL
  Hickory, PECAN
  Light-wooded, BALSA
  Malayan, TERAP
  Mediterranean, CAROB
  Mexican, ABETO
  Mexican pine, OCOTE
  New Zealand, MAIRE
  Philippine, ALMON
  Rain, SAMAN
  South American, UMBRA
  Tamarack, LARCH
  Tamarisk salt, ATLEE
  West Indian, ACANA
Trout, CHARR
Troy, ILION, ILIUM
Twin: Siamese, CHANG
Vestment: Ecclesiastical, STOLE
Violin: Famous, AMATI, STRAD
Volcano: Mud, SALSE
Wampum, PEAGE
War cry: Greek, ALALA
Wavy (heraldry), UNDEE
Weight: Jewish, GERAH
Wen, TALPA
Wheat, SPELT
Wheel: Persian water, NORIA
Whitefish, CISCO
Willow, OSIER
Window: Bay, ORIEL
Wine, MEDOC, RHINE, TINTA, TOKAY
Winged, ALATE
Woman (French), FEMME
Year: Excess of solar over lunar, EPACT
Zoroastrian, PARSI

Words of Six or More Letters

Agave, MAGUEY
Alkaloid: Crystalline, ESERIN, ESERINE
Alligator, CAYMAN
Amphibole, EDENITE, URALITE
Ant: White, TERMITE
Antelope: African, DIKDIK, DUIKER, GEMSBOK, IMPALA,
  KOODOO
  European, CHAMOIS
  Indian, NILGAI, NILGAU, NILGHAI, NILGHAU
Ape: Asian or East Indian, GIBBON
Appendage: Leaf, STIPEL, STIPULE
Armadillo, PELUDO, TATOUAY
Arrowroot, ARARAO
Ascetic: Jewish, ESSENE
Ass: Asian wild, ONAGER
Avatar: Of Vishnu, KRISHNA
Babylonian, ELAMITE
Badge: Shoulder, EPAULET
Baldness, ALOPECIA

Barracuda, SENNET
Bark: Aromatic, SINTOC
Bearlike, URSINE
Beetle, ELATER
Bible: Zoroastrian, AVESTA
Bird: Sea, PETREL
  South American, SERIEMA
  Wading, AVOCET, AVOSET
Bone: Leg, FIBULA
Branched, RAMATE
Brother (Latin), FRATER
Bunting: European, ORTOLAN
Call: Trumpet, SENNET
Canoe: Eskimo, BAIDAR, OOMIAK
Caravansary, IMARET
Cat: Asian or African, CHEETAH
  Leopardlike, OCELOT
Cenobite: Jewish, ESSENE
Centerpiece: Table, EPERGNE

Cetacean, DOLPHIN, PORPOISE
Chariot, ESSEDA, ESSEDE
Chief: Seminole, OSCEOLA
Claim: Release as (law), REMISE
Clock: Water, CLEPSYDRA
Cloud, CUMULUS, NIMBUS
Coach: French hackney, FIACRE
Coin: Czech, KORUNA
  Ethiopian, TALARI
  Finnish, MARKKA
  German, THALER
  Greek, DRACHMA
  Haitian, GOURDE
  Honduran, LEMPIRA
  Hungarian, FORINT
  Indo-Chinese, PIASTER
  Netherlands, GUILDER
  Panamanian, BALBOA
  Paraguayan, GUARANI
  Portuguese, ESCUDO
  Russian, COPECK, KOPECK, ROUBLE
  Spanish, PESETA
  Venezuelan, BOLIVAR
Communion: Last holy, VIATICUM
Conceal (law), ELOIGN
Confection, PRALINE
Construction: Sentence, SYNTAX
Convexity: Shaft of column, ENTASIS
Court: Anglo-Saxon, GEMOTE
Cow: Sea, DUGONG, MANATEE
Cylindrical, TERETE
Dagger, STILETTO
  Malay, CREESE, KREESE
Date: Roman, CALENDS, KALENDS
Deer, CARIBOU, WAPITI
Disease: Plant, ERINOSE
Doorkeeper, OSTIARY
Dragonflies: Order of, ODANATA
Drink: Of gods, NECTAR
Drum: TABOUR
  Moorish, ATABAL, ATTABAL
Duck: Fish-eating, MERGANSER
  Sea, SCOTER
Dynasty: Chinese, MANCHU
Eel, CONGER
Edit, REDACT
Envelope: Flower, PERIANTH
Eskimo, AMERIND
Ether: Crystalline, APIOLE
Excuse (law), ESSOIN
Eyespots, OCELLI
Fabric, ESTAMENE, ESTAMIN, ETAMINE
Falcon: European, KESTREL
Figure: Used as column, CARYATID, TELAMON
Fine: For punishment, AMERCE
Fish: Asian fresh-water, GOURAMI
  Pikelike, BARRACUDA
Five: Group of, PENTAD
Fly: African, TSETSE
Foot: Metric, ANAPEST, IAMBUS
Foxlike, VULPINE
Frying pan, SPIDER
Fur, KARAKUL
Galley: Greek or Roman, BIREME, TRIREME
Game: Card, ECARTE
Garment: Greek, CHLAMYS
Gateway, GOPURA, TORANA
Genus: Birds (ravens, crows), CORVUS
  Eels, CONGER
  Fishes, ANABAS
  Foxes, VULPES
  Herbs, ANEMONE
  Insects, CICADA
  Lemurs, GALAGO
  Mints (incl. catnip), NEPETA
  Mollusks, ANOMIA, ASTARTE, TEREDO
  Mollusks (incl. oysters), OSTREA
  Monkeys (spider monkeys), ATELES
  Thrushes (incl. robins), TURDUS
  Trees (of elm family), CELTIS
  Trees (inc. dogwood), CORNUS
  Trees, tropical American, SAPOTA
  Wrens, NANNUS
Gibbon, SIAMANG, WOUWOU
Gland: Salivary, RACEMOSE
Goat: Bezoar, PASANG

Goatlike, CAPRINE
God: Assyrian, ASHSHUR, ASSHUR
  Babylonian, BABBAR, MARDUK, MERODACH, NANNAR, NERGAL, SHAMASH
  Hindu, BRAHMA, KRISHNA, VISHNU
  Tahitian, TAAROA
Goddess: Babylonian, ISHTAR
  Hindu, CHANDI, HAIMAVATI, LAKSHMI, PARVATI, SARASVATI, SARASWATI
Government, POLITY
Governor: Persian, SATRAP
Grandson (Scotch), NEPOTE
Group: Of five, PENTAD
  Of nine, ENNEAD
  Of seven, HEPTAD
Hare: in first year, LEVERET
Harpsichord, SPINET
Herb: Alpine, EDELWEISS
  Chinese, GINSENG
  South African, FREESIA
Hermit, EREMITE
Hero: Legendary, PALADIN
Heron, BITTERN
Horselike, EQUINE
Hound: Short-legged, BEAGLE
House (French), MAISON
Idiot, CRETIN
Implement: Stone, NEOLITH
Incarnation: Hindu, AVATAR
Indian, APACHE, COMANCHE, PAIUTE, SENECA
Inn: Turkish, IMARET
Insects: Order of, DIPTERA
Instrument: Japanese banjolike, SAMISEN
  Musical, CLAVIER, SPINET
Interstice, AREOLA
Ironwood, COLIMA
Juniper: Old Testament, RAETAM
Kettledrum, ATABAL
King: Fairy, OBERON
Kneecap, PATELLA
Knife, MACHETE
Langur: Sumatran, SIMPAI
Legislature: Spanish, CORTES
Lemur: African, GALAGO
  Madagascar, AYEAYE
Letter: Greek, EPSILON, LAMBDA, OMICRON, UPSILON
  Hebrew, DALETH, LAMEDH, SAMEKH
Lighthouse, PHAROS
Lizard, IGUANA
Llama, ALPACA
Lockjaw, TETANUS
Locust, CICADA, CICALA
Macaw: Brazilian, MARACAN
Maid: Of Astolat, ELAINE
Mammal: Madagascar, TENDRAC, TENREC
Man (Spanish), HOMBRE
Marmoset: South American, TAMARIN
Marsupial, BANDICOOT, WOMBAT
Massacre, POGROM
Mayor: Spanish, ALCALDE
Measure: Electric, AMPERE, COULOMB, KILOWATT
Medicine: Quack, NOSTRUM
Member: Religious order, CENOBITE
Molasses, TREACLE
Monkey: African, GRIVET, NISNAS
  Asian, LANGUR
  Philippine, MACHIN
  South American, PINCHE, SAIMIRI, SAMIRI, SAPAJOU
Monster, CHIMERA, GORGON
  (Comb. form), TERATO
  Cretan, MINOTAUR
Month: Jewish, HESHVAN, KISLEV, SHEBAT, TAMMUZ, TISHRI, VEADAR
Mountain: Asia Minor, ARARAT
Mulct, AMERCE
Musketeer, ARAMIS, PORTHOS
Nearsighted, MYOPIC
Net, TRAMMEL
New York City, GOTHAM
Nine: Group of, ENNEAD
Nobleman: Spanish, GRANDEE
Official: Roman, AEDILE
Onyx: Mexican, TECALI
Order: Dragonflies, ODANATA
  Insects, DIPTERA
Organ: Plant, PISTIL

Ornament: Shoulder, EPAULET
Overcoat: Military, CAPOTE
Ox: Wild, BANTENG
Oxidation: Bronze or copper, PATINA
Paralysis: Incomplete, PARESIS
Pear: Alligator, AVOCADO
Persimmon: Mexican, CHAPOTE
Pipe: Peace, CALUMET
Plaid (Scotch), TARTAN
Plain, PAMPAS, STEPPE, TUNDRA
Plant: Buttercup family, ANEMONE
    Century, MAGUEY
    On rocks, LICHEN
Plowing: Fit for, ARABLE
Poem: Heroic, EPOPEE
    Six-lined, SESTET
Point: Highest, ZENITH
Potion: Love, PHILTER, PHILTRE
Protozoan, AMOEBA
Punish, AMERCE
Purple (heraldry), PURPURE
Queen: Fairy, TITANIA
Race: Skiing, SLALOM
Rat, BANDICOOT, LEMMING
Retort, RIPOST, RIPOSTE
Ring: Harness, TERRET
    Little, ANNULET
Rodent: Jumping, JERBOA
    Spanish American, AGOUTI, AGOUTY
Sailor: East Indian, LASCAR
Salmon: Young, GRILSE
Salutation: Eastern, SALAAM
Sandpiper, PLOVER
Sandy, ARENOSE
Sapodilla, SAPOTA, SAPOTE
Saw: Surgical, TREPAN
Seven: Group of, HEPTAD
Sexes: Common to both, EPICENE
Shawl: Mexican, SERAPE
Sheathing: Flower, SPATHE
Sheep: Wild, AOUDAD, ARGALI
Shipworm, TEREDO
Shoes: Mercury's winged, TALARIA
Shortening: Syllable, SYSTOLE
Shrub, SPIRAEA
Sickle-shaped, FALCATE

Silver (heraldry), ARGENT
Snake, ANACONDA
Speech: Loss of, APHASIA
Spiral, HELICAL
Staff: Bishop's, CROSIER, CROZIER
Stalk: Plant, PETIOLE
State: Swiss, CANTON
Studio, ATELIER
Swan: Young, CYGNET
Swimming, NATANT
Sword-shaped, ENSATE
Terminal: Negative, CATHODE
Third (music), TIERCE
Thrust: Fencing, RIPOST, RIPOSTE
Tile: Pertaining to, TEGULAR
Tomb: Empty, CENOTAPH
Tooth (comb. form), ODONTO
Tower: Mohammedan, MINARET
Tree: African timber, BAOBAB
    Black gum, TUPELO
    East Indian, MARGOSA
    Locust, ACACIA
    Malayan, SINTOC
    Marmalade, SAPOTE
Urn: Tea, SAMOVAR
Vehicle, LANDAU, TROIKA
Verbose, PROLIX
Viceroy: Egyptian, KHEDIVE
Vulture: American, CONDOR
Warehouse (French), ENTREPOT
Whale: White, BELUGA
Whirlpool, VORTEX
Will: Addition to, CODICIL
    Having left, TESTATE
Wind, CHINOOK, MONSOON, SIMOOM, SIMOON, SIROCCO
Window: In roof, DORMER
Wine, BARBERA, BURGUNDY, CABERNET, CHABLIS, CHIANTI, CLARET, MUSCATEL, RIESLING, SAUTERNE, SHERRY, ZINFANDEL
Wolfish, LUPINE
Woman: Boisterous, TERMAGANT
Woolly, LANATE
Workshop, ATELIER
Zoroastrian, PARSEE

Old-Testament Names

(We do not pretend that this list is all-inclusive. We include only those names which in our opinion one meets most often in crossword puzzles.)

Aaron: First high priest of Jews; son of Amram; brother of Miriam and Moses; father of Abihu, Eleazer, Ithamar, and Nadab.
Abel: Son of Adam; slain by Cain.
Abigail: Wife of Nabal; later, wife of David.
Abihu: Son of Aaron.
Abimelech: King of Gerar.
Abner: Commander of army of Saul and Ishbosheth; slain by Joab.
Abraham (or Abram): Patriarch; forefather of the Jews; son of Terah; husband of Sarah; father of Isaac and Ishmael.
Absalom: Son of David and Maacah; revolted against David; slain by Joab.
Achish: King of Gath; gave refuge to David.
Achsa (or Achsah): Daughter of Caleb; wife of Othniel.
Adah: Wife of Lamech.
Adam: First man; husband of Eve; father of Cain, Abel, and Seth.
Adonijah: Son of David and Haggith.
Agag: King of Amalek; spared by Saul; slain by Samuel.
Ahasuerus: King of Persia; husband of Vashti and, later, Esther; sometimes identified with Xerxes the Great.
Ahijah: Prophet; foretold accession of Jeroboam.
Ahinoam: Wife of David.
Amasa: Commander of army of David; slain by Joab.
Amnon: Son of David and Ahinoam; ravished Tamar; slain by Absalom.
Amram: Husband of Jochebed; father of Aaron, Miriam and Moses.

Asenath: Wife of Joseph.
Asher: Son of Jacob and Zilpah.
Balaam: Prophet; rebuked by his donkey for cursing God.
Barak: Jewish captain; associated with Deborah.
Baruch: Secretary to Jeremiah.
Bathsheba: Wife of Uriah; later, wife of David.
Belshazzar: Crown prince of Babylon.
Benaiah: Warrior of David; proclaimed Solomon King.
Ben-Hadad: Name of several kings of Damascus.
Benjamin: Son of Jacob and Rachel.
Bezaleel: Chief architect of tabernacle.
Bilhah: Servant of Rachel; mistress of Jacob.
Bildad: Comforter of Job.
Boaz: Husband of Ruth; father of Obed.
Cain: Son of Adam and Eve; slayer of Abel; father of Enoch.
Cainan: Son of Enos.
Caleb: Spy sent out by Moses to visit Canaan; father of Achsa.
Canaan: Son of Ham.
Chilion: Son of Elimelech; husband of Orpah.
Cush: Son of Ham; father of Nimrod.
Dan: Son of Jacob and Bilhah.
Daniel: Prophet; saved from lions by God.
Deborah: Hebrew prophetess; helped Israelites conquer Canaanites.
Delilah: Mistress and betrayer of Samson.
Elam: Son of Shem.
Eleazar: Son of Aaron; succeeded him as high priest.

Eli: High priest and judge; teacher of Samuel; father of Hophni and Phinehas.

Eliakim: Chief minister of Hezekiah.

Eliezer: Servant of Abraham.

Elihu: Comforter of Job.

Elijah (or Elias): Prophet; went to heaven in chariot of fire.

Elimelech: Husband of Naomi; father of Chilion and Mahlon.

Eliphaz: Comforter of Job.

Elisha (or Eliseus): Prophet; successor of Elijah.

Elkanah: Husband of Hannah; father of Samuel.

Enoch: Son of Cain.

Enoch: Father of Methuselah.

Enos: Son of Seth; father of Cainan.

Ephraim: Son of Joseph.

Esau: Son of Isaac and Rebecca; sold his birthright to his brother Jacob.

Esther: Jewish wife of Ahasuerus; saved Jews from Haman's plotting.

Eve: First woman; created from rib of Adam.

Ezra (or Esdras): Hebrew scribe and priest.

Gad: Son of Jacob and Zilpah.

Gehazi: Servant of Elisha.

Gideon: Israelite hero; defeated Midianites.

Goliath: Philistine giant; slain by David.

Hagar: Handmaid of Sarah; concubine of Abraham; mother of Ishmael.

Haggith: Mother of Adonijah.

Ham: Son of Noah; father of Cush, Mizraim, Phut, and Canaan.

Haman: Chief minister of Ahasuerus; hanged on gallows prepared for Mordecai.

Hannah: Wife of Elkanah; mother of Samuel.

Hanun: King of Ammonites.

Haran: Brother of Abraham; father of Lot.

Hazael: King of Damascus.

Hephzi-Bah: Wife of Hezekiah; mother of Mannaseh.

Hiram: King of Tyre.

Holofernes: General of Nebuchadnezzar; slain by Judith.

Hophni: Son of Eli.

Isaac: Hebrew patriarch; son of Abraham and Sarah; half brother of Ishmael; husband of Rebecca; father of Esau and Jacob.

Ishmael: Son of Abraham and Hagar; half brother of Isaac.

Issachar: Son of Jacob and Leah.

Ithamar: Son of Aaron.

Jabal: Son of Lamech and Adah.

Jabin: King of Hazor.

Jacob: Hebrew patriarch, founder of Israel; son of Isaac and Rebecca; husband of Leah and Rachel; father of Asher, Benjamin, Dan, Gad, Issachar, Joseph, Judah, Levi, Naphtali, Reuben, Simeon, and Zebulun.

Jael: Slayer of Sisera.

Japheth: Son of Noah.

Jehoiada: High priest; husband of Jehoshabeath; revolted against Athaliah and made Joash King of Judah.

Jehoshabeath (or Jehosheba): Daughter of Jehoram of Judah; wife of Jehoiada.

Jephthah: Judge in Israel; sacrificed his only daughter because of vow.

Jesse: Son of Obed; father of David.

Jethro: Midianite priest; father of Zipporah.

Jezebel: Phoenician princess; wife of Ahab; mother of Ahaziah, Athaliah, and Jehoram.

Joab: Commander in chief under David; slayer of Abner, Absalom, and Amasa.

Job: Patriarch; underwent many afflictions; comforted by Bildad, Elihu, Eliphaz and Zophar.

Jochebed: Wife of Amram.

Jonah: Prophet; cast into sea and swallowed by great fish.

Jonathan: Son of Saul; friend of David.

Joseph: Son of Jacob and Rachel; sold into slavery by his brothers; husband of Asenath; father of Ephraim and Manassah.

Joshua: Successor of Moses; son of Nun.

Jubal: Son of Lamech and Adah.

Judah: Son of Jacob and Leah.

Judith: Slayer of Holofernes.

Kish: Father of Saul.

Laban: Father of Leah and Rachel.

Lamech: Son of Methuselah; father of Noah.

Lamech: Husband of Adah and Zillah; father of Jabal, Jubal, and Tubal-Cain.

Leah: Daughter of Laban; wife of Jacob.

Levi: Son of Jacob and Leah.

Lot: Son of Haran; escaped destruction of Sodom.

Maacah: Mother of Absalom and Tamar.

Mahlon: Son of Elimelech; first husband of Ruth.

Manasseh: Son of Joseph.

Melchizedek: King of Salem.

Methuselah: Patriarch; son of Enoch; father of Lamech.

Michal: Daughter of Saul; wife of David.

Miriam: Prophetess; daughter of Amram; sister of Aaron and Moses.

Mizraim: Son of Ham.

Mordecai: Uncle of Esther; with her aid, saved Jews from Haman's plotting.

Moses: Prophet and lawgiver; son of Amram; brother of Aaron and Miriam; husband of Zipporah.

Naaman: Syrian captain; cured of leprosy by Elisha.

Nabal: Husband of Abigail.

Naboth: Owner of vineyard; stoned to death because he would not sell it to Ahab.

Nadab: Son of Aaron.

Nahor: Father of Terah.

Naomi: Wife of Elimelech; mother-in-law of Ruth.

Naphtali: Son of Jacob and Bilhah.

Nathan: Prophet; reproved David for causing Uriah's death.

Nebuchadnezzar (or Nebuchadrezzar): King of Babylon; destroyer of Jerusalem.

Nehemiah: Jewish leader; empowered by Artaxerxes to rebuild Jerusalem.

Nimrod: Mighty hunter; son of Cush.

Noah: Patriarch; Son of Lamech; escaped Deluge by building Ark; father of Ham, Japheth and Shem.

Nun (or Non): Father of Joshua.

Obed: Son of Boaz; father of Jesse.

Og: King of Bashan.

Orpah: Wife of Chilion.

Othniel: Kenezite; judge of Israel; husband of Achsa.

Phinehas: Son of Eleazer.

Phinehas: Son of Eli.

Phut (or Put): Son of Ham.

Potiphar: Egyptian official; bought Joseph.

Rachel: Wife of Jacob.

Rebecca (or Rebekah): Wife of Isaac.

Reuben: Son of Jacob and Leah.

Ruth: Wife of Mahlon, later of Boaz; daughter-in-law of Naomi.

Samson: Judge of Israel; famed for strength; betrayed by Delilah.

Samuel: Hebrew judge and prophet; son of Elkanah.

Sarah (or Sara, Sarai): Wife of Abraham.

Sennacherib: King of Assyria.

Seth: Son of Adam; father of Enos.

Shem: Son of Noah; father of Elam.

Simeon: Son of Jacob and Leah.

Sisera: Canaanite captain; slain by Jael.

Tamar: Daughter of David and Maachah; ravished by Amnon.

Terah: Son of Nahor; father of Abraham.

Tubal-Cain: Son of Lamech and Zillah.

Uriah: Husband of Bathsheba; sent to death in battle by David.

Vashti: Wife of Ahasuerus; set aside by him.

Zadok: High priest during David's reign.

Zebulun (or Zabulon): Son of Jacob and Leah.

Zillah: Wife of Lamech.

Zilpah: Servant of Leah; mistress of Jacob.

Zipporah: Daughter of Jethro; wife of Moses.

Zophar: Comforter of Job.

Kings of Judah and Israel

Kings Before Division of Kingdom

Saul: First King of Israel; son of Kish; father of Ish-Bosheth, Jonathan and Michal.

Ish-Bosheth (or Eshbaal): King of Israel; son of Saul.

David: King of Judah; later of Israel; son of Jesse; husband of Abigail, Ahinoam, Bathsheba, Michal, etc.; father of Absalom, Adonijah, Amnon, Solomon, Tamar, etc.

Solomon: King of Israel and Judah; son of David; father of Rehoboam.

Rehoboam: Son of Solomon; during his reign the kingdom was divided into Judah and Israel.

Kings of Judah (Southern Kingdom)

Rehoboam: First King.

Abijah (or Abijam or Abia): Son of Rehoboam.

Asa: Probably son of Abijah.

Jehoshaphat: Son of Asa.

Jehoram (or Joram): Son of Jehoshaphat; husband of Athaliah.

Ahaziah: Son of Jehoram and Athaliah.

Athaliah: Daughter of King Ahab of Israel and Jezebel; wife of Jehoram.

Joash (or Jehoash): Son of Ahaziah.

Amaziah: Son of Joash.

Uzziah (or Azariah): Son of Amaziah.

Jotham: Regent, later King; son of Uzziah.

Ahaz: Son of Jotham.

Hezekiah: Son of Ahaz; husband of Hephzi-Bah.

Manasseh: Son of Hezekiah and Hephzi-Bah.

Amon: Son of Manasseh.

Josiah (or Josias): Son of Amon.

Jehoahaz (or Joahaz): Son of Josiah.

Jehoiachin: Son of Jehoiakim.

Jehoiakim: Son of Josiah.

Zedekiah: Son of Josiah; kingdom overthrown by Babylonians under Nebuchadnezzar.

Kings of Israel (Northern Kingdom)

Jeroboam I: Led secession of Israel.

Nadab: Son of Jeroboam I.

Baasha: Overthrew Nadab.

Elah: Son of Baasha.

Zimri: Overthrew Elah.

Omri: Overthrew Zimri.

Ahab: Son of Omri; husband of Jezebel.

Ahaziah: Son of Ahab.

Jehoram (or Joram): Son of Ahab.

Jehu: Overthrew Jehoram.

Jehoahaz (or Joahaz): Son of Jehu.

Jehoash (or Joash): Son of Jehoahaz.

Jeroboam II: Son of Jehoash.

Zechariah: Son of Jeroboam II.

Shallum: Overthrew Zechariah.

Menahem: Overthrew Shallum.

Pekahiah: Son of Menahem.

Pekah: Overthrew Pekahiah.

Hoshea: Overthrew Pekah; kingdom overthrown by Assyrians under Sargon II.

Prophets

Major.—Isaiah, Jeremiah, Ezekiel, Daniel.

Minor.—Hosea, Obadiah, Nahum, Haggai, Joel, Jonah, Habakkuk, Zechariah, Amos, Micah, Zephaniah, Malachi.

Greek and Roman Mythology

(Most of the Greek deities were adopted by the Romans, although in many cases there was a change of name. In the list below, information is given under the Greek name; the name in parentheses is the Latin equivalent. However, all Latin names are listed with cross references to the Greek ones. In addition, there are several deities which were exclusively Roman.)

Acheron: *See* Rivers.

Achilles: Greek warrior; slew Hector at Troy; slain by Paris, who wounded him in his vulnerable heel.

Actaeon: Hunter; surprised Artemis bathing; changed by her to stag and killed by his dogs.

Admetus: King of Thessaly; his wife, Alcestis, offered to die in his place.

Adonis: Beautiful youth loved by Aphrodite.

Aeacus: One of three judges of dead in Hades; son of Zeus.

Aeëtes: King of Colchis; father of Medea; keeper of Golden Fleece.

Aegeus: Father of Theseus; believing Theseus killed in Crete, he drowned himself, Aegean Sea named for him.

Aegisthus: Son of Thyestes; slew Atreus; with Clytemnestra, his paramour, slew Agamemnon; slain by Orestes.

Aegyptus: Brother of Danaus; his sons, except Lynceus, slain by Danaides.

Aeneas: Trojan; son of Anchises and Aphrodite; after fall of Troy, led his followers eventually to Italy; loved and deserted Dido.

Aeolus: *See* Winds.

Aesculapius: *See* Asclepius.

Aeson: King of Ioclus; father of Jason; overthrown by his brother Pelias; restored to youth by Medea.

Aether: Personification of sky.

Aethra: Mother of Theseus.

Agamemnon: King of Mycenae; son of Atreus; brother of Menelaus; leader of Greeks against Troy; slain on his return home by Clytemnestra and Aegisthus.

Agiaia: *See* Graces.

Ajax: Greek warrior; killed himself at Troy because Achilles' armor was awarded to Odysseus.

Alcestis: Wife of Admetus; offered to die in his place but saved from death by Hercules.

Alcmene: Wife of Amphitryon; mother by Zeus of Hercules.

Alcyone: *See* Pleiades.

Alecto: *See* Furies.

Alectryon: Youth changed by Ares into cock.

Althaea: Wife of Oeneus; mother of Meleager.

Amazons: Female warriors in Asia Minor; supported Troy against Greeks.

Amor: *See* Eros.

Amphion: Musician; husband of Niobe; charmed stones to build fortifications for Thebes.

Amphitrite: Sea goddess; wife of Poseidon.

Amphitryon: Husband of Alcmene.

Anchises: Father of Aeneas.

Ancile: Sacred shield that fell from heavens; palladium of Rome.

Andraemon: Husband of Dryope.

Andromache: Wife of Hector.

Andromeda: Daughter of Cepheus; chained to cliff for monster to devour; rescued by Perseus.

Anteia: Wife of Proetus; tried to induce Bellerophon to elope with her.

Anteros: God who avenged unrequited love.

Antigone: Daughter of Oedipus; accompanied him to Colonus; performed burial rite for Polynices and hanged herself.

Antinoüs: Leader of suitors of Penelope; slain by Odysseus.

Aphrodite (Venus): Goddess of love and beauty; daughter

of Zeus; mother of Eros.

Apollo: God of beauty, poetry, music; later identified with Helios as Phoebus Apollo; son of Zeus and Leto.

Aquilo: *See* Winds.

Arachne: Maiden who challenged Athena to weaving contest; changed to spider.

Ares (Mars): God of war; son of Zeus and Hera.

Argo: Ship in which Jason and followers sailed to Colchis for Golden Fleece.

Argus: Monster with hundred eyes; slain by Hermes; his eyes placed by Hera into peacock's tail.

Ariadne: Daughter of Minos; aided Theseus in slaying Minotaur; deserted by him on island of Naxos and married to Dionysus.

Arion: Musician; thrown overboard by pirates but saved by dolphin.

Artemis (Diana): Goddess of moon; huntress; twin sister of Apollo.

Asclepius (Aesculapius): Mortal son of Apollo; slain by Zeus for raising dead; later deified as god of medicine. Also known as Asklepios.

Astarte: Phoenician goddess of love; variously identified with Aphrodite, Selene, and Artemis.

Astraea: Goddess of Justice; daughter of Zeus and Themis.

Atalanta: Princess who challenged her suitors to a foot race; Hippomenes won race and married her.

Athena (Minerva): Goddess of wisdom; known poetically as Pallas Athene; sprang fully armed from head of Zeus.

Atlas: Titan; held world on his shoulders as punishment for warring against Zeus; son of Iapetus.

Atreus: King of Mycenae; father of Menelaus and Agamemnon; brother of Thyestes, three of whose sons he slew and served to him at banquet; slain by Aegisthus.

Atropos: *See* Fates.

Aurora: *See* Eos.

Auster: *See* Winds.

Avernus: Infernal regions; name derived from small vaporous lake near Vesuvius which was fabled to kill birds and vegetation.

Bacchus: *See* Dionysus.

Bellerophon: Corinthian hero; killed Chimera with aid of Pegasus; tried to reach Olympus on Pegasus and was thrown to his death.

Bellona: Roman goddess of war.

Boreas: *See* Winds.

Briareus: Monster of hundred hands; son of Uranus and Gaea.

Briseis: Captive maiden given to Achilles; taken by Agamemnon in exchange for loss of Chryseis, which caused Achilles to cease fighting, until death of Patroclus.

Cadmus: Brother of Europa; planter of dragon seeds from which first Thebans sprang.

Calliope: *See* Muses.

Calypso: Sea nymph; kept Odysseus on her island Ogygia for seven years.

Cassandra: Daughter of Priam; prophetess who was never believed; slain with Agamemnon.

Castor: *See* Dioscuri.

Celaeno: *See* Pleiades.

Centaurs: Beings half man and half horse; lived in mountains of Thessaly.

Cephalus: Hunter; accidentally killed his wife Procris with his spear.

Cepheus: King of Ethiopia; father of Andromeda.

Cerberus: Three-headed dog guarding entrance to Hades.

Ceres: *See* Demeter.

Chaos: Formless void; personified as first of gods.

Charon: Boatman on Styx who carried souls of dead to Hades; son of Erebus.

Charybdis: Female monster; personification of whirlpool.

Chimera: Female monster with head of lion, body of goat, tail of serpent; killed by Bellerophon.

Chiron: Most famous of centaurs.

Chronos: Personification of time.

Chryseis: Captive maiden given to Agamemnon; his refusal to accept ransom from her father Chryses caused Apollo to send plague on Greeks besieging Troy.

Circe: Sorceress; daughter of Helios; changed Odysseus' men into swine.

Clio: *See* Muses.

Clotho: *See* Fates.

Clytemnestra: Wife of Agamemnon, whom she slew with aid of her paramour, Aegisthus; slain by her son Orestes.

Cocytus: *See* Rivers.

Creon: Father of Jocasta; forbade burial of Polynices; ordered burial alive of Antigone.

Creüsa: Princess of Corinth, for whom Jason deserted Medea; slain by Medea, who sent her poisoned robe; also known as Glaüke.

Creusa: Wife of Aeneas; died fleeing Troy.

Cronus (Saturn): Titan; god of harvests; son of Uranus and Gaea; dethroned by his son Zeus.

Cupid: *See* Eros.

Cybele: Anatolian nature goddess; adopted by Greeks and identified with Rhea.

Cyclopes: Race of one-eyed giants (singular: Cyclops).

Daedalus: Athenian artificer; father of Icarus; builder of Labyrinth in Crete; devised wings attached with wax for him and Icarus to escape Crete.

Danae: Princess of Argos; mother of Perseus by Zeus, who appeared to her in form of golden shower.

Danaïdes: Daughters of Danaüs; at his command, all except Hypermnestra slew their husbands, the sons of Aegyptus.

Danaüs: Brother of Aegyptus; father of Danaïdes; slain by Lynceus.

Daphne: Nymph; pursued by Apollo; changed to laurel tree.

Decuma: *See* Fates.

Deino: *See* Graeae.

Demeter (Ceres): Goddess of agriculture; mother of Persephone.

Diana: *See* Artemis.

Dido: Founder and queen of Carthage; stabbed herself when deserted by Aeneas.

Diomedes: Greek hero; with Odysseus, entered Troy and carried off Palladium, sacred statue of Athena.

Diomedes: Owner of man-eating horses, which Hercules, as ninth labor, carried off.

Dione: Titan goddess; mother by Zeus of Aphrodite.

Dionysus (Bacchus): God of wine; son of Zeus and Semele.

Dioscuri: Twins Castor and Pollux; sons of Leda by Zeus.

Dis: *See* Hades.

Dryads: Wood nymphs.

Dryope: Maiden changed to Hamadryad.

Echo: Nymph who fell hopelessly in love with Narcissus; faded away except for her voice.

Electra: Daughter of Agamemnon and Clytemnestra; sister of Orestes; urged Orestes to slay Clytemnestra and Aegisthus.

Electra: *See* Pleiades.

Elysium: Abode of blessed dead.

Endymion: Mortal loved by Selene.

Enyo: *See* Graeae.

Eos (Aurora): Goddess of dawn.

Epimetheus: Brother of Prometheus; husband of Pandora.

Erato: *See* Muses.

Erebus: Spirit of darkness; son of Chaos.

Erinyes: *See* Furies.

Eris: Goddess of discord.

Eros (Amor or Cupid): God of love; son of Aphrodite.

Eteocles: Son of Oedipus, whom he succeeded to rule alternately with Polynices; refused to give up throne at end of year; he and Polynices slew each other.

Eumenides: *See* Furies.

Euphrosyne: *See* Graces.

Europa: Mortal loved by Zeus, who, in form of white bull, carried her off to Crete.

Eurus: *See* Winds.

Euryale: *See* Gorgons.

Eurydice: Nymph; wife of Orpheus.

Eurystheus: King of Argos; imposed twelve labors on Hercules.

Euterpe: *See* Muses.

Fates: Goddesses of destiny; Clotho (Spinner of thread of life), Lachesis (Determiner of length), and Atropos (Cutter of thread); also called Moirae. Identified by Romans with their goddesses of fate; Nona, Decuma, and Morta; called Parcae.

Fauns: Roman deities of woods and groves.
Faunus: *See* Pan.
Favonius: *See* Winds.
Flora: Roman goddess of flowers.
Fortuna: Roman goddess of fortune.
Furies: Avenging spirits; Alecto, Megaera, and Tisiphone; known also as Erinyes or Eumenides.
Gaea: Goddess of earth; daughter of Chaos; mother of Titans; known also as Ge, Gea, Gaia, etc.
Galatea: Statue of maiden carved from ivory by Pygmalion; given life by Aphrodite.
Galatea: Sea nymph; loved by Polyphemus.
Ganymede: Beautiful boy; successor to Hebe as cupbearer of gods.
Glaucus: Mortal who became sea divinity by eating magic grass.
Glauke: *See* Creüsa.
Golden Fleece: Fleece from ram that flew Phrixos to Colchis; Aeëtes placed it under guard of dragon; carried off by Jason.
Gorgons: Female monsters; Euryale, Medusa, and Stheno; had snakes for hair; their glances turned mortals to stone. *See* Medusa.
Graces: Beautiful goddesses: Aglaia (Brilliance), Euphrosyne (Joy), and Thalia (Bloom); daughters of Zeus.
Graeae: Sentinels for Gorgons; Deino, Enyo, and Pephredo; had one eye among them, which passed from one to another.
Hades (Dis): Name sometimes given Pluto; also, abode of dead, ruled by Pluto.
Haemon: Son of Creon; promised husband of Antigone; killed himself in her tomb.
Hamadryads: Tree nymphs.
Harpies: Monsters with heads of women and bodies of birds.
Hebe (Juventas): Goddess of youth; cupbearer of gods before Ganymede; daughter of Zeus and Hera.
Hecate: Goddess of sorcery and witchcraft.
Hector: Son of Priam; slayer of Patroclus; slain by Achilles.
Hecuba: Wife of Priam.
Helen: Fairest woman in world; daughter of Zeus and Leda; wife of Menelaus; carried to Troy by Paris, causing Trojan War.
Heliades: Daughters of Helios; mourned for Phaëthon and were changed to poplar trees.
Helios (Sol): God of sun; later identified with Apollo.
Helle: Sister of Phrixos; fell from ram of Golden Fleece; water where she fell named Hellespont.
Hephaestus (Vulcan): God of fire; celestial blacksmith; son of Zeus and Hera; husband of Aphrodite.
Hera (Juno): Queen of heaven; wife of Zeus.
Hercules: Hero and strong man; son of Zeus and Alcmene; performed twelve labors or deeds to be free from bondage under Eurystheus; after death, his mortal share was destroyed, and he became immortal. Also known as Herakles or Heracles. Labors: (1) killing Nemean lion; (2) killing Lernaean Hydra; (3) capturing Erymanthian boar; (4) capturing Cerynean hind; (5) killing man-eating Stymphalian birds; (6) procuring girdle of Hippolyte; (7) cleaning Augean stables; (8) capturing Cretan bull; (9) capturing man-eating horses of Diomedes; (10) capturing cattle of Geryon; (11) procuring golden apples of Hesperides; (12) bringing Cerberus up from Hades.
Hermes (Mercury): God of physicians and thieves; messenger of gods; son of Zeus and Maia.
Hero: Priestess of Aphrodite; Leander swam Hellespont nightly to see her; drowned herself at his death.
Hesperus: Evening star.
Hestia (Vesta): Goddess of hearth; sister of Zeus.
Hippolyte: Queen of Amazons; wife of Theseus.
Hippolytus: Son of Theseus and Hippolyte; falsely accused by Phaedra of trying to kidnap her; slain by Poseidon at request of Theseus.
Hippomenes: Husband of Atalanta, whom he beat in race by dropping golden apples, which she stopped to pick up.
Hyacinthus: Beautiful youth accidentally killed by Apollo, who caused flower to spring up from his blood.
Hydra: Nine-headed monster in marsh of Lerna; slain by Hercules.
Hygeia: Personification of health.

Hyman: God of marriage.
Hyperion: Titan; early sun god; father of Helios.
Hypermnestra: Daughter of Danaüs; refused to kill her husband Lynceus.
Hypnos (Somnus): God of sleep.
Iapetus: Titan; father of Atlas, Epimetheus, and Prometheus.
Icarus: Son of Daedalus; flew too near sun with wax-attached wings and fell into sea and was drowned.
Io: Mortal maiden loved by Zeus; changed by Hera into heifer.
Iobates: King of Lycia; sent Bellerophon to slay Chimera.
Iphigenia: Daughter of Agamemnon; offered as sacrifice to Artemis at Aulis; carried by Artemis to Tauris where she became priestess; escaped from there with Orestes.
Iris: Goddess of rainbow; messenger of Zeus and Hera.
Ismene: Daughter of Oedipus; sister of Antigone.
Iulus: Son of Aeneas.
Ixion: King of Lapithae; for making love to Hera he was bound to endlessly revolving wheel in Tartarus.
Janus: Roman god of gates and doors; represented with two opposite faces.
Jason: Son of Aeson; to gain throne of Ioclus from Pelias, went to Colchis and brought back Golden Fleece; married Medea; deserted her for Creüsa.
Jocasta: Wife of Laius; mother of Oedipus; unwittingly became wife of Oedipus; hanged herself when relationship was discovered.
Juno: *See* Hera.
Jupiter: *See* Zeus.
Juventas: *See* Hebe.
Lachesis: *See* Fates.
Laius: Father of Oedipus, by whom he was slain.
Laocoön: Priest of Apollo at Troy; warned against bringing wooden horse into Troy; destroyed with his two sons by serpents sent by Athena.
Lares: Roman ancestral spirits protecting descendants and homes.
Lavinia: Wife of Aeneas after defeat of Turnus.
Leander: Swam Hellespont nightly to see Hero; drowned in storm.
Leda: Mortal loved by Zeus in form of Swan; mother of Helen, Clytemnestra, Dioscuri.
Lethe: *See* Rivers.
Leto (Latona): Mother by Zeus of Artemis and Apollo.
Lucina: Roman goddess of childbirth; identified with Juno.
Lynceus: Son of Aegyptus; husband of Hypermnestra; slew Danaüs.
Maia: Daughter of Atlas; mother of Hermes.
Maia: *See* Pleiades.
Manes: Souls of dead Romans, particularly of ancestors.
Mars: *See* Ares.
Marsyas: Shepherd; challenged Apollo to music contest and lost; flayed alive by Apollo.
Medea: Sorceress; daughter of Aeëtes; helped Jason obtain Golden Fleece; when deserted by him for Creüsa, killed her children and Creüsa.
Medusa: Gorgon; slain by Perseus, who cut off her head.
Megaera: *See* Furies.
Meleager: Son of Althaea; his life would last as long as brand burning at his birth; Althaea quenched and saved it but destroyed it when Meleager slew his uncles.
Melpomene: *See* Muses.
Memnon: Ethiopian king; made immortal by Zeus; son of Tithonus and Eos.
Menelaus: King of Sparta; son of Atreus; brother of Agamemnon; husband of Helen.
Mercury: *See* Hermes.
Merope: *See* Pleiades.
Mezentius: Cruel Etruscan king; ally of Turnus against Aeneas; slain by Aeneas.
Midas: King of Phrygia; given gift of turning to gold all he touched.
Minerva: *See* Athena.
Minos: King of Crete; after death, one of three judges of dead in Hades; son of Zeus and Europa.
Minotaur: Monster, half man and half beast, kept in Labyrinth in Crete; slain by Theseus.

Mnemosyne: Goddess of memory; mother by Zeus of Muses.

Moirae: *See* Fates.

Momus: God of ridicule.

Morpheus: God of dreams.

Mors: *See* Thanatos.

Morta: *See* Fates.

Muses: Goddesses presiding over arts and sciences: Calliope (epic poetry), Clio (history), Erato (lyric and love poetry), Euterpe (music), Melpomene (tragedy), Polymnia or Polyhymnia (sacred poetry), Terpsichore (choral dance and song), Thalia (comedy and bucolic poetry), Urania (astronomy); daughters of Zeus and Mnemosyne.

Naiads: Nymphs of waters, streams, and fountains.

Napaeae: Wood nymphs.

Narcissus: Beautiful youth loved by Echo; in punishment for not returning her love, he was made to fall in love with his image reflected in pool; pined away and became flower.

Nemesis: Goddess of retribution.

Neoptolemus: Son of Achilles; slew Priam; also known as Pyrrhus.

Neptune: *See* Poseidon.

Nereids: Sea nymphs; attendants on Poseidon.

Nestor: King of Pylos; noted for wise counsel in expedition against Troy.

Nike: Goddess of victory.

Niobe: Daughter of Tantalus; wife of Amphion; her children slain by Apollo and Artemis; changed to stone but continued to weep for her loss.

Nona: *See* Fates.

Notus: *See* Winds.

Nox: *See* Nyx.

Nymphs: Beautiful maidens; inferior deities of nature.

Nyx (Nox): Goddess of night.

Oceanids: Ocean nymphs; daughters of Oceanus.

Oceanus: Eldest of Titans; god of waters.

Odysseus (Ulysses): King of Ithaca; husband of Penelope; wandered ten years after fall of Troy before arriving home.

Oedipus: King of Thebes; son of Laius and Jocasta; unwittingly murdered Laius and married Jocasta; tore his eyes out when relationship was discovered.

Oenone: Nymph of Mount Ida; wife of Paris, who abandoned her; refused to cure him when he was poisoned by arrow of Philoctetes at Troy.

Ops: *See* Rhea.

Oreads: Mountain nymphs.

Orestes: Son of Agamemnon and Clytemnestra; brother of Electra; slew Clytemnestra and Aegisthus; pursued by Furies until his purification by Apollo.

Orion: Hunter; slain by Artemis and made heavenly constellation.

Orpheus: Famed musician; son of Apollo and Muse Calliope; husband of Eurydice.

Pales: Roman goddess of shepherds and herdsmen.

Palinurus: Aeneas' pilot; fell overboard in his sleep and was drowned.

Pan (Faunus): God of woods and fields; part goat; son of Hermes.

Pandora: Opener of box containing human ills; mortal wife of Epimetheus.

Parcae: *See* Fates.

Paris: Son of Priam; gave apple of discord to Aphrodite, for which she enabled him to carry off Helen; slew Achilles at Troy; slain by Philoctetes.

Patroclus: Great friend of Achilles; wore Achilles' armor and was slain by Hector.

Pegasus: Winged horse that sprang from Medusa's body at her death; ridden by Bellerophon when he slew Chimera.

Pelias: King of Ioclus; seized throne from his brother Aeson; sent Jason for Golden Fleece; slain unwittingly by his daughters at instigation of Medea.

Pelops: Son of Tantalus; his father cooked and served him to gods; restored to life; Peloponnesus named for him.

Penates: Roman household gods.

Penelope: Wife of Odysseus; waited faithfully for him for ten years while putting off numerous suitors.

Pephredo: *See* Graeae.

Periphetes: Giant; son of Hephaestus; slain by Theseus.

Persephone (Proserpine): Queen of infernal regions; daughter of Zeus and Demeter; wife of Pluto.

Perseus: Son of Zeus and Danaë; slew Medusa; rescued Andromeda from monster and married her.

Phaedra: Daughter of Minos; wife of Theseus; caused the death of her stepson, Hippolytus.

Phaethon: Son of Helios; drove his father's sun chariot and was struck down by Zeus before he set world on fire.

Philoctetes: Greek warrior who possessed Hercules' bow and arrows; slew Paris at Troy with poisoned arrow.

Phineus: Betrothed of Andromeda; tried to slay Perseus but turned to stone by Medusa's head.

Phlegethon: *See* Rivers.

Phosphor: Morning star.

Phrixos: Brother of Helle; carried by ram of Golden Fleece to Colchis.

Pirithous: Son of Ixion; friend of Theseus; tried to carry off Persephone from Hades; bound to enchanted rock by Pluto.

Pleiades: Alcyone, Celaeno, Electra, Maia, Merope, Sterope or Asterope, Taygeta; seven daughters of Atlas; transformed into heavenly constellation, of which six stars are visible (Merope is said to have hidden in shame for loving a mortal).

Pluto (Dis): God of Hades; brother of Zeus.

Plutus: God of wealth.

Pollux: *See* Dioscuri.

Polymnia: *See* Muses.

Polynices: Son of Oedipus; he and his brother Eteocles killed each other; burial rite, forbidden by Creon, performed by his sister Antigone.

Polyphemus: Cyclops; devoured six of Odysseus' men; blinded by Odysseus.

Polyxena: Daughter of Priam; betrothed to Achilles, whom Paris slew at their betrothal; sacrificed to shade of Achilles.

Pomona: Roman goddess of fruits.

Pontus: Sea god; son of Gaea.

Poseidon (Neptune): God of sea; brother of Zeus.

Priam: King of Troy; husband of Hecuba; ransomed Hector's body from Achilles; slain by Neoptolemus.

Priapus: God of regeneration.

Procris: Wife of Cephalus, who accidentally slew her.

Procrustes: Giant; stretched or cut off legs of victims to make them fit iron bed; slain by Theseus.

Proetus: Husband of Anteia; sent Bellerophon to Iobates to be put to death.

Prometheus: Titan; stole fire from heaven for man. Zeus punished him by chaining him to rock in Caucasus where vultures devoured his liver daily.

Proteus: Sea god; assumed various shapes when called on to prophesy.

Psyche: Beloved of Eros; punished by jealous Aphrodite; made immortal and united with Eros.

Pygmalion: King of Cyprus; carved ivory statue of maiden which Aphrodite gave life as Galatea.

Pyramus: Babylonian youth; made love to Thisbe through hole in wall; thinking Thisbe slain by lion, killed himself.

Pyrrhus: *See* Neoptolemus.

Python: Serpent born from slime left by Deluge; slain by Apollo.

Quirinus: Roman war god.

Remus: Brother of Romulus; slain by him.

Rhadamanthus: One of three judges of dead in Hades; son of Zeus and Europa.

Rhea (Ops): Daughter of Uranus and Gaea; wife of Cronus; mother of Zeus; identified with Cybele.

Rivers of Underworld: Acheron (woe), Cocytus (wailing), Lethe (forgetfulness), Phlegethon (fire), Styx (across which souls of dead were ferried by Charon).

Romulus: Founder of Rome; he and Remus suckled in infancy by she-wolf; slew Remus; deified by Romans.

Sarpedon: King of Lycia; son of Zeus and Europa; slain by Patroclus at Troy.

Saturn: *See* Cronus.

Satyrs: Hoofed demigods of woods and fields; companions of Dionysus.

Sciron: Robber; forced strangers to wash his feet, then hurled them into sea where tortoise devoured them; slain by Theseus.

Scylla: Female monster inhabiting rock opposite Charybdis; menaced passing sailors.

Selene: Goddess of moon.

Semele: Daughter of Cadmus; mother by Zeus of Dionysus; demanded Zeus appear before her in all his splendor and was destroyed by his lightnings.

Sibyis: Various prophetesses; most famous, Cumaean sibyl, accompanied Aeneas into Hades.

Sileni: Minor woodland deities similar to satyrs (singular: silenus). Sometimes Silenus refers to eldest of satyrs, son of Hermes or of Pan.

Silvanus: Roman god of woods and fields.

Sinis: Giant; bent pines, by which he hurled victims against side of mountain; slain by Theseus.

Sirens: Minor deities who lured sailors to destruction with their singing.

Sisyphus: King of Corinth; condemned in Tartarus to roll huge stone to top of hill; it always rolled back down again.

Sol: *See* Helios.

Somnus: *See* Hypnos.

Sphinx: Monster of Thebes; killed those who could not answer her riddle; slain by Oedipus. Name also refers to other monsters having body of lion, wings, and head and bust of woman.

Sterope: *See* Pleiades.

Stheno: *See* Gorgons.

Styx: *See* Rivers.

Symplegades: Clashing rocks at entrance to Black Sea; Argo passed through, causing them to become forever fixed.

Syrinx: Nymph pursued by Pan; changed to reeds, from which he made his pipes.

Tantalus: Cruel king; father of Pelops and Niobe; condemned in Tartarus to stand chin-deep in lake surrounded by fruit branches; as he tried to eat or drink, water or fruit always receded.

Tartarus: Underworld below Hades; often refers to Hades.

Taygeta: *See* Pleiades.

Telemachus: Son of Odysseus; made unsuccessful journey to find his father.

Tellus: Roman goddess of earth.

Terminus: Roman god of boundaries and landmarks.

Terpsichore: *See* Muses.

Terra: Roman earth goddess.

Thalia: *See* Graces; Muses.

Thanatos (Mors): God of death.

Themis: Titan goddess of laws of physical phenomena; daughter of Uranus; mother of Prometheus.

Theseus: Son of Aegeus; slew Minotaur; married and deserted Ariadne; later married Phaedra.

Thisbe: Beloved of Pyramus; killed herself at his death.

Thyestes: Brother of Atreus; Atreus killed three of his sons and served them to him at banquet.

Tiresias: Blind soothsayer of Thebes.

Tisiphone: *See* Furies.

Titans: Early gods from which Olympian gods were derived; children of Uranus and Gaea.

Tithonus: Mortal loved by Eos; changed into grasshopper.

Triton: Demigod of sea; son of Poseidon.

Turnus: King of Rutuli in Italy; betrothed to Lavinia; slain by Aeneas.

Ulysses: *See* Odysseus.

Urania: *See* Muses.

Uranus: Personification of Heaven; husband of Gaea; father of Titans; dethroned by his son Cronus.

Venus: *See* Aphrodite.

Vertumnus: Roman god of fruits and vegetables; husband of Pomona.

Vesta: *See* Hestia.

Vulcan: *See* Hephaestus.

Winds: Aeolus (keeper of winds), Boreas (Aquilo) (north wind), Eurus (east wind), Notus (Auster) (south wind), Zephyrus (Favonius) (west wind).

Zephyrus: *See* Winds.

Zeus (Jupiter): Chief of Olympian gods; son of Cronus and Rhea; husband of Hera.

Norse Mythology

Aesir: Chief gods of Asgard.

Andvari: Dwarf; robbed of gold and magic ring by Loki.

Angerbotha (Angrbotha): Giantess; mother by Loki of Fenrir, Hel, and Midgard serpent.

Asgard (Asgarth): Abode of gods.

Ask (Aske, Askr): First man; created by Odin, Hoenir, and Lothur.

Asynjur: Goddesses of Asgard.

Atli: Second husband of Gudrun; invited Gunnar and Hogni to his court, where they were slain; slain by Gudrun.

Audhumia (Audhumbla): Cow that nourished Ymir, created Buri by licking ice cliff.

Balder (Baldr, Baldur): God of light, spring, peace, joy; son of Odin; slain by Hoth at instigation of Loki.

Bifrost: Rainbow bridge connecting Midgard and Asgard.

Bragi (Brage): God of poetry; husband of Ithunn.

Branstock: Great oak in hall of Volsungs; into it, Odin thrust Gram, which only Sigmund could draw forth.

Brynhild: Valkyrie; wakened from magic sleep by Sigurd; married Gunnar, instigated death of Sigurd; killed herself and was burned on pyre beside Sigurd.

Bur (Bor): Son of Buri; father of Odin, Hoenir, and Lothur.

Buri (Bori): Progenitor of gods; father of Bur; created by Audhumla.

Embla: First woman; created by Odin, Hoenir, and Lothur.

Fafnir: Son of Rodmar, whom he slew for gold in Otter's skin; in form of dragon, guarded gold; slain by Sigurd.

Fenrir: Wolf; offspring of Loki; swallows Odin at Ragnarok and is slain by Vitharr.

Forseti: Son of Balder.

Frey (Freyr): God of fertility and crops; son of Njorth; originally one of Vanir.

Freya (Freyja): Goddess of love and beauty; sister of Frey; originally one of Vanir.

Frigg (Frigga): Goddess of sky; wife of Odin.

Garm: Watchdog of Hel; slays, and is slain by, Tyr at Ragnarok.

Gimle: Home of blessed after Ragnarok.

Giuki: King of Nibelungs; father of Gunnar, Hogni, Guttorm, and Gudrun.

Glathsehim (Gladsheim): Hall of gods in Asgard.

Gram (meaning "Angry"): Sigmund's sword; rewelded by Regin; used by Sigurd to slay Fafnir.

Greyfell: Sigmund's horse; descended from Sleipnir.

Grimhild: Mother of Gudrun; administered magic potion to Sigurd which made him forget Brynhild.

Gudrun: Daughter of Giuki; wife of Sigurd; later wife of Atli and Jonakr.

Gunnar: Son of Giuki; in his semblance Sigurd won Brynhild for him; slain at hall of Atli.

Guttorm: Son of Giuki; slew Sigurd at Brynhild's request.

Heimdall (Heimdallr): Guardian of Asgard.

Hel: Goddess of dead and queen of underworld; daughter of Loki.

Hiordis: Wife of Sigmund; mother of Sigurd.

Hoenir: One of creators of Ask and Embla; son of Bur.

Hogni: Son of Giuki; slain at hall of Atli.

Hoth (Hoder, Hodur): Blind god of night and darkness; slayer of Balder at instigation of Loki.

Ithunn (Ithun, Iduna): Keeper of golden apples of youth; wife of Bragi.

Jonakr: Third husband of Gudrun.

Jormunrek: Slayer of Swanhild; slain by sons of Gudrun.

Jotunnheim (Jotunheim): Abode of giants.

Lif and Lifthrasir: First man and woman after Ragnarok.

Loki: God of evil and mischief; instigator of Balder's death.

Lothur (Lodur): One of creators of Ask and Embla.

Midgard (Midgarth): Abode of mankind; the earth.

Midgard Serpent: Sea monster; offspring of Loki; slays, and is slain by, Thor at Ragnarok.

Mimir: Giant; guardian of well in Jotunnheim at root of Yggdrasill; knower of past and future.

Mjollnir: Magic hammer of Thor.

Nagifar: Ship to be used by giants in attacking Asgard at

Ragnarok; built from nails of dead men.

Nanna: Wife of Balder.

Nibelungs: Dwellers in northern kingdom ruled by Giuki.

Niflheim (Nifelheim): Outer region of cold and darkness; abode of Hel.

Njorth: Father of Frey and Freya; originally one of Vanir.

Norns: Demigoddesses of fate: Urth (Urdur) (Past), Verthandi (Verdandi) (Present), Skuld (Future).

Odin (Othin): Head of Aesir; creator of world with Vili and Ve; equivalent to Woden (Wodan, Wotan) in Teutonic mythology.

Otter: Son of Rodmar; slain by Loki; his skin filled with gold hoard of Andvari to appease Rodmar.

Ragnarok: Final destruction of present world in battle between gods and giants; some minor gods will survive, and Lif and Lifthrasir will repeople world.

Regin: Blacksmith; son of Rodmar; foster-father of Sigurd.

Rerir: King of Huns; son of Sigi.

Rodmar: Father of Regin, Otter, and Fafnir; demanded Otter's skin be filled with gold; slain by Fafnir, who stole gold.

Sif: Wife of Thor.

Siggeir: King of Goths; husband of Signy; he and his sons slew Volsung and his sons, except Sigmund; slain by Sigmund and Sinflotli.

Sigi: King of Huns; son of Odin.

Sigmund: Son of Volsung; brother of Signy, who bore him Sinflotli; husband of Hiordis, who bore him Sigurd.

Signy: Daughter of Volsung; sister of Sigmund; wife of Siggeir; mother by Sigmund of Sinflotli.

Sigurd: Son of Sigmund and Hiordis; wakened Brynhild from magic sleep; married Gudrun; slain by Guttorm at instigation of Brynhild.

Sigyn: Wife of Loki.

Sinflotli: Son of Sigmund and Signy.

Skuld: *See* Norns.

Sleipnir (Sleipner): Eight-legged horse of Odin.

Surt (Surtr): Fire demon; slays Frey at Ragnarok.

Svartalfaheim: Abode of dwarfs.

Swanhild: Daughter of Sigurd and Gudrun; slain by Jormunrek.

Thor: God of thunder; oldest son of Odin; equivalent to Germanic deity Donar.

Tyr: God of war; son of Odin; equivalent to Tiu in Teutonic mythology.

Ull (Ullr): Son of Sif; stepson of Thor.

Urth: *See* Norns.

Valhalla (Valhall): Great hall in Asgard where Odin received souls of heroes killed in battle.

Vali: Odin's son; Ragnarok survivor.

Valkyries: Virgins, messengers of Odin, who selected heroes to die in battle and took them to Valhalla; generally considered as nine in number.

Vanir: Early race of gods; three survivors, Njorth, Frey, and Freya, are associated with Aesir.

Ve: Brother of Odin; one of creators of world.

Verthandi: *See* Norns.

Vili: Brother of Odin; one of creators of world.

Vingolf: Abode of goddesses in Asgard.

Vitharr (Vithar): Son of Odin; survivor of Ragnarok.

Volsung: Descendant of Odin, and father of Signy, Sigmund; his descendants were called Volsungs.

Yggdrasill: Giant ash tree springing from body of Ymir and supporting universe; its roots extended to Asgard, Jotunnheim, and Niffheim.

Ymir (Ymer): Primeval frost giant killed by Odin, Vili, and Ve; world created from his body; also, from his body sprang Yggdrasill.

Egyptian Mythology

Aaru: Abode of the blessed dead.

Amen (Amon, Ammdn): One of chief Theban deities; united with sun god under form of Amen-Ra.

Amenti: Region of dead where souls were judged by Osiris.

Anubis: Guide of souls to Amenti; son of Osiris; jackal-headed.

Apis: Sacred bull, an embodiment of Ptah; identified with Osiris as Osiris-Apis or Serapis.

Geb (Keb, Seb): Earth god; father of Osiris; represented with goose on head.

Hathor (Athor): Goddess of love and mirth; cow-headed.

Horus: God of day; son of Osiris and Isis; hawk-headed.

Isis: Goddess of motherhood and fertility; sister and wife of Osiris.

Khepera: God of morning sun.

Khnemu (Khnum, Chnuphis, Chnemu, Chnum): Ram-headed god.

Khonsu (Khensu, Khuns): Son of Amen and Mut.

Mentu (Ment): Solar deity, sometimes considered god of war; falcon-headed.

Min (Khem, Chem): Principle of physical life.

Mut (Maut): Wife of Amen.

Nephthys: Goddess of the dead; sister and wife of Set.

Nu: Chaos from which world was created, personified as a god.

Nut: Goddess of heavens; consort of Geb.

Osiris: God of underworld and judge of dead; son of Geb and Nut.

Ptah (Phtha): Chief deity of Memphis.

Ra: God of the Sun, the supreme god; son of Nut; Pharaohs claimed descent from him; represented as lion, cat, or falcon.

Serapis: God uniting attributes of Osiris and Apis.

Set (Seth): God of darkness or evil; brother and enemy of Osiris.

Shu: Solar deity; son of Ra and Hathor.

Tem (Atmu, Atum, Tum): Solar deity.

Thoth (Dhouti): God of wisdom and magic; scribe of gods; ibis-headed.

Modern Wedding Anniversary Gift List

Anniversary	Gift	Anniversary	Gift	Anniversary	Gift
1st	Gold jewelry	10th	Diamond jewelry	19th	Aquamarine
2nd	Garnet	11th	Turquoise	20th	Emerald
3rd	Pearls	12th	Jade	25th	Silver jubilee
4th	Blue topaz	13th	Citrine	30th	Pearl jubilee
5th	Sapphire	14th	Opal	35th	Emerald
6th	Amethyst	15th	Ruby	40th	Ruby
7th	Onyx	16th	Peridot	45th	Sapphire
8th	Tourmaline	17th	Watches	50th	Golden jubilee
9th	Lapis	18th	Cat's-eye	60th	Diamond jubilee

Source: Jewelry Industry Council.

Biotechnology: Geneticists in the Pasture

By George E. Seidel, Jr.

Popular articles about biotechnology tend to focus on its effects on humans and crops. Yet one of the biggest impacts will be on animal agriculture. In the next several years we can expect to see animals with genes from other species, offspring from either two female or two male parents, and animal clones numbering in the thousands. These creatures will resist diseases better, reproduce more efficiently, grow faster, and yield higher-quality products. Exotic as the methods sound, they will evolve from breeding practices that already have had dramatic benefits. For centuries farmers have used simple selection techniques to produce animals that differ greatly in size, food-production characteristics, and docility. In recent decades they have turned to biotechnology to improve upon the process. For example, artificial insemination, which became widespread about 35 years ago, has allowed U.S. farmers to produce more milk with 10 million cows than they did in 1945 with 25 million.

Most of the new methods will simply speed up the pace of genetic changes. While many critics question the impacts, the technologies likely will be environmentally sounder than current practices, and probably will enhance animal health. Food prices will continue to drop, although some farms and agribusinesses that cannot keep up with the changes will die out.

Most of the procedures are now being used on cattle, since they are too expensive to use on species such as sheep that bring in lower income per animal. But this will change as the industry becomes more experienced with the techniques and prices drop.

Mosquito Genes in Farm Animals

A new biotechnology procedure that could become commercially available in as little as two to four years is "transgenesis," which permits scientists to create an animal with specific traits by adding, removing, inactivating, or repairing genes in an embryo. The additional genes can come from any source. For example, if a gene of interest occurs in mosquitoes or alligators—say, one that codes for resistance to a certain disease—it can be removed and placed in the embryo of a farm animal. The several strains of commercially useful transgenic farm animals that will probably emerge in the next few years could include leaner pigs, poultry resistant to avian influenza and other deadly diseases, sheep with wool that is easier to wash, and goats that produce valuable pharmaceuticals in their milk.

The simplest way to make transgenic animals is to inject a gene into a one-cell embryo and then implant the embryo in another animal. Under the right conditions, the new gene joins one of the embryo's strands of genes. Each cell created as the embryo divides gets a copy of the new gene.

An alternative technique is to incorporate the gene into a type of virus known as a retrovirus that has been modified so it cannot reproduce itself after entering a cell. The virus, which cannot cause disease, delivers the gene to the cell's nucleus. Often this method is better than gene injection because a retrovirus always delivers just one gene, and the gene is always intact.

Yet another method is to add genes to undifferentiated embryonic cells, which are then placed in other embryos. But so far the difficulty of keeping the embryonic cells of farm animals from differentiating into various specialized cells has made it impossible to use this technique with these species.

An interesting use of transgenic technology relies on the gene responsible for producing casein, the major protein in milk. Like almost all genes, this one has a part that is structural: it carries the information needed to create the protein. Another part is regulatory: it determines when and in which cells casein is made—in mammary tissue and only during lactation. Joining the regulatory part of the casein gene with the structural part of genes that code for valuable pharmaceutical products can result in a farm animal whose milk contains medicines such as tPA—which dissolves blood clots after heart attacks—and human blood-clotting Factor IX—which hemophiliacs use.

Another technique that should become commercially available in the next decade is the transplantation of cellular nuclei. It could yield thousands of identical offspring. In many cases this offers clear advantages over sexual reproduction, which produces unpredictable results.

The technology is based on the fact that the nucleus of every undifferentiated cell in a single embryo contains the same genetic information. With this in mind, animal scientists can transplant the nucleus from each cell of a 32-cell embryo into 32 single-cell eggs whose original genetic information has been removed by suction using microsurgical methods. The nuclei and eggs are usually fused through a pulse of electrical current. If 10 percent of the eggs survive (the rate ranges from 0 to 30 percent), the result is 3 embryos, which then are allowed to develop to the 32-cell stage. The 96 identical nuclei from these 3 embryos can be transplanted to 96 single-cell eggs. With a 10 percent survival rate each time, repeating the procedure should yield approximately 9 embryos, then 28, 89, 284, and so on.

George E. Seidel, Jr., professor of physiology at Colorado State University, received his doctorate in reproductive physiology at Cornell University and did postdoctoral work at Harvard Medical School. He is conducting research funded by private industry on disease-resistant transgenic animals, and developed a commercial venture owned by his university that collects, freezes, splits, and transfers embryos. Seidel was raised on a dairy farm in Pennsylvania.

This article is reprinted with permission from *TECHNOLOGY REVIEW*. Copyright © 1989.

When enough embryos accumulate, some are transferred to animals for gestation. If the offspring are determined to be of superior quality, the remainder of the embryos, which have been frozen, are saved.

In the short time that scientists have worked with this procedure—the first article concerning its use with farm animals was published in 1986—they have obtained up to seven cloned calves from one embryo. As researchers continue to work with species other than laboratory animals in the next few years, success rates are likely to increase.

Still another biotechnology that is developing rapidly for farm animals is in vitro fertilization (IVF), which involves extracting an egg and sperm from animals and mixing them in a test tube to form an embryo. The embryo is then placed in another animal's reproductive tract to develop. Today this technique is much more widely used with humans than farm animals.

For animal agriculture an important advantage of IVF is that the eggs are very inexpensive, since they are collected at slaughterhouses. Moreover, in the future animal scientists may be able to save and use tens of thousands of eggs from each ovary.

IVF research will soon receive a huge infusion of resources because the number of cows in Europe has recently decreased, which has resulted in markedly higher beef prices. A neat solution to the demand for more animals is to have a high proportion of cows produce twins. This could be accomplished by fertilizing eggs in test tubes and then placing two embryos into each cow's reproductive tract.

Virgin Births

Two more exotic techniques show longer term promise, perhaps early in the next century. They are gynogenesis, in which an offspring is produced with only female parents, and androgenesis, in which two males are used to produce offspring. Androgenesis would be particularly valuable, since artificial insemination has revealed the genetic qualities of bulls with great precision. Superior offspring would be obtained by crossing two high-quality bulls rather than a superior bull with a female whose quality is uncertain.

Androgenesis exploits the egg's function as a processing device for sperm. The trick is to fertilize it with two sperm. A block that prevents a second sperm from entering the egg normally occurs upon fertilization, but scientists can cover an egg with so many sperm that two can enter simultaneously. Next researchers remove the egg's genetic material through suction. The genetic material from the two sperm then combines as that from one sperm and an egg normally would.

With gynogenesis, scientists fuse two eggs to start embryonic development. Electrical pulses are often used to join the eggs. Inactivated viruses can also do the job by breaking down the eggs' surfaces.

So far, poultry, fish, and amphibians have been produced by gynogenesis and androgenesis, although not for commercial purposes. In some high school biology classes students even produce frogs by a form of gynogenesis called parthenogenesis, which is Greek for virgin birth. This technique involves stimulating an egg so that two doses of genetic information from it join together.

These procedures are difficult to perform with mammals because their genetic material appears to change subtly as it passes through testes and ovaries. The subtle changes are complementary: both sexes are needed to develop an adequate placenta, blood supply, and fetus. Thus, mammalian gynogenetic embryos die after reaching a size of thousands of cells, while androgenetic embryos die even earlier.

At present, androgenetic embryos are difficult to save. It is possible, however, to rescue the gynogenetic embryos of mammals by mixing their cells with those of normal embryos, which already have a good placenta and blood supply. These embryos end up containing both normal and gynogenetic cells. Sometimes the resulting offspring can produce eggs containing genes from the animals used in gynogenesis, so that traits from valuable females can be passed on.

Today, nearly all experimental work in this field is done with mice, which may present more severe technical problems than farm animals. But it is virtually impossible to obtain funding for similar research on farm animals because the costs are so high. □

Atomic Energy

At the turn of the century, scientists began to wonder whether the atoms of the chemical elements might not be composed of smaller particles. This was actually a contradiction in terms, because the Greek word *atomos*, from which the word *atom* was derived, meant "indivisible." But there were some indications of particles smaller than an atom—the electrons. In 1907, Albert Einstein suggested that matter might just be "condensed energy" and gave the conversion formula $E = mc^2$, in which E represents the energy, m the mass, and c the velocity of light. According to this formula a small piece of matter should represent enormous amounts of energy.

Atomic energy can be released in two ways. One is the *fission* of elements with very heavy atoms, such as uranium and plutonium, which will split when struck by a neutron, a sub-atomic particle. The splitting of the heavy atom releases more neu-

trons, which are then available to split other atoms—the so-called chain reaction. The other way of obtaining atomic energy is *fusion*; four light atoms (hydrogen) are fused together into the next heavier element (helium). The fusion reaction requires enormous heat and very high pressures. These pressures, coupled with very high temperatures, can most easily be produced by exploding a fission bomb.

Just as the Space Age is said to have started with the orbiting of Sputnik I, the Atomic Age is said to have started with the explosion of a test bomb on July 16, 1945, near Alamogordo, N.M., at 5:30 A.M. local time. The bomb was placed on top of a steel tower, and observers were stationed in bunkers 10,000 yards away. The explosion vaporized the steel tower, produced a mushroom cloud rising to 40,000 feet, and melted the desert sand into glass for distances up to 800 yards from the tower.

Table of Geological Periods

It is now generally assumed that planets are formed by the accretion of gas and dust in a cosmic cloud, but there is no way of estimating the length of this process. Our earth acquired its present size, more or less, between 4,000 and 5,000 million years ago. Life on earth originated about 2,000 million years ago, but there are no good fossil remains from periods earlier than the Cambrian, which began about 550 million years ago. The largely unknown past before the Cambrian Period is referred to as the Pre-Cambrian and is subdivided into the Lower (or older) and Upper (or younger) Pre-Cambrian—also called the Archaeozoic and Proterozoic Eras.

The known geological history of the earth since the beginning of the Cambrian Period is subdivided into three "eras," each of which comprises a number of "periods." They, in turn, are subdivided into "subperiods." In a subperiod, a certain section may be especially well known because of rich fossil finds. Such a section is called a "formation," and it is usually identified by a place name.

Paleozoic Era

This era began 550 million years ago and lasted for 355 million years. The name was compounded from Greek *palaios* (old) and *zoön* (animal).

Period	Duration[1]	Subperiods	Events
Cambrian (from *Cambria*, Latin name for Wales)	70	Lower Cambrian Middle Cambrian Upper Cambrian	Invertebrate sea life of many types, proliferating during this and the following period
Ordovician (from Latin *Ordovices*, people of early Britain)	85	Lower Ordovician Upper Odovician	
Silurian (from Latin *Silures*, people of early Wales)	40	Lower Silurian Upper Silurian	First known fishes; gigantic sea scorpions
Devonian (from Devonshire in England)	50	Lower Devonian Upper Devonian	Proliferation of fishes and other forms of sea life, land still largely lifeless
Carboniferous (from Latin *carbo* = coal + *fero* = to bear)	85	Lower or Mississippian Upper of Pennsylvanian	Period of maximum coal formation in swampy forests; early insects and first known amphibians
Permian (from district of Perm in Russia)	25	Lower Permian Upper Permian	Early reptiles and mammals; earliest form of turtles

Mesozoic Era

This era began 195 million years ago and lasted for 135 million years. The name was compounded from Greek *mesos* (middle) and *zoön* (animal). Popular name: Age of Reptiles.

Period	Duration[1]	Subperiods	Events
Triassic (from *trias* = triad)	35	Lower or Buntsandstein (from German *bunt* = colorful + *Sandstein* = sandstone) Middle or Muschelkalk (from German *Muschel* = clam + *Kalk* = limestone) Upper or Keuper (old miners' term)	Early saurians
Jurassic (from Jura Mountains)	35	Lower or Black Jurassic, or Lias (from French *liais* = hard stone) Middle or Brown Jurassic, or Dogger (old provincial English for ironstone) Upper or White Jurassic, or Malm (Middle English for sand)	Many sea-going reptiles; early large dinosaurs; somewhat later, flying reptiles (pterosaurs), earliest known birds
Cretaceous (from Latin *creta* = chalk)	65	Lower Cretaceous Upper Cretaceous	Maximum development of dinosaurs; birds proliferating; oppossum-like mammals

Cenozoic Era

This era began 60 million years ago and includes the geological present. The name was compounded from Greek *kainos* (new) and *zoön* (animal). Popular name: Age of Mammals.

Period	Duration[1]	Subperiods	Events
Tertiary (originally thought to be the third of only three periods)	c. 60	Paleocene (from Greek *palaios* = old + *kainos* = new)	First mammals other than marsupials
		Eocene (from Greek *eos* = dawn + *kainos* = new)	Formation of amber; rich insect fauna; early bats
		Oligocene (from Greek *oligos* = few + *kainos* = new)	Steady increase of large mammals
		Miocene (from Greek *meios* = less + *kainos* = new)	
		Pliocene (from Greek *pleios* = more + *kainos* = new)	Mammals closely resembling present types; protohumans
Pleistocene (from Greek *pleistos* = most + *kainos* = new) (popular name: Ice Age)	1	Four major glaciations, named Günz, Mindel, Riss, and Würm, originally the names of rivers. Last glaciation ended 10,000 to 15,000 years ago	Various forms of early man
Holocene (from Greek *holos* = entire + *kainos* = new)		The present	The last 3,000 years are called "history"

1. In millions of years.

Chemical Elements

Element	Symbol	Atomic no.	Atomic weight	Specific gravity	Melting point °C	Boiling point °C	Number of isotopes[1]	Discoverer	Year
Actinium	Ac	89	227[2]	10.07[2]	1050	3200 ±300	11	Debierne	1899
Aluminum	Al	13	26.9815	2.6989	660.37	2467	8	Wöhler	1827
Americium	Am	95	243[6]	13.67	994 ±4	2607	13[3]	Seaborg et al.	1944
Antimony	Sb	51	121.75	6.691	630.74	1750	29	Early historic times	—
Argon	Ar	18	39.948	1.7837[4]	−189.2	−185.7	8	Rayleigh and Ramsay	1894
Arsenic (gray)	As	33	74.9216	5.73	817 (28 atm.)	613[5]	14	Albertus Magnus	1250?
Astatine	At	85	−210	—	302	337	21	Corson et al.	1940
Barium	Ba	56	137.34	3.5	725	1640	25	Davy	1808
Berkelium	Bk	97	247[6]	14.00[7]	—	—	8[3]	Seaborg et al.	1949
Beryllium	Be	4	9.01218	1.848	1278 ±5	2970 (5 mm.)	6	Vauquelin	1798
Bismuth	Bi	83	208.9806	9.747	271.3	1560 ±5	19	Geoffroy	1753
Boron	B	5	10.81	2.37[8]	2300	2550[5]	6	Gay-Lussac and Thénard; Davy	1808
Bromine	Br	35	79.904	3.12[4]	−7.2	58.78	19	Balard	1826
Cadmium	Cd	48	112.40	8.65	320.9	765	22	Stromeyer	1817
Calcium	Ca	20	40.08	1.55	839 ±2	1484	14	Davy	1808
Californium	Cf	98	251[6]	—	—	—	12[3]	Seaborg et al.	1950
Carbon	C	6	12.011	1.8–3.5[9]	−3550	4827	7	Prehistoric	—
Cerium	Ce	58	140.12	6.771	798 ±3	3257	19	Berzelius and Hisinger; Klaproth	1803
Cesium	Cs	55	132.9055	1.873	28.40	678.4	22	Bunsen and Kirchhoff	1860
Chlorine	Cl	17	35.453	1.56[4]	−100.98	−34.6	11	Scheele	1774
Chromium	Cr	24	51.996	7.18–7.20	1857 ±20	2672	9	Vauquelin	1797
Cobalt	Co	27	58.9332	8.9	1495	2870	14	Brandt	c.1735
Copper	Cu	29	63.546	8.96	1083.4±0.2	2567	11	Prehistoric	—
Curium	Cm	96	247[6]	13.51[2]	1340 ±40	—	13[3]	Seaborg et al.	1944
Dysprosium	Dy	66	162.50	8.540	1409	2335	21	Boisbaudran	1886
Einsteinium	Es	99	254[6]	—	—	—	12[3]	Ghiorso et al	1952
Erbium	Er	68	167.26	9.045	1522	2510	16	Mosander	1843
Europium	Eu	63	151.96	5.283	822 ±5	1597	21	Demarcay	1896
Fermium	Fm	100	257[6]	—	—	—	10[3]	Ghiorso et al	1953
Fluorine	F	9	18.9984	1.108[4]	−219.62	−188.14	6	Moissan	1886
Francium	Fr	87	223[6]	—	27[2]	677[2]	21	Perey	1939
Gadolinium	Gd	64	157.25	7.898	1311 ±1	3233	17	Marignac	1880
Gallium	Ga	31	69.72	5.904	29.78	2403	14	Boisbaudran	1875
Germanium	Ge	32	72.59	5.323	937.4	2830	17	Winkler	1886
Gold	Au	79	196.9665	19.32	1064.43	2807	21	Prehistoric	—
Hafnium	Hf	72	178.49	13.31	2227 ±20	4602	17	Coster and von Hevesy	1923
Helium	He	2	4.00260	0.1785[4]	−272.2 (26 atm.)	−268.934	5	Janssen	1868
Holmium	Ho	67	164.9303	8.781	1470	2720	29	Delafontaine and Soret	1878
Hydrogen	H	1	1.0080	0.070[4]	−259.14	−252.87	3	Cavendish	1766

Element	Symbol	Atomic no.	Atomic weight	Specific gravity	Melting point °C	Boiling point °C	Number of isotopes[1]	Discoverer	Year
Indium	In	49	114.82	7.31	156.61	2080	34	Reich and Richter	1863
Iodine	I	53	126.9045	4.93	113.5	184.35	24	Courtois	1811
Iridium	Ir	77	192.22	22.42	2410	4130	25	Tennant	1803
Iron	Fe	26	55.847	7.894	1535	2750	10	Prehistoric	—
Krypton	Kr	36	83.80	3.733[4]	−156.6	−152.30±0.10	23	Ramsay and Travers	1898
Lanthanum	La	57	138.9055	6.166	920 ±5	3454	19	Mosander	1839
Lawrencium	Lr	103	257[6]	—	—	—	20[3]	Ghiorso et al.	1961
Lead	Pb	82	207.2	11.35	327.502	1740	29	Prehistoric	—
Lithium	Li	3	6.941	0.534	180.54	1347	5	Arfvedson	1817
Lutetium	Lu	71	174.97	9.835	1656 ±5	3315	22	Urbain	1907
Magnesium	Mg	12	24.305	1.738	648.8±0.5	1090	8	Black	1755
Manganese	Mn	25	54.9380	7.21–7.44[10]	1244 ±3	1962	11	Gahn, Scheele, and Bergman	1774
Mendelevium	Md	101	256[6]	—	—	—	3[3]	Ghiorso et al.	1955
Mercury	Hg	80	200.59	13.546	−38.87	356.58	26	Prehistoric	—
Molybdenum	Mo	42	95.94	10.22	2617	4612	20	Scheele	1778
Neodymium	Nd	60	144.24	6.80 & 7.004[10]	1010	3127	16	von Welsbach	1885
Neon	Ne	10	20.179	0.89990 (g/l 0°C/1 atm)	−248.67	−246.048	8	Ramsay and Travers	1898
Neptunium	Np	93	237.0482	20.25	640 ±1	3902	15[3]	McMillan and Abelson	1940
Nickel	Ni	28	58.71	8.902	1453	2732	11	Cronstedt	1751
Niobium (Columbium)	Nb	41	92.9064	8.57	2468 ±10	4742	24	Hatchett	1801
Nitrogen	N	7	14.0067	0.808[4]	−209.86	−195.8	8	Rutherford	1772
Nobelium	No	102	254[6]	—	—	—	7[3]	Ghiorso et al.	1957
Osmium	Os	76	190.2	22.57	3045 ±30	5027 ±100	19	Tennant	1803
Oxygen	O	8	15.9994	1.14[4]	−218.4	−182.962	8	Priestley	1774
Palladium	Pd	46	106.4	12.02	1552	3140	21	Wollaston	1803
Phosphorus	P	15	30.9738	1.82 (white)	44.1	280	7	Brand	1669
Platinum	Pt	78	195.09	21.45	1772	3827 ±100	32	Ulloa	1735
Plutonium	Pu	94	244[6]	19.84	641	3232	16[3]	Seaborg et al.	1940
Poionium	Po	84	210[6]	9.32	254	962	34	Curie	1898
Potassium	K	19	39.102	0.862	63.65	774	10	Davy	1807
Praseodymium	Pr	59	140.9077	6.772	931 ±4	3212	15	von Welsbach	1885
Promethium	Pm	61	145[6]	—	≈1080	2460?	14	Marinsky et al.	1945
Protactinium	Pa	91	231.0359	15.37[2]	<1600	—	14	Hahn and Meitner	1917
Radium	Ra	88	226.0254	5.0?	700	1140	15	P. and M. Curie	1898
Radon	Rn	86	222[6]	4.4[4]	−71	−61.8	20	Dorn	1900
Rhenium	Re	75	186.2	21.02	3180	5627[7]	21	Noddack, Berg, and Tacke	1925
Rhodium	Rh	45	102.9055	12.41	1966 ±3	3727 ±100	20	Wollaston	1803
Rubidium	Rb	37	85.4678	1.532	38.89	688	20	Bunsen and Kirchoff	1861
Ruthenium	Ru	44	101.07	12.44	2310	3900	16	Klaus	1844
Samarium	Sm	62	150.4	7.536	1072 ±5	1778	17	Boisbaudran	1879
Scandium	Sc	21	44.9559	2.989	1539	2832	15	Nilson	1879
Selenium	Se	34	78.96	4.79 (gray)	217	684.9±1	20	Berzelius	1817
Silicon	Si	14	28.086	2.33	1410	2355	8	Berzelius	1824
Silver	Ag	47	107.868	10.50	961.93	2212	27	Prehistoric	—
Sodium	Na	11	22.9898	0.971	97.81±0.03	882.9	7	Davy	1807
Strontium	Sr	38	87.62	2.54	769	1384	18	Davy	1808
Sulfur	S	16	32.06	2.07[11]	112.8	444.674	10	Prehistoric	—
Tantalum	Ta	73	180.9479	16.654	2996	5425 ±100	19	Ekeberg	1801
Technetium	Tc	43	98.9062	11.50[2]	2172	4877	23	Perrier and Segrè	1937
Tellurium	Te	52	127.60	6.24	449.5±0.3	989.8±3.8	29	von Reichenstein	1782
Terbium	Tb	65	158.9254	8.234	1360 ±4	3041	24	Mosander	1843
Thallium	Tl	81	204.37	11.85	303.5	1457 ±10	28	Crookes	1861
Thorium	Th	90	232.0381	11.72	1750	4790	12	Berzelius	1828
Thulium	Tm	69	168.9342	9.314	1545 ±15	1727	18	Cleve	1879
Tin	Sn	50	118.69	7.31 (white)	231.9681	2270	28	Prehistoric	—
Titanium	Ti	22	47.90	4.55	1660 ±10	3287	9	Gregor	1791
Tungsten (Wolfram)	W	74	183.85	19.3	3410 ±20	5660	22	J. and F. d'Elhuyar	1783
Uranium	U	92	238.029	~18.95	1132.3±0.8	3818	15	Peligot	1841
Vanadium	V	23	50.9414	6.11	1890 ±10	3380	9	del Rio	1801
Xenon	Xe	54	131.30	3.52[4]	−111.9	−107.1±3	31	Ramsay and Travers	1898
Ytterbium	Yb	70	173.04	6.972	824 ±5	1193	16	Marignac	1878
Yttrium	Y	39	88.9059	4.457	1523 ±8	3337	21	Gadolin	1794
Zinc	Zn	30	65.38	7.133	419.58	907	15	Prehistoric	—
Zirconium	Zr	40	91.22	6.506[2]	1852 ±2	4377	20	Klaproth	1789

Elements No. 104, 105, and 106—See NOTE at end of footnotes.

1. Isotopes are different forms of the same element having the same atomic number but different atomic weights. 2. Calculated figure. 3. Artificially produced. 4. Liquid. 5. Sublimation point. 6. Mass number of the isotope of longest known life. 7. Estimated. 8. Amorphous. 9. Depending on whether amorphous, graphite or diamond. 10. Depending on allotropic form. 11. Rhombic. —Is approximately. < Is less than. NOTE: There is a dispute between groups at the Lawrence Berkeley Laboratory of the University of California and at the Dubna Laboratory in the Soviet Union concerning the discovery of elements 104, 105, and 106. The Lawrence Berkeley Laboratory claims that 104 and 105 were discovered in 1969 and 1970, respectively, by Ghiorso et al. and has suggested the names Rutherfordium and Hahnium. The U.S. laboratory claims also that Ghiorso et al. discovered element 106 in 1974. No name has yet been suggested for this element. Names will not be official until the controversy is resolved and they have been approved by the International Union of Pure and Applied Chemistry.

MAJOR ADVANCES OF SCIENCE

Text by Boyce Rensberger. Photos, illustrations, and biographies by Information Please Almanac unless otherwise noted.

Edwin Hubble

1. The Big Bang and the Expanding Universe

The universe as we know it is not ageless. It was born between 13 and 20 billion years ago. In 1929 Edwin Hubble, an American Astronomer, noticed certain peculiarities in the light from stars and galaxies, and realized that the only way to account for his observations was to conclude that these celestial structures were all flying away from each other at great speed. The universe, Hubble discovered, is expanding exactly as if it were exploding from one central point. The explosion came to be called the Big Bang, and by reckoning backward from the present scale of the universe, astronomers have been able to calculate when it started. In the beginning, all of what we know today as matter, energy, space, and time were contained, in some poorly understood primordial form, within a tiny speck. That speck exploded (nobody knows why), and under conditions of unimaginable temperature and pressure, the Big Bang brought forth everything from atoms to galaxies.

The resultant cosmos is organized into a variety of structures. Planets such as the Earth are among the tiniest of these. Larger forms include stars of several kinds, most of which are organized into galaxies. The universe also contains bizarre objects such as black holes, pulsars, and—perhaps most puzzling—quasars whose energy output seems to draw on a source millions of times more powerful than any that physicists can imagine.

Edwin Powell Hubble

Edwin Powell Hubble, the American astronomer who revolutionized our understanding of the universe was born in Marshfield, Mo., on Nov. 20, 1889. He studied physics at the University of Chicago and law at Oxford. After a brief practice at law, he returned to Chicago to work for a doctorate in astronomy.

Hubble did research at Yerkes Observatory, Williams Bay, Wis., from 1914 to 1917, and joined the Army following America's entrance in the war. He accepted a position on the staff of Mt. Wilson Observatory, Pasadena, Calif., in 1919 where at that time and up until 1948 the observatory's 100-inch Hooker reflector telescope was the most powerful in the world.

Hubble spend the rest of his life at Mt. Wilson and eventually became its director. He took time out from his work during World War II when he did research on ballistics (1942-1946).

During 1923-1924, Hubble studied the Andromeda nebula from photographs taken through the 100-inch telescope and discovered that it contained short-period variable stars. This observation led him to conclude that Andromeda was not part of our own Milky Way galaxy, but was an independent star system at a very great distance from our own. He went on to study more remote galaxies along with other astronomers, and in 1929 found the first observational evidence to support the theories that the universe is expanding. Hubble also classified galaxies according to their shapes and investigated many of their properties. He died at San Marino, Calif., on Sept. 28, 1953. □

2. The Copernican Revolution: The Heliocentric Solar System

The Earth, alas, is not at the center of the universe, nor is it even at the center of the solar system. We, like the other planets, orbit the sun. Though today it may seem a trivial discovery, this finding had a powerful impact on philosophies and theologies that proclaimed human beings to be the pinnacle or centerpiece of creation. Nicolaus Copernicus, a sixteenth-century Polish astronomer, proposed that the Earth circled the sun. A century later, Galileo Galilei, an Italian astronomer, used one of the first telescopes to find the evidence supporting Copernicus' proposal. Johannes Kepler, a German contemporary of Galileo, confirmed the finding and improved it by showing the planetary orbits to be ellipses, not perfect circles.

Quasars and Cosmology

Source: A Field Guide to the Stars and Planets, Donald H. Menzel and Jay M. Pasachoff.

The Milky Way in Sagittarius. Astronomers believe that there may be a large black hole at the center of our own galaxy, the Milky Way, 30,000 light years away.

Quasars

It came as a surprise in 1960 when some of the sources of celestial radio waves appeared to be pointlike—"quasi-stellar"—instead of looking like galaxies. These "quasi-stellar radio sources"—*quasars,* for short—were discovered three years later to be extremely far away, when Maarten Schmidt discovered that the spectrum of one of them showed an extreme redshift. A class of radio-quiet quasars—quasi-stellar objects with huge redshifts—has since been discovered. We now know of over a thousand quasars.

The redshift can be expressed as the fraction or percentage by which the wavelengths of light are shifted. For speeds much slower than the speed of light, this fraction is the same as the fraction that the recession speed of the quasar is of the speed of light. For example, a redshift (called z) of 0.2 means that the wavelengths of light are shifted toward the red by 0.2 times (20% of) the original wavelength. It is also true that the galaxy or quasar emitting such light is receding from us at 0.2 times the speed of light, or 60,000 km/sec. A quasar with redshift of 1.0 has its wavelengths shifted by 1.0 times (100% of) the original wavelength; each wavelength is doubled. But Einstein's formulas from the special theory of relativity must be used to calculate how fast the quasars are receding; their velocities are always less than the speed of light.

The most distant quasar is redshifted by $z = 3.78$.[1] Few quasars with redshifts greater than 3 (300%) have been found, even though instruments exist that would be sensitive enough to do so. The farther out the quasar is, the farther back in time the light reaching us was emitted. That few quasars of the largest redshifts are found indicates that we are seeing back to the instant at which the first quasars were formed—somewhat over 10 billion years ago.

Since quasars are so far away yet still send us some visible light and relatively strong radio radiation, the quasars must be astonishingly bright. Astronomers now agree that giant black holes are probably present in the centers of quasars. These black holes would contain millions of times the mass of the sun. As gas is sucked into the black holes, it heats up and gives off energy. Quasars may be a stage in the evolution of galaxies, for there is evidence that some quasars have structure around them not unlike that of galaxies. Since we see most quasars quite far away, we are seeing them far back in time, and we can conclude that the epoch at which quasars were brightest took place long ago.

Cosmology

Hubble's observations that the most distant galaxies are receding from us faster than closer galaxies can be explained if the universe were expanding in a way similar to the way a giant loaf of raisin bread rises. If you picture yourself as sitting on a raisin, all the other raisins will recede from you as the bread rises. Since there is more dough between you and the more distant raisins, the dough will expand more and the distant raisins will recede more rapidly than closer ones. Similarly, the universe is expanding. We have the same view no matter which raisin or galaxy we are on, so the fact that all raisins and galaxies seem to be receding doesn't say that we are at the center of the universe. Indeed, the universe has no center. (We would have to picture a loaf of raisin bread extending infinitely in all directions to get a more accurate analogy.)

Since the universe is uniformly expanding now, we can ask what happened in the past. As we go back in time, the universe must have been more compressed, until it was at quite a high density 15 billion or so years ago. Most models of the origin of the universe say that there then was a *big bang* that started the expansion. A new model—the *inflationary universe*—holds that the early universe grew larger rapidly for a short time before it settled down to its current rate of expansion. The big bang itself may not have occurred; the first matter could have formed as a chance fluctuation in the nothingness of space.

Astronomers ask what will happen to the universe in the future. The evidence is not all in. One possibility is that the universe is *open*—it will continue to expand forever. Another possibility is that the universe will eventually stop its expansion and begin to contract. We know that this cannot happen for at least 50 billion years more—at least three times longer than the current age of the universe—because we can observe the rate at which the universe is now expanding. Still, if the universe does contract in the long run, then we have a *closed universe* that will wind up in a *big crunch*. The inflationary model indicates that the universe will expand forever, but at a decreasing rate. ☐

1. In 1988, astronomers announced the discovery of a galaxy designated 4C41.17 which has a redshift of 3.8, making it the most distant galaxy observed.—Ed.

From A FIELD GUIDE TO THE STARS AND PLANETS, 2E, Revised by Donald Menzel and Jay Pasachoff. Copyright © 1983 by the Estate of Donald H. Menzel and by Jay M. Pasachoff. Reprinted by permission of Houghton Mifflin Company.

Galileo Galilei

Johannes Kepler

The great Italian scientist, Galileo Galilei, was born in Pisa on Feb. 15, 1564. He taught mathematics at the University of Pisa from 1589 to 1592. He discovered that all falling bodies, large or small, descend with an equal velocity, but the famous story that he demonstrated this by experimenting with weights dropped from the Leaning Tower of Pisa is believed not to be true. From 1592 to 1610, he was a professor of mathematics at the University of Padua. After hearing about a simple magnifying device that was constructed in Holland, he was able to make the first complete astronomical telescope in 1609. Within a year, Galileo made some spectacular discoveries from his celestial observations. They included the four largest moons of Jupiter, the phases of Venus, the mountains and craters of the Moon, and the finding that the Milky Way is made up of myriads of single stars. Galileo's discovery that Venus goes through a complete cycle of phases was a major proof of Copernicus's idea that the sun rather than the Earth is the center of the solar system. His support of Copernicus's views conflicted with church dogma and, in 1616, he was ordered to refrain from teaching Copernicus's heliocentric view of the heavens. Despite the warning, he continued to support Copernician ideas, and in 1633, was summoned to Rome and tried by the Holy Inquisition. Galileo was convicted and made to recant his "false" belief that the Earth moves round the Sun. He was placed in house arrest at his retreat at Arcetri near Florence, where he remained until his death on Jan. 8, 1642. □

Johannes Kepler

Johannes Kepler, German astronomer and mathematician, was the founder of modern astronomy. He was born on Dec. 27, 1571, in the village of Weil-der-Stadt in the Duchy of Württenberg, Swabia. He studied mathematics, philosophy, theology, and astronomy at the University of Tüblingen, earning his M.A. in 1591.

Kepler became a teacher of mathematics and astronomy at Gratz, the Austrian province of Styria from 1594 to 1600. His writings on celestial orbits impressed the famous Danish astronomer Tycho Brahe who invited Kepler to join him at Prague. Kepler accepted and assisted Tycho in preparing new planetary tables. When Brahe died in 1601, Kepler succeeded him as Imperial Mathematician. He had access to all of Tycho Brahe's papers and 20 years of precise observations which he used to form the foundation of his three laws of planetary motion *(Kepler's Laws)* published between 1609 and 1618.

They are: (1) the path of a planet is an ellipse with the sun at one focus; (2) a line from the sun to a planet sweeps out equal areas in equal time periods; and (3) the square of the orbital period of a planet is proportional to the cube of its average distance from the sun.

Kepler spent the latter part of his life as a professor of mathematics at Linz, Austria. He died at Regensburg, Bavaria, on Nov. 15, 1630. □

3. The Origin of the Earth, Plate Tectonics, and Geological Uniformitarianism

Four and a half billion years ago the Earth was little more than a flying heap of debris left over from the formation of the sun. Gradually, however, the debris organized itself into a dynamic planet. Heat at the center of the Earth melted the debris, allowing most of the heavier elements, such as iron, to sink to the planet's core, while lighter compounds, such as the silicates that make rock, floated to the top and hardened.

The heat-driven processes that shaped the primordial Earth have not stopped. They continue to remodel the planet's surface, pushing chunks of the Earth's crust (or plates) in different directions, with the result that continents move continually, sometimes splitting to open huge rift valleys, sometimes colliding and pushing up mountains, and sometimes rubbing against one another, triggering earthquakes.

Though sometimes sporadic, these processes represent a fundamentally uniform rate of geological activity that is constantly, gradually changing Earth's surface features. This idea, called uniformitarianism, was introduced in the nineteenth century as a radical challenge to the prevailing theory of catastrophism, which held that sudden major events, such as Noah's flood, shaped the Earth's surface.

Sir Isaac Newton

Sir Isaac Newton, the English mathematician and philosopher was born in Woolsthrope, Lincolnshire, on Christmas day 1642. He earned his B.A. degree at Trinity College, Cambridge University in 1665. During this time he made his first discovery on fluxions but did not publish it. However, it has been established that he devised calculus independently of the German philosopher and mathematician Gottfried W. Leibnitz.

In 1666, according to the popular story, he was working in his garden at Woolsthorpe, when he supposedly reflected on the fall of an apple and it suggested to him the law of universal gravitation.

Newton's subsequent investigations include the nature of light. He experimented with sunlight refracted through a prism in a darkened room and discovered that ordinary white light contains the colors of the rainbow. His study of the laws of refraction and reflection led him to construct the first reflecting telescope in 1668.

Newton's other achievements were in the field of mechanics with his discovery of the second and third laws of motion. He became a member of the Royal Society in 1672.

He published his greatest work, "The Mathematical Principle of Natural Philosophy" in 1687 which presented his law of gravitation and laws of motion. He was knighted by Queen Anne in 1705.

Newton was elected president of the Royal Society in 1703 and remained in that office until his death in London on Mar. 20, 1727. He was given a national funeral and was the first scientist to be buried in Westminster Abbey. □

4. Newton's Law of Universal Gravitation

All bodies in the universe exert a gravitational pull that affects all other bodies. This is the force that binds the moon to the Earth and the Earth to the sun. It is what holds galaxies together. The strength of the pull increases with the mass of the object exerting the pull, but diminishes the greater the distance from the object being pulled. Isaac Newton, a seventeenth-century English mathematician and physicist, worked out formulas to calculate how strong a gravitational pull should be for any given mass or distance.

5. Newton's Three Laws of Motion

These are the three principles of mechanics that govern virtually all moving objects within the everyday realm of experience. It is now known that these laws do not hold inside the atom or for objects moving at velocities near the speed of light, for which Einstein's relativity theory is more accurate. Newton didn't do any very extensive experiments in order to arrive at these laws. He simply condensed the accumulated observations of centuries into the simplest set of statements that could account for everything about moving objects. The laws state (1) that an object in motion or at rest will stay that way unless acted on by an outside force, (2) that a force is anything that changes the rate of motion of a body, and (3) that for every action of a force, there is an equal and opposite reaction.

6. Einstein's Theories of Relativity

In 1905 Albert Einstein, a German-Swiss-American theoretical physicist, put forth two theories of relativity—the special theory and the general theory. A brief summary is scarcely possible in this space. Suffice it to say here that the theory of relativity shows that Newton's laws do not hold for objects that are moving at an appreciable fraction of the speed of light. When objects go that fast, certain characteristics about them change in the eyes of a stationary observer. Fast-moving objects increase their mass and shrink in the dimension parallel to their motion. Also, time appears to slow down; an astronaut who flew about at nearly the speed of light for a year (as measured on his watch) could return to Earth and find that several years had elapsed there. Although these are called theories, there is no question that they are true. Every experimental test has confirmed Einstein's predictions. Perhaps the most dramatic test was the atomic bomb, which proved the relativity theory's assertion that matter and energy are the same thing in two different guises, each of which can be converted into the other. Nuclear bombs turn matter into energy. Particle accelerators turn energy into matter.

Perhaps the most counterintuitive of the theory's ideas is that there is really no force called gravity. Instead, Einstein said, space is curved. Just as a golf ball's path across a green is bent by the curvature of the ground, so the curvature of space bends the path of objects moving through space. The curvature of space results from concentration of mass. The Earth, an appreciable concentration of mass, curves the space all around it so that the path of any less massive object moving nearby is bent toward the ground. Gravity, Einstein said, is simply a human concept that makes it easier to understand the visible effects of curved space.

7. Atom Theory

Matter is made of very tiny particles called atoms. Although the Greeks first advanced this idea, it was not until Einstein, writing in 1905, that there was direct proof of the fact. Until then, many people argued that matter was some kind of continuous stuff, and that it wasn't grainy, as something made of small particles should be. Almost a century before Einstein, however, John Dalton, an English chemist, developed the first modern concept of atoms by asserting that each chemical element (iron, carbon, oxygen, etc.) was made of its own kind of atom. Chemistry, Dalton correctly said, was simply the business of binding or unbinding atoms in various combinations.

Second from left: Albert Einstein, third from left: Max Planck

Albert Einstein

Albert Einstein, one of the greatest intellects in the history of mankind, was born of Jewish parents in Ulm, Wurttemberg, Germany, on March 14, 1879. Contrary to a popular legend that he failed math in his youth, Einstein was a gifted student in mathematics and physics. He earned his doctorate at the University of Zurich, Switzerland, in 1905. During the same year, he published four papers of major importance in physics, which included his special and general theory of relativity.

He became a Swiss citizen and taught at the University of Zurich in 1909, the German University of Prague in 1911, and returned to Zurich in 1912. In 1913, Einstein accepted the posts of titular professor of physics and director of theoretical physics at the Kaiser Wilhelm Institute in Berlin and renewed his German citizenship.

One of his predictions on the general theory of relativity, which concerned the bending of light rays from stars by the sun as they passed on their way to the earth, was verified in 1919 by British scientists studying a solar eclipse and brought him international fame.

Einstein was awarded the 1921 Nobel Prize in Physics for his work on the photoelectric effect.

After Hitler's rise to power in 1933, he was persecuted by the Nazi government and he gave up his German citizenship. Fortunately, he had accepted the post as head of the school of mathematics at the Institute for Advanced Study at Princeton in 1933 and remained there until his death. He eventually became a U.S. citizen.

Although Einstein was an ardent pacifist, he wrote to President Roosevelt in 1939 to investigate the use of atomic energy in bombs. He did this at the request of other scientists including Niels Bohr who suspected that the Nazis were developing a nuclear-fission device. After the war, Einstein was a leader in seeking international govermental control of nuclear energy.

A Zionist, Einstein was offered the presidency of Israel by David Ben-Gurion in 1952, but declined. He died in Princeton, N.J., on April 18, 1955. ☐

8. Atomic Structure: Atoms are Made of Smaller Particles

Atoms, it turns out, are badly named. The word is Greek for "indivisible," but atoms can be divided. They consist of a nucleus (made of smaller particles called neutrons and protons) surrounded by orbiting electrons. Although electrons do orbit, they do not follow the neat circular paths shown in the old models that make an atom look like a solar system. The electrons stay in no clearly definable path, but instead move within cloudlike shells or regions. Even neutrons and protons, it turns out, are not indivisible. They are made of still smaller particles called quarks, of which there are six basic kinds. The so-called strong force binds the nuclear particles, and the electromagnetic force binds the negatively charged electrons to the oppositely charged nucleus.

9. The Nature of Chemical Bonding

Though the world around us is largely made of atoms, most of the matter we encounter is made of larger objects called molecules. Molecules are combinations of atoms that are bound together in regular and predictable ways. Although millions of kinds of molecules can be formed, there are only two fundamental processes that cause atoms to stick together to form molecules—covalent bonding and ionic bonding. Both involve the electrons that swarm around an atom's nucleus. Atoms that share electrons are bound to one another covalently; atoms that transfer them from one atom to another are bound ionically. The elucidation of the nature of chemical bonding, which grew out of the work of many researchers over at least two centuries, made it possible for scientists to begin to understand the fundamental nature of matter itself.

Max Planck

Max Carl Ernst Ludwig Planck was born on April 23, 1858, in Kiel, Germany. He studied at the University of Munich from 1874 to 1877. In 1877 he went to the University of Berlin where he received his Ph.D. for his dissertation on the second law of thermodynamics when he was 21 years old. He subsequently taught at the University of Munich and Kiel University.

In 1889, he became a professor at the University of Berlin, where he remained until 1928 when he retired.

While investigating the problem of black body[1] radiation, Planck discovered the algebraic equation that described it. Since his findings did not conform to the classical laws of physics, he continued to study the problem and, in 1900, announced his revolutionary theory that energy was not a continuous entity but came in discontinuous small bundles that he called quanta. His discovery had provided an understanding of the nature of light and of radiation in general.

Later research by scientists such as Albert Einstein and Niels Bohr confirmed his basic hypothesis and established the Quantum Theory of modern physics.

Planck was awarded the Nobel prize in physics in 1918 for his work on black body radiation. He died at the age of 89 on Oct. 3, 1947, in Göttingen.

1. Black body: a theoretically perfect absorber of all radiation falling on it, reflecting or transmitting none.

10. Quantum Theory and Quantum Mechanics

Along with Einstein's theory of relativity, quantum theory and its development into quantum mechanics is generally considered the greatest of the twentieth century's intellectual achievements. Introduced by Max Planck, the German physicist, and developed by Albert Einstein and Niels Bohr, the Danish physicist, quantum theory says that energy, like matter, comes in particles, or grains. In other words, energy is not a continuously variable thing; when you examine smaller and smaller units of energy, you finally come to the fundamental unit—the quantum—and although quanta come in different sizes, there is no such thing as half a quantum. Despite popular usage of the name to the contrary, a quantum is a very small piece of energy, its effect significant only within atoms. If a quantum of energy (be it light, heat, or any other form) enters an atom, it may be absorbed by an electron, with the result that the electron jumps up to a "higher" orbit around its nucleus. Since this position is unstable, the electron soon drops back to its normal orbit, nearer to the nucleus, and gives up the quantum, or emits it. Quanta are also known as photons, which are the fundamental particles of light. Photons having a certain fixed energy, or energy level (corresponding to an electromagnetic wave of a certain frequency, are perceived by the human eye as light. Since, according to relativity theory, matter and energy are interchangeable, quantum theory explains the behavior of all fundamental entities, whether they are described as quanta of energy or particles of matter.

Quantum mechanics is a development of quantum theory that explains the behavior of particles inside the atom.

11. The Unification of Magnetism and Electricity

Magnetism was known in ancient times as a curious property of a mineral called lodestone. Electricity was appreciated in the more recent past in the form of lightning, static electricity, and as the product of the battery which was invented in 1800. In the 1820s Michael Faraday, an English physicist, discovered that if you move a magnet near a wire (or vice versa), an electrical current will flow in the wire. Conversely, if an electrical current flows through a wire near a piece of iron, the iron will become a magnet. Magnetism and electricity are two different manifestations of one fundamental force called electromagnetism. James Clerk Maxwell, a Scottish physicist, worked out the mathematical relationships in Faraday's discoveries, producing what many consider to be the most elegant intellectual construction of the nineteenth century and paving the way for the making of electric motors and generators. In 1897, J.J. Thomson, an English physicist, established that electricity consists of a flow of particles called electrons.

12. The Nature of Light

Isaac Newton, the English physicist, said in the 1600s that light consisted of tiny particles. In this view, a beam of light was like a hail of machine-gun bullets. Newton's contemporary, Christiaan Huygens, a Dutch physicist, said that light was not particles but waves. In this view light is more like a ripple on a pond, in which the only thing that moves away from the source is a disturbance in the medium—in a water wave, for example, the water doesn't move horizontally. The wave-particle argument see-sawed for centuries until Albert Einstein argued early in this century that both were correct. He turned out to be right. Paradoxical as it seems, light has a dual nature, being both a particle (called a photon) and a wave (called electromagnetism)—a statement which concedes that our language is incapable of grasping the truth.

Subsequent discoveries show that light represents only a narrow portion of a much broader spectrum of electromagnetic waves that also includes radio waves, x-rays, and heat.

Michael Faraday

Michael Faraday, the distinguished English physicist and chemist, was born of poor parents in Newington Butts on Sept. 22, 1791. Due to his family's poverty, his formal education was only in reading, writing, and the rudiments of mathematics.

At the age of 13, Faraday was apprenticed to a bookbinder and, because of the opportunities given him while learning the trade, he was able to read extensively about science during his free time.

In 1812, he obtained employment as laboratory assistant to Sir Humphrey Davy, the celebrated chemist and inventor, and was launched on his scientific career that led to many important discoveries.

Faraday discovered electromagnetic induction and developed the first dynamo. It was a simple device consisting of a copper disk that rotated between the poles of a permanent magnet. He also formulated the laws of electrolysis. Faraday gave us the familiar terms: *electrode, cathode, anode, anion, cation, ion, ionization, electrolyte,* and *electrolysis.*

He became a member of the Royal Institution in 1823 and was made a Fellow of the Royal Society in 1824. He was offered knighthood, and the presidency of the Royal Society but declined both honors. Michael Faraday died at Hampton Court, near London, on Aug. 25, 1867.   □

Niels Henrik David Bohr

Niels Bohr, the founder of the modern theory of atomic structure was born in Copenhagen on Oct. 7, 1885. He received his Ph.D in physics from the University of Copenhagen in 1911. His thesis on the electron theory of metals remains a classic today.

From 1912 to 1916, Bohr worked at Manchester University with Ernest Rutherford (1871-1937) who in 1911 had introduced the nuclear model of the atom, i.e., a small positively charged nucleus surrounded by negatively charged electrons. Bohr applied Planck's quantum theory to Rutherford's atomic structure, and in 1913, proposed a radical new concept of atomic structure (known as the Bohr

Niels Bohr

atom) in which electrons travel around the nucleus in orbits that are determined by quantum conditions and not by classical laws alone. He left Manchester in 1916 to take a professorship at the University of Copenhagen, and in 1920 he assumed the directorship of the Institute of Theoretical Physics created for him at the University and remained in that position for the rest of his academic career.

His brilliant work on atomic structure won him the Nobel Prize for physics in 1922.

During World War II, Bohr escaped from the Nazi occupation of Denmark to Sweden in 1943, and from there to England. The same year, he visited the United States and made some technical contributions to atomic bomb research. However, he was greatly concerned for the future of the world and the control of these terrible weapons.

After the war, he returned to Denmark. He continued his efforts to further world peace and mutual understanding. He received the first Atoms for Peace award in 1957.

Bohr died in Copenhagen on Nov. 18, 1962.   □

13. The Conservation of Matter and Energy

Matter can neither be created nor destroyed; it can only be changed from one form to another. In its day, that was a bold insight, because even so simple an act as burning a log seemed to destroy matter. But Antoine Lavoisier, a French chemist, would set the record straight. He made very careful measurements in experiments in the late 1700s to show, for example, that the mass of an object that seems to be lost by burning simply goes somewhere else. John Dalton, an English chemist working in the early 1800s showed that not only was mass not destroyed, but that the original atoms were unchanged; they merely reassembled themselves into new combinations.

The equivalent observation for energy was developed independently by several people. Gottfried Leibniz, a German mathematician, put it forth as a philosophical postulate in the seventeenth century. Hermann von Helmholtz, a German physicist, made it more explicit in the nineteenth century. Everyday examples of such transformations include the conversion of chemical energy (as muscle cells burn food) into kinetic energy (as the muscles lift the arm) and thermal energy (as the muscle heats up). The kinetic energy of the arm, which holds a baseball bat, is transferred to the ball on impact. Some of this kinetic energy becomes heat at the moment of impact (both the ball and bat actually suddenly get warmer), but most of it propels the ball. Friction with the air saps some of the ball's kinetic energy, heating the air in its path. When the ball clears the fence and hits the bleacher seat, all the rest of its energy becomes heat.

Although both principles of conservation are true in the ordinary realm of human experience, Albert Einstein showed in the early 1900s that under special circumstances matter and energy can be converted into one another. Still, however, the total amount of matter and energy in the universe remains the same.

James Clerk Maxwell

James Clerk Maxwell, the British physicist and creator of the electromagnetic theory of light, was born in Edinburgh, Scotland, on June 13, 1831. He studied at the University of Edinburgh and Trinity College, Cambridge, graduating in 1854. In 1855, he became a Fellow of Trinity, and was appointed Professor of Natural Philosophy and Astronomy at King's College London in 1860. He left King's College in 1865 to retire to private life and devote himself to research and writing on electricity and magnetism.

In 1871, Maxwell became the first Cavendish professor of experimental physics at Cambridge and directed the organization of the Cavendish laboratory which opened in .1874.

Basing his own study and research on that of Michael Faraday, he developed the mathematical interpretation of Faraday's electromagnetic field concepts. He published his famous *Treatise on Electricity and Magnetism* in 1873 which expounded a set of four equations that were applicable to electricity, magnetism, and light.

Maxwell also made important contributions to theoretical physics in the kinetic theory of gases. He is also known for his studies of color and color blindness. He invented the "Maxwell" disk and color box. Maxwell showed that you could produce any given color from a combination of three selected colors taken from the spectrum.

James Clerk Maxwell's work on electromagnetic theory ranks next to Newton's work on mechanics. He died on Nov. 5, 1879, at Cambridge. □

Hermann von Helmholtz

Hermann Ludwig Ferdinand von Helmholtz, one of the 19th century's greatest scientists, was born in Potsdam, Germany, on Aug. 31, 1821. He studied medicine at the Royal Institute for Medicine and Surgery, Berlin, from 1838 to 1842. He later taught physics at the University of Berlin (1871-1894) and became the first director of the Physio-Technical Institute at Charlottenburg (1888-1894).

Helmholtz's studies led him to reject the doctrine of vitalism (*see* Vitalism, p. 454) and he concluded that all forces could be reduced ultimately to matter and motion. His famous paper, "On the Conservation of Force," published in 1847, included his mathematical formulation on the principle of conservation of energy, making him one of the originators of this idea.

Helmholtz also made many important contributions to physiology, optics, electrodynamics, and mathematics. He invented the opthalmoscope and opthalmometer.

He died in Charlottenburg on Sept. 8, 1894. □

14. The Nature of Heat and the Laws of Thermodynamics

Heat is in us and all around us. Even on the coldest day objects still have more than 300 degrees of heat, measuring from absolute zero. Although heat was once thought of as a mysterious fluid, physicists now realize that it is a form of energy that exists in matter as the motion of molecules vibrating and rotating, even as they make up part of the hardest solid. The more the molecules move, the higher the temperature of the matter. Any other form of energy can be converted to heat. Burning, for example, converts the energy stored in the chemical bonds of a fuel, such as wood, into heat. The principle involved is the one discussed in the previous section—the conservation of energy.

One of the fundamental relationships in classical physics is that of heat (the usual standard for measuring units of energy) and work. Physicists define work as a force moving through a distance. Turn the page and you are using the power of your muscles to exert a force that acts through the distance traveled by the moving page. Start your car and the energy locked in the molecular structure of gasoline begins to do work. It becomes heat, which expands the gases in the engine's combustion chamber, pushing the piston, which rotates the crankshaft, which, after a series of gears, turns the wheels, and the car moves. Heat (*therme* is Greek) has been turned into a force that makes the car move through a distance (*dynamikos* is Greek for power).

The study of the relationship between heat and work has produced the three classic laws of thermodynamics. The first law is simply a formulation of the idea that heat is a form of energy and that, while energy may change form, it is not entirely lost—a state of affairs known as the conservation of energy. The second law is the most famous, and is often paraphrased as, "there is no such thing as a free lunch." Basically, it says, that every time you use energy to do work, you lose some of the energy forever. It becomes heat and radiates away, and you can never recapture it.

15. The Law of Biogenesis: Life Arises Only from Life

Until two Italian scientists set the record straight in the seventeenth and eighteenth centuries, many people believed in the spontaneous generation of life. Heaps of manure seemed to give rise to worms, and rotting garbage caused maggots to come into existence. Francisco Redi, working in the 1600s, showed that if meat were protected from adult flies trying to lay eggs, no maggots would develop. In the next century Lorenzo Spallanzani did similar experiments to show the same thing for bacteria. Establishment of the law of biogenesis, which may seem trivial today, was a major, necessary step in thinking toward a theory of evolution, which works only because life is transmitted from one generation to the next.

16. Cell Theory: The Fundamental Unit of Life is the Cell

Although the term "cell" (as referring to microscopic structures) was coined in the 1600s, it was not until 1839 that these structures were appreciated as the smallest units of an organism that can be said to possess life. Until Theodor Schwann and Mathias Schleiden, two German biologists, put forth their ideas in that year, most scientists thought that the units of life were fibers and vessels that started small and just grew, rather like crystals. Rudolf Virchow, another German, soon modified the cell theory to include the view that growth is the result of existing cells duplicating themselves. Virchow's modification was a key step that led to an understanding of how organisms develop from a single, unspecialized cell—the fertilized egg—to billions of specialized cells.

17. Germ Theory: Microbes Cause Disease

Barely a century ago, Robert Koch, a German bacteriologist, became the first person to implicate a specific microbe—a bacterium—as the cause of a specific disease, anthrax, which afflicts hoofed ani-

mals. Koch went on to identify the bacterial species that causes tuberculosis. In so doing, he helped sweep away belief in evil spirits and other supernatural phenomena as causes of disease. The germ theory, as Koch's ideas have come to be called, led to a host of highly effective methods of dealing with much human suffering, from measures for preventing disease and ways to eliminate sources of bacteria to vaccines that render people immune and drugs that kill invading microbes.

Charles Darwin

Charles Robert Darwin, the English naturalist, was born in Shrewsbury, England, on Feb. 12, 1809. When he was sixteen, he attended Edinburgh University to study medicine and, in 1827, attended Christ's College, Cambridge, to prepare for the ministry. Although he received a B.A. degree in 1831, he was disinterested in both professions. However, while at Cambridge, he became keenly interested in natural history.

An important change took place in his life when, in 1831, he was able to obtain a position as official naturalist aboard the H.M.S. *Beagle* bound on an around-the-world scientific expedition. During the five-year voyage (1831-1836), Darwin saw many natural wonders and made many important observations which he recorded in voluminous notes. This great scientific adventure was the beginning of his career as one of England's leading biologists and provided him with the basis for his evolutionary theory of natural selection.

In 1859, he published his controversial book on the "Origin of Species." It soon received wide and stormy attention. His book on the "Descent of Man," published in 1871, proposed the idea that man descended from ape-like ancestors and added to the furor as it contradicted divine scripture.

When Charles Darwin died on April 19, 1882, many scientists had accepted his basic theories. He was buried at Westminster Abbey. ☐

18. Darwin's Theory of Evolution

The epochal contribution to science of Charles Darwin, the nineteenth-century English naturalist, should be divided into two parts. The first was his assertion that evolution had occurred; that the kinds of animals and plants we see today have not always existed, but have developed, through an accumulation of many small changes from remote ancestors. Others had suggested this in various forms, all the way back to the Greeks, but it was Darwin who marshaled the evidence finally to convince the world at large that it was true.

Darwin's second contribution was to suggest how the change happened. He pinned it all on what he called natural selection, which operates through four steps. First, organisms produce more offspring than can survive. Second, the offspring vary slightly in body and behavior. Third, the competition for food and mates will be won by the offspring with the more advantageous traits. And fourth, the winners will produce more offspring than will the losers, and so will pass those traits to a greater number of descendants. Darwin said that countless generations of such gradual change had caused one (or a few) original types of organisms to diversify into today's many forms. Some evolutionists today doubt that natural selection accounts for all evolutionary change. They hold that most species are not changing much during most of their existence; that major change can occur quickly in relatively few generations; and that random events can favor the survival of changed forms of a species as readily as can natural selection.

19. Mendel's Particle Theory of Inheritance

Few major advances in science have been the work of one person, but such is the case with the discoveries of Gregor Mendel, the nineteenth-century Austrian monk who found that hereditary traits are passed on through discrete particles. Mendel raised sweet peas in his monastery garden, crossbreeding different varieties, and keeping records of the traits that showed up in the offspring. Through a statistical analysis (among the first in all of science) of the likelihood of a given parental trait showing up in an offspring, Mendel deduced that hereditary factors (later called genes) come in pairs, with one parent contributing each member of the offspring's pairs. He found that organisms may carry genes for traits they themselves do not show but which may be passed on to offspring. Mendelian inheritance patterns turn out not to be the only kind, but Mendel's discovery (neglected for forty years and only rediscovered around 1900) was correct as far as it went, and opened the door to modern genetics research that continues to develop at an ever-quickening pace.

20. Genes Are Made of DNA and Carried on Chromosomes

Gregor Mendel had shown that genes exist, but actually finding them in a cell and knowing what they were took some forty years of fairly intensive research after the rediscovery of Mendel's work. Chromosomes (the word means "colored bodies") had long been known to exist as structures in the nuclei of cells, but nobody knew what they did until Walter S. Sutton, an American biologist, noticed around 1902 that they behaved rather like Mendel's genes. For example, they came in pairs that split up when the organism made sperm or eggs, and then formed new pairs when a sperm and an egg united to create the offspring. In the 1920s Thomas Hunt Morgan, another American, found that various traits were inherited in predictable groups, and his analysis showed these traits had to be carried in linear fashion on chromosomes. In the 1940s Oswald Avery, still another American, finally figured out what kind of molecule it was that constituted genes. It was DNA (deoxyribonucleic acid), an enormously long molecule that was made up of many much smaller links, each being one of only four different kinds of simpler molecules. If DNA contained the code of life, its four-letter alphabet hardly seemed adequate to spell out all the specifications for a living organism.

21. The Double Helix: How DNA Can Replicate

Perhaps the most famous discovery in modern biology was that of the molecular structure of DNA. In 1953 James Watson, an American, and Francis Crick, an Englishman, figured it out. Armed with only general knowledge, such as the relative amounts of the smaller molecules that are chained together to make DNA, the two played around with models made of balls and sticks and drawings on paper. The basic rules of chemistry dictated how long the stick, or chemical bond, should be between certain balls, or atoms, and what the angles should be between different sticks. When Watson and Crick hit on the fact that the DNA molecule consists of a double helix—two, single corkscrew-like strands entwined with one another—the structure immediately revealed how DNA duplicates itself so that a dividing cell can bequeath two identical sets of chromosomes. One of the most astonishing natural phenomena in all of chemistry, the self-replication of DNA turned out to have an elegantly simple explanation.

22. Cracking the Genetic Code: How Genes Work

The discovery of the DNA double helix did not explain what genes do or how they do it. In fact, the function of genes was worked out in the 1940s, a decade before the double helix, by two American biologists, George Beadle and Edward Tatum. In experiments with fruit flies and bread mold, they established that genes command cells to make specific chemicals, called proteins, of which there are thousands of kinds. They showed that each gene contains the genetic code for one kind of protein. Other researchers showed that each such code, preserved on the DNA in the cell's nucleus, was first transcribed into a similar molecule called RNA, which moves out of the nucleus. In the main body of the cell, special structures called ribosomes "read" the RNA code and accordingly assemble the proper protein molecule.

In the early 1960s, Francis Crick, who helped discover the double helix, and Sidney Brenner, a British molecular biologist, made the discovery that, more than the double helix, launched the modern era of molecular biology. They figured out how the seemingly simple four-letter alphabet of DNA could specify the proper sequence of protein sub-units, called amino acids (which come in twenty different kinds) to make up a specific kind of protein molecule. The answer: a group of three "letters" specifies one amino acid. Armed with this knowledge, other workers quickly deciphered the three-letter codes for each of the twenty amino acids, and by 1966, the genetic code had been completely cracked.

One of the most profound discoveries made during this period was that the code is exactly the same for all plants and animals. Although minor exceptions—slight variations in a few microbes—have been found recently, this finding not only vindicated the reliance on insects and molds as clues to human heredity, but provided powerful confirmation of Darwin's theory of evolution. Had all life

The Double Helix—DNA

not stemmed from one ancestor, we would expect to find many genetic codes.

23. The Modern Synthesis: Unifying Darwin and Mendel

Charles Darwin in England and Gregor Mendel in Austria were contemporaries who made their chief contributions in the mid-nineteenth century. Darwin showed that the diverse species on Earth had all descended from a common ancestor by acquiring various modifications in body plan and form. But he had no idea how those modifications were transmitted from parent to offspring. Mendel, on the other hand, showed how differences in body plan and form are transmitted across the generations—through the discrete particles that would someday be called genes. But Mendel had no idea what role these particles played in the larger drama of the evolution of life. There is no evidence that the two scientists ever knew of one another.

Not until 1900, after both men were dead, was Mendel's long-ignored work rediscovered. At first it seemed to conflict with certain elements of Darwinian theory but, beginning in the 1920s, a number of biologists saw how to reconcile the discoveries of both men. The reconciliation was called the "modern synthesis." Mendel's genes, everyone soon realized, were the means by which Darwin's modifications could be passed on.

24. The Evolution of Human Beings

A fitting climax to this sequence of science's greatest achievements—at the opposite end of the spectrum from the origin of everything in the Big Bang—would seem to be the modern understanding of how human beings originated. The appearance of our species in the world is, after all, a relatively recent event, having occurred only in the latest 0.01 percent of the time since the universe began.

Despite controversy among the paleoanthropologists who study this question, the story of human evolution is remarkably clear. We are, as Darwin said, descended from the animals, from small African primates that probably looked a little like modern apes but which weren't apes. (Apes descended from the same ancestors, changing as much as humans have since the two lineages parted. Thus it is as true to say that apes descended from human-like ancestors as vice versa.) By three and a half million years ago, we were walking on two legs but carrying brains the size of those in modern chimpanzees. By two million years ago, our bodies were almost completely modern in size and appearance, and our brains had grown to half their modern size. Our faces had lost much of their muzzle and our hands had found an ability to chip stones into tools. By one million years ago we had migrated out of Africa and through much of Asia and Europe. We had domesticated fire and made clothes to protect us in Eurasian winters. By 100,000 years ago our brains had reached fully modern size. Further evolution in brain and body produced only minor revisions until, by 40,000 years ago, fully modern human beings were on the scene.

Not until about 2,500 years ago did human beings begin the enterprise called science. It had only a brief life, however, and died out within a few centuries. Fortunately, human beings revived the practice of science about 500 years ago. □

INVENTIONS & TECHNOLOGY

A Chronology of Major Developments from 1450 to the Present

Text from AN ENCYCLOPEDIA OF WORLD HISTORY by William L. Langer, The Fifth Edition, Copyright 1940, 1948, 1952, and © 1967, 1972 by Houghton Mifflin Company. Reprinted by permission of Houghton Mifflin Company.

c. 1450. Printing with moveable type introduced into Europe by **Johannes Gutenberg** (?1400-1468). **Laurens Coster** (1440), cheapened and widened the diffusion of knowledge. This development accompanied an increased use of wood-block illustrations.

1485. Publication of **Leon Battista Alberti's** (1404-1472) *De re aedificora* exemplifies the extended interests of Renaissance architects and artists in the realm of applied science. A more famous example is **Leonardo da Vinci** (1452-1519), who was a military engineer and speculated on various types of machines. Structural theory did not advance until the work of **Galileo Galilei** (*Dialogues concerning Two New Sciences*, 1638), **Christopher Wren,** and **Robert Hooke.** The revival of interest in classical architecture, sparked by the rediscovery of the works of Vitruvius, led architects to develop new techniques, flat ceiling, and the dome. Some architects of the period were **Filippo Brunelleschi** (?1377-1446), **François Mansard** (1598-1666), **Claude Perrault** (1613-1688), **François Blondel** (1617-1686), **Inigo Jones** (1573-1652), and **Christopher Wren** (1632-1723).

1500. The expansion of trade brought a **development in ship construction.** Galleys were in use until the 17th century but the fully rigged ship with stern-post rudder developed during the 15th century, and by 1700 the four-masted galleon had evolved.

c. 1510. First of the handbooks on metallurgy appeared, *Probierbergbüchlein* on assaying, *Bergbüchlein* on mining. In 1540 **Vannocio Biringuccio's** (1480-1539) *Pyrotechnica* published, the first practical, comprehensive metallurgy text by a professional metallurgist. Included were descriptions of alloying and cannon-molding processes. In 1556 *De re metallica* of Agricola (Georg Bauer), a physician in the mining area of Saxony, appeared. It covered all aspects of mining from the survey of the site through the equipment and methods of mining to assaying, blast and glass furnace descriptions as well as the treatment of iron, copper, and glass. Agricola was concerned with miners' health, and described the diseases to which they are prone.

1520. Wheel lock invented, probably in Italy, one of the steps to a single-handed pistol. **Rifling** of the gun barrel was a known technique, 1525, and by 1697 **iron cannon** were cast directly from the blast furnace.

1533. The principle of **triangulation** in surveying discovered by **Gemma Frisius**, a German. More technical maps began to appear to replace the earlier Portalan maps (first **road map of Europe** appeared in Germany, 1511). **Maritime charts** were improved; in 1536 **Pedro Nuñez** (1492-1577) wrote on the errors in the plain charts used at sea. In 1569 **Gerhard Mercator** [Kremer] (1512-1594) devised the mercator chart; in 1600

The true Effigies of Iohn Guttemberg *Delineated from the Original Painting at Mentz in Germanie.*

Johannes Gutenberg.

the first seaman's calendar appeared. The **telescope**, invented c. 1590, and the back-staff (1595) of **John Davis** (?1550-1605), superseded the older navigational instruments, the astrolabe and cross-staff.

c. 1589. William Lee (d. 1610) invented the first frame **knitting machine,** slowly accepted during the 17th century.

1560-1660. Increased **use of coal,** especially in England, as a power source. The output of coal in Newcastle rose from 32,951 tons in 1563-1564 to 529,032 tons in 1658-1659. The use of coal was dictated by serious deforestation both in England and on the Continent. By 1615 wood-fired glass furnaces were illegal in England; thus technology was stimulated by the necessity of using coal.

1575-1680. The evolution of the **glass-maker's "chair."** Many new techniques were introduced into glass-making, including those of producing ruby glass (before 1620), lead and white glass (1679).

1603. Cannon were bored in Spain. By 1650 lead shot was molded by means of a split mold.

1698. Thomas Savery's (?1650-1715) steam engine.

The steam mill of **Giovanni Branca**, 1629, was ill conceived, and the engine of **Denis Papin**, 1688, was not developed and had no effect on the Industrial Revolution.

1700. By this date many **foods and crops** were exchanged between Europe, Asia, and the Americas. From the New World came the **potato** (in Spain c. 1570), maize, tea, chocolate, **tobacco**. **Coffee** grew wild in Ethiopia (known c. 1450) and was introduced into Europe (in England by 1650). By this date **sugar** was a common, cheap commodity in England; cane was shipped to America to form the basis of the industry in the Caribbean in the 18th century. **Cotton** was exported to America where it became an important crop.

Technical achievements of this century in agriculture, mining, metallurgy, and machinery (prime movers, textiles, and machine tools) laid the groundwork for the Industrial Revolution, commencing about the mid-century, which was markedly to change the nature of society and civilization. Industrialization, commencing first in England and first in the textile industry, was to urbanize society, transform the international power structure, and put its mark upon every aspect of modern life.

c. 1700. Christopher Polhem (1661-1751), the "Father of Swedish Technology," developed an improved **rolling mill** and utilized water power for primitive mass production.

1709-1717. Abraham Darby (1677-1717) produced iron from a **coke-fired blast furnace** at Coalbrookdale; despite shortage of charcoal, it took 50 years and improvements made in the method by his son Abraham Darby II before coke was regularly used for this purpose.

1712. Low pressure **steam pump** ("atmospheric engine") of **Thomas Newcomen** (1663-1729) used to pump water from mines. Newcomen utilized some features of **Denis Papin's** (1647-1714) atmospheric engine of 1695, but his invention was quite independent of **Thomas Savery's** (?1650-1715) first useful "fire-engine" of 1698. **John Smeaton** (1724-1792) made many empirical improvements of the Newcomen engine; he also designed bridges, harbors, canals, and the Eddystone Lighthouse (1759), and lowered the price of iron by his water-powered bellows (1761).

1716. Corps des Ponts et Chaussées established in France for civil engineering works; clear distinction made between civil engineer and architect. First improvements in **road-making** since Roman times with work of **P. M. J. Trésaguet** (1716-

1794) in France, and **John L. McAdam** (1756-1836) ("metalled" or "macadamized" roads) and **Thomas Telford** (1757-1834) in England. Trésaguet and Telford emphasized a road foundation of large stones, with smaller stones for top layer; McAdam stressed a roadtop impervious to water.

1722. First technical treatise on iron, *L'Art de convertir le fer forgé en acier et l'art d'adoucir le fer fondu*, by **René A. F. de Réaumur** (1683-1757). **Metallurgical techniques** developed during this century included **Benjamin Huntsman's** (1704-1776) crucible process for casting steel (1751), utilized for cutlery and instruments but not commercially successful until 1770; **Henry Cort's** (1740-1800) puddling process to produce wrought (bar) iron from cast iron in a reverberatory furnace (1784); and Cort's perfected rolling mill with grooved rollers (1784).

1732. Publication of **Jethro Tull's** (1674-1741) *New Horse Hoeing Husbandry* in which he described his innovations in **scientific cultivation**: seed drill (1701) to plant seed in rows rather than the older, casual method of tossing seeds; the horsehoe (introduced by Tull from France in 1714); and the technique of soil pulverization. **Robert Bakewell** (1725-1795) introduced selective breeding of livestock, and **Charles Townshend** (1674-1738) introduced useful new crops, turnips and clover, for winter fodder. The work of these pioneers in scientific cultivation, publicized by **Arthur Young** (1741-1820), helped to produce the **Agricultural Revolution**, which effected radical transformations in agricultural crops and techniques and a large increase in the production of foodstuffs and animal materials (wool, hides).

1733. John Kay (d. 1764?) patented the **flying shuttle**, the first of a series of inventions which were to transform the manufacture of textiles, substitute the factory system for the older method of domestic production, introduce power-driven machinery into manufacturing processes, and mark the first steps in the Industrial Revolution. Other landmarks in the industrialization of textile production were the **spinning jenny** invented (1764) by **James Hargreaves** (d. 1778); the spinning machine **(waterframe)** developed (1769) by **Richard Arkwright** (1732-1792), perhaps based on earlier machines for roller spinning (especially that devised by Lewis Paul in 1733 with some assistance from John Wyatt), and which made Arkwright Lancashire's largest cotton-manufacturer and one of England's richest

Major Developments 1450-1789

Development	See year	Development	See year	Development	See year
Architecture	1485	Flush toilet	1707	Roadmaps	1533
Agricultural developments	1732	Glassmaking	1575-1680	Rolling mill	1700
Blast furnace	1709-17	Knitting machines	1589	Ship construction	1500
Bleaching	1785	Lithography	1798	Semephore	1793
Boring mill	1774	Mapmaking	1533	Steam engines	1698,1776
Cannon	1520,1603	Marine chronometer	1797	Soda	1789
Canal building	1770	Metallurgy	c.1510,1722	Telescope	1533
Crops, New World	1700	Optical glass	1798	Textile production	1733
Ceramics	1753	Pumps	1712	Toolmaking	1797
		Road construction	1716	Wheel lock	1520

**Watt's steam engine, 1784. His improved engines
helped usher in the Industrial Revolution.**

men; the **spinning "mule"** (1784) of **Samuel
Crompton** (1753-1827); the power-loom (1785) of
Edmund Cartwright (1743-1823), and the cotton
gin (1793) of **Eli Whitney** (1765-1825).

1753. Publication by **Johann Heinrich Pott** of the
Lithogeoginoise pyrotechnique on the **ceramic
arts,** which developed during this period as Europeans sought to reproduce the much admired
Chinese porcelain introduced to Europe in the
later 17th century. First to produce quality china
were the **Meissen** works in Saxony (Dresden
China), followed by the French state manufac-
tory at **Sèvres** (1768). The English developed
bone-china (utilizing bone-ash as an ingredient).
Josiah Wedgwood (1730-1795) was appointed
royal potter (1762) and established his **Etruria**
works in 1769. By the 1750's The Potteries, a series of towns in Staffordshire, had become the
center of world production of inexpensive earth-
enware.

1754. Society for the Encouragement of Arts, Manufactures and Commerce (later, **The Royal Society of Arts**) established, inspiring the organization of similar societies in France, Netherlands,
and Russia. The first exhibition of the industrial
arts was held in Paris (1763). The French
Encyclopédie (1751-1772) provided a comprehensive treatise, with illustrations, of contemporary technology.

1770. Completion of the English **Grand Trunk
Canal** linking the Trent and the Mersey Rivers,
giving the industrial towns of the Midlands a direct water route for exports and initiating a
canal-building fever in England, which reached
America and France in the early 19th century.
Principal English canal engineers were **James
Brindley** (1716-1772), **John Rennie** (1761-1821),
and **Thomas Telford** (1757-1834).

1774. **John Wilkinson** (1728-1808) invented the
boring-mill. Originally designed to bore cannon,
this machine was to find its most important use
in the boring of cylinders for

1776. The **steam engine** of **James Watt** (1736-1819).
Based upon the older Newcomen engine, the

first working model (1768, patented 1769) contained the separate steam condenser. Put into
practical use in 1776, Watt's engine was not a
commercial success until 1785, when Watt went
into partnership with the entrepreneur **Matthew Boulton** (1728-1809) and only after further
improvements had been made: the epicyclic
(sun-and-planet) gear (1781) producing rotary
motion by the reciprocal piston action, and the
double-acting expansive engine (1782). (The
"steam engine," actually a two-cylinder atmospheric pressure engine, of the Russian **Polzunov**
[1729-1766] operated only for a short time
[1767] and had no influence on subsequent engine development.)

1785. Introduction of **chemical bleaching** with
chlorine *(eau de Javel)* by the French chemist **C.
L. Berthollet** (1748-1822).

1789. The **Leblanc process** for obtaining soda from
common salt invented by **Nicolas Leblanc** (1742-
1806) but first exploited in England.

1793. **Claude Chappe** (1763-1805) developed the
semaphore (visual telegraph); rapid spread after
success of first line from Paris-Lille.

1794. Establishment of **École Polytechnique,** premier institution of higher technological education in France; emphasis upon mathematics and
applied science.

1797. **Henry Maudslay** (1771-1831) designed a
screw-cutting lathe, made entirely of metal and
utilizing a slide-rest. This tool was the culmination of much previous precision tool development, including the drill and lathe (1768-1780)
of **Jacques de Vaucanson** (1709-1782), the screw-
cutting lathe (1770) of **Jesse Ramsden** (1735-
1800); the marine chronometer (1759) of **John
Harrison** (1693-1776); the spring-winding machine of **Joseph Bramah** (1748-1814), who also invented the modern water closet (1778) and a hydraulic press (1796).

1798. **P. L. Guinand** (1748-1824), a Swiss, patented
a stirring process for making optical glass which
became the foundation of the great German **optical industry** of the 19th century.

1798. **Aloys Senefelder** (1771-1834) of Prague invented **lithography.**

The Industrial Revolution

The Industrial Revolution, begun in the latter
half of the 18th century, expanded into new geographical areas, revolutionized older technologies,
created new ones, and continued to transform society and human life during the 19th and 20th centuries. Although historians might debate as to
whether several industrial revolutions occurred
during this two-century span, whether there were
different phases of the same revolution, or whether
industrialization had reached the point of a "continuing revolution," there was no doubt that technological advances from the mid-18th century to
the present had given man greatly increased mas-
tery over his environment, while at the same time
posing problems and even threats to man's continued existence.

The culmination of Britain's leadership in the Industrial Revolution was reached at the **Great Exhibition of 1851** in London; after that Britain's position declined relatively while new industrial giants,
America and Germany near the close of the 19th
century, and Russia in the 20th century, gained in
technological strength.

Drake's oil well. He struck oil on August 27, 1859, at a depth of 69 feet.

Energy and Power

1800. The **galvanic cell,** or Voltaic pile, of **Alessandro Volta** (1745-1827) was the first electric battery (converting chemical energy into electrical energy).

1802. Richard Trevithick (1771-1833) built the first **high-pressure steam engine,** although the American **Oliver Evans** (1755-1819) had patented one in the United States in 1797. Other advances in steam-engine technology included the compound engine (adding a high pressure cylinder to the original Watt engine) by **William McNaught** (1813-1881) in 1845.

1806. First gas-lighting of cotton mills. Improvements made in production and distribution of gas as heat source (**Bunsen burner,** 1855) and for illumination (**Welsbach gas-mantle,** 1885).

1827. Benoit Fourneyron (1802-1867) developed the **water-turbine.**

1832. The first mechanical generation of electricity by **Hippolyte Pixii.** Major improvements in **electric generators** followed: the improved armature (1856) designed by **Werner von Siemens** (1816-1892); and the ring-armature (1870) of **Zénobe T. Gramme** (1826-1901), which represented the first practical dynamo.

1854. Abraham Gesner (1797-1864) manufactured kerosene.

1859. William M. J. Rankine (1820-1872) published the first comprehensive manual of the steam engine. The steam engine stimulated theoretical studies in thermodynamics by Clapeyron, Clausius, Joule, Lord Kelvin, and Gibbs.

1859. Edwin L. Drake (1819-1880) drilled the first oil well in Titusville, Pennsylvania, opening up the Pennsylvania oil field and starting the large-scale commercial exploitation of petroleum. **First oil pipeline** (two-inch diameter, six miles long) constructed 1865 in Pennsylvania.

1876. Nicholas August Otto (1832-1891) built the first practical gas engine, working upon the so-called **Otto cycle,** which is now almost universally employed for all internal combustion engines. Otto's work was based upon previous engines of **Étienne Lenoir** (1822-1900) and **Alphonse Beau de Rochas** (1815-1891). The Otto cycle was employed in the gasoline engine patented (1885) by **Gottlieb Daimler** (1834-1900).

1882. The Pearl Street (New York City) electric generating station, a pioneer central power station designed by **Thomas A. Edison** (1847-1931), commenced operations a few months after Edison dynamos had been installed at Holborn Viaduct Station in England.

1884. Charles A. Parsons (1854-1931) patented the **steam turbine.** The steam turbine (1887) of the Swede **Gustav de Laval** (1845-1913) proved successful for engines of smaller power.

1886. Beginning of the first great **hydroelectric installation** at Niagara Falls.

1888. Nikola Tesla (1856-1943) invented the **alternating current electric motor;** he also made possible the polyphase transmission of power over long distances and pioneered the invention of radio.

1892. Rudolf Diesel (1858-1913) patented his heavy oil engine, first manufactured successfully in 1897.

1921. Tetraethyl lead, gasoline anti-knock additive, produced by **Thomas Midgley** (1889-1944).

1930-1937. Development of gas turbine unit for jet propulsion in aircraft by **Frank Whittle.**

1930-1935. Development of first commercially practicable **catalytic cracking** system for petroleum by **Eugene J. Houdry** (1892-1962).

1942. Dawn of the Nuclear Age. The first self-sustaining **nuclear chain reaction** achieved at Stagg Field, Chicago, by **Enrico Fermi** (1901-1954). The first full-scale use of nuclear fuel to produce electricity occurred at Calder Hall (England) in 1956.

1954. The **solar battery** developed by Bell Telephone Laboratories, making it possible to convert sunlight directly to electric power.

Major Developments in Energy and Power Sources

Development	See year	Development	See year	Development	See year
Catalytic Cracking	1930-35	Hydroelectric installation	1886	Tetracthyl lead	1921
Electric battery	1800	Kerosine	1854	Turbine, steam	1884
A.C. motor	1888	Diesel engine	1892	Turbine, jet-propulsion	1930-37
Electric generators	1832	Nuclear chain reaction	1942	Turbine, water	1827
Electric generating station	1882	Oil well	1859	Solar battery	1954
Gasoline engines	1876	Oil pipeline	1865		
Gas lightning	1806	Steam engine	1802, 1859		

Low-cost Bessemer steelmaking established the foundation of the modern steel industry.

Materials and Construction

1800. Pioneer **suspension bridge,** hung by iron chains, built by **James Finley** (c. 1762-1828) in Pennsylvania; wire suspension employed by **Marc Seguin** (1786-1875) in bridge near Lyons (1825). The American, **Ithiel Town** (1784-1844), patented his truss bridge (1820).

1817-1825. Building of the **Erie Canal,** the first great American civil engineering work.

1818. The **Institute of Civil Engineers** (London), the first professional engineering society, founded.

    Marc Isambard Brunel (1769-1849) patented the cast-iron **tunnel shield; Thomas Cochrane** (1830) used this shield to construct foundations on marshy ground.

1824. Joseph Aspdin (1779-1855) patented **Portland cement,** a hydraulic cement (impervious to water) as durable as that employed by the Romans.

1827. Gay-Lussac tower introduced in manufacture of sulfuric-acid, largely replacing John Roebuck's lead-chamber process (1746). **Herman Frasch** (1851-1914) developed process (1891) for mining sulfur (by superheated water and pumping to the surface).

1836. Galvanized iron introduced by Sorel in France. Galvanized fencing and barbed wire (c. 1880) helped to fence off large tracts of cattle land in American west during latter part of 19th century.

1839. Charles Goodyear (1800-1860) **vulcanized rubber.** Although introduced into Europe in 1615, rubber had not been commercially successful until a solvent for the latex was found (1765); bonding of rubber to cloth to produce raincoats (macintoshes) had been developed (1824) by **Charles Macintosh** (1766-1843).

1855. John A. Roebling (1806-1869) completed **wire cable bridge** at Niagara; Roebling utilized this same method for the **Brooklyn Bridge** (completed by his son, W.A. Roebling, in 1883), and it became standard construction technique for all great suspension bridges.

1856. Henry Bessemer (1813-1898) perfected the technique *(Bessemer process)* for converting pig iron into steel by directing an air blast upon the molten metal.

1856. *Mauve,* first of the **aniline** (coal-tar) **dyes,** discovered by **William H. Perkin** (1838-1907). Beginning of the synthetic dye industry, which was to develop greatly in Germany.

1861. Ernest Solvay (1838-1922) patented the Solvay ammonia process for the manufacture of soda.

1863. The **open-hearth process** for the manufacture of steel developed by the Martin brothers in France using the regenerative furnace devised (1856) by **Frederick Siemens** (1826-1904) (also known as the Siemens-Martin process).

1867. Alfred Nobel (1833-1896) manufactured **dynamite.** Guncotton and nitroglycerine both discovered in 1846, had previously been used for blasting purposes. In 1875 Nobel discovered blasting gelatine, from which arose the gelignite industry. Cordite, another explosive, patented 1889 by Frederick Abel and James Dewar.

1863. Henry Clifton Sorby (1826-1908) of Sheffield discovered the microstructure of steel, marking the beginning of **modern metallurgical science.**

1868. Robert F. Mushet (1811-1891) began the manufacture of **tungsten steel.** Other steel alloys also developed: chromium steel (France, 1877); manganese steel (Robert Hadfield, England, 1882); nickel steel (France, 1888); stainless steel (many inventors, 1911-1920).

Major Developments in Materials and Construction

Development	See year	Development	See year	Development	See year
Aluminum	1886	Dynamite	1867	Solvay ammonia process	1861
Aniline dyes	1856	Eiffel Tower	1889	Steelmaking, basic oxygen	1950
Bridge, wire cable	1855	Erie Canal	1817-25	Steelmaking, Bessemer	1856
Bridge, suspension	1800	Galvanized iron	1836	Steel-frame building	1928
Bridge, truss	1800	Institue of Civil Engineers	1818	Sulfuric acid	1827
Celluloid	1872	Modern metallurgy	1863	Tungsten steel	1868
Casting, shell molding	1941	Polymer	1909	Vulcanized rubber	1839
Cantilever technique,		Reinforced concrete	1947		
buildings	1947	Silicones	1945		

1872. John W. Hyatt (1837-1920) began commercial production of celluloid, discovered by Alexander Parkes (1855).

1877. Joseph Monier (1823-1906) patented a **reinforced concrete** beam. In the 1890s two other Frenchmen, Edmond Coignet and Francois Hennibique, utilized reinforced concrete for pipes, aqueducts, bridges, tunnels; E. L. Ransome employed it extensively in building construction.

1879. Percy Gilchrist (1851-1935) and **Sidney G. Thomas** (1850-1885) developed a method for making steel from phosphoric iron ores, thereby doubling in effect the world's potential steel production.

1886. Charles M. Hall (1863-1914) developed the electrolytic method of obtaining aluminum from its oxide (bauxite).

1889. Completion of the **Eiffel Tower;** wrought-iron superstructure on reinforced concrete base. Cast iron used for building construction earlier in the century by James Bogardus (1800-1874) for office buildings in New York and by Joseph Paxton (1801-1865) for Crystal Palace at Great Exhibition of 1851 (also employing wrought iron and glass, and prefabricated units). The first complete steel-frame structure was built in Chicago in 1890; steel made possible skyscrapers, as did the earlier invention (1854) of the elevator by **Elisha G. Otis** (1811-1861).

1902. Arthur D. Little (1863-1935) patented rayon, the **first cellulose fiber,** and also artificial silk. Earlier (1884) Louis, Count of Chardonet (1839-1924), had produced an artificial thread which was woven into a silk-like material. Cellophane developed by J. E. Brandenberger (1912); further developed by W.H. Church and K. E. Prindle (1926).

1909. The first polymer, **Bakelite,** discovered by **Leo H. Baekeland** (1863-1944). Subsequent development of polymers include neoprene, arising from work of Father Julius A. Nieuwland beginning in 1906; nylon, developed by Wallace H. Carothers and first manufactured in 1938; acrilan; orlon; dynel; and dacron (called terylene by its British inventors, J. R. Whinfield and J. T. Dickson, 1941). Synthetic polymers include elastomers, fibers, plastics. Silicon polymers developed c. 1945.

1928. The first steel-frame, glass-curtain-wall building completed. By 1960 this technique was practically universal for high buildings; developed particularly by **L. Mies van der Rohe** (1886-1969).

1941. Shell molding, a revolutionary process producing more accurate castings cheaply, invented by **Johannes Croning.** Powder metallurgy, although known since Wollaston's work at the beginning of the 19th century, achieved extensive application in mid-20th century.

1945. Industrial development of silicones proceeded apace for a wide variety of applications, including lubricants for exceedingly high and low temperatures; binding of fiberglass; water-repellent agents; etc.

1947. Frank Lloyd Wright (1869-1959) extended pure cantilever technique (earlier employed with iron and steel construction in bridges) by using concrete slab cantilevers for S. C. Johnson Research Building (Racine, Wisconsin).

1950. Basic-oxygen process for manufacture of steel developed in Austria.

Machines and Industrial Techniques

1800. Eli Whitney (1765-1825) credited with introduction of **interchangeable parts** for manufacturing muskets. Although it had European precedents, the system of interchangeable parts became known as "the American system" because it was most fully exploited in the United States and became the foundation of the mass production characteristic of American industry at a later date.

1801. Joseph M. Jacquard (1752-1834) invented a loom for figured silk fabrics, later introduced into the making of worsteds. **William Horrocks** (1776-1849) developed the power loom (1813), improved (1822) by **Richard Roberts** (1789-1864). Machine combing of wool developed (1845); ring spinning frame (1830); the Brussels power loom invented by Erastus B. Bigelow (1814-1879) of Massachusetts for the weaving of carpets (1845); and the loom of J. H. Northrop of Massachusetts (1892), which was almost completely automatic.

1810. Friedrich Koenig's (1774-1833) **power-driven press** in use, followed by the flat bed press (1811). Other developments leading to mass production of printed matter, especially newspapers, were the rotary press of Robert Hoe (1846) and the web printing press, allowing for printing on a continuous roll (web) of paper by a rotary press, invented (1865) by William A. Bullock. In 1885 the linotype of **Ottmar Mergenthaler** (1854-1899) replaced monotype.

Major Developments in Machines and Industrial Techniques

Development	See year	Development	See year	Development	See year
Adding machines	1884	Electric driven machinery	1873	Printing presses and	
Armament	1837	Interchangable manufacturing		automatic typsetting	1810
Automation	1947	parts	1849-54	Refrigeration	1895
Ballpoint pen	1938	Interchangeable firearm		Resistance welder	1877
Bottlemaking	1898	parts	1800	Razors	1895
Calculators	1823-43	Laser	1920	Screw gauge	1830
Computers	1944, 1953	Liquid air plant	1895	Sewing machines	1846
Continuous rolling,		Looms	1801	Steam hammer	1839
steel sheet	1923	Managerial techniques	1920	Tanks	1915
Electric appliances	1882	Milling machine	1855	Turret lathe	1855
Electric precipitation	1905-10	Mass production	1914	Zipper	1913

1823-1843. Charles Babbage (1792-1871) attempted to build calculating machines (following the lead of Thomas de Colmar, who built the first practical calculating machine in 1820); Babbage's machines were never completed, being too advanced for the technology of the time, but his theories formed a basis for later work in this field.

1830. Joseph Whitworth (1803-1887) developed the standard screw gauge and a machine to measure one-millionth of an inch, for standards. Made possible more precise machine tools for planing, gear-cutting, and milling.

1837. Rapid development of armament, keeping pace with improvements in metallurgy, machines, and explosives: **Henri J. Paixhans'** (1783-1854) shell-gun, adopted by France, 1837; rifled, breech-loading artillery used by Piedmont, 1845; the French '75, the first quick-firing artillery piece, firing both shrapnel and high explosive, 1898; the cast steel breech-loading Prussian artillery manufactured by the Krupps from 1849 on. In small arms, there was the Colt revolver (1835), the Dreyse needle-gun (1841), the Minié bullet (1849), Winchester repeating rifle (1860), Gatling machine gun (1861), French Chassepot (1866), and the Maxim gun (1884). The self-propelled torpedo was invented by Robert Whitehead (1823-1905) in 1864; smokeless powder appeared in 1884.

1839. Steam hammer invented by **James Nasmyth** (1808-1890). Also developments in drop-forging and die-stamping at this time.

1846. Elias Howe (1819-1867) invented the lockstitch sewing machine; in 1851 **Isaac M. Singer** (1811-1875) invented the first practical domestic sewing machine. This became the first major consumer appliance, soon followed by the carpet sweeper of M. R. Bissell (1876), and the vacuum cleaner (I. W. McGaffey, 1869; J. Thurman, 1899).

1849-1854. Exploiting the increasing accuracy of machine tools, **Samuel Colt** (1814-1862) and **Elisha Root** (1808-1865) developed a practical system for manufacturing interchangeable parts, especially in connection with Colt's revolver.

1855. Development of turret lathe by American machine-tool makers. First true universal milling machine designed (1862) by **Joseph R. Brown** (1810-1876). Other machine-tool improvements included Mushet's tool steel, increasing the cutting speed (high speed tool steel, 1898, by Taylor and White), gear-box mechanisms for better control, multiple-spindle lathes (1890), and tungsten carbide tools (1926).

1873. First use of electricity to drive machinery, Vienna. Quickly adopted, usually with the motor incorporated into the machine rather than separate.

1877. Elihu Thomson invented a resistance welder. N. W. Bernardos of Russia patented carbon-arc welding, although arc welding (most popularly employed process today) did not come into its own until invention of the coated electrode in the 1920s. Oxyacetylene torch (invented in 1900 by Edmund Fouche) and gas welding was the dominant process until recently. Development of inert-gas-shielded arc welding after 1942.

1882. Invention and use of electric appliances for consumer market: electric fan (S.S. Wheeler); flatiron (H. W. Seely, 1882); stove (W. S. Hadaway, 1896); separate attachable plug (H. Hubbell, 1904); sewing machine (Singer Co., 1889); washing machine (Hurling Co., 1907).

1884. Dorr E. Felt (1862-1930) made first accurate comptometer. **William S. Burroughs** (1857-1898) developed first successful recording adding machine (1888); Brunsviga calculating machine (1892).

1895. Carl Linde established liquid air plant. He had previously (1876) introduced the ammonia compressor machine (the first vapor compression machine invented by Jacob Perkins, 1834). Other refrigerating machines were: ammonia absorption machine (Carré, 1860), air refrigerator (Gorrie, 1845; improved by Kirk, 1862), open-cycle air machine (Giffard, 1873), and later by Bell and Coleman).

1895. King C. Gillette (1855-1932) invented safety razor with throwaway blades. **J. Schick** invented electric razor (1928). Stainless steel throwaway blades invented in Sweden (1962).

1898. M. J. Owens (1859-1923) invented automatic bottle-making machine.

1905-1910. Electric precipitation equipment for prevention of atmospheric pollution by industry, developed by Frederick G. Cottrell (1877-1948).

1913. G. Sundback invented a slide fastener (zipper); earlier version patented by W. L. Judson (1891).

1914. Conveyer-belt mass production employed in the United States most dramatically in Henry Ford's assembly line for Model T Ford automobile, which became the symbol for American industrial technique.

1915. Development of tank in warfare by British (Sir Ernest Swinton).

1920. Managerial techniques improved through development of "Scientific Management," whose principles were first enunciated by **Frederick W. Taylor** (1856-1915) in the first decade of the century. Taylor concentrated on time-motion studies. Other proponents of "rationalized" production were Frank Gilbreth and Charles Bedaux. Quality control developed 1926.

1920. J. C. Shaw developed a sensing device, controlled by a servomechanism, for a milling machine. Hydraulic trace of J. W. Anderson (1927) allowed the reproduction of complex shapes. Machine tools further supplemented by electrolytic and ultrasonic machines, and cutting machines guided by an electron beam. Development of laser (light amplification by simulated emission of radiation) by Theodore N. Maiman (1960), also used for precision cutting.

1923. First mill for hot continuous wide strip rolling of steel, based on work of John B. Tytus.

1938. Ladislao J. and George Biro patented the ball-point pen.

1944. Harvard IBM Automatic Sequence Controlled Calculator, the first automatic general-purpose digital computer, completed. ENIAC (electronic numerical integrator and calculator), the first electronic digital computer, built in 1946. Development of special purpose computers and data processor (1950), including programmed teaching machines.

1947. Word Automation coined by John Diebold and D. S. Harder, to define "self-powered, self-guiding and correcting mechanism," and later extended to include all elements of "automated factory" and extension to office and clerical procedures.

1953. Electronic computers with feedback mechanism (servomechanisms), made possible new field of Cybernetics, defined by **Norbert Wiener** (1953) as "the study of control and communication in the animal and the machine."

Major Developments in Agriculture and Food Technology

Development	See year	Development	See year	Development	See year
Artificial insemination	1940	DDT	1939	Plows	1837
Cream separator	1877	Evaporated milk	1860	Poultry farming	1950
Canning	1810	Farm implements	1850-80	Reapers	1834
Chemical fertilizers	1880	Frozen foods	1917	Refrigeration	1865
Cotton picker	1889	Hydrogenation	1902	Sugarbeet industry	1801
		Pasteurization	1861	Tractors	1892

Agricultural Production and Food Technology

1801. Franz K. Achard (1753-1821) built the first **sugar-beet factory** (Silesia). Sugar-beet cultivation and beet-sugar industry developed primarily in France and Germany.

1810. Nicolas Appert (c. 1750-1840) described system for food preservation by canning, using glass jars. Tin cans introduced 1811.

1834. Cyrus H. McCormick (1809-1884) patented his **reaper**, and began commercial manufacture c. 1840. Obed Hussey (1792-1860) invented a similar reaper simultaneously and independently.

1837. John Deere (1804-1886) introduced the **steel plow.** In 1819 Jethro Wood (1774-1834) had developed a cast-iron plow; and John Lane had introduced a steel-blade plowshare in 1833. James Oliver's (1823-1908) chilled plow of 1855 was improved by the Marsh brothers (1857). Mechanical power applied to plowing with the introduction of **cable plowing** (1859); by 1858 John Fowler had introduced the **steam plow.**

1850-1880. Improvements in farm implements included the revolving disc harrow (1847), binder (1850), corn planter (1853), two-horsestraddle-row cultivator (1856), combine harvester (1860), combine seed drill (1867), and sheaf-biding harvester (1878).

1860. Gail Borden (1801-1874) opened the first factory for the production of **evaporated milk.**

1861. After Louis Pasteur's work on microorganisms, **pasteurization** was introduced as a preservative for beer, wine, and milk.

1865. Development of **mechanical refrigeration** for preservation of food products, especially Thaddeus Lowe's (1832-1913) compression ice machine (1865) and Linde's ammonia compression refrigerator (1873).

1869. Transcontinental railway aided development of **meat-packing industry** in Chicago.

1877. Gustav de Laval (1845-1913) invented the centrifugal **cream separator.**

1880. Application of **chemical fertilizers** increased food production. J. B. Lawes manufactured superphosphates (1842); Chilean sodium nitrate beds exploited from c. 1870 until methods of fixing atmospheric nitrogen were developed after 1900 by Fritz Haber (1868-1934); use of potash as an inorganic fertilizer from Strassfurt deposits.

1889. Angus Campbell tested the first spindle type **cotton picker;** this type of machine was not fully developed and marketed successfully until the 1940s, competing with the machine devised by John and Mack Rust in 1924 and also commercially produced in the 1940s.

1892. Gasoline tractor came into use for farming. **Caterpillar tractor** developed 1931.

1902. W. Normann patented a process for hardening liquid fats by hydrogenation, making available an ample supply of solid fats for soap and food.

1917. Clarence Birdseye (1886-1956) began development of method for quick **freezing of foods** in small containers; placed on market in 1929.

1939. Paul Muller synthesized DDT for use as an insecticide. Othmar Zeidler had prepared DDT in 1874, but its insecticidal qualities had not been suspected.

1940. Development of **artificial insemination** to improve livestock breeding.

1945. Unit **packaging of foodstuffs** improved by development of plastic packaging films. Trend toward prepared "convenience" foods for household use.

1950. Mass-production, battery-raising of poultry increased production, lowered prices, and converted chicken and turkey from a holiday and Sunday luxury to an everyday food item.

Transportation and Communication

1802. Richard Trevithick (1771-1833) patented a steam carriage; earlier attempts to use steam power for transport purposes had been made by Nicolas Cugnot in France (1769); William Murdock in England (1785), and Oliver Evans in the United States. In 1804 Trevithick designed and built a locomotive to run on rails.

1807. Robert Fulton (1765-1815) sailed the *Clermont* from New York to Albany. This was by no means the first steamboat: the Marquis Claude de Jouffroy d'Abbans (1751-1832) had built a paddle-wheel steamer in France (1783); John Fitch (1743-1798) had launched a steamboat on the Delaware (1787); James Rumsey (1743-1792) on the Potomac (1787); and John Stevens (1749-1838) had designed a successful screw-propeller steamboat (1802). However, Fulton's boat was the first steamboat to represent a commercial success. By 1819 steam augmented sail on the first transatlantic steamship crossing of the *Savannah.*

Cugnot's steam carriage, 1770.

Stephenson's locomotive, the *Rocket*.

1814. George Stephenson (1781-1848) built his **first locomotive,** and in 1829 his *Rocket,* designed with the aid of his son Robert (1803-1859), won out in a competition with locomotives of other design and thereby set the pattern for future locomotive developments.

1825. Opening of the **Stockton-Darlington Railway,** the first successful railroad system, using a steam engine built by Stephenson. In 1829 the first railroads were opened in the United States (Pennsylvania) and France (Lyon-St. Étienne), both employing English-built locomotives. The first American locomotive was built (1830) by Peter Cooper (1791-1883).

1837. Charles Wheatstone (1802-1875) and William F. Cooke (1806-1879) patented the telegraph, which was also independently invented by the American Samuel F. B. Morse (1791-1872), whose **telegraphic code** was universally adopted. By 1866, Cyrus W. Field (1819-1892) succeeded in laying a **transatlantic cable,** after two previous failures and after overcoming tremendous financial and technical difficulties.

1839. Louis J. M. Daguerre (1787-1851) evolved the **daguerreotype photographic process,** based on the work of Joseph Nicéphore Niepce (1765-1833). Although William H. F. Talbot (1800-1877) produced paper positives (1841), the first fully practical medium for photography was the wet collodion plate process (1851) of Frederick S. Archer (1813-1857).

1860. Construction began on the **London underground railway** system, which was electrified in 1905. Construction began on the Paris *metro* in 1898, on New York City subway in 1900.

1864. George M. Pullman (1831-1897) built the first **sleeping car** specially constructed for that purpose.

1867. Ernest Michaux invented the **velocipede,** the first bicycle to put cranks and pedals directly on the front wheel; the "safety" bicycle with the geared chain-drive to rear wheel was introduced in 1885.

1869. Union Pacific and Central Pacific Railroads met to complete the **first transcontinental line** in America. The **Trans-Siberian Railway** was begun in 1891.

1869. Opening of the Suez Canal, the work of the French engineer **Ferdinand de Lesseps** (1805-1894).

1873. The Remington Company began manufacture of the **typewriter** patented by Christopher L. Sholes (1819-1890); shift-key system, with capital and small letters on same type bar, introduced in 1878.

1874. Stephen D. Field's (1846-1913) electrically powered **streetcar** began operation in New York City, replacing the horsecars introduced in 1832. The cable streetcar, invented by Andrew S. Hallidie (1836-1900), was put into use in San Francisco (1873). The first streetcars with overhead trolley lines were in use in Germany by 1884 and first installed in the United States at Richmond, Virginia, in 1888.

1876. Alexander Graham Bell (1847-1922) patented the **telephone.** The first telephone exchange installed in New Haven (1877) and an automatic switching system introduced in 1879. Much previous experimentation had been done on telephones, including that of Philip Reis of Germany (1861), Antonio Meucci of Italy (1857),

Bell demonstrating the long-distance capability of his invention at Salem, Mass., on March 15, 1877. A hook-up was made with Boston, 18 miles away, and an extended conversation took place between the two cities.

and Elisha Gray (simultaneously with Bell). The periodic insertion of loading coils (inductors), originated by M. I. Pupin (1899), made possible long distance transmission of telephone calls.

1878-1879. Joseph W. Swan (1828-1914) of England made the first successful carbon filament **electric lamp** in 1878; working independently Thomas A. Edison patented his **incandescent bulb** in 1879. Improved vacuum in the lamp bulb made possible by the high vacuum mercury pump developed by Hermann Springel (1865). At the same time successful experiments in public lighting were carried on with the use of arc lamps, the most successful systems being those of P. Jablochkoff (Paris, 1876) and Charles F. Brush (Cleveland, 1879). Tungsten filament lamp introduced in 1913.

1885. Karl Benz (1844-1929) produced the prototype of the **automobile** using an internal combustion motor operating on the Otto four-stroke cycle principle; the same year Gottlieb Daimler (1834-1900) also patented his **gasoline engine**, trying it first on a motorcycle, then on a four-wheeled vehicle. These may be said to have been the first automobiles, although there had been experiments with battery-powered electric automobiles from 1851 on and some previous internal combustion vehicles had been attempted by the Frenchman Étienne Lenoir (1859) and the Austrian Siegfried Marcus (1864). Other automobile pioneers included the Frenchmen Peugeot and Panhard. The first automobile patent in the United States was taken out by George B. Selden

(1879), but the Duryea (1895) was the first auto made for sale in the United States. **Henry Ford** (1863-1947) made his first car in 1896 and founded the Ford Motor Co. in 1903. Important in the development of the automobile was the invention (1888) of the **pneumatic tire** by John B. Dunlop (1840-1921).

1889-1890. Thomas Edison improved on his first **phonograph** (patented 1878) by substituting wax for the tinfoil-coated cylinders and by adding a loudspeaker to amplify the sounds produced by the diaphragm. Emile Berliner (1851-1929) improved the quality of sound reproduction (1890) by utilizing disk-records and better cutting technique.

1888. George Eastman (1854-1932) perfected the **hand camera** *(Kodak);* he had previously invented the first successful roll film (1880). Leo Backeland perfected (1893) a photographic paper *(Velox)* sufficiently sensitive to be printed by artificial light. Work of Rudolph Fischer and Siegrist in dye-coupler color processes (1910-1914) provided the basis for the development of a commercially practicable color film *(Kodachrome)* by Leopold Godowsky, Jr., and Leopold Mannes (1935).

1895. The first public **motion picture** showing in Paris, by **Louis** (1864-1948) and **Auguste** (1862-1954) **Lumière,** inventors of the **cinématographe.** This followed by a year the openeing of Edison's Kinetosceope Parlor (New York City) where the motion picture (peepshow) could be viewed by but one person at a time. Both these successful attempts at motion pictures had been preceded by earlier devices: the "thaumatrope" of J. A. Paris (1826); the magic lantern, devised by A. Kircher (1645) and improved by Pieter van Musschenbroek (1736); the multi-camera apparatus of Edward Muybridge (1872); the "photographic gun" of E. J. Marey (1882); the celluloid motion-picture film of William Friese-Green (1889). Prototype of the modern **film projector** was the Vitascope (1896), devised by **Charles Francis Jenkins** (1867-1934) and Thomas Armat on the basis of Edison's kinetoscope.

1895. Guglielmo Marconi (1874-1937) invented the **wireless telegraph**, based on the discovery (1887) of radio waves by Heinrich Hertz (1857-1894) (existence of these waves had been deduced by James Clerk Maxwell in 1873). Other contributors to wireless development were E. Branly, Thomas Edison, Alexander Popov (who contributed the aerial), Reginald E. Fessenden (improved transmitter, 1901). In 1901 Marconi succeeded in sending a wireless signal across the Atlantic.

1898. Valdemar Poulsen of Denmark invented the **magnetic recording of sound** (1898). F. Pfleumer of Germany replaced steel wire by plastic tape coated with magnetic material (1930's), and Marvin Camras of the United States made further developments in magnetic recording (1940s).

1904. John Ambrose Fleming (1849-1945) devised the diode thermionic valve (**radio tube**); **Lee de Forest** (1873-1961) invented the Audion (1906), a three-electrode vacuum tube (triode amplifier), thereby providing the basis for the development of **electronics.**

1911. Charles F. Kettering (1876-1958), who had previously invented lighting and ignition systems for the automobile, perfected the **electric self-starter.** The first fully **automatic transmission**, perfected by Earl A. Thompson, was introduced commercially in 1939. Harry Vickers and Francis W. Davis began work on hydraulic **power-assisted steering** systems in 1925 and 1926 respectively, and in 1951 power steering was introduced for passenger cars.

1913. Diesel-electric railway engines first used in Sweden. Coming into use in the United States during the later 1930's, they have largely replaced steam-locomotives.

1920. Frank Conrad (1874-1941) of the Westinghouse Co. began broadcasting radio programs in Pittsburgh, marking the **beginning of radio** as a mass communication medium.

1922. Herbert T. Kalmus developed **Technicolor,** first commercially successful color process for motion pictures.

1926. Sound Motion Pictures. Although Edison had attempted to put together his phonograph and motion picture inventions for sound movies as early as 1904, it was 1923 before de Forest successfully demonstrated his phono-film system for recording sound on the motion picture film. The first motion picture with sound accompaniment was publicly shown in 1926, the first talking picture in 1927.

1926. John L. Baird (1888-1946) successfully demonstrated **television** in England. His mechanical system of television, similar to that of C. F. Jenkins in the United States, was based on Paul von Nipkov's rotating disk (1886), but had technical limitations; modern electronic television developed from the cathode-ray tube (1897) of Ferdinand Braun and A. A. Campbell-Swinton's proposals (1911) for use of a cathode ray to scan an image. The crucial invention was the Iconoscope of the Russian-American **Vladimir Zworykin** (1889-1982), the device which transmits television images quickly and effectively. Philo Farnsworth of the United States contributed the image disector tube (1927). General broadcasting of television began in England in 1936, in the United States in 1941, but languished until after World War II. Peter C. Goldmark of Columbia Broadcasting System demonstrated (1940) sequential method of color television which gave way to compatible electronic system developed by R. C. A. in the 1950s.

1932. Edwin H. Land (1909-   ) invented the first practical synthetic light-polarizing material (**polaroid glass**), found useful in sunglasses, cameras, and scientific optical instruments. In 1947 he invented the **Polaroid Land camera,** which developed the film inside the camera and produced a photograph print within one minute; in 1962 he introduced color film for his camera.

1933. Fluorescent lamps introduced for floodlighting and advertising. Developments leading up to

Major Developments in Transportation and Communication

Development	See year	Development	See year	Development	See year
Aviation (see Aviation section)		Hand-held camera	1888	Sound recording	1898
Automobiles	1885	Polariod glass, camera	1932	Steam power	1802
Self-starter	1911	Radar	1940-45	Steamboat	1807
Bicycles	1867	Radio tube	1904	Streetcar	1874
Electric lamp	1878-79	Radio broadcasts	1920	Submarine, nuclear	1950
Fluorescent lamp	1933	FM (frequency modulation)	1933	Suez Canal	1869
Maser	1954	Railroad system, first	1825	Telegraph	1837
Motion pictures	1895	Diesel-electric engines	1913	Wireless	1895
Technicolor	1922	Sleeping car	1864	Telephone	1876
3-D films	1953	Locomotive	1814	Television	1926
Cinerama	1953	London railway system	1860	Transistor	1948
Phonograph	1888-90	Transcontinental, first	1869	Typewriter	1873
Long-playing records	1948	Space (see Space section)		Xerography	1937
Photography, Daguerrotype	1839	Satellite	1957		

The world's first liquid-fuel rocket, 1926 (Smithsonian Institution photo)

this included experiments by George Stokes (1852) and Alexandre Becquerel (1859) to excite fluorescent materials by ultraviolet rays or in a discharge tube; Peter Cooper-Hewitt's invention of the mercury vapor lamp (1901); the introduction of the **Neon lamp** by Georges Claude and the work on cathodes by D. M. Moore and Wehnelt in the 1900's; and J. Risler's application of powder to the outside of tubular discharge lamps (1923). Subsequent developments have included increased cathode life and improved fluorescent powders.

1933. Edwin H. Armstrong (1890-1954), pioneer radio inventor (regenerative, i.e., feedback, circuit, 1912, and superheterodyne circuit, 1918), perfected **frequency modulation (FM)** providing static-free radio reception.

1937. Chester Carlson patented a new dry photographic process *(Xerography)* based upon principles of photoconductivity and electrostatics.

1939. Igor Sikorsky (1889-1972) flew the first **helicopter** of his design. The first helicopter capable of flight was the work of Ellehammer of Denmark (1912), based on C. Rendard's articulated rotor blade (1904) and G. A. Croco's cyclic pitch control (1906). Juan de la Cierva invented the autogiro (1922), differing from the helicopter in that its rotor auto-rotated and the engine drove a normal propeller. Further development work was done (1934-1936) by Louis Breguet and Heinrich Focke.

1939. First test flight of a **turbo-jet airplane** (Heinkel) with an engine designed by Hans von Ohain.

Simultaneous and parallel work on jet airplanes in Britain, based on turbo-jet engine designed by Frank Whittle (1930). (Also see special section on Aviation for additional information.)

1940-1945. Development of radar ("radio-detection-and-ranging") stimulated by World War II, for detection of aircraft, blind-bombing techniques, and naval search equipment. Based on Heinrich Hertz's demonstration (1887) that radio waves are reflected similarly to light rays, the technique was first applied by Edward Appleton in Britain (1924) and G. Breit and M. A. Tuve in the United States (1925) for investigating ionization in the upper atmosphere. Robert A. Watson-Watt showed the possibilities of employing radio waves to detect aircraft (1935); J. T. Randall and H. A. H. Boot developed the cavity magnetron for high-power microwave transmission. Simultaneously, radar development had been going on in Germany and the United States, including the development of equipment by Robert H. Page of the Naval Laboratory. After 1940 Britain and the United States co-operated in radar development, much of the work being done at the Radiation Laboratory in Cambridge, Mass.

1941-1945. Construction of 2,500 miles of large diameter (20-inch-24-inch) **pipelines** to deliver petroleum from oil-producing regions in Southwest United States to East Coast depots. Development of welding of steelpipe sections (1913-1914) cut leakage and made possible large-scale pipeline construction.

1948. Long-playing phonograph record introduced, based on Peter Goldmark's development of the narrow-groove vinyl plastic record, a lightweight pickup, and a slow-speed (33-1/3 r.p.m.), silent turntable.

1948. Basic research in semi-conductors at the Bell Telephone Laboratories resulted in the invention of the **transistor** by a group which included William Shockley, John Bardeen, and Walter H. Brattain. This tiny, rugged, amplifying device was increasingly used to replace vacuum tubes in electronic instruments. In 1954 the silicon transistor was developed.

1950. Development of **nuclear propulsion** for submarines and surface ships. The United States submarine *Nautilus* (1955), built under the stimulus exerted by Admiral Hyman Rickover, was the first submarine to pass under the North Polar ice cap. The Soviet icebreaker *Lenin* was the first nuclear-powered surface vessel.

1953. "Cinerama" system (invented and developed by Fred Waller) to produce three-dimensional films, released for commercial exhibition. At about the same time Cinemascope, employing a single large concave screen, and stereophonic sound were introduced for motion picture exhibition.

1954. Charles H. Townes (1915-   ) invented the **maser** (microwave amplification by the simulated emission of radiation), making it possible to transmit signals over great distances.

1957. Launching of first **man-made satellite**, *Sputnik I*, by Russia (Oct. 4) marked the beginning of the **Space Age**. This was the product of millennia of human dreams but, more materially, of the rocket researches of **Robert H. Goddard** (1882-1945) of the United States (first liquid-fuel rocket launched, 1926), the theoretical studies of the Russian **Konstantin Tsiolkovsky** (1903), and the German **Herman Oberth** (1923). (Also see special section on Space for additional information.)

Selected Scientific Inventions, Discoveries, and Theories

Abacus: *See* Calculating machine

Adding machine: *See* Calculating machine; Computer

Adrenaline: (isolation of) John Jacob Abel, U.S., 1897

Anesthetic: (first use of anesthetic—ether—on man) Crawford W. Long, U.S., 1842

Antibiotics: (first demonstration of antibiotic effect) Louis Pasteur, Jules-François Joubert, France, 1887; (penicillin, first modern antibiotic) Alexander Fleming, England, 1928

Antiseptic: (surgery) Joseph Lister, England, 1867

Antitoxin, diphtheria: Emil von Behring, Germany, 1890

Atomic theory: (ancient) Leucippus, Democritus, Greece, c.500 B.C.; Lucretius, Rome, c.100 B.C.; (modern) John Dalton, England, 1808

Bacteria: Anton van Leeuwenhoek, The Netherlands, 1683

Barometer: Evangelista Torricelli, Italy, 1643

Bicycle: Karl D. von Sauerbronn, Germany, 1816; (first modern model) James Starley, England, 1884

Bifocal lens: *See* Lens, bifocal

Blood, circulation of: William Harvey, England, 1628

Braille: Louis Braille, France, 1829

Bullet: (conical) Claude Minié, France, 1849

Calculating machine: (Abacus) China, c.190; (logarithms: made multiplying easier and thus calculators practical) John Napier, Scotland, 1614; (slide rule) William Oughtred, England, 1632; (digital calculator) Blaise Pascal, France, 1642; (multiplication machine) Gottfried Leibnitz, Germany, 1671; (important 19th-century contributors to modern machine) Frank S. Baldwin, Jay R. Monroe, Dorr E. Felt, W. T. Ohdner, William Burroughs, all U.S.; ("analytical engine" design, included concepts of programming, taping) Charles Babbage, England, 1835. *See also* Computer

Classification of plants and animals: (by genera and species) Carolus Linnaeus, Sweden, 1737–53

Clock, pendulum: Christian Huygens, The Netherlands, 1656

Combustion: (nature of) Antoine Lavoisier, France, 1777

Computer: (differential analyzer, mechanically operated) Vannevar Bush, U.S., 1928; (Mark I, first information-processing digital computer) Howard Aiken, U.S., 1944; (ENIAC, Electronic Numerical Integrator and Calculator, first all-electronic) J. Presper Eckert, John W. Mauchly, U.S., 1946; (stored-program concept) John von Neumann, U.S., 1947

Conditioned reflex: Ivan Pavlov, Russia, c.1910

Cosmetics: Egypt, c.4000 B.C.

Crossbow: China, c.300 B.C.

Cyclotron: Ernest O. Lawrence, U.S., 1931

Deuterium: (heavy hydrogen) Harold Urey, U.S., 1931

DNA: (deoxyribonucleic acid) Friedrich Meischer, Germany, 1869; (determination of double-helical structure) F. H. Crick, England, James D. Watson, U.S., 1953

Electromagnet: William Sturgeon, England, 1823

Electron: Sir Joseph J. Thompson, England, 1897

E = mc²: (equivalence of mass and energy) Albert

Section of Charles Babbage's Difference Engine an ingenious calculating machine.

Einstein, Switzerland, 1907

Evolution: (by natural selection) Charles Darwin, England, 1859

Falling bodies, law of: Galileo Galilei, Italy, 1590

Fermentation: (micro-organisms as cause of) Louis Pasteur, France, c.1860

Geometry, elements of: Euclid, Alexandria, Egypt, c.300 B.C.

Gravitation, law of: Sir Isaac Newton, England, c. 1665 (published 1687)

Gunpowder: China, c.700

Gyrocompass: Elmer A. Sperry, U.S., 1905

Gyroscope: Léon Foucault, France, 1852

Helium first observed on sun: Sir Joseph Lockyer, England, 1868

Heredity, laws of: Gregor Mendel, Austria, 1865

Induction, electric: Joseph Henry, U.S., 1828

Insulin: Sir Frederick G. Banting, J. J. R. MacLeod, Canada, 1922

Intelligence testing: Alfred Binet, Theodore Simon, France, 1905

Isotopes: (concept of) Frederick Soddy, England, 1912; (stable isotopes) J. J. Thompson, England, 1913; (existence demonstrated by mass spectrography) Francis W. Ashton, 1919

Laser: (theoretical work on) Charles H. Townes, Arthur L. Schawlow, U.S., N. Basov, A. Prokhorov, U.S.S.R., 1958; (first working model) T. H. Maiman, U.S., 1960

Lens, bifocal: Benjamin Franklin, U.S., c.1760

Light, nature of: (wave theory) Christian Huygens, The Netherlands, 1678; (electromagnetic theory) James Clerk Maxwell, England, 1873

Light, speed of: (theory that light has finite velocity) Olaus Roemer, Denmark, 1675

Lightning rod: Benjamin Franklin, U.S., 1752

Logarithms: *See* Calculating machine

Loom: (horizontal, two-beamed) Egypt, c.4400 B.C.; (Jacquard drawloom, pattern controlled by punch cards) Jacques de Vaucanson, France, 1745, Joseph-Marie Jacquard, 1801; (flying shuttle) John Kay, England, 1733; (power-driven loom) Edmund Cartwright, England, 1785

Machine gun: James Puckle, England, 1718; Richard J. Gatling, U.S., 1861

Match: (phosphorus) François Derosne, France, 1816; (friction) Charles Sauria, France, 1831; (safety) J. E. Lundstrom, Sweden, 1855

Mendelian law: *See* Heredity

Microscope: (compound) Zacharias Janssen, The Netherlands, 1590; (electron) Vladimir Zworykin et al., U.S., Canada, Germany, 1932–1939

Neptunium: (first transuranic element, synthesis of) Edward M. McMillan, Philip H. Abelson, U.S., 1940

Neutron: James Chadwick, England, 1932

Neutron-induced radiation: Enrico Fermi et al., Italy, 1934

Nuclear fission: Otto Hahn, Fritz Strassmann, Germany, 1938

Ohm's law: (relationship between strength of electric current, electromotive force, and circuit resistance) Georg S. Ohm, Germany, 1827

Ozone: Christian Schönbein, Germany, 1839

Paper: China, c.100 B.C.

Parachute: Louis S. Lenormand, France, 1783

Pen: (fountain) Lewis E. Waterman, U.S., 1884; (ball-point, for marking on rough surfaces) John H. Loud, U.S., 1888; (ball-point, for handwriting) Lazlo Biro, Argentina, 1944

Penicillin: *See* Antibiotics

Periodic law: (that properties of elements are functions of their atomic weights) Dmitri Mendeleev, Russia, 1869

Periodic table: (arrangement of chemical elements based on periodic law) Dmitri Mendeleev, Russia, 1869

Plow, forked: Mesopotamia, before 3000 B.C.

Plutonium, synthesis of: Glenn T. Seaborg, Edwin M. McMillan, Arthur C. Wahl, Joseph W. Kennedy, U.S., 1941

Polio, vaccine against: (vaccine made from dead virus strains) Jonas E. Salk, U.S., 1954; (vaccine made from live virus strains) Albert Sabin, U.S., 1960

Positron: Carl D. Anderson, U.S., 1932

Pressure cooker: (early version) Denis Papin, France, 1679

Printing: (block) Japan, c.700; (movable type) Korea, c.1400; Johann Gutenberg, Germany, c.1450 (lithography, offset) Aloys Senefelder, Germany, 1796; (rotary press) Richard Hoe, U.S., 1844; (linotype) Ottmar Mergenthaler, U.S. 1884

Programming, information: *See* Calculating machine

Propeller, screw: Sir Francis P. Smith, England, 1836; John Ericsson, England, worked independently of and simultaneously with Smith, 1837

Proton: Ernest Rutherford, England, 1919

Psychoanalysis: Sigmund Freud, Austria, c.1904

Quantum theory: Max Planck, Germany, 1901

Rabies immunization: Louis Pasteur, France, 1885

Radioactivity: (X-rays) Wilhelm K. Roentgen, Germany, 1895; (radioactivity of uranium) Henri Becquerel, France, 1896; (radioactive elements, radium and polonium in uranium ore) Marie Sklodowska-Curie, Pierre Curie, France, 1898; (classification of alpha and beta particle radiation) Pierre Curie, France, 1900; (gamma radiation) Paul Ulrich Villard, France, 1900; (carbon dating) Willard F. Libby et al., U.S., 1955

Relativity: (special and general theories of) Albert Einstein, Switzerland, Germany, U.S., 1905–53

Roller bearing: (wooden for cartwheel) Germany or France, c.100 B.C.

Safety match: *See* Match

Solar system, universe: (sun-centered universe) Nicolaus Copernicus, Warsaw, 1543; (establishment of planetary orbits as elliptical) Johannes Kepler, Germany, 1609; (infinity of universe) Giordano Bruno, Italian monk, 1584

Spectrum: (heterogeneity of light) Sir Isaac Newton, England, 1665–66

Spermatozoa: Anton van Leeuwenhoek, The Netherlands, 1683

Spinning: (spinning wheel) India, introduced to Europe in Middle Ages; (Saxony wheel, continuous spinning of wool or cotton yarn) England, c.1500–1600; (spinning jenny) James Hargreaves, England, 1764; (spinning frame) Sir Richard Arkwright, England, 1769; (spinning mule, completed mechanization of spinning, permitting production of yarn to keep up with demands of modern looms) Samuel Crompton, England, 1779

Sulfa drugs: (parent compound, para-aminobenzenesulfanomide) Paul Gelmo, Austria, 1908; (antibacterial activity) Gerhard Domagk, Germany, 1935

Syphilis, test for: *See* Wassermann test

Thermometer: (open-column) Galileo Galilei, c.1593; (clinical) Santorio Santorio, Padua, c.1615; (mercury, also Fahrenheit scale) Gabriel D. Fahrenheit, Germany, 1714; (centigrade scale) Anders Celsius, Sweden, 1742; (absolute-temperature, or Kelvin, scale) William Thompson, Lord Kelvin, 1848

Toilet, flush: Product of Minoan civilization, Crete, c.2000 B.C. Alleged invention by "Thomas Crapper" is untrue.

Tractor: Benjamin Holt, U.S., 1900

Transformer, electric: William Stanley, U.S., 1885

Uncertainty principle: (that position and velocity of an object cannot both be measured exactly, at the same time) Werner Heisenberg, Germany, 1927

Vaccination: Edward Jenner, England, 1796

Van Allen (radiation) Belt: (around the earth) James Van Allen, U.S., 1958

Vitamins: (hypothesis of disease deficiency) Sir F. G. Hopkins, Casimir Funk, England, 1912; (vitamin A) Elmer V. McCollum, M. Davis, U.S., 1912–14; (vitamin B) Elmer V. McCollum, U.S., 1915–16; (thiamin, B_1) Casimir Funk, England, 1912; (riboflavin, B_2) D. T. Smith, E. G. Hendrick, U.S., 1926; (niacin) Conrad Elvehjem, U.S., 1937; (B_6) Paul Gyorgy, U.S., 1934; (vitamin C) C. A. Hoist, T. Froelich, Norway, 1912; (vitamin D) Elmer V. McCollum, U.S., 1922; (folic acid) Lucy Wills, England, 1933

Wassermann test: (for syphilis) August von Wassermann, Germany, 1906

Weaving, cloth: *See* Loom

Wheel: (cart, solid wood) Mesopotamia, c.3800–3600 B.C.

Windmill: Persia, c.600

X-ray: *See* Radioactivity

Zero: India, c.600; (absolute zero, cessation of all molecular energy) William Thompson, Lord Kelvin, England, 1848

1989 Environmental Quality Index

Source Copyright 1989 by the National Wildlife Federation.

Reprinted from the February-March issue of *National Wildlife Magazine*.

National Wildlife's annual Environmental Quality Index is a subjective analysis of the state of the nation's natural resources. The information included in each section is based on personal interviews, news reports, and the most current scientific studies. The judgments on resource trends represent the collective thinking of the editors and the National Wildlife Federation staff, based on consultation with government experts, private specialists, and academic researchers.

Wildlife: Worse. The plight of wildlife in many areas of the United States worsened dramatically during the drought of 1988, but most conservationists were more concerned about the long-term effects of human activity on habitat than the harsh weather. Ducks and other waterfowl were the hardest hit when fully 40 percent of the prairie potholes—their breeding grounds—evaporated under drought conditions. This only compounded the real threat to North American waterfowl—wetland drainage for agriculture and other kinds of development. On a positive note, the long stalemate that had delayed the extension and revision of the federal Endangered Species Act finally was broken last year and President Reagan signed it. Also the Environmental Protection Agency indicated it would reject a controversial plan to build a recreation area at Lake Alma in southern Georgia that would have ruined important wetlands and other habitat and fined three developers thousands of dollars for illegally filling marshlands in Illinois.

Air: Worse. During the long, hot summer of 1988, much of America's air turned thick and rancid with smog—ozone pollution created by the action of sunlight on such emissions as automobile exhaust. The worst air pollution measured in a decade, the smog obscured some heartening statistics on the continuing reduction of lead and carbon monoxide from the nation's environment. However, late last year the federal government weakened the automobile fuel efficiency standards. The year brought new attempts to face up to the consequences of acid rain, along with several indications that delays in dealing with the problem are creating perilous conditions. A study reported that more than 25 percent of the lakes in New York's Adirondack Mountains are now so acidic that fish cannot live in them. By October, the last hope for legislation to reduce acid precipitation and urban smog died as Congress again failed to complete a much needed overhaul of the Clean Air Act.

Water: Worse. There were enormous offshore algae blooms that were strangling fish by the millions, and toxins that were shutting down shellfish operations along U.S. coastlines. Yet it was the pollution that appeared last summer on the country's beaches that grabbed the headlines. In the West water-supply problems dominated, whereas in the Upper Midwest water quality continued to be a much more serious problem than supply. The Great Lakes remained in trouble. Scientists have found traces of some 400 toxic chemicals in the water. For the 117 million Americans who rely on underground wells for drinking water, EPA data show pesticides have percolated into well water in some 34 states with harmful levels found in at least one out of every nine wells tested. Meanwhile, another source of groundwater contamination—leading hazardous waste sites—continued to threaten the nation in 1988.

Energy: Same. There was no perceptible change in the country's energy situation in 1988, but there were significant changes in perception. The International Energy Agency announced in January that it had been underestimating the world oil consumption by more than a million barrels of oil per day. A few months later the U.S. Geological Survey announced another revision. Using a new method of analysis, the agency concluded the nation has little more than half the undiscovered crude oil projected earlier. A report on the impact on the Alaskan environment of development of the Prudhoe Bay oil field indicated that environmental damage at Prudhoe Bay has been vastly greater than predicted, thereby adding another factor in the debate over oil exploration in Alaska's Arctic National Wildlife Reserve. As 1988 came to a close, the country still lacked a clear national policy linking the nation's energy future to the efficient use of fossile fuels and the development of benign alternatives to such fuels.

Forests: Borderline Same/Worse. In the nation's forests, as elsewhere, natural disaster was the hallmark for 1988. Some four million acres in seven western states and Alaska had been burned over. But fires did not replace the principal threat to the well-being of America's forests: the world's seemingly limitless appetite for more wood products. Demand from the timber industry for wood from the national forests continues to be high. In 1987, nearly 13 billion board feet of timber were cut on national forest lands—an all-time record. In planning for the next half-century, the Forest Service projected high levels of logging and extension road building to open up remote areas to logging in 19 national forests of the Pacific Northwest. On the positive side, the Forest Service agreed to halt logging operations in some areas of Idaho not already served by logging roads and canceled a timber sale near Idaho's Lake Pend Oreille.

Soil: Worse. Only three times since the 1930s have the farms and ranches of the Great Plains lost more topsoil to drought and winds than they did in the spring of 1988. The government recorded excessive soil erosion on 13 million acres during the spring. Cumulative effects of the damage are of grave concern. The lack of crop residue on the dusty fields meant that more severe wind erosion is likely to occur in the future; water erosion by winter rains and spring runoff was expected to be worse than normal; and farmlands were strewn with a variety of agricultural chemicals that had not been activated by water or decomposed by growth. Meanwhile the U.S. Soil Conservation Service was undercutting application of the soil-conservation and "swampbuster" provisions of the 1985 federal farm bill.

Quality of Life: Worse. Throughout 1988 most Americans did not have to travel far to see grim reminders of how environmental contamination is

affecting their lives. In New York sportsmen who purchased state fishing licenses were warned that any fish caught should be consumed sparingly, if at all. Along the Gulf Coast nearly a third of Lousiana's oyster beds and half of Texas' shell fish beds were either temporarily closed or declared permanently off limits due to contamination. On the East Coast pollution-caused beach closings were more prevalent than in any year in recent history. In Washington, D.C. Environmental Protection Agency workers picketed the agency's headquarters building, charging that the air inside was so contaminated it caused fatigue, dizziness, and made breathing difficult. An estimated one-fifth to one-third of all U.S. buildings are now considered "sick."

Some Endangered and Threatened Species of the World[1]

Common name	Scientific name	Listed range
MAMMALS		
Bear, brown	*Ursus arctos pruinosus*	China (Tibet)
Bear, brown or grizzly[2]	*Ursus arctos horribilis*	Western U.S. (not Alaska)
Cat, leopard	*Felis bengalensis bengalensis*	Eastern Asia
Cat, tiger	*Felis tigrinus*	Costa Rica to northern Argentina
Cheetah	*Acinonyx jubatus*	Africa to India
Chimpanzee[2]	*Pan troglodytes*	Western and Central Africa
Chinchilla	*Chinchilla brevicaudata boliviana*	Bolivia
Deer, Columbian white-tailed	*Odocoileus virginianus leucurus*	U.S. (Ore., Wash.)
Deer, marsh	*Blastocerus dichotomus*	Argentina, Uruguay, Bolivia Paraguay, Brazil
Deer, musk	*Moschus moschiferus moschiferus*	Central and East Asia
Elephant, Asian	*Elephas maximus*	Southcentral and Southeast Asia
Gazelle, Clark's (Dibatag)	*Ammodorcas clarkei*	Somalia, Ethiopia
Gazelle, slender-horned (Rhim)	*Gazella leptoceros*	Sudan, Algeria, Egypt, Libya
Gorilla	*Gorilla gorilla*	Central and western Africa
Ibex, Walia	*Capra walie*	Ethiopia
Jaguar	*Panthera onca*	Central and South America, including Mexico
Kangaroo, red[2]	*Macropus (=Megaleia) rufus*	Australia
Leopard	*Panthera pardus*	Africa and Asia
Leopard, snow	*Panthera uncia*	Central Asia
Lion, Asiatic	*Panthera leo persica*	Turkey to India
Mandrill	*Papio sphinx*	Equatorial West Africa
Monkey, black howler[2]	*Alouatta pigra*	Mexico, Guatemala, Belize
Ocelot	*Felis pardalis*	Central and South America, Ariz., Texas
Orangutan	*Pongo pygmaeus*	Borneo, Sumatra
Otter, southern sea[2]	*Enhydra lutris nereis*	West coast U.S. (Wash., Ore., Calif.), south to Mexico (Baja Calif.)
Panther, Florida	*Felis concolor coryi*	U.S. (La. and Ark., east to S.C. and Fla.)
Prairie dog, Utah[2]	*Cynomys parvidens*	U.S. (Utah)
Pronghorn, Sonoran	*Antilocapra americana sonoriensis*	U.S. (Ariz.), Mexico
Rat, Morro Bay kangaroo	*Dipodomys heermanni morroensis*	U.S. (Calif.)
Rhinoceros, great Indian	*Rhinoceros unicornis*	India, Nepal
Sloth, Brazilian three-toed	*Bradypus torquatus*	Brazil
Tiger	*Panthera tigris*	Temperate and tropical Asia
Whale, humpback	*Megaptera novaeangliae*	Oceanic
Wolf, gray	*Canis lupus*	U.S. (48 conterminous other than Minn.[2]), Mexico
Zebra, mountain	*Equus zebra zebra*	South Africa
BIRDS		
Albatross, short-tailed	*Diomedea albatrus*	North Pacific Ocean: Japan, U.S.S.R

Common name	Scientific name	Listed Range
Condor, Andean	*Vultur gryphus*	Colombia to Chile and Argentina
Eagle, bald	*Haliaeetus leucocephalus*	Conterminous U.S. (except Wash., Ore., Minn., Wis., Mich.²)
Falcon, Eurasian peregrine	*Falco peregrinus peregrinus*	Europe, Eurasia south to Africa and Mideast
Parakeet, paradise (=beautiful)	*Psephotus pulcherrimus*	Australia
Pelican, brown	*Pelecanus occidentalis*	U.S. (La., Miss., Texas, Calif.), West Indies, Central and South America, coastal
Penguin, Galápagos	*Spheniscus mendiculus*	Ecuador (Galápagos Islands)
Stork, oriental white	*Ciconia ciconia boyciana*	China, Japan, Korea, U.S.S.R.
REPTILES		
Crocodile, American	*Crocodylus acutus*	U.S. (Fla.), Mexico, South America, Central America, Caribbean
Iguana, Anegada ground	*Cyclura pinguis*	West Indies, British Virgin Is. (Anegada Is.)
Python, Indian	*Python molurus molurus*	Sri Lanka, India
Snake, Atlantic salt marsh²	*Nerodia fasciata taeniata*	U.S. (Fla.)
AMPHIBIANS		
Frog, Israel painted	*Discoglossus nigriventer*	Israel
Toad, African viviparous	*Nectophrynoides* spp.	Tanzania, Guinea, Ivory Coast, Cameroon, Liberia, Ethiopia
FISH		
Catfish, giant	*Pangasianodon gigas*	Thailand
Trout, greenback cutthroat²	*Salmo clarki stomias*	U.S. (Colo.)

1. Due to space limitations, does not include all mammals, birds, reptiles, amphibians, and fish or any clams, crustaceans, snails, insects, and plants. For a complete list, write Publications Unit, U.S. Fish and Wildlife Service, Washington, D.C. 20240. 2. Threatened. *Source:* Department of the Interior, Fish and Wildlife Service.

Animal Group Terminology

Source: James Doherty, Curator of Mammals, N.Y. Zoological Society, and *Information Please* data.

ants: colony
bears: sleuth, sloth
bees: grist, hive, swarm
birds: flight, volery
cattle: drove
cats: clutter, clowder
chicks: brood, clutch
clams: bed
cranes: sedge, seige
crows: murder
doves: dule
ducks: brace, team
elephants: herd
elks: gang
finches: charm
fish: school, shoal, draught
foxes: leash, skulk
geese: flock, gaggle, skein
gnats: cloud, horde
goats: trip

gorillas: band
hares: down, husk
hawks: cast
hens: brood
hogs: drift
horses: pair, team
hounds: cry, mute, pack
kangaroos: troop
kittens: kindle, litter
larks: exaltation
lions: pride
locusts: plague
magpies: tidings
mules: span
nightingales: watch
oxen: yoke
oysters: bed
parrots: company
partridges: covey

peacocks: muster, ostentation
pheasants: nest, bouquet
pigs: litter
ponies: string
quail: bevy, covey
rabbits: nest
seals: pod
sheep: drove, flock
sparrows: host
storks: mustering
swans: bevy, wedge
swine: sounder
toads: knot
turkeys: rafter
turtles: bale
vipers: nest
whales: gam, pod
wolves: pack, route
woodcocks: fall

Animal Names: Male, Female, and Young

Animal	Male	Female	Young	Animal	Male	Female	Young	Animal	Male	Female	Young
Ass	Jack	Jenny	Foal	Duck	Drake	Duck	Duckling	Sheep	Ram	Ewe	Lamb
Bear	Boar	Sow	Cub	Elephant	Bull	Cow	Calf	Swan	Cob	Pen	Cygnet
Cat	Tom	Queen	Kitten	Fox	Dog	Vixen	Cub	Swine	Boar	Sow	Piglet
Cattle	Bull	Cow	Calf	Goose	Gander	Goose	Gosling	Tiger	Tiger	Tigress	Cub
Chicken	Rooster	Hen	Chick	Horse	Stallion	Mare	Foal	Whale	Bull	Cow	Calf
Deer	Buck	Doe	Fawn	Lion	Lion	Lioness	Cub	Wolf	Dog	Bitch	Pup
Dog	Dog	Bitch	Pup	Rabbit	Buck	Doe	Bunny				

Source: James Doherty, Curator of Mammals, N.Y. Zoological Society.

Speed of Animals

Most of the following measurements are for maximum speeds over approximate quarter-mile distances. Exceptions—which are included to give a wide range of animals—are the lion and elephant, whose speeds were clocked in the act of charging; the whippet, which was timed over a 200-yard course; the cheetah over a 100-yard distance; man for a 15-yard segment of a 100-yard run; and the black mamba, six-lined race runner, spider, giant tortoise, three-toed sloth, and garden snail, which were measured over various small distances.

Animal	Speed mph	Animal	Speed mph	Animal	Speed mph
Cheetah	70	Mongolian wild ass	40	Man	27.89
Pronghorn antelope	61	Greyhound	39.35	Elephant	25
Wildebeest	50	Whippet	35.5	Black mamba snake	20
Lion	50	Rabbit (domestic)	35	Six-lined race runner	18
Thomson's gazelle	50	Mule deer	35	Squirrel	12
Quarter horse	47.5	Jackal	35	Pig (domestic)	11
Elk	45	Reindeer	32	Chicken	9
Cape hunting dog	45	Giraffe	32	Spider (Tegenearia atrica)	1.17
Coyote	43	White-tailed deer	30	Giant Tortoise	0.17
Gray fox	42	Wart hog	30	Three-toed sloth	0.15
Hyena	40	Grizzly bear	30	Garden snail	0.03
Zebra	40	Cat (domestic)	30		

Source: Natural History Magazine, March 1974, copyright 1974. The American Museum of Natural History; and James Doherty, Curator of Mammals, N.Y. Zoological Society.

Gestation, Incubation, and Longevity of Certain Animals

Animal	Gestation or incubation, in days & (average)	Longevity, in years & (record exceptions)	Animal	Gestation or incubation, in days & (average)	Longevity, in years & (record exceptions)
Ass	365	18–20 (63)	Horse	329–345 (336)	20–25 (50+)
Bear	180–240 [1]	15–30 (47)	Kangaroo	32–39 [1]	4–6 (23)
Cat	52–69 (63)	10–12 (26+)	Lion	105–113 (108)	10 (29)
Chicken	22	7–8 (14)	Man	253–303	[2]
Cow	c. 280	9–12 (39)	Monkey	139–270 [1]	12–15 [1] (29)
Deer	197–300 [1]	10–15 (26)	Mouse	19–31 [1]	1–3 (4)
Dog	53–71 (63)	10–12 (24)	Parakeet (Budgerigar)	17–20 (18)	8 (12+)
Duck	21–35 [1] (28)	10 (15)	Pig	101–130 (115)	10 (22)
Elephant	510–730 (624) [1]	30–40 (71)	Pigeon	11–19	10–12 (39)
Fox	51–63 [1]	8–10 (14)	Rabbit	30–35 (31)	6–8 (15)
Goat	136–160 (151)	12 (17)	Rat	21	3 (5)
Groundhog	31–32	4–9	Sheep	144–152 (151) [1]	12 (16)
Guinea pig	58–75 (68)	3 (6)	Squirrel	44	8–9 (15)
Hamster, golden	15–17	2 (8)	Whale	365–547 [1]	
Hippopotamus	220–255 (240)	30 (49+)	Wolf	60–63	10–12 (16)

1. Depending on kind. 2. For life expectancy charts, see Index. Source: James Doherty, Curator of Mammals, N.Y. Zoological Society.

Zoological Gardens

North America abounds in zoos from Canada to Mexico. The Metro Toronto Zoo, opened in 1974, is one of the largest in the world. Its six pavilions simulate the animals' natural habitats. So does the Calgary Zoo which also has a children's zoo. Mexico City's Chapultepec Park includes a large zoo featuring one of the few pairs of pandas outside of Red China, and a children's zoo.

The first zoological garden in the United States was established in Philadelphia in 1874. Since that time nearly every large city in the country has acquired a zoo. Among the largest are San Diego's on the West Coast; Chicago's Brookfield Zoo and those of St. Louis and Kansas City in the Middle West; New Orleans' Audubon Park and Zoological Garden in the South; and in the East the New York Zoological Society's park in the Bronx. The National Zoological Park in Washington, D.C., in a beautiful setting of hills, woods, and streams, was established in 1890 by an act of Congress. The major U.S. zoos now have created large natural-habitat areas for their collections.

In Europe, zoological gardens have long been popular public institutions. The modern concept of zoo keeping may be dated from 1752 with the founding of the Imperial Menagerie at the Schönbrunn Palace in Vienna. It was opened to the public in 1765 and is still in operation. In 1793 the zoological collection of the Jardin des Plantes was established in Paris in the Bois de Boulogne. At

Antwerp the Royal Zoological Society founded a large menagerie in 1843. Now its aviary is noted for the principle of lighted and darkened spaces for confining the birds. Germany's famous Tiergarten zoo, in West Berlin, was founded in 1841 and officially opened in 1844. East Berlin has founded its own zoo.

In the British Isles, the Zoological Society of London established its collection in Regent's Park in 1828. It was also responsible for the establishment of the prototype of the open-range zoo, Whipsnade Park, in 1932. Edinburgh's zoo is famous for its collection of penguins, the largest colony in captivity.

U.S. Zoos and Aquariums

Source: The facilities listed are members of, and accredited by, the American Association of Zoological Parks and Aquariums to ensure that they are maintaining professional standards.

Abilene Zoological Gardens, Texas
Alexandria Zoological Park, La.
Arizona-Sonora Desert Museum, Tucson
Audubon Park and Zoological Garden, New Orleans
John Ball Zoological Gardens, Grand Rapids, Mich.
Baltimore Zoo, Md.
Beardsley Zoological Gardens, Bridgeport, Conn.
Belle Isle Zoo and Aquarium, Detroit
Binder Park Zoo, Battle Creek, Mich.
Birmingham Zoo, Ala.
Blank Park Zoo of Des Moines, Iowa
Brandywine Zoo, Wilmington, Del.
Brookgreen Gardens, Murrells Inlet, S.C.
Buffalo Zoological Gardens, N.Y.
Burnet Park Zoo, Rochester, N.Y.
Busch Gardens, Tampa, Fla.
Caldwell Zoo, Texas
Central Florida Zoological Park, Lake Monroe, Fla.
Central Texas Zoo, Waco, Texas
Cheyenne Mountain Zoological Park, Colorado Springs
Chicago Zoological Park, Brookfield, Ill.
Cincinnati Zoo and Botanical Garden, Ohio
Cleveland Metroparks Zoo, Ohio
Columbus Zoological Gardens, Ohio
Dallas Aquarium, Texas
Dallas Zoo, Texas
Denver Zoological Gardens, Colo.
Detroit Zoological Park, Mich.
Dickerson Park Zoo, Springfield, Mo.
Discovery Island, Buena Vista, Fla.
Dreher Park Zoo, West Palm Beach, Fla.
El Paso Zoological Park, Texas
Emporia Zoo, Kan.
Erie Zoo, Pa.
Florida Cypress Gardens, Inc., Fla.
Fort Wayne Children's Zoo, Ind.
Fort Worth Zoological Park, Texas
Fossil Rim Wildlife Ranch, Fort Worth, Texas
Fresno Zoo, Calif.
Glen Oak Zoo, Ill.
Greater Baton Rouge Zoo, La.
Greenville Zoo, S.C.
Hogle Zoological Gardens, Salt Lake City, Utah
Honolulu Zoo, Hawaii
Houston Zoological Gardens, Texas
Indianapolis Zoo, Ind.
International Crane Foundation, Baraboo, Wis.
Jacksonville Zoological Park, Fla.
Kansas City Zoological Gardens, Mo.
Knoxville Zoological Park, Tenn.
Lake Superior Zoological Gardens, Duluth, Minn.
Lincoln Park Zoological Gardens, Chicago
Little Rock Zoological Gardens, Ark.
Living Desert, The, Palm Desert, Calif.
Los Angeles Zoo, Calif.
Louisville Zoological Garden, Ky.
Marine World Africa USA, Redwood City, Calif.
Memphis Zoological Gardens and Aquarium, Tenn.

Mesker Park Zoo, Evansville, Ind.
Miami Metrozoo, Fla.
Miller Park Zoo, Bloomington, Ill.
Milwaukee County Zoological Gardens, Wis.
Minnesota Zoological Garden, Apple Valley, Minn.
Monkey Jungle, Inc., Miami, Fla.
Monterey Bay Aquarium, Calif.
Montgomery Zoo, Ala.
Mystic Marinelife Aquarium, Mystic, Conn.
National Aquarium in Baltimore, Md.
National Zoological Park, Washington, D.C.
New England Aquarium, Boston
New York Aquarium, Brooklyn, N.Y.
New York Zoological Park, Bronx, N.Y.
North Carolina Zoological Park, Asheboro, N.C.
Northwest Trek Wildlife Park, Eatonville, Wash.
Oakland Zoo, Calif.
Oglebay's Good Children's Zoo, Wheeling, W.Va.
Oklahoma City Zoological Park, Okla.
Omaha's Henry Doorly Zoo, Neb.
Parrot Jungle, Inc., Miami, Fla.
Clyde Peeling's Reptiland Ltd., Williamsport, Pa.
Philadelphia Zoological Garden, Pa.
Phoenix Zoo, Ariz.
Pittsburgh Aviary, Pa.
Pittsburgh Zoo, Pa.
Point Defiance Zoo and Aquarium, Tacoma, Wash.
Gladys Porter Zoo, Brownsville, Texas
Potawatomi Zoo, South Bend, Ind.
Potter Park Zoo, Lansing, Mich.
Racine Zoological Gardens, Wis.
Reid Park Zoo, Tucson, Ariz.
Lee Richardson Zoo, Garden City, Kan.
Rio Grande Zoological Park, Albuquerque, N.M.
Riverbanks Zoological Park, Columbia, S.C.
Henson Robinson Zoo, Springfield, Ill.
Roosevelt Zoo, Minot, N.D.
Ross Park Zoo, Binghamton, N.Y.
Sacramento Zoo, Calif.
St. Augustine Alligator Farm, Fla.
St. Louis Zoological Park, Mo.
St. Paul's Como Zoo, Minn.
Salisbury Zoological Park, Md.
San Antonio Zoological Gardens and Aquarium, Texas
San Diego Wild Animal Park, Calif.
San Diego Zoo, Calif.
San Francisco Zoological Gardens, Calif.
Santa Ana Zoo, Calif.
Santa Barbara Zoological Gardens, Calif.
Sante Fe Teaching Zoo, Fla.
Sea Life Park, Waimanalo, Hawaii
Sea World of California, San Diego
Sea World of Florida, Orlando
Sea World of Ohio, Aurora
The Seattle Aquarium, Wash.
Sedgwick County Zoo and Botanical Garden, Wichita, Kan.
Seneca Park Zoo, Rochester, N.Y.

John G. Shedd Aquarium, Chicago
Staten Island Zoo, N.Y.
Toledo Zoological Gardens, Ohio
Topeka Zoological Park, Kan.
Ellen Trout Zoo, Lufkin, Texas
Tulsa Zoological Park, Okla.
Utica Zoo, N.Y.
Van Saun Park Zoo, Paramus, N.J.
Henry Vilas Zoo, Madison, Wis.
Virginia Zoological Park, Norfolk, Va.
Waikiki Aquarium, Hawaii

Washington Park Zoo, Portland, Ore.
Wild Animal Habitat, Kings Island, Ohio
Wildlife Safari, Inc. Winston, Ore.
Wildlife World Zoo, Litchfield Park, Ariz.
Roger Williams Park Zoo, Providence, R.I.
Woodland Park Zoological Gardens, Seattle
The Zoo, Gulf Breeze, Fla.
Zoo Atlanta, Ga.
ZOOAMERICA North American Wildlife Park, Hershey, Pa.

The National Park System

Source: Department of the Interior, National Park Service.

The National Park System of the United States is administered by the National Park Service, a bureau of the Department of the Interior. Started with the establishment of Yellowstone National Park in 1872, the system includes not only the most extraordinary and spectacular scenic exhibits in the United States but also a large number of sites distinguished either for their historic or prehistoric importance or scientific interest, or for their superior recreational assets. The number and extent of the various types of areas that make up the system follow.

Type of area	Number	Total acreage[1]	Type of area	Number	Total acreage[1]
International Historic Site	1	35.39	National Monument	79	4,884,610.12
National Battlefield	11	12,771.90	National Park	50	47,319,321.07
National Battlefield Park	3	8,767.39	National Parkway	4	168,618.32
National Battlefield Site	1	1.00	National Preserve	14	22,155,497.84
National Capital Park	1	6,468.88	National Recreation Area	18	3,686,923.39
National Historic Site	68	18,503.10	National Rivers[2]	14	553,226.73
National Historical Park	29	151,632.86	National Scenic Trail	3	172,202.61
National Lakeshore	4	227,244.37	National Seashore	10	597,096.47
National Mall	1	146.35	Park (other)	10	40,120.70
National Memorial	23	7,949.16	White House	1	18.07
National Military Park	9	34,046.72	**Total**	**354**	**80,005,167.05**

1. Acreages as of December 31, 1988. 2. National Park System units and components of the Wild & Scenic Rivers System.

National Parks

Name, location, and year authorized	Acreage	Outstanding characteristics
Acadia (Maine), 1919	41,408.63	Rugged seashore on Mt. Desert Island and adjacent mainland
Arches (Utah), 1971	73,378.98	Unusual stone arches, windows, pedestals caused by erosion
Badlands (S.D.), 1978	243,244.48	Arid land of fossils, prairie, bison, deer, bighorn, antelope
Big Bend (Tex.), 1935	802,541.30	Mountains and desert bordering the Rio Grande
Biscayne (Fla.), 1980	173,039.39	Aquatic, coral reef park south of Miami was a national monument, 1968–80
Bryce Canyon (Utah), 1924	35,835.08	Area of grotesque eroded rocks brilliantly colored
Canyonlands (Utah), 1964	337,570.43	Colorful wilderness with impressive red-rock canyons, spires, arches
Capitol Reef (Utah), 1971	241,904.26	Highly colored sedimentary rock formations in high, narrow gorges
Carlsbad Caverns (N.M.), 1930	46,755.33	The world's largest known caves
Channel Islands (Calif.) 1980	249,353.77	Area is rich in marine mammals, sea birds, endangered species and archeology
Crater Lake (Ore.), 1902	183,224.05	Deep blue lake in heart of inactive volcano
Denali (Alaska), 1917	4,716,726.00	Mt. McKinley National Park was renamed and enlarged by Act of Dec. 2, 1980. Contains Mt. McKinley, N. America's highest mountain (20,320 ft)
Everglades (Fla.), 1934	1,398,938.40	Subtropical area with abundant bird and animal life
Gates of the Arctic (Alaska), 1980	7,523,888.00	Diverse north central wilderness contains part of Brooks Range
Glacier (Mont.), 1910	1,013,572.42	Rocky Mountain scenery with many glaciers and lakes
Glacier Bay (Alaska), 1980	3,225,284.00	Park was a national monument (1925–1980) popular for wildlife, whale-watching, glacier-calving, and scenery
Grand Canyon (Ariz.), 1919	1,218,375.24	Mile-deep gorge, 4 to 18 miles wide, 217 miles long

Grand Teton (Wyo.), 1929	309,993.93	Picturesque range of high mountain peaks
Great Basin (Nev.), 1986	77,109.15	Exceptional scenic, biologic, and geologic attractions
Great Smoky Mts. (N.C.-Tenn), 1926	520,269.44	Highest mountain range east of Black Hills; luxuriant plant life
Guadalupe Mountains (Tex.), 1966	86,416.01	Contains highest point in Texas: Guadalupe Peak (8,751 ft)
Haleakala (Hawaii), 1960	28,655.25	World-famous 10,023-ft. Haleakala volcano (dormant)
Hawaii Volcanoes (Hawaii), 1916	229,177.03	Spectacular volcanic area; luxuriant vegetation at lower levels
Hot Springs (Ark.), 1921	5,839.24	47 mineral hot springs said to have therapeutic value
Isle Royale (Mich.), 1931	571.790.11	Largest wilderness island in Lake Superior; moose, wolves, lakes
Katmai (Alaska), 1980	3,716,000.00	Expansion may assure brown bear's preservation. Park was national monument 1918–80; is known for fishing, 1912 eruption, bears
Kenai Fjords (Alaska), 1980	669,541.00	Mountain goats, marine mammals, birdlife are features at this seacoast park near Seward
Kings Canyon (Calif.), 1940	461,901.20	Huge canyons; high mountains; giant sequoias
Kobuk Valley (Alaska), 1980	1,750,421.00	Native culture and anthropology center around the broad Kobuk River in northwest Alaska
Lake Clark (Alaska), 1980	2,636,839.00	Park provides scenic and wilderness recreation across Cook Inlet from Anchorage
Lassen Volcanic (Calif.), 1916	106,372.36	Exhibits of impressive volcanic phenomena
Mammoth Cave (Ky.), 1926	52,419.00	Vast limestone labyrinth with underground river
Mesa Verde (Colo.), 1906	52,085.14	Best-preserved prehistoric cliff dwellings in United States
Mount Rainier (Wash.), 1899	235,404.00	Single-peak glacial system; dense forests, flowered meadows
North Cascades (Wash.), 1968	504,780.94	Roadless Alpine landscape; jagged peaks; mountain lakes; glaciers
Olympic (Wash.), 1938	921,942.14	Finest Pacific Northwest rain forest; scenic mountain park
Petrified Forest (Ariz.), 1962	93,532.57	Extensive natural exhibit of petrified wood
Redwood (Calif.), 1968	110,132.40	Coastal redwood forests; contains world's tallest known tree (369.2 ft)
Rocky Mountain (Colo.), 1915	265,200.07	Section of the Rocky Mountains; 107 named peaks over 10,000 ft
Samoa (American Samoa)	6,000.00	Samoa National Park, American Samoa: two rain forest preserves and a coral reef on the island of Ofu are home to unique tropical animals. The park also includes several thousand acres on the islands of Tutuila and Ta'u.
Sequoia (Calif.), 1890	402,482.38	Giant sequoias; magnificent High Sierra scenery, including Mt. Whitney
Shenandoah (Va.), 1926	195,382.13	Tree-covered mountains; scenic Skyline Drive
Theodore Roosevelt (N.D.), 1978	70,416.39	Scenic valley of Little Missouri River; T.R. Ranch; Wildlife
Virgin Islands (U.S. V.I.), 1956	14,688.87	Beaches; lush hills; prehistoric Carib Indian relics
Voyageurs (Minn.), 1971	218,035.93	Wildlife, canoeing, fishing, and hiking
Wind Cave (S.D.), 1903	28,292.08	Limestone caverns in Black Hills; buffalo herd
Wrangell-St. Elias (Alaska), 1980	8,331,604.00	Largest Park System area has abundant wildlife, second highest peak in U.S. (Mt. St. Elias); adjoins Canadian park
Yellowstone (Wyo.-Mont.-Idaho), 1872	2,219,790.71	World's greatest geyser area; abundant falls, wildlife, and canyons
Yosemite (Calif.), 1890	761,170.20	Mountains; inspiring gorges and waterfalls; giant sequoias
Zion (Utah), 1919	146,597.64	Multicolored gorge in heart of southern Utah desert

NATIONAL HISTORICAL PARKS

Name and location	Total acreage
Appomattox Court House (Va.)	1,325.08
Boston (Mass.)	41.03
Chaco Culture (N.M.)	33,974.29
Chesapeake and Ohio Canal (Md.-W.Va.-D.C.)	20,781.00
Colonial (Va.)	9,327.37
Cumberland Gap (Ky.-Tenn.-Va.)	20,274.42
George Rogers Clark (Ind.)	26.17
Harpers Ferry (W.Va.-Md.)	2,238.60
Independence (Pa.)	44.85
Jean Lafitte (La.)	20,020.00
Kalaupapa (Hawaii)	10,778.88
Klondike Goldrush (Alaska, Wash.)	13,191.35
Kaloko-Honokohau (Hawaii)	1,160.91
Lowell (Mass.)	136.04
Lyndon B. Johnson (Tex.)	1,570.61
Minute Man (Mass.)	750.00
Morristown (N.J.)	1,670.61

Name and location	Total acreage
Natchez (Miss.)	0.00
Nez Perce (Idaho)	2,108.89
Púuchonua o Honaunau (Hawaii)	181.80
San Antonio Missions (Tex.)	492.66
San Franisco Maritime (Calif.)	50.00
San Juan Island (Wash.)	1,751.99
Saratoga (N.Y.)	3,392.82
Sitka (Alaska)	106.83
Valley Forge (Pa.)	3,468.06
War in the Pacific (Guam)	1,960.15
Women's Rights (N.Y.)	5.54
Zuni-Cibola (N.M.)	800.00

NATIONAL MONUMENTS

Agate Fossil Beds (Neb.)	3,055.22
Alibates Flint Quarries (Tex.)	1,370.97
Aniakchak (Alaska)	137,176.00
Aztec Ruins (N.M.)	319.03
Bandelier (N.M.)	32,737.20

Name and location	Total acreage
Black Canyon (Colo.)	20,766.14
Booker T. Washington (Va.)	223.92
Buck Island Reef (U.S. V.I.)	880.00
Cabrillo (Calif.)	143.94
Canyon de Chelly (Ariz.)	83,840.00
Cape Krusenstern (Alaska)	659,807.00
Capulin Volcano (N.M.)	792.84
Casa Grande (Ariz.)	472.50
Castillo de San Marcos (Fla.)	20.48
Castle Clinton (N.Y.)	1.00
Cedar Breaks (Utah)	6,154.60
Chiricahua (Ariz.)	11,984.80
Colorado (Colo.)	20,453.93
Congaree Swamp (S.C.)	22,200.00
Craters of the Moon (Idaho)	53,545.05
Custer Battlefield (Mont.)	765.34
Death Valley (Calif.-Nev.)	2,067,627.68
Devils Postpile (Calif.)	798.46
Devils Tower (Wyo.)	1,346.91
Dinosaur (Utah-Colo.)	211,141.69
Effigy Mounds (Iowa)	1,481.39
El Malpais (N.M.)	114,716.28
El Morro (N.M.)	1,278.72
Florissant Fossil Beds (Colo.)	5,998.09
Fort Frederica (Ga.)	216.35
Fort Jefferson (Fla.)	64,700.00
Fort Matanzas (Fla.)	227.76
Fort McHenry (Md.)	43.26
Fort Pulaski (Ga.)	5,623.10
Fort Stanwix (N.Y.)	15.52
Fort Sumter (S.C.)	196.75
Fort Union (N.M.)	720.60
Fossil Butte (Wyo.)	8,198.00
George Washington Birthplace (Va.)	538.23
George Washington Carver (Mo.)	210.00
Gila Cliff Dwellings (N.M.)	533.13
Grand Portage (Minn.)	709.97
Great Sand Dunes (Colo.)	38,662.18
Hagerman Fossil Beds (Idaho)	4,394.00
Hohokam Pima (Ariz.)	1,690.00
Homestead (Neb.)	194.57
Hovenweep (Utah-Colo.)	784.93
Jewel Cave (S.D.)	1,273.51
John Day Fossil Beds (Ore.)	14,014.10
Joshua Tree (Calif.)	559,954.50
Lava Beds (Calif.)	46,559.87
Montezuma Castle (Ariz.)	857.69
Mound City Group (Ohio)	270.20
Muir Woods (Calif.)	553.55
Natural Bridges (Utah)	7,636.49
Navajo (Ariz.)	360.00
Ocmulgee (Ga.)	683.48
Oregon Caves (Ore.)	487.98
Organ Pipe Cactus (Ariz.)	330,688.86
Pecos (N.M.)	364.80
Pinnacles (Calif.)	16,265.44
Pipe Spring (Ariz.)	40.00
Pipestone (Minn.)	281.78
Poverty Point	910.85
Rainbow Bridge (Utah)	160.00
Russell Cave (Ala.)	310.45
Saguaro (Ariz.)	83,573.88
Salinas (N.M.)	1,076.94
Scotts Bluff (Neb.)	2,997.08
Statue of Liberty (N.Y.-N.J.)	58.38
Sunset Crater (Ariz.)	3,040.00
Timpanogos Cave (Utah)	250.00
Tonto (Ariz.)	1,120.00
Tumacacori (Ariz.)	16.52
Tuzigoot (Ariz.)	800.62
Walnut Canyon (Ariz.)	2,249.46
White Sands (N.M.)	143,732.92
Wupatki (Ariz.)	35,253.24

Name and location	Total acreage
Yucca House (Colo.)	10.00

NATIONAL PRESERVES

Aniakchak (Alaska)	465,603.00
Bering Land Bridge (Alaska)	2,784,960.00
Big Cypress (Fla.)	716,000.00
Big Thicket (Tex.)	85,732.85
City of Rock, (Idaho)	14,320.00
Denali (Alaska)	1,311,365.00
Gates of the Arctic (Alaska)	948,629.00
Glacier Bay (Alaska)	57,884.00
Katmai (Alaska)	374,000.00
Lake Clark (Alaska)	1,407,293.00
Noatak (Alaska)	6,574,481.00
Timucuan Ecological and Historic Preserve (Fla.)	35,000.00
Wrangell-St. Elias (Alaska)	4,856,720.99
Yukon-Charley (Alaska)	2,523,509.00

NATIONAL MILITARY PARKS

Chickamauga and Chattanooga (Ga.-Tenn.)	8,106.04
Fredericksburg and Spotsylvania (Va.)	5,907.45
Gettysburg (Pa.)	3,895.70
Guilford Courthouse (N.C.)	220.25
Horseshoe Bend (Ala.)	2,040.00
Kings Mountain (S.C.)	3,945.29
Pea Ridge (Ark.)	4,300.35
Shiloh (Tenn.)	3,837.50
Vicksburg (Miss.)	1,619.89

NATIONAL BATTLEFIELDS

Antietam (Md.)	3,244.42
Big Hole (Mont.)	655.61
Cowpens (S.C.)	841.56
Fort Donelson (Tenn.)	536.66
Fort Necessity (Pa.)	902.80
Monocacy (Md.)	1,647.01
Moores Creek (N.C.)	86.52
Petersburg (Va.)	2,735.38
Stones River (Tenn.)	330.86
Tupelo (Miss.)	1.00
Wilson's Creek (Mo.)	1,749.91

NATIONAL BATTLEFIELD PARKS

Kennesaw Mountain (Ga.)	2,884.52
Manassas (Va.)	5,113.71
Richmond (Va.)	769.16

NATIONAL BATTLEFIELD SITE

Brices Cross Roads (Miss.)	1.00

NATIONAL HISTORIC SITES

Abraham Lincoln Birthplace (Ky.)	116.50
Adams (Mass.)	9.82
Allegheny Portage Railroad (Pa.)	1,246.97
Andersonville (Ga.)	475.72
Andrew Johnson (Tenn.)	16.68
Bent's Old Fort (Colo.)	799.80
Boston African American (Mass.)	0.00
Carl Sandburg Home (N.C.)	263.52
Charles Pinckney (S.C.)	25.00
Christiansted (V.I.)	27.15
Clara Barton (Md.)	8.59
Edgar Allan Poe (Pa.)	0.52
Edison (N.J.)	21.25
Eisenhower (Pa.)	690.46
Eleanor Roosevelt (N.Y.)	180.50
Eugene O'Neill (Calif.)	13.19
Ford's Theatre (Lincoln Museum) (D.C.)	0.29
Fort Bowie (Ariz.)	1,000.00
Fort Davis (Tex.)	460.00
Fort Laramie (Wyo.)	832.85

Name and location	Total acreage
Fort Larned (Kan.)	718.39
Fort Point (Calif.)	29.00
Fort Raleigh (N.C.)	157.27
Fort Scott (Kan.)	16.69
Fort Smith (Ark.-Okla.)	75.00
Fort Union Trading Post (N.D.-Mont.)	442.45
Fort Vancouver (Wash.)	208.89
Frederick Douglass Home (D.C.)	8.53
Frederick Law Olmsted (Mass.)	1.75
Friendship Hill (Pa.)	674.56
Golden Spike (Utah)	2,735.28
Grant-Kohrs Ranch (Mont.)	1,498.65
Hampton (Md.)	62.04
Harry S Truman (Mo.)	0.78
Herbert Hoover (Iowa)	186.80
Home of F. D. Roosevelt (N.Y.)	290.34
Hopewell Furnace (Pa.)	848.06
Hubbell Trading Post (Ariz.)	160.09
James A. Garfield (Ohio)	7.82
Jefferson National Expansion Memorial (Mo.)	190.58
Jimmy Carter (Ga.)	69.55
John F. Kennedy (Mass.)	0.09
John Muir (Calif.)	338.90
Knife River Indian Villages (N.D.)	1,293.35
Lincoln Home (Ill.)	12.24
Longfellow (Mass.)	1.98
Maggie L. Walker (Va.)	1.29
Martin Luther King, Jr. (Ga.)	23.18
Martin Van Buren (N.Y.)	39.58
Ninety Six (S.C.)	989.14
Palo Alto Battlefield (Tex.)	50.00
Pennsylvania Avenue (D.C.)	0.00
Puukohola Heiau (Hawaii)	80.47
Sagamore Hill (N.Y.)	83.02
Saint-Gaudens (N.H.)	148.23
Saint Paul's Church (N.Y.)	6.13
Salem Maritime (Mass.)	8.95
San Juan (P.R.)	75.13
Saugus Iron Works (Mass.)	8.51
Springfield Armory (Mass.)	54.93
Steamtown (Pa.)	42.30
Theodore Roosevelt Birthplace (N.Y.)	0.11
Theodore Roosevelt Inaugural (N.Y.)	1.03
Thomas Stone (Md.)	328.25
Tuskegee Institute (Ala.)	74.39
Vanderbilt Mansion (N.Y.)	211.65
Whitman Mission (Wash.)	98.15
William Howard Taft (Ohio)	3.07

NATIONAL MEMORIALS

Arkansas Post (Ark.)	389.18
Arlington House, the Robert E. Lee Memorial (Va.)	27.91
Chamizal (Tex.)	54.90
Coronado (Ariz.)	4,750.22
De Sota (Fla.)	26.84
Federal Hall (N.Y.)	0.45
Fort Caroline (Fla.)	138.39
Fort Clatsop (Ore.)	125.20
General Grant (N.Y.)	0.76
Hamilton Grange (N.Y.)	0.11
John F. Kennedy Center for Performing Arts (D.C.)	17.50
Johnstown Flood (Pa.)	164.12
Lincoln Boyhood (Ind.)	199.65
Lincoln Memorial (D.C.)	109.63
Lyndon Baines Johnson Memorial Grove on the Potomac (D.C.)	17.00
Mount Rushmore (S.D.)	1,278.45
Roger Williams (R.I.)	4.56
Thaddeus Kosciuszko (Pa.)	0.02

Name and location	Total acreage
Theodore Roosevelt Island (D.C.)	88.50
Thomas Jefferson Memorial (D.C.)	18.36
USS Arizona Memorial (Hawaii)	0.00
Washington Monument (D.C.)	106.01
Wright Brothers (N.C.)	431.40

NATIONAL CEMETERIES[1]

Antietam (Md.)	11.36
Battleground (D.C.)	1.03
Fort Donelson (Tenn.)	15.34
Fredericksburg (Va.)	12.00
Gettysburg (Pa.)	20.58
Poplar Grove (Va.)	8.72
Shiloh (Tenn.)	10.05
Stones River (Tenn.)	20.09
Vicksburg (Miss.)	116.28
Yorktown (Va.)	2.91

NATIONAL SEASHORES

Assateague Island (Md.-Va.)	39,630.93
Canaveral (Fla.)	57,661.69
Cape Cod (Mass.)	43,557.24
Cape Hatteras (N.C.)	30,319.43
Cape Lookout (N.C.)	28,414.74
Cumberland Island (Ga.)	36,415.09
Fire Island (N.Y.)	19,578.55
Gulf Islands (Fla.-Miss.)	139,775.46
Padre Island (Tex.)	130,696.83
Point Reyes (Calif.)	71,046.51

NATIONAL PARKWAYS

Blue Ridge (Va.-N.C.)	85,954.83
George Washington Memorial (Va.-Md.)	7,130.63
John D. Rockefeller, Jr., Memorial (Wyo.)	23,777.22
Natchez Trace (Miss.-Tenn.-Ala.)	51,755.64

NATIONAL LAKESHORES

Apostle Islands (Wis.)	69,371.89
Indiana Dunes (Ind.)	13,841.16
Pictured Rocks (Mich)	72,898.86
Sleeping Bear Dunes (Mich.)	71,132.46

NATIONAL SCENIC RIVERS AND RIVERWAYS

Alagnak Wild River (Alaska)	24,038.00
Big South Fork National River & Recreation Area (Ky.-Tenn.)	122,960.00
Bluestone National Scenic River (W. Va.)	0.00
Buffalo (Ark.)	94,218.57
Delaware (N.Y.-N.J.-Pa.)	1,973.33
Lower St. Croix (Minn.-Wis.)	9,474.93
Mississippi National River & Recreation Area (Minn.)	0.00
Missouri National Recreational River (Neb., S.D.)	0.00
New River Gorge (W. Va.)	62,663.00
Obed Wild & Scenic River (Tenn.)	5,077.02
Ozark (Mo.)	80,788.34
Rio Grande Wild & Scenic (Tex.)	9,600.00
St. Croix (Minn.-Wis.)	67,433.54
Upper Delaware (N.Y., N.J.-Pa.)	75,000.00

NATIONAL CAPITAL PARKS

National Capital Parks (D.C.-Va.-Md.)	6,467.85

WHITE HOUSE

White House (D.C.)	18.07

1. The National Cemeteries are not independent areas of the National Park System; each is part of a military park, battlefield, etc., except Battleground. Their acreage is kept separately. Arlington National Cemetery is under the Department of the Army. *See* Index.

OTHER PARKS

Catoctin Mountain (Md.)	5,770.22
Constitution Gardens, (D.C.)	52.00

Fort Washington Park (Md.)	341.00
Greenbelt Park (Md.)	1,175.99
Perry's Victory and International Peace Memorial (Ohio)	25.38
Piscataway (Md.)	4,262.52
Prince William Forest (Va.)	18,571.55
Rock Creek Park (D.C.)	1,754.37
Vietnam Veterans Memorial (D.C.)	2.00
Wolf Trap Farm Park for the Performing Arts (Va.)	130.28

NATIONAL RECREATION AREAS

Amistad (Tex.)	57,292.44
Bighorn Canyon (Wyo.-Mont.)	120,296.22
Chattahoochee River (Ga.)	9,264.74
Chickasaw (Okla.)	9,521.91
Coulee Dam (Wash.)	100,390.31
Curecanti (Colo.)	42,114.47
Cuyahoga Valley (Ohio)	32,460.19
Delaware Water Gap (Pa.-N.J.)	66,651.86
Gateway (N.Y.-N.J.)	26,310.93
Gauley River (W. Va.)	0.00
Glen Canyon (Ariz.-Utah)	1,236,880.00
Golden Gate (Calif.)	73,080.16
Lake Chelan (Wash.)	61,889.46
Lake Mead (Ariz.-Nev.)	1,495,665.52
Lake Meredith (Tex.)	44,977.63
Ross Lake (Wash.)	117,574.09
Santa Monica Mountains (Calif.)	150,050.00
Whiskeytown-Shasta-Trinity (Calif.)	42,503.46

NATIONAL SCENIC TRAIL

Appalachian (Maine, N.H., Vt., Mass., Conn., N.Y., N.J., Pa., Md., W.Va., Va., N.C., Tenn., Ga.)	161,207.61
Natchez Trace (Ga.-Ala.-Tenn.)	10,995.00
Potomac Heritage (D.C.-Md.-Va.-Pa.)	0.00

NATIONAL MALL

National Mall (D.C.)	146.35

INTERNATIONAL HISTORIC SITE

Saint Croix Island (Maine)	35.39

AFFILIATED AREAS

(National Historic Sites unless otherwise noted.)

American Memorial Park (N. Mariana Is.)	0.00
Benjamin Franklin (Pa.)[1]	0.00
Blackstone River Valley National Heritage Corridor (Mass., R.I.)	0.00
Chicago Portage (Ill.)	91.20
Chimney Rock (Neb.)	83.36
David Berger (Ohio)[1]	0.00
Delaware and Lehigh Navigation Canal National Heritage Corridor (Pa.)	0.00
Ebey's Landing (Wash.)	0.00
Father Marquette (Mich.)[1]	52.00
Gloria Dei Church (Pa.)	3.71
Green Springs Historic District (Va.)	5,490.59
Historic Camden (S.C.)	0.00
Ice Age Scenic Trail (Wisc.)	0.00
Ice Age (Wis.)[2]	32,500.00
Iditarod National Historic Trail (Alaska)	0.00
Illinois and Michigan Canal National Heritage Corridor	322,000.00
International Peace Garden (N.D.)	2,330.30
Jamestown (Va.)	20.63
Lewis & Clark Natl. Historic Trail (Ill., Mo., Kan., Neb., Iowa, Idaho, S.D., N.D., Mont., Ore., Wash.)	0.00
M. McLeod Bethune Council House (D.C.)	0.00
McLoughlin House (Ore.)	0.63
Mormon Pioneer Natl. Historic Trail (Ill., Iowa, Neb., Wyo., Utah)	0.00
North Country Nat'l Scenic Trail (N.Y., Pa., Ohio, Mich., Wis., Minn., N.D.)	0.00
Oregon Natl. Historic Trail (Mo., Kan., Neb., Wyo., Idaho, Ore., Wash.)	0.00
Overmountain Victory Trail (Mo. to Ore.)	0.00
Pinelands Natl. Reserve (N.J.)	0.00
Red Hill Patrick Henry (Va.)[1]	0.00
Roosevelt-Campobello International Park (Canada)	2,721.50
Sewell-Belmont House National Historic Site (D.C.)	0.35
Touro Synagogue (R.I.)	0.23

1. National Memorial. 2. National Scientific Reserve.

Water Supply of the World[1]

The Antarctic Icecap is the largest supply of fresh water, nearly 2 percent of the world's total of fresh and salt water. As can be seen from the table below, the amount of water in our atmosphere is over ten times as large as the water in all the rivers taken together. The fresh water actually available for human use in lakes and rivers and the accessible ground water amounts to only about one third of one percent of the world's total water supply.

	Surface area (square miles)	Volume (cubic miles)	Percentage of total
Salt Water			
The oceans	139,500,000	317,000,000	97.2
Inland seas and saline lakes	270,000	25,000	0.008
Fresh Water			
Freshwater lakes	330,000	30,000	0.009
All rivers (average level)	—	300	0.0001
Antarctic Icecap	6,000,000	6,300,000	1.9
Arctic Icecap and glaciers	900,000	680,000	0.21
Water in the atmosphere	197,000,000	3,100	0.001
Ground water within half a mile from surface	—	1,000,000	0.31
Deep-lying ground water	—	1,000,000	0.31
Total (rounded)	—	326,000,000	100.00

1. All figures are estimated. *Source:* Department of the Interior, Geological Survey.

Congressional Committees Dealing with Environmental Issues

Source: *Conservation 89*, May 10, 1989, National Wildlife Federation.

HOUSE COMMITTEES

House Committee on Agriculture
Phone: (202) 225-2171
   Jurisdiction includes: forests and related forest resources, soil conservation, pesticides, wetlands conservation, wilderness.

Subcommittees:
   Conservation, Credit, and Rural Development; Forests, Family Farms, and Energy.

House Committee on Appropriations
Phone: (202) 225-2771
   Approves government spending bills.

Subcommittees:
   Energy and Water Development; Foreign Operations; Interior and Related Agencies.

House Committee on Energy and Commerce
Phone: (202) 255-2927
   Jurisdiction includes: clean air, toxics, oil, gas, and coal production, water projects, energy conservation.

Subcommittees:
   Energy and Power; Health and the Environment; Transportation, Tourism, and Hazardous Materials.

House Committee on Interior and Insular Affairs
Phone: (202) 255-2761
   Jurisdiction includes: national parks, wild and scenic rivers, forests and lands administered by the Bureau of Land Management and the Bureau of Reclaimation, mineral development, grazing, irrigation, fish and wildlife.

Subcommittees:
   Energy and The Environment; Mining and Natural Resources; National Parks and Public Lands; Water and Power Resources.

House Committee on Merchant Marine and Fisheries
Phone: (202) 255-4047
   Jurisdiction includes: fisheries, coastal barriers, marine mammals, aquatic life, waterfowl, wildlife refuges, wetlands conservation, endangered species.

Subcommittees:
   Fisheries and Wildlife Conservation, and the Environment; Merchant Marine; Oceanography.

House Committee on Public Works and Transportation
Phone: (202) 255-4472
   Jurisdiction includes: water projects, water pollution, billboard control, scenic highways, wetlands conservation.

Subcommittees:
   Surface Transportation; Water Resources.

SENATE COMMITTEES

Senate Committee on Agriculture, Nutrition, and Forestry
Phone: (202) 224-2035
   Jurisdiction includes: forests, soil conservation, pesticides, wetlands conservation, wilderness, fresh water resources.

Subcommittees:
   Agriculture Research and General Legislation; Conservation and Forestry.

Senate Committee on Appropriations
Phone: (202) 224-3471
   Approves government spending bills.

Subcommittees:
   Energy and Water Development; Interior and Related Agencies.

Senate Committee on Commerce, Science, and Transportation
Phone: (202) 224-5115
   Jurisdiction includes: coastal zone management, water projects, fisheries, ocean policy.

Subcommittees:
   Merchant Marine; National Ocean Policy Study; Surface Transportation

Senate Committee on Energy and Natural Resources
Phone: (202) 224-4971
   Jurisdiction includes: mining of coal, oil, gas; energy development, regulation and conservation, national parks, forests, wild and scenic rivers, wilderness and lands administered by the Bureau of Land Management, and Bureau of Reclamation.

Subcommittees:
   Energy Regulation and Conservation; Mineral Resources, Development, and Production; Public Lands, National Parks, and Forests; Water and Power.

Senate Committee on Environment and Public Works
Phone: (202) 224-6176
   Jurisdiction includes: air and water pollution, toxics, nuclear energy, wildlife refuges, fish and wildlife, water projects, wetlands conservation, endangered species, coastal barriers, solid waste disposal, recycling, billboards and scenic highways.

Subcommittees:
   Environmental Protection; Water Resources, Transportation, and Infrastructure; Superfund, Ocean, and Water Protection; Nuclear Regulation; Toxic Substances, Environmental Oversight, Research and Development.

CALENDAR & HOLIDAYS

1990

JANUARY

S	M	T	W	T	F	S
—	1	2	3	4	5	6
7	8	9	10	11	12	13
14	15	16	17	18	19	20
21	22	23	24	25	26	27
28	29	30	31			

FEBRUARY

S	M	T	W	T	F	S
—	—	—	—	1	2	3
4	5	6	7	8	9	10
11	12	13	14	15	16	17
18	19	20	21	22	23	24
25	26	27	28			

MARCH

S	M	T	W	T	F	S
—	—	—	—	1	2	3
4	5	6	7	8	9	10
11	12	13	14	15	16	17
18	19	20	21	22	23	24
25	26	27	28	29	30	31

APRIL

S	M	T	W	T	F	S
①	2	3	4	5	6	7
8	9	10	11	12	13	14
15	16	17	18	19	20	21
22	23	24	25	26	27	28
29	30					

U.S. Census Day

JANUARY
- 1—New Year's Day
- 6—Epiphany
- 15—Martin Luther King's Birthday

FEBRUARY
- 2—Ground-hog Day
- 12—Lincoln's Birthday
- 14—St. Valentine's Day
- 19—Washington's Birthday Observed
- 28—Ash Wednesday

MARCH
- 11—Purim
- 17—St. Patrick's Day
- 28—1st Day of Ramadan

APRIL
- 1—U.S. Census Day & Daylight Savings Time begins
- 8—Palm Sunday
- 10—1st Day of Passover
- 13—Good Friday
- 15—Easter

MAY

S	M	T	W	T	F	S
—	—	1	2	3	4	5
6	7	8	9	10	11	12
13	14	15	16	17	18	19
20	21	22	23	24	25	26
27	28	29	30	31		

JUNE

S	M	T	W	T	F	S
—	—	—	—	—	1	2
3	4	5	6	7	8	9
10	11	12	13	14	15	16
17	18	19	20	21	22	23
24	25	26	27	28	29	30

JULY

S	M	T	W	T	F	S
1	2	3	4	5	6	7
8	9	10	11	12	13	14
15	16	17	18	19	20	21
22	23	24	25	26	27	28
29	30	31				

AUGUST

S	M	T	W	T	F	S
—	—	—	1	2	3	4
5	6	7	8	9	10	11
12	13	14	15	16	17	18
19	20	21	22	23	24	25
26	27	28	29	30	31	

MAY
- 13—Mother's Day
- 24—Ascension Day
- 30—Memorial Day & 1st Day of Shavuot

JUNE
- 3—Pentecost
- 14—Flag Day
- 17—Father's Day

JULY
- 1—Canada Day
- 4—Independence Day

SEPTEMBER

S	M	T	W	T	F	S
—	—	—	—	—	—	1
2	3	4	5	6	7	8
9	10	11	12	13	14	15
16	17	18	19	20	21	22
23	24	25	26	27	28	29
30						

OCTOBER

S	M	T	W	T	F	S
—	1	2	3	4	5	6
7	8	9	10	11	12	13
14	15	16	17	18	19	20
21	22	23	24	25	26	27
28	29	30	31			

NOVEMBER

S	M	T	W	T	F	S
—	—	—	—	1	2	3
4	5	6	7	8	9	10
11	12	13	14	15	16	17
18	19	20	21	22	23	24
25	26	27	28	29	30	

DECEMBER

S	M	T	W	T	F	S
—	—	—	—	—	—	1
2	3	4	5	6	7	8
9	10	11	12	13	14	15
16	17	18	19	20	21	22
23	24	25	26	27	28	29
30	31					

SEPTEMBER
- 3—Labor Day
- 20—1st Day of Rosh Hashana
- 29—Yom Kippur

OCTOBER
- 8—Thanksgiving Day (Canada)
- 12—Columbus Day
- 28—Daylight Savings Time ends
- 31—Halloween

NOVEMBER
- 1—All Saint's Day
- 6—Election Day
- 11—Veteran's Day
- 22—Thanksgiving

DECEMBER
- 2—1st Sunday of Advent
- 12—1st Day of Hanukkah
- 25—Christmas

Seasons for the Northern Hemisphere, 1990

Eastern Standard Time

March 20, 4:19 p.m., sun enters sign of Aries; spring begins

June 21, 10:33 a.m., sun enters sign of Cancer; summer begins

Sept. 23, 1:55 a.m., sun enters sign of Libra; fall begins

Dec. 21, 10:07 p.m., sun enters sign of Capricorn; winter begins

1989

JANUARY						
S	M	T	W	T	F	S
1	2	3	4	5	6	7
8	9	10	11	12	13	14
15	16	17	18	19	20	21
22	23	24	25	26	27	28
29	30	31				

FEBRUARY						
S	M	T	W	T	F	S
—	—	—	1	2	3	4
5	6	7	8	9	10	11
12	13	14	15	16	17	18
19	20	21	22	23	24	25
26	27	28				

MARCH						
S	M	T	W	T	F	S
—	—	—	1	2	3	4
5	6	7	8	9	10	11
12	13	14	15	16	17	18
19	20	21	22	23	24	25
26	27	28	29	30	31	

APRIL						
S	M	T	W	T	F	S
—	—	—	—	—	—	1
2	3	4	5	6	7	8
9	10	11	12	13	14	15
16	17	18	19	20	21	22
23	24	25	26	27	28	29
30						

MAY						
S	M	T	W	T	F	S
—	1	2	3	4	5	6
7	8	9	10	11	12	13
14	15	16	17	18	19	20
21	22	23	24	25	26	27
28	29	30	31			

JUNE						
S	M	T	W	T	F	S
—	—	—	—	1	2	3
4	5	6	7	8	9	10
11	12	13	14	15	16	17
18	19	20	21	22	23	24
25	26	27	28	29	30	

JULY						
S	M	T	W	T	F	S
—	—	—	—	—	—	1
2	3	4	5	6	7	8
9	10	11	12	13	14	15
16	17	18	19	20	21	22
23	24	25	26	27	29	29
30	31					

AUGUST						
S	M	T	W	T	F	S
—	—	1	2	3	4	5
6	7	8	9	10	11	12
13	14	15	16	17	18	19
20	21	22	23	24	25	26
27	28	29	30	31		

SEPTEMBER						
S	M	T	W	T	F	S
—	—	—	—	—	1	2
3	4	5	6	7	8	9
10	11	12	13	14	15	16
17	18	19	20	21	22	23
24	25	26	27	28	29	30

OCTOBER						
S	M	T	W	T	F	S
1	2	3	4	5	6	7
8	9	10	11	12	13	14
15	16	17	18	19	20	21
22	23	24	25	26	27	28
29	30	31				

NOVEMBER						
S	M	T	W	T	F	S
—	—	—	1	2	3	4
5	6	7	8	9	10	11
12	13	14	15	16	17	18
19	20	21	22	23	24	25
26	27	28	29	30		

DECEMBER						
S	M	T	W	T	F	S
—	—	—	—	—	1	2
3	4	5	6	7	8	9
10	11	12	13	14	15	16
17	18	19	20	21	22	23
24	25	26	27	28	29	30
31						

1991

JANUARY						
S	M	T	W	T	F	S
—	—	1	2	3	4	5
6	7	8	9	10	11	12
13	14	15	16	17	18	19
20	21	22	23	24	25	26
27	28	29	30	31		

FEBRUARY						
S	M	T	W	T	F	S
—	—	—	—	—	1	2
3	4	5	6	7	8	9
10	11	12	13	14	15	16
17	18	19	20	21	22	23
24	25	26	27	28		

MARCH						
S	M	T	W	T	F	S
—	—	—	—	—	1	2
3	4	5	6	7	8	9
10	11	12	13	14	15	16
17	18	19	20	21	22	23
24	25	26	27	28	29	30
31						

APRIL						
S	M	T	W	T	F	S
—	1	2	3	4	5	6
7	8	9	10	11	12	13
14	15	16	17	18	19	20
21	22	23	24	25	26	27
28	29	30				

MAY						
S	M	T	W	T	F	S
—	—	—	1	2	3	4
5	6	7	8	9	10	11
12	13	14	15	16	17	18
19	20	21	22	23	24	25
26	27	28	29	30	31	

JUNE						
S	M	T	W	T	F	S
—	—	—	—	—	—	1
2	3	4	5	6	7	8
9	10	11	12	13	14	15
16	17	18	19	20	21	22
23	24	25	26	27	28	29
30						

JULY						
S	M	T	W	T	F	S
—	1	2	3	4	5	6
7	8	9	10	11	12	13
14	15	16	17	18	19	20
21	22	23	24	25	26	27
28	29	30	31			

AUGUST						
S	M	T	W	T	F	S
—	—	—	—	1	2	3
4	5	6	7	8	9	10
11	12	13	14	15	16	17
18	19	20	21	22	23	24
25	26	27	28	29	30	31

SEPTEMBER						
S	M	T	W	T	F	S
1	2	3	4	5	6	7
8	9	10	11	12	13	14
15	16	17	18	19	20	21
22	23	24	25	26	27	28
29	30					

OCTOBER						
S	M	T	W	T	F	S
—	—	1	2	3	4	5
6	7	8	9	10	11	12
13	14	15	16	17	18	19
20	21	22	23	24	25	26
27	28	29	30	31		

NOVEMBER						
S	M	T	W	T	F	S
—	—	—	—	—	1	2
3	4	5	6	7	8	9
10	11	12	13	14	15	16
17	18	19	20	21	22	23
24	25	26	27	28	29	30

DECEMBER						
S	M	T	W	T	F	S
1	2	3	4	5	6	7
8	9	10	11	12	13	14
15	16	17	18	19	20	21
22	23	24	25	26	27	28
29	30	31				

Pre-Columbian Calendar Systems

The Mayans and the Aztecs both used two calendars—a sacred or ceremonial calendar of 260 days and a 365-day secular calendar that was divided into 18 months of 20 days each. An additional five days were added to complete the 365-day year.

The Mayans were able to approximate the true length of the tropical year with a greater accuracy than does the Gregorian calendar year we now use.

The tropical year is 365.2422 days. The Mayans determined it to be 365.2420 days, whereas the Gregorian calendar year is 365.2425.

Very little is known about the Inca calendar. Because the Incas did not have a written language, early reports about their calendar cannot be verified.

PERPETUAL CALENDAR

1800 ..4	1844 ..9	1888 ..8	1932 .13	1976 .12	2020 .11
1801 ..5	1845 ..4	1889 ..3	1933 ..1	1977 ..7	2021 ..6
1802 ..6	1846 ..5	1890 ..4	1934 ..2	1978 ..1	2022 ..7
1803 ..7	1847 ..6	1891 ..5	1935 ..3	1979 ..2	2023 ..1
1804 ..8	1848 .14	1892 .13	1936 .11	1980 .10	2024 ..9
1805 ..3	1849 ..2	1893 ..1	1937 ..6	1981 ..5	2025 ..4
1806 ..4	1850 ..3	1894 ..2	1938 ..7	1982 ..6	2026 ..5
1807 ..5	1851 ..4	1895 ..3	1939 ..1	1983 ..7	2027 ..6
1808 .13	1852 .12	1896 .11	1940 ..9	1984 ..8	2028 .14
1809 ..1	1853 ..7	1897 ..6	1941 ..4	1985 ..3	2029 ..2
1810 ..2	1854 ..1	1898 ..7	1942 ..5	1986 ..4	2030 ..3
1811 ..3	1855 ..2	1899 ..1	1943 ..6	1987 ..5	2031 ..4
1812 .11	1856 .10	1900 ..2	1944 .14	1988 .13	2032 .12
1813 ..6	1857 ..5	1901 ..3	1945 ..2	1989 ..1	2033 ..7
1814 ..7	1858 ..6	1902 ..4	1946 ..3	1990 ..2	2034 ..1
1815 ..1	1859 ..7	1903 ..5	1947 ..4	1991 ..3	2035 ..2
1816 ..9	1860 ..8	1904 .13	1948 .12	1992 .11	2036 .10
1817 ..4	1861 ..3	1905 ..1	1949 ..7	1993 ..6	2037 ..5
1818 ..5	1862 ..4	1906 ..2	1950 ..1	1994 ..7	2038 ..6
1819 ..6	1863 ..5	1907 ..3	1951 ..2	1995 ..1	2039 ..7
1820 .14	1864 .13	1908 .11	1952 .10	1996 ..9	2040 ..8
1821 ..2	1865 ..1	1909 ..6	1953 ..5	1997 ..4	2041 ..3
1822 ..3	1866 ..2	1910 ..7	1954 ..6	1998 ..5	2042 ..4
1823 ..4	1867 ..3	1911 ..1	1955 ..7	1999 ..6	2043 ..5
1824 .12	1868 .11	1912 ..9	1956 ..8	2000 .14	2044 .13
1825 ..7	1869 ..6	1913 ..4	1957 ..3	2001 ..2	2045 ..1
1826 ..1	1870 ..7	1914 ..5	1958 ..4	2002 ..3	2046 ..2
1827 ..2	1871 ..1	1915 ..6	1959 ..5	2003 ..4	2047 ..3
1828 .10	1872 ..9	1916 .14	1960 .13	2004 .12	2048 .11
1829 ..5	1873 ..4	1917 ..2	1961 ..1	2005 ..7	2049 ..6
1830 ..6	1874 ..5	1918 ..3	1962 ..2	2006 ..1	2050 ..7
1831 ..7	1875 ..6	1919 ..4	1963 ..3	2007 ..2	2051 ..1
1832 ..8	1876 .14	1920 .12	1964 .11	2008 .10	2052 ..9
1833 ..3	1877 ..2	1921 ..7	1965 ..6	2009 ..5	2053 ..4
1834 ..4	1878 ..3	1922 ..1	1966 ..7	2010 ..6	2054 ..5
1835 ..5	1879 ..4	1923 ..2	1967 ..1	2011 ..7	2055 ..6
1836 .13	1880 .12	1924 .10	1968 ..9	2012 ..8	2056 .14
1837 ..1	1881 ..7	1925 ..5	1969 ..4	2013 ..3	2057 ..2
1838 ..2	1882 ..1	1926 ..6	1970 ..5	2014 ..4	2058 ..3
1839 ..3	1883 ..2	1927 ..7	1971 ..6	2015 ..5	2059 ..4
1840 .11	1884 .10	1928 ..8	1972 .14	2016 .13	2060 .12
1841 ..6	1885 ..5	1929 ..3	1973 ..2	2017 ..1	2061 ..7
1842 ..7	1886 ..6	1930 ..4	1974 ..3	2018 ..2	2062 ..1
1843 ..1	1887 ..7	1931 ..5	1975 ..4	2019 ..3	2063 ..2

DIRECTIONS: The number given with each year in the key above is number of calendar to use for that year

---

The page displays twelve monthly-grid calendars, numbered **1** through **6** in two side-by-side columns. Each numbered calendar contains the twelve months (JANUARY, FEBRUARY, MARCH, APRIL, MAY, JUNE, JULY, AUGUST, SEPTEMBER, OCTOBER, NOVEMBER, DECEMBER) with the day-of-week column headings **S M T W T F S** and the corresponding day numbers arranged beneath them.

Perpetual calendars (dominical number shown before each full-year calendar).

7 — Common year, January 1 = Saturday

```
JANUARY                 FEBRUARY                MARCH                   APRIL
S  M  T  W  T  F  S      S  M  T  W  T  F  S      S  M  T  W  T  F  S      S  M  T  W  T  F  S
               1               1  2  3  4  5               1  2  3  4  5                     1  2
 2  3  4  5  6  7  8      6  7  8  9 10 11 12      6  7  8  9 10 11 12      3  4  5  6  7  8  9
 9 10 11 12 13 14 15     13 14 15 16 17 18 19     13 14 15 16 17 18 19     10 11 12 13 14 15 16
16 17 18 19 20 21 22     20 21 22 23 24 25 26     20 21 22 23 24 25 26     17 18 19 20 21 22 23
23 24 25 26 27 28 29     27 28                    27 28 29 30 31           24 25 26 27 28 29 30
30 31

MAY                     JUNE                    JULY                    AUGUST
S  M  T  W  T  F  S      S  M  T  W  T  F  S      S  M  T  W  T  F  S      S  M  T  W  T  F  S
 1  2  3  4  5  6  7            1  2  3  4                     1  2         1  2  3  4  5  6
 8  9 10 11 12 13 14      5  6  7  8  9 10 11      3  4  5  6  7  8  9      7  8  9 10 11 12 13
15 16 17 18 19 20 21     12 13 14 15 16 17 18     10 11 12 13 14 15 16     14 15 16 17 18 19 20
22 23 24 25 26 27 28     19 20 21 22 23 24 25     17 18 19 20 21 22 23     21 22 23 24 25 26 27
29 30 31                 26 27 28 29 30           24 25 26 27 28 29 30     28 29 30 31
                                                  31

SEPTEMBER               OCTOBER                 NOVEMBER                DECEMBER
S  M  T  W  T  F  S      S  M  T  W  T  F  S      S  M  T  W  T  F  S      S  M  T  W  T  F  S
            1  2  3                     1               1  2  3  4  5               1  2  3
 4  5  6  7  8  9 10      2  3  4  5  6  7  8      6  7  8  9 10 11 12      4  5  6  7  8  9 10
11 12 13 14 15 16 17      9 10 11 12 13 14 15     13 14 15 16 17 18 19     11 12 13 14 15 16 17
18 19 20 21 22 23 24     16 17 18 19 20 21 22     20 21 22 23 24 25 26     18 19 20 21 22 23 24
25 26 27 28 29 30        23 24 25 26 27 28 29     27 28 29 30              25 26 27 28 29 30 31
                         30 31
```

8 — Leap year, January 1 = Sunday

```
JANUARY                 FEBRUARY                MARCH                   APRIL
S  M  T  W  T  F  S      S  M  T  W  T  F  S      S  M  T  W  T  F  S      S  M  T  W  T  F  S
 1  2  3  4  5  6  7            1  2  3  4               1  2  3         1  2  3  4  5  6  7
 8  9 10 11 12 13 14      5  6  7  8  9 10 11      4  5  6  7  8  9 10      8  9 10 11 12 13 14
15 16 17 18 19 20 21     12 13 14 15 16 17 18     11 12 13 14 15 16 17     15 16 17 18 19 20 21
22 23 24 25 26 27 28     19 20 21 22 23 24 25     18 19 20 21 22 23 24     22 23 24 25 26 27 28
29 30 31                 26 27 28 29              25 26 27 28 29 30 31     29 30

MAY                     JUNE                    JULY                    AUGUST
S  M  T  W  T  F  S      S  M  T  W  T  F  S      S  M  T  W  T  F  S      S  M  T  W  T  F  S
       1  2  3  4  5                  1  2         1  2  3  4  5  6  7               1  2  3  4
 6  7  8  9 10 11 12      3  4  5  6  7  8  9      8  9 10 11 12 13 14      5  6  7  8  9 10 11
13 14 15 16 17 18 19     10 11 12 13 14 15 16     15 16 17 18 19 20 21     12 13 14 15 16 17 18
20 21 22 23 24 25 26     17 18 19 20 21 22 23     22 23 24 25 26 27 28     19 20 21 22 23 24 25
27 28 29 30 31           24 25 26 27 28 29 30     29 30 31                 26 27 28 29 30 31

SEPTEMBER               OCTOBER                 NOVEMBER                DECEMBER
S  M  T  W  T  F  S      S  M  T  W  T  F  S      S  M  T  W  T  F  S      S  M  T  W  T  F  S
                  1         1  2  3  4  5  6               1  2  3                        1
 2  3  4  5  6  7  8      7  8  9 10 11 12 13      4  5  6  7  8  9 10      2  3  4  5  6  7  8
 9 10 11 12 13 14 15     14 15 16 17 18 19 20     11 12 13 14 15 16 17      9 10 11 12 13 14 15
16 17 18 19 20 21 22     21 22 23 24 25 26 27     18 19 20 21 22 23 24     16 17 18 19 20 21 22
23 24 25 26 27 28 29     28 29 30 31              25 26 27 28 29 30        23 24 25 26 27 28 29
30                                                                         30 31
```

9 — Leap year, January 1 = Monday

```
JANUARY                 FEBRUARY                MARCH                   APRIL
S  M  T  W  T  F  S      S  M  T  W  T  F  S      S  M  T  W  T  F  S      S  M  T  W  T  F  S
    1  2  3  4  5  6            1  2  3               1  2         1  2  3  4  5  6
 7  8  9 10 11 12 13      4  5  6  7  8  9 10      3  4  5  6  7  8  9      7  8  9 10 11 12 13
14 15 16 17 18 19 20     11 12 13 14 15 16 17     10 11 12 13 14 15 16     14 15 16 17 18 19 20
21 22 23 24 25 26 27     18 19 20 21 22 23 24     17 18 19 20 21 22 23     21 22 23 24 25 26 27
28 29 30 31              25 26 27 28 29           24 25 26 27 28 29 30     28 29 30
                                                  31

MAY                     JUNE                    JULY                    AUGUST
S  M  T  W  T  F  S      S  M  T  W  T  F  S      S  M  T  W  T  F  S      S  M  T  W  T  F  S
          1  2  3  4                     1         1  2  3  4  5  6               1  2  3
 5  6  7  8  9 10 11      2  3  4  5  6  7  8      7  8  9 10 11 12 13      4  5  6  7  8  9 10
12 13 14 15 16 17 18      9 10 11 12 13 14 15     14 15 16 17 18 19 20     11 12 13 14 15 16 17
19 20 21 22 23 24 25     16 17 18 19 20 21 22     21 22 23 24 25 26 27     18 19 20 21 22 23 24
26 27 28 29 30 31        23 24 25 26 27 28 29     28 29 30 31              25 26 27 28 29 30 31
                         30

SEPTEMBER               OCTOBER                 NOVEMBER                DECEMBER
S  M  T  W  T  F  S      S  M  T  W  T  F  S      S  M  T  W  T  F  S      S  M  T  W  T  F  S
 1  2  3  4  5  6  7            1  2  3  4  5                  1  2         1  2  3  4  5  6  7
 8  9 10 11 12 13 14      6  7  8  9 10 11 12      3  4  5  6  7  8  9      8  9 10 11 12 13 14
15 16 17 18 19 20 21     13 14 15 16 17 18 19     10 11 12 13 14 15 16     15 16 17 18 19 20 21
22 23 24 25 26 27 28     20 21 22 23 24 25 26     17 18 19 20 21 22 23     22 23 24 25 26 27 28
29 30                    27 28 29 30 31           24 25 26 27 28 29 30     29 30 31
```

10 — Leap year, January 1 = Tuesday

```
JANUARY                 FEBRUARY                MARCH                   APRIL
S  M  T  W  T  F  S      S  M  T  W  T  F  S      S  M  T  W  T  F  S      S  M  T  W  T  F  S
       1  2  3  4  5                  1  2                        1               1  2  3  4  5
 6  7  8  9 10 11 12      3  4  5  6  7  8  9      2  3  4  5  6  7  8      6  7  8  9 10 11 12
13 14 15 16 17 18 19     10 11 12 13 14 15 16      9 10 11 12 13 14 15     13 14 15 16 17 18 19
20 21 22 23 24 25 26     17 18 19 20 21 22 23     16 17 18 19 20 21 22     20 21 22 23 24 25 26
27 28 29 30 31           24 25 26 27 28 29        23 24 25 26 27 28 29     27 28 29 30
                                                  30 31

MAY                     JUNE                    JULY                    AUGUST
S  M  T  W  T  F  S      S  M  T  W  T  F  S      S  M  T  W  T  F  S      S  M  T  W  T  F  S
          1  2  3      1  2  3  4  5  6  7            1  2  3  4  5                  1  2
 4  5  6  7  8  9 10      8  9 10 11 12 13 14      6  7  8  9 10 11 12      3  4  5  6  7  8  9
11 12 13 14 15 16 17     15 16 17 18 19 20 21     13 14 15 16 17 18 19     10 11 12 13 14 15 16
18 19 20 21 22 23 24     22 23 24 25 26 27 28     20 21 22 23 24 25 26     17 18 19 20 21 22 23
25 26 27 28 29 30 31     29 30                    27 28 29 30 31           24 25 26 27 28 29 30
                                                                           31

SEPTEMBER               OCTOBER                 NOVEMBER                DECEMBER
S  M  T  W  T  F  S      S  M  T  W  T  F  S      S  M  T  W  T  F  S      S  M  T  W  T  F  S
    1  2  3  4  5  6            1  2  3  4                        1            1  2  3  4  5  6
 7  8  9 10 11 12 13      5  6  7  8  9 10 11      2  3  4  5  6  7  8      7  8  9 10 11 12 13
14 15 16 17 18 19 20     12 13 14 15 16 17 18      9 10 11 12 13 14 15     14 15 16 17 18 19 20
21 22 23 24 25 26 27     19 20 21 22 23 24 25     16 17 18 19 20 21 22     21 22 23 24 25 26 27
28 29 30                 26 27 28 29 30 31        23 24 25 26 27 28 29     28 29 30 31
                                                  30
```

11 — Leap year, January 1 = Wednesday

```
JANUARY                 FEBRUARY                MARCH                   APRIL
S  M  T  W  T  F  S      S  M  T  W  T  F  S      S  M  T  W  T  F  S      S  M  T  W  T  F  S
          1  2  3  4                        1      1  2  3  4  5  6  7            1  2  3  4
 5  6  7  8  9 10 11      2  3  4  5  6  7  8      8  9 10 11 12 13 14      5  6  7  8  9 10 11
12 13 14 15 16 17 18      9 10 11 12 13 14 15     15 16 17 18 19 20 21     12 13 14 15 16 17 18
19 20 21 22 23 24 25     16 17 18 19 20 21 22     22 23 24 25 26 27 28     19 20 21 22 23 24 25
26 27 28 29 30 31        23 24 25 26 27 28 29     29 30 31                 26 27 28 29 30

MAY                     JUNE                    JULY                    AUGUST
S  M  T  W  T  F  S      S  M  T  W  T  F  S      S  M  T  W  T  F  S      S  M  T  W  T  F  S
                  1  2      1  2  3  4  5  6            1  2  3  4                        1
 3  4  5  6  7  8  9      7  8  9 10 11 12 13      5  6  7  8  9 10 11      2  3  4  5  6  7  8
10 11 12 13 14 15 16     14 15 16 17 18 19 20     12 13 14 15 16 17 18      9 10 11 12 13 14 15
17 18 19 20 21 22 23     21 22 23 24 25 26 27     19 20 21 22 23 24 25     16 17 18 19 20 21 22
24 25 26 27 28 29 30     28 29 30                 26 27 28 29 30 31        23 24 25 26 27 28 29
31                                                                         30 31

SEPTEMBER               OCTOBER                 NOVEMBER                DECEMBER
S  M  T  W  T  F  S      S  M  T  W  T  F  S      S  M  T  W  T  F  S      S  M  T  W  T  F  S
       1  2  3  4  5            1  2  3      1  2  3  4  5  6  7            1  2  3  4  5
 6  7  8  9 10 11 12      4  5  6  7  8  9 10      8  9 10 11 12 13 14      6  7  8  9 10 11 12
13 14 15 16 17 18 19     11 12 13 14 15 16 17     15 16 17 18 19 20 21     13 14 15 16 17 18 19
20 21 22 23 24 25 26     18 19 20 21 22 23 24     22 23 24 25 26 27 28     20 21 22 23 24 25 26
27 28 29 30              25 26 27 28 29 30 31     29 30                    27 28 29 30 31
```

12 — Leap year, January 1 = Thursday

```
JANUARY                 FEBRUARY                MARCH                   APRIL
S  M  T  W  T  F  S      S  M  T  W  T  F  S      S  M  T  W  T  F  S      S  M  T  W  T  F  S
             1  2  3      1  2  3  4  5  6  7            1  2  3  4  5  6               1  2  3
 4  5  6  7  8  9 10      8  9 10 11 12 13 14      7  8  9 10 11 12 13      4  5  6  7  8  9 10
11 12 13 14 15 16 17     15 16 17 18 19 20 21     14 15 16 17 18 19 20     11 12 13 14 15 16 17
18 19 20 21 22 23 24     22 23 24 25 26 27 28     21 22 23 24 25 26 27     18 19 20 21 22 23 24
25 26 27 28 29 30 31     29                       28 29 30 31              25 26 27 28 29 30

MAY                     JUNE                    JULY                    AUGUST
S  M  T  W  T  F  S      S  M  T  W  T  F  S      S  M  T  W  T  F  S      S  M  T  W  T  F  S
                     1            1  2  3  4  5               1  2  3      1  2  3  4  5  6  7
 2  3  4  5  6  7  8      6  7  8  9 10 11 12      4  5  6  7  8  9 10      8  9 10 11 12 13 14
 9 10 11 12 13 14 15     13 14 15 16 17 18 19     11 12 13 14 15 16 17     15 16 17 18 19 20 21
16 17 18 19 20 21 22     20 21 22 23 24 25 26     18 19 20 21 22 23 24     22 23 24 25 26 27 28
23 24 25 26 27 28 29     27 28 29 30              25 26 27 28 29 30 31     29 30 31
30 31

SEPTEMBER               OCTOBER                 NOVEMBER                DECEMBER
S  M  T  W  T  F  S      S  M  T  W  T  F  S      S  M  T  W  T  F  S      S  M  T  W  T  F  S
          1  2  3  4                  1  2         1  2  3  4  5  6            1  2  3  4
 5  6  7  8  9 10 11      3  4  5  6  7  8  9      7  8  9 10 11 12 13      5  6  7  8  9 10 11
12 13 14 15 16 17 18     10 11 12 13 14 15 16     14 15 16 17 18 19 20     12 13 14 15 16 17 18
19 20 21 22 23 24 25     17 18 19 20 21 22 23     21 22 23 24 25 26 27     19 20 21 22 23 24 25
26 27 28 29 30           24 25 26 27 28 29 30     28 29 30                 26 27 28 29 30 31
                         31
```

13 — Leap year, January 1 = Friday

```
JANUARY                 FEBRUARY                MARCH                   APRIL
S  M  T  W  T  F  S      S  M  T  W  T  F  S      S  M  T  W  T  F  S      S  M  T  W  T  F  S
                1  2         1  2  3  4  5  6         1  2  3  4  5                     1  2
 3  4  5  6  7  8  9      7  8  9 10 11 12 13      6  7  8  9 10 11 12      3  4  5  6  7  8  9
10 11 12 13 14 15 16     14 15 16 17 18 19 20     13 14 15 16 17 18 19     10 11 12 13 14 15 16
17 18 19 20 21 22 23     21 22 23 24 25 26 27     20 21 22 23 24 25 26     17 18 19 20 21 22 23
24 25 26 27 28 29 30     28 29                    27 28 29 30 31           24 25 26 27 28 29 30
31

MAY                     JUNE                    JULY                    AUGUST
S  M  T  W  T  F  S      S  M  T  W  T  F  S      S  M  T  W  T  F  S      S  M  T  W  T  F  S
 1  2  3  4  5  6  7            1  2  3  4                     1  2            1  2  3  4  5  6
 8  9 10 11 12 13 14      5  6  7  8  9 10 11      3  4  5  6  7  8  9      7  8  9 10 11 12 13
15 16 17 18 19 20 21     12 13 14 15 16 17 18     10 11 12 13 14 15 16     14 15 16 17 18 19 20
22 23 24 25 26 27 28     19 20 21 22 23 24 25     17 18 19 20 21 22 23     21 22 23 24 25 26 27
29 30 31                 26 27 28 29 30           24 25 26 27 28 29 30     28 29 30 31
                                                  31

SEPTEMBER               OCTOBER                 NOVEMBER                DECEMBER
S  M  T  W  T  F  S      S  M  T  W  T  F  S      S  M  T  W  T  F  S      S  M  T  W  T  F  S
            1  2  3                     1               1  2  3  4  5               1  2  3
 4  5  6  7  8  9 10      2  3  4  5  6  7  8      6  7  8  9 10 11 12      4  5  6  7  8  9 10
11 12 13 14 15 16 17      9 10 11 12 13 14 15     13 14 15 16 17 18 19     11 12 13 14 15 16 17
18 19 20 21 22 23 24     16 17 18 19 20 21 22     20 21 22 23 24 25 26     18 19 20 21 22 23 24
25 26 27 28 29 30        23 24 25 26 27 28 29     27 28 29 30              25 26 27 28 29 30 31
                         30 31
```

14 — Leap year, January 1 = Saturday

```
JANUARY                 FEBRUARY                MARCH                   APRIL
S  M  T  W  T  F  S      S  M  T  W  T  F  S      S  M  T  W  T  F  S      S  M  T  W  T  F  S
                     1            1  2  3  4  5               1  2  3  4                        1
 2  3  4  5  6  7  8      6  7  8  9 10 11 12      5  6  7  8  9 10 11      2  3  4  5  6  7  8
 9 10 11 12 13 14 15     13 14 15 16 17 18 19     12 13 14 15 16 17 18      9 10 11 12 13 14 15
16 17 18 19 20 21 22     20 21 22 23 24 25 26     19 20 21 22 23 24 25     16 17 18 19 20 21 22
23 24 25 26 27 28 29     27 28 29                 26 27 28 29 30 31        23 24 25 26 27 28 29
30 31                                                                      30

MAY                     JUNE                    JULY                    AUGUST
S  M  T  W  T  F  S      S  M  T  W  T  F  S      S  M  T  W  T  F  S      S  M  T  W  T  F  S
    1  2  3  4  5  6            1  2  3                     1            1  2  3  4  5
 7  8  9 10 11 12 13      4  5  6  7  8  9 10      2  3  4  5  6  7  8      6  7  8  9 10 11 12
14 15 16 17 18 19 20     11 12 13 14 15 16 17      9 10 11 12 13 14 15     13 14 15 16 17 18 19
21 22 23 24 25 26 27     18 19 20 21 22 23 24     16 17 18 19 20 21 22     20 21 22 23 24 25 26
28 29 30 31              25 26 27 28 29 30        23 24 25 26 27 28 29     27 28 29 30 31
                                                  30 31

SEPTEMBER               OCTOBER                 NOVEMBER                DECEMBER
S  M  T  W  T  F  S      S  M  T  W  T  F  S      S  M  T  W  T  F  S      S  M  T  W  T  F  S
                1  2      1  2  3  4  5  6  7            1  2  3  4                     1  2
 3  4  5  6  7  8  9      8  9 10 11 12 13 14      5  6  7  8  9 10 11      3  4  5  6  7  8  9
10 11 12 13 14 15 16     15 16 17 18 19 20 21     12 13 14 15 16 17 18     10 11 12 13 14 15 16
17 18 19 20 21 22 23     22 23 24 25 26 27 28     19 20 21 22 23 24 25     17 18 19 20 21 22 23
24 25 26 27 28 29 30     29 30 31                 26 27 28 29 30           24 25 26 27 28 29 30
                                                                           31
```

The Calendar

History of the Calendar

The purpose of a calendar is to reckon time in advance, to show how many days have to elapse until a certain event takes place—the harvest, a religious festival, or whatever. The earliest calendars, naturally, were crude, and they must have been strongly influenced by the geographical location of the people who made them. In the Scandinavian countries, for example, where the seasons are pronounced, the concept of the year was determined by the seasons, specifically by the end of winter. The Norsemen, before becoming Christians, are said to have had a calendar consisting of ten months of 30 days each.

But in warmer countries, where the seasons are less pronounced, the Moon became the basic unit for time reckoning; an old Jewish book actually makes the statement that "the Moon was created for the counting of the days." All the oldest calendars of which we have reliable information were lunar calendars, based on the time interval from one new moon to the next—a so-called "lunation." But even in a warm climate there are annual events that pay no attention to the phases of the Moon. In some areas it was a rainy season; in Egypt it was the annual flooding of the Nile. It was, therefore, necessary to regulate daily life and religious festivals by lunations, but to take care of the annual event in some other manner.

The calendar of the Assyrians was based on the phases of the Moon. The month began with the first appearance of the lunar crescent, and since this can best be observed in the evening, the day began with sunset. They knew that a lunation was 29 1/2 days long, so their lunar year had a duration of 354 days, falling eleven days short of the solar year.[1] After three years such a lunar calendar would be off by 33 days, or more than one lunation. We know that the Assyrians added an extra month from time to time, but we do not know whether they had developed a special rule for doing so or whether the priests proclaimed the necessity for an extra month from observation. If they made every third year a year of 13 lunations, their three-year period would cover 1,091 1/2 days (using their value of 29 1/2 days for one lunation), or just about four days too short. In one century this mistake would add up to 133 days by their reckoning (in reality closer to 134 days), requiring four extra lunations per century.

We now know that an eight-year period, consisting of five years with 12 months and three years with 13 months would lead to a difference of only 20 days per century, but we do not know whether such a calendar was actually used.

The best approximation that was possible in antiquity was a 19-year period, with seven of these 19 years having 13 months. This means that the period contained 235 months. This, still using the old value for a lunation, made a total of 6,932 1/2 days, while 19 solar years added up to 6,939.7 days, a difference of just one week per period and about five weeks per century. Even the 19-year period required constant adjustment, but it was the period that became the basis of the religious calendar of

the Jews. The Arabs used the same calendar at first, but Mohammed forbade shifting from 12 months to 13 months, so that the Islamic religious calendar, even today, has a lunar year of 354 days. As a result the Islamic religious festivals run through all the seasons of the year three times per century.

The Egyptians had a traditional calendar with 12 months of 30 days each. At one time they added five extra days at the end of every year. These turned into a five-day festival because it was thought to be unlucky to work during that time.

When Rome emerged as a world power, the difficulties of making a calendar were well known, but the Romans complicated their lives because of their superstition that even numbers were unlucky. Hence their months were 29 or 31 days long, with the exception of February, which had 28 days. However, four months of 31 days, seven months of 29 days, and one month of 28 days added up to only 355 days. Therefore, the Romans invented an extra month called Mercedonius of 22 or 23 days. It was added every second year.

Even with Mercedonius, the Roman calendar was so far off that Caesar, advised by the astronomer Sosigenes, ordered a sweeping reform in 45 B.C. One year, made 445 days long by imperial decree, brought the calendar back in step with the seasons. Then the solar year (with the value of 365 days and 6 hours) was made the basis of the calendar. The months were 30 or 31 days in length, and to take care of the six hours, every fourth year was made a 366-day year. Moreover, Caesar decreed, the year began with the first of January, not with the vernal equinox in late March.

This was the Julian calendar, named after Julius Caesar. It is still the calendar of the Eastern Orthodox churches.

However, the year is 11 1/2 minutes shorter than the figure written into Caesar's calendar by Sosigenes, and after a number of centuries, even 11 1/2 minutes add up. *See* table.

While Caesar could decree that the vernal equinox should not be used as the first day of the new year, the vernal equinox is still a fact of Nature that could not be disregarded. One of the first (as far as we know) to become alarmed about this was Roger Bacon. He sent a memorandum to Pope Clement IV, who apparently was not impressed. But Pope Sixtus IV (reigned 1471 to 1484) decided that another reform was needed and called the German astronomer Regiomontanus to Rome to advise him. Regiomontanus arrived in 1475, but one year later he died in an epidemic, one of the recurrent outbreaks of the plague. The Pope himself survived, but his reform plans died with Regiomontanus.

Less than a hundred years later, in 1545, the Council of Trent authorized the then Pope, Paul III, to reform the calendar once more. Most of the mathematical and astronomical work was done by Father Christopher Clavius, S.J. The immediate correction, advised by Father Clavius and ordered by Pope Gregory XIII, was that Thursday, Oct. 4, 1582, was to be the last day of the Julian calendar. The next day was Friday, with the date of October 15. For long-range accuracy, a formula suggested by the Vatican librarian Aloysius Giglio (latinized into Lilius) was adopted: every fourth year is a leap year *unless* it is a century year like 1700 or 1800. Century years can be leap years *only* when they are divisible by 400 (e.g., 1600). This rule elim-

---

1. The correct figures are: lunation: 29 d, 12 h, 44 min, 2.8 sec (29.530585 d); solar year: 365 d, 5 h, 48 min, 46 sec (365.242216 d); 12 lunations: 354 d, 8 h, 48 min, 34 sec (354.3671 d).

Drift of the Vernal Equinox in the Julian Calendar

Date	Julian year	Date	Julian year	Date	Julian year
March 21	325 A.D.	March 17	837 A.D.	March 13	1349 A.D.
March 20	453 A.D.	March 16	965 A.D.	March 12	1477 A.D.
March 19	581 A.D.	March 15	1093 A.D.	March 11	1605 A.D.
March 18	709 A.D.	March 14	1221 A.D.		

inates three leap years in four centuries, making the calendar sufficiently correct for all ordinary purposes.

Unfortunately, all the Protestant princes in 1582 chose to ignore the papal bull; they continued with the Julian calendar. It was not until 1698 that the German professor Erhard Weigel persuaded the Protestant rulers of Germany and of the Netherlands to change to the new calendar. In England the shift took place in 1752, and in Russia it needed the revolution to introduce the Gregorian calendar in 1918.

The average year of the Gregorian calendar, in spite of the leap year rule, is about 26 seconds longer than the earth's orbital period. But this discrepancy will need 3,323 years to build up to a single day.

Modern proposals for calendar reform do not aim at a "better" calendar, but at one that is more convenient to use, especially for commercial purposes. A 365-day year cannot be divided into equal halves or quarters; the number of days per month is haphazard; the months begin or end in the middle of a week; a holiday fixed by date (e.g., the Fourth of July) will wander through a week; a holiday fixed in another manner (e.g., Easter) can fall on thirty-five possible dates. The Gregorian calendar, admittedly, keeps the calendar dates in reasonable unison with astronomical events, but it still is full of minor annoyances. Moreover, you need a calendar every year to look up dates; an ideal calendar should be one that you can memorize for one year and that is valid for all other years, too.

In 1834 an Italian priest, Marco Mastrofini, suggested taking one day out of every year. It would be made a holiday and *not* be given the name of a weekday. That would make every year begin with January 1 as a Sunday. The leap-year day would be treated the same way, so that in leap years there would be two unnamed holidays at the end of the year.

About a decade later the philosopher Auguste Comte also suggested a 364-day calendar with an extra day, which he called Year Day.

Since then there have been other unsuccessful attempts at calendar reform.

Time and Calendar

The two natural cycles on which time measurements are based are the year and the day. The year is defined as the time required for the Earth to complete one revolution around the Sun, while the day is the time required for the Earth to complete one turn upon its axis. Unfortunately the Earth needs 365 days plus about six hours to go around the Sun once, so that the year does not consist of so and so many days; the fractional day has to be taken care of by an extra day every fourth year.

But because the Earth, while turning upon its axis, also moves around the Sun there are two kinds of days. A day may be defined as the interval between the highest point of the Sun in the sky on two successive days. This, averaged out over the year, produces the customary 24-hour day. But one might also define a day as the time interval between the moments when a certain point in the sky, say a conveniently located star, is directly overhead. This is called:

Sidereal time. Astronomers use a point which they call the "vernal equinox" for the actual determination. Such a sidereal day is somewhat shorter than the "solar day," namely by about 3 minutes and 56 seconds of so-called "mean solar time."

Apparent solar time is the time based directly on the Sun's position in the sky. In ordinary life the day runs from midnight to midnight. It begins when the Sun is invisible by being 12 hours from its zenith. Astronomers use the so-called "Julian Day," which runs from noon to noon; the concept was invented by the astronomer Joseph Scaliger, who named it after his father Julius. To avoid the problems caused by leap-year days and so forth, Scaliger picked a conveniently remote date in the past and suggested just counting days without regard to weeks, months, and years. The Julian Day for 0^h Jan. 31, 1990 is 244 7922.5. The reason for having the Julian Day run from noon to noon is the practical one that astronomical observations usually extend across the midnight hour, which would require a change in date (or in the Julian Day number) if the astronomical day, like the civil day, ran from midnight to midnight.

Mean solar time, rather than apparent solar time, is what is actually used most of the time. The mean solar time is based on the position of a fictitious "mean sun." The reason why this fictitious sun has to be introduced is the following: the Earth turns on its axis regularly; it needs the same number of seconds regardless of the season. But the movement of the Earth around the Sun is not regular because the Earth's orbit is an ellipse. This has the result (as explained in the section The Seasons) that the Earth moves faster in January and slower in July. Though it is the Earth that changes velocity, it looks to us as if the Sun did. In January, when the Earth moves faster, the *apparent* movement of the Sun looks faster. The "mean sun" of time measurements, then, is a sun that moves regularly all year round; the real Sun will be either ahead of or behind the "mean sun." The difference between the real Sun and the fictitious mean sun is called the *equation of time.*

When the real Sun is west of the mean sun we have the "sun fast" condition, with the real Sun crossing the meridian ahead of the mean sun. The opposite is the "sun slow" situation when the real Sun crosses the meridian after the mean sun. Of course, what is observed is the real Sun. The equation of time is needed to establish mean solar time, kept by the reference clocks.

But if all clocks were actually set by mean solar time we would be plagued by a welter of time differences that would be "correct" but a major nuisance. A clock on Long Island, correctly showing mean solar time for its location (this would be *local*

The Names of the Days

Latin	Saxon	English	French	Italian	Spanish	German
Dies Solis	Sun's Day	Sunday	Dimanche	domenica	domingo	Sonntag
Dies Lunae	Moon's Day	Monday	Lundi	lunedi	lunes	Montag
Dies Martis	Tiw's Day	Tuesday	Mardi	martedi	martes	Dienstag
Dies Mercurii	Woden's Day	Wednesday	Mercredi	mercoledi	miércoles	Mittwoch
Dies Jovis	Thor's Day	Thursday	Jeudi	giovedi	jueves	Donnerstag
Dies Veneris	Frigg's Day	Friday	Vendredi	venedri	viernes	Freitag
Dies Saturni	Seterne's Day	Saturday	Samedi	sabato	sábado	Sonnabend

NOTE: The Romans gave one day of the week to each planet known, the Sun and Moon being considered planets in this connection. The Saxon names are a kind of translation of the Roman names: Tiw was substituted for Mars, Woden (Wotan) for Mercury, Thor for Jupiter (Jove), Frigg for Venus, and Seterne for Saturn. The English names are adapted Saxon. The Spanish and Italian names, which are normally not capitalized, and the French are derived from the Latin. The German names follow the Saxon pattern with two exceptions: Wednesday is Mittwoch (Middle of the Week), and Saturday is Sonnabend (Sunday's Eve).

civil time), would be slightly ahead of a clock in Newark, N.J. The Newark clock would be slightly ahead of a clock in Trenton, N.J., which, in turn, would be ahead of a clock in Philadelphia. This condition actually prevailed in the past until 1883, when *standard time* was introduced. Standard time is the correct mean solar time for a designated meridian, and this time is used for a certain area to the east and west of this meridian. In the U.S. four meridians have been designated to supply standard times; they are 75°, 90°, 105°, and 120° west of Greenwich. The 75° meridian determines Eastern Standard Time. It happens to run through Camden, N.J., where standard time, therefore, is also mean solar time and local civil time. The 90° meridian (which happens to pass through the western part of Memphis, Tenn.) determines Central Standard Time, the 105° meridian (passing through Denver) determines Mountain Standard Time, and the 120° meridian (which runs through Lake Tahoe) determines Pacific Standard Time.

Canada, extending over more territory from west to east, adds one time zone on either side: Atlantic Standard Time (based on 60° west of Greenwich) for New Brunswick, Nova Scotia, and Quebec, and Yukon Standard Time (determined by the 135° meridian) for its extreme West. Alaska, extending still farther to the west, adds two more time zones, Alaska Standard Time (determined by the 150° meridian that passes through Anchorage) and Nome Standard Time, based on the 165° meridian just east of Nome.

In general the Earth is divided into 24 such time zones, which run one hour apart. For practical purposes the time zones sometimes show indentations, and there are a few "subzones" that differ from the neighboring zone by only half an hour, e.g., Newfoundland.

The date line. While the time zones are based on the natural event of the Sun crossing the meridian, the date must be an arbitrary decision. The meridians are traditionally counted from the meridian of the observatory of Greenwich in England, which is called the zero meridian. The logical place for changing the date is 12 hours, or 180° from Greenwich. Fortunately, the 180th meridian runs mostly through the open Pacific. The date line makes a zigzag in the north to incorporate the eastern tip of Siberia into the Siberian time system and then another one to incorporate a number of islands into the Alaska time system. In the south there is a similar zigzag for the purpose of tying a number of British-owned islands to the New Zealand time system. Otherwise the date line is the same as 180° from Greenwich. At points to the east of the date line the calendar is one day earlier than at points to the west of it. A traveller going eastward across the date line from one island to another would not have to re-set his watch because he would stay inside the time zone (provided he does so where the date line does *not* coincide with the 180° meridian), but it would be the same time of the previous day.

The Seasons

The seasons are caused by the tilt of the Earth's axis (23.4°) and not by the fact that the Earth's orbit around the Sun is an ellipse. The average distance of the Earth from the Sun is 93 million miles; the difference between aphelion (farthest away) and perihelion (closest to the Sun) is 3 million miles, so that perihelion is about 91.4 million miles from the Sun. The Earth goes through the perihelion point a few days after New Year, just when the northern hemisphere has winter. Aphelion is passed during the first days in July. This by itself shows that the

The Names of the Months

January: named after Janus, protector of the gateway to heaven

February: named after Februalia, a time period when sacrifices were made to atone for sins

March: named after Mars, the god of war, presumably signifying that the campaigns interrupted by the winter could be resumed

April: from *aperire*, Latin for "to open" (buds)

May: named after Maia, the goddess of growth of plants

June: from *juvenis*, Latin for "youth"

July: named after Julius Caesar

August: named after Augustus, the first Roman Emperor

September: from *septem*, Latin for "seven"

October: from *octo*, Latin for "eight"

November: from *novem*, Latin for "nine"

December: from *decem*, Latin for "ten"

NOTE: The earliest Latin calendar was a 10-month one; thus September was the seventh month, October, the eighth, etc. July was originally called Quintilis, as the fifth month; August was originally called Sextilis, as the sixth month.

distance from the Sun is not important within these limits. What is important is that when the Earth passes through perihelion, the northern end of the Earth's axis happens to tilt away from the Sun, so that the areas beyond the Tropic of Cancer receive only slanting rays from a Sun low in the sky.

The tilt of the Earth's axis is responsible for four lines you find on every globe. When, say, the North Pole is tilted away from the Sun as much as possible, the farthest points in the North which can still be reached by the Sun's rays are 23 1/2° from the pole. This is the Arctic Circle. The Antarctic Circle is the corresponding limit 23.4° from the South Pole; the Sun's rays cannot reach beyond this point when we have mid-summer in the North.

When the Sun is vertically above the equator, the day is of equal length all over the Earth. This happens twice a year, and these are the "equinoxes" in March and in September. After having been over the equator in March, the Sun will seem to move northward. The northernmost point where the Sun can be straight overhead is 23.4° north of the equator. This is the Tropic of Cancer; the Sun can never be vertically overhead to the north of this line. Similarly the Sun cannot be vertically overhead to the south of a line 23.4° south of the equator—the Tropic of Capricorn.

This explains the climatic zones. In the belt (the Greek word *zone* means "belt") between the Tropic of Cancer and the Tropic of Capricorn, the Sun can be straight overhead; this is the tropical zone. The two zones where the Sun cannot be overhead but will be above the horizon every day of the year are the two temperate zones; the two areas where the Sun will not rise at all for varying lengths of time are the two polar areas, Arctic and Antarctic.

Holidays

Religious and Secular, 1990

Since 1971, by federal law, Washington's Birthday, Memorial Day, Columbus Day, and Veterans' Day have been celebrated on Mondays to create three-day weekends for federal employees. Many states now observe these holidays on the same Mondays. The dates given for the holidays listed below are the traditional ones.

New Year's Day, Monday, Jan. 1. A legal holiday in all states and the District of Columbia, New Year's Day has its origin in Roman Times, when sacrifices were offered to Janus, the two-faced Roman deity who looked back on the past and forward to the future.

Epiphany, Saturday, Jan. 6. Falls the twelfth day after Christmas and commemorates the manifestation of Jesus as the Son of God, as represented by the adoration of the Magi, the baptism of Jesus, and the miracle of the wine at the marriage feast at Cana. Epiphany originally marked the beginning of the carnival season preceding Lent, and the evening (sometimes the eve) is known as Twelfth Night.

Martin Luther King, Jr.'s Birthday, Monday, Jan. 15. Honors the late civil rights leader. Became a legal public holiday in 1986.

Ground-hog Day, Friday, Feb. 2. Legend has it that if the ground-hog sees his shadow, he'll return to his hole, and winter will last another six weeks.

Lincoln's Birthday, Monday, Feb. 12. A legal holiday in many states, this day was first formally observed in Washington, D.C., in 1866, when both houses of Congress gathered for a memorial address in tribute to the assassinated President.

St. Valentine's Day, Wednesday, Feb. 14. This day is the festival of two third-century martyrs, both named St. Valentine. It is not known why this day is associated with lovers. It may derive from an old pagan festival about this time of year, or it may have been inspired by the belief that birds mate on this day.

Washington's Birthday, Thursday, Feb. 22. The birthday of George Washington is celebrated as a legal holiday in every state of the Union, the District of Columbia, and all territories. The observance began in 1796.

Shrove Tuesday, Feb. 27. Falls the day before Ash Wednesday and marks the end of the carnival season, which once began on Epiphany but is now usually celebrated the last three days before Lent. In France, the day is known as Mardi Gras (Fat Tuesday), and Mardi Gras celebrations are also held in several American cities, particularly in New Orleans. The day is sometimes called Pancake Tuesday by the English because fats, which were prohibited during Lent, had to be used up.

Ash Wednesday, Feb. 28. The first day of the Lenten season, which lasts 40 days. Having its origin sometime before A.D. 1000, it is a day of public penance and is marked in the Roman Catholic Church by the burning of the palms blessed on the previous year's Palm Sunday. With his thumb, the priest then marks a cross upon the forehead of each worshipper. The Anglican Church and a few Protestant groups in the United States also observe the day, but generally without the use of ashes.

Purim (Feast of Lots), Sunday, March 11. A day of joy and feasting celebrating deliverance of the Jews from a massacre planned by the Persian Minister Haman. The Jewish Queen Esther interceded with her husband, King Ahasuerus, to spare the life of her uncle, Mordecai, and Haman was hanged on the same gallows he had built for Mordecai. The holiday is marked by the reading of the Book of Esther (megillah), and by the exchange of gifts, donations to the poor, and the presentation of Purim plays.

St. Patrick's Day, Saturday, March 17. St. Patrick, patron saint of Ireland, has been honored in America since the first days of the nation. There are many dinners and meetings but perhaps the most notable part of the observance is the annual St. Patrick's Day parade on Fifth Avenue in New York City.

Palm Sunday, April 8. Is observed the Sunday before Easter to commemorate the entry of Jesus into Jerusalem. The procession and the ceremonies introducing the benediction of palms probably had their origin in Jerusalem.

First Day of Passover (Pesach), Tuesday, April 10. The Feast of the Passover, also called the Feast of Unleavened Bread, commemorates the escape of the Jews from Egypt. As the Jews fled they ate unleavened bread, and from that time the Jews have allowed no leavening in the houses during Passover, bread being replaced by matzoh.

Good Friday, April 13. This day commemorates the Crucifixion, which is retold during services from the Gospel according to St. John. A feature in Roman Catholic churches is the Liturgy of the Passion; there is no Consecration, the Host having been consecrated the previous day. The eating of hot cross buns on this day is said to have started in England.

Easter Sunday, April 15. Observed in all Christian churches, Easter commemorates the Resurrection of Jesus. It is celebrated on the first Sunday after the full moon which occurs on or next after March 21 and is therefore celebrated between March 22 and April 25 inclusive. This date was fixed by the Council of Nicaea in A.D. 325. The Orthodox Church celebrates Easter on April 15, 1990.

Mother's Day, Sunday, May 13. Observed the second Sunday in May, as proposed by Anna Jarvis of Philadelphia in 1907.

Ascension Day, Thursday, May 24. Took place in the presence of His apostles 40 days after the Resurrection of Jesus. It is traditionally held to have occurred on Mount Olivet in Bethany.

Memorial Day, Wednesday, May 30. Also known as Decoration Day, Memorial Day is a legal holiday in most of the states and in the territories, and is also observed by the armed forces. In 1868, Gen. John A. Logan, Commander in Chief of the Grand Army of the Republic, issued an order designating the day as one in which the graves of soldiers would be decorated. The holiday was originally devoted to honoring the memory of those who fell in the Civil War, but is now also dedicated to the memory of all war dead.

First Day of Shavuot (Hebrew Pentecost), Wednesday, May 30. This festival, sometimes called the Feast of Weeks, or of Harvest, or of the First Fruits, falls 50 days after Passover and originally celebrated the end of the seven-week grain harvesting season. In later tradition, it also celebrated the giving of the Law to Moses on Mount Sinai.

Pentecost (Whitsunday), June 3. This day commemorates the descent of the Holy Ghost upon the apostles 50 days after the Resurrection. The sermon by the Apostle Peter, which led to the baptism of 3,000 who professed belief, originated the ceremonies that have since been followed. "Whitsunday" is believed to have come from "white Sunday" when, among the English, white robes were worn by those baptized on the day.

Flag Day, Thursday, June 14. This day commemorates the adoption by the Continental Congress on June 14, 1777, of the Stars and Stripes as the U.S. flag. Although it is a legal holiday only in Pennsyl-

vania, President Truman, on Aug. 3, 1949, signed a bill requesting the President to call for its observance each year by proclamation.

Father's Day, Sunday, June 19. Observed the third Sunday in June. First celebrated June 19, 1910.

Independence Day, Wednesday, July 4. The day of the adoption of the Declaration of Independence in 1776, celebrated in all states and territories. The observance began the next year in Philadelphia.

Labor Day, Monday, Sept. 3. Observed the first Monday in September in all states and territories, Labor Day was first celebrated in New York in 1882 under the sponsorship of the Central Labor Union, following the suggestion of Peter J. McGuire, of the Knights of Labor, that the day be set aside in honor of labor.

First Day of Rosh Hashana (Jewish New Year), Thursday, Sept. 20. This day marks the beginning of the Jewish year 5751 and opens the Ten Days of Penitence closing with Yom Kippur.

Yom Kippur (Day of Atonement), Saturday, Sept. 29. This day marks the end of the Ten Days of Penitence that began with Rosh Hashana. It is described in *Leviticus* as a "Sabbath of rest," and synagogue services begin the preceding sundown, resume the following morning, and continue to sundown.

First Day of Sukkot (Feast of Tabernacles) Thursday, Oct. 4. This festival, also known as the Feast of the Ingathering, originally celebrated the fruit harvest, and the name comes from the booths or tabernacles in which the Jews lived during the harvest, although one tradition traces it to the shelters used by the Jews in their wandering through the wilderness. During the festival many Jews build small huts in their back yards or on the roofs of their houses.

Simhat Torah (Rejoicing of the Law), Friday, Oct. 12. This joyous holiday falls on the eighth day of Sukkot. It marks the end of the year's reading of the Torah (Five Books of Moses) in the synagogue every Saturday and the beginning of the new cycle of reading.

Columbus Day, Friday, Oct. 12. A legal holiday in many states, commemorating the discovery of America by Columbus in 1492. Quite likely the first celebration of Columbus Day was that organized in 1792 by the Society of St. Tammany, or Columbian Order, widely known as Tammany Hall.

United Nations Day, Wednesday, Oct. 24. Marking the founding of the United Nations.

Halloween, Wednesday, Oct. 31. Eve of All Saints' Day, formerly called All Hallows and Hallowmass. Halloween is traditionally associated in some countries with old customs such as bonfires, masquerading, and the telling of ghost stories. These are old Celtic practices marking the beginning of winter.

All Saints' Day, Thursday, Nov. 1. A Roman Catholic and Anglican holiday celebrating all saints, known and unknown.

Election Day, (legal holiday in certain states), Tuesday, Nov. 6. Since 1845, by Act of Congress, the rst Tuesday after the first Monday in November s the date for choosing Presidential electors. State lections are also generally held on this day.

Veterans Day, Sunday, Nov. 11. Armistice Day was established in 1926 to commemorate the signing n 1918 of the Armistice ending World War I. On une 1, 1954, the name was changed to Veterans Day to honor all men and women who have served America in its armed forces.

Thanksgiving, Thursday, Nov. 22. Observed nationally on the fourth Thursday in November by Act of Congress (1941), the first such national proclamation having been issued by President Lincoln n 1863, on the urging of Mrs. Sarah J. Hale, editor of *Godey's Lady's Book.* Most Americans believe that the holiday dates back to the day of thanks ordered by Governor Bradford of Plymouth Colony n New England in 1621, but scholars point out that days of thanks stem from ancient times.

First Sunday of Advent, Dec. 2. Advent is the season in which the faithful must prepare themselves for the advent of the Saviour on Christmas. The four Sundays before Christmas are marked by special church services.

First Day of Hanukkah (Festival of Lights), Wednesday, Dec. 12. This festival was instituted by Judas Maccabeus in 165 B.C. to celebrate the purification of the Temple of Jerusalem, which had been desecrated three years earlier by Antiochus Epiphanes, who set up a pagan altar and offered sacrifices to Zeus Olympius. In Jewish homes, a light is lighted on each night of the eight-day festival.

Christmas (Feast of the Nativity), Tuesday, Dec. 25. The most widely celebrated holiday of the Christian year, Christmas is observed as the anniversary of the birth of Jesus. Christmas customs are centuries old. The mistletoe, for example, comes from the Druids, who, in hanging the mistletoe, hoped for peace and good fortune. Use of such plants as holly comes from the ancient belief that such plants blossomed at Christmas. Comparatively recent is the Christmas tree, first set up in Germany in the 17th century, and the use of candles on trees developed from the belief that candles appeared by miracle on the trees at Christmas. Colonial Manhattan Islanders introduced the name Santa Claus, a corruption of the Dutch name for the 4th-century Asia Minor St. Nicholas.

State Observances

January 6, Three Kings' Day: Puerto Rico.
January 8, Battle of New Orleans Day: Louisiana.
January 11, De Hostos' Birthday: Puerto Rico.
January 19, Robert E. Lee's Birthday: Arkansas, Florida, Kentucky, Louisiana, South Carolina, **(third Monday)** Alabama, Mississippi.
January 19, Confederate Heroes Day: Texas.
January (third Monday): Lee-Jackson-King Day: Virginia.
January 30, F.D.Roosevelt's Birthday: Kentucky.
February 15, Susan B. Anthony's Birthday: Florida, Minnesota.
March (first Tuesday), Town Meeting Day: Vermont.
March 2, Texas Independence Day: Texas.
March (first Monday), Casimir Pulaski's Birthday: Illinois.
March 17, Evacuation Day: Massachusetts (in Suffolk County).
March 20 (First Day of Spring), Youth Day: Oklahoma.
March 22, Abolition Day: Puerto Rico.
March 25, Maryland Day: Maryland.
March 26, Prince Jonah Kuhio Kalanianaole Day: Hawaii.
March (last Monday), Seward's Day: Alaska.
April 2, Pascua Florida Day: Florida
April 13, Thomas Jefferson's Birthday: Alabama, Oklahoma.
April 16, De Diego's Birthday: Puerto Rico.
April (third Monday), Patriots' Day: Maine, Massachusetts.
April 21, San Jacinto Day: Texas.
April 22, Arbor Day: Nebraska.
April 22, Oklahoma Day: Oklahoma.
April 26, Confederate Memorial Day: Florida, Georgia.
April (fourth Monday), Fast Day: New Hampshire.
April (last Monday), Confederate Memorial Day: Alabama, Mississippi.
May 1, Bird Day: Oklahoma.
May 8, Truman Day: Missouri.
May 11, Minnesota Day: Minnesota.

May 20, Mecklenburg Independence Day: North Carolina.
June (first Monday), Jefferson Davis's Birthday: Alabama, Mississippi.
June 3, Jefferson Davis's Birthday: Florida, South Carolina.
June 3, Confederate Memorial Day: Kentucky, Louisiana.
June 9, Senior Citizens Day: Oklahoma.
June 11, King Kamehameha I Day: Hawaii.
June 15, Separation Day: Delaware.
June 17, Bunker Hill Day: Massachusetts (in Suffolk County).
June 19, Emancipation Day: Texas.
June 20, West Virginia Day: West Virginia.
July 17, Muñoz Rivera's Birthday: Puerto Rico.
July 24, Pioneer Day: Utah.
July 25, Constitution Day: Puerto Rico.
July 27, Barbosa's Birthday: Puerto Rico.
August (first Sunday), American Family Day: Arizona.
August (first Monday), Colorado Day: Colorado.
August (second Monday), Victory Day: Rhode Island.
August 16, Bennington Battle Day: Vermont.
August (third Friday), Admission Day: Hawaii.
August 27, Lyndon B. Johnson's Birthday: Texas.
August 30, Huey P. Long Day: Louisiana.
September 9, Admission Day: California.
September 12, Defenders' Day: Maryland.
September 16, Cherokee Strip Day: Oklahoma.
September (first Saturday after full moon), Indian Day: Oklahoma.
October 10, Leif Erickson Day: Minnesota.
October 10, Oklahoma Historical Day: Oklahoma.
October 18, Alaska Day: Alaska.
October 31, Nevada Day: Nevada.
November 4, Will Rogers Day: Oklahoma.
November (week of the 16th), Oklahoma Heritage Week: Oklahoma.
November 19, Discovery Day: Puerto Rico.
December 7, Delaware Day: Delaware.

Movable Holidays, 1990–1993

CHRISTIAN AND SECULAR

Year	Ash Wednesday	Easter	Pentecost	Labor Day	Election Day	Thanksgiving	1st Sun. Advent
1990	Feb. 28	April 15	June 3	Sept. 3	Nov. 6	Nov. 22	Dec. 2
1991	Feb. 13	March 31	May 19	Sept. 2	Nov. 5	Nov. 28	Dec. 1
1992	March 4	April 19	June 7	Sept. 7	Nov. 3	Nov. 26	Nov. 29
1993	Feb. 24	April 11	May 30	Sept. 6	Nov. 2	Nov. 25	Nov. 28

Shrove Tuesday: 1 day before Ash Wednesday
Palm Sunday: 7 days before Easter
Maundy Thursday: 3 days before Easter
Good Friday: 2 days before Easter

Holy Saturday: 1 day before Easter
Ascension Day: 10 days before Pentecost
Trinity Sunday: 7 days after Pentecost
Corpus Christi: 11 days after Pentecost

NOTE: Easter is celebrated on April 15, 1990, by the Orthodox Church.

JEWISH

Year	Purim[1]	1st day Passover[2]	1st day Shavuot[3]	1st day Rosh Hashana[4]	Yom Kippur[5]	1st day Sukkot[6]	Simhat Torah[7]	1st day Hanukkah[8]
1990	March 11	April 10	May 30	Sept. 20	Sept. 29	Oct. 4	Oct. 12	Dec. 12
1991	Feb. 28	March 30	May 19	Sept. 9	Sept. 18	Sept. 23	Oct. 1	Dec. 2
1992	March 14	April 18	June 7	Sept. 28	Oct. 7	Oct. 12	Oct. 20	Dec. 20
1993	March 7	April 6	May 26	Sept. 16	Sept. 25	Sept. 30	Oct. 8	Dec. 9

1. Feast of Lots. 2. Feast of Unleavened Bread. 3. Hebrew Pentecost; or Feast of Weeks, or of Harvest, or of First Fruits. 4. Jewish New Year. 5. Day of Atonement. 6. Feast of Tabernacles, or of the Ingathering. 7. Rejoicing of the Law. 8. Festival of Lights.

Length of Jewish holidays (O=Orthodox, C=Conservative, R=Reform):

Passover: O & C, 8 days (holy days: first 2 and last 2); R, 7 days (holy days: first and last)
Shavuot: O & C, 2 days; R, 1 day
Rosh Hashana: O & C, 2 days; R, 1 day.
Yom Kippur: All groups, 1 day

Sukkot: All groups, 7 days (holy days: O & C, first 2; R, first only)
O & C observe two additional days: Shemini Atseret (Eighth Day of the Feast) and Simhat Torah. R observes Shemini Atseret but not Simhat Torah
Hanukkah: All groups, 8 days

NOTE: All holidays begin at sundown on the evening before the date given.

Islamic 1990

March 29 First day of the month of Ramadan
April 28 'Id al Fitr (Festival of end of Ramadan)
July 5 'Id al-Adha (Festival of Sacrifice at time of annual pilgrimage to Mecca)

July 24 First day of month of Muharram (beginning of liturgical year)
Oct. 3 Mawlid al-Nabi (Anniversary of Prophet Mohammed's birthday)

NOTE: All holidays begin at sundown on the evening before the date given.

Chinese Calendar

The Chinese lunar year is divided into 12 months of 29 or 30 days. The calendar is adjusted to the length of the solar year by the addition of extra months at regular intervals.

The years are arranged in major cycles of 60 years. Each successive year is named after one of 12 animals. These 12-year cycles are continuously repeated. The Chinese New Year is celebrated at the first new moon after the sun enters Aquarius—sometime between Jan. 21 and Feb. 19.

Rat	Ox	Tiger	Cat (Rabbit)	Dragon	Snake	Horse	Sheep (Goat)	Monkey	Rooster	Dog	Pig
1864	1865	1866	1867	1868	1869	1870	1871	1872	1873	1874	1875
1876	1877	1878	1879	1880	1881	1882	1883	1884	1885	1886	1887
1888	1889	1890	1891	1892	1893	1894	1895	1896	1897	1898	1899
1900	1901	1902	1903	1904	1905	1906	1907	1908	1909	1910	1911
1912	1913	1914	1915	1916	1917	1918	1919	1920	1921	1922	1923
1924	1925	1926	1927	1928	1929	1930	1931	1932	1933	1934	1935
1936	1937	1938	1939	1940	1941	1942	1943	1944	1945	1946	1947
1948	1949	1950	1951	1952	1953	1954	1955	1956	1957	1958	1959
1960	1961	1962	1963	1964	1965	1966	1967	1968	1969	1970	1971
1972	1973	1974	1975	1976	1977	1978	1979	1980	1981	1982	1983
1984	1985	1986	1987	1988	1989	1990	1991	1992	1993	1994	1995

National Holidays Around the World, 1990

Country	Date	Country	Date	Country	Date
Afghanistan	April 27	Ghana	March 6	Peru	July 28
Albania	Nov. 29	Greece	March 25	Philippines	June 12
Algeria	Nov. 1	Grenada	Feb. 7	Poland	July 22
Angola	Nov. 11	Guatemala	Sept. 15	Portugal	June 10
Antigua and Barbuda	Nov. 1	Guinea	Oct. 2	Qatar	Sept. 3
Argentina	May 25	Guinea-Bissau	Sept. 24	Romania	Aug. 23
Australia	Jan. 26	Guyana	Feb. 23	Rwanda	July 1
Austria	Oct. 26	Haiti	Jan. 1	St. Kitts and Nevis	Sept. 19
Bahamas	July 10	Honduras	Sept. 15	St. Lucia	Feb. 22
Bahrain	Dec. 16	Hungary	April 4	St. Vincent and	
Bangladesh	March 26	Iceland	June 17	the Grenadines	Oct. 27
Barbados	Nov. 30	India	Jan. 26	São Tomé and Príncipe	July 12
Belgium	July 21	Indonesia	Aug. 17	Saudi Arabia	Sept. 23
Belize	Sept. 21	Iran	Feb. 11	Senegal	April 4
Benin	Nov. 30	Iraq	July 17	Seychelles	June 5
Bhutan	Dec. 17	Ireland	March 17	Sierra Leone	April 27
Bolivia	Aug. 6	Israel	April 30[1]	Singapore	Aug. 9
Botswana	Sept. 30	Italy	June 2	Solomon Islands	July 7
Brazil	Sept. 7	Ivory Coast	Dec. 7	Somalia	Oct. 21
Brunei	Feb. 23	Jamaica	Aug. 6[2]	South Africa	May 31
Bulgaria	Sept. 9	Japan	April 29	Spain	Oct. 12
Burkina Faso	Aug. 4	Jordan	May 25	Sri Lanka	Feb. 4
Burma	Jan. 4	Kenya	Dec. 12	Sudan	Jan. 1
Burundi	July 1	Kuwait	Feb. 25	Suriname	Nov. 25
Cambodia	April 17	Laos	Dec. 2	Swaziland	Sept. 6
Cameroon	May 20	Lebanon	Nov. 22	Sweden	June 6
Canada	July 1	Lesotho	Oct. 4	Switzerland	Aug. 1
Cape Verde	Sept. 12	Liberia	July 26	Syria	April 17
Central African Republic	Dec. 1	Libya	Sept. 1	Tanzania	April 26
Chad	June 7	Luxembourg	June 23	Thailand	Dec. 5
Chile	Sept. 18	Madagascar	June 26	Togo	April 27
China	Oct. 1	Malawi	July 6	Trinidad and Tobago	Aug. 31
Colombia	July 20	Malaysia	Aug. 31	Tunisia	June 1
Comoros	July 6	Maldives	July 26	Turkey	Oct. 29
Congo	Aug. 15	Mali	Sept. 22	Uganda	Oct. 9
Costa Rica	Sept. 15	Malta	March 31	U.S.S.R.	Nov. 7
Cuba	Jan. 1	Mauritania	Nov. 28	United Arab Emirates	Dec. 2
Cyprus	Oct. 1	Mauritius	March 12	United Kingdom	June 9[3]
Czechoslovakia	May 9	Mexico	Sept. 16	United States	July 4
Denmark	April 16	Mongolia	July 11	Uruguay	Aug. 25
Djibouti	June 27	Morocco	March 3	Vanuatu	July 30
Dominica	Nov. 3	Mozambique	June 25	Venezuela	July 5
Dominican Republic	Feb. 27	Nepal	Dec. 28	Viet Nam	Sept. 2
Ecuador	Aug. 10	Netherlands	April 30	Western Samoa	June 1
Egypt	July 23	New Zealand	Feb. 6	Yemen, People's Dem.	
El Salvador	Sept. 15	Nicaragua	Sept. 15	Republic of	Oct. 14
Equatorial Guinea	Oct. 12	Niger	Dec. 18	Yemen Arab Republic	Sept. 26
Ethiopia	Sept. 12	Nigeria	Oct. 1	Yugoslavia	Nov. 29
Fiji	Oct. 10	Norway	May 17	Zaire	June 30
Finland	Dec. 6	Oman	Nov. 18	Zambia	Oct. 24
France	July 14	Pakistan	March 23	Zimbabwe	April 18
Gabon	Aug. 17	Panama	Nov. 3		
Gambia	Feb. 18	Papua New Guinea	Sept. 16		
Germany, East	Oct. 7	Paraguay	May 14		

1. Changes yearly according to Hebrew calendar. 2. Celebrated on first Monday in August. 3. Celebrated the second Saturday in June. *Source:* United Nations.

The Basic Unit of the World Calendar

Days	First month					Second month					Third month				
Sunday	1	8	15	22	29	—	5	12	19	26	—	3	10	17	24
Monday	2	9	16	23	30	—	6	13	20	27	—	4	11	18	25
Tuesday	3	10	17	24	31	—	7	14	21	28	—	5	12	19	26
Wednesday	4	11	18	25	—	1	8	15	22	29	—	6	13	20	27
Thursday	5	12	19	26	—	2	9	16	23	30	—	7	14	21	28
Friday	6	13	20	27	—	3	10	17	24	—	1	8	15	22	29
Saturday	7	14	21	28	—	4	11	18	25	—	2	9	16	23	30

Some Old Ideas About New Calendars

Several clever schemes have been devised to make the calendar easier-to-use. Two of these attempts are presented here for your information only. This is not intended to suggest that *Information Please Almanac* is interested in or advocates calendar reform.

The French philosopher Auguste Comte (1798-1857) suggested a 364-day calendar with an extra day, which he called Year Day. He intended to do away with the uneven months and suggested 13 months of 28 days each. This would result in a scheme valid for every one of the 13 months, as shown in the table.

Another suggestion was the World Calendar proposed around 1900. It also contains the extra holiday, but it does produce a very simple calendar, constructed with a quarter year as the basic unit.

In the World Calendar, each quarter begins the first month with a Sunday and has 31 days. The second and third months have 30 days each and the last day of the third month is a Saturday, so that the next quarter begins with a Sunday again.

The first month of the quarter therefore has five Sundays and the other two months have four each, so that every month, all year round, has 26 weekdays. The total number of days per quarter is 91 and the total number of weeks per quarter is 13.

The 364-day calendar is, of course, incomplete. In order to correct this, it was proposed that a day be added on to the end of the year (as December 31st) and called the Year-End World Holiday. In addition, it was suggested that every four years another day be added on to the end of the first half of the year (as June 31st) and named the Leap-Year Holiday. The calendar would thus be balanced.

In this simplified calendar each date in the year could be compared to the corresponding date in every other year and the calendar could be memorized.

The 13-Month Calendar of Auguste Comte

Monday	Tuesday	Wednesday	Thursday	Friday	Saturday	Sunday
1	2	3	4	5	6	7
8	9	10	11	12	13	14
15	16	17	18	19	20	21
22	23	24	25	26	27	28

World's Timekeepers Slowed Their Clocks

The U.S. Naval Observatory added an extra second to the official U.S. time scale at midnight (Universal Time), Dec. 31, 1987. The 'leap second' made the last day in December have 61 seconds rather than 60. This was done world-wide by an international scientific agreement in an effort to keep atomic time closely matched to solar time, or the rotation of the Earth.

The official United States time scale is determined by the Master Clock at the U.S. Naval Observatory, Washington, D.C. This scale is obtained by averaging 25 cesium beam 'atomic' clocks. For as long as man has kept time, he has set his clock by marking the passage of the Sun and the stars across the skies. Unfortunately, the Earth rotates irregularly, sometimes speeding up, but usually slowing down. The leap seconds are inserted to keep to a minimum the difference between the time as kept by the Earth's rotation and the time as kept by the independent atomic clock.

The atomic clock system is accurate to within a billionth of a second per day, while the Earth's rotation is only uniform to within one thousandth of a second per day. The two time standards will drift apart, and usually after 12 to 18 months the difference has reached eight tenths of a second. To coordinate the two, the 'leap second' is inserted. The last 'leap second' was inserted on June 30, 1985.

Although the Earth's rotation rate sometimes speeds up, the long-term trend is to slow down. According to the U.S. Naval Observatory, the present day's length is about two hours longer than a day's length 150 million years ago. Some 300 million years ago, the day lasted only about 20 hours. Think about that for a second.

The Cross-Quarter Days

(Source: U.S. Naval Observatory.)

There are four astronomical days in the year when the Earth is midway between the Equinoxes and the Solstices. The first is Groundhog Day, February 2; the second is Mayday, May 1; the next is called Lammas, August 1; and the last is Halloween, October 31.

Auto Rentals: How To Avoid Getting Taken For A Ride

Reprinted with permission, Department of Consumer Affairs, The City of New York

Shopping for a rental car is one of the more complicated tasks you may face as a consumer. When looking to rent a car, you are confronted with a variety of rental plans, insurance fees, fuel charges, etc. Even though the information you get appears very confusing, you have to sort out and understand your options, or you could end up choosing the wrong plan and spending lots of extra dollars or getting poor service.

Q. How can I get the best deal on a rental car?

A. In order to get the best deal, it is essential to *comparison shop. Rental plans* and prices vary with respect to car size and rental period. They also vary depending on the specific dates of the rental, for there may be different rates for holidays or promotional specials. Additionally, plans and prices for the same car size, rental period, and rental date vary widely among rental firms and the individual branches of each firm, with some establishments even offering consumers a choice between various plans for the same type of rental. Rental plans generally have two main factors: the rental fee and the mileage charge.

The *rental fee* is the amount you are charged per day, week, or weekend, no matter how far you drive the car. The *mileage charge*, on the other hand, accumulates with the number of miles you drive; it is based on a per-mile fee. Not only do the amounts of the rental fee and mileage charge vary, but so does the type of mileage plan offered. The most common types of mileage plans offer a certain number of free miles and then a per-mile charge for anything over; some plans, however, offer unlimited mileage, an option which is usually paired with a higher rental fee. When looking to rent a car, choose the overall plan that best fits your needs. For example, if you are planning to travel only a short distance, look for a plan that saves you money on the rental fee rather than on mileage.

Q. Does it make any difference whether I call a firm's national toll-free number or an individual branch directly?

A. It often does. Many national auto rental companies offer a central toll-free number at which you can get price quotes and make reservations for a car to be picked up at a particular local branch. Even though many people assume they will get the same price quotes whether they call the individual branch or the toll-free number, information given by the two is often inconsistent. Therefore, whenever you call for price quotes, it is best to confirm information given to you by a national firm's central number by calling the individual branch from which you want to rent the car. If the two numbers give you different prices, tell each office you were given different estimates, and find out which will be honored when you make your reservation.

Q. Can I rely upon advertisements in choosing which company to rent from?

A. Be wary of all advertisements, especially advertised specials. The advertised rates that you see in big numerals do not tell the whole story. There are a host of "hidden charges," usually in fine print at the bottom of the ad, such as insurance fees, gasoline charges, younger driver surcharges, and fees for dropping the car off in other cities, that are not part of the basic advertised rate, but which you may be liable for. Because of these hidden charges, your total bill might be more than double the rental rates advertised in large numbers. Therefore, it is important to read *all* the fine print and call the auto rental firm to find out about all hidden charges. Also, when you see an ad for an advertised special, make sure the special applies in your particular area.

Q. Should I take out the insurance offered by the rental company?

A. Not necessarily. Rental companies offer you, for an extra charge, a number of insurance-like plans, all of which are usually optional. These include medical coverage for passengers in the rental vehicle, liability insurance for damages to persons or property caused by the rental vehicle, and personal effects insurance, which covers you for any of your property which is stolen from the rental car. However, the most commonly-known insurance-like plan offered by the rental companies is the collision damage waiver, or CDW. The CDW will, in most cases, free you of any financial responsibility you have to the rental company in case you damage the car. Many firms will hold customers who don't take the CDW liable for up to the full value of the car, though some companies still have lower limits on customer liability. Some firms even require that their customers take out the CDW.

In those cases where the firm tells you that one or more of their insurance plans are required, make sure that these plans are actually mandatory and not just "strongly recommended," for you might not want to take out the insurance plans if they are optional—the insurance can significantly increase the cost of your rental. You might nevertheless feel that it is wiser to pay the extra dollars now rather than risk thousands of dollars in damages, but before you go ahead and pay any insurance fees, consider the following:

● You may already have one or more of the insurance plans being offered as part of your own coverage. Check your own auto insurance policy. If your own auto insurance covers you for damages to a rental car, you will first have to pay the rental company for any damages, and then your insurance company will reimburse you.

● If you have a credit card, your credit card company may cover at least part of your liability for damage to the rental car in case of an accident, whether or not you take out the CDW. Check with your credit card issuer.

● If you are a member of certain organizations, such as the American Automobile Association

(AAA), your organization may have an agreement with one or more rental companies limiting its members' damage liability to the rental company in case of an accident, whether or not you take out the CDW. Again, check with the organizations to which you belong.

Q. If I do take out the collision damage waiver, am I totally covered for any damage to the rental car?

A. Not in all cases. Most rental companies have a number of conditions which will invalidate the coverage you have just purchased. These generally include driving recklessly, driving off paved roads, driving under the influence of drugs or alcohol, or driving while drowsy. In addition, some companies require that you pay for the first several hundred dollars of damage to the car even if you have purchased the CDW.

Q. Will a rental company allow me to drop the car off in another city?

A. A large number of rental companies do not allow "one-way rentals"—driving the car to an-

other city and dropping it off there. On the other hand, many companies do allow such rentals. However, if you take advantage of their policy, you should expect to be in for heavy drop-off fees totaling as high as several hundred dollars. In addition, your daily or weekly rental fee might be significantly raised.

Q. Is there anything else I should know before I actually drive away in a rented car?

A. Before agreeing to take any rental car, look it over for dents, damages, or any defects which a visual examination would reveal. You should start the car and see if the headlights, brakes, and other easily checked equipment work. Try to avoid taking a car with any defect and, of course, never take a car with a safety-related defect. If you must take a car with a dent, scratch, or some other defect that does not affect safety, make sure the car's condition is clearly and specifically noted on the rental contract. Otherwise, you risk being charged for damage you did not cause when you come to return the car. □

Copyrights

Source: Library of Congress, Copyright Office.

U.S. is Now a Member of the Berne Union

On March 1, 1989, the United States joined the Berne Union by entering into an international treaty called the Berne Convention, whose full title is the Berne Convention for the Protection of Literary and Artistic Works. Also on that date, amendments to the U.S. copyright law that satisfy U.S. treaty obligations under the Convention took effect and some of them are listed herein. Contact the U.S. copyright office for details of Berne Convention obligations.

The U.S. Law continues to govern the protection and registration of works in the United States.

Beginning March 1, 1989, copyright in the works of U.S. authors is protected automatically in all member nations of the Berne Union and the works of foreign authors who are nationals of a Berne Union country, and works first published in a Berne Union country are automatically protected in the United States.

In order to fulfill its Berne Convention obligations, the United States made certain changes in its copyright law by passing the Berne Convention Implementation Act of 1988. These changes are not retroactive and are effective only on and after March 1, 1989.

The copyright law (Title 17 of the United States Code) was amended by the enactment of a statute for its general revision, Public Law 94–553 (90 Stat. 2541), which was signed by the President on October 19, 1976. The new law superseded the copyright act of 1909, as amended, which remained effective until the new enactment took effect on January 1, 1978.

Under the new law, all copyrightable works, whether published or unpublished, are subject to a single system of statutory protection which gives a copyright owner the exclusive right to reproduce the copyrighted work in copies or phonorecords and distribute them to the public by sale, rental, lease, or lending. Among the other rights given to

the owner of a copyright are the exclusive rights to prepare derivative works based upon the copyrighted work, to perform the work publicly if it be literary, musical, dramatic, choreographic, a pantomime, motion picture, or other audiovisual work, and in the case of literary, musical, dramatic, and choreographic works, pantomimes, and pictorial, graphic, or sculptural works, including the individual images of a motion picture or other audiovisual work, to display the copyrighted work publicly. All of these rights are subject to certain exceptions, including the principle of "fair use" which the new statute specifically recognizes.

Special provisions are included which permit compulsory licensing for the recording of musical compositions, noncommercial transmissions by public broadcasters of published musical and graphic works, performances of copyrighted music by jukeboxes, and the secondary transmission of copyrighted works on cable television systems.

Copyright protection under the new law extends to original works of authorship fixed in any tangible medium of expression, now known or later developed, from which they can be perceived, reproduced, or otherwise communicated, either directly or with the aid of a machine or device. Works of authorship include books, periodicals and other literary works, musical compositions with accompanying lyrics, dramas and dramatico-musical compositions, pantomimes and choreographic works, motion pictures and other audiovisual works, and sound recordings.

As a mandatory condition of copyright protection under the law in effect before 1978, all published copies of a work were required to bear a copyright notice. The 1976 Act provides for a notice on published copies, but omission or errors will not immediately result in forfeiture of the copyright, and can be corrected within certain time limits. Innocent infringers misled by the omission or error will be shielded from liability.

In accordance with the Berne agreement, mandatory notice of copyright has been abolished for works published for the first time on or after March

1, 1989. Failure to place a notice of copyright on copies or phonorecords of such works can no longer result in the loss of copyright.

Voluntary use of notice is encouraged. Placing a notice of copyright on published works is still strongly recommended. One of the benefits is that an infringer will not be able to claim that he or she "innocently infringed" a work. (A successful innocent infringement claim may result in a reduction in damages for infringement that the copyright owner would otherwise receive.)

A sample notice of copyright is: © 1989 John Brown.

The notice requirement for works incorporating a predominant portion of U.S. government work has been eliminated as of March 1, 1989. For these works to receive the evidentiary benefit of voluntary notice, in addition to the notice, a statement is required on the copies identifying what is copyrighted.

A sample is: © 1989 Jane Brown. Copyright claimed in Chapters 7-10, exclusive of U.S. government maps.

Notice Unchanged for Works Published Before March 1, 1989

The Berne Convention Implementation Act is not retroactive. Thus, the notice requirements that were in place before March 1, 1989, govern all works first published during that period (regardless of national origin).

● Works first published between January 1, 1978, and February 28, 1989: If a work was first published without notice during this period, it is still necessary to register the work before or within five years after publication and add the notice to copies distributed in the United States after discovery of the omission.

● Works first published before January 1, 1978: If a work was first published without the required notice before 1978, copyright was lost immediately (except for works seeking "ad interim" protection). Once copyright is lost, it can never be restored in the United States, except by special legislation.

Registration in the Copyright Office is not a condition of copyright protection but will be a prerequisite to bringing an action in a court of law for infringement. With certain exceptions, the remedies of statutory damages and attorney's fees will not be available for infringements occurring before registration. Copies or phonorecords published in the United States with notice of copyright are required to be deposited for the collections of the Library of Congress, not as a condition of copyright protection, but under provisions of the law subjecting the copyright owner to certain penalties for failure to deposit after a demand by the Register of Copyrights. Registration is permissive, but may be made either at the time the depository requirements are satisfied or at any other time during the subsistence of the copyright.

For works already under statutory protection, the new law retains the present term of copyright of 28 years from first publication (or from registration in some cases), renewable by certain persons for a second period of protection, but it increases the length of the second period to 47 years. Copyrights in their first term on January 1, 1978, must still be renewed during the last (28th) year of the original copyright term to receive the maximum statutory term of 75 years (a first term of 28 years plus a renewal term of 47 years).

Copyrights in their second term on January 1, 1978, are automatically extended up to a maximum of 75 years, without the need for further renewal. Unpublished works that are already in existence on January 1, 1978, but are not protected by statutory copyright and have not yet gone into the public domain, will generally obtain automatic Federal copyright protection for the author's life, plus an additional 50 years after the author's death, but in any event, for a minimal term of 25 years (that is, until December 31, 2002), and if the work is published before that date, then for an additional term of 25 years, through the end of 2027.

For works created on or after January 1, 1978, the new law provides a term lasting for the author's life, plus an additional 50 years after the author's death. For works made for hire, and for anonymous and pseudonymous works (unless the author's identity is revealed in Copyright Office records), the new term will be 75 years from publication or 100 years from creation, whichever is shorter. The new law provides that all terms of copyright will run through the end of the calendar year in which they would otherwise expire. This will not only affect the duration of copyrights, but also the time-limits for renewal registrations.

Works already in the public domain cannot be protected under the new law. The 1976 Act provides no procedure for restoring protection to works in which copyright has been lost for any reason. In general, works published before January 1, 1914, are not under copyright protection in the United States, at least insofar as any version published before that date is concerned.

The new law requires that all visually perceptible copies published in the United States or elsewhere bear a notice of copyright affixed in such manner and location as to give reasonable notice of the claim of copyright. (Abolished in or after March 1, 1989, according to the Berne agreement) The notice consists of the symbol © (the letter C in a circle), the word "Copyright," or the abbreviation "Copr.," and the year of first publication of the work, and the name of the owner of copyright in the work. EXAMPLE: © *1989 John Doe.*

The notice of copyright prescribed for sound recordings consists of the symbol ℗ (the letter P in a circle), the year of first publication of the sound recording, and the name of the owner of copyright in the sound recording, placed on the surface of the phonorecord, or on the phonorecord label or container, in such manner and location as to give reasonable notice of the claim of copyright EXAMPLE: ℗ *1989 Doe Records, Inc.*

According to the Berne Agreement, copyright owners must deposit in the Copyright Office two complete copies or phonorecords of the best edition of all works subject to copyright that are publicly distributed in the United States, whether or not the work contains a notice of copyright. In general, this deposit requirement may be satisfied by registration. For more information about mandatory deposit, request Circular 7d.

Renewal Is Still Required

Works first federally copyrighted before 1978 must still be renewed in the 28th year in order to receive the second term of 47 years. If such a work is not timely renewed, it will fall into the public domain in the United States at the end of the 28th year.

Recordation

Recordation as a Prerequisite to an Infringement Suit. The copyright owner no longer has to record a transfer before bringing a copyright lawsuit in that owner's name.

Benefits of recordation. The benefits of recordation in the Copyright Office are unchanged:
 • Under certain conditions, recordation establishes priorities between conflicting transfers and nonexclusive licenses;
 • Under certain conditions, recordation establishes priority between conflicting transfers; and,
 • Recordation establishes a public record of the contents of the transfer or document.

Jukebox Licenses

Section 116 of the 1976 Copyright Act provides for a compulsory license to publicly perform nondramatic musical works by means of coin-operated phonorecord players (jukeboxes). The Berne Convention Implementation Act amends the law to provide for negotiated licenses between the user (the jukebox operator) and the copyright owner. If necessary, the parties are encouraged to submit to arbitration to facilitate negotiated licenses. Such licenses take precedence over the compulsory license.

For detailed information about the admendments to U.S. copyright law under the Berne Convention agreement, request circulars 93, "Highlights of U.S. Adherence to the Berne Convention," and 93a, "The United States Joins The Berne Union" from the Copyright Office.

For publications, call the Forms and Publications Hotline, 202-707-9100, or write:
Copyright Office
Publications Section, LM-455
Library of Congress
Washington, D.C. 20559
To speak with an information specialist or to request further information, call 202-479-0700, or write:
Copyright Office
Information Section, LM-401
Library of Congress
Washington, D.C. 20559

Counterfeit Products

Source: U.S. Office of Consumer Affairs.

Counterfeit products include any product bearing an unauthorized representation of a manufacturer's trademark or trade name. Examples of products which have been counterfeited include prescription and over-the-counter drugs, clothing, credit cards, watches, pacemakers, and machine and automobile replacement parts. Because counterfeit products are often of sub-standard quality, there are potential safety risks which may cause personal injury as well as economic loss.

Avoiding counterfeit products takes practice. The following are usually associated with counterfeit products:
 • incorrect, smeared or blurred product packaging
 • incorrect spelling of brand name
 • no warranty or guarantee available
 • "unbelievably" low prices

Unemployment Insurance

Unemployment insurance is managed jointly by the states and the federal government. Most states began paying benefits in 1938 and 1939.

Under What Conditions Can the Worker Collect?

The laws vary from state to state. In general, a waiting period of one week is required after a claim is filed before collecting unemployment insurance; the worker must be able to work, must not have quit without good cause or have been discharged for misconduct; he must not be involved in a labor dispute; above all, he must be ready and willing to work. He may be disqualified if he refuses, without good cause, to accept a job which is suitable for him in terms of his qualifications and experience, unless the wages, hours and working conditions offered are substantially less favorable than those prevailing for similar jobs in the community.

The unemployed worker must go to the local state employment security office and register for work. If that office has a suitable opening available, he must accept it or lose his unemployment payments, unless he has good cause for the refusal. If a worker moves out of his own state, he can still collect at his new residence; the state in which he is now located will act as agent for the other state, which will pay his benefits.

Benefits are paid only to unemployed workers who have had at least a certain amount of recent

past employment or earnings in a job covered by the state law. The amount of employment or earnings, and the period used to measure them, vary from state to state, but the intent of the various laws is to limit benefits to workers whose recent records indicate that they are members of the labor force. The amount of benefits an unemployed worker may receive for any week is also determined by application to his past wages of a formula specified in the law. The general objective is to provide a weekly benefit which is about half the worker's customary weekly wages, up to a maximum set by the law (see table). In a majority of states, the total benefits a worker may receive in a 12-month period is limited to a fraction of his total wages in a prior 12-month period, as well as to a stated number of weeks. Thus, not all workers in a state are entitled to benefits for the number of weeks shown in the table.

Who Pays for the Insurance?

The total cost is borne by the employer in all but a few states. Each state has a sliding scale of rates. The standard rate is set at 6.2% of taxable payroll in most states. But employers with records of less unemployment (that is, with fewer unemployment benefits paid to their former workers) are rewarded with rates lower than the standard state rate.

During periods of high unemployment in a state,

federal-state extended benefits are available to workers who have exhausted their regular benefits. An unemployed worker may receive benefits equal to the weekly benefit he received under the state program for one half the weeks of his basic entitlement to benefits up to a maximum (including regular benefits) of 39 weeks.

Federal Programs

Amendments to the Social Security Act provided unemployment insurance for Federal civilian employees (1954) and for ex-servicemen (1958). Benefits under these programs are paid by state employment security agencies as agents of the federal government under agreements with the Secretary of Labor. For federal civilian employees, eligibility for benefits and the amount of benefits paid are determined according to the terms and conditions of the applicable state unemployment insurance law. Ex-servicemen are subject to specific eligibility and benefit payment provisions: benefits are not payable before the fifth week subsequent to the week of release or discharge from service and such benefits are limited to 13 weeks of duration.

State Unemployment Compensation Maximums, 1989

State	Weekly benefit[1]	Maximum duration, weeks	State	Weekly benefit[1]	Maximum duration, weeks
Alabama	145	26	Nebraska	134	26
Alaska	188–260	26	Nevada	184	26
Arizona	145	26	New Hampshire	156	26
Arkansas	209	26	New Jersey	258	26
California	166	26	New Mexico	166	26
Colorado	214	26	New York	245	26
Connecticut	234–284	26	North Carolina	228	26
Delaware	205	26	North Dakota	183	26
D.C.	283	26	Ohio	169–268	26
Florida	200	26	Oklahoma	197	26
Georgia	165	26	Oregon	229	26
Hawaii	239	26	Pennsylvania	266–274	26
Idaho	193	26	Puerto Rico	110	20
Illinois	187–244	26	Rhode Island	240–300	26
Indiana	96–161	26	South Carolina	147	26
Iowa	174–214	26	South Dakota	140	26
Kansas	210	26	Tennessee	155	26
Kentucky	166	26	Texas	210	26
Louisiana	181	26	Utah	208	26
Maine	171–256	26	Vermont	169	26
Maryland	205	26	Virgin Islands	162	26
Massachusetts	255–382	30	Virginia	176	26
Michigan	263	26	Washington	209	30
Minnesota	254	26	West Virginia	225	26
Mississippi	145	26	Wisconsin	200	26
Missouri	150	26	Wyoming	200	26
Montana	185	26			

1. Maximum amounts. When two amounts are shown, higher includes dependents' allowances. *Source:* Department of Labor, Employment and Training Administration.

Trademarks

Source: Department of Commerce, Patent and Trademark Office.

A trademark may be defined as a word, letter, device, or symbol, as well as some combination of these, which is used in connection with merchandise and which points distinctly to the origin of the goods.

Certificates of registration of trademarks are issued under the seal of the Patent and Trademark Office and may be registered by the owner if he is engaged in interstate or foreign commerce, since any Federal jurisdiction over trademarks arises under the commerce clause of the Constitution. Trademarks may be registered by foreign owners who comply with our law, as well as by citizens of foreign countries with which the U.S. has treaties relating to trademarks. American citizens may register trademarks in foreign countries by complying with the laws of those countries. The right to registration and protection of trademarks in many foreign countries is guaranteed by treaties.

General jurisdiction in trademark cases involving Federal Registrations is given to Federal courts. Adverse decisions of examiners on applications for registration are appealable to the Trademark Trial and Appeal Board, whose affirmances, and decisions in *inter partes* proceedings, are subject to court review. Before adopting a trademark, a person should make a search of prior marks to avoid infringing unwittingly upon them.

The duration of a trademark registration is 20 years, but it may be renewed indefinitely for 20-year periods, provided the trademark is still in use at the time of expiration.

The application fee is $200.

Patents

Source: Department of Commerce, Patent and Trademark Office.

A patent, in the most general sense, is a document issued by a government, conferring some special right or privilege. The term is now restricted mainly to patents for inventions; occasionally, land patents.

The grant of a patent for an invention gives the inventor the privilege, for a limited period of time, of excluding others from making, using, or selling a certain article. However, it does not give him the right to make, use, or sell his own invention if it is an improvement on some unexpired patent whose claims are infringed thereby.

In the U.S., the law provides that a patent may be granted, for a term of 17 years, to any person who has invented or discovered any new and useful art, machine, manufacture, or composition of matter, as well as any new and useful improvements thereof. A patent may also be granted to a person who has invented or discovered and asexually reproduced a new and distinct variety of plant (other than a tuber-propagated one) or has invented a new, original and ornamental design for an article of manufacture.

A patent is granted only upon a regularly filed application, complete in all respects; upon payment of the fees; and upon determination that the disclosure is complete and that the invention is new, useful, and, in view of the prior art, unobvious to one skilled in the art. The disclosure must be of such nature as to enable others to reproduce the invention.

A complete application, which must be addressed to the Commissioner of Patents and Trademarks, Washington, D.C. 20231, consists of a specification with one or more claims; oath or declaration; drawing (whenever the nature of the case admits of it); and a basic filing fee of $185.00[1] The filing fee is not returned to the applicant if the patent is refused. If the patent is allowed, another fee of $310.00[1] is required before the patent is issued. The fee for design patent application is $110.00[1]; the issue fee is $150.00[1]. Maintenance fees are required on utility patents at stipulated intervals.

Applications are ordinarily considered in the order in which they are received. Patents are not granted for printed matter, for methods of doing business, or for devices for which claims contrary to natural laws are made. Applications for a perpetual-motion machine have been made from time to time, but until a working model is presented that actually fulfills the claim, no patent will be issued.

1. Fees quoted are for small entities. Fees are double for corporations.

Beware of Illegal Patent Services

It is illegal under patent law (35 USC 33) for anyone to hold himself out as qualified to prepare and prosecute patent applications unless he is registered with the Patent Office. Also, Patent Office regulations forbid registered practitioners advertising for patent business. Some inventors, unaware of this, enter into binding contracts with persons and firms which advertise their assistance in making patent searches, preparing drawings, specifications, and patent applications, only to discover much later that their applications require the services of fully qualified agents or attorneys.

Birthstones

Month	Stone	Month	Stone
January	Garnet	July	Ruby or Star Ruby
February	Amethyst	August	Peridot or Sardonyx
March	Aquamarine or Bloodstone	September	Sapphire or Star Sapphire
April	Diamond	October	Opal or Tourmaline
May	Emerald	November	Topaz
June	Pearl or Alexandrite	December	Turquoise or Zircon

Source: Jewelry Industry Council.

Additional Consumer Sources

Consult the following special sections of *Information Please Almanac* for specific consumer information

State Consumer Protection Offices

Source: U.S. Office of Consumer Affairs.

State consumer protection offices resolve individual consumer complaints, conduct informational and educational programs, and enforce consumer protection and fraud laws. Most of these offices require complaints in writing. Call to find out the correct procedure for filing a complaint and what sales documents are needed. Phone numbers are subject to change.

Alabama
Montgomery (205) 261-7334
1 (800) 392-5658 (Alabama only)

Alaska
Anchorage (907) 279-0428
Fairbanks (907) 456-8588

Arizona
Phoenix (602) 255-3702 (fraud only)
1 (800) 352-8431 (Arizona only)

Arkansas
Little Rock (501) 371-2341
1 (800) 482-8982 (Arkansas only)

California
Sacramento-Consumer Affairs
(916) 445-0660 (complaint assistance)
(916) 445-1254 (consumer information)
(916) 322-3360 (Attorney General)
1 (800) 952-5225 (California only)
(916) 366-5055 (auto repairs)
1 (800) 952-5210 (California only-auto repairs)
Los Angeles (213) 620-4360

Colorado
Denver (303) 866-5167
(303) 866-3561 (agriculture)

Connecticut
Hartford (203) 566-4999
1 (800) 842-2649 (Connecticut only)

Delaware
Wilmington (302) 571-3250
(302) 571-3849 (economic crime)

District of Columbia
Washington, DC (202) 727-7000

Florida
Tallahassee (904) 488-2226
1 (800) 327-3382 (education)
Miami (305) 377-5619

Georgia
Atlanta (404) 656-7000
1 (800) 282-5808 (Georgia only)

Hawaii
Honolulu (808) 548-2560 (legal-Hawaii only)
(808) 548-2540 (complaints-Hawaii only)
Hilo (808) 961-7433
Lihue (808) 245-4365
Wailuku (808) 244-4387

Illinois
Springfield (217) 782-0244
1 (800) 642-3112 (Illinois only)
Chicago (312) 917-3580
(312) 917-3289 (citizens rights)

Indiana
Indianapolis (317) 232-6330
1 (800) 382-5516 (Indiana only)

Iowa
Des Moines (515) 281-3592
1 (800) 358-5510 (Iowa only)
(515) 281-5926 (consumer protection)

Kansas
Topeka (913) 296-3751
1 (800) 432-2310 (Kansas only)

Kentucky
Frankfort (502) 564-2200
1 (800) 432-9257 (Kentucky only)

Louisiana
Baton Rouge (504) 342-7013
New Orleans (504) 568-5472

Maine
Augusta (207) 289-3731
(207) 289-3716 (9 a.m.-1 p.m.)
Portland (207) 797-8978 (1 p.m.-4 p.m.)

Maryland
Baltimore (301) 528-8662 (9 a. m.-1 p.m.)
Hagerstown (301) 791-4780
Glen Burnie (301) 768-7420
Salisbury (301) 543-6620

Massachusetts
Boston (617) 727-8400 (information & referral only)
(617) 727-7780 (information & referral only)
Springfield (413) 785-1951

Michigan
Lansing (517) 373-1140
(517) 373-0947 (Consumers Council)
(517) 373-7858 (automotive regulation)
1 (800) 292-4204 (Michigan only)

Minnesota
Duluth (218) 723-4891
St. Paul (612) 296-2331

Mississippi
Jackson (601) 354-6018
(601) 359-3680
(601) 359-3648 (agriculture and commerce)

Missouri
Jefferson City (314) 751-4962
(314) 751-2616 (trade offenses)
1 (800) 392-8222 (Missouri only)

Montana
Helena (406) 444-4312

Nebraska
Lincoln (402) 471-2682

Nevada
Carson City (702) 885-4340
Las Vegas (702) 486-4150

New Hampshire
Concord (603) 271-3641

New Jersey
Newark (201) 648-4010 (consumer affairs)

(201) 648-4730 (Attorney General)
Trenton (609) 292-7087
1 (800) 792-8600 (New Jersey only)

New Mexico
Santa Fe (505) 872-6910
1 (800) 432-2070 (New Mexico only)

New York
Albany (518) 474-8583
(518) 474-5481
New York (212) 587-4482
(212) 341-2300

North Carolina
Raleigh
(919) 733-7741

North Dakota
Bismarck (701) 224-2210
(701) 224-3404 (Consumer Fraud)
1 (800) 472-2600 (North Dakota only)

Ohio
Columbus (614) 466-8831, 4986
1 (800) 282-0515 (Ohio only)
(614) 466-9605 (Consumers' Counsel)
1 (800) 282-9448 (Ohio only)

Oklahoma
Oklahoma City (405) 521-3921
(405) 521-3653

Oregon
Salem (503) 378-4320

Pennsylvania
Allentown (215) 821-6690
Erie (814) 871-4371
Harrisburg (717) 787-9707
1 (800) 441-2555 (Pennsylvania only)
(717) 783-5048 (utilities only)
(717) 787-7109 (consumer protection)
Scranton (717) 963-4913
Philadelphia (215) 560-2414
Pittsburgh (412) 565-5135

Puerto Rico
Old San Juan (809) 721-2900
Santurce (809) 722-7555

Rhode Island
Providence (401) 277-2104
(401) 277-2764

South Carolina
Columbia (803) 734-3970 (fraud)
(803) 734-9452 (Consumer affairs)
1 (800) 922-1594 (South Carolina only)
(803) 734-0457, 0467 (State Ombudsman)

South Dakota
Pierre (605) 773-4400

Tennessee
Nashville (615) 741-2672 (consumer protection)

(615) 741-4737 (consumer affairs)
1 (800) 342-8385 (Tennessee only)

Texas
Austin (512) 463-2070
Dallas (214) 742-8944
El Paso (915) 533-3484
Houston (713) 223-5886
Lubbock (806) 747-5238
McAllen (512) 682-4547
San Antonio (512) 225-4191

Utah
Salt Lake City (801) 530-6601
(801) 533-5319 (consumer affairs)

Vermont
Montpelier (802) 828-3171
(802) 828-2436 (agriculture)

Virgin Islands
St. Croix (809) 774-3130

Virginia
Richmond (804) 786-2115
(804) 786-2042 (agriculture)
1 (800) 552-9963 (Virginia only)

Washington
Olympia (206) 753-6210
Seattle (206) 464-7744
1 (800) 551-4636 (Washington only)
Spokane (509) 456-3123
Tacoma (206) 593-2904

West Virginia
Charleston (304) 348-8986
1 (800) 368-8808 (West Virginia only)

St. Albans (304) 727-5781

Wisconsin
Altoona (715) 839-3848
Green Bay (414) 436-4087 (agriculture)
Milwaukee (414) 438-4844 (agriculture)
(414) 227-4948
Madison (608) 266-1852 (Consumer protection)
1 (800) 362-8189 (Wisconsin only)
(608) 266-9836 (agriculture)
1 (800) 362-3020 (Wisconsin only)

Wyoming
Cheyenne (307) 377-777-7841, 6286

How to Write a Complaint Letter

Source: United States Office of Consumer Affairs.

- Include your name, address, and home and work phone numbers.
- Type your letter if possible. If it is handwritten, make sure it is neat and easy to read.
- Make your letter brief and to the point. Include all important facts about your purchase, including the date and place where you made the purchase and any information you can give about the product or service such as serial or model numbers or specific type of service.

- State exactly what you want done about the problem and how long you are willing to wait to get it resolved. Be reasonable.
- Include all documents regarding your problem. Be sure to send COPIES, not originals.
- Avoid writing an angry, sarcastic, or threatening letter. The person reading your letter probably was not responsible for your problem, but may be very helpful in resolving it.
- Keep a copy of the letter for your records.

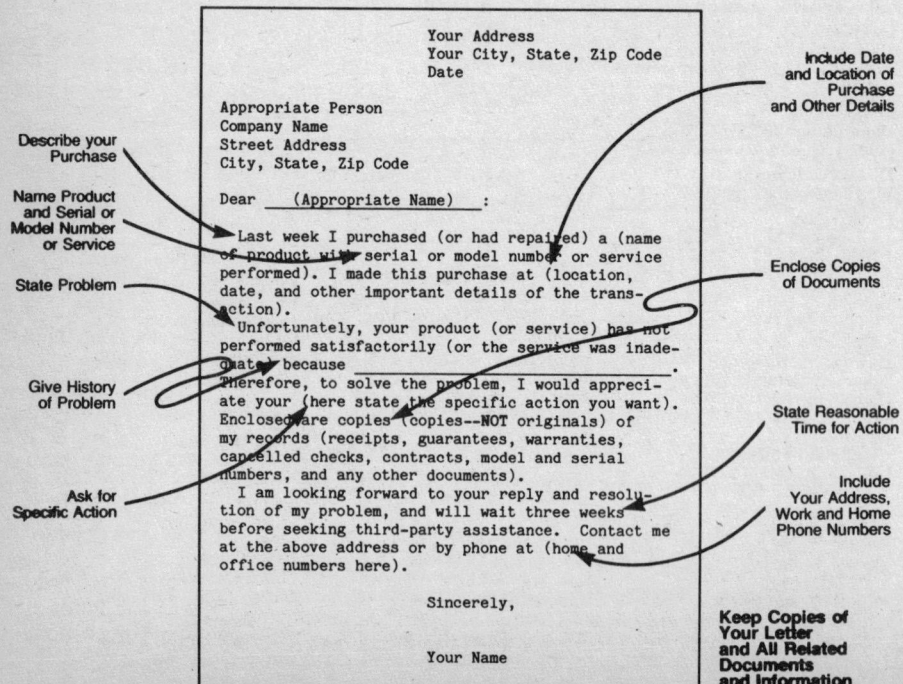

CONSUMER ASSISTANCE

This special section is intended to help you identify the address and phone number of over 300 company headquarters. When writing, please address your complaint to the attention of the Consumer Affairs Department. If you do not find a product in this listing, check Standard & Poor's Register of Corporations, Directors, and Executives, the Trade Names Directory, and the Standard Directory of Advertisers. Also see the Thomas Register of American Manufactures. These books can be found in most libraries. NOTE: Addresses and phone numbers are subject to change.

Consumer Assistance Directory

AAMCO Transmissions, Inc., One Presidential Blvd., Bala Cynwyd, PA 19004. (215) 668-2900; 1 (800) 523-0401 (toll free).

A.H. Robins Co., Inc., 3800 Cutshaw Ave., Richmond, VA 23230. (804) 257-2720.

AMTRAK, 400 North Capitol St., N.W., Washington, DC 20001. (202) 383-2121; 1 (800) 562-6960 (toll free TDD in Pennsylvania); 1 (800) 523-6590 (toll free TDD outside Pennsylvania).

AT&T, 295 North Maple Ave., Rm. 2353 G1, Basking Ridge, NJ 07920. (201) 221-7015.

Admiral. See Maycor

Alaska Airlines, P.O. Box 68900, Seattle, WA 98168. (206) 431-7286.

Alberto-Culver Co., 2525 Armitage Ave., Melrose Park, IL 60160. (312) 450-3163.

Allied Van Lines, P.O. Box 4403, Chicago, IL 60680 (312) 681-8000.

Allstate Insurance Company, Allstate Plaza, Northbrook, IL 60062. (312) 291-6719.

Aloha Airlines, P.O. Box 30028, Honolulu, HI 96820. (808) 836-4293.

Amana Refrigeration, Inc., Amana, IA 52204. (319) 622-5511.

America West Airlines, 222 South Mill Ave., Tempe, AZ 85281. (602) 921-5055.

American Airlines, Dallas/Fort Worth Airport, P.O. Box 619616 5E12, Dallas/Fort Worth, TX 75261. (817) 355-2114.

American Cyanamid Co., 697 Route 46, Clifton, NJ 07015. 1 (800) 932-2732 (toll free).

American Express Co., American Express Tower, World Financial Center, New York, N.Y. 10285. (212) 640-5619; 1 (800) 528-4800 (toll free—green card inquiries); 1 (800) 327-2177 (toll free—gold card inquiries); 1 (800) 525-3355 (toll free—platinum card inquiries).

American Greetings Corp., 10500 American Rd., Cleveland, OH 44144. (216) 252-7300; 1 (800) 321-3040 (toll free outside Ohio).

American Home Foods, 685 Third Ave., New York, NY 10017. (212) 878-6865.

American Standard, Inc., P.O. Box 6820, Piscataway, NJ 08855. 1 (800) 223-0651 (toll free in New Jersey); 1 (800) 223-0068 (toll free outside New Jersey).

American Stores Co., P.O. Box 27447, Salt Lake City, UT 84127. (801) 539-0112.

American Tourister, Inc., 91 Main St., Warren, RI 02885. (401) 245-2100 (Rhode Island); 1(800) 538-3383 (toll free outside Rhode Island).

Amerongen, Inc. See Budget Rent-A-Car Corp.

Amoco Oil Co., 200 East Randolph, Chicago, IL 60601. (312) 856-5894.

Anheuser-Busch, Inc., One Busch Place, St. Louis, MO 63118. (314) 577-3093.

Apple Computer, Inc., 20525 Mariani Ave., Mail Stop 37-S, Cupertino, CA 95014. (408) 973-2244 (complaints and questions); 1 (800) 538-9696 (toll free for dealer information).

Aramis, Inc. See Estee Lauder, Inc.

Arm & Hammer. See Church & Dwight Co., Inc.

Armstrong Tire Co., 500 Sargent Dr., New Haven, CT 06536. 1 (800) 243-0167 (toll free).

Armstrong World Industries, P.O. Box 3001, Lancaster, PA 17604. (717) 396-4401; 1 (800) 233-3823 (toll free).

Armour Processed Meat Co., 15101 North Scottsdale Rd., Scottsdale, AZ 85254. (602) 998-6186.

Arrow Shirts. See West Point-Pepperell

Atlantic Richfield Co., 515 South Flower St., Rm. 2059, Los Angeles, CA 90071. (213) 486-0265; 1 (800) 322-2726 (toll free).

Avis Rent-A-Car System, 900 Old Country Rd., Garden City, NY 11530. (516) 222-4200.

Avon Products, Inc., 9 West 57th St., New York, NY 10019. (212) 546-7777.

Averst Labs, 685 Third Ave., New York, NY 10017. (212) 878-6087.

B-F Beverage Co., P.O. Box 1080, Louisville, KY 40201. (502) 585-1100.

BIC Corporation, Wiley St., Milford, CT 06460. (203) 783-2000.

Bali. See Kitchens of Sara Lee

Bank of America, NT & SA, Bank of America Ctr., 555 California St., Dept. 353B, San Francisco, CA 94104. (415) 622-6081.

Bausch and Lomb Personal Products Div., Contact Lens Solutions, 1400 North Goodman St., Rochester, NY 14609. 1 (800) 227-4670 (toll free in New York); 1 (800) 553-5340 (toll free outside New York).

Bausch and Lomb Professional Products Div., Contact Lenses, 1400 North Goodman St., Rochester, NY 14609. (716) 338-6000.

Bausch and Lomb Sunglasses Div., 465 Paul Rd., Rochester, NY 14624. 1 (800) 462-4893 (toll free in New York); 1 (800) 828-1430 (toll free outside New York).

Becton Dickinson and Company, One Becton Dr., Franklin Lakes, NJ 07417. (201) 848-6800.

Beatrice Companies, Inc., 2 North LaSalle St., Chicago. IL 60602. (312) 558-3755.

Beecham Group, P.O. Box 1467, Pittsburgh, PA 15230. 1 (800) 242-1718 (toll free in Pennsylvania); 1 (800) 245-1040 (toll free outside Pennsylvania).

Beiersdorf, Inc., P.O. Box 5529, Norwalk, CT 06856. (203) 853-8008 (Connecticut); 1 (800) 233-2340 (toll free outside Connecticut).

Best Western International, P.O. Box 10203, Phoenix, AZ 85064. (602) 957-4200.

Birds Eye. See General Foods

Black and Decker Home Appliances, 6 Armstrong Rd., Shelton, CT 06484. (203) 926-3218.

Black and Decker Power Tools, 10 North Park Dr., Hunt Valley, MD 21030. (301) 683-7100.

Block Drug Co., Inc., 257 Cornelison Ave., Jersey City, NJ 07302. (201) 434-3000, ext. 308; 1 (800) 526-6040 (toll free outside New Jersey).

Blue Bell, Inc., P.O. Box 21488, Greensboro, NC 27420. (919) 373-3564.

Blue Cross and Blue Shield Association, 1709 New York Ave., N.W., Suite 303, Washington, DC 20006. (202) 783-6222.

Borden, Inc., 180 East Broad St., Columbus, OH 43215. (614) 225-4511.

Bradlees Stores, One Bradlees Circle, Braintree, MA 02184. (617) 770-5468.

Braniff, Inc., P.O. Box 7035, Dallas, TX 75209. (214) 358-7404.

Breck Hair Care Products. See American Cyanamid Co.

Bristol-Myers Co., 345 Park Ave., New York, NY 10154. (212) 546-4000.

British Airways, 245 Park Ave., New York, NY 10167. (212) 878-4500.

Brock Hotel Corp., 4441 West Airport Freeway, Irving, TX 75062. (214) 258-8500.

Brown Group, Inc., P.O. Box 354, St. Louis, MO 63166. (314) 854-2797.

Budget Rent-A-Car Corp., 3350 Boyington Dr., Carrollton, TX 75006. (312) 580-5000; 1 (800) 621-2855 (toll free in Texas); 1 (800) 621-2844 (toll free outside Texas).

Bulova Watch Co., 26-15 Brooklyn Queens Expressway East, Woodside, NY 11377. (718) 204-3300 (consumer relations); (718) 204-3222 (repairs).

Burlington Industries, P.O. Box 21207, Greensboro, NC 27420. (919) 379-2331.

Burroughs Wellcome Company, 330 Cornwallis Rd., Research Triangle Park, NC 27709. (919) 248-3000.

CBS Broadcast Group, 51 West 52nd St., New York, NY 10019. (212) 975-3166.

CIBA-GEIGY Corp., Pharmaceuticals Div., 556 Morris Ave., Summit, NJ 07901. (201) 277-5000.

CIBA Vision Corporation, 2910 Amwiler Ct., Atlanta, GA 30360. 1 (800) 241-5999 (toll free).

CVS, One CVS Dr., Woonsocket, RI 02895. (401) 765-1500.

Cadbury Schweppes Confections Div., Route 63 New Haven Rd., Naugatuck, CT 06770. (203) 729-0221.

Caloric Modern Maid Corp., 403 North Main St., Topton, PA 19562. (215) 682-4211.

Calvin Klein Industries, Inc., 205 West 39th St., 10th Floor, New York, NY 10018. (212) 719-2600.

Campbell Soup Co., Campbell Place, Camden, NJ 08101. (609) 342-3714.

Canon USA, Inc., 1 Jerricho Plaza, Jerricho, NY 11753. (516) 933-6300.

Carnation Co., 5045 Wilshire Blvd., Los Angeles, CA 90036. (213) 932-6000.

Carrier Air Conditioning Co., P.O. Box 4808, Syracuse, NY 13221. (315) 432-0761; 1 (800) 227-7437 (toll free outside New York).

Casio, Inc., 570 Mount Pleasant Ave., Dover, NJ 07801. (201) 361-5400.

Chesebrough-Pond's, Inc., 33 Benedict Place, Greenwich, CT 06830. 1 (800) 852-8558 (toll free in Connecticut); 1 (800) 243-5804 (toll free outside Connecticut).

Chevron U.S.A., P.O. Box H, Concord, CA 94524. (415) 827-6412.

Chuck E. Cheese. See Brock Hotel Corp.

Citizen Watch Co. of America, Inc., 8506 Osage Ave., Los Angeles, CA 90045. (213) 215-9660; 1 (800) 458-3300 (toll free in California); 1

(800) 321-3173 (toll free outside California).

Clinique Laboratories, Inc. See Estee Lauder, Inc.

Clorox Co., P.O. Box 24305, Oakland, CA 94623. (415) 271-7283.

Coca-Cola Co., Drawer 1734, Atlanta, GA 30301. 1 (800) 438-2653 (toll free).

Coleco Industries, Inc., P.O. Box 460, Amsterdam, NY 12010. (518) 843-4390.

Colgate-Palmolive Co., 300 Park Ave., New York, NY 10022. (212) 310-2653.

Commerce Drug Div. See Del Laboratories, Inc.

Commodore Business Machines, Inc., 1200 Wilson Dr., West Chester, PA 19380. (215) 431-9100.

Compaq Computer Corp., 20555 FM 149, Houston, TX 77070. (713) 370-0412.

Congoleum Corp., 195 Belgrove Dr., Kearny, NJ 07032. (201) 991-1000.

Consumers Products Group. See Commodore Business Machines, Inc.

Continental Airlines, P.O. Box 4607, Houston, TX 77210. (713) 442-4700.

Continental Baking Co., Checkerboard Square, St. Louis, MO 63104. (314) 982-4953.

Control Data Corp., 8100 34th Ave. South, Minneapolis, MN 55440. (612) 853-3400; 1 (800) 232-1985 (toll free).

Coppertone. See Plough, Inc.

Corning Glass Works, 1300 Hopeman Parkway, Waynesboro, VA 22980. (703) 942-3500.

Cosmair, Inc., P.O. Box 98, Westfield, NJ 07091. 1 (800) 631-7358 (toll free).

Cotter & Co., 2740 North Clybourn Ave., Chicago, IL 60614. (312) 975-2700.

Crown Books, 3300 75th Ave., Landover, MD 20785. (301) 731-1200.

Cuisinarts, Inc., P.O. Box 2150, Greenwich, CT 06836. (202) 622-4600; 1 (800) 243-8540 (toll free).

DHL Corp., 333 Twin Dolphin Dr., Redwood City, CA 94065. (415) 593-7474.

Dannon Company, Inc., 11 Westchester Ave., White Plains, NY 10604. (914) 697-9700.

Danskin, P.O. Box M 16, York, PA 17405. (717) 846-4874.

Dayton Hudson Department Store Co., 700 Nicollet Mall, Minneapolis, MN 55402. (612) 375-6802.

Del Monte Corp., P.O. Box 3575, San Francisco, CA 94119. (415) 942-4803.

Delta Airlines, Hartsfield Atlanta International Airport, Atlanta, GA 30320. (404) 765-2600.

The Dial Corp., Greyhound Tower, Station 316, Phoenix, AZ 85077. (602) 248-2595.

Diners Club International, 183 Inverness Dr. West, Englewood, CO 80112. (303) 790-2433; 1 (800) 525-9135 (toll free).

Discover Credit Card. See Sears, Roebuck and Co.

Dole Food Products, 50 California St., San Francisco, CA 94111. (415) 986-3000, ext. 4272; 1 (800) 232-8888 (toll free in California); 1 (800) 232-8800 (toll free outside California).

Doubleday Co., Inc., 501 Franklin Ave., Garden City, NY 11530. (516) 873-4628.

Dow Consumer Products, Food Care Div., P.O. Box 68511, Indianapolis, IN 46268. 1 (800) 428-4795 (toll free).

Dow Consumer Products, Texize Household Products Div., P.O. Box 368, Greenville, SC 29602. (803) 297-3400.

Dr. Pepper Co., 5523 East Mockingbird Lane, Dallas, TX 75206. (214) 824-0331.

Dunlop Tire Corp., P.O. Box 1109, Buffalo, NY 14240. (716) 879-8258.

E.I. DuPont De Nemours & Co., 1007 Market St., Wilmington, DE 19898. 1 (800) 441-7515 (toll free).

Eastern Airlines, Miami International Airport, Miami, FL 33148. (305) 873-3450.

Eastman Kodak Co., 343 State St., Rochester, NY 14650. 1 (800) 242-2424 (toll free).

Edward Lowe Industries, Inc., 919 North Michigan Ave., Suite 2002, Chicago, IL 60611. (312) 642-0888.

E.F. Hutton & Co., Inc., One Battery Park Plaza, 19th Floor, New York, NY 10004. (212) 742-7164.

Electrolux Corp., 3003 Summer St., Stamford, CT 06905. (203) 359-3600; 1 (800) 892-5678 (toll free).

Eli Lilly & Co., Lilly Corporate Center, Indianapolis, IN 46285. (317) 276-2339.

Emerson Electric Co., 8000 West Florissant Ave., St. Louis, MO 63136. (314) 553-3800.

Emery Worldwide, Old Danbury Rd., Wilton, CT 06897. (203) 762-8601.

Encyclopedia Britannica, Inc., 310 S. Michigan Ave., Chicago, IL 60604. (312) 347-7230.

Esprit, 900 Minnesota St., San Francisco, CA 94107. 1 (800) 4-ESPRIT (toll free).

Estee Lauder, Inc., 767 Fifth Ave., New York, NY 10153. (212) 572-4200.

Ethan Allen, Inc., Ethan Allen Dr., Danbury, CT 06811. (203) 743-8546.

Exxon Corp., P.O. Box 2180, Houston, TX 77252. (713) 656-3151.

Faultless Starch/Bon Ami Co., 1025 West Eighth St., Kansas City, MO 64101. (816) 842-1230.

Fayva Shoe Stores. *See* Morse Shoe Co.

Federal Express Corp., P.O. Box 727, Dept. 2640, Memphis, TN 38194. (901) 922-5642.

Federated Department Stores, 7 West Seventh St., Cincinnati, OH 45202. (513) 579-7000.

Fieldcrest Cannon, Inc., 60 West 40th St., New York, NY 10018. (212) 536-1284.

Firestone Tire & Rubber Co., P.O. Box 26602, Akron, OH 44319. 1 (800) 321-1252 (toll free).

First National Supermarkets, Inc., 17000 Rockside Rd., Cleveland, OH 44137. (216) 587-7100.

Fisher. *See* SFS Corp.

Fisher Price. *See* Quaker Oats Co.

Florists Transworld Delivery Association (FTD), 29200 Northwestern Hwy., P.O. Box 2227, Southfield, MI 48037. (313) 355-9300 (Southfield); 1 (800) 355-9300 (toll free).

Florsheim Shoe Co., 130 South Canal St., Chicago, IL 60606. (312) 559-7456.

Forbes, Inc., 60 Fifth Ave., New York, NY 10011. (212) 620-2248.

Fotomat Corp., 205 9th St., St. Petersburg, FL 33701. (813) 823-2027; 1 (800) 237-0307, ext. 0523 (toll free).

Freeman Shoes, Men's Div., 1 Freeman Lane, Beloit, WI 53511. 1 (800) 356-5400 (toll free).

French Shriner Shoes, 1 Freeman Lane, Beloit, WI 53511. (608) 364-1200.

Frigidaire Appliances. *See* White Consolidated Industries.

Frontier Airlines. *See* Continental Airlines.

Fruit of the Loom, Inc., One Fruit of the Loom Dr., Bowling Green, KY 42102. (502) 781-6400.

Fuji Photo Film U.S.A., Inc., 800 Central Blvd., Carlstadt, NJ 07072. 1 (800) 526-9030 (toll free).

Fuller Brush Co. *See* Kitchens of Sara Lee.

GTE Corp., One Stamford Forum, Stamford, CT 06904. (203) 965-2630.

General Electric Co. For information on GE Consumer Products and Services, call: GE ANSWER CENTER, 1 (800) 626-2000 (toll free).

General Foods Corp., 250 North St., White Plains, NY 10625. (914) 335-2500; 1 (800) 431-

1001 (toll free—desserts); 1 (800) 431-1002 (toll free—beverages); 1 (800) 431-1003 (toll free—main meals and beverages); 1 (800) 431-1004 (toll free—Maxwell House and Bird's Eye).

General Mills, Inc., P.O. Box 1113, Minneapolis, MN 55440. (612) 540-4295; 1 (800) 328-6787 (toll free).

General Tire & Rubber Co., One General St., Akron, OH 44329. 1 (800) 426-4889 (toll free in Ohio); 1 (800) 847-3349 (toll free outside Ohio).

George A. Hormel and Co., 501 16th Ave. N.E., Austin, MN 55912. (507) 437-5611.

Gerber Products, 445 State St., Fremont, MI 49412. (616) 928-2000; (800) 4-GERBER (toll free).

Giant Food, Inc., P.O. Box 1804, Dept. 597, Washington, DC 20013. (301) 341-4365; (301) 341-4327 (TDD).

Gibbons Greenvan. *See* Budget Rent-A-Car Corp.

Gibson Appliances. *See* White Consolidated Industries.

Gillette Co., Prudential Tower Bldg., 24th Floor, Boston, MA 02199. (617) 421-7315.

Glenbrook Laboratories. *See* Sterling Drug Inc.

The Glidden Co., 925 Euclid Ave., Cleveland, OH 44115. (216) 344-8000.

Goodyear Tire & Rubber Co., 1144 East Market St., Akron, OH 44313. (216) 796-4940.

Greyhound Lines, Inc., 901 Main St., Suite 2500, Dallas, TX 75202. (214) 744-6509.

H&R Block, Inc., 4410 Main St., Kansas City, MO 64111. (816) 753-6900.

H.J. Heinz Co., 1062 Progress St., Pittsburgh, PA 15212. (412) 237-5740.

HVR Co. *See* Clorox Co.

Hallmark Cards, Inc., P.O. Box 580, Kansas City, MO 64141. (816) 274-5697.

Halston. *See* Revlon.

Hanes. *See* Kitchens of Sara Lee.

Hardwick. *See* Maycor.

Hartz Mountain Corp. 700 South Fourth St., Harrison, NJ 07029. (201) 481-4800 (collect calls accepted).

Hasbro, Inc., 1027 Newport Ave., Pawtucket, RI 02861. (401) 727-5000; 1 (800) 237-0063 (toll free).

Hathaway Shirts. *See* Warnaco Men's Apparel.

Hawaiian Airlines, Honolulu International Airport, Honolulu, HI 96820. (808) 836-7230.

Helene Curtis Industries, 325 North Wells St., Chicago, IL 60610. (312) 661-0222.

Hershey Foods Corp., P.O. Box 815, Hershey, PA 17033. 1 (800) 468-1714 (toll free).

Hertz Corp., 660 Madison Ave., New York, NY 10021. (212) 980-2979; 1 (800) 654-3131 (toll free).

Hilton Hotels Corp., 9336 Civic Center Dr., Beverly Hills, CA 90210. (213) 278-4321.

Hitachi, Ltd., Hitachi Sales Corp. of America, 401 West Artesia Blvd., Compton, CA 90220. (213) 537-8383.

Holiday Inns, 3781 Lamar Ave., Memphis, TN 38195. (901) 362-4827.

Holly Farms, P.O. Box 88, Wilkesboro, NC 28697. (919) 838-2171.

Honeywell, Inc., 1885 Douglas Dr., Golden Valley, MN 55422. (612) 542-7354; 1 (800) 328-8194 (toll free).

Hoover Co., 101 East Maple, North Canton, OH 44720. (216) 499-9200, ext. 2294.

Hormel. *See* George A. Hormel and Co.

Hostess. *See* Continental Baking Co.

Howard Johnson Lodging, 710 Route 46 East, Fairfield, NJ 07007. (201) 882-1880.

Hyatt Hotels & Resorts, 3424 North 90th St., Omaha, NE 68134. 1 (800) 228-3336 (toll free).

IBM Corp., Old Orchard Rd., Armonk, NY 10504. (914) 765-5546.

J.C. Penney Co., 1301 Avenue of the Americas, New York, NY 10019. (212) 957-7282.

JVC Company of America, 41 Slater Dr., Elmwood Park, NJ 07407. (201) 794-3900.

Jenn-Air Co. *See* Maycor.

Jet America Airlines, 3521 East Spring St., Long Beach, CA 90806. (213) 492-6046.

Jhirmack. *See* Playtex, Inc.

John Hancock Financial Services, P.O. Box 111, Boston, MA 02117. (617) 572-6272.

Johnson & Johnson Baby Products Co., Grandview Rd., Skillman, NJ 08558. 1 (800) 526-3967 (toll free).

Johnson & Johnson Products, Inc., 501 George St., New Brunswick, NJ 08903. 1 (800) 526-2433 (toll free).

Jordache Enterprises, Inc., 498 7th Ave., New York, NY 10018. (212) 279-7343.

K Mart Corp., 3100 West Big Beaver Rd., Troy, MI 48084. (313) 643-1643.

Karastan Mills, P.O. Box 130, Eden, NC 27288. (919) 627-3400; 1 (800) 334-1181 (toll free).

Kayser-Roth Hosiery, Inc., 2306 West Meadowview Rd., Greensboro, NC 27407. (919) 852-6300.

Keebler Co., Inc., One Hollow Tree Lane, Elmhurst, IL 60126. (312) 833-2900.

Kellogg Co., P.O. Box 3599, Battle Creek, MI 49016. (616) 961-2277.

Kelvinator Appliance Co. *See* White Consolidated Industries.

The Kelly Springfield Tire Co., Willowbrook Rd., Cumberland, MD 21502. (301) 777-6016.

Kimberly-Clark Corp., P.O. Box 2020, Neenah, WI 54956. (414) 721-5604.

Kingsford Products Co. *See* Clorox Co.

Kitchens of Sara Lee, 500 Waukegan Rd., Deerfield, IL 60015. (312) 948-6138.

Kraft, Inc., Kraftcourt, Glenview, IL 60025. 1 (800) 323-0768 (toll free).

Kroger Co., 1014 Vine St., Cincinnati, OH 45201. (513) 762-1532; 1 (800) 632-6900 (toll free—meat and seafood).

Land O'Lakes, Inc., P.O. Box 116, Minneapolis, MN 55440. 1 (800) 328-4155 (toll free).

Lane Furniture, P.O. Box 151, Altavista, VA 24170. (804) 369-5641.

Lee Apparel Co., Inc., P.O. Box 2940, Shawnee Mission, KS 66201. (913) 384-4000.

L'Eggs Brands, Inc., P.O. Box 748, Rural Hall, NC 27098. (919) 744-4213.

Lennox Industries, P.O. Box 809000, Dallas, TX 75380. (214) 980-6000.

Lever Brothers Corp., 390 Park Ave., New York, NY 10022. (800) 451-6679 (toll free).

Levi Strauss & Co., 1155 Battery St., San Francisco, CA 94111. 1 (800) 227-5600 (toll free).

Liberty Mutual Insurance Group, 175 Berkeley St., Boston, MA 02117. (617) 357-9500.

Litton Microwave Cooking Products, P.O. Box 1976, Memphis, TN 38101. (901) 366-3300.

L'Oreal. *See* Cosmair, Inc.

Lorillard, Ltd., 2525 East Market St., Greensboro, NC 27420. (919) 373-6669.

Lucky Stores, Inc., P.O. Box BB, Dublin, CA 94568. (415) 833-6000.

M&M/Mars, Inc., High St., Hackettstown, NJ 07840. (201) 852-1000.

MCA, Inc., 100 Universal City Plaza, Universal City, CA 91608. (818) 777-1000.

MTV Networks, Inc. See Viacom International, Inc.

Magic Chef. *See* Maycor.

Magnavox. *See* NAP Consumer Electronics Corp.

Mannington Mills, Inc., P.O. Box 30, Salem, NJ 08079. (609) 935-3000.

Marion Labs, Consumer Products Div., Marion Park Dr., Kansas City, MO 64134. (816) 966-5000.

Marriott Corp., One Marriott Dr., Washington, DC 20058. (301) 294-3601.

MasterCard International. (Contact issuing bank.)

Matsushita Servicing Co., 50 Meadowlands Pkwy., Secaucus, NJ 07094. (201) 348-7000.

Mattel Toys, Inc., 5150 Rosecrans, Hawthorne, CA 90250. (213) 978-6127; 1 (800) 421-2887 (toll free outside California).

Max Factor. *See* Revlon.

Maxicare Health Plans, Inc., 5200 West Century Blvd., Los Angeles, CA 90045. (213) 568-9000 (after 12 noon EST).

Maxwell House. *See* General Foods.

May Department Stores Co., 611 Olive St., St. Louis, MO 63101. (314) 342-4336.

Maybelline. *See* Plough, Inc.

Maycor Appliance, Parts, and Service Co., 240 Edwards St., S.E., Cleveland, TN 37311. (615) 472-3333.

Maytag. *See* Maycor.

McCormick & Co., Inc., 414 Light St., Baltimore, MD 21202. (301) 547-6273.

McCrory Stores, 2955 East Market St., York, PA 17402. (717) 757-8181.

McDonald's Corporation, McDonald's Plaza, Oak Brook, IL 60521. (312) 575-6198.

McGraw-Hill, Inc., Princeton Rd., Highstown, NJ 08520. (609) 426-7600.

McKee Baking Co., P.O. Box 750, Collegedale, TN 37315. (615) 238-7111.

McNeil Consumer Products Company, Camp Hill Rd., Fort Washington, PA 19034. (215) 233-7000.

Mennen Company, Morristown, NJ 07960. (201) 631-9000.

Merrill Lynch, Pierce, Fenner & Smith, Inc., 165 Broadway, New York, NY 10080. (212) 637-0891.

Metropolitan Life and Affiliated Companies, One Madison Ave., New York, NY 10010. (212) 578-2544.

Michelin Tire Corp., Patewood Executive Plaza, Two Patewood Court, Greenville, SC 29602. (803) 234-5000.

Midway Airlines, 5700 South Cicero, Chicago, IL 60638. (312) 838-4494.

Milton Bradley Co., 443 Shaker Rd., East Long Meadow, MA 01028. (413) 525-6411.

Minnetonka Corp., Jonathan Industrial Park, Chaska, MN 55318. (612) 448-4181; 1 (800) 247-8428 (toll free outside Minnesota).

Minolta Corp., 101 Williams Dr., Ramsey, NJ 07446. (201) 825-4000.

Minwax Wood Products, 102 Chestnut Ridge Plaza, Montvale, NJ 07645. 1 (800) 526-0495 (toll free).

Mitsubishi Electric Sales of America, Inc., 5757 Plaza Dr., P.O. Box 6007, Cypress, CA 90630. (714) 220-2500; 1 (800) 262-1299 (toll free in California); 1 (800) 421-1140 (toll free outside California).

Mobil Oil Corp., 3225 Gallows Rd., Fairfax, VA 22037. (703) 849-3986.

Monet Jewelers, Number Two Lonsdale Ave., Pawtucket, RI 02860. (401) 728-9800; (401) 212-7254.

Monsanto Co., 800 North Lindbergh Blvd., St.

Louis, MO 63167. (314) 694-2883.

Montgomery Ward, One Montgomery Ward Plaza, Chicago, IL 60671. (312) 467-2628.

Morse Shoe Co., 555 Turnpike St., Canton, MA 02021. (617) 828-9300.

Morton Salt, 110 North Wacker Dr., Chicago, IL 60606. (312) 807-2694.

Motorola, Inc., 1303 East Algonquin Rd., Schaumburg, IL 60196. (312) 397-5000.

NAP Consumer Electronics Corp., P.O. Box 555, Jefferson City, TN 37760. (615) 475-3801.

NBC, Inc., 30 Rockefeller Plaza, New York, NY 10112. (212) 664-2333.

NEC Home Electronics USA, 1255 Michael Dr., Wood Dale, IL 60191. (312) 860-9500; 1 (800) 323-1728 (toll free outside Illinois).

Nabisco Brands, Inc., East Hanover, NJ 07936. (201) 884-4000.

National Car Rental System, Inc., 7700 France Ave., South Minneapolis, MN 55435. (612) 830-2121; 1 (800) 367-6767 (toll free outside Minnesota).

National Presto Industries, Inc., 3925 North Hastings Way, Eau Claire, WI 54703. (715) 839-2121.

Neiman-Marcus, 2620 North Haskell Ave., P.O. Box 2142, Dallas, TX 75262. (214) 821-4000; 1 (800) 442-2274 (toll free in Texas); 1 (800) 527-1767 (toll free outside Texas).

Nestle Foods Corp., 100 Manhattanville Rd., Purchase, NY 10577. (914) 251-3000.

Neutrogena Corp., 5755 West 96th St., Los Angeles, CA 90045. (213) 642-1150; 1 (800) 421-6857 (toll free outside California).

New York Air. *See* Continental Airlines.

New York Times Co., 229 West 43rd St., New York, NY 10036. (212) 556-7171.

Newsweek, Inc., P.O. Box 404, Livingston, NJ 07039. (212) 350-4000; 1 (800) 631-1040 (toll free subscriber service only).

Nike, Inc., 9300 Nimbus Rd., Beaverton, OR 97005. (503) 644-9000; 1 (800) 344-6453 (toll free outside Oregon).

No Nonsense. See Kayser-Roth Hosiery, Inc.

Norge. *See* Maycor.

North American Philips, Consumer Electronics Div., P.O. Box 555, Jefferson City, TN 37760. (615) 475-3801.

North American Watch Corp., 650 Fifth Ave., New York, NY 10019. (212) 397-7800.

Northwest Airlines, M/S A5100 Minneapolis/St. Paul International Airport, St. Paul, MN 55111. (612) 726-2046.

Noxell Corp., 11050 York Rd., Hunt Valley, MD 21030. (301) 785-4411.

Nu Tone. *See* Scoville, Inc.

Ocean Spray Cranberries Inc., 225 Water St., Plymouth, MA 02360. (617) 747-7407.

O'Keefe & Merit Appliances. See White Consolidated Industries.

Olympus Optical Co., Ltd., 145 Crossways Park, Woodbury, NY 11797. (516) 364-3000; 1 (800) 433-0880 (toll free—information).

Oneida, Ltd., Kenwood Station, Oneida, NY 13421. (315) 361-3000.

Orville Redenbacher. *See* Beatrice Companies, Inc.

OSCO Drugs. *See* American Stores Co.

Oster Co., 5055 North Lydell Ave., Milwaukee, WI 53217. (414) 332-8300; 1 (800) 356-7837 (toll free).

Owens-Corning Fiberglas Corp., Fiberglas Tower, Toledo, OH 43659. (419) 248-8000.

Pacific Southwest Airlines, P.O. Box 85385, San Diego, CA 92138. (619) 574-2314.

PaineWebber, Inc., 120 Broadway, New York, NY 10271. (212) 437-2087.

Pan American World Airways, 200 Park Ave., Pan Am Bldg., New York, NY 10166. (212) 880-6139.

Panasonic. *See* Matsushita Servicing Co.

Parke-Davis. *See* Warner-Lambert Co.

Pennzoil Products Co., P.O. Box 2967, Houston, TX 77252. (713) 546-4262.

Peoples Drug Stores, Inc., 6315 Bren Mar Dr., Alexandria, VA 22312. 1 (800) 572-0267 (toll free inside Virginia); 1 (800) 336-4990 (toll free outside Virginia).

People Express. *See* Continental Airlines.

Pepperidge Farm, Inc., Westport Ave., Norwalk, CT 06856. (203) 846-7276.

Pepsi Cola Co., Route 35 and 100, Somers, NY 10589. (914) 767-7218.

Perdue Farms, P.O. Box 1537, Salisbury, MD 21801. (301) 543-3000; 1 (800) 638-1150.

Personal Products Company, Van Liew Ave., Milltown, NJ 08850. 1 (800) 631-5249 (toll free).

Pet Incorporated, P.O. Box 392, St. Louis, MO 63166. (314) 621-5400.

Pet Incorporated, Frozen/Bakery Group, P.O. Box 392, St. Louis, MO 63166. (314) 621-5400.

Pet Incorporated, Grocery Group, P.O. Box 392, St. Louis, MO 63166. (314) 621-5400.

Pfizer Consumer Products, 235 East 42nd St., New York, NY 10017. (212) 573-2323.

Pillsbury Co., 2821 Pillsbury Center, Minneapolis, MN 55402. (612) 330-4728.

Philco. *See* NAP Consumer Electronics Corp.

Phillips Petroleum Co., 16 Phillips Bldg., Bartlesville, OK 74004. (918) 661-1215.

Piaget. *See* North American Watch Corp.

Piedmont Airlines, Inc., Customer Relations, 1 Piedmont Plaza, Winston-Salem, NC 27156. (919) 770-8206.

Pierre Cardin. *See* American Cyanamid Co.

Pioneer Electronics Service, Inc., P.O. Box 1760, Long Beach, CA 90801. 1 (800) 421-1404 (toll free).

Playskool. *See* Hasbro, Inc.

Playtex, Inc., 215 College Rd., P.O. Box 728, Paramus, NJ 07652. (201) 265-8000; 1 (800) 624-0825 (toll free in New Jersey); 1 (800) 222-0453 (toll free outside New Jersey).

Plough, Inc., 3030 Jackson Ave., Memphis, TN 38151. (901) 320-2386.

Polaroid Corp., 784 Memorial Dr., Cambridge, MA 02139. (617) 577-2000 (collect calls within Massachusetts); 1 (800) 343-5000 (toll free outside Massachusetts).

Princeton Pharmaceutical Products. *See* Squibb Corp.

Procter & Gamble Co., P.O. Box 599, Cincinnati, OH 45201. (513) 562-2200.

Prudential Insurance Company of America, One Washington Bldg., Newark, NJ 07101. (201) 877-7340.

Publishers Clearing House, 382 Channel Dr., Port Washington, NY 11050. (516) 883-5432; 1 (800) 645-9242 (toll free outside New York).

Publix Supermarkets, 1936 George Jenkins Blvd., P.O. Box 407, Lakeland, FL 33802. (813) 688-1188; 1 (800) 282-4168 (toll free in Florida).

Purolator Courier Corp., 131 Marstown Rd., Basking Ridge, NJ 07920. 1 (800) 653-3333 (toll free).

Quaker Oats Co., P.O. Box 9003, Chicago, IL 60604. (312) 222-7843.

Quaker State Corp., P.O. Box 989, Oil City, PA 16301. (814) 676-7676.

Quasar Co., 1325 Pratt Blvd., Elk Grove Village, IL 60007. (312) 228-6366.

Radio Shack. *See* Tandy Corp.

Ralston Purina Co., Checkerboard Square, St. Louis, MO 63164. (314) 982-4566.

Ramada, Inc., P.O. Box 29004, Phoenix, AZ 85038. (602) 273-4000.

Reader's Digest Association, Inc., Pleasantville, NY 10570. 1 (800) 262-2627 (toll free in New York); 1 (800) 431-1246 (toll free outside New York).

Reebok, 150 Royall St., Canton, MA 02021. (617) 821-2800; 1 (800) 843-4444 (toll free outside Massachusetts).

The Regina Co., 313 Regina Ave., Rahway, NJ 07065. (201) 381-1000; 1 (800) 847-8336 (toll free outside New Jersey).

Remington Products, Inc., 60 Main St., Bridgeport, CT 06602. (203) 367-4400.

Remington Rifle. *See* E.I. duPont de Nemours & Co.

Revlon, 767 Fifth Ave., New York, NY 10153. (212) 326-5682.

Reynolds Metals Co., 6603 West Broad St., Richmond, VA 23230. (804) 281-4104.

Richardson-Vicks, Inc., Healthcare & Personal Products Div., 10 Westport Rd., Wilton, CT 06897. (203) 834-5000.

Rockport. *See* Reebok.

Rolex Watch U.S.A., Inc., 665 Fifth Ave., New York, NY 10022. (212) 758-7700.

Rorer Group Inc., 500 Virginia Dr., Fort Washington, PA 19034. (215) 628-6416.

Ross Laboratories, 625 Cleveland Ave., Columbus, OH 43215. (614) 227-3758.

Rubbermaid, Inc., 1147 Akron Rd., Wooster, OH 44691. (216) 264-6464.

Rustler Jeans. *See* Blue Bell, Inc.

Ryder Truck Rental, P.O. Box 020816, Miami, FL 33102. 1 (800) 327-7777 (toll free outside Florida).

7-Eleven Food Stores. *See* The Southland Corp.

SFS Corporation, Customer Information Center, 1 (800) 421-5013 (toll free).

STP Corporation, 39 Old Ridgebury Rd., Danbury, CT 06817. (203) 794-3930.

Safeway Stores, Inc., Oakland, CA 94660. (415) 891-3267.

Samsonite. *See* Beatrice Companies, Inc.

Sandoz Company, Hwy. 56 and Interstate 80, P.O. Box 83288, Lincoln, NE 68501. (402) 464-6311.

Sanyo Electric Inc. *See* SFS Corp.

Sara Lee. *See* Kitchens of Sara Lee.

Schwinn Bicycle Co., 217 North Jefferson St., Chicago, IL 60606. (312) 454-7400.

Scott Paper Co., Scott Plaza Two, Philadelphia, PA 19113. (215) 522-6170; 1 (800) 835-7268 (toll free outside Pennsylvania).

Scoville, Inc., Madison and Red Bank Rds., Cincinnati, OH 45227. (513) 527-5100; 1 (800) 582-2030 (toll free in Ohio); 1 (800) 543-8687 (toll free outside Ohio).

Sealy Mattress Manufacturing Co., 1300 East Ninth St., Cleveland, OH 44114. (216) 522-1310.

Seaman Furniture Store, 70 Charles Lindbergh Blvd., Uniondale, NY 11553. (516) 222-6011.

G.D. Searle and Co., Consumer Products Div., P.O. Box 5110, Chicago, IL 60680. 1 (800) 942-5686 (toll free in Illinois); 1 (800) 323-1157 (toll free outside Illinois).

G.D. Searle and Co., Nutrasweet, P.O. Box C-1115, Skokie, IL 60076. (312) 982-7972; 1 (800) 321-7254 (toll free outside Illinois).

G.D. Searle and Co., Pharmaceuticals, P.O. Box 5110, Chicago, IL 60680. 1 (800) 942-2566 (toll free in Illinois); 1 (800) 323-1603 (toll free outside Illinois).

Sears, Roebuck and Co., Dept. 731 A, Sears Tower, Chicago, IL 60684 (312) 875-5188.

Sedgefield Jeans. See Blue Bell, Inc.

Seiko Time Corp., 1111 MacGauther Blvd., Mahwah, NJ 07430. (201) 529-3311.

The Seven-Up Co., P.O. Box 655086, Dallas, TX 75265. (214) 824-0331.

Seventeen Magazine. *See* Triangle Publications, Inc.

Sharp Electronics Corp., Sharp Plaza, P.O. Box 650, Mahwah, NJ 07430. (201) 529-9140.

Shell Oil Co., P.O. Box 2463, Houston, TX 77001. (713) 241-2281.

Sherwin-Williams Co., 101 Prospect Ave., N.W., Cleveland, OH 44101. (216) 566-2068.

Shop Rite Supermarket, 600 York St., Elizabeth, NJ 07207. (201) 527-3342.

ShowBiz Pizza. *See* Brock Hotel Corp.

Simmons U.S.A., P.O. Box 95465, Atlanta, GA 30347. (404) 321-3030.

Simonize, 39 Old Ridgebury Rd., Danbury, CT 06817. (203) 794-3930.

Singer Sewing Co., 155 Raritan Center Pkwy., Edison, NJ 08837. (201) 527-6000.

Skaggs Co. *See* American Stores Co.

SmithKline Consumer Products, One Franklin Plaza, P.O. Box 8082, Philadelphia, PA 19101. (215) 751-4324.

J.M. Smucker Co., Strawberry Lane, Orrville, OH 44667. (216) 682-0015.

Sonesta International Hotels Corp., 200 Clarendon St., Boston, MA 02116. (617) 421-5413.

Sony Corp. of America, Sony Service Co., Sony Dr., Park Ridge, NJ 07656. (201) 930-7669.

Southwest Airlines, Love Field, P.O. Box 37611, Dallas, TX 75235. (214) 353-6145.

Spalding & Evenflo, Inc., Meadow St., Chicopee, MA 01021. 1 (800) 332-9662 (toll free in Massachusetts); 1 (800) 225-6601 (toll free outside Massachusetts).

Speed Queen Co., P.O. Box 990, Ripon, WI 54971. (414) 748-3121.

Spiegel, Inc., Regency Towers, 1515 West 22nd St., Oak Brook, IL 60522. (312) 954-2772.

Squibb Corp., P.O. Box 4000, Princeton, NJ 08540. (609) 921-4279.

Stanley Hardware, Div. Stanley Works, 195 Lake St., New Britain, CT 06050. (203) 225-5111.

Sterling Drug Inc., 90 Park Ave., New York, NY 10016. (212) 907-2000, 3149.

Stop & Shop Supermarkets, P.O. Box 1942, Boston, MA 02105. (617) 770-8895.

Stouffer Foods Corp., 5750 Harper Rd., Solon, OH 44139. (216) 248-3600.

Stouffer Restaurant Company, 30050 Chagrin Bldg., Pepper Pike, OH 44124. (216) 464-6606.

Sun-Diamond Growers of California, P.O. Box 1727, Stockton, CA 95201. (209) 466-4851.

Sunbeam Appliance Co., 1333 Butterfield Rd., P.O. Box 1576, Downers Grove, IL 60515. (312) 719-5000.

Supermarkets General Corp., 301 Blair Rd., Woodbridge, NJ 07095. (201) 499-3500.

Swatch Watch USA, 1704 Hempstead Lane, Lancaster, PA 17601. 1 (800) SWATCH-1 (toll free).

Sylvania Television. *See* NAP Consumer Electronics Corp.

3M, 3M Center, Bldg. 225-5N-04, St. Paul, MN 55144. (612) 733-1871.

T.V. Guide. *See* Triangle Publications, Inc.

Tandy Corp./Radio Shack, 1600 One Tandy Center,

Fort Worth, TX 76102. (817) 390-3218.

Tappan Co., Inc. See White Consolidated Industries

Target Stores, 33 South 6th St., P.O. Box 1392, Minneapolis, MN 55440. (612) 370-6006.

Technics. *See* Matsushita Servicing Co.

Teledyne, Inc., 1730 East Prospect St., Fort Collins, CO 80525. (303) 484-1352; 1 (800) 525-2774 (toll free except Alaska & Hawaii).

Tenneco, Inc., P.O. Box 2511, Houston, TX 77001. (713) 757-2777.

Tetley, Inc., 100 Commerce Dr., Shelton, CT 06484. (203) 929-9342.

Texaco Refining and Marketing, P.O. Box 2000, Bellarie, TX 77401. (713) 432-2235, 2018.

Texas Instruments, Inc., P.O. Box 53, Lubbock, TX 79408. 1 (800) 232-3200 (Dallas, TX).

Thom McAn Shoe Co., 67 Millbrook St., Worcester, MA 01606. (617) 791-3811.

Thrift Drug Co., 615 Alpha Dr., Pittsburgh, PA 15238. (412) 781-5373.

Time Inc., Rockefeller Center, New York, N.Y. 10020. (212) 522-1212.

Timex Corp., P.O. Box 2740, Little Rock, AR 72203. (501) 372-1111.

Tonka Corp., 6000 Clearwater Dr., Minnetonka, MN 55343. (612) 936-3300.

Toshiba Corp., 82 Totowa Rd., Wayne, NJ 07470. (201) 628-8000 (consumer products).

Totes, Inc., 10078 East Kemper Rd., Loveland, OH 45140. (513) 583-2300.

Tourneau, Inc., 515 Madison Ave., New York, NY 10022. (212) 758-3265; 1 (800) 223-1288 (toll free outside New York).

Toys R Us, 395 West Passaic, Rochelle Park, NJ 07662. (201) 368-5528.

Trane/Cac, Inc. See American Standard, Inc.

Trans World Airlines, 605 Third Ave., New York, NY 10158. (212) 692-3311.

Triangle Publications, Inc., Four Radnor Corporate Center, Radnor, PA 19088. (215) 293-8500.

True Value Hardware Stores. *See* Cotter & Co.

Tupperware, P.O. Box 2353, Orlando, FL 32802. (305) 847-3111; 1 (800) 858-7221 (toll free outside Florida).

Turner Broadcasting System, Inc., P.O. Box 7500 (WTBS), Atlanta, GA 30357. 1 (800) 257-1234 (toll free outside Georgia).

Tyson Foods, Inc., 2210 W. Oaklawn Dr., P.O. Drawer E, Springdale, AR 72764. (501) 756-4000.

U-Haul International, 2727 N. Central Ave., Phoenix, AZ 85004. (602) 263-6771; 1 (800) 528-0463 (toll free outside Arizona).

USAir, Hangar 12, Washington National Airport, Washington, DC 20001. (703) 892-7020.

U.S. Shoe Corp., One Eastwood Dr., Cincinnati, OH 45227. (513) 527-7590.

US West, Inc., Orchard Falls Bldg., Englewood, CO 80111. (303) 793-6660.

Uniroyal Goodrich Co., 600 S. Main St., Akron, OH 44397. (216) 374-3796; 1 (800) 521-9796 (toll free).

United Airlines, P.O. Box 66100, Chicago, IL 60666. (312) 952-5341.

United Parcel Service of America, Inc., 51 Weaver St., Greenwich, CT 16836. (203) 622-7012.

United Van Lines, One United Dr., Fenton, MO 63026. 1 (800) 325-3870 (toll free).

Universal Match Corp., 1224 Fern Ridge Pkwy., St. Louis, MO 63141. (314) 469-3655.

Upjohn Co., 7000 Portage Rd., Kalamazoo, MI 49001. (616) 323-6004.

Valvoline Oil Co., P.O. Box 12918, Lexington, KY 40512. (606) 268-7389.

Van Heusen Co., 281 Centennial Ave., Piscataway, NJ 08854. (201) 885-5000; 1 (800) 631-5809 (toll free outside New Jersey).

Vanity Fair, 640 Fifth Ave., New York, NY 10019. (212) 582-6767.

Viacom International, Inc., 1211 Avenue of the Americas, New York, NY 10036. (212) 719-7556.

Visa USA, Inc., P.O. Box 8999, San Francisco, CA 94128. (415) 570-3200.

Wal-Mart Stores, Inc., P.O. Box 116, Bentonville, AR 72716. (501) 273-4000.

Walgreen, 200 Wilmot Rd., Deerfield, IL 60015. (312) 940-2500.

Wamsutta Pacific, 111 W. 40th St., 16th Floor, New York, NY 10018. (212) 930-5594.

Wang Laboratories Inc., One Industrial Ave., Lowell, MA 01851. (617) 967-4068.

Warnaco Men's Apparel, 10 Water St., Waterville, ME 04901. (207) 873-4241.

Warner-Lambert Company, 201 Tabor Rd., Morris Plains, NJ 07950. (201) 540-2458.

Wells Fargo & Co., 201 Third St., MAC 0187-020, San Francisco, CA 94163. (415) 477-5005.

West Bend Co., 400 Washington St., West Bend, WI 53095. (414) 334-2311.

West Point-Pepperell, 1221 Avenue of the Americas, New York, NY 10020. (212) 382-5000.

Western Union Telegraph Co., One Lake St., Upper Saddle River, NJ 07458. (201) 825-5937.

Whirlpool Corp., 2000 M 63 North, Benton Harbor, MI 49022. (616) 926-5101; 1 (800) 253-1301 (toll free).

White Consolidated Industries, 300 Phillipi Rd., Columbus, OH 43288. (614) 272-4100; 1 (800) 245-0600 (toll free outside Ohio).

Frigidaire Appliances. 1 (800) 451-7007 (toll free).

Gibson Appliances. 1 (800) 458-1445 (toll free).

Kelvinator Appliance Co. 1 (800) 323-7773 (toll free).

O'Keefe & Merit Appliances. 1 (800) 537-5530 (toll free).

Tappan Co., Inc. 1 (800) 537-5530 (toll free).

White Westinghouse. 1 (800) 245-0600 (toll free).

White Westinghouse. *See* White Consolidated Industries.

Winthrop Consumer Products. *See* Sterling Drug Inc.

F.W. Woolworth Co., 233 Broadway, Rm. 2638, New York, NY 10279. (212) 553-2202.

Wrangler Jeans. *See* Blue Bell, Inc.

Wm. Wrigley Jr. Co., 410 N. Michigan Ave., Chicago, IL 60611. (312) 645-4071.

Xerox Corp., 100 Clinton Ave. S., Rochester, NY 14644. (716) 423-5480.

Yamaha Motor Corp., 6555 Katella Ave., Cypress, CA 90630. (714) 761-7439.

Zenith Electronics Corp., 1000 Milwaukee Ave., Glenview, IL 60025. (312) 391-8100.

Free Consumer Catalog

The Consumer Information Catalog lists over 200 free or low-cost Federal booklets on a variety of topics including careers and education, child care, Federal benefits, financial planning, gardening, health, housing, small business, travel, hobbies, etc.

The free catalog is published quarterly by the Consumer Information Center and may be ordered by sending your name and address to: Consumer Information Center, Pueblo, CO 81009.

TOLL-FREE NUMBERS

There are thousands of toll-free numbers available to consumers. However, very few of them can be used in all states. Most toll-free numbers are for local use only and are listed in your telephone directory.

The following is a selection of "800" numbers known to *Information Please Almanac* that can be used by readers throughout the United States.

AIDS
AIDS Hotline
U.S. Public Health Service
1-800-342-2437
SIDA (Spanish line) 1-800-344-7432
TTY (hearing impaired) 1-800-243-7889
Hours: 24 hours, 7 days

Provides the latest information to the public about Acquired Immune Deficiency Syndrome (AIDS).

AIDS Drugs Hotline
National Institute of Allergies and Infectious Diseases
1-800-874-2572
Hours: 9 a.m.–7 p.m., Mon.-Fri.
Callers learn the status of research and how to get into an FDA clinical trial.

ALZHEIMER'S DISEASE
Alzheimer's Disease and Related Disorders Association, Inc.
1-800-621-0379
1-800-572-6037 (Illinois)
Hours: 24 hours, 7 days

Information and referral service. Provides support for patients and their families, aids research efforts, etc.

AUTOMOBILE
Auto Safety Hotline
National Highway Traffic Safety Administration
202-366-0123 (Washington, D.C.)
1-800-424-9393 (Elsewhere)
Hours: 8:00–4:00, EST Mon.–Fri.
Answering service after hours.

Handles complaints on safety-related defects, and receives reports of vehicle safety problems. Provides information and in some cases literature on:
- motor vehicle safety recalls
- car seats
- automobile equipment
- tires
- motor homes
- drunk driving
- gas mileage

BANKING
Federal Deposit Insurance Corporation
202-898-3536 (Washington, D.C.)
1-800-424-5488 (Elsewhere)
Hours: 9:00–4:00, EST Mon.–Fri.

Provides general banking information on consumer banking laws. Will refer consumer to proper regulatory agency that supervises institution complaint is being filed against.

Federal Home Loan Bank Board
202-377-6988 (Washington, D.C.)
1-800-424-5405 (Elsewhere)
Hours: 24-hour recording

Provides information on federal adjustable mortgage rates.

BOATING SAFETY HOTLINE
U.S. Coast Guard
1-800-368-5647
1-202-267-0972 (Washington, D.C.)
Hours: 8:00—4:00 EST Mon.-Fri.

Provides information on boats, safe boating, and associated equipment involved in safety defect (recall) campaigns for past five model years. Takes complaints about possible safety defects. Cannot resolve non-safety problems between consumer and manufacturer and cannot recommend or endorse specific boats or products.

BLIND
National Federation of the Blind
1-800-638-7518, 8-5 EST, Mon.-Fri.
1-301-659-9314 (Maryland)

Provides job information. Concerned about the rights of the blind. Free package of information about blindness.

CHEMICALS
Chemical Referral Center
1-800-262-8200
In Washington, D.C. call locally.
Hours: 9:00-6:00, EST, Mon.-Fri.

Refers callers to health and safety contacts at chemical manufacturers.

CHILD ABUSE
Parents Anonymous
1-800-352-0386 (California)
1-800-421-0353 (Elsewhere)
Hours: 8:30–5:00 Mon.–Fri., PST
Has a 24-hour hotline.

American Child Protective Association, Inc.
1-800-KID-WATCH
Hours: 24 hours, 7 days.

"Kid Watch Radio Alert Program" presents information through the radio stations to the public that a missing child situation exists. The Kid Watch Public Awareness Program has helped fingerprint over 40,000 children.

COCAINE ABUSE
National Cocaine Hotline
1-800-COCAINE
Hours: 24 hours—7days

Provides information on cocaine and drug-related problems for cocaine abusers.

CIVIL RIGHTS HOTLINE
Office of Civil Rights
1-800-368-1019
Hours: 9:00—5:30, EST Mon.-Fri. Answering machine after 5:30 p.m., including weekends.

Accepts complaints regarding discrimination on the basis of race, color, national origin, handicap, or age occurring in Health and Human Services programs, i.e. in admission to hospitals, nursing homes, day care centers, or federally funded state health care assistance.

DEPARTMENT OF DEFENSE
1-800-424-9098 (Washington, D.C.)
223-5080 (Autovon Line)
593-5080 (FTS)
Hours: 8:00–4:30, EST

Operated for citizens to report suspected cases of fraud and waste involving the Department of Defense. The anonymity of callers will be respected.

DRUG ABUSE
National Institute on Drug Abuse
1-800-662-HELP
Hours: 9:00–3:00 Monday to Friday), 12:00–3:00 Saturday & Sunday).

Provides information on drug abuse, and treatment referrals.

ELECTIONS
Federal Election Commission
Clearinghouse on Election Administration
1-800-424-9530
202-376-3120 (Wash. D.C., Alaska, and Hawaii)
Hours: 8:30—5:30, EST Mon.-Fri.

Provides information on campaign financing.

ENERGY
Conservation and Renewable Energy Inquiry and Referral Service
1-800-233-3071 (Alaska and Hawaii)
1-800-523-2929 (Elsewhere)
Hours: 9:00–5:00, EST Mon.–Fri.

Provides non-technical information on solar, wind, and other energy heating and cooling technologies, energy conservation, and alcohol fuels.

ENVIRONMENT
Hazardous Waste
RCRA Superfund Hotline
Environmental Protection Agency
202-382-3000 (Washington, D.C.)
1-800-424-9346 (Elsewhere)
Hours: 8:30–4:30, EST Mon.–Fri.

Provides information and interpretation of federal hazardous waste regulations. Will provide referrals regarding other hazardous waste matters.

Pesticide Hotline
National Pesticide Telecommunications Network
1-800-858-7378
Hours: 24 hours—7 days

Provides information on health hazards, cleanup and disposal of pesticides. Will refer callers to human and animal poison control centers in their states if necessary.

GAY-LESBIAN HOTLINE
National Gay/Lesbian Crisisline/AIDS 800 (NGLC)
1-800-SOS-GAYS
Hours: 5:00–10:00 p.m., EST, M–F; (Sept.–May, Sat., 1–5)

Provides information on gay/lesbian life styles, AIDS; referrals to resources and gay/lesbian events in the caller's community.

HEALTH CARE
Cancer Information Service
National Cancer Institute
National Institutes of Health
Department of Health & Human Services
808-524-1234 (Hawaii) (neighboring islands call collect)
1-800-638-6070 (Alaska)
1-800-638-6694 (National Cancer Institute)
1-800-4-Cancer (Elsewhere)
Hours: 9:00–4:30, EST Mon.–Fri. (NCI number rings 4:30–10:30 p.m.)

Provides information on cancer, prevention, treatment and ongoing research; fills requests for pamphlets and other literature on cancer.

National Health Information Center
Department of Health & Human Services
301-565-4167 (Maryland)
1-800-336-4797 (Elsewhere)
Hours: 9:00–5:00 EST Mon.–Fri.

Provides referrals to sources of information on health-related issues.

Second Surgical Opinion Hotline for Non-Emergency Surgery
Sponsored by Health Care Financing Administration
Department of Health and Human Services
1-800-638-6833
1-800-492-6603 (Maryland)
Hours: 8:00–12:00, EST 7 days

Callers will be given a free referral to an agency that maintains listing of physicians in their area who will give a second opinion before an operation is performed. Brochures mailed upon request.

HOUSING
Fair Housing Discrimination Hotline
Fair Housing and Equal Opportunity
Department of Housing and Urban Development
202-426-3500 (Washington, D.C.) (9–5, M-F)
1-800-424-8590 (Elsewhere)
Hours: 24 hours, 7 days

Receives housing discrimination complaints due to race, color, religion, sex, familial status, handicap, or national origin.

HOUSEHOLD APPLIANCES
Major Appliance Consumer Action Panel (MACAP)
1-800-621-0477
1-312-984-5858 (Illinois)
Hours: 9:00—5:00, CST Mon.-Fri.

An independent mediation group that offers to help users of major household appliances resolve complaints if they have been unsuccessful in getting satisfaction from the manufacturer. The Panel's recommendations are not binding to either party.

INSURANCE
Federal Crime Insurance
Federal Emergency Management Administration
301-251-1660 (Maryland)
1-800-638-8780 (Elsewhere)
Hours: 8:30–5:00, EST Mon.–Fri.
Answering service after hours.

Provides information on federal crime insurance for both homes and businesses which have been robbed or burglarized.

National Flood Insurance
1-800-492-6605 (Maryland)
1-800-638-6831 (Alaska, Hawaii, Puerto Rico, Virgin Islands, Guam)
1-800-638-6620 (Elsewhere)
Hours: 8:00–8:00, EST Mon.–Fri.

Provides information on community participation in the flood program (emergency or regular). If the community does not have a program, it is not eligible for government-subsidized insurance relief. Complaints are referred to the proper office within the agency.

ORGAN DONOR INFORMATION
The Living Bank
1-800-528-2971
Hours: 8:00—5:00, CST Mon.-Fri. Has 24 hour answering service.

The Living Bank International is a nonprofit service organization dedicated to helping those who, after death, wish to donate organs or body tissues for transplantation, therapy, medical research, or anatomical studies. It provides information and donor registration material. NOTE: The Bank does not receive donated organs and bodies and is not a storage facility for them.

The American Liver Foundation
1-800-223-0179
Hours: 8:30-4:30, EST, Mon.-Fri.
201-256-2550 (New Jersey)
Hours: 24 hour recording

Answers questions and keeps list of liver transplant centers. Doctor referral list.

PRODUCT SAFETY
Consumer Product Safety Commission
1-800-638-2772
Hours: 10:30-4:00, EST Mon.-Fri.

Provides recorded information on the safety of consumer products. Receives reports of product related deaths, illnesses, and injuries. Products are not rated or recommended.

RUNAWAYS
1-800-231-6946 (U.S.A. except Texas)
1-800-392-3352 (Texas)
Hours: 24 hours, 7 days

Helps runaways by referring them to shelters, clinics, local hotlines. Will relay messages from the runaway to the parent.

SOCIAL SECURITY AND MEDICARE FRAUD
Inspector General Hotline
Department of Health and Human Services
1-800-368-5779
Hours: 10:00–4:00, EST Mon.-Fri.

Takes calls on fraud in Social Security payments or abuse, Medicaid and Medicare fraud and other HHS programs. Recording machine after hours.

VIETNAM VETERANS
Vietnam Veterans of America
1-800-424-7275 (answering machine)
202-332-2700 (Washington, D.C.)
Hours: 9:00–5:30, EST Mon.-Fri.

Answering machine takes messages for information and help. Provides information on Agent Orange. Will answer questions on direct line.

Veteran's of the Vietnam War, Inc.
1-800-VIETNAM
Hours: 8 a.m.–6 p.m., Mon.-Fri., service after hours

Provides information on filing claims against the Agent Orange Settlement, filing claims for veterans benefits with the VA, how to take the VA to court, and information on MIAs and POWs. Veterans newsletter is available, also provides Veterans location services.

Choosing Long Distance Telephone Service

Make sure the one you choose provides service to the areas you call most frequently. Check if long distance carrier gives credit for uncompleted calls, wrong numbers, or calls that are unanswered. Ask about one-time only and regular charges. Find out if there is a subscription fee? Monthly service fee?

Monthly minimum charge?
A trial period may help you decide. Before signing up, be sure you understand the terms of the carrier's cancellation policy, and the costs involved in switching to another carrier.

Your Right to Federal Records

The Freedom of Informaction Act (FOIA) guarantees any person the right, enforceable in court, to look at all Federal agency records except for those exempted in the Act. FOIA applies only to records of the executive branch of the Federal Government, not to those of the Congress or the Federal courts. It also does not apply to records of any State or local government or any private entity.

The Act contains one very important provision concerning privacy—Exemption 6. It may.protect you from others seeking information about you, but may block you if you seek information about others. FOIA Exemption 6 permits an agency to withold information about individuals if disclosing it would be a "clearly unwarranted invasion of personal privacy." This includes, for example, most of

the information in medical and personnel files.

The Privacy Act gives citizens the right to see files about themselves and the right to sue the Government for permitting others to see their files without their knowledge and permission. You may order a copy of the Privacy Act, Public Law 93-579, from the Superintendent of Documents, U.S. Government Printing Office, for $2.50. Please specify stock number 022-003-90866-8.

You can purchase a booklet, "A Citizen's Guide on How To Use the Freedom of Information Act and the Privacy Act in Requesting Government Documents," for $1.75. from the Superintendent of Documents, U.S. Government Printing Office, Washington, D.C. 20402. Please specify stock number 052-071-00540-4.

U.S. Telephone Area Codes and Time Zones

POSTAL REGULATIONS

Domestic Mail Service

First Class

First-class consists of letters and written and sealed matter. The rate is 25¢ for the first oz; 20¢ for each additional oz, or fraction of an oz, up to 12 oz. Pieces over 12 oz are subject to priority-mail (heavy pieces) rates. Single postcards, 15¢; double postcards, 30¢ (15¢ for each half). The post office sells prestamped single and double postal cards. Consult your postmaster for information on business-reply mail and presort rates.

The weight limit for first-class mail is 70 lb.

Weight	Rates
First oz	$ .25
Over 1 oz, but not over 2	.45
Over 2 oz, but not over 3	.65
Over 3 oz, but not over 4	.85
Over 4 oz, but not over 5	1.05
Over 5 oz, but not over 6	1.25
Over 6 oz, but not over 7	1.45
Over 7 oz, but not over 8	1.65
Over 8 oz, but not over 9	1.85
Over 9 oz, but not over 10	2.05
Over 10 oz, but not over 11	2.25
Over 11 oz, but not over 12	2.45
Over 12 oz, *see* Priority Mail	

Priority Mail (over 12 oz to 70 lb)

The zone rate applies to mailable matter over 12 oz of any class carried by air. Your local post office will supply free official zone tables appropriate to your location.

Airmail

First-class and priority mail receive airmail service.

Express Mail

Express Mail Service is available for any mailable article up to 70 lb in weight and 108 in. in combined length and girth. Flat rates: letter rate (up to 8 ounces), $8.75; up to 2 lb, $12.00; over 2 lb and up to 5 lb, $15.25; 6 to 70 pound rates vary by weight and distance (zones).

Articles received by 5 p.m. at a postal facility offering Express Mail Service will be delivered by 3 p.m. the next day or, if you prefer, your shipment can be picked up as early as 10 a.m. the next business day. Rates include Insurance, Shipment Receipt, and Record of Delivery at the destination post office.

Consult Postmaster for other Express Mail Services and rates.

The Postal Service will refund, upon application to originating office, the postage for any Express

Mail shipments not meeting the service standard except for those delayed by strike or work stop page.

Second Class

Second-class mail is used primarily by newspapers, magazines, and other periodicals with second-class mailing privileges. For copies mailed by the public, the rate is the applicable single piece third- or fourth-class rate.

Third Class (under 16 oz)

Third-class mail is used for circulars, books printed matter, merchandise, seeds, cuttings bulbs, roots, scions, and plants, and all other mailable matter not in first or second class. There are two rate structures for this class, a single-piece and a bulk rate.

Many community organizations, as well as businesses, find it economical to use this service. Because of the number of categories of third-class mail, you should consult your postmaster for the one best suited to your needs.

Third-Class, Single-Piece Rates

Weight	Rates	Weight	Rates
0 to 1 oz	$ .25	Over 8 to 10 oz	$ 1.20
Over 1 to 2 oz	.45	Over 10 to 12 oz	1.30
Over 2 to 3 oz	.65	Over 12 to 14 oz	1.40
Over 3 to 4 oz	.85	Over 14 but less	
Over 4 to 6 oz	1.00	than 16 oz	1.50
Over 6 to 8 oz	1.10		

Fourth Class (Parcel Post— 16 oz and over)

Fourth-class mail is used for merchandise, books, printed matter, and all other mailable matter not in first, second, or third class. Special fourth-class rates apply to books, library books, publications or records for the blind, and certain controlled-circulation publications.

Packages should be taken to your local post office, where the postage will be determined according to the weight of the package and the distance it is being sent. Information on weight and size limits for fourth-class mail may be obtained there.

Special Services

Registered Mail. When you use registered mail service, you are buying security—the safest way to send valuables. The full value of your mailing must be declared when mailed. You receive a receipt and the movement of your mail is controlled throughout the postal system. For an additional

...ee, a return receipt showing to whom, when, and ...here delivered may be obtained.

Fees for articles (in addition to postage)

Value			With insurance	Without insurance
0.01	to	$ 100	$4.50	$4.40
100.01	to	500	4.85	4.70
500.01	to	1,000	5.25	5.05

...or higher values, consult your postmaster.

Certified Mail. Certified mail service provides for receipt to the sender and a record of delivery at the post office of address. No record is kept at the post office where mailed. It is handled in the ordinary mails and no insurance coverage is provided. Fee in addition to postage, 85¢.

Return Receipts. Requested at time of mailing:

Showing to whom and date delivered	$ .90
Showing to whom, date, and address where delivered	1.20
Requested after mailing:	
Showing to whom and date delivered	5.00

C.O.D. Mail. Consult your postmaster for fees and conditions of mailing.

Insured Mail. Fees, in addition to postage, for coverage against loss or damage:

Liability			Fees
.01	to	$50	$ .70
50.01	to	$100	1.50
100.01	to	$150	1.90
150.01	to	$200	2.20
200.01	to	$300	3.15
300.01	to	$400	4.30
400.01	to	500	5.00

Special Delivery. The payment of the special-delivery fee entitles mail to the most expeditious transportation and delivery. The fee is in addition to the regular postage.

Weight/Fees

Class of mail	Not more than 2 lb	More than 2 lb but not more than 10 lb	More than 10 lb
First-class	$5.35	$5.75	$7.25
All other classes	5.65	6.50	8.10

Special Handling. Payment of the special-handling fee entitles third- and fourth-class matter to the most expeditious handling and transportation, but not special delivery. The fee is in addition to the regular postage.

Weight	Fees
Not more than 10 lb	$1.55
More than 10 lb	2.25

Money Orders. Money orders are used for the safe transmission of money.

Amount of money order			Fees
$ .01	to	$35	$ .75
$ 35.01	to	$700	1.00

Minimum Mail Sizes

All mail must be at least 0.007 in. thick and mail that is 1/4 in. or less in thickness must be at least 3 1/2 in. in height, at least 5 in. long, and rectangular in shape (except keys and identification devices). NOTE: Pieces greater than 1/4 in. thick can be mailed even if they measure less than 3 1/2 by 5 inches.

Adhesive Stamps Available

Purpose	Form	Denomination and prices
Ordinary postage	Single or sheet	1, 2, 3, 4, 5, 6, 7, 8, 9, 10, 11, 14, 15, 17, 18, 19, 20, 21, 22, 23, 25, 28, 30, 40, 45, 50, 65¢, $1, $2, $5, and $8.75.
	Books	20 at 25 cents ($5.00), 6 at 25 cents ($1.50), 12 at 25 cents ($3.00), Commemorative stamps, 20 at 25 cents ($5.00).
	Coil of 100	17, 20, 22, and 25¢. (dispenser and stamp affixer for use with these coils are also available).
	Coil of 500	1, 2, 3, 4, 5, 6, 9, 10, 11, 12, 14, 15, 17, 18, 20, 21, 22, 25¢ and $1.
	Coil of 3000	1, 2, 3, 4, 5, 6, 9, 10, 11, 12, 14, 15, 17, 18, 20, 21, 22, 25¢ and $1.
International airmail postage	Single or sheet	36 and 45¢

Note: Denominations listed are currently in stock. Others may be available until supplies are exhausted.

Non-Standard Mail

All first-class mail weighing one ounce or less and all single-piece rate third-class mail weighing one ounce or less is nonstandard (and subject to a 10¢ surcharge in addition to the applicable postage and fees) if any of the following dimensions are exceeded: length—11 1/2 inches; height—6 1/8 inches; thickness—1/4 inch, or the piece has a height to length (aspect) ratio which does not fall between 1 to 1.3 and 1 to 2.5 inclusive. (The aspect ratio is found by dividing the length by the height. If the answer is between 1.3 and 2.5 inclusive, the piece has a standard aspect ratio).

International Mail Service

Letters and Letter Packages

Items of mail containing personal handwritten or typewritten communications having the character of current correspondence must be sent as letters or letter packages. Unless prohibited by the country of destination, dutiable merchandise may be transmitted in packages prepaid at the letter rate of postage. Weight limit for all countries, 4 pounds. For rates, consult your local post office.

Post and Postal Cards

Canada $0.21 All other—surface $0.28
Mexico $0.15 All other—air $0.36

Aerogrammes—$0.39 each.

Canada and Mexico—Surface Rates

Letters and Letter Packages

Weight not over		Canada	Mexico	Weight not over		Canada	Mexico
Lb	Oz			Lb	Oz		
0	1	$.30	$.25	0	11	2.50	2.25
0	2	.52	.45	0	12	2.72	2.45
0	3	.74	.65	1	0	3.08	3.25
0	4	.96	.85	1	8	3.70	4.05
0	5	1.18	1.05	2	0	4.32	4.85
0	6	1.40	1.25	2	8	4.94	5.65
0	7	1.62	1.45	3	0	5.56	6.45
0	8	1.84	1.65	3	8	6.18	7.25
0	9	2.06	1.85	4	0	6.80	8.05
0	10	2.28	2.05				
			Weight Limit—4 Pounds*				

Note: Mail paid at this rate receives First-Class service in the United States and air service in Canada and Mexico. *Registered letters to Canada may weigh up to 66 pounds. The rate for over 4 pounds to 66 pounds is $1.24 per pound or fraction of a pound.

Letters and Letter Packages— Airmail Rates

All Countries other than Canada & Mexico

Weight not over	Rate	Weight not over	Rate
Oz		Oz	
0.5	$ 0.45	24.5	$20.70
1.0	0.90	25.0	21.12
1.5	1.35	25.5	21.54
2.0	1.80	26.0	21.96
2.5	2.22	26.5	22.38
3.0	2.64	27.0	22.80
3.5	3.06	27.5	23.22
4.0	3.48	28.0	23.64
4.5	3.90	28.5	24.06
5.0	4.32	29.0	24.48
5.5	4.74	29.5	24.90
6.0	5.16	30.0	25.32
6.5	5.58	30.5	25.74
7.0	6.00	31.0	26.16
7.5	6.42	31.5	26.58
8.0	6.84	32.0	27.00
8.5	7.26	33	27.42
9.0	7.68	34	27.84
9.5	8.10	35	28.26
10.0	8.52	36	28.68
10.5	8.94	37	29.10
11.0	9.36	38	29.52
11.5	9.78	39	29.94
12.0	10.20	40	30.36
12.5	10.62	41	30.78
13.0	11.04	42	31.20
13.5	11.46	43	31.62
14.0	11.88	44	32.04
14.5	12.30	45	32.46
15.0	12.72	46	32.88
15.5	13.14	47	33.30
16.0	13.56	48	33.72
16.5	13.98	49	34.14
17.0	14.40	50	34.56
17.5	14.82	51	34.98
18.0	15.24	52	35.40
18.5	15.66	53	35.82
19.0	16.08	54	36.24
19.5	16.50	55	36.66
20.0	16.92	56	37.08
20.5	17.34	57	37.50
21.0	17.76	58	37.92
21.5	18.18	59	38.34
22.0	18.60	60	38.76
22.5	19.02	61	39.18
23.0	19.44	62	39.60
23.5	19.86	63	40.02
24.0	20.28	64	40.44

Countries Other Than Canada and Mexico—Surface Rates

Letters and Letter Packages

Weight not over		Rate	Weight not over		Rate
Lb	Oz		Lb	Oz	
0	1	0.40	0	11	3.80
0	2	0.63	0	12	3.80
0	3	0.86	1	0	3.80
0	4	1.09	1	8	5.20
0	5	1.32	2	0	6.60
0	6	1.55	2	8	7.60
0	7	1.78	3	0	8.60
0	8	2.01	3	8	9.60
0	9	3.80	4	0	10.60
0	10	3.80			

Weight limit—4 pounds.

International Surface Parcel Post

Other Than Canada

Weight through lb	Mexico, Central America, Caribbean Islands, Bahamas, Bermuda, St. Pierre and Miquelon	All other countries
2	$ 4.40 $1.40 each additional lb or fraction	$ 4.60 $1.50 each additional lb or fraction

Consult your postmaster for weight/size limits of individual countries.

For other international services and rates consult your local postmaster.

Canada Surface Parcel Post

Up to 2lb $3.95, $1.20 for each additional lb up to the maximum weight of 66lb. Minimum weight is 1 lb.

International Money Order Fees

This service available only to certain countries. Consult post office.

United Nations Stamps

United Nations stamps are issued in three different currencies, namely, U.S. dollars, Swiss francs, and Austrian schillings. Stamps in all three currencies are available at face value at each of the U.N. Postal Administration offices in New York, Geneva, and Vienna. They may be purchased over the counter, by mail, or by opening a Customer Deposit Account.

Mail orders for mint (unused) stamps and postal stationery may be sent to the U.N. Postal Administration in New York, Geneva, and Vienna. Write to: United Nations Postal Administration, P.O. Box 5900, Grand Central Station, New York, N.Y. 10017.

How to Complain About a Postal Problem

When you have a problem with your mail service, complete a Consumer Service Card which is available from letter carriers and at post offices. This will help your postmaster respond to your problem. If you wish to telephone a complaint, a postal employee will fill out the card for you.

The Consumer Advocate represents consumers at the top management level in the Postal Service. If your postal problems cannot be solved by your local post office, then write to the Consumer Advocate. His staff stands ready to serve you. Write to:

The Consumer Advocate, U.S. Postal Service, Washington, D.C. 20260-6320. Or phone: 1-202-268-2284.

The Mail Order Merchandise Rule

The mail order rule adopted by the Federal Trade Commission in October 1975 provides that when you order by mail:

You must receive the merchandise when the seller says you will.

If you are not promised delivery within a certain time period, the seller must ship the merchandise to you no later than 30 days after your order comes in.

If you don't receive it shortly after that 30-day period, you can cancel your order and get your money back.

How the Rule Works

The seller must notify you if the promised delivery date (or the 30-day limit) cannot be met. The seller must also tell you what the new shipping date will be and give you the option to cancel the order and receive a full refund or agree to the new shipping date. The seller must also give you a free way to send back your answer, such as a stamped envelope or a postage-paid postcard. *If you don't answer, it means that you agree to the shipping delay.*

The seller must tell you if the shipping delay is going to be more than 30 days. You then can agree to the delay or, if you do not agree, the seller must return your money by the end of the first 30 days of the delay.

If you cancel a prepaid order, the seller must mail you the refund within seven business days. Where there is a credit sale, the seller must adjust your account within one billing cycle.

It would be impossible, however, for one rule to apply uniformly to such a varied field as mail order merchandising. For example, the rule does not apply to mail order photo finishing, magazine subscriptions, and other serial deliveries (except for the initial shipment); to mail order seeds and growing plants; to COD orders; or to credit orders where the buyer's account is not charged prior to shipment of the merchandise.

Authorized 2-Letter State Abbreviations

When the Post Office instituted the ZIP Code for mail in 1963, it also drew up a list of two-letter abbreviations for the states which would gradually replace the traditional ones in use. Following is the official list, including the District of Columbia, Guam, Puerto Rico, and the Virgin Islands (note that only capital letters are used):

State	Abbr.	State	Abbr.	State	Abbr.
Alabama	AL	Kentucky	KY	Ohio	OH
Alaska	AK	Louisiana	LA	Oklahoma	OK
Arizona	AZ	Maine	ME	Oregon	OR
Arkansas	AR	Maryland	MD	Pennsylvania	PA
California	CA	Massachusetts	MA	Puerto Rico	PR
Colorado	CO	Michigan	MI	Rhode Island	RI
Connecticut	CT	Minnesota	MN	South Carolina	SC
Delaware	DE	Mississippi	MS	South Dakota	SD
Dist. of Columbia	DC	Missouri	MO	Tennessee	TN
Florida	FL	Montana	MT	Texas	TX
Georgia	GA	Nebraska	NE	Utah	UT
Guam	GU	Nevada	NV	Vermont	VT
Hawaii	HI	New Hampshire	NH	Virginia	VA
Idaho	ID	New Jersey	NJ	Virgin Islands	VI
Illinois	IL	New Mexico	NM	Washington	WA
Indiana	IN	New York	NY	West Virginia	WV
Iowa	IA	North Carolina	NC	Wisconsin	WI
Kansas	KS	North Dakota	ND	Wyoming	WY

STRUCTURES

The Seven Wonders of the World

(Not all classical writers list the same items as the Seven Wonders, but most of them agree on the following.)

The Pyramids of Egypt. A group of three pyramids, *Khufu, Khafra,* and *Menkaura* at Giza, outside modern Cairo, is often called the first wonder of the world. The largest pyramid, built by Khufu (Cheops), a king of the fourth Dynasty, had an original estimated height of 482 ft (now approximately 450 ft). The base has sides 755 ft long. It contains 2,300,000 blocks; the average weight of each is 2.5 tons. Estimated date of construction is 2800 B.C. Of all the Seven Wonders, the pyramids alone survive.

Hanging Gardens of Babylon. Often listed as the second wonder, these gardens were supposedly built by Nebuchadnezzar about 600 B.C. to please his queen, Amuhia. They are also associated with the mythical Assyrian Queen, Semiramis. Archeologists surmise that the gardens were laid out atop a vaulted building, with provisions for raising water. The terraces were said to rise from 75 to 300 ft.

The Walls of Babylon, also built by Nebuchadnezzar, are sometimes referred to as the second (or the seventh) wonder instead of the Hanging Gardens.

Statue of Zeus (Jupiter) at Olympia. The work of Phidias (5th century B.C.), this colossal figure in gold and ivory was reputedly 40 ft high. All trace of it is lost, except for reproductions on coins.

Temple of Artemis (Diana) at Ephesus. A beautiful structure, begun about 350 B.C. in honor of a non-Hellenic goddess who later became identified with the Greek goddess of the same name. The temple, with Ionic columns 60 ft high, was destroyed by invading Goths in A.D. 262.

Mausoleum at Halicarnassus. This famous monument was erected by Queen Artemisia in memory of her husband, King Mausolus of Caria in Asia Minor, who died in 353 B.C. Some remains of the structure are in the British Museum. This shrine is the source of the modern word "mausoleum."

Colossus at Rhodes. This bronze statue of Helios (Apollo), about 105 ft high, was the work of the sculptor Chares, who reputedly labored for 12 years before completing it in 280 B.C. It was destroyed during an earthquake in 224 B.C.

Pharos of Alexandria. The seventh wonder was the Pharos (lighthouse) of Alexandria, built by Sostratus of Cnidus during the 3rd century B.C. on the island of Pharos off the coast of Egypt. It was destroyed by an earthquake in the 13th century.

Famous Structures

Ancient

The *Great Sphinx of Egypt,* one of the wonders of ancient Egyptian architecture, adjoins the pyramids of Giza and has a length of 240 ft. It was built in the 4th dynasty.

Other Egyptian buildings of note include the *Temples of Karnak* and *Edfu* and the *Tombs at Beni Hassan.*

The *Parthenon of Greece,* built on the Acropolis in Athens, was the chief temple to the goddess Athena. It was believed to have been completed by 438 B.C. The present temple remained intact until the 5th century A.D. Today, though the Parthenon is in ruins, its majestic proportions are still discernible.

Other great structures of ancient Greece were the *Temples at Paestum* (about 540 and 420 B.C.); the *Temple of Poseidon* (about 460 B.C.); the *Temple of Apollo* at Corinth (about 540 B.C.); the *Temple of Apollo* at Bassae (about 450–420 B.C.); the famous *Erechtheum* atop the Acropolis (about 421–405 B.C.); the *Temple of Athena Niké* at Athens (about 426 B.C.); the *Olympieum* at Athens (174 B.C.–A.D. 131); the *Athenian Treasury* at Delphi (about 515 B.C.); the *Propylaea* of the Acropolis at Athens (437–432 B.C.); the *Theater of Dionysus* at Athens (about 350–325 B.C.); the *House of Cleopatra* at Delos (138 B.C.) and the *Theater* at Epidaurus (about 325 B.C.).

The *Colosseum (Flavian Amphitheater) of Rome,* the largest and most famous of the Roman amphitheaters, was opened for use A.D. 80. Elliptical in shape, it consisted of three stories and an upper gallery, rebuilt in stone in its present form in the third century A.D. Its seats rise in tiers, which in turn are buttressed by concrete vaults and stone piers. It could seat between 40,000 and 50,000 spectators. It was principally used for gladiatorial combat.

The *Pantheon* at Rome, begun by Agrippa in 27 B.C. as a temple, was rebuilt in its present circular form by Hadrian (A.D. 110–25). Literally the Pantheon was intended as a temple of "all the gods." It is remarkable for its perfect preservation today, and it has served continuously for 20 centuries as a place of worship.

Famous Roman arches include the *Arch of Constantine* (about A.D. 315) and the *Arch of Titus* (about A.D. 80).

Later European

St. Mark's Cathedral in Venice (1063–67), one of the great examples of Byzantine architecture, was begun in the 9th century. Partly destroyed by fire in 976, it was later rebuilt as a Byzantine edifice.

Other famous Byzantine examples of architecture are *St. Sophia* in Istanbul (A.D. 532–37); *San Vitale* in Ravenna (542); *St. Paul's Outside the Walls,* Rome (5th century); the *Kremlin* baptism and marriage church, Moscow (begun in 1397); and *St. Lorenzo Outside the Walls,* Rome, begun in 588.

The *Cathedral Group* at Pisa (1067–1173), one of the most celebrated groups of structures built in Romanesque-style, consists of the cathedral, the cathedral's baptistery, and the *Leaning Tower.* This trio forms a group by itself in the northwest corner of the city. The cathedral and baptistery are built in varicolored marble. The campanile *(Leaning Tower)* is 179 ft. high and leans more than 16 ft out of the perpendicular. There is little reason to believe that the architects intended to have the tower lean.

Other examples of Romanesque architecture include the *Vézelay Abbey* in France (1130); the *Church of Notre-Dame-du-Port* at Clermont-Ferrand in France (1100); the *Church of San Zeno* (begun in 1138) at Verona, and *Durham Cathedral* in England.

The *Alhambra* (1248–1354), located in Granada, Spain, is universally esteemed as one of the greatest masterpieces of Moslem architecture. Designed as a palace and fortress for the Moorish monarchs of Granada, it is surrounded by a heavily fortified wall more than a mile in perimeter. The location of the Alhambra in the Sierra Nevada provides a magnificent setting for this jewel of Moorish Spain.

The *Tower of London* is a group of buildings and towers covering 13 acres along the north bank of the Thames. The central *White Tower,* begun in 1078 during the reign of William the Conqueror, was originally a fortress and royal residence, but was later used as a prison. The *Bloody Tower* is associated with Anne Boleyn and other notables.

Westminster Abbey, in London, was begun in 1045 and completed in 1065. It was rebuilt and enlarged in 1245–50.

Notre-Dame de Paris (begun in 1163), one of the great examples of Gothic architecture, is a twin-towered church with a steeple over the crossing and immense flying buttresses supporting the masonry at the rear of the church.

Other famous Gothic structures are *Chartres Cathedral* (12th century); *Sainte Chapelle,* Paris (1246–48); *Laon Cathedral,* France (1160–1205); *Reims Cathedral* (about 1210–50; rebuilt after its almost complete destruction in World War I); *Rouen Cathedral* (13th–16th centuries); *Amiens Cathedral* (1218–69); *Beauvais Cathedral* (begun 1247); *Salisbury Cathedral* (1220–60); *York Minster* or the *Cathedral of St. Peter* (begun in the 7th century); *Milan Cathedral* (begun 1386); and *Cologne Cathedral* (13th–19th centuries); badly damaged in World War II.

The *Duomo* (cathedral) in Florence was founded in 1298, completed by Brunelleschi and consecrated in 1436. The oval-shaped dome dominates the entire structure.

The *Vatican* is a group of buildings in Rome comprising the official residence of the Pope. The *Basilica of St. Peter,* the largest church in the Christian world, was begun in 1450. The *Sistine Chapel,* begun in 1473, is noted for the art masterpieces of Michelangelo, Botticelli, and others. The *Basilica of the Savior* (known as *St. John Lateran*) is the first-ranking Catholic Church in the world, for it is the cathedral of the Pope.

Other examples of Renaissance architecture are the *Palazzo Riccardi,* the *Palazzo Pitti* and the *Palazzo Strozzi* in Florence; the *Farnese Palace* in Rome; *Palazzo Grimani* (completed about 1550) in Venice; the *Escorial* (1563–93) near Madrid; the *Town Hall* of Seville (1527–32); the *Louvre,* Paris;

the *Château* at Blois, France; *St. Paul's Cathedral,* London (1675–1710; badly damaged in World War II); the *École Militaire,* Paris (1752); the *Pazzi Chapel,* Florence, designed by Brunelleschi (1429); the *Palace of Fontainebleau* and the *Château de Chambord* in France.

The *Palace of Versailles,* containing the famous Hall of Mirrors, was built during the reign of Louis XIV and served as the royal palace until 1793.

Outstanding European buildings of the 18th and 19th centuries are the *Superga* at Turin, the *Hôtel-Dieu* in Lyons, the *Belvedere Palace* at Vienna, the *Royal Palace* of Stockholm, the *Opera House* of Paris (1863–75); the *Bank of England,* the *British Museum,* the *University of London,* and the *Houses of Parliament,* all in London; the *Panthéon,* the *Church of the Madeleine,* the *Bourse,* and the *Palais de Justice* in Paris.

The *Eiffel Tower,* in Paris, was built for the Exposition of 1889 by Alexandre Eiffel. It is 984 ft high.[1]

1. 1,056 ft, including the television tower.

Asiatic and African

The *Taj Mahal* (1632–50), at Agra, India, built by Shah Jahan as a tomb for his wife, is considered by some as the most perfect example of the Mogul style and by others as the most beautiful building in the world. Four slim white minarets flank the building, which is topped by a white dome; the entire structure is of marble.

Other examples of Indian architecture are the temples at Benares and Tanjore.

Among famed Moslem edifices are the *Dome of the Rock* or *Mosque of Omar,* Jerusalem (A.D. 691); the *Citadel* (1166), and the *Tombs of the Mamelukes* (15th century), in Cairo; the *Tomb of Humayun* in Delhi; the *Blue Mosque* (1468) at Tabriz, and the *Tamerlane Mausoleum* at Samarkand.

Angkor Wat, outside the city of Angkor Thom, Cambodia, is one of the most beautiful examples of Cambodian or Khmer architecture. The sanctuary was built during the 12th century.

Great Wall of China (228 B.C.?), designed specifically as a defense against nomadic tribes, has large watch towers which could be called buildings. It was erected by Emperor Ch'in Shih Huang Ti and is 1,400 miles long. Built mainly of earth and stone, it varies in height between 18 and 30 ft.

Typical of Chinese architecture are the pagodas or temple towers. Among some of the better-known pagodas are the *Great Pagoda of the Wild Geese* at Sian (founded in 652); *Nan t'a* (11th century) at Fang Shan; the *Pagoda of Sung Yueh Ssu* (A.D. 523) at Sung Shan, Honan.

Other well-known Chinese buildings are the *Drum Tower* (1273), the *Three Great Halls* in the Purple Forbidden City (1627), *Buddha's Perfume Tower* (19th century), the *Porcelain Pagoda,* and the *Summer Palace,* all at Peking.

United States

Rockefeller Center, in New York City, extends from 5th Ave. to the Avenue of the Americas between 48th and 52nd Sts. (and halfway to 7th Ave. between 47th and 51st Sts.). It occupies more than 22 acres and has 19 buildings.

The Cathedral of St. John the Divine, at 112th St. and Amsterdam Ave. in New York City, was begun in 1892 and is now in the final stages of completion. When completed, it will be the largest cathedral in the world: 601 ft long, 146 ft wide at the nave, 320 ft wide at the transept. The east end is designed in Romanesque-Byzantine style, and the nave and west end are Gothic.

St. Patrick's Cathedral, at Fifth Ave. and 50th St. in New York City, has a seating capacity of 2,500. The nave was opened in 1877, and the cathedral was dedicated in 1879.

Louisiana Superdome, in New Orleans, is the largest arena in the history of mankind. The main area can accommodate up to 95,000 people. It is the world's largest steel-constructed room. Unob structed by posts, it covers 13 acres and reaches 2? stories at its peak.

World Trade Center, in New York City, was dedi cated in 1973. Its twin towers are 110 stories high (1,350 ft), and the complex contains over 9 million sq ft of office space. A restaurant is on the 107th floor of the North Tower.

World's Highest Dams

Name	River, Country or State	Structural height		Gross reservoir capacity		Year completed
		feet	meters	thousands of acre feet	millions of cubic meters	
Rogun	Vakhsh, U.S.S.R.	1066	325	9,404	11,600	1985
Nurek	Vakhsh, U.S.S.R.	984	300	8,512	10,500	1980
Grande Dixence	Dixence, Switzerland	935	285	324	400	1962
Inguri	Inguri, U.S.S.R.	892	272	801	1,100	1984
Chicoasén	Grijalva, Mexico	869	265	1,346	1,660	1981
Vaiont	Vaiont, Italy	869	265	137	169	1961
Tehri	Bhagirathi, India	856	261	2,869	3,540	UC
Kinshau	Tons, India	830	253	1,946	2,400	1985
Guavio	Orinoco, Colombia	820	250	811	1,000	UC
Mica	Columbia, Canada	794	242	20,000	24,670	1972
Sayano-Shushensk	Yenisei, U.S.S.R.	794	242	25,353	31,300	1980
Mihoesti	Aries, Romania	794	242	5	6	1983
Chivor	Batá, Colombia	778	237	661	815	1975
Mauvoisin	Drance de Bagnes, Switzerland	777	237	146	180	1957
Oroville	Feather, California	770	235	3,538	4,299	1968
Chirkey	Sulak, U.S.S.R.	764	233	2,252	2,780	1977
Bhakra	Sutlej, India	741	226	8,002	9,870	1963
El Cajón	Humuya, Honduras	741	226	4,580	5,650	1984
Hoover	Colorado, Arizona/Nevada	726	221	28,500	35,154	1936
Contra	Verzasca, Switzerland	722	220	70	86	1965
Dabaklamm	Dorferbach, Austria	722	220	191	235	UC
Mratinje	Piva, Yugoslavia	722	220	713	880	1973
Dworshak	N. Fk. Clearwater, Idaho	717	219	3,453	4,259	1974
Glen Canyon	Colorado, Arizona	710	216	27,000	33,304	1964
Toktogul	Naryn, U.S.S.R.	705	215	15,800	19,500	1978
Daniel Johnson	Manicouagan, Canada	703	214	115,000	141,852	1968
San Roque	Agno, Philippines	689	210	803	990	UC
Luzzone	Brenno di Luzzone, Switzerland	682	208	71	87	1963
Keban	Firat, Turkey	679	207	25,110	31,000	1974
Dez	Dez, Abi, Iran	666	203	2,707	3,340	1963
Almendra	Tormes, Spain	662	202	2,148	2,649	1970
Kölnbrein	Malta, Austria	656	200	166	205	1977
Karūn	Karun, Iran	656	200	2,351	2,900	1976
Altinkaya	Kizil Irmak, Turkey	640	195	4,672	5,763	1986
New Bullards Bar	No. Yuba, California	637	194	960	1,184	1968
Lakhwar	Yamuna, India	630	192	470	580	1985
New Melones	Stanislaus, California	625	191	2,400	2,960	1979
Itaipu	Paraná, Brazil/Paraguay	623	190	23,510	29,000	1982
Kurobe 4	Kurobe, Japan	610	186	162	199	1964
Swift	Lewis, Washington	610	186	756	932	1958
Mossyrock	Cowlitz, Washington	607	185	1,300	1,603	1968
Oymopinar	Manavgat, Turkey	607	185	251	310	1983
Atatürk	Firat, Turkey	604	184	39,482	48,700	UC
Shasta	Sacramento, California	602	183	4,550	5,612	1945
Bennett WAC	Peace, Canada	600	183	57,006	70,309	1967
Karakaya	Firat, Turkey	591	180	7,767	9,580	1986
Tignes	Isère, France	591	180	186	230	1952
Amir Kabir (Karad)	Karadj, Iran	591	180	166	205	1962
Tachien	Tachia, Taiwan	591	180	188	232	1974
Dartmouth	Mitta-Mitta, Australia	591	180	3,243	4,000	1978
Özköy	Gediz, Turkey	591	180	762	940	1983
Emosson	Barberine, Switzerland	590	180	184	225	1974
Zillergründl	Ziller, Austria	590	180	73	90	1986
Los Leones	Los Leones, Chile	587	179	86	106	1986
New Don Pedro	Tuolumne, California	585	178	2,030	2,504	1971
Alpa-Gera	Cormor, Italy	584	178	53	65	1965

Name	River, country, or state	Structural height feet	Structural height meters	Gross reservoir capacity Thousands of acre feet	Gross reservoir capacity millions of cubic meters	Year completed
Kopperston Tailings 3	Jones Branch, West Virginia	580	177	—	—	1963
Takase	Takase, Japan	577	176	62	76	1979
Nader Shah	Marun, Iran	574	175	1,313	1,620	1978
Hasan Ugurlu	Yesil Irmak, Turkey	574	175	874	1,078	1980
Pauti-Mazar	Mazar, Ecuador	540	165	405	500	1984
Hungry Horse	S.Fk., Flathead, Montana	564	172	3,470	4,280	1953
Longyangxia	Huanghe, China	564	172	20,025	24,700	1983
Cabora Bassa	Zambezi, Mozambique	561	171	51,075	63,000	1974
Maqarin	Yarmuk, Jordan	561	171	259	320	1987
Amaluza	Paute, Ecuador	558	170	81	100	1982
Idikki	Periyar, India	554	169	1,618	1,996	1974
Charvak	Chirchik, U.S.S.R.	552	168	1,620	2,000	1970
Gura Apelor Retezat	Riul Mare, Romania	552	168	182	225	1980
Grand Coulee	Columbia, Washington	550	168	9,390	11,582	1942
Boruca	Terraba, Costa Rica	548	167	12,128	14,960	UC
Vidraru	Arges, Romania	545	166	380	465	1965
Kremasta (King Paul)	Achelöus, Greece	541	165	3,850	4,750	1965

NOTE: UC = under construction. *Source:* Department of the Interior, Bureau of Reclamation and *International Water Power and Dam Construction.*

World's Largest Dams

Dam	Location	Volume (thousands) Cubic meters	Volume (thousands) Cubic yards	Year completed
New Cornelia Tailings	Arizona	209,500	274,015	1973
Pati (Chapetón)	Argentina	200,000	261,590	UC
Tarbela	Pakistan	121,720	159,203	1976
Fort Peck	Montana	96,049	125,628	1940
Atatürk	Turkey	84,500	110,522	UC
Yacyretá-Apipe	Paraguay/Argentina	81,000	105,944	UC
Guri (Raul Leoni)	Venezuela	78,000	102,014	1986
Rogun	U.S.S.R.	75,500	98,750	1985
Oahe	South Dakota	70,339	92,000	1963
Mangla	Pakistan	65,651	85,872	1967
Gardiner	Canada	65,440	85,592	1968
Afsluitdijk	Netherlands	63,400	82,927	1932
Oroville	California	59,639	78,008	1968
San Luis	California	59,405	77,700	1967
Nurek	U.S.S.R.	58,000	75,861	1980
Garrison	North Dakota	50,843	66,500	1956
Cochiti	New Mexico	48,052	62,850	1975
Tabka (Thawra)	Syria	46,000	60,168	1976
Bennett W.A.C.	Canada	43,733	57,201	1967
Tucurui	Brazil	43,000	56,242	1984
Boruca	Costa Rica	43,000	56,242	UC
High Aswan (Sadd-el-Aali)	Egypt	43,000	56,242	1970
San Roque	Philippines	43,000	56,242	UC
Kiev	U.S.S.R.	42,841	56,034	1964
Dantiwada Left Embankment	India	41,040	53,680	1965
Saratov	U.S.S.R.	40,400	52,843	1967
Mission Tailings 2	Arizona	40,088	52,435	1973
Fort Randall	South Dakota	38,227	50,000	1953
Kanev	U.S.S.R.	37,860	49,520	1976
Mosul	Iraq	36,000	47,086	1982
Kakhovka	U.S.S.R.	35,640	46,617	1955
Itumbiara	Brazil	35,600	46,563	1980
Lauwerszee	Netherlands	35,575	46,532	1969
Beas	India	35,418	46,325	1974
Oosterschelde	Netherlands	35,000	45,778	1986

NOTE: UC = under construction. *Source:* Department of the Interior, Bureau of Reclamation and *International Water Power and Dam Construction.*

World's Largest Hydroelectric Plants

Name of dam	Location	Rated capacity (MW)		Year of initial operation
		Present	Ultimate	
Itaipu	Brazil/Paraguay	1,400	12,600	1984
Grand Coulee	Washington	6,480	10,080	1942
Guri (Raul Leoni)	Venezuela	2,800	10,060	1968
Tucuruí	Brazil	—	7,500	1985
Sayano-Shushensk	U.S.S.R.	—	6,400	1980
Krasnoyarsk	U.S.S.R.	6,096	6,096	1968
Corpus-Posadas	Argentina/Paraguay	—	6,000	UC
LaGrande 2	Canada	5,328	5,328	1982
Churchill Falls	Canada	5,225	5,225	1971
Bratsk	U.S.S.R.	4,100	4,600	1964
Ust'—Ilimsk	U.S.S.R.	3,675	4,500	1974
Cabora Bassa	Mozambique	2,075	4,150	1974
Yacyretá-Apipe	Argentina/Paraguay	—	4,050	UC
Rogun	U.S.S.R.	—	3,600	1985
Paulo Afonso	Brazil	3,409	3,409	1954
Salto Santiago	Brazil	1,332	3,333	1980
Pati (Chapetón)	Argentina	—	3,300	UC
Brumley Gap	Virginia	3,200	3,200	1973
Ilha Solteira	Brazil	3,200	3,200	1973
Inga I	Zaire	360	2,820	1974
Gezhouba	China	965	2,715	1981
John Day	Oregon/Washington	2,160	2,700	1969
Nurek	U.S.S.R.	900	2,700	1976
Revelstoke	Canada	900	2,700	1984
São Simao	Brazil	2,680	2,680	1979
LaGrande 4	Canada	2,637	2,637	1984
Mica	Canada	1,736	2,610	1976
Volgograd—22nd Congress	U.S.S.R.	2,560	2,560	1958
Fos do Areia	Brazil	2,511	2,511	1983
Itaparica	Brazil	—	2,500	1985
Bennett W.A.C.	Canada	2,116	2,416	1969
Chicoasén	Mexico	—	2,400	1980
Atatürk	Turkey	—	2,400	UC
LaGrande 3	Canada	2,310	2,310	1982
Volga—V.I. Lenin	U.S.S.R.	2,300	2,300	1955
Iron Gates I	Romania/Yugoslavia	2,300	2,300	1970
Iron Gates II	Romania/Yugoslavia	270	2,160	1983
Bath County	Virginia	—	2,100	1985
High Aswan (Saad-el-Aali)	Egypt	2,100	2,100	1967
Tarbela	Pakistan	1,400	2,100	1977
Piedra del Aquila	Argentina	—	2,100	UC
Itumbiara	Brazil	2,080	2,080	1980
Chief Joseph	Washington	2,069	2,069	1956
McNary	Oregon	980	2,030	1954
Green River	North Carolina	—	2,000	1980
Tehri	India	—	2,000	UC
Cornwall	New York	—	2,000	1978
Ludington	Michigan	1,979	1,979	1973
Robert Moses—Niagara	New York	1,950	1,950	1961
Salto Grande	Argentina/Uruguay	—	1,890	1979

Note: MW = Megawatts, UC = under construction. *Source:* Department of the Interior, Bureau of Reclamation and *International Water Power and Dam Construction.*

The First Skyscraper

A ten-story building isn't anyone's idea of a skyscraper today, but it was in fact the first skyscraper. It was not its height that gave it that distinction but its construction. It was the first building in the world to employ steel skeleton construction and thus became the prototype for the skyscraper.

Designed by William Le Baron Jenny for the Home Insurance Company of New York, it was erected at the corner of La Salle and Adams streets in Chicago. Construction began on May 1, 1884, and was completed in the fall of 1885. It was built of marble and flanked by four columns of polished granite supporting a marble balcony. A steel frame supported the weight of the walls, rather than the walls themselves bearing the weight. Two additional stories were added later.

Four years after completion of the Home Insurance Company Building, the steel-framed skyscraper had totally evolved in Chicago earning it the distinction of being its birth place.

Notable U.S. Skyscrapers

City	Building	Stories	Height ft	Height m	City	Building	Stories	Height ft	Height m
Chicago	Sears Tower	110	1,454	443	San Francisco	Bank of America	52	779	237
New York	World Trade Center	110	1,377	419	Minneapolis	IDS Tower	57	775	236
New York	Empire State	102	1,250	381	New York	One Liberty Plaza	54	775	236
Chicago	Standard Oil (Indiana)	80	1,136	346	New York	One Penn Plaza	57	774	236
Chicago	John Hancock Center	100	1,127	343	Miami	Southeast Financial Centre	55	765	233
New York	Chrysler	77	1,046	319	Atlanta	Peachtree Plaza	73	754	230
Houston	Texas	75	1,002	305	New York	Exxon	54	750	229
Houston	Allied Bank	71	985	300	Boston	Prudential Tower	52	750	229
New York	American International	66	952	290	Detroit	Detroit Plaza Hotel	73	747	228
New York	Citicorp Center	59	915	279	Dallas	First International	55	744	227
New York	40 Wall Tower	71	900	274	Los Angeles	Security Pacific Plaza	55	743	226
Chicago	Water Tower Place	74	859	262	New York	One Astor Plaza	54	730	222
Los Angeles	United California Bank	62	858	261	Houston	Gulf Tower	52	725	221
San Francisco	Transamerica Pyramid	61	853	260	New York	Marine Midland	52	724	221
Chicago	First National Bank	60	851	259	Houston	One Shell Plaza	50	714	218
New York	RCA	70	850	259	Dallas	First International	56	710	216
Pittsburgh	U.S. Steel Headquarters	64	841	256	Cleveland	Terminal Tower	52	708	216
New York	Chase Manhattan	60	813	248	New York	Union Carbide	52	707	215
New York	Pan Am	59	808	246	New York	General Motors	50	705	215
New York	Woolworth	55	792	241	New York	Metropolitan Life	50	700	213
Boston	John Hancock Tower	60	790	241					

NOTE: Height does not include TV towers and antennas. *Source: Information Please* questionnaires to building managements.

Notable Tunnels

Name	Location	Length mi.	Length km	Year completed
Railroad, excluding subways				
Seikan	Tsugara Strait, Japan	33.1	53.3	1983
Simplon (I and II)	Alps, Switzerland-Italy	12.3	19.8	1906 & 1922
Apennine	Genoa, Italy	11.5	18.5	1934
St. Gotthard	Swiss Alps	9.3	14.9	1881
Lötschberg	Swiss Alps	9.1	14.6	1911
Mont Cénis	French Alps	8.5[1]	13.7	1871
New Cascade	Cascade Mountains, Washington	7.8	12.6	1929
Vosges	Vosges, France	7.0	11.3	1940
Arlberg	Austrian Alps	6.3	10.1	1884
Moffat	Rocky Mountains, Colorado	6.2	9.9	1928
Shimuzu	Shimuzu, Japan	6.1	9.8	1931
Rimutaka	Wairarapa, New Zealand	5.5	8.9	1955
Vehicular				
St. Gotthard	Alps, Switzerland	10.2	16.4	1980
Mt. Blanc	Alps, France-Italy	7.5	12.1	1965
Mt. Ena	Japan Alps, Japan	5.3	8.5	1976[2]
Great St. Bernard	Alps, Switzerland-Italy	3.4	5.5	1964
Mount Royal	Montreal, Canada	3.2	5.1	1918
Lincoln	Hudson River, New York-New Jersey	2.5	4.0	1937
Queensway Road	Mersey River, Liverpool, England	2.2	3.5	1934
Brooklyn-Battery	East River, New York City	2.1	3.4	1950
Holland	Hudson River, New York-New Jersey	1.7	2.7	1927
Fort McHenry	Baltimore, Maryland	1.7	2.7	1985
Hampton Roads	Norfolk, Virginia	1.4	2.3	1957
Queens-Midtown	East River, New York City	1.3	2.1	1940
Liberty Tubes	Pittsburgh, Pennsylvania	1.2	1.9	1923
Baltimore Harbor	Baltimore, Maryland	1.2	1.9	1957
Allegheny Tunnels	Pennsylvania Turnpike	1.2	1.9	1940[3]

1. Lengthened to its present 8.5 miles in 1881. 2. Parallel tunnel begun in 1976. 3. Parallel tunnel built in 1965, twin tunnel in 1966. NOTE: UC = under construction. *Source:* American Society of Civil Engineers and International Bridge, Tunnel & Turnpike Association.

Notable Modern Bridges

Name	Location	Length of main span, ft	Length of main span, m	Year completed
Suspension				
Humber	Hull, Britain	4,626	1,410	1981
Verrazano-Narrows	Lower New York Bay	4,260	1,298	1964
Golden Gate	San Francisco Bay	4,200	1,280	1937
Mackinac Straits	Michigan	3,800	1,158	1957
Bosporus	Istanbul	3,524	1,074	1973
George Washington	Hudson River at New York City	3,500	1,067	1931
Ponte 25 de Abril	Tagus River at Lisbon	3,323	1,013	1966
Forth Road	Queensferry, Scotland	3,300	1,006	1964
Severn	Severn River at Beachley, England	3,240	988	1966
Tacoma Narrows	Puget Sound at Tacoma, Wash.	2,800	853	1950
Kanmon Strait	Kyushu-Honshu, Japan	2,336	712	1973
Angostura	Orinoco River at Ciudad Bolivar, Venezuela	2,336	712	1967
Transbay (twin spans)	San Francisco Bay	2,310	704	1936
Bronx-Whitestone	East River, New York City	2,300	701	1939
Pierre Laporte	St. Lawrence River at Quebec, Canada	2,190	668	1970
Delaware Memorial (twin bridges)	Delaware River near Wilmington, Del.	2,150	655	1951, 1968
Seaway Skyway	St. Lawrence River at Ogdensburg, N.Y.	2,150	655	1960
Gas Pipe Line	Atchafalaya River, Louisiana	2,000	610	1951
Walt Whitman	Delaware River at Philadelphia	2,000	610	1957
Tancarville	Seine River at Tancarville, France	1,995	608	1959
Lillebaelt	Lillebaelt Strait, Denmark	1,969	600	1970
Ambassador International	Detroit River at Detroit	1,850	564	1929
Throgs Neck	East River, New York City	1,800	549	1961
Benjamin Franklin	Delaware River at Philadelphia	1,750	533	1926
Skjomen	Narvik, Norway	1,722	525	1972
Kvalsund	Hammerfest, Norway	1,722	525	1977
Kleve-Emmerich	Rhine River at Emmerich, West Germany	1,640	500	1965
Bear Mountain	Hudson River at Peekskill, N.Y.	1,632	497	1924
Wm. Preston Lane, Jr., Memorial (twin bridges)	Near Annapolis, Md.	1,600	488	1952, 1973
Williamsburg	East River, New York City	1,600	488	1903
Newport	Narragansett Bay at Newport, R.I.	1,600	488	1969
Brooklyn	East River, New York City	1,595	486	1883
Cantilever				
Quebec Railway	St. Lawrence River at Quebec, Canada	1,800	549	1917
Forth Railway (twin spans)	Queensferry, Scotland	1,710	521	1890
Minato Ohashi	Osaka, Japan	1,673	510	1974
Commodore John Barry	Chester, Pa.	1,644	501	1974
Greater New Orleans (twin spans)	Mississippi River, Louisiana	1,576	480	1958
Howrah	Hooghly River at Calcutta	1,500	457	1943
Transbay Bridge	San Francisco Bay	1,400	427	1936
Baton Rouge	Mississippi River, Louisiana	1,235	376	1968
Tappan Zee	Hudson River at Tarrytown, N.Y.	1,212	369	1955
Longview	Columbia River at Longview, Wash.	1,200	366	1930
Patapsco River	Baltimore Outer Harbor Crossing	1,200	366	1976
Queensboro	East River, New York City	1,182	360	1909
Steel Arch				
New River Gorge	Fayetteville, W. Va.	1,700	518	1977
Bayonne	Kill Van Kull at Bayonne, N.J.	1,675	510	1931
Sydney Harbor	Sydney, Australia	1,670	509	1932
Fremont	Portland, Ore.	1,255	383	1973
Zdákov	Vltava River, Czechoslovakia	1,244	380	1967
Port Mann	Fraser River at Vancouver, British Columbia	1,200	366	1964
Thatcher Ferry	Panama Canal, Panama	1,128	344	1962
Laviolette	St. Lawrence River, Trois Rivieres, Quebec	1,100	335	1967
Runcorn-Widnes	Mersey River, England	1,082	330	1961
Birchenough	Sabi River at Fort Victoria, Rhodesia	1,080	329	1935

Name	Location	Length of main span, ft	m	Year completed
Cable-Stayed				
Annacis	Vancouver, B.C., Canada	1525	465	1986
Yokohama-ko-odan	Kanagawa, Japan	1509	460	UC
Second Hooghly	Calcutta, India	1500	457	UC
Chao Phya	Thailand	1476	450	1986
Barrios de Luna	Spain	1444	440	1983
Iwaguroshima	Kagawa, Japan	1378	420	UC
Shizakuishishima	Kagawa, Japan	1378	420	UC
Meiko Nishi	Aichi, Japan	1329	405	1985
St. Nazaire	Loire River, St. Nazaire, France	1325	404	1975
Rande	Rande, Spain	1312	400	1977
Dame Point	Jacksonville, Florida, U.S.A.	1300	396	1988
Houston Ship Channel	Baytown, Texas	1250	381	UC
Hale Boggs Memorial	Luling, Louisiana, U.S.A.	1222	373	1983
Dusseldorf Flehe	West Germany	1207	368	1979
Tjörn	Sweden	1200	366	1981
Sunshine Skyway	Tampa, Florida, U.S.A.	1200	366	1987
Continuous Truss				
Astoria	Columbia River at Astoria, Oregon	1,232	376	1966
Oshima	Oshima Island, Japan	1,066	325	1976
Croton Reservoir	Croton, N.Y.	1,052	321	1970
Tenmon	Kumamoto, Japan	984	300	1966
Kuronoseto	Nagashima-Kyushu, Japan	984	300	1974
Ravenswood	Ohio River, Ravenswood, W. Va.	902	275	1981
Dubuque	Mississippi River at Dubuque, Iowa	845	258	1943
Braga Memorial	Taunton River at Somerset, Mass.	840	256	1966
Graf Spee	Germany	839	256	1936
Cooper River	Charleston, S.C.	800	244	UC
Concrete Arch				
Jesse H. Jones Memorial	Houston Ship Channel, Texas	1,500	455	1982
KRK	Zagreb, Yugoslavia	1,280	390	1979
Gladesville	Parramatta River at Sydney, Australia	1,000	305	1964
Amizade	Paraná River at Foz do Iguassu, Brazil	951	290	1964
Arrábida	Porto, Portugal	886	270	1963
Sandö	Angerman River at Kramfors, Sweden	866	264	1943
Shibenik	Krka River, Yugoslavia	808	246	1966
Fiumarella	Catanzaro, Italy	758	231	1961
Zaporozhe	Old Dnepr River, U.S.S.R.	748	228	1952
Novi Sad	Danube River, Yugoslavia	692	211	1961

1. Concrete bridge. NOTE: UC = under construction. *Source: Encyclopaedia Britannica,* American Society of Civil Engineers, and Bridge Division, Federal Highway Administration.

Famous Ship Canals

Name	Location	Length (miles)[1]	Width (feet)	Depth (feet)	Locks	Year opened
Albert	Belgium	80.0	53.0	16.5	6	1939
Amsterdam-Rhine	Netherlands	45.0	164.0	41.0	3	1952
Beaumont-Port Arthur	United States	40.0	200.0	34.0	—	1916
Chesapeake and Delaware	United States	19.0	250.0	27.0	—	1927
Houston	United States	43.0	300.0	34.0	—	1914
Kiel (Nord-Ostsee Kanal)	Germany	61.3	144.0	36.0	4	1895
Panama	Canal Zone	50.7	110.0	41.0	12	1914
St. Lawrence Seaway	U.S. and Canada	2,400.0 [2]	(3)	—	—	1959
Montreal to Prescott	U.S. and Canada	11.5	80.0	30.0	7	1959
Welland	Canada	27.5	80.0	27.0	8	1931
Sault Ste. Marie	Canada	1.2	60.0	16.8	1	1895
Sault Ste. Marie	United States	1.6	80.0	25.0	4	1915
Suez	Egypt	100.6 [4]	197.0	36.0	—	1869

1. Statute miles. 2. From Montreal to Duluth. 3. 442–550 feet; there are 11.5 miles of locks, 80 feet wide and 30 feet deep. 4. From Port Said lighthouse to entrance channel in Suez roads. *Source:* American Society of Civil Engineers.

U.S. HISTORY & GOVERNMENT

THE DECLARATION OF INDEPENDENCE

In Congress, July 4, 1776

The unanimous Declaration of the thirteen united States of America.

When in the Course of human events it becomes necessary for one people to dissolve the political bands which have connected them with another, and to assume among the powers of the earth, the separate and equal station to which the Laws of Nature and of Nature's God entitle them, a decent respect to the opinions of mankind requires that they should declare the causes which impel them to the separation.

We hold these truths to be self-evident, that all men are created equal, that they are endowed by their Creator with certain unalienable Rights, that among these are Life, Liberty and the pursuit of Happiness.—That to secure these rights, Governments are instituted among Men, deriving their just powers from the consent of the governed,— That whenever any Form of Government becomes destructive of these ends, it is the Right of the People to alter or to abolish it, and to institute new Government, laying its foundation on such principles and organizing its powers in such form, as to them shall seem most likely to effect their Safety and Happiness. Prudence, indeed, will dictate that Governments long established should not be changed for light and transient causes; and accordingly all experience hath shewn that mankind are more disposed to suffer, while evils are sufferable, than to right themselves by abolishing the forms to which they are accustomed. But when a long train of abuses and usurpations, pursuing invariably the same Object evinces a design to reduce them under absolute Despotism, it is their right, it is their duty, to throw off such Government, and to provide new Guards for their future security.— Such has been the patient sufferance of these Colonies; and such is now the necessity which constrains them to alter their former Systems of Government. The history of the present King of Great Britain is a history of repeated injuries and usurpations, all having in direct object the establishment of an absolute Tyranny over these States. To prove this, let Facts be submitted to a candid world.

He has refused his Assent to Laws, the most wholesome and necessary for the public good.

He has forbidden his Governors to pass Laws of immediate and pressing importance, unless suspended in their operation till his Assent should be obtained; and when so suspended, he has utterly neglected to attend to them.

He has refused to pass other Laws for the accommodation of large districts of people, unless those people would relinquish the right of Representation in the Legislature, a right inestimable to them and formidable to tyrants only.

He has called together legislative bodies at places unusual, uncomfortable, and distant from the depository of their Public Records, for the sole purpose of fatiguing them into compliance with his measures.

He has dissolved Representative Houses repeatedly, for opposing with manly firmness his invasions on the rights of the people.

He has refused for a long time, after such dissolutions, to cause others to be elected; whereby the Legislative Powers, incapable of Annihilation, have returned to the People at large for their exercise; the State remaining in the mean time exposed to all the dangers of invasion from without, and convulsions within.

He has endeavoured to prevent the population of these States; for that purpose obstructing the Laws for Naturalization of Foreigners; refusing to pass others to encourage their migrations hither, and raising the conditions of new Appropriations of Lands.

He has obstructed the Administration of Justice, by refusing his Assent to Laws for establishing Judiciary Powers.

He has made Judges dependent on his Will alone, for the tenure of their offices, and the amount and payment of their salaries.

He has erected a multitude of New Offices, and sent hither swarms of Officers to harass our people, and eat out their substance.

He has kept among us, in times of peace, Standing Armies without the Consent of our legislatures.

He has affected to render the Military independent of and superior to the Civil Power.

He has combined with others to subject us to a jurisdiction foreign to our constitution, and unacknowledged by our laws; giving his Assent to their Acts of pretended Legislation:

For quartering large bodies of armed troops among us:

For protecting them, by a mock Trial, from punishment for any Murders which they should commit on the Inhabitants of these States:

For cutting off our Trade with all parts of the

NOTE: On April 12, 1776, the legislature of North Carolina authorized its delegates to the Continental Congress to join with others in a declaration of separation from Great Britain; the first colony to instruct its delegates to take the actual initiative was Virginia on May 15. On June 7, 1776, Richard Henry Lee of Virginia offered a resolution to the Congress to the effect "that these United Colonies are, and of right ought to be, free and independent States. . . ." A committee, consisting of Thomas Jefferson, John Adams, Benjamin Franklin, Robert R. Livingston, and Roger Sherman was organized to "prepare a declaration to the effect of the said first resolution." The Declaration of Independence was adopted on July 4, 1776.

Most delegates signed the Declaration August 2, but George Wythe (Va.) signed August 27; Richard Henry Lee (Va.), Elbridge Gerry (Mass.), and Oliver Wolcott (Conn.) in September; Matthew Thornton (N.H.), not a delegate until September, in November; and Thomas McKean (Del.), although present on July 4, not until 1781 by special permission, having served in the army in the interim.

world:

For imposing Taxes on us without our Consent:

For depriving us in many cases, of the benefits of Trial by Jury:

For transporting us beyond Seas to be tried for pretended offences:

For abolishing the free System of English Laws in a neighbouring Province, establishing therein an Arbitrary government, and enlarging its Boundaries so as to render it at once an example and fit instrument for introducing the same absolute rule into these Colonies:

For taking away our Charters, abolishing our most valuable Laws and altering fundamentally the Forms of our Governments:

For suspending our own Legislatures, and declaring themselves invested with power to legislate for us in all cases whatsoever.

He has abdicated Government here, by declaring us out of his Protection and waging War against us.

He has plundered our seas, ravaged our Coasts, burnt our towns, and destroyed the lives of our people.

He is at this time transporting large Armies of foreign Mercenaries to compleat the works of death, desolation, and tyranny, already begun with circumstances of Cruelty & Perfidy scarcely paralleled in the most barbarous ages, and totally unworthy the Head of a civilized nation.

He has constrained our fellow Citizens taken Captive on the high Seas to bear Arms against their Country, to become the executioners of their friends and Brethren, or to fall themselves by their Hands.

He has excited domestic insurrections amongst us, and has endeavoured to bring on the inhabitants of our frontiers, the merciless Indian Savages, whose known rule of warfare, is an undistinguished destruction of all ages, sexes and conditions.

In every stage of these Oppressions We have Petitioned for Redress in the most humble terms: Our repeated Petitions have been answered only by repeated injury. A Prince, whose character is thus marked by every act which may define a Tyrant, is unfit to be the ruler of a free people.

Nor have We been wanting in attentions to our Brittish brethren. We have warned them from time to time of attempts by their legislature to extend an unwarrantable jurisdiction over us. We have reminded them of the circumstances of our emigration and settlement here. We have appealed to their native justice and magnanimity, and we have conjured them by the ties of our common kindred to disavow these usurpations, which would inevitably interrupt our connections and correspondence. They too have been deaf to the voice of justice and of consanguinity. We must, therefore, acquiesce in the necessity, which denounces our Separation, and hold them, as we hold the rest of mankind, Enemies in War, in Peace Friends.

We, therefore, the Representatives of the United States of America, in General Congress, Assembled, appealing to the Supreme Judge of the world for the rectitude of our intentions, do, in the Name, and by Authority of the good People of these Colonies, solemnly publish and declare, That these United Colonies are, and of Right ought to be Free and Independent States; that they are Absolved from all Allegiance to the British Crown, and that all political connection between them and the State of Great Britain, is and ought to be totally dissolved; and that as Free and Independent States, they have full Power to levy War, conclude Peace, contract Alliances, establish Commerce, and to do all other Acts and Things which Independent States may of right do.—And for the support of this Declaration, with a firm reliance on the protection of Divine Providence, we mutually pledge to each other our Lives, our Fortunes and our sacred Honor.

—John Hancock

New Hampshire
Josiah Bartlett
Wm. Whipple
Matthew Thornton

Rhode Island
Step. Hopkins
William Ellery

Connecticut
Roger Sherman
Sam'el Huntington
Wm. Williams
Oliver Wolcott

New York
Wm. Floyd
Phil. Livingston
Frans. Lewis
Lewis Morris

New Jersey
Richd. Stockton
Jno. Witherspoon
Fras. Hopkinson
John Hart
Abra. Clark

Pennsylvania
Robt. Morris
Benjamin Rush
Benj. Franklin
John Morton
Geo. Clymer
Jas. Smith
Geo. Taylor
James Wilson
Geo. Ross

Massachusetts-Bay
Saml. Adams
John Adams
Robt. Treat Paine
Elbridge Gerry

Delaware
Caesar Rodney
Geo. Read
Tho. M'Kean

Maryland
Samuel Chase
Wm. Paca
Thos. Stone
Charles Carroll of Carrollton

Virginia
George Wythe
Richard Henry Lee
Th. Jefferson
Benj. Harrison
Ths. Nelson, Jr.
Francis Lightfoot Lee
Carter Braxton

North Carolina
Wm. Hooper
Joseph Hewes
John Penn

South Carolina
Edward Rutledge
Thos. Heyward, Junr.
Thomas Lynch, Junr.
Arthur Middleton

Georgia
Button Gwinnett
Lyman Hall
Geo. Walton

Constitution of the United States of America

(Historical text has been edited to conform to contemporary American usage.
The bracketed words are designations for your convenience; they are not part of the Constitution.)

The oldest federal constitution in existence was framed by a convention of delegates from twelve of the thirteen original states in Philadelphia in May, 1787, Rhode Island. failing to send a delegate. George Washington presided over the session, which lasted until September 17, 1787. The draft (originally a preamble and seven Articles) was submitted to all thirteen states and was to become effective when ratified by nine states. It went into effect on the first Wednesday in March, 1789, having been ratified by New Hampshire, the ninth state to approve, on June 21, 1788. The states ratified the Constitution in the following order:

Delaware	December 7, 1787	South Carolina	May 23, 1788
Pennsylvania	December 12, 1787	New Hampshire	June 21, 1788
New Jersey	December 18, 1787	Virginia	June 25, 1788
Georgia	January 2, 1788	New York	July 26, 1788
Connecticut	January 9, 1788	North Carolina	November 21, 1789
Massachusetts	February 6, 1788	Rhode Island	May 29, 1790
Maryland	April 28, 1788		

[Preamble]

We the people of the United States, in order to form a more perfect Union, establish justice, insure domestic tranquility, provide for the common defence, promote the general welfare, and secure the blessings of liberty to ourselves and our posterity, do ordain and establish this Constitution for the United States of America.

Article I

Section 1

[**Legislative powers vested in Congress.**] All legislative powers herein granted shall be vested in a Congress of the United States, which shall consist of a Senate and House of Representatives.

Section 2

[**Composition of the House of Representatives.— 1.**] The House of Representatives shall be composed of members chosen every second year by the people of the several States, and the electors in each State shall have the qualifications requisite for electors of the most numerous branch of the State Legislature.

[**Qualifications of Representatives.—2.**] No Person shall be a Representative who shall not have attained to the age of twenty-five years, and been seven years a citizen of the United States, and who shall not, when elected, be an inhabitant of that State in which he shall be chosen.

[**Apportionment of Representatives and direct taxes—census.'—3.**] (Representatives and direct taxes shall be apportioned among the several States which may be included within this Union, according to their respective numbers, which shall be determined by adding to the whole number of free persons, including those bound to service for a term of years, and excluding Indians not taxed, three fifths of all other persons.) The actual enumeration shall be made within three years after the first meeting of the Congress of the United States, and within every subsequent term of ten years, in such manner as they shall by law direct. The number of Representatives shall not exceed one for every thirty thousand, but each State shall have at least one Representative; and until such enumeration shall be made, the State of New Hampshire shall be entitled to choose three, Massachusetts

eight, Rhode-Island and Providence Plantations one, Connecticut five, New York six, New Jersey four, Pennsylvania eight, Delaware one, Maryland six, Virginia ten, North Carolina five, South Carolina five, and Georgia three.

[**Filling of vacancies in representation.—4.**] When vacancies happen in the representation from any State, the Executive Authority thereof shall issue writs of election to fill such vacancies.

[**Selection of officers; power of impeachment.— 5.**] The House of Representatives shall choose their Speaker and other officers; and shall have the sole power of impeachment.

Section 3[2]

[**The Senate.—1.**] The Senate of the United States shall be composed of two Senators from each State, chosen by the Legislature thereof, for six years; and each Senator shall have one vote.

[**Classification of Senators; filling of vacancies.— 2.**] Immediately after they shall be assembled in consequence of the first election, they shall be divided as equally as may be into three classes. The seats of the Senators of the first class shall be vacated at the expiration of the second year, of the second class at the expiration of the fourth year, and of the third class at the expiration of the sixth year, so that one-third may be chosen every second year; and if vacancies happen by resignation, or otherwise, during the recess of the Legislature of any State, the Executive thereof may make temporary appointments (until the next meeting of the Legislature, which shall then fill such vacancies).

[**Qualification of Senators.—3.**] No person shall be a Senator who shall not have attained to the age of thirty years, and been nine years a citizen of the United States, and who shall not, when elected, be an inhabitant of that State for which he shall be chosen.

[**Vice President to be President of Senate.—4.**] The Vice President of the United States shall be President of the Senate, but shall have no vote, unless they be equally divided.

[**Selection of Senate officers; President pro tempore.—5.**] The Senate shall choose their other officers, and also a President pro tempore, in the absence of the Vice President, or when he shall exercise the office of President of the United States.

[**Senate to try impeachments.—6.**] The Senate

shall have the sole power to try all impeachments. When sitting for that purpose, they shall be on oath or affirmation. When the President of the United States is tried, the Chief Justice shall preside: and no person shall be convicted without the concurrence of two thirds of the members present.

[Judgment in cases of Impeachment.—7.] Judgment in cases of impeachment shall not extend further than to removal from office, and disqualification to hold and enjoy any office of honor, trust, or profit under the United States: but the party convicted shall nevertheless be liable and subject to indictment, trial, judgment and punishment, according to Law.

Section 4

[Control of congressional elections.—1.] The times, places, and manner of holding elections for Senators and Representatives, shall be prescribed in each State by the Legislature thereof; but the Congress may at any time by law make or alter such regulations, except as to the places of choosing Senators.

[Time for assembling of Congress.³—2.] The Congress shall assemble at least once in every year, and such meeting shall be on the first Monday in December, unless they shall by law appoint a different day.

Section 5

[Each house to be the judge of the election and qualifications of its members; regulations as to quorum.—1.] Each House shall be the judge of the elections, returns, and qualifications of its own members, and a majority of each shall constitute a quorum to do business; but a smaller number may adjourn from day to day, and may be authorized to compel the attendance of absent members, in such manner, and under such penalties as each House may provide.

[Each house to determine its own rules.—2.] Each House may determine the rules of its proceedings, punish its members for disorderly behavior, and, with the concurrence of two thirds, expel a member.

[Journals and yeas and nays.—3.] Each House shall keep a journal of its proceedings, and from time to time publish the same, excepting such parts as may in their judgment require secrecy; and the yeas and nays of the members of either House on any question shall, at the desire of one fifth of those present, be entered on the journal.

[Adjournment.—4.] Neither House, during the session of Congress, shall, without the consent of the other, adjourn for more than three days, nor to any other place than that in which the two Houses shall be sitting.

Section 6

[Compensation and privileges of members of Congress.—1.] The Senators and Representatives shall receive a compensation for their services, to be ascertained by law, and paid out of the Treasury of the United States. They shall in all cases, except treason, felony, and breach of the peace, be privileged from arrest during their attendance at the session of their respective Houses, and in going to and returning from the same; and for any speech or debate in either House, they shall not be questioned in any other place.

[Incompatible offices; exclusions.—2.] No Senator or Representative shall, during the time for which he was elected, be appointed to any civil office under the authority of the United States, which shall have been created, or the emoluments whereof shall have been increased during such time; and no person holding any office under the United States shall be a member of either House during his continuance in office.

Section 7

[Revenue bills to originate in House.—1.] All bills for raising revenue shall originate in the House of Representatives; but the Senate may propose or concur with amendments as on other bills.

[Manner of passing bills; veto power of President.—2.] Every bill which shall have passed the House of Representatives and the Senate, shall, before it becomes a law, be presented to the President of the United States; if he approve he shall sign it, but if not he shall return it, with his objections to that House in which it shall have originated, who shall enter the objections at large on their journal, and proceed to reconsider it. If after such reconsideration two thirds of that House shall agree to pass the bill, it shall be sent, together with the objections, to the other House, by which it shall likewise be reconsidered, and if approved by two thirds of that House, it shall become a law. But in all such cases the votes of both Houses shall be determined by yeas and nays, and the names of the persons voting for and against the bill shall be entered on the journal of each house, respectively. If any bill shall not be returned by the President within ten days (Sundays excepted) after it shall have been presented to him, the same shall be a law, in like manner as if he had signed it, unless the Congress by their adjournment prevent its return, in which case it shall not be a law.

[Concurrent orders or resolutions, to be passed by President.—3.] Every order, resolution, or vote to which the concurrence of the Senate and House of Representatives may be necessary (except on a question of adjournment) shall be presented to the President of the United States; and before the same shall take effect, shall be approved by him, or being disapproved by him, shall be repassed by two thirds of the Senate and House of Representatives, according to the rules and limitations prescribed in the case of a bill.

Section 8

[General powers of Congress.⁴]
[Taxes, duties, imposts, and excises.—1.] The Congress shall have power to lay and collect taxes, duties, imposts and excises, to pay the debts and provide for the common defense and general welfare of the United States; but all duties, imposts and excises shall be uniform throughout the United States;

[Borrowing of money.—2.] To borrow money on the credit of the United States;

[Regulation of commerce.—3.] To regulate commerce with foreign nations, and among the several States, and with the Indian tribes;

[Naturalization and bankruptcy.—4.] To establish a uniform rule of naturalization, and uniform laws on the subject of bankruptcies throughout the United States;

[Money, weights and measures.—5.] To coin money, regulate the value thereof, and of foreign coin, and fix the standard of weights and measures;

[Counterfeiting.—6.] To provide for the punishment of counterfeiting the securities and current coin of the United States;

[Post offices.—7.] To establish post offices and post roads;

[Patents and copyrights.—8.] To promote the

progress of science and useful arts, by securing for limited times to authors and inventors the exclusive right to their respective writings and discoveries;

[**Inferior courts.—9.**] To constitute tribunals inferior to the Supreme Court;

[**Piracies and felonies.—10.**] To define and punish piracies and felonies committed on the high seas, and offences against the law of nations;

[**War; marque and reprisal.—11.**] To declare war, grant letters of marque and reprisal, and make rules concerning captures on land and water;

[**Armies.—12.**] To raise and support armies, but no appropriation of money to that use shall be for a longer term than two years;

[**Navy.—13.**] To provide and maintain a navy;

[**Land and naval forces.—14.**] To make rules for the government and regulation of the land and naval forces;

[**Calling out militia.—15.**] To provide for calling forth the militia to execute the laws of the Union, suppress insurrections, and repel invasions.

[**Organizing, arming, and disciplining militia.—16.**] To provide for organizing, arming, and disciplining, the militia, and for governing such part of them as may be employed in the service of the United States, reserving to the States, respectively, the appointment of the officers, and the authority of training the militia according to the discipline prescribed by Congress;

[**Exclusive legislation over District of Columbia.—17.**] To exercise exclusive legislation in all cases whatsoever, over such district (not exceeding ten miles square) as may, by cession of particular States, and the acceptance of Congress, become the seat of the Government of the United States, and to exercise like authority over all places purchased by the consent of the Legislature of the State in which the same shall be, for the erection of forts, magazines, arsenals, dock-yards, and other needful buildings;—And

[**To enact laws necessary to enforce Constitution.—18.**] To make all laws which shall be necessary and proper for carrying into execution the foregoing powers, and all other powers vested by this Constitution in the Government of the United States, or in any department or officer thereof.

Section 9

[**Migration or importation of certain persons not to be prohibited before 1808.—1.**] The migration or importation of such persons as any of the States now existing shall think proper to admit, shall not be prohibited by the Congress prior to the year one thousand eight hundred and eight, but a tax or duty may be imposed on such importation, not exceeding ten dollars for each person.

[**Writ of habeas corpus not to be suspended; exception.—2.**] The privilege of the writ of habeas corpus shall not be suspended, unless when in cases of rebellion or invasion the public safety may require it.

[**Bills of attainder and ex post facto laws prohibited.—3.**] No bill of attainder or ex post facto law shall be passed.

[**Capitation and other direct taxes.—4.**] No capitation, or other direct, tax shall be laid, unless in proportion to the census or enumeration herein before directed to be taken.[5]

[**Exports not to be taxed.—5.**] No tax or duty shall be laid on articles exported from any State.

[**No preference to be given to ports of any States; interstate shipping.—6.**] No preference shall be given by any regulation of commerce or revenue to the ports of one State over those of another: nor shall vessels bound to, or from, one State, be obliged to enter, clear, or pay duties in another.

[**Money, how drawn from treasury; financial statements to be published.—7.**] No money shall be drawn from the Treasury, but in consequence of appropriations made by law; and a regular statement and account of the receipts and expenditures of all public money shall be published from time to time.

[**Titles of nobility not to be granted; acceptance by government officers of favors from foreign powers.—8.**] No title of nobility shall be granted by the United States: and no person holding any office of profit or trust under them, shall, without the consent of the Congress, accept of any present, emolument, office, or title, of any kind whatever, from any king, prince, or foreign state.

Section 10

[**Limitations of the powers of the several States.—1.**] No State shall enter into any treaty, alliance, or confederation; grant letters of marque and reprisal; coin money; emit bills of credit; make any thing but gold and silver coin a tender in payment of debts; pass any bill of attainder, ex post facto law, or law impairing the obligation of contracts, or grant any title of nobility.

[**State imposts and duties.—2.**] No State shall, without the consent of the Congress, lay any imposts or duties on imports or exports, except what may be absolutely necessary for executing its inspection laws; and the net produce of all duties and imposts, laid by any State on imports or exports, shall be for the use of the Treasury of the United States; and all such laws shall be subject to the revision and control of the Congress.

[**Further restrictions on powers of States.—3.**] No State shall, without the consent of Congress, lay any duty of tonnage, keep troops, or ships of war in time of peace, enter into any agreement or compact with another state, or with a foreign power, or engage in war, unless actually invaded, or in such imminent danger as will not admit of delay.

Article II

Section 1

[**The President; the executive power.—1.**] The executive power shall be vested in a President of the United States of America. He shall hold his office during the term of four years, and, together with the Vice President, chosen for the same term, be elected, as follows

[**Appointment and qualifications of presidential electors.—2.**] Each State shall appoint, in such manner as the Legislature thereof may direct, a number of electors, equal to the whole number of Senators and Representatives to which the State may be entitled in the Congress: but no Senator or Representative, or person holding an office of trust or profit under the United States, shall be appointed an elector.

[**Original method of electing the President and Vice President.[6]**] (The electors shall meet in their respective States, and vote by ballot for two persons, of whom one at least shall not be an inhabitant of the same State with themselves. And they shall make a list of all the persons voted for, and of the number of votes for each; which list they shall sign and certify, and transmit sealed to the seat of the Government of the United States, directed to the

President of the Senate. The President of the Senate shall, in the presence of the Senate and House of Representatives, open all the certificates, and the votes shall then be counted. The person having the greatest number of votes shall be the President, if such number be a majority of the whole number of electors appointed; and if there be more than one who have such majority, and have an equal number of votes, then the House of Representatives shall immediately choose by ballot one of them for President; and if no person have a majority, then from the five highest on the list the said House shall in like manner choose the President. But in choosing the President, the votes shall be taken by States, the representation from each State having one vote; A quorum for this purpose shall consist of a member or members from two thirds of the States, and a majority of all the states shall be necessary to a choice. In every case, after the choice of the President, the person having the greatest number of votes of the electors shall be the Vice President. But if there should remain two or more who have equal votes, the Senate should choose from them by ballot the Vice President.)

[Congress may determine time of choosing electors and day for casting their votes.—3.] The Congress may determine the time of choosing the electors, and the day on which they shall give their votes; which day shall be the same throughout the United States.

[Qualifications for the office of President.[7]—4.] No person except a natural born citizen, or a citizen of the United States, at the time of the adoption of this Constitution, shall be eligible to the office of President; neither shall any person be eligible to that office who shall not have attained to the age of thirty-five years, and been fourteen years a resident within the United States.

[Filling vacancy in the office of President.[8]—5.] In case of the removal of the President from office, or of his death, resignation, or inability to discharge the powers and duties of the said office, the same shall devolve on the Vice President, and the Congress may by law provide for the case of removal, death, resignation or inability, both of the President and Vice President, declaring what officer shall then act as President, and such officer shall act accordingly, until the disability be removed, or a President shall be elected.

[Compensation of the President.—6.] The President shall, at stated times, receive for his services, a compensation, which shall neither be increased nor diminished during the period for which he shall have been elected, and he shall not receive within that period any other emolument from the United States, or any of them.

[Oath to be taken by the President.—7.] Before he enter on the execution of his office, he shall take the following oath or affirmation:—"I do solemnly swear (or affirm) that I will faithfully execute the office of President of the United States, and will to the best of my ability, preserve, protect, and defend the Constitution of the United States."

Section 2

[The President to be commander in chief of army and navy and head of executive departments; may grant reprieves and pardons.—1.] The President shall be Commander in Chief of the Army and Navy of the United States, and of the militia of the several States, when called into the actual service of the United States; he may require the opinion, in writing, of the principal officer in each of the executive departments, upon any subject relating to the duties of their respective offices, and he shall have power to grant reprieves and pardons for offences against the United States, except in cases of impeachment.

[President may, with concurrence of Senate, make treaties, appoint ambassadors, etc.; appointment of inferior officers, authority of Congress over.—2.] He shall have power, by and with the advice and consent of the Senate, to make treaties, provided two thirds of the Senators present concur; and he shall nominate, and by and with the advice and consent of the Senate, shall appoint ambassadors, other public ministers and consuls, judges of the Supreme Court, and all other officers of the United States, whose appointments are not herein otherwise provided for, and which shall be established by law: but the Congress may by law vest the appointment of such inferior officers, as they think proper, in the President alone, in the courts of law, or in the heads of departments.

[President may fill vacancies in office during recess of Senate.—3.] The President shall have power to fill up all vacancies that may happen during the recess of the Senate, by granting commissions which shall expire at the end of their session.

Section 3

[President to give advice to Congress; may convene or adjourn it on certain occasions; to receive ambassadors, etc.; have laws executed and commission all officers.] He shall from time to time give to the Congress information of the state of the Union, and recommend to their consideration such measures as he shall judge necessary and expedient; he may, on extraordinary occasions, convene both Houses, or either of them, and in case of disagreement between them, with respect to the time of adjournment, he may adjourn them to such time as he shall think proper; he shall receive ambassadors and other public ministers: he shall take care that the laws be faithfully executed, and shall commission all the officers of the United States.

Section 4

[All civil officers removable by impeachment.] The President, Vice President, and all civil officers of the United States shall be removed from office on impeachment for, and conviction of, treason, bribery, or other high crimes and misdemeanors.

Article III

Section 1

[Judicial powers; how vested; term of office and compensation of judges.] The judicial Power of the United States, shall be vested in one Supreme Court, and in such inferior courts as the Congress may from time to time ordain and establish. The judges, both of the supreme and inferior courts, shall hold their offices during good behavior, and shall, at stated times, receive for their services, a compensation, which shall not be diminished during their continuance in office.

Section 2

[Jurisdiction of Federal courts.[9]—1.] The judicial power shall extend to all cases, in law and equity, arising under this Constitution, the laws of the United States, and treaties made, or which shall be made, under their authority; to all cases affecting ambassadors, other public ministers and consuls; to all cases of admiralty and maritime jurisdiction; to controversies to which the United States, shall be a party; to controversies between two or more States; between a State and citizens of another State; between citizens of different States; between citizens of the same State claiming lands under grants of different states, and between a State, or the citizens thereof, and foreign states, citizens, or subjects.

[**Original and appellate jurisdiction of Supreme Court.—2.**] In all cases affecting ambassadors, other public ministers and consuls, and those in which a State shall be party, the Supreme Court shall have original jurisdiction. In all the other cases before mentioned, the Supreme Court shall have appellate jurisdiction, both as to law and fact, with such exceptions, and under such regulations, as the Congress shall make.

[**Trial of all crimes, except impeachment, to be by jury.—3.**] The trial of all crimes, except in cases of impeachment, shall be by jury; and such trial shall be held in the State where the said crimes shall have been committed; but when not committed within any State, the trial shall be at such place or places as the Congress may by law have directed.

Section 3

[**Treason defined; conviction of.—1.**] Treason against the United States, shall consist only in levying war against them, or, in adhering to their enemies, giving them aid and comfort. No person shall be convicted of treason unless on the testimony of two witnesses to the same overt act, or on confession in open court.

[**Congress to declare punishment for treason; proviso.—2.**] The Congress shall have power to declare the punishment of treason, but no attainder of treason shall work corruption of blood, or forfeiture except during the life of the person attained.

Article IV

Section 1

[**Each State to give full faith and credit to the public acts and records of other States.**] Full faith and credit shall be given in each State to the public acts, records, and judicial proceedings of every other State. And the Congress may by general laws prescribe the manner in which such acts, records, and proceedings shall be proved, and the effect thereof.

Section 2

[**Privileges of citizens.—1.**] The citizens of each State shall be entitled to all privileges and immunities of citizens in the several States.

[**Extradition between the several States.—2.**] A person charged in any State with treason, felony, or other crime, who shall flee from justice, and be found in another State, shall on demand of the Executive authority of the State from which he fled, be delivered up, to be removed to the State having jurisdiction of the crime.

[**Persons held to labor or service in one State, fleeing to another, to be returned.—3.**] No person held to service or labor in one State, under the laws thereof, escaping into another, shall, in conse-

quence of any law or regulation therein, be discharged from such service or labor, but shall be delivered up on claim of the party to whom such service or labor may be due.

Section 3

[**New States.—1.**] New States may be admitted by the Congress into this Union; but no new State shall be formed or erected within the jurisdiction of any other State; nor any State be formed by the junction of two or more States, or parts of States, without the consent of the Legislatures of the States concerned as well as of the Congress.

[**Regulations concerning territory.—2.**] The Congress shall have power to dispose of and make all needful rules and regulations respecting the territory or other property belonging to the United States; and nothing in this Constitution shall be so construed as to prejudice any claims of the United States, or of any particular State.

Section 4

[**Republican form of government and protection guaranteed the several States.**] The United States shall guarantee to every State in this Union a Republican form of government, and shall protect each of them against invasion; and on application of the Legislature, or of the Executive (when the Legislature cannot be convened) against domestic violence.

Article V

[**Ways in which the Constitution can be amended.**] The Congress, whenever two thirds of both Houses shall deem it necessary, shall propose amendments to this Constitution, or, on the application of the Legislatures of two thirds of the several States shall call a convention for proposing amendments, which, in either case, shall be valid to all intents and purposes, as part of this Constitution, when ratified by the Legislatures of three fourths of the several States, or by conventions in three fourths thereof, as the one or the other mode of ratification may be proposed by the Congress; provided that no amendment which may be made prior to the year one thousand eight hundred and eight shall in any manner affect the first and fourth clauses in the ninth Section of the first Article; and that no State, without its consent, shall be deprived of its equal suffrage in the Senate.

Article VI

[**Debts contracted under the confederation secured.—1.**] All debts contracted and engagements entered into, before the adoption of this Constitution, shall be as valid against the United States under this Constitution, as under the Confederation.

[**Constitution, laws, and treaties of the United States to be supreme.—2.**] This Constitution, and the laws of the United States which shall be made in pursuance thereof; and all treaties made, or which shall be made, under the authority of the United States, shall be the supreme law of the land; and the judges in every State shall be bound thereby, any thing in the Constitution or laws of

1. The clause included in parentheses is amended by the 14th Amendment, Section 2. 2. The first paragraph of this section and the part of the second paragraph included in parentheses are amended by the 17th Amendment. 3. Amended by the 20th Amendment, Section 2. 4. By the 16th Amendment, Congress is given the power to lay and collect taxes on income. 5. See the 16th Amendment. 6. This clause has been superseded by the 12th Amendment. 7. For qualifications of the Vice President, see 12th Amendment. 8. Amended by the 20th Amendment, Sections 3 and 4. 9. This section is abridged by the 11th Amendment. 10. See the 13th Amendment.

any State to the contrary notwithstanding.

[**Who shall take constitutional oath; no religious test as to official qualification.—3.**] The Senators and Representatives before mentioned, and the members of the several State Legislatures, and all executive and judicial officers, both of the United States and of the several States, shall be bound by oath or affirmation, to support this Constitution; but no religious test shall ever be required as a qualification to any office or public trust under the United States.

Article VII

[**Constitution to be considered adopted when ratified by nine States.**] The ratification of the conventions of nine States shall be sufficient for the establishment of this Constitution between the States so ratifying the same.

Done in convention by the unanimous consent of the States present the seventeenth day of September in the year of our Lord one thousand seven hundred and eighty seven and of the independence of the United States of America the Twelfth. In witness whereof we have hereunto subscribed our names.

GEORGE WASHINGTON
President and Deputy from Virginia

NEW HAMPSHIRE
John Langdon   Nicholas Gilman

MASSACHUSETTS
Nathaniel Gorham   Rufus King

CONNECTICUT
Wm. Saml. Johnson   Roger Sherman

NEW YORK
Alexander Hamilton

NEW JERSEY
Wil. Livingston   Wm. Paterson
David Brearley   Jona. Dayton

PENNSYLVANIA
B. Franklin   Thomas Mifflin
Robt. Morris   Geo. Clymer
Thos. FitzSimons   Jared Ingersoll
James Wilson   Gouv. Morris

DELAWARE
Geo. Read   Gunning Bedford Jun.
John Dickinson   Richard Bassett
Jaco. Broom

MARYLAND
James McHenry   Dan. of St. Thos. Jenifer
Danl. Carroll

VIRGINIA
John Blair   James Madison, Jr.

NORTH CAROLINA
Wm. Blount   Richd Dobbs Spaight
Hu. Williamson

SOUTH CAROLINA
J. Rutledge   Charles Cotesworth
Charles Pinckney   Pinckney
                                 Pierce Butler

GEORGIA
William Few   Abr. Baldwin
Attest: William Jackson, Secretary

Amendments to the Constitution of the United States

(Amendments I to X inclusive, popularly known as the Bill of Rights, were proposed and sent to the states by the first session of the First Congress. They were ratified Dec. 15, 1791.)

Article I

[**Freedom of religion, speech, of the press, and right of petition.**] Congress shall make no law respecting an establishment of religion, or prohibiting the free exercise thereof; or abridging the freedom of speech, or of the press; or the right of the people peaceably to assemble, and to petition the Government for a redress of grievances.

Article II

[**Right of people to bear arms not to be infringed.**] A well regulated militia, being necessary to the security of a free State, the right of the people to keep and bear arms, shall not be infringed.

Article III

[**Quartering of troops.**] No soldier shall, in time of peace be quartered in any house, without the consent of the owner, nor in time of war, but in a manner to be prescribed by law.

Article IV

[**Persons and houses to be secure from unreasonable searches and seizures.**] The right of the people to be secure in their persons, houses, papers, and effects, against unreasonable searches and seizures, shall not be violated, but upon probable cause, supported by oath or affirmation, and particularly describing the place to be searched, and the persons or things to be seized.

Article V

[**Trials for crimes; just compensation for private property taken for public use.**] No person shall be held to answer for a capital, or otherwise infamous crime, unless on a presentment or indictment of a Grand Jury, except in cases arising in the land or naval forces, or in the militia, when in actual service in time of war or public danger; nor shall any person be subject for the same offence to be twice put in jeopardy of life or limb; nor shall be compelled in any criminal case to be a witness, against himself, nor be deprived of life, liberty, or property, without due process of law; nor shall private property be taken for public use, without just compensation.

Article VI

[Civil rights in trials for crimes enumerated.] In all criminal prosecutions, the accused shall enjoy the right to a speedy and public trial, by an impartial jury of the State and district wherein the crime shall have been committed, which district shall have been previously ascertained by law, and to be informed of the nature and cause of the accusation; to be confronted with the witnesses against him; to have compulsory process for obtaining witnesses in his favor, and to have the assistance of counsel for his defense.

Article VII

[Civil rights in civil suits.] In suits at common law, where the value in controversy shall exceed twenty dollars, the right of trial by jury shall be preserved, and no fact tried by a jury, shall be otherwise re-examined in any court of the United States, than according to the rules of the common law.

Article VIII

[Excessive bail, fines, and punishments prohibited.] Excessive bail shall not be required, nor excessive fines imposed, nor cruel and unusual punishments inflicted.

Article IX

[Reserved rights of people.] The enumeration in the Constitution, of certain rights, shall not be construed to deny or disparage others retained by the people.

Article X

[Powers not delegated, reserved to states and people respectively.] The powers not delegated to the United States by the Constitution, nor prohibited by it to the States, are reserved to the States, respectively, or to the people.

Article XI

(The proposed amendment was sent to the states Mar. 5, 1794, by the Third Congress. It was ratified Feb. 7, 1795.)

[Judicial power of United States not to extend to suits against a State.] The judicial power of the United States shall not be construed to extend to any suit in law or equity, commenced or prosecuted against one of the United States by citizens of another State, or by citizens or subjects of any foreign state.

Article XII

(The proposed amendment was sent to the states Dec. 12, 1803, by the Eighth Congress. It was ratified July 27, 1804.)

[Present mode of electing President and Vice-President by electors.[1]] The electors shall meet in their respective states, and vote by ballot for President and Vice President, one of whom, at least, shall not be an inhabitant of the same state with themselves; they shall name in their ballots the person voted for as President, and in distinct ballots the person voted for as Vice President, and they shall make distinct lists of all persons voted for as President, and of all persons voted for as Vice President, and of the number of votes for each, which lists they shall sign and certify, and transmit sealed to the seat of the government of the United States, directed to the President of the Senate; the President of the Senate shall, in the presence of the Senate and House of Representatives, open all the certificates and the votes shall then be counted; the person having the greatest number of votes for President, shall be the President, if such number be a majority of the whole number of electors appointed; and if no person have such majority, then from the persons having the highest numbers not exceeding three on the list of those voted for as President, the House of Representatives shall choose immediately, by ballot, the President. But in choosing the President, the votes shall be taken by states, the representation from each State having one vote; a quorum for this purpose shall consist of a member or members from two thirds of the states, and a majority of all the states shall be necessary to a choice. And if the House of Representatives shall not choose a President whenever the right of choice shall devolve upon them, before the fourth day of March next following, then the Vice President shall act as President, as in the case of the death or other constitutional disability of the President. The person having the greatest number of votes as Vice President, shall be the Vice President, if such number be a majority of the whole number of electors appointed, and if no person have a majority, then from the two highest numbers on the list, the Senate shall choose the Vice President; a quorum for the purpose shall consist of two thirds of the whole number of Senators, and a majority of the whole number shall be necessary to a choice. But no person constitutionally ineligible to the office of President shall be eligible to that of Vice President of the United States.

Article XIII

(The proposed amendment was sent to the states Feb. 1, 1865, by the Thirty-eighth Congress. It was ratified Dec. 6, 1865.)

Section 1

[Slavery prohibited.] Neither slavery nor involuntary servitude, except as a punishment for crime whereof the party shall have been duly convicted, shall exist within the United States, or any place subject to their jurisdiction.

Section 2

[Congress given power to enforce this article.] Congress shall have power to enforce this article by appropriate legislation.

Article XIV

(The proposed amendment was sent to the states June 16, 1866, by the Thirty-ninth Congress. It was ratified July 9, 1868.)

Section 1

[Citizenship defined; privileges of citizens.] All persons born or naturalized in the United States, and subject to the jurisdiction thereof, are citizens of the United States and of the State wherein they reside. No State shall make or enforce any law which shall abridge the privileges or immunities of citizens of the United States; nor shall any State deprive any person of life, liberty, or property, without due process of law; nor deny to any person within its jurisdiction the equal protection of the laws.

Section 2

[**Apportionment of Representatives.**] Representatives shall be apportioned among the several States according to their respective numbers, counting the whole number of persons in each State, excluding Indians not taxed. But when the right to vote at any election for the choice of electors for President and Vice President of the United States, Representatives in Congress, the executive and judicial officers of a State, or the members of the Legislature thereof, is denied to any of the male inhabitants of such State, being twenty-one years of age, and citizens of the United States, or in any way abridged, except for participation in rebellion, or other crime, the basis of representation therein shall be reduced in the proportion which the number of such male citizens shall bear to the whole number of male citizens twenty-one years of age in such State.

Section 3

[**Disqualification for office; removal of disability.**] No person shall be a Senator or Representative in Congress, or elector of President and Vice President, or hold any office, civil or military, under the United States, or under any State, who, having previously taken an oath, as a member of Congress, or as an officer of the United States, or as a member of any State Legislature, or as an executive or judicial officer of any State, to support the Constitution of the United States, shall have engaged in insurrection or rebellion against the same, or given aid or comfort to the enemies thereof. But Congress may be a vote of two thirds of each House, remove such disability.

Section 4

[**Public debt not to be questioned; payment of debts and claims incurred in aid of rebellion forbidden.**] The validity of the public debt of the United States, authorized by law, including debts incurred for payment of pensions and bounties for services in suppressing insurrection or rebellion, shall not be questioned. But neither the United States nor any State shall assume or pay any debt or obligation incurred in aid of insurrection or rebellion against the United States, or any claim for the loss or emancipation of any slave; but all such debts, obligations, and claims shall be held illegal and void.

Section 5

[**Congress given power to enforce this article.**] The Congress shall have power to enforce, by appropriate legislation, the provisions of this article.

Article XV

(The proposed amendment was sent to the states Feb. 27, 1869, by the Fortieth Congress. It was ratified Feb. 3, 1870.)

Section 1

[**Right of certain citizens to vote established.**] The right of citizens of the United States to vote shall not be denied or abridged by the United States or by any State on account of race, color, or previous condition of servitude.

Section 2

[**Congress given power to enforce this article.**] The Congress shall have power to enforce this article by appropriate legislation.

Article XVI

(The proposed amendment was sent to the states July 12, 1909, by the Sixty-first Congress. It was ratified Feb. 3, 1913.)

[**Taxes on income; Congress given power to lay and collect.**] The Congress shall have power to lay and collect taxes on incomes, from whatever source derived, without apportionment among the several States, and without regard to any census or enumeration.

Article XVII

(The proposed amendment was sent to the states May 16, 1912, by the Sixty-second Congress. It was ratified April 8, 1913.)

[**Election of United States Senators; filling of vacancies; qualifications of electors.**] The Senate of the United States shall be composed of two Senators from each State, elected by the people thereof, for six years; and each Senator shall have one vote. The electors in each State shall have the qualifications requisite for electors of the most numerous branch of the State Legislatures.

When vacancies happen in the representation of any State in the Senate, the executive authority of such State shall issue writs of election to fill such vacancies: Provided, that the legislature of any State may empower the executive thereof to make temporary appointment until the people fill the vacancies by election as the legislature may direct.

This amendment shall not be so construed as to affect the election or term of any Senator chosen before it becomes valid as part of the Constitution.

Article XVIII[2]

(The proposed amendment was sent to the states Dec. 18, 1917, by the Sixty-fifth Congress. It was ratified by three quarters of the states by Jan. 16, 1919, and became effective Jan. 16, 1920.)

Section 1

[**Manufacture, sale, or transportation of intoxicating liquors, for beverage purposes, prohibited.**] After one year from the ratification of this article the manufacture, sale, or transportation of intoxicating liquors within, the importation thereof into, or the exportation thereof from the United States and all territory subject to the jurisdiction thereof for beverage purposes is hereby prohibited.

Section 2

[**Congress and the several States given concurrent power to pass appropriate legislation to enforce this article.**] The Congress and the several States shall have concurrent power to enforce this article by appropriate legislation.

Section 3

[**Provisions of article to become operative, when adopted by three fourths of the States.**] This article shall be inoperative unless it shall have been ratified as an amendment to the Constitution by the legislatures of the several States, as provided in the Constitution, within seven years from the date of the submission hereof to the States by Congress.

Article XIX

(The proposed amendment was sent to the states June 4, 1919, by the Sixty-sixth Congress. It was ratified Aug. 18, 1920.)

[The right of citizens to vote shall not be denied because of sex.] The right of citizens of the United States to vote shall not be denied or abridged by the United States or by any State on account of sex.

[Congress given power to enforce this article.] Congress shall have power to enforce this article by appropriate legislation.

Article XX

(The proposed amendment, sometimes called the "Lame Duck Amendment," was sent to the states Mar. 3, 1932, by the Seventy-second Congress. It was ratified Jan. 23, 1933; but, in accordance with Section 5, Sections 1 and 2 did not go into effect until Oct. 15, 1933.)

Section 1

[Terms of President, Vice President, Senators, and Representatives.] The terms of the President and Vice President shall end at noon on the twentieth day of January, and the terms of Senators and Representatives at noon on the third day of January, of the years in which such terms would have ended if this article had not been ratified; and the terms of their successors shall then begin.

Section 2

[Time of assembling Congress.] The Congress shall assemble at least once in every year, and such meeting shall begin at noon on the third day of January, unless they shall by law appoint a different day.

Section 3

[Filling vacancy in office of President.] If, at the time fixed for the beginning of the term of the President, the President-elect shall have died, the Vice President-elect shall become President. If a President shall not have been chosen before the time fixed for the beginning of his term, or if the President-elect shall have failed to qualify, then the Vice President shall have qualified; and the Congress may by law provide for the case wherein neither a President-elect nor a Vice President-elect shall have qualified, declaring who shall then act as President, or the manner in which one who is to act shall be selected, and such person shall act accordingly until a President or Vice President shall have qualified.

Section 4

[Power of Congress in Presidential succession.] The Congress may by law provide for the case of the death of any of the persons from whom the House of Representatives may choose a President whenever the right of choice shall have devolved upon them, and for the case of the death of any of the persons from whom the Senate may choose a Vice President whenever the right of choice shall have devolved upon them.

Section 5

[Time of taking effect.] Sections 1 and 2 shall take effect on the 15th day of October following the ratification of this article.

Section 6

[Ratification.] This article shall be inoperative unless it shall have been ratified as an amendment to the Constitution by the legislatures of three fourths of the several States within seven years from the date of its submission.

Article XXI

(The proposed amendment was sent to the states Feb. 20, 1933, by the Seventy-second Congress. It was ratified Dec. 5, 1933.)

Section 1

[Repeal of Prohibition Amendment.] The eighteenth article of amendment to the Constitution of the United States is hereby repealed.

Section 2

[Transportation of intoxicating liquors.] The transportation or importation into any State, territory, or possession of the United States for delivery or use therein of intoxicating liquors, in violation of the laws thereof, is hereby prohibited.

Section 3

[Ratification.] This article shall be inoperative unless it shall have been ratified as an amendment to the Constitution by convention in the several States, as provided in the Constitution, within seven years from the date of the submission thereof to the States by the Congress.

Article XXII

(The proposed amendment was sent to the states Mar. 21, 1947, by the Eightieth Congress. It was ratified Feb. 27, 1951.)

Section 1

[Limit to number of terms a President may serve.] No person shall be elected to the office of the President more than twice, and no person who has held the office of President, or acted as President, for more than two years of a term to which some other person was elected President shall be elected to the office of the President more than once. But this article shall not apply to any person holding the office of President when this article was proposed by the Congress, and shall not prevent any person who may be holding the office of President, or acting as President, during the term within which this article becomes operative from holding the office of President or acting as President during the remainder of such term.

Section 2

[Ratification.] This article shall be inoperative unless it shall have been ratified as an amendment to the Constitution by the legislatures of three fourths of the several States within seven years from the date of its submission to the States by the Congress.

Article XXIII

(The proposed amendment was sent to the states June 16, 1960, by the Eighty-sixth Congress. It was ratified March 29, 1961.)

Section 1

[Electors for the District of Columbia.] The District constituting the seat of Government of the United States shall appoint in such manner as the Congress may direct:

A number of electors of President and Vice President equal to the whole number of Senators and Representatives in Congress to which the District would be entitled if it were a State, but in no event more than the least populous State; they shall be in addition to those appointed by the States, but

they shall be considered, for the purposes of the election of President and Vice President, to be electors appointed by a State; and they shall meet in the District and perform such duties as provided by the twelfth article of amendment.

Section 2

[Congress given power to enforce this article.] The Congress shall have the power to enforce this article by appropriate legislation.

Article XXIV

(The proposed amendment was sent to the states Aug. 27, 1962, by the Eighty-seventh Congress. It was ratified Jan. 23, 1964.)

Section 1

[Payment of poll tax or other taxes not to be prerequisite for voting in federal elections.] The right of citizens of the United States to vote in any primary or other election for President or Vice President, for electors for President or Vice President, or for Senator or Representative in Congress, shall not be denied or abridged by the United States or any State by reasons of failure to pay any poll tax or other tax.

Section 2

[Congress given power to enforce this article.] The Congress shall have the power to enforce this article by appropriate legislation.

Article XXV

(The proposed amendment was sent to the states July 6, 1965, by the Eighty-ninth Congress. It was ratified Feb. 10, 1967.)

Section 1

[Succession of Vice President to Presidency.] In case of the removal of the President from office or of his death or resignation, the Vice President shall become President.

Section 2

[Vacancy in office of Vice President.] Whenever there is a vacancy in the office of the Vice President, the President shall nominate a Vice President who shall take office upon confirmation by a majority vote of both Houses of Congress.

Section 3

[Vice President as Acting President.] Whenever the President transmits to the President pro tempore of the Senate and the Speaker of the House of Representatives his written declaration that he is unable to discharge the powers and duties of his office, and until he transmits to them a written declaration to the contrary, such powers and duties shall be discharged by the Vice President as Acting President.

Section 4

[Vice President as Acting President.] Whenever the Vice President and a majority of either the principal officers of the executive departments or of such other body as Congress may by law provide, transmit to the President pro tempore of the Senate and the Speaker of the House of Representatives their written declaration that the President is unable to discharge the powers and duties of his office, the Vice President shall immediately assume the powers and duties of the office as Acting President.

Thereafter, when the President transmits to the President pro tempore of the Senate and the Speaker of the House of Representatives his written declaration that no inability exists, he shall resume the powers and duties of his office unless the Vice President and a majority of either the principal officers of the executive department or of such other body as Congress may by law provide, transmit within four days to the President pro tempore of the Senate and the Speaker of the House of Representatives their written declaration that the President is unable to discharge the powers and duties of his office. Thereupon Congress shall decide the issue, assembling within forty-eight hours for that purpose if not in session. If the Congress, within twenty-one days after receipt of the latter written declaration, or, if Congress is not in session, within twenty-one days after Congress is required to assemble, determines by two thirds vote of both Houses that the President is unable to discharge the powers and duties of his office, the Vice President shall continue to discharge the same as Acting President; otherwise, the President shall resume the powers and duties of his office.

Article XXVI

(The proposed amendment was sent to the states Mar. 23, 1971, by the Ninety-second Congress. It was ratified July 1, 1971.)

Section 1

[Voting for 18-year-olds.] The right of citizens of the United States, who are 18 years of age or older, to vote shall not be denied or abridged by the United States or by any state on account of age.

Section 2

[Congress given power to enforce this article.] The Congress shall have power to enforce this article by appropriate legislation.

1. Amended by the 20th Amendment, Sections 3 and 4. 2. Repealed by the 21st Amendment.

The White House

Source: Department of the Interior, U.S. National Park Service.

The White House, the official residence of the President, is at 1600 Pennsylvania Avenue in Washington, D.C. The site, covering about 18 acres, was selected by President Washington and Pierre Charles L'Enfant, and the architect was James Hoban. The design appears to have been influenced by Leinster House, Dublin, and James Gibb's *Book of Architecture.* The cornerstone was laid Oct. 13, 1792, and the first residents were President and Mrs. John Adams in November 1800. The building was fired by the British in 1814.

From December 1948 to March 1952, the interior of the White House was rebuilt, and the outer walls were strengthened.

The rooms for public functions are on the first floor; the second and third floors are used as the residence of the President and First Family. The most celebrated public room is the East Room, where formal receptions take place. Other public rooms are the Red Room, the Green Room, and the Blue Room. The State Dining Room is used for formal dinners. There are 132 rooms.

The Mayflower Compact

On Sept. 6, 1620, the *Mayflower*, a sailing vessel of about 180 tons, started her memorable voyage from Plymouth, England, with about 100[1] pilgrims aboard, bound for Virginia to establish a private permanent colony in North America. Arriving at what is now Provincetown, Mass., on Nov. 11 (Nov. 21, new style calendar), 41 of the passengers signed the famous "Mayflower Compact" as the boat lay at anchor in that Cape Cod harbor. A small detail of the pilgrims, led by William Bradford, assigned to select a place for permanent settlement landed at what is now Plymouth, Mass., on Dec. 21 (n.s.).

The text of the compact follows:

In the name of God, Amen. We, whose names are underwritten, the Loyal Subjects of our dread Sovereign Lord, King *James*, by the Grace of God, of *Great Britain, France and Ireland*, King, *Defender of the Faith, &*

Having undertaken for the Glory of God, and Advancement of the Christian Faith, and the Honour of our King and Country, a voyage to plant the first colony in the northern Parts of Virginia; do by these Presents, solemnly and mutually in the Presence of God and one of another, covenant and combine ourselves together into a civil Body Politick, for our better Ordering and Preservation, and Furtherance of the Ends aforesaid; And by Virtue hereof to enact, constitute, and frame, such just and equal Laws, Ordinances, Acts, Constitutions and Offices, from time to time, as shall be thought most meet and convenient for the General good of the Colony; unto which we promise all due Submission and Obedience.

In Witness whereof we have hereunto subscribed our names at *Cape Cod* the eleventh of *November*, in the Reign of our Sovereign Lord, King *James* of *England, France* and *Ireland*, the eighteenth, and of *Scotland* the fifty-fourth. *Anno Domini*, 1620

John Carver	William Mullins	John Billington	Peter Brown
Digery Priest	Thomas English	Thomas Tinker	John Turner
William Brewster	John Howland	Samuel Fuller	Edward Tilly
Edmund Margesson	Stephen Hopkins	Richard Clark	John Craxton
John Alden	Edward Winslow	John Allerton	Thomas Rogers
George Soule	Gilbert Winslow	Richard Warren	John Goodman
James Chilton	Miles Standish	Edward Liester	Edward Fuller
Francis Cooke	Richard Bitteridge	William Bradford	Richard Gardiner
Moses Fletcher	Francis Eaton	Thomas Williams	William White
John Ridgate	John Tilly	Isaac Allerton	Edward Doten
Christopher Martin			

1. Historians differ as to whether 100, 101, or 102 passengers were aboard.

The Monroe Doctrine

The Monroe Doctrine was announced in President James Monroe's message to Congress, during his second term on Dec. 2, 1823, in part as follows:

"In the discussions to which this interest has given rise, and in the arrangements by which they may terminate, the occasion has been deemed proper for asserting as a principle in which rights and interests of the United States are involved, that the American continents, by the free and independent condition which they have assumed and maintain, are henceforth not to be considered as subjects for future colonization by any European power. . . . We owe it, therefore, to candor and to the amicable relations existing between the United States and those powers to declare that we should consider any attempt on their part to extend their system to any portion of this hemisphere as dangerous to our peace and safety. With the existing colonies or dependencies of any European power we have not interfered and shall not interfere. But with the governments who have declared their independence and maintain it, and whose independence we have, on great consideration and on just principles, acknowledged, we could not view any interposition for the purpose of oppressing them or controlling in any other manner their destiny by any European power in any other light than as the manifestation of an unfriendly disposition toward the United States."

Order of Presidential Succession

1. The Vice President
2. Speaker of the House
3. President pro tempore of the Senate
4. Secretary of State
5. Secretary of the Treasury
6. Secretary of Defense
7. Attorney General
8. Secretary of the Interior
9. Secretary of Agriculture
10. Secretary of Commerce
11. Secretary of Labor
12. Secretary of Health and Human Services
13. Secretary of Housing and Urban Development
14. Secretary of Transportation
15. Secretary of Energy
16. Secretary of Education

NOTE: An official cannot succeed to the Presidency unless that person meets the Constitutional requirements.

The Star-Spangled Banner

Francis Scott Key, 1814

O say, can you see, by the dawn's early light,
What so proudly we hail'd at the twilight's last gleaming?
Whose broad stripes and bright stars, thro' the perilous fight,
O'er the ramparts we watch'd, were so gallantly streaming?
And the rockets' red glare, the bombs bursting in air,
Gave proof thro' the night that our flag was still there.
O say, does that star-spangled banner yet wave
O'er the land of the free and the home of the brave?

On the shore dimly seen thro' the mists of the deep,
Where the foe's haughty host in dread silence reposes,
What is that which the breeze, o'er the towering steep,
As it fitfully blows, half conceals, half discloses?
Now it catches the gleam of the morning's first beam,
In full glory reflected, now shines on the stream:
'T is the star-spangled banner: O, long may it wave
O'er the land of the free and the home of the brave!

And where is that band who so vauntingly swore
That the havoc of war and the battle's confusion,
A home and a country should leave us no more?
Their blood has wash'd out their foul footsteps' pollution.
No refuge could save the hireling and slave
From the terror of flight or the gloom of the grave:
And the star-spangled banner in triumph doth wave
O'er the land of the free and the home of the brave.

O thus be it ever when free-men shall stand
Between their lov'd home and the war's desolation;
Blest with vict'ry and peace, may the heav'n-rescued land
Praise the Pow'r that hath made and preserv'd us a nation!
Then conquer we must, when our cause it is just,
And this be our motto: "In God is our trust!"
And the star-spangled banner in triumph shall wave
O'er the land of the free and the home of the brave!

On Sept. 13, 1814, Francis Scott Key visited the British fleet in Chesapeake Bay to secure the release of Dr. William Beanes, who had been captured after the burning of Washington, D.C. The release was secured, but Key was detained on ship overnight during the shelling of Fort McHenry, one of the forts defending Baltimore. In the morning, he was so delighted to see the American flag still flying over the fort that he began a poem to commemorate the occasion. First published under the title "Defense of Fort M'Henry," and later as "The Star-Spangled Banner," the poem soon attained wide popularity as sung to the tune "To Anacreon in Heaven." The origin of this tune is obscure, but it may have been written by John Stafford Smith, a British composer born in 1750. "The Star-Spangled Banner" was officially made the National Anthem by Congress in 1931, although it had been already adopted as such by the Army and the Navy.

The Emancipation Proclamation

January 1, 1863

By the President of the United States of America:

A Proclamation.
Whereas on the 22d day of September, A.D. 1862, a proclamation was issued by the President of the United States, containing, among other things, the following, to wit:
"That on the 1st day of January, A.D. 1863, all persons held as slaves within any State or designated part of a State the people whereof shall then be in rebellion against the United States shall be then, thenceforward, and forever free; and the executive government of the United States, including the military and naval authority thereof, will recognize and maintain the freedom of such persons, or will do not act or acts to repress such persons, or any of them, in any efforts they may make for their actual freedom.

"That the executive will on the 1st day of January aforesaid, by proclamation, designate the States and parts of States, if any, in which the people thereof, respectively, shall then be in rebellion against the United States; and the fact that any State or the people thereof shall on that day be in good faith represented in the Congress of the United States by members chosen thereto at elections wherein a majority of the qualified voters of such States shall have participated shall, in the absence of strong countervailing testimony, be deemed conclusive evidence that such State and the people thereof are not then in rebellion against the United States."
Now, therefore, I, Abraham Lincoln, President

of the United States, by virtue of the power in me vested as Commander-in-Chief of the Army and Navy of the United States in time of actual armed rebellion against the authority and government of the United States, and as a fit and necessary war measure for suppressing said rebellion, do, on this 1st day of January, A.D. 1863, and in accordance with my purpose so to do, publicly proclaimed for the full period of one hundred days from the first day above mentioned, order and designate as the States and parts of States wherein the people thereof, respectively, are this day in rebellion against the United States the following, to wit:

Arkansas, Texas, Louisiana (except the parishes of St. Bernard, Plaquemines, Jefferson, St. John, St. Charles, St. James, Ascension, Assumption, Terrebonne, Lafourche, St. Mary, St. Martin, and Orleans, including the city of New Orleans), Mississippi, Alabama, Florida, Georgia, South Carolina, North Carolina, and Virginia (except the forty-eight counties designated as West Virginia, and also the counties of Berkeley, Accomac, Northhampton, Elizabeth City, York, Princess Anne, and Norfolk, including the cities of Norfolk and Portsmouth), and which excepted parts are for the present left

precisely as if this proclamation were not issued.

And by virtue of the power and for the purpose aforesaid, I do order and declare that all persons held as slaves within said designated States and parts of States are, and henceforward shall be, free; and that the Executive Government of the United States, including the military and naval authorities thereof, will recognize and maintain the freedom of said persons.

And I hereby enjoin upon the people so declared to be free to abstain from all violence, unless in necessary self-defense; and I recommend to them that, in all cases when allowed, they labor faithfully for reasonable wages.

And I further declare and make known that such persons of suitable condition will be received into the armed service of the United States to garrison forts, positions, stations, and other places, and to man vessels of all sorts in said service.

And upon this act, sincerely believed to be an act of justice, warranted by the Constitution upon military necessity, I invoke the considerate judgment of mankind and the gracious favor of Almighty God.

The Confederate States of America

State	Seceded from Union	Readmitted to Union[1]	State	Seceded from Union	Readmitted to Union[1]
1. South Carolina	Dec. 20, 1860	July 9, 1868	7. Texas	March 2, 1861	March 30, 1870
2. Mississippi	Jan. 9, 1861	Feb. 23, 1870	8. Virginia	April 17, 1861	Jan. 26, 1870
3. Florida	Jan. 10, 1861	June 25, 1868	9. Arkansas	May 6, 1861	June 22, 1868
4. Alabama	Jan. 11, 1861	July 13, 1868	10. North Carolina	May 20, 1861	July 4, 1868
5. Georgia	Jan. 19, 1861	July 15, 1870[2]	11. Tennessee	June 8, 1861	July 24, 1866
6. Louisiana	Jan. 26, 1861	July 9, 1868			

1. Date of readmission to representation in U.S. House of Representatives. 2. Second readmission date. First date was July 21, 1868, but the representatives were unseated March 5, 1869. NOTE: Four other slave states—Delaware, Kentucky, Maryland, and Missouri—remained in the Union.

Lincoln's Gettysburg Address

The Battle of Gettysburg, one of the most noted battles of the Civil War, was fought on July 1, 2, and 3, 1863. On Nov. 19, 1863, the field was dedicated as a national cemetery by President Lincoln in a two-minute speech that was to become immortal. At the time of its delivery the speech was relegated to the inside pages of the papers, while a two-hour address by Edward Everett, the leading orator of the time, caught the headlines.

The following is the text of the address revised by President Lincoln from his own notes:

Fourscore and seven years ago our fathers brought forth on this continent a new nation conceived in liberty and dedicated to the proposition that all men are created equal. Now we are engaged in a great civil war testing whether that nation, or any nation so conceived and so dedicated, can long endure. We are met on a great battlefield of that war. We have come to dedicate a portion of that field as a final resting-place for those who here gave their lives that that nation might live. It is altogether fitting and proper that we should do this. But, in a larger sense, we cannot dedicate, we cannot consecrate, we cannot hallow this ground. The brave men, living and dead, who struggled here have consecrated it far above our poor power to add or detract. The world will little note nor long remember what we say here, but it can never forget what they did here. It is for us the living rather to be dedicated here to the unfinished work which they who fought here have thus far so nobly advanced. It is rather for us to be here dedicated to the great task remaining before us—that from these honored dead we take increased devotion to that cause for which they gave the last full measure of devotion—that we here highly resolve that these dead shall not have died in vain, that this nation under God shall have a new birth of freedom, and that government of the people, by the people, for the people shall not perish from the earth.

The Early Congresses

At the urging of Massachusetts and Virginia, the First Continental Congress met in Philadelphia on Sept. 5, 1774, and was attended by representatives of all the colonies except Georgia. Patrick Henry of Virginia declared: "The distinctions between Pennsylvanians, New Yorkers and New Englanders are no more. I am not a Virginian but an American." This Congress, which adjourned Oct. 26, 1774, passed intercolonial resolutions calling for extensive boycott by the colonies against British trade.

The following year, most of the delegates from the colonies were chosen by popular election to attend the Second Continental Congress, which assembled in Philadelphia on May 10. As war had already begun between the colonies and England, the chief problems before the Congress were the procuring of military supplies, the establishment of an army and proper defenses, the issuing of continental bills of credit, etc. On June 15, 1775, George Washington was elected to command the Conti-

nental army. Congress adjourned Dec. 12, 1776.

Other Continental Congresses were held in Baltimore (1776–77), Philadelphia (1777), Lancaster, Pa. (1777), York, Pa. (1777–78), and Philadelphia (1778–81).

In 1781, the Articles of Confederation, although establishing a league of the thirteen states rather than a strong central government, provided for the continuance of Congress. Known thereafter as the Congress of the Confederation, it held sessions in Philadelphia (1781–83), Princeton, N.J. (1783), Annapolis, Md. (1783–84), and Trenton, N.J. (1784). Five sessions were held in New York City between the years 1785 and 1789.

The Congress of the United States, established by the ratification of the Constitution, held its first meeting on March 4, 1789, in New York City. Several sessions of Congress were held in Philadelphia, and the first meeting in Washington, D.C., was on Nov. 17, 1800.

Presidents of the Continental Congresses

Name	Elected	Birth and Death Dates	Name	Elected	Birth and Death Dates
Peyton Randolph, Va.	9/5/1774	c.1721-1775	John Hanson, Md.	11/5/1781	1715-1783
Henry Middleton, S.C.	10/22/1774	1717-1784	Elias Boudinot, N.J.	11/4/1782	1740-1821
Peyton Randolph, Va.	5/10/1775	c.1721-1775	Thomas Mifflin, Pa.	11/3/1783	1744-1800
John Hancock, Mass.	5/24/1775	1737-1793	Richard Henry Lee, Va.	11/30/1784	1732-1794
Henry Laurens, S.C.	11/1/1777	1724-1792	John Hancock, Mass.[1]	11/23/1785	1737-1793
John Jay, N.Y.	12/10/1778	1745-1829	Nathaniel Gorham, Mass.	6/6/1786	1738-1796
Samuel Huntington, Conn.	9/28/1779	1731-1796	Arthur St. Clair, Pa.	2/2/1787	1734-1818
Thomas McKean, Del.	7/10/1781	1734-1817	Cyrus Griffin, Va.	1/22/1788	1748-1810

1. Resigned May 29, 1786, never having served, because of continued illness.

The Great Seal of the U.S.

On July 4, 1776, the Continental Congress appointed a committee consisting of Benjamin Franklin, John Adams, and Thomas Jefferson "to bring in a device for a seal of the United States of America." After many delays, a verbal description of a design by William Barton was finally approved by Congress on June 20, 1782. The seal shows an American bald eagle with a ribbon in its mouth bearing the device *E pluribus unum* (One out of many). In its talons are the arrows of war and an olive branch of peace. On the reverse side it shows an unfinished pyramid with an eye (the eye of Providence) above it. Although this description was adopted in 1782, the first drawing was not made until four years later, and no die has ever been cut.

The American's Creed

William Tyler Page

"I believe in the United States of America as a government of the people, by the people, for the people; whose just powers are derived from the consent of the governed; a democracy in a republic; a sovereign Nation of many sovereign States; a perfect union, one and inseparable; established upon those principles of freedom, equality, justice, and humanity for which American patriots sacrificed their lives and fortunes.

"I therefore believe it is my duty to my country to love it, to support its Constitution, to obey its laws, to respect its flag, and to defend it against all enemies."

NOTE: William Tyler Page, Clerk of the U.S. House of Representatives, wrote "The American's Creed" in 1917. It was accepted by the House on behalf of the American people on April 3, 1918.

U.S. Capitol

When the French architect and engineer Maj. Pierre L'Enfant first began to lay out the plans for a new Federal city (now Washington, D.C.), he noted that Jenkins' Hill, overlooking the area, seemed to be "a pedestal waiting for a monument." It was here that the U.S. Capitol would be built. The basic structure as we know it today evolved over a period of more than 150 years. In 1792 a competition was held for the design of a capitol building. Dr. William Thornton, a physician and amateur architect, submitted the winning plan, a simple, low-lying structure of classical proportions with a shallow dome. Later, internal modifications were made by Benjamin Henry Latrobe. After the building was burned by the British in 1814, Latrobe and architect Charles Bulfinch were responsible for its reconstruction. Finally, under Thomas Walter, who was Architect of the Capitol from 1851 to 1865, the House and Senate wings and the imposing cast iron dome topped with the Statue of Freedom were added, and the Capitol assumed the form we see today. It was in the old Senate chamber that Daniel Webster cried out, "Liberty and Union, now and forever, one and inseparable!" In Statuary Hall, which used to be the old House chamber, a small disk on the floor marks the spot where John Quincy Adams was fatally stricken after more than 50 years of service to his country. A whisper from one side of this room can be heard across the vast space of the hall. Visitors can see the original Supreme Court chamber a floor below the Rotunda.

In addition to its historical association, the Capitol Building is also a vast artistic treasure house. The works of such famous artists as Gilbert Stuart, Rembrandt Peale, and John Trumbull are displayed on the walls. The Great Rotunda, with its 180-foot- (54.9-m-) high dome, is decorated with a massive fresco by Constantino Brumidi, which extends some 300 feet (90 m) in circumference. Throughout the building are many paintings of events in U.S. history and sculptures of outstanding Americans. The Capitol itself is situated on a 68-acre (27.5-ha) park designed by the 19th-century landscape architect Frederick Law Olmsted. There are free guided tours of the Capitol, which include admission to the House and Senate galleries. Those who wish to visit the visitors' gallery in either wing without taking the tour may obtain passes from their Senators or Congressmen. Visitors may ride on the monorail subway that joins the House and Senate wings of the Capitol with the Congressional office buildings.

Washington Monument

Construction of this magnificent Washington, D.C., monument, which draws some two million visitors a year, took nearly a century of planning, building, and controversy. Provision for a large equestrian statue of George Washington was made in the original city plan, but the project was soon dropped. After Washington's death it was taken up again, and a number of false starts and changes of design were made. Finally, in 1848, work was begun on the monument that stands today. The design, by architect Robert Mills, then featured an ornate base. In 1854, however, political squabbling and a lack of money brought construction to a halt. Work was resumed in 1880, and the monument was completed in 1884 and opened to the public in 1888. The tapered shaft, faced with white marble and rising from walls 15 feet thick (4.6 m) at the base was modeled after the obelisks of ancient Egypt. The monument, one of the tallest masonry constructions in the world, stands just over 555 feet (169 m). Memorial stones from the 50 States, foreign countries, and organizations line the interior walls. The top, reached only by elevator, commands a panoramic view of the city.

The Liberty Bell

The Liberty Bell was cast in England in 1752 for the Pennsylvania Statehouse (now named Independence Hall) in Philadelphia. It was recast in Philadelphia in 1753. It is inscribed with the words, "Proclaim liberty throughout all the land unto all the inhabitants thereof" (Lev. 25:10). The bell was rung on July 8, 1776, for the first public reading of the Declaration of Independence. Hidden in Allentown during the British occupation of Philadelphia, it was replaced in Independence Hall in 1778. The bell cracked on July 8, 1835, while tolling the death of Chief Justice John Marshall. In 1976 the Liberty Bell was moved to a special exhibition building near Independence Hall.

Arlington National Cemetery

Arlington National Cemetery occupies 612 acres in Virginia on the Potomac River, directly opposite Washington. This land was part of the estate of John Parke Custis, Martha Washington's son. His son, George Washington Parke Custis, built the mansion which later became the home of Robert E. Lee. In 1864, Arlington became a military cemetery. More than 200,000 servicemembers and their dependents are buried there. Expansion of the cemetery began in 1966, using a 180-acre tract of land directly east of the present site.

In 1921, an Unknown American Soldier of World War I was buried in the cemetery; the monument at the Tomb was opened to the public without ceremony in 1932. Two additional Unknowns, one from World War II and one from the Korean War, were buried May 30, 1958. The Unknown Serviceman of Vietnam was buried on May 28, 1984. The inscription carved on the Tomb of the Unknowns reads:

HERE RESTS IN
HONORED GLORY
AN AMERICAN
SOLDIER
KNOWN BUT TO GOD

History of the Flag

Source: Encyclopaedia Britannica.

The first official American flag, the Continental or Grand Union flag, was displayed on Prospect Hill, Jan. 1, 1776, in the American lines besieging Boston. It had 13 alternate red and white stripes, with the British Union Jack in the upper left corner.

On June 14, 1777, the Continental Congress adopted the design for a new flag, which actually was the Continental flag with the red cross of St. George and the white cross of St. Andrew replaced on the blue field by 13 stars, one for each state. No rule was made as to the arrangement of the stars, and while they were usually shown in a circle, there were various other designs. It is uncertain when the new flag was first flown, but its first official announcement is believed to have been on Sept. 3, 1777.

The first public assertion that Betsy Ross made the first Stars and Stripes appeared in a paper read before the Historical Society of Pennsylvania on March 14, 1870, by William J. Canby, a grandson. However, Mr. Canby on later investigation found no official documents of any action by Congress on the flag before June 14, 1777. Betsy Ross's own story, according to her daughter, was that Washington, Robert Morris, and George Ross, as representatives of Congress, visited her in Philadelphia in June 1776, showing her a rough draft of the flag and asking her if she could make one. However, the only actual record of the manufacture of flags by Betsy Ross is a voucher in Harrisburg, Pa., for 14 pounds and some shillings for flags for the Pennsylvania navy.

On Jan. 13, 1794, Congress voted to add two stars and two stripes to the flag in recognition of the admission of Vermont and Kentucky to the Union. By 1818, there were 20 states in the Union, and as it was obvious that the flag would soon become unwieldy, Congress voted April 18 to return to the original 13 stripes and to indicate the admission of a new state simply by the addition of a star the following July 4. The 49th star, for Alaska, was added July 4, 1959; and the 50th star, for Hawaii, was added July 4, 1960.

The first Confederate flag, adopted in 1861 by the Confederate convention in Montgomery, Ala., was called the Stars and Bars; but because of its similarity in colors to the American flag, there was much confusion in the Battle of Bull Run. To remedy this situation, Gen. G. T. Beauregard suggested a battle flag, which was used by the Southern armies throughout the war. The flag consisted of a red field on which was placed a blue cross of St. Andrew separated from the field by a white fillet and adorned with 13[1] white stars for the Confederate states. In May 1863, at Richmond, an official flag was adopted by the Confederate Congress. This flag was white and twice as long as wide; the union, two-thirds the width of the flag, contained the battle flag designed for Gen. Beauregard. A broad transverse stripe of red was added Feb. 4, 1865, so that the flag might not be mistaken for a signal of truce.

1. 11 states formally seceded, and unofficial groups in Kentucky and Missouri adopted ordinances of secession. On this basis, these two states were admitted to the Confederacy, although the official state governments remained in the Union.

The Pledge of Allegiance[1] to the Flag

"I pledge allegiance to the Flag of the United States of America, and to the Republic for which it stands, one Nation under God,[2] indivisible, with liberty and justice for all."

1. The original pledge was published in the Sept. 8, 1892, issue of *The Youth's Companion* in Boston. For years, the authorship was in dispute between James B. Upham and Francis Bellamy of the magazine's staff. In 1939, after a study of the controversy, the United States Flag Association decided that authorship be credited to Bellamy. 2. The phrase "under God" was added to the pledge on June 14, 1954.

The Statue of Liberty

The Statue of Liberty ("Liberty Enlightening the World") is a 225-ton, steel-reinforced copper female figure, 152 ft in height, facing the ocean from Liberty[1] Island in New York Harbor. The right hand holds aloft a torch, and the left hand carries a tablet upon which is inscribed: "July IV MDCCLXXVI."

The statue was designed by Frédéric Auguste Bartholdi of Alsace as a gift to the United States from the people of France to memorialize the alliance of the two countries in the American Revolution and their abiding friendship. The French people contributed the $250,000 cost.

The 150-foot pedestal was designed by Richard M. Hunt and built by Gen. Charles P. Stone, both Americans. It contains steel underpinnings designed by Alexander Eiffel of France to support the statue. The $270,000 cost was borne by popular subscription in this country. President Grover Cleveland accepted the statue for the United States on Oct. 28, 1886.

On Sept. 26, 1972, President Richard M. Nixon dedicated the American Museum of Immigration, housed in structural additions to the base of the statue. In 1984 scaffolding went up for a major restoration and the torch was extinguished on July 4. It was relit with much ceremony July 4, 1986 to mark its centennial.

On a tablet inside the pedestal is engraved the following sonnet, written by Emma Lazarus (1849–1887):

The New Colossus

Not like the brazen giant of Greek fame.
With conquering limbs astride from land to land;
Here at our sea-washed, sunset gates shall stand
A mighty woman with a torch, whose flame
Is the imprisoned lightning, and her name
Mother of Exiles. From her beacon-hand
Glows world-wide welcome; her mild eyes command
The air-bridged harbor that twin cities frame.
"Keep, ancient lands, your storied pomp!" cries she
With silent lips. "Give me your tired, your poor,
Your huddled masses yearning to breathe free,
The wretched refuse of your teeming shore.
Send these, the homeless, tempest-tost to me,
I lift my lamp beside the golden door!"

1. Called Bedloe's Island prior to 1956.

Presidents

Name and (party)[1]	Term	State of birth	Born	Died	Religion	Age at inaug.	Age at death
1. Washington (F)[2]	1789–1797	Va.	2/22/1732	12/14/1799	Episcopalian	57	67
2. J. Adams (F)	1797–1801	Mass.	10/30/1735	7/4/1826	Unitarian	61	90
3. Jefferson (DR)	1801–1809	Va.	4/13/1743	7/4/1826	Deist	57	83
4. Madison (DR)	1809–1817	Va.	3/16/1751	6/28/1836	Episcopalian	57	85
5. Monroe (DR)	1817–1825	Va.	4/28/1758	7/4/1831	Episcopalian	58	73
6. J. Q. Adams (DR)	1825–1829	Mass.	7/11/1767	2/23/1848	Unitarian	57	80
7. Jackson (D)	1829–1837	S.C.	3/15/1767	6/8/1845	Presbyterian	61	78
8. Van Buren (D)	1837–1841	N.Y.	12/5/1782	7/24/1862	Reformed Dutch	54	79
9. W. H. Harrison (W)[3]	1841	Va.	2/9/1773	4/4/1841	Episcopalian	68	68
10. Tyler (W)	1841–1845	Va.	3/29/1790	1/18/1862	Episcopalian	51	71
11. Polk (D)	1845–1849	N.C.	11/2/1795	6/15/1849	Methodist	49	53
12. Taylor (W)[3]	1849–1850	Va.	11/24/1784	7/9/1850	Episcopalian	64	65
13. Fillmore (W)	1850–1853	N.Y.	1/7/1800	3/8/1874	Unitarian	50	74
14. Pierce (D)	1853–1857	N.H.	11/23/1804	10/8/1869	Episcopalian	48	64
15. Buchanan (D)	1857–1861	Pa.	4/23/1791	6/1/1868	Presbyterian	65	77
16. Lincoln (R)[4]	1861–1865	Ky.	2/12/1809	4/15/1865	Liberal	52	56
17. A. Johnson (U)[5]	1865–1869	N.C.	12/29/1808	7/31/1875	([6])	56	66
18. Grant (R)	1869–1877	Ohio	4/27/1822	7/23/1885	Methodist	46	63
19. Hayes (R)	1877–1881	Ohio	10/4/1822	1/17/1893	Methodist	54	70
20. Garfield (R)[4]	1881	Ohio	11/19/1831	9/19/1881	Disciples of Christ	49	49
21. Arthur (R)	1881–1885	Vt.	10/5/1830	11/18/1886	Episcopalian	50	56
22. Cleveland (D)	1885–1889	N.J.	3/18/1837	6/24/1908	Presbyterian	47	71
23. B. Harrison (R)	1889–1893	Ohio	8/20/1833	3/13/1901	Presbyterian	55	67
24. Cleveland (D)[7]	1893–1897	—	—	—	—	55	—
25. McKinley (R)[4]	1897–1901	Ohio	1/29/1843	9/14/1901	Methodist	54	58
26. T. Roosevelt (R)	1901–1909	N.Y.	10/27/1858	1/6/1919	Reformed Dutch	42	60
27. Taft (R)	1909–1913	Ohio	9/15/1857	3/8/1930	Unitarian	51	72
28. Wilson (D)	1913–1921	Va.	12/28/1856	2/3/1924	Presbyterian	56	67
29. Harding (R)[3]	1921–1923	Ohio	11/2/1865	8/2/1923	Baptist	55	57
30. Coolidge (R)	1923–1929	Vt.	7/4/1872	1/5/1933	Congregationalist	51	60
31. Hoover (R)	1929–1933	Iowa	8/10/1874	10/20/1964	Quaker	54	90
32. F. D. Roosevelt (D)[3]	1933–1945	N.Y.	1/30/1882	4/12/1945	Episcopalian	51	63
33. Truman (D)	1945–1953	Mo.	5/8/1884	12/26/1972	Baptist	60	88
34. Eisenhower (R)	1953–1961	Tex.	10/14/1890	3/28/1969	Presbyterian	62	78
35. Kennedy (D)[4]	1961–1963	Mass.	5/29/1917	11/22/1963	Roman Catholic	43	46
36. L. B. Johnson (D)	1963–1969	Tex.	8/27/1908	1/22/1973	Disciples of Christ	55	64
37. Nixon (R)[8]	1969–1974	Calif.	1/9/1913	—	Quaker	56	—
38. Ford (R)	1974–1977	Neb.	7/14/1913	—	Episcopalian	61	—
39. Carter (D)	1977–1981	Ga.	10/1/1924	—	Southern Baptist	52	—
40. Reagan (R)	1981–1989	Ill.	2/6/1911	—	Disciples of Christ	69	—
41. Bush (R)	1989–	Mass.	6/12/24	—	Episcopalian	64	—

1. F—Federalist; DR—Democratic-Republican; D—Democratic; W—Whig; R—Republican; U—Union. 2. No party for first election. The party system in the U.S. made its appearance during Washington's first term. 3. Died in office. 4. Assassinated in office. 5. The Republican National Convention of 1864 adopted the name Union Party. It renominated Lincoln for President; for Vice President it nominated Johnson, a War Democrat. Although frequently listed as a Republican Vice President and President, Johnson undoubtedly considered himself strictly a member of the Union Party. When that party broke apart after 1868, he returned to the Democratic Party. 6. Johnson was not a professed church member; however, he admired the Baptist principles of church government. 7. Second nonconsecutive term. 8. Resigned Aug. 9, 1974.

Vice Presidents

Name and (party)[1]	Term	State of birth	Birth and death dates	President served under
1. John Adams (F)[2]	1789–1797	Massachusetts	1735–1826	Washington
2. Thomas Jefferson (DR)	1797–1801	Virginia	1743–1826	J. Adams
3. Aaron Burr (DR)	1801–1805	New Jersey	1756–1836	Jefferson
4. George Clinton (DR)[3]	1805–1812	New York	1739–1812	Jefferson and Madison
5. Elbridge Gerry (DR)[3]	1813–1814	Massachusetts	1744–1814	Madison
6. Daniel D. Tompkins (DR)	1817–1825	New York	1774–1825	Monroe
7. John C. Calhoun[4]	1825–1832	South Carolina	1782–1850	J. Q. Adams and Jackson
8. Martin Van Buren (D)	1833–1837	New York	1782–1862	Jackson
9. Richard M. Johnson (D)	1837–1841	Kentucky	1780–1850	Van Buren
10. John Tyler (W)[5]	1841	Virginia	1790–1862	W. H. Harrison
11. George M. Dallas (D)	1845–1849	Pennsylvania	1792–1864	Polk
12. Millard Fillmore (W)[5]	1849–1850	New York	1800–1874	Taylor
13. William R. King (D)[3]	1853	North Carolina	1786–1853	Pierce
14. John C. Breckinridge (D)	1857–1861	Kentucky	1821–1875	Buchanan

Name and (party)[1]	Term	State of birth	Birth and death dates	President served under
15. Hannibal Hamlin (R)	1861–1865	Maine	1809–1891	Lincoln
16. Andrew Johnson (U)[5]	1865	North Carolina	1808–1875	Lincoln
17. Schuyler Colfax (R)	1869–1873	New York	1823–1885	Grant
18. Henry Wilson (R)[3]	1873–1875	New Hampshire	1812–1875	Grant
19. William A. Wheeler (R)	1877–1881	New York	1819–1887	Hayes
20. Chester A. Arthur (R)[5]	1881	Vermont	1830–1886	Garfield
21. Thomas A. Hendricks (D)[3]	1885	Ohio	1819–1885	Cleveland
22. Levi P. Morton (R)	1889–1893	Vermont	1824–1920	B. Harrison
23. Adlai E. Stevenson (D)	1893–1897	Kentucky	1835–1914	Cleveland
24. Garret A. Hobart (R)[3]	1897–1899	New Jersey	1844–1899	McKinley
25. Theodore Roosevelt (R)[5]	1901	New York	1858–1919	McKinley
26. Charles W. Fairbanks (R)	1905–1909	Ohio	1852–1918	T. Roosevelt
27. James S. Sherman (R)[3]	1909–1912	New York	1855–1912	Taft
28. Thomas R. Marshall (D)	1913–1921	Indiana	1854–1925	Wilson
29. Calvin Coolidge (R)[5]	1921–1923	Vermont	1872–1933	Harding
30. Charles G. Dawes (R)	1925–1929	Ohio	1865–1951	Coolidge
31. Charles Curtis (R)	1929–1933	Kansas	1860–1936	Hoover
32. John N. Garner (D)	1933–1941	Texas	1868–1967	F. D. Roosevelt
33. Henry A. Wallace (D)	1941–1945	Iowa	1888–1965	F. D. Roosevelt
34. Harry S. Truman (D)[5]	1945	Missouri	1884–1972	F. D. Roosevelt
35. Alben W. Barkley (D)	1949–1953	Kentucky	1877–1956	Truman
36. Richard M. Nixon (R)	1953–1961	California	1913–	Eisenhower
37. Lyndon B. Johnson (D)[5]	1961–1963	Texas	1908–1973	Kennedy
38. Hubert H. Humphrey (D)	1965–1969	South Dakota	1911–1978	Johnson
39. Spiro T. Agnew (R)[6]	1969–1973	Maryland	1918–	Nixon
40. Gerald R. Ford (R)[7]	1973–1974	Nebraska	1913–	Nixon
41. Nelson A. Rockefeller (R)[8]	1974–1977	Maine	1908–1979	Ford
42. Walter F. Mondale (D)	1977–1981	Minnesota	1928–	Carter
43. George Bush (R)	1981–1989	Massachusetts	1924–	Reagan
44. J. Danforth Quayle (R)	1989–	Indiana	1947–	Bush

1. F—Federalist; DR—Democratic-Republican; D—Democratic; W—Whig; R—Republican; U—Union. 2. No party for first election. The party system in the U.S. made its appearance during Washington's first term as President. 3. Died in office. 4. Democratic-Republican with J. Q. Adams; Democratic with Jackson. Calhoun resigned in 1832 to become a U.S. Senator. 5. Succeeded to presidency on death of President. 6. Resigned Oct. 10, 1973, after pleading no contest to Federal income tax evasion charges. 7. Nominated by Nixon on Oct. 12, 1973, under provisions of 25th Amendment. Confirmed by Congress on Dec. 6, 1973, and was sworn in same day. He became President Aug. 9, 1974, upon Nixon's resignation. 8. Nominated by Ford Aug. 20, 1974; confirmed by Congress on Dec. 19, 1974, and was sworn in same day.

Burial Places of the Presidents

President	Burial place	President	Burial place
Washington	Mt. Vernon, Va.	Grant	New York City
J. Adams	Quincy, Mass.	Hayes	Fremont, Ohio
Jefferson	Charlottesville, Va.	Garfield	Cleveland, Ohio
Madison	Montpelier Station, Va.	Arthur	Albany, N.Y.
Monroe	Richmond, Va.	Cleveland	Princeton, N.J.
J. Q. Adams	Quincy, Mass.	B. Harrison	Indianapolis
Jackson	The Hermitage, nr. Nashville, Tenn.	McKinley	Canton, Ohio
		T. Roosevelt	Oyster Bay, N.Y.
Van Buren	Kinderhook, N.Y.	Taft	Arlington National Cemetery
W. H. Harrison	North Bend, Ohio	Wilson	Washington National Cathedral
Tyler	Richmond, Va.	Harding	Marion, Ohio
Polk	Nashville, Tenn.	Coolidge	Plymouth, Vt.
Taylor	Louisville, Ky.	Hoover	West Branch, Iowa
Fillmore	Buffalo, N.Y.	F. D. Roosevelt	Hyde Park, N.Y.
Pierce	Concord, N.H.	Truman	Independence, Mo.
Buchanan	Lancaster, Pa.	Eisenhower	Abilene, Kan.
Lincoln	Springfield, Ill.	Kennedy	Arlington National Cemetery
A. Johnson	Greeneville, Tenn.	L. B. Johnson	Stonewall, Tex.

"In God We Trust"

"In God We Trust" first appeared on U.S. coins after April 22, 1864, when Congress passed an act authorizing the coinage of a 2-cent piece bearing this motto. Thereafter, Congress extended its use to other coins. On July 30, 1956, it became the national motto.

Wives and Children of the Presidents

President	Wife's name	Year and place of wife's birth	Married	Wife died	Children of President[1]	
					Sons	Daughters
Washington	Martha Dandridge Custis	1732, Va.	1759	1802	—	—
John Adams	Abigail Smith	1744, Mass.	1764	1818	3	2
Jefferson	Martha Wayles Skelton	1748, Va.	1772	1782	1	5
Madison	Dorothy "Dolley" Payne Todd	1768, N.C.	1794	1849	—	—
Monroe	Elizabeth "Eliza" Kortright	1768, N.Y.	1786	1830	—	2
J. Q. Adams	Louisa Catherine Johnson	1775, England	1797	1852	3	1
Jackson	Mrs. Rachel Donelson Robards	1767, Va.	1791	1828	—	—
Van Buren	Hannah Hoes	1788, N.Y.	1807	1819	4	—
W. H. Harrison	Anna Symmes	1775, N.J.	1795	1864	6	4
Tyler	Letitia Christian	1790, Va.	1813	1842	3	4
	Julia Gardiner	1820, N.Y.	1844	1889	5	2
Polk	Sarah Childress	1803, Tenn.	1824	1891	—	—
Taylor	Margaret Smith	1788, Md.	1810	1852	1	5
Fillmore	Abigail Powers	1798, N.Y.	1826	1853	1	1
	Caroline Carmichael McIntosh	1813, N.J.	1858	1881	—	—
Pierce	Jane Means Appleton	1806, N.H.	1834	1863	3	—
Buchanan	(Unmarried)	—	—	—	—	—
Lincoln	Mary Todd	1818, Ky.	1842	1882	4	—
A. Johnson	Eliza McCardle	1810, Tenn.	1827	1876	3	2
Grant	Julia Dent	1826, Mo.	1848	1902	3	1
Hayes	Lucy Ware Webb	1831, Ohio	1852	1889	7	1
Garfield	Lucretia Rudolph	1832, Ohio	1858	1918	5	2
Arthur	Ellen Lewis Herndon	1837, Va.	1859	1880	2	1
Cleveland	Frances Folsom	1864, N.Y.	1886	1947	2	3
B. Harrison	Caroline Lavinia Scott	1832, Ohio	1853	1892	1	1
	Mary Scott Lord Dimmick	1858, Pa.	1896	1948	—	1
McKinley	Ida Saxton	1847, Ohio	1871	1907	—	2
T. Roosevelt	Alice Hathaway Lee	1861, Mass.	1880	1884	—	1
	Edith Kermit Carow	1861, Conn.	1886	1948	4	1
Taft	Helen Herron	1861, Ohio	1886	1943	2	1
Wilson	Ellen Louise Axson	1860, Ga.	1885	1914	—	3
	Edith Bolling Galt	1872, Va.	1915	1961	—	—
Harding	Florence Kling DeWolfe	1860, Ohio	1891	1924	—	—
Coolidge	Grace Anna Goodhue	1879, Vt.	1905	1957	2	—
Hoover	Lou Henry	1875, Iowa	1899	1944	2	—
F. D. Roosevelt	Anna Eleanor Roosevelt	1884, N.Y.	1905	1962	5	1
Truman	Bess Wallace	1885, Mo.	1919	1982	—	1
Eisenhower	Mamie Geneva Doud	1896, Iowa	1916	1979	2	—
Kennedy	Jacqueline Lee Bouvier	1929, N.Y.	1953	—	2	1
L. B. Johnson	Claudia Alta "Lady Bird" Taylor	1912, Tex.	1934	—	—	2
Nixon	Thelma Catherine "Pat" Ryan	1912, Nev.	1940	—	—	2
Ford	Elizabeth "Betty" Bloomer Warren	1918, Ill.	1948	—	3	1
Carter	Rosalynn Smith	1928, Ga.	1946	—	3	1
Reagan	Jane Wyman	1914, Mo.	1940[2]	—	1[3]	1
	Nancy Davis	1921 (?)[4], N.Y.	1952	—	1	1
Bush	Barbara Pierce	1925, N.Y.	1945	—	4	2

1. Includes children who died in infancy. 2. Divorced in 1948. 3. Adopted. 4. Birthday officially given as 1923 but her high school and college records show 1921 for year of birth.

Elections

How a President Is Nominated and Elected

The National Conventions of both major parties are held during the summer of a presidential-election year. Earlier, each party selects delegates by primaries, conventions, committees, etc.

For their 1988 National Convention, the Republicans allow each state a base of 6 delegates at large; the District of Columbia, 14; Puerto Rico, 14; Guam and the Virgin Islands, 4 each. In addition, each state receives 3 district delegates for each representative it has in the House of Representatives, regardless of political affiliation. This did not apply to the District of Columbia, Puerto Rico, Guam and the Virgin Islands.

Each state is awarded additional delegates at large on the basis of having supported the Republican candidate for President in 1984 and electing Republican candidates for Senator, Governor, and U.S. Representative between 1984 and 1987 inclusive.

The number of delegates at the 1988 convention, held in New Orleans starting August 15, was 2,277.

Following was the apportionment of delegates:

Alabama	38	Florida	82	Kentucky	38	Montana	20	Ohio	88	Texas	111
Alaska	19	Georgia	48	Louisiana	41	Nebraska	25	Oklahoma	36	Utah	26
Arizona	33	Guam	4	Maine	22	Nevada	20	Oregon	32	Vermont	17
Arkansas	27	Hawaii	20	Maryland	41	N.H.	23	Pa.	96	V.I.	4
California	175	Idaho	22	Mass.	52	N. Jersey	64	P.R.	14	Virginia	50
Colorado	36	Illinois	92	Michigan	77	New Mexico	26	R.I.	21	Washington	41
Connecticut	35	Indiana	51	Minnesota	31	New York	136	S.C.	37	W. Va.	28
Delaware	17	Iowa	37	Mississippi	31	N.C.	54	S.D.	18	Wisconsin	47
D.C.	14	Kansas	34	Missouri	47	N.D.	16	Tennessee	45	Wyoming	18

The Democrats base the number of delegates on a state's showing in the 1984 and 1986 elections. At the 1988 convention, held in Atlanta starting July 18, there were 4,203[1][2] delegates casting 4,161 votes. Following is the apportionment by states:

Alabama	65	Florida	154	Kentucky	65	Montana	28	Ohio	183	Texas	212
Alaska	17	Georgia	94	Louisiana	76	Nebraska	30	Oklahoma	56	Utah	28
Arizona	43	Guam	10[1]	Maine	29	Nevada	23	Oregon	54	Vermont	20
Arkansas	48	Hawaii	28	Maryland	84	N. H.	22	Pa.	202	V.I.	11
California	368[1]	Idaho	24	Mass.	119	New Jersey	125	P.R.	61[1]	Virginia	86
Colorado	55	Illinois	200	Michigan	162	New Mexico	30	R.I.	28	Washington	77
Connecticut	63	Indiana	91[1]	Minnesota	91	New York	292	S.C.	53	W. Va.	47
Delaware	19	Iowa	61	Mississippi	47	N.C.	95	S.D.	20	Wisconsin	91
D. C.	24	Kansas	45	Missouri	88	N.D.	22	Tennessee	84	Wyoming	18

1. Fractional votes. 2. Includes 22[1] delegates for Democrats Abroad and 12[1] for American Samoa.

The Conventions

At each convention, a temporary chairman is chosen. After a credentials committee seats the delegates, a permanent chairman is elected. The convention then votes on a platform, drawn up by the platform committee.

By the third or fourth day, presidential nominations begin. The chairman calls the roll of states alphabetically. A state may place a candidate in nomination or yield to another state.

Voting, again alphabetically by roll call of states, begins after all nominations have been made and seconded. A simple majority is required in each party, although this may require many ballots.

Finally, the vice-presidential candidate is selected. Although there is no law saying that the candidates *must* come from different states, it is, practically, necessary for this to be the case. Otherwise, according to the Constitution (*see* Amendment XII), electors from that state could vote for only one of the candidates and would have to cast their other vote for some person of another state. This could result in a presidential candidate's receiving a majority electoral vote and his running mate's failing to.

The Electoral College

The next step in the process is the nomination of electors in each state, according to its laws. These electors must not be Federal office holders. In the November election, the voters cast their votes for electors, not for President. In some states, the ballots include only the names of the presidential and vice-presidential candidates; in others, they include only names of the electors. Nowadays, it is rare for electors to be split between parties. The last such occurrence was in North Carolina in 1968[1]; the last before that, in Tennessee in 1948.

On three occasions (1824, 1876, and 1888), the presidential candidate with the largest popular vote failed to obtain an electoral-vote majority.

Each state has as many electors as it has Senators and Representatives. For the 1984 election, the total electors were 538, based on 100 Senators, 435 Representatives, plus 3 electoral votes from the District of Columbia as a result of the 23rd Amendment to the Constitution.

On the first Monday after the second Wednesday in December, the electors cast their votes in their respective state capitols. Constitutionally they may vote for someone other than the party candidate but usually they do not since they are pledged to one party and its candidate on the ballot. Should the presidential or vice-presidential candidate die between the November election and the December meetings, the electors pledged to vote for him could vote for whomever they pleased. However, it seems certain that the national committee would attempt to get an agreement among the state party leaders for a replacement candidate.

The votes of the electors, certified by the states, are sent to Congress, where the president of the Senate opens the certificates and has them counted in the presence of both Houses on January 6. The new President is inaugurated at noon on January 20.

Should no candidate receive a majority of the electoral vote for President, the House of Representatives chooses a President from among the three highest candidates, voting, not as individuals, but as states, with a majority (now 26) needed to elect. Should no vice-presidential candidate obtain the majority, the Senate, voting as individuals, chooses from the highest two.

1. In 1956, 1 of Alabama's 11 electoral votes was cast for Walter B. Jones. In 1960, 6 of Alabama's 11 electoral votes and 1 of Oklahoma's 8 electoral votes were cast for Harry Flood Byrd. (Byrd also received all 8 of Mississippi's electoral votes.)

National Political Conventions Since 1856

Opening date	Party	Where held	Opening date	Party	Where held
June 17, 1856	Republican	Philadelphia	June 10, 1924	Republican	Cleveland
June 2, 1856	Democratic	Cincinnati	June 24, 1924[2]	Democratic	New York City
May 16, 1860	Republican	Chicago	June 12, 1928	Republican	Kansas City
April 23, 1860	Democratic	Charleston and Baltimore	June 26, 1928	Democratic	Houston
June 7, 1864	Republican[1]	Baltimore	June 14, 1932	Republican	Chicago
Aug. 29, 1864	Democratic	Chicago	June 27, 1932	Democratic	Chicago
May 20, 1868	Republican	Chicago	June 9, 1936	Republican	Cleveland
July 4, 1868	Democratic	New York City	June 23, 1936	Democratic	Philadelphia
June 5, 1872	Republican	Philadelphia	June 24, 1940	Republican	Philadelphia
June 9, 1872	Democratic	Baltimore	July 15, 1940	Democratic	Chicago
June 14, 1876	Republican	Cincinnati	June 26, 1944	Republican	Chicago
June 28, 1876	Democratic	St. Louis	July 19, 1944	Democratic	Chicago
June 2, 1880	Republican	Chicago	June 21, 1948	Republican	Philadelphia
June 23, 1880	Democratic	Cincinnati	July 12, 1948	Democratic	Philadelphia
June 3, 1884	Republican	Chicago	July 17, 1948	(3)	Birmingham
July 11, 1884	Democratic	Chicago	July 22, 1948	Progressive	Philadelphia
June 19, 1888	Republican	Chicago	July 7, 1952	Republican	Chicago
June 6, 1888	Democratic	St. Louis	July 21, 1952	Democratic	Chicago
June 7, 1892	Republican	Minneapolis	Aug. 20, 1956	Republican	San Francisco
June 21, 1892	Democratic	Chicago	Aug. 13, 1956	Democratic	Chicago
June 16, 1896	Republican	St. Louis	July 25, 1960	Republican	Chicago
July 7, 1896	Democratic	Chicago	July 11, 1960	Democratic	Los Angeles
June 19, 1900	Republican	Philadelphia	July 13, 1964	Republican	San Francisco
July 4, 1900	Democratic	Kansas City	Aug. 24, 1964	Democratic	Atlantic City
June 21, 1904	Republican	Chicago	Aug. 5, 1968	Republican	Miami Beach
July 6, 1904	Democratic	St. Louis	Aug. 26, 1968	Democratic	Chicago
June 16, 1908	Republican	Chicago	July 10, 1972	Democratic	Miami Beach
July 7, 1908	Democratic	Denver	Aug. 21, 1972	Republican	Miami Beach
June 18, 1912	Republican	Chicago	July 12, 1976	Democratic	New York City
June 25, 1912	Democratic	Baltimore	Aug. 16, 1976	Republican	Kansas City, Mo.
June 7, 1916	Republican	Chicago	Aug. 11, 1980	Democratic	New York City
June 14, 1916	Democratic	St. Louis	July 14, 1980	Republican	Detroit
June 8, 1920	Republican	Chicago	Aug. 20, 1984	Republican	Dallas
June 28, 1920	Democratic	San Francisco	July 16, 1984	Democratic	San Francisco
			July 18, 1988	Democratic	Atlanta
			Aug. 15, 1988	Republican	New Orleans

1. The Convention adopted name Union party to attract War Democrats and others favoring prosecution of war. 2. In session until July 10, 1924. 3. States' Rights delegates from 13 Southern states.

National Committee Chairmen Since 1944

Chairman and (state)	Term	Chairman and (state)	Term
REPUBLICAN		**DEMOCRATIC**	
Herbert Brownell, Jr. (N.Y.)	1944–46	Robert E. Hannegan (Mo.)	1944–47
Carroll Reece (Tenn.)	1946–48	J. Howard McGrath (R.I.)	1947–49
Hugh D. Scott, Jr. (Pa.)	1948–49	William M. Boyle, Jr. (Mo.)	1949–51
Guy G. Gabrielson (N.J.)	1949–52	Frank E. McKinney (Ind.)	1951–52
Arthur E. Summerfield (Mich.)	1952–53	Stephen A. Mitchell (Ill.)	1952–54
Wesley Roberts (Kan.)	1953–	Paul M. Butler (Ind.)	1955–60
Leonard W. Hall (N.Y.)	1953–57	Henry M. Jackson (Wash.)	1960–61
Meade Alcorn (Conn.)	1957–59	John M. Bailey (Conn.)	1961–68
Thruston B. Morton (Ky.)	1959–61	Lawrence F. O'Brien (Mass.)	1968–69
William E. Miller (N.Y.)	1961–64	Fred R. Harris (Okla.)	1969–70
Dean Burch (Ariz.)	1964–65	Lawrence F. O'Brien (Mass.)	1970–72
Ray C. Bliss (Ohio)	1965–69	Jean Westwood (Utah)	1972
Rogers C. B. Morton (Md.)	1969–71	Robert S. Strauss (Tex.)	1972–77
Robert Dole (Kan.)	1971–73	Kenneth M. Curtis (Me.)	1977
George H. Bush (Tex.)	1973–74	John C. White (Tex.)	1977–81
Mary Louise Smith (Iowa)	1974–77	Charles T. Manatt (Calif.)	1981–85
William E. Brock III (Tenn.)	1977–81	Paul G. Kirk, Jr. (Mass.)	1985–89
Richard Richards (Utah)	1981–83	Ronald H. Brown (D.C.)	1989
Frank J. Fahrenkopf, Jr. (Nevada)	1983–89		
Lee Atwater (S.C.)	1989–		

Republican National Committee: 310 First St., S.E., Washington, D. C. 20003.
Democratic National Committee: 430 South Capitol St., S.E., Washington, D.C. 20003.

Presidential Elections, 1789 to 1988

For the original method of electing the President and the Vice President (elections of 1789, 1792, 1796, and 1800), see Article II, Section 1, of the Constitution. The election of 1804 was the first one in which the electors voted for President and Vice President on separate ballots. (See Amendment XII to the Constitution.)

Year	Presidential candidates	Party	Electoral vote	Year	Presidential candidates	Party	Electoral vote
1789[1]	George Washington	(no party)	69	1796	John Adams	Federalist	71
	John Adams	(no party)	34		Thomas Jefferson	Dem.-Rep.	68
	Scattering	(no party)	35		Thomas Pinckney	Federalist	59
	Votes not cast		8		Aaron Burr	Dem.-Rep.	30
					Scattering		48
1792	George Washington	Federalist	132				
	John Adams	Federalist	77	1800[2]	Thomas Jefferson	Dem.-Rep.	73
	George Clinton	Anti-Federalist	50		Aaron Burr	Dem.-Rep.	73
	Thomas Jefferson	Anti-Federalist	4		John Adams	Federalist	65
	Aaron Burr	Anti-Federalist	1		Charles C. Pinckney	Federalist	64
	Votes not cast		6		John Jay	Federalist	1

Year	Presidential candidates	Party	Electoral vote	Vice-presidential candidates	Party	Electoral vote
1804	Thomas Jefferson	Dem.-Rep.	162	George Clinton	Dem.-Rep.	162
	Charles C. Pinckney	Federalist	14	Rufus King	Federalist	14
1808	James Madison	Dem.-Rep.	122	George Clinton	Dem.-Rep.	113
	Charles C. Pinckney	Federalist	47	Rufus King	Federalist	47
	George Clinton	Dem.-Rep.	6	John Langdon	Ind. (no party)	9
	Votes not cast		1	James Madison	Dem.-Rep.	3
				James Monroe	Dem.-Rep.	3
				Votes not cast		1
1812	James Madison	Dem.-Rep.	128	Elbridge Gerry	Dem.-Rep.	131
	De Witt Clinton	Federalist	89	Jared Ingersoll	Federalist	86
	Votes not cast		1	Votes not cast		1
1816	James Monroe	Dem.-Rep.	183	Daniel D. Tompkins	Dem.-Rep.	183
	Rufus King	Federalist	34	John E. Howard	Federalist	22
	Votes not cast		4	James Ross	Ind. (no party)	5
				John Marshall	Federalist	4
				Robert G. Harper	Ind. (no party)	3
				Votes not cast		4
1820	James Monroe	Dem-Rep	231	Daniel D. Tompkins	Dem.-Rep.	218
	John Quincy Adams	Ind. (no party)	1	Richard Stockton	Ind. (no party)	8
	Votes not cast		3	Daniel Rodney	Ind. (no party)	4
				Richard Rush	Ind. (no party)	1
				Robert G. Harper	Ind. (no party)	1
				Votes not cast		3
1824[3]	John Quincy Adams	(no party)	84	John C. Calhoun	(no party)	182
	Andrew Jackson	(no party)	99	Nathan Sanford	(no party)	30
	William H. Crawford	(no party)	41	Nathaniel Macon	(no party)	24
	Henry Clay	(no party)	37	Andrew Jackson	(no party)	13
				Martin Van Buren	(no party)	9
				Henry Clay	(no party)	2
				Votes not cast		1
1828	Andrew Jackson	Democratic	178	John C. Calhoun	Democratic	171
	John Quincy Adams	Natl. Rep.	83	Richard Rush	Natl. Rep.	83
				William Smith	Democratic	7
1832	Andrew Jackson	Democratic	219	Martin Van Buren	Democratic	189
	Henry Clay	Natl. Rep.	49	John Sergeant	Natl. Rep.	49
	John Floyd	Ind. (no party)	11	Henry Lee	Ind. (no party)	11
	William Wirt	Antimasonic[4]	7	Amos Ellmaker	Antimasonic	7
	Votes not cast		2	William Wilkins	Ind. (no party)	30
				Votes not cast		2

Year	Presidential candidates	Party	Electoral vote	Vice-presidential candidates	Party	Electoral vote
1836	Martin Van Buren	Democratic	170	Richard M. Johnson[5]	Democratic	147
	William H. Harrison	Whig	73	Francis Granger	Whig	77
	Hugh L. White	Whig	26	John Tyler	Whig	47
	Daniel Webster	Whig	14	William Smith	Ind. (no party)	23
	W. P. Mangum	Ind. (no party)	11			
1840	William H. Harrison[6]	Whig	234	John Tyler	Whig	234
	Martin Van Buren	Democratic	60	Richard M. Johnson	Democratic	48
				L. W. Tazewell	Ind. (no party)	11
				James K. Polk	Democratic	1
1844	James K. Polk	Democratic	170	George M. Dallas	Democratic	170
	Henry Clay	Whig	105	Theo. Frelinghuysen	Whig	105
1848	Zachary Taylor[7]	Whig	163	Millard Fillmore	Whig	163
	Lewis Cass	Democratic	127	William O. Butler	Democratic	127
1852	Franklin Pierce	Democratic	254	William R. King	Democratic	254
	Winfield Scott	Whig	42	William A. Graham	Whig	42
1856	James Buchanan	Democratic	174	John C. Breckinridge	Democratic	174
	John C. Fremont	Republican	114	William L. Dayton	Republican	114
	Millard Fillmore	American[8]	8	A. J. Donelson	American[8]	8
1860	Abraham Lincoln	Republican	180	Hannibal Hamlin	Republican	180
	John C. Breckinridge	Democratic	72	Joseph Lane	Democratic	72
	John Bell	Const. Union	39	Edward Everett	Const. Union	39
	Stephen A. Douglas	Democratic	12	H. V. Johnson	Democratic	12
1864	Abraham Lincoln[9]	Union[10]	212	Andrew Johnson	Union[15]	212
	George B. McClellan	Democratic	21	G. H. Pendleton	Democratic	21
1868	Ulysses S. Grant	Republican	214	Schuyler Colfax	Republican	214
	Horatio Seymour	Democratic	80	Francis P. Blair, Jr.	Democratic	80
	Votes not counted[11]		23	Votes not counted[11]		23

Year	Presidential candidates	Party	Electoral vote	Popular vote	Vice-presidential candidates and party
1872	Ulysses S. Grant	Republican	286	3,597,132	Henry Wilson—R
	Horace Greeley	Dem., Liberal Rep.	([12])	2,834,125	B. Gratz Brown—D, LR—(47)
	Thomas A. Hendricks	Democratic	42		Scattering—(19)
	B. Gratz Brown	Dem., Liberal Rep.	18		Votes not counted—(14)
	Charles J. Jenkins	Democratic	2		
	David Davis	Democratic	1		
	Votes not counted		17		
1876[13]	Rutherford B. Hayes	Republican	185	4,033,768	William A. Wheeler—R
	Samuel J. Tilden	Democratic	184	4,285,992	Thomas A. Hendricks—D
	Peter Cooper	Greenback	0	81,737	Samuel F. Cary—G
1880	James A. Garfield[14]	Republican	214	4,449,053	Chester A. Arthur—R
	Winfield S. Hancock	Democratic	155	4,442,035	William H. English—D
	James B. Weaver	Greenback	0	308,578	B. J. Chambers—G
1884	Grover Cleveland	Democratic	219	4,911,017	Thomas A. Hendricks—D
	James G. Blaine	Republican	182	4,848,334	John A. Logan—R
	Benjamin F. Butler	Greenback	0	175,370	A. M. West—G
	John P. St. John	Prohibition	0	150,369	William Daniel—P
1888	Benjamin Harrison	Republican	233	5,440,216	Levi P. Morton—R
	Grover Cleveland	Democratic	168	5,538,233	A. G. Thurman—D
	Clinton B. Fisk	Prohibition	0	249,506	John A. Brooks—P
	Alson J. Streeter	Union Labor	0	146,935	Charles E. Cunningham—UL
1892	Grover Cleveland	Democratic	277	5,556,918	Adlai E. Stevenson—D
	Benjamin Harrison	Republican	145	5,176,108	Whitelaw Reid—R
	James B. Weaver	People's[15]	22	1,041,028	James G. Field—Peo
	John Bidwell	Prohibition	0	264,133	James B. Cranfill—P

Year	Presidential candidates	Party	Electoral vote	Popular vote	Vice-presidential candidates and party
1896	William McKinley	Republican	271	7,035,638	Garret A. Hobart—R
	William J. Bryan	Dem., People's[15]	176	6,467,946	Arthur Sewall—D—(149)
					Thomas E. Watson—Peo—(27)
	John M. Palmer	Natl. Dem.	0	133,148	Simon B. Buckner—ND
	Joshua Levering	Prohibition	0	132,007	Hale Johnson—P
1900	William McKinley[16]	Republican	292	7,219,530	Theodore Roosevelt—R
	William J. Bryan	Dem., People's[15]	155	6,358,071	Adlai E. Stevenson—D, Peo
	Eugene V. Debs	Social Democratic	0	94,768	Job Harriman—SD
1904	Theodore Roosevelt	Republican	336	7,628,834	Charles W. Fairbanks—R
	Alton B. Parker	Democratic	140	5,084,491	Henry G. Davis—D
	Eugene V. Debs	Socialist	0	402,400	Benjamin Hanford—S
1908	William H. Taft	Republican	321	7,679,006	James S. Sherman—R
	William J. Bryan	Democratic	162	6,409,106	John W. Kern—D
	Eugene V. Debs	Socialist	0	402,820	Benjamin Hanford—S
1912	Woodrow Wilson	Democratic	435	6,286,214	Thomas R. Marshall—D
	Theodore Roosevelt	Progressive	88	4,126,020	Hiram Johnson—Prog
	William H. Taft	Republican	8	3,483,922	Nicholas M. Butler—R[17]
	Eugene V. Debs	Socialist	0	897,011	Emil Seidel—S
1916	Woodrow Wilson	Democratic	277	9,129,606	Thomas R. Marshall—D
	Charles E. Hughes	Republican	254	8,538,221	Charles W. Fairbanks—R
	A. L. Benson	Socialist	0	585,113	G. R. Kirkpatrick—S
1920	Warren G. Harding[18]	Republican	404	16,152,200	Calvin Coolidge—R
	James M. Cox	Democratic	127	9,147,353	Franklin D. Roosevelt—D
	Eugene V. Debs	Socialist	0	917,799	Seymour Stedman—S
1924	Calvin Coolidge	Republican	382	15,725,016	Charles G. Dawes—R
	John W. Davis	Democratic	136	8,385,586	Charles W. Bryan—D
	Robert M. LaFollette	Progressive, Socialist	13	4,822,856	Burton K. Wheeler—Prog S
1928	Herbert Hoover	Republican	444	21,392,190	Charles Curtis—R
	Alfred E. Smith	Democratic	87	15,016,443	Joseph T. Robinson—D
	Norman Thomas	Socialist	0	267,420	James H. Maurer—S
1932	Franklin D. Roosevelt	Democratic	472	22,821,857	John N. Garner—D
	Herbert Hoover	Republican	59	15,761,841	Charles Curtis—R
	Norman Thomas	Socialist	0	884,781	James H. Maurer—S
1936	Franklin D. Roosevelt	Democratic	523	27,751,597	John N. Garner—D
	Alfred M. Landon	Republican	8	16,679,583	Frank Knox—R
	Norman Thomas	Socialist	0	187,720	George Nelson—S
1940	Franklin D. Roosevelt	Democratic	449	27,244,160	Henry A. Wallace—D
	Wendell L. Willkie	Republican	82	22,305,198	Charles L. McNary—R
	Norman Thomas	Socialist	0	99,557	Maynard C. Krueger—S
1944	Franklin D. Roosevelt[19]	Democratic	432	25,602,504	Harry S. Truman—D
	Thomas E. Dewey	Republican	99	22,006,285	John W. Bricker—R
	Norman Thomas	Socialist	0	80,518	Darlington Hoopes—S
1948	Harry S. Truman	Democratic	303	24,179,345	Alben W. Barkley—D
	Thomas E. Dewey	Republican	189	21,991,291	Earl Warren—R
	J. Strom Thurmond	States' Rights Dem.	39	1,176,125	Fielding L. Wright—SR
	Henry A. Wallace	Progressive	0	1,157,326	Glen Taylor—Prog
	Norman Thomas	Socialist	0	139,572	Tucker P. Smith—S
1952	Dwight D. Eisenhower	Republican	442	33,936,234	Richard M. Nixon—R
	Adlai E. Stevenson	Democratic	89	27,314,992	John J. Sparkman—D
1956	Dwight D. Eisenhower	Republican	457	35,590,472	Richard M. Nixon—R
	Adlai E. Stevenson	Democratic	73[20]	26,022,752	Estes Kefauver—D
1960	John F. Kennedy[22]	Democratic	303	34,226,731	Lyndon B. Johnson—D
	Richard M. Nixon	Republican	219[21]	34,108,157	Henry Cabot Lodge—R

Year	Presidential candidates	Party	Electoral vote	Popular vote	Vice-presidential candidates and party
1964	Lyndon B. Johnson	Democratic	486	43,129,484	Hubert H. Humphrey—D
	Barry M. Goldwater	Republican	52	27,178,188	William E. Miller—R
1968	Richard M. Nixon	Republican	301	31,785,480	Spiro T. Agnew—R
	Hubert H. Humphrey	Democratic	191	31,275,166	Edmund S. Muskie—D
	George C. Wallace	American Independent	46	9,906,473	Curtis F. LeMay—AI
1972	Richard M. Nixon[23]	Republican	520[24]	47,169,911	Spiro T. Agnew—R
	George McGovern	Democratic	17	29,170,383	Sargent Shriver—D
	John G. Schmitz	American	0	1,099,482	Thomas J. Anderson—A
1976	Jimmy Carter	Democratic	297	40,830,763	Walter F. Mondale—D
	Gerald R. Ford	Republican	240[25]	39,147,973	Robert J. Dole—R
	Eugene J. McCarthy	Independent	0	756,631	None
1980	Ronald Reagan	Republican	489	43,899,248	George Bush—R
	Jimmy Carter	Democratic	49	36,481,435	Walter F. Mondale—D
	John B. Anderson	Independent	0	5,719,437	Patrick J. Lucey—I
1984	Ronald Reagan	Republican	525	54,455,075	George Bush—R
	Walter F. Mondale	Democratic	13	37,577,185	Geraldine A. Ferraro—D
1988	George H. Bush	Republican	426	48,886,097	J. Danforth Quayle—R
	Michael S. Dukakis	Democratic	111[26]	41,809,074	Lloyd Bentsen—D

1. Only 10 states participated in the election. The New York legislature chose no electors, and North Carolina and Rhode Island had not yet ratified the Constitution. 2. As Jefferson and Burr were tied, the House of Representatives chose the President. In a vote by states, 10 votes were cast for Jefferson, 4 for Burr; 2 votes were not cast. 3. As no candidate had an electoral-vote majority, the House of Representatives chose the President from the first three. In a vote by states, 13 votes were cast for Adams, 7 for Jackson, and 4 for Crawford. 4. The Antimasonic Party on Sept. 26, 1831, was the first party to hold a nominating convention to choose candidates for President and Vice-President. 5. As Johnson did not have an electoral-vote majority, the Senate chose him 33–14 over Granger, the others being legally out of the race. 6. Harrison died April 4, 1841, and Tyler succeeded him April 6. 7. Taylor died July 9, 1850, and Fillmore succeeded him July 10. 8. Also known as the Know-Nothing Party. 9. Lincoln died April 15, 1865, and Johnson succeeded him the same day. 10. Name adopted by the Republican National Convention of 1864. Johnson was a War Democrat. 11. 23 Southern electoral votes were excluded. 12. See Election of 1872 in *Unusual Voting Results* under Elections, Presidential, in Index. 13. See Election of 1876 in *Unusual Voting Results* under Elections, Presidential, in Index. 14. Garfield died Sept. 19, 1881, and Arthur succeeded him Sept. 20. 15. Members of People's Party were called Populists. 16. McKinley died Sept. 14, 1901, and Roosevelt succeeded him the same day. 17. James S. Sherman, Republican candidate for Vice President, died Oct. 30, 1912, and the Republican electoral votes were cast for Butler. 18. Harding died Aug. 2, 1923, and Coolidge succeeded him Aug. 3. 19. Roosevelt died April 12, 1945, and Truman succeeded him the same day. 20. One electoral vote from Alabama was cast for Walter B. Jones. 21. Sen. Harry F. Byrd received 15 electoral votes. 22. Kennedy died Nov. 22, 1963, and Johnson succeeded him the same day. 23. Nixon resigned Aug. 9, 1974, and Gerald R. Ford succeeded him the same day. 24. One electoral vote from Virginia was cast for John Hospers, Libertarian Party. 25. One electoral vote from Washington was cast for Ronald Reagan. 26. One electoral vote from West Virginia was cast for Lloyd Bentsen.

Qualifications for Voting

The Supreme Court decision of March 21, 1972, declared lengthy requirements for voting in state and local elections unconstitutional and suggested that 30 days was an ample period. Most of the states have changed or eliminated their durational residency requirements to comply with the ruling, as shown.

NO DURATIONAL RESIDENCY REQUIREMENT

Alabama,[6] Arkansas, Connecticut,[13] Delaware,[12] District of Columbia,[16] Florida,[5] Georgia,[2] Hawaii,[2] Iowa,[6] Maine, Maryland, Massachusetts,[3] Missouri,[4] Nebraska,[9] New Hampshire,[17] New Mexico,[7] North Carolina, Oklahoma, South Carolina,[2] South Dakota,[10] Tennessee, Texas, Virginia, West Virginia,[2] Wyoming[2]

30-DAY RESIDENCY REQUIREMENT

Alaska,[18] Arizona,[11] Idaho, Illinois, Indiana, Kentucky,[2] Louisiana,[8] Michigan, Mississippi,[2] Montana, Nevada, New Jersey, New York, North Dakota,[3] Ohio, Pennsylvania, Rhode Island, Utah, Washington

OTHER

California,[19] Colorado,[1] Kansas, Minnesota[15] and Oregon, 20 days; Vermont, 17 days;[14] Wisconsin, 10 days

1. 32 days. 2. 30-day registration requirement. 3. No residency required to register to vote. 4. Must be registered by the fourth Wednesday prior to election. 5. 30-day registration requirement for national elections; 30-day for state elections. 6. 10-day registration requirement. In-person registration by 5 PM, eleven days before election date. 7. Must register 28 days before election. 8. 24 days prior to any election. 9. Registration requirement, 2nd Friday prior to elections. 10. 15-day registration requirement. 11. Residency in the state 50 days next preceding the election except 30 days for presidential election. 12. Must reside in Delaware and register by the last day that the books are open for registration. 13. Registration deadline 21st day before election; registration and party enrollment deadline the day before primary; unaffiliated voters may vote in Republican primaries for *some* offices. 14. Administrative cut-off date for processing applications. 15. Permits registration and voting on election day with approved ID. 16. Registration stops 30 days before any election and until 15 days after. Voters must inform Board of Elections of change of address within 30 days of moving. 17. Registration requirement, 10 days prior

to elections. 18. If otherwise qualified but has not been a resident of the election district for at least 30 days preceding the date of a presidential election, is entitled to register and vote for presidential and vice-presidential candidates. 19. 29 days before an election. *Source: Information Please* questionnaires to the states.

Unusual Voting Results

Election of 1872

The presidential and vice-presidential candidates of the Liberal Republicans and the northern Democrats in 1872 were Horace Greeley and B. Gratz Brown. Greeley died Nov. 29, 1872, before his 66 electors voted. In the electoral balloting for President, 63 of Greeley's votes were scattered among four other men, including Brown.

Election of 1876

In the election of 1876 Samuel J. Tilden, the Democratic candidate, received a popular majority but lacked one undisputed electoral vote to carry a clear majority of the electoral college. The crux of the problem was in the 22 electoral votes which were in dispute because Florida, Louisiana, South Carolina, and Oregon each sent in two sets of election returns. In the three southern states, Republican election boards threw out enough Democratic votes to certify the Republican candidate, Hayes. In Oregon, the Democratic governor disqualified a Republican elector, replacing him with a Democrat. Since the Senate was Republican and the House of Representatives Democratic, it seemed useless to refer the disputed returns to the two houses for solution. Instead Congress appointed an Electoral Commission with five representatives each from the Senate, the House, and the Supreme Court. All but one Justice was named, giving the Commission seven Republican and seven Democratic members. The naming of the fifth Justice was left to the other four. He was a Republican who first favored Tilden but, under pressure from his party, switched to Hayes, ensuring his election by the Commission voting 8 to 7 on party lines.

Minority Presidents

Fifteen candidates have become President of the United States with a popular vote less than 50% of the total cast. It should be noted, however, that in elections before 1872, presidential electors were not chosen by popular vote in all states. Adams' election in 1824 was by the House of Representatives, which chose him over Jackson, who had a plurality of both electoral and popular votes, but not a majority in the electoral college.

Besides Jackson in 1824, only two other candidates receiving the largest popular vote have failed to gain a majority in the electoral college—Samuel J. Tilden (D) in 1876 and Grover Cleveland (D) in 1888.

The "minority" Presidents follow:

Vote Received by Minority Presidents

Year	President	Electoral Percent	Popular vote Percent
1824	John Q. Adams	31.8	29.8
1844	James K. Polk (D)	61.8	49.3
1848	Zachary Taylor (W)	56.2	47.3
1856	James Buchanan (D)	58.7	45.3
1860	Abraham Lincoln (R)	59.4	39.9
1876	Rutherford B. Hayes (R)	50.1	47.9
1880	James A. Garfield (R)	57.9	48.3
1884	Grover Cleveland (D)	54.6	48.8
1888	Benjamin Harrison (R)	58.1	47.8
1892	Grover Cleveland (D)	62.4	46.0
1912	Woodrow Wilson (D)	81.9	41.8
1916	Woodrow Wilson (D)	52.1	49.3
1948	Harry S. Truman (D)	57.1	49.5
1960	John F. Kennedy (D)	56.4	49.7
1968	Richard M. Nixon (R)	56.1	43.4

How a Bill Becomes a Law

When a Senator or a Representative introduces a bill, he sends it to the clerk of his house, who gives it a number and title. This is the *first reading*, and the bill is referred to the proper committee.

The committee may decide the bill is unwise or unnecessary and *table* it, thus killing it at once. Or it may decide the bill is worthwhile and hold hearings to listen to facts and opinions presented by experts and other interested persons. After members of the committee have debated the bill and perhaps offered amendments, a vote is taken; and if the vote is favorable, the bill is sent back to the floor of the house.

The clerk reads the bill sentence by sentence to the house, and this is known as the *second reading*. Members may then debate the bill and offer amendments. In the House of Representatives, the time for debate is limited by a *cloture rule*, but there is no such restriction in the Senate for cloture, where 60 votes are required. This makes possible a *filibuster*, in which one or more opponents hold the floor to defeat the bill.

The *third reading* is by title only, and the bill is put to a vote, which may be by voice or roll call, depending on the circumstances and parliamentary rules. Members who must be absent at the time but who wish to record their vote may be paired if each negative vote has a balancing affirmative one.

The bill then goes to the other house of Congress, where it may be defeated, or passed with or without amendments. If the bill is defeated, it dies. If it is passed with amendments, a joint Congressional committee must be appointed by both houses to iron out the differences.

After its final passage by both houses, the bill is sent to the President. If he approves, he signs it, and the bill becomes a law. However, if he disapproves, he *vetoes* the bill by refusing to sign it and sending it back to the house of origin with his reasons for the veto. The objections are read and debated, and a roll-call vote is taken. If the bill receives less than a two-thirds vote, it is defeated and goes no farther. But if it receives a two-thirds vote or greater, it is sent to the other house for a vote. If that house also passes it by a two-thirds vote, the President's veto is *overridden*, and the bill becomes a law.

Should the President desire neither to sign nor to veto the bill, he may retain it for ten days, Sundays excepted, after which time it automatically becomes a law without signature. However, if Congress has adjourned within those ten days, the bill is automatically killed, that process of indirect rejection being known as a *pocket veto*.

Government Officials
Cabinet Members With Dates of Appointment

Although the Constitution made no provision for a President's advisory group, the heads of the three executive departments (State, Treasury, and War) and the Attorney General were organized by Washington into such a group; and by about 1793, the name "Cabinet" was applied to it. With the exception of the Attorney General up to 1870 and the Postmaster General from 1829 to 1872, Cabinet members have been heads of executive departments.

A Cabinet member is appointed by the President, subject to the confirmation of the Senate; and as his term is not fixed, he may be replaced at any time by the President. At a change in Administration, it is customary for him to tender his resignation, but he remains in office until a successor is appointed.

The table of Cabinet members lists only those members who actually served after being duly commissioned.

The dates shown are those of appointment. "Cont." indicates that the term continued from the previous Administration for a substantial amount of time.

With the creation of the Department of Transportation in 1966, the Cabinet consisted of 12 members. This figure was reduced to 11 when the Post Office Department became an independent agency in 1970 but, with the establishment in 1977 of a Department of Energy, became 12 again. Creation of the Department of Education in 1980 raised the number to 13. Creation of the Department of Veterans' Affairs in 1989 raised the number to 14.

WASHINGTON

Secretary of State	Thomas Jefferson 1789
	Edmund Randolph 1794
	Timothy Pickering 1795
Secretary of the Treasury	Alexander Hamilton 1789
	Oliver Wolcott, Jr. 1795
Secretary of War	Henry Knox 1789
	Timothy Pickering 1795
	James McHenry 1796
Attorney General	Edmund Randolph 1789
	William Bradford 1794
	Charles Lee 1795

J. ADAMS

Secretary of State	Timothy Pickering (Cont.)
	John Marshall 1800
Secretary of the Treasury	Oliver Wolcott, Jr. (Cont.)
	Samuel Dexter 1801
Secretary of War	James McHenry (Cont.)
	Samuel Dexter 1800
Attorney General	Charles Lee (Cont.)
Secretary of the Navy	Benjamin Stoddert 1798

JEFFERSON

Secretary of State	James Madison 1801
Secretary of the Treasury	Samuel Dexter (Cont.)
	Albert Gallatin 1801
Secretary of War	Henry Dearborn 1801
Attorney General	Levi Lincoln 1801
	Robert Smith 1805
	John Breckinridge 1805
	Caesar A. Rodney 1807
Secretary of the Navy	Benjamin Stoddert (Cont.)
	Robert Smith 1801

MADISON

Secretary of State	Robert Smith 1809
	James Monroe 1811
Secretary of the Treasury	Albert Gallatin (Cont.)
	George W. Campbell 1814
	Alexander J. Dallas 1814
	William H. Crawford 1816
Secretary of War	William Eustis 1809
	John Armstrong 1813

	James Monroe 1814
	William H. Crawford 1815
Attorney General	Caesar A. Rodney (Cont.)
	William Pinckney 1811
	Richard Rush 1814
Secretary of the Navy	Paul Hamilton 1809
	William Jones 1813
	B. W. Crowninshield 1814

MONROE

Secretary of State	John Quincy Adams 1817
Secretary of the Treasury	William H. Crawford (Cont.)
Secretary of War	John C. Calhoun 1817
Attorney General	Richard Rush (Cont.)
	William Wirt 1817
Secretary of the Navy	B. W. Crowninshield (Cont.)
	Smith Thompson 1818
	Samuel L. Southard 1823

J. Q. ADAMS

Secretary of State	Henry Clay 1825
Secretary of the Treasury	Richard Rush 1825
Secretary of War	James Barbour 1825
	Peter B. Porter 1828
Attorney General	William Wirt (Cont.)
Secretary of the Navy	Samuel L. Southard (Cont.)

JACKSON

Secretary of State	Martin Van Buren 1829
	Edward Livingston 1831
	Louis McLane 1833
	John Forsyth 1834
Secretary of the Treasury	Samuel D. Ingham 1829
	Louis McLane 1831
	William J. Duane 1833
	Roger B. Taney[3] 1833
	Levi Woodbury 1834
Secretary of War	John H. Eaton 1829
	Lewis Cass 1831
Attorney General	John M. Berrien 1829
	Roger B. Taney 1831
	Benjamin F. Butler 1833
Postmaster General	William T. Barry 1829
	Amos Kendall 1835
Secretary of the Navy	John Branch 1829
	Levi Woodbury 1831
	Mahlon Dickerson 1834

VAN BUREN

Secretary of State	John Forsyth (Cont.)
Secretary of the Treasury	Levi Woodbury (Cont.)
Secretary of War	Joel R. Poinsett 1837
Attorney General	Benjamin F. Butler (Cont.)
	Felix Grundy 1838
	Henry D. Gilpin 1840
Postmaster General	Amos Kendall (Cont.)
	John M. Niles 1840
Secretary of the Navy	Mahlon Dickerson (Cont.)
	James K. Paulding 1838

W. H. HARRISON

Secretary of State	Daniel Webster 1841
Secretary of the Treasury	Thomas Ewing 1841
Secretary of War	John Bell 1841
Attorney General	John J. Crittenden 1841
Postmaster General	Francis Granger 1841
Secretary of the Navy	George E. Badger 1841

TYLER

Secretary of State	Daniel Webster (Cont.)
	Abel P. Upshur 1843
	John C. Calhoun 1844
Secretary of the Treasury	Thomas Ewing (Cont.)
	Walter Forward 1841
	John C. Spencer[3] 1843
	George M. Bibb 1844
Secretary of War	John Bell (Cont.)
	John C. Spencer 1841
	James M. Porter[3] 1843
	William Wilkins 1844
Attorney General	John J. Crittenden (Cont.)
	Hugh S. Legaré 1841
	John Nelson 1843
Postmaster General	Francis Granger (Cont.)
	Charles A. Wickliffe 1841
Secretary of the Navy	George E. Badger (Cont.)
	Abel P. Upshur 1841
	David Henshaw[3] 1843
	Thomas W. Gilmer 1844
	John Y. Mason 1844

POLK

Secretary of State	James Buchanan 1845
Secretary of the Treasury	Robert J. Walker 1845
Secretary of War	William L. Marcy 1845
Attorney General	John Y. Mason 1845
	Nathan Clifford 1846
	Isaac Toucey 1848
Postmaster General	Cave Johnson 1845
Secretary of the Navy	George Bancroft 1845
	John Y. Mason 1846

TAYLOR

Secretary of State	John M. Clayton 1849
Secretary of the Treasury	William M. Meredith 1849
Secretary of War	George W. Crawford 1849
Attorney General	Reverdy Johnson 1849
Postmaster General	Jacob Collamer 1849
Secretary of the Navy	William B. Preston 1849
Secretary of the Interior	Thomas Ewing 1849

FILLMORE

Secretary of State	Daniel Webster 1850
	Edward Everett 1852
Secretary of the Treasury	Thomas Corwin 1850
Secretary of War	Charles M. Conrad 1850
Attorney General	John J. Crittenden 1850
Postmaster General	Nathan K. Hall 1850
	Samuel D. Hubbard 1852
Secretary of the Navy	William A. Graham 1850
	John P. Kennedy 1852
Secretary of the Interior	Thos. M. T. McKennan 1850
	Alex. H. H. Stuart 1850

PIERCE

Secretary of State	William L. Marcy 1853
Secretary of the Treasury	James Guthrie 1853
Secretary of War	Jefferson Davis 1853
Attorney General	Caleb Cushing 1853
Postmaster General	James Campbell 1853
Secretary of the Navy	James C. Dobbin 1853
Secretary of the Interior	Robert McClelland 1853

BUCHANAN

Secretary of State	Lewis Cass 1857
	Jeremiah S. Black 1860
Secretary of the Treasury	Howell Cobb 1857
	Philip F. Thomas 1860
	John A. Dix 1861
Secretary of War	John B. Floyd 1857
	Joseph Holt 1861
Attorney General	Jeremiah S. Black 1857
	Edwin M. Stanton 1860
Postmaster General	Aaron V. Brown 1857
	Joseph Holt 1859
	Horatio King 1861
Secretary of the Navy	Isaac Toucey 1857
Secretary of the Interior	Jacob Thompson 1857

LINCOLN

Secretary of State	William H. Seward 1861
Secretary of the Treasury	Salmon P. Chase 1861
	William P. Fessenden 1864
	Hugh McCulloch 1865
Secretary of War	Simon Cameron 1861
	Edwin M. Stanton 1862
Attorney General	Edward Bates 1861
	James Speed 1864
Postmaster General	Montgomery Blair 1861
	William Dennison 1864
Secretary of the Navy	Gideon Welles 1861
Secretary of the Interior	Caleb B. Smith 1861
	John P. Usher 1863

A. JOHNSON

Secretary of State	William H. Seward (Cont.)
Secretary of the Treasury	Hugh McCulloch (Cont.)
Secretary of War	Edwin M. Stanton (Cont.)
	John M. Schofield 1868
Attorney General	James Speed (Cont.)
	Henry Stanbery 1866
	William M. Evarts 1868
Postmaster General	William Dennison (Cont.)
	Alexander W. Randall 1866
Secretary of the Navy	Gideon Welles (Cont.)
Secretary of the Interior	John P. Usher (Cont.)
	James Harlan 1865
	Orville H. Browning 1866

GRANT

Secretary of State	Elihu B. Washburne 1869
	Hamilton Fish 1869
Secretary of the Treasury	George S. Boutwell 1869
	William A. Richardson 1873
	Benjamin H. Bristow 1874
	Lot M. Morrill 1876
Secretary of War	John A. Rawlins 1869
	William W. Belknap 1869
	Alphonso Taft 1876
	James D. Cameron 1876
Attorney General	Ebenezer R. Hoar 1869
	Amos T. Akerman 1870
	George H. Williams 1871
	Edwards Pierrepont 1875
	Alphonso Taft 1876
Postmaster General	John A. J. Creswell 1869
	Marshall Jewell 1874
	James N. Tyner 1876
Secretary of the Navy	Adolph E. Borie 1869
	George M. Robeson 1869
Secretary of the Interior	Jacob D. Cox 1869
	Columbus Delano 1870
	Zachariah Chandler 1875

HAYES

Secretary of State	William M. Evarts 1877
Secretary of the Treasury	John Sherman 1877
Secretary of War	George W. McCrary 1877
	Alexander Ramsey 1879
Attorney General	Charles Devens 1877
Postmaster General	David M. Key 1877
	Horace Maynard 1880

Secretary of the Navy	Richard W. Thompson 1877
	Nathan Goff, Jr. 1881
Secretary of the Interior	Carl Schurz 1877

GARFIELD

Secretary of State	James G. Blaine 1881
Secretary of the Treasury	William Windom 1881
Secretary of War	Robert T. Lincoln 1881
Attorney General	Wayne MacVeagh 1881
Postmaster General	Thomas L. James 1881
Secretary of the Navy	William H. Hunt 1881
Secretary of the Interior	Samuel J. Kirkwood 1881

ARTHUR

Secretary of State	James G. Blaine (Cont.)
	F. T. Frelinghuysen 1881
Secretary of the Treasury	William Windom (Cont.)
	Charles J. Folger 1881
	Walter Q. Gresham 1884
	Hugh McCulloch 1884
Secretary of War	Robert T. Lincoln (Cont.)
Attorney General	Wayne MacVeagh (Cont.)
	Benjamin H. Brewster 1881
Postmaster General	Thomas L. James (Cont.)
	Timothy O. Howe 1881
	Walter Q. Gresham 1883
	Frank Hatton 1884
Secretary of the Navy	William H. Hunt (Cont.)
	William E. Chandler 1882
Secretary of the Interior	Samuel J. Kirkwood (Cont.)
	Henry M. Teller 1882

CLEVELAND

Secretary of State	Thomas F. Bayard 1885
Secretary of the Treasury	Daniel Manning 1885
	Charles S. Fairchild 1887
Secretary of War	William C. Endicott 1885
Attorney General	Augustus H. Garland 1885
Postmaster General	William F. Vilas 1885
	Don M. Dickinson 1888
Secretary of the Navy	William C. Whitney 1885
Secretary of the Interior	Lucius Q. C. Lamar 1885
	William F. Vilas 1888
Secretary of Agriculture	Norman J. Colman 1889

B. HARRISON

Secretary of State	James G. Blaine 1889
	John W. Foster 1892
Secretary of the Treasury	William Windom 1889
	Charles Foster 1891
Secretary of War	Redfield Proctor 1889
	Stephen B. Elkins 1891
Attorney General	William H. H. Miller 1889
Postmaster General	John Wanamaker 1889
Secretary of the Navy	Benjamin F. Tracy 1889
Secretary of the Interior	John W. Noble 1889
Secretary of Agriculture	Jeremiah M. Rusk 1889

CLEVELAND

Secretary of State	Walter Q. Gresham 1893
	Richard Olney 1895
Secretary of the Treasury	John G. Carlisle 1893
Secretary of War	Daniel S. Lamont 1893
Attorney General	Richard Olney 1893
	Judson Harmon 1895
Postmaster General	Wilson S. Bissell 1893
	William L. Wilson 1895
Secretary of the Navy	Hilary A. Herbert 1893
Secretary of the Interior	Hoke Smith 1893
	David R. Francis 1896
Secretary of Agriculture	Julius Sterling Morton 1893

McKINLEY

Secretary of State	John Sherman 1897
	William R. Day 1898
	John Hay 1898
Secretary of the Treasury	Lyman J. Gage 1897
Secretary of War	Russell A. Alger 1897
	Elihu Root 1899
Attorney General	Joseph McKenna 1897
	John W. Griggs 1898
	Philander C. Knox 1901
Postmaster General	James A. Gary 1897
	Charles E. Smith 1898
Secretary of the Navy	John D. Long 1897
Secretary of the Interior	Cornelius N. Bliss 1897
	Ethan A. Hitchcock 1898
Secretary of Agriculture	James Wilson 1897

T. ROOSEVELT

Secretary of State	John Hay (Cont.)
	Elihu Root 1905
	Robert Bacon 1909
Secretary of the Treasury	Lyman J. Gage (Cont.)
	Leslie M. Shaw 1902
	George B. Cortelyou 1907
Secretary of War	Elihu Root (Cont.)
	William H. Taft 1904
	Luke E. Wright 1908
Attorney General	Philander C. Knox (Cont.)
	William H. Moody 1904
	Charles J. Bonaparte 1906
Postmaster General	Charles E. Smith (Cont.)
	Henry C. Payne 1902
	Robert J. Wynne 1904
	George B. Cortelyou 1905
	George von L. Meyer 1907
Secretary of the Navy	John D. Long (Cont.)
	William H. Moody 1902
	Paul Morton 1904
	Charles J. Bonaparte 1905
	Victor H. Metcalf 1906
	Truman H. Newberry 1908
Secretary of the Interior	Ethan A. Hitchcock (Cont.)
	James R. Garfield 1907
Secretary of Agriculture	James Wilson (Cont.)
Secretary of Commerce and Labor	George B. Cortelyou 1903
	Victor H. Metcalf 1904
	Oscar S. Straus 1906

TAFT

Secretary of State	Philander C. Knox 1909
Secretary of the Treasury	Franklin MacVeagh 1909
Secretary of War	Jacob M. Dickinson 1909
	Henry L. Stimson 1911
Attorney General	George W. Wickersham 1909
Postmaster General	Frank H. Hitchcock 1909
Secretary of the Navy	George von L. Meyer 1909
Secretary of the Interior	Richard A. Ballinger 1909
	Walter L. Fisher 1911
Secretary of Agriculture	James Wilson (Cont.)
Secretary of Commerce and Labor	Charles Nagel 1909

WILSON

Secretary of State	William J. Bryan 1913
	Robert Lansing 1915
	Bainbridge Colby 1920
Secretary of the Treasury	William G. McAdoo 1913
	Carter Glass 1918
	David F. Houston 1920
Secretary of War	Lindley M. Garrison 1913
	Newton D. Baker 1916
Attorney General	James C. McReynolds 1913
	Thomas W. Gregory 1914
	A. Mitchell Palmer 1919
Postmaster General	Albert S. Burleson 1913
Secretary of the Navy	Josephus Daniels 1913
Secretary of the Interior	Franklin K. Lane 1913
	John B. Payne 1920
Secretary of Agriculture	David F. Houston 1913
	Edwin T. Meredith 1920
Secretary of Commerce	William C. Redfield 1913
	Joshua W. Alexander 1919
Secretary of Labor	William B. Wilson 1913

HARDING

Secretary of State	Charles E. Hughes 1921
Secretary of the Treasury	Andrew W. Mellon 1921
Secretary of War	John W. Weeks 1921
Attorney General	Harry M. Daugherty 1921
Postmaster General	Will H. Hays 1921

	Hubert Work 1922
	Harry S. New 1923
Secretary of the Navy	Edwin Denby 1921
Secretary of the Interior	Albert B. Fall 1921
	Hubert Work 1923
Secretary of Agriculture	Henry C. Wallace 1921
Secretary of Commerce	Herbert Hoover 1921
Secretary of Labor	James J. Davis 1921

COOLIDGE

Secretary of State	Charles E. Hughes (Cont.)
	Frank B. Kellogg 1925
Secretary of the Treasury	Andrew W. Mellon (Cont.)
Secretary of War	John W. Weeks (Cont.)
	Dwight F. Davis 1925
Attorney General	Harry M. Daugherty (Cont.)
	Harlan F. Stone 1924
	John G. Sargent 1925
Postmaster General	Harry S. New (Cont.)
Secretary of the Navy	Edwin Denby (Cont.)
	Curtis D. Wilbur 1924
Secretary of the Interior	Hubert Work (Cont.)
	Roy O. West 1928
Secretary of Agriculture	Henry C. Wallace (Cont.)
	Howard M. Gore 1924
	William M. Jardine 1925
Secretary of Commerce	Herbert Hoover (Cont.)
	William F. Whiting 1928
Secretary of Labor	James J. Davis (Cont.)

HOOVER

Secretary of State	Frank B. Kellogg (Cont.)
	Henry L. Stimson 1929
Secretary of the Treasury	Andrew W. Mellon (Cont.)
	Ogden L. Mills 1932
Secretary of War	James W. Good 1929
	Patrick J. Hurley 1929
Attorney General	William D. Mitchell 1929
Postmaster General	Walter F. Brown 1929
Secretary of the Navy	Charles F. Adams 1929
Secretary of the Interior	Ray Lyman Wilbur 1929
Secretary of Agriculture	Arthur M. Hyde 1929
Secretary of Commerce	Robert P. Lamont 1929
	Roy D. Chapin 1932
Secretary of Labor	James J. Davis (Cont.)
	William N. Doak 1930

F. D. ROOSEVELT

Secretary of State	Cordell Hull 1933
	E. R. Stettinius, Jr. 1944
Secretary of the Treasury	William H. Woodin 1933
	Henry Morgenthau, Jr. 1934
Secretary of War	George H. Dern 1933
	Harry H. Woodring 1936
	Henry L. Stimson 1940
Attorney General	Homer S. Cummings 1933
	Frank Murphy 1939
	Robert H. Jackson 1940
	Francis Biddle 1941
Postmaster General	James A. Farley 1933
	Frank C. Walker 1940
Secretary of the Navy	Claude A. Swanson 1933
	Charles Edison 1940
	Frank Knox 1940
	James Forrestal 1944
Secretary of the Interior	Harold L. Ickes 1933
Secretary of Agriculture	Henry A. Wallace 1933
	Claude R. Wickard 1940
Secretary of Commerce	Daniel C. Roper 1933
	Harry L. Hopkins 1938
	Jesse H. Jones 1940
	Henry A. Wallace 1945
Secretary of Labor	Frances Perkins 1933

TRUMAN

Secretary of State	E. R. Stettinius, Jr. (Cont.)
	James F. Byrnes 1945
	George C. Marshall 1947
	Dean Acheson 1949
Secretary of the Treasury	Henry Morgenthau, Jr. (Cont.)
	Frederick M. Vinson 1945
	John W. Snyder 1946

Secretary of Defense	James Forrestal 1947
	Louis A. Johnson 1949
	George C. Marshall 1950
	Robert A. Lovett 1951
Attorney General	Francis Biddle (Cont.)
	Tom C. Clark 1945
	J. Howard McGrath 1949
	James P. McGranery 1952
Postmaster General	Frank C. Walker (Cont.)
	Robert E. Hannegan 1945
	Jesse M. Donaldson 1947
Secretary of the Interior	Harold L. Ickes (Cont.)
	Julius A. Krug 1946
	Oscar L. Chapman 1949
Secretary of Agriculture	Claude R. Wickard (Cont.)
	Clinton P. Anderson 1945
	Charles F. Brannan 1948
Secretary of Commerce	Henry A. Wallace (Cont.)
	W. Averell Harriman 1946
	Charles Sawyer 1948
Secretary of Labor	Frances Perkins (Cont.)
	Lewis B. Schwellenbach 1945
	Maurice J. Tobin 1948
Secretary of War[2]	Henry L. Stimson (Cont.)
	Robert P. Patterson 1945
	Kenneth C. Royall 1947
Secretary of the Navy[2]	James Forrestal (Cont.)

EISENHOWER

Secretary of State	John Foster Dulles 1953
	Christian A. Herter 1959
Secretary of the Treasury	George M. Humphrey 1953
	Robert B. Anderson 1957
Secretary of Defense	Charles E. Wilson 1953
	Neil H. McElroy 1957
	Thomas S. Gates, Jr. 1959
Attorney General	Herbert Brownell, Jr. 1953
	William P. Rogers 1958
Postmaster General	Arthur E. Summerfield 1953
Secretary of the Interior	Douglas McKay 1953
	Frederick A. Seaton 1956
Secretary of Agriculture	Ezra Taft Benson 1953
Secretary of Commerce	Sinclair Weeks 1953
	Lewis L. Strauss[3] 1958
	Frederick H. Mueller 1959
Secretary of Labor	Martin P. Durkin 1953
	James P. Mitchell 1953
Secretary of Health, Education, and Welfare	Oveta Culp Hobby 1953
	Marion B. Folsom 1955
	Arthur S. Flemming 1958

KENNEDY

Secretary of State	Dean Rusk 1961
Secretary of the Treasury	C. Douglas Dillon 1961
Secretary of Defense	Robert S. McNamara 1961
Attorney General	Robert F. Kennedy 1961
Postmaster General	J. Edward Day 1961
	John A. Gronouski 1963
Secretary of the Interior	Stewart L. Udall 1961
Secretary of Agriculture	Orville L. Freeman 1961
Secretary of Commerce	Luther H. Hodges 1961
Secretary of Labor	Arthur J. Goldberg 1961
	W. Willard Wirtz 1962
Secretary of Health, Education, and Welfare	Abraham A. Ribicoff 1961
	Anthony J. Celebrezze 1962

L. B. JOHNSON

Secretary of State	Dean Rusk (Cont.)
Secretary of the Treasury	C. Douglas Dillon (Cont.)
	Henry H. Fowler 1965
	Joseph W. Barr[4] 1968
Secretary of Defense	Robert S. McNamara (Cont.)
	Clark M. Clifford 1968
Attorney General	Robert F. Kennedy (Cont.)
	N. de B. Katzenbach 1965
	Ramsey Clark 1967
Postmaster General	John A. Gronouski (Cont.)
	Lawrence F. O'Brien 1965
	W. Marvin Watson 1968
Secretary of the Interior	Stewart L. Udall (Cont.)
Secretary of Agriculture	Orville L. Freeman (Cont.)

Secretary of Commerce	Luther H. Hodges (Cont.)
	John T. Connor 1964
	A. B. Trowbridge 1967
	C. R. Smith 1968
Secretary of Labor	W. Willard Wirtz (Cont.)
Secretary of Health, Education,	
and Welfare	Anthony J. Celebrezze (Cont.)
	John W. Gardner 1965
	Wilbur J. Cohen 1968
Secretary of Housing and Urban	
Development	Robert C. Weaver 1966
	Robert C. Wood[4] 1969
Secretary of Transportation	Alan S. Boyd 1966

NIXON

Secretary of State	William P. Rogers 1969
	Henry A. Kissinger 1973
Secretary of the Treasury	David M. Kennedy 1969
	John B. Connally 1971
	George P. Shultz 1972
	William E. Simon 1974
Secretary of Defense	Melvin R. Laird 1969
	Elliot L. Richardson 1973
	James R. Schlesinger 1973
Attorney General	John N. Mitchell 1969
	Richard G. Kleindienst 1972
	Elliot L. Richardson 1973
	William B. Saxbe 1974
Postmaster General[5]	William M. Blount 1969
Secretary of the Interior	Walter J. Hickel 1969
	Rogers C. B. Morton 1971
Secretary of Agriculture	Clifford M. Hardin 1969
	Earl L. Butz 1971
Secretary of Commerce	Maurice H. Stans 1969
	Peter G. Peterson 1972
	Frederick B. Dent 1973
Secretary of Labor	George P. Shultz 1969
	James D. Hodgson 1970
	Peter J. Brennan 1973
Secretary of Health, Education,	
and Welfare	Robert H. Finch 1969
	Elliot L. Richardson 1970
	Caspar W. Weinberger 1973
Secretary of Housing and Urban	
Development	George Romney 1969
	James T. Lynn 1973
Secretary of Transportation	John A. Volpe 1969
	Claude S. Brinegar 1973

FORD

Secretary of State	Henry A. Kissinger (Cont.)
Secretary of the Treasury	William E. Simon (Cont.)
Secretary of Defense	James R. Schlesinger (Cont.)
	Donald H. Rumsfeld 1975
Attorney General	William B. Saxbe (Cont.)
	Edward H. Levi 1975
Secretary of the Interior	Rogers C. B. Morton (Cont.)
	Stanley K. Hathaway 1975
	Thomas S. Kleppe 1975
Secretary of Agriculture	Earl L. Butz (Cont.)
	John Knebel 1976
Secretary of Commerce	Frederick B. Dent (Cont.)
	Rogers C. B. Morton 1975
	Elliot L. Richardson 1976
Secretary of Labor	Peter J. Brennan (Cont.)
	John T. Dunlop 1975
	William J. Usery, Jr. 1976
Secretary of Health, Education,	
and Welfare	Caspar W. Weinberger (Cont.)
	F. David Mathews 1975
Secretary of Housing and Urban	
Development	James T. Lynn (Cont.)
	Carla A. Hills 1975
Secretary of Transportation	Claude S. Brinegar (Cont.)
	William T. Coleman, Jr. 1975

CARTER

Secretary of State	Cyrus R. Vance 1977
	Edmund S. Muskie 1980

Secretary of the Treasury	W. Michael Blumenthal 1977
	G. William Miller 1979
Secretary of Defense	Harold Brown 1977
Attorney General	Griffin B. Bell 1977
	Benjamin R. Civiletti 1979
Secretary of the Interior	Cecil D. Andrus 1977
Secretary of Agriculture	Bob S. Bergland 1977
Secretary of Commerce	Juanita M. Kreps 1977
	Philip M. Klutznick 1979
Secretary of Labor	F. Ray Marshall 1977
Secretary of Health and Human	
Services[6]	Joseph A. Califano, Jr. 1977
	Patricia Roberts Harris 1979
Secretary of Housing and Urban	
Development	Patricia Roberts Harris 1977
	Moon Landrieu 1979
Secretary of Transportation	Brock Adams 1977
	Neil E. Goldschmidt 1979
Secretary of Energy	James R. Schlesinger 1977
	Charles W. Duncan, Jr. 1979
Secretary of Education	Shirley Mount Hufstedler 1979

REAGAN

Secretary of State	Alexander M. Haig, Jr. 1981
	George P. Shultz 1982
Secretary of the Treasury	Donald T. Regan 1981
	James A. Baker 3rd 1985
	Nicholas F. Brady 1988
Secretary of Defense	Caspar W. Weinberger 1981
	Frank C. Carlucci 1987
Attorney General	William French Smith 1981
	Edwin Meese 3rd 1985
	Richard L. Thornburgh 1988
Secretary of the Interior	James G. Watt 1981
	William P. Clark 1983
	Donald P. Hodel 1985
Secretary of Agriculture	John R. Block 1981
	Richard E. Lyng 1986
Secretary of Commerce	Malcolm Baldrige 1981
	C. William Verity, Jr. 1987
Secretary of Labor	Raymond J. Donovan 1981
	William E. Brock 1985
	Ann Dore McLaughlin 1987
Secretary of Health and Human	
Services	Richard S. Schweiker 1981
	Margaret M. Heckler 1983
	Otis R. Bowen 1985
Secretary of Housing and Urban	
Development	Samuel R. Pierce, Jr. 1981
Secretary of Transportation	Andrew L. Lewis, Jr. 1981
	Elizabeth H. Dole 1983
	James H. Burnley 4th 1987
Secretary of Energy	James B. Edwards 1981
	Donald P. Hodel 1983
	John S. Herrington 1985
Secretary of Education	T. H. Bell 1981
	William J. Bennett 1985
	Lauro F. Cavazos 1988

BUSH

Secretary of State	James A. Baker 3d 1989
Secretary of the Treasury	Nicholas F. Brady (Cont.)
Secretary of Defense	Richard Cheney 1989
Attorney General	Richard L. Thornburgh (Cont.)
Secretary of the Interior	Manuel Lujan Jr. 1989
Secretary of Agriculture	Clayton K. Yeutter 1989
Secretary of Commerce	Robert A. Mosbacher Sr. 1989
Secretary of Labor	Elizabeth H. Dole 1989
Secretary of Health and Human	
Services	Louis W. Sullivan 1989
Secretary of Housing and Urban	
Development	Jack F. Kemp 1989
Secretary of Transportation	Samuel K. Skinner 1989
Secretary of Energy	James D. Watkins 1989
Secretary of Education	Lauro F. Cavazos (Cont.)
Secretary of Veterans	
Affairs	Edward J. Derwinski 1989

1. The Postmaster General did not become a Cabinet member until 1829. Earlier Postmasters General were: Samuel Osgood (1789), Timothy Pickering (1791), Joseph Habersham (1795), Gideon Granger (1801), Return J. Meigs, Jr. (1814), and

John McLean (1823). 2. On July 26, 1947, the Departments of War and of the Navy were incorporated into the Department of Defense. 3. Not confirmed by the Senate. 4. Recess appointment. 5. The Postmaster General is no longer a Cabinet member. 6. Known as Department of Health, Education, and Welfare until May 1980.

Figures and Legends in American Folklore

Appleseed, Johnny (John Chapman, 1774–1847): Massachusetts-born nurseryman; reputed to have spread seeds and seedlings from which rose orchards of the Midwest.

Billy the Kid (William H. Bonney, 1859–1881): New York-born desperado; killed his first man before he reached his teens; after short life of crime in Wild West, was gunned down by Sheriff Pat Garrett; symbol of lawless West.

Boone, Daniel (1734–1820): Frontiersman and Indian fighter, about whom legends of early America have been built; figured in Byron's *Don Juan*.

Brodie, Steve (1863–1901): Reputed to have dived off Brooklyn Bridge on July 23, 1886. (Whether he actually did so has never been proved.)

Buffalo Bill (William F. Cody, 1846–1917): Buffalo hunter and Indian scout; much of legend about him and Wild West stems from his own Wild West show, which he operated in late 19th century.

Bunyan, Paul: Mythical lumberjack; subject of tall tales throughout timber country (that he dug Grand Canyon, for example).

Crockett, David (1786–1836): Frontiersman and member of U.S. Congress, about whom legends have been built of heroic feats; died in defense of Alamo.

Fritchie (or Frietchie), Barbara: Symbol of patriotism; in ballad by John Greenleaf Whittier, 90-year-old Barbara Fritchie defiantly waves Stars and Stripes as "Stonewall" Jackson's Confederate troops march through Frederick, Md.

James, Jesse (1847–1882): Bank and train robber; folklore has given him quality of American Robin Hood.

Jones, Casey (John Luther Jones, 1863–1900): Example of heroic locomotive engineer given to feats of prowess; died in wreck with his hand on brake lever when his Illinois Central "Cannonball" express hit freight train at Vaughan, Miss.

Ross, Betsy (1752–1836): Member of Philadelphia flag-making family; reported to have designed and sewn first American flag. (Report is without confirmation.)

Uncle Sam: Personification of United States and its people; origin uncertain; may be based on inspector of government supplies in Revolutionary War and War of 1812.

Assassinations and Attempts in U. S. Since 1865

Cermak, Anton J. (Mayor of Chicago): Shot Feb. 15, 1933, in Miami by Giuseppe Zangara, who attempted to assassinate Franklin D. Roosevelt; Cermak died March 6.

Ford, Gerald R. (President of U.S.): Escaped assassination attempt Sept. 5, 1975, in Sacramento, Calif., by Lynette Alice (Squeaky) Fromm, who pointed but did not fire .45-caliber pistol. Escaped assassination attempt in San Francisco, Calif., Sept. 22, 1975, by Sara Jane Moore, who fired one shot from a .38-caliber pistol that was deflected.

Garfield, James A. (President of U.S.): Shot July 2, 1881, in Washington, D.C., by Charles J. Guiteau; died Sept. 19.

Jordan, Vernon E., Jr. (civil rights leader): Shot and critically wounded in assassination attempt May 29, 1980, in Fort Wayne, Ind.

Kennedy, John F. (President of U.S.): Shot Nov. 22, 1963, in Dallas, Tex., allegedly by Lee Harvey Oswald; died same day. Injured was Gov. John B. Connally of Texas. Oswald was shot and killed two days later by Jack Ruby.

Kennedy, Robert F. (U.S. Senator from New York): Shot June 5, 1968, in Los Angeles by Sirhan Bishara Sirhan; died June 6.

King, Martin Luther, Jr. (civil rights leader): Shot April 4, 1968, in Memphis by James Earl Ray; died same day.

Lincoln, Abraham (President of U.S.): Shot April 14, 1865, in Washington, D.C., by John Wilkes Booth; died April 15.

Long, Huey P. (U.S. Senator from Louisiana): Shot Sept. 8, 1935, in Baton Rouge by Dr. Carl A. Weiss; died Sept. 10.

McKinley, William (President of U.S.): Shot Sept. 6, 1901, in Buffalo by Leon Czolgosz; died Sept. 14.

Reagan, Ronald (President of U.S.): Shot in left lung in Washington by John W. Hinckley, Jr., on March 30, 1981; three others also wounded.

Roosevelt, Franklin D. (President-elect of U.S.): Escaped assassination unhurt Feb. 15, 1933, in Miami. *See* Cermak.

Roosevelt, Theodore (ex-President of U.S.): Escaped assassination (though shot) Oct. 14, 1912, in Milwaukee while campaigning for President.

Seward, William H. (Secretary of State): Escaped assassination (though injured) April 14, 1865, in Washington, D.C., by Lewis Powell (or Paine), accomplice of John Wilkes Booth.

Truman, Harry S. (President of U.S.): Escaped assassination unhurt Nov. 1, 1950, in Washington, D.C., as 2 Puerto Rican nationalists attempted to shoot their way into Blair House.

Wallace, George C. (Governor of Alabama): Shot and critically wounded in assassination attempt May 15, 1972, at Laurel, Md., by Arthur Herman Bremer. Wallace paralyzed from waist down.

Members of the Supreme Court of the United States

Name; apptd. from	Service Term	Yrs	Birth Place	Date	Died	Religion
CHIEF JUSTICES						
John Jay, N.Y.	1789-1795	5	N.Y.	1745	1829	Episcopal
John Rutledge, S.C.	1795	0	S.C.	1739	1800	Church of England
Oliver Ellsworth, Conn.	1796-1800	4	Conn.	1745	1807	Congregational
John Marshall, Va.	1801-1835	34	Va.	1755	1835	Episcopal
Roger B. Taney, Md.	1836-1864	28	Md.	1777	1864	Roman Catholic
Salmon P. Chase, Ohio	1864-1873	8	N.H.	1808	1873	Episcopal
Morrison R. Waite, Ohio	1874-1888	14	Conn.	1816	1888	Episcopal
Melville W. Fuller, Ill.	1888-1910	21	Me.	1833	1910	Episcopal
Edward D. White, La.	1910-1921	10	La.	1845	1921	Roman Catholic
William H. Taft, Conn.	1921-1930	8	Ohio	1857	1930	Unitarian
Charles E. Hughes, N.Y.	1930-1941	11	N.Y.	1862	1948	Baptist
Harlan F. Stone, N.Y.	1941-1946	4	N.H.	1872	1946	Episcopal
Frederick M. Vinson, Ky.	1946-1953	7	Ky.	1890	1953	Methodist
Earl Warren, Calif.	1953-1969	15	Calif.	1891	1974	Protestant
Warren E. Burger, Va.	1969-1986	17	Minn.	1907	—	Presbyterian
William H. Rehnquist, Ariz.	1986-		Wis.	1924	—	Lutheran
ASSOCIATE JUSTICES						
James Wilson, Pa.	1789-1798	8	Scotland	1742	1798	Episcopal
John Rutledge, S.C.	1790-1791	1	S.C.	1739	1800	Church of England
William Cushing, Mass.	1790-1810	20	Mass.	1732	1810	Unitarian
John Blair, Va.	1790-1796	5	Va.	1732	1800	Presbyterian
James Iredell, N.C.	1790-1799	9	England	1751	1799	Episcopal
Thomas Johnson, Md.	1792-1793	0	Md.	1732	1819	Episcopal
William Paterson, N.J.	1793-1806	13	Ireland	1745	1806	Protestant
Samuel Chase, Md.	1796-1811	15	Md.	1741	1811	Episcopal
Bushrod Washington, Va.	1799-1829	30	Va.	1762	1829	Episcopal
Alfred Moore, N.C.	1800-1804	3	N.C.	1755	1810	Episcopal
William Johnson, S.C.	1804-1834	30	S.C.	1771	1834	Presbyterian
Brockholst Livingston, N.Y.	1807-1823	16	N.Y.	1757	1823	Presbyterian
Thomas Todd, Ky.	1807-1826	18	Va.	1765	1826	Presbyterian
Gabriel Duval, Md.	1811-1835	23	Md.	1752	1844	French Protestant
Joseph Story, Mass.	1812-1845	33	Mass.	1779	1845	Unitarian
Smith Thompson, N.Y.	1823-1843	20	N.Y.	1768	1843	Presbyterian
Robert Trimble, Ky.	1826-1828	2	Va.	1777	1828	Protestant
John McLean, Ohio	1830-1861	31	N.J.	1785	1861	Methodist-Epis.
Henry Baldwin, Pa.	1830-1844	14	Conn.	1780	1844	Trinity Church
James M. Wayne, Ga.	1835-1867	32	Ga.	1790	1867	Protestant
Philip P. Barbour, Va.	1836-1841	4	Va.	1783	1841	Episcopal
John Catron, Tenn.	1837-1865	28	Pa.	1786	1865	Presbyterian
John McKinley, Ala.	1837-1852	14	Va.	1780	1852	Protestant
Peter V. Daniel, Va.	1841-1860	18	Va.	1784	1860	Episcopal
Samuel Nelson, N.Y.	1845-1872	27	N.Y.	1792	1873	Protestant
Levi Woodbury, N.H.	1845-1851	5	N.H.	1789	1851	Protestant
Robert C. Grier, Pa.	1846-1870	23	Pa.	1794	1870	Presbyterian
Benjamin R. Curtis, Mass.	1851-1857	5	Mass.	1809	1874	(2)
John A. Campbell, Ala.	1853-1861	8	Ga.	1811	1889	Episcopal
Nathan Clifford, Maine	1858-1881	23	N.H.	1803	1881	(1)
Noah H. Swayne, Ohio	1862-1881	18	Va.	1804	1884	Quaker
Samuel F. Miller, Iowa	1862-1890	28	Ky.	1816	1890	Unitarian
David Davis, Ill.	1862-1877	14	Md.	1815	1886	(4)
Stephen J. Field, Calif.	1863-1897	34	Conn.	1816	1899	Episcopal
William Strong, Pa.	1870-1880	10	Conn.	1808	1895	Presbyterian
Joseph P. Bradley, N.J.	1870-1892	21	N.Y.	1813	1892	Presbyterian
Ward Hunt, N.Y.	1872-1882	9	N.Y.	1810	1886	Episcopal
John M. Harlan, Ky.	1877-1911	33	Ky.	1833	1911	Presbyterian
William B. Woods, Ga.	1880-1887	6	Ohio	1824	1887	Protestant
Stanley Matthews, Ohio	1881-1889	7	Ohio	1824	1889	Presbyterian
Horace Gray, Mass.	1882-1902	20	Mass.	1828	1902	(3)
Samuel Blatchford, N.Y.	1882-1893	11	N.Y.	1820	1893	Presbyterian
Lucius Q. C. Lamar, Miss.	1888-1893	5	Ga.	1825	1893	Methodist
David J. Brewer, Kan.	1889-1910	20	Asia Minor	1837	1910	Protestant
Henry B. Brown, Mich.	1890-1906	15	Mass.	1836	1913	Protestant
George Shiras, Jr., Pa.	1892-1903	10	Pa.	1832	1924	Presbyterian
Howell E. Jackson, Tenn.	1893-1895	2	Tenn.	1832	1895	Baptist
Edward D. White, La.	1894-1910	16	La.	1845	1921	Roman Catholic
Rufus W. Peckham, N.Y.	1895-1909	13	N.Y.	1838	1909	Episcopal
Joseph McKenna, Calif.	1898-1925	26	Pa.	1843	1926	Roman Catholic

Name; apptd. from	Service		Birth			
	Term	Yrs	Place	Date	Died	Religion
Oliver W. Holmes, Mass.	1902-1932	29	Mass.	1841	1935	Unitarian
William R. Day, Ohio	1903-1922	19	Ohio	1849	1923	Protestant
William H. Moody, Mass.	1906-1910	3	Mass.	1853	1917	Episcopal
Horace H. Lurton, Tenn.	1909-1914	4	Ky.	1844	1914	Episcopal
Charles E. Hughes, N.Y.	1910-1916	5	N.Y.	1862	1948	Baptist
Willis Van Devanter, Wyo.	1910-1937	26	Ind.	1859	1941	Episcopal
Joseph R. Lamar, Ga.	1910-1916	4	Ga.	1857	1916	Ch. of Disciples
Mahlon Pitney, N.J.	1912-1922	10	N.J.	1858	1924	Presbyterian
James C. McReynolds, Tenn.	1914-1941	26	Ky.	1862	1946	Disciples of Christ
Louis D. Brandeis, Mass.	1916-1939	22	Ky.	1856	1941	Jewish
John H. Clarke, Ohio	1916-1922	5	Ohio	1857	1945	Protestant
George Sutherland, Utah	1922-1938	15	England	1862	1942	Episcopal
Pierce Butler, Minn.	1923-1939	16	Minn.	1866	1939	Roman Catholic
Edward T. Sanford, Tenn.	1923-1930	7	Tenn.	1865	1930	Episcopal
Harlan F. Stone, N.Y.	1925-1941	16	N.H.	1872	1946	Episcopal
Owen J. Roberts, Pa.	1930-1945	15	Pa.	1875	1955	Episcopal
Benjamin N. Cardozo, N.Y.	1932-1938	6	N.Y.	1870	1938	Jewish
Hugo L. Black, Ala.	1937-1971	34	Ala.	1886	1971	Baptist
Stanley F. Reed, Ky.	1938-1957	19	Ky.	1884	1980	Protestant
Felix Frankfurter, Mass.	1939-1962	23	Austria	1882	1965	Jewish
William O. Douglas, Conn.	1939-1975	36	Minn.	1898	1980	Presbyterian
Frank Murphy, Mich.	1940-1949	9	Mich.	1890	1949	Roman Catholic
James F. Byrnes, S.C.	1941-1942	1	S.C.	1879	1972	Episcopal
Robert H. Jackson, Pa.	1941-1954	13	N.Y.	1892	1954	Episcopal
Wiley B. Rutledge, Iowa	1943-1949	6	Ky.	1894	1949	Unitarian
Harold H. Burton, Ohio	1945-1958	13	Mass.	1888	1964	Unitarian
Tom C. Clark, Tex.	1949-1967	17	Tex.	1899	1977	Presbyterian
Sherman Minton, Ind.	1949-1956	7	Ind.	1890	1965	Roman Catholic
John M. Harlan, N.Y.	1955-1971	16	Ill.	1899	1971	Presbyterian
William J. Brennan, Jr., N.J.	1956-	—	N.J.	1906	—	Roman Catholic
Charles E. Whittaker, Mo.	1957-1962	5	Kan.	1901	1973	Methodist
Potter Stewart, Ohio	1958-1981	23	Mich.	1915	1985	Episcopal
Byron R. White, Colo.	1962-	—	Colo.	1917	—	Episcopal
Arthur J. Goldberg, Ill.	1962-1965	2	Ill.	1908	—	Jewish
Abe Fortas, Tenn.	1965-1969	3	Tenn.	1910	1982	Jewish
Thurgood Marshall, N.Y.	1967-	—	Md.	1908	—	Episcopalian
Harry A. Blackmun, Minn.	1970-	—	Ill.	1908	—	Methodist
Lewis F. Powell, Jr., Va.	1972-1987	15	Va.	1907	—	Presbyterian
William H. Rehnquist, Ariz.	1972-1986	14	Wis.	1924	—	Lutheran
John Paul Stevens, Ill.	1975-	—	Ill.	1920	—	Protestant
Sandra Day O'Connor, Ariz.	1981-	—	Tex.	1930	—	Episcopal
Antonin Scalia, D.C.	1986-	—	N.J.	1936	—	Roman Catholic
Anthony M. Kennedy, Calif.	1988-	—	Calif.	1936	—	n.a.

1. Congregational; later Unitarian. 2. Unitarian; then Episcopal. 3. Unitarian or Congregational. 4. Not a member of any church.
NOTE: n.a.=not available.

Impeachments of Federal Officials

Source: Congressional Directory

The procedure for the impeachment of Federal officials is detailed in Article I, Section 3, of the Constitution. See Index.

The Senate has sat as a court of impeachment in the following cases:

William Blount, Senator from Tennessee; charges dismissed for want of jurisdiction, January 14, 1799.

John Pickering, Judge of the U.S. District Court for New Hampshire; removed from office March 12, 1804.

Samuel Chase, Associate Justice of the Supreme Court; acquitted March 1, 1805.

James H. Peck, Judge of the U.S. District Court for Missouri; acquitted Jan. 31, 1831.

West H. Humphreys, Judge of the U.S. District Court for the middle, eastern, and western districts of Tennessee; removed from office June 26, 1862.

Andrew Johnson, President of the United States; acquitted May 26, 1868.

William W. Belknap, Secretary of War; acquitted Aug. 1, 1876.

Charles Swayne, Judge of the U.S. District Court for the northern district of Florida; acquitted Feb. 27, 1905.

Robert W. Archbald, Associate Judge, U.S. Commerce Court; removed Jan. 13, 1913.

George W. English, Judge of the U.S. District Court for eastern district of Illinois; resigned Nov. 4, 1926; proceedings dismissed.

Harold Louderback, Judge of the U.S. District Court for the northern district of California; acquitted May 24, 1933.

Halsted L. Ritter, Judge of the U.S. District Court for the southern district of Florida; removed from office April 17, 1936.

Harry E. Claiborne, Judge of the U.S. District Court for the district of Nevada; removed from office October 9, 1986.

Executive Departments and Agencies

Source: Congressional Directory, 1989–1990
Unless otherwise indicated, addresses shown are in Washington, D.C.

CENTRAL INTELLIGENCE AGENCY (CIA)
Washington, D.C. (20505).
Established: 1947.
Director: William H. Webster.
COUNCIL OF ECONOMIC ADVISERS (CEA)
Executive Office Bldg. (20500).
Members: 3.
Established: Feb. 20, 1946.
Chairman: Michael J. Boskin
COUNCIL ON ENVIRONMENTAL QUALITY
722 Jackson Pl., N.W. (20006).
Members: 3.
Established: 1969.
Chairman: A. Alan Hill.
NATIONAL SECURITY COUNCIL (NSC)
Old Executive Office Bldg. (20506).
Members: 4.
Established: July 26, 1947.
Chairman: The President.
Other members: Vice President; Secretary of State; Secretary of Defense.
OFFICE OF ADMINISTRATION
Old Executive Office Bldg. (20500).
Established: Dec. 12, 1977.
Director: Paul Bateman
OFFICE OF MANAGEMENT AND BUDGET
Executive Office Bldg. (20503).
Established: July 1, 1970.
Director: Richard Darman
OFFICE OF SCIENCE AND TECHNOLOGY POLICY
Old Executive Office Building (20506).
Established: May 11, 1976
Director: William R. Graham
OFFICE OF THE UNITED STATES TRADE REPRE-SENTATIVE
600 17th St., N.W. (20506).
Established: Jan. 15, 1963.
Trade Representative: Carla A. Hills
OFFICE OF POLICY DEVELOPMENT
1600 Pennsylvania Ave., N.W. (20500).
Established: Jan. 21, 1981.
Director: Bill Roper
OFFICE OF NATIONAL DRUG CONTROL POLICY
Suite 1011, 1825 Connecticut Ave., N.W. (20009)
Established: March 13, 1989
Director: William J. Bennett

Executive Departments

DEPARTMENT OF STATE
2201 C St., N.W. (20520).
Established: 1781 as Department of Foreign Affairs; reconstituted, 1789, following adoption of Constitution; name changed to Department of State Sept. 15, 1789.
Secretary: James A. Baker III
Deputy Secretary: Lawrence S. Eagleburger
Chief Delegate to U.N.: Vernon A. Walters.
DEPARTMENT OF THE TREASURY
15th St. & Pennsylvania Ave., N.W. (20220).
Established: Sept. 2, 1789.
Secretary: Nicholas F. Brady
Deputy Secretary: M. Peter McPherson
Treasurer of the U.S.: Catalina Vasquez Villalpando
Comptroller of the Currency: Robert L. Clarke.
DEPARTMENT OF DEFENSE
The Pentagon (20301).
Established: July 26, 1947, as National Depart-ment Establishment; name changed to Department of Defense on Aug. 10, 1949. Subordinate to Secretary of Defense are Secretaries of Army, Navy, Air Force.
Secretary: Richard Cheney
Deputy Secretary: Donald J. Atwood
Secretary of Army: Richard L. Armitage
Secretary of Navy: H. Lawrence Garrett III
Secretary of Air Force: Donald B. Rice
Commandant of Marine Corps: Gen. Alfred M. Gray.
Joint Chiefs of Staff: Adm. William J. Crowe, Jr. Chairman; Adm. Carlisle A. H. Trost, Navy; Gen. Larry D. Welch, Air Force: Gen. Carl E. Vuono, Army; Gen. Alfred M. Gray, Marine Corps.
DEPARTMENT OF JUSTICE
Constitution Ave. between 9th & 10th Sts., N.W. (20530).
Established: Office of Attorney General was created Sept. 24, 1789. Although he was one of original Cabinet members, he was not executive department head until June 22, 1870, when Department of Justice was established.
Attorney General: Richard L. Thornburgh
Deputy Attorney General: Harold G. Christensen
Solicitor General: Charles Fried.
Director of FBI: William Steele Sessions.
DEPARTMENT OF THE INTERIOR
C St. between 18th & 19th Sts., N.W. (20240).
Established: March 3, 1849.
Secretary: Manuel Lujan, Jr.
Under Secretary: Frank A. Bracken
DEPARTMENT OF AGRICULTURE
Independence Ave. between 12th & 14th Sts., S.W. (20250).
Established: May 15, 1862. Administered by Commissioner of Agriculture until 1889, when it was made executive department.
Secretary: Clayton Yeutter
Deputy Secretary: Jack C. Parnell
DEPARTMENT OF COMMERCE
14th St. between Constitution Ave. & E St., N.W. (20230).
Established: Department of Commerce and Labor was created Feb. 14, 1903. On March 4, 1913, all labor activities were transferred out of Department of Commerce and Labor and it was renamed Department of Commerce.
Secretary: Robert A. Mosbacher
Deputy Secretary: Thomas J. Murrin
DEPARTMENT OF LABOR
200 Constitution Ave., N.W. (20210).
Established: Bureau of Labor was created in 1884 under Department of the Interior; later became independent department without executive rank. Returned to bureau status in Department of Commerce and Labor, but on March 4, 1913, became independent executive department under its present name.
Secretary: Elizabeth H. Dole
Deputy Secretary: Dennis E. Whitfield.
DEPARTMENT OF HEALTH AND HUMAN SERVICES[1]
200 Independence Ave., S.W. (20201).
Established: April 11, 1953, replacing Federal Security Agency created in 1939.
Secretary: Louis W. Sullivan

Surgeon General: Vacant

1. Originally Department of Health, Education and Welfare. Name changed in May 1980 when Department of Education was activated.

DEPARTMENT OF HOUSING AND URBAN DEVELOPMENT
451 7th St., S.W. (20410).
   Established: 1965, replacing Housing and Home Finance Agency created in 1947.
   Secretary: Jack Kemp
   Under Secretary: Alfred A. DelliBovi

DEPARTMENT OF TRANSPORTATION
400 7th St., S.W. (20590).
   Established: Oct. 15, 1966, as result of Department of Transportation Act, which became effective April 1, 1967.
   Secretary: Samuel K. Skinner
   Deputy Secretary: Elaine L. Chao

DEPARTMENT OF ENERGY
1000 Independence Ave., S.W. (20585).
   Established: Aug. 1977.
   Secretary: James D. Watkins
   Deputy Secretary: W. Henson Moore

DEPARTMENT OF EDUCATION
400 Maryland Avenue, S.W. (20202).
   Established: Oct. 17, 1979.
   Secretary: Lauro F. Cavazos
   Under Secretary: John T. Sanders

DEPARTMENT OF VETERANS' AFFAIRS
810 Vermont Avenue, N.W. (20420).
   Established: March 15, 1989, replacing Veterans Administration created in 1930.
   Secretary: Edward J. Derwinski
   Deputy Secretary: Anthony J. Principi

Major Independent Agencies

ACTION
806 Connecticut Ave., N.W. (20525).
   Established: July 1, 1971.
   Director: Donna M. Alvarado.

CONSUMER PRODUCT SAFETY COMMISSION
5401 Westbard Ave., Bethesda, Md. (20207).
   Members: 5.
   Established: Oct. 27, 1972.
   Chairman: Anne M. Graham (acting)

ENVIRONMENTAL PROTECTION AGENCY (EPA)
401 M St., S.W. (20460).
   Established: Dec. 2, 1970.
   Administrator: Lee M. Thomas.

EQUAL EMPLOYMENT OPPORTUNITY COMMISSION (EEOC)
2401 E St., N.W. (20506).
   Members: 5.
   Established: July 2, 1965.
   Chairman: Clarence Thomas.

FARM CREDIT ADMINISTRATION (FCA)
1501 Farm Credit Dr., McLean, Va. (22102).
   Members: 13.
   Established: July 17, 1916.
   Chairman of Federal Farm Credit Board: Marvin R. Duncan (acting)

FEDERAL COMMUNICATIONS COMMISSION (FCC)
1919 M St., N.W. (20554).
   Members: 7.
   Established: 1934.
   Chairman: Dennis R. Patrick.

FEDERAL DEPOSIT INSURANCE CORPORATION (FDIC)
550 17th St., N.W. (20429).
   Members: 3.
   Established: June 16, 1933.
   Chairman: L. William Seidman.

FEDERAL ELECTION COMMISSION (FEC)
999 E St., N.W. (20463).
   Members: 6.
   Established: 1974.
   Chairman: Danny L. McDonald

FEDERAL MARITIME COMMISSION
1100 L St., N.W. (20573).
   Members: 5.
   Established: Aug. 12, 1961.
   Chairman: James J. Carey (acting)

FEDERAL MEDIATION AND CONCILIATION SERVICE (FMCS)
2100 K St., N.W. (20427).
   Established: 1947.
   Director: Kay McMurray.

FEDERAL RESERVE SYSTEM (FRS), BOARD OF GOVERNORS OF
20th St. & Constitution Ave., N.W. (20551).
   Members: 7.
   Established: Dec. 23, 1913.
   Chairman: Alan Greenspan.

FEDERAL TRADE COMMISSION (FTC)
Pennsylvania Ave. at 6th St., N.W. (20580).
   Members: 5.
   Established: Sept. 26, 1914.
   Chairman: Daniel Oliver

GENERAL SERVICES ADMINISTRATION (GSA)
18th and F Sts., N.W. (20405).
   Established: July 1, 1949.
   Administrator: Richard G. Austin (acting)

INTERSTATE COMMERCE COMMISSION (ICC)
12th St. & Constitution Ave., N.W. (20423).
   Members: 7.
   Established: Feb. 4, 1887.
   Chairman: Heather J. Gradison.

NATIONAL AERONAUTICS AND SPACE ADMINISTRATION (NASA)
400 Maryland Ave., S.W. (20546).
   Established: 1958.
   Administrator: Rear Adm. Richard H. Truly

NATIONAL FOUNDATION ON THE ARTS AND THE HUMANITIES
1100 Pennsylvania Ave., N.W., (20506).
   Established: 1965.
   Chairmen: National Endowment for the Arts, Hugh Southern (acting); National Endowment for the Humanities, Lynne V. Cheney

NATIONAL LABOR RELATIONS BOARD (NLRB)
1717 Pennsylvania Ave., N.W. (20570).
   Members: 5.
   Established: July 5, 1935.
   Chairman: James M. Stephens

NATIONAL MEDIATION BOARD
1425 K St., N.W. (20572).
   Members: 3
   Established: June 21, 1934.
   Chairman: Walter C. Wallace

NATIONAL SCIENCE FOUNDATION (NSF)
1800 G St., N.W. (20550).
   Established: 1950.
   Director: Erich Bloch

NATIONAL TRANSPORTATION SAFETY BOARD
800 Independence Ave., S.W. (20594).
   Members: 5
   Established: April 1, 1975.
   Chairman: James L. Kolstad (acting)

NUCLEAR REGULATORY COMMISSION (NRC)
1717 H St., N.W. (20555).
   Members: 5.
   Established: Jan. 19, 1975.
   Chairman: Lando W. Zech, Jr.

OFFICE OF PERSONNEL MANAGEMENT (OPM)
1900 E St., N.W. (20415).
  Members: 3
  Established: Jan. 1, 1979.
  Director: Constance B. Newman

SECURITIES AND EXCHANGE COMMISSION (SEC)
450 5th St., N.W. (20549).
  Members: 5.
  Established: July 2, 1934
  Chairman: David S. Ruder.

SELECTIVE SERVICE SYSTEM (SSS)
National Headquarters (20435).
  Established: Sept. 16, 1940.
  Director: Gen. Samuel K. Lessey, Jr.

SMALL BUSINESS ADMINISTRATION (SBA)
1441 L St., N.W. (20416).
  Established: July 30, 1953.
  Administrator: Susan S. Engeleiter

TENNESSEE VALLEY AUTHORITY (TVA)
400 West Summit Hill Drive, Knoxville, Tenn. (37902).
Washington office: Capitol Hill Office Bldg., 412 First St., S.E. (20444).
  Members of Board of Directors: 3.
  Established: May 18, 1933.
  Chairman: Marvin Runyon

U.S. AGENCY FOR INTERNATIONAL DEVELOPMENT
320 21st St., N.W. (20523).
  Established: Oct. 1, 1979.
  Administrator: Alan Woods

U.S. ARMS CONTROL AND DISARMAMENT AGENCY
320 21st St., N.W., (20451).
  Established: Sept. 26, 1961.
  Director: Ronald F. Lehman II

U.S. COMMISSION ON CIVIL RIGHTS
1121 Vermont Avenue, N.W. (20425).
  Members: 8.
  Established: 1957.
  Chairman: William B. Allen

U.S. INFORMATION AGENCY
301 Fourth St., S.W. (20547).
  Established: April 1, 1978.
  Director: Bruce Gelb

U.S. INTERNATIONAL TRADE COMMISSION
701 E St., N.W. (20436).
  Members: 6.
  Established: Sept. 8, 1916.
  Chairman: Anne E. Brunsdale (Acting)

U.S. POSTAL SERVICE
475 L'Enfant Plaza West, S.W. (20260).
  Postmaster General: Anthony M. Frank
  Deputy Postmaster General: Michael S. Coughlin.
  Established: Office of Postmaster General and temporary post office system created in 1789. Act of Feb. 20, 1792, made detailed provisions for Post Office Department. In 1970 became independent agency headed by 11-member board of governors.

Other Independent Agencies

Administrative Conference of the United States—2120 L St., N.W. (20037).

American Battle Monuments Commission—5127 Pulaski Bldg. 20 Massachusetts Ave. (20314).

Appalachian Regional Commission—1666 Connecticut Ave., N.W. (20235).

Board for International Broadcasting—Suite 400, 1201 Connecticut Ave., N.W. (20036).

Commission of Fine Arts—708 Jackson Place, N.W. (20006).

Commodity Futures Trading Commission—2033 K St., N.W. (20581).

Export-Import Bank of the United States—811 Vermont Ave., N.W. (20571).

Federal Emergency Management Agency—500 C St., S.W. (20472).

Federal Home Loan Bank Board—1700 G St., N.W. (20552).

Federal Labor Relations Authority—500 C St., S.W. (20424).

Inter-American Foundation—1515 Wilson Blvd., Arlington, Va. (22209).

Merit Systems Protection Board—1120 Vermont Ave., N.W. (20419).

National Commission on Libraries and Information Science—7th & D Sts., S.W. (20024).

National Credit Union Administration—1776 G St., N.W. (20456).

Occupational Safety and Health Review Commission—1825 K St., N.W. (20006).

Panama Canal Commission—2000 L St., N.W. (20036).

Peace Corps—806 Connecticut Ave., N.W. (20526).

Pension Benefit Guaranty Corporation—2020 K St., N.W. (20006).

Postal Rate Commission—1333 H St., N.W. (20268).

President's Committee on Employment of the Handicapped—1111 20th St., N.W. (20036).

President's Council on Physical Fitness and Sports—450 5th St., S.W. (20001).

Railroad Retirement Board (RRB)—844 Rush St., Chicago, Ill. (60611); Washington Liaison Office: Suite 558, 2000 L St. (20036).

U.S. Parole Commission—5550 Friendship Blvd., Chevy Chase, Md. (20815).

Legislative Department

Architect of the Capitol—U.S. Capitol Building (20515)

General Accounting Office (GAO)—441 G St., N.W. (20548)

Government Printing Office (GPO)—North Capitol & H Sts., N.W. (20401)

Library of Congress—10 First St. S.E. (20540)

Office of Technology Assessment—600 Pennsylvania Ave., S.E. (20510)

United States Botanic Garden—Office of Director, 245 First St., S.W. (20024)

Quasi-Official Agencies

American National Red Cross—430 17th St., N.W. (20006).

Legal Services Corporation—400 Virginia Ave. S.W. (20024).

National Academy of Sciences, National Academy of Engineering, National Research Council, Institute of Medicine—2101 Constitution Ave., N.W. (20418).

National Railroad Passenger Corporation (Amtrak)—400 N. Capitol St., N.W. (20001).

Smithsonian Institution—1000 Jefferson Dr., S.W. (20560).

U.S. Railway Association—955 L'Enfant Plaza North, S.W. (20595).

Biographies of the Presidents

GEORGE WASHINGTON was born on Feb. 22, 1732 (Feb. 11, 1731/2, old style) in Westmoreland County, Va. While in his teens, he trained as a surveyor, and at the age of 20 he was appointed adjutant in the Virginia militia. For the next three years, he fought in the wars against the French and Indians, serving as Gen. Edward Braddock's aide in the disastrous campaign against Fort Duquesne. In 1759, he resigned from the militia, married Martha Dandridge Custis, a widow, and settled down as a gentleman farmer at Mount Vernon, Va.

As a militiaman, Washington had been exposed to the arrogance of the British officers, and his experience as a planter with British commercial restrictions increased his anti-British sentiment. He opposed the Stamp Act of 1765 and after 1770 became increasingly prominent in organizing resistance. A delegate to the Continental Congress, Washington was selected as commander in chief of the Continental Army and took command at Cambridge, Mass., on July 3, 1775.

Inadequately supported and sometimes covertly sabotaged by the Congress, in charge of troops who were inexperienced, badly equipped, and impatient of discipline, Washington conducted the war on the policy of avoiding major engagements with the British and wearing them down by harrassing tactics. His able generalship, along with the French alliance and the growing weariness within Britain, brought the war to a conclusion with the surrender of Cornwallis at Yorktown, Va., on Oct. 19, 1781.

The chaotic years under the Articles of Confederation led Washington to return to public life in the hope of promoting the formation of a strong central government. He presided over the Constitutional Convention and yielded to the universal demand that he serve as first President. He was inaugurated on April 30, 1789, in New York, the first national capital. In office, he sought to unite the nation and establish the authority of the new government at home and abroad. Greatly distressed by the emergence of the Hamilton-Jefferson rivalry, Washington worked to maintain neutrality but actually sympathized more with Hamilton. Following his unanimous re-election in 1792, his second term was dominated by the Federalists. His Farewell Address on Sept. 17, 1796 (published but never delivered) rebuked party spirit and warned against "permanent alliances" with foreign powers.

He died at Mount Vernon on Dec. 14, 1799.

JOHN ADAMS was born on Oct. 30 (Oct. 19, old style), 1735, at Braintree (now Quincy), Mass. A Harvard graduate, he considered teaching and the ministry but finally turned to law and was admitted to the bar in 1758. Six years later, he married Abigail Smith. He opposed the Stamp Act, served as lawyer for patriots indicted by the British, and by the time of the Continental Congresses, was in the vanguard of the movement for independence. In 1778, he went to France as commissioner. Subsequently he helped negotiate the peace treaty with Britain, and in 1785 became envoy to London. Resigning in 1788, he was elected Vice President under Washington and was re-elected in 1792.

Though a Federalist, Adams did not get along with Hamilton, who sought to prevent his election to the presidency in 1796 and thereafter intrigued against his administration. In 1798, Adam's independent policy averted a war with France but completed the break with Hamilton and the right-wing Federalists; at the same time, the enactment of the Alien and Sedition Acts, directed against foreigners and against critics of the government, exasperated the Jeffersonian opposition. The split between Adams and Hamilton resulted in Jefferson's becoming the next President. Adams retired to his home in Quincy. He and Jefferson died on the same day, July 4, 1826, the 50th anniversary of the signing of the Declaration of Independence.

His *Defence of the Constitutions of Government of the United States* (1787) contains original and striking, if conservative, political ideas.

THOMAS JEFFERSON was born on April 13 (April 2, old style), 1743, at Shadwell in Goochland (now Albemarle) County, Va. A William and Mary graduate, he studied law, but from the start showed an interest in science and philosophy. His literary skill and political clarity brought him to the forefront of the revolutionary movement in Virginia. As delegate to the Continental Congress, he drafted the Declaration of Independence. In 1776, he entered the Virginia House of Delegates and initiated a comprehensive reform program for the abolition of feudal survivals in land tenure and the separation of church and state.

In 1779, he became governor, but constitutional limitations on his power, combined with his own lack of executive energy, caused an unsatisfactory administration, culminating in Jefferson's virtual abdication when the British invaded Virginia in 1781. He retired to his beautiful home at Monticello, Va., to his family. His wife, Martha Wayles Skelton, whom he married in 1772, died in 1782.

Jefferson's *Notes on Virginia* (1784–85) illustrate his many-faceted interests, his limitless intellectual curiosity, his deep faith in agrarian democracy. Sent to Congress in 1783, he helped lay down the decimal system and drafted basic reports on the organization of the western lands. In 1785 he was appointed minister to France, where the Anglo-Saxon liberalism he had drawn from John Locke, the British philosopher, was stimulated by contact with the thought that would soon ferment in the French Revolution. In 1789, Washington appointed him Secretary of State. While favoring the Constitution and a strengthened central government, Jefferson came to believe that Hamilton contemplated the establishment of a monarchy. Growing differences resulted in Jefferson's resignation on Dec. 31, 1793.

Elected vice president in 1796, Jefferson continued to serve as spiritual leader of the opposition to Federalism, particularly to the repressive Alien and Sedition Acts. He was elected President in 1801 by the House of Representatives as a result of Hamilton's decision to throw the Federalist votes to him rather than to Aaron Burr, who had tied him in electoral votes. He was the first President to be inaugurated in Washington, which he had helped to design.

The purchase of Louisiana from France in 1803, though in violation of Jefferson's earlier constitutional scruples, was the most notable act of his administration. Re-elected in 1804, with the Federalist Charles C. Pinckney opposing him, Jefferson tried desperately to keep the United States out of the Napoleonic Wars in Europe, employing to this end the unpopular embargo policy.

After his retirement to Monticello in 1809, he developed his interest in education, founding the University of Virginia and watching its development with never-flagging interest. He died at Monticello on July 4, 1826. Jefferson had an enormous variety of interests and skills, ranging from education and science to architecture and music.

JAMES MADISON was born in Port Conway, Va., on March 16, 1751 (March 5, 1750/1, old style). A Princeton graduate, he joined the struggle for independence on his return to Virginia in 1771. In the 1770s and 1780s he was active in state politics, where he championed the Jefferson reform program, and in the Continental Congress. Madison was influential in the Constitutional Convention as leader of the group favoring a strong central government and as recorder of the debates; and he subsequently wrote, in collaboration with Alexander Hamilton and John Jay, the *Federalist* papers to aid the campaign for the adoption of the Constitution.

Serving in the new Congress, Madison soon emerged as the leader in the House of the men who opposed Hamilton's financial program and his pro-British leanings in foreign policy. Retiring from Congress in 1797, he continued to be active in Virginia and drafted the Virginia Resolution protesting the Alien and Sedition Acts. His intimacy with Jefferson made him the natural choice for Secretary of State in 1801.

In 1809, Madison succeeded Jefferson as President, defeating Charles C. Pinckney. His attractive wife, Dolley Payne Todd, whom he married in 1794, brought a new social sparkle to the executive mansion. In the meantime, increasing tension with Britain culminated in the War of 1812—a war for which the United States was unprepared and for which Madison lacked the executive talent to clear out incompetence and mobilize the nation's energies. Madison was re-elected in 1812, running against the Federalist De Witt Clinton. In 1814, the British actually captured Washington and forced Madison to flee to Virginia.

Madison's domestic program capitulated to the Hamiltonian policies that he had resisted 20 years before and he now signed bills to establish a United States Bank and a higher tariff.

After his presidency, he remained in retirement in Virginia until his death on June 28, 1836.

JAMES MONROE was born on April 28, 1758, in Westmoreland County, Va. A William and Mary graduate, he served in the army during the first years of the Revolution and was wounded at Trenton. He then entered Virginia politics and later national politics under the sponsorship of Jefferson. In 1786, he married Elizabeth (Eliza) Kortright.

Fearing centralization, Monroe opposed the adoption of the Constitution and, as senator from Virginia, was highly critical of the Hamiltonian program. In 1794, he was appointed minister to France, where his ardent sympathies with the Revolution exceeded the wishes of the State Department. His troubled diplomatic career ended with his recall in 1796. From 1799 to 1802, he was governor of Virginia. In 1803, Jefferson sent him to France to help negotiate the Louisiana Purchase and for the next few years he was active in various negotiations on the Continent.

In 1808, Monroe flirted with the radical wing of the Republican Party, which opposed Madison's candidacy; but the presidential boom came to naught and, after a brief term as governor of Virginia in 1811, Monroe accepted Madison's offer to become Secretary of State. During the War of 1812, he vainly sought a field command and instead served as Secretary of War from September 1814 to March 1815.

Elected President in 1816 over the Federalist Rufus King, and re-elected without opposition in 1820, Monroe, the last of the Virginia dynasty, pursued the course of systematic tranquilization that won for his administrations the name "the era of good feeling." He continued Madison's surrender to the Hamiltonian domestic program, signed the Missouri Compromise, acquired Florida, and with the able assistance of his Secretary of State, John Quincy Adams, promulgated the Monroe Doctrine in 1823, declaring against foreign colonization or intervention in the Americas. He died in New York City on July 4, 1831, the third president to die on the anniversary of Independence.

JOHN QUINCY ADAMS was born on July 11, 1767, at Braintree (now Quincy), Mass., the son of John Adams, the second President. He spent his early years in Europe with his father, graduated from Harvard, and entered law practice. His anti-Jeffersonian newspaper articles won him political attention. In 1794, he became minister to the Netherlands, the first of several diplomatic posts that occupied him until his return to Boston in 1801. In 1797, he married Louisa Catherine Johnson.

In 1803, Adams was elected to the Senate, nominally as a Federalist, but his repeated displays of independence on such issues as the Louisiana Purchase and the embargo caused his party to demand his resignation and ostracize him socially. In 1809, Madison rewarded him for his support of Jefferson by appointing him minister to St. Petersburg. He helped negotiate the Treaty of Ghent in 1814, and in 1815 became minister to London. In 1817 Monroe appointed him Secretary of State where he served with great distinction, gaining Florida from Spain without hostilities and playing an equal part with Monroe in formulating the Monroe Doctrine.

When no presidential candidate received a majority of electoral votes in 1824, Adams, with the support of Henry Clay, was elected by the House in 1825 over Andrew Jackson, who had the original plurality. Adams had ambitious plans of government activity to foster internal improvements and promote the arts and sciences, but congressional obstructionism, combined with his own unwillingness or inability to play the role of a politician, resulted in little being accomplished. After being defeated for re-election by Jackson in 1828, he successfully ran for the House of Representatives in 1830. There though nominally a Whig, he pursued as ever an independent course. He led the fight to force Congress to receive antislavery petitions and fathered the Smithsonian Institution.

Stricken on the floor of the House, he died on Feb. 23, 1848. His long and detailed *Diary* gives a unique picture of the personalities and politics of the times.

ANDREW JACKSON was born on March 15, 1767, in what is now generally agreed to be Waxhaw, S.C. After a turbulent boyhood as an orphan and a British prisoner, he moved west to Tennessee, where he soon qualified for law practice but found time for such frontier pleasures as horse racing, cock-fighting, and dueling. His marriage to Rachel Donelson Robards in 1791 was complicated by subsequent legal uncertainties about the status of her divorce. During the 1790s, Jackson served in the Tennessee Constitutional Convention, the United States House of Representatives and Senate, and on the Tennessee Supreme Court.

After some years as a country gentleman, living at the Hermitage near Nashville, Jackson in 1812 was given command of Tennessee troops sent against the Creeks. He defeated the Indians at Horseshoe Bend in 1814; subsequently he became a major general and won the Battle of New Orleans over veteran British troops, though after the treaty of peace had been signed at Ghent. In 1818, Jackson invaded Florida, captured Pensacola, and hanged two Englishmen named Arbuthnot and Ambrister, creating an international incident. A presidential boom began for him in 1821, and to foster it, he returned to the Senate (1823–25). Though he won a plurality of electoral votes in 1824, he lost in the House when Clay threw his strength to Adams. Four years later, he easily defeated Adams.

As President, Jackson greatly expanded the power and prestige of the presidential office and carried through an unprecedented program of domestic reform, vetoing the bill to extend the United States Bank, moving toward a hard-money currency policy, and checking the program of federal internal improvements. He also vindicated federal authority against South Carolina with its doctrine of nullification and against France on the question of debts. The support given his policies by the workingmen of the East as well as by the farmers of the East, West, and South resulted in his triumphant re-election in 1832 over Clay.

After watching the inauguration of his hand-picked successor, Martin Van Buren, Jackson retired to the Hermitage, where he maintained a lively interest in national affairs until his death on June 8, 1845.

MARTIN VAN BUREN was born on Dec. 5, 1782, at Kinderhook, N.Y. After graduating from the village school, he became a law clerk, entered practice in 1803, and soon became active in state politics as state senator and attorney general. In 1820, he was elected to the United States Senate. He threw the support of his efficient political organization, known as the Albany Regency, to William H. Crawford in 1824 and to Jackson in 1828. After leading the opposition to Adams's administration in the Senate, he served briefly as governor of New York (1828–29) and resigned to become Jackson's Secretary of State. He was soon on close personal terms with Jackson and played an important part in the Jacksonian program.

In 1832, Van Buren became vice president; in 1836, President. The Panic of 1837 overshadowed his term. He attributed it to the overexpansion of the credit and favored the establishment of an independent treasury as repository for the federal funds. In 1840, he established a 10-hour day on public works. Defeated by Harrison in 1840, he was the leading contender for the Democratic nomination in 1844 until he publicly opposed immediate annexation of Texas, and was subsequently beaten by the Southern delegations at the Baltimore convention. This incident increased his growing misgivings about the slave power.

After working behind the scenes among the antislavery Democrats, Van Buren joined in the movement that led to the Free-Soil Party and became its candidate for President in 1848. He subsequently returned to the Democratic Party while continuing to object to its pro-Southern policy. He died in Kinderhook on July 24, 1862. His *Autobiography* throws valuable sidelights on the political history of the times.

His wife, Hannah Hoes, whom he married in 1807, died in 1819.

WILLIAM HENRY HARRISON was born in Charles City County, Va., on Feb. 9, 1773. Joining the army in 1791, he was active in Indian fighting in the Northwest, became secretary of the Northwest Territory in 1798 and governor of Indiana in 1800. He married Anna Symmes in 1795. Growing discontent over white encroachments on Indian lands led to the formation of an Indian alliance under Tecumseh to resist further aggressions. In 1811, Harrison won a nominal victory over the Indians at Tippecanoe and in 1813 a more decisive one at the Battle of the Thames, where Tecumseh was killed.

After resigning from the army in 1814, Harrison had an obscure career in politics and diplomacy, ending up 20 years later as a county recorder in Ohio. Nominated for President in 1835 as a military hero whom the conservative politicians hoped to be able to control, he ran surprisingly well against Van Buren in 1836. Four years later, he defeated Van Buren but caught penumonia and died in Washington on April 4, 1841, a month after his inauguration. Harrison was the first president to die in office.

JOHN TYLER was born in Charles City County, Va., on March 29, 1790. A William and Mary graduate, he entered law practice and politics, serving in the House of Representatives (1817–21), as governor of Virginia (1825–27), and as senator (1827–36). A strict constructionist, he supported Crawford in 1824 and Jackson in 1828, but broke with Jackson over his United States Bank policy and became a member of the Southern state-rights group that cooperated with the Whigs. In 1836, he resigned from the Senate rather than follow instructions from the Virginia legislature to vote for a resolution expunging censure of Jackson from the Senate record.

Elected vice president on the Whig ticket in 1840, Tyler succeeded to the presidency on Harrison's death. His strict-constructionist views soon caused a split with the Henry Clay wing of the Whig party and a stalemate on domestic questions. Tyler's more considerable achievements were his support of the Webster-Ashburton Treaty with Britain and his success in bringing about the annexation of Texas.

After his presidency he lived in retirement in Virginia until the outbreak of the Civil War, when he emerged briefly as chairman of a peace convention and then as delegate to the provisional Congress of the Confederacy. He died on Jan. 18, 1862. He married Letitia Christian in 1813 and, two years after her death in 1842, Julia Gardiner.

JAMES KNOX POLK was born in Mecklenburg County, N.C., on Nov. 2, 1795. A graduate of the University of North Carolina, he moved west to Tennessee, was admitted to the bar, and soon became prominent in state politics. In 1825, he was elected to the House of Representatives, where he opposed Adams and, after 1829, became Jackson's floor leader in the fight against the Bank. In 1835, he became Speaker of the House. Four years later, he was elected governor of Tennessee, but was beaten in tries for re-election in 1841 and 1843.

The supporters of Van Buren for the Democratic

nomination in 1844 counted on Polk as his running mate; but, when Van Buren's stand on Texas alienated Southern support, the convention swung to Polk on the ninth ballot. He was elected over Henry Clay, the Whig candidate. Rapidly disillusioning those who thought that he would not run his own administration, Polk proceeded steadily and precisely to achieve four major objectives—the acquisition of California, the settlement of the Oregon question, the reduction of the tariff, and the establishment of the independent treasury. He also enlarged the Monroe Doctrine to exclude all non-American intervention in American affairs, whether forcible or not, and he forced Mexico into a war that he waged to a successful conclusion.

His wife, Sarah Childress, whom he married in 1824, was a woman of charm and ability. Polk died in Nashville, Tenn., on June 15, 1849.

ZACHARY TAYLOR was born at Montebello, Orange County, Va., on Nov. 24, 1784. Embarking on a military career in 1808, Taylor fought in the War of 1812, the Black Hawk War, and the Seminole War, meanwhile holding garrison jobs on the frontier or desk jobs in Washington. A brigadier general as a result of his victory over the Seminoles at Lake Okeechobee (1837), Taylor held a succession of Southwestern commands and in 1846 established a base on the Rio Grande, where his forces engaged in hostilities that precipitated the war with Mexico. He captured Monterrey in September 1846 and, disregarding Polk's orders to stay on the defensive, defeated Santa Anna at Buena Vista in February 1847, ending the war in the northern provinces.

Though Taylor had never cast a vote for president, his party affiliations were Whiggish and his availability was increased by his difficulties with Polk. He was elected president over the Democrat Lewis Cass. During the revival of the slavery controversy, which was to result in the Compromise of 1850, Taylor began to take an increasingly firm stand against appeasing the South; but he died in Washington on July 9, 1850, during the fight over the Compromise. He married Margaret Mackall Smith in 1810. His bluff and simple soldierly qualities won him the name Old Rough and Ready.

MILLARD FILLMORE was born at Locke, Cayuga County, N.Y., on Jan. 7, 1800. A lawyer, he entered politics with the Anti-Masonic Party under the sponsorship of Thurlow Weed, editor and party boss, and subsequently followed Weed into the Whig Party. He served in the House of Representatives (1833–35 and 1837–43) and played a leading role in writing the tariff of 1842. Defeated for governor of New York in 1844, he became State comptroller in 1848, was put on the Whig ticket with Taylor as a concession to the Clay wing of the party, and became president upon Taylor's death in 1850.

As president, Fillmore broke with Weed and William H. Seward and associated himself with the pro-Southern Whigs, supporting the Compromise of 1850. Defeated for the Whig nomination in 1852, he ran for president in 1856 as candidate of the American, or Know-Nothing Party, which sought to unite the country against foreigners in the alleged hope of diverting it from the explosive slavery issue. Fillmore opposed Lincoln during the Civil War. He died in Buffalo on March 8, 1874.

He was married in 1826 to Abigail Powers, who died in 1853, and in 1858 to Caroline Carmichael McIntosh.

FRANKLIN PIERCE was born at Hillsboro, N.H., on Nov. 23, 1804. A Bowdoin graduate, lawyer, and Jacksonian Democrat, he won rapid political advancement in the party, in part because of the prestige of his father, Gov. Benjamin Pierce. By 1831 he was Speaker of the New Hampshire House of Representatives; from 1833 to 1837, he served in the federal House and from 1837 to 1842 in the Senate. His wife, Jane Means Appleton, whom he married in 1834, disliked Washington and the somewhat dissipated life led by Pierce; in 1842 Pierce resigned from the Senate and began a successful law practice in Concord, N.H. During the Mexican War, he was a brigadier general.

Thereafter Pierce continued to oppose antislavery tendencies within the Democratic Party. As a result, he was the Southern choice to break the deadlock at the Democratic convention of 1852 and was nominated on the 49th ballot. In the election, Pierce overwhelmed Gen. Winfield Scott, the Whig candidate.

As president, Pierce followed a course of appeasing the South at home and of playing with schemes of territorial expansion abroad. The failure of his foreign and domestic policies prevented his renomination; and he died in Concord on Oct. 8, 1869, in relative obscurity.

JAMES BUCHANAN was born near Mercersburg, Pa., on April 23, 1791. A Dickinson graduate and a lawyer, he entered Pennsylvania politics as a Federalist. With the disappearance of the Federalist Party, he became a Jacksonian Democrat. He served with ability in the House (1821–31), as minister to St. Petersburg (1832–33), and in the Senate (1834–45), and in 1845 became Polk's Secretary of State. In 1853, Pierce appointed Buchanan minister to Britain, where he participated with other American diplomats in Europe in drafting the expansionist Ostend Manifesto.

He was elected president in 1856, defeating John C. Frémont, the Republican candidate, and former President Millard Fillmore of the American Party. The growing crisis over slavery presented Buchanan with problems he lacked the will to tackle. His appeasement of the South alienated the Stephen Douglas wing of the Democratic Party without reducing Southern militancy on slavery issues. While denying the right of secession, Buchanan also denied that the federal government could do anything about it. He supported the administration during the Civil War and died in Lancaster, Pa., on June 1, 1868.

The only president to remain a bachelor throughout his term, Buchanan used his charming niece, Harriet Lane, as White House hostess.

ABRAHAM LINCOLN was born in Hardin (now Larue) County, Ky., on Feb. 12, 1809. His family moved to Indiana and then to Illinois, and Lincoln gained what education he could along the way. While reading law, he worked in a store, managed a mill, surveyed, and split rails. In 1834, he went to the Illinois legislature as a Whig and became the party's floor leader. For the next 20 years he practiced law in Springfield, except for a single term (1847–49) in Congress, where he denounced the Mexican War. In 1855, he was a candidate for senator annd the next year he joined the new Republican Party.

A leading but unsuccessful candidate for the vice-presidential nomination with Frémont, Lincoln gained national attention in 1858 when, as

Republican candidate for senator from Illinois, he engaged in a series of debates with Stephen A. Douglas, the Democratic candidate. He lost the election, but continued to prepare the way for the 1860 Republican convention and was rewarded with the presidential nomination on the third ballot. He won the election over three opponents.

From the start, Lincoln made clear that, unlike Buchanan, he believed the national government had the power to crush the rebellion. Not an abolitionist, he held the slavery issue subordinate to that of preserving the Union, but soon perceived that the war could not be brought to a successful conclusion without freeing the slaves. His administration was hampered by the incompetence of many Union generals, the inexperience of the troops, and the harassing political tactics both of the Republican Radicals, who favored a hard policy toward the South, and the Democratic Copperheads, who desired a negotiated peace. The Gettysburg Address of Nov. 19, 1863, marks the high point in the record of American eloquence. Lincoln's long search for a winning combination finally brought Generals Ulysses S. Grant and William T. Sherman on the top; and their series of victories in 1864 dispelled the mutterings from both Radicals and Peace Democrats that at one time seemed to threaten Lincoln's re-election. He was re-elected in 1864, defeating Gen. George B. McClellan, the Democratic candidate. His inaugural address urged leniency toward the South: "With malice toward none, with charity for all . . . let us strive on to finish the work we are in; to bind up the nation's wounds . . ." This policy aroused growing opposition on the part of the Republican Radicals, but before the matter could be put to the test, Lincoln was shot by the actor John Wilkes Booth at Ford's Theater, Washington, on April 14, 1865. He died the next morning.

Lincoln's marriage to Mary Todd in 1842 was often unhappy and turbulent, in part because of his wife's pronounced instability.

ANDREW JOHNSON was born at Raleigh, N.C., on Dec. 29, 1808. Self-educated, he became a tailor in Greeneville, Tenn., but soon went into politics, where he rose steadily. He served in the House of Representatives (1843–54), as governor of Tennessee (1853–57), and as a senator (1857–62). Politically he was a Jacksonian Democrat and his specialty was the fight for a more equitable land policy. Alone among the Southern Senators, he stood by the Union during the Civil War. In 1862, he became war governor of Tennessee and carried out a thankless and difficult job with great courage. Johnson became Lincoln's running mate in 1864 as a result of an attempt to give the ticket a nonpartisan and nonsectional character. Succeeding to the presidency on Lincoln's death, Johnson sought to carry out Lincoln's policy, but without his political skill. The result was a hopeless conflict with the Radical Republicans who dominated Congress, passed measures over Johnson's vetoes, and attempted to limit the power of the executive concerning appointments and removals. The conflict culminated with Johnson's impeachment for attempting to remove his disloyal Secretary of War in defiance of the Tenure of Office Act which required senatorial concurrence for such dismissals. The opposition failed by one vote to get the two thirds necessary for conviction.

After his presidency, Johnson maintained an interest in politics and in 1875 was again elected to the Senate. He died near Carter Station, Tenn., on July 31, 1875. He married Eliza McCardle in 1827.

ULYSSES SIMPSON GRANT was born (as Hiram Ulysses Grant) at Point Pleasant, Ohio, on April 27, 1822. He graduated from West Point in 1843 and served without particular distinction in the Mexican War. In 1848 he married Julia Dent. He resigned from the army in 1854, after warnings from his commanding officer about his drinking habits, and for the next six years held a wide variety of jobs in the Middle West. With the outbreak of the Civil War, he sought a command and soon, to his surprise, was made a brigadier general. His continuing successes in the western theaters, culminating in the capture of Vicksburg, Miss., in 1863, brought him national fame and soon the command of all the Union armies. Grant's dogged, implacable policy of concentrating on dividing and destroying the Confederate armies brought the war to an end in 1865. The next year, he was made full general.

In 1868, as Republican candidate for president, Grant was elected over the Democrat, Horatio Seymour. From the start, Grant showed his unfitness for the office. His Cabinet was weak, his domestic policy was confused, many of his intimate associates were corrupt. The notable achievement in foreign affairs was the settlement of controversies with Great Britain in the Treaty of London (1871), negotiated by his able Secretary of State, Hamilton Fish.

Running for re-election in 1872, he defeated Horace Greeley, the Democratic and Liberal Republican candidate. The Panic of 1873 graft scandals close to the presidency created difficulties for his second term.

After retiring from office, Grant toured Europe for two years and returned in time to accede to a third-term boom, but was beaten in the convention of 1880. Illness and bad business judgment darkened his last years, but he worked steadily at the *Personal Memoirs*, which were to be so successful when published after his death at Mount McGregor, near Saratoga, N.Y., on July 23, 1885.

RUTHERFORD BIRCHARD HAYES was born in Delaware, Ohio, on Oct. 4, 1822. A graduate of Kenyon College and the Harvard Law School, he practiced law in Lower Sandusky (now Fremont) and then in Cincinnati. In 1852 he married Lucy Webb. A Whig, he joined the Republican party in 1855. During the Civil War he rose to major general. He served in the House of Representatives from 1865 to 1867 and then confirmed a reputation for honesty and efficiency in two terms as Governor of Ohio (1868–72). His election to a third term in 1875 made him the logical candidate for those Republicans who wished to stop James G. Blaine in 1876, and he was nominated.

The result of the election was in doubt for some time and hinged upon disputed returns from South Carolina, Louisiana, Florida, and Oregon. Samuel J. Tilden, the Democrat, had the larger popular vote but was adjudged by the strictly partisan decisions of the Electoral Commission to have one fewer electoral vote, 185 to 184. The national acceptance of this result was due in part to the general understanding that Hayes would pursue a conciliatory policy toward the South. He withdrew the troops from the South, took a conservative position on financial and labor issues, and urged civil service reform.

Hayes served only one term by his own wish and

spent the rest of his life in various humanitarian endeavors. He died in Fremont on Jan. 17, 1893.

JAMES ABRAM GARFIELD, the last president to be born in a log cabin, was born in Cuyahoga County, Ohio, on Nov. 19, 1831. A Williams graduate, he taught school for a time and entered Republican politics in Ohio. In 1858, he married Lucretia Rudolph. During the Civil War, he had a promising career, rising to major general of volunteers; but he resigned in 1863, having been elected to the House of Representatives, where he served until 1880. His oratorical and parliamentary abilities soon made him the leading Republican in the House, though his record was marred by his unorthodox acceptance of a fee in the DeGolyer paving contract case and by suspicions of his complicity in the Crédit Mobilier scandal.

In 1880, Garfield was elected to the Senate, but instead became the presidential candidate on the 36th ballot as a result of a deadlock in the Republican convention. In the election, he defeated Gen. Winfield Scott Hancock, the Democratic candidate. Garfield's administration was barely under way when he was shot by Charles J. Guiteau, a disappointed office seeker, in Washington on July 2, 1881. He died in Elberton, N.J., on Sept. 19.

CHESTER ALAN ARTHUR was born at Fairfield, Vt., on Oct. 5, 1830. A graduate of Union College, he became a successful New York lawyer. In 1859, he married Ellen Herndon. During the Civil War, he held administrative jobs in the Republican state administration and in 1871 was appointed collector of the Port of New York by Grant. This post gave him control over considerable patronage. Though not personally corrupt, Arthur managed his power in the interests of the New York machine so openly that President Hayes in 1877 called for an investigation and the next year Arthur was suspended.

In 1880 Arthur was nominated for vice president in the hope of conciliating the followers of Grant and the powerful New York machine. As president upon Garfield's death, Arthur, stepping out of his familiar role as spoilsman, backed civil service reform, reorganized the Cabinet, and prosecuted political associates accused of post office graft. Losing machine support and failing to gain the reformers, he was not nominated for a full term in 1884. He died in New York City on Nov. 18, 1886.

STEPHEN GROVER CLEVELAND was born at Caldwell, N.J., on March 18, 1837. He was admitted to the bar in Buffalo, N.Y., in 1859 and lived there as a lawyer, with occasional incursions into Democratic politics, for more than 20 years. He did not participate in the Civil War. As mayor of Buffalo in 1881, he carried through a reform program so ably that the Democrats ran him successfully for governor in 1882. In 1884 he won the Democratic nomination for President. The campaign contrasted Cleveland's spotless public career with the uncertain record of James G. Blaine, the Republican candidate, and Cleveland received enough Mugwump (independent Republican) support to win.

As president, Cleveland pushed civil service reform, opposed the pension grab and attacked the high tariff rates. While in the White House, he married Frances Folsom in 1886. Renominated in 1888, Cleveland was defeated by Benjamin Harrison, polling more popular but fewer electoral votes. In 1892, he was elected over Harrison. When the Panic of 1893 burst upon the country, Cleveland's attempts to solve it by sound-money measures alienated the free-silver wing of the party, while his tariff policy alienated the protectionists. In 1894, he sent troops to break the Pullman strike. In foreign affairs, his firmness caused Great Britain to back down in the Venezuela border dispute.

In his last years Cleveland was an active and much-respected public figure. He died in Princeton, N.J., on June 24, 1908.

BENJAMIN HARRISON was born in North Bend, Ohio, on Aug. 20, 1833, the grandson of William Henry Harrison, the ninth president. A graduate of Miami University in Ohio, he took up the law in Indiana and became active in Republican politics. In 1853, he married Caroline Lavinia Scott. During the Civil War, he rose to brigadier general. A sound-money Republican, he was elected senator from Indiana in 1880. In 1888, he received the Republican nomination for President on the eighth ballot. Though behind on the popular vote, he won over Grover Cleveland in the electoral college by 233 to 168.

As President, Harrison failed to please either the bosses or the reform element in the party. In foreign affairs he backed Secretary of State Blaine, whose policy foreshadowed later American imperialism. Harrison was renominated in 1892 but lost to Cleveland. His wife died in the White House in 1892 and Harrison married her niece, Mary Scott (Lord) Dimmick, in 1896. After his presidency, he resumed law practice. He died in Indianapolis on March 13, 1901.

WILLIAM McKINLEY was born in Niles, Ohio, on Jan. 29, 1843. He taught school, then served in the Civil War, rising from the ranks to become a major. Subsequently he opened a law office in Canton, Ohio, and in 1871 married Ida Saxton. Elected to Congress in 1876, he served there until 1891, except for 1883–85. His faithful advocacy of business interests culminated in the passage of the highly protective McKinley Tariff of 1890. With the support of Mark Hanna, a shrewd Cleveland businessman interested in safeguarding tariff protection, McKinley became governor of Ohio in 1892 and Republican presidential candidate in 1896. The business community, alarmed by the progressivism of William Jennings Bryan, the Democratic candidate, spent considerable money to assure McKinley's victory.

The chief event of McKinley's administration was the war with Spain, which resulted in our acquisition of the Philippines and other islands. With imperialism an issue, McKinley defeated Bryan again in 1900. On Sept. 6, 1901, he was shot at Buffalo, N.Y., by Leon F. Czolgosz, an anarchist, and he died there eight days later.

THEODORE ROOSEVELT was born in New York City on Oct. 27, 1858. A Harvard graduate, he was early interested in ranching, in politics, and in writing picturesque historical narratives. He was a Republican member of the New York State Assembly in 1882–84, an unsuccessful candidate for mayor of New York in 1886, a U.S. Civil Service Commissioner under Benjamin Harrison, Police Commissioner of New York City in 1895, and Assistant Secretary of the Navy under McKinley in 1897. He resigned in 1898 to help organize a volunteer regiment, the Rough Riders, and take a more direct part in the war with Spain. He was elected governor of New York in 1898 and vice president in 1900, in spite of lack of enthusiasm on the part of the bosses.

Assuming the presidency of the assassinated McKinley in 1901, Roosevelt embarked on a wideranging program of government reform and conservation of natural resources. He ordered antitrust suits against several large corporations, threatened to intervene in the anthracite coal strike of 1902, which prompted the operators to accept arbitration, and, in general, championed the rights of the "little man" and fought the "malefactors of great wealth." He was also responsible for such progressive legislation as the Elkins Act of 1901, which outlawed freight rebates by railroads; the bill establishing the Department of Commerce and Labor; the Hepburn Act, which gave the I.C.C. greater control over the railroads; the Meat Inspection Act; and the Pure Food and Drug Act.

In foreign affairs, Roosevelt pursued a strong policy, permitting the instigation of a revolt in Panama to dispose of Colombian objections to the Panama Canal and helping to maintain the balance of power in the East by bringing the Russo-Japanese War to an end, for which he won the Nobel Peace Prize, the first American to achieve a Nobel prize in any category. In 1904, he decisively defeated Alton B. Parker, his conservative Democratic opponent.

Roosevelt's increasing coldness toward his successor, William Howard Taft, led him to overlook his earlier disclaimer of third-term ambitions and to re-enter politics. Defeated by the machine in the Republican convention of 1912, he organized the Progressive Party (Bull Moose) and polled more votes than Taft, though the split brought about the election of Woodrow Wilson. From 1915 on, Roosevelt strongly favored intervention in the European war. He became deeply embittered at Wilson's refusal to allow him to raise a volunteer division. He died in Oyster Bay, N.Y., on Jan. 6, 1919. He was married twice: in 1880 to Alice Hathaway Lee, who died in 1884, and in 1886 to Edith Kermit Carow.

WILLIAM HOWARD TAFT was born in Cincinnati on Sept. 15, 1857. A Yale graduate, he entered Ohio Republican politics in the 1880s. In 1886 he married Helen Herron. From 1887 to 1890, he served on the Ohio Superior Court; 1890–92, as solicitor general of the United States; 1892–1900, on the federal circuit court. In 1900 McKinley appointed him president of the Philippine Commission and in 1901 governor general. Taft had great success in pacifying the Filipinos, solving the problem of the church lands, improving economic conditions, and establishing limited self-government. His period as Secretary of War (1904–08) further demonstrated his capacity as administrator and conciliator, and he was Roosevelt's hand-picked successor in 1908. In the election, he polled 321 electoral votes to 162 for William Jennings Bryan, who was running for the presidency for the third time.

Though he carried on many of Roosevelt's policies, Taft got into increasing trouble with the progressive wing of the party and displayed mounting irritability and indecision. After his defeat in 1912, he became professor of constitutional law at Yale. In 1921 he was appointed Chief Justice of the

United States. He died in Washington on March 8, 1930.

THOMAS WOODROW WILSON was born in Staunton, Va., on Dec. 28, 1856. A Princeton graduate, he turned from law practice to post-graduate work in political science at Johns Hopkins University, receiving his Ph.D. in 1886. He taught at Bryn Mawr, Wesleyan, and Princeton, and in 1902 was made president of Princeton. After an unsuccessful attempt to democratize the social life of the university, he welcomed an invitation in 1910 to be the Democratic gubernatorial candidate in New Jersey, and was elected. His success in fighting the machine and putting through a reform program attracted national attention.

In 1912, at the Democratic convention in Baltimore, Wilson won the nomination on the 46th ballot and went on to defeat Roosevelt and Taft in the election. Wilson proceeded under the standard of the New Freedom to enact a program of domestic reform, including the Federal Reserve Act, the Clayton Antitrust Act, the establishment of the Federal Trade Commission, and other measures designed to restore competition in the face of the great monopolies. In foreign affairs, while privately sympathetic with the Allies, he strove to maintain neutrality in the European war and warned both sides against encroachments on American interests.

Re-elected in 1916 as a peace candidate, he tried to mediate between the warring nations; but when the Germans resumed unrestricted submarine warfare in 1917, Wilson brought the United States into what he now believed was a war to make the world safe for democracy. He supplied the classic formulations of Allied war aims and the armistice of Nov. 11, 1918 was negotiated on the basis of Wilson's Fourteen Points. In 1919 he strove at Versailles to lay the foundations for enduring peace. He accepted the imperfections of the Versailles Treaty in the expectation that they could be remedied by action within the League of Nations. He probably could have secured ratification of the treaty by the Senate if he had adopted a more conciliatory attitude toward the mild reservationists; but his insistence on all or nothing eventually caused the diehard isolationists and diehard Wilsonites to unite in rejecting a compromise.

In September 1919 Wilson suffered a paralytic stroke that limited his activity. After leaving the presidency he lived on in retirement in Washington, dying on Feb. 3, 1924. He was married twice—in 1885 to Ellen Louise Axson, who died in 1914, and in 1915 to Edith Bolling Galt.

WARREN GAMALIEL HARDING was born in Morrow County, Ohio, on Nov. 2, 1865. After attending Ohio Central College, Harding became interested in journalism and in 1884 bought the *Marion* (Ohio) *Star.* In 1891 he married a wealthy widow, Florence Kling De Wolfe. As his paper prospered, he entered Republican politics, serving as state senator (1899–1903) and as lieutenant governor (1904–06). In 1910, he was defeated for governor, but in 1914 was elected to the Senate. His reputation as an orator made him the keynoter at the 1916 Republican convention.

When the 1920 convention was deadlocked between Leonard Wood and Frank O. Lowden, Harding became the dark-horse nominee on his solemn affirmation that there was no reason in his past that he should not be. Straddling the League question, Harding was easily elected over James M. Cox, his Democratic opponent. His Cabinet contained some able men, but also some manifestly unfit for public office. Harding's own intimates were mediocre when they were not corrupt. The impending disclosure of the Teapot Dome scandal in the Interior Department and illegal practices in the Justice Department and Veterans' Bureau, as well as political setbacks, profoundly worried him. On his return from Alaska in 1923, he died unexpectedly in San Francisco on Aug. 2.

JOHN CALVIN COOLIDGE was born in Plymouth, Vt., on July 4, 1872. An Amherst graduate, he went into law practice at Northampton, Mass., in 1897. He married Grace Anna Goodhue in 1905. He entered Republican state politics, becoming successively mayor of Northampton, state senator, lieutenant governor and, in 1919, governor. His use of the state militia to end the Boston police strike in 1919 won him a somewhat undeserved reputation for decisive action and brought him the Republican vice-presidential nomination in 1920. After Harding's death Coolidge handled the Washington scandals with care and finally managed to save the Republican Party from public blame for the widespread corruption.

In 1924, Coolidge was elected without difficulty, defeating the Democrat, John W. Davis, and Robert M. La Follette running on the Progressive ticket. His second term, like his first, was characterized by a general satisfaction with the existing economic order. He stated that he did not choose to run in 1928.

After his presidency, Coolidge lived quietly in Northampton, writing an unilluminating *Autobiography* and conducting a syndicated column. He died there on Jan. 5, 1933.

HERBERT CLARK HOOVER was born at West Branch, Iowa, on Aug. 10, 1874, the first president to be born west of the Mississippi. A Stanford graduate, he worked from 1895 to 1913 as a mining engineer and consultant throughout the world. In 1899, he married Lou Henry. During World War I, he served with distinction as chairman of the American Relief Committee in London, as chairman of the Commission for Relief in Belgium, and as U.S. Food Administrator. His political affiliations were still too indeterminate for him to be mentioned as a possibility for either the Republican or Democratic nomination in 1920, but after the election he served Harding and Coolidge as Secretary of Commerce.

In the election of 1928, Hoover overwhelmed Gov. Alfred E. Smith of New York, the Democratic candidate and the first Roman Catholic to run for the presidency. He soon faced the worst depression in the nation's history, but his attacks upon it were hampered by his devotion to the theory that the forces that brought the crisis would soon bring the revival and then by his belief that there were too many areas in which the federal government had no power to act. In a succession of vetoes, he struck down measures proposing a national employment system or national relief, he reduced income tax rates, and only at the end of his term did he yield to popular pressure and set up agencies such as the Reconstruction Finance Corporation to make emergency loans to assist business.

After his 1932 defeat, Hoover returned to private business. In 1946, President Truman charged him with various world food missions; and from 1947 to 1949 and 1953 to 1955, he was head of the Commission on Organization of the Executive Branch of the Government. He died in New York City on Oct. 20, 1964.

FRANKLIN DELANO ROOSEVELT was born in Hyde Park, N.Y., on Jan. 30, 1882. A Harvard graduate, he attended Columbia Law School and was admitted to the New York bar. In 1910, he was elected to the New York State Senate as a Democrat. Re-elected in 1912, he was appointed Assistant Secretary of the Navy by Woodrow Wilson the next year. In 1920, his radiant personality and his war service resulted in his nomination for vice president as James M. Cox's running mate. After his defeat, he returned to law practice in New York. In August 1921, Roosevelt was stricken with infantile paralysis while on vacation at Campobello, New Brunswick. After a long and gallant fight, he recovered partial use of his legs. In 1924 and 1928, he led the fight at the Democratic national conventions for the nomination of Gov. Alfred E. Smith of New York, and in 1928 Roosevelt was himself induced to run for governor of New York. He was elected, and was re-elected in 1930.

In 1932, Roosevelt received the Democratic nomination for president and immediately launched a campaign that brought new spirit to a weary and discouraged nation. He defeated Hoover by a wide margin. His first term was characterized by an unfolding of the New Deal program, with greater benefits for labor, the farmers, and the unemployed, and the progressive estrangement of most of the business community.

At an early stage, Roosevelt became aware of the menace to world peace posed by totalitarian fascism, and from 1937 on he tried to focus public attention on the trend of events in Europe and Asia. As a result, he was widely denounced as a warmonger. He was re-elected in 1936 over Gov. Alfred M. Landon of Kansas by the overwhelming electoral margin of 523 to 8, and the gathering international crisis prompted him to run for an unprecedented third term in 1940. He defeated Wendell L. Willkie.

Roosevelt's program to bring maximum aid to Britain and, after June 1941, to Russia was opposed, until the Japanese attack on Pearl Harbor restored national unity. During the war, Roosevelt shelved the New Deal in the interests of conciliating the business community, both in order to get full production during the war and to prepare the way for a united acceptance of the peace settlements after the war. A series of conferences with Winston Churchill and Joseph Stalin laid down the bases for the postwar world. In 1944 he was elected to a fourth term, running against Gov. Thomas E. Dewey of New York.

On April 12, 1945, Roosevelt died of a cerebral hemorrhage at Warm Springs, Ga., shortly after his return from the Yalta Conference. His wife, Anna Eleanor Roosevelt, whom he married in 1905, was a woman of great ability who made significant contributions to her husband's policies.

HARRY S. TRUMAN was born on a farm near Lamar, Mo., on May 8, 1884. During World War I, he served in France as a captain with the 129th Field Artillery. He married Bess Wallace in 1919. After engaging briefly and unsuccessfully in the haberdashery business in Kansas City, Mo., Truman entered local politics. Under the sponsorship of Thomas Pendergast, Democratic boss of Missouri, he held a number of local offices, preserving his personal honesty in the midst of a notoriously corrupt political machine. In 1934, he was elected to the Senate and was re-elected in 1940. During his first term he was a loyal but quiet supporter of the New Deal, but in his second term, an appointment as head of a Senate committee to investigate war production brought out his special qualities of honesty, common sense, and hard work, and he won widespread respect.

Elected vice president in 1944, Truman became president upon Roosevelt's sudden death in April 1945 and was immediately faced with the problems of winding down the war against the Axis and preparing the nation for postwar adjustment.

The years 1947–48 were distinguished by civil-rights proposals, the Truman Doctrine to contain the spread of Communism, and the Marshall Plan to aid in the economic reconstruction of war-ravaged nations. Truman's general record, highlighted by a vigorous Fair Deal campaign, brought about his unexpected election in 1948 over the heavily favored Thomas E. Dewey.

Truman's second term was primarily concerned with the Cold War with the Soviet Union, the implementing of the North Atlantic Pact, the United Nations police action in Korea, and the vast rearmament program with its accompanying problems of economic stabilization.

On March 29, 1952, Truman announced that he would not run again for the presidency. After leaving the White House, he returned to his home in Independence, Mo., to write his memoirs. He further busied himself with the Harry S. Truman Library there. He died in Kansas City, Mo., on Dec. 26, 1972.

DWIGHT DAVID EISENHOWER was born in Denison, Tex., on Oct. 14, 1890. His ancestors lived in Germany and emigrated to America, settling in Pennsylvania, early in the 18th century. His father, David, had a general store in Hope, Kan., which failed. After a brief time in Texas, the family moved to Abilene, Kan.

After graduating from Abilene High School in 1909, Eisenhower did odd jobs for almost two years. He won an appointment to the Naval Academy at Annapolis, but was too old for admittance. Then he received an appointment in 1910 to West Point, from which he graduated as a second lieutenant in 1915.

He did not see service in World War I, having been stationed at Fort Sam Houston, Tex. There he met Mamie Geneva Doud, whom he married in Denver on July 1, 1916, and by whom he had two sons: Doud Dwight (died in infancy) and John Sheldon Doud.

Eisenhower served in the Philippines from 1935 to 1939 with Gen. Douglas MacArthur. Afterward, Gen. George C. Marshall, the Army Chief of Staff, brought him into the War Department's General Staff and in 1942 placed him in command of the invasion of North Africa. In 1944, he was made Supreme Allied Commander for the invasion of Europe.

After the war, Eisenhower served as Army Chief of Staff from November 1945 until February 1948, when he was appointed president of Columbia University.

In December 1950, President Truman recalled Eisenhower to active duty to command the North Atlantic Treaty Organization forces in Europe. He held his post until the end of May 1952.

At the Republican convention of 1952 in Chicago, Eisenhower won the presidential nomination on the first ballot in a close race with Senator Robert A. Taft of Ohio. In the election, he defeated Gov. Adlai E. Stevenson of Illinois.

Through two terms, Eisenhower hewed to moderate domestic policies. He sought peace through Free World strength in an era of new nationalisms, nuclear missiles, and space exploration. He fostered alliances pledging the United States to resist Red aggression in Europe, Asia, and Latin America. The Eisenhower Doctrine of 1957 extended commitments to the Middle East.

At home, the popular president lacked Republican Congressional majorities after 1954, but he was re-elected in 1956 by 457 electoral votes to 73 for Stevenson.

While retaining most Fair Deal programs, he stressed "fiscal responsibility" in domestic affairs. A moderate in civil rights, he sent troops to Little Rock, Ark., to enforce court-ordered school integration.

With his wartime rank restored by Congress, Eisenhower returned to private life and the role of elder statesman, with his vigor hardly impaired by a heart attack, an ileitis operation, and a mild stroke suffered while in office. He died in Washington on March 28, 1969.

JOHN FITZGERALD KENNEDY was born in Brookline, Mass., on May 29, 1917. His father, Joseph P. Kennedy, was Ambassador to Great Britain from 1937 to 1940.

Kennedy was graduated from Harvard University in 1940 and joined the Navy the next year. He became skipper of a PT boat that was sunk in the Pacific by a Japanese destroyer. Although given up for lost, he swam to a safe island, towing an injured enlisted man.

After recovering from a war-aggravated spinal injury, Kennedy entered politics in 1946 and was elected to Congress. In 1952, he ran against Senator Henry Cabot Lodge, Jr., of Massachusetts, and won.

Kennedy was married on Sept. 12, 1953, to Jacqueline Lee Bouvier, by whom he had three children: Caroline, John Fitzgerald, Jr., and Patrick Bouvier (died in infancy).

In 1957 Kennedy won the Pulitzer Prize for a book he had written earlier, *Profiles in Courage.*

After strenuous primary battles, Kennedy won the Democratic presidential nomination on the first ballot at the 1960 Los Angeles convention. With a plurality of only 118,574 votes, he carried the election over Vice President Richard M. Nixon and became the first Roman Catholic president.

Kennedy brought to the White House the dynamic idea of a "New Frontier" approach in dealing with problems at home, abroad, and in the dimensions of space. Out of his leadership in his first few months in office came the 10-year Alliance for Progress to aid Latin America, the Peace Corps, and accelerated programs that brought the first Americans into orbit in the race in space.

Failure of the U.S.-supported Cuban invasion in April 1961 led to the entrenchment of the Communist-backed Castro regime, only 90 miles from United States soil. When it became known that Soviet offensive missiles were being installed in Cuba in 1962, Kennedy ordered a naval "quarantine" of the island and moved troops into position to eliminate this threat to U.S. security. The world seemed on the brink of a nuclear war until Soviet Premier Khrushchev ordered the removal of the missiles.

A sudden "thaw," or the appearance of one, in the cold war came with the agreement with the Soviet Union on a limited test-ban treaty signed in Moscow on Aug. 6, 1963.

In his domestic policies, Kennedy's proposals for medical care for the aged, expanded area redevelopment, and aid to education were defeated, but on minimum wage, trade legislation, and other measures he won important victories.

Widespread racial disorders and demonstrations led to Kennedy's proposing sweeping civil rights legislation. As his third year in office drew to a close, he also recommended an $11-billion tax cut to bolster the economy. Both measures were pending in Congress when Kennedy, looking forward to a second term, journeyed to Texas for a series of speeches.

While riding in a procession in Dallas on Nov. 22, 1963, he was shot to death by an assassin firing from an upper floor of a building. The alleged assassin, Lee Harvey Oswald, was killed two days later in the Dallas city jail by Jack Ruby, owner of a striptease place.

At 46 years of age, Kennedy became the fourth president to be assassinated and the eighth to die in office.

LYNDON BAINES JOHNSON was born in Stonewall, Tex., on Aug. 27, 1908. On both sides of his family he had a political heritage mingled with a Baptist background of preachers and teachers. Both his father and his paternal grandfather served in the Texas House of Representatives.

After his graduation from Southwest Texas State Teachers College, Johnson taught school for two years. He went to Washington in 1932 as secretary to Rep. Richard M. Kleberg. During this time, he married Claudia Alta Taylor, known as "Lady Bird." They had two children: Lynda Bird and Luci Baines.

In 1935, Johnson became Texas administrator for the National Youth Administration. Two years later, he was elected to Congress as an all-out supporter of Franklin D. Roosevelt, and served until 1949. He was the first member of Congress to enlist in the armed forces after the attack on Pearl Harbor. He served in the Navy in the Pacific and won a Silver Star.

Johnson was elected to the Senate in 1948 after he had captured the Democratic nomination by only 87 votes. He was 40 years old. He became the Senate Democratic leader in 1953. A heart attack in 1955 threatened to end his political career, but he recovered fully and resumed his duties.

At the height of his power as Senate leader, Johnson sought the Democratic nomination for president in 1960. When he lost to John F. Kennedy, he surprised even some of his closest associates by accepting second place on the ticket.

Johnson was riding in another car in the motorcade when Kennedy was assassinated in Dallas on Nov. 22, 1963. He took the oath of office in the presidential jet on the Dallas airfield.

With Johnson's insistent backing, Congress finally adopted a far-reaching civil-rights bill, a voting-rights bill, a Medicare program for the aged, and measures to improve education and conservation. Congress also began what Johnson described as "an all-out war" on poverty.

Amassing a record-breaking majority of nearly 16 million votes, Johnson was elected president in his own right in 1964, defeating Senator Barry Goldwater of Arizona.

The double tragedy of a war in Southeast Asia and urban riots at home marked Johnson's last two years in office. Faced with disunity in the nation and challenges within his own party, Johnson surprised the country on March 31, 1968, with the announcement that he would not be a candidate for re-election. He died of a heart attack suffered at his LBJ Ranch on Jan. 22, 1973.

RICHARD MILHOUS NIXON was born in Yorba Linda, Calif., on Jan. 9, 1913, to Midwestern-bred parents, Francis A. and Hannah Milhous Nixon, who raised their five sons as Quakers.

Nixon was a high school debater and was undergraduate president at Whittier College in California, where he was graduated in 1934. As a scholarship student at Duke University Law School in North Carolina, he graduated third in his class in 1937.

After five years as a lawyer, Nixon joined the Navy in August 1942. He was an air transport officer in the South Pacific and a legal officer stateside before his discharge in 1946 as a lieutenant commander.

Running for Congress in California as a Republican in 1946, Nixon defeated Rep. Jerry Voorhis. As a member of the House Un-American Activities Committee, he made a name as an investigator of Alger Hiss, a former high State Department official, who was later jailed for perjury. In 1950, Nixon defeated Rep. Helen Gahagan Douglas, a Democrat, for the Senate. He was criticized for portraying her as a Communist dupe.

Nixon's anti-Communism, his Western base, and his youth figured in his selection in 1952 to run for vice president on the ticket headed by Dwight D. Eisenhower. Demands for Nixon's withdrawal followed disclosure that California businessmen had paid some of his Senate office expenses. He televised rebuttal, known as "the Checkers speech" (named for a cocker spaniel given to the Nixons), brought him support from the public and from Eisenhower. The ticket won easily in 1952 and again in 1956.

Eisenhower gave Nixon substantive assignments, including missions to 56 countries. In Moscow in 1959, Nixon won acclaim for his defense of U.S. interests in an impromptu "kitchen debate" with Soviet Premier Nikita S. Khrushchev.

Nixon lost the 1960 race for the presidency to John F. Kennedy.

In 1962, Nixon failed in a bid for California's governorship and seemed to be finished as a national candidate. He became a Wall Street lawyer, but kept his old party ties and developed new ones through constant travels to speak for Republicans.

Nixon won the 1968 Republican presidential nomination after a shrewd primary campaign, then made Gov. Spiro T. Agnew of Maryland his surprise choice for vice president. In the election, they edged out the Democratic ticket headed by Vice President Hubert H. Humphrey by 510,314 votes out of 73,212,065 cast.

Committed to wind down the U.S. role in the Vietnamese War, Nixon pursued "Vietnamization"—training and equipping South Vietnamese to do their own fighting. American ground combat forces in Vietnam fell steadily from 540,000 when Nixon took office to none in 1973 when the military draft was ended. But there was heavy continuing use of U.S. air power.

Nixon improved relations with Moscow and re-opened the long-closed door to mainland China with a good-will trip there in February 1972. In May of that year, he visited Moscow and signed agreements on arms limitation and trade expansion and approved plans for a joint U.S.-Soviet space mission in 1975.

Inflation was a campaign issue for Nixon, but he failed to master it as president. On Aug. 15, 1971, with unemployment edging up, Nixon abruptly announced a new economic policy: a 90-day wage-price freeze, stimulative tax cuts, a temporary 10% tariff, and spending cuts. A second phase, imposing guidelines on wage, price and rent boosts, was announced October 7.

The economy responded in time for the 1972 campaign, in which Nixon played up his foreign-policy achievements. Played down was the burglary on June 17, 1972, of Democratic national headquarters in the Watergate apartment complex in Washington. The Nixon-Agnew re-election campaign cost a record $60 million and swamped the Democratic ticket headed by Senator George McGovern of South Dakota with a plurality of 17,999,528 out of 77,718,554 votes. Only Massachusetts, with 14 electoral votes, and the District of Columbia, with 3, went for McGovern.

In January 1973, hints of a cover-up emerged at the trial of six men found guilty of the Wtergate burglary. With a Senate investigation under way, Nixon announced on April 30 the resignations of his top aides, H. R. Haldeman and John D. Ehrlichman, and the dismissal of White House counsel John Dean III. Dean was the star witness at televised Senate hearings that exposed both a White House cover-up of Watergate and massive illegalities in Republican fund-raising in 1972.

The hearings also disclosed that Nixon had routinely tape-recorded his office meetings and telephone conversations.

On Oct. 10, 1973, Agnew resigned as vice president, then pleaded no-contest to a negotiated federal charge of evading income taxes on alleged bribes. Two days later, Nixon nominated the House minority leader, Rep. Gerald R. Ford of Michigan, as the new vice president. Congress confirmed Ford on Dec. 6, 1973.

In June 1974, Nixon visited Israel and four Arab nations. Then he met in Moscow with Soviet leader Leonid I. Brezhnev and reached preliminary nuclear arms limitation agreements.

But, in the month after his return, Watergate ended the Nixon regime. On July 24 the Supreme Court ordered Nixon to surrender subpoenaed tapes. On July 30, the Judiciary Committee referred three impeachment articles to the full membership. On August 5, Nixon bowed to the Supreme Court and released tapes showing he halted an FBI probe of the Watergate burglary six days after it occurred. It was in effect an admission of obstruction of justice, and impeachment appeared inevitable.

Nixon resigned on Aug. 9, 1974, the first president ever to do so. A month later, President Ford issued an unconditional pardon for any offenses Nixon might have committed as president, thus forestalling possible prosecution.

In 1940, Nixon married Thelma Catherine (Pat) Ryan. They had two daughters, Patricia (Tricia) Cox and Julie, who married Dwight David Eisenhower II, grandson of the former president.

GERALD RUDOLPH FORD was born in Omaha, Neb., on July 14, 1913, the only child of Leslie and Dorothy Gardner King. His parents were divorced in 1915. His mother moved to Grand Rapids, Mich., and married Gerald R. Ford. The boy was renamed for his stepfather.

Ford captained his high school football team in Grand Rapids, and a football scholarship took him to the University of Michigan, where he starred as varsity center before his graduation in 1935. A job as assistant football coach at Yale gave him an opportunity to attend Yale Law School, from which he graduated in the top third of his class in 1941.

He returned to Grand Rapids to practice law, but entered the Navy in April 1942. He saw wartime service in the Pacific on the light aircraft carrier *Monterey* and was a lieutenant commander when he returned to Grand Rapids early in 1946 to resume law practice and dabble in politics.

Ford was elected to Congress in 1948 for the first of his 13 terms in the House. He was soon assigned to the influential Appropriations Committee and rose to become the ranking Republican on the subcommittee on Defense Department appropriations and an expert in the field.

As a legislator, Ford described himself as "a moderate on domestic issues, a conservative in fiscal affairs, and a dyed-in-the-wool internationalist." He carried the ball for Pentagon appropriations, was a hawk on the war in Vietnam, and kept a low profile on civil-rights issues.

He was also dependable and hard-working and popular with his colleagues. In 1963, he was elected chairman of the House Republican Conference. He served in 1963–64 as a member of the Warren Commission that investigated the assassination of John F. Kennedy. A revolt by dissatisfied younger Republicans in 1965 made him minority leader.

Ford shelved his hopes for the Speakership on Oct. 12, 1973, when Nixon nominated him to fill the vice presidency left vacant by Agnew's resignation under fire. It was the first use of the procedures for filling vacancies in the vice presidency laid down in the 25th Amendment to the Constitution, which Ford had helped enact.

Congress confirmed Ford as vice president on Dec. 6, 1973. Once in office, he said he did not believe Nixon had been involved in the Watergate scandals, but criticized his stubborn court battle against releasing tape recordings of Watergate-related conversations for use as evidence.

The scandals led to Nixon's unprecedented resignation on Aug. 9, 1974, and Ford was sworn in immediately as the 38th president, the first to enter the White House without winning a national election.

Ford assured the nation when he took office that "our long national nightmare is over" and pledged "openness and candor" in all his actions. He won a warm response from the Democratic 93rd Congress when he said he wanted "a good marriage" rather than a honeymoon with his former colleagues. In December 1974 Congressional majorities backed his choice of former New York Gov. Nelson A. Rockefeller as his successor in the again-vacant vice presidency.

The cordiality was chilled by Ford's announcement on Sept. 8, 1974, that he had granted an unconditional pardon to Nixon for any crimes he might have committed as president. Although no formal charges were pending, Ford said he feared "ugly passions" would be aroused if Nixon were brought to trial. The pardon was widely criticized.

To fight inflation, the new president first proposed fiscal restraints and spending curbs and a 5% tax surcharge that got nowhere in the Senate and House. Congress again rebuffed Ford in the spring of 1975 when he appealed for emergency military aid to help the governments of South Vietnam and Cambodia resist massive Communist offensives.

In November 1974, Ford visited Japan, South Korea, and the Soviet Union, where he and Soviet leader Leonid I. Brezhnev conferred in Vladivostok and reached a tentative agreement to limit the number of strategic offensive nuclear weapons. It was Ford's first meeting as president with Brezhnev, who planned a return visit to Washington in the fall of 1975.

Politically, Ford's fortunes improved steadily in the first half of 1975. Badly divided Democrats in Congress were unable to muster votes to override his vetoes of spending bills that exceeded his budget. He faced some right-wing opposition in his own party, but moved to pre-empt it with an early announcement—on July 8, 1975—of his intention to be a candidate in 1976.

Early state primaries in 1976 suggested an easy victory for Ford despite Ronald Reagan's bitter attacks on administration foreign policy and defense programs. But later Reagan primary successes threatened the President's lead. At the Kansas City convention, Ford was nominated by the narrow margin of 1,187 to 1,070. But Reagan had moved the party to the right, and Ford himself was regarded as a caretaker president lacking in strength and vision. He was defeated in November by Jimmy Carter.

In 1948, Ford married Elizabeth Anne (Betty) Bloomer. They had four children, Michael Gerald, John Gardner, Steven Meigs, and Susan Elizabeth.

JAMES EARL CARTER, JR., was born in the tiny village of Plains, Ga., Oct. 1, 1924, and grew up on the family farm at nearby Archery. Both parents were fifth-generation Georgians. His father, James Earl Carter, was known as a segregationist, but treated his black and white workers equally. Carter's mother, Lillian Gordy, was a matriarchal presence in home and community and opposed the then-prevailing code of racial inequality. The future President was baptized in 1935 in the conservative Southern Baptist Church and spoke often of being a "born again" Christian, although committed to the separation of church and state.

Carter married Rosalynn Smith, a neighbor, in 1946. Their first child, John William, was born a year later in Portsmouth, Va. Their other children are James Earl III, born in Honolulu in 1950; Donnel Jeffrey, born in New London, Conn., in 1952, and Amy Lynn, born in Plains in 1967.

In 1946 Carter was graduated from the U.S. Naval Academy at Annapolis and served in the nuclear-submarine program under Adm. Hyman G. Rickover. In 1954, after his father's death, he resigned from the Navy to take over the family's flourishing warehouse and cotton gin, with several thousand acres for growing seed peanuts.

Carter was elected to the Georgia Senate in 1962. In 1966 he lost the race for Governor, but was elected in 1970. His term brought a state government reorganization, sharply reduced agencies, increased economy and efficiency, and new social programs, all with no general tax increase. In 1972 the peanut farmer-politician set his sights on the Presidency and in 1974 built a base for himself as he criss-crossed the country as chairman of the Democratic Campaign Committee, appealing for revival and reform. In 1975 his image as a typical Southern white was erased when he won support of most of the old Southern civil-rights coalition after endorsement by Rep. Andrew Young, black Democrat from Atlanta, who had been the closest aide to the Rev. Martin Luther King, Jr. At Carter's 1971 inauguration as Governor he had called for an end to all forms of racial discrimination.

In the 1976 spring primaries, he won 19 out of 31 with a broad appeal to conservatives and liberals, black and white, poor and well-to-do. Throughout his campaigning Carter set forth his policies in his soft Southern voice, and with his electric-blue stare faced down skeptics who joked about "Jimmy Who?" His toothy smile became his trademark. He was nominated on the first roll-call vote of the 1976 Bicentennial Democratic National Convention in New York, and defeated Gerald R. Ford in November. Likewise, in 1980 he was renominated on the first ballot after vanquishing Senator Edward M. Kennedy of Massachusetts in the primaries. At the convention he defeated the Kennedy forces in their attempt to block a party rule that bound a large majority of pledged delegates to vote for Carter. In the election campaign, Carter attacked his rivals, Ronald Reagan and John B. Anderson, independent, with the warning that a Reagan Republican victory would heighten the risk of war and impede civil rights and economic opportunity. In November Carter lost to Reagan, who won 489 Electoral College votes and 51% of the popular tally, to 49 electoral votes and 41% for Carter.

In his one term, Carter fought hard for his programs against resistance from an independent-minded Democratic Congress that frustrated many pet projects although it overrode only two vetoes. Many of his difficulties were traced to his aides' brusqueness in dealing with Capitol Hill and insensitivity to Congressional feelings and tradition. Observers generally viewed public dissatisfaction with the "stagflation" economy as a principal factor in his defeat. Others included his jittery performance in the debate Oct. 28 with Reagan and the final uncertainties in the negotiations for freeing the Iranians' hostages, along with earlier staff problems, friction with Congress, long gasoline lines, and the months-long Iranian crisis, including the abortive sally in April 1980 to free the hostages. The President, however, did deflect criticism resulting from the activities of his brother, Billy. Yet, assessments of his record noted many positive elements. There was, for one thing, peace throughout his term, with no American combat deaths and with a brake on the advocates of force. Regarded as perhaps his greatest personal achievements were the Camp David accords between Israel and Egypt and the resulting treaty—the first between Israel and an Arab neighbor. The treaty with China and the Panama Canal treaties were also major achievements. Carter worked for nuclear-arms control. His concern for international human rights was credited with saving lives and reducing torture, and he supported the British policy that ended internecine warfare in Rhodesia, now Zimbabwe. Domestically, his environmental record was a major accomplishment. His judicial appointments won acclaim; the Southerner who had forsworn racism made 265 choices for the Federal bench that included minority members and women. On energy, he ended by price decontrols the practice of holding U.S. petroleum prices far below world levels.   —*A.P.R., Jr.*

RONALD WILSON REAGAN rode to the Presidency in 1980 on a tide of resurgent right-wing sentiment among an electorate battered by winds of unwanted change, longing for a distant, simpler era.

He left office in January 1989 with two-thirds of the American people approving his performance during his two terms. It was the highest rating for any retiring President since World War II. In his farewell speech, Reagan exhorted the nation to cling to the revival of patriotism that he had fostered. And he spoke proudly of the economic recovery during his Administrations, although regretting the huge budget deficit, for which, in part, many blamed his policies.

Reagan had retained the public's affection as he applied his political magic to policy goals. His place in history will rest, perhaps, on the short- and intermediate-range missile treaty consummated on a cordial visit to the Soviet Union that he had once reviled as an "evil empire." Its provisions, including a ground-breaking agreement on verification inspection, were formulated in four days of summit talks in Moscow in May 1988 with the Soviet leader, Mikhail S. Gorbachev.

And Reagan can point to numerous domestic achievements: sharp cuts in income tax rates, sweeping tax reform; creating economic growth without inflation, reducing the unemployment rate, among others. He failed, however, to win the "Reagan Revolution" on such issues as abortion and school prayer, and he seemed aloof from "sleazy" conduct by some top officials.

In his final months Reagan campaigned aggressively to win election as President for his two-term Vice President, George Bush.

Reagan's popularity with the public dipped sharply in 1986 when the Iran-Contra scandal broke, shortly after the Democrats gained control of the Senate. Observers agreed that Reagan's presidency had been weakened, if temporarily, by the two unrelated events. Then the weeks-long Congressional hearings in the summer of 1987 heard an array of Administration officials, present and former, tell their tales of a White House riven by deceit and undercover maneuvering. Yet no breath of illegality touched the President's personal reputation; on Aug. 12, 1987, he told the nation that he had not known of questionable activities but agreed that he was "ultimately accountable."

Ronald Reagan, actor turned politician, New Dealer turned conservative, came to the films and politics from a thoroughly Middle-American background—middle class, Middle West and small town. He was born in Tampico, Ill., Feb. 6, 1911, the second son of John Edward Reagan and Nelle Wilson Reagan, and the family later moved to Dixon, Ill. The father, of Irish descent, was a shop clerk and merchant with Democratic sympathies. It was an impoverished family; young Ronald sold homemade popcorn at high school games and worked as a lifeguard to earn money for his college tuition. When the father got a New Deal WPA job, the future President became an ardent Roosevelt Democrat.

Reagan won a B.A. degree in 1932 from Eureka (Ill.) College, where a photographic memory aided in his studies and in debating and college theatricals. In a Depression year, he was making $100 a week as a sports announcer for radio station WHO in Des Moines, Iowa, from 1932 to 1937. His career as a film and TV actor stretched from 1937 to 1966, and his salary climbed to $3,500 a week. As a World War II captain in Army film studios, Reagan re-

coiled from what he saw as the laziness of Civil Service workers, and moved to the Right. As president of the Screen Actors Guild, he resisted what he considered a Communist plot to subvert the film industry. With advancing age, Reagan left leading-man roles and became a television spokesman for the General Electric Company at $150,000.

With oratorical skill his trademark, Reagan became an active Republican. At the behest of a small group of conservative Southern California businessmen, he ran for governor with a pledge to cut spending, and was elected by almost a million votes over the political veteran, Democratic Gov. Edmund G. Brown, father of the later governor.

In the 1980 election battle against Jimmy Carter, Reagan broadened his appeal by espousing moderate policies, gaining much of his support from disaffected Democrats and blue-collar workers. The incoming Administration immediately set out to "turn the government around" with a new economic program. Over strenuous Congressional opposition, Reagan triumphed on his "supply side" theory to stimulate production and control inflation through tax cuts and sharp reductions in government spending.

The President won high acclaim for his nomination of Sandra Day O'Connor as the first woman on the Supreme Court. His later nominations met increasing opposition but did much to tilt the Court's orientation to the Right.

In 1982, the President's popularity had slipped as the economy declined into the worst recession in 40 years, with persistent high unemployment and interest rates. Initial support for "supply side" economics faded but the President won crucial battles in Congress.

Internationally, Reagan confronted numerous critical problems in his first term. The successful invasion of Grenada accomplished much diplomatically. But the intervention in Lebanon and the withdrawal of Marines after a disastrous terrorist attack were regarded as military failures.

The popular President won reelection in the 1984 landslide, with the economy improving and inflation under control. Domestically, a tax reform bill that Reagan backed became law. But the constantly growing budget deficit remained a constant irritant, with the President and Congress persistently at odds over priorities in spending for defense and domestic programs. His foreign policy met stiffening opposition, with Congress increasingly reluctant to increase spending for the Nicarguan "Contras" and the Pentagon and to expand the development of the MX missile. But even severe critics praised Reagan's restrained but decisive handling of the crisis following the hijacking of an American plane in Beirut by Moslem extremists. The attack on Libya in April 1986 galvanized the nation, although it drew scathing disapproval from the NATO alliance.

Barely three months into his first term, Reagan was the target of an assassin's bullet; his courageous comeback won public admiration.

Reagan is devoted to his wife, Nancy, whom he married after his divorce from the screen actress Jane Wyman. The children of the first marriage are Maureen, his daughter by Miss Wyman, and Michael, an adopted son. In the present marriage the children are Patricia and Ron.   —*A.P.R. Jr.*

GEORGE H. BUSH entered the Presidency on January 20, 1989, with his theme harmony and conciliation after the often turbulent Reagan years. Indeed, with his calm and unassuming manner he emerged from his subordinate Vice-Presidential role with an air of quiet authority. His Inaugural address emphasized, "A new breeze is blowing, and the old bipartisanship must be made new again."

His equanimity survived even the tempestuous Senate over the frustrated Tower nomination and the House turmoil that resulted in the replacement of the Speaker.

In his first months, the 65-year-old President, the nation's 41st in the office, established himself as his own man and all but erased memories of what many had regarded as his fiercely abrasive Presidential election campaign of 1988 and questionable tactics against his Democratic opponent. People liked his easy style and readiness to compromise even as he remained a staunch conservative, although that readiness had made some orthodox conservatives uneasy. And he still clung to his campaign slogan of "no new taxes."

Bush's Cabinet choices reflected a pragmatic desire for an efficient nonideological Government, most of them the "inside the Beltway" type so favored in Washington. Three conservatives, but with flexible viewpoints, were among his close associates: Jack F. Kemp, to be Secretary of Housing and Urban Development; former Gov. John H. Sununu of New Hampshire, White House Chief of Staff; and William J. Bennett, coordinator of the antidrug campaign. James A. Baker 3rd, Secretary of State, is a veteran White House pro. The Cabinet also includes a black, two Hispanics, and two women.

At home and abroad, Bush, a World War II hero, won plaudits for his confident, competent conduct at the NATO 40th anniversary summit meeting at Brussels, the Paris economic conference, and on his tour of Eastern Europe, all in his first few months. Perhaps the gravest challenge as the first year drew on was the Lebanon hostage crisis, sharpened by the execution killing of a United States Marine officer. Another grave issue was the ongoing war on the drug traffic, at home and worldwide.

The dramatically changing events in Poland represented a major challenge, to which the Bush Administration responded with caution, and with restrained language on events in Eastern Europe.

In his European dealings, particularly at Brussels, the reaction of the Allies as well as that in Washington was highly favorable. Observers felt that he had scored with new proposals for discussions on conventional arms, such as the inclusion of aircraft, and with fending off a breach in the European alliance.

Domestically, the President had to cope with such issues as the Exxon oil spill in Alaska and the dispute over flag burning following the Supreme Court decision establishing the free speech right of that form of political protest, a decision that "disturbed" him.

In the flurry of the traditional "100 days" assessment in April, the President told newspaper publishers that he noted a "good start" in domestic and foreign policy undertakings. Among matters he cited were a bipartisan budget agreement with Congress, moves to stabilize the beleaguered savings and loan industry and on education, hazardous wastes, and the third world debt.

Bush, scion of an aristocratic New England family, came to the White House after a long career in public service, in which he held top positions in national and international organizations. As Ronald Reagan's Vice President, he avoided the appearance of direct involvement in the Iran-Contra affair while not seeming to shy away from the President.

Earlier, in the 1960s, Bush won two contests for a Texas Republican seat in the House of Representatives, but lost two bids for a Senate seat and one for the Presidency. After his second race for the Senate, President Nixon appointed him U.S. delegate to the United Nations with the rank of Ambassador and he later became Republican National Chairman. He headed the United States liaison office in Beijing before becoming Director of Central Intelligence.

In 1980 Bush became Reagan's running mate despite earlier criticism of Reagan "voodoo economics" and by the 1984 election had won acclaim for devotion to Reagan's conservative agenda despite his own reputation as somewhat more liberally inclined. Nevertheless, die-hard right-wingers could find satisfaction in Bush's war record and his Government service, particularly with the C.I.A. Throughout he remained influential in White House decisions, particularly in foreign affairs.

In the 1988 campaign, Bush's choice of Senator Dan Quayle of Indiana for Vice President surprised his friends and provoked criticism and ridicule that continued even after the Administration was established in office. Nonetheless Bush strongly defended his choice against charges against Quayle of youth and inexperience.

The future President joined the Navy after war broke out and at 18 became the Navy's youngest commissioned pilot, serving from 1942 to 1945. The man later derided by some as a "wimp" fought the Japanese on 58 missions and was shot down once. He won the Distinguished Flying Cross.

Throughout his whole career, Bush had the backing of an established family, headed by his father, the autocratic and wealthy Prescott Bush, who was elected to the Senate from Connecticut in 1952. And his family helped the young patrician became established in his early business ventures, a rich uncle raising most of the capital required for founding a new oil company in Texas.

George Herbert Walker Bush was born June 12, 1924, in Milton, Mass., to Prescott and Dorothy Bush. The family later moved to Connecticut. The youth studied at the élite Phillips Academy in Andover, Mass., before entering the Navy.

After the war, Bush earned an economics degree and a Phi Beta Kappa key in two and a half years at Yale University. While there he captained the baseball team and was initiated into "Skull and Bones," the prestigious Yale secret society.

In 1945 Bush married Barbara Pierce of Rye, N.Y., daughter of a magazine publisher. With his bride, Bush moved to Texas instead of entering his father's investment banking business. There he founded his oil company and in 1980 reported an estimated wealth of $1.4 million.

The Bushes have lived in 17 cities and more than a score of homes and have traveled in as many countries. In her husband's frequent absences during the early years, Mrs. Bush was often matriarch of a family of four boys and a girl. Bush is close to his immediate family and to 10 grandchildren, a sister, and three brothers.

Bush sold his Houston home several years ago and moved from the Vice President's dwelling to the White House, and lives there and at the family estate at Kennebunkport, Maine.

—Arthur P. Reed, Jr.

WEATHER & CLIMATE

Weather Skills

By Stephen Strauss

When humans and intelligent alien life first meet, the climates on their respective planets could be so different as to defy comparison. But the beings will still joke about the universal inability of forecasters to predict the weather.

Despite such jibes, North American weather services are increasingly able to anticipate "skillfully" what will happen in the future. In May 1988, Canada's national weather bureau joined its U.S. counterpart in offering the public a 30-day forecast. While the U.S. Weather Service has been issuing 30-day forecasts since 1947 and 90-day forecasts since 1972, only recently have they qualified these with indications of the skill of the projections. Canada will issue 90-day forecasts within a year, says Amir Shabbar of the Canadian Atmospheric Environment Service in Toronto. The Canadian skill levels were recognized after predictions were analyzed over a three-year period starting in 1985, says Shabbar.

Climatologists studying long-term patterns say their new confidence is not based on any major breakthrough in understanding the high-altitude winds and circulation patterns that create most weather. Rather, incremental advances in computer modeling and collecting historical data have helped scientists revise the concept of "skill" in forecasting. The result could be major economic benefits for certain areas at certain times of the year.

Along with his colleagues, Robert Livezey, chief scientist of the prediction branch of the U.S. Climate Analysis Center in Washington, D.C., has led the way in defining the elements of a "skillful" forecast. He believes unskilled predictions have often hidden behind ambiguous language. He says the *Farmer's Almanac*, which began issuing monthly mean forecasts for 16 U.S. regions in the mid-1970s, is a classic beneficiary of verbal vagueness. The almanac makes its predictions based on a secret formula first derived in 1818. According to editor Ray Geiger, it is partially based on sunspot activity and the position of planets.

In 1981 University of Illinois atmospheric scientists John Walsh and D. Allen analyzed the almanac's predictive ability over a five-year period and found that it was right about half the time. In fact, until recently forecasters had assumed they showed some degree of skill if they were right more than half the time, but Livezey says that record demonstrates "no measurable skill" and actually masks ignorance. He points out that some predictions must be right almost all the time to be useful. For example, a prophecy that the Arizona desert will be dry in July means little. Similarly, most of the world's precipitation occurs in infrequent downpours, so daily predictions of below-average rain incorrectly appear wise.

Meteorologists have also eliminated numerous subtle errors in compiling information that biased previous forecasting efforts. Weather data has often been collected at airports, where "microclimates" tend to get significantly warmer when houses are built around them. Consequently, predictions of higher-than-normal temperatures could appear right even when they aren't.

Weather Cents

Taking factors like these into account, meteorologists now say that a forecaster in the Arizona case must be right more than 87 percent of the time to be considered skillful. In addition, they have created a new sliding scale—the "skill rate"—that compares predictions to chance guesses. By this standard, a score of 94 percent or higher would mark a skillful forecast.

Climatologists studying long-term trends have also begun to uncover hidden pockets of skill. For example, they have found they have a much better record predicting temperature than precipitation. And they know that predictions of North American temperature patterns in winter have been right more often than those for summers, in part because warm air is less stable than cold air.

Such knowledge has led to analyses showing how relatively small improvements in long-range forecasting—so small as to seem insignificant to outsiders—might have a dramatic impact. Atmospheric scientist Allan Murphy and his associates at Oregon State University in Corvallis have found that dry-land farmers could earn $10 more a hectare if the rainfall forecast around Havre, Mont., were merely a half percent better than chance. Murphy says farmers make decisions about whether to plant spring wheat based on soil-moisture conditions and some feeling about future rain. Forecasts 10 percent better might yield returns of $120 per hectare.

Livezey adds that many potential users of forecasts are unaware of the money to be saved by trusting weather reports. Meteorologists have learned much about where and when predictions are reliable, and although the Great Plains remains a forecaster's nightmare, parts of the Carolinas are much easier to deal with. Large-scale heating-oil consumers there could reap benefits since long-range temperature forecasts are right three-fourths of the time. Livezey suggests that fuel companies could allocate supplies in advance more efficiently if they knew future temperature conditions. □

Stephen Strauss is a science reporter for the *Globe and Mail* in Toronto. Reprinted with permission from *Technology Review*, copyright © 1988.

About That Drought ...

By Richard R. Heim, Jr.

. . ., while the drought of 1988 afflicted a large part of the United States, it was not as bad as the droughts of the 1930s and 1950s—and probably other droughts that occurred before weather records were kept.

Drought Detective Work

Comprehensive weather records for the nation as a whole generally go back only to the 1890s. Other sources have to be sought to reconstruct the drought picture for earlier times—sources such as newspaper reports, crop-harvest statistics, and the width of growth rings in trees (generally, tree rings are wide when there is abundant rain and narrow when there isn't enough rain to support normal growth).

While studying tree rings from Nebraska, for example, dendroclimatologist Harry Weakly found 12 droughts (from 1220 to 1957) that lasted 10 years or more. The drought that began in 1276 *lasted 38 years.* Climatologist Reid Bryson attributes the disappearance of several Indian civilizations in the Great Plains and Southwest to a shift to a drier climate between 1200 and 1400.

According to climatologist Ivan Tannehill, very little contemporary information is available for droughts prior to the Civil War. Climate historian David M. Ludlum has summarized what we do know in the *Weather Record Book.* As noted by Ludlum, drought plagued the colonists almost from the first day of settlement. The Pilgrims' crops were threatened by a lack of rain in 1621 and 1623, while fields of grain caught fire in eastern New England during severe droughts in 1749, 1761, and 1762. The eastern states were also very dry in 1805 and 1822.

In California, in the record dry season of 1850 and 1851, only 33 percent of normal rain fell at Sacramento and San Francisco, while the summer of 1854 brought widespread drought and crop failures from New York to Missouri. In the next decade, the two extremely dry seasons of 1862-63 and 1863-64 put an end to the extensive cattle industry in southern California.

According to a paper by climatologist Dean Bark, the years around 1860 were very dry in the central Plains and Midwest—the area including Kansas, Missouri, Illinois, Iowa, Minnesota, and Wisconsin. Professor Tannehill notes that the drought of 1860 was "the most severe recorded in this country up to that time."

Rainfall was plentiful in the Great Plains from the mid-1860s to the mid-1880s, and a lot of farmers migrated to the area. Prolonged dry weather returned to the Plains in the late 1880s, however, culminating in a complete crop failure in 1894. Ludlum notes that fully half the settlers of Nebraska and western Kansas deserted the area during this drought.

Richard R. Heim, Jr., is the meterologist in charge of the Drought Information Center at the National Climatic Data Center in Asheville, North Carolina. Reprinted from *Weatherwise,* Copyright © 1988 by the Helen Dwight Reid Educational Foundation.

The entire country east of the Mississippi River was hit by drought in 1881. . . . Even the water supply of New York City failed and it was necessary to find new water sources.

Severe drought occurred in the southwestern and southeastern corners of the country around the turn of the century. Drought struck again, in the southern Plains, northern Plains, and northeastern region in 1910 and 1911 (1910 is still the driest year for the nation as a whole since 1895), and in the southern Plains in 1917 and 1918. The Far West was hit by extensive drought in 1924, as was the Southeast in 1925. These were generally short-lived events compared to those of the late 1800s and what was soon to follow.

The Greatest Weather Disaster in American History?

The drought of the 1930s has been called by Ludlum "the greatest disaster in American history attributable to meteorological factors." Drought dominated the entire decade, causing what hydrologist Luna Leopold called the period of lowest streamflow in the United States since river records began. It is the longest drought of the 20th century, afflicting some part of the country from 1930 to 1941. It also affected parts of Canada and Mexico.

The 1930s drought spread across large parts of the country during several peak periods—1930, 1934, 1936, and 1939 and 1940. During 1934 the dry region stretched solidly from New York and Pennsylvania across the Great Plains to the California coast, covering fully 61 percent of the country. A great "dust bowl" was created in the south-central Plains, covering some 50 million acres at its greatest extent, during the winter of 1935-1936. . . .

As plants withered and the ground cracked, strong winds blew the soil into huge dust storms. "Occasionally dust storms raged for days, and twice they overspread nearly half the United States," according to Lylyan Block, writing in a 1934 edition of the *Bulletin of the American Meteorological Society.* And once again there was "tremendous emigration from the Plains region."

The 1940s brought generally wet weather to most of the nation, but widespread drought returned in the 1950s. During 1953 and 1954, severe drought stretched from the Southeast across the Ohio Valley and into the central Rockies and Great Basin, at its peak covering 51 percent of the country. The dry area expanded again in 1956, covering the southern and central Plains. . . . Dust storms once again swirled across the Great Plains.

Drought in the Midst of Moisture

Generally speaking, the United States has been in an overall *wet spell* since the 1950s. Indeed, eight of the twenty wettest years for the country as a whole have occurred in the 1970s and 1980s, based on records going back to 1895. (In comparison, the 1930s had six of the twenty driest years and the 1950s four of the 20 driest years.)

In spite of the relative overall wetness, significant regional droughts did occur in the 1960s and 1970s. The northern Rockies were dry during 1960 and 1961, as was much of the Midwest in 1963 and 1964. Moderate drought appeared in the Northeast in 1961, then worsened into the extreme category during 1964 to 1966. Water shortages developed when New York City reservoirs dropped to about 30 percent of capacity, and forest fires were widespread by the autumn of 1963.

Severe drought returned briefly to the Southwest and the southern Plains in 1971 and again in 1972 and 1974. Extreme drought occurred during 1976 and 1977 in the Far West and northern Plains-Great Lakes region. For some of the people in these areas, the 1976 and 1977 drought was their most *severe* drought of this century (as measured by the Palmer Drought Severity Index). Low rainfall and reservoir records were set in many parts of California.

Drought appeared briefly during 1980 and 1981 in scattered areas across the country. The drought of 1988, however, is the major drought of the 1980s. This summer, [1988] the Mississippi River reached near-record low levels at many gaging stations, restricting barge and towboat traffic. At Memphis, the river level was the lowest since 1872, the year records for Memphis begin.

Reservoir levels in California were also down,

though not as low as in the 1970s. Farmers in the Plains and Midwest were suffering what *U.S. News and World Report* magazine called "potentially the worst crop disaster since the 1930s." Parts of the Southeast were experiencing the worst drought of the century.

The current drought has been going on in the West since 1987 and in the Southeast since 1984. It was the dryness of the 1987-1988 winter and following spring, however, that brought the regions together to form the national drought of 1988.

* * *

Those Record-High Temperatures

* * *

While 1988 has been hot, the 1930s set temperature records that still stand: most of the Great Plains and Midwest had their hottest June and July period in the 1930s. When temperatures are averaged across the entire country for the whole year, the 1930s show six of the twenty warmest years since 1895.

The 1988 drought has produced some of the driest and hottest weather of the twentieth century. When put into historical perspective, however, it is simply the latest in a long series of similar fluctuations that characterize the climatic history of our country. □

Weather Glossary

blizzard: storm characterized by strong winds, low temperatures, and large amounts of snow.
blowing snow: snow lifted from ground surface by wind; restricts visibility.
cold wave warning: indicates that a change to abnormally cold weather is expected; greater than normal protective measures will be required.
cyclone: circulation of winds rotating counterclockwise in the northern hemisphere and clockwise in the southern hemisphere. Hurricanes and tornadoes are both examples of cyclones.
drifting snow: strong winds will blow loose or falling snow into significant drifts.
drizzle: uniform close precipitation of tiny drops with diameter of less than .02 inch.
flash flood: dangerous rapid rise of water levels in streams, rivers, or over land area.
freezing rain or drizzle: rain or drizzle that freezes on contact with the ground or other objects forming a coating of ice on exposed surfaces.
gale warning: winds in the 33–48 knot (38–55 mph) range forecast.
hail: small balls of ice falling separately or in lumps; usually associated with thunderstorms and temperatures that may be above freezing.
hazardous driving warnings: indicates that drizzle, freezing rain, snow, sleet, or strong winds make driving conditions difficult.
heavy snow warnings: issued when 4 inches or more of snow are expected to fall in a 12-hour period or when 6 inches or more are anticipated in a 24-hour period.
hurricane: devastating cyclonic storm; winds over 74 mph near storm center; usually tropical in origin; called cyclone in Indian Ocean, typhoon in the Pacific.
hurricane warning: winds in excess of 64 knots (74 mph) in connection with hurricane.

rain: precipitation of liquid particles with diameters larger than .02 inch.
sleet: translucent or transparent ice pellets; frozen rain; generally a winter phenomenon.
small craft warning: indicates winds as high as 33 knots (38 mph) and sea conditions dangerous to small boats.
snow flurries: snow falling for a short time at intermittent periods; accumulations are usually small.
snow squall: brief, intense falls of snow, usually accompanied by gusty winds.
storm warnings: winds greater than 48 knots (55 mph) are forecast.
temperature-humidity index (THI): measure of personal discomfort based on the combined effects of temperature and humidity. Most people are uncomfortable when the THI is 75. A THI of 80 produces acute discomfort for almost everyone.
tidal waves: series of ocean waves caused by earthquakes; can reach speeds of 600 mph; they grow in height as they reach shore and can crest as high as 100 feet.
thunder: the sound produced by the rapid expansion of air heated by lightning.
tornado: dangerous whirlwind associated with the cumulonimbus clouds of severe thunderstorms; winds up to 300 mph.
tornado warning: tornado has actually been detected by radar or sighted in designated area.
tornado watch: potential exists in the watch area for storms that could contain tornadoes.
travelers' warning: *see* hazardous driving warning.
tsunami: *see* tidal waves.
wind-chill factor: combined effect of temperature and wind speed as compared to equivalent temperature in calm air.

Climate of 100 Selected U.S. Cities

| City | Average Monthly Temperature (°F)[1] | | | | Precipitation | | Snowfall | |
	Jan.	April	July	Oct.	Average (in.)[1]	annual (days)[2]	Average annual (in.)[2]	Years[2]
Albany, N.Y.	21.1	46.6	71.4	50.5	35.74	134	65.5	38
Albuquerque, N.M.	34.8	55.1	78.8	57.4	8.12	59	10.6	45
Anchorage, Alaska	13.0	35.4	58.1	34.6	15.20	115	69.2	41[3]
Asheville, N.C.	36.8	55.7	73.2	56.0	47.71	124	17.5	20
Atlanta, Ga.	41.9	61.8	78.6	62.2	48.61	115	1.9	50
Atlantic City, N.J.	31.8	51.0	74.4	55.5	41.93	112	16.4	40[3]
Austin, Texas	49.1	68.7	84.7	69.8	31.50	83	0.9	43
Baltimore, Md.	32.7	54.0	76.8	56.9	41.84	113	21.8	34
Baton Rouge, La.	50.8	68.4	82.1	68.2	55.77	108	0.1	34[3]
Billings, Mont.	20.9	44.6	72.3	49.3	15.09	96	57.2	50
Birmingham, Ala.	42.9	62.8	80.1	62.6	54.52	117	1.3	41
Bismark, N.D.	6.7	42.5	70.4	46.1	15.36	96	40.3	45
Boise, Idaho	29.9	48.6	74.6	51.9	11.71	92	21.4	45
Boston, Mass.	29.6	48.7	73.5	54.8	43.81	127	41.8	49[3]
Bridgeport, Conn.	29.5	48.6	74.0	56.0	41.56	117	26.0	36
Buffalo, N.Y.	23.5	45.4	70.7	51.5	37.52	169	92.2	41
Burlington, Vt.	16.6	42.7	69.6	47.9	33.69	153	78.2	41
Caribou, Maine	10.7	37.3	65.1	43.1	36.59	160	113.3	45
Casper, Wyom.	22.2	42.1	70.9	47.1	11.43	95	80.5	34
Charleston, S.C.	47.9	64.3	80.5	65.8	51.59	113	0.6	42
Charleston, W.Va.	32.9	55.3	74.5	55.9	42.43	151	31.5	37
Charlotte, N.C.	40.5	60.3	78.5	60.7	43.16	111	6.1	45
Cheyenne, Wyom.	26.1	41.8	68.9	47.5	13.31	98	54.1	49
Chicago, Ill.	21.4	48.8	73.0	53.5	33.34	127	40.3	26
Cleveland, Ohio	25.5	48.1	71.6	53.2	35.40	156	53.6	43
Columbia, S.C.	44.7	63.8	81.0	63.4	49.12	109	1.9	37
Columbus, Ohio	27.1	51.4	73.8	53.9	36.97	137	28.3	37[3]
Concord, N.H.	19.9	44.1	69.5	48.3	36.53	125	64.5	43
Dallas–Ft. Worth, Texas	44.0	65.9	86.3	67.9	29.46	78	3.1	31
Denver, Colo.	29.5	47.4	73.4	51.9	15.31	88	59.8	50
Des Moines, Iowa	18.6	50.5	76.3	54.2	30.83	107	34.7	45
Detroit, Mich.	23.4	47.3	71.9	51.9	30.97	133	40.4	26
Dodge City, Kan.	29.5	54.3	80.0	57.7	20.66	78	19.5	42
Duluth, Minn.	6.3	38.3	65.4	44.2	29.68	135	77.4	41[3]
El Paso, Texas	44.2	63.6	82.5	63.6	7.82	47	5.2	45
Fairbanks, Alaska	−12.7	30.2	61.5	25.1	10.37	106	67.5	33
Fargo, N.D.	4.3	42.1	70.6	46.3	19.59	100	35.9	42
Grand Junction, Colo.	25.5	51.7	78.9	54.9	8.00	72	26.1	38
Grand Rapids, Mich.	22.0	46.3	71.4	50.9	34.35	143	72.4	21
Hartford, Conn.	25.2	48.8	73.4	52.4	44.39	127	50.0	30
Helena, Mont.	18.1	42.3	67.9	45.1	11.37	96	47.9	44
Honolulu, Hawaii	72.6	75.7	80.1	79.5	23.47	100	0.0	38[3]
Houston, Texas	51.4	68.7	83.1	69.7	44.76	105	0.4	50
Indianapolis, Ind.	26.0	52.4	75.1	54.8	39.12	125	23.1	53[3]
Jackson, Miss.	45.7	65.1	81.9	65.0	52.82	109	1.2	21
Jacksonville, Fla.	53.2	67.7	81.3	69.5	52.76	116	T	43
Juneau, Alaska	21.8	39.1	55.7	41.8	53.15	220	102.8	41
Kansas City, Mo.	28.4	56.9	80.9	59.6	29.27	98	20.0	43
Knoxville, Tenn.	38.2	59.6	77.6	59.5	47.29	127	12.3	42
Las Vegas, Nev.	44.5	63.5	90.2	67.5	4.19	26	1.4	36
Lexington, Ky.	31.5	55.1	75.9	56.8	45.68	131	16.3	40
Little Rock, Ark.	39.9	62.4	82.1	63.1	49.20	104	5.4	42
Long Beach, Calif.	55.2	60.9	72.8	67.5	11.54	32	T	41[3]
Los Angeles, Calif.	56.0	59.5	69.0	66.3	12.08	36	T	49
Louisville, Ky.	32.5	56.6	77.6	57.7	43.56	125	17.5	37
Madison, Wisc.	15.6	45.8	70.6	49.5	30.84	118	40.8	36
Memphis, Tenn.	39.6	62.6	82.1	62.9	51.57	107	5.5	34
Miami, Fla.	67.1	75.3	82.5	77.9	57.55	129	0.0	42
Milwaukee, Wisc.	18.7	44.6	70.5	50.9	30.94	125	47.0	44
Minneapolis-St. Paul, Minn.	11.2	46.0	73.1	49.6	26.36	115	48.9	46
Mobile, Ala.	50.8	68.0	82.2	68.5	64.64	123	0.3	43
Montgomery, Ala.	46.7	65.2	81.7	65.3	49.16	108	0.3	40
Mt. Washington, N.H.	5.1	22.4	48.7	30.5	89.92	209	246.8	52
Nashville, Tenn.	37.1	59.7	79.4	60.2	48.49	119	11.1	43
Newark, N.J.	31.2	52.1	76.8	57.2	42.34	122	28.2	43
New Orleans, La.	52.4	68.7	82.1	69.2	59.74	114	0.2	38[3]
New York, N.Y.	31.8	51.9	76.4	57.5	42.82	119	26.1	40[3]

City	Average Monthly Temperature (°F)[1]				Precipitation		Snowfall	
	Jan.	April	July	Oct.	Average (in.)[1]	annual (days)[2]	Average annual (in.)[2]	Years[2]
Norfolk, Va.	39.9	58.2	78.4	61.3	45.22	115	7.9	36
Oklahoma City, Okla.	35.9	60.2	82.1	62.3	30.89	82	9.0	45
Olympia, Wash.	37.2	47.3	63.0	50.1	50.96	164	18.0	43
Omaha, Neb.	20.2	52.2	77.7	54.5	30.34	98	31.1	49[3]
Philadelphia, Pa.	31.2	52.9	76.5	56.5	41.42	117	21.9	42[3]
Phoenix, Ariz.	52.3	68.1	92.3	73.4	7.11	36	T	47[3]
Pittsburgh, Pa.	26.7	50.1	72.0	52.5	36.30	154	44.6	32
Portland, Maine	21.5	42.8	68.1	48.5	43.52	128	72.4	44
Portland, Ore.	38.9	50.4	67.7	54.3	37.39	154	6.8	44
Providence, R.I.	28.2	47.9	72.5	53.2	45.32	124	37.1	31
Raleigh, N.C.	39.6	59.4	77.7	59.7	41.76	112	7.7	40
Reno, Nev.	32.2	46.4	69.5	50.3	7.49	51	25.3	42
Richmond, Va.	36.6	57.9	77.8	58.6	44.07	113	14.6	47
Roswell, N.M.	41.4	61.9	81.4	61.7	9.70	52	11.4	37[3]
Sacramento, Calif.	45.3	58.2	75.6	63.9	17.10	58	0.1	36[3]
Salt Lake City, Utah	28.6	49.2	77.5	53.0	15.31	90	59.1	56
San Antonio, Texas	50.4	69.6	84.6	70.2	29.13	81	0.4	42
San Diego, Calif.	56.8	61.2	70.3	67.5	9.32	43	T	44
San Francisco, Calif.	48.5	54.8	62.2	60.6	19.71	63	T	57
Savannah, Ga.	49.1	66.0	81.2	66.9	49.70	111	0.3	34
Seattle-Tacoma, Wash.	39.1	48.7	64.8	52.4	38.60	158	12.8	40
Sioux Falls, S.D.	12.4	46.4	74.0	49.4	24.12	96	39.9	39
Spokane, Wash.	25.7	45.8	69.7	47.5	16.71	114	51.5	37
Springfield, Ill.	24.6	53.3	76.5	56.0	33.78	114	24.5	37
St. Louis, Mo.	28.8	56.1	78.9	57.9	33.91	111	19.8	48[3]
Tampa, Fla.	59.8	71.5	82.1	74.4	46.73	107	T	38
Toledo, Ohio	23.1	47.8	71.8	51.7	31.78	137	38.3	29
Tucson, Ariz.	51.1	64.9	86.2	70.4	11.14	52	1.2	44
Tulsa, Okla.	35.2	61.0	83.2	62.6	38.77	89	9.0	46
Vero Beach, Fla.	61.9	71.7	81.1	75.2	51.41	n.a.	n.a.	0
Washington, D.C.	35.2	56.7	78.9	59.3	39.00	112	17.0	41[3]
Wilmington, Del.	31.2	52.4	76.0	56.3	41.38	117	20.9	37
Wichita, Kan.	29.6	56.3	81.4	59.1	28.61	85	16.4	31

1. Based on 30 year period 1951–80. Data latest available. 2. Data through 1984 based on number of years as indicated in Years column. 3. For snowfall data where number of years differ from that for precipitation data. T = trace. n.a. = not available. *Source:* National Oceanic and Atmospheric Administration.

Wind Chill Factors

Wind speed (mph)	Thermometer reading (degrees Fahrenheit)															
	35	30	25	20	15	10	5	0	−5	−10	−15	−20	−25	−30	−35	−40	−45
5	33	27	21	19	12	7	0	−5	−10	−15	−21	−26	−31	−36	−42	−47	−52
10	22	16	10	3	−3	−9	−15	−22	−27	−34	−40	−46	−52	−58	−64	−71	−77
15	16	9	2	−5	−11	−18	−25	−31	−38	−45	−51	−58	−65	−72	−78	−85	−92
20	12	4	−3	−10	−17	−24	−31	−39	−46	−53	−60	−67	−74	−81	−88	−95	−103
25	8	1	−7	−15	−22	−29	−36	−44	−51	−59	−66	−74	−81	−88	−96	−103	−110
30	6	−2	−10	−18	−25	−33	−41	−49	−56	−64	−71	−79	−86	−93	−101	−109	−116
35	4	−4	−12	−20	−27	−35	−43	−52	−58	−67	−74	−82	−89	−97	−105	−113	−120
40	3	−5	−13	−21	−29	−37	−45	−53	−60	−69	−76	−84	−92	−100	−107	−115	−123
45	2	−6	−14	−22	−30	−38	−46	−54	−62	−70	−78	−85	−93	−102	−109	−117	−125

NOTES: This chart gives equivalent temperatures for combinations of wind speed and temperatures. For example, the combination of a temperature of 10° Fahrenheit and a wind blowing at 10 mph has a cooling power equal to −9° F. Wind speeds of higher than 45 mph have little additional cooling effect.

Other Recorded Extremes

Highest average annual mean temperature (World): Dallol, Ethiopia (Oct. 1960-Dec. 1966), 94° F (35° C). **(U.S.):** Key West, Fla. (30-year normal), 78.2° F (25.7° C).

Lowest average annual mean temperature (Antarctica): Plateau Station −70° F (−57° C). **(U.S.):** Barrow, Alaska (30-year normal), 9.3° F (−13° C).

Greatest average yearly rainfall (U.S.): Mt. Waialeale, Kauai, Hawaii (32-year avg), 460 in. (1,168 cm). **(India):** Cherrapunji (74-year avg), 450 in. (1,143 cm).

Minimum average yearly rainfall (Chile): Arica (59-year avg), 0.03 in. (0.08 cm) (no rainfall for 14 consecutive years). **(U.S.):** Death Valley, Calif. (42-year avg), 1.63 in. (4.14 cm). Bagdad, Calif., holds the U.S. record for the longest period with no measurable rain, 767 days, from Oct. 3, 1912 to Nov. 8, 1914).

Hottest summer avg in Western Hemisphere (U.S.): Death Valley, Calif., 98° F (36.7° C).

Longest hot spell (W. Australia): Marble Bar, 100° F (38° C) (or above) for 162 consecutive days, Oct. 30, 1923-Apr. 7, 1924.

Largest hailstone (U.S.): Coffeyville, KS, 17.5 in. (44.5 cm), Sept. 3, 1979.

World and U.S. Extremes of Climate

Highest recorded temperature

	Place	Date	Degree Fahrenheit	Degree Centigrade
World (Africa)	El Azizia, Libya	Sept. 13, 1922	136	58
North America (U.S.)	Death Valley, Calif.	July 10, 1913	134	57
Asia	Tirat Tsvi, Israel	June 21, 1942	129	54
Australia	Cloncurry, Queensland	Jan. 16, 1889	128	53
Europe	Seville, Spain	Aug. 4, 1881	122	50
South America	Rivadavia, Argentina	Dec. 11, 1905	120	49
Canada	Midale and Yellow Grass, Saskatchewan	July 5, 1937	113	45
Persian Gulf (sea-surface)		August 5, 1924	96	36
South Pole		Dec. 27, 1978	7.5	−14
Antarctica	Vanda Station	Jan. 5, 1974	59	15

Lowest recorded temperature

	Place	Date	Degree Fahrenheit	Degree Centigrade
World (Antarctica)	Vostok	July 21, 1983	−129	−89
Asia	Verkhoyansk/Oimekon	Feb. 6, 1933	−90	−68
Greenland	Northice	Jan. 9, 1954	−87	−66
North America (excl. Greenland)	Snag, Yukon, Canada	Feb. 3, 1947	−81	−63
Alaska	Prospect Creek, Endicott Mts.	Jan. 23, 1971	−80	−62
U.S., excluding Alaska	Rogers Pass, Mont.	Jan. 20, 1954	−70	−56.5
Europe	Ust 'Shchugor, U.S.S.R.	n.a.	−67	−55
South America	Sarmiento, Argentina	Jan. 1, 1907	−27	−33
Africa	Ifrane, Morocco	Feb. 11, 1935	−11	−24
Australia	Charlotte Pass, N.S.W.	July 22, 1947	−8	−22
United States	Prospect Creek, Alaska	Jan. 23, 1971	−80	−62

Greatest rainfalls

	Place	Date	Inches	Centimeters
1 minute (World)	Unionville, Md.	July 4, 1956	1.23	3.1
20 minutes (World)	Curtea-de-Arges, Romania	July 7, 1889	8.1	20.5
42 minutes (World)	Holt, Mo.	June 22, 1947	12	30.5
12 hours (World)	Foc-Foc, La Reunion	Jan. 7-8, 1966	45	114
24 hours (World)	Foc-Foc, La Réunion	Jan. 7-8, 1966	72	182.5
24 hours (N. Hemisphere)	Paishih, Taiwan	Sept. 10-11, 1963	49	125
24 hours (Australia)	Bellenden Ker, Queensland	Jan. 4, 1979	44	114
24 hours (U.S.)	Alvin, Texas	July 25-26, 1979	43	109
24 hours (Canada)	Ucluelet Brynnor Mines, British Columbia	Oct. 6, 1967	19	49
5 days (World)	Commerson, La Réunion	Jan. 23-28, 1980	156	395
1 month (World)	Cherrapunji, India	July 1861	366	930
12 months (World)	Cherrapunji, India	Aug. 1860-Aug. 1861	1,042	2,647
12 months (U.S.)	Kukui, Maui, Hawaii	Dec. 1981-Dec. 1982	739	1878

Greatest snowfalls

	Place	Date	Inches	Centimeters
1 month (U.S.)	Tamarack, Calif.	Jan. 1911	390	991
24 hours (N. America)	Silver Lake, Colo.	April 14-15, 1921	76	192.5
24 hours (Alaska)	Thompson Pass	Dec. 29, 1955	62	157.5
19 hours (France)	Bessans	April 5-6, 1969	68	173
1 storm (N. America)	Mt. Shasta Ski Bowl, Calif.	Feb. 13-19, 1959	189	480
1 storm (Alaska)	Thompson Pass	Dec. 26-31, 1955	175	445.5
1 season (N. America)	Paradise Ranger Sta., Wash.	1971-1972	1,122	2,850
1 season (Alaska)	Thompson Pass	1952-1953	974.5	2,475
1 season (Canada)	Revelstoke Mt. Copeland, British Columbia	1971-1972	964	2,446.5

Source: U.S. Army Corps of Engineers, Engineer Topographic Laboratories.

Devastating North Atlantic Hurricanes of the 20th Century

The following is a selected list of North Atlantic hurricanes based on casualties, damage, and general public interest. Facts about each storm are taken from Weather records, although in some cases only estimates of wind speed are available. Data given in this list pertain only to U.S. land areas except where indicated otherwise.

Date	Areas hardest hit	Land stations with highest wind speed	Deaths (U.S. only)	Est. damage (millions)	Remarks
1900, Aug. 27–Sept. 15	Galveston, Tex.	Galveston, Tex. (120[1] mph)	6,000	$30	Damage due to both winds and storm wave. Galveston Is. inundated.
1909, Sept. 10–21	Louisiana and Mississippi	New Orleans, La. (53 mph)	350	5	Winds 50–75 mi. W of New Orleans, where deaths occurred, were stronger than 68 mph.
1915, Aug. 5–23	East Texas and Louisiana	Galveston, Tex. (120 mph)	275	50	Water 5–6 ft deep in Galveston business district. 90% of homes demolished. Warnings issued well ahead of time.
1915, Sept. 22–Oct. 1	Mid-Gulf Coast	Burrwood, La. (140 mph)	275	13	Many casualties due to persons insisting on staying in low-lying areas despite warnings.
1919, Sept. 2–15	Florida, Louisiana, and Texas	Sand Key, Fla. (84[1] mph)	287	22	488 persons drowned at sea.
1926, Sept. 11–22	Florida and Alabama	Miami, Fla. (138 mph)	243	112	Most deaths were in Miami area. Said to have been one of most destructive storms of century.
1928, Sept. 6–20	Southern Florida	Lake Okeechobee, Fla. (75[1] mph)	1,836	25	1,870 injured. Nearly all deaths were in Lake Okeechobee area. Winds estimated as high as 160 mph caused Lake to overflow into populated areas.
1935, Aug. 29–Sept. 10	Southern Florida	Tampa, Fla. (86 mph)	408	6	Sustained winds over Florida Keys est. 150–200 mph. Remembered as "Labor Day Storm."
1938, Sept. 10–22	Long Island and Southern New England	Blue Hills Obs., Mass. (183 mph)	600	306	Unusually destructive. Storm center moved as fast as 56 mph at times. 1,754 injured.
1944, Sept. 9–16	North Carolina to New England	Cape Henry, Va. (150[1] mph)	46	100	344 deaths at sea. Shipping lanes were crowded with war-time activity.
1944, Oct. 12–23	Florida	Dry Tortugas Is. (120 mph)	18	100	About 300 were killed in Cuba area before storm reached U.S. Evacuation of thousands from threatened areas in Fla. prevented higher toll.
1947, Sept. 4–21	Florida and Mid-Gulf Coast	Hillsboro Light, Fla. (155 mph)	51	110	Wind damage especially heavy along Gulf Coast and Florida east coast.
1954, Aug. 25–31	North Carolina to New England	Block Island, R.I. (135 mph)	60	461	"CAROL"—more damage than any other single storm to this date. Water and high waves flooded low-lying areas; 1,000 injuries in Long Island—New England area.
1954, Sept. 2–14	New Jersey to New England	Block Island, R.I. (87 mph)	21	40	"EDNA"—New England again heavily hit. Gusts of 120 mph at Martha's Vineyard, Mass.
1954, Oct. 5–18	South Carolina to New York	New York, N.Y. (113 mph) (See Remarks)	95	252	"HAZEL"—several N.C. localities had winds of 130–150 mph with unusually heavy wave damage resulting. Est. 400–1,000 casualties in Haiti. In Canada there were 78 deaths, mostly due to flooding.
1955, Aug. 7–21	North Carolina to New England	Wilmington, N.C. (83 mph)	184	832	"DIANE"—worst floods in history in Southern New England. 16 in. of rain in Hartford area.
1957, June 25–28	Texas to Alabama	Sabine/Pass, Tex. (100 mph)	390	150	"AUDREY"—gave an early start to the hurricane season and wiped out Cameron, La. Two weeks later "BERTHA" struck same area.

Date	Areas hardest hit	Land stations with highest wind speed	Deaths (U.S. only)	Est. damage (millions)	Remarks
1960, Aug. 29–Sept. 13	Florida to New England	Ft. Myers, Fla. (92 mph) Block Island, R.I. (130 mph) (See Remarks)	50	500	"DONNA"—hurricane winds from a single storm swept the entire Atlantic seaboard from Florida to New England for the first time in a 75-year record. Winds estimated near 140 mph with gusts 175–180 mph on Central Keys and lower southwest Florida coast. 115 deaths in Antilles, most from flash floods in Puerto Rico.
1961, Sept. 3–15	Texas coast	Port Lavaca, Tex. (145 mph)	46	408	"CARLA"—devastated Texas Gulf Coast Cities with 15-foot tides and 15-inch rains. Gusts to 175 mph at Port Lavaca.
1964, Aug. 20–Sept. 5	Southern Florida, Eastern Virginia	Miami, Fla. (110 mph)	3	129	"CLEO"—first hurricane in Miami area since 1950. Killed 214 in Caribbean Islands.
1964, Aug. 28–Sept. 16	Northeastern Florida, Southern Georgia	St. Augustine, Fla. (125 mph)	5	250	"DORA"—first storm of full hurricane force on record to move inland from east over northeastern Florida.
1965, Aug. 27–Sept. 12	Southern Florida and Louisiana	Port Sulphur, La. (136 mph)	75	1,420	"BETSY"—Damage in Louisiana, $1.2 billion. 27,000 homes destroyed, 17,500 injured or ill, 300,000 evacuated. Gusts of 165 mph at Pine Key, Fla.
1967, Sept. 5–22	Southern Texas	Brownsville, Texas (109 mph gust)	15	200	"BEULAH"—main damage was caused by torrential rains.
1969, Aug. 14–22	Mississippi, Louisiana, Alabama, Virginia, W. Virginia	Oil drilling rig east of Boothville, La. (172 mph)	256	1,420	"CAMILLE"—68 additional persons missing. One of most destructive killer storms ever to hit U.S.
1970, July 23–Aug. 5	Texas coast	Corpus Christi, Tex. (130 mph)	11	453.8	"CELIA"—Gusts of 161 mph recorded.
1972, June 14–23	Florida to New York	Key West, Fla. (43 mph)	117	2,100	"AGNES"—Devastating floods with many record-breaking river crests. Pa. hardest hit, with 50 deaths.
1975, Sept. 13–24	Florida and Southern Alabama	Ozark, Ala. (104 mph)	21	490	"ELOISE"—Structures destroyed from Panama City Beach, Fla., to Ft. Walton Beach, Fla. Major flooding from rainfall.
1976, Aug. 6–10	New York, New Jersey, and Southern New England	Bridgeport, Conn. (77 mph gust)	5	100	"BELLE"—Crop damage in the Northeast. Considerable Inland stream and road flooding.
1979, Aug. 25–Sept. 7	Florida to New England	Fort Pierce, Fla. (95 mph gust)	5	320	"DAVID"—1200 deaths in the Dominican Republic. Homes 80 percent destroyed in Dominica.
1979, Aug. 29–Sept. 14	Alabama and Mississippi	Dauphin Island, Alabama (145 mph gust)	5	2300	"FREDERIC"—highest dollar damage ever in the United States.
1980, Aug. 3–10	Caribbean Islands to Texas Gulf Coast	Port Mansfield, Texas (120 mph gust)	28	300	"ALLEN"—Highest tides in 61 years. Over 200 killed in Caribbean Islands. Extensive crop damage in Caribbean.
1983, Aug. 15–21	Texas Coast	Hobby Airport (94 mph)	21	2000	"ALICIA"—Extensive damage in Galveston/Houston area.
1985, Aug. 28–Sept. 4	Florida to Mississippi	Dauphin Island, Ala. (96 mph)	4	1,000	"ELENA"—one million persons evacuated.
1985, Sept. 16–27	North Carolina Outer Banks and Long Island, N.Y.	Chesapeake Bay Bridge (92 mph)	8	1,000	"GLORIA"—downed trees and power outages across southern New England.
1985, Oct. 26–Nov. 1	Louisiana	Pensacola, Fla. (63 mph gust)	12	1,500	"JUAN"—Serious damage to offshore oil rigs. Sustained flooding over SE Louisiana.

1. Wind-measuring equipment disabled at speed indicated. NOTE: Additional hurricanes may be listed in *Current Events*.
Source: Department of Commerce, National Oceanic and Atmospheric Administration.

Record Highest Temperatures by State

State	Temp, °F	Date	Station	Elevation, feet
Alabama	112	Sept. 5, 1925	Centerville	345
Alaska	100	June 27, 1915	Fort Yukon	est. 420
Arizona	127	July 7, 1905*	Parker	345
Arkansas	120	Aug. 10, 1936	Ozark	396
California	134	July 10, 1913	Greenland Ranch	−178
Colorado	118	July 11, 1888	Bennett	5,484
Connecticut	105	July 22, 1926	Waterbury	400
Delaware	110	July 21, 1930	Millsboro	20
Florida	109	June 29, 1931	Monticello	207
Georgia	113	May 27, 1978	Greenville	860
Hawaii	100	Apr. 27, 1931	Pahala	850
Idaho	118	July 28, 1934	Orofino	1,027
Illinois	117	July 14, 1954	E. St. Louis	410
Indiana	116	July 14, 1936	Collegeville	672
Iowa	118	July 20, 1934	Keokuk	614
Kansas	121	July 24, 1936*	Alton (near)	1,651
Kentucky	114	July 28, 1930	Greensburg	581
Louisiana	114	Aug. 10, 1936	Plain Dealing	268
Maine	105	July 10, 1911*	North Bridgton	450
Maryland	109	July 10, 1936*	Cumberland & Frederick	623;325
Massachusetts	107	Aug. 2, 1975	New Bedford & Chester	120;640
Michigan	112	July 13, 1936	Mio	963
Minnesota	114	July 6, 1936*	Moorhead	904
Mississippi	115	July 29, 1930	Holly Springs	600
Missouri	118	July 14, 1954*	Warsaw & Union	687;560
Montana	117	July 5, 1937	Medicine Lake	1,950
Nebraska	118	July 24, 1936*	Minden	2,169
Nevada	122	June 23, 1954*	Overton	1,240
New Hampshire	106	July 4, 1911	Nashua	125
New Jersey	110	July 10, 1936	Runyon	18
New Mexico	116	July 14, 1934*	Orogrande	4,171
New York	108	July 22, 1926	Troy	35
North Carolina	109	Sept. 7, 1954*	Weldon	81
North Dakota	121	July 6, 1936	Steele	1,857
Ohio	113	July 21, 1934*	Gallipolis (near)	673
Oklahoma	120	July 26, 1943*	Tishomingo	670
Oregon	119	Aug. 10, 1898	Pendleton	1,074
Pennsylvania	111	July 10, 1936*	Phoenixville	100
Rhode Island	104	Aug. 2, 1975	Providence	51
South Carolina	111	June 28, 1954*	Camden	170
South Dakota	120	July 5, 1936	Gannvalley	1,750
Tennessee	113	Aug. 9, 1930*	Perryville	377
Texas	120	Aug. 12, 1936	Seymour	1,291
Utah	116	June 28, 1892	Saint George	2,880
Vermont	105	July 4, 1911	Vernon	310
Virginia	110	July 15, 1954	Balcony Falls	725
Washington	118	Aug. 5, 1961*	Ice Harbor Dam	475
West Virginia	112	July 10, 1936*	Martinsburg	435
Wisconsin	114	July 13, 1936	Wisconsin Dells	900
Wyoming	114	July 12, 1900	Basin	3,500

*Also on earlier dates at the same or other places. *Source:* National Oceanic and Atmospheric Administration, Environmental Data and Information Service, National Climatic Center, Asheville, N.C.

HIGHEST TEMPERATURE OF RECORD AND LOCATIONS, BY STATES

Source: National Oceanic and Atmospheric Administration.

LOWEST TEMPERATURES OF RECORD AND LOCATIONS BY STATES

Record Lowest Temperatures by State

State	Temp, °F	Date	Station	Elevation, feet
Alabama	−27	Jan. 30, 1966	New Market	760
Alaska	−80	Jan. 23, 1971	Prospect Creek	1,100
Arizona	−40	Jan. 7, 1971	Hawley Lake	8,180
Arkansas	−29	Feb. 13, 1905	Pond	1,250
California	−45	Jan. 20, 1937	Boca	5,532
Colorado	−60	Jan. 1, 1979*	Maybell	5,920
Connecticut	−32	Feb. 16, 1943	Falls Village	585
Delaware	−17	Jan. 17, 1893	Millsboro	20
Florida	−2	Feb. 13, 1899	Tallahassee	193
Georgia	−17	Jan. 27, 1940	CCC Camp F-16	est. 1,000
Hawaii	14	Jan. 2, 1961	Haleakala, Maui Is	9,750
Idaho	−60	Jan. 18, 1943	Island Park Dam	6,285
Illinois	−35	Jan. 22, 1930	Mount Carroll	817
Indiana	−35	Feb. 2, 1951	Greensburg	954
Iowa	−47	Jan. 12, 1912	Washta	1,157
Kansas	−40	Feb. 13, 1905	Lebanon	1,812
Kentucky	−34	Jan. 28, 1963	Cynthiana	684
Louisiana	−16	Feb. 13, 1899	Minden	194
Maine	−48	Jan. 19, 1925	Van Buren	510
Maryland	−40	Jan. 13, 1912	Oakland	2,461
Massachusetts	−34	Jan. 18, 1957	Birch Hill Dam	840
Michigan	−51	Feb. 9, 1934	Vanderbilt	785
Minnesota	−59	Feb. 16, 1903*	Pokegama Dam	1,280
Mississippi	−19	Jan. 30, 1966	Corinth	420
Missouri	−40	Feb. 13, 1905	Warsaw	700
Montana	−70	Jan. 20, 1954	Rogers Pass	5,470
Nebraska	−47	Feb. 12, 1899	Camp Clarke	3,700
Nevada	−50	Jan. 8, 1937	San Jacinto	5,200
New Hampshire	−46	Jan. 28, 1925	Pittsburg	1,575
New Jersey	−34	Jan. 5, 1904	River Vale	70
New Mexico	−50	Feb. 1, 1951	Gavilan	7,350
New York	−52	Feb. 18, 1979*	Old Forge	1,720
North Carolina	−29	Jan. 30, 1966	Mt. Mitchell	6,525
North Dakota	−60	Feb. 15, 1936	Parshall	1,929
Ohio	−39	Feb. 10, 1899	Milligan	800
Oklahoma	−27	Jan. 18, 1930	Watts	958
Oregon	−54	Feb. 10, 1933*	Seneca	4,700
Pennsylvania	−42	Jan. 5, 1904	Smethport	est. 1,500
Rhode Island	−23	Jan. 11, 1942	Kingston	100
South Carolina	−20	Jan. 18, 1977	Caesars Head	3,100
South Dakota	−58	Feb. 17, 1936	McIntosh	2,277
Tennessee	−32	Dec. 30, 1917	Mountain City	2,471
Texas	−23	Feb. 8, 1933*	Seminole	3,275
Utah	−50	Jan. 5, 1913*	Strawberry Tunnel	7,650
Vermont	−50	Dec. 30, 1933	Bloomfield	915
Virginia	−29	Feb. 10, 1899	Monterey	—
Washington	−48	Dec. 30, 1968	Mazama & Winthrop	2,120;1,765
West Virginia	−37	Dec. 30, 1917	Lewisburg	2,200
Wisconsin	−54	Jan. 24, 1922	Danbury	908
Wyoming	−63	Feb. 9, 1933	Moran	6,770

*Also on earlier dates at the same or other places. *Source:* National Oceanic and Atmospheric Administration, Environmental Data and Information Service, National Climatic Center, Asheville, N.C.

Tropical Storms and Hurricanes, 1886–1988

	Jan.–April	May	June	July	Aug.	Sept.	Oct.	Nov.	Dec.	Total
Number of tropical storms (incl. hurricanes)	3	14	55	63	207	294	180	41	6	863
Number of tropical storms that reached hurricane intensity	1	3	23	33	145	185	90	21	3	504

Tornadoes That Caused Outstanding Damage

Date	Number of tornadoes	Deaths	Property losses	States in which storms occurred
1884, Feb. 19	60	800	(1)	Mississippi, Alabama, North and South Carolina, Tennessee, Kentucky, Indiana
1917, May 26–27	(1)	249	$5,555,000	Illinois, Indiana, Arkansas, Kentucky, Tennessee, Alabama, Mississippi
1920, April 20	6	220	3,525,000	Mississippi, Alabama, Tennessee
1924, April 29–30	22	115	4,372,300	Oklahoma, Arkansas, Alabama, Georgia, Louisiana, North and South Carolina, Virginia
1924, June 28	4	96	13,050,000	Ohio and Pennsylvania
1925, March 18	8	792	17,872,000	Missouri, Illinois, Indiana, Kentucky, Tennessee, Alabama
1927, May 8–9	36	227	7,877,000	Texas, Louisiana, Missouri, Nebraska, Indiana, Michigan
1932, March 21	27	321	5,514,000	Alabama, Mississippi, Georgia, Tennessee
1936, April 5–6	22	498	21,800,000	Arkansas, Alabama, Tennessee, Georgia, South Carolina
1944, June 23	4	153	5,160,000	Pennsylvania, West Virginia, Maryland
1947, April 9–10	8	167	10,030,750	Texas, Oklahoma, Kansas
1952, March 21–22	31	343	15,327,100	Arkansas, Tennessee, Missouri, Mississippi, Alabama, Kentucky
1953, June 7–9	12	234	93,230,840	Michigan, Ohio, and New England states
1953, May 11	1	114	39,500,000	Texas
1955, May 25	13	102	11,747,500	Oklahoma and Kansas
1965, April 11–12	47	257	200,000,000	Iowa, Illinois, Wisconsin, Michigan, Indiana, Ohio
1968, May 15	7	63	65,000,000	Arkansas, Iowa, Illinois
1970, May 11	1	26	135,000,000	Texas
1971, Feb. 21	(1)	117	17,000,000	Louisiana, Mississippi
1973, March 31	2	9	115,000,000	Georgia, South Carolina
1973, May 26–28	96	22	(1)	Hawaii and 18 states in South, Southwest, Midwest, and East
1974, April 3–4	144	307	500,000,000 +	13 states in East, South, and Midwest
1975, May 6	3	3	400,000,000 +	Nebraska
1977, April 4	7	22	15,000,000	Alabama
1978, Dec. 3	13	4	100,000,000 +	Louisiana and Arkansas
1979, April 10	10	54	(1)	Texas and Oklahoma
1979, Oct. 3	1	3	200,000,000	Connecticut
1980, May 13	1	5	40,000,000	Michigan
1980, Aug. 9–11	29	0	50,000,000 +	Texas
1981, April 4	1	3	12,900,000	Wisconsin
1983, July 3	22	0	11,000,000 +	Wisconsin
1984, April 26–27	47	16	n.a.	Iowa, Illinois, Kansas, Louisiana, Michigan, Minnesota, Missouri, Oklahoma, South Dakota, Wisconsin
1985, May 31	30	76	102,500,000 +	Ohio, Pennsylvania, New York
1986[2], Feb. 5	1	2	50,000,000	Texas
1988, Nov. 15	44	7	35,000,000 +	Arkansas, Illinois, Iowa, Kansas, Missouri, Oklahoma, Texas
1988, Nov. 28	1	2	100,000,000	Raleigh, N.C.

1. Not definitely known; believed to be large. 2. Preliminary. NOTE: Additional storms may be listed in the *Current Events* section. n.a. = not available. *Source:* Department of Commerce, National Oceanic and Atmospheric Administration and for 1986, *Weatherwise*, February 1987 issue from an article by Edward W. Ferguson, Frederick P. Ostby and Preston W. Leftwich, Jr. Copyright © 1987 by the Helen Dwight Reid Educational Foundation.

Hurricane Gilbert's Rampage

Between Sept. 10-18, 1988, Hurricane Gilbert rolled across the tropical Atlantic, the Caribbean, the Gulf of Mexico, and into Yucatan. It was the worst Atlantic hurricane ever recorded. The sea level pressure in the eye of Gilbert dropped to 888 millibars (26.22 inches of Mercury) on the evening of Sept. 13th, setting a new record for the Western Hemisphere. The maximum wind speed was 185 miles per hour.

When the storm subsided, an estimated 318 people had been killed. Estimated property damage in both Jamaica and Mexico was $2 billion and $50 million in the United States mainly due to tornadoes in Texas. Twenty-nine Texas tornadoes were the result of Gilbert.

The total estimated damage caused by Hurricane Gilbert is believed to be $5 billion. □

Temperature Extremes in The United States

Source: National Oceanic and Atmospheric Administration, Environmental Data and Information Service, and National Center Climatic Center

The Highest Temperature Extremes

Greenland Ranch, California, with 134° F (56.67° C) on July 10, 1913, holds the record for the highest temperature ever officially observed in the United States. This station was located in barren Death Valley, 178 feet below sea level. Death Valley is about 140 miles long, four to six miles wide, and oriented north to south in southwestern California. Much of the valley is below sea level and is flanked by towering mountain ranges with Mt. Whitney, the highest landmark in the 48 conterminous states, rising to 14,495 feet above sea level, less than 100 miles to the west. Death Valley has the hottest summers in the Western Hemisphere, and is the only known place in the United States where nighttime temperatures sometimes remain above 100° F (37.78° C).

The highest annual normal (1941-70 mean) temperature in the United States, 78.2° F (25.67° C), and the highest summer (June-August) normal temperature, 92.8° F (33.78° C), are for Death Valley, California. The highest winter (December-February) normal temperature is 72.8° F (22.67° C) for Honolulu, Hawaii.

Amazing temperature rises of 40° to 50° F (4.44 to 10° C) in a few minutes occasionally may be brought about by chinook winds.[1]

Some Outstanding Temperature Rises

In 12 hours: 83° F (46.11° C), Granville, N.D., Feb. 21, 1918, from −33° F to 50° F (−36.11 to 10° C) from early morning to late afternoon.

In 15 minutes: 42° F (23.34° C), Fort Assinniboine, Mont., Jan. 19, 1892, from −5° F to 37° F (−20.56 to 2.78° C).

In seven minutes: 34° F (1.11° C), Kipp, Mont., Dec. 1, 1896. The observer also reported that a total rise of 80° F (26.67° C) occurred in a few hours and that 30 inches of snow disappeared in one-half day.

In two minutes: 49° F (27.22° C), Spearfish, S.D., Jan. 22, 1943 from −4° F (20° C) at 7:30 a.m. to 45° F (7.22° C) at 7:32 a.m.

The Lowest Temperature Extremes

The lowest temperature on record in the United States, −79.8° F (−62.1° C), was observed at Pros-

pect Creek Camp in the Endicott Mountains of northern Alaska (latitude 66° 48′N, longitude 150° 40′W) on Jan. 23, 1971. The lowest ever recorded in the conterminous 48 states, −69.7° F (−56.5° C), occurred at Rogers Pass, in Lewis and Clark County, Mont., on Jan. 20, 1954. Rogers Pass is in mountainous and heavily forested terrain about one-half mile east of and 140 feet below the summit of the Continental Divide.

The lowest annual normal (1941-70 mean) temperature in the United States is 9.3° F (−12.68° C) for Barrow, Alaska, which lies on the Arctic coast. Barrow also has the coolest summers (June-August) with a normal temperature of 36.4° F (2.44° C). The lowest winter (December-February) normal temperature, is −15.7° F (−26.5° C) for Barter Island on the arctic coast of northeast Alaska.

In the 48 conterminous states, Mt. Washington, N.H. (elevation 6,262 feet) has the lowest annual normal temperature 26.9° F (−2.72° C) and the lowest normal summer temperature, 46.8° F (8.22° C). A few stations in the northeastern United States and in the upper Rocky Mountains have normal annual temperatures in the 30s; summer normal temperatures at these stations are in the low 50s. Winter normal temperatures are lowest in northeastern North Dakota, 5.6° F (−14.23° C) for Langdon Experiment Farm, and in northwestern Minnesota, 5.3° F (−14.83° C) for Hallock.

Some Outstanding Temperature Falls

In 24 hours: 100° F (55.57° C), Browing, Mont., Jan. 23-24, 1916, from 44° to −56° F (6.67° to −48.9° C).

In 12 hours: 84° F (46.67° C), Fairfield, Mont., Dec. 24, 1924, from 63° (17.22° C) at noon to −21° F (−29.45° C) at midnight.

In 2 hours: 62° F (34.45° C), Rapid City, S.D., Jan. 12, 1911, from 49° F (9.45° C) at 6:00 a.m. to −13° F (−25° C) at 8:00 a.m.

In 27 minutes: 58° F (32.22° C), Spearfish, S.D., Jan. 22, 1943, from 54° F (12.22° C) at 9:00 a.m. to −4° F (−20° C) at 9:27 a.m.

In 15 minutes: 63° F (26.11° C), Rapid City, S.D., Jan. 10, 1911, from 55° F (12.78° C) at 7:00 a.m. to 8° F (−13.33° C). at 7:15 a.m.

1. A warm, dry wind that descends from the eastern slopes of the Rocky Mountains, causing a rapid rise in temperature.

Winter Indoor Comfort and Relative Humidity

Compared to summer when the moisture content of the air (relative humidity) is an important factor of body discomfort, air moisture has a lesser effect on the human body during outdoor winter activities. But it is a big factor for winter indoor comfort because it has a direct bearing on health and energy consumption.

The colder the outdoor temperature, the more heat must be added indoors for body comfort.

However, the heat that is added will cause a drying effect and lower the indoor relative humidity, unless an indoor moisture source is present.

While a room temperature between 71° and 77° F may be comfortable for short periods of time under very dry conditions, prolonged exposure to dry air has varying effects on the human body and usually causes discomfort. The moisture content of the air is important, and by increasing the rela-

Average Indoor Relative Humidity, %, for January

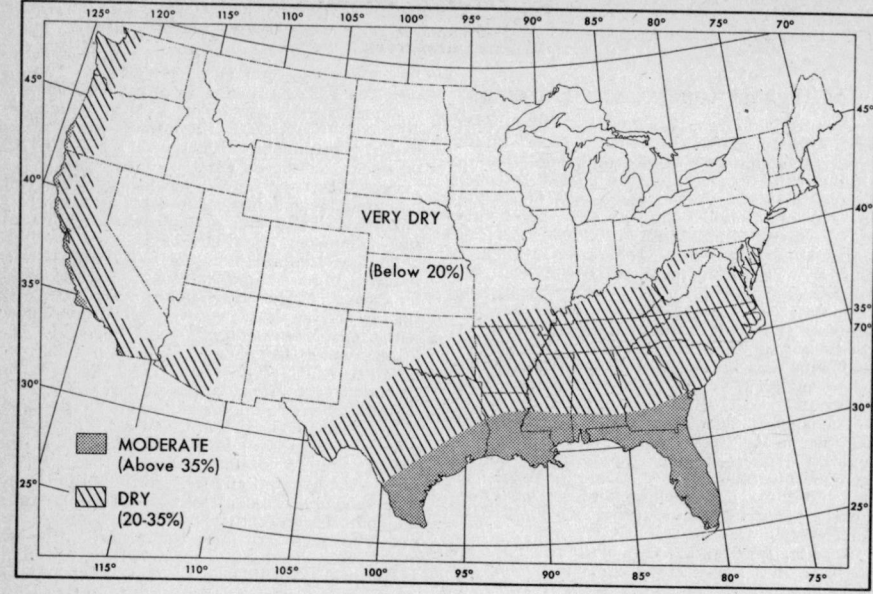

Source: National Oceanic and Atmospheric Administration, Environmental Data and Information Service, National Climatic Center.

tive humidity to above 50% within the above temperature range, 80% or more of all average dressed persons would feel comfortable.

Effects of Dry Air on the Body

Studies have shown that dry air has four main effects on the human body:

1. Breathing dry air is a potential health hazard which can cause such respiratory ailments as asthma, bronchitis, sinusitis, and nosebleeds, or general dehydration since body fluids are depleted during respiration.

2. Skin moisture evaporation can cause skin irritations and eye itching.

3. Irritative effects, such as static electricity which causes mild shocks when metal is touched, are common when the air moisture is low.

4. The "apparent temperature" of the air is lower than what the thermometer indicates, and the body "feels" colder.

These problems can be reduced by simply increasing the indoor relative humidity. This can be done through use of humidifiers, vaporizers, steam generators, sources such as large pans, or water containers made of porous ceramics. Even wet towels or water in a bathtub will be of some help. The lower the room temperature the easier the relative humidity can be brought to its desired level. A relative humidity indicator (hygrometer) may be of assistance in determining the humidity in the house.

Referring to item 4, a more detailed discussion is necessary. While the indoor temperature as read

from a thermometer may be 75° F, the apparent temperature (what it feels like) may be warmer or colder depending on the moisture content of the air. Apparent temperature can vary as much as 8° F within a relative humidity range of 10 to 80 percent (these limits are generally possible in a closed room). Because of evaporation the human body cools when exposed to dry air, and the sense of coldness increases as the humidity decreases. With a room temperature of 70° F, for example, a person will feel colder in a dry room than in a moist room; this is especially noticeable when entering a dry room after bathing.

The table on the following page gives apparent temperatures for various combinations of room temperature and relative humidity. As an example of how to read the table, a room temperature of 70° F combined with a relative humidity of 10% feels like 64° F, but at 80% it feels like 71° F.

Although degrees of comfort vary with age, health, activity, clothing, and body characteristics, the table can be used as a general guideline when raising the apparent temperature and the level of comfort through an increase in room moisture, rather than by an addition of heat to the room. This method of changing the apparent temperature can give the direct benefit of reducing heating costs because comfort can be maintained with a lower thermostat setting if moisture is added. For example, an apparent comfortable temperature can be maintained with a thermostat setting of 75° F with 20% relative humidity or with a 70° F setting with 80 percent humidity. A relative humidity of 20 percent is common for homes without a humidifier during winter in the northern United States.

Apparent Temperature for Values of Room Temperature and Relative Humidity

RELATIVE HUMIDITY (%)

ROOM TEMPERATURE (°F)	0	10	20	30	40	50	60	70	80	90	100
75	68	69	71	72	74	75	76	76	77	78	79
74	66	68	69	71	72	73	74	75	76	77	78
73	65	67	68	70	71	72	73	74	75	76	77
72	64	65	67	68	70	71	72	73	74	75	76
71	63	64	66	67	68	70	71	72	73	74	75
70	63	64	65	66	67	68	69	70	71	72	73
69	62	63	64	65	66	67	68	69	70	71	72
68	61	62	63	64	65	66	67	68	69	70	71
67	60	61	62	63	64	65	66	67	68	68	69
66	59	60	61	62	63	64	65	66	67	67	68
65	59	60	61	61	62	63	64	65	65	66	67
64	58	59	60	60	61	62	63	64	64	65	66
63	57	58	59	59	60	61	62	62	63	64	64
62	56	57	58	58	59	60	61	61	62	63	63
61	56	57	57	58	59	59	60	60	61	61	62
60	55	56	56	57	58	58	59	59	60	60	61

Source: National Oceanic and Atmospheric Administration, Environmental Data and Information Service and National Climatic Center.

PEOPLE

Many public figures not listed here may be found elsewhere in the *Information Please Almanac*.

46	Governors	907	Sports Personalities
632	Presidents	648	Supreme Court Justices
634	Presidents' Wives	632	Vice Presidents
39	Senators		

A name in parentheses is the original name or form of name. Localities are places of birth. Country name in parenthesis is the present-day name. Dates of birth appear as month/day/year. **Boldface** years in parentheses are dates of **(birth-death)**.
Information has been gathered from many sources, including the individuals themselves. However, the *Information Please Almanac* cannot guarantee the accuracy of every individual item.

A

Aalto, Alvar (architect); Kuortane, Finland **(1898-1976)**
Abbott, Bud (William) (comedian); Asbury Park, N.J. **(1898-1974)**
Abbott, George (stage producer); Forestville, N.Y., 6/25/1887
Abel, Walter (actor); St. Paul **(1898-1987)**
Abelard, Peter (theologian); nr. Nantes, France **(1079-1142)**
Abernathy, Ralph (civil rights leader); Linden, Ala., 3/11/1926
Acheson, Dean (statesman); Middletown, Conn. **(1893-1971)**
Acuff, Roy Claxton (musician); nr. Maynardsville, Tenn. 9/15/1903
Adams, Charles Francis (diplomat); Boston **(1807-1886)**
Adams, Don (actor); New York City, 4/19/1926
Adams, Edie (Edie Enke) (actress); Kingston, Pa., 4/16/1929
Adams, Franklin Pierce (columnist and author); Chicago **(1881-1960)**
Adams, Henry Brooks (historian); Boston **(1838-1918)**
Adams, Joey (comedian); New York City, 1/6/1911
Adams, Maude (Maude Kiskadden) (actress); Salt Lake City, **(1872-1953)**
Adams, Samuel (American Revolutionary patriot); Boston **(1722-1803)**
Adamson, Joy (naturalist); Troppau, Silesia **(1910-1980)**
Addams, Charles (cartoonist); Westfield, N.J., **(1912-1988)**
Addams, Jane (social worker); Cedarville, Ill. **(1860-1935)**
Adderley, Julian "Cannonball" (jazz saxophonist); Tampa, Fla. **(1928-1975)**
Ade, George (humorist); Kentland, Ind. **(1866-1944)**
Adenauer, Konrad (statesman); Cologne, Germany **(1876-1967)**
Adler, Alfred (psychoanalyst); Vienna **(1870-1937)**
Adler, Larry (musician); Baltimore, 2/10/1914
Adler, Richard (songwriter); New York City, 8/3/1921
Adoree, Renée (Renée La Fonte) (actress); Lille, France **(1898-1933)**
Aeschylus (dramatist); Eleusis (Greece) **(525-456** B.C.)
Aesop (fabulist); birthplace unknown **(lived c. 600** B.C.)
Aherne, Brian (actor); King's Norton, England **(1902-1986)**
Aiken, Conrad (poet); Savannah, Ga. **(1889-1973)**
Ailey, Alvin (choreographer); Rogers, Tex., 1/5/1931
Albanese, Licia (operatic soprano); Bari, Italy, 7/22/1913
Albee, Edward (playwright); Washington, D.C., 3/12/1928
Albers, Josef (painter); Bottrop, Germany **(1888-1976)**
Albert, Eddie (Edward Albert Heimberger) (actor); Rock Island, Ill., 4/22/1908
Albertson, Jack (actor); Malden, Mass. **(1910?-1981)**
Albright, Lola (actress); Akron, Ohio, 7/20/1925
Alcott, Louisa May (novelist); Germantown, Pa. **(1832-1888)**
Alda, Alan (actor); New York City, 1/28/1936
Alda, Robert (Alphonso d'Abruzzo) (actor); New York City **(1914-1986)**
Alden, John (American Pilgrim); England **(1599?-1687)**
Alexander the Great (monarch and conqueror); Pella, Macedonia (Greece) **(356-323** B.C.)
Alger, Horatio (author); Revere, Mass. **(1834-1899)**
Algren, Nelson (novelist); Detroit **(1909-1981)**
Allen, Ethan (American Revolutionary soldier); Litchfield, Conn. **(1738-1789)**
Allen, Fred (John Florence Sullivan) (comedian); Cambridge, Mass. **(1894-1956)**
Allen, Gracie (Grace Ethel Cecile Rosalie Allen) (comedienne); San Francisco **(1906-1964)**
Allen, Mel (Melvin Israel) (sportscaster); Birmingham, Ala., 2/14/1913
Allen, Steve (TV entertainer); New York City, 12/26/1921
Allen, Woody (Allen Stewart Konigsberg) (actor, writer, and director); Brooklyn, N.Y., 12/1/1935
Allison, Fran (TV entertainer); LaPorte City, Iowa, **(1908?-1989)**
Allman, Gregg (singer); Nashville, Tenn., 12/8/1947
Allyson, June (Jan Allyson) (actress); New York City, 10/7/1923
Alonso, Alicia (ballerina); Havana, 12/21/1921(?)

Alpert, Herb (band leader); Los Angeles, 3/31/1935(?)
Alsop, Joseph W., Jr. (journalist); Avon, Conn., 10/11/1910
Alsop, Stewart (journalist); Avon, Conn. **(1914-1974)**
Altman, Robert (film director); Kansas City, Mo., 2/20/1925
Amati, Nicola (violin maker); Cremona, Italy **(1596-1684)**
Ambler, Eric (suspense writer); London, 6/28/1909
Ameche, Don (Dominic Amici) (actor); Kenosha, Wis., 5/31/1908
Amis, Kingsley (novelist); London, 4/16/1922
Amory, Cleveland (writer and conservationist); Nahant, Mass., 9/2/1917
Amos (Freeman F. Gosden) (radio comedian); Richmond, Va., **(1899-1982)**
Amsterdam, Morey (actor); Chicago, 12/14/1914
Andersen, Hans Christian (author of fairy-tales); Odense, Denmark **(1805-1875)**
Anderson, Eddie. *See* Rochester
Anderson, Ib (ballet dancer); Copenhagen, 12/14/1954
Anderson, Jack (journalist); Long Beach, Calif., 10/19/1922
Anderson, Dame Judith (actress); Adelaide, Australia, 2/10/1898
Anderson, Lindsay (Gordon) (director); Bangalore, India, 4/17/1923
Anderson, Lynn (singer); Grand Forks, N.D., 9/26/1947
Anderson, Marian (contralto); Philadelphia, 2/17/1902
Anderson, Maxwell (dramatist); Atlantic, Pa. **(1888-1959)**
Anderson, Robert (playwright); New York City, 4/28/1917
Andersson, Bibi (actress); Stockholm, 11/11/1935
Andress, Ursula (actress); Switzerland, 3/19/1938
Andrews, Dana (actor); Collins, Miss., 1/1/1909
Andrews, Julie (Julia Wells) (actress and singer); Walton-on-Thames, England, 10/1/1935
Andrews, La Verne (singer); Minneapolis **(1916-1967)**
Andrews, Maxene (singer); Minneapolis, 1/3/1918
Andrews, Patti (singer); Minneapolis, 2/16/1920
Andy (Charles J. Correll) (radio comedian); Peoria, Ill. **(1890-1972)**
Angeles, Victoria de los (Victoria Gamez Cima) (operatic soprano); Barcelona, 11/1/1924
Anka, Paul (singer and composer); Ottawa, 7/30/1941
Ann-Margret (Ann-Margret Olsson) (actress); Valsjobyn, Sweden, 4/28/1941
Annabella (actress); Paris, 1912
Anouilh, Jean (playwright); Bordeaux, France **(1910-1987)**
Anthony, Susan Brownell (woman suffragist); Adams, Mass. **(1820-1906)**
Antonioni, Michelangelo (director); Ferrara, Italy, 9/29/1912
Antony, Mark (Marcus Antonius) (statesman); Rome **(83?-30** B.C.)
Anuszkiewicz, Richard (painter); Erie, Pa., 5/23/1930
Aquinas, St. Thomas (philosopher); nr. Aquino (Italy) **(1225?-1274)**
Arbuckle, Roscoe "Fatty" (actor and director); San Jose, Calif. **(1887-1933)**
Archimedes (physicist and mathematician); Syracuse, Sicily **(287?-212** B.C.)
Archipenko, Alexandre (sculptor); Kiev, Russia **(1887-1964)**
Arden, Elizabeth (Florence Nightingale Graham) (cosmetics executive); Woodbridge, Canada **(1891-1966)**
Arden, Eve (Eunice Quedens) (actress); Mill Valley, Calif., 4/30/1912
Arendt, Hannah (historian); Hannover, Germany **(1906-1975)**
Aristophanes (dramatist); Athens **448?-380** B.C.)
Aristotle (philosopher); Stagirus, Macedonia **(384-322** B.C.)
Arkin, Alan (actor and director); New York City, 3/26/1934
Arledge, Roone (TV executive); Forest Hills, N.Y., 7/8/1931
Arlen, Harold (Hyman Arluck) (composer); Buffalo, N.Y. **(1905-1986)**
Arlen, Richard (actor); Charlottesville, Va. **(1900-1976)**
Arliss, George (actor); London **(1868-1946)**
Armstrong, Louis ("Satchmo") (musician); New Orleans **(1900-1971)**
Armstrong-Jones, Anthony. *See* Snowdon, Earl of
Arnaz, Desi (Desiderio) (actor and producer); Santiago, Cuba **(1917-1986)**

Arness, James (James Aurness) (TV actor); Minneapolis, 5/26/1923
Arno, Peter (cartoonist); New York City (1904-1968)
Arnold, Benedict (American Revolutionary War general, charged with treason); Norwich, Conn. (1741-1801)
Arnold, Eddy (singer); Henderson, Tenn., 5/15/1918
Arnold, Edward (actor); New York City (1890-1956)
Arnold, Matthew (poet and critic); Laleham, England (1822-1888)
Arp, Jean (sculptor and painter); Strasbourg (France) (1887-1966)
Arquette, Cliff ("Charley Weaver") (actor); Toledo, Ohio (1905-1974)
Arrau, Claudio (pianist); Chillán, Chile, 2/6/1903
Arroyo, Martina (soprano); New York City, 2/2/1940
Arthur, Bea (Bernice Frankel) (actress); New York City, 5/13/1926(?)
Arthur, Jean (Gladys Greene) (actress); New York City, 10/17/1905
Asch, Sholem (novelist); Kutno, Poland (1880-1957)
Ashkenazy, Vladimir (concert pianist); Gorki, U.S.S.R., 7/6/1937
Ashley, Elizabeth (actress); Ocala, Fla., 8/30/1939
Ashton, Sir Frederick William Mallandaine (choreographer); Guayaquil, Ecuador (1904-1988)
Asimov, Isaac (author); Petrovichi, Russia, 1/2/1920
Asner, Edward (actor); Kansas City, Mo., 11/15/1929
Astaire, Fred (Frederick Austerlitz) (dancer and actor); Omaha, Neb. (1899-1987)
Astor, John Jacob (financier); Waldorf (Germany) (1763-1848)
Astor, Mary (Lucile Langhanke) (actress); Quincy, Ill. (1906-1987)
Atkins, Chet (guitarist); nr. Luttrell, Tenn., 6/20/1924
Atkinson, Brooks (drama critic); Melrose, Mass. (1894-1984)
Attenborough, Richard (actor-director) Cambridge, England, 8/29/1923
Attila (King of Huns, called "Scourge of God") (406?-453)
Attlee, Clement Richard (statesman); London (1883-1967)
Auchincloss, Louis (author); Lawrence, N.Y., 9/27/1917
Auden, W(ystan) H(ugh) (poet); York, England (1907-1973)
Audubon, John James (naturalist and painter); Haiti (1785-1851)
Auer, Leopold (violinist and teacher); Veszprém, Hungary (1845-1930)
Auer, Mischa (actor); St. Petersburg, Russia (1905-1967)
Augustine, Saint (Aurelius Augustinus) (theologian); Tagaste, Numidia (Algeria) (354-430)
Augustus (Gaius Octavius) (Roman emperor); Rome (63 B.C.-A.D. 14)
Aumont, Jean-Pierre (actor); Paris, 1/5/1913
Austen, Jane (novelist); Steventon, England (1775-1817)
Autry, Gene (singer and actor); Tioga, Tex., 9/29/1907
Avalon, Frankie (singer); Philadelphia, 9/18/1940
Avedon, Richard (photographer); New York City, 5/15/1923
Avery, Milton (painter); Altmar, N.Y. (1893-1965)
Ax, Emanuel (pianist); Lvov, U.S.S.R., 6/8/1949
Axelrod, George (playwright); New York City, 6/9/1922
Ayckbourn, Alan (playwright); London, 4/12/1939
Ayckroyd, Dan (actor); Ottawa, Ont., Canada, 7/1/1952
Ayres, Lew (actor); Minneapolis, 12/28/1908

B

Bacall, Lauren (Betty Joan Perske) (actress); New York City, 9/16/1924
Bach, Johann Sebastian (composer); Eisenach (East Germany) (1685-1750)
Bach, Karl Phillipp Emanuel (composer); Weimar (East Germany) (1714-1788)
Bacharach, Burt (songwriter); Kansas City, Mo., 5/12/1929
Backus, Jim (actor); Cleveland, (1913-1989)
Bacon, Francis (painter); Dublin, 1910
Bacon, Francis (philosopher and essayist); London (1561-1626)
Bacon, Roger (philosopher and scientist); Ilchester, England (1214?-1294)
Baedeker, Karl (travel-guidebook publisher); Essen (Germany) (1801-1859)
Baez, Joan (folk singer); Staten Island, N.Y., 1/9/1941
Bagnold, Enid (novelist); Rochester, England (1889-1981)
Bailey, F. Lee (lawyer); Waltham, Mass., 6/10/1933
Bailey, Pearl (singer); Newport News, Va., 3/29/1918
Bainter, Fay (actress); Los Angeles (1891-1968)
Baird, Bil (William B.) (puppeteer); Grand Island, Neb (1904-1987)
Baker, Anita (singer); Toledo, Ohio, 1958
Baker, Josephine (singer and dancer); St. Louis (1906-1975)
Baker, Russell (columnist); Loudoun County, Va., 8/14/1925
Balanchine, George (choreographer); St. Petersburg, Russia (1904-1983)
Balboa, Vasco Nuñez de (explorer); Jerez de los Caballeros (Spain) (1475-1517)
Baldwin, Faith (novelist); New Rochelle, N.Y. (1893-1978)
Baldwin, James (novelist); New York City (1924-1987)
Balenciaga, Cristóbal (fashion designer); Guetaria, Spain (1895-1972)
Ball, Lucille (Désirée) (actress and producer); Celoron (nr. James-

town), N.Y. (1911-1989)
Ballard, Kaye (Catherine Gloria Balotta) (actress); Cleveland, 11/20/1926
Balmain, Pierre (fashion designer); St.-Jean-de-Maurienne, France (1914-1982)
Balsam, Martin (actor); New York City, 11/4/1919
Balzac, Honoré de (novelist); Tours, France (1799-1850)
Bancroft, Anne (Annemarie Italiano) (actress); New York City, 9/17/1931
Bancroft, George (actor); Philadelphia (1882-1956)
Bankhead, Tallulah (actress); Huntsville, Ala. (1903-1963)
Banneker, Benjamin (almanacker and mathematician-astronomer on District of Columbia site survey); Ellicott, Md. (1731-1806)
Banting, Fredrick Grant (physiologist); Alliston, Ont., Canada (1891-1941)
Bara, Theda (Theodosia Goodman) (actress); Cincinnati (1890-1955)
Barber, Red (Walter Lanier) (sportscaster); Columbus, Miss., 2/17/1908
Barber, Samuel (composer); West Chester, Pa. (1910-1981)
Barca, Pedro Calderón del al (dramatist); Madrid (1600-1681)
Bardot, Brigitte (actress); Paris, 1935
Barenboim, Daniel (concert pianist and conductor); Buenos Aires, 11/15/1942
Barnard, Christiaan N. (heart surgeon); Beauford West, South Africa, 1923
Barnum, Phineas Taylor (showman); Bethel, Conn. (1810-1891)
Barr, Roseanne (actress), Salt Lake City, 11/3/1952
Barrie, Sir James Matthew (author); Kirriemuir, Scotland (1860-1937)
Barrie, Wendy (actress); Hong Kong (1913-1978)
Barry, Gene (Eugene Klass) (actor); New York City, 6/4/1922
Barry, John (naval officer); County Wexford, Ireland (1745-1803)
Barrymore, Diana (actress); New York City (1921-1960)
Barrymore, Ethel (Ethel Blythe) (actress); Philadelphia (1879-1959)
Barrymore, Georgiana Drew (actress); Philadelphia (1856-1893)
Barrymore, John (John Blythe) (actor); Philadelphia (1882-1942)
Barrymore, Lionel (Lionel Blythe) (actor); Philadelphia (1878-1954)
Barrymore, Maurice (Herbert Blythe) (actor and playwright); Agra, India (1847-1905)
Barthelme, Donald (novelist); Philadelphia (1931-1989)
Barthelmess, Richard (actor); New York City (1897-1963)
Bartholomew, Freddie (actor); London, 3/28/1924
Bartók, Béla (composer); Nagyszentmiklos (Romania) (1881-1945)
Barton, Clara (founder of American Red Cross); Oxford, Mass. (1821-1912)
Baruch, Bernard Mannes (statesman), Camden, S.C. (1870-1965)
Baryshnikov, Mikhail Nikolayevich (ballet dancer and artistic director); Riga, Latvia, 1/27/1948
Basehart, Richard (actor); Zanesville, Ohio (1914-1984)
Basie, Count (William) (band leader); Red Bank, N.J. (1904-1984)
Bassey, Shirley (singer); Cardiff, Wales, 1/8/1937
Batchelor, Clarence Daniel (political cartoonist); Osage City, Kan. (1888-1977)
Bates, Alan (actor); Allestree, England, 2/17/1934
Battle, Kathleen (soprano); Portsmouth, Ohio, 8/13/48
Baudelaire, Charles Pierre (poet); Paris (1821-1867)
Baudouin (King); Palace of Laeken, Belgium, 9/7/1930
Baxter, Anne (actress); Michigan City, Ind. (1923-1985)
Baxter, Warner (actor); Columbus, Ohio (1891-1951)
Bean, Orson (Dallas Frederick Burrows) (actor); Burlington, Vt., 7/22/1928
Beardsley, Aubrey Vincent (illustrator); Brighton, England (1872-1898)
Beaton, Cecil (photographer and designer); London (1904-1980)
Beatty, Warren (actor and producer); Richmond, Va., 3/30/1937
Beaumont, Francis (dramatist); Grace-Dieu, England (1584-1616)
Becket, Thomas à (Archbishop of Canterbury); London (1118?-1170)
Beckett, Samuel (playwright); Dublin, 4/13/1906
Beckmann, Max (painter); Leipzig, Germany (1884-1950)
Bede, Saint ("The Venerable Bede") (scholar); Monkwearmouth, England (673-735)
Beecham, Sir Thomas (conductor); St. Helens, England (1879-1961)
Beecher, Henry Ward (clergyman); Litchfield, Conn. (1813-1887)
Beerbohm, Sir Max (author); London (1872-1956)
Beery, Noah, Jr. (actor); New York City, 8/10/1916
Beery, Wallace (actor); Kansas City, Mo. (1886-1949)
Beethoven, Ludwig van (composer); Bonn (Germany) (1770-1827)
Begley, Ed (actor); Hartford, Conn. (1901-1970)
Belafonte, Harry (singer and actor); New York City, 3/1/1927
Belasco, David (dramatist and producer); San Francisco (1854-1931)
Bell, Alexander Graham (inventor); Edinburgh, Scotland (1847-1922)
Bellamy, Edward (author); Chicopee Falls, Mass. (1850-1898)
Bellamy, Ralph (actor); Chicago, 6/17/1904
Bellini, Giovanni (painter); Venice (c.1430-1516)
Bellow, Saul (novelist); Lachine, Quebec, Canada, 6/10/1915

Bellows, George Wesley (painter and lithographer); Columbus, Ohio **(1882-1925)**
Belmondo, Jean-Paul (actor); Neuilly-sur-Seine, France, 4/9/1933
Belushi, John (comedian, actor); Chicago **(1949-1982)**
Benchley, Peter Bradford (novelist); New York City, 5/8/1940
Benchley, Robert Charles (humorist); Worcester, Mass. **(1889-1945)**
Bendix, William (actor); New York City **(1906-1964)**
Benes, Eduard (statesman); Kozlany (Czechoslovakia) **(1884-1948)**
Benét, Stephen Vincent (poet and story writer); Bethlehem, Pa. **(1898-1943)**
Benét, William Rose (poet and novelist); Ft. Hamilton, Brooklyn, N.Y. **(1886-1950)**
Ben-Gurion, David (David Green) (statesman); Plónsk (Poland) **(1886-1973)**
Benjamin, Richard (actor); New York City, 5/22/1938
Bennett, Constance (actress); New York City **(1905-1965)**
Bennett, Enoch Arnold (novelist and dramatist); Hanley, England **(1867-1931)**
Bennett, James Gordon (editor); Keith, Scotland **(1795-1872)**
Bennett, Joan (actress); Palisades, N.J., 2/27/1910
Bennett, Robert Russell (composer); Kansas City, Mo., **(1894-1981)**
Bennett, Tony (Anthony Benedetto) (singer); Astoria, Queens, N.Y., 8/3/1926
Benny, Jack (Benjamin Kubelsky) (comedian); Chicago **(1894-1974)**
Bentham, Jeremy Heinrich (economist); London **(1748-1832)**
Benton, Thomas Hart (painter); Neosho, Mo. **(1889-1975)**
Berg, Alban (composer); Vienna **(1885-1935)**
Berg, Gertrude (writer and actress); New York City **(1899-1966)**
Bergen, Candice (actress); Beverly Hills, Calif., 5/9/1946
Bergen, Edgar (ventriloquist); Chicago, **(1903-1978)**
Bergen, Polly (actress and singer); Knoxville, Tenn., 7/14/1930
Bergerac, Cyrano de (poet); Paris **(1619-1655)**
Bergman, Ingmar (film director); Uppsala, Sweden, 7/14/1918
Bergman, Ingrid (actress); Stockholm **(1918-1982)**
Bergson, Henri (philosopher); Paris **(1859-1941)**
Berle, Milton (Milton Berlinger) (comedian); New York City, 7/12/1908
Berlin, Irving (Israel Baline) (songwriter); Temum, Russia, 5/11/1888
Berlioz, Louis Hector (composer); La Côte-Saint-André, France **(1803-1869)**
Berman, Lazar (concert pianist); Leningrad, 1930.
Berman, Shelley (Sheldon) (comedian); Chicago, 2/3/1926
Bernardi, Herschel (actor); New York City **(1922-1986)**
Bernhardt, Sarah (Rosine Bernard) (actress); Paris **(1844-1923)**
Bernini, Gian Lorenzo (sculptor and painter); Naples (Italy) **(1598-1680)**
Bernoulli, Jacques (scientist); Basel, Switzerland **(1654-1705)**
Bernstein, Leonard (conductor); Lawrence, Mass., 8/25/1918
Berry, Chuck (Charles Edward Berry) (singer); San Jose, Calif., 1/15/1926
Betjeman, Sir John (Poet Laureate); London **(1906-1984)**
Bickford, Charles (actor); Cambridge, Mass. **(1889-1967)**
Bierce, Ambrose Gwinnett (journalist); Meigs County, Ohio **(1842-1914?)**
Bikel, Theodore (actor and folk singer); Vienna, 5/2/1924
Bing, Sir Rudolf (opera manager); Vienna, 1/9/1902
Bingham, George Caleb (painter); Augusta Co., Va. **(1811-1879)**
Bishop, Joey (Joseph Gottlieb) (comedian); New York City, 2/3/1919
Bismarck-Schönhausen, Prince Otto Eduard Leopold von (statesman); Schönhausen (East Germany) **(1815-1898)**
Bisset, Jacqueline (actress); Weybridge, England, 9/13/1944
Bixby, Bill (actor); San Francisco, 1/22/1934
Bizet, Georges (Alexandre César Léopold Bizet) (composer); Paris **(1838-1875)**
Black, Cilla (singer and actress); Liverpool, England, 5/27/1943
Black, Karen (actress); Park Ridge, Ill., 7/1/1942
Black, Shirley Temple (former actress); Santa Monica, Calif., 4/23/1928
Blackmer, Sidney (actor); Salisbury, N.C. **(1898-1973)**
Blackstone, Sir William (jurist); London **(1723-1780)**
Blaine, Vivian (actress and singer); Newark, N.J., 11/21/1924
Blair, Janet (actress); Altoona, Pa., 4/23/1921
Blake, Amanda (Beverly Louise Neill) (actress); Buffalo, N.Y., 1931
Blake, Eubie (James Hubert) (pianist); Baltimore, **(1883-1983)**
Blake, Robert (Michael Gubitosi) (actor); Nutley, N.J., 9/18/1933
Blake, William (poet and artist); London **(1757-1827)**
Blanc, Mel(vin Jerome) (actor and voice specialist); San Francisco **(1908-1989)**
Blass, Bill (fashion designer); Fort Wayne, Ind., 6/22/1922
Bloch, Ernest (composer); Geneva **(1880-1959)**
Blondell, Joan (actress); New York City **(1909-1979)**
Bloom, Claire (actress); London, 2/15/1931
Bloomgarden, Kermit (producer); Brooklyn, N.Y. **(1904-1976)**
Blue, Monte (actor); Indianapolis **(1890-1963)**
Blyth, Ann (actress); New York City, 8/16/1928
Boccaccio, Giovanni (author); Paris **(1313-1375)**

Boccherini, Luigi (Rodolfo) (composer); Lucca, Italy **(1743-1805)**
Boccioni, Umberto (painter and sculptor); Reggio di Calabria, Italy **(1882-1916)**
Bock, Jerry (composer); New Haven, Conn., 11/23/1928
Bogarde, Dirk (Derek Van den Bogaerde) (film actor and director); London, 3/28/1921
Bogart, Humphrey DeForest (actor); New York City **(1899-1957)**
Bogdanovich, Peter (producer and director); Kingston, N.Y., 7/30/1939
Bohlen, Charles E. (diplomat); Clayton, N.Y. **(1904-1974)**
Bohr, Niels (atomic physicist); Copenhagen **(1885-1962)**
Bolger, Ray (dancer and actor); Dorchester, Mass **(1904-1987)**
Bolívar, Simón (South American liberator); Caracas, Venezuela **(1783-1830)**
Bologna, Giovanni da (sculptor); Douai (France) **(1529-1608)**
Bombeck, Erma (author, columnist); Dayton, Ohio 2/21/1927
Bonaparte, Napoleon (Emperor of the French); Ajaccio, Corsica (France) **(1769-1821)**
Bond, Julian (Georgia legislator); Nashville, Tenn., 1/14/1940
Bondi, Beulah (actress); Chicago **(1883-1981)**
Bonnard, Pierre (painter); Fontenayaux-Roses, France **(1867-1947)**
Bono, Sonny (Salvatore) (singer); Detroit, 2/16/1935
Boone, Daniel (frontiersman); nr. Reading, Pa. **(1734-1820)**
Boone, Pat (Charles) (singer); Jacksonville, Fla., 6/1/1934
Boone, Richard (actor); Los Angeles **(1917-1981)**
Booth, Edwin Thomas (actor); Bel Air, Md. **(1833-1893)**
Booth, Evangeline Cory (religious leader); London **(1865-1950)**
Booth, John Wilkes (actor; assassin of Lincoln); Harford County, Md. **(1838-1865)**
Booth, Shirley (Thelma Booth Ford) (actress); New York City, 8/30/1907
Bordoni, Irene (actress); Ajaccio (France) **(1895-1953)**
Borge, Victor (pianist and comedian); Copenhagen, 1/3/1909
Borgia, Cesare (nobleman and soldier); Rome **(1475?-1507)**
Borgia, Lucrezia (Duchess of Ferrara); Rome **(1480-1519)**
Borgnine, Ernest (actor); Hamden, Conn., 1/24/1917
Borromini, Francesco (architect); Bissone (Italy) **(1599-1667)**
Bosch, Hieronymus (Hieronymus van Aeken) (painter); Hertogenbosch (Netherlands) **(c.1450-1516)**
Bosley, Tom (actor); Chicago, 10/1/1927
Boswell, Connee (singer); New Orleans **(1907-1976)**
Boswell, James (diarist and biographer); Edinburgh, Scotland **(1740-1795)**
Botticelli, Sandro (Alessandro di Mariano dei Filipepi) (painter); Florence (Italy) **(1444?-1510)**
Boulez, Pierre (conductor); Montbrison, France, 3/26/1925
Bourke-White, Margaret (photographer); New York City **(1906-1971)**
Bow, Clara (actress); Brooklyn, N.Y. **(1905-1965)**
Bowen, Catherine Drinker (biographer); Haverford, Pa. **(1897-1973)**
Bowie, David (David Robert Jones) (actor and musician); London, 1/8/1947(?)
Bowie, James (soldier); Burke County, Ga. **(1799-1836)**
Bowles, Chester (diplomat); Springfield, Mass. **(1901-1986)**
Boyce, William (composer); London? **(1710-1779)**
Boyd, Bill (William) ("Hopalong Cassidy") (actor); Cambridge, Ohio **(1898-1972)**
Boyd, Stephen (Stephen Millar) (actor); Belfast, Northern Ireland **(1928-1977)**
Boyer, Charles (actor); Figeac, France **(1899-1978)**
Boy George (George Alan O'Dowd) (singer); London, 1961
Boyle, Robert (scientist); Lismore Castle, Munster, Ireland **(1627-1691)**
Bracken, Eddie (actor); Astoria, Queens, N.Y., 2/7/1920
Bradbury, Ray Douglas (science-fiction writer); Waukegan, Ill., 8/22/1920
Bradlee, Benjamin C. (editor); Boston, 8/26/1921
Bradley, Ed (broadcast journalist); Philadelphia, Pa., 6/22/1941
Bradley, Omar N. (5-star general); Clark, Mo. **(1893-1981)**
Brady, Scott (actor); Brooklyn, N.Y. **(1924-1985)**
Brahe, Tycho (astronomer); Knudstrup, Denmark **(1546-1601)**
Brahms, Johannes (composer); Hamburg **(1833-1897)**
Braille, Louis (inventor of blind); Coupvray, France **(1809-1862)**
Brailowsky, Alexander (pianist); Kiev, Russia **(1896-1976)**
Bramante, Donato D'Agnolo (architect); Monte Asdrualdo (now Fermignano, Italy) **(1444-1514)**
Brancusi, Constantin (sculptor); Pestisansi, Romania **(1876-1957)**
Brando, Marlon (actor); Omaha, Neb., 4/3/1924
Brandt, Willy (Herbert Frahm) (ex-Chancellor); Lübeck, Germany, 12/18/1913
Braque, Georges (painter); Argenteuil, France **(1882-1963)**
Brazzi, Rossano (actor); Bologna, Italy, 9/18/1916
Brecht, Bertolt (dramatist and poet); Augsburg, Bavaria **(1898-1956)**
Brel, Jacques (singer and composer); Brussels, **(1929-1978)**
Brennan, Walter (actor); Lynn, Mass. **(1894-1974)**
Brent, George (actor); Dublin **(1904-1979)**
Breslin, Jimmy (journalist); Jamaica, Queens, N.Y., 10/17/1930

Breuer, Marcel (architect and designer); Pécs, Hungary **(1902-1981)**
Brewer, Teresa (singer); Toledo, Ohio, 5/7/1931
Brewster, Kingman, Jr. (ex-president of Yale); Longmeadow, Mass. **(1919-1988)**
Brezhnev, Leonid I. (Communist Party Secretary); Dneprodzerzhinsk, Ukraine **(1906-1982)**
Brice, Fanny (Fannie Borach) (comedienne); New York City **(1892-1951)**
Bridges, Beau (actor); Los Angeles, 12/9/1941
Bridges, Lloyd (actor); San Leandro, Calif. 1/15/1913
Brinkley, David (TV newscaster); Wilmington, N.C., 7/10/1920
Britten, Benjamin (composer); Lowestoft, England **(1913-1976)**
Britton, Barbara (actress); Long Beach, Calif. **(1920-1980)**
Bromfield, Louis (novelist); Mansfield, Ohio **(1896-1956)**
Bronson, Charles (Charles Buchinsky) (actor); Ehrenfield, Pa., 11/3/1922(?)
Brontë, Charlotte (novelist); Thornton, England **(1816-1855)**
Brontë, Emily Jane (novelist); Thornton, England **(1818-1848)**
Bronzino, Agnolo (painter); Monticelli (Italy) **(1503-1572)**
Brook, Peter (director); London, 3/21/1925
Brooke, Rupert (poet); Rugby, England **(1887-1915)**
Brooks, Geraldine (Geraldine Stroock) (actress); New York City **(1925-1977)**
Brooks, Gwendolyn (poet); Topeka, Kan., 6/7/1917
Brooks, Mel (Melvin Kaminsky) (writer and film director); Brooklyn, N.Y., 1926(?)
Brothers, Joyce (Bauer) (psychologist, author, radio-TV personality); New York City, 1927(?)
Broun, Matthew Heywood Campbell (journalist); Brooklyn, N.Y. **(1888-1939)**
Brown, Helen Gurley (author); Green Forest, Ark., 2/18/1922
Brown, James (singer); Augusta, Ga., 5/3/1934
Brown, Joe E. (comedian); Holgate, Ohio **(1892-1973)**
Brown, John (abolitionist); Torrington, Conn. **(1800-1859)**
Brown, John Mason (critic); Louisville, Ky. **(1900-1969)**
Brown, Les (band leader); Reinerton, Pa., 1912
Brown, Pamela (actress); London **(1918-1975)**
Brown, Vanessa (Smylla Brind) (actress); Vienna, 3/24/1928
Browne, Jackson (singer and guitarist); Heidelberg, Germany, 10/9/late 1940s
Browning, Elizabeth Barrett (poet); Durham, England **(1806-1861)**
Browning, Robert (poet); London **(1812-1889)**
Brubeck, Dave (musician); Concord, Calif., 12/6/1920
Bruce, Lenny (comedian); Long Island, N.Y. **(1926-1966)**
Brueghel, Pieter (painter); nr. Breda, Flanders (Netherlands) **(1520?-1569)**
Bruhn, Erik (Belton Evers) (ballet dancer); Copenhagen **(1928-1986)**
Brunelleschi, Filippo (architect); Florence (Italy) **(1377-1446)**
Bruno, Giordano (philosopher); Nola, Italy **(1548-1600)**
Brutus, Marcus Junius (Roman politician); (85?-42 B.C.)
Bryan, William Jennings (orator and politician); Salem, Ill. **(1860-1925)**
Bryant, Anita (singer); Barnsdall, Okla., 3/25/1940
Bryant, William Cullen (poet and editor); Cummington, Mass. **(1794-1878)**
Brynner, Yul (Taidje Khan) (actor); Sakhalin Island, Russia **(1920-1985)**
Brzezinski, Zbigniew (ex-presidential adviser); Warsaw, 3/28/1928
Buber, Martin (philosopher and theologian); Vienna **(1878-1965)**
Buchanan, Edgar (actor); Humansville, Mo., **(1903-1979)**
Buchholz, Horst (actor); Berlin, 12/4/1933
Buchwald, Art (Arthur) (columnist); Mount Vernon, N.Y., 10/20/1925
Buck, Pearl S(ydenstricker) (author); Hillsboro, W. Va. **(1892-1973)**
Buckley, William F., Jr. (journalist); New York City, 11/24/1925
Buddha. See Gautama Buddha
Buffalo Bill (William Frederick Cody) (scout); Scott County, Iowa **(1846-1917)**
Bujold, Genevieve (actress); Montreal, 7/1/1942
Bujones, Fernando (ballet dancer); Miami, Fla., 3/9/1955
Bullins, Ed (playwright); Philadelphia, 7/2/1935
Bumbry, Grace (mezzo-soprano); St. Louis, 1/4/1937
Bunche, Ralph J. (statesman); Detroit **(1904-1971)**
Bundy, McGeorge (educator); Boston, 3/30/1919
Bundy, William Putnam (editor); Washington, D.C., 9/24/1917
Buñuel, Luis (film director); Calanda, Spain, **(1900-1983)**
Bunyan, John (preacher and author); Elstow, England **(1628-1688)**
Burbank, Luther (horticulturist); Lancaster, Mass. **(1849-1926)**
Burke, Adm. Arleigh A. (ex-Chief of Naval Operations); Boulder, Colo., 10/19/1901
Burke, Billie (comedienne); Washington, D.C. **(1885-1970)**
Burke, Edmund (statesman); Dublin **(1729-1797)**
Burne-Jones, Edward Coley (painter); Birmingham, England **(1833-1898)**
Burnett, Carol (comedienne); San Antonio, 4/26/1936
Burney, Fanny (Frances) (writer); King's Lynn, England **(1752-1840)**

Burns, George (Nathan Birnbaum) (comedian); New York City, 1/20/1896
Burns, Robert (poet); Alloway, Scotland **(1759-1796)**
Burr, Aaron (political leader); Newark, N.J. **(1756-1836)**
Burr, Raymond (William Stacey Burr) (actor); New Westminster, British Columbia, Canada, 5/21/1917
Burroughs, Edgar Rice (novelist); Chicago **(1875-1950)**
Burrows, Abe (playwright and director); New York City, **(1910-1985)**
Burstyn, Ellen (Edna Rae Gillooly) (actress); Detroit, 12/7/1932
Burton, Richard (Richard Jenkins) (actor); Pontrhydfen, Wales **(1925-1984)**
Bush, Vannevar (scientist); Everett, Mass. **(1890-1974)**
Bushman, Francis X. (actor); Baltimore **(1883-1966)**
Butler, Samuel (author); Langar, England **(1835-1902)**
Buttons, Red (Aaron Chwatt) (actor); New York City, 2/5/1919
Buzzi, Ruth (comedienne); Wequetequock, Conn., 7/24/1936
Byrd, Richard Evelyn (polar explorer); Winchester, Va. **(1888-1957)**
Byron, George Gordon (6th Baron Byron) (poet); London **(1788-1824)**

C

Caan, James (actor); The Bronx, N.Y., 3/26/1939
Cabot, John (Giovanni Caboto) (navigator); Genoa (?) **(1450-1498)**
Cabot, Sebastian (navigator); Venice **(1476?-1557)**
Cadmus, Paul (painter and etcher); New York City, 12/17/1904
Caesar, Gaius Julius (statesman); Rome (100?-44 B.C.)
Caesar, Sid (comedian); Yonkers, N.Y., 9/8/1922
Cagney, James (actor); New York City **(1899-1986)**
Cahn, Sammy (songwriter); New York City, 6/18/1913
Caine, Michael (Maurice J. Micklewhite) (actor); London, 3/14/1933
Calder, Alexander (sculptor); Lawnton, Pa. **(1898-1976)**
Caldwell, Erskine (novelist); White Oak, Ga **(1903-1987)** *
Caldwell, Sarah (opera director and conductor); Maryville, Mo., 1928
Caldwell, Taylor (novelist); Manchester, England **(1900-1985)**
Caldwell, Zoe (actress); Hawthorn, Australia, 9/14/1933
Calhern, Louis (Carl Henry Vogt) (actor); Brooklyn, N.Y. **(1895-1956)**
Calhoun, John Caldwell (statesman); nr. Calhoun Mills, S.C. **(1782-1850)**
Calisher, Hortense (novelist); New York City, 12/20/1911
Callas, Maria (Maria Calogeropoulos) (dramatic soprano); New York City **(1923-1977)**
Calloway, Cab (Cabell) (band leader); Rochester, N.Y., 12/25/1907
Calvet, Corinne (actress); Paris, 4/30/1926
Calvin, John (Jean Chauvin) (religious reformer); Noyon, Picardy **(1509-1564)**
Cambridge, Godfrey (comedian); New York City **(1933-1976)**
Cameron, Rod (Rod Cox) (actor); Calgary, Alberta, Canada, **(1912-1983)**
Campbell, Glen (singer); nr. Delight, Ark., 4/22/1938
Camus, Albert (author); Mondovi, Algeria **(1913-1960)**
Canaletto, (Giovanni Antonio Canale); (painter) Venice **(1697-1768)**
Caniff, Milton (cartoonist); Hillsboro, Ohio **(1907-1988)**
Cannon, Dyan (actress); Tacoma, Wash., 1/4/1937
Canova, Judy (comedienne); Jacksonville, Fla., **(1916-1983)**
Cantinflas (Mario Moreno) (comedian); Mexico City, 8/12/1911
Cantor, Eddie (Edward Iskowitz) (actor); New York City **(1892-1964)**
Cantrell, Lana (singer); Sydney, Australia, 1944
Capote, Truman (novelist); New Orleans **(1924-1984)**
Capp, Al (Alfred Gerald Caplin) (cartoonist); New Haven, Conn. **(1909-1979)**
Capra, Frank (film producer, director); Palermo, Italy, 5/18/1897
Caravaggio, Michelangelo Merisi da (painter); Caravaggio (Italy) **(1573-1610)**
Cardin, Pierre (fashion designer); nr. Venice, 7/7/1922
Cardinale, Claudia (actress); Tunis, Tunisia, 1939
Carey, Harry (actor); New York City **(1878-1947)**
Carey, Macdonald (actor); Sioux City, Iowa, 3/15/1913
Carlisle, Kitty (singer and actress); New Orleans, 9/3/1915
Carlson, Richard (actor); Albert Lea, Minn., **(1912-1977)**
Carlyle, Thomas (essayist and historian); Ecclefechan, Scotland **(1795-1881)**
Carmichael, Hoagy (Hoagland Howard) (songwriter); Bloomington, Ind. **(1899-1981)**
Carne, Judy (Joyce Botterill) (singer); Northampton, England, 1939
Carnegie, Andrew (industrialist); Dunfermline, Scotland **(1835-1919)**
Carney, Art (actor); Mt. Vernon, N.Y., 11/4/1918
Carnovsky, Morris (actor); St. Louis, 9/5/1897
Caron, Leslie (actress); Paris, 7/1/1931
Carr, Vikki (singer); El Paso, 7/19/1942
Carracci, Annibale (painter); Bologna (Italy) **(1560-1609)**
Carracci, Lodovico (painter); Bologna (Italy) **(1555-1619)**
Carradine, David (actor); Hollywood, Calif., 12/8/1936
Carradine, John (actor); New York City **(1906-1988)**

Carreras, José (tenor); Barcelona, Spain, 12/5/1946
Carrillo, Leo (actor); Los Angeles **(1881-1961)**
Carroll, Diahann (Carol Diahann Johnson) (singer and actress); Bronx, N.Y., 7/17/1935
Carroll, Leo G. (actor); Weedon, England **(1892-1972)**
Carroll, Lewis (Charles Lutwidge Dodgson) (author and mathematician); Daresbury, England **(1832-1898)**
Carroll, Madeleine (actress); West Bromwich, England **(1906-1987)**
Carroll, Pat (comedienne); Shreveport, La., 5/5/1927
Carson, Johnny (TV entertainer); Corning, Iowa, 10/23/1925
Carson, Kit (Christopher) (scout); Madison County, Ky. **(1809-1868)**
Carson, Rachel (biologist and author); Springdale, Pa. **(1907-1964)**
Carter, Jack (comedian); New York City, 1923
Cartier, Jacques (explorer); Saint-Malo, Brittany (France) **(1491-1557)**
Cartier-Brisson, Henri (photographer); Chanteloup, France, 8/22/1908
Cartland, Barbara (author); England, 7/9/1901
Caruso, Enrico (Errico) (tenor); Naples, Italy **(1873-1921)**
Carver, George Washington (botanist); Missouri **(1864-1943)**
Cary, Arthur Joyce Lunel (novelist); Londonderry, Ireland **(1888-1957)**
Casals, Pablo (cellist); Vendrell, Spain **(1876-1973)**
Casanova de Seingalt, Giovanni Jacopo (adventurer); Venice **(1725-1798)**
Cash, Johnny (singer); nr. Kingsland, Ark., 2/26/1932
Cass, Peggy (comedienne); Boston, 5/21/1924
Cassatt, Mary (painter); Allegheny, Pa. **(1844-1926)**
Cassavetes, John (actor and director); New York City **(1929-1989)**
Cassidy, David (singer); New York City, 4/12/1950
Cassidy, Jack (actor); Richmond Hill, Queens, N.Y. **(1927-1976)**
Cassini, Oleg (Oleg Lolewski-Cassini) (fashion designer); Paris, 4/11/1913
Castagno, Andrea del (painter); San Martino a Corella (Italy) **(c.1421-1457)**
Castellano, Richard (actor); New York City **(1934-1988)**
Castle, Irene (Irene Foote) (actress and dancer); New Rochelle, N.Y. **(1893-1969)**
Castle, Vernon Blythe (dancer and aviator); Norwich, England **(1887-1918)**
Castro Ruz, Fidel (Premier); Mayari, Oriente, Cuba, 8/13/1926
Cather, Willa Sibert (novelist); Winchester, Va. **(1876-1947)**
Cato, Marcus Porcius (called Cato the Elder) (statesman); Tusculum (Italy) (234-149 B.C.)
Catt, Carrie Chapman Lane (woman suffragist); Ripon, Wis. **(1859-1947)**
Catton, Bruce (historian); Petoskey, Mich. **(1899-1978)**
Cavaliaro, Carmen (band leader); New York City, 1913
Cavett, Dick (Richard) (TV entertainer); Gibbon, Neb., 11/19/1936
Cellini, Benvenuto (goldsmith and sculptor); Florence (Italy) **(1500-1571)**
Cervantes Saavedra, Miguel de (novelist); Alcalá de Henares, Spain **(1547-1616)**
Cézanne, Paul (painter); Aix-en-Provence, France **(1839-1906)**
Chagall, Marc (painter); Vitebsk, Russia, **(1887-1985)**
Chaliapin, Feodor Ivanovitch (operatic basso); Kazan, Russia **(1873-1938)**
Chamberlain, Arthur Neville (statesman); Edgbaston, England **(1869-1940)**
Chamberlain, Richard (actor); Los Angeles, 3/31/1935(?)
Champion, Gower (choreographer); Geneva, Ill. **(1921-1980)**
Champion, Marge (actress and dancer); Los Angeles, 9/2/1923
Champlain, Samuel de (explorer); nr. Rochefort, France **(1567?-1635)**
Chancellor, John (TV commentator); Chicago, 7/14/1927
Chandler, Raymond (writer); Chicago **(1883-1959)**
Chanel, "Coco" (Gabriel Bonheur) (fashion designer); Issoire, France **(1883-1971)**
Chaney, Lon (actor); Colorado Springs, Colo. **(1883-1930)**
Channing, Carol (actress); Seattle, 1/31/1923
Chaplin, Geraldine (actress); Santa Monica, Calif., 7/31/1944
Chaplin, Sir Charles (actor); London **(1889-1977)**
Charisse, Cyd (Tula Finklea) (dancer and actress); Amarillo, Tex., 3/8/1923
Charlemagne (Holy Roman Emperor); birthplace unknown **(742-814)**
Charles, Ray (Ray Charles Robinson) (pianist, singer, and songwriter); Albany Ga., 9/23/1930
Chase, Chevy (Cornelius Crane Chase) (comedian); New York City, 10/8/1943
Chase, Ilka (author and actress); New York City **(1905-1978)**
Chase, Lucia (founder Ballet Theatre [now American Ballet Theatre]); Waterbury, Conn. **(1907-1986)**
Chatterton, Ruth (actress); New York City **(1893-1961)**
Chaucer, Geoffrey (poet); London **(1340?-1400)**
Chávez, Carlos (composer); nr. Mexico City **(1899-1978)**
Chavez, Cesar (labor leader); nr. Yuma, Ariz., 3/31/1927

Chayefsky, Paddy (Sidney) (playwright); New York City, **(1923-1981)**
Checker, Chubby (Ernest Evans) (performer); Philadelphia, 10/3/1941
Cheever, John (novelist); Quincy, Mass. **(1912-1982)**
Chekhov, Anton Pavlovich (dramatist and short-story writer); Taganrog, Russia **(1860-1904)**
Cher (Cherilyn LaPiere) (singer); El Centro, Calif., 5/20/1946
Cherubini, Luigi (composer); Florence **(1760-1842)**
Chesterton, Gilbert Keith (author); Kensington, England **(1874-1936)**
Chevalier, Maurice (entertainer); Paris **(1888-1972)**
Chiang Kai-shek (Chief of State); Feng-hwa, China **(1887-1975)**
Child, Julia (food expert); Pasadena, Calif., 8/15/1912
Chippendale, Thomas (cabinet-maker); Otley, England **(1718?-1779)**
Chirico, Giorgio de (painter); Vólos, Greece, **(1888-1978)**
Chopin, Frédéric François (composer); nr. Warsaw **(1810-1849)**
Chou En-lai. *See* Zhou Enlai
Christian, Linda (Blanca Rosa Welter) (actress); Tampico, Mexico, 11/13/1924
Christie, Agatha (mystery writer); Torquay, England, **(1890-1976)**
Christie, Julie (actress); Chukua, India, 4/14/1941
Christopher, Jordon (actor and musician); Youngstown, Ohio, 1941
Christy, June (singer); Springfield, Ill., 1925
Churchill, Sir Winston Leonard Spencer (statesman); Blenheim Palace, Oxfordshire, England **(1874-1965)**
Cicero, Marcus Tullius (orator and statesman); Arpinum (Italy) (106-43 B.C.)
Cid, El (Rodrigo (or Ruy) Díez de Bivar) (Spanish national hero); nr. Burgos, Spain **(1040?-1099)**
Cilento, Diane (actress); Queensland, Australia, 10/5/1933
Cimabue, Giovanni (painter); Florence (Italy) **(c.1240-c.1302)**
Cimino, Michael (film director); New York City, 1943(?)
Clair, René (René Chomette) (film director); Paris **(1898-1981)**
Claire, Ina (Ina Fagan) (actress); Washington, D.C., **(1895-1985)**
Clapton, Eric (singer and guitarist); Ripley, England, 3/30/1945
Clark, Dick (TV personality); Mt. Vernon, N.Y., 11/30/1929
Clark, Mark W. (general); Madison Barracks, N.Y. **(1896-1984)**
Clark, Petula (singer); Epsom, England, 11/15/1934
Clark, Roy (country music artist); Meherrin, Va., 4/15/1933
Clark, William (explorer); Caroline County, Va. **(1770-1838)**
Clarke, Arthur C. (science fiction writer); Minehead, England, 12/16/1917
Claude Lorrain (Claude Gellée) (painter); Champagne, France **(1600-1682)**
Clausewitz, Karl von (military strategist); Burg (East Germany) **(1780-1831)**
Clay, Henry (statesman); Hanover County, Va. **(1777-1852)**
Clay, Lucius D. (banker, ex-general); Marietta, Ga. **(1897-1978)**
Clayburgh, Jill (actress); New York City, 4/30/1944
Clemenceau, Georges (statesman); Mouilleron-en-Pareds, Vondée, France **(1841-1929)**
Clemens, Samuel L. *See* Mark Twain
Cleopatra (Queen of Egypt); Alexandria, Egypt (69-30 B.C.)
Cliburn, Van (Harvey Lavan Cliburn, Jr.) (concert pianist); Shreveport, La., 7/12/1934
Clifford, Clark M. (ex-Secretary of Defense); Ft. Scott, Kan., 12/25/1906
Clift, Montgomery (actor); Omaha, Neb. **(1920-1966)**
Clooney, Rosemary (singer); Maysville, Ky., 5/23/1928
Close, Glenn (actress); Greenwich, Conn., 3/19/1947
Clurman, Harold (stage producer); New York City **(1901-1980)**
Cobb, Irvin Shrewsbury (humorist); Paducah, Ky. **(1876-1944)**
Cobb, Lee J. (Leo Jacob) (actor); New York City **(1911-1976)**
Coburn, Charles Douville (actor); Savannah, Ga. **(1877-1961)**
Coburn, James (actor); Laurel, Neb., 8/31/1928
Coca, Imogene (comedienne); Philadelphia, 11/18/1908
Cocker, Joe (John Robert Cocker) (singer); Sheffield, England, 5/20/1944
Coco, James (actor); New York City **(1929-1987)**
Cocteau, Jean (author); Maison-Lafitte, France **(1891-1963)**
Cody, W. F. *See* Buffalo Bill
Cohan, George Michael (actor and dramatist); Providence, R.I. **(1878-1942)**
Colbert, Claudette (Lily Chauchoin) (actress); Paris, 9/13/1903
Colby, William E. (ex-Director of CIA); St. Paul, 1/4/1920
Cole, Nat "King" (singer); Montgomery, Ala. **(1919-1965)**
Cole, Natalie (singer); Los Angeles, 2/6/1950
Cole, Thomas (painter); Lancashire, England **(1801-1848)**
Coleridge, Samuel Taylor (poet); Ottery St. Mary, England **(1772-1834)**
Colette (Sidonie-Gabrielle Colette) (novelist); St.-Sauveur, France **(c. 1873-1954)**
Collingwood, Charles (TV commentator); Three Rivers, Mich. **(1917-1985)**
Collins, Dorothy (Marjorie Chandler) (singer); Windsor, Ontario, Canada, 11/18/1926
Collins, Joan (actress); London 5/23/1933

Collins, Judy (singer); Seattle, 5/1/1939
Colman, Ronald (actor); Richmond, England **(1891-1958)**
Colonna, Jerry (comedian); Boston **(1905-1986)**
Columbus, Christopher (Cristoforo Colombo) (discoverer of America); Genoa (Italy) **(1451-1506)**
Comden, Betty (writer); New York City, 5/3/1919
Comenius, Johann Amos (educational reformer) Nivnice, Moravia (Czechoslovakia) **(1592-1670)**
Commager, Henry Steele (historian); Pittsburgh, 10/25/1902
Como, Perry (Pierino) (singer); Canonsburg, Pa., 5/18/1912
Compton, Karl Taylor (physicist); Wooster, Ohio **(1887-1954)**
Comte, August (philosopher); Montpellier, France **(1798-1857)**
Conant, James B. (educator and statesman); Dorchester, Mass. **(1893-1978)**
Condon, Eddie (jazz musician); Goodland, Ind. **(1905-1973)**
Confucius (K'ung Fu-tzu) (philosopher); Shantung province, China **(c. 551-479 B.C.)**
Congreve, William (dramatist); nr. Leeds, England **(1670-1729)**
Connelly, Marc (playwright); McKeesport, Pa. **(1890-1980)**
Connery, Sean (actor); Edinburgh, Scotland, 8/25/1930
Conniff, Ray (band leader); Attleboro, Mass., 11/6/1916
Connors, Chuck (actor); Brooklyn, N.Y., 4/10/1921
Connors, Mike (Krekor Ohanian) (actor); Fresno, Calif., 8/15/1925
Conrad, Joseph (Teodor Jozef Konrad Korzeniowski) (novelist); Berdichev, Ukraine **(1857-1924)**
Conrad, Robert (Conrad Robert Falk) (actor); Chicago, 3/1/1935
Conrad, William (actor); Louisville, Ky., 9/27/1920
Conried, Hans (Frank Foster) (actor); Baltimore **(1915-1982)**
Constable, John (painter); East Bergholt, Suffolk, England **(1776-1837)**
Constantine II (ex-king); Athens, 6/2/1940
Conte, Richard (actor); New York City **(1916-1975)**
Conti, Tom (actor); Paisley, Scotland, 11/22/1941
Converse, Frank (actor); St. Louis, 1938
Conway, Tim (comedian); Chagrin Falls, Ohio, 12/15/1933
Coogan, Jackie (actor); Los Angeles **(1914-1984)**
Cooke, Alistair (Alfred Alistair); (TV narrator and journalist); Manchester, England, 11/20/1908
Cooley, Denton A(rthur) (heart surgeon); Houston, Tex., 8/22/1920
Coolidge, Rita (singer); Nashville, Tenn., 1944
Cooper, Alice (Vincent Furnier) (rock musician); Detroit, 2/4/1948
Cooper, Gary (Frank James Cooper) (actor); Helena, Mont. **(1901-1961)**
Cooper, Jackie (actor and director); Los Angeles, 9/15/1922
Cooper, James Fenimore (novelist); Burlington, N.J. **(1789-1851)**
Cooper, Peter (industrialist and philanthropist); New York City **(1791-1883)**
Copernicus, Nicolaus (Mikolaj Kopernik) (astronomer); Thorn, Poland **(1473-1543)**
Copland, Aaron (composer); Brooklyn, N.Y., 11/14/1900
Copley, John Singleton (painter); Boston, Mass. **(1738-1815)**
Coppola, Francis Ford (film director); Detroit, 4/7/1939
Corelli, Arcangelo (composer); Fusignano, Italy **(1653-1713)**
Corelli, Franco (operatic tenor); Ancona, Italy, 4/8/1923
Corneille, Pierre (dramatist); Rouen, France **(1606-1684)**
Cornell, Katharine (actress); Berlin **(1893-1974)**
Coret, Jean Baptiste Camille (painter); Paris **(1796-1875)**
Correggio, Antonio Allegri da (painter); Correggio (Italy) **(1494-1534)**
Corsaro, Frank (opera director); New York harbor, 12/22/1924
Cortés (or Cortez), Hernando (explorer); Medellin, Spain **(1485-1547)**
Cosby, Bill (actor); Philadelphia, 7/12/1937
Cosell, Howard (Howard Cohen) (sportscaster); Winston-Salem, N.C., 3/25/1920
Costa-Gavras, Henri (Kostantinos Gavras) (film director); Athens, 1933
Costello, Elvis (Declan Patrick McManus) (singer-musician-songwriter); London, 1954
Costello, Lou (comedian); Paterson, N.J. **(1908-1959)**
Cotten, Joseph (actor); Petersburg, Va., 5/15/1905
Couperin, François (composer); Paris **(1668-1733)**
Courbet, Gustave (painter); Ornans, France **(1819-1877)**
Courrèges, André (fashion designer); Pau, France, 3/9/1923
Courtenay, Tom (actor); Hull, England, 2/25/1937
Cousins, Norman (publisher); Union Hill, N.J., 6/24/1915
Cousteau, Jacques-Yves (marine explorer); St. André-de-Cubzac, France, 6/11/1910
Coward, Sir Noel (playwright and actor); Teddington, England **(1899-1973)**
Cowles, Gardner, Jr. (newspaper publisher); Algona, Iowa, **(1903-1985)**
Cowper, William (poet); Great Berkhamstead, England **(1731-1800)**
Cozzens, James Gould (novelist); Chicago **(1903-1978)**
Crabbe, Buster (Clarence) (actor); Oakland, Calif. **(1908-1983)**
Crain, Jeanne (actress); Barstow, Calif., 5/25/1925

Cranach, Lucas, the elder (painter); Kronach (Germany) **(1472-1553)**
Crane, Hart (poet); Garrettsville, Ohio **(1899-1932)**
Crane, Stephen (novelist and poet); Newark, N.J. **(1871-1900)**
Cranmer, Thomas (churchman); Aslacton, England **(1489-1556)**
Crawford, Broderick (actor); Philadelphia **(1911-1986)**
Crawford, Cheryl (stage producer); Akron, Ohio **(1902-1986)**
Crawford, Joan (Lucille LeSueur) (actress and business executive); San Antonio **(1908-1977)**
Crenna, Richard (actor); Los Angeles, 11/30/1927
Crespin, Régine (operatic soprano); Marseilles, France, 2/23/1929
Crichton, (John) Michael (novelist); Chicago, 10/23/1942
Crisp, Donald (actor); London **(1880-1974)**
Croce, Benedetto (philosopher); Peseasseroli, Aquila, Italy **(1866-1952)**
Croce, Jim (singer); Philadelphia **(1942-1973)**
Crockett, Davy (David) (frontiersman); Greene County, Tenn. **(1786-1836)**
Cromwell, Oliver (statesman); Huntingdon, England **(1599-1658)**
Cronin, A. J. (Archibald J. Cronin) (novelist); Cardross, Scotland **(1896-1981)**
Cronkite, Walter (TV newscaster); St. Joseph, Mo., 11/4/1916
Cronyn, Hume (actor); London, Ontario, Canada, 7/18/1911
Crosby, Bing (Harry Lillis) (singer, actor); Tacoma, Wash. **(1904-1977)**
Crosby, Bob (musician); Spokane, Wash., 8/23/1913
Cross, Ben (Bernard) (actor); Paddington, England, 12/16/1947
Cross, Milton (opera commentator); New York City **(1897-1975)**
Crouse, Russel (playwright); Findlay, Ohio **(1893-1966)**
Cruise, Tom (actor); Syracuse, N.Y., 7/3/1962
Cugat, Xavier (band leader); Barcelona, Spain, 1/1/1900
Cukor, George (film director); New York City **(1899-1983)**
Cullen, Bill (William Lawrence Cullen) (radio and TV entertainer); Pittsburgh, 2/18/1920
Culp, Robert (actor); Berkeley, Calif., 8/16/1930
Cummings, E. E. (Edward Estlin Cummings) (poet); Cambridge, Mass. **(1894-1962)**
Cummings, Robert (actor); Joplin, Mo., 6/9/1910
Curie, Marie (Marja Sklodowska) (physical chemist); Warsaw **(1867-1934)**
Curie, Pierre (physicist); Paris **(1859-1906)**
Curtin, Phyllis (soprano); Clarksburg, W.Va., 12/3/1927
Curtis, Tony (Bernard Schwartz) (actor); Bronx, N.Y., 6/3/1925
Curzon, Clifford (concert pianist); London **(1907-1982)**
Custer, George Armstrong (army officer); New Rumley, Ohio **(1839-1876)**

D

da Gama, Vasco (explorer); Sines, Portugal **(1460-1524)**
Daguerre, Louis (photographic pioneer); nr. Paris **(1787-1851)**
Dahl, Arlene (actress); Minneapolis, 8/11/1928
Dailey, Dan (actor and dancer); New York City, **(1917-1978)**
Daley, Richard J. (Mayor of Chicago); Chicago **(1902-1976)**
Dali, Salvador (painter); Figueras, Spain **(1904-1989)**
Dalton, John (chemist); nr. Cockermouth, England **(1766-1844)**
Daly, James (actor); Wisconsin Rapids, Wis. **(1918-1978)**
Daly, John (radio and TV news analyst); Johannesburg, South Africa, 2/20/1914
d'Amboise, Jacques (ballet dancer); Dedham, Mass., 7/28/1934
Damone, Vic (Vito Farinola) (singer); Brooklyn, N.Y., 6/12/1928
Damrosch, Walter Johannes (orchestra conductor); Breslau (Poland) **(1862-1950)**
Dana, Charles Anderson (editor); Hinsdale, N.H. **(1819-1897)**
Dandridge, Dorothy (actress); Cleveland **(1923-1965)**
Dangerfield, Rodney (comedian); Babylon, L.I., N.Y., 1921
Daniels, Bebe (Virginia Daniels) (actress); Dallas **(1901-1971)**
Danilova, Alexandra (ballerina); Peterhof, Russia, 1/20/1904
Dannay, Frederic (novelist, pseudonym Ellery Queen); Brooklyn, N.Y. **(1905-1982)**
Danner, Blythe (actress); Philadelphia, 1944(?)
D'Annunzio, Gabriele (soldier and author); Francaville at Mare, Pescara, Italy **(1863-1938)**
Dante (or Durante) Alighieri (poet); Florence (Italy) **(1265-1321)**
Danton, Georges Jacques (French Revolutionary leader); Arcis-sur-Aube, France **(1759-1794)**
Darnell, Linda (actress); Dallas **(1921-1965)**
Darren, James (actor); Philadelphia, 6/8/1936
Darrieux, Danielle (actress); Bordeaux, France, 5/1/1917
Darrow, Clarence Seward (lawyer); Kinsman, Ohio **(1857-1938)**
Darwin, Charles Robert (naturalist); Shrewsbury, England **(1809-1882)**
daSilva, Howard (actor); Cleveland **(1909-1986)**
Dassin, Jules (film director); Middletown, Conn., 12/18/1911
Daumier, Honoré (caricaturist); Marseilles, France **(1808-1879)**

Dauphin, Claude (actor); Corbeil, France **(1903-1978)**
David, Jacques-Louis (painter); Paris **(1748-1825)**
David (King of Israel and Judah) **(died c. 973 B.C.)**
Davidson, John (singer and actor); Pittsburgh, 12/13/1941
Davies, Marion (Marion Douras) (actress); New York City **(1898?-1961)**
da Vinci, Leonardo (painter and scientist); Vinci, Tuscany (Italy) **(1452-1519)**
Davis, Bette (actress); Lowell, Mass., 4/5/1908
Davis, Elmer Holmes (radio commentator); Aurora, Ind. **(1890-1958)**
Davis, Jefferson (President of the Confederacy); Christian (now Todd) County, Ky. **(1808-1889)**
Davis, Mac (singer); Lubbock, Tex., 1/21/1942
Davis, Miles (jazz trumpeter); Alton, Ill., 5/25/1926
Davis, Ossie (actor and writer); Cogdell, Ga., 12/18/1917
Davis, Sammy, Jr. (actor and singer); New York City, 12/8/1925
Davis, Skeeter (Mary Francis Penick) (singer); Dry Ridge, Ky., 12/30/1931
Davis, Stuart (painter); Philadelphia **(1894-1964)**
Day, Dennis (singer); New York City **(1917-1988)**
Day, Doris (Doris von Kappelhoff) (singer and actress); Cincinnati, 4/3/1924
Day, Laraine (La Raine Johnson) (actress); Roosevelt, Utah, 10/13/1920
Dayan, Moshe (ex-Defense Minister of Israel); Dagania, Palestine **(1915-1981)**
Dean, James (actor); Marion, Ind. **(1931-1955)**
Dean, Jimmy (singer); Seth Ward, nr. Plainview, Tex., 8/10/1928
De Bakey, Michael E. (heart surgeon); Lake Charles, La., 9/7/1908
de Beauvoir, Simone (novelist and philosopher); Paris **(1908-1986)**
Debs, Eugene Victor (Socialist leader); Terre Haute, Ind. **(1855-1926)**
Debussy, Claude Achille (composer); St. Germain-en-Laye, France **(1862-1918)**
De Carlo, Yvonne (Peggy Yvonne Middleton) (actress); Vancouver, B.C., Canada, 9/1/1924
de Chirico, Giorgio (painter); Volos, Greece, **(1888-1978)**
Defoe, Daniel (novelist); London **(1659?-1731)**
Degas, Hilaire Germain Edgar (painter); Paris **(1834-1917)**
de Gaulle, Charles André Joseph Marie (soldier and statesman); Lille, France **(1890-1970)**
DeHaven, Gloria (actress); Los Angeles, 7/23/1925
de Havilland, Olivia (actress); Tokyo, 7/1/1916
Dekker, Albert (actor); Brooklyn, N.Y. **(1904-1968)**
de Kooning, Willem (painter); Rotterdam, 4/24/1904
Delacroix, Eugène (painter); Charenton-St. Maurice, France **(1798-1863)**
de la Renta, Oscar (fashion designer); Santo Domingo, Dominican Republic, 7/22/1932
Delaunay, Robert (painter); Paris **(1885-1941)**
De Laurentiis, Dino (film producer); Torre Annunziata, Bay of Naples, Italy, 8/8/1919
della Robbia, Andrea (sculptor) Florence **(1435-1525)**
della Robbia, Luca (sculptor); Florence **(1400-1482)**
Delon, Alain (actor); Sceaux, France, 11/8/1935
Del Rio, Dolores (Dolores Ansunsolo) (actress); Durango, Mexico **(1905-1983)**
DeLuise, Dom (comedian); Brooklyn, N.Y., 8/1/1933
Demarest, William (actor); St. Paul **(1892-1983)**
de Mille, Agnes (choreographer); New York City 9/18/1905
De Mille, Cecil Blount (film director); Ashfield, Mass. **(1881-1959)**
Demosthenes (orator); Athens **(385?-322 B.C.)**
Deneuve, Catherine (actress); Paris, 10/22/1943
De Niro, Robert (actor); New York City, 8/17/1943
Dennis, Sandy (actress); Hastings, Neb., 4/27/1937
Denver, John (Henry John Deutschendorf, Jr.) (singer); Roswell, N.M., 12/31/1943
De Palma, Brian (film director); Newark, N.J., 9/11/1940
Derain, André (painter); Chatou, Seine-et-Oise, France **(1880-1954)**
Dern, Bruce (actor); Chicago, 6/4/1936
Descartes, René (philosopher and mathematician); La Haye, France **(1596-1650)**
De Seversky, Alexander P. (aviator); Tiflis, Russia **(1894-1974)**
De Sica, Vittorio (film director); Sora, Italy **(1901-1974)**
Desmond, Johnny (composer); Detroit **(1921-1985)**
Desmond, William (actor); Dublin **(1878-1949)**
De Soto, Hernando (explorer); Barcarrota, Spain **(1500?-1542)**
De Valera, Eamon (ex-President of Ireland); New York City **(1882-1975)**
Devine, Andy (actor); Flagstaff, Ariz. **(1905-1977)**
DeVito, Danny (Daniel Michael); (actor, director); Neptune, N.J., 11/17/1944
De Vries, Peter (novelist); Chicago, 2/27/1910
Dewey, George (admiral); Montpelier, Vt. **(1837-1917)**
Dewey, John (philosopher and educator); Burlington, Vt. **(1859-1952)**
Dewey, Thomas E. (politician); Owosso, Mich. **(1902-1971)**

Dewhurst, Colleen (actress); Montreal, 1926(?)
Diamond, Neil (singer); Brooklyn, N.Y., 1/24/1941
Diana (Diana Frances Spencer) (Princess of Wales); Sandringham, England, 7/1/61
Dichter, Misha (pianist); Shanghai, 9/27/1945
Dickens, Charles John Huffam (novelist); Portsea, England **(1812-1870)**
Dickey, James (poet); Atlanta, 2/2/1923
Dickinson, Angie (Angeline Brown) (actress); Kulm, N.D., 9/30/1932
Dickinson, Emily Elizabeth (poet); Amherst, Mass. **(1830-1886)**
Diddley, Bo (Elias McDaniel) (guitarist); McComb, Miss., 12/30/1928
Diderot, Denis (encyclopedist); Langres, France **(1713-1784)**
Diefenbaker, John G. (ex-Prime Minister); Grey County, Ontario, Canada **(1895-1979)**
Dietrich, Marlene (Maria Magdalena von Losch) (actress); Berlin, 12/27/1901
Diggs, Dudley (actor); Dublin **(1879-1947)**
Diller, Phyllis (Phyllis Driver) (comedienne); Lima, Ohio, 7/17/1917
Dillman, Bradford (actor); San Francisco, 4/14/1930
Dine, Jim (painter); Cincinnati, 6/16/1935
Diogenes (philosopher); Sinope (Turkey) **(412?-323 B.C.)**
Dion (Dion DiMucci) (singer); Bronx, N.Y., 7/18/1939
Dior, Christian (fashion designer); Granville, France **(1905-1957)**
Disney, Walt(er) Elias (film animator and producer); Chicago **(1901-1966)**
Disraeli, Benjamin (Earl of Beaconsfield) (statesman); London **(1804-1881)**
Dix, Dorothea (civil rights reformer); Hampden, Me. **(1802-1887)**
Dix, Richard (Ernest Carlton Brimmer) (actor); St. Paul **(1894-1949)**
Dixon, Jeane (Jeane Pinckert) (seer); Medford, Wis., 1918
Dobbs, Mattiwilda (soprano); Atlanta, Ga., 7/11/1925
Doctorow, E(dgar) L(aurence) (novelist); New York City, 1/6/1931
Dodgson, C. L. *See* Carroll, Lewis.
Dolin, Anton (dancer); Slinfold, England **(1904-1983)**
Domingo, Placido (tenor); Madrid, 1/21/1941
Domino, Fats (Antoine) (musician); New Orleans, 2/26/1928
Donahue, Phil (television personality); Cleveland, 12/21/1935 ·
Donat, Robert (actor); Withington, England **(1905-1958)**
Donatello (Donato Niccolò di Betto Bardi) (sculptor); Florence **(c. 1386-1466)**
Donne, John (poet); London **(1573-1631)**
Doolittle, James H. (ex-Air Force general); Alameda, Calif., 12/14/1896
Dorati, Antal (orchestra conductor); Budapest **(1906-1988)**
Dorsey, Jimmy (band leader); Shenandoah, Pa. **(1904-1957)**
Dorsey, Tommy (band leader); Mahonoy Plains, Pa. **(1905-1956)**
Dos Passos, John (author); Chicago **(1896-1970)**
Dostoevski, Fyodor Mikhailovich (novelist); Moscow **(1821-1881)**
Douglas, Helen Gahagan (ex-Representative); Boonton, N.J. **(1900-1980)**
Douglas, Kirk (Issur Danielovitch) (actor); Amsterdam, N.Y., 12/9/1916
Douglas, Melvyn (Melvyn Hesselberg) (actor); Macon, Ga., **(1901-1981)**
Douglas, Michael (actor; movie producer); New Brunswick, N.J., 9/25/1944
Douglas, Mike (Michael D. Dowd, Jr.) (TV personality); Chicago, 8/11/1925
Douglas, Paul (actor); Philadelphia **(1907-1959)**
Douglas, Stephen Arnold (politician); Brandon, Vt. **(1813-1861)**
Dowling, Eddie (Edward Goucher) (actor and stage producer); Woonsocket, R.I., **(1894-1976)**
Downs, Hugh (TV entertainer); Akron, Ohio, 2/14/1921
Doyle, Sir Arthur Conan (novelist and spiritualist); Edinburgh, Scotland **(1859-1930)**
Drake, Alfred (singer and actor); New York City, 10/7/1914
Drake, Sir Francis (navigator); Tavistock, England **(1545-1596)**
Dreiser, Theodore (writer); Terre Haute, Ind. **(1871-1945)**
Dressler, Marie (Leila Koerber) (actress); Cobourg, Ontario, Canada **(1869-1934)**
Dreyfus, Alfred (French army officer); Mulhouse (France) **(1859-1935)**
Dreyfuss, Richard (actor); Brooklyn, N.Y., 10/29/1947
Drury, Allen (novelist); Houston, 9/2/1918
Dryden, John (poet); Northamptonshire, England **(1631-1700)**
Dubček, Alexander (ex-President of Czechoslovakia); Uhroved (Czechoslovakia), 11/27/1921
Dubinsky, David (David Dobnievski) (labor leader); Brest-Litovsk (U.S.S.R.) **(1892-1982)**
Duchamp, Marcel (painter); Blainville, France **(1887-1968)**
Duchin, Peter (pianist and band leader); New York City, 7/28/1937
Dufay, Guillaume (composer); Cambrai, France **(c. 1400-1474)**
Duff, Howard (actor); Bremerton, Wash., 11/24/1917
Dufy, Raoul (painter); Le Havre, France **(1877-1953)**
Duke, James B. (industrialist); nr. Durham, N.C. **(1856-1925)**
Duke, Patty (Anna Marie Duke) (actress); New York City, 12/14/1946

Dullea, Keir (actor); Cleveland, 5/30/1936(?)
Dulles, Allen Welsh (ex-Director of CIA); Watertown, N.Y. **(1893-1969)**
Dulles, John Foster (statesman); Washington, D.C. **(1888-1959)**
Dumas, Alexandre (called Dumas fils) (novelist); Paris **(1824-1895)**
Dumas, Alexandre (called Dumas père) (novelist); Villers-Cotterets, France **(1802-1870)**
du Maurier, Daphne (novelist); London **(1907-1989)**
du Maurier, George Louis Palmella Busson (novelist); Paris **(1834-1896)**
Dumont, Margaret (actress); **(1889-1965)**
Dunaway, Faye (actress); Bascom, Fla., 1/14/1941
Duncan, Isadora (dancer); San Francisco **(1878-1927)**
Duncan, Sandy (actress); Henderson, Tex., 2/20/1946
Dunn, James (actor); Santa Monica, Calif. **(1905-1967)**
Dunne, Irene (actress); Louisville, Ky., 12/20/1904
Dunnock, Mildred (actress); Baltimore, 1/25/1906
Duns Scotus, John (theologian); Duns, Scotland **(1265-1303)**
Du Pont, Pierre S. (economist); Paris **(1739-1817)**
Durante, Jimmy (comedian); New York City **(1893-1980)**
Durbin, Deanna (Edna Mae) (actress); Winnipeg, Canada, 12/4/1922
Dürer, Albrecht (painter and engraver); Nürnberg (Germany) **(1471-1528)**
Durrell, Lawrence George (novelist); Julundur, India, 2/27/1912
Duse, Eleonora (actress); Chioggia, Italy **(1859-1924)**
Duvalier, Jean-Claude (ex-President; son of "Papa Doc"); Port-au-Prince, Haiti, 7/3/1951
Duvall, Robert (actor); San Diego, Calif., 1931
Dvořák, Antonin (composer); Nelahozeves (Czechoslovakia) **(1841-1904)**
Dylan, Bob (Robert Zimmerman) (folk singer and composer); Duluth, Minn., 5/24/1941

E

Eagels, Joanne (actress); Kansas City, Mo. **(1894-1929)**
Eakins, Thomas (painter and sculptor); Philadelphia, **(1844-1916)**
Earhart, Amelia (aviator); Atchison, Kan. **(1898-1937)**
Eastman, George (inventor); Waterville, N.Y. **(1854-1932)**
Eastwood, Clint (actor); San Francisco, 5/31/1930
Ebsen, Buddy (Christian Ebsen, Jr.) (actor); Belleville, Ill., 4/2/1908
Eckstine, Billy (singer); Pittsburgh, 7/8/1914
Eddy, Mary Baker (founder of Christian Science Church); Bow, N.H. **(1821-1910)**
Eddy, Nelson (baritone and actor); Providence, R.I. **(1901-1967)**
Eden, Sir Anthony (Earl of Avon) (ex-Prime Minister); Durham, England **(1897-1977)**
Edison, Thomas Alva (inventor); Milan, Ohio **(1847-1931)**
Edwards, Blake (film writer-producer); Tulsa, Okla. 7/26/1922
Edwards, Jonathan (theologian); East Windsor, Conn. **(1703-1758)**
Edwards, Ralph (TV and radio producer); Merino, Colo., 1913
Edwards, Vincent (actor); Brooklyn, N.Y., 7/7/1928
Egan, Richard (actor); San Francisco, **(1923-1987)**
Eggar, Samantha (actress); London, 5/3/1939
Eglevsky, André (ballet dancer); Moscow **(1917-1977)**
Ehrlich, Paul (bacteriologist); Strzelin (Poland) **(1854-1915)**
Einstein, Albert (physicist); Ulm, Germany **(1879-1955)**
Eisenhower, Milton S. (educator); Abilene, Kan., **(1899-1985)**
Eisenstaedt, Alfred (photographer and photojournalist); Dirschau (Poland), 12/6/1898
Ekberg, Anita (actress); Malmö, Sweden, 9/29/1931
Eldridge, Florence (Florence McKechnie) (actress); Brooklyn, N.Y., **(1901-1988)**
Elgar, Sir Edward (composer); Worcester, England **(1857-1934)**
Elgart, Larry (band leader); New London, Conn., 3/20/1922
El Greco (Domenicos Theotocopoulos) (painter); Candia, Crete (Greece) **(c.1541-1614)**
Eliot, George (Mary Ann Evans) (novelist); Chilvers Coton, England **(1819-1880)**
Eliot, Thomas Stearns (poet); St. Louis **(1888-1965)**
Ellington, Duke (Edward Kennedy) (jazz musician); Washington, D.C. **(1899-1974)**
Elliot, "Mama" Cass (Ellen Naomi Cohen) (singer); Baltimore **(1941-1974)**
Elman, Mischa (violinist); Stalnoye, Ukraine **(1891-1967)**
Emerson, Ralph Waldo (philosopher and poet); Boston **(1803-1882)**
Enesco, Georges (composer); Dorohoi, Romania **(1881-1955)**
Engels, Friedrich (Socialist writer); Barmen (Germany) **(1820-1895)**
Entremont, Philippe (concert pianist); Rheims, France, 6/7/1934
Epicurus (philosopher); Samos (Greece) **(341-270 B.C.)**
Epstein, Sir Jacob (sculptor); New York City **(1880-1959)**
Erasmus, Desiderius (Gerhard Gerhards) (scholar); Rotterdam **(1466?-1536)**
Erhard, Ludwig (ex-Chancellor); Furth, Germany **(1897-1977)**

Erickson, Leif (actor); Alameda, Calif. **(1911-1986)**
Ericson, Leif (navigator); **(c. 10th century A.D.)**
Erikson, Erik H. (psychoanalyst); Frankfurt, Germany, 6/15/1902
Ernst, Max (painter); Bruhl, Germany **(1891-1976)**
Euclid (mathematician); Megara (Greece) **(c. 300 B.C.)**
Euier, Leonhard (mathematician); Basel, Switzerland **(1707-1783)**
Euripides (dramatist); Salamis (Greece) **(c.484-407 B.C.)**
Evans, Dale (Frances Butts) (actress and singer); Uvalde, Tex., 10/31/1912
Evans, Dame Edith (actress); London **(1888-1976)**
Evans, Linda (actress); Hartford, Conn., 11/18/1942
Evans, Maurice (actor); Dorchester, England **(1901-1989)**
Everett, Chad (actor); (Raymon Lee Cramton) South Bend, Ind., 6/11/1936
Evers, Charles (civil rights leader); Decatur, Miss., 9/14/1923(?)
Evers, Medgar (civil rights leader); Decatur, Miss. **(1925-1963)**
Ewell, Tom (Yewell Tompkins) (actor); Owensboro, Ky., 4/29/1909

F

Fabian (Fabian Anthony Forte) (singer); Philadelphia, 2/6/1943
Fabray, Nanette (Nanette Fabarés) (actress); San Diego, Calif., 10/27/1922
Fadiman, Clifton (literary critic); Brooklyn, N.Y., 5/15/1904
Fahrenheit, Gabriel (German physicist); Danzig (Poland); **(1686-1736)**
Fairbanks, Douglas (Douglas Ulman) (actor); Denver **(1883-1939)**
Fairbanks, Douglas, Jr. (actor); New York City, 12/9/1909
Faith, Percy (conductor); Toronto **(1908-1976)**
Falk, Peter (actor); New York City, 9/16/1927
Falla, Manuel de (composer); Cadiz, Spain **(1876-1946)**
Faraday, Michael (physicist); Newington, England **(1791-1867)**
Farber, Barry (radio-TV broadcaster); Baltimore, Md., 1930
Farentino, James (actor); Brooklyn, N.Y., 2/24/1938
Farmer, James (civil rights leader); Marshall, Tex., 1/12/1920
Farnum, William (actor); Boston **(1876-1953)**
Farrell, Charles (actor); Onset Bay, Mass., 1901
Farrell, Eileen (operatic soprano); Willimantic, Conn., 2/13/1920
Farrell, Glenda (actress); Enid, Okla. **(1904-1971)**
Farrell, James T. (novelist); Chicago **(1904-1979)**
Farrell, Suzanne (Roberta Sue Ficker) (ballerina); Cincinnati, 8/16/1945
Farrow, Mia (actress); Los Angeles, 2/9/1946
Fasanella, Ralph (painter); New York City, 9/2/1914
Fassbinder, Rainer Werner (film and stage director); Bad Wörishofen, West Germany **(1946-1982)**
Fast, Howard (novelist); New York City, 11/11/1914
Faulkner, William (novelist); New Albany, Miss. **(1897-1962)**
Fauré, Gabriel Urbain (composer); Pamiers, France **(1845-1924)**
Fawcett, Farrah (actress); Corpus Christi, Tex., 2/2/1947(?)
Faye, Alice (Ann Leppert) (actress); New York City, 5/5/1915
Feiffer, Jules (cartoonist); New York City, 1/26/1929
Feininger, Lyonel (painter); New York City **(1871-1956)**
Feldon, Barbara (actress); Pittsburgh, 3/12/1941
Feliciano, José (singer); Larez, Puerto Rico, 9/10/1945
Felker, Clay S. (editor and publisher); St. Louis, 10/2/1925(?)
Fellini, Federico (film director); Rimini, Italy, 1/20/1920
Fender, Freddie (Baldemar Huerta) (singer); San Benito, Tex., 1937
Ferber, Edna (novelist); Kalamazoo, Mich. **(1885-1968)**
Ferguson, Maynard (jazz trumpeter); Verdun, Quebec, Canada, 5/4/1928
Fermi, Enrico (atomic physicist); Rome **(1901-1954)**
Fernandel (Fernand Joseph Desire Contandin) (actor); Marseilles, France **(1903-1971)**
Ferrer, José (actor and director); Santurce, Puerto Rico, 1/8/1912
Ferrer, Mel (actor); Elberon, N.J., 8/25/1917
Fetchit, Stepin (Lincoln Theodore Perry) (comedian); Key West, Fla. **(1902-1985)**
Fiedler, Arthur (conductor); Boston **(1894-1979)**
Field, Eugene (poet); St. Louis **(1850-1895)**
Field, Marshall (merchant); nr. Conway, Mass. **(1834-1906)**
Field, Sally (actress); Pasadena, Calif., 11/6/1946
Fielding, Henry (novelist); nr. Glastonbury, England **(1707-1754)**
Fields, Gracie (comedienne); Rochdale, England **(1898-1979)**
Fields, Totie (comedienne); Hartford, Conn. **(1931-1978)**
Fields, W. C. (William Claude Dukenfield) (comedian); Philadelphia **(1880-1946)**
Fierstein, Harvey (Forbes) (playwright and actor); Brooklyn, 6/6/1954
Filene, Edward A. (merchant); **(1860-1937)**
Finch, Peter (actor); Kensington, England **(1916-1977)**
Finney, Albert (actor); Salford, England, 5/9/1936
Firkusny, Rudolf (pianist); Napajedla (Czechoslovakia), 2/11/1912

Fischer-Dieskau, Dietrich (baritone); Berlin, 5/28/1925
Fisher, Eddie (Edwin) (singer); Philadelphia, 8/10/1928
Fitzgerald, Barry (William Joseph Shields) (actor); Dublin **(1888-1961)**
Fitzgerald, Edward (radio broadcaster); Troy, N.Y. **(1898(?)-1982)**
Fitzgerald, Ella (singer); Newport News, Va., 4/25/1918
Fitzgerald, F. Scott (Francis Scott Key) (novelist); St. Paul, Minn. **(1896-1940)**
Fitzgerald, Geraldine (actress); Dublin, 11/24/1914
Fitzgerald, Pegeen (radio broadcaster); Norcatur, Kan. **(1910-1989)**
Flack, Roberta (singer); Black Mountain, N.C., 2/10/1940
Flagstad, Kirsten (Wagnerian soprano); Hamar, Norway **(1895-1962)**
Flatt, Lester Raymond (bluegrass musician); Overton County, Tenn. **(1914-1979)**
Flaubert, Gustave (novelist); Rouen, France **(1821-1880)**
Fleming, Sir Alexander (bacteriologist); Lochfield, Scotland **(1881-1955)**
Fleming, Rhonda (Marilyn Louis) (actress); Los Angeles, 8/10/1923
Fletcher, John (dramatist); Rye? England **(1579-1625)**
Flynn, Errol (actor); Hobart, Tasmania **(1909-1959)**
Foch, Nina (actress); Leyden, Netherlands, 4/20/1924
Fodor, Eugene (violinist); Turkey Creek, Colo., 3/5/1950
Fonda, Henry (actor); Grand Island, Neb. **(1905-1982)**
Fonda, Jane (actress); New York City, 12/21/1937
Fonda, Peter (actor); New York City, 2/23/1939
Fontaine, Frank (singer and comedian); Cambridge, Mass. **(1920-1979)**
Fontaine, Joan (Joan de Havilland) (actress); Tokyo, 10/22/1917
Fontanne, Lynn (actress); London, **(1887-1983)**
Fonteyn, Dame Margot (Margaret Hookham) (ballerina); Reigate, England, 5/18/1919
Forbes, Malcolm S(tevenson) (publisher and sportsman); Brooklyn, N.Y., 8/19/1919
Ford, Glenn (Gwyllyn Ford) (actor); Quebec, 5/1/1916
Ford, Harrison (actor); Chicago, 7/13/1942
Ford, Henry (industrialist); Greenfield, Mich. **(1863-1947)**
Ford, Henry, II (auto maker); Detroit **(1917-1987)**
Ford, John (film director); Cape Elizabeth, Me. **(1895-1973)**
Ford, Paul (actor); Baltimore **(1901-1976)**
Ford, Tennessee Ernie (Ernie Jennings Ford) (singer); Bristol, Tenn., 2/13/1919
Forrester, Maureen (contralto); Montreal, 7/25/1930
Forsythe, John (actor); Carney's Point, N.J., 1/29/1918
Fosdick, Harry Emerson (clergyman); Buffalo, N.Y. **(1878-1968)**
Fosse, Bob (Robert Louis) (choreographer and director); Chicago **(1927-1987)**
Foster, Preston (actor); Ocean City, N.J. **(1900-1970)**
Foster, Stephen Collins (composer); nr. Pittsburgh **(1826-1864)**
Fox, Michael J. (actor); Edmonton, Alta., Canada, 6/9/1961
Foxx, Redd (John Elroy Sanford) (actor and comedian); St. Louis, 12/9/1922
Foy, Eddie, Jr. (dancer and actor); New Rochelle, N.Y. **(1905-1983)**
Fra Angelico (Giovanni da Fiesole) (painter); Vicchio in the Mugello, Tuscany (Italy) **(c.1387-1455)**
Fracci, Carla (ballerina); Milan, Italy, 8/20/1936
Fragonard, Jean Honoré (painter); Grasse, France **(1732-1806)**
Frampton, Peter (rock musician); Beckenham, England, 4/20/1950
France, Anatole (Jacques Anatole François Thibault) (author); Paris **(1844-1924)**
Francescatti, Zino (violinist); Marseilles, France, 8/9/1905
Franciosa, Anthony (Anthony Papaleo) (actor); New York City, 10/25/1928
Francis, Arlene (Arlene Francis Kazanjian) (actress); Boston, 10/20/1908
Francis, Connie (Concetta Franconero) (singer); Newark, N.J., 12/12/1938
Francis, Kay (Katherine Edwina Gibbs) (actress); Oklahoma City **(1903-1968)**
Francis of Assisi, Saint (Giovanni Francesco Barnardone) (founder of Franciscans); Assisi, Italy **(1182-1226)**
Franck, César Auguste (composer); Liège (Belgium) **(1822-1890)**
Franco Bahamonde, Francisco (Chief of State); El Ferrol, Spain **(1892-1975)**
Franklin, Aretha (singer); Memphis, Tenn., 3/25/1942
Franklin, Benjamin (statesman and scientist); Boston **(1706-1790)**
Frazer, Sir James George (anthropologist); Glasgow, Scotland **(1854-1941)**
Freud, Sigmund (psychoanalyst); Moravia (Czechoslovakia) **(1856-1939)**
Friedan, Betty (Betty Naomi Goldstein) (feminist); Peoria, Ill., 2/4/1921
Fromm, Erich (psychoanalyst); Frankfurt-am-Main, Germany **(1900-1980)**
Frost, David (TV entertainer); Tenterden, England, 4/7/1939
Frost, Robert Lee (poet); San Francisco **(1874-1963)**
Fry, Christopher (playwright); Bristol, England, 12/18/1907

Frye, David (impressionist); Brooklyn, N.Y., 1934
Fugard, Athol (playwright); Middleburg, South Africa, 6/11/1932
Fuller, R(ichard) Buckminster (Jr.) (architect and educator); Milton, Mass. **(1895-1983)**
Fulton, Robert (inventor); Lancaster County, Pa. **(1765-1815)**
Funt, Allen (TV producer); Brooklyn, N.Y., 9/16/1914
Furness, Betty (Elizabeth) (ex-actress and consumer advocate); New York City, 1/3/1916

G

Gabel, Martin (actor and producer); Philadelphia **(1912-1986)**
Gabin, Jean (actor); Paris **(1904-1976)**
Gable, (William) Clark (actor); Cadiz, Ohio **(1901-1960)**
Gabo, Naum (sculptor); Briansk, Russia **(1890-1977)**
Gabor, Eva (actress); Budapest, 2/11/1926(?)
Gabor, Zsa Zsa (Sari) (actress); Budapest, 2/6/1919(?)
Gabrieli, Giovanni (composer); Venice **(c.1557-1612)**
Gainsborough, Thomas (painter); Sudbury, Suffolk, England **(1727-1788)**
Galbraith, John Kenneth (economist); Iona Station, Ontario, Canada, 10/15/1908
Galilei, Galileo (astronomer and physicist); Pisa (Italy) **(1564-1642)**
Gallico, Paul (novelist); New York City **(1897-1976)**
Gallup, George H. (poll taker); Jefferson, Iowa **(1901-1984)**
Galsworthy, John (novelist and dramatist); Coombe, England **(1867-1933)**
Galway, James (flutist); Belfast, Northern Ireland, 12/8/1939
Gambling, John A. (radio broadcaster); New York City, 1930
Gandhi, Indira (Indira Nehru) (Prime Minister); Allahabad, India **(1917-1984)**
Gandhi, Mohandas Karamchand (called Mahatma Gandhi) (Hindu leader); Porbandar, India **(1869-1948)**
Gannett, Frank E. (editor and publisher); **(1876-1957)**
Garagiola, Joe (Joseph Henry) (sportscaster); St. Louis, 2/12/1926
Garbo, Greta (Greta Gustafsson) (actress); Stockholm, 9/18/1905
Garcia Lorca, Frederico (author); Fuente Vaqueros, Spain **(1898-1936)**
Gardner, Ava (actress); Smithfield, N.C., 12/24/1922
Gardner, Erle Stanley (novelist); Malden, Mass. **(1889-1970)**
Garfield, John (Jules Garfinkle) (actor); New York City **(1913-1952)**
Garfunkel, Art (Arthur) (singer); Newark, N.J., 11/5/1941
Gargan, William (actor); Brooklyn, N.Y., **(1905-1979)**
Garibaldi, Giuseppe (Italian nationalist leader); Nice, France **(1807-1882)**
Garland, Judy (Frances Gumm) (actress and singer); Grand Rapids, Minn. **(1922-1969)**
Garner, Erroll (jazz pianist); Pittsburgh **(1921-1977)**
Garner, James (James Bumgarner) (actor); Norman, Okla., 4/7/1928
Garrett, Betty (actress); St. Joseph, Mo., 5/23/1919
Garrick, David (actor); Hereford, England **(1717-1779)**
Garrison, William Lloyd (abolitionist); Newburyport, Mass. **(1805-1879)**
Garroway, Dave (TV host); Schenectady, N.Y. **(1913-1982)**
Garson, Greer (actress); County Down, Northern Ireland, 9/29/1912(?)
Gary, John (singer); Watertown, N.Y., 11/29/1932
Gassman, Vittorio (film actor and director); Genoa, Italy, 9/1/1922
Gaudí, Antonio (architect); Reus, Spain **(1852-1926)**
Gauguin, Eugène Henri Paul (painter); Paris **(1848-1903)**
Gautama Buddha (Prince Siddhartha) (philosopher); Kapilavastu (India) **(563?-?483** B.C.)
Gavin, John (actor, diplomat); Los Angeles, 4/8/1935
Gayle, Crystal (Brenda Gayle Webb) (singer); Paintsville, Ky., 1/9/51
Gaynor, Janet (actress); Philadelphia **(1906-1984)**
Gaynor, Mitzi (Francesca Mitzi Marlene de Czanyi von Gerber) (actress); Chicago, 9/4/1931
Gazzara, Ben (Biago Anthony Gazzara) (actor); New York City, 8/28/1930
Gebel-Williams, Gunther (animal trainer); Schweidnitz (Poland), 1934
Geddes, Barbara Bel (actress); New York City, 10/31/1922
Genet, Jean (playwright); Paris **(1910-1986)**
Genghis Khan (Temujin) (conqueror); nr. Lake Baikal, Russia **(1162-1227)**
Gentry, Bobbie (Roberta Streeter) (singer); Chickasaw Co., Miss., 7/27/1944.
George, David Lloyd (statesman); Manchester, England **(1863-1945)**
Gere, Richard (actor); Philadelphia, 1950
Gericault, Jean Louis (painter); Rouen, France **(1791-1824)**
Geronimo (Goyathlay) (Apache chieftain); Arizona **(1829-1909)**
Gershwin, George (composer); Brooklyn, N.Y. **(1898-1937)**
Gershwin, Ira (lyricist); New York City **(1896-1983)**
Getty, J. Paul (oil executive); Minneapolis **(1892-1976)**
Getz, Stan (saxophonist); Philadelphia, 2/2/1927

Ghiberti, Lorenzo (goldsmith and sculptor); Florence **(1378-1455)**
Giacometti, Alberto (sculptor); Switzerland **(1901-1966)**
Giannini, Giancarlo (actor); La Spezia, Italy, 8/1/1942
Gibbon, Edward (historian); Putney, England **(1737-1794)**
Gibson, Charles Dana (illustrator); Roxbury, Mass. **(1867-1944)**
Gibson, Hoot (Edward) (actor); Tememah, Neb. **(1892-1962)**
Gide, André (author); Paris **(1869-1951)**
Gielgud, Sir John (actor); London, 4/14/1904
Gilbert, John (movie actor); Logan, Utah **(1897-1936)**
Gilbert, Sir William Schwenck (librettist); London **(1836-1911)**
Gilels, Emil (concert pianist); Odessa, Ukraine **(1916-1985)**
Gillespie, Dizzy (John Birks Gillespie) (jazz trumpeter); Cheraw, S.C., 10/21/1917
Gimbel, Bernard F. (merchant); Vincennes, Ind. **(1885-1966)**
Gingold, Hermione (actress and comedienne); London **(1897-1987)**
Ginsberg, Allen (poet); Newark, N.J., 6/3/1926
Giordano, Luca (painter); Naples, Italy **(1632-1705)**
Giorgione (painter); Castelfranco, (Italy) **(c.1477-1510)**
Giotto di Bondone (painter); Vespignamo (Italy) **(c.1266-1337)**
Giovanni, Nikki (poet); Knoxville, Tenn., 6/7/1943
Giroud, Françoise (French government official); Geneva, 9/21/1916
Gish, Dorothy (actress); Massillon, Ohio **(1898-1968)**
Gish, Lillian (Lillian de Guiche) (actress); Springfield, Ohio, 10/14/1896(?)
Givenchy, Hubert (fashion designer); Beauvais, France, 2/21/1927
Gladstone, William Ewart (statesman); Liverpool, England **(1809-1898)**
Glass, Philip (composer); Baltimore, 1/31/1937
Gleason, Jackie (comedian); Brooklyn, N.Y. **(1916-1987)**
Gleason, James (actor); New York City **(1886-1959)**
Gluck, Christoph Willibald (composer); Erasbach (Germany) **(1714-1787)**
Gobel, George (comedian); Chicago, 5/20/1920
Godard, Jean Luc (film director); Paris, 12/3/1930
Goddard, Robert Hutchings (father of modern rocketry); Worcester, Mass. **(1882-1945)**
Goddard, Paulette (Marion Levy) (actress); Great Neck, N.Y., 6/3/1911
Godfrey, Arthur (entertainer); New York City **(1903-1983)**
Godunov, Alexander (ballet dancer); Sakhalin, U.S.S.R. 11/28/1949
Goebbels, Joseph Paul (Nazi leader); Rheydt, Germany **(1897-1945)**
Goering, Hermann (Nazi leader); Rosenheim, Germany **(1893-1946)**
Goethals, George Washington (engineer); Brooklyn, N.Y. **(1858-1928)**
Goethe, Johann Wolfgang von (poet); Frankfurt-am-Main, Germany **(1749-1832)**
Gogol, Nikolai Vasilievich (novelist); nr. Mirgorod, Ukraine **(1809-1852)**
Goldberg, Rube (cartoonist); San Francisco **(1883-1970)**
Goldberg, Whoopi (actress); New York City, 1949 (?)
Golden, Harry (Harry Goldhurst) (author); New York City **(1902-1981)**
Goldsmith, Oliver (dramatist and poet); County Longford, Ireland **(1728-1774)**
Goldwyn, Samuel (Samuel Goldfish) (film producer); Warsaw **(1882-1974)**
Golenpaul, Dan (creator of Information Please radio show and editor of almanac of same name); New York City **(1900-1974)**
Gompers, Samuel (labor leader); London **(1850-1924)**
Goodall, Jane (Baroness van Lawick-Goodall) (ethologist); London, 4/3/1934
Goodman, Benny (clarinetist); Chicago **(1909-1986)**
Goodyear, Charles (inventor); New Haven, Conn. **(1800-1860)**
Gorbachev, Mikhail Sergeyevich (Soviet leader); Privolnoye, U.S.S.R., 3/2/1931
Gordimer, Nadine (novelist and short-story writer); Springs, South Africa, 12/20/1923
Gordon, Max (stage producer); New York City; **(1892-1978)**
Gordon, Ruth (actress); Wollaston, Mass. **(1896-1985)**
Gordy, Berry, Jr. (record company executive); Detroit, 11/28/1929
Gore, Lesley (singer); Tenafly, N.J., 1946
Goren, Charles H. (bridge expert); Philadelphia, 3/4/1901
Gorki, Maxim (Alexei Maximovich Peshkov) (author); Nizhni Novgorod, Russia **(1868-1936)**
Gorky, Arshile (painter); Armenia **(1904-1948)**
Gormé, Eydie (singer); Bronx, N.Y., 8/16/1932
Gorshin, Frank (actor); Pittsburgh, 4/5/1934
Gosden, Freeman F. *See* Amos
Gould, Chester (cartoonist); Pawnee, Okla. **(1900-1985)**
Gould, Elliott (Elliott Goldstein) (actor); Brooklyn, N.Y., 8/29/1938
Gould, Glenn (concert pianist); Toronto, **(1932-1982)**
Gould, Morton (composer); Richmond Hill, Queens, N.Y., 12/10/1913
Goulet, Robert (singer); Lawrence, Mass., 11/26/1933
Gounod, Charles François (composer); Paris **(1818-1893)**
Goya y Lucientes, Francisco José de (painter); Fuendetodos, Spain

(1746-1828)
Grable, Betty (actress); St. Louis **(1916-1973)**
Grace, Princess of Monaco (Grace Kelly) (ex-actress); Philadelphia **(1929-1982)**
Graham, Bill (Wolfgang Grajonca) (rock impresario); Berlin, 1931
Graham, Billy (William F.) (evangelist); Charlotte, N.C., 11/7/1918
Graham, Katharine Meyer (newspaper publisher); New York City, 6/16/1917
Graham, Martha (choreographer); Pittsburgh, 5/11/1894(?)
Grahame, Gloria (Gloria Hallwood) (actress); Los Angeles **(1929-1981)**
Grainger, Percy Aldridge (pianist and composer); Melbourne, Australia **(1882-1961)**
Gramm, Donald (Grambach) (bass-baritone); Milwaukee **(1927-1983)**
Granger, Farley (actor); San Jose, Calif., 7/1/1925
Granger, Stewart (James Stewart) (actor); London, 5/6/1913
Grant, Cary (Alexander Archibald Leach) (actor); Bristol, England **(1904-1986)**
Grant, Lee (Lyova Haskell Rosenthal) (actress); New York City, 10/31/1930
Granville, Bonita (actress); New York City **(1923-1988)**
Grass, Günter (novelist); Danzig (Poland), 10/16/1927
Grauer, Ben (radio and TV announcer); New York City **(1908-1977)**
Graves, Peter (Peter Arness) (actor); Minneapolis, 3/18/1926
Graves, Robert (writer); London **(1895-1985)**
Gray, Barry (Bernard Yaroslaw) (radio interviewer); Atlantic City, N.J., 7/2/1916
Gray, Dolores (singer and actress); Chicago, 6/7/1930
Gray, Thomas (poet); London **(1716-1771)**
Grayson, Kathryn (Zelma Hednick) (singer and actress); Winston-Salem, N.C., 2/9/1923
Greco, Buddy (singer); Philadelphia, 8/14/1926
Greco, José (dancer); Montorio nei Frentani, Itály, 12/23/1918
Greeley, Horace (journalist and politician); Amherst, N.H. **(1811-1872)**
Green, Adolph (actor and lyricist); New York City, 12/2/1915
Green, Al (singer); Forrest City, Ark., 4/13/1946
Greene, Graham (novelist); Berkhamsted, England, 10/2/1904
Greene, Lorne (actor); Ottawa **(1915-1987)**
Greene, Martyn (actor); London **(1899-1975)**
Greenstreet, Sydney (actor); Sandwich, England **(1879-1954)**
Greenwood, Joan (actress and director); London **(1921-1987)**
Greer, Germaine (feminist); Melbourne, 1/29/1939
Gregory, Cynthia (ballerina); Los Angeles, 7/8/1946
Gregory, Dick (comedian); St. Louis, 1932
Greuze, Jean-Baptiste (painter); Tournus, France **(1725-1805)**
Grey, Joel (Joel Katz) (actor); Cleveland, 4/11/1932
Grey, Zane (author); Zanesville, Ohio **(1875-1939)**
Grieg, Edvard Hagerup (composer); Bergen, Norway **(1843-1907)**
Grier, Roosevelt (entertainer and former athlete); Cuthbert, Ga., 7/14/1932
Griffin, Merv (TV entertainer); San Mateo, Calif., 7/6/1925
Griffith, Andy (actor); Mount Airy, N.C., 6/1/1926
Griffith, David Lewelyn Wark (film producer); La Grange, Ky. **(1875-1948)**
Grigorovich, Yuri (choreographer); Leningrad, 1/1/1927
Grimes, Tammy (actress); Lynn, Mass., 1/30/1934
Grimm, Jacob (author of fairy tales); Hanau (Germany) **(1785-1863)**
Grimm, Wilhelm (author of fairy tales); Hanau (Germany) **(1786-1859)**
Gris, Juan (José Victoriano González) (painter); Madrid **(1887-1927)**
Grizzard, George (actor); Roanoke Rapids, N.C., 4/1/1928
Gromyko, Andrei A. (diplomat); Starye Gromyki, Russia **(1909-1989)**
Gropius, Walter (architect); Berlin **(1883-1969)**
Gropper, William (painter, illustrator); New York City **(1897-1977)**
Grosz, George (painter); Germany **(1893-1959)**
Guardino, Harry (actor); New York City, 12/23/1925
Guggenheim, Meyer (capitalist); Langnau, Switzerland **(1828-1905)**
Guinness, Sir Alec (actor); London, 4/2/1914
Guitry, Sacha (Alexandre) (actor and film director); St. Petersburg, Russia **(1885-1957)**
Gumbel, Bryant Charles (TV newscaster); New Orleans, 9/29/1948
Gunther, John (author); Chicago **(1901-1970)**
Gutenberg, Johann (printer); Mainz (Germany) **(1400?-?1468)**
Guthrie, Arlo (singer); New York City, 7/10/1947
Guthrie, Woody (folk singer and composer); Okemah, Okla. **(1912-1967)**
Gwenn, Edmund (actor); London **(1875-1959)**

H

Hackett, Bobby (trumpeter); Providence, R.I. **(1915-1976)**
Hackett, Buddy (Leonard Hacker) (comedian and actor); Brooklyn,

N.Y., 8/31/1924
Hackman, Gene (actor); San Bernardino, Calif., 1/30/1931
Hagen, Uta (actress); Göttingen, Germany, 6/12/1919
Haggard, Merle (songwriter); Bakersfield, Calif., 4/6/1937
Hagman, Larry (actor); Weatherford, Tex., 1931
Haig, Alexander Meigs, Jr. (ex-Secretary of State and ex-general); Bala-Cynwyd, Pa., 12/2/1924
Haile Selassie (Ras Tafari Makonnen) (ex-Emperor); Ethiopia **(1892-1975)**
Hailey, Arthur (novelist); Luton, England, 4/5/1920
Halberstam, David (journalist); New York City, 4/10/1934
Hale, Edward Everett (clergyman and author); Boston **(1822-1909)**
Hale, Nathan (American Revolutionary officer); Coventry, Conn. **(1755-1776)**
Halevi, Judah (Jewish poet); Toledo, Spain **(1085-1140)**
Haley, Alex (writer); Ithaca, N.Y., 8/11/1921
Hall, Donald (Andrew, Jr.) (poet) New Haven, Conn., 9/20/1928
Hall, Monty (TV personality); Winnipeg, Canada, 1923
Halley, Edmund (astronomer); London **(1656-1742)**
Hals, Frans (painter); Antwerp (Netherlands) **(1580?-1666)**
Halsey, William Frederick, Jr. (naval officer); Elizabeth, N.J. **(1882-1959)**
Hamill, Pete (journalist); Brooklyn, N.Y., 6/24/1935
Hamilton, Alexander (statesman); Nevis, British West Indies **(1757?-1804)**
Hamilton, George (actor); Memphis, Tenn., 8/12/1939
Hamilton, Margaret (actress); Cleveland **(1902-1985)**
Hamlisch, Marvin (composer and pianist); New York City, 6/2/1944
Hammarskjöld, Dag (U.N. Secretary-General); Jönköping, Sweden **(1905-1961)**
Hammerstein, Oscar, II (librettist and stage producer); New York City **(1895-1960)**
Hampden, Walter (Walter Hampden Dougherty) (actor); Brooklyn, N.Y. **(1879-1955)**
Hampton, Lionel (vibraharpist and band leader); Birmingham, Ala., 4/12/1913
Hamsun, Knut (Knut Pedersen) (novelist); Lom, Norway **(1859-1952)**
Hancock, John (statesman); Braintree, Mass. **(1737-1793)**
Hand, Learned (jurist); Albany, N.Y. **(1872-1961)**
Handel, George Frederick (Georg Friedrich Händel) (composer); Halle (East Germany) **(1685-1759)**
Handy, William Christopher (blues composer); Florence, Ala. **(1873-1958)**
Hanks, Tom (actor); Concord, Calif., 7/9/1956
Hannibal (Carthaginian general); North Africa **(247-182 B.C.)**
Hanson, Howard (conductor); Wahoo, Neb., **(1896-1981)**
Harburg, E. Y. "Yip" (songwriter); New York City **(1896-1981)**
Harding, Ann (actress); San Antonio, Tex. **(1902-1981)**
Hardwicke, Sir Cedric (actor); Stourbridge, England **(1893-1964)**
Hardy, Oliver (comedian); Atlanta **(1892-1957)**
Hardy, Thomas (novelist); Dorsetshire, England **(1840-1928)**
Harkness, Edward S. (capitalist); Cleveland **(1874-1940)**
Harlow, Jean (Harlean Carpentier) (actress); Kansas City, Mo. **(1911-1937)**
Harnick, Sheldon (lyricist); Chicago, 4/30/1924
Harper, Valerie (actress); Suffern, N.Y., 8/22/1940(?)
Harrell, Lynn (cellist); New York City, 1/30/1944
Harriman, W. (William) Averell (ex-Governor of New York); New York City **(1891-1986)**
Harris, Barbara (actress); Evanston, Ill., 1935
Harris, Emmylou (singer); Birmingham, Ala., 1949
Harris, Julie (actress); Grosse Pointe Park, Mich., 12/2/1925
Harris, Phil (actor and band leader); Linton, Ind., 6/24/1906
Harris, Richard (actor); Limerick, Ireland, 10/1/1933
Harris, Rosemary (actress); Ashby, England, 9/19/1930
Harris, Roy (composer); Lincoln County, Okla. **(1898-1979)**
Harrison, George (singer and songwriter); Liverpool, England, 2/25/1943
Harrison, Rex (Reginald Carey) (actor); Huyton, England, 3/5/1908
Hart, Lorenz (lyricist); New York **(1895-1943)**
Hart, Moss (playwright); New York City **(1904-1961)**
Hart, William S. (actor); Newburgh, N.Y. **(1862-1946)**
Harte, Bret (Francis Brett Harte) (author); Albany, N.Y. **(1836-1902)**
Hartford, Huntington (George Huntington Hartford II) (A.&P. heir); New York City, 4/18/1911
Hartford, John (singer and banjoist); New York City, 12/30/1937
Hartman, David Downs (TV newscaster); Pawtucket, R.I., 5/19/1935
Hartman, Elizabeth (actress); Youngstown, Ohio **(1941-1987)**
Harvey, Laurence (Larushka Skikne) (actor); Joniskis, Lithuania **(1928-1973)**
Harvey, William (physician); Folkestone, England **(1578-1657)**
Hasso, Signe (actress); Stockholm, 8/15/1915
Havoc, June (June Hovick) (actress); Seattle, 1916
Haver, June (actress); Rock Island, Ill., 6/10/1926
Hawkins, Jack (actor); London **(1910-1973)**
Hawn, Goldie (actress); Washington, D.C., 11/21/1945

Haworth, Jill (actress); Sussex, England, 1945
Hawthorne, Nathaniel (novelist); Salem, Mass. **(1804-1864)**
Hay, John Milton (statesman); Salem, Ind. **(1838-1905)**
Hayakawa, Sessue (actor); Honshu, Japan **(1890-1973)**
Hayden, Melissa (ballerina); Toronto, 4/25/1923
Hayden, Sterling (Sterling Relyea Walter) (actor and writer); Montclair, N.J. **(1916-1986)**
Haydn, Franz Joseph (composer); Rohrau (Austria) **(1732-1809)**
Hayes, Helen (Helen Hayes Brown) (actress); Washington, D.C., 10/10/1900
Hayes, Isaac (composer); Covington, Tenn., 8/20/1942
Hayward, Louis (actor); Johannesburg, South Africa **(1909-1985)**
Hayward, Susan (Edythe Marrener) (actress); Brooklyn, N.Y. **(1919?-1975)**
Hayworth, Rita (Margarita Cansino) (actress); New York City **(1918-1987)**
Head, Edith (costume designer); Los Angeles **(1907-1981)**
Hearst, William Randolph (publisher); San Francisco **(1863-1951)**
Hearst, William Randolph, Jr. (publisher); New York City, 1/27/1908
Heath, Edward (ex-Prime Minister); Broadstairs, England, 7/9/1916
Heatherton, Joey (actress); Rockville Centre, N.Y., 9/14/1944
Hecht, Ben (author); New York City **(1894-1964)**
Heckart, Eileen (actress); Columbus, Ohio, 3/29/1919
Heflin, Van (Emmet Evan Heflin) (actor); Walters, Okla. **(1910-1971)**
Hefner, Hugh (publisher); Chicago, 4/9/1926
Hegel, Georg Wilhelm Friedrich (philosopher); Stuttgart (Germany) **(1770-1831)**
Heifetz, Jascha (concert violinist); Vilna, Russia **(1901-1987)**
Heine, Heinrich (Harry) (poet); Düsseldorf (Germany) **(1797-1856)**
Heinemann, Gustav (ex-President of Germany); Schweim, Germany **(1899-1976)**
Heisenberg, Werner Karl (physicist); Würzburg, Germany **(1901-1976)**
Heller, Joseph (novelist); Brooklyn, N.Y., 5/1/1923
Hellman, Lillian (playwright); New Orleans **(1905-1984)**
Hemingway, Ernest Miller (novelist); Oak Park, Ill. **(1899-1961)**
Hemmings, David (actor); Guilford, England, 11/2/1941
Henderson, Florence (actress); Dale, Ind., 2/14/1934
Henderson, Skitch (Lyle Russell Cedric) (conductor and pianist); Birmingham, England(?), 1/27/1918
Hendrix, Jimi (James Marshall Hendrix) (guitarist); Seattle **(1942-1970)**
Henley, Beth (playwright-actress); Jackson, Miss., 5/8/1952
Henning, Doug (magician and actor); Winnipeg, Canada, 1947(?)
Henreid, Paul (actor); Trieste, 1/10/1908
Henri, Robert (painter); Cincinnati **(1865-1926)**
Henry, O. (William Sydney Porter) (story writer); Greensboro, N.C. **(1862-1910)**
Henry, Patrick (statesman); Hanover County, Va. **(1736-1799)**
Henson, Jim (puppeteer); Greenville, Miss., 9/24/1936
Hepburn, Audrey (actress); Brussels, Belgium, 5/4/1929
Hepburn, Katharine (actress); Hartford, Conn., 11/8/1909
Hepplewhite, George (furniture designer); England **(?-1786)**
Hepworth, Barbara (sculptor); Wakefield, England **(1903-1975)**
Herachel, William (Frederich Wilhelm) (astronomer); Hanover, Germany **(1738-1822)**
Herbert, George (poet); Montgomery Castle, Wales **(1593-1633)**
Herbert, Victor (composer); Dublin **(1859-1924)**
Herblock (Herbert L. Block) (political cartoonist); Chicago, 10/13/1909
Herman, Woody (Woodrow Charles) (band leader); Milwaukee **(1913-1987)**
Herod (Herodes) (called Herod the Great) (King of Judea) **(73?-4 B.C.)**
Herodotus (historian); Halicarnassus, Asia Minor (Turkey) **(c. 484-425 B.C.)**
Herrick, Robert (poet); London? **(1591-1674)**
Hershfield, Harry (humorist and raconteur); Cedar Rapids, Iowa **(1885-1974)**
Hersholt, Jean (actor); Copenhagen **(1886-1956)**
Hesburgh, Theodore M. (educator); Syracuse, N.Y., 5/2/1917
Heston, Charlton (actor); Evanston, Ill., 10/4/1924
Heyerdahl, Thor (ethnologist and explorer); Larvik, Norway, 10/6/1914
Hildegarde (Hildegarde Loretta Sell) (singer); Adell, Wis., 2/1/1906
Hill, Arthur (actor); Melfort, Canada, 8/1/1922
Hillary, Sir Edmund (mountain climber); New Zealand, 7/20/1919
Hiller, Wendy (actress); Bramhall, England, 8/15/1912
Hilliard, Harriet. *See* Nelson, Harriet
Hindemith, Paul (composer); Hanau, Germany **(1895-1963)**
Hines, Earl "Fatha" (jazz pianist); Duquesne, Pa. **(1905-1983)**
Hines, Jerome (Jerome Heinz) (basso); Los Angeles, 11/8/1921
Hingle, Pat (actor); Denver, 7/19/1924
Hippocrates (physician); Cos, Greece **(c. 460-c. 377 B.C.)**
Hirohito (Emperor); Tokyo, **(1901-1989)**
Hiroshige, Ando (painter); Edo? (Tokyo) **(1797-1858)**

Hirsch, Judd (actor); New York City, 3/15/1935
Hirschfeld, Al (Albert) (cartoonist); St. Louis, 6/21/1903
Hirschhorn, Joseph Herman (financier, speculator, and art collector); Mitau, Latvia **(1899-1981)**
Hirt, Al (trumpeter); New Orleans, 11/7/1922
Hitchcock, Alfred J. (film director); London **(1899-1980)**
Hitler, Adolf (German dictator); Braunau, Austria **(1889-1945)**
Hitzig, William Maxwell (physician); Austria, 12/15/1904
Hobbes, Thomas (philosopher); Westport, England **(1588-1679)**
Hobson, Laura Z. (Laura K. Zametkin) (novelist); New York City **(1900-1986)**
Hockney, David (artist); Bradford, England, 7/9/1937
Hodges, Eddie (actor); Hattiesburg, Miss., 3/5/1947
Hoffa, James R(iddle) (labor leader); Brazil, Ind. **(1913-75?)** presumed murdered.
Hoffman, Dustin (film actor and director); Los Angeles, 8/8/1937
Hofmann, Hans (painter); Germany **(1880-1966)**
Hogan, Paul (actor); Lightning Ridge, NSW, Australia, 1941 (?)
Hogarth, William (painter and engraver); London **(1697-1764)**
Hokusai, Katauhika (artist); Yedo, Japan **(1760-1849)**
Holbein, Hans (the Elder) (painter); Augsburg (Germany) **(1465?-1524)**
Holbein, Hans (the Younger) (painter); Augsburg (Germany) **(1497?-1543)**
Holbrook, Hal (actor); Cleveland, 2/17/1925
Holden, William (William Franklin Beedle, Jr.) (actor); O'Fallon, Ill. **(1918-1981)**
Holder, Geoffrey (dancer); Port-of-Spain, Trinidad, 8/1/1930
Holiday, Billie (Eleanora Fagan) (jazz-blues singer); Baltimore **(1915-1959)**
Holliday, Judy (Judith Tuvim) (comedienne); New York City **(1922-1965)**
Holloway, Stanley (actor); London **(1890-1982)**
Holloway, Sterling (actor); Cedartown, Ga., 1905
Holm, Celeste (actress); New York City, 4/29/1919
Holmes, Oliver Wendell (jurist); Boston **(1841-1935)**
Holt, Jack (actor); Winchester, Va. **(1888-1951)**
Holtz, Lou (comedian); San Francisco **(1898-1980)**
Home, Lord (Alexander Frederick Douglas-Home) (diplomat); London, 7/2/1903
Homeier, Skip (George Vincent Homeier) (actor); Chicago, 10/5/1930
Homer, Winslow (painter); Boston, Mass. **(1836-1910)**
Homer (Greek poet) **(c.850 B.C.?)**
Homolka, Oscar (actor); Vienna **(1898-1978)**
Honegger, Arthur (composer); Le Havre, France **(1892-1955)**
Hook, Sidney (philosopher); New York City, **(1902-1989)**
Hoover, J. Edgar (FBI director); Washington, D.C. **(1895-1972)**
Hope, Bob (Leslie Townes Hope) (comedian); London, 5/29/1903
Hopkins, Anthony (actor); Port Talbot, Wales, 12/31/1937
Hopkins, Gerald Manley (poet); Stratford, England **(1844-1899)**
Hopkins, Johns (financier); Anne Arundel County, Md. **(1795-1873)**
Hopkins, Miriam (actress); Bainbridge, Ga. **(1902-1972)**
Hopper, Dennis (actor); Dodge City, Kan., 5/17/1936
Hopper, Edward (painter); Nyack, N.Y. **(1882-1967)**
Horace (Quintus Horatius Flaccus) (poet); Venosa (Italy) **(65-8 B.C.)**
Horne, Lena (singer); Brooklyn, N.Y., 6/30/1917
Horne, Marilyn (mezzo-soprano); Bradford, Pa., 1/16/1934
Horowitz, Vladimir (pianist); Kiev, Russia, 10/1/1904
Horton, Edward Everett (comedian); Brooklyn, N.Y. **(1887-1970)**
Houdini, Harry (Ehrich Weiss) (magician); Appleton, Wis. **(1874-1926)**
Houseman, John (Jacques Haussmann) (producer, director, and actor); Bucharest **(1902-1988)**
Housman, A(lfred) E(dward) (poet); Fockburg, England **(1859-1936)**
Houston, Samuel (political leader); Rockbridge County, Va. **(1793-1863)**
Howard, Leslie (Leslie Stainer) (actor); London **(1893-1943)**
Howard, Trevor (actor); Kent, England **(1916-1988)**
Howe, Elias (inventor); Spencer, Mass. **(1819-1867)**
Howe, Irving (literary critic); New York City, 6/11/1920
Howe, Julia Ward (poet and reformer); New York City **(1819-1910)**
Howes, Sally Ann (actress); London, 7/20/1934
Hudson, Henry (English navigator) **(?-1611)**
Hudson, Rock (born Roy Scherer, Jr.; took Roy Fitzgerald as legal name) (actor); Winnetka, Ill., **(1925-1985)**
Hughes, Charles Evans (jurist); Glens Falls, N.Y. **(1862-1948)**
Hughes, Howard (industrialist and film producer); Houston **(1905-1976)**
Hughes, Langston (poet); Joplin, Mo. **(1902-1967)**
Hugo, Victor Marie (author); Besançon, France **(1802-1885)**
Hume, David (philosopher); Edinburgh, Scotland **(1711-1776)**
Humperdinck, Engelbert (Arnold Dorsey) (singer); Madras, India, 5/2/1936
Humperdinck, Engelbert (composer); Siegburg (Germany) **(1854-1921)**

Hunt, H. L. (industrialist); nr. Vandalia, Ill. **(1889-1974)**
Hunt, Marsha (actress); Chicago, 10/17/1917
Hunter, Kim (Janet Cole) (actress); Detroit, 11/12/1922
Hunter, Tab (Arthur Andrew Gelien) (actor); New York City, 7/11/1931
Huntley, Chet (TV newscaster); Cardwell, Mont. **(1911-1974)**
Hurok, Sol (Solomon) (impresario); Pogar, Russia **(1884-1974)**
Hurst, Fannie (novelist); Hamilton, Ohio **(1889-1968)**
Hurt, John (actor); Shirebrook, England, 1/22/1940
Hus, Jan (Bohemian religious reformer); Husinetz, nr. Budweis (Czechoslovakia) **(c.1369-1415)**
Hussein I (King); Jordan, 11/14/1935
Huston, John (film director and writer); Nevada, Mo. **(1906-1987)**
Huston, Walter (Walter Houghston) (actor); Toronto **(1884-1950)**
Hutchins, Robert M. (educator); Brooklyn, N.Y. **(1899-1977)**
Hutton, Barbara (Woolworth heiress); New York City **(1912-1979)**
Hutton, Betty (Betty Thornburg) (actress); Battle Creek, Mich., 2/26/1921
Hutton, Timothy (actor); Los Angeles, 8/16/1960
Huxley, Aldous (author); Godalming, England **(1894-1963)**
Huxley, Sir Julian S. (biologist and author); London **(1887-1975)**
Huxley, Thomas Henry (biologist); Ealing, England **(1825-1895)**

I

Ian, Janis (singer); New York City, 5/7/1951
Ibsen, Henrik (dramatist); Skien, Norway **(1828-1906)**
Inge, William (playwright); Independence, Kan. **(1913-1973)**
Ingres, Jean Auguste Dominique (painter); Montauban, France **(1780-1867)**
Inness, George (painter); nr. Newburgh, N.Y. **(1825-1894)**
Ionesco, Eugene (playwright); Slatina, Romania, 11/26/1912
Ireland, John (actor); Vancouver, B.C., Canada, 1/30/1915
Irons, Jeremy (actor); Cowes, Isle of Wight, England, 9/19/1948
Irving, Amy (actress); Palo Alto, Calif., 9/10/1953
Irving, John (Winslow) (writer); Exeter, N.H., 3/2/1942
Irving, Washington (author); New York City **(1783-1859)**
Isherwood, Christopher (novelist and playwright); nr. Dilsey and High Lane, England **(1904-1986)**
Iturbi, José (concert pianist); Valencia, Spain **(1895-1980)**
Ives, Burl (Icle Ivanhoe) (singer); Hunt, Ill., 6/14/1909
Ives, Charles E(dward) (composer); Danbury, Conn. **(1874-1954)**

J

Jackson, Anne (actress); Millvale, Pa., 9/3/1926
Jackson, Glenda (actress); Hoylake, England, 1937(?)
Jackson, Rev. Jesse (civil rights leader); Greenville, S.C., 10/8/1941
Jackson, Kate (actress); Birmingham, Ala., 10/29/1949
Jackson, Mahalia (gospel singer); New Orleans **(1912-1972)**
Jackson, Michael (singer); Gary, Ind., 8/19/1958
Jackson, Thomas Jonathan ("Stonewall") (general); Clarksburg, Va. (now W. Va.) **(1824-1863)**
Jacobs, Jane (urbanologist); Scranton, Pa., 5/1/1916
Jaffe, Sam (actor); New York City **(1891-1984)**
Jagger, Dean (actor); Lima, Ohio, 11/7/1903
Jagger, Mick (Michael Phillip) (singer); Dartford, England, 7/26/1944
James, Harry (trumpeter); Albany, Ga. **(1916-1983)**
James, Henry (novelist); New York City **(1843-1916)**
James, Jesse Woodson (outlaw); Clay County, Mo. **(1847-1882)**
James, William (psychologist); New York City **(1842-1910)**
Jameson, (Margaret) Storm (novelist); Whitby, England **(1897-1986)**
Janis, Byron (pianist); McKeesport, Pa., 3/24/1928
Jannings, Emil (actor); Brooklyn, N.Y. **(1886-1950)**
Janssen, David (David Meyer) (actor); Naponee, Neb. **(1930-1980)**
Jay, John (statesman and jurist); New York City **(1745-1829)**
Jeanmaire, Renée (dancer); Paris, 4/29/1924
Jenner, Edward (physician); Berkeley, England **(1749-1823)**
Jennings, Waylon (singer); Littlefield, Tex., 1937
Jessel, George (entertainer); New York City **(1898-1981)**
Jessup, Philip C. (diplomat); New York City, 1/5/1897
Jiang Qing (political leader); Chucheng, China, 1913 (?)
Joan of Arc (Jeanne d'Arc) (saint and patriot); Domremy-la-Pucelle, France **(1412-1431)**
Joel, Billy (singer); New York City, 5/9/1949
Joffrey, Robert (Abdullah Jaffa Bey Khan) (choreographer); Seattle **(1930-1988)**
John, Elton (Reginald Kenneth Dwight) (singer and pianist); Pinner, England, 3/25/1947
Johns, Glynis (actress); Pretoria, South Africa, 10/5/1923
Johns, Jasper (painter and sculptor); Augusta, Ga., 5/15/1930
Johnson, James Weldon (author and educator); Jacksonville, Fla.

(1871-1938)
Johnson, Philip Cortalyou (architect); Cleveland, Ohio, 7/8/1906
Johnson, Samuel (lexicographer and author); Lichfield, England **(1709-1784)**
Johnson, Van (actor); Newport, R.I., 8/20/1916
Joliot-Curie, Frédéric (physicist); Paris **(1900-1958)**
Joliot-Curie, Irène (Irène Curie) (physicist); France **(1897-1956)**
Jolliet (or Joliet), Louis (explorer); Beaupré, Canada **(1645-1700)**
Jolson, Al (Asa Yoelson) (actor and singer); St. Petersburg, Russia **(1886-1950)**
Jones, Carolyn (singer and actress); Amarillo, Tex., **(1933-1983)**
Jones, Dean (actor); Morgan County, Ala., 1/25/1935
Jones, George (singer); Saratoga, Tex., 9/12/1931
Jones, Inigo (architect); London **(1573-1652)**
Jones, James (novelist); Robinson, Ill. **(1921-1977)**
Jones, James Earl (actor); Arkabutla, Miss., 1/17/1931
Jones, Jennifer (Phyllis Isley) (actress); Tulsa, Okla., 3/2/1919
Jones, John Paul (John Paul) (naval officer); Scotland **(1747-1792)**
Jones, Quincy (composer); Chicago, 3/14/1933
Jones, Shirley (singer and actress); Smithtown, Pa., 3/31/1934
Jones, Tom (Thomas Jones Woodward) (singer); Pontypridd, Wales, 6/7/1940
Jong, Erica (writer); New York City, 3/26/1942
Jonson, Ben (Benjamin) (poet and dramatist); Westminster, England **(1572-1637)**
Joplin, Janis (singer); Port Arthur, Tex. **(1943-1970)**
Jory, Victor (actor); Dawson City, Yukon, Canada **(1902-1982)**
Josquin des Prés (usually known as Josquin) (composer); Conde-sur-L'Escaut?, Hainaut (France or Belgium) **(c.1445-1521)**
Jourdan, Louis (Louis Gendre) (actor); Marseilles, France, 6/19/1920
Joyce, James (novelist); Dublin **(1882-1941)**
Juárez, Benito Pablo (statesman); Guelatao, Mexico **(1806-1872)**
Julia, Raul (Raúl Rafael Carlos Julia y Arcelay) (actor); San Juan, Puerto Rico, 3/9/1940
Juliana (Queen); The Hague, Netherlands, 4/30/1909
Jung, Carl Gustav (psychoanalyst); Basel, Switzerland **(1875-1961)**
Jurado, Katy (actress); Guadalajara, Mexico, 1927

K

Kabalevsky, Dmitri (composer); St. Petersburg, Russia **(1904-1987)**
Kafka, Franz (author); Prague **(1883-1924)**
Kádár, János (Communist Party leader); Hungary, 1912
Kahn, Gus (songwriter); Coblenz, Germany **(1886-1941)**
Kahn, Louis I. (architect); Oesel Island, Estonia **(1901-1974)**
Kahn, Madeline (actress); Boston, 9/29/1942
Kaminska, Ida (actress); Odessa, Russia **(1899-1980)**
Kandinsky, Wassily (painter); Moscow **(1866-1944)**
Kanin, Garson (playwright); Rochester, N.Y., 11/24/1912
Kant, Immanuel (philosopher); Königsberg (Kaliningrad, U.S.S.R.) **(1724-1804)**
Kantor, MacKinlay (novelist); Webster City, Iowa **(1904-1977)**
Kaplan, Gabe (Gabriel) (actor); Brooklyn, N.Y., 3/31/1945
Karloff, Boris (William Henry Pratt) (actor); London **(1887-1969)**
Kaufman, George S. (playwright); Pittsburgh **(1889-1961)**
Kaye, Danny (David Daniel Kominski) (comedian); Brooklyn, N.Y. **(1913-1987)**
Kaye, Sammy (band leader); Cleveland **(1910-1987)**
Kazan, Elia (director); Constantinople, Turkey, 9/7/1909
Kazan, Lainie (Levine) (singer); New York City, 5/15/1940
Keach, Stacy (actor); Savannah, Ga., 6/2/1941
Keaton, Buster (Joseph Frank Keaton) (comedian); Piqua, Kan. **(1896-1966)**
Keaton, Diane (actress); Los Angeles, 1/5/1946
Keats, John (poet); London **(1795-1821)**
Keel, Howard (singer and actor); Gillespie, Ill., 4/13/1919
Keeler, Ruby (Lehy Keeler) (actress and dancer); Halifax, Nova Scotia, Canada, 8/25/1910
Kefauver, Estes (legislator); Madisonville, Tenn. **(1903-1963)**
Keith, Brian (actor); Bayonne, N.J., 11/14/1921
Keller, Helen Adams (author and educator); Tuscumbia, Ala. **(1880-1968)**
Kellerman, Sally (actress); Long Beach, Calif., 6/2/1938
Kelly, Emmett (clown); Sedan, Kan., **(1898-1979)**
Kelly, Gene (dancer and actor); Pittsburg, 8/23/1912
Kelly, Grace. *See* Grace, Princess of Monaco.
Kelly, Patsy (actress and comedienne); Brooklyn, N.Y. **(1910-1981)**
Kelly, Walt (cartoonist); Philadelphia **(1913-1973)**
Kemal Ataturk (Mustafa Kemal) (Turkish soldier and statesman); Salonika (Greece) **(1881-1938)**
Kempis, Thomas a (mystic); Kempis, Prussia (Germany) **(1380-1471)**
Kennan, George F. (diplomat); Milwaukee, 2/16/1904
Kennedy, Arthur (actor); Worcester, Mass., 2/17/1914

Kennedy, George (actor); New York City, 2/18/1925
Kennedy, Jacqueline. *See* Onassis, Jacqueline
Kennedy, Joseph P. (financier); Boston **(1888-1969)**
Kennedy, Robert Francis (legislator); Brookline, Mass. **(1925-1968)**
Kennedy, Rose Fitzgerald (President's mother); Boston, 7/22/1890
Kent, Rockwell (painter); Tarrytown Heights, N.Y. **(1882-1971)**
Kenton, Stan (Stanley Newcomb) (jazz musician); Wichita, Kan. **(1912-1979)**
Kepler, Johannes (astronomer); Weil (Germany) **(1571-1630)**
Kerensky, Alexander Fedorovich (statesman); Simbirks, Russia **(1881-1970)**
Kern, Jerome David (composer); New York City **(1885-1945)**
Kerr, Deborah (actress); Helensburgh, Scotland, 9/30/1921
Kettering, Charles F. (engineer and inventor); nr. Loudonville, Ohio **(1876-1958)**
Key, Francis Scott (lawyer and author of national anthem); Frederick (now Carroll) County, Md. **(1779-1843)**
Keyes, Frances Parkinson (novelist); Charlottesville, Va. **(1885-1970)**
Keynes (1st Baron of Tilton) (John Maynard Keynes) (economist); Cambridge, England **(1883-1946)**
Khachaturian, Aram (composer); Tiflis, Russia **(1903-1978)**
Khrushchev, Nikita S. (Soviet leader); Kalinovka, nr. Kursk, Ukraine **(1894-1971)**
Kibbee, Guy (actor); El Paso **(1886-1956)**
Kidd, Michael (choreographer); Brooklyn, N.Y., 1917
Kidd, William (called Captain Kidd) (pirate); Greenock, Scotland **(1645?-1701)**
Kieran, John (writer); New York City **(1892-1981)**
Kierkegaard, Sören Aalys (philosopher); Copenhagen **(1813-1855)**
Kiesinger, Kurt Georg (diplomat); Ebingen, Germany **(1904-1988)**
Kiley, Richard (actor and singer); Chicago, 3/31/1922
Kilmer, Alfred Joyce (poet); New Brunswick, N.J. **(1886-1918)**
King, Alan (Irwin Alan Kniberg) (entertainer); Brooklyn, N.Y., 12/26/1927
King, B.B. (Riley King) (guitarist); Itta Bena, Miss., 9/16/1925
King, Carole (singer and songwriter); Brooklyn, N.Y., 2/9/1941
King, Coretta Scott (civil rights leader); Marion, Ala., 4/27/1927
King, Martin Luther, Jr. (civil rights leader); Atlanta **(1929-1968)**
King, Pee Wee (Frank) (singer); Abrams, Wis., 2/18/1914
King, Stephen (writer); Portland, Maine, 9/21/1947
Kingsley, Ben (Krishna Bhanji) (actor); Snainton, England, 12/31/1943
Kingsley, Sidney (Sidney Kirschner) (playwright); New York City, 10/18/1906
Kinski, Nastassja (Nastassja Nakszynski) (actress); West Berlin, 1/24/1961
Kipling, Rudyard (author); Bombay **(1865-1936)**
Kipnis, Alexander (basso); Ukraine, **(1891-1978)**
Kirby, George (comedian); Chicago, **1923(?)**
Kirk, Grayson (educator); Jeffersonville, Ohio, 10/12/1903
Kirk, Lisa (actress and singer); Charleroi, Pa., 1925
Kirk, Phyllis (actress); Plainfield, N.J., 9/18/1930
Kirkland, Gelsey (ballerina); Bethlehem, Pa., 12/29/1952
Kirkpatrick, Jeane Jordan (educator-public affairs); Duncan, Okla., 11/19/1926
Kirkpatrick, Ralph (harpsichordist); Leominster, Mass. **(1911-1984)**
Kirkwood, James (actor); Grand Rapids, Mich. **(1883-1963)**
Kirsten, Dorothy (soprano); Montclair, N.J., 7/6/1919
Kissinger, Henry (Heinz Alfred Kissinger) (ex-Secretary of State); Furth, Germany, 5/27/1923
Kitt, Eartha (singer); North, S.C., 1/26/1928
Klee, Paul (painter); Münchenbuchsee, nr. Bern, Switzerland **(1879-1940)**
Klein, Calvin (fashion designer); Bronx, N.Y., 11/19/1942
Klein, Robert (comedian); New York City, 2/8/1942
Kleist, Henrich von (poet); Frankfurt an der Oder (East Germany) **(1777-1811)**
Klemperer, Otto (conductor); Breslau (Poland) **(1885-1973)**
Klemperer, Werner (actor); Cologne, Germany, 3/22/1920
Klugman, Jack (actor); Philadelphia, 4/27/1924
Knievel, Evel (Robert Craig) (daredevil motorcyclist); Butte, Mont., 10/17/1938
Knight, Gladys (singer); Atlanta, 5/28/1944
Knight, Ted (Tadeus Wladyslaw Konopka) (actor); Terryville, Conn., **(1923-1986)**
Knight, John S. (publisher); Bluefield, W. Va. **(1894-1981)**
Knopf, Alfred A. (publisher); New York City, **(1892-1984)**
Knotts, Don (actor); Morgantown, W.Va., 7/21/1924
Knox, John (religious reformer); Haddington, East Lothian, Scotland **(1505-1572)**
Koch, Robert (physician); Klausthal (Germany) **(1843-1910)**
Koestler, Arthur (novelist); Budapest **(1905-1983)**
Kokoschka, Oskar (painter); Pöchlarn Austria **(1886-1980)**
Kooper, Al (singer and pianist); Brooklyn, N.Y., 2/5/1944
Korman, Harvey (actor); Chicago, 2/15/1927
Kosciusko, Thaddeus (Tadeusz Andrzej Bonawentura Kosciuszko)

(military officer); Grand Duchy of Lithuania **(1746-1817)**

Kossuth, Lajos (patriot); Monok, Hungary **(1802-1894)**

Kostelanetz, André (orchestra conductor); St. Petersburg, Russia **(1901-1980)**

Kosygin, Aleksei N. (Premier); St. Petersburg, Russia **(1904-1980)**

Koussevitzky, Serge (Sergei) Alexandrovitch (orchestra conductor); Vishni Volochek, Tver, Russia **(1874-1951)**

Kovacs, Ernie (comedian); Trenton, N.J. **(1919-1962)**

Kramer, Stanley E. (film producer and director); New York City, 9/29/1913

Kràus, Lili (pianist); Budapest **(1905-1986)**

Kreisler, Fritz (violinist and composer); Vienna **(1875-1962)**

Kresge, S. S. (merchant); Bald Mount, Pa. **(1867-1966)**

Krips, Josef (orchestra conductor); Vienna **(1902-1974)**

Kristofferson, Kris (singer); Brownsville, Tex., 6/22/1936

Kruger, Otto (actor); Toledo, Ohio **(1885-1974)**

Krupa, Gene (drummer); Chicago **(1909-1973)**

Krupp, Alfred (munitions magnate); Essen, Germany **(1812-1887)**

Kubelik, Rafael (conductor); Bychory (Czechoslovakia), 6/29/1914

Kublai Khan (Mongol conqueror) **(1216-1294)**

Kubrick, Stanley (producer and director); New York City, 7/26/1928

Kuralt, Charles (TV journalist); Wilmington, N.C., 9/10/1934

Kurosawa, Akira (film director); Tokyo, 3/23/1910

Kurtz, Efrem (conductor); St. Petersburg, Russia, 11/7/1900

Ky, Nguyen Cao (ex-Vice President of South Vietnam); Son Tay (Vietnam), 9/8/1930

L

Ladd, Alan (actor); Hot Springs, Ark. **(1913-1964)**

Ladd, Cheryl (Cheryl Stoppelmoor) (actress); Huron, S.D., 7/12/1951

Lafayette, Marquis de (Marie Joseph Paul Yves Roch Gilbert du Motier) (military officer); Auvergne, France **(1757-1834)**

Lafitte, Jean (pirate); Bayonne? France **(1780-1826)**

La Follette, Robert Marin (politician); Primrose, Wis. **(1855-1925)**

La Guardia, Fiorello Henry (Mayor of New York); New York City **(1882-1947)**

Lahr, Bert (Irving Lahrheim) (comedian); New York City **(1895-1967)**

Laine, Frankie (Frank Paul LoVecchio) (singer); Chicago, 3/30/1913

Laird, Melvin (ex-Secretary of Defense); Omaha, Neb., 9/1/1922

Lamarck, Chevalier de (Jean Baptiste Pierre Antoine de Monet) (naturalist); Bazantin, France **(1744-1829)**

Lamarr, Hedy (Hedwig Kiesler) (actress); Vienna, 1915

Lamb, Charles (Elia) (essayist); London **(1775-1834)**

L'Amour, Louis (author); Jamestown, N.D., **(1908-1988)**

Lamour, Dorothy (Dorothy Kaumeyer) (actress); New Orleans, 10/10/1914

Lancaster, Burt (actor); New York City, 11/2/1913

Lanchester, Elsa (Elsa Sullivan) (actress); London **(1902-1986)**

Landau, Martin (actor); Brooklyn, N.Y. 1934

Landers, Ann (columnist); Sioux City, Iowa, 7/4/1918

Landon, Michael (Eugene Maurice Orowitz) (actor); Forest Hills, Queens, N.Y., 10/31/1936(?)

Lane, Abbe (singer); New York City, 1933

Lang, Fritz (film director); Vienna **(1890-1976)**

Lang, Paul Henry (music critic); Budapest, 8/28/1901

Lange, Hope (actress); Redding Ridge, Conn., 11/28/1933

Langella, Frank (actor); Bayonne, N.J., 1/1/1940

Langford, Frances (singer); Lakeland, Fla., 4/4/1913

Langmuir, Irving (chemist); Brooklyn, N.Y. **(1881-1957)**

Langtry, Lillie (Emily Le Breton) (actress); Island of Jersey **(1852-1929)**

Lansbury, Angela (actress); London, 10/16/1925

Lansing, Robert (Robert Howell Brown) (actor); San Diego, Calif., 6/5/1928

Lanza, Mario (Alfred Arnold Cocozza) (singer and actor); Philadelphia **(1925-1959)**

Lao-Tzu (or Lao-Tse) (Li Erh) (philosopher); Honan Province, China (c. 604-531 B.C.)

Lardner, Ring (Ringgold Wilmar Lardner) (story writer); Niles, Mich. **(1885-1933)**

La Rouchefoucauld, Francois duc de (author); Paris **(1613-1680)**

La Salle, Sieur de (Robert Cavelier) (explorer); Rouen, France **(1643-1687)**

Lasser, Louise (actress); New York City, 1940(?)

Lauder, Sir Harry (Harry MacLennan) (singer); Portobello, Scotland **(1870-1950)**

Laughton, Charles (actor); Scarborough, England **(1899-1962)**

Lauper, Cyndi (singer); New York City, 6/20/53

Laurel, Stan (Arthur Jefferson) (comedian); Ulverston, England **(1890-1965)**

Laurents, Arthur (playwright); New York City, 7/14/1918

Laurie, Piper (Rosetta Jacobs) (actress); Detroit, 1/22/1932

Lavoisier, Antoine-Laurent (chemist); Paris **(1743-1794)**

Lawford, Peter (actor); London **(1923-1984)**

Lawrence, David Herbert (novelist); Nottingham, England **(1885-1930)**

Lawrence, Gertrude (Gertrud Klasen) (actress); London **(1900-1952)**

Lawrence, Marjorie (singer); Deans Marsh, Australia **(1908-1979)**

Lawrence, Steve (Sidney Leibowitz) (singer); Brooklyn, N.Y., 7/8/1935

Lawrence of Arabia (Thomas Edward Lawrence, later changed to Shaw) (author and soldier); Tremadoc, Wales **(1888-1935)**

Leachman, Cloris (actress); Des Moines, Iowa, 4/30/1926(?)

Lean, David (film director); Croydon, England, 3/25/1908

Lear, Edward (nonsense poet); London **(1812-1888)**

le Carré, John (David John Moore Cornwell) (novelist); Poole, England, 10/19/1931

Le Corbusier (Charles Edouard Jeanneret) (architect); La Chaux-de-Fonds, Switzerland **(1887-1965)**

Lederer, Francis (actor); Prague, 11/6/1906

Lee, Christopher (actor); London, 5/27/1922

Lee, Gypsy Rose (Rose Louise Hovick) (entertainer); Seattle **(1914-1970)**

Lee, Manfred B. (novelist, pseudonym Ellery Queen); Brooklyn, N.Y. **(1905-1971)**

Lee, Peggy (Norma Engstrom) (singer); Jamestown, N.D., 5/26/1920

Lee, Robert Edward (Confederate general); Stratford Estate, Va. **(1807-1870)**

Leeuwenhoek, Anton van (zoologist); Delft (Netherlands) **(1632-1723)**

Le Gallienne, Eva (actress); London, 1/11/1899

Lehár, Franz (composer); Komárom (Czechoslovakia) **(1870-1948)**

Lehman, Herbert H. (Governor and Senator); New York City **(1878-1963)**

Lehmann, Lotte (soprano); Perleberg (Germany) **(1888-1976)**

Leibniz, Gottfried W. von (scientist); Leipzig (East Germany) **(1646-1716)**

Leigh, Janet (Jeanetta Morrison) (actress); Merced, Calif., 7/6/1927

Leigh, Vivien (Vivien Mary Hartley) (actress); Darjeeling, India **(1913-1967)**

Leighton, Margaret (actress); nr. Birmingham, England **(1922-1976)**

Leinsdorf, Erich (conductor); Vienna, 2/4/1912

Lemmon, Jack (actor); Boston, 2/8/1925

Lenin, Vladimir (Vladimir Ilich Ulyanov) (Soviet leader); Simbirsk, Russia **(1870-1924)**

Lennon, John (singer and songwriter); Liverpool, England **(1940-1980)**

Leno, Jay (comedian); New Rochelle, N.Y., 4/28/1950

Lenya, Lotte (Karoline Blamauer) (singer and actress); Vienna, Austria **(1898-1981)**

Leonard, Sheldon (actor and director); New York City, 2/22/1907

Lerner, Alan Jay (lyricist); New York City **(1918-1986)**

Lerner, Max (columnist); Minsk, Russia, 12/20/1902

Le Roy, Mervyn (film producer); San Francisco **(1900-1987)**

Leslie, Joan (actress); Detroit, 1/26/1925

Lessing, Doris (novelist); Kermanshah, Iran, 10/22/1919

Lester, Mark (actor); Richmond, England, 1958

Letterman, David (TV personality); Indianapolis, 1947

Levant, Oscar (pianist); Pittsburgh **(1906-1972)**

Levene, Sam (actor); New York City **(1905-1980)**

Levenson, Sam (humorist); New York City **(1911-1980)**

Levi, Carlo (novelist); Turin, Italy **(1902-1975)**

Levine, James (music director, Metropolitan Opera); Cincinnati, 6/23/1943

Levine, Joseph E. (film producer); Boston **(1905-1987)**

Lewis, Jerry (Joseph Levitch) (comedian and film director); Newark, N.J., 3/16/1926

Lewis, Jerry Lee (singer); Ferriday, La., 9/29/1935

Lewis, John Llewellyn (labor leader); Lucas, Iowa **(1880-1969)**

Lewis, Meriwether (explorer); Albemarle Co., Va. **(1774-1809)**

Lewis, Shari (Shari Hurwitz) (puppeteer); New York City, 1/17/1934

Lewis, Sinclair (novelist); Sauk Centre, Minn. **(1885-1951)**

Lewis, Ted (entertainer); Circleville, Ohio **(1891-1971)**

Ley, Willy (science writer); Berlin **(1906-1969)**

Liberace (Wladziu Liberace) (pianist); West Allis, Wis. **(1919-1987)**

Lichtenstein, Roy (painter); New York City, 10/27/1923

Lie, Trygve Halvdan (first U.N. Secretary-General); Oslo **(1896-1968)**

Lightfoot, Gordon (singer and songwriter); Orillia, Ontario, Canada, 11/17/1938

Lillie, Beatrice (Lady Peel) (actress and comedienne); Toronto **(1898-1989)**

Lin Yutang (author); Changchow, China **(1895-1976)**

Lind, Jenny (Johanna Maria Lind) (soprano); Stockholm **(1820-1887)**

Lindbergh, Anne Morrow (author); Englewood, N.J., 6/22/1906

Lindbergh, Charles A. (aviator); Detroit **(1902-1974)**

Linden, Hal (Harold Lipshitz) (actor); New York City, 3/20/1931

Lindsay, Howard (playwright); Waterford, N.Y. **(1889-1968)**

Lindsay, John Vliet (ex-Mayor of New York City); New York City,

11/24/1921
Lindstrom, Pia (TV newscaster); Stockholm, 11/?/1938
Linkletter, Art (radio-TV personality); Moose Jaw, Saskatchewan, Canada, 7/17/1912
Linnaeus, Carolus (Carl von Linné) (botanist); Råshult, Sweden **(1707-1778)**
Lipchitz, Jacques (sculptor); Druskieniki, Latvia **(1891-1973)**
Lippi, Fra Filippo (painter); Florence **(1406-1469)**
Lippmann, Walter (columnist, author, and political analyst); New York City **(1889-1974)**
Lister, (1st Baron of Lyme Regis) (Joseph Lister) (surgeon); Upton, England **(1827-1912)**
Liszt, Franz (composer and pianist); Raiding (Hungary) **(1811-1886)**
Little, Cleavon (actor and comedian); Chickasha, Okla., 6/1/1939
Little, Rich (impressionist); Ottawa, 11/26/1938
Livesey, Roger (actor); Barry, Wales **(1906-1976)**
Livingstone, David (missionary and explorer); Lanarkshire, Scotland **(1813-1873)**
Livingstone, Mary (Sadye Marks) (comedienne); Seattle **(1909-1983)**
Llewellyn, Richard (novelist); St. David's, Wales **(1906-1983)**
Lloyd, Harold (comedian); Burchard, Neb. **(1894-1971)**
Lloyd George, David (Earl of Dwyfor) (statesman); Manchester, England **(1863-1945)**
Lloyd Webber, Andrew (composer); London, England, 3/22/1948
Locke, John (philosopher); Somersetshire, England **(1632-1704)**
Lockhart, Gene (actor); London, Ontario, Canada **(1891-1957)**
Lockhart, June (actress); New York City, 6/25/1925
Lockwood, Margaret (actress); Karachi (Pakistan), 9/15/1916
Lodge, Henry Cabot (legislator); Boston **(1850-1924)**
Lodge, Henry Cabot, Jr. (diplomat); Nahant, Mass. **(1902-1985)**
Loesser, Frank (composer); New York City **(1910-1969)**
Loewe, Frederick (composer); Vienna **(1901-1988)**
Logan, Joshua (director and producer); Texarkana, Tex. **(1908-1988)**
Lollobrigida, Gina (actress); Subiaco, Italy, 1928
Lombard, Carole (Carol Jane Peters) (actress); Ft. Wayne, Ind. **(1908-1942)**
Lombardo, Guy (band leader); London, Ontario, Canada **(1902-1977)**
London, George (baritone); Montreal **(1920-1985)**
London, Jack (John Griffith London) (novelist); San Francisco **(1876-1916)**
London, Julie (Julie Peck) (singer and actress); Santa Rosa, Calif., 9/26/1926
Long, Huey Pierce (politician); Winnfield, La. **(1893-1935)**
Longfellow, Henry Wadsworth (poet); Portland, Me. **(1807-1882)**
Longworth, Alice Roosevelt (social figure); New York City **(1884-1980)**
Loos, Anita (novelist); Sissons, Calif., **(1888-1981)**
Lopez, Vincent (band leader); Brooklyn, N.Y. **(1895-1975)**
Lord, Jack (John Joseph Ryan) (actor); New York City, 12/30/1930
Loren, Sophia (Sofia Scicolone) (actress); Rome, 9/20/1934
Lorre, Peter (Laszlo Löewenstein) (actor); Rosenberg (Czechoslovakia) **(1904-1964)**
Loudon, Dorothy (actress, singer); Boston, 9/17/1933
Louise, Tina (actress); New York City, 2/11/1937
Lovecraft, Howard Phillips (author); Providence, R.I., **(1890-1937)**
Lowell, Amy (poet); Brookline, Mass. **(1874-1925)**
Lowell, James Russell (poet); Cambridge, Mass. **(1819-1891)**
Lowell, Robert (poet); Boston **(1917-1977)**
Loy, Myrna (Myrna Williams) (actress); nr. Helena, Mont., 8/2/1905
Loyola, St. Ignatius of (Iñigo de Oñez y Loyola) (founder of Jesuits); Gúipuzcoa Province, Spain **(1491-1556)**
Lubitsch, Ernst (film director); Berlin **(1892-1947)**
Luce, Clare Boothe (playwright and former Ambassador); New York City **(1903-1987)**
Luce, Henry Robinson (editor and publisher); Tengchow, China **(1898-1967)**
Ludlum, Robert (author); New York City, 5/25/1927
Lugosi, Bela (Bela Lugosi Blasko) (actor); Logos, Hungary **(1888-1956)**
Lukas, Paul (actor); Budapest **(1895-1971)**
Lully, Jean Baptiste (French composer); Florence **(1639-1687)**
Lumet, Sidney (film and TV director); Philadelphia, 6/25/1924
Lunt, Alfred (actor); Milwaukee **(1892-1977)**
Lupino, Ida (actress and director); London, 2/4/1918
LuPone, Patti (actress; singer); Northport, N.Y., 4/21/1949
Luther, Martin (religious reformer); Eisleben (East Germany) **(1483-1546)**
Lynde, Paul (comedian); Mt. Vernon, Ohio **(1926-1982)**
Lynn, Jeffrey (actor); Auburn, Mass., 1909
Lynn, Loretta (singer); Butcher's Hollow, Ky., 4/14/1935

M

Ma, Yo-Yo (cellist); Paris, 10/7/1955
Maazel, Lorin (conductor); Neuilly, France, 3/5/1930

MacArthur, Charles (playwright); Scranton, Pa. **(1895-1956)**
MacArthur, Douglas (five-star general); Little Rock Barracks, Ark. **(1880-1964)**
MacArthur, James (actor); Los Angeles, 12/8/1937
Macaulay, Thomas Babington (author); Rothley Temple, England **(1800-1859)**
MacDermot, Galt (composer); Montreal, 12/19/1928
MacDonald, James Ramsay (statesman); Lossiemouth, Scotland **(1866-1937)**
MacDonald, Jeanette (actress and soprano); Philadelphia **(1907-1965)**
Macdonald, Ross (Kenneth Millar) (mystery writer); Los Gatos, Calif. **(1915-1983)**
MacDowell, Edward Alexander (composer); New York City **(1861-1908)**
Macfadden, Bernarr (physical culturist); nr. Mill Spring, Mo. **(1868-1955)**
MacGraw, Ali (actress); New York City, 4/1/1939
Machaut, Guillaume de (composer); Marchault, France **(1300-1377)**
Machiavelli, Niccolò (political philosopher); Florence (Italy) **(1469-1527)**
Mack, Ted (TV personality); Greeley, Colo. **(1904-1976)**
MacKenzie, Gisele (Marie Marguerite Louise Gisele LaFleche) (singer and actress); Winnipeg, Manitoba, Canada, 1/10/1927
MacLaine, Shirley (Shirley MacLean Beatty) (actress); Richmond, Va., 4/24/1934
MacLeish, Archibald (poet); Glencoe, Ill. **(1892-1982)**
Macmillan, Harold (ex-Prime Minister); London **(1894-1986)**
MacMurray, Fred (actor); Kankakee, Ill., 8/30/1908
MacNeil, Cornell (baritone); Minneapolis, 1925
MacRae, Gordon (singer); East Orange, N.J. **(1921-1986)**
Madison, Guy (Robert Moseley) (actor); Bakersfield, Calif., 1/19/1922
Madonna (Madonna Louise Ciccone) (singer); Bay City, Mich. 1960
Maeterlinck, Count Maurice (author); Ghent, Belgium **(1862-1949)**
Magellan, Ferdinand (Fernando de Magalhaes) (navigator); Sabrosa, Portugal **(1480?-1521)**
Magnani, Anna (actress); Rome **(1908-1973)**
Magritte, René (painter); Belgium **(1898-1967)**
Magsaysay, Ramón (statesman); Iba, Luzon, Philippines **(1907-1957)**
Mahan, Alfred Thayer (naval historian); West Point, N.Y. **(1840-1914)**
Mahler, Gustav (composer and conductor); Kalischt (Czechoslovakia) **(1860-1911)**
Mailer, Norman (novelist); Long Branch, N.J., 1/31/1923
Maillol, Aristide (sculptor); Banyuls-sur-Mer, Rousillion, France **(1861-1944)**
Maimonides, Moses (Jewish philosopher); Cordoba, Spain **(1135-1204)**
Main, Marjorie (Mary Tomlinson Krebs) (actress); Acton, Ind. **(1890-1975)**
Mainbocher (Main Rousseau Bocher) (fashion designer); Chicago **(1891-1976)**
Majors, Lee (actor); Wyandotte, Mich., 4/23/1940
Makarova, Natalia (ballerina); Leningrad, 11/21/1940
Makeba, Miriam (singer); Johannesburg, South Africa, 3/4/1932
Malamud, Bernard (novelist); Brooklyn, N.Y., **(1914-1986)**
Malden, Karl (Miaden Sekulovich) (actor); Chicago, 3/22/1913
Malone, Dorothy (actress); Chicago, 1/30/1925
Malraux, André (author); Paris **(1901-1976)**
Malthus, Thomas Robert (economist); nr. Dorking, England **(1766-1834)**
Mamet, David (playwright); Chicago, 11/30/1947
Manchester, Melissa (singer); Bronx, N.Y., 2/15/1951
Manchester, William (writer); Attleboro, Mass., 4/1/1922
Mancini, Henry (composer and conductor); Cleveland, 4/16/1924
Mandela, Winnie (Nomzamo) (South African political activist); Pondoland district of the Transkei, 1936(?)
Mandrell, Barbara (singer); Houston, 12/25/1948
Manet, Edouard (painter); Paris **(1832-1883)**
Mangano, Silvana (actress); Rome, 4/21/1930
Mangione, Chuck (hornist, pianist, and composer); Rochester, N.Y., 11/29/1940
Manilow, Barry (singer); Brooklyn, N.Y., 6/17/1946
Mankiewicz, Frank F. (columnist); New York City, 5/16/1924
Mankiewicz, Joseph L. (film writer and director); Wilkes-Barre, Pa., 2/11/1909
Mann, Horace (educator); Franklin, Mass. **(1796-1859)**
Mann, Thomas (novelist); Lübeck, Germany **(1875-1955)**
Mannes, Marya (writer); New York City, 11/14/1904
Mansfield, Jayne (Jayne Palmer) (actress); Bryn Mawr, Pa. **(1932-1967)**
Mansfield, Katherine (story writer); Wellington, New Zealand **(1888-1923)**
Mantovani, Annunzio (conductor); Venice **(1905-1980)**
Mao Zedong (Tse-tung) (Chinese leader); Shao Shan, China **(1893-**

1976)
Marat, Jean Paul (French revolutionist); Boudry, Neuchâtel, Switzerland **(1743-1793)**
Marceau, Marcel (mime); Strasbourg, France, 3/22/1923
March, Fredric (Frederick Bickel) (actor); Racine, Wis. **(1897-1975)**
Marconi, Guglielmo (inventor); Bologna, Italy **(1874-1937)**
Marcus Aurelius (Marcus Annius Verus) (Roman emperor); Rome **(121-180)**
Marcuse, Herbert (philosopher); Berlin, **(1898-1979)**
Margaret Rose (Princess); Glamis Castle, Angus, Scotland, 8/21/1930
Margrethe II (Queen); Copenhagen, 4/16/1940
Marie Antoinette (Josephe Jeanne Marie Antoinette) (Queen of France); Vienna **(1755-1793)**
Marisol (sculptor); Venezuela, 1930
Markham, Edwin (poet); Oregon City, Ore. **(1852-1940)**
Markova, Dame Alicia (Lilian Alice Marks) (ballerina); London, 12/1/1910
Marley, Bob (reggae singer and songwriter); Kingston, Jamaica **(1945-1981)**
Marlowe, Christopher (dramatist); Canterbury, England **(1564-1593)**
Marlowe, Julia (Sarah Frances Frost) (actress); Cumberlandshire, England **(1866-1950)**
Marquand, J(ohn) P(hillips) (novelist); Wilmington, Del. **(1893-1960)**
Marquette, Jacques (missionary and explorer); Laon, France **(1637-1675)**
Marriner, Neville (conductor); Lincoln, England, 4/15/1924
Marsh, Jean (actress); Stoke Newington, England, 7/1/1934
Marshall, E.G. (actor); Owatonna, Minn., 6/18/1910
Marshall, George Catlett (general); Uniontown, Pa. **(1880-1959)**
Marshall, Herbert (actor); London **(1890-1968)**
Marshall, John (jurist); nr. Germantown, Va. **(1755-1835)**
Marshall, Penny (actress); New York City, 10/15/1942
Martin, Dean (Dino Crocetti) (singer and actor); Steubenville, Ohio, 6/17/1917
Martin, Mary (singer and actress); Weatherford, Tex., 12/1/1913
Martin, Steve (comedian); Waco, Tex., 1945(?)
Martin, Tony (Alvin Morris) (singer); San Francisco, 12/25/1913
Martinelli, Giovanni (tenor); Montagnana, Italy **(1885-1969)**
Martins, Peter (dancer-choreographer); Copenhagen, 10/27/1945
Marvell, Andrew (poet); Winestead, England **(1621-1678)**
Marvin, Lee (actor); New York City **(1924-1987)**
Marx, Chico (Leonard) (comedian); New York City **(1891-1961)**
Marx, Groucho (Julius) (comedian); New York City **(1890-1977)**
Marx, Harpo (Arthur) (comedian); New York City **(1893-1964)**
Marx, Karl (Socialist writer); Treves (Germany) **(1818-1883)**
Marx, Zeppo (Herbert) (comedian); New York City **(1901-1979)**
Mary Stuart (Queen of Scotland); Linlithgow, Scotland **(1542-1587)**
Masaryk, Jan Garrigue (statesman); Prague (Czechoslovakia) **(1886-1948)**
Masaryk, Thomas Garrigue (statesman); Hodonin (Czechoslovakia) **(1850-1937)**
Masefield, John (poet); Ledbury, England **(1878-1967)**
Masekela, Hugh (trumpeter); Wilbank, South Africa, 4/4/1939
Mason, James (actor); Huddersfield, England **(1909-1984)**
Massenet, Jules Emile Frédéric (composer); Montaud, France **(1842-1912)**
Massey, Raymond (actor); Toronto, **(1896-1983)**
Massine, Léonide (choreographer); Moscow, **(1895-1979)**
Masters, Edgar Lee (poet); Garnett, Kan. **(1869-1950)**
Mastroianni, Marcello (actor); Fontana Liri, Italy, 9/28/1924
Mather, Cotton (clergyman); Boston **(1663-1728)**
Mathis, Johnny (singer); San Francisco, 9/30/1935
Matisse, Henri (painter); Le Cateau, France **(1869-1954)**
Matthau, Walter (Walter Matuschanskayasky) (actor); New York City, 10/1/1920
Mature, Victor (actor); Louisville, Ky., 1/19/1916
Maugham, W(illiam) Somerset (author); Paris **(1874-1965)**
Mauldin, Bill (political cartoonist); Mountain Park, N.M., 10/29/1921
Maupassant, Henri René Albert Guy de (story writer); Normandy, France **(1850-1893)**
Maurois, André (Emile Herzog) (author); Elbauf, France **(1885-1967)**
Maximilian (Ferdinand Maximilian Joseph) (Emperor of Mexico); Vienna **(1832-1867)**
Maxwell, James Clerk (physicist); Edinburgh, Scotland **(1831-1879)**
May, Elaine (Elaine Berlin) (entertainer-writer); Philadelphia, 4/21/1932
May, Rollo (psychologist); Ada, Ohio, 4/21/1909
Mayall, John (singer and songwriter); Manchester, England, 11/29/1933
Mayo, Charles H. (surgeon); Rochester, Minn. **(1865-1939)**
Mayo, Charles W. (surgeon); Rochester, Minn. **(1898-1968)**
Mayo, Virginia (Jones) (actress); St. Louis, 1920
Mayo, William J. (surgeon); Le Sueur, Minn. **(1861-1939)**
Mazzini, Giuseppe (patriot); Genoa **(1805-1872)**
McBride, Mary Margaret (radio personality); Paris, Mo. **(1899-1976)**

McBride, Patricia (ballerina); Teaneck, N.J., 8/23/1942
McCallum, David (actor); Glasgow, Scotland, 9/19/1933
McCambridge, Mercedes (actress); Joliet, Ill., 3/17/1918
McCarthy, Eugene J. (ex-Senator); Watkins, Minn., 3/29/1916
McCarthy, Joseph Raymond (Senator); Grand Chute, Wis. **(1908-1957)**
McCarthy, Kevin (actor); Seattle, 2/15/1914
McCarthy, Mary (novelist); Seattle, 6/21/1912
McCartney, Paul (singer and songwriter); Liverpool, England, 6/18/1942
McClellan, George Brinton (general); Philadelphia **(1826-1885)**
McClintock, Barbara (geneticist); Hartford, Conn., 6/16/1902
McCloy, John J. (lawyer and banker); Philadelphia, 3/31/1895
McClure, Doug (actor); Glendale, Calif., 5/11/1938
McCormack, John (tenor); Athlone, Ireland **(1884-1945)**
McCormack, John W. (ex-Speaker of House); Boston **(1891-1980)**
McCormack, Patty (actress); New York City, 8/21/1945
McCormick, Cyrus Hall (inventor); Rockbridge County, Va. **(1809-1884)**
McCoy, Col. Tim (actor); Saginaw, Mich. **(1891-1978)**
McCracken, James (dramatic tenor); Gary, Ind. **(1926-1988)**
McCrea, Joel (actor); Los Angeles, 11/5/1905
McCullers, Carson (novelist); Columbus, Ga. **(1917-1967)**
McDowall, Roddy (actor); London, 9/17/1928
McDowell, Malcolm (actor); Leeds, England, 6/19/1943
McGavin, Darren (actor); San Joaquin, Calif., 5/7/1922
McGinley, Phyllis (poet and writer); Ontario, Ore. **(1905-1978)**
McGoohan, Patrick (actor); Astoria, Queens, N.Y., 1928
McGuire, Dorothy (actress); Omaha, Neb. 6/14/1919
McKellen, Ian (actor); Burnley, England, 5/25/1939
McKenna, Siobhan (actress); Belfast, Northern Ireland **(1923-1986)**
McKuen, Rod (singer and composer); Oakland, Calif., 4/29/1933
McLaglen, Victor (actor); Tunbridge Wells, Kent, England **(1886-1959)**
McLaughlin, John (guitarist); Yorkshire, England, 1942
McLean, Don (singer and songwriter); New Rochelle, N.Y., 10/2/1945
McLuhan, Marshall (Herbert Marshall) (communications writer); Edmonton, Canada **(1911-1980)**
McMahon, Ed (TV personality); Detroit, 3/6/1923
McNamara, Robert S. (former president of World Bank); San Francisco, 6/9/1916
McQueen, Steve (Terence Stephen McQueen) (actor); Indianapolis **(1930-1980)**
Mead, Margaret (anthropologist); Philadelphia, **(1901-1978)**
Meadows, Audrey (actress); Wu Chang, China, 1922(?)
Meadows, Jayne (actress); Wu Chang, China 9/27/1926
Meany, George (labor leader); New York City **(1894-1980)**
Meara, Anne (actress); New York City, 1929
Medici, Lorenzo de' (called Lorenzo the Magnificent) (Florentine ruler); Florence (Italy) **(1449-1492)**
Meeker, Ralph (Ralph Rathgeber) (actor); Minneapolis, **(1920-1988)**
Mehta, Zubin (conductor); Bombay, 4/29/1936
Meir, Golda (Golda Myerson, nee Mabovitz) (ex-Premier of Israel); Kiev, Russia **(1898-1978)**
Melanie (Melanie Safka) (singer and songwriter); New York City, 2/3/1947
Melba, Dame Nellie (Helen Porter Mitchell) (soprano); nr. Melbourne **(1861-1931)**
Melchior, Lauritz (Lebrecht Hommel) (heroic tenor); Copenhagen **(1890-1973)**
Mellon, Andrew William (financier); Pittsburgh **(1855-1937)**
Melville, Herman (novelist); New York City **(1819-1891)**
Mencken, Henry Louis (writer); Baltimore **(1880-1956)**
Mendel, Gregor Johann (geneticist); Heinzendorf, Austrian Silesia **(1822-1884)**
Mendeleyev, Dmitri Ivanovich (chemist); Tobolsk, Russia **(1834-1907)**
Mendelssohn-Bartholdy, Jakob Ludwig Felix (composer); Hamburg **(1809-1847)**
Mendès-France, Pierre (ex-Premier); Paris **(1905-1982)**
Menjou, Adolphe (actor); Pittsburgh **(1890-1963)**
Mennin, Peter (Peter Mennini) (composer); Erie, Pa. **(1923-1983)**
Menninger, William C. (psychiatrist); Topeka, Kan. **(1899-1966)**
Menotti, Gian Carlo (composer); Cadegliano, Italy, 7/7/1911
Menuhin, Yehudi (violinist and conductor); New York City, 4/22/1916
Menzies, Robert Gordon (ex-Prime Minister); Jeparit, Australia **(1894-1978)**
Mercer, Johnny (songwriter); Savannah, Ga. **(1909-1976)**
Mercer, Mabel (singer); Burton-on-Trent, England **(1900-1984)**
Mercouri, Melina (actress); Athens, 10/18/1925
Meredith, Burgess (actor); Cleveland, 11/16/1908
Merkel, Una (actress); Covington, Ky. **(1903-1986)**
Merman, Ethel (Ethel Zimmerman) (singer and actress); Astoria, Queens, N.Y. **(1909-1984)**
Merrick, David (David Margulois) (stage producer); St. Louis, 11/27/1912

Merrill, Dina (actress); New York City, 12/9/1925
Merrill, Gary (actor); Hartford, Conn., 8/2/1914
Merrill, Robert (baritone); Brooklyn, N.Y., 6/4/1919
Merton, Thomas (clergyman and writer); France (1915-1968)
Mesmer, Franz Anton (physician); Itzmang, nr. Constance (Germany) (1733-1815)
Mesta, Perle (social figure); Sturgis, Mich. (1889-1975)
Metternich, Prince Klemens Wenzel Nepomuk Lothar von (statesman); Coblenz (Germany) (1773-1859)
Michelangelo Buonarreti (painter, sculptor, and architect); Caprese (Italy) (1475-1564)
Michener, James A. (novelist); New York City, 2/3/1907
Mickiewicz, Adam (Polish poet); Zozie, Belorussia (U.S.S.R.) (1798-1855)
Midler, Bette (singer); Honolulu, 1945
Mielziner, Jo (stage designer); Paris (1901-1976)
Mies van der Rohe, Ludwig (architect and designer); Aachen, Germany (1886-1969)
Mikoyan, Anastas I. (diplomat); Sanain, Armenia, (1895-1978)
Miles, Sarah (actress); Essex, England, 12/31/1943
Miles, Sylvia (actress); New York City, 9/9/1932
Miles, Vera (Vera Ralston) (actress); nr. Boise City, Okla., 8/23/1930
Milhaud, Darius (composer); Aix-en-Provence, France (1892-1974)
Mill, John Stuart (philosopher); London, (1806-1873)
Milland, Ray (Reginald Truscott-Jones) (actor); Neath, Wales (1907-1986)
Millay, Edna St. Vincent (poet); Rockland, Me. (1892-1950)
Miller, Ann (Lucille Ann Collier) (dancer and actress); Cherino, Tex., 4/12/1923
Miller, Arthur (playwright); New York City, 10/17/1915
Miller, Glenn (band leader); Clarinda, Iowa (1904-1944)
Miller, Henry (novelist); New York City (1891-1980)
Miller, Jason (John Miller) (playwright); New York City, 1939(?)
Miller, Mitch (Mitchell) (musician); Rochester, N.Y., 7/4/1911
Miller, Roger (singer); Fort Worth, 1/2/1936
Millet, Jean François (painter); Gruchy, France (1814-1875)
Millett, Kate (feminist); St. Paul, 9/14/1934
Millikan, Robert A. (physicist); Morrison, Ill. (1869-1953)
Mills, Hayley (actress); London, 4/18/1946
Mills, John (actor); Felixstowe, England, 2/22/1908
Milne, A(lan) A(lexander) (author); London (1882-1956)
Milstein, Nathan (concert violinist); Odessa, Russia, 12/31/1904
Milton, John (poet); London (1608-1674)
Mimieux, Yvette (actress); Hollywood, Calif., 1/8/1941
Mineo, Sal (actor); New York City (1939-1976)
Minnelli, Liza (singer and actress); Hollywood, Calif., 3/12/1946
Minnelli, Vincente (film director); Chicago (1913-1986)
Minuit, Peter (Governor of New Amsterdam); Wesel (Germany) (1580-1638)
Miranda, Carmen (Maria do Carmo da Cunha) (singer and dancer); Lisbon (1913-1955)
Miró, Joan (painter); Barcelona (1893-1983)
Mitchell, Cameron (actor); Dallastown, Pa., 4/11/1918
Mitchell, Guy (actor); Detroit, 2/27/1927
Mitchell, John N. (former Attorney General); Detroit (1913-1988)
Mitchell, Joni (Roberta Joan Anderson) (singer and songwriter); Ft. Macleod, Canada, 11/7/1943
Mitchell, Margaret (novelist); Atlanta (1900-1949)
Mitchum, Robert (actor); Bridgeport, Conn., 8/6/1917
Mitropoulos, Dimitri (orchestra conductor); Athens (1896-1960)
Mix, Tom (actor); Mix Run, Pa. (1880-1940)
Modigliani, Amedeo (painter); Leghorn, Italy (1884-1920)
Moffo, Anna (soprano); Wayne, Pa., 6/27/1934
Mohammed (prophet); Mecca (Saudi Arabia) (570-632)
Molière (Jean Baptiste Poquelin) (dramatist); Paris (1622-1673)
Molnar, Ferenc (dramatist); Budapest (1878-1952)
Molotov, Vyacheslav M. (V. M. Skryabin) (diplomat); Kukarka, Russia (1890-1986)
Mondrian, Piet (painter); Amersfoort, Netherlands (1872-1944)
Monet, Claude (painter); Paris (1840-1926)
Monk, Meredith (choreographer-composer-performing artist); Lima, Peru, 11/20/1942
Monk, Thelonious (pianist); Rocky Mount, N.C. (1918-1982)
Monroe, Marilyn (Norma Jean Mortenson or Baker) (actress); Los Angeles (1926-1962)
Monroe, Vaughn (Wilton) (band leader); Akron, Ohio (1912-1973)
Monsarrat, Nicholas (novelist); Liverpool, England, (1910-1979)
Montaigne, Michel Eyquem de (essayist); nr. Bordeaux, France (1533-1592)
Montalban, Ricardo (actor); Mexico City, 11/25/1920
Montand, Yves (Yvo Montand Livi) (actor and singer); Monsummano, Italy, 10/13/1921
Montesquieu, Charles-Louis de Secondat, baron de La Brède and de, (philosopher) nr. Borleaux, France (1689-1755)
Monteverdi, Claudio (composer); Cremona? Italy (1567-1643)
Montez, Maria (actress); Dominican Republican (1918-1951)

Montezuma II (Aztec emperor); Mexico (1480?-1520)
Montgomery, Elizabeth (actress); Hollywood, Calif., 4/15/1933
Montgomery, George (George Montgomery Letz) (actor); Brady, Mont., 8/29/1916
Montgomery, Robert (Henry, Jr.) (actor); Beacon, N.Y. (1904-1981)
Montgomery of Alamein, 1st Viscount of Hindhead (Sir Bernard Law Montgomery) (military leader); London (1887-1976)
Montoya, Carlos (guitarist); Madrid, 12/13/1903
Moore, Clement Clarke (author); New York City (1779-1863)
Moore, Dudley (actor-writer-musician); Dagenham, England, 4/19/1935
Moore, Garry (Thomas Garrison Morfit) (TV personality); Baltimore, 1/31/1915
Moore, Grace (soprano); Jellico, Tenn. (1901-1947)
Moore, Henry (sculptor); Castleford, England (1898-1986)
Moore, Marianne (poet); Kirkwood, Mo. (1887-1972)
Moore, Mary Tyler (actress); Brooklyn, N.Y., 12/29/1937
Moore, Melba (Beatrice) (singer and actress); New York City, 10/27/1945
Moore, Roger (actor); London, 10/14/1927(?)
Moore, Thomas (poet); Dublin (1779-1852)
Moore, Victor (actor); Hammonton, N.J. (1876-1962)
Moorehead, Agnes (actress); Clinton, Mass. (1906-1974)
More, Henry (philosopher); Grantham, England (1614-1687)
More, Sir Thomas (statesman and author); London (1478-1535)
Moreau, Jeanne (actress); Paris, 1/23/1928
Moreno, Rita (Rosita Dolores Alverio) (actress); Humacao, Puerto Rico, 12/11/1931
Morgan, Dennis (actor); Prentice, Wis., 12/10/1920
Morgan, Harry (actor); Detroit, 4/10/1915
Morgan, Helen (singer); Danville, Ohio (1900?-1941)
Morgan, Henry (comedian); New York City, 3/31/1915
Morgan, Jane (Florence Currier) (singer); Boston, 1920
Morgan, John Pierpont (financier); Hartford, Conn. (1837-1913)
Moriarty, Michael (actor); Detroit, 4/5/1941
Morini, Erica (concert violinist); Vienna, 1/5/1910
Morison, Samuel Eliot (historian); Boston (1887-1976)
Morley, Christopher Darlington (novelist); Haverford, Pa. (1890-1957)
Morley, Robert (actor); Semley, England, 5/26/1908
Morrison, Jim (James Douglas Morrison) (singer and songwriter); Melbourne, Fla. (1943-1971)
Morse, Marston (mathematician); Waterville, Me. (1892-1977)
Morse, Robert (actor); Newton, Mass., 5/18/1931
Morse, Samuel Finley Breese (painter and inventor); Charlestown, Mass. (1791-1872)
Moses, Grandma (Mrs. Anna Mary Robertson Moses) (painter); Greenwich, N.Y. (1860-1961)
Moses, Robert (urban planner); New Haven, Conn., (1888-1981)
Mostel, Zero (Samuel Joel Mostel) (actor); Brooklyn, N.Y. (1915-1977)
Moussorgsky, Modest Petrovich (composer); Karev, Russia (1839-1881)
Moyers, Bill D. (Billy Don) (journalist); Hugo, Okla., 6/5/1934
Moynihan, Daniel Patrick (New York Senator); Tulsa, Okla., 3/16/1927
Mozart, Wolfgang Amadeus (Johannes Chrysostomus Wolfgangus Theophilus Mozart) (composer); Salzburg (Austria) (1756-1791)
Mudd, Roger (TV newscaster); Washington, D.C., 2/9/1928
Muggeridge, Malcolm (Thomas) (writer); Croydon, England, 3/24/1903
Muhammad, Elijah (Elijah Poole) (religious leader); Sandersville, Ga. (1897-1975)
Mulgrew, Kate (actress); Dubuque, Iowa, 4/?/1929
Mulhare, Edward (actor); Ireland, 1923
Mumford, Lewis (cultural historian and city planner); Flushing, Queens, N.Y., 10/19/1895
Munch, Edvard (painter); Löten, Norway (1863-1944)
Munchhausen, Karl Friedrick Hieronymus, baron von (anecdotist); Hanover, Germany (1720-1797)
Muni, Paul (Muni Weisenfreund) (actor); Lemburg (Ukraine) (1895-1967)
Munsel, Patrice (soprano); Spokane, Wash., 5/14/1925
Murdoch, Iris (novelist); Dublin, 7/15/1919
Murdoch, Rupert (publisher); Melbourne, 3/11/1931
Murillo, Bartolomé Esteban (painter); Seville, Spain (1617-1682)
Murphy, Audie (actor and war hero); Kingston, Tex. (1924-1971)
Murphy, Eddie (actor-comedian); Brooklyn, N.Y. 4/3/61
Murphy, George (actor, dancer, and ex-Senator); New Haven, Conn., 7/4/1902
Murray, Arthur (dance teacher); New York City, 4/4/1895
Murray, Bill (actor-comedian); Wilmette, Ill. 9/21/1950
Murray, Kathryn (dance teacher); Jersey City, N.J., 1906
Murray, Ken (Don Court) (producer); Nyack, N.Y. (1903-1988)
Murray, Mae (Marie Adrienne Koenig) (actress); Portsmouth, Va. (1890-1965)

Murrow, Edward R. (commentator and government official); Greensboro, N.C. **(1908-1965)**
Mussolini, Benito (Italian dictator); Dovia, Forli, Italy **(1883-1945)**
Myerson, Bess (consumer advocate); Bronx, N.Y., 1924
Myrdal, Gunnar (sociologist and economist); Gustaf Parish, Sweden **(1898-1987)**

N

Nabokov, Vladimir (novelist); St. Petersburg, Russia **(1899-1977)**
Nabors, Jim (actor and singer); Sylacauga, Ala., 6/12/1932
Nader, Ralph (consumer advocate); Winsted, Conn., 2/27/1934
Nagel, Conrad (actor); Keokuk, Iowa **(1897-1970)**
Naish, J. Carrol (actor); New York City **(1900-1973)**
Naldi, Nita (Anita Donna Dooley) (actress); New York City **(1899-1961)**
Napoleon Bonaparte. *See* Bonaparte, Napoleon
Nash, Graham (singer); Blackpool, England, 1942
Nash, Ogden (poet); Rye, N.Y. **(1902-1971)**
Nasser, Gamal Abdel (statesman); Beni Mor, Egypt **(1918-1970)**
Nast, Thomas (cartoonist); Landau (Germany) **(1840-1902)**
Nation, Carry Amelia (temperance leader); Garrard County, Ky. **(1846-1911)**
Natwick, Mildred (actress); Baltimore, 6/19/1908
Nazimova, Alla (actress); Yalta, Crimea, Russia **(1879-1945)**
Neagle, Anna (Marjorie Robertson) (actress); London **(1908-1986)**
Neal, Patricia (actress); Packard, Ky., 1/20/1926
Neff, Hildegarde (actress); Ulm, Germany, 12/28/1925
Negri, Pola (Apolina Mathias-Chalupec) (actress); Bromberg (Poland) **(1899-1987)**
Nehru, Jawaharlal (first Prime Minister of India); Allahabad, India **(1889-1964)**
Nelson, Barry (Neilsen) (actor); San Francisco, 1920
Nelson, David (actor); New York City, 10/24/1936
Nelson, Harriet Hilliard (Peggy Lou Snyder) (actress); Des Moines, Iowa, 1914
Nelson, Ozzie (Oswald) (actor); Jersey City, N.J. **(1907-1975)**
Nelson, Ricky (Eric) (singer and actor); Teaneck, N.J. **(1940-1985)**
Nelson, Viscount Horatio (naval officer); Burnham Thorpe, England **(1758-1805)**
Nelson, Willie (singer); Waco, Texas, 4/30/1933
Nenni, Pietro (Socialist leader); Faenza, Italy **(1891-1980)**
Nero (Nero Claudius Caesar Drusus Germanicus) (Roman emperor); Antium (Italy) **(37-68)**
Nero, Peter (pianist); New York City, 5/22/1934
Nesbitt, Cathleen (actress); Cheshire, England **(1889-1982)**
Nevelson, Louise (sculptor); Kiev, Russia **(1899-1988)**
Newhart, Bob (entertainer); Chicago, 9/5/1929
Newhouse, Samuel I. (publisher); New York City **(1895-1979)**
Newley, Anthony (actor and song writer); London, 9/24/1931
Newman, Edwin (news commentator); New York City, 1/25/1919
Newman, John Henry (prelate); London **(1801-1890)**
Newman, Paul (actor and director); Cleveland, 1/26/1925
Newman, Randy (singer); Los Angeles, 11/28/1943
Newton, Huey (black activist); New Orleans, 2/17/1942
Newton, Sir Isaac (mathematician and scientist); nr. Grantham, England **(1642-1727)**
Newton, Wayne (singer); Norfolk, Va., 4/3/1942
Newton-John, Olivia (singer); Cambridge, England, 9/26/1948
Nichols, Mike (Michael Peschkowsky) (stage and film director); Berlin, 11/6/1931
Nicholson, Jack (actor); Neptune, N.J., 4/22/1937
Nietzsche, Friedrich Wilhelm (philosopher); nr. Lützen Saxony (East Germany) **(1844-1900)**
Nightingale, Florence (nurse); Florence (Italy) **(1820-1910)**
Nijinsky, Vaslav (ballet dancer); Warsaw **(1890-1950)**
Nilsson, Birgit (soprano); West Karup, Sweden, 5/17/1923
Nilsson, Harry (singer and songwriter); Brooklyn, N.Y., 6/15/1941
Nimitz, Chester W. (naval officer); Fredericksburg, Tex. **(1885-1966)**
Nimoy, Leonard (actor); Boston, 3/26/1931
Nin, Anaïs (author and diarist); Neuilly, France **(1903-1977)**
Niven, David (actor); Kirriemuir, Scotland, **(1910-1983)**
Nizer, Louis (lawyer and author); London, 2/6/1902
Nobel, Alfred Bernhard (industrialist); Stockholm **(1833-1896)**
Noguchi, Isamu (sculptor); Los Angeles **(1904-1988)**
Nolan, Lloyd (actor); San Francisco **(1902-1985)**
Nolte, Nick (actor); Omaha, Neb., 1942
Norell, Norman (Norman Levinson) (fashion designer); Noblesville, Ind. **(1900-1972)**
Norman, Marsha (Marsha Williams) (playwright); Louisville, Ky., 9/21/1947
Norstad, Gen. Lauris (ex-commander of NATO forces); Minneapolis

(1907-1988)
North, John Ringling (circus director); Baraboo, Wis. **(1903-1985)**
North, Sheree (actress); Los Angeles, 1/17/1933
Norton, Eleanor Holmes (New York City government official, lawyer); Washington, D.C., 6/13/1937
Nostradamus (Michel de Notredame) (astrologer); St. Rémy, France **(1503-1566)**
Novaes, Guiomar (pianist); São João de Boa Vista, Brazil **(1895-1979)**
Novak, Kim (Marilyn Novak) (actress); Chicago, 2/13/1933
Novarro, Ramon (Ramon Samaniegoes) (actor); Durango, Mexico **(1899-1968)**
Nugent, Elliott (actor and director); Dover, Ohio, **(1899-1980)**
Nureyev, Rudolf (ballet dancer); U.S.S.R., 3/17/1938
Nuyen, France (actress); Marseilles, France, 7/31/1939
Nyro, Laura (singer and songwriter); Bronx, N.Y., 1947

O

Oakie, Jack (actor); Sedalia, Mo. **(1903-1978)**
Oates, Joyce Carol (novelist); Lockport, N.Y., 6/16/1938
Oberon, Merle (Estelle Merle O'Brien Thompson) (actress); Tasmania **(1911-1979)**
O'Brian, Hugh (Hugh J. Krampe) (actor); Rochester, N.Y., 4/19/1930
O'Brien, Edmond (actor); New York City **(1915-1985)**
O'Brien, Margaret (Angela Maxine O'Brien) (actress); San Diego, Calif., 1/15/1937
O'Brien, Pat (William Joseph O'Brien, Jr.) (actor); Milwaukee, **(1899-1983)**
O'Casey, Sean (playwright); Dublin **(1881-1964)**
Ochs, Adolph Simon (publisher); Cincinnati **(1858-1935)**
O'Connor, Carroll (actor); New York City, 8/2/1924
O'Connor, Donald (actor); Chicago, 8/28/1925
Odets, Clifford (playwright); Philadelphia **(1906-1963)**
Odetta (Odetta Holmes) (folk singer and actress); Birmingham, Ala., 12/31/1930
Offenbach, Jacques (composer); Cologne, Germany **(1819-1880)**
O'Hara, John (novelist); Pottsville, Pa. **(1905-1970)**
O'Hara, Maureen (Maureen FitzSimons) (actress); Dublin, 8/17/1921
Ohlsson, Garrick (pianist); Bronxville, N.Y., 4/3/1948
Ohrbach, Jerry (actor-singer); Bronx, N.Y., 10/20/1935
Oistrakh, David (concert violinist); Odessa, Russia **(1908-1974)**
O'Keeffe, Georgia (painter); Sun Prairie, Wis. **(1887-1986)**
Oland, Warner (actor); Umea, Sweden **(1880-1938)**
Olav V (King of Norway); Sandringham, England, 7/2/1903
Oldenburg, Claes (painter); Stockholm, Sweden, 1/28/1929
Olivier, Lord (Laurence) (actor); Dorking, England **(1907-1989)**
Olmsted, Frederick Law (landscape architect); Hartford, Conn. **(1822-1903)**
Olsen, Ole (John Sigvard Olsen) (comedian); Peru, Ind. **(1892-1963)**
Omar Khayyam (poet and astronomer); Nishapur (Iran) **(died c. 1123)**
Onassis, Aristotle (shipping executive); Smyrna, Turkey **(1906-1975)**
Onassis, Christina (shipping executive); New York City **(1950-1988)**
Onassis, Jacqueline Kennedy (Jacqueline Bouvier) (President's widow); Southampton, N.Y., 7/28/1929
O'Neal, Ryan (Patrick) (actor); Los Angeles, 4/20/1941
O'Neal, Tatum (actress); Los Angeles, Calif., 11/5/1963
O'Neill, Eugene Gladstone (playwright); New York City **(1888-1953)**
O'Neill, Jennifer (actress); Rio de Janeiro, 2/20/1949
Oppenheimer, J. Robert (nuclear physicist); New York City **(1904-1967)**
Orff, Carl (composer); Munich, Germany **(1895-1982)**
Orlando, Tony (Michael Anthony Orlando Cassavitis) (singer); New York City, 4/3/1944
Ormandy, Eugene (conductor); Budapest **(1899-1985)**
Orozco, José Clemente (painter); Zapotlán, Jalisco, Mexico **(1883-1949)**
Orwell, George (Eric Arthur Blair) (British author); Motihari, India **(1903-1950)**
Osborn, Paul (playwright); Evansville, Ind. **(1901-1988)**
Osborne, John (playwright); London, 12/12/1929
Osler, Sir William (physician); Bondhead, Ontario, Canada **(1849-1919)**
Osmond, Donny (singer); Ogden, Utah, 12/9/1957
Osmond, Marie (singer); Ogden, Utah, 1959
O'Sullivan, Maureen (actress); County Roscommon, Ireland, 5/17/1911
Otis, Elisha (inventor); Halifax, Vt. **(1811-1861)**
O'Toole, Peter (actor); Connemara, Ireland, 8/2/1933
Ovid (Publius Ovidius Naso) (poet); Sulmona (Italy) **(43** B.C.-?A.D. **17)**
Owens, Buck (Alvis Edgar Owens) (singer); Sherman, Tex., 8/12/1929

P

Paar, Jack (TV personality); Canton, Ohio, 5/1/1918

Pacino, Al (Alfred) (actor); New York City, 4/25/1940

Packard, Vance (author); Granville Summit, Pa., 5/22/1914

Paderewski, Ignace Jan (pianist and statesman); Kurylowka, Russian Podolia (1860-1941)

Paganini, Nicolò (violinist); Genoa (Italy) (1782-1840)

Page, Geraldine (actress); Kirksville, Mo. (1924-1987)

Page, Patti (Clara Ann Fowler) (singer and entertainer); Claremore, Okla., 11/8/1927

Paige, Janis (actress); Tacoma, Wash., 9/16/1922

Paine, Thomas (political philosopher); Thetford, England (1737-1809)

Palance, Jack (Walter Palanuik) (actor); Lattimer, Pa., 2/18/1920

Palestrina, Giovanni Pierluigi da (composer); Palestrina, Italy (1526-1594)

Paley, William S. (broadcasting executive); Chicago, 9/28/1901

Palladio, Andrea (architect); Padua or Vicenza (Italy) (1508-1580)

Palmer, Betsy (actress); East Chicago, Ind., 1929

Palmer, Lilli (Lilli Peiser) (actress); Posen (Germany) (1914-1986)

Palmerston, Henry John Templeton (3rd Viscount) (statesman); Broadlands, England (1784-1865)

Papanicolaou, George N. (physician); Coumi, Greece (1883-1962)

Papas, Irene (actress); Chiliomodion, Greece, 1929

Papp, Joseph (Joseph Papirofsky) (stage producer and director); Brooklyn, N.Y., 6/22/1921

Paracelsus, Philippus (Aureolus Theophrastus Bombastus von Hohenheim) (physican); Einsiedeln, Switzerland (1493-1541)

Park, Chung Hee (President of South Korea); Sangmo-ri, Korea (1917-1979)

Parker, Dorothy (Dorothy Rothschild) (author); West End, N.J. (1893-1967)

Parker, Eleanor (actress); Cedarville, Ohio, 6/26/1922

Parker, Fess (actor); Fort Worth, Tex., 1925

Parker, Suzy (model and actress); San Antonio, 10/28/1933

Parkinson, C(yril) Northcote (historian); Durham, England, 7/30/1909

Parks, Bert (Bert Jacobson) (entertainer); Atlanta, 12/30/1914

Parks, Gordon (film director); Ft. Scott, Kan., 11/30/1912

Parnell, Charles Stewart (statesman); Avondale, Ireland (1846-1891)

Parnis, Mollie (Mollie Parnis Livingston) (fashion designer); New York City, 3/18/1905

Parsons, Estelle (actress); Marblehead, Mass., 11/20/1927

Parton, Dolly (singer); Locust Ridge, Tenn. 1/19/1946

Pascal, Blaise (philosopher); Clermont, France (1623-1662)

Pasternak, Boris Leonidovich (author); Moscow (1890-1960)

Pasternak, Joseph (film producer); Silagy-Somlyo, Romania, 9/19/1901

Pasteur, Louis (chemist); Dôle, France (1822-1895)

Paton, Alan (author); Pietermaritzburg, South Africa (1903-1988)

Patton, George Smith, Jr. (general); San Gabriel, Calif., (1885-1945)

Paul, Les (Lester William Polfus) (guitarist); Waukesha, Wis., 6/9/1915

Paul VI (Giovanni Battista Montini) (Pope); Concesio, nr. Brescia, Italy (1897-1978)

Pauley, Jane (TV newscaster); Indianapolis, 10/31/1950

Pauling, Linus Carl (chemist); Portland, Ore., 2/28/1901

Pavarotti, Luciano (tenor); Modena, Italy, 10/12/1935

Pavlov, Ivan Petrovich (physiologist); Ryazan district, Russia (1849-1936)

Pavlova, Anna (ballerina); St. Petersburg, Russia (1885-1931)

Payne, John (actor); Roanoke, Va., 1912

Peale, Norman Vincent (clergyman); Bowersville, Ohio, 5/31/1898

Pearl, Minnie (Sarah Ophelia Colley Cannon) (comedienne and singer); Centerville, Tenn., 10/25/1912

Pears, Peter (tenor); Farnham, England (1910-1986)

Pearson, Drew (Andrew Russel Pearson) (columnist); Evanston, Ill. (1897-1969)

Pearson, Lester B. (statesman); Toronto (1897-1972)

Peary, Robert Edwin (explorer); Cresson, Pa. (1856-1920)

Peck, Gregory (actor); La Jolla, Calif., 4/5/1916

Peckinpah, Sam (film director); Fresno, Calif. (1925-1984)

Peerce, Jan (tenor); New York City (1904-1984)

Pegler, (James) Westbrook (columnist); Minneapolis, (1894-1969)

Pei, I(eoh) M(ing) (architect); Canton, China, 4/26/1917

Penn, Arthur (stage and film director); Philadelphia, 9/27/1922

Penn, William (American colonist); London (1644-1718)

Penney, James C. (merchant); Hamilton, Mo. (1875-1971)

Peppard, George (actor); Detroit, 10/1/1928

Pepys, Samuel (diarist); Bampton, England (1633-1703)

Perelman, S(idney) J(oseph) (writer); Brooklyn, N.Y. (1904-1979)

Pergolesi, Giovanni Battista (composer); Jesi, Italy (1710-1736)

Pericles (statesman); Athens (died 429 B.C.)

Perkins, Osgood (actor); West Newton, Mass. (1892-1937)

Perkins, Tony (Anthony) (actor); New York City, 4/14/1932

Perlman, Itzhak (violinist); Tel Aviv, Israel, 8/31/1945

Perón, Isabel (María Estela Martínez Cartas) (former chief of state); La Rioja, Argentina, 2/4/1931

Perón, Juan D. (statesman); nr. Lobos, Argentina (1895-1974)

Perón, Maria Eva Duarte de (political leader); Los Toldos, Argentina (1919-1952)

Perrine, Valerie (actress and dancer); Galveston, Tex., 9/3/1943

Pershing, John Joseph (general); Linn County, Mo. (1860-1948)

Pestalozzi, Johann (educator); Zurich, Switzerland (1746-1827)

Peters, Bernadette (Bernadette Lazzara) (actress); New York City, 2/28/1944

Peters, Brock (actor-singer); New York City, 7/2/1927

Peters, Jean (actress); Canton, Ohio, 10/15/1926

Peters, Roberta (Roberta Peterman) (soprano); New York City, 5/4/1930

Petit, Roland (choreographer and dancer); Villemombe, France, 1924

Petrarch (Francesco Petrarca) (poet); Arezzo (Italy) (1304-1374)

Philip (Philip Mountbatten) (Duke of Edinburgh); Corfu, Greece, 6/10/1921

Piaf, Edith (Edith Gassion) (chanteuse); Paris (1916-1963)

Piatigorsky, Gregor (cellist); Ekaterinoslav, Russia (1903-1976)

Piazza, Ben (actor); Little Rock, Ark., 7/30/1934

Piazza, Marguerite (soprano); New Orleans, 5/6/1926

Picasso, Pablo (painter and sculptor); Málaga, Spain (1881-1973)

Pickford, Jack (Jack Smith) (actor); Toronto (1896-1933)

Pickford, Mary (Gladys Mary Smith) (actress); Toronto (1893-1979)

Picon, Molly (actress); New York City, 6/1/1898

Pidgeon, Walter (actor); East St. John, New Brunswick, Canada (1898-1984)

Pinter, Harold (playwright); London, 10/10/1930

Pinza, Ezio (basso); Rome (1892-1957)

Pirandello, Luigi (dramatist and novelist); nr. Girgenti, Italy (1867-1936)

Piranesi, Giambattista (artist); Mestre, Italy (1720-1778)

Pissaro, Camille Jacob (painter); St. Thomas (U.S. Virgin Islands) (1830-1903)

Piston, Walter (composer); Rockland, Me. (1894-1976)

Pitman, Sir (Isaac) James (educator and publisher); Bath, England, 8/14/1901

Pitt, William ("Younger Pitt") (statesman); nr. Bromley, England (1759-1806)

Pitts, ZaSu (actress); Parsons, Kan. (1898-1963)

Pius XII (Eugenio Pacelli) (Pope); Rome (1876-1958)

Pizarro, Francisco (explorer); Trujillo, Spain (1470?-1541)

Planck, Max (physicist); Kiel, Germany (1858-1947)

Plato (Aristocles) (philosopher); Athens (?) (427?-347 B.C.)

Pleasence, Donald (actor); Worksop, England, 10/5/1919

Pleshette, Suzanne (actress); New York City, 1/31/1937

Plimpton, George (author); New York City, 3/18/1927

Plisetskaya, Maya (ballerina); Moscow, 11/20/1925

Plowright, Joan (actress); Brigg, England, 10/28/1929

Plummer, Christopher (actor); Toronto, 12/13/1929

Plutarch (biographer); Chaeronea (Greece) (46?-?120)

Pocahontas (Matoaka) (American Indian princess); Virginia (?) (1595?-1617)

Podhoretz, Norman (author); Brooklyn, N.Y., 1/16/1930

Poe, Edgar Allan (poet and story writer); Boston, Mass. (1809-1849)

Poitier, Sidney (film actor and director); Miami, Fla., 2/20/1927

Polanski, Roman (film director); Paris, 8/18/1933

Pollard, Michael J. (actor); Passaic, N.J., 5/30/1939

Pollock, Jackson (painter); Cody, Wyo. (1912-1956)

Polo, Marco (traveler); Venice (1254?-?1324)

Pompadour, Mme. de (Jeanne Antoinette Poisson) (courtesan); Versailles (1721-1764)

Pompey (Gnaeus Pompeius Magnus) (general); Rome (?) (106-48 B.C.)

Ponce de León, Juan (explorer); Servas, Spain (1460?-1521)

Pons, Lily (coloratura soprano); Cannes, France (1904-1976)

Ponti, Carlo (director); Milan, Italy, 12/11/1913

Pope, Alexander (poet); London (1688-1744)

Porter, Cole (songwriter); Peru, Ind. (1892?-1964)

Porter, Katherine Anne (novelist); Indian Creek, Tex. (1891-1980)

Post, Wiley (aviator); Grand Plain, Tex. (1900-1935)

Poston, Tom (actor); Columbus, Ohio, 10/17/1927

Potëmkin, Grigori Aleksandrovich, Prince (statesman); Khizovo (Khizov, Belorussia, U.S.S.R.) (1739-1791)

Potok, Chaim (author); New York City, 2/17/1929

Poulenc, Francis (composer); Paris (1899-1963)

Pound, Ezra (poet); Hailey, Idaho (1885-1972)

Poussin, Nicolas (painter); Villers, France (1594-1665)

Powell, Adam Clayton, Jr. (Congressman); New Haven, Conn. (1908-1972)

Powell, Dick (actor); Mt. View, Ark. (1904-1963)

Powell, Eleanor (actress and tap dancer); Springfield, Mass. **(1912-1982)**
Powell, Jane (Suzanne Burce) (actress and singer); Portland, Ore., 4/1/1929
Powell, William (actor); Pittsburgh, **(1892-1984)**
Power, Tyrone (actor); Cincinnati, Ohio **(1914-1958)**
Powers, Stephanie (Taffy Paul) (actress); Hollywood, Calif., 11/12/1942
Praxiteles (sculptor); Athens **(c.370-c.330** B.C.)
Preminger, Otto (film director and producer); Vienna **(1906-1986)**
Prentiss, Paula (Paula Ragusa) (actress); San Antonio, 1939
Presley, Elvis (singer and actor); Tupelo, Miss. **(1935-1977)**
Preston, Robert (Robert Preston Meservey) (actor); Newton Highlands, Mass **(1918-1987)**
Previn, André (conductor); Berlin, 4/6/1929
Previn, Dory (singer); Rahway, N.J., 10/22/1929(?)
Price, Leontyne (Mary) (soprano); Laurel, Miss., 2/10/1927
Price, Ray (country music artist); Perryville, Tex., 1/12/1926
Price, Vincent (actor); St. Louis, 5/27/1911
Pride, Charley (singer); Sledge, Miss., 3/18/1938(?)
Priestley, J. B. (John B.) (author); Bradford, England **(1894-1984)**
Priestley, Joseph (chemist); nr. Leeds, England **(1733-1804)**
Primrose, William (violist); Glasgow, Scotland **(1904-1982)**
Prince (Prince Roger Nelson) (singer); Minneapolis, 6/7/58
Prince, Harold (stage producer); New York City, 1/30/1928
Prinze, Freddie (actor); New York City **(1954-1977)**
Pritchett, V(ictor) S(awdon) (literary critic); Ipswich, England, 12/16/1900
Procter, William (scientist); Cincinnati **(1872-1951)**
Prokofiev, Sergei Sergeevich (composer); St. Petersburg, Russia **(1891-1953)**
Proust, Marcel (novelist); Paris **(1871-1922)**
Provine, Dorothy (actress); Deadwood, S. Dak., 1/20/1937
Prowse, Juliet (actress); Bombay, 9/25/1936
Pryor, Richard (comedian); Peoria, Ill., 12/1/1940
Ptolemy (Claudius Ptolemaeus) (astronomer and geographer); Ptolemais Hermii (Egypt) **(2nd century** A.D.)
Pucci, Emilio (Marchese di Barsento) (fashion designer); Naples, Italy, 11/20/1914
Puccini, Giacomo (composer); Lucca, Italy **(1858-1924)**
Puente, Tito (band leader); New York City, 4/20/1923
Pulaski, Casimir (military officer); Podolia, Poland **(1748-1779)**
Pulitzer, Joseph (publisher); Makó (Hungary) **(1847-1911)**
Pullman, George (inventor); Brockton, N.Y. **(1831-1897)**
Purcell, Henry (composer); London **(1658-1695)**
Pusey, Nathan M. (educator); Council Bluffs, Iowa, 4/4/1907
Pushkin, Alexander Sergeevich (poet and dramatist); Moscow **(1799-1837)**
Puzo, Mario (novelist); New York City, 10/15/1921
Pyle, Ernest Taylor (journalist); Dana, Ind. **(1900-1945)**
Pythagoras (mathematician and philosopher); Samos (Greece) **(6th century** B.C.)

Q

Quayle, Anthony (actor); Ainsdale, England, 9/7/1913
Queen, Ellery: pen name of the late Frederic Dannay and the late Manfred B. Lee
Queler, Eve (conductor); New York City, 1/1/1936
Quennell, Peter Courtney (biographer); Bromley, England, 3/9/1905
Quinn, Anthony (actor); Chihuahua, Mexico, 4/21/1916

R

Rabe, David (playwright); Dubuque, Iowa, 3/10/1940
Rabelais, François (satirist); nr. Chinon, France **(1494?-1553)**
Rabi, I(sidor) I(saac) (physicist); Rymanow (Poland) **(1898-1988)**
Rachmaninoff, Sergei Wassilievitch (pianist and composer); Oneg Estate, Novgorod, Russia **(1873-1943)**
Racine, Jean Baptiste (dramatist); La Ferté-Milon, France **(1639-1699)**
Radner, Gilda (comedienne); Detroit **(1946-1989)**
Raft, George (actor); New York City **(1895-1980)**
Rainer, Luise (actress); Vienna, 1912
Raines, Ella (actress); Snoqualmie Falls, Wash. **(1921-1988)**
Rainier III (Prince); Monaco, 5/31/1923
Rains, Claude (actor); London **(1889-1967)**
Raitt, Bonnie (singer); Burbank, Calif., 11/8/1949
Raleigh, Sir Walter (courtier and navigator); London **(1552?-1618)**
Rameau, Jean-Philippe (composer); Dijon? France **(1683-1764)**
Randall, Tony (Leonard Rosenberg) (actor); Tulsa, Okla., 2/26/1920
Randolph, A(sa) Philip (labor leader); Crescent City, Fla. **(1889-1979)**
Raphael (Raffaello Santi) (painter and architect); Urbino (Italy) **(1483-**

1520)
Rasputin, Grigori Efimovich (monk); Tobolsk Province, Russia **(1871?-1916)**
Rathbone, Basil (actor); Johannesburg, South Africa **(1892-1967)**
Rather, Dan (TV newscaster); Wharton, Tex., 10/31/1931
Ratoff, Gregory (film director); St. Petersburg, Russia **(1897-1960)**
Rattigan, Terence (playwright); London **(1911-1977)**
Rauschenberg, Robert (painter); Port Arthur, Tex., 10/22/1925
Ravel, Maurice Joseph (composer); Ciboure, France **(1875-1937)**
Rawls, Lou (singer); Chicago, 12/1/1935
Ray, Man (painter); Philadelphia **(1890-1976)**
Ray, Satyajat (film director); Calcutta, 5/2/1922
Rayburn, Gene (TV personality); Christopher, Ill., 12/22/1917
Raye, Martha (Margie Yvonne Reed) (comedienne and actress); Butte, Mont., 8/27/1916
Raymond, Gene (actor); New York City, 8/13/1908
Reasoner, Harry (TV commentator); Dakota City, Iowa, 4/17/1923
Redding, Otis (singer); Dawson, Ga. **(1941-1967)**
Reddy, Helen (singer); Melbourne, 10/25/1941
Redford, Robert (Charles Robert Redford, Jr.) (actor); Santa Monica, Calif., 8/18/1937
Redgrave, Lynn (actress); London, 3/8/1943
Redgrave, Sir Michael (actor); Bristol, England **(1908-1985)**
Redgrave, Vanessa (actress); London, 1/30/1937
Reed, Donna (actress); Denison, Iowa **(1921-1986)**
Reed, Rex (critic); Ft. Worth, 10/2/1940
Reed, Walter (army surgeon); Belroi, Va. **(1851-1902)**
Reese, Della (Deloreese Patricia Early) (singer); Detroit, 7/6/1932
Reeves, Jim (singer); Panola County, Tex. **(1923-1964)**
Reich, Steve (composer); New York City, 10/3/1936
Reid, Wallace (actor); St. Louis **(1891-1923)**
Reiner, Carl (actor); New York City, 3/20/1922
Reiner, Fritz (conductor); Budapest **(1888-1963)**
Reiner, Robert (actor); Bronx, N.Y., 1945
Reinhardt, Max (Max Goldmann) (theater producer); nr. Vienna **(1873-1943)**
Remarque, Erich Maria (novelist); Osnabrük, Germany **(1898-1970)**
Rembrandt (Rembrandt Harmensz van Rijn) (painter); Leyden (Netherlands) **(1605-1669)**
Remick, Lee (Ann) (actress); Boston, 12/14/1935
Rennert, Günther (opera director and producer); Essen, Germany, 4/1/1911
Rennie, Michael (actor); Bradford, England **(1909-1971)**
Renoir, Jean (film director and writer); Paris, **(1894-1979)**
Renoir, Pierre Auguste (painter); Limoges, France **(1841-1919)**
Resnais, Alain (film director); Vannes, France, 6/3/1922
Resnik, Regina (mezzo-soprano); New York City, 8/30/1922
Respighi, Ottorino (composer); Bologna, Italy **(1879-1936)**
Reston, James (journalist); Clydebank, Scotland, 11/3/1909
Reuther, Walter (labor leader); Wheeling, W. Va. **(1907-1970)**
Revere, Paul (silversmith and hero of famous ride); Boston **(1735-1818)**
Revson, Charles (business executive); Boston **(1906-1975)**
Reynolds, Burt (actor); Waycross, Ga., 2/11/1936
Renolds, Debbie (Marie Frances Reynolds) (actress); El Paso, 4/1/1932
Reynolds, Sir Joshua (painter); nr. Plymouth, England **(1723-1792)**
Rhodes, Cecil John (South African statesman); Bishop Stortford, England **(1853-1902)**
Rice, Elmer (playwright); New York City **(1892-1967)**
Rice, Grantland (sports writer); Murfreesboro, Tenn. **(1880-1954)**
Rich, Buddy (Bernard) (drummer); Brooklyn, N.Y. **(1917-1987)**
Rich, Charlie (singer); Colt, Ark., 12/14/1932
Richardson, Elliot L. (ex-Cabinet member); Boston, 7/20/1920
Richardson, Sir Ralph (actor); Cheltenham, England **(1902-1983)**
Richardson, Tony (director); Shipley, England, 6/5/1928
Richelieu, Duc de (Armand Jean du Plessis) (cardinal); Paris **(1585-1642)**
Richie, Lionel (singer-songwriter); Tuskegee, Ala., 1949 (?)
Richter, Charles Francis (seismologist); Hamilton, Canada **(1900-1985)**
Richter, Sviatosiav (pianist); Zhitomir, Ukraine, 3/20/1914
Rickenbacker, Edward V. (aviator); Columbus, Ohio **(1890-1973)**
Rickles, Don (comedian); New York City, 5/8/1926
Rickover, Vice Admiral Hyman G. (atomic energy expert); Russia **(1900-1986)**
Riddle, Nelson (composer); Hackensack, N.J. **(1921-1985)**
Ride, Sally K(risten) (astronaut, astrophysicist); Encino, Calif., 5/26/1951
Ridgway, General Matthew B. (ex-Army Chief of Staff); Ft. Monroe, Va., 3/3/1895
Rigg, Diana (actress); Doncaster, England, 7/20/1938
Riley, James Whitcomb (poet); Greenfield, Ind. **(1849-1916)**
Rimsky-Korsakov, Nikolai Andreevich (composer); Tikhvin, Russia **(1844-1908)**
Rinehart, Mary (née Roberts) (novelist); Pittsburgh **(1876-1958)**

Ritchard, Cyril (actor and director); Sydney, Australia (1898-1977)
Ritter, John (Jonathan) (actor); Burbank, Calif., 9/17/1948
Ritter, Tex (Woodward Maurice Ritter) (singer); Panola County, Tex., (1905-1973)
Rivera, Chita (Dolores Figuero del Rivero) (dancer-actress-singer); Washington, D.C. 1/23/1933
Rivera, Diego (painter); Guanajuato, Mexico (1886-1957)
Rivera, Geraldo (Miguel) (TV newscaster); New York City, 7/3/1943
Rivers, Joan (comedienne); Brooklyn, N.Y., 6/8/1933
Rivers, Larry (Yitzroch Loiza Grossberg) (painter); New York City, 8/17/1923
Robards, Jason, Jr. (actor); Chicago, 7/26/1922
Robards, Jason, Sr. (actor); Hillsdale, Mich. (1892-1963)
Robbins, Harold (Harold Rubin) (novelist); New York City, 5/21/1916
Robbins, Jerome (Jerome Rabinowitz) (choreographer); New York City, 10/11/1918
Robbins, Marty (singer); Glendale, Ariz., (1925-1982)
Roberts, (Granville) Oral (evangelist and publisher); nr. Ada, Okla., 1/24/1918
Robertson, Cliff (actor); La Jolla, Calif., 9/9/1925
Robertson, Dale (Dayle) (actor); Oklahoma City, 7/14/1923
Robeson, Paul (singer and actor); Princeton, N.J., (1898-1976)
Robespierre, Maximilien François Marie Isidore de (French Revolutionist); Arras, France (1758-1794)
Robinson, Bill "Bojangles" (Luther) (dancer); Richmond, Va. (1878-1949)
Robinson, Edward G. (Emanuel Goldenberg) (actor); Bucharest (1893-1973)
Robinson, Edwin Arlington (poet); Head Tide, Me. (1869-1935)
Robson, Dame Flora (actress); South Shields, England (1902-1984)
Rochester (Eddie Anderson) (actor); Oakland, Calif. (1905-1977)
Rockefeller, David (banker); New York City, 6/12/1915
Rockefeller, John Davison (capitalist); Richford, N.Y. (1839-1937)
Rockefeller, John Davison, Jr. (industrialist); Cleveland (1874-1960)
Rockefeller, John D., 3rd (philanthropist); New York City (1906-1978)
Rockefeller, Laurance S. (conservationist); New York City, 5/26/1910
Rockwell, Norman (painter and illustrator); New York City, (1894-1978)
Rodgers, Jimmie (singer); Meridian, Miss. (1897-1933)
Rodgers, Richard (composer); New York City (1902-1979)
Rodin, François Auguste René (sculptor); Paris (1840-1917)
Roentgen, Wilhelm Konrad (physicist); Lennep, Prussia (1845-1923)
Rogers, Buddy (Charles) (actor); Olathe, Kan., 8/13/1904
Rogers, Ginger (Virginia McMath) (dancer and actress); Independence, Mo., 7/16/1911
Rogers, Kenny (singer); Houston, 1939(?)
Rogers, Roy (Leonard Slye) (actor); Cincinnati, 11/5/1912
Rogers, Will (William Penn Adair Rogers) (humorist); Oologah, Okla. (1879-1935)
Rogers, William P. (ex-Secretary of State); Norfolk, N.Y., 6/23/1913
Roland, Gilbert (actor); Juarez, Mexico, 12/11/1905
Rolland, Romain (author); Clamecy, France (1866-1944)
Rollins, Sonny (saxophonist); New York City, 9/7/1930
Romberg, Sigmund (composer); Szeged (Hungary) (1887-1951)
Rome, Harold (composer); Hartford, Conn., 5/27/1908
Romero, Cesar (actor); New York City, 2/15/1907
Romney, George W. (ex-Secretary of HUD); Chihuahua, Mexico, 7/8/1907
Romulo, Carlos P. (diplomat and educator); Manila (1899-1985)
Ronsard, Pierre de (poet); La Possonniere nr. Couture (Couture-sur-Loir, France) (1524-1585)
Ronstadt, Linda (singer); Tucson, Ariz., 7/30/1946
Rooney, Andy (TV personality); Albany, N.Y., 1/14/1919
Rooney, Mickey (Joe Yule, Jr.) (actor); Brooklyn, N.Y., 9/23/1920
Roosevelt, Anna Eleanor (reformer and humanitarian); New York City (1884-1962)
Rorem, Ned (composer); Richmond, Ind., 10/23/23
Rose, Billy (showman); New York City (1899-1966)
Rose, Leonard (concert cellist); Washington, D.C. (1918-1984)
Ross, Betsy (Betsey Griscom) (flagmaker); Philadelphia (1752-1836)
Ross, Diana (singer); Detroit, 3/26/1944
Ross, Katharine (actress); Hollywood, Calif., 1/29/1943
Rossellini, Isabella (model, actress); Rome, Italy, 6/18/1952
Rossellini, Roberto (film director); Rome (1906-1977)
Rossetti, Dante Gabriel (painter and poet); London (1828-1882)
Rossini, Gioacchino Antonio (composer); Pesaro (Italy) (1792-1868)
Rostand, Edmond (dramatist); Marseilles, France (1868-1918)
Rostow, Walt Whitman (economist); New York City, 10/7/1916
Rostropovich, Mstislav (cellist and conductor); Baku, U.S.S.R., 3/27/1927
Roth, Lillian (singer); Boston (1910-1980)
Roth, Philip (novelist); Newark, N.J., 3/19/1933
Rothko, Mark (Marcus Rothkovich) (painter); Russia (1903-1970)
Rouault, Georges (painter); Paris (1871-1958)

Roundtree, Richard (actor); New Rochelle, N.Y., 9/7/1942
Rousseau, Henri (painter); Laval, France (1844-1910)
Rousseau, Jean Jacques (philosopher); Geneva (1712-1778)
Rovere, Richard H. (journalist); Jersey City, N.J., 5/5/1915
Rowan, Dan (comedian); Beggs, Okla. (1922-1987)
Rowlands, Gena (actress); Cambria, Wis., 6/19/1936(?)
Rubens, Sir Peter Paul (painter); Siegen (Germany) (1577-1640)
Rubinstein, Arthur (concert pianist); Lódz (Poland) (1887-1982)
Rubinstein, Helena (cosmetics executive); Krakow (Poland) (1882?-1965)
Rudel, Julius (conductor); Vienna, 3/6/1921
Ruggles, Charles (actor); Los Angeles (1892-1970)
Rule, Janice (actress); Norwood, Ohio, 8/15/1931
Runcie, Robert (Alexander Kennedy) (Archbishop of Canterbury); Liverpool, England, 10/2/1921
Runyon, (Alfred) Damon (journalist); Manhattan, Kan. (1884-1945)
Rusk, Dean (ex-Sec. of State); Cherokee County, Ga., 2/9/1909
Ruskin, John (art critic); London (1819-1900)
Russell, Lord Bertrand (Arthur William) (mathematician and philosopher); Trelleck, Wales (1872-1970)
Russell, Jane (actress); Bemidji, Minn., 6/21/1921
Russell, Leon (pianist and singer); Lawton, Okla., 4/2/1941
Russell, Lillian (Helen Louise Leonard) (soprano); Clinton, Iowa (1861-1922)
Russell, Nipsy (comedian); Atlanta, 1924(?)
Russell, Rosalind (actress); Waterbury, Conn. (1912-1976)
Rustin, Bayard (civil rights leader); West Chester, Pa. (1910-1987)
Rutherford, Dame Margaret (actress); London (1892-1972)
Ryan, Robert (actor); Chicago (1909-1973)
Rydell, Bobby (singer); Philadelphia, 1942
Rysanek, Leonie (dramatic soprano); Vienna, 11/14/1928

S

Saarinen, Eero (architect); Finland (1910-1961)
Sabin, Albert B. (polio researcher); Bialystok (Poland), 8/26/1906
Sadat, Anwar el- (President); Egypt (1918-1981)
Sade, Marquis de (Donatien Alphonse Francois, Comte de Sade) (libertine and writer); Paris (1740-1814)
Safer, Morley (TV newscaster); Toronto, 11/8/1931
Sagan, Carl (Edward) (astronomer, astrophysicist); New York City, 11/9/1934
Sagan, Francoise (novelist); Cajarc, France, 6/21/1935
Sahl, Mort (Morton Lyon Sahl) (comedian); Montreal, 5/11/1927
Saint, Eva Marie (actress); Newark, N.J., 7/4/1924
Saint-Gaudens, Augustus (sculptor); Dublin (1848-1907)
St. James, Susan (Susan Miller) (actress); Los Angeles, 8/14/1946
St. John, Jill (actress); Los Angeles, 8/19/1940
St. Johns, Adela Rogers (journalist and author); Los Angeles (1894-1988)
Saint-Laurent, Yves (Henri Donat Mathieu) (fashion designer); Oran, Algeria, 8/1/1936
Saint-Saens, Charles Camille (composer); Paris (1835-1921)
Sainte-Marie, Buffy (Beverly) (folk singer); Craven, Saskatchewan, Canada, 2/20/1942(?)
Salinger, J(erome) D(avid) (novelist); New York City, 1/1/1919
Salisbury, Harrison L. (journalist); Minneapolis, 11/14/1908
Salk, Jonas (polio researcher); New York City, 10/28/1914
Salk, Leo (psychologist); New York City, 1926
Salomon, Haym (American Revolution financier); Leszno, Poland (1740-1785)
Sand, George (Amandine Lucille Aurore Dudevant, née Dupin) (novelist); Paris (1804-1876)
Sandburg, Carl (poet and biographer); Galesburg, Ill. (1878-1967)
Sanders, George (actor); St. Petersburg, Russia (1906-1972)
Sands, Tommy (singer); Chicago, 8/27/1937
Sanger, Margaret (birth control leader); Corning, N.Y. (1883-1966)
Santayana, George (philosopher); Madrid (1863-1952)
Sappho (poet); Lesbos (Greece) (lived c. 600 B.C.)
Sargent, John Singer (painter); Florence, Italy (1856-1925)
Sarnoff, David (radio executive); Minsk, Russia (1891-1971)
Saroyan, William (novelist); Fresno, Calif. (1908-1981)
Sarrazin, Michael (actor); Quebec, 5/22/1940
Sarto, Andrea del (Andrea Domenico d'Agnolo di Francesco) (painter); Florence (Italy) (1486-1531)
Sartre, Jean-Paul (existentialist writer); Paris (1905-1980)
Sassoon, Vidal (hair stylist); London, 1/(?)/1928
Saul (King of Israel) (11th century B.C.)
Savalas, Telly (Aristoteles) (actor); Garden City, N.Y., 1/21/1924(?)
Savonarola, Girolamo (religious reformer); Ferrara, Italy (1452-1498)
Sayão, Bidú (soprano); Rio de Janeiro, 5/11/1902
Scaasi, Arnold (Arnold Isaacs) (fashion designer); Montreal
Scarlatti, Alessandro (composer); Palermo, Italy (1659-1725)

Scarlatti, Domenico (composer); Naples, Italy **(1685-1757)**
Scavullo, Francesco (photographer); Staten Island, N.Y. 1/16/1929
Schary, Dore (producer and writer); Newark, N.J. **(1905-1980)**
Schell, Maria (actress); Vienna, 1/15/1926
Schell, Maximilian (actor); Vienna, 12/8/1930
Schiaparelli, Elsa (fashion designer); Rome **(1890?-1973)**
Schiff, Dorothy (newspaper publisher); New York City, 3/11/1903
Schildkraut, Joseph (actor); Vienna **(1896-1964)**
Schiller, Johann Christoph Friedrich von (dramatist and poet); Marbach (Germany) **(1759-1805)**
Schippers, Thomas (conductor); Kalamazoo, Mich. **(1930-1977)**
Schlegel, Friedrich von (philosopher); Hanover? Germany **(1772-1829)**
Schlesinger, Arthur M., Jr. (historian); Columbus, Ohio, 10/15/1917
Schneider, Romy (Rose-Marie Albach) (actress); Vienna **(1938-1982)**
Schoenberg, Arnold (composer); Vienna **(1874-1951)**
Schopenhauer, Arthur (philosopher); Danzig (Poland) **(1788-1860)**
Schubert, Franz Peter (composer); Vienna **(1797-1828)**
Schulberg, Budd (novelist); New York City, 3/27/1914
Schulz, Charles M. (cartoonist); Minneapolis, 11/26/1922
Schuman, Robert (statesman); Luxembourg **(1886-1963)**
Schuman, William (composer); New York City, 8/4/1910
Schumann, Robert Alexander (composer); Zwickau (East Germany) **(1810-1856)**
Schwartz, Arthur (song writer); Brooklyn, N.Y. **(1900-1984)**
Schwarzkopf, Elisabeth (soprano); Jarotschin, Poznán (Poland), 12/9/1915
Schweitzer, Albert (humanitarian); Kaysersburg, Upper Alsace **(1875-1965)**
Scofield, Paul (actor); Hurstpierpoint, England, 1/21/1922
Scorsese, Martin (film director); Flushing, N.Y., 11/17/1942
Scott, George C. (actor); Wise, Va., 10/18/1927
Scott, Lizabeth (Emma Matso) (actress); Scranton, Pa., 1923
Scott, Martha (actress); Jamesport, Mo., 9/22/1914
Scott, Randolph (Randolph Crane) (actor); Orange County, Va **(1898-1987)**
Scott, Robert Falcon (explorer); Devonport, England **(1868-1912)**
Scott, Sir Walter (novelist); Edinburgh, Scotland **(1771-1832)**
Scott, Zachary (actor); Austin, Tex. **(1914-1965)**
Scotto, Renata (operatic soprano); Savona, Italy, 2/?/1936?
Scruggs, Earl Eugene (bluegrass musician); Cleveland County, N.C., 1/6/1924
Sebastian, John (composer); New York City, 3/17/1944
Seberg, Jean (actress); Marshalltown, Iowa **(1938-1979)**
Sedaka, Neil (singer); Brooklyn, N.Y., 3/13/1939
Seeger, Pete (folk singer); New York City, 5/3/1919
Segal, Erich (novelist); Brooklyn, N.Y., 6/16/1937
Segal, George (actor); New York City, 2/13/1936
Segovia, Andrés (guitarist); Linares, Spain **(1893-1987)**
Selleck, Tom (actor); Detroit, 1/29/1945
Sellars, Peter (theater director); Pittsburgh, Pa., 1958 (?)
Sellers, Peter (actor); Southsea, England **(1925-1980)**
Selznick, David O. (film producer); Pittsburgh **(1902-1965)**
Sendak, Maurice (Bernard) (children's book author and illustrator); Brooklyn, N.Y., 6/10/1928
Sennett, Mack (Michael Sinnott) (film producer); Richmond, Quebec, Canada **(1880-1960)**
Serkin, Peter (pianist); New York City, 7/24/1947
Serkin, Rudolf (pianist); Eger (Hungary), 3/28/1903
Serling, Rod (story writer); Syracuse, N.Y. **(1924-1975)**
Sessions, Roger (composer); Brooklyn, N.Y. **(1896-1985)**
Seurat, Georges (painter); Paris **(1859-1891)**
Seuss, Dr. (Theodor Seuss Geisel) (author and illustrator); Springfield, Mass., 3/2/1904
Sevareid, Eric (TV commentator); Velva, N.D., 11/26/1912
Severinsen, Doc (Carl) (band leader); Arlington, Ore., 7/7/1927
Sexton, Anne (poet); Newton, Mass. **(1928-1974)**
Shaffer, Peter (playwright); Liverpool, England, 5/15/1926
Shahn, Ben(jamin) (painter); Kaunas, Lithuania **(1898-1969)**
Shakespeare, William (dramatist); Stratford on Avon, England **(1564-1616)**
Shandling, Garry (comedian); Chicago, Ill., 1950
Shankar, Ravi (sitar player); Benares, India, 4/7/1920
Shanker, Albert (labor leader); New York City, 9/14/1928
Sharif, Omar (Michael Shalhoub) (actor); Alexandria, Egypt, 4/10/1932
Shatner, William (actor); Montreal, 3/22/1931
Shaw, Artie (Arthur Arshawsky) (band leader); New York City, 5/23/1910
Shaw, George Bernard (dramatist); Dublin, **(1856-1950)**
Shaw, Irwin (novelist); Brooklyn, N.Y. **(1913-1984)**
Shaw, Robert (actor); Lancashire, England **(1927-1978)**
Shaw, Robert (chorale conductor); Red Bluff, Calif., 4/30/1916
Shearer, Moira (ballerina); Dunfermline, Scotland, 1/17/1926
Shearer, Norma (actress); Montreal, **(1902?-1983)**
Shearing, George (pianist); London, 8/13/1920

Sheen, Fulton J. (Peter Sheen) (Roman Catholic bishop); El Paso, Ill. **(1895-1979)**
Sheen, Martin (Ramon Estevez) (actor); Dayton, Ohio, 8/3/1940
Shelley, Percy Bysshe (poet); nr. Horsham, England **(1792-1822)**
Shepard, Sam (playwright); Ft. Sheridan, Ill. 11/5/1943
Sheraton, Thomas (furniture designer); Stockton-on-Tees, England **(1751-1806)**
Sheridan, Ann (actress); Denton, Tex. **(1915-1967)**
Sheridan, Philip (army officer); Albany, N.Y. **(1831-1888)**
Sheridan, Richard Brinsley (dramatist); Dublin, **(1751-1816)**
Sherman, William Tecumseh (army officer); Lancaster, Ohio **(1820-1891)**
Sherwood, Robert Emmet (playwright); New Rochelle, N.Y. **(1896-1955)**
Shevardnadze, Eduard Amvrosiyevich (Minister of Foreign Affairs, U.S.S.R.); Mamati, Georgia, U.S.S.R. 1/25/1928
Shields, Brooke (actress); New York City, 5/31/1965
Shirer, William L. (journalist and historian); Chicago, 2/23/1904
Sholokhov, Mikhail (novelist); Veshenskaya, Russia **(1905-1984)**
Shore, Dinah (Frances Rose Shore) (singer); Winchester, Tenn., 3/1/1917(?)
Short, Bobby (Robert Waltrip Short) (singer and pianist); Danville, Ill., 9/15/1924
Shostakovich, Dmitri (composer); St. Petersburg, Russia **(1906-1975)**
Shriver, Sargent (Robert Sargent Shriver, Jr.) (business executive); Westminster, Md., 11/9/1915
Shulman, Max (novelist); St. Paul **(1919-1988)**
Sibelius, Jean (Johann Julius Christian Sibelius) (composer); Tavastehus (Finland) **(1865-1957)**
Sidney, Sylvia (actress); New York City, 8/8/1910
Siepi, Cesare (basso); Milan, Italy, 2/10/1923
Signoret, Simone (Simone Kaminker) (actress); Wiesbaden, Germany **(1921-1985)**
Sikorsky, Igor I. (inventor); Kiev, Russia **(1889-1972)**
Sills, Beverly (Belle Silverman) (soprano, opera director); Brooklyn, N.Y., 5/25/1929
Silone, Ignazio (Secondo Tranquilli) (novelist); Pescina del Marsi, Italy **(1900-1978)**
Silverman, Fred (broadcasting executive); New York City, 9/13/1937
Silvers, Phil (Philip Silversmith) (comedian); Brooklyn, N.Y. **(1912-1985)**
Sim, Alastair (actor); Edinburgh, Scotland **(1900-1976)**
Simenon, Georges (Georges Sim) (mystery writer); Liège, Belgium, 2/13/1903
Simmons, Jean (actress); Crouch Hill, London, 1/31/1929
Simon, Carly (singer and songwriter); New York City, 6/25/1945
Simon, Neil (playwright); Bronx, N.Y., 7/4/1927
Simon, Norton (business executive); Portland, Ore., 2/5/1907
Simon, Paul (singer and songwriter); Newark, N.J., 11/5/1942
Simone, Nina (Eunice Kathleen Waymoa) (singer and pianist); Tryon, N.C., 2/21/1933
Sinatra, Frank (Francis Albert) (singer and actor); Hoboken, N.J., 12/12/1915
Sinclair, Upton Beall (novelist); Baltimore **(1878-1968)**
Singer, Isaac Bashevis (novelist); Radzymin (Poland), 7/14/1904
Siqueiros, David (painter); Chihuahua, Mexico **(1896-1974)**
Sisley, Alfred (painter); Paris **(1839-1899)**
Sitting Bull (Prairie Sioux Indian Chief); on Grand River, S.D. **(c. 1835-1890)**
Skelton, Red (Richard) (comedian); Vincennes, Ind., 7/18/1913
Skinner, B(urrhus) F(rederic) (psychologist); Susquehanna, Pa., 3/20/1904
Skinner, Cornelia Otis (writer and actress); Chicago, **(1901-1979)**
Skinner, Otis (actor); Cambridge, Mass. **(1858-1942)**
Slatkin, Leonard (conductor); Los Angeles, 9/1/1944
Slezak, Walter (actor); Vienna **(1902-1983)**
Sloan, Alfred P., Jr. (industrialist); New Haven, Conn. **(1875-1965)**
Sloan, John (painter); Lock Haven, Pa. **(1871-1951)**
Smetana, Bedrich (composer); Litomysl (Czechoslovakia) **(1824-1884)**
Smith, Adam (economist); Kirkaldy, Scotland **(1723-1790)**
Smith, Alexis (actress); Penticon, Canada, 6/8/1921
Smith, Alfred Emanuel (politician); New York City **(1873-1944)**
Smith, David (sculptor); Decatur, Ind. **(1906-1965)**
Smith, H. Allen (humorist); McLeansboro, Ill. **(1907-1976)**
Smith, Howard K. (TV commentator); Ferriday, La., 5/12/1914
Smith, John (American colonist); Willoughby, Lincolnshire, England **(1580-1631)**
Smith, Joseph (religious leader); Sharon, Vt. **(1805-1844)**
Smith, Kate (Kathryn) (singer); Greenville, Va. **(1909-1986)**
Smith, Maggie (actress); Ilford, England, 12/28/1934
Smith, Red (Walter) (sports columnist); Green Bay, Wis. **(1905-1982)**
Smollet, Tobias (novelist); Dalquhurn, Scotland **(1721-1771)**
Smothers, Dick (Richard) (comedian); Governors Island, New York City, 11/20/1939

Smothers, Tom (Thomas) (comedian); Governors Island, New York City, 2/2/1937

Snow, Lord (Charles Percy) (author); Leicester, England **(1905-1980)**

Snowdon, Earl of (Anthony Armstrong-Jones) (photographer); London, 3/7/1930

Snyder, Tom (TV personality); Milwaukee, 5/12/1936

Socrates (philosopher); Athens **(469-399** B.C.**)**

Solomon (King of Israel); Jerusalem (?) **(died c. 933** B.C.**)**

Solon (lawgiver); Salamis (Greece) **(638?-559** B.C.**)**

Solti, Sir Georg (conductor); Budapest, 10/21/1912

Solzhenitsyn, Aleksandr (novelist); Kislovodsk, Russia, 12/11/1918

Somers, Suzanne (Suzanne Mahoney) (actress); San Bruno, Calif., 10/16/1946

Sommer, Elke (Elke Schletz) (actress); Berlin, 11/5/1942

Sondheim, Stephen (composer); New York City, 3/22/1930

Sontag, Susan (author and film director); New York City, 1/28/1933

Sophocles (dramatist); nr. Athens **(496?-406** B.C.**)**

Sothern, Ann (Harriette Lake) (actress); Valley City, N.D., 1/22/1909

Sousa, John Philip (composer); Washington, D.C. **(1854-1932)**

Soyer, Raphael (painter); Borisoglebsk, Russia **(1899-1987)**

Spaak, Paul-Henri (statesman); Brussels **(1899-1972)**

Spacek, Sissy (Mary Elizabeth) (actress); Quitman, Tex., 12/25/1949

Spark, Muriel (novelist); Edinburgh, Scotland, 2/1/1918

Spector, Phil (rock producer); Bronx, N.Y., 12/25/1940

Spencer, Herbert (philosopher); Derby, England **(1820-1903)**

Spender, Stephen (poet); nr. London, 2/28/1909

Spengler, Oswald (philosopher); Blankenburg, (East Germany) **(1880-1936)**

Spenser, Edmund (poet); London **(1552?-1599)**

Spewack, Bella (playwright); Hungary, 3/25/1899

Spiegel, Sam (producer); Jaroslaw (Poland) **(1901-1985)**

Spielberg, Steven (film director); Cincinnati, 12/18/1947

Spillane, Mickey (Frank Spillane) (mystery writer); Brooklyn, N.Y., 3/9/1918

Spinoza, Baruch (philosopher); Amsterdam (Netherlands) **(1632-1677)**

Spivak, Lawrence (TV producer); Brooklyn, N.Y., 1900

Spock, Benjamin (pediatrician); New Haven, Conn., 5/2/1903

Springsteen, Bruce (singer and songwriter); Freehold, N.J., 9/23/1949

Sproul, Robert G. (educator); San Francisco **(1891-1975)**

Stack, Robert (actor); Los Angeles, 1/13/1919

Stafford, Jo (singer); Coalinga, Calif., 1918

Stalin, Joseph Vissarionovich (Iosif V. Dzhugashvili) (Soviet leader); nr. Tiflis, Russia **(1879-1953)**

Stalina, Svetlana Alliluyeva (Stalin's daughter); Moscow, 2/28/1926

Stallone, Sylvester (actor and writer); New York City, 7/6/1946

Stamp, Terrence (actor); London, 1938

Stang, Arnold (comedian); Chelsea, Mass., 1925

Stanislavski (Konstantin Sergeevich Alekseev) (stage producer); Moscow **(1863-1938)**

Stanley, Sir Henry Morton (John Rowlands) (explorer); Denbigh, Wales **(1841-1904)**

Stanley, Kim (Patricia Reid) (actress); Tularosa, N.M., 2/11/1925

Stans, Maurice H. (ex-Secretary of Commerce); Shakope, Minn., 3/22/1908

Stanton, Frank (broadcasting executive); Muskegon, Mich., 3/20/1908

Stanwyck, Barbara (Ruby Stevens) (actress); Brooklyn, N.Y., 7/16/1907

Stapleton, Jean (Jeanne Murray) (actress); New York City, 1/19/1923

Stapleton, Maureen (actress); Troy, N.Y., 6/21/1925

Starker, Janós (cellist); Budapest 7/5/1926

Starr, Kay (Starks) (singer); Dougherty, Okla., 7/21/1922

Starr, Ringo (Richard Starkey) (singer and songwriter); Liverpool, England, 7/7/1940

Stassen, Harold E. (ex-government official); West St. Paul, Minn., 4/13/1907

Steegmuller, Francis (biographer); New Haven, Conn., 7/3/1906

Steele, Tommy (singer); London, 12/17/1936

Stegner, Wallace (Earle) (novelist and critic); Lake Mills, Iowa, 2/18/1909

Steichen, Edward Jean (photographer, artist); Luxembourg **(1879-1973)**

Steiger, Rod (Rodney) (actor); Westhampton, N.Y., 4/14/1925

Stein, Gertrude (author); Allegheny, Pa. **(1874-1946)**

Steinbeck, John Ernst (novelist); Salinas, Calif. **(1902-1968)**

Steinberg, David (comedian); Winnipeg, Manitoba, Canada, 8/19/1942

Steinberg, William (conductor); Cologne, Germany **(1899-1978)**

Steinem, Gloria (feminist); Toledo, Ohio, 3/25/1934

Steinmetz, Charles (electrical engineer); Breslau (Poland) **(1865-1923)**

Stendhal (Marie Henri Beyle) (novelist); Grenoble, France **(1783-1842)**

Sterling, Jan (actress); New York City, 4/3/1923

Stern, Isaac (concert violinist); Kreminlecz, Russia, 7/21/1920

Sterne, Laurence (novelist); Clonmel, Ireland **(1713-1768)**

Stevens, Cat (Steven Georgiou) (singer and songwriter); London 7/?/1947

Stevens, Connie (Concetta Ingolia) (singer); Brooklyn, N.Y., 8/8/1938

Stevens, George (film director); Oakland, Calif. **(1905-1975)**

Stevens, Risë (mezzo-soprano); New York City, 6/11/1913

Stevens, Stella (actress); Yazoo City, Miss., 10/1/1936

Stevenson, Adlai Ewing (statesman); Los Angeles **(1900-1965)**

Stevenson, McLean (actor); Bloomington, Ill., 11/14/1929(?)

Stevenson, Robert Louis Balfour (novelist and poet); Edinburgh, Scotland **(1850-1894)**

Stewart, James (actor); Indiana, Pa., 5/20/1908

Stewart, Rod (Roderick David) (singer); London, 1/10/1945

Stickney, Dorothy (actress); Dickinson, N.D. 6/21/1903

Stieglitz, Alfred (photographer); Hoboken, N.J. **(1864-1946)**

Stills, Stephen (singer and songwriter); Dallas, 1/3/1945

Sting (Gordon Matthew Sumner) (singer and composer); Wallsend England, 10/2/1951

Stokes, Carl (TV newscaster); Cleveland, 6/21/1927

Stokowski, Leopold (conductor); London **(1882-1977)**

Stone, Edward Durell (architect); Fayetteville, Ark. **(1902-1978)**

Stone, Ezra (actor and producer); New Bedford, Mass., 12/2/1917

Stone, I(sidor) F(einstein) (journalist); Philadelphia **(1907-1989)**

Stone, Irving (Irving Tennenbaum) (novelist); San Francisco, 7/14/1903

Stone, Lewis (actor); Worcester, Mass. **(1879-1953)**

Stone, Lucy (woman suffragist); nr. West Brookfield, Mass. **(1818-1893)**

Stone, Sly (Sylvester) (rock musician); 1944

Stoppard, Tom (Thomas Straussler) (playwright); Zlin, Czechoslovakia, 7/3/1937

Storm, Gale (actress); Bloomington, Tex., 1922

Stout, Rex (mystery writer); Noblesville, Ind. **(1886-1975)**

Stowe, Harriet Elizabeth Beecher (novelist); Litchfield, Conn. **(1811-1896)**

Stradivari, Antonio (violinmaker); Cremona (Italy) **(1644-1737)**

Strasberg, Lee (stage director); Budanov, Austria **(1901-1982)**

Strasberg, Susan (actress); New York City, 5/22/1938

Straus, Oskar (composer); Vienna **(1870-1954)**

Strauss, Johann (composer); Vienna **(1825-1899)**

Strauss, Lewis L. (naval officer and scientist); Charleston, W. Va. **(1896-1974)**

Strauss, Richard (composer); Munich, Germany **(1864-1949)**

Stravinsky, Igor (composer); Orlenbaum, Russia **(1882-1971)**

Streep, Meryl (Mary Louise) (actress); Summit, N.J., 6/22/1949

Streisand, Barbra (singer and actress); Brooklyn, N.Y., 4/24/1942

Stritch, Elaine (actress); Detroit, 2/2/1925(?)

Struthers, Sally Ann (actress); Portland, Ore., 7/28/1948

Stuart, Gilbert Charles (painter); Rhode Island **(1755-1828)**

Stuart, James Ewell Brown (known as Jeb) (Confederate army officer); Patrick County, Va. **(1833-1864)**

Stuyvesant, Peter (Governor of New Amsterdam); West Friesland (Netherlands) **(1592-1672)**

Styne, Jule (Julius Kerwin Stein) (songwriter); London, 12/31/1905

Styron, William (William Clark Styron, Jr.) (novelist); Newport News, Va., 6/11/1925

Sullavan, Margaret Brooke (actress); Norfolk, Va. **(1911-1960)**

Sullivan, Sir Arthur Seymour (composer); London **(1842-1900)**

Sullivan, Barry (Patrick Barry) (actor); New York City, 8/29/1912

Sullivan, Ed (columnist and TV personality); New York City **(1901-1974)**

Sullivan, Frank (Francis John) (humorist); Saratoga Springs, N.Y. **(1892-1976)**

Sullivan, Louis Henry (architect); Boston, Mass. **(1856-1924)**

Sulzberger, Arthur Ochs (newspaper publisher); New York City, 2/5/1926

Sumac, Yma (singer); Ichocan, Peru, 9/10/1927

Summer, Donna (La Donna Andrea Gaines) (singer); Boston, 12/31/1948

Sun Yat-sen (statesman); nr. Macao **(1866-1925)**

Susann, Jacqueline (novelist); Philadelphia **(1926?-1974)**

Susskind, David (TV producer); New York City **(1920-1987)**

Sutherland, Joan (soprano); Sydney, Australia, 11/7/1926

Suzuki, Pat (actress); Cressey, Calif., 1931

Swados, Elizabeth (composer, playwright); Buffalo, N.Y., 2/5/1951

Swanson, Gloria (Gloria May Josephine Svensson) (actress); Chicago, **(1899-1983)**

Swarthout, Gladys (soprano); Deepwater, Mo. **(1904-1969)**

Swayze, John Cameron (news commentator); Wichita, Kan., 4/4/1906

Swendenborg, Emanuel (scientist, philosopher, mystic); Stockholm **(1688-1772)**

Swift, Jonathan (satirist); Dublin **(1667-1745)**

Swinburne, Algernon Charles (poet); London **(1837-1909)**
Swope, Herbert Bayard (journalist); St. Louis **(1882-1958)**
Sydow, von, Max (Carl Adolf von Sydow) (actor); Lund, Sweden, 4/10/1929
Synge, John Millington (dramatist); nr. Dublin **(1871-1909)**
Szilard, Leo (physicist); Budapest **(1898-1964)**

T

Taft, Robert Alphonso (legislator); Cincinnati **(1889-1953)**
Tagore, Sir Rabindranath (poet); Calcutta **(1861-1941)**
Tallchief, Maria (ballerina); Fairfax, Okla., 1/24/1925
Talleyrand-Périgord, Charles Maurice de (statesman); Paris **(1754-1838)**
Talmadge, Norma (actress); Niagara Falls, N.Y. **(1897-1957)**
Talvela, Martti (basso); Hiitola, Finalnd **(1935-1989)**
Tamerlane (Timur) (Mongol conqueror); nr. Samarkand (U.S.S.R.) **(1336?-1405)**
Tandy, Jessica (actress); London, 6/7/1909
Tarkington, (Newton) Booth (novelist); Indianapolis **(1869-1946)**
Tate, Allen (John Orley) (poet and critic); Winchester, Ky., **(1899-1979)**
Tate, Sharon (actress); Dallas **(1943-1969)**
Tati, Jacques (Jacques Tatischeff) (actor); Pecq, France **(1908-1982)**
Taylor, Elizabeth (actress); London, 2/27/1932
Taylor, Estelle (actress); Wilmington, Del. **(1899-1958)**
Taylor, Harold (educator); Toronto, 9/28/1914
Taylor, James (singer and songwriter); Boston, 3/12/1948
Taylor, (Joseph) Deems (composer); New York City **(1885-1966)**
Taylor, Laurette (Laurette Cooney) (actress); New York City **(1884-1946)**
Taylor, Gen. Maxwell D. (former Army Chief of Staff); Keytesville, Mo **(1901-1987)**
Taylor, Robert (Spangler Arlington Brugh) (actor); Filley, Neb. **(1911-1969)**
Taylor, Rod (actor); Sydney, Australia, 1/11/1930
Tchaikovsky, Peter (Pëtr) Ilich (composer); Votkinsk, Russia **(1840-1893)**
Teasdale, Sara (poet); St. Louis **(1884-1933)**
Tebaldi, Renata (lyric soprano); Pesaro, Italy, 1/2/1922
Tecumseh (Shawnee Indian chief); nr. Springfield, Ohio **(1768?-1813)**
Telemann, Georg Philipp (composer); Magdeburg (East Germany) **(1681-1767)**
Teller, Edward (atomic physicist); Budapest, 1/15/1908
Temple, Shirley. *See* Black, Shirley Temple
Tennyson, Alfred (1st Baron Tennyson) (poet); Somersby, England **(1809-1892)**
Terhune, Albert Payson (novelist and journalist); Newark, N.J. **(1872-1942)**
Terkel, Studs (writer-interviewer); New York City, 5/16/1912
Terry, Ellen Alicia (actress); Coventry, England **(1848-1928)**
Terry-Thomas (Thomas Terry Hoar Stevens) (actor); London, 7/14/1911
Tesla, Nikola (electrical engineer and inventor); Smiljan (Yugoslavia) **(1856-1943)**
Thackeray, William Makepeace (novelist); Calcutta **(1811-1863)**
Thant, U (U.N. statesman); Pantanaw (Burma) **(1909-1974)**
Tharp, Twyla (dancer and choreographer); Portland, Ind., 7/1/1941(?)
Thatcher, Margaret (Prime Minister); Grantham, England, 10/13/1925
Thaxter, Phyllis (actress); Portland, Me., 1921
Thebom, Blanche (mezzo-soprano); Monessen, Pa., 9/19/1919
Theodorakis, Mikis (composer); Chios, Greece, 7/29/1925
Thieu, Nguyen Van (ex-President of South Vietnam); Trithuy (Vietnam) 4/5/1923
Thomas, Danny (Amos Jacobs) (entertainer and TV producer); Deerfield, Mich., 1/6/1914
Thomas, Dylan Marials (poet); Carmarthenshire, Wales **(1914-1953)**
Thomas, Lowell (explorer, commentator); Woodington, Ohio **(1892-1981)**
Thomas, Marlo (actress); Detroit, 11/21/1943
Thomas, Michael Tilson (conductor); Hollywood, Calif., 12/21/1944
Thomas, Norman Mattoon (Socialist leader); Marion, Ohio **(1884-1968)**
Thomas, Richard (actor); New York City, 6/13/1951
Thompson, Dorothy (writer); Lancaster, N.Y. **(1894-1961)**
Thompson, Hunter (Stockton) (writer); Louisville, Ky. 7/18/1939
Thoreau, Henry David (naturalist and author); Concord, Mass. **(1817-1862)**
Thorndike, Dame Sybil (actress); Gainsborough, England **(1882-1976)**
Thurber, James Grover (author and cartoonist); Columbus, Ohio

(1894-1961)
Tibbett, Lawrence (baritone); Bakersfield, Calif. **(1896-1960)**
Tierney, Gene (actress); Brooklyn, N.Y., 11/20/1920
Tiffin, Pamela (actress); Oklahoma City, 10/13/1942
Tillstrom, Burr (puppeteer); Chicago **(1917-1985)**
Tintoretto, Il (Jacopo Robusti) (painter); Venice **(1518-1594)**
Tiny Tim (Herbert Khaury) (entertainer); New York City, 1923(?)
Tiomkin, Dmitri (composer); St. Petersburg, Russia **(1894-1979)**
Titian (Tiziano Vecelli) (painter); Pieve di Cadore (Italy) **(1477-1576)**
Tito (Josip Broz or Brozovich) (President of Yugoslavia); Croatia (Yugoslavia) **(1892-1980)**
Tocqueville, Alexis de (writer); Verneuil, France **(1805-1859)**
Todd, Thelma (actress); Lawrence, Mass. **(1905-1935)**
Tolstoi, Count Leo (Lev) Nikolaevich (novelist); Tula Province, Russia **(1828-1910)**
Tomlin, Lily (comedienne); Detroit, 1939(?)
Tone, Franchot (actor); Niagara Falls, N.Y. **(1905-1968)**
Tormé, Mel (Melvin) (singer); Chicago, 9/13/1925
Torn, Rip (Elmore Torn, Jr.) (actor and director); Temple, Tex., 2/6/1931
Torquamada, Tomás de (Spanish Inquisitor); Valladolid, Spain **(1420-1498)**
Toscanini, Arturo (orchestra conductor); Parma, Italy **(1867-1957)**
Toulouse-Lautrec (Henri Marie Raymond de Toulouse-Lautrec Monfa) (painter); Albi, France **(1864-1901)**
Toynbee, Arnold J. (historian); London **(1889-1975)**
Tracy, Spencer (actor); Milwaukee **(1900-1967)**
Traubel, Helen (Wagnerian soprano); St. Louis **(1903-1972)**
Travolta, John (actor); Englewood, N.J., 2/18/1954
Treacher, Arthur (actor); Brighton, England **(1894-1975)**
Trevor, Claire (actress); New York City, 1911
Trigère, (Pauline (fashion designer); Paris, 11/4/1912
Trilling, Lionel (author and educator); New York City **(1905-1975)**
Trotsky, Leon (Lev Davidovich Bronstein) (statesman); Elisavetgrad, Russia **(1879-1940)**
Trudeau, Garry (cartoonist); New York City, 1948
Trudeau, Pierre Elliott (former Prime Minister); Montreal, 10/18/1919
Truffaut, François (film director); Paris **(1932-1984)**
Trujillo y Molina, Rafael Leonidas (Dominican Republic dictator); San Cristóbal, Dominican Republic **(1891-1961)**
Truman, Margaret (author); Independence, Mo., 2/17/1924
Tryon, Thomas (actor and novelist); Hartford, Conn., 1/14/1926
Tsiolkovsky, Konstantin E. (father of cosmonautics); Izhevskoye, Russia **(1857-1935)**
Tucker, Forrest (actor); Plainfield, Ind. **(1919-1986)**
Tucker, Richard (tenor); New York City **(1914-1975)**
Tucker, Sophie (Sophie Abuza) (singer); Europe **(1884?-1966)**
Tudor, Antony (choreographer); London **(1909-1987)**
Tune, Tommy (dancer-choreographer); Wichita Falls, Tex., 2/28/1939
Turgenev, Ivan Sergeevich (novelist); Orel, Russia **(1818-1883)**
Turner, Joseph M.W. (painter); London **(1775-1851)**
Turner, Kathleen (actress); Springfield, Mo., 1956 (?)
Turner, Lana (Julia Jean Mildred Frances Turner) (actress); Wallace, Idaho, 2/8/1920
Turner, Nat (civil rights leader); Southampton County, Va. **(1800-1831)**
Turner, Tina (Annie Mae Bullock) (singer); Brownsville, Tex., 1939
Turpin, Ben (comedian); New Orleans **(1874-1940)**
Tushingham, Rita (actress); Liverpool, England, 3/14/1942
Twain, Mark (Samuel Langhorne Clemens) (author); Florida, Mo. **(1835-1910)**
Tweed, William Marcy (politician); New York City **(1823-1878)**
Twining, Gen. Nathan F. (former Air Force Chief of Staff); Monroe, Wis. **(1897-1982)**
Twitty, Conway (Harold Lloyd Jenkins) (singer and guitarist); Friars Point, Miss., 9/1/1933
Tyson, Cicely (actress); New York City, 12/19/1939(?)

U

Udall, Stewart L. (ex-Secretary of the Interior); St. Johns, Ariz., 1/31/1920
Uggams, Leslie (singer and actress); New York City, 5/25/1943
Ulanova, Galina (ballerina); St. Petersburg, Russia, 1/10/1910
Ullmann, Liv (actress); Tokyo, 12/16/1939
Ulric, Lenore (actress); New Ulm, Minn. **(1894-1970)**
Untermeyer, Louis (anthologist and poet); New York City **(1885-1977)**
Updike, John (novelist); Shillington, Pa., 3/18/1932
Urey, Harold C. (physicist); Walkerton, Ind. **(1893-1981)**
Uris, Leon (novelist); Baltimore, 8/3/1924
Ustinov, Peter (actor and producer); London, 4/16/1921
Utrillo, Maurice (painter); Paris **(1883-1955)**

V

Vaccaro, Brenda (actress); Brooklyn, N.Y., 11/18/1939
Vadim, Roger (Roger Vadim Plemiannikov) (film director); Paris, 1/26/1928
Valentine, Karen (actress); Santa Rosa, Calif., 1947
Valentino, Rudolph (Rodolpho d'Antonguolla) (actor); Castellaneta, Italy **(1895-1926)**
Valentino (Valentino Garavani) (fashion designer); nr. Milan, Italy, 5/11/1932
Vallee, Rudy (Hubert Prior Rudy Vallée) (band leader and singer); Island Pond, Vt. **(1901-1986)**
Valli, Frankie (Frank Castellaccio) (singer); Newark, N.J., 5/3/1937
Van Allen, James Alfred (space physicist); Mt. Pleasant, Iowa, 9/7/1914
Van Buren, Abigail (Mrs. Morton Phillips) (columnist); Sioux City, Iowa, 7/4/1918
Vance, Vivian (actress); Cherryvale, Kan. **(1912-1979)**
Vanderbilt, Alfred G. (sportsman); London, 9/22/1912
Vanderbilt, Cornelius (financier); Port Richmond, N.Y. **(1794-1877)**
Vanderbilt, Gloria (fashion designer) New York City, 2/20/1924
Van Doren, Carl (writer and educator); Hope, Ill. **(1885-1950)**
Van Doren, Mamie (actress); Rowena, S.D., 2/6/1933
Van Dyke, Dick (actor); West Plains, Mo., 12/13/1925
Vandyke (or Van Dyck), Sir Anthony (painter); Antwerp (Belgium) **(1599-1641)**
Van Eyck, Jan (painter); Maeseyck (Belgium) **(c.1390-1441)**
van Gogh, Vincent (painter); Groot Zundert, Brabant **(1853-1890)**
Van Hamel, Martine (ballerina); Brussels, 11/16/1945
Van Heusen, Jimmy (Edward Chester Babcock) (songwriter); Syracuse, N.Y., 1/26/1913
Van Peebles, Melvin (playwright); Chicago, 9/21/1932
Vaughan, Sarah (singer); Newark, N.J., 3/27/1924
Vaughan Williams, Ralph (composer); Down Ampney, England **(1872-1958)**
Vaughn, Robert (actor); New York City, 11/22/1932
Velázquez, Diego Rodriguez de Silva y (painter); Seville, Spain **(1599-1660)**
Velez, Lupe (Guadalupe Velez de Villalobos) (actress); San Luis Potosi, Mexico **(1908-1944)**
Venturi, Robert (Charles) (architect); Philadelphia, 6/25/1925
Verdi, Giuseppe (composer); Roncole (Italy) **(1813-1901)**
Verdon, Gwen (actress); Culver City, Calif., 1/13/1925
Vereen, Ben (actor and singer); Miami, Fla., 10/10/1946
Vermeer, Jan (or Jan van der Meer van Delft) (painter); Delft (Netherlands) **(1632-1675)**
Verne, Jules (author); Nantes, France **(1828-1905)**
Veronese, Paolo (Paolo Cagliari) (painter); Verona **(1528-1588)**
Verrazano, Giovanni da (navigator); Florence (Italy) **(1485?-1528)**
Verrett, Shirley (mezzo-soprano); New Orleans, 5/31/1933
Vesalius, Andreas (anatomist); Brussels, Belgium **(1515-1564)**
Vespucci, Amerigo (navigator); Florence (Italy) **(1454-1512)**
Vickers, Jon (tenor); Prince Albert, Sask, Canada, 10/29/1926
Vico, Giovanni Battista (philosopher); Naples, Italy **(1668-1744)**
Vidal, Gore (novelist); West Point, N.Y., 10/3/1925
Vidor, King (film director and producer); Galveston, Tex. **(1895-1982)**
Villa, Pancho (Doroteo Arango) (bandit); Rio Grande, Mexico **(1877-1923)**
Villella, Edward (ballet dancer); Bayside, Queens, N.Y., 10/1/1936
Villon, François (François de Montcorbier) (poet); Paris **(1431-1463)**
Vinton, Bobby (singer); Canonsburg, Pa., 4/16/1935(?)
Virgil (or Vergil) (Publius Vergilius Maro) (poet); nr. Mantua (Italy) **(70-19 B.C.)**
Vishnevskaya, Galina (soprano); Leningrad, 10/25/1926
Vivaldi, Antonio (composer); Venice **(1678-1741)**
Vlaminck, Maurice de (painter); Paris **(1876-1958)**
Voight, Jon (actor); Yonkers, N.Y., 12/29/1938
Volta, Alessandro (scientist); Como, Italy **(1745-1827)**
Voltaire (François Marie Arouet) (author); Paris **(1694-1778)**
von Braun, Wernher (rocket scientist); Wirsitz, Germany **(1912-1977)**
von Aroldingen, Karin (Karin Awny Hannelore Reinbold von Aroedingen and Eltzinger) (ballet dancer); Greiz (East Germany) 7/9/1941
von Furstenberg, Betsy (Elizabeth Caroline Maria Agatha Felicitas Therese von Furstenberg-Hedringen) (actress); Nelheim-Heusen, Germany, 8/16/1935
von Fürstenberg, Diane (Diane Simone Michelle Halfin) (fashion designer); Brussels, 12/31/1946
von Hindenburg, Paul (statesman); Posen (Poland) **(1847-1934)**
von Karajan, Herbert (conductor); Salzburg (Austria) **(1908-1989)**
Vonnegut, Kurt, Jr. (novelist); Indianapolis, 11/11/1922
Von Stroheim, Erich Oswald Hans Carl Maria von Nordenwall (film actor and director); Vienna **(1885-1957)**
Vreeland, Diana (Diana Dalziel) (fashion journalist and museum consultant); Paris, 1903(?)

W

Wagner, Lindsay (actress); Los Angeles, 6/22/1949
Wagner, Robert (actor); Detroit, 2/10/1930
Wagner, Robert F. (ex-Mayor of New York City); New York City, 4/20/1910
Wagner, Wilhelm Richard (composer); Leipzig (East Germany) **(1813-1883)**
Waldheim, Kurt (ex-U.N. Secretary-General); St. Andrae-Wörden, Austria, 12/21/1918
Walker, Clint (actor); Hartford, Ill., 5/30/1927
Walker, Nancy (Ann Myrtle Swoyer); (actress and comedienne); Philadelphia, 5/10/1922
Wallace, DeWitt (publisher); St. Paul **(1889-1981)**
Wallace, Irving (novelist); Chicago, 3/19/1916
Wallace, Mike (Myron Wallace) (TV interviewer and commentator); Brookline, Mass., 5/9/1918
Wallach, Eli (actor); Brooklyn, N.Y., 12/7/1915
Waller, Thomas "Fats" (pianist); New York City **(1904-1943)**
Wallis, Hal (film producer); Chicago **(1899-1986)**
Walpole, Horace (statesman and novelist); London **(1717-1797)**
Waltari, Mika (novelist); Helsinki, Finland, **(1903-1979)**
Walter, Bruno (Bruno Walter Schlesinger) (orchestra conductor); Berlin **(1876-1962)**
Walters, Barbara (TV commentator); Boston, 9/25/1931
Walton, Izaak (author); Stafford, England **(1593-1683)**
Wambaugh, Joseph (author and screenwriter); East Pittsburgh, Pa., 1/22/1937
Wanamaker, John (merchant); Philadelphia **(1838-1922)**
Ward, Barbara (economist); York, England **(1914-1981)**
Warhol, Andy (artist and producer); Pennsylvania **(1928(?)-1987)**
Waring, Fred (band leader); Tyrone, Pa., **(1900-1984)**
Warner, H. B. (Henry Bryan Warner Lickford) (actor); London **(1876-1958)**
Warren, Robert Penn (novelist); Guthrie, Ky., 4/24/1905
Warwick, Dionne (singer); East Orange, N.J., 1941
Washington, Booker Taliaferro (educator); Franklin County, Va. **(1856-1915)**
Waters, Ethel (actress and singer); Chester, Pa. **(1896-1977)**
Waters, Muddy (McKinley Morganfield) (singer and guitarist); Rolling Fork, Miss. **(1915-1983)**
Watson, Thomas John (industrialist); Campbell, N.Y. **(1874-1956)**
Watt, James (inventor); Greenock, Scotland **(1736-1819)**
Watteau, Jean-Antoine (painter); Valanciennes, France **(1684-1721)**
Watts, André (concert pianist); Nuremberg, Germany, 6/20/1946
Waugh, Alec (Alexander Raban Waugh) (novelist); London **(1898-1981)**
Waugh, Evelyn (satirist); London **(1903-1966)**
Wayne, Anthony (military officer); Waynesboro (family farm), nr. Paoli, Pa. **(1745-1796)**
Wayne, David (David McMeekan); (actor); Traverse City, Mich., 1/30/1914
Wayne, John (Marion Michael Morrison) (actor); Winterset, Iowa, **(1907-1979)**
Weaver, Dennis (actor); Joplin, Mo., 6/4/1925
Weaver, Sigourney (actress); New York City, 10/8/1949
Webb, Clifton (Webb Parmelee Hollenbeck) (actor); Indianapolis **(1893-1966)**
Webb, Jack (film actor and producer); Santa Monica, Calif. **(1920-1982)**
Weber, Karl Maria Friedrich Ernst von (composer); nr. Lübeck (Germany) **(1786-1826)**
Webster, Daniel (statesman); Salisbury, N.H. **(1782-1852)**
Webster, Noah (lexicographer); West Hartford, Conn. **(1758-1843)**
Weill, Kurt (composer); Dessau, (East Germany) **(1900-1950)**
Weir, Peter (film director); Sydney, Australia, 8/21/1944
Weizmann, Chaim (statesman); Grodno Province, Russia **(1874-1952)**
Welch, Raquel (Raquel Tejada) (actress); Chicago, 9/5/1942
Weld, Tuesday (Susan) (actress); New York City, 8/27/1943
Welk, Lawrence (band leader); Strasburg, N.D., 3/11/1903
Welles, Orson (actor and producer); Kenosha, Wis. **(1915-1985)**
Wellington, Duke of (Arthur Wellesley) (statesman); Ireland **(1769-1852)**
Wells, H(erbert) G(eorge) (author); Bromley, England **(1866-1946)**
Welty, Eudora (novelist); Jackson, Miss., 4/13/1909
Werfel, Franz (novelist); Prague **(1890-1945)**
Werner, Oskar (Josef Schliessmayer) (film actor and director); Vienna **(1922-1984)**
Wertmuller, Lina (film director); Rome, 1926(?)
Wesley, John (religious leader); Epworth Rectory, Lincolnshire, England **(1703-1791)**
West, Dame Rebecca (Cicily Fairfield); (novelist); County Kerry, Ireland **(1892-1983)**
West, Jessamyn (novelist); nr. North Vernon, Ind. **(1902-1984)**
West, Mae (actress); Brooklyn, N.Y. **(1893-1980)**

West, Nathanael (Nathan Weinstein) (novelist); New York City **(1902-1940)**

Westheimer, Ruth (Karola Ruth Siegel) (psychologist, author, broadcaster); Frankfurt, Germany, 1928

Westinghouse, George (inventor); Central Bridge, N.Y. **(1846-1914)**

Westmoreland, William Childs (ex-Army Chief of Staff); Saxon, S.C., 3/26/1914

Wharton, Edith Newbold (née Jones) (novelist); New York City **(1862-1937)**

Wheeler, Bert (Albert Jerome Wheeler) (comedian); Paterson, N.J. **(1895-1968)**

Whistler, James Abbott McNeill (painter and etcher); Lowell, Mass. (1834-1903)

White, E(lwyn) B(rooks) (author); Mt. Vernon, N.Y. **(1899-1985)**

White, Stanford (architect); New York City **(1853-1906)**

White, Theodore H. (historian); Boston **(1915-1986)**

White, Vanna (TV personality); Conway, S.C., 2/18/1957

White, William Allen (journalist); Emporia, Kan. **(1868-1944)**

Whitehead, Alfred North (mathematician and philosopher); Isle of Thanet, England **(1861-1947)**

Whiteman, Paul (band leader); Denver **(1891-1967)**

Whitman, Walt (Walter) (poet); West Hills, N.Y. **(1819-1892)**

Whitmore, James (actor); White Plains, N.Y., 10/1/1921

Whitney, Cornelius Vanderbilt (sportsman); New York City, 2/20/1899

Whitney, Eli (inventor); Westboro, Mass. **(1765-1825)**

Whitney, John Hay (publisher); Ellsworth, Me. **(1904-1982)**

Whittier, John Greenleaf (poet); Haverhill, Mass. **(1807-1892)**

Widmark, Richard (actor); Sunrise, Minn., 12/26/1914

Wiesel, Elie (Eliezer) (author); Signet, Romania, 9/30/1928

Wilde, Cornel (film actor and producer); New York City, 10/13/1918

Wilde, Oscar Fingal O'Flahertie Wills (author); Dublin **(1854-1900)**

Wilder, Billy (film producer and director); Vienna, 6/22/1906

Wilder, Gene (Jerome Silberman) (actor); Milwaukee, 6/11/1935(?)

Wilder, Thornton (author); Madison, Wis. **(1897-1975)**

Wilding, Michael (actor); Westcliff, England **(1912-1979)**

Wilkins, Roy (civil rights leader); St. Louis **(1901-1981)**

Williams, Andy (singer); Wall Lake, Iowa, 12/3/1930

Williams, Billy Dee (actor); New York City, 4/6/1937

Williams, Cindy (actress); Van Nuys, Calif., 8/22/(?)

Williams, Edward Bennett (lawyer); Hartford, Conn. **(1920-1988)**

Williams, Emlyn (actor and playwright); Mostyn, Wales **(1905-1987)**

Williams, Gluyas (cartoonist); San Francisco **(1888-1982)**

Williams, Hank, Sr. (Hiram King Williams) (singer); Georgiana, Ala. **(1923-1953)**

Williams, Joe (singer); Cordele, Ga., 12/12/1918

Williams, Paul (singer, composer, actor); Omaha, Neb., 9/19/1940

Williams, Robin (comedian); Chicago, 7/?/1952

Williams, Roger (clergyman); London **(1603?-1683)**

Williams, Tennessee (Thomas L. Williams) (playwright); Columbus, Miss. **(1911-1983)**

Williams, William Carlos (physician and poet); Rutherford, N.J. **(1883-1963)**

Willkie, Wendell Lewis (lawyer); Elwood, Ind. **(1892-1944)**

Willis, Bruce (actor); Germany, 3/19/1955

Willson, Meredith (composer); Mason City, Iowa **(1902-1984)**

Wilson, August (poet, writer, playwright); Pittsburgh, Pa., 1945

Wilson, Don (radio and TV announcer); Lincoln, Neb. **(1900-1982)**

Wilson, Edmund (literary critic and author); Red Bank, N.J. **(1895-1972)**

Wilson, Flip (Clerow) (comedian); Jersey City, N.J., 12/8/1933

Wilson, Harold (ex-Prime Minister); Huddersfield, England, 3/11/1916

Wilson, Nancy (singer); Chillicothe, Ohio, 2/20/1937

Wilson, Sloan (novelist); Norwalk, Conn., 5/8/1920

Winchell, Walter (columnist); New York City **(1897-1972)**

Windsor, Duchess of (Bessie Wallis Warfield); Blue Ridge Summit, Pa. **(1896-1986)**

Windsor, Duke of (formerly King Edward VIII of England); Richmond Park, England **(1894-1972)**

Winfrey, Oprah (talk show hostess, actress); Kosciuska, Miss., 1/29/1954

Winkler, Henry (actor); New York City, 10/30/1945

Winter, Johnny (guitarist); Leland, Miss., 2/23/1944

Winters, Jonathan (comedian); Dayton, Ohio, 11/11/1925

Winters, Shelley (Shirley Schrift) (actress); East St. Louis, Ill., 8/18/1922

Winthrop, John (first Governor, Massachusetts Bay Colony); Suffolk, England **(1588-1649)**

Wise, Stephen Samuel (rabbi); Budapest **(1874-1949)**

Withers, Jane (actress); Atlanta, 1927

Wittgenstein, Ludwig (Josef Johann) (philosopher); Vienna **(1889-1951)**

Wodehouse, P(elham) G(renville) (novelist); Guildford, England **(1881-1975)**

Wolfe, Thomas Clayton (novelist); Asheville, N.C. **(1900-1938)**

Wolfe, Tom (journalist); Richmond, Va., 3/2/1931

Wolsey, Thomas (prelate and statesman); Ipswich, England **(1475?-1530)**

Wonder, Stevie (Steveland Judkins, later Steveland Morris) (singer and songwriter); Saginaw, Mich., 5/13/1950

Wong, Anna May (Lu Tsong Wong) (actress); Los Angeles **(1907-1961)**

Wood, Grant (painter); Anamosa, Iowa **(1892-1942)**

Wood, Natalie (Natasha Gurdin) (film actress); San Francisco **(1938-1981)**

Woodhouse, Barbara (Blackburn) (dog trainer, author, TV personality); Rathfarnham, Ireland **(1910-1988)**

Woodward, Joanne (film actress); Thomasville, Ga., 2/27/1930

Woolf, Adeline Virginia (née Stephens) (novelist); London **(1882-1941)**

Woollcott, Alexander (author-critic); Phalanx, N.J. **(1887-1943)**

Woolley, Monty (Edgar Montillion Woolley) (actor); New York City **(1888-1963)**

Woolworth, Frank (merchant); Rodman, N.Y. **(1852-1919)**

Wordsworth, William (poet); Cockermouth, England **(1770-1850)**

Wouk, Herman (novelist); New York City, 5/27/1915

Wray, Fay (actress); Alberta, Canada, 1907

Wren, Sir Christopher (architect); East Knoyle, England **(1632-1723)**

Wright, Frank Lloyd (architect); Richland Center, Wis. **(1869-1959)**

Wright, Orville (inventor); Dayton, Ohio **(1871-1948)**

Wright, Richard (novelist); nr. Natchez, Miss. **(1908-1960)**

Wright, Teresa (actress); New York City, 10/27/1918

Wright, Wilbur (inventor); Millville, Ind. **(1867-1912)**

Wyatt, Jane (film actress); Campgaw, N.J., 8/12/1912

Wycliffe, John (church reformer); Hipswell, England **(1320-1384)**

Wyeth, Andrew (painter); Chadds Ford, Pa., 7/12/1917

Wyler, William (film director); Mulhouse (France), **(1902-1981)**

Wyman, Jane (Sarah Jane Fulks) (actress); St. Joseph, Mo., 1/4/1914

Wynette, Tammy (Wynette Pugh) (singer); Tupelo, Miss. 5/5/1942

Wynn, Ed (Isaiah Edwin Leopold) (comedian); Philadelphia **(1886-1966)**

Wynn, Keenan (actor); New York City **(1916-1986)**

X

Xavier, St. Francis (Jesuit missionary); Pamplona, Navarre (Spain) **(1506-1552)**

Xenophon (soldier, historian and essayist); Athens, Greece, **(434(?)-355(?) B.C.)**

Xerxes, the Great (king); Persian Empire, **(519(?)-465 B.C.)**

Y

Yeats, William Butler (poet); nr. Dublin **(1865-1939)**

Yevtushenko, Yevgeny (poet); Zima, U.S.S.R., 7/18/1933

York, Alvin Cullun (Sergeant York, World War I hero); Tennessee **(1887-1964)**

York, Michael (actor); Fulmer, England, 3/27/1942

York, Susannah (Fletcher) (actress); London, 1/9/1942

Yorty, Samuel W. (ex-Mayor of Los Angeles); Lincoln, Neb., 10/1/1909

Young, Alan (actor); North Shield, England, 11/19/1919

Young, Brigham (religious leader); Whitingham, Vt. **(1801-1877)**

Young, Gig (Byron Barr) (actor); St. Cloud, Minn. **(1917-1978)**

Young, Loretta (Gretchen Young) (actress); Salt Lake City, Utah, 1/6/1913

Young, Neil (singer and songwriter); Toronto, 11/12/1945

Young, Robert (actor); Chicago, 2/22/1907

Youngman, Henny (comedian); Liverpool, England, 1/12/1906

Z

Zanuck, Darryl F. (film producer); Wahoo, Neb. **(1902-1979)**

Zeffirelli, Franco (director); Florence, Italy, 2/12/1923

Zenger, John Peter (printer and journalist); Germany, **(1697-1746)**

Zhou Enlai (Premier); Hualyin, China **(1898-1976)**

Ziegfeld, Florenz (theatrical producer); Chicago **(1869-1932)**

Zimbalist, Efrem (concert violinist); Rostov-on-Don, Russia **(1889-1985)**

Zimbalist, Efrem, Jr. (actor); New York City, 11/30/1923

Zola, Emile (novelist); Paris **(1840-1902)**

Zoroaster (religious leader); Persian Empire **(c. 6th century B.C.)**

Zukerman, Pinchas (violinist); Tel Aviv, Israel 7/16/1948

Zweig, Stefan (author); Vienna **(1881-1942)**

Zwingli, Huldrych (humanist); Wildaus, Switzerland **(1484-1531)**

AWARDS

Nobel Prizes

The Nobel prizes are awarded under the will of Alfred Bernhard Nobel, Swedish chemist and engineer, who died in 1896. The interest of the fund is divided annually among the persons who have made the most outstanding contributions in the fields of physics, chemistry, and physiology or medicine, who have produced the most distinguished literary work of an idealist tendency, and who have contributed most toward world peace.

In 1968, a Nobel Prize of economic sciences was established by Riksbank, the Swedish bank, in celebration of its 300th anniversary. The prize was awarded for the first time in 1969.

The prizes for physics and chemistry are awarded by the Swedish Academy of Science in Stockholm, the one for physiology or medicine by the Caroline Medical Institute in Stockholm, that for literature by the academy in Stockholm, and that for peace by a committee of five elected by the Norwegian Storting. The distribution of prizes was begun on December 10, 1901, the anniversary of Nobel's death. The amount of each prize varies with the income from the fund and currently is about $190,000. No Nobel prizes were awarded for 1940, 1941, and 1942; prizes for Literature were not awarded for 1914, 1918, and 1943.

PEACE

1901 Henri Dunant (Switzerland); Frederick Passy (France)
1902 Elie Ducommun and Albert Gobat (Switzerland)
1903 Sir William R. Cremer (England)
1904 Institut de Droit International (Belgium)
1905 Bertha von Suttner (Austria)
1906 Theodore Roosevelt (U.S.)
1907 Ernesto T. Moneta (Italy) and Louis Renault (France)
1908 Klas P. Arnoldson (Sweden) and Frederik Bajer (Denmark)
1909 Auguste M. F. Beernaert (Belgium) and Baron Paul H. B. B. d'Estournelles de Constant de Rebecque (France)
1910 Bureau International Permanent de la Paix (Switzerland)
1911 Tobias M. C. Asser (Holland) and Alfred H. Fried (Austria)
1912 Elihu Root (U.S.)
1913 Henri La Fontaine (Belgium)
1915 No award
1916 No award
1917 International Red Cross
1919 Woodrow Wilson (U.S.)
1920 Léon Bourgeois (France)
1921 Karl H. Branting (Sweden) and Christian L. Lange (Norway)
1922 Fridtjof Nansen (Norway)
1923 No award
1924 No award
1925 Sir Austen Chamberlain (England) and Charles G. Dawes (U.S.)
1926 Aristide Briand (France) and Gustav Stresemann (Germany)
1927 Ferdinand Buisson (France) and Ludwig Quidde (Germany)
1928 No award
1929 Frank B. Kellogg (U.S.)
1930 Lars O. J. Söderblom (Sweden)
1931 Jane Addams and Nicholas M. Butler (U.S.)
1932 No award
1933 Sir Norman Angell (England)
1934 Arthur Henderson (England)
1935 Karl von Ossietzky (Germany)
1936 Carlos de S. Lamas (Argentina)
1937 Lord Cecil of Chelwood (England)
1938 Office International Nansen pour les Réfugiés (Switzerland)
1939 No award
1944 International Red Cross
1945 Cordell Hull (U.S.)
1946 Emily G. Balch and John R. Mott (U.S.)

1947 American Friends Service Committee (U.S.) and British Society of Friends' Service Council (England)
1948 No award
1949 Lord John Boyd Orr (Scotland)
1950 Ralph J. Bunche (U.S.)
1951 Léon Jouhaux (France)
1952 Albert Schweitzer (French Equatorial Africa)
1953 George C. Marshall (U.S.)
1954 Office of U.N. High Commissioner for Refugees
1955 No award
1956 No award
1957 Lester B. Pearson (Canada)
1958 Rev. Dominique Georges Henri Pire (Belgium)
1959 Philip John Noel-Baker (England)
1960 Albert John Luthuli (South Africa)
1961 Dag Hammarskjöld (Sweden)
1962 Linus Pauling (U.S.)
1963 Intl. Comm. of Red Cross; League of Red Cross Societies (both Geneva)
1964 Rev. Dr. Martin Luther King, Jr. (U.S.)
1965 UNICEF (United Nations Children's Fund)
1966 No award
1967 No award
1968 René Cassin (France)
1969 International Labour Organization
1970 Norman E. Borlaug (U.S.)
1971 Willy Brandt (West Germany)
1972 No award
1973 Henry A. Kissinger (U.S.); Le Duc Tho (North Vietnam)[1]
1974 Eisaku Sato (Japan); Sean MacBride (Ireland)
1975 Andrei D. Sakharov (U.S.S.R.)
1976 Mairead Corrigan and Betty Williams (both Northern Ireland)
1977 Amnesty International
1978 Menachem Begin (Israel) and Anwar el-Sadat (Egypt)
1979 Mother Teresa of Calcutta (India)
1980 Adolfo Pérez Esquivel (Argentina)
1981 Office of the United Nations High Commissioner for Refugees
1982 Alva Myrdal (Sweden) and Alfonso García Robles (Mexico)
1983 Lech Walesa (Poland)
1984 Bishop Desmond Tutu (South Africa)
1985 International Physicians for the Prevention of Nuclear War
1986 Elie Wiesel (U.S.)
1987 Oscar Arias Sánchez (Costa Rica)

1. Le Duc Tho refused prize, charging that peace had not yet been really established in South Vietnam.

1988 U.N. Peacekeeping Forces

LITERATURE

1901 René F. A. Sully Prudhomme (France)
1902 Theodor Mommsen (Germany)
1903 Björnstjerne Björnson (Norway)
1904 Frédéric Mistral (France) and José Echegaray (Spain)
1905 Henryk Sienkiewicz (Poland)
1906 Giosuè Carducci (Italy)
1907 Rudyard Kipling (England)
1908 Rudolf Eucken (Germany)
1909 Selma Lagerlöf (Sweden)
1910 Paul von Heyse (Germany)
1911 Maurice Maeterlinck (Belgium)
1912 Gerhart Hauptmann (Germany)
1913 Rabindranath Tagore (India)
1915 Romain Rolland (France)
1916 Verner von Heidenstam (Sweden)
1917 Karl Gjellerup (Denmark) and Henrik Pontoppidan (Denmark)
1919 Carl Spitteler (Switzerland)
1920 Knut Hamsun (Norway)
1921 Anatole France (France)
1922 Jacinto Benavente (Spain)
1923 William B. Yeats (Ireland)
1924 Wladyslaw Reymont (Poland)
1925 George Bernard Shaw (England)
1926 Grazia Deledda (Italy)
1927 Henri Bergson (France)
1928 Sigrid Undset (Norway)
1929 Thomas Mann (Germany)
1930 Sinclair Lewis (U.S.)
1931 Erik A. Karlfeldt (Sweden)
1932 John Galsworthy (England)
1933 Ivan G. Bunin (Russia)
1934 Luigi Pirandello (Italy)
1935 No award
1936 Eugene O'Neill (U.S.)
1937 Roger Martin du Gard (France)
1938 Pearl S. Buck (U.S.)
1939 Frans Eemil Sillanpää (Finland)
1944 Johannes V. Jensen (Denmark)
1945 Gabriela Mistral (Chile)
1946 Hermann Hesse (Switzerland)
1947 André Gide (France)
1948 Thomas Stearns Eliot (England)
1949 William Faulkner (U.S.)
1950 Bertrand Russell (England)
1951 Pär Lagerkvist (Sweden)
1952 François Mauriac (France)
1953 Sir Winston Churchill (England)
1954 Ernest Hemingway (U.S.)
1955 Halldór Kiljan Laxness (Iceland)
1956 Juan Ramón Jiménez (Spain)
1957 Albert Camus (France)
1958 Boris Pasternak (U.S.S.R.) (declined)
1959 Salvatore Quasimodo (Italy)
1960 St-John Perse (Alexis St.-Léger Léger) (France)
1961 Ivo Andric (Yugoslavia)
1962 John Steinbeck (U.S.)
1963 Giorgios Seferis (Seferiades) (Greece)
1964 Jean-Paul Sartre (France) (declined)
1965 Mikhail Sholokhov (U.S.S.R.)
1966 Shmuel Yosef Agnon (Israel) and Nelly Sachs (Sweden)
1967 Miguel Angel Asturias (Guatemala)
1968 Yasunari Kawabata (Japan)
1969 Samuel Beckett (France)
1970 Aleksandr Solzhenitsyn (U.S.S.R.)
1971 Pablo Neruda (Chile)
1972 Heinrich Böll (Germany)
1973 Patrick White (Australia)

1974 Eyvind Johnson and Harry Martinson (both Sweden)
1975 Eugenio Montale (Italy)
1976 Saul Bellow (U.S.)
1977 Vicente Aleixandre (Spain)
1978 Isaac Bashevis Singer (U.S.)
1979 Odysseus Elytis (Greece)
1980 Czeslaw Milosz (U.S.)
1981 Elias Canetti (Bulgaria)
1982 Gabriel García Márquez (Colombia)
1983 William Golding (England)
1984 Jaroslav Seifert (Czechoslovakia)
1985 Claude Simon (France)
1986 Wole Soyinka (Nigeria)
1987 Joseph Brodsky (U.S.)
1988 Naguib Mahfouz (Egypt)

PHYSICS

1901 Wilhelm K. Roentgen (Germany), for discovery of Roentgen rays
1902 Hendrik A. Lorentz and Pieter Zeeman (Netherlands), for work on influence of magnetism upon radiation
1903 A. Henri Becquerel (France), for work on spontaneous radioactivity; and Pierre and Marie Curie (France), for study of radiation
1904 John Strutt (Lord Rayleigh) (England), for discovery of argon in investigating gas density
1905 Philipp Lenard (Germany), for work with cathode rays
1906 Sir Joseph Thomson (England), for investigations on passage of electricity through gases
1907 Albert A. Michelson (U.S.), for spectroscopic and metrologic investigations
1908 Gabriel Lippmann (France), for method of reproducing colors by photography
1909 Guglielmo Marconi (Italy) and Ferdinand Braun (Germany), for development of wireless
1910 Johannes D. van der Waals (Netherlands), for work with the equation of state for gases and liquids
1911 Wilhelm Wien (Germany), for his laws governing the radiation of heat
1912 Gustaf Dalén (Sweden), for discovery of automatic regulators used in lighting lighthouses and light buoys
1913 Heike Kamerlingh-Onnes (Netherlands), for work leading to production of liquid helium
1914 Max von Laue (Germany), for discovery of diffraction of Roentgen rays passing through crystals
1915 Sir William Bragg and William L. Bragg (England), for analysis of crystal structure by X rays
1916 No award
1917 Charles G. Barkla (England), for discovery of Roentgen radiation of the elements
1918 Max Planck (Germany), discoveries in connection with quantum theory
1919 Johannes Stark (Germany), discovery of Doppler effect in Canal rays and decomposition of spectrum lines by electric fields
1920 Charles E. Guillaume (Switzerland), for discoveries of anomalies in nickel steel alloys
1921 Albert Einstein (Germany), for discovery of the law of the photoelectric effect
1922 Niels Bohr (Denmark), for investigation of structure of atoms and radiations emanating from them
1923 Robert A. Millikan (U.S.), for work on elementary charge of electricity and photoelectric phenomena
1924 Karl M. G. Siegbahn (Sweden), for investigations in X-ray spectroscopy

1925 James Franck and Gustav Hertz (Germany), for discovery of laws governing impact of electrons upon atoms

1926 Jean B. Perrin (France), for work on discontinous nous structure of matter and discovery of the equilibrium of sedimentation

1927 Arthur H. Compton (U.S.), for discovery of Compton phenomenon; and Charles T. R. Wilson (England), for method of perceiving paths taken by electrically charged particles

1928 In 1929, the 1928 prize was awarded to Sir Owen Richardson (England), for work on the phenomenon of thermionics and discovery of the Richardson Law

1929 Prince Louis Victor de Broglie (France), for discovery of the wave character of electrons

1930 Sir Chandrasekhara Raman (India), for work on diffusion of light and discovery of the Raman effect

1931 No award

1932 In 1933, the prize for 1932 was awarded to Werner Heisenberg (Germany), for creation of the quantum mechanics

1933 Erwin Schrödinger (Austria) and Paul A. M. Dirac (England), for discovery of new fertile forms of the atomic theory

1934 No award

1935 James Chadwick (England), for discovery of the neutron

1936 Victor F. Hess (Austria), for discovery of cosmic radiation; and Carl D. Anderson (U.S.), for discovery of the positron

1937 Clinton J. Davisson (U.S.) and George P. Thomson (England), for discovery of diffraction of electrons by crystals

1938 Enrico Fermi (Italy), for identification of new radioactivity elements and discovery of nuclear reactions effected by slow neutrons

1939 Ernest Orlando Lawrence (U.S.), for development of the cyclotron

1943 Otto Stern (U.S.), for detection of magnetic momentum of protons

1944 Isidor Isaac Rabi (U.S.), for work on magnetic movements of atomic particles

1945 Wolfgang Pauli (Austria), for work on atomic fissions

1946 Percy Williams Bridgman (U.S.), for studies and inventions in high-pressure physics

1947 Sir Edward Appleton (England), for discovery of layer which reflects radio short waves in the ionosphere

1948 Patrick M. S. Blackett (England), for improvement on Wilson chamber and discoveries in cosmic radiation

1949 Hideki Yukawa (Japan), for mathematical prediction, in 1935, of the meson

1950 Cecil Frank Powell (England), for method of photographic study of atom nucleus, and for discoveries about mesons

1951 Sir John Douglas Cockcroft (England) and Ernest T. S. Walton (Ireland), for work in 1932 on transmutation of atomic nuclei

1952 Edward Mills Purcell and Felix Bloch (U.S.), for work in measurement of magnetic fields in atomic nuclei

1953 Fritz Zernike (Netherlands), for development of "phase contrast" microscope

1954 Max Born (England), for work in quantum mechanics; and Walther Bothe (Germany), for work in cosmic radiation

1955 Polykarp Kusch and Willis E. Lamb, Jr. (U.S.), for atomic measurements

1956 William Shockley, Walter H. Brattain, and John Bardeen (U.S.), for developing electronic transistor

1957 Tsung Dao Lee and Chen Ning Yang (China), for disproving principle of conservation of parity

1958 Pavel A. Cherenkov, Ilya M. Frank, and Igor E. Tamm (U.S.S.R.), for work resulting in development of cosmic-ray counter

1959 Emilio Segre and Owen Chamberlain (U.S.), for demonstrating the existence of the anti-proton

1960 Donald A. Glaser (U.S.), for invention of "bubble chamber" to study subatomic particles

1961 Robert Hofstadter (U.S.), for determination of shape and size of atomic nucleus; Rudolf Mössbauer (Germany), for method of producing and measuring recoil-free gamma rays

1962 Lev D. Landau (U.S.S.R.), for his theories about condensed matter

1963 Eugene Paul Wigner, Maria Goeppert Mayer (both U.S.), and J. Hans D. Jensen (Germany), for research on structure of atom and its nucleus

1964 Charles Hard Townes (U.S.), Nikolai G. Basov, and Aleksandr M. Prochorov (both U.S.S.R.), for developing maser and laser principle of producing high-intensity radiation

1965 Richard P. Feynman, Julian S. Schwinger (both U.S.), and Shinichiro Tomonaga (Japan), for research in quantum electrodynamics

1966 Alfred Kastler (France), for work on energy levels inside atom

1967 Hans A. Bethe (U.S.), for work on energy production of stars

1968 Luis Walter Alvarez (U.S.), for study of subatomic particles

1969 Murray Gell-Mann (U.S.), for study of subatomic particles

1970 Hannes Alfvén (Sweden), for theories in plasma physics; and Louis Néel (France), for discoveries in antiferromagnetism and ferrimagnetism

1971 Dennis Gabor (England), for invention of holographic method of three-dimensional imagery

1972 John Bardeen, Leon N. Cooper, and John Robert Schrieffer (all U.S.), for theory of superconductivity, where electrical resistance in certain metals vanishes above absolute zero temperature

1973 Ivar Giaever (U.S.), Leo Esaki (Japan), and Brian D. Josephson (U.K.), for theories that have advanced and expanded the field of miniature electronics

1974 Antony Hewish (England), for discovery of pulsars; Martin Ryle (England), for using radio-telescopes to probe outer space with high degree of precision

1975 James Rainwater (U.S.) and Ben Mottelson and Aage N. Bohr (both Denmark), for showing that the atomic nucleus is asymmetrical

1976 Burton Richter and Samuel C. C. Ting (both U.S.), for discovery of subatomic particles known as J and psi

1977 Philip W. Anderson and John H. Van Vleck (both U.S.), and Nevill F. Mott (U.K.), for work underlying computer memories and electronic devices

1978 Arno A. Penzias and Robert W. Wilson (both U.S.), for work in cosmic microwave radiation; Piotr L. Kapitsa (U.S.S.R.), for basic inventions and discoveries in low-temperature physics

1979 Steven Weinberg and Sheldon L. Glashow (both U.S.) and Abdus Salam (Pakistan), for developing theory that electromagnetism and the "weak" force, which causes radioactive decay in some atomic nuclei, are facets of the same phenomenon

1980 James W. Cronin and Val L. Fitch (both U.S.), for work concerning the assymetry of subatomic particles

1981 Nicolaas Bloembergen and Arthur L. Schawlow (both U.S.) and Kai M. Siegbahn (Sweden), for developing technologies with lasers and other devices to probe the secrets of complex forms of matter

1982 Kenneth G. Wilson (U.S.), for analysis of changes in matter under pressure and temperature

1983 Subrahmanyam Chandrasekhar and William A. Fowler (both U.S.) for complementary research on processes involved in the evolution of stars

1984 Carlo Rubbia (Italy) and Simon van der Meer (Netherlands), for their role in discovering three subatomic particles, a step toward developing a single theory to account for all natural forces

1985 Klaus von Klitzing (Germany), for developing an exact way of measuring electrical conductivity

1986 Ernst Ruska, Gerd Binnig (both Germany) and Heinrich Rohrer (Switzerland) for work on microscopes

1987 K. Alex Müller (Switzerland) and J. Georg Bednorz (Germany) for their discovery of high-temperature superconductors.

1988 Leon M. Lederman, Melvin Schwartz, and Jack Steinberger (all U.S.) for research that improved the understanding of elementary particles and forces.

CHEMISTRY

1901 Jacobus H. van't Hoff (Netherlands), for laws of chemical dynamics and osmotic pressure in solutions

1902 Emil Fischer (Germany), for experiments in sugar and purin groups of substances

1903 Svante A. Arrhenius (Sweden), for his electrolytic theory of dissociation

1904 Sir William Ramsay (England), for discovery and determination of place of inert gaseous elements in air

1905 Adolf von Baeyer (Germany), for work on organic dyes and hydroaromatic combinations

1906 Henri Moissan (France), for isolation of fluorine, and introduction of electric furnace

1907 Eduard Buchner (Germany), discovery of cell-less fermentation and investigations in biological chemistry

1908 Sir Ernest Rutherford (England), for investigations into disintegration of elements

1909 Wilhelm Ostwald (Germany), for work on catalysis and investigations into chemical equilibrium and reaction rates

1910 Otto Wallach (Germany), for work in the field of alicyclic compounds

1911 Marie Curie (France), for discovery of elements radium and polonium

1912 Victor Grignard (France), for reagent discovered by him; and Paul Sabatier (France), for methods of hydrogenating organic compounds

1913 Alfred Werner (Switzerland), for linking up atoms within the molecule

1914 Theodore W. Richards (U.S.), for determining atomic weight of many chemical elements

1915 Richard Willstätter (Germany), for research into coloring matter of plants, especially chlorophyll

1916 No award

1917 No award

1918 Fritz Haber (Germany), for synthetic production of ammonia

1919 No award

1920 Walther Nernst (Germany), for work in thermochemistry

1921 Frederick Soddy (England), for investigations into origin and nature of isotopes

1922 Francis W. Aston (England), for discovery of isotopes in nonradioactive elements and for discovery of the whole number rule

1923 Fritz Pregl (Austria), for method of microanalysis of organic substances discovered by him

1924 No award

1925 In 1926, the 1925 prize was awarded to Richard Zsigmondy (Germany), for work on the heterogeneous nature of colloid solutions

1926 Theodor Svedberg (Sweden), for work on disperse systems

1927 In 1928, the 1927 prize was awarded to Heinrich Wieland (Germany), for investigations of bile acids and kindred substances

1928 Adolf Windaus (Germany), for investigations on constitution of the sterols and their connection with vitamins

1929 Sir Arthur Harden (England) and Hans K. A. S. von Euler-Chelpin (Sweden), for research of fermentation of sugars

1930 Hans Fischer (Germany), for work on coloring matter of blood and leaves and for his synthesis of hemin

1931 Karl Bosch and Friedrich Bergius (Germany), for invention and development of chemical high-pressure methods

1932 Irving Langmuir (U.S.), for work in realm of surface chemistry

1933 No award

1934 Harold C. Urey (U.S.), for discovery of heavy hydrogen

1935 Frédéric and Irène Joliot-Curie (France), for synthesis of new radioactive elements

1936 Peter J. W. Debye (Netherlands), for investigations on dipole moments and diffraction of X rays and electrons in gases

1937 Walter N. Haworth (England), for research on carbohydrates and Vitamin C; and Paul Karrer (Switzerland), for work on carotenoids, flavins, and Vitamins A and B

1938 Richard Kuhn (Germany), for carotinoid study and vitamin research (declined)

1939 Adolf Butenandt (Germany), for work on sexual hormones (declined the prize); and Leopold Ruzicka (Switzerland), for work with polymethylenes

1943 Georg Hevesy De Heves (Hungary), for work on use of isotopes as indicators

1944 Otto Hahn (Germany), for work on atomic fission

1945 Artturi Illmari Virtanen (Finland), for research in the field of conservation of fodder

1946 James B. Sumner (U.S.), for crystallizing enzymes; John H. Northrop and Wendell M. Stanley (U.S.), for preparing enzymes and virus proteins in pure form

1947 Sir Robert Robinson (England), for research in plant substances

1948 Arne Tiselius (Sweden), for biochemical discoveries and isolation of mouse paralysis virus

1949 William Francis Giauque (U.S.), for research in thermodynamics, especially effects of low temperature

1950 Otto Diels and Kurt Alder (Germany), for discovery of diene synthesis enabling scientists to study structure of organic matter

1951 Glenn T. Seaborg and Edwin H. McMillan (U.S.), for discovery of plutonium

1952 Archer John Porter Martin and Richard Laurence Millington Synge (England), for development of partition chromatography

1953 Hermann Staudinger (Germany), for research in giant molecules

1954 Linus C. Pauling (U.S.), for study of forces holding together protein and other molecules

1955 Vincent du Vigneaud (U.S.), for work on pituitary hormones

1956 Sir Cyril Hinshelwood (England) and Nikolai N. Semenov (U.S.S.R.), for parallel research on chemical reaction kinetics

1957 Sir Alexander Todd (England), for research with chemical compounds that are factors in heredity

1958 Frederick Sanger (England), for determining molecular structure of insulin

1959 Jaroslav Heyrovsky (Czechoslovakia), for development of polarography, an electrochemical method of analysis

1960 Willard F. Libby (U.S.), for "atomic time clock" to measure age of objects by measuring their radioactivity

1961 Melvin Calvin (U.S.), for establishing chemical steps during photosynthesis

1962 Max F. Perutz and John C. Kendrew (England), for mapping protein molecules with X-rays

1963 Carl Ziegler (Germany) and Giulio Natta (Italy), for work in uniting simple hydrocarbons into large molecule substances

1964 Dorothy Mary Crowfoot Hodgkin (England), for determining structure of compounds needed in combating pernicious anemia

1965 Robert B. Woodward (U.S.), for work in synthesizing complicated organic compounds

1966 Robert Sanderson Mulliken (U.S.), for research on bond holding atoms together in molecule

1967 Manfred Eigen (Germany), Ronald G. W. Norrish, and George Porter (both England), for work in high-speed chemical reactions

1968 Lars Onsager (U.S.), for development of system of equations in thermodynamics

1969 Derek H. R. Barton (England) and Odd Hassel (Norway), for study of organic molecules

1970 Luis F. Leloir (Argentina), for discovery of sugar nucleotides and their role in biosynthesis of carbohydrates

1971 Gerhard Herzberg (Canada), for contributions to knowledge of electronic structure and geometry of molecules, particularly free radicals

1972 Christian Boehmer Anfinsen, Stanford Moore, and William Howard Stein (all U.S.), for pioneering studies in enzymes

1973 Ernst Otto Fischer (W. Germany) and Geoffrey Wilkinson (U.K.), for work that could solve problem of automobile exhaust pollution

1974 Paul J. Flory (U.S.), for developing analytic methods to study properties and molecular structure of long-chain molecules

1975 John W. Cornforth (Australia) and Vladimir Prelog (Switzerland), for research on structure of biological molecules such as antibiotics and cholesterol

1976 William N. Lipscomb, Jr. (U.S.), for work on the structure and bonding mechanisms of boranes

1977 Ilya Prigogine (Belgium), for contributions to nonequilibrium thermodynamics, particularly the theory of dissipative structures

1978 Peter Mitchell (U.K.), for contributions to the understanding of biological energy transfer

1979 Herbert C. Brown (U.S.) and Georg Wittig (West Germany), for developing a group of substances that facilitate very difficult chemical reactions

1980 Paul Berg and Walter Gilbert (both U.S.) and Frederick Sanger (England), for developing methods to map the structure and function of DNA, the substance that controls the activity of the cell

1981 Roald Hoffmann (U.S.) and Kenichi Fukui (Japan), for applying quantum-mechanics theories to predict the course of chemical reactions

1982 Aaron Klug (U.K.), for research in the detailed structures of viruses and components of life

1983 Henry Taube (U.S.), for research on how electrons transfer between molecules in chemical reactions

1984 R. Bruce Merrifield (U.S.) for research that revolutionized the study of proteins

1985 Herbert A. Hauptman and Jerome Karle (both U.S.) for their outstanding achievements in the development of direct methods for the determination of crystal structures

1986 Dudley R. Herschback, Yuan T. Lee (both U.S.), and John C. Polanyi (Canada) for their work on "reaction dynamics"

1987 Donald J. Cram and Charles J. Pedersen (both U.S.) and Jean-Marie Lehn (France), for wide-ranging research that has included the creation of artificial molecules that can mimic vital chemical reactions of the processes of life.

1988 Johann Deisenhofer, Robert Huber, and Hartmut Michel (all West Germany) for unraveling the structure of proteins that play a crucial role in photosynthesis.

PHYSIOLOGY OR MEDICINE

1901 Emil A. von Behring (Germany), for work on serum therapy against diptheria

1902 Sir Ronald Ross (England), for work on malaria

1903 Niels R. Finsen (Denmark), for his treatment of lupus vulgaris with concentrated light rays

1904 Ivan P. Pavlov (U.S.S.R.), for work on the physiology of digestion

1905 Robert Koch (Germany), for work on tuberculosis

1906 Camillo Golgi (Italy) and Santiago Ramón y Cajal (Spain), for work on structure of the nervous system

1907 Charles L. A. Laveran (France), for work with protozoa in the generation of disease

1908 Paul Ehrlich (Germany), and Elie Metchnikoff (U.S.S.R.), for work on immunity

1909 Theodor Kocher (Switzerland), for work on the thyroid gland

1910 Albrecht Kossel (Germany), for achievements in the chemistry of the cell

1911 Allvar Gullstrand (Sweden), for work on the dioptrics of the eye

1912 Alexis Carrel (France), for work on vascular ligature and grafting of blood vessels and organs

1913 Charles Richet (France), for work on anaphylaxy

1914 Robert Bárány (Austria), for work on physiology and pathology of the vestibular system

1915-1918 No award

1919 Jules Bordet (Belgium), for discoveries in connection with immunity

1920 August Krogh (Denmark), for discovery of regulation of capillaries' motor mechanism

1921 No award

1922 In 1923, the 1922 prize was shared by Archibald V. Hill (England), for discovery relating to heat-production in muscles; and Otto Meyerhof (Germany), for correlation between consumption of oxygen and production of lactic acid in muscles

1923 Sir Frederick Banting (Canada) and John J. R. Macleod (Scotland), for discovery of insulin

1924 Willem Einthoven (Netherlands), for discovery of the mechanism of the electrocardiogram

1925 No award

1926 Johannes Fibiger (Denmark), for discovery of the Spiroptera carcinoma

1927 Julius Wagner-Jauregg (Austria), for use of malaria inoculation in treatment of dementia paralytica

1928 Charles Nicolle (France), for work on typhus exanthematicus

1929 Christiaan Eijkman (Netherlands), for discovery of the antineuritic vitamins; and Sir Frederick Hopkins (England), for discovery of growth-promoting vitamins

1930 Karl Landsteiner (U.S.), for discovery of human blood groups

1931 Otto H. Warburg (Germany), for discovery of the character and mode of action of the respiratory ferment

1932 Sir Charles Sherrington (England) and Edgar D. Adrian (U.S.), for discoveries of the function of the neuron

1933 Thomas H. Morgan (U.S.), for discoveries on hereditary function of the chromosomes

1934 George H. Whipple, George R. Minot, and William P. Murphy (U.S.), for discovery of liver therapy against anemias

1935 Hans Spemann (Germany), for discovery of the organizer-effect in embryonic development

1936 Sir Henry Dale (England) and Otto Loewi (Germany), for discoveries on chemical transmission of nerve impulses

1937 Albert Szent-Györgyi von Nagyrapolt (Hungary), for discoveries on biological combustion

1938 Corneille Heymans (Belgium), for determining importance of sinus and aorta mechanisms in the regulation of respiration

1939 Gerhard Domagk (Germany), for antibacterial effect of prontocilate

1943 Henrik Dam (Denmark) and Edward A. Doisy (U.S.), for analysis of Vitamin K

1944 Joseph Erlanger and Herbert Spencer Gasser (U.S.), for work on functions of the nerve threads

1945 Sir Alexander Fleming, Ernst Boris Chain, and Sir Howard Florey (England), for discovery of penicillin

1946 Herman J. Muller (U.S.), for hereditary effects of X-rays on genes

1947 Carl F. and Gerty T. Cori (U.S.), for work on animal starch metabolism; Bernardo A. Houssay (Argentina), for study of pituitary

1948 Paul Mueller (Switzerland), for discovery of insect-killing properties of DDT

1949 Walter Rudolf Hess (Switzerland), for research on brain control of body; and Antonio Caetano de Abreu Freire Egas Moniz (Portugal), for development of brain operation

1950 Philip S. Hench, Edward C. Kendall (both U.S.), and Tadeus Reichstein (Switzerland), for discoveries about hormones of adrenal cortex

1951 Max Theiler (South Africa), for development of anti-yellow-fever vaccine

1952 Selman A. Waksman (U.S.), for co-discovery of streptomycin

1953 Fritz A. Lipmann (Germany-U.S.) and Hans Adolph Krebs (Germany-England), for studies of living cells

1954 John F. Enders, Thomas H. Weller, and Frederick C. Robbins (U.S.), for work with cultivation of polio virus

1955 Hugo Theorell (Sweden), for work on oxidation enzymes

1956 Dickinson W. Richards, Jr., André F. Cournand (both U.S.), and Werner Forssmann (Germany), for new techniques in treating heart disease

1957 Daniel Bovet (Italy), for development of drugs to relieve allergies and relax muscles during surgery

1958 Joshua Lederberg (U.S.), for work with genetic mechanisms; George W. Beadie and Edward L. Tatum (U.S.), for discovering how genes transmit hereditary characteristics

1959 Severo Ochoa and Arthur Kornberg (U.S.), for discoveries related to compounds within chromosomes, which play a vital role in heredity

1960 Sir Macfarlane Burnet (Australia) and Peter Brian Medawar (England), for discovery of acquired immunological tolerance

1961 Georg von Bekesy (U.S.), for discoveries about physical mechanisms of stimulation within cochlea

1962 James D. Watson (U.S.), Maurice H. F. Wilkins, and Francis H. C. Crick (England), for determining structure of deoxyribonucleic acid (DNA)

1963 Alan Lloyd Hodgkin, Andrew Fielding Huxley (both England), and Sir John Carew Eccles (Australia), for research on nerve cells

1964 Konrad E. Bloch (U.S.) and Feodor Lynen (Germany), for research on mechanism and regulation of cholesterol and fatty acid metabolism

1965 François Jacob, André Lwolff, and Jacques Monod (France), for study of regulatory activities in body cells

1966 Charles Brenton Huggins (U.S.), for studies in hormone treatment of cancer of prostate; Francis Peyton Rous (U.S.), for discovery of tumor-producing viruses

1967 Haldan K. Hartline, George Wald, and Ragnar Granit (U.S.), for work on human eye

1968 Robert W. Holley, Har Gobind Khorana, and Marshall W. Nirenberg (U.S.), for studies of genetic code

1969 Max Delbruck, Alfred D. Hershey, and Salvador E. Luria (U.S.), for study of mechanism of virus infection in living cells

1970 Julius Axelrod (U.S.), Ulf S. von Euler (Sweden), and Sir Bernard Katz (England), for studies of how nerve impulses are transmitted within the body

1971 Earl W. Sutherland, Jr. (U.S.), for research on how hormones work

1972 Gerald M. Edelman (U.S.), and Rodney R. Porter (U.K.), for research on the chemical structure and nature of antibodies

1973 Karl von Frisch and Konrad Lorenz (Austria), and Nikolaas Tinbergen (Netherlands), for their studies of individual and social behavior patterns

1974 George E. Palade and Christian de Duve (both U.S.) and Albert Claude (Belgium), for contributions to understanding inner workings of living cells

1975 David Baltimore, Howard M. Temin, and Renato Dulbecco (all U.S.), for work in interaction between tumor viruses and genetic material of the cell

1976 Baruch S. Blumberg and D. Carleton Gajdusek (U.S.), for discoveries concerning new mechanisms for the origin and dissemination of infectious diseases

1977 Rosalyn S. Yalow, Roger C. L. Guillemin, and Andrew V. Schally (all U.S.), for research in role of hormones in chemistry of the body

1978 Daniel Nathans and Hamilton Smith (both U.S.) and Werner Arber (Switzerland), for discovery of restriction enzymes and their application to problems of molecular genetics

1979 Allan McLeod Cormack (U.S.) and Godfrey Newbold Hounsfield (England), for developing computed axial tomography (CAT scan) X-ray technique

1980 Baruj Benacerraf and George D. Snell (both U.S.) and Jean Dausset (France), for discoveries that explain how the structure of cells relates to organ transplants and diseases

1981 Roger W. Sperry and David H. Hubel (both U.S.) and Torsten N. Wiesel (Sweden), for studies vital to understanding the organization and functioning of the brain

1982 Sune Bergstrom and Bengt Samuelsson (Sweden) and John R. Vane (U.K.), for research in prostaglandins, a hormonelike substance involved in a wide range of illnesses

1983 Barbara McClintock (U.S.), for her discovery of mobile genes in the chromosomes of a plant that change the future generations of plants they produce

1984 Cesar Milstein (U.K./Argentina) Georges J.F. Kohler (West Germany), and Niels K. Jerne (U.K./Denmark) for their work in immunology

1985 Michael S. Brown and Joseph L. Goldstein (both U.S.) for their work which has drastically widened our understanding of the cholesterol metabolism and increased our possibilities to prevent and treat atherosclerosis and heart attacks

1986 Rita Levi-Montalcini (dual U.S./Italy) and Stanley Cohen (U.S.) for their contributions to the understanding of substances that influence cell growth

1987 Susumu Tonegawa (Japan), for his discoveries of how the body can suddenly marshal its immunological defenses against millions of different disease agents that it has never encountered before.

1988 Gertrude B. Elion, George H. Hitchings (both U.S.) and Sir James Black (U.K.) for their discoveries of important principles for drug treatment.

ECONOMIC SCIENCE

1969 Ragnar Frisch (Norway) and Jan Tinbergen (Netherlands), for work in econometrics (application of mathematics and statistical methods to economic theories and problems)

1970 Paul A. Samuelson (U.S.), for efforts to raise the level of scientific analysis in economic theory

1971 Simon Kuznets (U.S.), for developing concept of using a country's gross national product to determine its economic growth

1972 Kenneth J. Arrow (U.S.) and Sir John R. Hicks (U.K.), for theories that help to assess business risk and government economic and welfare policies

1973 Wassily Leontief (U.S.), for devising the input-output technique to determine how different sectors of an economy interact

1974 Gunnar Myrdal (Sweden) and Friedrich A. von Hayek (U.K.), for pioneering analysis of the interdependence of economic, social and institutional phenomena

1975 Leonid V. Kantorovich (U.S.S.R.) and Tjalling C. Koopmans (U.S.), for work on the theory of optimum allocation of resources

1976 Milton Friedman (U.S.), for work in consumption analysis and monetary history and theory, and for demonstration of complexity of stabilization policy

1977 Bertil Ohlin (Sweden) and James E. Meade (U.K.), for contributions to theory of international trade and international capital movements

1978 Herbert A. Simon (U.S.), for research into the decision-making process within economic organizations

1979 Sir Arthur Lewis (England) and Theodore Schultz (U.S.), for work on economic problems of developing nations

1980 Lawrence R. Klein (U.S.), for developing models for forecasting economic trends and shaping policies to deal with them

1981 James Tobin (U.S.), for analyses of financial markets and their influence on spending and saving by families and businesses

1982 George J. Stigler (U.S.), for work on government regulation in the economy and the functioning of industry

1983 Gerard Debreu (U.S.), in recognition of his work on the basic economic problem of how prices operate to balance what producers supply with what buyers want.

1984 Sir Richard Stone (U.K.), for his work to develop the systems widely used to measure the performance of national economics

1985 Franco Modigliani (U.S.) for his pioneering work in analyzing the behavior of household savers and the functioning of financial markets

1986 James M. Buchanan (U.S.) for his development of new methods for analyzing economic and political decision-making

1987 Robert M. Solow (U.S.), for seminal contributions to the theory of economic growth.

1988 Maurice Allais (France) for his pioneering development of theories to better understand market behavior and the efficient use of resources.

1989 Bancroft Prizes in American History

Reconstruction: America's Unfinished Revolution 1863-1877, by Eric Foner (Harper & Row)
Inventing the People: The Rise of Popular Sover-

eignty in England and America, by Edmund S. Morgan (W.W. Norton & Co.)

Motion Picture Academy Awards (Oscars)

1928

Picture: *Wings,* Paramount
Director: Frank Borzage, *Seventh Heaven;* Lewis Milestone, *Two Arabian Nights*
Actress: Janet Gaynor, *Seventh Heaven, Street Angel, Sunrise*
Actor: Emil Jannings, *The Way of All Flesh, The Last Command*

1929

Picture: *The Broadway Melody,* M-G-M
Director: Frank Lloyd, *The Divine Lady*
Actress: Mary Pickford, *Coquette*
Actor: Warner Baxter, *In Old Arizona*

1930

Picture: *All Quiet on the Western Front,* Universal
Director: Lewis Milestone, *All Quiet on the Western Front*
Actress: Norma Shearer, *The Divorcee*
Actor: George Arliss, *Disraeli*

1931

Picture: *Cimarron:* RKO Radio
Director: Norman Taurog, *Skippy*
Actress: Marie Dressler, *Min and Bill*
Actor: Lionel Barrymore, *A Free Soul*

1932

Picture: *Grand Hotel,* M-G-M
Director: Frank Borzage, *Bad Girl*
Actress: Helen Hayes, *The Sin of Madelon Claudet*
Actor: Fredric March, *Dr. Jekyll and Mr. Hyde,* and Wallace Beery, *The Champ*

1933

Picture: *Cavalcade,* Fox
Director: Frank Lloyd, *Cavalcade*
Actress: Katharine Hepburn, *Morning Glory*
Actor: Charles Laughton, *The Private Life of Henry VIII*

1934

Picture: *It Happened One Night,* Columbia
Director: Frank Capra, *It Happened One Night*
Actress: Claudette Colbert, *It Happened One Night*
Actor: Clark Gable, *It Happened One Night*

1935

Picture: *Mutiny on the Bounty,* M-G-M
Director: John Ford, *The Informer*
Actress: Bette Davis, *Dangerous*
Actor: Victor McLaglen, *The Informer*

1936

Picture: *The Great Ziegfeld,* M-G-M
Director: Frank Capra, *Mr. Deeds Goes to Town*
Actress: Luise Rainer, *The Great Ziegfeld*
Actor: Paul Muni, *The Story of Louis Pasteur*
Supporting Actress: Gale Sondergaard, *Anthony Adverse*
Supporting Actor: Walter Brennan, *Come and Get It*

1937

Picture: *The Life of Emile Zola,* Warner Bros.
Director: Leo McCarey, *The Awful Truth*
Actress: Luise Rainer, *The Good Earth*
Actor: Spencer Tracy, *Captains Courageous*
Supporting Actress: Alice Brady, *In Old Chicago*
Supporting Actor: Joseph Schildkraut, *The Life of Emile Zola*

1938

Picture: *You Can't Take It with You,* Columbia
Director: Frank Capra, *You Can't Take It with You*
Actress: Bette Davis, *Jezebel*
Actor: Spencer Tracy, *Boys Town*
Supporting Actress: Fay Bainter, *Jezebel*
Supporting Actor: Walter Brennan, *Kentucky*

1939

Picture: *Gone with the Wind,* Selznick-M-G-M
Director: Victor Fleming, *Gone with the Wind*
Actress: Vivien Leigh, *Gone with the Wind*
Actor: Robert Donat, *Goodbye, Mr. Chips*
Supporting Actress: Hattie McDaniel, *Gone with the Wind*
Supporting Actor: Thomas Mitchell, *Stagecoach*

1940

Picture: *Rebecca,* Selznick-UA
Director: John Ford, *The Grapes of Wrath*
Actress: Ginger Rogers, *Kitty Foyle*
Actor: James Stewart, *The Philadelphia Story*
Supporting Actress: Jane Darwell, *The Grapes of Wrath*
Supporting Actor: Walter Brennan, *The Westerner*

1941

Picture: *How Green Was My Valley,* 20th Century-Fox
Director: John Ford, *How Green Was My Valley*
Actress: Joan Fontaine, *Suspicion*
Actor: Gary Cooper, *Sergeant York*
Supporting Actress: Mary Astor, *The Great Lie*
Supporting Actor: Donald Crisp, *How Green Was My Valley*

1942

Picture: *Mrs. Miniver,* M-G-M
Director: William Wyler, *Mrs. Miniver*
Actress: Greer Garson, *Mrs. Miniver*
Actor: James Cagney, *Yankee Doodle Dandy*
Supporting Actress: Teresa Wright, *Mrs. Miniver*
Supporting Actor: Van Heflin, *Johnny Eager*

1943

Picture: *Casablanca,* Warner Bros.
Director: Michael Curtiz, *Casablanca*
Actress: Jennifer Jones, *The Song of Bernadette*
Actor: Paul Lukas, *Watch on the Rhine*
Supporting Actress: Katina Paxinou, *For Whom the Bell Tolls*
Supporting Actor: Charles Coburn, *The More the Merrier*

1944

Picture: *Going My Way,* Paramount
Director: Leo McCarey, *Going My Way*
Actress: Ingrid Bergman, *Gaslight*
Actor: Bing Crosby, *Going My Way*
Supporting Actress: Ethel Barrymore, *None But the Lonely Heart*
Supporting Actor: Barry Fitzgerald, *Going My Way*

1945

Picture: *The Lost Weekend,* Paramount
Director: Billy Wilder, *The Lost Weekend*
Actress: Joan Crawford, *Mildred Pierce*
Actor: Ray Milland, *The Lost Weekend*
Supporting Actress: Anne Revere, *National Velvet*
Supporting Actor: James Dunn, *A Tree Grows in Brooklyn*

1946

Picture: *The Best Years of Our Lives,* Goldwyn-RKO Radio
Director: William Wyler, *The Best Years of Our Lives*
Actress: Olivia de Havilland, *To Each His Own*
Actor: Fredric March, *The Best Years of Our Lives*
Supporting Actress: Anne Baxter, *The Razor's Edge*
Supporting Actor: Harold Russell, *The Best Years of Our Lives*

1947

Picture: *Gentleman's Agreement,* 20th Century-Fox
Director: Elia Kazan, *Gentleman's Agreement*
Actress: Loretta Young, *The Farmer's Daughter*
Actor: Ronald Colman, *A Double Life*
Supporting Actress: Celeste Holm, *Gentleman's Agreement*
Supporting Actor: Edmund Gwenn, *Miracle on 34th Street*

1948

Picture: *Hamlet,* Rank-Two Cities-U-I
Director: John Huston, *Treasure of Sierra Madre*
Actress: Jane Wyman, *Johnny Belinda*
Actor: Laurence Olivier, *Hamlet*
Supporting Actress: Claire Trevor, *Key Largo*
Supporting Actor: Walter Huston, *Treasure of Sierra Madre*

1949

Picture: *All the King's Men,* Rossen-Columbia
Director: Joseph L. Mankiewicz, *A Letter to Three Wives*
Actress: Olivia de Havilland, *The Heiress*
Actor: Broderick Crawford, *All the King's Men*
Supporting Actress: Mercedes McCambridge, *All the King's Men*
Supporting Actor: Dean Jagger, *Twelve O'Clock High*

1950

Picture: *All About Eve,* 20th Century-Fox
Director: Joseph L. Mankiewicz, *All About Eve*
Actress: Judy Holliday, *Born Yesterday*
Actor: José Ferrer, *Cyrano de Bergerac*
Supporting Actress: Josephine Hull, *Harvey*
Supporting Actor: George Sanders, *All About Eve*

1951

Picture: *An American in Paris,* M-G-M
Director: George Stevens, *A Place in the Sun*
Actress: Vivien Leigh, *A Streetcar Named Desire*
Actor: Humphrey Bogart, *The African Queen*
Supporting Actress: Kim Hunter, *A Streetcar Named Desire*
Supporting Actor: Karl Malden, *A Streetcar Named Desire*

1952

Picture: *The Greatest Show on Earth,* DeMille-Paramount
Director: John Ford, *The Quiet Man*
Actress: Shirley Booth, *Come Back, Little Sheba*
Actor: Gary Cooper, *High Noon*
Supporting Actress: Gloria Grahame, *The Bad and the Beautiful*
Supporting Actor: Anthony Quinn, *Viva Zapata!*

1953

Picture: *From Here to Eternity,* Columbia
Director: Fred Zinnemann, *From Here to Eternity*
Actress: Audrey Hepburn, *Roman Holiday*

Actor: William Holden, *Stalag 17*
Supporting Actress: Donna Reed, *From Here to Eternity*
Supporting Actor: Frank Sinatra, *From Here to Eternity*

1954

Picture: *On the Waterfront,* Horizon-American Corp., Columbia
Director: Elia Kazan, *On the Waterfront*
Actress: Grace Kelly, *The Country Girl*
Actor: Marlon Brando, *On the Waterfront*
Supporting Actress: Eva Marie Saint, *On the Waterfront*
Supporting Actor: Edmond O'Brien, *The Barefoot Contessa*

1955

Picture: *Marty,* Hecht and Lancaster, United Artists
Director: Delbert Mann, *Marty*
Actress: Anna Magnani, *The Rose Tattoo*
Actor: Ernest Borgnine, *Marty*
Supporting Actress: Jo Van Fleet, *East of Eden*
Supporting Actor: Jack Lemmon, *Mister Roberts*

1956

Picture: *Around the World in 80 Days,* Michael Todd Co., Inc.-U.A.
Director: George Stevens, *Giant*
Actress: Ingrid Bergman, *Anastasia*
Actor: Yul Brynner, *The King and I*
Supporting Actress: Dorothy Malone, *Written on the Wind*
Supporting Actor: Anthony Quinn, *Lust for Life*

1957

Picture: *The Bridge on the River Kwai,* Horizon Picture, Columbia
Director: David Lean, *The Bridge on the River Kwai*
Actress: Joanne Woodward, *The Three Faces of Eve*
Actor: Alec Guinness, *The Bridge on the River Kwai*
Supporting Actress: Miyoshi Umeki, *Sayonara*
Supporting Actor: Red Buttons, *Sayonara*

1958

Picture: *Gigi,* Arthur Freed Productions, Inc., M-G-M
Director: Vincente Minnelli, *Gigi*
Actress: Susan Hayward, *I Want to Live!*
Actor: David Niven, *Separate Tables*
Supporting Actress: Wendy Hiller, *Separate Tables*
Supporting Actor: Burl Ives, *The Big Country*

1959

Picture: *Ben-Hur,* M-G-M
Director: William Wyler, *Ben-Hur*
Actress: Simone Signoret, *Room at the Top*
Actor: Charlton Heston, *Ben-Hur*
Supporting Actress: Shelley Winters, *The Diary of Anne Frank*
Supporting Actor: Hugh Griffith, *Ben-Hur*

1960

Picture: *The Apartment,* Mirisch Co., Inc., United Artists
Director: Billy Wilder, *The Apartment*
Actress: Elizabeth Taylor, *Butterfield 8*
Actor: Burt Lancaster, *Elmer Gantry*
Supporting Actress: Shirley Jones, *Elmer Gantry*
Supporting Actor: Peter Ustinov, *Spartacus*

1961

Picture: *West Side Story,* Mirisch Pictures, Inc., and B and P Enterprises, Inc., United Artists

Director: Robert Wise and Jerome Robbins, *West Side Story*
Actress: Sophia Loren, *Two Women*
Actor: Maximillian Schell, *Judgment at Nuremberg*
Supporting Actress: Rita Moreno, *West Side Story*
Supporting Actor: George Chakiris, *West Side Story*

1962

Picture: *Lawrence of Arabia,* Horizon Pictures, Ltd.-Columbia
Director: David Lean, *Lawrence of Arabia*
Actress: Anne Bancroft, *The Miracle Worker*
Actor: Gregory Peck, *To Kill a Mockingbird*
Supporting Actress: Patty Duke, *The Miracle Worker*
Supporting Actor: Ed Begley, *Sweet Bird of Youth*

1963

Picture: *Tom Jones,* A Woodfall Production, UA-Lopert Pictures
Director: Tony Richardson, *Tom Jones*
Actress: Patricia Neal, *Hud*
Actor: Sidney Poitier, *Lilies of the Field*
Supporting Actress: Margaret Rutherford, *The V.I.P.s*
Supporting Actor: Melvyn Douglas, *Hud*

1964

Picture: *My Fair Lady,* Warner Bros.
Director: George Cukor, *My Fair Lady*
Actress: Julie Andrews, *Mary Poppins*
Actor: Rex Harrison, *My Fair Lady*
Supporting Actress: Lila Kedrova, *Zorba the Greek*
Supporting Actor: Peter Ustinov, *Topkapi*

1965

Picture: *The Sound of Music,* Argyle Enterprises Production, 20th Century-Fox
Director: Robert Wise, *The Sound of Music*
Actress: Julie Christie, *Darling*
Actor: Lee Marvin, *Cat Ballou*
Supporting Actress: Shelley Winters, *A Patch of Blue*
Supporting Actor: Martin Balsam, *A Thousand Clowns*

1966

Picture: *A Man for All Seasons,* Highland Films, Ltd., Production, Columbia
Director: Fred Zinnemann, *A Man for All Seasons*
Actress: Elizabeth Taylor, *Who's Afraid of Virginia Woolf?*
Actor: Paul Scofield, *A Man for All Seasons*
Supporting Actress: Sandy Dennis, *Who's Afraid of Virginia Woolf?*
Supporting Actor: Walter Matthau, *The Fortune Cookie*

1967

Picture: *In the Heat of the Night,* Mirisch Corp. Productions, United Artists
Director: Mike Nichols, *The Graduate*
Actress: Katharine Hepburn, *Guess Who's Coming to Dinner*
Actor: Rod Steiger, *In the Heat of the Night*
Supporting Actress: Estelle Parsons, *Bonnie and Clyde*
Supporting Actor: George Kennedy, *Cool Hand Luke*

1968

Picture: *Oliver!,* Columbia Pictures
Director: Sir Carol Reed, *Oliver!*
Actress: Katharine Hepburn, *The Lion in Winter* and Barbara Streisand, *Funny Girl*
Actor: Cliff Robertson, *Charly*

Supporting Actress: Ruth Gordon, *Rosemary's Baby*
Supporting Actor: Jack Albertson, *The Subject Was Roses*

1969

Picture: *Midnight Cowboy,* Jerome Hellman-John Schlesinger Production, United Artists
Director: John Schlesinger, *Midnight Cowboy*
Actress: Maggie Smith, *The Prime of Miss Jean Brodie*
Actor: John Wayne, *True Grit*
Supporting Actress: Goldie Hawn, *Cactus Flower*
Supporting Actor: Gig Young, *They Shoot Horses Don't They?*

1970

Picture: *Patton,* Frank McCarthy-Franklin J. Schaffner Production, 20th Century Fox
Director: Franklin J. Schaffner, *Patton*
Actress: Glenda Jackson, *Women in Love*
Actor: George C. Scott, *Patton*
Supporting Actress: Helen Hayes, *Airport*
Supporting Actor: John Mills, *Ryan's Daughter*

1971

Picture: *The French Connection,* D'Antoni Productions, 20th Century-Fox
Director: William Friedkin, *The French Connection*
Actress: Jane Fonda, *Klute*
Actor: Gene Hackman, *The French Connection*
Supporting Actress: Cloris Leachman, *The Last Picture Show*
Supporting Actor: Ben Johnson, *The Last Picture Show*

1972

Picture: *The Godfather,* Albert S. Ruddy Production, Paramount
Director: Bob Fosse, *Cabaret*
Actress: Liza Minnelli, *Cabaret*
Actor: Marlon Brando, *The Godfather*
Supporting Actress: Eileen Heckart, *Butterflies Are Free*
Supporting Actor: Joel Gray, *Cabaret*

1973

Picture: *The Sting,* Universal-Bill-Phillips-George Roy Hill Production, Universal
Director: George Roy Hill, *The Sting*
Actress: Glenda Jackson, *A Touch of Class*
Actor: Jack Lemmon, *Save the Tiger*
Supporting Actress: Tatum O'Neal, *Paper Moon*
Supporting Actor: John Houseman, *The Paper Chase*

1974

Picture: *The Godfather, Part II,* Coppola Co. Production, Paramount
Director: Francis Ford Coppola, *The Godfather, Part II*
Actress: Ellen Burstyn, *Alice Doesn't Live Here Anymore*
Actor: Art Carney, *Harry and Tonto*
Supporting Actress: Ingrid Bergman, *Murder on the Orient Express*
Supporting Actor: Robert De Niro, *The Godfather, Part II*

1975

Picture: *One Flew Over the Cuckoo's Nest,* Fantasy Films Production, United Artists
Director: Milos Forman, *One Flew Over the Cuckoo's Nest*
Actress: Louise Fletcher, *One Flew Over the Cuckoo's Nest*

Actor: Jack Nicholson, *One Flew Over the Cuckoo's Nest*
Supporting Actress: Lee Grant, *Shampoo*
Supporting Actor: George Burns, *The Sunshine Boys*

1976

Picture: *Rocky,* Robert Chartoff-Irwin Winkler Production, United Artists
Director: John G. Avildsen, *Rocky*
Actress: Faye Dunaway, *Network*
Actor: Peter Finch, *Network*
Supporting Actress: Beatrice Straight, *Network*
Supporting Actor: Jason Robards, *All the President's Men*

1977

Picture: *Annie Hall,* Jack Rollins-Charles H. Joffe Production, United Artists
Director: Woody Allen, *Annie Hall*
Actress: Diane Keaton, *Annie Hall*
Actor: Richard Dreyfuss, *The Goodbye Girl*
Supporting Actress: Vanessa Redgrave, *Julia*
Supporting Actor: Jason Robards, *Julia*

1978

Picture: *The Deer Hunter,* Michael Cimino Film Production, Universal
Director: Michael Cimino, *The Deer Hunter*
Actress: Jane Fonda, *Coming Home*
Actor: Jon Voight, *Coming Home*
Supporting Actress: Maggie Smith, *California Suite*
Supporting Actor: Christopher Walken, *The Deer Hunter*

1979

Picture: *Kramer vs. Kramer,* Stanley Jaffe Production, Columbia Pictures
Director: Robert Benton, *Kramer vs. Kramer*
Actress: Sally Field, *Norma Rae*
Actor: Dustin Hoffman, *Kramer vs. Kramer*
Supporting Actress: Meryl Streep, *Kramer vs. Kramer*
Supporting Actor: Melvyn Douglas, *Being There*

1980

Picture: *Ordinary People,* Wildwood Enterprises Production, Paramount
Director: Robert Redford, *Ordinary People*
Actress: Sissy Spacek, *Coal Miner's Daughter*
Actor: Robert De Niro, *Raging Bull*
Supporting Actress: Mary Steenburgen, *Melvin and Howard*
Supporting Actor: Timothy Hutton, *Ordinary People*

1981

Picture: *Chariots of Fire,* Enigma Productions, Ladd Company/Warner Bros.
Director: Warren Beatty, *Reds*
Actress: Katharine Hepburn, *On Golden Pond*
Actor: Henry Fonda, *On Golden Pond*
Supporting Actress: Maureen Stapleton, *Reds*
Supporting Actor: John Gielgud, *Arthur*

1982

Picture: *Gandhi,* Indo-British Films Production/Columbia
Director: Richard Attenborough, *Gandhi*
Actress: Meryl Streep, *Sophie's Choice*
Actor: Ben Kingsley, *Gandhi*
Supporting Actress: Jessica Lange, *Tootsie*
Supporting Actor: Louis Gossett, Jr., *An Officer and a Gentleman*

1983

Picture: *Terms of Endearment,* Paramount
Director: James L. Brooks, *Terms of Endearment*
Actress: Shirley MacLaine, *Terms of Endearment*
Actor: Robert Duvall, *Tender Mercies*
Supporting Actress: Linda Hunt, *The Year of Living Dangerously*
Supporting Actor: Jack Nicholson, *Terms of Endearment*

1984

Picture: *Amadeus,* Orion Pictures
Director: Milos Forman, *Amadeus*
Actress: Sally Field, *Places in the Heart*
Actor: F. Murray Abraham, *Amadeus*
Supporting Actress: Dame Peggy Ashcroft, *A Passage to India*
Supporting Actor: Haing S. Ngor, *The Killing Fields*

1985

Picture: *Out of Africa,* Universal
Director: Sydney Pollack, *Out of Africa*
Actress: Geraldine Page, *The Trip to Bountiful*
Actor: William Hurt, *Kiss of the Spider Woman*
Supporting Actress: Anjelica Huston, *Prizzi's Honor*
Supporting Actor: Don Ameche, *Cocoon*

1986

Picture: *Platoon,* Orion Pictures
Director: Oliver Stone, *Platoon*
Actress: Marlee Matlin, *Children of a Lesser God*
Actor: Paul Newman, *The Color of Money*
Supporting Actress: Dianne Wiest, *Hannah and Her Sisters*
Supporting Actor: Michael Caine, *Hannah and Her Sisters*

1987

Picture: *The Last Emperor,* Columbia Pictures
Director: Bernardo Bertolucci, *The Last Emperor*
Actress: Cher, *Moonstruck*
Actor: Michael Douglas, *Wall Street*
Supporting Actress: Olympia Dukakis, *Moonstruck*
Supporting Actor: Sean Connery, *The Untouchables*

1988

Picture: *Rain Man,* United Artists
Director: Barry Levinson, *Rain Man*
Actress: Jodie Foster, *The Accused*
Actor: Dustin Hoffman, *Rain Man*
Supporting Actress: Geena Davis, *The Accidental Tourist*
Supporting Actor: Kevin Kline: *A Fish Named Wanda*

Other Academy Awards for 1988

Art direction: Stuart Craig, art direction, and Gerard James, set decoration, *Dangerous Liaisons*
Cinematography: Peter Bizlou, *Mississippi Burning*
Costume Design: James Acheson, *Dangerous Liaisons*
Documentary (feature): *Hotel Terminus: The Life and Times of Klaus Barbie;* **(short subject):** *You Don't Have To Die*
Editing: Arthur Schmidt, *Who Framed Roger Rabbit*
Foreign-language film: *Pelle the Conqueror,* Denmark
Makeup: Ve Neill, Steve La Porte, and Robert Short, *Beetlejuice*
Music (original score): Dave Grusin, *The Milagro*

Beanfield War

Screenplay (original): Ronald Bass and Barry Marrow, *Rain Man;* **(adaption):** Christopher Hampton, *Dangerous Liaisons*

Short subject (live-action): *The Appointments of Dennis Jennings;* **(animated):** *Tin Toy*

Song: Carly Simon, *Let the River Run* from *Working Girl*

Sound: Les Fresholtz, Dick Alexander, Vern Poore, and Willie D. Burton, *Bird*

Sound-effects editing: Charles L. Campbell and

Louis L. Edemann, *Who Framed Roger Rabbit*

Visual Effects: Ken Ralston, Richard Williams, Edward Jones, and George Gibbs, *Who Framed Roger Rabbit*

Honorary Awards: The National Film Board of Canada and Eastman Kodak Company

Special Achievement: Richard Williams

Merit Award: Ray Dolby and Ioan Allen of Dolby Laboratories

Gordon E. Sawyer Award: Gordon Henry Cook

National Society of Film Critics Awards, 1988

Best Film: *The Unbearable Lightness of Being,* Philip Kaufman

Best Actress: Judy Davis, *High Tide*

Best Actor: Michael Keaton, *Beetlejuice* and *Clean and Sober*

Best Supporting Actress: Mercedes Ruehl, *Married to the Mob*

Best Supporting Actor: Dean Stockwell, *Married to the Mob*

Best Director: Philip Kaufman, *The Unbearable Lightness of Being*

Best Screenplay: *Bull Durham,* Ron Shelton

Best Cinematography: Henri Alekan, *Wings of Desire*

Best Documentary: *Thin Blue Line,* Errol Morris

Special Award for His Originality: Pedro Almodovar, director of *Women on the Verge of a Nervous Breakdown* and *Matador*

George Foster Peabody Awards for Broadcasting, 1988

Radio

WHAS Louisville, Ky.: *A Matter of Time: The Crisis in Kentucky Corrections*

WBUR, Boston: *Speaking for Everyman: Ian McKellen Celebrates Shakespeare's Birthday*

KMOX, St. Louis: *Hate Crimes: America's Cancer*

National Public Radio, Washington, D.C.: *Cowboys on Everest*

BBC World Service for Africa, London: *Nothing Political/Mandela at 70*

KTAR, Phoenix: *The Impeachment of Evan Mecham*

Television

WPLG, Miami: *Caution: Precious Cargo*

MacNeil/Lehrer Productions, New York: *The MacNeil/Lehrer NewsHour: Election '88 Coverage*

Frontline, Boston: *Frontline: The Choice*

CBS News, New York: *Abortion Battle* and *On Runaway Street* from *48 Hours*

KCBS, Los Angeles: *MCA and the Mob*

CBS Entertainment and Telecom Entertainment in association with **Yorkshire Television:** *The Attic: The Hiding of Anne Frank*

BBC, London and WNET/13, New York: *The Singing Detective*

NBC, New York: *The Murder of Mary Phagam*

ABC, New York, and the Bedford Falls Company in association with **MGM/UA Television:** *thirtysomething*

The Children's Television Workshop, New York: *3-2-1 CONTACT Extra: I Have AIDS, A Teen-ager's*

Story

The South Carolina ETV Network, Columbia, S.C.: *Children's Express NEWSMAGAZINE: Campaign '88*

The Christian Science Monitor Reports, New York: *Islam in Turmoil*

WTTW, Chicago, in association with **Chloe Productions Inc.:** *. . . And the Pursuit of Happiness*

HBO, New York: *Dear America: Letters Home From Vietnam*

HBO, in association with **Pro Image Productions:** *Suzi's Story*

WBRZ, Baton Rouge, La.: *The Best Insurance Commissioner Money Can Buy*

Turner Network Television, Atlanta: *The Making of a Legend: Gone With The Wind*

CBS News: *Mr. Snow Goes to Washington,* from *60 Minutes*

WJLA, Washington, D.C.: *The Radon Watch Campaign*

Public Affaris Television, New York: *Bill Moyers' World of Ideas*

Personal Awards

Walter Annenberg, publisher, for his philanthropic role in support of the educational uses of radio and television.

Don Hewitt, CBS News, for exceptional contributions to television news for 40 years.

Jim McKay, ABC-TV, for pioneering efforts and accomplishments in televised sports.

Enrico Fermi Award

Named in honor of Enrico Fermi, the atomic pioneer, the $100,000 award is given in recognition of "exceptional and altogether outstanding" scientific and technical achievement in atomic energy.

1954 Enrico Fermi	1969 Walter H. Zinn	Neddermeyer
1956 John von Neumann	1970 Norris E. Bradbury	1983 Alexander Hollaender and
1957 Ernest O. Lawrence	1971 Shields Warren and Stafford	John Lawrence
1958 Eugene P. Wigner	L. Warren	1984 Robert R. Wilson and Georges
1959 Glenn T. Seaborg	1972 Manson Benedict	Vendryès
1961 Hans A. Bethe	1976 William L. Russell	1985 Norman C. Rasmussen and Marshall
1962 Edward Teller	1978 Harold M. Agnew and Wolfgang	N. Rosenblath
1963 J. Robert Oppenheimer	K.H. Panofsky	1986 Ernest D. Courant and M. Stanley Livingston
1964 Hyman G. Rickover	1980 Alvin M. Weinberg and Rudolf	
1966 Otto Hahn, Lise Meitner, and	E. Peirls	1987 Luis W. Alvarez and Gerald F. Tape
Fritz Strassman	1981 W. Bennett Lewis	1988 Richard B. Setlow and Victor F.
1968 John A. Wheeler	1982 Herbert Anderson and Seth	Weisskopf

Pulitzer Prize Awards

(For years not listed, no award was made.)

Source: Columbia University.

Pulitzer Prizes in Journalism

MERITORIOUS PUBLIC SERVICE

1918 *New York Times;* also special award to Minna Lewinson and Henry Beetle Hough
1919 *Milwaukee Journal*
1921 *Boston Post*
1922 *New York World*
1923 *Memphis Commercial Appeal*
1924 *New York World*
1926 *Columbus* (Ga.) *Enquirer Sun*
1927 *Canton* (Ohio) *Daily News*
1928 *Indianapolis Times*
1929 *New York Evening World*
1931 *Atlanta Constitution*
1932 *Indianapolis News*
1933 *New York World-Telegram*
1934 *Medford* (Ore.) *Mail Tribune*
1935 *Sacramento Bee*
1936 *Cedar Rapids* (Iowa) *Gazette*
1937 *St. Louis Post-Dispatch*
1938 *Bismarck* (N.D.) *Tribune*
1939 *Miami Daily News*
1940 *Waterbury* (Conn.) *Republican* and *American*
1941 *St. Louis Post-Dispatch*
1942 *Los Angeles Times*
1943 *Omaha World-Herald*
1944 *New York Times*
1945 *Detroit Free Press*
1946 *Scranton* (Pa.) *Times*
1947 *Baltimore Sun*
1948 *St. Louis Post-Dispatch*
1949 *(Lincoln) Nebraska State Journal*
1950 *Chicago Daily News;* and *St. Louis Post-Dispatch*
1951 *Miami Herald;* and *Brooklyn Eagle*
1952 *St. Louis Post-Dispatch*
1953 *Whiteville* (N.C.) *News Reporter;* and *Tabor City* (N.C.) *Tribune*
1954 *Newsday* (Garden City, L.I.)
1955 *Columbus* (Ga.) *Ledger* and *Sunday Ledger-Enquirer*
1956 *Watsonville* (Calif.) *Register-Pajaronian*
1957 *Chicago Daily News*
1958 *(Little Rock) Arkansas Gazette*
1959 *Utica* (N.Y.) *Observer Dispatch* and *Utica Daily Press*
1960 *Los Angeles Times*
1961 *Amarillo* (Tex.) *Globe-Times*
1962 *Panama City* (Fla.) *News-Herald*
1963 *Chicago Daily News*
1964 *St. Petersburg* (Fla.) *Times*
1965 *Hutchinson* (Kan.) *News*
1966 *Boston Globe*
1967 *Louisville Courier-Journal* and *Milwaukee Journal*
1968 *Riverside* (Calif.) *Press-Enterprise*
1969 *Los Angeles Times*
1970 *Newsday* (Garden City, L.I.)
1971 *Winston-Salem* (N.C.) *Journal and Sentinel*
1972 *New York Times*
1973 *Washington Post*
1974 *Newsday* (Garden City, L.I.)
1975 *Boston Globe*
1976 *Anchorage* (Alaska) *Daily News*
1977 *Lufkin* (Tex.) *News*
1978 *Philadelphia Inquirer*

1979 *Point Reyes* (Calif.) *Light*
1980 Gannett News Service
1981 *Charlotte* (N.C.) *Observer*
1982 *Detroit News*
1983 *Jackson* (Miss.) *Clarion-Ledger*
1984 *Los Angeles Times*
1985 *The Fort Worth Star-Telegram*
1986 *Denver Post*
1987 Andrew Schneider and Matthew Brelis, *Pittsburgh Press*
1988 *Charlotte* (N.C.) *Observer*
1989 *Anchorage Daily News*

EDITORIAL

1917 *New York Tribune*
1918 *Louisville Courier-Journal*
1920 Harvey E. Newbranch *(Omaha Evening World-Herald)*
1922 Frank M. O'Brien *(New York Herald)*
1923 William Allen White *(Emporia* [Kan.] *Gazette)*
1924 *Boston Herald* (Frank Buxton); special prize: Frank I. Cobb *(New York World)*
1925 *Charleston* (S.C.) *News and Courier*
1926 *New York Times* (Edward M. Kingsbury)
1927 *Boston Herald* (F. Lauriston Bullard)
1928 Grover Cleveland Hall *(Montgomery* [Ala.] *Advertiser)*
1929 Louis Isaac Jaffe *(Norfolk Virginian-Pilot)*
1931 Charles S. Ryckman *(Fremont* [Neb.] *Tribune)*
1933 *Kansas City* (Mo.) *Star*
1934 E. P. Chase *(Atlantic* [Iowa] *News Telegraph)*
1936 Felix Morley *(Washington Post);* George B. Parker (Scripps-Howard Newspapers)
1937 John W. Owens *(Baltimore Sun)*
1938 W. W. Waymack *(Des Moines Register and Tribune)*
1939 Ronald G. Callvert *(Portland Oregonian)*
1940 Bart Howard *(St. Louis Post-Dispatch)*
1941 Reuben Maury *(New York Daily News)*
1942 Geoffrey Parsons *(New York Herald Tribune)*
1943 Forrest W. Seymour *(Des Moines Register and Tribune)*
1944 *Kansas City* (Mo.) *Star* (Henry J. Haskell)
1945 George W. Potter *(Providence* [R.I.] *Journal-Bulletin)*
1946 Hodding Carter *([Greenville, Miss.] Delta Democrat-Times)*
1947 William H. Grimes *(Wall Street Journal)*
1948 Virginius Dabney *(Richmond Times-Dispatch)*
1949 John H. Crider *(Boston Herald);* Herbert Elliston *(Washington Post)*
1950 Carl M. Saunders *(Jackson* [Mich.] *Citizen Patriot)*
1951 William H. Fitzpatrick *(New Orleans States)*
1952 Louis LaCoss *(St. Louis Globe-Democrat)*
1953 Vermont C. Royster *(Wall Street Journal)*
1954 *Boston Herald* (Don Murray)
1955 *Detroit Free Press* (Royce Howes)
1956 Lauren K. Soth *(Des Moines Register and Tribune)*
1957 Buford Boone *(Tuscaloosa* [Ala.] *News)*
1958 Harry S. Ashmore *(Arkansas Gazette)*
1959 Ralph McGill *(Atlanta Constitution)*
1960 Lenoir Chambers *(Virginian-Pilot)*
1961 William J. Dorvillier *(San Juan* [P.R.] *Star)*

1962 Thomas M. Storke *(Santa Barbara* [Calif.] *News-Press)*
1963 Ira B. Harkey, Jr. *(Pascagoula* [Miss.] *Chronicle)*
1964 Hazel Brannon Smith *(Lexington* [Miss.] *Advertiser)*
1965 John R. Harrison *(Gainesville* [Fla.] *Daily Sun)*
1966 Robert Lasch *(St. Louis Post-Dispatch)*
1967 Eugene Patterson *(Atlanta Constitution)*
1968 John S. Knight (Knight Newspapers)
1969 Paul Greenberg *(Pine Bluff* [Ark.] *Commercial)*
1970 Phillip L. Geyelin *(Washington Post)*
1971 Horance G. Davis, Jr. *(Gainesville* [Fla.] *Sun)*
1972 John Strohmeyer *(Bethlehem* [Pa.] *Globe Times)*
1973 Roger Bourne Linscott *(Berkshire Eagle* [Pittsfield, Mass.])
1974 F. Gilman Spencer *(Trenton* [N.J.] *Trentonian)*
1975 John Daniell Maurice *(Charleston* [W. Va.] *Daily Mail)*
1976 Philip P. Kerby *(Los Angeles Times)*
1977 Warren L. Lerude, Foster Church and Norman F. Cardoza *(Reno* [Nev.] *Gazette* and *Nevada State Journal)*
1978 Meg Greenfield *(Washington Post)*
1979 Edwin M. Yoder, Jr. *(Washington Star)*
1980 Robert L. Bartley *(Wall Street Journal)*
1981 Not awarded
1982 Jack Rosenthal *(New York Times)*
1983 *Miami Herald*
1984 Albert Scardino *(Georgia Gazette)*
1985 Richard Aregood *(Philadelphia Daily News)*
1986 Jack Fuller *(Chicago Tribune)*
1987 Jonathan Freedman *(San Diego Tribune)*
1988 Jane E. Healy *(Orlando* Fla. *Sentinel)*
1989 Lois Wille *(Chicago Tribune)*

CORRESPONDENCE

1929 Paul Scott Mowrer *(Chicago Daily News)*
1930 Leland Stowe *(New York Herald Tribune)*
1931 H. R. Knickerbocker *(Philadelphia Public Ledger* and *New York Evening Post)*
1932 Walter Duranty *(New York Times);* Charles G. Ross *(St. Louis Post-Dispatch)*
1933 Edgar Ansel Mowrer *(Chicago Daily News)*
1934 Frederick T. Birchall *(New York Times)*
1935 Arthur Krock *(New York Times)*
1936 Wilfred C. Barber *(Chicago Tribune)*
1937 Anne O'Hare McCormick *(New York Times)*
1938 Arthur Krock *(New York Times)*
1939 Louis P. Lochner *(Associated Press)*
1940 Otto D. Tolischus *(New York Times)*
1941 Group award[1]
1942 Carlos P. Romulo *(Philippines Herald)*
1943 Hanson W. Baldwin *(New York Times)*
1944 Ernie Pyle (Scripps-Howard Newspaper Alliance)
1945 Harold V. (Hal) Boyle (Associated Press)
1946 Arnaldo Cortesi *(New York Times)*
1947 Brooks Atkinson *(New York Times)*
1948 Discontinued

EDITORIAL CARTOONING

1922 Rollin Kirby *(New York World)*
1924 Jay Norwood Darling *(New York Tribune)*
1925 Rollin Kirby *(New York World)*
1926 D. R. Fitzpatrick *(St. Louis Post-Dispatch)*
1927 Nelson Harding *(Brooklyn Eagle)*
1928 Nelson Harding *(Brooklyn Eagle)*
1929 Rollin Kirby *(New York World)*

1930 Charles R. Macauley *(Brooklyn Eagle)*
1931 Edmund Duffy *(Baltimore Sun)*
1932 John T. McCutcheon *(Chicago Tribune)*
1933 H. M. Talburt *(Washington Daily News)*
1934 Edmund Duffy *(Baltimore Sun)*
1935 Ross A. Lewis *(Milwaukee Journal)*
1937 C. D. Batchelor *(New York Daily News)*
1938 Vaughn Shoemaker *(Chicago Daily News)*
1939 Charles G. Werner *(Daily Oklahoman* [Oklahoma City])
1940 Edmund Duffy *(Baltimore Sun)*
1941 Jacob Burck *(Chicago Times)*
1942 Herbert L. Block (NEA Service)
1943 Jay Norwood Darling *(New York Herald Tribune)*
1944 Clifford K. Berryman *(Washington Evening Star)*
1945 Bill Mauldin (United Features Syndicate)
1946 Bruce Alexander Russell *(Los Angeles Times)*
1947 Vaughn Shoemaker *(Chicago Daily News)*
1948 Reuben L. Goldberg *(New York Sun)*
1949 Lute Pease *(Newark Evening News)*
1950 James T. Berryman *(Washington Evening Star)*
1951 Reg (Reginald W.) Manning *(Arizona Republic* [Phoenix])
1952 Fred L. Packer *(New York Mirror)*
1953 Edward D. Kuekes *(Cleveland Plain Dealer)*
1954 Herbert L. Block *(Washington Post* and *Times-Herald)*
1955 Daniel R. Fitzpatrick *(St. Louis Post-Dispatch)*
1956 Robert York *(Louisville Times)*
1957 Tom Little *(Nashville Tennessean)*
1958 Bruce M. Shanks *(Buffalo Evening News)*
1959 Bill Mauldin *(St. Louis Post-Dispatch)*
1961 Carey Orr *(Chicago Tribune)*
1962 Edmund S. Valtman *(Hartford Times)*
1963 Frank Miller *(Des Moines Register)*
1964 Paul Conrad (formerly of *Denver Post,* later on *Los Angeles Times)*
1966 Don Wright *(Miami News)*
1967 Patrick B. Oliphant *(Denver Post)*
1968 Eugene Gray Payne *(Charlotte* [N.C.] *Observer)*
1969 John Fischetti *(Chicago Daily News)*
1970 Thomas F. Darcy *(Newsday* [Garden City, L.I.])
1971 Paul Conrad *(Los Angeles Times)*
1972 Jeffrey K. MacNelly *(Richmond* [Va.] *News Leader)*
1974 Paul Szep *(Boston Globe)*
1975 Garry Trudeau (Universal Press Syndicate)
1976 Tony Auth *(Philadelphia Inquirer)*
1977 Paul Szep *(Boston Globe)*
1978 Jeffrey K. MacNelly *(Richmond* [Va.] *News Leader)*
1979 Herbert L. Block *(Washington Post)*
1980 Don Wright *(Miami News)*
1981 Mike Peters *(Dayton* [Ohio] *Daily News)*
1982 Ben Sargent *(Austin* [Tex.] *American-Statesman)*
1983 Richard Locher *(Chicago Tribune)*
1984 Paul Conrad *(Los Angeles Times)*
1985 Jeff MacNelly *(Chicago Tribune)*
1986 Jules Feiffer *(Village Voice)*
1987 Berke Breathed *(Washington Post* Writers Group)
1988 Doug Marlette *(Atlanta Constitution* and *Charlotte* [N.C.] *Observer)*
1989 Jack Higgins *(Chicago Sun-Times)*

NEWS PHOTOGRAPHY

1942 Milton Brooks *(Detroit News)*
1943 Frank Noel (Associated Press)
1944 Frank Filan (Associated Press); Earle L. Bunker *(Omaha World-Herald)*
1945 Joe Rosenthal (Associated Press)

1. For the public services and the individual achievements of American news reporters in the war zones.

1947 Arnold Hardy
1948 Frank Cushing *(Boston Traveler)*
1949 Nat Fein *(New York Herald Tribune)*
1950 Bill Crouch *(Oakland Tribune)*
1951 Max Desfor (Associated Press)
1952 John Robinson and Don Ultang *(Des Moines Register & Tribune)*
1953 William M. Gallagher *(Flint* [Mich.] *Journal)*
1954 Mrs. Walter M. Schau
1955 John L. Gaunt, Jr. *(Los Angeles Times)*
1956 *New York Daily News*
1957 Harry A. Trask *(Boston Traveler)*
1958 William C. Beall *(Washington Daily News)*
1959 William Seaman *(Minneapolis Star)*
1960 Andrew Lopez (United Press International)
1961 Yasushi Nagao (Mainichi Newspapers, Tokyo)
1962 Paul Vathis (Harrisburg [Pa.] bureau of Associated Press)
1963 Hector Rondon (*La Republica,* Caracas, Venezuela)
1964 Robert H. Jackson *(Dallas Times Herald)*
1965 Horst Faas (Associated Press)
1966 Kyoichi Sawada (United Press International)
1967 Jack R. Thornell (Associated Press)
1968 News: Rocco Morabito *(Jacksonville* [Fla.] *Journal);* features: Toshio Sakai (United Press International)
1969 Spot news: Edward T. Adams (Associated Press); features: Moneta Sleet, Jr.
1970 Spot news: Steve Starr (Associated Press); features: Dallas Kinney *(Palm Beach Post)*
1971 Spot news: John Paul Filo *(Valley Daily News and Daily Dispatch* [Tarentum and New Kensington, Pa.]); features: Jack Dykinga *(Chicago Sun-Times)*
1972 Spot news: Horst Faas and Michel Laurent (Associated Press); features: Dave Kennerly (United Press International)
1973 Spot news: Huynh Cong Ut *(Associated Press);* features: Brian Lanker *(Topeka Capital-Journal)*
1974 Spot news: Anthony K. Roberts (Associated Press); features: Slava Veder (Associated Press)
1975 Spot news: Gerald H. Gay *(Seattle Times);* features: Matthew Lewis *(Washington Post)*
1976 Spot news: Stanley J. Forman *(Boston Herald-American);* features: photographic staff of *Louisville Courier-Journal* and *Times*
1977 Spot news: Neal Ulevich (Associated Press) and Stanley J. Forman *(Boston Herald-American);* features: Robin Hood *(Chattanooga News-Free Press)*
1978 Spot news: John Blair, freelance, Evansville, Ind.; features: J. Ross Baughman (Associated Press)
1979 Spot news: Thomas J. Kelly, 3rd *(Pottstown* [Pa.] *Mercury);* features: photographic staff of *Boston Herald-American*
1980 Features: Erwin H. Hagler *(Dallas Times Herald)*
1981 Spot news: Larry C. Price *(Fort Worth Star-Telegram);* features: Taro M. Yamasaki *(Detroit Free Press)*
1982 Spot news: Ron Edmonds (Associated Press); features: John H. White *(Chicago Sun-Times)*
1983 Spot news: Bill Foley (Associated Press); features: James B. Dickman *(Dallas Times Herald)*
1984 Spot news: Stan Grossfeld *(Boston Globe);* features: Anthony Suau *(Denver Post)*
1985 Spot news: photographic staff of *Register,* Santa Ana, Calif.; features: Stan Grossfeld *(Boston Globe)*
1986 Spot news: Michel duCille and Carol Guzy *(Miami Herald);* features: Tom Gralish *(Philadelphia Inquirer)*
1987 Spot news: Kim Komenich *(San Francisco Examiner);* features: David Peterson *(Des Moines Register)*
1988 Spot news: Scott Shaw *(Odessa* [Texas] *American);* features: Michel duCille *(Miami Herald)*
1989 Spot news: Ron Olshwanger *(St. Louis Post-Dispatch);* features: Manny Crisostomo *(Detroit Free Press)*

NATIONAL TELEGRAPHIC REPORTING

1942 Louis Stark *(New York Times)*
1944 Dewey L. Fleming *(Baltimore Sun)*
1945 James Reston *(New York Times)*
1946 Edward A. Harris *(St. Louis Post-Dispatch)*
1947 Edward T. Folliard *(Washington Post)*

NATIONAL REPORTING

1948 Bert Andrews *(New York Herald Tribune);* Nat S. Finney *(Minneapolis Tribune)*
1949 C. P. Trussel *(New York Times)*
1950 Edwin O. Guthman *(Seattle Times)*
1952 Anthony Leviero *(New York Times)*
1953 Don Whitehead (Associated Press)
1954 Richard Wilson (Cowles Newspapers)
1955 Anthony Lewis *(Washington Daily News)*
1956 Charles L. Bartlett *(Chattanooga Times)*
1957 James Reston *(New York Times)*
1958 Relman Morin (Associated Press) and Clark Mollenhoff *(Des Moines Register & Tribune)*
1959 Howard Van Smith *(Miami News)*
1960 Vance Trimble (Scripps-Howard Newspaper Alliance)
1961 Edward R. Cony *(Wall Street Journal)*
1962 Nathan G. Caldwell and Gene S. Graham *(Nashville Tennessean)*
1963 Anthony Lewis *(New York Times)*
1964 Merriman Smith (United Press International)
1965 Louis M. Kohlmeier *(Wall Street Journal)*
1966 Haynes Johnson *(Washington Evening Star)*
1967 Stanley Penn and Monroe Karmin *(Wall Street Journal)*
1968 Howard James *(Christian Science Monitor);* Nathan K. (Nick) Kotz *(Des Moines Register* and *Minneapolis Tribune)*
1969 Robert Cahn *(Christian Science Monitor)*
1970 William J. Eaton *(Chicago Daily News)*
1971 Lucinda Franks and Thomas Powers (United Press International)
1972 Jack Anderson *(United Feature Syndicate)*
1973 Robert Boyd and Clark Hoyt *(Knight Newspapers)*
1974 Jack White *(Providence* [R.I.] *Journal-Bulletin);* and James R. Polk *(Washington Star-News)*
1975 Donald L. Barlett and James B. Steele *(Philadelphia Inquirer)*
1976 James Risser *(Des Moines Register)*
1977 Walter Mears (Associated Press)
1978 Gaylord D. Shaw *(Los Angeles Times)*
1979 James Risser *(Des Moines Register)*
1980 Bette Swenson Orsini and Charles Stafford *(St. Petersburg Times)*
1981 John M. Crewdson *(New York Times)*
1982 Rick Atkinson *(Kansas City* [Mo.] *Times)*
1983 *Boston Globe*
1984 John N. Wilford *(New York Times)*
1985 Thomas J. Knudson *(Des Moines Register)*
1986 Craig Flournoy and George Rodrigue *(Dallas Morning News)* and Arthur Howe *(Philadelphia Inquirer)*
1987 *Miami Herald,* staff; *New York Times,* staff
1988 Tim Weiner *(Philadelphia Inquirer)*
1989 Donald L. Barlett and James B. Steele *(Philadel-*

phia Inquirer)

INTERNATIONAL TELEGRAPHIC
REPORTING

1942 Laurence Edmund Allen (Associated Press)
1943 Ira Wolfert (North American Newspaper Alliance, Inc.)
1944 Daniel De Luce (Associated Press)
1945 Mark S. Watson *(Baltimore Sun)*
1946 Homer W. Bigart *(New York Herald Tribune)*
1947 Eddy Gilmore (Associated Press)

INTERNATIONAL REPORTING

1948 Paul W. Ward *(Baltimore Sun)*
1949 Price Day *(Baltimore Sun)*
1950 Edmund Stevens *(Christian Science Monitor)*
1951 Keyes Beech and Fred Sparks *(Chicago Daily News);* Homer Bigart and Marguerite Higgins *(New York Herald Tribune);* Relman Morin and Don Whitehead (Associated Press)
1952 John M. Hightower (Associated Press)
1953 Austin C. Wehrwein *(Milwaukee Journal)*
1954 Jim G. Lucas (Scripps-Howard Newspapers)
1955 Harrison E. Salisbury *(New York Times)*
1956 William Randolph Hearst, Jr. and Frank Conniff (Hearst Newspapers) and Kingsbury Smith (INS)
1957 Russell Jones (United Press)
1958 *New York Times*
1959 Joseph Martin and Philip Santora *(New York Daily News)*
1960 A. M. Rosenthal *(New York Times)*
1961 Lynn Heinzerling (Associated Press)
1962 Walter Lippmann (New York Herald Tribune Syndicate)
1963 Hal Hendrix *(Miami News)*
1964 Malcolm W. Browne (Associated Press) and David Halberstam *(New York Times)*
1965 J. A. Livingston *(Philadelphia Bulletin)*
1966 Peter Arnett (Associated Press)
1967 R. John Hughes *(Christian Science Monitor)*
1968 Alfred Friendly *(Washington Post)*
1969 William Tuohy *(Los Angeles Times)*
1970 Seymour M. Hersh (Dispatch News Service)
1971 Jimmie Lee Hoagland *(Washington Post)*
1972 Peter R. Kann *(Wall Street Journal)*
1973 Max Frankel *(New York Times)*
1974 Hedrick Smith *(New York Times)*
1975 William Mullen and Ovie Carter *(Chicago Tribune)*
1976 Sydney H. Schanberg *(New York Times)*
1978 Henry Kamm *(New York Times)*
1979 Richard Ben Cramer *(Philadelphia Inquirer)*
1980 Joel Brinkley and Jay Mather *(Louisville Courier-Journal)*
1981 Shirley Christian *(Miami Herald)*
1982 John Darnton *(New York Times)*
1983 Thomas L. Friedman *(New York Times)*
1984 Karen E. House *(Wall Street Journal)*
1985 Josh Friedman, Dennis Bell, and Ozier Muhammad *(Newsday)*
1986 Lewis M. Simons, Pete Carey, and Katherine Ellison *(San Jose Mercury News)*
1987 Michael Parks *(Los Angeles Times)*
1988 Thomas L. Friedman *(New York Times)*
1989 Bill Keller *(New York Times);* Glenn Frankel *(Washington Post)*

REPORTING

1917 Herbert B. Swope *(New York World)*
1918 Harold A. Littledale *(New York Evening Post)*
1920 John J. Leary, Jr. *(New York World)*
1921 Louis Seibold *(New York World)*

1922 Kirke L. Simpson (Associated Press)
1923 Alva Johnston *(New York Times)*
1924 Magner White *(San Diego Sun)*
1925 James W. Mulroy and Alvin H. Goldstein *(Chicago Daily News)*
1926 William Burke Miller *(Louisville Courier-Journal)*
1927 John T. Rogers *(St. Louis Post-Dispatch)*
1929 Paul Y. Anderson *(St. Louis Post-Dispatch)*
1930 Russell D. Owen *(New York Times);* special award: W. O. Dapping *(Auburn* [N.Y.] *Citizen)*
1931 A. B. MacDonald *(Kansas City* [Mo.] *Star)*
1932 W. C. Richards, D. D. Martin, J. S. Pooler, F. D. Webb, J. N. W. Sloan (all of *Detroit Free Press)*
1933 Francis A. Jamieson (Associated Press)
1934 Royce Brier *(San Francisco Chronicle)*
1935 William H. Taylor *(New York Herald Tribune)*
1936 Lauren D. Lyman *(New York Times)*
1937 John J. O'Neill *(New York Herald Tribune);* William Leonard Laurence *(New York Times);* Howard W. Blakeslee (Associated Press); Gobind Behari Lal (Universal Service); David Dietz (Scripps-Howard Newspapers)
1938 Raymond Sprigle *(Pittsburg Post-Gazette)*
1939 Thomas L. Stokes *(New York World-Telegram)*
1940 S. Burton Heath *(New York World-Telegram)*
1941 Westbrook Pegler *(New York World-Telegram)*
1942 Stanton Delaplane *(San Francisco Chronicle)*
1943 George Weller *(Chicago Daily News)*
1944 Paul Schoenstein and associates *(New York Journal-American)*
1945 Jack S. McDowell *(San Francisco Call-Bulletin)*
1946 William Leonard Laurence *(New York Times)*
1947 Frederick Woltman *(New York World-Telegram)*
1948 George E. Goodwin *(Atlanta Journal)*
1949 Malcolm Johnson *(New York Sun)*
1950 Meyer Berger *(New York Times)*
1951 Edward S. Montgomery *(San Francisco Examiner)*
1952 George de Carvalho *(San Francisco Chronicle)*
1953 Editorial staff *(Providence Journal and Evening Bulletin);*[1] Edward J. Mowery *(New York World-Telegram and Sun)*[2]
1954 *Vicksburg* (Miss.) *Sunday Post-Herald;*[1] Alvin Scott McCoy *(Kansas City* [Mo.] *Star)*[2]
1955 Mrs. Caro Brown *(Alice* [Tex.] *Daily Echo);*[1] Roland Kenneth Towery *(Cuero* [Tex.] *Record)*[2]
1956 Lee Hills *(Detroit Free Press);*[1] Arthur Daley *(New York Times)*[2]
1957 *Salt Lake Tribune;*[1] Wallace Turner and William Lambert *(Portland Oregonian)*[2]
1958 *Fargo* [N.D.] *Forum;*[1] George Beveridge *(Washington* [D.C.] *Evening Star)*[2]
1959 Mary Lou Werner *(Washington* [D.C.] *Evening Star);*[1] John Harold Brislin *(Scranton* [Pa.] *Tribune & Scrantonian)*[2]
1960 Jack Nelson *(Atlanta Constitution);*[1] Miriam Ottenberg *(Washington Evening Star)*[2]
1961 Sanche de Gramont *(New York Herald Tribune);*[1] Edgar May *(Buffalo Evening News)*[2]
1962 Robert D. Mullins *(Deseret News,* Salt Lake City);[1] George Bliss *(Chicago Tribune)*[2]
1963 Sylvan Fox, Anthony Shannon, and William Longgood *(New York World-Telegram and Sun);*[1] Oscar Griffin, Jr. (former editor of *Pecos* [Tex.] *Independent and Enterprise,* now on staff of *Houston Chronicle)*[2]

GENERAL LOCAL REPORTING

1964 Norman C. Miller *(Wall Street Journal)*

1. Reporting under pressure of edition deadlines. 2. Reporting not under pressure of edition deadlines.

1965 Melvin H. Ruder (*Hungry Horse News,* Columbia Falls, Mont.)
1966 Staff of *Los Angeles Times*
1967 Robert V. Cox *(Chambersburg* [Pa.] *Public Opinion)*
1968 Staff of *Detroit Free Press*
1969 John Fetterman (*Louisville Times* and *Courier-Journal)*
1970 Thomas Fitzpatrick *(Chicago Sun-Times)*
1971 Staff of *Akron* (Ohio) *Beacon*
1972 Richard Cooper and John Machacek *(Rochester* [N.Y.] *Times-Union)*
1973 *Chicago Tribune*
1974 Arthur M. Petacque and Hugh F. Hough *(Chicago Sun-Times)*
1975 *Xenia* (Ohio) *Daily Gazette*
1976 Gene Miller *(Miami Herald)*
1977 Margo Huston *(Milwaukee Journal)*
1978 Richard Whitt *(Louisville Courier-Journal)*
1979 Staff of *San Diego* (Calif.) *Evening Tribune*
1980 Staff of *Philadelphia Inquirer*
1981 *Longview* (Wash.) *Daily News*
1982 *Kansas City* (Mo.) *Star* and *Kansas City* (Mo.) *Times*
1983 *Fort Wayne* (Ind.) *News-Sentinel*
1984 *Newsday*

GENERAL NEWS REPORTING

1985 Thomas Turcol (*Virginian-Pilot and Ledger-Star)*
1986 Edna Buchanan *(Miami Herald)*
1987 *Akron Beacon Journal,* staff
1988 *Alabama Journal* (Montgomery), staff, *Lawrence* (Mass.) *Eagle-Tribune,* staff
1989 *Louisville Courier-Journal* staff

SPECIAL LOCAL REPORTING

1964 James V. Magee, Albert V. Gaudiosi, and Frederick A. Meyer *(Philadelphia Bulletin)*
1965 Gene Goltz *(Houston Post)*
1966 John A. Frasca *(Tampa Tribune)*
1967 Gene Miller *(Miami Herald)*
1968 J. Anthony Lukas *(New York Times)*
1969 Albert L. Delugach and Denny Walsh *(St. Louis Globe-Democrat)*
1970 Harold Eugene Martin *(Montgomery Advertiser)*
1971 William Hugh Jones *(Chicago Tribune)*
1972 Timothy Leland, Gerard N. O'Neill, Stephen A. Kurkjian, and Ann DeSantis *(Boston Globe)*
1973 Sun Newspapers of Omaha, Neb.
1974 William Sherman *(New York Daily News)*
1975 *Indianapolis Star*
1976 *Chicago Tribune*
1977 Acel Moore and Wendell Rawls, Jr. *(Philadelphia Inquirer)*
1978 Anthony R. Dolan *(Stamford* [Conn.] *Advocate)*
1979 Gilbert M. Gaul and Elliot G. Jaspin *(Pottsville* [Pa.] *Republican)*
1980 Nils J. Bruzelius, Alexander B. Hawes, Jr., Stephen A. Kurkjian, Robert M. Porterfield, and Joan Vennochi *(Boston Globe)*
1981 Clark Hallas and Robert B. Lowe (*Arizona Daily Star,* Tucson)
1982 Paul Henderson *(Seattle Times)*
1983 Loretta Tofani *(Washington Post)*
1984 *Boston Globe*

INVESTIGATIVE REPORTING

1985 Lucy Morgan and Jack Reed (*St. Petersburg* [Fla.] *Times*) and William K. Marimow *(Philadelphia Inquirer)*
1986 Jeffrey A. Marx and Michael M. York *(Lexington* [Ky.] *Herald Leader)*

1987 Daniel R. Biddle, H.G. Bissinger, and Fredric N. Tulsky *(Philadelphia Inquirer)*
1988 Dean Baquet, William C. Gaines, and Ann Marie Lipinski *(Chicago Tribune)*
1989 Bill Dedman *(Atlanta Journal and Constitution)*

FEATURE WRITING

1979 Jon D. Franklin *(Baltimore Evening Sun)*
1980 Madeleine Blais *(Miami Herald)*
1981 Teresa Carpenter (*Village Voice,* New York)
1982 Saul Pett (Associated Press)
1983 Nan Robertson *(New York Times)*
1984 Peter M. Rinearson *(Seattle Times)*
1985 Alice Steinbach *(Baltimore Sun)*
1986 John Camp *(St. Paul Pioneer Press and Dispatch)*
1987 Steve Twomey *(Philadelphia Inquirer)*
1988 Jacqui Banaszynski *(St. Paul Pioneer Press Dispatch)*
1989 David Zucchino *(Philadelphia Inquirer)*

COMMENTARY

1970 Marquis W. Childs *(St. Louis Post-Dispatch)*
1971 William A. Caldwell (*Record* [Hackensack, N.J.])
1972 Mike Royko *(Chicago Daily News)*
1973 David S. Broder *(Washington Post)*
1974 Edwin A. Roberts, Jr. *(National Observer)*
1975 Mary McGrory *(Washington Star)*
1976 Walter W. (Red) Smith *(New York Times)*
1977 George F. Will (*Washington Post* Writers Group)
1978 William Safire *(New York Times)*
1979 Russell Baker *(New York Times)*
1980 Ellen H. Goodman *(Boston Globe)*
1981 Dave Anderson *(New York Times)*
1982 Art Buchwald (*Los Angeles Times* Syndicate)
1983 Claude Sitton *(Raleigh* [N.C.] *News & Observer)*
1984 Vermont Royster *(Wall Street Journal)*
1985 Murray Kempton *(Newsday)*
1986 Jimmy Breslin *(New York Daily News)*
1987 Charles Krauthammer (*Washington Post* Writers Group)
1988 Dave Barry *(Miami Herald)*
1989 Clarence Page *(Chicago Tribune)*

CRITICISM

1970 Ada Louise Huxtable *(New York Times)*
1971 Harold C. Schonberg *(New York Times)*
1972 Frank Peters, Jr. *(St. Louis Post-Dispatch)*
1973 Ronald Powers *(Chicago Sun-Times)*
1974 Emily Genauer (Newsday Syndicate)
1975 Roger Ebert *(Chicago Sun-Times)*
1976 Alan M. Kriegsman *(Washington Post)*
1977 William McPherson *(Washington Post)*
1978 Walter Kerr *(New York Times)*
1979 Paul Gapp *(Chicago Tribune)*
1980 William A. Henry, 3rd *(Boston Globe)*
1981 Jonathan Yardley *(Washington Star)*
1982 Martin Bernheimer *(Los Angeles Times)*
1983 Manuela Hoelterhoff *(Wall Street Journal)*
1984 Paul Goldberger *(New York Times)*
1985 Howard Rosenberg *(Los Angeles Times)*
1986 Donal Henahan *(New York Times)*
1987 Richard Eder *(Los Angeles Times)*
1988 Tom Shales *(Washington Post)*
1989 Michael Skube *(News and Observer,* Raleigh, N.C.)

EXPLANATORY JOURNALISM

1985 Jon Franklin *(Baltimore Evening Sun)*
1986 *New York Times*
1987 Jeff Lyon and Peter Gorner *(Chicago Tribune)*
1988 Daniel Hertzberg and James B. Stewart *(Wall

Street Journal)
1989 David Hanners, William Snyder, and Karen Blessen *(Dallas Morning News)*

SPECIALIZED REPORTING

1985 Randall Savage and Jackie Crosby *(Macon* [Ga.] *Telegraph and News)*
1986 Andrew Schneider and Mary Pat Flaherty *(Pittsburgh Press)*
1987 Alex S. Jones *(New York Times)*
1988 Walt Bogdanich *(Wall Street Journal)*
1989 Edward Humes *(Orange County Register)*

SPECIAL CITATIONS

1938 *Edmonton* (Alberta) *Journal,* special bronze plaque for editorial leadership in defense of freedom of press in Province of Alberta.
1941 *New York Times* for the public educational value of its foreign news report.
1944 Byron Price, Director of the Office of Censorship, for the creation and administration of the newspaper and radio codes. Mrs. William Allen White, for her husband's interest and services during the past seven years as a member of the Advisory Board of the Graduate School of Journalism, Columbia University. Richard Rodgers and Oscar Hammerstein II for their musical *Oklahoma!*
1945 The cartographers of the American press for their war maps.
1947 (Pulitzer centennial year.) Columbia University and the Graduate School of Journalism for their efforts to maintain and advance the high standards governing the Pulitzer Prize awards. The *St. Louis Post-Dispatch* for its unswerving adherence to the public and professional ideals of its founder and its leadership in American journalism.
1948 Dr. Frank D. Fackenthal for his interest and service.
1951 Cyrus L. Sulzberger *(New York Times)* for his exclusive interview with Archbishop Stepinac in a Yugoslav prison.
1952 *Kansas City Star* for coverage of 1951 floods; Max Kase *(New York Journal-American)* for exposures of bribery in college basketball.
1953 *New York Times* for its 17-year publication of "News of the Week in Review"; and Lester Markel, its founder.
1957 Kenneth Roberts for his historical novels.
1958 Walter Lippmann *(New York Herald Tribune)* for his "wisdom, perception and high sense of responsibility" in his commentary on national and international affairs.
1960 Garrett Mattingly, for *The Armada.*
1961 *American Heritage Picture History of the Civil War,* as distinguished example of American book publishing.
1964 Gannett Newspapers, Rochester, N.Y.
1973 James Thomas Flexner for his biography *George Washington.*
1974 Roger Sessions for his "life's work in music."
1976 John Hohenberg for "services for 22 years as administrator of the Pulitzer Prizes"; Scott Joplin for his contributions to American music.
1977 Alex Haley for his novel, *Roots.*
1978 E.B. White of *New Yorker* magazine and Richard L. Strout of *Christian Science Monitor.*
1982 Milton Babbitt, "for his life's work as a distinguished and seminal American composer."
1984 Theodor Seuss Geisel (Dr. Seuss) for "books full of playful rhymes, nonsense words and strange illustrations."
1985 William H. Schuman for "more than a half century of contribution to American music as a composer and educational leader."
1987 Joseph Pulitzer Jr., "for extraordinary services to American journalism and letters during his 31 years as chairman of the Pulitzer Prize Board and for his accomplishments as an editor and publisher."

Pulitzer Prizes in Letters

FICTION[1]

1918 *His Family.* Ernest Poole
1919 *The Magnificent Ambersons.* Booth Tarkington
1921 *The Age of Innocence.* Edith Wharton
1922 *Alice Adams.* Booth Tarkington
1923 *One of Ours.* Willa Cather
1924 *The Able McLaughlins.* Margaret Wilson
1925 *So Big.* Edna Ferber
1926 *Arrowsmith.* Sinclair Lewis
1927 *Early Autumn.* Louis Bromfield
1928 *The Bridge of San Luis Rey.* Thornton Wilder
1929 *Scarlet Sister Mary.* Julia Peterkin
1930 *Laughing Boy.* Oliver La Farge
1931 *Years of Grace.* Margaret Ayer Barnes
1932 *The Good Earth.* Pearl S. Buck
1933 *The Store.* T. S. Stribling
1934 *Lamb in His Bosom.* Caroline Miller
1935 *Now in November.* Josephine Winslow Johnson
1936 *Honey in the Horn.* Harold L. Davis
1937 *Gone With the Wind.* Margaret Mitchell
1938 *The Late George Apley.* John Phillips Marquand
1939 *The Yearling.* Marjorie Kinnan Rawlings
1940 *The Grapes of Wrath.* John Steinbeck
1942 *In This Our Life.* Ellen Glasgow
1943 *Dragon's Teeth.* Upton Sinclair

1. Before 1948, award was for novels only.

1944 *Journey in the Dark.* Martin Flavin
1945 *A Bell for Adano.* John Hersey
1947 *All the King's Men.* Robert Penn Warren
1948 *Tales of the South Pacific.* James A. Michener
1949 *Guard of Honor.* James Gould Cozzens
1950 *The Way West.* A. B. Guthrie, Jr.
1951 *The Town.* Conrad Richter
1952 *The Caine Mutiny.* Herman Wouk
1953 *The Old Man and the Sea.* Ernest Hemingway
1955 *A Fable.* William Faulkner
1956 *Andersonville.* MacKinlay Kantor
1958 *A Death in the Family.* James Agee
1959 *The Travels of Jaimie McPheeters.* Robert Lewis Taylor
1960 *Advise and Consent.* Allen Drury
1961 *To Kill a Mockingbird.* Harper Lee
1962 *The Edge of Sadness.* Edwin O'Connor
1963 *The Reivers.* William Faulkner
1965 *The Keepers of the House.* Shirley Ann Grau
1966 *Collected Stories of Katherine Anne Porter.* Katherine Anne Porter
1967 *The Fixer.* Bernard Malamud
1968 *The Confessions of Nat Turner.* William Styron
1969 *House Made of Dawn.* N. Scott Momaday
1970 *Collected Stories.* Jean Stafford
1972 *Angle of Repose.* Wallace Stegner
1973 *The Optimist's Daughter.* Eudora Welty
1975 *The Killer Angels.* Michael Shaara
1976 *Humboldt's Gift.* Saul Bellow

1978 *Elbow Room.* James Alan McPherson
1979 *The Stories of John Cheever.* John Cheever
1980 *The Executioner's Song.* Norman Mailer
1981 *A Confederacy of Dunces.* John Kennedy Toole
1982 *Rabbit Is Rich.* John Updike
1983 *The Color Purple.* Alice Walker
1984 *Ironweed.* William Kennedy
1985 *Foreign Affairs,* Alison Lurie
1986 *Lonesome Dove,* Larry McMurtry
1987 *A Summons to Memphis,* Peter Taylor
1988 *Beloved,* Toni Morrison
1989 *Breathing Lessons,* Anne Tyler

DRAMA

1918 *Why Marry?* Jesse Lynch Williams
1920 *Beyond the Horizon.* Eugene O'Neill
1921 *Miss Lulu Bett.* Zona Gale
1922 *Anna Christie.* Eugene O'Neill
1923 *Icebound.* Owen Davis
1924 *Hell-Bent Fer Heaven.* Hatcher Hughes
1925 *They Knew What They Wanted.* Sidney Howard
1926 *Craig's Wife.* George Kelly
1927 *In Abraham's Bosom.* Paul Green
1928 *Strange Interlude.* Eugene O'Neill
1929 *Street Scene.* Elmer L. Rice
1930 *The Green Pastures.* Marc Connelly
1931 *Alison's House.* Susan Glaspell
1932 *Of Thee I Sing.* George S. Kaufman, Morrie Ryskind, and Ira Gershwin
1933 *Both Your Houses.* Maxwell Anderson
1934 *Men in White.* Sidney Kingsley
1935 *The Old Maid.* Zöe Akins
1936 *Idiot's Delight.* Robert E. Sherwood
1937 *You Can't Take It With You.* Moss Hart and George S. Kaufman
1938 *Our Town.* Thornton Wilder
1939 *Abe Lincoln in Illinois.* Robert E. Sherwood
1940 *The Time of Your Life.* William Saroyan
1941 *There Shall Be No Night.* Robert E. Sherwood
1943 *The Skin of Our Teeth.* Thornton Wilder
1945 *Harvey.* Mary Chase
1946 *State of the Union.* Russel Crouse and Howard Lindsay
1948 *A Streetcar Named Desire.* Tennessee Williams
1949 *Death of a Salesman.* Arthur Miller
1950 *South Pacific.* Richard Rodgers, Oscar Hammerstein II, and Joshua Logan
1952 *The Shrike.* Joseph Kramm
1953 *Picnic.* William Inge
1954 *The Teahouse of the August Moon.* John Patrick
1955 *Cat on a Hot Tin Roof.* Tennessee Williams
1956 *The Diary of Anne Frank.* Frances Goodrich and Albert Hackett
1957 *Long Day's Journey Into Night.* Eugene O'Neill
1958 *Look Homeward, Angel.* Ketti Frings
1959 *J.B.* Archibald MacLeish
1960 *Fiorello!* George Abbott, Jerome Weidman, Jerry Bock, and Sheldon Harnick
1961 *All the Way Home.* Tad Mosel
1962 *How to Succeed in Business Without Really Trying.* Frank Loesser and Abe Burrows
1965 *The Subject Was Roses.* Frank D. Gilroy
1967 *A Delicate Balance.* Edward Albee
1969 *The Great White Hope.* Howard Sackler
1970 *No Place to Be Somebody.* Charles Gordone
1971 *The Effect of Gamma Rays on Man-in-the-Moon Marigolds.* Paul Zindel
1973 *That Championship Season.* Jason Miller
1975 *Seascape.* Edward Albee
1976 *A Chorus Line.* Conceived by Michael Bennett
1977 *The Shadow Box.* Michael Cristofer
1978 *The Gin Game.* Donald L. Coburn
1979 *Buried Child.* Sam Shepard

1980 *Talley's Folly.* Lanford Wilson
1981 *Crimes of the Heart.* Beth Henley
1982 *A Soldier's Play.* Charles Fuller
1983 *'Night, Mother.* Marsha Norman
1984 *Glengarry Glen Ross.* David Mamet
1985 *Sunday in the Park with George.* Stephen Sondheim and James Lapine
1987 *Fences.* August Wilson
1988 *Driving Miss Daisy.* Alfred Uhry
1989 *The Heidi Chronicles,* Wendy Wasserstein

HISTORY OF UNITED STATES

1917 *With Americans of Past and Present Days.* J. J. Jusserand, Ambassador of France to United States
1918 *A History of the Civil War, 1861–1865.* James Ford Rhodes
1920 *The War With Mexico.* Justin H. Smith
1921 *The Victory at Sea.* William Sowden Sims in collaboration with Burton J. Hendrick
1922 *The Founding of New England.* James Truslow Adams
1923 *The Supreme Court in United States History.* Charles Warren
1924 *The American Revolution—A Constitutional Interpretation.* Charles Howard McIlwain
1925 *A History of the American Frontier.* Frederic L. Paxson
1926 *The History of the United States.* Edward Channing
1927 *Pinckney's Treaty.* Samuel Flagg Bemis
1928 *Main Currents in American Thought.* Vernon Louis Parrington
1929 *The Organization and Administration of the Union Army, 1861–1865.* Fred Albert Shannon
1930 *The War of Independence.* Claude H. Van Tyne
1931 *The Coming of the War: 1914.* Bernadotte E. Schmitt
1932 *My Experiences in the World War.* John J. Pershing
1933 *The Significance of Sections in American History.* Frederick J. Turner
1934 *The People's Choice.* Herbert Agar
1935 *The Colonial Period of American History.* Charles McLean Andrews
1936 *The Constitutional History of the United States.* Andrew C. McLaughlin
1937 *The Flowering of New England.* Van Wyck Brooks
1938 *The Road to Reunion, 1865–1900.* Paul Herman Buck
1939 *A History of American Magazines.* Frank Luther Mott
1940 *Abraham Lincoln: The War Years.* Carl Sandburg
1941 *The Atlantic Migration, 1607–1860.* Marcus Lee Hansen
1942 *Reveille in Washington.* Margaret Leech
1943 *Paul Revere and the World He Lived In.* Esther Forbes
1944 *The Growth of American Thought.* Merle Curti
1945 *Unfinished Business.* Stephen Bonsal
1946 *The Age of Jackson.* Arthur M. Schlesinger, Jr.
1947 *Scientists Against Time.* James Phinney Baxter, 3rd
1948 *Across the Wide Missouri.* Bernard DeVoto
1949 *The Disruption of American Democracy.* Roy Franklin Nichols
1950 *Art and Life in America.* Oliver W. Larkin
1951 *The Old Northwest, Pioneer Period 1815–1840.* R. Carlyle Buley
1952 *The Uprooted.* Oscar Handlin
1953 *The Era of Good Feelings.* George Dangerfield

1954 *A Stillness at Appomattox.* Bruce Catton
1955 *Great River: The Rio Grande in North American History.* Paul Horgan
1956 *The Age of Reform.* Richard Hofstadter
1957 *Russia Leaves the War: Soviet-American Relations, 1917–1920.* George F. Kennan
1958 *Banks and Politics in America: From the Revolution to the Civil War.* Bray Hammond
1959 *The Republican Era: 1869–1901.* Leonard D. White, assisted by Jean Schneider
1960 *In the Days of McKinley.* Margaret Leech
1961 *Between War and Peace: The Potsdam Conference.* Herbert Feis
1962 *The Triumphant Empire, Thunder-Clouds Gather in the West.* Lawrence H. Gipson
1963 *Washington, Village and Capital, 1800–1878.* Constance McLaughlin Green
1964 *Puritan Village: The Formation of a New England Town.* Sumner Chilton Powell
1965 *The Greenback Era.* Irwin Unger
1966 *Life of the Mind in America.* Perry Miller
1967 *Exploration and Empire: The Explorer and Scientist in the Winning of the American West.* William H. Goetzmann
1968 *The Ideological Origins of the American Revolution.* Bernard Bailyn
1969 *Origins of the Fifth Amendment.* Leonard W. Levy
1970 *Present at the Creation: My Years in the State Department.* Dean Acheson
1971 *Roosevelt: The Soldier of Freedom.* James McGregor Burns
1972 *Neither Black Nor White. Slavery and Race Relations in Brazil and the United States.* Carl N. Degler
1973 *People of Paradox: An Inquiry Concerning the Origin of American Civilization.* Michael Kammen
1974 *The Americans: The Democratic Experience, Vol. 3.* Daniel J. Boorstin
1975 *Jefferson and His Time.* Dumas Malone
1976 *Lamy of Santa Fe.* Paul Horgan
1977 *The Impending Crisis: 1841–1861.* David M. Potter (posth)
1978 *The Invisible Hand: The Managerial Revolution in American Business.* Alfred D. Chandler, Jr.
1979 *The Dred Scott Case: Its Significance in Law and Politics.* Don E. Fehrenbacher
1980 *Been in the Storm So Long.* Leon F. Litwack
1981 *American Education: The National Experience; 1783–1876.* Lawrence A. Cremin
1982 *Mary Chestnut's Civil War.* C. Vann Woodward, editor
1983 *The Transformation of Virginia, 1740–1790.* Rhys L. Isaac
1985 *The Prophets of Regulation.* Thomas K. McCraw
1986 *. . . the Heavens and the Earth: A Political History of the Space Age.* Walter A. McDougall
1987 *Voyagers to the West: A Passage in the Peopling of America on the Eve of the Revolution.* Bernard Bailyn
1988 *The Launching of Modern American Science 1846-1876.* Robert V. Bruce
1989 *Parting the Waters,* Taylor Branch; *Battle Cry of Freedom,* James M. McPherson

BIOGRAPHY OR AUTOBIOGRAPHY

1917 *Julia Ward Howe.* Laura E. Richards and Maude Howe Elliott, assisted by Florence Howe Hall
1918 *Benjamin Franklin, Self-Revealed.* William Cabell Bruce
1919 *The Education of Henry Adams.* Henry Adams
1920 *The Life of John Marshall.* Albert J. Beveridge

1921 *The Americanization of Edward Bok.* Edward Bok
1922 *A Daughter of the Middle Border.* Hamlin Garland
1923 *The Life and Letters of Walter H. Page,* Burton J. Hendrick
1924 *From Immigrant to Inventor.* Michael Idvorsky Pupin
1925 *Barrett Wendell and His Letters.* M. A. DeWolfe Howe
1926 *The Life of Sir William Osler.* Harvey Cushing
1927 *Whitman.* Emory Holloway
1928 *The American Orchestra and Theodore Thomas.* Charles Edward Russell
1929 *The Training of an American. The Earlier Life and Letters of Walter H. Page.* Burton J. Hendrick
1930 *The Raven.* Marquis James
1931 *Charles W. Eliot.* Henry James
1932 *Theodore Roosevelt.* Henry F. Pringle
1933 *Grover Cleveland.* Allan Nevins
1934 *John Hay.* Tyler Dennett
1935 *R. E. Lee.* Douglas S. Freeman
1936 *The Thought and Character of William James.* Ralph Barton Perry
1937 *Hamilton Fish.* Allan Nevins
1938 *Pedlar's Progress.* Odell Shepard; *Andrew Jackson.* Marquis James
1939 *Benjamin Franklin.* Carl Van Doren
1940 *Woodrow Wilson. Life and Letters,* Vols. VII and VIII. Ray Stannard Baker
1941 *Jonathan Edwards.* Ola E. Winslow
1942 *Crusader in Crinoline.* Forrest Wilson
1943 *Admiral of the Ocean Sea.* Samuel Eliot Morison
1944 *The American Leonardo: The Life of Samuel F. B. Morse.* Carleton Mabee
1945 *George Bancroft: Brahmin Rebel.* Russel Blaine Nye
1946 *Son of the Wilderness.* Linnie Marsh Wolfe
1947 *The Autobiography of William Allen White*
1948 *Forgotten First Citizen: John Bigelow.* Margaret Clapp
1949 *Roosevelt and Hopkins.* Robert E. Sherwood
1950 *John Quincy Adams and the Foundations of American Foreign Policy.* Samuel Flagg Bemis
1951 *John C. Calhoun: American Portrait.* Margaret Louise Coit
1952 *Charles Evans Hughes.* Merlo J. Pusey
1953 *Edmund Pendleton, 1721–1803.* David J. Mays
1954 *The Spirit of St. Louis.* Charles A. Lindbergh
1955 *The Taft Story.* William S. White
1956 *Benjamin Henry Latrobe.* Talbot F. Hamlin
1957 *Profiles in Courage.* John F. Kennedy
1958 *George Washington.* Douglas Southall Freeman (Vols. 1–6) and John Alexander Carroll and Mary Wells Ashworth (Vol. 7)
1959 *Woodrow Wilson, American Prophet.* Arthur Walworth
1960 *John Paul Jones.* Samuel Eliot Morison
1961 *Charles Sumner and the Coming of the Civil War.* David Donald
1963 *Henry James: Vol. II, The Conquest of London, 1870–1881; Vol. III, The Middle Years, 1881–1895.* Leon Edel
1964 *John Keats.* Walter Jackson Bate
1965 *Henry Adams* (3 Vols.). Ernest Samuels
1966 *A Thousand Days.* Arthur M. Schlesinger, Jr.
1967 *Mr. Clemens and Mark Twain.* Justin Kaplan
1968 *Memoirs, 1925–1950.* George F. Kennan
1969 *The Man From New York.* B. L. Reid
1970 *Huey Long.* T. Harry Williams
1971 *Robert Frost: The Years of Triumph, 1915–*

1938. Lawrence Thompson
1972 *Eleanor and Franklin: The Story of Their Relationship Based on Eleanor Roosevelt's Private Papers.* Joseph P. Lash
1973 *Luce and His Empire.* W. A. Swanberg
1974 *O'Neill, Son and Artist.* Louis Sheaffer
1975 *The Power Broker: Robert Moses and the Fall of New York.* Robert A. Caro
1976 *Edith Wharton: A Biography.* Richard W. B. Lewis
1977 *A Prince of Our Disorder.* John E. Mack
1978 *Samuel Johnson.* Walter Jackson Bate
1979 *Days of Sorrow and Pain: Leo Baeck and the Berlin Jews.* Leonard Baker
1980 *The Rise of Theodore Roosevelt.* Edmund Morris
1981 *Peter the Great.* Robert K. Massie
1982 *Grant: A Biography.* William S. McFeely
1983 *Growing Up.* Russell Baker
1984 *Booker T. Washington.* Louis R. Harlan
1985 *The Life and Times of Cotton Mather,* Kenneth Silverman
1986 *Louise Bogan: A Portrait,* Elizabeth Frank
1987 *Bearing the Cross: Martin Luther King Jr. and the Southern Christian Leadership Conference,* David J. Garrow
1988 *Look Homeward: A Life of Thomas Wolfe.* David Herbert Donald
1989 *Oscar Wilde.* Richard Ellmann

POETRY[1]

1918 *Love Songs.* Sara Teasdale
1919 *Old Road to Paradise.* Margaret Widdemer; *Corn Huskers.* Carl Sandburg
1922 *Collected Poems.* Edwin Arlington Robinson
1923 *The Ballad of the Harp-Weaver; A Few Figs from Thistles; eight sonnets in American Poetry, 1922, A Miscellany.* Edna St. Vincent Millay
1924 *New Hampshire: A Poem With Notes and Grace Notes.* Robert Frost
1925 *The Man Who Died Twice.* Edwin Arlington Robinson
1926 *What's O'Clock.* Amy Lowell
1927 *Fiddler's Farewell.* Leonora Speyer
1928 *Tristram.* Edwin Arlington Robinson
1929 *John Brown's Body.* Stephen Vincent Benét
1930 *Selected Poems.* Conrad Aiken
1931 *Collected Poems.* Robert Frost
1932 *The Flowering Stone.* George Dillon
1933 *Conquistador.* Archibald MacLeish
1934 *Collected Verse.* Robert Hillyer
1935 *Bright Ambush.* Audrey Wurdemann
1936 *Strange Holiness.* Robert P. T. Coffin
1937 *A Further Range.* Robert Frost
1938 *Cold Morning Sky.* Marya Zaturenska
1939 *Selected Poems.* John Gould Fletcher
1940 *Collected Poems.* Mark Van Doren
1941 *Sunderland Capture.* Leonard Bacon
1942 *The Dust Which Is God.* William Rose Benét
1943 *A Witness Tree.* Robert Frost
1944 *Western Star.* Stephen Vincent Benét
1945 *V-Letter and Other Poems.* Karl Shapiro
1947 *Lord Weary's Castle.* Robert Lowell
1948 *The Age of Anxiety.* W. H. Auden
1949 *Terror and Decorum.* Peter Viereck
1950 *Annie Allen.* Gwendolyn Brooks
1951 *Complete Poems.* Carl Sandburg
1952 *Collected Poems.* Marianne Moore
1953 *Collected Poems, 1917–1952.* Archibald MacLeish

1. This prize was established in 1922. The 1918 and 1919 awards were made from gifts provided by the Poetry Society.

1954 *The Waking.* Theodore Roethke
1955 *Collected Poems.* Wallace Stevens
1956 *Poems—North & South.* Elizabeth Bishop
1957 *Things of This World.* Richard Wilbur
1958 *Promises: Poems, 1954–1956.* Robert Penn Warren
1959 *Selected Poems, 1928–1958.* Stanley Kunitz
1960 *Heart's Needle.* William Snodgrass
1961 *Times Three: Selected Verse From Three Decades.* Phyllis McGinley
1962 *Poems.* Alan Dugan
1963 *Pictures From Breughel.* William Carlos Williams
1964 *At the End of the Open Road.* Louis Simpson
1965 *77 Dream Songs.* John Berryman
1966 *Selected Poems.* Richard Eberhart
1967 *Live or Die.* Anne Sexton
1968 *The Hard Hours.* Anthony Hecht
1969 *Of Being Numerous.* George Oppen
1970 *Untitled Subjects.* Richard Howard
1971 *The Carrier of Ladders.* William S. Merwin
1972 *Collected Poems.* James Wright
1973 *Up Country.* Maxine Winokur Kumin
1974 *The Dolphin.* Robert Lowell
1975 *Turtle Island.* Gary Snyder
1976 *Self-Portrait in a Convex Mirror.* John Ashbery
1977 *Divine Comedies.* James Merrill
1978 *Collected Poems.* Howard Nemerov
1979 *Now and Then: Poems, 1976-1978.* Robert Penn Warren
1980 *Selected Poems.* Donald Rodney Justice
1981 *The Morning of the Poem.* James Schuyler
1982 *The Collected Poems.* Sylvia Plath
1983 *Selected Poems.* Galway Kinnell
1984 *American Primitive.* Mary Oliver
1985 *Yin,* Carolyn Kizer
1986 *The Flying Change,* Henry Taylor
1987 *Thomas and Beulah,* Rita Dove
1988 *Partial Accounts: New and Selected Poems.* William Meredith
1989 *New and Collected Poems.* Richard Wilbur

GENERAL NONFICTION

1962 *The Making of the President, 1960.* Theodore H. White
1963 *The Guns of August.* Barbara W. Tuchman
1964 *Anti-Intellectualism in American Life.* Richard Hofstadter
1965 *O Strange New World.* Howard Mumford Jones
1966 *Wandering Through Winter.* Edwin Way Teale
1967 *The Problem of Slavery in Western Culture.* David Brion Davis
1968 *Rousseau and Revolution.* Will and Ariel Durant
1969 *So Human an Animal.* Rene Jules Dubos; *The Armies of the Night.* Norman Mailer
1970 *Gandhi's Truth.* Erik H. Erikson
1971 *The Rising Sun.* John Toland
1972 *Stilwell and the American Experience in China, 1911–1945.* Barbara W. Tuchman
1973 *Fire in the Lake: The Vietnamese and the Americans in Vietnam.* Frances FitzGerald; and *Children of Crisis* (Vols. 1 and 2). Robert M. Coles
1974 *The Denial of Death.* Ernest Becker
1975 *Pilgrim at Tinker Creek.* Annie Dillard
1976 *Why Survive? Being Old in America.* Robert N. Butler
1977 *Beautiful Swimmers: Watermen, Crabs and the Chesapeake Bay.* William W. Warner
1978 *The Dragons of Eden.* Carl Sagan
1979 *On Human Nature.* Edward O. Wilson
1980 *Gödel, Escher, Bach: An Eternal Golden Braid.* Douglas R. Hofstadter
1981 *Fin-de-Siecle Vienna: Politics and Culture.* Carl E. Schorske

1982 *The Soul of a New Machine*. Tracy Kidder
1983 *Is There No Place on Earth for Me?* Susan Sheehan
1984 *Social Transformation of American Medicine*. Paul Starr
1985 *The Good War: An Oral History of World War II*, Studs Terkel
1986 *Move Your Shadow: South Africa, Black and White*, Joseph Lelyveld; *Common Ground: A Turbulent Decade in the Lives of Three American Families*, J. Anthony Lukas
1987 *Arab and Jew: Wounded Spirits in a Promised Land*, David K. Shipler
1988 *The Making of the Atomic Bomb*. Richard Rhodes
1989 *A Bright Shining Lie*. Neil Sheehan

PULITZER PRIZES IN MUSIC

1943 *Secular Cantata No. 2, A Free Song*. William Schuman
1944 *Symphony No. 4* (Op. 34). Howard Hanson
1945 *Appalachian Spring*. Aaron Copland
1946 *The Canticle of the Sun*. Leo Sowerby
1947 *Symphony No. 3*. Charles Ives
1948 *Symphony No. 3*. Walter Piston
1949 *Louisiana Story* music. Virgil Thomson
1950 *The Consul*. Gian Carlo Menotti
1951 Music for opera *Giants in the Earth*. Douglas Stuart Moore
1952 *Symphony Concertante*. Gail Kubik
1954 *Concerto for Two Pianos and Orchestra*. Quincy Porter
1955 *The Saint of Bleecker Street*. Gian Carlo Menotti
1956 *Symphony No. 3*. Ernst Toch
1957 *Meditations on Ecclesiastes*. Norman Dello Joio
1958 *Vanessa*. Samuel Barber
1959 *Concerto for Piano and Orchestra*. John La Montaine
1960 *Second String Quartet*. Elliott Carter
1961 *Symphony No. 7*. Walter Piston
1962 *The Crucible*. Robert Ward
1963 *Piano Concerto No. 1*. Samuel Barber
1966 *Variations for Orchestra*. Leslie Bassett
1967 *Quartet No. 3*. Leon Kirchner
1968 *Echoes of Time and the River*. George Crumb
1969 *String Quartet No. 3*. Karel Husa
1970 *Time's Encomium*. Charles Wuorinen
1971 *Synchronisms No. 6 for Piano and Electronic Sound*. Mario Davidovsky
1972 *Windows*. Jacob Druckman
1973 *String Quartet No. 3*. Elliott Carter
1974 *Notturno*. Donald Martino
1975 *From the Diary of Virginia Woolf*. Dominick Argento
1976 *Air Music*. Ned Rorem
1977 *Visions of Terror and Wonder*. Richard Wernick
1978 *Déjà Vu for Percussion Quartet and Orchestra*. Michael Colgrass
1979 *Aftertones of Infinity*. Joseph Schwantner
1980 *In Memory of a Summer Day*. David Del Tredici
1981 Not awarded
1982 *Concerto for Orchestra*. Roger Sessions
1983 *Three Movements for Orchestra*. Ellen T. Zwilich
1984 *Canti del Sole*. Bernard Rands
1985 *Symphony RiverRun*, Stephen Albert
1986 *Wind Quintet IV*, George Perle
1987 *The Flight Into Egypt*, John Harbison
1988 *12 New Etudes for Piano*. William Bolcom
1989 *Whispers Out of Time*, Roger Reynolds

Poets Laureate of the United States

The post was established in 1985. Appointment is for a one-year term, but is renewable.

Robert Penn Warren	1986-1987	Howard Nemerov	1988-
Richard Wilbur	1987-1988		

New York Drama Critics' Circle Awards

1935–36
Winterset, Maxwell Anderson
1936–37
High Tor, Maxwell Anderson
1937–38
Of Mice and Men, John Steinbeck
Shadow and Substance, Paul Vincent Carroll[1]
1938–39
(No award) *The White Steed*, Paul Vincent Carroll[1]
1939–40
The Time of Your Life, William Saroyan
1940–41
Watch on the Rhine, Lillian Hellman
The Corn Is Green, Emlyn Williams[1]
1941–42
(No award) *Blithe Spirit*, Noel Coward[1]
1942–43
The Patriots, Sidney Kingsley
1943–44
(No award) *Jacobowsky and the Colonel*. Franz Werfel and S. N. Behrman[1]
1944–45
The Glass Menagerie, Tennessee Williams
1945–46
(No award) *Carousel*, Richard Rodgers and Oscar Hammerstein II[2]
1946–47
All My Sons, Arthur Miller

No Exit, Jean-Paul Sartre[1]
Brigadoon, Alan Jay Lerner and Frederick Loewe[2]
1947–48
A Streetcar Named Desire, Tennessee Williams
The Winslow Boy, Terence Rattigan[1]
1948–49
Death of a Salesman, Arthur Miller
The Madwoman of Chaillot, Jean Giraudoux and Maurice Valency[1]
South Pacific, Richard Rodgers, Oscar Hammerstein II, and Joshua Logan[2]
1949–50
The Member of the Wedding, Carson McCullers
The Cocktail Party, T. S. Eliot[1]
The Consul, Gian Carlo Menotti[2]
1950–51
Darkness at Noon, Sidney Kingsley[3]
The Lady's Not for Burning, Christopher Fry[1]
Guys and Dolls, Abe Burrows, Jo Swerling, and Frank Loesser[2]
1951–52
I Am a Camera, John Van Druten[4]
Venus Observed, Christopher Fry[1]
Pal Joey, Richard Rodgers, Lorenz Hart, and John O'Hara[2]
Don Juan in Hell, George B. Shaw[5]
1952–53
Picnic, William Inge

The Love of Four Colonels, by Peter Ustinov[1]
Wonderful Town, Joseph Fields, Jerome Chodorov, Betty Comden, Adolph Green, and Leonard Bernstein[2]
1953–54
The Teahouse of the August Moon, John Patrick
Ondine, Jean Giraudoux[1]
The Golden Apple, John Latouche and Jerome Moross[2]
1954–55
Cat on a Hot Tin Roof, Tennessee Williams
Witness for the Prosecution, Agatha Christie[1]
The Saint of Bleecker Street, Gian Carlo Menotti[2]
1955–56
The Diary of Anne Frank, Frances Goodrich and Albert Hackett
Tiger at the Gates, Jean Giraudoux and Christopher Fry[1]
My Fair Lady, Frederick Loewe and Alan Jay Lerner[2]
1956–57
Long Day's Journey Into Night, Eugene O'Neill
Waltz of the Toreadors, Jean Anouilh[1]
The Most Happy Fella, Frank Loesser[2 6]
1957–58
Look Homeward, Angel, Ketti Frings[7]
Look Back in Anger, John Osborne[1]
The Music Man, Meredith Willson[2]
1958–59
A Raisin in the Sun, Lorraine Hansberry
The Visit, Friedrich Duerrenmatt-Maurice Valency[1]
La Plume de ma Tante, Robert Dhery and Gerard Calvi[2]
1959–60
Toys in the Attic, Lillian Hellman
Five Finger Exercise, Peter Shaffer[1]
Fiorello!, Jerome Weidman, George Abbott, Jerry Bock, and Sheldon Harnick[2]
1960–61
All the Way Home, Tad Mosel[3]
A Taste of Honey, Shelagh Delaney[1]
Carnival, Michael Stewart[2]
1961–62
The Night of the Iguana, Tennessee Williams
A Man for All Seasons, Robert Bolt[1]
How to Succeed in Business Without Really Trying, Abe Burrows, Jack Weinstock, Willie Gilbert, and Frank Loesser[2 9]
1962–63
Who's Afraid of Virginia Woolf?, Edward Albee
Beyond the Fringe, Alan Bennett, Peter Cook, Jonathan Miller, and Dudley Moore[10]
1963–64
Luther, John Osborne
Hello, Dolly!, Michael Stewart and Jerry Herman[2 11]
The Trojan Women, Euripides[10 12]
1964–65
The Subject Was Roses, Frank D. Gilroy
Fiddler on the Roof, Joseph Stein, Jerry Bock, and Sheldon Harnick[2 13]
1965–66
The Persecution and Assassination of Marat as Performed by the Inmates of the Asylum of Charenton Under the Direction of the Marquis de Sade, Peter Weiss
The Man of La Mancha, Dale Wasserman, Mitch Leigh, and Joe Darion
1966–67
The Homecoming, Harold Pinter
Cabaret, Joe Masteroff, John Kander, and Fred Ebb[2 14]
1967–68
Rosencrantz and Guildenstern Are Dead, Tom Stoppard
Your Own Thing, Donald Driver, Hal Hester, and Danny Apolinar[2]
1968–69
The Great White Hope, Howard Sackler
1776, Sherman Edwards and Peter Stone[2]
1969–70
Borstal Boy, Frank McMahon[15]
The Effect of Gamma Rays on Man-in-the-Moon Marigolds, Paul Zindel[16]
Company, George Furth and Stephen Sondheim[2]
1970–71
Home, David Storey
The House of Blue Leaves, John Guare[16]
Follies, James Goldman and Stephen Sondheim[2]
1971–72
That Championship Season, Jason Miller
Two Gentlemen of Verona, adapted by John Guare and Mel Shapiro[2]
The Screens, Jean Genet[1]
1972–73
The Changing Room, David Storey
The Hot l Baltimore, by Lanford Wilson[16]
A Little Night Music, Hugh Wheeler and Stephen Sondheim[2]
1973–74
The Contractors, David Storey
Short Eyes, Miguel Piñero[16]
Candide, Leonard Bernstein, Hugh Wheeler, and Richard Wilbur[2]
1974–75
Equus, Peter Shaffer
The Taking of Miss Janie, Ed Bullins[16]
A Chorus Line, James Kirkwood and Nicholas Dante[2]
1975–76
Travesties, Tom Stoppard
Streamers, David Rabe[16]
Pacific Overtures, Stephen Sondheim, John Weidman, and Hugh Wheeler[2]
1976–77
Otherwise Engaged, Simon Gray
American Buffalo, David Mamet[16]
Annie, Thomas Meehan, Charles Strouse, and Martin Charnin[2]
1977–78
Da, Hugh Leonard
Ain't Misbehavin', conceived by Richard Maltby, Jr.[2]
1978–79
The Elephant Man, Bernard Pomerance
Sweeney Todd, Hugh Wheeler and Stephen Sondheim[2]
1979–80
Talley's Folly, Lanford Wilson
Evita,[2] Andrew Lloyd Webber and Tim Rice
Betrayal, Harold Pinter[1]
1980–81
A Lesson From Aloes, Athol Fugard
Crimes of the Heart, Beth Henley[16]
1981–82
The Life and Adventures of Nicholas Nickleby, adapted by David Edgar
A Soldier's Play, Charles Fuller[16]
1982–83
Brighton Beach Memoirs, Neil Simon
Plenty, David Hare[1]
Little Shop of Horrors, Alan Menken and Howard Ashman[2 17]
1983–84
The Real Thing, Tom Stoppard
Glengarry Glen Ross, David Mamet[16]
Sunday in the Park with George, Stephen W Sondheim and James Lapine[2]

1984-85
Ma Rainey's Black Bottom, August Wilson
(No award for best musical or foreign play)
1985-86
Lie of the Mind, Sam Shepard
Benefactors, Michael Frayn[1]
The Search for Signs of Intelligent Life in the Universe, Lily Tomlin and Jane Wagner[18]
(No award for best musical)
1986-87
Fences, August Wilson
Les Liaisons Dangereuses, Christopher Hampton[1]
Les Miserables, Claude-Michel Schonberg and Alain Boublil[2]
1987-88
Joe Turner's Come and Gone, August Wilson
The Road to Mecca, Athol Fugard[1]
Into the Woods, Stephen Sondheim and James Lapine[2]

1988-89
The Heidi Chronicles, Wendy Wasserstein
Aristocrats, Brian Friel[1]
Largely New York, Bill Irwin[18]
(No award for best musical)

1. Citation for best foreign play. 2. Citation for best musical. 3. Based on a novel by Arthur Koestler. 4. Based on Christopher Isherwood's *Berlin Stories*. 5. For "distinguished and original contribution to the theater." 6. Based on Sidney Howard's *They Knew What They Wanted*. 7. Based on a novel by Thomas Wolfe. 8. Based on James Agee's *A Death in the Family*. 9. Based on a book by Shepherd Mead. 10. Special citation. 11. Based on Thornton Wilder's *The Matchmaker*. 12. Translated by Edith Hamilton. 13. Based on Sholem Aleichem's Tevye stories, translated by Arnold Perl. 14. Based on John Van Druten's *I Am a Camera*, which won the award for the best play in 1951–52. 15. Based on Brendan Behan's autobiography. 16. Citation for best American play. 17. Based on a story by Roger Corman. 18. Special citation.

Antoinette Perry (Tony) Awards, 1989

Dramatic Play: *The Heidi Chronicles*, Wendy Wasserstein
Musical: *Jerome Robbins's Broadway*
Actor (play): Philip Bosco, *Lend Me a Tenor*
Actress (play): Pauline Collins, *Shirley Valentine*
Actor, featured (play): Boyd Gaines, *The Heidi Chronicles*
Actress, featured (play): Christine Baranski, *Rumors*
Actor (musical): Jason Alexander, *Jerome Robbins's Broadway*
Actress (musical): Ruth Brown, *Black and Blue*
Actor, featured (musical): Scott Wise, *Jerome Robbins's Broadway*
Actress, featured (musical): Debbie Shapiro, *Jerome Robbins's Broadway*
Director (play): Jerry Zaks, *Lend Me a Tenor*
Director (musical): Jerome Robbins, *Jerome Robbins's Broadway*
Scenic design: Santo Loquasto, *Cafe Crown*
Costume design: Claudie Segovia and Hector Orezzoli, *Black and Blue*
Lighting: Jennifer Tipton, *Jerome Robbins's Broadway*
Choreography: Cholly Atkins, Henry LeTang, Frankie Manning, and Fayard Nicholas, *Black and Blue*
Revivial of play or musical: *Our Town*
Special Award: The Hartford Stage Company for best regional theater.

1989 Obie Award Winners

Sustained Achievement: Irene Worth
Performance: Mark Blum, *Gus and Al;* Niall Buggy, *Aristocrats;* William Converse-Roberts, *Love's Labor's Lost;* Fyvush Finkel, *Cafe Crown;* Gloria Foster, *The Forbidden City;* Paul Hecht, *Enrico IV;* Nancy Marchand, *The Cocktail Hour;* Tim McDonnell, *Diary of a Madman;* Will Patton, *What Did He See?;* Lonny Price, *The Immigrant;* Everett Quinton, *A Tale of Two Cities;* Rocco Sisto, *The Winter's Tale;* Kathy Najimy and Mo Gaffney, *The Kathy and Mo Show*
Direction: Ingar Bergman, *Hamlet;* Peter Stein, *Falstaff*
Sustained Excellence of Direction: Rene Buch
Sustained Excellence of Set Design: Donald Eastman
Sustained Excellence of Costume Design: Gabriel Berry and Susan Young
Citations: Leo Bassi, *Nero's Last Folly;* Dance Theater Workshop; The Dramatists Guild for The Young Playwrights Festival; Janie Geiser, *Stories From Here;* Rachel Rosenthal, *Rachel's Brain;* Tamamatsu Yoshida, *The Warrior Ant;* Paul Zaloom, *The House of Horror*
Cash Grants: Cucaracha Warehouse Theater, The Living Theater
Playwriting Workshop Grants: Intar Hispanic Playwrights-in-Residence Laboratory and The Frank Silvera Writers Workshop

Winners of Bollingen Prize in Poetry

($5,000[1] award is given biennially. It is administered by Yale University and the Bollingen Foundation.)

1949	Ezra Pound	1963	Robert Frost
1950	Wallace Stevens	1965	Horace Gregory
1951	John Crowe Ransom	1967	Robert Penn Warren
1952	Marianne Moore	1969	John Berryman and Karl Shapiro
1953	Archibald MacLeish and William Carlos Williams	1971	Richard Wilbur and Mona Van Duyn
1954	W. H. Auden	1973	James Merrill
1955	Léonie Adams and Louise Bogan	1975	Archie Randolph Ammons
1956	Conrad Aiken	1977	David Ignatow
1957	Allen Tate	1979	W. S. Merwin
1958	E.E. Cummings	1981	Howard Nemerov and May Swenson
1959	Theodore Roethke	1983	Anthony Hecht and John Hollander
1960	Delmore Schwartz	1985	John Ashbery and Fred Chappell
1961	Yvor Winters	1987	Stanley Kunitz
1962	John Hall Wheelock and Richard Eberhart	1989	Edgar Bowers

1. Beginning 1989 award increased to $10,000.

Awards of the Society of Professional Journalists, 1988

(Sigma Delta Chi)

General reporting: Gary Thatcher, Timothy Aeppel, Peter Grier, and George Moffett III, *Christian Science Monitor* (circulation more than 100,000); Peggy O'Crowley, *News Tribune,* (Woodbridge, N.J.) (circulation less than 100,000)

Editorial writing: Chuck Green, Fred Brown, and Jack Cox, *The Denver Post*

Washington correspondence: James O'Shea, *Chicago Tribune*

Foreign correspondence: Douglas Farah, *Washington Post*

News photography: Joe Cavaretta, *Albuquerque Tribune*

Editorial cartooning: Jack Higgins, *Chicago Sun-Times*

Public service in newspaper journalism: *The Philadelphia Inquirer* (circulation more than 100,000); *Anchorage Daily News* (circulation less than 100,000)

Magazine reporting: Jacqueline E. Sharkey, *Common Cause Magazine*

Public service in magazine journalism: *Atlanta Magazine*

Radio spot-news reporting: KRRI-FM staff, Boulder City, Nev.

Public service in radio journalism: KNX News Radio, Los Angeles

Editorializing on radio: G. Donald Gale, KSL, Salt Lake City

Television spot-news reporting: WTHR staff, Indianapolis

Public service in television journalism: ABC's *Nightline* (stations in the top 50 markets); WBRZ, Baton Rouge, La. (small-market stations)

Editorializing on television: John Beatty, Paul Sands, and Ed Quinn, KGTV News, San Diego

Research about journalism: Thomas B. Littlewood, *Coals of Fire: The Alton Telegraph Libel Case*

Bicentennial broadcast award: Jeff Friedman, New Jersey Network

Alfred I. du Pont-Columbia University Broadcast News Awards

Gold Baton Award: *60 Minutes,* CBS

Silver Baton Awards: *CBS Evening News,* for coverage of final weeks of the Iran-Iraq War; *NBC News* for Tom Brokaw's interview with Mikhail S. Gorbachev; *Nightline,* ABC for coverage of the Middle East conflict; WWOR, Secaucus, N.J. for local investagation reporting; WCVB of Boston for work of David Ropeik who followed a trial through the eyes of a sequestered jury; WUSA, Washington, D.C. for interviews with Justice Thurgood Marshall by Carl Rowan; WSMV, Nashville for stories on sewage overflows by Erin Hays; KING, Seattle for forming a team of seven local television stations to produce biographies of the 13 Presidential candidates; WCAX, Burlington, Vt. for a five-part series, *The Politics of Pollution;* WBRZ, Baton Rouge, La. and John Camp for investigations; Public Affairs Television and Alvin H. Perlmutter for *Joseph Campbell and the Power of Myth*

Silver Baton Award for Radio News: Nina Totenberg, National Public Radio for coverage of Supreme Court nominations

National Book Critics Circle Awards, 1989

Fiction: *The Middleman and Other Stories* by Bharati Mukherjee (Grove Press)

General nonfiction: *Parting the Waters,* Taylor Branch (Simon & Schuster)

Poetry: *The One Day,* Donald Hall (Ticknor & Fields)

Criticism: *Works and Lives: The Anthropologist as Author,* Clifford Geertz (Stanford University Press)

Biography/Autobiography: *Oscar Wilde,* Richard Ellmann (Alfred A. Knopf)

American Library Association Awards for Children's Books, 1988

John Newbery Medal for best book: *Joyful Noise: Poems for Two Voices,* Paul Fleischman (Charlotte Zolotow/Harper & Row)

Newbery Honor Books: *In the Beginning: Creation Stories From Around the World,* Virginia Hamilton (Harcourt Brace Jovanovich); *Scorpions,* Walter Dean Myers (Harper & Row)

Randolph Caldecott Medal for best picture book: *Song and Dance Man,* illustrated by Stephen Gammeli, written by Karen Ackerman (Alfred A. Knopf)

Caldecott Honor Books: *The Boy of the Three Year Nap,* illustrated by Allen Say, written by Dianne Snyder (Houghton Mifflin); *Free Fall,* illustrated by David Wiesner (Lothrop, Lee & Shepard); *Goldilocks and the Three Bears,* illustrated by James Marshall (Dial Books); *Mirandy and Brother Wind,* illustrated by Jerry Pinkney, written by Patricia C. McKissack (Alfred A. Knopf)

Laura Ingall Wilder Award (given every three years for a body of work) Elizabeth George Spear

National Book Awards, 1988

Established by Association of American Publishers

(American Book Awards 1980-86. Reverted to original name in 1987.)

Fiction: *Paris Trout* by Pete Dexter (Random House)

Nonfiction: *A Bright Shining Lie: John Paul Vann and America in Vietnam* by Neil Sheehan (Random House)

First Annual National Book Awards for Distinguished Contribution to American Letters: Jason Eptein, editorial director of Random House

Major Grammy Awards for Recording in 1988

Source: National Academy of Recording Arts and Sciences.

Record: "Don't Worry Be Happy," Bobby McFerrin (EMI/USA)

Album: "Faith," George Michael (Columbia/CBS)

Song: "Don't Worry Be Happy," Bobby McFerrin (EMI/USA)

New Artist: Tracy Chapman (Elektra)

Pop Vocalists: Tracy Chapman, "Fast Car" (Elektra); Bobby McFerrin, "Don't Worry Be Happy" (EMI/USA)

Pop Duo or Group: Manhattan Transfer, "Brasil" (Atlantic)

Pop Instrumental: David Sanborn, "Close-Up" (Reprise)

New Age: Shadowfax, "Folksongs for a Nuclear Village" (Capitol)

Rock Vocalists: Tina Turner, "Tina Turner in Europe" (Capitol); Robert Palmer, "Simply Irresistible" (EMI/Manhattan)

Rock Group: U2, "Desire" (Island)

Rock Instrumentalist: Carlos Santana, "Blues for Salvador" (Columbia/CBS)

Rhythm and Blues Vocalists: Anita Baker, "Giving You the Best That I Got" (Elektra); Terence Trent D'Arby, "Introducing the Hardline According to Terence Trent D'Arby" (Columbia/CBS)

Rhythm and Blues Group: Gladys Knight and The Pips, "Love Overboard" (MCA)

Rhythm and Blues Instrumental: Chick Corea, "Light Years" track from GRP Super Live in Concert, Vols. 1 & 2 (GRP)

Rhythm and Blues Song: Anita Baker, Skip Scarborough, and Randy Holland, "Giving You the Best I Got" (Elektra)

Traditional Blues: "Hidden Charms," Willie Dixon (Bug/Capitol)

Contemporary Blues: "Don't Be Afraid of the Dark," The Robert Cray Band (Mercury)

Country Vocalists: K.T. Oslin, "Hold Me" track from This Woman (RCA); Randy Travis, "Old 8×10" (Warner Bros.)

Country Duo or Group: The Judds, "Give a Little Love" track from Greatest Hits (RCA)

Country Instrumental: Asleep at the Wheel, "Sugarfoot Rag" track from Western Standard Time (Epic)

Country Song: "Hold Me," K.T. Oslin (RCA)

Jazz Vocalists: Betty Carter, "Look What I Got!" (Verve); Bobby McFerrin, "Brothers" track from Rob Wasserman's Duets (MCA)

Jazz Instrumentalists: Soloist, Michael Brecker, "Don't Try This at Home" (MCA Impluse); group, McCoy Tyner, Pharoah Sanders, David Murray, Cecil McBee, and Roy Haynes, "Blues for Coltrane: A Tribute to John Coltrane" (MCA Impluse)

Jazz, Big Band: Gil Evans & The Monday Night Orchestra, "Bud & Bird" (Intersound)

Jazz Fusion: Yellowjackets, "Politics" (MCA)

Gospel Vocalists: Amy Grant, "Lead Me On" (A&M); Larnelle Harris, "Christmas" (Benson)

Gospel Duo or Group: The Winans, "The Winans Live at Carnegie Hall" (QWest)

Soul Gospel Vocalists: Aretha Franklin, "One Lord, One Faith, One Baptism" (Arista); Bebe Winans, "Abundant Life" track from Ron Winans Family & Friends Choir (Selah Records)

Soul Gospel Duo or Group: Take 6, "Take Six" (Reprise)

Traditional Folk: "Folkways: A Vision Shared—A Tribute to Woody Guthrie and Leadbelly," Don DeVito, Joe McEwen, Harold Leventhal, and Ralph Rinzler, album producers (Columbia/CBS)

Reggae: "Conscious Party," Ziggy Marley and The Melody Makers (Virgin)

Latin Pop: Roberto Carlos, "Roberto Carlos" (Discos CBS International)

Tropical Latin: Ruben Blades, "Antecedente" (Elektra)

Mexican/American: Linda Ronstadt, "Canciones de Mi Padre (Elektra)

For Children: "Pecos Bill," Robin Williams, narration; Ry Cooder, music (Windham Hill)

Comedy: "Good Morning Vietnam," Robin Williams (A&M)

Spoken Word: Speech by Rev. Jesse Jackson (July 27) track from Aretha Franklin's One Lord, One Faith, One Baptism, Rev. Jesse Jackson (Arista)

Instrumental Composition: Mike Post, "The Theme from L.A. Law" (Polydor)

Instrumental Arrangement: Roger Kellaway, "Memos from Paradise" (GRP)

Cast Show Album: "Into the Woods," Jay David Saks, album producer; lyricist and composer, Stephen Sondheim (RCA)

Performance Music Video: "Where the Streets Have No Name," U2 (Island)

Concept Music Video: "I'm Fat," "Weird Al" Yankovic (Rock 'n' Roll/Epic)

Historical Album: "Crossroads," Bill Levenson, Album producer (Polydor)

Classical Album: "Verdi: Requiem & Operatic Choruses, "Robert Shaw conducting Atlanta Symphony Orchestra & Chorus. Robert Woods, album producer (Telarc)

Classical Orchestral Recording: "Rorem: String Symphony; Sunday Morning; Eagles," Robert Shaw conducting "String Symphony"; Louis Lane conducting "Sunday Morning" and "Eagles." Atlanta Symphony Orchestra. Robert Woods, album producer (New World)

Classical Soloist with Orchestra: Vladimir Horowitz (Carlo Maria Giulini conducting LaScala Opera Orchestra), "Mozart: Piano Concerto No. 23 in A" (Deutsche Grammophon); **Without Orchestra:** Alicia de Larrocha, "Albeniz: Iberia; Navarra; Suite Espagnola" (London)

Chamber Music: Murray Perahia & Sir Georg Solti, pianos with David Corkhill & Evelyn Glennie, percussion, "Bartok: Sonata for Two Pianos & Percussion/Brahms: Variations on a Theme by Joseph Haydn for Two Pianos" (CBS Masterworks)

Classical Vocal Soloist: Luciano Pavarotti, Luciano Pavarotti in Concert (CBS Masterworks)

Classical Choral: "Verdi: Requiem & Operatic Choruses," Robert Shaw, conductor, Atlanta Symphony Chorus and Orchestra (Telarc)

Opera: "Wagner: Lohengrin," Sir Georg Solti, conductor, Vienna State Opera Choir & Vienna Philharmonic (London)

Contemporary Composition: "Adams: Nixon in China," John Adams (Elektra/Nonesuch)

Producers: Non-Classical, Neil Dorfsman; **Classical,** Robert Woods

Presidential Medal of Freedom

The nation's highest civilian award, the Presidential Medal of Freedom, was established in 1963 by President John F. Kennedy to continue and expand Presidential recognition of meritorious service which, since 1945, had been granted as the Medal of Freedom. Kennedy selected the first recipients, but was assassinated before he could make the presentations. They were made by President Johnson. NOTE: An asterisk following a year denotes a posthumous award.

SELECTED BY PRESIDENT KENNEDY

Marian Anderson (contralto)	1963
Ralph J. Bunche (statesman)	1963
Ellsworth Bunker (diplomat)	1963
Pablo Casals (cellist)	1963
Genevieve Caulfield (educator)	1963
James B. Conant (educator)	1963
John F. Enders (bacteriologist)	1963
Felix Frankfurter (jurist)	1963
Karl Horton (youth authority)	1963
Robert J. Kiphuth (athletic director)	1963
Edwin H. Land (inventor)	1963
Herbert H. Lehman (statesman)	1963*
Robert A. Lovett (statesman)	1963
J. Clifford MacDonald (educator)	1963*
John J. McCloy (banker and statesman)	1963
George Meany (labor leader)	1963
Alexander Meiklejohn (philosopher)	1963
Ludwig Mies van der Rohe (architect)	1963
Jean Monnet (European statesman)	1963
Luis Muñoz-Marin (Governor of Puerto Rico)	1963
Clarence B. Randall (industrialist)	1963
Rudolf Serkin (pianist)	1963
Edward Steichen (photographer)	1963
George W. Taylor (educator)	1963
Alan T. Waterman (scientist)	1963
Mark S. Watson (journalist)	1963
Annie D. Wauneka (public health worker)	1963
E. B. White (author)	1963
Thornton N. Wilder (author)	1963
Edmund Wilson (author and critic)	1963
Andrew Wyeth (artist)	1963

AWARDED BY PRESIDENT JOHNSON

Dean G. Acheson (statesman)	1964
Eugene R. Black (banker)	1969
Detlev W. Bronk (neurophysiologist)	1964
McGeorge Bundy (government service)	1969
Ellsworth Bunker (diplomat)	1968
Clark Clifford (statesman)	1969
Aaron Copland (composer)	1964
Michael E. DeBakey (surgeon)	1969
Willem de Kooning (artist)	1964
Walt Disney (cartoon film producer)	1964
J. Frank Dobie (author)	1964
David Dubinsky (labor leader)	1969
Lena F. Edwards (physician and humanitarian)	1964
Thomas Stearns Eliot (poet)	1964
Ralph Ellison (author)	1969
Lynn Fontanne (actress)	1964
Henry Ford II (industrialist)	1969
John W. Gardner (educator)	1964
W. Averell Harriman (statesman)	1969
Rev. Theodore M. Hesburgh (educator)	1964
Bob Hope (comedian)	1969
John XXIII (Pope)	1963*
Clarence L. Johnson (aircraft engineer)	1964
Edgar F. Kaiser (industrialist)	1969
Frederick R. Kappel (telecommunications executive)	1964
Helen A. Keller (educator)	1964
John Fitzgerald Kennedy (U.S. President)	1963*
Robert W. Komer (government service)	1968
Mary Lasker (philanthropist)	1969
John L. Lewis (labor leader)	1964
Walter Lippmann (journalist)	1964
Eugene M. Locke (diplomat)	1968

Alfred Lunt (actor)	1964
John W. Macy, Jr. (government service)	1969
Ralph McGill (journalist)	1964
Robert S. McNamara (government service)	1968
Samuel Eliot Morison (historian)	1964
Lewis Mumford (urban planner and critic)	1964
Edward R. Murrow (radio-TV commentator)	1964
Reinhold Niebuhr (theologian)	1964
Gregory Peck (actor)	1969
Leontyne Price (soprano)	1964
A. Philip Randolph (labor leader)	1964
Laurance S. Rockefeller (conservationist)	1969
Walt Whitman Rostow (government service)	1969
Dean Rusk (statesman)	1969
Carl Sandburg (poet and biographer)	1964
Merriman Smith (journalist)	1969
John Steinbeck (author)	1964
Helen B. Taussig (pediatrician)	1964
Cyrus R. Vance (government service)	1969
Carl Vinson (legislator)	1964
Thomas J. Watson, Jr. (industrialist)	1964
James E. Webb (NASA administrator)	1968
Paul Dudley White (physician)	1964
William S. White (journalist)	1969
Roy Wilkins (social welfare executive)	1969
Whitney M. Young, Jr. (social welfare executive)	1969

AWARDED BY PRESIDENT NIXON

Edwin E. Aldrin (astronaut)	1969
Apollo 13 Mission Operations Team	1970
Neil A. Armstrong (astronaut)	1969
Earl Charles Behrens (journalist)	1970
Manlio Brosio (NATO secretary general)	1971
Michael Collins (astronaut)	1969
Edward K. (Duke) Ellington (musician)	1969
Edward T. Folliard (journalist)	1970
John Ford (film director)	1973
Samuel Goldwyn (film producer)	1971
Fred Wallace Haise, Jr. (astronaut)	1970
William M. Henry (journalist)	1970*
Paul G. Hoffman (statesman)	1974
William J. Hopkins (White House service)	1971
Arthur Krock (journalist)	1970
Melvin R. Laird (government service)	1974
David Lawrence (journalist)	1970
George Gould Lincoln (journalist)	1970
James A. Lovell, Jr. (astronaut)	1970
Dr. Charles L. Lowman (orthopedist)	1974
Raymond Moley (journalist)	1970
Eugene Ormandy (conductor)	1970
William P. Rogers (diplomat)	1973
Adela Rogers St. Johns (journalist)	1970
John Leonard Swigert, Jr. (astronaut)	1970
John Paul Vann (adviser, Vietnam war)	1972*
DeWitt and Lila Wallace (founders, *Reader's Digest*)	1972

AWARDED BY PRESIDENT FORD

I. W. Abel (labor leader)	1977
John Bardeen (physicist)	1977
Irving Berlin (composer)	1977
Norman Borlaug (agricultural scientist)	1977
Gen. Omar N. Bradley (soldier)	1977
David K. E. Bruce (diplomat)	1976
Arleigh Burke (national security)	1977
Alexander Calder (sculptor)	1977
Bruce Catton (historian)	1977

Joseph P. DiMaggio (baseball star)	1977
Ariel Durant (author)	1977
Will Durant (author)	1977
Arthur Fiedler (conductor)	1977
Henry J. Friendly (jurist)	1977
Martha Graham (dancer-choreographer)	1976
Claudia "Lady Bird" Johnson (service to U.S. scenic beauty)	1977
Henry A. Kissinger (statesman)	1977
Archibald MacLeish (poet)	1977
James A. Michener (author)	1977
Georgia O'Keeffe (artist)	1977
Jesse Owens (track champion)	1976
Nelson A. Rockefeller (government service)	1977
Norman Rockwell (illustrator)	1977
Arthur Rubinstein (pianist)	1976
Donald H. Rumsfeld (government service)	1977
Katherine Filene Shouse (service to the performing arts)	1977
Lowell Thomas (radio-TV commentator)	1977
James D. Watson (biochemist)	1977

AWARDED BY PRESIDENT CARTER

Ansel Adams (photographer)	1980
Horace M. Albright (government service)	1980
Roger Baldwin (civil libertarian)	1981
Harold Brown (government service)	1981
Zbigniew Brzezinski (government service)	1981
Rachel Carson (author)	1980*
Lucia Chase (ballet director)	1980
Warren M. Christopher (government service)	1981
Walter Cronkite (TV newscaster)	1981
Kirk Douglas (actor)	1981
Arthur J. Goldberg (government service)	1978
Hubert H. Humphrey (government service)	1980*
Archbishop Iakovos (churchman)	1980
Lyndon B. Johnson (U.S. President)	1980*
Rev. Dr. Martin Luther King, Jr. (civil rights leader)	1977*
Margaret Craig McNamara (educator)	1981
Margaret Mead (anthropologist)	1979*
Karl Menninger (psychiatrist)	1981
Clarence Mitchell, Jr. (civil rights leader)	1980
Edmund S. Muskie (government service)	1981
Esther Peterson (government service)	1981
Roger Tory Peterson (ornithologist)	1980
Adm. Hyman Rickover (national security)	1980
Jonas Salk (medical research)	1977
Beverly Sills (opera singer)	1980
Gerard C. Smith (government service)	1981
Robert S. Strauss (government service)	1981
Elbert Parr Tuttle (government service)	1981
Earl Warren (government service)	1981*
Robert Penn Warren (author and poet)	1980
John Wayne (actor)	1980*
Eudora Welty (author)	1980
Tennessee Williams (playwright)	1980
Andrew M. Young (government service)	1981

AWARDED BY PRESIDENT REAGAN

Walter H. Annenberg (publisher and diplomat)	1986
Anne L. Armstrong (diplomat)	1987
Howard H. Baker, Jr. (government service)	1984
George Balanchine (choreographer)	1983
Malcolm Baldrige (government service)	1988*
Count Basie (jazz pianist)	1985*
Pearl Bailey Bellson (entertainer and humanitarian)	1988
Earl (Red) Blaik (football coach)	1986
James H. (Eubie) Blake (composer-pianist)	1981
Irving Brown (labor leader)	1988
Paul W. (Bear) Bryant (football coach)	1983*
Warren Burger (former Chief Justice)	1987
James Burnham (editor-historian)	1983
James Francis Cagney (actor)	1984

The Right Honorable Lord Carrington (Secretary General of NATO)	1988
Whittaker Chambers (public servant)	1984*
James Cheek (educator)	1983
Leo Cherne (economist-humanitarian)	1984
Terence Cardinal Cooke, His Eminence (theologian)	1984*
Denton Arthur Cooley, M.D. (heart surgeon)	1984
Jacques-Yves Cousteau (marine explorer)	1985
Justin W. Dart Sr. (businessman)	1987*
Tennessee Ernie Ford (singer)	1984
Milton Friedman (economist)	1988
R. Buckminster Fuller (architect-geometrician)	1983
Hector P. Garcia, M.D. (humanitarian)	1984
Barry Goldwater (government service)	1986
Gen. Andrew J. Goodpaster (soldier-diplomat)	1984
Rev. Billy Graham (evangelist)	1983
Ella T. Grasso (Connecticut governor)	1981*
Philip C. Habib (diplomat)	1982
Bryce N. Harlow (government service)	1981
Helen Hayes (actress)	1986
Eric Hoffer (philosopher-longshoreman)	1983
Jerome Holland (educator and ambassador)	1985*
Sidney Hook (philosopher-educator)	1985
Vladimir Horowitz (pianist)	1985
Henry Martin Jackson (government service)	1984*
Jacob K. Javits (government service)	1983
Walter H. Judd (government service)	1981
Irving Kaufman (jurist)	1987
Danny Kaye (actor)	1987*
Jeane J. Kirkpatrick (government service)	1985
Lincoln Kirstein (ballet director)	1984
Louis L'Amour (author)	1984
Morris I. Leibman (lawyer)	1981
Gen. Lyman L. Lemnitzer (soldier)	1987
George M. Low (educator and administrator NASA)	1985*
Clare Booth Luce (author-diplomat)	1983
Joseph M.A.H. Luns (diplomat-NATO)	1984
Jean Faircloth MacArthur (patriot)	1988
Dumas Malone (historian)	1983
Michael Mansfield (government service)	1989
J. Willard Marriott (businessman)	1988*
John A. McCone (government service)	1987
Mabel Mercer (jazz singer)	1983
Paul Nitz (government service)	1985
David Packard (public service, businessman)	1988
Frederick Patterson (educator)	1987
Norman Vincent Peale (theologian)	1984
Nathan Perlmutter (public service)	1987
Simon Ramo (industrialist)	1983
Frank Reynolds (TV anchor)	1985*
Gen. Matthew B. Ridgway (soldier)	1986
S. Dillon Ripley (cultural and public service)	1985
Jack Roosevelt Robinson (baseball player)	1984*
Gen. Carlos P. Romulo (Philippino statesman)	1984
Mstislav Rostropovich (cellist-conductor)	1987
Vermont Royster (journalist)	1986
Albert B. Sabin (medical research)	1986
Mohamed Anwar el-Sadat (statesman)	1984*
George P. Shultz (gov. service)	1989
Eunice Kennedy Shriver (humanitarian)	1984
Frank Sinatra (entertainer)	1985
Kate Smith (singer)	1982
Roger L. Stevens (theatrical producer)	1988
James Stewart (actor)	1985
Mother Teresa (humanitarian)	1985
Charles B. Thornton (industrialist)	1981
William B. Walsh (humanitarian)	1987
Gen. Albert Coady Wedemeyer (national security)	1985
Casper W. Weinberger (government service)	1987
Meredith Willson (composer)	1987*
Albert and Roberta Wohlstetter (government service)	1985
Charles E. Yeager (public service)	1985

Recipients of Kennedy Center Honors

The Kennedy Center for the Performing Arts in Washington, D.C., created its Honors awards in 1978 to recognize the achievements of five distinguished contributors to the performing arts. Following are the recipients:

1978: Marian Anderson (contralto), Fred Astaire (dancer-actor), Richard Rodgers (Broadway composer), Arthur Rubinstein (pianist), George Balanchine (choreographer).

1979: Ella Fitzgerald (jazz singer), Henry Fonda (actor), Martha Graham (dancer-choreographer), Tennessee Williams (playwright), Aaron Copland (composer).

1980: James Cagney (actor), Leonard Bernstein (composer-conductor), Agnes de Mille (choreographer), Lynn Fontanne (actress), Leontyne Price (soprano).

1981: Count Basie (jazz composer-pianist), Cary Grant (actor), Helen Hayes (actress), Jerome Robbins (choreographer), Rudolf Serkin (pianist).

1982: George Abbott (Broadway producer), Lillian Gish (actress), Benny Goodman (jazz clarinetist), Gene Kelly (dancer-actor), Eugene Ormandy (conductor).

1983: Katherine Dunham (dancer-choreographer), Elia Kazan (director-author), James Stewart (actor), Virgil Thomson (music critic-composer), Frank Sinatra (singer).

1984: Lena Horne (singer), Danny Kaye (comedian-actor), Gian Carlo Menotti (composer), Arthur Miller (playwright), Isaac Stern (violinist).

1985: Merce Cunningham (dancer-choreographer), Irene Dunne (actress), Bob Hope (comedian), Alan Jay Lerner (lyricist-playwright), Frederick Loewe (composer), Beverly Sills (soprano and opera administrator).

1986: Lucille Ball (comedienne), Ray Charles (musician), Yehudi Menuhin (violinist), Antony Tudor (choreographer), Hume Cronyn and Jessica Tandy (husband-and-wife acting team).

1987: Perry Como (singer), Bette Davis (actress), Sammy Davis Jr. (entertainer), Nathan Milstein (violinist), Alwin Nikolais (choreographer).

1988: Alvin Ailey (choreographer), George Burns (comedian-actor), Myrna Loy (actress), Alexander Schneider (violinist), Roger L. Stevens (theatrical producer and the Kennedy Center's founding chairman).

1989 Christopher Awards

Adult Books

Alicia: My Story, by Alicia Appleman-Jurman (Bantam)

Balm in Gilead: Journey of a Healer, by Sara Lawrence Lightfoot (Addison Wesley/A Merloyd Lawrence Book)

Battle Cry of Freedom: The Civil War Era, by James M. McPherson (Oxford University Press)

Beyond the Frozen Sea: Visions of Antarctica, by Edwin Mickleburg (St. Martin's Press)

Fear No Evil, by Natan Sharansky (Random House)

Getting Better: Inside Alcoholics Anonymous, by Nan Robertson (William Morrow)

Grey Is the Color of Hope, by Irina Ratushinskaya, translated by Alyona Kojevnikov (Alfred A. Knopf)

Morning Glory Babies: Children with Aids and the Celebration of Life, by Tolbert McCarroll (St. Martin's Press)

Murdered in Central America: The Stories of Eleven U.S. Missionaries, by Donna Whitson Brett and Edward T. Brett (Orbis Books)

No Place But Here: A Teacher's Vocation in a Rural Community, by Garret Keizer (Viking)

Parting the Waters: America in the King Years 1954-63, by Taylor Branch (Simon & Schuster)

Rachel and Her Children: Homeless Families in America, by Jonathan Kozol (Crown)

With All Our Heart & Mind: The Spiritual Works of

Mercy in a Psychological Age, by Sidney Callahan (Crossroad)

Young People's Books

The Good-Bye Book, by Judith Viorst, illustrated by Kay Chorao (Macmillan)

Family Farm, by Thomas Locker (Dial Books)

Lies, Deception and Truth, by Ann E. Weiss (Houghton Mifflin)

Looking the Tiger in the Eye: Confronting the Nuclear Threat, by Carl B. Feldbaum and Ronald J. Bee (Harper & Row)

Television Specials

American Playhouse: The Revolt of Mother (PBS)

The Attic: The Hiding of Anne Frank (CBS)

Drugs: Why This Plague? An ABC News Special

Evil in Clear River (ABC)

Go Toward the Light (CBS)

The Murder of Mary Phagan (NBC)

A Place at the Table: An NBC Family Special

Films

Babette's Feast (Orion Classics)

Little Dorrit (Cannon Screen Entertainment)

Stand and Deliver (Warner Bros.)

The James Keller Youth Award

Joan Ganz Cooney

Poets Laureate of England

Edmund Spenser	1591–1599	Laurence Eusden	1718-1730	Alfred Lord Tennyson	1850-1892
Samuel Daniel	1599–1619	Colley Cibber	1730-1757	Alfred Austin	1896-1913
Ben Jonson	1619–1637	William Whitehead	1757-1785	Robert Bridges	1913-1930
William Davenant	1638–1668	Thomas Warton	1785-1790	John Masefield	1930-1967
John Dryden[1]	1670–1689	Henry James Pye	1790-1813	C. Day Lewis	1967-1972
Thomas Shadwell	1689–1692	Robert Southey	1813-1843	Sir John Betjeman	1972-1984
Nahum Tate	1692–1715	William Wordsworth	1843-1850	Ted Hughes	1984-
Nicholas Rowe	1715-1718				

1. First to bear the title officially. *Source: Encyclopaedia Britannica.*

ENTERTAINMENT & CULTURE

TV of the Future

By Hugh Carter Donahue

Cable and VCRs transformed television in the 1970s and 1980s, providing unheard of variety and flexibility in programming. High-definition television promises to have even greater impact in the 1990s. HDTV sets will show high-resolution pictures on large, extra-wide screens, and will produce the crystal-clear sound of a compact disc. They may also be smart enough to store and retrieve electronic still pictures, allow two-way video communication, and receive programming in different formats from broadcasters, cable, satellites, and perhaps even fiber-optic phone lines.

The HDTV race is on in Japan, Europe, and the United States. At stake is more than just each country's share of the consumer electronics market. Because the new receivers could use much more sophisticated gadgetry than today's sets, they present a huge potential market for microprocessors, memory chips, and other devices. So leadership in HDTV might dramatically boost a country's standing in other key areas.

By virtue of seniority, the Japanese are leading the pack. NHK, the Japanese Broadcasting System, began developing high-definition television in the 1970s. Together with electronics giants such as Sony, Matsushita, and Hitachi, NHK demonstrated a working system in 1981 with 1,125 scanning lines—more than twice the 525 lines that form a conventional U.S. television picture. The Japanese initiative encompassed equipment like cameras, picture tubes, a video recorder, and a scanner for transferring films to videotape.

Europe is not far behind. At a 1986 meeting of the Comité Consultatif International de Radiodiffusion—a worldwide standard-setting organization—European representatives turned down Japan's bid to make the NHK system the international standard. Eureka, Europe's 19-nation technology development program, then mobilized to create its own high-definition format for European markets. Experimental satellite transmissions are planned for later this year [1989]; full HDTV satellite and cable service, for 1995.

The United States is bringing up the rear. The combination of less public-private cooperation, stricter antitrust regulation, and fewer major TV manufacturers (one, to be exact) has led to a slower start in developing HDTV. And with 160 million television receivers and 1,300 broadcasters—far more than Japan or Europe—the United States has to overcome a lot of inertia in switching to a new standard.

Some Americans argue that Japan's and Europe's lead is too great for the United States to become a serious player in HDTV. Better, they say, to concentrate on software and video programming and concede receiver manufacturing to the frontrunners. But the United States does stand a chance. Because they started so early, the Japanese are building upon dated 1970s technology. They are "ahead" only because they can demonstrate working prototypes. European firms, though eager to market HDTV wares in the United States, are building primarily for Europe. And their equipment is tailored to European TV's 50 images per second, so they would have to modify it to fit the U.S. standard of 59.94.

HDTV presents an opportunity for the United States to leapfrog the Japanese and challenge the Europeans. But first, U.S. television interests must decide what standard or standards they are going to follow. Since the 1940s, American transmitters and receivers have been based on a scheme set by the National Television System Committee (NTSC). Last September [1988], the Federal Communications Commission ruled that a high-definition system could not render NTSC equipment obsolete overnight. The FCC mandated a transition period of unspecified length during which viewers will have a choice of watching conventional pictures on their old sets or buying new HDTV sets.

A Sharper Image

HDTV improves on NTSC in some big ways. Instead of the current 525 lines, it can have as many as 1,050 or 1,125 lines. And although some proposed systems display pictures the same way as NTSC, which interlaces two half-images, or fields, in quick succession (transmitting first the odd-numbered lines, then the even-numbered lines, and letting the mind's eye do the rest), many use "progressive" scanning. That is, they scan the whole picture in one continuous sequence, simultaneously boosting resolution and cutting flicker. If the system also shows twice the number of lines, resolution is further increased.

HDTV also clears up some of the annoying defects of broadcast television. For example, information for light and color in NTSC is interleaved on the same signal. Because the two types of information overlap slightly, today's receivers can mix up color and light, especially in detailed patterns. That's why a herringbone coat often shows up with splashes of rainbow color in it. With twice or four times the resolution, HDTV greatly reduces this defect—as well as problems such as flickering around the borders of objects.

The improved picture will permit the use of much larger and wider screens. The aspect ratio, or ratio of width to height, of a conventional screen is 4:3, the format for movies in 1936 when the National Television Committee began setting parameters for TV. Since the 1930s, films have adopted a ratio of either 1.85:1 or 2.35:1 for greater impact. As a result, movies shown on TV must be cropped. Many HDTV developers plan to use an aspect ratio of 16:9, which will allow movies to be transmitted in a form much closer to their original composition. (Regular sets will show either a cropped version of the HDTV picture or a full version with black bands at top and bottom.) When this big, clear picture is combined with the CD-quality audio that most HDTV proponents are developing, watching TV should be just like going to the movies.

The Standards Race

Roughly 20 HDTV proponents are seeking FCC approval of their broadcast system as a national standard. A private-sector advisory committee to the FCC will begin tests on competing formats late this year. [1989] The committee has to assess proposed systems' compatibility with today's receivers, the number and bandwidth of channels required to carry the high-definition signal, display size, aspect ratio, and vertical, horizontal, and dynamic (motion) resolution. Because only proposals with prototype hardware will be tested, the many developers whose systems exist only as computer simulations are racing to build prototypes. By late 1990 or early 1991 the committee plans to report its findings to the FCC. In 1991 or 1992, the FCC should be ready to render a decision. ☐

Hugh Carter Donahue, who received a Ph.D. in communications and policy analysis from MIT in 1985, teaches journalism at Ohio State University. His book "The Battle to Control Broadcast News: Who Owns the First Amendment?" (MIT Press, 1989) chronicles the political uses of broadcasting from Coolidge to Bush.

This article is excerpted from "Choosing the TV of The Future" by Hugh Carter Donahue, and is reprinted with permission from *TECHNOLOGY REVIEW*, M.I.T. Alumni Association, copyright 1989.

Notable Books, 1988

This list has been compiled by the Notable Books Council, Reference and Adult Services, a division of the American Library Association for use by the general reader and by librarians who work with adult readers. The titles were selected for their significant contribution to the expansion of knowledge or for the pleasure they can provide to adult readers. Criteria include wide general appeal and literary merit.

Fiction

Allende, Isabel, **Eva Luna,** Knopf
Carver, Raymond, **Where I'm Calling From: New and Selected Stories,** Atlantic Monthly Press
DeLillo, Don, **Libra,** Viking
Dexter, Pete, **Paris Trout,** Random
Dubus, Andre, **Selected Stories,** Godine
Erdrich, Louise, **Tracks,** Holt
Garcia Marquez, Gabriel, **Love in the Time of Cholera,** Knopf
Greenberg, Joanne, **Of Such Small Differences,** Holt
Lessing, Doris, **The Fifth Child,** Knopf
Mukherjee, Bharati, **The Middleman and Other Stories,** Grove
Naylor, Gloria, **Mama Day,** Ticknor & Fields
Powers, J.F. **Wheat That Springeth Green,** Knopf
Sexton, Linda Gray, **Points of Light,** Little, Brown
Smith, Lee, **Fair and Tender Ladies,** Putnam
Spark, Muriel, **A Far Cry from Kensington,** Houghton Mifflin
Tyler, Anne, **Breathing Lessons,** Knopf

Nonfiction

Berton, Pierre, **The Arctic Grail: The Quest for the North West Passage and the North Pole, 1818-1909,** Viking
Cagin, Seth and Dray, Philip, **We Are Not Afraid: The Story of Goodman, Schwerner, and Chaney and the Civil Rights Campaign for Mississippi,** Macmillan
Ellmann, Richard, **Oscar Wilde,** Knopf
Gay, Peter, **Freud: A Life for Our Times,** Norton
Goodwin, Richard N., **Remembering America: A Voice From the Sixties,** Little Brown
Hansen, Eric, **Stranger in the Forest: On Foot across Borneo,** Houghton Mifflin
Lester, Julius, **Lovesong: Becoming a Jew,** Holt
McPherson, James M., **Battle Cry of Freedom: The Civil War Era,** Oxford
Maddox, Brenda **Nora: The Real Life of Molly Bloom,** Houghton Mifflin
Pagels, Elaine, **Adam, Eve, and the Serpent,** Random
Sharansky, Natan, **Fear No Evil,** Random

Source: Reprinted by permission of the American Library Association. Issued as a pamphlet by ALA, 50 E. Huron St., Chicago, Ill. 60611, annually in the spring for the preceding year. © American Library Association 1988.

Major U.S. Symphony Orchestras and Their Music Directors

Source: American Symphony Orchestra League.

Atlanta Symphony: Yoel Levi
Baltimore Symphony: David Zinman
Boston Symphony: Seiji Ozawa
Buffalo Philharmonic: Semyon Bychkov
Chicago Symphony: Daniel Barenboim[1]
Cincinnati Symphony: Jesus Lopez-Cobos
Cleveland Orchestra: Christoph von Dohnanyi
Columbus Symphony: Christian Badea
Dallas Symphony: Eduardo Mata
Denver Symphony: Sixten Ehrling[2]
Detroit Symphony: Gunther Herbig
Houston Symphony: Christoph Eschenbach
Indianapolis Symphony: Raymond Leppard
Los Angeles Philharmonic: André Previn[7]
Milwaukee Symphony: Zdenek Macal
Minnesota Orchestra: Edo de Waart
National Symphony: (D.C.): Mstislav Rostropovich

New Jersey Symphony: Hugh Wolff
New Orleans Symphony: Maxim Shostakovich
New York Philharmonic: Zubin Mehta[3]
Oregon Symphony: James DePreist
Philadelphia Orchestra: Riccardo Muti
Phoenix Symphony Orchestra: James Saderes
Pittsburgh Symphony: Lorin Maazel
Rochester Philharmonic: Jerzy Semkow[2,4]
Saint Louis Symphony: Leonard Slatkin
⁵Saint Paul Chamber Orchestra: Hugh Wolff[4]
San Antonio Symphony: Zdenek Macal[4,6]
San Diego Symphony: Lynn Harrell[2]
San Francisco Symphony: Herbert Blomstedt
Seattle Symphony: Gerard Schwarz
Syracuse Symphony: Kazuyoshi Akiyama
Utah Symphony: Joseph Silverstein

1. Starting 1990–91 season. 2. Music Advisor. 3. Through 1990–91. 4. Principal Conductor. 5. Artistic Commission also includes Christopher Hogwood, Director of Music and John Adams, Creative Chair. 6. Artistic Director. 7. Resigned as Music Director but continues as conductor. Esa-Pekka Salonen takes over as Music Director with the 1992–93 season.

Major Public Libraries

City (branches)	Volumes	Circulation	Budget (in millions)	City (branches)	Volumes	Circulation	Budget (in millions)
Akron-Summit County, Ohio (18)	1,205,000	2,727,252	$10.7	Louisville, Ky. (14)	903,084	2,835,115	6.6
Albuquerque, N.M. (9)	629,152	2,564,132	4.4	Madison, Wis. (7)	699,100	2,210,278	$4.9
Annapolis, Md. (13)	1,790,177	4,281,015	8.8	Memphis, Tenn. (22)	2,246,274	2,575,267	11.2
Atlanta-Fulton County (25)	1,574,218	2,104,745	14.8	Miami-Dade County, Fla. (28)*	2,386,204	4,200,000	21.0
Austin, Tex. (16)*				Milwaukee (12)	2,102,659	3,200,829	14.8
Baltimore (31)	2,148,625	1,505,323	15.5	Minneapolis (14)	1,854,649	2,801,573	12.3
Baton Rouge, La. (9)	581,557	1,689,707	7.3	Nashville-Davidson			
Birmingham, Ala. (19)	1,150,000	3,520,323	8.3	County, Tenn. (15)	627,732	1,856,676	6.1
Boston (25)	6,003,386	1,781,899	26.2	Newark, N.J. (11)	1,200,000	1,072,758	8.6
Buffalo-Erie County, N.Y. (58)	3,506,352	6,482,455	15.0	New Orleans (15)	1,008,606	1,113,035	6.0
Charleston-Kanawha				*New York City:*			
County, W.Va. (8)	545,000	1,035,831	3.1	†The New York Public Library			
Charlotte, N.C. (19)	1,057,879	3,279,594	9.9	Branches (82)	3,391,750	8,340,496	70.3
Chicago (88)	5,167,810	7,384,700	60.5	Research	9,496,024		50.1
Cincinnati (40)	3,831,856	7,663,921	22.7	Brooklyn (60)	4,685,109	8,287,569	30.4
Cleveland (31)	2,514,817	4,365,878	29.0	Queens (60)	7,809,126	12,138,604	40.2
Columbus-Franklin				Norfolk, Va. (11)	861,607	823,908	4.1
County, Ohio (20)	1,381,516	5,506,073	27.2	Oklahoma City-County (10)	875,279	3,350,113	8.1
Dallas (19)	2,871,497	4,237,153	16.2	Omaha, Neb. (10)	614,836	2,123,804	6.2
Dayton-Montgomery				Philadelphia (52)	4,795,981	4,798,575	38.5
County, Ohio (19)	1,509,623	5,153,578	11.9	Phoenix, Ariz. (10)	1,501,994	4,975,751	10.6
Denver (21)	3,820,000	3,253,673	13.4	Pittsburgh (20)	1,848,827	2,758,868	11.1
Des Moines, Iowa (5)	527,800	1,217,112	3.3	Portland-Multnomah			
Detroit (24)	2,716,058	1,803,262	21.0	County, Ore. (14)	1,209,595	4,241,377	9.8
D.C. (26)	1,550,630	1,949,455	18.1	Providence, R.I. (9)	1,103,421	901,053	3.9
El Paso (9)	455,000	1,268,435	4.0	Richmond, VA. (10)	764,732	840,000	3.1
Erie, Pa. (6)	500,000	1,433,142	2.3	Rochester, N.Y. (11)	1,463,265	1,594,528	9.2
Evansville-Vanderburgh				Sacramento, Calif. (24)	1,400,000	4,000,000	15.0
County, Ind. (7)	857,709	1,377,754	3.8	St. Louis (14)	1,162,510	1,262,505	5.7
Fairfax County, Va. (22)	2,300,000	8,200,000	18.7	St. Paul (12)	935,151	2,285,872	6.1
Fort Wayne-Allen				St. Petersburg, Fla. (5)*			
County, Ind. (12)	1,972,916	2,951,812	7.9	Salt Lake City-County,			
Fort Worth (8)	1,815,572	3,621,705	5.9	Utah (15)	1,038,381	3,417,016	10.0
Grand Rapids, Mich. (5)	1,006,186	1,018,013	3.3	San Antonio (17)	1,795,057	3,341,175	8.9
Greenville City-County, S.C. (11)	546,551	1,220,217	3.7	San Diego, Calif. (31)	1,631,121	4,879,053	18.3[2]
Hawaii State Public Library				San Francisco (26)	1,974,896	3,395,153	18.2
System (49)[1]	2,210,241	6,512,715	16.4	San Jose, Calif. (18)	1,121,601	3,724,583	14.3
Houston (33)	3,459,824	6,273,271	15.6	Seattle (22)	1,759,502	4,715,322	16.0
Independence, Mo. (26)	1,600,000	3,750,000	9.5	Springfield, Mass. (8)	678,254	1,317,931	5.0
Indianapolis-Marion				Tampa, Fla. (16)	1,840,000	2,855,963	12.3
County (21)	1,627,429	5,376,388	15.1	Tucson, Ariz. (17)	1,013,750	4,309,200	9.6
Jackson, Miss. (12)	500,000	803,058	2.3	Tulsa City-County, Okla. (20)	760,092	3,081,643	7.4
Jacksonville, Fla. (11)	1,862,377	2,442,064	9.5	Wichita, Kan. (11)	886,193	1,527,058	3.5
Kansas City, Mo. (9)	1,476,827	1,425,300	9.0	Winston-Salem-			
Knoxville, Tenn. (16)	643,757	1,594,373	3.5	Forsyth County, N.C. (8)	350,000	2,000,000	4.5
Lincoln, Neb. (7)	481,227	1,344,272	2.9	Worcester, Mass. (7)	565,139	775,636	3.2
Long Beach, Calif. (11)	920,103	2,763,731	10.7	Youngstown-			
Los Angeles (County) (102)	5,000,000+	12,217,107	60.0	Mahoning County, Ohio (21)	709,087	1,509,121	6.9

NOTE: n.a. = not available. 1. State-wide system. 2. Includes $4.7 million capital improvements. † Includes Manhattan, Bronx, and Staten Island. * Did not reply to questionnaire.

Glossary of Art Movements

Abstract Expressionism. American art movement of the 1940s that emphasized form and color within a nonrepresentational framework. Jackson Pollock initiated the revolutionary technique of splattering the paint directly on canvas to achieve the subconscious interpretation of the artist's inner vision of reality.

Art Deco. A 1920s style characterized by setbacks, zigzag forms, and the use of chrome and plastic ornamentation. New York's Chrysler Building is an architectural example of the style.

Art Nouveau. An 1890s style in architecture, graphic arts, and interior decoration characterized by writhing forms, curving lines, and asymmetrical

organization. Some critics regard the style as the first stage of modern architecture.

Ashcan School. A group of New York realist artists, formed in 1908, who abandoned decorous subject matter and portrayed the more common as well as the sordid aspects of city life.

Assemblage (Collage). Forms of modern sculpture and painting utilizing readymades, found objects, and pasted fragments to form an abstract composition. Louise Nevelson's boxlike enclosures, each with its own composition of assembled objects, illustrate the style in sculpture. Pablo Picasso developed the technique of cutting and pasting natural or manufactured materials to a painted or unpainted surface.

Barbizon School (Landscape Painting). A group of painters who, around the middle of the 19th century, reacted against classical landscape and advocated a direct study of nature. They were influenced by English and Dutch landscape masters. Theodore Rousseau, one of the principal figures of the group, led the fight for outdoor painting. In this respect, the school was a forerunner of Impressionism.

Baroque. European art and architecture of the 17th and 18th centuries. Giovanni Bernini, a major exponent of the style, believed in the union of the arts of architecture, painting, and sculpture to overwhelm the spectator with ornate and highly dramatized themes. Although the style originated in Rome as the instrument of the Church, it spread throughout Europe in such monumental creations as the Palace of Versailles.

Beaux Arts. Elaborate and formal architectural style characterized by symmetry and an abundance of sculptured ornamentation. New York's old Custom House at Bowling Green is an example of the style.

Black or Afro-American Art. The work of American artists of African descent produced in various styles characterized by a mood of protest and a search for identity and historical roots.

Classicism. A form of art derived from the study of Greek and Roman styles characterized by harmony, balance, and serenity. In contrast, the Romantic Movement gave free rein to the artist's imagination and to the love of the exotic.

Constructivism. A form of sculpture using wood, metal, glass, and modern industrial materials expressing the technological society. The mobiles of Alexander Calder are examples of the movement.

Cubism. Early 20th-century French movement marked by a revolutionary departure from representational art. Pablo Picasso and Georges Bracque penetrated the surface of objects, stressing basic abstract geometric forms that presented the object from many angles simultaneously.

Dada. A product of the turbulent and cynical post-World War I period, this anti-art movement extolled the irrational, the absurd, the nihilistic, and the nonsensical. The reproduction of Mona Lisa adorned with a mustache is a famous example. The movement is regarded as a precursor of Surrealism. Some critics regard HAPPENINGS as a recent development of Dada. This movement incorporates environment and spectators as active and important ingredients in the production of random events.

Expressionism. A 20th-century European art movement that stresses the expression of emotion and the inner vision of the artist rather than the exact representation of nature. Distorted lines and shapes and exaggerated colors are used for emotional impact. Vincent Van Gogh is regarded as the precursor of this movement.

Fauvism. The name "wild beasts" was given to the group of early 20th-century French painters because their work was characterized by distortion and violent colors. Henri Matisse and Georges Roualt were leaders of this group.

Futurism. This early 20th-century movement originating in Italy glorified the machine age and attempted to represent machines and figures in motion. The aesthetics of Futurism affirmed the beauty of technological society.

Genre. This French word meaning "type" now refers to paintings that depict scenes of everyday life without any attempt at idealization. Genre paintings can be found in all ages, but the Dutch productions of peasant and tavern scenes are typical.

Impressionism. Late 19th-century French school dedicated to defining transitory visual impressions painted directly from nature, with light and color of primary importance. If the atmosphere changed, a totally different picture would emerge. It was not the object or event that counted but the visual impression as caught at a certain time of day under a certain light. Claude Monet and Camille Pissarro were leaders of the movement.

Mannerism. A mid-16th century movement, Italian in origin, although El Greco was a major practitioner of the style. The human figure, distorted and elongated, was the most frequent subject.

Neoclassicism. An 18th-century reaction to the excesses of Baroque and Rococo, this European art movement tried to recreate the art of Greece and Rome by imitating the ancient classics both in style and subject matter.

Neoimpressionism. A school of painting associated with George Seurat and his followers in late 19th-century France that sought to make Impressionism more precise and formal. They employed a technique of juxtaposing dots of primary colors to achieve brighter secondary colors, with the mixture left to the eye to complete (pointillism).

Op Art. The 1960s movement known as Optical Painting is characterized by geometrical forms that create an optical illusion in which the eye is required to blend the colors at a certain distance.

Pop Art. In this return to representational art, the artist returns to the world of tangible objects in a reaction against abstraction. Materials are drawn from the everyday world of popular culture—comic strips, canned goods, and science fiction.

Realism. A development in mid-19th-century France lead by Gustave Courbet. Its aim was to depict the customs, ideas, and appearances of the time using scenes from everyday life.

Rococo. A French style of interior decoration developed during the reign of Louis XV consisting mainly of asymmetrical arrangements of curves in paneling, porcelain, and gold and silver objects. The characteristics of ornate curves, prettiness, and gaiety can also be found in the painting and sculpture of the period.

Surrealism. A further development of Collage, Cubism, and Dada, this 20th-century movement stresses the weird, the fantastic, and the dreamworld of the subconscious.

Symbolism. As part of a general European movement in the latter part of the 19th century, it was closely allied with Symbolism in literature. It marked a turning away from painting by observation to transforming fact into a symbol of inner experience. Gauguin was an early practitioner.

Top 10 Videocassettes Sales, 1988

1. **Lady and the Tramp** (Walt Disney Home Video)
2. **Callanetics** (MCA Home Video)
3. **Jane Fonda's Low Impact Aerobic Workout** (Lorimar Home Video)
4. **Star Trek IV: The Voyage Home** (Paramount Home Video)
5. **Start Up with Jane Fonda** (Lorimar Home Video)
6. **An American Tail** (MCA Home Video)
7. **Jane Fonda's New Workout** (Lorimar Home Video)
8. **Pink Floyd the Wall** (MGM/UA Home Video)
9. **Dirty Dancing** (Vestron Video)
10. **Sleeping Beauty** (Walt Disney Home Video)

Source: Billboard. © 1988 by Billboard Publications, Inc. Reprinted with permission.

Top 10 Classical Crossover Albums, 1988

1. **By Request . . . The Best of John Williams,** Boston Pops (Williams) (Philips)
2. **Beethoven or Bust,** Don Dorsey (Telarc)
3. **Hollywood's Greatest Hits,** Cincinnati Pops (Kunzel) (Telarc)
4. **Kiri Sings Gershwin,** Kiri Te Kanawa (Angel)
5. **Volare,** Luciano Pavarotti (Mancini) (London)
6. **Bach On Abbey Road,** John Bayless (ProArte)
7. **Flamenco Guitar,** Paco Pena (Nimbus)
8. **Gershwin: Of Thee I Sing/Let 'Em Eat Cake,** Orchestra of St. Luke's (Tilson Thomas) (CBS)
9. **James Galway's Greatest Hits,** James Galway (RCA)
10. **The Jazz Album,** London Sinfonietta (Rattle) (Angel)

Source: Billboard. © 1988 by Billboard Publications, Inc. Reprinted with permission.

Top 10 Pop Compact Discs, 1988

1. **Faith,** George Michael (Columbia)
2. **Dirty Dancing,** Soundtrack (RCA)
3. **Kick,** INXS (Atlantic)
4. **Hysteria,** Def Leppard (Mercury)
5. **Tracy Chapman,** Tracy Chapman (Elektra)
6. **. . . Nothing Like the Sun,** Sting (A&M)
7. **Appetite for Destruction,** Guns 'N Roses (Geffen)
8. **Now and Zen,** Robert Plant (EsParanza)
9. **Bad,** Michael Jackson (Epic)
10. **A Momentary Lapse of Reason,** Pink Floyd (Columbia)

Source: Billboard. © 1988 by Billboard Publications, Inc. Reprinted with permission.

VCR & TV Sales to Retailers, 1988

Television	
Color	20,200,000
Monochrome	2,570,000
Total TV[1]	22,770,000
Projection TV	301,000
Home VCR	12,792,000
Camcorders[2]	2,044,000

1. Excludes projection television. 2. Included in Home VCR.
Source: Electronic Industries Association Consumer Electronics Group.

Top 10 Videocassettes Rentals, 1988

1. **Dirty Dancing** (Vestron Video)
2. **Lethal Weapon** (Warner Home Video)
3. **Fatal Attraction** (Paramount Home Video)
4. **The Untouchables** (Paramount Home Video)
5. **The Witches of Eastwick** (Warner Home Video)
6. **No Way Out** (HBO Viedo)
7. **Outrageous Fortune** (Touchstone Home Video)
8. **Robocop** (Orion Home Video)
9. **Stakeout** (Touchstone Home Video)
10. **Tin Men** (Touchstone Home Video)

Source: Billboard. © 1988 Billboard Publications, Inc. Reprinted with permission.

Top 10 Music Videocassettes, 1988

1. **$19.98 Home Vid Cliff'Em All!** (Metallica) (Elektra Entertainment)
2. **Slippery When Wet** (PolyGram Video)
3. **Aerosmith's Video Scrapbook** (CBS-Fox Music Video)
4. **Sting: The Videos Part I** (A&M Video)
5. **One Night of Rapture** (Elektra Entertainment)
6. **CV** (Virgin Music Video)
7. **So Far** (6 West Home Video)
8. **Whitesnake: The Trilogy** (Geffen Home Video)
9. **Kick-The Video Flick** (Atlantic Video)
10. **The Cure in Orange** (Elektra Entertainment)

Source: Billboard. © 1988 by Billboard Publications, Inc. Reprinted with permission.

10 Top-grossing Concerts

1. **Grateful Dead,** $2,896,369, Madison Square Garden, New York, N.Y., Sept. 14-16, 18-20, 22-23.
2. **Van Halen's Monsters of Rock: Van Halen, Scorpions, Dokken, Metallica, Kingdom Come,** $2,665,797, Alpine Valley Music Theatre, East Troy, Wis., May 27-29.
3. **Human Rights Now! Tour: Bruce Springsteen, Sting, Peter Gabriel, Tracy Chapman, Youssou N'Dour, Joan Baez,** $2,621,220, John F. Kennedy Stadium, Philadelphia, Pa., Sept. 19.
4. **U2, Pretenders,** (Nov. 17-18), **Steve Jones** (Nov. 17), **BoDeans** (Nov. 18), $2,590,497, Los Angeles Memorial Coliseum, Los Angeles, Calif., Nov. 17-18.
5. **Pink Floyd,** $2,389,635, Giants Stadium, East Rutherford, N.J., June 3-4.
6. **Elton John,** $2,250,580, Madison Square Garden, New York, N.Y., Oct. 17-18, 20-22.
7. **Bruce Springsteen & the E Street Band,** $2,215,305, Madison Square Garden, New York, N.Y., May 16, 18-19, 22-23.
8. **U2, Pretenders, BoDeans,** $1,973,790, Oakland–Alameda County Coliseum, Oakland, Calif., Nov. 14-15.
9. **Human Rights Now! Tour: Bruce Springsteen, Sting, Peter Gabriel, Tracy Chapman, Youssou n'Dour, Joan Baez,** $1,973,790, Los Angeles Memorial Coliseum, Los Angeles, Calif., Sept. 21.
10. **Van Halen's Monsters Of Rock: Van Halen, Scorpions, Dokken, Metallica, Kingdom Come,** $1,943,900, Los Angeles Memorial Colisem, Los Angeles, Calif., July 24.

Source: Copyright 1988 by Amusement Business magazine. Reprinted by permission.

Top 10 Classical Albums, 1988

1. **Horowitz Plays Mozart,** Vladimir Horowitz (DG)
2. **Baroque Music for Trumpets,** Wynton Marsalis (CBS)
3. **Horowitz in Moscow,** Vladimir Horowitz (DG)
4. **Mendelssohn: Violin Concerto,** Nadja Salerno-Sonnenberg (Angel)
5. **Beethoven: Symphony No. 9,** London Classical Players (Norrington) (Angel)
6. **The Movies Go To the Opera,** Various Artists (Angel)
7. **Beethoven: Piano Concerto No. 5,** Murray Perahia (CBS)
8. **Wagner: The 'Ring' Without Words,** Berlin Philharmonic (Maazel) (Telarc)
9. **The Academy Plays Opera,** Academy of St. Martin-in-the-Fields (Angel)
10. **Brahms: Double Concerto,** Isaac Stern, Yo-Yo Ma (CBS)

Source: Billboard. © 1988 by Billboard Publications, Inc. Reprinted with permission.

Artists of the Year, 1988

Based on combined singles and albums chart performance—through sales and radio play—during the year.
Single of the Year: Faith, George Michael
Album of the Year: Faith, George Michael
Female Artist of the Year: Debbie Gibson
Male Artist of the Year: George Michael
Group of the Year: Def Leppard
New Artist of the Year: Guns N' Roses
Country Artist of the Year: Randy Travis
Black Artist of the Year: Michael Jackson
Adult Contemporary Artist of the Year: Steve Windwood
Jazz Artist of the Year: Wynton Marsalis
Classical Artist of the Year: Vladimir Horowitz
Soundtrack of the Year: Dirty Dancing

Source: Billboard. © 1988 by Billboard Publications, Inc. Reprinted with permission.

Top 10 Country Single Recordings, 1988

1. **Don't Close Your Eyes,** Keith Whitley (RCA)
2. **If You Change Your Mind,** Rosanne Cash (Columbia)
3. **Set 'Em Up Joe,** Vern Gosdin (Columbia)
4. **Strong Enough To Bend,** Tanya Tucker (Capitol)
5. **Bluest Eyes in Texas,** Restless Heart (RCA)
6. **It's Such a Small World,** Rodney Crowell & Rosanne Cash (Columbia)
7. **I Couldn't Leave You If I Tried,** Rodney Crowell (Columbia)
8. **If It Don't Come Easy,** Tanya Tucker (Capitol)
9. **I'm Gonna Get You,** Eddy Raven (RCA)
10. **Joe Knows How To Live,** Eddy Raven (RCA)

Source: Billboard. © 1988 by Billboard Publications, Inc. Reprinted by permission.

Top 10 Pop Single Recordings, 1988

1. **Faith,** George Michael (Columbia)
2. **Need You Tonight,** INXS (Atlantic)
3. **Got My Mind Set On You,** George Harrison (Dark Horse)
4. **Never Gonna Give You Up,** Rick Astley (RCA)
5. **Sweet Child O' Mine,** Guns 'N Roses (Geffen)
6. **So Emotional,** Whitney Houston (Arista)
7. **Heaven Is a Place On Earth,** Belinda Carlisle (MCA)
8. **Could've Been,** Tiffany (MCA)
9. **Hands To Heaven,** Breathe (A&M)
10. **Roll With It,** Steve Winwood (Virgin)

Source: Billboard. © 1988 by Billboard Publications, Inc. Reprinted with permission.

Top 10 Pop Albums, 1988

1. **Faith,** George Michael (Columbia)
2. **Dirty Dancing,** Soundtrack (RCA)
3. **Hysteria,** Def Leppard (Mercury)
4. **Kick,** INXS (Atlantic)
5. **Bad,** Michael Jackson (Epic)
6. **Appetite for Destruction,** Guns N' Roses (Geffen)
7. **Out of the Blue,** Debbie Gibson (Atlantic)
8. **Richard Marx,** Richard Marx (EMI)
9. **Tiffany,** Tiffany (MCA)
10. **Permanent Vacation,** Aerosmith (Geffen)

Source: Billboard. © 1988 by Billboard Publications, Inc. Reprinted by permission.

Manufacturers' Dollar[1] Shipments of Recordings

(in millions)

	1985	1986	1987	1988
Singles	281	228	203	180.4
LP's/EP's	1,281	983	793	532.3
CD's	390	930	1,593	2,089.9
Cassettes	2,412	2,500	2,959	3,385.1
Cassette singles[2]	—	—	14	57.3

1. List price value. 2. New configuration. *Source:* Recording Industry Association of America, Inc.

Top 10 Black Single Recordings, 1988

1. **I Want Her,** Keith Sweat (Vintertainment)
2. **Girlfriend,** Pebbles (MCA)
3. **Just Got Paid,** Johnny Kemp (Columbia)
4. **I Want To Be Your Man,** Roger (Reprise)
5. **Two Occasions,** The Deele (Solar)
6. **Love Changes,** Kashif & Meli'sa Morgan (Arista)
7. **Nite and Day,** Al B. Sure! (Warner Bros.)
8. **My Forever Love,** LeVert (Atlantic)
9. **Joy,** Teddy Pendergrass (Elektra)
10. **Love Overboard,** Gladys Knight & The Pips (MCA)

Source: Billboard. © 1988 by Billboard Publications, Inc. Reprinted with permission.

Top 15 Regularly Scheduled Network Programs, Nov. 1988

Rank	Program name (network)	Total percent of TV households
1.	Bill Cosby Show (NBC)	27.9
2.	A Different World (NBC)	23.4
3.	Cheers (NBC)	22.8
4.	Roseanne (ABC)	22.3
4.	Golden Girls (NBC)	22.3
6.	60 Minutes (CBS)	22.2
7.	Who's the Boss? (ABC)	20.8
8.	Growing Pains (ABC)	20.2
9.	Empty Nest (NBC)	19.8
10.	Murder, She Wrote (CBS)	19.3
11.	Dear John (NBC)	18.3
12.	Head of the Class (ABC)	18.2
13.	Hogan Family (NBC)	17.9
14.	L.A. Law (NBC)	17.8
15.	Alf (NBC)	17.5
	Total U.S. TV households	90,400,000

NOTE: Percentages are calculated from average audience viewings, 15 minutes or longer and 2 or more telecasts. *Source:* Nielsen Media Research, 1989 Nielsen Report on Television.

Top 15 Syndicated TV Programs 1988–'89 Season

Rank	Program	Rating (% U.S.)[1]
1.	Wheel of Fortune, M-F	15.7
2.	Jeopardy	13.2
3.	Cosby Show	11.7 [2]
4.	Oprah Winfrey Show	10.1
5.	Star Trek	10.0 [2]
6.	Universal Pictures Debut Network	9.6 [2]
7.	Wheel of Fortune, Weekend	9.5
8.	Tri Star Showcase	9.3
9.	Columbia Night at the Movies	9.0 [2]
10.	TV Net Movie	8.9 [2]
11.	MGM Premier Network III	8.0 [2]
12.	Entertainment Tonight	7.1 [2]
13.	National Geographic on Assignment	6.9 [2]
14.	Donahue	6.7
15.	Win, Lose or Draw	6.6 [2]

1. 8/29/88-2/19/89. 2. Includes multiple exposures. *Source:* Nielsen Syndication Service National TV Ratings.

Top Sports Shows 1988–89[1]*

Rank	Program name (network)	Rating (% of TV households)
1.	Super Bowl XXIII (NBC)	43.5
2.	NFC Championship Game (CBS)	31.9
3.	World Series Game 5 (NBC)	27.0
4.	AFC Championship Game (NBC)	26.1
5.	World Series Game 3 (NBC)	24.8

1. Sept. 19, 1988, through May 28, 1989.

Top Evening News Shows 1988–89[1]*

Rank	Program name (network)	Rating (% of TV households)
1.	CBS Evening News	11.0
2.	World News Tonight (ABC)	10.9
3.	NBC Nightly News	10.4

1. Sept. 19, 1988, through April 16, 1989.

Top Miniseries 1988–89[1,2]

Rank	Program name (network)	Rating (% of TV households)
1.	Lonesome Dove (CBS)	26.2
2.	War and Remembrance (Nov.) (ABC)	18.6
3.	Favorite Son (NBC)	16.0
4.	War and Remembrance (May) (ABC)	14.8

1. Sept. 19, 1988, through May 28, 1989. 2. Three or more parts.

Top Specials 1988–89[1]*

Rank	Program name (network)	Rating (% of TV households)
1.	61th Academy Awards (ABC)	29.8
2.	Barbara Walters (50th Special) (ABC)	24.8
3.	Barbara Walters Special with Roseanne Barr, Tom Hanks, and Tom Selleck (ABC)	24.4
4.	Devil Worship (NBC)	21.9

1. Sept. 19, 1988, through May 28, 1989.

Top Morning News Shows 1988–89[1]*

Rank	Program name (network)	Rating (% of TV households)
1.	Today (NBC)	4.4
2.	Good Morning America (ABC)	4.0
3.	CBS This Morning	2.4

1. Sept. 19, 1988, through April 16, 1989.

Top Soap Operas 1988–89[1]*

Rank	Program name (network)	Rating (% of TV households)
1.	The Young and the Restless (CBS)	8.1
2.	General Hospital (ABC)	7.5
3.	One Life to Live (ABC)	7.1
4.	All My Children (ABC)	6.7
5.	Days of Our Lives (NBC)	6.5

1. Sept. 19, 1988, through April 16, 1989.

*Reprinted with permission from *TV Guide*® magazine. Copyright © 1989 by News America Publications, Inc., Radnor, Pa.

Weekly TV Viewing by Age
(in hours and minutes)

	Time per week	
	Nov. 1988	Nov. 1987
Women 18–34 years old	28 h 53 min	28 h 43 min
Women 35–54	32 h 28 min	32 h 14 min
Women 55 and over	41 h 01 min	41 h 17 min
Men 18–34	25 h 44 min	26 h 15 min
Men 35–54	27 h 01 min	26 h 07 min
Men 55 and over	37 h 32 min	37 h 07 min
Female Teens	21 h 18 min	23 h 13 min
Male Teens	22 h 36 min	24 h 16 min
Children 6–11	23 h 17 min	22 h 46 min
Children 2–5	25 h 43 min	25 h 26 min
Total Persons (2+)	**29 h 40 min**	**29 h 40 min**

NOTE: All figures are estimates based on Nielsen Television Index NAD Report. *Source:* Nielsen Media Research, Nielsen Report on Television.

Television Network Addresses

American Broadcasting Companies (ABC)
1330 Avenue of the Americas
New York, N.Y. 10019
Canadian Broadcasting Corporation (CBC)
1500 Bronson Avenue
Ottawa, Ontario, Canada K1G 3J5
Columbia Broadcasting System (CBS)
51 W. 52nd Street
New York, N.Y. 10019
Fox Television (WNYW)
205 E. 67th Street
New York, N.Y. 10021
National Broadcasting Company (NBC)
30 Rockefeller Plaza
New York, N.Y. 10020
Public Broadcasting Service (PBS)
1320 Braddock Place
Alexandra, Va. 22314
Westinghouse Broadcasting (Group W)
90 Park Avenue
New York, N.Y. 10016

Persons Viewing Prime Time[1]
(in millions)

	Total persons
Monday	95.6
Tuesday	99.2
Wednesday	94.1
Thursday	95.5
Friday	89.1
Saturday	89.8
Sunday	106.4
Total average	**95.7**

1. Average minute audiences Nov. 1988. NOTE: Prime time is 8–11 p.m. (EST) except Sun. 7-11 p.m. Excludes unusual days. *Source:* Nielsen Media Research, Nielsen Report on Television.

Average Hours of Household TV Usage
(in hours and minutes per day)

	Yearly average	February	July
1980–81	6 h 44 min	7 h 32 min	6 h 03 min
1981–82	6 h 48 min	7 h 22 min	6 h 09 min
1982–83	6 h 55 min	7 h 33 min	6 h 23 min
1983–84	7 h 08 min	7 h 38 min	6 h 26 min
1984–85	7 h 07 min	7 h 49 min	6 h 34 min
1985–86	7 h 10 min	7 h 48 min	6 h 37 min
1986–87	7 h 05 min	7 h 35 min	6 h 32 min
1987–88	6 h 55 min	7 h 38 min	6 h 31 min

NOTE: Estimates are based on total U.S. TV households Sept.-Aug. 48 week average, excluding unusual days. *Source:* Nielsen Media Research, Nielsen Report on Television.

Audience Composition by Selected Program Type[1]
(Average Minute Audience)

	General drama	Suspense and mystery drama	Situation comedy	Adventure	Feature films	All regular network programs 7–11 p.m.
Women (18 and over)	11,170,000	8,820,000	11,310,000	7,280,000	10,250,000	9,780,000
Men (18 and over)	6,440,000	6,930,000	6,910,000	6,140,000	7,620,000	7,350,000
Teens (12–17)	910,000	940,000	2,070,000	1,020,000	1,380,000	1,320,000
Children (2–11)	1,480,000	1,260,000	3,460,000	1,460,000	1,670,000	2,010,000
Total persons (2+)	**20,000,000**	**17,950,000**	**23,750,000**	**15,900,000**	**20,920,000**	**20,460,000**

1. All figures are estimated for the period Nov. 1988. *Source:* Nielsen Media Research, 1988 Nielsen Report on Television.

Hours of TV Usage Per Week by Household Income

	Under $30,000	$30,000+	$40,000+	$50,000+	$60,000+
Nov. 1986	n.a.	51 h 40 min	51 h 31 min	n.a.	n.a.
Nov. 1987	n.a.	49 h 38 min	48 h 29 min	n.a.	n.a.
Nov. 1988	52 h 43 min	49 h 22 min	48 h 44 min	48 h 26 min	47 h 49 min

Source: Nielsen Media Research, Nielsen Report on Television. NOTE: n.a. = not available.

Source of Household Viewing—Prime Time
Pay Cable, Basic Cable, and Non-Cable Households
(Mon.-Sun. 8–11 pm)

	Nov. 1988			Nov. 1987			Nov. 1986		
	Pay cable	Basic cable	Non-cable	Pay cable	Basic cable	Non-cable	Pay cable	Basic cable	Non-cable
% TV Usage	67.7	63.1	57.7	68.7	59.3	56.8	68.7	65.6	59.2
Pay Cable	11.8	—	—	10.4	—	—	10.8	—	—
Cable-originated programming	13.5	13.1	—	10.8	10.1	—	7.9	8.8	—
Other-on-air stations	14.2	14.7	16.1	14.9	13.6	14.7	12.3	15.0	13.6
Network affiliated stations	38.1	40.9	46.0	42.6	39.6	46.7	46.2	47.4	49.8
Network share	(56)	(65)	(80)	(62)	(67)	(82)	(67)	(72)	(84)

Source: Nielsen Media Research, Nielsen Report on Television.

Major U.S. Fairs and Expositions

1853 Crystal Palace Exposition, New York City: modeled on similar fair held in London.

1876 Centennial Exposition, Philadelphia: celebrating 100th year of independence.

1893 World's Columbian Exposition, Chicago: commemorating 400th anniversary of Columbus' voyage to America.

1894 Midwinter International Exposition, San Francisco: promoting business revival after Depression of 1893.

1898 Trans-Mississippi and International Exposition, Omaha, Neb.: exhibiting products, resources, industries, and civilization of states and territories west of the Mississippi River.

1901 Pan-American Exposition, Buffalo, N.Y.: promoting social and commercial interest of Western Hemisphere nations.

1904 Louisiana Purchase Exposition, St. Louis: marking 100th anniversary of major land acquisition from France and opening up of the West.

1905 Lewis and Clark Centennial Exposition, Portland, Ore.: commemorating 100th anniversary of exploration of a land route to the Pacific.

1907 Jamestown Ter Centennial Exposition, Hampton Roads, Va.: marking 300th anniversary of first permanent English settlement in America.

1909 Alaska-Yukon-Pacific Exposition, Seattle: celebrating growth of the Puget Sound area.

1915-16 Panama-Pacific International Exposition, San Francisco: celebrating opening of the Panama Canal.

1915-16 Panama-California Exposition, San Diego: promoting resources and opportunities for development and commerce of the Western states.

1926 Sesquicentennial Exposition, Philadelphia: marking 150th year of independence.

1933-34 Century of Progress International Exposition, Chicago: celebrating 100th anniversary of incorporation of Chicago as a city.

1935 California Pacific International Exposition, San Diego: marking 400 years of progress since the first Spaniard landed on the West Coast.

1939-40 New York World's Fair, New York City: "The World of Tomorrow," symbolized by Trylon and Perisphere. Officially commemorating 150th anniversary of inauguration of George Washington as President in New York.

1939-40 Golden Gate International Exposition, Treasure Island, San Francisco: celebrating new Golden Gate Bridge and Oakland Bay Bridge.

1962 The Century 21 Exposition, Seattle: "Man in the Space Age," symbolized by 600-foot steel space needle.

1964-65 New York World's Fair, New York City: "Peace Through Understanding."

1974 Expo '74, Spokane: "Tomorrow's Fresh, New Environment."

1982 World's Fair, Knoxville, Tenn.: "Energy Turns the World," symbolized by the bronze-globed Sunsphere.

1984 Louisiana World Exposition, New Orleans: "The World of Rivers."

Longest Broadway Runs[1]

1. Oh, Calcutta (M) (1976-89)	5,959	
2. A Chorus Line (M) (1975-)	5,832	
3. 42nd Street (M) (1980-1989)	3,486	
4. Grease (M) (1972-80)	3,388	
5. Fiddler on the Roof (1964-72)	3,242	
6. Life with Father (1939-47)	3,224	
7. Tobacco Road (1933-41)	3,182	
8. Hello, Dolly! (M) (1964-71)	2,844	
9. Cats (M) (1982-)	2,861	
10. My Fair Lady (M) (1956-62)	2,717	
11. Annie (M) (1977-83)	2,377	
12. Oklahoma (M) (1943-48)	2,377	
13. Man of La Mancha (M) (1965-71)	2,328	
14. Abie's Irish Rose (1922-27)	2,327	
15. Pippin (M) (1971-77)	1,994	
16. South Pacific (M) (1949-54)	1,925	
17. Magic Show (M) (1974-78)	1,920	
18. Deathtrap (1978-82)	1,792	
19. Gemini (1977-81)	1,788	
20. Harvey (1944-49)	1,775	
21. Dancin' (M) (1978-82)	1,774	
22. Cage aux Folles (M) (1983-87)	1,761	
23. Hair (M) (1968-72)	1,750	
24. The Wiz (M) (1975-79)	1,672	
25. Born Yesterday (1946-49)	1,642	

1. As of Aug. 6, 1989. M = musical. Years are those of opening and closing.

Motion Picture Revenues

All-Time Top Money Makers[1]		Top Rentals 1988[2]	
1. E.T. The Extra-Terrestrial (Universal, 1982)	$228,618,939	1. Who Framed Roger Rabbit (Buena Vista)	$78,000,000
2. Star Wars (20th Century-Fox, 1977)	193,500,000	2. Coming To America (Paramount)	65,000,000
3. Return of the Jedi (20th Century-Fox, 1983)	168,002,414	3. Good Morning, Vietnam (1987)	58,103,000
4. The Empire Strikes Back (20th Century-Fox, 1980)	141,600,000	4. Crocodile Dundee II (Paramount)	57,300,000
		5. Big (20th Century-Fox)	50,800,000
5. Ghostbusters (Columbia, 1984)	130,211,324	6. Three Men and a Baby (Buena Vista)	36,300,000
6. Jaws (Universal, 1975)	129,549,325	7. Die Hard (20th Century-Fox)	35,000,000
7. Raiders of the Lost Ark (Paramount, 1981)	115,598,000	8. Cocktail (Buena Vista)	35,000,000
8. Indiana Jones and the Temple of Doom (Paramount, 1984)	109,000,000	9. Moonstruck (MGM/United Artists)	34,393,000
9. Beverly Hills Cop (Paramount, 1984)	108,000,000	10. Beetlejuice (Geffen/Warner Brothers)	33,200,000
10. Back to the Future (Universal, 1985)	104,408,738	11. Scrooged (Paramount)	33,000,000
11. Grease (Paramount, 1978)	96,300,000	12. Twins (Universal)	32,000,000
12. Tootsie (Columbia, 1982)	96,292,736	13. Rambo III (Tri-Star)	28,000,000
13. The Exorcist (Warner Brothers, 1973)	89,000,000	14. Willow (MGM/United Artists)	27,835,000
14. The Godfather (Paramount, 1972)	86,275,000	15. A Fish Called Wanda (MGM/United Artists)	26,000,000
15. Superman (Warner Brothers, 1978)	82,800,000	16. The Naked Gun (Paramount)	26,000,000
16. Close Encounters of the Third Kind (Columbia, 1977/1980)	82,750,000	17. A Nightmare On Elm Street 4: The Dream Master (New Line)	22,000,000
17. Three Men and a Baby (Buena Vista, 1977)	81,313,000	18. Bull Durham (Orion)	21,900,000
18. Beverly Hills Cop II (Paramount, 1987)	80,857,776	19. Colors (Orion)	21,200,000
19. The Sound of Music (20th Century-Fox, 1965)	79,748,000	20. Rain Man (MGM/United Artists)	21,000,000
20. Gremlins (Warner Brothers, 1984)	79,500,000	21. Young Guns (20th Century-Fox)	19,500,000
21. Top Gun (Paramount, 1986)	79,400,000	22. Biloxi Blues (Universal)	19,466,043
22. Rambo: First Blood Part II (Tri-Star, 1985)	78,919,250	23. The Great Outdoors (Universal)	19,104,434
23. The Sting (Universal, 1973)	78,212,000	24. The Dead Pool (Warner Brothers)	19,000,000
24. Who Framed Roger Rabbit (Buena Vista, 1988)	78,000,000	25. Bambi (reissue)	18,865,000
25. Gone With the Wind (MGM/United Artists, 1939)	77,641,106		

NOTE: United States and Canada only. 1. Figures are not to be confused with gross box-office receipts from sale of tickets. 2. Figures are total rentals collected by film distributors as of Dec. 31, 1988. *Source: Variety.*

Miss America Winners

1921 Margaret Gorman, Washington, D.C.
1922-23 Mary Campbell, Columbus, Ohio
1924 Ruth Malcolmson, Philadelphia, Pa.
1925 Fay Lamphier, Oakland, Calif.
1926 Norma Smallwood, Tulsa, Okla.
1927 Lois Delaner, Joliet, Ill.
1933 Marion Bergeron, West Haven, Conn.
1935 Henrietta Leaver, Pittsburgh, Pa.
1936 Rose Coyle, Philadelphia, Pa.
1937 Bette Cooper, Bertrand Island, N.J.
1938 Marilyn Meseke, Marion, Ohio
1939 Patricia Donnelly, Detroit, Mich.
1940 Frances Marie Burke, Philadelphia, Pa.
1941 Rosemary LaPlanche, Los Angeles, Calif.
1942 Jo-Caroll Dennison, Tyler, Texas
1943 Jean Bartel, Los Angeles, Calif.
1944 Venus Ramey, Washington, D.C.
1945 Bess Myerson, New York, N.Y.
1946 Marilyn Buferd, Los Angeles, Calif.
1947 Barbara Walker, Memphis, Tenn.
1948 BeBe Shopp, Hopkins, Minn.
1949 Jacque Mercer, Litchfield, Ariz.
1951 Yolande Betbeze, Mobile, Ala.
1952 Coleen Kay Hutchins, Salt Lake City, Utah
1953 Neva Jane Langley, Macon, Ga.
1954 Evelyn Margaret,Ay, Ephrata, Pa.
1955 Lee Meriwether, San Francisco, Calif.
1956 Sharon Ritchie, Denver, Colo.
1957 Marian McKnight, Manning, S.C.
1958 Marilyn Van Derbur, Denver, Colo.
1959 Mary Ann Mobley, Brandon, Miss.
1960 Lynda Lee Mead, Natchez, Miss.

1961 Nancy Fleming, Montague, Mich.
1962 Maria Fletcher, Asheville, N.C.
1963 Jacquelyn Mayer, Sandusky, Ohio
1964 Donna Axum, El Dorado, Ark.
1965 Vonda Kay Van Dyke, Phoenix, Ariz.
1966 Deborah Irene Bryant, Overland Park, Kan.
1967 Jane Anne Jayroe, Laverne, Okla.
1968 Debra Dene Barnes, Moran, Kan.
1969 Judith Anne Ford, Belvidere, Ill.
1970 Pamela Anne Eldred, Birmingham, Mich.
1971 Phyllis Ann George, Denton, Texas
1972 Laurie Lea Schaefer, Columbus, Ohio
1973 Terry Anne Meeuwsen, DePere, Wis.
1974 Rebecca Ann King, Denver, Colo.
1975 Shirley Cothran, Fort Worth, Texas
1976 Tawney Elaine Godin, Yonkers, N.Y.
1977 Dorothy Kathleen Benham, Edina, Minn.
1978 Susan Perkins, Columbus, Ohio
1979 Kylene Baker, Galax, Va.
1980 Cheryl Prewitt, Ackerman, Miss.
1981 Susan Powell, Elk City, Okla.
1982 Elizabeth Ward, Russellville, Ark.
1983 Debra Maffett, Anaheim, Calif.
1984 Vanessa Williams, Milwood, N.Y.[1]
    Suzette Charles, Mays Landing, N.J.
1985 Sharlene Wells, Salt Lake City, Utah
1986 Susan Akin, Meridian, Miss.
1987 Kellye Cash, Memphis, Tenn.
1988 Kaye Lani Rae Rafko, Toledo, Ohio
1989 Gretchen Elizabeth Carlson, Anoka, Minn.
1990 (*See* Current Events)
1. Resigned July 23, 1984.

States and Territories

State flower, bird, etc., are official unless otherwise indicated; dates in parentheses are those of adoption. Largest cities include incorporated places only. For secession and readmission dates of the former Confederate states, *see* Index. For lists of Governors, Senators, and Representatives, *see* Index. For additional state information, *see* the sections on "Business and the Economy," "Elections," "Taxes," and "U.S. Statistics." Source for 1987 est. population, percent population below age 15, age 65 and over, and immigrants from abroad, courtesy of Population Reference Bureau, Inc., Washington, D.C. Source for 1987 violent crimes: *Uniform Crime Reports, 1987,* U.S. Dept. of Justice, Federal Bureau of Investigation. Source for land area, *U.S. Statistical Abstract, 1980 Census.*

ALABAMA

Capital: Montgomery
Governor: Guy Hunt, R (to Jan. 1991)
Lieut. Governor: Jim E. Folsom, Jr., D (to Jan. 1991)
Secy. of State: Perry Hand, R (to Jan. 1991)
Comptroller: Robert Childree
Atty. General: Don Siegelman, D (to Jan. 1991)
Organized as territory: March 3, 1817
Entered Union & (rank): Dec. 14, 1819 (22)
Present constitution adopted: 1901
Motto: *Audemus jura nostra defendere* (We dare defend our rights)
State flower: Camellia (1959)
State bird: Yellowhammer (1927)
State song: "Alabama" (1931)
State tree: Southern pine (longleaf) (1949)
Nickname: Yellowhammer State
Origin of name: May come from Choctaw meaning "thicket-clearers" or "vegetation-gatherers"
1980 population (1980 census) & (rank): 3,893,888 (22)
1987 est. population (July 1) & (rank): 4,083,000 (22)
1980 land area & (rank): 50,767 sq mi. (131,487 sq km) (28)
Geographic center: In Chilton Co., 12 mi. SW of Clanton
Number of counties: 67
Largest cities (1980 census): Birmingham, 284,413; Mobile, 200,452; Montgomery, 178,157; Huntsville, 142,513; Tuscaloosa, 75,143; Gadsden, 47,565
State forests: 21 (48,000 ac.)
State parks: 22 (45,614 ac.)
1987 percent pop. below age 15: 22
1987 percent pop. age 65 and over: 12
1987 violent crimes per 100,000 pop.: 559.2
1984 (fiscal year) immigrants: 1,696

Spanish explorers are believed to have arrived at Mobile Bay in 1519, and the territory was visited in 1540 by the explorer Hernando de Soto. The first permanent European settlement in Alabama was founded by the French at Fort Louis in 1702. The British gained control of the area in 1763 by the Treaty of Paris, but had to cede almost all the Alabama region to the U.S. after the American Revolution. The Confederacy was founded at Montgomery in February 1861 and, for a time, the city was the Confederate capital.

During the last part of the 19th century, the economy of the state slowly improved. At Tuskegee Institute, founded in 1881 by Booker T. Washington, Dr. George Washington Carver carried out his famous agricultural research.

In the 1950s and '60s, Alabama was the site of such landmark civil-rights actions as the bus boycott in Montgomery (1955–56) and the "Freedom March" from Selma to Montgomery (1965).

Today paper, chemicals, rubber and plastics, apparel and textiles, and primary metals comprise the leading industries of Alabama. Continuing as a major manufacturer in coal, iron, and steel, Birmingham is also noted for its world-renowned medical center, especially for heart surgery. The state ranks high in the production of poultry, soybeans, milk, vegetables, livestock, wheat, cattle, cotton, peanuts, fruits, hogs, and corn.

Points of interest include the Space and Rocket Center at Huntsville, the White House of the Confederacy, and Shakespeare Festival Theater Complex in Montgomery, and Russell Cave near Bridgeport.

ALASKA

Capital: Juneau
Governor: Steve Cowper, D (to Dec. 1990)
Lieut. Governor: Stephen McAlpine, D (to Dec. 1990)
Commissioner of Administration: John Andrews, D (to Dec. 1990)
Atty. General: Douglas B. Baily (to Dec. 1990)
Organized as territory: 1912
Entered Union & (rank): Jan. 3, 1959 (49)
Constitution ratified: April 24, 1956
Motto: North to the Future
State flower: Forget-me-not
State tree: Sitka spruce
State bird: Willow ptarmigan
State fish: King salmon
State song: "Alaska's Flag"
Nickname: The state is commonly called "The Last Frontier" or "Land of the Midnight Sun"
Origin of name: Corruption of Aleut word meaning "great land" or "that which the sea breaks against"
1980 population (1980 census) & (rank): 401,851 (50)
1987 est. population (July 1) & (rank): 525,000 (49)
1980 land area & (rank): 570,833 sq mi. (1,478,458 sq km) (1)
Geographic center: 60 mi. NW of Mt. McKinley
Number of boroughs: 12
Largest cities (1988 est.): Anchorage, 246,139; Fairbanks, 27,141; Juneau, 29,946; Ketchikan (Borough), 12,982; Ketchikan (City), 7,601; Sitka, 8,102; Kodiak, 6,774; Bethel, 4,462
State forests: None
State parks: 5; 59 waysides and areas (3.3 million ac.)
1987 percent pop. below age 15: 28
1987 percent pop. age 65 and over: 4
1987 violent crimes per 100,000 pop.: 455.4
1984 (fiscal year) immigrants: 970

Vitus Bering, a Dane working for the Russians, and Alexei Chirikov discovered the Alaskan mainland and the Aleutian Islands in 1741. The tremendous land mass of Alaska—equal to one fifth of the continental U.S.—was unexplored in 1867 when Secretary of State William Seward arranged for its purchase from the Russians for $7,200,000. The transfer of the territory took place on Oct. 18, 1867. Despite a price of about two cents an acre, the purchase was widely ridiculed as "Seward's Folly." The first official census (1880) reported a total of 33,426 Alaskans, all but 430 being of aboriginal stock. The Gold Rush of 1898 resulted in a mass influx of more than 30,000 people. Since then, Alaska has returned billions of dollars' worth of products to the U.S.

In 1968, a large oil and gas reservoir near Prudhoe Bay on the Arctic Coast was found. The Prudhoe Bay reservoir, with an estimated recoverable 10 billion barrels of oil and 27 trillion cubic feet of gas, is twice as large as any other oil field in North America. The Trans-Alaska pipeline was completed in 1977 at a cost of $7.7 billion. On June 20, oil started flowing through the 800-mile-long pipeline from Prudhoe Bay to the port of Valdez.

Other industries important to Alaska's economy are fisheries, wood and wood products, and furs, and tourism.

Denali National Park and Mendenhall Glacier in North Tongass National Forest are of interest, as is the large totem pole collection at Sitka National Historical Park. The Katmai National Park includes the "Valley of Ten Thousand Smokes," an area of active volcanoes.

ARIZONA

Capital: Phoenix
Governor: Rose Mofford, D (to Jan. 1991)
Secy. of State: Jim Shumway, D (to Jan. 1991)
Atty. General: Bob Corbin, R (to Jan. 1991)
State Treasurer: Ray Rottas, R (to Jan. 1991)
Organized as territory: Feb. 24, 1863
Entered Union & (rank): Feb. 14, 1912 (48)
Present constitution adopted: 1911
Motto: *Ditat Deus* (God enriches)
State flower: Flower of saguaro cactus (1931)
State bird: Cactus wren (1931)
State colors: Blue and old gold (1915)
State song: "Arizona March Song" (1919)
State tree: Paloverde (1957)
Nickname: Grand Canyon State
Origin of name: From the Indian "Arizonac," meaning "little spring"
1980 population (1980 census) & (rank): 2,718,425 (29)
1987 est. population (July 1) & (rank): 3,386,000 (25)
1980 land area & (rank): 113,508 sq mi. (293,986 sq km) (6)
Geographic center: In Yavapai Co., 55 mi. ESE of Prescott
Number of counties: 15
Largest cities (1980 census): Phoenix, 789,704; Tucson, 330,537; Mesa, 152,453; Tempe, 106,743; Glendale, 97,172; Scottsdale, 86,622; Yuma, 42,481
State forests: None
State parks: 24
1987 percent pop. below age 15: 23
1987 percent pop. age 65 and over: 13
1987 violent crimes per 100,000 pop.: 612.6
1984 (fiscal year) immigrants: 5,289

Marcos de Niza, a Spanish Franciscan friar, was the first European to explore Arizona. He entered the area in 1539 in search of the mythical Seven Cities of Gold. Although he was followed a year later by another gold seeker, Francisco Vásquez de Coronado, most of the early settlement was for missionary purposes. In 1776 the Spanish established Fort Tucson. In 1848, after the Mexican War, most of the Arizona territory became part of the U.S., and the southern portion of the territory was added by the Gadsden Purchase in 1853.

In 1973 the world's biggest dam, the New Cornelia Tailings, was completed near Ajo.

Arizona history is rich in legends of America's Old West. It was here that the great Indian chiefs Geronimo and Cochise led their people against the frontiersmen. Tombstone, Ariz., was the site of the West's most famous shoot-out—the gunfight at the O.K. Corral. Today, Arizona has the largest U.S. Indian population; more than 14 tribes are represented on 19 reservations.

Manufacturing has become Arizona's most important industry. Principal products include electrical, communications, and aeronautical items. The state produces over half the country's copper. Agriculture is also important to the state's economy.

State attractions include such famous scenery as the Grand Canyon, the Petrified Forest, and the Painted Desert. Hoover Dam, Lake Mead, Fort Apache, and the reconstructed London Bridge at Lake Havasu City are of particular interest.

ARKANSAS

Capital: Little Rock
Governor: Bill Clinton, D (to Jan. 1990)
Lieut. Governor: Winston Bryant, D (to Jan. 1990)
Secy. of State: W. J. McCuen, D (to Jan. 1990)
Atty. General: Steve Clark (to Jan. 1990)
Auditor of State: Julia Hughes Jones, D (to Jan. 1990)
Treasurer of State: Jimmie Lou Fisher, D (to Jan. 1990)
Land Commissioner: Charles Daniels, D (to Jan. 1990)
Organized as territory: March 2, 1819
Entered Union & (rank): June 15, 1836 (25)
Present constitution adopted: 1874
Motto: *Regnat populus* (The people rule)
State flower: Apple Blossom (1901)
State tree: Pine (1939)
State bird: Mockingbird (1929)
State insect: Honeybee
State song: "Arkansas" (1963)
Nickname: The Natural State
Origin of name: From the Quapaw Indians
1980 population (1980 census) & (rank): 2,286,435 (33)
1987 est. population (July 1) & (rank): 2,388,000 (33)
1980 land area & (rank): 52,078 sq mi. (134,883 sq km) (27)
Geographic center: In Pulaski Co., 12 mi. NW of Little Rock
Number of counties: 75
Largest cities (1980 census): Little Rock, 158,461; Fort Smith, 71,626; North Little Rock, 64,288; Pine Bluff, 56,636; Fayetteville, 36,608; Hot Springs, 35,781
State forests: None
State parks: 44
1987 percent pop. below age 15: 22
1987 percent pop. age 65 and over: 15
1987 violent crimes per 100,000 pop.: 412.0
1984 (fiscal year) immigrants: 1,104

Hernando de Soto, in 1541, was among the early European explorers to visit the territory. It was a Frenchman, Henri de Tonti, who in 1686 founded the first permanent white settlement—the Arkansas Post. In 1803 the area was acquired by the U.S. as part of the Louisiana Purchase.

Food products are the state's largest employing sector, with lumber and wood products a close second. Arkansas is also a leader in the production of cotton, rice, and soybeans. The state produces 97% of the nation's high-grade domestic bauxite ore—the source of aluminum. It also has the country's only active diamond mine; located near Murfreesboro, it is operated as a tourist attraction.

Hot Springs National Park, and Buffalo River in the Ozarks are major state attractions.

Blanchard Springs Caverns, the Arkansas Territorial Capitol Restoration at Little Rock, and Dogpatch U.S.A. near Harrison are of interest.

CALIFORNIA

Capital: Sacramento
Governor: George Deukmejian, R (to Jan. 1991)
Lieut. Governor: Leo McCarthy, D (to Jan. 1991)
Secy. of State: March Fong Eu, D (to Jan. 1991)
Controller: Gray Davis, D (to Jan. 1991)
Atty. General: John Van de Kamp, D (to Jan. 1991)
Treasurer: Jesse M. Unruh, D (to Jan. 1991)
Entered Union & (rank): Sept. 9, 1850 (31)
Present constitution adopted: 1879
Motto: *Eureka* (I have found it)
State flower: Golden poppy (1903)
State tree: California redwoods *(Sequoia sempervirens & Sequoia gigantea)* (1937 & 1953)
State bird: California valley quail (1931)
State animal: California grizzly bear (1953)
State fish: California golden trout (1947)
State colors: Blue and gold (1951)
State song: "I Love You, California" (1951)
Nickname: Golden State
Origin of name: From a book, *Las Sergas de Esplandián*, by García Ordóñez de Montalvo, c. 1500
1987 population (1980 census) & (rank): 27,663,000 (1)
1987 est. population (July 1) & (rank): 26,365,000 (1)
1980 land area & (rank): 156,299 sq mi. (404,815 sq km) (3)
Geographic center: In Madera Co., 35 mi. NE of Madera
Number of counties: 58
Largest cities (1980 census): Los Angeles, 2,966,850; San Diego, 875,538; San Francisco, 678,974; San Jose, 629,442; Long Beach, 361,334; Oakland, 339,337
State forests: 8 (70,283 ac.)
State parks and beaches: 180 (723,000 ac.)
1987 percent pop. below age 15: 22
1987 percent pop. age 65 and over: 11
1987 violent crimes per 100,000 pop.: 918.0
1984 (fiscal year) immigrants: 140,289

Although California was sighted by Spanish navigator Juan Rodríguez Cabrillo in 1542, its first Spanish mission (at San Diego) was not established until 1769. California became a U.S. Territory in 1847 when Mexico surrendered it to John C. Frémont. On Jan. 24, 1848, James W. Marshall discovered gold at Sutter's Mill, starting the California Gold Rush and bringing settlers to the state in large numbers.

In 1964, the U.S. Census Bureau estimated that California had become the most populous state, surpassing New York. California also leads the country in personal income and consumer expenditures.

Leading industries include manufacturing (transportation equipment, machinery, and electronic equipment), agriculture, biotechnology, and tourism. Principal natural resources include timber, petroleum, cement, and natural gas.

More immigrants settle in California than any other state—27% of the nation's total in 1986. The influx was led by new arrivals from Mexico and the Philippines.

Death Valley, in the southeast, is 282 feet below sea level, the lowest point in the nation; and Mt. Whitney (14,495 ft) is the highest point in the contiguous 48 states. Lassen Peak is one of two active U.S. volcanos outside of Alaska and Hawaii; its last

eruptions were recorded in 1917. The General Sherman Tree in Sequoia National Park is estimated to be about 3,500 years old and a stand of bristlecone pine trees in the White Mountains may be over 4,000 years old.

Other points of interest include Yosemite National Park, Disneyland, Hollywood, the Golden Gate bridge, San Simeon State Park, and Point Reyes National Seashore.

COLORADO

Capital: Denver
Governor: Roy Romer, D (to Jan. 1991)
Lieut. Governor: Michael Callihan, D (to Jan. 1991)
Secy. of State: Natalie Meyer, R (to Jan 1991)
Treasurer: Gail Schoettler, D (to Jan. 1991)
Controller: James A. Stroup
Atty. General: Duane Woodard, D (to Jan. 1991)
Organized as territory: Feb. 28, 1861
Entered Union & (rank): Aug. 1, 1876 (38)
Present constitution adopted: 1876
Motto: *Nil sine Numine* (Nothing without Providence)
State flower: Rocky Mountain columbine (1899)
State tree: Colorado blue spruce (1939)
State bird: Lark bunting (1931)
State animal: Rocky Mountain bighorn sheep
State colors: Blue and white (1911)
State song: "Where the Columbines Grow" (1915)
Nickname: Centennial State
Origin of name: From the Spanish, "ruddy" or "red"
1980 population (1980 census) & (rank): 2,889,735 (28)
1987 est. population (July 1) & rank: 3,296,000 (26)
1980 land area & (rank): 103,595 sq mi. (268,311 sq km) (8)
Geographic center: In Park Co., 30 mi. NW of Pikes Peak
Number of counties: 63
Largest cities (1980 census): Denver, 492,365; Colorado Springs, 214,821; Aurora, 158,588; Lakewood, 113,808; Pueblo, 101,686; Arvada, 84,576; Boulder, 76,685
State forests: 1 (71,000 ac.)
1987 percent pop. below age 15: 22
1987 percent pop. age 65 and over: 9
1987 violent crimes per 100,000 pop.: 467.5
1984 (fiscal year) immigrants: 4,656

First visited by Spanish explorers in the 1500s, the territory was claimed for Spain by Juan de Ulibarri in 1706. The U.S. obtained eastern Colorado as part of the Louisiana Purchase in 1803, the central portion in 1845 with the admission of Texas as a state, and the western part in 1848 as a result of the Mexican War.

Colorado has the highest mean elevation of any state, with more than 1,000 Rocky Mountain peaks over 10,000 feet high and 54 towering above 14,000 feet. Pikes Peak, the most famous of these mountains, was discovered by U.S. Army Lieut. Zebulon M. Pike in 1806.

Once primarily a mining and agricultural state, Colorado's economy is now driven by the service-producing industries, which provide jobs for more than four-fifths of the state's non-farm work force. In addition, tourism is extremely important to the state's economy. The ski industry accounts for approximately one-third of the state's tourism market. The main tourist attractions in the state include Rocky Mountain National Park, Curecanti National Recreation Area, Mesa Verde National Park, and the Great Sand Dunes and Dinosaur National Monuments.

The two primary facets of Colorado's manufacturing industry are advanced technology and defense.

The mining industry, which includes oil and gas, coal, and metal mining, is still important to Colorado's economy, though it employs only 1.5 percent of the state's workforce. Gold production is growing in importance, and Denver is now home to companies that control half of the nation's gold production. The farm industry, which is primarily concentrated in livestock, is also an important element of the state's economy. The primary crops in Colorado are corn, hay, and wheat.

CONNECTICUT

Capital: Hartford
Governor: William A. O'Neill, D (to Jan. 1991)
Lieut. Governor: Joseph J. Fauliso, D (to Jan. 1991)
Secy. of State: Julia H. Tashjian, D (to Jan. 1991)
Comptroller: J. Edward Caldwell, D (to Jan. 1991)
Treasurer: Francisco L. Borges, D (to Jan. 1991)
Atty. General: Clarine Nardi Riddle, D (to Jan. 1991)
Entered Union & (rank): Jan. 9, 1788 (5)
Present constitution adopted: Dec. 30, 1965
Motto: *Qui transtulit sustinet* (He who transplanted still sustains)
State flower: Mountain laurel (1907)
State tree: White Oak (1947)
State animal: Sperm whale (1975)
State bird: American robin (1943)
State Hero: Nathan Hale (1985)
State insect: Praying mantis (1977)
State mineral: Garnet (1977)
State song: "Yankee Doodle" (1978)
State ship: USS Nautilus (SSN571) (1983)
Official designation: *Constitution State* (1959)
Nickname: Nutmeg State
Origin of name: From an Indian word (Quinnehtukqut) meaning "beside the long tidal river"
1980 population (1980 census) & (rank): 3,107,576 (25)
1987 est. population (July 1) & (rank): 3,211,000 (28)
1980 land area & (rank): 4,872 sq mi. (12,618 km) (48)
Geographic center: In Hartford Co., at East Berlin
Number of counties: 8
Largest cities (1980 census): Bridgeport, 142,546; Hartford, 136,392; New Haven, 126,109; Waterbury, 103,266; Stamford, 102,453; Norwalk, 77,767
State forests: 30 (138,682 ac.)
State parks: 91 (29,856 ac.)
1987 percent pop. below age 15: 19
1987 percent pop. age 65 and over: 13
1987 violent crimes per 100,000 pop.: 419.0
1984 (fiscal year) immigrants: 7,069

The Dutch navigator, Adriaen Block, was the first European of record to explore the area, sailing up the Connecticut River in 1614. In 1633, Dutch colonists built a fort and trading post near present-day Hartford, but soon lost control to English Puritans migrating south from the Massachusetts Bay Colony.

English settlements, established in the 1630s at Windsor, Wethersfield, and Hartford, united in 1639 to form the Connecticut Colony and adopted the *Fundamental Orders*, considered the world's first written constitution.

The colony's royal charter of 1662 was exceptionally liberal. When Gov. Edmund Andros tried to seize it in 1687, it was hidden in the Hartford Oak, commemorated in Charter Oak Place.

Connecticut played a prominent role in the Revolutionary War, serving as the Continental Army's major supplier. Sometimes called the "Arsenal of the Nation," the state became one of the most industrialized in the nation.

Today, Connecticut factories produce weapons, sewing machines, jet engines, helicopters, motors, hardware and tools, cutlery, clocks, locks, ball bearings, silverware, and submarines. Hartford, which has the oldest U.S. newspaper still being published—the *Courant*, established 1764—is the insurance capital of the nation.

Poultry, fruit, and dairy products account for the largest portion of farm income, and Connecticut shade-grown tobacco is acknowledged to be the nation's most valuable crop, per acre.

Connecticut is a popular resort area with its 250-mile Long Island Sound shoreline and many inland lakes. Among the major points of interest are Yale University's Gallery of Fine Arts and Peabody Museum. Other famous museums include the P.T. Barnum, Winchester Gun, and American Clock and Watch. The town of Mystic features a recreated 19th-century New England seaport and the Mystic Marinelife Aquarium.

DELAWARE

Capital: Dover
Governor: Michael N. Castle, R (to Jan. 1993)
Lieut. Governor: Dale E. Wolf, R (to Jan. 1993)
Secy. of State: Michael Harkins, R (Pleasure of Governor)
State Treasurer: Janet C. Rzewnicki, R (to Jan. 1991)
Atty. General: Charles M. Oberly III, D (to Jan. 1991)
Entered Union & (rank): Dec. 7, 1787 (1)
Present constitution adopted: 1897
Motto: Liberty and independence
State colors: Colonial blue and buff
State flower: Peach blossom
State tree: American holly
State bird: Blue Hen chicken
State insect: Ladybug
State song: "Our Delaware"
Nicknames: Diamond State; First State; Small Wonder
Origin of name: From Delaware River and Bay; named in turn for Sir Thomas West, Lord De La Warr
1980 population (1980 census) & (rank): 594,317 (47)
1987 est. population (July 1) & (rank): 644,000 (47)
1980 land area & (rank): 1,932 sq mi. (5,005 sq km) (49)
Geographic center: In Kent Co., 11 mi. S of Dover
Number of counties: 3
Largest cities (1980 census): Wilmington, 70,195; Newark, 25,247; Dover, 23,512; Elsmere, 6,493; Milford, 5,356; Seaford, 5,256; New Castle, 4,709; Lewes, 2,197
State forests: 3 (6,149 ac.)
State parks: 10
1987 percent pop. below age 15: 21
1987 percent pop. age 65 and over: 12
1987 violent crimes per 100,000 pop.: 430.7
1984 (fiscal year) immigrants: 592

Henry Hudson, sailing under the Dutch flag, is credited with Delaware's discovery in 1609. The following year, Capt. Samuel Argall of Virginia named Delaware for his colony's governor, Thomas West, Baron De La Warr. An attempted Dutch settlement failed in 1631. Swedish colonization began at Fort Christina (now Wilmington) in 1638, but New Sweden fell to Dutch forces led by New Netherlands' Gov. Peter Stuyvesant in 1655.

England took over the area in 1664 and it was transferred to William Penn as the southern Three Counties in 1682. Semiautonomous after 1704, Delaware fought as a separate state in the American Revolution and became the first state to ratify the constitution in 1787.

During the Civil War, although a slave state, Delaware did not secede from the Union.

In 1802, Éleuthère Irénée du Pont established a gunpowder mill near Wilmington that laid the foundation for Delaware's huge chemical industry. Delaware's manufactured products now also include vulcanized fiber, textiles, paper, medical supplies, metal products, machinery, machine tools, and automobiles.

Delaware also grows a great variety of fruits and vegetables and is a U.S. pioneer in the food-canning industry. Corn, soybeans, potatoes, and hay are important crops. Delaware's broiler chicken farms supply the big Eastern markets, fishing and dairy products are other important industries.

Points of interest include the Fort Christina Monument, Hagley Museum, Holy Trinity Church (erected in 1698, the oldest Protestant church in the United States still in use), and Winterthur Museum, in and near Wilmington; central New Castle, an almost unchanged late 18th-century capital; and the Delaware Museum of Natural History.

Popular recreation areas include Cape Henlopen, Delaware Seashore, Trapp Pond State Park, and Rehoboth Beach.

DISTRICT OF COLUMBIA

See listing at end of *50 Largest Cities of the United States.*

FLORIDA

Capital: Tallahassee
Governor: Bob Martinez, R (to Jan. 1991)
Lieut. Governor: Bobby Brantley, R (to Jan. 1991)
Secy. of State: George Firestone, D (to Jan. 1991)
Comptroller: Gerald Lewis, D (to Jan. 1991)
Commissioner of Agriculture: Doyle Connor, D (to Jan. 1991)
Atty. General: Bob Butterworth, D (to Jan. 1991)
Organized as territory: March 30, 1822
Entered Union & (rank): March 3, 1845 (27)
Present constitution adopted: 1969
Motto: In God we trust (1868)
State flower: Orange blossom (1909)
State bird: Mockingbird (1927)
State song: "Suwannee River" (1935)
Nickname: Sunshine State (1970)
Origin of name: From the Spanish, meaning "feast of flowers" (Easter)
1980 population (1980 census) & (rank): 9,746,342 (7)
1987 est. population (July 1) & (rank): 12,023,000 (4)
1980 land area & (rank): 54,153 sq mi. (140,256 sq km) (26)
Geographic center: In Hernando Co., 12 mi. NNW of Brooksville
Number of counties: 67
Largest cities (1984 est.): Jacksonville, 571,421; Miami, 383,027; Tampa, 275,512; St. Petersburg, 242,115; Fort Lauderdale, 152,053; Hialeah, 157,137
State forests: 3 (306,881 ac.)
State parks: 105 (215,820 ac.)
1987 percent pop. below age 15: 18
1987 percent pop. age 65 and over: 18
1987 violent crimes per 100,000 pop.: 1,024.4
1984 (fiscal year) immigrants: 32,364

In 1513, Ponce De Leon, seeking the mythical "Fountain of Youth," discovered and named Florida, claiming it for Spain. Later, Florida would be held at different times by Spain and England until Spain finally sold it to the United States in 1819. (Incidentally, France established a colony named Fort Caroline in 1564 in the state that was to become Florida.)

Florida's early 19th-century history as a U.S. territory was marked by wars with the Seminole Indians that did not end until 1842, although a treaty was actually never signed.

One of the nation's fastest-growing states, Florida's population has gone from 2.8 million in 1950 to more than 11.3 million in 1985.

Florida's economy rests on a solid base of tourism (in 1988 the state entertained more than 36.8 million visitors from all over the world), manufacturing, and agriculture.

In recent years, oranges and grapefruit lead Florida's crop list, followed by vegetables, potatoes, melons, strawberries, sugar cane, dairy products, cattle and calves, and forest products.

Major tourist attractions are Miami Beach, Palm Beach, St. Augustine (founded in 1565, thus the oldest permanent city in the U.S.), Daytona Beach, and Fort Lauderdale on the East Coast. West Coast resorts include Sarasota, Tampa, Key West and St. Petersburg. Disney World, located on a 27,000-acre site near Orlando, is a popular attraction.

Also drawing many visitors are the NASA Kennedy Space Center's Spaceport USA, located in the town of Kennedy Space Center, Everglades National Park, and the Epcot Center.

GEORGIA

Capital: Atlanta
Governor: Joe Frank Harris, D (to Jan. 1991)
Lieut. Governor: Zell Miller, D (to Jan. 1991)
Secy. of State: Max Cleland, D (to Jan. 1991)
Insurance Commissioner: Warren Evans, D (to Jan. 1991)
Atty. General: Michael J. Bowers, D (to Jan. 1991)
Entered Union & (rank): Jan. 2, 1788 (4)
Present constitution adopted: 1977
Motto: Wisdom, justice, and moderation
State flower: Cherokee rose (1916)
State tree: Live oak (1937)
State bird: Brown thrasher (1935)
State song: "Georgia on my Mind" (1922)
Nicknames: Peach State, Empire State of the South
Origin of name: In honor of George II of England
1980 population (1980 census) & (rank): 5,463,105 (13)
1987 est. population (July 1) & (rank): 6,222,000 (11)
1980 land area & (rank): 58,910 sq mi. (152,577 sq km) (21)
Geographic center: In Twiggs Co., 18 mi. SE of Macon
Number of counties: 159
Largest cities (1980 census): Atlanta, 425,022; Columbus, 169,441; Savannah, 141,634; Macon, 116,860; Albany, 74,550; Augusta, 47,532; Athens, 42,549; Warner Robins, 39,893
State forests: 25,258,000 ac. (67% of total state area)
State parks: 53 (42,600 ac.)
1987 percent pop. below age 15: 23
1987 percent pop. age 65 and over: 10
1985 violent crimes per 100,000 pop.: 576.5
1984 (fiscal year) immigrants: 4,690

Hernando de Soto, the Spanish explorer, first traveled parts of Georgia in 1540. British claims later conflicted with those of Spain. After obtaining a royal charter, Gen. James Oglethorpe established the first permanent settlement in Georgia in 1733 as a refuge for English debtors. In 1742, Oglethorpe defeated Spanish invaders in the Battle of Bloody Marsh.

A Confederate stronghold, Georgia was the scene of extensive military action during the Civil War. Union General William T. Sherman burned Atlanta and destroyed a 60-mile wide path to the coast where he captured Savannah in 1864.

The largest state east of the Mississippi, Georgia is typical of the changing South with an ever-increasing industrial development. Atlanta, largest city in the state, is the communications and transportation center for the Southeast and the area's chief distributor of goods.

Georgia leads the nation in the production of paper and board, tufted textile products, and processed chicken. Other major manufactured products are transportation equipment, food products, apparel, and chemicals.

Important agricultural products are corn, cotton, tobacco, soybeans, eggs, and peaches. Georgia produces twice as many peanuts as the next leading state. From its vast stands of pine come more than half the world's resins and turpentine and 74.4% of the U.S. supply. Georgia is also a leader in the production of marble, kaolin, barite, and bauxite.

Principal tourist attractions in Georgia include the Okefenokee National Wildlife Refuge, Andersonville Prison Park and National Cemetery, Chickamauga and Chattanooga National Military Park, the Little White House at Warm Springs where Pres. Franklin D. Roosevelt died in 1945, Sea Island, the enormous Confederate Memorial at Stone Mountain, Kennesaw Mountain National Battlefield Park, and Cumberland Island National Seashore.

HAWAII

Capital: Honolulu (on Oahu)
Governor: John Waihee, D (to Dec. 1990)
Lieut. Governor: Ben Cayetano, D (to Dec. 1990)
Comptroller: Russel S. Nagata, D (to Dec. 1990)
Atty. General: Warren Price, D (to Dec. 1990)
Organized as territory: 1900
Entered Union & (rank): Aug. 21, 1959 (50)
Motto: *Ua Mau Ke Ea O Ka Aina I Ka Pono* (The life of the land is perpetuated in righteousness)
State flower: Hibiscus
State song: "Hawaii Ponoi"
State bird: Nene (Hawaiian goose)
Nickname: Aloha State
Origin of name: Uncertain. The islands may have been named by Hawaii Loa, their traditional discoverer. Or they may have been named after Hawaii or Hawaiki, the traditional home of the Polynesians.
1980 population (1980 census) & (rank): 964,691 (39)
1987 est. population (July 1) & (rank): 1,083,000 (39)
1980 land area & (rank): 6,425 sq mi. (16,641 sq km) (47)
Geographic center: Between islands of Hawaii and Maui
Number of counties: 4 plus one non-functioning county (Kalawao)
Largest cities (1980 census): Honolulu, 365,048; Pearl City, 42,575; Kailua, 35,812; Hilo, 35,269[1]
State parks and historic sites: 76
1987 percent pop. below age 15: 22
1987 percent pop. age 65 and over: 10
1987 violent crimes per 100,000 pop.: 263.3
1987 (fiscal year) immigrants: 6,796

1. There are no political boundaries to Honolulu or any other place, but statistical boundaries are assigned under state law.

First settled by Polynesians sailing from other Pacific islands between 300 and 600 A.D., Hawaii was visited in 1778 by British Captain James Cook who called the group the Sandwich Islands.

Hawaii was a native kingdom throughout most of the 19th century when the expansion of the vital sugar industry (pineapple came after 1898) meant increasing U.S. business and political involvement. In 1893, Queen Liliuokalani was deposed and a year later the Republic of Hawaii was established with Sanford B. Dole as president. Then, following its annexation in 1898, Hawaii became a U.S. Territory in 1900.

The Japanese attack on the naval base at Pearl Harbor on Dec. 7, 1941, was directly responsible for U.S. entry into World War II.

Hawaii, 2,397 miles west-southwest of San Francisco, is a 1,523-mile chain of islets and eight main islands—Hawaii, Kahoolawe, Maui, Lanai, Molokai, Oahu, Kauai, and Niihau. The Northwestern Hawaiian Islands, other than Midway, are administratively part of Hawaii.

The temperature is mild and Hawaii's soil is fertile for tropical fruits and vegetables. Cane sugar and pineapple are the chief products. Hawaii also grows coffee, bananas and nuts. The tourist business is Hawaii's largest source of outside income.

Hawaii's highest peak is Mauna Kea (13,796 ft.). Mauna Loa (13,679 ft.) is the largest volcanic mountain in the world in cubic content.

Among the major points of interest are Hawaii Volcanoes National Park (Hawaii), Haleakala National Park (Maui), Puuhonua o Honaunau National Historical Park (Hawaii), Polynesian Cultural Center (Oahu), the U.S.S. *Arizona* Memorial at Pearl Harbor, and Iolani Palace (the only royal palace in the U.S.), Bishop Museum, and Waikiki Beach (all in Honolulu).

IDAHO

Capital: Boise
Governor: Cecil D. Andrus, D (to Jan. 1991)
Lieut. Governor: C. L. "Butch" Otter, R (to Jan. 1991)
Secy. of State: Pete T. Cenarrusa, R (to Jan. 1991)
State Auditor: J.D. Williams, D (to Jan. 1991)
Atty. General: James Jones, R (to Jan. 1991)
Treasurer: Lydia Justice Edwards, R (to Jan. 1991)
Organized as territory: March 3, 1863
Entered Union & (rank): July 3, 1890 (43)
Present constitution adopted: 1890
Motto: *Esto perpetua* (It is forever)
State flower: Syringa (1931)
State tree: White pine (1935)
State bird: Mountain bluebird (1931)
State horse: Appaloosa (1975)
State gem: Star garnet (1967)
State song: "Here We Have Idaho"
Nicknames: Gem State; Spud State; Panhandle State
Origin of name: Means "Gem of the Mountains"
1980 population (1980 census) & (rank): 944,038 (41)
1987 est. population (July 1) & (rank): 998,000 (42)
1980 land area & (rank): 82,412 sq mi. (213,449 sq km) (11)
Geographic center: In Custer Co., at Custer, SW of Challis
Number of counties: 44, plus small part of Yellowstone National Park
Largest cities (1986 est.): Boise, 108,390; Pocatello, 44,420; Idaho Falls, 42,830; Nampa, 28,250; Twin Falls, 27,750; Lewiston, 27,730; Coeur d'Alene, 24,690
State forests: 881,000 ac.
State parks: 21 (38,487) ac.
1987 percent pop. below age 15: 26
1987 percent pop. age 65 and over: 12

1987 violent crimes per 100,000 pop.: 214.2
1984 (fiscal year) immigrants: 741

After its acquisition by the U.S. as part of the Louisiana Purchase in 1803, the region was explored by Meriwether Lewis and William Clark in 1805–06. Northwest boundary disputes with Great Britain were settled by the Oregon Treaty in 1846 and the first permanent U.S. settlement in Idaho was established by the Mormons at Franklin in 1860.

After gold was discovered on Orofino Creek in 1860, prospectors swarmed into the territory, but left little more than a number of ghost towns.

In the 1870s, growing white occupation of Indian lands led to a series of battles between U.S. forces and the Nez Percé, Bannock, and Sheepeater tribes.

Mining, lumbering, and irrigation farming have been important for years. Idaho produces more than one third of all the silver mined in the U.S. It also ranks high among the states in antimony, lead, cobalt, garnet, phosphate rock, vanadium, zinc, and mercury.

Idaho's most impressive growth began when World War II military needs made processing agricultural products a big industry, particularly the dehydrating and freezing of potatoes. The state produces about one fourth of the nation's potato crop, as well as wheat, apples, corn, barley, sugar beets, and hops.

With the growth of winter sports, tourism now outranks mining in dollar revenue. Idaho's many streams and lakes provide fishing, camping, and boating sites. The nation's largest elk herds draw hunters from all over the world and the famed Sun Valley resort attracts thousands of visitors to its swimming and skiing facilities.

Other points of interest are the Craters of the Moon National Monument; Nez Percé National Historic Park, which includes many sites visited by Lewis and Clark; and the State Historical Museum in Boise.

ILLINOIS

Capital: Springfield
Governor: James R. Thompson, R (to Jan. 1991)
Lieut. Governor: George H. Ryan, R (to Jan. 1991)
Secy. of State: Jim Edgar, R (to Jan. 1991)
Comptroller: Roland J. Burris, D (to Jan. 1991)
Atty. General: Neil F. Hartigan, D (to Jan. 1991)
Treasurer: Jerry Cosentino, D (to Jan. 1991)
Organized as territory: Feb. 3, 1809
Entered Union & (rank): Dec. 3, 1818 (21)
Present constitution adopted: 1970
Motto: State sovereignty, national union
State flower: Violet (1908)
State tree: White oak (1973)
State bird: Cardinal (1929)
State animal: White-tailed deer (1982)
State fish: Bluegill (1987)
State insect: Monarch butterfly
State song: "Illinois" (1925)
State mineral: Fluorite (1965)
Nickname: Prairie State
Origin of name: From an Indian word and French suffix meaning "tribe of superior men"
1980 population (1980 census) & (rank): 11,426,596 (5)
1987 est. population (July 1) & (rank): 11,582,000 (6)
1980 land area & (rank): 55,645 sq mi. (144,120 sq km) (24)

Geographic center: In Logan County 28 mi. NE of Springfield
Number of counties: 102
Largest cities (1984 census): Chicago, 2,992,472; Rockford, 136,531; Peoria, 117,113; Springfield, 101,570; Decatur, 91,851; Aurora, 85,735
Public use areas: 187 (275,000 ac.), incl. state parks, memorials, forests and conservation areas
1987 percent pop. below age 15: 22
1987 percent pop. age 65 and over: 12
1987 violent crimes per 100,000 pop.: 796.2
1984 (fiscal year) immigrants: 26,617

French explorers Marquette and Joliet, in 1673, were the first Europeans of record to visit the region. In 1699 French settlers established the first permanent settlement at Cahokia, near present-day East St. Louis.

Great Britain obtained the region at the end of the French and Indian War in 1763. The area figured prominently in frontier struggles during the Revolutionary War and in Indian wars during the early 19th century.

Significant episodes in the state's early history include the growing migration of Eastern settlers following the opening of the Erie Canal in 1825; the Black Hawk War, which virtually ended the Indian troubles in the area; and the rise of Abraham Lincoln from farm laborer to President-elect.

Today, Illinois stands high in manufacturing, coal mining, agriculture, and oil production. The sprawling Chicago district (including a slice of Indiana) is a great iron and steel producer, meat packer, grain exchange, and railroad center. Chicago is also famous as a Great Lakes port.

Illinois ranks first in the nation in export of agricultural products and second in hog production. An important dairying state, Illinois is also a leader in corn, oats, wheat, barley, rye, truck vegetables, and the nursery products.

The state manufactures a great variety of industrial and consumer products: railroad cars, clothing, furniture, tractors, liquor, watches, and farm implements are just some of the items made in its factories and plants.

Central Illinois is noted for shrines and memorials associated with the life of Abraham Lincoln. In Springfield are the Lincoln Home, the Lincoln Tomb, and the restored Old State Capitol. Other points of interest are the home of Mormon leader Joseph Smith in Nauvoo and, in Chicago: the Art Institute, Field Museum, Museum of Science and Industry, Shedd Aquarium, Adler Planetarium, Merchandise Mart, and Chicago Portage National Historic Site.

INDIANA

Capital: Indianapolis
Governor: Birch Evans Bayh III, D (to Jan. 1993)
Lieut. Governor: Frank O'Bannon, D (to Jan. 1993)
Secy. of State: Joseph H. Hogsett, D (to Dec. 1990)
Treasurer: Marjorie H. O'Laughlin, R (to Feb. 1991)
Atty. General: Linley E. Pearson, R (to Jan. 1989)
Auditor: Ann G. Devore, R (to Dec. 1990)
Organized as territory: May 7, 1800
Entered Union & (rank): Dec. 11, 1816 (19)
Present constitution adopted: 1851
Motto: The Crossroads of America
State flower: Peony (1957)
State tree: Tulip tree (1931)
State bird: Cardinal (1933)

State song: "On the Banks of the Wabash, Far Away" (1913)
Nickname: Hoosier State
Origin of name: Meaning "land of Indians"
1980 population (1980 census) & (rank): 5,490,260 (12)
1987 est. population (July 1) & (rank): 5,531,000 (14)
1980 land area & (rank): 35,932 sq mi. (93,064 sq km) (38)
Geographic center: In Boone Co., 14 mi. NNW of Indianapolis
Number of Counties: 92
Largest cities (1980 census): Indianapolis, 700,807; Fort Wayne, 172,028; Gary, 151,953; Evansville, 130,496; South Bend, 109,727; Hammond, 93,714; Muncie, 77,216
State parks: 19 (54,126 ac.)
State memorials: 16 (941.977 ac.)
1987 percent pop. below age 15: 22
1987 percent pop. age 65 and over: 12
1987 violent crimes per 100,000 pop.: 328.5
1984 (fiscal year) immigrants: 2,398

First explored for France by La Salle in 1679–80, the region figured importantly in the Franco-British struggle for North America that culminated with British victory in 1763.

George Rogers Clark led American forces against the British in the area during the Revolutionary War and, prior to becoming a state, Indiana was the scene of frequent Indian uprisings until the victory of Gen. William Henry Harrison at Tippecanoe in 1811.

Indiana's 41-mile Lake Michigan waterfront—one of the world's great industrial centers—turns out iron, steel, and oil products. Products include automobile parts and accessories, mobile homes and recreational vehicles, truck and bus bodies, aircraft engines, farm machinery, and fabricated structural steel. Phonograph records, wood office furniture, and pharmaceuticals are also manufactured.

The state is a leader in agriculture with corn the principal crop. Hogs, soybeans, wheat, oats, rye, tomatoes, onions, and poultry also contribute heavily to Indiana's agricultural output. Much of the building limestone used in the U.S. is quarried in Indiana which is also a large producer of coal.

Wyandotte Cave, one of the largest in the U.S., is located in Crawford County in southern Indiana and West Baden and French Lick are well known for their mineral springs. Other attractions include Indiana Dunes National Lakeshore, Indianapolis Motor Speedway, Lincoln Boyhood National Memorial, and the George Rogers Clark National Historical Park.

IOWA

Capital: Des Moines
Governor: Terry E. Branstad, R (to Jan. 1991)
Lieut. Governor: Jo Ann Zimmerman, D (to Jan. 1991)
Secy. of State: Elaine Baxter, D (to Jan. 1991)
Treasurer: Michael L. Fitzgerald, D (to Jan. 1991)
Atty. General: Tom Miller, D (to Jan. 1991)
Organized as territory: June 12, 1838
Entered Union & (rank): Dec. 28, 1846 (29)
Present constitution adopted: 1857
Motto: Our liberties we prize and our rights we will maintain
State flower: Wild rose (1897)
State bird: Eastern goldfinch (1933)
State colors: Red, white, and blue (in state flag)
State song: "Song of Iowa"
Nickname: Hawkeye State

Origin of name: Probably from an Indian word meaning "I-o-w-a, this is the place," or "The Beautiful Land"
1980 population (1980 census) & (rank): 2,913,808 (27)
1987 est. population (July 1) & (rank): 2,834,000 (29)
1980 land area & (rank): 55,965 sq mi. (144,950 sq km) (25)
Geographic center: In Story Co., 5 mi. NE of Ames
Number of counties: 99
Largest cities (1980 census): Des Moines, 191,003; Cedar Rapids, 110,243; Davenport, 103,264; Sioux City, 82,003; Waterloo, 75,985; Dubuque, 62,321; Council Bluffs, 56,449; Iowa City, 50,508; Ames, 45,775
State forests: 5 (28,000 ac.)
State parks: 95 (49,237)
1985 percent pop. below age 15: 22
1985 percent pop. age 65 and over: 14
1987 violent crimes per 100,000 pop.: 231.2
1984 (fiscal year) immigrants: 1,564

The first Europeans to visit the area were the French explorers, Father Jacques Marquette and Louis Joliet in 1673. The U.S. obtained control of the area in 1803 as part of the Louisiana Purchase.

During the first half of the 19th century, there was heavy fighting between white settlers and Indians. Lands were taken from the Indians after the Black Hawk War in 1832 and again in 1836 and 1837.

When Iowa became a state in 1846, its capital was Iowa City; the more centrally located Des Moines became the new capital in 1857. At that time, the state's present boundaries were also drawn.

Although Iowa produces a tenth of the nation's food supply, the value of Iowa's manufactured products is three times that of its agriculture. Major industries are food and associated products, non-electrical machinery, electrical equipment, printing and publishing, and fabricated products.

Iowa stands in a class by itself as an agricultural state. Its farms sell over $9 billion worth of crops and livestock annually. Iowa is second in the nation in all livestock and hog marketings, with about 25.7% of the pork supply and 7.2% of the grain-fed cattle. Iowa's forests produce hardwood lumber, particularly walnut, and its mineral products include cement, limestone, sand, gravel, gypsum, and coal.

Tourist attractions include the Herbert Hoover birthplace and library near West Branch; the Amana Colonies; Fort Dodge Historical Museum, Fort, and Stockade; the Iowa State Fair at Des Moines in August; and the Effigy Mounds National Monument at Marquette, a prehistoric Indian burial site.

KANSAS

Capital: Topeka
Governor: Mike Hayden, R (to Jan. 1991)
Lieut. Governor: Jack D. Walker, R (to Jan. 1991)
Secy. of State: Bill Graves, R (to Jan. 1991)
Treasurer: Joan Finney, D (to Jan. 1991)
Atty. General: Robert T. Stephan, R (to Jan. 1991)
Organized as territory: May 30, 1854
Entered Union & (rank): Jan. 29, 1861 (34)
Present constitution adopted: 1859
Motto: *Ad astra per aspera* (To the stars through difficulties)
State flower: Sunflower (1903)
State tree: Cottonwood (1937)
State bird: Western meadow lark (1937)
State animal: Buffalo (1955)

State song: "Home on the Range" (1947)
Nicknames: Sunflower State; Jayhawk State
Origin of name: From a Siouan word meaning "people of the south wind"
1980 population (1980 census) & (rank): 2,364,236 (32)
1987 est. population (July 1) & (rank): 2,476,000 (32)
1980 land area & (rank): 81,778 sq mi. (211,805 sq km) (13)
Geographic center: In Barton Co., 15 mi. NE of Great Bend
Number of counties: 105
Largest cities (1980 census): Wichita, 279,835; Kansas City, 161,148; Topeka, 115,266; Overland Park, 81,784; Lawrence, 52,738; Salina, 41,843; Hutchinson, 40,284
State parks: 22 (14,394 ac.)
1987 percent pop. below age 15: 22
1987 percent pop. age 65 and over: 14
1987 violent crimes per 100,000 pop.: 360.7
1984 (fiscal year) immigrants: 2,609

Nickname: Bluegrass State
Origin of name: From an Iroquoian word "Ken-tah-ten" meaning "land of tomorrow"
1980 population (1980 census) & (rank): 3,660,777 (23)
1987 est. population (July 1) & (rank): 3,727,000 (23)
1980 land area & (rank): 39,669 sq mi. (102,743 sq km) (37)
Geographic center: In Marion Co., 3 mi. NNW of Lebanon
Number of counties: 120
Largest cities (1985 proj.): Louisville, 293,834; Lexington, 214,072; Owensboro, 56,419; Covington, 47,725; Bowling Green, 45,549; Paducah, 29,699; Hopkinsville, 30,406
State forests: 9 (44,173 ac.)
State parks: 43 (40,574 ac.)
1987 percent pop. below age 15: 22
1987 percent pop. age 65 and over: 12
1987 violent crimes per 100,000 pop.: 337.8
1984 (fiscal year) immigrants: 1,073

Spanish explorer Francisco de Coronado, in 1541, is considered the first European to have traveled this region. La Salle's extensive land claims for France (1682) included present-day Kansas. Ceded to Spain by France in 1763, the territory reverted back to France in 1800 and was sold to the U.S. as part of the Louisiana Purchase in 1803.

Lewis and Clark, Zebulon Pike, and Stephen H. Long explored the region between 1803 and 1819. The first permanent settlements in Kansas were outposts—Fort Leavenworth (1827), Fort Scott (1842), and Fort Riley (1853)—established to protect travelers along the Santa Fe and Oregon Trails.

Just before the Civil War, the conflict between the pro- and anti-slavery forces earned the region the grim title "Bleeding Kansas."

Today, wheat fields, oil well derricks, herds of cattle, and grain storage elevators are chief features of the Kansas landscape. A leading wheat-growing state, Kansas also raises corn, sorghums, oats, barley, soy beans, and potatoes. Kansas stands high in petroleum production and mines zinc, coal, salt, and lead. It is also the nation's leading producer of helium.

Wichita is one of the nation's leading aircraft manufacturing centers, ranking first in production of private aircraft. Kansas City is an important transportation, milling, and meat-packing center.

Points of interest include the new Kansas Museum of History at Topeka, the Eisenhower boyhood home and the new Eisenhower Memorial Museum and Presidential Library at Abilene, John Brown's cabin at Osawatomie, recreated Front Street in Dodge City, Fort Larned (once the most important military post on the Santa Fe Trail), and Fort Leavenworth and Fort Riley.

Kentucky was the first region west of the Allegheny Mountains settled by American pioneers. James Harrod established the first permanent settlement at Harrodsburg in 1774; the following year Daniel Boone, who had explored the area in 1767, blazed the Wilderness Trail and founded Boonesboro.

Politically, the Kentucky region was originally part of Virginia, but early statehood was gained in 1792.

During the Civil War, as a slaveholding state with a considerable abolitionist population, Kentucky was caught in the middle of the conflict, supplying both Union and Confederate forces with thousands of troops.

In recent years, manufacturing has shown important gains, but agriculture and mining are still vital to Kentucky's economy. Kentucky prides itself on producing some of the nation's best tobacco, horses, and whiskey. Corn, soybeans, wheat, fruit, hogs, cattle, and dairy farming are also important.

Among the manufactured items produced in the state are furniture, aluminum ware, brooms, shoes, lumber products, machinery, textiles, and iron and steel products. Kentucky also produces significant amounts of petroleum, natural gas, fluorspar, clay, and stone. However, coal accounts for 90% of the total mineral income.

Louisville, the largest city, famed for the Kentucky Derby at Churchill Downs, is also the location of a large state university, whiskey distilleries, and cigarette factories. The Bluegrass country around Lexington is the home of some of the world's finest race horses. Other attractions are Mammoth Cave, the George S. Patton, Jr., Military Museum at Fort Knox, and Old Fort Harrod State Park.

KENTUCKY

Capital: Frankfort
Governor: Wallace G. Wilkinson, D (to Dec. 1991)
Lieut. Governor: Brereton C. Jones, D (to Dec. 1991)
Secy. of State: Bremer Ehrler, D (to Jan. 1992)
State Treasurer: Robert Meade, D (to Jan. 1992)
State Auditor: Bob Babbage, D (to Jan. 1992)
Atty. General: Fred Cowan, D (to Jan. 1992)
Entered Union & (rank): June 1, 1792 (15)
Present constitution adopted: 1891
Motto: United we stand, divided we fall
State tree: Coffeetree
State flower: Goldenrod
State bird: Kentucky cardinal
State song: "My Old Kentucky Home"

LOUISIANA

Capital: Baton Rouge
Governor: Buddy Roemer, D (to March 1992)
Lieut. Governor: Paul J. Hardy, D (to March 1992)
Secy. of State: W. Fox McKeithen, D (to March 1992)
Treasurer: Mary Landrieu, D (to March 1992)
Atty. General: Gen. Wm. J. Guste, Jr., D (to March 1992)
Organized as territory: March 26, 1804
Entered Union & (rank): April 30, 1812 (18)
Present constitution adopted: 1974
Motto: Union, justice, and confidence
State flower: Magnolia (1900)
State tree: Bald cypress
State bird: Pelican

State song: "Give Me Louisiana," and "You Are My Sunshine"
Nicknames: Pelican State; Sportsman's Paradise; Creole State; Sugar State
Origin of name: In honor of Louis XIV of France
1980 population (1980 census) & (rank): 4,206,312 (19)
1987 est. population (July 1) & (rank): 4,461,000 (20)
1980 land area & (rank): 44,521 sq mi. (115,309 sq km) (33)
Geographic center: In Avoyelles Parish, 3 mi. SE of Marksville
Number of parishes (counties): 64
Largest cities (1980 census): New Orleans, 557,927; Baton Rouge, 219,419; Shreveport, 205,820; Lafayette, 81,961; Lake Charles, 75,226; Monroe, 57,597; Alexandria, 51,565
State forests: 1 (8,000 ac.)
State parks: 30 (13,932 ac.)
1987 percent pop. below age 15: 25
1987 percent pop. age 65 and over: 11
1987 violent crimes per 100,000 pop.: 693.0
1984 (fiscal year) immigrants: 5,403

Louisiana has a rich, colorful historical background. Early Spanish explorers were Piñeda, 1519; Cabeza de Vaca, 1528; and de Soto in 1541. La Salle reached the mouth of the Mississippi and claimed all the land drained by it and its tributaries for Louis XIV of France in 1682.

Louisiana became a French crown colony in 1731, was ceded to Spain in 1763, returned to France in 1800, and sold by Napoleon to the U.S. as part of the Louisiana Purchase (with large territories to the north and northwest) in 1803.

In 1815, Gen. Andrew Jackson's troops defeated a larger British army in the Battle of New Orleans, neither side aware that the treaty ending the War of 1812 had been signed.

As to total value of its mineral output, Louisiana is a leader in natural gas, salt, petroleum, and sulfur production. Much of the oil and sulfur comes from offshore deposits. The state also produces large crops of sweet potatoes, rice, sugarcane, pecans, soybeans, corn, and cotton.

Leading manufactures include chemicals, processed food, petroleum and coal products, paper, lumber and wood products, transportation equipment, and apparel.

Louisiana marshes supply most of the nation's muskrat fur as well as that of opossum, raccoon, mink, and otter, and large numbers of game birds.

Major points of interest include New Orleans with its French Quarter and Superdome, plantation homes near Natchitoches and New Iberia, Cajun country in the Mississippi delta region, Chalmette National Historical Park, and the state capital at Baton Rouge.

MAINE

Capital: Augusta
Governor: John R. McKernan, Jr., R (to Jan. 1991)
Secy. of State: Rodney F. Quinn, D (to Jan. 1989)
Controller: David A. Bourne, R (term indefinite)
Atty. General: James Tierney, D (to Jan. 1991)
Entered Union & (rank): March 15, 1820 (23)
Present constitution adopted: 1820
Motto: *Dirigo* (I direct)
State flower: White pine cone and tassel (1895)
State tree: White pine tree (1945)
State bird: Chickadee (1927)
State fish: Landlocked salmon (1969)

State mineral: Tourmaline (1971)
State song: "State of Maine Song" (1937)
Nickname: Pine Tree State
Origin of name: First used to distinguish the mainland from the offshore islands. It has been considered a compliment to Henrietta Maria, Queen of Charles I of England. She was said to have owned the province of Mayne in France.
1980 population (1980 census) & (rank): 1,125,027 (38)
1987 est. population (July 1) & (rank): 1,187,000 (38)
1980 land area & (rank): 30,995 sq mi. (80,277 sq km) (39)
Geographic center: In Piscataquis Co., 18 mi. N of Dover-Foxcroft
Number of counties: 16
Largest cities (1980 census): Portland, 61,572; Lewiston, 40,481; Bangor, 31,643; Auburn, 23,128; South Portland, 22,712; Augusta, 21,819; Biddeford, 19,638
State forests: 1 (21,000 ac.)
State parks: 26 (247,627 ac.)
State historic sites: 18 (403 ac.)
1987 percent pop. below age 15: 21
1987 percent pop. age 65 and over: 13
1987 violent crimes per 100,000 pop.: 152.1
1984 (fiscal year) immigrants: 798

John Cabot and his son, Sebastian, are believed to have visited the Maine coast in 1498. However, the first permanent English settlements were not established until more than a century later, in 1623.

The first naval action of the Revolutionary War occurred in 1775 when colonials captured the British sloop *Margaretta* off Machias on the Maine coast. In that same year, the British burned Falmouth (now Portland).

Long governed by Massachusetts, Maine became the 23rd state as part of the Missouri Compromise in 1820.

Maine produces 98% of the nation's low-bush blueberries. Farm income is also derived from apples, potatoes, dairy products, and vegetables, with poultry and eggs the largest items.

The state is one of the world's largest pulp-paper producers. It ranks fifth in boot-and-shoe manufacturing. With more than 90% of its area forested, Maine turns out wood products from boats to toothpicks.

Maine leads the world in the production of the familiar flat tins of sardines, producing more than 100 million of them annually. Lobstermen normally catch 80–90% of the nation's true total of lobsters.

A scenic seacoast, beaches, lakes, mountains, and resorts make Maine a popular vacationland. There are more than 2,500 lakes and 5,000 streams, plus 26 state parks, to attract hunters, fishermen, skiers, and campers.

Major points of interest are: Bar Harbor, Allagash National Wilderness Waterway, the Wadsworth-Longfellow House in Portland, Roosevelt Campobello International Park, and the St. Croix Island National Monument.

MARYLAND

Capital: Annapolis
Governor: William Donald Schaefer, D (to Jan. 1991)
Lieut. Gov.: Melvin A. Steinberg, D (to Jan. 1991)
Secy. of State: Winfield M. Kelly, Jr., D (appointed by governor)
Comptroller of the Treasury: Louis L. Goldstein, D (to Jan. 1991)

Treasurer: Lucille Maurer, D (to Jan. 1991)
Atty. General: J. Joseph Curran, Jr., D (to Jan. 1991)
Entered Union & (rank): April 28, 1788 (7)
Present constitution adopted: 1867
Motto: *Fatti maschii, parole femine* (Manly deeds, womanly words)
State flower: Black-eyed susan (1918)
State tree: White oak (1941)
State bird: Baltimore oriole (1947)
State dog: Chesapeake Bay retriever (1964)
State fish: Rockfish (1965)
State crustacean: Maryland Blue Crab (1989)
State insect: Baltimore checkerspot butterfly (1973)
State sport: Jousting (1962)
State song: "Maryland! My Maryland!" (1939)
Nicknames: Free State; Old Line State
Origin of name: In honor of Henrietta Maria (Queen of Charles I of England)
1980 population (1980 census) & (rank): 4,216,975 (18)
1987 est. population (July 1) & (rank): 4,535,000 (19)
1980 land area & (rank): 9,837 sq mi. (25,477 sq km) (42)
Geographic center: In Prince Georges Co., 4 1/2 mi. NW of Davidsonville
Number of counties: 23, and 1 independent city
Largest cities (1980 census): Baltimore, 786,775; Rockville, 43,811; Hagerstown, 34,132; Bowie, 33,695; Annapolis, 31,740; Frederick, 28,086; Gaithersburg, 26,424
State forests: 10 (120,921 ac.)
State parks: 42 (70,302 ac.)
1987 percent pop. below age 15: 20
1987 percent pop. age 65 and over: 11
1987 violent crimes per 100,000 pop.: 767.8
1984 (fiscal year) immigrants: 9,749

In 1608, Chesapeake Bay was explored by Capt. John Smith. Charles I granted a royal charter to Cecil Calvert, Lord Baltimore, in 1632 and English Roman Catholics landed on St. Clement's (now Blakistone Island) in 1634. Religious freedom, granted all Christians in the Toleration act passed by the Maryland assembly in 1649, was ended by a Puritan revolt, 1654–58.

In 1814, when the British unsuccessfully tried to capture Baltimore, the bombardment of Fort McHenry inspired Francis Scott Key to write *The Star Spangled Banner*.

Maryland is almost cut in two by the Chesapeake Bay, and the many estuaries and rivers create one of the longest waterfronts of any state. The Bay produces more seafood—oysters, crabs, clams, fin fish—than any comparable body of water. Important agricultural products, in order of cash value, are chickens, dairy products, corn, cattle, tobacco, and vegetables. Maryland is a leader in vegetable canning. Sand, gravel, lime and cement, stone, coal, and clay are the chief mineral products.

Manufacturing industries produce missiles, airplanes, steel, clothing, and chemicals. Baltimore, home of The Johns Hopkins University and Hospital, ranks as the nation's second port in foreign tonnage. Annapolis, site of the U.S. Naval Academy, has one of the earliest state houses (1772–79) still in regular use by a State government.

Among the popular attractions in Maryland are the Fort McHenry National Monument, Harpers Ferry and Chesapeake and Ohio Canal, National Aquarium, and Maryland Science Center at Baltimore's Inner Harbor, National Historical Parks, St. Marys City restoration near Leonardtown, USS *Constellation* at Baltimore, U.S. Naval Academy in Annapolis, Assateague Island National Seashore,

and Catoctin Mountain and Piscataway parks.

MASSACHUSETTS

Capital: Boston
Governor: Michael S. Dukakis, D (to Jan. 1991)
Lieut. Governor: Evelyn F. Murphy, D (to Jan. 1991)
Secy. of the Commonwealth: Michael Joseph Connolly, D (to Jan. 1991)
Treasurer & Receiver-General: Robert Q. Crane, D (to Jan. 1991)
Auditor of the Commonwealth: A. Joseph DeNucci, D (to Jan. 1991)
Atty. General: James M. Shannon, D (to Jan. 1991)
Entered Union & (rank): Feb. 6, 1788 (6)
Motto: *Ense petit placidam sub libertate quietem* (By the sword we seek peace, but peace only under liberty)
State flower: Mayflower (1918)
State tree: American elm (1941)
State bird: Chickadee (1941)
State colors: Blue and gold
State song: "All Hail to Massachusetts" (1966)
State beverage: Cranberry juice (1970)
State insect: Ladybug (1974)
Nicknames: Bay State; Old Colony State
Origin of name: From two Indian words meaning "Great mountain place"
1980 population (1980 census) & (rank): 9,258,344 (9)
1987 est. population (July 1) & (rank): 5,855,000 (13)
1980 land area & (rank): 7,824 sq mi. (20,265 sq km) (45)
Geographic center: In Worcester Co., in S part of city of Worcester
Number of counties: 14
Largest cities (1980 census): Boston, 562,994; Worcester, 161,799; Springfield, 152,319; New Bedford, 98,478; Cambridge, 95,322; Brockton, 95,172; Fall River, 94,574
State forests and parks: 129 (242,000 ac.)[1]
1987 percent pop. below age 15: 18
1987 percent pop. age 65 and over: 14
1987 violent crimes per 100,000 pop.: 564.6
1984 (fiscal year) immigrants: 13,418

1. The Metropolitan District Commission, an agency of the Commonwealth serving municipalities in the Boston area, has about 14,000 acres of parkways and reservations under its jurisdiction.

Massachusetts has played a significant role in American history since the Pilgrims, seeking religious freedom, founded Plymouth Colony in 1620.

As one of the most important of the 13 colonies, Massachusetts became a leader in resisting British oppression. In 1773, the Boston Tea Party protested unjust taxation. The Minutemen started the American Revolution by battling British troops at Lexington and Concord on April 19, 1775.

During the 19th century, Massachusetts was famous for the vigorous intellectual activity of famous writers and educators and for its expanding commercial fishing, shipping, and manufacturing interests.

Massachusetts pioneered in the manufacture of textiles and shoes. Today, these industries have been replaced in importance by activity in the electronics and communications equipment fields.

The state's cranberry crop is the nation's largest. Also important are dairy and poultry products, nursery and greenhouse produce, vegetables, and fruit.

Tourism has become an important factor in the economy of the state because of its numerous recreational areas and historical landmarks.

Cape Cod has summer theaters, water sports, and an artists' colony at Provincetown. Tanglewood, in the Berkshires, features the summer concerts of the Boston Symphony.

Among the many other points of interest are Old Sturbridge Village, Minute Man National Historical Park between Lexington and Concord, and, in Boston: Old North Church, Old State House, Faneuil Hall, the USS *Constitution* and the John F. Kennedy Library.

MICHIGAN

Capital: Lansing
Governor: James J. Blanchard, D (to Jan. 1991)
Lieut. Governor: Martha W. Griffiths, D (to Jan. 1991)
Secy. of State: Richard H. Austin, D (to Jan. 1991)
Atty. General: Frank J. Kelley, D (to Jan. 1991)
Organized as territory: Jan. 11, 1805
Entered Union & (rank): Jan. 26, 1837 (26)
Present constitution adopted: April 1, 1963, (effective Jan. 1, 1964)
Motto: *Si quaeris peninsulam amoenam circumspice* (If you seek a pleasant peninsula, look around you)
State flower: Apple blossom (1897)
State bird: Robin
State fish: Brook trout (1965)
State gem: Isle Royal Greenstone (Chlorastrolite) (1972)
State stone: Petoskey stone (1965)
Nickname: Wolverine State
Origin of name: From two Indian words meaning "great lake"
1980 population (1980 census) & (rank): 9,262,078 (8)
1987 est. population (July 1) & (rank): 9,200,000 (8)
1980 land area & (rank): 56,954 sq mi. (147,511 sq km) (22)
Geographic center: In Wexford Co., 5 mi. NNW of Cadillac
Number of counties: 83
Largest cities (1980 census): Detroit, 1,203,339; Grand Rapids, 181,843; Warren, 161,134; Flint, 159,611; Lansing, 130,414; Sterling Heights, 108,999; Ann Arbor, 107,966
State forests: 6 (3,762,184 ac.)
State parks and recreation areas: 92 (250,000)
1987 percent pop. below age 15: 22
1987 percent pop. age 65 and over: 12
1987 violent crimes per 100,000 pop.: 780.1
1986 (fiscal year) immigrants: 8,560

Indian tribes were living in the Michigan region when the first European, Etienne Brulé of France, arrived in 1618. Other French explorers, including Marquette, Joliet, and La Salle, followed, and the first permanent settlement was established in 1668 at Sault Ste. Marie. France was ousted from the territory by Great Britain in 1763, following the French and Indian War.

After the Revolutionary War, the U.S. acquired most of the region, which remained the scene of constant conflict between the British and U.S. forces and their respective Indian allies through the War of 1812.

Bordering on four of the five Great Lakes, Michigan is divided into Upper and Lower Peninsulas by the Straits of Mackinac, which link Lakes Michigan and Huron. The two parts of the state are connected by the Mackinac Bridge, one of the world's longest suspension bridges. To the north, connecting Lakes Superior and Huron are the busy Sault Ste. Marie Canals.

While Michigan ranks first among the states in production of motor vehicles and parts, it is also a leader in many other manufacturing and processing lines including prepared cereals, machine tools, airplane parts, refrigerators, hardware, steel springs, and furniture.

The state produces important amounts of iron, copper, iodine, gypsum, bromine, salt, lime, gravel, and cement. Michigan's farms grow apples, cherries, pears, grapes, potatoes, and sugar beets and the annual value of its forest products is estimated at $2 billion. With over 36,000 miles of streams, some 11,000 lakes, and a 2,000 mile shoreline, Michigan is a prime area for both commercial and sport fishing.

Points of interest are the automobile plants in Dearborn, Detroit, Flint, Lansing, and Pontiac; Mackinac Island; Pictured Rocks and Sleeping Bear Dunes National Lakeshores, Greenfield Village near Dearborn; and the many summer resorts along both the inland and Great Lakes.

MINNESOTA

Capital: St. Paul
Governor: Rudy Perpich, D (to Jan. 1991)
Lieut. Governor: Marlene Johnson, D (to Jan. 1991)
Secy. of State: Joan Growe, D (to Jan. 1991)
State Auditor: Arne Carlson, R (to Jan. 1991)
Atty. General: Hubert H. Humphrey III, D (to Jan. 1991)
State Treasurer: Michael McGrath, D (to Jan. 1991)
Organized as territory: March 3, 1849
Entered Union & (rank): May 11, 1858 (32)
Present constitution adopted: 1858
Motto: L'Etoile du Nord (The North Star)
State flower: Showy lady slipper (1902)
State tree: Red (or Norway) pine
State bird: Common loon (also called Great Northern Diver)
State song: "Hail Minnesota"
Nicknames: North Star State; Gopher State; Land of 10,000 Lakes
Origin of name: From a Dakota Indian word meaning "sky-tinted water"
1980 population (1980 census) & (rank): 4,075,970 (21)
1987 est. population (July 1) & (rank): 4,246,000 (21)
1980 land area & (rank): 79,548 sq mi. (206,030 sq km) (14)
Geographic center: In Crow Wing Co., 10 mi. SW of Brainerd
Number of counties: 87
Largest cities (1980 census): Minneapolis, 370,951; St. Paul, 270,230; Duluth, 92,811; Bloomington, 81,831; Rochester, 57,890; Edina, 46,073
State forests: 55 (2,984,000 ac.)
State parks: 92 (202,205 ac.)
1987 percent pop. below age 15: 22
1987 percent pop. age 65 and over: 13
1987 violent crimes per 100,000 pop.: 285.4
1984 (fiscal year) immigrants: 5,243

Following the visits of several French explorers, fur traders, and missionaries, including Marquette and Joliet and La Salle, the region was claimed for Louis XIV by Daniel Greysolon, Sieur Duluth, in 1679.

The U.S. acquired eastern Minnesota from Great Britain after the Revolutionary War and 20 years later bought the western part from France in the Louisiana Purchase of 1803. Much of the region was explored by U.S. Army Lt. Zebulon M. Pike before cession of the northern strip of Minnesota bordering Canada by Britain in 1818.

The state is rich in natural resources. A few square miles of land in the north in the Mesabi, Cuyuna, and Vermillion ranges, produce more than 60% of the nation's iron ore. The state's farms rank high in yields of corn, wheat, rye, alfalfa, and sugar beets. Other leading farm products include butter, eggs, milk, potatoes, green peas, barley, and livestock.

Minnesota's factory production includes non-electrical machinery, fabricated metals, flour-mill products, plastics, electronic computers, scientific instruments, and processed foods.

Minneapolis is the trade center of the Northwest; St. Paul is the nation's biggest publisher of calendars and law books. These "twin cities" are the nation's third largest trucking center. Duluth has the nation's largest inland harbor and now handles a significant amount of foreign trade. Rochester is the home of the Mayo Clinic, an internationally famous medical center.

Today, tourism is a major revenue producer in Minnesota, with fishing, hunting, water sports, and winter sports bringing in millions of visitors each year.

Among the most popular attractions are the St. Paul Winter Carnival; the Tyrone Guthrie Theatre, the Institute of Arts, Walker Art Center, and Minnehaha Park, in Minneapolis; Voyageurs National Park; North Shore Drive; and the Minnesota Zoological Gardens.

MISSISSIPPI

Capital: Jackson
Governor: Ray Mabus, D (to Jan. 1992)
Lieut. Governor: Brad Dye, D (to Jan. 1992)
Secy. of State: Dick Molpus, D (to Jan. 1992)
Treasurer: Marshall Bennett, D (to Jan. 1992)
Atty. General: Mike Moore, D (to Jan. 1992)
Organized as Territory: April 7, 1798
Entered Union & (rank): Dec. 10, 1817 (20)
Present constitution adopted: 1890
Motto: *Virtute et armis* (By valor and arms)
State flower: Flower or bloom of the magnolia or evergreen magnolia (1952)
State tree: Magnolia (1938)
State bird: Mockingbird (1944)
State song: "Go, Mississippi" (1962)
Nickname: Magnolia State
Origin of name: From an Indian word meaning "Father of Waters"
1980 population (1980 census) & (rank): 2,520,638 (31)
1987 est. population (July 1) & (rank): 2,625,000 (31)
1980 land area & (rank): 47,233 sq mi. (122,333 sq km) (31)
Geographic center: In Leake Co., 9 mi. WNW of Carthage
Number of counties: 82
Largest cities (1980 census): Jackson, 202,895; Biloxi, 49,311; Hattiesburg, 40,829; Greenville, 40,613; Gulfport, 39,676; Pascagoula, 29,318
State forests: 1 (1,760 ac.)
State parks: 27 (16,763 ac.)
1987 percent pop. below age 15: 25
1987 percent pop. age 65 and over: 12
1987 violent crimes per 100,000 pop.: 269.8
1984 (fiscal year) immigrants: 786

First explored for Spain by Hernando de Soto who discovered the Mississippi River in 1540, the region was later claimed by France. In 1699, a French group under Sieur d'Iberville established the first permanent settlement near present-day Biloxi.

Great Britain took over the area in 1763 after the French and Indian War, ceding it to the U.S. in 1783 after the Revolution. Spain did not relinquish its claims until 1798, and in 1810 the U.S. annexed West Florida from Spain, including what is now southern Mississippi.

For a little more than one hundred years, from shortly after the state's founding through the Great Depression, cotton was the undisputed king of Mississippi's largely agrarian economy. Over the last half-century, however, Mississippi has progressively deepened its commitment to diversification by balancing agricultural output with increased industrial activity.

Today, agriculture continues as a major segment of the state's economy. Soybeans have supplanted cotton as the largest crop—although Mississippi still ranks second only to Texas in cotton production—and the state's farmlands yield important harvests of corn, peanuts, pecans, rice, sugarcane, sweet potatoes, and hay, as well as poultry and eggs. Mississippi is also the world's leading producer of pond-raised catfish.

The state abounds in historical landmarks and is the home of the Vicksburg National Military Park. Other National Park Service areas are Brices Cross Roads National Battlefield Site, Tupelo National Battlefield, and part of Natchez Trace National Parkway. Pre-Civil War mansions are the special pride of Natchez, Oxford, Hattiesburg, and Jackson.

MISSOURI

Capital: Jefferson City
Governor: John D. Ashcroft, R (to Jan. 1993)
Lieut. Governor: Mel Carnahan, D (to Jan. 1993)
Secy. of State: Roy D. Blunt, R (to Jan. 1993)
Auditor: Margaret Kelly, R (to Jan. 1991)
Treasurer: Wendell Bailey, R (to Jan. 1993)
Atty. General: William L. Webster, R (to Jan. 1993)
Organized as territory: June 4, 1812
Entered Union & (rank): Aug. 10, 1821 (24)
Present constitution adopted: 1945
Motto: *Salus populi suprema lex esto* (The welfare of the people shall be the supreme law)
State flower: Hawthorn (1923)
State bird: Bluebird (1927)
State colors: Red, white, and blue (1913)
State song: "Missouri Waltz" (1949)
State rock: Mozarkite (1967)
State mineral: Galena (1967)
State insect: Honeybee (1985)
Nickname: Show-me State
Origin of name: Named after a tribe called Missouri Indians. "Missouri" means "town of the large canoes."
1980 population (1980 census) & (rank): 4,916,759 (15)
1987 est. population (July 1) & (rank): 5,103,000 (15)
1980 land area & (rank): 68,945 sq mi. (178,568 sq km) (18)
Geographic center: In Miller Co., 20 mi. SW of Jefferson City
Number of counties: 114, plus 1 independent city
Largest cities (1980 census): St. Louis, 453,085; Kansas City, 448,159; Springfield, 133,116; Independence, 111,806; St. Joseph, 76,961; Columbia, 62,061; Florissant, 55,372
State forests and Tower sites: 134 (308,978 ac.)
State parks: 73 (105,325 ac.)[1]
1987 percent pop. below age 15: 21
1987 percent pop. age 65 and over: 14
1987 violent crimes per 100,000 pop.: 544.6
1984 (fiscal year) immigrants: 3,186

1. Includes 45 historic sites.

De Soto visited the Missouri area in 1541. France's claim to the entire region was based on La Salle's travels in 1682. French fur traders established Ste. Genevieve in 1735 and St. Louis was first settled in 1764.

The U.S. gained Missouri from France as part of the Louisiana Purchase in 1803, and the territory was admitted as a state following the Missouri Compromise of 1820. Throughout the pre-Civil War period and during the war, Missourians were sharply divided in their opinions about slavery and in their allegiances, supplying both Union and Confederate forces with troops. However, the state itself remained in the Union.

Historically, Missouri played a leading role as a gateway to the West, St. Joseph being the eastern starting point of the Pony Express, while the much-traveled Santa Fe and Oregon Trails began in Independence. Now a popular vacationland, Missouri has 11 major lakes and numerous fishing streams, springs, and caves. Bagnell Dam, across the Osage River in the Ozarks, completed in 1931, created one of the largest man-made lakes in the world, covering 65,000 acres of surface area.

Manufacturing, paced by the aerospace industry, provides more income and jobs than any other segment of the economy. Missouri is also a leading producer of transportation equipment, shoes, lead, and beer. Among the major crops are corn, soybeans, wheat, oats, barley, potatoes, tobacco, and cotton.

Points of interest include Mark Twain's boyhood home and Mark Twain Cave (Hannibal), the Harry S. Truman Library and Museum (Independence), the house where Jesse James was killed in St. Joseph, Jefferson National Expansion Memorial (St. Louis), and the Ozark National Scenic Riverway.

MONTANA

Capital: Helena
Governor: Stan Stephens, R (to Jan. 1993)
Lieut. Governor: Allen Kolstad, R (to Jan. 1993)
Secy. of State: Mike Cooney, D (to Jan. 1993)
Auditor: Andrea Bennett, R (to Jan. 1993)
Atty. General: Marc Racicot, R (to Jan. 1993)
Organized as territory: May 26, 1864
Entered Union & (rank): Nov. 8, 1889 (41)
Present constitution adopted: 1972
Motto: *Oro y plata* (Gold and silver)
State flower: Bitterroot (1895)
State tree: Ponderosa pine (1949)
State stones: Sapphire and agate (1969)
State bird: Western meadow lark (1931)
State song: "Montana" (1945)
Nickname: Treasure State
Origin of name: Chosen from Latin dictionary by J. M. Ashley. It is a Latinized Spanish word.
1980 population (1980 census) & (rank): 786,900 (44)
1987 est. population (July 1) & (rank): 809,000 (44)
1980 land area & (rank): 145,388 sq mi. (376,564 sq km) (4)
Geographic center: In Fergus Co., 12 mi. W of Lewistown
Number of counties: 56, plus small part of Yellowstone National Park
Largest cities (1980 census): Billings, 66,824; Great Falls, 56,725; Butte-Silver Bow, 37,205; Missoula, 33,388; Helena, 23,938; Bozeman, 21,645; Havre, 10,891
State forests: 7 (214,000 ac.)
State parks and recreation areas: 110 (18,273 ac.)
1987 percent pop. below age 15: 23
1987 percent pop. age 65 and over: 13
1987 violent crimes per 100,000 pop.: 151.2
1984 (fiscal year) immigrants: 333

First explored for France by François and Louis-

Joseph Verendrye in the early 1740s, much of the region was acquired by the U.S. from France as part of the Louisiana Purchase in 1803. Before western Montana was obtained from Great Britain in the Oregon Treaty of 1846, American trading posts and forts had been established in the territory.

The major Indian wars (1867–1877) included the famous 1876 Battle of the Little Big Horn, better known as "Custer's Last Stand," in which Cheyennes and Sioux killed George A. Custer and more than 200 of his men in southeastern Montana.

Much of Montana's early history was concerned with mining with copper, lead, zinc, silver, coal, and oil as principal products.

Butte is the center of the area that once supplied half of the U.S. copper.

Fields of grain cover much of Montana's plains; it ranks high among the states in wheat and barley, with rye, oats, flaxseed, sugar beets, and potatoes other important crops. Sheep and cattle raising make significant contributions to the economy.

Tourist attractions include hunting, fishing, skiing, and dude ranching. Glacier National Park, on the Continental Divide, is a scenic and vacation wonderland with 60 glaciers, 200 lakes, and many streams with good trout fishing.

Other major points of interest include the Custer Battlefield National Monument, Virginia City, Yellowstone National Park, Museum of the Plains Indians at Browning, and the Fort Union Trading Post and Grant-Kohr's Ranch National Historic Sites.

NEBRASKA

Capital: Lincoln
Governor: Kay A. Orr, R (to Jan. 1991)
Lieut. Governor: Wm. Nichol, R (to Jan. 1991)
Secy. of State: Allen J. Beerman, R (to Jan. 1991)
Atty. General: Robert Spire, R (to Jan. 1991)
Auditor: Ray A. C. Johnson, R (to Jan. 1991)
Treasurer: Frank Marsh, R (to Jan. 1991)
Organized as territory: May 30, 1854
Entered Union & (rank): March 1, 1867 (37)
Present constitution adopted: Nov. 1, 1875 (extensively amended 1919–20)
Motto: Equality before the law
State flower: Goldenrod (1895)
State tree: Cottonwood (1972)
State bird: Western meadow lark (1929)
State insect: Honey Bee (1975)
State gem stone: Blue agate (1967)
State rock: Prairie agate (1967)
State fossil: Mammoth (1967)
State song: "Beautiful Nebraska" (1967)
Nicknames: Cornhusker State; Beef State; The Tree Planter State
Origin of name: From an Oto Indian word meaning "flat water"
1980 population (1980 census) & (rank): 1,570,006 (35)
1987 est. population (July 1) & (rank): 1,594,000 (36)
1980 land area & (rank): 76,644 sq mi. (198,508 sq km) (15)
Geographic center: In Custer Co., 10 mi. NW of Broken Bow
Number of counties: 93
Largest cities (1980 census): Omaha, 313,911; Lincoln, 171,932; Grand Island, 33,180; North Platte, 24,479; Fremont, 23,979; Hastings, 23,045; Bellevue, 21,813
State forests: None
State parks: 93 areas, 4 categories, 5 major areas
1987 percent pop. below age 15: 22
1987 percent pop. age 65 and over: 14

1987 violent crimes per 100,000 pop.: 251.2
1984 (fiscal year) immigrants: 984

French fur traders first visited Nebraska in the early 1700s. Part of the Louisiana Purchase in 1803, Nebraska was explored by Lewis and Clark in 1804–06.

Robert Stuart pioneered the Oregon Trail across Nebraska in 1812–13 and the first permanent settlement was established at Bellevue in 1823. Western Nebraska was acquired by treaty following the Mexican War in 1848. The Union Pacific began its transcontinental railroad at Omaha in 1865. In 1937, Nebraska became the only state in the Union to have a unicameral (one-house) legislature. Members are elected to it without party designation.

Nebraska is a leading grain-producer with bumper crops of rye, corn, and wheat. More varieties of grass, valuable for forage, grow in this state than in any other in the nation.

The state's sizable cattle and hog industries make Omaha with its surrounding area the nation's largest meat-packing center and the second-largest cattle market in the world.

Manufacturing has become diversified in Nebraska, strengthening the state's economic base. Firms making electronic components, auto accessories, pharmaceuticals, and mobile homes have joined such older industries as clothing, farm machinery, chemicals, and transportation equipment. Oil was discovered in 1939 and natural gas in 1949.

Among the principal attractions are Agate Fossil Beds, Homestead, and Scotts Bluff National Monuments; Chimney Rock National Historic Site; a recreated pioneer village at Minden; the Union stockyards in Omaha; the Stuhr Museum of the Prairie Pioneer with 57 original 19th-century buildings near Grand Island; and the Sheldon Memorial Art Gallery at the University of Nebraska in Lincoln.

NEVADA

Capital: Carson City
Governor (acting) and Lieut. Governor: Robert J. Miller (to Jan. 1991)
Secy. of State: Frankie Sue Del Papa, D (to Jan. 1991)
State Treasurer: Ken Santor, R (to Jan. 1991)
Controller: Darrel R. Daines, R (to Jan. 1991)
Atty. General: Brian McKay, R (to Jan. 1991)
Organized as territory: March 2, 1861
Entered Union & (rank): Oct. 31, 1864 (36)
Present constitution adopted: 1864
Motto: All for Our Country
State flower: Sagebrush (1967)
State tree: Single-leaf pinon (1953)
State bird: Mountain bluebird (1967)
State animal: Desert bighorn sheep (1973)
State colors: Silver and blue (unofficial)
State song: "Home Means Nevada" (1933)
Nicknames: Sagebrush State; Silver State; Battle-born State
Origin of name: Spanish: "snowcapped"
1980 population (1980 census) & (rank): 800,493 (43)
1987 est. population (July 1) & (rank): 1,007,000 (41)
1980 land area & (rank): 109,894 sq mi. (284,624 sq km) (7)
Geographic center: In Lander Co., 26 mi. SE of Austin
Number of counties: 16, plus 1 independent city
Largest cities (est. as of July 1, 1985): Las Vegas, 193,052; Reno, 115,464; North Las Vegas, 45,920; Sparks, 49,612; Carson City, 35,400; Henderson, 37,046; Boulder City, 11,425
State forests: None

State parks: 20 (150,000 ac., including leased lands)
1987 percent pop. below age 15: 21
1987 percent pop. age 65 and over: 11
1987 violent crimes per 100,000 pop.: 695.7
1984 (fiscal year) immigrants: 2,130

Trappers and traders, including Jedediah Smith, and Peter Skene Ogden, entered the Nevada area in the 1820s. In 1843–45, John C. Fremont and Kit Carson explored the Great Basin and Sierra Nevada.

In 1848 following the Mexican War, the U.S. obtained the region and the first permanent settlement was a Mormon trading post near present-day Genoa.

The driest state in the nation with an average annual rainfall of only 3.73 inches, much of Nevada is uninhabited, sagebrush-covered desert.

Nevada was made famous by the discovery of the fabulous Comstock Lode in 1859 and its mines have produced large quantities of gold, silver, copper, lead, zinc, mercury, barite, and tungsten. Oil was discovered in 1954. Gold now far exceeds all other minerals in value of production.

In 1931, the state created two industries, divorce and gambling. For many years, Reno and Las Vegas were the "divorce capitals of the nation." More liberal divorce laws in many states have ended this distinction, but Nevada is the gambling and entertainment capital of the U.S. State gambling taxes account for 45% of tax revenues. Although Nevada leads the nation in per capita gambling revenue, it ranks only fourth in total gambling revenue.

Near Las Vegas, on the Colorado River, stands Hoover Dam, which impounds the waters of Lake Mead, one of the world's largest artificial lakes.

The state's agricultural crop consists mainly of hay, alfalfa seed, barley, and wheat.

Nevada manufactures gaming devices, chemicals, forest products, suntan lotion, and stone-clay-glass products.

Major resort areas flourish in Lake Tahoe, Reno, and Las Vegas. Recreation areas include those at Pyramid Lake, Lake Tahoe, and Lake Mead and Lake Mohave, both in Lake Mead National Recreation Area. Among the other attractions are Hoover Dam, Virginia City, and Lehman Caves National Monument.

NEW HAMPSHIRE

Capital: Concord
Governor: Judd A. Gregg, R (to Jan. 1991)
Treasurer: Georgie A. Thomas, R (to Dec. 1990)
Secy. of State: William M. Gardner, D (to Dec. 1990)
Commissioner: George C. Jones, R
Atty. General: John R. Arnold, R (to March 1993)
Entered Union & (rank): June 21, 1788 (9)
Present constitution adopted: 1784
Motto: Live free or die
State flower: Purple lilac (1919)
State tree: White birch (1947)
State bird: Purple finch (1957)
State songs: "Old New Hampshire" (1949) and "New Hampshire, My New Hampshire" (1963)
Nickname: Granite State
Origin of name: From the English county of Hampshire
1980 population (1980 census) & (rank): 920,610 (42)
1987 est. population (July 1) & (rank): 1,057,000 (40)
1980 land area & (rank): 8,993 sq mi. (23,292 sq km) (44)

Geographic center: In Belknap Co., 3 mi. E of Ashland
Number of counties: 10
Largest cities (1987 est.): Manchester, 100,535; Nashua, 79,859; Concord, 35,803; Portsmouth, 29,014; Dover, 24,360; Rochester, 24,226; Keene, 22,422
State forests & parks: 175 (96,975 ac.)
1987 percent pop. below age 15: 21
1987 percent pop. age 65 and over: 12
1987 violent crimes per 100,000: 149.6
1984 (fiscal year) immigrants: 772

Under an English land grant, Capt. John Smith sent settlers to establish a fishing colony at the mouth of the Piscataqua River, near present-day Rye and Dover, in 1623. Capt. John Mason, who participated in the founding of Portsmouth in 1630, gave New Hampshire its name.

After a 38-year period of union with Massachusetts, New Hampshire was made a separate royal colony in 1679. As leaders in the revolutionary cause, New Hampshire delegates received the honor of being the first to vote for the Declaration of Independence on July 4, 1776. New Hampshire is the only state that ever played host at the formal conclusion of a foreign war when, in 1905, Portsmouth was the scene of the treaty ending the Russo-Japanese War.

Abundant water power early turned New Hampshire into an industrial state and manufacturing is the principal source of income in the state. The most important industrial products are electrical and other machinery, textiles, pulp and paper products, and stone and clay products.

Dairy and poultry farming and growing fruit, truck vegetables, corn, potatoes, and hay are the major agricultural pursuits.

Tourism, because of New Hampshire's scenic and recreational resources, now brings over $400 million into the state annually.

Vacation attractions include Lake Winnipesaukee, largest of 1,300 lakes and ponds; the 724,000-acre White Mountain National Forest; Daniel Webster's birthplace near Franklin; Strawbery Banke, restored building of the original settlement at Portsmouth; and the famous "Old Man of the Mountain" granite head profile, the state's official emblem, at Franconia.

NEW JERSEY

Capital: Trenton
Governor: Thomas H. Kean, R (to Jan. 1990)
Secy. of State: Jane Burgio, R (to Jan. 1990)
Treasurer: Feather O'Connor, R (to Jan. 1990)
Atty. General: Peter Perretti, Jr., R (to Jan. 1990)
Entered Union & (rank): Dec. 18, 1787 (3)
Present constitution adopted: 1947
Motto: Liberty and prosperity
State flower: Purple violet (1913)
State bird: Eastern goldfinch (1935)
State insect: Honeybee (1974)
State tree: Red oak (1950)
State animal: Horse (1977)
State colors: Buff and blue (1965)
Nickname: Garden State
Origin of name: From the Channel Isle of Jersey
1980 population (1980 census) & (rank): 7,364,823 (9)
1987 est. population (July 1) & (rank): 7,672,000 (9)
1980 land area & (rank): 7,468 sq mi. (19,342 sq km) (46)
Geographic center: In Mercer Co., 5 mi. SE of Trenton
Number of counties: 21
Largest cities (1980 census): Newark, 329,248; Jersey City, 223,532; Paterson, 137,970; Elizabeth, 106,201; Trenton, 92,124; Camden, 84,910; Clifton, 77,690
State forests: 11
State parks: 35 (67,111 ac.)
1987 percent pop. below age 15: 19
1987 percent pop. age 65 and over: 13
1987 violent crimes per 100,000 pop.: 541.0
1984 (fiscal year) immigrants: 27,148

New Jersey's early colonial history was involved with that of New York (New Netherlands), of which it was a part. One year after the Dutch surrender to England in 1664, New Jersey was organized as an English colony under Gov. Philip Carteret.

In the late 1600s the colony was divided between Carteret and William Penn; later it would be administered by the royal governor of New York. Finally, in 1738, New Jersey was separated from New York under its own royal governor, Lewis Morris.

Because of its key location between New York City and Philadelphia, New Jersey saw much fighting during the American Revolution.

Today, New Jersey, an area of wide industrial diversification, is known as the Crossroads of the East. Products from over 15,000 factories can be delivered overnight to almost 60 million people, representing 12 states and the District of Columbia. The greatest single industry is chemicals and New Jersey is one of the foremost research centers in the world. Many large oil refineries are located in northern New Jersey and other important manufactures are pharmaceuticals, instruments, machinery, electrical goods, and apparel.

Of the total land area, 37% is forested. Farmland is declining. In 1987 there were about 7,600 farms, with over 500,000 acres under harvest. The state ranks high in production of almost all garden vegetables. Tomatoes, asparagus, corn, and blueberries are important crops, and poultry farming and dairying make significant contributions to the state's economy.

Tourism is the second largest industry in New Jersey. The state has numerous resort areas on 127 miles of Atlantic coastline. In 1977, New Jersey voters approved legislation allowing legalized casino gambling in Atlantic City. Points of interest include the Walt Whitman House in Camden, the Delaware Water Gap, the Edison National Historic Site in West Orange, and Princeton University.

NEW MEXICO

Capital: Santa Fe
Governor: Garrey E. Carruthers, R (to Jan. 1990)
Lieut. Governor: Jack Stahl, R (to Jan. 1990)
Secy. of State: Rebecca Vigil-Giron, D (to Jan. 1990)
Atty. General: Hal Stratton, R (to Jan. 1990)
State Auditor: Harroll H. Adams, D (to Jan. 1990)
State Treasurer: James B. Lewis, D (to Jan. 1990)
Commissioner of Public Lands: William R. Humphries, R (to Jan. 1990)
Organized as territory: Sept. 9, 1850
Entered Union & (rank): Jan. 6, 1912 (47)
Present constitution adopted: 1911
Motto: *Crescit eundo* (It grows as it goes)
State flower: Yucca (1927)
State tree: Pinon (1949)
State animal: Black bear (1963)
State bird: Roadrunner (1949)
State fish: Cutthroat trout (1955)
State vegetables: Chile and frijol (1965)
State gem: Turquoise (1967)
State colors: Red and yellow of old Spain (1925)

State song: "O Fair New Mexico" (1917)
Spanish language state song: "Asi Es Nuevo Mejico" (1971)
Nicknames: Land of Enchantment; Sunshine State
Origin of name: From the country of Mexico
1980 population (1980 census) & (rank): 1,302,981 (37)
1987 est. population (July 1) & (rank): 1,500,000 (37)
1980 land area & (rank): 121,335 sq mi. (314,258 sq km) (5)
Geographic center: In Torrance Co., 12 mi. SSW of Willard
Number of counties: 33
Largest cities (July 1, 1984 est.): Albuquerque, 350,575; Santa Fe, 52,274; Las Cruces, 50,275; Roswell, 45,702; Farmington, 37,332; Hobbs, 35,029
State-owned forested land: 933,000 ac.
State parks: 29 (105,012 ac.)
1987 percent pop. below age 15: 25
1987 percent pop. age 65 and over: 10
1987 serious crimes per 100,000 pop.: 628.5
1984 (fiscal year) immigrants: 2,258

Francisco Vásquez de Coronado, Spanish explorer searching for gold, traveled the region that became New Mexico in 1540–42. In 1598 the first Spanish settlement was established on the Rio Grande River by Juan de Onate and in 1610 Santa Fe was founded and made the capital of New Mexico.

The U.S. acquired most of New Mexico in 1848, as a result of the Mexican War, and the remainder in the 1853 Gadsden Purchase. Union troops captured the territory from the Confederates during the Civil War. With the surrender of Geronimo in 1886, the Apache Wars and most of the Indian troubles in the area were ended.

Since 1945, New Mexico has been a leader in energy research and development with extensive experiments conducted at Los Alamos Scientific Laboratory and Sandia Laboratories in the nuclear, solar, and geothermal areas.

Minerals are the state's richest natural resource and New Mexico is one of the U.S. leaders in output of uranium and potassium salts. Petroleum, natural gas, copper, gold, silver, zinc, lead, and molybdenum also contribute heavily to the state's income.

The principal manufacturing industries include food products, chemicals, transportation equipment, lumber, electrical machinery, and stone-clay-glass products. More than two thirds of New Mexico's farm income comes from livestock products, especially sheep. Cotton, pecans, and sorghum are the most important field crops. Corn, peanuts, beans, onions, chile, and lettuce are also grown.

Tourist attractions in New Mexico include the Carlsbad Caverns National Park, Inscription Rock at El Morro National Monument, the ruins at Fort Union, Billy the Kid mementos at Lincoln, the White Sands and Gila Cliff Dwellings National Monuments, and the Chaco Culture National Historical Park.

NEW YORK

Capital: Albany
Governor: Mario M. Cuomo, D (to Jan. 1991)
Lieut. Governor: Stan Lundine, D (to Jan. 1991)
Secy. of State: Gail S. Shaffer, D (to Jan. 1991)
Comptroller: Edward V. Regan, R (to Jan. 1991)
Atty. General: Robert Abrams, D (to Jan. 1991)
Entered Union & (rank): July 26, 1788 (11)
Present constitution adopted: 1777 (last revised 1938)
Motto: *Excelsior* (Ever upward)
State animal: Beaver (1975)

State fish: Brook trout (1975)
State gem: Garnet (1969)
State flower: Rose (1955)
State tree: Sugar maple (1956)
State bird: Bluebird
State insect: Ladybug
State song: "I Love New York" (1980)
Nickname: Empire State
Origin of name: In honor of the English Duke of York
1980 population (1980 census) & (rank): 17,558,165 (2)
1987 est. population (July 1) & (rank): 17,825,000 (2)
1980 land area & (rank): 47,377 sq mi. (122,707 sq km) (30)
Geographic center: In Madison Co., 12 mi. S of Oneida and 26 mi. SW of Utica
Number of counties: 62
Largest cities (1986 est.): New York, 7,263,000; Buffalo, 324,820; Rochester, 235,970; Yonkers, 186,080; Syracuse, 160,750; Albany, 97,020; Utica, 69,440
State forest preserves: Adirondacks, 2,500,000 ac., Catskills, 250,000 ac.
State parks: 150 (250,000 ac.)
1987 percent pop. below age 15: 20
1987 percent pop. age 65 and over: 13
1987 violent crimes per 100,000 pop.: 1,008.1
1984 (fiscal year) immigrants: 107,056

Giovanni da Verrazano, Italian-born navigator sailing for France, discovered New York Bay in 1524. Henry Hudson, an Englishman employed by the Dutch, reached the bay and sailed up the river now bearing his name in 1609, the same year that northern New York was explored and claimed for France by Samuel de Champlain.

In 1624 the first permanent Dutch settlement was established at Fort Orange (now Albany); one year later Peter Minuit is said to have purchased Manhattan Island from the Indians for trinkets worth about $24 and founded the Dutch colony of New Amsterdam (now New York City), which was surrendered to the English in 1664.

For a short time, New York City was the U.S. capital and George Washington was inaugurated there as first President on April 30, 1789.

New York's extremely rapid commercial growth may be partly attributed to Governor De Witt Clinton, who pushed through the construction of the Erie Canal (Buffalo to Albany), which was opened in 1825. Today, the 559-mile Governor Thomas E. Dewey Thruway connects New York City with Buffalo and with Connecticut, Massachusetts, and Pennsylvania express highways. Two toll-free superhighways, the Adirondack Northway (linking Albany with the Canadian border) and the North-South-Expressway (crossing central New York from the Pennsylvania border to the Thousand Islands) have been opened.

New York, with the great metropolis of New York City, is the spectacular nerve center of the nation. It is a leader in manufacturing, foreign trade, commercial and financial transactions, book and magazine publishing, and theatrical production.

New York City is not only a national but an international leader. A leading seaport, its John F. Kennedy International Airport is one of the busiest airports in the world. The largest manufacturing center in the country, in 1982 its manufacturing establishments employed 529,000 persons. The apparel industry is the city's largest manufacturing employer, with printing and publishing second.

Nearly all the rest of the state's manufacturing is done on Long Island, along the Hudson River north to Albany and through the Mohawk Valley, Central New York, and Southern Tier regions to

Buffalo. The St. Lawrence seaway and power projects have opened the North Country to industrial expansion and have given the state a second seacoast.

The state ranks second in the nation in manufacturing with 1,221,900 employees in 1987. The principal industries are apparel, printing and publishing, leather products, instruments and electronic equipment.

The convention and tourist business is one of the state's most important sources of income.

New York farms are famous for raising cattle and calves, producing corn for grain, poultry, and the raising of vegetables and fruits. The state is a leading wine producer.

Among the major points of interest are Castle Clinton, Fort Stanwix, and Statue of Liberty National Monuments; Niagara Falls; U.S. Military Academy at West Point; National Historic Sites that include homes of Franklin D. Roosevelt at Hyde Park and Theodore Roosevelt in Oyster Bay and New York City; National Memorials, including Grant's Tomb and Federal Hall in New York City; Fort Ticonderoga; the Baseball Hall of Fame in Cooperstown; and the United Nations, skyscrapers, museums, theaters, and parks in New York City.

NORTH CAROLINA

Capital: Raleigh
Governor: James G. Martin, R (to Jan. 1993)
Lieut. Governor: James C. Gardner, R (to Jan. 1993)
Secy. of State: Rufus L. Edmisten, D (to Jan. 1993)
Treasurer: Harlan E. Boyles (to Jan. 1993)
Auditor: Edward Renfrow, D (to Jan. 1993)
Atty. General: Lacey H. Thornburg, D (to Jan. 1993)
Entered Union & (rank): Nov. 21, 1789 (12)
Present constitution adopted: 1971
Motto: *Esse quam videri* (To be rather than to seem)
State flower: Dogwood (1941)
State tree: Pine (1963)
State bird: Cardinal (1943)
State mammal: Gray Squirrel (1969)
State insect: Honeybee (1973)
State Reptile: Turtle (1979)
State gem stone: Emerald (1973)
State shell: Scotch bonnet (1965)
State song: "The Old North State" (1927)
State colors: Red and blue (1945)
Nickname: Tar Heel State
Origin of name: In honor of Charles I of England
1980 population (1980 census) & (rank): 5,881,766 (10)
1987 est. population (July 1) & (rank): 6,413,000 (10)
1980 land area & (rank): 48,843 sq mi. (126,504 sq km) (29)
Geographic center: In Chatham Co., 10 mi. NW of Sanford
Number of counties: 100
Largest cities (est. as of July 1, 1984): Charlotte, 338,107; Raleigh, 180,559; Greensboro, 159,744; Winston-Salem, 146,886; Durham, 106,115; High Point, 66,380
State forests: 1
State parks: 30 (125,000 ac.)
1987 percent pop. below age 15: 21
1987 percent pop. age 65 and over: 12
1987 violent crimes per 100,000 pop.: 484.0
1984 (fiscal year) immigrants: 3,207

English colonists, sent by Sir Walter Raleigh, unsuccessfully attempted to settle Roanoke Island in 1585 and 1587. Virginia Dare, born there in 1587, was the first child of English parentage born in America.

In 1653 the first permanent settlements were established by English colonists from Virginia near the Roanoke and Chowan Rivers.

The region was established as an English proprietary colony in 1663–65 and its early history was the scene of Culpepper's Rebellion (1677), the Quaker-led Cary Rebellion of 1708, the Tuscarora Indian War in 1711–13, and many pirate raids.

During the American Revolution, there was relatively little fighting within the state, but many North Carolinians saw action elsewhere. Despite considerable pro-Union, anti-slavery sentiment, North Carolina joined the Confederacy.

North Carolina is the nation's largest furniture, tobacco, brick, and textile producer. It holds second place in the Southeast in population and first place in the value of its industrial and agricultural production. This production is highly diversified, with metalworking, chemicals, and paper constituting enormous industries. Tobacco, corn, cotton, hay, peanuts, and truck and vegetable crops are of major importance. It is the country's leading producer of mica and lithium.

Tourism is also important, with travelers and vacationers spending more than $1 billion annually in North Carolina. Sports include year-round golfing, skiing at mountain resorts, both fresh and salt water fishing, and hunting.

Among the major attractions are the Great Smoky Mountains, the Blue Ridge National Parkway, the Cape Hatteras and Cape Lookout National Seashores, the Wright Brothers National Memorial at Kitty Hawk, Guilford Courthouse and Moores Creek National Military Parks, Carl Sandburg's home near Hendersonville, and the Old Salem Restoration in Winston-Salem.

NORTH DAKOTA

Capital: Bismarck
Governor: George A. Sinner, D (to Dec. 1992)
Lieut. Governor: Lloyd Omdahl, D (to Jan. 1993)
Secy. of State: Jim Kusler, D (to Jan. 1993)
Auditor: Robert W. Peterson, R (to Jan. 1993)
State Treasurer: Robert Hanson, D (to Jan. 1993)
Atty. General: Nicholas Spaeth, D (to Jan. 1993)
Organized as territory: March 2, 1861
Entered Union & (rank): Nov. 2, 1889 (39)
Present constitution adopted: 1889
Motto: Liberty and union, now and forever: one and inseparable
State tree: American Elm (1947)
State bird: Western meadow lark (1947)
State song: "North Dakota Hymn" (1947)
Nickname: Sioux State; Flickertail State, Peace Garden State
Origin of name: From the Dakotah tribe, meaning "allies"
1980 population (1980 census) & (rank): 652,717 (46)
1987 est. population (July 1) & (rank): 672,000 (46)
1980 land area & (rank): 70,665 sq mi. (183,022 sq km) (17)
Geographic center: In Sheridan Co., 5 mi. SW of McClusky
Number of counties: 53
Largest cities (1980 census): Fargo, 61,383; Bismarck, 44,485; Grand Forks, 43,765; Minot, 32,843; Jamestown, 16,280; Dickinson, 15,924; Mandan, 15,513
State forests: None
State parks: 14 (14,922.6 ac.)
1987 percent pop. below age 15: 24
1987 percent pop. age 65 and over: 13
1987 violent crimes per 100,000 pop.: 56.8
1984 (fiscal year) immigrants: 385

North Dakota was explored in 1738–40 by French Canadians led by Vérendrye. In 1803, the

U.S. acquired most of North Dakota from France in the Louisiana Purchase. Lewis and Clark explored the region in 1804–06 and the first settlements were made at Pembina in 1812 by Scottish and Irish families while this area was still in dispute between the U.S. and Great Britain.

In 1818, the U.S. obtained the northeastern part of North Dakota by treaty with Great Britain and took possession of Pembina in 1823.

North Dakota is the most rural of all the states, with farms covering more than 90% of the land. Only Kansas produces more wheat, and the state's coal and oil reserves are plentiful.

Other agricultural products include barley, rye, oats, and flaxseed, sugar beets, and hay; beef cattle, sheep, and hogs.

Recently, manufacturing industries have grown, especially food processing and farm equipment. The state also produces natural gas, lignite, salt, clay, sand, and gravel.

The Garrison Dam on the Missouri River provides extensive irrigation and produces 400,000 kilowatts of electricity for the Missouri Basin areas.

Known for its waterfowl, grouse, and deer hunting and bass, trout, and northern pike fishing, North Dakota has 20 state parks and recreation areas. Points of interest include the International Peace Garden near Dunseith, Fort Union Trading Post National Historic Site, the State Capitol at Bismarck, the Badlands, and Fort Lincoln, now a state park, from which Gen. George Custer set out on his last campaign in 1876.

OHIO

Capital: Columbus
Governor: Richard F. Celeste, D (to Jan. 1991)
Lieut. Governor: Paul Leonard, D (to Jan. 1991)
Secy. of State: Sherrod Brown, D (to Jan. 1991)
Auditor: Thomas E. Ferguson, D (to Jan. 1991)
Treasurer: Mary Ellen Withrow, D (to Jan. 1991)
Atty. General: Anthony J. Celebrezze, Jr., D (to Jan. 1991)
Entered Union & (rank): March 1, 1803 (17)
Present constitution adopted: 1851
Motto: With God, all things are possible
State flower: Scarlet carnation (1904)
State tree: Buckeye (1953)
State bird: Cardinal (1933)
State insect: Ladybug (1975)
State gem stone: Flint (1965)
State song: "Beautiful Ohio"
State drink: Tomato juice (1965)
Nickname: Buckeye State
Origin of name: From an Iroquoian word meaning "great river"
1980 population (1980 census) & (rank): 10,797,624 (6)
1987 est. population (July 1) & (rank): 10,784,000 (7)
1980 land area & (rank): 41,004 sq mi. (106,201 sq km) (35)
Geographic center: In Delaware Co., 25 mi. NNE of Columbus
Number of counties: 88
Largest cities (1980 census): Cleveland, 573,822; Columbus, 565,032; Cincinnati, 385,457; Toledo, 354,635; Akron, 237,177; Dayton, 203,371; Youngstown, 115,436
State forests: 19 (172,744 ac.)
State parks: 71 (198,027 ac.)
1987 percent pop. below age 15: 21
1987 percent pop. age 65 and over: 13
1987 violent crimes per 100,000 pop.: 421.3
1986 (fiscal year) immigrants: 7,289

First explored for France by La Salle in 1669, the Ohio region became British property after the French and Indian War. Ohio was acquired by the U.S. after the Revolutionary War in 1783 and, in 1788, the first permanent settlement was established at Marietta, capital of the Northwest Territory.

The 1790s saw severe fighting with the Indians in Ohio; a major battle was won by Maj. Gen. Anthony Wayne at Fallen Timbers in 1794. In the War of 1812, Commodore Oliver H. Perry defeated the British in the Battle of Lake Erie on Sept. 10, 1813.

Ohio is one of the nation's industrial leaders, ranking third in the value of manufactured products. Important manufacturing centers are located in or near Ohio's major cities. Akron is known for rubber; Canton for roller bearings; Cincinnati for jet engines and machine tools; Cleveland for auto assembly and parts, refining, and steel; Dayton for office machines, refrigeration, and heating and auto equipment; Youngstown and Steubenville for steel; and Toledo for glass and auto parts.

The state's thousands of factories almost overshadow its importance in agriculture and mining. Its fertile soil produces soybeans, corn, oats, grapes, and clover. More than half of Ohio's farm receipts come from dairying and sheep and hog raising. Ohio is the top state in lime production and among the leaders in coal, clay, salt, sand, and gravel. Petroleum, gypsum, cement, and natural gas are also important.

Tourism is a valuable revenue producer, bringing in over $3 billion annually. Attractions include the Indian burial grounds at Mound City Group National Monument, Perry's Victory International Peace Memorial, the Pro Football Hall of Fame at Canton, and the homes of Presidents Grant, Taft, Hayes, Harding, and Garfield.

OKLAHOMA

Capital: Oklahoma City
Governor: Henry Bellmon, R (to Jan. 1991)
Lieut. Governor: Robert S. Kerr, III, D (to Jan. 1991)
Secy. of State: Hannah Diggs Atkins, D (to Jan. 1991)
Treasurer: Ellis Edwards, D (to Jan. 1991)
Atty. General: Robert Henry, D (to Jan. 1991)
Organized as territory: May 2, 1890
Entered Union & (rank): Nov. 16, 1907 (46)
Present constitution adopted: 1907
Motto: *Labor omnia vincit* (Labor conquers all things)
State flower: Mistletoe (1893)
State tree: Redbud (1937)
State bird: Scissor-tailed flycatcher (1951)
State animal: Bison (1972)
State reptile: Mountain boomer lizard (1969)
State stone: Rose Rock (barite rose) (1968)
State colors: Green and white (1915)
State song: "Oklahoma" (1953)
Nickname: Sooner State
Origin of name: From two Choctaw Indian words meaning "red people"
1980 population (1980 census) & (rank): 3,025,290 (26)
1987 est. population (July 1) & (rank): 3,272,000 (27)
1980 land area & (rank): 68,655 sq mi. (177,817 sq km) (19)
Geographic center: In Oklahoma Co., 8 mi. N of Oklahoma City
Number of counties: 77
Largest cities (1980 census): Oklahoma City, 403,213; Tulsa, 360,919; Lawton, 80,054; Norman, 68,020; Enid, 50,363; Midwest City, 49,559; Muskogee, 40,011

State forests: None
State parks: 36 (57,487 ac.)
1987 percent pop. below age 15: 23
1987 percent pop. age 65 and over: 13
1987 violent crimes per 100,000 pop.: 417.6
1984 (fiscal year) immigrants: 4,915

Francisco Vásquez de Coronado first explored the region for Spain in 1541. The U.S. acquired most of Oklahoma in 1803 in the Louisiana Purchase from France; the Western Panhandle region became U.S. territory with the annexation of Texas in 1845.

Set aside as Indian Territory in 1834, the region was divided into Indian Territory and Oklahoma Territory on May 2, 1890. The two were combined to make a new state, Oklahoma, on Nov. 16, 1907.

On April 22, 1889, the first day homesteading was permitted, 50,000 people swarmed into the area. Those who tried to beat the noon starting gun were called "Sooners." Hence the state's nickname.

Oil made Oklahoma a rich state, but natural gas production has now surpassed it. Oil refining, meat packing, food processing, and machinery manufacturing (especially construction and oil equipment) are important industries.

Other minerals produced in Oklahoma include helium, gypsum, zinc, cement, coal, copper, and silver.

Oklahoma's rich plains produce bumper yields of wheat, as well as large crops of sorghum, hay, cotton, and peanuts. More than half of Oklahoma's annual farm receipts are contributed by livestock products, including cattle, dairy products, and poultry.

Tourist attractions include the National Cowboy Hall of Fame in Oklahoma City, the Will Rogers Memorial in Claremore, the Cherokee Cultural Center with a restored Cherokee village, the restored Fort Gibson Stockade near Muskogee, and the Lake Texoma recreation area.

OREGON

Capital: Salem
Governor: Neil Goldschmidt, D (to Jan. 1991)
Secy. of State: Barbara Roberts, R (to Jan. 1993)
Treasurer: Tony Meeker, R (to Jan. 1993)
Atty. General: David B. Frohnmayer, R (to Jan. 1993)
Organized as territory: Aug. 14, 1848
Entered Union & (rank): Feb. 14, 1859 (33)
Present constitution adopted: 1859
Motto: "Alis volat Propriis" ("She flies with her own wings") (1987)
State flower: Oregon grape (1899)
State tree: Douglas fir (1939)
State animal: Beaver (1969)
State bird: Western meadow lark (1927)
State fish: Chinook salmon (1961)
State rock: Thunderegg (1965)
State colors: Navy blue and gold (1959)
State song: "Oregon, My Oregon" (1927)
Nickname: Beaver State
Poet Laureate: William E. Stafford (1974)
Origin of name: Unknown. However, it is generally accepted that the name, first used by Jonathan Carver in 1778, was taken from the writings of Maj. Robert Rogers, an English army officer.
1980 population (1980 census) & (rank): 2,633,105 (30)
1987 est. population (July 1) & (rank): 2,724,000 (30)
1980 land area & (rank): 96,184 sq mi. (249,117 sq km) (10)

Geographic center: In Crook Co., 25 mi. SSE of Prineville
Number of counties: 36
Largest cities (est. as of July 1, 1985): Portland, 379,000; Eugene, 106,100; Salem, 94,600; Medford, 41,975; Springfield, 40,690
State forests: 820,000 ac.
State parks: 240 (93,330 ac.)
1985 percent pop. below age 15: 21
1985 percent pop. age 65 and over: 14
1987 violent crimes per 100,000 pop.: 539.5
1984 (fiscal year) immigrants: 4,342

Spanish and English sailors are believed to have sighted the Oregon coast in the 1500s and 1600s. Capt. James Cook, seeking the Northwest Passage, charted some of the coastline in 1778. In 1792, Capt. Robert Gray, in the *Columbia*, discovered the river named after his ship and claimed the area for the U.S.

In 1805 the Lewis and Clark expedition explored the area and John Jacob Astor's fur depot, Astoria, was founded in 1811. Disputes for control of Oregon between American settlers and the Hudson Bay Company were finally resolved in the 1846 Oregon Treaty in which Great Britain gave up claims to the region.

Oregon has a five-billion-dollar wood processing industry. Its salmon-fishing industry is one of the world's largest.

In agriculture, the state leads in growing peppermint, winter pears, fresh plums, prunes, blackberries, boysenberries, filberts, Blue Lake beans, and cover seed crops, and also raises strawberries, hops, wheat and other grains, sugar beets, potatoes, green peas, fiber flax, dairy products, livestock and poultry, apples, pears, and cherries. Oregon is the source of all the nickel produced in the U.S.

With the low-cost electric power provided by Bonneville Dam, McNary Dam, and other dams in the Pacific Northwest, Oregon has developed steadily as a manufacturing state. Leading manufactures are lumber and plywood, metalwork, machinery, aluminum, chemicals, paper, food packing, and electronic equipment.

Crater Lake National Park, Mount Hood, and Bonneville Dam on the Columbia are major tourist attractions. Oregon Dunes National Recreation Area has been established near Florence. Other points of interest include the Oregon Caves National Monument, Cape Perpetua in Siuslaw National Forest, Columbia River Gorge between The Dalles and Troutdale, and Hells Canyon.

PENNSYLVANIA

Capital: Harrisburg
Governor: Robert P. Casey, D (to Jan. 1991)
Lieut. Governor: Mark S. Singel, D (to Jan. 1991)
Secy. of the Commonwealth: James J. Haggerty, D (at the pleasure of the Governor)
Auditor General: Barbara Hafe, R (to Jan. 1993)
Atty. General: Ernest D. Preate, Jr., R (to Jan. 1993)
Entered Union & (rank): Dec. 12, 1787 (2)
Present constitution adopted: 1874
Motto: Virtue, liberty, and independence
State flower: Mountain laurel (1933)
State tree: Hemlock (1931)
State bird: Ruffed grouse (1931)
State dog: Great Dane (1965)
State colors: Blue and gold
State song: None
Nickname: Keystone State

Origin of name: In honor of Adm. Sir. William Penn, father of William Penn. It means "Penn's Woodland."
1980 population (1980 census) & (rank): 11,863,895 (4)
1987 est. population (July 1) & (rank): 11,936,000 (5)
1980 land area & (rank): 44,888 sq mi. (116,260 sq km) (32)
Geographic center: In Centre Co., 2 1/2 mi. SW of Bellefonte
Number of counties: 67
Largest cities (1980 census): Philadelphia, 1,688,210; Pittsburgh, 423,959; Erie, 119,123; Allentown, 103,758; Scranton, 88,117; Reading, 78,686; Bethlehem, 70,419
State forests: 1,930,108 ac.
State parks: 120 (297,438 ac.)
1987 percent pop. below age 15: 19
1987 percent pop. age 65 and over: 15
1987 violent crimes per 100,000 pop.: 369.4
1984 (fiscal year) immigrants: 9,801

Rich in historic lore, Pennsylvania territory was disputed in the early 1600s among the Dutch, the Swedes, and the English. England acquired the region in 1664 with the capture of New York and in 1681 Pennsylvania was granted to William Penn, a Quaker, by King Charles II.

Philadelphia was the seat of the federal government almost continuously from 1776 to 1800; there the Declaration of Independence was signed in 1776 and the U.S. Constitution drawn up in 1787. Valley Forge, of Revolutionary War fame, and Gettysburg, the turning-point of the Civil War, are both in Pennsylvania. The Liberty Bell is located in a glass pavilion across from Independence Hall in Philadelphia.

With the decline of the coal, steel and railroad industries, Pennsylvania's industry has diversified, though the state still leads the country in the production of specialty steel. Pennsylvania is a leader in the production of chemicals, food, and electrical machinery and produces 10% of the nation's cement. Also important are brick and tiles, glass, limestone, and slate. Data processing is also increasingly important.

Pennsylvania's nine million agricultural acres produce a wide variety of crops. Leading products are milk, poultry and eggs, a variety of fruits, sweet corn, potatoes, mushrooms, cheese, beans, and even Christmas trees.

Tourists now spend approximately $6 billion in Pennsylvania annually. Among the chief attractions: the Gettysburg National Military Park, Valley Forge National Historical Park, Independence National Historical Park in Philadelphia, the Pennsylvania Dutch region, the Eisenhower farm near Gettysburg, and the Delaware Water Gap National Recreation Area.

RHODE ISLAND

Capital: Providence
Governor: Edward D. DiPrete, R (to Jan. 1991)
Lieut. Governor: Roger N. Begin (to Jan. 1991)
Secy. of State: Kathleen S. Connell, D (to Jan. 1991)
Controller: Lawrence Franklin, Jr. (civil service)
Atty. General: James E. O'Neil, D (to Jan. 1991)
Entered Union & (rank): May 29, 1790 (13)
Present constitution adopted: 1843
Motto: Hope
State flower: Violet (unofficial)
State tree: Red maple (official)
State bird: Rhode Island Red (official)

State colors: Blue, white, and gold (in state flag)
State song: "Rhode Island" (1946)
Nickname: The Ocean State
Origin of name: From the Greek Island of Rhodes
1980 population (1980 census) & (rank): 947,154 (40)
1987 est. population (July 1) & (rank): 986,000 (43)
1980 land area & (rank): 1,055 sq mi. (2,732 sq km) (50)
Geographic center: In Kent Co., 1 mi. SSW of Crompton
Number of counties: 5
Largest cities (1980 census): Providence, 156,804; Warwick, 87,123; Cranston, 71,992; Pawtucket, 71,204; East Providence, 50,980; Woonsocket, 45,914
State forests: 11 (20,900 ac.)
State parks: 17 (8,200 ac.)
1987 percent pop. below age 15: 19
1987 percent pop. age 65 and over: 15
1987 violent crimes per 100,000 pop.: 359.7
1984 (fiscal year) immigrants: 2,666

From its beginnings, Rhode Island has been distinguished by its support for freedom of conscience and action, started by Roger Williams, who was exiled by the Massachusetts Bay Colony Puritans in 1636, and was the founder of the present state capital, Providence. Williams was followed by other religious exiles who founded Pocasset, now Portsmouth, in 1638 and Newport in 1639.

The first Baptist church in the U.S. was established in Providence in 1638 and Rhode Island provided a haven for Quakers in 1657 and for Jews from Holland in 1659.

Rhode Island's rebellious, authority-defying nature was further demonstrated by the burnings of the British revenue cutters *Liberty* and *Gaspee* prior to the Revolution, by its early declaration of independence from Great Britain in May 1776, its refusal to participate actively in the War of 1812, and by Dorr's Rebellion of 1842, which protested property requirements for voting.

Rhode Island, smallest of the 50 states, is densely populated and highly industrialized. The state pioneered in the manufacture of jewelry and silverware and still retains first place in the U.S. Other leading industries are primary metal processing, metal products, machinery, rubber and plastics, food processing, chemicals, transportation equipment and electronic equipment.

With more than eight tenths of the population living in urban areas, adjacent areas of the state are involved in dairying and poultry and truck farming. Nursery and greenhouse products, potatoes, corn, apples, oats, and hay lead the crop list.

Newport became famous as the summer capital of society in the mid-19th century. Touro Synagogue (1763) is the oldest in the U.S. Other points of interest include the Roger Williams National Memorial in Providence, Samuel Slater's Mill in Pawtucket, the General Nathaniel Greene Homestead in Coventry and Block Island.

SOUTH CAROLINA

Capital: Columbia
Governor: Carroll Campbell, R (to Jan. 1991)
Lieut. Governor: Nick Theodore, D (to Jan. 1991)
Secy. of State: John T. Campbell, D (to Jan. 1991)
Comptroller General: Earl E. Morris, Jr. (to Jan. 1991)
Atty. General: T. Travis Medlock, D (to Jan. 1991)
Entered Union & (rank): May 23, 1788 (8).
Present constitution adopted: 1895
Mottoes: *Animis opibusque parati* (Prepared in mind and

resources) and *Dum spiro spero* (While I breathe, I hope)
State flower: Carolina yellow jessamine (1924)
State tree: Palmetto tree (1939)
State bird: Carolina wren (1948)
State song: "Carolina" (1911)
Nickname: Palmetto State
Origin of name: In honor of Charles I of England
1980 population (1980 census) & (rank): 3,121,833 (24)
1987 est. population (July 1) & (rank): 3,425,000 (24)
1980 land area & (rank): 30,203 sq mi. (78,227 sq km) (40)
Geographic center: In Richland Co., 13 mi. SE of Columbia
Number of counties: 46
Largest cities (1980 census): Columbia, 100,385; Charleston, 69,510; North Charleston, 62,534; Greenville, 58,242; Spartanburg, 43,826; Rock Hill, 35,344
State forests: 4 (124,052 ac.)
State parks: 50 (61,726 ac.)
1987 percent pop. age 15: 23
1987 percent pop. age 65 and over: 11
1987 violent crimes per 100,000 pop.: 664.9
1984 (fiscal year) immigrants: 1,677

Following exploration of the coast in 1521 by De Gordillo, the Spanish tried unsuccessfully to establish a colony near present-day Georgetown in 1526 and the French also failed to colonize Parris Island near Fort Royal in 1562.

The first English settlement was made in 1670 at Albemarle Point on the Ashley River, but poor conditions drove the settlers to the site of Charleston (originally called Charles Town). South Carolina, officially separated from North Carolina in 1729, was the scene of extensive military action during the Revolution and again during the Civil War. The Civil War began in 1861 as South Carolina troops fired on federal Fort Sumter in Charleston Harbor and the state was the first to secede from the Union.

Once primarily agricultural, South Carolina has built so many large textile and other mills that today its factories produce eight times the output of its farms in cash value. Charleston makes asbestos, wood, pulp, and steel products; chemicals, machinery, and apparel are also important.

Farms have become fewer but larger in recent years. South Carolina grows more peaches than any other state except California; it ranks fourth in tobacco. Other farm products include cotton, peanuts, sweet potatoes, soybeans, corn, and oats. Poultry and dairy products are also important revenue producers.

Points of interest include Fort Sumter National Monument, Fort Moultrie, Fort Johnson, and aircraft carrier USS *Yorktown* in Charleston Harbor; the Middleton, Magnolia, and Cypress Gardens in Charleston; Cowpens National Battlefield; and the Hilton Head resorts.

SOUTH DAKOTA

Capital: Pierre
Governor: George S. Mickelson, R (to Jan. 1991)
Lieut. Governor: Walter Dale Miller, R (to Jan. 1991)
Atty. General: Roger Tellinghuisen, R (to Jan. 1991)
Secy. of State: Joyce Hazeltine, R (to Jan. 1991)
State Auditor: Vern Larson, R (to Jan. 1991)
State Treasurer: David L. Volk, R (to Jan. 1991)
Organized as territory: March 2, 1861
Entered Union & (rank): Nov. 2, 1889 (40)

Present constitution adopted: 1889
Motto: Under God the people rule
State flower: American pasqueflower (1903)
State grass: Western wheat grass (1970)
State tree: Black Hills spruce (1947)
State bird: Ring-necked pheasant (1943)
State insect: Honeybee (1978)
State animal: Coyote (1949)
State mineral stone: Rose quartz (1966)
State gem stone: Fairburn agate (1966)
State colors: Blue and gold (in state flag)
State song: "Hail! South Dakota" (1943)
State fish: Walleye (1982)
Nicknames: Sunshine State; Coyote State
Origin of name: Same as for North Dakota
1980 population (1980 census) & (rank): 690,768 (45)
1987 est. population (July 1) & (rank): 709,000 (45)
1980 land area & (rank): 75,952 sq mi. (196,715 sq km) (16)
Geographic center: In Hughes Co., 8 mi. NE of Pierre
Number of counties: 67 (64 county governments)
Largest cities (1980 census): Sioux Falls, 81,343; Rapid City, 46,492; Aberdeen, 25,851; Watertown, 15,649; Brookings, 14,951; Mitchell, 13,916; Huron, 13,000
State forests: None[1]
State parks: 13 plus 39 recreational areas (87,269 ac.)[2]
1987 percent pop. below age 15: 23
1987 percent pop. age 65 and over: 14
1987 violent crimes per 100,000 pop.: 119.7
1984 (fiscal year) immigrants: 293

1. No designated state forests; about 13,000 ac. of state land is forestland. 2. Acreage includes 39 recreation areas and 80 roadside parks, in addition to 12 state parks.

Exploration of this area began in 1743 when Louis-Joseph and François Verendrye came from France in search of a route to the Pacific.

The U.S. acquired the region as part of the Louisiana Purchase in 1803 and it was explored by Lewis and Clark in 1804–06. Fort Pierre, the first permanent settlement, was established in 1817 and, in 1831, the first Missouri River steamboat reached the fort.

Settlement of South Dakota did not begin in earnest until the arrival of the railroad in 1873 and the discovery of gold in the Black Hills the following year.

In 1988, South Dakota ranked first in rye production. It also ranked among the top five states in sheep and lambs, lamb crop, durum wheat, spring wheat, flaxseed, sunflower seeds, all hay, alfalfa hay, oats, and honey. In 1987, the state boasted 3,500,000 cattle, 610,000 sheep, and 1,520,000 hogs.

South Dakota is the nation's second leading producer of gold (Nevada ranks first) and the Homestake Mine is the richest in the U.S. Other minerals produced include berylium, bentonite, granite, silver, petroleum, and uranium.

Processing of foods produced by farms and ranches is the largest South Dakota manufacturing industry, followed by lumber, wood products, and machinery, including farm equipment.

The Black Hills are the highest mountains east of the Rockies. Mt. Rushmore, in this group, is famous for the likenesses of Washington, Jefferson, Lincoln, and Theodore Roosevelt, which were carved in granite by Gutzon Borglum. The Badlands offer scenic masses of bare rock and clay unrelieved by any vegetation. Other points of interest are Deadwood, where Wild Bill Hickok was killed in 1876; the Crazy Horse Memorial near Custer; and the Corn Palace in Mitchell.

TENNESSEE

Capital: Nashville
Governor: Ned Ray McWherther, D (to Jan. 1991)
Lieut. Governor: John S. Wilder, D (to Jan. 1991)
Secy. of State: Gentry Crowell, D (to Jan. 1991)
Atty. General: Charles W. Burson, D (Jan. 1991)
State Treasurer: Steve Adams, D (to Jan. 1991)
Entered Union & (rank): June 1, 1796 (16)
Present constitution adopted: 1870; amended 1953
   1960, 1966, 1972, 1978
Motto: "Tennessee—America at its best!" (1965)
State flower: Iris (1933)
State tree: Tulip poplar (1947)
State bird: Mockingbird (1933)
State horse: Tennessee walking horse
State animal: Raccoon
State wild flower: Passion flower
State song: "Tennessee Waltz" (1965)
Nickname: Volunteer State
Origin of name: Of Cherokee origin; the exact meaning is
   unknown
1980 population (1980 census) & (rank): 4,591,120 (17)
1987 est. population (July 1) & (rank): 4,855,000 (16)
1980 land area & (rank): 41,155 sq mi. (106,591 sq km)
   (34)
Geographic center: In Rutherford Co., 5 mi. NE of
   Murfreesboro
Number of counties: 95
Largest cities (1980 census): Memphis, 646,174;
   Nashville, 455,651; Knoxville, 175,045; Chattanooga,
   169,558; Clarksville, 54,777; Jackson, 49,131
State forests: 14 (155,752 ac.)
State parks: 21 (130,000 ac.)
1987 percent pop. below age 15: 21
1987 percent pop. age 65 and over: 12
1987 violent crimes per 100,000 pop.: 533.5
1984 (fiscal year) immigrants: 2,065

First visited by the Spanish explorer de Soto in 1541, the Tennessee area would later be claimed by both France and England as a result of the 1670s and 1680s explorations of Marquette and Joliet, La Salle, and the Englishmen James Needham and Gabriel Arthur.

Great Britain obtained the region following the French and Indian War in 1763 and it was rapidly occupied by settlers moving in from Virginia and the Carolinas.

During 1784–87, the settlers formed the "state" of Franklin, which was disbanded when the region was allowed to send representatives to the North Carolina legislature. In 1790 Congress organized the territory south of the Ohio River and Tennessee joined the Union in 1796.

Although Tennessee joined the Confederacy during the Civil War, there was much pro-Union sentiment in the state, which was the scene of extensive military action.

The state is now predominantly industrial; in 1970, 58.8% of its population lived in urban areas. Among the most important products are chemicals, textiles, apparel, electrical machinery, furniture, and leather goods. Other lines include food processing, lumber, primary metals, and metal products. The state is known as the U.S. hardwood-flooring center and ranks first in the production of marble, zinc, pyrite, and ball clay.

Tennessee is one of the leading tobacco-producing states in the nation and its farming income is also derived from livestock and dairy products as well as corn, cotton, and soybeans.

With six other states, Tennessee shares the extensive federal reservoir developments on the Tennessee and Cumberland River systems. The Tennessee Valley Authority operates a number of dams and reservoirs in the state.

Among the major points of interest: the Andrew Johnson National Historic Site at Greenville, American Museum of Atomic Energy at Oak Ridge, Great Smoky Mountains National Park, The Hermitage (home of Andrew Jackson near Nashville), Rock City Gardens near Chattanooga, and three National Military Parks.

TEXAS

Capital: Austin
Governor: William P. Clements, R (to Jan. 1991)
Lieut. Governor: William P. Hobby, D (to Jan. 1991)
Secy. of State: George Bayoud, R (Apptd. by Govr.)
Treasurer: Ann W. Richards, D (to Jan. 1991)
Comptroller: Bob Bullock, D (to Jan. 1991)
Atty. General: Jim Mattox, D (to Jan. 1991)
Entered Union & (rank): Dec. 29, 1845 (28)
Present constitution adopted: 1876
Motto: Friendship
State flower: Bluebonnet (1901)
State tree: Pecan (1919)
State bird: Mockingbird (1927)
State song: "Texas, Our Texas" (1930)
State fish: Guadalupe bass (1989)
State seashell: Lightning whelk (1987)
Nickname: Lone Star State
Origin of name: From an Indian word meaning "friends"
1980 population (1980 census) & (rank): 14,229,288 (3)
1987 est. population (July 1) & (rank): 16,789,000 (3)
1980 land area & (rank): 262,017 sq mi. (678,623 sq
   km) (2)
Geographic center: In McCulloch Co., 15 mi. NE of Brady
Number of counties: 254
Largest cities (1980 census): Houston, 1,595,138; Dallas,
   904,078; San Antonio, 785,023; El Paso, 425,259; Fort
   Worth, 385,164; Austin, 345,496
State forests: 4 (6,306 ac.)
State parks: 83 (64 developed)
1987 percent pop. below age 15: 25
1987 percent pop. age 65 and over: 10
1987 violent crimes per 100,000 pop.: 631.1
1984 (fiscal year) immigrants: 42,180

Spanish explorers, including Cabeza de Vaca and Coronado, were the first to visit the region in the 16th and 17th centuries, settling at Ysleta near El Paso in 1682. In 1685, La Salle established a short-lived French colony at Matagorda Bay.

Americans, led by Stephen F. Austin, began to settle along the Brazos River in 1821 when Texas was controlled by Mexico, recently independent from Spain. In 1836, following a brief war between the American settlers in Texas and the Mexican government, and famous for the battles of the Alamo and San Jacinto, the Independent Republic of Texas was proclaimed with Sam Houston as president.

After Texas became the 28th U.S. state in 1845, border disputes led to the Mexican War of 1846–48.

Today, Texas, second only to Alaska in land area, leads all other states in such categories as oil, cattle, sheep, and cotton. Possessing enormous natural resources, Texas is a major agricultural state and an industrial giant.

Sulfur, salt, helium, asphalt, graphite, bromine, natural gas, cement, and clays give Texas first place in mineral production. Chemicals, oil refining, food processing, machinery, and transportation equipment are among the major Texas manufacturing industries.

Texas ranches and farms produce beef cattle, poultry, rice, pecans, peanuts, sorghum, and an extensive variety of fruits and vegetables.

Millions of tourists spend well over $2 billion annually visiting more than 70 state parks, recreation areas, and points of interest such as the Gulf Coast resort area, the Lyndon B. Johnson Space Center in Houston, the Alamo in San Antonio, the state capital in Austin, and the Big Bend and Guadalupe Mountains National Parks.

UTAH

Capital: Salt Lake City
Governor: Norman H. Bangerter, R (to Jan. 1993)
Lieut. Governor: W. Val Oveson, R (to Jan. 1993)
Atty. General: David Wilkinson, R (to Jan. 1993)
Organized as territory: Sept. 9, 1850
Entered Union & (rank): Jan. 4, 1896 (45)
Present constitution adopted: 1896
Motto: Industry
State flower: Sego lily (1911)
State tree: Blue spruce (1933)
State bird: Seagull (1955)
State emblem: Beehive
State song: "Utah, We Love Thee"
Nickname: Beehive State
Origin of name: From the Ute tribe, meaning "people of the mountains"
1970 population & (rank): 1,059,273 (36)
1980 population (1980 census) & (rank): 1,461,037 (36)
1987 est. population (July 1) & (rank): 1,680,000 (35)
1980 land area & (rank): 82,073 sq mi. (212,569 sq km) (12)
Geographic center: In Sanpete Co., 3 mi. N. of Manti
Number of counties: 29
Largest cities (1980 census): Salt Lake City, 163,697; Provo, 52,210; Ogden, 64,407; Orem, 52,399; Sandy City, 52,210; Bountiful, 32,877; West Jordan, 27,192; Logan, 26,844; Murray, 25,750
State forests: None
State parks: 44 (64,097 ac.)
1987 percent pop. below age 15: 32
1987 percent pop. age 65 and over: 8
1987 violent crimes per 100,000 pop.: 229.8
1984 (fiscal year) immigrants: 2,746

The region was first explored for Spain by Franciscan friars, Escalante and Dominguez in 1776. In 1824 the famous American frontiersman Jim Bridger discovered the Great Salt Lake.

Fleeing the religious persecution encountered in eastern and middle-western states, the Mormons reached the Great Salt Lake in 1847 and began to build Salt Lake City. The U.S. acquired the Utah region in the treaty ending the Mexican War in 1848 and the first transcontinental railroad was completed with the driving of a golden spike at Promontory Point in 1869.

Mormon difficulties with the federal government about polygamy did not end until the Mormon Church renounced the practice in 1890, six years before Utah became a state.

In recent years, manufacturing has become Utah's most important industry, ahead of mining, agriculture, and tourism. The state's factories produce transportation equipment, food products, machinery, metal products, and electrical equipment. Utah has also become an important aerospace research and production center and is a leading warehousing and distribution point for much of the western U.S.

Rich in natural resources, Utah has long been a leading producer of copper, gold, silver, lead, zinc, and molybdenum. Oil has also become a major product; with Colorado and Wyoming, Utah shares what have been called the world's richest oil shale deposits.

Ranked eighth among the states in number of sheep in 1973, Utah also produces large crops of apricots and cherries as well as sugar beets, potatoes, onions, alfalfa, winter wheat, and beans. Utah's farmlands and crops require extensive irrigation.

Utah is a great vacationland with 11,000 miles of fishing streams and 147,000 acres of lakes and reservoirs. Among the many tourist attractions are Arches, Bryce Canyon, Canyonlands, Capitol Reef, and Zion National Parks; Dinosaur, Natural Bridges, and Rainbow Bridge National Monuments; the Mormon Tabernacle in Salt Lake City; and Monument Valley.

VERMONT

Capital: Montpelier
Governor: Madeleine M. Kunin, D (to Jan. 1991)
Lieut. Governor: Howard B. Dean, D (to Jan. 1991)
Secy. of State: James H. Douglas, R (to Jan. 1991)
Treasurer: Paul W. Ruse, Jr., D (to Jan. 1991)
Auditor of Accounts: Alexander V. Acebo, R (to Jan. 1991)
Atty. General: Jeffrey L. Amestoy, R (to Jan. 1991)
Entered Union & (rank): March 4, 1791 (14)
Present constitution adopted: 1793
Motto: Vermont, Freedom, and Unity
State flower: Red clover (1894)
State tree: Sugar maple (1949)
State bird: Hermit thrush (1941)
State animal: Morgan horse (1961)
State insect: Honeybee (1978)
State song: "Hail, Vermont!" (1938)
Nickname: Green Mountain State
Origin of name: From the French "vert mont," meaning "green mountain"
1980 population (1980 census) & (rank): 511,456 (48)
1987 est. population (July 1) & (rank): 548,000 (48)
1980 land area & (rank): 9,273 sq mi. (24,017 sq km) (43)
Geographic center: In Washington Co., 3 mi. E of Roxbury
Number of counties: 14
Largest cities (1980 census): Burlington, 37,712; Rutland, 18,436; South Burlington, 10,679; Barre, 9,824; Montpelier, 8,241; St. Albans, 7,308; Winooski, 6,318
State forests: 34 (113,953 ac.)
State parks: 45 (31,325 ac.)
1987 percent pop. below age 15: 21
1987 percent pop. age 65 and over: 12
1987 violent crimes per 100,000 pop.: 136.5
1984 (fiscal year) immigrants: 406

The Vermont region was explored and claimed for France by Samuel de Champlain in 1609 and the first French settlement was established at Fort Ste. Anne in 1666. The first English settlers moved into the area in 1724 and built Fort Drummer on the site of present-day Brattleboro. England gained control of the area in 1763 after the French and Indian War.

First organized to drive settlers from New York out of Vermont, the Green Mountain Boys, led by Ethan Allen, won fame by capturing Fort Ticonderoga from the British on May 10, 1775, in the early days of the Revolution.

In 1777 Vermont adopted its first constitution abolishing slavery and providing for universal male suffrage without property qualifications. In 1791 Vermont became the first state after the original 13 to join the Union.

Vermont leads the nation in the production of monument granite, marble, and maple syrup. It is also a leader in the production of asbestos and talc.

In ratio to population, Vermont keeps more dairy cows than any other state. Vermont's soil is devoted to dairying, truck farming, and fruit growing because the rugged, rocky terrain discourages extensive farming.

Principal industrial products include electrical equipment, fabricated metal products, printing and publishing, and paper and allied products.

Tourism is a major industry in Vermont. Vermont's many famous ski areas include Stowe, Killington, Mt. Snow, Bromley, Jay Peak, and Sugarbush. Hunting and fishing also attract many visitors to Vermont each year. Among the many points of interest are the Green Mountain National Forest, Bennington Battle Monument, the Calvin Coolidge Homestead at Plymouth, and the Marble Exhibit in Proctor.

VIRGINIA

Capital: Richmond
Governor: Gerald L. Baliles, D (to Jan. 1990)
Lieut. Governor: L. Douglas Wilder, D (to Jan. 1990)
Secy. of the Commonwealth: Sandra D. Bowen (apptd. by governor)
Comptroller: Edward J. Mazur (apptd. by governor)
Atty. General: Mary Sue Terry, D (to Jan. 1990)
Entered Union & (rank): June 25, 1788 (10)
Present constitution adopted: 1970
Motto: *Sic semper tyrannis* (Thus always to tyrants)
State flower: American dogwood (1918)
State bird: Cardinal (1950)
State dog: American foxhound (1966)
State shell: Oyster shell
State song: "Carry Me Back to Old Virginia" (1940)
Nicknames: The Old Dominion; Mother of Presidents
Origin of name: In honor of Elizabeth "Virgin Queen" of England
1980 population (1980 census) & (rank): 5,346,818 (14)
1987 est. population (July 1) & (rank): 5,904,000 (12)
1980 land area & (rank): 39,704 sq mi. (102,832 sq km) (36)
Geographic center: In Buckingham Co., 5 mi. SW of Buckingham
Number of counties: 95, plus 41 independent cities
Largest cities (1980 census): Norfolk, 266,979; Virginia Beach, 262,199; Richmond, 219,214; Newport News, 144,903; Hampton, 122,617; Chesapeake, 114,486
State forests: 8 (49,566 ac.)
State parks and recreational parks: 27, plus 3 in process of acquisition and/or development (42,722 ac.)[1]
1987 percent pop. below age 15: 20
1987 percent pop. age 65 and over: 11
1987 violent crimes per 100,000 pop.: 295.0
1984 (fiscal year) immigrants: 9,528

1. Does not include portion of Breaks Interstate Park (Va.-Ky., 1,200 ac.) which lies in Virginia.

The history of America is closely tied to that of Virginia, particularly in the Colonial period. Jamestown, founded in 1607, was the first permanent English settlement in North America and slavery was introduced there in 1619. The surrenders ending both the American Revolution (Yorktown) and the Civil War (Appomattox) occurred in Virginia. The state is called the "Mother of Presidents" be-

cause eight chief executives of the United States were born there.

Today, Virginia has a large number of diversified manufacturing industries including transportation equipment, textiles, food processing and electric and electronic equipment. Other important lines are chemicals, printing, apparel, and lumber and wood products.

Agriculture remains an important sector in the Virginia economy and the state ranks among the leaders in the U.S. in tobacco, peanuts, apples, and sweet potatoes. Other crops include corn, vegetables, barley, and peaches. Famous for its turkeys and Smithfield hams, Virginia also has a large dairy industry.

Coal mining accounts for roughly 70% of Virginia's mineral output, and lime, zinc, and stone are also mined.

Points of interest include Mt. Vernon and other places associated with George Washington; Monticello, home of Thomas Jefferson; Stratford, home of the Lees; Richmond, capital of the Confederacy and of Virginia; and Williamsburg, the restored Colonial capital.

The Chesapeake Bay Bridge-Tunnel spans the mouth of Chesapeake Bay, connecting Cape Charles with Norfolk. Consisting of a series of low trestles, two bridges and two mile-long tunnels, the complex is 18 miles (29 km) long. It was opened in 1964.

Other attractions are the Shenandoah National Park, Fredericksburg and Spotsylvania National Military Park, the Booker T. Washington birthplace near Roanoke, Arlington House (the Robert E. Lee Memorial), the Skyline Drive, and the Blue Ridge National Parkway.

WASHINGTON

Capital: Olympia
Governor: Booth Gardner, D (to 1989)
Lieut. Governor: Joel Pritchard, D (to 1991)
Secy. of State: Ralph Munro (to 1991)
State Treasurer: Daniel K. Grimm (to 1991)
Atty. General: Kenneth O. Eikenberry (to 1991)
Organized as territory: March 2, 1853
Entered Union & (rank): Nov. 11, 1889 (42)
Present constitution adopted: 1889
Motto: *Al-Ki* (Indian word meaning "by and by")
State flower: Rhododendron (1949)
State tree: Western hemlock (1947)
State bird: Willow goldfinch (1951)
State fish: Steelhead trout (1969)
State gem: Petrified wood (1975)
State colors: Green and gold (1925)
State song: "Washington, My Home" (1959)
State dance: Square dance (1979)
Nicknames: Evergreen State; Chinook State
Origin of name: In honor of George Washington
1980 population (1980 census) & (rank): 4,538,000 (18)
1987 est. population (July 1) & (rank): 4,409,000 (19)
1980 land area & (rank): 66,511 sq mi (172,264 sq km) (20)
Geographic center: In Chelan Co., 10 mi. WSW of Wenatchee
Number of counties: 39
Largest cities (1980 census): Seattle, 493,846; Spokane, 171,300; Tacoma, 158,501; Bellevue, 73,903; Everett, 54,413; Yakima, 49,826; Bellingham, 45,794
State forest lands: 1,922,880 ac.
State parks: 202 (171,700 ac.)[1]
1987 percent pop. below age 15: 21
1987 percent pop. age 65 and over: 12

1987 violent crimes per 100,000 pop.: 439.5
1984 (fiscal year) immigrants: 9,234

1. Parks and undeveloped areas administered by Parks and Recreation Dept. Game Dept. administers wildlife and recreation areas totaling 762,895 acres.

As part of the vast Oregon Country, Washington territory was visited by Spanish, American, and British explorers—Bruno Heceta for Spain in 1775, the American Capt. Robert Gray in 1792, and Capt. George Vancouver for Britain in 1792–94. Lewis and Clark explored the Columbia River region and coastal areas for the U.S. in 1805–06.

Rival American and British settlers and conflicting territorial claims threatened war in the early 1840s. However, in 1846 the Oregon Treaty set the boundary at the 49th parallel and war was averted.

Washington is a leading lumber producer. Its rugged surface is rich in stands of Douglas fir, hemlock, ponderosa and white pine, spruce, larch, and cedar. The state holds first place in apples, blueberries, hops, and red raspberries and it ranks high in potatoes, winter wheat, pears, grapes, apricots, and strawberries. Livestock and livestock products make important contributions to total farm revenue and the commercial fishing catch of salmon, halibut, and bottomfish makes a significant contribution to the state's economy.

Manufacturing industries in Washington include aircraft and missiles, shipbuilding and other transportation equipment, lumber, food processing, metals and metal products, chemicals, and machinery.

The Columbia River contains one third of the potential water power in the U.S., harnessed by such dams as the Grand Coulee, one of the greatest power producers in the world. Washington has 90 dams throughout the state built for irrigation, power, flood control, and water storage. Its abundance of electrical power makes Washington the nation's largest producer of refined aluminum.

Among the major points of interest: Mt. Rainier, Olympic, and North Cascades. In 1980, Mount St. Helens, a peak in the Cascade Range in Southwestern Washington erupted on May 18th. Also of interest are National Parks; Whitman Mission and Fort Vancouver National Historic Sites; and the Pacific Science Center and Space Needle in Seattle.

WEST VIRGINIA

Capital: Charleston
Governor: Gaston Caperton, D (to Jan. 1993)
Secy. of State: Ken Heckler, D (to Jan. 1993)
State Auditor: Glen Gainer (to Jan. 1993)
Atty. General: Charlie Brown, D (to Jan. 1993)
Entered Union & (rank): June 20, 1863 (35)
Present constitution adopted: 1872
Motto: *Montani semper liberi* (Mountaineers are always free)
State flower: Rhododendron (1903)
State tree: Sugar maple (1949)
State bird: Cardinal (1949)
State animal: Black bear
State colors: Blue and gold (unofficial)
State songs: "West Virginia, My Home Sweet Home," "The West Virginia Hills," and "This Is My West Virginia" (adopted by Legislature in 1947, 1961 and 1963 as official state songs)
Nickname: Mountain State
Origin of name: Same as for Virginia
1980 population (1980 census) & (rank): 1,950,279 (34)

1987 est. population (July 1) & (rank): 1,897,000 (34)
1980 land area & (rank): 24,119 sq mi. (62,468 sq km) (41)
Geographic center: In Braxton Co., 4 mi. E of Sutton
Number of counties: 55
Largest cities (1980 census): Charleston, 63,968; Huntington, 63,684; Wheeling, 43,070; Parkersburg, 39,967; Morgantown, 27,605; Weirton, 25,371
State forests: 9 (77,000 ac.)
State parks: 34 (65,861 ac.)
1987 percent pop. below age 15: 21
1987 percent pop. age 65 and over: 14
1987 violent crimes per 100,000 pop.: 137.3
1984 (fiscal year) immigrants: 628

West Virginia's early history from 1609 until 1863 is largely shared with Virginia, of which it was a part until Virginia seceded from the Union in 1861. Then the delegates of 40 western counties formed their own government, which was granted statehood in 1863.

First permanent settlement dates from 1731 when Morgan Morgan founded Mill Creek. In 1742 coal was discovered on the Coal River, an event that would be of great significance in determining West Virginia's future.

The state usually ranks 3rd in bituminous coal production with about 15% of the U.S. total. It also is a leader in steel, glass, aluminum, and chemical manufactures; natural gas, oil, quarry products, and hardwood lumber.

Major cash farm products are poultry and eggs, dairy products, apples, and feed crops. More than 80% of West Virginia is covered with forests.

Tourism is increasingly popular in mountainous West Virginia and visitors spend over $1.4 billion annually. More than a million acres have been set aside in 34 state parks and recreation areas and in 9 state forests.

Major points of interest include Harpers Ferry and New River Gorge National River, The Greenbrier and Berkeley Springs resorts, the scenic railroad at Cass, and the historic homes in the Eastern Panhandle.

WISCONSIN

Capital: Madison
Governor: Tommy G. Thompson, R (to Jan. 1991)
Lieut. Governor: Scott McCallum, R (to Jan. 1991)
Secy. of State: Douglas J. La Follette, D (to Jan. 1991)
State Treasurer: Charles P. Smith, D (to Jan. 1991)
Atty. General: Donald J. Hanaway, R (to Jan. 1991)
Superintendent of Public Instruction: Herbert J. Grover, Nonpartisan (to July 1989)
Organized as territory: July 4, 1836
Entered Union & (rank): May 29, 1848 (30)
Present constitution adopted: 1848
Motto: Forward
State flower: Wood violet
State tree: Sugar maple
State bird: Robin
State animal: Badger; "wild life" animal: white-tailed deer; "domestic" animal: dairy cow
State insect: Honeybee (1977)
State fish: Musky (Muskellunge)
State song: "On Wisconsin"
State mineral: Galena (1971)
State rock: Red Granite (1971)
Nickname: Badger State

Origin of name: French corruption of an Indian word whose meaning is disputed
1980 population (1980 census) & (rank): 4,705,521 (16)
1987 est. population (July 1) & (rank): 4,807,000 (17)
1980 land area & (rank): 54,426 sq mi. (140,964 sq km) (25)
Geographic center: In Wood Co., 9 mi. SE of Marshfield
Number of counties: 72
Largest cities (1980 census): Milwaukee, 636,236; Madison, 170,616; Green Bay, 87,899; Racine, 85,725; Kenosha, 77,685; West Allis, 63,982; Appleton, 58,913
State forests: 9 (476,004 ac.)
State parks & scenic trails: 49 parks, 13 trails (66,185 ac.)
1987 percent pop. below age 15: 22
1987 percent pop. age 65 and over: 13
1987 violent crimes per 100,000 pop.: 249.9
1984 (fiscal year) immigrants: 2,469

The Wisconsin region was first explored for France by Jean Nicolet, who landed at Green Bay in 1634. In 1660 a French trading post and Roman Catholic mission were established near present-day Ashland.

Great Britain obtained the region in settlement of the French and Indian War in 1763; the U.S. acquried it in 1783 after the Revolutionary War. However, Great Britain retained actual control until after the War of 1812. The region was successively governed as part of the territories of Indiana, Illinois, and Michigan between 1800 and 1836, when it became a separate territory.

Wisconsin leads the nation in milk and cheese production. In 1987 the state ranked first in the number of milk cows (1,790,000) and produced 17% of the nation's total output of milk. Other important farm products are peas, beans, corn, potatoes, oats, hay, and cranberries.

The chief industrial products of the state are automobiles, machinery, furniture, paper, beer, and processed foods. Wisconsin ranks second among the 47 paper-producing states.

Wisconsin pioneered in social legislation, providing pensions for the blind (1907), aid to dependent children (1913), and old-age assistance (1925). In labor legislation, the state was the first to enact an unemployment compensation law (1932) and the first in which a workman's compensation law actually took effect. Wisconsin had the first state-wide primary-election law and the first successful income-tax law. In April 1984, Wisconsin became the first state to adopt the Uniform Marital Property Act. The act took effect on January 1, 1986.

The state has over 8,500 lakes, of which Winnebago is the largest. Water sports, ice-boating, and fishing are popular, as are skiing and hunting. Public parks and forests take up one seventh of the land, with 49 state parks, 9 state forests, 13 state trails, 3 recreational areas, and 2 national forests.

Among the many points of interest are the Apostle Islands National Lakeshore; Ice Age National Scientific Reserve; the Circus World Museum at Baraboo; the Wolf, St. Croix, and Lower St. Croix national scenic riverways; and the Wisconsin Dells.

WYOMING

Capital: Cheyenne
Governor: Michael J. Sullivan, D (to Jan. 1991)
Secy. of State: Kathy Karpan, D (to Jan. 1991)
Auditor: Jack Sidi, R (to Jan. 1991)
Treasurer: Stanford S. Smith, R (to Jan. 1991)
Atty. General: Joseph B. Meyer, D (apptd. by Governor)
Organized as territory: May 19, 1869
Entered Union & (rank): July 10, 1890 (44)
Present constitution adopted: 1890
Motto: Equal rights (1955)
State flower: Indian paintbrush (1917)
State tree: Cottonwood (1947)
State bird: Meadow lark (1927)
State gemstone: Jade (1967)
State insignia: Bucking horse (unofficial)
State song: "Wyoming" (1955)
Nickname: Equality State
Origin of name: From the Delaware Indian word, meaning "mountains and valleys alternating"; the same as the Wyoming Valley in Pennsylvania
1980 population (1980 census) & (rank): 490,000 (50)
1987 est. population (July 1) & (rank): 509,000 (50)
1980 land area & (rank): 96,989 sq mi. (251,201 sq km) (9)
Geographic center: In Fremont Co., 58 mi. ENE of Lander
Number of counties: 23, plus Yellowstone National Park
Largest cities (1980 census): Casper, 51,016; Cheyenne, 47,283; Laramie, 24,410; Rock Springs, 19,458; Sheridan, 15,146; Green River, 12,807; Gillette, 12,134
State forests: None
State parks: 9 (44,732 ac.)
1987 percent pop. below age 15: 26
1987 percent pop. age 65 and over: 9
1987 violent crimes per 100,000 pop. 283.1
1984 (fiscal year) immigrants: 271

The U.S. acquired the territory from France as part of the Louisiana Purchase in 1803. John Colter, a fur-trapper, is the first white man known to have entered present Wyoming. In 1807 he explored the Yellowstone area and brought back news of its geysers and hot springs.

Robert Stuart pioneered the Oregon Trail across Wyoming in 1812–13 and, in 1834, Fort Laramie, the first permanent trading post in Wyoming, was built. Western Wyoming was obtained by the U.S. in the 1846 Oregon Treaty with Great Britain and as a result of the treaty ending the Mexican War in 1848.

When the Wyoming Territory was organized in 1869 Wyoming women became the first in the nation to obtain the right to vote. In 1925 Mrs. Nellie Tayloe Ross was elected first woman governor in the United States.

Wyoming's towering mountains and vast plains provide spectacular scenery, grazing lands for sheep and cattle, and rich mineral deposits.

Mining, particularly oil and natural gas, is the most important industry. In 1986, Wyoming led the nation in sodium carbonate (natrona) and bentonite production, and was second in uranium.

Wyoming ranks second among the states in wool production. In January 1987, its sheep numbered 775,000, exceeded only by Texas and California; it also had 1,300,000 cattle. Principal crops include wheat, oats, sugar beets, corn, potatoes, barley, and alfalfa.

Second in mean elevation to Colorado, Wyoming has many attractions for the tourist trade, notably Yellowstone National Park. Cheyenne is famous for its annual "Frontier Days" celebration. Flaming Gorge, the Fort Laramie National Historic Site, and Devils Tower and Fossil Butte National Monuments are other National points of interest.

Self-Governing Areas

PUERTO RICO

Capital: San Juan
Governor: Rafael Hernández-Colón, Popular Democratic Party
Song: "La Borinqueña"
1970 population: 2,712,033
1980 population: 3,196,520
Largest cities (1980 census): San Juan, 424,600; Bayamón, 185,087; Ponce, 161,739; Carolina, 147,835, Caguas, 87,214; Mayagüez, 82,968

Puerto Rico is an island about 100 miles long and 35 miles wide at the northeastern end of the Caribbean Sea. It is a self-governing Commonwealth freely and voluntarily associated with the U.S. Under its Constitution, a Governor and a Legislative Assembly are elected by direct vote for a four-year period. The judiciary is vested in a Supreme Court and lower courts established by law. The people elect a Resident Commissioner to the U.S. House of Representatives, where he has a voice but no vote. The island was formerly an unincorporated territory of the U.S. after being ceded by Spain as a result of the Spanish-American War.

The Commonwealth, established in 1952, has one of the highest standards of living in Latin America. Featuring Puerto Rican economic development is Operation Bootstrap. There are now over 1,600 manufacturing plants which have been created by this program. It has also greatly increased transportation and communications facilities, electric power, housing, and other industries.

The island's chief exports are chemicals, apparel, fish products and electronic products.

Columbus discovered the island on his second voyage to America in 1493.

GUAM

Capital: Agaña
Governor: Joseph F. Ada
1950 population: 59,498
1960 population: 67,044
1970 population: 84,996
1990 population (projected): 132,137
1980 land area: 209 sq mi. (541 sq km)

Guam, the largest of the Mariana Islands, is independent of the trusteeship assigned to the U.S. in 1947. It was acquired by the U.S. from Spain in 1898 (occupied 1899) and was placed under the Navy Department.

In World War II, Guam was seized by the Japanese on Dec. 11, 1941; but on July 21, 1944, it was once more in U.S. hands.

On Aug. 1, 1950, President Truman signed a bill which granted U.S. citizenship to the people of Guam and established self-government. However, the people do not vote in national elections. In 1972 Guam elected its first delegate to the U.S. Congress. The Executive Branch of the Guam government is under the general supervision of the U.S. Secretary of the Interior. In November 1970, Guam elected its first Governor.

Military installations and tourism are important factors in Guam's economy.

Non-Self-Governing Territories

AMERICAN SAMOA

Capital: Pago Pago
Governor: Peter T. Coleman
Lieut. Governor: Galeai Poumele
1960 population: 20,051
1970 population: 27,159
1986 population: 36,260
1980 land area: 77 sq mi (199 sq km)

American Samoa, a group of five volcanic islands and two coral atolls located some 2,600 miles south of Hawaii in the South Pacific Ocean, is an unincorporated, unorganized territory of the U.S., administered by the Department of the Interior.

By the Treaty of Berlin, signed Dec. 2, 1899, and ratified Feb. 16, 1900, the U.S. was internationally acknowledged to have rights extending over all the islands of the Samoa group east of longitude 171° west of Greenwich. On April 17, 1900, the chiefs of Tutuila and Aunu'u ceded those islands to the U.S. In 1904, the King and chiefs of Manu'a ceded the islands of Ofu, Olosega and Tau (composing the Manu'a group) to the U.S. Swains Island, some 214 miles north of Samoa, was included as part of the territory by Act of Congress March 4, 1925; and on Feb. 20, 1929, Congress formally accepted sovereignty over the entire group and placed the responsibility for administration in the hands of the President. From 1900 to 1951, by Presidential direction, the Department of the Navy governed the territory. On July 1, 1951, administration was transferred to the Department of the Interior. The first Constitution for the territory was signed on April 27, 1960, and became effective on Oct. 17, 1960. It was revised in 1967.

Congress has provided for a non-voting delegate to sit in the House of Representatives in 1981.

The principal products are canned tuna, pet food, fish meal, mats, and handicrafts.

BAKER, HOWLAND, AND JARVIS ISLANDS

These Pacific islands were not to play a role in the extraterritorial plans of the U.S. until May 13, 1936. President F. D. Roosevelt, at that time, placed them under the control and jurisdiction of the Secretary of the Interior for administration purposes.

Baker Island is a saucer-shaped atoll with an area of approximately one square mile. It is about 1,650 miles from Hawaii.

Howland Island, 36 miles to the northeast, is approximately one and a half miles long and half a mile wide.

Jarvis Island is several hundred miles to the east and is approximately two miles long by one and an eighth miles wide.

Baker, Howland, and Jarvis have been uninhabited since 1942. In 1974, these islands became part of the National Wildlife Refuge System, administered by the U.S. Fish & Wildlife Service, Department of the Interior.

CANTON AND ENDERBURY ISLANDS

Canton and Enderbury islands, the largest of the Phoenix group, are jointly administered by the U.S. and Great Britain after an agreement signed April 6, 1939. The status of Canton and Enderbury was the subject of negotiations between the U.S., U.K., and Gilbert Islands Governments in 1979. The negotiations resulted in the signing on September 20, 1979, of a Treaty of Friendship between the U.S. and the Republic of Kiribati. The Republic of Kiribati declared its independence on July 12, 1979.

Canton is triangular in shape and the largest of the eight islands of this group. It lies about 1,600 miles southwest of Hawaii and was discovered at the turn of the 18th century by U.S. whalers. After World War II it served as an aviation support facility, and later as a missile tracking station.

Enderbury is rectangular in shape and is 3.5 miles long by 1.5 miles wide. It is unpopulated and lies about 32 miles southeast of Canton.

JOHNSTON ATOLL

Johnston is a coral atoll about 700 miles southwest of Hawaii. It consists of four small islands—Johnston Island, Sand Island, Hikina Island, and Akau Island—which lie on a reef about 9 miles long in a northeast-southwest direction.

The atoll was discovered by Capt. Charles James Johnston of *H.M.S. Cornwallis* in 1807. In 1858 it was claimed by Hawaii, and later became a U.S. possession.

Johnston Atoll is a Naval Defense Sea Area and Airspace Reservation and is closed to the public. The administration of Johnston Atoll is under the jurisdiction of the Defense Nuclear Agency, Commander, Johnston Atoll (FCDNA), APO San Francisco, CA 96305.

KINGMAN REEF

Kingman Reef, located about 1,000 miles south of Hawaii, was discovered by Capt. E. Fanning in 1798, but named for Capt. W. E. Kingman, who rediscovered it in 1853. The reef, drying only on its northeast, east and southeast edges, is of atoll character. The reef is triangular in shape, with its apex northward; it is about 9.5 miles long, east and west, and 5 miles wide, north and south, within the 100-fathom curve.

A United States possession, Kingman Reef is a Naval Defense Sea Area and Airspace Reservation, and is closed to the public. The Airspace Entry Control has been suspended, but is subject to immediate reinstatement without notice. No vessel, except those authorized by the Secretary of the Navy, shall be navigated in the area within the 3-mile limit.

MIDWAY ISLANDS

Midway Islands, lying about 1,150 miles westnorthwest of Hawaii, were discovered by Captain N. C. Brooks of the Hawaiian bark *Gambia* on July 5, 1859, in the name of the United States. The atoll was formally declared a U.S. possession in 1867, and in 1903 Theodore Roosevelt made it a naval reservation.

Midway Islands consist of a circular atoll, 6 miles in diameter, and enclosing two islands. Eastern Island, on its southeast side, is triangular in shape, and about 1.2 miles long. Sand Island on its south side, is about 2 miles long in a northeast-southwest direction.

The Midway Islands are within a Naval Defense Sea Area. The Navy Department maintains an installation and has jurisdiction over the atoll. Permission to enter the Naval Defense Sea Area must be obtained in advance from the Commander Third Fleet (N31), Pearl Harbor, HI 96860.

U.S. VIRGIN ISLANDS

Capital: Charlotte Amalie (on St. Thomas)
Governor: Alexander A. Farrelly
1980 population: 96,569
1986 population: 109,800 (St. Croix, 52,260; St. Thomas, 52,260; St. John, 2,940)
1980 land area: 132 sq mi (342 sq km): St. Croix, 84 sq. mi. (207 sq km), St. Thomas, 32 sq mi (83 sq km), St. John, 20 sq mi. (52 sq km)

The Virgin Islands, consisting of nine main islands and some 75 islets, were discovered by Columbus in 1493. Since 1666, England has held six of the main islands; the other three (St. Croix, St. Thomas, and St. John), as well as about 50 of the islets, were eventually acquired by Denmark, which named them the Danish West Indies. In 1917, these islands were purchased by the U.S. from Denmark for $25 million.

Congress granted U.S. citizenship to Virgin Islanders in 1927; and, in 1931, administration was transferred from the Navy to the Department of the Interior. Universal suffrage was given in 1936 to all persons who could read and write the English language. The Governor was elected by popular vote for the first time in 1970; previously he had been appointed by the President of the U.S. A unicameral 15-man legislature serves the Virgin Islands, and Congressional legislation gave the islands a non-voting Representative in Congress.

The "Constitution" of the Virgin Islands is the Revised Organic Act of 1954 in which the U.S. Congress defines the three branches of the territorial government, i.e., the Executive Branch, the Legislative Branch, and the Judicial Branch. Residents of the islands substantially enjoy the same rights as those enjoyed by mainlanders with one important exception: citizens of the U.S. who are residents may not vote in presidential elections.

About 80% of the population is black, and there is limited farming, fishing, and cattle raising. Industrial products include rum, watches, costume jewelry, pharmaceuticals, and petroleum products. Tourism is the principal industry.

WAKE ISLAND

Wake Island, about halfway between Midway and Guam, is an atoll comprising the three islets of Wilkes, Peale, and Wake. They were discovered by the British in 1796 and annexed by the U.S. in 1899. The entire area comprises 3 square miles and has no native population. In 1938, Pan American Airways established a seaplane base and Wake Island has been used as a commercial base since then. On Dec. 8, 1941, it was attacked by the Japanese, who finally took possession on Dec. 23. It was surrendered by the Japanese on Sept. 4, 1945.

The President, acting pursuant to the Hawaii Omnibus Act, assigned responsibility for Wake to the Secretary of the Interior in 1962. The Department of Transportation exercised civil administration of Wake through an agreement with the Department of the Interior until June 1972, at which time the Department of the Air Force assumed responsibility for the Territory.

Trust Territory of the Pacific Islands (Micronesia)

In 1885, Germany assumed a protectorate over the Marshall Islands; and, in 1899, she purchased the Northern Mariana and Caroline Islands from Spain. These islands were occupied by the Japanese in 1914 and were mandated to Japan by the League of Nations in 1919. On April 2, 1947, the U. N. Security Council approved a trusteeship agreement proposed by the U.S. under which the Northern Mariana, Caroline, and Marshall Islands became a Strategic Trust Territory under the administration of the U.S. The measure was approved by the President, with the agreement of Congress, on July 18, 1947. Administration was transferred from the Navy to the Department of the Interior on July 1, 1951. However, during 1953, administration of the islands of the Northern Marianas, except Rota, was transferred back to the Navy. The Department of the Interior again took over administration of these islands in July, 1962. The 1980 population of the Northern Marianas was 16,780.

In February 1975 a covenant was signed by the U.S. and the Marianas Political Status Commission that would make the 14 islands in the Northern Marianas a commonwealth under American sovereignty. The covenant was overwhelmingly ratified by the people of the islands and was approved by President Ford on March 24, 1976.

On April 9, 1978, in Hilo, Hawaii, the heads of the three Micronesian political status commissions and the U.S. negotiator signed a statement of agreed principles which is intended to form the basis of a free association relationship between the U.S. and Micronesia. Compact of Free Association was signed by the U.S. and the Micronesian commissions in 1982. The terms of the Compact of Free Association between the United States and the Federated States of Micronesia became effective as of November 3, 1986.

The entire group with a 1980 population of 116,149 comprises more than 2,000 islands, but the total land area is only 533 sq mi. (1,381 sq km), many of the islands being only tiny coral reefs.

The Micronesians are the main ethnic group; however, the inhabitants of two outlying islands, Kapingamarangi and Nukuoro, are Polynesian. The population of the Trust Territory in 1980 was estimated to be 116,974.

CAROLINE ISLANDS

The Caroline Islands, east of the Philippines and south of the Marianas, include the Yap, Truk, and the Palau groups and the islands of Ponape and Kosrae, as well as many coral atolls.

The islands are composed chiefly of volcanic rock, and their peaks rise 2,000 to 3,000 feet above sea level. Chief exports of the islands are copra, fish products, and handicrafts.

MARIANA ISLANDS

The Mariana Islands, east of the Philippines and south of Japan, include the islands of Guam, Rota, Saipan, Tinian, Pagan, Guguan, Agrihan, and Aguijan. Guam, the largest, is independent of the trusteeship, having been acquired by the U.S. from Spain in 1898. (For more information, *see* the entry on Guam in this section.) The remaining islands, referred to as the Commonwealth of the Northern Mariana Islands became part of the Unites States pursuant to P.L. 94-241 as of November 3, 1986.

Chief crops are copra and fresh fruits and vegetables.

REPUBLIC OF THE MARSHALL ISLANDS

The Government of the United States and the Republic of the Marshall Islands signed a Compact of Free Association on October 15, 1986, which became effective as of October 21, 1986. The termination of the Trusteeship Agreement became effective on November 3, 1986.

The Marshall Islands, east of the Carolines, are divided into two chains: the western or Ralik group, including the atolls Jaluit, Kwajalein, Wotho, Bikini, and Enewetak; and the eastern or Ratak group, including the atolls Mili, Majuro, Maloelap, Wotje, and Likiep.

The islands are of the coral-reef type and rise only a few feet above sea level. The chief crop is coconuts; exports include copra, tortoise shell, mother-of-pearl, etc.

Bikini and Enewetak were the scene of several atom-bomb tests after World War II. In April 1977, some 55 original inhabitants, the forerunner of 450 returnees, were resettled after an absence of 30 years.

Tabulated Data on State Governments

State	Governor		Legislature[1]					Highest Court[2]		
	Term, years	Annual salary	Membership		Term, yrs.		Salaries of members[5]	Members	Term, years	Annual salary[6]
			U[3]	L[4]	U[3]	L[4]				
Alabama	4[10]	70,222[16]	35	105	4	4	45.00 per diem[22]	9	6	83,880[6]
Alaska	4	81,648	20	40	4	2	22,140 per annum	5	(8)	85,278
Arizona	4	75,000	30	60	2	2	15,000 per annum	5	6	75,000
Arkansas	4	35,000	35	100	4	2	7,500 per annum[25]	7	8	67,660[6]

State	Governor Term, years	Annual salary	Legislature[1] Member-ship U[3]	L[4]	Term, yrs. U[3]	L[4]	Salaries of members[5]	Highest Court[2] Mem-bers	Term, years	Annual salary[6]
California[30]*	4	85,000	40	80	4	2	40,816 [32] per annum	7	12	103,469 [6]
Colorado	4	70,000	35	65	4	2	17,500 per annum	7	10	72,000 [6]
Connecticut	4	78,000	36	151	2	2	30,400 per biennium	7	8	86,835 [6]
Delaware	4 [9]	80,000	21	41	4	2	22,173 per annum	5	12	97,300
Florida	4 [10]	98,904	40	120	4	2	20,748 per annum	7	6	92,882
Georgia	4 [9]	86,706	56	180	2	2	10,251 per annum	7	6	80,514
Hawaii	4	80,000	25	51	4	2	27,000 [33] per year	5	10	78,500 [6]
Idaho	4	55,000	42	84	2	2	30 per diem[34]	5	6	62,737
Illinois	4	93,266	59	118	4-2	2	35,661 per annum	7	10	93,266
Indiana	4 [10]	77,200	50	100	4	2	11,600 per annum	5	([24])	66,000 [6]
Iowa	4	70,000	50	100	4	2	14,600 per annum	9	8	65,200 [6]
Kansas	4	65,000	40	125	4	2	120 per diem[22]	7	6	59,143 [31]
Kentucky	4 [7]	69,731	38	100	4	2	100 per diem[22]	7	8	72,358 [6]
Louisiana	4	73,440	39	105	4	4	16,800 per annum	7	10	66,566
Maine	4	70,000 [16]	35	151	2	2	16,500 per biennium[16]	7	7	77,300
Maryland	4 [10]	85,000	47	141	4	4	24,000 per annum	7	10	86,900
Massachusetts	4	85,000	40	160	2	2	39,040 per annum	7	([13])	65,000
Michigan	4	106,690 [16]	38	110	4	2	45,450 [16] per annum[16]	7	8	106,610
Minnesota*	4	91,460	67	134	4	2	22,244 per annum[16]	9	6	73,981 [6]
Mississippi	4	63,000	52	122	4	4	10,000 per session[5]	9	8	59,000
Missouri	4 [10]	83,790	34	163	4	2	21,211 per annum[5]	7	12	81,009
Montana	4	50,452	50	100	4	2	59.12 per diem[16]	6	8	50,452 [6]
Nebraska	4 [10]	58,000	49 [11]	—	4 [11]	—	([37])	7	6	49,764
Nevada	4	77,500	21	42	4	2	7,800 per biennium	5	6	73,500
New Hampshire	2	72,146	24	([12])	2	2	200 per biennium	5	([13])	70,102 [6]
New Jersey	4 [10]	85,000	40	80	4 [14]	2	35,000 [35,36] per annum	7	7 [15]	93,000 [6]
New Mexico	4 [7]	63,000	42	70	4	2	75 per diem	5	8	60,375
New York	4	130,000	61	150	2	2	57,500 per annum	7	14	115,000 [6]
North Carolina	4 [9]	109,728 [16]	50	120	2	2	11,124 per annum[16]	7	8	81,348 [6]
North Dakota	4	60,862 [16]	53	106	4	2	90 per diem[16 23]	5	10	59,140 [6]
Ohio*	4	65,000	33	99	4	2	36,300 per annum	7	6	83,250
Oklahoma	4	70,000	48	101	4	2	32,000 [16] per annum	([19])	6	71,406 [6]
Oregon	4 [10]	75,000	30	60	4	2	937 [31] per annum	7	6	74,172 [6]
Pennsylvania	4 [10]	105,000	50	203	4	2	47,000 per annum	7	10	91,500
Rhode Island	2	69,900	50	100	2	2	5 per diem[17]	5	([18])	90,697
South Carolina	4	84,897	46	124	4 [2]	2	10,000 per annum	5	10	83,883 [6]
South Dakota	4 [10]	60,816	35	70	2	2	8,000 per biennium	5	3 [27]	58,684
Tennessee	4	85,000 [26]	33	99	4	2	16,500 per annum	5	8	60,000 [26]
Texas	4	91,600	31	150	4	2	7,200 [5] per annum	([20])	9	79,310
Utah*	4	60,000	29	75	4	2	65 per diem[16]	5	10	64,000 [6]
Vermont	2	71,200	30	150	2	2	340 per week[21]	5	6	63,900 [6]
Virginia	4 [7]	108,000	40	100	4	2	18,000 per annum	7	12	94,907 [6]
Washington	4	93,900	49	98	4	2	15,000 per annum	9	6	82,700
West Virginia	4 [10]	72,000	34	100	4	2	7,200 per annum	5	12	55,000
Wisconsin	4	86,149	33	99	4	2	31,236 per annum	7	10	76,859
Wyoming	4	70,000	30	62	4	2	60 [16] per diem[16]	5	8	63,500

1. General Assembly in Ark., Colo., Conn., Del., Ga., Ind., Ky., Md., Mo., N.C., Ohio, Pa., R.I., S.C., Tenn., Vt., Va., Legislative Assembly in N.D., Ore.; General Court in Mass., N.H.; Legislature in other states. Meets biennially in Calif., Ky., Me., Mont., Nev., N.J., N.C., N.D., Ore., Pa., Texas, Wash. Wyo Legislature meets annually. Regular general session on odd numbered years and a budget session on even numbered years. Ark. G.A. meets every other year for 60 days in odd numbered years.; meets annually in other states. 2. Court of Appeals in Md., N.Y., Supreme Court of Virginia in Va., Supreme Judicial Court in Me., Mass.; Supreme Court in other states. 3. Upper house: Senate in all states. 4. Lower house: Assembly in Calif., Nev., N.Y., Wis.; House of Delegates in Md., Va., W.Va.; General Assembly in N.J.; House of Representatives in other states. 5. Does not include additional payments for expenses, mileage, special sessions, etc., or additional per diem payments beyond salary shown. 6. In some states, Chief Justice receives a higher salary. 7. Cannot succeed himself. 8. Appointed for 3 years; thereafter subject to approval or rejection on a nonpartisan ballot for 10-year term. 9. May serve only 2 terms, consecutive or otherwise. 10. May not serve 3rd consecutive term. 11. Unicameral legislature. 12. Constitutional number: 375–400. 13. Until 70 years old. 14. When term begins in Jan. of 2nd year following U.S. census, term may be 2 years. 15. 2nd term receive tenure, mandatory retirement at 70. 16. Plus additional expenses. 17. For 60 days only. 18. Term of good behavior. 19. 9 members in Supreme Court, highest in civil cases; 5 in Court of Criminal Appeals. 20. 9 members in Supreme Court, highest in civil cases; 9 in Court of Criminal Appeals. 21. To limit of $11,000 per biennium; $2,000 for special session. 22. When in session. 23. Plus $180 per month when not in session. 24. Appointed for 2 years; thereafter elected popularly for 10-year term. 25. To receive cost of living increase not to exceed 10% in the two year period. 26. Adjusted annually according to increase in Consumer Price Index. 27. Subsequent terms, 8 years. 28. Plus $600 per month whether legislature is in session or not. 29. As of July 1, 1986. 30. Plus $600 per month when not in session. 31. Plus $400 monthly when not in session and per diem allowance when in session. 32. As of Dec. 5, 1988. 33. As of Jan. 1, 1989. 34. $30 per day while in session and $15 per day otherwise, plus per diem and mileage. 35. Plus $75,000 allowance for entertaining and other expenses. 36. Each legislator receives $60,000 annually for appointment of personal staff aides. 37. Salary not to exceed one thousand dollars per month. NOTE: An asterisk (*) indicates that up-to-date information has not been provided. Source: Information Please questionnaires to the states.

50 Largest Cities of the United States

(According to population estimates, July 1986)

Data supplied by Bureau of the Census and by the cities in response to *Information Please* questionnaires. Ranking of 50 largest cities latest available census data published as of August 1989. Civilian labor force (SMA, Jan. 1989); Percent employed and unemployed (SMA Jan. 1989); Per capita personal income (SMA Jan. 1987).

ALBUQUERQUE, N.M.

Incorporated as city: 1891
Mayor: Ken Schultz (to Dec. 1989)
1980 population (1980 census) & (rank): 332,336 (46)
1986 est. population & rank: 366,750 (40)
Land area: 95.3 sq mi. (247 sq km)
Altitude: 4,958 ft.
Location: Central part of state on Rio Grande River
County: Bernalillo
Churches: 211
City-owned parks: 135
Radio stations: 30
Television stations: 7
1980 CENSUS: Population 65 and over, 8.4%; **under 18,** 27.8%; **Black,** 2.5%; **Spanish, origin,** 33.8%
CIVILIAN LABOR FORCE: 257,800
Unemployed: 13,600, **Percent:** 5.3
Per capita personal income: $14,305
Chamber of Commerce: Greater Albuquerque Chamber of Commerce, 401 2nd St., N.W., Albuquerque, N.M. 87102. Albuquerque Hispano Chamber of Commerce, 1520 Central Ave., S.E., Albuquerque, N.M. 87106

ATLANTA, GA.

Incorporated as city: 1847
Mayor: Andrew Young (to Jan. 1990)
1980 population (1980 census) & (rank): 425,022 (29)
1986 est. population & (rank): 421,910 (32)
City land area: 136 sq mi. (352.2 sq km)
Altitude: Highest, 1,050 ft; lowest, 940
Location: In northwest central part of state, near Chattahoochee River
Counties: Fulton and DeKalb
Churches (18-county area): 1,500+
City-owned parks: 277 (3,178 ac.)
Radio stations (18-county area): AM, 7; FM, 20
Television stations (18-county area): 7 commercial; 2 PBS
1980 CENSUS: Population 65 and over, 11.5%; **under 18,** 26.8%; **Black,** 66.6%; **Spanish, origin** 1.4%
CIVILIAN LABOR FORCE: 1,521,500
Unemployed: 74,100, **Percent:** 4.9
Per capita personal income: $17,293
Chamber of Commerce: Atlanta Chamber of Commerce, 235 International Blvd., Atlanta, Ga. 30301 Information is gathered on 2 geographic areas:
City of Atlanta, and 18 county MSA

AUSTIN, TEX.

Incorporated as city: 1839
Mayor: Lee Cooke (to May 1991)
1980 population (1980 census) & (rank): 372,564 (35)
1986 est. population & rank: 466,550 (27)
1990 proj. population: 506,900
Land area: 116.0 sq mi. (300 sq km)
Altitude: From 425 ft. to over 1000 ft. elevation
Location: In south central part of state, on the Colorado River
County: Seat of Travis Co.
Churches: 353 churches, representing 45 denominations
City-owned parks and playgrounds: 160 (10,000 ac.)
Radio stations: AM, 6; FM, 12
Television stations: 3 commercial; 1 PBS; 1 independent
1980 CENSUS: Population 65 and over, 7.5%; **under 18,** 24.5%; **Black,** 12.2%; **Spanish, origin** 18.7%
CIVILIAN LABOR FORCE: 418,100
Unemployed: 25,300, **Percent:** 6.1
Per capita personal income: $15,027
Chamber of Commerce: Austin Chamber of Commerce, P.O. Box 1967, Austin, Tex. 78767

BALTIMORE, MD.

Incorporated as city: 1797
Mayor: Kurt L. Schmoke (to Dec. 1991)
1980 population (1980 census) & (rank): 786,741 (11)
1986 est. population & (rank): 752,800 (11)
1987 est. population: 753,300
Land area: 80.3 sq mi. (208 sq km)
Altitude: Highest, 490 ft; lowest, sea level
Location: On Patapsco River, about 12 mi. from Chesapeake Bay
County: Independent city
Churches: Roman Catholic, 72; Jewish, 50; Protestant and others, 344
City-owned parks: 347 park areas and tracts (6,314 ac.)
Radio stations: AM, 11; FM, 9
Television stations: 7
1980 CENSUS: Population 65 and over, 12.8%; **under 18,** 26.9%; **Black,** 54.8%; **Spanish, origin,** 1.0%
CIVILIAN LABOR FORCE: 1,188,900
Unemployed: 51,700, **Percent:** 4.4
Per capita personal income: $17,776
Chamber of Commerce: Greater Baltimore Committee, 111 S. Calvert St., Ste. 1500, Baltimore, MD 21202

BOSTON, MASS.

Incorporated as city: 1822
Mayor: Raymond L. Flynn (to Jan. 1992)
1980 population (1980 census) & (rank): 562,994 (20)
1986 est. population & (rank): 573,600 (19)
Land area: 47.2 sq mi. (122 sq km)
Altitude: Highest, 330 ft; lowest, sea level
Location: On Massachusetts Bay, at mouths of Charles and Mystic Rivers
County: Seat of Suffolk Co.
Churches: Protestant, 187; Roman Catholic, 72; Jewish, 28; others, 100
City-owned parks, playgrounds, etc.: 2,276.36 ac.
Radio stations: AM, 9; FM, 12
Television stations: 10
1980 CENSUS: Population 65 and over, 12.7%; **under 18,** 21.6%; **Black,** 22.4%; **Spanish, origin,** 6.4%
CIVILIAN LABOR FORCE: 1,554,300
Unemployed: 47,800, **Percent:** 3.1
Per capita personal income: $20,239

Chamber of Commerce: Boston Chamber of Commerce, 600 Atlantic Ave., Boston, Mass. 02210

BUFFALO, N.Y.

Incorporated as city: 1832
Mayor: James Griffin (to Dec. 1989)
1980 population (1980 census) & (rank): 357,870 (40)
1986 est. population & (rank): 324,820 (48)
Land area: 42.67 sq. mi. (109 sq. km)
Altitude: Highest 705 ft; lowest 571.84 ft;
Location: At east end of Lake Erie, on Niagara River
County: Seat of Erie Co.
Churches: 60 denominations, with over 1,100 churches
County-owned parks: 9 public parks (3,000 ac.)
Radio stations: AM 10; FM 13
Television stations: 8 (plus reception from 3 Canadian Stations)
1980 CENSUS: Population 65 and over, 15.0%; **under 18,** 25.2%; **Black,** 26.6%; **Spanish, origin,** 2.7%
CIVILIAN LABOR FORCE: 457,700
Unemployed: 32,300, **Percent:** 7.1
Per capita personal income: $15,349
Chamber of Commerce: Greater Buffalo Chamber of Commerce, 107 Delaware Avenue, Buffalo, NY 14202

CHARLOTTE, N.C.

Incorporated as city: 1768
Mayor: Sue Myrick (to Nov. 1989)
1980 population (1980 census) & (rank): 326,330 (48)
1989 est. population: 380,000
1986 est. population & rank: 352,070 (44)
Land area: 162.3 sq mi. (420 sq km)
Altitude: 765 ft
Location: In the southern part of state near the border of South Carolina
County: Seat of Mecklenburg Co.
Churches: Protestant, over 400; Roman Catholic, 8; Jewish, 3; Greek Orthodox, 1
City-owned parks and parkways: 87
Radio stations: AM, 8; FM, 12
Television stations: 4 commercial; 2 PBS
1980 CENSUS: Population 65 and over, 8.6%; **under 18,** 27.8%; **Black,** 31.0%; **Spanish, origin,** 1.1%
CIVILIAN LABOR FORCE: 648,900
Unemployed: 23,700, **Percent:** 3.7
Per capita personal income: $15,267
Chamber of Commerce: Charlotte Chamber, P.O. Box 32785, Charlotte, N.C., 28232

CHICAGO, ILL.

Incorporated as city: 1837
Mayor: Richard M. Daley (to April 1991)
1980 population (1980 census) & (rank): 3,005,072 (2)
1986 est. population & (rank): 3,009,530 (3)
Land area: 228.1 sq mi. (591 sq km)
Altitude: Highest, 672 ft; lowest, 578.5
Location: On lower west shore of Lake Michigan
County: Seat of Cook Co.
Churches: Protestant, 850; Roman Catholic, 263; Jewish, 51
City-owned parks: 560
Radio stations: AM, 20; FM, 16
Television stations: 10
1980 CENSUS: Population 65 and over, 11.4%; **under 18,** 28.4%; **Black,** 39.8%; **Spanish, origin,** 14.0%
CIVILIAN LABOR FORCE: 3,181,200
Unemployed: 180,100, **Percent:** 5.7
Per capita personal income: $17,733
Chamber of Commerce: Chicago Association of Commerce & Industry, 200 N. LaSalle, Chicago, Ill. 60602

CINCINNATI, OHIO

Incorporated as city: 1819
Mayor: Charles Luken (to Nov. 1989)
City Manager: Scott Johnson
1980 population (1980 census) & (rank): 385,410 (33)
1986 est. population & (rank): 369,750 (39)
Land area: 78.1 sq mi. (202 sq km)
Altitude: Highest, 960 ft; lowest, 441
Location: In southwestern corner of state on Ohio River
County: Seat of Hamilton Co.
Churches: 850
City-owned parks: 96 (4,345 ac.)
Radio stations: AM, 9; FM, 15 (Greater Cincinnati)
Television stations: 6
1980 CENSUS: Population 65 and over, 14.5%; **under 18,** 25.2%; **Black,** 33.8%; **Spanish, origin,** 0.8%
CIVILIAN LABOR FORCE: 771,200
Unemployed: 40,300, **Percent:** 5.2
Per capita personal income: $15,472
Chamber of Commerce: Cincinnati Chamber of Commerce, 120 W Fifth St., Cincinnati, Ohio 45202

CLEVELAND, OHIO

Incorporated as city: 1836
Mayor: George V. Voinovich (to Dec. 1989)
1980 population (1980 census) & (rank): 573,822 (18)
1986 est. population & (rank): 535,830 (22)
Land area: 79.0 sq mi. (205 sq km)
Altitude: Highest, 1048 ft.; lowest, 573
Location: On Lake Erie at mouth of Cuyahoga River
County: Seat of Cuyahoga Co.
Churches: [1] Protestant, 980; Roman Catholic, 187; Jewish, 31; Eastern Orthodox, 22
City-owned parks: 41 (1,930 ac.)
Radio stations: AM, 15; FM, 17
Television stations: 7
1980 CENSUS: Population 65 and over, 13.0%; **under 18,** 27.8%; **Black,** 43.8%; **Spanish, origin,** 3.1%
CIVILIAN LABOR FORCE: 940,300
Unemployed: 56,400, **Percent:** 6.0
Per capita personal income: $16,898
Chamber of Commerce: Greater Cleveland Growth Association, 690 Union Commerce Building, Cleveland, Ohio 44115
1. 100-mile area.

COLUMBUS, OHIO

Incorporated as city: 1834
Mayor: Dana G. Rinehart (to Jan. 1992)
1980 population (1980 census) & (rank): 565,032 (19)
1987 est. population: 611,344
1986 est. population & (rank): 566,030 (20)
Land area: 192.976 sq mi. (499.81 sq km)
Altitude: Highest, 902 ft; lowest, 702
Location: In central part of state, on Scioto River
County: Seat of Franklin Co.
Churches: Protestant, 436; Roman Catholic, 62; Jewish, 5;

Other, 8
City-owned parks: 407 (12,070 ac.)
Radio stations: AM, 8; FM, 12
Television stations: 8 commercial, 3 PBS
1980 CENSUS: Population 65 and over, 8.9%; under 18, 25.8%; Black, 22.1%; Spanish, origin, 0.8%
CIVILIAN LABOR FORCE: 724,300
Unemployed: 41,700, Percent: 5.8
Per capita personal income: $15,308
Chamber of Commerce: Columbus Area Chamber of Commerce, P.O. Box 1527, Columbus, Ohio 43216

DALLAS, TEX.

Incorporated as city: 1856
Mayor: Annette Strauss (to April 1991)
City Manager: Richard Knight, Jr. (apptd. Oct. 1986)
1980 population (1980 census) & (rank): 904,599 (7)
1986 est. population & (rank): 1,003,520 (8)
Land area: 378 sq mi. (979 sq km)
Altitude: Highest, 750 ft; lowest, 375
Location: In northeastern part of state, on Trinity River
County: Seat of Dallas Co.
Churches: 1,974 (in Dallas Co.)
City-owned parks: 296 (47,025 ac.)
Radio stations: AM, 19; FM, 30
Television stations: 10 commercial, 1 PBS
1980 CENSUS: Population 65 and over, 9.5%; under 18, 27.0%; Black, 29.4%; Spanish, origin, 12.3%
CIVILIAN LABOR FORCE: 1,432,500
Unemployed: 84,400, Percent: 5.9
Per capita personal income: $17,748
Chamber of Commerce: Dallas Chamber of Commerce. 1507 Pacific, Dallas, Tex. 75201

DENVER, COLO.

Incorporated as city: 1861
Mayor: Federico Pena (to July 1991)
1980 population (1980 census) & (rank): 492,694 (24)
1986 est. population & rank: 505,000 (23)
Land area: 110.6 sq mi. (287 sq km)
Altitude: Highest, 5,470 ft; lowest, 5,130
Location: In northeast central part of state, on South Platte River
County: Coextensive with Denver Co.
Churches:[1] Protestant, 815; Roman Catholic, 63; Jewish, 13
City-owned parks: 155 (3,600 ac.)
City-owned mountain parks: 40 (13,448 ac.)
Radio stations: AM, 18; FM, 13[1]
Television stations: 5
1980 CENSUS: Population 65 and over, 12.6%; under 18, 22.5%; Black, 12.0%; Spanish, origin, 18.8%
CIVILIAN LABOR FORCE: 865,100
Unemployed: 57,100, Percent: 6.6
Per capita personal income: $17,214
Chamber of Commerce: Denver Chamber of Commerce, 1301 Welton, Denver, Colo. 80204
1. Metropolitan area. 2. Excluding school district. 3. Latest figures available.

DETROIT, MICH.

Incorporated as city: 1815
Mayor: Coleman A. Young (to Jan. 1990)
1980 population (1980 census) & (rank): 1,203,369 (6)
1986 est. population & rank: 1,086,220 (6)
Land area: 143 sq mi. (370 sq km)
Altitude: Highest, 685 ft; lowest, 574
Location: In southeastern part of state, on Detroit River
County: Seat of Wayne Co.
Churches:[1] Protestant, 1,165; Roman Catholic, 113; Jewish, 2
City-owned parks: 52 parks (3,843 ac.); 350 sites (5,838 ac.)
Radio stations: AM, 12; FM, 21[2] (includes 1 in Windsor, Ont.)
Television stations: 8[2] (includes 1 in Windsor, Ont.)
1980 CENSUS: Population 65 and over, 11.7%; under 18, 30.3%; Black, 63.1%; Spanish, origin, 2.4%
CIVILIAN LABOR FORCE: 2,206,600
Unemployed: 163,600, Percent: 7.4
Per capita personal income: $17,241
Chamber of Commerce: Greater Detroit Chamber of Commerce, 622 W. Lafayette, Detroit, Mich. 48226
1. Six-county metropolitan area. 2. Within three counties of Metro Detroit.

EL PASO, TEX.

Incorporated as city: 1873
Mayor: Suzanne F. Azar (to June 1991)
1980 population (1980 census) & (rank): 425,259 (28)
1989 est. population: 519,690
1986 est. population & rank: 491,800 (24)
Land area: 247.4 sq mi. (641 sq km)
Altitude: 4,000 ft
Location: In far western part of state, on Rio Grande
County: Seat of El Paso Co.
Churches: Protestant, 320; Roman Catholic, 39; Jewish, 3; others, 20
City-owned parks: 115[1] (1,663 ac.)
Radio Stations: AM, 17; FM, 17
Television stations: 6
1980 CENSUS: Population 65 and over, 6.9%; under 18, 35.0%; Black, 3.2%; Spanish, origin, 62.5%
CIVILIAN LABOR FORCE: 239,300
Unemployed: 26,300, Percent: 11.0
Per capita personal income: $9,484
Chamber of Commerce: El Paso Chamber of Commerce, 10 Civic Center Plaza, El Paso, Tex. 79944
1. Includes 108 developed and 7 undeveloped parks.

FORT WORTH, TEX.

Incorporated as city: 1873
Mayor: Bob Bolen (to May 1991)
City Manager: Douglas Harman
1980 population (1980 census) & (rank): 385,164 (34)
1986 est. population & (rank): 429,550 (30)
Land area: 293.03 sq mi. (758.96 sq km)
Altitude: Highest, 780 ft; lowest, 520
Location: In north central part of state, on Trinity River
County: Seat of Tarrant Co.
Churches: Protestant, 392; Roman Catholic, 16; Jewish, 2
City-owned parks: 136 (8,189 ac.; 3,500 ac. in Nature Center)
Radio stations: AM, 6; FM, 8
Television stations: 6 (2 local)
1980 CENSUS: Population 65 and over, 11.8%; under 18, 27.1%; Black, 22.8%; Spanish, origin, 12.6%
CIVILIAN LABOR FORCE: 676,100
Unemployed: 42,100, Percent: 6.2
Per capita personal income: $15,890

Chamber of Commerce: Fort Worth Chamber of Commerce, 700 Throckmorton, Fort Worth, Tex. 76102

HONOLULU, HAWAII

Incorporated as city and county: 1907
Mayor: Frank F. Fasi (to Jan. 1993)
1980 population (1980 census) & (rank): 367,878 (37)
1986 est. population & (rank): 372,330 (38)
Land area: 600 sq mi. (1,554 sq km)[1]
Altitude: Highest, 4,025 ft; lowest, sea level
Location: The city and county government's jurisdiction includes the entire island of Oahu
Churches: Roman Catholic, 34; Buddhist, 34; Jewish, 2; Protestant and others, 329
City-owned parks: 5,386 ac.
Radio stations: AM, 16; FM, 14
Television stations: 10
1980 CENSUS: Population 65 and over, 10.4%; **under 18,** 23.1%; **Black,** 1.2%; **Spanish, origin,** 5.2%
CIVILIAN LABOR FORCE: 379,200
Unemployed: 11,500, **Percent:** 3.0
Per capita personal income: $16,412
Chamber of Commerce: Chamber of Commerce of Hawaii, 735 Bishop St., Honolulu, Hawaii 96813
1. City and county area. The census bureau does not include the entire city and county in its census of Honolulu. If it did, the 1980 census and rank would be 762,565 (12), and the estimated population and rank would be 830,600 (12).

HOUSTON, TEX.

Incorporated as city: 1837
Mayor: Kathryn J. Whitmire (to Dec. 1989)
1980 population (1980 census) & (rank): 1,611,382 (5)
1986 est. population & (rank): 1,728,910 (4)
1988 est. population & (rank): 1,730,000 (4)
Land area: 579.58 sq mi. (1501.12 sq km)
Altitude: Highest, 120 ft; lowest, sea level
Location: In southeastern part of state, near Gulf of Mexico
County: Seat of Harris Co.
Churches: 1,750[2]
City-owned parks: 324 (32,500 ac.)
Radio stations: AM, 23; FM, 24[1]
Television stations: 11 commercial, 1 PBS
Poet Laureate: HUY-LUC Khoi Tien Bui
1980 CENSUS: Population 65 and over, 6.9%; **under 18,** 28.4%; **Black,** 27.6%; **Spanish, origin,** 17.6%
CIVILIAN LABOR FORCE: 1,607,600
Unemployed: 106,000, **Percent:** 6.6
Per capita personal income: $15,200
Chamber of Commerce: Houston Chamber of Commerce, 1100 Milam Building, 25th Fl., Houston, Tex. 77002
1. Includes annexations since 1970. 2. Harris County.

INDIANAPOLIS, IND.

Incorporated as city: 1832 (reincorporated 1838)
Mayor: William H. Hudnut III (to Jan. 1992)
1980 population (1980 census) & (rank): 700,807 (12)
1986 est. population & (rank): 719,820 (13)
Land area: 352.0 sq mi. (912 sq km)
Altitude: Highest, 840 ft; lowest, 700
Location: In central part of the state, on West Fork of White River
County: Seat of Marion Co.
Churches: 1,200[1]
City-owned parks: 134 (10,753 ac.)
Radio stations: AM, 9; FM, 18

Television stations: 7[1]
1980 CENSUS: Population 65 and over, 10.3%; **under 18,** 28.6%; **Black,** 21.8%; **Spanish, origin,** 0.9%
CIVILIAN LABOR FORCE: 672,500
Unemployed: 27,700, **Percent:** 4.1
Per capita personal income: $15,809
Chamber of Commerce: Indianapolis Chamber of Commerce, 320 N Meridian St., Indianapolis, Ind. 46202
1. Marion County.

JACKSONVILLE, FLA.

Incorporated as city: 1822
Mayor: Tommy Hazouri (to July 1, 1991)
1980 population (1980 census) & (rank): 540,920 (22)
1986 est. population & rank: 609,860 (17)
Land area: 759.6 sq mi. (1,967 sq km)
Altitude: Highest, 71 ft; lowest, sea level
Location: On St. Johns River, 20 miles from Atlantic Ocean
County: Duval
Churches: Protestant, 608; Roman Catholic, 20; Jewish, 5; others, 23
City-owned parks and playgrounds: 138 (1,522 ac.)
Radio stations: AM, 16; FM, 12
Television stations: 6 commercial, 1 PBS
1980 CENSUS: Population 65 and over, 9.6%; **under 18,** 28.8%; **Black,** 25.4%; **Spanish, origin,** 1.8%
CIVILIAN LABOR FORCE: 448,900
Unemployed: 28,500, **Percent:** 6.4
Per capita personal income: $14,611
Chamber of Commerce: Jacksonville Area Chamber of Commerce, Jacksonville, Fla. 32202

KANSAS CITY, MO.

Incorporated as city: 1850
Mayor: Richard L. Berkley (April 10, 1991)
City Manager: David H. Olson (apptd. Nov. 1984)
1980 population (1980 census) & (rank): 448,028 (27)
1986 est. population & (rank): 441,170 (29)
Land area: 316.41 sq mi. (819 sq km)
Altitude: Highest, 1,014 ft; lowest, 722
Location: In western part of state, at juncture of Missouri and Kansas Rivers
County: Located in Jackson, Clay, and Platte Co.
Churches: 1,100 churches of all denominations
City-owned parks and playgrounds: 177 (7,646 ac.)
Radio stations: AM, 14; FM, 13[1]
Television stations: 6[1]
1980 CENSUS: Population 65 and over, 12.3%; **under 18,** 26.5%; **Black,** 27.4%; **Spanish, origin,** 3.3%
CIVILIAN LABOR FORCE: 849,400
Unemployed: 49,700, **Percent:** 5.8
Per capita personal income: $16,309
Chamber of Commerce: Chamber of Commerce of Greater Kansas City, 920 Main St., Kansas City, Mo. 64105
1. Metropolitan area.

LONG BEACH, CALIF.

Incorporated as city: 1888
Mayor: Ernie Kell (to third Tuesday of 1990)

City Manager: James C. Hankla
1980 population (1980 census) & (rank): 361,496 (38)
1986 est. population & rank: 396,280 (33)
1988 est. population: 415,808
Land area: 49.8 sq mi. (129 sq km)
Altitude: Highest, 170 ft; lowest, sea level
Location: On San Pedro Bay, south of Los Angeles
County: Los Angeles
Churches: 236
City-owned parks: 42 (1,182 ac.)
Radio stations: AM, 2; FM, 2
Television stations: 1 (cable)
1980 CENSUS: Population 65 and over, 14.0%; under 18,
    22.9%; Black, 11.3%; Spanish, origin, 14.0%
CIVILIAN LABOR FORCE: 4,168,100[1]
Unemployed: 184,300,[1] Percent: 4.4[1]
Per capita personal income: $17,863[1]
Chamber of Commerce: Long Beach Area Chamber of
    Commerce, P.O. Box 690, Long Beach, CA 90801, (213)
    436-1251
1. Los Angeles-Long Beach MSA.

LOS ANGELES, CALIF.

Incorporated as city: 1850
Mayor: Tom Bradley (to June 1993)
1980 population (1980 census) & (rank): 2,968,528 (3)
1988 est. population: 3,361,500
1986 est. population & rank: 3,259,340 (2)
Land area: 470 sq mi. (1,217 sq km)
Altitude: Highest, 5,081 ft; lowest, sea level
Location: In southwestern part of state, on Pacific Ocean
County: Seat of Los Angeles Co.
Churches: 2,000 of all denominations
City-owned parks: 354 (15,002 ac.)
Radio stations: AM, 33; FM, 41
Television stations: 18
1980 CENSUS: Population 65 and over, 10.6%; under 18,
    25.1%; Black, 17.0%; Spanish, origin, 27.5%
CIVILIAN LABOR FORCE: 4,168,100[1]
Unemployed: 184,300,[1] Percent: 4.4[1]
Per capita personal income: $17,863[1]
Chamber of Commerce: Los Angeles Chamber of
    Commerce, 404 S Bixel St., Los Angeles, Calif. 90017
1. Los Angeles-Long Beach MSA.

MEMPHIS, TENN.

Incorporated as city: 1826
Mayor: Richard C. Hackett (to Dec. 1991)
1980 population (1980 census) & (rank): 646,356 (14)
1986 est. population & (rank): 652,640 (15)
Land area: 281 sq mi. (751.30 sq km)
Altitude: Highest, 331 ft
Location: In southwestern corner of state, on Mississippi
    River
County: Seat of Shelby Co.
Churches: 800
Parks and playgrounds: 175 (5,600 ac.)
Radio stations: AM, 12; FM, 8
Television stations: 6
1980 CENSUS: Population 65 and over, 10.4%; under 18,
    29.1%; Black, 47.6%; Spanish, origin, 0.8%
CIVILIAN LABOR FORCE: 443,400
Unemployed: 25,000, Percent: 5.6
Per capita personal income: $14,271
Chamber of Commerce: Memphis Area Chamber of
    Commerce, P.O. Box 224, Memphis, Tenn. 38103
1. Includes all Governmental Fund types and Expendable
Trust Funds.

MIAMI, FLA.

Incorporated as city: 1896
Mayor: Xavier L. Suarez (to Nov. 1989)
City manager: Cesar Odio (apptd. Dec. 1985)
1980 population (1980 census) & (rank): 346,681 (42)
1987 est. population: 380,000
1986 est. population & rank: 373,940 (36)
Land area: 34.3 sq mi. (89 sq km)
Altitude: Average, 12 ft
Location: In southeastern part of state, on Biscayne Bay
County: Seat of Dade Co.
Churches: Protestant, 592; Roman Catholic, 53; Jewish, 48
City-owned parks: 103
Radio stations: AM, 18; FM, 20
Television stations: 8 commercial, 2 PBS
1980 CENSUS: Population 65 and over, 17.0%; under 18,
    21.4%; Black, 25.1%; Spanish, origin, 55.9%
CIVILIAN LABOR FORCE: 929,500[1]
Unemployed: 58,200,[1] Percent: 6.3[1]
Per capita personal income: $15,689[1]
Chamber of Commerce: Greater Miami Chamber of
    Commerce, 1601 Biscayne Blvd., Miami, Fla. 33132
1. Miami-Hialeah MSA.

MILWAUKEE, WIS.

Incorporated as city: 1846
Mayor: John O. Norquist (to April 1992)
1980 population (1980 census) & (rank): 636,298 (16)
1986 est. population & (rank): 605,090 (18)
Land area: 95.8 sq mi. (248 sq km)
Altitude: 580.60 ft
Location: In southeastern part of state, on Lake Michigan
County: Seat of Milwaukee Co.
Churches: 411
County-owned parks: 14,758 ac.
Radio stations: AM, 15; FM, 8
Television stations: 10
1980 CENSUS: Population 65 and over, 12.5%; under 18,
    27.0%; Black, 23.1%; Spanish, origin, 4.1%
CIVILIAN LABOR FORCE: 770,000
Unemployed: 28,800, Percent: 4.6
Per capita personal income: $16,686
Chamber of Commerce: Metropolitan Milwaukee Association
    of Commerce, 828 N. Broadway, Milwaukee, Wis. 53202

MINNEAPOLIS, MINN.

Incorporated as city: 1867
Mayor: Donald M. Fraser (to Jan. 1990)
1980 population (1980 census) & (rank): 370,951 (36)
1986 est. population & (rank): 356,840 (43)
Land area: 55.1 sq mi. (143 sq km)
Altitude: Highest, 945 ft; lowest, 695
Location: In southeast central part of state, on Mississippi
    River
County: Seat of Hennepin Co.
Churches: 419
City-owned parks: 153
Radio stations: AM, 17; FM, 15 (metro area)
Television stations: 6 (metro area)
1980 CENSUS: Population 65 and over, 15.4%; under 18,
    20.0%; Black, 7.7%; Spanish, origin, 1.3%
CIVILIAN LABOR FORCE: 1,389,100[1]
Unemployed: 54,800,[1] Percent: 3.9[1]
Per capita personal income: $18,277[1]
Chamber of Commerce: Greater Minneapolis Chamber of
    Commerce, 15 S Fifth Street, Minneapolis, Minn. 55402
1. Minneapolis-St. Paul MSA.

NASHVILLE-DAVIDSON, TENN.

Incorporated as city: 1806
Mayor: Bill Boner (to August, 1991)
1980 population (1980 census) & (rank): 455,651 (25)
1986 est. population & (rank): 473,670 (26)
Land area: 533 sq mi. (1,380 sq km)
Altitude: Highest, 1,100 ft; lowest, approx. 400 ft
Location: In north central part of state, on Cumberland River
County: Davidson
Churches: Protestant, 739; Roman Catholic, 15; Jewish, 3
City-owned parks: 72 (6,650 ac.)
Radio stations: AM, 11; FM, 8
Television stations: 7
1980 CENSUS: Population 65 and over, 11.0%; **under 18,** 25.0%; **Black,** 23.3%; **Spanish, origin,** 0.8%
CIVILIAN LABOR FORCE: 516,900
Unemployed: 23,900, **Percent:** 4.6
Per capita personal income: $15,253
Chamber of Commerce: Nashville Area Chamber of Commerce, 161 Fourth Ave. North, Nashville, Tenn. 37219

NEWARK, N.J.

Incorporated as city: 1836
Mayor: Sharpe James (to June 1990)
1980 population (1980 census) & (rank): 329,248 (47)
1986 est. population & (rank): 316,240 (50)
Land area: 24.1 sq mi. (62 sq km)
Altitude: Highest, 273.4 ft; lowest, sea level
Location: In northeastern part of state, on Passaic River and Newark Bay
County: Seat of Essex Co.
Churches: Roman Catholic, 37; Jewish, 2; Protestant and others, 250
City-owned parks: 40 (and 20 mini parks); (39.3 ac.)
County-governed parks in city: 7 (743.97 ac.)
Radio stations: AM, 2; FM, 4
Television stations: 3
1980 CENSUS: Population 65 and over, 8.8%; **under 18,** 34.1%; **Black,** 58.2%; **Spanish, origin,** 18.6%
CIVILIAN LABOR FORCE: 961,600
Unemployed: 43,700, **Percent:** 4.5
Per capita personal income: $21,061
Chamber of Commerce: Greater Newark Chamber of Commerce, 40 Clinton St., Newark, N.J. 07102

NEW ORLEANS, LA.

Incorporated as city: 1805
Mayor: Sidney J. Barthelemy (to May 1990)
1980 population (1980 census) & (rank): 557,927 (21)
1988 est. population: 546,325
1986 est. population & rank: 554,500 (21)
Land area: 199.4 sq mi. (516 sq km)
Altitude: Highest, 15 ft; lowest, −4
Location: In southeastern part of state, between Mississippi River and Lake Ponchartrain
Parish: Seat of Orleans Parish
Churches: 644
City-owned parks: 266 (4,460 ac.)
Radio stations: AM, 12; FM, 13
Television stations: 7
1980 CENSUS: Population 65 and over, 11.7%; **under 18,** 28.8%; **Black,** 55.3%; **Spanish, origin,** 3.4%
CIVILIAN LABOR FORCE: 584,800
Unemployed: 57,100, **Percent:** 9.8
Per capita personal income: $13,130
Chamber of Commerce: New Orleans and the River Region

Chamber of Commerce, 301 Camp Street, New Orleans, La. 70130

NEW YORK, N.Y.

Chartered as "Greater New York": 1898
Mayor: Edward I. Koch (to Dec. 31, 1989)
Borough Presidents: Bronx, Fernando Ferrer; Brooklyn, Howard Golden; Manhattan, David N. Dinkins; Queens, Claire Shulman; Staten Island, Ralph J. Lamberti
1980 population (1980 census) & (rank): 7.071,639 (1)[1]
1986 est. population & (rank): 7,262,700 (1)[1]
Land area: 314.7 sq mi. (815 sq km) (Queens, 112.83; Brooklyn, 74.45; Staten Island, 60.06; Bronx, 43.63; Manhattan, 23.73)
Altitude: Highest, 410 ft; lowest, sea level
Location: In south of state, at mouth of Hudson River (also known as the North River as it passes Manhattan)
Counties: Consists of 5 counties: Bronx, Kings (Brooklyn), New York (Manhattan), Queens, Richmond (Staten Island)
Churches: Protestant, 1,766; Jewish, 1,256; Roman Catholic, 437; Orthodox, 66
City-owned parks: 1,701 (26,138 ac.)
Radio stations: AM, 13, FM, 18
Television stations: 6 commercial, 1 public
1980 CENSUS: Population 65 and over, 13.5%; **under 18,** 25.0%; **Black,** 25.2%; **Spanish, origin,** 19.9%
CIVILIAN LABOR FORCE: 3,264,100
Unemployed: 184,600, **Percent:** 5.7
Per capita personal income: $19,185
Chamber of Commerce: New York Chamber of Commerce and Industry, 65 Liberty St., New York, N.Y. 10005

1. For population of boroughs, *see* Index.

OAKLAND, CALIF.

Incorporated as city: 1854
Mayor: Lionel J. Wilson (to Jan., 1991)
City Manager: Henry L. Gardner (apptd. June 1981)
1980 population (1980 census) & (rank): 339,337 (44)
1986 est. population & rank: 356,960 (42)
Land area: 53.9 sq mi.
Altitude: Highest, 1,700 ft; lowest, sea level
Location: In west central part of state, on east side of San Francisco Bay
County: Seat of Alameda Co.
Churches: 374, representing over 78 denominations in the City; over 500 churches in Alameda County
City-owned parks: 2,196 ac.
Radio stations: AM, 3; FM, 2
Television stations: 9 commercial; 3 PBS
1980 CENSUS: Population 65 and over, 13.2%; **under 18,** 24.3%; **Black,** 46.9%; **Spanish, origin,** 9.6%
CIVILIAN LABOR FORCE: 1,087,700
Unemployed: 49,000, **Percent:** 4.5
Per capita personal income: $19,896
Chamber of Commerce: Oakland Chamber of Commerce, 475 Fourteenth St., Oakland, Calif. 94612-1928

OKLAHOMA CITY, OKLA.

Incorporated as city: 1890
Mayor: Ron Norick
City Manager: Terry Childers
1980 population (1980 census) & (rank): 404,014 (31)
1986 est. population & (rank): 446,120 (28)

Land area: 648.3 sq mi. (1,679.1 sq km)
Altitude: Highest, 1,320 ft; lowest, 1,140
Location: In central part of state, on North Canadian River
County: Seat of Oklahoma Co.
Churches: Roman Catholic, 15; Jewish, 2; Protestant and others, 741
City-owned parks: 138 (3,944 ac.)
Television stations: 8
Radio stations: AM, 10; FM, 14
1980 CENSUS: Population 65 and over, 11.3%; **under 18,** 27.0%; **Black,** 14.6%; **Spanish, origin,** 2.8%
CIVILIAN LABOR FORCE: 491,300
Unemployed: 26,300, **Percent:** 5.3
Per capita personal income: $13,735
Chamber of Commerce: Oklahoma City Chamber of Commerce, 1 Santa Fe Plaza, Oklahoma City, Okla. 73102

OMAHA, NEB.

Incorporated as city: 1857
Mayor: P.J. Morgan (to June 1993)
1980 population (1980 census) & (rank): 342,786 (43)
1986 est. population & rank: 349,270 (45)
Land area: 90.9 sq mi. (235 sq km)
Altitude: Highest, 1,270 ft
Location: In eastern part of state, on Missouri River
County: Seat of Douglas Co.
Churches: Protestant, 246; Roman Catholic, 44; Jewish, 4
City-owned parks: 99 (3,671.6 ac.)
Radio stations: AM, 7; FM, 6
Television stations: 4
1980 CENSUS: Population 65 and over, 12.2%; **under 18,** 27.5%; **Black,** 12.0%; **Spanish, origin,** 2.3%
CIVILIAN LABOR FORCE: 330,600
Unemployed: 12,300, **Percent:** 3.7
Per capita personal income: $15,033
Chamber of Commerce: Omaha Chamber of Commerce, 1301 Harway St., Omaha, Neb. 68102

PHILADELPHIA, PA.

First charter as city: 1701
Mayor: W. Wilson Goode (to Nov. 1991)
1980 population (1980 census) & (rank): 1,688,210 (4)
1986 est. population & (rank): 1,642,900 (5)
Land area: 136.0 sq mi. (352 sq km)
Altitude: Highest, 440 ft; lowest, sea level
Location: In southeastern part of state, at junction of Schuylkill and Delaware Rivers
County: Seat of Philadelphia Co. (coterminous)
Churches: Roman Catholic, 133; Jewish, 55; Protestant and others, 830
City-owned parks: 630 (10,252 ac.)
Radio stations: AM, 10; FM, 22
Television stations: 8
1980 CENSUS: Population 65 and over, 14.1%; **under 18,** 25.9%; **Black,** 37.8%; **Spanish, origin,** 3.8%
CIVILIAN LABOR FORCE: 2,465,000
Unemployed: 99,200, **Percent:** 4.0
Per capita personal income: $17,294
Chamber of Commerce: Philadelphia Chamber of Commerce, 1346 Chestnut St., Suite 800, Philadelphia, Pa. 19107

PHOENIX, ARIZ.

Incorporated as city: 1881
Mayor: Terry Goddard (to Jan. 1990)
City Manager: Marvin A. Andrews (appt. Oct. 1976)
1980 population (1980 census) & (rank): 790,183 (10)
1986 est. population & (rank): 894,070 (10)
1988 est. population & rank: 965,808 (10)
Land area: 403.4 sq mi. (1,044 sq km)
Altitude: Highest, 2,740 ft.; lowest, 1,017
Location: In center of state, on Salt River
County: Seat of Maricopa Co.
City-owned parks: 135 (29,925 ac.)
Radio stations: AM, 18; FM, 17
Television stations: 9 commercial; 1 PBS
1980 CENSUS: Population 65 and over, 9.3%; **under 18,** 29.0%; **Black,** 4.8%; **Spanish, origin,** 14.8%
CIVILIAN LABOR FORCE: 1,030,000
Unemployed: 49,400, **Percent:** 4.8
Per capita personal income: $16,077
Chamber of Commerce: Phoenix Chamber of Commerce, 34 W. Monroe St., Phoenix, Ariz. 85003

PITTSBURGH, PA.

Incorporated as city: 1816
Mayor: Sophie Masloff (to Jan. 1990)
1980 population (1980 census) & (rank): 423,960 (30)
1986 est. population & (rank): 387,490 (35)
Land area: 55.5 sq mi. (144 sq km)
Altitude: Highest, 1,240 ft; lowest, 715
Location: In southwestern part of state, at beginning of Ohio River
County: Seat of Allegheny Co.
Churches: Protestant, 348; Roman Catholic, 86; Jewish, 28; Orthodox, 26
City-owned parks and playgrounds: 270 (2,572 ac.)
Radio stations: AM, 18; FM, 9
Television stations: 8
1980 CENSUS: Population 65 and over, 16.0%; **under 18,** 21.4%; **Black,** 24.0%; **Spanish, origin,** 0.8%
CIVILIAN LABOR FORCE: 975,000
Unemployed: 52,800, **Percent:** 5.4
Per capita personal income: $15,419
Chamber of Commerce: The Chamber of Commerce of Greater Pittsburgh, 3 Gateway Center, Pittsburgh, Pa. 15222

PORTLAND, ORE.

Incorporated as city: 1851
Mayor: John (Bud) Clark (till Jan. 1993)
1980 est. population (1980 census) & rank: 396,666 (32)
1988 est. population: 429,415
1986 est. population & rank: 387,870 (34)
Land area: 135 sq. mi. (350 sq. km.)
Altitude: Highest, 1073 ft. lowest, sea level
Location: In northwestern part of the state on Willamette River
County: Seat of Multnomah Co.
Churches: Protestant, 450; Roman Catholic, 48; Jewish, 9, Buddhist, 6; other, 190
City-owned parks: 200 (over 9,400 ac.)
Radio stations: AM: 14, FM: 14
Television stations: 5 commercial, 1 public
1980 CENSUS: Population 65 and over, 15.3%; **under 18,** 21.8%; **Black,** 7.6%; **Spanish, origin,** 2.1%
CIVILIAN LABOR FORCE: 653,900

Unemployed: 30,100, Percent: 4.6
Per capita personal income: $15,732
Chamber of Commerce: Portland Chamber of Commerce, 221 NW 2nd Ave., Portland, Ore. 97209

Per capita personal income: $12,291
Chamber of Commerce: Greater San Antonio Chamber of Commerce, P.O. Box 1628, 602 E Commerce, San Antonio, Tex. 78296

SACRAMENTO, CALIF.

Incorporated as city: 1849
Mayor: Anne Rudin (to Sept. 1991)
1980 population (1980 census) & rank: 275,741 (52)
1986 est. population & rank: 326,400 (49)
Land area: 98 sq mi. (249 sq km)
County: Seat of Sacramento Co.
City park & recreational facilities: 120+ (2,000+ ac.)
Television stations: 7
1980 CENSUS: Population 65 and over, 13.6%; under 18, 24.6%; Black, 13.4%; Spanish, origin, 14.2%
CIVILIAN LABOR FORCE: 719,000
Unemployed: 40,800, Percent: 5.7
Per capita personal income: $16,300
Chamber of Commerce: Sacramento Chamber of Commerce, 917 7th St., Sacramento, Calif. 95814; West Sacramento Chamber of Commerce, 834-C Jefferson Blvd., Sacramento, Calif. 95691

ST. LOUIS, MO.

Incorporated as city: 1822
Mayor: Vincent Schoemehl, Jr. (to April 1989)
1980 population (1980 census) & (rank): 452,804 (26)
1987 est. population: 435,900
1986 est. population & rank: 426,300 (31)
Land area: 61.4 sq mi. (159 sq km)
Altitude: Highest, 616 ft; lowest, 413
Location: In east central part of state, on Mississippi River
County: Independent city
Churches: 900[1]
City-owned parks: 89 (2,639 ac.)
Radio stations: AM, 21; FM 27 (Metro area)[1]
Television stations: 6 commercial; 1 PBS
1980 CENSUS: Population 65 and over, 17.6%; under 18, 26.1%; Black, 45.6%; Spanish, origin, 1.2%
CIVILIAN LABOR FORCE: 1,256,000
Unemployed: 78,700, Percent: 6.3
Per capita personal income: $16,706
Chamber of Commerce: St. Louis Regional Commerce and Growth Association, 100 S. Fourth St., Ste. 500, St. Louis, Mo. 63102
1. Metropolitan area.

SAN ANTONIO, TEX.

Incorporated as city: 1837
Mayor: Lila Cockrell (to May 1991)
City Manager: Louis J. Fox (apptd. Jan. 1982)
1980 population (1980 census) & (rank): 810,353 (9)
1986 est. population & (rank): 914,350 (9)
Land area: 328.53 sq mi. (841.89 sq km)
Altitude: 700 ft
Location: In south central part of state, on San Antonio River
County: Seat of Bexar Co.
City-owned parks: Approximately 6,235.9 ac.
Radio stations: AM, 13; FM, 12
Television stations: 5
1980 CENSUS: Population 65 and over, 9.5%; under 18, 32.2%; Black, 7.3%; Spanish, origin, 53.7%
CIVILIAN LABOR FORCE: 599,100
Unemployed: 48,000, Percent: 8.0

SAN DIEGO, CALIF.

Incorporated as city: 1850
Mayor: Maureen O'Connor (to Dec. 11, 1992)
City Manager: John Lockwood (apptd. Sept. 1986)
1980 population (1980 census) & (rank): 875,538 (8)
1986 est. population & rank: 1,015,190 (7)
1988 est, population: 1,058,700 (7)
Land area: 403.4 sq miles (1,045 sq km)
Altitude: Highest, 1,591 ft; lowest, sea level
Location: In southwesternmost part of state, on San Diego Bay
County: Seat of San Diego Co.
Churches: Roman Catholic, 98; Jewish, 17; Protestant, 334 Eastern Orthodox, 7; other, 6
City park and recreation facilities: 147 (16,453 ac.)
Radio stations: AM, 14; FM, 22
Television stations: 7
1980 CENSUS: Population 65 and over, 9.7%; under 18, 24.1%; Black, 8.9%; Spanish, origin, 14.9%
CIVILIAN LABOR FORCE: 1,142,700
Unemployed: 46,200, Percent: 4.0
Per capita personal income: $16,633
Chamber of Commerce: San Diego Chamber of Commerce, 110 West C St., Ste. 1600, San Diego, Calif. 92101

SAN FRANCISCO, CALIF.

Incorporated as city: 1850
Mayor: Art Agnos (to Jan. 1992)
1980 population (1980 census) & (rank): 678,974 (13)
1986 est. population & (rank): 749,000 (12)
Land area: 46.1 sq mi. (120 sq km)
Altitude: Highest, 925 ft; lowest, sea level
Location: In northern part of state between Pacific Ocean and San Francisco Bay
County: Coextensive with San Francisco Co.
Churches: 540 of all denominations
City-owned parks and squares: 225
Radio stations: 29
Television stations: 10
1980 CENSUS: Population 65 and over, 15.4%; under 18, 17.2%; Black, 12.7%; Spanish, origin, 12.3%
CIVILIAN LABOR FORCE: 889,300
Unemployed: 31,500, Percent: 3.5
Per capita personal income: $24,593
Chamber of Commerce: Greater San Francisco Chamber of Commerce, 465 California St., San Francisco, Calif. 94104

SAN JOSE, CALIF.

Incorporated as city: 1850
Mayor: Thomas McEnery (to Dec. 31, 1990)
City Manager: Leslie R. White (apptd. May 1989)
1980 population (1980 census) & (rank): 629,402 (17)
1989 est. population: 738,399
1986 est. population & rank: 712,080 (14)
Land area: 172.2 sq mi. (446 sq km)
Altitude: Highest, 4,372 ft; lowest, sea level
Location: In northern part of state, on south San Francisco Bay, 50 miles from San Francisco
County: Seat of Santa Clara County

Churches: 403
City-owned parks and playgrounds: 152 (3,136 ac.)
Radio stations: 14
Television stations: 4
1980 CENSUS: Population 65 and over, 6.2%; **under 18,** 31.0%; **Black,** 4.6%; **Spanish, origin,** 22.3%
CIVILIAN LABOR FORCE: 850,200
Unemployed: 33,900, **Percent:** 4.0
Per capita personal income: $21,510
Chamber of Commerce: San Jose Chamber of Commerce, One Paseo de San Antonio, San Jose, Calif. 95113

SEATTLE, WASH.

Incorporated as city: 1869
Mayor: Charles Royer (to Dec. 1989)
1980 population (1980 census) & (rank): 493,846 (23)
1986 est. population & (rank): 486,200 (25)
Land area: 144.6 sq mi. (375 sq km)
Altitude: Highest, 540 ft; lowest, sea level
Location: In west central part of state, on Puget Sound
County: Seat of King Co.
Churches: Roman Catholic, 36; Jewish, 13; Protestant and others, 535
City-owned parks, playgrounds, etc.: 278 (4,773.4 ac.)
Radio stations: AM, 22; FM, 26
Television stations: 3 commercial; 1 educational
1980 CENSUS: Population 65 and over, 15.4%; **under 18,** 17.6%; **Black,** 9.5%; **Spanish, origin,** 2.6%
CIVILIAN LABOR FORCE: 1,057,200
Unemployed: 52,800, **Percent:** 5.0
Per capita personal income: $18,610
Chamber of Commerce: Seattle Chamber of Commerce, 1200 One Union Square, Seattle, Wash. 98101

TOLEDO, OHIO

Incorporated as city: 1837
Mayor: Donna Owens (to Dec. 1989)
City Manager: Phillip Hawkey
1980 population (1980 census) & (rank): 354,635 (41)
1986 est. population & (rank): 340,680 (46)
Land area: 84.2 sq mi. (218 sq km)
Altitude: 630 ft
Location: In northwestern part of state, on Maumee River at Lake Erie
County: Seat of Lucas Co.
Churches: Protestant, 301; Roman Catholic, 55; Jewish, 4; others, 98
City-owned parks and playgrounds: 134 (2,650.90 ac.)
Radio stations: AM, 8; FM, 8
Television stations: 6
1980 CENSUS: Population 65 and over, 12.5%; **under 18,** 28.1%; **Black,** 17.4%; **Spanish, origin,** 3.0%
CIVILIAN LABOR FORCE: 317,100
Unemployed: 22,300, **Percent:** 7.0
Per capita personal income: $15,103
Chamber of Commerce: Toledo Area Chamber of Commerce, 218 Huron St., Toledo, Ohio 43604

TUCSON, ARIZ.

Incorporated as city: 1877
Mayor: Thomas J. Volgy (to Dec. 1991)
1980 population (1980 census) & (rank): 338,636 (45)

1987 est. population: 399,300
1986 est. population & (rank): 358,850 (41)
Land area: 130 sq mi. (336.7 sq km)
Altitude: 2,500 ft
Location: In southeastern part of state, on the Santa Cruz River
County: Seat of Pima Co.
Churches: Protestant, 325; Roman Catholic, 40; other, 74
City-owned parks and parkways: (25,349 ac.)
Radio stations: AM, 16; FM, 11
Television stations: 3 commercial; 1 educational; 4 other
1980 CENSUS: Population 65 and over, 11.7%; **under 18,** 25.5%; **Black,** 3.7%; **Spanish, origin,** 24.9%
CIVILIAN LABOR FORCE: 314,300
Unemployed: 14,800, **Percent:** 4.7
Per capita personal income: $13,845
Chamber of Commerce: Tucson Metropolitan Chamber of Commerce, P.O. Box 991, Tucson, Ariz. 85702

TULSA, OKLA.

Incorporated as city: 1898
Mayor: Rodger Randle (to May 1990)
1980 population (1980 census) & (rank): 360,919 (39)
1986 est. population & rank: 373,644 (37)
Land area: 192.459 sq mi. (499 sq km)
Altitude: 674 ft
Location: In northeastern part of state, on Arkansas River
County: Seat of Tulsa Co.
Churches: Protestant, 593; Roman Catholic, 32; Jewish, 2; others, 4
City parks and playgrounds: 113 (5,338 ac.)
Radio stations: AM, 7; FM, 8
Television stations: 5 commercial; 1 PBS; 1 cable
1980 CENSUS: Population 65 and over, 10.8%; **under 18,** 25.8%; **Black,** 11.8%; **Spanish, origin,** 1.7%
CIVILIAN LABOR FORCE: 338,100
Unemployed: 23,100, **Percent:** 6.8
Per capita personal income: $14,085
Chamber of Commerce: Metropolitan Tulsa Chamber of Commerce, 616 S Boston, Tulsa, Okla. 74119

VIRGINIA BEACH, VA.

Incorporated as city: 1963
Mayor: Meyera E. Obendorf (to June 30, 1992)
1980 population (1980 census) & (rank): 262,199 (56)
1989 est. population: 390,800
1986 est. population & rank: 333,400 (47)
Land area: 258.7 sq mi. (670 sq km)
Altitude: 12 ft
Location: Southeastern most portion of state, on Atlantic coastline
County: None
Churches: Protestant, 159; Catholic, 8; Jewish, 4
City-owned parks: 151 (1,748 ac.)
Radio stations: AM 18, FM 22
Television stations: 4 commercial, 1 PBS, 1 cable
1980 CENSUS: Population 65 and over, 4.5%; **under 18,** 30.7%; **Black,** 10.0%; **Spanish, origin,** 2.0%
CIVILIAN LABOR FORCE: 596,700[1]
Unemployed: 29,700[1], **Percent:** 5.0[1]
Per capita personal income: $14,462[1]
Chamber of Commerce: Hampton Roads Chamber of Commerce, 4512 Virginia Beach Blvd., Virginia Beach, Va., 23456

1. Norfolk-Virginia Beach-Newport News MSA.

WASHINGTON, D.C.

Land ceded to Congress: 1788 by Maryland; 1789 by Virginia (retroceded to Virginia Sept. 7, 1846)
Seat of government transferred to D. C.: Dec. 1, 1800
Created municipal corporation: Feb. 21, 1871
Mayor: Marion Barry, Jr. (to Jan. 1991)
Motto: *Justitia omnibus* (Justice to all)
Flower: American beauty rose
Tree: Scarlet oak
Origin of name: In honor of Columbus
1980 population (1980 census) & (rank): 638,432 (15)
1986 est. population & (rank): 626,000 (16)
Land area: 68.25 sq mi. (176.12 sq km)
Geographic center: Near corner of Fourth and L Sts., NW
Altitude: Highest, 420 ft; lowest, sea level
Location: Between Virginia and Maryland, on Potomac River
Churches: Protestant, 610; Roman Catholic, 45; Jewish, 15
City parks: 753 (7,725 ac.)
Radio stations: AM, 29; FM, 26
Television stations: 6 (including 2 UHF stations)
1980 CENSUS: Population 65 and over, 11.6%; **under 18,** 22.5%; **Black,** 70.3%; **Spanish, origin,** 2.8%
CIVILIAN LABOR FORCE: 2,212,400
Unemployed: 61,600, **Percent:** 2.8
Per capita personal income: $21,539
Chamber of Commerce: D.C. Chamber of Commerce, 1319 F St., NW, Washington, D.C. 20004

The District of Columbia—identical with the City of Washington—is the capital of the United States and the first carefully planned capital in the world.

D.C. history began in 1790 when Congress directed selection of a new capital site, 10 miles square, along the Potomac. When the site was determined, it included 30.75 square miles on the Virginia side of the river. In 1846, however, Congress returned that area to Virginia, leaving the 68.25 square miles ceded by Maryland.

The city was planned and partly laid out by Major Pierre Charles L. 'Enfant, a French engineer. This work was perfected and completed by Major Andrew Ellicott and Benjamin Banneker, a freeborn black man, who was an astronomer and mathematician. In 1814, during the War of 1812, a British force fired the capital, and it was from the white paint applied to cover fire damage that the President's home was called the White House.

Until Nov. 3, 1967, the District of Columbia was administered by three commissioners appointed by the President. On that day, a government consisting of a mayor-commissioner and a 9-member Council, all appointed by the President with the approval of the Senate, took office. On May 7, 1974, the citizens of the District of Columbia approved a Home Rule Charter, giving them an elected mayor and 13-member council—their first elected municipal government in more than a century. The District also has one non-voting member in the House of Representatives and an elected Board of Education.

On Aug. 22, 1978, Congress passed a proposed constitutional amendment to give Washington, D.C., voting representation in the Congress. The amendment had to be ratified by at least 28 state legislatures within seven years to become effective. As of 1985 it died.

A petition asking for the District's admission to the Union as the 51st State was filed in Congress on September 9, 1983. The District is continuing this drive for statehood.

Estimated Population of 50 Largest U.S. Cities—July 1986

City	Population	1986 Rank	1980 Rank	City	Population	1986 Rank	1980 Rank
New York, NY	7,262,700	1	1	Nashville–Davidson, TN	473,670	26	25
Los Angles, CA	3,259,340	2	3	Austin, TX	466,550	27	35
Chicago, IL	3,009,530	3	2	Oklahoma City, OK	446,120	28	31
Houston, TX	1,728,910	4	5	Kansas City, MO	441,170	29	27
Philadelphia, PA	1,642,900	5	4	Fort Worth, TX	429,550	30	34
Detroit, MI	1,086,220	6	6	St. Louis, MO	426,300	31	26
San Diego, CA	1,015,190	7	8	Atlanta, GA	421,910	32	29
Dallas, TX	1,003,520	8	7	Long Beach, CA	396,280	33	38
San Antonio, TX	914,350	9	9	Portland, OR	387,870	34	32
Phoenix, AZ[1]	894,070	10	10	Pittsburgh, PA	387,490	35	30
Baltimore, MD	752,800	11	11	Miami, FL	373,940	36	42
San Francisco, CA	749,000	12	13	Tulsa, OK	373,750	37	39
Indianapolis, IN	719,820	13	12	Honolulu, HI[2]	372,330	38	37
San Jose, CA	712,080	14	17	Cincinnati, OH	369,750	39	33
Memphis, TN	652,640	15	14	Albuquerque, NM	366,750	40	46
Washington, DC	626,000	16	15	Tucson, AZ[1]	358,850	41	45
Jacksonville, FL	609,860	17	22	Oakland, CA	356,960	42	44
Milwaukee, WI	605,090	18	16	Minneapolis, MN	356,840	43	36
Boston, MA	573,600	19	20	Charlotte, NC	352,070	44	48
Columbus, OH	566,030	20	19	Omaha, NE[1]	349,270	45	43
New Orleans, LA	554,500	21	21	Toledo, OH	340,680	46	41
Cleveland, OH	535,830	22	18	Virginia Beach, VA	333,400	47	56
Denver, CO	505,000	23	24	Buffalo, NY	324,820	48	40
El Paso, TX	491,800	24	28	Sacramento, CA	323,550	49	52
Seattle, WA	486,200	25	23	Newark, NJ	316,240	50	47

1. The 1980 count includes population annexed since January 1, 1980. 2. The city of Honolulu, coextensive with Honolulu County, is a Federal funding area not recognized as a city for census purposes. Honolulu census-designated place in 1980 had a population of 365,048. *Source:* U.S. Department of Commerce, Bureau of the Census.

Tabulated Data on City Governments

City	Mayor		City manager's salary[2]	Council or Commission			
	Term, years	Salary[1]		Name	Members	Term, years	Salary[3]
Albuquerque, N.M.	4	$52,600	52,500 [4]	Council	9	4	$5,260
Atlanta	4	90,000	62,928 [27]	Council	19	4	23,000
Austin, Tex.	3	26,000	100,000	Council	6	3	30,000
Baltimore	4	60,000	—	Council	19	4	29,000
Baton Rouge, La.	4	67,000	—	Council	12	4	3,600
Boston	4	100,000	—	Council	13	2	45,000
Buffalo, N.Y.	4	64,000	—	Council	13	2 [5]	34,000
Charlotte, N.C.	2	14,800	106,780	Council	11	2	8,000
Chicago	4	80,000	—	Council	50	4	40,000
Cincinnati	2	38,964	93,695	Council	9	2	35,464
Cleveland	4	67,318	—	Council	21	4	29,960
Columbus, Ohio	4	77,000	—	Council	7	4	25,000
Dallas	2	50 [6]	—	Council	11	2	50 [6]
Denver*	4	77,400	—	Council	13	4	28,680 [21, 28]
Detroit	4	125,350	—	Council	9	4	57,770 [29]
El Paso	2	25,000	—	Council	7 [7]	2	15,000
Fort Worth	2	10 [8]	100,000	Council	9	2	10 [8]
Honolulu	4	84,725	77,500 [9]	Council	9	4	35,000 [3]
Houston	2	105,000	—	Council	14	2	30,000
Indianapolis	4	79,042	—	Council	29	4	8,585 [10]
Jacksonville, Fla.	4	78,458	58,000 [11]	Council	19	4	18,666
Kansas City, Mo.	4	47,000	99,240	Council	13 [7]	4	19,500
Long Beach, Calif.	4	13,892 [25]	105,000	Council	9 [12]	4	13,892 [12]
Los Angeles	4	97,654	—	Council	15	4	58,592
Memphis, Tenn.	4	82,500	70,000 [5]	Council	13	4	6,000
Miami, Fla.	4	4,992 [13]	96,595.20	Commission	5 [7]	4	4,992
Milwaukee	4	81,770	—	Council	16	4	36,270
Minneapolis	4	63,000	76,284	Council	13	4	46,500
Nashville, Tenn.	4	79,935	—	Council	41	4	5,400
Newark, N.J.	4	77,215	80,143 [15]	Council	9	4	36,034 [23]
New Orleans	4	80,000	69,000	Council	7	4	44,625
New York	4	130,000	97,500 [14]	Council	35	4	55,000 [26]
Oakland, Calif.	4	80,000	90,000	Council	9 [7]	4	(16)
Oklahoma City	4	2,000	75,000	Council	8	4	20 [17]
Omaha, Neb.	4	60,900	—	Council	7	4	16,229 [3]
Philadelphia	4	84,550	62,500 [18]	Council	17	4	40,000
Phoenix, Ariz.	2	37,500	128,960	Council	9 [7]	2	18,000
Pittsburgh	4	64,425	—	Council	9	4	36,734
Portland, Ore.	4	63,928	—	Commission	4	4	55,557
Sacramento	4	8,100 [30]	107,000	Council	9 [12]	4	8,100 [31]
St. Louis	4	71,266	—	Board of Aldermen	29	4	18,500 [32]
San Antonio	2	3,000 [19]	100,000	Council	11 [7]	2	20 [20]
San Diego, Calif.	4	50,000	105,000	Council	8	4	45,000
San Francisco	4	122,356	121,212 [33]	Board of Supervisors	11	4	23,924
San Jose, Calif.	4	68,600	84,000	Council	10	4	45,750
Seattle	4	80,762	—	Council	9	4	54,815
Toledo, Ohio	4	85,000	80,000	Council	9 [12]	4	7,800
Tucson, Ariz.	4	24,000	111,000	Council	7	4	12,000
Tulsa, Okla.	2	50,000	—	Commission	4	2	38,500
Virginia Beach, Va.	2	17,000	90,000 [24]	Council	11	4	15,000
Washington, D.C.	4	85,000	79,500	Council	13	4	69,500 [22]

1. Annual salary unless otherwise indicated. 2. Annual salary. City Manager's term is indefinite and at will of Council (or Mayor). 3. Annual salary unless otherwise indicated. In some cities, President of Council receives a higher salary. 4. City Administrative Officer appointed by Mayor, approved by Council. 5. For 9 District Councilmen; 4 years for 3 Councilmen-at-Large. 6. Per Council meeting; not over $2,600 per year. 7. Including Mayor. 8. Per week and per Council meeting. 9. Managing Director appointed by Mayor; no Council approval required. 10. Plus $54 per meeting for three meetings a month. 11. Chief Administrative Officer appointed by Mayor; not subject to Council confirmation. 12. Including Mayor and Vice-Mayor. 13. Plus $2,500 expense account. 14. No City Manager; salary is for Deputy Mayor. 15. Business Administrator, appointed by Mayor and confirmed by Council. 16. Flat $1,800 per month, or $21,600 annually. 17. Per Council meeting; not to exceed 5 meetings a month. 18. Appointed by Mayor, with title of Managing Director. 19. Plus Council pay. 20. Per Council meeting; not over $1,040 per year. 21. Council President receives $28,992. 22. Council Chairman receives $79,500. 23. Annual allowance in lieu of expenses: Council members $13,000; Council President $15,000. 24. Plus $4,000 in travel expenses. 25. Plus $1,200 per month expense account. 26. Council President receives $105,000. 27. City Manager's salary up to $83,000. 28. Council President receives $33,680. 29. Council President receives $61,040. 30. Plus $4,500 annual expense account and $4,200 annual secretarial expense allowance. 31. Plus $3,000 annual expense account. 32. For 12 Aldermen $18,500, 16 Aldermen $21,460. 33. Chief Administrative Officer, $121,212. NOTE: An asterisk (*) indicates up-to-date information not provided. *Source: Information Please* questionnaires to the cities.

U.S. STATISTICS

The 1990 Census: 21 and Counting

An eminent French philosopher once said, "The United States presents in its history a phenomenon which has no parallel. It is that of a people who instituted the statistics of their country on the very day they founded their government." He made this observation because the U.S. Constitution, ratified in 1789, required an enumeration of the population at least every 10 years.

The 21st census will take a snapshot of America's estimated 250 million people, and may well be the nation's single most important source of information about ourselves. The results will tell us who we are and where and how we live. The data it collects will affect our lives for an entire decade.

Census accuracy has steadily improved during the 20th century but the bureau is still concerned about ensuring that the historically undercounted—for the most part segments of minority groups—are fully counted: The bureau is mounting special outreach and promotion efforts targeted for the American Indian, Asian, Black, and Hispanic communities to encourage full participation by these groups.

The 1990 census brings the additional challenge of counting millions of newly arrived persons of Asian and Hispanic descent as these communites have grown dramatically since the last census.

To aid in meeting this challenge, the Census Bureau has instituted the Local Review Program. The effort encourages officials in the nation's 39,000 local and tribal governments to voluntarily check Census Bureau maps and block-by-block housing unit counts compiled from a master list created and updated throughout the census period.

The Local Review Program is conducted in two phases. During the first phase, in November 1989, the Census Bureau will send preliminary housing unit counts, by block, to select governments in those areas of the nation where the census will be taken using the mail-out, mail-back method. These local officials have until January 5, 1990, to check the counts and return their comments to the bureau. If large discrepancies exist, then census workers will investigate them.

During the final phase of the Local Review Program after census day, all local and tribal governments will receive sets of maps and postcensus housing counts. The information will display the governments' boundaries as of January 1, 1990, based on the bureau's December 1989 Boundary and Annexation Survey.

After another period of local review, Census Bureau workers will recanvass those blocks where large discrepancies were discovered.

Aiding in the map preparation is a TIGER inside the computers at the Census Bureau.

TIGER is an acronym for the bureau's Topologically Integrated Geographic Encoding and Referencing System. Using TIGER the bureau has adapted computer-readable (digital) map information from the U.S. Geological Survey to produce the first complete, large-scale map set in U.S. history.

With the TIGER File, the bureau will produce maps for more than 300,000 field enumerators (census takers) to use in data collection activities for the 1990 census.

The TIGER system provides the capability of computer-assigning residential and business mailing addresses so that enumerators can validate mailing lists and visit households that do not respond to the census by mail. The system also provides the ability to rapidly update map features and boundaries when enumerators report new housing developments or local officials report changes in their boundaries.

All that most of us need worry about on Census Day, April 1, 1990, is to drop our completed questionnaires into a mailbox. If case you wonder what will become of them after that, here's the story:

Within 10 days following Census Day, some 70 million questionnaires are expected to flood back to the bureau by mail, creating a tidal wave of paper and data.

But the Census Bureau won't just stand there watching as millions of returning questionnaires accumulate. For years, the bureau has carefully prepared for "flow processing" that will enable it to place controls on each questionnaire the moment it arrives, earmarking each for editing or follow-up action, and finally sending them to the computers for extraction of data.

Flow processing is different from batch processing, the method used for the 1980 census. In batch processing, the collection offices stored questionnaires until several weeks after Census Day. The questionnaires than were trucked to one of three widely scattered processing sites to be converted into computerized data.

This is how flow processing will work:

Check in. Most questionnaires in their mail-back envelopes arrive at a census field office where the bar-coded number on the envelope is read by a laser wand, automatically recording its arrival. For several highly populated areas of the country, however, questionnaires are delivered to high-tech processing offices where high-speed, automated, sorters are used. All questionnaires then are extracted, unfolded, and stacked.

Filming. The stacks are sent to a processing office where they are filmed by a machine that is a combination page turner and camera.

Data capture. The film is developed and forwarded to a FOSDIC (Film Optical Sensing Device for Input to Computer) which scans answers and transmits the information to the Census Bureau's computers in a processing office.

How many people and how much equipment will flow processing take: A field force of some 300,000 workers. Throughout the decennial period, some 470,000 workers will have been hired. A complex of 484 temporary field offices, 13 regional census centers, and 7 processing centers. The "heavy" pieces will consist of some 530 mini and microcomputers, 12 laser-sorters, 72 camera/page turners, 21 microfilm processors, and 21 FOSDICS.

Costs for the years of planning (beginning in 1984), actual decennial census activities, and production of the results will total about $2.6 billion, or $10.40 per U.S. resident. □

Population
Colonial Population Estimates (in round numbers)

Year	Population	Year	Population	Year	Population	Year	Population
1610	350	1660	75,100	1710	331,700	1760	1,593,600
1620	2,300	1670	111,900	1720	466,200	1770	2,148,100
1630	4,600	1680	151,500	1730	629,400	1780	2,780,400
1640	26,600	1690	210,400	1740	905,600		
1650	50,400	1700	250,900	1750	1,170,800		

National Censuses[1]

Year	Resident population[2]	Land area, sq mi.	Pop. per sq mi.	Year	Resident population[2]	Land area, sq mi.	Pop. per sq mi.
1790	3,929,214	864,746	4.5	1890	62,947,714	2,969,640	21.2
1800	5,308,483	864,746	6.1	1900	75,994,575	2,969,834	25.6
1810	7,239,881	1,681,828	4.3	1910	91,972,266	2,969,565	31.0
1820	9,638,453	1,749,462	5.5	1920	105,710,620	2,969,451	35.6
1830	12,866,020	1,749,462	7.4	1930	122,775,046	2,977,128	41.2
1840	17,069,453	1,749,462	9.8	1940	131,669,275	2,977,128	44.2
1850	23,191,876	2,940,042	7.9	1950	150,697,361	2,974,726	50.7
1860	31,443,321	2,969,640	10.6	1960	179,323,175	3,540,911	50.6
1870	39,818,449	2,969,640	13.4	1970	203,302,031	3,540,023	57.4
1880	50,155,783	2,969,640	16.9	1980	226,545,805	3,618,770	62.6

1. Beginning with 1960, figures include Alaska and Hawaii. 2. Excludes armed forces overseas. NOTE: n.a. = not available.
Source: Department of Commerce, Bureau of the Census.

Population Distribution by Age, Race, Nativity, and Sex

		Age					Race and nativity				
							White[1]				
Year	Total	Under 5	5–19	20–44	45–62	65 and over	Total	Native born	Foreign born	Black	Other races[1]
PERCENT DISTRIBUTION											
1860[2]	100.0	15.4	35.8	35.7	10.4	2.7	85.6	72.6	13.0	14.1	0.3
1870[2]	100.0	14.3	35.4	35.4	11.9	3.0	87.1	72.9	14.2	12.7	0.2
1880[2]	100.0	13.8	34.3	35.9	12.6	3.4	86.5	73.4	13.1	13.1	0.3
1890[3]	100.0	12.2	33.9	36.9	13.1	3.9	87.5	73.0	14.5	11.9	0.3
1900	100.0	12.1	32.3	37.7	13.7	4.1	87.9	74.5	13.4	11.6	0.5
1910	100.0	11.6	30.4	39.0	14.6	4.3	88.9	74.4	14.5	10.7	0.4
1920	100.0	10.9	29.8	38.4	16.1	4.7	89.7	76.7	13.0	9.9	0.4
1930	100.0	9.3	29.5	38.3	17.4	5.4	89.8	78.4	11.4	9.7	0.5
1940	100.0	8.0	26.4	38.9	19.8	6.8	89.8	81.1	8.7	9.8	0.4
1950	100.0	10.7	23.2	37.6	20.3	8.1	89.5	82.8	6.7	10.0	0.5
1960	100.0	11.3	27.1	32.2	20.1	9.2	88.6	83.4	5.2	10.5	0.9
1970[2]	100.0	8.4	29.5	31.7	20.6	9.8	87.6	83.4	4.3	11.1	1.4
1980	100.0	7.2	24.8	37.1	19.6	11.3	83.1	n.a.	n.a.	11.7	5.2
MALES PER 100 FEMALES											
1860[2]	104.7	102.4	101.2	107.9	111.5	98.3	105.3	103.7	115.1	99.6	260.8
1870[2]	102.2	102.9	101.2	99.2	114.5	100.5	102.8	100.6	115.3	96.2	400.7
1880[2]	103.6	103.0	101.3	104.0	110.2	101.4	104.0	102.1	115.9	97.8	362.2
1890[3]	105.0	103.6	101.4	107.3	108.3	104.2	105.4	102.9	118.7	99.5	165.2
1900	104.4	102.1	100.9	105.8	110.7	102.0	104.9	102.8	117.4	98.6	185.2
1910	106.0	102.5	101.3	108.1	114.4	101.1	106.6	102.7	129.2	98.9	185.6
1920	104.0	102.5	100.8	102.8	115.2	101.3	104.4	101.7	121.7	99.2	156.6
1930	102.5	103.0	101.4	100.5	109.1	100.5	102.9	101.1	115.8	97.0	150.6
1940	100.7	103.2	102.0	98.1	105.2	95.5	101.2	100.1	111.1	95.0	140.5

| | | | Age | | | | Race and nativity | | | | |
| | | | | | | | | White[1] | | | |
Year	Total	Under 5	5–19	20–44	45–62	65 and over	Total	Native born	Foreign born	Black	Other races[1]
1950	98.6	103.9	102.5	96.2	100.1	89.6	99.0	98.8	102.0	93.7	129.7
1960	97.1	103.4	102.7	95.6	95.7	82.8	97.4	97.6	94.2	93.3	109.7
1970[2]	94.8	104.0	103.3	95.1	91.6	72.1	95.3	95.9	83.8	90.8	100.2
1980	94.5	104.7	104.0	98.1	90.7	67.6	94.8	n.a.	n.a.	89.6	100.3

1. The 1980 census data for white and other races categories are not directly comparable to those shown for the preceding years because of the changes in the way some persons reported their race, as well as changes in 1980 procedures relating to racial classification. 2. Excludes persons for whom age is not available. 3. Excludes persons enumerated in the Indian Territory and on Indian reservations. NOTES: Data exclude Armed Forces overseas. Beginning in 1960, includes Alaska and Hawaii, n.a. = not available. *Source:* Department of Commerce, Bureau of the Census.

Population and Rank of Large Metropolitan Areas, 1980–1987

(over 150,000)

Standard metropolitan statistical area	1987 Est. Number	1987 Est. Rank	1980 Census Number	1980 Census Rank	Change 1980–87 Number	Change 1980–87 %
Akron, Ohio	647,000	—	660,328	—	−13,300	−2.0
Albany–Schenectady–Troy, N.Y.	846,400	48	835,880	46	10,500	1.3
Albuquerque, N.M.	486,200	75	420,262	79	65,900	15.7
Allentown–Bethlehem, Pa.–N.J.	666,000	55	635,481	54	30,500	4.8
Amarillo, Texas	197,200	155	173,699	157	23,500	13.5
Anaheim–Santa Ana, Calif.	2,219,100	—	1,932,921	—	286,200	14.8
Anchorage, Alaska	222,600	144	174,431	156	48,200	27.6
Ann Arbor, Mich.	267,800	—	264,740	—	3,100	1.2
Appleton–Oshkosh–Neenah, Wis.	309,100	113	291,369	107	17,700	6.1
Asheville, N.C.	171,500	171	160,934	171	10,600	6.6
Atlanta	2,656,800	13	2,138,143	16	518,600	24.3
Atlantic City, N.J.	302,700	114	276,385	113	26,300	9.5
Augusta, Ga.–S.C.	392,500	90	345,923	95	46,600	13.5
Aurora–Elgin, Ill.	352,300	—	315,607	—	36,700	11.6
Austin, Texas	738,000	—	536,688	63	201,300	37.5
Bakersfield, Calif.	504,500	72	403,089	84	101,400	25.2
Baltimore	2,302,900	17	2,199,497	15	103,400	4.7
Baton Rouge, La.	538,300	68	494,151	69	44,100	8.9
Beaumont–Port Arthur, Texas	371,100	96	375,497	88	−2,200	−0.6
Beaver County, Pa.	191,000	—	204,441	—	−13,400	−6.6
Benton Harbor, Mich.	164,800	177	171,276	161	−6,400	−3.8
Bergen–Passaic, N.J.	1,294,200	—	1,292,970	—	1,200	0.1
Biloxi–Gulfport, Miss.	205,800	153	182,161	153	23,700	13.0
Binghamton, N.Y.	260,000	126	263,460	123	−3,400	−1.3
Birmingham, Ala.	916,900	45	884,014	42	32,900	3.7
Boise City, Idaho	195,700	156	173,125	158	22,600	13.0
Boston	2,841,700	—	2,805,911	—	35,700	1.3
Brandenton, Fla.	183,500	161	148,445	181	35,100	23.6
Brazoria, Texas	186,800	—	169,587	—	17,200	10.1
Bremerton, Wash.	174,300	167	147,152	182	27,200	18.5
Bridgeport–Milford, Conn.	443,800	—	438,557	—	5,200	1.2
Brockton, Mass.	185,400	—	182,891	—	2,500	1.3
Brownsville–Harlingen, Texas	263,600	124	209,727	138	53,900	25.7
Buffalo, N.Y.	958,300	—	1,015,472	—	−57,200	−5.6
Canton, Ohio	397,100	88	404,421	83	−7,300	−1.8
Cedar Rapids, Iowa	169,600	172	169,775	163	−200	−0.1
Champaign–Urbana–Rantoul, Ill.	172,700	169	168,392	164	4,300	2.5
Charleston, S.C.	502,100	74	430,346	76	71,800	16.7
Charleston, W. Va.	261,200	125	269,595	118	−8,400	−3.1
Charlotte–Gastonia–Rock Hill, N.C.-S.C.	1,091,000	35	971,447	36	119,500	12.3
Chattanooga, Tenn.–Ga.	431,500	82	426,540	77	5,100	1.2
Chicago	6,190,000	3	6,060,401	3	138,600	2.3
Chico, Calif.	169,000	173	143,851	184	25,100	17.5
Cincinnati, Ohio–Ky.–Ind.	1,438,300	—	1,401,471	—	36,800	2.6
Clarksville–Hopkinsville, Tenn.–Ky.	156,600	180	150,220	179	6,300	4.2
Cleveland	1,851,400	—	1,898,825	—	−47,400	−2.5
Colorado Springs, Colo.	389,900	91	309,424	105	80,500	26.0
Columbia, S.C.	451,400	78	409,955	82	41,400	10.1
Columbus, Ga.–Ala.	245,900	132	239,196	131	6,700	2.8
Columbus, Ohio	1,320,100	30	1,243,827	28	76,300	6.1

Standard metropolitan statistical area	1987 Est. Number	1987 Est. Rank	1980 Census Number	1980 Census Rank	Change, 1980–87 Number	Change, 1980–87 %
Corpus Christi, Texas	360,300	100	326,228	99	34,100	10.4
Dallas–Fort Worth	3,724,900	8	2,930,539	10	794,300	27.1
Danbury, Conn.	188,800	—	170,369	—	18,500	10.8
Davenport–Rock Island–Moline, Iowa–Ill.	366,600	97	384,749	86	−18,100	−4.7
Dayton–Springfield, Ohio	938,800	43	942,083	39	−3,300	−0.4
Daytona Beach, Fla.	331,900	108	258,762	124	73,200	28.3
Denver–Boulder, Colo.	1,861,300	22	1,618,461	21	242,800	15.0
Des Moines, Iowa	385,100	93	367,561	89	17,500	4.8
Detroit, Mich.	4,361,600	—	4,488,024	—	−126,400	−2.8
Duluth, Minn.–Wis.	241,700	135	266,650	119	−25,000	−9.4
El Paso, Texas	572,800	67	479,899	70	92,900	19.4
Erie, Pa.	278,700	121	279,780	111	−1,100	−0.4
Eugene–Springfield, Ore.	264,700	123	275,226	115	−10,500	−3.8
Evansville, Ind.–Ky.	281,000	120	276,252	114	4,700	1.7
Fall River, Mass.–R.I.	152,900	—	157,222	—	−4,300	−2.7
Fayetteville, N.C.	258,500	128	247,160	127	11,400	4.6
Flint, Mich.	435,100	81	450,449	73	−15,400	−3.4
Fort Collins–Loveland, Colo.	179,500	164	149,184	180	30,300	20.3
Fort Lauderdale–Hollywood–Pompano Beach, Fla.	1,162,600	—	1,018,257	—	144,400	14.2
Fort Myers–Cape Coral, Fla.	294,600	116	205,266	140	89,300	43.5
Fort Pierce, Fla.	215,400	147	151,196	178	64,200	42.5
Fort Smith, Ark.–Okla.	178,200	165	162,813	169	15,400	9.4
Fort Wayne, Ind.	364,400	98	354,156	93	10,200	2.9
Fresno, Calif.	597,400	64	514,621	67	82,800	16.1
Gainsville, Fla.	205,000	154	171,392	160	33,600	19.6
Galveston–Texas City, Texas	211,400	—	195,738	—	15,700	8.0
Gary–Hammond, Ind.	604,300	—	642,733	—	−38,400	−6.0
Grand Rapids, Mich.	657,000	57	601,680	56	55,300	9.2
Green Bay, Wis.	188,400	159	175,280	155	13,100	7.5
Greensboro–Winston-Salem–High Point, N.C.	915,700	46	851,444	44	64,200	7.5
Greenville–Spartanburg, S.C.	611,900	61	570,211	59	41,700	7.3
Hamilton–Middletown, Ohio	276,300	—	258,787	—	17,500	6.8
Harrisburg–Lebanon–Carlisle, Pa.	583,700	66	556,242	62	27,500	4.9
Hartford, Conn.	747,600	—	715,923	—	31,700	4.4
Hickory, N.C.	219,100	145	202,711	142	16,400	8.1
Honolulu	830,600	49	762,565	47	68,000	8.9
Houma–Thibodaux, La.	185,100	160	176,876	154	8,200	4.7
Houston, Texas	3,228,100	—	2,734,617	—	493,500	18.0
Huntington–Ashland, W.Va.–Ky.–Ohio	323,400	111	336,410	97	−13,000	−3.9
Huntsville, Ala.	231,500	139	196,966	144	34,500	17.5
Indianapolis	1,228,600	32	1,166,575	30	62,100	5.3
Jackson, Miss.	395,900	89	362,038	92	33,900	9.4
Jacksonville, Fla.	878,200	47	722,252	50	156,000	21.6
Jersey City, N.J.	547,200	—	556,972	—	−9,800	−1.8
Johnson City–Kingsport–Bristol, Tenn.–Va.	442,600	80	433,638	75	9,000	2.1
Johnstown, Pa.	252,200	131	264,506	121	−12,300	−4.7
Joliet, Ill.	377,300	—	355,042	—	22,300	6.3
Kalamazoo, Mich.	218,500	146	212,378	136	6,100	2.9
Kansas City, Mo.–Kan.	1,546,400	25	1,433,464	25	113,000	7.9
Killeen–Temple, Texas	234,000	137	214,587	135	19,400	9.0
Knoxville, Tenn.	594,000	65	565,970	60	28,100	5.0
Lafayette, La.	212,100	150	190,231	150	21,900	11.5
Lake Charles, La.	171,800	170	167,223	165	4,600	2.8
Lake County, Ill.	494,300	—	440,387	—	53,900	12.2
Lakeland–Winter Haven, Fla.	387,000	92	321,652	101	64,500	20.3
Lancaster, Pa.	403,700	86	362,346	91	41,400	11.4
Lansing–East Lansing, Mich.	427,800	83	419,750	80	8,100	1.9
Las Vegas, Nev.	599,900	63	463,087	72	136,800	29.5
Lawrence–Haverhill, Mass.–N.H.	375,000	—	339,090	—	35,900	10.6
Lexington–Fayette, Ky.	341,500	105	317,548	103	24,000	7.6
Lima, Ohio	155,600	182	154,795	175	800	0.5
Lincoln, Neb.	207,700	152	192,884	147	14,800	7.7
Little Rock–North Little Rock, Ark.	511,500	71	474,464	71	37,000	7.8
Longview–Marshall, Texas	166,900	174	151,760	176	15,100	10.0
Lorain–Elyria, Ohio	268,500	—	274,909	—	−6,400	−2.3
Los Angeles–Long Beach, Calif.	8,504,500	—	7,477,422	2	1,027,300	13.7
Louisville, Ky.–Ind.	966,500	41	956,486	38	10,100	1.1
Lowell, Mass.–N.H.	260,100	—	243,142	—	17,000	7.0
Lubbock, Texas	227,600	141	211,651	137	16,000	7.5
Macon–Warner Robins, Ga.	282,600	118	263,591	122	19,000	7.2
Madison, Wis.	347,400	102	323,545	100	23,900	7.4
McAllen–Edinburg–Mission, Texas	378,600	94	283,323	110	95,200	33.6

Standard metropolitan statistical area	1987 Est. Number	1987 Est. Rank	1980 Census Number	1980 Census Rank	Change, 1980–87 Number	Change, 1980–87 %
Melbourne–Titusville–Palm Bay, Fla.	374,900	95	272,959	116	101,900	37.3
Memphis, Tenn.–Ark.–Miss.	971,900	40	913,472	40	58,500	6.4
Merced, Calif.	165,800	176	134,557	197	31,300	23.2
Miami–Hialeah, Fla.	1,791,500	—	1,625,611	—	166,000	10.2
Middlesex–Somerset–Hunterdon, N.J.	966,300	—	886,383	—	79,900	9.0
Milwaukee, Wis.	1,389,100	—	1,397,020	—	−7,900	−0.6
Minneapolis–St. Paul, Minn.–Wis.	2,335,600	16	2,137,133	17	39,500	9.3
Mobile, Ala.	483,000	76	443,536	74	39,500	8.9
Modesto, Calif.	327,400	109	265,900	120	61,500	23.1
Monmouth–Ocean, N.J.	956,600	—	849,211	—	107,400	12.6
Montgomery, Ala.	297,400	115	272,687	117	24,800	9.1
Muskegon, Mich.	158,700	179	157,589	173	1,100	0.7
Nashua, N.H.	172,400	—	142,527	—	29,800	20.9
Nashville, Tenn.	956,200	42	850,505	45	105,700	12.4
Nassau–Suffolk, N.Y.	2,631,000	—	2,605,813	—	25,200	1.0
Newark, N.J.	1,890,800	—	1,879,147	—	11,600	0.6
New Bedford, Mass.	166,400	175	166,699	166	−300	−0.2
New Haven–Meriden, Conn.	519,000	69	500,462	68	18,500	3.7
New London–Norwich, Conn.–R.I.	258,600	127	250,839	125	7,800	3.1
New Orleans	1,321,000	29	1,256,668	27	64,300	5.1
New York, N.Y.	8,528,800	—	8,274,961	1	253,800	3.1
Niagara Falls, N.Y.	216,200	—	227,354	—	−11,100	−4.9
Norfolk–Virginia Beach–Newport News, Va.	1,346,100	27	1,160,311	31	185,800	16.0
Oakland, Calif.	1,968,000	—			206,300	11.7
Ocala, Fla.	181,300	163	122,488	212	58,900	48.1
Oklahoma City, Okla.	975,000	39	860,969	43	114,100	13.2
Olympia, Wash.	151,400	184			27,100	21.8
Omaha, Neb.–Iowa	616,400	60	585,122	57	31,300	5.3
Orange County, N.Y.	287,900	—	259,603	—	28,300	10.9
Orlando, Fla.	934,700	44	699,906	51	234,800	33.5
Oxnard–Ventura, Calif.	628,300	—	529,174	—	99,100	18.7
Parkersburg–Marietta, W.Va.–Ohio	155,800	172	157,889	172	−2,100	−1.3
Pawtucket–Woonsocket–Attleboro, R.I.–Mass.	322,100	—	307,403	—	14,700	4.8
Pensacola, Fla.	343,900	103	289,782	109	54,100	18.7
Peoria, Ill.	338,500	107	365,864	90	−27,300	−7.5
Philadelphia, Pa.–N.J.	4,866,500	—	4,716,559	—	149,900	3.2
Phoenix, Ariz.	1,959,600	21	1,509,262	24	450,400	29.8
Pittsburgh	2,105,400	—	2,218,870	—	−113,500	−5.1
Portland, Maine	209,900	151	193,831	145	16,100	8.3
Portland, Ore.	1,167,800	—	1,105,750	—	62,000	5.6
Portsmouth–Dover–Rochester, N.H.–Maine	215,300	148	190,938	148	24,400	12.8
Poughkeepsie, N.Y.	258,400	129	245,055	129	13,400	5.5
Providence, R.I.	642,700	—	618,514	—	24,200	3.9
Provo–Orem, Utah	241,800	134	218,106	134	23,700	10.9
Racine, Wis.	173,000	—	173,132	—	−100	−0.1
Raleigh–Durham, N.C.	665,400	56	560,774	61	104,600	18.7
Reading, Pa.	324,300	110	312,509	104	11,800	3.8
Reno, Nev.	232,100	138	193,623	146	38,500	19.9
Richmond–Petersburg, Va.	825,300	50	761,311	48	64,000	8.4
Riverside–San Bernardino, Calif.	2,119,000	—	1,558,215	—	560,800	36.0
Roanoke, Va.	224,200	142	220,393	133	3,800	1.7
Rochester, N.Y.	979,100	38	971,230	37	7,800	0.8
Rockford, Ill.	281,400	119	279,514	112	1,900	0.7
Sacramento, Calif.	1,336,500	28	1,099,814	32	236,700	21.5
Saginaw–Bay City–Midland, Mich.	404,400	85	421,518	78	−17,100	−4.1
St. Cloud, Minn.	177,400	166	163,256	168	14,200	8.7
St. Louis, Mo.–Ill.	2,458,100	14	2,376,971	14	81,100	3.4
Salem–Gloucester, Mass.	258,400	—	258,231	—	200	0.1
Salem, Ore.	265,800	122	249,895	126	15,900	6.4
Salinas–Seaside–Monterey, Calif.	343,100	104	290,444	108	52,600	18.1
Salt Lake City–Ogden, Utah	1,054,500	37	910,222	41	144,300	15.9
San Antonio, Texas	1,306,700	31	1,072,125	34	234,600	21.9
San Diego, Calif.	2,285,900	19	1,861,846	19	424,000	22.8
San Francisco–Oakland, Calif.	1,590,000	—	3,250,605	—	101,100	6.8
San Jose, Calif.	1,415,000	—	1,295,071	—	119,900	9.3
Santa Barbara–Santa Maria–Lompoc, Calif.	340,900	106	298,694	106	42,200	14.1
Santa Cruz, Calif.	221,700	—	188,141	—	33,500	17.8
Santa Rosa–Petaluma, Calif.	354,000	—	299,681	—	54,400	18.1
Sarasota, Fla.	255,600	130	202,251	143	53,300	26.4
Savannah, Ga.	241,400	136	220,553	132	20,900	9.5
Scranton–Wilkes-Barre, Pa.	730,900	54	728,796	49	2,200	0.3
Seattle, Wash.	1,795,900	—	1,607,618	—	188,300	11.7

Standard metropolitan statistical area	1987 Est.		1980 Census		Change, 1980–87	
	Number	Rank	Number	Rank	Number	%
Shreveport, La.	363,800	99	333,158	98	30,600	9.2
South Bend–Mishawaka, Ind.	242,400	133	241,617	130	700	0.3
Spokane, Wash.	355,300	101	341,835	96	13,500	3.9
Springfield, Ill.	191,000	157	187,770	151	3,200	1.7
Springfield, Mass.	516,700	70	515,259	66	1,400	0.3
Springfield, Mo.	229,000	140	207,704	139	21,300	10.2
Stamford, Conn.	192,800	—	198,854	—	−6,000	−3.0
Stockton, Calif.	443,500	79	347,342	94	96,100	27.7
Syracuse, N.Y.	647,000	58	642,971	53	4,100	0.6
Tacoma, Wash.	544,700	—	485,667	—	59,000	12.1
Tallahassee, Fla.	222,600	143	190,329	149	32,300	17.0
Tampa–St. Petersburg–Clearwater, Fla.	1,965,100	20	1,613,621	22	331,500	21.8
Toledo, Ohio	611,000	62	616,864	55	−5,900	−1.0
Topeka, Kan.	162,400	178	154,916	174	7,500	4.8
Trenton, N.J.	327,100	—	307,863	—	19,300	6.3
Tucson, Ariz.	619,400	59	531,443	64	87,900	16.5
Tulsa, Okla.	733,000	53	657,173	52	75,800	11.5
Tyler, Texas	152,600	183	128,366	206	24,200	18.9
Utica–Rome, N.Y.	313,900	112	320,180	102	−6,300	−2.0
Vallejo–Fairfield–Napa, Calif.	404,300	—	334,402	—	69,900	20.9
Vancouver, Wash.	215,600	—	192,227	—	23,400	12.2
Visalia–Tulare–Porterville, Calif.	291,600	117	245,738	128	45,800	18.6
Waco, Texas	189,400	158	170,755	162	18,700	10.9
Washington, D.C.–Md.–Va.	3,646,000	9	3,250,921	8	395,100	12.2
Waterbury, Conn.	213,400	149	204,968	141	8,500	4.1
West Palm Beach–Boca Raton–Delray Beach, Fla.	790,100	51	576,754	58	213,300	37.0
Wheeling, W.Va.–Ohio	172,800	168	185,566	152	−12,800	−6.9
Wichita, Kan.	474,700	77	411,870	81	32,300	7.3
Wilmington, Del.–N.J.–Md.	559,400	—	523,221	—	36,200	6.9
Worcester, Mass.	410,200	84	402,918	85	7,200	1.8
Yakima, Wash.	182,800	162	172,508	159	10,300	5.9
York, Pa.	403,600	87	381,255	87	22,400	5.9
Youngstown–Warren, Ohio	502,500	73	531,350	65	−28,800	−5.4

NOTE: A standard metropolitan statistical area (SMSA) is one of a large population nucleus together with adjacent communities that have a high degree of economic and social integration with that nucleus. — Source does not list rank separately. It is given for the Consolidated Metropolitan Statistical Area of which this area is a part. *Source:* Bureau of the Census.

Resident Population by Age, Sex, Race, and Hispanic Origin, 1987

(in thousands)

Age	White		Black		Other races		Hispanic origin		All persons	
	Male	Female	Male	Female	Male	Female	Male	Female	Male	Female
Under 5	7,567	7,187	1,393	1,352	381	371	1,047	1,005	9,341	8,910
5–9	7,305	6,935	1,383	1,395	349	344	970	930	9,037	8,625
10–14	6,803	6,442	1,314	1,275	332	318	905	871	8,450	8,035
15–19	7,664	7,350	1,406	1,384	341	313	861	830	9,412	9,047
20–24	8,238	8,129	1,334	1,428	343	321	1,008	930	9,915	9,878
25–29	9,313	9,121	1,334	1,477	362	372	1,097	978	11,009	10,971
30–34	9,071	8,903	1,215	1,378	375	393	912	845	10,661	10,674
35–39	7,994	7,974	964	1,144	315	347	690	685	9,273	9,465
40–44	6,696	6,809	699	846	243	273	508	531	7,639	7,928
45–49	5,239	5,392	594	729	192	204	389	417	6,025	6,326
50–54	4,612	4,825	523	646	151	170	323	353	5,285	5,641
55–59	4,673	5,063	506	607	120	154	281	316	5,298	5,823
60–64	4,507	5,139	455	557	105	134	232	267	5,068	5,831
65–69	4,028	4,796	381	491	86	107	157	193	4,495	5,394
70–74	3,000	3,992	266	380	62	77	103	146	3,329	4,450
75–79	2,038	3,173	180	285	45	55	n.a.	n.a.	2,264	3,513
80–84	1,116	2,111	88	157	22	30	n.a.	n.a.	1,225	2,298
85 and over	723	1,887	69	152	15	22	n.a.	n.a.	806	1,300
All ages	100,589	105,231	14,103	15,633	3,839	4,005	9,619	9,510	118,531	124,869
15 and over	78,913	84,666	10,012	11,661	2,778	2,972	6,697	6,704	91,703	99,300
20 and over	71,249	77,316	8,606	10,277	2,436	2,659	5,836	5,874	82,291	90,252
65 and over	10,905	15,960	984	1,465	230	291	396	551	12,119	17,716
75 and over	3,877	7,171	337	594	82	108	137	212	4,295	7,873
Median age	31.9	34.2	25.8	28.5	27.4	29.5	25.1	25.9	31.0	33.3

1. Persons of Hispanic origin may be of any race NOTE: n.a. = not available. Data latest available as of August 1989. *Source:* U.S. Bureau of the Census.

Population by State

State	1980	Percent change, 1970–80	Pop. per sq. mi., 1980	Pop. rank, 1980	1970	1950	1900	1790
Alabama	3,893,888	+13.1	76.7	22	3,444,354	3,061,743	1,828,697	—
Alaska	401,851	+32.8	0.7	50	302,583	128,643	63,592	—
Arizona	2,718,425	+53.1	23.9	29	1,775,399	749,587	122,931	—
Arkansas	2,286,435	+18.9	43.9	33	1,923,322	1,909,511	1,311,564	—
California	23,667,565	+18.5	151.4	1	19,971,069	10,586,223	1,485,053	—
Colorado	2,889,735	+30.8	27.9	28	2,209,596	1,325,089	539,700	—
Connecticut	3,107,576	+ 2.5	637.8	25	3,032,217	2,007,280	908,420	237,946
Delaware	594,317	+ 8.4	307.6	47	548,104	318,085	184,735	59,096
D.C.	638,432	−15.6	—	—	756,668	802,178	278,718	—
Florida	9,746,324	+43.5	180.0	7	6,791,418	2,771,305	528,542	—
Georgia	5,463,105	+19.1	94.1	13	4,587,930	3,444,578	2,216,331	82,548
Hawaii	964,691	+25.3	150.1	39	769,913	499,794	154,001	—
Idaho	944,038	+32.4	11.5	41	713,015	588,637	161,772	—
Illinois	11,426,518	+ 2.8	205.3	5	11,110,285	8,712,176	4,821,550	—
Indiana	5,490,260	+ 5.7	152.8	12	5,195,392	3,934,224	2,516,462	—
Iowa	2,913,808	+ 3.1	52.1	27	2,825,368	2,621,073	2,231,853	—
Kansas	2,364,236	+ 5.1	28.9	32	2,249,071	1,905,299	1,470,495	—
Kentucky	3,660,257	+13.7	92.3	23	3,220,711	2,944,806	2,147,174	73,677
Louisiana	4,206,312	+15.4	94.5	19	3,644,637	2,683,516	1,381,625	—
Maine	1,125,027	+13.2	36.3	38	993,722	913,774	694,466	96,540
Maryland	4,216,975	+ 7.5	428.7	18	3,923,897	2,343,001	1,188,044	319,728
Massachusetts	5,737,037	+ 0.8	733.3	11	5,689,170	4,690,514	2,805,346	378,787
Michigan	9,262,078	+ 4.3	162.6	8	8,881,826	6,371,766	2,420,982	—
Minnesota	4,075,970	+ 7.1	51.2	21	3,806,103	2,982,483	1,751,394	—
Mississippi	2,520,638	+13.7	53.4	31	2,216,994	2,178,914	1,551,270	—
Missouri	4,916,759	+ 5.1	71.3	15	4,677,623	3,954,653	3,106,665	—
Montana	786,690	+13.3	5.4	44	694,409	591,024	243,329	—
Nebraska	1,569,825	+ 5.7	20.5	35	1,485,333	1,325,510	1,066,300	—
Nevada	800,493	+63.8	7.3	43	488,738	160,083	42,335	—
New Hampshire	920,610	+24.8	102.4	42	737,681	533,242	411,588	141,885
New Jersey	7,364,823	+ 2.7	986.2	9	7,171,112	4,835,329	1,883,669	184,139
New Mexico	1,302,981	+28.1	10.7	37	1,017,055	681,187	195,310	—
New York	17,558,072	− 3.7	370.6	2	18,241,391	14,830,192	7,268,894	340,120
North Carolina	5,881,813	+15.7	120.4	10	5,084,411	4,061,929	1,893,810	393,751
North Dakota	652,717	+ 5.7	9.4	46	617,792	619,636	319,146	—
Ohio	10,797,624	+ 1.3	263.3	6	10,657,423	7,946,627	4,157,545	—
Oklahoma	3,025,290	+18.2	44.1	26	2,559,463	2,233,351	790,391[1]	—
Oregon	2,633,149	+25.9	27.4	30	2,091,533	1,521,341	413,536	—
Pennsylvania	11,863,895	+ 0.5	264.3	4	11,800,766	10,498,012	6,302,115	434,373
Rhode Island	947,154	− 0.3	897.8	40	949,723	791,896	428,556	68,825
South Carolina	3,121,833	+20.5	103.4	24	2,590,713	2,117,027	1,340,316	249,073
South Dakota	690,768	+ 3.7	9.1	45	666,257	652,740	401,570	—
Tennessee	4,591,120	+16.9	111.6	17	3,926,018	3,291,718	2,020,616	35,691
Texas	14,229,288	+27.1	54.3	3	11,198,655	7,711,194	3,048,710	—
Utah	1,461,037	+37.9	17.8	36	1,059,273	688,862	276,749	—
Vermont	511,456	+15.0	55.2	48	444,732	377,747	343,641	85,425
Virginia	5,346,818	+14.9	134.7	14	4,651,448	3,318,680	1,854,184	747,610[2]
Washington	4,132,180	+21.1	62.1	20	3,413,244	2,378,963	518,103	—
West Virginia	1,950,279	+11.8	80.8	34	1,744,237	2,005,552	958,800	—
Wisconsin	4,705,521	+ 6.5	86.5	16	4,417,821	3,434,575	2,069,042	—
Wyoming	469,557	+41.3	4.8	49	332,416	290,529	92,531	—
Total U.S.	226,545,805	+11.4	62.6	—	203,302,031	151,325,798	76,212,168	3,929,214

1. Includes population of Indian Territory: 1900, 392,960. 2. Until 1863, Virginia included what is now West Virginia. *Source:* Department of Commerce, Bureau of the Census.

The United States—A Nation of Urban Dwellers

Roughly half of the population of the United States lives in metropolitan areas with a population of at least one million, according to a recent Census Bureau report. There are 37 such metropolitan areas in which 119 million people live out of a total population of 243.4 million.

In addition, more than three of every four people live in the country's 282 designated metropolitan areas whose population totaled 187.1 million in 1987. During 1987 metropolitan population increased at twice the rate of that of nonmetropolitan territory.

Phoenix has been the fastest growing metro area of a million or more, followed by Dallas-Fort Worth. Among all metropolitan areas Naples and Ocala, Fla., lead in population growth since 1980. In fact 7 out of 10 fastest growing areas now are in Florida.

Incorporated Places Over 25,000 Population

Asterisk denotes more than one ZIP code for a city and refers to Postmaster. To find the ZIP code for a particular address, consult the ZIP code directory available in every post office. For latest population figures of many cities, see listing for individual states in the United States section.

City and major ZIP code	1980 census	1970 census	City and major ZIP code	1980 census	1970 census
Aberdeen, SD (57401)	25,851	26,476	Bellflower, CA (90706)	53,441	52,334
Abilene, TX (79604*)	98,315	89,653	Bell Gardens, CA (90201)	34,117	29,308
Addison, IL (60101)	29,759	24,482	Bellingham, WA (98225*)	45,794	39,375
Akron, OH (44309*)	237,177	275,425	Beloit, WI (53511)	35,207	35,729
Alameda, CA (94501)	63,852	70,968	Bergenfield, NJ (07621)	25,568	29,000
Albany, GA (31706*)	74,550	72,623	Berkeley, CA (94704*)	103,328	114,091
Albany, NY (12212*)	101,727	115,781	Berwyn, IL (60402)	46,840	52,502
Albany, OR (97321)	26,678	18,181	Bessemer, AL (35020*)	31,729	33,428
Albuquerque, NM (87101*)	331,767	244,501	Bethel Park, PA (15102)	34,755	34,758
Alexandria, LA (71301*)	51,565	41,811	Bethlehem, PA (18016*)	70,419	72,686
Alexandria, VA (22313*)	103,217	110,927	Bettendorf, IA (52722)	27,381	22,126
Alhambra, CA (91802*)	64,615	62,125	Beverly, MA (01915)	37,655	38,348
Allen Park, MI (48101)	34,196	40,747	Beverly Hills, CA (90213*)	32,367	33,416
Allentown, PA (18101*)	103,758	109,871	Billings, MT (59101*)	66,842	61,581
Alton, IL (62002)	34,171	39,700	Biloxi, MS (39530*)	49,311	48,486
Altoona, PA (16603*)	57,078	63,115	Binghamton, NY (13902*)	55,860	64,123
Amarillo, TX (79120*)	149,230	127,010	Birmingham, AL (35203*)	284,413	300,910
Ames, IA (50010)	45,775	39,505	Bismarck, ND (58501)	44,485	34,703
Amherst, MA (01002)	33,229	26,331	Blacksburg, VA (24060)	30,638	9,384
Anaheim, CA (92803*)	219,311	166,408	Blaine, MN (55433)	28,558	20,573
Anchorage, AK (99502*)	174,431	48,081	Bloomfield, NJ (07003)	47,792	52,029
Anderson, IN (46018*)	64,695	70,787	Bloomington, IL (61701)	44,189	39,992
Anderson, SC (29621*)	27,965	27,556	Bloomington, IN (47401)	52,044	43,262
Annapolis, MD (21401*)	31,740	30,095	Bloomington, MN (55420*)	81,831	81,970
Ann Arbor, MI (48106*)	107,966	100,035	Blue Springs, MO (64015)	25,927	6,779
Anniston, AL (36201*)	29,523	31,533	Boca Raton, FL (33432*)	49,505	28,506
Antioch, CA (94509)	42,683	28,060	Boise, ID (83708*)	102,160	74,990
Appleton, WI (54911*)	58,913	56,377	Bolingbrook, IL (60439)	37,261	7,651
Arcadia, CA (91006)	45,994	45,138	Bossier City, LA (71111*)	50,817	43,769
Arlington, TX (76010*)	160,113	90,229	Boston, MA (02205*)	562,994	641,071
Arlington Heights, IL (60004*)	66,116	65,058	Boulder, CO (80302*)	76,685	66,870
Arvada, CO (80001*)	84,576	49,844	Bountiful, UT (84010)	32,877	27,751
Asheville, NC (28810*)	53,583	57,820	Bowie, MD (20715*)	33,695	35,028
Ashland, KY (41101)	27,064	29,245	Bowling Green, KY (42101)	40,450	36,705
Athens, GA (30601*)	42,549	44,342	Bowling Green, OH (43402)	25,728	14,656
Atlanta, GA (30304*)	425,022	495,039	Boynton Beach, FL (33435*)	35,624	18,115
Atlantic City, NJ (08401*)	40,199	47,859	Bradenton, FL (33506*)	30,170	21,040
Attleboro, MA (02703)	34,196	32,907	Brea, CA (92621)	27,913	18,447
Auburn, AL (36830)	28,471	22,767	Bremerton, WA (98310*)	36,208	35,307
Auburn, NY (13021)	32,548	34,599	Bridgeport, CT (06602*)	142,546	156,542
Auburn, WA (98002*)	26,417	21,653	Bristol, CT (06010)	57,370	55,487
Augusta, GA (30901*)	47,532	59,864	Brockton, MA (02403*)	95,172	89,040
Aurora, CO (80010*)	158,588	74,974	Broken Arrow, OK (74012*)	35,761	11,018
Aurora, IL (60507*)	81,293	74,389	Brookfield, WI (53005)	34,035	31,761
Austin, TX (78710*)	345,496	253,539	Brooklyn Center, MN (55429*)	31,230	35,173
Azusa, CA (91702)	29,380	25,217	Brooklyn Park, MN (55007)	43,332	26,230
Bakersfield, CA (93302*)	105,735	69,515	Brook Park, OH (44142)	26,195	30,774
Baldwin Park, CA (91706)	50,554	47,285	Brownsville, TX (78520*)	84,997	52,522
Baltimore, MD (21233*)	786,775	905,787	Brunswick, OH (44212)	28,104	15,852
Bangor, ME (04401)	31,643	33,168	Bryan, TX (77801*)	44,337	33,719
Barberton, OH (44203)	29,751	33,052	Buena Park, CA (90622*)	64,165	63,646
Bartlesville, OK (74003*)	34,568	29,683	Buffalo, NY (14240*)	357,870	462,768
Baton Rouge, LA (70821*)	219,419	165,921	Burbank, CA (91505*)	84,625	88,871
Battle Creek, MI (49016*)	35,724	38,931	Burbank, IL (60459)	28,462	—
Bay City, MI (48706)	41,593	49,449	Burlingame, CA (94010)	26,173	27,320
Bayonne, NJ (07002)	65,047	72,743	Burlington, IA (52601)	29,529	32,366
Baytown, TX (77520*)	56,923	43,980	Burlington, NC (27215)	37,266	35,930
Beaumont, TX (77704*)	118,102	117,548	Burlington, VT (05401)	37,712	38,633
Beavercreek, OH (45401)	31,589	—	Burnsville, MN (55337)	35,674	19,940
Beaverton, OR (97005*)	30,582	18,577	Burton, MI (48502)	29,976	—
Bell, CA (90201)	25,450	21,836	Butte, MT (59701)	37,205	23,368
Belleville, IL (62220*)	41,580	41,223	Calumet City, IL (60409)	39,697	33,107
Belleville, NJ (07109)	35,367	37,629	Camarillo, CA (93010)	37,797	19,219
Bellevue, WA (98009*)	73,903	61,196	Cambridge, MA (02140)	95,322	100,361

City and major ZIP code	1980 census	1970 census	City and major ZIP code	1980 census	1970 census
Camden, NJ (08101*)	84,910	102,551	Cupertino, CA (95014)	34,015	17,895
Campbell, CA (95008)	27,067	23,797	Cuyahoga Falls, OH (44222*)	43,890	49,815
Canton, OH (44711*)	93,077	110,053	Cypress, CA (90630)	40,391	31,569
Cape Coral, FL (33910)	32,103	—	Dallas, TX (75260*)	904,078	844,401
Cape Girardeau, MO (63701)	34,361	31,282	Daly City, CA (94015*)	78,519	66,922
Carbondale, IL (62901)	26,414	22,816	Danbury, CT (06810*)	60,470	50,781
Carlsbad, CA (92008)	35,490	14,944	Danville, IL (61832)	38,985	42,570
Carlsbad, NM (88220)	25,496	21,297	Danville, VA (24541*)	45,642	46,391
Carrollton, TX (75006*)	40,595	13,855	Davenport, IA (52802*)	103,264	98,469
Carson, CA (90749)	81,221	71,150	Davis, CA (95616)	36,640	23,488
Carson City, NV (89701)	32,022	15,468	Dayton, OH (45401*)	193,444	243,023
Casper, WY (82601*)	51,016	39,361	Daytona Beach, FL (32015*)	54,176	45,327
Cedar Falls, IA (50613)	36,322	29,597	Dearborn, MI (48120*)	90,660	104,199
Cedar Rapids, IA (52401*)	110,243	110,642	Dearborn Heights, MI (48127)	67,706	80,069
Cerritos, CA (90701)	53,020	15,856	Decatur, AL (35602*)	42,002	38,044
Champaign, IL (61820*)	58,133	56,837	Decatur, IL (62521*)	94,081	90,397
Chandler, AZ (85224)	29,673	13,763	Deerfield Beach, FL (33441)	39,193	16,662
Chapel Hill, NC (27514)	32,421	26,199	De Kalb, IL (60115)	33,099	32,949
Charleston, SC (29423*)	69,510	66,945	Del City, OK (73155*)	28,424	27,133
Charleston, WV (25301*)	63,968	71,505	Delray Beach, FL (33444*)	34,325	19,915
Charlotte, NC (28228*)	314,447	241,420	Del Rio, TX (78840)	30,034	21,330
Charlottesville, VA (22906*)	39,916	38,880	Denton, TX (76201*)	48,063	39,874
Chattanooga, TN (37401*)	169,558	119,923	Denver, CO (80202*)	492,365	514,678
Chelsea, MA (02150)	25,431	30,625	Des Moines, IA (50318*)	191,003	201,404
Chesapeake, VA (23320*)	114,486	89,580	Des Plaines, IL (60018*)	53,568	57,239
Chester, PA (19013*)	45,794	56,331	Detroit, MI (48233*)	1,203,339	1,514,063
Cheyenne, WY (82001*)	47,283	41,254	Dothan, AL (36303*)	48,750	36,733
Chicago, IL (60607*)	3,005,072	3,369,357	Downers Grove, IL (60515*)	42,572	32,544
Chicago Heights, IL (60411)	37,026	40,900	Downey, CA (90241*)	82,602	88,573
Chico, CA (95926)	26,603	19,580	Dubuque, IA (52001)	62,321	62,309
Chicopee, MA (01021*)	55,112	66,676	Duluth, MN (55806*)	92,811	100,578
Chino, CA (91710)	40,165	20,411	Duncanville, TX (75138*)	27,781	14,105
Chula Vista, CA (92010*)	83,927	67,901	Dunedin, FL (33528)	30,203	17,639
Cicero, IL (60650)	61,232	67,058	Durham, NC (27701*)	100,538	95,438
Cincinnati, OH (45234*)	385,457	453,514	East Chicago, IN (46312)	39,786	49,982
Claremont, CA (91711)	30,950	24,776	East Cleveland, OH (44112)	36,957	39,660
Clarksville, TN (37041*)	54,777	31,719	East Detroit, MI (48021)	38,280	45,920
Clearwater, FL (33575*)	85,528	52,074	East Lansing, MI (48823)	51,392	47,540
Cleveland, OH (44101*)	573,822	750,879	Easton, PA (18042)	26,027	29,450
Cleveland, TN (37311)	26,415	21,446	East Orange, NJ (07019*)	77,690	75,471
Cleveland Heights, OH (44118)	56,438	60,767	East Point, GA (30364)	37,486	39,315
Clifton, NJ (07015*)	74,388	82,437	East Providence, RI (02914)	50,980	48,207
Clinton, IA (52732)	32,828	34,719	East St. Louis, IL (62201*)	55,200	70,169
Clovis, CA (93612)	33,021	13,856	Eau Claire, WI (54701*)	51,509	44,619
Clovis, NM (88101)	31,194	28,495	Edina, MN (55424*)	46,073	44,046
College Station, TX (77840)	37,272	17,676	Edmond, OK (73034)	34,637	16,633
Colorado Springs, CO (80901*)	214,821	135,517	Edmonds, WA (98020)	27,679	23,684
Columbia, MO (65201*)	62,061	58,812	El Cajon, CA (92020*)	73,892	52,273
Columbia, SC (29201*)	100,385	113,542	El Dorado, AR (71730)	25,270	25,283
Columbia, TN (38401)	26,571	21,471	Elgin, IL (60120)	63,798	55,691
Columbus, GA (31908*)	169,441	155,028	Elizabeth, NJ (07207*)	106,201	112,654
Columbus, IN (47201*)	30,614	26,457	Elk Grove, IL (60007)	28,907	20,346
Columbus, MS (39701*)	27,383	25,795	Elkhart, IN (46515*)	41,305	43,152
Columbus, OH (43216*)	565,032	540,025	Elmhurst, IL (60126)	44,276	46,392
Compton, CA (90220*)	81,286	78,547	Elmira, NY (14901*)	35,327	39,945
Concord, CA (94520*)	103,255	85,164	El Monte, CA (91734*)	79,494	69,892
Concord, NH (03301*)	30,400	30,022	El Paso, TX (79910*)	425,259	322,261
Coon Rapids, MN (55433)	35,826	30,505	Elyria, OH (44035*)	57,538	53,427
Coral Gables, FL (33114)	43,241	42,494	Emporia, KS (66801)	25,287	23,327
Coral Springs, FL (33065)	37,349	1,489	Englewood, CO (80110*)	30,021	33,695
Corona, CA (91720)	37,791	27,519	Enid, OK (73701)	50,363	44,986
Corpus Christi, TX (78408*)	231,999	204,525	Erie, PA (16515*)	119,123	129,265
Corvallis, OR (97333*)	40,960	35,056	Escondido, CA (92025*)	64,355	36,792
Costa Mesa, CA (92626*)	82,562	72,660	Euclid, OH (44117)	59,999	71,552
Council Bluffs, IA (51501)	56,449	60,348	Eugene, OR (97401*)	105,624	79,028
Covina, CA (91722*)	33,751	30,395	Evanston, IL (60204*)	73,706	80,113
Covington, KY (41011*)	49,563	52,535	Evansville, IN (47708*)	130,496	138,764
Cranston, RI (02910*)	71,992	74,287	Everett, MA (02149)	37,195	42,485
Crystal, MN (55428*)	25,543	30,925	Everett, WA (98201*)	54,413	53,622
Culver City, CA (90230)	38,139	34,451	Fairborn, OH (45324)	29,702	32,267
Cumberland, MD (21502*)	25,933	29,724	Fairfield, CA (94533)	58,099	44,146

City and major ZIP code	1980 census	1970 census	City and major ZIP code	1980 census	1970 census
Fairfield, OH (45014)	30,777	14,680	Gulfport, MS (39503*)	39,676	40,791
Fair Lawn, NJ (07410)	32,229	38,040	Hackensack, NJ (07602*)	36,039	36,008
Fall River, MA (02722*)	92,574	96,898	Hagerstown, MD (21740)	34,132	35,862
Fargo, ND (58102*)	61,383	53,365	Hallandale, FL (33009)	36,517	23,849
Farmington, NM (87401)	31,222	21,979	Haltom City, TX (76117)	29,014	28,127
Farmington Hills, MI (48024)	58,056	—	Hamilton, OH (45012*)	63,189	67,865
Fayetteville, AR (72701)	36,608	30,729	Hammond, IN (46320*)	93,714	107,983
Fayetteville, NC (28302*)	59,507	53,510	Hampton, VA (23670*)	122,617	120,779
Ferndale, MI (48220)	26,227	30,850	Hanover Park, IL (60103)	28,850	11,735
Findlay, OH (45840)	35,594	35,800	Harlingen, TX (78551*)	43,543	33,503
Fitchburg, MA (01420)	39,580	43,343	Harrisburg, PA (17105*)	53,264	68,061
Flagstaff, AZ (86001)	34,743	26,117	Hartford, CT (06101*)	136,392	158,017
Flint, MI (48502*)	159,611	193,317	Harvey, IL (60426)	35,810	34,636
Florence, AL (35631*)	37,029	34,031	Hattiesburg, MS (39401)	40,829	38,277
Florence, SC (29501)	29,176	25,997	Haverhill, MA (01830)	46,865	46,120
Florissant, MO (63033*)	55,372	65,908	Hawthorne, CA (90250)	56,447	53,304
Fond du Lac, WI (54935)	35,863	35,515	Hayward, CA (94544*)	94,342	93,058
Fontana, CA (92335)	37,107	20,673	Hazleton, PA (18201)	27,318	30,426
Fort Collins, CO (80521*)	65,092	43,337	Hempstead, NY (11551*)	40,404	39,411
Fort Dodge, IA (50501)	29,423	31,263	Hendersonville, TN (37075)	26,561	412
Fort Lauderdale, FL (33310*)	153,279	139,590	Hialeah, FL (33010*)	145,254	102,452
Fort Lee, NJ (07024)	32,449	30,631	Highland, IN (46322)	25,935	24,947
Fort Myers, FL (33906*)	36,638	27,351	Highland Park, IL (60035)	30,611	32,263
Fort Pierce, FL (33450*)	33,802	29,721	Highland Park, MI (48203)	27,909	35,444
Fort Smith, AR (72901*)	71,626	62,802	High Point, NC (27260*)	63,808	63,229
Fort Wayne, IN (46801*)	172,028	178,269	Hillsboro, OR (97123*)	27,664	14,675
Fort Worth, TX (76101*)	385,164	393,455	Hilo, HI (96720)	35,269	26,353
Fountain Valley, CA (92728)	55,080	31,886	Hobbs, NM (88240)	29,153	26,025
Frankfort, KY (40601)	25,973	21,902	Hoboken, NJ (07030)	42,460	45,380
Frederick, MD (21701)	28,086	23,641	Hoffman Estates, IL (60195)	37,272	22,238
Freeport, IL (61032)	26,266	27,736	Holland, MI (49423)	26,281	26,479
Freeport, NY (11520)	38,272	40,374	Hollywood, FL (33022*)	121,323	106,873
Fremont, CA (94538*)	131,945	100,869	Holyoke, MA (01040)	44,678	50,112
Fresno, CA (93706*)	218,202	165,655	Honolulu, HI (96820*)	365,048	324,871
Fridley, MN (55432)	30,228	29,233	Hopkinsville, KY (42240)	27,318	21,395
Fullerton, CA (92631*)	102,034	85,987	Hot Springs, AR (71901*)	35,781	35,631
Gadsden, AL (35901*)	47,565	53,928	Houma, LA (70360)	32,602	30,922
Gainesville, FL (32602*)	81,371	64,510	Houston, TX (77201*)	1,595,138	1,233,535
Gaithersburg, MD (20877*)	26,424	8,344	Huber Heights, OH (45424)	35,480	—
Galesburg, IL (61401)	35,305	36,290	Huntington, WV (25704*)	63,684	74,315
Galveston, TX (77553*)	61,902	61,809	Huntington Beach, CA (92647*)	170,505	115,960
Gardena, CA (90247*)	45,165	41,021	Huntington Park, CA (90255)	46,223	33,744
Garden City, MI (48135)	35,640	41,864	Huntsville, AL (35813*)	142,513	139,282
Garden Grove, CA (92640*)	123,307	121,155	Hurst, TX (76053)	31,420	27,215
Garfield, NJ (07026)	26,803	30,797	Hutchinson, KS (67501)	40,284	36,885
Garfield Heights, OH (44125)	34,938	41,417	Idaho Falls, ID (83401*)	39,590	35,776
Garland, TX (75040*)	138,857	81,437	Independence, MO (64051*)	111,806	111,630
Gary, IN (46401*)	151,953	175,415	Indianapolis, IN (46206*)	700,807	736,856
Gastonia, NC (28052)	47,333	47,322	Inglewood, CA (90311*)	94,245	89,985
Glendale, AZ (85301*)	97,172	36,228	Inkster, MI (48141)	35,190	38,595
Glendale, CA (91209*)	139,060	132,664	Iowa City, IA (52240*)	50,508	46,850
Glendora, CA (91740)	38,500	32,143	Irvine, CA (92713)	62,134	—
Glenview, IL (60025)	32,060	24,880	Irving, TX (75061*)	109,943	97,260
Gloucester, MA (01930)	27,768	27,941	Irvington, NJ (07111)	61,493	59,743
Goldsboro, NC (27530)	31,871	26,960	Ithaca, NY (14850)	28,732	26,226
Grand Forks, ND (58201)	43,765	39,008	Jackson, MI (49201*)	39,739	45,484
Grand Island, NE (68801)	33,180	32,358	Jackson, MS (39205*)	202,895	153,968
Grand Junction, CO (81501*)	27,956	20,170	Jackson, TN (38301*)	49,131	39,996
Grand Prairie, TX (75051*)	71,462	50,904	Jacksonville, AR (72076)	27,589	19,832
Grand Rapids, MI (49501*)	181,843	197,649	Jacksonville, FL (32203*)	540,920	504,265
Granite City, IL (62040)	36,815	40,685	Jamestown, NY (14701)	35,775	39,795
Great Falls, MT (59403*)	56,725	60,091	Janesville, WI (53545*)	51,071	46,426
Greeley, CO (80631*)	53,006	38,902	Jefferson City, MO (65101)	33,619	32,407
Green Bay, WI (54301*)	87,899	87,809	Jersey City, NJ (07303*)	223,532	260,350
Greenfield, WI (53220)	31,467	24,424	Johnson City, TN (37601)	39,753	33,770
Greensboro, NC (27420*)	155,642	144,076	Johnstown, PA (15901*)	35,496	42,476
Greenville, MS (38701*)	40,613	39,648	Joliet, IL (60436*)	77,956	78,827
Greenville, NC (27834)	35,740	29,063	Jonesboro, AR (72401)	31,530	27,050
Greenville, SC (29602*)	58,242	61,436	Joplin, MO (64801)	39,023	39,256
Gresham, OR (97030)	33,005	10,030	Kalamazoo, MI (49001*)	79,722	85,555

City and major ZIP code	1980 census	1970 census	City and major ZIP code	1980 census	1970 census
Kankakee, IL (60901)	30,141	30,944	Lorain, OH (44052*)	75,416	78,185
Kansas City, KS (66110*)	161,148	168,213	Los Altos, CA (94022)	25,769	25,062
Kansas City, MO (64108*)	448,159	507,330	Los Angeles, CA (90052*)	2,966,850	2,811,801
Kearny, NJ (07032)	35,735	37,585	Los Gatos, CA (95030)	26,906	22,613
Kenner, LA (70062*)	66,382	29,858	Louisville, KY (40231*)	298,840	361,706
Kennewick, WA (99336)	34,397	15,212	Loveland, CO (80537)	30,244	16,220
Kenosha, WI (53141*)	77,685	78,805	Lowell, MA (01853*)	92,418	94,239
Kent, OH (44240)	26,164	28,183	Lubbock, TX (79408*)	173,979	149,101
Kentwood, MI (49508)	30,438	20,310	Lufkin, TX (75901)	28,562	23,049
Kettering, OH (45429)	61,186	71,864	Lynchburg, VA (24506*)	66,743	54,083
Killeen, TX (76541*)	46,296	35,507	Lynn, MA (01901*)	78,471	90,294
Kingsport, TN (37662*)	32,027	31,938	Lynwood, CA (90262)	48,548	43,354
Kingsville, TX (78363)	28,808	28,915	Macon, GA (31213*)	116,896	122,423
Kinston, NC (28501)	25,234	23,020	Madison, WI (53707*)	170,616	171,809
Kirkwood, MO (63122)	27,987	31,679	Madison Heights, MI (48071)	35,375	38,599
Knoxville, TN (37901*)	175,045	174,587	Malden, MA (02148)	53,386	56,127
Kokomo, IN (46902*)	47,808	44,042	Manchester, NH (03103*)	90,936	87,754
La Crosse, WI (54601*)	48,347	50,286	Manhattan, KS (66502)	32,644	27,575
Lafayette, IN (47901*)	43,011	44,955	Manhattan Beach, CA (90266)	31,542	35,352
Lafayette, LA (70501*)	81,961	68,908	Manitowoc, WI (54220)	32,547	33,430
La Habra, CA (90631)	45,232	41,350	Mankato, MN (56001)	28,651	30,895
Lake Charles, LA (70601*)	75,226	77,998	Mansfield, OH (44901*)	53,927	55,047
Lakeland, FL (33802*)	47,406	42,803	Maple Heights, OH (44137)	29,735	34,093
Lakewood, CA (90714*)	74,654	83,025	Maplewood, MN (55109)	26,990	25,186
Lakewood, CO (80215)	113,808	92,743	Margate, FL (33063*)	35,900	8,867
Lakewood, OH (44107)	61,963	70,173	Marietta, GA (30060*)	30,829	27,216
Lake Worth, FL (33461*)	27,048	23,714	Marion, CA (46952*)	35,874	39,607
La Mesa, CA (92041)	50,308	39,178	Marion, OH (43302)	37,040	38,646
La Mirada, CA (90638)	40,986	30,808	Marlborough, MA (01752)	30,617	27,936
Lancaster, CA (93534*)	48,027	—	Marshalltown, IA (50158)	26,938	26,219
Lancaster, OH (43130)	34,953	32,911	Mason City, IA (50401)	30,144	30,279
Lancaster, PA (17604*)	54,725	57,690	Massillon, OH (44646)	30,557	32,539
Lansing, IL (60438)	29,039	25,805	Maywood, IL (60153)	27,998	29,019
Lansing, MI (48924*)	130,414	131,403	McAllen, TX (78501)	66,281	37,636
La Puente, CA (91747*)	30,882	31,092	McKeesport, PA (15134*)	31,012	37,977
Laredo, TX (78041*)	91,449	69,024	Medford, MA (02155)	58,076	64,397
Largo, FL (33540*)	58,977	24,230	Medford, OR (97501)	39,603	28,973
Las Cruces, NM (88001*)	45,086	37,857	Melbourne, FL (32901*)	46,536	40,236
Las Vegas, NV (89114*)	164,674	125,787	Melrose, MA (02176)	30,055	33,180
Lauderdale Lakes, FL (33313)	25,426	10,577	Memphis, TN (38101*)	646,174	623,988
Lauderhill, FL (33313)	37,271	8,465	Menlo Park, CA (94025)	26,369	26,826
Lawrence, IN (46226)	25,591	16,353	Menomonee Falls, WI (53051)	27,845	31,697
Lawrence, KS (66044)	52,738	45,698	Mentor, OH (44060)	42,065	36,912
Lawrence, MA (01842*)	63,175	66,915	Merced, CA (95340)	36,499	22,670
Lawton, OK (73501*)	80,054	74,470	Meriden, CT (06450)	57,118	55,959
Leavenworth, KS (66048)	33,656	25,147	Meridian, MS (39301)	46,577	45,083
Lebanon, PA (17042)	25,711	28,572	Merrillville, IN (46410)	27,677	—
Lee's Summit, MO (64063)	28,741	16,230	Mesa, AZ (85201*)	152,453	63,049
Leominster, MA (01453)	34,508	32,939	Mesquite, TX (75149*)	67,053	55,131
Lewiston, ID (83501)	27,986	26,068	Miami, FL (33152*)	346,865	334,859
Lewiston, ME (04240)	40,481	41,779	Miami Beach, FL (33139)	96,298	87,072
Lexington, KY (40511*)	204,165	108,137	Michigan City, IN (46360)	36,850	39,369
Lima, OH (45802*)	47,381	53,734	Middletown, CT (06457)	39,040	36,924
Lincoln, NE (68501*)	171,932	149,518	Middletown, OH (45042)	43,719	48,767
Lincoln Park, MI (48146)	45,105	52,984	Midland, MI (48640)	37,250	35,176
Linden, NJ (07036)	37,836	41,409	Midland, TX (79702*)	70,525	59,463
Lindenhurst, NY (11757)	26,919	28,359	Midwest City, OK (73140*)	49,559	48,212
Little Rock, AR (72231*)	158,461	132,483	Milford, CT (06460)	49,101	50,858
Littleton, CO (80120*)	28,631	26,466	Milpitas, CA (95035)	37,820	26,561
Livermore, CA (94550)	48,349	37,703	Milwaukee, WI (53201*)	636,236	717,372
Livonia, MI (48150*)	104,814	110,109	Minneapolis, MN (55401*)	370,951	434,400
Lodi, CA (95240)	35,221	28,691	Minnetonka, MN (55343)	38,683	35,776
Logan, UT (84321)	26,844	22,333	Minot, ND (58701)	32,843	32,290
Lombard, IL (60148)	37,295	34,043	Miramar, FL (33023)	32,813	23,997
Lompoc, CA (93436)	26,267	25,284	Mishawaka, IN (46544*)	40,201	36,060
Long Beach, CA (90809*)	361,334	358,879	Missoula, MT (59806*)	33,388	29,497
Long Beach, NY (11561)	34,073	33,127	Mobile, AL (36601*)	200,452	190,026
Long Branch, NJ (07740)	29,819	31,774	Modesto, CA (95350*)	106,602	61,712
Longmont, CO (80501)	42,942	23,209	Moline, IL (61265)	45,709	46,237
Longview, TX (75602*)	62,762	45,547	Monroe, LA (71203*)	57,597	56,374
Longview, WA (98632)	31,052	28,373	Monroeville, PA (15146)	30,977	29,011

City and major ZIP code	1980 census	1970 census
Monrovia, CA (91016)	30,531	30,562
Montclair, NJ (07042*)	38,321	44,043
Montebello, CA (90640)	52,929	42,807
Monterey, CA (93940)	27,558	26,302
Monterey Park, CA (91754)	54,338	49,166
Montgomery, AL (36119*)	177,857	133,386
Moore, OK (73153*)	35,063	18,761
Moorhead, MN (56560)	29,998	29,687
Morgantown, WV (26505)	27,605	29,431
Mountain View, CA (94042*)	58,655	54,132
Mount Prospect, IL (60056)	52,634	34,995
Mount Vernon, NY (10551*)	66,713	72,778
Muncie, IN (47302*)	77,216	69,082
Murfreesboro, TN (37130)	32,845	26,360
Murray, UT (84107)	25,750	21,206
Muskegon, MI (49440*)	40,823	44,631
Muskogee, OK (74401)	40,011	37,331
Nacogdoches, TX (75961)	27,149	22,544
Nampa, ID (83651)	25,112	20,768
Napa, CA (94558*)	50,879	36,103
Naperville, IL (60566*)	42,330	22,794
Nashua, NH (03061*)	67,865	55,820
Nashville, TN (37202*)	455,651	426,029
National City, CA (92050)	48,772	43,184
Naugatuck, CT (06770)	26,456	23,034
New Albany, IN (47150)	37,103	38,402
Newark, CA (94560)	32,126	27,153
Newark, DE (19711*)	25,247	21,298
Newark, NJ (07102*)	329,248	381,930
Newark, OH (43055)	41,200	41,836
New Bedford, MA (02741*)	98,478	101,777
New Berlin, WI (53151)	30,529	26,910
New Britain, CT (06050*)	73,840	83,441
New Brunswick, NJ (08901*)	41,442	41,885
New Castle, PA (16101*)	33,621	38,559
New Haven, CT (06511*)	126,109	137,707
New Iberia, LA (70560)	32,766	30,147
New London, CT (06320)	28,842	31,630
New Orleans, LA (70113*)	557,927	593,471
Newport, RI (02840)	29,259	34,562
Newport Beach, CA (92660*)	62,556	49,582
Newport News, VA (23607*)	144,903	138,177
New Rochelle, NY (10802*)	70,794	75,385
Newton, MA (02158)	83,622	91,263
New York, NY (10001*)	7,071,639	7,895,563
Bronx borough (10451*)	1,168,972	1,471,701
Brooklyn borough (11201*)	2,230,936	2,602,012
Manhattan borough (10001*)	1,428,285	1,539,233
Queens borough[1]	1,891,325	1,987,174
Staten Island borough (10314*)	352,121	295,443
Niagara Falls, NY (14302*)	71,384	85,615
Niles, IL (60648)	30,363	31,432
Norfolk, VA (23501*)	266,979	307,951
Normal, IL (61761)	35,672	26,396
Norman, OK (73070*)	68,020	52,117
Norristown, PA (19401*)	34,684	38,169
Northampton, MA (01060)	29,286	29,664
Northbrook, IL (60062)	30,778	25,422
North Charleston, SC (29406)	62,534	—
North Chicago, IL (60064)	38,774	47,275
Northglenn, CO (80233)	29,847	27,785
North Las Vegas, NV (89030)	42,739	46,067
North Little Rock, AR (72114*)	64,288	60,040
North Miami, FL (33161)	42,566	34,767
North Miami Beach, FL (33160)	36,553	30,544
North Olmsted, OH (44070)	36,486	34,861
North Richland Hills, TX (76118)	30,592	16,514
North Tonawanda, NY (14120)	35,760	36,012
Norwalk, CA (90650)	85,286	90,164
Norwalk, CT (06856*)	77,767	79,288
Norwich, CT (06360)	38,074	41,739
Norwood, OH (45212*)	26,342	30,420
Novato, CA (94947)	43,916	31,006
Nutley, NJ (07110)	28,998	31,913
Oak Forest, IL (60452)	26,096	19,271
Oakland, CA (94615*)	339,337	361,561
Oak Lawn, IL (60454*)	60,590	60,305
Oak Park, IL (60301*)	54,887	62,511
Oak Park, MI (48237)	31,537	36,762
Oak Ridge, TN (37830)	27,662	28,319
Ocala, FL (32678*)	37,170	22,583
Oceanside, CA (92054*)	76,698	40,494
Odessa, TX (79760*)	90,027	78,380
Ogden, UT (84401*)	64,407	69,478
Oklahoma City, OK (73125*)	403,136	368,164
Olathe, KS (66061*)	37,258	17,917
Olympia, WA (98501*)	27,447	23,296
Omaha, NE (68108*)	313,911	346,929
Ontario, CA (91761*)	88,820	64,118
Orange, CA (92667*)	91,788	77,365
Orange, NJ (07051*)	31,136	32,566
Orem, UT (84057*)	52,399	25,729
Orlando, FL (32802*)	128,291	99,006
Oshkosh, WI (54901)	49,620	53,082
Ottumwa, IA (52501)	27,381	29,610
Overland Park, KS (66204)	81,784	77,934
Owensboro, KY (43201)	54,450	50,329
Oxnard, CA (93030*)	108,195	71,225
Pacifica, CA (94044)	36,866	36,020
Paducah, KY (42001)	29,315	31,627
Palatine, IL (60067*)	32,166	26,050
Palm Springs, CA (92263*)	32,366	20,936
Palo Alto, CA (94303*)	55,225	56,040
Panama City, FL (32401*)	33,346	32,096
Paramount, CA (90723)	36,407	34,734
Paramus, NJ (07652)	26,474	28,381
Paris, TX (75460)	25,498	23,441
Parkersburg, WV (26101*)	39,967	44,208
Park Forest, IL (60466)	26,222	30,638
Park Ridge, IL (60068)	38,704	42,614
Parma, OH (44129)	92,548	100,216
Pasadena, CA (91109*)	118,550	112,951
Pasadena, TX (77501*)	112,560	89,957
Pascagoula, MS (39567)	29,318	27,264
Passaic, NJ (07055)	52,463	55,124
Paterson, NJ (07510*)	137,970	144,824
Pawtucket, RI (02860*)	71,204	76,984
Peabody, MA (01960)	45,976	48,080
Pembroke Pines, FL (33024)	35,776	15,496
Pensacola, FL (32501*)	57,619	59,507
Peoria, IL (61601*)	124,160	126,963
Perth Amboy, NJ (08861*)	38,951	38,798
Petaluma, CA (94952)	33,834	24,870
Petersburg, VA (23804*)	41,055	36,103
Phenix City, AL (36867)	26,928	25,281
Philadelphia, PA (19104*)	1,688,210	1,949,996
Phoenix, AZ (85026*)	789,704	584,303
Pico Rivera, CA (90660)	53,387	54,170
Pine Bluff, AR (71601*)	56,636	57,389
Pinellas Park, FL (33565)	32,811	22,287
Pittsburg, CA (94565)	33,034	21,423
Pittsburgh, PA (15219*)	423,959	520,089
Pittsfield, MA (01201)	51,974	57,020
Placentia, CA (92670)	35,041	21,948
Plainfield, NJ (07061*)	45,555	46,862
Plano, TX (75074*)	72,331	17,872
Plantation, FL (33318)	48,653	23,523
Pleasant Hill, CA (94523)	25,124	24,610
Pleasanton, CA (94566)	35,160	18,328

City and major ZIP code	1980 census	1970 census	City and major ZIP code	1980 census	1970 census
Plum, PA (15239)	25,390	21,932	St. Louis Park, MN (55426*)	42,931	48,883
Plymouth, MN (55447*)	31,615	18,077	St. Paul, MN (55101*)	270,230	309,866
Pocatello, ID (83201)	46,340	40,036	St. Petersburg, FL (33730*)	238,647	216,159
Pomona, CA (91766*)	92,742	87,384	Salem, MA (01970)	38,220	40,556
Pompano Beach, FL (33060*)	52,618	38,587	Salem, OR (97301*)	89,233	68,725
Ponca City, OK (74601*)	26,238	25,940	Salina, KS (67401)	41,843	37,714
Pontiac, MI (48056*)	76,715	85,279	Salinas, CA (93907*)	80,479	58,896
Portage, IN (46368)	27,409	19,127	Salt Lake City, UT (84119*)	163,697	175,885
Portage, MI (49081)	38,157	33,590	San Angelo, TX (76902*)	73,240	63,884
Port Arthur, TX (77640)	61,251	57,371	San Antonio, TX (78284*)	786,023	654,153
Port Huron, MI (48060)	33,981	35,794	San Bernardino, CA (92403*)	118,794	106,869
Portland, ME (04101*)	61,572	65,116	San Bruno, CA (94066)	35,417	36,254
Portland, OR (97208*)	366,383	379,967	San Buenaventura (Ventura), CA (93002*)	74,393	57,964
Portsmouth, NH (03801)	26,254	25,717	San Clemente, CA (92672)	27,325	17,063
Portsmouth, OH (45662)	25,943	27,633	San Diego, CA (92199*)	875,538	697,471
Portsmouth, VA (23705*)	104,577	110,963	Sandusky, OH (44870)	31,360	32,674
Poughkeepsie, NY (12601*)	29,757	32,029	Sandy City, UT (84070*)	52,210	6,438
Prichard, AL (36610*)	39,541	41,578	San Francisco, CA (94188*)	678,974	715,674
Providence, RI (02940*)	156,804	179,116	San Gabriel, CA (91776*)	30,072	29,336
Provo, UT (84603*)	74,108	53,131	San Jose, CA (95101*)	629,546	459,913
Pueblo, CO (81003*)	101,686	97,774	San Leandro, CA (94577*)	63,952	68,698
Quincy, IL (62301)	42,554	45,288	San Luis Obispo, CA (93401)	34,252	28,036
Quincy, MA (02269)	84,743	87,966	San Mateo, CA (94402*)	77,561	78,991
Racine, WI (53401*)	85,725	95,162	San Rafael, CA (94901*)	44,700	38,977
Rahway, NJ (07065*)	26,723	29,114	Santa Ana, CA (92711*)	204,023	155,710
Raleigh, NC (27611*)	150,255	122,830	Santa Barbara, CA (93102*)	74,414	70,215
Rancho Cucamonga, CA (91730)	55,250	—	Santa Clara, CA (95050*)	87,746	86,118
Rancho Palos Verdes, CA (90274)	36,577	—	Santa Cruz, CA (95060*)	41,483	32,076
Rapid City, SD (57701)	46,492	43,836	Santa Fe, NM (87501*)	48,953	41,167
Raytown, MO (64133*)	31,759	33,306	Santa Maria, CA (93456*)	39,685	32,749
Reading, PA (19603*)	78,686	87,643	Santa Monica, CA (90406*)	88,314	88,289
Redding, CA (96001*)	41,995	16,659	Santa Rosa, CA (95402*)	83,320	50,006
Redlands, CA (92373)	43,619	36,355	Sarasota, FL (33578*)	48,868	40,237
Redondo Beach, CA (90277*)	57,102	57,451	Saratoga, CA (95070)	29,261	26,810
Redwood City, CA (94064*)	54,951	55,686	Savannah, GA (31401*)	141,390	118,349
Reno, NV (89510*)	100,756	72,863	Sayreville, NJ (08872)	29,969	32,508
Renton, WA (98057*)	30,612	25,878	Schaumburg, IL (60194)	53,305	18,531
Revere, MA (02151)	42,423	43,159	Schenectady, NY (12301*)	67,972	77,958
Rialto, CA (92376)	37,474	28,370	Scottsdale, AZ (85251*)	88,622	67,823
Richardson, TX (75080*)	72,496	48,405	Scranton, PA (18505*)	88,117	102,696
Richfield, MN (55423)	37,851	47,231	Seal Beach, CA (90740)	25,975	24,441
Richland, WA (99352)	33,578	26,290	Seaside, CA (93955)	36,567	36,883
Richmond, CA (94802*)	74,676	79,043	Seattle, WA (98109*)	493,846	530,831
Richmond, IN (47374)	41,349	43,999	Selma, AL (36701)	26,684	27,379
Richmond, VA (23232*)	219,214	249,332	Shaker Heights, OH (44120)	32,487	36,306
Ridgewood, NJ (07451*)	25,208	27,547	Shawnee, KS (66202*)	29,653	20,946
Riverside, CA (92507*)	170,591	140,089	Shawnee, OK (74801)	26,506	25,075
Riviera Beach, FL (33404)	26,489	21,401	Sheboygan, WI (53081)	48,085	48,484
Roanoke, VA (24022*)	100,220	92,115	Shelton, CT (06484)	31,314	27,165
Rochester, MN (55901*)	57,890	53,766	Sherman, TX (75090)	30,413	29,061
Rochester, NY (14692*)	241,741	295,011	Shreveport, LA (71102*)	205,820	182,064
Rockford, IL (61125*)	139,712	147,370	Simi Valley, CA (93065*)	77,500	59,832
Rock Hill, SC (29730)	35,344	33,846	Sioux City, IA (51101*)	82,003	85,925
Rock Island, IL (61201)	47,036	50,166	Sioux Falls, SD (57101*)	81,343	72,488
Rockville, MD (20850*)	43,811	42,739	Skokie, IL (60076*)	60,278	68,322
Rockville Centre, NY (11570)	25,412	27,444	Slidell, LA (70458)	26,718	16,101
Rocky Mount, NC (27801)	41,283	34,284	Somerville, MA (02143)	77,372	88,779
Rome, GA (30161)	29,654	30,759	Somerville, NJ (08876)	29,969	32,508
Rome, NY (13440)	43,826	50,148	South Bend, IN (46624*)	109,727	125,580
Rosemead, CA (91770)	42,604	40,972	South Euclid, OH (44121)	25,713	29,579
Roseville, MI (48066)	54,311	60,529	Southfield, MI (48037*)	75,568	69,285
Roseville, MN (55113*)	35,820	34,438	South Gate, CA (90280)	66,784	56,909
Roswell, NM (88201)	39,676	33,908	Southgate, MI (48195)	32,058	33,909
Royal Oak, MI (48068*)	70,893	86,238	South San Francisco, CA (94080)	49,393	46,646
Sacramento, CA (95813*)	275,741	257,105	Sparks, NV (89431)	40,780	24,187
Saginaw, MI (48065*)	77,508	91,849	Spartanburg, SC (29301*)	43,826	44,546
St. Charles, MO (63301)	36,087	31,834	Spokane, WA (99210*)	171,300	170,516
St. Clair Shores, MI (48080*)	76,210	88,093	Springfield, IL (62703*)	100,054	91,753
St. Cloud, MN (56301)	42,566	39,691	Springfield, MA (01101*)	152,319	163,905
St. Joseph, MO (64501*)	76,691	72,748	Springfield, MO (65801*)	133,116	120,096
St. Louis, MO (63155*)	453,085	622,236			

City and major ZIP code	1980 census	1970 census	City and major ZIP code	1980 census	1970 census
Springfield, OH (45501*)	72,563	81,941	Visalia, CA (93277*)	49,729	27,130
Springfield, OR (97477*)	41,621	26,874	Vista, CA (92083)	35,834	24,688
Stamford, CT (06904*)	102,453	108,798	Waco, TX (76701*)	101,261	95,326
State College, PA (16801*)	36,130	32,833	Walla Walla, WA (99362)	25,618	23,619
Sterling Heights, MI (48077)	108,999	61,365	Walnut Creek, CA (94596*)	53,643	39,844
Steubenville, OH (43952)	26,400	30,771	Waltham, MA (02154)	58,200	61,582
Stillwater, OK (74074*)	38,268	31,126	Warner Robins, GA (31093)	39,893	33,491
Stockton, CA (95208*)	149,779	109,963	Warren, MI (48089*)	161,134	179,260
Stow, OH (44224)	25,303	20,061	Warren, OH (44481*)	56,629	63,494
Strongsville, OH (44136)	28,577	15,182	Warwick, RI (02887*)	87,123	83,694
Suffolk, VA (23434*)	47,621	9,858	Washington, DC (20013*)	638,432	756,668
Sunnyvale, CA (94086*)	106,618	95,976	Waterbury, CT (06701*)	103,266	108,033
Sunrise, FL (33338)	39,681	7,403	Waterloo, IA (50701*)	75,985	75,533
Superior, WI (54880)	29,571	32,237	Watertown, NY (13601)	27,861	30,787
Syracuse, NY (13220*)	170,105	197,297	Waukegan, IL (60085*)	67,653	65,134
Tacoma, WA (98413*)	158,501	154,407	Waukesha, WI (53186)	50,365	39,695
Tallahassee, FL (32301*)	81,548	72,624	Wausau, WI (54401)	32,426	32,806
Tamarac, FL (33320)	29,376	5,193	Wauwatosa, WI (53213)	51,308	58,676
Tampa, FL (33630*)	271,523	277,714	Weirton, WV (26062)	25,371	27,131
Taunton, MA (02780)	45,001	43,756	West Allis, WI (53213)	63,982	71,649
Taylor, MI (48180)	77,568	70,020	West Covina, CA (91793*)	80,291	68,034
Tempe, AZ (85282*)	106,743	63,550	Westfield, MA (01085)	36,465	31,433
Temple, TX (76501*)	42,354	33,431	Westfield, NJ (07091*)	30,447	33,720
Temple City, CA (91780)	28,972	31,034	West Haven, CT (06516)	53,184	52,851
Terre Haute, IN (47808*)	61,125	70,335	West Jordan, UT (84084)	27,192	4,221
Texarkana, TX (75501*)	31,271	30,497	Westland, MI (48185)	84,603	86,749
Texas City, TX (77590*)	41,403	38,908	West Memphis, AR (72301)	28,138	26,070
Thornton, CO (80229)	40,343	13,326	West Mifflin, PA (15122)	26,279	28,070
Thousand Oaks, CA (91360*)	77,072	35,873	Westminster, CA (92683)	71,133	60,076
Tinley Park, IL (60477)	26,171	12,572	Westminster, CO (80030*)	50,211	19,512
Titusville, FL (32780)	31,910	30,515	West New York, NJ (07093)	39,194	40,627
Toledo, OH (43601*)	354,635	383,062	West Orange, NJ (07052)	39,510	43,715
Topeka, KS (66603*)	115,266	125,011	West Palm Beach, FL (33401*)	63,305	57,375
Torrance, CA (90510*)	129,881	134,968	Wheaton, IL (60187)	43,043	31,138
Torrington, CT (06790)	30,987	31,952	Wheat Ridge, CO (80033)	30,293	29,778
Trenton, NJ (08650*)	92,124	104,786	Wheeling, WV (26003)	43,070	48,188
Troy, MI (48099*)	67,102	39,419	White Plains, NY (10602*)	46,999	50,346
Troy, NY (12180*)	56,638	62,918	Whittier, CA (90605*)	69,717	72,863
Tucson, AZ (85726*)	330,537	262,933	Wichita, KS (67276*)	279,835	276,554
Tulsa, OK (74101*)	360,919	330,350	Wichita Falls, TX (76307*)	94,201	96,265
Turlock, CA (95380)	26,287	13,992	Wilkes-Barre, PA (18701*)	51,551	58,856
Tuscaloosa, AL (35403*)	75,211	65,773	Williamsport, PA (17701)	33,401	37,918
Tustin, CA (92680)	32,317	22,313	Wilmette, IL (60091)	28,229	32,134
Twin Falls, ID (83301)	26,209	21,914	Wilmington, DE (19850*)	70,195	80,386
Tyler, TX (75712*)	70,508	57,770	Wilmington, NC (28402*)	44,000	46,169
Union City, CA (94587)	39,406	14,724	Wilson, NC (27893)	34,424	29,347
Union City, NJ (07087)	55,593	57,305	Winona, MN (55987)	25,075	26,438
University City, MO (63130)	42,738	47,527	Winston-Salem, NC (27102*)	131,885	133,683
Upland, CA (91786)	47,647	32,551	Woburn, MA (01801)	36,626	37,406
Upper Arlington, OH (43221)	35,648	38,727	Woodland, CA (95695)	30,235	20,677
Urbana, IL (61801)	35,978	33,976	Woonsocket, RI (02895)	45,914	46,820
Utica, NY (13504*)	75,632	91,373	Worcester, MA (01613*)	161,799	176,572
Vacaville, CA (95688)	43,367	21,690	Wyandotte, MI (48192)	34,006	41,061
Valdosta, GA (31601)	37,596	32,303	Wyoming, MI (49509)	59,616	56,560
Vallejo, CA (94590*)	80,303	71,710	Yakima, WA (98903*)	49,826	45,588
Valley Stream, NY (11580*)	35,769	40,413	Yonkers, NY (10701*)	195,351	204,297
Vancouver, WA (98661*)	42,834	41,859	Yorba Linda, CA (92686)	28,254	11,856
Vicksburg, MS (39180)	25,434	25,478	York, PA (17405*)	44,619	50,335
Victoria, TX (77901*)	50,695	41,349	Youngstown, OH (44501*)	115,436	140,909
Vineland, NJ (08360)	53,753	47,399	Yuma, AZ (85364*)	42,481	29,007
Virginia Beach, VA (23450*)	262,199	172,106	Zanesville, OH (43701)	28,655	33,045

1. Queens has four major ZIP codes: 11690*—Far Rockaway; 11351*—Flushing; 11431*—Jamaica; 11101*—Long Island City. *Sources:* Department of Commerce, Bureau of the Census; *National ZIP Code & Post Office Directory.*

Family Share of Households Is Declining

Between 1980 and 1988 the number of family households increased by 9 percent compared to nonfamily households which increased by 22 percent. Persons living alone account for most of the nonfamily households. Of the 25.9 million nonfamily households in 1988, approximately 21.9 million or 84 percent were persons living alone and more than half of them are women.

The Expansion of the UNITED STATES

CANADA

Atlantic Ocean

BAHAMA ISLANDS (British)

CUBA

Limit of British claim

St. Lawrence R.

L. Ontario

L. Erie

L. Huron

L. Superior

L. Michigan

THE UNITED STATES 1783

ORIGINAL THIRTEEN

St. Mary's R.

FLORIDA

Purchased from Spain, 1819

Claimed by Spain to 1795

Florida to 1819

Gulf of Mexico

Mississippi R.

LOUISIANA PURCHASE Purchased from France, 1803

Missouri R.

REPUBLIC OF TEXAS Annexed, 1845

Area claimed by Texas and ceded by Mexico 1848

Rio Grande

MEXICO

ROCKY MOUNTAINS

Ceded by Mexico ~ 1848

Gila R.

Gadsden Purchase 1853

Colorado R.

OREGON COUNTRY U.S. Claim recognized by Great Britain, by Treaty of 1846

Columbia R.

Pacific Ocean

Present State Boundaries

Scale of Miles
0 100 300 500

Territorial Expansion

Accession	Date	Area[1]
United States	—	3,618,770
Territory in 1790	—	891,364
Louisiana Purchase	1803	831,321
Florida	1819	69,866
Texas	1845	384,958
Oregon	1846	283,439
Mexican Cession	1848	530,706
Gadsden Purchase	1853	29,640
Alaska	1867	591,004
Hawaii	1898	6,471
Other territory	—	4,664
Philippines	1898	115,600 [2]
Puerto Rico	1899	3,515
Guam	1899	209
American Samoa	1900	77
Canal Zone[3]	1904	553
Virgin Islands of U.S.	1917	132
Trust Territory of Pacific Islands	1947	717 [4]
All other	—	14
Total, 1980	—	**3,623,434**

1. Total land and water area in square miles. 2. Became independent in 1946. 3. Reverted to Panama. 4. Land area only; includes Northern Mariana Islands. *Source:* Department of Commerce, Bureau of the Census.

Total Population

Area	1980	1970	1960
50 states of U.S.	226,545,805	203,302,031	179,323,175
48 coterminous	225,179,263	202,229,535	178,464,236
Alaska	401,851	302,583	226,167
Hawaii	964,691	769,913	632,772
American Samoa	32,297	27,159	20,051
Canal Zone	(¹)	44,198	42,122
Canton Island	—	n.a.	320
Corn Islands	—	(²)	1,872
Guam	105,979	84,996	67,044
Johnston Atoll	327	1,007	156
Midway	453	2,220	2,356
Puerto Rico	3,196,520	2,712,033	2,349,544
Swan Islands	n.a.	22	28
Trust Ter. of Pac. Is.	132,929 ³	90,940	70,724
Virgin Is. of U.S.	96,569	62,468	32,099
Wake Island	302	1,647	1,097
Population abroad	995,546	1,737,836	1,374,421
Armed forces	515,408	1,057,776	609,720
Other[4]	n.a.	n.a.	n.a.
Total	**231,106,727**	**208,066,557**	**183,285,009**

1. Granted independence on Oct. 1, 1979. 2. Returned to Nicaragua April 25, 1971. 3. Includes Northern Mariana Islands. 4. Includes Baker Island, Enderbury Island, Howland Island, and Jarvis Island, all uninhabited. NOTE: n.a. = unavailable. *Source:* Department of Commerce, Bureau of the Census.

Population by Race, 1980 Census

State	White	Black	Spanish origin	Other	State	White	Black	Spanish origin	Other
Ala.	2,869,688	995,623	33,100	24,750	Mont.	740,148	1,786	9,974	44,756
Alaska	308,455	13,619	9,497	78,407	Neb.	1,490,569	48,389	28,020	31,048
Ariz.	2,240,033	75,034	440,915	402,799	Nev.	699,377	50,791	53,786	49,016
Ark.	1,890,002	373,192	17,873	22,319	N.H.	910,099	3,990	5,587	6,521
Calif.	18,031,689	1,819,282	4,543,770	3,817,591	N.J.	6,127,090	924,786	491,867	312,282
Colo.	2,570,596	101,702	339,300	216,517	N.M.	976,465	24,042	476,089	299,461
Conn.	2,799,420	217,433	124,499	90,723	N.Y.	13,961,106	2,401,842	1,659,245	1,194,340
Del.	488,543	95,971	9,671	10,711	N.C.	4,453,010	1,316,050	56,607	105,369
D.C.	171,796	488,229	17,652	17,626	N.D.	625,536	2,568	3,903	24,591
Fla.	8,178,387	1,342,478	857,898	219,127	Ohio	9,597,266	1,076,734	119,880	123,419
Ga.	3,948,007	1,465,457	61,261	50,801	Okla.	2,597,783	204,658	57,413	222,825
Hawaii	318,608	17,352	71,479	629,040	Ore.	2,490,192	37,059	65,833	105,412
Idaho	901,641	2,716	36,615	39,578	Pa.	10,654,325	1,047,609	154,004	164,794
Ill.	9,225,575	1,675,229	635,525	517,657	R.I.	896,692	27,584	19,707	22,878
Ind.	5,004,567	414,732	87,020	70,880	S.C.	2,145,122	948,146	33,414	25,940
Iowa	2,838,805	41,700	25,536	32,882	S.D.	638,955	2,144	4,028	49,079
Kan.	2,167,752	126,127	63,333	69,329	Tenn.	3,835,078	725,949	34,081	29,723
Ky.	3,379,648	259,490	27,403	22,295	Tex.	11,197,663	1,710,250	2,985,643	1,320,470
La.	2,911,243	1,237,263	99,105	55,466	Utah	1,382,550	9,225	60,302	69,262
Me.	1,109,850	3,128	5,005	11,682	Vt.	506,736	1,135	3,304	3,585
Md.	3,158,412	958,050	64,740	99,984	Va.	4,229,734	1,008,311	79,873	108,234
Mass.	5,362,836	221,279	141,043	152,922	Wash.	3,777,296	105,544	119,986	247,323
Mich.	7,868,956	1,198,710	162,388	190,678	W. Va.	1,874,751	65,051	12,707	9,842
Minn.	3,936,948	53,342	32,124	86,858	Wis.	4,442,598	182,593	62,981	80,114
Miss.	1,615,190	887,206	24,731	18,242	Wyo.	447,716	3,364	24,499	19,736
Mo.	4,346,267	514,274	51,667	56,903	**Total**	**188,340,790**	**26,488,218**	**14,605,883**	**11,675,817**

Source: Department of Commerce, Bureau of the Census.

Suicides Among the Elderly on the Rise

After steadily declining for nearly 50 years, the suicide rate among the elderly has been on the increase in the 1980s. Between 1981 and 1986 the suicide rate for those 65 and older increased by 25 percent, to 21.6 per 100,000 people, as against a national rate of 12.8.

Although there is no official explanation for this surge of suicides, researches have noted a tendency among the elderly to choose "rational suicide" over a life of infirmity.

Immigration to U.S. by Country of Origin

(Figures are totals, not annual averages, and were tabulated as follows: 1820–67, alien passengers arrived; 1868–91 and 1895–97, immigrant aliens arrived; 1892–94 and 1898 to present, immigrant aliens admitted. Data before 1906 relate to country whence alien came; 1906-80, to country of last permanent residence; 1981 to present data based on country of birth.

Countries	1988	1820–1987	1971-80	1961-70	1951-60	1941-50	1931-40	1820–1930
Europe: Albania[1]	82	2,859	329	98	59	85	2,040	—
Austria[2]	514	4,321,424	9,478	20,621	67,106	24,860	3,563	3,658,978
Belgium	581	207,385	5,329	9,192	18,575	12,189	4,817	153,388
Bulgaria[3]	217	69,574	1,188	619	104	375	938	64,918
Czechoslovakia[1]	1,482	146,188	6,023	3,273	918	8,347	14,393	105,620
Denmark	558	368,605	4,439	9,201	10,984	5,393	2,559	332,466
Estonia[1]	11	1,249	91	163	185	212	506	—
Finland[1]	390	36,262	2,868	4,192	4,925	2,503	2,146	17,447
France	2,524	770,387	25,069	45,237	51,121	38,809	12,623	582,375
Germany[2]	6,755	7,040,414	74,414	190,796	477,765	226,578	114,058	5,907,893
Great Britain: England	13,228	5,050,304	137,374	174,452	156,171	112,252	21,756	2,619,435
Scotland	—	—	—	29,849	32,854	16,131	6,887	726,887
Wales	—	—	—	2,052	2,589	3,209	735	85,659
Not specified[4]	—	—	—	3,675	3,884	—	—	793,741
Greece	2,458	686,966	92,369	85,969	47,608	8,973	9,119	421,489
Hungary[2]	1,227	2,000	6,550	5,401	36,637	3,469	7,861	473,373
Ireland	5,058	4,702,425	11,490	37,461	57,332	26,967	13,167	4,578,941
Italy	2,949	5,329,602	129,368	214,111	185,491	57,661	68,028	4,651,195
Latvia[1]	31	2,848	207	510	352	361	1,192	—
Lithuania[1]	47	4,241	248	562	242	683	2,201	—
Luxembourg[1]	28	3,091	307	556	684	820	·565	—
Netherlands	1,187	370,148	10,492	30,606	52,277	14,860	7,150	246,609
Norway[5]	397	859,813	3,941	15,484	22,935	10,100	4,740	800,115
Poland[6]	9,507	575,329	37,234	53,539	9,985	7,571	17,026	397,729
Portugal	3,199	488,858	101,710	76,065	19,588	7,423	3,329	252,715
Romania[7]	3,875	199,852	12,393	2,531	1,039	1,076	3,871	153,074
Spain	1,483	275,494	34,141	44,659	7,894	2,898	3,258	166,865
Sweden[5]	1,156	1,280,238	6,531	17,116	21,697	10,665	3,960	1,213,488
Switzerland	751	355,282	8,235	18,453	17,675	10,547	5,512	290,168
U.S.S.R.[8]	2,949	3,430,256	38,961	2,336	584	548	1,356	3,341,991
Yugoslavia[3]	1,941	129,426	30,540	20,381	8,225	1,576	5,835	50,952
Other Europe	212	58,132	4,049	4,203	8,155	3,983	2,361	33,699
Total Europe	64,797	36,783,512	800,368	1,123,363	1,325,640	621,124	347,552	32,121,210
Asia: China[9]	38,387	799,361	124,326	34,764	9,657	16,709	4,928	377,245
India	26,268	378,661	164,154	27,189	1,973	1,761	496	9,377
Israel	3,640	120,661	—	—	—	—	—	—
Japan[10]	4,512	443,312	49,775	39,988	46,250	1,555	1,948	275,643
Turkey	1,642	403,820	13,399	10,142	3,519	798	1,065	360,171
Other Asia	190,016	3,149,904	1,236,544	315,688	88,707	11,537	7,644	35,895
Total Asia[11]	264,465	5,154,892	1,588,178	427,771	150,106	32,360	16,081	1,058,331
America: Canada and Newfoundland[12]	11,783	4,217,105	169,939	413,310	377,952	171,718	108,527	2,897,201
Central America	30,715	532,342	134,640	101,330	44,751	21,665	5,861	43,293
Mexico[13]	95,039	2,706,857	640,294	453,937	299,811	60,589	22,319	755,936
South America ·	41,007	1,058,681	295,741	257,954	91,628	21,831	7,803	113,499
West Indies	112,357	2,407,489	741,126	470,213	123,091	49,725	15,502	431,469
Other America[13]	115	110,154	789	19,630	59,711	29,276	25	31
Total America	219,016	10,987,943	1,982,529	1,716,374	996,944	354,804	160,037	4,241,429
Africa	18,882	269,524	80,779	28,954	14,092	7,367	1,750	24,310
Australia and New Zealand	2,024	136,780	23,788	19,562	11,506	13,805	2,231	52,301
Pacific Islands[14]	1,815	25,722	1,806	1,769	· 4,698	5,437	780	10,365
Countries not specified[15]	26	301,484	15,866	3,884	12,493	142	—	254,066
Total all countries	643,025	53,723,582	4,493,314	3,321,677	2,515,479	1,035,039	528,431	37,762,012

1. Countries established since beginning of World War I are included with countries to which they belonged. 2. Data for Austria-Hungary not reported until 1861. Austria and Hungary recorded separately after 1905, Austria included with Germany 1938–45. 3. Bulgaria, Serbia, Montenegro first reported in 1899. Bulgaria reported separately since 1920. In 1920, separate enumeration for Kingdom of Serbs, Croats, Slovenes; since 1922, recorded as Yugoslavia. 4. United Kingdom not specified; for 1901–51, included in "Other Europe." 5. Norway included with Sweden 1820–68. 6. Included with Austria-Hungary, Germany, and Russia 1899–1919. 7. No record of immigration until 1880. 8. From 1931–63, the U.S.S.R. was broken down into European U.S.S.R. and Asian U.S.S.R. Since 1964, total U.S.S.R. has been reported in Europe. 9. Beginning in 1957, China includes Taiwan. 10. No record of immigration until 1861. 11. From 1934, Asia included Philippines; before 1934, recorded in separate tables as insular travel. 12. Includes all British North American possessions, 1820–98. 13. No record of immigration, 1886–93. 14. Included with "Countries not specified" prior to 1925. 15. Includes 32,897 persons returning in 1906 to their homes in U.S. *Source:* Department of Justice, Immigration and Naturalization Service. NOTE: Data are latest available.

Immigrant and Nonimmigrant Aliens Admitted to U.S.

Period[1]	Immigrants	Non-immigrants	Total	Period[1]	Immigrants	Non-immigrants	Total
1901–10	8,795,386	1,007,909	9,803,295	1981	596,600	11,756,903	12,353,503
1911–20	5,735,811	1,376,271	7,112,082	1982	594,131	11,779,359	12,373,490
1921–30	4,107,209	1,774,896	5,882,090	1983[3]	559,763	9,849,458	10,409,221
1931–40	528,431	1,574,071	2,102,502	1984	543,903	9,426,759	9,970,662
1941–50	1,035,039	2,461,359	3,496,398	1985	570,009	9,675,650	10,245,659
1951–60	2,515,479	7,113,023	9,628,502	1986	601,708	10,471,024	11,072,732
1961–70	3,321,677	24,107,224	27,428,901	1987	601,516	12,272,866	12,874,382
1971–77	2,797,209	45,236,597	48,033,806	1988	643,025	14,591,735	15,234,760

1. Fiscal year ending June 30 prior to 1977. After 1977 for fiscal year ending Sept. 30, except as noted. 2. Figures for October 1978–June 1979. 3. Figures for calendar year 1983. Nonimmigrant aliens include visitors for business or pleasure, students, foreign government officials, and others temporarily in the U.S. NOTE: n.a. = not available. Source: Department of Justice, Immigration and Naturalization Service.

Persons Naturalized Since 1907

Period[1]	Civilian	Military	Total	Period[1]	Civilian	Military	Total
1907–30	2,713,389	300,506	3,013,895	1984	192,113	2,965	197,023[2]
1931–40	1,498,573	19,891	1,518,464	1985	238,394	3,266	244,717[3]
1941–50	1,837,229	149,799	1,987,028	1907–88	11,356,949	639,628	12,004,755[4]
1951–60	1,148,241	41,705	1,189,946	1986	275,352	2,901	280,623[5]
1961–70	1,084,195	36,068	1,120,263	1987	224,100	2,402	227,008[6]
1971–80	1,397,846	66,926	1,464,772	1988	239,541	2,296	242,063[7]

1. Fiscal year ending June 30. Starting 1977, Fiscal year ending Sept. 30. 2. Including 1,945 unidentified. 3. Including 3,057 unidentified. 4. Including 8,178 unidentified. 5. Including 2,370 unidentified. 6. Including 506 unidentified. 7. Including 226 unidentified. Source: Department of Justice, Immigration and Naturalization Service. NOTE: Data are latest available.

Population of Largest Indian Reservations, 1987

Navajo (Ariz., N.M., Utah)	173,018	Rosebud (S.D.)	11,685[1]	Zuni (N.M.)	8,135
Cherokee (Okla.)	58,232	Gila River (Ariz.)	10,688	Pawnee (Okla.)	7,657
Creek (Okla.)	54,606	Papago-Sells (Ariz.)	10,138	Northern Pueblos (N.M.)	7,651
Choctaw (Okla.)	21,858	Turtle Mountain (N.D.)	9,889	Shawnee (Okla., Texas)	7,263
Pine Ridge (S.D.)	19,246	Hopi (Ariz.)	9,040	Blackfeet (Mont.)	7,193
Southern Pueblos (N.M.)	17,079	Standing Rock (N.D., S.D.)	8,612	Yakima (Wash.)	6,846
Chicksaw (Okla.)	11,780	Fort Apache (Ariz.)	8,421	Wind River (Wyo.)	5,124

NOTE: The Bureau of Indian Affairs lists 861,500 Indians residing on or near Federal reservations as of January 1987. The total Indian population of the United States, according to the 1980 updated census, is 1,534,000, including Aleuts and Eskimos. Source: Department of the Interior, Bureau of Indian Affairs. 1. 1984 data. NOTE: Figures are most recent available.

Persons Below Poverty Level
by Age, Region, Race, and Hispanic Origin, 1987

Age and region	Number below poverty level (1,000)				Percent below poverty level			
	All races[2]	White	Black	Hispanic origin[1]	All races[2]	White	Black	Hispanic origin[1]
Under 16 years	11,859	7,290	4,007	2,493	21.2	16.2	46.7	40.6
16 to 21	3,455	2,148	1,144	565	15.9	12.1	36.0	27.5
22 to 44	9,596	6,470	2,647	1,628	10.7	8.5	25.1	21.2
45 to 64	4,145	2,905	1,077	536	9.1	7.4	23.5	20.4
65 and older	3,491	2,597	808	247	12.2	10.1	33.9	27.4
Northeast	5,476	3,860	1,391	1,232	11.0	8.9	28.8	36.6
Midwest	7,499	5,185	2,041	366	12.7	9.9	36.6	27.5
South	13,287	7,426	5,648	1,910	16.1	11.5	34.5	31.0
West	6,285	4,939	603	1,962	12.6	11.5	24.3	23.0
Total	32,546	21,409	9,683	5,470	13.5	10.5	33.1	28.2

1. Persons of Hispanic origin may be of any race. 2. Includes race not shown separately. Source: U.S. Bureau of the Census.

Revised Population Projections to 2080[1,2]

(in millions)

Sex, race, age group	2000	2050	2070	2080	Sex, race, age group	2000	2050	2070	2080
MALE, WHITE	108.8	110.3	105.6	103.6	FEMALE, BLACK	18.3	24.7	25.0	25.0
Up to 19 years	29.7	37.3	23.9	23.4	Up to 19 years	5.8	5.6	5.3	5.2
20 to 39 years	31.4	27.4	25.9	25.3	20 to 39 years	5.6	6.2	5.9	5.7
40 to 59 years	30.7	27.6	26.7	25.7	40 to 59 years	4.4	6.0	6.1	6.0
60 to 79 years	14.2	22.8	21.7	21.6	60 to 79 years	2.0	5.0	5.4	5.6
80 and over	2.8	7.4	7.5	7.6	80 and over	0.4	1.8	2.2	2.4
FEMALE, WHITE	112.7	116.2	110.9	108.7	TOTALS[3]	268.3	299.8	294.6	292.2
Up to 19 years	28.2	24.0	22.7	22.2	Up to 19 years	73.3	66.7	64.0	63.0
20 to 39 years	30.6	26.7	25.2	24.6	20 to 39 years	76.6	73.1	70.4	69.2
40 to 59 years	31.0	27.6	26.6	25.6	40 to 59 years	72.8	73.0	72.5	70.9
60 to 79 years	17.2	25.1	23.8	23.5	60 to 79 years	36.2	62.0	61.7	62.2
80 and over	5.7	12.9	12.5	12.7	80 and over	9.3	24.9	25.9	26.9
MALE, BLACK	16.7	22.4	22.7	22.6	Males	131.2	145.3	142.9	141.7
Up to 19 years	6.1	5.9	5.6	5.4	Females	137.1	154.5	151.7	150.5
20 to 39 years	5.2	5.8	5.5	5.4	White	221.5	226.6	216.5	212.3
40 to 59 years	3.7	5.3	5.4	5.3	Black	35.1	47.1	47.7	47.6
60 to 79 years	1.6	4.3	4.8	5.0	Median age	36.4	42.7	43.6	43.9
80 and over	0.2	1.1	1.4	1.5					

1. Based on Population Report issued January 1989 revising prior Report issued May 1984. 2. Based on average of 1.8 lifetime births per woman. 3. Includes all races. NOTE: Zero population growth is expected to be reached by 2050. Details may not add because of rounding. *Source:* Department of Commerce, Bureau of the Census.

Marriage and Divorce

Marriages and Divorces

Year	Marriage Number	Marriage Rate[2]	Divorce[1] Number	Divorce[1] Rate[2]	Year	Marriage Number	Marriage Rate[2]	Divorce[1] Number	Divorce[1] Rate[2]
1900	709,000	9.3	55,751	.7	1965	1,800,000	9.3	479,000	2.5
1905	842,000	10.0	67,976	.8	1966	1,857,000	9.5	499,000	2.5
1910	948,166	10.3	83,045	.9	1967	1,927,000	9.7	523,000	2.6
1915	1,007,595	10.0	104,298	1.0	1968	2,069,258	10.4	584,000	2.9
1920	1,274,476	12.0	170,505	1.6	1969	2,145,438	10.6	639,000	3.2
1925	1,188,334	10.3	175,449	1.5	1970	2,158,802	10.6	708,000	3.5
1930	1,126,856	9.2	195,961	1.6	1971	2,190,481	10.6	773,000	3.7
1935	1,327,000	10.4	218,000	1.7	1972	2,282,154	11.0	845,000	4.1
1940	1,595,879	12.1	264,000	2.0	1973	2,284,108	10.9	915,000	4.4
1945	1,612,992	12.2	485,000	3.5	1974	2,229,667	10.5	977,000	4.6
1950	1,667,231	11.1	385,144	2.6	1975	2,152,662	10.1	1,036,000	4.9
1952	1,539,318	9.9	392,000	2.5	1976	2,154,807	10.0	1,083,000	5.0
1953	1,546,000	9.8	390,000	2.5	1977	2,178,367	10.1	1,091,000	5.0
1954	1,490,000	9.2	379,000	2.4	1978	2,282,272	10.5	1,130,000	5.2
1955	1,531,000	9.3	377,000	2.3	1979	2,341,799	10.6	1,181,000	5.4
1956	1,585,000	9.5	382,000	2.3	1980	2,406,708	10.6	1,182,000	5.2
1957	1,518,000	8.9	381,000	2.2	1981	2,438,000	10.6	1,219,000	5.3
1958	1,451,000	8.4	368,000	2.1	1982	2,495,000	10.8	1,180,000	5.1
1959	1,494,000	8.5	395,000	2.2	1983	2,444,000	10.5	1,179,000	5.0
1960	1,523,000	8.5	393,000	2.2	1984	2,487,000	10.5	1,155,000	4.9
1961	1,548,000	8.5	414,000	2.3	1985	2,425,000	10.2	1,187,000	5.0
1962	1,577,000	8.5	413,000	2.2	1986	2,400,000	10.0	1,159,000	4.8
1963	1,654,000	8.8	428,000	2.3	1987	2,421,000	9.9	1,157,000	4.8
1964	1,725,000	9.0	450,000	2.4	1988[3]	2,389,000	9.7	1,183,000	4.8

1. Includes annulments. 2. Per 1,000 population. Divorce rates for 1941–46 are based on population including armed forces overseas. Marriage rates are based on population excluding armed forces overseas. 3. Provisional. NOTE: Marriage and divorce figures for most years include some estimated data. Alaska is included beginning 1959, Hawaii beginning 1960. *Source:* Department of Health and Human Services, National Center for Health Statistics.

Percent of Population Ever Married

Age group, years[1]	1988	1980	1970	1960	1950	1940	1930	1920	1910	1900
Males: 15 to 19	1.8	2.7	2.6	3.3	2.9	1.5	1.5	1.8	1.0	0.9
20 to 24	22.3	31.2	45.3	46.9	41.0	27.8	29.0	29.1	24.7	22.2
25 to 29	56.7	67.0	80.9	79.2	76.2	64.0	63.2	60.5	57.1	54.1
30 to 34	75.0	84.1	90.6	88.1	86.8	79.3	78.8	75.8	73.9	72.3
35 to 44	89.0	92.5	93.3	91.9	90.4	86.0	85.7	83.8	83.3	83.0
45 to 54	94.3	93.9	92.5	92.6	91.5	88.9	88.6	88.0	88.8	89.7
Females: 15 to 19	5.8	8.8	9.7	13.5	14.4	10.0	10.9	10.8	9.8	9.4
20 to 24	38.9	49.8	64.2	71.6	67.7	52.8	53.9	54.4	51.5	48.4
25 to 29	70.5	79.1	89.5	89.5	86.7	77.2	78.3	76.9	75.0	72.4
30 to 34	83.9	90.5	93.8	93.1	90.7	85.3	86.8	85.1	83.8	83.4
35 to 44	92.3	94.5	94.8	93.9	91.7	89.6	90.0	88.6	88.6	88.9
45 to 54	94.9	95.3	95.1	93.0	92.2	91.3	90.9	90.4	91.4	92.2

1. Prior to 1980 data are for persons 14 years and older. *Source:* Department of Commerce, Bureau of the Census.

Persons Living Alone, by Sex and Age
(numbers in thousands)

Sex and age[1]	1988 Number	1988 Percent	1980 Number	1980 Percent	1975 Number	1975 Percent	1970 Number	1970 Percent	1960 Number	1960 Percent
BOTH SEXES										
15 to 24 years	1,244	5.7	1,726	9.4	1,111	8.0	556	5.1	234	3.3
25 to 44 years	6,856	31.3	4,729	25.8	2,744	19.7	1,604	14.8	1,212	17.2
45 to 64 years	5,104	23.3	4,514	24.7	4,076	29.2	3,622	33.4	2,720	38.5
65 years and over	8,683	39.7	7,328	40.1	6,008	43.1	5,071	46.7	2,898	41.0
Total, 15 years and over	**21,889**	**100.0**	**18,296**	**100.0**	**13,939**	**100.0**	**10,851**	**100.0**	**7,063**	**100.0**
MALE										
15 to 24 years	653	7.4	947	13.6	610	4.4	274	2.5	124	1.8
25 to 44 years	4,145	47.2	2,920	41.9	1,689	12.1	933	8.6	686	9.7
45 to 64 years	2,077	23.6	1,613	23.2	1,329	9.5	1,152	10.6	965	13.7
65 years and over	1,913	21.8	1,486	21.3	1,290	9.3	1,174	10.8	853	12.1
Total, 15 years and over	**8,788**	**100.0**	**6,966**	**100.0**	**4,918**	**35.3**	**3,532**	**32.5**	**2,628**	**37.2**
FEMALE										
15 to 24 years	591	4.5	779	6.9	501	3.6	282	2.6	110	1.6
25 to 44 years	2,711	20.7	1,809	16.0	1,055	7.6	671	6.2	526	7.4
45 to 64 years	3,027	23.1	2,901	25.6	2,747	19.7	2,470	22.8	1,755	24.8
65 years and over	6,770	51.7	5,842	51.6	4,718	33.8	3,897	35.9	2,045	29.0
Total, 15 years and over	**13,101**	**100.0**	**11,330**	**100.0**	**9,021**	**64.7**	**7,319**	**67.5**	**4,436**	**62.8**

1. Prior to 1980, data are for persons 14 years and older. *Source:* Department of Commerce, Bureau of the Census.

Characteristics of Unmarried-Couple Households, 1988
(number in thousands)

Characteristics	Number	Percent	Characteristics	Number	Percent
Unmarried-couple households	2,588	100.0	Presence of children:		
			No children under 15 years	1,786	69.0
Age of householders:			Some children under 15 years	802	31.0
Under 25 years	510	19.7			
25–44 years	1,635	63.2	Sex of householders:		
45–64 years	325	12.6	Male	1,537	59.4
65 years and over	118	4.6	Female	1,051	40.6

Source: U.S. Bureau of the Census.

Households, Families, and Married Couples

Date	Households		Families		Married couples
	Number	Average population per household	Number	Average population per family	Number
June 1890	12,690,000	4.93	—	—	—
April 1930	29,905,000	4.11	—	—	25,174,000
April 1940	34,949,000	3.67	32,166,000	3.76	28,517,000
April 1950	43,554,000	3.37	39,303,000	3.54	36,091,000
April 1955	47,874,000	3.33	41,951,000	3.59	37,556,000
March 1960[1]	52,799,000	3.33	45,111,000	3.67	40,200,000
March 1965	57,436,000	3.29	47,956,000	3.70	42,478,000
March 1970	63,401,000	3.14	51,586,000	3.58	45,373,000
March 1975	71,120,000	2.94	55,712,000	3.42	47,547,000
March 1980	80,776,000	2.76	59,550,000	3.29	49,714,000
March 1985	86,789,000	2.69	62,706,000	3.23	51,114,000
March 1986	88,458,000	2.67	63,558,000	3.21	51,704,000
March 1987	89,479,000	2.66	64,491,000	3.19	52,286,000
March 1988	91,066,000	2.64	65,133,000	3.17	52,613,000

1. First year in which figures for Alaska and Hawaii are included. *Source:* Department of Commerce, Bureau of the Census.

Families Maintained by Women, With No Husband Present

(numbers in thousands)

	1988		1980		1975		1970		1960	
	Number	Percent	Number	Percent	Number	Percent	Number	Percent	Number	Percent
Age of women:										
Under 35 years	3,581	33.8	3,015	34.6	2,356	32.5	1,364	24.4	796	17.7
35 to 44 years	2,765	26.1	1,916	22.0	1,510	20.9	1,074	19.2	940	20.9
45 to 64 years	2,784	26.2	2,514	28.9	2,266	31.3	2,021	36.1	1,731	38.5
65 years and over	1,479	13.9	1,260	14.5	1,108	15.3	1,131	20.2	1,027	22.9
Median age	41.0	—	41.7	—	43.4	—	48.5	—	50.1	—
Presence of children:										
No own children under 18 years	4,335	40.9	3,260	37.4	2,838	39.2	2,665	47.7	2,397	53.3
With own children under 18 years	6,273	59.1	5,445	62.6	4,404	60.8	2,926	52.3	2,097	46.7
Total own children under 18 years	10,906	—	10,204	—	9,227	—	6,694	—	4,674	—
Average per family	1.03	—	1.17	—	1.27	—	1.20	—	1.04	—
Average per family with children	1.74	—	1.87	—	2.10	—	2.29	—	2.24	—
Race:										
White	7,235	68.2	6,052	69.5	5,212	72.0	4,165	74.5	3,547	78.9
Black[1]	3,074	29.0	2,495	28.7	1,940	26.8	1,382	24.7	947	21.1
Other	299	2.8	158	1.8	90	1.2	44	0.8	n.a.	n.a.
Marital status:										
Married, husband absent	1,922	18.1	1,769	20.3	1,647	22.7	1,326	23.7	1,099	24.5
Widowed	2,604	24.5	2,570	29.5	2,559	35.3	2,396	42.9	2,325	51.7
Divorced	3,833	36.1	3,008	34.6	2,110	29.1	1,259	22.5	694	15.4
Never married	2,250	21.2	1,359	15.6	926	12.8	610	10.9	376	8.4
Total families maintained by women	**10,608**	**100.0**	**8,705**	**100.0**	**7,242**	**100.0**	**5,591**	**100.0**	**4,494**	**100.0**

1. Includes other races in 1960. NOTE: n.a. = not available. (—) as shown in this table, means "not applicable." *Source:* Department of Commerce, Bureau of the Census.

Median Age at First Marriage

Year	Males	Females	Year	Males	Females	Year	Males	Females	Year	Males	Females
1900	25.9	21.9	1930	24.3	21.3	1960	22.8	20.3	1986	25.7	23.1
1910	25.1	21.6	1940	24.3	21.5	1970	23.2	20.8	1987	25.8	23.6
1920	24.6	21.2	1950	22.8	20.3	1980	24.7	22.0	1988	25.9	23.6

Source: Department of Commerce, Bureau of the Census.

Selected Family Characteristics

Characteristics[1]	1987 Number (thousands)	1987 Median income	Characteristics	1987 Number (thousands)	1987 Median income
ALL RACES			Tenure status		
All families	65,133	30,853	Owner occupies	46,680	35,854
Type of residence			Renter occupied	17,427	19,082
Nonfarm	63,705	30,972	Occupier paid no cash rent	1,027	18,529
Farm	1,428	26,016	Educational attainment of		
Location of residence			householder		
Inside metropolitan areas	49,967	33,131	Elementary	7,499	16,094
1,000,000 or more	27,011	35,448	High school	30,420	27,733
Inside central cities	10,449	27,458	College	24,288	43,357
Outside central cities	16,561	40,270	1 to 3 years	10,519	36,392
Under 1,000,000	22,957	31,021	4 years or more	13,769	50,115
Inside central cities	8,835	27,294	4 years	7,470	46,533
Outside central cities	14,122	33,192	5 years or more	6,299	54,491
Outside metropolitan areas	15,166	24,397	Total, 25 years and over	62,207	31,662
Region					
Northeast	13,382	33,938	**WHITE**		
North Central	15,905	30,991	All families	56,044	32,274
South	22,846	28,250	Type of residence		
West	13,000	32,026	Nonfarm	54,641	32,442
Type of family			Farm	1,403	26,122
Married-couple family	51,809	34,700	Location of residence		
Wife in paid labor force	29,112	40,422	Inside metropolitan areas	42,386	35,117
Wife not in paid labor force	22,698	26,652	1,000,000 or more	22,002	37,861
Male householder, no			Inside central cities	7,083	31,773
wife present	2,715	24,804	Outside central cities	14,919	40,807
Female householder, no			Under 1,000,000	20,384	32,266
husband present	10,608	14,620	Inside central cities	7,208	29,690
Number of earners[2]	64,228	30,951	Outside central cities	13,176	33,766
No earners	9,440	12,849	Outside metropolitan areas	13,658	25,736
1 earner	18,009	23,192	Region		
2 earners	27,748	36,990	Northeast	11,855	35,262
3 earners	6,329	46,961	North Central	14,240	32,149
4 earners	2,703	59,445	South	18,559	30,729
Size of family			West	11,389	32,521
2 persons	26,871	25,810	Type of family		
3 persons	15,410	32,125	Married-couple families	46,644	35,295
4 persons	13,729	36,812	Wife in paid labor force	25,800	41,023
5 persons	5,844	35,889	Wife not in paid labor		
6 persons	2,057	34,036	force	20,844	27,394
7 persons or more	1,222	30,551	Male householder, no wife		
Occupation group of longest[4]			present	2,165	26,230
job of householder	49,625	35,634	Female householder, no		
Executives, administrators			husband present	7,235	17,018
and managerial	7,386	50,575	Number of earners[2]	55,324	32,372
Professional specialty	6,387	49,514	No earners	7,803	14,924
Technical and related			1 earner	15,064	25,369
support	1,400	40,049	2 earners	24,559	37,731
Sales	5,537	38,553	3 earners	5,545	47,860
Administrative support,			4 earners or more	2,353	60,221
including clerical	4,316	31,554			
Precision production,			**BLACK**		
craft and repair	9,068	34,906	All families	7,177	18,098
Machine operators, assem-			Type of residence		
blers and inspectors	3,783	29,155	Nonfarm	7,154	18,105
Transportation and mater-			Farm	22	632
ial moving	3,109	31,246	Location of residence		
Handlers, equipment clean-			Inside metropolitan areas	5,934	19,579
ers, helpers, laborers	1,847	24,852	1,000,000 or more	3,904	20,659
Service workers	4,906	21,415	Inside central cities	2,763	18,255
Private household	216	11,445	Outside central cities	1,141	27,090
Other	4,690	21,920	Under 1,000,000	2,030	17,422
Farming, forestry and fishing	1,820	21,323	Inside central cities	1,375	17,015
			Outside central cities	654	18,381

Characteristics[1]	1987		Characteristics	1987	
	Number (thousands)	Median income		Number (thousands)	Median income
Outside metropolitan areas	1,243	12,861	Location of residence		
Region			Inside metropolitan areas	4,265	20,702
Northeast	1,189	20,678	1,000,000 or more	2,893	21,280
North Central	1,389	16,755	Inside central cities	1,721	17,430
South	3,972	17,302	Outside central cities	1,172	27,054
West	627	20,627	Under 1,000,000	1,372	19,271
Type of family			Inside central cities	784	17,919
Married-couple families	3,682	27,182	Outside central cities	588	23,045
Wife in paid labor force	2,424	33,333	Outside metropolitan areas	323	15,334
Wife not in paid labor force	1,258	16,822	Region		
Male householder, no wife			Northeast	916	16,750
present	421	17,455	North Central	306	21,985
Female householder, no			South	1,477	18,798
husband present	3,074	9,710	West	1,889	22,142
Number of earners[2]	7,030	17,999	Type of family		
No earners	1,396	5,528	Married-couple families	3,204	24,677
1 earner	2,396	13,774	Wife in paid labor force	1,655	31,354
2 earners	2,442	29,922	Wife not in paid labor force	1,549	17,967
3 earners	569	37,458	Male householder, no wife		
4 earners or more	227	49,929	present	312	19,411
			Female householder, no		
SPANISH ORIGIN OF			husband present	1,072	9,805
HOUSEHOLDER[3]			Number of earners[2]	4,514	20,264
All families	4,588	20,306	No earners	648	6,262
Type of residence			1 earner	1,458	15,148
Nonfarm	4,566	20,338	2 earners	1,791	27,201
Farm	22	(B)	3 earners	419	34,183
			4 earners or more	199	49,004

1. Family data are as of March 1988. 2. Excludes families with members in the Armed Forces. 3. Persons of Spanish origin may be of any race. 4. Includes persons whose longest job was in the Armed Forces. (B) Base less than 75,000. Statistics not given because of unreliability. *Source:* Department of Commerce, Bureau of the Census. NOTE: Data are the latest available.

Births

Live Births and Birth Rates

Year	Births[1]	Rate[2]	Year	Births[1]	Rate[2]	Year	Births[1]	Rate[2]
1910	2,777,000	30.1	1954[3]	4,078,000	25.3	1971[3]	3,555,970	17.2
1915	2,965,000	29.5	1955	4,104,000	25.0	1972	3,258,411	15.6
1920	2,950,000	27.7	1956[3]	4,218,000	25.2	1973	3,136,965	14.9
1925	2,909,000	25.1	1957[3]	4,308,000	25.3	1974	3,159,958	14.9
1930	2,618,000	21.3	1958[3]	4,255,000	24.5	1975	3,144,198	14.8
1935	2,377,000	18.7	1959[3]	4,295,000	24.3	1976	3,167,788	14.8
1940	2,559,000	19.4	1960[3]	4,257,850	23.7	1977	3,326,632	15.4
1944	2,939,000	21.2	1961[3]	4,268,326	23.3	1978	3,333,279	15.3
1945	2,858,000	20.4	1962[3]	4,167,362	22.4	1979	3,494,398	15.9
1946	3,411,000	24.1	1963[3]	4,098,020	21.7	1980	3,612,258	15.9
1947	3,817,000	26.6	1964[3]	4,027,490	21.0	1982	3,680,537	15.9
1948	3,637,000	24.9	1965[3]	3,760,358	19.4	1983	3,638,933	15.5
1949	3,649,000	24.5	1966[3]	3,606,274	18.4	1984	3,669,141	15.5
1950	3,632,000	24.1	1967[4]	3,520,959	17.8	1985	3,760,561	15.8
1951[3]	3,823,000	24.9	1968[3]	3,501,564	17.5	1986	3,731,000	15.5
1952[3]	3,913,000	25.1	1969[3]	3,600,206	17.8	1987	3,829,000	15.7
1953[3]	3,965,000	25.1	1970[3]	3,731,386	18.4	1988[5]	3,913,000	15.9

1. Figures through 1959 include adjustment for underregistration; beginning 1960, figures represent number registered. For comparison, the 1959 registered count was 4,245,000. 2. Rates are per 1,000 population estimated as of July 1 for each year except 1940, 1950, 1960, 1970, and 1980, which are as of April 1, the census date; for 1942–46 based on population including armed forces overseas. 3. Based on 50% sample of births. 4. Based on a 20 to 50% sample of births. 5. Provisional. NOTE: Alaska is included beginning 1959; Hawaii beginning 1960. Since 1972, based on 100% of births in selected states and on 50% sample in all other states. *Sources:* Department of Health and Human Services, National Center for Health Statistics.

Live Births by Age of Mother

Year[1] and race	Total	Under 15 yr	15–19 yr	20–24 yr	25–29 yr	30–34 yr	35–39 yr	40–44 yr	45 yr and over
1940	2,558,647	3,865	332,667	799,537	693,268	431,468	222,015	68,269	7,558
1945	2,858,449	4,028	298,868	832,746	785,299	554,906	296,852	78,853	6,897
1950	3,631,512	5,413	432,911	1,155,167	1,041,360	610,816	302,780	77,743	5,322
1955	4,014,112	6,181	493,770	1,290,939	1,133,155	732,540	352,320	89,777	5,430
1960	4,257,850	6,780	586,966	1,426,912	1,092,816	687,722	359,908	91,564	5,182
1965	3,760,358	7,768	590,894	1,337,350	925,732	529,376	282,908	81,716	4,614
1970	3,731,386	11,752	644,708	1,418,874	994,904	427,806	180,244	49,952	3,146
1975	3,144,198	12,642	582,238	1,093,676	936,786	375,500	115,409	26,319	1,628
1980	3,612,258	10,169	552,161	1,226,200	1,108,291	550,354	140,793	23,090	1,200
1983	3,638,933	9,752	489,286	1,160,274	1,147,720	624,516	180,353	25,882	1,150
1984	3,669,141	9,965	469,682	1,141,578	1,165,711	658,496	195,755	26,846	1,108
1985	3,760,561	10,220	467,485	1,141,320	1,201,350	696,354	214,336	28,334	1,162
1986	3,756,547	10,176	461,905	1,102,119	1,199,519	721,395	230,335	29,847	1,251
White	2,970,439	4,007	311,328	853,662	991,019	599,453	186,832	23,262	876
Black	621,221	5,877	135,729	208,882	155,640	82,657	28,142	4,099	195
Other	164,887	292	14,848	39,575	52,860	39,285	15,361	2,486	180

1. Data for 1940–55 are adjusted for underregistration. Beginning 1960, registered births only are shown. Data for 1960–70 based on a 50% sample of births. For 1972-84, based on 100% of births in selected states and on 50% sample in all other states. Beginning 1960, including Alaska and Hawaii. NOTE: Data refer only to births occurring within the U.S. Figures are shown to the last digit as computed for convenience in summation. They are not assumed to be accurate to the last digit. Figures for age of mother not stated are distributed. *Source:* Department of Health and Human Services, National Center for Health Statistics.

Births to Unmarried Women

(in thousands, except as indicated)

Age and race	1986	1985	1980	1975	1970	1965	1960	1955	1950
By age of mother:									
Under 15 years	9.4	9.4	9.0	11.0	9.5	6.1	4.6	3.9	3.2
15–19 years	280.7	270.9	262.8	222.5	190.4	123.1	87.1	68.9	56.0
20–24 years	316.1	300.4	237.3	134.0	126.7	90.7	68.0	55.7	43.1
25–29 years	165.7	152.0	99.6	50.2	40.6	36.8	32.1	28.0	20.9
30–34 years	74.9	67.3	41.0	19.8	19.1	19.6	18.9	16.1	10.8
35–39 years	27.0	24.0	13.2	8.1	9.4	11.4	10.6	8.3	6.0
40 years and over	4.6	4.1	2.9	2.3	3.0	3.7	3.0	2.4	1.7
By race:									
White	466.8	433.0	320.1	186.4	175.1	123.7	82.5	64.2	53.5
Black and other	411.7	395.2	345.7	261.6	223.6	167.5	141.8	119.2	88.1
Total of above births	878.5	828.2	665.8	447.9	398.7	291.2	224.3	183.4	141.6
Percent of all births[1]	23.4	22.0	18.4	14.2	10.7	7.7	5.3	4.5	3.9
Rate[2]	34.3	32.8	29.4	24.8	26.4	23.4	21.8	19.3	14.1

1. Through 1955, based on data adjusted for underregistration; thereafter, registered births. 2. Rate per 1,000 unmarried (never married, widowed, and divorced) women, 15–44 years old. *Source:* Department of Health and Human Services, National Center for Health Statistics. NOTE: Data are latest available.

More Women Return to Work After Giving Birth

According to a Census Bureau survey taken in June of 1988, the number of women who were in the labor force following the birth of a child had increased substantially since 1976. In that year 31 percent of the women with newborns were in the labor force compared to 51 percent for 1988.

Women with four or more years of college were more likely to be working than those who had completed less than 12 years of school—60 percent compared to 34 percent. Also older women with recent births were more likely to be in the labor force: 53 percent of women between the ages of

25 and 44 compared to 46 percent of women 18 to 24 years of age.

Women who gave birth for the first time were more likely to be in the labor force than those having additional children—58 percent to 47 percent, respectively. Greater job commitment or the ability to pay for child care services may account for the higher labor force rates for older or more educated mothers, while child care services may be more available and affordable for women with only one child.

Live Births and Birth Rates

State	1987[1] number	1987[1] rate	1986 number	1986 rate	State	1987[1] number	1987[1] rate	1986 number	1986 rate
Alabama	59,207	14.5	59,465	14.7	Montana	11,976	14.8	12,734	15.6
Alaska	11,441	21.8	12,167	22.9	Nebraska	23,657	14.8	24,426	15.3
Arizona	63,449	18.7	60,874	18.6	Nevada	16,279	16.2	15,897	16.4
Arkansas	33,375	14.0	34,393	14.5	New Hampshire	16,435	15.5	15,895	15.5
California	494,053	17.9	482,236	17.9	New Jersey	111,344	14.5	108,812	14.3
Colorado	54,314	16.5	55,151	16.9	New Mexico	30,169	16.2	27,392	18.5
Connecticut	46,547	14.5	44,850	14.0	New York	270,390	15.2	264,027	14.8
Delaware	10,032	15.6	9,718	15.4	North Carolina	93,405	14.6	90,254	14.3
D.C.	20,406	32.8	10,045	16.1	North Dakota	11,545	17.2	10,819	15.9
Florida	174,688	14.5	167,601	14.3	Ohio	156,900	14.5	158,026	14.7
Georgia	104,881	16.9	98,183	16.1	Oklahoma	45,535	13.9	50,640	15.3
Hawaii	18,602	17.2	18,297	17.2	Oregon	39,708	14.6	38,871	14.4
Idaho	15,956	16.0	16,448	16.4	Pennsylvania	166,287	13.9	160,970	13.5
Illinois	177,564	15.3	176,717	15.3	Rhode Island	14,519	14.7	13,444	13.8
Indiana	77,694	14.0	79,322	14.4	South Carolina	50,693	14.8	51,800	15.3
Iowa	38,736	13.7	38,771	13.6	South Dakota	11,514	16.2	11,615	16.4
Kansas	37,167	15.0	39,265	16.0	Tennessee	71,343	14.7	66,249	13.8
Kentucky	51,075	13.7	51,794	13.9	Texas	308,229	18.4	307,066	18.4
Louisiana	75,313	16.9	77,955	17.3	Utah	35,927	21.4	36,412	21.9
Maine	16,155	13.6	16,709	14.3	Vermont	7,226	13.2	8,139	15.0
Maryland	64,692	14.3	69,538	15.6	Virginia	87,002	14.7	87,183	15.0
Massachusetts	86,934	14.8	82,190	14.1	Washington	73,836	16.3	69,440	15.6
Michigan	136,374	14.8	137,631	15.1	West Virginia	23,572	12.4	23,236	12.1
Minnesota	64,068	15.1	65,784	15.6	Wisconsin	70,467	14.7	72,333	15.1
Mississippi	40,506	15.4	41,871	16.0	Wyoming	7,107	14.5	8,633	17.0
Missouri	75,950	14.9	75,259	14.9	**Total**	**3,804,244**	**15.7**	**3,756,547**	**15.6**

1. Provisional. NOTE: Provisional data by place of occurrence. Rates are per 1,000 population. *Source:* Department of Health and Human Services, National Center for Health Statistics.

Live Births by Race or National Origin

Race	1986	1985	Race	1986	1985
White	2,970,439	2,991,373	Chinese	18,284	17,880
Black	621,221	608,193	Filipino	22,490	21,482
American Indian[1]	42,645	42,646	Other[2]	68,844	66,452
Japanese	9,654	9,802	Total[3]	3,756,547	3,760,561

1. Includes Eskimos and Aleuts. 2. Hawaiian and other Asian or Pacific Islander. 3. Includes births of other races not shown separately. Data are latest available. *Source:* Department of Health and Human Services, National Center for Health Statistics.

Live Births by Sex and Sex Ratio[1]

	Total[2]			White			Black		
Year	Male	Female	Males per 1,000 females	Male	Female	Males per 1,000 females	Male	Female	Males per 1,000 females
1977[4]	1,705,916	1,620,716	1,053	1,383,440	1,307,630	1,058	275,556	268,665	1,026
1978[4]	1,709,394	1,623,885	1,053	1,378,222	1,302,894	1,058	279,598	271,942	1,028
1979[4]	1,791,267	1,703,131	1,052	1,442,981	1,365,439	1,057	293,013	284,842	1,029
1980[4]	1,852,616	1,759,642	1,053	1,490,140	1,408,592	1,058	299,033	290,583	1,029
1981[4]	1,860,272	1,768,966	1,052	1,494,451	1,414,232	1,057	297,864	289,923	1,027
1982[4]	1,885,676	1,794,861	1,051	1,509,704	1,432,350	1,054	301,121	291,520	1,033
1983[4]	1,865,553	1,773,380	1,052	1,492,385	1,411,865	1,057	297,011	289,016	1,028
1984[4]	1,879,490	1,789,651	1,050	1,500,326	1,423,176	1,054	300,951	291,794	1,031
1985[4]	1,927,983	1,832,578	1,052	1,536,645	1,454,727	1,056	308,575	299,618	1,030
1986[4]	1,924,868	1,831,679	1,051	1,523,914	1,446,525	1,041	315,788	305,443	1,034

1. Excludes births to nonresidents of U.S. 2. Includes races other than white and black. 3. Based on 50% sample of births. 4. Based on 100% of births for selected states and 50% sample in all others. *Source:* Department of Health and Human Services, National Center for Health Statistics. NOTE: Data are latest available.

Abortions and Abortion Rates

State	Numbers of abortions			Abortion occurence rate[1]			Change 1982-85
	1985	1984	1982	1985	1984	1982	
Alabama	19,380	19,210	19,930	20.2	20.3	21.6	−1.4
Alaska	3,450	3,170	1,930	27.7	26.2	17.0	+10.7
Arizona	22,330	21,190	15,830	29.9	29.2	23.4	+6.5
Arkansas	5,420	4,680	6,660	10.1	8.8	12.9	−2.8
California	304,130	297,730	265,740	47.9	47.8	44.5	+3.4
Colorado	24,350	24,600	25,170	28.8	29.8	32.2	−3.4
Connecticut	21,850	21,490	23,180	29.3	29.0	31.8	−2.5
Delaware	4,590	4,710	3,870	30.9	31.8	26.5	+4.4
District of Columbia	23,910	23,690	28,630	145.9	142.9	169.9	−24.0
Florida	76,650	75,800	76,910	31.8	32.3	34.8	−3.0
Georgia	38,340	38,710	38,480	26.1	26.8	27.7	−1.6
Hawaii	11,160	10,430	9,140	43.7	41.6	37.9	+5.8
Idaho	2,660	2,740	3,020	11.1	11.6	13.4	−2.3
Illinois	64,960	65,940	65,860	23.8	24.2	24.4	−0.6
Indiana	16,090	16,070	15,680	12.2	12.2	12.1	+0.1
Iowa	9,930	10,430	8,230	15.0	15.8	12.6	+2.4
Kansas	10,150	12,420	14,440	18.2	22.4	26.6	−8.4
Kentucky	9,820	10,090	10,830	11.0	11.4	12.5	−1.5
Louisiana	19,240	20,730	22,310	17.4	19.1	21.3	−3.9
Maine	4,960	5,180	5,470	18.6	19.6	21.1	−2.5
Maryland	29,480	29,120	34,810	26.9	26.8	32.7	−5.8
Massachusetts	40,310	36,340	41,250	29.3	26.4	30.2	−0.9
Michigan	64,390	66,010	64,190	28.7	29.6	29.0	−0.3
Minnesota	16,850	17,410	19,020	16.6	17.3	19.4	−2.8
Mississippi	5,890	5,490	5,500	9.7	9.1	9.3	+0.4
Missouri	20,100	22,140	19,780	17.3	19.2	17.4	−0.1
Montana	3,710	3,880	4,230	19.0	20.1	22.5	−3.5
Nebraska	6,680	6,730	6,580	18.2	18.4	18.3	−0.1
Nevada	9,910	9,370	9,960	40.5	39.8	46.0	−5.5
New Hampshire	7,030	6,740	5,600	29.0	28.3	24.5	+4.5
New Jersey	69,190	65,860	61,080	39.6	37.9	35.7	+3.9
New Mexico	6,110	5,380	7,470	17.4	15.6	22.8	−5.4
New York	195,120	192,020	182,700	47.4	46.6	44.5	+2.9
North Carolina	34,180	35,800	33,230	22.6	24.0	23.0	−0.4
North Dakota	2,850	2,940	3,350	18.5	19.3	22.4	−3.9
Ohio	57,360	58,040	61,440	22.4	22.7	24.3	−1.9
Oklahoma	13,100	12,630	12,690	17.1	16.8	17.6	−0.5
Oregon	15,230	15,310	16,350	22.3	22.8	25.2	−2.9
Pennsylvania	57,370	60,680	64,060	21.3	22.6	24.1	−2.8
Rhode Island	7,770	7,450	7,770	35.5	34.1	35.8	−0.3
South Carolina	11,200	11,280	16,140	13.7	14.0	20.7	−7.0
South Dakota	1,650	1,770	1,770	10.6	11.4	11.6	−1.0
Tennessee	22,350	22,570	26,100	19.1	19.5	23.3	−4.2
Texas	100,820	99,960	105,820	25.5	26.0	29.2	−3.7
Utah	4,440	4,240	4,180	11.1	10.9	11.4	−0.3
Vermont	3,430	3,450	3,710	26.2	26.7	29.4	−3.2
Virginia	34,180	31,670	34,880	24.0	22.6	25.7	−1.7
Washington	30,990	29,510	34,130	28.0	27.2	32.9	−4.9
West Virginia	4,590	4,680	3,420	10.1	10.4	7.7	+2.4
Wisconsin	17,830	18,640	20,380	15.7	16.6	18.5	−2.8
Wyoming	1,070	1,060	1,020	7.9	8.1	8.4	−0.5
Total	**1,588,550**	**1,577,180**	**1,573,920**	**28.0**	**28.1**	**28.8**	**−0.8**

1. Rate per 1,000 women aged 15–44. NOTES: Number of abortions are rounded to nearest 10. Rates are based on population estimates for July 1 of each year. *Source:* The Alan Guttmacher Institute. NOTE: Data latest available as of August 1989.

Contraceptive Failures Are Higher Than Expected

New research has revealed that failure rates among couples using various methods of family planning are nearly one-third higher than previously reported. More than three million unplanned pregnancies occur each year to American women, half of which are terminated in abortion. Nonusers of contraceptives account for 57 percent or 1.9 million of the unintended pregnancies, while users of contraceptives account for 43 percent or 1.5 million of the unintended pregnancies.

According to the new study, the likelihood of experiencing an unintended pregnancy while using a contraceptive method is generally lower with rising age, and higher among poor women, unmarried women, and minority women. This points up a leading factor in the failures, regardless of the method used—that is improper or inconsistent use.

Mortality
Death Rates for Selected Causes

	Death rates per 100,000							
Cause of death	1988[1]	1987[1]	1985	1980	1950	1945–49	1920–24[4]	1900–04[4]
Typhoid fever	n.a.	n.a.	—	0.0	0.1	0.2	7.3	26.7
Communicable diseases of childhood	n.a.	n.a.	n.a.	0.0	1.3	2.3	33.8	65.2
Measles	—	—	—	0.0	0.3	0.6	7.3	10.0
Scarlet fever	n.a.	n.a.	1.0	0.0	0.2	0.1	4.0	11.8
Whooping cough	—	—	—	0.0	0.7	1.0	8.9	10.7
Diphtheria	n.a.	n.a.	—	0.0	0.3	0.7	13.7	32.7
Pneumonia and influenza	31.5	28.8	27.9	23.3	31.3	41.3	140.3	184.3
Influenza	0.8	0.3	0.8	1.1	4.4	5.0	34.8	22.8
Pneumonia	30.7	28.6	27.1	22.0	26.9	37.2	105.5	161.5
Tuberculosis	0.8	0.7	0.7	0.8	22.5	33.3	96.7	184.7
Cancer	198.6	196.1	191.7	182.5	139.8	134.0	86.9	67.7
Diabetes mellitus	16.1	15.6	16.2	15.0	16.2	24.1	17.1	12.2
Major cardiovascular diseases	395.5	397.8	410.7	434.5	510.8	493.1	369.9	359.5
Diseases of the heart	312.2	313.4	325.0	335.2	356.8	325.1	169.8	153.0
Cerebrovascular diseases	61.1	61.3	64.0	74.6	104.0	93.8	93.5	106.3
Nephritis and nephrosis	8.9	9.5	9.4	7.6	16.4	48.4	81.5	84.3
Syphilis	0.0	0.0	0.0	0.1	5.0	8.4	17.6	12.9
Appendicitis	0.2	0.2	0.2	0.3	2.0	3.5	14.0	9.4
Accidents, all forms	20.4	20.1	38.6	46.0	60.6	67.6	70.8	79.2
Motor vehicle accidents	9.9	10.0	18.8	23.0	23.1	22.3	12.9	n.a.
Infant mortality[2]	6.3	6.5	10.6	12.5	29.2	33.3	76.7	n.a.
Neonatal mortality[2]	n.a.	n.a.	7.0	8.4	20.5	22.9	39.7	n.a.
Fetal mortality[3]	n.a.	n.a.	7.9	9.2	19.2	21.6	n.a.	n.a.
Maternal mortality[2]	n.a.	n.a.	0.1	0.1	0.8	1.4	6.9	n.a.
All causes	**883.0**	**874.0**	**890.8**	**883.4**	**960.1**	**1,000.6**	**1,157.4**	**1,621.6**

1. Based on a 10% sample of deaths. 2. Rates per 1,000 live births. 3. Ratio per 1,000 births. 4. Includes only deaths occurring within the registration areas. Beginning with 1940, area includes the entire United States; beginning with 1960, Alaska and Hawaii are included. Rates per 100,000 population residing in areas, enumerated as of April 1 for 1940, 1950 and 1980 and estimated as of July 1 for all other years. Due to changes in statistical methods, death rates are not strictly comparable. n.a. = not available. *Source:* Department of Health and Human Services, National Center for Health Statistics.

Accident Rates, 1987

Class of accident		One every	Class of accident		One every
All accidents	Deaths	6 minutes	Workers off-job	Deaths	15 minutes
	Injuries	4 seconds		Injuries	12 seconds
Motor-vehicle	Deaths	11 minutes	Home	Deaths	26 minutes
	Injuries	18 seconds		Injuries	10 seconds
Work	Deaths	47 minutes	Public non-motor-vehicle	Deaths	29 minutes
	Injuries	18 seconds		Injuries	14 seconds

NOTE: Data are latest available. *Source:* National Safety Council.

Improper Driving as Factor in Accidents, 1987

	Fatal accidents			Injury accidents			All accidents[1]		
Kind of improper driving	Total	Urban	Rural	Total	Urban	Rural	Total	Urban	Rural
Improper driving	62.0	60.6	62.6	70.9	71.9	69.2	67.3	67.7	66.4
Speed too fast[2]	27.2	25.7	28.0	24.2	21.4	28.9	18.8	16.2	24.3
Right of way	10.8	15.7	8.7	22.0	26.8	13.8	20.2	23.3	13.5
Drove left of center	8.5	3.7	10.5	2.8	1.1	5.8	2.2	1.0	5.0
Improper overtaking	3.9	3.3	4.1	1.8	1.4	2.3	2.2	2.0	2.7
Made improper turn	0.3	0.4	0.2	1.4	1.7	1.0	2.4	2.8	1.4
Followed too closely	0.7	0.7	0.7	5.0	6.0	3.5	5.4	6.0	3.9
Other improper driving	10.6	11.1	10.4	13.7	13.5	13.9	16.1	16.4	15.6
No improper driving stated	38.0	39.4	37.4	29.1	28.1	30.8	32.7	32.3	33.6
Total	100.0 %	100.0 %	100.0 %	100.0 %	100.0 %	100.0 %	100.0 %	100.0 %	100.0 %

1. Principally property-damage accidents, but also includes fatal and injury accidents. 2. Includes "speed too fast for conditions." *Source:* Urban and rural reports from six state traffic authorities to National Safety Council. NOTE: Figures are latest available.

Motor-Vehicle Deaths by Type of Accident

				Deaths from collisions with—					
Year	Pedes-trians	Other motor vehicles	Railroad trains	Street cars	Pedalcycles	Animal-drawn vehicle or animal	Fixed objects	Deaths from non-collision accidents	Total deaths[1]
1975	8,400	19,550	979	1	1,000	100	3,130	12,700	45,853
1980	9,700	23,000	739	1	1,200	100	3,700	14,700	53,172
1983	8,200	19,200	520	1	1,100	100	3,100	12,200	44,452
1984	8,500	20,000	630	0	1,100	100	3,200	12,700	46,263
1985	8,300	19,900	500	(2)	1,100	100	2,800	12,900	45,600
1986	8,300	20,500	600	(2)	1,200	100	3,300	13,900	47,900
1987	8,500	20,500	600	(2)	1,400	100	3,400	14,200	48,700

1. Totals do not equal sums of various types because totals are estimated. 2. Data not available for these years. NOTE: Figures are latest available. *Source:* National Safety Council.

Accidental Deaths by Principal Types

Year	Motor vehicle	Falls	Drown-ing	Fire burns	Ingestion of food or object	Fire-arms	Poison (solid, liquid)	Poison by gas
1980	53,172	13,294	7,257	5,822	3,249	1,955	3,089	1,242
1981	51,385	12,628	6,277	5,697	3,331	1,871	3,243	1,280
1982	45,779	12,077	6,351	5,210	3,254	1,756	3,474	1,259
1983	44,452	12,024	6,353	5,028	3,387	1,695	3,382	1,251
1984	46,263	11,937	5,388	5,010	3,541	1,668	3,808	1,103
1985	45,600	11,700	5,300	4,900	3,600	1,800	3,600	1,000
1986	47,900	11,000	5,600	4,800	3,600	1,800	4,000	900
1987	48,700	11,300	5,300	4,800	3,200	1,400	4,400	1,000

NOTE: Figures are latest available. *Source:* National Safety Council.

Deaths and Death Rates

State	Total deaths[1]		Motor vehicle traffic deaths[2]			State	Total deaths[1]		Motor vehicle traffic deaths[2]		
	1987 rate	1986 rate	1987 rate	1986 rate	1985 rate		1987 rate	1986 rate	1987 rate	1986 rate	1985 rate
Alabama	9.1	9.3	3.2	3.2	2.5	Montana	8.1	8.3	3.1	2.9	3.0
Alaska	4.0	3.9	2.0	2.5	3.1	Nebraska	9.5	9.2	2.4	2.3	2.0
Arizona	8.1	7.8	3.9	4.4	4.1	Nevada	8.5	7.7	3.0	2.9	3.4
Arkansas	9.8	10.1	3.5	3.4	3.1	New Hamshire	7.8	8.4	2.1	2.2	2.5
California	7.8	7.5	2.4	2.4	2.3	New Jersey	9.1	9.4	1.9	1.9	1.8
Colorado	6.5	6.4	2.3	2.3	2.2	New Mexico	7.0	6.8	4.1	3.8	4.0
Connecticut	8.8	8.8	1.8	1.9	2.0	New York	9.7	9.8	2.4	2.2	2.2
Delaware	8.8	8.9	2.5	2.4	2.0	North Carolina	8.6	8.6	3.0	3.1	3.0
D.C.	13.8	11.7	1.7	1.4	1.9	North Dakota	8.7	7.8	1.7	1.8	1.7
Florida	10.7	10.6	3.2	3.3	3.3	Ohio	9.1	9.3	2.1	2.1	2.2
Georgia	8.0	8.1	2.7	2.7	2.6	Oklahoma	8.5	9.1	1.9	2.3	2.4
Hawaii	5.9	5.5	1.9	1.7	1.9	Oregon	8.9	8.7	2.7	2.7	2.6
Idaho	7.0	7.4	3.3	3.3	3.3	Pennsylvania	10.5	10.5	2.5	2.5	2.4
Illinois	8.5	9.0	2.2	2.2	2.2	Rhode Island	10.0	10.0	1.8	2.1	1.8
Indiana	8.8	9.0	2.6	2.5	2.4	South Carolina	8.1	8.3	4.0	3.7	3.5
Iowa	9.5	9.5	2.3	2.2	2.3	South Dakota	9.4	9.3	2.2	2.1	2.1
Kansas	8.8	9.1	2.5	2.5	2.5	Tennessee	10.0	9.2	3.2	3.1	3.4
Kentucky	9.1	9.3	2.9	2.8	2.5	Texas	7.3	7.1	2.3	2.4	2.6
Louisiana	8.2	8.1	2.9	3.1	2.8	Utah	5.6	5.4	2.4	2.6	2.5
Maine	9.2	9.6	2.1	2.1	2.2	Vermont	8.2	8.8	2.4	2.3	2.5
Maryland	8.2	8.4	2.3	2.2	2.2	Virginia	7.8	8.0	1.9	2.2	2.0
Massachusetts	9.6	9.6	1.7	1.8	1.9	Washington	7.7	7.7	2.1	2.0	2.2
Michigan	8.6	8.8	2.2	2.3	2.3	West Virginia	10.5	10.4	3.6	3.3	3.3
Minnesota	8.2	8.3	1.6	1.7	1.9	Wisconsin	8.8	8.8	2.1	2.0	2.1
Mississippi	9.1	9.3	4.0	4.0	3.5	Wyoming	5.9	6.4	2.5	3.1	2.6
Missouri	10.7	9.9	2.5	2.7	2.4	**Total U.S.**		**8.7**	**2.6**	**2.6**	**2.6**

1. Provisional rates per 1,000 population, by place of occurrence. 2. Per 100 million vehicle-miles. *Sources:* Department of Health and Human Services, National Center for Health Statistics; National Safety Council.

Annual Death Rates

Year	Rate	Year	Rate	Year	Deaths	Rate
1900	17.2	1941	10.5	1965	1,828,136	9.4
1905	15.9	1942	10.3	1966	1,863,149	9.5
1910	14.7	1943	10.9	1967	1,851,323	9.4
1915	13.2	1944	10.6	1968	1,930,082	9.7
1918	18.1 [1]	1945	10.6	1969	1,921,990	9.5
1920	13.0	1946	10.0	1970[2]	1,921,031	9.5
1924	11.6	1947	10.1	1971	1,927,542	9.3
1925	11.7	1948	9.9	1972	1,963,944	9.4
1926	12.1	1949	9.7	1973	1,973,003	9.3
1927	11.3	1950	9.6	1974	1,934,388	9.1
1928	12.0	1951	9.7	1975	1,892,879	8.8
1929	11.9	1952	9.6	1976	1,909,440	8.8
1930	11.3	1953	9.6	1977	1,899,597	8.6
1931	11.1	1954	9.2	1978	1,927,788	8.7
1932	10.9	1955	9.3	1979	1,913,841	8.5
1933	10.7	1956	9.4	1980	1,989,841	8.7
1934	11.1	1957	9.6	1982	1,974,797	8.5
1935	10.9	1958	9.5	1983	2,019,201	8.6
1936	11.6	1959	9.4	1984	2,039,369	8.6
1937	11.3	1960	9.5	1985	2,086,440	8.7
1938	10.6	1962	9.5	1986	2,099,000	8.7
1939	10.6	1963	9.6	1987	2,127,000	8.7
1940	10.8	1964	9.4	1988[3]	2,171,000	8.8

1. Year of influenza epidemic. 2. First year for which deaths of nonresidents are excluded. 3. Provisional. NOTE: Includes only deaths occurring within the registration states. Beginning with 1933, area includes entire U.S.; with 1959 includes Alaska, and with 1960 includes Hawaii. Excludes fetal deaths. Rates per 1,000 population residing in area, as of April 1 for 1940, 1950, 1960, 1970, and 1980, and estimated as of July 1 for all other years. *Sources:* Department of Health and Human Services, National Center for Health Statistics.

Death Rates by Age, Race, and Sex

Age	1987[1]	1986	1985	1980[2]	1970	1960	1987[1]	1986	1985	1980[2]	1970[2]	1960
	White males						White females					
Under 1 year	9.4	9.8	10.4	12.3	21.1	26.9	7.3	7.6	7.9	9.6	16.1	20.1
1–4	0.5	5.2	0.5	0.7	0.8	1.0	0.4	0.4	0.4	0.5	0.8	0.9
5–14	0.3	0.3	0.3	0.4	0.5	0.5	0.2	0.2	0.2	0.2	0.3	0.3
15–24	1.5	1.5	1.4	1.7	1.7	1.7	1.4	0.5	0.5	0.5	0.6	0.5
25–34	1.7	1.7	1.6	1.7	1.8	1.6	0.6	0.6	0.6	0.7	0.8	0.9
35–44	2.5	2.5	2.4	2.6	3.4	3.3	1.1	1.2	1.2	1.2	1.9	1.9
45–54	5.8	6.0	6.0	7.0	8.8	9.3	3.3	3.3	3.4	3.7	4.6	4.6
55–64	15.5	15.7	16.1	17.3	22.0	22.3	8.6	8.5	8.6	8.8	10.1	10.8
65–74	35.8	36.3	37.1	40.4	48.1	48.5	20.1	20.3	20.3	20.7	24.7	27.8
75–84	82.0	83.4	85.0	88.3	101.0	103.0	50.7	51.0	51.8	54.0	67.0	77.0
85 and over	184.5	185.7	187.8	191.0	185.5	217.5	146.4	145.0	145.8	149.8	159.8	194.8

Age	1987[1]	1986	1985	1980[2]	1970	1960	1987[1]	1986	1985	1980[2]	1970[2]	1960
	All other males						All other females					
Under 1 year	19.2	19.1	18.9	23.5	40.2	51.9	15.3	15.2	15.5	19.4	31.7	40.7
1–4	0.8	0.8	0.8	1.0	1.4	2.1	0.5	0.7	0.6	0.8	1.2	1.7
5–14	0.4	0.4	0.4	0.4	0.6	0.8	0.2	0.3	0.3	0.3	0.4	0.5
15–24	1.7	1.8	1.6	2.0	3.0	2.1	0.6	0.6	0.6	0.7	1.1	1.1
25–34	3.1	3.3	3.0	3.6	5.0	3.9	1.2	1.3	1.2	1.4	2.2	2.6
35–44	5.5	5.5	5.3	5.9	8.7	7.3	2.5	2.5	2.4	2.9	4.9	5.5
45–54	10.4	10.7	10.9	13.1	16.5	15.5	5.6	5.7	5.7	6.9	9.8	11.4
55–64	21.8	22.5	23.4	26.1	30.5	31.5	12.7	12.9	13.3	14.2	18.9	24.1
65–74	40.8	43.0	42.2	47.5	54.7	56.6	25.5	25.9	26.6	28.6	36.8	39.8
75–84	82.6	84.6	85.4	86.9	89.8	86.6	53.7	56.0	57.4	58.6	63.9	67.1
85 and over	143.8	147.6	143.8	157.7	114.1	152.4	115.0	120.2	116.9	119.2	102.9	128.7

1. Provisional. Based on a 10% sample of deaths. 2. Excludes deaths of nonresidents of U.S. NOTE: Excludes fetal deaths. Rates are per 1,000 population in each group, enumerated as of April 1 for 1960, 1970, and 1980, and estimated as of July 1 for all other years. NOTE: Data are latest available. *Sources:* Department of Health and Human Services, National Center for Health Statistics.

Expectation of Life

Expectation of Life in the United States

Calendar period	Age								
	0	10	20	30	40	50	60	70	80
WHITE MALES									
1850[1]	38.3	48.0	40.1	34.0	27.9	21.6	15.6	10.2	5.9
1890[1]	42.50	48.45	40.66	34.05	27.37	20.72	14.73	9.35	5.40
1900–1902[2]	48.23	50.59	42.19	34.88	27.74	20.76	14.35	9.03	5.10
1909–1911[2]	50.23	51.32	42.71	34.87	27.43	20.39	13.98	8.83	5.09
1919–1921[3]	56.34	54.15	45.60	37.65	29.86	22.22	15.25	9.51	5.47
1929–1931	59.12	54.96	46.02	37.54	29.22	21.51	14.72	9.20	5.26
1939–1941	62.81	57.03	47.76	38.80	30.03	21.96	15.05	9.42	5.38
1949–1951	66.31	58.98	49.52	40.29	31.17	22.83	15.76	10.07	5.88
1959–1961	67.55	59.78	50.25	40.98	31.73	23.22	16.01	10.29	5.89
1969–1971	67.94	59.69	50.22	41.07	31.87	23.34	16.07	10.38	6.18
1979–1981	70.82	61.98	52.45	43.31	34.04	25.26	17.56	11.35	6.76
1984	71.8	62.8	53.3	44.0	34.7	25.8	18.0	11.6	6.9
1985	71.9	62.9	53.3	44.0	34.7	25.8	18.0	11.6	6.8
1986	72.0	62.9	53.4	44.2	34.9	26.1	18.2	11.7	6.9
WHITE FEMALES									
1850[1]	40.5	47.2	40.2	35.4	29.8	23.5	17.0	11.3	6.4
1890[1]	44.46	49.62	42.03	35.36	28.76	22.09	15.70	10.15	5.75
1900–1902[2]	51.08	52.15	43.77	36.42	29.17	21.89	15.23	9.59	5.50
1909–1911[2]	53.62	53.57	44.88	36.96	29.26	21.74	14.92	9.38	5.35
1919–1921[3]	58.53	55.17	46.46	38.72	30.94	23.12	15.93	9.94	5.70
1929–1931	62.67	57.65	48.52	39.99	31.52	23.41	16.05	9.98	5.63
1939–1941	67.29	60.85	51.38	42.21	33.25	24.72	17.00	10.50	5.88
1949–1951	72.03	64.26	54.56	45.00	35.64	26.76	18.64	11.68	6.59
1959–1961	74.19	66.05	56.29	46.63	37.13	28.08	19.69	12.38	6.67
1969–1971	75.49	66.97	57.24	47.60	38.12	29.11	20.79	13.37	7.59
1979–1981	78.22	69.21	59.44	49.76	40.16	30.96	22.45	14.89	8.65
1984	78.7	69.6	59.8	50.1	40.5	31.2	22.6	15.1	8.9
1985	78.7	69.6	59.8	50.1	40.4	31.1	22.6	15.0	8.7
1986	78.8	69.6	59.9	50.1	40.5	31.2	22.6	15.1	8.8
ALL OTHER MALES[4]									
1900–1902[2]	32.54	41.90	35.11	29.25	23.12	17.34	12.62	8.33	5.12
1909–1911[2]	34.05	40.65	33.46	27.33	21.57	16.21	11.67	8.00	5.53
1919–1921[3]	47.14	45.99	38.36	32.51	26.53	20.47	14.74	9.58	5.83
1929–1931	47.55	44.27	35.95	29.45	23.36	17.92	13.15	8.78	5.42
1939–1941	52.33	48.54	39.74	32.25	25.23	19.18	14.38	10.06	6.46
1949–1951	58.91	52.96	43.73	35.31	27.29	20.25	14.91	10.74	7.07
1959–1961	61.48	55.19	45.78	37.05	28.72	21.28	15.29	10.81	6.87
1969–1971	60.98	53.67	44.37	36.20	28.29	21.24	15.35	10.68	7.57
1979–1981	65.63	57.40	47.87	39.13	30.64	22.92	16.54	11.36	7.22
1984	67.4	58.9	49.3	40.3	31.6	23.7	16.9	11.5	7.2
1985	67.2	58.7	49.1	40.2	31.6	23.7	16.9	11.4	7.2
1986	67.2	58.7	49.1	40.3	31.8	23.9	17.0	11.5	7.1
ALL OTHER FEMALES[4]									
1900–1902[2]	35.04	43.02	36.89	30.70	24.37	18.67	13.60	9.62	6.48
1909–1911[2]	37.67	42.84	36.14	29.61	23.34	17.65	12.78	9.22	6.05
1919–1921[3]	46.92	44.54	37.15	31.48	25.60	19.76	14.69	10.25	6.58
1929–1931	49.51	45.33	37.22	30.67	24.30	18.60	14.22	10.38	6.90
1939–1941	55.51	50.83	42.14	34.52	27.31	21.04	16.14	11.81	8.00
1949–1951	62.70	56.17	46.77	38.02	29.82	22.67	16.95	12.29	8.15
1959–1961	66.47	59.72	50.07	40.83	32.16	24.31	17.83	12.46	7.66
1969–1971	69.05	61.49	51.85	42.61	33.87	25.97	19.02	13.30	9.01
1979–1981[5]	74.00	65.64	55.88	46.39	37.16	28.59	20.49	14.44	9.17
1984	75.0	66.5	56.7	47.1	37.8	29.1	21.3	14.6	9.1
1985	75.0	66.3	56.5	47.0	37.7	28.9	21.1	14.4	8.9
1986	75.1	66.4	56.6	47.1	37.8	29.1	21.2	14.5	8.9

1. Massachusetts only; white and nonwhite combined, the latter being about 1% of the total. 2. Original Death Registration States. 3. Death Registration States of 1920. 4. Data for periods 1900–1902 to 1929–1931 relate to blacks only. *Sources:* Department of Health and Human Services, National Center for Health Statistics.

Expectation of Life and Mortality Probabilities, 1986

Age	Expectation of life in years					Mortality probability per 1,000				
	Total persons	White		All other		Total persons	White		All other	
		Male	Female	Male	Female		Male	Female	Male	Female
0	74.8	72.0	78.8	67.2	75.1	10.4	10.0	7.8	17.3	14.0
1	74.6	71.7	78.4	67.4	75.1	0.7	0.8	0.6	1.1	.9
2	73.6	70.8	77.5	66.4	74.2	0.6	0.6	0.4	0.8	.7
3	72.7	69.8	76.5	65.5	73.2	0.4	0.4	0.3	0.7	.6
4	71.7	68.8	75.5	64.5	72.3	0.4	0.3	0.3	0.6	.5
5	70.7	67.8	74.6	63.6	71.3	0.3	0.3	0.2	0.5	.4
6	69.8	66.9	73.6	62.6	70.3	0.3	0.3	0.2	0.4	.3
7	68.8	65.9	72.6	61.6	69.4	0.2	0.3	0.2	0.4	.3
8	67.8	64.9	71.6	60.6	68.4	0.2	0.2	0.2	0.3	.2
9	66.8	63.9	70.6	59.7	67.4	0.2	0.2	0.1	0.3	.2
10	65.8	62.9	69.6	58.7	66.4	0.2	0.2	0.1	0.3	.2
11	64.8	61.9	68.6	57.7	65.4	0.2	0.2	0.1	0.3	.2
12	63.8	61.0	67.7	56.7	64.4	0.2	0.3	0.2	0.4	.2
13	62.9	60.0	66.7	55.7	63.4	0.3	0.4	0.2	0.5	.2
14	61.9	59.0	65.7	54.8	62.5	0.5	0.6	0.3	0.7	.3
15	60.9	58.0	64.7	53.8	61.5	0.6	0.9	0.4	0.8	.4
16	59.9	57.1	63.7	52.8	60.5	0.8	1.1	0.5	1.0	.4
17	59.0	56.1	62.8	51.9	59.5	0.9	1.3	0.5	1.2	.5
18	58.0	55.2	61.8	51.0	58.6	1.0	1.4	0.5	1.5	.5
19	57.1	54.3	60.8	50.0	57.6	1.0	1.5	0.5	1.7	.6
20	56.2	53.4	59.9	49.1	56.6	1.1	1.6	0.5	1.9	.6
21	55.2	52.5	58.9	48.2	55.7	1.2	1.6	0.5	2.2	.7
22	54.3	51.5	57.9	47.3	54.7	1.2	1.7	0.5	2.4	.8
23	53.3	50.6	56.9	46.4	53.7	1.2	1.7	0.5	2.5	.8
24	52.4	49.7	56.0	45.5	52.8	1.2	1.7	0.5	2.6	.9
25	51.5	48.8	55.0	44.7	51.8	1.2	1.6	0.5	2.7	.9
26	50.5	47.9	54.0	43.8	50.9	1.2	1.6	0.5	2.8	1.0
27	49.6	47.0	53.1	42.9	49.9	1.2	1.5	0.5	2.9	1.0
28	48.7	46.0	52.1	42.0	49.0	1.2	1.6	0.6	3.0	1.1
29	47.7	45.1	51.1	41.1	48.0	1.3	1.6	0.6	3.2	1.2
30	46.8	44.2	50.1	40.3	47.1	1.3	1.7	0.6	3.4	1.3
31	45.8	43.2	49.2	39.4	46.1	1.4	1.8	0.6	3.5	1.5
32	44.9	42.3	48.2	38.5	45.2	1.5	1.8	0.7	3.7	1.6
33	44.0	41.4	47.2	37.7	44.3	1.5	1.9	0.7	3.9	1.6
34	43.0	40.5	46.3	36.8	43.3	1.6	1.9	0.8	4.1	1.7
35	42.1	39.5	45.3	36.0	42.4	1.6	1.9	0.8	4.4	1.8
36	41.2	38.6	44.3	35.1	41.5	1.7	2.0	0.9	4.6	1.9
37	40.2	37.7	43.4	34.3	40.6	1.8	2.1	0.9	4.9	2.0
38	39.3	36.8	42.4	33.5	39.7	1.9	2.2	1.0	5.2	2.2
39	38.4	35.9	41.5	32.6	38.7	2.0	2.4	1.1	5.5	2.4
40	37.4	34.9	40.5	31.8	37.8	2.2	2.5	1.3	5.8	2.6
41	36.5	34.0	39.6	31.0	36.9	2.4	2.7	1.4	6.1	2.9
42	35.6	33.1	38.6	30.2	36.0	2.6	2.9	1.6	6.5	3.1
43	34.7	32.2	37.7	29.4	35.1	2.8	3.2	1.7	6.8	3.3
44	33.8	31.3	36.7	28.6	34.3	3.0	3.4	1.9	7.1	3.5
45	32.9	30.4	35.8	27.8	33.4	3.2	3.7	2.0	7.5	3.8
46	32.0	29.5	34.9	27.0	32.5	3.5	4.1	2.2	7.8	4.0
47	31.1	28.7	33.9	26.2	31.6	3.8	4.4	2.5	8.4	4.4
48	30.2	27.8	33.0	25.4	30.8	4.2	4.9	2.7	9.1	4.8
49	29.4	26.9	32.1	24.6	29.9	4.7	5.4	3.0	10.1	5.3
50	28.5	26.1	31.2	23.9	29.1	5.2	6.0	3.4	11.1	5.9
51	27.6	25.2	30.3	23.1	28.2	5.7	6.6	3.7	12.1	6.5
52	26.8	24.4	29.4	22.4	27.4	6.3	7.4	4.2	13.1	7.1
53	26.0	23.6	28.6	21.7	26.6	6.9	8.1	4.5	14.0	7.6
54	25.1	22.7	27.7	21.0	25.8	7.5	9.0	4.9	14.9	8.1
55	24.3	21.9	26.8	20.3	25.0	8.1	10.0	5.4	15.7	8.5
56	23.5	21.2	26.0	19.6	24.2	8.8	10.9	5.8	16.6	9.0
57	22.7	20.4	25.1	19.0	23.4	9.6	12.1	6.4	17.8	9.8
58	21.9	19.6	24.3	18.3	22.7	10.6	13.3	7.1	19.3	10.8
59	21.2	18.9	23.4	17.7	21.9	11.7	14.7	7.9	21.2	12.1
60	20.4	18.2	22.6	17.0	21.2	12.9	16.1	8.7	23.2	13.5
61	19.7	17.5	21.8	16.4	20.5	14.1	17.7	9.6	25.3	14.9
62	18.9	16.8	21.0	15.8	19.8	15.4	19.3	10.5	27.2	16.2
63	18.2	16.1	20.2	15.3	19.1	16.6	20.9	11.5	28.9	17.2
64	17.5	15.4	19.5	14.7	18.4	17.9	22.6	12.4	30.4	18.0
65	16.8	14.8	18.7	14.1	17.7	19.1	24.3	13.4	31.8	18.7

Age	Total persons	White Male	White Female	All other Male	All other Female	Total persons	White Male	White Female	All other Male	All other Female
		Expectation of life in years					Mortality probability per 1,000			
66	16.2	14.1	18.0	13.6	17.1	20.5	26.2	14.5	33.5	19.6
67	15.5	13.5	17.2	13.1	16.4	22.2	28.4	15.8	35.5	20.8
68	14.8	12.9	16.5	12.5	15.7	24.2	31.2	17.3	38.0	22.5
69	14.2	12.3	15.8	12.0	15.1	26.5	34.3	19.0	41.0	24.6
70	13.6	11.7	15.1	11.5	14.5	29.0	37.8	20.9	44.3	26.9
71	12.9	11.1	14.4	11.0	13.8	31.7	41.5	23.0	47.8	29.3
72	12.4	10.6	13.7	10.5	13.2	34.4	45.3	25.1	51.3	31.6
73	11.8	10.1	13.0	10.1	12.7	37.2	49.3	27.4	54.7	33.9
74	11.2	9.6	12.4	9.6	12.1	40.3	53.4	29.9	58.0	36.2
75	10.7	9.1	11.8	9.2	11.5	43.5	57.8	32.7	61.6	38.6
76	10.1	8.6	11.1	8.7	11.0	47.0	62.6	35.8	65.5	41.3
77	9.6	8.1	10.5	8.3	10.4	50.9	67.9	39.2	70.1	44.6
78	9.1	7.7	9.9	7.9	9.9	55.4	73.8	43.2	75.3	48.5
79	8.6	7.3	9.4	7.5	9.4	60.4	80.4	47.7	81.4	53.2
80	8.1	7.1	8.9	6.9	8.8	66.0	87.6	52.9	88.5	58.6
81	7.7	6.8	8.4	6.5	8.3	72.4	95.5	58.8	96.5	64.9
82	7.2	6.5	7.9	6.1	7.8	79.6	110.4	65.8	105.6	72.2
83	6.8	6.2	7.5	5.7	7.3	87.8	113.4	73.9	115.8	80.6
84	6.4	5.9	7.1	5.4	6.8	97.1	123.1	83.6	127.3	90.4
85	6.0	5.7	6.8	5.1	6.4	—	—	—	—	—

Source: Department of Health and Human Services, National Center for Health Statistics.

Law Enforcement and Crime

Full-Time Law Enforcement Employees, 1988

City	Officers	Civilians	Total	1987 Total	City	Officers	Civilians	Total	1987 Total
Atlanta	1,395	309	1,704	1,650	Minneapolis	730	98	828	827
Baltimore	2,993	553	3,546	3,472	New Orleans	1,360	276	1,636	1,736
Birmingham, Ala.	644	200	844	833	New York	26,723	9,304	36,027	34,764
Boston	1,927	691	2,618	2,567	Newark, N.J.	1,076	215	1,291	1,225
Buffalo, N.Y.	1,041	113	1,154	1,093	Norfolk, Va.	626	70	696	691
Chicago	12,163	1,670	13,833	14,042	Oakland, Calif.	590	234	824	904
Cincinnati	919	216	1,135	1,105	Oklahoma City	796	187	983	985
Cleveland	1,749	325	2,074	1,891	Omaha, Neb.	603	147	750	748
Columbus, Ohio	1,335	335	1,670	1,603	Philadelphia	6,063	872	6,935	7,566
Dallas	2,381	780	3,161	2,960	Phoenix, Ariz.	1,801	678	2,479	2,445
Denver	1,326	240	1,566	1,614	Pittsburgh	1,098	27	1,125	1,151
Detroit	3,572	691	4,263	5,674	Portland, Ore.	758	305	1,063	975
El Paso	677	209	886	891	Rochester, N.Y.	630	122	752	725
Fort Worth	950	293	1,243	1,247	St. Louis	1,528	587	2,115	2,076
Honolulu	1,706	378	2,084	2,052	St. Paul	512	130	642	646
Houston	4,270	1,001	5,271	5,555	San Antonio	1,451	318	1,769	1,695
Indianapolis	1,012	358	1,370	1,327	San Diego, Calif.	1,738	670	2,408	2,327
Jacksonville, Fla.	1,097	714	1,811	1,664	San Francisco	1,803	709	2,512	2,559
Kansas City, Mo.	1,117	580	1,697	1,708	San Jose, Calif.	1,013	216	1,229	1,224
Long Beach, Calif.	639	323	962	1,093	Seattle	1,179	396	1,575	1,511
Los Angeles	7,553	2,470	10,023	9,475	Tampa, Fla.	726	219	945	940
Louisville, Ky.	641	191	832	839	Toledo, Ohio	749	57	806	817
Memphis, Tenn.	1,269	427	1,696	1,658	Tucson, Ariz.	714	228	942	938
Miami, Fla.	1,038	320	1,358	1,400	Tulsa, Okla.	689	148	837	839
Milwaukee	1,947	387	2,334	2,317	Washington, D.C.	3,920	718	4,638	4,528

NOTE: As of Oct. 31, 1988. *Source:* Department of Justice, Federal Bureau of Investigation, *Uniform Crime Reports for the United States, 1989.*

Estimated Arrests, 1988[1]

Murder and non-negligent manslaughter	21,890	Weapons—carrying, possession, etc.	221,800
Forcible rape	38,610	Prostitution and commercial vice	104,100
Robbery	149,100	Sex offenses, except forcible rape	
Aggravated assault	416,300	and prostitution	106,300
Burglary	463,400	Drug abuse violations	1,155,200
Larceny—theft	1,571,200	Gambling	23,600
Motor vehicle theft	208,400	Offenses against family and children	69,900
Arson	19,700	Driving under the influence	1,792,500
Total violent crime	625,900	Liquor laws	699,600
Total property crime	2,262,700	Drunkenness	818,600
Other assaults	901,800	Disorderly conduct	760,500
Forgery and counterfeiting	101,700	Vagrancy	36,500
Fraud	366,300	All other offenses, except traffic	3,078,900
Embezzlement	15,500	Curfew and loitering law violations	72,200
Stolen property—buying, receiving, possessing	166,300	Runaways	166,900
Vandalism	295,300	**Total[2]**	**13,812,300**

1. Arrest totals based on all reporting agencies and estimates for unreported areas. 2. Because of rounding, items may not add to totals. *Source:* Department of Justice, Federal Bureau of Investigation, *Uniform Crime Reports for the United States,* 1989.

Number of Arrests by Sex and Age

	Male				Female			
	Total		Under 18		Total		Under 18	
Offense	1988	1987	1988	1987	1988	1987	1988	1987
Serious crimes	1,464,062	1,776,658	418,151	527,294	396,459	489,809	100,346	131,197
Murder[1]	12,865	14,629	1,498	1,454	1,767	2,085	112	138
Forcible rape	24,768	30,908	3,616	4,799	291	368	71	110
Robbery	93,241	113,342	20,766	25,779	8,735	9,964	1,698	1,903
Aggravated assault	234,590	261,548	28,836	32,640	36,391	40,186	5,156	6,006
Burglary—breaking or entering	263,638	345,169	88,328	122,391	24,726	29,794	7,238	9,771
Larceny—theft	701,437	865,432	221,892	282,329	309,177	391,120	80,043	106,459
Motor vehicle theft	122,698	132,542	48,048	52,387	13,726	14,211	5,528	6,186
Arson	10,825	13,088	4,807	5,515	1,646	2,081	500	624
All other								
Other assaults	509,516	570,689	66,111	75,648	92,348	101,249	19,966	22,232
Forgery and counterfeiting	41,679	51,732	3,562	4,729	21,443	27,085	1,698	2,368
Fraud	129,471	158,573	8,747	13,606	106,036	122,236	2,882	4,783
Embezzlement	6,344	6,582	522	578	3,985	4,057	371	330
Stolen property—buying, receiving, possessing	97,284	105,203	24,812	27,084	13,072	13,845	2,642	2,766
Vandalism	174,192	205,754	70,233	86,537	21,486	24,334	6,770	8,412
Weapons—carrying, possessing, etc.	133,333	153,001	22,472	23,818	11,235	12,649	1,607	1,835
Prostitution and commercialized v vice	23,051	35,525	460	688	51,238	65,425	853	1,447
Sex offenses, except forcible rape and prostitution	64,118	78,911	10,250	12,645	5,113	6,716	719	899
Drug abuse violations	632,282	689,853	58,283	66,081	117,186	121,225	8,406	9,956
Gambling	13,970	19,693	635	796	2,609	3,069	38	44
Offenses against family and children	34,975	39,663	1,285	1,590	7,555	8,339	736	977
Driving under the influence	965,956	1,245,446	12,668	17,032	129,470	164,951	1,941	2,685
Liquor laws	336,353	414,869	74,287	96,656	73,813	90,152	27,236	35,803
Drunkenness	479,411	635,961	12,172	17,083	49,448	64,701	2,360	3,271
Disorderly conduct	410,939	487,757	63,238	71,739	92,520	111,865	15,238	16,758
Vagrancy	24,918	28,757	1,856	2,013	3,283	3,761	366	439
All other offenses, except traffic	1,627,843	2,050,671	168,497	216,815	313,020	380,242	44,087	56,856
Curfew and loitering law violations	34,976	58,193	34,976	58,193	12,870	19,363	12,870	19,363
Runaways	46,734	58,061	46,734	58,061	59,237	77,574	59,237	77,574
Total	**7,251,407**	**8,881,528**	**1,100,491**	**1,380,748**	**1,583,426**	**1,914,341**	**310,369**	**400,492**

1. Includes non-negligent manslaughter. NOTE: 6,808 agencies reporting; 1987 estimated population 160,451,000. *Source:* Department of Justice, Federal Bureau of Investigation, *Uniform Crime Reports for the United States, 1989.*

Arrests by Race, 1988

Offense	White	Black	Other[1]	Total
Serious crimes				
Murder[2]	7,243	8,603	244	16,090
Forcible rape	14,775	12,853	408	28,036
Robbery	40,072	69,130	1,225	110,427
Aggravated assault	174,177	123,058	5,076	302,311
Burglary	220,998	103,249	5,565	329,812
Larceny-theft	758,752	372,574	25,824	1,151,150
Motor vehicle theft	89,115	59,984	2,620	15,719
Arson	10,559	3,591	224	14,374
All other				
Other assaults	423,697	247,839	11,646	683,182
Forgery and counterfeiting	47,156	24,902	802	72,860
Fraud	170,228	87,873	2,275	260,376
Embezzlement	7,388	3,926	153	11,467
Stolen property— buying, receiving, possessing	70,839	51,568	1,446	123,853
Vandalism	166,540	53,812	3,923	224,275
Weapons—carrying, possession, etc.	95,092	64,937	2,336	162,365
Prostitution and commercial vice	45,163	31,968	1,215	78,346
Sex offences, except forcible rape and prostitution	59,856	16,626	1,388	77,870
Drug abuse violation	503,125	334,015	7,160	844,300
Gambling	8,221	8,373	1,019	17,163
Offenses against family and children	31,572	16,444	1,627	49,643
Driving under the influence	1,279,121	130,375	23,639	1,279,121
Liquor laws	429,309	46,737	12,947	488,993
Drunkenness	478,479	104,459	16,357	599,295
Disorderly conduct	358,840	200,717	9,918	569,475
Vagrancy	16,351	10,882	736	27,969
All other offenses except traffic	2,197,185	755,704	41,626	2,197,185
Suspicion	5,811	5,600	106	11,517
Curfew and loitering law violations	44,219	8,766	1,862	54,847
Runaways	101,656	18,161	3,703	123,520
Total	6,903,070	2,977,266	187,111	10,067,447

1. Includes American Indian, Alaskan Native, and Asian or Pacific Islander. 2. Includes non-negligent manslaughter. NOTE: Figures represent arrests reported by 9,933 agencies serving a total 1988 population of 187,818,000 as estimated by FBI. *Source:* Department of Justice, Federal Bureau of Investigation, *Uniform Crime Reports for the United States, 1989.*

Total Arrests, by Age Groups, 1988

Age	Arrests	Age	Arrests	Age	Arrests	Age	Arrests	Age	Arrests
Under 15	526,421	18	499,454	22	419,466	30–34	1,379,390	50–54	181,896
15	291,045	19	480,274	23	419,160	35–39	881,397	55 and	
16	364,780	20	448,723	24	421,568	40–44	515,881	over	274,904
17	452,544	21	430,639	25–29	1,864,134	45–49	298,220	Total	10,149,896

NOTE: Based on reports furnished to the FBI by 9,970 agencies covering a 1988 estimated population of 188,928,000. *Source:* Department of Justice, Federal Bureau of Investigation, *Uniform Crime Reports for the United States, 1989.*

Federal Prosecutions of Public Corruption: 1977 to 1986

(Prosecution of persons who have corrupted public office in violation of Federal Criminal Statutes. As of Dec. 31, 1986)

Prosecution status	1986	1985	1984	1983	1982	1981	1980	1979	1978	1977
Total:[1] Indicted	1,192	1,182	936	1,073	729	878	721	687	557	507
Convicted	1,027	997	934	972	671	730	552	555	409	440
Awaiting trial	246	256	269	222	186	231	213	187	205	210
Federal officials: Indicted	596	563	408	460	158	198	123	128	133	129
Convicted	523	470	429	424	147	159	131	115	91	94
Awaiting trial	83	90	77	58	38	23	16	21	42	32
State officials: Indicted	88	79	58	81	49	87	72	58	55	50
Convicted	71	66	52	65	43	66	51	32	56	38
Awaiting trial	24	20	21	26	18	36	28	30	20	33
Local officials: Indicted	232	248	203	270	257	244	247	212	171	157
Convicted	207	221	196	226	232	211	168	156	127	164
Awaiting trial	55	49	74	61	58	102	82	67	72	62

1. Includes individuals who are neither public officials nor employees, but who were involved with public officials or employees in violating the law, now shown separately. NOTE: Figures are latest available. *Source:* U.S. Department of Justice, *Federal Prosecutions of Corrupt Public Officials, 1970–1980,* and *Report to Congress on the Activities and Operations of the Public Integrity Section,* annual.

Crime Rates for Population Groups and Selected Cities, 1987

(offenses known to the police per 100,000 population, as of July 1)

Group and city	Murder	Forcible rape	Robbery	Aggravated assault	Total	Burglary—breaking or entering	Larceny—theft	Motor vehicle theft	Total	Total all crimes
Total 7,721 Cities	10.2	46	315	446	868	1,602	3,968	709	6,279	7,560
MSA's (Metropolitan Statistical Areas)	9	42	269	400	720	1,485	3,444	646	5,574	6,294
Other Cities	5	24	50	272	351	1,042	3,303	203	4,548	4,898
Rural Areas	6	19	15	139	178	670	943	110	1,723	1,900
Selected Cities:										
Baltimore	29.5	78	976	785	1,869	1,762	3,964	976	1,762	8,570
Chicago	22.9	1	990	1,133	1	1,690	3,945	1,315	6,950	1
Dallas	32.0	125	900	932	1,989	3,885	8,442	1,968	14,294	16,283
Detroit	62.8	130	1,383	969	2,545	3,381	4,023	2,732	10,136	12,681
Houston	18.6	67	557	447	1,090	2,563	4,092	1,647	8,302	9,392
Indianapolis	11.9	90	279	568	949	1,827	2,786	780	5,393	6,342
Loas Angeles	24.3	65	784	1,307	1,910	1,584	3,431	1,709	6,723	8,634
Memphis	21.7	126	712	479	1,339	2,797	3,482	2,057	8,336	9,674
New York	23.0	48	1,083	882	2,036	1,694	3,969	1,313	6,977	9,013
Philadelphia, PA	20.5	67	564	404	1,055	1,217	2,533	929	4,679	5,734
Phoenix, AZ	11.9	54	245	566	877	2,270	5,219	632	8,121	8,997
San Antonio	18.9	92	354	197	662	3,591	7,194	1,480	12,264	12,926
San Diego	9.2	39	332	495	875	1,669	4,188	1,744	7,601	8,476
San Francisco	13.4	59	606	532	1,211	1,256	4,059	1,006	6,321	7,532
Washington, D.C.	36.2	39	717	817	1,610	1,807	4,014	1,012	6,833	8,444

1. The rates for 1987 forcible rape, violent crime, and total crime are not shown because the forcible rape figures were not in accordance with national Uniform Crime Reporting guidelines. *Source: Statistical Abstract of the United States 1989.*

Percent of Firearms Usage in Selected Crimes, by Region: 1986–1988

Region	Murder[1] 1988	1987	1986	Aggravated assault 1988	1987	1986	Robbery 1988	1987	1986
Northeast	57.3	54.8	49.4	15.9	14.9	13.3	27.1	25.3	27.3
Midwest	59.0	57.7	60.4	23.1	24.4	24.4	33.4	32.6	34.1
South	64.4	62.9	64.3	26.3	25.6	25.5	40.8	39.7	41.2
West	59.2	56.4	54.8	18.4	17.7	18.1	33.1	33.8	33.5
U.S. Total	60.7	59.1	59.1	21.1	21.4	21.3	33.4	33.0	34.3

1. Murder includes non-negligent manslaughter. *Source:* U.S. Federal Bureau of Investigation, *Crime in the United States,* annual.

Reported Child Neglect and Abuse Cases: 1983 to 1985

Division	Percent change 1984-85	Total number of reports (1,000) 1985	1984	1983	Reports per 1,000 population 1985	1984	1983
New England	8.5	59.9	55.2	58.5	4.7	5.8	4.7
Middle Atlantic	4.5	152.2	145.6	101.0	4.1	3.9	2.7
North Central	8.9	316.4	290.6	235.4	11.1	5.3	8.8
South Atlantic	9.5	225.5	205.4	228.5	5.6	4.5	5.9
South Central	19.6	249.9	209.0	165.3	12.9	4.6	8.2
Mountain	29.3	77.6	60.0	49.5	6.1	4.7	4.0
Pacific	15.0	218.4	189.8	163.3	6.2	5.7	4.9
U.S. Total	12.4	1,299.4	1,155.6	1,001.4	5.4	4.8	4.3

NOTE: Figures are latest available. *Source:* American Humane Association, *National Analysis of Official Child Neglect and Abuse Reporting,* annual.

Prisoners Under Sentence of Death

Characteristic	1987	1986	1985	Characteristic	1987	1986	1985
White	1,138	1,006	903	Marital status:			
Black and other	846	775	688	Never married	856	772	655
Under 20 years	10	19	13	Married	571	525	487
20–24 years	222	217	212	Divorced or separated[2]	557	484	449
25–34 years	969	872	804	Time elapsed since sentencing:			
35–54 years	744	639	531	Less than 12 months	295	293	273
55 years and over	39	34	31	12–47 months	804	757	739
				48–71 months	412	376	303
Schooling completed:				72 months and over	473	355	276
7 years or less	181	164	147	Legal status at arrest:			
8 years	183	174	159	Not under sentence	1,123	992	861
9–11 years	650	577	483	On parole or probation	480[3]	409[3]	350[3]
12 years	591	515	440	In prison or escaped	91	82	81
More than 12 years	168	143	127	Unknown	290	298	299
Unknown	211	208	235	**Total**	**1,984**	**1,781**	**1,591**[1]

1. Revisions to the total number of prisoners were not carried to the characteristics except for race. 2. Includes widows, widowers, and unknown. 3. Includes 20 persons on mandatory conditional release, work release, leave, AWOL, or bail for 1985 and 1986; 22 for 1987. NOTE: As of Dec. 31. Excludes prisoners under sentence of death confined in local correctional systems pending appeal or who had not been committed to prison. *Source:* U.S. Bureau of Justice Statistics, *Capital Punishment,* annual.

Methods of Execution[1]

State	Method	State	Method
Alabama[2]	Electrocution	Nevada[2]	Lethal injection
Alaska	No death penalty	New Hampshire[2]	Lethal injection
Arizona[2]	Lethal gas	New Jersey	Lethal injection
Arkansas[2]	Lethal injection	New Mexico	Lethal injection
California[4]	Lethal gas	New York	No death penalty
Colorado[2,7]	Lethal injection	North Carolina[2]	Lethal gas or injection
Connecticut[2]	Electrocution	North Dakota	No death penalty
Delaware	Lethal injection	Ohio[2]	Electrocution
D.C.	No death penalty	Oklahoma	Lethal injection
Florida	Electrocution	Oregon[5]	Lethal injection
Georgia[2]	Electrocution	Pennsylvania[2]	Electrocution
Hawaii	No death penalty	Rhode Island	No death penalty([3])
Idaho[2]	Lethal injection	South Carolina[2]	Electrocution
Illinois	Lethal injection	South Dakota	Lethal injection
Indiana[2]	Electrocution	Tennessee[2]	Electrocution
Iowa	No death penalty	Texas[2]	Lethal injection
Kansas	No death penalty	Utah[2]	Firing squad or lethal injection
Kentucky[2]	Electrocution	Vermont	Electrocution
Louisiana[2]	Electrocution	Virginia	Electrocution
Maine	No death penalty	Washington[2]	Hanging or lethal injection
Maryland[2]	Lethal gas	West Virginia	No death penalty
Massachusetts	No death penalty	Wisconsin	No death penalty
Michigan	No death penalty	Wyoming	Lethal injection
Minnesota	No death penalty	U.S. (Fed. Govt.)	([4])
Mississippi[2]	Lethal injection	American Samoa	No death penalty
Missouri	Lethal injection	Guam	No death penalty
Montana[2]	Hanging, or lethal injection[6]	Puerto Rico	No death penalty
Nebraska[2]	Electrocution	Virgin Islands	No death penalty

1. On July 1, 1976, by a 7-2 decision, the U.S. Supreme Court upheld the death penalty as not being "cruel or unusual." However, in another ruling the same day, the Court, by a 5-4 vote, stated that states may not impose "mandatory" capital punishment on every person convicted of murder. These decisions left uncertain the fate of condemned persons throughout the U.S. On Oct. 4, the Court refused to reconsider its July ruling, which allows some states to proceed with executions of condemned prisoners. The first execution in this country since 1967 was in Utah on Jan. 17, 1977. Gary Mark Gilmore was executed by shooting. 2. Voted to restore death penalty after June 29, 1972, Supreme Court decision ruling capital punishment unconstitutional. 3. Person shall be executed by gas if he commits murder while serving a prison term. 4. Is that of the state in which the execution takes place. 5. Death penalty has been passed, but not been used. 6. Defendant may choose between hanging and a lethal injection. 7. Applies to offenses committed on or after July, 1 1988. Prior to this date the method of execution was lethal gas. *Source: Information Please* questionnaires to the states. NOTE: An asterisk after the name of the state indicates non-reply.

Motor Vehicle Laws, 1989

State	Age for license		Age for driver's license[1]			Driver's license duration	Fee	Annual safety inspection required
	Motorcycle	Moped	Regular	Learner's	Restrictive			
Alabama	14	14	16	15[5]	14[11]	4 yrs.	$15.00	no[17]
Alaska	14	14	16	14[6]	14[11]	5	10.00	no[17]
Arizona	16	16	18	15 7 mo.[5,6]	16[6]	4	7	no[18,19]
Arkansas	16	10	16	(5)	14[6]	2 or 4	7/13.00	yes
California	18	15 1/2	18	15[4,7]	16[4]	4	10.00	no[19]
Colorado	16	16	21	15 1/2[5,8]	16[6]	4	6.50	no[19]
Connecticut	18	16	18		16[4]	2 or 4	24.75/38	yes[20,21]
Delaware	18	16	18	15 10 mo.	16[4,6]	5	12.50	yes
D. C.	16	16	18	(5)	16[6]	4	15.00	yes
Florida	15	15	16	15(5)	15[6]	4 or 6	15.00	no
Georgia	16	15	21	15	16[6]	4	5.00	no[20]
Hawaii	15	15	18	(5)	15[6]	4[13]	3-12.00	yes[23]
Idaho	16	16	16	(5)	14[4]	3	13.50	no
Illinois	18	16[4]	18	(5)	16[4,6]	4 or 5	8.00/10.00	no[24]
Indiana	16 1/2	15	18	15[8]	16 1 mo.[4,6]	4[15]	6.00	no
Iowa	18	14[4]	18	14	16[4]	6[16]	8.00/16.00	(17)
Kansas	14	14	16	(5)	14	4	8/12.00	(17)
Kentucky	16	16	18	(5)	16[6]	4	8.00	no
Louisiana	15	15	17[5]	(5)	15[6]	4[2]	9.00/15.50	yes
Maine	17	16	17	(5)	15[4]	4	18.00	yes
Maryland	18	18	18	15 9 mo.	16[4,6]	4	20.00	no[24]
Massachusetts	17	16	18	(5)	16 1/2[4,6]	4	25.00	yes[21]
Michigan	18	15	18		16[4,6]	2 or 4	12.00	no[17]
Minnesota	19	15	19	15[7,8]	16[4]	4	15.00	no[17]
Mississippi	15	15	15	(5)		4	13.00	yes
Missouri	16	16	16		15[4]	3	7.50	yes[19]
Montana	18	16	18	(5)	15[4,6]	4	12.00	no
Nebraska	16	16	16	15[5]	14	4	10.00	no
Nevada	16	16	16	15 1/2[5]	14[6,10]	4	10.00[16]	no[20,24]
New Hampshire	18	16	18[4]		16[4]	4	20.00	yes
New Jersey	17	15	17		16	4	16-17.50	yes
New Mexico	16	13	16	15	14[12]	4	10.00	no
New York	17[4]	16	17[4]		16[6]	4	17.50	yes[19]
North Carolina	18	16	18	15[4,6]		4	15.00	yes
North Dakota	16	14	16	(5)	14[4,6]	4	10.00	no[17]
Ohio	18	14	18	16[5,7]	14[3]	4	9.00	no[19]
Oklahoma	14		16	7	15 1/2[4]	4	18.00	yes
Oregon	16	16	16	15[5]	14	4	25.00	no[17,19]
Pennsylvania	16	16	18	16[6,7,5]	16[6]	4	5.00	yes[19]
Rhode Island	16[28]	16	16	(5)	16[4]	5	20.00	yes
South Carolina	16	14	16	15[9]	15	4	10.00	yes
South Dakota	14	14	16		14	4	6.00	no
Tennessee	16	14	16	15	15	4	14.00	no
Texas	18	15	16	15[7]	15	4	16.00	yes
Utah	16	16	16[4]	(5)		4	10.00	yes
Vermont	18	16	18	15[9]	16	2 or 4	10/16	yes
Virginia	18	16	18	15 8 mo.[5,6]	16[4,6]	5	12.00	yes
Washington	18	16	18	15[5,8]	16[4]	4	14.00	no[20]
West Virginia	16	16	18	(5)	16[6]	4	10.00	yes
Wisconsin	18	16	18	(5)	16[4]	4	9.00	no[17]
Wyoming	16	15	16	15[6,7]	14[6,7]	4	10.00	no

1. Full driving privileges at age given in "Regular" column. A license restricted or qualified in some manner may be obtained at age given in "Restricted" column. 2. 2 years, 70 or older. 3. Upon proof of hardship. 4. Must have completed approved driver education course. 5. Learner's permit required. 6. Guardian's or parental consent required. 7. Driver with learner's permit must be accompanied by locally licensed operator 18 years or older. 8. Must be enrolled in driver education course. 9. Driver with learner's permit must be accompanied by locally licensed operator 21 years or older. 10. To and from school or transporting handicapped. 11. Restricted to mopeds. 12. For use while enrolled in driver education course. Must be accompanied by instructor. 13. 2 years if 15-24 or over 65. 14. 3 years if over 75. 15. 2 years if under 18 or over 70. 16. 70 and older, $5.00. 17. State troopers are authorized to inspect at their discretion. 18. Arizona emission inspection fee $7.00. 19. Annual emissions test in some counties. 20. Used motor vehicles being registered in Connecticut from out-of-state are required to be inspected and approved and Connecticut cars 10 years old and older must be inspected upon being sold or transferred. 21. Annual emissions test. 22. If car is 10 years or older, every 6 months. 23. Trucks and buses only. 24. All used vehicles upon resale or transfer. 25. Up to 50cc. 26. May obtain instruction permit with motorcycle endorsement. 27. At night, under 18 must be accompanied by parent, guardian, or driving instructor. 28. Requires completion of motorcycle safety course. NOTES: A driver's license is required in every state. The national speed limit is 55 miles per hour. All states have an *implied consent* Chemical Test Law for alcohol. *Source:* American Automobile Association.

Law Enforcement Officers Killed or Assaulted: 1976 to 1987

(Covers officers killed feloniously and accidentally in line of duty; includes federal officers.)

	1987	1986	1985	1984	1983	1982	1981	1980	1979	1977
Northeast	24	15	19	21	20	17	17	31	21	14
Midwest	31	19	23	22	26	41	29	23	28	26
South	51	62	64	69	64	75	80	72	77	65
West	40	29	29	32	34	27	27	32	32	18
Puerto Rico	1	6	10	3	6	3	3	6	4	1
Total killed	**147**	**131**	**148**[6]	**147**	**152**[5]	**164**[4]	**157**[3]	**165**[1]	**164**[2]	**125**[3]
Assaults:										
Population (1,000)[7]	190,025	196,030	198,935	195,794	198,341	176,563	177,836	182,288	182,027	168,868
Number of—										
Agencies	8,957	9,755	9,906	10,002	9,908	8,829	9,019	9,235	9,638	8,742
Police officers	378,977	380,249	389,808	372,268	377,620	319,101	332,856	345,554	340,764	322,205
Firearm	2,789	2,852	2,793	2,654	3,067	2,642	3,330	3,295	3,237	2,809
Knife or cutting instrument	1,561	1,614	1,715	1,662	1,829	1,452	1,733	1,653	1,720	1,481
Other dangerous weapon	5,685	5,721	5,263	5,148	5,527	4,879	4,800	5,415	5,543	4,626
Hands, fists, feet, etc.	53,807	54,072	51,953	50,689	51,901	46,802	47,253	47,484	48,531	40,240
Total assaulted	**63,842**	**64,259**	**61,724**	**60,153**	**62,324**	**55,775**	**57,116**	**57,847**	**59,031**	**49,156**

1. Includes one officer in Virgin Islands. 2. Includes 2 officers in Guam. 3. Includes one officer in American Samoa. 4. Includes one officer in Mariana Islands. 5. Includes one officer each in Guam and Mariana Islands. 6. Includes one officer in Guam and 2 in foreign locations. 7. Represents the number of persons covered by agencies shown. *Source: Statistical Abstract of the United States, 1988.*

Minimum Legal Age for Purchase of Liquor, Wine, and Beer

State	Liquor	Wine	Beer	State	Liquor	Wine	Beer
Alabama	21	21	21	Montana	21	21	21
Alaska	21	21	21	Nebraska	21	21	21
Arizona	21	21	21	Nevada	21	21	21
Arkansas	21	21	21	New Hampshire	21	21	21
California	21	21	21	New Jersey	21	21	21
Colorado	21	21	21	New Mexico	21	21	21
Connecticut	21	21	21	New York	21	21	21
Delaware	21	21	21	North Carolina	21	21	21
D.C.	21	21	21	North Dakota	21	21	21
Florida	21	21	21	Ohio	21	21	21
Georgia	21	21	21	Oklahoma	21	21	21
Hawaii	21	21	21	Oregon	21	21	21
Idaho	21	21	21	Pennsylvania	21	21	21
Illinois	21	21	21	Rhode Island	21	21	21
Indiana	21	21	21	South Carolina	21	21	21
Iowa	21	21	21	South Dakota	21	21	21
Kansas	21	21	21	Tennessee	21	21	21
Kentucky	21	21	21	Texas	21	21	21
Louisiana	21	21	21	Utah	21	21	21
Maine	21	21	21	Vermont	21	21	21
Maryland	21	21	21	Virginia	21	21	21
Massachusetts	21	21	21	Washington	21	21	21
Michigan	21	21	21	West Virginia	21	21	21
Minnesota	21	21	21	Wisconsin	21	21	21
Mississippi	21	21	21	Wyoming	21	21	21
Missouri	21	21	21				

Source: Distilled Spirits Council of the United States.

Youthful Offenders

According to a Bureau of Justice Statistics survey of juveniles and young adults confined in long-term, state-operated juvenile institutions, nearly 40 percent (39.3%) were being held for a violent offense. A greater number, 45.6, were in for a property offense. While only 5.6 percent were in on a drug charge, more than 60 percent used drugs regularly and almost 40 percent were under the influence of drugs at the time of the crime, whatever its category.

Almost 43 percent of the juveniles had been arrested more than 5 times, with over 20 percent of them having been arrested more than 10 times in the past.

U.S. District Courts—Criminal Cases Commenced and Defendants Disposed of, by Nature of Offense: 1985 and 1987

[For years ending June 30]

| | | Disposition of Defendants, 1987 | | | | | | | | 1985 | |
| | | Not convicted | | Convicted | | | Sentenced | | | | De-fend-ants dis-posed of |
Nature of offense	1987 cases com-menced[1]	Total	Ac-quitted	Total	Guilty plea	Court or jury	Im-prison-ment	Proba-tion	Fine and other	Cases com-menced[1]	
General offenses:											
Homicide	146	41	13	115	74	41	95	5	15	160	170
Robbery	1,291	147	23	1,225	1,069	156	1,168	56	1	1,236	1,387
Assault	705	183	50	535	403	132	316	171	48	552	555
Burglary	119	28	0	105	97	8	75	26	4	158	165
Larceny—theft	3,451	801	88	3,229	2,965	264	1,377	1,604	248	3,571	4,108
Embezzlement and fraud	9,444	1,573	246	9,544	8,578	966	4,111	5,130	303	7,912	9,044
Auto theft	253	59	7	346	322	24	243	101	2	300	461
Forgery, counterfeiting	2,135	353	26	2,176	2,032	144	1,099	1,058	19	2,118	2,372
Sex offenses	359	62	15	272	231	41	168	101	3	266	200
DAPCA[3]	8,869	2,431	384	12,699	10,655	2,044	9,907	2,680	112	6,690	11,117
Misc. general offenses	15,384	4,548	590	13,696	12,014	1,682	4,785	5,091	3,820	15,583	17,721
Total[2]	42,156	10,226	1,442	43,942	38,440	5,502	23,344	16,023	4,575	38,546	47,360

1. Excludes transfers. 2. Includes items not shown separately. 3. All marijuana, narcotics, and controlled substances under the Drug, Abuse, Prevention and Control Act. *Source: Statistical Abstract of the United States, 1989.*

Murder Victims by Weapons Used

| | | Weapons used or cause of death | | | | | | |
| | | Guns | | Cutting or stabbing | Blunt object[1] | Strangu-lation and hands, fists, feet | Arson[3] | All other[2] |
Year	Murder victims, total	Total	Percent					
1965	8,773	5,015	57.2	2,021	505	894	226	112
1970	13,649	9,039	66.2	2,424	604	1,031	353	198
1971	16,183	10,712	66.2	3,017	645	1,295	314	200
1972	15,832	10,379	65.6	2,974	672	1,291	331	185
1973	17,123	11,249	65.7	2,985	848	1,445	173	423
1974	18,632	12,474	66.9	3,228	976	1,417	153	384
1975	18,642	12,061	64.7	3,245	1,001	1,646	193	496
1978	18,714	11,910	63.6	3,526	896	1,422	255	705
1979	20,591	13,040	63.3	3,954	997	1,557	276	767
1980	21,860	13,650	62.0	4,212	1,094	1,666	291	947
1981	20,053	12,523	62.4	3,886	1,038	1,469	258	658
1982	19,485	11,721	60.2	4,065	957	1,657	279	630
1983	18,673	10,895	58.0	4,075	1,062	1,656	216	769
1984	16,689	9,819	58.8	3,540	973	1,407	192	758
1985	17,545	10,296	58.7	3,694	972	1,491	243	849
1986	19,257	11,381	59.1	3,957	1,099	1,651	230	939
1987	17,859	10,556	59.1	3,619	1,039	1,519	199	927
1988	18,269	11,084	60.7	3,496	1,143	1,546	258	742

1. Refers to club, hammer, etc. 2. Includes poison, explosives, unknown, drowning, narcotics, and not stated. 3. Before 1973, includes drowning. *Source:* Department of Justice, Federal Bureau of Investigation, *Uniform Crime Reports for the United States, 1989.*

Recidivism

Of the 108,580 persons released from prisons in 11 states in 1983, representing more than half of all released state prisoners that year, an estimated 62.5 percent were arrested for a felony or serious misdemeanor within 3 years, 46.8 percent were re-convicted, and 41.4 percent returned to prison or jail. Before their release from prison, they had been arrested and charged with an average of more than 12 offenses each; nearly two-thirds had been ar-rested at least once in the past for a violent offense; and two-thirds had previously been in jail or prison. By year-end 1986, those prisoners who were rear-rested averaged an additional 4.8 new charges. An estimated 22.7 percent of all prisoners were rear-rested for a violent offense.

Firsts in America

This selection is based on our editorial judgment. Other sources may list different firsts.

Admiral in U.S. Navy: David Glasgow Farragut, 1866.

Air-mail route, first transcontinental: Between New York City and San Francisco, 1920.

Assembly, representative: House of Burgesses, founded in Virginia, 1619.

Bank established: Bank of North America, Philadelphia, 1781.

Birth in America to English parents: Virginia Dare, born Roanoke Island, N.C., 1587.

Botanic garden: Established by John Bartram in Philadelphia, 1728 and is still in existence in its original location.

Cartoon, colored: "The Yellow Kid," by Richard Outcault, in *New York World,* 1895.

College: Harvard, founded 1636.

College to confer degrees on women: Oberlin (Ohio) College, 1841.

College to establish coeducation: Oberlin (Ohio) College, 1833.

Electrocution of a criminal: William Kemmler in Auburn Prison, Auburn, N.Y., Aug. 6, 1890.

Five and Ten Cents Store: Founded by Frank Woolworth, Utica, N.Y., 1879 (moved to Lancaster, Pa., same year).

Fraternity: Phi Beta Kappa; founded Dec. 5, 1776, at College of William and Mary.

Law to be declared unconstitutional by U.S. Supreme Court: Judiciary Act of 1789. Case: *Marbury v. Madison,* 1803.

Library, circulating: Philadelphia, 1731.

Newspaper, illustrated daily: *New York Daily Graphic,* 1873.

Newspaper published daily: *Pennsylvania Packet and General Advertiser,* Philadelphia, Sept., 1784.

Newspaper published over a continuous period: *The Boston News-Letter,* April, 1704.

Newsreel: Pathé Frères of Paris, in 1910, circulated a weekly issue of their *Pathé Journal.*

Oil well, commercial: Titusville, Pa., 1859.

Panel quiz show on radio: *Information Please,* May 17, 1938.

Postage stamps issued: 1847.

Public School: Boston Latin School, Boston, 1635.

Railroad, transcontinental: Central Pacific and Union Pacific railroads, joined at Promontory, Utah, May 10, 1869.

Savings bank: The Provident Institute for Savings, Boston, 1816.

Science museum: Founded by Charleston (S.C.) Library Society, 1773.

Skyscraper: Home Insurance Co., Chicago, 1885 (10 floors, 2 added later).

Slaves brought into America: At Jamestown, Va., 1619, from a Dutch ship.

Sorority: Kappa Alpha Theta, at De Pauw University, 1870.

State to abolish capital punishment: Michigan, 1847.

State to enter Union after original 13: Vermont, 1791.

Steam-heated building: Eastern Hotel, Boston, 1845.

Steam railroad (carried passengers and freight): Baltimore & Ohio, 1830.

Strike on record by union: Journeymen Printers, New York City, 1776.

Subway: Opened in Boston, 1897.

"Tabloid" picture newspaper: *The Illustrated Daily News* (now *The Daily News*), New York City, 1919.

Vaudeville theater: Gaiety Museum, Boston, 1883.

Woman astronaut to ride in space: Dr. Sally K. Ride, 1983.

Woman astronaut to walk in space: Dr. Kathryn D. Sullivan, 1984.

Woman cabinet member: Frances Perkins, Secretary of Labor, 1933.

Woman candidate for President: Victoria Claflin Woodhull, nominated by National Woman's Suffrage Assn. on ticket of Nation Radical Reformers, 1872.

Woman candidate for Vice-President: Geraldine A. Ferraro, nominated by a major party on ticket of the Democratic Party, 1984.

Woman doctor of medicine: Elizabeth Blackwell; M.D. from Geneva Medical College of Western New York, 1849.

Woman elected governor of a state: Mrs. Nellie Tayloe Ross, Wyoming, 1925.

Woman elected to U.S. Senate: Mrs. Hattie Caraway, Arkansas; elected Nov., 1932.

Woman graduate of law school: Mrs. Ada H. Kepley, Union College of Law, Chicago, 1870.

Woman member of U.S. House of Representatives: Jeannette Rankin; elected Nov., 1916.

Woman member of U.S. Senate: Mrs. Rebecca Latimer Felton of Georgia; appointed Oct. 3, 1922.

Woman member of U.S. Supreme Court: Mrs. Sandra Day O'Connor; appointed July 1981.

Woman suffrage granted: Wyoming Territory, 1869.

Written constitution: *Fundamental Orders of Connecticut,* 1639.

U.S. SOCIETIES & ASSOCIATIONS

Source: Information Please questionnaires to organizations. Names are listed alphabetically according to key word in title; figure in parentheses is year of founding; other figure is membership. An asterisk (*) before a name indicates that up-to-date information has not been provided.

The following is a partial list selected for general readership interest. A comprehensive listing of approximately 20,000 national and international organizations can be found in the "Encyclopedia of Associations," 20th Ed., 1986, Vol. I, Parts 1-3 (Katherine Gruber, Editor; Iris Cloyd, Research Editor), published by Gale Research Company, Book Tower, Detroit, Mich. 48226, available in most public libraries.

Abortion Federation, National (1977): 1436 U St. N.W., Suite 103, Washington, D.C., 20009. 285. Phone: (202) 546-9060.

Abortion Rights Action League, National (1969): 1101 14th St. N.W., Washington, D.C. 20005. 250,000. Phone: (202) 371-0779.

Accountants, American Institute of Certified Public (1887): 1211 Avenue of the Americas, New York, N.Y. 10036. 284,000. Phone: (212) 575-6200.

Accountants, National Association of (1919): 10 Paragon Dr., Montvale, N.J., 07645-1760. 85,000. Phone: (201) 573-9000.

ACME, Inc.—The association of management consulting firms (1929): 230 Park Ave., New York, N.Y. 10169. 60 firms. Phone: (212) 697-9693.

Acoustical Society of America (1929): 500 Sunnyside Blvd., Woodbury, N.Y. 11797. 6,200. Phone: (516) 349-7800.

Actors' Equity Association (1913): 165 W. 46th St., New York, N.Y. 10036. Phone: (212) 869-8530.

Actuaries, Society of (1949): 475 N. Martingale Rd., Suite 800, Schaumburg, Ill. 60173-2226. 10,800. Phone: (312) 706-3500.

Adirondack Mountain Club (1922): RD 3, Box 3055, Luzerne Rd., Lake George, N.Y. 12845. 16,000. Phone: (518) 668-4447.

Aeronautic Association, National (1905): 1763 R St. N.W., Washington, D.C. 20009. 250,000. Phone: (202) 265-8720.

Aeronautics and Astronautics, American Institute of (1932): 370 L'Enfant Promenade S.W., Washington, D.C. 20024. 42,000. Phone: (202) 646-7400.

Aerospace Industries Association of America (1919): 1250 Eye St. N.W., Washington, D.C. 20005. 50 companies. Phone: (202) 371-8400.

Aerospace Medical Association (1929): 320 S. Henry St., Alexandria, Va. 22314-3524. 4,500. Phone: (703) 739-2240.

African-American Institute, The (1953): 833 United Nations Plaza, New York, N.Y. 10017. Phone: (212) 949-5666.

Afro-American Life and History, Association for the Study of (1915): 1407 14th St. N.W., Washington, D.C. 20005. 2,000. Phone: (202) 667-2822.

AFS Intercultural Programs (1947): 313 E. 43rd St., New York, N.Y. 10017. 100,000. Phone: (212) 949-4242 or (800) AFS-INFO.

Aging Association, American (1970): Univ. of Nebraska Medical Center, 42nd and Dewey Ave., Omaha, Neb. 68105. 500. Phone: (402) 559-4416.

Agricultural Engineers, American Society of (1907): 2950 Niles Rd., St. Joseph, Mich. 49085. 12,000. Phone: (616) 429-0300.

Agricultural History Society (1919): 1301 New York Ave. N.W., Washington, D.C. 20005. 1,400. Phone: (202) 786-3307.

Agronomy, American Society of (1907): 677 S. Segoe Rd., Madison, Wis. 53711-1086. 13,000. Phone: (608) 273-8080.

Air & Waste Management Association (formerly APCA) (1907): P.O. Box 2861, Pittsburgh, Pa. 15230. 10,000. Phone: (412) 232-3444.

Aircraft Association, Experimental (1953): Wittman Field, Oshkosh, Wis. 54903-3086. 125,000. Phone: (414) 426-4800.

Aircraft Owners and Pilots Association (1939): 421 Aviation Way, Frederick, Md. 21701. 290,000. Phone: (301) 695-2000.

Air Force Association (1946): 1501 Lee Highway, Arlington, Va., 22209. 231,000. Phone: (703) 247-5800.

Air Line Pilots Association (1931): 1625 Massachusetts Ave. N.W., Washington, D.C. 20036 and 535 Herndon Pkwy., Herndon, Va. 22070. 41,000. Phone: (703) 689-2270.

Air Transport Association of America (1936): 1709 New York Ave. N.W., Washington, D.C. 20006. 21 airlines. Phone: (202) 626-4000.

Al-Anon Family Group Headquarters, Inc. (1951): P.O. Box 862, Midtown Station, New York, N.Y. 10018-0862. 29,301 groups worldwide. Phone: (800) 356-9996.

Alcoholics Anonymous (1935): P.O. Box 459, Grand Central Station, New York, N.Y. 10163. 1,800,000. Address communications to General Service Office. Phone: (212) 686-1100.

Alcoholism, National Council on (1944): 12 W. 21st St., New York, N.Y. 10010. 190 affiliates. Phone: (212) 206-6770.

`Alcohol Problems, American Council on** (1895): 3426 Bridgeland Dr., Bridgeton, Mo. 63044. 3,500. Phone: (314) 739-5944.

Alexander Graham Bell Association for the Deaf (1890): 3417 Volta Place N.W., Washington, D.C. 20007. 6,000. Phone: (202) 337-5220.

Allergy and Immunology, American Academy of (1943): 611 E. Wells St., Milwaukee, Wis. 53202. 4,045. Phone: (414) 272-6071.

Alzheimer's Disease and Related Disorders Association, Inc., (1980): 70 E. Lake St., Chicago, Ill. 60601-5997. 200 Chapters and Affiliates, over 1,500 Family Support Groups. Toll-free information: 1-800-621-0379; in Illinois: 1 (800) 572-6037.

American Federation of Labor and Congress of Industrial Organizations (AFL-CIO) (1955): 815 16th St. N.W., Washington, D.C. 20006. 14,100,000. Phone: (202) 637-5010.

American Film and Video Association (formerly Educational Film Library Assn.) (1943): 920 Barnsdale Rd., Suite 152, La Grange Park, Ill. 60525. 1,400. Phone: (312) 482-4000.

American Friends Service Committee (1917): 1501 Cherry St., Philadelphia, Pa. 19102. Phone:

(215) 241-7000.

American Historical Association (1884): 400 A St. S.E., Washington, D.C. 20003. 15,000. Phone: (202) 544-2422.

American Indian Affairs, Association on (1923): 95 Madison Ave., New York, N.Y. 10016. 35,000. Phone: (212) 689-8720.

American Legion, The (1919): P.O. Box 1055, Indianapolis, Ind. 46206. 2,900,000. Phone: (317) 635-8411.

American Legion Auxiliary (1919): 777 N. Meridian St., Indianapolis, Ind. 46204. 950,000. Phone: (317) 635-6291.

American Mensa, Ltd. (1945): 2626 E. 14th St., Brooklyn, N.Y. 11235-3992. Phone: (718) 934-3700.

American Montessori Society (1960): 150 Fifth Ave., New York, N.Y. 10011. 12,000. Phone: (212) 924-3209.

American Planning Association (1978): 1776 Massachusetts Ave. N.W., Washington, D.C. 20036 (headquarters). 23,000. Phone: (202) 872-0611. Membership office: 1313 E. 60th St., Chicago, Ill. 60637. (312) 955-9100.

Americans for Democratic Action, Inc. (1947): 1511 "K" St. N.W., Suite 941, Washington, D.C. 20005. 40,000. Phone: (202) 638-6447.

American Society for Public Administration (ASPA) (1939): 1120 G St. N.W., Suite 500, Washington, D.C. 20005. 16,000. Phone: (202) 393-7878.

American Society of CLU & ChFC (1928): 270 Bryn Mawr Ave., Bryn Mawr, Pa. 19010. Phone: (215) 526-2500.

*****American States, Organization of** (1948): General Secretariat, Washington, D.C. 20006. 32 countries. Phone: (202) 458-3000.

American Universities, Association of (1900): One Dupont Circle N.W., Suite 730, Washington, D.C. 20036. Phone: (202) 466-5030.

AMIDEAST (America-Mideast Educational and Training Services) (1951): 1100 17th St. N.W., Washington, D.C. 20036-4601. 200. Phone: (202) 785-0022.

Amnesty International/USA (1961): 322 Eighth Ave., New York, N.Y. 10001. 355,000. Phone: (212) 807-8400.

AMVETS (American Veterans of World War II, Korea, and Vietnam) (1944): 4647 Forbes Blvd., Lanham, Md. 20706. 200,000. Phone: (301) 459-9600.

*****AMVETS National Auxiliary** (1946): 4647 Forbes Blvd., Lanham, Md. 20706. 75,000. Phone: (301) 459-6255.

Animal Protection Institute of America (1968): 2831 Fruitridge Rd., P.O. Box 22505, Sacramento, Calif. 95822. Phone: (916) 731-5521.

Animals, Fund For (1967): 200 W. 57th St., New York, N.Y. 10019. 175,000. Phone: (212) 246-2096.

Animals, The American Society for the Prevention of Cruelty to (ASPCA) (1866): 441 E. 92nd St., New York, N.Y. 10128. 300,000. Phone: (212) 876-7700..

Animal Welfare Institute (1951): P.O. Box 3650, Washington, D.C. 20007. 8,600. Phone: (202) 337-2332.

Anthropological Association, American (1902): 1703 New Hampshire Ave. N.W., Washington, D.C. 20009. 10,970. Phone: (202) 232-8800.

Anti-Defamation League of B'nai B'rith (1913): 823 United Nations Plaza, New York, N.Y. 10017. Phone: (212) 490-2525.

Antiquarian Society, American (1812): 185 Salisbury St., Worcester, Mass. 01609. 522. Phone: (508) 755-5221.

Anti-Vivisection Society, The American (1883): Suite 204, Noble Plaza, 801 Old York Rd., Jenkintown, Pa. 19046. 15,000. Phone: (215) 887-0816.

Appraisers, American Society of (1936): P.O. Box 17265, Washington, D.C. 20041. 5,500. Phone: (703) 478-2228.

Arbitration Association, American (1926): 140 W. 51st St., New York, N.Y. 10020. 5,500. Phone: (212) 484-4000.

Arboriculture, International Society of (1924): 303 W. University, Urbana, Ill. 61801-1746. 5,200. Phone: (217) 328-2032.

Archaeological Institute of America (1879): 675 Commonwealth Ave., Boston, Mass. 02215. 8,000. Phone: (617) 353-9361.

Archaeology, Institute of Nautical (1973): Texas A&M University, Drawer HG, College Station, Tex. 77841. 850. Phone: (409) 845-6694.

Architects, American Institute of (1857): 1735 New York Ave. N.W., Washington, D.C. 20006. 54,000. Phone: (202) 626-7300.

Architectural Historians, Society of (1940): 1232 Pine St., Philadelphia, Pa. 19107. 4,000. Phone: (215) 735-0224.

Army, Association of the United States (1950): 2425 Wilson Blvd., Arlington, Va. 22210-0860. 150,000. Phone: (703) 841-4300.

Arthritis Foundation (1948): 1314 Spring St., N.W., Atlanta, Ga. 30309. 72 local chapters. Phone: (404) 872-7100.

Arts, National Endowment for the (1965): 1100 Pennsylvania Ave. N.W., Washington, D.C. 20506. Phone: (202) 682-5400.

Arts, The American Federation of (1909): 41 E. 65th St., New York, N.Y. 10021. 1,400. Phone: (212) 988-7700. Museum Services Division: 270 Sutter St., San Francisco, Calif. 94108. Phone: (415) 392-9222.

Arts and Letters, American Academy and Institute of (1898): 633 W. 155th St., New York, N.Y. 10032. 250. Phone: (212) 368-5900.

ASM International (1913): Metals Park, Ohio 44073. 54,000. Phone: (216) 338-5151.

Astronomical Society, American (1899): Astronomy Program, University of Maryland, College Park, Md. 20742. 4,600. Phone: (301) 454-3001.

Atheists, American (1963): P.O. Box 2117, Austin, Tex. 78714-0195. 40,000 Families. Phone: (512) 458-1244.

Auctioneers Association, National (1949): 8880 Ballentine, Overland Park, Kan. 66214. 6,000. Phone: (913) 541-8084.

Audubon Society, National (1905): 950 Third Ave., New York, N.Y. 10022. 546,000. Phone: (212) 832-3200.

Authors League of America (1912): 234 W. 44th St., New York, N.Y. 10036. 14,000. Phone: (212) 391-9198.

Autism Society of America (1965): 1234 Massachusetts Ave. N.W., Washington, D.C. 20005. 7,000. Phone: (202) 783-0125.

Automobile Association, American (1902): 8111 Gatehouse Rd., Falls Church, Va. 22047. 30,000,000. Phone: (703) 222-6000.

Automobile Club, National (1924): Bayside Plaza, 188 The Embarcadero, #300, San Francisco, Calif. 94105. 300,000. Phone: (415) 777-4000.

Automobile Dealers Association, National (1917): 8400 Westpark Dr., McLean, Va. 22102. 20,

000. Phone: (703) 821-7100.

Automotive Engineers, Inc., Society of (1905): 400 Commonwealth Dr., Warrendale, Pa. 15096. 55,000. Phone: (412) 776-4841.

Automotive Hall of Fame (1939): P.O. Box 1727, Midland, Mich. 48641-1727. Phone: (517) 631-5760.

Bar Association, American (1878): 750 N. Lake Shore Dr., Chicago, Ill. 60611. 360,000. Phone: (312) 988-5000.

*****Bar Association, Federal** (1920): 1815 H St. N.W., Suite 408, Washington, D.C. 20006-3697. 15,000. Phone: (202) 638-0252.

Barber Shop Quartet Singing in America, Society for the Preservation and Encouragement of (1938): 6315 Third Ave., Kenosha, Wis., 53140-5199. 38,000. Phone: (414) 654-9111.

Better Business Bureaus, Council of (1970): 1515 Wilson Blvd., Arlington, Va. 22209. Phone: (703) 276-0100.

Bible Society, American (1816): 1865 Broadway, New York, N.Y. 10023. 320,000. Phone: (212) 581-7400.

Biblical Literature, Society of (1880): 819 Houston Mill Rd. N.E., Atlanta, Ga. 30329. Phone: (404) 636-4744.

Bibliographical Society of America (1904): P.O. Box 397, Grand Central Station, New York, N.Y. 10163. 1,400. Phone: (212) 481-9698.

Bide-A-Wee Home Association, Inc. (1903): 410 E. 38th St., New York, N.Y. 10016. 26,000. Phone: (212) 532-4455.

Big Brothers/Big Sisters of America (1977): 230 N. 13th St., Philadelphia, Pa. 19107. Phone: (215) 567-7000.

Biochemistry and Molecular Biology, American Society for (1906): 9650 Rockville Pike, Bethesda, Md. 20814. 8,000. Phone: (301) 530-7145.

Biological Sciences, American Institute of (1947): 730 11th St. N.W., Washington, D.C. 20001-4584. 12,500. Phone: (202) 628-1500.

Blind, American Council of the (1961): 1010 Vermont Ave. N.W., Suite 1100, Washington, D.C. 20005. 20,000. Phone: (202) 393-3666.

Blind, National Federation of the (1940): 1800 Johnson St., Baltimore, Md. 21230. 50,000. Phone: (301) 659-9314.

Blindness, National Society to Prevent (1908): 500 E. Remington Rd., Schaumburg, Ill. 60173-4557. 26 affiliates. Phone: (312) 843-2020.

Blindness, Research to Prevent (1960): 598 Madison Ave., New York, N.Y. 10022. 3,300. Phone: (212) 752-4333.

Blue Cross and Blue Shield Association (1946 and 1948): 676 N. St. Clair St., Chicago, Ill. 60611. 75 Plans. Phone: (312) 440-5955.

B'nai B'rith International (1843): 1640 Rhode Island Ave. N.W., Washington, D.C. 20036. 500,000. Phone: (202) 857-6500.

Booksellers Association, American (1900): 137 W. 25th St., New York, N.Y. 10001. 7,300. Phone: (212) 463-8450.

Botanical Gardens & Arboreta, American Association of (1971): P.O. Box 206, Swarthmore, Pa. 19081. 1,100. Phone: (215) 328-9145.

Boys Clubs of America (1906): 771 First Ave., New York, N.Y. 10017. 1,300,000. Phone: (212) 351-5900.

Boy Scouts of America (1910): 1325 Walnut Hill Lane, P.O. Box 152079, Irving, Tex. 75015-2079. 5,339,184. Phone: (214) 580-2000.

Bridge, Tunnel, and Turnpike Association, International (1932): 2120 L St. N.W., Suite 305, Washington, D.C. 20037. 215 agencies. Phone: (202) 659-4620.

*****Bridge League, American Contract** (1927): 2200 Democrat Rd., Memphis, Tenn. 38132. 200,000. Phone: (901) 332-5586.

Broadcasters, National Association of (1922): 1771 N St. N.W., Washington, D.C. 20036. 5,970. Phone: (202) 429-5300.

Brookings Institution, The (1927): 1775 Massachusetts Ave. N.W., Washington, D.C. 20036. Phone: (202) 797-6000.

Brooks Bird Club, Inc., The (1932): 707 Warwood Ave., Wheeling, W. Va. 26003. 1,000. Phone: (304) 547-5253.

*****Business Clubs, National Association of American** (1922): 3315 No. Main St., High Point, N.C. 27260. 6,800. Phone: (919) 869-2166.

Business Education Association, National (1946): 1914 Association Dr., Reston, Va. 22091. 18,000. Phone: (703) 860-8300.

*****Business Law Association, American** (1923): Dept. of Insurance, Legal Studies, and Real Estate, Univ. of Georgia, Athens, Ga. 30602. 1,200. Phone: (404) 542-3795.

Business Women's Association, American (1949): 9100 Ward Parkway, P.O. Box 8728, Kansas City, Mo. 64114. More than 100,000. Phone: (816) 361-6621.

Campers & Hikers Association, National (1949): 4804 Transit Rd., Bldg. 2, Depew, N.Y. 14043-4704. 28,000 families. Phone: (716) 668-6242.

Camp Fire, Inc. (1910): 4601 Madison Ave., Kansas City, Mo. 64112. 550,000. Phone: (816) 756-1950.

Camping Association, The American (1910): 5000 State Rd. 67 N., Martinsville, Ind. 46151. 5,500. Phone: (317) 342-8456.

Cancer Council, Inc., United (1959): 4010 W. 86th St., Suite H, Indianapolis, Ind. 46268-1704. 39 agencies. Phone: (317) 879-9900.

Cancer Society, American (1913): 1599 Clifton Rd., N.E., Atlanta Ga. 30329. 2,646,070 volunteers. Phone: (404) 320-3333.

CARE, Inc. (1945): 660 First Ave., New York, N.Y. 10016. 20 agencies plus 25 public members. Phone: (212) 686-3110.

Carnegie Endowment for International Peace (1910): 11 Du Pont Circle N.W., Washington, D.C. 20036. Phone: (202) 797-6400.

Cartoonists Society, National (1946): 9 Ebony Court, Brooklyn, N.Y. 11229. 450. Phone: (718) 743-6510.

*****Catholic Bishops, National Conference of** (1966): 1312 Massachusetts Ave. N.W., Washington, D.C. 20005. Phone: (202) 659-6774.

Catholic Charities USA (1910): 1319 F St. N.W., Washington, D.C. 20004. 4,000 individuals, 633 agencies and institutions. Phone: (202) 639-8400.

*****Catholic Conference, United States** (1966): 1312 Massachusetts Ave. N.W., Washington, D.C. 20005. Phone: (202) 659-6600.

Catholic Daughters of the Americas (1903): 10 W. 71st St., New York, N.Y. 10023. 155,000. Phone: (212) 877-3041.

Catholic Historical Society, American (1884): 263 S. Fourth St., Philadelphia, Pa. 19106. 950. Phone: (215) 925-5752.

Catholic War Veterans of the U.S.A. Inc. (1935): 419 N. Lee St., Alexandria, Va. 22314. 30,000. Phone: (703) 549-3622.

Ceramic Society, Inc., The American (1899): 757 Brooksedge Plaza Dr., Westerville, Ohio 43081-6136. Phone: (614) 890-4700; FAX (614) 899-6109; TWA: 7101109409.

Cerebral Palsy Associations, Inc., United (1949): 7 Penn Plaza, Suite 804, New York, N.Y. 10001. 180 affiliates. Phone: 1 (800) USA IUCP.

Chamber of Commerce of the U.S. (1912): 1615 H St. N.W., Washington, D.C. 20062. 180,000. Phone: (202) 659-6000.

Chemical Engineers, American Institute of (1908): 345 E. 47th St., New York, N.Y. 10017. 50,000. Phone: (212) 705-7338.

Chemical Manufacturers Association, Inc. (1872): 2501 M St. N.W., Washington, D.C. 20037. 175 companies. Phone: (202) 887-1100.

Chemical Society, American (1876): 1155 16th St. N.W., Washington, D.C. 20036. 137,500. Phone: (202) 872-4600.

Chemists, American Institute of (1923): 7315 Wisconsin Ave., Bethesda, Md. 20814. 7,000. Phone: (301) 652-2447.

Chess Federation, United States (1939): 186 Rt. 9W, New Windsor, N.Y. 12550. 60,000. Phone: (914) 562-8350.

Child Labor Committee, National (1904): 1501 Broadway, Rm. 1111, New York, N.Y. 10036. Phone: (212) 840-1801.

Children, American Association for Protecting (a Div. of the American Humane Association) (1877): 9725 E. Hampden, Denver, Colo. 80231. Phone: (303) 695-0811.

Children's Aid Society, The (1853): 105 E. 22nd St., New York, N.Y. 10010. 1,207. Phone: (212) 949-4800.

Children's Book Council (1945): 67 Irving Place, New York, N.Y. 10003. 61 publishing houses. Phone: (212) 254-2666.

Children Under Six, Southern Association on (1948): Box 5403, Brady Station, Little Rock, Ark. 72215. 15,500. Phone: (501) 663-0353.

Child Welfare League of America (1920): 440 First St. N.W., Suite 310, Washington, D.C. 20001. Phone: (202) 638-2952.

Chiropractic Association, American (1963): 1701 Clarendon Blvd., Arlington, Va. 22209. 21,300. Phone: (703) 276-8800.

Christians and Jews, National Conference of (1928): 71 Fifth Ave., New York, N.Y. 10003. 200,000. Phone: (212) 206-0006.

Churches of Christ in the USA, National Council of the (1950): 475 Riverside Drive, New York, N.Y. 10115. 32 Protestant and Orthodox communions. Phone: (212) 870-2200.

Cities, National League of (1924): 1301 Pennsylvania Ave. N.W., Washington, D.C. 20004. 16,000 cities and towns. Phone: (202) 626-3000.

Civil Air Patrol (1941): Maxwell AFB, Ala. 36112-5572. 72,000. Phone: (205) 293-7593.

Civil Engineers, American Society of (1852): 345 E. 47th St., New York, N.Y. 10017. 102,345. Phone: (212) 705-7496.

Civil Liberties Union, American (1920): 132 W. 43rd St., New York, N.Y. 10036. 275,000. Phone: (212) 944-9800.

Clinical Chemistry, Inc., American Association for (1948): 2029 K St., N.W., 7th Floor, Washington, D.C. 20006. 9,000. Phone (202) 857-0717.

Clinical Pathologists, American Society of (1922): 2100 W. Harrison St., Chicago, Ill. 60612. 34,000. Phone: (312) 738-1336.

Collectors Association, American (1939): Box 35106, Minneapolis, Minn. 55435-0106. Over 3,400 debt collection agencies. Phone: (612) 926-6547.

College Board, The (1900): 45 Columbus Ave., New York, N.Y. 10023. 2,600 institutions. Phone: (212) 713-8000.

College Placement Council (1956): 62 E. Highland Ave., Bethlehem, Pa. 18017. 2,800. Phone: (215) 868-1421.

***Colleges, Association of American** (1915): 1818 R St. N.W., Washington, D.C. 20009. 613 institutions. Phone: (202) 387-3760.

***Colored Women's Clubs, National Association of** (1896): 5808 16th St. N.W., Washington, D.C. 20011. 40,000. Phone: (202) 726-2044.

Common Cause (1970): 2030 M St. N.W., Washington, D.C. 20036. 280,000. Phone: (202) 833-1200.

Community and Junior Colleges, American Association of (1920): One Dupont Circle N.W., Suite 410, Washington, D.C. 20036-1176. 1,086 institutions. Phone: (202) 293-7050.

Community Cultural Center Association, American (1978): 19 Foothills Dr., Pompton Plains, N.J. 07444. Phone: (201) 835-2661.

Composers, Authors, and Publishers, American Society of (ASCAP) (1914): One Lincoln Plaza, New York, N.Y. 10023. 40,000. Phone: (212) 595-3050.

Composers/USA, National Association of (1932): P.O. Box 49652, Barrington Station, Los Angeles, Calif. 90049. 550. Phone: (213) 541-8213.

Concerned Scientists, Union of (1969): 26 Church St., Cambridge, Mass. 02238. Phone: (617) 547-5552.

Congress of Racial Equality (CORE) (1942): 1457 Flatbush Ave., Brooklyn, N.Y. 11210. Nationwide network of chapters. Phone: (718) 434-3580.

***Conscientious Objectors, Central Committee for** (1948): 2208 South St., Philadelphia, Pa. 19146. Phone: (215) 545-4626.

Conservation Engineers, Association of (1961): Alabama Dept. of Cons. & Natural Resources, Engineering Section, 64 N. Union St., Montgomery, Ala 36130. Phone: (205) 261-3476.

Consulting Chemists & Chemical Engineers, Inc., Association of (1928): 310 Madison Ave., Rm. 1423, New York, N.Y. 10017. 130. Phone: (212) 983-3160.

Consumer Federation of America (1968): 1424 16th St. N.W., Washington, D.C. 20036. 240 member organizations. Phone: (202) 387-6121.

Consumer Interests, American Council on (1953): 240 Stanley Hall, Univ. of Missouri, Columbia, Mo. 65211. 1,800. Phone: (314) 882-3817.

Consumers League, National (1899): 815 15th St. N.W., Suite 516, Washington, D.C. 20005. Phone: (202) 639-8140.

Consumers Union (1936): 256 Washington St., Mt. Vernon, N.Y. 10553. 3,800,000 subscribers to *Consumer Reports*. Phone: (914) 667-9400.

Cooperative Business Association, National (formerly Cooperative League of the U.S.A) (1916): 1401 New York Ave. N.W., Suite 1100, Washington, D.C. 20005. Phone: (202) 638-6222.

Counselors and Family Therapists, National Academy of (1972): 55 Morris Ave., Springfield, N.J. 07081-1422. Phone: (201) 379-7496.

Country Music Association (1958): Box 22299, Nashville, Tenn. 37202. 8,000. Phone: (615) 244-2840.

Credit Association, International (1912): P.O. Box 27357, St. Louis, Mo. 63141-1757. 13,000. Phone: (314) 991-3030.

Credit Management, National Association of (1896): 8815 Centre Park Dr., Suite 200, Columbia, Md. 21045. Phone: (301) 740-5560.

Credit Union National Association (1934): P.O. Box 431, Madison, Wis. 53701. 52 state leagues representing 16,000 credit unions. Phone: (608)

231-4000.

Crime and Delinquency, National Council on (1907): 77 Maiden Lane, San Francisco, Calif. 94108. Nationwide membership. Phone: (415) 956-5651.

Criminal Investigators Association, International (ICIA) (1982): P.O. Box 15350, Chevy Chase, Md. 20815. 1,000. Phone: (202) 293-9088.

*CSA/USA, Celiac Sprue Association/United States of America: 2313 Rocklyn Dr. #1, Des Moines, Iowa 50322. 6 regions in U.S., 18 chapters, 50 active resource units. Phone: (515) 270-9689.

Dairy Council, National (1915): 6300 N. River Rd., Rosemont, Ill. 60018. Phone: (312) 696-1020.

Daughters of the American Revolution, National Society (1890): 1776 D St. N.W., Washington, D.C. 20006. 200,000. Phone: (202) 628-1776.

Daughters of the Confederacy, United (1894): 328 N. Boulevard, Richmond, Va. 23220-4057. 27,000. Phone: (804) 355-1636.

Deaf, National Association of the (1880): 814 Thayer Ave., Silver Spring, Md. 20910. Phone: (301) 587-1788.

Defenders of Wildlife (1947): 1244 19th St. N.W., Washington, D.C. 20036. 80,000. Phone: (202) 659-9510.

Defense Preparedness Association, American (1919): Rosslyn Center, Suite 900, 1700 N. Moore St., Arlington, Va. 22209. 45,000 individual, 1,000 corporate. Phone: (703) 522-1820.

*Democratic Club, National (1834): The 60 East Club, 60 E. 42nd St., New York, N.Y. 10165. Phone: (212) 689-1313.

Dental Association, American (1859): 211 E. Chicago Ave., Chicago, Ill. 60611. 145,000. Phone: (312) 440-2500.

Diabetes Association, American (1940): 1660 Duke St., Alexandria, Va. 22314. Phone: (703) 549-1500.

Dignity (1969): 1500 Massachusetts Ave. N.W., Suite 11, Washington, D.C. 20005. 5,000. Phone: (202) 861-0017.

Disabled American Veterans (1920): 807 Maine Ave. S.W., Washington, D.C. 20024. Phone: (202) 554-3501.

Dowsers, Inc., The American Society of (1961): Danville, Vt. 05828. 3,500. Phone: (802) 684-3417.

Drug, Chemical, & Allied Trades Association, Inc., The (1890): 2 Roosevelt Ave., Syosset, N.Y. 11791. 504. Phone (516) 496-3317.

Ducks Unlimited, Inc. (1937): One Waterfowl Way, Long Grove, Ill. 60047. 550,000. Phone: (708) 438-4300.

Earthwatch (1970): 680 Mt. Auburn St., Box 403, Watertown, Mass. 02272. 40,000. Phone: (617) 926-8200.

Eastern Star, Order of, General Grand Chapter (1876): 1618 New Hampshire Ave. N.W., Washington, D.C. 20009. 2,500,000. Phone: (202) 667-4737.

Easter Seal Society, The National (1921): 70 E. Lake St., Chicago, Ill. 60601. 58 affiliated state societies and Puerto Rico. Phone: (312) 726-4258.

Economic Association, American (1885): 1313 21st Ave. So., Nashville, Tenn. 37212. 20,000 members, 5,500 inst. subscribers. Phone: (615) 322-2595.

Economic Development, Committee for (1942): 477 Madison Ave., New York, N.Y. 10022. 250 trustees. Phone: (212) 688-2063.

Edison Electric Institute (1933): 1111 19th St.

N.W., Washington, D.C. 20036-3691. 180. Phone: (202) 778-6400.

Education, American Council on (1918): One Dupont Circle N.W., Washington, D.C. 20036. 1,650 institutional members. Phone: (202) 939-9300.

Education, Council for Advancement and Support of (1974): 11 Dupont Circle N.W., Suite 400, Washington, D.C. 20036. 13,500. Phone: (202) 328-5900.

Educational Exchange, International, Council on (1947): 205 E. 42nd St., New York, N.Y. 10017. 198. Phone: (212) 661-1414.

Educational Research Association, American (1906): 1230 17th St. N.W., Washington, D.C. 20036. 15,000. Phone: (202) 223-9485.

Education Association, National (1857): 1201 16th St. N.W., Washington, D.C. 20036-3290. 1.8 million. Phone: (202) 833-4000.

Electrochemical Society, The (1902): 10 S. Main St., Pennington, N.J. 08534. 6,274. Phone: (609) 737-1902.

Electronic Industries Association (1924): 2001 Eye St. N.W., Washington, D.C. 20006. 1,000 member companies. Phone: (202) 457-4900.

Electroplaters and Surface Finishers Society, American (1909): 12644 Research Pkwy., Orlando, Fla. 32826. 10,000. Phone: (407) 281-6441.

Elks of the U.S.A., Benevolent and Protective Order of the (1868): 2750 Lake View Ave., Chicago, Ill. 60614. 1,500,000. Phone: (312) 477-2750.

Energy Engineers, Association of (1978): 4025 Pleasantdale Rd., Suite 420, Atlanta, Ga. 30340. 6,500. Phone: (404) 447-5083.

English-Speaking Union of the United States (1920): 16 E. 69th St., New York, N.Y. 10021. 25,000. Phone: (212) 879-6800.

Entomological Society of America (1889): 9301 Annapolis Rd., Lanham, Md. 20706. 9,000. Phone: (301) 731-4535.

Exceptional Children, The Council for (1922): 1920 Association Dr., Reston, Va. 22091. 53,000. Phone: (703) 620-3660.

Experimental Test Pilots, The Society of (1956): 44814 Elm St., Lancaster, Calif. 93534. 1,800. Phone: (805) 942-9574.

Exploration Geophysicists, Society of (1930): P.O. Box 702740, Tulsa, Okla. 74170. 15,000. Phone: (918) 493-3516.

Family Physicians, American Academy of (1947): 8880 Ward Pkwy., Kansas City, Mo. 64114. 65,000. Phone: (816) 333-9700.

Family Relations, National Council on (1938): 1910 W. County Rd. B, Suite 147, St. Paul, Minn. 55113. 4,000. Phone: (612) 633-6933.

Family Service America (1911): 11700 W. Lake Park Dr., Park Place, Milwaukee, Wis. 53224. Approx. 300 member agencies. Phone: (414) 359-2111.

Farm Bureau Federation, American (1919): 225 Touhy Ave., Park Ridge, Ill. 60068. 3.7 million member families. Phone: (312) 399-5700.

Farmer Cooperatives, National Council of (1929): 50 F St. N.W., Washington, D.C. 20001. 165. Phone: (202) 626-8700.

Federal Employees, National Federation of (1917): 1016 16th St. N.W., Washington, D.C. 20036. Rep. 150,000. Phone: (202) 862-4400.

Feline and Canine Friends, Inc. (1973): 505 N. Bush St., Anaheim, Calif. 92805. 1,000. Phone: (714) 635-7975.

Fellowship of Reconciliation (1915): Box 271, Nyack, N.Y. 10960. 35,000. Phone: (914) 358-

4601.

Female Executives, National Association for (1972): 127 W. 24th St., New York, N.Y. 10011. 190,000. Phone: (212) 645-0770.

FFA Organization, National (1928): 5632 Mt. Vernon Memorial Hwy., P.O. Box 15160, Alexandria, Va. 22309-0160. 404,900. Phone: (703) 360-3600.

Financial Analysts Federation (1947): 1633 Broadway, 16th floor, New York, N.Y. 10019. 17,500. Phone: (212) 957-2860.

Fire Protection Association, National (1896): Batterymarch Park, Quincy, Mass. 02269. 52,000. Phone: (617) 770-3000.

Flag Foundation, National (1968): Flag Plaza, Pittsburgh, Pa. 15219. 3,000+. Phone: (412) 261-1776.

Fleet Reserve Association (1924): 1303 New Hampshire Ave. N.W., Washington, D.C. 20036. 160,000. Phone: (202) 785-2768.

Flight Test Engineers, Society of (1968): P.O. Box 4047, Lancaster, Calif. 93539. 1,100. Phone: (805) 948-3067.

Flying Saucer Clubs of America, Amalgamated (1959): P.O. Box 39, Yucca Valley, Calif. 92286. 5,600. Phone: (619) 365-1141.

Foreign Policy Association (1918): 729 Seventh Ave., New York, N.Y. 10019. Phone: (212) 764-4050.

Foreign Relations, Council on (1921): 58 E. 68th St., New York, N.Y. 10021. 2,400. Phone: (212) 734-0400.

Foreign Student Affairs, National Association for (1948): 1860 19th St. N.W., Washington, D.C. 20009. 6,200. Phone: (202) 462-4811.

Foreign Study, American Institute for (1965): 102 Greenwich Ave., Greenwich, Conn. 06830. 325,000. Phone: (203) 869-9090.

Foreign Trade Council, Inc., National (1914): 100 E. 42nd St., New York, N.Y. 10017. Over 550 companies. Phone: (212) 867-5630. Also, 1625 K St. N.W., Washington, D.C. 20006. Phone: (202) 887-0278.

Forensic Sciences, American Academy of (1948): 218 E. Cache La Poudre/80903, P.O. Box 669, Colorado Springs, Colo. 80901-0669. 3,200. Phone: (719) 636-1100.

Forest Council, American (1932): 1250 Connecticut Ave. N.W., Suite 320, Washington, D.C. 20036. 100. Phone: (202) 463-2455.

Foresters, Society of American (1900): 5400 Grosvenor Lane, Bethesda, Md. 20814. 20,000. Phone: (301) 897-8720.

Forestry Association, American (1875): 1516 P St. N.W., Washington, D.C. 20005. 27,000. Phone: (202) 667-3300.

Fortean Organization, International (1965): P.O. Box 367, Arlington, Va. 22210-0367. 800. Phone: (703) 522-9232.

Foster Parents Plan International (1937). Box 804, East Greenwich, R.I. 02818. Phone: (401) 826-2500.

Foundrymen's Society, Inc., American (1896): Golf & Wolf Rds., Des Plaines, Ill. 60016-2277. 14,000. Phone: (312) 824-0181; or 1 (800) 537-4AFS.

4-H Program (early 1900s): Room 3860-S, U.S. Department of Agriculture, Washington, D.C. 20250. 4,300,000. Phone: (202) 447-5853.

Freedom of Information Center (1958): Box 858, Univ. of Missouri-Columbia, Columbia, Mo. 65205. Phone: (314) 882-4856.

French-American Chamber of Commerce in the U.S. Inc. (1896): 509 Madison Ave., Suite 1900,

New York, N.Y. 10022. 605. Trade Association. Phone: (212) 371-4466.

French Institute/Alliance Française (1911): 22 E. 60th St., New York, N.Y. 10022. 8,500. Phone: (212) 355-6100.

Friendship and Good Will, International Society of (Esperanto) (1978): 211 W. Fourth Ave., P.O. Box 2637, Gastonia, N.C. 28053-2637. 3,850 in 162 countries. Phone: (704) 864-7906.

Friends of Animals Inc. (1957): P.O. Box 1244, Norwalk, Conn. 06856. 104,000. Phone: (203) 866-5223. For low-cost spay/neuter info. call: 1 (800) 631-2212.

*Friends of the Earth (1969): 530 Seventh St. S.E., Washington, D.C. 20003. 18,000. Phone: (202) 543-4312.

Future Homemakers of America, Inc. (1945): 1910 Association Dr., Reston, Va. 22091. 285,000. Phone: (703) 476-4900.

Gamblers Anonymous: Box 17173, Los Angeles, Calif. 90017. Phone: (213) 386-8789.

Genealogical Society, National (1903): 4527 17th St. N., Arlington, Va. 22207. 10,000. Phone: (703) 525-0050.

Genetic Association, American (1903): P.O. Box 39, Buckeystown, Md. 21717. 1,600. Phone: (301) 695-9292.

Geographers, Association of American (1904): 1710 16th St. N.W., Washington, D.C. 20009. 6,000. Phone: (202) 234-1450.

Geographical Society, The American (1851): 156 Fifth Ave., Suite 600, New York, N.Y. 10010. 7,002. Phone: (212) 242-0214.

Geographic Education, National Council for (1915): Indiana University of Pennsylvania, Indiana, Pa. 15705. 3,200. Phone: (412) 357-6290.

Geographic Society, National (1888): 17th and M Sts. N.W., Washington, D.C. 20036. 10,500,000. Phone: (202) 857-7000.

Geological Institute, American (1948): 4220 King St., Alexandria, Va. 22302. 19 member societies representing 70,000 geoscientists. Phone: (703) 379-2480.

Geological Society of America, Inc. (1888): 3300 Penrose Pl., P.O. Box 9140, Boulder, Colo. 80301. 17,200. Phone: (303) 447-2020.

Geriatrics Society, American (1942): 770 Lexington Ave., Suite 400, New York, N.Y. 10021. 5,500. Phone: (212) 308-1414.

Gideons International, The (1889): 2900 Lebanon Rd., Nashville, Tenn. 37214. 95,000. Phone: (615) 883-8533.

Gifted, The Association for the (1958): The Council for Exceptional Children, 1920 Association Dr., Reston, Va. 22091. 2,200. Phone: (703) 620-3660.

Girls Clubs of America (1945): 30 E. 33rd St., New York, N.Y. 10016. 250,000. Phone: (212) 689-3700.

Girl Scouts of the U.S.A. (1912): 830 Third Ave., New York, N.Y. 10022. 3,051,956. Phone: (212) 940-7500.

Graphic Artists, Society of American (1916): 32 Union Square, Rm. 1214, New York, N.Y. 10003. Phone: (212) 260-5706.

Graphoanalysis Society, International (1929): 111 N. Canal St., Chicago, Ill. 60606. 10,000. Phone: (312) 930-9446.

Gray Panthers Project Fund (1970): 311 S. Juniper St., Suite 601, Philadelphia, Pa. 19107. Over 80 chapters. Phone: (215) 545-6555.

Greenpeace U.S.A. (1979): 1436 U St. N.W., Washington, D.C. 20009. 800,000. Phone: (202) 462-1177.

Group Psychotherapy Association, American (1942): 25 E. 21st St., 6th Floor, New York, N.Y. 10010. 3,500 Phone: (212) 477-2677.

Guide Dog Foundation for the Blind, Inc. (1946): 371 E. Jericho Turnpike, Smithtown, N.Y. 11787. 1,326.. Phone: (516) 265-2121; outside N.Y. state call 1 (800) 548-4337.

Hadassah, The Women's Zionist Organization of America (1912): 50 W. 58th St., New York, N.Y. 10019. 385,000. Phone: (212) 355-7900.

Handgun Control, Inc. (1974): 1225 Eye St. N.W., Washington, D.C. 20005. 175,000. Phone: (202) 898-0792.

Health, Physical Education, Recreation, and Dance, American Alliance for (1885): 1900 Association Dr., Reston, Va. 22091. 35,000. Phone: (703) 476-3400.

Heart Association, American (1924): 7320 Greenville Ave., Dallas, Tex. 75231. 2,000,000 volunteers. Phone: (214) 373-6300.

Heating, Refrigerating, and Air-Conditioning Engineers, Inc., American Society of (1894): 1791 Tullie Circle N.E., Atlanta, Ga. 30329. 50,000. Phone: (404) 636-8400.

Helicopter Association International (1948): 1619 Duke St., Alexandria, Va. 22314-3406. Phone: (703) 683-4646.

Hemispheric Affairs, Council on (1975): 1612 20th St. N.W., Washington, D.C. 20009. Phone: (202) 745-7000.

Historians, The Organization of American (1907): Indiana Univ., 112 N. Bryan St., Bloomington, Ind. 47408. 8,500. Phone: (812) 855-7311.

Historic Preservation, National Trust for (1949): 1785 Massachusetts Ave. N.W., Washington, D.C. 20036. 250,000. Phone: (202) 673-4000.

Home Economics Association, American (1909): 1555 King St., Alexandria, Va. 22314. 26,000. Phone: 1 (800) 424-8080.

Horse Council, Inc., American (1969): 1700 K St. N.W., Washington, D.C. 20006. More than 165 organizations and 2,100 individuals. Phone: (202) 296-4031.

Horse Shows Association, Inc., American (1917): 220 E. 42nd St., New York, N.Y. 10017-5806. 47,000. Phone: (212) 972-2472.

Horticultural Association, National Junior (1935): 441 E. Pine, Freemont, Mich. 49412. 12,500. Phone: (616) 924-5237.

Horticultural Society, American (1922): Box 0105, Mt. Vernon, Va. 22121. 20,000. Phone: (703) 768-5700.

Hospital Association, American (1898): 840 N. Lake Shore Dr., Chicago, Ill. 60611. 5,900 institutions. Phone: (312) 280-6000.

Humane Association, American (1877): 9725 E. Hampden, Denver, Colo. 80231. Phone: (303) 695-0811.

Humane Society of the United States (1954): 2100 L St. N.W., Washington, D.C. 20037. 900,000. Phone: (202) 452-1100.

Humanities, National Endowment for the (1965): 1100 Pennsylvania Ave. N.W., Washington, D.C. 20506. Phone: (202) 786-0438.

Hydrogen Energy, International Association for (1975): P.O. Box 248266, Coral Gables, Fla. 33124. 2,500. Phone: (305) 284-4666.

Illustrators, Society of (1901): 128 E. 63rd St., New York, N.Y. 10021. 975. Phone: (212) 838-2560.

*Industrial Engineers, Institute of (1948): 25 Technology Park/Atlanta, Norcross, Ga. 30092. 41,000. Phone: (404) 449-0460.

Interfraternity Conference, National (1909): 3901 W. 86th St., Suite 390, Indianapolis, Ind. 46268. 59. Phone: (317) 872-1112.

Iron and Steel Institute, American (1908): 1133 15th St. N.W., Washington, D.C. 20005-2701. 1,200. Phone: (202) 452-7100.

Izaak Walton League of America (1922): 1401 Wilson Blvd., Level B, Arlington, Va. 22209. 50,000. Phone: (703) 528-1818.

Jaycees, The United States (1920): P.O. Box 7, Tulsa, Okla. 74121. 227,401. Phone: (918) 584-2481.

Jewish Appeal, United (1939): 99 Park Ave., New York, N.Y. 10016. Phone: (212) 818-9100.

Jewish Committee, American (1906): 165 E. 56th St., New York, N.Y. 10022. 50,000. Phone: (212) 751-4000.

Jewish Community Centers, World Confederation of (1946): 12 Hess St., Jerusalem, Israel 94185. Phone: (02) 231 371.

Jewish Congress, American (1918): 15 E. 84th St., New York, N.Y. 10028. 50,000. Phone: (212) 879-4500.

Jewish Historical Society, American (1892): 2 Thornton Rd., Waltham, Mass. 02154. 3,500. Phone: (617) 891-8110.

Jewish War Veterans of the U.S.A. (1896): 1811 R St. N.W., Washington, D.C. 20009. Phone: (202) 265-6280.

Jewish Women, National Council of (1893): 53 W. 23rd St., New York, N.Y. 10010. 100,000. Phone: (212) 645-4048.

John Birch Society (1958): 395 Concord Ave., Belmont, Mass. 02178. Under 100,000. Phone: (617) 489-0600.

Journalists, Society of Professional, (1909): 53 W. Jackson Blvd., Suite 731, Chicago, Ill. 60604-3610. 20,000. Phone: (312) 922-7424.

Journalists and Authors, American Society of (1948): 1501 Broadway, Suite 1907, New York, N.Y. 10036. 750. Phone: (212) 997-0947.

Judaism, American Council for (1943): P.O. Box 9009, Alexandria, Va. 22304. 10,000. Phone: (703) 836-2546.

Junior Achievement Inc. (1919): 45 Clubhouse Dr., Colorado Springs, Colo. 80906. 9,201,108. Phone: (719) 540-8000.

Junior Leagues, Inc., Association of (1921): 660 First Ave., New York, N.Y. 10016. 273 Leagues, 180,000 members. Phone: (212) 683-1515.

Junior Statesmen of America (1934): 650 Bair Island Rd., Suite 201, Redwood City, Calif. 94063. 10,000. Phone: (415) 366-2700.

JWB (1917): 15 E. 26th St., New York, N.Y. 10010-1579. 275 affiliated Jewish Community Centers, YM-YWHAs, and camps. Phone: (212) 532-4949.

Kennel Club, American (1884): 51 Madison Ave., New York, N.Y. 10010. 457 member clubs. Phone: (212) 696-8234.

Kiwanis International (1915): 3636 Woodview Trace, Indianapolis, Ind. 46268-3196. 313,000. Phone: (317) 875-8755.

Knights of Columbus (1882): One Columbus Plaza, New Haven, Conn. 06507. 1,445,745. Phone: (203) 772-2130.

Knights of Pythias, Supreme Lodge (1864): 2785 E. Desert Inn Rd. #150, Las Vegas, Nev. 89121. 104,736. Phone: (702) 735-3302.

Knights Templar, Grand Encampment of (1816): 14 E. Jackson Blvd., Suite 1700, Chicago, Ill. 60604. 340,000. Phone: (312) 427-5670.

La Leche League International (1956): 9616 Minneapolis Ave., Franklin Park, Ill. 60131-8209. 40,000. Phone: (708) 455-7730.

Law, American Society of International (1906): 2223 Massachusetts Ave. N.W., Washington, D.C. 20008. 4,500. Phone: (202) 265-4313.

***League of Women Voters of the U.S.** (1920): 1730 M St. N.W., Washington, D.C. 20036. 114,000. Phone: (202) 429-1965.

Legal Aid and Defender Association, National (1911): 1625 K St. N.W., Suite 800, Washington, D.C. 20006. 5,000. Phone: (202) 452-0620.

Legal Secretaries, National Association of (1950): 2250 E. 73rd St., Suite 550, Tulsa, Okla. 74136-6864. 18,000. Phone: (918) 493-3540.

Leukemia Society of America (1949): 733 Third Ave., New York, N.Y. 10017. Phone: (212) 573-8484.

Library Association, American (1876): 50 E. Huron St., Chicago, Ill. 60611. 48,000. Phone: (312) 944-6780.

Life Insurance, American Council of (1976): 1001 Pennsylvania Ave. N.W., Washington, D.C. 20004-2599. 630. Phone: (202) 624-2000.

Life Underwriters, National Association of (1890): 1922 F St. N.W., Washington, D.C. 20006. Phone: (202) 331-6001.

Lions Clubs International (1917): 300 22nd St., Oak Brook, Ill. 60570. 1,356,703. Phone: (312) 571-5466.

Lung Association, American (1904): 1740 Broadway, New York, N.Y. 10019-4374. 138 constituent and affiliate associations. Phone: (212) 315-8700.

Magazine Editors, American Society of (1963): 575 Lexington Ave., New York, N.Y. 10022. 650. Phone: (212) 752-0055.

Magazine Publishers of America (1919): 575 Lexington Ave., New York, N.Y. 10022. 292 member companies; 1,250 publications. Phone: (212) 752-0055.

Management Association, American (1923): 135 W. 50th St., New York, N.Y. 10020. 75,000. Phone: (212) 586-8100.

Management Consultants, Institute of (1968): 230 Park Ave., Suite 544, New York, N.Y. 10169. 2,100. Phone: (212) 697-8262.

Manufacturers, National Association of (1895): 1331 Pennsylvania Ave. N.W., Suite 1500–North Lobby, Washington, D.C. 20004-1703. 13,500. Phone: (202) 637-3065.

Manufacturers' Agents National Association (MANA) (1947): 23016 Mill Creek Rd., P.O. Box 3467, Laguna Hills, Calif. 92654. 9,000. Phone: (714) 859-4040.

March of Dimes Birth Defects Foundation (1938): 1275 Mamaroneck Ave., White Plains, N.Y. 10605. 130 chapters. Phone: (914) 428-7100.

Marine Conservation, Center for (formerly Center for Environmental Education, est. 1972): 1725 De Sales St. N.W., Suite 500, Washington, D.C. 20036. 110,000. Phone: (202) 429-5609.

Marine Corps Association (1913): Box 1775 Marine Corps Base, Quantico, Va. 22134. 102,784. Phone: (703) 640-6161.

Marine Corps League (1923): 8626 Lee Hwy., Fairfax, Va. Correspondence address: P.O. Box 3070, Merrifield, Va. 22116. 30,000. Phone: (703) 207-9588 or (703) 207-9589.

Marine Technology Society (1963): 1825 K St. N.W., Suite 203, Washington, D.C. 20006. 2,500. Phone: (202) 775-5966.

Masons, Ancient and Accepted Scottish Rite, Northern Masonic Jurisdiction, Supreme Council 33 (1867): 33 Marrett Rd., Lexington, Mass. 02173. 435,497. Phone: (617) 862-4410.

Masons, Ancient and Accepted Scottish Rite, **Southern Jurisdiction, Supreme Council** (1801): 1733 16th St. N.W., Washington, D.C. 20009. 592,753. Phone: (202) 232-3579.

Masons, Royal Arch, General Grand Chapter International (1797): 1084 New Circle Rd. N.E., Lexington, Ky. 40505. 277,340. Phone: (606) 252-4618.

Massachusetts Audubon Society (1896): South Great Rd., Lincoln, Mass. 01773. 44,000 member households. Phone: (508) 259-9500.

Mathematical Association of America (1915): 1529 18th St. N.W., Washington, D.C. 20036. 27,000. Phone: (202) 387-5200.

Mathematical Society, American (1888): P.O. Box 6248, Providence, R.I. 02940. 22,611. Phone: (401) 272-9500.

Mathematical Statistics, Institute of (1935): 3401 Investment Blvd. #7, Hayward, Calif. 94545. 3,800. Phone: (415) 783-8141.

Mayflower Descendants, General Society of (1897): 4 Winslow St., P.O. Box 3297, Plymouth, Mass. 02361. 25,000. Phone: (508) 746-3188.

Mayors, U.S. Conference of (1932): 1620 Eye St. N.W., Washington, D.C. 20006. 8 standing committees. Phone: (202) 293-7330.

Mechanical Engineers, American Society of (1880): 345 E. 47th St., New York, N.Y. 10017. 117,000. Phone: (212) 705-7722.

Mechanics, American Academy of (1969): Dept. of Ames, R-011, University of Calif., San Diego, La Jolla, Calif. 92093. 1,200. Phone: (619) 534-4772.

Medical Association, American (1847): 535 N. Dearborn St., Chicago, Ill. 60610-4377. Phone: (312) 645-5000.

Medical Library Association (1898): Six N. Michigan Ave., Suite 300, Chicago, Ill. 60602. 5,000. Phone: (312) 419-9094.

***Mental Health Association, National** (1909): 1021 Prince St., Alexandria, Va., 22314-2971. 1,000,000. Phone: (703) 684-7722.

Meteorological Society, American (1919): 45 Beacon St., Boston, Mass. 02108. 10,000. Phone: (617) 227-2425.

Military Chaplains Association of the U.S.A. (1925): P.O. Box 645, Riverdale, Md. 20737. 1, 550. Phone: (302) 674-3306.

Mining, Metallurgical and Petroleum Engineers, American Institute of (1871): 345 E. 47th St., New York, N.Y. 10017. 4 Member Societies: Society of Mining Engineers, The Minerals, Metals and Materials Society, Iron & Steel Society, Society of Petroleum Engineers. Phone: (212) 705-7695.

Mining and Metallurgical Society of America (1910): 210 Post St., Suite 1102, San Francisco, Calif. 94108. Phone: (415) 398-6925.

Model Aeronautics, Academy of (1936): 1810 Samuel Morse Dr., Reston, Va. 22090. 150,000. Phone: (703) 435-0750.

Modern Language Association of America (1883): 10 Astor Place, New York, N.Y. 10003. 26,436. Phone: (212) 475-9500.

Modern Woodmen of America (1883): Mississippi River at 17th St., Rock Island, Ill. 61201. 550, 000. Phone: (309) 786-6481.

Moose, Loyal Order of (1888): Mooseheart, Ill. 60539. 1,788,885. Phone: (312) 859-2000.

Mothers Against Drunk Driving (MADD) (1980): 669 Airport Fwy., Suite 310, Hurst, Tex. 76053. 600,000. Phone: (817) 268-6233.

***Motion Picture & Television Engineers, Society of** (1916): 595 W. Hartsdale Ave., White Plains, N.Y. 10607. 9,000. Phone: (914) 761-1100.

Motion Picture Arts & Sciences, Academy of

(1927): 8949 Wilshire Blvd., Beverly Hills, Calif. 90211. Phone: (213) 278-8990.

Multiple Sclerosis Society, National (1946): 205 E. 42nd St., New York, N.Y. 10017. 370,000. Phone: (212) 986-3240.

Muscular Dystrophy Association (1950): 810 Seventh Ave., New York, N.Y. 10019. 2,300,000 volunteers. Phone: (212) 586-0808.

Museum of Natural History, American (1869): Central Park West at 79th St., New York, N.Y. 10024. 505,000. Phone: (212) 769-5000.

Museums, American Association of (1906): 1225 Eye St. N.W., Suite 200, Washington, D.C. 20005. 10,000. Phone: (202) 289-1818.

Music Council, National (1940): 40 W. 37th St., Fifth floor, New York, N.Y. 10018. 50 National Music Organizations. Phone: (212) 563-3734.

Musicians, American Federation of (1896): 1501 Broadway, Suite 600 Paramount Bldg., New York, N.Y. 10036. 230,000. Phone: (212) 869-1330.

Music Publishers Association, Inc., National (1917): 205 E. 42nd St., New York, N.Y. 10017. Trade Organization/Harry Fox Agency-Licensing Organization. Phone: (212) 370-5330.

Muzzle Loading Rifle Association, National (1933): P.O. Box 67, Friendship, Ind. 47021. 30,000. Phone: (812) 667-5131.

Narcolepsy and Cataplexy Foundation of America (1975): 1410 York Ave., Suite 2D, Mail Box 22, New York, N.Y. 10021. 3,991. Phone: (212) 628-6315.

*National Association for the Advancement of Colored People (1909): 4805 Mt. Hope Dr., Baltimore, Md. 21215. 450,000. Phone: (301) 358-8900.

National Grange, The (1867): 1616 H St. N.W., Washington, D.C. 20006. 345,000. Phone: (202) 628-3507.

National PTA (National Congress of Parents and Teachers) (1897): 700 N. Rush St., Chicago, Ill. 60611. 6.4 million. Phone: (312) 787-0977.

Natural Science for Youth Foundation (1961): 130 Azalea Dr., Roswell, Ga. 30075. 350. Phone: (404) 594-9367.

Nature Conservancy, The (1951): 1815 N. Lynn St., Arlington, Va. 22209. 400,000. Phone: (703) 841-5300.

Naval Architects and Marine Engineers, The Society of (1893): 601 Pavonia Ave., Jersey City, N.J. 07306. 12,200. Phone: (201) 798-4800.

Naval Engineers, American Society of (1888): 1452 Duke St., Alexandria, Va. 22314. 9,000. Phone: (703) 836-6727.

Naval Institute, United States (1873): Annapolis, Md. 21402. 110,000. Phone: (301) 268-6110.

*Navigation, The Institute of (1945): 815 15th St. N.W., Suite 832, Washington, D.C. 20005. 3,000. Phone: (202) 783-4121.

Navy League of the United States (1902): 2300 Wilson Blvd., Arlington, Va. 22201. 70,500; William G. Sizemore, Executive Director.

Neurofibromatosis Foundation, The National (1978): 141 Fifth Ave., Suite 7-S, New York, N.Y. 10010. 27,000. Phone: (212) 460-8980; toll-free outside N.Y. state 1 (800) 323-7938.

Newspaper Editors, American Society of (1922): P.O. Box 17004, Washington, D.C. 20041. 1,000. Phone: (703) 648-1144.

Newspaper Publishers Association, American (1887): The Newspaper Center, P.O. Box 17407, Dulles International Airport, Washington, D.C. 20041. 1,430. Phone: (703) 648-1000.

Nondestructive Testing, Inc., The American Society for (1941): 4153 Arlingate Plaza, P.O. Box 28518, Columbus, Ohio 43228-0518. 9,000. Phone: Natl. 1-800-222-ASNT; Ohio 1-800-NDT-OHIO.

Nuclear Society, American (1954): 555 N. Kensington Ave., La Grange Park, Ill. 60525. 16,000. Phone: (312) 352-6611.

Numismatic Association, American (1891): 818 N. Cascade Ave., Colorado Springs, Colo. 80903-3279. 34,000. Phone: (719) 632-2646; (800) 367-9723.

Nurses' Association, American (1896): 2420 Pershing Rd., Kansas City, Mo. 69108. 189,000. Phone: (816) 474-5720.

Nutrition, American Institute of (1930): 9650 Rockville Pike, Bethesda, Md. 20814. 2,400. Phone: (301) 530-7050.

Odd Fellows, Sovereign Grand Lodge, Independent Order of (1819): 422 N. Trade St., Winston-Salem, N.C. 27101. 700,000. Phone: (919) 725-5955.

Olympic Committee, United States (1921): 1750 East Boulder St., Colorado Springs, Colo. 80909. Phone: (719) 632-5551.

Optical Society of America (1916): 1816 Jefferson Place N.W., Washington, D.C. 20036. 10,000. Phone: (202) 223-8130.

Optometric Association, American (1898): 243 N. Lindbergh Blvd., St. Louis, Mo. 63141. 27,000. Phone: (314) 991-4100.

*Organization of American States, General Secretariat (1890): 1889 F St. N.W., Washington, D.C. 20006. 32 member nations. Phone: (202) 458-3000.

Ornithologists' Union, American (1883): c/o National Museum of Natural History, Smithsonian Institution, Washington, D.C. 20560. 5,000. Phone: (202) 357-1970.

ORT Federation, American (1922): 817 Broadway, New York, N.Y. 10003. 160,000. Phone: (212) 677-4400.

Osteopathic Association, American (1897): 142 E. Ontario St., Chicago, Ill. 60611-3269. 30,000. Phone: (312) 280-5800.

Overeaters Anonymous (1960): P.O. Box 92870, Los Angeles, Calif. 90009. 130,000. Phone: (213) 542-8363.

Parents Without Partners (1957): 8807 Colesville Rd., Silver Spring, Md. 20910. 130,000. Phone: (301) 588-9354 or 1 (800) 637-7974.

Parks & Conservation Association, National (1919): 1015 31st St. N.W., Washington, D.C. 20007. 85,000. Phone: (202) 944-8530.

Pathologists, American Association of (1976): 9650 Rockville Pike, Bethesda, Md. 20814. 2,500. Phone: (301) 530-7130.

People for the American Way (1980): 2000 M St. N.W., Suite 400, Washington, D.C. 20036. 270,000. Phone: (202) 467-4999.

Petroleum Geologists, American Association of (1917): P.O. Box 979, Tulsa, Okla. 74101-0979. 37,000. Phone: (918) 584-2555.

Pharmaceutical Association, American (1852): 2215 Constitution Ave. N.W., Washington, D.C. 20037. 40,000. Phone: (202) 628-4410.

Philatelic Society, American (1886): P.O. Box 8000, State College, Pa. 16803. 56,000. Phone: (814) 237-3803.

Philosophical Society, American (1743): 104 S. 5th St., Philadelphia, Pa. 19106-3387. 600. Phone: (215) 440-3400.

Photogrammetry and Remote Sensing, American Society for (1934): 210 Little Falls St., Falls Church, Va. 22046-4398. 8,000. Phone: (703) 534-6617.

Photographic Society of America (1934): 3000 United Founders Blvd., Suite 103, Oklahoma City, Okla. 73112. 10,500. Phone: (405) 843-1437.

Photography, International Center of (1974): 1130 Fifth Ave., New York, N.Y. 10128. Phone: (212) 860-1777.

Physical Society, American (1899): 335 E. 45th St., New York, N.Y. 10017. 39,000. Phone: (212) 682-7341.

Physical Therapy Association, American (APTA) (1921): 1111 N. Fairfax St., Alexandria, Va. 22314. 44,000. Phone: (703) 684-2782.

Physics, American Institute of (1931): 335 E. 45th St., New York, N.Y. 10017. 102,500. Phone: (212) 661-9404.

Pilot Club International (1921): Pilot International Bldg., 244 College St., P.O. Box 4844, Macon, Ga. 31213. 21,000. Phone: (912) 743-7403.

Planetary Society, The (1979): 65 N. Catalina Ave., Pasadena, Calif. 91106. 120,000. Phone: (818) 793-5100.

Planned Parenthood Federation of America, Inc., (1916): 810 Seventh Ave., New York, N.Y. 10019. 175 affiliates. Phone: (212) 541-7800.

Plastics Engineers, Society of (1942): 14 Fairfield Dr., Brookfield, Conn. 06804-0403. 32,000. Phone: (203) 775-0471.

Police, American Federation of (1966): Records Center, 1100 N.E. 125th St., North Miami, Fla. 33161. 55,000. Phone: (305) 891-1700.

Police, International Association of Chiefs of (1893): 1110 N. Glebe Rd., Suite 200, Arlington, Va. 22201. 14,500. Phone (703) 243-6500.

Police Hall of Fame, American (1960): 14600 S. Tamiami Trail, North Port, Fla. 33596. 55,000. Phone: (305) 891-1700.

Political and Social Science, American Academy of (1889): 3937 Chestnut St., Philadelphia, Pa. 19104. Phone: (215) 386-4594.

Political Science, Academy of (1880): 475 Riverside Dr., Suite 1274, New York, N.Y. 10115-0012. 10,000. Phone: (212) 870-2500.

Powder Metallurgy Institute, American (1958): 105 College Rd. East, Princeton, N.J. 08540. 2,400. Phone: (609) 452-7700.

*Practical Nurse Education and Service, National Association for (1951): 10801 Pear Tree Lane, Suite 151, St. Ann, Mo. 63074. Phone: (314) 426-2662.

Press Club, National (1908): National Press Bldg., 529 14th St. N.W., Washington, D.C. 20045. 4,800. Phone: (202) 662-7500.

Professional Engineers, National Society of (1934): 1420 King St., Alexandria, Va. 22314. 75,000. Phone: (703) 684-2800.

Professional Photographers of America, Inc. (1880): 1090 Executive Way, Des Plaines, Ill. 60018. 17,000. Phone: (312) 299-8161.

Psychiatric Association, American (1844): 1400 K St. N.W., Washington, D.C. 20005. 35,650. Phone: (202) 682-6000.

Psychoanalytic Association, The American (1911): 309 E. 49th St., New York, N.Y. 10017. 3,000 psychoanalysts. Phone: (212) 752-0450.

Psychological Association, American (1892): 1200 17th St. N.W., Washington, D.C. 20036. 96,000. Phone: (202) 955-7600.

Public Health Association, American (1872): 1015 15th St. N.W., Washington, D.C. 20005. 50,000+. Phone: (202) 789-5600.

Puppeteers of America (1937): 5 Cricklewood Path, Pasadena, Calif. 91107. Phone: (818) 797-5748.

Quality Control, The American Society for (1946):

310 W. Wisconsin Ave., Milwaukee, Wis. 53203. 57,000. Phone: (414) 272-8575.

Radio Relay League, American (amateur radio) (1914): 225 Main St., Newington, Conn. 06111. 150,000. Phone: (203) 666-1541.

Railroads, Association of American (1934): 50 F St. N.W., Washington, D.C. 20001. Phone: (202) 639-2100.

Recording Arts and Sciences, Inc., National Academy of (1958): 303 N. Glenoaks Blvd., Suite M-140, Burbank, Calif. 91502. 7,300. Phone: (213) 849-1313.

Red Cross, American (1881): 17th and D Sts. N.W., Washington, D.C. 20006. Over 2,800 chapters. Phone: (202) 737-8300.

Rehabilitation Association, National (1925): 633 S. Washington St., Alexandria, Va. 22314. 17,000. Phone: (703) 836-0850.

Research and Enlightenment, Association for (1931): 67th St. & Atlantic Ave. (P.O. Box 595), Virginia Beach, Va. 23451. 90,000. Phone: (804) 428-3588.

*Reserve Officers Association of the United States (1922): 1 Constitution Ave. N.E., Washington, D.C. 20002. 125,000. Phone: (202) 479-2200.

Retarded Citizens, Association for (1950): 2501 Avenue J, Arlington, Tex. 76006. 1,300 chapters. Phone: (817) 640-0204.

Retired Federal Employees, National Association of (1921): 1533 New Hampshire Ave. N.W., Washington, D.C. 20036. 495,000. Phone: (202) 234-0832.

Retired Persons, American Association of (1958): 1909 K St. N.W., Washington, D.C. 20049. 29,000,000. Phone: (202) 872-4700.

Reye's Syndrome Foundation, National (1974): 426 N. Lewis St., Bryan, Ohio 43506. Phone: (800) 233-7393. In Ohio: 1 (800) 231-7393.

RID-USA (Remove Intoxicated Drivers) (1978): Box 520, Schenectady, N.Y. 12301. Over 135/36 state chapters. Phone: (518) 372-0034.

Rifle Association of America, National (1871): 1600 Rhode Island Ave. N.W., Washington, D.C. 20036. 3,000,000. Phone: (202) 828-6000.

Right to Life, National Committee (1973): 419 7th St. N.W., Washington, D.C. 20004. Phone: (202) 626-8800.

Rotary International (1905): One Rotary Center, Evanston, Ill. 60201. 1,065,383 in 164 countries. Phone: (312) 866-3000.

Safety Council, National (1913): 444 N. Michigan Ave., Chicago, Ill. 60611. Phone: (312) 527-4800.

Salvation Army, The (1865): 799 Bloomfield Ave., Verona, N.J. 07044. 433,443. Phone: (201) 239-0606.

SANE/FREEZE: Campaign for Global Security (a merger of SANE and the Nuclear Weapons Freeze Campaign) (1957): 711 G St. S.E., Washington, D.C. 20003. 170,000. Phone: (202) 546-7100.

*Save Our Shores, Inc. (1969): P.O. Box 103, North Quincy, Mass. 02171. 50,000. Phone: (617) 328-1121.

Save-the-Redwoods League (1918): 114 Sansome St., San Francisco, Calif. 94104. 45,000. Phone: (415) 362-2352.

Savings Institutions, National Council of (1920): 1101 15th St. N.W., Suite 400, Washington, D.C. 20005. Phone: (202) 857-3100.

*Science, American Association for the Advancement of (1848): 1333 H St. N.W., Washington, D.C. 20005. 133,000. Phone: (202) 326-6400.

Science and Health, American Council on (1978):

1995 Broadway, 16th Floor, New York, N.Y. 10023. Phone: (212) 362-7004.

Science Fiction Society, World (1939): c/o Southern California Institute for Fan Interests, P.O. Box 8442, Van Nuys, Calif. 91409. 6,000. Phone: (213) 837-4708.

Science Writers, Inc., National Association of (1934): P.O. Box 294, Greenlawn, N.Y. 11740. 1,525. Phone: (516) 757-5664.

Scientists, Federation of American (FAS) (1945): 307 Massachusetts Ave. N.E., Washington, D.C. 20002..4,000. Phone: (202) 546-3300.

SCRABBLE® Crossword Game Players (1972): P.O. Box 700, Front Street Garden, Greenport, N.Y. 11944. 15,000. Phone: (516) 477-0033.

Screen Actors Guild (1933): 7065 Hollywood Blvd., Hollywood, Calif. 90028. 70,000. Phone: (213) 465-4600.

Sculpture Society, National (1893): 15 E. 26th St., New York, N.Y. 10010. 350. Phone: (212) 889-6960.

Seeing Eye Inc., The (1929): P.O. Box 375. Morristown, N.J. 07963-0375. Phone: (201) 539-4425.

Senior Citizens, National Alliance of (1974): 2525 Wilson Blvd., Arlington, Va. 22201. 2.2 million. Phone: (703) 528-4380.

Separationists, Society of (1963): P.O. Box 140195, Austin, Tex. 78714-0195. 37,216 families. Phone: (512) 458-1244.

Shrine of North America (Shriners Hospitals) (1872): Box 31356, Tampa, Fla. 33631-3356. 798,734. Phone: (813) 885-2575.

Sierra Club (1892): 730 Polk St., San Francisco, Calif. 94109. 500,000. Phone: (415) 776-2211.

SIETAR—The International Society for Intercultural Education, Training, and Research (1974): 1505 22nd St. N.W., Washington, D.C. 20037. 1, 500. Phone: (202) 296-4710.

Simon Wiesenthal Center (1978): 9760 W. Pico Blvd., Los Angeles, Calif. 90035. 361,000. Phone: (213) 553-9036.

Small Business United, National (1937): 1155 15th St. N.W., Washington, D.C. 20005. 50,000. Phone: (202) 293-8830.

Social Work Education, Council on (1919): 1744 R St. N.W., Washington, D.C. 20009. 5,000. Phone: (202) 667-2300.

Social Workers, National Association of (1955): 7981 Eastern Ave., Silver Spring, Md. 20910. Phone: (301) 565-0333.

Sociological Association, American (1905): 1722 N St. N.W., Washington, D.C. 20036. 12,000. Phone: (202) 833-3410.

Soil and Water Conservation Society (1945): 7515 N.E. Ankeny Rd., Ankeny, Iowa 50021. 13, 000. Phone: (515) 289-2331.

Songwriters Guild of America, The (1931): 276 Fifth Ave., New York, N.Y. 10001. 4,200. Phone: (212) 686-6820.

Sons of Italy in America, Order (1905): 219 E St. N.E., Washington, D.C. 20002. 100,000. Phone: (202) 547-2900.

Sons of the American Revolution, National Society of the (1889): 1000 S. 4th St., Louisville, Ky. 40203. 24,900. Phone: (502) 589-1776.

Soroptimist International of the Americas (1921): 1616 Walnut St., Philadelphia, Pa. 19103. 50, 000. Phone: (215) 732-0512.

*Southern Christian Leadership Conference (1957): 334 Auburn Ave. N.E., Atlanta, Ga. 30303. 1,000,000; 350 chapters, 260 affiliated organizations. Phone: (404) 522-1420.

Space Education Association, U.S. (1973): 746 Turnpike Rd., Elizabethtown, Pa. 17022-1161. 1,000. Phone: (717) 367-3265.

Space Society, National (1974): 922 Pennsylvania Ave. S.E., Washington, D.C. 20003. 20,000. Phone: (202) 543-1900.

Special Olympics International (1968): 1350 New York Ave. N.W., Suite 500, Washington, D.C., 20005. 1,000,000. Phone: (202) 628-3630.

Speech-Language-Hearing Association, American (1925): 10801 Rockville Pike, Rockville, Md. 20852. 46,000. Phone: (301) 897-5700.

Sports Car Club of America Inc. (1944): 9033 E. Easter Place, Englewood, Colo. 80112. 50,000. Phone: (303) 694-7222.

State Garden Clubs, Inc., National Council of (1929): 4401 Magnolia Ave., St. Louis, Mo. 63110. 308,623. Phone: (314) 776-7574.

State Governments, The Council of (1933): P.O. Box 11910, Iron Works Pike, Lexington, Ky. 40578. All state officials, all 50 states. Phone: (606) 252-2291.

Statistical Association, American (1839): 1429 Duke St., Alexandria, Va. 22314. 15,103.

Student Association, United States (1978): 1012 14th St. N.W., #207, Washington, D.C. 20005. Phone: (202) 347-8772.

Surgeons, American College of (1913): 55 E. Erie, St., Chicago, Ill. 60611. 50,000+. Phone: (312) 664-4050.

Surveying and Mapping, American Congress on (1941): 210 Little Falls St., Falls Church, Va. 22046. 10,700. Phone: (703) 241-2446.

Symphony Orchestra League, American (1942): 777 Fourteenth St. N.W., Suite 500, Washington, D.C. 20005. 4,713. Phone: (202) 628-0099.

TASH: The Association for Persons with Severe Handicaps (1973): 7010 Roosevelt Way, N.E., Seattle, Wash. 98115. 8,200. Phone: (206) 523-8446.

Tax Foundation, Inc. (1937): One Thomas Circle N.W., Suite 500, Washington, D.C. 20005. 600. Phone: (202) 822-9050.

Teachers, American Federation of (1916): 555 New Jersey Ave. N.W., Washington, D.C., 20001. 660,000. Phone: (202) 879-4400.

Television Arts and Sciences, National Academy of (1948): 111 W. 57th St., New York, N.Y., 10019. 15,000. Phone: (212) 586-8424.

Testing & Materials, American Society for (1898): 1916 Race St., Philadelphia, Pa. 19103. 32,000. Phone: (215) 299-5400.

Theatre Guild (1919): 226 W. 47th St., New York, N.Y. 10036. 105,000. Phone: (212) 869-5470.

Theosophical Society in America, The (1875): P.O. Box 270, Wheaton, Ill. 60189-0270. 5,600. Phone: (312) 668-1571; toll free (800) 654-9429.

Toastmasters International (1924): P.O. Box 10400, 2200 N. Grand Ave., Santa Ana, Calif., 92711. 142,500. Phone: (714) 542-6793.

TOUGHLOVE (1977): P.O. Box 1069, Doylestown, Pa. 18901. 2,000 groups internationally. Phone: (215) 348-7090.

TransAfrica Forum (1982): 545 Eighth St. S.E., Suite 200, Washington, D.C. 20003. Phone: (202) 547-2550.

Travel Agents, American Society of (ASTA) (1931): P.O. Box 23992, Washington, D.C. 20026-3992. 23,000. Phone: (703) 739-2782.

Travelers Aid Services (1905/1982); 2 Lafayette St., New York, N.Y. 10007. Lucy N. Friedman, Executive Director. (Result of merger of Travelers Aid Society of New York and Victim Services

Agency in 1982). Phone: (212) 577-7700.

Tuberous Sclerosis Association, National (1975): P.O. Box 612, Winfield, Ill. 60190. 5,000. Phone: (312) 668-0787.

UFOs, National Investigations Committee on (1967): 14617 Victory Blvd., Suite 4, Van Nuys, Calif. 91411. Phone: (818) 989-5942.

*UNICEF, U.S. Committee for (1947): 331 E. 38th St., New York, N.Y. 10016. 1,000,000 volunteers. Phone: (212) 686-5522.

United Negro College Fund Inc. (1944): 500 E. 62nd St., New York, N.Y. 10021. Phone: (212) 326-1100.

United Way of America (1918): 701 N. Fairfax St., Alexandria, Va. 22314. 2,300 local groups. Phone: (703) 836-7100.

University Foundation, International (1973): 1301 S. Noland Rd., Independence, Mo. 64055. 35,000. Phone: (816) 461-3633.

University Women, American Association of (1881): 2401 Virginia Ave. N.W., Washington, D.C. 20037. 140,000. Phone: (202) 785-7700.

Urban League, National (1910): 500 E. 62nd St., New York, N.Y. 10021. 116. Phone: (212) 310-9000.

USO (United Service Organizations) (1941): 601 Indiana Ave. N.W., Washington, D.C. 20004. Phone: (202) 783-8121.

Variety Clubs International (1927): 1560 Broadway, Suite 1209, New York, N.Y. 10036. 15,000. Phone: (212) 704-9872.

Veterans Committee, American (AVC) (1944): 1717 Massachusetts Ave. N.W., Suite 203, Washington, D.C. 20036. 25,000. Phone: (202) 667-0090.

Veterans of Foreign Wars of the U.S. (1899): V.F.W. Bldg., 34th and Broadway, Kansas City, Mo. 64111. V.F.W. and Auxiliary, 2,850,000. Phone: (816) 756-3390.

Veterinary Medical Association, American (1863): 930 N. Meacham Rd., Schaumburg, Ill. 60196. 47,500. Phone: (312) 605-8070.

Visually Handicapped, Division for the (1948): The Council for Exceptional Children, 1920 Association Dr., Reston, Va. 22091. 1,000. Phone: (703) 620-3660.

Volunteers of America (1896): 3813 N. Causeway Blvd., Metairie, La. 70002. services in over 200 communities. Phone: (504) 837-2652.

War Resisters League (1923): 339 Lafayette St., New York, N.Y. 10012. 18,000. Phone: (212) 228-0450.

Washington Legal Foundation (1976): 1705 N St. N.W., Washington, D.C. 20036. 200,000. Phone: (202) 857-0240.

Water Quality Association (1974): 4151 Naperville Rd., Lisle, Ill. 60532. Phone: (312) 369-1600.

Water Resources Association, American (1964): 5410 Grosvenor Lane, Suite 220, Bethesda, Md. 20814. 4,000. Phone: (301) 493-8600.

Welding Society, American (1919): 550 N.W. Le-Jeune Rd., Miami, Fla. 33126. 34,673. Phone: (305) 443-9353; toll free (800) 443-9353.

Wildlife Federation, National (1936): 1400 16th St. N.W., Washington, D.C. 20036. 5,100,000. Phone: (202) 797-6800.

Wildlife Fund, World (1961): 1250 24th St. N.W., Washington, D.C. 20037. 600,000. Phone: (202) 293-4800.

Woman's Christian Temperance Union, National (1874): 1730 Chicago Ave., Evanston, Ill. 60201. 100,000. Phone: (312) 864-1396.

Women, National Organization for (NOW) (1966): 1000 16th St. N.W., Suite 700, Washington, D.C. 20036-5705. 160,000. Phone: (202) 331-0066.

Women's American ORT (1927): 315 Park Ave. South, New York, N.Y. 10010. 145,000. Phone: (212) 505-7700.

Women's Clubs, General Federation of (1890): 1734 N St., N.W., Washington, D.C. 20036. 500,000. Phone: (202) 347-3168.

Women's Educational and Industrial Union (1877): 356 Boylston St., Boston, Mass. 02116. 2,200. Phone: (617) 536-5651.

Women's International League for Peace and Freedom (1915): 1213 Race St., Philadelphia, Pa. 19107. 15,000. Phone: (215) 563-7110.

*Women Strike for Peace (1961): 145 S. 13th St., Philadelphia, Pa. 19107. 9,000. Phone: (215) 923-0861.

World Future Society (1966): 4916 Saint Elmo Ave., Bethesda, Md. 20814. 30,000. Phone: (301) 656-8274.

World Health, American Association for (1951): 2001 S St. N.W., Washington, D.C. 20009. 900. Phone: (202) 265-0286.

World Peace, International Association of Educators for (1969): P.O. Box 3282, Mastin Lake Station, Huntsville, Ala. 35810. 20,000. Phone: (205) 534-5501.

Worldwatch Institute (1974): 1776 Massachusetts Ave. N.W., Washington, D.C. 20036. Research organization. Phone: (202) 452-1999.

World Peace Foundation (1910): 22 Batterymarch St., Boston, Mass. 02109. Phone: (617) 482-3875.

Writers Union, National (1983): 13 Astor Pl., 7th Fl., New York, NY 10003. 2,600. Phone: (212) 254-0279.

YMCA of the USA (1844): 101 N. Wacker Dr., Chicago, Ill. 60606. 13,500,000. Phone: (312) 977-0031.

Young Men's and Young Women's Hebrew Association (1874): 1395 Lexington Ave., New York, N.Y. 10128. 9,000. Phone: (212) 427-6000.

Young Women's Christian Association of the U.S.A. (1858 in U.S.A., 1855 in England): 726 Broadway, New York, N.Y. 10003. 2,030,922. Phone: (212) 614-2846.

Youth Hostels, Inc., American (1934): P.O. Box 37613, Washington, D.C. 20013-7613. 100,000. Phone: (202) 783-6161.

Zero Population Growth (1968): 1400 Sixteenth St. N.W., Suite 320, Washington, D.C. 20036. 28,000. Phone: (202) 332-2200.

Zionist Organization of America (1897): ZOA House, 4 E. 34th St., New York, N.Y. 10016. 135,000. Phone: (212) 481-1500.

Zoological Parks and Aquariums, American Association of (1924): Oglebay Park, Wheeling, W. Va. 26003. 5,100. Phone: (304) 242-2160.

Zoologists, American Society of (1890): 104 Sirius Circle, Thousand Oaks, Calif. 91360. 4,000. Phone: (805) 492-3585.

Conservation Hall of Fame

The new headquarters office of the National Wildlife Federation features a Conservation Hall of Fame which is open to the public Monday through Friday, 8:00 a.m. to 4:30 p.m.

The first person to be so honored was Theodore Roosevelt, the nation's 25th president.

Some Books Challenged or Banned in 1988-1989

Source: Selected from a list compiled by the American Library Association and reprinted by their permission.

Books Challenged or Banned as reported in the *Newsletter on Intellectual Freedom* **from May 1988 through May 1989.**

Alyson, Sasha, ed. *Young, Gay and Proud.* Alyson Pubns. Challenged at the Public Libraries of Saginaw, Mich. (1989) because the book promoted acts in violation of Michigan law and "appears to qualify as obscene material."

Angelou, Maya. *I Know Why the Caged Bird Sings.* Bantam; Random. Challenged at Mount Abram Regional High School in Strong, Maine (1988) because parents objected to a rape scene.

Auel, Jean. *Clan of the Cave Bear.* Coronet. Challenged at the Berrien Springs, Mich. High School for use in classrooms and libraries (1988) because the novel is "vulgar, profane, and sexually explicit."

Bach, Alice. *When the Sky Began to Roar.* Houghton. Challenged at the Seward, Neb. Public Library (1988) because it is "obscene."

Belpre, Pura. *Perez and Martina.* Warne. Challenged at the Multnomah County Library in Portland, Ore. (1988) because the death of a mouse in the story could upset children.

Bunn, Scott. *Just Hold On.* Delacorte. Banned at the Covington Junior High School in Vancouver, Wash. (1988) because the book is devoid of hope and positive role models.

Conroy, Pat. *The Prince of Tides.* Bantam; Houghton. Removed as a reading assignment for an advanced English class at the St. Andres Parish, S.C. public school (1988) because it is "trashy pulp pornography."

Davis, Jim. *Garfield: His Nine Lives.* Ballantine. Moved to the adult section of the Public Libraries of Saginaw, Mich. (1989) after patrons requested that children be denied access.

Golding, William. *Lord of the Flies.* Coward. A committee of the Toronto, Canada Board of Education ruled on June 23, 1988 that the novel is "racist and recommended that it be removed from all schools." Parents and members of the black community complained about a reference to "niggers" in the book and said it denigrates blacks.

Hedderwick, Mairi. *Katie Morag and the Tiresome Ted.* Little. Challenged at the Public Libraries of Saginaw, Mich. (1989) because on the last page of the story "the mother's sweater is open to fully expose her breast." The library was asked to cover the drawing with a marker.

Hoobler, Dorothy and Thomas. *Nelson and Winnie Mandela.* Watts. Challenged at the Hillsboro, Ore. Public Library (1988) by a patron who charged that the Mandelas and the African National Congress are Communist-backed and advocate violence.

Howe, Norma. *God, the Universe and Hot Fudge Sundaes.* Houghton. Challenged at the Canby, Ore. junior high school library (1988) because the book "pushes several items of the humanist agenda: death education, anti-God, pro-evolution, anti-Bible, anti-Christian, and logic over faith."

Huxley, Aldous. *Brave New World.* Harper. Challenged as required reading at the Yukon, Okla. High School (1988) because of "the book's language and moral content."

Johnson, Eric W. *Love and Sex in Plain Language.* Lippincott/Harper; Bantam. Challenged in the Williamsport, Penn. schools (1988) because of allegedly inaccurate and misleading information in the book.

Lightner, A. M. *Gods or Demons?* Fourwinds. Pr. Challenged at the Canby, Ore. junior high school library (1988) because the book "promotes a secular-humanistic belief in evolution and portrays the 'Bible as myth.'"

O'Connor, Jane. *Just Good Friends.* Dell; Harper. Removed from the Jefferson Middle School library in Eugene, Ore. (1988) because of the book's sexual references.

Peck, Robert Newton. *A Day No Pigs Would Die.* ABC-Clio; Dell; Knopf. Challenged in Jefferson County, Colo. school libraries (1988) because "it is bigoted against Baptists and women and depicts violence, hatred, animal cruelty, and murder."

Price, Susan. *The Devil's Piper.* Faber; Greenwillow. Challenged at the Canby, Ore. junior high school library (1988) because it "could encourage young minds to pursue occult, suicide, or adopt ill attitudes."

Pyle, Howard. *King Stork.* Little. Challenged at the Public Libraries of Saginaw, Mich. (1989) because it "would encourage boys beating girls" when the drummer beats the enchantress with a switch until she becomes a 'good' princess."

Sendak, Maurice. *In the Night Kitchen.* Harper. Challenged at the Robeson Elementary School in Champaign, Ill. (1988) because "gratuitous" nudity.

Shengold, Nina & Smith & Kraus, eds. *The Actor's Book of Contemporary Stage Monologues.* Penguin. Challenged at the Salem Junior High School in Virginia Beach, Va. (1988) because it contains racial slurs, profanity and lewd descriptions.

Silverstein, Shel. *A Light in the Attic.* Harper. The poem "Little Abigail and the Beautiful Pony" from this award-winning children's book was banned from second grade classes in Huffman, Texas (1989) because a mother protested that it "exposes children to the horrors of suicide."

Steinbeck, John. *Of Mice and Men.* Bantam; Penguin; Viking. Challenged in the Marion County, W. Va. schools (1988), at the Wheaton-Warrenville, Ill. Middle School (1988), and at the Berrien Springs, Mich. High School (1988) because the book contains profanity.

Twain, Mark [Samuel L. Clemens]. *The Adventures of Huckleberry Finn.* Bantam; Bobbs-Merrill; Grosset; Harper; Holt; Houghton; Longman; Macmillan; NAL; Norton; Penguin; Pocket Bks. Removed from the required reading in the Rockford, Ill. public schools (1988) because the book contains the word "nigger." Challenged at the Berrien Springs, Mich. High School (1988). Removed from a required reading list and school libraries in Caddo Parish, La. (1988) because of racially offensive passages. Challenged at the Sevier County High School in Sevierville, Tenn. (1989) because of racial slurs and dialect.

Watson, Jane Werner and Chambers, Sol. *The Golden Book of the Mysterious.* Golden. Challenged at the Winchester, Md. Elementary School (1988) because of the book's reference to witchcraft, sorcery and spells, fortunetelling, reincarnation, werewolves, vampires, and ghosts.

Wilde, Oscar, *The Happy Prince and Other Stories.* Penguin. Challenged at the Springfield, Ore. Public Library (1988) because the stories were "distressing and morbid."

Wright, Richard. *Native Son.* Harper. Challenged at the Berrien Springs, Mich. High School in classrooms and libraries (1988) because of the novel is "vulgar, profane, and sexually explicit."

NOTE: The opinions about the books stated here are not those of the Publisher or editorial staff of *Information Please Almanac.*

For further information on book censorship you may write: Office for Intellectual Freedom, American Library Association, 50 East Huron Street, Chicago, Ill. 60611.

EDUCATION

School Enrollment, October 1988
(in thousands)

Age	White		Black		Spanish origin[1]		All races	
	Enrolled	Percent	Enrolled	Percent	Enrolled	Percent	Enrolled	Percent
3 and 4 years	2,288	38.9	375	33.4	205	24.5	2,797	38.2
5 and 6 years	5,655	96.1	1,072	95.5	788	95.7	7,044	96.0
7 to 9 years	8,599	99.7	1,664	99.7	1,206	99.6	10,704	99.6
10 to 13 years	10,721	99.7	2,097	99.7	1,392	99.8	13,340	99.7
14 to 15 years	5,186	98.8	1,025	98.9	693	98.8	6,481	98.9
16 and 17 years	5,284	91.4	1,029	91.5	492	78.8	6,561	91.6
18 and 19 years	3,338	55.8	532	50.3	324	44.1	4,059	55.7
20 and 21 years	2,309	40.2	276	28.1	125	16.7	2,724	39.1
22 to 24 years	1,771	18.6	201	13.2	140	12.1	2,092	18.3
25 to 29 years	1,458	8.2	192	7.2	123	5.8	1,773	8.3
30 to 34 years	1,062	5.9	145	5.6	101	5.6	1,271	5.9
Total	47,672	48.0	8,608	50.6	5,589	46.0	58,846	48.7

1. Persons of Spanish origin may be of any race. NOTE: Figures include persons enrolled in nursery school, kindergarten, elementary school, high school, and college. *Source:* Department of Commerce, Bureau of the Census.

Persons Not Enrolled in School, October 1988
(in thousands)

Age	Population	Total not enrolled		High school graduate		Not high school graduate (dropouts)[1]	
		Number	Percent	Number	Percent	Number	Percent
14 and 15 years	6,555	74	1.1	5	0.1	69	1.1
16 and 17 years	7,160	599	8.4	117	1.6	482	6.7
18 and 19 years	7,294	3,235	44.4	2,172	29.8	1,063	14.6
20 and 21 years	6,974	4,250	61.0	3,232	46.4	1,018	14.6
22 to 24 years	11,465	9,373	81.8	7,705	67.2	1,668	14.6

1. Persons who are not enrolled in school and who are not high school graduates are considered dropouts. *Source:* Department of Commerce, Bureau of the Census.

School Enrollment by Grade, Control, and Race
(in thousands)

Grade level and type of control	White			Black			All races[1]		
	Oct. 1988[3]	Oct. 1980[4]	Oct. 1970	Oct. 1988[3]	Oct. 1980[4]	Oct. 1970	Oct. 1988[3]	Oct. 1980[4]	Oct. 1970
Nursery school: Public	651	432	198	168	180	129	868	633	333
Private	1,583	1,205	695	118	115	49	1,770	1,354	763
Kindergarten: Public	2,722	2,172	2,233	547	440	374	3,420	2,690	2,674
Private	471	423	473	44	50	53	538	486	536
Grades 1–8: Public	20,086	19,743	24,923	4,289	4,058	4,668	25,443	24,398	30,001
Private	2,455	2,768	3,715	250	202	200	2,778	3,051	3,949
Grades 9–12: Public	9,571	12,056[2]	11,599	2,016	2,200[2]	1,794	12,095	14,556[2]	13,545
Private	890	—	1,124	62	—	41	998	—	1,170
College: Public	7,302	8,875[2]	5,168	894	1,007[2]	422	8,663	10,180[2]	5,699
Private	1,940	—	1,591	220	—	100	2,278	—	1,714
Total: Public	40,332	—	44,121	7,914	—	7,387	50,489	—	52,225
Private	7,339	—	7,598	694	—	443	8,362	—	8,132
Grand Total	**47,671**	**47,673**	**51,719**	**8,608**	**8,251**	**7,830**	**58,851**	**57,348**	**60,357**

1. Includes persons of Spanish origin. 2. Total public and private. Breakdown not available. 3. Estimates controlled to 1980 census base. 4. Estimates controlled to 1970 census base. *Source:* Department of Commerce, Bureau of the Census.

State Compulsory School Attendance Laws

State	Enactment[1]	Age limits	State	Enactment[1]	Age limits
Alabama	1915	7–16	Montana[4]	1883	7–16
Alaska[2]	1929	7–16	Nebraska	1887	7–16
Arizona	1899	8–16	Nevada	1873	7–17
Arkansas	1909	7–17	New Hampshire	1871	6–16
California	1874	6–16	New Jersey	1875	6–16
Colorado	1889	7–16	New Mexico	1891	6–18
Connecticut	1872	7–16	New York[5]	1874	6–16
Delaware	1907	5–16	North Carolina	1907	7–16
D. C.	1864	7–17	North Dakota	1883	7–16
Florida	1915	6–16	Ohio	1877	6–18
Georgia	1916	7–16	Oklahoma	1907	7–18
Hawaii	1896	6–18	Oregon	1889	7–18
Idaho	1887	7–16	Pennsylvania	1895	8–17
Illinois	1883	7–16	Rhode Island	1883	7–16
Indiana	1897	7–16	South Carolina[6]	1915	5–17
Iowa	1902	7–16	South Dakota[4]	1883	7–16
Kansas	1874	7–16	Tennessee	1905	7–17
Kentucky[3]	1896	6–18	Texas[7]	1915	7–16
Louisiana	1910	7–16	Utah	1890	6–18
Maine	1875	7–17	Vermont	1867	7–16
Maryland	1902	6–16	Virginia	1908	5–17
Massachusetts	1852	6–16	Washington	1871	8–18
Michigan	1871	6–16	West Virginia	1897	6–16
Minnesota	1885	7–16	Wisconsin[8]	1879	6–18
Mississippi	1918	6–14	Wyoming	1876	7–16
Missouri	1905	7–16			

1. Date of enactment of first compulsory attendance law. 2. Ages 7 to 16 or high school graduation. 3. Must have parental signature for leaving school between ages of 16 and 18. 4. May leave after completion of eighth grade. 5. The ages are 6 to 17 for New York City and Buffalo. 6. Permits parental waiver of kindergarten at age 5. 7. Must complete academic year in which 16th birthday occurs. 8. Law specifies ages 6 to 18 unless excused or graduated. *Source:* Department of Education, National Center for Educational Statistics.

High School and College Graduates

Year of graduation	High School			College[1]		
	Men	Women	Total	Men	Women	Total
1900	38,075	56,808	94,883	22,173	5,237	27,410
1910	63,676	92,753	156,429	28,762	8,437	37,199
1920	123,684	187,582	311,266	31,980	16,642	48,622
1929–30	300,376	366,528	666,904	73,615	48,869	122,484
1939–40	578,718	642,757	1,221,475	109,546	76,954	186,500
1949–50	570,700	629,000	1,199,700	328,841	103,217	432,058
1959–60	898,000	966,000	1,864,000	254,063	138,377	392,440
1964–65	1,314,000	1,351,000	2,665,000	316,286	213,717	530,003
1967–68	1,341,000	1,361,000	2,702,000	390,507	276,203	666,710
1968–69	1,402,000	1,427,000	2,829,000	444,380	319,805	764,185
1969–70	1,433,000	1,463,000	2,896,000	484,174	343,060	827,234
1970–71	1,456,000	1,487,000	2,943,000	511,138	366,538	877,676
1971–72	1,490,000	1,518,000	3,008,000	541,313	389,371	930,684
1972–73	1,501,000	1,536,000	3,037,000	564,680	407,700	972,380
1973–74	1,515,000	1,565,000	3,080,000	575,843	423,749	999,592
1974–75	1,541,000	1,599,000	3,140,000	533,797	425,052	978,849
1975–76	1,554,000	1,601,000	3,155,000	557,817	430,578	988,395
1976–77	1,548,000	1,606,000	3,154,000	547,919	435,989	983,908
1977–78	1,535,000	1,599,000	3,134,000	487,000	434,000	921,000
1978–79	1,531,800	1,602,400	3,134,200	529,996	460,242	990,238
1979–80	1,500,000	1,558,000	3,058,000	526,327	473,221	999,548
1980–81	1,483,000	1,537,000	3,020,000	470,000	465,000	935,000
1981–82	1,474,000	1,527,000	3,001,000	473,000	480,000	953,000
1982–83	1,437,000	1,451,000	2,888,000	479,140	490,370	969,510
1983–84	n.a.	n.a.	2,767,000	482,319	491,990	974,309
1984–85	n.a.	n.a.	2,677,000	482,528	496,949	979,477
1985–86	n.a.	n.a.	2,642,000	485,923	501,900	987,823
1986–87	n.a.	n.a.	2,693,000[2]	475,000[2]	512,000[2]	987,000[2]

1. Includes bachelor's and first-professional degrees for years 1900–1960. 2. Estimated. n.a. = not available. NOTE: Includes graduates from public and private schools. Beginning in 1959–60, figures include Alaska and Hawaii. Because of rounding, details may not add to totals. Most recent data available. *Source:* Department of Education, Center for Education Statistics.

Federal Funds for Some Major Programs for Education, Fiscal Year 1990[1]

Program	Amount in thousands	Program	Amount in thousands
Elementary–secondary		Higher education facilities	22,744
Educationally disadvantaged	$ 4,730,441	Aid for institutional development	184,580
Special programs	1,200,670	**Vocational education**	7,148
Bilingual education	207,199	**Adult basic and secondary education**	170,000
School assistance in federally		**Education for the handicapped**	
affected areas	629,260	State grant program	1,525,614
Higher education		Preschool grants	247,000
Program development	52,768	Special populations	55,687
Student assistance		Training and information	74,568
Pell grants	4,680,368	All other	111,958
Work study/grants	610,497	**Indian education**	74,168
Direct loans to students	495,263	**Education research and improvement**	88,330
Special programs for the disadvantaged	228,168	**Total**	**$15,396,431**

1. Estimated outlay for fiscal year 1990. *Source: Budget of the United States Government,* Fiscal Year 1990.

Funding for Public Elementary and Secondary Education, 1979–80 to 1985–86

(In thousands except percent)

School year	Total	Federal	State	Local[1]	% Federal	% State	% Local[1]
1979–80	$ 96,881,165	$9,503,537	$45,348,814	$42,028,813	9.8	46.8	43.4
1980–81	105,949,087	9,768,262	50,182,659	45,998,166	9.2	47.4	43.4
1981–82	110,191,257	8,186,466	52,436,435	49,568,356	7.4	47.6	45.0
1982–83	117,497,502	8,339,990	56,282,157	52,875,354	7.1	47.9	45.0
1983–84	126,055,419	8,576,547	60,232,981	57,245,892	6.8	47.8	45.4
1984–85[2]	137,350,722	8,952,358	66,983,340	61,415,023	6.5	48.8	44.7
1984-85	137,294,678	9,105,569	67,168,684	61,020,425	6.6	48.9	44.4
1985-86	149,004,882	9,956,009	73,673,174	65,375,698	6.7	49.4	43.9

1. Includes a relatively small amount from nongovernmental sources (gifts and tuition and transportation fees from patrons) *Source:* U.S. Department of Education, National Center for Education Statistics.

Major U.S. College and University Libraries

(Top 50 based on number of volumes in library)

Institution	Volumes	Microforms[1]	Institution	Volumes	Microforms[1]
Harvard	11,496,906	4,902,955	New York	2,988,453	2,396,661
Yale	8,538,156	2,861,143	Pennsylvania State	2,965,695	2,925,368
U of Illinois-Urbana	7,377,051	3,198,912	Iowa	2,930,932	3,020,711
U of California-Berkeley	7,190,821	4,051,125	Johns Hopkins	2,728,347	1,449,195
U of Michigan	6,133,171	3,472,083	U of Pittsburgh	2,713,324	2,258,997
U of Texas	5,888,776	4,020,195	U of Florida	2,701,857	2,478,106
U of California-Los Angeles	5,812,163	5,137,087	U of Kansas	2,688,482	1,998,985
Columbia	5,740,832	3,694,261	U of Georgia	2,688,433	3,797,738
Stanford	5,740,162	3,104,714	Rochester	2,590,720	2,360,899
U of Chicago	4,970,720	1,454,193	U of Southern California	2,533,850	2,627,754
Cornell	4,924,421	4,530,771	SUNY-Buffalo	2,492,502	3,461,883
U of Wisconsin	4,804,386	3,018,515	U of Missouri	2,410,569	4,559,542
U of Washington	4,764,341	4,890,148	Arizona State	2,340,657	2,827,350
U of Minnesota	4,473,262	2,616,670	Louisiana State	2,327,869	1,943,977
Ohio State	4,254,266	2,971,011	U of South Carolina	2,292,721	2,368,227
Princeton	4,070,827	2,343,650	U of Massachusetts	2,275,822	1,636,005
Indiana	4,011,675	1,466,554	Syracuse	2,247,176	3,308,306
Duke	3,668,935	1,279,898	U of Hawaii	2,244,118	2,363,009
North Carolina	3,520,273	2,731,236	Wayne State	2,233,540	1,974,435
U of Pennsylvania	3,499,741	1,105,575	U of Oklahoma	2,230,257	2,657,805
Northwestern	3,346,817	1,855,577	U of California-Davis	2,227,255	2,656,808
U of Arizona	3,329,146	3,622,457	U of Colorado	2,185,565	1,073,961
Michigan State	3,301,739	3,256,021	Washington U-St. Louis	2,169,792	1,683,373
Rutgers	3,065,533	3,362,830	U of Connecticut	2,146,993	2,352,897
U of Virginia	3,003,066	3,923,464	Brown	2,123,050	1,062,880

1. Includes reels of microfilm and number of microcards, microprint sheets, and microfiches. *Source:* Association of Research Libraries.

College and University Endowments, 1987–88

(top 75 in millions of dollars)

Institution	Endowment (market value)	Voluntary support[1]	Expenditures[2]	Institution	Endowment (market value)	Voluntary support[1]	Expenditures[2]
Harvard U	$4,089.5	$155.1	$865.5	Grinnell C	$269.8	$3.6	$23.9
Princeton U	2,111.6	78.7	236.5	U of Delaware	267.9	13.1	183.3
Yale U	2,055.8	121.2	521.7	Purdue U	267.8	22.0	453.6
Stanford U	1,800.0	181.9	750.0	Carnegie–Mellon U	265.7	34.4	192.4
Columbia U	1,357.5	93.7	673.9	Wake Forest U	259.0	24.0	171.0
Texas A&M U	1,295.5	44.7	212.8	Texas Christian U	254.8	12.4	57.1
Washington U	1,141.3	50.6	423.3	George Washington U	251.5	16.3	218.9
Massachusetts Inst. of Tech.	1,139.1	96.9	526.7	Ohio State U	247.9	63.9	689.5
Northwestern U	930.5	65.9	483.2	Trinity U	247.2	6.9	35.7
U of Chicago	897.8	63.7	376.8	Wesleyan U	245.0	8.2	56.0
Rice U	873.1	19.2	93.9	U of Richmond	242.3	15.1	38.8
Emory U	773.9	48.1	247.5	Amherst C	242.2	12.4	39.8
Cornell U	770.5	142.0	780.6	Pomona C	242.0	33.7	32.2
U of Pennsylvania	664.6	106.1	655.6	Washington State U	239.7	20.8	n.a.
Dartmouth C	570.7	35.4	161.8	U of Pittsburgh	227.7	24.3	43.3
U of Rochester	540.0	34.0	282.2	Loyola U of Chicago	227.2	25.9	12.4
New York U	518.9	66.0	627.3	Loyola U–New Orleans	225.0	n.a.	41.2
Rockefeller U	503.3	20.7	83.1	Berea C	219.0	10.5	16.6
Johns Hopkins U	502.7	70.5	538.6	U of Wisconsin–Madison	218.3	89.0	683.3
Vanderbilt U	499.4	34.9	245.5	Baylor U	218.3	21.5	83.9
U of California–Berkeley	463.9	66.8	615.1	Oberlin C	216.0	15.4	52.2
U of Notre Dame	463.5	44.7	103.9	Georgetown U	215.9	29.0	225.3
Mayo Medical School	442.1	26.6	111.8	Vassar C	212.8	11.0	40.4
California Inst. of Tech.	425.5	97.4	161.0	Tulane U of Louisiana	200.9	25.7	175.1
U of Southern California	403.7	82.0	538.3	Boston C	200.4	14.6	133.8
U of Virginia	397.8	45.5	302.0	Middlebury C	197.6	9.4	34.7
U of Minnesota	394.1	109.5	847.4	Lehigh U	192.0	25.7	126.8
Duke U	392.9	85.9	358.9	Macalester C	190.0	6.1	24.4
Brown U	368.3	35.3	162.5	Indiana U	190.0	37.0	58.1
U of Michigan	346.3	68.0	783.0	Rensselaer Poly. Inst.	182.4	20.2	113.5
Case Western Reserve U	334.0	34.0	222.0	Lafayette C	176.3	7.5	31.9
Princeton Theol. Sem.	302.5	6.3	17.4	Boston U	175.7	30.0	419.4
U of Texas–Austin	299.5	32.5	462.8	Thomas Jefferson U	173.3	8.8	133.8
Smith C	294.5	27.9	73.3	U of Kansas	172.3	17.4	189.3
Wellesley C	293.3	19.1	49.6	U of Tennessee	160.9	29.6	521.1
Southern Methodist U	289.7	30.2	116.3	U of North Carolina at Chapel Hill	160.3	39.6	430.6
Williams C	279.7	14.5	44.1	Mount Holyoke C	153.1	15.4	37.7
Swarthmore C	273.5	12.5	37.5				

1. Gifts from business, alumni, religious denominations, and others. 2. Figure represents about 80% of typical operating budget. Does not include auxiliary enterprises and capital outlays. NOTE: C = College; U = University; n.a. = not available. *Source:* Council for Aid to Education.

Institutions of Higher Education—Average Salaries and Fringe Benefits for Faculty Members, 1970-1988[1]

(in thousands of dollars)

Control and Academic Rank	1988	1987	1986	1985	1984	1983	1982	1981	1980	1975	1970
Average Salaries											
Public: All ranks	37.2	35.8	33.4	31.2	29.4	28.6	26.2	23.9	22.1	16.6	13.1
Professor	47.2	45.3	42.3	39.6	37.1	36.0	33.7	31.0	28.8	21.7	17.3
Associate professor	35.6	34.2	32.2	30.2	28.4	27.5	25.7	23.4	21.9	16.7	13.2
Assistant professor	29.6	28.5	26.7	25.0	23.5	22.6	21.2	19.2	18.0	13.7	10.9
Instructor	22.2	21.8	20.9	19.5	19.1	17.7	16.7	15.1	14.8	11.2	9.1
Private:[2] All ranks	39.7	37.8	35.4	33.0	31.1	29.2	26.8	24.4	22.1	16.6	13.1
Professor	52.2	50.3	47.0	44.1	41.5	38.8	35.8	32.7	30.1	22.4	17.8
Associate professor	36.6	34.9	32.9	30.9	29.4	27.5	25.4	23.1	21.0	16.0	12.6
Assistant professor	30.1	28.3	26.8	25.0	23.7	22.1	20.4	18.4	17.0	13.0	10.3
Instructor	22.7	20.4	19.8	19.0	18.4	17.6	15.9	14.4	13.3	10.9	8.6
Average Fringe Benefits—All Ranks Combined											
Public	8.2	7.8	7.3	7.0	6.0	5.4	5.1	4.7	3.9	2.5	1.9
Private[2]	9.2	8.6	8.0	7.2	6.4	5.7	5.4	4.9	4.1	2.8	2.2

1. Figures are for 9 months teaching for full-time faculty members in four-year colleges and universities. 2. Excludes church-related colleges and universities. *Source:* U.S. Bureau of the Census, *Statistical Abstract of the United States: 1988.*

Accredited U.S. Senior Colleges and Universities

Source: The Guidance Information System™, a product of Houghton Mifflin Company, Software Division.

Schools listed are four-year institutions that offer at least a Bachelor's degree and are fully accredited by one of the institutional and professional accrediting associations. Included are accredited colleges outside the U.S.

Tuition, room, and board listed are average annual figures (including fees) subject to fluctuation, usually covering two semesters, two out of three trimesters, or three out of four quarters, depending on the school calendar.

For further information, write to the Registrar of the school concerned.

NOTE: n.a. = information not available. — = does not apply. Enrollment figures are approximate. (C) = Coeducational, (M) = primarily for men, (W) = primarily for women.

Abbreviations used for controls:

AB	American Baptist	GGF	Grace Gospel Fellowship
AC	Advent Christian	ID	Interdenominational
AG	Assemblies of God	Ind	Independent
AL	American Lutheran	L	Lutheran
AME	African Methodist Episcopal	LCA	Lutheran Church of America
B	Baptist	LDS	Latter Day Saints
BC	Brethren in Christ	M	Methodist
Br	Brethren	MB	Mennonite Brethren
CB	Church of Brethren	MC	Missionary Church
CC	Church of Christ	Men	Mennonite
CE	Christian Evangelical	Mor	Moravian
CG	Church of God	Naz	Nazarene
ChC	Christian Church	ND	Non-denominational
CMA	Christian & Missionary Alliance	OBS	Open Bible Standard
CME	Christian Methodist Episcopal	P	Private
CP	Cumberland Presbyterian	PH	Pentecostal Holiness
CR	Christian Reformed	Pub	Public
DC	Disciples of Christ	PUS	Presbyterian, U.S.
E	Episcopal	RC	Roman Catholic
EC	Evangelical Covenant	RCA	Reformed Church in America
EFC	Evangelical Free Church	RP	Reformed Presbyterian
EL	Evangelical Lutheran	SB	Southern Baptist
F	Friends	SDA	Seventh Day Adventist
FG	Foursquare Gospel	UCC	United Church of Christ
FM	Free Methodist	UM	United Methodist
FWB	Free Will Baptist	UP	United Presbyterian
		W	Wesleyan
		WM	Wesleyan Methodist

			Tuition ($)		Rm/Bd
Institution and location	Enrollment	Control	Res.	Nonres.	($)
Abilene Christian University; Abilene, Tex. 79699	3,723 (C)	P/CC	4,400	4,400	2,450
Academy of Art College; San Francisco, Calif. 94108	2,156 (C)	P/Ind	4,800	4,800	5,400
Academy of the New Church College; Bryn Athyn, Pa. 19009	139 (C)	P	2,637	2,637	2,511
Adams State College; Alamosa, Colo. 81102	2,021 (C)	Pub	1,292	3,256	2,580
Adelphi University; Garden City, N.Y. 11530	5,122 (C)	P	8,000	8,000	4,377
Adrian College; Adrian, Mich. 49221	1,229 (C)	P/UM	8,096	8,096	2,545
Aeronautics, College of; Flushing, N.Y. 11371	1,200 (C)	P	5,600	5,600	n.a.
Agnes Scott College; Decatur, Ga. 30030	526 (W)	P	9,780	9,780	3,905
Akron, University of; Akron, Ohio 44325	23,904 (C)	Pub	2,078	4,702	2,808
Alabama, University of; Tuscaloosa, Ala. 35487-0132	15,296 (C)	Pub	1,642	4,044	3,090
Alabama, University of–Birmingham; Birmingham, Ala. 35294	9,864 (C)	Pub	1,698	3,258	3,870
Alabama, University of–Huntsville; Huntsville, Ala. 35899	5,717 (C)	Pub	2,040	4,080	1,827
Alabama A&M University; Normal, Ala. 35762	2,454 (C)	Pub	1,134	2,026	2,236
Alabama State University; Montgomery, Ala. 36195	3,699 (C)	Pub	960	1,920	1,620
Alaska, University of–Anchorage; Anchorage, Alas. 99508	4,091 (C)	Pub	941	2,765	3,200
Alaska, University of–Fairbanks; Fairbanks, Alas. 99701	6,786 (C)	Pub	1,332	3,156	2,500
Alaska, University of–Juneau; Juneau, Alas. 99801	2,057 (C)	Pub	932	2,756	2,760
Alaska Bible College; Glennallen, Alas. 99588	90 (C)	P/ID	2,190	2,190	3,000
Alaska Pacific University; Anchorage, Alas. 99508	454 (C)	P/UM	5,900	5,900	3,770
Albany College of Pharmacy; Albany, N.Y. 12208	646 (C)	P	6,225	6,225	3,600
Albany State College; Albany, Ga. 31705	1,800 (C)	Pub	1,476	3,765	2,190
Albertus Magnus College; New Haven, Conn. 06511	500 (C)	P/RC	8,818	8,818	4,695
Albion College; Albion, Mich. 49224	1,664 (C)	P/UM	8,432	8,432	3,540
Albright College; Reading, Pa. 19603	1,326 (C)	P/UM	10,715	10,715	3,250
Alcorn State University; Lorman, Miss. 39096	2,757 (C)	Pub	1,670	2,852	1,630
Alderson–Broaddus College; Philippi, W. Va. 26416	760 (C)	P/AB	7,336	7,336	2,490
Alfred University; Alfred, N.Y. 14802	2,270 (C)	P	11,880	11,880	3,874
Alice Lloyd College; Pippa Passes, Ky. 41844	517 (C)	P	2,580	2,580	2,250

Institution and location	Enrollment	Control	Tuition ($) Res.	Tuition ($) Nonres.	Rm/Bd ($)
llegheny College; Meadville, Pa. 16335	1,990 (C)	P	11,540	11,540	3,600
llentown College of St. Francis de Sales; Center Valley, Pa. 18034	881 (C)	P/RC	6,530	6,530	3,600
lma College; Alma, Mich. 48801	1,198 (C)	P	9,132	9,132	3,390
lvernia College; Reading, Pa. 19607	1,076 (C)	P/RC	5,606	5,606	3,200
lverno College; Milwaukee, Wis. 53215	2,191 (W)	P	5,966	5,966	3,460
mber University; Garland, Tex. 75041	600 (C)	P	3,780	3,780	n.a.
merican Baptist College; Nashville, Tenn. 37207	163 (C)	P/B	1,650	1,650	1,486
merican University of Paris; 75007 Paris, France	972 (C)	P	11,080	11,080	n.a.
merican College of Switzerland; 1854 Leysin (HM), Switzerland	300 (C)	P	16,035	16,035	3,279
merican Conservatory of Music; Chicago, Ill. 60602	124 (C)	P	6,000	6,000	n.a.
merican International College; Springfield, Mass. 01109	1,391 (C)	P	6,850	6,850	3,300
merican University; Washington, D.C. 20016	7,335 (C)	P	11,436	11,436	5,158
merican University in Cairo; New York, N.Y. 10017	2,447 (C)	P	6,500	6,500	3,870
mherst College; Amherst, Mass. 01002	1,585 (C)	P	13,780	13,780	4,200
nderson University; Anderson, Ind. 46012	1,866 (C)	P/CG	6,680	6,680	2,370
ndrews University; Berrien Springs, Mich. 49104	1,884 (C)	P/SDA	7,660	7,660	2,916
ngelo State University; San Angelo, Tex. 76909	5,892 (C)	Pub	975	4,035	3,280
nna Maria College for Men and Women; Paxton, Mass. 01612	450 (C)	P	7,700	7,700	4,020
ntillian College; Mayaguez, P.R. 00709	815 (C)	P/SDA	2,550	2,550	1,440
ntioch College; Yellow Springs, Ohio 45387	568 (C)	P	11,460	11,460	3,330
ntioch Los Angeles; Marina Del Rey, Calif. 90292	182 (C)	P	6,300	6,300	n.a.
ntioch Santa Barbara; Santa Barbara, Calif. 93101	48 (C)	P	6,000	6,000	n.a.
ntioch School for Adult & Experiential Learning; Yellow Springs, Ohio 45387	167 (C)	P	4,032	4,032	n.a.
ntioch Seattle; Seattle, Wash. 98109	91 (C)	P	5,850	5,850	n.a.
ppalachian Bible College; Bradley, W. Va. 25818	182 (C)	P/Ind	3,140	3,140	2,600
ppalachian State University; Boone, N.C. 28608	10,206 (C)	Pub	968	4,806	2,060
quinas College; Grand Rapids, Mich. 49506	2,159 (C)	P/RC	7,494	7,494	3,484
rizona, University of; Tucson, Ariz. 85721	25,154 (C)	Pub	1,446	6,270	2,920
rizona College of the Bible; Phoenix, Ariz. 85021	177 (C)	P/ID	3,790	3,790	2,770
rizona State University; Tempe, Ariz. 85287	32,253 (C)	Pub	1,362	5,484	3,520
rkansas, Univ. of, Fayetteville; Fayetteville, Ark. 72701	15,000 (C)	Pub	1,290	3,190	2,500
rkansas, Univ. of-Little Rock; Little Rock, Ark. 72204	8,775 (C)	Pub	1,250	3,150	n.a.
rkansas, Univ. of-Monticello; Monticello, Ark, 71655	1,854 (C)	Pub	1,100	1,440	1,790
rkansas, Univ. of-Pine Bluff; Pine Bluff, Ark. 71601	3,333 (C)	Pub	1,080	2,550	1,760
rkansas College; Batesville, Ark. 72501	756 (C)	P/PUS	5,455	5,455	2,660
rkansas State University; State University, Ark. 72467	9,026 (C)	Pub	1,200	2,450	2,010
rkansas Tech. University; Russellville, Ark. 72801	3,453 (C)	Pub	1,100	2,150	1,940
rlington Baptist College; Arlington, Tex. 76012	209 (C)	P	1,920	1,920	2,057
rmstrong State College; Savannah, Ga. 31419	2,750 (C)	Pub	1,314	3,606	2,655
rmstrong College; Berkeley, Calif. 94704	251 (C)	P	4,057	4,057	n.a.
rnold & Marie Schwartz College of Pharmacy & Health Sciences. *See* Long Island University Center, Brooklyn Center					
rt Academy of Cincinnati; Cincinnati, Ohio 45202	250 (C)	P	5,825	5,825	n.a.
rt Center College of Design; Pasadena, Calif. 91103	1,257 (C)	P	9,035	9,035	n.a.
rt Institute of Chicago, School of the; Chicago, Ill. 60603	1,843 (C)	P	9,300	9,300	n.a.
rts, The University of the; Philadelphia, Pa. 19102	1,228 (C)	P	8,400	8,400	4,300
rt Institute of Southern California; Laguna Beach, Calif. 92651	115 (C)	P	6,250	6,250	n.a.
sbury College; Wilmore, Ky. 40390	993 (C)	P	6,308	6,308	2,127
shland College; Ashland, Ohio 44805	2,068 (C)	P/Br	8,474	8,474	3,726
ssumption College; Worcester, Mass. 01615-0005	1,750 (C)	P/RC	8,675	8,675	4,450
thens State College; Athens, Ala. 35611	1,392 (C)	Pub	864	1,728	2,075
tlanta Christian College; East Point, Ga. 30344	169 (C)	P	2,716	2,716	2,590
tlanta College of Art; Atlanta, Ga. 30309	340 (C)	P	6,250	6,250	3,400
tlantic, College of the; Bar Harbor, Maine 04609	200 (C)	P	9,600	9,600	3,700
tlantic Christian College; Wilson, N.C. 27893	1,354 (C)	P/DC	5,050	5,050	2,420
tlantic Union College; South Lancaster, Mass. 01561	610 (C)	P/SDA	8,185	8,185	2,800
uburn University; Auburn University, Ala. 36849	18,410 (C)	Pub	1,476	4,428	2,600
uburn University at Montgomery; Montgomery, Ala. 36193	4,450 (C)	Pub	1,095	3,285	2,600
ugsburg College; Minneapolis, Minn. 55454	2,554 (C)	P/AL	8,740	8,740	3,328
ugusta College; Augusta, Ga. 30910	3,934 (C)	Pub	1,296	3,585	3,195
ugustana College; Rock Island, Ill. 61201	2,013 (C)	P/LCA	8,751	8,751	2,994
ugustana College; Sioux Falls, S.D. 57197	1,963 (C)	P/AL	8,000	8,000	2,475
urora University; Aurora, Ill. 60506	1,523 (C)	P	7,500	7,500	3,345
ustin College; Sherman, Tex. 75090	1,210 (C)	P/PUS	8,020	8,020	3,219
ustin Peay State University; Clarksville, Tenn. 37040	4,784 (C)	Pub	1,150	3,886	2,340
verett College; Danville, Va. 24541-3692	900 (C)	P/SB	6,900	6,900	3,920
vila College; Kansas City, Mo. 64145	1,485 (C)	P/RC	6,030	6,030	2,750
zusa Pacific University; Azusa, Calif. 91702	1,567 (C)	P/Ind	7,900	7,900	3,550
abson College; Wellesley, Mass. 02157	1,546 (C)	P	11,392	11,392	4,888
aker University; Baldwin City, Kan. 66006	805 (C)	P/UM	5,820	5,820	2,990
aldwin-Wallace College; Berea, Ohio 44017	2,494 (C)	P/UM	8,625	8,625	3,501
all State University; Muncie, Ind. 47306	16,209 (C)	Pub	1,876	4,320	2,448
altimore, University of; Baltimore, Md. 21201	2,826 (C)	Pub	1,830	3,230	n.a.

Institution and location	Enrollment	Control	Tuition ($) Res.	Tuition ($) Nonres.	Rm/B (\$)
Baltimore Hebrew College; Baltimore, Md. 21215	432 (C)	P	1,800	1,800	n.a.
Baptist Bible College; Springfield, Mo. 65803	742 (C)	P/B	1,700	1,700	2,190
Baptist Bible College of Pennsylvania; Clarks Summit, Pa. 18411	494 (C)	P	4,747	4,747	2,600
Baptist Bible Institute; Graceville, Fla. 32440	370 (C)	P/SB	1,254	1,254	2,300
Baptist College at Charleston; Charleston, S.C. 29411	1,794 (C)	P/SB	5,554	5,554	2,764
Barat College; Lake Forest, Ill. 60045	674 (C)	P	7,020	7,020	3,000
Barber–Scotia College; Concord, N.C. 28025	370 (C)	P/UP	3,330	3,330	2,287
Bard College; Annandale-on-Hudson, N.Y. 12504	930 (C)	P	14,630	14,630	4,760
Barnard College of Columbia University; New York, N.Y. 10027	2,200 (W)	P	12,436	12,436	5,515
Barry University; Miami Shores, Fla. 33161	3,932 (C)	P	7,790	7,790	4,200
Bartlesville Wesleyan College; Bartlesville, Okla. 74003	496 (C)	P/W	4,670	4,670	2,700
Bassist College; Portland, Ore. 97201	208 (C)	P	7,100	7,100	3,850
Bates College; Lewiston, Maine 04240	1,500 (C)	P	18,430	18,430	—
Baylor University; Waco, Tex. 76706	10,243 (C)	P/SB	4,620	4,620	3,330
Beaver College; Glenside, Pa. 19038	1,194 (C)	P	8,460	8,460	3,600
Behrend College. *See* Pennsylvania State University					
Belhaven College; Jackson, Miss. 39202	693 (C)	P/PUS	5,370	5,370	2,040
Bellarmine College; Louisville, Ky. 40205	2,102 (C)	P/RC	5,500	5,500	2,220
Bellevue College; Bellevue, Neb. 68005	2,021 (C)	P	2,370	2,370	n.a.
Bellin College of Nursing; Green Bay, Wisc. 54305-5000	161 (C)	P	4,827	4,827	n.a.
Belmont Abbey College; Belmont, N.C. 28012	865 (C)	P/RC	4,260	5,360	2,886
Belmont College; Nashville, Tenn. 37203	2,414 (C)	P/SB	4,650	4,650	2,080
Beloit College; Beloit, Wis. 53511	1,192 (C)	P	10,902	10,902	2,958
Bemidji State University; Bemidji, Minn. 56601	4,566 (C)	Pub	1,721	2,599	2,130
Benedict College; Columbia, S.C. 29204	1,448 (C)	P/Ind	3,796	3,796	1,980
Benedictine College; Atchison, Kan. 66002	803 (C)	P/RC	6,560	6,560	2,805
Bennett College; Greensboro, N.C. 27401	549 (W)	P/UM	4,265	4,265	2,000
Bennington College; Bennington, Vt. 05201	593 (C)	P	16,495	16,495	3,480
Bentley College; Waltham, Mass. 02254	3,957 (C)	P	9,530	9,530	3,992
Berea College; Berea, Ky. 40404	1,527 (C)	P	170	170	2,205
Berklee College of Music; Boston, Mass. 02215	2,829 (C)	P	7,740	7,740	5,390
Bernard M. Baruch Coll. *See* New York, City Univ. of					
Berry College; Mount Berry, Ga. 30149	1,584 (C)	P	5,400	5,400	3,420
Bethany Bible College; Santa Cruz, Calif. 95066	533 (C)	P/AG	5,350	5,350	2,800
Bethany College; Lindsborg, Kan. 67456	722 (C)	P/LCA	5,992	5,992	2,912
Bethany College; Bethany, W. Va. 26032	844 (C)	P/DC	9,768	9,768	3,402
Bethel College; Mishawaka, Ind. 46545	539 (C)	P/MC	5,720	5,720	2,340
Bethel College; North Newton, Kan. 67117	614 (C)	P/Men	5,782	5,782	2,800
Bethel College; St. Paul, Minn. 55112	1,800 (C)	P/B	8,500	8,500	3,180
Bethel College; McKenzie, Tenn. 38201	469 (C)	P/CP	3,600	3,600	2,100
Bethune–Cookman College; Daytona Beach, Fla. 32015	1,860 (C)	P	4,134	4,134	2,545
Biola University; La Mirada, Calif. 90639	1,838 (C)	P/Ind	8,202	8,202	3,630
Birmingham–Southern College; Birmingham, Ala. 35254	1,757 (C)	P/UM	7,593	7,593	3,065
Black Hills State College; Spearfish, S.D. 57783	2,282 (C)	Pub	1,658	2,890	1,898
Blackburn College; Carlinville, Ill. 62626	469 (C)	P	6,800	6,800	3,400
Bloomfield College; Bloomfield, N.J. 07003	1,484 (C)	P	6,250	6,250	3,160
Bloomsburg State Coll. *See* Bloomsburg Univ. of Pennsylvania					
Bloomsburg University of Pennsylvania; Bloomsburg, Pa. 17815	6,352 (C)	Pub	2,290	3,712	2,064
Blue Mountain College; Blue Mountain, Miss. 38610	374 (W)	P/SB	3,180	3,180	1,940
Bluefield College; Bluefield, Va. 24605	366 (C)	P/SB	4,550	4,550	3,150
Bluefield State College; Bluefield, W. Va. 24701	2,487 (C)	Pub	1,170	2,770	n.a.
Bluffton College; Bluffton, Ohio 45817	608 (C)	P/Men	7,065	7,065	2,901
Boca Raton, College of; Boca Raton, Fla. 33431	1,150 (C)	P	10,000	10,000	4,000
Boise State University; Boise, Idaho 83725	10,401 (C)	Pub	1,180	3,080	2,400
Boricua College; New York, N.Y. 10032	1,072 (C)	P	4,300	4,300	n.a.
Borromeo College of Ohio; Wickliffe, Ohio 44092	45 (M)	P/RC	4,500	4,500	2,300
Boston Architecture Center School of Architecture; Boston, Mass. 02115	597 (C)	P	2,105	2,105	n.a.
Boston College; Chestnut Hill, Mass. 02167	8,752 (C)	P/RC	12,066	12,066	5,790
Boston Conservatory; Boston, Mass. 02215	385 (C)	P	8,210	8,210	4,900
Boston University; Boston, Mass. 02215	14,678 (C)	P	14,095	14,095	5,540
Bowdoin College; Brunswick, Maine 04011	1,350 (C)	P	14,060	14,060	4,920
Bowie State College; Bowie, Md. 20715	2,144 (C)	Pub	1,869	3,337	3,094
Bowling Green State University; Bowling Green, Ohio 43403	15,707 (C)	Pub	2,480	5,460	2,210
Bradford College; Bradford, Mass. 01835	450 (C)	P	9,850	9,850	5,050
Bradley University; Peoria, Ill. 61625	4,594 (C)	P	7,990	7,990	3,380
Brandeis University; Waltham, Mass. 02254	2,881 (C)	P	13,081	13,081	5,520
Brenau: The Women's College; Gainesville, Ga. 30501	489 (W)	P	6,018	6,018	4,982
Brescia College; Owensboro, Ky. 42301	666 (C)	P/RC	4,600	4,600	2,300
Brewton-Parker College; Mount Vernon, Ga. 30445	1,350 (C)	P	2,900	2,900	2,100
Briar Cliff College; Sioux City, Iowa 51104	1,103 (C)	P/RC	6,390	6,390	2,688
Bridgeport, University of; Bridgeport, Conn. 06601	3,146 (C)	P	9,444	9,444	4,410
Bridgeport Engineering Institute; Bridgeport, Conn. 06606	830 (C)	P	3,840	3,840	n.a.
Bridgewater College; Bridgewater, Va. 22812	800 (C)	P	7,650	7,650	3,750

Institution and location	Enrollment	Control	Tuition ($) Res.	Tuition ($) Nonres.	Rm/Bd ($)
Bridgewater State College; Bridgewater, Mass. 02325	5,270 (C)	Pub	1,402	3,898	2,810
Brigham Young University; Provo, Utah 84602	26,600 (C)	P/LDS	1,800	1,800	2,750
Brigham Young University–Hawaii; Laie, Oahu, Hawaii 96762	2,142 (C)	P/LDS	2,160	2,160	2,355
Brooklyn Center. See Long Island University Center					
Brooklyn College. See New York, City University of					
Bristol University; Bristol, Tenn. 37621	700 (C)	P	3,600	3,600	n.a.
Brooks Institute of Photography; Santa Barbara, Calif. 93108	645 (C)	P	7,050	7,050	n.a.
Brown University; Providence, R.I. 02912	5,804 (C)	P	14,375	14,375	4,590
Bryan College; Dayton, Tenn. 37321	402 (C)	P	5,210	5,210	3,200
Bryant College; Smithfield, R.I. 02917	2,897 (C)	P	8,719	8,719	5,401
Bryn Mawr College; Bryn Mawr, Pa. 19010	1,146 (W)	P	12,600	12,600	5,220
Bucknell University; Lewisburg, Pa. 17837	3,297 (C)	P	13,725	13,725	3,475
Buena Vista College; Storm Lake, Iowa 50588	1,086 (C)	P	8,953	8,953	3,944
Burlington College; Burlington, Vt. 05401	200 (C)	P	5,950	5,950	n.a.
Butler University; Indianapolis, Ind. 46208	2,375 (C)	P	7,992	7,992	3,032
Cabrini College; Radnor, Pa. 19087	720 (C)	P	5,885	5,885	4,100
Caldwell College; Caldwell, N.J. 07006	961 (C)	P	6,300	6,300	3,600
California, University of; Berkeley, Calif. 94720:					
UC–Berkeley; Berkeley, Calif. 94720	22,671 (C)	Pub	1,670	7,470	4,134
UC–Davis; Davis, Calif. 95616	16,545 (C)	Pub	1,531	6,337	3,990
UC–Irvine; Irvine, Calif. 92717	13,032 (C)	Pub	1,584	4,506	5,000
UC–Los Angeles; Los Angeles, Calif. 90024	23,883 (C)	Pub	1,634	7,433	3,700
UC–Riverside; Riverside, Calif. 92521	6,010 (C)	Pub	1,697	7,496	4,390
UC–San Diego; La Jolla, Calif. 92093	14,105 (C)	Pub	1,623	6,129	5,326
UC–Santa Barbara; Santa Barbara, Calif. 93106	15,777 (C)	Pub	1,319	4,086	5,853
UC–Santa Cruz; Santa Cruz, Calif. 95064	8,348 (C)	Pub	1,579	5,869	4,473
California Baptist College; Riverside, Calif. 92504	617 (C)	P	5,076	5,076	4,198
California College of Arts and Crafts; Oakland, Calif. 94618	1,044 (C)	P	8,580	8,580	3,700
California Institute of Technology; Pasadena, Calif. 91125	854 (C)	P	12,489	12,489	3,947
California Institute of the Arts; Valencia, Calif. 91355	625 (C)	P	9,200	9,200	3,200
California Lutheran University; Thousand Oaks, Calif. 91360	1,330 (C)	P/AL	8,350	8,350	3,700
California Maritime Academy; Vallejo, Calif. 94590	400 (C)	Pub	1,154	3,814	3,507
California Polytechnic State University; San Luis Obispo, Calif. 93407	14,973 (C)	Pub	780	5,010	3,425
California State Coll. (Pa.). See California Univ. of Pennsylvania					
California State Polytechnic University–Pomona; Pomona, Calif. 91768	17,338 (C)	Pub	750	4,710	3,960
California State University–Bakersfield; Bakersfield, Calif. 93311-1099	3,560 (C)	Pub	801	5,481	3,269
California State University–Chico; Chico, Calif. 95929	14,070 (C)	Pub	808	5,488	3,308
California St. Univ.–Dominguez Hills; Carson, Calif. 90747	5,159 (C)	Pub	771	4,515	3,632
California State Univ.–Fresno; Fresno, Calif. 93740	15,035 (C)	Pub	820	4,564	3,604
California State Univ.–Fullerton; Fullerton, Calif. 92634	20,488 (C)	Pub	922	6,592	3,650
California State Univ.–Hayward; Hayward, Calif. 94542	9,252 (C)	Pub	823	4,572	3,650
California State Univ.–Long Beach; Long Beach, Calif. 90840	28,729 (C)	Pub	862	5,670	4,200
California State Univ.–Los Angeles; Los Angeles, Calif. 90032	15,148 (C)	Pub	786	4,314	3,785
California State Univ.–Northridge; Northridge, Calif. 91330	25,420 (C)	Pub	876	4,620	4,108
California State Univ.–Sacramento; Sacramento, Calif. 95819	19,885 (C)	Pub	734	5,360	3,546
California State Univ.–San Bernardino; San Bernardino, Calif. 92407	5,979 (C)	Pub	837	4,581	3,160
California State Univ.–Stanislaus; Turlock, Calif. 95380	3,848 (C)	Pub	810	5,178	3,200
California Univ. of Pennsylvania; California, Pa. 15419	4,681 (C)	Pub	2,500	3,922	2,180
Calumet College of St. Joseph; Whiting, Ind. 46394	1,059 (C)	P/RC	3,240	3,240	n.a.
Calvary Bible College; Kansas City, Mo. 64147	328 (C)	P/Ind	3,220	3,220	2,320
Calvin College; Grand Rapids, Mich. 49506	4,368 (C)	P/CR	6,790	6,790	2,860
Cameron University; Lawton, Okla. 73505	5,700 (C)	Pub	1,040	2,525	1,810
Campbell University; Buie's Creek, N.C. 27506	2,631 (C)	P/SB	5,896	5,896	2,185
Campbellsville College; Campbellsville, Ky. 42718	671 (C)	P/SB	4,190	4,190	2,710
Canisius College; Buffalo, N.Y. 14208	3,107 (C)	P	7,300	7,300	3,800
Capital University; Columbus, Ohio 43209	3,069 (C)	P/AL	9,530	9,530	3,330
Capitol College; Laurel, Md. 20708	777 (C)	P	5,580	5,580	4,076
Cardinal Stritch College; Milwaukee, Wis. 53217	1,751 (C)	P/RC	6,040	6,040	2,950
Carleton College; Northfield, Minn. 55057	1,885 (C)	P	12,485	12,485	2,745
Carlow College; Pittsburgh, Pa. 15213	962 (W)	P/RC	7,940	7,940	4,000
Carnegie–Mellon University; Pittsburgh, Pa. 15213	4,259 (C)	P	13,080	13,080	4,320
Carroll College; Helena, Mont. 59625	1,414 (C)	P/RC	5,475	5,475	2,975
Carroll College; Waukesha, Wis. 53186	1,393 (C)	P/UP	9,360	9,360	3,070
Carson–Newman College; Jefferson City, Tenn. 37760	1,681 (C)	P/SB	5,030	5,130	2,210
Carthage College; Kenosha, Wis. 53140	959 (C)	P/LCA	8,700	8,700	3,200
Case Western Reserve University; Cleveland, Ohio 44106	3,017 (C)	P	12,000	12,000	4,300
Castleton State College; Castleton, Vt. 05735	1,370 (C)	Pub	2,920	5,900	3,920
Catawba College; Salisbury, N.C. 28144	1,032 (C)	P/UCC	6,800	6,800	3,200
Catholic University of America; Washington, D.C. 20064	2,950 (C)	P	10,150	10,150	5,060

Institution and location	Enrollment	Control	Tuition ($) Res.	Tuition ($) Nonres.	Rm/Bd ($)
Catholic University of Puerto Rico; Ponce, P.R. 00732	10,298 (C)	P/RC	2,213	2,213	2,200
Cayey University College. *See* Puerto Rico, University of					
Cedar Crest College; Allentown, Pa. 18104-6196	452 (W)	P	9,680	9,680	4,180
Cedarville College; Cedarville, Ohio 45314	1,879 (C)	P/B	4,972	4,972	3,090
Centenary College; Hackettstown, N.J. 07840	820 (C)	P	7,560	7,560	3,915
Centenary College of Louisiana; Shreveport, La. 71104	738 (C)	P/UM	6,000	6,000	2,910
Center for Creative Studies, College of Art and Design; Detroit, Mich. 48202	954 (C)	P	7,870	7,870	3,700
Central Arkansas, University of; Conway, Ark. 72032	5,924 (C)	Pub	1,080	2,130	1,920
Central Baptist College; Conway, Ark. 72032	182 (C)	P/B	2,085	2,085	1,700
Central Bible College; Springfield, Mo. 65803	886 (C)	P/AG	2,680	2,680	2,600
Central Christian College of the Bible; Moberly, Mo. 65270	79 (C)	P/ChC	1,984	1,984	1,920
Central College; Pella, Iowa 50219	1,680 (C)	P/RCA	7,938	7,938	3,075
Central Connecticut State University; New Britain, Conn. 06050	11,113 (C)	Pub	1,625	4,035	3,344
Central Florida, University of; Orlando, Fla. 32816	13,608 (C)	Pub	1,134	3,623	3,087
Central Methodist College; Fayette, Mo. 65248	714 (C)	P/UM	5,660	5,660	2,850
Central Michigan University; Mt. Pleasant, Mich. 48859	15,353 (C)	Pub	1,850	4,485	3,010
Central Missouri State University; Warrensburg, Mo. 64093	8,158 (C)	Pub	1,400	2,586	2,344
Central State University; Wilberforce, Ohio 45384	2,674 (C)	Pub	1,884	3,804	3,543
Central State University; Edmond, Okla. 73034	10,940 (C)	Pub	994	2,488	1,992
Central Texas, University of; Killeen, Tex. 76540	315 (C)	P	3,660	3,660	2,484
Central Washington University; Ellensburg, Wash. 98926	6,398 (C)	Pub	1,400	4,600	2,875
Central Wesleyan College; Central, S.C. 29630	418 (C)	P	5,240	5,240	2,436
Centre College; Danville, Ky. 40422	861 (C)	P	8,665	8,665	3,320
Chadron State College; Chadron, Neb. 69337	2,009 (C)	Pub	1,226	1,916	1,992
Chaminade University of Honolulu; Honolulu, Hawaii 96816	2,213 (C)	P/RC	5,250	5,250	3,300
Chapman College; Orange, Calif. 92666	1,539 (C)	P	10,600	10,600	3,800
Charleston, College of; Charleston, S.C. 29424	5,387 (C)	Pub	2,060	3,860	2,450
Charleston, University of; Charleston, W. Va. 25304	1,527 (C)	P	6,750	6,750	3,300
Charter Oak College; Farmington, Conn. 06032-1909	810 (C)	Pub	150	225	n.a.
Chatham College; Pittsburgh, Pa. 15232	696 (W)	P	9,290	9,290	4,100
Chestnut Hill College; Philadelphia, Pa. 19118-2695	620 (W)	P/RC	7,000	7,000	3,550
Cheyney University of Pennsylvania; Cheyney, Pa. 19319	1,473 (C)	Pub	2,340	3,762	2,556
Chicago, University of—The College; Chicago, Ill. 60637	3,257 (C)	P	13,815	13,815	5,170
Chicago State University; Chicago, Ill. 60628	4,644 (C)	Pub	1,472	4,136	n.a.
Christ College–Irvine; Irvine, Calif. 92715	577 (C)	P/L	6,735	6,735	3,570
Christian Brothers College; Memphis, Tenn. 38104	1,758 (C)	P/RC	6,260	6,260	3,020
Christian Heritage College; El Cajon, Calif. 92019	396 (C)	P/Ind	5,720	5,720	2,866
Christopher Newport College; Newport News, Va. 23606	4,650 (C)	Pub	1,630	2,660	n.a.
Church College of Hawaii. *See* Brigham Young University—Hawaii Campus					
Cincinnati, University of; Cincinnati, Ohio 45221	19,947 (C)	Pub	2,532	6,036	3,516
Cincinnati College of Mortuary Science Cohen Center; Cincinnati, Oh. 45212	130 (C)	P	4,340	4,340	n.a.
Circleville Bible College; Circleville, Ohio 43113	162 (C)	P/CC	3,514	3,514	2,580
Citadel–The Military College of South Carolina; Charleston, S.C. 29409	2,274 (M)	Pub	7,413	10,091	2,600
City College (NYC). *See* New York, City University of					
City University; Bellevue, Wash. 98008	1,728 (C)	P	4,725	4,725	n.a.
Claflin College; Orangeburg, S.C. 29115	756 (C)	P/UM	3,568	3,568	1,890
Claremont Colleges:					
Claremont McKenna College; Claremont, Calif. 91711	845 (C)	P	12,900	12,900	4,550
Claremont Men's College. *See* Claremont McKenna College					
Harvey Mudd College; Claremont, Calif. 91711	524 (C)	P	12,660	12,660	5,290
Pitzer College; Claremont, Calif. 91711	740 (C)	P	13,190	13,190	4,890
Pomona College; Claremont, Calif. 91711	1,325 (C)	P	13,130	13,130	5,200
Scripps College; Claremont, Calif. 91711	607 (W)	P	12,890	12,890	5,550
Clarion State College. *See* Clarion University of Pennsylvania					
Clarion University of Pennsylvania; Clarion, Pa. 16214	5,833 (C)	Pub	2,078	3,592	2,210
Clark College; Atlanta, Ga. 30314	1,883 (C)	P	4,974	4,974	2,310
Clark University; Worcester, Mass. 01610	2,262 (C)	P	12,170	12,170	3,900
Clarke College; Dubuque, Iowa 52001	777 (C)	P/RC	7,550	7,550	2,665
Clarkson College of Technology. *See* Clarkson University					
Clarkson University; Potsdam, N.Y. 13676	3,345 (C)	P	11,500	11,500	4,272
Clearwater Christian College; Clearwater, Fla. 33519	295 (C)	P	3,770	3,770	3,000
Cleary College; Ypsilanti, Mich. 48197	940 (C)	P	3,825	3,825	n.a.
Clemson University; Clemson, S.C. 29634	11,774 (C)	Pub	2,243	5,496	2,620
Cleveland Institute of Art; Cleveland, Ohio 44106	517 (C)	P	7,500	7,500	4,270
Cleveland Institute of Music; Cleveland, Ohio 44106	167 (C)	P	9,375	9,375	4,380
Cleveland State University; Cleveland, Ohio 44115	13,000 (C)	Pub	2,277	4,554	2,907
Clinch Valley College. *See* Virginia, University of					
Coe College; Cedar Rapids, Iowa 52402	1,242 (C)	P/UP	8,750	8,750	3,300
Cogswell College; Cupertino, Calif. 95014	245 (C)	P	6,240	8,160	n.a.

Institution and location	Enrollment	Control	Tuition ($) Res.	Tuition ($) Nonres.	Rm/Bd ($)
Coker College; Hartsville, S.C. 29550	626 (C)	P	6,660	6,660	3,228
Colby College; Waterville, Me. 04901	1,704 (C)	P	14,120	14,120	4,860
Colby–Sawyer College; New London, N.H. 03257	450 (W)	P	9,980	9,980	3,920
Coleman College; La Mesa, Calif. 92041	950 (C)	P	7,225	7,225	n.a.
Colgate University; Hamilton, N.Y. 13346	2,709 (C)	P	13,455	13,455	4,540
College for Human Services; New York, NY 10014. *See* Human Services, College for					
College Misericordia; Dallas, Pa. 18612	900 (C)	P/RC	6,880	6,880	3,700
College of Great Falls; Great Falls, Mont. 59405. *See* Great Falls, College of					
Colorado, University of; Boulder, Colo. 80309:					
U. of Colorado–Boulder; Boulder, Colo. 80309	18,927 (C)	Pub	2,000	4,000	3,500
U. of Colorado–Colorado Springs; Colorado Springs, Colo. 80933	4,092 (C)	Pub	1,497	4,531	n.a.
U. of Colorado–Denver; Denver, Colo. 80202	5,557 (C)	Pub	1,292	5,702	n.a.
Colorado Christian College; Lakewood, Colo. 80226	394 (C)	P	4,165	4,165	2,116
Colorado College; Colorado Springs, Colo. 80903	1,940 (C)	P	11,470	11,470	3,095
Colorado School of Mines; Golden, Colo. 80401	1,527 (C)	Pub	3,475	9,057	3,400
Colorado State University; Fort Collins, Colo. 80523	16,042 (C)	Pub	1,897	5,583	3,115
Colorado Technical College; Colorado Springs, Colo. 80907	900 (C)	P	5,200	5,200	n.a.
Colorado Women's College. *See* Denver, Univ. of					
Columbia Bible College and Seminary; Columbia, S.C. 29230	508 (C)	P	3,888	3,888	2,391
Columbia Christian College; Portland, Ore. 97216	268 (C)	P	4,560	4,560	2,474
Columbia College; Chicago, Ill. 60605	5,298 (C)	P	4,996	4,996	n.a.
Columbia College; Columbia, Mo. 65216	714 (C)	P	6,190	6,190	2,796
Columbia College; Columbia, S.C. 29203	1,218 (W)	P/UM	7,600	7,600	2,890
Columbia College–Hollywood; Los Angeles, Calif. 90038	225 (C)	P	4,050	4,050	n.a.
Columbia Union College; Takoma Park, Md. 20912	1,204 (C)	P/SDA	7,830	7,830	3,690
Columbia University–Columbia College; New York, N.Y. 10027	2,900 (C)	P	12,628	12,628	5,105
Columbus College; Columbus, Ga. 31993	3,350 (C)	Pub	1,488	3,777	n.a.
Columbus College of Art and Design; Columbus, Ohio 43215	1,355 (C)	P	6,900	6,900	4,000
Conception Seminary College; Conception, Mo. 64433	65 (M)	P/RC	4,160	4,160	2,820
Concord College; Athens, W. Va. 24712	2,450 (C)	Pub	990	2,570	2,528
Concordia College; Ann Arbor, Mich. 48105	548 (C)	P/L	6,326	6,326	3,290
Concordia College; Bronxville, N.Y. 10708	560 (C)	P/L	6,790	6,790	3,700
Concordia College; Moorhead, Minn. 56560	2,880 (C)	P/AL	7,625	7,625	2,375
Concordia College; Portland, Ore. 97211	458 (C)	P	6,585	6,585	2,770
Concordia College; River Forest, Ill. 60305	933 (C)	P/L	5,984	5,984	3,138
Concordia College; St. Paul, Minn. 55104	1,133 (C)	P/L	6,690	6,690	2,550
Concordia College–Wisconsin; Mequon, Wis. 53092	1,006 (C)	P/L	6,100	6,100	3,100
Concordia Lutheran College; Austin, Tex. 78705	507 (C)	P/L	4,740	4,740	3,000
Concordia Teachers College; Seward, Neb. 68434	750 (C)	P/L	6,100	6,100	2,450
Connecticut, University of; Storrs, Conn. 06269	13,978 (C)	Pub	2,623	6,803	3,660
Connecticut College; New London, Conn. 06320	1,591 (C)	P	12,900	12,900	3,850
Conservatory of Music of Puerto Rico; Hato Rey, P.R. 00918	264 (C)	Pub	210	210	n.a.
Converse College; Spartanburg, S.C. 29301	918 (W)	P	8,350	8,350	3,000
Cooper Union; New York, N.Y. 10003	948 (C)	P	300	300	n.a.
Coppin State College; Baltimore, Md. 21216	2,240 (C)	Pub	1,896	3,364	n.a.
Corcoran School of Art; Washington, D.C. 20006	280 (C)	P	6,840	6,840	4,400
Cornell College; Mt. Vernon, Iowa 52314	1,152 (C)	P	9,980	9,980	3,510
Cornell University; Ithaca, N.Y. 14853	12,633 (C)	P	13,140	13,140	4,320
Cornish College of the Arts; Seattle, Wash. 98102	549 (C)	P	6,890	6,890	n.a.
Corpus Christi State Univ.; Corpus Christi, Tex. 78412	1,902 (C)	Pub	840	3,960	1,850
Covenant College; Lookout Mountain, Tenn. 37350	467 (C)	P/RP	6,230	6,230	2,780
Creighton University; Omaha, Neb. 68178	4,053 (C)	P	7,436	7,436	3,300
Crichton College; Memphis, Tenn. 38182	318 (C)	P	3,384	3,384	2,780
Culver–Stockton College; Canton, Mo. 63435	1,032 (C)	P	5,900	5,900	2,190
Cumberland College; Williamsburg, Ky. 40769	1,904 (C)	P/SB	3,990	3,990	2,476
Cumberland University of Tennessee; Lebanon, Tenn. 37087	707 (C)	P	4,010	4,010	2,640
Curry College; Milton, Mass. 02186	978 (C)	P	9,650	9,650	4,750
Curtis Institute of Music; Philadelphia, Pa. 19103	110 (C)	P	125	125	n.a.
C. W. Post Center. *See* Long Island Univ. Center					
Daemen College; Amherst, N.Y. 14226	1,500 (C)	P	6,450	6,450	3,350
Dakota State College; Madison, S.D. 57042	1,131 (C)	Pub	1,678	1,844	1,900
Dakota Wesleyan University; Mitchell, S.D. 57301	631 (C)	P/UM	4,910	4,910	2,450
Dallas, University of; Irving, Tex. 75062	943 (C)	P/RC	6,780	6,780	3,540
Dallas Baptist University; Dallas, Tex. 75211	1,627 (C)	P/SB	3,360	3,360	2,887
Dallas Christian College; Dallas, Tex. 75234	114 (C)	P/ChC	2,040	2,040	2,500
Dana College; Blair, Neb. 68008	495 (C)	P/AL	6,080	6,080	2,520
Daniel Webster College; Nashua, N.H. 03063	544 (C)	P	8,360	8,360	3,725
Dartmouth College; Hanover, N.H. 03755	3,726 (C)	P	14,445	14,445	4,665
David Lipscomb College; Nashville, Tenn. 37203	2,132 (C)	P/CC	4,000	4,000	2,800
Davidson College; Davidson, N.C. 28036	1,406 (C)	P/PUS	11,327	11,327	3,567
Davis and Elkins College; Elkins, W. Va. 26241	811 (C)	P/PUS	6,800	6,800	3,500

Institution and location	Enrollment	Control	Tuition ($) Res.	Tuition ($) Nonres.	Rm/Bd ($)
Dayton, University of; Dayton, Ohio 45469	7,366 (C)	P/RC	6,920	6,920	3,290
Defiance College; Defiance, Ohio 43512	1,033 (C)	P/UCC	7,184	7,184	2,800
Delaware, University of; Newark, Del. 19716	14,975 (C)	P	2,738	6,478	2,740
Delaware State College; Dover, Del. 19901	2,510 (C)	Pub	1,000	2,550	2,300
Delaware Valley College of Science and Agriculture; Doylestown, Pa. 18901	1,200 (C)	P	7,475	7,475	3,215
Delta State University; Cleveland, Miss. 38732	3,008 (C)	Pub	1,470	2,652	1,490
Denison University; Granville, Ohio 43023	2,108 (C)	P	12,400	12,400	3,510
Denver, University of; Denver, Colo. 80208	2,798 (C)	P	10,944	10,944	4,500
CWC Campus Weekend College-Women's Program; Denver, Colo. 80220	453 (W)	P	6,300	6,300	n.a.
DePaul University; Chicago, Ill. 60604	9,198 (C)	P	8,000	8,000	3,500
DePauw University; Greencastle, Ind. 46135	2,450 (C)	P/UM	10,550	10,550	3,860
Deree College–Division of the American College of Greece; Athens, Greece GR-153 42	2,477 (C)	P	2,288	2,288	n.a.
Design Institute of San Diego; San Diego, Calif. 92121	170 (C)	P	4,800	4,800	n.a.
Detroit, University of; Detroit, Mich. 48221	3,436 (C)	P/RC	7,560	7,560	3,000
Detroit Bible College. *See* William Tyndale College					
Detroit College of Business; Dearborn, Mich. 48126	4,061 (C)	P	3,924	3,924	n.a.
DeVry Institute of Technology; Decatur, Ga. 30341	3,023 (C)	P	4,525	4,525	n.a.
DeVry Institute of Technology; Chicago, Ill. 60618	3,531 (C)	P	4,525	4,525	n.a.
DeVry Institute of Technology; City of Industry, Calif. 91744	2,479 (C)	P	4,525	4,525	n.a.
DeVry Institute of Technology; Columbus, Ohio 43209	2,934 (C)	P	4,525	4,525	n.a.
DeVry Institute of Technology; Irving, Tex. 75038	2,327 (C)	P	4,525	4,525	n.a.
DeVry Institute of Technology; Kansas City, Mo. 64131	1,632 (C)	P	4,525	4,525	n.a.
DeVry Institute of Technology; Lombard, Ill. 60148	2,746 (C)	P	4,525	4,525	n.a.
DeVry Institute of Technology; Phoenix, Ariz. 85021	2,700 (C)	P	4,525	4,525	n.a.
DeVry Technical Institute; Woodbridge, N.J. 07095	2,861 (C)	P	4,525	4,525	n.a.
Dickinson College; Carlisle, Pa. 17013	1,986 (C)	P/UM	13,300	13,300	4,000
Dickinson State University; Dickinson, N.D. 58601	1,417 (C)	Pub	1,299	2,979	1,750
Dillard University; New Orleans, La. 70122	1,200 (C)	P	4,800	4,800	2,900
District of Columbia, Univ. of the; Washington, D.C. 20008	9,084 (C)	Pub	664	2,464	n.a.
Divine Word College; Epworth, Iowa 52045	64 (M)	P/RC	4,800	4,800	2,900
Doane College; Crete, Neb. 68333	611 (C)	P/UCC	7,250	7,250	2,325
Dr. Martin Luther College; New Ulm, Minn. 56073	447 (C)	P/EL	2,985	2,985	1,590
Dominican College of Blauvelt; Orangeburg, N.Y. 10962	1,300 (C)	P	4,970	4,970	4,200
Dominican College of San Rafael; San Rafael, Calif. 94901	426 (C)	P/RC	8,500	8,500	4,580
Dominican School of Philosophy and Theology; Berkeley, Calif. 94709	8 (C)	P/RC	4,500	4,500	n.a.
Don Bosco College; Newton, N.J. 07860	42 (M)	P/RC	3,150	3,150	2,120
Dordt College; Sioux Center, Iowa 51250	987 (C)	P	6,400	6,400	2,040
Dowling College; Oakdale, N.Y. 11769	2,992 (C)	P	5,805	5,805	3,400
Drake University; Des Moines, Iowa 50311	3,979 (C)	P	9,250	9,250	3,650
Drew University–College of Liberal Arts; Madison, N.J. 07940	1,496 (C)	P/UM	14,102	14,102	4,032
Drexel University; Philadelphia, Pa. 19104	6,848 (C)	P	8,816	8,816	4,295
Drury College; Springfield, Mo. 65802	1,138 (C)	P/UCC	6,392	6,392	2,490
Dubuque, Univ. of; Dubuque, Iowa 52001	880 (C)	P/UP	6,875	6,875	2,625
Duke University; Durham, N.C. 27706	5,877 (C)	P	12,800	12,800	4,556
Duquesne University; Pittsburgh, Pa 15282	3,979 (C)	P/RC	7,350	7,350	3,526
Dyke College; Cleveland, Ohio 44115	1,380 (C)	P	4,020	4,020	n.a.
D'Youville College; Buffalo, N.Y. 14201	1,100 (C)	P	6,400	6,400	3,100
Earlham College; Richmond, Ind. 47374	1,200 (C)	P/F	11,610	11,610	3,393
East Carolina University; Greenville, N.C. 27834	12,982 (C)	Pub	878	4,716	2,260
East Central University; Ada, Okla. 74820-6899	3,845 (C)	Pub	1,200	4,140	1,988
Eastern College; St. Davids, Pa. 19087	958 (C)	P/AB	8,110	8,110	3,220
Eastern Connecticut State Univ.; Willimantic, Conn. 06226	4,104 (C)	Pub	1,616	4,042	3,014
Eastern Illinois University; Charleston, Ill. 61920	9,574 (C)	Pub	2,052	5,196	2,388
Eastern Kentucky University; Richmond, Ky. 40475	12,026 (C)	Pub	1,130	3,130	2,150
Eastern Mennonite College; Harrisonburg, Va. 22801	967 (C)	P/Men	6,240	6,240	2,880
Eastern Michigan University; Ypsilanti, Mich. 48197	17,643 (C)	Pub	1,643	4,200	3,015
Eastern Montana College; Billings, Mont. 59101	3,939 (C)	Pub	1,125	2,583	2,606
Eastern Nazarene College; Quincy, Mass. 02170	775 (C)	P/Naz	6,387	6,387	2,950
Eastern New Mexico University; Portales, N.M. 88130	3,147 (C)	Pub	1,030	3,664	1,014
Eastern Oregon State College; La Grande, Ore. 97850	1,563 (C)	Pub	1,500	1,500	2,682
Eastern Washington University; Cheney, Wash. 99004	7,543 (C)	Pub	1,317	4,584	2,830
Eastman School of Music; Rochester, N.Y. 14604	445 (C)	P	11,200	11,200	4,285
East Stroudsburg University of Pennsylvania; East Stroudsburg, Pa. 18301	4,311 (C)	Pub	2,258	3,732	2,438
East Tennessee State University; Johnson City, Tenn. 37614	9,245 (C)	Pub	1,192	3,928	2,200
East Texas Baptist University; Marshall, Tex. 75670	716 (C)	P/SB	3,600	3,600	2,495
East Texas State University; Commerce, Tex. 75428	4,083 (C)	Pub	870	3,990	2,757
East-West University; Chicago, Ill. 60605	320 (C)	P	4,830	4,830	n.a.
Eckerd College; St. Petersburg, Fla. 33733	1,325 (C)	P/PUS	10,895	10,895	3,030

Institution and location	Enrollment	Control	Tuition ($) Res.	Tuition ($) Nonres.	Rm/Bd ($)
Edgewood College; Madison, Wis. 53711	800 (C)	P/RC	5,990	5,990	2,900
Edinboro University of Pennsylvania; Edinboro, Pa. 16444	6,339 (C)	Pub	2,320	3,846	2,182
Electronic Data Processing College of Puerto Rico; Hato Rey, P.R. 00918	1,176 (C)	P	2,334	2,334	n.a.
Elizabeth City State University; Elizabeth City, N.C. 27909	1,641 (C)	Pub	1,024	3,740	2,144
Elizabethtown College; Elizabethtown, Pa. 17022	1,401 (C)	P/CB	9,700	9,700	3,500
Elmhurst College; Elmhurst, Ill. 60126	1,766 (C)	P/UCC	7,166	7,166	3,064
Elmira College; Elmira, N.Y. 14901	1,493 (C)	P	8,900	8,900	3,500
Elms College; Chicopee, Mass. 01013-2839	600 (W)	P	8,100	8,100	3,900
Elon College; Elon College, N.C. 27244	3,079 (C)	P/UCC	6,170	6,170	3,150
Embry–Riddle Aeronautical Univ.–Daytona Beach Campus; Daytona Beach, Fla. 32014	5,197 (C)	P	5,200	5,200	3,780
Prescott Campus; Prescott, Ariz. 86301	1,609 (C)	P	5,200	5,200	3,780
Emerson College; Boston, Mass. 02116	1,977 (C)	P	10,892	10,892	6,733
Emmanuel College; Boston, Mass. 02115	877 (W)	P/RC	9,185	9,185	4,666
Emmanuel College School of Christian Ministries; Franklin Springs, Ga. 30639	30 (C)	P/PH	3,210	3,210	2,385
Emory and Henry College; Emory, Va. 24327	788 (C)	P/UM	4,780	6,280	3,414
Emory University; Atlanta, Ga. 30322	5,193 (C)	P	12,410	12,410	3,850
Emporia State University; Emporia, Kan. 66801	3,881 (C)	Pub	1,285	3,179	2,370
Erskine College; Due West, S.C. 29639	494 (C)	P/RP	6,795	6,795	2,675
Esther Boyer College of Music, Temple University; Philadelphia, Pa. 19122	350 (C)	Pub	3,844	6,752	3,750
ETI Technical College; Cleveland, Ohio 44114	900 (C)	P	4,600	4,600	3,140
Eugene Bible College; Eugene, Ore. 97405	124 (C)	P/OBS	2,993	2,993	2,130
Eureka College; Eureka, Ill. 61530	481 (C)	P/DC	6,875	6,875	2,845
Evangel College; Springfield, Mo. 65802	1,564 (C)	P/AG	4,970	4,970	2,770
Evansville, University of; Evansville, Ind. 47722	3,141 (C)	P/UM	8,200	8,200	3,320
Evergreen State College; Olympia, Wash. 98505	2,715 (C)	Pub	1,317	4,581	3,100
Fairfield University; Fairfield, Conn. 06430	2,937 (C)	P/RC	10,570	10,570	4,750
Fairhaven College–Western Washington University; Bellingham, Wash. 98225	250 (C)	Pub	1,320	4,590	2,500
Fairleigh Dickinson Univ.–Madison; Madison, N.J. 07940	2,478 (C)	P	7,264	7,264	4,310
Fairleigh Dickinson Univ.–Rutherford; Rutherford, N.J. 07070	1,413 (C)	P	7,936	7,936	4,698
Fairleigh Dickinson Univ.–Teaneck; Teaneck, N.J. 07666	3,376 (C)	P	7,264	7,264	4,310
Fairmont State College; Fairmont, W. Va. 26554	5,747 (C)	Pub	990	2,570	2,400
Faith Baptist Bible College and Theological Seminary; Ankeny, Iowa 50021	283 (C)	P/B	3,500	3,500	2,612
Faulkner University; Montgomery, Ala. 36193	1,825 (C)	P	3,750	3,750	2,600
Fayetteville State University; Fayetteville, N.C. 28301	2,307 (C)	Pub	962	4,800	2,150
Felician College; Lodi, N.J. 07644	647 (C)	P/RC	5,700	5,700	n.a.
Ferris State University; Big Rapids, Mich. 49307	11,561 (C)	Pub	1,947	4,044	2,474
Ferrum College; Ferrum, Va. 24088	1,145 (C)	P/UM	6,500	6,500	3,000
Findlay, University of; Findlay, Ohio 45840	1,745 (C)	P/CG	7,345	7,345	3,186
Fisk University; Nashville, Tenn. 37203	520 (C)	P	4,600	4,600	2,285
Fitchburg State College; Fitchburg, Mass. 01420	5,671 (C)	Pub	1,244	3,440	2,400
Flagler College; St. Augustine, Fla. 32085	1,100 (C)	P	4,090	4,090	2,550
Flaming Rainbow University; Stilwell, Okla. 74960	227 (C)	P	3,630	3,630	n.a.
Florida, University of; Gainesville, Fla. 32611	26,498 (C)	Pub	1,144	3,632	3,200
Florida A&M University; Tallahassee, Fla. 32307	6,457 (C)	Pub	1,258	3,938	2,337
Florida Atlantic University; Boca Raton, Fla. 33431	8,067 (C)	Pub	1,258	3,938	2,337
Florida Christian College; Kissimmee, Fla. 32743	130 (C)	P	2,777	2,777	2,999
Florida Institute of Technology; Melbourne, Fla. 32901	3,004 (C)	P	6,966	6,966	3,141
Florida International University; Miami, Fla. 33199	13,560 (C)	Pub	1,104	3,657	4,000
Florida Memorial College; Miami, Fla. 33054	1,750 (C)	P/AB	4,100	4,100	1,460
Florida Southern College; Lakeland, Fla. 33801	1,765 (C)	P/UM	5,600	5,600	3,660
Florida State University; Tallahassee, Fla. 32306	19,799 (C)	Pub	1,100	3,589	2,800
Fontbonne College; St. Louis, Mo. 63105	684 (C)	P/RC	6,725	6,725	3,296
Fordham Univ.–Rose Hill Campus; New York, N.Y. 10458	6,481 (C)	P	9,365	9,365	4,900
Forsyth School for Dental Hygienists; Boston, Mass. 02115	120 (C)	P	9,295	9,295	5,505
Fort Hays State University; Hays, Kan. 67601	3,750 (C)	Pub	1,275	2,955	2,196
Fort Lauderdale College; Fort Lauderdale, Fla. 33301	500 (C)	P	4,400	4,400	4,200
Fort Lewis College; Durango, Colo. 81301	3,842 (C)	Pub	1,286	4,440	2,388
Fort Valley State College; Fort Valley, Ga. 31030	1,748 (C)	Pub	1,404	3,606	2,040
Fort Wayne Bible College; Fort Wayne, Ind. 46807	356 (C)	P/MC	5,420	5,420	2,570
Framingham State College; Framingham, Mass. 01701	3,359 (C)	Pub	1,561	4,057	2,594
Francis Marion College; Florence, S.C. 29501	3,596 (C)	Pub	1,550	3,100	2,830
Franciscan University of Steubenville; Steubenville, Ohio 43952	1,093 (C)	P	5,670	5,670	3,250
Franklin College; Sorengo, Switzerland	200 (C)	P	10,400	10,400	6,000
Franklin and Marshall College; Lancaster, Pa. 17604-3003	1,926 (C)	P/UCC	13,690	13,690	3,980
Franklin College; Franklin, Ind. 46131	769 (C)	P/AB	7,710	7,710	2,825
Franklin Pierce College; Rindge, N.H. 03461	1,183 (C)	P	9,600	9,600	3,880

Institution and location	Enrollment	Control	Tuition ($) Res.	Tuition ($) Nonres.	Rm/Bd ($)
Franklin University; Columbus, Ohio 43215-5399	4,061 (C)	P	3,816	3,816	n.a.
Freed–Hardeman College; Henderson, Tenn. 38340	1,169 (C)	P/CC	4,260	4,260	2,670
Free Will Baptist Bible College; Nashville, Tenn. 37205	332 (C)	P/FWB	2,641	2,641	2,456
Fresno Pacific College; Fresno, Calif. 93702	464 (C)	P/MB	6,100	6,100	2,880
Friends Bible College; Haviland, Kan. 67059	92 (C)	P/F	4,350	4,350	2,200
Friends University; Wichita, Kan. 67213	990 (C)	P/F	6,225	6,225	2,352
Frostburg State University; Frostburg, Md. 21532	3,927 (C)	Pub	1,862	3,389	3,275
Furman University; Greenville, S.C. 29613	2,529 (C)	P/SB	9,156	9,156	3,504
Gallaudet University; Washington, D.C. 20002	1,558 (C)	P	3,304	3,304	3,735
Gannon University; Erie, Pa. 16541	3,975 (C)	P/RC	5,600	5,600	3,200
Gardner–Webb College; Boiling Springs, N.C. 28017	2,139 (C)	P/SB	5,770	5,770	3,086
General Motors Institute. *See* GMI Engineering and Management Institute					
Geneva College; Beaver Falls, Pa. 15010	1,411 (C)	P/RP	6,670	6,670	3,250
George Fox College; Newberg, Ore. 97132	705 (C)	P/F	6,750	6,750	2,960
George Mason University; Fairfax, Va. 22030	12,575 (C)	Pub	2,040	4,236	4,056
Georgetown College; Georgetown, Ky. 40324	1,028 (C)	P/SB	5,050	5,050	3,000
Georgetown University; Washington, D.C. 20057	5,920 (C)	P/RC	13,250	13,250	5,460
George Washington University; Washington, D.C. 20052	6,337 (C)	P	11,500	11,500	3,400
Georgia, University of; Athens, Ga. 30602	26,547 (C)	Pub	1,849	4,875	2,682
Georgia College; Milledgeville, Ga. 31061	3,539 (C)	Pub	1,395	3,684	1,755
Georgia Institute of Technology; Atlanta, Ga. 30332	9,213 (C)	Pub	1,887	5,589	3,780
Georgia Southern College; Statesboro, Ga. 30458	7,801 (C)	Pub	1,446	3,735	2,295
Georgia Southwestern College; Americus, Ga. 31709	1,726 (C)	Pub	1,395	3,684	1,950
Georgia State University; Atlanta, Ga. 30303	15,600 (C)	Pub	1,586	5,276	n.a.
Georgian Court College; Lakewood, N.J. 08701	1,509 (W)	P/RC	6,255	6,255	3,550
Gettysburg College; Gettysburg, Pa. 17325	1,900 (C)	P/L	13,625	13,625	3,160
Glassboro State College; Glassboro, N.J. 08028	5,500 (C)	Pub	1,770	2,370	3,600
Glenville State College; Glenville, W. Va. 26351	2,204 (C)	Pub	974	2,554	2,560
GMI Engineering & Management Institute; Flint, Mich. 48504	2,569 (C)	P	6,882	6,882	2,350
Goddard College; Plainfield, Vt. 05667	225 (C)	P	13,166	13,166	–
God's Bible School and College; Cincinnati, Ohio 45210	232 (C)	P	2,340	2,340	2,050
Golden Gate University; San Francisco, Calif. 94105	2,253 (C)	P	4,148	4,148	n.a.
Goldey Beacom College; Wilmington, Del. 19808	1,800 (C)	P	4,500	4,500	3,800
Gonzaga University; Spokane, Wash. 99258	2,592 (C)	P	8,750	8,750	3,350
Gordon College; Wenham, Mass. 01984	1,183 (C)	P	9,299	9,299	3,696
Goshen College; Goshen, Ind. 46526	1,082 (C)	P/Men	6,610	6,610	2,890
Goucher College; Baltimore, Md. 21204	812 (C)	P	10,800	10,800	4,900
Governors State University; University Park, Ill. 60466	2,553 (C)	Pub	1,396	4,108	n.a.
Grace Bible College; Grand Rapids, Mich. 49509	130 (C)	P/GGF	3,300	3,300	2,350
Grace College; Winona Lake, Ind. 46590	757 (C)	P	6,002	6,002	3,004
Grace College of the Bible; Omaha, Neb. 68108	239 (C)	P/Ind	2,654	2,654	2,300
Graceland College; Lamoni, Iowa 50140	909 (C)	P	6,770	6,770	2,420
Grambling State University; Grambling, La. 71245	5,518 (C)	Pub	1,508	2,858	2,346
Grand Canyon College; Phoenix, Ariz. 85017	1,813 (C)	P/SB	3,928	3,928	2,280
Grand Rapids Baptist College; Grand Rapids, Mich. 49505	779 (C)	P/B	4,846	4,846	3,330
Grand Valley State University; Allendale, Mich. 49401	7,311 (C)	Pub	1,794	4,200	2,940
Grand View College; Des Moines, Iowa 50316	1,349 (C)	P/LCA	5,190	5,190	2,220
Gratz College; Philadelphia, Pa. 19141	92 (C)	P	2,100	2,100	n.a.
Great Falls, College of; Great Falls, Mont. 59405	1,127 (C)	P/RC	3,670	3,670	n.a.
Great Lakes Bible College; Lansing, Mich. 48901	127 (C)	P/CC	3,108	3,108	3,850
Green Mountain College; Poultney, Vt. 05764	550 (C)	P	6,775	6,775	3,900
Greensboro College; Greensboro, N.C. 27401	967 (C)	P/UM	5,646	5,646	2,906
Greenville College; Greenville, Ill. 62246	753 (C)	P/FM	7,164	7,164	3,211
Griffin College; Seattle, Wash. 98121	1,000 (C)	P	3,600	3,600	n.a.
Grinnell College; Grinnell, Iowa 50112	1,276 (C)	P	11,708	11,708	3,380
Grove City College; Grove City, Pa. 16127	2,148 (C)	P	4,050	4,050	2,220
Guam, University of; Mangilao, Guam 96913	1,788 (C)	Pub	1,408	2,136	2,905
Guilford College; Greensboro, N.C. 27410	1,250 (C)	P/F	8,530	8,530	8,530
Gustavus Adolphus College; St. Peter, Minn. 56082	2,389 (C)	P/LCA	10,100	10,100	2,700
Gwynedd–Mercy College; Gwynedd Valley, Pa. 19437	1,741 (C)	P/RC	6,650	6,650	3,500
Hahnemann University School of Health Sciences and Humanities; Philadelphia, Pa. 19102	741 (C)	P	7,000	7,000	5,000
Hamilton College; Clinton, N.Y. 13323	1,620 (C)	P	14,050	14,050	4,150
Hamline University; St. Paul, Minn. 55104	1,236 (C)	P/UM	9,860	9,860	3,224
Hampden–Sydney College; Hampden–Sydney, Va. 23943	937 (M)	P/PUS	10,155	10,155	3,280
Hampshire College; Amherst, Mass. 01002	1,232 (C)	P	13,845	13,845	3,585
Hampton University; Hampton, Va. 23668	5,000 (C)	P	4,800	4,800	3,450
Hannibal-LeGrange College; Hannibal, Mo. 63401	830 (C)	P/SB	4,300	4,300	1,900
Hanover College; Hanover, Ind. 47243	1,070 (C)	P/UP	5,330	5,330	2,370
Harding University; Searcy, Ark. 72143	3,204 (C)	P/CC	4,000	4,000	2,407
Hardin-Simmons University; Abilene, Tex. 79698	1,615 (C)	P	6,737	6,737	2,687

Institution and location	Enrollment	Control	Tuition ($) Res.	Tuition ($) Nonres.	Rm/Bd ($)
Harrington Institute of Interior Design; Chicago, Ill. 60605	411 (C)	P	6,390	6,390	n.a.
Harris–Stowe State College; St. Louis, Mo. 63103	1,400 (C)	Pub	1,170	2,293	n.a.
Hartford, University of; West Hartford, Conn. 06117	5,824 (C)	P	10,992	10,992	4,766
Hartwick College; Oneonta, N.Y. 13820	1,480 (C)	P	11,100	11,100	3,750
Harvard and Radcliffe Colleges; Cambridge, Mass. 02138	6,620 (C)	P	13,665	13,665	4,545
Harvey Mudd College. See Claremont Colleges					
Hastings College; Hastings, Neb. 68901	911 (C)	P/UP	6,990	6,990	2,610
Haverford College; Haverford, Pa. 19041	1,132 (C)	P	13,900	13,900	4,700
Hawaii, Univ. of–Hilo Colleges of Arts and Sciences and Agriculture; Hilo, Hawaii 96720-4091	1,232 (C)	Pub	400	2,310	2,525
Hawaii, University of–Manoa; Honolulu, Hawaii 96822	12,890 (C)	Pub	1,230	3,680	3,072
Hawaii, University of–West Oahu College; Pearl City, Hawaii 96782	492 (C)	Pub	830	2,480	n.a.
Hawaii Loa College; Kaneohe, Hawaii 96744	490 (C)	P	7,300	7,300	4,000
Hawaii Pacific College; Honolulu, Hawaii 96813	3,952 (C)	P	4,300	4,300	n.a.
Health Sciences, University of–School of Related Health Sciences; North Chicago, Ill. 60064	58 (C)	P	6,031	6,031	n.a.
Heidelberg College; Tiffin, Ohio 44883	1,087 (C)	P	10,001	10,001	3,220
Hellenic College; Brookline, Mass. 02146	49 (C)	P	5,100	5,100	3,410
Henderson State University; Arkadelphia, Ark. 71923	3,027 (C)	Pub	1,050	2,100	1,800
Hendrix College; Conway, Ark. 72032	1,029 (C)	P/UM	6,210	6,210	2,475
Herbert H. Lehman College. See New York, City University of					
Heritage College; Toppenish, Wash. 98948	309 (C)	P	3,088	3,088	n.a.
High Point College; High Point, N.C. 27261	1,917 (C)	P/UM	5,640	5,640	2,880
Hillsdale College; Hillsdale, Mich. 49242	1,050 (C)	P	8,600	8,600	3,600
Hiram College; Hiram, Ohio 44234	866 (C)	P	10,339	10,339	3,248
Hobart and William Smith Colleges; Geneva, N.Y. 14456	1,950 (C)	P	13,785	13,785	4,946
Hofstra University; Hempstead, N.Y. 11550	8,495 (C)	P	7,350	7,350	4,360
Hollins College; Roanoke, Va. 24020	850 (W)	P	9,900	9,900	4,100
Holy Apostles College and Seminary; Cromwell, Conn. 06416	85 (C)	P/RC	3,000	3,000	3,820
Holy Cross, College of the; Worcester, Mass. 01610	2,564 (C)	P/RC	12,870	12,870	5,200
Holy Family College; Philadelphia, Pa. 19114	761 (C)	P	5,990	5,990	n.a.
Holy Names College; Oakland, Calif. 94619	450 (C)	P/RC	7,810	7,810	3,870
Hood College; Frederick, Md. 21701	1,100 (W)	P	10,650	10,650	5,345
Hope College; Holland, Mich. 49423	2,781 (C)	P/RCA	8,520	8,520	3,416
Houghton College; Houghton, N.Y. 14744	1,164 (C)	P/W	7,468	7,468	2,900
Houghton College–Buffalo Suburban Campus; West Seneca, N.Y. 14225	86 (C)	P	6,874	6,874	2,816
Houston, Univ. of; Houston, Tex. 77004	18,684 (C)	Pub	930	4,050	3,300
Houston, Univ. of–Clear Lake; Houston, Tex. 77058	3,547 (C)	Pub	914	4,154	n.a.
Houston, Univ. of–Downtown; Houston, Tex. 77002	7,213 (C)	Pub	890	4,010	3,034
Houston, Univ. of–Victoria; Victoria, Tex. 77901	480 (C)	Pub	900	4,020	n.a.
Houston Baptist University; Houston, Tex. 77074	1,940 (C)	P	4,290	4,290	2,220
Howard Payne University; Brownwood, Tex. 76801	1,000 (C)	P/SB	3,520	3,520	2,210
Howard University; Washington, D.C. 20059	9,039 (C)	P	5,005	5,005	3,500
Human Services, College for; New York, N.Y. 10014	708 (C)	P	7,200	7,200	n.a.
Humboldt State University; Arcata, Calif. 95521	6,245 (C)	Pub	843	4,587	3,421
Hunter College. See New York, City University of					
Huntingdon College; Montgomery, Ala. 36194	866 (C)	P/UM	5,160	5,160	2,900
Huntington College; Huntington, Ind. 46750	534 (C)	P/BC	6,900	6,900	2,720
Huron College; Huron, S.D. 57350	510 (C)	P	5,500	5,500	2,618
Husson College; Bangor, Me. 04401	1,518 (C)	P	6,800	6,800	3,400
Huston–Tillotson College; Austin, Tex. 78702	502 (C)	P	3,950	3,950	2,669
Idaho, College of; Caldwell, Idaho 83605	578 (C)	P	7,850	7,850	2,675
Idaho, University of; Moscow, Idaho 83843	6,303 (C)	Pub	1,048	3,048	2,272
Idaho State University; Pocatello, Idaho 83209	6,047 (C)	Pub	1,000	2,900	2,358
Illinois, Univ. of, at Chicago; Chicago, Ill. 60680	15,940 (C)	Pub	2,697	6,237	4,000
Illinois, Univ. of, at Urbana–Champaign; Urbana, Ill. 61801	26,859 (C)	Pub	2,698	6,238	3,538
Illinois Benedictine College; Lisle, Ill. 60532	1,462 (C)	P/RC	6,900	6,900	3,180
Illinois College; Jacksonville, Ill. 62650	842 (C)	P	5,500	5,500	3,100
Illinois Institute of Technology; Chicago, Ill. 60616	2,612 (C)	P	10,500	10,500	3,942
Illinois State University; Normal, Ill. 61761	19,358 (C)	Pub	2,187	5,615	2,479
Illinois Wesleyan University; Bloomington, Ill. 61702	1,708 (C)	P	8,506	8,506	3,085
Immaculata College; Immaculata, Pa. 19345	1,900 (W)	P/RC	6,150	6,150	3,750
Incarnate Word College; San Antonio, Tex. 78209	1,770 (C)	P/RC	6,198	6,198	3,160
Indiana Institute of Technology; Fort Wayne, Ind. 46803	800 (C)	P	5,100	5,100	2,770
Indianapolis, University of; Indianapolis, Ind. 46227	2,725 (C)	P	7,590	7,590	3,050
Indiana State University; Terre Haute, Ind. 47809	10,106 (C)	Pub	1,874	4,424	2,592
Indiana University of Pennsylvania; Indiana, Pa. 15705	11,131 (C)	Pub	2,488	3,910	2,320
Indiana University–Bloomington; Bloomington, Ind. 47405	25,386 (C)	Pub	1,887	5,448	2,700
Indiana University–East; Richmond, Ind. 47374	1,498 (C)	Pub	1,590	3,938	n.a.
Indiana University–Kokomo; Kokomo, Ind. 46902	2,857 (C)	Pub	1,272	3,150	n.a.
Indiana University–Northwest; Gary, Ind. 46408	4,210 (C)	Pub	1,590	3,938	n.a.

Institution and location	Enrollment	Control	Tuition ($) Res.	Tuition ($) Nonres.	Rm/Bd ($)
Indiana University–Purdue University at Fort Wayne; Fort Wayne, Ind. 46805	9,998 (C)	Pub	1,272	3,150	n.a.
Indiana University–Purdue University at Indianapolis; Indianapolis, Ind. 46202	17,203 (C)	Pub	1,475	4,132	4,791
Indiana University–South Bend; South Bend, Ind. 46634	4,985 (C)	Pub	1,635	3,990	n.a.
Indiana University–Southeast; New Albany, Ind. 47150	4,931 (C)	Pub	1,318	3,200	n.a.
Indiana Wesleyan University; Marion, Ind. 46953	1,105 (C)	P	6,420	6,420	2,930
Insurance, College of; New York, N.Y. 10007	96 (C)	P	6,600	6,600	6,200
Inter-American University–Arecibo Regional College; Arecibo, P.R. 00612	3,715 (C)	P	1,760	1,760	n.a.
International Training, School for; Brattleboro, Vt. 05301	75 (C)	P	8,200	8,200	2,850
International Institute of the Americas of World University; Hato Rey, P.R. 00917	4,600 (C)	P	2,280	2,280	n.a.
Iona College; New Rochelle, N.Y. 10801	3,496 (C)	P	7,310	7,310	4,600
Iowa, University of; Iowa City, Iowa 52242	20,667 (C)	Pub	1,826	5,982	2,580
Iowa State University; Ames, Iowa 50011	21,086 (C)	Pub	2,739	8,973	3,720
Iowa Wesleyan College; Mount Pleasant, Iowa 52641	652 (C)	P/UM	6,500	6,500	2,750
Ithaca College; Ithaca, N.Y. 14850	5,493 (C)	P	9,200	9,200	4,000
ITT Technical Institute; West Covina, Calif. 91790-2767	700 (C)	P	6,490	6,490	n.a.
Jackson College for Women. *See* Tufts University					
Jackson State University; Jackson, Miss. 39217	6,500 (C)	Pub	1,500	2,676	2,094
Jacksonville State University; Jacksonville, Ala. 36265	6,679 (C)	Pub	1,100	1,500	1,850
Jacksonville University; Jacksonville, Fla. 32211	1,927 (C)	P	6,300	6,300	3,160
James Madison University; Harrisonburg, Va. 22807	9,434 (C)	Pub	2,702	5,054	3,178
Jamestown College; Jamestown, N.D. 58401	733 (C)	P/UP	6,170	6,170	2,980
Jarvis Christian College; Hawkins, Tex. 75765	560 (C)	P	3,780	3,780	2,712
Jersey City State College; Jersey City, N.J. 07305	5,345 (C)	Pub	1,823	2,423	3,820
Jewish Theological Seminary of America; New York, N.Y. 10027	145 (C)	P	4,945	4,945	5,000
John Brown University; Siloam Springs, Ark. 72761	874 (C)	P	4,500	4,500	2,680
John Carroll University; University Heights, Ohio 44118	3,400 (C)	P/RC	7,424	7,424	4,230
John F. Kennedy University–Evenings; Orinda, Calif. 94563	395 (C)	P	4,920	4,920	n.a.
John Jay Coll. of Criminal Justice. *See* New York, City Univ. of					
Johns Hopkins University; Baltimore, Md. 21218	2,710 (C)	P	14,360	14,360	5,180
Johnson and Wales University; Providence, R.I. 02903	7,019 (C)	P	7,194	7,194	3,150
Johnson Bible College; Knoxville, Tenn. 37998	395 (C)	P/ChC	2,750	2,750	3,100
Johnson C. Smith University; Charlotte, N.C. 28216	1,197 (C)	P	4,448	4,448	2,186
Johnson State College; Johnson, Vt. 05656	1,200 (C)	Pub	2,605	5,389	3,666
Johnston College, Calif. *See* Redlands, University of					
John Wesley College; High Point, N.C. 27260	56 (C)	P/ID	3,000	3,000	2,400
Jones College–Jacksonville; Jacksonville, Fla. 32211	1,700 (C)	P	3,240	3,240	n.a.
Judson College; Marion, Ala. 36756	411 (W)	P/SB	3,500	3,500	2,490
Judson College; Elgin, Ill. 60120	498 (C)	P/B	6,690	6,690	3,590
Juilliard School; New York, N.Y. 10023	490 (C)	P	8,650	8,650	n.a.
Juniata College; Huntingdon, Pa. 16652	1,134 (C)	P	10,600	10,600	3,240
Kalamazoo College; Kalamazoo, Mich. 49007	1,255 (C)	P/AB	10,736	10,736	3,516
Kansas, University of; Lawrence, Kan. 66045	19,602 (C)	Pub	1,355	3,785	2,240
Kansas, University of, Medical Center; Kansas City, Kan. 66103	621 (C)	Pub	1,156	3,586	n.a.
Kansas City Art Institute; Kansas City, Mo. 64111	533 (C)	P	9,150	9,150	3,150
Kansas Newman College; Wichita, Kan. 67213	691 (C)	P	4,800	4,800	2,450
Kansas State University; Manhattan, Kan. 66506	15,611 (C)	Pub	1,430	3,982	2,340
Kansas Wesleyan; University; Salina, Kan. 67401	550 (C)	P/UM	5,720	5,720	2,800
Kean College of New Jersey; Union, N.J. 07083	13,000 (C)	Pub	1,673	2,273	2,745
Kearney State College; Kearney, Neb. 68849	6,614 (C)	Pub	1,031	1,583	1,950
Keene State College; Keene, N.H. 03431	3,098 (C)	Pub	2,050	5,400	2,792
Kendall College; Evanston, Ill. 60201	387 (C)	P	5,901	5,901	3,777
Kendall College of Art and Design; Grand Rapids, Mich. 49503	746 (C)	P	6,900	6,900	n.a.
Kennesaw College; Marietta, Ga. 30061	7,955 (C)	Pub	1,248	3,537	n.a.
Kent State University; Kent, Ohio 44242	18,527 (C)	Pub	2,630	4,830	2,738
Kentucky, University of; Lexington, Ky. 40506	17,260 (C)	Pub	1,540	4,260	2,400
Kentucky Christian College; Grayson, Ky. 41143	491 (C)	P/ChC	2,806	2,806	2,620
Kentucky State University; Frankfort, Ky. 40601	2,116 (C)	Pub	1,160	3,240	2,284
Kentucky Wesleyan College; Owensboro, Ky. 42301	837 (C)	P/UM	5,000	5,000	2,900
Kenyon College; Gambier, Ohio 43022	1,553 (C)	P	13,585	13,585	3,215
Keuka College; Keuka Park, N.Y. 14478	600 (C)	P	7,000	7,000	3,030
King College; Bristol, Tenn. 37620	600 (C)	P/PUS	5,550	5,550	3,050
King's College; Wilkes-Barre, Pa. 18711	2,304 (C)	P/RC	6,950	6,950	3,500
Kings College; Briarcliff Manor, N.Y. 10510	508 (C)	P/ND	6,670	6,670	3,262
Knox College; Galesburg, Ill. 61401	1,030 (C)	P	10,746	10,746	3,216
Knoxville College; Knoxville, Tenn. 37921	500 (C)	P	4,800	4,800	3,400
Kutztown Univ.; Kutztown, PA 19530	6,519 (C)	Pub	2,322	3,744	2,250
Laboratory Institute of Merchandising; New York, N.Y. 10022	258 (C)	P	6,940	6,940	n.a.
Lafayette College; Easton, Pa. 18042	2,039 (C)	P	13,050	13,050	4,300

Institution and location	Enrollment	Control	Tuition ($) Res.	Tuition ($) Nonres.	Rm/Bd ($)
LaGrange College; LaGrange, Ga. 30240	964 (C)	P/UM	4,725	4,725	2,715
Lake Erie College; Painesville, Ohio 44077	568 (C)	P	7,360	7,360	3,630
Lake Forest College; Lake Forest, Ill. 60045	1,126 (C)	P	12,780	12,780	2,870
Lakeland College; Sheboygan, Wis. 53082	1,535 (C)	P/UCC	6,995	6,995	2,950
Lake Superior State University; Sault Ste. Marie, Mich. 49783	2,959 (C)	Pub	1,851	3,507	3,016
Lamar University; Beaumont, Tex. 77710	10,347 (C)	Pub	782	3,278	2,500
Lambuth College; Jackson, Tenn. 38301	767 (C)	P/UM	4,182	4,182	2,600
Lancaster Bible College; Lancaster, Pa. 17601	387 (C)	P	5,080	5,080	2,570
Lander College; Greenwood, S.C. 29646	2,376 (C)	Pub	1,970	2,870	2,300
Lane College; Jackson, Tenn. 38301	501 (C)	P/CME	3,704	3,704	2,242
Langston University; Langston, Okla. 73050	2,103 (C)	Pub	828	2,016	1,900
Laredo State University; Laredo, Tex. 78040-9960	541 (C)	Pub	1,338	4,398	n.a.
La Roche College; Pittsburgh, Pa. 15237	1,625 (C)	P	5,910	5,910	3,320
La Salle University; Philadelphia, Pa. 19141	3,202 (C)	P/RC	8,200	8,200	4,710
La Verne, University of; La Verne, Calif. 91750	1,532 (C)	P/Ind.	9,145	9,145	3,542
Lawrence Technological University; Southfield, Mich. 48075	5,400 (C)	P	3,780	3,780	3,400
Lawrence University; Appleton, Wis. 54912	1,242 (C)	P	12,620	12,620	3,015
Lebanon Valley College; Annville, Pa. 17003	840 (C)	P/UM	9,800	9,800	3,875
Lee College; Cleveland, Tenn. 37311	1,331 (C)	P	3,450	3,450	2,426
Lee College of the University of Judaism; Los Angeles, Calif. 90077	69 (C)	P	5,700	5,700	4,175
Lehigh University; Bethlehem, Pa. 18015	4,453 (C)	P	13,550	13,550	4,370
Le Moyne College; Syracuse, N.Y. 13214-1399	1,830 (C)	P	7,480	7,480	3,390
LeMoyne–Owen College; Memphis, Tenn. 38126	955 (C)	P	3,380	3,380	n.a.
Lenoir–Rhyne College; Hickory, N.C. 28603	1,465 (C)	P/LCA	7,250	7,250	2,890
Lesley College; Cambridge, Mass. 02138-2790	525 (W)	P	9,490	9,490	4,600
LeTourneau College; Longview, Tex. 75607	768 (C)	P	5,714	5,714	3,320
Lewis and Clark College; Portland, Ore. 97219	1,920 (C)	P	10,197	10,197	3,798
Lewis–Clark State College; Lewiston, Idaho 83501	2,275 (C)	Pub	1,040	2,940	2,720
Lewis University; Romeoville, Ill. 60441	2,912 (C)	P/RC	6,784	6,784	3,350
Liberty University; Lynchburg, Va. 24506	6,130 (C)	P/B	3,880	3,880	3,400
L.I.F.E. Bible College; Los Angeles, Calif. 90026	459 (C)	P/FG	2,880	2,880	2,169
Limestone College; Gaffney, S.C. 29340	295 (C)	P	5,597	5,597	2,700
Lincoln Christian College; Lincoln, Ill. 62656	327 (C)	P/CC	3,040	3,040	2,200
Lincoln Memorial University; Harrogate, Tenn. 37752	1,425 (C)	P	3,980	3,980	2,400
Lincoln University; Jefferson City, Mo. 65101	2,470 (C)	Pub	1,200	2,400	2,698
Lincoln University; Lincoln University, Pa. 19352	1,057 (C)	Pub	2,732	3,832	2,615
Lindenwood College; St. Charles, Mo. 63301	500 (C)	P	6,150	6,150	3,000
Linfield College; McMinnville, Ore. 97128	1,283 (C)	P	9,380	9,380	3,050
Livingstone College; Salisbury, N.C. 28144	640 (C)	P/AME	3,317	3,317	2,268
Livingston University; Livingston, Ala. 35470	1,421 (C)	Pub	1,263	1,263	1,836
Lock Haven University of Pennsylvania; Lock Haven, Pa. 17745	2,890 (C)	Pub	2,130	3,552	1,993
Loma Linda University; Loma Linda, Calif. 92350	2,322 (C)	P/SDA	8,550	8,550	3,235
Loma Linda University–La Sierra; Riverside, Calif. 92515	1,592 (C)	P/SDA	8,550	8,550	3,066
Long Island University; Greenvale, N.Y. 11548:					
Brooklyn Campus; Brooklyn, N.Y. 11201	3,441 (C)	P	7,500	7,500	5,400
C.W. Post Campus; Greenvale, N.Y. 11548	5,281 (C)	P	7,880	7,880	4,000
Southampton Campus; Southampton, N.Y. 11968	1,184 (C)	P	8,450	8,450	4,922
Longwood College; Farmville, Va. 23901	2,875 (C)	Pub	2,598	4,384	2,900
Loras College; Dubuque, Iowa 52001	1,933 (C)	P	7,345	7,345	2,760
Louisiana College; Pineville, La. 71359	1,017 (C)	P/SB	3,247	3,247	3,062
Louisiana State Univ. and A&M Coll.; Baton Rouge, La. 70803	22,256 (C)	Pub	1,814	5,014	2,400
LSU–Shreveport; Shreveport, La. 71115	3,995 (C)	Pub	1,320	3,240	n.a.
Louisiana Tech University; Ruston, La. 71272	9,070 (C)	Pub	1,602	2,544	2,025
Louisville, University of; Louisville, Ky. 40292	21,900 (C)	Pub	1,488	4,248	1,680
Lourdes College; Sylvania, Ohio 43560	773 (C)	P/RC	4,660	4,660	n.a.
Lowell, University of; Lowell, Mass. 01854	11,555 (C)	Pub	1,541	4,445	2,552
Loyola College; Baltimore, Md. 21210	3,007 (C)	P/RC	7,975	7,975	4,300
Loyola Marymount University; Los Angeles, Calif. 90045	4,046 (C)	P/RC	9,431	9,431	4,464
Loyola University; New Orleans, La. 70118	3,594 (C)	P/RC	7,775	7,775	4,000
Loyola University of Chicago; Chicago, Ill. 60611	5,655 (C)	P	6,980	6,980	4,174
Lubbock Christian Univ.; Lubbock, Tex. 79407	1,079 (C)	P/CC	4,700	4,700	2,180
Lutheran Bible Institute of Seattle; Issaquah, Wash. 98027	143 (C)	P/L	4,495	4,495	2,875
Luther College; Decorah, Iowa 52101	2,214 (C)	P/AL	9,025	9,025	2,675
Lycoming College; Williamsport, Pa. 17701	1,163 (C)	P	9,280	9,280	3,400
Lynchburg College; Lynchburg, Va. 24501	1,600 (C)	P	8,800	8,800	4,300
Lyndon State College; Lyndonville, Vt. 05851	948 (C)	Pub	2,700	5,484	3,666
Macalester College; St. Paul, Minn. 55105	1,847 (C)	P	10,508	10,508	3,292
MacMurray College; Jacksonville, Ill. 62650	650 (C)	P/UM	7,200	7,200	3,000
Madonna College; Livonia, Mich. 48150	3,782 (C)	P	3,110	3,110	2,525
Maharishi International University; Fairfield, Iowa 52556	298 (C)	P	6,448	6,448	2,304
Maine, Univ. of, at Farmington; Farmington, Me. 04938	2,427 (C)	Pub	1,560	3,780	2,900
Maine, Univ. of, at Fort Kent; Fort Kent, Me. 04743-1292	611 (C)	Pub	1,560	3,780	2,875

Institution and location	Enrollment	Control	Tuition ($) Res.	Tuition ($) Nonres.	Rm/Bd ($)
Maine, Univ. of, at Machias; Machias, Me. 04654	851 (C)	Pub	1,560	3,780	2,995
Maine, Univ. of, at Orono; Orono, Me. 04469	10,682 (C)	Pub	1,970	5,030	3,390
Maine, Univ. of, at Presque Isle; Presque Isle, Me. 04769	1,294 (C)	Pub	1,560	3,780	2,900
Maine Maritime Academy; Castine, Me. 04420	479 (C)	Pub	2,900	5,030	3,200
Mallinckrodt College of the North Shore; Wilmette, Ill. 60091	272 (C)	P/RC	3,750	3,750	n.a.
Malone College; Canton, Ohio 44709	1,048 (C)	P/F	6,634	6,634	2,800
Manchester College; North Manchester, Ind. 46962	931 (C)	P/CB	7,260	7,260	2,810
Manhattan Christian College; Manhattan, Kan. 66502	189 (C)	P/CC	2,700	2,700	2,210
Manhattan College; Riverdale, N.Y. 10471	3,400 (C)	P	9,100	9,100	4,800
Manhattan School of Music; New York, N.Y. 10027	403 (C)	P	8,900	8,900	n.a.
Manhattanville College; Purchase, N.Y. 10577	1,050 (C)	P	9,846	9,846	4,676
Mankato State University; Mankato, Minn. 56001	14,206 (C)	Pub	1,774	2,710	2,140
Mannes College of Music; New York, N.Y. 10024	120 (C)	P	8,500	8,500	4,900
Mansfield University of Pennsylvania; Mansfield, Pa. 16933	2,661 (C)	Pub	2,330	3,752	2,556
Marian College; Indianapolis, Ind. 46222	1,233 (C)	P/RC	5,866	5,866	2,570
Marian College of Fond du Lac; Fond du Lac, Wis. 54935	714 (C)	P/RC	6,200	6,200	2,610
Marietta College; Marietta, Ohio 45750	1,285 (C)	P	10,250	10,250	3,000
Marist College; Poughkeepsie, N.Y. 12601	2,900 (C)	P	7,100	7,100	4,122
Marlboro College; Marlboro, Vt. 05344	240 (C)	P	13,290	13,290	4,470
Marquette University; Milwaukee, Wis. 53233	9,163 (C)	P	7,500	7,500	3,450
Mars Hill College; Mars Hill, N.C. 28754	1,116 (C)	P/SB	5,650	5,650	2,650
Marshall University; Huntington, W. Va. 25705	9,941 (C)	Pub	1,132	2,952	3,200
Martin Center College; Indianapolis, Ind. 42605	255 (C)	P	3,750	3,750	n.a.
Mary, University of; Bismarck, N.D. 58504	1,190 (C)	P	4,800	4,800	2,260
Mary Baldwin College; Staunton, Va. 24401	648 (W)	P/PUS	8,050	8,050	5,500
Marycrest College; Davenport, Iowa 52804	1,081 (C)	P/RC	7,200	7,200	2,700
Marygrove College; Detroit, Mich. 48221	1,014 (C)	P/RC	5,170	5,170	2,900
Mary Hardin–Baylor, University of; Belton, Tex. 76513	1,307 (C)	P/SB	4,185	4,185	2,625
Maryland, Univ. of–Baltimore County; Baltimore, Md. 21228	8,693 (C)	Pub	2,016	5,402	3,360
Maryland, Univ. of–College Park; College Park, Md. 20742	27,902 (C)	Pub	1,906	5,292	3,732
Maryland, Univ. of–Eastern Shore; Princess Anne, Md. 21853	1,484 (C)	Pub	1,880	5,160	3,224
Maryland, Univ. of, University College; College Park, Md. 20742	11,466 (C)	Pub	2,910	2,910	n.a.
Maryland Institute–College of Art; Baltimore, Md. 21217	850 (C)	P	9,650	9,650	3,825
Marylhurst College; Marylhurst, Ore. 97036	1,564 (C)	P	5,655	5,655	n.a.
Marymount College; Tarrytown, N.Y. 10591	1,247 (W)	P	8,750	8,750	4,996
Marymount Manhattan College; New York, N.Y. 10021	1,484 (W)	P	7,150	7,150	4,900
Marymount Univ.; Arlington, Va. 22207	1,878 (C)	P	8,400	8,400	4,332
Maryville College; Maryville, Tenn. 37801	787 (C)	P	6,995	6,995	3,395
Maryville College—St. Louis; St. Louis, Mo. 63141	2,377 (C)	P	6,300	6,300	3,300
Mary Washington College; Fredericksburg, Va. 22401	3,352 (C)	Pub	2,264	4,592	3,642
Marywood College; Scranton, Pa. 18509	2,072 (C)	P/RC	6,300	6,300	3,100
Massachusetts, Univ. of–Amherst; Amherst, Mass. 01003	19,853 (C)	Pub	2,350	5,860	3,000
Massachusetts, Univ. of–Boston; Boston, Mass. 02125	10,399 (C)	Pub	2,139	6,429	n.a.
Massachusetts College of Art; Boston, Mass. 02115	1,112 (C)	Pub	1,594	4,150	n.a.
Massachusetts College of Pharmacy and Allied Health Sciences; Boston, Mass. 02115	785 (C)	P	7,824	7,824	5,570
Massachusetts Institute of Technology; Cambridge, Mass. 02139	4,225 (C)	P	13,400	13,400	4,640
Massachusetts Maritime Academy; Buzzards Bay, Mass. 02532	600 (C)	Pub	1,544	4,100	3,150
Master's College, The; Newhall, Calif. 91322	814 (C)	P/B	5,850	5,850	3,690
Mayville State University; Mayville, N. D. 58257	761 (C)	Pub	1,299	2,859	1,920
McKendree College; Lebanon, Ill. 62258	1,038 (C)	P/UM	5,216	5,216	2,830
McMurry College; Abilene, Tex. 79697	1,703 (C)	P/UM	4,260	4,260	2,080
McNeese State University; Lake Charles, La. 70609	6,371 (C)	Pub	1,396	2,746	1,700
McPherson College; McPherson, Kan. 67460	469 (C)	P/CB	5,940	5,940	2,950
Medaille College; Buffalo, N.Y. 14214	1,053 (C)	P	5,550	5,550	n.a.
Medical College of Georgia; Augusta, Ga. 30912	696 (C)	Pub	1,712	4,748	3,060
Medical University of South Carolina; Charleston, S.C. 29425	915 (C)	Pub	1,750	3,500	3,300
Memphis College of Art; Memphis, Tenn. 38112	254 (C)	P	6,750	6,750	4,000
Memphis State University; Memphis, Tenn. 38152	16,179 (C)	Pub	1,319	4,043	2,490
Menlo College; Atherton, Calif. 94025	590 (C)	P	10,552	10,552	5,738
Mercer University; Macon, Ga. 31207	2,596 (C)	P/SB	7,309[1]	7,309	3,278
Mercer University–Atlanta; Atlanta, Ga. 30341	1,405 (C)	P/SB	5,468	5,468	n.a.
Mercy College; Dobbs Ferry, N.Y. 10522	6,267 (C)	P	5,490	5,490	n.a.
Mercy College of Detroit; Detroit, Mich. 48219	2,325 (C)	P/RC	5,489	5,489	1,800
Mercyhurst College; Erie, Pa. 16546	2,067 (C)	P/RC	7,100	7,100	2,875
Meredith College; Raleigh, N.C. 27607	1,935 (W)	P	4,910	4,910	2,470
Merrimack College; North Andover, Mass. 01845	2,357 (C)	P/RC	8,900	8,900	4,900
Mesa State College; Grand Junction, Colo. 81502	3,958 (C)	Pub	1,268	3,258	2,654
Messiah College; Grantham, Pa. 17027	2,179 (C)	P	7,380	7,380	3,680
Methodist College; Fayetteville, N.C. 28311-1499	1,502 (C)	P	6,650	6,650	2,850
Metropolitan State College; Denver, Colo. 80204	15,150 (C)	Pub	1,332	4,340	n.a.
Metropolitan State University; St. Paul, Minn. 55101	5,535 (C)	Pub	1,440	2,314	n.a.

Institution and location	Enrollment	Control	Tuition ($) Res.	Tuition ($) Nonres.	Rm/Bd ($)
Miami, University of; Coral Gables, Fla. 33124	8,805 (C)	P	11,875	11,875	4,730
Miami Christian College; Miami, Fla. 33167	155 (C)	P/ID	4,300	4,300	2,880
Miami University; Oxford, Ohio 45056	14,528 (C)	Pub	3,036	6,540	2,700
Michigan, Univ. of–Ann Arbor; Ann Arbor, Mich. 48109	35,216 (C)	Pub	2,876	9,888	3,425
Michigan, Univ. of–Dearborn; Dearborn, Mich. 48128	6,474 (C)	Pub	1,990	5,982	n.a.
Michigan, Univ. of–Flint; Flint, Mich. 48502	6,305 (C)	Pub	1,954	3,130	n.a.
Michigan State University; East Lansing, Mich. 48824	42,695 (C)	Pub	4,242	8,262	2,733
Michigan Technological University; Houghton, Mich. 49931	6,037 (C)	Pub	2,262	5,067	2,846
Mid–America Bible College; Oklahoma City, Okla. 73170	259 (C)	P/CG	3,924	3,924	2,100
Mid–America Nazarene College; Olathe, Kan. 66061	1,121 (C)	P	4,656	4,656	2,848
Middlebury College; Middlebury, Vt. 05753	1,900 (C)	P	19,160	19,160	–
Midland Lutheran College; Fremont, Neb. 68025	910 (C)	P/L	6,900	6,900	2,400
Middle Tennessee State Univ.; Murfreesboro, Tenn. 37132	11,850 (C)	Pub	1,142	3,878	1,750
Midwestern State University; Wichita Falls, Tex. 76308	4,711 (C)	Pub	960	4,080	2,242
Miles College; Birmingham, Ala. 35208	566 (C)	P/CME	3,760	3,760	2,300
Millersville University of Pennsylvania; Millersville, Pa. 17551	6,560 (C)	Pub	2,130	3,552	2,550
Milligan College; Milligan College, Tenn. 37682	600 (C)	P	5,416	5,416	2,458
Millikin University; Decatur, Ill. 62522	1,625 (C)	P	8,421	8,421	3,329
Mills College; Oakland, Calif. 94613	810 (W)	P	12,205	12,205	5,100
Millsaps College; Jackson, Miss. 39210	1,174 (C)	P/UM	8,250	8,250	3,080
Milwaukee Institute of Art and Design; Milwaukee, Wis. 53202	407 (C)	P	6,320	6,320	n.a.
Milwaukee School of Engineering; Milwaukee, Wis. 53201-0644	1,842 (C)	P	7,800	7,800	3,000
Minneapolis Coll. of Art and Design; Minneapolis, Minn. 55404	629 (C)	P	8,650	8,650	3,400
Minnesota, Univ. of–Duluth; Duluth, Minn. 55812	7,365 (C)	Pub	2,105	4,880	2,850
Minnesota, Univ. of–Morris; Morris, Minn. 56267	2,021 (C)	Pub	2,268	5,292	2,650
Minnesota, Univ. of–Twin Cities; Minneapolis, Minn. 55455	29,278 (C)	Pub	2,412	5,327	2,650
Minnesota Bible College; Rochester, Minn. 55902	90 (C)	P/CC	2,700	2,700	2,860
Minot State University; Minot, N.D. 58701	2,950 (C)	Pub	1,257	2,937	1,620
Mississippi, University of; University, Miss. 38677	7,589 (C)	Pub	1,790	2,972	2,204
Mississippi, Univ. of, Medical Center; Jackson, Miss. 39216	472 (C)	Pub	1,595	2,777	2,324
Mississippi College; Clinton, Miss. 39058	1,880 (C)	P	4,432	4,432	2,250
Mississippi State University; Mississippi State, Miss. 39762	10,576 (C)	Pub	1,794	2,976	2,500
Mississippi University for Women; Columbus, Miss. 39701	2,024 (C)	Pub	1,580	2,772	2,092
Mississippi Valley State University; Itta Bena, Miss. 38941	1,848 (C)	Pub	1,660	2,842	1,675
Missouri, Univ. of–Columbia; Columbia, Mo. 65211	17,525 (C)	Pub	1,801	5,173	2,667
Missouri, Univ. of–Kansas City; Kansas City, Mo. 64110	7,141 (C)	Pub	1,851	4,944	2,678
Missouri, Univ. of–Rolla; Rolla, Mo. 65401	4,212 (C)	Pub	2,023	5,395	3,180
Missouri, Univ. of–St. Louis; St. Louis, Mo. 63121	10,069 (C)	Pub	1,822	5,194	n.a.
Missouri Baptist College; St. Louis, Mo. 63141	951 (C)	P/SB	4,600	4,600	2,100
Missouri Southern State College; Joplin, Mo. 64801	5,504 (C)	Pub	1,072	2,144	2,080
Missouri Valley College; Marshall, Mo. 65340	564 (C)	P	6,750	6,750	3,510
Missouri Western State College; St. Joseph, Mo. 64507	4,153 (C)	Pub	1,154	2,174	1,924
Mobile College; Mobile, Ala. 36613	901 (C)	P/SB	3,192	3,192	2,718
Molloy College; Rockville Centre, N.Y. 11570	1,385 (C)	P/RC	6,700	6,700	n.a.
Monmouth College; Monmouth, Ill. 61462	676 (C)	P/UP	9,795	9,795	2,850
Monmouth College; West Long Branch, N.J. 07764	3,097 (C)	P	8,000	8,000	4,000
Montana, University of; Missoula, Mont. 59812	7,353 (C)	Pub	1,363	3,200	2,858
Montana College of Mineral Science and Technology; Butte, Mont. 59701	1,696 (C)	Pub	1,091	2,909	2,700
Montana State University; Bozeman, Mont. 59717	10,024 (C)	Pub	1,343	3,161	2,800
Montclair State College; Upper Montclair, N.J. 07043	10,224 (C)	Pub	1,875	2,595	3,556
Monterey Institute of Intl. Studies; Monterey, Calif. 93940	99 (C)	P	9,545	9,545	n.a.
Montevallo, University of; Montevallo, Ala. 35115	2,379 (C)	Pub	1,500	2,460	2,318
Montreat–Anderson College; Montreat, N.C. 28757	386 (C)	P	4,787	4,784	2,872
Moody Bible Institute; Chicago, Ill. 60610	1,410 (C)	P/ID	500	500	3,500
Moore College of Art; Philadelphia, Pa. 19103	647 (W)	P	9,100	9,100	4,700
Moorhead State University; Moorhead, Minn. 56560	8,752 (C)	Pub	1,824	2,760	2,100
Moravian College; Bethlehem, Pa. 18018	1,219 (C)	P/MOR	10,805	10,805	3,515
Morehead State University; Morehead, Ky. 40351	5,962 (C)	Pub	1,190	3,310	2,330
Morehouse College; Atlanta, Ga. 30314	2,166 (M)	P	5,550	5,550	3,600
Morgan State University; Baltimore, Md. 21239	3,449 (C)	Pub	1,778	3,544	3,980
Morningside College; Sioux City, Iowa 51106	1,126 (C)	P/UM	7,566	7,566	2,590
Morris Brown College; Atlanta, Ga. 30314	1,500 (C)	P/AME	4,650	4,650	2,600
Morris College; Sumter, S.C. 29150	700 (C)	P	3,127	3,127	2,158
Morrison College Reno Business College; Reno, Nev. 89503	300 (C)	P	5,000	5,000	n.a.
Mount Angel Seminary; St. Benedict, Ore. 97373	25 (M)	P/RC	3,030	3,030	2,800
Mount Holyoke College; South Hadley, Mass. 01075	1,954 (W)	P	12,840	12,840	3,720
Mount Marty College; Yankton, S.D. 57078	488 (C)	P/RC	5,775	5,775	2,460
Mount Mary College; Milwaukee, Wis. 53222	1,333 (W)	P/RC	5,750	5,750	2,375
Mount Mercy College; Cedar Rapids, Iowa 52402	1,568 (C)	P	6,490	6,490	2,655
Mount Olive College; Mount Olive, N.C. 28365	997 (C)	P	4,995	4,995	2,550
Mount St. Joseph, College of; Mount St. Joseph, Ohio 45051	2,343 (C)	P/RC	6,940	6,940	3,550
Mount Saint Mary College; Newburgh, N.Y. 12550	1,106 (C)	P	5,650	5,650	3,300

Institution and location	Enrollment	Control	Tuition ($) Res.	Tuition ($) Nonres.	Rm/Bd ($)
Mount Saint Mary's College; Emmitsburg, Md. 21727	1,411 (C)	P/RC	8,525	8,525	4,900
Mount St. Clare College; Clinton, Iowa 52732	335 (C)	P	6,080	6,080	2,800
Mount St. Mary's College; Los Angeles, Calif. 90049	938 (W)	P/RC	8,120	8,120	4,088
Mount Saint Vincent, College of; New York, N.Y. 10471	936 (C)	P	7,350	7,350	4,250
Mount Senario College; Ladysmith, Wis. 54848	489 (C)	P	5,600	5,600	2,300
Mount Union College; Alliance, Ohio 44601	1,227 (C)	P	10,070	10,070	2,930
Mount Vernon College; Washington, D.C. 20007	528 (W)	P	9,582	9,582	5,216
Mount Vernon Nazarene College; Mount Vernon, Ohio 43050	1,087 (C)	P	5,052	5,052	2,720
Muhlenberg College; Allentown, Pa. 18104	1,616 (C)	P/L	13,115	13,115	3,675
Multnomah School of the Bible; Portland, Ore. 97220	569 (C)	P	4,650	4,650	2,600
Mundelein College; Chicago, Ill. 60660	1,010 (W)	P/RC	7,020	7,020	3,090
Murray State University; Murray, Ky. 42071	6,302 (C)	Pub	1,160	3,280	2,160
Museum of Fine Arts, School of the-Tufts University; Boston, Mass. 02115	664 (C)	P	8,350	8,350	n.a.
Museum Art School, Portland. *See* Pacific Northwest Coll. of Art					
Muskingum College; New Concord, Ohio 43762	1,140 (C)	P/UP	10,120	10,120	3,080
Naropa Institute; Boulder, Colo. 80302	285 (C)	P	7,580	7,580	n.a.
Nathaniel Hawthorne College. *See* Hawthorne College					
National College; Rapid City, S.D. 57709	678 (C)	P	5,460	5,460	2,790
National College-Albuquerque; Albuquerque, N.M. 87108	198 (C)	P	4,548	4,548	n.a.
National College, Colorado Springs Branch; Colorado Springs, Colo. 80909	320 (C)	P	3,800	3,800	n.a.
National College of Education; Evanston, Ill. 60201	2,226 (C)	P	6,525	6,525	3,795
National University; San Diego, Calif. 92108	7,121 (C)	P	5,405	5,405	n.a.
Nazareth College in Kalamazoo; Nazareth, Mich. 49001-1282	615 (C)	P	7,156	7,156	3,082
Nazareth College of Rochester; Rochester, N.Y. 14610	1,479 (C)	P	7,200	7,200	3,770
Nebraska, University of-Lincoln; Lincoln, Neb. 68588-0415	19,755 (C)	Pub	1,703	4,200	2,310
Nebraska, University of-Omaha; Omaha, Neb. 68182	14,829 (C)	Pub	1,368	3,524	n.a.
Nebraska Christian College; Norfolk, Neb. 68701	148 (C)	P	2,240	2,240	2,090
Nebraska Wesleyan University; Lincoln, Neb. 68504	1,576 (C)	P/UM	7,188	7,188	2,570
Neumann College; Aston, Pa. 19014	1,073 (C)	P	6,100	6,100	n.a.
Nevada, University of-Las Vegas; Las Vegas, Nev. 89154	15,000 (C)	Pub	1,500	4,500	3,500
Nevada, University of-Reno; Reno, Nev. 89557	7,444 (C)	Pub	1,280	4,280	2,600
Newberry College; Newberry, S.C. 29108	686 (C)	P/LCA	6,600	6,600	2,600
New College of California; San Francisco, Calif. 94110	400 (C)	P	4,600	4,600	n.a.
New College of the University of South Florida; Sarasota, Fla. 34243-2197	497 (C)	Pub	1,311	4,298	2,940
New England, University of; Biddeford, Me. 04005	690 (C)	P	8,550	8,550	3,830
New England College; Henniker, N.H. 03242	1,087 (C)	P	9,020	9,020	3,880
New England College-Arundel Campus; Sussex BN18 ODA, England	211 (C)	P	9,020	9,020	3,880
New England Conservatory of Music; Boston, Mass. 02115	428 (C)	P	11,100	11,100	5,400
New England Institute of Technology; Warwick, R.I. 02886	1,950 (C)	P	6,225	6,225	n.a.
New Hampshire, University of; Durham, N.H. 03824	9,496 (C)	Pub	2,767	7,947	3,000
New Hampshire College; Manchester, N.H. 03104	1,600 (C)	P	8,280	8,280	4,380
New Haven, University of; West Haven, Conn. 06516	1,755 (C)	P	7,720	7,720	3,900
New Jersey Institute of Technology; Newark, N.J. 07102	4,704 (C)	Pub	3,220	5,820	4,095
New Mexico, University of; Albuquerque, N.M. 87131	19,746 (C)	Pub	1,222	4,572	2,850
New Mexico Highlands University; Las Vegas, N.M. 87701	1,563 (C)	Pub	1,003	3,576	1,724
New Mexico Inst. of Mining & Technology; Socorro, N.M. 87801	939 (C)	Pub	804	3,972	2,740
New Mexico State University; Las Cruces, N.M. 88003-0001	13,284 (C)	Pub	1,284	4,980	2,100
New Orleans, University of; New Orleans, La. 70148	16,109 (C)	Pub	1,666	4,138	2,368
New Rochelle, College of-School of Arts & Sciences and School of Nursing; New Rochelle, N.Y. 10801	622 (W)	P	7,650	7,650	3,700
New School for Social Research Eugene Lang College; New York, N.Y. 10011	250 (C)	P	8,230	8,230	5,405
New York, City University of; New York, N.Y. 10021:					
Bernard M. Baruch College; New York, N.Y. 10010	12,628 (C)	Pub	1,301	4,102	n.a.
Brooklyn College; Brooklyn, N.Y. 11210	11,940 (C)	Pub	1,351	4,155	n.a.
City College; New York, N.Y. 10031	10,179 (C)	Pub	1,345	4,145	n.a.
College of Staten Island; Staten Island, N.Y. 10301	9,679 (C)	Pub	1,344	4,144	n.a.
Hunter College; New York, N.Y. 10021	16,091 (C)	Pub	1,250	2,550	2,135
John Jay College of Criminal Justice; New York, N.Y. 10019	6,769 (C)	Pub	1,350	4,200	n.a.
Herbert H. Lehman College; Bronx, N.Y. 10468	10,000 (C)	Pub	1,301	4,102	n.a.
Queens College; Flushing, N.Y. 11367	16,000 (C)	Pub	1,430	4,232	n.a.
York College; Jamaica, N.Y. 11451	4,826 (C)	Pub	1,347	4,122	n.a.
New York, State University of; Albany, N.Y. 12246:					
SUNY-Albany; Albany, N.Y. 12222	11,788 (C)	Pub	1,478	4,700	3,103
SUNY-Buffalo; Buffalo, N.Y. 14214	19,278 (C)	Pub	1,474	3,324	3,590
SUNY-Purchase; Purchase, N.Y. 10577	3,864 (C)	Pub	1,495	4,095	3,286
SUNY-Stony Brook; Stony Brook, N.Y. 11794	11,210 (C)	Pub	1,495	4,095	3,720
SUNY-College at Brockport; Brockport, N.Y. 14420	6,788 (C)	Pub	1,490	4,090	3,440
SUNY-College at Buffalo; Buffalo, N.Y. 14222	10,684 (C)	Pub	1,465	3,315	3,030
SUNY-College at Cortland; Cortland, N.Y. 13045	3,467 (C)	Pub	1,375	3,225	3,125
SUNY-College at Fredonia; Fredonia, N.Y. 14063	4,626 (C)	Pub	1,487	3,347	3,160

Institution and location	Enrollment	Control	Tuition ($) Res.	Tuition ($) Nonres.	Rm/Bd ($)
SUNY–College at Geneseo; Geneseo, N.Y. 14454-1471	4,892 (C)	Pub	1,350	3,200	2,700
SUNY–College at New Paltz; New Paltz, N.Y. 12561	4,696 (C)	Pub	1,495	4,095	3,360
SUNY–College at Old Westbury; Old Westbury, N.Y. 11568	3,942 (C)	Pub	1,445	3,950	4,907
SUNY–College at Oneonta; Oneonta, N.Y. 13820	5,501 (C)	Pub	1,545	3,400	2,800
SUNY–College at Oswego; Oswego, N.Y. 13126	6,622 (C)	Pub	1,350	3,950	3,102
SUNY–College at Plattsburgh; Plattsburgh, N.Y. 12901	5,754 (C)	Pub	1,485	3,335	3,166
SUNY–College at Potsdam; Potsdam, N.Y. 13676	3,686 (C)	Pub	1,475	3,325	3,156
SUNY–College of Environmental Science and Forestry; Syracuse, N.Y. 13210	905 (C)	Pub	1,440	3,290	4,000
SUNY–College of Technology, Marcy Campus; Utica, N.Y. 13504	2,416 (C)	Pub	1,475	4,075	n.a.
SUNY–Empire State College; Saratoga Springs, N.Y. 12866	5,862 (C)	Pub	1,387	3,237	n.a.
SUNY–Fashion Institute of Technology; New York, N.Y. 10001-5992	4,017 (C)	Pub	1,560	3,250	4,355
SUNY–Health Science Center at Syracuse; Syracuse, N.Y. 13210	276 (C)	Pub	1,440	4,040	3,493
SUNY–Maritime College; Fort Schuyler, Bronx, N.Y. 10465	760 (C)	Pub	1,495	4,135	3,450
SUNY–University Center at Binghamton; Binghamton, N.Y. 13901	9,355 (C)	Pub	1,503	4,103	3,672
New York City Technical Coll. *See* New York, City Univ. of					
New York Institute of Technology Central Islip Campus; Central Islip, N.Y. 11722	1,616 (C)	P	6,232	6,232	n.a.
New York Institute of Technology; Old Westbury, N.Y. 11568	6,428 (C)	P	6,232	6,232	n.a.
New York Institute of Technology, Metropolitan Center; New York, N.Y. 10023	2,841 (C)	P	6,232	6,232	n.a.
New York School of Interior Design; New York, N.Y. 10022	809 (C)	P	6,850	6,850	n.a.
New York University; New York, N.Y. 10003	14,608 (C)	P	12,200	12,200	5,850
New York, University of the State of, Regents College Degrees; Albany, N.Y. 12230	14,372 (C)	Pub	375	375	n.a.
Niagara University; Niagara University, N.Y. 14109	2,500 (C)	P	7,640	7,640	3,617
Nicholls State University; Thibodaux, La. 70310	6,511 (C)	Pub	1,390	2,740	1,980
Nichols College; Dudley, Mass. 01570	791 (C)	P	6,600	6,600	3,800
Norfolk State University; Norfolk, Va. 23504	7,047 (C)	Pub	1,606	3,156	2,730
North Adams State College; North Adams, Mass. 01247	2,100 (C)	Pub	1,500	4,000	3,000
North Alabama, University of; Florence, Ala. 35632	4,636 (C)	Pub	1,152	1,612	2,202
North Carolina, Univ. of–Asheville; Asheville, N.C. 28804	3,152 (C)	Pub	852	4,224	2,720
North Carolina, Univ. of–Chapel Hill; Chapel Hill, N.C. 27514	15,251 (C)	Pub	876	4,830	3,200
North Carolina, Univ. of–Charlotte; Charlotte, N.C. 28223	11,032 (C)	Pub	821	4,659	2,402
North Carolina, Univ. of–Greensboro; Greensboro, N.C. 27412	8,441 (C)	Pub	1,128	5,082	2,905
North Carolina, Univ. of–Wilmington; Wilmington, N.C. 28403	6,288 (C)	Pub	953	4,453	2,520
North Carolina Agricultural and Technical State University; Greensboro, N.C. 27411	5,396 (C)	Pub	899	4,737	2,188
North Carolina Central University; Durham, N.C. 27707	3,532 (C)	Pub	983	4,821	2,536
North Carolina School of the Arts; Winston–Salem, N.C. 27127-2189	502 (C)	Pub	1,191	5,523	2,727
North Carolina State University–Raleigh; Raleigh, N.C. 27695	24,021 (C)	Pub	922	4,876	2,770
North Carolina Wesleyan College; Rocky Mount, N.C. 27801	1,516 (C)	P/UM	6,400	6,400	3,100
North Central Bible College; Minneapolis, Minn. 55404	1,167 (C)	P	4,420	4,420	2,750
North Central College; Naperville, Ill. 60566	2,081 (C)	P	7,590	7,590	3,117
North Dakota, University of; Grand Forks, N.D. 58202	10,140 (C)	Pub	1,472	3,356	2,104
North Dakota State University; Fargo, N.D. 58105	8,606 (C)	Pub	1,389	3,273	2,010
North Georgia College; Dahlonega, Ga. 30597	1,909 (C)	Pub	1,401	3,690	2,025
North Park College; Chicago, Ill. 60625	1,083 (C)	P/EC	7,007	7,007	3,084
North Texas, University of; Denton, Tex. 76203	18,171 (C)	Pub	1,010	4,130	2,967
Northeast Louisiana University; Monroe, La. 71209	9,442 (C)	Pub	1,413	2,553	2,250
Northeast Missouri State University; Kirksville, Mo. 63501	5,432 (C)	Pub	1,398	2,658	2,152
Northeastern Bible College; Essex Fells, N.J. 07021	193 (C)	P	4,880	4,880	2,740
Northeastern Illinois University; Chicago, Ill. 60625	7,267 (C)	Pub	1,656	4,334	n.a.
Northeastern State Univ.; Tahlequah, Okla. 74464	6,009 (C)	Pub	1,255	3,268	1,880
Northeastern University; Boston, Mass. 02115	15,497 (C)	P	8,670	8,670	5,160
Northern Arizona University; Flagstaff, Ariz. 86011	11,647 (C)	Pub	1,412	5,004	2,358
Northern Colorado, University of; Greeley, Colo. 80639	7,967 (C)	Pub	1,944	4,524	2,952
Northern Illinois University; DeKalb, Ill. 60115	18,122 (C)	Pub	2,072	5,000	2,472
Northern Iowa, University of; Cedar Falls, Iowa 50614	10,517 (C)	Pub	1,810	4,650	2,150
Northern Kentucky University; Highland Heights, Ky. 41076	8,592 (C)	Pub	1,140	3,260	3,836
Northern Michigan University; Marquette, Mich. 49855	7,493 (C)	Pub	1,842	3,762	2,983
Northern Montana College; Havre, Mont. 59501	1,686 (C)	Pub	1,051	2,370	2,400
Northern State College; Aberdeen, S.D. 57401	2,560 (C)	Pub	2,144	2,816	1,651
North Florida, University of; Jacksonville, Fla. 32216	6,085 (C)	Pub	1,100	3,600	2,800
Northland College; Ashland, Wis. 54806	547 (C)	P	6,850	6,850	3,240
Northrop University; Los Angeles, Calif. 90045	1,181 (C)	P	9,120	9,120	8,402
Northwest Christian College; Eugene, Ore. 97401	279 (C)	P/DC	5,237	5,237	2,788
Northwest College; Kirkland, Wash. 98083-0579	687 (C)	P	5,145	5,145	2,300
Northwest Missouri State University; Maryville, Mo. 64468	4,600 (C)	Pub	1,320	2,415	2,300
Northwest Nazarene College; Nampa, Idaho 83651	1,095 (C)	P/Naz	5,823	5,823	2,529
Northwestern College; Orange City, Iowa 51041	953 (C)	P/RCA	6,900	6,900	2,475
Northwestern College; St. Paul, Minn. 55113	977 (C)	P/ID	7,575	7,575	2,510
Northwestern Oklahoma State University; Alva, Okla. 73717	1,957 (C)	Pub	1,056	2,640	1,574

Institution and location	Enrollment	Control	Tuition ($) Res.	Tuition ($) Nonres.	Rm/Bd ($)
Northwestern State Univ. of Louisiana; Natchitoches, La. 71497	5,757 (C)	Pub	1,459	2,809	1,964
Northwestern University; Evanston, Ill. 60201-3060	7,405 (C)	P	12,996	12,996	4,380
Northwood Institute of Florida; West Palm Beach, Fla. 33409	450 (C)	P	7,080	7,080	4,515
Northwood Institute of Michigan; Midland, Mich. 48640	1,851 (C)	P	6,780	6,780	3,345
Northwood Institute of Texas; Cedar Hill, Tex. 75104	215 (C)	P	6,780	6,780	3,645
Norwich University; Northfield, Vt. 05663	1,653 (C)	P	11,200	11,200	4,300
Notre Dame, College of; Belmont, Calif. 94002	591 (C)	P/RC	8,400	8,400	4,300
Notre Dame, University of; Notre Dame, Ind. 46556	7,500 (C)	P	11,500	11,500	3,200
Notre Dame College; Manchester, N.H. 03104	520 (C)	P/RC	6,100	6,100	3,578
Notre Dame College of Ohio; Cleveland, Ohio 44121	757 (W)	P/RC	5,750	5,750	2,930
Notre Dame of Maryland, College of; Baltimore, Md. 21210	617 (W)	P/RC	8,100	8,100	4,400
Nova University; Ft. Lauderdale, Fla. 33314	2,400 (C)	P	5,550	5,550	4,100
Nyack College; Nyack, N.Y. 10960	519 (C)	P/CMA	6,380	6,380	3,080
O'More College of Design; Franklin, Tenn. 37604	156 (C)	P	5,000	5,000	n.a.
Oakland City College; Oakland City, Ind. 47660	625 (C)	P/B	5,990	5,990	2,430
Oakland University; Rochester, Mich. 48063	9,952 (C)	Pub	1,542	4,044	2,873
Oakwood College; Huntsville, Ala. 35896	1,000 (C)	P/SDA	5,331	5,331	3,051
Oberlin College; Oberlin, Ohio 44074	2,850 (C)	P	14,220	14,220	4,620
Oblate College; Washington, D.C. 20017	5² (C)	P/RC	3,550	3,550	n.a.
Occidental College; Los Angeles, Calif. 90041	1,677 (C)	P	13,044	13,044	4,860
Oglethorpe University; Atlanta, Ga. 30319	972 (C)	P	8,350	8,350	3,750
Ohio Dominican College; Columbus, Ohio 43219	1,331 (C)	P/RC	5,990	5,990	3,320
Ohio Institute of Technology, Columbus. See DeVry Institute of Technology, Columbus					
Ohio Northern University; Ada, Ohio 45810	2,241 (C)	P/UM	9,600	9,600	3,015
Ohio State University; Columbus, Ohio 43210	40,538 (C)	Pub	2,040	5,628	3,726
Ohio University; Athens, Ohio 45701	14,000 (C)	Pub	2,394	4,953	3,159
Ohio University–Zanesville; Zanesville, Ohio 43701	985 (C)	Pub	1,941	4,500	n.a.
Ohio Wesleyan University; Delaware, Ohio 43015	1,775 (C)	P/UM	11,128	11,128	4,230
Oklahoma, University of–Health Sciences Center; Oklahoma City, Okla. 73190	986 (C)	Pub	1,419	4,581	n.a.
Oklahoma, University of–Norman; Norman, Okla. 73019	16,375 (C)	Pub	1,000	3,004	2,772
Oklahoma Baptist University; Shawnee, Okla. 74801	1,967 (C)	P/B	3,586	3,586	2,300
Oklahoma Christian College; Oklahoma City, Okla. 73136-1100	1,611 (C)	P/CC	3,540	3,540	2,300
Oklahoma City University; Oklahoma City, Okla. 73106	1,573 (C)	P/UM	4,228	4,228	2,830
Oklahoma Panhandle State University; Goodwell, Okla. 73939	1,276 (C)	Pub	885	2,370	1,580
Oklahoma State University; Stillwater, Okla. 74078	16,323 (C)	Pub	1,522	4,478	2,620
Old Dominion University; Norfolk, Va. 23508	11,514 (C)	Pub	2,414	4,622	3,858
Olivet College; Olivet, Mich. 49076	784 (C)	P/UCC	6,860	6,860	2,715
Olivet Nazarene University; Kankakee, Ill. 60901	1,566 (C)	P/Naz	5,548	5,548	3,078
Oral Roberts University; Tulsa, Okla. 74171	3,564 (C)	P	5,100	5,100	3,250
Oregon Art Institute–Pacific Northwest College of Art; Portland, Ore. 97205	191 (C)	P	4,750	4,750	n.a.
Oregon, University of; Eugene, Ore. 97403	13,794 (C)	Pub	1,649	4,517	2,486
Oregon Coll. of Education. See Western Oregon State Coll.					
Oregon Health Sciences University; Portland, Ore. 97201	400 (C)	Pub	2,061	4,929	2,849
Oregon Institute of Technology; Klamath Falls, Ore. 97601	3,026 (C)	Pub	1,606	4,481	2,688
Oregon State University; Corvallis, Ore. 97331	12,890 (C)	Pub	1,604	4,472	2,772
Orlando College; Orlando, Fla. 32810	810 (C)	P	3,037	3,037	n.a.
Otis Art Institute of Parsons School of Design; Los Angeles, Calif. 90057	704 (C)	P	9,140	9,140	2,150
Ottawa University; Ottawa, Kan. 66067	476 (C)	P/AB	5,600	5,600	2,760
Ottawa University–Phoenix Center; Phoenix, Ariz. 85021	415 (C)	P	2,760	2,760	n.a.
Otterbein College; Westerville, Ohio 43081	2,051 (C)	P/UM	9,261	9,261	3,414
Ouachita Baptist University; Arkadelphia, Ark. 71923	1,428 (C)	P/B	4,410	4,410	2,000
Our Lady of Angels College. See Neumann College					
Our Lady of Holy Cross College; New Orleans, La. 70131-7399	606 (C)	P/RC	4,600	4,600	n.a.
Our Lady of the Lake–University of San Antonio; San Antonio, Tex. 78285	1,779 (C)	P/RC	5,186	5,186	2,734
Ozarks, School of the; Point Lookout, Mo. 65726	1,243 (C)	P	7,650	7,650	3,216
Ozarks, University of the; Clarksville, Ark. 72830	711 (C)	P/UP	2,810	2,810	2,110
Pace University; New York, N.Y. 10038	7,239 (C)	P	7,180	7,180	4,116
Pace University–College of White Plains; White Plains, N.Y. 10603	1,561 (C)	P	7,180	7,180	4,116
Pace University–Pleasantville–Briarcliff; Pleasantville, N.Y. 10570	4,104 (C)	P	7,180	7,180	4,116
Pacific, University of the; Stockton, Calif. 95211	3,600 (C)	P	12,772	12,772	4,598
Pacific Christian College; Fullerton, Calif. 92631	489 (C)	P/ChC	5,000	5,000	2,800
Pacific Lutheran University; Tacoma, Wash. 98447	3,351 (C)	P	9,360	9,360	3,600
Pacific Oaks College; Pasadena, Calif. 91103	50 (C)	P	8,200	8,200	n.a.
Pacific Union College; Angwin, Calif. 94508	1,537 (C)	P/SDA	7,980	7,980	2,880
Pacific University; Forest Grove, Ore. 97116	832 (C)	P/UCC	8,700	8,700	3,700
Paier College of Art, Inc.; Hamden, Conn. 06511	312 (C)	P	8,610	8,610	n.a.
Paine College; Augusta, Ga. 30910	708 (C)	P/UM	4,500	4,500	2,350
Palm Beach Atlantic College; West Palm Beach, Fla. 33401	1,153 (C)	P/SB	4,800	4,800	2,500

Institution and location	Enrollment	Control	Tuition ($) Res.	Tuition ($) Nonres.	Rm/Bd ($)
Pan American University; Edinburg, Tex. 78539	9,000 (C)	Pub	972	4,716	2,080
Park College; Parkville, Mo. 64152	479 (C)	P/LDS	5,500	5,500	2,600
Parks College of St. Louis University; Cahokia, Ill. 62206	1,100 (C)	P/RC	5,280	5,280	3,100
Parsons School of Design; New York, N.Y. 10011	1,740 (C)	P	10,110	10,110	4,950
Patten College; Oakland, Calif. 94601	228 (C)	P/CE	3,150	3,150	3,790
Paul Quinn College; Waco, Tex. 76704	509 (C)	P	2,900	2,900	2,750
Peabody Conservatory of Music; Baltimore, Md. 21202	256 (C)	P	10,425	10,425	4,230
Pembroke State University; Pembroke, N.C. 28372	2,231 (C)	Pub	716	4,088	1,770
Pennsylvania, University of; Philadelphia, Pa. 19104	9,175 (C)	P	12,750	12,750	5,050
Pennsylvania State Erie–Behrend College; Erie, Pa. 16563	2,667 (C)	Pub	3,610	7,248	3,170
Pennsylvania State Harrisburg–The Capital College; Middletown, Pa. 17057	1,937 (C)	Pub	3,610	7,248	3,170
Pennsylvania State University—Park; University Park, Pa. 16802	31,251 (C)	Pub	3,610	7,248	3,170
Pepperdine University School of Business and Management; Culver City, Calif. 90230	600 (C)	P	12,500	12,500	n.a.
Pepperdine University–Seaver College; Malibu, Calif. 90265	2,562 (C)	P	13,210	13,210	5,520
Peru State College; Peru, Neb. 68421	1,700 (C)	Pub	1,375	1,955	2,150
Pfeiffer College; Misenheimer, N.C. 28109	811 (C)	P/UM	5,535	5,535	2,710
Pharmacy, School of (Ga.). *See* Mercer Univ.					
Philadelphia College of Bible; Langhorne, Pa. 19047	591 (C)	P	5,515	5,515	3,200
Philadelphia College of Pharmacy and Science; Philadelphia, Pa. 19104	1,522 (C)	P	7,000	7,000	3,600
Philadelphia College of Textiles and Science; Philadelphia, Pa. 19144	1,820 (C)	P	6,950	6,950	3,650
Philander Smith College; Little Rock, Ark. 72202	572 (C)	P/UM	2,236	2,236	2,300
Phillips University; Enid, Okla. 73702	808 (C)	P	4,918	4,918	2,318
Phoenix, University of; Phoenix, Ariz. 85040	3,023 (C)	P	5,478	5,478	n.a.
Piedmont Bible College; Winston–Salem, N.C. 27101	268 (C)	P	2,800	2,800	2,100
Piedmont College; Demorest, Ga. 30535	555 (C)	P/Ind	2,736	2,736	2,680
Pikeville College; Pikeville, Ky. 41501	753 (C)	P/UP	3,700	3,700	2,300
Pillsbury Baptist Bible College; Owatonna, Minn. 55060	394 (C)	P	3,600	3,600	2,450
Pine Manor College; Chestnut Hill, Mass. 02167	578 (W)	P	10,900	10,900	5,800
Pittsburgh, University of; Pittsburgh, Pa. 15260	18,861 (C)	Pub	3,836	7,516	3,174
Pittsburgh, University of–Bradford; Bradford, Pa. 16701-2898	954 (C)	Pub	3,810	7,490	3,160
Pittsburgh, University of–Greensburg; Greensburg, Pa. 15601	1,452 (C)	Pub	3,710	7,390	2,230
Pittsburgh, University of–Johnstown; Johnstown, Pa. 15904	3,270 (C)	Pub	3,780	7,460	3,136
Pittsburg State University; Pittsburg, Kan. 66762	4,165 (C)	Pub	1,236	3,130	2,470
Pitzer College. *See* Claremont Colleges					
Plymouth State College; Plymouth, N.H. 03264	3,400 (C)	Pub	2,006	5,356	2,826
Point Loma Nazarene College; San Diego, Calif. 92106	2,165 (C)	P/Naz	6,405	6,405	3,225
Point Park College; Pittsburgh, Pa. 15222	2,713 (C)	P	6,860	6,860	3,390
Polytechnic University; Brooklyn, N.Y. 11201	1,879 (C)	P	11,180	11,180	1,800
Pomona College. *See* Claremont Colleges					
Pontifical College Josephinum; Columbus, Ohio 43235-1498	97 (M)	P/RC	2,815	2,815	2,240
Portland, University of; Portland, Ore. 97203	1,972 (C)	P	7,000	7,000	2,980
Portland School of Art; Portland, Me. 04101	300 (C)	P	7,550	7,550	4,018
Portland State University; Portland, Ore. 97207	12,494 (C)	Pub	1,545	4,329	4,600
Post College; Waterbury, Conn. 06708	1,654 (C)	P	7,400	7,400	3,650
Potsdam Coll. of Arts & Science. *See* New York, State Univ. of					
Prairie View A&M University; Prairie View, Tex. 77446	4,834 (C)	Pub	866	3,986	2,998
Pratt Institute; Brooklyn, N.Y. 11205	2,784 (C)	P	9,460	9,460	4,805
Presbyterian College; Clinton, S.C. 29325	1,112 (C)	P	7,807	7,807	2,793
Prescott College; Prescott, Ariz. 86301	284 (C)	P	6,200	6,200	n.a.
Princeton University; Princeton, N.J. 08544	4,564 (C)	P	14,390	14,390	4,817
Principia College; Elsah, Ill. 62028	639 (C)	P	10,065	10,065	4,090
Providence College; Providence, R.I. 02918	3,727 (C)	P	9,450	9,450	4,300
Puerto Rico, University of–Cayey University College; Cayey, P.R. 00633	3,357 (C)	Pub	662	2,000	n.a.
Puerto Rico, University of–Humacao University College; Humacao, P.R. 00661	3,825 (C)	Pub	684	1,680	n.a.
Puerto Rico, University of–Mayaguez Campus; Mayaguez, P.R. 00708	9,001 (C)	Pub	590	2,890	n.a.
Puerto Rico, University of–Medical Science; San Juan, P.R. 00936	962 (C)	Pub	([3])	([4])	n.a.
Puget Sound, University of; Tacoma, Wash. 98416	3,042 (C)	P	10,300	10,300	3,600
Puget Sound Christian College; Edmonds, Wash. 98020	88 (C)	P	3,885	3,885	2,700
Purdue University; West Lafayette, Ind. 47907	28,904 (C)	Pub	1,916	5,800	2,950
Purdue University–Calumet; Hammond, Ind. 46323	6,578 (C)	Pub	1,539	3,779	n.a.
Queens College; Charlotte, N.C. 28274	1,178 (C)	P/PUS	7,550	7,550	3,850
Queens College (NYC). *See* New York, City University of					
Quincy College; Quincy, Ill. 62301	1,425 (C)	P/RC	7,000	7,000	2,910
Quinnipiac College; Hamden, Conn. 06518	2,784 (C)	P	8,300	8,300	4,000
Radcliffe College. *See* Harvard and Radcliffe Colleges					
Rabbinical College of America; Morristown, N.J. 07960	230 (M)	P	3,800	3,800	3,200

Institution and location	Enrollment	Control	Tuition ($) Res.	Tuition ($) Nonres.	Rm/Bd ($)
Rabbinical Seminary of America; Forest Hills, N.Y. 11375	200 (M)	P	3,000	3,000	3,000
Radford University; Radford, Va. 24142	7,544 (C)	Pub	2,076	3,474	3,370
Ramapo College of New Jersey; Mahwah, N.J. 07430	4,058 (C)	Pub	2,145	2,745	3,900
Randolph–Macon College; Ashland, Va. 23005	1,052 (C)	P	8,375	8,375	3,620
Randolph–Macon Woman's College; Lynchburg, Va. 24503	765 (W)	P/UM	10,060	10,060	4,500
Redlands, University of; Redlands, Calif. 92373-0999	1,220 (C)	P	11,890	11,890	4,740
Reed College; Portland, Ore. 97202	1,263 (C)	P	12,750	12,750	3,780
Reformed Bible College; Grand Rapids, Mich. 49506	166 (C)	P	3,960	3,960	2,500
Regis College; Denver, Colo. 80221	1,015 (C)	P/RC	8,660	8,660	4,200
Regis College; Weston, Mass. 02193	1,025 (W)	P/RC	9,080	9,080	4,520
Rensselaer Polytechnic Institute; Troy, N.Y. 12180	4,458 (C)	P	13,250	13,250	4,300
Research College of Nursing; Kansas City, Mo. 64132	133 (C)	P	6,850	6,850	3,200
Rhode Island, University of; Kingston, R.I. 02881	11,938 (C)	Pub	2,331	6,257	3,796
Rhode Island, University of, College of Continuing Education; Providence, R.I. 02908-5090	3,819 (C)	Pub	(⁵)	(⁶)	n.a.
Rhode Island College; Providence, R.I. 02908	6,429 (C)	Pub	1,584	4,134	3,650
Rhode Island School of Design; Providence, R.I. 02903	1,817 (C)	P	11,350	11,350	4,835
Rhodes College Memphis; Memphis, Tenn. 38112	1,346 (C)	P/PUS	10,660	10,660	3,824
Rice University; Houston, Tex. 77251	2,600 (C)	P	6,100	6,100	4,375
Richmond, University of; Richmond, Va. 23173	2,819 (C)	P/B	9,900	9,900	2,615
Richmond College; Surrey, TW10 6JP England	995 (C)	P	8,565	8,565	4,500
Rider College; Lawrenceville, N.J. 08648	3,032 (C)	P	9,000	9,000	4,000
Ringling School of Art and Design; Sarasota, Fla. 34234	457 (C)	P	6,600	6,600	3,800
Rio Grande College and Community College; Rio Grande, Ohio 45674	1,680 (C)	P	1,953	4,470	2,700
Ripon College; Ripon, Wis. 54971	859 (C)	P	11,104	11,104	2,635
Rivier College; Nashua, N.H. 03060	550 (W)	P/RC	7,350	7,350	3,780
Roanoke Bible College; Elizabeth City, N.C. 27909	130 (C)	P	2,000	2,000	2,000
Roanoke College; Salem, Va. 24153	1,594 (C)	P/LCA	9,400	9,400	3,600
Robert Morris College; Coraopolis, Pa. 15108	5,083 (C)	P	4,200	4,200	3,000
Roberts Wesleyan College; Rochester, N.Y. 14624	820 (C)	P/FM	7,548	7,548	2,650
Rochester, University of; Rochester, N.Y. 14627	4,795 (C)	P	12,305	12,305	4,878
Rochester Institute of Technology; Rochester, N.Y. 14623	11,692 (C)	P	10,150	10,150	4,470
Rockford College; Rockford, Ill. 61108	1,198 (C)	P	8,030	8,030	3,000
Rockhurst College; Kansas City, Mo. 64110	3,085 (C)	P/RC	6,280	6,280	3,240
Rocky Mountain College; Billings, Mont. 59102	705 (C)	P	5,800	5,800	2,900
Roger Williams College; Bristol, R.I. 02809	2,000 (C)	P	7,800	7,800	4,300
Rollins College; Winter Park, Fla. 32789	1,400 (C)	P	11,950	11,950	3,815
Roosevelt University; Chicago, Ill. 60605	4,112 (C)	P	6,240	6,240	3,900
Rosary College; River Forest, Ill. 60305-1099	969 (C)	P/RC	6,850	6,850	3,150
Rose–Hulman Institute of Technology; Terre Haute, Ind. 47803	1,310 (M)	P	9,360	9,360	3,090
Rosemont College; Rosemont, Pa. 19010	613 (W)	P/RC	7,800	7,800	4,800
Rush University Colleges of Nursing and Health Sciences; Chicago, Ill. 60612	175 (C)	P	6,360	6,360	2,435
Russell Sage College; Troy, N.Y. 12180	1,227 (W)	P	8,970	8,970	3,700
Rust College; Holly Springs, Miss. 38635	915 (C)	P	3,000	3,000	1,448
Rutgers University–Camden College of Arts and Sciences; Camden, N.J. 08102	3,063 (C)	Pub	2,628	4,908	3,370
Rutgers University–College of Engineering; New Brunswick, N.J. 08903	2,567 (C)	Pub	2,994	5,524	3,319
Rutgers University–College of Nursing–Newark; Newark, N.J. 07102	412 (C)	Pub	2,604	4,884	3,293
Rutgers University–College of Pharmacy; New Brunswick, N.J. 08903	774 (C)	Pub	2,870	5,276	3,319
Rutgers University–Cook College; New Brunswick, N.J. 08903	3,009 (C)	Pub	2,860	5,266	3,319
Rutgers University–Douglass College; New Brunswick, N.J. 08903	3,341 (W)	Pub	2,728	5,008	3,319
Rutgers University–Livingston College; New Brunswick, N.J. 08903	3,576 (C)	Pub	2,759	5,039	3,319
Rutgers University–Mason Gross School of the Arts; New Brunswick, N.J. 08903	420 (C)	Pub	2,744	5,024	3,319
Rutgers University–Newark College of Arts and Sciences; Newark, N.J. 07102	3,621 (C)	Pub	2,611	4,891	n.a.
Rutgers University–Rutgers College; New Brunswick, N.J. 08903	8,563 (C)	Pub	2,744	5,024	3,319
Rutgers University—University College–Camden; Camden, N.J. 08102	973 (C)	Pub	(⁷)	(⁸)	n.a.
Rutgers University—University College–New Brunswick; New Brunswick, N. J. 08903	3,101 (C)	Pub	(⁷)	(⁸)	n.a.
Rutgers University—University College–Newark; Newark, N.J. 07102	1,978 (C)	Pub	(⁷)	(⁸)	n.a.
Sacred Heart, Univ. of the; Santurce, P.R. 00924	7,198 (C)	P/RC	2,930	2,930	3,140
Sacred Heart Seminary; Detroit, Mich. 48206	554 (C)	P/RC	2,850	2,850	2,350
Sacred Heart University; Bridgeport, Conn. 06606	3,407 (C)	P	6,500	6,500	n.a.
Saginaw Valley State University; University Center, Mich. 48710	4,769 (C)	Pub	2,031	4,030	2,855

Institution and location	Enrollment	Control	Tuition ($) Res.	Tuition ($) Nonres.	Rm/Bd ($)
St. Alphonsus College; Suffield, Conn. 06078	43 (M)	P/RC	3,300	3,300	2,100
St. Ambrose University; Davenport, Iowa 52803	1,650 (C)	P/RC	7,320	7,320	3,010
St. Andrews Presbyterian College; Laurinburg, N.C. 28352	833 (C)	P/PUS	7,650	7,650	3,455
Saint Anselm College; Manchester, N.H. 03102	1,833 (C)	P	7,870	7,870	4,050
St. Augustine's College; Raleigh, N.C. 27611	1,716 (C)	P/E	4,250	4,250	2,800
St. Benedict, College of; St. Joseph, Minn. 56374-2099	1,852 (W)	P/RC	8,810	8,810	3,160
St. Bonaventure University; St. Bonaventure, N.Y. 14778	2,368 (C)	P	7,085	7,085	3,683
St. Catherine, College of; St. Paul, Minn. 55105	2,541 (W)	P/RC	8,544	8,544	3,140
St. Cloud State University; St. Cloud, Minn. 56301	14,429 (C)	Pub	1,766	2,702	2,115
St. Edward's University; Austin, Tex. 78704	2,417 (C)	P/RC	6,108	6,108	2,900
St. Elizabeth, College of; Convent Station, N.J. 07961	969 (W)	P	7,250	7,250	3,400
St. Francis, College of; Joliet, Ill. 60435	1,105 (C)	P/RC	6,110	6,110	3,020
St. Francis College; Fort Wayne, Ind. 46808	897 (C)	P/RC	4,416	4,416	3,100
St. Francis College; Brooklyn Heights, N.Y. 11201	1,248 (C)	P	5,120	5,120	n.a.
St. Francis College; Loretto, Pa. 15940	1,037 (C)	P/RC	7,360	7,360	3,600
St. Hyacinth College and Seminary; Granby, Mass. 01033	50 (M)	P/RC	3,600	3,600	4,000
St. John Fisher College; Rochester, N.Y. 14618	1,571 (C)	P	7,275	7,275	3,540
St. John Vianney College Seminary; Miami, Fla. 33165	50 (M)	P	5,500	5,500	3,000
St. John's College; Annapolis, Md. 21404	418 (C)	P	11,880	11,880	3,996
St. John's Seminary College; Camarillo, Calif. 93010	86 (M)	P/RC	4,012	4,012	—
St. John's College; Santa Fe, N.M. 87501	389 (C)	P	11,880	11,880	3,996
St. John's Seminary College of Liberal Arts; Brighton, Mass. 02135	70 (M)	P/RC	3,600	3,600	2,600
St. John's University; Collegeville, Minn. 56321	1,917 (M)	P/RC	8,810	8,810	3,315
St. John's University Queens–Staten Island; Jamaica, N.Y. 11439	14,380 (C)	P/RC	6,340	6,340	n.a.
St. Joseph in Vermont, College of; Rutland, Vt. 05701	460 (C)	P/RC	5,350	5,350	3,200
St. Joseph College; West Hartford, Conn. 06117	696 (W)	P/RC	8,900	8,900	4,040
St. Joseph Seminary College; St. Benedict, La. 70457	59 (M)	P	3,800	3,800	3,000
St. Joseph's College; Brooklyn, N.Y. 11205	794 (C)	P	5,200	5,200	n.a.
Saint Joseph's College; Rensselaer, Ind. 47978	1,001 (C)	P/RC	7,950	7,950	3,180
St. Joseph's College–Suffolk; Patchogue, N.Y. 11772	1,766 (C)	P	5,286	5,286	n.a.
Saint Joseph's College; Windham, Me. 04062-1198	622 (C)	P/RC	6,825	6,825	3,700
Saint Joseph's University; Philadelphia, Pa. 19131	2,400 (C)	P/RC	8,900	8,900	4,500
St. Lawrence University; Canton, N.Y. 13617	2,263 (C)	P	13,505	13,505	4,345
Saint Leo College; Saint Leo, Fla. 33574	1,118 (C)	P/RC	6,450	6,450	3,200
St. Louis Christian College; Florissant, Mo. 63033	137 (C)	P	2,560	2,560	1,860
St. Louis College of Pharmacy; St. Louis, Mo. 63110	723 (C)	P	4,700	4,700	3,200
St. Louis Conservatory of Music; St. Louis, Mo. 63130	70 (C)	P	7,750	7,750	n.a.
St. Louis University; St. Louis, Mo. 63103	6,850 (C)	P	7,080	7,080	3,600
St. Martin's College; Lacey, Wash. 98503	577 (C)	P	7,690	7,690	3,194
St. Mary, College of; Omaha, Neb. 68124	1,133 (W)	P/RC	6,600	6,600	2,800
Saint Mary College; Leavenworth, Kan. 66048	448 (C)	P	5,360	5,360	2,910
St. Mary of the Plains College; Dodge City, Kan. 67801	911 (C)	P/RC	5,310	5,310	2,800
St. Mary-of-the-Woods Coll.; St. Mary-of-the-Woods, Ind. 47876	858 (W)	P/RC	7,635	7,635	3,135
St. Mary's College; Notre Dame, Ind. 46556	1,826 (W)	P/RC	8,459	8,459	3,636
St. Mary's College; Orchard Lake, Mich. 48033	307 (C)	P	3,325	3,325	2,700
St. Mary's College; Winona, Minn. 55987	1,263 (C)	P	8,005	8,005	2,800
St. Mary's College of California; Moraga, Calif. 94575	2,000 (C)	P/RC	8,486	8,486	4,318
St. Mary's College of Maryland; St. Mary's City, Md. 20686	1,585 (C)	Pub	2,500	4,100	3,800
St. Mary's University of San Antonio; San Antonio, Tex. 78284	2,404 (C)	P/RC	6,133	6,133	2,780
Saint Meinrad College; St. Meinrad, Ind. 47577	127 (M)	P/RC	4,013	4,013	3,924
Saint Michael's College; Winooski, Vt. 05404	1,694 (C)	P/RC	9,110	9,110	3,880
St. Norbert College; De Pere, Wis. 54115	1,809 (C)	P/RC	8,455	8,455	3,485
St. Olaf College; Northfield, Minn. 55057	3,048 (C)	P/AL	10,150	10,150	3,000
St. Paul Bible College; Bible College, Minn. 55375	528 (C)	P/CMA	5,560	5,560	3,010
Saint Paul's College; Lawrenceville, Va. 23868	736 (C)	P	3,950	3,950	2,855
St. Peter's College; Jersey City, N.J. 07306	3,146 (C)	P/RC	5,346	5,346	3,940
Saint Rose, The College of; Albany, N.Y. 12203	2,209 (C)	P	7,184	7,184	4,250
St. Scholastica, College of; Duluth, Minn. 55811	1,535 (C)	P/RC	7,932	7,932	2,796
St. Thomas, College of; St. Paul, Minn. 55105	4,848 (C)	P	8,992	8,992	3,136
St. Thomas, University of; Houston, Tex. 77006	1,032 (C)	P/RC	4,464	4,464	3,040
St. Thomas Aquinas College; Sparkill, N.Y. 10968	1,879 (C)	P	5,000	5,000	3,150
Saint Thomas University; Miami, Fla. 33054	2,100 (C)	P/RC	6,300	6,300	3,400
Saint Vincent College; Latrobe, Pa. 15650	1,193 (C)	P/RC	6,758	6,758	2,996
St. Xavier College; Chicago, Ill. 60655	2,171 (C)	P/RC	6,540	6,540	2,765
Salem College; Winston-Salem, N.C. 27108	682 (W)	P	8,300	8,300	5,300
Salem College; Salem, W. Va. 26426	714 (C)	P	6,083	6,083	3,580
Salem State College; Salem, Mass. 01970	5,334 (C)	Pub	1,374	3,870	2,652
Salisbury State University; Salisbury, Md. 21801	4,715 (C)	Pub	2,188	3,710	3,590
Salve Regina College; Newport, R.I. 02840-4192	1,756 (C)	P	9,700	9,700	4,850
Sam Houston State University; Huntsville, Tex. 77341	10,047 (C)	Pub	940	4,060	2,350
Samford University; Birmingham, Ala. 35229	4,089 (C)	P/SB	5,500	5,500	2,964
San Diego, University of; San Diego, Calif. 92110	3,400 (C)	P/RC	9,420	9,420	5,070

Institution and location	Enrollment	Control	Tuition ($) Res.	Tuition ($) Nonres.	Rm/Bd ($)
San Diego State University; San Diego, Calif. 92182	29,056 (C)	Pub	802	4,546	3,750
Imperial Valley Campus; Calexico, Calif. 92231	200 (C)	Pub	772	5,452	n.a.
San Francisco, University of; San Francisco, Calif. 94117	2,664 (C)	P/RC	9,102	9,102	4,562
San Francisco Art Institute; San Francisco, Calif. 94133	514 (C)	P	11,550	11,550	n.a.
San Francisco Conservatory of Music, The; San Francisco, Calif. 94122	147 (C)	P	7,800	7,800	n.a.
San Francisco State Univ.; San Francisco, Calif. 94132	21,458 (C)	Pub	750	5,160	3,198
San Jose Bible College; San Jose, Calif. 95108	169 (C)	P/ChC	4,449	4,449	2,310
San Jose State University; San Jose, Calif. 95192-0009	22,748 (C)	Pub	936	5,472	4,500
Sangamon State University; Springfield, Ill. 62708	2,234 (C)	Pub	1,824	4,944	5,530
Santa Clara University; Santa Clara, Calif. 95053	3,777 (C)	P/RC	9,618	9,618	4,686
Santa Fe, College of; Santa Fe, N.M. 87501	1,482 (C)	P/RC	2,788	2,788	1,167
Sarah Lawrence College; Bronxville, N.Y. 10708	850 (C)	P	12,990	12,990	3,550
Savannah College of Art and Design; Savannah, Ga. 31401	1,293 (C)	P	6,150	6,150	4,150
Savannah State College; Savannah, Ga. 31404	1,754 (C)	Pub	1,461	3,603	2,025
Schiller International University; 6900 Heidelberg, W. Ger.	1,311 (C)	P	8,350	8,350	5,500
Schreiner College; Kerrville, Tex. 78028	603 (C)	P	6,330	6,330	4,270
Science and Arts, University of, of Oklahoma; Chickasha, Okla. 73018	1,373 (C)	Pub	1,080	2,784	1,700
Scranton, University of; Scranton, Pa. 18510	3,423 (C)	P/RC	7,184	7,184	3,330
Scripps College. *See* Claremont Colleges					
Seattle Pacific University; Seattle, Wash. 98119	2,400 (C)	P/FM	9,050	9,050	3,432
Seattle University; Seattle, Wash. 98122	3,262 (C)	P/RC	8,955	8,955	3,723
Seaver College. *See* Pepperdine University					
Seton Hall University; South Orange, N.J. 07079	5,138 (C)	P/RC	8,400	8,400	4,866
Seton Hill College; Greensburg, Pa. 15601	870 (W)	P	7,500	7,500	3,280
Shaw University; Raleigh, N.C. 27611	1,500 (C)	P	4,300	4,300	3,200
Shawnee State University; Portsmouth, Ohio 45662	2,900 (C)	Pub	1,269	1,569	n.a.
Sheldon Jackson College; Sitka, Alaska 99835	290 (C)	P/UP	4,896	4,896	4,100
Shenandoah College and Conservatory; Winchester, Va. 22601-9986	892 (C)	P	10,000	10,000	3,000
Shepherd College; Shepherdstown, W. Va. 25443	4,010 (C)	Pub	990	2,570	2,996
Shimer College; Waukegan, Ill. 60085	100 (C)	P	7,950	7,950	3,145
Shippensburg University of Pennsylvania; Shippensburg, Pa. 17257	5,324 (C)	Pub	2,396	3,818	2,282
Shorter College; Rome, Ga. 30161	832 (C)	P	4,930	4,930	3,770
Siena College; Loudonville, N.Y. 12211	3,481 (C)	P	6,890	6,890	3,860
Siena Heights College; Adrian, Mich. 49221	1,511 (C)	P	6,090	6,090	3,300
Sierra Nevada College; Incline Village, Nev. 89450	297 (C)	P	5,250	5,250	3,600
Silver Lake College; Manitowoc, Wis. 54220	719 (C)	P/RC	6,100	6,100	n.a.
Simmons College; Boston, Mass. 02115	1,451 (W)	P	12,132	12,132	5,248
Simon's Rock of Bard College; Great Barrington, Mass. 01230	298 (C)	P	13,280	13,280	4,430
Simpson College; San Francisco, Calif. 94134	163 (C)	P/CMA	5,304	5,304	3,000
Simpson College; Indianola, Iowa 50125	1,710 (C)	P	8,105	8,105	2,860
Sioux Falls College; Sioux Falls, S.D. 57105	900 (C)	P/B	6,210	6,210	2,485
Skidmore College; Saratoga Springs, N.Y. 12866	2,155 (C)	P	13,275	13,275	4,725
Slippery Rock State College. *See* Slippery Rock University of Pennsylvania					
Slippery Rock Univ. of Pennsylvania; Slippery Rock, Pa. 16057	6,822 (C)	Pub	2,338	3,864	2,470
Smith College; Northampton, Mass. 01063	2,721 (W)	P	13,380	13,380	5,170
Sojourner-Douglass College; Baltimore, Md. 21205	402 (C)	P	4,515	4,515	n.a.
Sonoma State University; Rohnert Park, Calif. 94928	4,983 (C)	Pub	822	4,350	3,256
South, University of the; Sewanee, Tenn. 37375	1,111 (C)	P/E	11,690	11,690	3,010
South Alabama, University of; Mobile, Ala. 36688	9,044 (C)	Pub	1,725	2,325	2,463
Southampton College. *See* Long Island Univ. Center					
South Carolina, University of; Columbia, S.C. 29208	15,011 (C)	Pub	2,228	4,848	2,603
South Carolina, Univ. of-Aiken; Aiken, S.C. 29801	2,528 (C)	Pub	1,600	3,340	2,330
South Carolina, Univ. of-Coastal Carolina; Conway, S.C. 29526	3,989 (C)	Pub	1,660	3,320	2,120
South Carolina, Univ. of-Spartanburg; Spartanburg, S.C. 29303	3,247 (C)	Pub	1,600	3,440	2,750
South Carolina State College; Orangeburg, S.C. 29117	3,531 (C)	Pub	1,450	2,980	2,286
South Dakota, University of; Vermillion, S.D. 57069	4,167 (C)	Pub	1,804	3,260	2,102
South Dakota School of Mines and Technology; Rapid City, S.D. 57701	1,794 (C)	Pub	2,093	3,640	1,964
South Dakota State University; Brookings, S.D. 57007	6,063 (C)	Pub	1,742	3,198	1,648
South Florida, University of; Tampa, Fla. 33620	20,604 (C)	Pub	1,250	3,850	2,750
Southeast Missouri State Univ.; Cape Girardeau, Mo. 63701	8,200 (C)	Pub	1,390	3,510	2,100
Southeastern Baptist College; Laurel, Miss. 39440	79 (C)	P	2,080	2,080	1,600
Southeastern Bible College; Birmingham, Ala. 35243	296 (C)	P/ID	3,400	3,400	2,400
Southeastern College; Lakeland, Fla. 33801	1,155 (C)	P/AG	2,500	2,500	1,800
Southeastern Louisiana University; Hammond, La. 70402	7,873 (C)	Pub	1,389	2,829	2,110
Southeastern Massachusetts University; North Dartmouth, Mass. 02747	5,500 (C)	Pub	1,520	4,424	3,700
Southeastern Oklahoma State Univ.; Durant, Okla. 74701	3,616 (C)	Pub	804	1,992	1,704
Southeastern University; Washington, D.C. 20024	559 (C)	P	5,487	5,487	n.a.
Southern Arkansas University; Magnolia, Ark. 71753	2,165 (C)	Pub	1,050	1,680	1,900

Institution and location	Enrollment	Control	Tuition ($) Res.	Tuition ($) Nonres.	Rm/Bd ($)
Southern California, Univ. of; Los Angeles, Calif. 90089	16,528 (C)	P	12,540	12,540	4,850
Southern California College; Costa Mesa, Calif. 92626	866 (C)	P/AG	6,170	6,170	3,100
Southern California Institute of Architecture; Santa Monica, Calif. 90404	310 (C)	P	7,960	7,960	n.a.
Southern College of Seventh–Day Adventists; Collegedale, Tenn. 37315	1,443 (C)	P/SDA	6,200	6,200	2,722
Southern College of Technology; Marietta, Ga. 30060	3,675 (C)	Pub	1,323	3,612	2,825
Southern Colorado, University of; Pueblo, Colo. 81001	3,800 (C)	Pub	1,412	2,474	3,142
Southern Connecticut State Univ.; New Haven, Conn. 06515	6,222 (C)	Pub	1,420	3,830	3,324
Southern Illinois Univ.–Carbondale; Carbondale, Ill. 62901	20,126 (C)	Pub	2,166	5,286	2,636
Southern Illinois Univ.–Edwardsville; Edwardsville, Ill. 62026	8,552 (C)	Pub	1,798	4,720	4,520
Southern Indiana, University of; Evansville, Ind. 47714	5,265 (C)	Pub	1,523	3,638	2,750
Southern Maine, University of; Gorham, Me. 04038	9,424 (C)	Pub	1,726	4,786	3,290
Southern Methodist University; Dallas, Tex. 75275	5,749 (C)	P/UM	8,764	8,764	4,498
Southern Missionary College. See Southern College of Seventh-Day Adventists					
Southern Mississippi, Univ. of; Hattiesburg, Miss. 39406	9,379 (C)	Pub	1,684	2,866	2,150
Southern Nazarene Univ.; Bethany, Okla. 73008	1,165 (C)	P	4,200	4,200	2,688
Southern Oregon State College; Ashland, Ore. 97520	4,494 (C)	Pub	1,596	4,050	3,000
Southern University–New Orleans; New Orleans, La. 70126	3,200 (C)	Pub	1,372	2,930	n.a.
Southern University–Baton Rouge; Baton Rouge, La. 70813	9,448 (C)	Pub	1,354	2,876	2,370
Southern Utah State College; Cedar City, Utah 84720	3,000 (C)	Pub	1,245	3,328	2,059
Southern Vermont College; Bennington, Vt. 05201	635 (C)	P	5,850	5,850	3,280
Southwest, College of the; Hobbs, N.M. 88240	215 (C)	P	2,230	2,230	2,750
Southwest Baptist University; Bolivar, Mo. 65613	2,909 (C)	P	6,750	6,750	1,930
Southwest Missouri State Univ.; Springfield, Mo. 65804	17,681 (C)	Pub	1,322	2,618	2,280
Southwest State University; Marshall, Minn. 56258	2,475 (C)	Pub	1,800	3,000	2,300
Southwest Texas State Univ.; San Marcos, Tex. 78666	20,511 (C)	Pub	982	4,102	2,227
Southwestern Adventist College; Keene, Tex. 76059	764 (C)	P	6,224	6,224	3,178
Southwestern Assemblies of God College; Waxahachie, Tex. 75165	622 (C)	P	2,600	2,600	2,500
Southwestern College; Winfield, Kan. 67156	663 (C)	P/UM	4,152	4,152	2,464
Southwestern Conservative Baptist Bible College; Phoenix, Ariz. 85032	163 (C)	P/B	4,090	4,090	1,850
Southwestern Louisiana, University of; Lafayette, La. 70504	14,092 (C)	Pub	1,263	2,913	1,908
Southwestern Oklahoma State Univ.; Weatherford, Okla. 73096	5,478 (C)	Pub	762	2,180	1,380
Southwestern University; Georgetown, Tex. 78626	1,171 (C)	P/UM	7,600	7,600	3,650
Spalding University; Louisville, Ky. 40203	804 (C)	P/RC	5,100	5,100	2,560
Spelman College; Atlanta, Ga. 30314	1,742 (W)	P	4,792	4,792	4,130
Spertus College of Judaica; Chicago, Ill. 60605	100 (C)	P	3,600	3,600	n.a.
Spring Arbor College; Spring Arbor, Mich. 49283	782 (C)	P	6,890	6,890	2,533
Springfield College; Springfield, Mass. 01109	2,350 (C)	P	7,854	7,854	3,600
Spring Garden College; Philadelphia, Pa. 19119	1,224 (C)	P	7,300	7,300	4,000
Spring Hill College; Mobile, Ala. 36608	932 (C)	P/RC	7,800	7,800	3,700
Stanford University; Stanford, Calif. 94305	6,457 (C)	P	13,569	13,569	5,595
Staten Island, Coll. of (NYC). See New York, City Univ. of					
Stephen F. Austin State Univ.; Nacogdoches, Tex. 75962	10,800 (C)	Pub	900	4,000	2,800
Stephens College; Columbia, Mo. 65215	1,256 (W)	P	9,850	9,850	3,900
Sterling College; Sterling, Kan. 67579	503 (C)	P/PUS	5,500	5,500	2,800
Stetson University; Deland, Fla. 32720	2,113 (C)	P	8,440	8,440	3,600
Stevens Institute of Technology; Hoboken, N.J. 07030	1,400 (C)	P	11,900	11,900	4,000
Stillman College; Tuscaloosa, Ala. 35403	791 (C)	P/PUS	3,550	3,550	2,450
Stockton State College; Pomona, N.J. 08240	5,297 (C)	Pub	1,808	2,448	3,500
Stonehill College; North Easton, Mass. 02357	1,964 (C)	P/RC	8,771	8,771	4,460
Strayer College; Washington, D.C. 20005	1,185 (C)	P	3,645	3,645	n.a.
Suffolk University; Boston, Mass. 02108	2,791 (C)	P	7,328	7,328	n.a.
Susquehanna University; Selinsgrove, Pa. 17870	1,465 (C)	P/L	9,565	9,565	3,375
Swarthmore College; Swarthmore, Pa. 19081	1,300 (C)	P	14,530	14,530	4,920
Sweet Briar College; Sweet Briar, Va. 24595	600 (W)	P	10,890	10,890	4,000
Syracuse University; Syracuse, N.Y. 13210	14,145 (C)	P	11,035	11,035	4,860
Tabor College; Hillsboro, Kan. 67063	476 (C)	P/MB	5,650	5,650	2,550
Talladega College; Talladega, Ala. 35160	528 (C)	P	3,512	3,512	2,030
Tampa, University of; Tampa, Fla. 33606	2,136 (C)	P	9,260	9,260	3,600
Tampa College; Tampa, Fla. 33614	1,264 (C)	P	3,600	3,600	n.a.
Tarkio College; Tarkio, Mo. 64491	784 (C)	P/UP	6,300	6,300	3,200
Tarleton State University; Stephenville, Tex. 76402	4,951 (C)	Pub	956	4,076	2,348
Taylor University; Upland, Ind. 46989	1,608 (C)	P/ID	8,007	8,007	3,142
Temple University; Philadelphia, Pa. 19122	22,336 (C)	Pub	3,514	6,172	3,596
Temple University–Ambler; Ambler, Pa. 19002	3,774 (C)	Pub	3,844	6,752	3,750
Tennessee, Univ. of–Chattanooga; Chattanooga, Tenn. 37402	6,208 (C)	Pub	1,282	4,016	3,394
Tennessee, Univ. of–Knoxville; Knoxville, Tenn. 37996	19,578 (C)	Pub	1,466	4,200	2,990
Tennessee, Univ. of–Martin; Martin, Tenn. 38238	4,475 (C)	Pub	1,260	3,994	2,130
Tennessee, Univ. of–Memphis, Health Science Center; Memphis, Tenn. 38163	326 (C)	Pub	1,644	4,650	2,892

Institution and location	Enrollment	Control	Tuition ($) Res.	Tuition ($) Nonres.	Rm/Bd ($)
Tennessee State University; Nashville, Tenn. 37203	7,012 (C)	Pub	1,202	3,938	2,246
Tennessee Technological Univ.; Cookeville, Tenn. 38505	7,044 (C)	Pub	1,269	4,005	2,613
Tennessee Temple University; Chattanooga, Tenn. 37404	1,400 (C)	P/B	3,560	3,560	2,800
Tennessee Wesleyan College; Athens, Tenn. 37303	572 (C)	P/UM	4,190	4,190	2,764
Texas, University of–Arlington; Arlington, Tex. 76019	19,796 (C)	Pub	778	3,274	2,600
Texas, University of–Austin; Austin, Tex. 78712	35,007 (C)	Pub	830	3,730	3,288
Texas, University of–Dallas; Richardson, Tex. 75083	4,311 (C)	Pub	886	3,990	n.a.
Texas, University of–El Paso; El Paso, Tex. 79968	12,618 (C)	Pub	900	3,960	2,600
Texas, University of–Health Science Center–San Antonio; San Antonio, Tex. 78284	691 (C)	Pub	504	3,000	n.a.
Texas, University of, Medical Branch–Galveston; Galveston, Tex. 77550	668 (C)	Pub	864	5,760	5,400
Texas, University of–Permian Basin; Odessa, Tex. 79762	1,203 (C)	Pub	855	3,975	2,900
Texas, University of–San Antonio; San Antonio, Tex. 78285	11,736 (C)	Pub	930	4,050	2,850
Texas, University of Southwestern Medical Ctr. at Dallas; Dallas, Tex. 75235	324 (C)	Pub	987	5,439	n.a.
Texas, University of–Tyler; Tyler, Tex. 75701	2,335 (C)	Pub	861	3,695	n.a.
Texas A&I University–Kingsville; Kingsville, Tex. 78363	4,448 (C)	Pub	840	4,000	2,625
Texas A&M University; College Station, Tex. 77843	31,843 (C)	Pub	1,200	4,320	3,734
Texas A&M University at Galveston; Galveston, Tex. 77553	742 (C)	Pub	683	3,803	2,986
Texas Christian University; Fort Worth, Tex. 76129	5,846 (C)	P/DC	4,480	4,480	2,400
Texas College; Tyler, Tex. 75702	450 (C)	P/CME	1,130	1,130	2,300
Texas Lutheran College; Seguin, Tex. 78155	1,034 (C)	P	5,300	5,300	2,640
Texas Southern University; Houston, Tex. 77004	6,498 (C)	Pub	752	3,248	3,320
Texas Tech University; Lubbock, Tex. 79409	20,481 (C)	Pub	746	2,306	2,918
Texas Wesleyan College; Fort Worth, Tex. 76105	1,502 (C)	P/UM	4,500	4,500	3,350
Texas Woman's University; Denton, Tex. 76204	4,167 (W)	Pub	904	4,024	2,625
Thiel College; Greenville, Pa. 16125	941 (C)	P/LCA	7,730	7,730	3,800
Thomas A. Edison State College; Trenton, N.J. 08625	6,844 (C)	Pub	185	300	n.a.
Thomas Aquinas College; Santa Paula, Calif. 93060	150 (C)	P/RC	9,000	9,000	4,430
Thomas College; Waterville, Me. 04901	375 (C)	P	6,750	6,750	3,670
Thomas Jefferson University, College of Allied Health Sciences; Philadelphia, Pa. 19107	991 (C)	P	9,200	9,200	3,200
Thomas More College; Crestview Hills, Ky. 41017	1,097 (C)	P	6,400	6,400	2,980
Tiffin University; Tiffin, Ohio 44883	777 (C)	P	5,000	5,000	2,845
Toccoa Falls College; Toccoa Falls, Ga. 30598	769 (C)	P	3,910	3,910	2,530
Toledo, University of; Toledo, Ohio 43606	19,665 (C)	Pub	1,908	4,338	2,496
Tougaloo College; Tougaloo, Miss. 39174	672 (C)	P	3,999	3,999	1,550
Touro College; New York, N.Y. 10036	4,298 (C)	P	5,580	5,580	5,300
Towson State University; Towson, Md. 21204-7097	13,906 (C)	Pub	1,990	3,530	4,040
Transylvania University; Lexington, Ky. 40508	816 (C)	P/DC	8,302	8,302	3,498
Trenton State College; Trenton, N.J. 08650	6,760 (C)	Pub	2,080	2,880	4,243
Trevecca Nazarene College; Nashville, Tenn. 37210	781 (C)	P	3,990	3,990	2,368
Tri–State University; Angola, Ind. 46703	997 (C)	P	6,366	6,366	2,820
Trinity Bible College; Ellendale, N.D. 58436	456 (C)	P	3,950	3,950	2,988
Trinity Christian College; Palos Heights, Ill. 60463	550 (C)	P/CR	6,080	6,080	2,605
Trinity College; Burlington, Vt. 05401	970 (W)	P/RC	8,040	8,040	4,140
Trinity College; Deerfield, Ill. 60015	824 (C)	P/EFC	7,300	7,300	3,370
Trinity College; Hartford, Conn. 06106	1,754 (C)	P	13,000	13,000	3,960
Trinity College; Washington, D.C. 20017	906 (W)	P/RC	9,425	9,425	5,700
Trinity University; San Antonio, Tex. 78284	2,280 (C)	P	9,006	9,006	3,760
Troy State University; Troy, Ala. 36082	3,642 (C)	Pub	1,260	1,890	2,147
Troy State University–Dothan; Dothan, Ala. 36301	1,192 (C)	Pub	1,254	1,614	n.a.
Troy State University–Montgomery; Montgomery, Ala. 36195	1,944 (C)	Pub	1,170	1,755	n.a.
Tufts University; Medford, Mass. 02155	4,792 (C)	P	13,975	13,975	5,120
Tulane University; New Orleans, La. 70118	7,170 (C)	P	14,000	14,000	5,200
Tulsa, University of; Tulsa, Okla. 74104	2,951 (C)	P	7,400	7,400	3,100
Tusculum College; Greeneville, Tenn. 37743	777 (C)	P/UP	5,056	5,056	2,800
Tuskegee University; Tuskegee, Ala. 36088	3,398 (C)	P	4,850	4,850	2,350
UECU (Union for Experimenting Colleges and Universities); Cincinnati, Ohio 45202-2407	200 (C)	P	6,500	6,500	n.a.
Union College; Barbourville, Ky. 40906	782 (C)	P	4,850	4,850	2,150
Union College; Lincoln, Neb. 68506	645 (C)	P/SDA	6,670	6,670	2,270
Union College; Schenectady, N.Y. 12308	2,083 (C)	P	13,513	13,513	4,695
Union University; Jackson, Tenn. 38305	2,017 (C)	P/SB	3,900	3,900	2,030
U.S. Air Force Academy; Colorado Springs, Colo. 80840	4,501 (C)	Pub	1,000	1,000	—
U.S. Coast Guard Academy; New London, Conn. 06320	899 (C)	Pub	1,500	1,500	—
U.S. International University; San Diego, Calif. 92131	1,361 (C)	P	7,650	7,650	3,840
U.S. Merchant Marine Academy; Kings Point, N.Y. 11024	844 (C)	Pub	850	850	—
U.S. Military Academy; West Point, N.Y. 10996	4,500 (C)	Pub	1,000	1,000	—
U.S. Naval Academy; Annapolis, Md. 21402	4,500 (C)	Pub	1,500	1,500	—
United Wesleyan College; Allentown, Pa. 18103	148 (C)	P	5,090	5,090	2,600
Unity College; Unity, Me. 04988	370 (C)	P	4,946	6,128	3,521

Institution and location	Enrollment	Control	Tuition ($) Res.	Tuition ($) Nonres.	Rm/Bd ($)
Universidad de las Americas—Puebla; Puebla, Mexico 72820	4,250 (C)	P	2,430	2,430	650
Upper Iowa University; Fayette, Iowa 52142	1,299 (C)	P	7,540	7,540	1,860
Upsala College; East Orange, N.J. 07019	1,228 (C)	P	8,065	8,065	3,550
Urbana Univ.; Urbana, Ohio 43078	411 (C)	P	5,512	5,512	2,895
Ursinus College; Collegeville, Pa. 19426	1,237 (C)	P	10,500	10,500	3,970
Ursuline College; Pepper Pike, Ohio 44124	427 (C)	P/RC	4,440	4,440	2,850
Utah, University of; Salt Lake City, Utah 84112	19,373 (C)	Pub	1,517	4,187	1,499
Utah State University; Logan, Utah 84322	9,840 (C)	Pub	1,374	3,810	2,295
Utica College of Syracuse University; Utica, N.Y. 13502	2,431 (C)	P	8,500	8,500	3,700
Valdosta State College; Valdosta, Ga. 31698	5,775 (C)	Pub	1,422	3,711	2,070
Valley City State University; Valley City, N.D. 58072	1,154 (C)	Pub	1,278	2,958	1,791
Valley Forge Christian College; Phoenixville, Pa. 19460	511 (C)	P/AG	3,135	3,135	2,494
Valparaiso University; Valparaiso, Ind. 46383	3,431 (C)	P/L	8,238	8,238	2,530
Vanderbilt University; Nashville, Tenn. 37212	5,199 (C)	P	11,500	11,500	4,500
VanderCook College of Music; Chicago, Ill. 60616	91 (C)	P	7,150	7,150	3,855
Vassar College; Poughkeepsie, N.Y. 12601	2,250 (C)	P	13,600	13,600	4,700
Vennard College; University Park, Iowa 52595	143 (C)	P	3,869	3,869	2,050
Vermont, University of; Burlington, Vt. 05401-3596	8,032 (C)	Pub	3,726	10,450	3,848
Villa Julie College; Stevenson, Md. 21153	1,279 (C)	P	4,990	4,990	n.a.
Villa Maria College; Erie, Pa. 16505	699 (W)	P	5,980	5,980	3,100
Villanova University; Villanova, Pa. 19085	6,400 (C)	P	8,400	8,400	4,500
Virgin Islands, University of the; St. Thomas, V.I. 00802	2,471 (C)	Pub	970	2,730	3,024
Virginia, University of; Charlottesville, Va. 22906	11,197 (C)	Pub	3,950	7,750	3,000
Virginia, University of–Clinch Valley College; Wise, Va. 24293	1,688 (C)	Pub	1,574	2,534	2,680
Virginia Commonwealth University; Richmond, Va. 23284-2526	14,801 (C)	Pub	2,415	5,545	3,130
Virginia Intermont College; Bristol, Va. 24201	450 (C)	P/B	5,400	5,400	3,600
Virginia Military Institute; Lexington, Va. 24450	1,300 (M)	Pub	3,705	7,155	2,835
Virginia Polytechnic Institute and State University; Blacksburg, Va. 24061	18,149 (C)	Pub	2,544	5,184	3,346
Virginia State University; Petersburg, Va. 23803	3,284 (C)	Pub	2,926	4,890	3,430
Virginia Union University; Richmond, Va. 23220	1,112 (C)	P/B	5,311	5,311	2,634
Virginia Wesleyan College; Norfolk, Va. 23502	1,261 (C)	P/UM	7,400	7,400	3,900
Visual Arts, School of; New York, N.Y. 10010	2,058 (C)	P	7,900	7,900	3,050
Viterbo College; La Crosse, Wis. 54601	1,022 (C)	P/RC	6,460	6,460	2,750
Voorhees College; Denmark, S.C. 29042	574 (C)	P/E	3,000	3,000	5,402
Wabash College; Crawfordsville, Ind. 47933	872 (M)	P	8,825	8,825	3,325
Wadhams Hall Seminary—College; Ogdensburg, N.Y. 13669	50 (M)	P	3,195	3,195	3,200
Wagner College; Staten Island, N.Y. 10301	1,407 (C)	P/L	8,680	8,680	4,700
Wake Forest University; Winston–Salem, N.C. 27109	3,541 (C)	P/B	8,800	8,800	3,115
Walla Walla College; College Place, Wash. 99324	1,294 (C)	P/SDA	7,350	7,350	2,655
Walsh College; Canton, Ohio 44720	1,277 (C)	P/RC	5,190	5,190	2,900
Walsh College of Accountancy and Business Administration; Troy, Mich. 48007	1,734 (C)	P	3,852	3,852	n.a.
Warner Pacific College; Portland, Ore. 97215	390 (C)	P/CG	6,200	6,200	2,295
Warner Southern College; Lake Wales, Fla. 33853	318 (C)	P/CG	4,610	4,610	2,580
Warren Wilson College; Swannanoa, N.C. 28778	470 (C)	P	6,650	6,650	812
Wartburg College; Waverly, Iowa 50677	1,329 (C)	P/AL	8,130	8,130	2,810
Washburn University of Topeka; Topeka, Kan. 66621	5,557 (C)	Pub	2,100	2,940	2,575
Washington, University of; Seattle, Wash. 98195	24,447 (C)	Pub	2,797	4,998	3,448
Washington and Jefferson College; Washington, Pa. 15301	1,192 (C)	P	10,740	10,740	3,090
Washington and Lee University; Lexington, Va. 24450	1,592 (C)	P	10,205	10,205	3,680
Washington Bible College; Lanham, Md. 20706	313 (C)	P	3,651	3,651	3,020
Washington College; Chestertown, Md. 21620	902 (C)	P	9,600	9,600	4,000
Washington State University; Pullman, Wash. 99164	13,255 (C)	Pub	1,798	4,998	2,900
Washington University; St. Louis, Mo. 63130	4,925 (C)	P	13,600	13,600	4,610
Wayland Baptist University; Plainview, Tex. 79072	1,726 (C)	P	3,180	3,180	2,321
Wayne State College; Wayne, Neb. 68787	2,291 (C)	Pub	1,272	1,962	2,112
Wayne State University; Detroit, Mich. 48202	19,751 (C)	Pub	2,100	4,600	2,700
Waynesburg College; Waynesburg, Pa. 15370	973 (C)	P	6,630	6,630	2,780
Webb Institute of Naval Architecture; Glen Cove, N.Y. 11542	80 (C)	P	—	—	3,450
Webber College; Babson Park, Fla. 33827	196 (C)	P	5,020	5,020	2,655
Weber State College; Ogden, Utah 84408	12,002 (C)	Pub	1,200	3,219	2,202
Webster University; St. Louis, Mo. 63119	2,034 (C)	P	5,900	5,900	3,010
Wellesley College; Wellesley, Mass. 02181	2,200 (W)	P	13,510	13,510	5,285
Wells College; Aurora, N.Y. 13026	420 (W)	P	10,160	10,160	3,740
Wentworth Institute of Technology; Boston, Mass. 02115	3,800 (C)	P	7,079	7,079	5,334
Wesley College; Dover, Del. 19901	1,270 (C)	P	6,425	6,425	3,675
Wesley College; Florence, Miss. 39073	75 (C)	P/M	1,700	1,700	2,000
Wesleyan College; Macon, Ga. 31297	544 (W)	P/M	8,255	8,255	3,550
Wesleyan University; Middletown, Conn. 06457	2,669 (C)	P	14,070	14,070	4,695
West Chester Univ. of Pennsylvania; West Chester, Pa. 19383	9,770 (C)	Pub	2,298	3,772	2,294
West Coast Christian College; Fresno, Calif. 93710	274 (C)	P/CG	2,880	2,880	2,640

Institution and location	Enrollment	Control	Tuition ($) Res.	Nonres.	Rm/Bd ($)
West Coast University; Los Angeles, Calif. 90020	850 (C)	P	6,750	6,750	n.a.
Western Baptist College; Salem, Ore. 97301	328 (C)	P/B	5,622	5,622	2,943
Western Carolina University; Cullowhee, N.C. 28723	4,782 (C)	Pub	986	4,824	2,090
Western Connecticut State University; Danbury, Conn. 06810	5,202 (C)	Pub	1,632	4,042	3,002
Western Illinois University; Macomb, Ill. 61455	9,724 (C)	Pub	1,791	4,455	2,445
Western International University; Phoenix, Ariz. 85021	500 (C)	P	3,960	3,960	n.a.
Western Kentucky University; Bowling Green, Ky. 42101	12,009 (C)	Pub	1,160	3,280	2,470
Western Maryland College; Westminster, Md. 21157	1,326 (C)	P	10,584	10,584	3,946
Western Michigan University; Kalamazoo, Mich. 49008	18,703 (C)	Pub	1,776	4,440	2,917
Western Montana College; Dillon, Mont. 59725	1,097 (C)	Pub	1,193	2,651	2,630
Western New England College; Springfield, Mass. 01119	2,872 (C)	P	7,010	7,010	4,244
Western New Mexico University; Silver City, N.M. 88061	1,441 (C)	Pub	904	3,802	2,030
Western Oregon State College; Monmouth, Ore. 97361	3,199 (C)	Pub	1,569	4,020	2,568
Western State College of Colorado; Gunnison, Colo. 81230	2,500 (C)	Pub	1,454	3,920	2,528
Western Washington University; Bellingham, Wash. 98225	9,832 (C)	Pub	1,410	4,840	3,200
Westfield State College; Westfield, Mass. 01085	3,043 (C)	Pub	1,413	3,909	2,822
West Florida, University of; Pensacola, Fla. 32514	5,924 (C)	Pub	1,200	3,900	3,700
West Georgia College; Carrollton, Ga. 30118	5,333 (C)	Pub	1,455	3,744	2,010
West Liberty State College; West Liberty, W. Va. 26074	2,435 (C)	Pub	936	2,446	2,570
West Los Angeles, University of, School of Paralegal Studies; Los Angeles, Calif. 90066	318 (C)	P	2,604	2,604	n.a.
Westmar College; LeMars, Iowa 51031	559 (C)	P/UM	7,268	7,268	2,948
Westminster Choir College; Princeton, N.J. 08540	226 (C)	P	9,900	9,900	4,250
Westminster College; Fulton, Mo. 65251	677 (C)	P	6,850	6,850	3,150
Westminster College; New Wilmington, Pa. 16142	1,321 (C)	P/UP	7,700	7,700	2,450
Westminster Coll. of Salt Lake City; Salt Lake City, Utah 84105	1,813 (C)	P	6,060	6,060	4,040
Westmont College; Santa Barbara, Calif. 93108	1,290 (C)	P	9,750	9,750	4,276
West Oahu College. See Hawaii, University of.					
West Texas State University; Canyon, Tex. 79016	4,667 (C)	Pub	952	4,072	2,508
West Virginia Institute of Technology; Montgomery, W. Va. 25136	2,946 (C)	Pub	1,110	2,840	2,870
West Virginia State College; Institute, W. Va. 25112	4,509 (C)	Pub	1,092	2,672	2,450
West Virginia University; Morgantown, W. Va. 26506	13,769 (C)	Pub	1,400	3,530	3,380
West Virginia Wesleyan College; Buckhannon, W. Va. 26201	1,484 (C)	P/UM	8,430	8,430	3,000
Wheaton College; Norton, Mass. 02766	1,172 (C)	P	13,320	13,320	4,660
Wheaton College; Wheaton, Ill. 60187	2,229 (C)	P	8,350	8,350	3,380
Wheeling Jesuit College; Wheeling, W. Va. 26003	1,068 (C)	P	7,515	7,515	3,550
Wheelock College; Boston, Mass. 02215	669 (C)	P	9,696	9,696	4,680
White Plains, Coll. of, of Pace Univ. See Pace Univ.					
Whitman College; Walla Walla, Wash. 99362	1,240 (C)	P	10,694	10,694	3,930
Whittier College; Whittier, Calif. 90608	1,063 (C)	P	11,672	11,672	4,300
Whitworth College; Spokane, Wash. 99251	1,321 (C)	P/UP	8,975	8,975	3,425
Wichita State University; Wichita, Kan. 67208	13,720 (C)	Pub	1,422	3,852	2,695
Widener University; Chester, Pa. 19013	2,616 (C)	P	8,290	8,290	3,700
Wilberforce University; Wilberforce, Ohio 45384	739 (C)	P/AME	5,330	5,330	2,904
Wiley College; Marshall, Tex. 75670	557 (C)	P	3,946	3,946	2,544
Wilkes College; Wilkes-Barre, Pa. 18766	1,886 (C)	P	7,185	7,185	3,410
Willamette University; Salem, Ore. 97301	1,514 (C)	P	9,480	9,480	3,350
William and Mary, College of; Williamsburg, Va. 23185	5,300 (C)	Pub	2,966	7,812	3,404
William Carey College; Hattiesburg, Miss. 39401	1,546 (C)	P	2,885	2,885	2,000
William Jewell College; Liberty, Mo. 64068	1,426 (C)	P/B	6,820	6,820	2,500
William Paterson College; Wayne, N.J. 07470	7,441 (C)	Pub	1,776	2,376	3,316
William Penn College; Oskaloosa, Iowa 52577	500 (C)	P/F	7,500	7,500	2,550
William Smith College. See Hobart and William Smith Colleges					
William Tyndale College; Farmington Hills, Mich. 48018	431 (C)	P	4,270	4,270	3,000
William Woods College; Fulton, Mo. 65251	730 (W)	P	7,100	7,100	2,900
Williams College; Williamstown, Mass. 01267	1,989 (C)	P	12,850	12,850	4,340
Wilmington College; New Castle, Del. 19720	1,036 (C)	P	4,100	4,100	2,880
Wilmington College of Ohio; Wilmington, Ohio 45177	825 (C)	P/F	7,480	7,480	2,900
Wilson College; Chambersburg, Pa. 17201-1285	665 (W)	P/UP	9,414	9,414	4,102
Wingate College; Wingate, N.C. 28174	1,692 (C)	P/SB	5,070	5,070	2,550
Winona State University; Winona, Minn. 55987	6,000 (C)	Pub	1,800	2,700	2,300
Winston-Salem State University; Winston-Salem, N.C. 27110	2,532 (C)	Pub	896	4,268	2,265
Winthrop College; Rock Hill, S.C. 29733	4,400 (C)	Pub	2,078	3,682	2,124
Wisconsin, University of–Eau Claire; Eau Claire, Wis. 54701	10,573 (C)	Pub	1,638	4,720	2,170
Wisconsin, University of–Green Bay; Green Bay, Wis. 54302	4,991 (C)	Pub	1,587	4,668	2,300
Wisconsin, University of–La Crosse; La Crosse, Wis. 54601	8,654 (C)	Pub	1,658	4,740	1,860
Wisconsin, University of–Madison; Madison, Wis. 53706	29,727 (C)	Pub	1,857	5,639	3,050
Wisconsin, University of–Milwaukee; Milwaukee, Wis. 53201	21,535 (C)	Pub	1,917	5,699	2,590
Wisconsin, University of–Oshkosh; Oshkosh, Wis. 54901	9,521 (C)	Pub	1,580	4,662	1,920
Wisconsin, University of–Parkside; Kenosha, Wis. 53141	4,896 (C)	Pub	1,595	4,677	2,436
Wisconsin, University of–Platteville; Platteville, Wis. 53818	5,080 (C)	Pub	1,658	4,740	2,030
Wisconsin, University of–River Falls; River Falls, Wis. 54022	5,420 (C)	Pub	1,638	4,720	2,235

Institution and location	Enrollment	Control	Tuition ($) Res.	Tuition ($) Nonres.	Rm/Bd ($)
Wisconsin, University of–Stevens Point; Stevens Point, Wis. 54481	9,387 (C)	Pub	1,670	4,752	2,360
Wisconsin, University of–Stout; Menomonie, Wis. 54751	7,092 (C)	Pub	1,721	4,832	2,103
Wisconsin, University of–Superior; Superior, Wis. 54880	2,438 (C)	Pub	1,577	4,659	2,048
Wisconsin, University of–Whitewater; Whitewater, Wis. 53190	9,293 (C)	Pub	1,652	4,734	2,004
Wittenberg University; Springfield, Ohio 45501	2,250 (C)	P	11,100	11,100	4,263
Wofford College; Spartanburg, S.C. 29301	1,135 (C)	P/UM	7,135	7,135	3,400
Woodbury University; Burbank, Calif. 91504-1099	702 (C)	P	7,695	7,695	5,100
Wooster, College of; Wooster, Ohio 44691	1,913 (C)	P	15,230	15,230	—
Worcester Polytechnic Institute; Worcester, Mass. 01609	2,593 (C)	P	13,080	13,080	4,310
Worcester State College; Worcester, Mass. 01602	3,600 (C)	Pub	1,296	3,792	2,680
World College West; Petaluma, Calif. 94952	135 (C)	P	7,500	7,500	3,600
Wright State University; Dayton, Ohio 45435	13,546 (C)	Pub	2,124	4,248	3,330
Wyoming, University of; Laramie, Wyo. 82071	8,561 (C)	Pub	1,003	3,039	2,960
Xavier University; Cincinnati, Ohio 45207	3,779 (C)	P	7,650	7,650	3,690
Xavier University of Louisiana; New Orleans, La. 70125	2,226 (C)	P	5,000	5,000	2,800
Yale University; New Haven, Conn. 06520	5,191 (C)	P	12,960	12,960	5,100
Yeshiva University; New York, N.Y. 10033-3299	1,773 (C)	P	9,420	9,420	4,800
York College (NYC). See New York, City University of					
York College of Pennsylvania; York, Pa. 17405	2,586 (C)	P	3,760	3,760	2,598
Youngstown State Univ.; Youngstown, Ohio 44555	13,521 (C)	Pub	1,800	2,925	2,700

1. In-city, $4,185. 2. Graduate School only. 3. $15 per credit. 4. $50 per credit. 5. $74 per credit. 6. $238 per credit. 7. $74 per credit. 8. $148 per credit.

Tips on Choosing a College

Begin by making a list of college characteristics that are important to you: location, type (two-year, four-year, public, private, Ivy League, Big Ten), student makeup (same sex, co-ed), religious affiliation, size, major course offerings, student activities and athletics, competitive or noncompetitive atmosphere, social life, and cost.

Consult a college guidebook. They contain profiles of colleges across the country, including information about size, curriculum, and campus setting.

Write to the admissions office of the schools that interest you and ask for a catalog, an admissions application, and a financial aid application, if you need one.

Visit campuses that interest you. Talk to students and faculty members. Pick up a copy of the school paper. Arrange for an admissions interview, if one is required, during this visit.

Ask the admissions office to put you in touch with alumni or other representatives in your area for you to talk to, if you're unable to visit.

Above all, don't rule out any college because of cost restrictions. Although federal student aid has leveled off, financial aid for students who want to attend college is still available in various forms.

The Ivy League

The Ivy League consists of a group of colleges and universities in the northeastern United States widely regarded as high in academic and social prestige. It includes Harvard (established in 1636), Yale (1701), Pennsylvania (1740), Princeton (1746),

Columbia (1754), Brown (1764), Dartmouth (1769), and Cornell (1853). Although competition between the colleges dates back to football meetings in the 1870s, the Ivy League was not formally organized as an athletic conference until 1956.

Future Job Outlook for College Graduates Improves

According to the Bureau of Labor Statistics projections covering the period from 1986 to 2000, the number of college graduates entering the labor force will be nearly in balance with the number of job openings that require four or more years of college education. On average, about 19 out of every 20 graduates who enter the labor force over the 1986–2000 period are expected to find college-level jobs.

The number of jobs requiring four or more years of college will increase by more than 50 percent compared to the 19 percent growth projected for all jobs. Projected growth rates for occupational groups in which the largest number of graduates were employed in 1986 follow:

Jobs in professional occupations requiring a college degree are expected to grow by more than 40 percent, with the most rapid growth occurring among engineers, computer systems analysts, and health occupations. About one out of five college-level job openings is expected to be in elementary and secondary school teaching.

College-level jobs in managerial and management-related occupations are expected to increase nearly 60 percent, with the most rapid growth occurring among accountants and auditors and management analysts.

Jobs for college-trained technicians are expected to increase by about 70 percent. Rapid growth will occur in college-level jobs in computer programmer and health technologist occupations.

Jobs in marketing and sales occupations that require a college degree are expected to grow more than 75 percent, the largest percentage increase for any group. College-level marketing and sales jobs are concentrated in insurance, real estate, securities and financial services, and other non-retail marketing and sales occupations.

College-level jobs in administrative support, service, and blue-collar occupations—although very small in number—are expected to grow by more than half.

Selected Degree Abbreviations

A.B. Bachelor of Arts
AeEng. Aeronautical Engineer
A.M.T. Master of Arts in Teaching
B.A. Bachelor of Arts
B.A.E. Bachelor of Arts in Education, or Bachelor of Art Education, Aeronautical Engineering, Agricultural Engineering, or Architectural Engineering
B.Ag. Bachelor of Agriculture
B.A.M. Bachelor of Applied Mathematics
B.Arch. Bachelor of Architecture
B.B.A. Bachelor of Business Administration
B.C.E. Bachelor of Civil Engineering
B.Ch.E. Bachelor of Chemical Engineering
B.C.L. Bachelor of Canon Law
B.D. Bachelor of Divinity
B.E. Bachelor of Education or Bachelor of Engineering
B.E.E. Bachelor of Electrical Engineering
B.F. Bachelor of Forestry
B.F.A. Bachelor of Fine Arts
B.J. Bachelor of Journalism
B.L.S. Bachelor of Liberal Studies or Bachelor of Library Science
B.Litt. Bachelor of Literature
B.M. Bachelor of Medicine or Bachelor of Music
B.M.S. Bachelor of Marine Science
B.N. Bachelor of Nursing
B.Pharm. Bachelor of Pharmacy
B.R.E. Bachelor of Religious Education
B.S. Bachelor of Science
B.S.Ed. Bachelor of Science in Education
C.E. Civil Engineer
Ch.E. Chemical Engineer
D.B.A. Doctor of Business Administration
D.C. Doctor of Chiropractic
D.D. Doctor of Divinity[1]
D.D.S. Doctor of Dental Surgery or Doctor of Dental Science
D.L.S. Doctor of Library Science
D.M.D. Doctor of Dental Medicine
D.O. Doctor of Osteopathy
D.M.S. Doctor of Medical Science
D.P.A. Doctor of Public Administration[2]
D.P.H. Doctor of Public Health
D.R.E. Doctor of Religious Education
D.S.W. Doctor of Social Welfare or Doctor of Social Work
D.Sc. Doctor of Science[3]
D.V.M. Doctor of Veterinary Medicine
Ed.D. Doctor of Education[2]
Ed.S. Education Specialist
E.E. Electrical Engineer

E.M. Engineer of Mines
E.Met. Engineer of Metallurgy
I.E. Industrial Engineer or Industrial Engineering
J.D. Doctor of Laws[2]
J.S.D. Doctor of Juristic Science
L.H.D. Doctor of Humane Letters[3]
Litt.B. Bachelor of Letters
Litt.M. Master of Letters[4]
LL.B. Bachelor of Laws
LL.D. Doctor of Laws[3]
LL.M. Master of Laws
M.A. Master of Arts
M.Aero.E. Master of Aeronautical Engineering
M.B.A. Master of Business Administration
M.C.E. Master of Christian Education or Master of Civil Engineering
M.C.S. Master of Computer Science
M.D. Doctor of Medicine
M.Div. Master of Divinity
M.E. Master of Engineering
M.Ed. Master of Education
M.Eng. Master of Engineering
M.F.A. Master of Fine Arts
M.H.A. Master of Hospital Administration
M.L.S. Master of Library Science
M.M. Master of Music
M.M.E. Master of Mechanical Engineering or Master of Music Education
M.Mus. Master of Music
M.N. Master of Nursing
M.R.E. Master of Religious Education
M.S. Master of Science
M.S.W. Master of Social Work
M.Th. Master of Theology
Nuc.E. Nuclear Engineer
O.D. Doctor of Optometry
Pharm.D. Doctor of Pharmacy[2]
Ph.B. Bachelor of Philosophy
Ph.D. Doctor of Philosophy
S.B. Bachelor of Science
Sc.D. Doctor of Science[3]
S.J.D. Doctor of Juridical Science or Doctor of the Science of Law
S.Sc.D Doctor of Social Science
S.T.B. Bachelor of Sacred Theology
S.T.D. Doctor of Sacred Theology
S.T.M. Master of Sacred Theology
Th.B. Bachelor of Theology
Th.D. Doctor of Theology
Th.M. Master of Theology

1. Honorary. 2. Earned and honorary. 3. Usually honorary.
4. Sometimes honorary.

Academic Costume: Colors Associated With Fields

Field	Color	Field	Color
Agriculture	Maize	Medicine	Green
Arts, Letters, Humanities	White	Music	Pink
Commerce, Accountancy, Business	Drab	Nursing	Apricot
		Oratory (Speech)	Silver gray
Dentistry	Lilac	Pharmacy	Olive Green
Economics	Copper	Philosophy	Dark blue
Education	Light Blue	Physical Education	Sage Green
Engineering	Orange	Public Admin. including Foreign Service	Peacock blue
Fine Arts, Architecture	Brown	Public Health	Salmon pink
Forestry	Russet	Science	Golden yellow
Journalism	Crimson	Social Work	Citron
Law	Purple	Theology	Scarlet
Library Science	Lemon	Veterinary Science	Gray

THE OLYMPIC GAMES

(W)—Site of Winter Games. (S)—Site of Summer Games

1896	Athens	1936	Berlin (S)	1972	Sapporo, Japan (W)
1900	Paris	1948	St. Moritz (W)	1972	Munich (S)
1904	St. Louis	1948	London (S)	1976	Innsbruck, Austria (W)
1906	Athens	1952	Oslo (W)	1976	Montreal (S)
1908	London	1952	Helsinki (S)	1980	Lake Placid (W)
1912	Stockholm	1956	Cortina d'Ampezzo, Italy (W)	1980	Moscow (S)
1920	Antwerp	1956	Melbourne (S)	1984	Sarajevo, Yugoslavia (W)
1924	Chamonix (W)	1960	Squaw Valley, Calif. (W)	1984	Los Angeles (S)
1924	Paris (S)	1960	Rome (S)	1988	Calgary, Alberta (W)
1928	St. Moritz (W)	1964	Innsbruck, Austria (W)	1988	Seoul, South Korea (S)
1928	Amsterdam (S)	1964	Tokyo (S)	1992	Albertville, France (W)
1932	Lake Placid (W)	1968	Grenoble, France (W)	1992	Barcelona, Spain (S)
1932	Los Angeles (S)	1968	Mexico City (S)	1994	Lillehammer, Norway (W)
1936	Garmisch-Partenkirchen (W)				

The first Olympic Games of which there is record were held in 776 B.C., and consisted of one event, a great foot race of about 200 yards held on a plain by the River Alpheus (now the Ruphia) just outside the little town of Olympia in Greece. It was from that date that the Greeks began to keep their calendar by "Olympiads," the four-year spans between the celebrations of the famous games.

The modern Olympic Games, which started in Athens in 1896, are the result of the devotion of a French educator, Baron Pierre de Coubertin, to the idea that, since young people and athletics have gone together through the ages, education and athletics might go hand-in-hand toward a better international understanding.

The principal organization responsible for the staging of the Games every four years is the International Olympic Committee (IOC). Other important roles are played by the National Olympic Committees in each participating country, international sports federations, and the organizing committee of the host city.

The headquarters of the 89-member International Olympic Committee are in Lausanne, Switzerland. The president of the IOC is Juan Antonio Samaranch of Spain.

The Olympic motto is "Citius, Altius, Fortius,"— "Faster, Higher, Stronger." The Olympic symbol is five interlocking circles colored blue, yellow, black, green, and red, on a white background, representing the five continents. At least one of those colors appears in the national flag of every country.

The ideal of peaceful international athletic competition has been severely tested the past four Olympiads, dating back to the 1972 raid by Arab terrorists on the Olympic village in Munich, Germany. Eleven Israelis, five terrorists, and a German police officer were all killed in the seige.

In 1976, political problems kept one-quarter of the IOC-member nations from competing. The most pressing was the conflict over recognition of Taiwan or Mainland China as the correct representative of that country. An additional 31 nations withdrew over the failure to bar New Zealand, which had a soccer team touring apartheid South Africa.

A total of 66 nations, including the United States, did not participate in 1980, over the Soviet Union's invasion of Afghanistan. Those Summer Games were scheduled for Moscow.

Considering this action, it was almost inevitable that the Soviet Union would take some similar action for the 1984 games, held in Los Angeles. Officially, the Soviet Union, and nearly the entire Soviet-communist bloc, withdrew over dissatisfaction with security measures in Los Angeles.

The 1988 Summer Olympics were held in Seoul, South Korea. For the first time since 1976, all the Eastern bloc countries competed against the nations of the West.

Winter Games

FIGURE SKATING—MEN

1908	Ulrich Salchow, Sweden
1920	Gillis Grafstrom, Sweden
1924	Gillis Grafstrom, Sweden
1928	Gillis Grafstrom, Sweden
1932	Karl Schaefer, Austria
1936	Karl Schaefer, Austria
1948	Richard Button, United States
1952	Richard Button, United States
1956	Hayes Alan Jenkins, United States
1960	David Jenkins, United States
1964	Manfred Schnelldorfer, Germany
1968	Wolfgang Schwartz, Austria
1972	Ondrej Nepela, Czechoslovakia
1976	John Curry, Great Britain
1980	Robin Cousins, Great Britain
1984	Scott Hamilton, United States
1988	Brian Boitano, United States

FIGURE SKATING—WOMEN

1908	Madge Syers, Britain
1920	Magda Julin–Maurey, Sweden
1924	Herma Szabo-Planck, Austria
1928	Sonja Henie, Norway
1932	Sonja Henie, Norway
1936	Sonja Henie, Norway
1948	Barbara Ann Scott, Canada
1952	Jeannette Altwegg, Great Britain
1956	Tenley Albright, United States
1960	Carol Heiss, United States
1964	Sjoukje Dijkstra, Netherlands
1968	Peggy Fleming, United States

1972	Beatrix Schuba, Austria
1976	Dorothy Hamill, United States
1980	Anett Poetzsch, East Germany
1984	Katarina Witt, East Germany
1988	Katarina Witt, East Germany

1988

SPEED SKATING—MEN

(U.S. winners only)

500 Meters

1924	Charles Jewtraw	44.0
1932	John A. Shea	43.4
1952	Kenneth Henry	43.2
1964	Terrence McDermott	40.1
1980	Eric Heiden	38.03

1,000 Meters

1976	Peter Mueller	1:19.32
1980	Eric Heiden	1:15.18

1,500 Meters

1932	John A. Shea	2:57.5
1980	Eric Heiden	1:55.44

5,000 Meters

1932	Irving Jaffee	9:40.8
1980	Eric Heiden	7:02.29

10,000 Meters

1932	Irving Jaffee	19:13.6
1980	Eric Heiden	14:28.13

1988

SPEED SKATING—WOMEN

500 Meters

1972	Anne Henning	43.33
1976	Sheila Young	42.76
1988	Bonnie Blair,	39.10[1]

1,500 Meters

1972	Dianne Holum	2:20.85

1. World Record

SKIING, ALPINE—MEN

Downhill

1948	Henri Oreiller, France	2m55.0s
1952	Zeno Colo, Italy	2m30.8s
1956	Anton Sailer, Austria	2m52.2s
1960	Jean Vuarnet, France	2m06.2s
1964	Egon Zimmermann, Austria	2m18.16s
1968	Jean-Claude Killy, France	1m59.85s
1972	Bernhard Russi, Switzerland	1m51.43s
1976	Franz Klammer, Austria	1m45.72s
1980	Leonhard Stock, Austria	1m45.50s
1984	Bill Johnson, United States	1m45.59s
1988	Pirmin Zurbriggen, Switzerland	1m59.63s

Slalom

1948	Edi Reinalter, Switzerland	2m10.3s
1952	Othmar Schneider, Austria	2m00.0s

DISTRIBUTION OF MEDALS
1988 WINTER GAMES

(Calgary, Alberta)

	Gold	Silver	Bronze	Total
Soviet Union	11	9	9	29
East Germany	9	10	6	25
Switzerland	5	5	5	15
Austria	3	5	2	10
West Germany	2	4	2	8
Finland	4	1	2	7
Netherlands	3	2	2	7
Sweden	4	0	2	6
United States	2	1	3	6
Italy	2	1	2	5
Norway	0	3	2	5
Canada	0	2	3	5
Yugoslavia	0	2	1	3
Czechoslovakia	0	1	2	3
France	1	0	1	2
Japan	0	0	1	1
Liechtenstein	0	0	0	1

1956	Anton Sailer, Austria	194.7 pts.
1960	Ernst Hinterseer, Austria	2m08.9s
1964	Josef Stiegler, Austria	2m10.13
1968	Jean-Claude Killy, France	1m39.73s
1972	Francisco Fernandez Ochoa, Spain	1m49.27s
1976	Piero Gros, Italy	2m03.29s
1980	Ingemar Stenmark, Sweden	1m44.26s
1984	Phil Mahre, United States	1m39.41s
1988	Alberto Tomba, Italy	1m39.47s

Giant Slalom

1952	Stein Eriksen, Norway	2m25.0s
1956	Anton Sailer, Austria	3m00.1s
1960	Roger Staub, Switzerland	1m48.3s
1964	François Bonlieu, France	1m46.71s
1968	Jean-Claude Killy, France	3m29.28s
1972	Gustavo Thoeni, Italy	3m09.52s
1976	Heini Hemmi, Switzerland	3m26.97s
1980	Ingemar Stenmark, Sweden	2m40.74s
1984	Max Julen, Switzerland	1m20.54s
1988	Alberto Tomba, Italy	2m06.37s

SKIING, ALPINE—WOMEN

Downhill

1948	Hedi Schlunegger, Switzerland	2m28.3s
1952	Trude Jochum-Beiser, Austria	1m47.1s
1956	Madeleine Berthod, Switzerland	1m40.1s
1960	Heidi Biebl, Germany	1m37.6s
1964	Christl Haas, Austria	1m55.39s
1968	Olga Pall, Austria	1m40.87s
1972	Marie-Therese Nadig, Switzerland	1m36.68s
1976	Rosi Mittermeier, West Germany	1m46.16s
1980	Annemarie Proell Moser, Austria	1m37.52s
1984	Michela Figini, Switzerland	1m13.36s
1988	Marina Kiehl, West Germany	1m25.86s

Slalom

1948	Gretchen Fraser, United States	1m57.2s
1952	Andrea Mead Lawrence, United States	2m10.6s
1956	Renee Colliard, Switzerland	112.3 pts.
1960	Anne Heggtveigt, Canada	1m49.6s
1964	Christine Goitschel, France	1m29.86s
1968	Marielle Goitschel, France	1m25.86s
1972	Barbara Cochran, United States	1m31.24s

1976	Rosi Mittermeier, West Germany	1m30.54s
1980	Hanni Wenzel, Liechtenstein	1m25.09s
1984	Paoletta Magoni, Italy	1m36.47s
1988	Vreni Schneider, Switzerland	1m36.69s

Giant Slalom

1952	Andrea M. Lawrence, United States	2m06.8s
1956	Ossi Reichert, Germany	1m56.5s
1960	Yvonne Ruegg, Switzerland	1m39.9s
1964	Marielle Goitschel, France	1m52.24s
1968	Nancy Greene, Canada	1m51.97s
1972	Marie-Therese Nadig, Switzerland	1m29.90s
1976	Kathy Kreiner, Canada	1m29.13s
1980	Hanni Wenzel, Liechtenstein	2m41.66s
1984	Debbie Armstrong, United States	2m20.98s
1988	Vreni Schneider, Switzerland	2m06.49s

SKIING, NORDIC, JUMPING

90-Meter Hill

		Points
1924	Jacob T. Thams, Norway	227.5
1928	Alfred Andersen, Norway	230.5
1932	Birger Ruud, Norway	228.0
1936	Birger Ruud, Norway	232.0
1948	Peter Hugsted, Norway	228.1
1952	A. Bergmann, Norway	226.0
1956	Antti Hyvarinen, Finland	227.0
1960	Helmut Recknagel, Germany	227.2
1964	Toralf Engan, Norway	230.7
1968	Vladimir Beloussov, U.S.S.R.	231.3
1972	Wojciech Fortuna, Poland	219.9
1976	Karl Schnabl, Austria	234.8
1980	Jouko Tormanen, Finland	271.0
1984	Matti Nykanen, Finland	231.2
1988	Matti Nykanen, Finland	224.0

Small Hill (70 meters)

1964	Veikko Kankkonen, Finland	229.9
1968	Jiri Raska, Czechoslovakia	216.5
1972	Yukio Kasaya, Japan	244.2
1976	Hans-Georg Aschenbach, East Germany	252.0
1980	Anton Innauer, Austria	266.3
1984	Jens Weissflog, East Germany	215.2
1988	Matti Nykanen, Finland	229.1

ICE HOCKEY

1920	Canada	1960	United States
1924	Canada	1964	U.S.S.R.
1928	Canada	1968	U.S.S.R.
1932	Canada	1972	U.S.S.R.
1936	Great Britain	1976	U.S.S.R.
1948	Canada	1980	United States
1952	Canada	1984	U.S.S.R.
1956	U.S.S.R.	1988	U.S.S.R.

FINAL OVER-ALL 1988 OLYMPIC HOCKEY STANDINGS

	W	L	T	Pts	GF	GA
1.Soviet Union	4	1	0	8	25	7
2.Finland	3	1	1	7	18	10
3.Sweden	2	1	2	6	16	18
Canada	2	2	1	5	17	14
West Germany	1	4	0	2	8	26
Czechoslovakia	1	4	0	2	12	22

1. won gold medal 2. won silver medal 3. won bronze medal

Championship

Soviet Union 7, Sweden 1

Second Place

Finland 2, Soviet Union 1

Third Place

Sweden 3, West Germany 2

Fourth Place

Canada 6, Czechoslovakia 3

Seventh Place

United States 8, Switzerland 4

Ninth Place

Austria 3, Poland 2

Other 1988 Winter Olympic Games Champions

Biathlon

10-kilometer—Frank-Peter Roetsch, East Germany
20 kilometer—Frank-Peter Roetsch, East Germany
30-kilometer relay—Soviet Union

Bobsledding

2-man—U.S.S.R. I
4-man—Switzerland I

Figure Skating

Pairs—Ekaterina Gordeeva and Sergeir Grinkov, U.S.S.R.
Dance—Natalia Bestemianova and Andrei Boukine, U.S.S.R.

Speed Skating—Men

500m—Jens-Uew Mey, East Germany
1,000m—Nikolai Gouliaev, U.S.S.R.
1,500m—Andre Hoffmann, East Germany
5,000m—Tomas Gustafson, Sweden
10,000m—Tomas Gustafson, Sweden

Speed Skating—Women

500m—Bonnie Blair, United States
1,000m—Christa Rothenberger, East Germany

1,500m—Yvonne Van Gennip, The Netherlands
3,000m—Yvonne Van Gennip, The Netherlands
5,000m—Yvonne Van Gennip, The Netherlands

Luge

Men's singles—Jens Mueller, East Germany
Men's doubles—Joerg Hoffmann and Jochen Pietzsch, East Germany

Skiing, Nordic—Men

Combined team—West Germany
Combined—Hippolyt Kempf, Switzerland
Men's 15-kilometer—Mikhail Deviatiarov, U.S.S.R.
Men's 30-kilometer—Alexei Prokourorov, U.S.S.R.
Men's 50-kilometer—Gunde Svan, Sweden
40-kilometer relay—Sweden
70-m jump—Matti Nykaenen, Finland
90-m jump—Matti Nykaenen, Finland

Skiing, Nordic—Women

Women's 5-kilometer—Marjo Matikainen, Finland
Women's 10-kilometer—Vida Ventsene, U.S.S.R.
Women's 20-kilometer—Tamara Tikhonova, U.S.S.R.
20-kilometer relay—U.S.S.R.

Summer Games

TRACK AND FIELD—MEN

100-Meter Dash

1896	Thomas Burke, United States	12s
1900	Francis W. Jarvis, United States	10.8s
1904	Archie Hahn, United States	11s
1906	Archie Hahn, United States	11.2s
1908	Reginald Walker, South Africa	10.8s
1912	Ralph Craig, United States	10.8s
1920	Charles Paddock, United States	10.8s
1924	Harold Abrahams, Great Britain	10.6s
1928	Percy Williams, Canada	10.8s
1932	Eddie Tolan, United States	10.3s
1936	Jesse Owens, United States	10.3s[1]
1948	Harrison Dillard, United States	10.3s
1952	Lindy Remigino, United States	10.4s
1956	Bobby Morrow, United States	10.5s
1960	Armin Hary, Germany	10.2s
1964	Robert Hayes, United States	10s
1968	James Hines, United States	9.9s
1972	Valery Borzov, U.S.S.R.	10.14s
1976	Hasely Crawford, Trinidad and Tobago	10.06s
1980	Allan Wells, Britain	10.25s
1984	Carl Lewis, United States	9.99s
1988	Carl Lewis, United States	9.92s[2]

1. Wind assisted. 2. Lewis was awarded the gold medal when Ben Johnson of Canada, the original winner in 09.79s, was stripped of his medal after testing positive for steroid use.

200-Meter Dash

1900	John Tewksbury, United States	22.2s
1904	Archie Hahn, United States	21.6s
1908	Robert Kerr, Canada	22.6s
1912	Ralph Craig, United States	21.7s
1920	Allan Woodring, United States	22s
1924	Jackson Scholz, United States	21.6s
1928	Percy Williams, Canada	21.8s
1932	Eddie Tolan, United States	21.2s
1936	Jesse Owens, United States	20.7s
1948	Melvin E. Patton, United States	21.1s
1952	Andrew Stanfield, United States	20.7s
1956	Bobby Morrow, United States	20.6s
1960	Livio Berruti, Italy	20.5s
1964	Henry Carr, United States	20.3s
1968	Tommie Smith, United States	19.8s
1972	Valery Borzov, U.S.S.R.	20s
1976	Don Quarrie, Jamaica	20.23s
1980	Pietro Mennea, Italy	20.19s
1984	Carl Lewis, United States	19.80s
1988	Joe DeLoach, United States	19.75s

400-Meter Dash

1896	Thomas Burke, United States	54.2s
1900	Maxwell Long, United States	49.4s
1904	Harry Hillman, United States	49.2s
1906	Paul Pilgrim, United States	53.2s
1908	Wyndham Halswelle, Great Britain (walkover)	50s
1912	Charles Reidpath, United States	48.2s
1920	Bevil Rudd, South Africa	49.6s
1924	Eric Liddell, Great Britain	47.6s
1928	Ray Barbuti, United States	47.8s
1932	William Carr, United States	46.2s
1936	Archie Williams, United States	46.5s
1948	Arthur Wint, Jamaica, B.W.I.	46.2s
1952	George Rhoden, Jamaica, B.W.I.	45.9s
1956	Charles Jenkins, United States	46.7s
1960	Otis Davis, United States	44.9s
1964	Mike Larrabee, United States	45.1s
1968	Lee Evans, United States	43.8s
1972	Vincent Matthews, United States	44.66s
1976	Alberto Juantorena, Cuba	44.26s
1980	Viktor Markin, U.S.S.R.	44.60s
1984	Alonzo Babers, United States	44.27s
1988	Steve Lewis, United States	43.87s

800-Meter Run

1896	Edwin Flack, Australia	2m11s
1900	Alfred Tysoe, Great Britain	2m1.4s
1904	James Lightbody, United States	1m56s
1906	Paul Pilgrim, United States	2m1.2s
1908	Mel Sheppard, United States	1m52.8s
1912	Ted Meredith, United States	1m51.9s
1920	Albert Hill, Great Britain	1m53.4s
1924	Douglas Lowe, Great Britain	1m52.4s
1928	Douglas Lowe, Great Britain	1m51.8s
1932	Thomas Hampson, Great Britain	1m49.8s
1936	John Woodruff, United States	1m52.9s
1948	Malvin Whitfield, United States	1m49.2s
1952	Malvin Whitfield, United States	1m49.2s
1956	Tom Courtney, United States	1m47.7s
1960	Peter Snell, New Zealand	1m46.3s
1964	Peter Snell, New Zealand	1m45.1s
1968	Ralph Doubell, Australia	1m44.3s
1972	David Wottle, United States	1m45.9s
1976	Alberto Juantorena, Cuba	1m43.5s
1980	Steve Ovett, Britain	1m45.4s
1984	Joaquin Cruz, Brazil	1m43.0s
1988	Paul Ereng, Kenya	1m43.45s

1,500-Meter Run

1896	Edwin Flack, Australia	4m33.2s
1900	Charles Bennett, Great Britain	4m6s
1904	James Lightbody, United States	4m5.4s
1906	James Lightbody, United States	4m12s
1908	Mel Sheppard, United States	4m3.4s
1912	Arnold Jackson, Great Britain	3m56.8s
1920	Albert Hill, Great Britain	4m1.8s
1924	Paavo Nurmi, Finland	3m53.6s
1928	Harry Larva, Finland	3m53.2s
1932	Luigi Beccali, Italy	3m51.2s
1936	Jack Lovelock, New Zealand	3m47.8s
1948	Henri Eriksson, Sweden	3m49.8s
1952	Joseph Barthel, Luxembourg	3m45.2s
1956	Ron Delany, Ireland	3m41.2s
1960	Herb Elliott, Australia	3m35.6s
1964	Peter Snell, New Zealand	3m38.1s
1968	Kipchoge Keino, Kenya	3m34.9s
1972	Pekka Vasala, Finland	3m36.3s
1976	John Walker, New Zealand	3m39.17s
1980	Sebastian Coe, Britain	3m38.4s
1984	Sebastian Coe, Britain	3m32.53s
1988	Peter Rono, Kenya	3m35.96s

5,000-Meter Run

1912	Hannes Kolehmainen, Finland	14m36.6s
1920	Joseph Guillemot, France	14m55.6s
1924	Paavo Nurmi, Finland	14m31.2s
1928	Willie Ritola, Finland	14m38s
1932	Lauri Lehtinen, Finland	14m30s
1936	Gunnar Hockert, Finland	14m22.2s
1948	Gaston Reiff, Belgium	14m17.6s
1952	Emil Zatopek, Czechoslovakia	14m6.6s
1956	Vladimir Kuts, U.S.S.R.	13m39.6s
1960	Murray Halberg, New Zealand	13m43.4s
1964	Bob Schul, United States	13m48.8s
1968	Mohamed Gammoudi, Tunisia	14m.05s
1972	Lasse Viren, Finland	13m26.4s
1976	Lasse Viren, Finland	13m24.76s
1980	Miruts Yifter, Ethiopia	13m21s
1984	Saud Aouita, Morocco	13m5.59s

1988	John Ngugi, Kenya	13m11.70s

10,000-Meter Run

1912	Hannes Kolehmainen, Finland	31m20.8s
1920	Paavo Nurmi, Finland	31m45.8s
1924	Willie Ritola, Finland	30m23.2s
1928	Paavo Nurmi, Finland	30m18.8s
1932	Janusz Kusocinski, Poland	30m11.4s
1936	Ilmari Salminen, Finland	30m15.4s
1948	Emil Zatopek, Czechoslovakia	29m59.6s
1952	Emil Zatopek, Czechoslovakia	29m17s
1956	Vladimir Kuts, U.S.S.R.	28m45.6s
1960	Peter Bolotnikov, U.S.S.R.	28m32.2s
1964	Billy Mills, United States	28m24.4s
1968	Naftali Temu, Kenya	29m27.4s
1972	Lasse Viren, Finland	27m38.4s
1976	Lasse Viren, Finland	27m40.38s
1980	Miruts Yifter, Ethiopia	27m42.7s
1984	Alberto Cova, Italy	27m47.5s
1988	Mly Brahim Boutaib, Morocco	27m21.46s

Marathon

1896	Spiridon Loues, Greece	2h58m50s
1900	Michel Teato, France	2h59m45s
1904	Thomas Hicks, United States	3h28m53s
1906	William J. Sherring, Canada	2h51m23.65s
1908	John J. Hayes, United States	2h55m18.4s
1912	Kenneth McArthur, South Africa	2h36m54.8s
1920	Hannes Kolehmainen, Finland	2h32m35.8s
1924	Albin Stenroos, Finland	2h41m22.6s
1928	A. B. El Quafi, France	2h32m57s
1932	Juan Zabala, Argentina	2h31m36s
1936	Kitei Son, Japan	2h29m19.2s
1948	Delfo Cabrera, Argentina	2h34m51.6s
1952	Emil Zatopek, Czechoslovakia	2h23m3.2s
1956	Alain Mimoun, France	2h25m
1960	Abebe Bikila, Ethiopia	2h15m16.2s
1964	Abebe Bikila, Ethiopia	2h12m11.2s
1968	Mamo Wold, Ethiopia	2h20m26.4s
1972	Frank Shorter, United States	2h12m19.8s
1976	Walter Cierpinski, East Germany	2h09m55s
1980	Walter Cierpinski, East Germany	2h11m3s
1984	Carlos Lopes, Portugal	2hr9m.55s
1988	Gelindo Bordin, Italy	2hr10m47s

110-Meter Hurdles

1896	Thomas Curtis, United States	17.6s
1900	Alvin Kraenzlein, United States	15.4s
1904	Frederick Schule, United States	16s
1906	R. G. Leavitt, United States	16.2s
1908	Forrest Smithson, United States	15s
1912	Frederick Kelly, United States	15.1s
1920	Earl Thomson, Canada	14.8s
1924	Daniel Kinsey, United States	15s
1928	Sydney Atkinson, South Africa	14.8s
1932	George Saling, United States	14.6s
1936	Forrest Towns, United States	14.2s
1948	William Porter, United States	13.9s
1952	Harrison Dillard, United States	13.7s
1956	Lee Calhoun, United States .	13.5s
1960	Lee Calhoun, United States	13.8s
1964	Hayes Jones, United States	13.6s
1968	Willie Davenport, United States	13.3s
1972	Rodney Milburn, United States	13.24s
1976	Guy Drut, France	13.30s
1980	Thomas Munkelt, East Germany	13.39s
1984	Roger Kingdom, United States	13.20s
1988	Roger Kingdom, United States	12.98s

200-Meter Hurdles

1900	Alvin Kraenzlein, United States	25.4s
1904	Harry Hillman, United States	24.6s

400-Meter Hurdles

1900	John Tewksbury, United States	57.6s
1904	Harry Hillman, United States	53s
1908	Charles Bacon, United States	55s
1920	Frank Loomis, United States	54s
1924	F. Morgan Taylor, United States	52.6s
1928	Lord David Burghley, Great Britain	53.4s
1932	Robert Tisdall, Ireland	51.8s[1]
1936	Glenn Hardin, United States	52.4s
1948	Roy Cochran, United States	51.1s
1952	Charles Moore, United States	50.8s
1956	Glenn Davis, United States	50.1s
1960	Glenn Davis, United States	49.3s
1964	Rex Cawley, United States	49.6s
1968	David Hemery, Great Britain	48.1s
1972	John Akii-Bua, Uganda	47.8s
1976	Edwin Moses, United States	47.64s
1980	Volker Beck, East Germany	48.70s
1984	Edwin Moses, United States	47.75s
1988	Andre Phillips, United States	47.19s

1. Record not allowed.

2,500-Meter Steeplechase

1900	George Orton, United States	7m34s
1904	James Lightbody, United States	7m39.6s

3,000-Meter Steeplechase

1920	Percy Hodge, Great Britain	10m0.4s
1924	Willie Ritola, Finland	9m33.6s
1928	Toivo Loukola, Finland	9m21.8s
1932	Volmari Iso-Hollo, Finland	10m33.4s[1]
1936	Volmari Iso-Hollo, Finland	9m3.8s
1948	Thure Sjoestrand, Sweden	9m4.6s
1952	Horace Ashenfelter, United States	8m45.4s
1956	Chris Brasher, Great Britain	8m41.2s
1960	Zdzislaw Krzyskowiak, Poland	8m34.2s
1964	Gaston Roelants, Belgium	8m30.8s
1968	Amos Biwott, Kenya	8m51s
1972	Kipchoge Keino, Kenya	8m23.6s
1976	Anders Gardervd, Sweden	8m08.02s
1980	Bronislaw Malinowski, Poland	8m9.7s
1984	Julius Korir, Kenya	8m11.80s
1988	Julius Karluki, Kenya	8m05.51s

1. About 3,450 meters—extra lap by error.

10,000-Meter Walk

1912	George Goulding, Canada	46m28.4s
1920	Ugo Frigerio, Italy	48m6.2s
1924	Ugo Frigerio, Italy	47m49s
1948	John Mikaelsson, Sweden	45m13.2s
1952	John Mikaelsson, Sweden	45m2.8s

20,000-Meter Walk

1956	Leonid Spirin, U.S.S.R.	1h31m27.4s
1960	Vladimir Golubnichy, U.S.S.R.	1h34m7.2s
1964	Ken Mathews, Great Britain	1h29m34s
1968	Vladimir Golubnichy, U.S.S.R.	1h33m58.4s
1972	Peter Frenkel, East Germany	1h26m42.4s
1976	Daniel Bautista, Mexico	1h24m40.6s
1980	Maurizio Damiliano, Italy	1h23m35.5s
1984	Ernesto Conto, Mexico	1m23.13s
1988	Jozef Pribilinec, Czechoslovakia	1h19m57s

50,000-Meter Walk

1932	Thomas W. Green, Great Britain	4h50m10s
1936	Harold Whitlock, Great Britain	4h30m41.1s
1948	John Ljunggren, Sweden	4h41m52s
1952	Giuseppe Dordoni, Italy	4h28m7.8s
1956	Norman Read, New Zealand	4h30m42.8s
1960	Donald Thompson, Great Britain	4h25m30s
1964	Abdon Pamich, Italy	4h11m12.4s
1968	Christoph Hohne, East Germany	4h20m13.6s
1972	Bern Kannernberg, West Germany	3h56m11.6s

1980	Hartwig Gauder, East Germany	3h49m24s
1984	Raul Gonzalez, Mexico	3hr47m26s
1988	Viacheslau Ivanenko, U.S.S.R.	3hr38m29s

400-Meter Relay (4 × 100)

1912	Great Britain	42.4s
1920	United States	42.2s
1924	United States	41s
1928	United States	41s
1932	United States	40s
1936	United States	39.8s
1948	United States	40.6s
1952	United States	40.1s
1956	United States	39.5s
1960	Germany	39.5s
1964	United States	39s
1968	United States	38.2s
1972	United States	38.19s
1976	United States	38.33s
1980	U.S.S.R.	38.26s
1984	United States	37.83s
1988	U.S.S.R.	38.19s

1,600-Meter Relay (4 × 400)

1912	United States	3m16.6s
1920	Great Britain	3m22.2s
1924	United States	3m16s
1928	United States	3m14.2s
1932	United States	3m8.2s
1936	Great Britain	3m9s
1948	United States	3m10.4s
1952	Jamaica, B.W.I.	3m3.9s
1956	United States	3m4.8s
1960	United States	3m2.2s
1964	United States	3m0.7s
1968	United States	2m56.1s
1972	Kenya	2m59.8s
1976	United States	2m58.65s
1980	U.S.S.R.	3m01.1s
1984	United States	2m57.91s
1988	United States	2m56.16s

Team Race

		Pts
1900	Great Britain (5,000 meters)	26
1904	United States (4 miles)	27
1908	Great Britain (3 miles)	6
1912	United States (3,000 meters)	9
1920	United States (3,000 meters)	10
1924	Finland (3,000 meters)	9

Standing High Jump

1900	Ray Ewry, United States	5 ft 5 in.
1904	Ray Ewry, United States	4 ft 11 in.
1906	Ray Ewry, United States	5 ft 1 5/8 in.
1908	Ray Ewry, United States	5 ft 2 in.
1912	Platt Adams, United States	5 ft 4 1/8 in.

Running High Jump

1896	Ellery Clark, United States	5 ft 11 1/4 in.
1900	Irving Baxter, United States	6 ft 2 3/4 in.
1904	Samuel Jones, United States	5 ft 11 in.
1906	Con Leahy, Ireland	5 ft 9 7/8 in.
1908	Harry Porter, United States	6 ft 3 in.
1912	Alma Richards, United States	6 ft 4 in.
1920	Richmond Landon, United States	6 ft 4 1/4 in.
1924	Harold Osborn, United States	6 ft 5 15/16 in.
1928	Robert W. King, United States	6 ft 4 3/8 in.
1932	Duncan McNaughton, Canada	6 ft 5 5/8 in.
1936	Cornelius Johnson, United States	6 ft 7 15/16 in.
1948	John Winter, Australia	6 ft 6 in.
1952	Walter Davis, United States	6 ft 8 5/16 in.
1956	Charles Dumas, United States	6 ft 11 1/4 in.
1960	Robert Shavlakadze, U.S.S.R.	7 ft 1 in.

1964	Valeri Brumel, U.S.S.R.	7 ft 1 3/4 in.
1968	Dick Fosbury, United States	7 ft 4 1/4 in.
1972	Yuri Tarmak, U.S.S.R.	7 ft 3 3/4 in.
1976	Jacek Wszola, Poland	(2.25m) 7 ft 4 1/2 in.
1980	Gerd Wessig, East Germany	7 ft 8 3/4 in.
1984	Dietmar Mogenburg, West Germany	7 ft 8 1/2 in.
1988	Guennadi Avdeenko, U.S.S.R.	7 ft 9 1/2 in.

Long Jump

1896	Ellery Clark, United States	20 ft 9 3/4 in.
1900	Alvin Kraenzlein, United States	23 ft 6 7/8 in.
1904	Myer Prinstein, United States	24 ft 1 in.
1906	Myer Prinstein, United States	23 ft 7 1/2 in.
1908	Frank Irons, United States	24 ft 6 1/2 in.
1912	Albert Gutterson, United States	24 ft 11 1/4 in.
1920	William Petterssen, Sweden	23 ft 5 1/2 in.
1924	DeHart Hubbard, United States	24 ft 5 1/8 in.
1928	Edward B. Hamm, United States	25 ft 4 3/4 in.
1932	Edward Gordon, United States	25 ft 3/4 in.
1936	Jesse Owens, United States	26 ft. 5 5/16 in.
1948	Willie Steele, United States	25 ft 8 in.
1952	Jerome Biffle, United States	24 ft 10 in.
1956	Gregory Bell, United States	25 ft 8 1/4 in.
1960	Ralph Boston, United States	26 ft 7 3/4 in.
1964	Lynn Davies, Great Britain	26 ft 5 3/4 in.
1968	Bob Beamon, United States	29 ft 2 1/2 in.
1972	Randy Williams, United States	27 ft 1 1/2 in.
1976	Arnie Robinson, United States	(8.35m) 24 ft 7 3/4 in.
1980	Lutz Dombrowski, E. Germany	28 ft 1/4 in.
1984	Carl Lewis, United States	28 ft 1/4 in.
1988	Carl Lewis, United States	28 ft 7 1/4 in.

Triple Jump

1896	James B. Connolly, United States	45 ft
1900	Myer Prinstein, United States	47 ft 4 1/4 in.
1904	Myer Prinstein, United States	47 ft
1906	P. G. O'Connor, Ireland	46 ft 2 in.
1908	Timothy Ahearne, Great Britain	48 ft 11 1/4 in.
1912	Gustaf Lindblom, Sweden	48 ft 5 1/8 in.
1920	Vilho Tuulos, Finland	47 ft 6 7/8 in.
1924	Archie Winter, Australia	50 ft 11 1/8 in.
1928	Mikio Oda, Japan	49 ft 10 13/16 in.
1932	Chuhei Nambu, Japan	51 ft 7 in.
1936	Naoto Tajima, Japan	52 ft 5 7/8 in.
1948	Arne Ahman, Sweden	50 ft 6 1/4 in.
1952	Adhemar da Silva, Brazil	53 ft 2 1/2 in.
1956	Adhemar da Silva, Brazil	53 ft 7 1/2 in.
1960	Jozef Schmidt, Poland	55 ft 1 3/4 in.
1964	Jozef Schmidt, Poland	55 ft 3 1/4 in.
1968	Viktor Saneyev, U.S.S.R.	57 ft 3/4 in.
1972	Viktor Saneyev, U.S.S.R.	56 ft 11 in.
1976	Viktor Saneyev, U.S.S.R.	(17.29m) 56 ft 8 3/4 in.
1980	Jaak Uudmae, U.S.S.R.	56 ft 11 1/8 in.
1984	Al Joyner, United States	56 ft 7 1/2 in.
1988	Hristo Markov, Bulgaria	57 ft 9 1/4 in.

Pole Vault

1896	William Hoyt, United States	10 ft 9 3/4 in.
1900	Irving Baxter, United States	10 ft 9 7/8 in.
1904	Charles Dvorak, United States	11 ft 6 in.
1906	Fernand Gouder, France	11 ft 6 in.
1908	Alfred Gilbert, United States, and Edward Cook, United States (tie)	12 ft 2 in.
1912	Harry Babcock, United States	12 ft 11 1/2 in.
1920	Frank Foss, United States	13 ft 5 9/16 in.
1924	Lee Barnes, United States	12 ft 11 1/2 in.
1928	Sabin W. Carr, United States	13 ft 9 3/8 in.
1932	William Miller, United States	14 ft 1 7/8 in.
1936	Earle Meadows, United States	14 ft 3 1/4 in.
1948	Guinn Smith, United States	14 ft 1 1/4 in.
1952	Robert Richards, United States	14 ft 11 1/8 in.
1956	Robert Richards, United States	14 ft 11 1/2 in.
1960	Don Bragg, United States	15 ft 5 1/8 in.

1964	Fred Hansen, United States	16 ft 8 3/4 in.
1968	Bob Seagren, United States	17 ft 8 1/2 in.
1972	Wolfgang Nordwig, East Germany	18 ft 1/2 in.
1976	Tadeusz Slusarski, Poland	(5.50m) 18 ft 1/2 in.
1980	Wladyslaw Kozakiewicz, Poland	18 ft 11 1/2 in.
1984	Pierre Quinon, France	18 ft 10 1/4 in.
1988	Sergei Bubka, U.S.S.R.	19 ft. 4 1/4 in.

16-lb Shot-Put

1896	Robert Garrett, United States	36 ft 9 3/4 in.
1900	Richard Sheldon, United States	46 ft 3 1/8 in.
1904	Ralph Rose, United States	48 ft 7 in.
1906	Martin Sheridan, United States	40 ft 4 4/5 in.
1908	Ralph Rose, United States	46 ft 7 1/2 in.
1912	Pat McDonald, United States	50 ft 4 in.
1920	Ville Porhola, Finland	48 ft 7 1/8 in.
1924	Clarence Houser, United States	49 ft 2 1/2 in.
1928	John Kuck, United States	52 ft 11 11/16 in.
1932	Leo Sexton, United States	52 ft 6 3/16 in.
1936	Hans Woellke, Germany	53 ft 1 3/4 in.
1948	Wilbur Thompson, United States	56 ft 2 in.
1952	Parry O'Brien, United States	57 ft 1 1/2 in.
1956	Parry O'Brien, United States	60 ft 11 in.
1960	Bill Nieder, United States	64 ft 6 3/4 in.
1964	Dallas Long, United States	66 ft 8 1/4 in.
1968	Randy Matson, United States	67 ft 4 3/4 in.
1972	Wladyslaw Komar, Poland	69 ft 6 in.
1976	Udo Beyer, East Germany	(21.05m) 69 ft 3/4 in.
1980	Vladimir Klselyov, U.S.S.R.	70 ft 1/2 in.
1984	Alessandro Andrei, Italy	69 ft 9 in.
1988	Uhf Timmerman, East Germany	73 ft 8 3/4 in.

Discus Throw

1896	Robert Garrett, United States	95 ft 7 1/2 in.
1900	Rudolf Bauer, Hungary	118 ft 2 7/8 in.
1904	Martin Sheridan, United States	128 ft 10 1/2 in.
1906	Martin Sheridan, United States	136 ft 1/8 in.
1908	Martin Sheridan, United States	134 ft 2 in.
1912	Armas Taipale, Finland	145 ft 9/16 in.
1920	Elmer Niklander, Finland	146 ft 7 in.
1924	Clarence Houser, United States	151 ft 5 1/4 in.
1928	Clarence Houser, United States	155 ft 2 4/5 in.
1932	John Anderson, United States	162 ft 4 7/8 in.
1936	Ken Carpenter, United States	165 ft 7 3/8 in.
1948	Adolfo Consolini, Italy	173 ft 2 in.
1952	Simeon Iness, United States	180 ft 6 1/2 in.
1956	Al Oerter, United States	184 ft 10 1/2 in.
1960	Al Oerter, United States	194 ft 2 in.
1964	Al Oerter, United States	200 ft 1 1/2 in.
1968	Al Oerter, United States	212 ft 6 in.
1972	Ludvik Danek, Czechoslovakia	211 ft 3 in.
1976	Mac Wilkins, United States	(67.5m) 221 ft 5 in.
1980	Viktor Rashchupkin, U.S.S.R.	218 ft 8 in.
1984	Rolf Dannenberg, West Germany	218 ft 6 in.
1988	Jurgen Schult, East Germany	225 ft 9 1/4 in.

Javelin Throw

1906	Eric Lemming, Sweden	175 ft 6 in.
1908	Eric Lemming, Sweden	179 ft 10 1/2 in.
1912	Eric Lemming, Sweden	198 ft 11 1/4 in.
1920	Jonni Myyra, Finland	215 ft 9 3/4 in.
1924	Jonni Myyra, Finland	206 ft 6 3/4 in.
1928	Eric Lundquist, Sweden	218 ft 6 1/8 in.
1932	Matti Jarvinen, Finland	238 ft 7 in.
1936	Gerhard Stoeck, Germany	235 ft 8 5/16 in.
1948	Kaj Rautavaara, Finland	228 ft 10 1/2 in.
1952	Cy Young, United States	242 ft 3/4 in.
1956	Egil Danielsen, Norway	281 ft 2 1/4 in.
1960	Viktor Tsibulenko, U.S.S.R.	277 ft 8 3/8 in.
1964	Pauli Nevala, Finland	271 ft 2 1/4 in.
1968	Janis Lusis, U.S.S.R.	295 ft 7 in.
1972	Klaus Wolfermann, West Germany	296 ft 10 in.
1976	Miklos Nemeth, Hungary	(94.58m) 310 ft 4 in.

1980	Dainis Kula, U.S.S.R.	299 ft 2 3/8 in.
1984	Arto Haerkoenen, Finland	284 ft 8 in.
1988	Tapio Korjus, Finland	276 ft 6 in.

16-lb Hammer Throw

1900	John Flanagan, United States	167 ft 4 in.
1904	John Flanagan, United States	168 ft 1 in.
1908	John Flanagan, United States	170 ft 4 1/4 in.
1912	Matt McGrath, United States	179 ft 7 1/8 in.
1920	Pat Ryan, United States	173 ft 5 5/8 in.
1924	Fred Tootell, United States	174 ft 10 1/4 in.
1928	Patrick O'Callaghan, Ireland	168 ft 7 1/2 in.
1932	Patrick O'Callaghan, Ireland	176 ft 11 1/8 in.
1936	Karl Hein, Germany	185 ft 4 in.
1948	Imre Nemeth, Hungary	183 ft 11 1/2 in.
1952	Jozsef Csermak, Hungary	197 ft 11 9/16 in.
1956	Harold Connolly, United States	207 ft 2 3/4 in.
1960	Vasily Rudenkov, U.S.S.R.	220 ft 1 5/8 in.
1964	Romuald Klim, U.S.S.R.	228 ft 9 1/2 in.
1968	Gyula Zsivotzky, Hungary	240 ft 8 in.
1972	Anatoly Bondarchuk, U.S.S.R.	247 ft 8 in.
1976	Yuri Sedykh, U.S.S.R.	(77.52m) 254 ft 4 in.
1980	Yuri Sedykh, U.S.S.R.	(81.80m) 268 ft 4 1/2 in.
1984	Juha Tiainen, Finland	256 ft 2 in.
1988	Sergei Litvinov, U.S.S.R.	278 ft 2 1/2 in.

Decathlon

1912	Jim Thorpe, United States	—
	Hugo Wieslander, Sweden	—
1920	Helge Lovland, Norway	6,804.35 pts.
1924	Harold Osborn, United States	7,710.775 pts.
1928	Paavo Yrjola, Finland	8,053.29 pts.
1932	James Bausch, United States	8,462.23 pts.
1936	Glenn Morris, United States	7,900 pts.[1]
1948	Robert B. Mathias, United States	7,139 pts.
1952	Robert B. Mathias, United States	7,887 pts.
1956	Milton Campbell, United States	7,937 pts.
1960	Rafer Johnson, United States	8,392 pts.
1964	Willi Holdorf, Germany	7,887 pts.[1]
1968	Bill Toomey, United States	8,193 pts.
1972	Nikolai Avilov, U.S.S.R.	8,454 pts.
1976	Bruce Jenner, United States	8,618 pts.
1980	Daley Thompson, Britain	8,495 pts.
1984	Daley Thompson, Britain	8,797 pts.
1988	Christian Schenk, East Germany	8,488 pts.

1. Point system revised.

TRACK AND FIELD—WOMEN

100-Meter Dash

1928	Elizabeth Robinson, United States	12.2s
1932	Stella Walsh, Poland	11.9s
1936	Helen Stephens, United States	11.5s
1948	Fanny Blankers-Koen, Netherlands	11.9s
1952	Marjorie Jackson, Australia	11.5s
1956	Betty Cuthbert, Australia	11.5s
1960	Wilma Rudolph, United States	11s
1964	Wyomia Tyus, United States	11.4s
1968	Wyomia Tyus, United States	11s
1972	Renate Stecher, East Germany	11.07s
1976	Annegret Richter, West Germany	11.08s
1980	Lyudmila Kondratyeva, U.S.S.R.	11.06s
1984	Evelyn Ashford, United States	10.97s
1988	Florence Griffith-Joyner, United States	10.54s

200-Meter Dash

1948	Fanny Blankers-Koen, Netherlands	24.4s
1952	Marjorie Jackson, Australia	23.7s
1956	Betty Cuthbert, Australia	23.4s
1960	Wilma Rudolph, United States	24s
1964	Edith McGuire, United States	23s

1968	Irena Szewinska, Poland	22.5s
1972	Renate Stecher, East Germany	22.4s
1976	Baerbel Eckert, East Germany	22.37s
1980	Barbara Wockel, East Germany	22.03s
1984	Valerie Brisco-Hooks, United States	21.81s
1988	Florence Griffith-Joyner, United States	21.34s

400-Meter Dash

1964	Betty Cuthbert, Australia	52s
1968	Colette Besson, France	52s
1972	Monika Zehrt, East Germany	51.08s
1976	Irena Szewinska, Poland	49.29s
1980	Marita Koch, East Germany	48.88s
1984	Valerie Brisco-Hooks, United States	48.83s
1988	Olga Bryzguina, U.S.S.R.	48.65s

800-Meter Run

1928	Lina Radke, Germany	2m16.8s
1960	Ljudmila Shevcova, U.S.S.R.	2m4.3s
1964	Ann Packer, Great Britain	2m1.1s
1968	Madeline Manning, United States	2m0.9s
1972	Hildegard Falck, West Germany	1m58.6s
1976	Tatiana Kazankina, U.S.S.R.	1m54.94s
1980	Nadezhda Olizarenko, U.S.S.R.	1m53.5s
1984	Doina Melinte, Romania	1m57.60s
1988	Sigrun Wodars, East Germany	1m56.10s

1,500-Meter Run

1972	Ludmila Bragina, U.S.S.R.	4m01.4s
1976	Tatiana Kazankina, U.S.S.R.	4m05.48s
1980	Tatiana Kazankina, U.S.S.R.	3m56.6s
1984	Gabriella Dorio, Italy	4m03.25s
1988	Paula Ivan, Romania	3m53.96s

3,000-Meter Run

1984	Maricica Puica, Romania	8m35.96s
1988	Tatiana Samolenko, U.S.S.R.	8m26.53s

80-Meter Hurdles

1932	Mildred Didrikson, United States	11.7s
1936	Trebisonda Valla, Italy	11.7s
1948	Fanny Blankers-Koen, Netherlands	11.2s
1952	Shirley S. de la Hunty, Australia	10.9s
1956	Shirley S. de la Hunty, Australia	10.7s
1960	Irina Press, U.S.S.R.	10.8s
1964	Karin Balzer, Germany	10.5s[1]
1968	Maureen Caird, Australia	10.3s

1. Wind assisted.

100-Meter Hurdles

1972	Annelie Ehrhardt, East Germany	12.59s
1976	Johanna Schaller, East Germany	12.77s
1980	Vera Komisova, U.S.S.R.	12.56s
1984	Benita Fitzgerald-Brown, United States	12.84s
1988	Jordanka Donkova, Bulgaria	12.38s

400-Meter Hurdle

1984	Nawai El Moutawakel, Morocco	54.61s
1988	Debra Flintoff-King, Australia	53.17s

400-Meter Relay

1928	Canada	48.4s
1932	United States	47s
1936	United States	46.9s
1948	Netherlands	47.5s
1952	United States	45.9s
1956	Australia	44.5s
1960	United States	44.5s
1964	Poland	43.6s
1968	United States	42.8s
1972	West Germany	42.81s

1976	East Germany	42.55s
1980	East Germany	41.60s
1984	United States	41.65s
1988	United States	41.98s

1,600-Meter Relay

1972	East Germany	3m23s
1976	East Germany	3m19.23s
1980	U.S.S.R.	3m20.2s
1984	United States	3m18.29s
1988	U.S.S.R.	3m15.18s

Marathon

1984	Joan Benoit, United States	2 hr 24 m 52s
1988	Rosa Mota, Portugal	2 hr 25 m 40s

Running High Jump

1928	Ethel Catherwood, Canada	5 ft 3 in.
1932	Jean Shiley, United States	5 ft 5 1/4 in.
1936	Ibolya Csak, Hungary	5 ft 3 in.
1948	Alice Coachman, United States	5 ft 6 1/8 in.
1952	Ester Brand, South Africa	5 ft 5 3/4 in.
1956	Mildred McDaniel, United States	5 ft 9 1/4 in.
1960	Iolanda Balas, Romania	6 ft 3/4 in.
1964	Iolanda Balas, Romania	6 ft 2 3/4 in.
1968	Miloslava Rezkova, Czechoslovakia	5 ft 11 3/4 in.
1972	Ulrike Meyfarth, West Germany	6 ft 3 5/8 in.
1976	Rosemarie Ackerman, E. Germany	(1.93m) 6 ft 4 in.
1980	Sara Simeoni, Italy	6 ft 5 1/2 in.
1984	Ulrike Meyfarth, West Germany	6 ft 7 1/2 in.
1988	Louise Ritter, United States	6 ft 8 in.

Long Jump

1948	Olga Gyarmati, Hungary	18 ft 8 1/4 in.
1952	Yvette Williams, New Zealand	20 ft 5 3/4 in.
1956	Elzbieta Krzesinska, Poland	20 ft 9 3/4 in.
1960	Vera Krepkina, U.S.S.R.	20 ft 10 3/4 in.
1964	Mary Rand, Great Britain	22 ft 2 in.
1968	Viorica Ciscopoleanu, Romania	22 ft 4 1/2 in.
1972	Heidemarie Rosendahl, West Germany	22 ft 3 in.
1976	Angela Voigt, East Germany	(6.72m) 22 ft 1/2 in.
1980	Tatiana Kolpakova, U.S.S.R.	23 ft 2 in.
1984	Anisoara Stanciu, Romania	22 ft 10 in.
1988	Jackie Joyner-Kersee, United States	24 ft 3 1/2 in.

Shot-Put

1948	Micheline Ostermeyer, France	45 ft 1 1/2 in.
1952	Galina Zybina, U.S.S.R.	50 ft 1 1/2 in.
1956	Tamara Tishkyevich, U.S.S.R.	54 ft 5 in.
1960	Tamara Press, U.S.S.R.	56 ft 9 7/8 in.
1964	Tamara Press, U.S.S.R.	59 ft 6 in.
1968	Margitta Gummel, East Germany	64 ft 4 in.
1972	Nadezhda Chizhova, U.S.S.R.	69 ft
1976	Ivanka Christova, Bulgaria	(21.16m) 69 ft 5 in.
1980	Ilona Sluplanek, East Germany	73 ft 6 in.
1984	Claudia Losch, West Germany	67 ft 2 1/4 in.
1988	Natalya Lisovskaya, U.S.S.R.	72 ft 11 1/2 in.

Discus Throw

1928	Helena Konopacka, Poland	129 ft 11 7/8 in.
1932	Lillian Copeland, United States	133 ft 2 in.
1936	Gisela Mauermayer, Germany	156 ft 3 3/16 in.
1948	Micheline Ostermeyer, France	137 ft 6 1/2 in.
1952	Nina Romaschkova, U.S.S.R.	168 ft 8 7/16 in.
1956	Olga Fikotova, Czechoslovakia	176 ft 1 1/2 in.
1960	Nina Ponomareva, U.S.S.R.	180 ft 8 1/4 in.
1964	Tamara Press, U.S.S.R.	187 ft 10 3/4 in.
1968	Lia Manoliu, Romania	191 ft 2 1/2 in.
1972	Faina Melnik, U.S.S.R.	218 ft 7 in.

1976	Evelin Schlaak, East Germany	(69.0m) 226 ft 4 in.
1980	Evelin Jahl, East Germany	229 ft 6 1/2 in.
1984	Ria Stalman, Netherlands	214 ft 5 in.
1988	Martina Hellmann, East Germany	237 ft 2 1/4 in.

Javelin Throw

1932	Mildred Didrikson, United States	143 ft 4 in.
1936	Tilly Fleischer, Germany	148 ft 2 3/4 in.
1948	Herma Bauma, Austria	149 ft 6 in.
1952	Dana Zatopek, Czechoslovakia	165 ft 7 in.
1956	Inessa Janzeme, U.S.S.R.	176 ft 8 in.
1960	Elvira Ozolina, U.S.S.R.	183 ft 8 in.
1964	Mihaela Penes, Romania	198 ft 7 1/2 in.
1968	Angela Nemeth, Hungary	198 ft 0 in.
1972	Ruth Fuchs, East Germany	209 ft 7 in.
1976	Ruth Fuchs, East Germany	(65.94m) 216 ft 4 in.
1980	Maria Colon, Cuba	224 ft 5 in.
1984	Tessa Sanderson, Britain	228 ft 2 in.
1988	Petra Felke, East Germany	245 ft

Pentathlon

1964	Irina Press, U.S.S.R.	5,246 pts.
1968	Ingrid Becker, West Germany	5,098 pts.
1972	Mary Peters, Britain	4,801 pts.
1976	Siegrun Siegl, East Germany	4,745 pts.
1980	Nadyezhda Tkachenko, U.S.S.R.	5,083 pts.
1984	Daniele Masala, Italy	5,469 pts.
1988	Jackie Joyner-Kersee, United States	7,291 pts.

SWIMMING—MEN

50 Meter Freestyle

| 1988 | Matt Biondi, United States | 22.14s |

100 Meter Freestyle

1896	Alfred Hajos, Hungary	1m22.2s
1904	Zoltan de Halmay, Hungary	1m2.8s[1]
1906	Charles Daniels, United States	1m13s
1908	Charles Daniels, United States	1m5.6s
1912	Duke P. Kahanamoku, United States	1m3.4s
1920	Duke P. Kahanamoku, United States	1m1.4s
1924	John Weissmuller, United States	59s
1928	John Weissmuller, United States	58.6s
1932	Yasuji Miyazaki, Japan	58.2s
1936	Ferenc Csik, Hungary	57.6s
1948	Walter Ris, United States	57.3s
1952	Clarke Scholes, United States	57.4s
1956	Jon Henricks, Australia	55.4s
1960	John Devitt, Australia	55.2s
1964	Don Schollander, United States	53.4s
1968	Michael Wenden, Australia	52.2s
1972	Mark Spitz, United States	51.22s
1976	Jim Montgomery, United States	49.99s
1980	Jorg Woithe, East Germany	50.40s
1984	Rowdy Gaines, United States	49.80s
1988	Matt Brondi, United States	48.63s

1. 100 yards.

200-Meter Freestyle

1900	Frederick Lane, Australia	2m25.2s
1904	Charles Daniels, United States	2m44.2s[1]
1968	Michael Wenden, Australia	1m55.2s
1972	Mark Spitz, United States	1m52.78s
1976	Bruce Furniss, United States	1m50.29s
1980	Sergei Kopliakov, U.S.S.R.	1m49.81s
1984	Michael Gross, West Germany	1m47.44s
1988	Duncan Armstrong, Australia	1m47.25s

1. 220 yards.

400-Meter Freestyle

1896	Paul Neumann, Austria	8m12.6s[1]
1904	Charles Daniels, United States	6m16.2s[2]
1906	Otto Sheff, Austria	6m23.8s
1908	Henry Taylor, Great Britain	5m36.8s
1912	George Hodgson, Canada	5m24.4s

1920	Norman Ross, United States	5m26.8s
1926	Jonn Weissmuller, United States	5m4.2s
1928	Albert Zorilla, Argentina	5m1.6s
1932	Clarence Crabbe, United States	4m48.4s
1936	Jack Medica, United States	4m44.5s
1948	William Smith, United States	4m41s
1952	Jean Boiteux, France	4m30.7s
1956	Murray Rose, Australia	4m27.3s
1960	Murray Rose, Australia	4m18.3s
1964	Don Schollander, United States	4m12.2s
1968	Mike Burton, United States	4m9s
1972	Bradford Cooper, Australia	4m00.27s[3]
1976	Brian Goodell, United States	3m51.93s
1980	Vladimir Salnikov, U.S.S.R.	3m51.31s
1984	George DiCarlo, United States	3m51.23s
1988	Uwe Dassier, East Germany	3m46.95s

1. 500 meters. 2. 440 yards. 3. Rick DeMont, United States, won but was disqualified following day for medical reasons.

1,500 Meter Freestyle

1904	Emil Rausch, Germany	27m18.2s[1]
1906	Henry Taylor, Great Britain	28m28s[2]
1908	Henry Taylor, Great Britain	22m48.4s
1912	George Hodgson, Canada	22m
1920	Norman Ross, United States	22m23.2s
1924	Andrew Charlton, Australia	20m6.6s
1928	Arne Borg, Sweden	19m51.8s
1932	Kusuo Kitamura, Japan	19m12.4s
1936	Noboru Terada, Japan	19m13.7s
1948	James McLane, United States	19m18.5s
1952	Ford Konno, United States	18m30s
1956	Murray Rose, Australia	17m58.9s
1960	Jon Konrads, Australia	17m19.6s
1964	Robert Windle, Australia	17m1.7s
1968	Michael Burton, United States	16m38.9s
1972	Michael Burton, United States	15m52.58s
1976	Brian Goodell, United States	15m02.4s
1980	Vladimir Salnikov, U.S.S.R.	14m58.27s
1984	Michael O'Brien, United States	15m05.2s
1988	Vladimir Salnikov, U.S.S.R.	15m00.4s

1. One mile. 2. 1,600 meters

100-Meter Backstroke

1904	Walter Brack, Germany	1m16.8s[1]
1908	Arno Bieberstein, Germany	1m24.6s
1912	Harry Hebner, United States	1m21.2s
1920	Warren Kealoha, United States	1m15.2s
1924	Warren Kealoha, United States	1m13.2s
1928	George Kojac, United States	1m8.2s
1932	Masaji Kiyokawa, Japan	1m8.6s
1936	Adolph Kiefer, United States	1m5.9s
1948	Allen Stack, United States	1m6.4s
1952	Yoshinobu Oyakawa, United States	1m5.4s
1956	David Thiele, Australia	1m2.2s
1960	David Thiele, Australia	1m1.9s
1968	Roland Matthes, East Germany	58.7s
1972	Roland Matthes, East Germany	56.58s
1976	John Naber, United States	55.49s
1980	Bengt Baron, Sweden	56.53s
1984	Rick Carey, United States	55.79s
1988	Daichi Suzuki, Japan	55.05s

1. 100 yards

200-Meter Backstroke

1900	Ernst Hoppenberg, Germany	2m47s
1964	Jed Graef, United States	2m10.3s
1968	Roland Matthes, East Germany	2m9.6s
1972	Roland Matthes, East Germany	2m2.82s
1976	John Naber, United States	1m59.19s
1980	Sandor Wladar, Hungary	2:01.93s
1984	Rick Carey, United States	2m00.23s
1988	Igor Polianski, U.S.S.R.	1m59.37s

100-Meter Breaststroke

1968	Donald McKenzie, United States	1m7.7s
1972	Nobutaka Taguchi, Japan	1m4.94s
1976	John Hencken, United States	1m03.11s
1980	Duncan Goodhew, Britain	1m03.34s
1984	Steve Lindquist, United States	1m01.65s
1988	Adrian Moorhouse, Great Britain	1m02.04s

200-Meter Breaststroke

1908	Frederick Holman, Great Britain	3m9.2s
1912	Walter Bathe, Germany	3m1.8s
1920	Haken Malmroth, Sweden	3m4.4s
1924	Robert Skelton, United States	2m56.6s
1928	Yoshiyuki Tsuruta, Japan	2m48.8s
1932	Yoshiyuki Tsuruta, Japan	2m45.4s
1936	Tetsuo Hamuro, Japan	2m41.5s
1948	Joseph Verdeur, United States	2m39.3s
1952	John Davies, Australia	2m34.4s
1956	Masura Furukawa, Japan	2m34.7s
1960	Bill Mulliken, United States	2m37.4s
1964	Ian O'Brien, Australia	2m27.8s
1968	Felipe Munoz, Mexico	2m28.7s
1972	John Hencken, United States	2m21.55s
1976	David Willkie, Britain	2m15.11s
1980	Robertas Zulpa, U.S.S.R.	2m15.85s
1984	Victor Davis, Canada	2m13.34s
1988	Jozsef Szabo, Hungary	2m13.52s

100-Meter Butterfly

1968	Douglas Russell, United States	55.9s
1972	Mark Spitz, United States	54.27s
1976	Matt Vogel, United States	54.35s
1980	Par Arvidsson, Sweden	54.92s
1984	Michael Gross, West Germany	53.08s
1988	Anthony Nesty, Surinam	53.0s

200-Meter Butterfly

1956	Bill Yorzyk, United States	2m19.3s
1960	Mike Troy, United States	2m12.8s
1964	Kevin Berry, Australia	2m6.6s
1968	Carl Robie, United States	2m8.7s
1972	Mark Spitz, United States	2m00.7s
1976	Mike Bruner, United States	1m59.23s
1980	Sergei Fesenko, U.S.S.R.	1m59.76s
1984	Jon Sieben, Australia	1m57.0s
1988	Michael Gross, East Germany	1m56.94s

200-Meter Individual Medley

1968	Charles Hickcox, United States	2m12s
1972	Gunnar Larsson, Sweden	2m7.17s
1988	Tamas Darnyi, Hungary	2m0.17s

400-Meter Individual Medley

1964	Dick Roth, United States	4m45.4s
1968	Charles Hickcox, United States	4m48.4s
1972	Gunnar Larsson, Sweden	4m31.98s
1976	Rod Strachan, United States	4m23.68s
1980	Aleksandr Sidorenko, U.S.S.R.	4m22.8s
1984	Alex Baumann, Canada	4m17.41s
1988	Tamas Darnyi, Hungary	4m14.75s

400-Meter Freestyle Relay

1964	United States	3m32.2s
1968	United States	3m31.7s
1972	United States	3m26.42s
1988	United States	3m16.53s

800-Meter Freestyle Relay

1908	Great Britain	10m55.6s
1912	Australia	10m11.2s
1920	United States	10m4.4s
1924	United States	9m53.4s
1928	United States	9m36.2s
1932	Japan	8m58.4s
1936	Japan	8m51.5s
1948	United States	8m46s
1952	United States	8m31.1s
1956	Australia	8m23.6s
1960	United States	8m10.2s
1964	United States	7m52.1s
1968	United States	7m52.3s
1972	United States	7m35.78s
1976	United States	7m23.22s
1980	U.S.S.R.	7m23.50s
1984	United States	7m16.59s
1988	United States	7m12.51s

400-Meter Medley Relay

1960	United States	4m5.4s
1964	United States	3m58.4s
1968	United States	3m54.9s
1972	United States	3m48.16s
1976	United States	3m42.22s
1980	Australia	3m45.70s
1984	United States	3m39.30s
1988	United States	3m36.93s

Springboard Dive

		Points
1908	Albert Zuerner, Germany	85.5
1912	Paul Guenther, Germany	79.23
1920	Louis Kuehn, United States	675
1924	Albert White, United States	696.4
1928	Pete Desjardins, United States	185.04
1932	Michael Galitzen, United States	161.38
1936	Richard Degener, United States	163.57
1948	Bruce Harlan, United States	163.64
1952	David Browning, United States	205.59
1956	Robert Clotworthy, United States	159.56
1960	Gary Tobian, United States	170.00
1964	Ken Sitzberger, United States	159.90
1968	Bernard Wrightson, United States	170.15
1972	Vladimir Vasin, U.S.S.R.	594.09
1976	Phil Boggs, United States	619.05
1980	Alexsandr Portnov, U.S.S.R.	905.02
1984	Greg Louganis, United States	754.41
1988	Greg Louganis, United States	730.80

Platform Dive

		Points
1904	G. E. Sheldon, United States	12.75
1906	Gottlob Walz, Germany	156
1908	Hialmar Johansson, Sweden	83.75
1912	Erik Adlerz, Sweden	73.94
1920	Clarence Pinkston, United States	100.67
1924	Albert White, United States	487.3
1928	Pete Desjardins, United States	98.74
1932	Harold Smith, United States	124.80
1936	Marshall Wayne, United States	113.58
1948	Samuel Lee, United States	130.05
1952	Samuel Lee, United States	156.28
1956	Joaquin Capilla, Mexico	152.44
1960	Bob Webster, United States	165.56
1964	Bob Webster, United States	148.58
1968	Klaus Dibiasi, Italy	164.18
1972	Klaus Dibiasi, Italy	504.12
1976	Klaus Dibiasi, Italy	600.51
1980	Falk Hoffman, E. Germany	835.65
1984	Greg Louganis, United States	710.91
1988	Greg Louganis, United States	638.61

SWIMMING—WOMEN

50-Meter Freestyle

1988	Kristin Otto, East Germany	25.49s

100-Meter Freestyle

1912	Fanny Durack, Australia	1m22.2s

1920	Ethelda Bleibtrey, United States	1m13.6s
1924	Ethel Lackie, United States	1m12.4s
1928	Albina Osipowich, United States	1m11s
1932	Helene Madison, United States	1m6.8s
1936	Hendrika Mastenbroek, Netherlands	1m5.9s
1948	Greta Andersen, Denmark	1m6.3s
1952	Katalin Szoke, Hungary	1m6.8s
1956	Dawn Fraser, Australia	1m2s
1960	Dawn Fraser, Australia	1m1.2s
1964	Dawn Fraser, Australia	59.5s
1968	Marge Jan Henne, United States	1m
1972	Sandra Neilson, United States	58.59s
1976	Kornelia Ender, East Germany	55.65s
1980	Barbara Krause, East Germany	54.79s
1984	Carrie Steinseifer, United States	55.92s
1988	Kristin Otto, East Germany	54.93s

200-Meter Freestyle

1968	Debbie Meyer, United States	2m10.5s
1972	Shane Gould, Australia	2m3.56s
1976	Kornelia Ender, East Germany	1m59.26s
1980	Barbara Krause, East Germany	1m58.33s
1984	Mary Wayle, United States	1m59.23s
1988	Heike Friedrich, East Germany	1m57.65s

400-Meter Freestyle

1920	Ethelda Bleibtrey, United States	4m34s[1]
1924	Martha Norelius, United States	6m2.2s
1928	Martha Norelius, United States	5m42.8s
1932	Helene Madison, United States	5m28.5s
1936	Hendrika Mastenbroek, Netherlands	5m26.4s
1948	Ann Curtis, United States	5m17.8s
1952	Valerie Gyenge, Hungary	5m12.1s
1956	Lorraine Crapp, Australia	4m54.6s
1960	Chris von Saltza, United States	4m50.6s
1964	Ginny Duenkel, United States	4m43.3s
1968	Debbie Meyer, United States	4m31.8s
1972	Shane Gould, Australia	4m19.04s
1976	Petra Thumer, East Germany	4m09.89s
1980	Ines Diers, East Germany	4m08.76s
1984	Tiffany Cohen, United States	4m07.10s
1988	Janet Evans, United States	4m03.85s

1. 300 meters.

800-Meter Freestyle

1968	Debbie Meyer, United States	9m24s
1972	Keena Rothhammer, United States	8m53.68s
1976	Petra Thumer, East Germany	8m37.14s
1980	Michelle Ford, Australia	8m28.90s
1984	Tiffany Cohen, United States	8m24.95s
1988	Janet Evans, United States	8m20.20s

100-Meter Backstroke

1924	Sybil Bauer, United States	1m23.2s
1928	Marie Braun, Netherlands	1m22s
1932	Eleanor Holm, United States	1m19.4s
1936	Dina Senff, Netherlands	1m18.9s
1948	Karen Harup, Denmark	1m14.4s
1952	Joan Harrison, South Africa	1m14.3s
1956	Judy Grinham, Great Britain	1m12.9s
1960	Lynn Burke, United States	1m9.3s
1964	Cathy Ferguson, United States	1m7.7s
1968	Kaye Hall, United States	1m6.2s
1972	Melissa Belote, United States	1m5.78s
1976	Ulrike Richter, East Germany	1m01.83s
1980	Rica Reinisch, East Germany	1m00.86s
1984	Theresa Andrews, United States	1m02.55s
1988	Kristin Otto, East Germany	1m0.89s

200-Meter Backstroke

1968	Pokey Watson, United States	2m24.8s
1972	Melissa Belote, United States	2m19.19s
1976	Ulrike Richter, East Germany	2m13.43s
1980	Rica Reinisch, East Germany	2m11.77s
1984	Jolanda DeRover, Netherlands	2m12.38s
1988	Krisztina Egerszegi, Hungary	2m09.29s

100-Meter Breaststroke

1968	Djurdjica Bjedov, Yugoslavia	1m15.8s
1972	Catherine Carr, United States	1m13.58s
1976	Hannelore Anke, East Germany	1m11.16s
1980	Ute Geweniger, East Germany	1m10.22s
1984	Petra Van Staveren, Netherlands	1m09.88s
1988	Tania Dangalakova, Bulgaria	1m07.95s

200-Meter Breaststroke

1924	Lucy Morton, Great Britain	3m33.2s
1928	Hilde Schrader, Germany	3m12.6s
1932	Clare Dennis, Australia	3m6.3s
1936	Hideko Maehata, Japan	3m3.6s
1948	Nel van Vliet, Netherlands	2m57.2s
1952	Eva Szekely, Hungary	2m51.7s
1956	Ursala Happe, Germany	2m53.1s
1960	Anita Lonsborough, Great Britain	2m49.5s
1964	Galina Prozumenschikova, U.S.S.R.	2m46.4s
1968	Sharon Wichman, United States	2m44.4s
1972	Beverly Whitfield, Australia	2m41.71s
1976	Marina Koshevaia, U.S.S.R.	2m33.35s
1980	Lina Kachushite, U.S.S.R.	2m29.54s
1984	Anne Ottenbrite, Canada	2m30.38s
1988	Silke Hoerner, East Germany	2m26.71s

100-Meter Butterfly

1956	Shelley Mann, United States	1m11s
1960	Carolyn Schuler, United States	1m9.5s
1964	Sharon Stouder, United States	1m4.7s
1968	Lynn McClements, Australia	1m5.5s
1972	Mayumi Aoki, Japan	1m3.34s
1976	Kornelia Ender, East Germany	1m00.13s
1980	Caren Metschuck, East Germany	1m00.42s
1984	Mary Meagher, United States	59.26s
1988	Kristin Otto, East Germany	59s

200-Meter Butterfly

1968	Ada Kok, Netherlands	2m24.7s
1972	Karen Moe, United States	2m15.57s
1976	Andrea Pollack, East Germany	2m11.41s
1980	Ines Geissler, East Germany	2m10.44s
1984	Mary Meagher, United States	2m06.90s
1988	Kathleen Nord, East Germany	2m9.51s

200-Meter Individual Medley

1968	Claudia Kolb, United States	2m24.7s
1972	Shane Gould, Australia	2m23.07s
1984	Tracy Caulkins, United States	1m12.64s
1988	Daniela Hunger, East Germany	2m12.59s

400-Meter Individual Medley

1964	Donna de Varona, United States	5m18.7s
1968	Claudia Kolb, United States	5m8.5s
1972	Gail Neall, Australia	5m2.97s
1976	Ulrike Tauber, East Germany	4m42.77s
1980	Petra Schneider, East Germany	4m36.29s
1984	Tracy Caulkins, United States	4m39.21s
1988	Janet Evans, United States	4m37.76s

400-Meter Freestyle Relay

1912	Great Britain	5m52.8s
1920	United States	5m11.6s
1924	United States	4m58.8s
1928	United States	4m47.6s
1932	United States	4m38s
1936	Netherlands	4m36s
1948	United States	4m29.2s

1952	Hungary	4m24.4s
1956	Australia	4m17.1s
1960	United States	4m8.9s
1964	United States	4m3.8s
1968	United States	4m2.5s
1972	United States	3m55.19s
1976	United States	3m44.82s
1980	East Germany	3m42.71s
1984	United States	3m44.43s
1988	East Germany	3m40.63s

400-Meter Medley Relay

1960	United States	4m41.1s
1964	United States	4m33.9s
1968	United States	4m28.3s
1972	United States	4m20.75s
1976	East Germany	4m07.95s
1980	East Germany	4m06.67s
1984	United States	4m08.34s
1988	East Germany	4m03.74s

Springboard Dive

		Points
1920	Aileen Riggin, United States	539.90
1924	Elizabeth Becker, United States	474.5
1928	Helen Meany, United States	78.62
1932	Georgia Coleman, United States	87.52
1936	Marjorie Gestring, United States	89.27
1948	Victoria M. Draves, United States	108.74
1952	Patricia McCormick, United States	147.30
1956	Patricia McCormick, United States	142.36
1960	Ingrid Kramer, Germany	155.81
1964	Ingrid Kramer Engel, Germany	145.00
1968	Sue Gossick, United States	150.77
1972	Micki King, United States	450.03
1976	Jennifer Chandler, United States	506.19
1980	Irina Kalinina, U.S.S.R.	725.91
1984	Sylvie Bernier, Canada	530.70
1988	Gao Min, China	580.23

Platform Dive

		Points
1912	Greta Johansson, Sweden	39.9
1920	Stefani Fryland, Denmark	34.60
1924	Caroline Smith, United States	166
1928	Elizabeth B. Pinkston, United States	31.60
1932	Dorothy Poynton, United States	40.26
1936	Dorothy Poynton Hill, United States	33.92
1948	Victoria M. Draves, United States	68.87
1952	Patricia McCormick, United States	79.37
1956	Patricia McCormick, United States	84.85
1960	Ingrid Kramer, Germany	91.28
1964	Lesley Bush, United States	99.80
1968	Milena Duchkova, Czechoslovakia	109.59
1972	Ulrika Knape, Sweden	390.00
1976	Elena Vaytsekhovskaia, U.S.S.R.	406.59
1980	Martina Jaschke, East Germany	596.25
1984	Zhou Jihong, China	435.51
1988	Xu Yanmei, China	445.20

BASKETBALL—MEN

1904	United States	1968	United States
1936	United States	1972	U.S.S.R.
1948	United States	1976	United States
1952	United States	1980	Yugoslavia
1956	United States	1984	United States
1960	United States	1988	U.S.S.R.
1964	United States		

BASKETBALL—WOMEN

1976	U.S.S.R.	1984	United States
1980	U.S.S.R.	1988	United States

DISTRIBUTION OF MEDALS
1988 SUMMER GAMES

Country	Gold	Silver	Bronze	Total
Soviet Union	55	31	46	132
East Germany	37	35	30	102
United States	36	31	27	94
West Germany	11	14	15	40
Bulgaria	10	12	13	35
South Korea	12	10	11	33
China	5	11	12	28
Romania	7	11	6	24
Britain	5	10	9	24
Hungary	11	6	6	23
France	6	4	6	16
Poland	2	5	9	16
Italy	6	4	4	14
Japan	4	3	7	14
Australia	3	6	5	14
New Zealand	3	2	8	13
Yugoslavia	3	4	5	12
Sweden	0	4	7	11
Canada	3	2	5	10
Kenya	5	2	2	9
The Netherlands	2	2	5	9
Czechoslovakia	3	3	2	8
Brazil	1	2	3	6
Norway	2	3	0	5
Denmark	2	1	1	4
Finland	1	1	2	4
Spain	1	1	2	4
Switzerland	0	2	2	4
Morocco	1	0	2	3
Turkey	1	1	0	2
Jamaica	0	2	0	2
Argentina	0	1	1	2
Belgium	0	0	2	2
Mexico	0	0	2	2
Austria	1	0	0	1
Portugal	1	0	0	1
Suriname	1	0	0	1
Chile	0	1	0	1
Costa Rica	0	1	0	1
Indonesia	0	1	0	1
Iran	0	1	0	1
Neth. Antilles	0	1	0	1
Peru	0	1	0	1
Senegal	0	1	0	1
Virgin Islands	0	1	0	1
Colombia	0	0	1	1
Djibouti	0	0	1	1
Greece	0	0	1	1
Mongolia	0	0	1	1
Pakistan	0	0	1	1
Philippines	0	0	1	1
Thailand	0	0	1	1

BOXING

(U.S. winners only)

(U.S. boycotted Olympics in 1980)

Flyweight—112 pounds (51 kilograms)

1904	George V. Finnegan	1952	Nate Brooks
1920	Frank De Genaro	1976	Leo Randolph
1924	Fidel La Barba	1984	Steve McCrory

Bantamweight—119 (54 kg)

1904	O.L. Kirk	1988	Kennedy McKinney

Featherweight—126 pounds (57 kg)

1904	O.L. Kirk	1984	Meldrick Taylor
1924	Jackie Fields		

Lightweight—132 pounds (60 kg)

1904	H.J. Spanger	1976	Howard Davis
1920	Samuel Mosberg	1984	Pernell Whitaker
1968	Ronnie Harris		

Light Welterweight—140 pounds (63.5 kg)

| 1952 | Charles Adkins | 1976 | Ray Leonard |
| 1972 | Ray Seales | 1984 | Jerry Page |

Welterweight—148 pounds (67 kg)

| 1904 | Al Young | 1984 | Mark Breland |
| 1932 | Edward Flynn | | |

Light Middleweight—157 pounds (71 kg)

| 1960 | Wilbert McClure | 1984 | Frank Tate |

Middleweight—165 pounds (75 kg)

1904	Charles Mayer	1960	Eddie Cook
1932	Carmen Barth	1976	Michael Spinks
1952	Floyd Patterson		

Light Heavyweight—179 pounds (81 kg)

1920	Edward Eagan	1960	Cassius Clay
1952	Norvel Lee	1976	Leon Spinks
1956	James Boyd	1988	Andrew Maynard

Heavyweight—201 pounds

1904	Sam Berger	1968	George Foreman
1952	Edward Sanders	1984	Henry Tillman
1956	Pete Rademacher	1988	Ray Mercer
1964	Joe Frazier		

Super Heavyweight (unlimited)

| 1984 | Tyrell Biggs |

Sixty-one Nations Competed in Seoul Paralympics

The Games of the 8th Seoul Paralympics opened at the Seoul Olympic Stadium on Oct. 15, 1988, with the attendance of 4,278 disabled athletes from 61 nations, the largest turnout in the event's history.

The sports competition for the disabled took place at the games venues in Seoul Sports Complex, Olympic Park and Kyonggi-do area under the ideals of "challenge and overcoming," "peace and friendship," and "participation and equality."

They competed in 16 sports including archery, track and field, fencing, judo, cycling, shooting, soccer, swimming and pingpong.

Other competitions were basketball, weightlifting and powerlifting, lawn bowling, boccia, goal ball, and snooker.

Among the participating nations, the United States fielded the largest number of participants with 376 in 12 games, followed by Britain with 242 in 15 games and host Korea with 239 in 16 games.

The nations participating in the Seoul Paralympics included the Soviet Union, China, Yugoslavia, Hungary, Bulgaria, Poland, and Czechoslovakia.

Koh Kwi-Nam, president of the Seoul Paralympics Organizing Committee (SPOC), said 8,325 people including physically handicapped citizens and their family members as well as those suffering other plights were invited to the Opening Ceremony.

The Seoul Paralympics served as an occasion to enhance the recognition by the Korean people of the physically handicapped and cement friendly relationships among the disabled from around the world, he said.

The Athletes Village for the Seoul Paralympics, consisting of 1,316 apartments in 10 buildings, was built at a 57,666-square-meter site, about 4 kilometers away from the Olympic Stadium.

A total of 5,911 volunteers worked for the Games as interpreter-guides for foreign athletes and officials, and assistants in competition operation, administration, logistics, security, and medical services. ☐

Coubertin Founded Modern Olympics

In the late 1880s, Baron Pierre de Coubertin of France conceived the idea of holding a modern olympics every four years to diminish tensions between world nations through the ennoblement of amateur sports and the general spirit of competition. Accordingly, he organized a conference in Paris in 1884 for this purpose. Thirteen countries sent representatives and 21 other nations sent their messages of support.

Baron de Coubertin wanted the first modern olympics to be held in Paris, but a motion was passed to hold them in Athens, Greece in 1896. At that time, most of the games consisted of track and field events.

De Coubertin died in Geneva in 1937, but his heart was buried near the Temple of Hera at Olympia. In honor of this remarkable man who shaped the ideals of the modern games, each olympic torch bearer must visit de Courbertin's tomb with the lighted torch before beginning the run to the host city.

JIM THORPE'S OLYMPIC MEDALS

More than 70 years after he won the pentathlon and decathlon at Stockholm, Sweden, Jim Thorpe's Olympic gold medals were returned posthumously to him by the International Olympic Committee. Thorpe, an Oklahoma Sac and Fox Indian, became one of the greatest all-around athletes ever produced in America. He was an all-American football player at the Carlisle Institute, an Indian trade school in Pennsylvania, and starred in baseball and track and field. After winning the medals in the 1912 Olympics, he was forced to give them up when he admitted he had played two seasons for money as a semipro baseball player in 1909 and 1910. Under the rules, he had lost his amateur status by taking money and thus was theoretically ineligible for the Olympics. In October of 1982, after many years of vigorous efforts by his family and other officials in athletics, the I.O.C. reinstated Thorpe in its archives as a co-winner of the two events. At ceremonies in Los Angeles in January 1983, Antonio Samaranch, president of the I.O.C. presented Thorpe's children with gold medals to replace those he had turned back. Thorpe, who later in his career played major-league baseball and pro football, died at the age of 65 in 1953.

Other 1988 Summer Olympic Games Champions

Archery
Men—Jay Barrs, United States
Men's Team—South Korea
Women—Kim Soo-nyung, South Korea
Women's Team—South Korea

Baseball
Men—United States

Canoeing
500 m—Olaf Heukrodt, East Germany
1,000 m—Ivan Klementiev, U.S.S.R.
500-m pairs—U.S.S.R. (Victor Reneiski and Nikolai Jouravski)
1,000-m pairs—U.S.S.R. (Victor Reneiski and Nikolai Jouravski)

Kayak—Women
500 m—Vania Guecheva, Bulgaria
500-m pairs—East Germany (Birgit Schmidt and Anke Nothnagel)
500-m fours—East Germany

Kayak—Men
500 m—Zsolt Gyulay, Hungary
500-m pairs—New Zealand (Ian Ferguson and Paul MacDonald)
1,000 m—Greg Barton, United States
1,000-m pairs—United States (Greg Barton and Norman Bellingham)
1,000-m fours—Hungary

Cycling—Men
196.9-km Individual road race—Olaf Ludwig, East Germany
Individual time trial—Alexander Kirichenko, U.S.S.R.
100-km Team time trial—East Germany
4,000-m Individual pursuit—Gintaoutas Umaras, U.S.S.R.
Match sprint—Lutz Hesslich, East Germany
4,000-m Team, Pursuit—U.S.S.R.
Points race—Dan Frost, Denmark

Cycling—Women
Sprint—Erika Salumiae, U.S.S.R.
Individual road race—Monique Knol, Holland

Equestrian
Dressage—Nicole Uphoff, West Germany
Dressage team—West Germany
Jumping—Pierre Durand, France
Jumping team—West Germany
Three-day event—Mark Todd, New Zealand
Team three-day event—West Germany

Fencing
Foil—Stefano Cerioni, Italy
Team foil—U.S.S.R.
Epee—Arnd Schmitt, West Germany
Team epee—France
Sabre—Jeanfrancois Lamour, France
Team sabre—Hungary
Women's foil—Anja Fichtel, West Germany
Women's team foil—West Germany

Gymnastics—Men
All-around—Vladimir Artemov, U.S.S.R.
Floor exercise—Sergei Kharikov, U.S.S.R.
Horizontal bar—Vladimir Artemov, U.S.S.R.
Parallel bars—Vladimir Artemov, U.S.S.R.
Pommel horse—Zsolt Borkai, Hungary; Dmitri Bilozertchev, U.S.S.R.; Lyubomir Gueraskov, Bulgaria

Rings—Holger Berendt, East Germany; Dmitri Bilozertchev, U.S.S.R.
Vault—Lou Yun, China
Team—U.S.S.R.

Gymnastics—Women
All-around—Elena Shoushounova, U.S.S.R.
Balance beam—Daniela Silivas, Romania
Floor exercise—Daniela Silivas, Romania
Rhythmic Gymnastics—Marina Lobatch, U.S.S.R.
Uneven bars—Daniela Silivas, Romania
Vault—Svetlana Boguinskaia, U.S.S.R.
Team—U.S.S.R.

Judo
133 lb—Kim Jae-Yup, South Korea
143 lb—Lee Kyung-keun, South Korea
156 lb—Marc Alexandre, France
171 lb—Waldemar Legien, Poland
189 lb—Peter Seisenbacher, Austria
209 lb—Aurelio Miguel, Brazil
Over 209 lb—Hitoshi Saito, Japan

Modern Pentathlon
Individual—Janos Martinek, Hungary
Team—Hungary

Rowing—Men
Singles—Thomas Lange, East Germany
Doubles—Holland
Quadruples—Italy
Pairs—Great Britain
Pairs with coxswain—Italy
Fours—East Germany
Fours with coxswain—East Germany
Eights—West Germany

Rowing—Women
Singles—Jutta Behrendt, East Germany
Doubles—East Germany
Pairs—Romania
Fours with coxswain—East Germany
Quadruple sculls—East Germany
Eights—East Germany

Shooting—Men
Free pistol—Sorin Babii, Romania
Rapid-fire pistol—Afanasi Kouzming, U.S.S.R.
Small-bore rifle—Miroslav Varga, Czechoslovakia
Small-bore rifle, 3-position—Malcolm Cooper, Great Britain
Rifle running game target—Tor Heiestad, Norway
Trap—Dimitri Monakov, U.S.S.R.
Air rifle—Goran Maksimovic, Yugoslavia

Shooting—Women
Air rifle—Irina Chilova, U.S.S.R.
Small-bore rifle—Silvia Sperber, West Germany
Air pistol—Jasna Sekaric, Yugoslavia
Rapid-fire pistol—Nino Saloukvadze, U.S.S.R.

Synchronized Swimming
Solo—Carolyn Waldo, Canada
Duet—Canada (Carolyn Waldo and Michelle Cameron)

Table Tennis
Men's singles—Yoo Nam-kyu, South Korea
Men's doubles—China (Chen Longcan and Wei Qingguang)

Women's singles—Chen Jing, China
Women's doubles—South Korea (Hyun Jung-hwa and Yang Young-ja)

Tennis
Men's singles—Miloslav Mecir, Czechoslovakia
Men's doubles—United States (Ken Flach and Robert Seguso)
Women's singles—Steffi Graf, West Germany
Women's doubles—United States (Pam Shriver and Zina Garrison)

Weight Lifting
115 lb—Sevdalin Marinov, Bulgaria
126 lb—Oxen Mirzoian, U.S.S.R.
132 lb—Naim Suleymanoglu, Turkey
149 lb—Joachim Kunz, East Germany
165 lb—Borislav Guidikov, Bulgaria
182 lb—Israil Arsamakov, U.S.S.R.
198 lb—Anatoli Khrapatyi, U.S.S.R.
220 lb—Pavel Kousnetzov, U.S.S.R.
242 lb—Yuri Zacharevich, U.S.S.R.
Over 242—Alexandre Kurlovich, U.S.S.R.

Wrestling—Freestyle
105.5 lb—Takashi Kobayashi, Japan
114.5 lb—Mitsuru Sato, Japan
125.5 lb—Sergei Beloglazov, U.S.S.R.
136.5 lb—John Smith, United States
149.5 lb—Arsen Fadzaev, U.S.S.R.
162.5 lb—Kenneth Monday, United States
180 lb—Han Myung-woo, South Korea
198 lb—Makharbek Khadartsev, U.S.S.R.
220 lb—Vasile Puscasu, Romania
286 lb—David Gobedjichvili, U.S.S.R.

Wrestling—Greco-Roman
105.5 lb—Vincenzo Maenza, Italy
114.5 lb—Jon Ronningen, Norway
125.5 lb—Andras Sike, Hungary
135.25 lb—Kamandar Madjivov, U.S.S.R.
149.5 lb—Levon Djoulfalakian, U.S.S.R.
162.75 lb—Kim Young-nam, South Korea
180.25 lb—Mikhail Mamiachvili, U.S.S.R.
198 lb—Atanas Komchev, Bulgaria
220 lb—Andrzej Wronski, Poland
286 lb—Alexandre Kareline, U.S.S.R.

Yachting
Board sailing—Bruce Kendall, New Zealand
Finn—Jose Luis Doreste, Spain
Flying Dutchman—Denmark (Jorgen Bojsen-Moller and Christian Gronborg)
470 Class—France (Thierry Peponnet and Luc Pillot)
Soling—East Germany
Star—Great Britain (Michael McIntyre and Pmilip Bryn Vaile)
Tornado—France (Jean Yves Le Deroff and Nicolas Henard)
Women's 470—United States (Allison Jolly and Lynne Jewell)

Team Champions
Field hockey, men—Great Britain
Field hockey, women—Australia
Handball, men—U.S.S.R.
Handball, women—South Korea
Soccer—U.S.S.R.
Volleyball, men—United States
Volleyball—U.S.S.R.
Water polo—Yugoslavia

FOOTBALL

The pastime of kicking around a ball goes back beyond the limits of recorded history. Ancient savage tribes played football of a primitive kind. There was a ball-kicking game played by Athenians, Spartans, and Corinthians 2500 years ago, which the Greeks called *Episkuros*. The Romans had a somewhat similar game called *Harpastum* and are supposed to have carried the game with them when they invaded the British Isles in the First Century, B.C.

Undoubtedly the game known in the United States as Football traces directly to the English game of Rugby, though the modifications have been many. Informal football was played on college lawns well over a century ago, and an annual Freshman-Sophomore series of "scrimmages" began at Yale in 1840. The first formal intercollegiate football game was the Princeton-Rutgers contest at New Brunswick, N.J., on Nov. 6, 1869, with Rutgers winning by 6 goals to 4.

In those days, games were played with 25, 20, 15, or 11 men on a side. In 1880, there was a convention at which Walter Camp of Yale persuaded the delegates to agree to a rule calling for 11 players on a side. The game grew so rough that it was attacked as brutal, and some colleges abandoned the sport. Conditions were so bad in 1906 that President Theodore Roosevelt called a meeting of Yale, Harvard, and Princeton representatives at the White House in the hope of reforming and improving the game. The outcome was that the game, with the forward pass introduced and some other modifications of the rules inserted, became faster and cleaner.

The first professional game was played in 1895 at Latrobe, Pa. The National Football League was founded in 1921. The All-American Conference went into action in 1946. At the end of the 1949 season the two circuits merged, retaining the name of the older league. In 1960, the American Football League began operations. In 1970, the leagues merged. The United States Football League played its first season in 1983, from March to July. It suspended spring operation after the 1985 season, and planned a 1986 move to fall, but suspended operations again. It did not function as a league through 1987.

College Football

NATIONAL COLLEGE FOOTBALL CHAMPIONS

The "National Collegiate A. A. Football Guide" recognizes as unofficial national champion the team selected each year by press association polls. Where The Associated Press poll (of writers) does not agree with the United Press International poll (of coaches), the guide lists both teams selected.

1937	Pittsburgh	1949	Notre Dame	1959	Syracuse	1969	Texas	1978 Alabama and
1938	Texas Christian	1950	Oklahoma	1960	Minnesota	1970	Texas and Ne-	So. California
1939	Texas A & M	1951	Tennessee	1961	Alabama		braska	1979 Alabama
1940	Minnesota	1952	Michigan State	1962	So. California	1971	Nebraska	1980 Georgia
1941	Minnesota	1953	Maryland	1963	Texas	1972	So. California	1981 Clemson
1942	Ohio State	1954	Ohio State and	1964	Alabama	1973	Notre Dame and	1982 Penn State
1943	Notre Dame		U.C.L.A.	1965	Alabama and		U. of Alabama	1983 Miami
1944	Army	1955	Oklahoma		Michigan	1974	Oklahoma and	1984 Brigham Young
1945	Army	1956	Oklahoma		State		So. California	1985 Oklahoma
1946	Notre Dame	1957	Auburn and Ohio	1966	Notre Dame	1975	Oklahoma	1986 Penn State
1947	Notre Dame		State	1967	So. California	1976	Pittsburgh	1987 Miami
1948	Michigan	1958	Louisiana State	1968	Ohio State	1977	Notre Dame	1988 Notre Dame

RECORD OF ANNUAL MAJOR BOWL COLLEGE FOOTBALL GAMES

Rose Bowl
(At Pasadena, Calif.)

1902	Michigan 49, Stanford 0	1931	Alabama 24, Washington State 0	1950	Ohio State 17, California 14
1916	Washington State 14, Brown 0	1932	So. California 21, Tulane 12	1951	Michigan 14, California 6
1917	Oregon 14, Pennsylvania 0	1933	So. California 35, Pittsburgh 0	1952	Illinois 40, Stanford 7
1918	Mare Island Marines 19, Camp Lewis 7	1934	Columbia 7, Stanford 0	1953	So. California 7, Wisconsin 0
		1935	Alabama 29, Stanford 13	1954	Michigan State 28, U.C.L.A. 20
1919	Great Lakes 17, Mare Island Marines 0	1936	Stanford 7, So. Methodist 0	1955	Ohio State 20, So. California 7
		1937	Pittsburgh 21, Washington 0	1956	Michigan State 17, U.C.L.A. 14
1920	Harvard 7, Oregon 6	1938	California 13, Alabama 0	1957	Iowa 35, Oregon State 19
1921	California 28, Ohio State 0	1939	So. California 7, Duke 3	1958	Ohio State 10, Oregon 7
1922	Washington and Jefferson 0, California 0	1940	So. California 14, Tennessee 0	1959	Iowa 38, California 12
		1941	Stanford 21, Nebraska 13	1960	Washington 44, Wisconsin 8
1923	So. California 14, Penn State 3	1942	Oregon State 20, Duke 16[1]	1961	Washington 17, Minnesota 7
1924	Navy 14, Washington 14	1943	Georgia 9, U.C.L.A. 0	1962	Minnesota 21, U.C.L.A. 3
1925	Notre Dame 27, Stanford 10	1944	So. California 29, Washington 0	1963	So. California 42, Wisconsin 37
1926	Alabama 20, Washington 19	1945	So. California 25, Tennessee 0	1964	Illinois 17, Washington 7
1927	Alabama 7, Stanford 7	1946	Alabama 34, So. California 14	1965	Michigan 34, Oregon State 7
1928	Stanford 7, Pittsburgh 6	1947	Illinois 45, U.C.L.A. 14	1966	U.C.L.A. 14, Michigan State 12
1929	Georgia Tech 8, California 7	1948	Michigan 49, So. California 0	1967	Purdue 14, So. California 13
1930	So. California 47, Pittsburgh 14	1949	Northwestern 20, California 14	1968	So. California 14, Indiana 3

1969 Ohio State 27, So. California 16
1970 So. California 10, Michigan 3
1971 Stanford 27, Ohio State 17
1972 Stanford 13, Michigan 12
1973 So. California 42, Ohio State 17
1974 Ohio State 42, So. California 21
1975 So. California 18, Ohio State 17
1976 U.C.L.A. 23, Ohio State 10
1977 So. California 14, Michigan 6
1978 Washington 27, Michigan 20
1979 So. California 17, Michigan 10
1980 So. California 17, Ohio State 16
1981 Michigan 23, Washington 6
1982 Washington 28, Iowa 0
1983 U.C.L.A. 24, Michigan 14
1984 U.C.L.A. 45, Illinois 9
1985 USC 20, Ohio St. 17
1986 U.C.L.A. 45, Iowa 28
1987 Arizona State 22, Michigan 15
1988 Michigan State 20, USC 17
1989 Michigan 22, So. California 14
1. Played at Durham, N.C.

Orange Bowl
(At Miami)

1933 Miami (Fla.) 7, Manhattan 0
1934 Duquesne 33, Miami (Fla.) 7
1935 Bucknell 26, Miami (Fla.) 0
1936 Catholic 20, Mississippi 0
1937 Duquesne 13, Mississippi State 12
1938 Auburn 6, Michigan State 0
1939 Tennessee 17, Oklahoma 0
1940 Georgia Tech 21, Missouri 7
1941 Mississippi State 14, Georgetown 7
1942 Georgia 40, Texas Christian 26
1943 Alabama 37, Boston College 21
1944 Louisiana State 19, Texas A&M 14
1945 Tulsa 26, Georgia Tech 12
1946 Miami (Fla.) 13, Holy Cross 6
1947 Rice 8, Tennessee 0
1948 Georgia Tech 20, Kansas 14
1949 Texas 41, Georgia 28
1950 Santa Clara 21, Kentucky 13
1951 Clemson 15, Miami (Fla.) 14
1952 Georgia Tech 17, Baylor 14
1953 Alabama 61, Syracuse 6
1954 Oklahoma 7, Maryland 0
1955 Duke 34, Nebraska 7
1956 Oklahoma 20, Maryland 6
1957 Colorado 27, Clemson 21
1958 Oklahoma 48, Duke 21
1959 Oklahoma 21, Syracuse 6
1960 Georgia 14, Missouri 0
1961 Missouri 21, Navy 14
1962 Louisiana State 25, Colorado 7
1963 Alabama 17, Oklahoma 0
1964 Nebraska 13, Auburn 7
1965 Texas 21, Alabama 17
1966 Alabama 39, Nebraska 28
1967 Florida 27, Georgia Tech 12
1968 Oklahoma 26, Tennessee 24
1969 Penn State 15, Kansas 14
1970 Penn State 10, Missouri 3
1971 Nebraska 17, Louisiana State 12
1972 Nebraska 38, Alabama 6
1973 Nebraska 40, Notre Dame 6
1974 Penn State 16, Louisiana State 9
1975 Notre Dame 13, Alabama 11
1976 Oklahoma 14, Michigan 6
1977 Ohio State 27, Colorado 10
1978 Arkansas 31, Oklahoma 6
1979 Oklahoma 31, Nebraska 24
1980 Oklahoma 24, Florida State 7
1981 Oklahoma 18, Florida State 17

1982 Clemson 22, Nebraska 15
1983 Nebraska 21, Louisiana State 20
1984 Miami 31, Nebraska 30
1985 Washington 28, Oklahoma 17
1986 Oklahoma 25, Penn St. 10
1987 Oklahoma 42, Arkansas 8
1988 Miami 20, Oklahoma 14
1989 Miami 23, Nebraska 3

Sugar Bowl
(At New Orleans)

1935 Tulane 20, Temple 14
1936 Texas Christian 3, Louisiana State 2
1937 Santa Clara 21, Louisiana State 14
1938 Santa Clara 6, Louisiana State 0
1939 Texas Christian 15, Carnegie Tech 7
1940 Texas A & M 14, Tulane 13
1941 Boston College 19, Tennessee 13
1942 Fordham 2, Missouri 0
1943 Tennessee 14, Tulsa 7
1944 Georgia Tech 20, Tulsa 18
1945 Duke 29, Alabama 26
1946 Oklahoma A & M 33, St. Mary's
      (Calif.) 13
1947 Georgia 20, North Carolina 10
1948 Texas 27, Alabama 7
1949 Oklahoma 14, North Carolina 6
1950 Oklahoma 35, Louisiana State 0
1951 Kentucky 13, Oklahoma 7
1952 Maryland 28, Tennessee 13
1953 Georgia Tech 24, Mississippi 7
1954 Georgia Tech 42, West Virginia 19
1955 Navy 21, Mississippi 0
1956 Georgia Tech 7, Pittsburgh 0
1957 Baylor 13, Tennessee 7
1958 Mississippi 39, Texas 7
1959 Louisiana State 7, Clemson 0
1960 Mississippi 21, Louisiana State 0
1961 Mississippi 14, Rice 6
1962 Alabama 10, Arkansas 3
1963 Mississippi 17, Arkansas 13
1964 Alabama 12, Mississippi 7
1965 Louisiana State 13, Syracuse 10
1966 Missouri 20, Florida 18
1967 Alabama 34, Nebraska 7
1968 Louisiana State 20, Wyoming 13
1969 Arkansas 16, Georgia 2
1970 Mississippi 27, Arkansas 22
1971 Tennessee 34, Air Force Academy 13
1972 Oklahoma 40, Auburn 22
1973 Oklahoma 14, Penn State 0
1974 Notre Dame 24, Alabama 23
1975 Nebraska 13, Florida 10
1976 Alabama 13, Penn State 6
1977 Pittsburgh 27, Georgia 3
1978 Alabama 35, Ohio State 6
1979 Alabama 14, Penn State 7
1980 Alabama 24, Arkansas 9
1981 Georgia 17, Notre Dame 10
1982 Pittsburgh 24, Georgia 20
1983 Penn State 27, Georgia 23
1984 Auburn 9, Michigan 7
1985 Nebraska 28, LSU 10
1986 Tennessee 35, Miami, Fla. 7
1987 Nebraska 30, Louisiana State 15
1988 Syracuse 16, Auburn 16 (tie)
1989 Florida State 13, Auburn 7

Cotton Bowl
(At Dallas)

1937 Texas Christian 16, Marquette 6
1938 Rice 28, Colorado 14
1939 St. Mary's (Calif.) 20, Texas Tech. 13
1940 Clemson 6, Boston College 3

1941 Texas A & M 13, Fordham 12
1942 Alabama 29, Texas A & M 21
1943 Texas 14, Georgia Tech 7
1944 Randolph Field 7, Texas 7
1945 Oklahoma A & M 34, Texas
      Christian 0
1946 Texas 40, Missouri 27
1947 Louisiana State 0, Arkansas 0
1948 So. Methodist 13, Penn State 13
1949 So. Methodist 21, Oregon 13
1950 Rice 27, North Carolina 13
1951 Tennessee 20, Texas 14
1952 Kentucky 20, Texas Christian 7
1953 Texas 16, Tennessee 0
1954 Rice 28, Alabama 6
1955 Georgia Tech 14, Arkansas 6
1956 Mississippi 14, Texas Christian 13
1957 Texas Christian 28, Syracuse 27
1958 Navy 20, Rice 7
1959 Air Force 0, Texas Christian 0
1960 Syracuse 23, Texas 14
1961 Duke 7, Arkansas 6
1962 Texas 12, Mississippi 7
1963 Louisiana State 13, Texas 0
1964 Texas 28, Navy 6
1965 Arkansas 10, Nebraska 7
1966 Louisiana State 14, Arkansas 7
1967 Georgia 24, So. Methodist 9
1968 Texas A & M 20, Alabama 16
1969 Texas 36, Tennessee 13
1970 Texas 21, Notre Dame 17
1971 Notre Dame 24, Texas 11
1972 Penn State 30, Texas 6
1973 Texas 17, Alabama 13
1974 Nebraska 19, Texas 3
1975 Penn State 41, Baylor 20
1976 Arkansas 31, Georgia 10
1977 Houston 30, Maryland 21
1978 Notre Dame 38, Texas 10
1979 Notre Dame 35, Houston 34
1980 Houston 17, Nebraska 14
1981 Alabama 30, Baylor 2
1982 Texas 14, Alabama 12
1983 Southern Methodist 7, Pittsburgh 3
1984 Georgia 10, Texas 9
1985 Boston College 45, Houston 28
1986 Texas A & M 36, Auburn 16
1987 Ohio State 28, Texas A & M 12
1988 Texas A & M 35, Notre Dame 10
1989 UCLA 17, Arkansas 3

Gator Bowl
(At Jacksonville, Fla. Played on
Saturday nearest New Year's Day of
year indicated)

1953 Florida 14, Tulsa 13
1954 Texas Tech 35, Auburn 13
1955 Auburn 33, Baylor 13
1956 Vanderbilt 25, Auburn 13
1957 Georgia Tech 21, Pittsburgh 14
1958 Tennessee 3, Texas A & M 0
1959 Mississippi 7, Florida 3
1960 Arkansas 14, Georgia Tech 7
1961 Florida 13, Baylor 12
1962 Penn State 30, Georgia Tech 15
1963 Florida 17, Penn State 7
1964 No. Carolina 35, Air Force 0
1965 Florida State 36, Oklahoma 19
1966 Georgia Tech 31, Texas Tech 21
1967 Tennessee 18, Syracuse 12
1968 Penn State 17, Florida State 17
1969 Missouri 35, Alabama 10
1970 Florida 14, Tennessee 13
1971 Auburn 35, Mississippi 28

1972	Georgia 7, North Carolina 3	1978	Pittsburgh 34, Clemson 3	1984	Florida 14, Iowa 6
1973	Auburn 24, Colorado 3	1979	Clemson 17, Ohio State 15	1985	Oklahoma St. 21, South Carolina 14
1974	Texas Tech 28, Tennessee 19	1980	North Carolina 17, Michigan 15	1986	Florida State 34, Oklahoma St. 23
1975	Auburn 27, Texas 3	1981	Pittsburgh 37, South Carolina 9	1987	Clemson 27, Stanford 21
1976	Maryland 13, Florida 0	1982	North Carolina 31, Arkansas 27	1987	LSU 30, South Carolina 13
1977	Notre Dame 20, Penn State 9	1983	Florida State 31, West Virginia 12	1989	Georgia 34, Michigan St. 27

RESULTS OF OTHER 1988 SEASON BOWL GAMES

All-American (Birmingham, Ala., Dec. 29)—Florida 14, Illinois 10
Aloha (Honolulu, Dec. 25)—Washington St. 24, Houston 22
California (Fresno, Dec. 10)—Fresno State 35, Western Michigan 30
Fiesta (Tempe, Ariz., Jan 2)—Notre Dame 34, West Virginia 21
Florida Citrus (Orlando, Jan. 2)—Clemson 13, Oklahoma 6
Freedom (Anaheim, Calif., Dec. 29)—Brigham Young 20, Colorado 17
Hall of Fame (Tampa, Fla., Jan. 2)—Syracuse 23, Louisiana State 10

Holiday (San Diego, Dec. 30)—Oklahoma State 62, Wyoming 14
Independence (Shreveport, La., Dec. 23)—Southern Mississippi 38, Texas El Paso 18
Liberty (Memphis, Dec. 28)—Indiana 34, South Carolina 10
Peach (Atlanta, Dec. 31)—North Carolina State 28, Iowa 23
Sun (El Paso, Tex., Dec. 24)—Alabama 29, Army 28

HEISMAN MEMORIAL TROPHY WINNERS

The Heisman Memorial Trophy is presented annually by the Downtown Athletic Club of New York City to the nation's outstanding college football player, as determined by a poll of sportswriters and sportscasters.

1935	Jay Berwanger, Chicago	1953	Johnny Lattner, Notre Dame	1971	Pat Sullivan, Auburn
1936	Larry Kelley, Yale	1954	Alan Ameche, Wisconsin	1972	Johnny Rodgers, Nebraska
1937	Clinton Frank, Yale	1955	Howard Cassady, Ohio State	1973	John Cappelletti, Penn State
1938	Davey O'Brien, Texas Christian	1956	Paul Hornung, Notre Dame	1974-75	Archie Griffin, Ohio State
1939	Nile Kinnick, Iowa	1957	John Crow, Texas A & M	1976	Tony Dorsett, Pittsburgh
1940	Tom Harmon, Michigan	1958	Pete Dawkins, Army	1977	Earl Campbell, Texas
1941	Bruce Smith, Minnesota	1959	Billy Cannon, Louisiana State	1978	Billy Sims, Oklahoma
1942	Frank Sinkwich, Georgia	1960	Joe Bellino, Navy	1979	Charles White, Southern California
1943	Angelo Bertelli, Notre Dame	1961	Ernie Davis, Syracuse	1980	George Rogers, South Carolina
1944	Leslie Horvath, Ohio State	1962	Terry Baker, Oregon State	1981	Marcus Allen, Southern California
1945	Felix Blanchard, Army	1963	Roger Staubach, Navy	1982	Hershel Walker, Georgia
1946	Glenn Davis, Army	1964	John Huarte, Notre Dame	1983	Mike Rozier, Nebraska
1947	Johnny Lujack, Notre Dame	1965	Mike Garrett, Southern California	1984	Doug Flutie, Boston College
1948	Doak Walker, So. Methodist	1966	Steve Spurrier, Florida	1985	Bo Jackson, Auburn
1949	Leon Hart, Notre Dame	1967	Gary Beban, U.C.L.A.	1986	Vinnie Testeverde, Miami
1950	Vic Janowicz, Ohio State	1968	O. J. Simpson, Southern California	1987	Tim Brown, Notre Dame
1951	Dick Kazmaier, Princeton	1969	Steve Owens, Oklahoma	1988	Barry Sanders, Oklahoma State
1952	Billy Vessels, Oklahoma	1970	Jim Plunkett, Stanford		

1988 N.C.A.A. CHAMPIONSHIP PLAYOFFS

DIVISION I-AA
Quarterfinals
Idaho 38, Northwestern Louisiana 30
Furman 13, Marshall 9
Georgia Southern 27, S.F. Austin 6
Eastern Kentucky 41, Western Kentucky 24
Semifinals
Furman 38, Idaho 7
Georgia Southern 21, Eastern Kentucky 17
Championship
Furman 17, Georgia Southern 12

DIVISION II
Quarterfinals
North Dakota State 36, Millersville 26
California-Sacramento 56, North Carolina Central 7
Texas A&I 34, Tennessee Martin 0
Portland State 20, Jacksonville 13
Semifinals
North Dakota State 42, California-Sacramento 20
Portland State 35, Texas A&I 27
Championship
North Dakota State 35, Portland State 21

DIVISION III
Quarterfinals
Ithaca 24, Cortland State 17
Ferrum 49, Moravian 28
Augustana 28, Wittenberg 14
Central Iowa 16, Wisconsin-Whitewater 13
Semifinals
Ithaca 62, Ferrum 28
Central Iowa 23, Augustana 17 (2 OT)
Championship
Ithaca 39, Central Iowa 24

NATIONAL ASSOCIATION OF INTERCOLLEGIATE ATHLETICS 1988 CHAMPIONSHIPS

DIVISION I
Quarterfinals
Central State, Ohio 14, Hillsdale, Mich 7
Carson-Newman, Tennessee 42, Moorhead State, Minnesota 6
Adams State, Colorado 38, Southeastern Oklahoma State 7
Pittsburg State, Kansas 23, Arkansas-Monticello 7
Semifinals
Carson-Newman 13, Central State 0
Adams State 13, Pittsburg 10
Championship
Carson-Newman 56, Adams State 21

DIVISION II
Quarterfinals
Westminster, Pa. 40, Bluffton 7
Wisconsin-LaCrosse 46, Northwestern, Iowa 38
Evangel, Mo. 33, Bethany, Kansas 10
Oregon Tech 70, Carroll, Montana 35
Semifinals
Westminster, Pa. 26, Evangel, Mo. 9
Wisconsin-La Crosse 37, Oregon Tech 24
Championship
Westminster 21, Wisconsin-La Crosse 14

COLLEGE FOOTBALL HALL OF FAME

(Kings Island, Interstate 71, Kings Mills, Ohio)

(Date given is player's last year of competition)

Players

Abell, Earl—Colgate, 1915
Agase, Alex—Purdue/Illinois, 1946
Agganis, Harry—Boston Univ., 1952
Albert, Frank—Stanford, 1941
Aldrich, Chas. (Ki)—T.C.U., 1938
Aldrich, Malcolm—Yale, 1921
Alexander, John—Syracuse, 1920
Alworth, Lance—Arkansas, 1961
Ameche, Alan (Horse)—Wisconsin, 1954
Amling, Warren—Ohio State, 1946
Anderson, Danny—Texas Tech, 1965
Anderson, H. (Hunk)—Notre Dame, 1921
Atkins, Doug—Tennessee, 1952
Bacon, C. Everett—Wesleyan, 1912
Bagnell, Francis (Reds)—Penn, 1950
Baker, Hobart (Hobey)—Princeton, 1913
Baker, John—So. Calif., 1931
Baker, Terry—Oregon State, 1962
Ballin, Harold—Princeton, 1914
Banker, Bill—Tulane, 1929
Banonis, Vince—Detroit, 1941
Barnes, Stanley—S. California, 1921
Barrett, Charles—Cornell, 1915
Baston, Bert—Minnesota, 1916
Battles, Cliff—W. Va. Wesleyan, 1931
Baugh, Sammy—Texas Christian U., 1936
Baughan, Maxie—Georgia Tech, 1959
Bausch, James—Kansas, 1930
Beagle, Ron—Navy, 1955
Beban, Gary—UCLA, 1967
Beckett, John—Oregon, 1913
Bednarik, Chuck—Pennsylvania, 1948
Behm, Forrest—Nebraska, 1940
Bellino, Joe—Navy, 1960
Below, Marty—Wisconsin, 1923
Benbrook, A.—Michigan, 1911
Bertelli, A.—Notre Dame, 1943
Berry, Charlie—Lafayette, 1924
Berwanger, John (Jay)—Chicago, 1935
Bettencourt, Larry—St. Mary's, 1927
Blanchard, Felix (Doc)—Army, 1946
Bock, Ed—Iowa State, 1938
Bomar, Lynn—Vanderbilt, 1924
Bomeisler, Doug (Bo)—Yale, 1913
Booth, Albie—Yale, 1931
Borries, Fred—Navy, 1934
Bosely, Bruce—West Virginia, 1955
Bottari, Vic—California, 1939
Boynton, Ben—Williams, 1920
Bozis, Al—Georgetown, 1941
Brewer, Charles—Harvard, 1895
Bright, John—Drake, 1951
Brodie, John—Stanford, 1956
Brooke, George—Pennsylvania, 1895
Brown, George—Navy, San Diego St., 1947
Brown, Gordon—Yale, 1900
Brown, John, Jr.—Navy, 1913
Brown, Johnny Mack—Alabama, 1925
Brown, Raymond (Tay)—So. California, 1932
Bunker, Paul—Army, 1902
Butkus, Dick—Illinois, 1964
Butler, Robert—Wisconsin, 1912
Cafego, George—Tennessee, 1939
Cagle, Chris—SW La./Army, 1929
Cain, John—Alabama, 1932
Cameron, Eddie—Wash. & Lee, 1924
Campbell, David C.—Harvard, 1901
Cannon, Billy—L.S.U., 1959
Cannon, Jack—Notre Dame, 1929
Carideo, Frank—Notre Dame, 1930
Caroline, J.C.—Illinois, 1954
Carney, Charles—Illinois, 1921
Carpenter, Bill—Army, 1959
Carpenter, C. Hunter—VPI, 1905
Carroll, Charles—Washington, 1928
Casey, Edward L.—Harvard, 1919
Cassady, Howard—Ohio State, 1955
Chamberlain, Guy—Nebraska, 1915
Chapman, Sam—Cal.-Berkeley, 1938

Chappuis, Bob—Michigan, 1947
Christman, Paul—Missouri, 1940
Clark, Earl (Dutch)—Colo. College, 1929
Cleary, Paul—USC, 1947
Clevenger, Zora—Indiana, 1903
Cochran, Gary—Princeton, 1895
Cody, Josh—Vanderbilt, 1920
Coleman, Don—Mich. State, 1951
Conerly, Chuck—Mississippi, 1947
Connor, George—Notre Dame, 1947
Corbin, W.—Yale, 1888
Corbus, William—Stanford, 1933
Cowan, Hector—Princeton, 1889
Coy, Edward H. (Tad)—Yale, 1909
Crawford, Fred—Duke, 1933
Crow, John D.—Texas A&M, 1957
Crowley, James—Notre Dame, 1924
Csonka, Larry—Syracuse, 1967
Cutter, Slade—Navy, 1934
Czarobski, Ziggie—Notre Dame, 1947
Dale, Carroll—Virginia Tech, 1959
Dalrymple, Gerald—Tulane, 1931
Daniell, James—Ohio State, 1941
Dalton, John—Navy, 1912
Daly, Charles—Harvard/Army, 1902
Daniell, Averell—Pittsburgh, 1936
Davies, Tom—Pittsburgh, 1921
Davis, Ernest—Syracuse, 1961
Davis, Glenn—Army, 1946
Davis, Robert T.—Georgia Tech, 1947
Dawkins, Pete—Army, 1958
De Rogatis, Al—Duke, 1940
DesJardien, Paul—Chicago, 1914
Devino, Aubrey—Iowa, 1921
DeWitt, John—Princeton, 1903
Ditka, Mike—Pittsburgh, 1960
Dobbs, Glenn—Tulsa, 1942
Dodd, Bobby—Tennessee, 1930
Donan, Holland—Princeton, 1950
Donchess, Joseph—Pittsburgh, 1929
Dougherty, Nathan—Tennessee, 1909
Drahos, Nick—Cornell, 1940
Driscoll, Paddy—Northwestern, 1917
Drury, Morley—So. California, 1927
Dudley, William (Bill)—Virginia, 1941
Eckersall, Walter—Chicago, 1906
Edwards, Turk—Washington State, 1931
Edwards, William—Princeton, 1900
Eichenlaub, R.—Notre Dame, 1913
Elliott, Chalmers—Purdue, 1944 &
    Michigan, 1947
Evans, Ray—Kansas, 1947
Exendine, Albert—Carlisle, 1908
Falaschi, Nello—Santa Clara, 1937
Fears, Tom—Santa Clara/UCLA, 1947
Feathers, Beattie—Tennessee, 1933
Fenimore, Robert—Oklahoma State, 1947
Fenton, G.E. (Doc)—La. State U., 1910
Ferraro, John—So. California, 1944
Fesler, Wesley—Ohio State, 1930
Fincher, Bill—Georgia Tech, 1920
Fischer, Bill—Notre Dame, 1948
Fish, Hamilton—Harvard, 1909
Fisher, Robert—Harvard, 1911
Flowers, Abe—Georgia Tech, 1920
Fortmann, Daniel—Colgate, 1935
Francis, Sam—Nebraska, 1936
Franco, Edmund (Ed)—Fordham, 1937
Frank, Clint—Yale, 1937
Franz, Rodney—California, 1949
Friedman, Benny—Michigan, 1926
Gabriel, Roman—North Carolina St., 1961
Gain, Bob—Kentucky, 1950
Galiffa, Arnold—Army, 1949
Gallarneau, Hugh—Stanford, 1940
Garbisch, Edgar—Army, 1924
Garrett, Mike—USC, 1965
Gelbert, Charles—Pennsylvania, 1896
Geyer, Forest—Oklahoma, 1915

Giel, Paul—Minnesota, 1953
Gifford, Frank—So. California, 1951
Gilbert, Walter—Auburn, 1936
Gipp, George—Notre Dame, 1920
Gladchuk, Chet—Boston College, 1940
Glass, Bill—Baylor, 1956
Goldberg, Marshall—Pittsburgh, 1938
Goodreault, Gene—Boston College, 1940
Gordon, Walter—California, 1918
Governale, Paul—Columbia, 1942
Graham, Otto—Northwestern, 1943
Grange, Harold (Red)—Illinois, 1925
Grayson, Robert—Stanford, 1935
Green, Joe—North Texas State, 1968
Griese, Bob—Purdue, 1966
Griffin, Archie—Ohio State, 1975
Gulick, Merel—Hobart, 1929
Guyon, Joe—Georgia Tech, 1919
Hale, Edwin—Mississippi Col, 1921
Hamilton, Robert (Bones)—Stanford, 1935
Hamilton, Tom—Navy, 1925
Hanson, Vic—Syracuse, 1926
Hardwick, H. (Tack)—Harvard, 1914
Hare, T. Truxton—Pennsylvania, 1900
Harley, Chick—Ohio State, 1919
Harmon, Tom—Michigan, 1940
Harpster, Howard—Carnegie Tech, 1928
Hart, Edward J.—Princeton, 1911
Hart, Leon—Notre Dame, 1949
Hartman, Bill—Georgia, 1937
Hazel, Homer—Rutgers, 1924
Healey, Ed—Dartmouth, 1916
Heffelfinger, W. (Pudge)—Yale, 1891
Hein, Mel—Washington State, 1930
Heinrich, Don—Washington, 1952
Hendricks, Ted—Miami, 1968
Henry, Wilber—Wash. & Jefferson, 1919
Herschberger, Clarence—Chicago, 1899
Herwig, Robert—California, 1937
Heston, Willie—Michigan, 1904
Hickman, Herman—Tennessee, 1931
Hickok, William—Yale, 1895
Hill, Dan—Duke, 1938
Hillebrand, A.R. (Doc)—Princeton, 1900
Hinkey, Frank—Yale, 1894
Hinkle, Carl—Vanderbilt, 1937
Hinkle, Clark—Bucknell, 1932
Hirsch, Elroy—Wis./Mich., 1943
Hitchcock, James—Auburn, 1932
Hoffman, Frank—Notre Dame, 1931
Hogan, James J.—Yale, 1904
Holland, Jerome (Brud)—Cornell, 1938
Holleder, Don—Army, 1955
Hollenbeck, William—Penn., 1908
Holovak, Michael—Boston College, 1942
Holub, E.J.—Texas Tech, 1960
Hornung, Paul—Notre Dame, 1956
Horrell, Edwin—California, 1924
Horvath, Les—Ohio State, 1944
Howe, Arthur—Yale, 1911
Howell, Millard (Dixie)—Alabama, 1934
Hubbard, Cal—Centenary, 1926
Hubbard, John—Amherst, 1906
Hubert, Allison—Alabama, 1925
Huff, Robert Lee (Sam)—W. Va., 1955
Humble, Weldon G.—Rice, 1946
Hunt, Joel—Texas A&M, 1927
Huntington, Ellery—Colgate, 1914
Hutson, Don—Alabama, 1934
Ingram, James—Navy, 1906
Isbell, Cecil—Purdue, 1937
Jablonsky, Harvey—Wash. U./Army, 1933
Janowicz, Vic—Ohio State, 1951
Jenkins, Darold—Missouri, 1941
Jensen, Jack—Cal-Berkeley, 1948
Joesting, Herbert—Minnesota, 1927
Johnson, James—Carlisle, 1903
Johnson, Robert—Tennessee, 1967
Jones, Calvin—Iowa, 1955

Jones, Gomer—Ohio State, 1935
Jordan, Lee Roy—Alabama, 1962
Juhan, Frank—Univ. of South, 1910
Justice, Charlie—North Carolina, 1949
Kaer, Mort—So. California, 1926
Kavanaugh, Kenneth—La. State U., 1939
Kaw, Edgar—Cornell, 1922
Kazmaier, Richard—Princeton, 1951
Keck, James—Princeton, 1921
Kelley, Larry—Yale, 1936
Kelly, William—Montana, 1926
Kenna, Ed—Syracuse, 1966
Kern, George—Boston College, 1941
Ketcham, Henry—Yale, 1913
Killinger, William—Penn State, 1922
Kimbrough, John—Texas A&M, 1940
Kinard, Frank—Mississippi, 1937
King, Phillip—Princeton, 1893
Kinnick, Nile—Iowa, 1939
Kipke, Harry—Michigan, 1923
Kirkpatrick, John Reed—Yale, 1910
Kitzmiller, John—Oregon, 1929
Koch, Barton—Baylor, 1931
Kitner, Malcolm—Texas, 1942
Kramer, Ron—Michigan, 1956
Krueger, Charlie—Texas A&M, 1957
Kwalick, Ted—Penn State, 1968
Lach, Steve—Duke, 1941
Lane, Myles—Dartmouth, 1927
Lattner, Joseph J.—Notre Dame, 1953
Lauricella, Hank—Tennessee, 1952
Lautenschlaeger—Tulane, 1925
Layden, Elmer—Notre Dame, 1924
Layne, Bobby—Texas, 1947
Lea, Langdon—Princeton, 1895
LeBaron, Eddie—Univ. of Pacific, 1949
Leech, James—Va. Mil. Inst., 1920
Lester, Darrell—Texas Christian, 1935
Lilly, Bob—Texas Christian, 1960
Little, Floyd—Syracuse, 1966
Lio, Augie—Georgetown, 1940
Locke, Gordon—Iowa, 1922
Lourie, Don—Princeton, 1921
Lucas, Richard—Penn State, 1959
Luckman, Sid—Columbia, 1938
Lujack, John—Notre Dame, 1947
Lund, J.L. (Pug)—Minnesota, 1934
Macomber, Bart—Illinois, 1915
MacLeod, Robert—Dartmouth, 1938
Maegle, Dick—Rice, 1954
Mahan, Edward W.—Harvard, 1915
Majors, John—Tennessee, 1956
Mallory, William—Yale, 1893
Mann, Gerald—So. Methodist, 1927
Manning, Archie—Mississippi, 1970
Manske, Edgar—Northwestern, 1933
Markov, Vic—Washington, 1937
Marshall, Robert—Minnesota, 1907
Matson, Ollie—San Fran. U., 1952
Matthews, Ray—Texas Christ. U., 1928
Maulbetsch, John—Michigan, 1914
Mauthe, J.L. (Pete)—Penn State, 1912
Maxwell, Robert—Chi./Swarthmore, 1906
McAfee, George—Duke, 1939
McColl, William F.—Stanford, 1951
McCormick, James B.—Princeton, 1907
McDonald, Tom—Oklahoma, 1956
McDowall, Jack—No. Car. State, 1927
McElhenny, Hugh—Washington, 1951
McEver, Gene—Tennessee, 1931
McEwan, John—Minn./Army, 1916
McFadden, J.B.—Clemson, 1939
McFadin, Bud—Texas, 1950
McClung, Thomas L.—Yale, 1891
McGinley, Edward—Pennsylvania, 1924
McGovern, J.—Minnesota, 1910
McGraw, Thurman—Colorado State, 1949
McKeever, Mike—USC, 1960
McLaren, George—Pittsburgh, 1918
McMillan, Dan—U.S.C./Calif., 1922
McMillin, A.N. (Bo)—Centre, 1921
McWhorter, Robert—Georgia, 1913
Mercer, Leroy—Pennsylvania, 1912
Meredith, Don—Southern Methodist, 1959
Metzger, Bert—Notre Dame, 1930
Mickal, Abe—La. State U., 1935

Miller, Creighton—Notre Dame, 1943
Miller, Don—Notre Dame, 1925
Miller, Edgar (Rip)—Notre Dame, 1924
Miller, Eugene—Penn State, 1913
Miller, Fred—Notre Dame, 1928
Milstead, Century—Wabash, Yale, 1923
Minds, John—Pennsylvania, 1897
Minisi, Anthony—Navy, Pennsylvania, 1947
Moffat, Alex—Princeton, 1884
Montgomery, Cliff—Columbia, 1933
Moomaw, Donn—U.C.L.A., 1952
Morley, William—Columbia, 1903
Morris, George—Georgia Tech, 1952
Morton, William—Dartmouth, 1931
Moscrip, Monk—Stanford, 1935
Muller, Harold (Brick)—Calif., 1922
Nagurski, Bronko—Minnesota, 1929
Nevers, Ernie—Stanford, 1925
Newell, Marshall—Harvard, 1893
Newman, Harry—Michigan, 1932
Nobis, Tommy—Texas, 1965
Nomellini, Leo—Minnesota, 1949
Oberlander, Andrew—Dartmouth, 1925
O'Brien, Davey—Texas Christ. U., 1938
O'Dea, Pat—Wisconsin, 1899
O'Hearn, J.—Cornell, 1915
Olds, Robin—Army, 1942
Oliphant, Elmer—Purdue/Army, 1917
Olsen, Merlin—Utah State, 1961
Oosterbaan, Ben—Michigan, 1927
O'Rourke, Charles—Boston College, 1940
Orsi, John—Colgate, 1931
Osgood, W.D.—Cornell/Penn, 1895
Osmanski, William—Holy Cross, 1938
Owen, George—Harvard, 1922
Owens, Jim—Oklahoma, 1949
Pardee, Jack—Texas A & M, 1956
Parilli, Vito (Babe)—Kentucky, 1951
Parker, Clarence (Ace)—Duke, 1936
Parker, Jackie—Miss. State, 1953
Parker, James—Ohio State, 1956
Pazzetti, V.J.—Wes./Lehigh, 1912
Peabody, Endicott—Harvard, 1941
Peck, Robert—Pittsburgh, 1916
Pennock, Stanley B.—Harvard, 1914
Pfann, George—Cornell, 1923
Phillips, H.D.—U. of South, 1904
Pingel, John—Michigan State, 1938
Pihos, Pete—Indiana, 1945
Pinckert, Ernie—So. California, 1931
Poe, Arthur—Princeton, 1899
Pollard, Fritz—Brown, 1916
Poole, Barney—Miss./Army, 1947
Pregulman, Merv—Michigan, 1943
Price, Eddie—Tulane, 1949
Pund, Henry—Georgia Tech, 1928
Ramsey, Gerrard—Wm. & Mary, 1942
Reeds, Claude—Oklahoma, 1913
Reid, Mike—Penn St. 1970
Reid, Steve—Northwestern, 1936
Reid, William—Harvard, 1900
Renfro, Mel—Oregon, 1963
Rentner, Ernest—Northwestern, 1932
Reynolds, Robert—Nebraska, 1952
Reynolds, Robert—Stanford, 1935
Richter, Les—California, 1951
Riley, John—Northwestern, 1931
Rinehart, Charles—Lafayette, 1897
Rodgers, Ira—West Virginia, 1919
Rogers, Edward L.—Minnesota, 1903
Romig, Joe—Colorado, 1961
Rosenberg, Aaron—So. California, 1934
Rote, Kyle—So. Methodist, 1950
Routt, Joe—Texas A&M, 1937
Salmon, Louis—Notre Dame, 1904
Sauer, George—Nebraska, 1933
Sayers, Gale—Kansas, 1964
Scarbath, Jack—Maryland, 1952
Scarlett, Hunter—Pennsylvania, 1909
Schloredt, Bob—Washington, 1960
Schoonover, Wear—Arkansas, 1929
Schreiner, Dave—Wisconsin, 1942
Schultz, Adolf (Germany)—Mich., 1908
Schwab, Frank—Lafayette, 1922
Schwartz, Marchmont—Notre Dame, 1931
Schwegler, Paul—Washington, 1931

Scott, Clyde—Arkansas, 1949
Scott, Richard—Navy 1947
Scott, Tom—Virginia, 1953
Seibels, Henry—Sewanee, 1899
Sellers, Ron—Florida State, 1968
Selmon, Lee Roy—Oklahoma, 1975
Shakespeare, Bill—Notre Dame, 1935
Shelton, Murray—Cornell, 1915
Shevlin, Tom—Yale, 1905
Shively, Bernie—Illinois, 1926
Simons, Claude—Tulane, 1934
Simpson, O.J.—So. Calif., 1968
Sington, Fred—Alabama, 1930
Sinkwich, Frank—Georgia, 1942
Sitko, Emil—Notre Dame, 1949
Skladany, Joe—Pittsburgh, 1933
Slater, F.F. (Duke)—Iowa, 1921
Smith, Bruce—Minnesota, 1941
Smith, Bubba—Michigan State, 1966
Smith, Ernie—So. California, 1932
Smith, Harry—So. California, 1939
Smith, Jim Ray—Baylor, 1954
Smith, John (Clipper)—Notre Dame, 1927
Smith, Riley—Alabama, 1935
Smith, Vernon—Georgia, 1931
Snow, Neil—Michigan, 1901
Sparlis, Al—U.C.L.A., 1945
Spears, Clarence W.—Dartmouth, 1915
Spears, W.D.—Vanderbilt, 1927
Sprackling, William—Brown, 1911
Sprague, M. (Bud)—Texas/Army, 1928
Spurrier, Steve—Florida, 1966
Stafford, Harrison—Texas, 1932
Stagg, Amos Alonzo—Yale, 1889
Staubach, Roger—Navy, 1963
Steffen, Walter—Chicago, 1908
Steffy, Joe—Army, 1947
Stein, Herbert—Pittsburgh, 1921
Steuber, Robert—Missouri, 1943
Stevens, Mal—Yale, 1923
Stinchcomb, Gaylord—Ohio State, 1920
Stevenson, Vincent—Pennsylvania, 1905
Strom, Brock—Air Force, 1959
Strong, Ken—New York Univ., 1928
Strupper, George—Georgia Tech, 1917
Stuhldreher, Harry—Notre Dame, 1924
Stydahar, Joe—West Virginia, 1935
Suffridge, Robert—Tennessee, 1940
Suhey, Steve—Pennsylvania State, 1947
Sundstrom, Frank—Cornell, 1923
Swanson, Clarence—Nebraska, 1921
Swiacki, Bill—Holy Cross/Colombia, 1947
Swink, Jim—Texas Christian, 1956
Taliaferro, George—Indiana, 1948
Tarkenton, Fran—Georgia, 1960
Taylor, Charles—Stanford, 1942
Thomas, Aurelius—Ohio St., 1957
Thompson, Joe—Pittsburgh, 1907
Thorne, Samuel B.—Yale, 1906
Thorpe, Jim—Carlisle, 1912
Ticknor, Ben—Harvard, 1930
Tigert, John—Vanderbilt, 1904
Tinsley, Gaynell—La. State U., 1936
Tipton, Eric—Duke, 1938
Tonnemaker, Clayton—Minnesota, 1949
Torrey, Robert—Pennsylvania, 1906
Travis, Ed Tarkio—Missouri, 1920
Trippi, Charles—Georgia, 1946
Tryon, J. Edward—Colgate, 1925
Utay, Joe—Texas A&M, 1907
Van Brocklin, Norm—Oregon, 1948
Van Sickel, Dale—Florida, 1929
Van Surdam, Henderson—Wesleyan, 1905
Very, Dexter—Penn State, 1912
Vessels, Billy—Oklahoma, 1952
Vick, Ernie—Michigan, 1921
Wagner, Huber—Pittsburgh, 1913
Walker, Doak—So. Methodist, 1949
Wallace, Bill—Rice, 1935
Walsh, Adam—Notre Dame, 1924
Warburton, I. (Cotton)—So. Calif., 1934
Ward, Robert (Bob)—Maryland, 1951
Warner, William—Cornell, 1903
Washington, Ken—U.C.L.A., 1939
Webster, George—Michigan St. 1966
Wedemeyer, Herman J.—St. Mary's, 1947

Weekes, Harold—Columbia, 1902
Weir, Ed—Nebraska, 1925
Welch, Gus—Carlisle, 1914
Weller, John—Princeton, 1935
Wendell, Percy—Harvard, 1913
West, D. Belford—Colgate, 1919
Westfall, Bob—Michigan, 1941
Weyand, Alex—Army, 1915
Wharton, Charles—Pennsylvania, 1896
Wheeler, Arthur—Princeton, 1894
White, Byron (Whizzer)—Colorado, 1937
Whitmire, Don—Alabama/Navy, 1944

Wickhorst, Frank—Navy, 1926
Widseth, Ed—Minnesota, 1936
Wildung, Richard—Minnesota, 1942
Williams, Bob—Notre Dame, 1950
Williams, James—Rice, 1949
Willis, William—Ohio State, 1945
Wilson, George—Washington, 1925
Wilson, George—Lafayette, 1928
Wilson, Harry—Penn State/Army, 1923
Wistert, Albert A.—Michigan, 1942
Wistert, Al—Michigan, 1949
Wistert, Frank (Whitey)—Mich., 1933

Wood, Barry—Harvard, 1931
Wojciechowicz, Alex—Fordham, 1936
Wyant, Andrew—Bucknell/Chicago, 1894
Wyatt, Bowden—Tennessee, 1938
Wyckoff, Clint—Cornell, 1896
Yarr, Tom—Notre Dame, 1931
Yary, Ron—USC, 1968
Yoder, Lloyd—Carnegie Tech, 1926
Young, Claude (Buddy)—Illinois, 1946
Young, Harry—Wash. & Lee, 1916
Young, Walter—Oklahoma, 1938
Zarnas, Gus—Ohio State, 1937

Coaches

Bill Alexander
Dr. Ed Anderson
Ike Armstrong
Matty Bell
Hugo Bezdek
Dana X. Bible
Bernie Bierman
Bob Blackman
Earl (Red) Blaik
Frank Broyles
Paul "Bear" Bryant
Charles W. Caldwell
Walter Camp
Len Casanova
Frank Cavanaugh
Fritz Crisler
Duffy Daugherty
Bob Devaney
Dan Devine
Gil Dobie
Michael Donohue
Gus Dorais

Bill Edwards
Charles (Rip) Engle
Don Faurot
Jake Gaither
Sid Gillman
Ernest Godfrey
Andy Gustafson
Jack Harding
Edward K. Hall
Richard Harlow
Jesse Harper
Percy Haughton
Woody Hayes
John W. Heisman
R. A. (Bob) Higgins
Orin E. Hollingberry
Frank Howard
William Ingram
Morley Jennings
Howard Jones
L. (Biff) Jones

Thomas (Tad) Jones
Ralph (Shug) Jordan
Andy Kerr
Frank Leahy
George E. Little
Lou Little
El (Slip) Madigan
Charley McClendon
Herbert McCracken
Daniel McGugin
John McKay
DeOrmond (Tuss) Mc-
  Laughry
L. R. (Dutch) Meyer
Bernie Moore
Scrappy Moore
Jack Mollenkopf
Ray Morrison
George A. Munger
Clarence Munn
Frank Murray

William Murray
Ed (Hooks) Mylin
Earle (Greasy) Neale
Jess Neely
David Nelson
Robert Neyland
Homer Norton
Frank (Buck) O'Neill
Bennie Owen
Ara Parseghian
Doyt Perry
James Phalea
E. N. Robinson
Knute Rockne
E. L. (Dick) Romney
William W. Roper
Darrell Royal
George F. Sanford
Francis A. Schmidt
Floyd (Ben) Schwartz-
  walder

Clark Shaughnessy
Buck Shaw
Andrew L. Smith
Carl Snavely
Amos A. Stagg
Jock Sutherland
James Tatum
Frank W. Thomas
Thad Vann
John H. Vaught
Wallace Wade
Lynn Waldorf
Glenn (Pop) Warner
E. E. (Tad) Wieman
John W. Wilce
Bud Wilkinson
Henry L. Williams
George W. Woodruff
Warren Woodson
Fielding H. Yost
Robert Zuppke

NFL TEAM NICKNAMES AND HOME FIELD CAPACITIES

AMERICAN CONFERENCE
Eastern Division

Buffalo Bills	Rich Stadium (AT)	80,020
Indianapolis Colts[1]	Hoosier Dome (AT)	61,500
Miami Dolphins	Joe Robbie Stadium (G)	75,000
New England Patriots	Sullivan Stadium (ST)	61,297
New York Jets[2]	Giants Stadium (AT)	76,891

Central Division

Cincinnati Bengals	Riverfront Stadium (AT)	59,754
Cleveland Browns	Municipal Stadium (G)	80,322
Houston Oilers	Astrodome (AT)	50,496
Pittsburgh Steelers	Three Rivers Stadium (AT)	59,000

Western Division

Denver Broncos	Mile High Stadium (G)	75,103
Kansas City Chiefs	Arrowhead Stadium (TT)	78,067
Los Angeles Raiders[3]	Memorial Coliseum (G)	92,498
San Diego Chargers	Jack Murphy Stadium (G)	53,675
Seattle Seahawks	Kingdome (AT)	64,757

1. Moved franchise from Baltimore prior to 1984 season. 2. Moved to Giants Stadium; East Rutherford, N.J. prior to 1984 season. 3. Moved franchise to Los Angeles for 1982 season. Shift is still being argued in courts, as city of Oakland tries to regain franchise.

NATIONAL CONFERENCE
Eastern Division

Dallas Cowboys	Texas Stadium (TT)	65,101
New York Giants	Giants Stadium (AT)[1]	76,891
Philadelphia Eagles	Veterans Stadium (AT)	72,204
Phoenix Cardinals	Sun Devil Stadium (G)	70,491
Washington Redskins	R.F. Kennedy Stadium (G)	55,045

Central Division

Chicago Bears	Soldier Field (AT)	65,793
Detroit Lions	Pontiac Silverdome (AT)	80,638
Green Bay Packers	Lambeau Field (G)	56,189
	Milwaukee Stadium (G)	55,958
Minnesota Vikings	Hubert Humphrey Metrodome (ST)	62,212
Tampa Bay Buccaneers	Tampa Stadium (G)	72,812

Western Division

Atlanta Falcons	Atlanta-Fulton Stadium (G)	60,748
Los Angeles Rams	Anaheim Stadium (G)	69,007
New Orleans Saints	Louisiana Superdome (AT)	71,330
San Francisco 49ers	Candlestick Park (G)	61,185

1. At East Rutherford, N.J. NOTE: Stadium playing surfaces in parentheses: (AT) Astro Turf; (G) Grass; (ST) Super Turf; (TT) Tartan Turf.

Professional Football

NATIONAL FOOTBALL LEAGUE FINAL STANDING 1988

AMERICAN CONFERENCE
Eastern Division

	W	L	T	Pct	Pts	Op
Buffalo	12	4	0	.750	329	237
Indianapolis	9	7	0	.563	354	315
New England	9	7	0	.563	250	284
New York Jets	8	7	1	.531	372	354
Miami	6	10	0	.375	319	380

Central Division

	W	L	T	Pct	Pts	Op
Cincinnati	12	4	0	.750	448	329
Cleveland[1]	10	6	0	.625	304	288
Houston[1]	10	6	0	.625	424	365
Pittsburgh	5	11	0	.313	336	421

Western Division

	W	L	T	Pct	Pts	Op
Seattle	9	7	0	.563	339	329
Denver	8	8	0	.500	327	352
Los Angeles Raiders	7	9	0	.438	325	369
San Diego	6	10	0	.375	231	332
Kansas City	4	11	1	.281	254	320

1. Wild card qualifier for playoffs.

Playoffs: Houston 24, Cleveland 23; Buffalo 17, Houston 10, Cincinnati 21, Seattle 13.
Conference championship: Cincinnati 21, Buffalo 10.

NATIONAL CONFERENCE
Eastern Division

	W	L	T	Pct	Pts	Op
Philadelphia	10	6	0	.625	379	319
New York Giants	10	6	0	.625	359	304
Washington	7	9	0	.438	345	387
Phoenix	7	9	0	.438	344	398
Dallas	3	13	0	.188	265	381

Central Division

	W	L	T	Pct	Pts	Op
Chicago	12	4	0	.750	312	215
Minnesota[1]	11	5	0	.688	406	233
Tampa Bay	5	11	0	.313	261	350
Detroit	4	12	0	.250	220	313
Green Bay	4	12	0	.250	240	315

Western Division

	W	L	T	Pct	Pts	Op
San Francisco	10	6	0	.625	369	294
Los Angeles Rams[1]	10	6	0	.625	407	293
New Orleans	10	6	0	.625	312	283
Atlanta	5	11	0	.313	244	315

1. Wild card qualifier for playoffs.

Playoffs: Minnesota 28, Los Angeles Rams 17; San Francisco 34, Minnesota 9; Chicago 20, Philadelphia 12.
Conference championship: San Francisco 28, Chicago 3.

LEAGUE CHAMPIONSHIP—SUPER BOWL XXIII

(January 22, 1989, at Joe Robbie Stadium, Miami, Fla.; Attendance: 75,179)

Scoring

	1st Q	2nd Q	3rd Q	4th Q	Final
Cincinnati (AFC)	0	3	10	3	- 16
San Francisco (NFC)	3	0	3	14	- 20

Scoring—San Francisco: Touchdowns: Rice, 14-yard pass from Montana (Cofer kick); Taylor, 10-yard pass from Montana (Cofer kick); Field goals: Cofer (2) 41, 32. **Cincinnati:** Touchdowns: Jennings, 93-yard kickoff return (Breech kick). Field goals: Breech (3) 34, 43, 40.

Statistics of the Game

	Cincinnati	San Francisco
First downs	13	23
Third down conversions	4-13	4-13
Yards gained rushing	28-106	28-111
Yards gained passing	123	343
Passes completed	11	23
Passes attempted	25	36
Passes intercepted by	0	1
Punts	5-44.6	4-37.0
Fumbles lost	0	1
Yards penalized	7-65	4-32
Time of possession	32:43	27:17

SUPER BOWLS I–XXIII

Game	Date	Winner	Loser	Site	Attendance
XXIII	Jan. 22, 1989	San Francisco (NFC) 20	Cincinnati (AFC) 16	Joe Robbie Stadium, Miami, Fla.	75,179
XXII	Jan. 31, 1988	Washington (NFC) 42	Denver (AFC) 10	Jack Murphy Stadium, San Diego, Calif.	73,302
XXI	Jan. 25, 1987	Giants (NFC) 39	Denver (AFC) 20	Rose Bowl, Pasadena, Calif.	101,063
XX	Jan. 26, 1986	Chicago (NFC) 46	New England (AFC) 10	Superdome, New Orleans	73,818
XIX	Jan. 20, 1985	San Francisco (NFC) 38	Miami (AFC) 16	Stanford Stadium, Palo Alto, Calif.	84,059
XVIII	Jan. 22, 1984	Los Angeles Raiders (AFC) 38	Washington (NFC) 9	Tampa Stadium, Tampa, Fla	72,920
XVII	Jan. 30, 1983	Washington (NFC) 27	Miami (AFC) 17	Rose Bowl, Pasadena, Calif.	103,667
XVI	Jan. 24, 1982	San Francisco (NFC) 26	Cincinnati (AFC) 21	Silverdome, Pontiac, Mich.	81,270
XV	Jan. 25, 1981	Oakland (AFC) 27	Philadelphia (NFC) 10	Superdome, New Orleans	75,500
XIV	Jan. 20, 1980	Pittsburgh (AFC) 31	Los Angeles (NFC) 19	Rose Bowl, Pasadena	103,985
XIII	Jan. 21, 1979	Pittsburgh (AFC) 35	Dallas (NFC) 31	Orange Bowl, Miami	79,484
XII	Jan. 15, 1978	Dallas (NFC) 27	Denver (AFC) 10	Superdome, New Orleans	75,583
XI	Jan. 9, 1977	Oakland (AFC) 32	Minnesota (NFC) 14	Rose Bowl, Pasadena	103,424
X	Jan. 18, 1976	Pittsburgh (AFC) 21	Dallas (NFC) 17	Orange Bowl, Miami	80,187
IX	Jan. 12, 1975	Pittsburgh (AFC) 16	Minnesota (NFC) 6	Tulane Stadium, New Orleans	80,997
VIII	Jan. 13, 1974	Miami (AFC) 24	Minnesota (NFC) 7	Rice Stadium, Houston	71,882

VII	Jan. 14, 1973	Miami (AFC) 14	Washington (NFC) 7	Memorial Coliseum, Los Angeles	90,182
VI	Jan. 16, 1972	Dallas (NFC) 24	Miami (AFC) 3	Tulane Stadium, New Orleans	81,591
V	Jan. 17, 1971	Baltimore (AFC) 16	Dallas (NFC) 13	Orange Bowl, Miami	79,204
IV	Jan. 11, 1970	Kansas City (AFL) 23	Minnesota (NFL) 7	Tulane Stadium, New Orleans	80,562
III	Jan. 12, 1969	New York (AFL) 16	Baltimore (NFL) 7	Orange Bowl, Miami	75,389
II	Jan. 14, 1968	Green Bay (NFL) 33	Oakland (AFL) 14	Orange Bowl, Miami	75,546
I	Jan. 15, 1967	Green Bay (NFL) 35	Kansas City (AFL) 10	Memorial Coliseum, Los Angeles	61,946

1. Super Bowls I to IV were played before the American Football League and National Football League merged into the NFL, which was divided into two conferences, the NFC and AFC.

NATIONAL LEAGUE CHAMPIONS

Year	Champion (W-L-T)	Year	Champion (W-L-T)	Year	Champion (W-L-T)
1921	Chicago Bears (Staley's) (10-1-1)	1925	Chicago Cardinals (11-2-1)	1929	Green Bay Packers (12-0-1)
1922	Canton Bulldogs (10-0-2)	1926	Frankford Yellow Jackets (14-1-1)	1930	Green Bay Packers (10-3-1)
1923	Canton Bulldogs (11-0-1)	1927	New York Giants (11-1-1)	1931	Green Bay Packers (12-2-0)
1924	Cleveland Indians (7-1-1)	1928	Providence Steamrollers (8-1-2)	1932	Chicago Bears (7-1-6)

Year	Eastern Conference winners (W-L-T)	Western Conference winners (W-L-T)	League champion playoff results
1933	New York Giants (11-3-0)	Chicago Bears (10-2-1)	Chicago Bears 23, New York 21
1934	New York Giants (8-5-0)	Chicago Bears (13-0-0)	New York 30, Chicago Bears 13
1935	New York Giants (9-3-0)	Detroit Lions (7-3-2)	Detroit 26, New York 7
1936	Boston Redskins (7-5-0)	Green Bay Packers (10-1-1)	Green Bay 21, Boston 6
1937	Washington Redskins (8-3-0)	Chicago Bears (9-1-1)	Washington 28, Chicago Bears 21
1938	New York Giants (8-2-1)	Green Bay Packers (8-3-0)	New York 23, Green Bay 17
1939	New York Giants (9-1-1)	Green Bay Packers (9-2-0)	Green Bay 27, New York 0
1940	Washington Redskins (9-2-0)	Chicago Bears (8-3-0)	Chicago Bears 73, Washington 0
1941	New York Giants (8-3-0)	Chicago Bears (10-1-1)²	Chicago Bears 37, New York 9
1942	Washington Redskins (10-1-1)	Chicago Bears (11-0-0)	Washington 14, Chicago Bears 6
1943	Washington Redskins (6-3-1)²	Chicago Bears (8-1-1)	Chicago Bears 41, Washington 21
1944	New York Giants (8-1-1)	Green Bay Packers (8-2-0)	Green Bay 14, New York 7
1945	Washington Redskins (8-2-0)	Cleveland Rams (9-1-0)	Cleveland 15, Washington 14
1946	New York Giants (7-3-1)	Chicago Bears (8-2-1)	Chicago Bears 24, New York 14
1947	Philadelphia Eagles (8-4-0)²	Chicago Cardinals (9-3-0)	Chicago Cardinals 28, Philadelphia 21
1948	Philadelphia Eagles (9-2-1)	Chicago Cardinals (11-1-0)	Philadelphia 7, Chicago Cardinals 0
1949	Philadelphia Eagles (11-1-0)	Los Angeles Rams (8-2-2)	Philadelphia 14, Los Angeles 0
1950¹	Cleveland Browns (10-2-0)²	Los Angeles Rams (9-3-0)²	Cleveland 30, Los Angeles 28
1951¹	Cleveland Browns (11-1-0)	Los Angeles Rams (8-4-0)	Los Angeles 24, Cleveland 17
1952¹	Cleveland Browns (8-4-0)	Detroit Lions (9-3-0)²	Detroit 17, Cleveland 7
1953	Cleveland Browns (11-1-0)	Detroit Lions (10-2-0)	Detroit 17, Cleveland 16
1954	Cleveland Browns (9-3-0)	Detroit Lions (9-2-1)	Cleveland 56, Detroit 10
1955	Cleveland Browns (9-2-1)	Los Angeles Rams (8-3-1)	Cleveland 38, Los Angeles 14
1956	New York Giants (8-3-1)	Chicago Bears (9-2-1)	New York 47, Chicago Bears 7
1957	Cleveland Browns (9-2-1)	Detroit Lions (8-4-0)³	Detroit 59, Cleveland 14
1958	New York Giants (9-3-0)²	Baltimore Colts (9-3-0)	Baltimore 23, New York 17³
1959	New York Giants (10-2-0)	Baltimore Colts (9-3-0)	Baltimore 31, New York 16
1960	Philadelphia Eagles (10-2-0)	Green Bay Packers (8-4-0)	Philadelphia 17, Green Bay 13
1961	New York Giants (10-3-1)	Green Bay Packers (11-3-0)	Green Bay 37, New York 0
1962	New York Giants (12-2-0)	Green Bay Packers (13-1-0)	Green Bay 16, New York 7
1963	New York Giants (11-3-0)	Chicago Bears (11-1-2)	Chicago 14, New York 10
1964	Cleveland Browns (10-3-1)	Baltimore Colts (12-2-0)	Cleveland 27, Baltimore 0
1965	Cleveland Browns (11-3-0)	Green Bay Packers (11-3-1)²	Green Bay 23, Cleveland 12
1966	Dallas Cowboys (10-3-1)	Green Bay Packers (12-2-0)	Green Bay 34, Dallas 27
1967	Dallas Cowboys (9-5-0)²	Green Bay Packers (9-4-1)²	Green Bay 21, Dallas 17
1968	Cleveland Browns (10-4-0)²	Baltimore Colts (13-1-0)²	Baltimore 34, Cleveland 0
1969	Cleveland Browns (10-3-1)²	Minnesota Vikings (12-2-0)²	Minnesota 27, Cleveland 7

1. League was divided into American and National Conferences, 1950–52 and again in 1970, when leagues merged. 2. Won divisional playoff. 3. Won at 8:15 of sudden death overtime period.

NATIONAL CONFERENCE CHAMPIONS

Year	Eastern Division	Central Division	Western Division	Champion
1970	Dallas Cowboys (10-4-0)	Minnesota Vikings (12-2-0)	San Francisco 49ers (10-3-1)	Dallas
1971	Dallas Cowboys (11-3-0)	Minnesota Vikings (11-3-0)	San Francisco 49ers (9-5-0)	Dallas
1972	Washington Redskins (11-3-0)	Green Bay Packers (10-4-0)	San Francisco 49ers (8-5-1)	Washington
1973	Dallas Cowboys (10-4-0)	Minnesota Vikings (12-2-0)	Los Angeles Rams (12-2-0)	Minnesota
1974	St. Louis Cardinals (10-4-0)	Minnesota Vikings (10-4-0)	Los Angeles Rams (10-4-0)	Minnesota
1975	St. Louis Cardinals (11-3-0)	Minnesota Vikings (12-2-0)	Los Angeles Rams (12-2-0)	Dallas
1976	Dallas Cowboys (11-3-0)	Minnesota Vikings (11-2-1)	Los Angeles Rams (10-3-1)	Minnesota
1977	Dallas Cowboys (12-2-0)	Minnesota Vikings (9-5-0)	Los Angeles Rams (10-4-0)	Dallas

1978	Dallas Cowboys (12–4–0)	Minnesota Vikings (8–7–1)	Los Angeles Rams (12–4–0)	Dallas
1979	Dallas Cowboys (11–5–0)	Tampa Bay Buccaneers (10–6–0)	Los Angeles Rams (9–7–0)	Los Angeles
1980	Philadelphia Eagles (12–4–0)	Minnesota Vikings (9–7–0)	Atlanta Falcons (12–4–0)	Philadelphia
1981	Dallas Cowboys (12–4–0)	Tampa Bay Buccaneers (9–7–0)	San Francisco 49ers (13–3–0)	San Francisco
1982*	Washington Redskins won conference title and also had best regular-season record (8–1–0)			
1983	Washington Redskins (14–2–0)	Detroit Lions (8–8–0)	San Francisco 49ers (10–6–0)	Washington
1984	Washington Redskins (11–5–0)	Chicago Bears (10–6–0)	San Francisco 49ers (15–1)	San Francisco
1985	Dallas Cowboys (10-6-0)	Chicago Bears (15-1-0)	Los Angeles Rams (11-5-0)	Chicago
1986	New York Giants (14–2–0)	Chicago Bears (14–2–0)	San Francisco 49ers (10–5–1)	New York
1987	Washington Redskins (11–4–0)	Chicago Bears (11–4–0)	San Francisco 49ers (13–2–0)	Washington
1988	Philadelphia Eagles (10–6–0)	Chicago Bears (12–4–0)	San Francisco 49ers (10–6–0)	San Francisco

*Schedule reduced to 9 games from usual 16, with no standings kept in Eastern, Central, and Western Divisions, because of 57-day player strike.

AMERICAN CONFERENCE CHAMPIONS

Year	Eastern Division	Central Division	Western Division	Champion
1970	Baltimore Colts (11–2–1)	Cincinnati Bengals (8–6–0)	Oakland Raiders (8–4–2)	Baltimore
1971	Miami Dolphins (10–3–1)	Cleveland Browns (9–5–0)	Kansas City Chiefs (10–3–1)	Miami
1972	Miami Dolphins (14–0–0)	Pittsburgh Steelers (11–3–0)	Oakland Raiders (10–3–1)	Miami
1973	Miami Dolphins (12–2–0)	Cincinnati Bengals (10–4–0)	Oakland Raiders (9–4–1)	Miami
1974	Miami Dolphins (11–3–0)	Pittsburgh Steelers (10–3–1)	Oakland Raiders (12–2–0)	Pittsburgh
1975	Baltimore Colts (10–4–0)	Pittsburgh Steelers (12–2–0)	Oakland Raiders (12–2–0)	Pittsburgh
1976	Baltimore Colts (11–3–0)	Pittsburgh Steelers (10–4–0)	Oakland Raiders (13–1–0)	Oakland
1977	Baltimore Colts (11–3–0)	Pittsburgh Steelers (9–5–0)	Denver Broncos (12–2–0)	Denver
1978	New England Patriots (11–5–0)	Pittsburgh Steelers (14–2–0)	Denver Broncos (10–6–0)	Pittsburgh
1979	Miami Dolphins (10–6–0)	Pittsburgh Steelers (12–4–0)	San Diego Chargers (12–4–0)	Pittsburgh
1980	Buffalo Bills (11–5–0)	Cleveland Browns (11–5–0)	San Diego Chargers (11–5–0)	Oakland
1981	Miami Dolphins (11–4–1)	Cincinnati Bengals (12–4–0)	San Diego Chargers (10–6–0)	Cincinnati
1982*	Miami Dolphins won the conference title, but the Los Angeles Raiders had best regular-season record (8–1–0).			
1983	Miami (12–4–0)	Pittsburgh (10–6–0)	Los Angeles Raiders (12–4–0)	Los Angeles Raiders
1984	Miami (14–2–0)	Pittsburgh (9–7–0)	Denver (13–3–0)	Miami
1985	Miami (12-4-0)	Cleveland (8-8)	Los Angeles Raiders (12-4-0)	New England
1986	New England (11–5–0)	Cleveland (12–4–0)	Denver (11–5–0)	Denver
1987	Indianapolis Colts (9–6–0)	Cleveland Browns (10–5–0)	Denver Broncos (10–4–1)	Denver
1988	Buffalo Bills (12–4–0)	Cincinnati Bengals (12–4–0)	Seattle Seahawks (9–7–0)	Cincinnati

*Schedule reduced to 9 games from usual 16, with no standings kept in Eastern, Central, and Western Divisions, because of 57-day player strike.

AMERICAN LEAGUE CHAMPIONS

Year	Eastern Division (W-L-T)	Western Division (W-L-T)	League champion, playoff results
1960	Houston Oilers (10-4-0)	Los Angeles Chargers (10-4-0)	Houston 24, Los Angeles 16
1961	Houston Oilers (10-3-1)	San Diego Chargers (12-2-0)	Houston 10, San Diego 3
1962	Houston Oilers (11-3-0)	Dallas Texans (11-3-0)	Dallas 20, Houston 17[1]
1963	Boston Patriots (8-6-1)[2]	San Diego Chargers (11-3-0)	San Diego 51, Boston 10
1964	Buffalo Bills (12-2-0)	San Diego Chargers (8-5-1)	Buffalo 20, San Diego 7
1965	Buffalo Bills (10-3-1)	San Diego Chargers (9-2-3)	Buffalo 23, San Diego 0
1966	Buffalo Bills (9-4-1)	Kansas City Chiefs (11-2-1)	Kansas City 31, Buffalo 7
1967	Houston Oilers (9-4-1)	Oakland Raiders (13-1-0)	Oakland 40, Houston 7
1968	New York Jets (11-3-0)	Oakland Raiders (12-2-0)[2]	New York 27, Oakland 23
1969	New York Jets (10-4-0)	Oakland Raiders (12-1-1)	Kansas City 17, Oakland 7[3]

1. Won at 2:45 of second sudden death overtime period. 2. Won divisional playoff. 3. Kansas City defeated New York, 13–6, and Oakland defeated Houston, 56–7, in interdivisional playoffs.

PRO FOOTBALL HALL OF FAME

(National Football Museum, Canton, Ohio)

Teams named are those with which player is best identified; figures in parentheses indicate number of playing seasons.

Adderley, Herb, defensive back, Packers, Cowboys (12)	1961–72
Alworth, Lance, wide receiver, Chargers, Cowboys (11)	1962–72
Atkins, Doug, defensive end, Browns, Bears, Saints (17)	1953–69
Badgro, Morris, end, N.Y. Yankees, Giants, Bklyn. Dodgers (8)	1927, 1930–36
Battles, Cliff, back, Redskins (6)	1932–37
Baugh, Sammy, quarterback, Redskins (16)	1937–52
Bednarik, Chuck, center-lineback, Eagles (14)	1949–62
Bell, Bert, N.F.L. founder, owner Eagles and	

N.F.L. INDIVIDUAL LIFETIME, SEASON, AND GAME RECORDS

(American Football League records were incorporated into N.F.L. records after merger of the leagues)

All-Time Leading Touchdown Scorers

	Yrs	Rush	Pass rec	Returns	TD
Jim Brown	9	106	20	0	126
Walter Payton	13	110	15	0	125
John Riggins	14	104	12	0	116
Lenny Moore	12	63	48	2	113
Don Hutson	11	3	99	3	105
Franco Harris	12	91	9	0	100
Jim Taylor	10	83	10	0	93
Bobby Mitchell	11	18	65	8	91
Leroy Kelly	10	74	13	3	90
Charley Taylor	13	11	79	0	90

All-Time Leading Receivers

Rank	Player	Yrs	Pass rec	Yds	Avg	TD
1.	STEVE LARGENT	13	791	12,686	16.0	97
2.	Charlie Joiner	18	750	12,146	16.2	65
3.	*Charley Taylor*	13	649	9110	14.0	79
4.	Don Maynard	15	633	11,834	18.7	88
5.	*Raymond Berry*	13	631	9275	14.7	68
6.	OZZIE NEWSOME	11	610	7416	12.2	44
7.	JAMES LOFTON	11	599	11,085	18.5	54
8.	Harold Carmichael	14	590	8985	15.2	79
9.	*Fred Biletnikoff*	14	589	8974	15.2	76
10.	Harold Jackson	16	579	10,372	17.9	76

Active players in capitals, Pro Football Hall of Fame members in italics.

All-Time Leading Passers
(Minimum 1500 attempts)

Rank	Player	Yrs	Att	Comp	Yds	TD	Int	Rating pts
1.	JOE MONTANA	-10	3673	2322	27,533	190	99	92.0
2.	DAN MARINO	6	3100	1866	23,856	196	103	91.5
3.	*Otto Graham*	10	2626	1464	23,584	174	135	86.6
4.	BOOMER ESIASON	5	1830	1038	14,825	98	65	86.2
5.	DAVE KRIEG	9	2344	1358	17,549	148	96	85.5
6.	KEN O'BRIEN	5	1990	1183	14,243	84	50	85.0
7.	*Roger Staubach*	11	2958	1685	22,700	153	109	83.4
8.	NEIL LOMAX	8	3153	1817	22,771	136	90	82.7
9.	*Sonny Jurgensen*	18	4262	2433	32,224	255	189	82.6
10.	Len Dawson	19	3741	2136	28,711	239	183	82.6
11.	Ken Anderson	16	4475	2654	32,838	197	160	81.9
12.	DANNY WHITE	13	2950	1761	21,959	155	132	81.7
13.	*Bart Starr*	16	3149	1808	24,718	152	138	80.5
14.	JIM McMAHON	7	1513	874	11,203	67	56	80.4
15.	*Fran Tarkenton*	18	6467	3686	47,003	342	266	80.4
16.	Dan Fouts	15	5604	3297	43,040	254	242	80.2
17.	Bert Jones	10	2551	1430	18,190	124	101	78.2
18.	*Johnny Unitas*	18	5186	2830	40,239	290	253	78.2
19.	Frank Ryan	13	2133	1090	16,042	149	111	77.6
20.	Joe Theismann	12	3602	2044	25,206	160	138	77.4

NOTE: Active Players in capitals. Hall of Fame members in italics.

All-Time Leading Scorers

Rank	Player	Yrs	TD	PAT	FG	Pts
1.	*George Blanda*	26	9	943	335	2002
2.	Jan Stenerud	19	0	580	373	1699
3.	*Lou Groza*	21	1	810	264	1608
4.	Jim Turner	16	1	521	304	1439
5.	Mark Moseley	16	0	482	300	1382
6.	Jim Bakken	17	0	534	282	1380
7.	Fred Cox	15	0	519	282	1365
8.	PAT LEAHY	15	0	467	241	1190
9.	CHRIS BAHR	13	0	461	224	1133
10.	Gino Cappelletti	11	42	350	176	1130
11.	Ray Wersching	15	0	456	222	1122
12.	Don Cockroft	13	0	432	216	1080
13.	Garo Yepremian	14	0	444	210	1074
14.	Bruce Gossett	11	0	374	219	1031
15.	Sam Baker	15	2	428	179	977

Active players in capitals, Pro Football Hall of Fame members in italics.

All-Time Leading Rushers

Rank	Player	Yrs	Att	Yds	Avg	TD
1.	Walter Payton	13	3838	16,726	4.4	110
2.	TONY DORSETT	12	2936	12,739	4.3	77
3.	*Jim Brown*	9	2359	12,312	5.2	106
4.	Franco Harris	13	2949	12,120	4.1	91
5.	John Riggins	14	2916	11,352	3.9	104
6.	*O.J. Simpson*	11	2404	11,236	4.7	61
7.	ERIC DICKERSON	6	2136	9915	4.6	75
8.	*Joe Perry*	16	1929	9723	5.0	71
9.	Earl Campbell	8	2187	9407	4.3	74
10.	*Jim Taylor*	10	1941	8597	4.4	83
11.	O.J. ANDERSON	10	1949	8294	4.3	55
12.	*Larry Csonka*	11	1891	8081	4.3	64
13.	Mike Pruitt	11	1844	7378	4.0	51
14.	Leroy Kelly	10	1727	7274	4.2	74
15.	George Rogers	7	1692	7176	4.2	54

Active players in capitals, Hall of Fame members in italics.

Scoring

Most points scored, lifetime—2,002, George Blanda, Chicago Bears, 1949-58; Baltimore, 1950; Houston, 1960-66; Oakland, 1967-75 (9tds, 943 pat, 335 fgs).

Most points, season—176, Paul Hornung, Green Bay, 1960 (15 td, 41 pat, 15 fg).

Most points, game—40, Ernie Nevers, Chicago Cardinals, 1929 (6 td, 4 pat).

Most points, per quarter—29, Don Hutson, Green Bay, 1945 (4 td, 5 pat).

Most touchdowns, lifetime—126, Jim Brown, Cleveland, 1957-65.

Most touchdowns, season—24, John Riggins, Washington, 1983.

Most touchdowns, game—6, Ernie Nevers, Chicago Cardinals, 1929; William Jones, Cleveland, 1951; Gale Sayers, Chicago Bears, 1965.

Most points after touchdown, lifetime—943, George Blanda, Chicago Bears, 1949–58; Baltimore, 1950; Houston, 1960–66; Oakland, 1967–75.

Most points after touchdown, game—9, Pat Harder, Chicago Cardinals, 1948; Bob Waterfield, Los Angeles, 1950; Charlie Gogolak, Washington, 1966.

Most consecutive points after touchdown—234, Tommy Davis, San Francisco, 1959–65.

Most points after touchdown, no misses, season—56, Danny Villanueva, Dallas, 1966.

Most field goals, lifetime—373, Jan Stenerud, Kansas City Chiefs, 1967–79; Green Bay Packers, 1980–84; Minnesota Vikings, 1985.

Most field goals, season—35, Ali Haji-Sheikh, N.Y. Giants, 1983.

Most field goals, game—7, Jim Bakken, St. Louis, 1967.

Longest field goal—63 yards, Tom Dempsey, New Orleans, 1970.

Rushing

Most yards gained, lifetime—16,726, Walter Payton, Chicago Bears, 1975–1987.

Most yards gained, season—2,105, Eric Dickerson, Los Angeles, 1983-still active.

Most yards gained, game—275, Walter Payton, Chicago, 1977.

Most touchdowns, lifetime—110, Walter Payton, Chicago, 1975–1987.

Most touchdowns, season—24, John Riggins, Washington, 1983.

Most touchdowns, game—6, Ernie Nevers, Chicago Cardinals, 1929.

Longest run from scrimmage—99 yards, Tony Dorsett, Dallas, 1982 (touchdown).

Most yards gained, game—554, Norm Van Brocklin, Los Angeles, 1951.

Passing

Most touchdown passes, lifetime—342, Fran Tarkenton, Minnesota, 1961–66, 72–78; New York Giants, 1967–71.

Most touchdown passes, season—48, Dan Marino, Miami, 1984.

Most touchdown passes, game—7, Sid Luckman, Chicago Bears, 1943; Adrian Burk, Philadelphia, 1954; George Blanda, Houston 1961; Y.A. Tittle, New York Giants, 1963; Joe Kapp, Minnesota, 1969.

Most consecutive games, touchdown passes—47, John Unitas, Baltimore.

Most consecutive passes attempted, none intercepted—294, Bart Starr, Green Bay, 1964–65.

Longest pass completion—99 yards, Frank Filchock (to Andy Farkas), Washington, 1939; George Izo (to Bob Mitchell), Washington, 1963; Karl Sweetan (to Pat Studstill), Detroit, 1966; Sonny Jurgensen (to Gerry Allen), Washington, 1968, (all for touchdowns).

NATIONAL FOOTBALL LEAGUE GOVERNMENT

Commissioner's Office: Pete Rozelle, Commissioner; Jay Moyer, Executive V.P./Counsel to Commissioner; Don Weiss, Executive Director; Joe Rhein, Director of Administration; John Schoemer, Treasurer; Jan Van Duser, Director of Operations; Joe Browne, Director of Communications; Jim Heffernan, Jr., Director of Public Relations; Val Pinchbeck, Jr., Director of Broadcasting; Nancy Dehar, Asst. Dir. of Broadcasting; Warren Welsh, Director of Security; Charles R. Jackson, Assistant Director of Security; Joel Bussert, Director of Player Personnel; Art McNally, Supervisor of Officials; Jack Reader, Assistant Supervisor of Officials; Jim Steeg, Director of Special Events; Susan McCann-Minogue, Asst. Dir. of Special Events; Bill Granholm, Director of Special Projects; Tom Sullivan, Controller; Dave Cornwell, Asst. Counsel/Dir. of Equal Employment; Mel Blount, Director of Player Relations.

Receiving

Most pass receptions, lifetime—792, Steve Largent, Seattle Seahawks, 1976–current (still active).

Most pass receptions, season—106, Art Monk, Washington, 1984.

Most pass receptions, game—18, Tom Fears, Los Angeles, 1950.

Most consecutive games, pass receptions—153, Steve Largent, 1976–current.

Most yards gained, pass receptions, lifetime—12,146, Charlie Joiner, Houston 1964–79, Cincinnati 1972–75, San Diego 1976–86.

Most yards gained receptions, season—1,746, Charley Hennigan, Houston, 1961.

Most yards gained receptions, game—309, Stephone Paige, Kansas City, 1985.

Most touchdown pass receptions, lifetime—99, Don Hutson, Green Bay, 1935–45.

Most touchdown pass receptions, season—22, Jerry Rice, San Francisco 49ers, 1987.

Most touchdown pass receptions, game—5, Bob Shaw, Chicago Cards, 1950 and Kellen Winslow, San Diego Chargers, 1981.

Most consecutive games, touchdown pass receptions—13, Jerry Rice, San Francisco 49ers, 1986–87.

Most pass interceptions, lifetime—81, Paul Krause, Washington, 1964–67; Minnesota, 1968–79.

Most pass interceptions, season—14, Richard (Night Train) Lane, Los Angeles, 1952.

Most pass interceptions, game—4, by 15 players.

Longest pass interception return—102 yards, Bob Smith, Chicago Bears, 1949; Erich Barnes, New York Giants, 1961; Gary Barbaro, Kansas City, 1977; Louis Breeden, Cincinnati, 1981.

Kicking

Longest punt—98 yards, Steve O'Neal, New York Jets, 1969.

Highest average punting, lifetime—45.16 yards, Rohn Stark, Indianapolis, 1982–current.

Longest punt return—98 yards, Gil LeFebvre, Cincinnati Reds, 1933; Charlie West, Minnesota, 1968; Dennis Morgan, Dallas, 1974.

Longest kick-off return—106 yards, Roy Green, St. Louis, 1979; Al Carmichael, Green Bay, 1956; Noland Smith, Kansas City, 1967.

Passing

Most passes completed, lifetime—3,686, Fran Tarkenton, Minnesota, 1961–66, 72–78; New York Giants, 1967–71.

Most passes completed, season—378, Dan Marino, 1986.

Most passes completed, game—42, Richard Todd, New York Jets, 1980.

Most consecutive passes completed—20, Ken Anderson, Cincinnati, 1983.

Most yards gained, lifetime—47,003, Fran Tarkenton, Minnesota, 1961–66, 72–78; New York Giants, 1967–71.

Most yards gained, season—5,084, Dan Marino, Miami, 1984.

American Football Conference: Lamar Hunt, President; Roger Goodell, Assistant to the President; Pete Abitante, Director of Information.

National Football Conference: Wellington Mara, President; James Noel, Assistant to the President; Dick Maxwell, Director of Information.

Canadian Football League—1988 Final Standing

Eastern Division

	W	L	T	Pts	Off	Def
Toronto	14	4	0	28	571	326
Winnipeg	9	9	0	18	407	458
Hamilton	9	9	0	18	478	465
Ottawa	2	16	0	4	278	618

Western Division

	W	L	T	Pts	Off	Def
Edmonton	11	7	0	22	477	408
Saskatchewan	11	7	9	22	525	452
British Columbia	10	8	0	20	489	417
Calgary	6	12	0	12	395	476

BASKETBALL

Basketball may be the one sport whose exact origin is definitely known. In the winter of 1891–92, Dr. James Naismith, an instructor in the Y.M.C.A. Training College (now Springfield College) at Springfield, Mass., deliberately invented the game of basketball in order to provide indoor exercise and competition for the students between the closing of the football season and the opening of the baseball season. He affixed peach baskets overhead on the walls at opposite ends of the gymnasium and organized teams to play his new game in which the purpose was to toss an association (soccer) ball into one basket and prevent the opponents from tossing the ball into the other basket. The game is fundamentally the same today, though there have been improvements in equipment and some changes in rules.

Because Dr. Naismith had eighteen available players when he invented the game, the first rule was; "There shall be nine players on each side." Later the number of players became optional, depending upon the size of the available court, but the five-player standard was adopted when the game spread over the country. United States soldiers brought basketball to Europe in World War I, and it soon became a world-wide sport.

College Basketball

NATIONAL COLLEGIATE A.A. CHAMPIONS

1939	Oregon	1951	Kentucky	1963	Loyola (Chicago)	1981	Indiana
1940	Indiana	1952	Kansas	1964	U.C.L.A.	1982	North Carolina
1941	Wisconsin	1953	Indiana	1965	U.C.L.A.	1983	North Carolina State
1942	Stanford	1954	La Salle	1966	Texas Western	1984	Georgetown
1943	Wyoming	1955	San Francisco	1967–73	U.C.L.A.	1985	Villanova
1944	Utah	1956	San Francisco	1974	No. Carolina State	1986	Louisville
1945	Oklahoma A & M	1957	North Carolina	1975	U.C.L.A.	1987	Indiana
1946	Oklahoma A & M	1958	Kentucky	1976	Indiana	1988	Kansas
1947	Holy Cross	1959	California	1977	Marquette	1989	Michigan
1948	Kentucky	1960	Ohio State	1978	Kentucky		
1949	Kentucky	1961	Cincinnati	1979	Michigan State		
1950	C.C.N.Y.	1962	Cincinnati	1980	Louisville		

NATIONAL INVITATION TOURNAMENT (NIT) CHAMPIONS

1939	Long Island U.	1953	Seton Hall	1966	Brigham Young	1979	Indiana
1940	Colorado	1954	Holy Cross	1967	So. Illinois	1980	Virginia
1941	Long Island U.	1955	Duquesne	1968	Dayton	1981	Tulsa
1942	West Virginia	1956	Louisville	1969	Temple	1982	Bradley
1943–44	St. John's (N.Y.C.)	1957	Bradley	1970	Marquette	1983	Fresno State
1945	DePaul	1958	Xavier (Cincinnati)	1971	North Carolina	1984	Michigan
1946	Kentucky	1959	St. John's (N.Y.C.)	1972	Maryland	1985	U.C.L.A.
1947	Utah	1960	Bradley	1973	Virginia Tech	1986	Ohio State
1948	St. Louis	1961	Providence	1974	Purdue	1987	Southern Mississippi
1949	San Francisco	1962	Dayton	1975	Princeton	1988	Connecticut
1950	C.C.N.Y.	1963	Providence	1976	Kentucky	1989	St. John's
1951	Brigham Young	1964	Bradley	1977	St. Bonaventure		
1952	La Salle	1965	St. John's (N.Y.C.)	1978	Texas		

N.C.A.A. MAJOR COLLEGE INDIVIDUAL SCORING RECORDS

Single Season Averages

Player, Team	Year	G	FG	FT	Pts	Avg
Pete Maravich, Louisiana State	1969–70	31	522 [1]	337	1381 [1]	44.5 [1]
Pete Maravich	1968–69	26	433	282	1148	44.2
Pete Maravich	1967–68	26	432	274	1138	43.8
Frank Selvy, Furman	1953–54	29	427	355 [1]	1209	41.7
Johnny Neumann, Mississippi	1970–71	23	366	191	923	40.1
Freeman Williams, Portland State	1976–77	26	417	176	1010	38.8
Billy McGill, Utah	1961–62	26	394	221	1009	38.8
Calvin Murphy, Niagara	1967–68	24	337	242	916	38.2
Austin Carr, Notre Dame	1969–70	29	444	218	1106	38.1

1. Record.

N.C.A.A. CAREER SCORING TOTALS

Division I

Player, Team	Last year	G	FG	FT	Pts	Avg
Pete Maravich, Louisiana State	1970	83	1387 [1]	893 [1]	3667 [1]	44.2 [1]
Austin Carr, Notre Dame	1971	74	1017	526	2560	34.6
Oscar Robertson, Cincinnati	1960	88	1052	869	2973	33.8
Calvin Murphy, Niagara	1970	77	947	654	2548	33.1
Dwight Lamar [2]	1973	57	768	326	1862	32.7
Frank Selvy, Furman	1954	78	922	694	2538	32.5
Rick Mount, Purdue	1970	72	910	503	2323	32.3
Darrel Floyd, Furman	1956	71	868	545	2281	32.1
Nick Werkman, Seton Hall	1964	71	812	649	2273	32.0

1. Record. 2. Also played two seasons in college division.

Division II

Player, Team	Last year	G	FG	FT	Pts	Avg
Travis Grant, Kentucky State	1972	121	1760 [1]	525	4045 [1]	33.4 [1]
John Rinka, Kenyon	1970	99	1261	729	3251	32.8
Florindo Vierira, Quinnipiac	1957	69	761	741	2263	32.8
Willie Shaw, Lane	1964	76	960	459	2379	31.3
Mike Davis, Virginia Union	1969	89	1014	730	2758	31.0
Henry Logan, Western Carolina	1968	107	1263	764	3290	30.7
Willie Scott, Alabama State	1969	103	1277	601	3155	30.6
Gregg Northington, Alabama State	1972	75	894	403	2191	29.2
Bob Hopkins, Grambling	1956	126	1403	953	3759	29.8

1. Record.

TOP SINGLE-GAME SCORING MARKS

Player, Team (Opponent)	Yr	Pts	Player, Team (Opponent)	Yr	Pts
Selvy, Furman (Newberry)	1954	100 [1]	Floyd, Furman (Morehead)	1955	67
Williams, Portland State (Rocky Mtn.)	1978	81	Maravich, LSU (Tulane)	1969	66
Mikvy, Temple (Wilkes)	1951	73	Handlan, W & L (Furman)	1951	66
Williams, Portland State (So. Oregon)	1977	71	Roberts, Oral Roberts (N.C. A&T)	1977	66
Maravich, LSU (Alabama)	1970	69	Williams, Portland State (Geo. Fox Coll.)	1978	66
Murphy, Niagara (Syracuse)	1969	68	Roberts, Oral Roberts (Oregon)	1977	65

1. Record.

MEN'S N.C.A.A. BASKETBALL CHAMPIONSHIPS—1989

DIVISION I

First Round—East

Minnesota 86, Kansas State 75
Siena 80, Stanford 78
West Virginia 84, Tennessee 68
Duke 90, South Carolina State 69
North Carolina State 81, South Carolina 66
Iowa 87, Rutgers 73
Georgetown 50, Princeton 49
Notre Dame 81, Vanderbilt 65

First Round—Southeast

Louisiana Tech 83, LaSalle 74
Oklahoma 72, East Tennessee State 71
Virginia 100, Providence 97
Middle Tennessee State 97, Florida State 83
Michigan 92, Xavier (Ohio) 87
South Alabama 84, Alabama 84
North Carolina 93, Southern, 79
UCLA 84, Iowa State 74

First Round—Midwest

Louisville 76, Arkansas—Little Rock 71
Arkansas 120, Loyola, Calif. 101
Illinois 77, McNeese State 71
Ball State 68, Pittsburgh 64
Syracuse 104, Bucknell 81
Colorado State 68, Florida 46
Missouri 85, Creighton 69
Texas 76, Georgia Tech 70

First Round—West

Arizona 94, Robert Morris 60
Clemson 83, St. Mary's (Calif.) 70
Nevada—Las Vegas 68, Idaho 56
DePaul 66, Memphis State 63
Evansville 94, Oregon State 90 (OT)
Seton Hall 60, Southwest Missouri State 51
Indiana 99, George Mason 85
Texas—El Paso 85, Louisiana State 74

Second Round—East

Duke 70, West Virginia 63
Minnesota 80, Siena 67
Georgetown 81, Notre Dame 74
North Carolina State 102, Iowa 96

Second Round—Southeast

Virginia 104, Middle Tennessee State 88
Oklahoma 124, Louisiana Tech 81
Michigan 91, South Alabama 82
North Carolina 88, UCLA 81

Second Round—Midwest

Louisville 93, Arkansas 84
Illinois 72, Ball State 60
Missouri 108, Texas 89
Syracuse 65, Colorado State 50

Second Round—West

Nevada—Las Vegas 85, Depaul 70
Arizona 94, Clemson 68
Seton Hall 87, Evansville 73
Indiana 92, Texas—El Paso 69

Third Round—East

Duke 87, Minnesota 70
Georgetown 69, North Carolina State 61

Third Round—Southeast

Virginia 86, Oklahoma 80
Michigan 92, North Carolina 87

Third Round—Midwest

Illinois 83, Louisville 69
Syracuse 83, Missouri 80

Third Round—West

Seton Hall 78, Indiana 65
Nevada—Las Vegas 68, Arizona 67

Regional Finals

East—Duke 85, Georgetown 77
Southeast—Michigan 102, Virginia 65
Midwest—Illinois 89, Syracuse 86
West—Seton Hall 84, Nevada—Las Vegas 61

National Semifinals

(Saturday, April 1, 1989, at Seattle, Wash.)

Seton Hall 95, Duke 78
Michigan 83, Illinois 81

National Final

(Monday, April 3, 1989, at Seattle, Wash.)

Michigan 80, Seton Hall 79

DIVISION II
Semifinals

North Carolina Central 90, Jacksonville State 70
Southeast Missouri State 84, Riverside 83

Championship

North Carolina Central 73, Southeast Missouri State 46

DIVISION III
Semifinals

Trenton State 84, Southern Maine 62
Wisconsin—Whitewater 88, Centre 81

Championship

Wisconsin—Whitewater 94, Trenton State 86

WOMEN'S NCAA BASKETBALL CHAMPIONSHIPS—1989

DIVISION I
First Round—East

LaSalle 72, Connecticut 63
West Virginia 66, Western Kentucky 57
James Madison 94, Providence 74
St. Joseph's 82, Vanderbilt 68

First Round—Mideast

Temple 90, Holy Cross 80
Georgia 90, Tennessee—Chattanooga 69
Old Dominion 66, Villanova 41
Rutgers 95, Southern Mississippi 73

First Round—Midwest

Oklahoma St. 93, Miami, Fla. 69
Purdue 91, Arkansas 63
Tennessee Tech 77, South Carolina 73
Illinois State 100, Northwestern Louisiana 79

First Round—West

Bowling Green 69, Cincinnati 59
Washington 87, Hawaii 79
Nevada—Las Vegas 67, Utah 53
Montana 82, California—Fullerton 67

Second Round—East

Tennessee 91, LaSalle 61
Virginia 81, West Virginia 68
Ohio State 81, James Madison 66
Long Beach State 84, St. Joseph's 65

Second Round—Mideast

Auburn 88, Temple 54
Clemson 78, Georgia 65
Mississippi 74, Old Dominion 58
North Carolina State 75, Rutgers 73

Second Round—Midwest

Louisiana Tech 103, Oklahoma State 78
Louisiana State 54, Purdue 53
Iowa 77, Tennessee Tech 75
Stanford 105, Illinois State 77

Second Round—West

Maryland 78, Bowling Green 65
S.F. Austin State 73, Washington 63
Nevada—Las Vegas 84, Colorado 74
Texas 83, Montana 54

Third Round—East

Long Beach State 89, Ohio State 83
Tennessee 80, Virginia 47

Third Round—Mideast

Mississippi 68, North Carolina State 63
Auburn 71, Clemson 60

Third Round—Midwest

Stanford 98, Iowa 74
Louisiana Tech 85, Louisiana State 68

Third Round—West

Maryland 89, S.F. Austin 54
Texas 88, Nevada—Las Vegas 77

Regional—Finals

East—Tennessee 94, Long Beach State 80
Mideast—Auburn 77, Mississippi 51
Midwest—Louisiana Tech 85, Stanford 75
West—Maryland 79, Texas 71

National Semifinals

(Friday, March 31, 1989 at Tacoma, Wash.)

Auburn 76, Louisiana Tech 71
Tennessee 77, Maryland 65

National Championship

(Sunday, April 2, 1989 at Tacoma, Wash.)

Tennessee 76, Auburn 60

DIVISION II
Semifinals

Cal-Poly Pomona 84, Bentley 83 (2OT)
Delta State 94, Central Missouri State 73

Championship

Delta State 88, Cal-Poly Pomona 58

DIVISION III
Semifinals

California—St. Stanislaus 89, Clarkson 74
Elizabethtown 73, Centre 64

Championship

Elizabethtown 66, California—St. Stanislaus 65

LEADING N.C.A.A. SCORERS—1988–1989

Division I

	FG	3-PT FG	FT	Pts	Avg
1. Hank Gathers, Loyola (Cal.)	419	0	177	1015	32.7
2. Chris Jackson, Louisiana St.	359	84	163	965	30.2
3. Lionel Simmons, La Salle	349	21	189	908	28.4
4. Gerald Glass, Mississippi	326	41	148	841	28.0
5. Blue Edwards, East Caro.	297	25	154	773	26.7
6. Raymond Dudley, Air Force	262	105	117	746	26.6
7. Bimbo Coles, Virginia Tech	249	62	157	717	26.6
8. Michael Smith, Brigham Young	286	33	160	765	26.4
9. Stacey King, Oklahoma	324	0	211	859	26.0
10. John Taft, Marshall	245	52	159	701	26.0
11. Jeff Martin, Murray St.	266	65	148	745	25.7
12. Glen Rice, Michigan	363	99	124	949	25.6
13. Kurk Lee, Towson St.	243	80	170	736	25.4
14. Tom Davis, Delaware St.	276	0	154	706	25.2
15. Eric Brown, Miami (Fla.)	255	9	246	765	24.7
16. Terry Brooks, Alabama St.	254	9	195	712	24.6
17. Scott Haffner, Evansville	263	98	136	760	24.5
18. Bailey Alston, Liberty	267	14	97	645	23.9
19. Dana Barros, Boston College	230	112	120	692	23.9
20. Chris Cheeks, Va. Commonwealth	246	49	126	667	23.8
21. John Rankin, Drexel	266	0	130	662	23.6
22. Jim Barton, Dartmouth	205	98	103	611	23.5
23. Sydney Grider, Southwestern La.	222	122	114	680	23.4
24. Jay Taylor, Eastern Ill.	271	56	150	748	23.4
25. Jeff Sanders, Ga. Southern	279	0	116	674	23.2

NATIONAL ASSOCIATION OF INTERCOLLEGIATE ATHLETICS—1989

MEN'S TOURNAMENT
Round of 16

St. Mary's (Texas), 56, Cumberland (Ky) 40
East Central (Okla) 83, Wayland Baptist 68
Wisconsin—Eau Claire 86, Washburn (Kan) 71
Central Washington 66, Charleston (SC) 55
Idaho 68, Western Montana 63
Siena Heights (Mich) 78, St. Ambrose 75
Wheeling Jesuit (W.Va.) 99, Drury (Mo.) 72
Hastings (Neb) 73, Auburn-Montgomery 63

Quarterfinals

St. Mary's (Texas) 81, Idaho 68
East Central (Okla.) 77, Siena Heights (Mich.) 67
Wisconsin—Eau Claire 88, Hastings (Neb.) 73
Central Washington 87, Wheeling Jesuit 78

Semifinals

St. Mary's (Texas) 60, Central Washington 58
East Central (Okla.) 58, Wisconsin—Eau Claire 54

Championship

St. Mary's (Texas) 61, East Central (Okla.) 58

WOMEN'S TOURNAMENT
Round of 16

St. Ambrose (Iowa) 111, St. Thomas Aquinas (N.Y.) 75
Claflin (S.C.) 114, Glenville State (W.Va.) 59

Arkansas Tech 80, Fresno Pacific (Calif.) 40
Doane (Neb.) 68, Wingate (N.C.) 65
Central State (Ohio) 73, Washburn (Kan) 67
Western Washington 89, Minnesota—Duluth 73
Wayland Baptist (Texas) 81, Union (Tenn) 70
Southern Nazarene (Okla) 87, Tri State (Ind) 67

Quarterfinals

St. Ambrose 90, Doane 69
Claflin 91, Central State 85
Arkansas Tech 78, Wayland Baptist 66
Southern Nazarene 92, Western Washington 68

Semifinals

Claflin 90, St. Ambrose 89
Southern Nazarene 73, Arkansas Tech 57

Championship

Southern Nazarene 98, Claflin 96

NATIONAL INVITATION TOURNAMENT (N.I.T.)—1989

Semifinals

(March 27, 1989, at Madison Square Garden, N.Y.)

St. John's 76, Alabama—Birmingham 65
St. Louis 74, Michigan State 64

Championships

(March 29, 1989, at Madison Square Garden, N.Y.)

St. John's 73, St. Louis 65

N.C.A.A. LEADING REBOUNDERS—1988-1989

	Games	No.	Avg
1. Hank Gathers, Loyola (Cal.)	31	426	13.7
2. Tyrone Hill, Xavier (Ohio)	33	403	12.2
3. Ron Draper, American	28	336	12.0
4. Daryl Battles, Southern-B.R.	31	360	11.6
5. Lionel Simmons, La Salle	32	365	11.4
6. Derrick Coleman, Syracuse	37	422	11.4
7. Fred Burton, LIU-Brooklyn	28	309	11.0
8. Rodney Mack, South Caro. St.	33	361	10.9
9. Kenny Sanders, George Mason	30	326	10.9
10. Rico Washington, Weber St.	28	303	10.8
11. Hakim Shahid, South Fla.	28	302	10.8
12. Clarence Weatherspoon, Southrn Miss	27	289	10.7
13. Rondey Robinson, Wright St.	28	299	10.7
14. Ed Horton, Iowa	33	350	10.6
15. Shaun Vandiver, Colorado	28	295	10.5
16. Randy White, Louisiana Tech	32	337	10.5
17. Anthony Bonner, St. Louis	37	386	10.4
18. Demetrius Laffitte, U.S. Int'l	27	280	10.4
19. Kerry Hammonds, Middle Tenn. St.	31	319	10.3
20. Warren Bradley, Cleveland St.	28	287	10.3
21. Stanley Brundy, DePaul	33	336	10.2
22. Eric McArthur, UC Santa Barb.	30	304	10.1
23. Anthony Smith, Western Ky.	28	282	10.1
24. Stacey King, Oklahoma	33	332	10.1
25. Larry Stewart, Coppin St.	28	280	10.0

Professional Basketball

NATIONAL BASKETBALL ASSOCIATION CHAMPIONS

Source: Matt Winick, Director of Media Information, National Basketball Association.

The National Basketball Association was originally the Basketball Association of America. It took its current name in 1949 when it merged with the National Basketball League.

Season	Eastern Conference (W-L)	Western Conference (W-L)	Playoff Champions[1]
1946–47	Washington Capitols (49–11)	Chicago Stags (39–22)	Philadelphia Warriors
1947–48	Philadelphia Warriors (27–21)	St. Louis Bombers (29–19)	Baltimore Bullets
1948–49	Washington Capitols (38–22)	Rochester Royals (45–15)	Minneapolis Lakers
1949–50	Syracuse Nationals (51–13)	Indianapolis Olympians (39–25)	Minneapolis Lakers
1950–51	Philadelphia Warriors (40–26)	Minneapolis Lakers (44–24)	Rochester Royals
1951–52	Syracuse Nationals (40–26)	Rochester Royals (41–25)	Minneapolis Lakers
1952–53	New York Knickerbockers (47–23)	Minneapolis Lakers (48–22)	Minneapolis Lakers
1953–54	New York Knickerbockers (44–28)	Minneapolis Lakers (46–26)	Minneapolis Lakers
1954–55	Syracuse Nationals (43–29)	Ft. Wayne Pistons (43–29)	Syracuse Nationals
1955–56	Philadelphia Warriors (45–27)	Ft. Wayne Pistons (37–35)	Philadelphia Warriors
1956–57	Boston Celtics (44–28)	St. Louis Hawks (38–34)	Boston Celtics
1957–58	Boston Celtics (48–23)	St. Louis Hawks (41–31)	St. Louis Hawks
1958–59	Boston Celtics (52–20)	St. Louis Hawks (49–23)	Boston Celtics
1959–60	Boston Celtics (59–16)	St. Louis Hawks (46–29)	Boston Celtics
1960–61	Boston Celtics (57–22)	St. Louis Hawks (51–28)	Boston Celtics
1961–62	Boston Celtics (60–20)	Los Angeles Lakers (54–26)	Boston Celtics
1962–63	Boston Celtics (58–22)	Los Angeles Lakers (53–27)	Boston Celtics
1963–64	Boston Celtics (59–21)	San Francisco Warriors (48–32)	Boston Celtics
1964–65	Boston Celtics (62–18)	Los Angeles Lakers (49–31)	Boston Celtics
1965–66	Philadelphia 76ers (55–25)	Los Angeles Lakers (45–35)	Boston Celtics
1966–67	Philadelphia 76ers (68–13)	San Francisco Warriors (44–37)	Philadelphia 76ers
1967–68	Philadelphia 76ers (62–20)	St. Louis Hawks (56–26)	Boston Celtics
1968–69	Baltimore Bullets (57–25)	Los Angeles Lakers (55–27)	Boston Celtics
1969–70	New York Knickerbockers (60–22)	Atlanta Hawks (48–34)	New York Knicks
1970–71	Baltimore Bullets (42–40)	Milwaukee Bucks (66–16)	Milwaukee Bucks
1971–72	New York Knickerbockers (48–34)	Los Angeles Lakers (69–13)	Los Angeles Lakers
1972–73	New York Knickerbockers (57–25)	Los Angeles Lakers (69–22)	New York Knicks
1973–74	Boston Celtics (56–26)	Milwaukee Bucks (59–23)	Boston Celtics
1974–75	Washington Bullets (60–22)	Golden State Warriors (48–34)	Golden State Warriors
1975–76	Boston Celtics (54–28)	Phoenix Suns (42–40)	Boston Celtics

Season	Eastern Conference (W-L)	Western Conference (W-L)	Playoff Champions[1]
1976–77	Philadelphia 76ers (50–32)	Portland Trail Blazers (49–33)	Portland Trail Blazers
1977–78	Washington Bullets (44–38)	Seattle Super Sonics (47–35)	Washington Bullets
1978–79	Washington Bullets (54–28)	Seattle Super Sonics (52–30)	Seattle Super Sonics
1979–80	Philadelphia 76ers (59–23)	Los Angeles Lakers (60–22)	Los Angeles Lakers
1980–81	Boston Celtics (62–20)	Phoenix Suns (57–25)	Boston Celtics
1981–82	Boston Celtics (63–19)	Houston Rockets (46–36)	Boston Celtics
1982–83	Philadelphia 76ers (65–17)	Los Angeles Lakers (58–24)	Philadelphia 76ers
1983–84	Boston Celtics (56–26)	Los Angeles Lakers (58–24)	Boston Celtics
1984–85	Boston Celtics (63–19)	Los Angeles Lakers (62–20)	Los Angeles Lakers
1985–86	Boston Celtics (67–15)	Houston Rockets (51–31)	Boston Celtics
1986–87	Boston Celtics (59–23)	Los Angeles Lakers (65-17)	Los Angeles Lakers
1987–88	Detroit Pistons (54–28)	Los Angeles Lakers (62–20)	Los Angeles Lakers
1988–89	Detroit Pistons (63–18)	Los Angeles Lakers (57–25)	Detroit Pistons

1. Playoffs may involve teams other than conference winners.

INDIVIDUAL N.B.A. SCORING CHAMPIONS

Season	Player, Team	G	FG	FT	Pts	Avg
1953–54	Neil Johnston, Philadelphia Warriors	72	591	577	1759	24.4
1954–55	Neil Johnston, Philadelphia Warriors	72	521	589	1631	22.7
1955–56	Bob Pettit, St. Louis Hawks	72	646	557	1849	25.7
1956–57	Paul Arizin, Philadelphia Warriors	71	613	591	1817	25.6
1957–58	George Yardley, Detroit Pistons	72	673	655	2001	27.8
1958–59	Bob Pettit, St. Louis Hawks	72	719	667	2105	29.2
1959–60	Wilt Chamberlain, Philadelphia Warriors	72	1065	577	2707	37.6
1960–61	Wilt Chamberlain, Philadelphia Warriors	79	1251	531	3033	38.4
1961–62	Wilt Chamberlain, Philadelphia Warriors	80	1597	835	4029	50.4
1962–63	Wilt Chamberlain, San Francisco Warriors	80	1463	660	3586	44.8
1963–64	Wilt Chamberlain, San Francisco Warriors	80	1204	540	2948	36.9
1964–65	Wilt Chamberlain, San Francisco Warriors-Phila. 76ers	73	1063	408	2534	34.7
1965–66	Wilt Chamberlain, Philadelphia 76ers	79	1074	501	2649	33.5
1966–67	Rick Barry, San Francisco Warriors	78	1011	753	2775	35.6
1967–68	Dave Bing, Detroit Pistons	79	835	472	2142	27.1
1968–69	Elvin Hayes, San Diego Rockets	82	930	467	2327	28.4
1969–70	Jerry West, Los Angeles Lakers	74	831	647	2309	31.2
1970–71	Lew Alcindor,[1] Milwaukee Bucks	82	1063	470	2596	31.7
1971–72	Kareem Abdul-Jabbar, Milwaukee Bucks	81	1159	504	2822	34.8
1972–73	Nate Archibald, Kansas City-Omaha Kings	80	1028	663	2719	34.0
1973–74	Bob McAdoo, Buffalo Braves	74	901	459	2261	30.8
1974–75	Bob McAdoo, Buffalo Braves	82	1095	641	2831	34.5
1975–76	Bob McAdoo, Buffalo Braves	78	934	559	2427	31.1
1976–77	Pete Maravich, New Orleans Jazz	73	886	501	2273	31.1
1977–78	George Gervin, San Antonio Spurs	82	864	504	2232	27.2
1978–79	George Gervin, San Antonio	80	947	471	2365	29.6
1979–80	George Gervin, San Antonio	78	1024	505	2585	33.1
1980–81	Adrian Dantley, Utah Jazz	80	909	632	2452	30.7
1981–82	George Gervin, San Antonio	79	993	555	2551	32.3
1982–83	Alex English, Denver Nuggets	82	959	406	2326	28.4
1983–84	Adrian Dantley, Utah Jazz	79	802	813	2418	30.6
1984–85	Bernard King, New York Knicks	55	691	426	1809	32.9
1985–86	Dominique Wilkins, Atlanta Hawks	78	888	527	2366	30.3
1986–87	Michael Jordan, Chicago Bulls[2]	82	1098	833	3041	37.1
1987–88	Michael Jordan, Chicago Bulls[3]	82	1069	723	2868	35.0
1988–89	Michael Jordan, Chicago Bulls[4]	81	966	674	2633	32.5

1. (Kareem Abdul-Jabbar). 2. Also had 12 3-point field goals. 3. Also had 7 3-point field goals. 4. Also had 27 3-point field goals.

N.B.A. LIFETIME LEADERS
(Through 1988–1989 season)

Scoring

	Yrs	FG	FT	Pts
Kareem Abdul Jabbar	20	15,837	6,712	38,387
Wilt Chamberlain	14	12,681	5,356	31,419
Julius Erving*	16	11,818	6,256	30,026
Dan Issel*	15	10,421	6,591	27,482
Elvin Hayes	16	10,976	5,356	27,313
Oscar Robertson	14	9,508	7,694	26,710
George Gervin*	14	11,362	2,737	26,595
John Havlicek	16	10,513	5,369	26,395
Moses Malone*	15	9,272	7,414	25,511
Rick Barry*	14	9,695	5,713	25,279
Jerry West	14	9,016	7,160	25,192
Artis Gilmore*	17	9,431	6,132	24,941
(a) Alex English	13	9,702	3,997	23,417
Elgin Baylor	14	8,693	5,763	23,149
(a) Adrian Dantley	13	7,919	6,614	22,458
Hal Greer	15	8,504	4,578	21,686
Walt Bellamy	14	7,914	5,113	20,941
Bob Petit	11	7,349	6,182	20,880
Dolph Shayes	16	6,135	6,979	19,249
Gail Goodrich	14	7,431	4,319	19,181

*Includes games played in the American Basketball Association. (a) Active player.

Scoring Average
(400 games or 10,000 points minimum)

	Games	Pts	Avg
(a) Michael Jordan	345	11,263	32.6
Wilt Chamberlain	1,045	31,419	30.1
Elgin Baylor	846	23,149	27.4
Jerry West	932	25,192	27.0
Bob Petit	792	20,880	26.4
(a) Dominique Wilkins	559	14,557	26.0
Oscar Robertson	1,040	26,710	25.7
George Gervin*	1,060	26,595	25.1
(a) Larry Bird	717	17,899	25.0
(a) Adrian Dantley	900	22,458	25.0

(a) Active player. *Includes games played in the American Basketball Association.

Free Throw Percentage
(1,200 free throws made, minimum)

	FTA	FTM	Pct
Rick Barry	6,317	5,713	.904
Calvin Murphy	3,864	3,445	.892
Bill Sharman	3,559	3,143	.883
(a) Larry Bird	3,783	3,328	.880
(a) Kiki Vanderweghe	3,514	3,058	.870
Mike Newlin	3,456	3,005	.870
(a) Jeff Malone	1,938	1,682	.868
(a) John Long	1,996	1,719	.861
Fred Brown	2,211	1,896	.858
Ricky Pierce	1,498	1,284	.857

(a) Active player. *Includes games played in the American Basketball Association.

Rebounds

Wilt Chamberlain	23,924
Bill Russell	21,620
Kareem Abdul Jabbar	17,440
Artis Gilmore*	16,330
Elvin Hayes	16,279
(a) Moses Malone*	15,293
Nate Thurmond	14,644
Walt Bellamy	14,241
Wes Unseld	13,769
Jerry Lucas	12,942

(a) Active player. *Includes games played in the American Basketball Association.

Field Goal Percentage
(2,000 field goals minimum)

	FGA	FGM	Pct
(a) James Donaldson	4,015	2,356	.587
Artis Gilmore*	16,158	9,403	.582
(a) Charles Barkley	5,252	3,032	.577
(a) Steve Johnson	4,810	2,759	.574
(a) Darryl Dawkins	6,079	3,477	.572
(a) Kevin McHale	8,958	5,057	.565
(a) Jeff Ruland	3,685	2,080	.564
(a) Kareem Abdul-Jabbar	28,307	15,837	.559
(a) Larry Nance	7,329	4,081	.557
(a) James Worthy	7,464	4,151	.556

*Includes games played in the American Basketball Association. (a) Active player.

Assists

Oscar Robertson	9,887
(a) Earvin Johnson	8,025
Len Wilkins	7,211
Bob Cousy	6,955
Guy Rodgers	6,917
Nate Archibald	6,476
(a) Norm Nixon	6,386
Jerry West	6,238
(a) Isiah Thomas	6,220
(a) John Lucas	6,216

(a) Active player.

N.B.A. MOST VALUABLE PLAYERS

1956	Bob Pettit
1957	Bob Cousy
1958	Bill Russell
1959	Bob Pettit
1960	Wilt Chamberlain
1961–63	Bill Russell
1964	Oscar Robertson
1965	Bill Russell
1966–68	Wilt Chamberlain
1969	Wes Unseld
1970	Willis Reed

1971–72	Lew Alcindor (Kareem Abdul-Jabbar)
1973	Dave Cowens
1974	Kareem Abdul-Jabbar, Milwaukee
1975	Bob McAdoo, Buffalo
1976–77	Kareem Abdul-Jabbar, Los Angeles
1978	Bill Walton, Portland
1979	Moses Malone, Houston
1980	Kareem Abdul-Jabbar, Los Angeles

1981	Julius Erving, Philadelphia
1982	Moses Malone, Houston
1983	Moses Malone, Philadelphia
1984	Larry Bird, Boston
1985	Larry Bird, Boston
1986	Larry Bird, Boston
1987	Earvin Johnson, Los Angeles
1988	Michael Jordan, Chicago
1989	Earvin Johnson, Los Angeles

N.B.A. TEAM RECORDS

Most points, game—186, Detroit vs. Denver, 3 overtimes, 1983
Most points, quarter—58, Buffalo vs. Boston, 1968
Most points, half—97, Atlanta vs. San Diego, 1970
Most points, overtime period—22, Detroit vs. Cleveland, 1973
Most field goals, game—74, Detroit, 1983
Most field goals, quarter—23, Boston, 1959; Buffalo, 1972
Most field goals, half—40, Boston, 1959; Syracuse, 1963; Atlanta, 1979
Most assists, game—53, Milwaukee, 1978
Most rebounds, game—109, Boston 1960
Most points, both teams, game—370

(Detroit 186, Denver 184) 3 overtimes, Denver, December 13, 1983
Most points, both teams, quarter—96 (Boston 52, Minneapolis 44), 1959; (Detroit 53, Cincinnati 43), 1972
Most points, both teams, half—170 (Philadelphia 90, Cincinnati 80), Philadelphia, 1971
Longest winning streak—33, Los Angeles, 1971–72
Longest losing streak—20, Philadelphia, 1973
Longest winning streak at home—36, Philadelphia, 1966–67
Most games won, season—69, Los Angeles, 1971–72
Most games lost, season—73, Philadelphia, 1972–73
Highest average points per game—126.5, Denver, 1981–82

N.B.A. INDIVIDUAL RECORDS

Most points, game—100, Wilt Chamberlain, Philadelphia vs. New York at Hershey, Pa., 1962

Most points, quarter—33, George Gervin, San Antonio, 1978

Most points, half—59, Wilt Chamberlain, Philadelphia, 1962

Most free throws, game—28, Wilt Chamberlain, Philadelphia, vs. New York at Hershey, Pa. 1962; 28, Adrian Dantley, Utah, vs. Houston, 1984

Most free throws, quarter—14, Rick Barry, San Francisco, 1966

Most free throws, half—19, Oscar Robertson, Cincinnati, 1964

Most field goals, game—36, Wilt Chamberlain, Philadelphia, 1962

Most consecutive field goals, game—18, Wilt Chamberlain, San Francisco, 1963; Wilt Chamberlain, Philadelphia, 1967

Most assists, game—29, Kevin Porter, New Jersey Nets, 1978

Most rebounds, game—55, Wilt Chamberlain, Philadelphia, 1963

NATIONAL BASKETBALL ASSOCIATION
FINAL STANDINGS OF THE CLUBS—1988-1989

EASTERN CONFERENCE
Atlantic Division

	W	L	Pct	Games behind
New York Knicks	52	30	.634	—
Philadelphia 76ers	46	36	.561	6
Boston Celtics	42	40	.512	10
Washington Bullets	40	42	.488	12
New Jersey Nets	26	56	.317	26
Charlotte Hornets	20	62	.244	32

Central Division

	W	L	Pct	Games behind
Detroit Pistons	63	19	.768	—
Cleveland Cavaliers	57	25	.695	6
Atlanta Hawks	52	30	.634	11
Milwaukee Bucks	49	33	.598	14
Chicago Bulls	47	35	.573	16
Indiana Pacers	28	54	.341	35

WESTERN CONFERENCE
Midwest Division

	W	L	Pct	Games behind
Utah Jazz	51	31	.622	—
Houston Rockets	45	37	.549	6
Denver Nuggets	44	38	.537	7
Dallas Mavericks	38	44	.463	13
San Antonio Spurs	21	61	.256	30
Miami Heat	15	67	.183	36

Pacific Division

	W	L	Pct	Games behind
Los Angeles Lakers	57	25	.695	—
Phoenix Suns	55	27	.671	2
Seattle SuperSonics	47	35	.573	10
Golden State Warriors	43	39	.524	14
Portland Trail Blazers	39	43	.476	18
Sacramento Kings	27	55	.329	30
Los Angeles Clippers	21	61	.256	36

N.B.A. PLAYOFFS—1989

EASTERN CONFERENCE
First Round

New York defeated Philadelphia, 3 games to 0
Detroit defeated Boston, 3 games to 0
Milwaukee defeated Atlanta, 3 games to 2
Chicago defeated Cleveland, 3 games to 2

Semifinal Round

Chicago defeated New York, 4 games to 2
Detroit defeated Milwaukee, 4 games to 0

Conference Finals

Detroit defeated Chicago, 4 games to 2
May 21—Chicago 94, Detroit 88
May 23—Detroit 100, Chicago 91
May 27—Chicago 99, Detroit 97
May 29—Detroit 86, Chicago 80
May 31—Detroit 94, Chicago 85
June 2—Detroit 103, Chicago 94

WESTERN CONFERENCE
First Round

Los Angeles Lakers defeated Portland, 3 games to 0
Utah defeated Golden State, 3 games to 0
Phoenix defeated Denver, 3 games to 0
Seattle defeated Houston, 3 games to 1

Semifinal Round

Phoenix defeated Golden State, 4 games to 1
Los Angeles Lakers defeated Seattle, 4 games to 0

Conference Finals

Los Angeles Lakers defeated Phoenix, 4 games to 0
May 20—Los Angeles 127, Phoenix 119
May 23—Los Angeles 101, Phoenix 95
May 26—Los Angeles 110, Phoenix 107
May 28—Los Angeles 122, Phoenix 117

CHAMPIONSHIP

Detroit defeated Los Angeles, 4 games to 0
June 6—Detroit 109, Los Angeles 97
June 8—Detroit 108, Los Angeles 105
June 11—Detroit 114, Los Angeles 110
June 13—Detroit 105, Los Angeles 97

LEADING SCORERS—1988–1989

	G	FG	FT	Pts	Avg
Michael Jordan, Chicago	81	966	674	2633	32.5
Karl Malone, Utah	80	809	703	2326	29.1
Dale Ellis, Seattle	82	857	377	2253	27.5
Clyde Drexler, Portland	78	829	438	2123	27.2
Chris Mullin, Golden State	82	830	493	2176	26.5
Alex English, Denver	82	924	325	2175	26.5
Dominique Wilkins, Atlanta	80	814	442	2099	26.2
Charles Barkley, Philadelphia	79	700	602	2037	25.8
Tom Chambers, Phoenix	81	774	509	2085	25.7
Akeem Olajuwon, Houston	82	790	454	2034	24.8
Terry Cummings, Milwaukee	80	730	362	1829	22.9
Patrick Ewing, New York	80	727	361	1815	22.7
Kelly Tripuka, Charlotte	71	568	440	1606	22.6
Kevin McHale, Boston	78	661	436	1758	22.5
Magic Johnson, L.A. Lakers	77	579	513	1730	22.5
Mitch Richmond, Golden State	79	649	410	1741	22.0
Jeff Malone, Washington	76	677	296	1851	21.7
Chuck Person, Indiana	80	711	243	1728	21.6
Eddie Johnson, Phoenix	70	608	217	1504	21.5
Bernard King, Washington	81	654	361	1674	20.7

STEALS LEADERS—1988–1989

(Minimum 70 games or 125 steals)

	G	Stl	Avg
John Stockton, Utah	82	263	3.21
Alvin Robertson, San Antonio	65	197	3.03
Michael Jordan, Chicago	81	234	2.89
Fats Lever, Denver	71	195	2.75
Clyde Drexler, Portland	78	213	2.73
Akeem Olajuwon, Houston	82	213	2.60
Glenn Rivers, Atlanta	76	181	2.38
Ron Harper, Cleveland	82	185	2.26
Garland, Golden State	79	175	2.22
Lester Conner, New Jersey	82	181	2.21

ASSISTS LEADERS—1988–1989

(Minimum 70 games or 400 assists)

	G	No.	Avg
John Stockton, Utah	82	1118	13.6
Magic Johnson, L.A. Lakers	77	988	12.8
Ken Johnson, Phoenix	81	991	12.2
Terry Porter, Portland	81	770	9.5
Nate McMillian, Seattle	75	696	9.3
Sleepy Floyd, Houston	82	709	8.6
Mark Jackson, New York	72	619	8.6
Mark Price, Cleveland	75	631	8.4
Isiah Thomas, Detroit	80	663	8.3
Michael Jordan, Chicago	81	650	8.0

BLOCKED-SHOTS LEADERS—1988–1989

(Minimum 70 games or 100 blocked shots)

	G	No.	Avg
Manute Bol, Golden State	80	345	4.31
Mark Eaton, Utah	82	315	3.84
Patrick Ewing, New York	80	281	3.51
Akeem Olajuwon, Houston	82	282	3.44
Larry Nance, Cleveland	73	206	2.82
Benoit Benjamin, L.A. Clippers	79	221	2.80
Wayne Cooper, Denver	79	211	2.67
West, Phoenix	82	187	2.28
Alton Lister, Seattle	82	180	2.20
Smits, Indiana	82	151	1.84

FIELD-GOAL LEADERS—1988–1989

(Minimum 300 FG made)

	FG	Att	Pct
Dennis Rodman, Detroit	316	531	.595
Charles Barkley, Philadelphia	700	1,208	.579
Robert Parish, Boston	596	1,045	.570
Patrick Ewing, New York	727	1,282	.567
James Worthy, L.A. Lakers	702	1,282	.548
Kevin McHale, Boston	661	1,211	.546
Otis Thorpe, Houston	521	961	.542
Benoit Benjamin, L.A. Clippers	491	907	.541
Larry Nance, Cleveland	496	920	.539
John Stockton, Utah	497	923	.538

FREE-THROW LEADERS—1988–1989

(Minimum 125 FT made)

	FT	Att	Pct
Magic Johnson, L.A. Lakers	513	563	.911
Jack Sikma, Milwaukee	266	294	.905
Scott Skiles, Indiana	130	144	.903
Mark Price, Cleveland	263	292	.901
Chris Mullin, Golden State	493	553	.892
Ken Johnson, Phoenix	508	576	.882
Joe Kleine, Boston	134	152	.882
Walter Davis, Denver	175	199	.879
Mike Gminski, Philadelphia	297	341	.871
Jeff Malone, Washington	296	340	.871

REBOUND LEADERS—1988–1989

(Minimum 70 games or 800 rebounds)

	G	Off	Def	Total	Avg
Akeem Olajuwon, Houston	82	338	767	1105	13.5
Charles Barkley, Philadelphia	79	403	583	986	12.5
Robert Parrish, Boston	80	342	654	996	12.5
Moses Malone, Atlanta	81	386	570	956	11.8
Karl Malone, Utah	80	259	594	853	10.7
Charles Oakley, New York	82	343	518	861	10.5
Mark Eaton, Utah	82	227	616	843	10.3
Otis Thorpe, Houston	82	272	515	787	9.6
Bill Laimbeer, Detroit	81	138	638	776	9.6
Michael Cage, Seattle	80	276	489	765	9.6

3-POINT FIELD-GOAL LEADERS 1988–1989

(Minimum 25 made)

	FG	Att	Pct
Jon Sundvold, Miami	48	92	.522
Dale Ellis, Seattle	162	339	.478
Mark Price, Cleveland	93	211	.441
Hershey Hawkins, Philadelphia	71	166	.428
Craig Hodges, Chicago	75	180	.417
Eddie Johnson, Phoenix	71	172	.413
Berry, Sacramento	65	160	.406
Pressley, Sacramento	119	295	.403
Miller, Indiana	98	244	.402
Byron Scott, L.A. Lakers	77	193	.399

Sports Personalities

A name in parentheses is the original name or form of name. Localities are places of birth. Dates of birth appear as month/day/year. **Boldface** years in parentheses are dates of **(birth-death)**.
Information has been gathered from many sources, including the individuals themselves. However, the *Information Please Almanac* cannot guarantee the accuracy of every individual item.

Aaron, Hank (Henry) (baseball); Mobile, Ala., 2/5/1934
Aaron, Tommie (baseball); Mobile, Ala. **(1939–1984)**
Abdul-Jabbar, Kareem (Lewis Ferdinand Alcindor, Jr.) (basketball); New York City, 4/16/1947
Adderly, Herbert A. (football); Philadelphia, 6/8/1939
Affleck, Francis (auto racing) **(1951-1985)**
Alcindor, Lew. *See* Abdul-Jabbar
Ali, Muhammad (Cassius Clay) (boxing); Louisville, Ky., 1/18/1942
Allen, Dick (Richard Anthony) (baseball); Wampum, Pa., 3/8/1942
Allison, Bobby (Robert Arthur) (auto racing); Hueytown, Ala., 12/3/1937
Alston, Walter (baseball); Venice, Ohio **(1911-1984)**
Alworth, Lance (football); Houston, 8/3/1940
Ameche, Alan (football); Houston, Tex. **(1933-1988)**
Anderson, Donny (Gary Donny) (football); Brooklyn, N.Y., 4/3/1949
Anderson, Ken (football); Batavia, Ill., 2/15/1949
Anderson, Sparky (George) (baseball); Bridgewater, S.D., 2/22/1934
Andretti, Mario (auto racing); Montona, Trieste, Italy, 2/28/1940
Anthony, Earl (bowling); Kent, Wash., 4/27/1938
Appling, Luke (baseball); High Point, N.C., 4/2/1907
Arcaro, Eddie (George Edward) (jockey); Cincinnati, 2/19/1916
Ashe, Arthur (tennis); Richmond, Va., 7/10/1943
Austin, Tracy (tennis); Rolling Hills, Calif., 12/2/1962
Averill, Earl (baseball); Everett, Wash. **(1915–1983)**
Babashoff, Shirley (swimming); Whittier, Calif., 1/31/1957
Baer, Max (boxing); Omaha, Neb. **(1909-1959)**
Bakken, Jim (James Leroy) (football); Madison, Wis., 11/2/1940
Banks, Ernie (baseball); Dallas, 1/31/1931
Bannister, Roger (runner); Harrow, England, 3/24/1929
Barkley, Charles (basketball); Leeds, Ala., 2/20/1963
Barry, Rick (Richard) (basketball); Elizabeth, N.J., 3/28/1944
Bauer, Hank (Henry) (baseball); East St. Louis, Ill., 7/31/1922
Baugh, Sammy (football); Temple, Tex., 3/17/1914
Bayi, Filbert (runner); Karratu, Tanganyika, 6/23/1953
Baylor, Elgin (basketball); Washington, D.C., 9/16/1934
Beamon, Bob (long jumper); New York City, 8/2/1946
Becker, Boris (tennis); Leiman, W. Germany, 11/22/1967
Bee, Clair (basketball); Cleveland, Ohio **(1896–1983)**
Beliveau, Jean (hockey); Three Rivers, Quebec, Canada, 8/31/1931
Bell, Rickey (football); Inglewood, Calif. **(1949-1984)**
Beman, Deane (golf); Washington, D.C., 4/22/1938
Bench, Johnny (Johnny Lee) (baseball); Oklahoma City, 12/7/1947
Berg, Patty (Patricia Jane) (golf); Minneapolis, 2/13/1918
Berning, Susie Maxwell (golf); Pasadena, Calif., 7/22/1941
Berra, Yogi (Lawrence) (baseball); St. Louis, 5/12/1925
Biletnikoff, Frederick (football); Erie, Pa., 2/23/1943
Bird, Larry (basketball); French Lick, Ind., 12/7/1956
Blaik, Earl H. (football); Detroit, 2/15/1897
Blanda, George Frederick (football); Youngwood, Pa., 9/17/1927
Blue, Vida (baseball); Mansfield, La., 7/28/1949
Borg, Björn (tennis); Stockholm, 6/6/1956
Boros, Julius (golf); Fairfield, Conn., 3/3/1920
Bossy, Mike (hockey); Montreal, 1/22/1957
Boston, Ralph (long jumper); Laurel, Miss., 5/9/1939
Bradley, Bill (William Warren) (basketball); Crystal City, Mo., 7/28/1943
Bradshaw, Terry (football); Shreveport, La., 9/2/1948
Brathwaite, Chris (track); Eugene, Ore. **(1949-1984)**
Breedlove, Craig (Norman) (speed driving); Los Angeles, 3/23/1938
Brett, George (baseball); Glendale, W. Va., 5/15/1953
Brewer, James (Jim) (baseball); Merced, Calif. **(1937-1987)**
Brock, Louis Clark (baseball); El Dorado, Ark., 6/18/1939
Brown, Jimmy (football); St. Simon Island, Ga., 2/17/1936
Brown, Larry (football); Clairton, Pa., 9/19/1947
Brumel, Valeri (high jumper); Tolbuzino, Siberia, 4/14/1942
Bryant, Paul "Bear" (football); Tuscaloosa, Ala. **(1913–1983)**
Bryant, Rosalyn Evette (track); Chicago, 1/7/1956
Burton, Michael (swimming); Des Moines, Iowa, 7/3/1947
Butkus, Dick (Richard Marvin) (football); Chicago, 12/9/1942
Campanella, Roy (baseball); Homestead, Pa., 11/19/1921
Campbell, Earl (football); Tyler, Tex., 3/29/1955
Caponi, Donna Maria (golf); Detroit, 1/29/1945
Cappelletti, Gino (football); Keewatin, Minn., 3/26/1934
Carew, Rod (Rodney Cline) (baseball); Gatun, Panama, 10/1/1945
Carlos, John (sprinter); New York City, 6/5/1945

Carlton, Steven Norman (baseball); Miami, Fla., 12/22/1944
Carner, Joanne Gunderson (Mrs. Don) (golf); Kirkland, Wash., 3/4/1939
Casals, Rosemary (tennis); San Francisco, 9/16/1948
Casper, Billy (golf); San Diego, Calif., 6/24/1931
Caulkins, Tracy (swimming); Wimona, Minn., 1/11/63
Cauthen, Steve (jockey); Covington, Ky., 5/1/1960
Chamberlain, Wilt (Wilton) (basketball); Philadelphia, 8/21/1936
Chapot, Frank (equestrian); Camden, N.J., 2/24/1934
Chinaglia, Giorgio (soccer); Carrara, Italy, 1/24/1947
Clarke, Bobby (Robert Earle) (hockey); Flin Flon, Manitoba, Canada, 8/13/1949
Clay, Cassius. *See* Ali, Muhammad
Clemente, Roberto Walker (baseball); Carolina, Puerto Rico **(1934-1972)**
Cobb, Tyrus Raymond (Ty) (baseball); Narrows, Ga. **(1886-1961)**
Cochran, Barbara Ann (skiing); Claremont, N.H., 1/4/1951
Cochran, Marilyn (skiing); Burlington, Vt., 2/7/1950
Cochran, Robert (skiing); Claremont, N.H., 12/11/1951
Coe, Sebastian Newbold (track); London, England, 9/29/1956
Colavito, Rocky (Rocco Domenico) (baseball); New York City, 8/10/1933
Comaneci, Nadia (gymnast); Onesti, Romania, 11/12/1961
Connors, Jimmy (James Scott) (tennis); East St. Louis, Ill., 9/2/1952
Cordero, Angel (jockey); Santurce, Puerto Rico, 5/8/1942
Cournoyer, Yvan Serge (hockey); Drummondville, Quebec, Canada, 11/22/1943
Court, Margaret Smith (tennis); Albury, New South Wales, Australia, 7/16/1942
Cousy, Bob (basketball); New York City, 8/9/1928
Crabbe, Buster (swimming); Scottsdale, Ariz. **(1908–1983)**
Crenshaw, Ben (golf); Austin, Tex., 1/11/1952
Cronin, Joe (baseball); San Francisco, **(1906–1984)**
Cruyff, Johan (soccer); Amsterdam, Netherlands, 4/25/47
Csonka, Larry (Lawrence Richard) (football); Stow, Ohio, 12/25/1946
Dancer, Stanley (harness racing); New Egypt, N.J., 7/25/1927
Dantley, Adrian (basketball); Washington, D.C., 2/28/1956
Dark, Alvin (baseball); Comanche, Okla., 1/7/1922
Davenport, Willie (track); Troy, Ala., 6/6/1943
Dawson, Leonard Ray (football); Alliance, Ohio, 6/20/1935
Dean, Dizzy (Jay Hanna) (baseball); Lucas, Ark. **(1911-1974)**
DeBusschere, Dave (basketball); Detroit, 10/16/1940
Delvecchio, Alex Peter (hockey); Fort William, Ontario, Canada, 12/4/1931
Demaret, Jim (golf); Houston **(1910-1983)**
Dempsey, Jack (William H.) (boxing); Manassa, Colo. **(1895-1983)**
DeVicenzo, Roberto (golf); Buenos Aires, 4/14/1923
Dibbs, Edward George (tennis); Brooklyn, New York, 2/23/1951
Dietz, James W. (rowing); New York, N.Y., 1/12/1949
DiMaggio, Joe (baseball); Martinez, Calif., 11/25/1914
Dionne, Marcel (hockey); Drummondville, Quebec, Canada, 8/3/1951
Dominguín, Luis Miguel (matador); Madrid, 12/9/1926
Dorsett, Tony (football); Rochester, Pa., 4/7/1954
Dryden, Kenneth (hockey); Hamilton, Ontario, Canada, 8/4/1947
Drysdale, Don (baseball); Van Nuys, Calif., 7/23/1936
Duran, Roberto (boxing); Panama City, 6/16/1951
Durocher, Leo (baseball); West Springfield, Mass., 7/27/1906
Durr, François (tennis); Algiers, Algeria, 12/25/1942
El Cordobés, (Manuel Benítez Pérez) (matador); Palma del Río, Córdoba, Spain, 5/4/1936(?)
Elder, Lee (golf); Dallas, 7/14/1934
Emerson, Roy (tennis); Kingsway, Australia, 11/3/1936
Ender, Kornelia (swimming); Plauen, East Germany, 10/25/1958
Erving, Julius (Dr. J) (basketball); Roosevelt, N.Y., 2/22/1950
Espinosa, Nino (baseball); Villa Altagracia, Dominican Republic **(1953-1988)**
Esposito, Phil (Philip Anthony) (hockey); Sault Ste. Marie, Ontario, Canada, 2/20/1942
Evans, Lee (runner); Mandena, Calif., 2/25/1947
Ewbank, Weeb (football); Richmond, Ind., 5/6/1907
Ewing, Patrick (basketball); Kingston, Jamaica, 8/5/1962
Feller, Robert (Bobby) (baseball); Van Meter, Iowa, 11/3/1918
Feuerbach, Allan Dean (track); Preston, Iowa, 1/12/1948
Finley, Charles O. (sportsman); Ensley, Ala., 2/22/1918
Fischer, Bobby (chess); Chicago, 3/9/1943

Fitzsimmons, Bob (Robert Prometheus) (boxing); Cornwall, England (1862-1917)
Fleming, Peggy Gale (ice skating); San Jose, Calif., 7/27/1948
Ford, Whitey (Edward) (baseball); New York City, 10/21/1928
Foreman, George (boxing); Marshall, Tex., 1/10/1949
Fosbury, Richard (high jumper); Portland, Ore., 3/6/1947
Fox, Nellie (Jacob Nelson) (baseball); St. Thomas, Pa. (1927-1975)
Foxx, James Emory (baseball); Sudlersville, Md., (1907-1967)
Foyt, A. J. (auto racing); Houston, 1/16/1935
Francis, Emile (hockey); North Battleford, Sask., 9/13/1926
Fratianne, Linda (figure skating); Los Angeles, 8/2/1960
Frazier, Joe (boxing); Beauford, S.C., 1/17/1944
Frazier, Walt (basketball); Atlanta, 3/29/1945
Frick, Ford C. (baseball); Wawaka, Ind., (1894-1978)
Furniss, Bruce (swimming); Fresno, Calif., 5/27/1957
Gable, Dan (wrestling); Waterloo, Iowa, 10/25/1948
Gabriel, Roman (football); Wilmington, N.C., 8/5/1940
Gallagher, Michael Donald (skiing); Yonkers, N.Y., 10/3/1941
Garms, Debs (baseball); Glen Rose, Tex. (1908-1984)
Garvey, Steve (baseball); Tampa, Fla., 12/22/1948
Gehrig, Lou (Henry Louis) (baseball); New York City (1903-1941)
Gehringer, Charlie (baseball); Fowlerville, Mich., 5/11/1903
Geoffrion, Bernie (Boom Boom) (hockey); Montreal, 2/14/1931
Gerulaitis, Vitas (tennis); Brooklyn, N.Y., 7/26/1954
Giacomin, Ed (hockey); Sudbury, Ontario, Canada, 6/6/1939
Gibson, Bob (baseball); Omaha, Neb., 11/9/1935
Gifford, Frank (football); Santa Monica, Calif., 8/16/1930
Gilbert, Rod (Rodrique) (hockey); Montreal, 7/1/1941
Giles, Warren (baseball executive); Tiskilwa, Ill. (1896–1979)
Gilmore, Artis (basketball); Chipley, Fla., 9/21/1949
Glance, Harvey (track); Phenix City, Ala., 3/28/1957
Gonzalez, Pancho (tennis); Los Angeles, 5/9/1928
Goodell, Brian Stuart (swimming); Stockton, Calif., 4/2/1959
Gooden, Dwight (baseball); Tampa, Fla., 11/16/1964
Goodrich, Gail (basketball); Los Angeles, 4/23/1943
Goolagong Cawley, Evonne (tennis); Griffith, Australia, 7/31/1951
Gossage, Rich (Goose) (baseball); Colorado Springs, Colo., 4/5/1951
Gottfried, Brian (tennis); Baltimore, Md., 1/27/1952
Graf, Steffi (tennis); Mannheim, W. Germany, 6/14/1969
Graham, David (golf); Windson, Australia, 5/23/1946
Graham, Otto Everett (football); Waukegan, Ill., 12/6/1921
Grange, Red (Harold) (football); Forksville, Pa., 6/13/1904
Green, Hubert (golf); Birmingham, Ala., 12/28/1946
Greene, Charles E. (sprinter); Pine Bluff, Ark., 3/21/1945
Greene, Joe (Mean); (football); Temple, Tex., 9/24/1946
Gretzky, Wayne (hockey); Brantford, Ont., 1/26/1961
Griese, Bob (Robert Allen) (football); Evansville, Ind., 2/3/1945
Groebli, Werner (Mr. Frick) (ice skating); Basil, Switzerland, 4/21/1915
Grove, Lefty (Robert Moses) (baseball); Lonaconing, Md., (1900-1975)
Groza, Lou (football); Martins Ferry, Ohio, 1/25/1924
Guidry, Ronald Ames (baseball); Lafayette, La., 8/28/1950
Gunter, Nancy Richey (tennis); San Angelo, Tex., 8/23/1942
Halas, George (football); Chicago (1895-1983)
Hall, Gary (swimming); Fayetteville, N.C., 8/7/1951
Hamill, Dorothy (figure skating); Chicago, 1956(?)
Hamilton, Scott (figure skating); Bowling Green, Ohio, 8/28/1958
Hammond, Kathy (runner); Sacramento, Calif., 11/2/1951
Harris, Franco (football); Ft. Dix, N.J., 3/7/1950
Hartack, William, Jr. (jockey); Colver, Pa., 12/9/1932
Haughton, William (harness racing); Gloversville, N.Y. (1923-1986)
Havlicek, John (basketball); Martins Ferry, Ohio, 4/8/1940
Hayes, Elvin (basketball); Rayville, La., 11/17/1945
Hayes, Woody (football) Upper Arlington, Ohio (1913-1987)
Haynie, Sandra (golf); Fort Worth, 6/4/1943
Heiden, Eric (speed skating); Madison, Wis., 6/14/1958
Hencken, John (swimming); Culver City, Calif., 5/29/1954
Henderson, Rickey (baseball); Chicago, 12/25/1958
Henie, Sonja (ice skater); Oslo (1912-1969)
Herman, Floyd Caves (Babe) (baseball); Buffalo, N.Y. (1903-1987)
Hernandez, Keith (baseball); San Francisco, 10/20/1953
Hershiser, Orel (baseball); Buffalo, N.Y., 9/16/1958
Hickcox, Charles (swimming); Phoenix, Ariz., 2/6/1947
Hines, James (sprinter); Dumas, Ark., 9/10/1946
Hodges, Gil (baseball); Princeton, Ind. (1924-1972)
Hogan, Ben (golf); Dublin, Tex., 8/13/1912
Holmes, Larry (boxing); Cuthert, Ga., 11/3/1949
Hornsby, Rogers (baseball); Winters, Tex. (1896-1963)
Hornung, Paul (football); Louisville, Ky., 12/23/1935
Houk, Ralph (baseball); Lawrence, Kan., 8/9/1919
Howard, Elston (baseball); St. Louis (1929-1980)
Howe, Gordon (hockey); Floral, Sask., Canada, 3/31/1928
Howell, Jim Lee (football); Lonoke, Ark., 9/27/1914
Howser, Dick (baseball) Miami, Fla. (1937-1987)
Hubbell, Carl (baseball); Carthage, Mo., 6/22/1903

Huff, Sam (Robert Lee) (football); Morgantown, W. Va., 10/4/1934
Hull, Bobby (hockey); Point Anne, Ontario, Canada, 1/3/1939
Hunter, Jim (Catfish) (baseball); Hertford, N.C., 4/8/1946
Huntley, Joni (track); McMinnville, Ore., 8/4/1956
Hutson, Donald (football); Pine Bluff, Ark., 1/31/1913
Insko, Del (harness racing); Amboy, Minn., 7/10/1931
Irwin, Hale (golf); Joplin, Mo., 6/3/1945
Jackson, Reggie (baseball); Wyncote, Pa., 5/18/1946
Jeffries, James J. (boxing); Carroll, Ohio (1875-1953)
Jenkins, Ferguson Arthur (baseball); Chatham, Ontario, Canada, 12/13/1943
Jenner, (W.) Bruce (track); Mt. Kisco, N.Y., 10/28/1949
Jezek, Linda (swimming); Palo Alto, Calif., 3/10/1960
Johnson, Earvin (Magic) (basketball); E. Lansing, Mich., 8/14/1959
Johnson, Anthony (rowing); Washington, D.C., 11/16/1940
Johnson, Jack (John Arthur) (boxing); Galveston, Tex. (1876-1946)
Johnson, Rafer (decathlon); Hillsboro, Tex., 8/18/1935
Johnson, Wilham Julius (Judy) (baseball); Wilmington, Del. (1899-1989)
Jones, Deacon (David) (football); Eatonville, Fla., 12/9/1938
Juantoreno, Alberto (track); Santiago, Cuba, 12/3/1951
Jurgensen, Sonny (football); Wilmington, N.C., 8/23/1934
Kaat, Jim (baseball); Zeeland, Mich., 11/7/1938
Kaline, Al (Albert) (baseball); Baltimore, 12/19/1934
Keino, Kipchoge (runner); Kapchemoiymo, Kenya, 1/?/1940
Kelly, Leroy (football); Philadelphia, 5/20/1942
Kelly, Red (Leonard Patrick) (hockey); Simcoe, Ontario, Canada, 7/9/1927
Killebrew, Harmon (baseball); Payette, Idaho, 6/29/1936
Killy, Jean-Claude (skiing); Saint-Cloud, France, 8/30/1943
Kilmer, Bill (William Orland) (football); Topeka, Kan., 9/5/1939
King, Billie Jean (Billie Jean Moffitt) (tennis); Long Beach, Calif., 11/22/1943
Kinsella, John (swimming); Oak Park, Ill., 8/26/1952
Kluszewski, Ted (baseball); Argo, Ill. (1924-1988)
Kodes, Jan (tennis); Prague, 3/1/1946
Kolb, Claudia (swimming); Hayward, Calif., 12/19/1949
Koosman, Jerry Martin (baseball); Appleton, Minn., 12/23/1942
Korbut, Olga (gymnast); Grodno, Byelorussia, U.S.S.R., 5/16/1955
Koufax, Sandy (Sanford) (baseball); Brooklyn, N.Y., 12/30/1935
Kramer, Jack (tennis); Las Vegas, Nev., 8/1/1921
Kramer, Jerry (football); Jordan, Mont., 1/23/1936
Kuenn, Harvey (baseball); West Allis, Wis. (1930-1988)
Kuhn, Bowie Kent (baseball); Takoma Park, Md., 10/28/1926
Kwalik, Ted (Thaddeus John) (football); McKees Rocks, Pa., 4/15/1947
Lafleur, Guy Damien (hockey); Thurson, Quebec, Canada, 8/20/1951
Laird, Ronald (walker); Louisville, Ky., 5/31/1935
Lamonica, Daryle (football); Fresno, Calif., 7/17/1941
Landis, Kenesaw Mountain (1st baseball commissioner); Millville, Ohio (1866-1944)
Landry, Tom (football); Mission, Tex., 9/11/1924
Landy, John (runner); Australia, 4/4/1930
Larrieu, Francie (track); Palo Alto, Calif., 11/28/1952
Lasorda, Tom (baseball); Norristown, Pa., 9/22/1927
Laver, Rod (tennis); Rockhampton, Australia, 8/9/1938
Layne, Bobby (football) Lubbock, Texas (1927-1986)
Lemieux, Mario (hockey); Montreal, Que., Canada, 10/5/1965
Lendl, Ivan (tennis); Prague, 3/7/1960
Leonard, Benny (Benjamin Leiner) (boxing); New York City (1896-1947)
Leonard, Sugar Ray (boxing); Wilmington, N.C., 5/17/1956
Lewis, Carl (track); Willingboro, N.J., 7/1/1961
Linehan, Kim (swimming); Bronxville, N.Y., 12/11/1962
Liquori, Marty (runner); Montclair, N.J., 9/11/1949
Little, Floyd Douglas (football); New Haven, Conn., 7/4/1942
Little, Lou (football); Leominster, Mass., (1893-1979)
Littler, Gene (golf); La Jolla, Calif., 7/21/1930
Lloyd, Chris Evert (Christine Marie) (tennis); Fort Lauderdale, Fla., 12/21/1954
Lombardi, Vince (football); Brooklyn, N.Y. (1913-1970)
Longden, Johnny (horse racing); Wakefield, England, 2/14/1907
Lopez, Al (baseball); Tampa, Fla., 8/20/1908
Lopez, Nancy (golf); Torrance, Calif., 1/6/1957
Louis, Joe (Joe Louis Barrow) (boxing); Lafayette, Ala. (1914-1981)
Lynn, Frederic Michael (baseball); Chicago, Ill., 2/3/1952
Lynn, Janet (figure skating); Rockford, Ill., 4/6/1953
Mack, Connie (Cornelius Alexander McGillicuddy) (baseball executive); East Brookfield, Mass. (1862-1956)
Mackey, John (football); New York City, 9/24/1941
Mahovlich, Frank (Francis William) (hockey); Timmins, Ontario, Canada, 1/10/1938
Mahre, Phil (skiing); White Pass, Wash., 5/10/1957
Malone, Moses (basketball); Petersburg, Va. 3/23/1955
Mandlikova, Hana (tennis); Prague, Czechoslovakia, 2/1962
Mann, Carol (golf); Buffalo, N.Y., 2/3/1941

Manning, Madeline (runner); Cleveland, 1/11/1948
Mantle, Mickey Charles (baseball); Spavinaw, Okla., 10/20/1931
Maravich, Peter (Pistol Pete); Aliquippa, Pa. **(1948-1988)**
Marciano, Rocky (boxing); Brockton, Mass. **(1923-1969)**
Marichal, Juan (baseball); Laguna Verde, Montecristi, Dominican Republic, 10/20/1937
Maris, Roger (baseball); Hibbing, Minn. **(1934-1985)**
Martin, Billy (Alfred Manuel) (baseball); Berkeley, Calif., 5/16/1928
Martin, Rick (Richard Lionel) (hockey); Verdun, Quebec, Canada, 7/26/1951
Mathews, Ed (Edwin) (baseball); Texarkana, Tex., 10/13/1931
Matson, Randy (shot putter); Kilgore, Tex., 3/5/1945
Mays, Willie (baseball); Westfield, Ala., 5/6/1931
McAdoo, Bob (basketball); Greensboro, N.C., 9/25/1951
McCarthy, Joe (Joseph Vincent) (baseball); Philadelphia **(1887-1978)**
McCovey, Willie Lee (baseball); Mobile, Ala., 1/10/1938
McDonald, Lanny (hockey); Hanna, Alberta, Canada, 2/16/1953
McEnroe, John Patrick, Jr. (tennis); Wiesbaden, Germany, 2/16/1959
McGraw, John Joseph (baseball); Truxton, N.Y. **(1873-1934)**
McLain, Dennis (baseball); Chicago, 3/24/1944
McMillan, Kathy Laverne (track); Raeford, N.C., 11/7/1957
Merrill, Janice (track); New London, Conn., 6/18/1962
Meyer, Deborah (swimming); Haddonfield, N.J., 8/14/1952
Middlecoff, Cary (golf); Halls, Tenn., 1/6/1921
Mikita, Stan (hockey); Sokolce, Czechoslovakia, 5/20/1940
Milburn, Rodney, Jr. (hurdler); Opelousas, La., 5/18/1950
Miller, Johnny (golf); San Francisco, 4/29/1947
Montgomery, Jim (swimming); Madison, Wis., 1/24/1955
Moore, Archie (boxing); Benoit, Miss., 12/13/1916
Morgan, Joe Leonard (baseball); Bonham, Tex., 9/19/1943
Morrall, Earl (football); Muskegon, Mich., 5/17/1934
Morton, Craig L. (football); Flint, Mich., 2/5/1943
Mosconi, Willie (pocket billiards); Philadelphia, 6/27/1913
Moser, Annemarie. *See* Proell, Annemarie
Moses, Edward Corley (track); Dayton, Ohio, 8/31/1958
Mungo, Van Lingo (baseball); Pageland, S.C. **(1911-1985)**
Munson, Thurman (baseball); Akron, Ohio, **(1947-1979)**
Murphy, Calvin (basketball); Norwalk, Conn., 5/9/1948
Musial, Stan (baseball); Donora, Pa., 11/21/1920
Myers, Linda (archery); York, Pa., 6/19/1947
Naber, John (swimming); Evanston, Ill., 1/20/1956
Namath, Joe (Joseph William) (football); Beaver Falls, Pa., 5/31/1943
Nastase, Ilie (tennis); Bucharest, 7/19/1946
Navratilova, Martina (tennis); Prague, 10/18/1956
Nehemiah, Renaldo (track); Newark, N.J., 3/24/1959
Nelson, Cindy (skiing); Lutsen, Minn., 8/19/1955
Newcombe, John (tennis); Sydney, Australia, 5/23/1943
Niekro, Phil (baseball); Lansing, Ohio, 4/1/1939
Nicklaus, Jack (golf); Columbus, Ohio, 1/21/1940
North, Lowell (yachting); Springfield, Mo., 12/2/1929
Oerter, Al (discus thrower); New York City, 9/19/1936
Okker, Tom (tennis); Amsterdam, 2/22/1944
Oldfield, Barney (racing driver); Fulton County, Ohio **(1878-1946)**
Oliva, Tony (Pedro) (baseball); Pinar Del Rio, Cuba, 7/20/1940
Olsen, Merlin Jay (football); Logan, Utah, 9/15/1940
O'Malley, Walter (baseball executive); New York City **(1903–1979)**
Orantes, Manuel (tennis); Granada, Spain, 2/6/1949
Orr, Bobby (hockey); Parry Sound, Ontario, Canada, 3/20/1948
Ovett, Steve (track); Brighton, England, 10/9/1955
Owens, Jesse (track); Decatur, Ala. **(1914-1980)**
Pace, Darrell (archery); Cincinnati, 10/23/1956
Paige, Satchel (Leroy) (baseball); Mobile, Ala., **(1906-1982)**
Palmer, Arnold (golf); Latrobe, Pa., 9/10/1929
Palmer, James Alvin (baseball); New York City, 10/15/1945
Parent, Bernard Marcel (hockey); Montreal, 4/3/1945
Park, Brad (Douglas Bradford) (hockey); Toronto, Ontario, Canada, 7/6/1948
Parseghian, Ara (football); Akron, Ohio, 5/21/1923
Pasarell, Charles (tennis); San Juan, Puerto Rico, 2/12/1944
Patterson, Floyd (boxing); Waco, N.C., 1/4/1935
Peete, Calvin (golf); Detroit, Mich., 7/18/1943
Pelé (Edson Arantes do Nascimento) (soccer); Tres Coracoes, Brazil, 10/23/1940
Perry, Gaylord (baseball); Williamston, N.C., 9/15/1938
Perry, Jim (baseball); Williamston, N.C., 9/15/1938
Pettit, Bob (basketball); Baton Rouge, La., 12/12/1932
Petty, Richard Lee (auto racing); Randleman, N.C., 7/2/1937
Pincay, Laffit, Jr. (jockey); Panama City, Panama, 12/29/1946
Plager, Barclay (ice hockey); Kirkland Lake, Ontario **(1941-1988)**
Plante, Jacques (hockey); Shawinigan Falls, Quebec, Canada, 1/17/1929
Player, Gary (golf); Johannesburg, South Africa, 11/1/1935
Plunkett, Jim (football); San Jose, Calif., 12/5/1947

Potvin, Denis Charles (hockey); Hull, Quebec, Canada, 10/29/1953
Powell, Boog (John) (baseball); Lakeland, Fla., 8/17/1941
Prefontaine, Steve Roland (runner); Coos Bay, Ore. **(1951-1975)**
Prince, Bob (baseball announcer); Pittsburgh **(1917-1985)**
Proell, Annemarie Moser (Alpine skier); Kleinarl, Austria, 3/27/1953
Ralston, Dennis (tennis); Bakersfield, Calif., 7/27/1942
Rankin, Judy Torluemke (golf); St. Louis, Mo., 2/18/1945
Raschi, Vic (baseball); West Springfield, Mass. **(1919-1988)**
Ratelle, Jean (Joseph Gilbert Yvon Jean) (hockey); St. Jean, Quebec, Canada, 10/29/1953
Rawls, Betsy (Elizabeth Earle) (golf); Spartanburg, S.C., 5/4/1928
Reed, Willis (basketball); Hico, La., 6/25/1942
Reese, Pee Wee (Harold) (baseball); Ekron, Ky., 7/23/1919
Resch, Glenn "Chico" (hockey); Moose Jaw, Saskatchewan, Canada, 7/10/1948
Richard, Maurice (hockey); Montreal, 8/14/1924
Riessen, Martin (tennis); Hinsdale, Ill., 12/4/1941
Rigney, William (baseball); Alameda, Calif., 1/29/1918
Rizzuto, Phil (baseball); New York City, 9/25/1918
Roark, Helen Wills Moody (tennis); Centerville, Calif., 10/6/1906
Robertson, Oscar (basketball); Charlotte, Tenn., 11/24/1938
Robinson, Arnie (track); San Diego, Calif., 4/7/1948
Robinson, Brooks (baseball); Little Rock, Ark., 5/18/1937
Robinson, Frank (baseball); Beaumont, Tex., 8/31/1935
Robinson, Jackie (baseball); Cairo, Ga. **(1919-1972)**
Robinson, Larry Clark (hockey); Marvelville, Ontario, Canada, 6/2/1951
Robinson, (Sugar) Ray (boxing); Detroit **(1920-1989)**
Rockne, Knute Kenneth (football); Voss, Norway **(1888-1931)**
Rockwell, Martha (skiing); Providence, R.I., 4/26/1944
Rono, Harry (track); Kiptaragon, Kenya, 2/12/1952
Rooney, Art (football); Pittsburgh, Pa. **(1901-1988)**
Rose, Pete (Peter Edward) (baseball); Cincinnati, 4/14/1942
Rosenbloom, Maxie (boxing); New York City **(1904-1976)**
Rosewall, Ken (tennis); Sydney, Australia, 11/2/1934
Rote, Kyle (football); San Antonio, 10/27/1928
Roush, Edd (baseball); Oakland City, Ind. **(1893-1988)**
Rozelle, Pete (Alvin Ray) (commissioner of National Football League); South Gate, Calif., 3/1/1926
Rudolph, Wilma Glodean (sprinter); St. Bethlehem, Tenn., 6/23/1940
Russell, Bill (basketball); Monroe, La., 2/12/1934
Ruth, Babe (George Herman Ruth) (baseball); Baltimore **(1895-1948)**
Rutherford, Johnny (auto racing); Fort Worth, 3/12/1938
Ryan, Nolan (Lynn Nolan, Jr.) (baseball); Refugio, Tex., 1/31/1947
Ryon, Luann (archery); Long Beach, Calif., 1/13/1953
Ryun, Jim (runner); Wichita, Kan., 4/29/1947
Salazar, Alberto (track); Havana, 8/7/1958
Samuels, Howard (horse racing, soccer); New York City **(1920-1984)**
Santana, Manuel (Manuel Santana Martinez) (tennis); Chamartin, Spain, 5/10/1938
Sayers, Gale (football); Wichita, Kan., 5/30/1943
Schmidt, Mike (baseball); Dayton, Ohio, 9/27/1949
Schoendienst, Al (Albert) (baseball); Germantown, Ill., 2/2/1923
Schollander, Donald (swimming); Charlotte, N.C., 4/30/1946
Seagren, Bob (Robert Lloyd) (pole vaulter); Pomona, Calif., 10/17/1946
Seaver, Tom (baseball); Fresno, Calif., 11/17/1944
Seidler, Maren (track); Brooklyn, N.Y., 6/11/1962
Selke, Frank (ice hockey); Canada **(1893-1985)**
Shepherd, Lee (auto racing) **(1945-1985)**
Shoemaker, Willie (jockey); Fabens, Tex., 8/19/1931
Shore, Eddie (ice hockey); Saskatchewan, Canada **(1902-1985)**
Shorter, Frank (runner); Munich, Germany, 10/31/1947
Shriver, Pam (tennis); Baltimore, 7/4/1962
Shula, Don (Donald Francis) (football); Grand River, Ohio, 1/4/1930
Silvester, Jay (discus thrower); Tremonton, Utah, 2/27/1937
Simpson, O. J. (Orenthal James) (football); San Francisco, 7/9/1947
Sims, Billy (football); St. Louis, 9/18/1955
Smith, Bubba (Charles Aaron) (football); Orange, Tex., 2/28/1945
Smith, Ronnie Ray (sprinter); Los Angeles, 3/28/1949
Smith, Stanley Roger (tennis); Pasadena, Calif., 12/14/1946
Smith, Tommie (sprinter); Clarksville, Tex., 6/5/1944
Smoke, Marcia Jones (canoeing); Oklahoma City, 7/18/1941
Snead, Sam (golf); Hot Springs, Va., 5/27/1912
Sneva, Tom (auto racing); Spokane, Wash., 6/1/1948
Snider, Duke (Edwin) (baseball); Los Angeles, 9/19/1926
Solomon, Harold (tennis); Washington, D.C., 9/17/1952
Spahn, Warren (baseball); Buffalo, N.Y., 4/23/1921
Speaker, Tristram (baseball); Hubbard City, Tex. **(1888-1958)**
Spencer, Brian (ice hockey); Fort St. James, British Columbia **(1949-1988)**
Spinks, Leon (boxing); St. Louis, 7/11/1953
Spitz, Mark (swimming); Modesto, Calif., 2/10/1950
Stabler, Kenneth (football); Foley, Ala., 12/25/1945
Stagg, Amos Alonzo (football); West Orange, N.J. **(1862-1965)**
Stargell, Willie (Wilver Dornell) (baseball); Earlsboro, Okla., 3/6/1941

Starr, Bart (football); Montgomery, Ala., 1/9/1934
Staub, Daniel (Rusty) (baseball); New Orleans, 4/4/1944
Staubach, Roger (football); Cincinnati, 2/5/1942
Steinkraus, William C. (equestrian); Cleveland, 10/12/1925
Stenerud, Jan (football); Fetsund, Norway, 11/26/1942
Stengel, Casey (Charles Dillon) (baseball); Kansas City, Mo. **(1891-1975)**
Stenmark, Ingemar (Alpine skier); Tarnaby, Sweden, 3/18/1956
Stockton, Richard LaClede (tennis); New York City, 2/18/1951
Stones, Dwight Edwin (track); Los Angeles, 12/6/1953
Strawberry, Darryl (baseball); Los Angeles, 3/12/1962
Sullivan, John Lawrence (boxing); Boston **(1858-1918)**
Sutton, Don (Donald Howard) (baseball); Clio, Ala., 4/2/1945
Swann, Lynn (football); Alcoa, Tenn., 3/7/1952
Tanner, Leonard Roscoe III (tennis); Chattanooga, Tenn., 10/15/1951
Tarkenton, Fran (Francis) (football); Richmond, Va., 2/3/1940
Tebbetts, Birdie (George R.) (baseball); Nashua, N.H., 11/10/1914
Theismann, Joe (football); New Brunswick, N.J., 9/9/1946
Thoeni, Gustavo (Alpine skier); Trafoi, Italy, 2/28/1951
Thompson, David (basketball); Shelby, N.C., 7/13/1954
Thorpe, Jim (James Francis) (all-around athlete); nr. Prague, Okla. **(1888-1953)**
Tilden, William Tatem II (tennis); Philadelphia **(1893-1953)**
Tittle, Y. A. (Yelberton Abraham) (football); Marshall, Tex., 10/24/1926
Toomey, William (decathlon); Philadelphia, 1/10/1939
Trevino, Lee (golf); Dallas, 12/1/1939
Trottier, Bryan (hockey); Val Marie, Sask., Canada, 7/17/1956
Tunney, Gene (James J.) (boxing); New York City **(1898-1978)**
Tyus, Wyomia (runner); Griffin, Ga., 8/29/1945
Ueberroth, Peter (baseball); Evanston, Ill., 9/2/1937
Unitas, John (football); Pittsburgh, 5/7/1933
Unser, Al (auto racing); Albuquerque, N. Mex., 5/29/1939
Unser, Bobby (auto racing); Albuquerque N. Mex., 2/20/1934
Valenzuela, Fernando (baseball); Sonora, Mexico, 11/1/1960
Van Brocklin, Norm (football); Eagle Butte, S. Dak. **(1926-1983)**
Vilas, Guillermo (tennis); Mar del Plata, Argentina, 8/17/1952
Viren, Lasse (track); Myrskyla, Finland, 7/12/1949
Wade, Virginia (tennis); Bournemouth, England, 7/10/1945

Wagner, Honus (John Peter Honus) (baseball); Carnegie, Pa. **(1867-1955)**
Waitz, Grete (Andersen) (running); Oslo, Norway, 10/1/1953
Wakefield, Dick (baseball); Chicago **(1921-1985)**
Walcott, Jersey Joe (Arnold Cream) (boxing); Merchantville, N.J., 1/31/1914
Walsh, Adam (football) **(1902-1985)**
Walton, Bill (basketball); La Mesa, Calif., 11/5/1952
Waterfield, Bob (football); Burbank, Calif. **(1921–1983)**
Watson, Martha Rae (track); Long Beach, Calif., 8/19/1946
Watson, Tom (golf); Kansas City, Mo., 9/4/1949
Weaver, Earl (baseball); St. Louis, 8/14/1930
Webster, Alex (football); Kearny, N.J., 4/19/1931
Weiskopf, Tom (golf); Massillon, Ohio, 11/9/1942
Weiss, George (baseball executive); New Haven, Conn. **(1895-1972)**
Weissmuller, Johnny (swimmer and actor); Windber, Pa. **(1904-1984)**
Weld, Philip (sailing); Cambridge, Mass. **(1915-1984)**
West, Jerry (basketball); Cheylan, W. Va., 5/28/1938
White, Willye B. (long jumper); Money, Miss., 1/1/1936
Whitworth, Kathy (golf); Monahans, Tex., 9/27/1939
Widing, Juha (ice hockey); Vancouver, Canada **(1948-1985)**
Wilkens, Mac Maurice (track); Eugene, Ore., 11/15/1950
Wilkins, Lennie (basketball); 11/25/1937
Wilkinson, Bud (football); Minneapolis, 4/23/1916
Williams, Del (football); New Orleans **(1945-1984)**
Williams, Dick (baseball); St. Louis, 5/7/1929
Williams, Ted (baseball); San Diego, Calif., 8/30/1918
Wills, Maury (baseball); Washington, D.C., 10/2/1932
Winfield, Dave (baseball); St. Paul, Minn., 10/3/1951
Wohlhuter, Richard C. (runner); Geneva, Ill. 12/23/1945
Wood, Joseph (Smokey) (baseball); Kansas City, Mo. **(1890-1985)**
Woodhead, Cynthia (swimming); Riverside, Calif., 2/7/1964
Wottle, David James (runner); Canton, Ohio, 8/7/1950
Wright, Mickey (Mary Kathryn) (golf); San Diego, Calif., 2/14/1935
Yarborough, Cale (William Caleb) (auto racing); Timmonsville, S.C., 3/27/1939
Yarbrough, Leeroy (auto racing); Jacksonville, Fla. **(1938-1984)**
Yastrzemski, Carl (baseball); Southampton, N.Y., 8/22/1939
Young, Cy (Denton True) (baseball); Gilmore, Ohio **(1867-1955)**
Young, Sheila (speed skater, bicycle racer); Detroit, 10/14/1950

Yachting

The word "yacht" is of Dutch origin and the first "yacht race" of record in the English language was a sailing contest from Greenwich to Gravesend and return in 1662 between a Dutch yacht and an English yacht designed and, at some part of the race, sailed by Charles II of England. The royal yacht won the contest.

The first yacht club was organized at Cork, Ireland, in 1720 under the name of the Cork Harbour Water Club, later changed to the Royal Cork Yacht Club. The Royal Yacht Squadron was organized at Cowes in 1812 and the name changed to the Royal Yacht Club in 1820. The New York Yacht Club was organized aboard the Stevens schooner "Gimcrack" on July 30, 1844, and a clubhouse erected at Elysian Fields, Hoboken, N.J., the following year.

From that time until the Civil War, races were held over courses starting from the water off the yacht club promontory. One course was to the Sandy Hook Lightship and return. (*See* Yachting records, page 954.)

Bowling

The game of bowling that is the favorite sport of millions in the United States is an indoor modification of the more ancient outdoor game. The outdoor game is prehistoric in origin and probably goes back to Primitive Man and round stones that were rolled at some target. It is believed that a game something like nine-pins was popular among the Dutch, Swiss, and Germans as long ago as 1200 A.D., at which time the game was played outdoors with an alley consisting of a single plank 12 to 18 inches wide along which was rolled a ball toward three rows of three pins each placed at the far end of the alley. When the first indoor alleys were built and how the game was modified from time to time are matters of dispute. Much of the confusion arises from a lack of certainty as to which game is meant, "bowls" or "bowling," one with a "jack" and the other with "pins," in historical passages.

It is supposed that the early settlers of New Amsterdam (New York City) being Dutch, they brought their two bowling games with them. About a century ago the game of nine-pins was flourishing in the United States but so corrupted by gambling on matches that it was barred by law in New York and Connecticut. Since the law specifically barred "nine-pins," it was eventually evaded by adding another pin and thus legally making it a new game. The genius who thought up that simple method of outwitting the law and putting a popular game in motion once more remained modestly anonymous. With the increase in the number of pins, the old diamond formation of nine-pins was abandoned for the triangle set-up of ten-pins that remains the rule to this day. Various organizations were formed to make rules for bowling and supervise competition in the United States but none was successful until the American Bowling Congress, organized Sept. 9, 1895, became the ruling body. (*See* Bowling records, pages 914–16.)

HOCKEY

Ice hockey, by birth and upbringing a Canadian game, is an offshoot of field hockey. Some historians say that the first ice hockey game was played in Montreal in December 1879 between two teams composed almost exclusively of McGill University students, but others assert that earlier hockey games took place in Kingston, Ontario, or Halifax, Nova Scotia. In the Montreal game of 1879, there were fifteen players on a side, who used an assortment of crude sticks to keep the puck in motion. Early rules allowed nine men on a side, but the number was reduced to seven in 1886 and later to six.

The first governing body of the sport was the Amateur Hockey Association of Canada, organized in 1887. In the winter of 1894–95, a group of college students from the United States visited Canada and saw hockey played. They became enthused over the game and introduced it as a winter sport when they returned home. The first professional league was the International Hockey League, which operated in northern Michigan in 1904–06.

Until 1910, professionals and amateurs were allowed to play together on "mixed teams," but this arrangement ended with the formation of the first "big league," the National Hockey Association, in eastern Canada in 1910. The Pacific Coast League was organized in 1911 for western Canadian hockey. The league included Seattle and later other American cities. The National Hockey League replaced the National Hockey Association in 1917. Boston, in 1924, was the first American city to join that circuit. The league expanded to include western cities in 1967. The Stanley Cup was competed for by "mixed teams" from 1894 to 1910, thereafter by professionals. It was awarded to the winner of the N.H.L. playoffs from 1926–67 and now to the league champion. The World Hockey Association was organized in October 1972 and was dissolved after the 1978–79 season when the N.H.L. absorbed four of the teams.

STANLEY CUP WINNERS

Emblematic of World Professional Championship; N.H.L. Championship after 1967

1894	Montreal A.A.A.	1923	Ottawa Senators	1951	Toronto Maple Leafs
1895	Montreal Victorias	1924	Montreal Canadiens	1952	Detroit Red Wings
1896	Winnipeg Victorias	1925	Victoria Cougars	1953	Montreal Canadiens
1897–99	Montreal Victorias	1926	Montreal Maroons	1954–55	Detroit Red Wings
1900	Montreal Shamrocks	1927	Ottawa Senators	1956–60	Montreal Canadiens
1901	Winnipeg Victorias	1928	N.Y. Rangers	1961	Chicago Black Hawks
1902	Montreal A.A.A.	1929	Boston Bruins	1962–64	Toronto Maple Leafs
1903–05	Ottawa Silver Seven	1930–31	Montreal Canadiens	1965–66	Montreal Canadiens
1906	Montreal Wanderers	1932	Toronto Maple Leafs	1967	Toronto Maple Leafs
1907	Kenora Thistles[1]	1933	N.Y. Rangers	1968–69	Montreal Canadiens
1907	Mont. Wanderers[2]	1934	Chicago Black Hawks	1970	Boston Bruins
1908	Montreal Wanderers	1935	Montreal Maroons	1971	Montreal Canadiens
1909	Ottawa Senators	1936–37	Detroit Red Wings	1972	Boston Bruins
1910	Montreal Wanderers	1938	Chicago Black Hawks	1973	Montreal Canadiens
1911	Ottawa Senators	1939	Boston Bruins	1974–75	Philadelphia Flyers
1912–13	Quebec Bulldogs	1940	N.Y. Rangers	1976–79	Montreal Canadiens
1914	Toronto	1941	Boston Bruins	1980–83	New York Islanders
1915	Vancouver Millionaires	1942	Toronto Maple Leafs	1984	Edmonton Oilers
1916	Montreal Canadiens	1943	Detroit Red Wings	1985	Edmonton Oilers
1917	Seattle Metropolitans	1944	Montreal Canadiens	1986	Montreal Canadiens
1918	Toronto Arenas	1945	Toronto Maple Leafs	1987	Edmonton Oilers
1919	No champion	1946	Montreal Canadiens	1988	Edmonton Oilers
1920–21	Ottawa Senators	1947–49	Toronto Maple Leafs	1989	Calgary Flames
1922	Toronto St. Patricks	1950	Detroit Red Wings	1. January. 2. March.	

NATIONAL HOCKEY LEAGUE YEARLY TROPHY WINNERS

The Hart Trophy—Most Valuable Player

1924	Frank Nighbor, Ottawa	1942	Tom Anderson, New York Americans
1925	Billy Burch, Hamilton	1943	Bill Cowley, Boston
1926	Nels Stewart, Montreal Maroons	1944	Babe Pratt, Toronto
1927	Herb Gardiner, Montreal Canadiens	1945	Elmer Lach, Montreal Canadiens
1928	Howie Morenz, Montreal Canadiens	1946	Max Bentley, Chicago
1929	Roy Worters, New York Americans	1947	Maurice Richard, Montreal Canadiens
1930	Nels Stewart, Montreal Maroons	1948	Buddy O'Connor, New York Rangers
1931–32	Howie Morenz, Montreal Canadiens	1949	Sid Abel, Detroit
1933	Eddie Shore, Boston	1950	Chuck Rayner, New York Rangers
1934	Aurel Joliat, Montreal Canadiens	1951	Milt Schmidt, Boston
1935–36	Eddie Shore, Boston	1952–53	Gordon Howe, Detroit
1937	Babe Siebert, Montreal Canadiens	1954	Al Rollins, Chicago
1938	Eddie Shore, Boston	1955	Ted Kennedy, Toronto
1939	Toe Blake, Montreal Canadiens	1956	Jean Belveau, Montreal Canadiens
1940	Ebbie Goodfellow, Detroit	1957–58	Gordon Howe, Detroit
1941	Bill Cowley, Boston	1959	Andy Bathgate, New York Rangers

1960	Gordon Howe, Detroit
1961	Bernie Geoffrion, Montreal Canadiens
1962	Jacques Plante, Montreal Canadiens
1963	Gordon Howe, Detroit
1964	Jean Beliveau, Montreal Canadiens
1965–66	Bobby Hull, Chicago
1967–68	Stan Mikita, Chicago
1969	Phil Esposito, Boston
1970–72	Bobby Orr, Boston
1973	Bobby Clarke, Philadelphia
1974	Phil Esposito, Boston
1975–76	Bobby Clarke, Philadelphia
1977–78	Guy Lafleur, Montreal
1979	Bryan Trottier, N.Y. Islanders
1980	Wayne Gretzky, Edmonton
1981	Wayne Gretzky, Edmonton
1982	Wayne Gretzky, Edmonton
1983	Wayne Gretzky, Edmonton
1984	Wayne Gretzky, Edmonton
1985	Wayne Gretzky, Edmonton
1986	Wayne Gretzky, Edmonton
1987	Wayne Gretzky, Edmonton
1988	Mario Lemieux, Pittsburgh
1989	Wayne Gretzky

Vezina Trophy—Leading Goalkeeper

1956–60	Jacques Plante, Montreal
1961	Johnny Bower, Toronto
1962	Jacques Plante, Montreal
1963	Glenn Hall, Chicago
1964	Charlie Hodge, Montreal
1965	Terry Sawchuk—Johnny Bower, Toronto
1966	Lorne Worsley—Charlie Hodge, Montreal
1967	Glenn Hall—Denis DeJordy, Chicago
1968	Lorne Worsley—Rogatien Vachon, Montreal
1969	Glenn Hall—Jacques Plante, St. Louis
1970	Tony Esposito, Chicago
1971	Ed Giacomin—Gilles Villemure, New York
1972	Tony Esposito—Gary Smith, Chicago
1973	Ken Dryden, Montreal
1974	Bernie Parent, Philadelphia, and Tony Esposito, Chicago
1975	Bernie Parent, Philadelphia
1976	Ken Dryden, Montreal
1977–79	Ken Dryden—Michel Larocque, Montreal
1980	Bob Sauve—Don Edwards, Buffalo
1981	Richard Sevigny, Denis Herron and Michel Larocque, Montreal
1982	Billy Smith, New York Islanders
1983	Pete Peeters, Boston
1984	Tom Barrasso, Buffalo
1985	Pelle Lindbergh, Philadelphia
1986	John Vanbiesbrouck, New York Rangers
1987	Ron Hextall, Philadelphia
1988	Grant Fuhr, Edmonton
1989	Patrick Roy, Montreal

James Norris Trophy—Defenseman

1954	Red Kelly, Detroit
1955–58	Doug Harvey, Montreal
1959	Tom Johnson, Montreal
1960–62	Doug Harvey, Montreal, New York (62)
1963–65	Pierre Pilote, Chicago
1966	Jacques Laperriere, Montreal
1967	Harry Howell, New York
1968–75	Bobby Orr, Boston
1976	Denis Potvin, N.Y. Islanders
1977	Larry Robinson, Montreal
1978	Denis Potvin, N.Y. Islanders
1980	Larry Robinson, Montreal
1981	Randy Carlyle, Pittsburgh
1982	Doug Wilson, Chicago
1983–84	Rod Langway, Washington
1985	Paul Coffey, Edmonton
1986	Paul Coffey, Edmonton
1987	Ray Bourque, Boston
1988	Ray Bourque, Boston
1989	Chris Chelios, Montreal

Lady Byng Trophy—Sportsmanship

1960	Don McKenney, Boston
1961	Red Kelly, Detroit
1962–63	Dave Keon, Toronto
1964	Ken Wharram, Chicago
1965	Bobby Hull, Chicago
1966	Alex Delvecchio, Detroit
1967–68	Stan Mikita, Chicago
1969	Alex Delvecchio, Detroit
1970	Phil Goyette, St. Louis
1971	John Bucyk, Boston
1972	Jean Ratelle, New York
1973	Gil Perreault, Buffalo
1974	John Buyck, Boston
1975	Marcel Dionne, Detroit
1976	Jean Ratelle, N.Y. Rangers–Boston
1977	Marcel Dionne, Los Angeles
1978	Butch Goring, Los Angeles
1979	Bob MacMillan, Atlanta
1980	Wayne Gretzky, Edmonton
1981	Rick Kehoe, Pittsburgh
1982	Rick Middleton, Boston
1983–84	Mike Bossy, N.Y. Islanders
1985	Jari Kurri, Edmonton
1986	Mike Bossy, N.Y. Islanders

Calder Trophy—Rookie

1962	Bobby Rousseau, Montreal
1963	Kent Douglas, Toronto
1964	Jacques Laperriere, Montreal
1965	Roger Crozier, Detroit
1966	Brit Selby, Toronto
1967	Bobby Orr, Boston
1968	Derek Sanderson, Boston
1969	Danny Grant, Minnesota
1970	Tony Esposito, Chicago
1971	Gilbert Perreault, Buffalo
1972	Ken Dryden, Montreal
1973	Steve Vickers, New York Rangers
1974	Denis Potvin, N.Y. Islanders
1975	Eric Vail, Atlanta
1976	Bryan Trottier, N.Y. Islanders
1977	Willi Plett, Atlanta
1978	Mike Bossy, N.Y. Islanders
1979	Bobby Smith, Minnesota
1980	Ray Bourque, Boston
1981	Peter Stastny, Quebec
1982	Dale Hawerchuk, Winnipeg
1983	Steve Larmer, Chicago
1984	Tom Barrasso, Buffalo
1985	Mario Lemieux, Pittsburgh
1986	Gary Suter, Calgary
1987	Luc Robitaille, Los Angeles
1988	Joe Nievwendyk, Calgary

Art Ross Trophy—Leading scorer

1955	Bernie Geoffrion, Montreal
1956	Jean Beliveau, Montreal
1957	Gordie Howe, Detroit
1958–59	Dickie Moore, Montreal
1960	Bobby Hull, Chicago
1961	Bernie Geoffrion, Montreal
1962	Bobby Hull, Chicago
1963	Gordie Howe, Detroit
1964–65	Stan Mikita, Chicago
1966	Bobby Hull, Chicago
1967–68	Stan Mikita, Chicago
1969	Phil Esposito, Boston
1970	Bobby Orr, Boston
1971–74	Phil Esposito, Boston
1975	Bobby Orr, Boston
1976–78	Guy Lafleur, Montreal
1979	Bryan Trottier, N.Y. Islanders
1980	Marcel Dionne, Los Angeles
1981–87	Wayne Gretzky, Edmonton
1988	Mario Lemieux, Pittsburgh
1989	Mario Lemieux, Pittsburgh

N.H.L. CHAMPIONS
Prince of Wales Trophy

1939	Boston	1956	Montreal
1940	Boston	1957	Detroit
1941	Boston	1958–62	Montreal
1942	New York	1963	Toronto
1943	Detroit	1964	Montreal
1944–47	Montreal	1965	Detroit
1948	Toronto	1966	Montreal
1948–55	Detroit	1967	Chicago

Eastern Division

1968–69	Montreal	1972	Boston
1970	Chicago	1973	Montreal
1971	Boston	1974	Boston

Prince of Wales Conference

1975	Buffalo
1976–79	Montreal
1980	Buffalo
1981	Montreal
1982	New York Islanders

1983	New York Islanders
1984	New York Islanders
1985	Philadelphia
1986	Montreal
1987	Philadelphia
1988	Boston
1989	Montreal

CAMPBELL BOWL
Western Division

1968	Philadelphia	1971–73	Chicago
1969	St. Louis	1974	Philadelphia
1970	St. Louis		

Clarence Campbell Conference

1975	Philadelphia
1976–77	Philadelphia
1978–79	N.Y. Islanders
1980	Philadelphia
1981	New York Islanders
1982	Edmonton
1983	Edmonton
1984	Edmonton
1985	Edmonton
1986	Calgary
1987	Edmonton
1988	Edmonton Oilers
1989	Calgary

NATIONAL HOCKEY LEAGUE
Final Standing of the Clubs—1988–89

PRINCE OF WALES CONFERENCE
Patrick Division

	W	L	T	GF	GA	Pts
Washington Capitals	41	29	10	305	259	92
Pittsburgh Penguins	40	33	7	347	349	87
New York Rangers	37	35	8	310	307	82
Philadelphia Flyers	36	36	8	307	285	80
New Jersey Devils	27	41	12	281	325	66
New York Islanders	28	47	5	265	325	61

Adams Division

	W	L	T	GF	GA	Pts
Montreal Canadiens	53	18	9	351	218	115
Boston Bruins	37	29	14	289	256	88
Buffalo Sabres	38	35	7	291	299	83
Hartford Whalers	37	38	5	299	290	79
Quebec Nordiques	27	46	7	269	342	61

CLARENCE CAMPBELL CONFERENCE
Norris Division

	W	L	T	GF	GA	Pts
Detroit Red Wings	34	34	12	313	316	80
St. Louis Blues	33	35	12	275	285	78
Minnesota North Stars	27	37	16	258	278	70
Chicago Black Hawks	27	41	12	297	335	66
Toronto Maple Leafs	28	46	6	259	342	62

Smythe Division

	W	L	T	GF	GA	Pts
Calgary Flames	54	17	9	354	226	117
Los Angeles Kings	42	31	7	376	335	91
Edmonton Oilers	38	34	8	325	306	84
Vancouver Canucks	33	39	8	251	253	74
Winnipeg Jets	26	42	12	300	355	64

Stanley Cup Playoffs—1989

Division Semifinals
Patrick Division

Pittsburgh Penguins defeated New York Rangers, 4 games to 0
Philadelphia Flyers defeated Washington Capitals, 4 games to 2

Adams Division

Montreal Canadiens defeated Hartford Whalers, 4 games to 0
Boston Bruins defeated Buffalo Sabres, 4 games to 1

Norris Division

Chicago Black Hawks defeated Detroit Red Wings, 4 games to 2
St. Louis Blues defeated Minnesota North Stars, 4 games to 1

Smythe Division

Calgary Flames defeated Vancouver Canucks, 4 games to 3
Los Angeles Kings defeated Edmonton Oilers, 4 games to 3

Division Finals
Patrick Division

Philadelphia Flyers defeated Pittsburgh Penguins, 4 games to 3

Adams Division

Montreal Canadiens defeated Boston Bruins, 4 games to 1

Norris Division

Chicago Black Hawks defeated St. Louis Blues, 4 games to 1

Smythe Division

Calgary Flames defeated Los Angeles Kings, 4 games to 0

Conference Finals (League semifinals)
Prince of Wales Conference

Montreal Canadiens defeated Philadelphia Flyers, 4 games to 2
(Home team in caps)
May 1—Philadelphia 3, MONTREAL 1
May 3—MONTREAL 3, Philadelphia 0
May 5—Montreal 5, PHILADELPHIA 1
May 7—Montreal 3, PHILADELPHIA 0
May 9—Philadelphia 2, MONTREAL 1 (OT)
May 11—Montreal 4, PHILADELPHIA 2

Clarence Campbell Conference

Calgary Flames defeated Chicago Black Hawks, 4 games to 1
(Home team in caps)
May 2—CALGARY 3, Chicago 0
May 4—Chicago 4, CALGARY 2
May 6—Calgary 5, CHICAGO 2
May 8—Calgary 2, CHICAGO 1 (OT)
May 10—CALGARY 3, Chicago 1

Stanley Cup Championship Finals

Calgary Flames defeated Montreal Canadiens, 4 games to 2
(Home team in caps)
May 14—CALGARY 3, Montreal 2
May 17—Montreal 4, CALGARY 2
May 10—MONTREAL 4, Calgary 3 (2OT)
May 21—Calgary 4, MONTREAL 2
May 23—CALGARY 3, Montreal 2
May 25—Calgary 4, MONTREAL 2

N.H.L. LEADING GOALTENDERS—1988–89
(Minimum 1,400 minutes played)

	Min	GA	ShO	Avg
Patrick Roy, Montreal	2744	113	4	2.47
Mike Vernon, Calgary	2938	130	0	2.65
Pete Peters, Washington	1854	88	4	2.85
Brian Hayward, Montreal	2091	101	1	2.90
Rick Wamsley, Calgary	1927	95	2	2.96
Steve Weeks, Vancouver	2056	102	0	2.98
Rejean Lemelin, Boston	2392	120	0	3.01
Peter Sidorkiewicz, Hartford	2635	133	4	3.03
Jon Casey, Minnesota	2961	151	1	3.06
Kirk McLean, Vancouver	2477	127	4	3.08

Andy Moog, Boston	2482	133	1	3.22	Kevin Dineen, Hartford	79	45	44	89
Ron Hextall, Philadelphia	3756	202	0	3.23	Mike Ridley, Washington	80	41	48	89
Clint Malarchuk, Wash.-Buff.	2748	154	2	3.36	Tim Kerr, Philadelphia	69	48	40	88
Daren Puppa, Buffalo	1908	107	1	3.36	Pat LaFontaine, N.Y. Islanders	79	45	43	88
Greg Millen, St. Louis	3019	170	6	3.38	Pierre Turgeon, Buffalo	80	34	54	88
Kari Takko, Minnesota	1604	93	0	3.48	Tomas Sandstrom, N.Y. Rangers	79	32	56	88
Bill Ranford, Edmonton	1509	88	1	3.50	Thomas Steen, Winnipeg	80	27	61	88
Alain Chevrier, Chicago	1573	92	0	3.51	Steve Larmer, Chicago	80	43	44	87
Vincent Riendeau, St. Louis	1842	108	0	3.52	John MacLean, New Jersey	74	42	45	87
Greg Hanlon, Detroit	2092	124	1	3.56					

Other NHL Awards—1989

Conn Smythe Trophy (Most valuable in playoffs)—Al MacInnis, Calgary
Selke (Top defensive forward)—Guy Carbonneau, Montreal

N.H.L. LEADING SCORERS—1988–89

	GP	G	A	Pts
Mario Lemieux, Pittsburgh	76	85	114	199
Wayne Gretzky, Los Angeles	78	54	114	168
Steve Yzerman, Detroit	80	65	90	155
Bernie Nicholls, Los Angeles	79	70	80	150
Rob Brown, Pittsburgh	68	49	66	115
Paul Coffey, Pittsburgh	75	30	83	113
Joe Mullen, Calgary	79	51	59	110
Jari Kurri, Edmonton	76	44	58	102
Jimmy Carson, Edmonton	80	49	51	100
Luc Robitaille, Los Angeles	78	46	52	98
Dale Hawerchuk, Winnipeg	75	41	55	96
Dan Quinn, Pittsburgh	79	34	60	94
Mark Messier, Edmonton	72	33	61	94
Gerrard Gallant, Detroit	76	39	54	93
Ed Olczyk, Toronto	80	38	52	90

N.H.L. CAREER SCORING LEADERS

(Listed in order of total points scored; figures in parentheses indicate Top 10 in goals scored.)

	Yrs	Games	G	A	Pts
Gordie Howe (1)	26	1,767	801	1,049	1,850
Wayne Gretzky (2)[1]	10	774	637	1,200	1,837
Marcel Dionne (3)[1]	17	1,348	731	1,040	1,771
Phil Esposito (4)	18	1,282	717	873	1,590
Stan Mikita (7)	22	1,394	541	926	1,467
John Bucyk (6)	23	1,540	556	813	1,369
Gil Perreault	16	1,171	503	807	1,310
Alex Delvecchio	24	1,549	456	825	1,281
Jean Ratelle	21	1,281	491	776	1,267
Guy Lafleur (9)	14	961	518	728	1,246
Norm Ullman	20	1,410	490	739	1,229
Jean Beliveau (10)	20	1,215	507	712	1,219
Bobby Clarke	15	1,144	358	852	1,210
Bobby Hull (5)	16	1,063	610	560	1,170
Darryl Sittler	15	1,096	484	637	1,121
Frank Mahovlich (8)	18	1,181	533	570	1,103
Henri Richard	20	1,256	358	688	1,046
Rod Gilbert	18	1,065	406	615	1,021

1. Still active in the N.H.L.

BOWLING

AMERICAN BOWLING CONGRESS CHAMPIONS

Year	Singles	All-events	Year	Singles	All-events
1959	Ed Lubanski	Ed Lubanski	1975	Jim Setser	Bobby Meadows
1960	Paul Kulbaga	Vince Lucci	1976	Mike Putzer	Jim Lindquist
1961	Lyle Spooner	Luke Karen	1977	Frank Gadaleto	Bud Debenham
1962	Andy Renaldo	Billy Young	1978	Rich Mersek	Chris Cobus
1963	Fred Delello	Bus Owalt	1979	Rick Peters	Bob Basacchi
1964	Jim Stefanich	Les Zikes, Jr.	1980	Mike Eaton	Steve Fehr
1965	Ken Roeth	Tom Hathaway	1981	Rob Vital	Rod Toft
1966	Don Chapman	John Wilcox	1982	Bruce Bohm	Rich Wonders
1967	Frank Perry	Gary Lewis	1983	Rick Kendrick	Tony Cariello
1968	Wayne Kowalski	Vince Mazzanti	1984	Bob Antczak and	Bob Goike
1969	Greg Campbell	Eddie Jackson		Neal Young (tie)	
1970	Jake Yoder	Mike Berlin	1985	Glen Harbison	Barry Asher
1971	Al Cohn	Al Cohn	1986	Jess Mackey	Ed Marazka
1972	Bill Pointer	Mac Lowry	1987	Terry Taylor	Ryan Schafer
1973	Ed Thompson	Ron Woolet	1988	Steve Hutkowski	Rick Steelsmith
1974	Gene Krause	Bob Hart	1989	Paul Tetreault	George Hall

PROFESSIONAL BOWLERS ASSOCIATION

National Championship Tournament

1960	Don Carter	1969	Mike McGrath	1977	Tommy Hudson	1985	Mike Aulby
1961	Dave Soutar	1970	Mike McGrath	1978	Warren Nelson	1986	Tom Crites
1962	Carmen Salvino	1971	Mike Lemongello	1979	Mike Aulby	1987	Randy Pedersen
1963	Billy Hardwick	1972	Johnny Guenther	1980	Johnny Petraglia	1988	Brian Voss
1964	Bob Strampe	1973	Earl Anthony	1981	Earl Anthony	1989	Pete Weber
1965	Dave Davis	1974	Earl Anthony	1982	Earl Anthony		
1966	Wayne Zahn	1975	Earl Anthony	1983	Earl Anthony		
1967	Dave Davis	1976	Paul Colwell	1984	Bob Chamberlain		
1968	Wayne Zahn						

BOWLING PROPRIETORS' ASSOCIATION OF AMERICA—MEN

United States Open[1]

1971	Mike Lemongello	1976	Paul Moser	1981	Marshall Holman	1986	Steve Cook
1972	Don Johnson	1977	Johnny Petraglia	1982	Dave Husted	1987	Del Ballard
1973	Mike McGrath	1978	Nelson Burton, Jr.	1983	Gary Dickinson	1988	Pete Weber
1974	Larry Laub	1979	Joe Berardi	1984	Mark Roth	1989	Mike Aulby
1975	Steve Neff	1980	Steve Martin	1985	Marshall Holman		

1. Replaced All-Star tournament and is rolled as part of B.P.A. tour.

WOMEN'S INTERNATIONAL BOWLING CONGRESS CHAMPIONS

Year	Singles	All-events	Year	Singles	All-events
1959	Mae Bolt	Pat McBride	1975	Barbara Leicht	Virginia Norton
1960	Marge McDaniels	Judy Roberts	1976	Bev Shonk	Betty Morris
1961	Elaine Newton	Evelyn Teal	1977	Akiko Yamaga	Akiko Yamaga
1962	Martha Hoffman	Flossie Argent	1978	Mae Bolt	Annese Kelly
1963	Dot Wilkinson	Helen Shablis	1979	Betty Morris	Betty Morris
1964	Jean Havlish	Jean Havlish	1980	Betty Morris	Cheryl Robinson
1965	Doris Rudell	Donna Zimmerman	1981	Virginia Norton	Virginia Norton
1966	Gloria Bouvia	Kate Helbig	1982	Gracie Freeman	Aleta Rzepecki
1967	Gloria Paeth	Carol Miller	1983	Aleta Rzepecki	Virginia Norton
1968	Norma Parks	Susie Reichley	1984	Freida Gates	Shinobu Saitoh
1969	Joan Bender	Helen Duval	1985	Polly Schwarzel	Aleta Sill
1970	Dorothy Fothergill	Dorothy Fothergill	1986	Dana Stewart	Robin Romeo
1971	Mary Scruggs	Lorrie Nichols			Maria Lewis (tie)
1972	D. D. Jacobson	Mildred Martorella	1987	Regi Junak	Leanne Barrette
1973	Bobby Buffaloe	Toni Calvery	1988	Michelle Meyer-Welty	Lisa Wagner
1974	Shirley Garms	Judy C. Soutar	1989	Lorraine Anderson	Nancy Fehn

WIBC QUEENS TOURNAMENT CHAMPIONS

1961	Janet Harman	1969	Ann Feigel	1977	Dana Stewart	1985	Aleta Sill
1962	Dorothy Wilkinson	1970	Mildred Martorella	1978	Loa Boxberger	1986	Cora Fiebig
1963	Irene Monterosso	1971	Mildred Martorella	1979	Donna Adamek	1987	Cathy Almeida
1964	D.D. Jacobson	1972	Dorothy Fothergill	1980	Donna Adamek	1988	Wendy McPherson
1965	Betty Kuczynski	1973	Dorothy Fothergill	1981	Katsuko Sugimoto	1989	Carol Gianotti
1966	Judy Lee	1974	Judy Soutar	1982	Katsuko Sugimoto		
1967	Mildred Martorella	1975	Cindy Powell	1983	Aleta Rzepecki		
1968	Phyllis Massey	1976	Pamela Buckner	1984	Kazue Inahashi		

BOWLING PROPRIETORS' ASSOCIATION OF AMERICA—WOMEN

United States Open

1971	Paula Carter	1976	Patty Costello (Pa.)	1981	Donna Adamek	1986	Wendy MacPherson
1972	Lorrie Nichols	1977	Betty Morris	1982	Shinobu Saitoh	1987	Carol Nurman
1973	Mildred Martorella	1978	Donna Adamek	1983	Dana Miller	1988	Lisa Wagner
1974	Pat Costello (Calif.)	1979	Diana Silva	1984	Karen Ellingsworth	1989	Robin Romeo
1975	Paula Carter	1980	Pat Costello (Calif.)	1985	Pat Mercatanti		

WOMEN'S INTERNATIONAL BOWLING CONGRESS TOURNAMENT—1989

(Bismark and Mandan, North Dakota, April 5–June 12, 1989)

Open Division

Singles—Lorraine Anderson, Northville, Mich.	683
Doubles—Diana Goodman, Chino Hill, Calif., and Rene Fleming, Oklahoma City, Okla.	1,283
All-Events—Nancy Fehr, Cincinnati, Ohio	1,911
Team—Robby's, Glendale, Calif.	3,000

Division I

Singles—Sandy Flint, Sioux Falls, S.D.	694
Doubles—Carole Feverborn, Otathe, Kan., and Leeta Swede, Garnett, Kan.	1,208
All-Events—Sandy Flint, Sioux Falls, S.D.	1,801
Team—Wheaton, Wheaton, Minn.	2,768

Division II

Singles—Beverly Tays, Crawfordsville, Ind.	689
Doubles—Marianna Verdugo and Wandy Lundy, Tucson, Ariz.	1,127
All-Events—Del Pkach, Bismark, N.D.	1,671
Team—The Crickets, Minneapolis, Minn.	2,627

PROFESSIONAL BOWLERS ASSOCIATION CHAMPIONSHIP—1989
(Toledo, March 12-18, 1989)

Winner—Pete Weber, St. Louis, defeated Dave Ferraro, Kingston, N.Y., 221-216
Third place—Amelto Monacelli, Venezuela
Fourth place—Jim Johnson, Jr., Wilmington, Del.
Fifth place—Mark Baker, Garden Grove, Calif.

WIBC QUEENS TOURNAMENT—1989
(Bismark, N.D., May 10-17, 1989)

Winner—Carol Gianotti, Perth, Australia, defeated Sandra Jo Shiery, Bronson, Mich., 207-177 in final
Third place—Aleta Sill, Dearborn, Mich.
Fourth place—Cynthia Kesterson, Council Bluffs, Iowa
Fifth place—Betty Morris, Stockton, Calif.

AMERICAN BOWLING CONGRESS TOURNAMENT—1989
(Wichita, Kan., Feb. 11–May 25, 1989)

Regular Division

Singles—Paul Tetreault, Lebanon, N.H.	813
Doubles—Gus Yannaras & Gary Daroszewski, Milwaukee, Wisc.	1,499
All-Events—George Hall, Mundelein, Ill.	2,227
Team—Chilton Vending, Wichita, Kansas	3,481
Team All-Events—Browning Pontiac No. 2, Cincinnatti, Ohio	10,107

Booster Division

National By-Products, Wichita, Kan.	2,813

SKIING

ALPINE WORLD CUP OVERALL WINNERS

Year	Men	Women	Team
1967	Jean-Claude Killy, France	Nancy Greene, Canada	France
1968	Jean-Claude Killy, France	Nancy Greene, Canada	France
1969	Karl Schranz, Austria	Gertrude Gabl, Austria	Austria
1970	Karl Schranz, Austria	Michel Jacot, France	France
1971	Gustavo Thoeni, Italy	Annemarie Proell, Austria	France
1972	Gustavo Thoeni, Italy	Annemarie Proell, Austria	France
1973	Gustavo Thoeni, Italy	Annemarie Proell Moser, Austria	Austria
1974	Piero Gros, Italy	Annemarie Proell Moser, Austria	Austria
1975	Gustavo Thoeni, Italy	Annemarie Proell Moser, Austria	Austria
1976	Ingemar Stenmark, Sweden	Rosi Mittermaier, West Germany	Austria
1977	Ingemar Stenmark, Sweden	Lise-Marie Morerod, Switzerland	Austria
1978	Ingemar Stenmark, Sweden	Hanni Wenzel, Liechtenstein	Austria
1979	Peter Luescher, Switzerland	Annemarie Proell Moser, Austria	Austria
1980	Andreas Wenzel, Liechtenstein	Hanni Wenzel, Liechtenstein	Liechtenstein
1981	Phil Mahre, United States	Marie-Theres Nadig, Switzerland	Switzerland
1982	Phil Mahre, United States	Erika Hess, Switzerland	Austria
1983	Phil Mahre, United States	Tamara McKinney, United States	
1984	Pirman Zurbriggen, Switzerland	Erika Hess, Switzerland	
1985	Marc Girardelli, Luxembourg	Michela Figini, Switzerland	
1986	Marc Girardelli, Luxembourg	Maria Walliser, Switzerland	Switzerland
1987	Pirmin Zubriggen, Switzerland	Maria Walliser, Switzerland	Switzerland
1988	Pirmin Zubriggen, Switzerland	Michela Figini, Switzerland	Switzerland
1989	Marc Giradelli, Luxembourg	Vreni Schneider, Switzerland	Switzerland

UNITED STATES CHAMPIONSHIPS—1989

ALPINE
Men's Events

Downhill—Jeff Olson	1:23.78
Slalom—Felix McGrath	1:31.45
Giant Slalom—Kyle Wieche	2:31.72
Super Giant Slalom—Tommy Moe	1:31.65

Women's Events

Downhill—Hillary Lindh	1:21.69
Slalom—Diann Roffe	1:21.76
Giant Slalom—Diann Roffe	2:42.51
Super Giant Slalom—Kristin Krone	1:39.03

NORDIC
Men's Cross Country

10 kilometers—Avdun Endestad	:30:55.3
15 kilometers—Todd Boonstra	:45:27.1
30 kilometers—Todd Boonstra	1:29:41.2
3 × 15 kilometer relay—Joe Galanes, Bill Spencer & Todd Boonstra	35:44.3

Women's Cross Country

5 kilometers—Nancy Fiddler	:16:57.6
10 kilometers—Nancy Fiddler	:34:16.9
15 kilometers—Leslie Thompson	:51:39.5
3×3 kilometer relay—Ingrid Butts, Betsy Youngman & Leslie Thompson	:24:45.8

NORDIC WORLD CUP—1989

Overall Men
Cross Country

1. Gunde Suan, Sweden	170
2. Vegard Ulvang, Norway	154
3. Torgny Mogren, Sweden	140
4. Pal G. Mikkelsplass, Norway	134
5. Vladimir Smirnov, Soviet Union	74

Overall Women
Cross Country

1. Jelena Valbe, Soviet Union	167

2. Alzbeta Haurancikova, Czechoslovakia   105
3. Tamara Tichonova, Soviet Union   93
4. Manuela Di Centa, Italy   91
5. Larisa Lazutina, Soviet Union   89

Nordic Men's Combined

1. Trond Arne Bredesen, Norway   119
2. Klaus Sulzenbacher, Austria   109
3. Hippolyt Kempf, Switzerland   94
4. Baard Jorgen Elden, Norway   89
5. Knul-Tore Apeland, Norway   83

ALPINE WORLD CUP—1989

Overall—Men

1. Marc Giradelli, Luxembourg   407
2. Primin Zurbriggen, Switzerland   309
3. Alberto Tomba, Italy   189
4. Ole Christian Furuseth, Norway   188
5. Markus Wasmeier, Belgium   166

Overall Women

1. Vreni Schneider, Switzerland   376
2. Maria Walliser, Switzerland   261
3. Michela Figini, Switzerland   242
4. Carole Merle, France   206
5. Anita Wachter, Austria   157

Event Leaders—Men

Downhill—Marc Girardelli, Luxembourg   139
2. Helmut Hoeflehner, Austria   112
3. Daniel Mahrer, Switzerland   102
Slalom—Armin Bittner, Belgium   117
2. Alberto Tomba, Italy   112
3. Marc Girardelli, Luxembourg   106
Ole Christian Furuseth, Norway   106
Best American finish—Felix McGrath (9th, 43 points)
Giant Slalom—Ole Christian Furuseth, Norway   82
2. Pirmin Zurbriggen, Switzerland   82
3. Rudolf Nierlich, Austria   79
Best American finish—Kyle Wieche (14th, 13 points)
Super Giant Slalom—Pirmin Zurbriggen, Switzerland   62
2. Lars-Boerje Eriksson, Sweden   51
3. Franck Piccard, France   49

Event Leaders—Women

Downhill—Michela Figini, Switzerland   176
2. Maria Walliser, Switzerland   142
3. Michaela Gerg, Belgium   91

Best American Finish—Hilary Lindh   (28th, 8 points)
Slalom—Vreni Schneider, Switzerland   175
2. Monika Maierhofer, Austria   85
3. Tamara McKinney, United States   77
Giant Slalom—Vreni Schneider, Switzerland   165
2. Mateja Svet, East Germany   106
3. Maria Walliser, Switzerland   87
Super Giant Slalom—Carole Merle, France   75
2. Sigrid Wolf, Austria   71
3. Anita Wachter, Austria   56
Best American finish—Kristin Krone   (29th, 2 points)

WORLD CUP JUMPING—1989

1. Jan Bokloev, Sweden   247
2. Jens Weissflog, Denmark   192
3. Dieter Thoma, Belgium   167
4. O. Cunnar Fidjestoel, Norway   145
5. Ari Pekka Nikkola, Finland   136

UNITED STATES JUMPING CHAMPIONSHIPS—1989

Nordic Combined—Joe Holland   432.23
70-meter—Joe Holland   221.5
Big Hill Special—Mike Holland   112.0
Small Hill Special—Mike Holland   219.2
Masters—Scott Immens   170.7
Nordic Combined, 15 kilometer—Jeff Graves   375.60

NCAA RESULTS—1989

Men

Slalom—Robert MacLeod, Middlebury   1:30.35
Giant Slalom—Ian Wilter, Colorado   2:16.30
Diagonal cross country—Hans Sjulsad, Utah   30:03.8
Freestyle cross country—Per Jakobsen, Colorado   56:17.6

Women

Slalom—Gabriella Hamberg, Vermont   1:32.66
Giant Slalom—Anke Freidrich, Utah   1:19.98
Diagonal cross country—Sari Argillander, Vermont   19.39.9
Freestyle cross country—Sari Argillander, Vermont   49:47.8

Team (men & women)

1. Vermont,   672
2. Utah,   668
3. Colorado,   608 1/2

COLLEGE SOCCER

(1988 NCAA Playoffs)

DIVISION I
MEN

Quarterfinals

Howard 3, Virginia 2 (2OT)
South Carolina 1, Southern Methodist 0
Indiana 3, Seton Hall 1
Portland 2, Fresno State 0

Semifinals

Howard 2, South Carolina 0
Indiana 1, Portland 0

Championship
(at Indiana University, Bloomington, Ind., Dec. 4, 1988)
Indiana 1, Howard 0

WOMEN
Quarterfinals

North Carolina 2, Central Florida 1
Wisconsin 2, Massachusetts 1
California 2, Colorado College 1 (2OT)

North Carolina State 1, George Mason 0 (2OT)

Semifinals

North Carolina 3, Wisconsin 0
North Carolina State 1, California 0

Championship
(November 20, 1989 at University of North Carolina, Chapel Hill, N.C.)
North Carolina 4, North Carolina State 1

FISHING

SELECTED WORLD ALL-TACKLE FISHING RECORDS

Caught with Rod and Reel in Fresh Water (as of July 12, 1989)

Source: International Game Fish Association.

Species	lb-oz	Where caught	Year	Angler
Bass, Largemouth	22-4	Montgomery Lake, Ga.	1932	George W. Perry
Bass, Peacock	26-8	Mataveni River, Columbia	1982	Rod Neubert
Bass, Redeye	8-3	Flint River, Ga.	1977	David A. Hubbard
Bass, Rock	3-0	York River, Ontario	1974	Peter Gulgin
Bass, Smallmouth	11-15	Dale Hollow Lake, Ky.	1955	David L. Hayes
Bass, Spotted	9-4	Parris Lake, Calif.	1987	Steven West[1] & Gilbert Rowe
Bass, Striped	60-8	Anderson County, Tenn.	1988	Gary Everett Helms
Bass, Striped (landlocked)	66-0	O'Neill Forebay, Los Banos, Calif.	1988	Ted Furnish
Bass, White	5-14	Kerr Lake, N.C.	1986	Jim King
Bass, Whiterock	22-6	Augusta, Ga.	1986	Jerry Adams
Bass, Yellow	2-4	Lake Monroe, Ind.	1977	Donald L. Stalker
Bluegill	4-12	Ketona Lake, Ala.	1950	T.S. Hudson
Bowfin	21-8	Florence, S.C.	1980	Robert L. Harmon
Buffalo, Bigmouth	70-5	Bussey Brake, Bastrop, La.	1980	Delbert Sisk
Buffalo, Smallmouth	68-8	Lake Hamilton, Ark.	1984	Jerry L. Dolezal
Bullhead, Black	8-0	Lake Waccabuc, N.Y.	1951	Kani Evans
Bullhead, Brown	5-8	Veal Pond, Ga.	1975	Jimmy Andrews
Burbot	18-4	Pickford, Mich.	1980	Tom Courtemanche
Carp	57-13	Potomac River, Wash.-D.C.	1983	David Nikolow
Catfish, Blue	97-0	Missouri River, S.D.	1959	Edward B. Elliott
Catfish, Channel	58-0	Santee–Cooper Res., S.C.	1964	W.B. Whaley
Catfish, Flathead	98-0	Lewisville, Tex.	1986	William Stevens
Char, Arctic	32-9	Tree River, Canada	1981	Jeffery Ward
Crappie, Black	4-8	Kerr Lake, Va.	1981	L. Carl Herring, Jr.
Crappie, White	5-3	Enid Dam, Mississippi	1957	Fred L. Bright
Dolly Varden	12-0	Noatak River, Alaska	1987	Kenneth Alt
Drum, Freshwater	54-8	Nickajack Lake, Tenn.	1972	Benny E. Hull
Gar, Alligator	279	Rio Grande River, Tex.	1951	Bill Valverde
Gar, Longnose	50-5	Trinity River, Texas	1954	Townsend Miller
Gar, Shortnose	5-0	Vian, Okla.	1985	Buddy Croslin
Inconnu	38-2	Kobuk River, Alaska	1982	Mark L. Feldman
Muskellunge	69-15	St. Lawrence River, N.Y.	1957	Arthur Lawton
Muskellunge, Tiger	51-3	Lac-Vieux-Desert, Wisc.-Mich.	1919	John A. Knobla
Perch, White	4-12	Messalonskee Lake, Maine	1949	Mrs. Earl Small
Perch, Yellow	4-3	Bordentown, N.J.	1865	Dr. C.C. Abbot
Pickerel, Eastern Chain	9-6	Homerville, Ga.	1961	Baxley McQuaig, Jr.
Redhorse, Northern	3-11	Missouri River, S.D.	1977	Phillip Laumeyer
Redhorse, Silver	11-7	Plum Creek, Wisconsin	1985	Neal D.G. Long
Salmon, Atlantic	79-2	Tana River, Norway	1928	Henrik Henriksen
Salmon, Chinook	97-4	Kenai River, Alaska	1985	Les Anderson
Salmon, Chum	27-3	Raymond Cove, Alaska	1977	Robert A. Jahnke
Salmon, Coho	31-0	Cowichan Bay, B.C., Canada	1947	Mrs. Lee Hallberg
Salmon, Landlocked	22-8	Sebago Lake, Maine	1907	Edward Blakely
Salmon, Pink	12-9	Moose & Kenai Rivers, Alaska	1974	Steven Alan Lee
Salmon, Sockeye	15-3	Kenai River, Alaska	1987	Stan Roach
Shad, American	11-1	Delaware River, N.J.	1984	Charles J. Mower
Sturgeon	468-0	Benicia, Calif.	1983	Joey Pallotta III
Sturgeon, White	380-0	Snake River, Idaho	1973	Del Canty
Sunfish, Green	2-2	Stockton Lake, Missouri	1971	Paul M. Dilley
Sunfish, Redbreast	1-12	Suwannee River, Fla.	1984	Alvin Buchanan
Sunfish, Redear	4-10	Mill Pond, Fla.	1985	C.L. Windham
Tigerfish	61-11	Lake Tanganyika, Zambia	1984	Don Hunter
Trout, Brook	14-8	Nipigon River, Ontario	1916	Dr. W.J. Cook
Trout, Brown	35-15	Nahuel Huapi, Argentina	1952	Eugenio Cavaglia
Trout, Bull	32-0	Lake Pend Orielle, Idaho	1949	N.L. Higgins
Trout, Cutthroat	41-0	Pyramid Lake, Nev.	1925	John Skimmerhorn
Trout, Golden	11-0	Cook's Lake, Wyoming	1948	Charles S. Reed
Trout, Lake	65-0	Great Bear Lake, N.W.T., Canada	1970	Larry Daunis
Trout, Rainbow	42-2	Bell Island, Alaska	1970	David Robert White
Trout, Tiger	20-13	Lake Michigan, Wisc.	1978	Peter M. Friedland
Walleye	25-0	Old Hickory Lake, Tenn.	1960	Mabry Harper
Whitefish, Lake	14-6	Meaford, Ontario, Canada	1984	Dennis M. Laycock
Whitefish, Mountain	5-0	Athabasca River, Alberta, Canada	1963	Orville Welch
Whitefish, Round	6-0	Putahow River, Manitoba, Canada	1984	Allan J. Ristori

1. West and Rowe caught same size record spotted bass in 1987 in same location, Parris Lake, Calif. 3 months apart—West in Feb. and Rowe in April.

Caught With Rod and Reel in Salt Water (as of July 12, 1989)

Source: International Game Fish Association.

Species	lb-oz	Where caught	Year	Angler
Albacore	88-2	Canary Islands	1977	Siegfried Dickemann
Amberjack	155-10	Challenger Bank, Bermuda	1981	Joseph Dawson
Barracuda	83	Lagos, Nigeria	1952	K. J. W. Hackett
Bass, Black Sea	9-8	Virginia Beach, Va.	1987	Joe Mizelle, Jr.
Bass, Giant Sea	563-8	Anacapa Island, Calif.	1968	J. D. McAdam, Jr.
Bass, Striped	78-8	Atlantic City, N.J.	1982	Albert R. McReynolds
Blackfish (Tautog)	21-8	Wachapreague, Virginia	1984	Tommy Wood
Bluefish	31-12	North Carolina	1972	James M. Hussey
Bonefish	19	Zululand, S. Africa	1962	Brian W. Batchelor
Bonito, Atlantic	18-4	Fayal Island, Azores	1984	D. Gama Higgs
Bonito, Pacific	23-8	Victoria, Mahe	1975	Mrs. Anne Cochain
Cobia	135-9	Shark Bay, Australia	1985	Peter Goulding
Cod, Atlantic	98-12	Isle of Shoals, N.H.	1969	Alphonse Bielevich
Cod, Pacific	30-0	Andrew Bay, Alaska	1984	Donald R. Vaughn
Conger	102-8	Plymouth, Devon, England	1983	Raymond Ewart Street
Dolphin	87	Papagallo Gulf, Costa Rica	1976	Manual Salazar
Drum, Black	113-1	Lewes, Del.	1975	G. M. Townsend
Drum, Red	94-2	Avon, North Carolina	1984	David G. Deuel
Flounder, Summer	22-7	Montauk, N.Y.	1975	Charles Nappi
Haddock	9-15	Perkins Cove, Maine	1988	Jim Donohue
Halibut, Atlantic	250	Gloucester, Mass.	1981	Louis P. Sirard
Halibut, California	53-4	Santa Rosa Island, Calif.	1988	Russ Harmon
Hailbut, Pacific	350	Homer, Alaska	1982	Vern S. Foster
Jack, Crevalle	54-7	Port Michel, Gabon	1982	Thomas F. Gibson, Jr.
Jack, Horse-eye	24-8	Miami, Fla.	1982	Tito Schnau
Jack, Pacific Crevalle	24-0	Cabo San Lucas, Mexico	1987	Sharon Swanson
Jewfish	680	Fernandina Beach, Fla.	1961	Lynn Joyner
Lingcod	64-0	Elfin Cove, Alaska	1988	David Bauer
Mackerel, King	90	Key West, Florida	1976	Norton I. Thomton
Mackerel, Spanish	13-0	Ocracoke Inlet, N.C.	1987	Robert Cranton
Marlin, Atlantic Blue	1282	St. Thomas, Virgin Islands	1977	Larry Martin
Marlin, Black	1560	Cabo Blanco, Peru	1953	A. C. Glassel, Jr.
Marlin, Pacific Blue	1376	Kaaiwi Point, Kona, Hawaii	1982	Jay Wm. deBeaubien
Marlin, Striped	494	Tutukaka, New Zealand	1986	Bill Boniface
Marlin, White	181-14	Victoria, Brazil	1979	Evandro Luiz Coser
Permit	51-8	Lake Worth, Fla.	1978	William M. Kenney
Pollack	26-7	Salcombe, England	1984	Robert Perry
Pollack (virens)	46-7	Brielle, N.J.	1975	John T. Holton
Pompano, African	41-8	Fort Lauderdale, Fla.	1979	Wayne Sommers
Sailfish, Atlantic	128-1	Luanda, Angola, Africa	1974	Harm Steyn
Sailfish, Pacific	221	Santa Cruz Is., Galapagos Is.	1947	C. W. Stewart
Seabass, White	83-12	San Felipe, Mexico	1953	L. C. Baumgardner
Shark, Blue	437	Catherine Bay, Australia	1976	Peter Hyde
Shark, Hammerhead	991	Sarasota, Fla.	1982	Allen Ogle
Shark, Mako	1115-0	Black River, Mauritius	1988	Patrick Guillanton
Shark, Porbeagle	465	Padstow, Cornwall, England	1976	Jorge Potier
Shark, Thresher	802	Tutukaka, New Zealand	1981	Dianne North
Shark, Tiger	1780	Cherry Grove, S.C.	1964	Walter Maxwell
Shark, White	2664	South Australia	1959	Alfred Dean
Snapper, Cubera	121-8	Cameron, La.	1982	Mike Hebert
Snook	53-10	Costa Rica	1978	Gilbert Ponzi
Spearfish	90-13	Madeira Island, Portugal	1980	Joseph Larkin
Swordfish	1182	Iquique, Chile	1953	L. E. Marron
Tanguigue	99	Scottburgh, Natal, South Africa	1982	Michael John Wilkin-son
Tarpon	283	Lake Maracalbo, Venezuela	1956	M. Salazar
Trevally, Bigeye	15-0	Isla Coiba, Panama	1984	Sally S. Timms
Trevally, Giant	137-9	McKenzie State Park, Hawaii	1983	Roy K. Gushiken
Tuna, Atlantic Bigeye	375-8	Ocean City, Md.	1977	Cecil Browne
Tuna, Blackfin	42	Bermuda	1978	Alan J. Card
Tuna, Bluefin	1496	Nova Scotia, Canada	1979	Ken Fraser
Tuna, Dog-tooth	194	Kwan-Tall Island, Korea	1980	Kim Chul
Tuna, Longtail	79-2	Montague Island, Australia	1982	Tim Simpson
Tuna, Pacific Big-Eyed	435	Cobo Blanco, Peru	1957	R.V. A. Lee
Tuna, Skipjack	41-12	Black River, Mauritius	1982	Bruno de Ravel
Tuna, Southern Bluefin	348-5	Whakatane, New Zealand	1981	Rex Wood
Tuna, Yellowfin	388-12	Mexico	1977	Curt Wiesenmutter
Wahoo	149	Cat Cay, Bahamas	1962	John Pirovano
Weakfish	19-2	Jones Beach Inlet, N.Y.	1984	Dennis Roger Rooney
Yellowtail, California	78-0	Rocas Alijos, Mexico	1987	Richard Cresswell
Yellowtail, Southern	114-10	Tauranga, New Zealand	1984	Mike Godfrey

SPEED SKATING

U.S. OUTDOOR CHAMPIONS

Men

1959-60	Ken Bartholomew	1982	Greg Oly	1972	Ruth Moore, Nancy Thorne
1961	Ed Rudolph	1983	Michael Ralston	1973	Nancy Class
1962	Floyd Bedbury	•1984	Michael Ralston	1974	Kris Garbe
1963	Tom Gray	1985	Andy Gabel	1975	Nancy Swider
1964	Neil Blatchford	1986	Eric Klein	1976	Connie Carpenter
1965-66	Rich Wurster	1987	Dave Paulicic	1977	Liz Crowe
1967	Mike Passarella	1988	Patrick Wentland	1978	Paula Class, Betsy Davis
1968-70	Peter Cefalu	1989	Matt Trimble	1979	Gretchen Byrnes
1971	Jack Walters	**Women**		1980	Shari Miller
1972	Barth Levy	1960	Mary Novak	1981	Lisa Merrifield
1973	Mike Woods	1961	Jean Ashworth	1982	Lisa Merrifield
1974	Leigh Barczewski, Mike Passarella	1962	Jean Omelenchuk	1983	Janet Hainstock
		1963	Jean Ashworth	1984	Janet Hainstock
1975	Rich Wurster	1964	Diane White	1985	Betsy Davis
1976	John Wurster	1965	Jean Omelenchuk	1986	Deb Perkins
1977	Jim Chapin	1966	Diane White	1987	Laura Zuckerman
1978	Bill Heinkel	1967	Jean Ashworth	1988	Elise Brinich
1979	Erik Henriksen	1968	Helen Lutsch	1989	Liza Merrifield
1980	Greg Oly	1969	Sally Blatchford		
1981	Tom Grannes	1970-71	Sheila Young		

WORLD SPEED SKATING RECORDS

Men

Distance	Time	Skater	Place	Year
500m	0:36.45	Jens-Uwe Mey, East Germany	Calgary, Canada	1988
1000m	1:12.58	Pavel Pegov, Soviet Union	Medeo, U.S.S.R.	1983
1000m	1:12.58	Igor Zhelezovski	Heerenveea, The Netherlands	1989
1500m	1:52.50	Andre Hoffmann, East Germany	Calgary, Canada	1988
3000m	3:59.27	Leo Visser, Netherlands	Heerenveen, The Netherlands	1987
5000m	6:44.63	Tomas Gustafson, Sweden	Calgary, Canada	1988
10,000m	13:48:20	Tomas Gustafson, Sweden	Calgary, Canada	1988
All-around	160.807	Victor Shasherin, Soviet Union	Medeo, U.S.S.R.	1984

Women

Distance	Time	Skater	Place	Year
500m	0:39.10	Bonnie Blair, United States	Calgary, Canada	1988
1000m	1:17.65	Christa Rothenburger, E. Germany	Calgary, Canada	1988
1500m	2:00.68	Yvonne Van Gennip, Netherlands	Calgary, Canada	1988
3000m	4:11.94	Yvonne Van Gennip, Netherlands	Calgary, Canada	1988
5000m	7:14:13	Yvonne Van Gennip, Netherlands	Calgary, Canada	1988
All-around	171.760	Andrea Schone, East Germany	Medeo, U.S.S.R.	1984

U.S. INDOOR CHAMPIONS—1989

Men—Andy Gabel, Northbrook, Ill.
Women—Janie Eickhoff, Los Alamitos, Calif.
Intermediate Men—Jeff Benjamin, Highland Park, Ill.
Intermediate Women—Kristen Tulbot, Schuylerville, N.Y.
Junior Boys—David Tamburrino, Saratoga Springs, N.Y.
Junior Girls—Tricia Stennes, Arden Hills, Minn.

U.S. OUTDOOR CHAMPIONS—1989

Men—Matt Trimble, Iowa City
Women—Liza Merrifield, Butte, Montana
Intermediate Men—Don Foley, Butte, Montana
Intermediate Women—Julie Kriskovich, Butte, Montana
Junior Boys—Heath Hafter, White Bear Lake, Minn.
Junior Girls—Debra Cohen, Northbrook, Ill.

World Sprint Championships—1989

(Heerenveen, Holland, Feb. 25-26, 1989)

Men

500m—Igor Zhelezouski, Soviet Union	0:36.52
Vwe-Jens Mey, East Germany	0:36.46
1000m—Igor Zhelezouski, Soviet Union	1:12.58
Igor Zhelezouski, Soviet Union	1:12.61
Overall—Igor Zhelezouski, Soviet Union	145.945 pts

Women

500m—Bonnie Blair, Champaign, Ill.	0:39.47
Bonnie Blair, Champaign, Ill.	0:39.54
1000m—Christa Luding, East Germany	1:20.11
Christa Luding, East Germany	1:20.15
Overall—Bonnie Blair, Champaign, Ill.	159.435 pts*

*World record.

World Championships—1989

Men

(Oslo, Norway, Feb 11-12, 1989)

Overall champion—Leo Visser, Netherlands	165.698 pts.
500m—Nicolai Guljajev, USSR	0:38.12
1500m—Leo Visser, Netherlands	2:00.06
5000m—Leo Visser, Netherlands	7:03.52
10,000m—Geir Karlstad, Norway	14:33.72

Women

(Lake Placid, N.Y. Feb 4-5, 1989)

Overall—Constance Moser, East Germany	181.389 pts
500m—Seiko Hashimoto, Japan	0:42.59
1500m—Elena Lapuga, USSR	2:10.23
3000m—Constance Moser, East Germany	4:39.56
5000m—Gunda Kleemann, East Germany	7:58.27

FIGURE SKATING

WORLD CHAMPIONS

Men

1960	Alain Giletti, France
1961	No competition
1962	Donald Jackson, Canada
1963	Don McPherson, Canada
1964	Manfred Schnelldorfer, West Germany
1965	Alain Calmat, France
1966-68	Emmerich Danzer, Austria
1969-70	Tim Wood, United States
1971-73	Ondrej Nepela, Czechoslovakia
1974	Jan Hoffman, East Germany
1975	Sergei Yolkov, U.S.S.R.
1976	John Curry, Britain
1977	Vladimir Kovalev, U.S.S.R.
1978	Charles Tickner, United States
1979	Vladimir Kovalev, U.S.S.R.
1980	Jan Hoffman, East Germany
1981	Scott Hamilton, United States
1982	Scott Hamilton, United States
1983	Scott Hamilton, United States
1984	Scott Hamilton, United States
1985	Alexandr Fadeev, U.S.S.R.
1986	Brian Boitano, United States
1987	Brian Orser, Canada
1988	Brian Boitano, United States
1989	Kurt Browning, Canada

Women

1956-60	Carol Heiss, United States
1961	No competition
1962-64	Sjoukje Dijkstra, Netherlands
1965	Petra Burka, Canada
1966-68	Peggy Fleming, United States
1969-70	Gabriele Seyfert, East Germany
1971-72	Beatrix Schuba, Austria
1973	Karen Magnusson, Canada
1974	Christine Errath, East Germany
1975	Dianne de Leeuw, Netherlands
1976	Dorothy Hamill, United States
1977	Linda Fratianne, United States
1978	Anett Poetzsch, East Germany
1979	Linda Fratianne, United States
1980	Anett Poetzsch, East Germany
1981	Denise Beillmann, Switzerland
1982	Elaine Zayak, United States
1983	Rosalynn Sumners, United States
1984	Katarina Witt, East Germany
1985	Katarina Witt, East Germany
1986	Debi Thomas, United States
1987	Katarina Witt, East Germany
1988	Katarina Witt, East Germany
1989	Midori Ito, Japan

U.S. CHAMPIONS

Men

1946-52	Richard Button
1953-56	Hayes Jenkins
1957-60	David Jenkins
1961	Bradley Lord
1962	Monty Hoyt
1963	Tommy Liz
1964	Scott Allen
1965	Gary Visconti
1966	Scott Allen
1967	Gary Visconti
1968-70	Tim Wood
1971	John M. Petkevich
1972	Ken Shelley
1973-75	Gordon McKellen
1976	Terry Kubicka
1977-80	Charles Tickner
1981	Scott Hamilton
1982	Scott Hamilton
1983	Scott Hamilton
1984	Scott Hamilton
1985	Brian Boitano
1986	Brian Boitano
1987	Brian Boitano
1988	Brian Boitano
1989	Christopher Bowman

Women

1943-48	Gretchen Merrill
1949-50	Yvonne Sherman
1951	Sonya Klopfer
1952-56	Tenley Albright
1957-60	Carol Heiss
1961	Laurence Owen
1962	Barbara Roles Pursley
1963	Lorraine Hanlon
1964-68	Peggy Fleming
1969-73	Janet Lynn
1974-76	Dorothy Hamill
1977-80	Linda Fratianne
1981	Elaine Zayak
1982	Rosalynn Sumners
1983	Rosalynn Sumners
1984	Rosalynn Sumners
1985	Tiffany Chin
1986	Debi Thomas
1987	Jill Trenary
1988	Debi Thomas
1989	Jill Trenary

UNITED STATES CHAMPIONSHIPS—1989

(Baltimore, Md., Feb. 7-12, 1989)

Men's singles—Christopher Bowman, Los Angeles Figure Skating Club
Women's Singles—Jill Trenary, Broadmoor Skating Club
Pairs—Kristi Yamaguchi and Rudi Galindo, St. Moritz Ice Skating Club
Dance—Susan Wynne, Broadmoor Skating Club, and Joseph Druar, Seattle Skating Club
Junior Men's singles—Shepard Clark, Broadmoor Skating Club
Junior women's singles—Kyoko Ina, Skating Club of New York
Junior pairs—Jennifer Heurlin and John Frederiksen, Broadmoor Skating Club
Junior dance—Rachel Mayer and Peter Breen, Skating Club of Boston
Novice men—Philip Dulebohn, Baltimore Figure Skating Club
Novice women—Casey Link, Las Vegas Figure Skating Club

WORLD CHAMPIONS—1989

(Paris, France, March 14-19, 1989)

Men's singles—Kurt Browning, Canada
Women's singles—Midori Ito, Japan
Pairs—Ekaterina Gordeeva and Sergei Grinkov, Soviet Union
Dance—Marina Klimova and Sergei Ponomarenko, Soviet Union

VOLLEYBALL

1989 U.S. OPEN VOLLEYBALL CHAMPIONSHIPS

(June 5-10, Toledo, Ohio)

Men's Club—1st, Kenneth Allen Volleyball Club—Chicago, IL; 2nd, Washington Volleyball Club—Springfield, VA; 3rd, Nike/Molten/Billauer Chiropractic—Carson, CA
Women's Club—1st, Burmy's—Long Beach, CA; 2nd, Molten-Hawaii—Honolulu, HI; 3rd, Longhorn Consultants Realtors—Austin, TX
Women's Open—1st, Plymouth Californians—Hayward, CA; 2nd, ICU Sportswear/Spikers—Seattle, WA; 3rd, Power Angle/Club Sportswear—Kansas City, MO
Men's Senior—1st, Silverado—San Diego, CA; 2nd, Sojourners—Birmingham, AL; 3rd, Network VBC—South Bend, IN
Women's Senior—1st, Colorado Connection—Denver, CO; 2nd, Mavericks-Nike—Los Angeles, CA; 3rd, Nick's Prime Time Players—Chicago, IL
Men's Masters—1st, Lehman, Lucchesi & Walker—Denver, CO; 2nd, Outrigger Canoe Club—Honolulu, HI; 3rd, Arnie's Saloon—Villa Hills, KY
Men's Golden Masters—1st, Outrigger Canoe Club—Honolulu, HI; 2nd, DTF—Fort Wayne, IN; 3rd, I Dig-Legends—Los Alamitos, CA

NCAA CHAMPIONSHIPS

Men

(May 5-6, UCLA, Los Angeles, California)

Final—UCLA defeated Stanford, 15-1, 15-13, 4-15, 15-12, in final match

Women

Division I—Texas defetaed Hawaii, 15-4, 16-14, 15-13 in final
Division II—Portland State defeated California State-Northbridge, 15-6, 15-8, 15-6 in final
Division III—California-San Diego defeated Illinois Benedictine, 14-16, 15-6, 6-15, 15-10, 15-2 in final

SWIMMING

WORLD RECORDS—MEN

(Through September 1, 1989)
Approved by the International Swimming Federation (F.I.N.A.)
(F.I.N.A. discontinued acceptance of records in yards in 1968)
Source: United States Swim Team.

Distance	Record	Holder	Country	Date
Freestyle				
50 meters	0:22.12	Tom Jager	United States	Aug. 20, 1989
100 meters	0:48.42	Matt Biondi	United States	August 9, 1988
200 meters	1:46.69	Georgio Lamberti	Italy	Aug. 15, 1989
400 meters	3:46.95	Uwe Dussler	East Germany	Sept. 23, 1988
800 meters	7:50.64	Vladimir Salnikov	Soviet Union	July 4, 1986
1,500 meters	14:54.76	Vladimir Salnikov	Soviet Union	Feb. 22, 1983
Backstroke				
100 meters	0:54.51	David Berkoff	United States	Sept. 24, 1988
200 meters	1:58.14	Igor Poliansky	Soviet Union	March 1, 1985
Breaststroke				
100 meters	1:01.49	Adrian Moorehouse	West Germany	Aug. 15, 1989
200 meters	2:13.09	Mike Barrowman	United States	Aug. 20, 1989
Butterfly				
100 meters	0:52.84	Pablo Morales	United States	June 23, 1986
200 meters	1:56.65	Michael Gross	West Germany	Aug. 10, 1985
Individual Medley				
200-meter individual medley	2:00.11	David Wharton	United States	Aug. 20, 1989
400-meter individual medley	4:15.42	Tamas Darnyi	Hungary	Sept. 21, 1988
Freestyle Relay				
400 meters	3:16.53	United States	National Team	Sept. 23, 1988
800-meters	7:12.51	United States	National Team	Sept. 21, 1988
Medley Relay				
400 meters	3:36.93	United States	National Team	Sept. 25, 1988

WORLD RECORDS—WOMEN

Distance	Record	Holder	Country	Date
Freestyle				
50 Meters	0:24.98	Yang Wenyi	China	April 11, 1988
100 Meters	0:54.73	Kristin Otto	East Germany	Aug. 19, 1986
200 Meters	1:57.55	Heike Friedrich	East Germany	June 16, 1986
400 Meters	4:03.85	Janet Evans	United States	Sept. 22, 1988
800 Meters	8:16.22	Janet Evans	United States	Aug. 20, 1989
1,500 Meters	15:52.10	Janet Evans	United States	March 26, 1988
Backstroke				
100 Meters	1:00.59	Ina Kleber	East Germany	Aug. 24, 1984
200 Meters	2:08.60	Betsy Mitchell	United States	June 27, 1986
Breaststroke				
100 Meters	1:07.91	Silke Hoerner	East Germany	Aug. 21, 1987
200 Meters	2:26.71	Silke Hoerner	East Germany	Sept. 21, 1988
Butterfly				
100 Meters	0:57.93	Mary T. Meagher	United States	Aug. 16, 1982
200 Meters	2:05.96	Mary T. Meagher	United States	Aug. 13, 1982
Individual Medley				
200 Meters	2:11.73	Ute Geweniger	East Germany	July 4, 1981
400 Meters	4:36.10	Petra Schneider	East Germany	Aug. 1, 1982

Freestyle

400 Meters	3:40.57	East German National Team	East Germany	Aug. 19, 1986
800 Meters	7:55.47	East German National Team	East Germany	Aug. 18, 1987

Medley Relay

400 Meters	4:03.69	East German National Team	East Germany	Aug. 24, 1984

U.S. SHORT-COURSE SWIMMING RECORDS

Source: United States Swimming Team.

MEN
Freestyle

50 yards—Matt Biondi, 1987	0:19.15
100 yards—Matt Biondi, 1987	0:41.80
200 yards—Matt Biondi, 1987	1:33.03
500 yards—Mike O'Brien, 1985	4:13.06
1,000 yards—Mike O'Brien, 1985	8:47.38
1,650 yards—Jeff Kostoff, 1986	14:37.87

Backstroke

100 yards—David Berkoff, 1989	0:47.02
200 yards—Rick Carey, 1983	1:44.43

Breaststroke

100 yards—Steve Lundquist, 1983	0:52.48
200 yards—Steve Lundquist, 1981	1:55.01

Butterfly

100 yards—Pablo Morales, 1986	0:46.26
200 yards—Pablo Morales, 1987	1:42.60

Individual Medley

200 yards—David Wharton, 1989	1:44.70
400 yards—David Wharton, 1988	3:42.23

Relays

200-yard freestyle—Mission Viejo, 1981	1:18.55
400-yard freestyle—University of Texas, 1988	2:52.01
800-yard freestyle—University of Texas, 1988	6:23.47
400-yard medley—Stanford, 1985	3:10.92

WOMEN
Freestyle

50 yards—Leanne Fetter, 1989	0:22.05
100 yards—Angel Meyers, 1988	0:48.20
200 yards—Cynthia Woodhead, 1979	1:44.10
500 yards—Tracy Caulkins, 1979	4:36.25
1000 yards—Janet Evans, 1989	9:25.49
1,650 yards—Janet Evans, 1989	15:44.98

Backstroke

100 yards—Betsy Mitchell, 1987	0:53.98
200 yards—Betsy Mitchell, 1987	1:55.16

Breaststroke

100 yards—Mary Ellen Blanchard, 1989	1:00.66
200 yards—Mary Ellen Blanchard, 1989	2:09.06

Butterfly

100 yards—Mary T. Meagher, 1987	0:52.42
200 yards—Mary T. Meagher, 1981	1:52.99

Individual Medley

200 yards—Tracy Caulkins, 1984	1:57.06
400 yards—Tracy Caulkins, 1981	4:04.63

Relays

200-yard freestyle—Texas, 1989	1:28.90
400-yard freestyle—Texas, 1989	3:19.15
800-yard freestyle—Florida, 1988	7:06.56
200-yard medley—Texas, 1987	1:39.88
400-yard medley—Stanford, 1987	3:38.17

U.S. SHORT COURSE CHAMPIONSHIPS

(Chapel Hill, N.C., March 21–25, 1989)

Women's Events

50-yard freestyle—Jenny Thompson	0:22.70
100-yard freestyle—Jenny Thompson	0:49.67
200-yard freestyle—Whitney Hedgepeth	1:46.56
500-yard freestyle—Janet Evans	4:41.31
1,000-yard freestyle—Janet Evans	9:25.49
1,650-yard freestyle—Julie Kole	16:06.60
100-yard backstroke—Anne Mahoney	0:55.91
200-yard backstroke—Dede Trimble	1:59.28
100-yard breaststroke—Mary Ellen Blanchard	1:01.08
200-yard breaststroke—Mary Ellen Blanchard	2:09.06
100-yard butterfly—Whitney Hedgepeth	0:54.62
200-yard butterfly—Summer Sanders	1:57.96
200-yard individual medley—Mary Ellen Blanchard	1:59.92
400-yard individual medley—Janet Evans	4:13.24
400-yard freestyle relay—Longhorn	3:22.84
800-yard freestyle relay—Mission Viejo "A"	7:18.32
400-yard medley relay—Longhorn	3:42.41
Team Standings: 1. Dynamo	276.0
2. Longhorn	236.0
3. Virginia Association	207.0

Men's Events

50-yard freestyle—Steve Crocker	0:19.60
100-yard freestyle—Doug Boyd	0:43.79
200-yard freestyle—John Keppeler	1:36.26
500-yard freestyle—Norbert Agh	4:23.34
1,000-yard freestyle—Chad Hundeby	9:01.53
1,650-yard freestyle—Jean-Marie Arnould	15:11.26
100-yard backstroke—Geoff Cronin	0:49.67
200-yard backstroke—Derekl Weatherford	1:46.28
100-yard breaststroke—Todd Torres	0:54.88
200-yard breaststroke—J.J. Freitag	1:59.52
100-yard butterfly—Anthony Nesty	0:47.52
200-yard butterfly—Anthony Nesty	1:46.52
200-yard individual medley—Tom Darnyi	1:48.87
400-yard individual medley—Chas Morton	3:52.90
400-yard freestyle relay—Little Rock	2:57.14
800-yard freestyle relay—Pine Crest Swim Club	6:34.31
400-yard medley relay—Longhorn	3:19.24
Team Standings: 1. Little Rock	230.0
2. Santa Clara	227.0
3. Longhorn	220.0

U.S. LONG COURSE CHAMPIONSHIPS

(Los Angeles, Calif., July 31–Aug. 4, 1989)

Women's Events

50-meter freestyle—Leanne Fetter	0:25.55
100-meter freestyle—Nicole Haislett	0:56.15
200-meter freestyle—Julie Kole	2:00.95
400-meter freestyle—Janet Evans	4:06.73
800-meter freestyle—Janet Evans	8:22.11
1,500-meter freestyle—Julie Kole	16:14.12
100-meter backstroke—Betsy Mitchell	1:02.37
200-meter backstroke—Kristen Linehan	2:14.01
100-meter breaststroke—Tracey McFarlane	1:09.88
200-meter breaststroke—Mary Ellen Blanchard	2:31.59
100-meter butterfly—Pamela Minthorn	1:01.12
200-meter butterfly—Pamela Minthorn	2:11.88
200-meter individual medley—Janet Evans	2:15.15
400-meter individual medley—Janet Evans	4:39.36
400-meter freestyle relay—Longhorn "A"	3:45.92
800-meter freestyle relay—Longhorn "A"	8:11.54
400-meter medley relay—Longhorn "A"	4:13.73

Men's Events

50-meter freestyle—Matt Biondi	0:22.36
100-meter freestyle—Brent Lang	0:50.17
200-meter freestyle—Doug Gjersten	1:48.70
400-meter freestyle—Daniel Jorgensen	3:50.88
800-meter freestyle—Daniel Jorgensen	7:56.61
1,500-meter freestyle—Lars Jorgensen	15:17.33
100-meter backstroke—Geoff Cronin	0:56.14
200-meter backstroke—Dan Veatch	2:02.09
100-meter breaststroke—Rich Schroeder	1:02.46
200-meter breaststroke—Mike Barrowman	2:14.74
100-meter butterfly—Wade King	0:53.72
200-meter butterfly—Melvin Stewart	1:57.94
200-meter individual medley—Dave Wharton	2:01.48
400-meter individual medley—David Wharton	4:15.93
400-meter freestyle relay—Longhorn "A"	3:22.00
800-meter freestyle relay—Longhorn "A"	7:22.78
400-meter medley relay—Ft. Lauderdale "A"	3:45.26

NATIONAL COLLEGIATE ATHLETIC ASSOCIATION

MEN'S CHAMPIONSHIPS—1989

(Indianapolis, Ind., March 30–April 1, 1989)

50-yard freestyle—Brent Lang, Michigan	0:19.68
100-yard freestyle—Shaun Jordan, Texas	0:42.98
200-yard freestyle—Artur Wojdat, Iowa	1:33.82
500-yard freestyle—Artur Wojdat, Iowa	4:12.24
1,650-yard freestyle—Mariusz Podkoscielny, Arizona	14:38.09
100-yard backstroke—David Berkoff, Harvard	0:47.02
200-yard backstroke—Jeff Rouse, Stanford	1:44.87
100-yard breaststroke—Kirk Stackle, Texas	0:54.02
200-yard breaststroke—Mike Barrowman, Michigan	1:55.72
100-yard butterfly—Jay Mortenson, Stanford	0:47.14
200-yard butterfly—Melvin Stewart, Tennessee	1:44.30
200-yard individual medley—David Wharton, USC	1:44.70
400-yard individual medley—David Wharton, USC	3:44.69
400-yard medley relay—Texas	3:11.60
400-yard freestyle relay—Texas	2:52.94
800-yard freestyle relay—Texas	6:22.51
1-meter diving—Mark Lenzi, Indiana	602.55 points
3-meter diving—Pat Evans, Cincinnati	649.55 points
10-meter diving—Scott Donie, Southern Methodist	757.45 points
Team standings—1. Texas	475
2. Stanford	396
3. Michigan	315

WOMEN'S CHAMPIONSHIPS—1989

(Indianapolis, Ind., March 16-18, 1989)

50-yard freestyle—Leanne Fetter, Texas	0:22.05
100-yard freestyle—Leanne Fetter, Texas	0:48.68
200-yard freestyle—Mitzi Kramer, Clemson	1:44.78
500-yard freestyle—Mitzi Kramer, Clemson	4:39.18
1,650-yard freestyle—Erika Hansen, Georgia	16:00.04
100-yard backstroke—Kristen Linehan, Florida	0:54.98
200-yard backstroke—Kristen Linehan, Florida	1:57.89
100-yard breaststroke—Stephanie Zunich, Florida	1:02.10
200-yard breaststroke—Ann Colloton, Michigan	2:12.96
100-yard butterfly—Jenna Johnson, Stanford	0:53.24
200-yard butterfly—Julia Gorman, Florida	1:56.94
200-yard individual medley—Angel Myers, Furman	1:59.49
400-yard individual medley—Michelle Griglione, Stanford	4:12.29
200-yard medley relay—Florida	1:41.08
400-yard medley relay—Florida	3:38.38
200-yard freestyle relay—Texas	1:28.90
400-yard freestyle relay—Texas	3:15.48
800-yard freestyle relay—Florida	7:07.82
1-meter diving—Alison Maisch, Louisiana State	479.10 points
3-meter diving—Kelly Jenkins, Texas	534.55 points
Team standings—1. Stanford	610.5
2. Texas	547
3. Flordia	536

U.S. DIVING CHAMPIONSHIPS—1989

INDOOR
(Boca Raton, Fla., April 19-23, 1989)
Men's Events

1-meter—Pat Evans, Stingrays	614.52
3-meter—Kent Ferguson, Mission Bay	629.88
Platform—Matt Scoggin, Longhorns	616.77

Women's Events

1-meter—Julie Farrell, Spartans	454.35
3-meter—Kelly McCormick, Ohio State	507.66
Platform—Wendy Wyland, Mission Bay	428.01

OUTDOOR
(Raleigh, N.C., Aug. 15-19, 1989)
Men's Events

1-meter—Kent Ferguson, Mission Bay	577.20
3-meter—Kent Ferguson, Mission Bay	671.82
Platform—Matt Scoggin, Longhorn	612.45

Women's Events

1-meter—Wendy Lucero, Kimball Divers	472.05
3-meter—Wendy Lucero, Kimball Divers	502.77
Platform—Wendy Wyland, Mission Bay	412.68

Swimming History

The famous British poet, Lord Byron, was a noted swimmer and swam one leg of the Hellspont, Sestos to Abydos, on May 3, 1810, in 1 hour and 10 minutes. Once in an endurance trial at Venice, Byron was in the water for 4 hours and 10 minutes. Distance swimming was an early type of competition. Captain Matthew Webb was the first to swim the English Channel—Dover to Calais—in August 1875, in 21 hours and 45 minutes. The first woman to swim the English Channel was Gertrude Ederle, of New York City, on Aug. 6, 1926, in 14 hours and 34 minutes.

The modern sport of swimming was developed in England during the 1800s. Contests using the breaststroke were held in London in 1837. A group of London swimming clubs met in 1869 and formed the London Swimming Association which later became the Amateur Swimming Association. The United States Amateur Athletic Union (AAU), formed in 1888, assumed supervision of swimming along with other sports.

BOXING

Whether it be called pugilism, prize fighting or boxing, there is no tracing "the Sweet Science" to any definite source. Tales of rivals exchanging blows for fun, fame or money go back to earliest recorded history and classical legend. There was a mixture of boxing and wrestling called the "pancratium" in the ancient Olympic Games and in such contests the rivals belabored one another with hands fortified with heavy leather wrappings that were sometimes studded with metal. More than one Olympic competitor lost his life at this brutal exercise.

There was little law or order in pugilism until Jack Broughton, one of the early champions of England, drew up a set of rules for the game in 1743. Broughton, called "the father of English box-

ing," also is credited with having invented boxing gloves. However, these gloves—or "mufflers" as they were called—were used only in teaching "the manly art of self-defense" or in training bouts. All professional championship fights were contested with "bare knuckles" until 1892, when John L. Sullivan lost the heavyweight championship of the world to James J. Corbett in New Orleans in a bout in which both contestants wore regulation gloves.

The Broughton rules were superseded by the London Prize Ring Rules of 1838. The 8th Marquis of Queensberry, with the help of John G. Chambers, put forward the "Queensberry Rules" in 1866, a code that called for gloved contests. Amateurs took quickly to the Queensberry Rules, the professionals slowly.

HISTORY OF WORLD HEAVYWEIGHT CHAMPIONSHIP FIGHTS

(Bouts in which a new champion was crowned)

Source: Nat Fleischer's Ring *Boxing Encyclopedia and Record Book*, published and copyrighted by The Ring Book Shop, Inc., 120 West 31st St., New York, N.Y. 10001.

Date	Where held	Winner, weight, age	Loser, weight, age	Rounds	Referee
Sept. 7, 1892	New Orleans, La.	James J. Corbett, 178 (26)	John L. Sullivan, 212 (33)	21	Prof. John Duffy
March 17, 1897	Carson City, Nev.	Bob Fitzsimmons, 167 (34)	James J. Corbett, 183 (30)	KO 14	George Siler
June 9, 1899	Coney Island, N.Y.	James J. Jeffries, 206 (24)[1]	Bob Fitzsimmons, 167 (37)	KO 11	George Siler
Feb. 23, 1906	Los Angeles	Tommy Burns, 180 (24)[2]	Marvin Hart, 188 (29)	20	James J. Jeffries
Dec. 26, 1908	Sydney, N.S.W.	Jack Johnson, 196 (30)	Tommy Burns, 176 (27)	KO 14	Hugh McIntosh
April 5, 1915	Havana, Cuba	Jess Willard, 230 (33)	Jack Johnson, 205 1/2 (37)	KO 26	Jack Welch
July 4, 1919	Toledo, Ohio	Jack Dempsey, 187 (24)	Jess Willard, 245 (37)	KO 3	Ollie Pecord
Sept. 23, 1926	Philadelphia	Gene Tunney, 189 (28)[3]	Jack Dempsey, 190 (31)	10	Pop Reilly
June 12, 1930	New York	Max Schmeling, 188 (24)	Jack Sharkey, 197 (27)	WF 4	Jim Crowley
June 21, 1932	Long Island City	Jack Sharkey, 205 (29)	Max Schmeling, 188 (26)	15	Gunboat Smith
June 29, 1933	Long Island City	Primo Carnera, 260 1/2 (26)	Jack Sharkey, 201 (30)	KO 6	Arthur Donovan
June 14, 1934	Long Island City	Max Baer, 209 1/2 (25)	Primo Carnera, 263 1/4 (27)	KO 11	Arthur Donovan
June 13, 1935	Long Island City	Jim Braddock, 193 3/4 (29)	Max Baer, 209 1/2 (26)	15	Jack McAvoy
June 22, 1937	Chicago	Joe Louis, 197 1/4 (23)	Jim Braddock, 197 (31)	KO 8	Tommy Thomas
June 22, 1949	Chicago	Ezzard Charles, 181 3/4 (27)[4]	Joe Walcott, 195 1/2 (35)	15	Davey Miller
Sept. 27, 1950	New York	Ezzard Charles, 184 1/2 (29)[5]	Joe Louis, 218 (36)	15	Mark Conn
July 18, 1951	Pittsburgh	Joe Walcott, 194 (37)	Ezzard Charles, 182 (30)	KO 7	Buck McTiernan
Sept. 23, 1952	Philadelphia	Rocky Marciano, 184 (29)[6]	Joe Walcott, 196 (38)	KO 13	Charley Daggert
Nov. 30, 1956	Chicago	Floyd Patterson, 182 1/4 (21)	Archie Moore, 187 3/4 (42)	KO 5	Frank Sikora
June 26, 1959	New York	Ingemar Johansson, 196 (26)	Floyd Patterson, 182 (24)	KO 3	Ruby Goldstein
June 20, 1960	New York	Floyd Patterson, 190 (25)	Ingemar Johansson, 194 3/4 (27)	KO 5	Arthur Mercante
Sept. 25, 1962	Chicago	Sonny Liston, 214 (28)	Floyd Patterson, 189 (27)	KO 1	Frank Sikora
Feb. 25, 1964	Miami Beach, Fla.	Cassius Clay, 210 (22)[7]	Sonny Liston, 218 (30)	KO 7	Barney Felix
March 4, 1968	New York	Joe Frazier, 204 1/2 (24)[8]	Buster Mathis, 243 1/2 (23)	KO 11	Arthur Mercante
April 27, 1968	Oakland, Calif.	Jimmy Ellis, 197 (28)[9]	Jerry Quarry, 195 (22)	15	Elmer Costa
Feb. 16, 1970	New York	Joe Frazier, 205 (26)[10]	Jimmy Ellis, 201 (29)	KO 5	Tony Perez
Jan. 22, 1973	Kingston, Jamaica	George Foreman, 217 1/2 (24)	Joe Frazier, 214 (29)	KO 2	Arthur Mercante
Oct. 30, 1974	Kinshasa, Zaire	Muhammad Ali, 216 1/2 (32)	George Foreman, 220 (26)	KO 8	Zack Clayton
Feb. 15, 1978	Las Vegas, Nev.	Leon Spinks, 197 (25)	Muhammad Ali, 224 1/2 (36)	15	Howard Buck
June 9, 1978	Las Vegas, Nev.	Larry Holmes, 212 (28)[11]	Ken Norton, 220 (32)	15	Mills Lans
Sept. 15, 1978	New Orleans	Muhammad Ali, 221 (36)[12]	Leon Spinks, 201 (25)	15	Lucien Joubert
Oct. 20, 1979	Pretoria, S. Africa	John Tate, 240 (24)[13]	Gerrie Coetzee, 222 (24)	15	Carlos Berrocal
March 31, 1980	Knoxville, Tenn.	Mike Weaver, 207 1/2 (27)	John Tate, 232 (25)	KO 15	Ernesto Magana Ansorena
Dec. 10, 1982	Las Vegas, Nev.	Michael Dokes, 216 (24)	Mike Weaver, 209 1/2 (30)	KO 1	Joey Curtis
Sept. 23, 1983	Richfield, Ohio	Gerrie Coetzee, 215 (28)	Michael Dokes, 217 (25)	KO 10	Tony Perez
March 9, 1984	Las Vegas, Nev.	Tim Witherspoon, 220 1/2 (26)[14]	Greg Page, 239 1/2 (25)	12	Mills Lane
August 31, 1984	Las Vegas, Nev.	Pinklon Thomas, 216 (26)	Tim Witherspoon, 217 (26)	12	Richard Steele
Nov. 9, 1984	Las Vegas, Nev.	Larry Holmes, 221 1/2 (35)[15]	James Smith 227 (31)	KO 12	Dave Pearl
Dec. 1, 1984	Sun City, S. Africa	Greg Page, 236 (25)[16]	Gerrie Coetzee, 217 (29)	KO 8	unavailable
April 29, 1985	Buffalo, N.Y.	Tony Tubbs, 229 (25)[16]	Greg Page, 239 1/2 (26)	15	unavailable.
Sept. 21,1985	Las Vegas, Nev.	Michael Spinks, 200 (29)	Larry Holmes, 221 (35)	15	Carlos Padilla
Jan. 17, 1986	Atlanta, Ga.	Tim Witherspoon, 227 (28)	Tony Tubbs, 229 (27)	15	unavailable
Nov. 23, 1986	Las Vegas, Nev.	Mike Tyson, 217 (20)[17]	Trevor Berbick, 220 (29)	KO2	unavailable
Dec. 12, 1986	New York, N.Y.	James Smith, 230 (33)[16]	Tim Witherspoon, 218 (29)	KO1	unavailable
March 7, 1987	Las Vegas, Nev.	Mike Tyson, 217 (20)[16]	James Smith, 230 (33)	12	unavailable

1. Jeffries retired as champion in March 1905. He named Marvin Hart and Jack Root as leading contenders and agreed to referee their fight in Reno, Nev., on July 3, 1905, with the stipulation that he would term the winner the champion. Hart, 190 (28), knocked out Root, 171 (29), in the 12th round. 2. Burns claimed the title after defeating Hart. 3. Tunney retired as champion after defeating Tom Heeney on July 26, 1928. 4. After Louis announced his retirement as champion on March 1, 1949, Charles won recognition from the National Boxing Association as champion by defeating Walcott. 5. Charles gained undisputed recognition as champion by defeating Louis, who came out of retirement. 6. Retired as Champion April 27, 1956. 7. The World Boxing Association later withdrew its recognition of Clay as champion and declared the winner of a bout between Ernie Terrell and Eddie Machen would gain its version of the title. Terrell, 199 (25), won a 15-round decision from Machen, 192 (32), in Chicago on March 5, 1965. Clay, 212 1/4 (25) and Terrell, 212 1/2 (27) met in Houston on Feb. 6, 1967. Clay winning a 15-round decision. 8. Winner recognized by New York, Massachusetts, Maine, Illinois, Texas and Pennsylvania to fill vacated title when Clay was stripped of championship for failing to accept U. S. Induction. 9. Bout was final of eight-man tournament to fill Clay's place and is recognized by World Boxing Association. 10. Bout settled controversy over title. 11. Holmes won World Boxing Council title after WBC had withdrawn recognition of Spinks, March 18, 1978, and awarded its title to Norton, WBC, said Spinks had reneged on agreement to fight Norton 12. Ali regained World Boxing Association championship. 13. Tate won WBA title after Ali retired and left it vacant. 14. Tim Witherspoon and Greg Page fought for the WBC heavyweight title vacated by Larry Holmes, who could not come to agreement on a deal to fight Page, the No. 1 contender. Holmes declared he would fight under the banner of the International Boxing Federation. Several dates were set and postponed for fights between Holmes and Gerry Coetzee, the WBA champ, the latest being Nov. 16, 1984.15. First fight under banner of International Boxing Federation. 16. New W.B.A. champion. 17. New W.B.C. champion.

OTHER WORLD BOXING TITLEHOLDERS
(Through Aug. 1, 1989)

Light Heavyweight

1903	Jack Root, George Gardner	1968	Dick Tiger, Bob Foster	1981	Matthew Saad Muhammad (WBC), Eddie Mustafa Muhammad (WBA), Michael Spinks (WBA), Dwight Braxton (WBC)
1903–05	Bob Fitzsimmons	1969–70	Bob Foster		
1905–12	Philadelphia Jack O'Brien[1]	1971	Vicente Rondon (WBA), Bob Foster (WBC)		
1912–16	Jack Dillon				
1916–20	Battling Levinsky	1972–73	Bob Foster (WBA, WBC)		
1920–22	Georges Carpentier	1974	John Conteh (WBA), Bob Foster (WBC)[14]	1982	Dwight Braxton (WBC), Michael Spinks (WBA)
1923	Battling Siki				
1923–25	Mike McTigue	1975–76	Victor Galindez (WBA), John Conteh (WBC)	1983	Michael Spinks (undisputed)
1925–26	Paul Berlenbach			1984	Michael Spinks (undisputed)
1926–27	Jack Delaney[2]	1977	Victor Galindez (WBA), John Conteh (WBC)[4], Miguel Cuello (WBC)	1985	Michael Spinks (undisputed)[5]
1927	Mike McTigue			1986	Marvin Johnson (WBA), Dennis Andries (WBC)
1927–29	Tommy Loughran				
1930	Jimmy Slattery	1978	Victor Galindez (WBA), Mike Rossman (WBA), Miguel Cuello (WBC), Mate Parlov (WBC), Marvin Johnson (WBC)	1987	Thomas Hearns (WBC), Virgil Hill (WBA), Bobby Czyz (IBF)
1930–34	Maxie Rosenbloom				
1934–35	Bob Olin				
1935–39	John Henry Lewis				
1939	Melio Bettina			1988	Charles Williams (IBF), Virgil Hill (WBA), Donny LaLonde (WBC), Sugar Ray Leonard (WBC)
1939–41	Billy Conn[2]	1979	Mike Rossman (WBA), Vict Galindez (WBA), Marvin Johnson (WBC), Matthew (Franklin) Saad Muhammad (WBC)		
1941	Anton Christoforidis (NBA)				
1941–48	Gus Lesnevich				
1948–50	Freddie Mills				
1950–52	Joey Maxim			1989	Dennis Andries (WBC), Virgil Hill (WBA), Charles Williams (IBF)
1952–61	Archie Moore[3]	1980	Matthew Saad Muhammad (WBC), Marvin Johnson (WBA), Eddie (Gregory) Mustafa Muhammad (WBA)		
1961–63	Harold Johnson				
1963–65	Willie Pastrano				
1965–66	José Torres				
1966–67	Dick Tiger				

1. Retired. 2. Abandoned title. 3. NBA withdrew recognition in 1961, New York Commission in 1962; recognized thereafter only by California and Europe. 4. WBC withdrew recognition. 5. Spinks relinquished title in 1985 to fight for heavyweight title.

Middleweight

			Freddy Steele, Al Hostak, Solly Kreiger, Fred Apostoli, Cerferino Garcia, Ken Overlin, Billy Soose, Tony Zale[4]	1962	Paul Pender[1]
1867–72	Tom Chandler			1962–63	Dick Tiger
1872–81	George Rooke			1963–65	Joey Giardello
1881–82	Mike Donovan[1]			1965–66	Dick Tiger
1884–91	Jack (Nonpareil) Dempsey			1966	Emile Griffith
1891–97	Bob Fitzsimmons[2]	1941–47	Tony Zale	1967	Nino Benvenuti, Emile Griffith
1908	Stanley Ketchel, Billy Papke	1947–48	Rocky Graziano	1968	Emile Griffith, Nino Benvenuti
1908–10	Stanley Ketchel[3]	1948	Tony Zale	1969	Nino Benvenuti
1913	Frank Klaus	1948–49	Marcel Cerdan	1970	Nino Benvenuti, Carlos Monzon
1913–14	George Chip	1949–51	Jake LaMotta		
1914–17	Al McCoy	1952	Ray Robinson, Randy Turpin	1971–73	Carlos Monzon
1917–20	Mike O'Dowd	1951–52	Ray Robinson[1]	1974–75	Carlos Monzon (WBA), Rodrigo Valdez (WBC)
1920–23	Johnny Wilson	1953–55	Carl Olson		
1923–26	Harry Greb	1955–57	Ray Robinson[5]	1976	Carlos Monzon (WBA, WBC), Rodrigo Valdez (WBC)
1926	Tiger Flowers	1957	Gene Fullmer, Ray Robinson		
1926–31	Mickey Walker[2]	1957–58	Carmen Basilio	1977	Carlos Monzon (WBA, WBC)[1], Rodrigo Valdez (WBA, WBC)
1931–41	Gorilla Jones, Ben Jeby, Marcel Thil, Lou Brouillard, Vince Dundee, Teddy Yarosz, Babe Risko,	1958–60	Ray Robinson[6]		
		1960–61	Paul Pender[7]		
		1959–62	Gene Fullmer (NBA)	1978	Rodrigo Valdez, Hugo Corro
		1961–62	Terry Downes[1]	1979	Hugo Corro, Vito Antuofermo

Sports—Boxing 927

1980	Vito Antuofermo, Alan Minter, Marvin Hagler		Sugar Ray Leonard (undisputed)		James Kinchen (NABF)
1981	Marvin Hagler	1988	Sumbu Kalambay (WBA), Thomas Hearns (WBC), Iran Barkley (WBC), Frank Tate (IBF), Michael Nunn (IBF),	1989	Michael Nunn (IBF), Mike McCallum (WBA), Iran Barkley (WBC)
1982-86	Marvelous Marvin Hagler (undisputed)				
1987	Marvin Hagler (undisputed)				

1. Retired. 2. Abandoned title. 3. Died. 4. National Boxing Association and New York Commission disagreed on champions. Those listed were accepted by one or the other until Zale gained world-wide recognition. 5. Ended retirement in 1954. 6. NBA withdrew recognition. 7. Recognized by New York, Massachusetts, and Europe.

Welterweight

1892-94	Mysterious Billy Smith	1940-41	Fritzie Zivic	1977-78	José Cuevas (WBA), Carlos Palomino (WBC)
1894-96	Tommy Ryan	1941-46	Freddie Cochrane	1979	José Cuevas (WBA), Carlos Palomino (WBC), Wilfredo Benitez (WBC)
1896	Kid McCoy[2]	1946	Marty Servo[1]		
1896-1900	Mysterious Billy Smith	1946-51	Ray Robinson[2]		
1900	Rube Ferns	1951	Johnny Bratton (NBA)	1980	José Cuevas (WBA), Ray Leonard (WBC), Roberto Duran (WBC), Thomas Hearns (WBA)
1900-01	Matty Matthews	1951-54	Kid Gavilan		
1901	Ruby Ferns	1954-55	Johnny Saxton		
1901-04	Joe Walcott	1955	Tony DeMarco	1981	Ray Leonard (WBC), Thomas Hearns (WBA), Ray Leonard (WBC,WBA)
1904	Dixie Kid[2]	1955-56	Carmen Basilio		
1904-06	Joe Walcott	1956	Johnny Saxton		
1906-07	Honey Mellody	1956-57	Carmen Basilio[2]	1982	Ray Leonard
1907	Mike (Twin) Sullivan[2]	1958	Virgil Akins	1983-85	Donald Curry (WBA)
1915-19	Ted Lewis	1959-60	Don Jordan	1983-85	Milton McCrory (WBC)
1919-22	Jack Britton	1960-61	Benny (Kid) Paret	1985-86	Donald Curry (undisputed)
1922-26	Mickey Walker	1961	Emile Griffith	1987	Mark Breland (WBA), Marlon Starling (WBA), Lloyd Honeychan (IBF)
1926-27	Pete Latzo	1961-62	Benny (Kid) Paret		
1927-29	Joe Dundee	1962-63	Emile Griffith, Luis Rodriguez		
1929-30	Jackie Fields	1963-66	Emile Griffith[2]	1988	Marlon Starling (WBA), Tomas Molinares (WBA), Lloyd Honeyghan (WBC), Simon Brown (IBF)
1930	Young Jack Thompson	1966-69	Curtis Cokes		
1930-31	Tommy Freeman	1969	Curtis Cokes, José Napoles		
1931	Young Jack Thompson	1970	José Napoles, Billy Backus		
1931-32	Lou Brouillard	1971	Billy Backus, José Napoles	1989	Mark Breland (WBA), Marlon Starling (WBC), Simon Brown (IBF)
1932-33	Jackie Fields	1972-74	José Napoles		
1933	Young Corbett 3rd	1975	José Napoles (WBA, WBC)[3], Angel Espada (WBA), John Stracey (WBC)		
1933-34	Jimmy McLarnin, Barney Ross				
1934-35	Jimmy McLarnin	1976	Angel Espada (WBA), José Cuevas (WBA), John Stracey (WBC), Carlos Palomino		
1935-38	Barney Ross				
1938-40	Henry Armstrong				

1. Retired. 2. Abandoned title. 3. WBA withdrew recognition.

Lightweight

1869-99	Kid Lavigne		Juan Zurita (NBA), Ike Williams (NBA)		Rodolfo Gonzalez (WBC))
1899-1902	Frank Erne	1947-51	Ike Williams	1974	Roberto Duran (WBA), Rodolfo Gonzalez (WBC), Guts Ishimatsu (WBC)
1902-08	Joe Gans	1951-52	James Carter		
1908-10	Battling Nelson	1952	Lauro Salas		
1910-12	Ad Wolgast	1952-54	James Carter	1975	Roberto Duran (WBA), Guts Ishimatsu (WBC)
1912-14	Willie Ritchie	1954	Paddy DeMarco		
1914-17	Freddy Welsh	1954-55	James Carter	1976	Roberto Duran (WBA), Guts Ishimatsu (WBC), Esteban De Jesus (WBC)
1917-25	Benny Leonard[1]	1955-56	Wallace Smith		
1925	Jimmy Goodrich	1956-62	Joe Brown		
1925-26	Rocky Kansas	1962-65	Carlos Ortiz	1977	Roberto Duran (WBA), Esteban De Jesus (WBC)
1926-30	Sammy Mandell	1965	Ismael Laguna		
1930	Al Singer	1965-68	Carlos Ortiz	1978	Roberto Duran (WBA, WBC)
1930-33	Tony Canzoneri	1968	Teo Cruz		
1933-35	Barney Ross[2]	1969	Teo Cruz, Mando Ramos	1979	Roberto Duran[2], Jim Watt (WBC), Ernesto Espana (WBA)
1935-36	Tony Canzoneri	1970	Mando Ramos, Ismael Laguna, Ken Buchanan		
1936-38	Lou Ambers			1980	Ernesto Espana (WBA), Hilmer Kenty (WBA), Jim Watt (WBC)
1938-39	Henry Armstrong	1971	Ken Buchanan (WBA), Mando Ramos (WBC), Pedro Carrasco (WBC)		
1939-40	Lou Ambers				
1940-41	Lew Jenkins	1972	Ken Buchanan (WBA), Roberto Duran (WBA), Pedro Carrasco (WBC), Mando Ramos (WBC), Chango Carmona (WBC), Rodolfo Gonzalez (WBC)	1981	Hilmer Kenty (WBA), Sean O'Grady (WBA), James Watt (WBC), Alexis Arguello (WBC), Arturo Frias (WBA)
1941-42	Sammy Angott[1]				
1943-47	Beau Jack (N.Y.), Bob Montgomery (N.Y.), Sammy Angott (NBA),				
				1982	Arturo Frias (WBA), Ray Mancini (WBA), Alexis Arguello (WBC)
		1973	Roberto Duran (WBA),	1983	Edwin Rosario (WBC),

1. Retired. 2. Abandoned title.

1984	Ray Mancini (WBA), Edwin Rosario (WBC), Livingstone Bramble (WBA)	1986	Hector Camacho (WBC), Livingstone Bramble (WBA), Jim Paul (IBF)	1988	Jose Luis Ramirez (WBC), Julio Cesar Chavez (WBA), Greg Haugen (IBF), Julius Cesar Chavez (WBC & WBA title unified)
1985	Jose Luis Ramirez (WBC), Hector Camacho (WBC), Livingstone Bramble (WBA)	1987	Edwin Rosario (WBA), Jose Luis Ramirez (WBC), Greg Haugen (IBF)	1989	Pernell Whitaker (IBF), Edwin Rosario (WBA)

Featherweight

1889	Dal Hawkins[1]		Legra,[3] Paul Rojas (WBA), Sho Saijo (WBA)	1978	Rafael Ortega (WBA), Cecilio Lastra (WBA), Eusebio Pedroza (WBA), Danny Lopez (WBC)
1890	Billy Murphy	1969	Sho Saijo (WBA), Johnny Famechon[3]		
1892–1900	George Dixon	1970	Sho Saijo (WBA), Johnny Famechon,[3] Vicente Salvidar,[3] Kuniaki Shibata[3]	1979	Eusebio Pedroza (WBA), Danny Lopez (WBC)
1900–01	Terry McGovern				
1901	Young Corbett[1]			1980	Eusebio Pedroza (WBA), Danny Lopez (WBC), Salvador Sanchez (WBC)
1901–12	Abe Attell	1971	Sho Saijo (WBA), Antonio Gomez (WBA), Kuniaki Shibata (WBC)		
1912–23	Johnny Kilbane			1981	Eusebio Pedroza (WBA), Salvador Sanchez (WBC)
1923	Eugene Criqui	1972	Antonio Gomez (WBA), Ernesto Marcel (WBA), Kuniaki Shibata (WBC), Clemente Sanchez (WBC), José Legra (WBC)	1982	Eusebio Pedroza (WBA), Salvador Sanchez (WBC)[4]
1923–25	Johnny Dundee[1]				
1925–27	Louis (Kid) Kaplan[1]			1983	Juan Laporte (WBC), Eusebio Pedroza (WBA)
1927–28	Benny Bass				
1928	Tony Canzoneri	1973	Ernesto Marcel (WBA), José Legra (WBC), Eder Jofre (WBC)	1984	Wilfred Gomez (WBC), Eusebio Pedroza (WBA)
1928–29	Andre Routis				
1929–32	Battling Battalino[1]	1974	Ernesto Marcel (WBA)[2], Ruben Olivares (WBA), Alexis Arguello (WBA), Eder Jofre (WBC), Bobby Chacon (WBC)	1985	Eusebio Pedroza (WBA), Barry McGuigan (WBA), Azumah Nelson (WBC)
1932	Tommy Paul (NBA), Kid Chocolate (N.Y.)				
1933–36	Freddie Miller				
1936–37	Petey Sarron			1986	Barry McGuigan (WBA), Stevie Cruz (WBA), Azumah Nelson (WBC)
1937–38	Henry Armstrong[1]	1975	Alexis Arguello (WBA), Bobby Chacon (WBC), Ruben Olivares (WBC), David Kotey (WBC)		
1938–40	Joey Archibald			1987	Azumah Nelson (WBC), Antonio Esparragoza (WBA)
1940–41	Harry Jefra, Joey Archibald				
1941–42	Chalky Wright	1976	Alexis Arguello (WBA),[2] David Kotey (WBC), Danny Lopez (WBC)	1988	Calvin Grove (IBF), Jorge Paez (IBF), Antonio Esparragoza (WBA), Jeff French (WBC)
1942–48	Willie Pep				
1948–49	Sandy Saddler[2]				
1949–50	Willie Pep	1977	Rafael Ortega (WBA), Danny Lopez (WBC)	1989	Jorge Paez (IBF), Antonio Esparragoza (WBA), Jeff French (WBC)
1950-57	Sandy Saddler				
1957–59	Kid Bassey				
1959–63	Davey Moore				
1963–64	Sugar Ramos				
1964–67	Vicente Saldivar[2]				
1968	Howard Winstone, José				

1. Abandoned title. 2. Retired. 3. Recognized in Europe, Mexico, and Orient. 4. Killed in auto accident.

Bantamweight

1890–92	George Dixon[1]	1937	Sixto Escobar, Harry Jeffra	1972	Ruben Olivares, Rafael Herrera, Enrique Pinder
1894–99	Jimmy Barry[2]	1938	Harry Jeffra, Sixto Escobar		
1899–1900	Terry McGovern[1]	1939–40	Sixto Escobar[2]	1973	Enrique Pinder (WBA), Romeo Anaya (WBA), Arnold Taylor (WBA), Rodolfo Martinez (WBC), Rafael Herrera
1901	Harry Harris[1]	1940–42	Lou Salica		
1902–03	Harry Forbes	1942–46	Manuel Ortiz		
1903–04	Frankie Neil	1947	Manuel Ortiz, Harold Dade	1974	Arnold Taylor (WBA), Soo Hwan Hong (WBA), Rafael Herrera (WBC), Rodolfo Martinez (WBC)
1904	Joe Bowker[1]	1948–50	Manuel Ortiz		
1905–07	Jimmy Walsh[1]	1950–52	Vic Toweel		
1910–14	Johnny Coulon	1952–54	Jimmy Carruthers[2]	1975	Soo Hwan Hong (WBA), Alfonso Zamora (WBA), Rodolfo Martinez (WBC)
1914–17	Kid Williams	1954–55	Robert Cohen		
1917–20	Pete Herman	1956	Robert Cohen, Mario D'Agata, Raul Macias (NBA)		
1920	Joe Lynch			1976	Alfonso Zamora (WBA), Rodolfo Martinez (WBC), Carlos Zarate (WBC)
1920–21	Joe Lynch, Pete Herman, Johnny Buff	1957	Mario D'Agata, Alphonse Halimi		
1922	Johnny Buff, Joe Lynch	1958–59	Alphonse Halimi	1977	Alfonso Zamora (WBA), Jorge Lujan (WBA), Carlos Zarate (WBC)
1923	Joe Lynch	1959–60	Jose Becerra[2]		
1924	Joe Lynch, Abe Goldstein	1960–61	Alphonse Halimi[4]	1978	Jorge Lujan (WBA), Carlos Zarate (WBC)
1924	Abe Goldstein, Eddie (Cannonball) Martin	1961–62	Johnny Caldwell[4]		
		1961–65	Eder Jofre	1979	Jorge Lujan (WBA), Carlos Zarate (WBC), Lupe Pinto (WBC)
1925	Eddie (Cannonball) Martin, Charlie (Phil) Rosenberg[3]	1965–68	Masahika (Fighting) Harada		
		1968	Masahika (Fighting) Harada, Lionel Rose	1980	Jorge Lujan (WBA), Lupe Pintor (WBC), Julian Solis
1927–28	Bud Taylor (NBA)[1]				
1929–34	Al Brown	1969	Lionel Rose, Ruben Olivares		
1935	Al Brown, Baltazar Sangchili	1970	Ruben Olivares, Chucho Castillo		
1936	Baltazar Sangchili, Tony Marino, Sixto Escobar	1971	Chucho Castillo, Ruben Olivares		

1. Abandoned title. 2. Retired. 3. Deprived of title for failing to make weight. 4. Recognized in Europe.

	(WBA), Jeff Chandler (WBA)		Albert Dauila (WBC)		Miguel Lora (WBC)
1981	Lupe Pintor (WBC), Jeff Chandler (WBA)	1985	Richard Sandoval (WBA) Daniel Zaragoza (WBC) Miguel Lora (WBC)	1988	Wilfred Vasquez (WBA), Jibaro Perez (WBC), Moon Sung-gil (WBA), Orlando Canizales (IBF)
1982	Lupe Pintor (WBC), Jeff Chandler (WBA)	1986	Richard Sandoval (WBA) Bernardo Pinango (WBA) Jeff Fenech (IBF)	1989	Jibaro Perez (WBC), Moon Sung-gil (WBA), Orlando Canizales (IBF)
1983	Jeff Chandler (WBA), Albert Dauila (WBC)	1987	Bernardo Pinango (WBA) Takuya Muguruma (WBA)		
1984	Richie Sandqual (WBA),				

Flyweight

1916–23	Jimmy Wilde		Chartvanchai (WBA), Masao Ohba (WBA)		Miguel Canto (WBC), Park Chan-Hee (WBA)
1923–25	Pancho Villa[1]				
1925	Frankie Genaro	1971	Masao Ohba (WBA), Erbito Salavarria (WBC)	1980	Luis Ibarra (WBA), Kim Tae Shik (WBA), Park Chan-Hee (WBC), Shoji Oguma (WBC)
1925–27	Fidel La Barba[2]				
1927–31	Corporal Izzy Schwartz, Frankie Genaro, Emile (Spider) Pladner, Midget Wolgast, Young Perez[3]	1972	Masao Ohba (WBA), Erbito Salavarria (WBC), Betulio Gonzalez (WBC), Venice Borkorsor (WBC)	1983	Frank Cedeno (WBC), Santos Lacia (WBA)
1932–35	Jackie Brown	1973	Masao Ohba (WBA), Chartchai Chionoi (WBA), Venice Borkorsor (WBC), Betulio Gonzalez (WBC)	1984	Koji Kobayashy (WBA), Gabriel Bernal (WBC), Santos Laciar (WBA)
1935–38	Bennie Lynch[4]				
1939	Peter Kane[4]				
1943–47	Jackie Paterson[1]	1974	Chartchai Chionoi (WBA), Susumu Hanagata (WBA), Betulio Gonzalez (WBC), Shoji Oguma (WBC)	1985	Sot Chitalasa (WBC), Santos Laciar (WBA)
1947–50	Rinty Monaghan[2]				
1950	Terry Allen			1986	Hilario Zapata (WBA), Julio Cesar-Chevez (WBC)
1950–52	Dado Marino				
1952–54	Yoshio Shirai				
1954–60	Pascual Perez	1975	Susumu Hanagata (WBA), Erbito Salavarria (WBA), Shoji Oguma (WBC), Miguel Canto (WBC)	1987	Shin Hi Sop (IBF), Chang Ho Choi (IBF), Sot Hitalada (WBC)
1960–62	Pone Kingpetch				
1962–63	Masahika (Fighting) Harada				
1963–64	Hiroyuki Ebihara			1988	Sot Chitalada (WBC), Kim Young Kang (WBC), Duke McKenzie (IBF), Fidel Bassa (WBA)
1964–65	Pone Kingpetch	1976	Erbito Salavarria (WBA), Alfonso Lopez (WBA), Guty Espadas (WBA), Miguel Canto (WBC)		
1965–66	Salvatore Burrini				
1966	Walter McGown, Chartchai Chionoi	1977	Guty Espadas (WBA), Miguel Canto (WBC)	1989	Kim Young-gang (WBC), Sot Chitdada (WBC), Lee Yol-woo (WBA), Duke McKenzie (IBF), Dave McAuley (IBF)
1966–68	Charchai Chionoi	1978	Guty Espadas (WBA), Betulio Gonzalez (WBA), Miguel Canto (WBC)		
1969	Bernabe Villacampa, Efran Torres (WBA)				
1970	Bernabe Villacampa, Chartchai Chionoi, Erbito Salavarria, Berkrerk	1979	Betulio Gonzalez (WBA),		

1. Died. 2. Retired. 3. Claimants to NBA and New York Commission titles. 4. Abandoned title.

FENCING

WORLD CHAMPIONS—1989

Men's epee—Manual Pereira, Spain
Men's foil—Alexander Koch, Finland
Men's sabre—Grigory Kirienko, Soviet Union
Women's foil—Olga Velitchko, Soviet Union
Women's epee—Anja Straub, Switzerland
Men's foil team—Soviet Union
Men's epee team—Italy
Men's sabre team—Soviet Union
Women's epee team—Hungary

UNITED STATES CHAMPIONS—1989

Source: U.S. Fencing Association.

Men's foil

Division I—Peter Lewison, Metro New York
Division II—Philip Adam Leary, New Jersey
Under 19—Al Carter, Philadelphia

Men's Epee

Division I—Robert Stull, South Texas
Division II—James Preston Elgart, Northern California
Under 19—Scott Rush, Illinois

Men's Sabre

Division I—Peter Westbrook, Metro New York
Division II—Edward Baguer, New Jersey
Under 19—Edward Baguer, New Jersey

Women's Foil

Division I—Caitlin K. Bilodeau, Metro New York
Division II—Marijoy Clinton, Western New York
Under 19—Sarah Isenberg, New England

Women's Epee

Division I—Cathy McClellan, New England
Division II—Amy Dunham Reiban, Philadelphia
Under 19—Rachel Haugh, Indiana
Men's foil team—Fairmount Park Fencing Center, Philadelphia Division
Men's epee team—Halberstadt Fencers, Northern California Division
Men's sabre team—New York Athletic Club, Metro New York Division
Women's foil team—Tanner City Fencers, New England Division
Women's epee team—Salle Auriol, Oregon Division

HORSE RACING

Ancient drawings on stone and bone prove that horse racing is at least 3000 years old, but Thoroughbred Racing is a modern development. Practically every thoroughbred in training today traces its registered ancestry back to one or more of three sires that arrived in England about 1728 from the Near East and became known, from the names of their owners, as the Byerly Turk, the Darley Arabian, and the Godolphin Arabian. The Jockey Club (English) was founded at Newmarket in 1750 or 1751 and became the custodian of the Stud Book as well as the court of last resort in deciding turf affairs.

Horse racing took place in this country before the Revolution, but the great lift to the breeding industry came with the importation in 1798, by Col. John Hoomes of Virginia, of Diomed, winner of the Epsom Derby of 1780. Diomed's lineal descendants included such famous stars of the American turf as American Eclipse and Lexington. From 1800 to the time of the Civil War there were race courses and breeding establishments plentifully scattered through Virginia, North Carolina, South Carolina, Tennessee, Kentucky, and Louisiana.

The oldest stake event in North America is the Queen's Plate, a Canadian fixture that was first run in the Province of Quebec in 1836. The oldest stake event in the United States is The Travers, which was first run at Saratoga in 1864. The gambling that goes with horse racing and trickery by jockeys, trainers, owners, and track officials caused attacks on the sport by reformers and a demand among horse racing enthusiasts for an honest and effective control of some kind, but nothing of lasting value to racing came of this until the formation in 1894 of The Jockey Club.

"TRIPLE CROWN" WINNERS IN THE UNITED STATES[1]
(Kentucky Derby, Preakness and Belmont Stakes)

Year	Horse	Owner	Year	Horse	Owner
1919	Sir Barton	J. K. L. Ross	1946	Assault	Robert J. Kleberg
1930	Gallant Fox	William Woodward	1948	Citation	Warren Wright
1935	Omaha	William Woodward	1973	Secretariat	Meadow Stable
1937	War Admiral	Samuel D. Riddle	1977	Seattle Slew	Karen Taylor
1941	Whirlaway	Warren Wright	1978	Affirmed	Louis Wolfson
1943	Count Fleet	Mrs. John Hertz			

1. Statistics relative to thoroughbred racing in this publication are reproduced from the *American Racing Manual*, by special permission of the copyright owners. TRIANGLE PUBLICATIONS, INC. Reproduction prohibited.

KENTUCKY DERBY
Churchill Downs; 3-year-olds; 1 1/4 miles.

Year	Winner	Jockey	Wt.	Win val.	Year	Winner	Jockey	Wt.	Win val.
1875	Aristides	O. Lewis	100	$2,850	1909	Wintergreen	V. Powers	117	$4,850
1876	Vagrant	R. Swim	97	2,950	1910	Donau	F. Herbert	117	4,850
1877	Baden Baden	W. Walker	100	3,300	1911	Meridian	G. Archibald	117	4,850
1878	Day Star	J. Carter	100	4,050	1912	Worth	C. H. Shilling	117	4,850
1879	Lord Murphy	C. Schauer	100	3,550	1913	Donerail	R. Goose	117	5,475
1880	Fonso	G. Lewis	105	3,800	1914	Old Rosebud	J. McCabe	114	9,125
1881	Hindoo	J. McLaughlin	105	4,410	1915	Regret	J. Notler	112	11,450
1882	Apollo	B. Hurd	102	4,560	1916	George Smith	J. Loftus	117	9,750
1883	Leonatus	W. Donohue	105	3,760	1917	Omar Khayyam	C. Borel	117	16,600
1884	Buchanan	I. Murphy	110	3,990	1918	Exterminator	W. Knapp	114	14,700
1885	Joe Cotton	E. Henderson	110	4,630	1919	Sir Barton	J. Loftus	112 1/2	20,825
1886	Ben Ali	P. Duffy	118	4,890	1920	Paul Jones	T. Rice	126	30,375
1887	Montrose	I. Lewis	118	4,200	1921	Behave Yourself	C. Thompson	126	38,450
1888	Macbeth II	G. Covington	115	4,740	1922	Morvich	A. Johnson	126	46,775
1889	Spokane	T. Kiley	118	4,970	1923	Zev	E. Sande	126	53,600
1890	Riley	I. Murphy	118	5,460	1924	Black Gold	J. D. Mooney	126	52,775
1891	Kingman	I. Murphy	122	4,680	1925	Flying Ebony	E. Sande	126	52,950
1892	Azra	A. Clayton	122	4,230	1926	Bubbling Over	A. Johnson	126	50,075
1893	Lookout	E. Kunze	122	4,090	1927	Whiskery	L. McAtee	126	51,000
1894	Chant	F. Goodale	122	4,020	1928	Reigh Count	C. Lang	126	55,375
1895	Halma	J. Perkins	122	2,970	1929	Clyde Van Dusen	L. McAtee	126	53,950
1896	Ben Brush	W. Simms	117	4,850	1930	Gallant Fox	E. Sande	126	50,725
1897	Typhoon H	F. Garner	117	4,850	1931	Twenty Grand	C. Kurtsinger	126	48,725
1898	Plaudit	W. Simms	117	4,850	1932	Burgoo King	E. James	126	52,350
1899	Manuel	F. Taral	117	4,850	1933	Brokers Tip	D. Meade	126	48,925
1900	Lieut. Gibson	J. Boland	117	4,850	1934	Cavalcade	M. Garner	126	28,175
1901	His Eminence	J. Winkfield	117	4,850	1935	Omaha	W. Saunders	126	39,525
1902	Alan-a-Dale	J. Winkfield	117	4,850	1936	Bold Venture	I. Hanford	126	37,725
1903	Judge Himes	H. Booker	117	4,850	1937	War Admiral	C. Kurtsinger	126	52,050
1904	Elwood	F. Prior	117	4,850	1938	Lawrin	E. Arcaro	126	47,050
1905	Agile	J. Martin	122	4,850	1939	Johnstown	J. Stout	126	46,350
1906	Sir Huon	R. Troxler	117	4,850	1940	Gallahadion	C. Bierman	126	60,150
1907	Pink Star	A. Minder	117	4,850	1941	Whirlaway	E. Arcaro	126	61,275
1908	Stone Street	A. Pickens	117	4,850	1942	Shut Out	W. D. Wright	126	64,225

Year	Winner	Jockey	Wt.	Win val.	Year	Winner	Jockey	Wt.	Win val.
1943	Count Fleet	J. Longden	126	$ 60,725	1967	Proud Clarion	R. Ussery	126	$119,700
1944	Pensive	C. McCreary	126	64,675	1968	Forward Pass[1]	I. Valenzuela	126	122,600
1945	Hoop Jr.	E. Arcaro	126	64,850	1969	Majestic Prince	W. Hartack	126	113,200
1946	Assault	W. Mehrtens	126	96,400	1970	Dust Commander	M. Manganello	126	127,800
1947	Jet Pilot	E. Guerin	126	92,160	1971	Canonero II	G. Avila	126	145,500
1948	Citation	E. Arcaro	126	83,400	1972	Riva Ridge	R. Turcotte	126	140,300
1949	Ponde	S. Brooks	126	91,600	1973	Secretariat	R. Turcotte	126	155,050
1950	Middleground	W. Boland	126	92,650	1974	Cannonade	A. Cordero, Jr.	126	274,000
1951	Count Turf	C. McCreary	126	98,050	1975	Foolish Pleasure	J. Vasquez	126	209,600
1952	Hill Gail	E. Arcaro	126	96,300	1976	Bold Forbes	A. Cordero, Jr.	126	165,200
1953	Dark Star	H. Moreno	126	90,050	1977	Seattle Slew	J. Cruguet	126	214,700
1954	Determine	R. York	126	102,050	1978	Affirmed	S. Cauthen	126	186,900
1955	Swaps	W. Shoemaker	126	108,400	1979	Spectacular Bid	R. Franklin	126	228,650
1956	Needles	D. Erb	126	123,450	1980	Genuine Risk	J. Vasquez	126	250,550
1957	Iron Liege	W. Hartack	126	107,950	1981	Pleasant Colony	J. Velasquez	126	317,200
1958	Tim Tam	I. Valenzuela	126	116,400	1982	Gato del Sol	E. Delahoussaye	126	417,600
1959	Tomy Lee	W. Shoemaker	126	119,650	1983	Sunny's Halo	E. Delahoussaye	126	426,000
1960	Venetian Way	W. Hartack	126	114,850	1984	Swale	L. Pincay, Jr.	126	537,400
1961	Carry Back	J. Sellers	126	120,500	1985	Spend a Buck	A. Cordero, Jr.	126	406,800
1962	Decidedly	W. Hartack	126	119,650	1986	Ferdinand	W. Shoemaker	126	609,400
1963	Chateauguay	B. Baeza	126	108,900	1987	Alysheba	C. McCarron	126	618,600
1964	Northern Dancer	W. Hartack	126	114,300	1988	Winning Colors	Gary Stevens	126	611,200
1965	Lucky Debonair	W. Shoemaker	126	112,000	1989	Sunday Silence	Patrick Valenzuela	126	574,200
1966	Kauai King	D. Brumfield	126	120,500					

1. Dancer's Image finished first but was disqualified after traces of drug were found in system.

PREAKNESS STAKES

Pimlico; 3-year-olds; 1 3/16 miles; first race 1873.

Year	Winner	Jockey	Wt.	Win Val.	Year	Winner	Jockey	Wt.	Win Val.
1919	Sir Barton	J. Loftus	126	$24,500	1960	Bally Ache	R. Ussery	126	$121,000
1930	Gallant Fox	E. Sande	126	51,925	1961	Carry Back	J. Sellers	126	126,200
1931	Mate	G. Ellis	126	48,225	1962	Greek Money	J. Rotz	126	135,800
1932	Burgoo King	E. James	126	50,375	1963	Candy Spots	W. Shoemaker	126	127,500
1933	Head Play	C. Kurtsinger	126	26,850	1964	Northern Dancer	W. Hartack	126	124,200
1934	High Quest	R. Jones	126	25,175	1965	Tom Rolfe	R. Turcotte	126	128,100
1935	Omaha	W. Saunders	126	25,325	1966	Kauai King	D. Brumfield	126	129,000
1936	Bold Venture	G. Woolf	126	27,325	1967	Damascus	W. Shoemaker	126	141,500
1937	War Admiral	C. Kurtsinger	126	45,600	1968	Forward Pass	I. Valenzuela	126	142,700
1938	Dauber	M. Peters	126	51,875	1969	Majestic Prince	W. Hartack	126	129,500
1939	Challedon	G. Seabo	126	53,710	1970	Personality	E. Belmonte	126	151,300
1940	Bimelech	F.A. Smith	126	53,230	1971	Canonero II	G. Avila	126	137,400
1941	Whirlaway	E. Arcaro	126	49,365	1972	Bee Bee Bee	E. Nelson	126	135,300
1942	Alsab	B. James	126	58,175	1973	Secretariat	R. Turcotte	126	129,900
1943	Count Fleet	J. Longden	126	43,190	1974	Little Current	M. Rivera	126	156,000
1944	Pensive	C. McCreary	126	60,075	1975	Master Derby	D. McHargue	126	158,100
1945	Polynesian	W.D. Wright	126	66,170	1976	Elocutionist	J. Lively	126	129,700
1946	Assault	W. Mehrtens	126	96,620	1977	Seattle Slew	J. Cruguet	126	138,600
1947	Faultless	D. Dodson	126	98,005	1978	Affirmed	S. Cauthen	126	136,200
1948	Citation	E. Arcaro	126	91,870	1979	Spectacular Bid	R. Franklin	126	165,300
1949	Capot	T. Atkinson	126	79,985	1980	Codex	A. Cordero	126	180,600
1950	Hill Prince	E. Arcaro	126	56,115	1981	Pleasant Colony	J. Velasquez	126	270,800
1951	Bold	E. Arcaro	126	83,110	1982	Aloma's Ruler	J. Kaenel	126	209,900
1952	Blue Man	C. McCreary	126	86,135	1983	Deputed Testimony	D. Miller	126	251,200
1953	Native Dancer	E. Guerin	126	65,200	1984	Gate Dancer	A. Cordero	126	243,600
1954	Hasty Road	J. Adams	126	91,600	1985	Tank's Prospect	Pat Day	126	423,200
1955	Nashua	E. Arcaro	126	67,550	1986	Snow Chief	A. Solis	126	411,900
1956	Fabius	W. Hartack	126	84,250	1987	Alysheba	C. McCarron	126	421,100
1957	Bold Ruler	E. Arcaro	126	65,250	1988	Risen Star	E. Delahoussaye	126	413,700
1958	Tim Tam	I. Valenzuela	126	97,900	1989	Sunday Silence	P. Valenzuela	126	438,230
1959	Royal Orbit	W. Harmatz	126	136,200					

BELMONT STAKES

Belmont Park; 3-year-olds; 1 1/2 miles.

Run at Jerome Park 1867 to 1890; at Morris Park 1890–94; at Belmont Park 1905–62; at Aqueduct 1963–67. Distance 1 5/8 miles prior to 1874; reduced to 1 1/2 miles, 1874; reduced to 1 1/4 miles, 1890; reduced to 1 1/8 miles, 1893; increased to 1 1/4 miles, 1895; increased to 1 3/8 miles, 1896; reduced to 1 1/4 miles in 1904; increased to 1 1/2 miles, 1926.

Year	Winner	Jockey	Wt.	Win val.	Year	Winner	Jockey	Wt.	Win val.
1919	Sir Barton	J. Loftus	126	$11,950	1930	Gallant Fox	E. Sande	126	66,040

Year	Winner	Jockey	Wt.	Win val.	Year	Winner	Jockey	Wt.	Win val.
1931	Twenty Grand	C. Kurtsinger	126	$58,770	1961	Sherluck	B. Baeza	126	$104,900
1932	Faireno	T. Malley	126	55,120	1962	Jaipur	W. Shoemaker	126	109,550
1933	Hurryoff	M. Garner	126	49,490	1963	Chateaugay	B. Baeza	126	101,700
1934	Peace Chance	W.D. Wright	126	43,410	1964	Quadrangle	M. Ycaza	126	110,850
1935	Omaha	W. Saunders	126	35,480	1965	Hail to All	J. Sellers	126	104,150
1936	Granville	J. Stout	126	29,800	1966	Amberoid	W. Boland	126	117,700
1937	War Admiral	C. Kurtsinger	126	38,020	1967	Damascus	W. Shoemaker	126	104,950
1938	Pasteurized	J. Stout	126	34,530	1968	Stage Door Johnny	H. Gustines	126	117,700
1939	Johnstown	J. Stout	126	37,020	1969	Arts and Letters	B. Baeza	126	104,050
1940	Bimelech	F.A. Smith	126	35,030	1970	High Echelon	J. Rotz	126	115,000
1941	Whirlaway	E. Arcaro	126	39,77-	1971	Pass Catcher	R. Blum	126	97,710
1942	Shut Out	E. Arcaro	126	44,520	1972	Riva Ridge	R. Turcotte	126	93,540
1943	Count Fleet	J. Longden	126	35,340	1973	Secretariat	R. Turcotte	126	90,120
1944	Bounding Home	G.L. Smith	126	55,000	1974	Little Current	M. Rivera	126	101,970
1945	Pavot	E. Arcaro	126	56,675	1975	Avatar	W. Shoemaker	126	116,160
1946	Assault	W. Mehrtens	126	75,400	1976	Bold Forbes	A. Cordero, Jr.	126	117,000
1947	Phalanx	R. Donoso	126	78,900	1977	Seattle Slew	J. Cruguet	126	109,080
1948	Citation	E. Arcaro	126	77,700	1978	Affirmed	S. Cauthen	126	110,580
1949	Capot	T. Atkinson	126	60,990	1979	Coastal	R. Hernandez	126	161,400
1950	Middleground	W. Boland	126	61,350	1980	Temperence Hill	E. Maple	126	176,220
1951	Counterpoint	D. Gorman	126	82,000	1981	Summing	G. Martens	126	170,580
1952	One Count	E. Arcaro	126	82,400	1982	Conquistador Cielo	L. Pincay, Jr.	126	159,720
1953	Native Dancer	E. Guerin	126	82,500	1983	Caveat	L. Pincay, Jr.	126	215,100
1954	High Gun	E. Guerin	126	89,000	1984	Swale	L. Pincay, Jr.	126	310,020
1955	Nashua	E. Arcaro	126	83,700	1985	Creme Fraiche	Eddie Maple	126	307,740
1956	Needles	D. Erb	126	83,600	1986	Danzig Connection	C. McCarron	126	338,640
1957	Gallant Man	W. Shoemaker	126	77,300	1987	Bet Twice	C. Perret	126	329,160
1958	Cavan	P. Anderson	126	73,440	1988	Risen Star	E. Delahoussaye	126	303,720
1959	Sword Dancer	W. Shoemaker	126	93,525	1989	Easy Goer	P. Day	126	413,520
1960	Celtic Ash	W. Hartack	126	96,785					

TRIPLE CROWN RACES—1989

Kentucky Derby (Churchill Downs, Lousville, Ky., May 6, 1989). Gross purse: $749,200. Distance: 1 1/4 miles. Order of finish: 1. Sunday Silence (Valenzuela), mutuel return: $8.20, $3.00, $3.60. 2. Easy Goer (Day) $2.60, $3.40. 3. Awe Inspiring (Perret) $2.60, $3.40 (head). 4. Dansil (Snyder). 5. Hawkster (Castaneda). 6. Northern Wolf (Ladner). 7. Irish Actor (Howard). 8. Houston (Pincay). 9. Triple Buck (Santos). 10. Shy Tom (Antley). 11. Wind Splitter (Miller). 12. Flying Continental (Black). 13. Clever Trevor (Pettinger). 14. Faultless Ensign (DeCarlo). 15. Western Playboy (Romero). Winner's purse: $574,200. Margin of victory: 2 1/2 lengths. Time of race: 2:05.00. Attendance: 122,653

Preakness Stakes (Pimlico, Md., May 20, 1989). Gross purse: $674,200. Distance 1 3/16 miles. Order of finish: 1. Sunday Silence (Valenzuela), mutuel returns: $6.20, $3.00, $3.20; 2. Easy Goer (Day) $2.40, $2.40. 3. Rock Point (Antley) $3.60. 4. Dansil (Snyder). 5. Hawkster (Castaneda). 6. Houston (Cordero). 7. Pulverizing (Stacey). 8. Northern Wolf (Ladner). Winner's purse: $438,230. Margin of victory: A nose. Time of race: 1:53 4/5. Attendance: 90,145.

Belmont Stakes (Elmont, N.Y., June 10, 1989) Gross purse: $1,689,200. Distance: 1 1/2 miles. Order of finish: 1. Easy Goer (Day), mutuel return: $5.20, $2.80, $2.40. 2. Sunday Silence (Valenzuela) $3.00, $2.60. 3. Le Voyageur (Romero) $4.60. 4. Awe Inspiring (Perret). 5. Hawkster (Castaneda). 6. Rock Point (Antley). 7. Imbibe (Cordero). 8. Irish Actor (Maple). 9. Triple Buck (Santos). 10. Fire Maker (Bailey). Winner's purse: $413,520. Margin of victory. Eight lengths. Time of race: 2:26.00. Attendance: 64,959.

ECLIPSE AWARDS—1988

Horse of the Year	Alysheba
Two-year-old colt	Easy Goer
Two-year-old filly	Open Mind
Three-year-old colt	Risen Star
Three-year-old filly	Winning Colors
Older male horse	Alysheba
Older filly or mare	Personal Ensign
Male turf horse	Sunshine Forever
Female turf horse	Miesque
Sprinter	Gulch
Steeplechaser	Jimmy Lorenzo
Owner	Ogden Phipps
Trainer	Claude McGaughey
Jockey	Jose Santos
Breeder	Ogden Phipps
Apprentice jockey	Steve Capanas

RODEO

PROFESSIONAL RODEO COWBOY ASSOCIATION, ALL AROUND COWBOY

1953	Bill Linderman	1966–70	Larry Mahan	1981	Jimmie Cooper
1954	Buck Rutherford	1971–72	Phil Lyne	1982	Chris Lybbert
1955	Casey Tibbs	1973	Larry Mahan	1983	Roy Cooper
1956–59	Jim Shoulders	1974	Tom Ferguson	1984	Dee Pickett
1960	Harry Tompkins	1975	Leo Camarillo and	1985	Lewis Field
1961	Benny Reynolds		Tom Ferguson	1986	Lewis Field
1962	Tom Nesmith	1976–79	Tom Ferguson	1987	Lewis Field[1]
1963–65	Dean Oliver	1980	Paul Tierney	1988	Dave Appleton

1. Next championship scheduled December 1989, in Las Vegas, Nev., after *Information Please Almanac* went to press.

TRACK AND FIELD

Running, jumping, hurdling and throwing weights—track and field sports, in other words—are as natural to young people as eating, drinking and breathing. Unorganized competition in this form of sport goes back beyond the Cave Man era. Organized competition begins with the first recorded Olympic Games in Greece, 776 B.C., when Coroebus of Elis won the only event on the program, a race of approximately 200 yards. The Olympic Games, with an ever-widening program of events, continued until "the glory that was Greece" had faded and "the grandeur that was Rome" was tarnished, and finally were abolished by decree of Emperor Theodosius I of Rome in A.D. 394. The Tailteann Games of Ireland are supposed to have antedated the first Olympic Games by some centuries, but we have no records of the specific events and winners thereof.

Professional contests of speed and strength were popular at all times and in many lands, but the widespread competition of amateur athletes in track and field sports is a comparatively modern development. The first organized amateur athletic meet of record was sponsored by the Royal Military Academy at Woolwich, England, in 1849. Oxford and Cambridge track and field rivalry began in 1864, and the English amateur championships were established in 1866. In the United States such organizations as the New York Athletic Club and the Olympic Club of San Francisco conducted track and field meets in the 1870s, and a few colleges joined to sponsor a meet in 1874. The success of the college meet led to the formation of the Intercollegiate Association of Amateur Athletes of America and the holding of an annual set of championship games beginning in 1876. The Amateur Athletic Union, organized in 1888, has been the ruling body in American amateur athletics since that time. In 1980, The Athletics Congress of the U.S.A. took over the governing of track and field from the A.A.U.

WORLD RECORDS—MEN

(Through Sept. 1, 1989)
Recognized by the International Athletic Federation.
The I.A.A.F. decided late in 1976 not to recognize records in yards except for the one-mile run.
The I.A.A.F. also requires automatic timing for all records for races of 400 meters or less.

Event	Record	Holder	Home Country	Where Made	Date
Running					
100 m	0:09.83	Ben Johnson	Canada	Rome	August 30, 1987
200 m	0:19.72	Pietro Mennea	Italy	Mexico City	Sept. 17, 1979
400 m	0:43.29	Butch Reynolds	United States	Indianapolis, Ind.	Aug. 17, 1988
800 m	1:41.8	Sebastian Coe	England	Florence, Italy	June 10, 1981
1,000 m	2:12.40	Sebastian Coe	England	Oslo, Norway	July 11, 1981
1,500 m	3:29.45	Said Aouita	Morocco	Berlin	August 23, 1985
1 mile	3:46.31	Steve Cram	Great Britain	Oslo	July 27, 1985
2,000 m	4:50.81	Said Aouita	Morocco	Paris	July 16, 1987
3,000 m	7:29.45	Said Aouita	Morocco	Cologne, W. Germany	Aug. 20, 1989
3,000 m steeplechase	8:05.35	Peter Koech	Kenya	Stockholm	July 3, 1989
5,000 m	12:58.39	Said Aouita	Morocco	Rome	July 22, 1987
10,000 m	27:08.23	Arturo Barrios	Mexico	Berlin	Aug. 18, 1989
25,000 m	1:13:55.8	Toshihiko Seko	Japan	Christchurch, N.Z.	March 22, 1981
30,000 m	1:29:18.8	Toshihiko Seko	Japan	Christchurch, N.Z.	March 22, 1981
20,000 m	57:24.2	Jos Hermans	Netherlands	Papandal, Neth.	May 1, 1976
1 hour	13 mi. 24 yd	Jos Hermans	Netherlands	Papandal, Neth.	May 1, 1976
Marathon	2:06.50	Belayneh Densimo	Ethiopia	Rotterdam	April 17, 1988
Walking					
20,000 m	1:18:39.9	Ernesto Canto	Mexico	Fana, Norway	May 5, 1984
2 hours	17 mi. 1,092 yd	Ralph Kowalsky	East Germany	East Berlin	March 28, 1982
30,000 m	2:06:27.0	Maurizio Damilano	Italy	Milanese, Italy	May 5, 1985
50,000 m	3:41.39	Raul Gonzales	Mexico	Bergen, Norway	May 25, 1979
Hurdles					
110 m	0:12.92	Roger Kingdom	United States	Berlin	Aug. 16, 1989
400 m	0:47.02	Edwin Moses	U.S.	Koblenz, W. Ger.	Aug. 31, 1983
Relay Races					
400 m (4×100)	0:37.83	Olympic Team	U.S.	Los Angeles, Ca.	Aug. 11, 1984
800 m (4×200)	1:20.26	So. California	U.S.	Tempe, Ariz.	May 27, 1978
(Joel Andrews, James Sanford, Billy Mullins, Clancy Edwards)					
1,600 m (4×400)	2:56.16	National Team	U.S.	Mexico City	Oct. 20, 1968
(Vince Matthews, Ron Freeman, Larry James, Lee Evans)					
1,600 m (4×400)	2:56.16	Olympic Team	United States	Seoul, South Korea	Oct. 1, 1988
3,200 m (4×800)	7:03.89	National Team	Britain	London	Aug. 30, 1982
(Peter Elliot, Garry Cook, Steve Cram, Sebastian Coe)					

Field Events

High Jump	8 ft 0 in.	Javier Sotomayor	Cuba	San Juan, P.R.	July 29, 1989
Long jump	29 ft 2 1/2 in.	Bob Beamon	U.S.	Mexico City	Oct. 18, 1968
Triple Jump	58 ft 11 1/2 in.	Willie Banks	Los Angeles, Calif.	Indianapolis	June 16, 1985
Pole vault	19 ft 10 1/2 in.	Sergey Bubka	U.S.S.R.	Niece, France	July 9, 1988
Shot-put	75 ft 8 in.	Ulf Timmerman	East Germany	Chania, Crete	May 22, 1988
Discus throw	243 ft 0 in.	Juergen Schult	East Germany	Neubrandenburg	June 6, 1986
Hammer throw	284 ft 7 in.	Yuriy Syedikh	U.S.S.R.	Stuttgart	Aug. 28, 1986
Javelin throw	343 ft 10 in.	Uwe Hohn	E. Germany	Oslo, Norway	July 20, 1984
Decathlon	8,798pts.	Jurgen Hingsen	W. Germany	Mannheim, W. Ger.	June 8–9, 1984

WORLD RECORDS—WOMEN

(Through Oct. 1, 1988—includes 1988 Summer Olympic Records)

Event	Record	Holder	Home Country	Where Made	Date
Running					
100 m	0:10.49	Florence Griffith-Joyner	United States	Indianapolis, Ind.	July 16, 1988
200 m	0:21.56	Florence Griffith-Joyner	United States	Seoul, South Korea	Oct. 1, 1988
400 m	0:47.99	Jarmila Kratochvilova	Czechoslovakia	Helsinki, Fin.	Aug. 10, 1983
800 m	1:53.28	Jarmila Kratochvilova	Czechoslovakia	Munich, W. Ger.	July 26, 1983
1,500 m	3:52.47	Tatyana Kazankina	U.S.S.R.	Zurich, Switz.	Aug. 13, 1980
1 mile	4:15.61	Paula Ivan	Romania	Nice, Italy	July 10, 1989
3,000 m	8:22.62	Tatyana Kazankina	U.S.S.R.	Moscow	Aug. 26, 1984
5,000 m	14:37.33	Ingrid Kristiansen	Norway	Stockholm	Aug. 5, 1986
10,000 m	30:13.74	Ingrid Kristiansen	Norway	Oslo	July 5, 1986
Marathon	2:21:06.0	Ingrid Kristiansen	Norway	London	April 21, 1985
Walking					
5000 m	20:27.59	Illeana Salvador	Italy	Trente	June 3, 1989
10,000 m	42:39.2	Illeana Salvador	Italy	Rome	June 18, 1989
Hurdles					
100-m hurdles	0:12.25	Ginka Zagorcheva	Bulgaria	Greece	August 8, 1987
400 m	0:53.33	Maria Stepanova	U.S.S.R.	Stuttgart	Aug. 28, 1986
Relay Races					
400 m (4×100)	0:41.53	East Germany	E. Germany	Berlin, E. Ger.	July 31, 1983
800 m (4×200)	1:28.15	East Germany	E. Germany	Jena, E. Ger.	Aug. 9, 1980
1,600 m (4×400)	3:15.18	Soviet Union	Soviet Union	Seoul, South Korea	Oct. 1, 1988
3,200 m (4×800)	7:52.3	U.S.S.R.	U.S.S.R.	Podolsk, U.S.S.R.	Aug. 16, 1976
Field Events					
High jump	6 ft 10 1/4 in.	Stefka Kostadinova	Bulgaria	Rome	August 30, 1987
Long jump	24 ft 8 1/4 in.	Galina Chistyakova	Soviet Union	Leningrad	June 11, 1988
Triple jump	45 ft 5 1/4 in.	Sheila Hudson	USA	San Jose	June 26, 1987
Shot-put	74 ft 3 in.	Natalya Lisovskaya	U.S.S.R.	Moscow	June 7, 1987
Discus throw	252 ft 0 in.	Gabriele Reinsch	East Germany	Neubrandenburg, E. Germany	July 9, 1988
Javelin throw	262 ft 5 in.	Petra Felke	East Germany	Potsdam	Sept. 9, 1988
Heptathlon	7,291 pts	Jackie Joyner-Kersee	United States	Seoul, South Korea	Sept. 24, 1988

AMERICAN RECORDS—MEN

(Through Sept. 1, 1989)
Officially approved by The Athletics Congress.

Event	Record	Holder	Where Made	Date
Running				
100 m	0:09.92	Carl Lewis	Seoul, South Korea	Sept. 24, 1988
200 m	0:19.75	Carl Lewis	Indianapolis, Ind.	June 19, 1983
400 m	0:43.29	Butch Reynolds	Indianapolis, Ind.	Aug. 17, 1988
800 m	1:42.60	Johnny Gray	Koblenz, W. Ger.	Aug. 29, 1985
1,000 m	2:13.9	Richard Wohlhuter	Oslo, Norway	July 30, 1974
1,500 m	3:29.77	Sydney Maree	Cologne, W. Ger.	Aug. 25, 1985
1 mile	3:47.69	Steve Scott	Oslo, Norway	July 7, 1982
2,000 m	4:54.71	Steve Scott	Ingelhelm, W. Ger.	Aug. 31, 1982
3,000 m	7:35.84	Doug Padilla	Oslo, Norway	July 9, 1983
5,000 m	13:01.15	Sydney Maree	Oslo, Norway	July 27, 1985
10,000 m	27:20.56	Mark Nenow	Brussels	Sept. 5, 1986
20,000 m	58:15.0	Bill Rodgers	Boston, Mass.	Aug. 9, 1977
25,000 m	1:14:11.8	Bill Rodgers	Saratoga, Cal.	Feb. 21, 1979
30,000 m	1:31.49	Bill Rodgers	Saratoga, Cal.	Feb. 21, 1979
1 hour	12 mi., 1351 yds	Bill Rodgers	Boston, Mass.	Aug. 9, 1977
3,000-m steeplechase	8:09.17	Henry Marsh	Koblenz, W. Ger.	Aug. 29, 1985

Hurdles

110 m	0:12.92	Roger Kingdom	Berlin	Aug. 16, 1989
400 m	0:47.02	Edwin Moses	Koblenz, W. Ger.	Aug. 31, 1983

Relay Races

400 m (4×100)	0:37.83	U.S. Olympic Team	Los Angeles, Cal.	Aug. 11, 1984
800 m (4×200)	1:20.26	Southern California	Tempe, Ariz.	May 27, 1978
1,600 m (4×400)	2:56.16	U.S. Olympic Team	Seoul, South Korea	Oct. 1, 1988
3,200 m (4×800)	7:06.50	Santa Monica Track Club	Walnut	Apr. 26, 1986

Field Events

High jump	7 ft 10 in.	Hollis Conway	Norman, Okla.	July 30, 1989
Long jump	29 ft 2 1/2 in.	Bob Beamon	Mexico City	Oct. 18, 1968
Triple jump	58 ft 11 1/2 in.	Willie Banks	Indianapolis, Ind.	June 16, 1985
Pole vault	19 ft 6 1/2 in.	Joe Dial	Norman	June 18, 1987
Shot-put	73 ft 10 3/4 in.	John Brenner	Walnut	April 26, 1987
Discus throw	237 ft 4 in.	Ben Plucknett	Stockholm, Swe.	July 7, 1981
Javelin throw	280 ft 1 in.	Tom Petranoff	Helsinki	July 7, 1986
Hammer throw	268 ft 8 in.	Judd Logan	University Park, Pa.	April 23, 1988
Decathlon	8,634 pts	Bruce Jenner	Montreal, Can.	July 29–30, 1976

AMERICAN RECORDS—WOMEN
(Through Sept. 1, 1989)

Event	Record	Holder	Where Made	Date
Running				
100 m	0:10.49	Florence Griffith-Joyner	Indianapolis, Ind.	July 16, 1988
200 m	0:21.56	Florence Griffith-Joyner	Seoul, South Korea	Oct. 1, 1988
400 m	0:48.83	Valerie Brisco-Hooks	Los Angeles, Cal.	Aug. 6, 1984
800 m	1:56.90	Mary Decker Slaney	Bern	Aug. 16, 1985
1,500 m	3:57.12	Mary Decker Slaney	Stockholm, Swe.	July 26, 1983
1000 m	2:34.8	Mary Decker Slaney	Eugene, Ore.	July 4, 1985
1 mile	4:16.71	Mary Decker Slaney	Zurich	Aug. 21, 1985
3,000 m	8:29.69	Mary Decker Slaney	Cologne	Aug. 25, 1985
5,000 m	14:59.99	PattiSue Plummer	Stockholm	July 3, 1989
10,000 m	31:35.3	Mary Decker Slaney	Eugene, Ore.	July 16, 1982
Hurdles				
100 m hurdles	0:12.61	Jackie Joyner-Kersee	San Jose, Calif.	May 28, 1988
400 m hurdles	0:53.37	Sandra Farmer-Patrick	New York	July 23, 1989
Relay Races				
400 m (4×100)	0:41.61	U.S. National Team	Colorado Springs, Col.	July 3, 1983
800 m (4×200)	1:32.57	Louisiana State	Des Moines, Iowa	April 28, 1989
1,600 m (4×400)	3:15.51	U.S. Olympic Team	Seoul, South Korea	Oct. 1, 1988
Field Events				
High jump	6 ft 8 in.	Louise Ritter	Austin, Tex.	July 9, 1988
Long jump	24 ft. 5 1/2 in.	Jackie Joyner-Kersee	Indianapolis	August 12, 1987
Triple jump	45 ft. 5 1/4 in.	Sheila Hudson	San Jose	June 26, 1987
Shot-put	66 ft. 2 1/2 in.	Ramon Pagel	San Diego, Calif.	June 25, 1988
Discus throw	216 ft 10 in.	Carol Cady	San Jose, Calif.	May 31, 1986
Javelin throw	227 ft 5 in.	Kate Schmidt	Furth, W. Ger.	Sept. 10, 1977
Heptathlon	7,291 pts	Jackie Joyner-Kersee	Seoul, South Korea	Sept. 23–24, 1988

HISTORY OF THE RECORD FOR THE MILE RUN

Time	Athlete	Country	Year	Location
4:36.5	Richard Webster	England	1865	England
4:29.0	William Chinnery	England	1868	England
4:28.8	Walter Gibbs	England	1868	England
4:26.0	Walter Slade	England	1874	England
4:24.5	Walter Slade	England	1875	London

4:23.2	Walter George	England	1880	London
4:21.4	Walter George	England	1882	London
4:18.4	Walter George	England	1884	Birmingham, England
4:18.2	Fred Bacon	Scotland	1894	Edinburgh, Scotland
4:17.0	Fred Bacon	Scotland	1895	London
4:15.6	Thomas Conneff	United States	1895	Travers Island, N.Y.
4:15.4	John Paul Jones	United States	1911	Cambridge, Mass.
4:14.4	John Paul Jones	United States	1913	Cambridge, Mass.
4:12.6	Norman Taber	United States	1915	Cambridge, Mass.
4:10.4	Paavo Nurmi	Finland	1923	Stockholm
4:09.2	Jules Ladoumegue	France	1931	Paris
4:07.6	Jack Lovelock	New Zealand	1933	Princeton, N.J.
4:06.8	Glenn Cunningham	United States	1934	Princeton, N.J.
4:06.4	Sydney Wooderson	England	1937	London
4:06.2	Gundar Hägg	Sweden	1942	Göteborg, Sweden
4:06.2	Arne Andersson	Sweden	1942	Stockholm
4:04.6	Gunder Hägg	Sweden	1942	Stockholm
4:02.6	Arne Andersson	Sweden	1943	Göteborg, Sweden
4:01.6	Arne Andersson	Sweden	1944	Malmö, Sweden
4:01.4	Gunder Hägg	Sweden	1945	Malmö, Sweden
3:59.4	Roger Bannister	England	1954	Oxford, England
3:58.0	John Landy	Australia	1954	Turku, Finland
3:57.2	Derek Ibbotson	England	1957	London
3:54.5	Herb Elliott	Australia	1958	Dublin
3:54.4	Peter Snell	New Zealand	1962	Wanganui, N.Z.
3:54.1	Peter Snell	New Zealand	1964	Auckland, N.Z.
3:53.6	Michel Jazy	France	1965	Rennes, France
3:51.3	Jim Ryun	United States	1966	Berkeley, Calif.
3:51.1	Jim Ryun	United States	1967	Bakersfield, Calif.
3:51.0	Filbert Bayi	Tanzania	1975	Kingston, Jamaica
3:49.4	John Walker	New Zealand	1975	Göteborg, Sweden
3:49.0	Sebastian Coe	England	1979	Oslo
3:48.8	Steve Ovett	England	1980	Oslo
3:48.53	Sebastian Coe	England	1981	Zurich, Switzerland
3:48.40	Steve Ovett	England	1981	Koblenz, W. Ger.
3:47.33	Sebastian Coe	England	1981	Brussels
3:46.31	Steve Cram	England	1985	Oslo

TOP TEN WORLD'S FASTEST OUTDOOR MILES

Time	Athlete	Country	Date	Location
3:46.31	Steve Cram	England	July 27, 1985	Oslo
3:47.33	Sebastian Coe	England	Aug. 28, 1981	Brussels
3:47.69	Steve Scott	United States	July 7, 1982	Oslo
3:47.79	Jose Gonzalez	Spain	July 27, 1985	Oslo
3:48.40	Steve Ovett	England	Aug. 26, 1981	Koblenz, W. Ger.
3:48.53	Sebastian Coe	England	Aug. 19, 1981	Zurich
3:48.53	Steve Scott	United States	June 26, 1982	Oslo
3:48.8	Steve Ovett	England	July 1, 1980	Oslo
3:48.83	Sydney Maree	United States	Sept. 9, 1981	Rieti, Italy
3:48.85	Sydney Maree[1]	United States	June 26, 1982	Oslo

1. Finished second. NOTE: Professional marks not included.

TOP TEN WORLD'S FASTEST INDOOR MILES

Time	Athlete	Country	Date	Location
3:49.78	Eamonn Coghlan	Ireland	Feb. 27, 1983	East Rutherford, N.J.
3:50.6	Eamonn Coghlan	Ireland	Feb. 20, 1981	San Diego
3:50.94	Marcus O'Sullivan	Ireland	Feb. 13, 1988	East Rutherford, N.J.
3:51.2	Ray Flynn[1]	Ireland	Feb. 27, 1983	East Rutherford, N.J.
3:51.66	Marcus O'Sullivan	Ireland	Feb. 10, 1989	East Rutherford, N.J.
3:51.8	Steve Scott[1]	United States	Feb. 20, 1981	San Diego
3:52.28	Steve Scott[2]	United States	Feb. 27, 1983	East Rutherford, N.J.
3:52:30	Frank O'Mara	Ireland	Feb. , 1986	New York
3:52.37	Eamonn Coughlan	Ireland	Feb. 9, 1985	East Rutherford, N.J.
3:52.40	Sydney Maree	United States	Feb. 9, 1985	East Rutherford, N.J.

1. Finished second. 2. Finished third.

TOP TEN POLE VAULT DISTANCES

(Some of early dates are the winning heights of A.A.U. champion for that year, used to show progression from one foot level to the next. Figures from A.A.U. records and *Track & Field News*.)

Fiberglas Poles

1988	Sergey Bubka	19 ft 10 1/2 in.	1984	Thierry Vigneron	19 ft 4 3/4 in.
1987	Sergey Bubka	19 ft 9 1/4 in.	1984	Sergey Bubka	19 ft 4 1/4 in.
1986	Sergey Bubka	19 ft 8 1/2 in.	1984	Sergey Bubka	19 ft 3 1/2 in.
1985	Sergey Bubka	19 ft 8 1/4 in.	1984	Sergey Bubka	19 ft 2 1/4 in.
1984	Sergey Bubka	19 ft 5 3/4 in.	1989	Rodion Gataullin	19 ft 2 1/4 in.

THE ATHLETICS CONGRESS NATIONAL CHAMPIONSHIPS INDOOR

(Madison Square Garden, New York, February 24, 1989)

Men's Events

(Running events in meters)

55 m—Leroy Burrell, University of Houston	0:06.15
400 m—Antonio McKay, New York Athletic Club	0:47.03
500 m—Mark Rowe, Accusplit Sports Club	1:01.59
800 m—Ray Brown, Atlantic Coast Club	1:46.77
Mile—Frank O'Mara, Reebok Track Club	3:58.58
3,000 m—Steve Scott, Asics Tiger Track Club	7:53.69
55 m hurdles—Tonie Campbell, Bee-Fit Track Club	0:06.98
5,000 m walk—Tim Lewis, unaffiliated	20:00.46
4 × 400 m relay—Atlantic Coast Club	3:14.70
4 × 800 m relay—Atlantic Cost Club	7:28.70
High jump—Troy Kemp, unaffiliated	7 ft 6 1/2 in.
Pole Vault—Rodion Gataullin, Soviet Union	19 ft 2 1/4 in.
Long jump—Larry Myricks, Goldwin Track Club	27 ft 0 in.
Triple jump—Mike Conley, Tyson Foods Track Club	56 ft 10 in.
Shot-put—Randy Barnes, Mazda Track Club	68 ft 6 in.
35-pound weight throw—Lance Deal, New York Athletic Club	73 ft 8 1/4 in.

Team—New York Athletic Club
Outstanding athlete—Ray Brown

Women's Events

(Running events in meters)

55 m—Gwen Torrence, Athletics West	0:06.61
200 m—Alice Jackson, Coca Cola Track Club	0:23.64
400 m—Diane Dixon, Athletics West	0:53.28
800 m—Joetta Clark, Athletics West	2:02.60
Mile—Linda Sheskey, Athletics West	4:43.09
3000 m—Elaine VanBlunk, Nike Running Room	9:16.46
55 m hurdles—Kim McKenzie, Mazda Track Club	0:07.39
3,000 m walk—Teresa Vaill, Walk USA	13:12.34
4 × 400 m relay—Rice University	3:44.56
High jump—Louise Ritter, Mazda Track Club	6 ft 5 in.
Long jump—Jennifer Inniss, Athletics West	21 ft 1/2 in.
Shot-put—Ramona Pagel, Mazda Track Club	62 ft 6 1/2 in.
20-pound weight throw—Virginia Young, St. John's University	60 ft 2 in.

Team—Athletics West
Outstanding athlete—Kim McKenzie

THE ATHLETICS CONGRESS NATIONAL CHAMPIONSHIPS—OUTDOOR

(Houston, Texas, June 13-17, 1989)

Men's Events

100m—Leroy Burrell, University of Houston	0:09.94
200m—Floyd Heard, Santa Monica Track Club	0:20.09
400m—Antonio Pettigrew, Atlantic Coast Club	0:44.27
800m—Johnny Gray, Santa Monica Track Club	1:46.17
1500m—Terrance Herrington, Clemson University	3:46.83
3000 m steeplechase—Brian Diemer, Athletics West	8:26.45
5000 m—Tim Hacker, Athletics West	13:39.75
10,000 m—Pat Porter, Athletics West	24:45.78
110 m hurdles—Roger Kingdom, Adidas Track Club	0:13.22
400 m hurdles—David Patrick, Fl-Jo International	0:48.83
20 k walk—Tim Lewis, Reebok Racing Club	1:27:19
High jump—Brian Brown, unaffiliated	7 ft 7 1/4 in.
Pole vault—Kory Tarpenning, Pacific Coast Club	19 ft 0 in.
Long jump—Larry Myricks, Goldwin Track Club	28 ft 6 1/2 in.
Triple jump—Michael Conley, Tyson International Track Club	57 ft 5 in.
Shot-put—Randy Barnes, Mazda Track Club	70 ft 9 1/2 in.
Discus throw—Kamy Keshmiri, una-filiated	218 ft 2 in.
Hammer throw—Lance Deal, New York Athletic Club	252 ft 5 in.
Javelin throw—Mike Barnett, New York Athletic Club	256 ft 9 in.

Team—Athletics West

Women's Events

100m—Dawn Sowell, Flo-Jo International	0:10.91
200 m—Danette Young, Reebok Racing Club	0:22.29
400 m—Rochelle Stevens, Atlantic Coast Club	0:50.75
800 m—Joetta Clark, Athletics West	2:01.42
1,500 m—Regina Jacobs, Team New Balance	4:11.80
3,000 m—Patti Sue Palmer, Athletics West	9:00.05
5,000 m—Mindy Rowand, Dominos Racing Team	16:12.36
10,000 m—Nan Davis, Athletics West	32:34.59
100 m hurdles—Lynda Tolbert, Nike Coast Track Club	0:12.75
400 m hurdles—Sandra Farmer-Patrick, Flo-Jo International	0:53.75
10 k walk—Lynn Weil, Walk-USA	46:44.1
High jump—Jan Wohlschlag, Nike Coast Track Club	6 ft 4 in.
Long jump—Claire Connor, LS United	21 ft 6 in.
Triple jump—Sheila Hudson, Nike Coast Track Club	45 ft 6 1/2 in.
Shot-put—Ramona Pagel, Mazda Track Club	62 ft 6 in.
Discus—Connie Price, Athletics West	201 ft 11 in.
Javelin—Laverne Eve, LS United	212 ft 6 in.

Team—Athletics West

N.C.A.A. CHAMPIONSHIPS—1989

INDOOR

(Indianapolis, Ind. March 10-11, 1989)

Men's Events

55 m—Raymond Stewart, Texas Christian	0:06:07
55 m hurdles—Earl Diamond, Florida	0:07.2
200 m—Michael Johnson, Baylor	0:20.59
400 m—Tyrone Kemp, Florida	0:46.03
800 m—Paul Ereng, Virginia	1:47.69
Mile—Joe Falcon, Arkansas	3:58.06
3,000 m—Greg Whitely, Brown	7:57.14
5000 m—John Scherer, Michigan	14:18.05
1,600 m relay—Florida	3:06.96[1]
3,200 m relay—Clemson	7:17.45[1]
High jump—Hollis Conway, Southwestern Louisiana	7 ft 9 1/4 in.
Pole Vault—Dean Starkey, Illinois	18 ft 6 1/2 in.
Long jump—Leroy Burrell, Houston	26 ft 6 1/4 in.
Triple jump—Edrick Floreal, Arkansas	56 ft 2 3/4 in.
Shot-put—Mike Stulce, Texas A&M	68 ft 3 1/4 in.
35-pound weight throw—Chris Koch, Northeast Louisiana	69 ft. 5 1/2 in.
Team 1. Arkansas	34 points
2. Florida	31
3. Texas A & M	23

1. Meet record.
DIVISION II champion—St. Augustine's College, Raleigh, N.C.
DIVISION III champion—North Central College, Naperville, Ill.

Women's Events

55 m—Dawn Sowell, Louisiana State	0;06.62
55 m hurdles—Tananjalyn Stanley, Lousiana State	0:07.47[1]
200 m—Dawn Sowell, Louisiana State	0:22.96[1]
400 m—Natasha Kaiser, Missouri	0:51.92[1]
800 m—Edith Nakiyingi, Iowa State	2:05.68[1]
Mile—Suzanne Favor, Wisconsin	4:30.63[1]
3,000 m—Vicki Huber, Villanova	8:55.29[1]
5,000 m—Jackie Goodman, Oklahoma State	15:52.77[1]
1,600 m relay—Louisiana State	3:33.98[1]
3,200 m relay—Villanova	8:34.54
High jump—Paula John, Weber State	6 ft. 0 in.
Long jump—Beatrice Utunde, Texas Southern	20 ft. 11 1/4 in.
Triple jump—Florence Hyacinth, Alabama	44 ft. 1 1/4 in.
Shot-put—Carla Garrett, Arizona	54 ft, 1 in.
Team—1. Louisiana State	61 points
2. Villanova	34
3. Texas	
Alabama (tie)	24

DIVISION II champions—Abilene Christian University, Abilene, Texas
DIVISION III champions—Christopher Newport College, Newport News, Va.

1. Meet record.

OUTDOOR

(Brigham Young University, Provo, Utah, May 31-June 3, 1989)

Men's Events

100 m—Raymond Stewart, Texas Christian	0:09.97
200 m—Dennis Mitchell, Florida	0:20.09
400 m—Raymond Pierre, Baylor	0:44.59
800 m—Paul Ereng, Virginia	1:47.50
1,500 m—Kip Cheruiyot, Mount St. Mary's (Md.)	3:42.06
3000 m steeplechase—Tom Nohilly, Florida	8:45.24
5,000 m—Marc Davis, Arizona	14:07.88
10,000 m—John Scherer, Michigan	29:48.95
110 m hurdles—Robert Reading, Southern California	0:13.19
400 m hurdles—Winthrop Graham, Texas	0:48.55
1,600 m relay—Texas A & M	3:00.91
400 m relay—Texas Christian	0:38.23[1]
High jump—Hollis Conway, Southwestern Louisiana	7 ft 9 1/2 in.[1]

Pole vault—Tim McMichael, Oklahoma	18 ft 6 1/2 in.[2]	
Long jump—Joe Greene, Ohio State	27 ft 7 1/4 in.[2]	
Triple jump—Edrick Floreal, Arkansas	56 ft 8 3/4 in.	
Shot put—Mike Stulce, Texas A & M	68 ft 11 3/4 in.	
Discus throw—John Nichols, Louisiana St.	208 ft 1 in.	
Hammer throw—Chris Koch, Northeast Louisiana	233 ft 2 in.	
Javelin throw—Patrik Boden, Texas	255 ft 4 in.	
Decathlon—Derek Huff, Arizona	8,020 points	
Team—1. Louisiana State	53 points	
2. Texas A&M	51	
3. Florida	39	

DIVISION II champion—St. Augustine College, Raleigh, N.C.
DIVISION III champion—Christopher Newport College, Newport News, Va.

Women's Events

100 m—Dawn Sowell, Louisiana State	0:10.78[2]	
200 m—Dawn Sowell, Louisiana State	0:22.04[2]	
400 m—Pauline Davis, Alabama	0:50.18[1]	
800 m—Meredith Rainey, Harvard	2:03.90	
1,500 m—Suzanne Favor, Wisconsin	4:15.83	
3,000 m—Vicki Huber, Villanova	9:06.96	
5,000 m—Valerie McGovern, Kentucky	16:17.20	
10,000 m—Jackie Goodman, Oklahoma St.	33:42.35	
100 m hurdles—Tananjalyn Stanley, Louisiana State	0:12.70	
400 m hurdles—Janeene Vickers, UCLA	0:55.27	
400 m relay—Louisiana State	0:42.50[1]	
1600 m relay—Texas	3:31.18	
High jump—Melinda Clark, Texas A&M	6 ft 3/4 in.	
Long jump—Christy Opara, Brigham Young	21 ft 2 1/2 in.	
Triple jump—Renita Robinson, Nebraska	44 ft 7 1/2 in.[2]	
Shot-put—Carla Garrett, Arizona	54 ft 8 in.	
Discus throw—Carla Garrett, Arizona	190 ft 4 in	
Javelin throw—Kim Engel, Georgia	196 ft 8 in.	
Heptathlon—Jolanda Jones, Houston	6,022 points	
Team—1. Louisiana State	86 points	
2. UCLA	47	
3. Nebraska	37	

DIVISION II CHAMPIONS—California Polytechnic, San Luis Obispo, Calif.
DIVISION III CHAMPIONS—Christopher Newport College, Newport News, Va.

1. Meet record. 2. Wind-aided.

UNITED STATES DECATHLON CHAMPIONSHIPS—1989

(June 13-14, 1989, Houston, Texas)

Final Standings

	Pts
1. David Johnson, New York Athletic Club	8,549
2. Sheldon Blockburger, Oregon International	8,248
3. Gary Kinder, New York Athletic Club	8,155
4. Derek Huff, Stars & Stripes Track Club	8,018
5. Kip Janvrin, K&K Track Club	7,994

UNITED STATES HEPTATHLON CHAMPIONSHIPS—1989

(June 13-14, Houston, Texas)

Final Standings

	Pts
1. Jolanda Jones, Houston Track Club	6,006
2. Gea Johnson, Nike Coast Track Club	5,990
3. Sharon Hanson, Nike Coast Track Club	5,983
4. Cathey Tyree, Stars & Stripes Track Club	5,873
5. Teri LeBlanc, University of Missouri	5,805

SPORTS ORGANIZATIONS AND BUREAUS

(Note: Addresses are subject to change)

Amateur Athletic Union of the U.S. 3400 West 86th St., P.O. Box 68207, Indianapolis, Ind. 46268-0207

Amateur Basketball Association. 1750 East Boulder St., Colorado Springs, Colo. 80909

Amateur Hockey Association of the U.S. Inc.; USA Hockey 2997 Broadmoor Valley Road, Colorado Springs, Colo. 80906

Amateur Softball Association. 2801 N.E. 50th St., Oklahoma City, Okla. 73111

American Amateur Racquetball Association. 815 North Weber St., Suite 101, Colorado Springs, Colo. 80903

American Association of Professional Baseball Clubs. P.O. Box 608, 3860 Broadway, Grove City, Ohio 43123

American Bowling Congress. 5301 South 76th St., Greendale, Wis. 53129-0500

American Hockey League. 218 Memorial Ave., West Springfield, Mass. 01089

American Horse Shows Association. 220 E. 42nd St., New York, N.Y. 10017-5806

American Kennel Club Inc. 51 Madison Ave., New York, N.Y. 10010

American League (baseball). 350 Park Ave., New York, N.Y. 10022

Athletics Congress/USA, The. 200 South Capital Ave., Suite 140, Indianapolis, Ind. 46225.

Baseball Hall of Fame. P.O. Box 590, Cooperstown, N.Y. 13326

Football Hall of Fame (college). Kings Island, Ohio 45034

(Big Ten) Conference (1896). 1111 Plaza Dr., Suite 600, Schaumburg, Ill. 60173-4990

International Game Fish Association. 3000 East Las Olas Blvd., Fort Lauderdale, Fla. 33316

International League (baseball). Box 608, Grove City, Ohio 43123

International Olympic Committee. Chateau de Vidy, 1007 Lausanne, Switzerland

International Tennis Hall of Fame. National Historic Landmark, Newport Casino, Newport, R.I. 02840

Ladies Professional Golf Association. 4675 Sweetwater Blvd., Sugar Land, Texas, 77479

Little League Baseball. P.O. Box 3485 Williamsport, Pa. 17701

National Archery Association. 1750 E. Boulder St., Colorado Springs, Colo. 80909

National Association for Stock Car Auto Racing. P.O. Box K, Daytona Beach, Fla. 32015—9947

National Association of Intercollegiate Athletics. 1221 Baltimore St., Kansas City, Mo. 64105

National Baseball Congress. P.O. Box 1420, Wichita, Kan. 67201

National Collegiate Athletic Association. P.O. Box 1906, Mission, Kan. 66201

National Duckpin Bowling Congress. 4609 Horizon Circle, Baltimore, Md. 21208

National Field Archery Association. 31407 Outer I-10, Redlands, Calif. 92373

National Football Foundation. 1865 Palmer Ave., Larchmont, N.Y. 10538. *See also:* Football Hall of Fame (college)

National Football League. 410 Park Ave., New York, N.Y. 10022

National Hockey League. 1155 Metcalfe St., Suite 960, Montreal, Que., Canada H3B 2W2

National Horseshoe Pitchers Association. Box 278, Munroe Falls, Ohio 44262

National Hot Rod Association. P.O. Box 5555, Glendora, Calif. 91740

National Junior College Athletic Association. P.O. Box 7305, Colorado Springs, Colo. 80933—7305

National Rifle Association of America. 1600 Rhode Island Ave., N.W., Washington, D.C. 20036

National Shuffleboard Association. Box 5441, Trailer Estates, Bradenton, Fla. 34281-5441

National Skeet Shooting Association. P.O. Box 680007, San Antonio, Tex. 78268-0007

New York Racing Association. P.O. Box 90, Jamaica, N.Y. 11417

New York State Athletic Commission (boxing and wrestling). 270 Broadway, New York, N.Y. 10007

North American Yacht Racing Union. *See* United States Yacht Racing Union

PGA TOUR, Inc., 112 TPC Blvd., Sawgrass, Ponte Vedra, Fla. 32082

Pro Football Hall of Fame. Canton, Ohio 44708

Roller Skating Rink Operators Association. P.O. Box 81846, Lincoln, Neb. 68501

Thoroughbred Racing Assns. of N. America. 3000 Marcus Ave., Lake Success, N.Y. 11042

United States Amateur Confederation of Roller Skating. P.O. Box 6579 Lincoln, Neb. Lincoln, Neb. 68506

United States Auto Club. 4910 West 16th St., Speedway, Ind. 46224

United States Gymnastics Federation. 201 S. Capitol, Ste. 300, Indianapolis, Ind. 46225

United States-International Professional Shuffleboard 1901 S.W. 87th Terrace, Fort Lauderdale, Fla. 33324

U.S. Baseball Federation. 2160 Greenwood Ave., Trenton, N.J. 08609

U.S. Chess Federation. 186 Route 9W, New Windsor, N.Y. 12550

U.S. Cycling Federation. 1750 East Boulder St., Colorado Springs, Colo. 80909

U.S. Fencing Assn. 1750 E. Boulder St., Colorado Springs, Colo. 80909

U.S. Figure Skating Association. 20 First Street, Colorado Springs, Colo. 80906

U.S. Football League. P.O. Box 936, Dover, N.J. 07801-0936

U.S. Golf Association. Golf House, P.O. Box 708, Far Hills, N.J. 07931-0708

U.S. Handball Association. 930 N. Benton Ave., Tucson, Ariz. 85711

U.S. Olympic Committee. 1750 East Boulder Street, Colorado Springs, Colo. 80909

U.S. Orienteering Federation. Box 1444, Forest Park, Ga. 30051

U.S. Rowing Assn. Pan American Plaza, 201 S. Capitol Ave., Ste. 400, Indianapolis, Ind. 46225

U.S. Soccer Federation. 1750 East Boulder St., Colorado Springs, Colo. 80909—5791

U.S. Tennis Association. 1212 Avenue of the Americas, New York, N.Y. 10036

U.S. Trotting Association. 750 Michigan Ave., Columbus, Ohio 43215

U.S. Yacht Racing Union. P.O. Box 209, Goat Island, Newport, R.I. 02840

USA Amateur Boxing Federation. 1750 East Boulder St., Colorado Springs, Colo. 80909

Women's International Bowling Congress. 5301 S. 76th St., Greendale, Wis. 53129

TENNIS

Lawn tennis is a comparatively modern modification of the ancient game of court tennis. Major Walter Clopton Wingfield thought that something like court tennis might be played outdoors on lawns, and in December, 1873, at Nantclwyd, Wales, he introduced his new game under the name of *Sphairistike* at a lawn party. The game was a success and spread rapidly, but the name was a total failure and almost immediately disappeared when all the players and spectators began to refer to the new game as "lawn tennis." In the early part of 1874, a young lady named Mary Ewing Outerbridge returned from Bermuda to New York, bringing with her the implements and necessary equipment of the new game, which she had obtained from a British Army supply store in Bermuda. Miss Outerbridge and friends played the first game of lawn tennis in the United States on the grounds of the Staten Island Cricket and Baseball Club in the spring of 1874.

For a few years, the new game went along in haphazard fashion until about 1880, when standard measurements for the court and standard equipment within definite limits became the rule. In 1881, the U.S. Lawn Tennis Association (whose name was changed in 1975 to U.S. Tennis Association) was formed and conducted the first national championship at Newport, R.I. The international matches for the Davis Cup began with a series between the British and United States players on the courts of the Longwood Cricket Club, Chestnut Hill, Mass., in 1900, with the home players winning.

Professional tennis, which got its start in 1926 when the French star Suzanne Lenglen was paid $50,000 for a tour, received full recognition in 1968. Staid old Wimbledon, the London home of what are considered the world championships, let the pros compete. This decision ended a long controversy over open tennis and changed the format of the competition. The United States championships were also opened to the pros and the site of the event, long held at Forest Hills, N.Y., was shifted to the National Tennis Center in Flushing Meadows, N.Y., in 1978. Pro tours for men and women became worldwide in play that continued throughout the year.

DAVIS CUP CHAMPIONSHIPS

No matches in 1901, 1910, 1915–18, and 1940–45.

1900	United States 3, British Isles 0	1932	France 3, United States 2	1964	Australia 3, United States 2
1902	United States 3, British Isles 0	1933	Great Britain 3, France 2	1965	Australia 4, Spain 1
1903	British Isles 4, United States 1	1934	Great Britain 4, United States 1	1966	Australia 4, India 1
1904	British Isles 5, Belgium 0	1935	Great Britain 5, United States 0	1967	Australia 4, Spain 1
1905	British Isles 5, United States 0	1936	Great Britain 3, Australia 2	1968	United States 4, Australia 1
1906	British Isles 5, United States 0	1937	United States 4, Great Britain 1	1969	United States 5, Romania 0
1907	Australasia 3, British Isles 2	1938	United States 3, Australia 2	1970	United States 5, West Germany 0
1908	Australasia 3, United States 2	1939	Australia 3, United States 2	1971	United States 3, Romania 2
1909	Australasia 5, United States 0	1946	United States 5, Australia 0	1972	United States 3, Romania 2
1911	Australasia 5, United States 0	1947	United States 4, Australia 1	1973	Australia 5, United States 0
1912	British Isles 3, Australasia 2	1948	United States 5, Australia 0	1974	South Africa (Default by India)
1913	United States 3, British Isles 2	1949	United States 4, Australia 1	1975	Sweden 3, Czechoslovakia 2
1914	Australasia 3, United States 2	1950	Australia 4, United States 1	1976	Italy 4, Chile 1
1919	Australasia 4, British Isles 1	1951	Australia 3, United States 2	1977	Australia 3, Italy 1
1920	United States 5, Australasia 0	1952	Australia 4, United States 1	1978	United States 4, Britain 1
1921	United States 5, Japan 0	1953	Australia 3, United States 2	1979	United States 5, Italy 0
1922	United States 4, Australasia 1	1954	United States 3, Australia 2	1980	Czechoslovakia 4, Italy 2
1923	United States 4, Australasia 1	1955	Australia 5, United States 0	1981	United States 3, Argentina 1
1924	United States 5, Australasia 0	1956	Australia 5, United States 0	1982	United States 3, France 0
1925	United States 5, France 0	1957	Australia 3, United States 2	1983	Australia 3, Sweden 2
1926	United States 4, France 1	1958	United States 3, Australia 2	1984	Sweden 4, United States 1
1927	France 3, United States 2	1959	Australia 3, United States 2	1985	Sweden 3, West Germany 2
1928	France 4, United States 1	1960	Australia 4, Italy 1	1986	Australia 3, Sweden 2
1929	France 3, United States 2	1961	Australia 5, Italy 0	1987	Sweden 5, Austria 0
1930	France 4, United States 1	1962	Australia 5, Mexico 0	1988	West Germany 4, Sweden 1
1931	France 3, Great Britain 2	1963	United States 3, Australia 2		

FEDERATION CUP CHAMPIONSHIPS

World team competition for women conducted by International Lawn Tennis Federation.

1963	United States 2, Australia 1	1972	South Africa 2, Britain 1	1981	United States 3, Britain 0
1964	Australia 2, United States 1	1973	Australia 3, South Africa 0	1982	United States 3, West Germany 0
1965	Australia 2, United States 1	1974	Australia 2, United States 1	1983	Czechoslovakia 2, West Germany 1
1966	United States 3, West Germany 0	1975	Czechoslovakia 3, Australia 0	1984	Czechoslovakia 2, Australia 1
1967	United States 2, Britain 0	1976	United States 2, Australia 1	1985	Czechoslovakia 2, United States 1
1968	Australia 3, Netherlands 0	1977	United States 2, Australia 1	1986	United States 3, Czechoslovakia 0
1969	United States 2, Australia 1	1978	United States 2, Australia 1	1987	West Germany 2, United States 1 [1]
1970	Australia 3, West Germany 0	1979	United States 3, Australia 0	1988	Czechoslovakia 2, Soviet Union 1
1971	Australia 3, Britain 0	1980	United States 3, Australia 0		

U.S. CHAMPIONS
Singles—Men

NATIONAL

1881–87	Richard D. Sears	1917–18	R. Lindley Murray[2]
1888–89	Henry Slocum, Jr.	1919	William Johnston
1890–92	Oliver S. Campbell	1920–25	Bill Tilden
1893–94	Robert D. Wrenn	1926–27	Jean Rene Lacoste
1895	Fred H. Hovey	1928	Henri Cochet
1896–97	Robert D. Wrenn	1929	Bill Tilden
1898–		1930	John H. Doeg
1900	Malcolm Whitman	1931–32	Ellsworth Vines
1901–02	William A. Larned	1933–34	Fred J. Perry
1903	Hugh L. Doherty	1935	Wilmer L. Allison
1904	Holcombe Ward	1936	Fred J. Perry
1905	Beals C. Wright	1937–38	Don Budge
1906	William J. Clothier	1939	Robert L. Riggs
1907–11	William A. Larned	1940	Donald McNeill
1912–13	Maurice McLoughlin	1941	Robert L. Riggs
		1942	Fred Schroeder
1914	R. N. Williams II	1943	Joseph Hunt
1915	William Johnston	1944–45	Frank Parker
1916	R. N. William II	1946–47	Jack Kramer

1948–49	Richard Gonzales	**OPEN**	
1950	Arthur Larsen	1968	Arthur Ashe
1951–52	Frank Sedgman	1969	Rod Laver
1953	Tony Trabert	1970	Ken Rosewall
1954	Vic Seixas	1971	Stan Smith
1955	Tony Trabert	1972	Ilie Nastase
1956	Ken Rosewall	1973	John Newcombe
1957	Mal Anderson	1974	Jimmy Connors
1958	Ashley Cooper	1975	Manuel Orantes
1959–60	Neale Fraser	1976	Jimmy Connors
1961	Roy Emerson	1977	Guillermo Vilas
1962	Rod Laver	1978	Jimmy Connors
1963	Rafael Osuna	1979	John McEnroe
1964	Roy Emerson	1980–81	John McEnroe
1965	Manuel Santana	1982	Jimmy Connors
1966	Fred Stolle	1983	Jimmy Connors
1967	John Newcombe	1984	John McEnroe
1968	Arthur Ashe	1985–87	Ivan Lendl
1969	Rod Laver	1988	Mats Wilander
		1989	Boris Becker

Singles—Women

NATIONAL

1887	Ellen F. Hansel	1906	Helen Homans
1888–89	Bertha Townsend	1907	Evelyn Sears
1890	Ellen C. Roosevelt	1908	Maud
1891–92	Mabel E. Cahill		Bargar-Wallach
1893	Aline M. Terry	1909–11	Hazel V.
1894	Helen R. Helwig		Hotchkiss
1895	Juliette P.	1912–14	Mary K. Browne
	Atkinson	1915–18	Molla Bjurstedt
1896	Elisabeth H.	1919	Hazel Hotchkiss
	Moore		Wightman
1897–98	Juliette P.	1920–22	Molla Bjurstedt
	Atkinson		Mallory
1899	Marion Jones	1923–25	Helen N. Wills
1900	Myrtle McAteer	1926	Molla B. Mallory
1901	Elisabeth H.	1927–29	Helen N. Wills
	Moore	1930	Betty Nuthall
1902	Marion Jones	1931	Helen Wills Moody
1903	Elisabeth H. Moore	1932–35	Helen Jacobs
1904	May Sutton	1936	Alice Marble
1905	Elisabeth H. Moore	1937	Anita Lizana

1938–40	Alice Marble	1968–69	Margaret Smith
1941	Sarah Palfrey		Court[3]
	Cooke	**OPEN**	
1942–44	Pauline Betz	1968	Virginia Wade
1945	Sarah Cooke	1969–70	Margaret Court
1946	Pauline Betz	1971–72	Billie Jean King
1947	Louise Brough	1973	Margaret Court
1948–50	Margaret Osborne	1974	Billie Jean King
	duPont	1975–78	Chris Evert
1951–53	Maureen Connolly	1979	Tracy Austin
1954–55	Doris Hart	1980	Chris Evert-Lloyd
1956	Shirley Fry	1981	Tracy Austin
1957–58	Althea Gibson	1982	Chris Evert-Lloyd
1959	Maria Bueno	1983–84	Martina Navratilova
1960–61	Darlene Hard	1985	Hana Mandlikova
1962	Margaret Smith	1986–87	Martina Navratilova
1963–64	Maria Bueno	1988	Steffi Graf
1965	Margaret Smith	1989	Steffi Graf
1966	Maria Bueno		
1967	Billie Jean King		

Doubles—Men

NATIONAL

1920	Bill Johnston–C. J. Griffin	1938	Don Budge–Gene Mako
1921–22	Bill Tilden–Vincent Richards	1939	A. K. Quist–J. E. Bromwich
1923	Bill Tilden–B. I. C. Norton	1940–41	Jack Kramer–F. R. Schroeder
1924	H. O. Kinsey–R. G. Kinsey	1942	Gardnar Mulloy–Bill Talbert
1925–26	Vincent Richards–R. N. Williams II	1943	Jack Kramer–Frank Parker
		1944	Don McNeill–Bob Falkenburg
1927	Bill Tilden–Frank Hunter	1945	Gardnar Mulloy–Bill Talbert
1928	G. M. Lott, Jr.-V. Hennessy	1946	Gardnar Mulloy–Bill Talbert
1929–30	G. M. Lott, Jr.-J. H. Doeg	1947	Jack Kramer–Fred Schroeder
1931	W. L. Allison–John Van Ryn	1948	Gardnar Mulloy–Bill Talbert
1932	E. H. Vines, Jr.–Keith Gledh	1949	John Bromwich–William Sidwell
1933–34	G. M. Lott, Jr.-L. R. Stoefen	1950	John Bromwich–Frank Sedgman
1935	W. L. Allison–John Van Ryn	1951	Frank Sedgman–Ken McGregor
1936	Don Budge–Gene Mako	1952	Vic Seixas–Mervyn Rose
1937	G. von Cramm–H. Henkel	1953	Mervyn Rose–Rex Hartwig

1954	Vic Seixas–Tony Trabert
1955	Kosei Kamo–Atsushi Miyagi
1956	Lewis Hoad–Ken Rosewall
1957	Ashley Cooper–Neale Fraser
1958	Ham Richardson–Alex Olmedo
1959–60	Neale Fraser–Roy Emerson
1961	Chuck McKinley–Dennis Ralston
1962	Rafael Osuna–Antonio Palafox
1963–64	Chuck McKinley–Dennis Ralston
1965–66	Fred Stolle–Roy Emerson
1967	John Newcombe–Tony Roche
1968	Stan Smith–Bob Lutz[3]
1969	Richard Crealy–Allan Stone[3]

OPEN

1968	Stan Smith–Bob Lutz	1976	Marty Riessen–Tom Okker	1984	John Fitzgerald–Tomas Smid
1969	Fred Stolle–Ken Rosewall	1977	Frew McMillan–Bob Hewitt	1985	Ken Flach–Robert Seguso
1970	Nikki Pilic–Fred Barthes	1978	Bob Lutz–Stan Smith	1986	Andres Gomez–Slobodan Zivo-jinovic
1971	John Newcombe–Roger Taylor	1979	John McEnroe–Peter Fleming		
1972	Cliff Drysdale–Roger Taylor	1980	Stan Smith–Bob Lutz	1987	Stefan Edberg–Anders Jarryd
1973	John Newcombe–Owen Davidson	1981	John McEnroe–Peter Fleming	1988	Sergio Casal–Emilio Sanchez
1974	Bob Lutz–Stan Smith	1982	Kevin Curren–Steve Denton	1989	John McEnroe—Mark Woodforde
1975	Jimmy Connors–Ilie Nastase	1983	John McEnroe–Peter Fleming		

1. Challenge round abandoned in 1912. 2. Patriotic Tournament in 1917. 3. With the inaugural of the Open Tournament in 1968, the United States Lawn Tennis Association held a national championship at Longwood, Chestnut Hill, Mass. which barred contract professionals in 1968 and 1969.

Doubles—Women

NATIONAL

1924	G. W. Wightman–Helen Wills	1951–54	Doris Hart–Shirley Fry	1971	Rosemary Casals–Judy Dalton
1925	Mary K. Browne–Helen Wills	1955–57	A. Louise Brough–Margaret O. duPont	1972	Francoise Durr–Betty Stove
1926	Elizabeth Ryan–Eleanor Goss			1973	Margaret Court–Virginia Wade
1927	L. A. Godfree–Ermyntrude Harvey	1958–59	Darlene Hard–Jeanne Arth	1974	Billie Jean King–Rosemary Casals
1928	Hazel Hotchkiss Wightman–Helen Wills	1960	Darlene Hard–Maria Bueno	1975	Margaret Court–Virginia Wade
		1961	Darlene Hard–Lesley Turner	1976	Linky Boshoff–Ilana Kloss
1929	Phoebe Watson–L. R. C. Michell	1962	Darlene Hard–Maria Bueno	1977	Martina Navratilova–Betty Stove
1930	Betty Nuthall–Sarah Palfrey	1963	Margaret Smith–Robyn Ebbern	1978	Billie Jean King–Martina Navra-tilova
1931	Betty Nuthall–E. B. Wittingstall	1964	Karen Hantze Susman–Billie Jean Moffitt		
1932	Helen Jacobs–Sarah Palfrey			1979	Betty Stove–Wendy Turnbull
1933	Betty Nuthall–Freda James	1965	Nancy Richey–Carole Caldwell Graebner	1980	Billie Jean King–Martina Navra-tilova
1934	Helen Jacobs–Sarah Palfrey				
1935	Helen Jacobs–Sarah Palfrey Fabyan	1966	Nancy Richey–Maria Bueno	1981	Kathy Jordan–Anne Smith
		1967	Billie Jean King–Rosemary Casals	1982	Rosemary Casals–Wendy Turnbull
1936	Marjorie G. Van Ryn–Carolin Bab-cock	1968	Margaret Court–Maria Bueno[3]	1983–84	Martina Navratilova–Pam Shriver
		1969	Margaret Court–Virginia Wade[3]	1985	Claudia Khode-Kilsch–Helena Sukova
1937–40	Sarah Palfrey Fabyan–Alice Marble				
1941	Sarah Palfrey Cooke–Margaret Os-borne			1986–87	Martina Navratilova–Pam Shriver
		OPEN		1988	Gigi Fernandez–Robin White
1942–47	A. Louise Brough–Margaret Os-borne	1968	Maria Bueno–Margaret Court	1989	Hana Mandlikova–Martina Navra-tilova
		1969	Darlene Hard–Francoise Durr		
1948–50	A. Louise Brough–Margaret O. duPont	1970	Margaret Court–Judy Dalton		

1. Challenge round abandoned in 1912. 2. Patriotic Tournament in 1917. 3. With the inaugural of the Open Tournament in 1968, the United States Lawn Tennis Association held a national championship at Longwood, Chestnut Hill, Mass. which barred contract professionals in 1968 and 1969.

U.S. INDOOR CHAMPIONS

Singles—Men

1964	Charles McKinley	1978–79	Jimmy Connors
1965	Erik Lundquist	1980	John McEnroe
1966	Charles Pasarell	1981	Gene Mayer
1967	Charles Pasarell	1982	Johan Kriek
1968	Cliff Richey	1983–84	Jimmy Connors
1969	Stan Smith	1985	Stefan Edberg
1970	Ilie Nastase	1986	Brad Gilbert
1971	Clark Graebner	1987	Stefan Edberg
1972	Stan Smith	1988	Andre Agassi
1973–75	Jimmy Connors	1989	Brad Gilbert
1976	Ilie Nastase		
1977	Bjorn Borg		

Singles—Women

1964	Mary Ann Eisel	1977	Chris Evert
1965	Nancy Richey	1978	Chris Evert
1966	Billie Jean King	1979	Evonne Goolagong
1967	Billie Jean King	1980	Tracy Austin
1968	Billie Jean King	1981	Martina Navratilova
1969	Mary Ann Eisel	1982	Barbara Potter
1970	Mary Ann Curtis	1983	Kim Shaefer
1971	Billie Jean King	1984	Martina Navratilova
1972	Not held	1985	Hana Mandlikova
1973	Evonne Goolagong	1986	Martina Navratilova
1974	Billie Jean King	1987	Helena Sukova
1975	Martina Navratilova	1988	Steffi Graf
1976	Virginia Wade	1989	Steffi Graf

Doubles—Men

1967	Arthur Ashe–Charles Pasarell	1978	Brian Gottfried–Raul Ramirez
1968	Thomas Koch–Tom Okker	1979	Wojtek Fibak–Tom Okker
1969	Stan Smith–Bob Lutz	1980	John McEnroe–Brian Gottfried
1970	Arthur Ashe–Stan Smith	1981	Gene Mayer–Sandy Mayer
1971	Manuel Orantes–Juan Gisbert	1982	Kevin Curren–Steve Denton
1972	Manuel Orantes–Andres Gimeno	1983	Peter McNamara–Paul McNamee
1973	Juan Gisbert–Jurgen Fassbender	1984	Fritz Bushning–Peter Fleming
1974	Jimmy Connors–Frew McMillan	1985	Pavel Slozil–Tomas Smid
1975	Jimmy Connors–Ilie Nastase	1986	Ken Flach–Robert Seguso
1976–77	Sherwood Stewart–Fred McNair	1987	Anders Jarryd–Jonas Svensson

1988	Kevin Curren–David Pate		
1989	Paul Annacone–Christo Van Rens-bury		

Doubles—Women

1967	Carol Aucamp–Mary Ann Eisel
1968	Rosemary Casals–Billie Jean King
1969	Mary Ann Eisel–Valerie Ziegen-fuss

970	Peaches Bartkowicz–Nancy Richey	1976	Rosemary Casals–Francoise Durr	1982	Rosemary Casals–Wendy Turnbull
971	Billie Jean King–Rosemary Casals	1977	Martina Navratilova–Betty Stove	1983	Billie Jean King–Sharon Walsh
972	Not held	1978	Kerry Reid–Wendy Turnbull	1984–85	Martina Navratilova–Pam Shriver
973	Olga Morozova–Marina Kroshina	1979	Billie Jean King–Martina Navratilova	1986	Kathy Jordan–Elizabeth Smylie
974	Not held	1980	Ann Kiyomura–Candy Reynolds	1987	Gigi Fernandez–Lori McNeil
975	Billie Jean King–Rosemary Casals	1981	Martina Navratilova–Pam Shriver	1988	Helena Sukova–Lori McNeil
				1989	Katrina Adams–Pam Shriver

BRITISH (WIMBLEDON) CHAMPIONS

(Amateur from inception in 1877 through 1967)

Singles—Men

908–09	Arthur Gore	1931	S. B. Wood	1954	Jaroslav Drobny	1973	Jan Kodes
910–13	A. F. Wilding	1932	Ellsworth Vines	1955	Tony Trabert	1974	Jimmy Connors
914	N. E. Brookes	1933	J. H. Crawford	1956–57	Lewis Hoad	1975	Arthur Ashe
919	G. L. Patterson	1934–36	Fred Perry	1958	Ashley Cooper	1976–80	Bjorn Borg
920–21	Bill Tilden	1937–38	Don Budge	1959	Alex Olmedo	1981	John McEnroe
922	G. L. Patterson	1939	Robert L. Riggs	1960	Neale Fraser	1982	Jimmy Connors
923	William Johnston	1946	Yvon Petra	1961–62	Rod Laver	1983–84	John McEnroe
924	Jean Borotra	1947	Jack Kramer	1963	Chuck McKinley	1985–86	Boris Becker
925	Rene Lacoste	1948	R. Falkenburg	1964–65	Roy Emerson	1987	Pat Cash
926	Jean Borotra	1949	Fred Schroeder	1966	Manuel Santana	1988	Stefan Edberg
927	Henri Cochet	1950	Budge Patty	1967	John Newcombe	1989	Boris Becker
928	Rene Lacoste	1951	Richard Savitt	1968–69	Rod Laver		
929	Jean Cochet	1952	Frank Sedgman	1970–71	John Newcombe		
930	Bill Tilden	1953	Vic Siexas	1972	Stan Smith		

Singles—Women

919–23	Lenglen	1938	Helen Wills Moody	1962	Karen Susman	1976	Chris Evert
924	Kathleen McKane	1939	Alice Marble	1963	Margaret Smith	1977	Virginia Wade
925	Lenglen	1946	Pauline M. Betz	1964	Maria Bueno	1978–79	Martina Navratilova
926	Godfree	1947	Margaret Osborne	1965	Margaret Smith	1980	Evonne Goolagong Cawley
927–29	Helen Wills	1948–50	A. Louise Brough	1966–67	Billie Jean King		
930	Helen Wills Moody	1951	Doris Hart	1968	Billie Jean King	1981	Chris Evert-Lloyd
931	Frl. C. Aussen	1952–54	Maureen Connolly	1969	Ann Jones	1982–87	Martina Navratilova
932–33	Helen Wills Moody	1955	A. Louise Brough	1970	Margaret Court	1988-89	Steffi Graf
934	D. E. Round	1956	Shirley Fry	1971	Evonne Goolagong		
935	Helen Wills Moody	1957–59	Althea Gibson	1972–73	Billie Jean King		
936	Helen Jacobs	1959–60	Maria Bueno	1974	Chris Evert		
937	D. E. Round	1961	Angela Mortimer	1975	Billie Jean King		

Doubles—Men

953	K. Rosewall–L. Hoad	1965	John Newcombe–Tony Roche	1979	Peter Fleming–John McEnroe
954	R. Hartwig–M. Rose	1966	John Newcombe–Ken Fletcher	1980	Peter McNamara–Paul McNamee
955	R. Hartwig–L. Hoad	1967	Bob Hewitt–Frew McMillan	1981	John McEnroe–Peter Fleming
956	L. Hoad–K. Rosewall	1968–70	John Newcombe–Tony Roche	1982	Paul McNamee–Peter McNamara
957	Gardnar Mulloy–Budge Patty	1971	Rod Laver–Roy Emerson	1983–84	John McEnroe–Peter Fleming
958	Sven Davidson–Ulf Schmidt	1972	Bob Hewitt–Frew McMillan	1985	Heinz Gunthardt–Balazs Taroczy
959	Roy Emerson–Neale Fraser	1973	Jimmy Connors–Ilie Nastase	1986	Joakim Nystrom–Mats Wilander
960	Dennis Ralston–Rafael Osuna	1974	John Newcombe–Tony Roche	1987	Ken Flach–Robert Seguso
961	Roy Emerson–Neale Fraser	1975	Vitas Gerulaitis–Sandy Mayer	1988	Ken Flach–Robert Seguso
962	Fred Stolle–Bob Hewitt	1976	Brian Gottfried–Raul Ramirez	1989	John Fitzgerald–Anders Jarryd
963	Rafael Osuna–Antonio Palafox	1977	Ross Case–Geoff Masters		
964	Fred Stolle–Bob Hewitt	1978	Fred McMillan–Bob Hewitt		

Doubles—Women

956	Althea Gibson–Angela Buxton	1966	Nancy Richey–Maria Bueno	1979	Billie Jean King–Martina Navratilova
957	Althea Gibson–Darlene Hard	1967–68	Billie Jean King–Rosemary Casals		
958	Althea Gibson–Maria Bueno	1969	Margaret Court–Judy Tegart	1980	Kathy Jordan–Anne Smith
959	Darlene Hard–Jeanne Arth	1970–71	Billie Jean King–Rosemary Casals	1981	Martina Navratilova–Pam Shriver
960	Darlene Hard–Maria Bueno	1972	Billie Jean King–Betty Stove	1982–84	Pam Shriver–Martina Navratilova
961	Karen Hantze–Billie Jean Moffitt	1973	Billie Jean King–Rosemary Casals	1985	Kathy Jordan–Elizabeth Smylie
962	Karen Hantze Susman–Billie Jean Moffitt	1974	Evonne Goolagong–Peggy Michel	1986	Pam Shriver–Martina Navratilova
		1975	Ann Kiyomura–Kazuko Sawamatsu	1987	Claudia Khode-Kilsch–Helena Sukova
963	Darlene Hard–Maria Bueno	1976	Chris Evert–Martina Navratilova		
964	Margaret Smith–Les Turnerley	1977	Helen Cawley–JoAnne Russell	1988	Steffi Graf–Gabriela Sabatini
965	Billie Jean Moffitt–Maria Bueno	1978	Wendy Turnbull–Kerry Reid	1989	Jana Novotna–Helena Sukova

UNITED STATES CHAMPIONS—1989

United States Open

(Flushing Meadow, Aug. 28-Sept. 10, 1989)

(seedings in parentheses)

Men's singles—Boris Becker (2), West Germany, defeated Ivan Lendl (1), Czechoslovakia, 7-6 (7-2), 1-6, 6-3, 7-6 (7-4).

Men's doubles—John McEnroe, Cove Neck, N.Y., and Mark Woodforde, Australia (7), defeated Ken Flach, St. Louis, and Robert Seguso, Boca Raton, Fla. (4), 6-4, 4-6, 6-3, 6-3.

Women's singles—Steffi Graf (1), West Germany, defeated Martina Navratilova (2), Fort Worth, Texas, 3-6, 7-5, 6-1.

Women's doubles: Hana Mandlikova, Australia, and Martina Navratilova, Fort Worth, Texas (6), defeated Mary Joe Fernandez, Miami, and Pam Shriver, Lutherville, Md. (5)., 5-7, 6-4, 6-4.

Mixed doubles—Robin White, San Diego, and Shelby Cannon, Gainesville, Fla., defeated Meredith McGrath, Midland, Mich., and Rick Leach, Laguna Beach, Calif., 3-6, 6-2, 7-5.

Senior men's singles—Hank Pfister (2), Bakersfield, Calif., defeated Sandy Mayer (4), Los Altos, Calif., 3-6, 6-4, 6-3.

Senior men's doubles—Tom Gullikson, Palm Coast, Fla., and Dick Stockton, Dallas (2), defeated Bob Lutz, San Clemente, Calif., and Sandy Mayer, Los Altos, Calif. (3), 6-4, 3-6, 6-2.

Senior women's doubles—Wendy Turnbull, Australia, and Virginia Wade, Britain (1), defeated Joanne Russell, Kingsmill, Va., and Olga Morozova, Soviet Union (4), 6-1, 6-0.

Tournament of Champions

(May 3-8, 1989)

Men's singles final—Ivan Lendl, Czechoslovakia, defeated Jamie Yzaga, Peru, 6-2, 6-1.

Men's doubles final—Rick Leach, Laguna Beach, Calif., and Jim Pugh, Palos Verdes, Calif., defeated Jim Currier, Dade City, Fla., and Pete Sampras, Palos Verdes, Calif., 6-4, 6-2.

U.S. Clay Courts

(May 8-14, 1989, Isle of Palms, S.C.)

Men's singles final—Jay Berger, Plantation, Fla., defeated Lawson Duncan, Asheville, N.C., 6-4, 6-3.

Men's doubles final—Mikael Pernfors and Tobais Svantesson, Sweden, defeated Agustin Moreno and Ygaza, Mexico, 6-4, 4-6, 7-5.

Hall of Fame Championships

(July 10-17, Newport, R.I.)

Singles final—Jim Pugh, Palos Verdes, Calif., defeated Peter Lundgren, Sweden, 6-4, 4-6, 6-2

Doubles final—Pat Galbraith and Brian Garrow, United States, defeated Neil Broad and Stefan Kruger, South Africa, 3-6, 7-5, 6-4.

U.S. Pro Indoor

(Philadelphia, Pa., Feb. 20-26, 1989)

Singles final—Boris Becker, West Germany, defeated Tim Mayotte, Boston, Mass., 7-6, 6-2, 6-3.

Doubles final—Paul Annacone, Knoxville, Tenn., and Christo van Rensburg, South Africa, defeated Rick Leach, Laguna Beach, Calif., and Jim Pugh, Palos Verdes, Calif., 6-3, 7-5.

International Players Championships

(March 20-April 2, 1989, Key Biscayne, Fla.)

Men's singles—Ivan Lendl, Czechoslovakia, declared winner by injury default after Thomas Muster of Australia was in an auto accident before the finals.

Women's singles—Gabriela Sabatini, Argentina, defeated Chris Evert, Boca Raton, Fla., 6-1, 4-6, 6-2.

Men's doubles—Jakob Hlasek, Switzerland, and Anders Jarryd, Sweden, defeated Patrick McEnroe, Oyster Bay, N.Y., and Jim Grabb, Tucson, Ariz., 6-3, injury default

Women's doubles—Jana Novotna and Helena Sukova, Czechoslovakia, defeated Lori McNeil and Gigi Fernandez, Miami, Fla., 7-6, 6-4.

OTHER 1989 CHAMPIONS

Wimbledon Open

Men's singles—Boris Becker, West Germany, defeated Stefan Edberg, Sweden, 6-0, 7-6 (7-1), 6-4.

Women's singles—Steffi Graf, West Germany, defeated Martina Navratilova, Fort Worth, Texas, 6-2, 6-7 (1-7), 6-1.

Men's doubles—John Fitzgerald, Australia, and Anders Jarryd, Sweden, defeated Rick Leach, Laguna Beach, Calif., and Jim Pugh, Palos Verdes, Calif., 3-6, 7-6 (7-4), 6-4, 7-6 (7-4).

Women's doubles—Jana Novotna and Helena Sukova, Czechoslovakia, defeated Larissa Savchenko and Natalie Zvereva, Soviet Union, 6-1, 6-2.

Mixed doubles—Jim Pugh, Palos Verdes, Calif., and Jana Novotna, Czechoslovakia, defeated Mark Kratzmann and Jenny Byrne, Australia, 6-4, 5-7, 6-4.

French Open

Men's singles—Michael Chang, Placentia, Calif., defeated Stefan Edberg, Sweden, 6-1, 3-6, 4-6, 6-4, 6-2.

Women's singles—Arantxa Sanchez, Spain, defeated Steffi Graf, West Germany, 7-6 (8-6), 3-6, 7-5.

Men's doubles—Patrick McEnroe, Oyster Bay, N.Y., and Jim Grabb, Tucson, Ariz., defeated Eric Winogradsky, France, and Mansour Bahrami, Iran, 6-4, 2-6, 6-4, 7-6 (7-5).

Women's doubles—Natalia Zvereva and Larisa Savchenko, Soviet Union, defeated Steffi Graf, West Germany, and Gabriela Sabatini, Argentina, 6-4, 6-4.

Mixed doubles—Manon Bollegraf and Tom Nijssen, The Netherlands, defeated Arantxa Sanchez, Spain, and Horacio de la Pena, Argentina, 6-3, 6-7 (3-7), 6-2.

Australian Open

Men's singles—Ivan Lendl, Czechoslovakia, defeated Miloslav Mecir, Czechoslovakia, 6-2, 6-2, 6-2.

Women's singles—Steffi Graf, West Germany, defeated Helena Sukova, Czechoslovakia, 6-4, 6-4.

Men's doubles—Jim Pugh, Palos Verdes, Calif., and Rick Leach, Laguna Beach, Calif., defeated Darren Cahill and Mark Kratzmann, Australia, 6-4, 6-4, 6-4.

Women's doubles—Martina Navratilova, Ft. Worth, Texas, and Pam Shriver, Lutherville, Md., defeated Patty Fendick, Sacramento, Calif., and Jill Hetherington, Canada, 3-6, 6-3, 6-2.

Mixed doubles—Jim Pugh, Palos Verdes, Calif., and Jana Novotna, Czechoslovakia, defeated Sherwood Stewart and Zina Garrison, Houston, Texas, 6-3, 6-4.

DAVIS CUP RESULTS—1988

West Germany 4, Sweden 1 (at Goteberg, Sweden, Dec. 16-18, 1988)

Singles—Carl-Uwe Steeb, West Germany, defeated Mats Wilander, Sweden, 8-10, 1-6, 6-2, 6-2, 8-6; Stefan Edberg, Sweden, defeated Carl-Uwe Steeb, 6-4, 8-6.; Boris Becker, West Germany, defeated Stefan Edberg, Sweden, 6-3, 6-1, 6-4.

Doubles—Boris Becker and Eric Jelen, West Germany, defeated Anders Jarryd and Stefan Edberg, Sweden, 3-6, 2-6, 7-5, 6-3, 6-2; Sweden forfeited final match to West Germany, with championship already decided.

MENS FINAL TENNIS EARNINGS—1988

Player and amount: Mats Wilander, $1,726,731; Boris Becker, $1,696,953; Stefan Edberg, $1,402,802; Ivan Lendl, $983,938; Andre Agassi, $822,062; Jakob Hlasek, $624,716; Emilio Sanchez, $555,146; Andre LeConte, $554,491; Kent Carlsson, $516,539; Tim Mayotte, $505,754.

WOMEN'S FINAL TENNIS EARNINGS—1988

Player and amount: Steffi Graf, $1,378,128; Martina Navratilova, $1,333,782; Gabriela Sabatini, $995,399; Chris Evert, $698,649; Pam Shriver, $621,327; Zina Garrison, $419,035; Helena Sukova, $388,317; Natalia Zvereva, $361,354; Lori McNeil, $358,043; Manuela Maleva, $256,174.

ROWING

Rowing goes back so far in history that there is no possibility of tracing it to any particular aboriginal source. The oldest rowing race still on the calendar is the "Doggett's Coat and Badge" contest among professional watermen of the Thames (England) that began in 1715. The first Oxford-Cambridge race was held at Henley in 1829. Competitive rowing in the United States began with matches between boats rowed by professional oarsmen of the New York water front. They were oarsmen who rowed the small boats that plied as ferries from Manhattan Island to Brooklyn and return, or who rowed salesmen down the harbor to meet ships arriving from Europe. Since the first salesman to meet an incoming ship had some advantage over his rivals, there was keen competition in the bidding for fast boats and the best oarsmen. This gave rise to match races.

Amateur boat clubs sprang up in the United States between 1820 and 1830 and seven students of Yale joined together to purchase a four-oared lap-streak gig in 1843. The first Harvard-Yale race was held Aug. 3, 1852, on Lake Winnepesaukee, N.H. The first time an American college crew went abroad was in 1869 when Harvard challenged Oxford and was defeated on the Thames. There were early college rowing races on Lake Quinsigamond, near Worcester, Mass., and on Saratoga Lake, N.Y., but the Intercollegiate Rowing Association in 1895 settled on the Hudson, at Poughkeepsie, as the setting for the annual "Poughkeepsie Regatta." In 1950 the I.R.A. shifted its classic to Marietta, Ohio, and in 1952 it was moved to Syracuse, N.Y. The National Association of Amateur Oarsmen, organized in 1872, has conducted annual championship regattas since that time.

INTERCOLLEGIATE ROWING ASSOCIATION REGATTA

(Varsity Eight-Oared Shells)

Rowed at 4 miles, Poughkeepsie, N.Y., 1895–97, 1899–1916, 1925–32, 1934–41. Rowed at 3 miles, Saratoga, N.Y., 1898; Poughkeepsie, 1921–24, 1947–49; Syracuse, N.Y., 1952–1963, 1965–67. Rowed at 2,000 meters, Syracuse, N.Y., 1964 and from 1968 on. Rowed at 2 miles, Ithaca, N.Y., 1920; Marietta, Ohio, 1950–51. Suspended 1917–19, 1933, 1942–46.

Year	Time	First	Second	Year	Time	First	Second
1895	21:25	Columbia	Cornell	1948	14:06 2/5	Washington	California
1896	19:59	Cornell	Harvard	1949	14:42 3/5	California	Washington
1897	20:47 4/5	Cornell	Columbia	1950	8:07.5	Washington	California
1898	15:51 1/2	Pennsylvania	Cornell	1951	7:50.5	Wisconsin	Washington
1899	20:04	Pennsylvania	Wisconsin	1952	15:08.1	Navy	Princeton
1900	19:44 3/5	Pennsylvania	Wisconsin	1953	15:29.6	Navy	Cornell
1901	18:53 1/5	Cornell	Columbia	1954	16:04.4	Navy[1]	Cornell
1902	19:03 3/5	Cornell	Wisconsin	1955	15:49.9	Cornell	Pennsylvania
1903	18:57	Cornell	Georgetown	1956	16:22.4	Cornell	Navy
1904	20:22 3/5	Syracuse	Cornell	1957	15:26.6	Cornell	Pennsylvania
1905	20:29	Cornell	Syracuse	1958	17:12.1	Cornell	Navy
1906	19:36 4/5	Cornell	Pennsylvania	1959	18:01.7	Wisconsin	Syracuse
1907	20:02 2/5	Cornell	Columbia	1960	15:57	California	Navy
1908	19:24 1/5	Syracuse	Columbia	1961	16:49.2	California	Cornell
1909	19:02	Cornell	Columbia	1962	17:02.9	Cornell	Washington
1910	20:42 1/5	Cornell	Pennsylvania	1963	17:24	Cornell	Navy
1911	20:10 4/5	Cornell	Columbia	1964	6:31.1	California	Washington
1912	19:31 2/5	Cornell	Wisconsin	1965	16:51.3	Navy	Cornell
1913	19:28 3/5	Syracuse	Cornell	1966	16:03.4	Wisconsin	Navy
1914	19:37 4/5	Columbia	Pennsylvania	1967	16:13.9	Pennsylvania	Wisconsin
1915	19:36 3/5	Cornell	Stanford	1968	6:15.6	Pennsylvania	Washington
1916	20:15 2/5	Syracuse	Cornell	1969	6:30.4	Pennsylvania	Dartmouth
1920	11:02 3/5	Syracuse	Cornell	1970	6:39.3	Washington	Wisconsin
1921	14:07	Navy	California	1971	6:06	Cornell	Washington
1922	13:33 3/5	Navy	Washington	1972	6:22.6	Pennsylvania	Brown
1923	14:03 1/5	Washington	Navy	1973	6:21	Wisconsin	Brown
1924	15:02	Washington	Wisconsin	1974	6:33	Wisconsin	Mass. Inst. of Technology
1925	19:24 4/5	Navy	Washington				
1926	19:28 3/5	Washington	Navy	1975	6:08.2	Wisconsin	M.I.T.
1927	20:57	Columbia	Washington	1976	6:31	California	Princeton
1928	18:35 4/5	California	Columbia	1977	6:32.4	Cornell	Pennsylvania
1929	22:58	Columbia	Washington	1978	6:39.5	Syracuse	Brown
1930	21:42	Cornell	Syracuse	1979	6:26.4	Brown	Wisconsin
1931	18:54 1/5	Navy	Cornell	1980	6:46	Navy	Northeastern
1932	19:55	California	Cornell	1981	5:57.3	Cornell	Navy
1934	19:44	California	Washington	1982	5:57.5	Cornell	Princeton
1935	18:52	California	Cornell	1983	6:14.4	Brown	Navy
1936	19:09 3/5	Washington	California	1984	5:54.7	Navy	Pennsylvania
1937	18:33 3/5	Washington	Navy	1985	5:49.9	Princeton	Brown
1938	18:19	Navy	California	1986	5:50.2	Brown	Pennsylvania
1939	18:12 3/5	California	Washington	1987	6:02.9	Brown	Wisconsin
1940	22:42	Washington	Cornell	1988	6:14.0	Northeastern	Brown
1941	18:53 3/10	Washington	California	1989	5:56.0	Penn	Wisconsin
1947	13:59 1/5	Navy	Cornell				

1. Disqualified.

HARNESS RACING

Oliver Wendell Holmes, the famous Autocrat of the Breakfast Table, wrote that the running horse was a gambling toy but the trotting horse was useful and, furthermore, "horse-racing is not a republican institution; horse-trotting is." Oliver Wendell Holmes was a born-and-bred New Englander, and New England was the nursery of the harness racing sport in America. Pacers and trotters were matters of local pride and prejudice in Colonial New England, and, shortly after the Revolution, the Messenger and Justin Morgan strains produced many winners in harness racing "matches" along the turnpikes of New York, Connecticut, Rhode Island, Massachusetts, Vermont, and New Hampshire.

There was English thoroughbred blood in Messenger and Justin Morgan, and, many years later, it was blended in Rysdyk's Hambletonian, foaled in 1849. Hambletonian was not particularly fast under harness but his descendants have had almost a monopoly of prizes, titles, and records in the harness racing game. Hambletonian was purchased as a foal with its dam for a total of $124 by William Rysdyk of Goshen, N.Y., and made a modest fortune for the purchaser.

Trotters and pacers often were raced under saddle in the old days, and, in fact, the custom still survives in some places in Europe. Dexter, the great trotter that lowered the mile record from 2:19 3/4 to 2:17 1/4 in 1867, was said to handle just as well under saddle as when pulling a sulky. But as sulkies were lightened in weight and improved in design, trotting under saddle became less common and finally faded out in this country.

WORLD RECORDS
Established in a Race or Against Time at One Mile
Source: United States Trotting Association
(Through September 11, 1989)

Trotting on Mile Track

	Record	Holder	Driver	Where Made	Year
All Age	1:52 1/5	Mack Lobell	John Campbell	Springfield, Ill.	1987
	1:52 4/5	Peace Corps	John Campbell	Du Quoin, Ill.	1989
	*1:54	Arndon	Del Miller	Lexington, Ky.	1982
	*1:55 1/4	Greyhound	Sep Palin	Lexington, Ky.	1938
2-year-old	1:55 3/5	Mack Lobell	John Campbell	Lexington, Ky.	1986
	*1:55	Noxie Hanover	Jim Simpson	Lexington, Ky.	1988
	1:58	Tarport Ramey	Del Miller	Indianapolis, Ind.	1986
3-year-old	1:52 1/5	Mack Lobell	John Campbell	Springfield, Ill.	1987
	1:52 4/5	Peace Corps	John Campbell	Du Quoin, Ill.	1989
	1:56	Nuclear Arsenal	Dave Magee	Springfield, Ill.	1989
4-year-old	1:53	Express Ride	Berndt Lindstedt	Lexington, Ky.	1987
	*1:55 2/5	Classical Way	John Simpson Jr.	Lexington, Ky.	1980
	1:56	Delray Lobell	John Campbell	East Rutherford, N.J.	1989
5-year-old and older	1:54 1/5	Napoletano	Stig Johansson	East Rutherford, N.J.	1989
	1:55	Franconia	John Campbell	East Rutherford, N.J.	1987
	*1:55 1/4	Greyhound	Sep Palin	Lexington, Ky.	1938

Trotting on Five Eighths-Mile Track

All Age	1:54 1/5	Mack Lobell	John Campbell	Pompano Beach, Fla.	1987
2-year-old	1:58 1/5	Valley Victory	Bill O'Donnell	Pompano Beach, Fla.	1988
3-year-old	1:54 1/5	Mack Lobell	John Campbell	Pompano Beach, Fla.	1987
4-year-old	1:54 4/5	Mack Lobell	John Campbell	Solvalla, Sweden	1988
5-year-old and older	1:55	Minou Du Donjon	Olle Goop	Solvalla, Sweden	1985

Trotting on Half-Mile Track

All Age	1:56	Mack Lobell	John Campbell	Saratoga Springs, N.Y.	1988
2-year-old	1:58 3/5	Petri Kosmos	Jan Nordin	Delaware, Ohio	1987
3-year-old	1:56 4/5	Editor In Chief	John Campbell	Delaware, Ohio	1988
4-year-old	1:56	Mack Lobell	John Campbell	Saratoga Springs, N.Y.	1988
5-year-old and older	1:57 4/5	Lakewater Glory	Valery Tanishin	Northfield, Ohio	1989

Pacing on a Mile Track

All-Age	*1:48 2/5	Matt's Scooter	Michel Lachance	Lexington, Ky.	1988
	*1:50 4/5	Fan Hanover	Glen Garnsey	Lexington, Ky.	1982
	1:51 1/5	Indian Alert	Jack Moiseyev	East Rutherford, N.J.	1988
2-year-old	1:52	L Dees Trish	Michel Lachance	Lexington, Ky.	1988
	1:52 1/5	Raque Bogart	Bill Fahy	Lexington, Ky.	1988
3-year-old	*1:48 2/5	Matt's Scooter	Michel Lachance	Lexington, Ky.	1988
	*1:51 2/5	Trini Hanover	Ron Waples	Springfield, Ill.	1987
	1:51 4/5	Indian Alert	Larry Noggle	Lexington, Ky.	1987
4-year-old	*1:49 2/5	Jaguar Spur	Dick Stillings	Lexington, Ky.	1988
	*1:50 4/5	Fan Hanover	Glen Garnsey	Lexington, Ky.	1982
	1:51 1/5	Indian Alert	Jack Moiseyev	East Rutherford, N.J.	1988
5-year-old and older	1:50 1/5	Ramblin' Storm	Michel Lachance	East Rutherford, N.J.	1988

Pacing on Five-Eighths-Mile Track

All-Age	1:51 3/5	Falcon Seelster	Tom Harmer	Meadows, Pa.	1986
2-year-old	1:53 2/5	Kentucky Spur	Dick Stillings	Pompano Beach, Fla.	1988
3-year-old	1:52 1/5	Marauder	Dick Richardson Jr.	Meadows, Pa.	1985
	1:52 1/5	Towner's Big Guy	Steve Warrington	Meadows, Pa.	1986
	1:51 1/5	Goalie Jeff	Michel Lachance	Montreal, Canada	1989
4-year-old	1:51	Falcon Seelster	Tom Harmer	Meadow Lands, Pa.	1986
5-year-old and older	1:52 2/5	Ring of Light	James Morand	Laurel, Md.	1988

Pacing on a Half-Mile Track

All Age	1:51	Falcon Seelster	Tom Harmer	Delaware, Ohio	1985
2-year-old	* 1:55	Rowleyalla	Kevin Rivett	Sydney, Aust.	1987
	1:55 1/5	Albert Albert	Chris Boring	Louisville, Ky.	1987
	1:55 1/5	Kentucky Spur	Dick Stilling	Louisville, Ky.	1988
3-year-old	1:51	Falcon Seelster	Tom Harmer	Delaware, Ohio	1985
4-year-old	1:53 1/5	Falcon Seelster	Tom Harmer	Maywood, Ill.	1986
5-year-old and older	1:54 1/5	Port Stanley	John Reese	Mawood, Ill.	1988

*Set in a time trial.

HARNESS RACING RECORDS FOR THE MILE

Trotters			**Pacers**		
Time	Trotter, age, driver	Year	Time	Pacer, age, driver	Year
2:00	Lou Dillon, 5, Millard Sanders	1903	2:00 1/2	John R. Gentry, 7, W.J. Andrews	1896
1:58 1/2	Lou Dillon, 5, Millard Sanders	1903	1:59 1/4	Star Pointer, 8, D. McClary	1897
1:58	Uhlan, 8, Charles Tanner	1912	1:59	Dan Patch, 7, M. E. McHenry	1903
1:58	Peter Manning, 5, T. W. Murphy	1921	1:56 1/4	Dan Patch, 7, M. E. McHenry	1903
1:57 3/4	Peter Manning, 5, T. W. Murphy	1921	1:56	Dan Patch, 8, H. C. Hersey	1904
1:57	Peter Manning, 6, T. W. Murphy	1922	1:55	Billy Direct, 4, Vic Fleming	1938
1:56 3/4	Peter Manning, 6, T. W. Murphy	1922	1:55	Adios Harry, 4, Luther Lyons	1955
1:56 3/4	Greyhound, 5, Sep Palin	1937	1:54 3/5	Adios Butler, 4, Paige West	1960
1:56	Greyhound, 5, Sep Palin	1937	1:54	Bret Hanover, 4, Frank Ervin	1966
1:55 1/4	Greyhound, 6, Sep Palin	1938	1:53 3/5	Bret Hanover, 4, Frank Ervin	1966
1:54 4/5	Nevele Pride, 4, Stanley Dancer	1969	1:52	Steady Star, 4, Joe O'Brien	1971
1:54 4/5	Lindy's Crown, 4, Howard Beissinger	1980	1:49 1/5	Niatross, 3, Clint Galbraith	1980
1:54	Arndon, 3, Del Miller	1982	1:48 2/5	Matt's Scooter, 3, Michel Lachance	1989
1:52 1/5	Mack Lobell, 3, John Campbell	1987			

HISTORY OF TRADITIONAL HARNESS RACING STAKES

The Hambletonian

Three-year-old trotters. One mile. Guy McKinney won first race at Syracuse in 1926; held at Goshen, N.Y., 1930–1942, 1944–1956; at Yonkers, N.Y., 1943; at Du Quoin, Ill., 1957–1980. Since 1981, the race has been held at The Meadowland in East Rutherford, N.J.

Year	Winner	Driver	Best time	Total purse
1967	Speedy Streak	Del Cameron	2:00	$ 122,650
1968	Nevele Pride	Stanley Dancer	1:59 2/5	116,190
1969	Lindy's Pride	Howard Beissinger	1:57 3/5	124,910
1970	Timothy T.	John Simpson, Jr.	1:58 2/5[1]	143,630
1971	Speedy Crown	Howard Beissinger	1:57 2/5	129,770
1972	Super Bowl	Stanley Dancer	1:56 2/5	119,090
1973	Flirth	Ralph Baldwin	1:57 1/5	144,710
1974	Christopher T	Billy Haughton	1:58 3/5	160,150
1975	Bonefish	Stanely Dancer	1:59[2]	232,192
1976	Steve Lobell	Billy Haughton	1:56 2/5	263,524
1977	Green Speed	Billy Haughton	1:55 3/5	284,131
1978	Speedy Somolli	Howard Beissinger	1:55[3]	241,280
1979	Legend Hanover	George Sholty	1:56 1/5	300,000
1980	Burgomeister	Billy Haughton	1:56 3/5	293,570
1981	Shiaway St. Pat	Ray Remmen	2:01 1/5[4]	838,000
1982	Speed Bowl	Tommy Haughton	1:56 4/5	875,750
1983	Duenna	Stanley Dancer	1:57 2/5	1,000,000
1984	Historic Free	Ben Webster	1:56 2/5	1,219,000
1985	Prakas	Bill O'Donnell	1:54 3/5	1,272,000
1986	Nuclear Kosmos	Ulf Thoresen	1:56	1,172,082
1987	Mack Lobell	John Campbell	1:53 3/5	1,046,300
1988	Armbro Goal	John Campbell	1:54 3/5	1,156,800
1989	Park Avenue Joe	Ron Wayples	1:55 3/5	1,131,000

1. By Formal Notice. 2. By Yankee Bambino. 3. By Speedy Somolli and Florida Pro. 4. By Super Juan.

Little Brown Jug

Three-year-old pacers. One Mile. Raced at Delaware County Fair Grounds, Delaware, Ohio.

Year	Winner	Driver	Best time	Total purse
1967	Best of All	Jim Hackett	1:59[1]	$ 84,778
1968	Rum Customer	Billy Haughton	1:59 3/5	104,226
1969	Laverne Hanover	Billy Haughton	2:00 2/5	109,731
1970	Most Happy Fella	Stanley Dancer	1:57 1/5	100,110
1971	Nansemond	Herve Filion	1:57 2/5	102,994
1972	Strike Out	Keith Waples	1:56 3/5	104,916
1973	Melvin's Woe	Joe O'Brien	1:57 3/5	120,000
1974	Ambro Omaha	Billy Haughton	1:57	132,630
1975	Seatrain	Ben Webster	1:57[2]	147,813
1976	Keystone Ore	Stanley Dancer	1:56 4/5[3]	153,799

Year	Winner	Driver	Best time	Total purse
1977	Governor Skipper	John Chapman	1:56 1/5	150,000
1978	Happy Escort	William Popfinger	1:55 2/5[4]	186,760
1979	Hot Hitter	Herve Filion	1:55 3/5	226,455
1980	Niatross	Clint Galbraith	1:54 4/5	207,361
1981	Fan Hanover	Glen Garnsey	1:56[5]	243,799
1982	Merger	John Campbell	1:56 3/5	328,900
1983	Ralph Hanover	Ron Waples	1:55 3/5	358,800
1984	Colt 46	Norman Boring	1:53 3/5	366,717
1985	Nihilator	Bill O'Donnell	1:52 1/5	350,730
1986	Barberry Spur	Bill O'Donnell	1:52 4/5	407,684
1987	Jaguar Spur	Richard Stillings	1:55 3/5	412,330
1988	B.J. Scoot	Michel Lachance	1:52 3/5	486,050
1989	Goalie Jeff	Michel Lachance	1:54 1/5	500,200

1. By Nardin's Byrd. 2. By Armbro Ranger. 3. By Falcon Almahurst. 4. By Falcon Almahurst. 5. By Seahawk Hanover.

HARNESS HORSE OF THE YEAR

Chosen in poll conducted by United States Trotting Association in conjunction with the U.S. Harness Writers Assn.

1959 Bye Bye Byrd, Pacer	1969 Nevele Pride, Trotter	1979 Niatross, Pacer
1960 Adios Butler, Pacer	1970 Fresh Yankee, Trotter	1980 Niatross, Pacer
1961 Adios Butler, Pacer	1971 Albatross, Pacer	1981 Fan Hanover, Pacer
1962 Su Mac Lad, Trotter	1972 Albatross, Pacer	1982 Cam Fella, Pacer
1963 Speedy Scot, Trotter	1973 Sir Dalrae, Pacer	1983 Cam Fella, Pacer
1964 Bret Hanover, Pacer	1974 Delmonica Hanover, Trotter	1984 Fancy Crown, Trotter
1965 Bret Hanover, Pacer	1975 Savoir, Trotter	1985 Nihilator, Trotter
1966 Bret Hanover, Pacer	1976 Keystone Ore, Pacer	1986 Forrest Skipper
1967 Nevele Pride, Trotter	1977 Green Speed, Trotter	1987 Mack Lobell
1968 Nevele Pride, Trotter	1978 Abercrombie, Pacer	1988 Mack Lobell

WRESTLING

U.S.A. NATIONAL CHAMPIONSHIPS—1989

Freestyle

(April 14-16, 1989, Topeka, Kansas)

105.5 lb (48 kg)—Tim Vannie, Tempe, Ariz.
114.4 lb (52 kg)—Zeke Jones, Tempe, Ariz.
125.5 lb (57 kg)—Brad Penrith, Iowa City, Iowa
136.5 lb (62 kg)—John Smith, Del City, Okla.
149.5 lb (68 kg)—Nate Carr, Morgantown, W.Va.
163.0 lb (74 kg)—Rob Koll, New York, N.Y.
180.5 lb (82 kg)—Rico Chiapparelli, Iowa City, Iowa
198.0 lb (90 kg)—Jim Scherr, Chicago, Ill.
220.0 lb (100 kg)—Bill Scherr, Bloomington, Ind.
Unlimited—Bruce Baumgartner, Cambridge Springs, Pa.
Outstanding Wrestler—Jim Scherr, Chicago

Greco-Roman

(April 14-16, 1989, Topeka, Kansas)

105.5 lb (48 kg)—Lewis Dorrance, Triangle, Va.
114.5 lb (52 kg)—Mark Fuller, Salt Lake City, Utah
125.5 lb (57 kg)—Gogi Parseghian, Glendale, Calif.
136.5 lb (62 kg)—Ike Anderson, Albany, N.Y.
149.5 lb (68 kg)—Andy Seres, Schenectady, N.Y.
163.0 lb (74 kg)—David Butler, El Cajon, Calif.
180.5 lb (82 kg)—John Morgan, St. Paul, Minn.
198.0 lb (90 kg)—Michael Foy, Minneapolis, Minn.
Unlimited—Craig Pittman, Quantico, Va.

N.C.A.A. CHAMPIONSHIPS

(March 16-18, 1989, Oklahoma City, Okla.)

118 lb—Jack Cuvo, East Stroudsburg
126 lb—Kendall Cross, Oklahoma State
134 lb—Sean O'Day, Edinboro
142 lb—Pat Santoro, Pittsburgh
150 lb—Tim Krieger, Iowa State
158 lb—Dan St. John, Arizona State
167 lb—Dave Lee, Wisconsin
177 lb—Chris Barnes, Oklahoma State
190 lb—Eric Voelker, Iowa State
Heavyweight—Carlton Haselrig, Pittsburgh-Johnstown
Outstanding Wrestler—Tim Krieger, Iowa State

Team Standings

1. Oklahoma State, 91 1/4 pts
2. Arizona State, 70 1/2 pts
3. Iowa State, 63 pts

WORLD CUP—1987

(New York, N.Y., November, 1987)

105.5 lb (48 kg)—Sergey Karamtchakov, Soviet Union
114.5 lb (52 kg)—Joe Gonzales, United States
125.5 lb (57 kg)—Ruslan Karaev, Soviet Union
136.5 lb (62 kg)—Joe McFarland, United States
149.5 lb (68 kg)—Abdulla Magomedov, Soviet Union
163.0 lb (74 kg)—Alberto Rodriguez, Cuba
180.5 lb (82 kg)—Aleksandr Tamboutsev, Soviet Union
190.0 lb (90 kg)—Makharbek Khadartsev, Soviet Union
220.0 lb (100 kg)—Akhmed Atavov, Soviet Union
Unlimited—David Gobedjichili, Soviet Union
Team Standings:
1. Soviet Union   4. Korea
2. United States   5. Australia
3. Cuba

GOLF

It may be that golf originated in Holland—historians believe it did—but certainly Scotland fostered the game and is famous for it. In fact, in 1457 the Scottish Parliament, disturbed because football and golf had lured young Scots from the more soldierly exercise of archery, passed an ordinance that "futeball and golf be utterly cryit doun and nocht usit." James I and Charles I of the royal line of Stuarts were golf enthusiasts, whereby the game came to be known as "the royal and ancient game of golf."

The golf balls used in the early games were leather-covered and stuffed with feathers. Clubs of all kinds were fashioned by hand to suit individual players. The great step in spreading the game came with the change from the feather ball to the guttapercha ball about 1850. In 1860, formal competition began with the establishment of an annual tournament for the British Open championship. There are records of "golf clubs" in the United States as far back as colonial days but no proof of actual play before John Reid and some friends laid out six holes on the Reid lawn in Yonkers, N.Y., in 1888 and played them there with golf balls and clubs brought over from Scotland by Robert Lockhart. This group then formed the St. Andrews Golf Club of Yonkers, and golf was established in this country.

However, it remained a rather sedate and almost aristocratic pastime until a 20-year-old ex-caddy, Francis Ouimet of Boston, defeated two great British professionals, Harry Vardon and Ted Ray, in the United States Open championship at Brookline, Mass., in 1913. This feat put the game and Francis Ouimet on the front pages of the newspapers and stirred a wave of enthusiasm for the sport. The greatest feat so far in golf history is that of Robert Tyre Jones, Jr., of Atlanta, who won the British Open, the British Amateur, the U.S. Open, and the U.S. Amateur titles in one year, 1930.

THE MASTERS TOURNAMENT WINNERS

Augusta National Golf Club, Augusta, Ga.

Year	Winner	Score	Year	Winner	Score	Year	Winner	Score
1934	Horton Smith	284	1954	Sam Snead[1]	289	1972	Jack Nicklaus	286
1935	Gene Sarazen[1]	282	1955	Cary Middlecoff	279	1973	Tommy Aaron	283
1936	Horton Smith	285	1956	Jack Burke	289	1974	Gary Player	278
1937	Byron Nelson	283	1957	Doug Ford	283	1975	Jack Nicklaus	276
1938	Henry Picard	285	1958	Arnold Palmer	284	1976	Ray Floyd	271
1939	Ralph Guldahl	279	1959	Art Wall, Jr.	284	1977	Tom Watson	276
1940	Jimmy Demaret	280	1960	Arnold Palmer	282	1978	Gary Player	277
1941	Craig Wood	280	1961	Gary Player	280	1979	Fuzzy Zoeller[1]	280
1942	Byron Nelson[1]	280	1962	Arnold Palmer[1]	280	1980	Severiano Ballesteros	275
1943–45	No Tournaments		1963	Jack Nicklaus	286	1981	Tom Watson	280
1946	Herman Keiser	282	1964	Arnold Palmer	276	1982	Craig Stadler[1]	284
1947	Jimmy Demaret	281	1965	Jack Nicklaus	271	1983	Severiano Ballesteros	280
1948	Claude Harmon	279	1966	Jack Nicklaus[1]	288	1984	Ben Crenshaw	277
1949	Sam Snead	282	1967	Gay Brewer, Jr.	280	1985	Bernhard Langer	282
1950	Jimmy Demaret	283	1968	Bob Goalby	277	1986	Jack Nicklaus	279
1951	Ben Hogan	280	1969	George Archer	281	1987	Larry Mize[1]	285
1952	Sam Snead	286	1970	Billy Casper[1]	279	1988	Sandy Lyle	281
1953	Ben Hogan	274	1971	Charles Coody	279	1989	Nick Faldo[1]	283

1. Winner in playoff.

U.S. OPEN CHAMPIONS

Year	Winner	Score	Where played	Year	Winner	Score	Where played
1895	Horace Rawlins	173	Newport	1919	Walter Hagen[2]	301	Brae Burn
1896	James Foulis	152	Shinnecock Hills	1920	Edward Ray	295	Inverness
1897	Joe Lloyd	162	Chicago	1921	Jim Barnes	289	Columbia
1898[3]	Fred Herd	328	Myopia	1922	Gene Sarazen	288	Skokie
1899	Willie Smith	315	Baltimore	1923	R. T. Jones, Jr.[1][2]	296	Inwood
1900	Harry Vardon	313	Chicago	1924	Cyril Walker	297	Oakland Hills
1901	Willie Anderson[1]	331	Myopia	1925	Willie Macfarlane[1]	291	Worcester
1902	Laurie Auchterlonie	307	Garden City	1926	R. T. Jones, Jr.[2]	293	Scioto
1903	Willie Anderson[1]	307	Baltusrol	1927	Tommy Armour[1]	301	Oakmont
1904	Willie Anderson	303	Glen View	1928	Johnny Farrell[1]	294	Olympia Fields
1905	Willie Anderson	314	Myopia	1929	R. T. Jones, Jr.[1][2]	294	Winged Foot
1906	Alex Smith	295	Onwentsia	1930	R. T. Jones, Jr.[2]	287	Interlachen
1907	Alex Ross	302	Philadelphia	1931	Billy Burke[1]	292	Inverness
1908	Fred McLeod[1]	322	Myopia	1932	Gene Sarazen	286	Fresh Meadow
1909	George Sargent	290	Englewood	1933	John Goodman[2]	287	North Shore
1910	Alex Smith[1]	298	Philadelphia	1934	Olin Dutra	293	Merion
1911	John McDermott[1]	307	Chicago	1935	Sam Parks, Jr.	299	Oakmont
1912	John McDermott	294	Buffalo	1936	Tony Manero	282	Baltusrol
1913	Francis Ouimet[1][2]	304	Brookline	1937	Ralph Guldahl	281	Oakland Hills
1914	Walter Hagen	290	Midlothian	1938	Ralph Guldahl	284	Cherry Hills
1915	Jerome D. Travers[2]	297	Baltusrol	1939	Byron Nelson[1]	284	Philadelphia
1916	Charles Evans, Jr.[2]	286	Minikahda	1940	Lawson Little[1]	287	Canterbury
1917–18	No tournaments[4]			1941	Craig Wood	284	Colonial

Year	Winner	Score	Where played	Year	Winner	Score	Where played
1942–45	No tournaments[5]			1968	Lee Trevino	275	Oak Hill
1946	Lloyd Mangrum[1]	284	Canterbury	1969	Orville Moody	281	Champions G. C.
1947	Lew Worsham[1]	282	St. Louis	1970	Tony Jacklin	281	Hazeltine
1948	Ben Hogan	276	Riviera	1971	Lee Trevino[1]	280	Merion
1949	Cary Middlecoff	286	Medinah	1972	Jack Nicklaus	290	Pebble Beach
1950	Ben Hogan[1]	287	Merion	1973	Johnny Miller	279	Oakmont
1951	Ben Hogan	287	Oakland Hills	1974	Hale Irwin	287	Winged Foot
1952	Julius Boros	281	Northwood	1975	Lou Graham[1]	287	Medinah
1953	Ben Hogan	283	Oakmont	1976	Jerry Pate	277	Atlanta A.C.
1954	Ed Furgol	284	Baltusrol	1977	Hubert Green	278	Southern Hills
1955	Jack Fleck[1]	287	Olympic	1978	Andy North	285	Cherry Hills
1956	Cary Middlecoff	281	Oak Hill	1979	Hale Irwin	284	Inverness
1957	Dick Mayer[1]	298	Inverness	1980	Jack Nicklaus	272	Baltusrol
1958	Tommy Bolt	283	Southern Hills	1981	David Graham	273	Merion
1959	Bill Casper, Jr.	282	Winged Foot	1982	Tom Watson	282	Pebble Beach
1960	Arnold Palmer	280	Cherry Hills	1983	Larry Nelson	280	Oakmont
1961	Gene Littler	281	Oakland Hills	1984	Fuzzy Zoeller[1]	276	Winged Foot
1962	Jack Nicklaus[1]	283	Oakmont	1985	Andy North[1]	279	Oakland Hills
1963	Julius Boros[1]	293	Country Club	1986	Ray Floyd	279	Shinnecock Hills
1964	Ken Venturi	278	Congressional	1987	Scott Simpson	277	Olympic Golf Club
1965	Gary Player[1]	282	Bellerive				
1966	Bill Casper[1]	278	Olympic	1988	Curtis Strange[1]	278	The Country Club
1967	Jack Nicklaus	275	Baltusrol	1989	Curtis Strange	278	Oak Hill Country Club

1. Winner in playoff. 2. Amateur. 3. In 1898, competition was extended to 72 holes. 4. In 1917, Jock Hutchison, with a 292, won an Open Patriotic Tournament for the benefit of the American Red Cross at Whitemarsh Valley Country Club. 5. In 1942, Ben Hogan, with a 271 won a Hale American National Open Tournament for the benefit of the Navy Relief Society and USO at Ridgemoor Country Club.

U.S. AMATEUR CHAMPIONS

1895	Charles B. Macdonald	1922	Jess W. Sweetser	1949	Charles Coe	1970	Lanny Wadkins
1896–97	H. J. Whigham	1923	Max R. Marston	1950	Sam Urzetta	1971	Gary Cowan
1898	Findlay S. Douglas	1924–25	R. T. Jones, Jr.	1951	Billy Maxwell	1972	Vinny Giles 3d
1899	H. M. Harriman	1926	George Von Elm	1952	Jack Westland	1973[3]	Craig Stadler
1900–01	Walter J. Travis	1927–28	R. T. Jones, Jr.	1953	Gene Littler	1974	Jerry Pate
1902	Louis N. James	1929	H. R. Johnston	1954	Arnold Palmer	1975	Fred Ridley
1903	Walter J. Travis	1930	R. T. Jones, Jr.	1955–56	Harvie Ward	1976	Bill Sander
1904–05	H. Chandler Egan	1931	Francis Ouimet	1957	Hillman Robbins	1977	John Fought
1906	Eben M. Byers	1932	Ross Somerville	1958	Charles Coe	1978	John Cook
1907–08	Jerome D. Travers	1933	G. T. Dunlap, Jr.	1959	Jack Nicklaus	1979	Mark O'Meara
1909	Robert A. Gardner	1934–35	Lawson Little	1960	Deane Beman	1980	Hal Sutton
1910	W. C. Fownes, Jr.	1936	John W. Fischer	1961	Jack Nicklaus	1981	Nathaniel Crosby
1911	Harold H. Hilton	1937	John Goodman	1962	Labron Harris, Jr.	1982	Jay Sigel
1912–13	Jerome D. Travers	1938	Willie Turnesa	1963	Deane Beman	1983	Jay Sigel
1914	Francis Ouimet	1939	Marvin H. Ward	1964	Bill Campbell	1984	Scott Verplank
1915	Robert A. Gardner	1940	R. D. Chapman	1965[2]	Robert Murphy, Jr.	1985	Sam Randolph
1916	Charles Evans, Jr.	1941	Marvin H. Ward	1966	Gary Cowan[1]	1986	Buddy Alexander
1919	S. D. Herron	1946	Ted Bishop	1967	Bob Dickson	1987	Bill Mayfair
1920	Charles Evans, Jr.	1947	Robert Riegel	1968	Bruce Fleisher	1988	Eric Meeks
1921	Jesse P. Guilford	1948	Willie Turnesa	1968	Steven Melnyk	1989	Chris Patton

1. Winner in playoff. 2. Tourney switched to medal play through 1972. 3. Return to match play.

U.S. P.G.A. CHAMPIONS

1916	Jim Barnes	1941	Victor Ghezzi	1959	Bob Rosburg	1976	Dave Stockton
1919	Jim Barnes	1942	Sam Snead	1960	Jay Hebert	1977	Lanny Wadkins[1]
1920	Jock Hutchison	1944	Bob Hamilton	1961	Jerry Barber[1]	1978	John Mahaffey
1921	Walter Hagen	1945	Byron Nelson	1962	Gary Player	1979	David Graham[1]
1922–23	Gene Sarazen	1946	Ben Hogan	1963	Jack Nicklaus	1980	Jack Nicklaus
1924–27	Walter Hagen	1947	Jim Ferrier	1964	Bobby Nichols	1981	Larry Nelson
1928–29	Leo Diegel	1948	Ben Hogan	1965	Dave Marr	1982	Ray Floyd
1930	Tommy Armour	1949	Sam Snead	1966	Al Geiberger	1983	Hal Sutton
1931	Tom Creavy	1950	Chandler Harper	1967	Don January[1]	1984	Lee Trevino
1932	Olin Dutra	1951	Sam Snead	1968	Julius Boros	1985	Hubert Green
1933	Gene Sarazen	1952	Jim Turnesa	1969	Ray Floyd	1986	Bob Tway
1934	Paul Runyan	1953	Walter Burkemo	1970	Dave Stockton	1987	Larry Nelson
1935	Johnny Revolta	1954	Chick Harbert	1971	Jack Nicklaus	1988	Jeff Sluman
1936–37	Denny Shute	1955	Doug Ford	1972	Gary Player	1989	Payne Stewart
1938	Paul Runyan	1956	Jack Burke, Jr.	1973	Jack Nicklaus		
1939	Henry Picard	1957	Lionel Hebert	1974	Lee Trevino		
1940	Byron Nelson	1958[2]	Dow Finsterwald	1975	Jack Nicklaus		

1. Winner in playoff. 2. Switched to medal play.

U.S. WOMEN'S AMATEUR CHAMPIONS

1916	Alexa Stirling	1938	Patty Berg	1959	Barbara McIntire	1975	Beth Daniel
1919–20	Alexa Stirling	1939–40	Betty Jameson	1960	JoAnne Gunderson	1976	Donna Horton
1921	Marion Hollins	1941	Mrs. Frank Newell	1961	Anne Quast Decker	1977	Beth Daniel
1922	Glenna Collett	1946	Mildred Zaharias	1962	JoAnne Gunderson	1978	Cathy Sherk
1923	Edith Cummings	1947	Louise Suggs	1963	Anne Quast Welts	1979	Carolyn Hill
1924	Dorothy Campbell Hurd	1948	Grace Lenczyk	1964	Barbara McIntire	1980	Juli Inkster
		1949	Mrs. D. G. Porter	1965	Jean Ashley	1981	Juli Inkster
1925	Glenna Collett	1950	Beverly Hanson	1966	JoAnne Gunderson	1982	Juli Inkster
1926	Helen Stetson	1951	Dorothy Kirby	1967	Lou Dill	1983	Joanne Pacillo
1927	Mrs. M. B. Horn	1952	Jacqueline Pung	1968	JoAnne G. Carner	1984	Deb Richard
1928–30	Glenna Collett	1953	Mary Lena Faulk	1969	Catherine LaCoste	1985	Michiko Hattori
1931	Helen Hicks	1954	Barbara Romack	1970	Martha Wilkinson	1986	Kay Cockerill
1932–34	Virginia Van Wie	1955	Patricia Lesser	1971	Laura Baugh	1987	Kay Cockerill
1935	Glenna Collett Vare	1956	Marlene Stewart	1972	Mary Ann Budke	1988	Pearl Sinn
1936	Pamela Barton	1957	JoAnne Gunderson	1973	Carol Semple	1989	Vicki Goetze
1937	Mrs. J. A. Page, Jr.	1958	Anne Quast	1974	Cynthia Hill		

U.S. WOMEN'S OPEN CHAMPIONS

Year	Winner	Score	Year	Winner	Score	Year	Winner	Score
1946	Patty Berg (match play)	—	1961	Mickey Wright	293	1976	JoAnne Carner	292
1947	Betty Jameson	295	1962	Murle Lindstrom	301	1977	Hollis Stacy	292
1948	Mildred D. Zaharias	300	1963	Mary Mills	289	1978	Hollis Stacy	289
1949	Louise Suggs	291	1964	Mickey Wright[1]	290	1979	Jerilyn Britz	284
1950	Mildred D. Zaharias	291	1965	Carol Mann	290	1980	Amy Alcott	280
1951	Betsy Rawls	293	1966	Sandra Spuzich	297	1981	Pat Bradley	279
1952	Louise Suggs	284	1967	Catherine LaCoste	294	1982	Janet Alex	283
1953	Betsy Rawls[1]	302	1968	Susie Berning	289	1983	Jan Stephenson	290
1954	Mildred D. Zaharias	291	1969	Donna Caponi	294	1984	Hollis Stacy	290
1955	Fay Crocker	299	1970	Donna Caponi	287	1985	Kathy Baker	280
1956	Katherine Cornelius[1]	302	1971	JoAnne Carner	288	1986	Jane Geddes	287
1957	Betsy Rawls	299	1972	Susie Berning	299	1987	Laura Davies	285
1958	Mickey Wright	290	1973	Susie Berning	290	1988	Liselotte Neumann	277
1959	Mickey Wright	287	1974	Sandra Haynie	295	1989	Betsy King	278
1960	Betsy Rawls	291	1975	Sandra Palmer	295			

1. Winner in playoff. 2. Amateur.

BRITISH OPEN CHAMPIONS

(First tournament, held in 1860, was won by Willie Park, Sr.)

Year	Winner	Score	Year	Winner	Score	Year	Winner	Score
1920	George Duncan	303	1948	Henry Cotton	283	1970	Jack Nicklaus[1]	283
1921	Jock Hutchison[1]	296	1949	Bobby Locke[1]	283	1971	Lee Trevino	278
1922	Walter Hagen	300	1950	Bobby Locke	279	1972	Lee Trevino	278
1923	A. G. Havers	295	1951	Max Faulkner	285	1973	Tom Weiskopf	276
1924	Walter Hagen	301	1952	Bobby Locke	287	1974	Gary Player	282
1925	Jim Barnes	300	1953	Ben Hogan	282	1975	Tom Watson[1]	279
1926	R. T. Jones, Jr.	291	1954	Peter Thomson	283	1976	Johnny Miller	279
1927	R. T. Jones, Jr.	285	1955	Peter Thomson	281	1977	Tom Watson	268
1928	Walter Hagen	292	1956	Peter Thomson	286	1978	Jack Nicklaus	281
1929	Walter Hagen	292	1957	Bobby Locke	279	1979	Severiano Ballesteros	283
1930	R. T. Jones, Jr.	291	1958	Peter Thomson[1]	278	1980	Tom Watson	271
1931	Tommy Armour	296	1959	Gary Player	284	1981	Bill Rogers	276
1932	Gene Sarazen	283	1960	Kel Nagle	278	1982	Tom Watson	284
1933	Denny Shute[1]	292	1961	Arnold Palmer	284	1983	Tom Watson	275
1934	Henry Cotton	283	1962	Arnold Palmer	276	1984	Severiano Ballesteros	276
1935	A. Perry	283	1963	Bob Charles[1]	277	1985	Sandy Lyle	282
1936	A. H. Padgham	287	1964	Tony Lema	279	1986	Greg Norman	280
1937	Henry Cotton	290	1965	Peter Thomson	285	1987	Nick Faldo	279
1938	R. A. Whitcombe	295	1966	Jack Nicklaus	282	1988	Seve Ballesteros	273
1939	R. Burton	290	1967	Roberto de Vicenzo	278	1989	Mark Calcavecchia	275
1940	Sam Snead	290	1968	Gary Player	289			
1947	Fred Daly	294	1969	Tony Jacklin	280			

1. Winner in playoff.

OTHER 1989 PGA TOUR WINNERS
(Through September 3, 1989)

Tournament of Champions—Steve Jones (279)	$135,000
Bob Hope Classic—Steve Jones (343)	180,000
Phoenix Open—Mark Calcavecchia (263)	126,000
Pebble Beach National Pro-Am—Mark O'Meara (277)	180,000
Los Angeles Open—Mark Calcavecchia (272)	180,000
Hawaiian Open—Gene Savers (197)	135,000
Shearson-Lehman Hutton Open—Greg Twiggs (271)	126,000
Doral Open—Bill Glasson (275)	234,000
Honda Classic—Blaine McAllister (266)	144,000
Nestle Invitational—Tom Kite (278)	144,000
The Players Championship—Tom Kite (279)	243,000
USF&G Classic—Tim Simpson (274)	135,000
Heritage Classic—Payne Stewart (268)	144,000
Greater Greensboro Open—Ken Green (277)	180,000
Las Vegas Invitational—Scott Hoch (336)	225,000
Byron Nelson Classic—Jodie Mudd (265)	180,000
Colonial National—Ian Baker-Finch (270)	180,000
Atlanta Classic—Scott Simpson (278)	162,000
Kemper Open—Tom Byrom (268)	162,000
Westchester Classic—Wayne Grady (277)	180,000
Canadian Open—Steve Jones (271)	162,000
Western Open—Mark McCumber (275)	180,000
Greater Hartford Open—Paul Azinger (267)	180,000
Busch Classic—Mike Donald (268)	153,000
Hardee's Classic—Curt Byrum (268)	126,000
Buick Open—Leonard Thompson (273)	180,000
St. Jude Classic—John Mahaffey (272)	180,000
International—Greg Norman (+13)	180,000
World Series of Golf—David Frost (276)	180,000
Milwaukee Open—Greg Norman (269)	144,000

OTHER 1989 LPGA TOUR WINNERS
(Through Sept. 3, 1989)

Jamaica Classic—Betsy King (202)	$75,000
Oldsmobile Classic—Dottie Mochrie (279) playoff	45,000
Hawaiian Open—Sherri Turner (205)	45,000
Kemper Open—Betsy King (202)	60,000
Daikin Orchid Ladies Golf—Patti Rizzo (211)	62,000
Tucson Open—Lori Garbacz (274)	45,000
Turquoise Classic—Allison Finney (282)	60,000
Dinah Shore—Juli Inkster (279)	80,000
Al-Star-Centinela Hospital Classic—Pat Bradley (208)	67,500
USX Classic—Betsy King (275)	37,500
Sara Lee Classic—Kathy Postlewait (203)	63,750
Crestar Classic—Juli Inkster (210)	45,000
Chrysler-Plymouth Classic—Cindy Rarick (214)	41,250
Mazda Championship—Nancy Lopez (274)	75,000
Corning Classic—Ayako Okameto (272)	48,750
Rochester International—Patty Sheehan (278)	45,000
Pat Bradley International—Robin Hood (Plus-16)	62,500
Lady Keystone Open—Laura Davies (207)	45,000
McDonald's Championships—Betsy King (272)	82,500
du Maurier Classic—Tammie Green (279)	90,000
Jamie Farr Classic—Penny Hammel (206)	41,250
U.S. Women's Open—Betsy King (278)	80,000
Boston Five Classic—Amy Alcott (272)	52,500
Atlantic City Classic—Nancy Lopez (206)	33,750
Greater Washington Open—Beth Daniel (205)	45,000
LPGA World Championship—Betsy King (275)	83,500
Rail Charity Classic—Beth Daniel (203)	41,250

JAMES E. SULLIVAN MEMORIAL AWARD WINNERS
(Amateur Athlete of Year Chosen in Amateur Athletic Union Poll)

1930	Robert Tyre Jones, Jr.	Golf	1960	Rafer Johnson	Track and field
1931	Bernard E. Berlinger	Track and field	1961	Wilma Rudolph Ward	Track and field
1932	James A. Bausch	Track and field	1962	Jim Beatty	Track and field
1933	Glenn Cunningham	Track and field	1963	John Pennel	Track and field
1934	William R. Bonthron	Track and field	1964	Don Schollander	Swimming
1935	W. Lawson Little, Jr.	Golf	1965	Bill Bradley	Basketball
1936	Glenn Morris	Track and field	1966	Jim Ryun	Track and field
1937	J. Donald Budge	Tennis	1967	Randy Matson	Track and field
1938	Donald R. Lash	Track and field	1968	Debbie Meyer	Swimming
1939	Joseph W. Burk	Rowing	1969	Bill Toomey	Decathlon
1940	J. Gregory Rice	Track and field	1970	John Kinsella	Swimming
1941	Leslie MacMitchell	Track and field	1971	Mark Spitz	Swimming
1942	Cornelius Warmerdam	Track and field	1972	Frank Shorter	Marathon
1943	Gilbert L. Dodds	Track and field	1973	Bill Walton	Basketball
1944	Ann Curtis	Swimming	1974	Rick Wohlhuter	Track
1945	Felix (Doc) Blanchard	Football	1975	Tim Shaw	Swimming
1946	Y. Arnold Tucker	Football	1976	Bruce Jenner	Track and field
1947	John B. Kelly, Jr.	Rowing	1977	John Naber	Swimming
1948	Robert B. Mathias	Track and field	1978	Tracy Caulkins	Swimming
1949	Richard T. Button	Figure skating	1979	Kurt Thomas	Gymnastics
1950	Fred Wilt	Track and field	1980	Eric Heiden	Speed skating
1951	Robert E. Richards	Track and field	1981	Carl Lewis	Track and field
1952	Horace Ashenfelter	Track and field	1982	Mary Decker Tabb	Track and field
1953	Major Sammy Lee	Diving	1983	Edwin Moses	Track and field
1954	Malvin Whitfield	Track and field	1984	Greg Louganis	Diving
1955	Harrison Dillard	Track and field	1985	Joan Benoit–Samuelson	Marathon
1956	Patricia McCormick	Diving	1986	Jackie Joyner–Kersee	Heptathlon
1957	Bobby Jo Morrow	Track and Field	1987	Jim Abbott	Baseball
1958	Glenn Davis	Track and field	1988	Florence Griffith–Joyner	Track and field
1959	Parry O'Brien	Track and field			

SOCCER

WORLD CUP

1930	Uruguay	1950	Uruguay	1970	Brazil	1990	To be held in Italy
1934	Italy	1954	West Germany	1974	West Germany	1994	To be held in United
1938	Italy	1958	Brazil	1978	Argentina		States
1942	No competition	1962	Brazil	1982	Italy		
1946	No competition	1966	England	1986	Argentina		

WORLD CUP—1986

SEMIFINALS

1. (at Guadalajara, Mexico, June 25, 1986)

West Germany 2, France 0

2. (at Mexico City, Mexico, June 25, 1986)

Argentina 2, Belgium 0

THIRD PLACE

(at Puebla, Mexico, June 28, 1986)

France 4, Belgium 2 (overtime)

The following are the results of matches played by the four teams which reached the semifinals:

FINALS

(at Mexico City, Mexico, June 29, 1986)

Argentina 3, West Germany 2

Argentina (Group A)
Argentina 3, South Korea 1
Argentina 1, Italy 1
Argentina 2, Bulgaria 0
Argentina 1, Uruguay 0
Argentina 2, England 1

West Germany (Group E)
West Germany 1, Uruguay 1
West Germany 2, Scotland 1
Denmark 2, West Germany 0
West Germany 1, Morocco 0
West Germany 4, Mexico 1

France (Group C)
France 1, Canada 0
France 1, Soviet Union 1
France 3, Hungary 0
France 2, Italy 0*
France 5, Brazil 4

*Italy was defending champion.

Belgium (Group B)
Mexico 2, Belgium 1
Belgium 2, Iraq 1
Belgium 2, Paraguay 2
Belgium 4, Soviet Union 3 (Overtime)
Belgium 6, Spain 5

A capacity crowd of 114,500 fans filled Aztec Stadium in Mexico City on Sunday, June 29, and another 500 million were estimated to have watched on television, as Argentina defeated West Germany, 3–2, for the championship of the 13th World Cup Tournament.

Argentina's Diego Maradona was the star of the tournament. His pass to teammate Jorge Burruchaga led to the winning goal, after Argentina had squandered a 2–0 lead. He was the only unanimous selection to the post-tournament all-star team.

More than 140 world nations play soccer. The World Cup, the most popular and best attended sporting event in the world, is a quadrennial event, and will next be played in 1990. Two years of elimination precede the 52-game championship tournament.

Once again, the United States was eliminated from the 1986 tourney during preliminary play. In early action, the American team defeated the Netherlands-Antilles and Trinidad-Tobago, but on May 31, 1985, lost a 1–0 game to Costa Rica and was eliminated.

That marked the ninth consecutive World Cup tournament the United States had failed to qualify for. Not since 1950 has an American squad been part of the world's most prestigious sporting event.

UNITED STATES GAINS 1994 WORLD CUP

It was both fitting and a bit ironic that the Federation Internationale de Football Association picked July 4, 1989, to award the United States the 1994 World Cup competition.

The World Cup, arguably the No. 1 sports event in the world, thus comes to a country where soccer has struggled for a national foothold.

The 1990 World Cup was to be held in Italy, and 113 countries from around the world were entered in the qualifying competition, including the United States.

The right to stage the World Cup is a prize the United States Soccer Federation had been seeking for many years. In 1983, the U.S. Federation bid for the 1986 tournament, but it was rejected by FIFA, which did not feel the necessary fan support existed in the United States.

What likely put the United States over the top was the total attendance of more than 1.4 million for soccer at the 1984 Summer Olympics in Los Angeles.

A new organization, World Cup USA 1994 was formed, with Paul Stiehl as director and financial backing from sponsors including Coca-Cola, Gillette, Anheuser-Busch, and American Express.

MAJOR INDOOR SOCCER LEAGUE—1989
FINAL STANDING[1]

	W	L	Pct	GB
Baltimore Blast	29	19	.604	—
San Diego Sockers	27	21	.563	2
Dallas Sidekicks	24	24	.500	5
Tacoma Stars	23	25	.479	6
Wichita Wings	23	25	.479	6
Los Angeles Lazers	21	27	.438	8
Kansas City Comets	21	27	.438	8

1. For the 1989 season, the Major Indoor Soccer League was reduced to a seven-team, one-division league, as teams in Minnesota, Cleveland, Chicago, and St. Louis either folded or went on a year's hiatus.

CHAMPIONSHIP PLAYOFFS

Wild Card (Between fourth and fifth place teams to qualify for semifinals)
Wichita defeated Tacoma, 3 games to 1

Semifinals

San Diego defeated Dallas, 4 games to 3
Baltimore defeated Wichita, 4 games to 2

Championship

San Diego defeated Baltimore, 4 games to 3 for third title in four years

NORTH AMERICAN SOCCER LEAGUE CHAMPIONS

1968—Atlanta Chiefs	1971—Dallas Tornado
1969—Kansas City Stars	1972—New York Cosmos
1970—Rochester Lancers	1973—Philadelphia Atoms

1974—Los Angeles Aztecs	1980—New York Cosmos
1975—Tampa Bay Rowdies	1981—Chicago Sting
1976—Toronto Metro–Croatia	1982—New York Cosmos
1977—New York Cosmos	1983—Tulsa Roughnecks
1978—New York Cosmos	1984—Chicago Sting
1979—Vancouver Whitecaps	

YACHTING

AMERICA'S CUP RECORD

First race in 1851 around Isle of Wight, Cowes, England. First defense and all others through 1920 held 30 miles off New York Bay. Races since 1930 held 30 miles off Newport, R.I. Conducted as one race only in 1851 and 1870; best four-of-seven basis, 1871; best two-of-three, 1876–1887; best three-of-five, 1893–1901; best four-of-seven, since 1930. Figures in parentheses indicate number of races won.

Year	Winner and owner	Loser and owner
1851	AMERICA (1), John C. Stevens, U.S.	AURORA, T. Le Marchant, England[1]
1870	MAGIC (1), Franklin Osgood, U.S.	CAMBRIA, James Ashbury, England[2]
1871	COLUMBIA (2), Franklin Osgood, U.S.[3]	LIVONIA (1), James Ashbury, England
	SAPPHO (2), William P. Douglas, U.S.	
1876	MADELEINE (2), John S. Dickerson, U.S.	COUNTESS OF DUFFERIN, Chas. Gifford, Canada
1881	MISCHIEF (2), J. R. Busk, U.S.	ATALANTA, Alexander Cuthbert, Canada
1885	PURITAN (2), J. M. Forbes-Gen. Charles Paine, U.S.	GENESTA, Sir Richard Sutton, England
1886	MAYFLOWER (2), Gen. Charles Paine, U.S.	GALATEA, Lt. William Henn, England
1887	VOLUNTEER (2), Gen. Charles Paine, U.S.	THISTLE, James Bell et al., Scotland
1893	VIGILANT (3), C. Oliver Iselin et al., U.S.	VALKYRIE II, Lord Dunraven, England
1895	DEFENDER (3), C. O. Iselin-W. K. Vanderbilt-E. D. Morgan, U.S.	VALKYRIE III, Lord Dunraven-Lord Lonsdale-Lord Wolverton, England
1899	COLUMBIA (3), J. P. Morgan-C. O. Iselin, U.S.	SHAMROCK I, Sir Thomas Lipton, Ireland
1901	COLUMBIA (3), Edwin D. Morgan, U.S.	SHAMROCK II, Sir Thomas Lipton, Ireland
1903	RELIANCE (3), Cornelius Vanderbilt et al., U.S.	SHAMROCK III, Sir Thomas Lipton, Ireland
1920	RESOLUTE (3), Henry Walters et al., U.S.	SHAMROCK IV (2), Sir Thomas Lipton, Ireland
1930	ENTERPRISE (4), Harold S. Vanderbilt et al., U.S.	SHAMROCK V, Sir Thomas Lipton, Ireland
1934	RAINBOW (4), Harold S. Vanderbilt, U.S.	ENDEAVOUR (2), T. O. M. Sopwith, England
1937	RANGER (4), Harold S. Vanderbilt, U.S.	ENDEAVOUR II, T. O. M. Sopwith, England
1958	COLUMBIA (4), Henry Sears et al., U.S.	SCEPTRE, Hugh Goodson et al., England
1962	WEATHERLY (4), Henry D. Mercer et al., U.S.	GRETEL (1), Sir Frank Packer et al., Australia
1964	CONSTELLATION (4), New York Y.C. Syndicate, U.S.	SOVEREIGN (0), J. Anthony Bowden, England
1967	INTREPID (4), New York Y.C. Syndicate, U.S.	DAME PATTIE (0), Sydney (Aust.) Syndicate
1970	INTREPID (4), New York Y.C. Syndicate, U.S.	GRETEL II (1), Sydney (Aust.) Syndicate
1974	COURAGEOUS (4), New York, N.Y. Syndicate, U.S.	SOUTHERN CROSS (0), Sydney (Aust.) Syndicate
1977	COURAGEOUS (4), New York, N.Y. Syndicate, U.S.	AUSTRALIA (0), Sun City (Aust.) Syndicate
1980	FREEDOM (4), New York, N.Y. Syndicate, U.S.	AUSTRALIA (1), Alan Bond et al., Australia
1983	AUSTRALIA II (4) Alan Bond et al., Australia,	LIBERTY (3) New York, N.Y. Syndicate, U.S.
1987	STARS & STRIPES (4), Dennis Conner et al., United States	KOOKABURRA III (0), Iain Murray et al., Australia
1988[4]	NEW ZEALAND Michael Fay, et al., New Zealand	STARS & STRIPES, Dennis Conner, et al., United States

1. Fourteen British yachts started against America; Aurora finished second. 2. Cambria sailed against 23 U.S. yachts and finished tenth. 3. Columbia was disabled in the third race, after winning the first two; Sappho substituted and won the fourth and fifth. 4. Shortly after Dennis Conner and his 60-foot, twin-hulled catamaran easily defeated the challenge of the New Zealand, a 133-foot, single-hulled yacht in the waters off San Diego in early September 1988, a New York State Supreme Court judge ruled that the Americans did not live up to the America's Cup Deed of Gift, which means competing boats must be similar. The judge ruled that the Americans had an unfair advantage over the monohulled ship, and awarded the Cup to New Zealand. However, an Appeal awarded the Cup to the United States.

WEIGHTLIFTING

U.S. WEIGHTLIFTING FEDERATION
MEN'S NATIONAL CHAMPIONSHIPS

(Houston, Texas, April 29, 1989)

	Snatch	C&J[1]	Total[2]
52 kg—Steven Womble	67.5	92.5	160.0
56 kg—Timothy McRae	90.0	117.5	207.5
60 kg—Thanh Nguyen	102.5	135.0	237.5
67.5 kg—Michael Jacques	120.0	152.5	272.5
75 kg—Michael Tom Listro	132.5	160.0	292.5
82.5 kg—Roberto Urrutia	145.0	170.0	315.0
90 kg—Derrick Crass	150.0	190.0	340.0
100 kg—Richard Schutz	162.5	185.0	347.5
110 kg—Jeffery T. Michels	165.0	182.5	347.5
Over 110 kg—Mario Martinez	162.5	195.0	357.5

WOMEN'S NATIONAL CHAMPIONSHIPS

(Houston, Texas, April 28, 1989)

	Snatch	C&J[1]	Total[2]
44 kg—Andrea Tibeau	40.0	52.5	92.5
48 kg—Sibby Flowers	47.5	60.0	107.5
52 kg—Robin Byrd	65.0	75.0	140.0
56 kg—Melanie Getz	62.5	72.5	135.0
60 kg—Colleene Colley	77.5	97.5	175.0
67.5 kg—Diana Fuhrman	80.0	100.0	180.0
75 kg—Arlys Kovach	92.5	110.0	202.5
82.5 kg—Carol Cady	82.5	115.0	197.5
Over 82.5 kg—Karyn Marshall	102.5	130.0	232.5

1. Clean and jerk. 2. All results in kilograms.

AUTO RACING

INDIANAPOLIS 500

Year	Winner	Car	Time	mph	Second place
1911	Ray Harroun	Marmon	6:42:08	74.59	Ralph Mulford
1912	Joe Dawson	National	6:21:06	78.72	Teddy Tetzloff
1913	Jules Goux	Peugeot	6:35:05	75.93	Spencer Wishart
1914	René Thomas	Delage	6:03:45	82.47	Arthur Duray
1915	Ralph DePalma	Mercedes	5:33:55.51	89.84	Dario Resta
1916[1]	Dario Resta	Peugeot	3:34:17	84.00	Wilbur D'Alene
1919	Howard Wilcox	Peugeot	5:40:42.87	88.05	Eddie Hearne
1920	Gaston Chevrolet	Monroe	5:38:32	88.62	René Thomas
1921	Tommy Milton	Frontenac	5:34:44.65	89.62	Roscoe Sarles
1922	Jimmy Murphy	Murphy Special	5:17:30.79	94.48	Harry Hartz
1923	Tommy Milton	H. C. S. Special	5:29:50.17	90.95	Harry Hartz
1924	L. L. Corum–Joe Boyer	Dusenberg Special	5:05:23.51	98.23	Earl Cooper
1925	Peter DePaolo	Dusenberg Special	4:56:39.45	101.13	Dave Lewis
1926[2]	Frank Lockhart	Miller Special	4:10:14.95	95.904	Harry Hartz
1927	George Souders	Dusenberg Special	5:07:33.08	97.54	Earl DeVore
1928	Louis Meyer	Miller Special	5:01:33.75	99.48	Lou Moore
1929	Ray Keech	Simplex Special	5:07:25.42	97.58	Louis Meyer
1930	Billy Arnold	Miller–Hartz Special	4:58:39.72	100.448	Shorty Cantlon
1931	Louis Schneider	Bowes Special	5:10:27.93	96.629	Fred Frame
1932	Fred Frame	Miller–Hartz Special	4:48:03.79	104.144	Howard Wilcox
1933	Louis Meyer	Tydol Special	4:48:00.75	104.162	Wilbur Shaw
1934	Bill Cummings	Boyle Products Special	4:46:05.20	104.863	Mauri Rose
1935	Kelly Petillo	Gilmore Special	4:42:22.71	106.240	Wilbur Shaw
1936	Louis Meyer	Ring Free Special	4:35:03.39	109.069	Ted Horn
1937	Wilbur Shaw	Shaw–Gilmore Special	4:24:07.80	113.580	Ralph Hepburn
1938	Floyd Roberts	Burd Piston Ring Special	4:15:58.40	117.200	Wilbur Shaw
1939	Wilbur Shaw	Boyle Special	4:20:47.39	115.035	Jimmy Snyder
1940	Wilbur Shaw	Boyle Special	4:22:31.17	114.277	Rex Mays
1941	Floyd Davis–Mauri Rose	Noc–Out Hose Clamp Special	4:20:36.24	115.117	Rex Mays
1946	George Robson	Thorne Engineering Special	4:21:26.71	114.820	Jimmy Jackson
1947	Mauri Rose	Blue Crown Special	4:17:52.17	116.338	Bill Holland
1948	Mauri Rose	Blue Crown Special	4:10:23.33	119.814	Bill Holland
1949	Bill Holland	Blue Crown Special	4:07:15.97	121.327	Johnny Parsons
1950[3]	Johnnie Parsons	Wynn's Friction Proof Special	2:46:55.97	124.002	Bill Holland
1951	Lee Wallard	Belanger Special	3:57:38.05	126.244	Mike Nazaruk
1952	Troy Ruttman	Agajanian Special	3:52:41.88	128.922	Jim Rathmann
1953	Bill Vukovich	Fuel Injection Special	3:53:01.69	128.740	Art Cross
1954	Bill Vukovich	Fuel Injection Special	3:49:17.27	130.840	Jim Bryan
1955	Bob Sweikert	John Zink Special	3:53:59.13	128.209	Tony Bettenhausen
1956	Pat Flaherty	John Zink Special	3:53:28.84	128.490	Sam Hanks
1957	Sam Hanks	Belond Exhaust Special	3:41:14.25	135.601	Jim Rathmann
1958	Jimmy Bryan	Belond A–P Special	3:44:13.80	133.791	George Amick
1959	Rodger Ward	Leader Card 500 Roadster	3:40:49.20	135.857	Jim Rathmann
1960	Jim Rathmann	Ken–Paul Special	3:36:11.36	138.767	Rodger Ward
1961	A. J. Foyt	Bowes Special	3:35:37.49	139.130	Eddie Sachs
1962	Rodger Ward	Leader Card Special	3:33:50.33	140.293	Len Sutton
1963	Parnelli Jones	Agajanian Special	3:29:35.40	143.137	Jim Clark
1964	A. J. Foyt	Offenhauser Special	3:23:35.83	147.350	Rodger Ward
1965	Jim Clark	Lotus–Ford	3:19:05.34	150.686	Parnelli Jones
1966	Graham Hill	Lola–Ford	3:27:52.53	144.317	Jim Clark
1967[4]	A. J. Foyt	Coyote–Ford	3:18:24.22	151.207	Al Unser
1968	Bobby Unser	Eagle–Offenhauser	3:16:13.76	152.882	Dan Gurney
1969	Mario Andretti	STP Hawk–Ford	3:11:14.71	156.867	Dan Gurney
1970	Al Unser	P. J. Colt–Ford	3:12:37.04	155.749	Mark Donohue
1971	Al Unser	P. J. Colt–Ford	3:10:11.56	157.735	Peter Revson
1972	Mark Donohue	McLaren–Offenhauser	3:04:05.54	162.962	Al Unser
1973[5]	Gordon Johncock	Eagle–Offenhauser	2:05:26.59	159.036	Bill Vukovich
1974	Johnny Rutherford	McLaren–Offenhauser	3:09:10.06	158.589	Bobby Unser
1975[6]	Bobby Unser	Eagle–Offenhauser	2:54:55.08	149.213	Johnny Rutherford
1976[7]	Johnny Rutherford	McLaren–Offenhauser	1:42:52.48	148.725	A. J. Foyt
1977	A. J. Foyt	Coyote–Foyt	3:05:57.16	161.331	Tom Sneva
1978	Al Unser	Lola–Cosworth	3:05:54.99	161.363	Tom Sneva
1979	Rick Mears	Penske–Cosworth	3:08:27.97	158.899	A. J. Foyt
1980	Johnny Rutherford	Chaparral–Cosworth	3:29:59.56	142.862	Tom Sneva
1981[8]	Bobby Unser	Eagle–Offenhauser	3:35:41.78	139.029	Mario Andretti
1982	Gordon Johncock	Wildcat–Cosworth	3:05:09.14	162.029	Rick Mears
1983	Tom Sneva	March–Cosworth	3:05:03.06	162.117	Al Unser
1984	Rick Mears	March–Cosworth	3:03:21.00	162.962	Roberto Guerrero

1985	Danny Sullivan	March–Cosworth	3:16:06.069	152.982	Mario Andretti
1986	Bobby Rahal	March–Cosworth	2:55:43.48	170.722	Kevin Cogan
1987	Al Unser, Sr.	March–Cosworth	3:04:59.147	162.175	Roberto Guerrero
1988	Rick Mears	March–Cosworth	3:27:10.204	144.809	Emerson Fittipaldi
1989	Emerson Fittipaldi	P.C.–18 Chevrolet	2:59:01.04	167.581	Al Unser, Jr.

1. 300 miles. 2. Race ended at 400 miles because of rain. 3. Race ended at 345 miles because of rain. 4. Race, postponed after 18 laps because of rain on May 30, was finished on May 31. 5. Race postponed May 28 and 29 was cut to 332.5 miles because of rain, May 30. 6. Race ended at 435 miles because of rain. 7. Race ended at 255 miles because of rain. 8. Andretti was awarded the victory the day after the race after Bobby Unser, whose car finished first, was penalized one lap and dropped from first place to second for passing other cars illegally under a yellow caution flag. Unser appealed the decision to the U.S. Auto Club and was upheld. A panel ruled the penalty was too severe and instead fined Unser $40,000, but restored the victory to him.

U.S. AUTO CLUB
NATIONAL CHAMPIONS

1910	Ray Harroun	1926	Harry Hartz	1950	Henry Banks	1970	Al Unser
1911	Ralph Mulford	1927	Peter DePaolo	1951	Tony Bettenhausen	1971–72	Joe Leonard
1912	Ralph DePalma	1928–29	Louis Meyer	1952	Chuck Stevenson	1973	Roger McCluskey
1913	Earl Cooper	1930	Billy Arnold	1953	Sam Hanks	1974	Bobby Unser
1914	Ralph DePalma	1931	Louis Schneider	1954	Jimmy Bryan	1975	A. J. Foyt
1915	Earl Cooper	1932	Bob Carey	1955	Bob Sweikert	1976	Gordon Johncock
1916	Dario Resta	1933	Louis Meyer	1956–57	Jimmy Bryan	1977–78	Tom Sneva
1917	Earl Cooper	1934	Bill Cummings	1958	Tony Bettenhausen	1979	A. J. Foyt
1918	Ralph Mulford	1935	Kelly Petillo	1959	Rodger Ward	1980	Johnny Rutherford
1919	Howard Wilcox	1936	Mauri Rose	1960–61	A. J. Foyt	1981–82	George Snider
1920	Gaston Chevrolet	1937	Wilbur Shaw	1962	Rodger Ward	1983	Tom Sneva
1921	Tommy Milton	1938	Floyd Roberts	1963–64	A. J. Foyt	1984	Rick Mears
1922	James Murphy	1939	Wilbur Shaw	1965–66	Mario Andretti	1985	Danny Sullivan
1923	Eddie Hearne	1940–41	Rex Mays	1967	A. J. Foyt	1986	Bobby Rahal
1924	James Murphy	1946–48	Ted Horn	1968	Bobby Unser	1987	Al Unser, Sr.
1925	Peter DePaolo	1949	Johnnie Parsons	1969	Mario Andretti	1988	Rick Mears

NATIONAL ASSOCIATION FOR STOCK CAR AUTO RACING
(NASCAR) GRAND NATIONAL CHAMPIONS

1949	Red Byron	1958–59	Lee Petty	1968–69	David Pearson	1981	Darrell Waltrip
1950	Bill Rexford	1960	Rex White	1970	Bobby Isaac	1982	Darrell Waltrip
1951	Herb Thomas	1961	Ned Jarrett	1971–72	Richard Petty	1983	Bobby Allison
1952	Tim Flock	1962–63	Joe Weatherly	1973	Benny Parsons	1984	Terry Labonte
1953	Herb Thomas	1964	Richard Petty	1974–75	Richard Petty	1985	Darrell Waltrip
1954	Lee Petty	1965	Ned Jarrett	1976–78	Cale Yarborough	1986	Dale Earnhardt
1955	Tim Flock	1966	David Pearson	1979	Richard Petty	1987	Dale Earnhardt
1956–57	Buck Baker	1967	Richard Petty	1980	Dale Earnhardt	1988	Bill Elliott

WORLD GRAND PRIX DRIVER CHAMPIONS

1950	Giuseppe Farina, Italy, Alfa Romeo	1970	Jochen Rindt, Austria, Lotus-Ford
1951	Juan Fangio, Argentina, Alfa Romeo	1971	Jackie Stewart, Scotland, Tyrrell-Ford
1952	Alberto Ascari, Italy, Ferrari	1972	Emerson Fittipaldi, Brazil, Lotus-Ford
1953	Alberto Ascari, Italy, Ferrari	1973	Jackie Stewart, Scotland, Tyrrell-Ford
1955	Juan Fangio, Argentina, Maserati, Mercedes-Benz	1974	Emerson Fittipaldi, Brazil, McLaren-Ford
1955	Juan Fangio, Argentina, Mercedes-Benz	1975	Niki Lauda, Austria, Ferrari
1956	Juan Fangio, Argentina, Lancia-Ferrari	1976	James Hunt, Britain, McLaren-Ford
1957	Juan Fangio, Argentina, Maserati	1977	Niki Lauda, Austria, Ferrari
1958	Mike Hawthorn, England, Ferrari	1978	Mario Andretti, Nazareth, Pa., Lotus
1959	Jack Brabham, Australia, Cooper	1979	Jody Scheckter, South Africa
1960	Jack Brabham, Australia, Cooper	1980	Alan Jones, Australia
1961	Phil Hill, United States, Ferrari	1981	Nelson Piquet, Brazil
1962	Graham Hill, England, BRM	1982	Kiki Rosberg, Finland
1963	Jim Clark, Scotland, Lotus-Ford	1983	Nelson Piquet, Brazil
1964	John Surtees, England, Ferrari	1984	Nikki Lauda, Austria
1965	Jim Clark, Scotland, Lotus-Ford	1985	Alain Prost, France
1966	Jack Brabham, Australia, Brabham-Repco	1986	Alain Prost, France
1967	Denis Hulme, New Zealand, Brabham-Repco	1987	Nelson Piquet, Brazil
1968	Graham Hill, England, Lotus-Ford	1988	Ayrton Senna, Brazil
1969	Jackie Stewart, Scotland, Matra-Ford		

1988 NASCAR LEADING MONEY WINNERS

1. Bill Elliot — $1,554,639
2. Rusty Wallace — 1,411,567
3. Dale Earnhardt — 1,214,089
4. Terry Labonte — 950,781
5. Davey Allison — 844,532
6. Darrell Waltrip — 731,659
7. Ken Schrader — 631,544
8. Geoff Bodine — 570,643
9. Phil Parsons — 532,043
10. Sterling Marlin — 521,464

FINAL 1988 WINSTON CUP GRAND NATIONAL POINT LEADERS

Pos.	Driver name	Points			
1.	Bill Elliott	4488	11.	Ricky Rudd	3547
2.	Rusty Wallace	4464	12.	Bobby Hillin, Jr.	3446
3.	Dale Earnhardt	4256	13.	Kyle Petty	3296
4.	Terry Labonte	4007	14.	Alan Kulwicki	3176
5.	Ken Schrader	3858	15.	Mark Martin	3142
6.	Geoff Bodine	3799	16.	Neil Bonnett	3040
7.	Darrell Waltrip	3764	17.	Lake Speed	2984
8.	Davey Allison	3631	18.	Michael Waltrip	2949
9.	Phil Parsons	3630	19.	Dave Marcis	2854
10.	Sterling Marlin	3621	20.	Brett Bodine	2828

1989 MAJOR RACES

Indianapolis 500 (Indianapolis Motor Speedway, May 28, 1989, 500 miles)—1. Emerson Fittipaldi, Brazil, PC-18 Chevrolet; 200 laps. Time: 2:59:01.04. Average speed: 167.581 mph; First place prize: $1,001,604. 2. Al Unser, Jr., Albuquerque, N.M., Lola-Chevrolet, 198 laps, $390,453. 3. Raul Boesei, Brazil, Lola-Judd, 194 laps, $306,603. 4. Mario Andretti, Nazareth, Pa., Lola-Chevrolet, 193 laps, $193,853. 5. A.J. Foyt, Houston, Texas, Lola-Cosworth, 193 laps, $177,403.

Pocono 500 (Long Pond, Pa., Pocono International Raceway, July 23, 1989, 500 miles)—1. Bill Elliot, Dawsonville, Ga., Ford Thunderbird; 200 laps. Time: 4:14:31. Average speed: 117.870 mph. First place prize: $54,800. 2. Rusty Wallace, St. Louis, Pontiac Grand Prix, 200, $46,875; 3. Mark Martin, Batesville, Ark. Ford Thunderbird, 200, $26,300. 4. Darrell Waltrip, Franklin, Tenn., Chevrolet Lumina, 200, $23,850. 5. Harry Gant, Taylorsville, N.C., Oldsmobile Cutlass, 200, $20,350.

LACROSSE

NATIONAL INTERCOLLEGIATE CHAMPIONS

1946	Navy	1960	Navy	1976–77	Cornell
1947–48	Johns Hopkins	1961	Army, Navy	1978–80	Johns Hopkins
1949	Johns Hopkins, Navy	1962–66	Navy	1981	North Carolina
1950	Johns Hopkins	1967	Johns Hopkins, Maryland, Navy	1982	North Carolina
1951	Army, Princeton	1968	Johns Hopkins	1983	Syracuse
1952	Virginia, R.P.I.	1969	Army, Johns Hopkins	1984	Johns Hopkins
1953	Princeton	1970	Johns Hopkins, Navy, Virginia	1985	Johns Hopkins
1954	Navy	1971[1]	Cornell	1986	North Carolina
1955–56	Maryland	1972	Virginia	1987	Johns Hopkins
1957	Johns Hopkins	1973	Maryland	1988	Syracuse
1958	Army	1974	Johns Hopkins	1989	Syracuse
1959	Army, Johns Hopkins, Maryland	1975	Maryland		

1. First year of N.C.A.A. Championship Tournaments.

1989 N.C.A.A. LACROSSE

DIVISION I
Men's Championships
Quarterfinals

Syracuse 18, Navy 11
Maryland 12, Adelphi 11 (OT)
North Carolina 12, Loyola (Md) 5
Johns Hopkins 9, Massachusetts 4

Semifinals

Syracuse 18, Maryland 8
Johns Hopkins 10, North Carolina 6

Championship

(At the University of Maryland, College Park, Md., May 29, 1989)

Syracuse 13, Johns Hopkins 12

Women's Championships
Semifinals

Penn State 9, Temple 3
Harvard 7, Princeton 5

Championship

(at West Chester University, West Chester, Pa., May 21, 1989)

Penn State 7, Harvard 6

History of the One-Mile Speed Mark

The first recorded effort for one mile was made in 1898 by Chasseloup-Laubat, driving a Jentaud, in France. His average speed was 39.23 m.p.h. This was increased to 65.79 in 1899 by Jenatzy, also in France. The first man to travel better than 100 m. p.h. was Bigolly, in 1904, at 103.56 m.p.h., followed by Baras, with 104.53 in the same year.

The first over 200 m.p.h. was Major H.O.D. Segrave, who drove at 203.790 in 1927 at Daytona, Florida.

In 1947, John Cobb of London became the first person to travel more than 400 m.p.h. on land. The Englishman accomplished the feat on Sept. 16 at Bonneville, Utah, while raising the world mile record to 394.196 m.p.h. and the world kilometer (. 62137 of a mile) mark to 398.825 m.p.h.

QUARTER HORSE RACING—1988

All-American Futurity—Merganser
Champion of Champions—Shawnes Favorite

SOFTBALL

Source: Amateur Softball Association.

AMATEUR CHAMPIONS

1959	Aurora (Ill.) Sealmasters	1972	Raybestos Cardinals, Stratford, Conn.
1960	Clearwater (Fla.) Bombers		
1961	Aurora (Ill.) Sealmasters	1973	Clearwater (Fla.) Bombers
1962–63	Clearwater (Fla.) Bombers	1974	Santa Rosa (Calif.)
1964	Burch Gage & Tool, Detroit	1975	Rising Sun Hotel, Reading, Pa.
1965	Aurora (Ill.) Sealmasters	1976	Raybestos Cardinals, Stratford, Conn.
1966	Clearwater (Fla.) Bombers		
1967	Aurora (Ill.) Sealmasters	1977	Billard Barbell, Reading, Pa.
1968	Clearwater (Fla.) Bombers	1978	Reading, Pa.
1969	Raybestos Cardinals, Stratford, Conn.	1979	Midland, Mich.
		1980	Peterbilt Western, Seattle
1971	Welty Way, Cedar Rapids, Iowa	1981	Archer Daniels Midland, Decatur, Ill.

1982	Peterbilt Western, Seattle
1983	Franklin Cardinals, West Haven, Conn.
1984	California Coors Kings, Merced, Calif.
1985	Pay 'n Pak, Bellevue, Washington
1986	Pay 'n Pak, Bellevue, Washington
1987	Pay 'n Pak, Bellevue, Washington
1988	Trans-Aire, Elkhart, Ind.
1989	Penn Corp., Sioux City, Iowa

1989 National Tournament Champions

Men's major fast pitch—Penn Corp., Sioux City, IA
Women's major fast pitch—Southern California Whittier Raiders, Whittier, CA
Men's Class A fast pitch—Texas Flyers, Houston, TX
Women's Class A fast pitch—John DeWyse & Sons, Essexville, MI
Men's Class B fast pitch—Barber Pontiac, Bakersfield, CA
Women's Class B fast pitch—Burbank Hilton Sureshots, Burbank, CA
Men's Class C fast pitch—Serpa's Arco, Stockton, CA
Women's Class C fast pitch—Red Machine, Nashville, TN
Men's major modified pitch—Don Swann Sales, Atlanta, GA
Women's major modified pitch—Kulick's Keene, NH
Men's Class A modified pitch—All-Star Chevrolet, Wilmington, DE
Men's masters (40-over) fast pitch—Bank of Melrose, Melrose, WI
Men's super slow pitch—Ritch's Salvage, Harrisburg, NC
Men's major slow pitch—Ritch's Salvage, Harrisburg, NC
Women's major slow pitch—Canaan's Illusions, Houston, TX
Men's Class A slow pitch—Vernon's, Jacksonville, FL
Women's Class A slow pitch—Bally, Orlando, FL
Men's Class B slow pitch—Kenova Construction, West Palm Beach, FL
Women's Class B slow pitch—Nothing But The Truth, Virginia Beach, VA
Men's Class C slow pitch—CSX A's, Glen Burnie, MD
Women's Class C slow pitch—Outlaws, Tucson, AZ
Men's major industrial slow pitch—Delta Allstars, Atlanta, GA
Women's major industrial slow pitch—Provident Vets, Chattanooga, TN
Men's Class A industrial slow pitch—Textron-Lycoming, Stratford, CT
Women's Class A industrial slow pitch—Certain Teed Lady A's, Wichita Falls, TX
Men's major church slow pitch—Choto, Knoxville, TN
Women's major church slow pitch—First Baptist of Houston, Houston, TX
Men's Class A church slow pitch—First Baptist Hendersonville, Hendersonville, TN
Women's Class A church slow pitch—First Baptist Church, Muskogee, OK
Men's major 16-inch slow pitch—Whips, Chicago, IL
Men's Class A 16-inch slow pitch—Aces, Chicago, IL
Men's masters (35-over) slow pitch—Nothdurft Tool & Die, Mount Clemens, MI
Men's masters (45-over) slow pitch—Capitol Oil, Columbus, IN
Men's masters (55-over) slow pitch—The Masters 12, Harrison, OH
Coed slow pitch—Braves, Jacksonville, FL
Boys' 19-under fast pitch—Rookies, Ruthton, MN
Girls' 19-under fast pitch—Gordon's Panthers, LaPalma, CA
Boys' 16-under fast pitch—Northwest Honda, Pattonsburg, MO
Girls' 16-under fast pitch—Case XX Batbusters, Fountain Valley, CA
Boys' 14-under fast pitch—Rice Lake/Cameron Lancers, Rice Lake/Cameron, WI
Girls' 14-under fast pitch—Crackerjack, Santa Ana, CA
Boys' 19-under slow pitch—Orange Crush, Cleveland, TN
Girls' 19-under slow pitch—Lady Panthers, Atlanta, GA
Boys' 16-under slow pitch—Tifton Renegades, Tifton, GA
Girls' 16-under slow pitch—Lake Lytal Lazers, West Palm Beach, FL
Boys' 14-under slow pitch—Wranglers, Chula, GA
Girls' 14-under slow pitch—Thunder, Pembroke Pines, FL

HANDBALL

U.S.H.A. NATIONAL FOUR-WALL CHAMPIONS

Singles

1960	Jimmy Jacobs
1961	John Sloan
1962–63	Oscar Obert
1964–65	Jimmy Jacobs
1966–67	Paul Haber
1968	Simon (Stuffy) Singer
1969–71	Paul Haber
1972	Fred Lewis
1973	Terry Muck
1974	Fred Lewis
1975	Jay Bilyeu
1976	Vern Roberts, Jr.
1977	Naty Alvarado
1978	Fred Lewis
1979	Naty Alvarado
1980	Naty Alvarado

1981	Fred Lewis
1982	Naty Alvarado
1983	Naty Alvarado
1984	Naty Alvarado
1985	Naty Alvarado
1986	Naty Alvarado
1987	Naty Alvarado
1988	Naty Alvarado[1]
1989	Ponch Monreal

Doubles

1960	Jimmy Jacobs–Dick Weisman
1961	John Sloan–Vic Hershkowitz
1962–63	Jimmy Jacobs–Marty Decatur
1964	John Sloan–Phil Elbert
1965	Jimmy Jacobs–Marty Decatur
1966	Pete Tyson–Bob Lindsay
1967–68	Jimmy Jacobs–Marty Decatur
1969	Lou Kramberg–Lou Russo

1970	Karl and Ruby Obert
1971	Ray Neveau–Simie Fein
1972	Kent Fusselman–Al Drews
1973–74	Ray Neveau–Simie Fein
1975	Marty Decatur–Steve Lott
1976	Gary Rohrer–Dan O'Connor
1977	Skip McDowell–Matt Kelly
1978	Stuffy Singer–Marty Decatur
1979	Stuffy Singer–Marty Decatur
1980	Skip McDowell–Harry Robertson
1981	Tom Kopatich–Jack Roberts
1982	Naty Alvarado–Vern Roberts
1983	Naty Alvarado–Vern Roberts
1984	Naty Alvarado–Vern Roberts
1985	Naty Alvarado–Vern Roberts
1986–87	Jon Kemdler–Poncho Monreal
1988	Doug Glatt–Dennis Haynes
1989	Danny Bell–Charlie Kalil

1. 10th time—American record.

BASEBALL

The popular tradition that baseball was invented by Abner Doubleday at Cooperstown, N.Y., in 1839 has been enshrined in the Hall of Fame and National Museum of Baseball erected in that town, but research has proved that a game called "Base Ball" was played in this country and England before 1839. The first team baseball as we know it was played at the Elysian Fields, Hoboken, N.J., on June 19, 1846, between the Knickerbockers and the New York Nine. The next fifty years saw a gradual growth of baseball and an improvement of equipment and playing skill.

Historians have it that the first pitcher to throw a curve was William A. (Candy) Cummings in 1867. The Cincinnati Red Stockings were the first all-professional team, and in 1869 they played 64 games without a loss. The standard ball of the same size and weight, still the rule, was adopted in 1872. The first catcher's mask was worn in 1875. The National League was organized in 1876. The first chest protector was worn in 1885. The three-strike rule was put on the books in 1887, and the four-ball ticket to first base was instituted in 1889. The pitching distance was lengthened to 60 feet 6 inches in 1893, and the rules have been modified only slightly since that time.

The American League, under the vigorous leadership of B. B. Johnson, became a major league in 1901. Judge Kenesaw Mountain Landis, by action of the two major leagues, became Commissioner of Baseball in 1921, and upon his death (1944), Albert B. Chandler, former United States Senator from Kentucky, was elected to that office (1945). Chandler failed to obtain a new contract and was succeeded by Ford C. Frick (1951), the National League president. Frick retired after the 1965 season, and William D. Eckert, a retired Air Force lieutenant general, was named to succeed him. Eckert resigned under pressure in December, 1968. Bowie Kuhn, a New York attorney, became interim commissioner for one year in February. His appointment was made permanent with two seven-year contracts until August 1983. In August 1983, Kuhn's contract was not renewed, and a search begun for his successor. Peter Ueberroth was named new Commissioner and took office Oct. 1, 1984.

Ueberroth did not seek a new term in 1989 and was succeded by Bart Giamatti who died suddenly on Sept. 1, 1989. Francis T. Vincent, Jr., replaced him on Sept. 13, 1989.

MAJOR LEAGUE ALL-STAR GAME

Year	Date	Winning league and manager	Runs	Losing league and manager	Runs	Winning pitcher	Losing pitcher	Site	Paid attendance
1933	July 6	A.L. (Mack)	4	N.L. (McGraw)	2	Gomez	Hallahan	Chicago A.L.	47,595
1934	July 10	A.L. (Cronin)	9	N.L. (Terry)	7	Harder	Mungo	New York N.L.	48,363
1935	July 8	A.L. (Cochrane)	4	N.L. (Frisch)	1	Gomez	Walker	Cleveland A.L.	69,831
1936	July 7	N.L. (Grimm)	4	A.L. (McCarthy)	3	J. Dean	Grove	Boston N.L.	25,556
1937	July 7	A.L. (McCarthy)	8	N.L. (Terry)	3	Gomez	J. Dean	Washington A.L.	31,391
1938	July 6	N.L. (Terry)	4	A.L. (McCarthy)	1	Vander Meer	Gomez	Cincinnati N.L.	27,067
1939	July 11	A.L. (McCarthy)	3	N.L. (Hartnett)	1	Bridges	Lee	New York A.L.	62,892
1940	July 9	N.L. (McKechnie)	4	A.L. (Cronin)	0	Derringer	Ruffing	St. Louis N.L.	32,373
1941	July 8	A.L. (Baker)	7	N.L. (McKechnie)	5	E. Smith	Passeau	Detroit A.L.	54,674
1942	July 6	A.L. (McCarthy)	3	N.L. (Durocher)	1	Chandler	Cooper	New York N.L.	34,178
1943	July 13[1]	A.L. (McCarthy)	5	N.L. (Southworth)	3	Leonard	Cooper	Philadelphia A.L.	31,938
1944	July 11[1]	N.L. (Southworth)	7	A.L. (McCarthy)	1	Raffensberger	Hughson	Pittsburgh N.L.	29,589
1946	July 9	A.L. (O'Neill)	12	N.L. (Grimm)	0	Feller	Passeau	Boston A.L.	34,906
1947	July 8	A.L. (Cronin)	2	N.L. (Dyer)	1	Shea	Sain	Chicago N.L.	41,123
1948	July 13	A.L. (Harris)	5	N.L. (Durocher)	2	Raschi	Schmitz	St. Louis A.L.	34,009
1949	July 12	A.L. (Boudreau)	11	N.L. (Southworth)	7	Trucks	Newcombe	Brooklyn N.L.	32,577
1950	July 11	N.L. (Shotton)	4	A.L. (Stengel)	3[3]	Blackwell	Gray	Chicago A.L.	46,127
1951	July 10	N.L. (Sawyer)	8	A.L. (Stengel)	3	Maglie	Lopat	Detroit A.L.	52,075
1952	July 8	N.L. (Durocher)	3	A.L. (Stengel)	2[4]	Rush	Lemon	Philadelphia N.L.	32,785
1953	July 14	N.L. (Dressen)	5	A.L. (Stengel)	1	Spahn	Reynolds	Cincinnati N.L.	30,846
1954	July 13	A.L. (Stengel)	11	N.L. (Alston)	9	Stone	Conley	Cleveland A.L.	68,751
1955	July 12	N.L. (Durocher)	6	A.L. (Lopez)	5[3]	Conley	Sullivan	Milwaukee N.L.	45,643
1956	July 10	N.L. (Alston)	7	A.L. (Stengel)	3	Friend	Pierce	Washington A.L.	28,843
1957	July 9	A.L. (Stengel)	6	N.L. (Alston)	5	Bunning	Simmons	St. Louis A.L.	30,693
1958	July 8	A.L. (Stengel)	4	N.L. (Haney)	3	Wynn	Friend	Baltimore A.L.	48,829
1959[2]	July 7	N.L. (Haney)	5	A.L. (Stengel)	4	Antonelli	Ford	Pittsburgh N.L.	35,277
	Aug. 3	A.L. (Stengel)	5	N.L. (Haney)	3	Walker	Drysdale	Los Angeles N.L.	55,105
1960[2]	July 11	N.L. (Alston)	5	A.L. (Lopez)	3	Friend	Monbouquette	Kansas City A.L.	30,619
	July 13	N.L. (Alston)	6	A.L. (Lopez)	0	Law	Ford	New York A.L.	38,362
1961[2]	July 11	N.L. (Murtaugh)	5	A.L. (Richards)	4[6]	Miller	Wilhelm	San Francisco N.L.	44,115
	July 31	N.L (Murtaugh)	1	A.L. (Richards)	1[7]	—	—	Boston A.L.	31,851
1962[2]	July 10	N.L. (Hutchinson)	3	A.L. (Houk)	1	Marichal	Pascual	Washington A.L.	45,480
	July 30	A.L. (Houk)	9	N.L. (Hutchinson)	4	Herbert	Mahaffey	Chicago N.L.	38,359
1963	July 9	N.L. (Dark)	5	A.L. (Houk)	3	Jackson	Bunning	Cleveland A.L.	44,160
1964	July 7	N.L. (Alston)	7	A.L. (Lopez)	4	Marichal	Radatz	New York N.L.	50,850
1965	July 13	N.L. (March)	6	A.L. (Lopez)	5	Koufax	McDowell	Minnesota N.L.	46,706
1966	July 12	N.L. (Alston)	2	A.L. (Mele)	1[6]	Perry	Rickert	St. Louis N.L.	49,926
1967	July 11	N.L. (Alston)	2	A.L. (Bauer)	1[8]	Drysdale	Hunter	Anaheim A.L.	46,309
1968	July 9	N.L. (Schoendienst)	1	A.L. (Williams)	0	Drysdale	Tiant	Houston N.L.	48,321
1969	July 23	N.L. (Schoendienst)	9	A.L. (M. Smith)	3	Carlton	Stottlemyre	Washington A.L.	45,259
1970	July 14	N.L. (Hodges)	5	A.L. (Weaver)	4	Osteen	Wright	Cincinnati N.L.	51,838
1971	July 13	A.L. (Weaver)	6	N.L. (Anderson)	4	Blue	Ellis	Detroit A.L.	53,559

1972	July 25	N.L. (Murtaugh)	4	A.L. (Weaver)	3[6]	McGraw	McNally	Atlanta N.L.	53,107
1973	July 24[1]	N.L. (Anderson)	7	A.L. (Williams)	1	Wise	Blyleven	Kansas City A.L.	40,849
1974	July 23[1]	N.L. (Berra)	7	A.L. (Williams)	2	Brett	Tiant	Pittsburgh N.L.	50,706
1975	July 15[1]	N.L. (Alston)	6	A.L. (Dark)	3	Matlack	Hunter	Milwaukee A.L.	51,540
1976	July 13	N.L. (Anderson)	7	A.L. (D. Johnson)	1	R. Jones	Fidrych	Philadelphia N.L.	63,974
1977	July 19[1]	N.L. (Anderson)	7	A.L. (Martin)	5	Sutton	Palmer	New York A.L.	56,683
1978	July 11[1]	N.L. (Lasorda)	7	A.L. (Martin)	3	Sutter	Gossage	San Diego N.L.	51,549
1979	July 17[1]	N.L. (Lasorda)	7	A.L. (Lemon)	6	Sutter	Kern	Seattle A.L.	58,905
1980	July 8[1]	N.L. (Tanner)	4	A.L. (Weaver)	2	Reuss	John	Los Angeles N.L.	56,088
1981	Aug. 9[1]	N.L. (Green)	5	A.L. (Frey)	4	Blue	Fingers	Cleveland* A.L.	72,086
1982	July 13[1]	N.L. (Lasorda)	4	A.L. (Martin)	1	Rogers	Eckersley	Montreal N.L.	59,057
1983	July 6[1]	A.L. (Kuenn)	13	N.L. (Herzog)	3	Steib	Soto	Chicago A.L.	43,801
1984	July 11[1]	N.L. (Owens)	3	A.L. (Altobelli)	1	Leg	Steib	San Francisco, N.L.	57,756
1985	July 16[1]	N.L. (Williams)	6	A.L. (Anderson)	1	Hoyt	Morris	Minneapolis, A.L.	54,960
1986	July 15[1]	A.L. (Howser)	3	N.L. (Herzog)	2	Clemens	Gooden	Houston, N.L.	45,774
1987	July 14[1]	N.L. (Johnson)	2	A.L. (McNamara)	0	Smith	Howell	Oakland, A.L.	49,671
1988	July 12[1]	A.L. (Kelly)	2	N.L. (Herzog)	1	Viola	Gooden	Cincinnati, N.L	55,837
1989	July 11[1]	A.L. (LaRussa)	5	N.L. (Lasorda)	3	Ryan	Smoltz	California, A.L.	64,036

1. Night game. 2. Two games. 3. Fourteen innings. 4. Five innings, rain. 5. Twelve innings. 6. Ten innings. 7. Called because of rain after nine innings. 8. Fifteen innings. NOTE: No game in 1945. *Game was originally scheduled for July 14, but was put off because of players' strike.

NATIONAL BASEBALL HALL OF FAME

Cooperstown, N.Y.

Fielders

Member	Active years	Member	Active years	Member	Active years
Aaron, Henry (Hank)	1954–1976	Eyers, John	1902–1919	McGraw, John J.	1891–1906
Anson, Adrian (Cap)	1876–1897	Ewing, William	1880–1897	McCovey, Willie	1959–1980
Aparicio, Luis	1956–1973	Flick, Elmer	1898–1910	Medwick, Joseph	
Appling, Lucius (Luke)	1930–1950	Foxx, James	1925–1945	(Ducky)	1932–1948
Averill, H. Earl	1929–1941	Frisch, Frank	1919–1937	Mize, John (The Big Cat)	1936–1953
Baker, J. Frank		Gehrig, H. Louis (Lou)	1923–1939	Musial, Stanley	1941–1963
(Home Run)	1908–1922	Gehringer, Charles	1924–1942	O'Rourke, James	1876–1894
Bancroft, David	1915–1930	Gibson, Josh[1]	1929–1946	Ott, Melvin	1926–1947
Banks, Ernest	1953–1971	Goslin, Leon (Goose)	1921–1938	Reese, Harold (Pee Wee)	1940–1958
Beckley, Jacob	1888–1907	Greenberg, Henry		Rice, Edgar (Sam)	1915–1934
Bell, James		(Hank)	1933–1947	Robinson, Brooks	1955–1977
(Cool Papa)[1]	1920–1947	Hafey, Charles (Chick)	1924–1937	Robinson, Frank	1956–1976
Bench, John	1967–1983	Hamilton, William	1888–1901	Robinson, Jack	1947–1956
Berra, Lawrence (Yogi)	1946–1965	Hartnett, Charles		Robinson, Wilbert	1886–1902
Bottomley, James	1922–1937	(Gabby)	1922–1941	Roush, Edd	1913–1931
Boudreau, Louis	1938–1952	Heilmann, Harry	1914–1932	Ruth, George (Babe)	1914–1935
Bresnahan, Roger	1897–1915	Herman, William	1931–1947	Schalk, Raymond	1912–1929
Brock, Lou	1961–1980	Hooper, Harry	1909–1925	Schoendienst, Red	1945–1963
Brouthers, Dennis	1879–1896	Hornsby, Rogers	1915–1937	Sewell, Joseph	1920–1933
Burkett, Jesse	1890–1905	Irvin, Monford (Monte)[1]	1939–1956	Simmons, Al	1924–1944
Campanella, Roy	1948–1957	Jackson, Travis	1922–1936	Sisler, George	1915–1930
Carey, Max	1910–1929	Jennings, Hugh	1891–1918	Slaughter, Enos	1938–1959
Chance, Frank	1898–1914	Johnson, William (Judy)[1]	1921–1937	Snider, Edwin D. (Duke)	1947–1964
Charleston, Oscar[1]	1915–1954	Kaline, Albert W.	1953–1974	Speaker, Tristram	1907–1928
Clarke, Fred	1894–1915	Keeler, William		Stargell, Willie	1962–1982
Clemente, Roberto	1955–1972	(Wee Willie)	1892–1910	Terry, William	1923–1936
Cobb, Tyrus	1905–1928	Kell, George	1943–1957	Thompson, Samuel	1885–1906
Cochrane, Gordon		Kelley, Joseph	1891–1908	Tinker, Joseph	1902–1916
(Mickey)	1925–1937	Kelly, George	1915–1932	Traynor, Harold (Pie)	1920–1937
Collins, Edward	1906–1930	Kelly, Michael (King)	1878–1893	Vaughan, Arky	1932–1948
Collins, James	1895–1908	Killebrew, Harmon	1954–1975	Wagner, John (Honus)	1897–1917
Comiskey, Charles	1882–1894	Kiner, Ralph	1946–1955	Wallace, Roderick	
Combs, Earle	1924–1935	Klein, Charles H. (Chuck)	1928–1944	(Bobby)	1894–1918
Connor, Roger	1880–1897	Lajoie, Napoleon	1896–1916	Waner, Lloyd	1927–1945
Crawford, Samuel	1899–1917	Leonard, Walter (Buck)[1]	1933–1955	Waner, Paul	1926–1945
Cronin, Joseph	1926–1945	Lindstrom, Frederick	1924–1936	Ward, John (Monte)	1878–1894
Cuyler, Hazen (Kiki)	1921–1938	Lloyd, John Henry[1]	1905–1931	Wheat, Zachariah	1909–1927
Dandridge, Ray[1]	1933–1953	Lombardi, Ernie	1932–1947	Williams, Billy	1959–1976
Delahanty, Edward	1888–1903	Mantle, Mickey	1951–1968	Williams, Theodore	1939–1960
Dickey, William	1928–1946	Manush, Henry (Heinie)	1923–1939	Wilson, Lewis R. (Hack)	1923–1934
Dihigo, Martin[1]	1923–1945	Maranville, Walter (Rabbit)	1912–1935	Yastrzemski, Carl	1961–1983
DiMaggio, Joseph	1936–1951	Matthews, Edwin	1952–1968	Youngs, Ross (Pep)	1917–1926
Doerr, Bobby	1937–1951	Mays, Willie	1951–1973		
Duffy, Hugh	1888–1906	McCarthy, Thomas	1884–1896		

1. Negro League player selected by special committee.

Pitchers

Alexander, Grover	1911–1930
Bender, Charles (Chief)	1903–1925
Brown, Mordecai	
(3-Finger)	1903–1916
Chesbro, John	1899–1909
Clarkson, John	1882–1894
Coveleski, Stanley	1912–1928
Dean, Jerome (Dizzy)	1930–1947
Drysdale, Don	1956–1969
Faber, Urban (Red)	1914–1933
Feller, Robert	1936–1956
Ferrell, Rick	1929–1947
Ford, Edward (Whitey)	1950–1967
Foster, Andrew (Rube)	1897–1926
Galvin, James (Pud)	1876–1892
Gibson, Bob	1959–1975
Gomez, Vernon (Lefty)	1930–1943
Griffith, Clark	1891–1914
Grimes, Burleigh	1916–1934
Grove, Robert (Lefty)	1925–1941
Haines, Jesse	1918–1937
Hoyt, Waite	1918–1938
Hubbell, Carl	1928–1943
Hunter, Jim (Catfish)	1965–1979
Johnson, Walter	1907–1927
Joss, Adrian	1902–1910
Keefe, Timothy	1880–1893
Koufax, Sanford (Sandy)	1955–1966
Lemon, Robert	1946–1958
Lyons, Theodore	1923–1946
Marichal, Juan	1960–1975
Marquard, Richard	
(Rube)	1908–1924
Mathewson, Christopher	1900–1916
McGinnity, Joseph	1899–1908
Nichols, Charles (Kid)	1890–1906
Paige, Leroy (Satchel)[1]	1926–1965
Pennock, Herbert	1912–1934
Plank, Edward	1901–1917
Radbourn, Charles	
(Hoss)	1880–1891
Rixey, Eppa	1912–1933
Roberts, Robert (Robin)	1948–1966
Ruffing, Charles (Red)	1924–1947
Rusie, Amos	1889–1901
Spahn, Warren	1942–1965
Vance, Arthur (Dazzy)	1915–1935
Waddell, George	1897–1910
Walsh, Edward	1904–1917
Welch, Michael (Mickey)	1880–1892
Wilhelm, Hoyt	1952–1972
Wynn, Early	1939–1963
Young, Denton (Cy)	1890–1911

Officials and Others

Alston, Walter[2]	Evans, William G.[5][3]	Klem, William[5]	Spalding, Albert G.[5]
Barrow, Edward[2][3]	Frick, Ford C.[7][3]	Landis, Kenesaw M.[7]	Stengel, Charles D.[8]
Bulkeley, Morgan G.[3]	Giles, Warren C.[3]	Lopez, Alfonso R.[8]	Weiss, George M.[3]
Carey, Harry[9]	Gowdy, Curt[9]	Mack, Connie[2][3]	Wright, George[6]
Cartwright, Alexander[3]	Harridge, William[3]	MacPhail, Leland S.[3]	Wright, Harry[6][2]
Chadwick, Henry[4]	Harris, Stanley R.[8]	McCarthy, Joseph V.[2]	Yawkey, Thomas[3]
Chandler, A.B.[7]	Hubbard, R. Calvin[5]	McKechnie, William B.[2]	
Conlan, John[3]	Higgins, Miller J.[2]	Rickey, W. Branch[2][3]	
Connolly, Thomas[5]	Johnson, B. Bancroft[3]	Scully, Vin[9]	
Cummings, William A.[6]		Smith, Ken[10]	

1. Negro league player selected by special committee. 2. Manager. 3. Executive. 4. Writer-statistician. 5. Umpire. 6. Early player. 7. Commissioner. 8. Player-manager. 9. Broadcaster. 10. Sportswriter.

OTHER LIFETIME BATTING, PITCHING, AND BASE-RUNNING RECORDS

(An asterisk indicates active player)

Sources: Baseball Record Book, published and copyrighted by The Sporting News, St. Louis, Mo. 63166; *The Book of Baseball Records,* published and copyrighted by Seymour Siwoff, New York, N.Y. 10036; and *The Complete Handbook of Baseball,* published and copyrighted by New American Library, New York, N.Y. 10019. All records through 1989 unless noted.

HITS (3,000 or more)

Pete Rose	4,256
Ty Cobb	4,190
Henry Aaron	3,771
Stan Musial	3,630
Tris Speaker	3,515
Honus Wagner	3,430
Carl Yastrzemski	3,419
Eddie Collins	3,311
Willie Mays	3,283
Nap Lajoie	3,251
Paul Waner	3,152
Rod Carew	3,053
Lou Brock	3,023
Cap Anson	3,022
Al Kaline	3,007
Roberto Clemente	3,000

Earned Run Average[1]

Minimum 1,000 innings pitched (under 3.00)

Walter Johnson	2.37
Grover Alexander	2.56
Dwight Gooden*	2.62
Whitey Ford	2.74
Orel Hershiser*	2.77
Kent Tekulve*	2.77
Jim Palmer	2.83
Bruce Sutter	2.84

Tom Seaver	2.86
Stan Coveleski	2.88
Juan Marichal	2.89
Wilbur Cooper	2.89
Bob Gibson	2.91
Carl Mays	2.92
Goose Gossage*	2.92
Don Drysdale	2.95
Carl Hubbell	2.98
Gaylord Perry	2.99

1. Through 1988 season.
*Active through 1989.

Runs Scored

Ty Cobb	2,245
Henry Aaron	2,174
Babe Ruth	2,174
Pete Rose	2,165
Willie Mays	2,062
Stan Musial	1,949
Lou Gehrig	1,888
Tris Speaker	1,881
Mel Ott	1,859
Frank Robinson	1,829
Eddie Collins	1,816
Carl Yastrzemski	1,816
Ted Williams	1,798
Charlie Gehringer	1,774

Jimmie Foxx	1,751
Honus Wagner	1,740
Willie Keeler	1,720
Cap Anson	1,712
Jesse Burkett	1,708
Billy Hamilton	1,690
Mickey Mantle	1,677
John McPhee	1,674
George Van Haltren	1,650

Strikeouts, Pitching

Nolan Ryan**	5,076
Steve Carlton	4,136
Tom Seaver	3,640
Don Sutton	3,569
Bert Blyleven**	3,562
Gaylord Perry	3,534
Walter Johnson	3,509
Phil Niekro	3,342
Ferguson Jenkins	3,192
Bob Gibson	3,117
Jim Bunning	2,855
Mickey Lolich	2,832
Cy Young	2,819
Warren Spahn	2,583
Bob Feller	2,581
Tim Keefe	2,538
Christy Mathewson	2,505

**Active through 1989.

Home Runs (350 or More)

Henry Aaron	755
Babe Ruth	714
Willie Mays	660
Frank Robinson	586
Harmon Killebrew	573
Reggie Jackson	563
Mike Schmidt	548
Mickey Mantle	536
Jimmie Foxx	534
Ted Williams	521
Willie McCovey	521
Eddie Matthews	512
Ernie Banks	512
Mel Ott	511
Lou Gehrig	493
Stan Musial	475
Willie Stargell	475
Carl Yastrzemski	452
Dave Kingman	442
Billy Williams	426
Duke Snider	406
Al Kaline	399
Johnny Bench	389
Frank Howard	382
Orlando Cepeda	379
Norm Cash	377

Rocky Colavito	374	Ed Plank	64	Tony Perez	1,845	Ted Williams	2,019
Tony Perez	371	Warren Spahn	63	Bobby Bonds	1,757	Carl Yastrzemski	1,845
Gil Hodges	370	Tom Seaver	60	Lou Brock	1,730	Joe Morgan	1,799
Ralph Kiner	369	Ed Walsh	58	Mickey Mantle	1,710	Mickey Mantle	1,734
Joe DiMaggio	361	Don Sutton	58	Harmon Killebrew	1,699	Mel Ott	1,708
Lee May	360	James Galvin	57	Dick Allen	1,556	Eddie Yost	1,614
Johnny Mize	359	Bob Gibson	56	Lee May	1,552	Darrell Evans**	1,605
Yogi Berra	358	Steve Carlton	55	Willie McCovey	1,550	Stan Musial	1,599
Dick Allen	351	Bert Blyleven	55	Frank Robinson	1,532	Harmon Killebrew	1,559

*Active through 1989.

Jim Palmer	53	Willie Mays	1,526	Mike Schmidt	1,515
Gaylord Perry	53	Eddie Matthews	1,487	Lou Gehrig	1,508

Shutouts

Juan Marichal	52	Frank Howard	1,460	Willie Mays	1,464

Strikeouts, Batting

				Jim Wynn	1,427	Jimmie Foxx	1,452
Walter Johnson	110					Eddie Matthews	1,444
Grover Alexander	90	Reggie Jackson	2,459	**Bases on Balls**		Frank Robinson	1,420
Christy Mathewson	83	Willie Stargell	1,912			Henry Aaron	1,402
Cy Young	77	Mike Schmidt	1,910	Babe Ruth	2,056		

RECORD OF WORLD SERIES GAMES

(Through 1988)

Source: The Book of Baseball Records, published by Seymour Siwoff, New York City.

Figures in parentheses for winning pitchers (WP) and losing pitchers (LP) indicate the game number in the series.

1903—Boston A.L. 5 (Jimmy Collins); Pittsburgh N.L. 3 (Fred Clarke). WP—Bos.: Dinneen (2, 6, 8), Young (5, 7); Pitts.: Phillippe (1, 3, 4). LP—Bos.: Young (1), Hughes (3), Dinneen (4); Pitts.: Leever (2, 6), Kennedy (5), Phillippe (7, 8).

1904—No series.

1905—New York N.L. 4 (John J. McGraw); Philadelphia A.L. 1 (Connie Mack). WP—N.Y.: Mathewson (1, 3, 5); McGinnity (4); Phila.: Bender (2). LP—N.Y.: McGinnity (2); Phila.: Plank (1, 4), Coakley (3), Bender (5).

1906—Chicago A.L. 4 (Fielder Jones); Chicago N.L. 2 (Frank Chance). WP—Chi.: A.L.: Altrock (1), Walsh (3, 5), White (6); Chi.: N.L.: Reulbach (2), Brown (4). LP—Chi. A.L.: White (2), Altrock (4); Chi. N.L.: Brown (1, 6), Pfeister (3, 5).

1907—Chicago N.L. 4 (Frank Chance); Detroit A.L. 0 (Hugh Jennings). First game tied 3–3, 12 innings. WP—Pfeister (2), Reulbach (3), Overall (4), Brown (5). LP—Mullin (2, 5), Siever (3), Donovan (4).

1908—Chicago N.L. 4 (Frank Chance); Detroit A.L. 1 (Hugh Jennings). WP—Chi.: Brown (1, 4), Overall (2, 5); Det.: Mullin (3). LP—Chi.: Pfeister (3); Det.: Summers (1, 4), Donovan (2, 5).

1909—Pittsburgh N.L. 4 (Fred Clarke); Detroit A.L. 3 (Hugh Jennings). WP—Pitts.: Adams (1, 5, 7), Maddox (3); Det.: Donovan (2), Mullin (4, 6). LP—Pitts.: Camnitz (2), Leifield (4), Willis (6); Det.: Mullin (1), Summers (3, 5), Donovan (7).

1910—Philadelphia A.L. 4 (Connie Mack); Chicago N.L. 1 (Frank Chance). WP—Phila.: Bender (1), Coombs (2, 3, 5); Chi.: Brown (4). LP—Phila.: Bender (4); Chi.: Overall (1), Brown (2, 5), McIntyre (3).

1911—Philadelphia A.L. 4 (Connie Mack); New York N.L. 2 (John J. McGraw). WP—Phila.: Plank (2), Coombs (3), Bender (4, 6); N.Y.: Mathewson (1), Crandall (5). LP—Phila.: Bender (1), Plank (5); N.Y.: Marquard (2), Mathewson (3, 4), Ames (6).

1912—Boston A.L. 4 (J. Garland Stahl); New York N.L. 3 (John J. McGraw). Second game tied, 6–6, 11 innings. WP—Bos.: Wood (1, 4, 8), Bedient (5); N.Y.: Marquard (3, 6), Tesreau (7). LP—Bos.: O'Brien (3, 6), Wood (7); N.Y.: Tesreau (1, 4), Mathewson (5, 8).

1913—Philadelphia A.L. 4 (Connie Mack); New York N.L. 1 (John J. McGraw). WP—Phila.: Bender (1, 4), Bush (3), Plank (5); N.Y.: Mathewson (2). LP—Phila.: Plank (2); N.Y.: Marquard (1), Tesreau (3), Demaree (4), Mathewson (5).

1914—Boston N.L. 4 (George Stallings); Philadelphia A.L. 0 (Connie Mack). WP—Rudolph (1, 4), James (2, 3). LP—Bender (1), Plank (2), Bush (3), Shawkey (4).

1915—Boston A.L. 4 (Bill Carrigan); Philadelphia N.L. 1 (Pat Moran). WP—Bos.: Foster (2, 5), Leonard (3), Shore (4); Phila.: Alexander (1). LP—Bos.: Shore (1); Phila.: Mayer (2), Alexander (3), Chalmers (4), Rixey (5).

1916—Boston A.L. 4 (Bill Carrigan); Brooklyn N.L. 1 (Wilbert Robinson). WP—Bos.: Shore (1, 5), Ruth (2), Leonard (4); Bklyn.: Coombs (3). LP—Bos.: Mays (3); Bklyn.: Marquard (1, 4), Smith (2), Pfeffer (5).

1917—Chicago A.L. 4 (Clarence Rowland); New York N.L. 2 (John McGraw). WP—Chi.: Cicotte (1), Faber (2, 5, 6); N.Y.: Benton (3), Schupp (4). LP—Chi.: Cicotte (3), Faber (4); N.Y.: Sallee (1, 5), Anderson (2), Benton (6).

1918—Boston A.L. 4 (Ed Barrow); Chicago N.L. 2 (Fred Mitchell). WP—Bos.: Ruth (1, 4), Mays (3, 6); Chi.: Tyler (2), Vaughn (5). LP—Bos.: Bush (2), Jones (5); Chi.: Vaughn (1, 3), Douglas (4), Tyler (6).

1919—Cincinnati N.L. 5 (Pat Moran); Chicago A.L. 3 (William Gleason). WP—Cin.: Ruether (1), Sallee (2), Ring (4), Eller (5, 8); Chi.: Kerr (3, 6), Cicotte (7). LP—Cin.: Fisher (3), Ring (6), Sallee (7); Chi.: Cicotte (1, 4), Williams (2, 5, 8).

1920—Cleveland A.L. 5 (Tris Speaker); Brooklyn N.L. 2 (Wilbert Robinson). WP—Cleve.: Coveleski (1, 4, 7), Bagby (5), Mails (6); Bklyn.: Grimes (2), Smith (3). LP—Cleve.: Bagby (2), Caldwell (3). Bklyn.: Marquard (1), Cadore (4), Grimes (5, 7), Smith (6).

1921—New York N.L. 5 (John J. McGraw); New York A.L. 3 (Miller Huggins). WP—N.Y. N.L.: Barnes (3, 6), Douglas (4, 7), Nehf (8); N.Y. A.L.: Mays (1), Hoyt (2, 5). LP—N.Y. N.L.: Nehf (2, 5), Douglas (1). N.Y. A.L.: Quinn (3), Mays (4, 7), Shawkey (6), Hoyt (8).

1922—New York N.L. 4 (John J. McGraw); New York A.L. 0 (Miller Huggins). Second game tied 3–3, 10 innings. WP—Ryan (1), Scott (3), McQuillan (4), Nehf (5). LP—Bush (1, 5), Hoyt (3), Mays (4).

1923—New York A.L. 4 (Miller Huggins); New York N.L. 2 (John J. McGraw). WP—N.Y. A.L.: Pennock (2, 6), Shawkey (4), Bush (5); N.Y. N.L.: Ryan (1), Nehf (3). LP—N.Y. A.L.: Bush (1), Jones (3); N.Y. N.L.: McQuillan (2), Scott (4), Bentley (5), Nehf (6).

1924—Washington A.L. 4 (Bucky Harris); New York N.L. 3 (John J. McGraw). WP—Wash.: Zachary (2, 6), Mogridge (4), Johnson (7); N.Y.: Nehf (1), McQuillan (3), Bentley (5). LP—Wash.: Johnson (1, 5), Marberry (3); N.Y.: Bentley (2, 7), Barnes (4), Nehf (6).

1925—Pittsburgh N.L. 4 (Bill McKechnie); Washington A.L. 3 (Bucky Harris). WP—Pitts.: Aldridge (2, 4), Kremer (6, 7); Wash.: Johnson (1, 4), Ferguson (3). LP—Pitts.: Meadows (1), Kremer (3), Yde (4); Wash.: Coveleski (2, 5), Ferguson (6), Johnson (7).

1926—St. Louis N.L. 4 (Rogers Hornsby); New York A.L. 3 (Miller Huggins). WP—St. L.: Alexander (2, 6), Haines (3, 7); N.Y.: Pennock (1, 5), Hoyt (4). LP—St. L.: Sherdel (1, 5), Reinhart (4); N.Y.: Shocker (2), Ruether (3), Shawkey (6), Hoyt (7).

1927—New York A.L. 4 (Miller Huggins); Pittsburgh N.L. 0 (Donie Bush). WP—Hoyt (1), Pipgras (2), Pennock (3), Moore (4). LP—Kremer (1), Aldridge (2), Meadows (3), Miljus (4).

1928—New York A.L. 4 (Miller Huggins); St. Louis N.L. 0 (Bill McKechnie). WP—Hoyt (1, 4), Pipgras (2), Zachary (3). LP—Sherdel (1, 4), Alexander (2), Haines (3).

1929—Philadelphia A.L. 4 (Connie Mack); Chicago N.L. 1 (Joe McCarthy). WP—Phila.: Ehmke (1), Earnshaw (2), Rommel (4), Walberg (5); Chi.: Bush (3). LP—Phila.: Earnshaw (3) Chi.: Root (1), Malone (2, 5), Blake (4).

1930—Philadelphia A.L. 4 (Connie Mack); St. Louis N.L. 2 (Gabby Street). WP—Phila.: Grove (1, 5), Earnshaw (2, 6); St. L.: Hallahan (3), Haines (4). LP—Phila.: Walberg (3), Grove (4); St. L.: Grimes (1, 5), Rhem (2), Hallahan (6).

1931—St. Louis N.L. 4 (Gabby Street); Philadelphia A.L. 3 (Connie Mack). WP—St. L.: Hallahan (2, 5), Grimes (3, 7); Phila.: Grove (1, 6), Earnshaw (4). St. L.: Derringer (1, 6), Johnson (4); Phila.: Earnshaw (2, 7), Grove (3), Hoyt (5).

1932—New York A.L. 4 (Joe McCarthy); Chicago N.L. 0 (Charles Grimm). WP—Ruffing (1), Gomez (2), Pipgras (3), Moore (4). LP—Bush (1), Warneke (2), Root (3), May (4).

1933—New York N.L. 4 (Bill Terry); Washington A.L. 1 (Joe Cronin.). WP—N.Y.: Hubbell (1, 4), Schumacher (2), Luque (5); Wash.: Whitehill (3). LP—N.Y.: Fitzsimmons (3); Wash.: Stewart (1), Crowder (2), Weaver (4), Russell (5).

1934—St. Louis N.L. 4 (Frank Frisch); Detroit A.L. 3 (Mickey Cochrane). WP—St. L.: J. Dean (1, 7), P. Dean (3, 6); Det.: Rowe (2), Auker (4), Bridges (5). LP—St. L.: W. Walker (2, 4), J. Dean (5); Det.: Crowder (1), Bridges (3), Rowe (6), Auker (7).

1935—Detroit A.L. 4 (Mickey Cochrane); Chicago N.L. 2 (Charles Grimm). WP—Det.: Bridges (2, 6), Rowe (3), Crowder (4); Chi.: Warneke (1, 5); LP—Det.: Rowe (1, 5), Chi.: Root (2), French (3, 6), Carleton (4).

1936—New York A.L. 4 (Joe McCarthy); New York N.L. 2 (Bill Terry). WP—N.Y. A.L.: Gomez (2, 6), Hadley (4), Pearson (4); N.Y. N.L.: Hubbell (1), Schumacher (5); LP—N.Y. A.L.: Ruffing (1), Malone (5); N.Y. N.L.: Schumacher (2), Fitzsimmons (3, 6), Hubbell (4).

1937—New York A.L. 4 (Joe McCarthy); New York N.L. 1 (Bill Terry). WP—N.Y. A.L.: Gomez (1, 5), Ruffing (2), Pearson (3); N.Y. N.L.: Hubbell (4). LP—N.Y. A.L.: Hadley (4); N.Y. N.L.: Hubbell (1), Melton (2, 5), Schumacher (3).

1938—New York A.L. 4 (Joe McCarthy); Chicago N.L. 0 (Gabby Hartnett). WP—Ruffing (1, 4), Gomez (2), Pearson (3) LP—Lee (1, 4), Dean (2), Bryant (3).

1939—New York A.L. 4 (Joe McCarthy); Cincinnati N.L. 0 (Bill McKechnie). WP—Ruffing (1), Pearson (2), Hadley (3), Murphy (4). LP—Derringer (1), Walters (2, 4), Thompson (3).

1940—Cincinnati N.L. 4 (Bill McKechnie); Detroit A.L. 3 (Del Baker). WP—Cin.: Walters (2, 6), Derringer (4, 7); Det.: Newsom (1, 5), Bridges (3) LP—Cin.: Derringer (1), Turner (3), Thompson (5); Det.: Rowe (2, 6), Trout (4), Newsom (7).

1941—New York A.L. 4 (Joe McCarthy); Brooklyn N.L. 1 (Leo Durocher). WP—N.Y.: Ruffing (1), Russo (3), Murphy (4), Bonham (5); Bklyn: Wyatt (2). LP—N.Y.: Chandler (1); Bklyn: Davis (1), Casey (3, 4), Wyatt (5).

1942—St. Louis N.L. 4 (Billy Southworth); New York A.L. 1 (Joe McCarthy). WP—St. L.: Beazley (2, 5), White (3), Lanier (4); N.Y.: Ruffing (1). LP—St. L.: Cooper (1); N.Y.: Bonham (2), Chandler (3), Donald (4), Ruffing (5).

1943—New York A.L. 4 (Joe McCarthy); St. Louis N.L. 1 (Billy Southworth). WP—N.Y.: Chandler (1, 5), Borowy (3), Russo (4); St. L.: Cooper (2). LP—N.Y.: Bonham (2); St. L.: Lanier (1), Brazle (3), Brecheen (4), Cooper (5).

1944—St. Louis N.L. 4 (Billy Southworth); St. Louis A.L. 2 (Luke Sewell). WP—St. L. N.L.: Donnelly (2), Brecheen (4), Cooper (5), Lanier (6); St. L. A.L.: Galehouse (1), Kramer (3). LP—St. L. N.L.: Cooper (1), Wilks (3); St. L. A.L.: Muncrief (2), Jakucki (4), Galehouse (6), Potter (6).

1945—Detroit A.L. 4 (Steve O'Neill); Chicago N.L. 3 (Charles Grimm). WP—Det.: Trucks (2), Trout (4), Newhouser (5, 7); Chi.: Borowy (1, 6), Passeau (3). LP—Det.: Newhouser (1), Overmire (3), Trout (6); Chi.: Wyse (2), Prim (4), Borowy (5, 7).

1946—St. Louis N.L. 4 (Eddie Dyer); Boston A.L. 3 (Joe Cronin). WP—St. L.: Brecheen (2, 6, 7), Munger (4); Bos.: Johnson (1), Ferriss (3), Dobson (5). LP—St. L.: Pollet (1), Dickson (3), Brazle (5); Bos.: Harris (2, 6), Hughson (4), Klinger (7).

1947—New York A.L. 4 (Bucky Harris); Brooklyn N.L. 3 (Burt Shotton). WP—N.Y.: Shea (1, 5), Reynolds (2), Page (7); Bklyn.: Casey (3, 4), Branca (6). LP—N.Y.: Newsom (3), Bevens (4), Page (6); Bklyn.: Branca (1), Lombardi (2), Barney (5), Gregg (7).

1948—Cleveland A.L. 4 (Lou Boudreau); Boston N.L. 2 (Billy Southworth). WP—Cleve.: Lemon (2, 6), Bearden (3), Gromek (4); Bos.: Sain (1), Spahn (5). LP—Cleve.: Feller (1, 5); Bos.: Spahn (2), Bickford (3), Sain (4), Voiselle (6).

1949—New York A.L. 4 (Casey Stengel); Brooklyn N.L. 1 (Burt Shotton). WP—N.Y.: Reynolds (1), Page (3), Lopat (4), Raschi (5); Bklyn.: Roe (2). LP—N.Y.: Raschi (2); Bklyn.: Newcombe (1, 4), Branca (3), Barney (5).

1950—New York A.L. 4 (Casey Stengel); Philadelphia N.L. 0 (Eddie Sawyer). WP—Raschi (1), Reynolds (2), Ferrick (3), Ford (4). LP—Konstanty (1), Roberts (2), Meyer (3), Miller (4).

1951—New York A.L. 4 (Casey Stengel); New York N.L. 2 (Leo Durocher). WP—N.Y. A.L.: Lopat (2, 5), Reynolds (4), Raschi (6); N.Y. N.L.: Koslo (1), Hearn (3). LP—N.Y. A.L.: Reynolds (1), Raschi (3); N.Y. N.L.: Jansen (2, 5), Maglie (4), Koslo (6).

1952—New York A.L. 4 (Casey Stengel); Brooklyn N.L. 3 (Chuck Dressen). WP—N.Y.: Raschi (2, 6), Reynolds (4, 7); Bklyn.: Black (1), Roe (3), Erskine (5). LP—N.Y.: Reynolds (1), Lopat (3), Sain (5); Bklyn.: Erskine (2), Black (4, 7), Loes (6).

1953—New York A.L. 4 (Casey Stengel); Brooklyn N.L. 2 (Chuck Dressen). WP—N.Y.: Sain (1), Lopat (2), McDonald (5), Reynolds (6); Bklyn.: Erskine (3), Loes (4). LP—N.Y.: Raschi (3), Ford (4); Bklyn.: Labine (1, 6), Roe (2), Podres (5).

1954—New York N.L. 4 (Leo Durocher); Cleveland A.L. 0 (Al Lopez). WP—Grissom (1), Antonelli (2), Gomez (3), Liddle (4). LP—Lemon (1, 4), Wynn (2), Garcia (3).

1955—Brooklyn N.L. 4 (Walter Alston); New York A.L. 3 (Casey Stengel). WP—Bklyn.: Podres (3, 7), Labine (4), Craig (5); N.Y.: Ford (1, 6), Byrne (2). LP—Bklyn.: Newcombe (1), Loes (2), Spooner (6); N.Y.: Turley (3), Larsen (4), Grim (5), Byrne (7).

1956—New York A.L. 4 (Casey Stengel); Brooklyn N.L. 3 (Walter Alston). WP—N.Y.: Ford (3), Sturdivant (4), Larsen (5), Kucks (7); Bklyn.: Maglie (1), Bessent (2), Labine (6). LP—N.Y.: Ford (1), Morgan (2), Turley (6); Bklyn.: Craig (3), Erskine (4), Maglie (5), Newcombe (7).

1957—Milwaukee N.L. 4 (Fred Haney); New York A.L. 3 (Casey Stengel). WP—Mil.: Burdette (2, 5, 7), Spahn (4); N.Y.: Ford (1), Larsen (3), Turley (6). LP—Mil.: Spahn (1), Buhl (3), Johnson (6); N.Y.: Shantz (2), Grim (4), Ford (5), Larsen (7).

1958—New York A.L. 4 (Casey Stengel); Milwaukee N.L. 3 (Fred Haney). WP—N.Y.: Larsen (3), Turley (5, 7), Duren (6); Mil.: Spahn (1, 4), Burdette (2). LP—N.Y.: Duren (1), Turley (2), Ford (4); Mil.: Rush (3), Burdette (5, 7), Spahn (6).

1959—Los Angeles N.L. 4 (Walter Alston); Chicago A.L. 2 (Al Lopez). WP—L.A.: Podres (2), Drysdale (3), Sherry (4, 6); Chi.: Wynn (1), Shaw (5). LP—L.A.: Craig (1), Koufax (5); Chi.: Shaw (2), Donovan (3), Staley (4), Wynn (6).

1960—Pittsburgh N.L. 4 (Danny Murtaugh); New York A.L. 3 (Casey Stengel). WP—Pitts.: Law (1, 4), Haddix (5, 7); N.Y.: Turley (2), Ford (3, 6). LP—Pitts.: Friend (2, 6), Mizell (3); N.Y.: Ditmar (1, 5), Terry (4, 7).

1961—New York A.L. 4 (Ralph Houk); Cincinnati N.L. 1 (Fred Hutchinson). WP—N.Y.: Ford (1, 4), Arroyo (3), Daley (5); Cin.: Jay (2). LP—N.Y.: Terry (2); Cin.: O'Toole (1, 4), Purkey (3), Jay (5).

1962—New York A.L. 4 (Ralph Houk); San Francisco N.L. 3 (Al Dark). WP—N.Y.: Ford (1), Stafford (3), Terry (5, 7); S.F. Sanford (2), Larsen (4), Pierce (6). LP—N.Y.: Terry (2), Coates (4), Ford (6); S.F.: O'Dell (1), Pierce (3), Sanford (5, 7).

1963—Los Angeles N.L. 4 (Walter Alston); New York A.L. 0 (Ralph Houk). WP—Koufax (1, 4), Podres (2), Drysdale (3). LP—Ford (1, 4), Downing (2), Bouton (3).

1964—St. Louis N.L. 4 (Johnny Keane); New York A.L. 3 (Yogi Berra). WP—St. L.: Sadecki (1), Craig (4), Gibson (5, 7); N.Y.: Stottlemyre (2), Bouton (3, 6). LP—St. L.: Gibson (2), Schultz (3), Simmons (6); N.Y.: Ford (1), Downing (4), Mikkelsen (5), Stottlemyre (7).

1965—Los Angeles N.L. 4 (Walter Alston); Minnesota A.L. 3 (Sam Mele). WP—L.A.: Osteen (3), Drysdale (4), Koufax (5, 7); Minn.: Grant (1, 6), Kaat (2). LP—L.A.: Drysdale (1), Koufax (2), Osteen (6); Minn.: Pascual (3), Grant (4), Kaat (5, 7).

1966—Baltimore A.L. 4 (Hank Bauer); Los Angeles N.L. 0 (Walter Alston). WP—Drabowsky (1), Palmer (2), Bunker (3), McNally (4). LP—Drysdale (1, 4), Koufax (2), Osteen (3).

1967—St. Louis N.L. 4 (Red Schoendienst); Boston A.L. 3 (Dick Williams). WP—St. L.: Gibson (1, 4, 7), Briles (3); Bos.: Lonborg (2, 5); Wyatt (6). LP—St. L.: Hughes (2), Carlton (5), Lamabe (6); Bos.: Santiago (1, 4), Bell (3), Lonborg (7).

1968—Detroit A.L. 4 (Mayo Smith); St. Louis N.L. 3 (Red Schoendienst). WP—Det.: Lolich (2, 5, 7), McLain (6); St. L.: Gibson (1, 4), Washburn (3), LP—Det.: McLain (1, 4), Wilson (3); St. L.: Briles (2), Hoerner (5), Washburn (6), Gibson (7).

1969—New York N.L. 4 (Gil Hodges); Baltimore A.L. 1 (Earl Weaver). WP—N.Y.: Koosman (2, 5), Gentry (3), Seaver (4); Balt.: Cuellar (1). LP—N.Y.: Seaver (1); Balt.: McNally (2), Palmer (3), Hall (4), Watt (5).

1970—Baltimore A.L. 4 (Earl Weaver); Cincinnati N.L. 1 (Sparky Anderson) 1. WP—Balt.: Palmer (1), Phoebus (2), McNally (3), Cuellar (5); Cin.: Carroll (4). LP—Cin.: Nolan (1), Wilcox (2), Cloninger (3), Merritt (5); Balt.: Watt (4).

1971—Pittsburgh N.L. 4 (Danny Murtaugh); Baltimore A.L. 3 (Earl Weaver). WP—Pitts.: Blass (3, 7), Kison (4), Briles (5); Balt.: McNally (1, 6), Palmer (2). LP—Pitts.: Ellis (1), R. Johnson (2), Miller (6); Balt.: Cuellar (3, 7), Watt (4) McNally (5).

1972—Oakland A.L. 4 (Dick Williams); Cincinnati N.L. (Sparky Anderson) 3. WP—Oakland: Holtzman (1), Hunter (2, 7), Fingers (4); Cincinnati: Billingham (3), Grimsley (5, 6). LP—Oakland: Odom (3), Fingers (5), Blue (6); Cincinnati: Nolan (1), Grimsley (2), Carroll (4), Borbon (7).

1973—Oakland A.L. 4 (Dick Williams): New York N.L. 3 (Yogi Berra). WP—Oakland: Holtzman (1, 7), Lindblad (3), Hunter (6). New York: McGraw (2), Matlack (4), Koosman (3). LP—Oakland: Fingers (2), Holtzman (4), Blue (5). New York: Matlack (1, 7) Parker (3), Seaver (6).

1974—Oakland A.L. 4 (Al Dark); Los Angeles·N.L. 1 (Walter Alston). WP—Oakland: Fingers (1), Hunter (3), Holtzman (4), Odom (5), Los Angeles: Sutton (2). LP—Oakland: Blue (2), Los Angeles: Messersmith (1, 4), Downing (3), Marshall (5).

1975—Cincinnati N.L. 4 (Sparky Anderson); Boston A.L. 3 (Darrell Johnson). WP—Cincinnati: Eastwick (2–3), Gullett (5), Carroll (7); Boston: Tiant (1–4), Wise (6). LP—Cincinnati: Gullett (1), Norman (4), Darcy (6); Boston: Drago (2), Willoughby (3), Cleveland (5), Burton (7).

1976—Cincinnati N.L. 4 (Sparky Anderson); New York A.L. 0 (Billy Martin). WP—Gullett (1), Billingham (2), Zachry (3), Nolan (4). LP—Alexander (1), Hunter (2), Ellis (3), Figueroa (4).

1977—New York A.L. 4 (Billy Martin); Los Angeles N.L. 2 (Tom Lasorda). WP—New York: Lyle (1), Torrez (3, 6), Guidry (4); Los Angeles: Hooton (2), Sutton (5). LP—New York: Hunter (2), Gullett (5); Los Angeles: Rhoden (1), John (3), Rau (4), Hooton (6).

1978—New York A.L. 4 (Bob Lemon), Los Angeles N.L. 2 (Tom Lasorda). WP—New York: Guidry (3), Gossage (4); Beattie (5),

Hunter (6); Los Angeles: John (1), Hooton (2). LP—New York: Figuero (1), Hunter (2); Los Angeles: Sutton (3–6), Welch (4), Hooton (5).

1979—Pittsburgh N.L. 4 (Chuck Tanner), Baltimore A.L. 3 (Earl Weaver); WP—Pittsburgh: D. Robinson (2), Blyleven (5), Candelaria (6), Jackson (7); Baltimore: Flanagan (1), McGregor (3), Stoddard (4). LP—Pittsburgh: Kison (1), Candelaria (3), Tekulve (4); Baltimore: Stanhouse (2), Flanagan (5), Palmer (6), McGregor (7).

1980—Philadelphia N.L. 4 (Dallas Green), Kansas City A.L. 2 (Jim Frey); WP—Philadelphia: Walk (1), Carlton (2), McGraw (5), Carlton (6); Kansas City: Quisenberry (3), Leonard (4). LP—Philadelphia: McGraw (3), Christenson (4); Kansas City: Leonard (1), Quisenberry (2), Quisenberry (5), Gale (6).

1981—Los Angeles N.L. 4 (Tom Lasorda), New York A.L. 2 (Bob Lemon); WP—Los Angeles: Valenzuela (3), Howe (4), Reuss (5), Hooton (6); New York: Guidry (1), John (2). LP—Los Angeles: Reuss (1), Hooton (2); New York: Frazier (3), Frazier (4), Guidry (5), Frazier (6).

1982—St. Louis N.L. 4 (Whitey Herzog), Milwaukee A.L. (Harvey Kuenn); WP—St. Louis: Sutter (2), Andujar (3), Stuper (6), Andujar (7). Milwaukee: Caldwell (1), Slaton (4), Caldwell (5). LP—St. Louis: Forsch (1), Bair (4), Forsch (5). Milwaukee: McClure (2), Vuckovich (3), Sutton (6), McClure (7).

1983—Baltimore A.L. 4 (Joe Altobelli), Philadelphia N.L. 1 (Paul Owens); WP—Baltimore: Boddicker (2), Palmer (3), Davis (4), McGregor (5). Philadelphia: Denny (1).

1984—Detroit A.L. 4 (Sparky Anderson), San Diego N.L. 1 (Dick Williams); WP—Det.: Morris (1,4), Wilcox (3), Lopez (5), San Diego: Hawkins (2). LP—Det.: Petry (2), San Diego: Thurmond (1), Lollar (3), Show (4), Hawkins (5).

1985—Kansas City A.L. 4 (Dick Howser), St. Louis N.L. 3 (Whitey Herzog); WP—KC: Saberhagen (3,7) Quisenberry (6), Jackson (5). St. Louis: Tudor (1,4) Dayley (2). LP—KC: Jackson (1), Leibrandt (2), Black (4); St. Louis: Andujar (3), Forsch (5), Worrell (6), Tudor (7).

1986—New York N.L. 4 (Dave Johnson); Boston A.L. (John McNamara) 3 WP—N.Y.—Ojeda (3), Darling (4), Aguilera (6), McDowell (7), Bos: Hurst (1), (5), Crawford (2). LP—N.Y. Darling (1), Gooden (2, 5).

1987—Minnesota, A.L. 4 (Tom Kelly); St. Louis N.L. (Whitey Herzog) 3. WP—Minn. Viola (1, 7), Blyleuin (2), Schatzeder (6), St. Louis: Tudor (1), Forsch (4), Cox (5). LP—Minn. Berenguer (3), Viola (4), Blyleuin (5); St. Louis: Magrane (1), Cox (2, 7), Tudor (6).

1988—Los Angeles N.L. 4 (Tommy Lasorda); Oakland A.L. (Tony LaRussa) 1. WP—Los Angeles: Hershiser (2, 5), Pena (1), Belcher (4); Oakland: Honeycutt (3). LP—Los Angeles: Howell (1); Oakland: Davis (2, 5), Eckersley (1), Stewart (4).

BASEBALL SUFFERS THROUGH TWO STRIKES, A THIRD THREATENED

Major League baseball, endured a strike by players for the second time since 1981 in August 1985. Unlike the 1981 strike, which lasted seven weeks and canceled 713 games, this one was ended quickly. The players walked on Aug. 6, and were back on the field three days later.

While in 1981 the major issue was over compensation for free agent signings to the club losing players, the 1985 strike was primarily over the pension fund, and how much of the reported $1.1 billion the owners receive through network television agreements would go into the plan.

The players were seeking an increase of $45 million over the $15 million they'd been receiving under the contract signed in 1981. The owners were adamant in refusing such a large increase.

There were other matters at question, including the issue of arbitration. Under the 1981 agreement, a player with two years of major league service who couldn't come to terms with ownership could take his case to binding arbitration. The owners were looking to increase the number of years vested service required to three years, and pointed

to substantial operating losses caused, in part, by large salaries granted by arbitrators and the increasing spiral of free agent salaries.

In the end, the players wound up with approximately $35 million for their pension fund, and the owners got their desired three years for arbitration, albeit the rule did not take effect until 1987.

The games canceled by the strike were rescheduled for later in the season, unlike the 1981 affair when far too many games were lost to be made up.

The 1981 strike settlement had been complicated by the decision to play a split season—awarding divisional championships to the teams in first place before the strike began, and starting a new second season to crown four additional champions. Those eight teams played off in a preliminary series. The survivors played for the league title and the right to move on to the World Series.

With the contract up at the end of the 1989 season, there was serious threat of another strike before the 1990 season.

WORLD SERIES CLUB STANDING
(Through 1988)

	Series	Won	Lost	Pct.		Series	Won	Lost	Pct.
Oakland (A)	4	3	1	.758	Detroit (A)	9	4	5	.444
Pittsburgh (N)	7	5	2	.714	New York (N-Giants)	14	5	9	.357
New York (A)	33	22	11	.667	Washington (A)	3	1	2	.333
Cleveland (A)	3	2	1	.667	Philadelphia (N)	4	1	3	.250
New York (N-Mets)	3	2	1	.667	Chicago (N)	10	2	8	.200
Philadelphia (A)	8	5	3	.625	Brooklyn (N)	9	1	8	.111
St. Louis (N)	15	9	6	.600	St. Louis (A)	1	0	1	.000
Boston (A)	9	5	4	.550	San Francisco (N)	1	0	1	.000
Los Angeles (N)	9	5	4	.550	Kansas City (A)	2	1	1	.500
Milwaukee (N)	2	1	1	.500	Milwaukee (A)	1	0	1	.000
Boston (N)	2	1	1	.500	San Diego (N)	1	0	1	.000
Chicago (A)	4	2	2	.500					
Cincinnati (N)	8	4	4	.500	**Recapitulation**				
Baltimore (A)	6	3	3	.500					
Minnesota (A)	2	1	1	.500					

Recapitulation

	Won
American League	48
National League	35

SINGLE GAME AND SINGLE SERIES RECORDS
(Through 1988)

Most hits game—5, Paul Molitor, Milwaukee A.L., first game vs. St. Louis, N.L., 1982.

Most 4-hit games, series—2, Robin Yount, Milwaukee A.L., first and fifth games vs. St. Louis N.L., 1982.

Most hits inning—2, held by many players.

Most hits series—13 (7 games) Bobby Richardson, New York A.L., 1964; Lou Brock, St. Louis N.L., 1968; 12 (6 games) Billy Martin, New York A.L., 1953; 12 (8 games) Buck Herzog, New York, N.L., 1912; Joe Jackson, Chicago A.L., 1919; 10 (4 games) Babe Ruth, New York A.L., 1928; 9 (5 games) held by 8 players.

Most home runs, series—5 (6 games) Reggie Jackson, New York A.L., 1977; 4 (7 games) Babe Ruth, New York A.L., 1926; Duke Snider, Brooklyn N.L., 1952, 1955; Hank Bauer, New York A.L., 1958; Gene Tenace, Oakland A.L., 1972; 4 (4 games) Lou Gehrig, New York A.L., 1928; 3 (6 games) Babe Ruth, New York A.L., 1923; Ted Kluszewski, Chicago A.L., 1959; 3 (5 games) Donn Clendenon, New York Mets N.L., 1969.

Most home runs, game—3, Babe Ruth, New York A.L., 1926 and 1928; Reggie Jackson, New York A.L., 1977.

Most strikeouts, series—12 (6 games) Willie Wilson, Kansas City A.L., 1980; 11 (7 games) Ed Mathews, Milwaukee N.L., 1958; Wayne Garrett, New York N.L., 1973; 10 (8 games) George Kelly, New York N.L., 1921; 9 (6 games) Jim Bottomley, St. Louis N.L., 1930;

9 (5 games) Carmelo Martinez, San Diego, N.L., 1984; Duke Snider, Brooklyn N.L., 1949; 7 (4 games) Bob Muesel, New York A.L., 1927.

Most stolen bases, game—3, Honus Wagner, Pittsburgh N.L., 1909; Willie Davis, Los Angeles N.L., 1965; Lou Brock, St. Louis N.L., 1967 and 1968.

Most strikeouts by pitcher, game—17, Bob Gibson, St. Louis N.L. 1968.

Most strikeouts by pitcher in succession—6, Horace Eller, Cincinnati N.L., 1919; Moe Drabowsky, Baltimore A.L., 1966.

Most strikeouts by pitcher, series—35 (7 games) Bob Gibson, St. Louis N.L., 1968; 28 (8 games) Bill Dinneen, Boston A.L., 1903; 23 (4 games) Sandy Koufax, Los Angeles, 1963; 20 (6 games) Chief Bender, Philadelphia A.L., 1911; 18 (5 games) Christy Mathewson, New York N.L., 1905.

Most bases on balls, series—11 (7 games) Babe Ruth, New York A.L., 1926; Gene Tenace, Oakland A.L., 1973; 9 (6 games) Willie Randolph, New York A.L., 1981; 7 (5 games) James Sheckard, Chicago N.L., 1910; Mickey Cochrane, Philadelphia A.L., 1929; Joe Gordon, New York A.L., 1941; 7 (4 games) Hank Thompson, New York N.L., 1954.

Most consecutive scoreless innings one series—27, Christy Mathewson, New York N.L., 1905.

LIFETIME WORLD SERIES RECORDS
(Through 1988)

Most hits—71, Yogi Berra, New York A.L., 1947, 1949–53, 1955–58, 1960–63.

Most runs—42, Mickey Mantle, New York A.L., 1951–53, 1955–58, 1960–64.

Most runs batted in—40, Mickey Mantle, New York A.L., 1951–53, 1955–58, 1960–64.

Most home runs—18, Mickey Mantle, New York A.L., 1951–53, 1955–58, 1960–64.

Most bases on balls—43, Mickey Mantle, New York A.L., 1951–53, 1955–58, 1960–64.

Most strikeouts—54, Mickey Mantle, New York A.L., 1951–53, 1955–58, 1960–64.

Most stolen bases—14, Eddie Collins, Philadelphia A.L. 1910–11, 13–14; Chicago A.L., 1917, 1919. Lou Brock, St. Louis N.L., 1964, 67–68.

Most victories, pitcher—10, Whitey Ford, New York A.L., 1950, 1953, 1955–58, 1960–64.

Most times member of winning team—10, Yogi Berra, New York A.L., 1947, 1949–53, 1956, 1958, 1961–62.

Most victories, no defeats—6, Vernon Gomez, New York A.L., 1932, 1936(2), 1937(2), 1938.

Most shutouts—4, Christy Mathewson, New York N.L., 1905 (3), 1913.

Most innings pitched—146, Whitey Ford, New York A.L., 1950, 1953, 1955–58, 1960–1964.

Most consecutive scoreless innings—33 2/3, Whitey Ford, New York A.L., 1960 (18), 1961 (14), 1962 (1 2/3).

Most strikeouts by pitcher—94, Whitey Ford, New York A.L., 1950, 1953, 1955–58, 1960–64.

AMERICAN LEAGUE HOME RUN CHAMPIONS

Year	Player, team	No.	Year	Player, team	No.	Year	Player, team	No.
1901	Nap Lajoie, Phila.	13	1932	Jimmy Foxx, Phila.	58	1964	Harmon Killebrew, Minn.	49
1902	Ralph Seybold, Phila.	16	1933	Jimmy Foxx, Phila.	48	1965	Tony Conigliaro, Bost.	32
1903	Buck Freeman, Bost.	13	1934	Lou Gehrig, N.Y.	49	1966	Frank Robinson, Balt.	49
1904	Harry Davis, Phila.	10	1935	Jimmy Foxx, Phila., and		1967	Carl Yastrzemski, Bost., and	
1905	Harry Davis, Phila.	8		Hank Greenberg, Det.	36		Harmon Killebrew, Minn.	44
1906	Harry Davis, Phila.	12	1936	Lou Gehrig, N.Y.	49	1968	Frank Howard, Wash.	44
1907	Harry Davis, Phila.	8	1937	Joe DiMaggio, N.Y.	46	1969	Harmon Killebrew, Minn.	49
1908	Sam Crawford, Det.	7	1938	Hank Greenberg, Det.	58	1970	Frank Howard, Wash.	44
1909	Ty Cobb, Det.	9	1939	Jimmy Foxx, Bost.	35	1971	Bill Melton, Chicago	33
1910	J. Garland Stahl, Bost.	10	1940	Hank Greenberg, Det.	41	1972	Dick Allen, Chicago	37
1911	Franklin Baker, Phila.	9	1941	Ted Williams, Bost.	37	1973	Reggie Jackson, Oak.	32
1912	Franklin Baker, Phila.	10	1942	Ted Williams, Bost.	36	1974	Dick Allen, Chicago	32
1913	Franklin Baker, Phila.	12	1943	Rudy York, Det.	34	1975	Reggie Jackson, Oak., and	
1914	Franklin Baker, Phila., and		1944	Nick Etten, N.Y.	22		George Scott, Mil.	36
	Sam Crawford, Det.	8	1945	Vern Stephens, St. L.	24	1976	Graig Nettles, N.Y.	32
1915	Robert Roth, Chi.-Cleve.	7	1946	Hank Greenberg, Det.	44	1977	Jim Rice, Boston	39
1916	Wally Pipp, N.Y.	12	1947	Ted Williams, Bost.	32	1978	Jim Rice, Boston	46
1917	Wally Pipp, N.Y.	9	1948	Joe DiMaggio, N.Y.	39	1979	Gorman Thomas, Milwaukee	45
1918	Babe Ruth, Bost., and		1949	Ted Williams, Bost.	43	1980	Reggie Jackson, N.Y., and	
	Clarence Walker, Phila.	11	1950	Al Rosen, Cleve.	37		Ben Oglivie, Mil.	41
1919	Babe Ruth, Bost.	29	1951	Gus Zernial, Chi.-Phila.	33	1981*	Tony Armas, Oak., Dwight	
1920	Babe Ruth, N.Y.	54	1952	Larry Doby, Cleve.	32		Evans, Bost., Bobby Grich,	
1921	Babe Ruth, N.Y.	59	1953	Al Rosen, Cleve.	43		Calif., and Eddie Murray,	
1922	Ken Williams, St. L.	39	1954	Larry Doby, Cleve.	32		Balt. (tie)	22
1923	Babe Ruth, N.Y.	41	1955	Mickey Mantle, N.Y.	37	1982	Gorman Thomas, Mil., and	
1924	Babe Ruth, N.Y.	46	1956	Mickey Mantle, N.Y.	52		Reggie Jackson, Calif.	39
1925	Bob Meusel, N.Y.	33	1957	Roy Sievers, Wash.	42	1983	Jim Rice, Boston	39
1926	Babe Ruth, N.Y.	47	1958	Mickey Mantle, N.Y.	42	1984	Tony Armas, Boston	43
1927	Babe Ruth, N.Y.	60	1959	Rocky Colavito, Cleve., and		1985	Darrell Evans, Detroit	40
1928	Babe Ruth, N.Y.	54		Harmon Killebrew, Wash.	42	1986	Jesse Barfield, Toronto	40
1929	Babe Ruth, N.Y.	46	1960	Mickey Mantle, N.Y.	40	1987	Mark McGwire, Oakland	49
1930	Babe Ruth, N.Y.	49	1961	Roger Maris, N.Y.	61	1988	Jose Canseco, Oakland	42
1931	Lou Gehrig, N.Y., and		1962	Harmon Killebrew, Minn.	48	1989	Fred McGriff	36
	Babe Ruth, N.Y.	46	1963	Harmon Killebrew, Minn.	45			

AMERICAN LEAGUE BATTING CHAMPIONS

Year	Player, team	Avg	Year	Player, team	Avg	Year	Player, team	Avg.
1901	Nap Lajoie, Phila.	.422	1931	Al Simmons, Phila.	.390	1961	Norman Cash, Det.	.361
1902	Ed Delahanty, Wash.	.376	1932	Dale Alexander, Det.-Bost.	.367	1962	Pete Runnels, Bost.	.326
1903	Nap Lajoie, Cleve.	.355	1933	Jimmy Foxx, Phila.	.356	1963	Carl Yastrzemski, Bost.	.321
1904	Nap Lajoie, Cleve.	.381	1934	Lou Gehrig, N.Y.	.363	1964	Tony Oliva, Minn.	.323
1905	Elmer Flick, Cleve.	.306	1935	Buddy Myer, Wash.	.349	1965	Tony Oliva, Minn.	.321
1906	George Stone, St. L.	.358	1936	Luke Appling, Chi.	.388	1966	Frank Robinson, Balt.	.316
1907	Ty Cobb, Det.	.350	1937	Charley Gehringer, Det.	.371	1967	Carl Yastrzemski, Bost.	.326
1908	Ty Cobb, Det.	.324	1938	Jimmy Foxx, Bost.	.349	1968	Carl Yastrzemski, Bost.	.301
1909	Ty Cobb, Det.	.377	1939	Joe DiMaggio, N.Y.	.381	1969	Rod Carew, Minn.	.332
1910	Ty Cobb, Det.	.385	1940	Joe DiMaggio, N.Y.	.352	1970	Alex Johnson, Calif.	.329
1911	Ty Cobb, Det.	.420	1941	Ted Williams, Bost.	.406	1971	Tony Oliva, Minn.	.337
1912	Ty Cobb, Det.	.410	1942	Ted Williams, Bost.	.356	1972	Rod Carew, Minn.	.318
1913	Ty Cobb, Det.	.390	1943	Luke Appling, Chi.	.328	1973	Rod Carew, Minn.	.350
1914	Ty Cobb, Det.	.368	1944	Lou Boudreau, Cleve.	.327	1974	Rod Carew, Minn.	.364
1915	Ty Cobb, Det.	.369	1945	George Sternweiss, N.Y.	.309	1975	Rod Carew, Minn.	.359
1916	Tris Speaker, Cleve.	.386	1946	Mickey Vernon, Wash.	.353	1976	George Brett, Kansas City	.333
1917	Ty Cobb, Det.	.383	1947	Ted Williams, Bost.	.343	1977	Rod Carew, Minn.	.388
1918	Ty Cobb, Det.	.382	1948	Ted Williams, Bost.	.369	1978	Rod Carew, Minn.	.333
1919	Ty Cobb, Det.	.384	1949	George Kell, Det.	.343	1979	Fred Lynn, Boston	.333
1920	George Sisler, St. L.	.407	1950	Billy Goodman, Bost.	.354	1980	George Brett, Kansas City	.390
1921	Harry Heilmann, Det.	.394	1951	Ferris Fain, Phila.	.344	1981*	Carney Lansford, Bost.	.336
1922	George Sisler, St. L.	.420	1952	Ferris Fain, Phila.	.327	1982	Willie Wilson, Kansas City	.332
1923	Harry Heilmann, Det.	.403	1953	Mickey Vernon, Wash.	.337	1983	Wade Boggs, Boston	.361
1924	Babe Ruth, N.Y.	.378	1954	Bobby Avila, Cleve.	.341	1984	Don Mattingly, New York	.343
1925	Harry Heilmann, Det.	.393	1955	Al Kaline, Det.	.340	1985	Wade Boggs, Boston	.368
1926	Heinie Manush, Det.	.378	1956	Mickey Mantle, N.Y.	.353	1986	Wade Boggs, Boston	.357
1927	Harry Heilmann, Det.	.398	1957	Ted Williams, Bost.	.388	1987	Wade Boggs, Boston	.363
1928	Goose Goslin, Wash.	.379	1958	Ted Williams, Bost.	.328	1988	Wade Boggs, Boston	.366
1929	Lew Fonseca, Cleve.	.369	1959	Harvey Kuenn, Det.	.353	1989	Kirby Puckett, Minnesota	.339
1930	Al Simmons, Phila.	.381	1960	Pete Runnels, Bost.	.320			

*Split season because of player strike.

NATIONAL LEAGUE HOME RUN CHAMPIONS

Year	Player, team	No.
1876	George Hall, Phila. Athletics	5
1877	George Shaffer, Louisville	3
1878	Paul Hines, Providence	4
1879	Charles Jones, Bost.	9
1880	James O'Rourke, Bost., and Harry Stovey, Worcester	6
1881	Dan Brouthers, Buffalo	8
1882	George Wood, Det.	7
1883	William Ewing, N.Y.	10
1884	Ed Williamson, Chi.	27
1885	Abner Dalrymple, Chi.	11
1886	Arthur Richardson, Det.	11
1887	Roger Conoor, N.Y., and Wm. O'Brien, Wash.	17
1888	Roger Connor, N.Y.	14
1889	Sam Thompson, Phila.	20
1890	Tom Burns, Bklyn, and Mike Tiernan, N.Y.	13
1891	Harry Stovey, Bost., and Mike Tiernan, N.Y.	16
1892	Jim Holliday, Cin.	13
1893	Ed Delahanty, Phila.	19
1894	Hugh Duffy, Bost., and Robert Lowe, Bost.	18
1895	Bill Joyce, Wash.	17
1896	Ed Delahnty, Phila., and Sam Thompson, Phila.	13
1897	Nap Lajoie, Phila.	10
1898	James Colins, Bost.	14
1899	John Freeman, Wash.	25
1900	Herman Long, Bost.	12
1901	Sam Crawford, Con.	16
1902	Tom Leach, Pitts.	6
1903	James Sheckard, Bklyn.	9
1904	Harry Lumley, Bklyn.	9
1905	Fred Odwell, Cin.	9
1906	Tim Jordan, Bklyn	12
1907	David Brain, Bost.	10
1908	Tim Jordan, Bklyn.	12
1909	John Murray, N.Y.	7
1910	Fred Beck, Bost., and Frank Schulte, Chi.	10
1911	Frank Schulte, Chi.	21
1912	Henry Zimmerman, Chi.	14
1913	Cliff Cravath, Phila.	19
1914	Cliff Cravath, Phila.	19
1915	Cliff Cravath, Phila.	24
1916	Davis Robertson, N.Y., and Fred Williams, Chi.	12
1917	Davis Robertson, N.Y., and Cliff Cravath, Phila.	12
1918	Cliff Cravath, Phila.	8
1919	Cliff Cravath, Phila.	12
1920	Cy Williams, Phila.	15
1921	George Kelly, N.Y.	23
1922	Rogers Hornsby, St. L.	42
1923	Cy Williams, Phila.	41
1924	Jacques Fournier, Bklyn.	27
1925	Rogers Hornsby, St. L.	39
1926	Hack Wilson, Chi.	21
1927	Hack Wilson, Chi., and Cy Williams, Phila.	30
1928	Hack Wilson, Chi., and Jim Bottomley, St. L.	31
1929	Chuck Klein, Phila.	43
1930	Hack Wilson, Chi.	56
1931	Chuck Klein, Phila.	31
1932	Chuck Klein, Phila., and Mel Ott, N.Y.	38
1933	Chuck Klein, Phila.	28
1934	Mel Ott, N.Y., and Rip Collins, St. L.	35
1935	Wally Berger, Bost.	34
1936	Mel Ott, N.Y.	33
1937	Mel Ott, N.Y., and Joe Medwick, St. L.	31
1938	Mel Ott, N.Y.	36
1939	John Mize, St. L.	28
1940	John Mize, St. L.	43
1941	Dolph Camilli, Bklyn.	34
1942	Mel Ott, N.Y.	30
1943	Bill Nicholson, Chi.	29
1944	Bill Nicholson, Chi.	33
1945	Tommy Holmes, Bost.	28
1946	Ralph Kiner, Pitts.	23
1947	Ralph Kiner, Pitts., and John Mize, N.Y.	51
1948	Ralph Kiner, Pitts., and John Mize, N.Y.	40
1949	Ralph Kiner, Pitts.	54
1950	Ralph Kiner, Pitts.	47
1951	Ralph Kiner, Pitts.	42
1952	Ralph Kiner, Pitts., and Hank Sauer, Chi.	37
1953	Ed Mathews, Mil.	47
1954	Ted Kluszewski, Cin.	49
1955	Willie Mays, N.Y.	51
1956	Duke Snider, Bklyn.	43
1957	Henry Aaron, Mil.	44
1958	Ernie Banks, Chi.	47
1959	Ed Mathews, Mil.	46
1960	Ernie Banks, Chi.	41
1961	Orlando Cepeda, San Fran.	46
1962	Willie Mays, San Fran.	49
1963	Henry Aaron, Mil., and Willie McCovey, San Fran.	44
1964	Willie Mays, San Fran.	47
1965	Willie Mays, San Fran.	52
1966	Henry Aaron, Atlanta	44
1967	Henry Aaron, Atlanta	39
1968	Willie McCovey, San Fran.	36
1969	Willie McCovey, San Fran.	45
1970	Johnny Bench, Cin.	45
1971	Willie Stargell, Pitts.	48
1972	Johnny Bench, Cin.	40
1973	Willie Stargell, Pitts.	44
1974	Mike Schmidt, Phila.	36
1975	Mike Schmidt, Phila.	38
1976	Mike Schmidt, Phila.	38
1977	George Foster, Cin.	52
1978	George Foster, Cin.	40
1979	Dave Kingman, Chicago	48
1980	Mike Schmidt, Phila.	48
1981*	Mike Schmidt, Phila.	31
1982	Dave Kingman, N.Y.	37
1983	Mike Schmidt, Phila.	40
1984	Mike Schmidt, Phila. and Dale Murphy, Atlanta	36
1985	Dale Murphy, Atlanta	37
1986	Mike Schmidt, Phila.	37
1987	Andre Dawson, Chicago	49
1988	Darryl Strawberry, N.Y.	39
1989	Kevin Mitchell, San Francisco	47

*Split season because of player strike.

NATIONAL LEAGUE BATTING CHAMPIONS

Year	Player, Team	Avg
1876	Roscoe Barnes, Chicago	.404
1877	Jim White, Boston	.385
1878	Abner Dalrymple, Mil.	.356
1879	Cap Anson, Chicago	.407
1880	George Gore, Chicago	.365
1881	Cap Anson, Chicago	.399
1882	Dan Brouthers, Buffalo	.367
1883	Dan Brouthers, Buffalo	.371
1884	James O'Rourke, Buffalo	.350
1885	Roger Connor, N. Y.	.371
1886	King Kelly, Chicago	.388
1887	Cap Anson, Chicago	.421
1888	Cap Anson, Chicago	.343
1889	Dan Brouthers, Boston	.373
1890	John Glasscock, N. Y.	.336
1891	William Hamilton, Phila.	.338
1892	Dan Brouthers, Bklyn., and Clarence Childs, Cleve.	.335
1893	Hugh Duffy, Boston	.378
1894	Hugh Duffy, Boston	.438
1895	Jesse Burkett, Cleveland	.423
1896	Jesse Burkett, Cleveland	.410
1897	Willie Keeler, Baltimore	.432
1898	Willie Keeler, Baltimore	.379
1899	Ed Delahanty, Phila.	.408
1900	Honus Wagner, Pittsburgh	.381
1901	Jesse Burkett, St. Louis	.382
1902	Clarence Beaumont, Pitts.	.357
1903	Honus Wagner, Pittsburgh	.355
1904	Honus Wagner, Pittsburgh	.349
1905	Cy Seymour, Cincinnati	.377
1906	Honus Wagner, Pittsburgh	.339
1907	Honus Wagner, Pittsburgh	.350
1908	Honus Wagner, Pittsburgh	.354
1909	Honus Wagner, Pittsburgh	.339
1910	Sherwood Magee, Philadelphia	.331
1911	Honus Wagner, Pittsburgh	.334
1912	Henry Zimmerman, Chicago	.372
1913	Jake Daubert, Brooklyn	.350
1914	Jake Daubert, Brooklyn	.329
1915	Larry Doyle, New York	.320
1916	Hal Chase, Cincinnati	.339
1917	Edd Roush, Cincinnati	.341
1918	Jack Wheat, Brooklyn	.335
1919	Edd Roush, Cincinnati	.321
1920	Rogers Hornsby, St. Louis	.370
1921	Rogers Hornsby, St. Louis	.397
1922	Rogers Hornsby, St. Louis	.401
1923	Rogers Hornsby, St. Louis	.384
1924	Rogers Hornsby, St. Louis	.424
1925	Rogers Hornsby, St. Louis	.403
1926	Gene Hargrave, Cincinnati	.353
1927	Paul Waner; Pittsburgh	.380
1928	Rogers Hornsby, Boston	.387
1929	Lefty O'Doul, Phila.	.398
1930	Bill Terry, N.Y.	.401

Year	Player, Team	Avg	Year	Player, Team	Avg	Year	Player, Team	Avg
1931	Chick Hafey, St. Louis	.349	1951	Stan Musial, St. Louis	.355	1971	Joe Torre, St. Louis	.363
1932	Lefty O'Doul, Brooklyn	.368	1952	Stan Musial, St. Louis	.336	1972	Billy Williams, Chicago	.333
1933	Chuck Klein, Phila.	.368	1953	Carl Furillo, Brooklyn	.344	1973	Pete Rose, Cincinnati	.338
1934	Paul Waner, Pittsburgh	.362	1954	Willie Mays, N. Y.	.345	1974	Ralph Garr, Atlanta	.353
1935	Arky Vaughan, Pittsburgh	.385	1955	Richie Ashburn, Phila.	.338	1975	Bill Madlock, Chicago	.354
1936	Paul Waner, Pittsburgh	.373	1956	Henry Aaron, Mil.	.328	1976	Bill Madlock, Chicago	.339
1937	Joe Medwick, St. Louis	.374	1957	Stan Musial, St. Louis	.351	1977	Dave Parker, Pittsburgh	.338
1938	Ernie Lombardi, Cin.	.342	1958	Richie Ashburn, Phila.	.350	1978	Dave Parker, Pittsburgh	.334
1939	John Mize, St. Louis	.349	1959	Henry Aaron, Mil.	.355	1979	Keith Hernandez, St. Louis	.344
1940	Debs Garms, Pittsburgh	.355	1960	Dick Groat, Pittsburgh	.325	1980	Bill Buckner, Chicago	.324
1941	Pete Reiser, Brooklyn	.343	1961	Roberto Clemente, Pitts.	.351	1981*	Bill Madlock, Pittsburgh	.341
1942	Ernie Lombardi, Boston	.330	1962	Tommy Davis, L. A.	.346	1982	Al Oliver, Montreal	.331
1943	Stan Musial, St. Louis	.357	1963	Tommy Davis, L. A.	.326	1983	Bill Madlock, Pittsburgh	.323
1944	Dixie Walker, Brooklyn	.357	1964	Roberto Clemente, Pitts.	.339	1984	Tony Gwynn, San Diego	.351
1945	Phil Cavarretta, Chicago	.355	1965	Roberto Clemente, Pitts.	.329	1985	Willie McGee, St. Louis	.353
1946	Stan Musial, St. Louis	.365	1966	Matty Alou, Pittsburgh	.342	1986	Tim Raines, Montreal	.334
1947	Harry Walker, St. L.-Phila.	.363	1967	Roberto Clemente, Pitts.	.357	1987	Tony Gwynn, San Diego	.370
1948	Stan Musial, St. Louis	.376	1968	Pete Rose, Cincinnati	.335	1988	Tony Gwynn, San Diego	.313
1949	Jackie Robinson, Brooklyn	.342	1969	Pete Rose, Cincinnati	.348	1989	Tony Gwynn, San Diego	.336
1950	Stan Musial, St. Louis	.346	1970	Rico Carty, Atlanta	.366			

AMERICAN LEAGUE PENNANT WINNERS

Year	Club	Manager	Won	Lost	Pct	Year	Club	Manager	Won	Lost	Pct
1901	Chicago	Clark C. Griffith	83	53	.610	1947[1]	New York	Stanley R. Harris	97	57	.630
1902	Philadelphia	Connie Mack	83	53	.610	1948[1]	Cleveland	Lou Boudreau	97	58	.626
1903[1]	Boston	Jimmy Collins	91	47	.659	1949[1]	New York	Casey Stengel	97	57	.630
1904[2]	Boston	Jimmy Collins	95	59	.617	1950[1]	New York	Casey Stengel	98	56	.636
1905	Philadelphia	Connie Mack	92	56	.622	1951[1]	New York	Casey Stengel	98	56	.636
1906[1]	Chicago	Fielder A. Jones	93	58	.616	1952[1]	New York	Casey Stengel	95	59	.617
1907	Detroit	Hugh A. Jennings	92	58	.613	1953[1]	New York	Casey Stengel	99	52	.656
1908	Detroit	Hugh A. Jennings	90	63	.588	1954	Cleveland	Al Lopez	111	43	.721
1909	Detroit	Hugh A. Jennings	98	54	.645	1955	New York	Casey Stengel	96	58	.623
1910[1]	Philadelphia	Connie Mack	102	48	.680	1956[1]	New York	Casey Stengel	97	57	.630
1911[1]	Philadelphia	Connie Mack	101	50	.669	1957	New York	Casey Stengel	98	56	.636
1912[1]	Boston	J. Garland Stahl	105	47	.691	1958[1]	New York	Casey Stengel	92	62	.597
1913[1]	Philadelphia	Connie Mack	96	57	.627	1959	Chicago	Al Lopez	94	60	.610
1914	Philadelphia	Connie Mack	99	53	.651	1960	New York	Casey Stengel	97	57	.630
1915[1]	Boston	William F. Carrigan	101	50	.669	1961[1]	New York	Ralph Houk	109	53	.673
1916[1]	Boston	William F. Carrigan	91	63	.591	1962[1]	New York	Ralph Houk	96	66	.593
1917[1]	Chicago	Clarence H. Rowland	100	54	.649	1963	New York	Ralph Houk	104	57	.646
1918[1]	Boston	Ed Barrow	75	51	.595	1964	New York	Yogi Berra	99	63	.611
1919	Chicago	William Gleason	88	52	.629	1965	Minnesota	Sam Mele	102	60	.630
1920[1]	Cleveland	Tris Speaker	98	56	.636	1966[1]	Baltimore	Hank Bauer	97	63	.606
1921	New York	Miller J. Huggins	98	55	.641	1967	Boston	Dick Williams	92	70	.568
1922	New York	Miller J. Huggins	94	60	.610	1968[1]	Detroit	Mayo Smith	103	59	.636
1923[1]	New York	Miller J. Huggins	98	54	.645	1969	Baltimore[3]	Earl Weaver	109	53	.673
1924[1]	Washington	Stanley R. Harris	92	62	.597	1970[3]	Baltimore[3]	Earl Weaver	108	54	.667
1925	Washington	Stanley R. Harris	96	55	.636	1971	Baltimore[4]	Earl Weaver	101	57	.639
1926	New York	Miller J. Huggins	91	63	.591	1972[1]	Oakland[5]	Dick Williams	93	62	.600
1927[1]	New York	Miller J. Huggins	110	44	.714	1973[1]	Oakland[6]	Dick Williams	94	68	.580
1928[1]	New York	Miller J. Huggins	101	53	.656	1974[1]	Oakland[6]	Alvin Dark	90	72	.556
1929[1]	Philadelphia	Connie Mack	104	46	.693	1975	Boston[4]	Darrell Johnson	95	65	.594
1930[1]	Philadelphia	Connie Mack	102	52	.662	1976	New York[7]	Billy Martin	97	62	.610
1931	Philadelphia	Connie Mack	107	45	.704	1977[1]	New York[7]	Billy Martin	100	62	.617
1932[1]	New York	Joseph V. McCarthy	107	47	.695	1978[1]	New York[7]	Billy Martin			
1933	Washington	Joseph E. Cronin	99	53	.651			and Bob Lemon	100	63	.613
1934	Detroit	Gordon Cochrane	101	53	.656	1979	Baltimore[8]	Earl Weaver	102	57	.642
1935[1]	Detroit	Gordon Cochrane	93	58	.616	1980	Kansas City[9]	Jim Frey	97	65	.599
1936[1]	New York	Joseph V. McCarthy	102	51	.667	1981	New York[10]	Gene Michael-Bob			
1937[1]	New York	Joseph V. McCarthy	102	52	.662			Lemon	59	48	.551*
1938[1]	New York	Joseph V. McCarthy	99	53	.651	1982	Milwaukee[11]	Harvey Kuenn	95	67	.586
1939[1]	New York	Joseph V. McCarthy	106	45	.702	1983[1]	Baltimore[12]	Joe Altobelli	98	64	.605
1940	Detroit	Delmar D. Baker	90	64	.584	1984	Detroit[13]	Sparky Anderson	104	58	.642
1941[1]	New York	Joseph V. McCarthy	101	53	.656	1985[1]	Kansas City[14]	Dick Howser	91	71	.562
1942	New York	Joseph V. McCarthy	103	51	.669	1986	Boston[11]	John McNamara	95	66	.590
1943[1]	New York	Joseph V. McCarthy	98	56	.636	1987	Minnesota[15]	Tom Kelly	85	77	.525
1944	St. Louis	Luke Sewell	89	65	.578	1988	Oakland[16]	Tony LaRussa	104	58	.642
1945[1]	Detroit	Steve O'Neill	88	65	.575	1989	Oakland[17]	Tony LaRussa	99	63	.611
1946	Boston	Joseph E. Cronin	104	50	.675						

*Split season because of player strike. 1. World Series winner. 2. No World Series. 3. Defeated Minnesota, Western Division winner, in playoff. 4. Defeated Oakland, Western Division Leader, in playoff. 5. Defeated Detroit, Eastern Division winner, in playoff. 6. Defeated Baltimore, Eastern Division winner, in playoff. 7. Defeated Kansas City, Western Division winner, in playoff. 8. Defeated California, Western Division winner, in playoff. 9. Defeated New York, Eastern Division winner, in playoff. 10. Defeated Oakland, Western Division winner, in playoff. 11. Defeated California, Western Division winner, in playoff. 12. Defeated Chicago, Western Division winner, in playoff. 13. Defeated Kansas City, Western Division winner, in playoff. 14. Defeated Toronto, Eastern Division winner, in playoff. 15. Defeated Detroit, Eastern winner, in playoff. 16. Defeated Boston, Eastern division winner, in playoffs. 17. Defeated Toronto, Eastern Division winner, in playoffs.

NATIONAL LEAGUE PENNANT WINNERS

Year	Club	Manager	Won	Lost	Pct	Year	Club	Manager	Won	Lost	Pct
1876	Chicago	Albert G. Spalding	52	14	.788	1933	New York[1]	William H. Terry	91	61	.599
1877	Boston	Harry Wright	31	17	.646	1934	St. Louis[1]	Frank F. Frisch	95	58	.621
1878	Boston	Harry Wright	41	19	.683	1935	Chicago	Charles J. Grimm	100	54	.649
1879	Providence	George Wright	55	23	.705	1936	New York	William H. Terry	92	62	.597
1880	Chicago	Adrian C. Anson	67	17	.798	1937	New York	William H. Terry	95	57	.625
1881	Chicago	Adrian C. Anson	56	28	.667	1938	Chicago	Gabby Hartnett	89	63	.586
1882	Chicago	Adrian C. Anson	55	29	.655	1939	Cincinnati	William B. McKechnie	97	57	.630
1883	Boston	John F. Morrill	63	35	.643	1940	Cincinnati[1]	William B. McKechnie	100	53	.654
1884	Providence	Frank C. Bancroft	84	28	.750	1941	Brooklyn	Leo E. Durocher	100	54	.649
1885	Chicago	Adrian C. Anson	87	25	.777	1942	St. Louis[1]	William H. Southworth	106	48	.688
1886	Chicago	Adrian C. Anson	90	34	.726	1943	St. Louis[1]	William H. Southworth	105	49	.682
1887	Detroit	W. H. Watkins	79	45	.637	1944	St. Louis[1]	William H. Southworth	105	49	.682
1888	New York	James J. Mutrie	84	47	.641	1945	Chicago	Charles J. Grimm	98	56	.636
1889	New York	James J. Mutrie	83	43	.659	1946	St. Louis[1]	Edwin H. Dyer	98	58	.628
1890	Brooklyn	William H. McGunnigle	86	43	.667	1947	Brooklyn	Burton E. Shotton	94	60	.610
1891	Boston	Frank G. Selee	87	51	.630	1948	Boston	William H. Southworth	91	62	.595
1892	Boston	Frank G. Selee	102	48	.680	1949	Brooklyn	Burton E. Shotton	97	57	.630
1893	Boston	Frank G. Selee	86	44	.662	1950	Philadelphia	Edwin M. Sawyer	91	63	.591
1894	Baltimore	Edward H. Hanlon	89	39	.695	1951	New York	Leo E. Durocher	98	59	.624
1895	Baltimore	Edward H. Hanlon	87	43	.669	1952	Brooklyn	Charles W. Dressen	96	57	.630
1896	Baltimore	Edward H. Hanlon	90	39	.698	1953	Brooklyn	Charles W. Dressen	105	49	.682
1897	Boston	Frank G. Selee	93	39	.705	1954	New York[1]	Leo E. Durocher	97	57	.630
1898	Boston	Frank G. Selee	102	47	.685	1955	Brooklyn[1]	Walter Alston	98	55	.641
1899	Brooklyn	Edward H. Hanlon	88	42	.677	1956	Brooklyn	Walter Alston	93	61	.604
1900	Brooklyn	Edward H. Hanlon	82	54	.603	1957	Milwaukee[1]	Fred Haney	95	59	.617
1901	Pittsburgh	Fred C. Clarke	90	49	.647	1958	Milwaukee	Fred Haney	92	62	.597
1902	Pittsburgh	Fred C. Clarke	103	36	.741	1959	Los Angeles[1]	Walter Alston	88	68	.564
1903	Pittsburgh	Fred C. Clarke	91	49	.650	1960	Pittsburgh[1]	Danny Murtaugh	95	59	.617
1904	New York[2]	John J. McGraw	106	47	.693	1961	Cincinnati	Fred Hutchinson	93	61	.604
1905	New York[1]	John J. McGraw	105	48	.686	1962	San Francisco	Alvin Dark	103	62	.624
1906	Chicago	Frank L. Chance	116	36	.763	1963	Los Angeles[1]	Walter Alston	99	63	.611
1907	Chicago[1]	Frank L. Chance	107	45	.704	1964	St. Louis[1]	Johnny Keane	93	69	.574
1908	Chicago[1]	Frank L. Chance	99	55	.643	1965	Los Angeles[1]	Walter Alston	97	65	.599
1909	Pittsburgh[1]	Fred C. Clarke	110	42	.724	1966	Los Angeles	Walter Alston	95	67	.586
1910	Chicago	Frank L. Chance	104	50	.675	1967	St. Louis[1]	Red Schoendienst	101	60	.627
1911	New York	John J. McGraw	99	54	.647	1968	St. Louis	Red Schoendienst	97	65	.599
1912	New York	John J. McGraw	103	48	.682	1969	New York[1][3]	Gil Hodges	100	62	.617
1913	New York	John J. McGraw	101	51	.664	1970	Cincinnati[4]	Sparky Anderson	102	60	.630
1914	Boston[1]	George T. Stallings	94	59	.614	1971	Pittsburgh[1][5]	Danny Murtaugh	97	65	.599
1915	Philadelphia	Patrick J. Moran	90	62	.592	1972	Cincinnati[4]	Sparky Anderson	95	59	.617
1916	Brooklyn	Wilbert Robinson	94	60	.610	1973	New York[6]	Yogi Berra	82	79	.509
1917	New York	John J. McGraw	98	56	.636	1974	Los Angeles[6]	Walter Alston	102	60	.630
1918	Chicago	Fred L. Mitchell	84	45	.651	1975	Cincinnati[1][4]	Sparky Anderson	108	54	.667
1919	Cincinnati[1]	Patrick J. Moran	96	44	.686	1976	Cincinnati[7][1]	Sparky Anderson	102	60	.630
1920	Brooklyn	Wilbert Robinson	93	61	.604	1977	Los Angeles[7]	Tom Lasorda	98	64	.605
1921	New York[1]	John J. McGraw	94	59	.614	1978	Los Angeles[7]	Tom Lasorda	95	67	.586
1922	New York[1]	John J. McGraw	93	61	.604	1979[1]	Pittsburgh[6]	Chuck Tanner	98	64	.605
1923	New York	John J. McGraw	95	58	.621	1980[1]	Philadelphia[4]	Dallas Green	91	71	.562
1924	New York	John J. McGraw	93	60	.608	1981	Los Angeles[1][9]	Tom Lasorda	63	47	.573*
1925	Pittsburgh[1]	William B. McKechnie	95	58	.621	1982[1]	St. Louis[10]	Whitey Herzog	92	70	.568
1926	St. Louis[1]	Rogers Hornsby	89	65	.578	1983	Philadelphia[11]	Paul Owens	90	72	.556
1927	Pittsburgh	Donie Bush	94	60	.610	1984	San Diego[12]	Dick Williams	92	70	.568
1928	St. Louis	William B. McKechnie	95	59	.617	1985	St. Louis[11]	Whitey Herzog	101	61	.623
1929	Chicago	Joseph V. McCarthy	98	54	.645	1986	New York[8]	Dave Johnson	108	54	.667
1930	St. Louis	Gabby Street	92	62	.597	1987	St. Louis[13]	Whitey Herzog	95	67	.586
1931	St. Louis[1]	Gabby Street	101	53	.656	1988	Los Angeles[14]	Tommy Lasorda	94	67	.584
1932	Chicago	Charles J. Grimm	90	64	.584	1989	San Francisco[15]	Roger Craig	92	70	.568

*Split season because of player strike. 1. World Series winner. 2. No World Series. 3. Defeated Atlanta, Western Division winner, in playoff. 4. Defeated Pittsburgh, Eastern Division winner, in playoff. 5. Defeated San Francisco, Western Division winner, in playoff. 6. Defeated Cincinnati, Western Division winner, in playoff. 7. Defeated Philadelphia, Eastern Division winner, in playoff. 8. Defeated Houston, Western Division winner, in playoff. 9. Defeated Montreal, Eastern Division winner, in playoff. 10. Defeated Atlanta, Western Division winner, in playoff. 11. Defeated Los Angeles, Western Division in playoff. 12. Defeated Chicago, Eastern Division champion in playoff. 13. Defeated San Francisco, Western winner, in playoff. 14. Defeated New York, Eastern Division champion in playoff. 15. Defeated Chicago, Eastern Division champion in playoff.

MOST VALUABLE PLAYERS
(Baseball Writers Association selections)

American League

1931	Lefty Grove, Philadelphia
1932–33	Jimmy Foxx, Philadelphia
1934	Mickey Cochrane, Detroit
1935	Hank Greenberg, Detroit
1936	Lou Gehrig, New York
1937	Charlie Gehringer, Detroit
1938	Jimmy Foxx, Boston
1939	Joe DiMaggio, New York
1940	Hank Greenberg, Detroit
1941	Joe DiMaggio, New York
1942	Joe Gordon, New York
1943	Spurgeon Chandler, New York
1944–45	Hal Newhouser, Detroit
1946	Ted Williams, Boston
1947	Joe DiMaggio, New York
1948	Lou Boudreau, Cleveland
1949	Ted Williams, Boston
1950	Phil Rizzuto, New York
1951	Yogi Berra, New York
1952	Bobby Shantz, Philadelphia
1953	Al Rosen, Cleveland
1954–55	Yogi Berra, New York
1956–57	Mickey Mantle, New York
1958	Jackie Jensen, Boston
1959	Nellie Fox, Chicago
1960–61	Roger Maris, New York
1962	Mickey Mantle, New York
1963	Elston Howard, New York
1964	Brooks Robinson, Baltimore
1965	Zoilo Versalles, Minnesota
1966	Frank Robinson, Baltimore
1967	Carl Yastrzemski, Boston
1968	Dennis McLain, Detroit
1969	Harmon Killebrew, Minnesota
1970	John (Boog) Powell, Baltimore
1971	Vida Blue, Oakland
1972	Dick Allen, Chicago
1973	Reggie Jackson, Oakland
1974	Jeff Burroughs, Texas
1975	Fred Lynn, Boston
1976	Thurman Munson, New York
1977	Rod Carew, Minnesota
1978	Jim Rice, Boston
1979	Don Baylor, California
1980	George Brett, Kansas City
1981	Rollie Fingers, Milwaukee
1982	Robin Yount, Milwaukee
1983	Cal Ripken, Jr., Baltimore
1984	Willie Hernandez, Detroit
1985	Don Mattingly, New York
1986	Roger Clemens, Boston
1987	George Bell, Toronto
1988	Jose Canseco, Oakland

National League

1931	Frank Frisch, St. Louis
1932	Chuck Klein, Philadelphia
1933	Carl Hubbell, New York
1934	Dizzy Dean, St. Louis
1935	Gabby Hartnett, Chicago
1936	Carl Hubbell, New York
1937	Joe Medwick, St. Louis
1938	Ernie Lombardi, Cincinnati
1939	Bucky Walters, Cincinnati
1940	Frank McCormick, Cincinnati
1941	Dolph Camilli, Brooklyn
1942	Mort Cooper, St. Louis
1943	Stan Musial, St. Louis
1944	Marty Marion, St. Louis
1945	Phil Cavarretta, Chicago
1946	Stan Musial, St. Louis
1947	Bob Elliott, Boston
1948	Stan Musial, St. Louis
1949	Jackie Robinson, Brooklyn
1950	Jim Konstanty, Philadelphia

1951	Roy Campanella, Brooklyn
1952	Hank Sauer, Chicago
1953	Roy Campanella, Brooklyn
1954	Willie Mays, New York
1955	Roy Campanella, Brooklyn
1956	Don Newcombe, Brooklyn
1957	Henry Aaron, Milwaukee
1958–59	Ernie Banks, Chicago
1960	Dick Groat, Pittsburgh
1961	Frank Robinson, Cincinnati
1962	Maury Wills, Los Angeles
1963	Sandy Koufax, Los Angeles
1964	Ken Boyer, St. Louis
1965	Willie Mays, San Francisco
1966	Roberto Clemente, Pittsburgh
1967	Orlando Cepeda, St. Louis
1968	Bob Gibson, St. Louis
1969	Willie McCovey, San Francisco
1970	Johnny Bench, Cincinnati
1971	Joe Torre, St. Louis
1972	Johnny Bench, Cincinnati
1973	Pete Rose, Cincinnati
1974	Steve Garvey, Los Angeles
1975–76	Joe Morgan, Cincinnati
1977	George Foster, Cincinnati
1978	Dave Parker, Pittsburgh
1979	Willie Stargell, Pittsburgh
1979	Keith Hernandez, St. Louis
1980	Mike Schmidt, Philadelphia
1981	Mike Schmidt, Philadelphia
1982	Dale Murphy, Atlanta
1983	Dale Murphy, Atlanta
1984	Ryne Sandberg, Chicago
1985	Willie McGee, St. Louis
1986	Mike Schmidt, Philadelphia
1987	Andre Dawson, Chicago
1988	Kirk Gibson, Los Angeles

CY YOUNG AWARD

1956	Don Newcombe, Brooklyn N.L.
1957	Warren Spahn, Milwaukee N.L.
1958	Bob Turley, New York A.L.
1959	Early Wynn, Chicago A.L.
1960	Vernon Law, Pittsburgh, N.L.
1961	Whitey Ford, New York A.L.
1962	Don Drysdale, Los Angeles N.L.
1963	Sandy Koufax, Los Angeles N.L.
1964	Dean Chance, Los Angeles A.L.
1965	Sandy Koufax, Los Angeles N.L.
1966	Sandy Koufax, Los Angeles N.L.
1967	Jim Lonborg, Boston A.L.; Mike McCormick, San Francisco N.L.
1968	Dennis, McLain, Detroit A.L.; Bob Gibson, St. Louis N.L.
1969	Mike Cuellar, Baltimore, and Dennis McLain, Detroit, tied in A.L.; Tom Seaver, N.Y. N.L.
1970	Jim Perry, Minnesota A.L; Bob Gibson, St. Louis N.L.

1971	Vida Blue, Oakland A.L.; Ferguson Jenkins, Chicago N.L.
1972	Gaylord Perry, Cleveland A.L.; Steve Carlton, Phila. N.L.
1973	Jim Palmer, Baltimore A.L.; Tom Seaver, New York N.L.
1974	Catfish Hunter, Oakland A.L.; Mike Marshall, Los Angeles N.L.
1975	Jim Palmer, Baltimore A.L.; Tom Seaver, New York N.L.
1976	Jim Palmer, Baltimore A.L.; Randy Jones, San Diego N.L.
1977	Sparky Lyle, N.Y., A.L.; Steve Carlton, Philadelphia N.L.
1978	Ron Guidry, N.Y., A.L.; Gaylord Perry, San Diego N.L.
1979	Mike Flanagan, Baltimore, A.L.; Bruce Sutter, Chicago, N.L.
1980	Steve Stone, Baltimore, A.L.;

	Steve Carlton, Philadelphia, N.L.
1981	Rollie Fingers, Milwaukee, A.L.; Fernando Valenzuela, Los Angeles, N.L.
1982	Pete Vuckovich, Milwaukee, A.L.; Steve Carlton, Philadelphia, N.L.
1983	LaMarr Hoyt, Chicago, A.L.; John Denny, Philadelphia, N.L.
1984	Willie Hernandez, Detroit, A.L.; Rick Sutcliffe, Chicago, N.L.
1985	Bret Saberhagen, A.L.; Dwight Gooden, N.L.
1986	Roger Clemens, A.L.; Mike Scott, N.L.
1987	Roger Clemens, A.L.; Steve Bedrosian, N.L.
1988	Frank Viola, A.L.; Orel Hershiser, N.L.

ROOKIE OF THE YEAR
(Baseball Writers Association selections)

American League

1949	Roy Sievers, St. Louis
1950	Walt Dropo, Boston
1951	Gil McDougald, New York
1952	Harry Byrd, Philadelphia
1953	Harvey Kuenn, Detroit
1954	Bob Grim, New York

1955	Herb Score, Cleveland
1956	Luis Aparicio, Chicago
1957	Tony Kubek, New York
1958	Albie Pearson, Washington
1959	Bob Allison, Washington
1960	Ron Hansen, Baltimore

1961	Don Schwall, Boston
1962	Tom Tresh, New York
1963	Gary Peters, Chicago
1964	Tony Oliva, Minnesota
1965	Curt Blefary, Baltimore
1966	Tommy Agee, Chicago

1967	Rod Carew, Minnesota
1968	Stan Bahnsen, New York
1969	Lou Piniella, Kansas City
1970	Thurman Munson, New York
1971	Chris Chambliss, Cleveland
1972	Carlton Fisk, Boston
1973	Alonzo Bumbry, Baltimore
1974	Mike Hargrove, Texas
1975	Fred Lynn, Boston
1976	Mark Fidrych, Detroit
1977	Eddie Murray, Baltimore
1978	Lou Whitaker, Detroit
1979	Alfredo Griffin, Toronto
1979	John Castino, Minnesota
1980	Joe Charboneau, Cleveland
1981	Dave Righetti, New York
1982	Cal Ripken, Jr., Baltimore
1983	Ron Kittle, Chicago
1984	Alvin Davis, Seattle
1985	Ozzie Guillen, Chicago
1986	Jose Canseco, Oakland
1987	Mark McGwire, Oakland
1988	Walter Weiss, Oakland

National League

1949	Don Newcombe, Brooklyn
1950	Sam Jethroe, Boston
1951	Willie Mays, New York
1952	Joe Black, Brooklyn
1953	Jim Gilliam, Brooklyn
1954	Wally Moon, St. Louis
1955	Bill Virdon, St. Louis
1956	Frank Robinson, Cincinnati
1957	Jack Sanford, Philadelphia
1958	Orlando Cepeda, San Francisco
1959	Willie McCovey, San Francisco
1960	Frank Howard, Los Angeles
1961	Billy Williams, Chicago
1962	Ken Hubbs, Chicago
1963	Pete Rose, Cincinnati
1964	Richie Allen, Philadelphia
1965	Jim Lefebvre, Los Angeles
1966	Tommy Helms, Cincinnati
1967	Tom Seaver, New York
1968	Johnny Bench, Cincinnati

1969	Ted Sizemore, Los Angeles
1970	Carl Morton, Montreal
1971	Earl Williams, Atlanta
1972	Jon Matlack, New York
1973	Gary Matthews, San Francisco
1974	Bake McBride, St. Louis
1975	John Montefusco, San Francisco
1976	Pat Zachry, Cincinnati
1977	Andre Dawson, Montreal
1978	Bob Horner, Atlanta
1979	Rick Sutcliffe, Los Angeles
1980	Steve Howe, Los Angeles
1981	Fernando Valenzuela, Los Angeles
1982	Steve Sax, Los Angeles
1983	Darryl Strawberry, New York
1984	Dwight Gooden, New York
1985	Vince Coleman, St. Louis
1986	Todd Worrell, St. Louis
1987	Benito Santiago, San Diego
1988	Tim Belcher, Los Angeles

BASEBALL'S PERFECTLY PITCHED GAMES[1]

(no opposing runner reached base)

John Richmond—Worcester vs. Cleveland (NL) June 12, 1880 (1-0)
John M. Ward—Providence vs. Buffalo (NL) June 17, 1880 (5-0)
Cy Young—Boston vs. Philadelphia (AL) May 5, 1904 (3-0)
Addie Joss—Cleveland vs. Chicago (AL) Oct. 2, 1908 (1-0)
Ernest Shore[2]—Boston vs. Washington (AL) June 23, 1917 (4-0)
Charles Robertson—Chicago vs. Detroit (AL) April 30, 1922 (2-0)

Don Larsen[3]—New York (AL) vs. Brooklyn (NL) Oct. 8, 1956 (2-0)
Jim Bunning—Philadelphia vs. New York (NL) June 21, 1964 (6-0)
Sandy Koufax—Los Angeles vs. Chicago (NL) Sept. 9, 1965 (1-0)
Jim Hunter—Oakland vs. Minnesota (AL) May 8, 1968 (4-0)
Len Barker—Cleveland vs. Toronto (AL) May 15, 1981 (3-0)
Mike Witt—California vs. Texas (AL) Sept. 30, 1984 (1-0)

1. Harvey Haddix, of Pittsburgh, pitched 12 perfect innings against Milwaukee (NL), May 26, 1959 but lost game in 13th on error and hit. 2. Shore, relief pitcher for Babe Ruth who walked first batter before being ejected by umpire, retired 26 batters who faced him and baserunner was out stealing. 3. World Series.

MAJOR LEAGUE LIFETIME RECORDS

Source: The Book of Baseball Records, published and copyrighted by Seymour Siwoff, New York, N.Y. 10036.

Leading Batters, by Average
(Minimum 10 major league seasons and 4,000 at bats)

	Years	At Bats	Hits	Avg
Ty Cobb	24	11,436	4,190	.366
Rogers Hornsby	23	8,173	2,930	.358
Joe Jackson	13	4,981	1,774	.356
Pete Browning	13	4,795	1,664	.347
Ed Delahanty	16	7,493	2,593	.346
Willie Keeler	19	8,570	2,955	.345
Billy Hamilton	14	6,262	2,157	.344
Ted Williams	19	7,706	2,654	.344
Tris Speaker	22	10,208	3,515	.344
Dan Brouthers	19	6,682	2,288	.342
Jesse Burkett	16	8,389	2,872	.342
Babe Ruth	22	8,399	2,873	.342
Harry Heilmann	17	7,787	2,660	.342
Bill Terry	14	6,428	2,193	.341
George Sisler	15	8,267	2,812	.340
Lou Gehrig	17	8,001	2,721	.340
Nap Lajoie	21	9,590	3,251	.339
Riggs Stephenson	14	4,508	1,515	.336
Al Simmons	20	8.761	2,927	.334
Cap Anson	22	9,067	3,022	.333
Paul Waner	20	9,459	3,152	.333
Eddie Collins	25	9,949	3,311	.333
Sam Thompson	15	5,972	1,984	.332
Stan Musial	22	10,972	3,630	.331
Heinie Manush	17	7,653	2,524	.330
Hugh Duffy	17	7,026	2,313	.329
Honus Wagner	21	10,427	3,430	.329
Rod Carew	19	9,315	3,053	.328

	Years	At Bats	Hits	Avg
Top O'Neill	10	4,254	1,389	.327
Jimmie Foxx	20	8,134	2,646	.325
Earle Combs	12	5,748	1,866	.325
Joe DiMaggio	13	6,821	2,214	.325

Leading Pitchers
(More than 250 career victories)

	Years	W	L	Pct
Cy Young	22	511	315	.619
Walter Johnson	21	416	279	.599
Christy Mathewson	17	374	187	.667
Grover Cleveland Alexander	20	373	208	.642
Warren Spahn	21	363	245	.597
James Galvin	15	361	309	.542
Kid Nichols	17	361	208	.634
Tim Keefe	14	341	224	.604
Steve Carlton	24	329	244	.574
John Clarkson	12	327	176	.650
Eddie Plank	17	325	193	.627
Don Sutton	24	324	256	.559
Phil Niekro	24	318	274	.537
Gaylord Perry	22	314	265	.542
Tom Seaver	20	311	205	.603
Mickey Welch	13	309	209	.597
Hoss Radbourne	21	308	191	.617
Lefty Grove	20	300	141	.680
Early Wynn	23	300	244	.551

	Years	W	L	Pct
Nolan Ryan**	22	289	263	.523
Tommy John	27	288	231	.555
Robin Roberts	19	286	245	.539
Tony Mullane	14	286	213	.573
Ferguson Jenkins	19	284	226	.557
Jim Kaat	25	283	236	.545
Red Ruffing	22	273	225	.548
Bert Blyleven**	20	271	231	.540
Burleigh Grimes	19	270	212	.560
Jim Palmer	18	268	149	.643

	Years	W	L	Pct
Bob Feller	18	266	162	.621
Eppa Rixey	21	266	251	.515
Gus Weyhing	14	266	229	.537
Jim McCormick	10	264	214	.562
Ted Lyons	21	260	230	.531
Red Faber	20	254	212	.545
Carl Hubbell	16	253	154	.622
Bob Gibson	17	251	174	.591

**Active through 1989.

MAJOR LEAGUE ALL-TIME PITCHING RECORDS

(Through 1989)

Most Games Won—511, Cy Young, Cleveland N.L., 1890–98, St. Louis N.L., 1899–1900, Boston A.L., 1901–08, Cleveland A.L., 1909–11, Boston N.L., 1911.

Most Games Won, Season—60, Hoss Radbourne, Providence N.L., 1884. (Since 1900—41, Jack Chesbro, New York A.L., 1904.)

Most Consecutive Games Won—24, Carl Hubbell, New York N.L., 1936 (16) and 1937 (8).

Most Consecutive Games Won, Season—19, Tim Keefe, New York N.L., 1888; Rube Marquard, New York N.L., 1912.

Most Years Won 20 or More Games—16, Cy Young, Cleveland N.L., 1891–98, St. Louis N.L., 1899–1900, Boston A.L., 1901–04, 1907–08.

Most Shutouts—113, Walter Johnson, Wash. A.L., 1907–27.

Most Shutouts, Season—16, Grover Alexander, Philadelphia N.L., 1916.

Most Consecutive Shutouts—6, Don Drysdale, Los Angeles, N.L., 1968.

Most Consecutive Scoreless Innings—59, Orel Hershiser, Los Angeles Dodgers, 1988.

Most Strikeouts—5,076, Nolan Ryan, New York N.L., California A.L., Houston N.L., 1968–1987 Texas, 1989 (Still active).

Most Strikeouts, Season—505, Matthew Kilroy, Baltimore A.A., 1886. (Since 1900—383, Nolan Ryan, California, A.L., 1973.)

Most Strikeouts, Game—21, Tom Cheney, Washington A.L., 1962, 16 innings. Nine innings: 20, Roger Clemens, Boston, A.L., 1986; 19, Charles McSweeney, Providence N.L., 1884; Hugh Dailey, Chicago U.A., 1884. (Since 1900—19, Steve Carlton, St. Louis N.L. vs. New York, Sept. 15, 1969; Tom Seaver, New York N.L. vs. San Diego, April 22, 1970; Nolan Ryan, California A.L. vs. Boston, Aug. 12, 1974.)

Most Consecutive Strikeouts—10, Tom Seaver, New York N.L. vs. San Diego, April 22, 1970.

Most Games, Season—106, Mike Marshall, Los Angeles, N.L., 1974.

Most Complete Games, Season—74, William White, Cincinnati N.L., 1879. (Since 1900—48, Jack Chesbro, New York A.L., 1904.)

MAJOR LEAGUE INDIVIDUAL ALL-TIME RECORDS

(Through 1989)

Highest Batting Average—442, James O'Neill, St. Louis, A.A., 1887; .438, Hugh Duffy, Boston, N.L., 1894 (Since 1900—.424, Rogers Hornsby, St. Louis, N.L., 1924; .422, Nap Lajoie, Phil., A.L., 1901)

Most Times at Bat—12,364, Henry Aaron, Milwaukee N.L., 1954–65; Atlanta N.L., 1966–74; Milwaukee A.L., 1975–76.

Most Years Batted .300 or Better—23, Ty Cobb, Detroit A.L., 1906–26, Philadelphia A.L., 1927–28.

Most hits—4,256, Pete Rose, Cincinnati 1963–79, Philadelphia 1980–83, Montreal 1984, Cincinnati 1984 (still active)

Most Hits, Season—257, George Sisler, St. Louis A.L., 1920.

Most Hits, Game (9 innings)—7, Wilbert Robinson, Baltimore N.L., 6 singles, 1 double, 1892. Rennie Stennett, Pittsburgh N.L., 4 singles, 2 doubles, 1 triple, 1975.

Most Hits, Game (extra innings)—9, John Burnett, Cleveland A.L., 18 innings, 7 singles, 2 doubles, 1932.

Most Hits in Succession—12, Mike Higgins, Boston A.L., in four games, 1938; Walt Dropo, Detroit A.L., in three games, 1952.

Most Consecutive Games Batted Safely—56, Joe DiMaggio, New York A.L., 1941.

Most Runs—2,244, Ty Cobb, Detroit A.L., 1905–26, Philadelphia A.L., 1927–28.

Most Runs, Season—196, William Hamilton, Philadelphia N.L., 1894. (Since 1900—177, Babe Ruth, New York A.L., 1921.)

Most Runs, Game—7, Guy Hecker, Louisville A.A., 1886. (Since 1900—6, by Mel Ott, New York N.L., 1934, 1944; Johnny Pesky, Boston A.L., 1946; Frank Torre, Milwaukee N.L., 1957.)

Most Runs Batted in—2,297, Henry Aaron, Milwaukee N.L., 1954–1965; Atlanta N.L., 1966–74; Milwaukee A.L., 1975–76.

Most Runs Batted in, Season—190, Hack Wilson, Chicago N.L., 1930.

Most Runs Batted In, Game—12, Jim Bottomley, St. Louis N.L., 1924.

Most Home Runs—755, Henry Aaron, Milwaukee N.L., 1954–1965; Atlanta N.L., 1966–74; Milwaukee A.L., 1975–76.

Most Home Runs, Season—61, Roger Maris, New York A.L., 1961 (162-game season); 60, Babe Ruth, New York A.L., 1927 (154-game season)

Most Home Runs with Bases Filled—23, Lou Gehrig, New York A.L., 1927–39.

Most 2-Base Hits—793, Tris Speaker, Boston A.L., 1907–15, Cleveland A.L., 1916–26, Washington A.L., 1927, Philadelphia A.L., 1928.

Most 2-Base Hits, Season—67, Earl Webb, Boston A.L., 1931.

Most 2-base Hits, Game—4, by many.

Most 3-Base Hits—312, Sam Crawford, Cincinnati N.L., 1899–1902, Detroit A.L., 1903–17.

Most 3-Base Hits, Season—36, Owen Wilson, Pittsburgh N.L., 1912.

Most 3-Base Hits, Game—4, George Strief, Philadelphia A.A., 1885; William Joyce, New York N.L., 1897. (Since 1900—3, by many.)

Most Games Played—3,298, Henry Aaron, Milwaukee N.L., 1954–1965; Atlanta N.L., 1966–74; Milwaukee A.L., 1975–76.

Most Consecutive Games Played—2,130, Lou Gehrig, New York A.L., 1925–39.

Most Bases on Balls—2,056, Babe Ruth, Boston A.L., 1914–19; New York A.L., 1920–34, Boston N.L., 1935.

Most Bases on Balls, Season—170, Babe Ruth, New York A.L., 1923.

Most bases on Balls, Game—6, Jimmy Foxx, Boston A.L., 1938.

Most Strikeouts, Season—189, Bobby Bonds, San Francisco N.L., 1970.

Most Strikeouts, Game (9 innings)—5, by many.

Most Strikeouts, Game (extra innings)—6, Carl Weilman, St. Louis A.L., 15 innings, 1913; Don Hoak, Chicago N.L., 17 innings, 1956; Fred Reichardt, California A.L., 17, innings, 1966; Billy Cowan, California A.L., 20, 1971; Cecil Cooper, Boston A.L., 15, 1974.

Most pinch—hits, lifetime—150, Manny Mota, S.F., 1962; Pitt., 1963–68; Montreal, 1969; L.A., 1969–80, N.L.

Most Pinch-hits, season—25, Jose Morales, Montreal N.L., 1976.

Most consecutive pinch-hits—9, Dave Philley, Phil., N.L., 1958 (8), 1959 (1).

Most pinch-hit home runs, lifetime—18, Gerald Lynch, Pitt.-Cin. N.L., 1957–66.

Most pinch-hit home runs, season—6, Johnny Frederick, Brooklyn, N.L., 1932.

Most stolen bases, lifetime (since 1900)—938, Lou Brock, Chicago N.L. 1961–64; St. Louis, N.L. 1964–79.

Most stolen bases, season—156, Harry Stovey, Phil., A.A., 1888. Since 1900: 130, Rickey Henderson, Oak., A.L., 1982; 118, Lou Brock, St. Lou., 1974.

Most stolen bases, game—7, George Gore, Chicago N.L. 1881; William Hamilton, Philadelphia N.L. 1894. (Since 1900—6, Eddie Collins, Philadelphia A.L., 1912.)

Most time stealing home, lifetime—35, Ty Cobb, Detroit-Phil. A.L., 1905–28.

MAJOR LEAGUE ATTENDANCE RECORDS

(Through 1989)

Single game—78,672, San Francisco at Los Angeles (N.L.), April 18, 1958. (At Memorial Coliseum.)

Doubleheader—84,587, New York at Cleveland (A.L.), Sept. 12, 1954.

Night—78,382, Chicago at Cleveland (A.L.), Aug. 20, 1948.

Season, home—3,608,881, Los Angeles (N.L.), 1982.

Season, road—2,461,240, New York (A.L.), 1980.

Season, league—29,848,782, American League, 1989.

Season, both leagues—55,174,745, 1989.

World Series, single game—92,706, Chicago (A.L.) at Los Angeles (N.L.), Oct. 6, 1959.

World Series, all games (6)—420,784, Chicago (A.L.) and Los Angeles (N.L.), 1959.

MOST HOME RUNS IN ONE SEASON

(45 or More)

HR	Player/Team	Year	HR	Player/Team	Year
61	Roger Maris, New York (AL)	1961	48	Jimmy Foxx, Philadelphia (AL)	1933
60	Babe Ruth, New York (AL)	1927	48	Harmon Killebrew, Minnesota (AL)	1962
59	Babe Ruth, New York (AL)	1921	48	Willie Stargell, Pittsburgh (NL)	1971
58	Jimmy Foxx, Philadelphia (AL)	1932	48	Dave Kingman, Chicago (NL)	1979
58	Hank Greenberg, Detroit (AL)	1938	48	Mike Schmidt, Philadelphia (NL)	1980
56	Hack Wilson, Chicago (NL)	1930	47	Babe Ruth, New York (AL)	1926
54	Babe Ruth, New York (AL)	1920	47	Ralph Kiner, Pittsburgh (NL)	1950
54	Babe Ruth, New York (AL)	1928	47	Ed Mathews, Milwaukee (NL)	1953
54	Ralph Kiner, Pittsburgh (NL)	1949	47	Ernie Banks, Chicago (NL)	1958
54	Mickey Mantle, New York (AL)	1961	47	Willie Mays, San Francisco (NL)	1964
52	Mickey Mantle, New York (AL)	1956	47	Henry Aaron, Atlanta (NL)	1971
52	Willie Mays, San Francisco (NL)	1965	47	Reggie Jackson, Oakland (AL)	1969
52	George Foster, Cincinnati (NL)	1977	47	George Bell, Toronto (AL)	1987
51	Ralph Kiner, Pittsburgh (NL)	1947	47	Kevin Mitchell, San Francisco (NL)	1989
51	John Mize, New York (NL)	1947	46	Babe Ruth, New York (AL)	1924
51	Willie Mays, New York (NL)	1955	46	Babe Ruth, New York, (AL)	1929
50	Jimmy Foxx, Boston (AL)	1938	46	Babe Ruth, New York (AL)	1931
49	Babe Ruth, New York (AL)	1930	46	Lou Gehrig, New York (AL)	1931
49	Lou Gehrig, New York (AL)	1934	46	Joe DiMaggio, New York (AL)	1937
49	Lou Gehrig, New York (AL)	1936	46	Ed Mathews, Milwaukee (NL)	1959
49	Ted Kluszewski, Cincinnati (NL)	1954	46	Orlando Cepeda, San Francisco (NL)	1961
49	Willie Mays, San Francisco (NL)	1962	46	Jim Rice, Boston (AL)	1978
49	Harmon Killebrew, Minnesota (AL)	1964	45	Harmon Killebrew, Minnesota (AL)	1963
49	Frank Robinson, Baltimore (AL)	1966	45	Willie McCovey, San Francisco (NL)	1969
49	Harmon Killebrew, Minnesota (AL)	1969	45	Johnny Bench, Cincinnati (NL)	1970
49	Mark McGwire, Oakland (AL)	1987	45	Gorman Thomas, Milwaukee (AL)	1979
49	Andre Dawson, Chicago (NL)	1987	45	Henry Aaron, Milwaukee (NL)	1962

MAJOR LEAGUE BASEBALL EXPANDS PLAYOFFS TO BEST 4-OF-7

After 16 years of five-game league championship playoffs, baseball expanded to a seven-game format in 1985 for the purpose of reaping a reported additional $9 million in network television revenue.

An agreement was reached between management and players to expand the series for 1985. The decision immediately increased baseball's revenue from $20 to $29 million for the playoffs.

The formula for splitting that money was part of the agreement with the players which settled the Aug. 6–8 major league players strike.

The playoffs had been a best 3-of-5 affair since 1969, when divisional play was first initiated. The World-Series remained a best 4-of-7 format.

STANDARD MEASUREMENTS IN SPORTS

BASEBALL

Home plate to pitcher's box: 60 feet 6 inches.
Plate to second base: 127 feet 3 3/8 inches.
Distance from base to base (home plate included): 90 feet.
Size of bases: 15 inches by 15 inches.
Pitcher's plate: 24 inches by 6 inches.
Batter's box: 4 feet by 6 feet.
Home plate: 17 inches by 12 inches by 12 inches, cut to a point at rear.
Home plate to backstop: Not less than 60 feet (recommended).
Weight of ball: Not less than 5 ounces nor more than 5 1/4 ounces.
Circumference of ball: Not less than 9 inches nor more than 9 1/4 inches.
Bat: Must be round, not over 2 3/4 inches in diameter at thickest part, nor more than 42 inches in length, and of solid wood in one piece or laminated wood.

BASKETBALL

(National Collegiate A.A. Men's Rules)

Playing court: College: 94 feet long by 50 feet wide (ideal dimensions). High School: 84 feet long by 50 feet wide (ideal inside dimensions).
Baskets: Rings 18 inches in inside diameter, with white cord 12-mesh nets, 15 to 18 inches in length. Each ring is made of metal, is not more than 5/8 of an inch in diameter, and is bright orange in color.
Height of basket: 10 feet (upper edge).
Weight of ball: Not less than 20 ounces nor more than 22.
Circumference of ball: No greater than 30 inches and not less than 29 1/2.
Free-throw line: 15 feet from the face of the backboard, 2 inches wide.
Three-point field goal line: 19 feet, 9 inches from the face of the backboard. In the National Basketball Association, the distance is 23 feet.

BOWLING

Lane dimensions: Overall length 62 feet 10 3/16 inches, measuring from foul line to pit (not including tail plank), with + or − 1/2 inch tolerance permitted. Foul line to center of No. 1 pinspot 60 feet, with + or − 1/2 inch tolerance permitted. Lane width, 41 1/2 inches with a tolerance of + or − 1/2 inch permitted. Approach, not less than 15 feet. Gutters, 9 5/16 inches wide with plus 3/16 or minus 5/16 tolerances permitted.
Ball: Circumference, not more than 27.002 inches. Weight, 16 pounds maximum.

BOXING

Ring: Professional matches take place in an area not less than 18 nor more than 24 feet square including apron. It is enclosed by four covered ropes, each not less than one inch in diameter. The floor has a 2-inch padding of Ensolite (or equivalent) underneath ring cover that extends at least 6 inches beyond the roped area in the case of elevated rings. For USA/ABF or amateur boxing, not less than 16 nor more than 20 feet square within the ropes. The floor must extend beyond the ring ropes not less than 2 feet. The ring posts shall be connected to the four ring ropes with the extension not shorter than 18 inches and must be properly padded.
Gloves: In professional fights, not less than 8-ounce gloves generally are used. USA/ABF, 10 ounces for 106 pounds through 156 pounds; 12-ounce for 165 pounds through +201 pounds; for international competition, 8 ounces for lighter classes, 10 ounces for heavier divisions.
Headguards: Mandatory in amateur boxing.

FOOTBALL

(N.C.A.A.)

Length of field: 120 yards. (including 10 yards of end zone at each end).
Width of field: 53 1/3 yards (160 feet).
Height of goal posts: At least 30 feet.
Height of crossbar: 10 feet.
Width of goal posts (above crossbar): 23 feet 4 inches, inside to inside, and not more than 24 feet, outside to outside.
Length of ball: 10 7/8 to 11 7/16 inches (long axis).
Circumference of ball: 20 3/4 to 21 1/4 inches (middle); 27 3/4 to 28 1/2 inches (long axis).

GOLF

The ball, specifications: Broadened to require that the ball be designed to perform as if it were spherically symmetrical. The weight of the ball shall not be greater than 1.620 ounces avoirdupois, and the size shall be not less than 1.680 inches in diameter.
Velocity of ball: Not greater than 250 feet per second when tested on U.S.G.A. apparatus, with 2 percent tolerance.
Hole: 4 1/4 inches in diameter and at least 4 inches deep.
Clubs: 14 is the maximum number permitted.
Overall distance standard: A brand of ball shall not exceed a distance of 280 yards plus 6% when tested on USGA apparatus under specified conditions, on an outdoor range at USGA Headquarters.

HOCKEY

Size of rink: 200 feet long by 85 feet wide surrounded by a wooden wall not less than 40 inches and not more than 48 inches above level of ice.
Size of goal: 6 feet wide by 4 feet in height.
Puck: 1 inch thick and 3 inches in diameter, made of vulcanized rubber; weight 5 1/2 to 6 ounces.
Length of stick: Not more than 60 inches from heel to end of shaft nor 12 1/2 inches from heel to end of blade. Blade should not be more than 3 inches in width but not less than 2 inches, except goal keeper's stick, which shall not exceed 3 1/2 inches in width except at the heel, where it must not exceed 4 1/2 inches nor shall the goalkeeper's stick exceed 15 1/2 inches from the heel to the end of the blade.

TENNIS

Size of court: Rectangle 78 feet long and 27 feet wide (singles); 78 feet long and 36 feet wide (doubles).
Height of net: 3 feet in center, gradually rising to reach 3-foot 6-inch posts at a point 3 feet outside each side of court.
Ball: Shall be more than 2 1/2 inches and less than 2 5/8 inches in diameter and weigh more than 2 ounces and less than 2 1/16 ounces.
Service line: 21 feet from net.

BOXING—AMATEUR

NATIONAL GOLDEN GLOVES CHAMPIONSHIPS—1989

(May 8-13, 1989, Knoxville, Tenn)

106 lb—Eric Griffin, Houston, Texas
112 lb—Sandtanner Lewis, Miami, Fla.
119 lb—John West, Nashville, Tenn.
125 lb—Oscar De Lahoya, Los Angeles, Calif.
132 lb—Tonga McClaine, Racine, Wis.
139 lb—Victor McKinnis, Fort Carson, Colo.
147 lb—Jesse Lucero, Camp Lejeune, N.C.
156 lb—Mario Munoz, Denver, Colo.
165 lb—Ray Lathon, St. Louis, Mo.
178 lb—Terry McGroom, Chicago, Ill.
201 lb—Boris Powell, St. Louis, Mo.
Over 201 lb—Larry Donald, Cincinnati

MAJOR LEAGUE BASEBALL—1989

AMERICAN LEAGUE
(Final Standing—1989)

EASTERN DIVISION

Team	W	L	Pct	GB
Toronto Blue Jays	89	73	.549	—
Baltimore Orioles	87	75	.537	2
Boston Red Sox	83	79	.512	6
Milwaukee Brewers	81	81	.500	8
New York Yankees	74	87	.460	14 1/2
Cleveland Indians	73	89	.451	16
Detroit Tigers	59	103	.364	30

WESTERN DIVISION

Team	W	L	Pct	GB
Oakland Athletics	99	63	.611	—
Kansas City Royals	92	70	.568	7
California Angels	91	71	.562	8
Texas Rangers	83	79	.512	16
Minnesota Twins	80	82	.494	19
Seattle Mariners	73	89	.451	26
Chicago White Sox	69	92	.429	29 1/2

AMERICAN LEAGUE LEADERS—1989

Batting—Kirby Puckett, Minnesota	.339
Runs—Wade Boggs, Boston	
Ricky Henderson, N.Y.-Oak, (tie)	113
Hits—Kirby Puckett, Minnesota	215
Runs batted in—Ruben Sierra, Texas	119
Triples—Ruben Sierra, Texas	14
Doubles—Wade Boggs, Boston	51
Home runs—Fred McGriff, Toronto	36
Stolen bases—Ricky Henderson, N.Y.-Oak.	77
Total bases—Ruben Sierra, Texas	344
Slugging percentage—Ruben Sierra, Texas	.543
On-base percentage—Wade Boggs, Boston	.430

Pitching

Victories—Bret Saberhagen, Kansas City	23
Earned run average—Bret Saberhagen	2.16
Strikeouts—Nolan Ryan, Texas	301
Shutouts—Bert Blyleven, California	5
Complete games—Bret Saberhagen, Kansas City	12
Saves—Jeff Russell, Texas	38
Inning pitched—Bret Saberhagen, Kansas City	262 1/3

AMERICAN LEAGUE AVERAGES—1989

Batting—Club

	AB	R	H	HR	RBI	Pct
Boston	5666	774	1571	108	717	.277
Minnesota	5581	740	1542	117	691	.276
Chicago	5505	693	1492	94	661	.271
Yankees	5458	698	1469	130	657	.269
Texas	5458	695	1432	122	653	.262
Oakland	5413	712	1412	127	658	.261
Kansas City	5475	690	1428	101	653	.261
Toronto	5581	731	1449	142	685	.260
Milwaukee	5473	707	1416	126	661	.259
Seattle	5512	694	1417	132	653	.257
California	5544	669	1422	145	624	.256
Baltimore	5438	708	1368	129	659	.252
Cleveland	5463	604	1340	127	567	.245
Detroit	5432	617	1315	116	564	.242

Batting Leaders
(100 or more at bats)

Player/Team	AB	R	H	HR	RBI	Pct
Velarde NY	100	12	34	2	11	.340
Puckett Min	635	75	215	9	85	.339

NATIONAL LEAGUE
(Final Standing—1989)

EASTERN DIVISION

Team	W	L	Pct	GB
Chicago Cubs	93	69	.571	—
New York Mets	87	75	.537	6
St. Louis Cardinals	86	76	.531	7
Montreal Expos	81	81	.500	12
Pittsburgh Pirates	74	88	.457	19
Philadelphia Phillies	67	95	.414	26

WESTERN DIVISION

Team	W	L	Pct	GB
San Francisco Giants	92	70	.568	—
San Diego Padres	89	73	.549	3
Houston Astros	86	76	.531	6
Los Angeles Dodgers	77	83	.481	14
Cincinnati Reds	75	87	.463	17
Atlanta Braves	63	97	.394	28

NATIONAL LEAGUE LEADERS—1989

Batting—Tony Gwynn, San Diego	.336
Runs—Howard Johnson, New York	
Will Clark, San Francisco	
Ryne Sandberg, Chicago (tie)	104
Hits—Tony Gwynn, San Diego	203
Runs batted in—Kevin Mitchell, San Francisco	125
Triples—Robbie Thompson, San Francisco	11
Doubles—Pedro Guerrero, St. Louis	
Tim Wallach, Montreal (tie)	42
Home Runs—Kevin Mitchell, San Francisco	47
Stolen bases—Vince Coleman, St. Louis	65
Total bases—Kevin Mitchell, San Francisco	345
Slugging percentage—Kevin Mitchell, San Francisco	.635
On-base percentage—Lonnie Smith, Atlanta	.415

Pitching

Victories—Mike Scott, Houston	20
Earned run average—Scott Garrelts, San Francisco	2.28
Strikeouts—Jose DeLeon, St. Louis	201
Shutouts—Tim Belcher, Los Angeles	8
Complete games—Tim Belcher, Los Angeles	10
Saves—Mark Davis, San Diego	44
Innings pitched—Orel Hershiser, Los Angeles	256 2/3

Lansford Oak	551	81	185	2	52	.336
Boggs Bsn	621	113	205	3	54	.330
Harper Min	385	43	125	8	57	.325
Yount Mil	614	101	195	21	103	.318
Dwyer Min	225	34	71	3	23	.316
Franco Tex	548	80	173	13	92	.316
Sax NY	651	88	206	5	63	.316
Molitor Mil	615	84	194	11	56	.315
Baines Tex	505	73	156	16	72	.309
Greenwell Bsn	578	87	178	14	95	.308
James Cle	245	26	75	4	29	.306
Sierra Tex	634	101	194	29	119	.306
ADavis Sea	498	84	152	21	95	.305
Petralli Tex	184	18	56	4	23	.304
Burks Bsn	399	73	121	12	61	.303
Mtngly NY	631	79	191	23	113	.303
Daughrty Tex	106	15	32	1	10	.302
Kelly NY	441	65	133	9	48	.302
Kittle Chi	169	26	51	11	37	.302
CMartinez Chi	350	44	105	5	32	.300
Heep Bsn	320	36	96	5	49	.300
LJohnson Chi	180	28	54	0	16	.300
Polonia NY	433	70	130	3	46	.300

Reynolds Sea	613	87	184	0	43	.300
Browne Cle	598	83	179	5	45	.299
MWilson Tor	238	32	71	2	17	298

Leading Pitchers
(4 or more decisions)

Player/Club	IP	H	BB	SO	W	L	ERA
Montgmry KC	92	66	25	93	7	3	1.37
McClure Cal	52	39	15	36	6	1	1.55
Eckersley Oak	58	32	3	55	4	0	1.56
Olsen Blt	85	57	46	90	5	2	1.69
Dubois Det	36	29	17	13	0	4	1.75
Henke Tor	89	66	25	116	8	3	1.92
Russell Tex	73	45	24	77	6	4	1.98
Orosco Cle	78	54	26	79	3	4	2.08
Sabrhgn KC	262	209	43	193	23	6	2.16
Minton Cal	90	76	37	42	4	3	2.20
Burns Oak	96	66	28	49	6	5	2.24
Lamp Bsn	112	96	27	61	4	2	2.32
DJones Cle	81	76	13	65	7	10	2.34
Hncytt Oak	77	56	26	52	2	2	2.35
Plesac Mil	61	47	17	52	3	4	2.35
BJones Chi	30	22	8	17	3	2	2.37
Wells Tor	86	66	28	78	7	4	2.40
Gtrmn NY	103	98	26	51	5	5	2.45
CFinley Cal	200	171	82	156	16	9	2.57
GrHarris Bsn	28	21	15	25	2	2	2.57
Moore Oak	242	193	83	172	19	11	2.61
Blyleven Cal	241	225	44	131	17	5	2.73
Murphy Bsn	105	97	41	107	5	7	2.74
Schooler Sea	77	81	19	69	1	7	2.81
Tibbs Blt	54	62	20	30	5	0	2.82

Pitching—Club

	ERA	H	ER	BB	SO	ShO	SA
Oakland	3.13	1287	504	511	930	20	57
Calif.	3.28	1384	530	465	894	20	38
K.C.	3.55	1414	573	455	976	13	38
Toronto	3.59	1409	585	478	848	12	38
Cleve.	3.64	1423	588	453	843	13	38
Milw.	3.80	1461	605	457	812	8	45
Texas	3.95	1278	629	654	1110	7	44
Boston	4.01	1448	651	548	1053	9	43
Seattle	4.01	1421	641	560	895	10	44
Balt.	4.01	1518	646	486	675	7	44
Chicago	4.26	1472	673	539	778	5	46
Minn.	4.28	1495	680	500	849	8	38
Detroit	4.54	1514	720	652	829	4	26
N.Y.	4.54	1549	714	521	787	9	44

NATIONAL LEAGUE AVERAGES—1989
Batting—Club

	AB	R	H	HR	RBI	Pct
Chicago	5513	702	1438	124	653	.261
StLouis	5491	632	1418	73	587	.258
San Diego	5422	642	1360	120	598	.251
S.F.	5469	699	1362	141	648	.249
Montreal	5483	632	1352	99	588	.247
Cincinnati	5520	632	1362	128	588	.247
New York	5489	632	1351	147	633	.246
Philadelphia	5447	629	1323	122	593	.243
Pittsburgh	5539	637	1333	95	582	.241
Los Angeles	5464	554	1313	89	513	.240
Houston	5516	647	1316	97	599	.239
Atlanta	5463	584	1281	128	544	.234

Batting Leaders
(100 or more at bats)

Player/Team	AB	R	H	HR	RBI	Pct
Larkin Cin	325	47	111	4	36	.342

TGwynn SD	604	82	203	4	62	.336
WClark SF	588	104	196	23	111	.333
DwSmith Chi	343	52	111	9	52	.324
LVlliere Pit	190	15	60	2	23	.316
LSmith Atl	482	89	152	21	79	.315
Grace Chi	510	74	160	13	79	.314
Guerrero StL	570	60	177	17	117	.311
Carreon Mets	133	20	41	6	16	.308
OMcDll Atl	280	56	864	7	24	.307
Roberts SD	329	81	99	3	25	.301
Bass Htn	313	426	94	5	44	.300
Kruk Phi	357	52	107	8	44	.300
MHatcher LA	224	18	66	2	25	.295
RAlomar SD	623	82	184	7	56	.295
Walton Chi	475	64	139	5	46	.293
KMitchell SF	543	100	158	47	125	.291
Oquendo StL	556	59	162	1	48	.291
Sasser Mets	182	17	53	1	22	.291
Stubbs LA	103	11	30	4	14	.291
MThmpsn StL	545	60	158	4	68	.290
Sandberg Chi	606	104	176	30	76	.290
Trevino Htn	131	15	38	2	16	.290
HJhnsn Mets	571	104	164	36	101	.287
Herr Phi	561	65	161	2	37	.287

Leading Pitchers
(4 or more decisions)

Player/Team	IP	H	BB	SO	W	L	ERA
Lancaster Chi	73	60	15	56	4	2	1.36
Andersen Htn	88	63	24	85	4	4	1.54
JHowell LA	80	60	22	55	5	3	1.58
Landrum Pit	81	60	28	51	2	3	1.67
MaDavis SD	93	66	31	92	4	3	1.85
RMcDwll Phi	92	79	33	47	4	8	1.96
Dibble Cin	99	62	39	141	10	5	2.09
Combs Phi	39	36	6	30	4	0	2.09
APena LA	76	62	18	75	4	3	2.13
Bair Pit	67	52	28	56	2	3	2.27
Garrelts SF	193	149	46	119	14	5	2.28
Hershiser LA	257	226	77	178	15	15	2.31
Aguilera Mets	69	59	21	79	6	6	2.34
Myers Mets	84	62	40	88	7	4	2.35
Darwin Htn	122	92	33	64	11	4	2.36
Langston Mon	177	138	93	175	12	9	2.39
DiPino StL	88	73	20	44	9	0	2.45
Morgan LA	153	130	33	72	8	11	2.53
Burke Mon	85	68	22	54	9	3	2.55
GHarris SD	135	106	52	106	8	9	2.60
DaSmith Htn	58	49	19	31	3	4	2.64
Quisnbry StL	78	78	14	37	3	1	2.64
Whitson SD	227	198	48	117	16	11	2.66
Acker Atl	98	84	20	67	0	6	2.67
Hurst SD	245	214	66	179	15	11	2.69

Pitching—Club

	ERA	H	ER	BB	SO	ShO	SA
L.A.	2.94	1278	478	504	1051	19	36
S.F.	3.30	1320	534	471	800	16	47
New York	3.30	1260	533	532	1105	12	38
StLouis	3.36	1328	546	482	844	17	44
S.D.	3.40	1359	551	481	932	11	52
Chicago	3.44	1369	558	533	917	10	55
Montreal	3.48	1344	568	519	1058	13	35
Houston	3.63	1379	597	551	964	12	38
Pitt.	3.64	1392	602	539	825	8	40
Atlanta	3.71	1369	596	468	962	8	33
Cinn.	3.75	1403	610	559	981	9	38
Phila.	4.08	1408	650	613	899	10	33

MAJOR LEAGUE BASEBALL—1989

AMERICAN LEAGUE PLAYOFFS—1989

1st game, Oakland, Calif., Oct. 3, 1989

Toronto	020	100	000	— 3	5	1
Oakland	010	013	02x	— 7	11	0

Stieb, Acker, Ward; Stewart, Eckersley.
Winner: Stewart. Loser: Stieb. Attendance: 49,435.

2nd game, Oakland, Calif., Oct. 4, 1989

Toronto	001	000	020	— 3	5	1
Oakland	000	203	10x	— 6	9	1

Stottlemyre, Ackers, Wells, Henke, Cerutti; Moore, Honeycutt, Eckersley.
Winner: Moore. Loser: Stottlemyre. Attendance: 49,444.

3rd game, Toronto, Canada, Oct. 6, 1989

Oakland	101	100	000	— 3	8	1
Toronto	000	400	30x	— 7	8	0

Davis, Honeycutt, Nelson, M. Young; Key, Acker, Henke.
Winner: Key. Loser: Davis. Attendance: 50,268.

4th game, Toronto, Canada, Oct. 7, 1989

Oakland	003	020	100	— 6	11	1
Toronto	000	101	120	— 5	13	0

Welch, Honeycutt, Eckersley; Flanagan, Ward, Cerutti, Acker.
Winner: Welch. Loser: Flanagan. Attendance: 50,076.

5th game, Toronto, Canada, Oct. 8, 1989

Oakland	101	000	200	— 4	4	0
Toronto	000	000	012	— 3	9	0

Stewart, Eckersley; Stieb, Acker, Henke.
Winner: Stewart. Loser: Stieb. Attendance: 50,027.

Oakland wins series, 4 games to 1.

NATIONAL LEAGUE PLAYOFFS—1989

1st game, Chicago, Ill., Oct. 4, 1989

San Francisco	301	400	030	— 11	13	0
Chicago	201	000	000	— 3	10	1

Garrelts, Brantley, Hammaker; Maddux, Kilgus, Wilson.
Winner: Garrelts. Loser: Maddux. Attendance: 39,195.

2nd game, Chicago, Ill., Oct. 5, 1989

San Francisco	000	200	021	— 5	10	0
Chicago	600	003	00x	— 9	11	0

Reuschel, Downs, Lefferts, Brantley, Bedrosian; Bielecki, Assenmacher, Lancaster.
Winner: Lancaster. Loser: Reuschel. Attendance: 39,195.

3rd game, San Francisco, Calif., Oct. 7, 1989

Chicago	200	100	100	— 4	10	0
San Francisco	300	000	20x	— 5	8	3

Sutcliffe, Assenmacher, Lancaster; LaCoss, Brantley, Robinson, Lefferts, Bedrosian.
Winner: Robinson. Loser: Lancaster. Attendance: 62,065.

4th game, San Francisco, Calif., Oct. 8, 1989

Chicago	110	020	000	— 4	12	1
San Francisco	102	120	00x	— 6	9	1

Maddux, Wilson, Sanderson, M. Williams; Garrelts, Downs, Bedrosian.
Winner: Downs. Loser: Wilson. Attendance: 62,078.

5th game, San Francisco, Calif., Oct. 9, 1989

Chicago	001	000	001	— 2	10	1
San Francisco	000	000	12x	— 3	4	1

Bielecki, M. Williams, Lancaster; Reuschel, Bedrosian.
Winner: Reuschel. Loser: Bielecki. Attendance: 62,084.

San Francisco wins series, 4 games to 1.

PETE ROSE, BASEBALL'S ALL-TIME HIT LEADER, BANNED FOR GAMBLING

Pete Rose, who broke Ty Cobb's all-time major league hit record in 1985 and retired with a record number of 4,256, was banned from the game of baseball by Commissioner A. Bartlett Giamatti for gambling.

The banning, announced on Thursday, August 24, was made with the stipulation that it was a lifetime ban, but that Rose would be able to reapply for admission one year later.

Giamatti, who died suddenly of a heart problem just eight days later, said at the banning announcement press conference: "I conclude that he bet on baseball." Rose has always denied betting on baseball, but has admitted betting on other sports, including college football and basketball and pro football.

"Obviously, I made mistakes," Rose said. "But one of my mistakes was not betting on baseball."

Rose and Giamatti reached the agreement to end a long legal battle that had cast a shadow over baseball for nearly two seasons. Rose, manager of the Cincinnati Reds at the time of the banning, continued to have legal troubles outside of baseball. The Internal Revenue Service was investigating his tax records, particularly money earned at numerous baseball memorabilia shows. And, Rose was named in gambling cases involving reputed bookies and gamblers.

Tommy Helms was named interim manager to replace Rose on August 25. He was not likely to be offered Rose's job on a permanent basis.

The scandal overshadowed the record Rose compiled on the field in 24 seasons as a player, and some argued that despite his many records, he should not be elected into the Baseball Hall of Fame when he becomes eligible in 1992. The voting is done by members of the Baseball Writers Association of America.

Among the records Rose holds are most games (3,562), most at-bats (14,053), most singles (3,215), only player to play more than 500 games at five different positions (first base, second base, third base, left field, right field), Most years played in the National League (24), longest National League hitting streak (44 games, June 14-July 31, 1978), and most National League hitting streaks of 20 games or more (7).

He was National League Rookie of the Year in 1963, Most Valuable Player in the National League in 1973, the World Series Most Valuable Player with the Cincinnati Reds in 1975, and led the National League in batting three times—1968, 1969, and 1973. He was named to the National League All-Star team 17 times.

WORLD SERIES—1989
Oakland Athletics (A) vs. San Francisco Giants (N)

World Series postponed due to northern California earthquake on October 17. Game 3 was rescheduled for October 27 after *Information Please Almanac* went to press.

1st Game—Oakland, Oct. 14

SAN FRANCISCO (N)	AB	R	H	BI	OAKLAND (A)	AB	R	H	BI
Butler, cf	4	0	0	0	R. Henderson, lf	5	0	2	1
Thompson, 2b	4	0	0	0	Lansford, 3b	5	0	1	0
Clark, 1b	4	0	2	0	Gallego, 2b	0	0	0	0
Mitchell, lf	4	0	2	0	Canseco, rf	3	0	0	0
Williams, 3b	4	0	0	0	Parker, dh	4	1	1	1
Riles, dh	4	0	0	0	D. Henderson, cf	3	1	0	0
Maldonado, rf	4	0	0	0	McGwire, 1b	4	0	3	0
Kennedy, c	3	0	0	0	Steinbach, c	4	1	1	0
Uribe, ss	2	0	1	0	Phillips, 2b	4	1	2	1
Oberkfell, 3b	0	0	0	0	Weiss, ss	4	1	1	1
Totals	33	0	5	0	Totals	36	5	11	4

San Francisco 000 000 000 — 0
Oakland 031 100 00x — 5

E—Stewart, Kennedy. LOB—San Francisco 7, Oakland 9. 2B—Clark. HR—Parker (1), Weiss (1).

San Francisco	IP	H	R	ER	BB	SO
Garrells L, 0-1	4	7	5	4	1	5
Hammaker	1 2-3	3	0	0	0	2
Brantley	1 1-3	1	0	0	1	0
LaCoss	1	0	0	0	0	1
Oakland						
Stewart W, 1-0	9	5	0	0	1	6

PB—Steinbach. Time of Game—2:45. Attendance—49,385.

HENDERSON OF A'S SETS STOLEN-BASES RECORD

Rickey Henderson of the Oakland A's broke the major league record for stolen bases in one season on Aug. 27, 1982, at Milwaukee when he stole his 119th base in the third inning. The previous record of 118 was held by Lou Brock of St. Louis and was set in 1974. Henderson had broken the American League stolen-bases mark in 1980 when he surpassed Ty Cobb's record of 96, set in 1915. Henderson finished the 1980 season with 100 stolen bases. In 1982 he completed the season with 130. The major league record for career stolen bases is held by Brock with 938.

Cheating Becomes an Issue

Three major league baseball players were suspended for cheating incidents during the 1987 season. Minnesota Twins pitcher Joe Niekro and Philadelphia Phillies pitcher Kevin Gross both were issued 10-day suspensions for having an emery board and sandpaper, respectively, which could be used to doctor the baseball. In addition, Houston Astros outfielder Billy Hatcher was suspended for 10 days when a bat he was using broke and revealed illegal cork inside.

While those three were the only players actually caught, cheating was a major league-wide issue in 1987, prompting Commissioner Peter Ueberroth in institute a rule allowing each manager to check one opposing hitter's bat per game.

2nd Game—Oakland, Oct. 15

SAN FRANCISCO (N)	AB	R	H	BI	OAKLAND (A)	AB	R	H	BI
Butler, cf	2	0	1	0	R. Henderson, lf	3	1	3	0
Thompson, 2b	3	0	0	1	Lansford, 3b	3	0	1	1
Clark, 1b	4	0	0	0	Canseco, rf	2	1	0	0
Mitchell, lf	4	0	1	0	Parker, dh	4	1	1	1
Williams, 3b	4	0	0	0	D. Henderson, cf	3	1	0	0
Riles, dh	3	0	0	0	McGwire, 1b	4	0	1	0
Maldonado, rf	3	0	0	0	Steinbach, c	4	1	1	3
Kennedy, c	3	0	1	0	Phillips, 2b	3	0	0	0
Uribe, ss	2	1	0	0	Weiss, ss	3	0	0	0
Oberkfell 3b	1	0	1	0					
Totals	29	1	4	1	Totals	29	5	7	5

San Francisco 001 000 000 — 1
Oakland 100 400 00x — 5

DP—San Francisco 2, Oakland 1. LOB—San Francisco 4, Oakland 5. 2B—Lansford, Parker, McGwire. 3B—R. Henderson. HR—Steinbach (1). SB—R. Henderson (1), Butler 2 (2). SF—Thompson.

San Francisco	IP	H	R	ER	BB	SO
Reuschel L, 0-1	4	5	5	5	4	2
Downs	2	1	0	0	0	2
Lefferts	1	1	0	0	1	1
Bedrosian	1	0	0	0	0	2
Oakland						
Moore W, 1-0	7	4	1	1	2	7
Honeycutt	1 1-3	0	0	0	0	1
Eckersley	2-3	0	0	0	0	0

Reuschel pitched to 2 batters in the 5th, Moore pitched to 1 batter in the 8th. WP—Moore 2. Time of Game—2:47. Attendance—49,388.

NOLAN RYAN BREAKS 5,000 STRIKEOUT MARK

Strikeout No. 5,000, as so many of the other 4,999 had before, came on a blazing fastball past Oakland Athletics outfielder Ricky Henderson on Tuesday night, Aug. 22, 1989, in Arlington, Texas.

Ryan, who had broken the 4,000 strikout barrier for the first time in baseball history in 1985 (Danny Heep of the New York Mets was the victim then), was pitching for the Texas Rangers—his first year with that team.

Ryan first came into the Major Leagues with the New York Mets in 1966. He subsequently pitched for the California Angels and Houston Astros before signing with the Rangers as a free agent before the start of the 1989 season.

Ryan, who turns 43 in January 1990, announced in October that he would return for his 23rd year next season. In 1989 he went 16-10 with a league-leading 301 strikouts. The previous season he had led the National League in strikeouts with 228.

Ryan also holds the record for most strikeouts in a season at 383, and has hurled five no-hitters. Five times during the 1989 season he took no-hitters into the seventh inning.

Florence Griffith Joyner Retires From Track

Shortly after winning the Jesse Owens International Trophy as the outstanding performer in track and field for 1988, Florence Griffith Joyner announced she was retiring from active competition.

Joyner, who turned 29 in 1989, set the women's world record for the 100 meters (10.49 seconds) and the 200 meters (21.34 seconds) and won three gold medals and a silver at the 1988 Summer Olympics in Seoul, South Korea.

Joyner said she would retire to pursue a career in acting and writing.

1,000 Stakes Race Victories for Shoemaker, Who Announces Retirement at End of 1989

Jockey Bill Shoemaker, who rode his first stakes race winning horse on Oct. 26, 1949, became the first jockey ever to ride 1,000 stakes winners in a career in 1989.

The 1000th win came aboard Peace, a 39-1 shot, by one length in the $110,700 Premiere Handicap at Hollywood Park, California.

Shoemaker, 58, also announced his retirement after 40 years as a jockey. He is the winningest jockey in the history of horse racing.

Ben Johnson Admits Steroid Use, Stripped of Records

Ben Johnson, who was clocked at 9.79 seconds for the fastest 100-meter race in history in the Summer Olympics in Seoul, South Korea, in September 1988, but was stripped of the gold medal in the event when he tested positive for the steroid stanozolol, was also stripped of all of his world records by the International Amateur Athletic Federation in September 1989.

Johnson lost his record of 9.83 seconds in the 100-meters, set at the 1987 World Championships of Track & Field in Rome. He was also stripped of the 60-meter mark he set at Indianapolis of 6.41 seconds in 1987.

Those records now belong to Carl Lewis (9.92 seconds) and Lee McRae (6.5 seconds), respectively.

Johnson was also banned from competition for two years by the International Amateur Athletic Federation.

INDIVIDUAL WORLD SHOOTING RECORDS

(as ratified by the International Shooting Union)
Max-Score

Free Rifle	300m	3 × 40 shots	1200-1166	Malcolm Cooper (GB)	Zurich, Switz, 1987
		60 shots prone	600-599	Malcolm Cooper (GB)	Skouder, Sweden, 1986
Standard Rifle	300m	3 × 20 shots	600-583	Malcolm Cooper (GB)	Zurich, Switz, 1985
Small-Bore Rifle	50m	3 × 40 shots	1200-1183	Peter Kurká (Czech)	Seoul, Korea, 1987
	50m	60 shots prone	600-600	Alistair Allan (GB)	Titograd, Yugo, 1981
			600	Ernest Van de Zande (US)	Rio de Janeiro, 1981
			600	Kiril Ivanov (USSR)	Mexico City, 1987
Free Pistol	50m	60 shots	600-581	Aleksandr Melentev (USSR)	Moscow, 1980
Rapid-Fire Pistol	25m	60 shots	600-599	Igor Puzyrev (USSR)	Titograd, Yugo, 1981
Center-Fire Pistol	25m	60 shots	600-597	Thomas D. Smith (US)	São Paulo, Brazil, 1963
Standard Pistol	25m	60 shots	600-584	Eric Buijong (US)	Caracas, Venez, 1983
Running Game Target	50m	60 shots "normal runs"	600-595	Igor Sokolov (USSR)	Miskulc, Hungary, 1981
Olympic Trap	—	200 birds	200-200	Danny Carlisle (US)	Caracas, Venez, 1983
Olympic Skeet	—	200 birds	200-200	Matthew Dryke (US)	São Paulo, Brazil, 1981
			200	Jan Hula (Czech)	Zaragossa, Spain, 1984
Air Rifle	10m	60 shots	600-596	Jean-Pierre Amat (France)	Zurich, Switz, 1987
Air Pistol	10m	60 shots	600-591	Vladas Tourla (USSR)	Caracas, Venez, 1983

CHESS

WORLD CHAMPIONS

1894–1921	Emanuel Lasker, Germany
1921–27	Jose R. Capablanca, Cuba
1927–35	Alexander A. Alekhine, U.S.S.R.
1935–37	Dr. Max Euwe, Netherlands
1937–46	Alexander A. Alekhine, U.S.S.R.[1]
1948–57	Mikhail Botvinnik, U.S.S.R.
1957–58	Vassily Smyslov, U.S.S.R.
1958–60	Mikhail Botvinnik, U.S.S.R.
1960–61	Mikhail Tal, U.S.S.R.
1961–63	Mikhail Botvinnik, U.S.S.R.
1963–68	Tigran Petrosian, U.S.S.R.
1969–71	Boris Spassky, U.S.S.R.
1972–74	Bobby Fischer, Los Angeles
1975	Bobby Fischer[2], Anatoly Karpov, U.S.S.R.
1976–85	Anatoly Karpov, U.S.S.R.[3]
1985–89	Gary Kasparov, U.S.S.R.

1. Alekhine, a French citizen, died while champion. 2. Relinquished title. 3. In 1978, Karpov defeated Viktor Korchnoi 6 games to 5.

UNITED STATES CHAMPIONS

1909–36	Frank J. Marshall, New York
1936–44	Samuel Reshevsky, New York[1]
1944–46	Arnold S. Denker, New York
1946	Samuel Reshevsky, Boston
1948	Herman Steiner, Los Angeles
1951–52	Larry Evan, New York

1954–57	Arthur Bisguier, New York
1958–61	Bobby Fischer, Brooklyn, N.Y.
1962	Larry Evans, New York
1963–67	Bobby Fischer, New York
1968	Larry Evans, New York
1969–71	Samuel Reshevsky, Spring Valley, N.Y.
1972	Robert Byrne, Ossining, N.Y.
1973	Lubomir Kavelek, Washington; John Grefe, San Francisco
1974–77	Walter Browne, Berkeley, Calif.
1978–79	Lubomir Kavelek, New York
1980	Tie, Walter Browne, Berkeley, Calif. Larry Christiansen, Modesto, Calif. Larry Evans, Reno, Nev.
1981–82[2]	Tie, Walter Browne, Berkeley, Calif. Yasser Seirawan, Seattle, Wash.
1983	Tie, Walter Browne, Berkeley, Calif. Larry Christiansen, Los Angeles, Calif., Roman Dzindzichashvili, Corona, N.Y.
1984–85	Lev Alburt, New York City
1986	Yasser Seirawan, Seattle, Wash.[3]
1987	TIE—Nick Defirmian, San Francisco, and Joel Benjamin, Brooklyn, N.Y.[3]
1988	Michael Wilder, Princeton, N.J.

1. In 1942, Isaac I. Kashdan of New York was co-champion for a while because of a tie with Reshevsky in that year's tournament. Reshevsky won the play-off. 2. Championship not contested in 1982. 3. 1989, Championships were scheduled Nov. 9–Dec. 3, 1989, after Information Please went to press.

GYMNASTICS

AMERICAN CUP CHAMPIONSHIPS—1989

(Fairfax, Va., March 4-5, 1989)

Men's Events

	Pts
All-around—Vitali Marinich, Soviet Union	58.200
Floor exercise—Makoto Aihara, Japan	9.750
Parallel bars—Vitali Marinich, Soviet Union	9.800
Pommel horse—Vitali Marinich, Soviet Union	9.750
Still rings—Alfonso Rodriguez, Spain and Vitali Marinich, Soviet Union	9.650
Vault—Li Jing, China	9.650
Horizontal bars—Lance Ringnald, United States	9.800

Women's Events

All around—Brandy Johnson, United States	39.649
Floor exercise—Brandy Johnson, United States	9.912
Vault—Phoebe Mills, United States	9.925
Uneven bars—Brandy Johnson, United States	9.900
Balance beam—Brandy Johnson, United States	9.937

WORLD CHAMPIONSHIPS—1987[1]

(Rotterdam, The Netherlands, Oct. 18-25, 1987)

Men's Events

	Pts
All-Around—Dimitri Bilozertchev, Soviet Union	118.375
Floor exercise—Yun Lou, China	19.875
High bar—Dimitri Bilozertchev, Soviet Union	19.825

Still rings—Yuri Korolev, Soviet Union	19.875
Pommel horse—Zsolt Borkai, Soviet Union	19.775
Parallel bars—Vladimir Artemov, Soviet Union	19.800
Vault—Yun Lou, China & Sylvio Kroll, East Germany (tie)	19.938
Team—Soviet Union	589.750

Women's Events

	Pts
All-Around—Aurelia Dobre, Romania	79.650
Floor exercise—Elena Shoushounova, Soviet Union	19.737
Balance beam—Aurelia Dobre, Romania	19.950
Uneven bars—Daniela Silivas, Romania	19.925
Vault—Elena Shoushounova, Soviet Union	19.894
Team—Romania	395.400

1. World Gymnastics championships are held every other year. The next were scheduled for Oct. 14–22, 1989, Stuttgart, West Germany, after Information Please went to Press.

CURLING

UNITED STATES CHAMPIONSHIPS—1989

Men (Detroit, Mich., March 5-11)—Seattle, Wash, Jim Vulcich, skip (defeated Madison, Wis., Steve Brown, skip, 6-4 in final)
Women (Detroit, Mich., March 5-11)—Rolla, N.D, Jan Lagasse, skip (defeated Fairbanks, Alaska, Gayle Hazen, skip, 6-4 in final)

WORLD CHAMPIONSHIPS—1989

Men (April 3-9, 1989, at Milwaukee, Wis.)—Canada, Pat Ryan, skip (defeated Switzerland, Patrick Huerlimann, skip, 5-4 in final)
Women (April 3-9, 1989, at Milwaukee, Wis.)—Canada, Heather Houston, skip (defeated Norway, Trine Trulsen, skip, 8-5 in final)

CURRENT EVENTS

What Happened in 1989

Highlights of the important events of the year from January to October 1989, organized month by month, in three categories for easy reference. The Countries of the World section (starting on page 151) covers specific international events, country by country.

1989

January 1989

International

Fifty-One Drown Off Rio De Janeiro (Jan. 1): Excursion boat sinks on way to Copacabana Beach fireworks display.

U.S. Planes Shoot Down Two Libyan Fighters (Jan. 4): Washington says Libyan aircraft displayed "clear hostile intent" over international waters in Mediterranean. **(Jan. 5):** U.S. displays video tapes from Navy F-14 showing four missiles under one of Libyan MIG-23s.

Emperor Hirohito Dead at 87 (Jan. 7): Japan mourns 124th and longest-reigning monarch, last of World War II leaders. Under him nation embraced militarism, conquered much of Asia, and waged war on U.S. and other Allied powers.

Soviet to Trim Chemical Arms (Jan. 8): Announces it will destroy stocks estimated at 300,000 tons or more.

Airliner Crash Kills 44 in England (Jan. 9): More than 80 survive as British Midland Boeing 737-400 hurtles to earth near major highway after both engines fail.

Conference Condemns Chemical Weapons (Jan. 11): Paris meeting of more than 140 nations calls for treaty to ban development, production, and possession.

Train Crash Kills 70 in Bangladesh (Jan. 15): Express smashes into mail train jammed with pilgrims.

Broad Human Rights Pact Adopted (Jan. 16): Accord by 35 nations at Vienna conference calls for freedom of assocation, religion, travel, and emigration.

Soviet Mudslide Deaths Set at 274 (Jan. 23): Hundreds injured after earthquake in mountainous Central Asia destroys several villages.

Soviet Deficit Set at $165 Billion (Jan. 25): Official economic adviser reports it is nearly three times official estimate and nation's greatest problem.

Austerity Ordered for Nicaragua (Jan. 30): President Ortega cuts budget in half, restricts credit, and slashes capital investment in move to raise production.

National

First Indictments in Pentagon Fraud (Jan. 6): Federal grand jury names contractor, former Pentagon official, and five others in two-year inquiry into fraud and bribery. Another contractor and two former executives plead guilty.

State Taxation of Interstate Calls Upheld (Jan. 10): Supreme Court rejects challenge to 5 percent Illinois excise.

Reagan Bids Farewell to Office (Jan. 11): In good-bye speech, retiring President speaks of economic recovery and "recovery of our morale."

U.S. Raises Soviet Refugee Quota (Jan. 11): Reagan increases number 39 percent, offset by reduction in places reserved for Southeast Asians.

Court Dismisses Key North Counts (Jan. 13): Federal judge drops main criminal conspiracy charges against Oliver L. North in Iran-Contra case, saying he is powerless without classified documents that the Administration ordered withheld.

Reagan Leaves With High Popular Rating (Jan. 17): Poll shows two-thirds of people approve performance, highest rating of any President at end of term since World War II.

Banks Admitted Into Bond Trading (Jan. 18): Federal Reserve breaks 50-year separation and allows banking companies to raise money for corporations.

George Bush Inaugurated (Jan. 20): Republican, 64, takes office as 41st U.S. President at ceremony in Washington. His inaugural, delivered before tens of thousands, promises new effort to heal social wounds and end two decades of divisiveness between White House and Congress. Bush stresses urgency of dealing with Federal budget deficit and calls on Democrats in Congress to join in coping with crime and poverty.

Supreme Court Limits Aid to Minorities (Jan. 23): Rules 6-3, that Richmond, Va., ordinance channeling share of public works funds to minority-owned construction companies violates constitutional rights of white contractors. Casts doubt on wide variety of non-Federal governmental hiring and contract programs to aid minorities.

General

Long-Running "42d Street" Closes (Jan. 8): Broadway era at end after 3,486 performances, a near record.

Violence Erupts in Miami Black Area (Jan. 16): Angry residents overturn cars, set fires, and throw bottles in Overtown district after Hispanic police officer fatally shoots black motorcyclist. **(Jan. 17):** Disorder spreads and looting breaks out; police use tear gas to disperse crowds. **(Jan. 19):** Violence ebbs. Damage to buildings put at less than $1 million. **(Jan. 23):** Police officer who shot cyclist is arrested.

Gunman Kills Five Children in Schoolyard (Jan. 17): Wounds 29 others and teacher, then kills himself at Stockton, Calif. Victims were Southeast Asia refugees.

Muitiple Killer Executed (Jan. 24): Ted Bundy electrocuted in Florida after trail of murder across nation in which at least 30 young women perished.

Woman Cleared as Episcopal Bishop (Jan. 25): Majority of 118 diocesan heads approve Massachusetts diocese choice of Rev. Barbara C. Harris. She will be first female bishop in world Anglican communion.

Lyndon H. LaRouche, Jr., Sentenced (Jan. 27): Political extremist, 66, meted 15 years in prison by Federal judge for scheming to defraud Internal Revenue Service and defaulting on $30 million in loans from supporters.

Alaska Suffers Record Cold Wave (Jan. 28): Temperatures slide to range lower than 70 degrees below zero.

February 1989

International

Two Koreas to Join in Project (Feb. 1): North and South agree to cooperate in developing tourist site. It is first such agreement in 43 years of hostility.

Party Leader Quits in South Africa (Feb. 2): President P.W. Botha, 73, recuperating from stroke, resigns as head of long-governing National Party.

Stalin's Victims Set at 20 Million (Feb. 3): Soviet weekly publishes detailed account of deaths in labor camps, forced collectivization, famine, and executions. Number equal to World War II toll.

Coup Ousts Paraguay's Dictator (Feb. 3): President Alfredo Stroessner overthrown after 35 years in office, with scores killed or wounded. Coup leader, Gen. Andrés Rodriguez, his second in command, sworn in as President with new nine-member Cabinet.

Soviet Ends Afghan War (Feb. 5): Troops complete withdrawal from capital of Kabul. (Feb. 15): Russians fulfill deadline pledge as commander of Soviet forces is last soldier to leave Afghanistan. War of nearly 10 years a domestic burden and international embarrassment for Moscow.

Plane Crash Kills 144 in Azores (Feb. 8): U.S. Boeing 707 carrying Italian vacationers hits mountain in fog. (Feb. 18): Inquiry focuses on human error.

Vatican Condemns Racism (Feb. 11): Major document touches on apartheid, anti-Semitism, tribal conflicts, rights of aboriginal peoples, and discrimination against migrants.

Furor Over "The Satanic Verses" Rages (Feb. 14): Iran's Ayatollah Ruhollah Khomeini declares author, Salman Rushdie, and publishers of novel he regards as offensive are "sentenced to death." Book has prompted widespread fatal rioting and violent protests by Islamic Fundamentalists over allusions regarded as blasphemous. In U.S. many booksellers temporarily withdraw book. (Feb. 19): Khomeini rejects Rushdie's expression of regret and renews death threat. (Feb. 20): Twelve European Community nations recall diplomats from Teheran in protest. (Feb. 22): President Bush brands death threat against author "deeply offensive."

Accord on Contra Bases Reached (Feb. 14): Presidents of five Central American nations agree Nicaraguan rebel centers in Honduras will be closed in return for open elections in Nicaragua. Prisoners to be released.

Bhopal Payments Set at $470 Million (Feb. 14): Indian Supreme Court orders Union Carbide to pay damages for gas leak that killed about 3,500 Dec. 2, 1984. Criminal charges and civil suits dismissed.

Winnie Mandela Repudiated (Feb. 16): Leaders of Antiapartheid movement expel her, blaming her for creating reign of terror by bodyguards in which a 14-year-old youth was killed.

Prague Court Convicts Dissident Playwright (Feb. 21): Finds Vaclav Havel, 52, guilty of inciting illegal protests and sentences him to nine months.

Bush Attends Hirohito Funeral (Feb. 22): At stop in Alaska on way to Tokyo, President reasserts determination of U.S. to remain a Pacific power. (Feb. 24): Bush joins world leaders at ancient rites for Japanese emperor, a showcase for peaceful, affluent Japan society. He confers with other leaders on East-West relations and military tensions. (Feb. 27): President home after five-day visit to Japan, China, and South Korea. He says trip underscores strong relationship with Congress, and that America is and will remain a Pacific power.

Nine Lost in Pacific Air Accident (Feb. 24): Passengers sucked out of United Airlines Boeing 747 as part of outer fuselage rips away. Twenty-four injured.

Rightists Reject Duarte Peace Bid (Feb. 27): Proposal for cease-fire and meeting with leftist guerrillas spurned by key political party and by the political allies of El Salvador rebels.

Venezuelans Killed in Price Rioting (Feb. 28): Dozens perish and hundreds are wounded in fighting over Government's economic measures to satisfy creditors.

National

AIDS Patients Allowed to Use Unproved Drugs (Feb. 2): F.D.A. discloses permission for administration of aerosol pentamidine, thought to prevent deadly pneumonia by blocking organisms.

Four Savings Units Taken Over (Feb. 7): Federal regulators assume control of large insolvent associations in first phase of President's plan for crisis.

Congress Kills Pay Increase Plan (Feb. 7): Senate and House reject 51 percent rise proposed by Federal panel, leaving political problems.

President Bush Addresses Congress (Feb. 9): Calls on joint session to work with him on budget to reduce deficit, give less emphasis to military and more to children and the disadvantaged.

Black Named Democrats' Leader (Feb. 10): Ronald H. Brown, Washington lawyer, elected chairman of National Committee, first of race to head major political party.

High Court Limits Obscenity Prosecution (Feb. 21): Justices unanimously rule First Amendment bars seizure of book store inventory before trial finds it obscene.

Court Rules on Child Abuse Intervention (Feb. 22): Justices, 6-2, declare Constitution does not mandate state and local protection in private attacks.

Senate Group Rejects Tower (Feb. 23): Armed Services Committee, 11-9, votes against nomination of John G. Tower as Secretary of Defense after allegations of drinking, sexual misbehavior, and financial ties to defense industry.

General

Apple Chemical Reported Dangerous (Feb. 1): E.P.A. finds risk of cancer in daminozide, used chiefly on 5 percent of nation's apples.

New National League President (Feb. 3): Bill White, 55, former major leaguer and baseball broadcaster, named to succeed Bart Giamatti.

Harvard Names Woman to Top Board (Feb. 6): Judith Richards Hope, a lawyer, first of sex in university's 353 years to serve on Harvard Corporation.

Kitty Dukakis Enters Alcohol Clinic (Feb. 6): Wife of Massachusetts Governor treated for drinking problem that followed husband's November defeat.

Birth of Pulsar Observed (Feb. 9): Astronomers report glimpsing extremely dense star spinning nearly 2,000 times a second inside stellar debris.

Three Added to Basketball Hall of Fame (Feb. 10): K.C. Jones and Benny Wilkens, guards noted for defense, honored along with William (Pop) Gates.

First Woman Episcopal Bishop Consecrated (Feb. 11): Rev. Barbara Clementine Harris, 55, a priest, acclaimed by thousands at ceremony in Boston.

Threat to Arctic Ozone Reported (Feb. 17): Expedition finds chemicals in stratosphere that threatened substantial destruction of shield from harmful radiation.

March 1989

International

Europeans Move to Protect Ozone (March 2): Twelve European Community nations agree to eliminate by end of century production and use of chemicals harmful to atmosphere's shield.

Computer Spy Ring Broken Up (March 2): West German police arrest five charged with working with Soviet agents to steal U.S. military passwords and software.

Poland Blames Soviet for Wartime Massacre (March 7): In policy shift, charges Russians were at fault in killing of 4,443 Polish officers at Katyn Forest.

Iran Breaks Ties With Britain (March 7): Severs diplomatic relations week after demanding that London renounce Salman Rushdie and "The Satanic Verses."

Sea Collision Kills 130 Refugees (March 8): Japanese supertanker collides with fishing boat carrying Vietnamese. **(March 23):** Tanker commander says other ships failed to respond to calls for help.

Vatican Receives U.S. Catholic Bishops (March 11): Four-day conference with Pope and aides ends with expressions that misunderstandings have been counteracted.

Gorbachev Asks New Farm Policy (March 15): In call for radical reversal of 60-year Soviet history of centralized agriculture, he proposes immediate dismantling of state agricultural bureaucracy and gradual introduction of free markets.

Suitcase Pieces Linked to Bombing of Jet (March 17): Scottish investigators report recovering shards of container of plastic explosive that destroyed Pan Am jet with 259 aboard and killed 11 on ground at Lockerbie, Scotland.

Soviet Ban on Solzhenitsyn Broken (March 19): Obscure magazine publishes essay by exiled writer.

Salvador Rightist Elected (March 20): Alfredo Cristiani of Nationalist Republican Alliance declared winner to succeed José Napoleón Duarte.

Soviet Election Upsets Party Officials (March 27): Nationwide balloting, first free vote since 1917, defeats Politburo member and several senior Communist Party officials running without opposition. Candidates promising more rapid change elected to new powerful Congress of People's Deputies. Opposition is first since time of Lenin.

National

Robert C. McFarlane Fined $20,000 (March 3): President Reagan's national security adviser also sentenced to two years' probation for withholding information from Congress about Iran-Contra affair.

Senate Rejects John Tower (March 9): Vote of 53-47 decides against Bush nominee for Secretary of Defense after weeks of inquiry into allegations about drinking, his private life, and conflict of interest. It is first time in 30 years that President has been denied choice of Cabinet nominee.

Secretary of Defense Approved (March 10): President chooses Rep. Dick Cheney of Wyoming, 48, popular Republican, in swift move after Tower rejection. **(March 17):** Senate, 92-0, approves choice. Also confirms Lawrence S. Eagleburger to be Deputy Secretary of State.

U.S. Settles With Teamsters (March 13): Agreement ending Government's racketeering suit calls for sweeping changes in election of national union officers and the way corruption is policed.

Imports of Assault Rifles Banned (March 14): Administration orders indefinite action pending review of sporting use of military-style weapons.

High Court Backs Some Drug Testing (March 21): Justices uphold Reagan Administration program for rail industry and in most respects for Customs Service employees.

House G.O.P. Names Firebrand as Whip (March 22): Chooses Rep. Newt Gingrich of Georgia as No. 2 leader.

Bipartisan Policy on Contra Aid (March 24): Administration and Congress leaders announce agreement to help Nicaraguan rebels and support Central American peace efforts. Four Congressional committees gain virtual veto power over continued aid.

Air Force Grounds B-1s (March 28): Entire fleet withdrawn after movable wing on one of $280-million aircraft punctures a fuel tank.

North Judge Bars Reagan Testimony (March 31): Rebuffs attempt to call former President as defense witness for Oliver L. North as not required.

General

Strike Paralyzes Eastern Airlines (March 4): Nearly 90 percent of planes grounded as pilots and flight attendants support machinists' walkout. Thousands of passengers left without flights. **(March 6):** Eastern slashes all but three routes as strike spreads, laying off 5,000 workers. **(March 9):** Airline files for bankruptcy protection in U.S. Court.

Time Inc. and Warner Communications Merging (March 4): Plan creation of Time Warner Inc. with stock market value of $15.2 billion, largest media and entertainment conglomerate in the world.

G.O.P. Head Quits Howard U. Board (March 7): Lee Atwater resigns as university trustee after students stage sit-in charging racial overtones in Republican chairman's management of Bush campaign.

Terrorist Blamed in Car Blast (March 10): Wife of captain of *U.S.S. Vincennes* hurt in explosion in San Diego. Husband, Will C. Rogers 3rd, had ordered attack on Iranian airliner.

Space Shuttle Discovery a Success (March 13): Five astronauts fly into orbit, third since *Challenger* disaster in 1986 and 28th in shuttle program. Flight's commander is Navy Capt. Michael L. Coats, 43. Crew includes: Air Force Col. John E. Blaha, 46, pilot; Marine Col. James F. Buchli, 43, mission specialist; Marine Col. Robert C. Springer, 46, mission specialist, and Dr. James P. Bagian, 37, a physician and mission specialist. **(March 18):** The $1.2-billion craft lands flawlessly at Edwards Air Force Base, Calif., to cheers of 450,000. Success of mission lifts NASA's hopes for six more flights planned this year.

Ruptured Tanker Spills Oil Into Alaskan Waters (March 24): Exxon *Valdez* runs aground 25 miles from Trans Alaska Pipeline terminus, sending 250,000 barrels into Prince William Sound, largest tanker spill in U.S. history. **(March 26):** Third mate, uncertified as pilot for area, was in command during grounding. **(March 27):** Lack of equipment, organizational mix-ups, and high winds hamper clean-up. **(March 28):** Fishermen and state officials take charge of fighting spread of fast-moving slick and protecting salmon nurseries. **(March 29):** Exxon admits failure to contain slick. **(March 30):** Blood tests show captain of tanker had been drinking. Coast Guard moves to file charges against him.

U.S. Indicts Wall Street Executive (March 29): Charges Michael R. Millken, 42, of Drexel Burnham Lambert Inc. with violating securities laws.

April 1989

International

Army Coup Fails in Haiti (April 2): Government reports it blocked attempt by rebel officers to overthrow military leader, Lieut. Gen. Prosper Avril.

Castro Welcomes Gorbachev to Cuba (April 2): Greets Soviet leader with bear hug as Havana crowds turn out. **(April 4):** Gorbachev signs friendship treaty with Cuba, asks end to outside military aid to Latin America.

Poland Decides on Free, Open Elections (April 5): Leaders of Solidarity sign accord with Government restoring banned union's legal status and providing for major changes in nation's political system.

Vietnam Announces Cambodia Withdrawal (April 5): Plans to end occupation 10 years and three months after invasion installed new government in Phnom Penh.

Soviet Nuclear Sub Sinks After Blaze (April 7): Catches fire while submerged, surfaces, then disappears in Norwegian Sea. Forty-two sailors killed. **(April 8):** Moscow denies danger of nuclear contamination of environment. **(April 11):** Soviet Navy announces plans to recover submarine. Western experts say she contains latest Soviet undersea technology.

Police Kill 16 in Soviet Georgia Rioting (April 9): More than 200 hurt when thousands of nationalists in Tbilisi, capital, refuse to disperse. Crisis is latest nationalist outbreak to face Gorbachev.

Mexico Seizes Drug Leader (April 10): Arrests Miguel Angel Félix Gallardo, 43, head of international cocaine ring. Also captures nearly entire police force of his base city of Culiacán.

Bombing Kills 38 in Sri Lanka (April 13): Tamil separatists set off blast in taxi among holiday shoppers in crowded marketplace.

Stadium Crush Kills 94 in Britain (April 15): Nearly 200 injured as soccer fans surge forward in overcrowded stands at match in Sheffield.

Spanish Ambassador Killed in Beirut (April 16): Sixteen others also die in day of intensive shelling by warring Christian and Moslem factions.

Bush Announces Aid to Poland (April 17): Economic relief program acknowledges agreement on free elections.

Swiss Seize Saudi Financier (April 18): Hold Adnan M. Khashoggi, international arms dealer, for trial in U.S. on racketeering and fraud charges.

Bomb Kills Salvadoran Attorney General (April 19): Roberto Garcia Alvadora, 53, a rightist, is victim of suspected left-wing guerrillas.

Thousands of Chinese Students Protest (April 19 et seq.): Tens of thousands take over Beijing's central square in rally for democracy. Protests are greatest since end of Maoist era more than a dozen years previously. Rallies grow in succeeding days as marchers defy police. **(April 27):** More than 150,000 defy official warnings and troop concentration to march for 14 hours through capital, repeatedly breaking police and troop lines. Government, humiliated, agrees to discuss demands for democracy and against corruption. Officials worried as crowds of cheering workers line parade route and applaud marching students.

Japanese Prime Minister Resigning (April 25): Noboru Takashita seeks to take responsibility for "political distrust" stemming from bribery and influence peddling scandal that has paralyzed government.

Kohl Launches New Arms Policy (April 27): West German affirms new call for talks with Moscow on short-range weapons, a challenge to U.S. and NATO.

Mobil Quitting South Africa (April 28): Corporation agrees to sell operations. Blames "foolish" U.S. laws.

U.S. and Japan Agree on Jet Fighter (April 28): Bush reports $7-billion project to produce new plane in U.S. "strategic and commercial interests."

National

Justices Back Airport Detentions (April 3): Supreme Court, 7-2, rules Constitution permits questioning of passengers with traits resembling those of drug couriers.

Thousands Rally for Abortion Rights (April 9): Marchers parade in Washington to grassy mall of Capitol, many carrying coat hangers to recall days of illegal operations. They wave banners urging Supreme Court to keep abortion "safe and legal."

Two Guilty in Pentagon Trial (April 13): Federal jury in Washington convicts George H. Kaub and Eugene R. Sullivan, officials of Teledyne Electronics, of conspiracy and wire fraud in first criminal trial of inquiry into Pentagon procurement fraud.

Ethics Inquiry Accuses House Speaker (April 17): House committee charges James Wright with plotting to evade limits on outside income and taking $145,000 in improper gifts over previous decade.

U.S. Warns of Two Heart Drugs (April 25): F.D.A. advises doctors to stop prescribing Tambocor and Enkaid for mild or moderate rhythmic irregularities.

General

Black Control of Chicago Ends (April 4): Richard M. Daley, son of old Democratic boss, elected over black rival. Support comes almost entirely from whites.

Tanker Captain Surrenders (April 5): Joseph J. Hazelwood, former skipper of Exxon *Valdez*, involved in Alaska oil spill, gives himself up on Long Island. Bail set at $1 million. **(April 16):** Another court frees him after cutting bail to $25,000.

U.S. Jury Convicts Two Sports Agents (April 13): Finds Norby Walters and Lloyd Bloom guilty of fraud and racketeering in payments to college football players, who then became ineligible.

Ritual-Murder Cult Kills 13 (April 13): Mexican officials dig up bodies of alleged victims of Cuban leader of drug-smuggling and ritual-killing ring.

Records Fall in Wheelchair Race (April 17): Five competitors surpass world-best performances five years after first such contest in Boston Marathon.

Close Call in Space (April 19): Astronomers report huge asteroid passed within half million miles of Earth, in closest approach of such object in 50 years.

Blast Kills 47 on Battleship Iowa (April 19): Many injured in explosion and fire in one of three 16-inch gun turrets. **(April 20):** *Iowa* steams to her Norfolk, Va., home port as nation mourns.

New Test Detects Viral Hepatitis (April 21): Experts find it in extensive tests highly effective against last major threat to blood supplies.

Herbert von Karajan, 81, Resigns (April 24): Quits after 34 years as chief conductor and artistic director of Berlin Philharmonic. Cites health and dispute.

First Inaugural Re-Enacted (April 30): Two-hour parade fills narrow lower Manhattan streets in celebration of 200th anniversary of Washington's taking oath as first President.

May 1989

International

Eighty Nations Back Move to Save Ozone (May 2): Helsinki conference approves ban by end of century on harmful substances destroying ozone layer.

Bush Approves Soviet Wheat Sale Subsidy (May 2): Approves deal for 1.5 million metric tons.

U.S. Reports Berlin Spy Post Crippled (May 6): Inquiry says court-martialed Army warrant officer damaged electronic eavesdropping operations aimed at Eastern Europe and Soviet Union.

Panamanian Election Declared Fraud (May 8): Jimmy Carter says armed forces prevented opposition from being declared winner. **(May 10):** Paramilitary squads attack opposition presidential and vice-presidential candidates as soldiers stand by.

Peronist Elected in Argentina (May 14): Carlos Saúl Menem, 59, wins on tradition of state largesse but faces prostrate economy.

Thousands Demonstrate in China (Mid-May et seq.): Three thousand young hunger strikers galvanize the people to provoke political crisis. More than million pour into streets of Beijing, capital, to put pressure on Government for more democracy. Crowds demand resignations of Deng Xiaoping, senior leader, and Prime Minister Li Peng. Chaos spreads across nation. Li and party leader, Zhao Ziyang, visit Tiananmen Square in capital to visit hunger strikers. More than million swarm streets to defy martial law and block troops from center of capital. Workers and students block convoys. Zhao stripped of powers after urging moderate line toward students.

Sunni Religious Leader Killed in Lebanon (May 16): Car bomb kills Sheik Hassan Khaled instantly and 21 others in Muslim-controlled West Beirut.

Chinese and Soviet Cement Ties (May 16): Deng Xiaoping and Mikhail S. Gorbachev shake hands to signal end of three decades of hostility. As four-day conference begins, the leaders agree to discuss possible military contacts. Meeting overshadowed by vast pro-democracy demonstration in center of Beijing capital.

Lebanese Guilty in Hijacking (May 17): Mohammed Ali Hamadei, pro-Iranian militant, sentenced to life in German court for murdering American hostage on Trans World Airlines jet in 1985.

Czechs Release Playwright (May 17): Vaclav Havel, dissident, had served half of eight-month term for role in Prague rally marking protesting student's death.

French Seize Pro-Nazi Fugitive (May 24): Arrest Paul Touvier, 74, military intelligence head for Nazis in Lyons, at Roman Catholic priory.

Gorbachev Named Soviet President (May 25): But faces rough questioning at opening of Congress of Peoples Deputies, first national assembly in seven decades with competitive elections. Deputy likens him to Napoleon, and Mrs. Gorbachev is ridiculed.

Swedes Charge Assassination Suspect (May 29): Accuse Carl Gustav Christer Pettersson, 42, laborer with criminal record, in 1986 killing of Prime Minister Olof Palme.

Maverick Communist Wins Moscow Seat (May 29): Congress yields to public indignation and votes seat for Boris N. Yeltsin in a new legislature.

Most Allies Back Bush Arms Plan (May 29): President offers four-part proposal for Vienna talks with Soviet on conventional-arms control. Britain and France cool about some aspects when Bush presents "revolutionary" program in address to conference at Brussels marking 40th anniversary of North Atlantic Treaty Organization.

National

Justices Aid Plaintiffs in Bias Suits (May 1): Supreme Court, 6-3, rules employers have legal burden of proving refusal to hire or promote employees is not based on discriminatory reasons.

Nation's Schools Get Low Marks (May 3): Administration report calls performance "merely average" and "stagnant." State officials challenge statistical base.

U.S. Jury Convicts Oliver L. North (May 4): Finds former Marine lieutenant colonel guilty of shredding documents and two other crimes stemming from role as President Reagan's covert agent to aid Nicaraguan rebels while aide to National Security Council. Key points of Government case rejected. **(May 5):** Jurors say they saw North as scapegoat blamed unfairly for following orders, despite judge's instructions.

Bush Denies Part in Contra Aid Plan (May 4): Says he had no role in 1985 White House arrangement for Honduras to get aid as "quid pro quo" for support of rebels fighting Government of Nicaragua.

Top Aide of Speaker Wright Resigns (May 11): John P. Mack quits after revelations of his attack on woman 16 years previously.

Repairs to Aging Airliners Ordered (May 18): F.A.A. starts program that will take several years.

U. of Kentucky Penalized (May 19): National Collegiate Athletic Association places basketball program on three-year probation for recruiting violations.

Secretary Baker Pleads With Israel (May 22): Bids nation reach out to Palestinians as neighbors who deserve "political rights." Blunt speech calls for concessions from both sides.

No. 3 Democrat Quits House (May 26): Rep. Tony Coelho of California resigns rather than put party and colleagues through long inquiry into finances.

House Speaker Resigns Under Cloud (May 31): Jim Wright announces decision to quit post and Congress after 34-year career. In bitter speech, he defends conduct against charges of ethics violations and attacks accusing House Ethics Committee.

General

Shuttle Atlantis Rockets Into Orbit (May 4): Astronauts release *Magellan*, 7,700-pound spacecraft, for flight to Venus in first American planetary exploration in 11 years. The five crew members are: Navy Capt. David M. Walker, mission commander; Air Force Col. Ronald J. Grabe, pilot; Dr. Norman E. Thagard, M.D.; Mary L. Cleave, Ph.D., and Air Force Maj. Mark C. Lee, mission specialists. **(May 8):** *Atlantis* lands safely in stiff breeze at Edwards Air Force Base, Calif.

Voodoo Cult Leader Slain (May 7): Adolfo de Jesús Constanzo orders member to kill him. Group blamed for 15 ritualist murders in Mexico.

Seventeen Dead as Storm Rips South (May 7): Tornadoes wreck homes and cars in several states.

Bush Offers "Open Skies" Plan (May 12): Texas speech revives Eisenhower proposal for NATO and Warsaw pact planes to survey each others' territories.

Apple Industry Drops Chemical Alar (May 15): Reports $50-million loss after U.S. found cancer peril.

Inquiry Blames Aloha Line (May 23): U.S. agency finds inspection and maintenance failures caused 1988 accident in which top of Boeing 737 jet tore away, causing death of flight attendant.

June 1989

International

China Cracks Down on Protestors (June 4 et seq.): Hundreds, possibly thousands, killed as tens of thousands of troops retake center of Beijing from pro-democracy demonstrators. Submachine guns kill and wound students and workers trying to resist. Soldiers and police also killed. U.S. and other nations order evacuation of diplomatic families. Clashes between Chinese military units reported. **(June 9):** Deng Xiaoping, senior leader, and other top officials, take hard line toward protests. **(June 10):** More than 400 protesters arrested. Wave of executions begins.

Solidarity Sweeps Polish Election (June 4): Communists concede "decisive majority" to opposition movement. Call on Solidarity to join in coalition government. **(June 8):** Official returns show ballot sweep in 92 of Solidarity's candidates to 100-seat Senate. Communist leaders humiliated.

Scores Dead in Eastern Uzbekistan Violence (June 5): Thousands of Soviet troops sent to restore order in conflict between Uzbeks and Meskhetian ethnic minority.

Hundreds Dead in Urals Gas Explosion (June 5): Hundreds also missing or hospitalized after gas leak erupts as two passenger trains pass in opposite directions near city of Asha. Operators accused of negligence.

Ayatollah Buried Amidst Frenzied Mourning (June 6): Ruhollah Khomeini, 87, revolutionary Shiite Moslem leader, dominated Iran for decade. At one point hysterical crowd seizes body and carries it off. Crowds estimated as high as 3 million.

Salvadoran Adviser Assassinated (June 9): Leftist Guerrillas accused in death of José Antonio Rodriguez Porth, 73, top staff assistant to newly elected President Alfredo Crsitiani.

New Soviet-West German Accord (June 13): Gorbachev and Chancellor Helmut Kohl sign declaration of new stage in relations. In Bonn speech, Soviet President calls for much closer economic cooperation.

Hungarians Honor Executed Leader of '56 Revolt (June 16): Imre Nagy receives hero's funeral in Budapest's largest square and is reburied after body is taken from mass grave. Four companions honored likewise. Communist Party leaders join in tribute.

Greek Voters Repudiate Premier (June 18): Andreas Papandreou loses control of Parliament. Scandal had dogged leader of moderate Socialists. **(June 19):** Conservatives fail to form coalition Government.

U.S. Suspends Talks With Chinese (June 20): High-level meetings canceled to express American anger at crackdown on pro-democracy movement.

Soviet-Iran Ties Renewed (June 20): Gorbachev welcomes Speaker of Iranian Parliament with appeal for closer relations. **(June 21):** Gorbachev announces restoration of railway service across border.

Cease-Fire Reached in Angola (June 22): Government and rebel forces agree to halt in fighting that has cost hundreds of thousands of lives over 14 years.

New Chinese Leadership Named (June 24): General Secretary Zhao Ziyang dismissed from party posts. Communists name officials likely to back new economic and political developments and ready to crack down harshly on political protests.

Polish Leader Bars Election Bid (June 30): Gen. Wojciech Jaruzelski, Communist chief and president for eight years, announces decision after Solidarity victory arouses hard-liners.

Civilian Regime Ousted in Sudan (June 30): Armed Forces overthrow Government of Prime Minister Sadiq al-Mahdi after friction over crippled economy.

National

U.S. Approves New Anemia Drug (June 1): F.D.A. finds genetically engineered form of hormone erythropoietin useful in treating kidney patients and might help in combating AIDS.

Thomas S. Foley New House Speaker (June 6): Washington State Democrat is 49th in post, succeeding Jim Wright, who resigned in face of ethics investigation. **(June 7):** Bush rebukes key Republican campaign aide over innuendo attacking Foley.

Bush Urges Stronger Fight on Air Pollution (June 12): offers costly program to cut sulfur dioxide in acid rain and require other efforts to combat urban smog and reduce emissions of toxic chemicals.

Bush Vetoes $4.55 Minimum Wage (June 13): Warns that increase from $3.35 an hour would accelerate inflation. **(June 14):** House Democrats fail to override veto.

House Democrats Choose Leaders (June 14): Elect Richard A. Gephardt of Missouri as majority leader and William H. Gray 3rd of Pennsylvania as whip. With new Speaker, Thomas S. Foley, they vow to put ethics struggle behind. Gray is first black in top leadership post in Congress.

High Court Upholds 1866 Rights Law (June 15): But rules, 5-4, that statute bars discrimination in hiring but not unfair treatment on job.

High Court Modifies Rights Litigation (June 12): Justices, 5-4, in tilt to right, rule court-approved affirmative action settlements are open to subsequent legal challenges by white workers. A second ruling places time limit on legal challenges to discriminatory seniority systems.

Air Controllers Get 20% Bonus (June 19): Transportation Department moves to bolster ranks.

Justices Uphold Right to Burn Flag (June 21): In rare 5-4 coalition, Supreme Court declares unconstitutional Federal and state laws in cases of peaceful expression of opinion. Ruling blurs ideological lines.

High Court Backs Seizure of Assets (June 22): Rules, 5-4, that Government can act before trial when assets are deemed proceeds of the crime.

Death Sentences Upheld (June 26): Supreme Court, 5-4, rules Constitution permits states to doom mentally retarded and youths who were under 16 when they committed their crime.

Nofziger Verdict Overturned (June 27): U.S. Appeals Court rules Government had not shown criminal intent in ethics case against Lyn Nofziger, close adviser to President Reagan.

General

Voters Shut Down Nuclear Power Plant (June 6): In national first, Sacramento, Calif., ballot causes closing of atomic utility as being uneconomic.

Corporate Raider Convicted (June 9): Paul A. Bilzerian, 38, Singer Company chairman, convicted in U.S. Court on nine counts, including securities fraud.

Four Golfers Shoot Hole-in-One (June 16): Doug Weaver, Mark Wiebe, Jerry Pate, and Nick Price set record in second round of U.S. Open at Pittsford, N.Y.

Three Oil Spills Stir Alarm (June 27): New concerns about clean-up technology arise after weekend spills in Rhode Island, Delaware, and Texas, but threat to environment is less than feared. **(June 28):** Captain of Greek tanker involved in spill off Rhode Island arrested and charged with violations of U.S. antipollution laws.

July 1989

International

Greek Coalition Cabinet Formed (July 1): Communists and conservatives join in Government, after long enmity, to prosecute high officials accused of wrongdoing.

Four Cuban Officers Executed (July 7): Sentenced by military court to die for drug trafficking. **(July 13):** Officers are executed by firing squad.

Bush Visits East European Nations (July 9): Arrives in Warsaw on "delicate" mission to unsettled Poland. **(July 10):** Announces six-part program of U.S. aid. **(July 12):** President offers Hungary modest measures of economic aid to support political and social change. Tells audience U.S. will send Peace Corps volunteers to teach English. **(July 13):** Bush in Paris after five-day trip to Poland and Hungary. Calls changes in Eastern Europe "absolutely amazing."

Soviet Coal Miners Strike (July 10): Tens of thousands walk out in Siberia and Ukraine. Many in Siberian coal region claim victory after nine-day wildcat walkout paralyzes mines and brings unexpected economic and industrial concessions from Government. First large groups vote to return. **(July 23):** President Gorbachev says he is greatly "inspired" by miners' taking things into their own hands to force changes he views as necessary. **(July 25):** Striking Ukrainian miners return to work.

Gen. Jaruzelski Named Polish President (July 19): Elected by new Parliament with minimum number of votes as Solidarity opposition shows vigorous strength. **(July 21):** General urges Solidarity to join Communists in coalition Government to deal with nation's dire economic situation.

Gorbachev Calls for Sweeping Purge of Party (July 21): Leaders alarmed about loss of control as labor and nationalist unrest spreads. **(July 24):** Gorbachev moves to advance elections for sweeping changes in local governments. **(July 27):** Soviet legislature approves plan of Lithuania and Estonia for drastic economic experiments.

Japan's Ruling Party Defeated (July 24): Setback for conservatives is worst in 34 years as Liberal Democratic Party is defeated by Socialist Party in election to upper house of Parliament. Prime Minister Sousuke Uno announces intention to resign.

Killer of Swedish Prime Minister Convicted (July 27): Swedish drifter, Carl Gustav Christer Pettersson, 42, sentenced to life for death of Olof Palme.

Israelis Abduct Pro-Iranian Leader (July 28): Commandos seize Sheik Abdul Karim Obeid at home in south Lebanon. Sheik heads Party of God.

Terrorists Report Hanging Hostage U.S. Marine (July 31): Lebanese Shiite Muslim group distributes videotape said to show body of Lieut. Col. William R. Higgins. Hostage was kidnapped Feb. 17, 1988, while serving with U.N. peacekeeping mission. Organization of Oppressed on Earth had threatened action after Israelis abducted Shiite leader. Bush confers with national security leaders, and says nation is "shocked right to the core."

National

High Court Upholds Curbs on Abortions (July 3): Justices, 5-4, give states right to impose sharp new restrictions, upholding Missouri law. Ruling indicates majority no longer considers abortion a fundamental constitutional right. Court stops short of overturning 1973 Roe v. Wade decision that established right.

Justices Rule on Religious Displays (July 3): Court, 5-4, finds Constitution does not permit Nativity display in Allegheny County, Pa., courthouse. But Justices, 6-3, uphold display of Hanukkah menorah next to Christmas tree as recognition of joint Christmas-Hanukkah part of same wintertime season that has attained "secular stature."

Oliver L. North Sentenced (July 5): U.S. Court fines former Marine Lieutenant Colonel $150,000 for crimes in Iran-Contra affair, but says a prison term "would only harden your misconceptions" about Government service. Court places North on probation for two years and orders 1,200 hours of community service in new anti-drug program. North could have faced 10 years in prison and $750,000 fine.

Bus Plunge in Israel Kills 14 (July 6): Packed vehicle with 43 aboard crashes into ravine as Arab seizes steering wheel. **(July 7):** Islamic Holy War claims responsibility for terrorist act.

Stealth Bomber Flies (July 17): B-2, radar-avoiding plane, takes off on first flight. **(July 20):** House Armed Services chairman seeks to freeze spending on Stealth in 1990 and force Pentagon to scale back its $70-billion project.

Bush Calls for Base on Moon (July 20): Also urges expedition to Mars and "permanent settlement in space" in speech celebrating 20th anniversary of man's landing on Moon. Space experts estimate cost of reaching both Moon and Mars at $400 billion.

President Offers Clean-Air Program (July 21): Bush sends Congress bill calling for reducing pollution from automobiles and other sources of urban smog.

I.R.S. Officials Accused of Misconduct (July 25): House panel charges breaches of ethical standards after year inquiry into Internal Revenue Service.

A.T.&T. Wins Data Publishing Right (July 28): Federal judge lifts restriction on giant phone company that prohibited publishing services.

General

Reagan Injured Falling Off Horse (July 4): Former President suffers minor injuries in Mexico accident.

Jumbo Jet Crash Kills 111 (July 19): United Airlines DC-10, crippled and uncontrollable because of hydraulic failure, crashes short of runway at Sioux City, Iowa, and bursts into flames. There were 185 survivors. Captain joined by four pilots in trying to control aircraft. Huge fan in tail engine believed to have disintegrated and sliced through system that powers flight controls. **(Aug. 19):** 112th passenger dies of injuries suffered in the crash.

Time Inc. Acquires Warner Communications (July 24): Delaware Supreme Court removes final obstacle to creation of one of world's largest communications and entertainment companies. Paramount, rebuffed by court, drops $12.2-billion offer for Time.

Student Indicted in Computer Crippling (July 26): Robert Tappan Morris, 24, Cornell graduate student, charged by U.S. grand jury with harming nationwide network with rogue software program.

Nissan Workers Rebuff U.A.W. (July 27): Workers at Smyrna, Tenn., plant overwhelmingly turn down representation in setback for union.

Major Drug Companies to Merge (July 27): Bristol-Myers and Squibb agree on $12.3-billion deal to create world's second largest pharmaceutical company.

AUGUST 1989

International

U.S. Works to Free Hostages (Aug. 1): Negotiates with Arab nations and Soviet Union to prevent further killings after Shiite Muslim group in Lebanon reprieves prisoner. (**Aug. 4**): Iran's new President, Hojatolislam Hashemi Rafsanjani, offers help to end crisis. (**Aug. 5**): Iran and pro-Iranian group in Labanon rebuff U.S. and Israel in move to free hostages, refusing to accept "message" through third country.

Disbanding of Contras Ordered (Aug. 7): Presidents of five Central American countries agree on timetable for dissolution of American-sponsored Nicaraguan rebels no later than Dec. 8.

New Japanese Prime Minister (Aug. 9): Toshiki Kaifu, 58, becomes nation's 19th postwar leader after governing Liberal Democratic Party names him its new head.

Congressman Dies in Ethiopia Crash (Aug. 13): Wreckage of plane found on remote mountainside. Victims are Rep. Mickey Leland, Democrat of Texas; eight other Americans, and seven Ethiopians. Leland, 44, a leader in fight on world hunger, and his party on way to inspect refugee camp.

P.W. Botha Quits as South Africa's President (Aug. 14): Official, 73, complains that Cabinet ministers ignored him. (**Aug. 15**): F.W. de Kierk, Botha's successor as National Party leader, sworn in as acting President. Reaffirms promise to phase out white rule.

Non-Communist Polish Prime Minister (Aug. 19): President Jaruzelski names a senior Solidarity official, Tadeusz Mazowiecki, 62, a leading journalist and devout Roman Catholic, and a close adviser to Solidarity leader Lech Walesa. Move, after decisive election victories over Communists, is first major Governmental change in Soviet bloc since World War II. (**Aug. 22**): After call from Soviet leader Gorbachev, Communists drop threat not to join coalition government and agree to cooperate to aid economic recovery through political reform.

Toll Is High in Thames Shipwreck (Aug. 20): Dozens believed drowned as barge sinks pleasure vessel with 100 young people aboard. Captain and second mate of barge arrested for possible criminal investigation.

Colombia Fights Drug Traffickers (Aug. 20): Police and military round up nearly 4,000 suspects in slaying of a Presidential candidate. (**Aug. 21**): Police seize 134 aircraft suspected of belonging to drug traffickers and capture a top figure wanted in U.S. (**Aug. 24**): Drug forces dynamite political party offices in reprisals. (**Aug. 25**): President Bush announces $65-million U.S. emergency aid.

Woman Gets Top Post in Japan (Aug. 25): Mayumi Moriyama, head of Environment Agency, becomes first of sex to hold influential position of Chief Cabinet Secretary. She replaces one of Prime Minister Toshiki Kaifu's close aides, who resigned after admitting affair with bar hostess.

Cambodia Conference Breaks Down (Aug. 30): Warring factions blame each other for failure of Paris talks.

National

Senate Rejects Bush Nomination for Rights Post (Aug. 1): Judiciary Committee refuses to endorse William C. Lucas, a black, to be assistant attorney general. Many black and civil rights groups had opposed him.

Congress Votes Savings and Loan Rescue (Aug. 5): Adjourns after House and Senate give final approval to President's $166-billion program for ailing industry. Action viewed as session's one of few successes. (**Aug. 9**): Bush signs legislation, under which hundreds of S. & L.'s will be closed or taken over with tighter control and stricter financial requirements.

Black Gets Top Military Post (Aug. 9): President picks Army Gen. Colin L. Powell to be Chairman of Joint Chiefs of Staff, first of race in post. Powell, 52, among youngest four-star peacetime generals.

William C. Lucas Gets Justice Post (Aug. 11): Picked by Attorney General as personal representative in law enforcement. Lucas, a black, had been rejected by Senate as top civil rights enforcement officer.

Bomb Detectors Ordered for Airlines (Aug. 30): U.S. moves to have new device check luggage at all major airports in this country and abroad.

Use of Benzene Limited (Aug. 31): E.P.A. restricts industrial use of chemical linked to leukemia.

General

Telephone Workers Strike (Aug. 5-6): About 160,000 operators, installers, and other employees walk off job in 15 states as talks break down.

Shuttle Columbia Lands Safely (Aug. 8): Oldest manned spacecraft soars into orbit at Cape Canaveral, Fla., on secret military mission. Commander is Col. Brewster H. Shaw, Jr., of Air Force, 44, veteran of two shuttle missions. Others in crew: Navy Comdrs. Richard N. Richards, 42, and David C. Leestma, 40; Lieut. Col. James C. Adamson, 43, and Maj. Mark N. Brown, 37, both of Air Force. (**Aug. 13**): *Columbia* lands at Edwards Air Force Base, Calif., after five-day mission, longest solely military one. Astronauts deployed 10-ton spy satellite and conducted experiments on antimissile shield.

Woman Heads West Point Corps of Cadets (Aug. 8): Kristin M. Baker, 20, daughter of Army colonel, is first of sex selected to be First Captain.

Protector of Lions Slain in Kenya (Aug. 20): George Adamson, 83, shot dead by poachers with two Kenyan assistants. Adamson and his wife, Joy, created legend of Elsa, the lion of "Born Free." Mrs. Adamson slain in 1980. The couple had separated.

Huey Newton Shot Dead on Coast (Aug. 22): Body of cofounder of Black Panther Party, aged 47, and a leader of a generation of blacks in 1960s, found in Oakland, Calif., neighborhood.

Pete Rose Banned From Baseball (Aug. 24): Commissioner A. Bartlett Giamatti announces agreement, saying he believed Rose bet on baseball games, including those of teams he managed. Rose was manager of the Cincinnati Reds.

Voyager 2 Answers Key Questions (Aug. 29): Spacecraft speeds beyond Neptune and environs after 12-year mission through outer solar system. Proud scientists sum up achievement by reporting six answers, among them that Neptune has eight moons and is a pale blue object glowing with auroras and crackling from radio noises of charged particles trapped by magnetic fields. Three distinct rings found around planet. Neptune's largest moon, Triton, is brightly glazed with methane and nitrogen ices with signs of icy volcanism. Little had previously been known of planet, which is 2.8 billion miles from Earth.

Leona Helmsley Convicted (Aug. 30): Self-styled "Queen" of hotel empire found guilty by U.S. jury of evading $1.2 million in Federal income taxes.

SEPTEMBER 1989

International

Anti-Sandinistas Pick Candidate (Sept. 3): Violeta Barros de Chamorro, 59, publisher of *La Prensa*, chief opposition newspaper, chosen by leaders of 14 opposition parties after heated debate.

Cuban Airline Crash Kills at Least 125 (Sept. 3): Soviet Ilushin 62-M clips runway fence in storm and plummets in flames onto village. Several houses destroyed. Disaster worst such in Cuban history.

Chinese Culture Minister Dismissed (Sept. 4): Wang Meng, 54, noted novelist, rose to power in government three years previously. Advocated renewed literary freedom.

Brazilian Airliner Crashes in Jungle (Sept. 5): Thirteen of 54 aboard Varig Boeing 737 reported to have perished. (**Sept. 6**): Survivors attribute rescue to youth, 19, unemployed passenger, who proves to be schooled in ways of rain forest.

U.S. Evacuates Beirut Embassy (Sept. 6): Removes personnel after Lebanese Christian army commander reportedly threatened to take Americans hostage.

Governing Party Set Back in Pretoria (Sept. 6): National Party, in power for 41 years, severely battered by conservatives and liberal challengers. (**Sept. 7**): Acting President F.W. de Kierk sees mandate to advance change in system of racial segregation.

Thousands of East Germans Flee to West (Sept. 10): Hungary suspends 20-year agreement with East Germany to allow refugees free passage to "country of choice." (**Sept. 11**): Even more thousands arrive in West Germany. Thousands more head for Hungary to attempt to join mass exodus.

Rumanian Ship Carrying 179 Sinks (Sept. 10): Capsizes after colliding with Bulgarian tugboat on Danube. Heavy casualty toll is reported.

Apartheid Foes March in South Africa (Sept. 13): Thousands stage multiracial demonstration in Cape Town, biggest such display since emergency rules were imposed three years previously. (**Sept. 15**): Government permits illegal mass demonstration in Johannesburg. About 20,000 apartheid foes, mostly black, march. Similar protest held in Pretoria, seat of Government. (**Sept. 27**): Johannesburg opens swimming pools and recreational centers to all races.

Blast Kills 171 on French Airliner (Sept. 19): DC-10 disappears in North Africa on flight from Chad to France. (**Sept. 20**): French airline blames bombing by terrorists for midair explosion.

Czechs Clear East Germans for West (Sept. 30): Thousands allowed to leave West German Prague Embassy and board buses on first stage of journey.

National

Bush Unveils Drug War Plan (Sept. 5): President proposes national strategy focussing on increased law enforcement against drug dealers and users. Plan shifts focus from stopping drugs at border to targeting narcotics enforcement on the street.

Bush Doubles Polish Food Aid (Sept. 14): Under pressure from Congress, he agrees to provide $100 million in new assistance for next fiscal year.

Mismanagement on Iowa Reported (Sept. 7): Formal Navy findings on explosion fatal to 47 sailors on battleship say "sabotage" most probably was the cause.

Bush Calls for End of Chemical Arms (Sept. 25): Tells U.N. that U.S. would destroy 80 percent of weapons if Soviet Union cuts stockpile to American level. (**Sept. 26**): Soviet welcomes proposal but suggests banning production of advanced type of arms that Washington wants to keep.

Conferees Reject Strict Art Curbs (Sept. 29): Senate-House committee votes only mild restrictions on National Endowment for the Arts.

General

Miss America Receives Crown (Sept. 16): Debbye Turner, a veterinary student at the University of Missouri, becomes the 1989 title-holder. She is from Mexico, Mo.

Hurricane Rakes Caribbean, Hits U.S. (Sept. 18): Storm Hugo wreaks destruction on tourist islands and Puerto Rico. Many killed or injured. Damage in billions. (**Sept. 19**): Hugo spares Bahamas. (**Sept. 20**): President Bush orders troops to Virgin Islands after looting and shooting. (**Sept. 21**): Hurricane lashes coastal communities in Georgia and the Carolinas with winds up to 135 miles an hour. (**Sept. 22**): Full impact hits Charlotte, N.C., and Charleston, S.C. Hurricane rated most powerful to hit U.S. in two decades. Death toll high, thousands homeless and suffer power blackout.

America's Cup Back in U.S. (Sept. 19): New York appeals court rules San Diego Yacht Club can keep trophy awarded New Zealand in legal dispute over vessel.

Irving Berlin Dies (Sept. 22): America's legendary composer of popular songs dies at the age of 101.

Vast Cocaine Hoard Seized in Los Angeles (Sept. 29): Drug agents break padlock on unguarded warehouse and take 20-ton cache and more than $10 million in cash. It is largest drug haul in history.

Major Emmy Awards for TV, 1989

(September 17)

Drama series: *L.A. Law* (NBC)
    Actress: Dana Delany, *China Beach* (ABC)
    Actor: Carroll O'Connor, *In the Heat of the Night* (NBC)
    Supporting actress: Melanie Mayron, *thirtysomething* (ABC)
    Supporting actor: Larry Drake, *L.A. Law* (NBC)
Comedy series: *Cheers* (NBC)
    Actress: Candice Bergen, *Murphy Brown* (CBS)
    Actor: Richard Mulligan, *Empty Nest* (NBC)
    Supporting actress: Rhea Perlman, *Cheers* (NBC)
    Supporting actor: Woody Harrelson, *Cheers* (NBC)
Variety music or comedy program: *The Tracey Ullman Show* (Fox)
Mini-Series: *War and Remembrance* (ABC)
Drama-Comedy special (tie): *Day One* (CBS); *Roe vs. Wade* (NBC)
Actress in a Mini-series or special: Holly Hunter, *Roe vs. Wade* (NBC)
Actor in a Mini-Series or special: James Woods, *Hallmark Hall of Fame: My Name is Bill W.* (ABC)
Supporting actress in a Mini-Series or special: Colleen Dewhurst, *Those She Left Behind* (NBC)
Supporting actor in a Mini-Series or special: Derek Jacobi, *Hallmark Hall of Fame: The Tenth Man* (ABC)
Individual performance in a variety or music program: Linda Ronstadt, *Great Performances: Canciones de mio Padre* (PBS)
Governor's Award: Posthumously to Lucille Ball
Network totals: NBC 12, ABC 6, CBS 5, HBO 2, Fox 1, PBS 1

OCTOBER 1989
(Through October 20)

International

U.S.-Mexico Sign Pact (Oct. 3): Presidents Bush and Carlos Salinas de Gortari sign an agreement to enlarge trade and investment between their countries.

Coup to Overthrow Noriega Fails (Oct. 3): Troops loyal to the Panamanian leader recapture a central military headquarters captured earlier by dissident officers, ending the rebellion.

East Germany Closes Czech Border (Oct. 3): After agreeing to allow refugees already in Czechoslovakia to leave for the West, it closes border to stop further exodus.

Hungarian Communist Party Congress Accepts Change (Oct. 7): Delegates agree to the leadership's proposal to transform the party into a socialist organization along traditional European lines and change its name to the Socialist Party. **(Oct. 9):** Rezso Nyers is elected head of the new party.

East Germany Celebrates 40th Anniversary Amid Protests (Oct. 8): The Government's efforts to celebrate 40 years of Communist rule sparks demonstrations in East Berlin, Dresden, Leipzig and elsewhere, leading to clashes between the protesters, the police and security forces. **(Oct. 9):** Fifty thousand East Germans march through Leipzig without interference from the police, although they were on hand. Before the start of the demonstration local party leaders offer dialogue with those demanding change.

South Africa to Release Black Leaders (Oct. 10): President F.W. de Klerk says that Walter Sisulu and other leaders of the banned African National Congress will be released as soon as formalities are completed. However, Nelson R. Mandela will not be freed at this time. **(Oct. 15):** Prisoners freed and call for release of Nelson Mandela.

East German Party Replaces Honecker (Oct. 18): Egan Krenz, his protege, assumes the posts of party chief, head of state, and chairman of the Defense Council.

National

House and Senate Fight Over Medicare (Oct. 4): The House of Representatives votes to repeal the Medicare Catastrophic Coverage Act. **(Oct. 6):** The Senate votes against repealing the program but voted unanimously to scale back the plan and eliminate the surtax that finances it.

Administration Admits Mishandling of Coup (Oct. 5): Senior officials admit American military had played a role in the Panamanian uprising and that the Administration's team performed badly in handling the affair. John H. Sununu orders a study on how the coup was handled.

Florida Legislators Rebuff Call for Abortion Curbs (Oct. 10): The State Legislature kills three of five of the Governor's proposals for tighter restrictions on abortion. **(Oct. 11):** Legislature ends special session after killing every proposal for tougher state laws.

House Votes to Restore Aid for Abortions (Oct. 11): In a policy reversal, the House votes to allow the Federal Government to pay for abortions for poor women whose pregnancies result from rape or incest. The measure goes to the Senate where it is expected to win final passage. Bush urged to veto the bill.

House Passes Flag Desecration Ban (Oct. 12): By an overwhelming margin, the House passes the bill as amended by the Senate that declares that burning or otherwise defacing the flag is punishable by a fine and imprisonment up to one year. The bill now goes to the White House.

General

Jim Bakker Is Guilty (Oct. 5): A jury convicts him on all 24 fraud and conspiracy counts. Sentencing is set for October 24. His lawyers say they will appeal the verdict.

Manufacturer To Give Away AIDS Drug (Oct. 11): Executives of Lyphomed, the maker of the drug pentamidine, which prevents pneumonia in AIDS patients, announce that they will provide the drug to health care providers who would give it to patients who lack insurance that covers its cost.

Stock Market Plunges (Oct. 13): The Dow Jones industrial average falls 190 points, the second largest decline in history.

Major Quake Hits Northern California (Oct. 17): At the start of the evening rush hour a quake, measuring 6.9 on the Richter scale, kills scores of people, causes major damage to the Bay Bridge, collapse of a section of the Nemitz Freeway in Oakland, and fires in San Francisco, Oakland, and Berkely. **(Oct. 18):** Quake dead estimate is put at more than 270, and injured at 1,400. **(Oct. 19):** Death toll on collapsed highway may be lower than first estimates because traffic was lighter than normal.

Shuttle Takes Off (Oct. 18): Atlantis launches Galileo spacecraft on its trip to Jupiter.

1989 Nobel Prize Winners

Peace: The Dalai Lama in recognition of his nonviolent campaign to end China's domination of Tibet.

Medicine: Dr. J. Michael Bishop and Dr. Harold E. Varmus (Americans) both cancer researchers at the University of California Medical School in San Francisco for their unifying theory of cancer development.

Economics: Trygve Haavelmo (Norwegian), professor emeritus at the University of Oslo, for his pioneering work in methods for testing economic theories that helped pave the way for modern economic forecasting.

Physics: Norman F. Ramsey (American) of Harvard University for his work that led to the development of the atomic clock and Hans G. Dehmelt (American) of the University of Washington and Wolfgang Paul (West German) of the University of Bonn for developments of methods to isolate atoms and subatomic particles for study.

Chemistry: Thomas R. Cech of the University of Colorado and Sidney Altman of Yale (both Americans) for the discovery, which they made independently, that RNA, a crucial genetic substance, was not merely a passive carrier of genetic information but could actively aid chemical reactions in the cells.

Literature: Camilo José Cela (Spanish), novelist, "for a rich and intensive prose, which with restrained compassion forms a challenging vision of man's vulnerability."

Deaths in 1988–1989

(As of September 1, 1989)

Adamson, George, 83: protector of lions and their environment in Kenya. Aug. 20, 1989.

Addams, Charles, 76: cartoonist, noted for his macabre humor, whose work appeared in *The New Yorker* magazine for five decades. Sept. 29, 1988.

Allison, Fran, 81: singer and radio comedian who was the human of the early popular television puppet show "Kukla, Fran, and Ollie." June 13, 1989.

Alsop, Joseph, 78: syndicated Washington columnist read throughout country for five decades. Column believed to have been longest-running syndicated feature of its kind. Aug. 28, 1989.

Alvarez, Luis W., 77: physicist, member of team that developed atomic bomb and winner of 1968 Nobel Prize in Physics. Sept. 1, 1988.

Armstrong, Henry, 75: only boxer ever to hold three world titles simultaneously—featherweight, lightweight, and welterweight. Oct. 24, 1988.

Attwood, William, 69: author, journalist, former publisher of *Newsday,* named by President Kennedy as Ambassador to Guinea in 1961. April 15, 1989.

Backus, Jim, 76: actor and writer in theater, radio, and television. Booming voice gave life to cartoon character "Mr. Magoo." July 3, 1989.

Ball, Lucille, 77: Hollywood veteran and star of television comedy for nearly quarter century. Best known for "I Love Lucy." April 26, 1989.

Barthelme, Donald, 58: short story writer and novelist. July 23, 1989.

Beadle, George W., 85: geneticist who won Nobel Prize in 1958 for work in demonstrating how genes control basic chemistry of living cell. President of University of Chicago from 1961 to 1968. June 9, 1989.

Blaik, Earl (Red), 92: head football coach at U.S. Military Academy for 18 seasons, 1941 to 1958. May 6, 1989.

Blanc, Mel, 81: actor who provided voices for many film cartoon characters, such as Bugs Bunny and Woody Woodpecker. July 10, 1989.

Brewster, Kingman, Jr., 69: President of Yale University from 1963 to 1977. Ambassador to Britain from 1977 to 1981. Nov. 8, 1988.

Brickwedde, Ferdinand, 86: physicist who in 1931 produced first measurable amounts of heavy hydrogen. March 29, 1989.

Brico, Antonia, 87: woman conductor who led own orchestras in 1930s and had devoted herself to fighting prejudice against women in orchestral field. Aug. 3, 1989.

Brodie, Dr. Bernard Beryl, 81: a leading researcher on drug therapy Feb. 27, 1989.

Carradine, John, 82: character actor who appeared in more than 200 films. Nov. 27, 1988.

Carter, Billy, 51: brother of President Jimmy Carter. Sept. 25, 1988.

Castellano, Richard, 55: character actor on stage and in films. Dec. 10, 1988.

Chrysler, Walter P., Jr., 79: son of founder of Chrysler Corporation. One of country's leading art collectors. Sept. 17, 1988.

Cotton, Norris, 88: staunch conservative Republican Senator from New Hampshire for 20 years. Feb. 24, 1989.

Cowley, Malcolm, 90: literary critic, historian, editor, poet, and essayist. March 27, 1989.

Dali, Salvador, 84: pioneer of European surrealistic painting and controversial figure in international art world. Jan. 23, 1989.

Daniel, Yuli M., 63: Soviet satirist and poet who attracted worldwide attention at trial in Moscow crackdown on dissidents. Dec. 30, 1988.

Daniels, Billy, 73: veteran nightclub performer, actor, and big-band singer. Won fame with recording of "That Old Black Magic." Oct. 7, 1988.

Dart, Raymond A., 95: anatomist who discovered early human fossil in Africa in 1922, revolutionizing study of human origins. Nov. 22, 1988.

Dorati, Antal, 82: internationally known orchestral conductor. Nov. 13, 1988.

du Maurier, Dame Daphne, 81: author of "Rebecca" and other popular Gothic and romantic novels. April 19, 1989.

Eldridge, Roy, 78: jazz trumpeter whose style linked the pioneering Louis Armstrong and innovator Dizzy Gillespie. Feb. 27, 1989.

Evans, Maurice, 87: one of best-known Shakespearean actors of 1930s and 1940s. Highly popular in performances of Shakespeare on Broadway and in productions that toured United States. March 12, 1989.

Fox, Ruth, 93: pioneer in chemical treatment of alcoholism, first medical director of National Council on Alcoholism. March 24, 1989.

Genda, Gen. Minoru, 85: Japanese officer who planned attack on Pearl Harbor. Early advocate of naval air power. Aug. 15, 1989.

Gomez, Vernon (Lefty), 80: pitcher for powerful Yankee baseball team half century previously. Feb. 17, 1989.

Green, Dr. Richard R., 52: New York City's first black school chancellor. May 10, 1989.

Gromyko, Andrei A., 79: former Soviet Foreign Minister, having served for 28 years. Spoke for intransigent Soviet foreign policy in postwar era. July 2, 1989.

Harding, Lord John, 92: commander of British forces in North Africa during World War II. Jan. 20, 1989.

Harrington, Michael, 61: co-chairman of Democratic Socialists of America and author of "The Other America." July 30, 1989.

Hirohito, Emperor, 87: Japan's 124th and longest-reigning monarch, on throne 62 years. Jan. 7, 1989.

Hoffman, Abbie (Abbott), 52: symbol of radical activism, writer, and antiwar protester who founded Yippie movement (Youth International Party) in 1960s. April 12, 1989.

Hook, Sidney, 86: philosopher who wrote many books on Marxism, public policy, and education. Known as vigorous anti-Communist. July 12, 1989.

Houseman, John, 86: spent half century in theater as influential producer and director. Won fame at 71 as crusty law professor in "The Paper Chase" on films and TV. Oct. 31, 1988.

Hubbell, Carl, 85: pitcher in Baseball Hall of Fame who won 253 games for New York Giants with delivery of screwball. Nov. 21, 1988.

Jorgensen, Christine, 62: underwent surgery and hormone treatments in 1952 to change sex from male to female. May 3, 1989.

Kadar, Janos, 77: leader of Hungarian Communist Party after Soviet Army crushed 1956 uprising until being replaced in May 1988. July 6, 1989.

Khomeini, Ayatollah Ruhollah, 87: revolutionary Shiite Moslem leader. Dominated Iran for a decade. June 3, 1989.

Kimbrough, Emily, 90: author, lecturer, and former

radio commentator. Feb. 11, 1989.

Lattimore, Owen, 88: Far East scholar and authority on history, culture, and politics of Central Asia. May 30, 1989.

Lekachman, Robert, 68: professor of economics, known for unorthodox views. Jan. 14, 1989.

Leland, Mickey, 44: Representative in Congress from Texas and one of most prominent black legislators, committed to ending world hunger. Circa. Aug. 10, 1989, in Ethiopia plane crash.

Lillie, Beatrice, 94: British comedienne, in half-century theatrical career, was called "funniest woman in the world." Jan. 20, 1989.

Magnuson, Warren G., 84: one of most powerful Senators, representing Washington state for 44 years in Congress. May 20, 1989.

Mangelsdorf, Paul C., 90: botanist with world reputation for cross-breeding of corn and other grains. July 22, 1989.

Manning, Timothy Cardinal, 79: served 15 years as Archbishop of Los Angeles. June 23, 1989.

McCloy, John J., 93: Lawyer and diplomat, adviser to Presidents from Franklin D. Roosevelt to Ronald Reagan. U.S. High Commissioner in postwar Germany. March 11, 1989.

Milanov, Zinka, 83: leading dramatic soprano for Metropolitan Opera for nearly 30 years. May 30, 1989.

Mitchell, John N., 75: President Nixon's Attorney General. Jailed for role in Watergate scandals. Nov. 9, 1988.

Newhouse, Mitzi E., 87: widow of publisher, donated $87 million to continue operation of theaters at New York's Lincoln Center. June 29, 1989.

Newton, Dr. Huey, 47: co-founder of Black Panther Party, a leader of generation of blacks in 1960s. Aug. 22, 1989.

Noguchi, Isamu, 84: versatile Japanese sculptor who worked in various mediums, bridging East and West. Dec. 30, 1988.

Norris, Clarence, 75: last survivor of "Scottsboro boys" rape case. Jan. 23, 1989.

Norstad, Gen. Lauris, 81: commander of North Atlantic Treaty forces and U.S. forces in Europe during Berlin crisis. Sept. 12, 1988.

Olivier, Sir Laurence, 82: one of greatest classical actors of all time. Also a movie star and film director acclaimed for Shakespearean adaptations. July 11, 1989.

Onassis, Christina, 37: part heiress to shipping and real estate empire founded by father, Aristotle S. Onassis. Nov. 19, 1988.

Panchen Lama, 50: Tibet's most important spiritual leader after Dalai Lama. Jan. 28, 1989.

Pepper, Claude, 88: Liberal Representative in Congress and former Senator who championed rights of elderly in 60-year political career. May 30, 1989.

Pride, Adm. Alfred M., 91: pioneer of aircraft carrier operations. Dec. 24, 1988.

Prinz, Dr. Joachim, 86: former president of American Jewish Congress and a leader in civil-rights causes. Sept. 30, 1988.

Radner, Gilda, 42: Emmy Award-winning comedian who created television characters on "Saturday Night Live." May 20, 1989.

Raposo, Joseph G., 51: a creator of children's television show "Sesame Street" and a composer. Feb. 1, 1989.

Richter, Curt Paul, 94: retired professor at Johns Hopkins Medical Institutions, pioneer in discovery and study of biorhythms, and conceived the "biological clock." Dec. 21, 1988.

Robinson, Sugar Ray (nee Walker Smith, Jr.), 67: five-time world middleweight boxing champion. April 12, 1989.

Said el-Mufti, 90: Former Prime Minister of Jordan, who helped nation become independent kingdom. March 25, 1989.

Schaffner, Franklin James, 69: Academy Award-winning film director. Seven Oscars awarded for his film "Patton." July 2, 1989.

Schiff, Dorothy, 86: owner of *New York Post* for 37 years, having used family money to gain control. Aug. 30, 1989.

Shockley, William B., 79: shared Nobel Prize in physics for role in creating transistor. Center of criticism for views on genetic differences among races. Aug. 12, 1989.

Sitwell, Sir Sacheverell, 90: British poet and art critic, brother of Sir Osbert and Dame Edith Sitwell. Oct. 1, 1988.

Sopwith, Sir Thomas, 101: aircraft designer, aviator, and aircraft manufacturing executive. Jan. 27, 1989.

Steloff, Frances, 101: founder of New York's Gotham Book Mart, an international literary haven. April 15, 1989.

Stephenson, Sir William, 93: British World War II chief of intelligence in Western Hemisphere with code name Intrepid. Jan. 31, 1989.

Stone, I.F., 81: independent, radical journalist on eight publications, mostly left of center. June 18, 1989.

Stone, Irving, 86: prolific and scholarly author of biographical novels, including "Lust for Life." Aug. 26, 1989.

Strauss, Franz Josef, 73: Bavarian premier. Helped found conservative Christian Social Union. Oct. 3, 1988.

Studebaker, John Ward, 102: U.S. Commissioner of Education for 14 years. Developed five-year program that trained 12 million for military industries in World War II. July 26, 1989.

Symington, Stuart, 87: former Missouri Democratic Senator who twice sought Presidential nomination. Dec. 16, 1988.

Tarras, Dave, 95: clarinetist who was one of America's most important klezmer musicians. Feb. 13, 1989.

Tinbergen, Nikolaas, 81: Dutch-born British zoologist who shared 1973 Nobel Prize in Medicine for discoveries in animal behavior. Dec. 21, 1988.

Tuchman, Barbara W., 77: prominent writer who won two Pulitzer prizes for "The Guns of August" and "Stilwell and the American Experience in China, 1911-45." Feb. 6, 1989.

Uhlenbeck, George E., 87: co-discoverer of electron's spin, former president of American Physical Society. Oct. 31, 1988.

Von Karajan, Herbert, 81: world's best-known orchestral conductor, a powerful figure in classical music. July 16, 1989.

Vreeland, Diana, in late 80's: fashion editor and creator of spectacular fashion exhibitions at Metropolitan Museum of Art. Aug. 22, 1989.

Wankel, Felix, 86: German inventor of rotary engine and other automotive and aeronautical equipment. Oct. 9, 1988.

Weeks, Edward A., 91: author and essayist. Editor of *Atlantic Monthly* for 28 years. March 11, 1989.

Yakovlev, Aleksandr S., 84: Soviet designer of World War II airplanes and modern passenger jets. Aug. 22, 1989.

Zita, 96: last Empress of Austria-Hungary. A princess of House of Bourbon-Parma and consort of Karl I, of the Hapsburg dynasty, the last Emperor. March 14, 1989.